ROBERT NORTH S.J.

ELENCHUS OF BIBLICA

1988

EDITRICE PONTIFICIO ISTITUTO BIBLICO
ROMA 1991

ROBERT NORTH S.J.

ELENCHUS OF BIBLICA

1988

EDITRICE PONTIFICIO ISTITUTO BIBLICO
ROMA 1991

ISBN 88-7653-594-2

Editrice Pontificio Istituto Biblico
Piazza della Pilotta, 35 - 00187 Roma

Finito di stampare il 15 febbraio 1991
Tipografia Poliglotta della Pontificia Università Gregoriana
Piazza della Pilotta, 4 – 00187 Roma

In memoriam, et...

*Abhinc decem annos,
ita functus est R. Pater
ETRUS NOBER, SJ, post
riginta annos redactionis
ujus* Elenchi *in forma
tilissima cujus erat ipse
erus fundator. Jam pro-
it hoc decimum volumen
ost privationem ejus di-
ectionis sollertissimae.*

*Intenti semper ad con-
ervationem linearum es-
entialium ejus directionis,
amen in spiritu ejus intro-
uximus etiam aliquas
modificationes, praesertim
nclusionem omnium com-
pilationum inter* Biblio-
raphica *in ipso initio, ad
uas deinde → fieri pos-
et.*

*Aliae novae dispositio-
es praesertim Evangelio-
um possunt conspici 'sy-
optice' in Indice Syste-
matico.*

*Praecipua innovatio hu-
us anni adumbratur tan-
um in* N° 6419-7999 *'non
dhibitis hoc anno'. Nam
ncepimus longum labo-
em redactionis cum
Theologia* N° 8000, *ita ut
materia recentior et abun-
dantior, interim collecta,
ossit locupletare potius
ectiones proprie exegeti-
as E-F-G.*

*Hoc anno demum redu-
ximus ad biennium illud
ntervallum quod necessa-
io intercedit inter scripta
itata et tempus publica-
ionis; tamen hic pro-
ressus non est nisi sta-
dium intermedium versus
erte necessariam majo-
em automationem, nunc
ub judice.*

A remembrance... and a prospect

Just ten years have passed since the death of Father PETER NOBER, S.J. (13.VIII.1912-27.IX.1980), the thirty-years editor and real founder of the *Elenchus bibliographicus biblicus*, at least in the form and amplitude which the exegetical world has found so useful. This is now the tenth volume which has had to appear without his valuable skill and experience.

We have striven to remain faithful to his guidelines which had proved so effective. But included among those guidelines was a willingness to adapt and change where it seemed desirable. Perhaps the major change which has been introduced since his death was the renvoi (→) to item-number especially of compilations within the same volume; and in view of this, the amplification and re-ordering of the very first section, entitled *Bibliographica*. The section on 'Jesus Christ' also was divided between Gospels and Biblical Theology; and the Gospels section itself was re-ordered to take account of current uniting of 'Luke- Acts' and 'the Johannine Corpus'.

Lesser changes also have been noted year by year as they occurred. They have been highlighted by boldface italic type in the Table of Contents or 'systematic index' now at the front, where on two facing pages can be seen in one 'synoptic' look the connection among all the topics treated in the volume.

With this 1988 volume a behind-the-scenes change has been introduced, not evident in the text except in the notation of p. 409, "The numbers 6419 to 7999 are not used this year". This was because we have readjusted our editing procedures in order to do first (after the essential Bibliographica) all those sections which are really peripheral to biblical exegesis. Since the editing takes about six months, during which also new materials are constantly being gathered, it has been a source of frustration that there has been a greater and more recent abundance among the less-relevant materials toward the end. With this volume we have begun the editing with section H, 'Biblical Theology' and done only at the end the strictly exegetical sections E-F-G, which thus contain all the material most recently made available. Not knowing in advance how many items would be involved, we left free all the numbers up to 8000. As we can now see, 7000 would have been enough.

With this volume also, we have finally reduced to two years the interval between materials cited and time of publication. It seems profitless to speculate whether this interval can be maintained or further diminished, since the future of the *Elenchus* must lie along the lines of greater computerization, now being studied.

December 1990.   R. N.

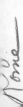

Index systematicus – Contents

AA	Ann Arbor
Amst	Amsterdam
B	Berlin
Ba/BA	Basel/Buenos Aires
Barc	Barcelona
Bo/Bru	Bologna/Brussel
CasM	Casale Monferrato
CinB	Cinisello Balsamo
C	Cambridge, England
CM	Cambridge, Mass.
Ch	Chicago
Da: Wiss	Darmstadt, WissBuchg
DG	Downers Grove, IL
Dü	Düsseldorf
E	Edinburgh
ENJ	EnglewoodCliffs NJ
F	Firenze
FrB/FrS	Freiburg-Br/Schw
Fra	Frankfurt/M
GCNY	Garden City NY
Gö	Göttingen
GR	Grand Rapids MI
Gü	Gütersloh
Ha	Hamburg
Heid	Heidelberg
Hw	Harmondsworth
J	Jerusalem
K	København
L	London
LA	Los Angeles
Lp	Leipzig
Lv(N)	Leuven (L-Neuve)
M/Mi	Madrid/Milano
Mü	München
N	Napoli
ND	NotreDame IN
Neuk	Neukirchen/Verlag
NHv	New Haven
Nv	Nashville
NY	New York
Ox	Oxford
P	Paris
Pd	Paderborn
Ph	Philadelphia
R	Roma
Rg	Regensburg
SF	San Francisco
Sto	Stockholm
Stu	Stuttgart
T/TA	Torino/Tel Aviv
Tü	Tübingen
U/W	Uppsala/Wien
Wmr	Warminster
Wsb	Wiesbaden
Wsh	Washington
Wsz	Warszawa
Wu	Wuppertal
Wü	Würzburg
Z	Zürich

Citando hinc
Adhibemus:
Intra titulum **;**
ante subtitulum
[**non** *sicut originale*]

Semper
'[" "]'
non , ' *vel* « ».

Pretium numero
rotundo: $20 *pro*
$19.95, *etiam*
contra *fontem*
ibidem citatum.

Annus voluminis
late interpretandus;
sub 1988
etiam 1988-9, *vel*
1988 *tarde*
editum, vel
(*numerus voluminis*
sine anno) *pro*
fonte *libri* 1988.

Datur tendentia
movendi titulos
non biblicos ab
initio versus
finem libri;
sic
compilationes
post primam
mentionem.

Index systematicus
(*et synopticus*)
monstrat
innovationes;
e.g. nunc
B4.4-6 de influxu
biblico in
litteraturam.

Nota Bene – in citing titles from this Elenchu

1. We strive to give the original form of the title as accurately and identically as possible. But every bibliography has certain 'conventions' or adaptations in the interest of its own internal clarity and consistency; thus for example a title is never given in ALL CAPITALS even when it is so in the original. Our major warning is this: we use the **semicolon** [**;**] to set off the **subtitle** where the original uses a colon, dot, or separate line. Also, like many bibliography and library catalogues, we do **not** capitalize every word in English-language titles.

For **quotation-marks**, we are following always British usage:

Normally ' ';
Quotes-within-quotes " "
even where the original may have „ " or « ».

2. The **price** is rounded off, in the interest of brevity, clarity, and coping with inflation. Thus $12.95 will appear as $13 even where the cited source has $12.95. Less often: £20 for 19.90; DM 50 for 49,80.

3. In principle each volume contains only books and articles published **within that year** or earlier; thus this volume 4 contains the writings dated 1988. However, to be as up-to-date as possible, we include: *a*) periodicals officially dated 1988 even though published late; *b*) periodical-volumes including **partly** 1988, but also the part published in 1989 (= 1988s); *c*) Source for 1988 books, usually by volume-number (without year-number) of a later periodical [thus TDig 36,182; but BL 90,35 since it has no volume-numbers]; so also for **dissertations**.

4. We have progressively been moving **away from the front** those materials which are less directly biblical. Thus a book given in A-section for its first appearance (so that its number can be used for → renvoi), if repeated in later volumes (with book-reviews), will be in the section where it fits best. — 'Summary reports of meetings' (not needed for renvoi) are now shunted from A2.2 to Y7.2. 'Revelation', formerly B3.2, is now H1.7. Hermeneutic materials not strictly biblical have been moved from B2 to J9 (linguistic analysis).

5. The Table of Contents (systematic index, p. 4-5) prints in **boldface** those categories which have been relocated, or new categories which have just been introduced: thus the former B4.5, 'The Bible as Literature', has now been sudivided into B4.4 'The Bible itself as literature'; B4.5, 'Biblical influence on secular literature in general'; B4.6, 'Bible-influence on individual authors'.

Acronyms: Periodica - Series (small).
8 fig. = ISSN; *10 fig.* = ISBN; *6/7* = DissA.

Ⓐ: *arabice,* in Arabic.

AAR [Aids]: American Academy of Religion (→ JAAR, not PAAR) [Aids for the Study of Religion; Chico CA].

AAS: Acta Apostolicae Sedis; Vaticano. 0001-5199.

AASOR: Annual of the American Schools of Oriental Research; CM.

Abh: Abhandlungen Gö Lp Mü etc.; → DOG / DPV.

AbhChrJüDial: Abhandlungen zum christlich-jüdischen Dialog; Mü, Kaiser.

AbrNahr: Abr-Nahrain; Leiden.

AcAANorv: Acta ad archaeologiam et artium historiam spectantia, Inst. Norvegiae; Roma.

AcBg: Académie royale de Belgique; Bru.

Acme; Mi, Fac. Lett. Filos. 0001-494X.

AcNum: Acta Numismatica; Barc. 0211-8386 [15 (1985)].

AcSém: Actes sémiotiques; Paris [5 (1983)].

Act: Actes/Acta (Congrès, Colloque).

ActAntH: Acta Antiqua Academiae Scientiarum Hungaricae; Budapest.

Acta PIB: Acta Pontificii Instituti Biblici: Roma.

ActArchH/K: Acta Archaeologica; Hungarica, Budapest. 0001-5210 / København. 0065-101X.

ActClasSAfr: Acta Classica; Cape Town.

ActIran: Acta Iranica; Téhéran/Leiden.

ActOrH/K: Acta Orientalia: Budapest, Academia Scientiarum Hungarica; 0044-5975 / K (Societates Orientales Danica, Norveigica). 0001-6438.

ActPraeh: Acta Praehistorica et Archaeologica; B.

ActSum: Acta Sumerologica; Hiroshima, Univ. Linguistics. 0387-8082.

ActuBbg: Actualidad Bibliográfica; Barc. 0211-4143.

ADAJ: Annual of the Department of Antiquities, Jordan; 'Amman.

ADPF: Association pour la diffusion de la pensée française; Paris → RCiv.

Aeg: Aegyptus; Milano. 0001-9046.

ÄgAbh: Ägyptologische Abhandlungen; Wb.

ÄgAT: Ägypten und Altes Testament; Wiesbaden. 0720-9061.

AegHelv: Aegyptiaca Helvetica: Basel Univ. Äg. Sem. (Univ. Genève).

AevA: Aevum Antiquum; Mi, Univ. Cattolica/ViPe. [1 (1988)]. 88-348-1701-5.

Aevum; Milano [anche Univ. Catt.].

AfER: African Ecclesial Review; Eldoret, Kenya.

AfJB: African Journal of Biblical, Studies; Ibadan. [1,1 (1986)].

AfO: Archiv für Orientforschung; Graz. 3-85028-141-8.

AfTJ: Africa Theological Journal; Arusha, Tanzania. 0856-0048.

AGJU: Arbeiten zur Geschichte des Antiken Judentums und des Urchristentums; Leiden.

AIBL: Académie des Inscriptions et Belles-Lettres; P → CRAI. – **AIEMA** → BMosA.

AION [-Clas]: Annali (dell')Istituto Universitario Orientale [Classico] → ArchStorAnt di Napoli.

AIPHOS: Annuaire de l'Institut de Philologie et d'Histoire Orientales et Slaves; Bru. 2-8004-0881-2.

AJA: American Journal of Archaeology; Princeton NJ. 0002-9114.

AJS: Association for Jewish Studies Review; CM 0364-0094 [6 (1981); Newsletter (10, 1985) 0278-4033].

Akkadica; Bruxelles/Brussel.

al.: et alii, and other(s).

ALGHJ: Arbeiten zur Literatur und Geschichte des hellenistischen Judentums; Leiden.

Al-Kibt, The Copts, die Kopten; Ha.

ALLC: Association for Literary and Linguistic Computing Bulletin; Stockport, Cheshire.

Altertum (Das); oB. 0002-6646.

AltOrF: Altorientalische Forschungen; B. 0232-8461.

AltsprU: Der altsprachliche Unterricht.

AmBapQ: American Baptist Quarterly; Valley Forge PA. 0015-8992.

AmBenR: American Benedictine Review; Richardton ND. 0002-7650.

Ambrosius, bollettino liturgico; Milano. 0392-5757.

America; NY. 0002-7049.

AmHR: American Historical Review; NY.

AmJAncH: American Journal of Ancient History; CM.

AmJPg: American Journal of Philology; Baltimore. 0002-9475.

AmJTPh: American Journal of Theology and Philosophy; W. Lafayette IN.

AmMessianJ: The American Messianic Jew; Ph [68 (1983)].

AmNumM: American Numismatic Society Museum Notes; NY.

AmPhTr: Transactions of the American Philosophical Society; Ph.

AmSci: American Scientist; New Haven. 0003-0996.

AmstCah: Amsterdamse cahiers voor exegese en bijbelse theologie; Kampen.

AmstMed ➤ Mededelingen.

AmStPapyr: American Studies in Papyrology; NHv.

AnAASyr: Annales Archéologiques Arabes Syriennes; Damas.

Anadolu; Ankara, Univ.

Anagénnēsis (none Ⓖ), papyrology; Athēnai [2 (1982)].

Anatolica; Istanbul. 0066-1554.

AnatSt: Anatolian Studies; London.

AnAug: Analecta Augustiniana; R.

ANaut: Archaeonautica; Paris. 0154-1854 [4 (1984)].

AnBib: Analecta Biblica. Investigationes scientificae in res biblicas; R. 0066-135X.

AnBoll: Analecta Bollandiana; Bruxelles. 0003-2468.

AnBritAth: Annual of the British School at Athens; London.

AnCalas: Analecta Calasanctiana (religioso–cultural–histórica); Salamanca. 0569-9789.

AnCÉtRel: Annales du Centre d'Études des Religions; Bru.

AncHB: Ancient History Bullettin; Calgary/Chicago Loyola Univ. [1, 1(-6) (1987-)].

AnChile: Anales de la Facultad de Teología; Santiago, Univ. Católica.

AnchorB: Anchor Bible; Garden City NY.

AncHRes: Ancient History ['Ancient Society' through ‹17 (1987)], Resources for Teachers; Macquaries Univ. 0310-5814.

AnCist: Analecta Cisterciensia; Roma. 0003-2476.

AnClas: Annales Universitatis, sectio classica; Budapest.

AnClémOchr: Annuaire de l'Académie de théologie 'St. Clément d'Ochrida' [27 (1977s) paru 1982].

AnCracov: Analecta Cracoviensia (Polish Theol. Soc.); Kraków. 0209-0864.

AncSoc: Ancient Society. Katholieke Universiteit; Leuven. 0066-1619.

AnCTS: Annual Publication of the College Theological Society; Chico CA [not = ➤ ProcC(ath)TS].

AncW: The Ancient World; Chicago. 0160-9645.

AndrUnS: Andrews University Seminary Studies; Berrien Springs, Mich. 0003-2980.

AnEgBbg: Annual Egyptological Bibliography; Leiden.

AnÉPH: Annuaire ➤ ÉPHÉ.

AnÉth: Annales d'Éthiopie; Addis-Ababa.

AnFac: Let: Annali della facoltà di lettere, Univ. (Bari/Cagliari/Perugia).

— **Ling/T:** Annal(es) Facultat(is); linguarum, theologiae.

AnFg: Anuario de Filología; Barc.

Ang: Angelicum; Roma. 0003-3081.

AnglTR: Anglican Theological Review; Evanston IL. 0003-3286.

AnGreg: Analecta (Pont. Univ.) Gregoriana; Roma. 0066-1376.

AnHArt: Annales d'histoire de l'art et d'archéologie: Bru.

AnHConc: Annuarium Historiae Conciliorum; Paderborn.

ANilM: Archéologie du Nil Moyen; Lille. 0299-8130 [1 (1986)].

AnItNum: Annali (dell')Istituto Italiano di Numismatica; Roma.

AnJapB: Annual of the Japanese Biblical Institute; Tokyo Ⓙ ➤ Sei-Ron.

AnLetN: Annali della Facoltà di lettere e filosofia dell'Univ.; Napoli.

AnLovBOr: Analecta Lovaniensia Biblica et Orientalia; Lv.

AnnTh: Annales Theologici; Roma [1,1 (1987) 88-384-4000-6].

AnOr: Analecta Orientalia: Roma.

AnOrdBas: Analecta Ordinis S. Basilii Magni; Roma.

AnPg: L'Année Philologique; Paris.

AnPisa: Annali della Scuola Normale Superiore; Pisa.

AnPraem: Analecta Praemonstratensia; Averbode.

AnRIM: Annual Review of the Royal Inscriptions of Mesopotamia Project; Toronto. 0822-2525.

AnRSocSR: Annual Review of the Social Sciences of Religion; The Hague. 0066-2062.

ANRW: Aufstieg und Niedergang der römischen Welt → 782.

AnSacTar: Analecta Sacra Tarraconensia; Barcelona.

AnSemClas: Annali del Seminario di Studi del Mondo Classico, sezione Archeologia e Storia Antica; Napoli, Ist. Univ. Orientale [5 (1983)].

AnStoEseg: Annali di Storia dell'Esegesi; Bologna. 88-10-20255-4.

AntAb: Antike und Abendland; Berlin. 0003-5696.

AntAfr: Antiquités africaines; Paris. 0066-4871.

AntClas: L'Antiquité Classique; Bru.

AntClCr: Antichità classica e cristiana; Brescia.

Anthropos; 1. Fribourg/Suisse. 0003-5572. / [2. Rivista sulla famiglia; Roma 1 (1985)].

Anthropotes; R, Città Nuova [3 (1987)].

AntiqJ: Antiquaries Journal; London. 0003-5815.

Antiquity; Gloucester. 0003-5982.

Ant/ka: ⑥ Anthropologiká; Thessaloniki.

AntKu: Antike Kunst; Basel. 0003-5688.

Anton: Antonianum; Roma. 0003-6064.

AntRArch: Antiqua, Rivista d'Archeologia e d'Architettura; Roma.

AnTVal: Anales de la Cátedra de Teología en la Universidad de Valencia [1 (1984)].

AntWelt: Antike Welt; Feldmeilen.

Anvil, Anglican Ev. theol.; Bramcote, Nottingham. 0003-6226.

AnzAltW: Anzeiger für die Altertumswissenschaft; Innsbruck. 0003-6293.

AnzW: Anzeiger der österreichischen Akademie (phil./hist.); Wien. 0378-8652.

AOAT: Alter Orient und Altes Testament: Kevelaer/Neukirchen.

AOtt: Univ. München, Arbeiten zu Text und Sprache im AT; St. Ottilien.

Apollonia: Afro-Hellenic studies, under patronage of Alexandria Patriarchate; Johannesburg, Rand Afrikaans Univ. [1 (1982)].

ArBegG: Archiv für Begriffsgeschichte (Mainz, Akad.); Bonn.

ArbGTL: Arbeiten zur Geschichte und Theologie des Luthertums, Neue Folge; B.

ArbKiG: Arbeiten zur Kirchengeschichte; B.

ArbNTJud: Arbeiten zum NT und zum Judentum: Frankfurt/M. 0170-8856.

ArbNtTextf: Arbeiten zur Neutestamentlichen Textforschung; B/NY.

ArbT: Arbeiten zur Theologie (Calwer); Stu.

ARCE → J[News] AmEg.

Archaeología; Wrocław. 0066-605X.

Archaeology; Boston. 0003-8113.

Archaeometry; L. 0003-813X.

Archaiognōsía ⑥; Athenai [2 (1981)].

ArchAnz: Archäologischer Anzeiger; Berlin. 0003-8105.

ArchAth: ⑥ Archaiología; Athēna [sic; 1 (1981); 2-5 (1982)].

ArchBbg: Archäologische Bibliographie zu JbDAI; Berlin.

ArchClasR: Archeologia Classica; R.

Archeo, attualità del passato; Milano [1-10 (1985)].

Archéo-Log: archéologie informatique; Liège, Univ. groupe Diapré. [1 (1986)].

Archéologia; (ex-Paris) Dijon, Faton. 0570-6270 → Dossiers.

ArchEph: ⑥ Archaiologikē Ephēmeris; Athēnai.

ArchInf: Archäologische Informationen; Bonn. 3-7749-2202-0.

Architectura; München. 0044-863X.

ArchMIran: Archäologische Mitteilungen aus Iran, N.F.; Berlin.

ArchNews: Archaeological News; Tallahassee FL. 0194-3413. [13 (1984)].

ArchRCamb: Archaeological Reviews from Cambridge (Eng.). 0261-4332.

ArchRep: Archaeological Reports; Wmr, British Sch. Athens. 0570-6084.

ArchStorAnt: [= a third AION] Archeologia e Storia Antica; Napoli, Univ. Ist. Or./Cl. 0393-070X.

Arctos, Acta Philologica Fennica; Helsinki. 0570-734X.

Areopagus: Hong Kong [1 (1987) incorporates vol. 11 of Aarhus Dialog].

ArEspArq: Archivo Español de Arqueología; Madrid. 0066-6742.

Arethusa... wellspring of Western man; Buffalo NY. 0004-0975.

ArFrancHist: Archivum Franciscanum Historicum; Grottaferrata.

ArGlottIt: Archivio Glottologico Italiano; Firenze. 0004-0207.

ArHPont: Archivum Historiae Pontificiae; Roma.

ArKulturg: Archiv für Kulturgeschichte; Köln. 0003-9233.

ArLtgW: Archiv für Liturgiewissenschaft; Regensburg. 0066-6386.

ArOr: Archiv Orientální; Praha. 0044-8699.

ArPapF: Archiv für Papyrusforschung; Leipzig. 0066-6459.

ArRefG: Archiv für Reformationsgeschichte; Gütersloh.

ArchRep: Archaeological Reports; Wmr, British School at Athens. 0570-6084.

ArSSocRel: Archives de Sciences Sociales des Religions; Paris.

ARTANES: Aids and Research Tools in Ancient Near Eastern Studies; Malibu.

ArTGran: Archivo Teológico Granadino; Granada. 0210-1629.

ArztC: Arzt und Christ; Salzburg.

ASAE: Annales du Service des Antiquités de l'Égypte; Le Caire.

AsbTJ: Asbury Theological Journal; Wilmore, KY.

AshlandTJ: Theological J. (Ohio).

AsiaJT: Asia Journal of Theology; Tokyo.

AsMis: Assyriological Miscellanies; K, Univ. [1 (1980)].

ASOR: American Schools of Oriental Research; CM (**diss.**: Dissertation Series).

Asprenas... Scienze Teologiche; Napoli.

ASTI: Annual of the [Jerusalem] Swedish Theological Institute; Leiden.

At[AcBol/Tor/Tosc]: Atti [dell'Accademia... di Bologna / di Torino / Toscana].

ATANT: Abhandlungen zur Theologie des Alten & Neuen Testaments; Zürich.

ATD: Das Alte Testament Deutsch. Neues Göttinger Bibelwerk; Gö.

AteDial: Ateismo e Dialogo; Vaticano.

AtenRom: Atene e Roma; Firenze. 0004-6493.

Athenaeum: Letteratura e Storia dell'antichità; Pavia.

ʾAtiqot, English edition; J, Dept. Ant.

AtKap: Ateneum Kapłańskie; Włocławek. 0208-9041.

ATLA: American Theological Library Association; Menuchen, NJ.

AtSGlot: Atti Sodalizio Glottologico; Mi.

Atualização, Revista de Divulgação Teológica; Belo Horizonte, MG.

AuCAfr: Au cœur de l'Afrique; Burundi [22 (1982)].

AugL: Augustinus-Lexikon ➤ 783.

AugLv: Augustiniana; Leuven.

AugM: Augustinus; Madrid.

AugR: Augustinianum; Roma.

AugSt: Augustinian Studies; Villanova PA.

AulaO: Aula Orientalis; Barc [1 (1983)].

AusgF: Ausgrabungen und Funde; B.

AustinSB: Austin (TX) Sem. Bulletin.

AustralasCR: Australasian Catholic Record; Sydney. 0727-3215.

AustralBR: Australian Biblical Review; Melbourne.

AVA: ➤ Bei AVgA.

BA: Biblical Archaeologist; CM. 0006-0895.

Babel, international organ of translation; Budapest, Akad.

BaBernSt: Basler und Berner Studien zur historischen und systematischen Theologie; Bern.

Babesch: Bulletin Antieke Beschaving; Haag. 0165-9367.

BaghMit: Baghdader Mitteilungen DAI; Berlin.

BAH: Bibliothèque Archéologique et Historique (IFA-Beyrouth).

BAngIsr: Bulletin of the Anglo-Israel Archaeological Soc.; L. 0266-2442.

BangTF: Bangalore Theological Forum. [18 (1986)].

BaptQ: Baptist [Historical Soc.] Quarterly; Oxford. 0005-576X.

BArchAfr: Bulletin archéologique des travaux historiques et scientifiques (A. Antiquités nationales) B. Afrique du Nord: P.

BArchAlg: Bulletin d'Archéologie Algérienne; Alger.

BarIlAn: Bar-Ilan Annual; Ramat-Gan. 0067-4109.

BAR (-Int): British Archaeology Reports; Oxford.

BAR-W: Biblical Archaeology Review; Washington. 0098-9444.

BArte: Bollettino d'Arte; Roma.

BAsEspOr: Boletín de la Asociación Española de Orientalistas; Madrid.

BASOR: Bulletin of the American Schools of Oriental Research; CM. 0003-097X.

BASP: Bulletin, American Society of Papyrologists; NY. 0003-1186.

BAusPrax: Biblische Auslegung für die Praxis; Stuttgart.

Bazmaveb (Pazmavep; Armenian); Venezia.

BBArchäom: Berliner Beiträge zur Archäometrie; Berlin. 0344-5098. [6 (1985)].

BBB: ➤ BiBasB & BoBB.

BbbOr: Bibbia e Oriente; Bornato BS.

BBelgRom: Bulletin de l'Institut Historique Belge de Rome; R. 0073-8530. [59 (1989)].

BBudé: Bulletin de l'Association G. Budé; Paris.

BCanadB: Bulletin of the Canadian Society of Biblical Studies; Ottawa.

BCanMed: Bulletin of the Canadian Mediterranean Institute [= BCIM].

BCentPrei: Bollettino del Centro Camuno di Studi Preistorici; Brescia. 0057-2168.

BCentProt: Bulletin du Centre Protestant d'Études; Genève.

BCH: Bulletin de Correspondance Hellénique; Paris. 0007-4217.

BChinAc: Bulletin of the China Academy; Taipei.

BCILL: Bibliothèque des Cahiers de l'Institut de Linguistique; Lv, Peeters/P, Cerf.

BCNH-T: Bibliothèque Copte de Nag Hammadi -Textes; Québec.

BEcuT: Bulletin of ecumenical theology; Enugu, Nigeria [2,1 (1989)].

Bedi Kartlisa, (44) ➤ RÉtGC (1).

BeerSheva: ❹ Annual: Bible/ANE; J.

BÉF: Bibliothèque des Écoles françaises d'Athènes et de Rome; R. ➤ MÉF.

BEgS: Bulletin of the Egyptological Seminar; NY.

BeiATJ: Beiträge zur Erforschung des Alten Testaments und des Antiken Judentums; Bern. 0722-0790.

BeiAVgArch: Beiträge zur allgemeinen und vergleichenden Archäologie; Mü, Beck.

BeiBibExT: Beiträge zur biblischen Exegese und Theologie [ipsi: BET]; Frankfurt/M.

BeiEvT: Beiträge zur evangelischen Theologie; München.

BeiGbEx: Beiträge zur Geschichte der biblischen Exegese; Tübingen.

BeiHistT: Beiträge zur Historischen Theologie; Tübingen.

BeiNam: Beiträge zur Namenforschung N. F.; Heid. 0005-8114.

BeiÖkT: Beiträge zur ökumenischen Theologie: München, Schöningh. 0067-5172.

BeiRelT: Beiträge zur Religionstheologie; Mödling.

BeiSudan: Beiträge zur Sudanforschung; Wien, Univ.

Belleten (Türk Tarih Kurumu); Ankara.

Benedictina; Roma.

Berytus (Amer. Univ. Beirut); København.

BethM: ❸ Beth Mikra; Jerusalem. 0005-979X.

BÉtOr: Bulletin d'Études Orientales; Damas, IFAO.

BFaCLyon: Bulletin des Facultés Catholiques; Lyon. 0180-5282.

Bib ➤ Biblica; Roma. 0006-0887.

BibAfr: La Bible en Afrique [francophone]; Lomé, Togo.

BiBasB: Biblische Basis Bücher; Kevelaer/Stuttgart.

BiBei: Biblische Beiträge, Schweizerisches Kath. Bibelwerk; Fribourg.

BibFe: Biblia y Fe; Bibel Heute; Stu, KBW, M. 0210-5209.

BibIll: Biblical Illustrator; Nv.

BibKonf: Biblische Konfrontationen; Stu, Kohlhammer.

Bible Bhashyam: Kottayam. 0970-2288.

BiblEscB/EstB: Biblioteca Escuela Bíblica; M / de Estudios Bíblicos, Salamanca.

BiblETL: Bibliotheca, ETL; Leuven.

BiblHumRef: Bibliotheca Humanistica et Reformatorica; Nieuwkoop, de Graaf.

BiblHumRen: Bibliothèque d'Humanisme et Renaissance; Genève/ Paris.

Biblica: commentarii Pontificii Instituti Biblici; Roma. 0006-0887.

Biblica-Lisboa (Capuchinos: given also as Revista Bíblica).

BiblMesop: Bibliotheca Mesopotamica; Malibu CA.

Biblos 1. Coimbra; 2. Wien.

BiblScRel: Biblioteca di Scienze religiose; Roma, Salesiana.

BibNot: Biblische Notizen; Bamberg. 0178-2967.

BibOrPont: Biblica et Orientalia, Pontificio Istituto Biblico; Roma.

BibTB: Biblical Theology Bulletin; St. Bonaventure NY. 0146-1079.

BibTPaid: Biblioteca Teologica; Brescia, Paideia.

BibTSt: Biblisch-Theologische Studien; Neukirchen-Vluyn. 0930-4800.

BibUnt: Biblische Untersuchungen; Regensburg.

BICLyon: Bulletin de l'Institut Catholique de Lyon [cf. → RICathP].

BIFAO: Bulletin de l'Institut Français d'Archéologie Orientale; Le Caire. 0255-0962.

Bijd: Bijdragen, Filosofie en Theologie; Nijmegen.

BijH: Bijbels Handboek; Kampen → 784, = World of the Bible; GR → 3, 847.

BiKi: Bibel und Kirche; Stuttgart.

BInfWsz: Bulletin d'Information de l'Académie de Théologie Catholique; Warszawa. 0137-7000.

BInstArch: Bulletin of the Institute of Archaeology; London. 0076-0722.

BIP[Br]: Books in Print, U.S., annual; NY, Bowker [British, L, Whitaker].

BiRes: Biblical Research; Chicago. 0067-6535.

Biserica ... Ortodoxă Română; Bucureşti.

BIstFGrec: Bollettino dell'Istituto di Filologia Greca, Univ. di Padova; Roma.

Bits and bytes review; Whitefish MT.

BiWelt: Die Bibel in der Welt; Stu.

BJG: Bulletin of Judaeo-Greek Studies; Cambridge Univ. [1 (1987)].

BJRyL: Bulletin of the John Rylands Library; Manchester. 0301-102X.

BKAT: Biblischer Kommentar AT; Neuk.

BL: Book List, The Society for Old Testament Study. 0-905495-04-7.

BLCéramEg: Bulletin de liaison ... céramique égyptienne; Le Caire, IFAO. 0255-0903 [10 (1985)].

BLitEc [Chr]: Bulletin de Littérature Ecclésiastique [Chronique]. Toulouse. 0007-4322 [0495-9396].

BLtg: Bibel und Liturgie; Wien-Klosterneuburg.

BMB: Bulletin du Musée de Beyrouth.

BMes: Bulletin, the Society for Mesopotamian Studies; Toronto [2-4 (1982)].

BMonde → CahTrB.

BMosA [ipsi AIEMA]: Bulletin d'information de l'Association internationale pour l'étude de la mosaïque antique; Paris. 0761-8808.

BO: Bibliotheca Orientalis; Leiden. 0006-1913.

BoBB: Bonner Biblische Beiträge; Königstein.

BogSmot: Bogoslovska Smotra; Zagreb. 0352-3101.

BogTrud: ☉ Bogoslovskiye Trudi; Moskva.

BogVest: Bogoslovni Vestnik; Ljubljana [46 (1986)].

BonnJb: Bonner Jahrbücher.

Boreas [1. Uppsala, series]; 2. Münsterische Beiträge zur Archäologie. 0344-810X.

BOriento: Biblia kaj Oriento (Esperanto) [1 (1986)].

BPast: Biblical pastoral bulletin; Nairobi, BICAM. [6 (1987)].

BR: Bible Review; Wsh. 8755-6316 [1 (1985)].

BREF: Bibliographie religieuse en français; Dourgne → 1,1042*.

BRevuo → BOriento.

BritJREd: British Journal of Religious Education; London [5 (1983)].

BS: Bibliotheca Sacra; Dallas, TX. 0006-1921.

BSAA: Boletín del Seminario de Estudios de Arte y Arqueología; Valladolid.

BSAC: Bulletin de la Société d'Archéologie Copte; Le Caire.

BSeptCog: Bulletin of the International Organization for Septuagint and Cognate Studies; ND.

BSignR: Bulletin Signalétique, religions; Paris. 0180-9296.

BSLP: Bulletin de la Société de Linguistique; Paris.

BSNAm: Biblical Scholarship in North America; Atlanta, SBL.

BSNEJap ➤ Oriento.

BSOAS: Bulletin of the School of Oriental and African Studies; London. 0041-977X.

BSoc[Fr]Ég: Bulletin de la Société [Française] d'Égyptologie; Genève [Paris].

BSoGgIt: Bollettino della Società Geografica Italiana; R. 0037-8755.

BSpade: Bible and Spade; Ballston NY.

BSSulp: Bulletin [annuel] de Saint-Sulpice; Paris.

BStLat: Bollettino di Studi Latini; N.

BStor: Biblioteca di storia e storiografia dei tempi biblici; Brescia.

BSumAg: Bulletin on Sumerian Agriculture; Cambridge. 0267-0658.

BTAfr: Bulletin de Théologie Africaine; Kinshasa.

BTAM: Bulletin de Théologie Ancienne et Médiévale; Louvain. ➤ RTAM.

BThemT: Bibliothek Themen der Theologie; Stuttgart.

BToday: The Bible Today; Collegeville MN. 0006-0836.

BTrans: The Bible Translator [Technical/ Practical, each 2 annually]; Stuttgart. 0260-0943.

BtSt: Biblisch-theologische Studien (ex-Biblische Studien); Neukirchen.

BTT: Bible de tous les temps; P.

BTZ: Berliner Theologische Zeitschrift; Berlin. 0724-6137.

BUBS: Bulletin of the United Bible Societies; Stu.

BudCSt: Buddhist-Christian Studies; Honolulu, Univ. 0882-0945 [4 (1984)].

Burgense; Burgos.

BurHist: Buried History; Melbourne.

BVieChr: Bible et Vie Chrétienne NS; Paris.

BViewp: Biblical Viewpoint; Greenville SC, B. Jones Univ. 0006-0925.

BWANT: Beiträge zur Wissenschaft vom Alten und Neuen Testament; Stuttgart.

BySlav: Byzantinoslavica; Praha. 0007-7712.

ByZ: Byzantinische Zeitschrift; München. 0007-7704.

Ⓖ Byzantina; Thessaloniki.

Byzantion; Bruxelles.

ByzFor: Byzantinische Forschungen; Amsterdam. 90-256-0619-9.

BZ: Biblische Zeitschrift; Paderborn. 0006-2014.

BZA[N]W: Beihefte zur ➤ ZAW[ZNW].

CAD: [Chicago] Assyrian Dictionary; Glückstadt. ➤ 890.

CADIR: Centre pour l'Analyse du Discours Religieux; Lyon ➤ SémBib.

CAH: Cambridge Ancient History [rev]; Cambridge Univ. ➤ 785.

CahArchéol: Cahiers Archéologiques; Paris. 2-7084-0131-9.

CahCMéd: Cahiers de Civilisation Médiévale; Poitiers.

CahDAFI: Cahiers de la Délégation Archéologique Française en Iran; Paris. 0765-104X.

CahÉv: Cahiers Évangile; Paris. 0222-8741.

CahHist: Cahiers d'Histoire; Lyon.

CahIntSymb: Cahiers Internationaux de Symbolique; Mons, Belgique.

CahLV: Cahiers voor Levensverdieping; Averbode.

CahRechScRel: Cahiers de Recherche en Sciences de la Religion; Québec.

CahRenan: Cahiers du Cercle Ernest Renan; Paris.

CahSpIgn: Cahiers de spiritualité ignatienne; Québec.

CahSPR: Cahiers de l'École des Sciences Philosophiques et Religieuses, Fac. Univ. St-Louis; Bru [3s (1988)].

CahTrB: Cahiers de traduction biblique; Pierrefitte France. 0755-1371.

CahTun: Les Cahiers (de la Faculté des Lettres) de Tunisie; Tunis.

CalvaryB: Calvary Baptist Theological Journal; Lansdale PA. 8756-0429 [1 (1985)].

CalvinT: Calvin Theological Journal; Grand Rapids MI. 0008-1795.

CalwTMon: Calwer Theologische Monographien (A: Biblisch); Stuttgart.

CamCW: Cambridge Commentary on Writings of the Jewish and Christian World 200 BC to AD 200: C. 0-521-28554-2.

CanadCR: Canadian Catholic Review; Saskatoon.

Carmel: Tilburg.

Carmelus: Roma. 0008-6673.

CARNES: Computer-aided research in Near Eastern Studies; Malibu CA. 0742-2334.

Carthaginensia; Murcia, Inst. Teol. 0213-4381 [1 (1985)].

CathCris: Catholicism in crisis; ND.

CathHR: Catholic Historical Review; Wsh. 0008-8080.

Catholica (Moehler-Institut, Paderborn); Münster.

Catholicisme: Paris ➤ 786.

Catholic Studies, Tokyo ➤ Katorikku.

CathTR: Catholic Theological Review; Clayton, Australia (NTAbs 30,150: Hong Kong) [6 (1984)].

CathTSocAmPr: ➤ PrCTSAm [AnCTS].

CATSS: Computer assisted tools for Septuagint studies: Atlanta ➤ SBL.

CBQ: Catholic Biblical Quarterly; Washington, DC. 0008-7912.

CC: La Civiltà Cattolica; R. 0009-8167.

CCGraec/Lat/Med: Corpus Christianorum, series graeca / latina / continuatio mediaev.; Turnhout.

CdÉ: Chronique d'Égypte; Bruxelles.

CédCarthB: Centre d'Études et de Documentation de la Conservation de Carthage, Bulletin; Tunis.

Center Journal; Notre Dame.

CERDAC: (Atti) Centro di Ricerca e Documentazione Classica; Milano.

CETÉDOC: Centre de Traitement Électronique des Documents; Lv.

CGL: Coptic Gnostic Library ➤ NHS.

CGMG: Christlicher Glaube in moderner Gesellschaft; FrB.

ChCu: Church and Culture; Vatican [1 (1984)].

ChH: Church History; Berne, Ind.

CHH: Center for Hermeneutical Studies in Hellenistic and Modern Culture; Berkeley CA.

Chiea [ChAfC]: Nairobi, Catholic Higher Institute of Eastern Africa.

Chiron: Geschichte, Epigraphie; München.

CHistEI: ❸ Cathedra, History of Eretz-Israel; Jerusalem.

CHist-J: Jerusalem Cathedra.

CHJud: Cambridge History of Judaism; C ➤ 789.

Chm: Churchman 1. (Anglican); London: 0009-661X / 2. (Humanistic); St. Petersburg FL: 0009-6628.

ChrCent: Christian Century; Chicago. Christus; 1. Paris; 2. México.

ChrJRel: Christian Jewish Relations; L.

ChrNIsr: Christian News from Israel; J.

ChrOost: Het Christelijk Oosten; Nijmegen.

ChrSchR: Christian Scholar's Review; Houston TX.

ChrT: Christianity Today; Carol Stream IL. 0009-5761.

ChSt: Chicago Studies; Mundelein IL.

Church: NY, Nat. Pastoral Life.

ChWoman: The Church Woman [Protestant, Roman Catholic, Orthodox, other Christian]; NY. 0009-6598.

CistSt: Cistercian Studies; ed. Getsemani KY; pub. Chimay, Belgium.

Citeaux; Achel, Belgium. 0009-7497.

Cithara: Essays in the Judaeo-Christian Tradition; St. Bonaventure (NY) Univ.

CiTom: Ciencia Tomista; Salamanca.

CiuD: Ciudad de Dios; M. 0009-7756.

CivClCr: Civiltà classica e cristiana; Genova. 0392-8632.

CiVit: Città di Vita; Firenze. [0]009-7632.

Claret: Claretianum; Roma.

ClasA: [formerly California Studies in] Classical Antiquity; Berkeley.

ClasB: Classical Bulletin; Ch. 0009-8137.

ClasJ: Classical Journal; Greenville SC. 0009-8353.

ClasMed: Classica et Mediaevalia; København. 0106-5815.

ClasModL: Classical and Modern Literature; Terre Haute IN.

ClasOutl: The Classical Outlook; Ch [ed. Miami Univ. OH]. 0009-8361.

ClasPg: Classical Philology; Chicago. 0009-8361.

ClasQ: Classical Quarterly NS; Oxford. 0009-8388.

ClasR: Classical Review NS; Oxford. 0009-840X.

ClasWo: Classical World; Pittsburgh. 0009-8148.

CLehre: Die Christenlehre; Berlin.

CleR: Clergy Rev. [➤ PrPeo 1 (1987)].

ClubH: Club des Hébraïsants; Boran.

CMatArch: Contributi e materiali di archeologia orientale; Roma, Univ. [1 (1986)].

CNRS: Conseil National de Recherche Scientifique; Paris.

CogF: Cogitatio Fidei; Paris.

ColcCist: Collectanea Cisterciensia; Forges, Belgique.

ColcFranc: Collectanea Franciscana; Roma. 0010-0749.

ColcT: Collectanea Theologica; Warszawa. 0137-6985.

ColcTFu: Collectanea theol. Universitatis Fujen = *Shenhsileh Lunchi*; Taipei.

CollatVL: Collationes, Vlaams ... Theologie en Pastoraal; Gent.

Colloquium; Auckland, Sydney.

ColStFen: Collezione di Studi Fenici; Roma, Univ.

ComLtg: Communautés et Liturgies; Ottignies (Belgique).

Commentary; NY. 0010-2601.

CommBras: Communio Brasiliensis: Rio de Janeiro.

CommND: Communio USA; Notre Dame. 0094-2065.

CommRevue: Communio [various languages, not related to **ComSev**]: revue catholique internationale; Paris.

CommStrum: Communio, strumento internazionale per un lavoro teologico; Milano.

Communio deutsch ➤ **IkaZ.**

ComOT: Commentaar op het Oude Testament. Kampen.

CompHum: Computers and the Humanities; Osprey FL. 0010-4817.

ComplNT: Compendium rerum Iudaicarum ad NT; Assen.

Compostellanum; Santiago de Compostela.

ComRatisbNT: Comentario de Ratisbona; Barc.

ComRelM: Commentarium pro Religiosis et Missionariis; Roma.

ComSev: Communio; Sevilla. 0010-3705.

ComSpirAT/NT: Commenti spirituali dell'Antico / Nuovo Testamento; Roma.

ComTeolNT: Commentario Teologico del NT; Brescia.

ComViat: Communio Viatorum; Praha. 0010-7133.

ConBib: Coniectanea Biblica OT/NT; Malmö.

Conc: Concilium, variis linguis; P,E, etc. [deutsch = ➤ IZT].

ConcordJ: Concordia Journal; St. Louis. 0145-7233.

ConcordTQ: Concordia Theological Quarterly; Fort Wayne.

ConoscRel: Conoscenza religiosa; Firenze.

Consensus: Canadian Lutheran; Winnipeg.

ConsJud: Conservative Judaism; NY. 0010-6542.

Contracts/Orthodoxe, de théologie et spiritualité; P. 0045-8325.

ContrIstStorAnt: Contributi dell'Istituto di Storia Antica; Milano, Univ. Sacro Cuore.

Coptologia [also for Egyptology]: Thunder Bay ONT, Lakehead Univ.

CouStR: Council for the Study of Religion Bulletin; Macon GA, Mercer Univ.

CovQ: Covenant Quarterly; Chicago.

CRAI: Comptes rendus de l'Académie des Inscriptions et Belles-Lettres; Paris.

Creation; Oakland CA.

Cretan Studies; Amst. [1 (1988) 90-256-0949-X; 52-X].

CRIPEL: Cahiers de Recherches de l'Institut de Papyrologie et d'Égyptologie de Lille [7 (1985)].

CriswT: Criswell Theological Review; Dallas [1 (1986)].

Criterio; Buenos Aires. 0011-1473.

CrkvaSv: Crkva u Svijetu; Split.

CrNSt: Cristianesimo nella Storia; Bologna. 0393-3598.

CroatC: Croatica Christiana; Zagreb.

CrossC: Cross Currents; West Nyack NJ. 0011-1953.

Crux: Vancouver. 0011-2186.

CSacSN: Corpus Sacrae Scripturae Neerlandicae Medii Aevi; Leiden.

CSCO: Corpus Scriptorum Christianorum Orientalium; Lv. 0070-0401.

CuadJer: Cuadernos Bíblicos, Institución S. Jerónimo; Valencia.

CuadFgClás: Cuadernos de Filología Clásica; M, Univ.

CuadTeol: Cuadernos de Teología; Buenos Aires [6,3 (1983)].

CuadTrad: Cuadernos de Traducción y Interpretación; Barc.

CuBíb: Cultura Bíblica; M: AFEBE. 0211-2493.

CuesT: Cuestiones Teológicas; Medellín [14 (1987)].

CurrTMiss: Currents in Theology and Mission; St. Louis. 0098-2113.

CyrMeth: Cyrillomethodianum; Thessaloniki.

ᴰ: director (in Indice etiam *auctor*) Dissertationis.

DAFI: Délégation Archéologique Française en Iran (Mém); Paris.

DAI: Deutsches Archäologisches Institut (Baghdad etc.) → Mi(tt).

DanTTs: Dansk Teologisk Tidsskrift; København.

DanVMed/Skr: Det Kongelige Danske Videnskabornes Selskap, Historisk-Filosofiske Meddelelser / Skriften; K.

DBS [= SDB], Dictionnaire de la Bible, Supplément; P → 809.

Dedalo: São Paulo.

DeltChr: Deltion tes christianikēs archaiologikēs hetaireias: Athēna [4,12 (for 1984: 1986)].

DeltVM: ⓖ Deltío vivlikôn meletôn (= Bulletin des Études Bibliques); Athēnai.

DHGE: Dictionnaire d'Histoire et de Géographie Ecclésiastiques; P → 790.

Diachronica, international journal for historical linguistics; Hildesheim [1 (1984)].

Diakonia; Mainz/Wien [13 (1982)] 0341-9592; Stu [8 (1982)].

DialArch: Dialoghi di Archeologia; Mi.

DiálEcum: Diálogo Ecuménico; Salamanca. 0210-2870.

Dialog; Minneapolis. 0012-2033.

DialTP: Diálogo teológico; El Paso TX.

DictSpir: Dictionnaire de Spiritualité; P. → 852.

Didascalia; Rosario ARG.

Didaskalia; Lisboa.

DielB: Dielheimer Blätter zum Alten Testament [ipsi DBAT]; Heid.

Dionysius: Halifax, Dalhousie University. 0705-1085.

Direction; Fresno CA.

DiscEg: Discussions in Egyptology; Oxford. 0268-3083 [1 (1985)].

Disciple, the (Disciples of Christ); St. Louis. 0092-8372.

Diss [= ᴰ, etiam Director]: Dissertation.

DissA: Dissertation Abstracts International; AA/L. -A [= US]: 0419-4209 [C = Europe. 0307-6075].

DissHRel: Dissertationes ad historiam religionum (supp. Numen); Leiden.

Divinitas, Pont. Acad. Theol. Rom. (Lateranensis); Vaticano. 0012-4222.

DivThom: Divus Thomas; Piacenza. 0012-4257.

DJD: Discoveries in the Judaean Desert; Oxford.

DLZ: Deutsche Literaturzeitung; Berlin. 0012-043X.

DMA: Dictionary of the Middle Ages; NY.

DocCath: Documentation Catholique; Paris.

DoctCom: Doctor Communis; Vaticano.

DoctLife: Doctrine and Life; Dublin.

DOG: Deutsche Orient-Gesellschaft: B.

Dor: Dor le Dor; J, World Jewish.

DosB: Les dossiers de la Bible; P.

DossHA: Histoire et archéologie, les dossiers; Dijon.

DowR: Downside Review; Bath. 0012-5806.

DPA: Dizionario patristico e di antichità cristiane; Casale Monferrato → 793.

DrevVost: ⓥ Drevnij Vostok; Moskva.

DrewG: The Drew [Theological School] Gateway; Madison NJ.

DumbO: Dumbarton Oaks Papers; CM. 0070-7546.

DutchMgA: Dutch Monographs in Ancient History and Archaeology; Amst.

ᴱ: editor, Herausgeber, *a cura di*.

EAfJE: East African Journal of Evangelical Theology; Machakos, Kenya.

EAsJT: East Asia Journal of Theology [combining NE & SE AJT]; Tokyo. 0217-3859.

EAPast: East Asian Pastoral Review; Manila. 0040-0564.

ÉcAnn: Écoutez et Annoncez, mensuel; Lomé, Togo [6 (1984)].

ÉchMClas: Échos du Monde Classique/ Classical Views; Calgary. 0012-9356.

ÉchSM: Les Échos de Saint-Maurice; Valais, Abbaye.

EcOr: Ecclesia Orans, periodica de scientiis liturgicis; R, Anselmiano [1,1 (1984)].

ÉcoutBib: Écouter la Bible; Paris.

EcuR: Ecumenical Review; Geneva. 0013-0790.

EfMex: Efemerides Mexicana; Tlalpan.

Egb: Ergänzungsband.

ÉglRur après 488 (1987) ➤ Sève.

ÉglT: Église et Théologie; Ottawa.

EgVO: Egitto e Vicino Oriente; Pisa.

ÉHRel: Études d'histoire des religions.

Einzb: Einzelband.

EkK [Vor]: Evangelischer-katholischer Kommentar zum NT; Z/Köln; Neukirchen-Vluyn ['Vorarbeiten'].

EkkT: Ⓖ Ekklēsía kaì Theología; L.

Elenchos, ... pensiero antico; Napoli.

Elliniká; Ⓖ Thessaloniki.

Emerita: (lingüística clásica); M.

Emmanuel: St. Meinrads IN/NY. 0013-6719.

Enc. Biblica ➤ EnșMiqr.

EncHebr: Ⓗ Encyclopaedia Hebraica; J/TA.

Enchoria, Demotistik/Koptologie; Wiesbaden. 3-447-02807-6.

EncIran: Encyclopaedia Iranica; London [I,1 (1982)] ➤ 874.

EncIslam: Encyclopédie de l'Islam. Nouvelle édition; Leiden/P ➤ 794.

EncKat: Encyklopedia Katolicka; Lublin ➤ 2,584*.

Encounter (theol.); Indianapolis.

EncRel: (1) E*Eliade* M., The encyclopedia of religion; NY ➤ 795; (2) Enciclopedia delle Religioni; Firenze.

EnșMiqr: Ⓗ Enșiqlopediya miqrā'ît, Encyclopaedia Biblica; Jerusalem.

Entschluss: Wien. 0017-4602.

EnzMär: Enzyklopädie des Märchens; B ➤ 3, 860.

EOL: Ex Oriente Lux ➤ 1.Jb/2. Phoenix.

Eos, ... philologia; Wsz. 0012-7825.

EpAnat: Epigraphica anatolica; Bonn.

ÉPHÉ[H/R]: École Pratique des Hautes-Études, Annuaire [Hist.-Pg. / Sc. Rel.]; Paris.

EpHetVyzSpoud: Ⓖ Ephēmeris tēs Hetaireías tōn Vyzantinōn Spoudōn; Athēnai.

EphLtg: Ephemerides Liturgicae; R.

EphMar: Ephemerides Mariologicae; Madrid.

ÉPR: Études préliminaires aux religions orientales dans l'Empire romain; Leiden.

Eranos[/Jb]: Acta Philologica Suecana; Uppsala / Jahrbuch; Frankfurt/M (< Z).

ErbAuf: Erbe und Auftrag; Beuron.

Eretz-Israel (partly Ⓗ), 'annual'; Jerusalem. 0071-108X.

ErfTSt/Schr: Erfurter Theologische Studien/ Schriften.

ErtFor: Ertrag der Forschung; Da, Wiss. 0174-0695.

EscrVedat: Escritos del Vedat [del Torrente]; Valencia. 0210-3133.

EsprVie: Esprit et Vie: 1. [< Ami du Clergé]; Langres; 2. (series) Chambray.

EstAgust: Estudio Agustiniano; Valladolid.

EstBíb: Estudios Bíblicos; Madrid. 0014-1437.

EstDeusto: Estudios Universidad Deusto: Madrid.

EstE: Estudios Eclesiásticos; Madrid. 0210-1610.

EstFranc: Estudios Franciscanos; Barcelona.

EsTGuat: Estudios Teológicos; Guatemala.

EstJos: Estudios Josefinos; Valladolid.

EstLul: Estudios Lulianos; Mallorca.

EstMar: Estudios Marianos; Madrid.

EstMonInstJer: Estudios y Monografias, Institución S. Jerónimo (bíblica); Valencia.

EstTrin: Estudios Trinitarios; Salamanca.

EstudosB: Estudos Bíblicos; Petrópolis [no longer part of **REB**].

ÉtBN: Études Bibliques, Nouvelle Série; Paris. 0760-3541.

ÉtClas: Les études classiques; Namur. 0014-200X.

Eternity; Philadelphia [34 (1983)].

ÉtFranc: Études Franciscaines; Blois.

ÉtIndE: Études Indo-Européennes; Lyon.

ETL: Ephemerides Theologicae Lovanienses; Leuven. 0013-9513.

ÉtPapyr: Études [Société Égyptienne] de Papyrologie; Le Caire.

ÉtPgHist: Études de Philologie et d'Histoire; Genève, Droz.

ÉTRel: Études Théologiques et Religieuses; Montpellier. 0014-2239.

ÉtTrav: Études et Travaux; Varsovie.

Études; Paris. 0014-1941.

Euhemer (**Ⓟ** hist. rel.); Warszawa. 0014-2298

EuntDoc: Euntes Docete; Roma.

EurHS: Europäische Hochschulschriften / Publ. Universitaires Européennes; Bern.

Evangel; Edinburgh. 0265-4547.

EvErz: Der evangelische Erzieher; Frankfurt/M. 0014-3413.

EvJ: Evangelical Journal; Myerstown PA [3 (1985)].

EvKL: Evangelisches Kirchenlexikon; → 798.

EvKom: Evangelische Kommentare; Stuttgart. 0300-4236.

EvQ[RT]: Evangelical Quarterly [Review of Theology]; Exeter.

EvT: Evangelische Theologie, NS; München. 0014-3502.

EWest: East and West | 1. L / 2. R.

EWSp: Encyclopedia of World Spirituality; NY/L.

ExAud: Ex auditu, ongoing symposium annual: Princeton (sb. Pickwick) 0883-0053 → 567.

ExcSIsr: Excavations and Surveys in Israel → Ḥadašot; Jerusalem. [Winona Lake: Eisenbrauns $10]. 0334-1607.

Expedition (archaeol., anthrop.); Philadelphia. 0014-4738.

Explor [sic]; Evanston. 0362-0876.

ExpTim: The Expository Times; Edinburgh. 0014-5246.

F&R: Faith and Reason; Front Royal VA. 0098-5449.

FascBíb: Fascículos bíblicos; Madrid.

Faventia: classica; Barc. 0210-7570.

fg./fil.: filologico, filosofico.

FgNt: Filologia neotestamentaria; Córdoba, Univ. [1 (1988)].

FidH: Fides et Historia; Longview TX [20 (1988)].

FilRTSt: Filosofia della Religione, Testi e Studi; Brescia.

FilT: Filosofia e teologia; Napoli. [2 (1988)].

Fønix [6 (1982)].

FoiTemps: La Foi et le Temps. NS; Tournai.

FoiVie: Foi et Vie; Paris. 0015-5357.

FolOr: Folia Orientalia, Polska Akademia Nauk; Kraków. 0015-5675.

Fondamenti; Brescia, Paideia [4 (1986)].

ForBib: Forschung zur Bibel; Wü/Stu.

ForBMusB: Forschungen und Berichte, Staatliche Museen zu Berlin.

ForGLehrProt: Forschungen zur Geschichte und Lehre des Protestantismus; Mü.

ForJüdChrDial: Forschungen zum jüdisch-christlichen Dialog; Neuk.

ForKiDG: Forschungen zur Kirchen- und Dogmengeschichte; Gö.

Fornvännen (Svensk Antikvarisk Forskning); Lund. 0015-7813.

ForSystÖ: Forschungen zur Systematischen & Ökumenischen Theologie; Gö.

ForTLing: Forum Theologiae Linguisticae; Bonn.

Forum [= Foundations & Facets]; Bonner MT. 0883-4970.

ForumKT: Forum Katholische Theologie; Münster. 0178-1626 [1 (1985)].

FOTLit: Forms of OT Literature; GR, Eerdmans.

FraJudBei: Frankfurter Judaistische Beiträge: Fra.

FranBog: Franciscanum, ciencias del espíritu; Bogotá. 0120-1468.

FrancSt: Franciscan Studies; St. Bonaventure, NY. 0080-5459.

FranzSt: Franziskanische Studien; Pd.

FraTSt: Frankfurter Theologische Studien; Fra, S. Georgen.

FreibRu: Freiburger Rundbrief. ... christlich-jüdische Begegnung; FrB.

FreibTSt: Freiburger Theologische Studien; Freiburg/Br.

FreibZ: Freiburger Zeitschrift für Philosophie und Theologie; Fribourg/Suisse.

FRLANT: Forschungen zur Religion und Literatur des Alten und NTs; Gö.

FutUo: Il futuro dell'uomo; Firenze, Assoc. Teilhard. 0390-217X [12 (1985)].

Ⓖ *Graece*; title in Greek.

GCS: Die Griechischen Christlichen Schriftsteller der ersten Jahrhunderte; oBerlin.

GDE / UTET: Grande dizionario enciclopedico; Torino, Unione Tipografica.

GdT: Giornale di Teologia; Brescia.

GeistL: Geist und Leben; Wü.

Genava (archéologie, hist. art); Genève. 0072-0585.

GenLing: General Linguistics; University Park PA.

Georgica: Jena/Tbilissi. 0232-4490.

GerefTTs: Gereformeerd Theologisch Tijdschrift; Kampen. 0016-8610.

Gerión, revista de Historia Antigua; Madrid, Univ. 0213-0181.

GGA: Göttingische Gelehrte Anzeigen; Göttingen. 0017-1549.

GidsBW: Gidsen bij de Bijbelwetenschap; Kampen, Kok.

GItFg: Giornale italiano di filologia; Napoli. 0017-0461.

GLÉCS: (Comptes rendus) Groupe Linguistique d'Études Chamito-Sémitiques; Paris.

GLern: Glaube und Lernen; Zeitschrift für theologische Urteilsbildung; Göttingen, VR [2 (1987)].

GLeven: Geest en leven [continuing OnsGLev] 65 (1988); Eindhoven.

GLNT: Grande Lessico del NT (< TWNT); Brescia → 862*.

Glotta: griech.-lat.; Göttingen. 0017-1298.

Gnomon; klass. Altertum; München. 0017-1417.

GöMiszÄg: Göttinger Miszellen ... zur ägyptologischen Diskussion; Göttingen. 0344-385X.

GöOrFor: Göttinger Orientforschungen; Würzburg.

GöTArb: Göttinger Theologische Arbeiten; Göttingen.

GraceTJ: Grace Theological Journal; Winona Lake IN. 0198-666X.

GraecChrPrim: Graecitas Christianorum Primaeva; Nijmegen, van der Vegt.

Grail, ecumenical quarterly; Waterloo ONT, St. Jerome's College [1,1 (1985)].

GrArab: Graeco-Arabica; Athenai.

GreeceR: Greece and Rome; Oxford.

Greg[LA]: Gregorianum; R, Pontificia Universitas Gregoriana [Liber Annualis].

GrenzfTP: Grenzfragen zwischen Theologie und Philosophie; Köln.

GRIC: Groupe de recherches islamo-chrétien; P.

GrOrTR: Greek Orthodox Theological Review; Brookline MA. 0017-3894.

GrPT: Growing Points in Theology.

GrRByz: Greek, Roman and Byzantine Studies; CM. 0017-3916.

GrSinal: Grande Sinal, revista de espiritualidade; Petrópolis.

Gymn: Gymnasium; Heid. 0342-5231.

Ⓗ *(Neo-)hebraice*; (modern) Hebrew.

HaBeiA: Hamburger Beiträge zur Archäologie. 0341-3152.

Ḥadašôt arkeologiyôt **Ⓗ** [News]; J, Education ministry museum dept. → ExcSIsr.

HalleB: Hallesche Beiträge zur Orientwissenschaft; Halle. 0233-2205.

Hamdard Islamicus [research]; Pakistan. 0250-7196.

Handes Amsorya [armen.]; Wien.

HarvSemMon/Ser: Harvard Semitic Monographs / (Museum) Series; CM.

HarvStClasPg: Harvard Studies in Classical Philology; CM.

HarvTR: The Harvard Theological Review; CM. 0017-8160.

HbAltW: Handbuch der Altertumswissenschaft; München.

HbAT/NT: Handbuch zum Alten/Neuen Testament; Tübingen.

HbDG: Handbuch der Dogmengeschichte; Freiburg/B.; → 1,896.

HbDTG: Handbuch der Dogmen- und Theologiegeschichte; Göttingen → 799.

HbOr: Handbuch der Orientalistik; Leiden.

HbRelG: Handbuch der Religionsgeschichte; Göttingen.

HDienst: Heiliger Dienst; Salzburg. 0017-9620.

HebAnR: Hebrew Annual Review; Columbus, Ohio State Univ.

HebBWJud: Hebräische Beiträge zur Wissenschaft des Judentums deutsch angezeigt: Heidelberg. [1/1s (1985)].

HebSt: Hebrew Studies; Madison WI. 0146-4094.

Helikon (Tradizione e Cultura Classica, Univ. Messina); Roma.
Hellenika; Bochum. 0018-0084; ➤ *Elliniká*.
Helmántica (humanidades clásicas, Univ.); Salamanca.
Henceforth, journal for Advent Christian thought; Lenox MA [14 (1985s)].
Henoch (ebraismo): Torino (Univ.).
Hephaistos, Theorie / Praxis Arch.; Ha.
HerdKor: Herder-Korrespondenz; Freiburg/Br. 0018-0645.
HerdTKom, NT: Herders Theologischer Kommentar zum NT; FrB.
Heresis, revue d'hérésiologie médiévale; Villegly/Carcassonne, Centre Nat. Ét. Cathares. 0758-3737 [4s (1985)].
Hermathena; Dublin. 0018-0750.
Hermeneus, antieke cultuur; Amersfoort.
Hermeneutica; Urbino, Univ.
Hermes, Klassische Philologie; Wiesbaden. 0018-0777.
HermUnT: Hermeneutische Untersuchungen zur Theologie; Tü. 0440-7180.
HervTS: Hervormde Teologiese Studies; Pretoria.
Hesperia (American School of Classical Studies at Athens); Princeton. 0018-098X.
Hethitica. Travaux édités; Lv.
HeythJ: Heythrop Journal; London. 0018-1196.
HistJ: Historical Journal; Cambridge.
HistJb: Historisches Jahrbuch; Mü.
Historia; 1. Baden-Baden: 0018-2311; 2. Santiago, Univ. Católica Chile.
HistRel: History of Religions; Chicago. 0018-2710.
HLand[S]: Das Heilige Land (Deutscher Verein) Köln [(Schw. Verein); Luzern].
Hokhma; Lausanne. 0379-7465.
HolyL: Holy Land: J, OFM. 0333-4851 [5 (1985)]. ➤ **TerraS.**
Homoousios (consustancial); Buenos Aires, Ortodoxía antioquena [1 (1986)].
HomPastR: Homiletic and Pastoral Review; New York. 0018-4268.
HomRel: Homo religiosus (histoire des religions); Louvain-la-Neuve.

HorBibT: Horizons in Biblical Theology (Old & NT); Pittsburgh. 0195-9085.
Horeb: Histoire Orientation Recherche Exégèse Bible; Sèvres.
Horizons (College Theology Society); Villanova PA. 0360-9669.
Hsientai Hsüehyüan (= Universitas); Taipei.
HSprF: Historische Sprachforschung ab 101 (1988) = **ZvglSpr.** 0044-3646.
HUC|A: Hebrew Union College [+ Jewish Institute of Religion] Annual; Cincinnati.
Humanitas; 1. Brescia; 2. Tucuman.
HumT: Humanística e Teologia; Porto [6 (1985)].
HWomenRel: History of women religious, news and notes; St. Paul MN. [1,3 (1988)].
Hydra, Middle Bronze Age studies; Uppsala, Univ. [1 (1985)].
Hypom: Hypomnemata; Göttingen, VR.
HZ: Historische Zeitschrift; München. 0018-2613.
IAJS: ➤ **RAMBI.**
IBMiss: International (formerly Occasional) Bulletin of Missionary Research; Minneapolis (Lutheran).
ICC: International Critical Commentary; Edinburgh.
ICI: Informations Catholiques Internationales; Paris.
IClasSt: Illinois Classical Studies; Urbana. 0363-1923 [11 (1985)].
IFA: Institut Français d'Archéologie (Orientale, Le Caire / Beyrouth).
IglV: Iglesia Viva; Valencia/Madrid.
IkaZ: Internationale Kath. Zeitschrift, Communio; Rodenkirchen. 0341-8693.
IkiZ: Internationale kirchliche Zeitschrift; Bern. 0020-9252.
ILN: Illustrated London News; London. 0019-2422.
Immanuel (ecumenical); J. 0302-8127.
Index Jewish Studies ➤ **RAMBI.**
IndIranJ: Indo-Iranian Journal; (Canberra-) Leiden. 0019-7246.
IndJT: Indian Journal of Theology; Serampore.
IndMissR: Indian Missiological Review; Shillong. [7 (1985)].

IndogF: Indogermanische Forschungen; Berlin. 0019-7262.

IndTSt: Indian Theological Studies; Bangalore, St. Peter's.

InnsBeiKultW/SpraW/TS: Innsbrucker Beiträge zur Kulturwissenschaft / Sprachwissenschaft / Theologische Studien.

Inst. Jerón. ➤ EstMon.

IntBbg[R/Z]: Internationale Bibliographie | der Rezensionen wissenschaftlicher Literatur [10 (1980)] / der Zeitschriftenliteratur aus allen Gebieten des Wissens [16 (1980)]; Osnabrück.

IntCathRCom ➤ CommND.

Interp: Interpretation; Richmond VA. 0020-9643.

IntJNaut: International Journal of Nautical Archaeology L/NY. 0305-7445.

IntJPhR: International Journal for the Philosophy of Religion; The Hague.

IntJSport: International Journal of the history of sport; L. [5 (1988)].

IntRMiss: International Review of Mission; London. 0020-8582.

Iran; London, British Institute Persian Studies. 0578-6967.

IrAnt: Iranica Antiqua; Leiden.

Iraq; L, British School of Archaeology. 0021-0889.

IrBSt: Irish Biblical Studies; Belfast. 0268-6112.

Irén: Irénikon; Chevetogne. 0021-0978.

IrTQ: Irish Theological Quarterly; Maynooth. 0021-1400.

ISBEnc: International Standard Bible Encyclopedia³; GR, Eerdmans ➤ 801.

Islam, Der: Berlin. 0021-1818.

Islamochristiana; Roma, Pontificio Istituto di Studi Arabi. 0392-7288.

IsrEJ: Israel Exploration Journal; Jerusalem. 0021-2059.

IsrJBot/Zool: Israel Journal of Botany 0021-213X / Zoology 0021-2210: Jerusalem.

IsrLawR: Israel Law Review; Jerusalem. 0021-2237.

IsrMusJ: Israel Museum Journal; Jerusalem.

IsrNumJ[SocB]: Israel Numismatic Journal, J [Society Bulletin: TA].

IsrOrSt: Israel Oriental Studies; Tel Aviv.

Istina; Paris. 0021-2423.

IVRA (Jura); Napoli.

IZBG: Internationale Zeitschriftenschau für Bibelwissenschaft und Grenzgebiete; Pd. 0074-9745.

IZT: Internationale Zeitschrift für Theologie [= Concilium deutsch].

JAAR: Journal of the American Academy of Religion; Atlanta. 0002-7189.

J[News]AmEg: Journal [Newsletter] of the American Research Center in Egypt; Winona Lake IN.

JAmScAff: Journal of the American Scientific Affiliation (evang.); Ipswich MA. 0003-0988.

JANES: Journal of the Ancient Near Eastern Society; NY, Jewish Theol. Sem. 0010-2016.

JanLing[Pract]: Janua Linguarum [Series Practica]; The Hague / Paris.

JAOS: Journal of the American Oriental Society; NHv. 0003-0279.

JapJRelSt: Japanese Journal of Religious Studies; Nagoya.

JapRel: Japanese Religions; Tokyo.

JArchSc: Journal of Archaeological Science; London/New York.

JAs: Journal Asiatique; P. 0021-762X.

JAsAf: Journal of Asian and African Studies (York Univ., Toronto); Leiden.

Javeriana ➤ TXav.

Jb: Jahrbuch [Heid, Mainz...]; Jaarbericht.

JbAC: Jahrbuch für Antike und Christentum; Münster i. W.

JbBerlMus: Jahrbücher der Berliner Museen; wBerlin.

JbBTh: Jahrbuch für biblische Theologie; Neukirchen.

JbEOL: Jaarbericht van het Vooraziatisch-Egyptisch Genootschap Ex Oriente Lux; Leiden.

JBL: Journal of Biblical Literature; Atlanta. 0021-9231.

JBlackT: Journal of Black Theology; Atteridgeville SAf. [1 (1987)].

JbLtgH: Jahrbuch für Liturgik und Hymnologie; Kassel. [3-7982-0182-X: 4 (1984)].

JbNumG: Jahrbuch für Numismatik und Geldgeschichte; Regensburg.

JbÖsByz: Jahrbuch der Österreichischen Byzantinistik; W. 0378-8660.

JbRP: Jahrbuch der Religionspädagogik; Neukirchen [2 (1985)].

JChrEd: Journal of Christian Education; Sydney. 0021-9657 [82s (1985)].

JCS: Journal of Cuneiform Studies; CM. 0022-0256.

JDharma: Journal of Dharma; Bangalore.

JdU: Judentum und Umwelt; Frankfurt/M.

JEA: Journal of Egyptian Archaeology; London. 0307-5133.

JEcuSt: Journal of Ecumenical Studies; Ph, Temple Univ. 0022-0558.

Jeevadhara; Alleppey, Kerala.

JEH: Journal of Ecclesiastical History; Cambridge. 0022-0469.

JEmpT: Journal of empirical theology; Kampen. [1 (1988)].

JerusSt: Jerusalem studies in Jewish thought; Jerusalem [2 (1982)].

JESHO: Journal of Economic and Social History of the Orient; Leiden.

JEvTS: Journal of the Evangelical Theological Society; Wheaton IL.

JewishH: Jewish History; Leiden. 0334-701X [4 (1989)].

JFemR: Journal of Feminist Studies in Religion; Chico CA. 8755-4178.

JField: Journal of Field Archaeology; Boston, Univ. 0093-4690.

JGlass: Journal of Glass Studies; Corning, NY. 0075-4250.

JHistId: Journal of the History of Ideas; Ph, Temple Univ. 0022-5037.

JHMR: Judaica, Hermeneutics, Mysticism, and Religion; Albany, SUNY.

JhÖsA: Jahreshefte des Österreichischen Archäologischen Institutes; Wien. 0078-3579.

JHS: Journal of Hellenic Studies; London. 0075-4269.

JIndEur: Journal of Indo-European Studies; Hattiesburg, Miss.

JIntdenom: Journal of the Interdenominational Theological Center; Atlanta GA.

JIntdis: Journal of the Society for Interdisciplinary History; CM, MIT.

JJC: Jésus et Jésus-Christ; Paris.

JJS: Journal of Jewish Studies; Oxford. 0022-2097.

JJurPap: Journal of Juristic Papyrology; Warszawa [revived 19 (1983)].

JLawA: Jewish Law Annual (Oxford).

JLawRel: Journal of Law and Religion; St. Paul. [3 (1985)].

JMeditArch: Journal of Mediterranean Archeol.; Sheffield. 0952-7648.

JMedRenSt: Journal of Medieval and Renaissance Studies; Durham NC.

JMoscPatr: [Engl.] Journal of the Moscow Patriarchate; Moscow.

JNES: Journal of Near Eastern Studies; Chicago, Univ. 0022-2968.

JNWS: Journal of Northwest Semitic Languages; Leiden.

Journal für Geschichte; Braunschweig.

JPrehRel: Journal of Prehistoric Religion; Göteborg. 0283-8486 [1 (1987)].

JPseud: Journal for the Study of the Pseudepigrapha; Sheffield. 0951-8207 [1 (1987)].

JPsy&C: Journal of Psychology and Christianity; Farmington Hills MI. 0733-4273.

JPsy&Jud: Journal of Psychology and Judaism; New York.

JPsy&T: Journal of Psychology and Theology; La Mirada / Rosemead CA.

JQR: Jewish Quarterly Review (Ph, Dropsie Univ.); Winona Lake IN. 0021-6682.

JRAS: Journal of the Royal Asiatic Society; London.

JRefJud: Journal of Reform Judaism; NY. 0149-712X.

JRel: Journal of Religion; Chicago. 0022-4189.

JRelAf: Journal of Religion in Africa; Leiden. 0022-4200.

JRelEth: Journal of Religion and Ethics; ND (ᴱRutgers). 0384-9694.

JRelHealth: The Journal of Religion and Health; New York.

JRelHist: Journal of Religious History; Sydney, Univ. 0022-4227.

JRelPsyR: Journal of Religion and Psychical Research; Bloomfield CT.

JRelSt: Journal of Religious Studies; Cleveland.

JRelTht: Journal of Religious Thought; Washington DC.

JRit: Journal of ritual studies; Pittsburgh/Waterloo ON.

JRPot: Journal of Roman Pottery Studies: Ox. [2 (1989)].

JRS: Journal of Roman Studies; London. 0075-4358.

JSArm: Journal of the Society for Armenian Studies; LA [1 (1984)].

JSav: Journal des Savants: Paris.

JScStR: Journal for the Scientific Study of Religion; NHv. 0021-8294.

JSHZ: Jüdische Schriften aus hellenistischer und römischer Zeit; Gütersloh.

JSS: Journal of Semitic Studies; Manchester. 0022-4480.

JSStEg: Journal of the Society for the Study of Egyptian Antiquities [ipsi SSEA]; Toronto. 0383-9753.

JStJud: Journal for the Study of Judaism in the Persian, Hellenistic, & Roman Periods; Leiden. 0047-2212.

JStJTht: Jerusalem Studies in Jewish Thought.

JStNT/OT: Journal for the Study of the NT/OT; Sheffield, Univ. 0142-064X / 0309-0892. → JPseud.

JStRel: Journal for the study of religion [formerly Religion in Southern Africa]; Pietermaritzburg, Natal [1,1 (1988)].

JTS: Journal of Theological Studies, N.S.: Oxford/London. 0022-5185.

JTSAfr: Journal of Theology for Southern Africa; Rondebosch.

Judaica; Zürich.

Judaism; NY. 0022-5762.

JudTSt: Judaistische Texte und Studien; Hildesheim.

JWarb: Journal of the Warburg and Courtauld Institutes; London.

JwHist: Jewish History; Haifa.

JWomen&R: Journal of Women and Religion; Berkeley [4,2 (1985)].

JyskR: Religionsvidenskabeligt Tidsskrift; Århus, Jysk [Jutland] Selskap.

Kadmos; Berlin. 0022-7498.

Kairos (Religionswiss.); Salzburg.

Karawane (Die); Ludwigsburg.

Karthago (archéologie africaine); P.

KAT: Kommentar zum AT: Gütersloh.

KatBlät: Katechetische Blätter; Mü.

KatKenk: Katorikku Kenkyu < Shingaku; Tokyo, Sophia. 0387-3005.

KBW: Katholisches Bibelwerk; Stu [bzw. Österreich, Schweiz].

KeK: Kritisch-exegetischer Kommentar über das NT; Göttingen.

KerDo: Kerygma und Dogma; Göttingen. 0023-0707.

KerkT: Kerk en Theologie; Wageningen. 0165-2346.

Kernos, religion grecque; Liège [1 (1988)].

Kerygma (on Indian missions); Ottawa. 0023-0693.

KGaku: ❺ Kirisutokyo Gaku (Christian Studies NS; Tokyo St. Paul's Univ. 0387-6810 [29 (1987)].

KingsTR: King's College Theological Review; London.

KirSef: ❻ Kiryat Sefer, Bibliographical Quarterly; J, Nat.-Univ. Libr. 0023-1851. → Rambi.

KIsr: Kirche und Israel, theologische Zeitschrift; Neukirchen. 0179-7239. [1 (1986)].

KkKS: Konfessionskundliche und Kontroverstheologische Studien; Pd. Bonifacius.

KkMat: Konfessionskundliches Institut, Materialdienst; Bensheim [39 (1988)].

KleinÄgTexte: Kleine ägyptische Texte; Wb.

Kler: ❻ Klēronomia (patristica); Thessaloniki.

Klio: oBerlin. 0075-6334.

KLK: Katholisches Leben und Kirchenreform im Zeitalter der Glaubensspaltung; Münster.

KölnJbVFG: Kölner Jahrbuch für Vor- und Frühgeschichte; Berlin, Mann. 0075-6512.

KomBeiANT: Kommentare und Beiträge zum Alten und N.T.; Düsseldorf, Patmos.

KosmosŒ: Kosmos en Œkumene: Amsterdam.

Kratylos (Sprachwissenschaft); Wsb.

KřestR [TPřil]: Křest'anská revue [Theologická Příloha]; Praha.

KTB/KUB: Keilschrifttexte/urkunden aus Boghazköi; wB,Mann/oB,Akademie.

Ktema; Strasbourg, CEDEX.

KuGAW: Kulturgeschichte der Antiken Welt; Mainz.

KvinnerA: Kvinner i [women in] arkeologi i Norge; Bergen, Historisk Museum [1 (1985)].

KZg: Kirchliche Zeitgeschichte; Gö [1 (1988)].

LA: ➤ Greg; SBF; [Libro Anual] México; Urug.

Labeo, diritto romano; N. 0023-6462.

Landas: Journal of Loyola School of Theology; Manila. [1,1 (1987)].

Language; Baltimore.

LAPO: Littératures Anciennes du Proche-Orient; Paris, Cerf. 0459-5831.

Lateranum; R, Pont. Univ. Lateranense.

Latomus (Ét. latines); Bru. 0023-8856.

Laur: Laurentianum; R. 0023-902X.

LavalTP: Laval Théologique et Philosophique; Québec.

LDiv: Lectio Divina; Paris, Cerf.

LebSeels: Lebendige Seelsorge; Wü/FrB.

LebZeug: Lebendiges Zeugnis; Paderborn. 0023-9941.

Lĕšonénu (Hebrew Language); J.

LetPastB: Lettura pastorale della Bibbia; Bologna, Dehoniane.

Levant (archeology); London.

LexÄg: Lexikon der Ägyptologie; Wb ➤ 802.

LexMA: Lexikon des Mittelalters; Mü/Z ➤ 803.

LexTQ: Lexington [KY] Theological Quarterly. 0024-1628.

LIAO: Lettre d'Information Archéologie Orientale; Valbonne, CNRS. 0750-6279.

LIGHT: Laughter in God, History, and Theology; Fort Worth.

LIMC: Lexicon iconographicum mythologiae classicae; Z. ➤ 852.

LimnOc: Limnology & Oceanography; AA.

LinceiR/Scavi/BClas: Accademia Nazionale dei Lincei. Rendiconti / Notizie degli Scavi / Bollettino Classico. 0391-8270: Roma.

LingBib: Linguistica Biblica; Bonn. 0342-0884.

Lire la Bible; P, Cerf. 0588-2257.

Listening: Oak Park IL.

LitLComp: Literary and Linguistic Computing; Ox. 0268-1145. [4 (1989)].

LitRelFrühjud: Literatur und Religion des Frühjudentums; Wü/Gü.

LitTOx: Literature and theology; Oxford. [1,1 (1987)].

LivLight: The Living Light (US Cath. Conf.); Huntington. 0024-5275.

LivWord: Living Word; Alwaye, Kerala.

LOB: Leggere oggi la Bibbia; Brescia, Queriniana.

LogosPh: Logos, philosophic issues in Christian perspective; Santa Clara, Univ. [5 (1984)].

Logotherapie, Zeitschrift der Deutschen Gesellschaft für ∼; Bremen [1 (1986); ColcT 58,1 (1988) 153-8].

LOrA: Langues orientales anciennes, philologie et linguistique; Lv. 0987-7738. [1 (1988)].

LStClas: London studies in classical philology [8, Corolla Londiniensis 1]; Amst.

LtgJb: Liturgisches Jahrbuch; Münster/Wf.

Lucentum; prehistoria, arqueología e historia antigua; Alicante, Univ.

LumenK: Lumen; København.

LumenVr: Lumen; Vitoria.

LumièreV: Lumière et Vie; Lyon. 0024-7359.

Luther (Gesellschaft) [Jb]; Hamburg. 0340-6210 [Gö 3-525-87419-7].

LuthMonh: Lutherische Monatshefte; Hamburg. 0024-7618.

LuthTJ: Lutheran Theological Journal; North Adelaide, S. Australia.

LuthTKi: Lutherische Theologie und Kirche; Oberursel. 0170-3846.

LVitae: Lumen Vitae; Bru. 0024-7324.

LvSt: Louvain Studies.

Ⓜ magyar: *hungarice*, en hongrois.

ᴹ: *mentio, de eo*; author commented upon.

Maarav; Winona Lake IN. 0149-5712.

MadMitt [B/F]: DAI Madrider Mitteilungen (Mainz: 3-8053-0831-0) [Beiträge/Forschungen].

MAGA: Mitteilungen zur Alten Geschichte und Archäologie; oB [13 (1985)].

Maia (letterature classiche); Messina. 0025-0538.

MaisD: La Maison-Dieu; P. 0025-0937.

MANE: Monographs on the Ancient Near East; 1. Leiden; 2. Malibu.

Manresa (espiritualidad ignaciana); Azpeitia-Guipúzcoa.

Manuscripta; St. Louis.

Mara: tijdschrift voor feminisme en theologie; [1: TsTNijm 27 (1987) 396].

MarbTSt: Marburger Theologische Studien; Marburg.

MARI: Mari, Annales de Recherches Interdisciplinaires; Paris [2 (1983)].

Marianum; Roma.

MariolSt: Mariologische Studien; Essen.

MarŠipri; Boston, Baghdad ASOR [1 (1988)].

MarSt: Marian Studies; Washington.

Masca: Museum Applied Science Center for Archaeology Journal; Ph, Univ. [3 (1984s)].

MasSt: (SBL) Masoretic Studies; Chico CA.

MatKonfInst: Materialdienst des konfessionskundlichen Instituts; Bensheim.

MatPomWykBib: Materiały pomocznicze do wykładów z biblistyki; Lublin.

Mayéutica (Agustinos Recoletos); Marcilla (Navarra).

MDOG: Mitteilungen der Deutschen Orientgesellschaft; B. 0342-118X.

Meander: Wsz Akad. 0025-6285.

Med: Mededelingen [Amst, ...]; Meddelander.

MedHum: Mediaevalia et Humanistica (Denton, N. Texas Univ.); Totowa NJ.

MeditHistR: Mediterranean historical review of Tel Aviv Univ.; London. 0951-8967 [3 (1988)].

MeditLg: Mediterranean Language Review: Wiesbaden [1 (1983)].

MÉF [= MélÉcFrR]: Mélanges de l'École Française de Rome/Ath; Ant. 0223-5102.

MélSR: Mélanges de Science Religieuse; Lille.

Mém: Mémoires ➤ AIBL ... AcSc, T...

MenQR: Mennonite Quarterly Review; Goshen, Ind.

Meroit: Meroitic Newsletter / Bulletin d'informations méroitiques: Paris, CNRS [24 (1985)].

MESA: Middle East Studies Association (Bulletin); Tucson, Univ. AZ.

MesopK: Mesopotamia: Copenhagen Studies in Assyriology; København.

MesopT: Mesopotamia (Archeologia, Epigrafia, Storia ... Torino); (pub. F).

Mesorot [Language-tradition researches]; Jerusalem [1983s: Lešonenu 50 (1985s) 252-260].

MESt: Middle Eastern Studies; L.

MetB: Metropolitan Museum Bulletin; New York. 0026-1521.

MethT: Method and theory in the study of religion; Toronto [1,1 (1989)].

Mêtis, Revue d'anthropologie du monde grec ancien; Philologie — histoire — archéologie; P. [1 (1986)].

Mg: Monograph (-ie, -fia); ➤ CBQ, SBL, SNTS.

MHT: Materialien zu einem hethitischen Thesaurus; Heidelberg.

MiDAI-A/K/M/R: Mitteilungen des Deutschen Archäologischen Instituts: Athen / Kairo 3-8053-0885-X. / Madrid / Rom 0342-1287.

MidAmJT: Mid-America Journal of Theology: Orange City, Iowa [4 (1988)].

Mid-Stream, Disciples of Christ; Indianapolis. – Midstream (Jewish); NY. 0026-332X.

Mikael; Paraná, Arg. (Seminario).

MilltSt: Milltown Studies (philosophy, theology); Dublin. 0332-1428.

Minerva: filología clásica; Valladolid [1 (1987)].

Minos (Filología Egea); Salamanca. 0544-3733.

MiscCom: Miscelánea Comillas, estudios históricos; M. 0210-9522.

MiscFranc: Miscellanea Francescana; Roma (OFM Conv.).

Mishkan, a theological forum on Jewish evangelism; Jerusalem, United Christian Council [1 (1984)].

Missiology; Scottdale PA.

MissHisp: Missionalia hispanica; Madrid, CSIC Inst. E. Flores [40,117 (1983)].

Mitt: Mitteilungen [Gö Septuaginta; Berliner Museen ...]; ➤ MiDAI.

Mnemosyne, Bibliotheca Classica Batava [+ Supplements]; Leiden.

ModChm: Modern Churchman; Leominster, Herf.

ModT: Modern Theology, quarterly review; Oxford, Blackwell [1,1 (1984)].

Mon ➤ Mg.

MonastSt: Monastic Studies; Montreal [14 (1983)].
MondeB: Le Monde de la Bible: 1. P. 0154-9049. – 2. Genève.
Monde Copte, Le: 0399-905X.
MonStB: Monographien und Studienbücher; Wu/Giessen.
Month (Christian Thought and World Affairs); London. 0027-0172.
Moralia; Madrid [6 (1984)].
MsME: Manuscripts of the Middle East; Leiden. 0920-0401. [1 (1986)].
MüÄgSt: Münchener Ägyptologische Studien; München/Berlin.
MüBei[T]PapR: Münchener Beiträge zur [Theologie] Papyruskunde und antiken Rechtsgeschichte; Mü.
MünstHand: Münsterische Beiträge zur Antiken Handelsgeschichte; St. Katharinen. 0722-4532.
MüStSprW: Münchener Studien zur Sprachwissenschaft; Mü. ➤ AOtt.
MüTZ: Münchener Theologische Zeitschrift; St. Ottilien. 0580-1400.
Mundus (German Research, in English); Stuttgart. 0027-3392.
Mus: Le Muséon; LvN. 0771-6494.
MusHelv: Museum Helveticum; Basel.
MusTusc: Museum Tusculanum; København. 0107-8062.
MuzTA: ⊕ Muzeon Ha-Areş NS; TA.
NachGö: Nachrichten der Akademie der Wissenschaften; Göttingen.
Naos: notes and materials for the linguistic study of the sacred; Pittsburgh Univ. [3,1 (1987)].
NarAzAfr: ⊕ Narody: Peoples of Asia and Africa; Moskva.
NatGeog: National Geographic; Washington. 0027-9358.
NatGrac: Naturaleza y Gracia; Salamanca (OFM Cap.).
NBL: Neues Bibel-Lexikon 1988 ➤ 804.
NBlackfr: New Blackfriars; London. 0028-4289.
NCent: The New Century Bible Commentary (reedited); Edinburgh / GR.
NChrIsr: Nouvelles Chrétiennes d'Israël: Jérusalem.
NduitseGT: Nederduits-Gereformeerde Teologiese Tydskrif; Kaapstad. 0028-2006.

NedTTs: Nederlands Theologisch Tijdschrift; Wageningen. 0028-212X.
Neotestamentica; Pretoria; NTWerk.
NEphS: Neue Ephemeris für semitische Epigraphik; Wiesbaden.
Nestor, Classical Antiquity, Indiana Univ.; Bloomington. 0028-2812.
NESTR: Near East School of Theology Review; Beirut.
News: Newsletter: Anat[olian Studies; NHv]; Targ[umic and Cognate Studies; Toronto]; ASOR [CM]; Ug[aritic Studies; Calgary]; ➤ JAmEg.
NewTR: New theology review: Ch, Catholic Theological Union [publ. Wilmington, Glazier [1,1 (1988)]. 0896-4297.
NHC: Nag Hammadi Codices, Egypt UAR Facsimile edition; Leiden.
NHL/S: Nag Hammadi Library in English / Studies; Leiden.
NHLW: Neues Handbuch der Literaturwissenschaft: Wb, Athenaion.
Nicolaus (teol. ecumenico-patristica); Bari.
NICOT: New International Commentary OT; Grand Rapids, Eerdmans.
NigJT: The Nigerian Journal of Theology; Owerri [1,4 (1988)].
NIGT: New International Greek Testament Commentary; Exeter/GR, Paternoster/Eerdmans.
NorJ: Nordisk Judaistik.
NorTTs: Norsk Teologisk Tidsskrift; Oslo. 0029-2176.
NotSocTLv: Notes de la Société Théologique de Louvain; Lv-N.
NOxR: New Oxford Review; Berkeley.
NRT: Nouvelle Revue Théologique; Tournai. 0029-4845.
NS [NF]: Nova series, nouvelle série.
NSys: Neue Zeitschrift für systematische Theologie und Religionsphilosophie; Berlin. 0028-3517.
NT: Novum Testamentum; Leiden. 0048-1009.
NTAbh: Neutestamentliche Abhandlungen. [N.F.]; Münster.
NTAbs: New Testament Abstracts; CM. 0028-6877.
NTDt: Das Neue Testament deutsch; Gö.
NTS: New Testament Studies; L (SNTS).

NubChr: Nubia Christiana; Warszawa, Akad. Teol. Kat. [1 (1983)].
NumC: Numismatic Chronicle; London. 0078-2696.
Numisma; Madrid. 0029-0015.
NumZ: Numismatische Zeitschrift; Wien. 0250-7838.
Numen (International Association for the History of Religions); Leiden.
NuovaUm: Nuova Umanità; Roma.
Nuovo Areopago (Il), trimestrale di cultura; Bologna, CSEO [1,1.2 (1982)].
NVFr/Z: Nova et Vetera; 1. Fribourg S. / 2. Zamora [10 (1985)].
NYarm: Newsletter of the Institute of Archaeology and Anthropology, Yarmuk Univ.; Irbid [1 (1987)].
NZMissW: Neue Zeitschrift für Missionswissenschaft; Beckenried, Schweiz. 0028-3495.
NZSysT → NSys.
ObnŽiv: Obnovljeni Život (Erneuertes religiöses Leben); Zagreb.
OBO: Orbis Biblicus et Orientalis: FrS/Gö.
OEIL: Office d'édition et d'impression du livre; Paris.
ÖkRu: Ökumenische Rundschau; Stuttgart. 0029-8654.
ÖkTbKom, NT: Ökumenischer Taschenbuchkommentar; Gütersloh / Würzburg.
ÖsterrBibSt: Österreichische Biblische Studien; Klosterneuburg.
Offa, ... Frühgeschichte; Neumünster. 0078-3714.
Ohio → JRelSt: Cleveland.
OIC/P/Ac: Oriental Institute Communications / Publications / Acquisitions; Ch.
OikBud: Oikumene; historia antiqua classica et orientalis; Budapest.
Olivo (El), diálogo jud.-cr.: Madrid.
OLZ: Orientalistische Literaturzeitung; ab 1987 Berlin. 0030-5383.
OMRO: Oudheidkundige Mededelingen, Rijksmuseum van Oudheden; Leiden.
OneInC: One in Christ (Catholic Ecumenical); Turvey, Bedfordshire.
OnsGErf: Ons Geestelijk Erf; Antwerpen.
OnsGLev: Ons Geestelijk Leven; ab 65 (1988) → GLeven.
OpAth/Rom: Opuscula Atheniensia 91-

85086-80-0 / Romana 91-7042-099-8; Swedish Inst.
OPTAT: Occasional Papers in Translation and Textlinguistics: Dallas [1,1 (1987)].
Opus, rivista internazionale per la storia economica e sociale dell'antichità (Siena); R.
Or: → Orientalia; Roma.
OraLab: Ora et Labora; Roriz, Portugal.
OrAnt[Coll]: Oriens Antiquus [Collectio]; Roma.
OrBibLov: Orientalia et Biblica Lovaniensia; Lv.
OrChr: Oriens Christianus; Wiesbaden. 3-447-02532-8.
OrChrPer[An]: Orientalia Christiana Periodica [Analecta]; R, Pontificium Inst. Orientalium Stud. 0030-5375.
OrGand: Orientalia Gandensia; Gent.
Orientalia (Ancient Near East); Rome, Pontifical Biblical Institute. 0030-5367.
Orientierung; Zürich. 0030-5502.
Orient-Japan: Orient, Near Eastern Studies Foreign Language Annual; Tokyo. 0743-3851; cf. ❶ Oriento. 0030-5219.
Origins; Washington Catholic Conference. 0093-609X.
OrJog: Orientasi, Annual ... Philosophy and Theology; Jogjakarta.
OrLovPer[An]: Orientalia Lovaniensia Periodica [Analecta]; Lv.
OrMod: Oriente Moderno; Napoli. 0030-5472.
OrOcc: Oriente-Occidente. Buenos Aires, Univ. Salvador.
OrPast: Orientamenti Pastorali; Roma.
Orpheus; Catania.
OrSuec: Orientalia Suecana; Uppsala.
OrtBuc: Ortodoxia; Bucureşti.
OrthF: Orthodoxes Forum; München, Univ. [1,1 (1987)].
OrTrad: Oral Tradition; Columbia MO, Univ. [1 (1986)].
OrVars: Orientalia Varsoviensia; Wsz. 0860-5785. [1 (1987)].
OstkSt: Ostkirchliche Studien; Würzburg. 0030-6487.
OTAbs: Old Testament Abstracts; Washington. 0364-8591.

OTEssays: Old Testament essays; Pretoria. 1010-9919. [1,1 (1988)].

OTS: Oudtestamentische Studiën; Leiden. 0169-9555.

OTWerkSuidA: Die Ou Testamentiese Werkgemeenskap Suid-Afrika; Pretoria.

OudKMed: Oudheidkundige Mededelingen uit het Rijksmuseum van Oudheden; Leiden.

OvBTh: Overtures to Biblical Theology; Philadelphia.

Overview; Ch St. Thomas More Asn.

OxJArch: Oxford Journal of Archaeology; Ox. 0262-5253.

𝗣: *polonice*, in Polish.

p./pa./pl.: page(s)/paperback/plate(s).

PAAR: Proceedings of the American Academy for Jewish Research; Ph.

Pacifica: Australian theological studies; Melbourne Brunswick East [1,1 (1988)].

PacTR: Pacific theological review: SanAnselmo, SF Theol.Sem. 21, 1 (1987).

Palaeohistoria; Haarlem.

PalCl: Palestra del Clero; Rovigo.

PaléOr: Paléorient; Paris.

PalSb: ◉ Palestinski Sbornik; Leningrad.

PapBritSR: Papers of the British School at Rome; London.

PAPS: Proceedings of the American Philosophical Society; Ph.

PapTAbh: Papyrologische Texte und Abhandlungen; Bonn, Habelt.

PapyrolColon: Papyrologica Coloniensia; Opladen. 0078-9410.

Parabola (Myth and the Quest for Meaning); New York.

Paradigms; Louisville KY [1 (1985)].

ParOr: Parole de l'Orient; Kaslik [12 (1984s)].

ParPass: Parola del Passato; Napoli. 0031-2355.

ParSpV: Parola, Spirito e Vita, quaderni di lettura biblica; Bo, Dehoniane.

ParVi: Parole di Vita; T-Leumann.

PasT: Pastoraltheologie; Göttingen.

PastScPast: Pastoral / Sciences pastorales; psych.sociol.théol.; Ottawa, St. Paul Univ. [5 (1986)].

PatByzR: Patristic and Byzantine Review; Kingston NY [1 (1982)].

Patr&M: Patristica et Mediaevalia; Buenos Aires [I. 1975; ... II. 1981 - VII. 1986: RHE 83,491].

PatrStudT: Patristische Studien und Texte; B. 0553-4003.

PBSB: Petite bibliothèque des sciences bibliques; Paris, Desclée.

PenséeC: La Pensée Catholique; P.

PEQ: Palestine Exploration Quarterly; London. 0031-0328.

PerAz: Peredneaziatskij Sbornik; Moskva.

Persica: Leiden.

PerspRelSt: Perspectives in Religious Studies (Baptist); Danville VA.

PerspT: Perspectiva Teológica; Belo Horizonte [before 1981 São Leopoldo].

Pg/Ph: philolog-/philosoph-.

PgOrTb: Philologia Orientalis (Georgian Ac. Sc.); Tbilisi.

Phase; Barcelona.

PhilipSa: Philippiniana Sacra; Manila.

Philologus; oB. 0031-7985.

Phoenix; Toronto. 0031-8299.

PhoenixEOL; Leiden (not = JbEOL). 0031-8329.

Phronema: St. Andrew's Greek Orthodox Theological College, Australia [annual; 1 (1986) TAth 58 (1987) 645s].

Phronesis; Assen. 0031-8868.

PiTMon: Theological Monograph Series; Pittsburgh.

PJungG: Projekte und Modelle zum Dialog mit der jungen Generation; Stu.

Pneuma, Pentecostal Studies; Pasadena [7 (1985)].

PoinT: Le Point Théologique; P.

Polin: Polish-Jewish Studies; Oxford [1 (1986)].

PontAcc, R/Mem: Atti della Pontificia Accademia Romana di Archeologia, Rendiconti/Memorie; Vaticano.

PrPeo [< CleR]: Priests and People; L.

PracArch: Prace Archeologiczne; Kraków, Univ. 0083-4300.

PraehZ: Praehistorische Zeitschrift; Berlin. 0079-4848.

PrakT: Praktische theologie ... pastorale wetenschappen; Zwolle.

PraktArch: ◉ Praktika, Archeology Society Athens.

PrAmPhilSoc: ➔ PAPS.

PrCambPg: Proceedings of the Cambridge Philological Society; England. 0068-6735.

PrCTSAm: Proceedings Catholic Theological Society of America; Villanova.

PredikOT/NT: De Prediking van het OT / van het NT; Nijkerk.

Presbyteri (Spiritualità pastorale); Trento.

Presbyterion; St. Louis.

PresPast: Presenza Pastorale; Roma.

PrêtreP: Prêtre et Pasteur; Montréal. 0385-8307.

Priest (The); Washington.

PrincSemB: Princeton Seminary Bulletin; Princeton NJ.

PrIrB: Proceedings of the Irish Biblical Association; Dublin, 'published annually'.

Prism; St. Paul, United Church of Christ [1 (1986)].

PrIsrAc: Proceedings of the Israel Academy of Sciences & Humanities; Jerusalem.

ProbHistChr: Problèmes de l'Histoire du Christianisme; Bruxelles, Univ.

ProcClas: Proceedings of the Classical Association; London [35 (1988)].

ProcCom: Proclamation Commentaries; Ph.

ProcGLM: Proceedings of the Eastern Great Lakes and Midwest Bible Societies; Buffalo.

Prooftexts; Baltimore.

PrOrChr: Proche-Orient Chrétien; Jérusalem. 0032-9622.

Prot: Protestantesimo; R. 0033-1767.

Proyección (Teología y mundo actual); Granada.

PrPrehS: Proceedings of the Prehistoric Society; Cambridge (Univ. Museum).

PrSemArab: Proceedings of the Seminar for Arabian Studies; London.

Prudentia (Hellenistic, Roman); Auckland.

PrzOr[Tom/Pow]: Przegląd Orientalistyczny, Wsz: [Tomisticzny 1 (1984) Wsz / Powszechny, Kraków].

PT: Philosophy/Theology: Milwaukee, Marquette Univ. [1 (1986)].

PubTNEsp: Publicaciones de la Facultad Teológica del Norte de España; Burgos.

PUF: Presses Universitaires de France; P.

Qadm: Qadmoniot ❺ Quarterly of Dept. of Antiquities; Jerusalem.

Qardom, ❺ mensuel pour la connaissance du pays; Jerusalem, Ariel.

QDisp: Quaestiones Disputatae; FrB.

Qedem: Monographs of the Institute of Archaeology: Jerusalem, Hebr. Univ.

QEtnR: Quaderni di etnologia religiosa; Milano.

QLtg: Questions Liturgiques; Lv.

QRMin: Quarterly Review [for] Ministry; Nv. 0270-9287.

QuadCatan / Chieti: Quaderni, Catania / Chieti [3 (1982)]; Univ.

QuadSemant: Quaderni di Semantica; Bologna.

QuadSemit: Quaderni di Semitistica; Firenze.

QuadUrb: Quaderni Urbinati di Cultura Classica; Urbino. 0033-4987.

Quaerendo (Low Countries: Manuscripts and Printed Books); Amst.

QuatreF: Les quatre fleuves; Paris.

QüestVidaCr: Qüestions de Vida Cristiana; Montserrat.

❺: *russice,* in Russian.

[R]: *recensio,* book-review(er).

RAC: Reallexikon für Antike und Christentum; Stuttgart ➔ 807.

Radiocarbon; NHv, Yale. 0033-8222.

RAfrT: Revue Africaine de Théologie; Kinshasa/Limete.

RAg: Revista Agustiniana [de Espiritualidad hacia 18 (1977)] Calahorra.

RAMBI: Rešimat Ma'amarim bemadda'ê ha-Yahedût, Index of articles on Jewish Studies; J. 0073-5817.

RaMIsr: Rassegna mensile di Israel; Roma.

RArchéol: Revue Archéologique; Paris. 0035-0737.

RArchéom: Revue d'Archéométrie; Rennes.

RArtLv: Revue des Archéologues et Historiens d'Art; Lv. 0080-2530.

RAss: Revue d'Assyriologie et d'Archéologie Orientale; P. 2-13-039142-7.

RasT: Rassegna di Teologia; Roma [ENapoli]. 0034-9644.

Raydan:

RazF: Razón y Fe; Madrid.

RB: Revue Biblique; J/P. 0035-0907.

RBén: Revue Bénédictine; Maredsous. 0035-0893.

RBgNum: Revue Belge de Numismatique et Sigillographie; Bruxelles.

RBgPg: Revue Belge de Philologie et d'Histoire; Bruxelles.

RBBras: Revista Bíblica Brasileira; Fortaleza [1 (1984)].

RBíbArg: Revista Bíblica; Buenos Aires. 0034-7078.

RBkRel: The Review of Books and Religion; Durham NC, Duke Univ. [10 c. 1984].

RCatalT: Revista Catalana de Teología; Barcelona, St. Pacià.

RCiv: Éditions Recherche sur les [Grandes] Civilisations [Mém(oires) 0291-1655]. Paris → ADPF.

RClerIt: Rivista del Clero Italiano; Mi.

RCuClaMed: Rivista di Cultura Classica e Medioevale; Roma.

RÉAnc: Revue des Études Anciennes; Bordeaux. 0035-2004.

RÉArmén: Revue des Études Arméniennes. 0080-2549.

RÉAug: Revue des Études Augustiniennes; Paris. 0035-2012.

REB: Revista Eclesiástica Brasileira; Petrópolis.

RÉByz: Revue des Études Byzantines; Paris.

RECAM: Regional Epigraphic Catalogues of Asia Minor [AnSt].

RechAug: Recherches Augustiniennes; Paris. 0035-2021.

RechSR: Recherches de Science Religieuse; Paris. 0034-1258.

RecTrPO: Recueil de travaux et communications de l'association des études du Proche-Orient ancien / Collected papers of the Society for Near Eastern Studies; Montréal [2 (1984)].

RefEgy: Református Egyház; Budapest. 0324-475X.

ReferSR: Reference Services Review; Dearborn MI, Univ.

RefF: Reformiertes Forum; Zürich.

RefGStT: Reformationsgeschichtliche Studien und Texten: Münster.

RefJ: The Reformed Journal; Grand Rapids. 0486-252X.

Reformatio; Zürich.

RefR: Reformed Review; New Brunswick NJ / Holland MI.

RefTR: Reformed Theological Review; Hawthorn, Australia. 0034-3072.

RefW: The Reformed World; Geneva.

RÉG: Revue des Études Grecques; Paris. 0035-2039.

RÉgp: Revue d'Égyptologie; Paris. 2-252-02201-9.

RÉJ: Revue des Études Juives; Paris. 0035-2055.

RÉLat: Revue des Études Latines; P.

RelCult: Religión y Cultura; M.

RelEd: Religious Education (biblical; Jewish-sponsored); Chicago.

RelHum: Religious Humanism; Yellow Springs OH.

Religion [... and Religions]; Lancaster. 0048-721X.

RelIntL: Religion and Intellectual Life; New Rochelle NY, College. 0741-0549 [2 (1985)].

RelPBei: Religionspädagogische Beiträge; Kaarst. [17 (1986)].

RelSoc: Religion and Society; B/Haag.

RelSt: Religious Studies; Cambridge. 0034-4125.

RelStR: Religious Studies Review; Waterloo, Ont. 0319-485X.

RelStT: Religious Studies [Bulletin, till 1985; now] and Theology; Edmonton.

RelTAbs: Religious and Theological Abstracts; Myerstown, Pa.

RelTrad: Religious Traditions; Brisbane. 0156-1650.

RencAssInt: Rencontre Assyriologique Internationale, Compte-Rendu.

RencChrJ: Rencontre Chrétiens et Juifs; Paris. 0233-5579.

Renovatio: 1. Zeitschrift für das interdisziplinäre Gespräch; Köln [38 (1982)]: 2. (teologia); Genova.

RepCyp: Report of the Department of Antiquities of Cyprus; Nicosia.

RepertAA: Répertoire d'art et d'archéologie; Paris. 0080-0953.

REPPAL: Revue d'Études Phéniciennes-Puniques et des Antiquités Libyques; Tunis [1 (1985)].

REspir: Revista de Espiritualidad; San Sebastián.

ResPLit: Res Publica Litterarum; Kansas.

RestQ: Restoration Quarterly; Abilene TX.

Résurrection, bimestriel catholique d'actualité et de formation [9-12 (1987)].

RET: Revista Española de Teología; Madrid.

RÉtGC: Revue des Études Géorgiennes et Caucasiennes; Paris. 0373-1537. [1 (1985) = Bedi Kartlisa 44].

RevCuBíb: Revista de Cultura Bíblica; São Paulo.

RevSR: Revue des Sciences Religieuses; Strasbourg. 0035-2217.

RExp: Review and Expositor; Louisville. 0034-6373.

RFgIC: Rivista di Filologia e di Istruzione Classica; Torino. 0035-6220.

RgStTh: Regensburger Studien zur Theologie; Fra/Bern, Lang.

RgVV: Religionsgeschichtliche Versuche und Vorarbeiten; B/NY, de Gruyter.

RHDroit: Revue historique de Droit français et étranger; Paris.

RHE: Revue d'Histoire Ecclésiastique; Louvain. 0035-2381.

RheinMus: Rheinisches Museum für Philologie; Frankfurt. 0035-449X.

Rhetorik [Jb]; Stu / Bad Cannstatt.

RHist: Revue Historique; Paris.

RHPR: Revue d'Histoire et de Philosophie Religieuses; Strasbourg. 0035-2403.

RHR: Revue de l'Histoire des Religions; Paris. 0035-1423.

RHS ➤ RUntHö; **RU** ➤ ZRUnt.

RHText: Revue d'Histoire des Textes; Paris. 0373-6075.

RIC: Répertoire bibliographique des institutions chrétiennes; Strasbourg, CERDIC.

RICathP: Revue de l'Institut Catholique de Paris. 0294-4308 [cf. ➤ BICLyon].

RicStorSocRel: Ricerche di Storia Sociale e Religiosa; Roma.

RIDA: Revue Internationale des Droits de l'Antiquité; Bruxelles.

RINASA: Rivista dell'Istituto Nazionale di Archeologia e Storia dell'Arte; Roma.

RitFg: Rivista italiana di Filologia Classica.

RItNum: Rivista Italiana di Numismatica e scienze affini; Milano.

RivArCr: Rivista di Archeologia Cristiana; Città del Vaticano. 0035-6042.

RivArV: Rivista di Archeologia, Univ. Venezia; Roma.

RivAscM: [non Nuova] Rivista di Ascetica e Mistica; Roma.

RivB: Rivista Biblica Italiana; (da 1985) Bo, Dehoniane. 0393-4853.

RivLtg: Rivista di Liturgia; T-Leumann.

RivPastLtg: Rivista di Pastorale Liturgica; Brescia. 0035-6395.

RivScR: Rivista di Scienze Religiose; Molfetta.

RivStoLR: Rivista di Storia e Letteratura Religiosa; F. 0035-6573.

RivStorA: Rivista Storica dell'Antichità; Bologna.

RivVSp: Rivista di Vita Spirituale; Roma. 0035-6638.

RLA: Reallexikon der Assyriologie & vorderasiatischen Archäologie; B ➤ 808.

RLatAmT: Revista Latinoamericana de Teología; El Salvador.

RNouv: La Revue Nouvelle; Bruxelles. 0035-3809.

RNum: Revue Numismatique; Paris.

RoczOr: Rocznik Orientalistyczny; Warszawa. 0080-3545.

RoczTK: Roczniki Teologiczno-Kanoniczne; Lublin. 0035-7723.

RömQ: Römische Quartalschrift für Christliche Altertumskunde...; Freiburg/Br. 0035-7812.

RomOrth: Romanian Orthodox Church News, French Version [sic]; Bucureşti.

RP: Revue de Philologie, de Littérature et d'Histoire anciennes; Paris, Klincksieck. 0035-1652.

RQum: Revue de Qumrân; P. 0035-1725.

RRéf: Revue Réformée; Saint-Germain-en-Laye.

RRel: Review for Religious; St. Louis. 0034-639X.

RRelRes: Review of Religious Research; New York. 0034-673X.

RRns: The Review of Religions; Wsh. 0743-5622.

RSO: Rivista degli Studi Orientali; Roma. 0392-4869.

RSocietà; Roma [1,1 (1986)].

RSPT: Revue des Sciences Philosophiques et Théologiques; [Le Saulchoir] Paris. 0035-2209.

RStFen: Rivista di Studi Fenici: R.

RStPomp: Rivista di Studi Pompeiani: Roma. [1 (1987)].

RTAM: Recherches de Théologie Ancienne et Médiévale; Louvain. 0034-1266. → BTAM.

RTBat: Revista Teológica (Sem. Batista); Rio de Janeiro.

RThom: Revue Thomiste; Toulouse/ Bru. 0035-4295.

RTLim: Revista Teológica; Lima.

RTLv: Revue théologique de Louvain. 0080-2654.

RTPhil: Revue de Théologie et de Philosophie; CH-1066 Épalinges. 0035-1784.

RuBi: Ruch Biblijny i Liturgiczny; Kraków. 0209-0872.

RUnivOtt: Revue de l'Université d'Ottawa.

RUntHö: Religionsunterricht an höheren Schulen; Düsseldorf.

RVidEsp: Revista vida espiritual [replacing Vida espiritual with 85 (1986)]; Bogotà.

RZaïrTP: Revue Zaïroise de Théologie Protestante; [2 (1988)].

SacEr: Sacris Erudiri; Steenbrugge.

Saeculum; FrB/Mü. 0080-5319.

SAfJud: South African Judaica; Johannesburg, Witwatersrand Univ. [1 (1984)].

Sales: Salesianum; Roma. 0036-3502.

Salm: Salmanticensis; Salamanca. 0036-3537.

SalT: Sal Terrae; Santander. 0211-4569.

Sandalion (Sassari); R, Herder.

SAOC: Studies in Ancient Oriental Civilization: Ch, Univ. 0081-7554.

Sap: Sapienza; Napoli. 0036-4711.

SapCro: La Sapienza della Croce; R.

sb.: subscription; price for members.

SBF/LA/Anal/Pub [min]: Studii Biblici Franciscani / Liber Annuus: 0081-8933 / Analecta / Publicationes series maior 0081-8971 [minor]; Jerusalem.

SBL [AramSt / CR / Mg / Diss / GRR / MasSt / NAm / SemP / TexTr]: Society of Biblical Literature: Aramaic Studies / Critical Review of Books in Religion / Monograph Series / Dissertation Series / Graeco-Roman Religion / Masoretic Studies / Biblical Scholarship in North America / Seminar Papers 0145-2711 / Texts and Translations. → JBL; CATSS.

SBS [KBW]: Stuttgarter Bibelstudien; Stuttgart, Katholisches Bibelwerk.

ScandJOT: Scandinavian Journal of the Old Testament; Aarhus.

ScEsp: Science et Esprit; Montréal. 0316-5345.

SCHN: Studia ad Corpus Hellenisticum NT; Leiden.

Schönberger Hefte; Fra.

Scholars Choice; Richmond VA.

SChr: Sources Chrétiennes; P. 0750-1978.

SciTHV: Science, technology and human values; NY [8 (1983)].

ScotBEv: The Scottish Bulletin of Evangelical Theology; E. 0265-4539.

ScotJT: Scottish Journal of Theology; Edinburgh. 0036-9306.

ScotR: Scottish Journal of Religious Studies; Stirling.

ScrCiv: Scrittura [scrivere] e Civiltà; T.

ScriptB: Scripture Bulletin; London. 0036-9780.

Scriptorium; Bruxelles.

ScripTPamp: Scripta theologica; Pamplona, Univ. Navarra. 0036-9764.

Scriptura; Stellenbosch.

ScriptVict: Scriptorium Victoriense; Vitoria, España.

ScrMedit: Scripta Mediterranea; Toronto, Univ. [3 (1982)].

ScuolC: La Scuola Cattolica; Venegono Inferiore, Varese. 0036-9810.

SDB [= DBS]: Supplément au Dictionnaire de la Bible; Paris → 809.

SDH: Studia et documenta historiae et iuris; Roma, Pont. Univ. Later.

SDJ: Studies on the Texts of the Desert of Judah; Leiden.

Search: Dublin [5 (1982)].

SecC: The Second Century; Malibu CA. 0276-7899.

Sefarad; Madrid. 0037-0894.

SEG: Supplementum epigraphicum graecum; Withoorn.

Segmenten; Amsterdam, Vrije Univ.

SeiRon: Seisho-gaku ronshū; Tokyo, Japanese Biblical Institute.

SelT: Selecciones de Teología; Barc.

SémBib: Sémiotique et Bible; Lyon → CADIR. 0154-6902.

Semeia (Biblical Criticism) [Supplements]; Chico CA, SBL. 0095-571X.

Seminarios ... sobre los ministerios en la Iglesia; Salamanca, Inst. Vocacional 'M. Ávila' [29 (1983)].

Seminarium; Roma.

Seminary Review; Cincinnati.

Semiotica; Amsterdam.

Semitica; Paris. 2-7200-1040-5.

Semitics; Pretoria. '84: 0-86981-312-9.

Sens; juifs et chrétiens; Paris.

SeptCogSt: → B[ulletin].

Servitium, quaderni di spiritualità; Bergamo, priorato S. Egidio; publ. Casale Monferrato. 88-211-9031-5.

SEST: South-Eastern [Baptist Sem.] Studies; Wake Forest NC.

Sevārtham; Ranchi (St. Albert's College).

Sève = Église aujourd'hui [non plus 'en monde rural' (→ ÉglRur) à partir du N° 488, mai 1987]; P. 0223-5854.

SGErm: ❺ Soobščeniya gosudarstvennovo Ermitaža, Reports of the State Hermitage Museum; Leningrad. 0432-1501.

ShinKen: ❹ *Shinyaku Kenkyū,* Studia Textus Novi Testamenti; Osaka.

ShnatM: ❺ Shnaton la-Mikra (Annual, Biblical and ANE Studies); Tel Aviv. → SMišpat.

SicArch: Sicilia archaeologica; Trapani.

SicGym: Siculorum Gymnasium; Catania.

Sidra, a journal for the study of Rabbinic literature; Ramat-Gan [1 (1985)].

SIMA: Studies in Mediterranean Archaeology; Göteborg.

SixtC: The Sixteenth Century Journal; St. Louis (Kirksville). 0361-0160.

SkK: Stuttgarter (KBW) kleiner Kommentar.

SkrifK: Skrif en Kerk; Pretoria, Univ.

SMEA: Studi Micenei ed Egeo-Ana-

tolici (Incunabula Graeca); Roma, Consiglio Naz.

SMišpat: Šnaton ha-Mišpaṭ ha-Ivri, Annual of the Institute for Research in Jewish Law [9s (1983)].

SMSR: Studi e Materiali di Storia delle religioni: Roma. [1977-82 'Studi Storico Religiosi'].

SNTS (Mg.): Studiorum Novi Testamenti Societas (Monograph Series); C.

SNTU-A/B: Studien zum NT und seiner Umwelt; Linz [Periodica / Series].

SocAnRel: Sociological analysis, a journal in the sociology of religion; Chicago [49 (1989)].

SocWB: The Social World of Biblical Antiquity; Sheffield.

Soundings; Nashville, Vanderbilt Univ. [65 (1983)].

SovArch: ❺ Sovyetskaja Archeologija; Moskva. 0038-5034.

Speculum (Medieval Studies); CM. 0038-7134.

SPg: Studia Philologica;

Spiritus; Paris. 0038-7665.

SpirLife: Spiritual Life; Washington. 0038-7630.

Sprache; Wien. 0038-8467.

SR: Studies in Religion / Sciences Religieuses; Waterloo, Ont. 0008-4298.

ST: (Vaticano) Studi e Testi.

ST: Studia Theologica; Oslo. 0039-338X.

StAChron: Studies in Ancient Chronology; London. 0952-4975 [1 (1987)].

Stadion, Geschichte des Sports; Sankt Augustin. 0178-4029.

StAltägK: Studien zur altägyptischen Kultur; Hamburg. 0340-2215.

StAns: Studia Anselmiana; Roma.

StANT: Studien zum Alten und Neuen Testament; München.

StAntCr: Studi di Antichità Cristiana; Città del Vaticano.

Star: St. Thomas Academy for Research; Bangalore.

StArchWsz: Studia archeologiczne; Warszawa, Univ.

Stauròs, Bollettino trimestrale sulla teologia della Croce: Pescara [7 (1981)].

StBEC: Studies in the Bible and Early Christianity; Lewiston NY.

StBib: Dehon/Paid/Leiden: Studi Biblici; Bo, Dehoniane / Brescia, Paideia / Studia Biblica; Leiden [1 (1983)].

StBoğT: Studien zu den Boğazköy-Texten; Wiesbaden.

STBuc: Studii Teologice; Bucureşti.

StCatt: Studi cattolici; Milano. 0039-2901.

StChHist: Studies in Church History; Oxford [21 (1984)].

StChrAnt: Studies in Christian Antiquity; Wsh.

StChrJud: Studies in Christianity and Judaism; Waterloo ON.

StClasBuc: Studii Clasice; Bucureşti.

StClasOr: Studi Classici e Orientali; P.

StCompRel: Studies in Comparative Religion; Bedfont, Middlesex.

StDelitzsch: Studia Delitzschiana (Institutum Judaicum Delitzschianum, Münster); Stuttgart. 0585-5071.

StEbl: Studi Eblaiti; Roma, Univ.

StEcum: Studi Ecumenici; Verona. 0393-3687 [2 (1984)].

StEgPun: Studi di Egittologia e di Antichità Puniche, Univ. Bologna: Pisa.

StEpL: Studi Epigrafici e Linguistici sul Vicino Oriente antico; Verona.

STEv: Studi di Teologia dell'Istituto Biblico Evangelico; Roma.

StFormSp: Studies in Formative Spirituality; Pittsburgh, Duquesne.

StGnes: Studia Gnesnensia; Gniezno.

StHCT: Studies in the History of Christian Thought; Leiden.

StHJewishP: Studies in the History of the Jewish People; Haifa.

StHPhRel: Studies in the History and Philosophy of Religion; CM.

StHRel [= Numen Suppl.] Studies in the History of Religions; Leiden.

StIran: Studia Iranica; Leiden.

StIsVArh: Studii şi cercetări de Istorie Veche şi arheologie; Bucureşti. 0039-4009.

StItFgC: Studi Italiani di Filologia Classica; Firenze.

StiZt: Stimmen der Zeit; FrB. 0039-1492.

StJudLA: Studies in Judaism in Late Antiquity; Leiden.

StLeg: Studium Legionense; León.

StLtg: Studia Liturgica; Nieuwendam.

StLuke: St. Luke's Journal of Theology; Sewanee TN.

StMiss: Studia Missionalia, Annual; Rome, Gregorian Univ.

StMor: Studia Moralia; R, Alphonsianum.

StNT [& W]: Studien zum Neuen Testament; Gütersloh; **STNT** ➤ Shin-Ken. / [Studies of the NT and its World; E].

StOr: Studia Orientalia; Helsinki, Societas Orientalis Fennica. 0039-3282.

StOrRel: Studies in Oriental Religions; Wiesbaden.

StOvet: Studium Ovetense; Oviedo ('La Asunción').

StPatav: Studia Patavina; Padova. 0039-3304.

StPatrist: Studia Patristica; oBerlin.

StPostB: Studia Post-Biblica; Leiden.

StPrace: Studia i Prace = Études et Travaux, Centre d'Archéologie Méditerranéenne; Warszawa [12 (1983)].

Streven: 1. cultureel maatschappelijk maandblad; Antwerpen [50 (1982s)] 0039-2324; 2. S.J., Amst [35 (1982)].

StRicOrCr: Studi e Ricerche dell'Oriente Cristiano; Roma [5 (1982)].

StRom: Studi Romani; Roma.

Stromata (< Ciencia y Fe); San Miguel, Argentina. 0049-2353.

StRz: Studia Religioznawcze (Filozofii i Socjologii); Wsz, Univ.

StSemLgLing: Studies in Semitic Language and Linguistics; Leiden.

StTGg: Studien zur Theologie und Geistesgeschichte des 19. Jdts.; Gö, VR.

StudiaBT: Studia Biblica et Theologica; Pasadena CA. 0094-2022.

Studies; Dublin. 0039-3495.

StudiesBT: Studies in Biblical Theology; L.

Studium; 1. Madrid; 2. R. 0039-4130.

StVTPseud: Studia in Veteris Testamenti Pseudepigrapha; Leiden.

STWsz: Studia theologica Varsaviensia; Warszawa.

SubsB: Subsidia Biblica; R, Pontifical Biblical Institute.

SudanTB: Sudan Texts Bulletin; Ulster, Univ. 0143-6554. [7 (1985)].

Sumer (Archaeology-History in the Arab World); Baghdad, Dir. Ant.

SUNT: Studien zur Umwelt des NTs; Göttingen.

SUNY: State University of New York; Albany etc.

Sup.: Supplement ➤ NT, JStOT, SDB, SEG.

Supplément, Le: autrefois 'de VSp'; P.

SvEx: Svensk Exegetisk Årsbok; U.

SVlad: St. Vladimir's Theological Quarterly; Tuckahoe NY. 0036-3227.

SvTKv: Svensk Teologisk Kvartalskrift; Lund.

SWJT: Southwestern [Baptist Seminary] Journal of Theology; Seminary Hill TX. 0038-4828.

Symbolae (graec-lat.); Oslo. 0039-7679.

Symbolon: 1. Ba/Stu; 2. Köln.

Synaxe, annuale dell'Istituto per la Documentazione e la Ricerca S. Paolo; Catania [1 (1983)].

Syria (Art Oriental, Archéologie); Paris, IFA Beyrouth.

SyrMesSt: Syro-Mesopotamian Studies (Monograph Journals); Malibu CA.

Szb: Sitzungsberichte [Univ.], phil.-hist. Klasse (Bayr./Mü. 0342-5991).

Szolgalat ⓜ ['Dienst']; Eisenstadt, Österreich.

➊: *lingua turca,* Turkish; – ᵀtranslator.

Tablet; London. 0039-8837.

TAik: Teologinen Aikakauskirja / Teologisk Tidskrift; Helsinki.

TaiwJT: Taiwan [Presbyterian Sem.] Journal of Theology; Taipei.

TAJ: Tel Aviv [Univ.] Journal of the Institute of Archaeology. 0334-4355.

TAn: Theology Annual; Hongkong.

ŢanţurYb: Ecumenical Institute for Theological Research Yearbook; J, Ţanţur.

TArb: Theologische Arbeiten; Stu/oB.

Tarbiẓ ⓗ (Jewish Studies); Jerusalem, Hebr. Univ. 0334-3650.

TArg: Teología; Buenos Aires.

TAth: ⓖ Theología; Athēnai, Synodos.

TAVO: Tübinger Atlas zum Vorderen Orient [Beih(efte)]: Wiesbaden.

TBei: Theologische Beiträge; Wuppertal.

TBer: Theologische Berichte: Z/Köln.

TBraga: Theologica; Braga.

TBud: Teologia; Budapest, Ac. Cath.

TBüch: Theologische Bücherei. (Neudrucke und Berichte 20. Jdt.); München.

TCN: Theological College of Northern Nigeria Research Bulletin; Bukuru.

TContext: Theology in Context, English ed. [5,1 (1988) ➤ **TKontext** 9,1]. 0176-1439.

TDeusto: Teología-Deusto; Bilbao/M [16 (1982)].

TDienst: Theologie und Dienst; Wuppertal.

TDig: Theology Digest; St. Louis. 0040-5728.

TDNT: Theological Dictionary of the NT [< TWNT]; Grand Rapids ➤ 811.

TDocStA: Testi e documenti per lo studio dell'Antichità; Milano, Cisalpino.

TDOT: Theological Dictionary of the Old Testament [< TWAT] GR ➤ 812.

TEdn: Theological Education; Vandalia OH [20 (1983s)].

TEdr: Theological Educator; New Orleans.

TEFS: Theological Education [Materials for Africa, Asia, Caribbean] Fund, Study Guide; London.

Telema (réflexion et créativité chrétiennes en Afrique); Kinshasa-Gombe.

Teocomunicação; [12 (1982)].

Teresianum [ex-EphCarm]; Roma.

TerraS / TerreS: Terra Santa: 0040-3784. / La Terre Sainte; J (Custodia OFM). ➤ **HolyL.**

TEspir: Teología Espiritual; Valencia.

TEV: Today's English Version (Good News for Modern Man); L, Collins.

TEvca: Theologia Evangelica; Pretoria, Univ. S. Africa.

TExH: Theologische Existenz heute; München.

Text; The Hague. 0165-4888.

TextEstCisn: Textos y Estudios 'Cardenal Cisneros'; Madrid, C.S.I.C.

TextPatLtg: Textus patristici et liturgici; Regensburg, Pustet.

Textus, Annual of the Hebrew Univ. Bible Project; J. 0082-3767.

TFor: Theologische Forschung; Hamburg.

TGegw: Theologie der Gegenwart in Auswahl; Münster, Regensberg-V.

TGL: Theologie und Glaube; Paderborn.

THandkNT: Theologischer Handkommentar zum NT; oB.

THAT: Theologisches Handwörterbuch zum AT; München. ➤ **1**,908.

Themelios; L. 0307-8388.

ThemTT: Themen und Thesen der Theologie; Dü.

Theokratia, Jahrbuch des Institutum Delitzschianum; Leiden/Köln.

Ho Theológos [sic], quadrimestrale Fac. Teol. Sicilia 'S. Giovanni Ev.'; Palermo [NS 1 (1983)].

30D: Thirty days in the Church and in the world [< Trenta giorni]; SF, Ignatius. [1,1 (1988)].

THist: Théologie Historique; P. 0563-4253.

This World; NY [3 (1982)].

Thomist, The; Wsh. 0040-6325.

Thought; Bronx NY, Fordham Univ.

TierraN: Tierra Nueva.

Tikkun; Oakland CA. [1,1 (1986)].

TimLitS: Times Literary Supplement; London.

TItSett: Teologia; Brescia (Fac. teol. Italia settentrionale).

TJb: Theologisches Jahrbuch; Leipzig.

TKontext: Theologie im Kontext; Aachen. 0724-1682. ➤ **TContext**.

TLond: Theology; London. 0040-571X.

TLZ: Theologische Literaturzeitung; Berlin. 0040-5671.

TolkNT: Tolkning [commentarius] av Nya Testamentet; Stockholm.

TorJT: Toronto Journal of Theology [1 (1985)].

TPast: Theologie en pastoraat; Zwolle.

TPhil: Theologie und Philosophie; Freiburg/Br. 0040-5655.

TPQ: Theologisch-praktische Quartalschrift; Linz, Ös. 0040-5663.

TPract: Theologia Practica; München/Hamburg. 0720-9525.

TR: Theologische Revue; Münster. 0040-568X.

Traces; annuel des religions; Turnhout. [1 (1986); 2 (1987)].

TradErn: Tradition und Erneuerung (religiös-liberales Judentum); Bern.

Traditio; Bronx NY, Fordham Univ.

Tradition, a journal of orthodox Jewish thought; New York.

TRE: Theologische Realenzyklopädie; Berlin ➤ 813.

TRef: Theologia Reformata; Woerden.

TRevNE: ➤ NESTR.

TRicScR: Testi e ricerche di scienze religiose; Brescia.

TrierTZ: Trierer Theologische Zeitschrift; Trier. 0041-2945.

TrinJ: Trinity Journal; Deerfield IL. 0360-3032.

TrinUn [St/Mon] Rel: Trinity University Studies [Monographs] in Religion, San Antonio TX.

Tripod; Hong Kong, Holy Spirit Study Centre [2 (1981)].

TRu: Theologische Rundschau; Tübingen. 0040-5698.

TS: Theological Studies; Baltimore. 0040-5639.

TsGesch: Tijdschrift voor Geschiedenis; Groningen.

TsLtg: Tijdschrift voor Liturgie; Lv.

TStAJud: Texte und Studien zum Antiken Judentum; Tübingen. 0721-8753.

TsTKi: Tidsskrift for Teologi og Kirke; Oslo. 0040-7194.

TsTNijm: Tijdschrift voor Theologie; Nijmegen (redactie). 0168-9959.

TSzem: Theologiai Szemle; Budapest. 0133-7599.

TTod: Theology Today; Princeton.

TU: Texte und Untersuchungen, Geschichte der altchristlichen Literatur; oBerlin.

Tü [ÄgBei] ThS: Tübinger [Ägyptologische Beiträge; Bonn, Habelt] Theologische Studien; Mainz, Grünewald.

[Tü]TQ: [Tübinger] Theologische Quartalschrift; Mü. 0342-1430.

TUmAT: Texte aus der Umwelt des ATs; Gütersloh ➤ 814.

TVers: Theologische Versuche; oB. 0437-3014.

TViat: Theologia Viatorum, Jb.; B; to 15 (1979s); ➤ BTZ.

TVida: Teología y Vida; Santiago, Chile. 0049-3449.

TWAT: Theologisches Wörterbuch zum Alten Testament; Stu ➤ 815.

TWiss: Theologische Wissenschaft, Sammelwerk für Studium und Beruf; Stu.

TWNT: Theologisches Wörterbuch zum NT; Stuttgart (➤ GLNT; TDNT).

TXav: Theologica Xaveriana; Bogotá.

TxK: Texte und Kontexte (Exegese); Stu.

Tyche, Beiträge zur alten Geschichte, Papyrologie und Epigraphik; Wien.
Tychique (Chemin Neuf); Lyon.
TyndB: Tyndale Bulletin; Cambridge.
TZBas: Theologische Zeitschrift; Basel.
UF: Ugarit-Forschungen; Kevelaer/ Neukirchen. 0342-2356.
Universitas; 1. Stuttgart. 0041-9079; 2. Bogotá. 0041-9060.
UnivT: Universale Teologica; Brescia.
UnSa: Una Sancta: 1. Augsburg-Meitingen; 2. Brooklyn.
UnSemQ: Union Seminary Quarterly Review; New York.
UPA: University Press of America; Wsh/ Lanham MD.
Update [new religious movements]; Aarhus [7 (1983)].
VAeg: Varia Aegyptiaca; San Antonio. 0887-4026 [1 (1985)].
VBGed: Verklaring van een Bijbelgedeelte; Kampen.
VChrét: Vie Chrétienne; P. 0767-3221.
VComRel: La vie des communautés religieuses; Montréal.
VDI: ❸ Vestnik Drevnej Istorii; Moskva. 0321-0391.
Veleia, (pre-) historia, arqueología filología clásicas; Vitoria-Gasteiz, Univ. País Vasco [1 (1984)].
Verbum; 1. SVD; R; 2. Nancy [5 (1983)].
Veritas; Porto Alegre, Univ. Católica.
VerkF: Verkündigung und Forschung; München.
VerVid: Verdad y Vida; Madrid.
VestB: Vestigia Biblica; Hamburg.
VetChr: Vetera Christianorum; Bari.
Vidyajyoti (Theological Reflection); Ranchi (Delhi, Inst. Rel.St.).
VieCons: La Vie Consacrée; P/Bru.
VigChr: Vigiliae Christianae; Leiden. 0042-6032.
ViMon: Vita Monastica; Camaldoli, Arezzo.
ViPe: Vita e Pensiero: Mi, Univ. S. Cuore.
VisLang: Visible Language; Cleveland.
VisRel: Visible Religion, annual for religious iconography; Leiden [3 (1984) 90-04-07496-1].
VitaCons: Vita Consacrata; Milano.

VizVrem: ❸ Vizantijskij Vremennik; Moskva. 0136-7358.
VO: Vicino Oriente; Roma.
Vocation; Paris.
VoxEvca: Vox Evangelica; London. 0263-6786.
VoxEvi: Vox Evangelii; Buenos Aires [NS 1 (1984)].
VoxRef: Vox Reformata; Geelong, Australia.
VoxTh: Vox Theologica; Assen.
VSp: La Vie Spirituelle; Paris. 0042-4935; **S(up).** 0083-5859.
VT: Vetus Testamentum; Leiden.
WDienst: Wort und Dienst; Bielefeld. 0342-3085.
WegFor: Wege der Forschung; Da, Wiss.
WeltOr: Welt des Orients; Göttingen. 0043-2547.
WesleyTJ: Wesleyan Theological Journal; Marion IN. 0092-4245.
WestTJ: Westminster Theological Journal; Philadelphia. 0043-4388.
WEvent: Word + Event, World Catholic Federation for the Biblical Apostolate; Stuttgart; printed in Hong Kong, also in Spanish ed.
WienerSt: Wiener Studien; Wien.
Wiss: Wissenschaftliche Buchhandlung; Da.
WissPrax: Wissenschaft und Praxis in Kirche und Gesellschaft; Göttingen.
WissWeish: Wissenschaft und Weisheit; Mü-Gladbach. 0043-678X.
WMANT: Wissenschaftliche Monographien zum Alten und Neuen Testament; Neukirchen.
WoAnt: Wort und Antwort; Mainz.
Word and Spirit; Still River MA.
WorldArch: World Archaeology; Henley.
World Spirituality ➤ EWSp.
Worship; St. John's Abbey, Collegeville, Minn. 0043-9414.
WrocST: Wrocławskie Studia Teologiczne / Colloquium Salutis; Wrocław. 0239-7714.
WUNT: Wissenschaftliche Untersuchungen zum NT: Tübingen.
WVDOG: Wissenschaftliche Veröffentlichungen der Deutschen Orient-Gesellschaft; Berlin.
WWorld: Word and World; St. Paul.

WZ: Wissenschaftliche Zeitschrift [...
Univ.].
WZKM: Wiener Zeitschrift für die
Kunde des Morgenlandes; Wien.
0084-0076.
YaleClas: Yale Classical Studies; NHv.
Yuval: Studies of the Jewish Music Re-
search Centre [incl. Psalms]; Jerusalem.
ZäSpr: Zeitschrift für Ägyptische
Sprache und Altertumskunde; Ber-
lin. 0044-216X.
ZAHeb: Zeitschrift für Althebraistik;
Stuttgart. 0932-4461 [1,1 (1988)].
ZAss: Zeitschrift für Assyriologie &
Vorderasiatische Archäologie; Ber-
lin. 0048-5299.
ZAW: Zeitschrift für die Alttestament-
liche Wissenschaft; Berlin. 0044-
2526.
ZDialT: Zeitschrift für dialektische
Theologie; Kampen [1 (1985)].
ZDMG: Zeitschrift der Deutschen
Morgenländischen Gesellschaft; Wies-
baden.
ZDPV: Zeitschrift des Deutschen Pa-
lästina-Vereins; Stu. 0012-1169.
ZeichZt: Die Zeichen der Zeit, Evan-
gelische Monatschrift; oBerlin.
Zeitwende (Die neue Furche); Gü.
ZeKUL: Zeszyty Naukowe Katolickiego
Uniwersytetu Lubelskiego; Lublin. 0044-
4405.
ZEthnol: Zeitschrift für Ethnologie;
Braunschweig. 0044-2666.
ZEvEthik: Zeitschrift für Evangelische
Ethik; Gütersloh. 0044-2674.

ZfArch: Zeitschrift für Archäologie:
oBerlin. 0044-233X.
ZGPred: Zeitschrift für Gottesdienst
und Predigt; Gü. [1 (1983)].
Zion: ❶; Jerusalem. 0044-4758.
ZIT: Zeitschriften Inhaltsdienst Theologie; Tübingen. 0340-8361.
ZKG: Zeitschrift für Kirchengeschich-
te; Stuttgart. 0044-2985.
ZkT: Zeitschrift für katholische Theo-
logie; Innsbruck. 0044-2895.
ZMissRW: Zeitschrift für Missions-
wissenschaft und Religionswissen-
schaft; Münster. 0044-3123.
ZNW: Zeitschrift für die Neutesta-
mentliche Wissenschaft und die
Kunde des Alten Christentums; Ber-
lin. 0044-2615.
ZPapEp: Zeitschrift für Papyrologie
und Epigraphik; Bonn. 0084-5388.
ZPraxRU: Zeitschrift für die Praxis
des Religionsunterrichts; Stu.
ZRGg: Zeitschrift für Religions- und
Geistesgeschichte; Köln. 0044-3441.
ZSavR: Zeitschrift der Savigny-
Stiftung (Romanistische) Rechtsge-
schichte: Weimar. 0323-4096.
ZSprW: Zeitschrift für Sprachwissen-
schaft; [3 (1984)].
ZTK: Zeitschrift für Theologie und
Kirche; Tübingen. 0513-9147.
ZvgSpr: Zeitschrift für vergleichende
Sprachforschung; ➤ HSpF ab 1988.
Zwingliana; Zürich [17 (1986-8) 3-
290-11532-1].
Zygon; Winter Park FL. 0044-5614.

| | I. Bibliographica |

A1   *Opera collecta*   .1 **Festschriften,** memorials.

1 Collected essays: CBQ 50 (1988) 152-163.342-353.551-557.739-748; –
Epp E. J. [*al.*], JBL 107 (1988) 169-182.365-373.573-7.777-783; – [E]*Ernst*
Juliette, Mélanges et recueils: AnPg 58 (1987) 812-820; *Langlamet* F.,
Recueils et mélanges: RB 95 (1988) 115-120.417-429.595-604.
2 ALONSO DÍAZ J., Palabra y vida, [E]**Vargas-Machuca** A., *Ruiz* G. 1984
➤ 64,2 ... 3,6: [R]AulaO 6 (1988) 138 (tit. pp.); JTS 39 (1988) 147-150 (A.
Chester: rich and rewarding tribute to a distinguished Spanish scholar);
TPhil 63 (1988) 590-2 (H. *Engel*: tit. pp.).

3 ALONSO SCHÖKEL Luis, El misterio de la palabra, ᴱCollado V., *Zurro* E.
   1983 ➤ 64,3; 65,7: ᴿAulaO 6 (1988) 131 (tit. pp.).
4 AMIET Pierre: Mélanges I = Iranica Antiqua 23 (Gent 1988). xxi-392 p.;
   portr.; bibliog. p. ix-xxi (L. *Vandenberghe*) [II = IrAnt 24 (1989)].
5 ARIELI Yehoshua: Religion, ideology and nationalism in Europe and
   America. J 1986, Shazar Center. 409 p. 30 sheqels. – ᴿRelStR 14 (1988)
   168 (J. D. *Sarna*: for Israel's chief expert on American history).
6 ASMUSSEN Jes P.: A green leaf, papers in honour of ~, ᴱDuchesne-
   Guillemin Jacques, *al.*: Acta Iranica 28. Leiden 1988, Brill. xxix-547 p.;
   xxv pl.; biobibliog. xv-xxvii. 90-6831-094-1. 51 art.; 7 infra.
6* ᶠAYALON David, Studies in Islamic history and civilization, ᴱSharon M.
   J/Leiden 1986, Cana/Brill. 611 p.; XVIII pl. *f* 145. 90-04-08473-8. –
   ᴿBSOAS 51 (1988) 622s (P. M. *Holt*); ZDMG 138 (1988) 422.
7 BÄUMER Remigius: Ecclesia militans; Studien zur Konzilien- und Reformationsgeschichte, ᴱBrandmüller Walter. Pd c. 1988, Schöningh. c. 580 +
   c. 720 p.; bibliog. II 715 ... [< ZIT 89,6 p. 426] 3-506-72195-x.
8 BARIGAZZI Adelmo: Studi in onore di ~, I [= Sileno per 1984 (II per
   1985)], ᴱCasanova Angelo. R 1986, Ateneo. xv-377 p. 41 art., 1 infra.
9 BEDESCHI Lorenzo: Studi: Modernismo, fonti e documenti 13. Urbino
   1984s, Univ. Ist. Storia [RHE 83, p. 50*].
10 BEESTON Alfred F. L.: Ṣayhadica; recherches sur les inscriptions de
   l'Arabie préislamique, ᴱRobin Christian, *Bâfaqîh* Muhammad. P 1987,
   Geuthner. xxxiv-180 + 12 p.; portr.; biobibliog. xv-xxxiv. 12 art., 1 infra.
11 BENZING Johannes: Kritische Beiträge zur Altaistik [Mundus 24,226:
   'Ancient Asiatics'] und Türkologie, ᴱJohanson Lars, *Schönig* Claus: Tur-
   cologica 3. Wsb 1988, Harrassowitz. 230 p.
11* BERLINGER Rudolph: Agora, zu Ehren von ~: Perspektiven der
   Philosophie 13. Amst/Wü 1987, Rodopi/Königshausen-Neumann. 464 p.
   [< AnPg 58,812: 'dépouillé'].
12 BERNHARD Marie-Louise; Études consacrées à ~: Études et Travaux 13.
   Wsz 1983, PWN. 420 p.; ill. 83-01-02408-9. 50 art., 9 infra.
13 BERTETTO Domenico: Virgo fidelis; miscellanea di studi mariani in onore
   di ~, ᴱBergamelli Ferdinando, *Cimosa* Mario: EphLtg Subsidia 43. R
   1988, 'C.L.V.'-Liturgiche. 594 p., portr.; biobibliog. p. 8-33. [Cartha-
   ginensia 5,294, J. M. *Lozano*]. 88-85918-33-6. – 8 art. infra.
14 BHANDARKAR Ramakrishna G. [150th b.], ᴱDandekar R. N. Annals of
   the Bhandarkar Oriental Research Institute 68 (1987). xii-671 p. 50 art.
14* BISCARDI Arnaldo: [I-V 1982-5 ➤ 1,19] VI. Mi 1987, Cisalpina. 567 p.
   [< AnPg 58 (1987) 812: dépouillé].
15 BØCKMAN Peter W.: Teologi på tidens torg: Relieff XXIII. Trondhjem
   1987, Tapir. 224 p. Nkr 150 [TsTKi 58,321].
16 Böhlig Alexander: Religion im Erbe Ägyptens; Beiträge zur spätantiken
   Religionsgeschichte, ᴱGörg Manfred: ÄgAT 14. Wsb 1988, Harrassowitz.
   xx-282 p.; portr.; bibliog. p. ix-xx. 14 art., infra. 3-447-02823-8 [OIAc].
17 BRAMBLE John: Homo viator; classical essays for ~, ᴱWhitby Michael, *al.*
   Bedminster/Oak Park IL 1987, Bristol Classical / Bolchazy-Carducci. xi-
   332 p. 0-86292-291-1; pa. 5-X / 0-86516-205-0; pa. 6-9. 33 art.; 4 infra. –
   ᴿClasR 102 (1988) 383-5 (N. *Horsfall*).
18 BREGLIA Laura: Studi per ~, *Panvini Rosati* F., present.: Bollettino di
   numismatica 4 Sup. R 1987, Ist. Poligrafico e Zecca 0392-971X.
   I. Numismatica greca, 286 p.; 23 art., 1 infra. – II. Numismatica romana e
   medievale, 278 p.; 24 art., 6 infra. – III. Archeologia e storia, 192 p.
   [Bibliog. Breglia, I, 11-15, *Caruso* Teresa].

19 BREUKELMAN Frans: Debharim, opstellen aangeboden aan ~, 70e verjaardag, Kampen 1986, Kok. 215 p. *f* 37,50. 90-242-0824-6. – ᴿNedTTs 42
(1988) 153s (M. J. *Mulder*).

20 CALLAWAY Joseph A. [† shortly after publication]: Benchmarks in time
and culture; an introduction to Palestinian archaeology, ᴱ**Drinkard** Joel
F.ᴶ, *al.*, : ASOR / SBL Archaeol. 1. Atlanta 1988, Scholars. xviii-487 p.;
maps; phot. p. 456; biobibliog. p. 457-464 (E. *Rust, al.*). $45. 1-55540-
172-4; pa 3-2. 22 art.; infra. [BL 89,26, J. R. *Bartlett*].

21 CAPONE Domenico. La coscienza morale oggi; omaggio al prof. ~, ᴱ**Na-**
lepa M., *Kennedy* T.: Quaestiones Morales 3. R 1987, Acad. Al-
phonsiana. 656 p.; portr.; bibliog. 27 art.; 4 on Scr. [NTAbs 32,362]. –
ᴿAntonianum 63 (1988) 616s (T. *Larrañaga*: anche per il 2º centenario
della morte di S. Alfonso LIGUORI); Salmanticensis 35 (1988) 438-441
(J.-R. *Flecha*).

22 CARMIGNAC Jean [1914-1986]: Mémorial, Études Qumrâniennes, ᴱ**García**
Martínez Florentino, *Puech* Émile = RQum 13,49-52 (1988). ix-692 p.;
biobibliog. p. 1-20; indices 657-689. F 950. 48 art., infra.

23 CHADWICK Henry: Christian authority, essays in honour of ~, ᴱ**Evans**
G. R. Ox 1988, Clarendon. x-355 p.; portr.; bibliog. p. 338-347. [TDig
36,53]. 0-19-826683-9. 15 art.; 12 infra.

24 CHEVALLIER Raymond: La mythologie, clef de lecture du monde classique, ᴱ**Martin** P. M., *Ternes* C. M. Tours 1986, Piganiol. [xiv-] 616 p.;
XLV p. pl. [2 vol.]. – ᴿLatomus 47 (1988) 232s (J. *Debergh*).

25 CHILDS Brevard S.: Canon, theology, and Old Testament interpretation;
essays in honor of ~, ᴱ**Tucker** C. M., *al.* Ph 1988, Fortress. xix-347 p.;
bibliog. p. 329-336 (*Trotti* John B.). $40. 0-8006-0854-2. 20 art., infra.
Church History centennial issue: 57 Sup. (1988), c. 140 p. [< ZIT].

26 COLBERT DE BEAULIEU J.-B.: Mélanges. P 1987, Léopard d'Or. 801 p.
76 art. [RBgNum 134 (1988) 193: *Naster* P., monnaies de Mésopotamie,
665-9, lire 'Abgar' pour 'Agbar'].

27 COLEIRO Edward: Laurea corona, Studies in honour of ~ ᴱ**Bonanno**
Anthony (*Vella* H. C. R.). Amst 1987, Grüner, xxiii-232 p.; portr.;
bibliog. p. xvii-xix. 90-6032-300-9. 29 art., 1 infra.

28 CONACHER D. J.: Greek tragedy and its legacy, ᴱ**Cropp** Martin, *al.*
Calgary ALB 1986, Univ. xiv-364 p.; 14 pl. – ᴿAmJPg 109 (1988) 594-7
(Ann N. *Michelini*); Phoenix 42,1 (Toronto 1988) 74-76 (Justina *Gregory*:
details).

28* COURTHIAL Pierre: I. Dieu parle! études sur la Bible et son interprétation, ᴱ*Wells* Paul. Aix-en-Provence 1984, Kerygma. [iv-] 188 p.;
portr. F 80. 13 art.; infra. – II. = RRéf 35[,3] (1984) ➔ 65,d766.
COWGILL Warren mem. 1987 ➔ 675.

29 CRAIGIE Peter C. mem.: Ascribe to the Lord; biblical and other studies,
ᴱ**Eslinger** Lyle M., *Taylor* Glen: JStOT Sup 67. Sheffield 1988, Academic. xv-633 p.; 603-7 bibliog; 593-7 biog. (H. G. *Coward*). £30.
1-85075-189-7 [BL 89,14: subjects; ZAW 101,452, tit. pp.]. 37 art., infra.

30 DAHLERUP Troels: Festskrift til ~, 60-årsdag: Historiske skrifter 5. Århus
1985, Arusia. 427 p. – ᴿTsTKi 58 (1987) 148 (A. B. *Amundsen*: historiker).

31 DE ANGELIS D'OSSAT Guglielmo: Saggi in onore, ᴱ**Benedetti** Sandro,
Miarelli Mariani Gaetano: Ist. Storia dell'Architettura, Quaderni NS 1-10
(1983-7). R 1987, Multigrafica. 616 p., ill.; bibliog. 5-12. 88-7597-042-4.
L'Antichità, 15 art., 2 infra.

31* DEICHMANN Friedrich W.: Studien zur spätantiken und byzantinischen
Kunst, I-III, ᴱ**Feld** Otto, *Peschlow* Urs: Röm/Germ.Vor/FrühGesch. 10.

Bonn 1986, Habelt. vii-285 p.; vi-183 p.; vi-143 p. [< AnPg 58,813: dépouillé].

32 DELLER Karlheinz; Ad bene et fideliter seminandum, Festgabe für ~, EMauer Gerlinde, Magen Ursula: AOAT 220. Kevelaer/Neuk 1988, Butzon & B./Neuk.-V. 332 p.; xvi pl.; Bibliog. p. 1-23. 3-7666-9483-9 / Neuk. 3-7887-1280-5. 14 art.; infra.

33 DESCHAMPS Jan: Miscellanea neerlandica, 70. anniv., ECockx-Indestege Elly, Hendrickx Frans. xi-542 p. portr.; x-470 p.; x-359 p.; ill. Fb 2400, 2000, 1600. – ROnsGErf 62 (1988) 366s (P. Verdeyen).

34 DÍEZ MACHO Alejandro mem., Salvación en la palabra, EMuñoz León D. 1986 → 2,21: RAulaO 6 (1988) 134s (tit. pp.).

35 DI FONZO Lorenzo: Contributi francescani, filosofia, teologia, storia R 1985, Misc. Franc. xliii-442 p.; portr. [Bibliog p. 3-31, Odoardi G., Danza B., anche a parte 1985; 75 p.]; vol. 2, 12 art.; 1 infra. – RColcFr 56 (1986) 162s (S. Gieben).

36 DRIJVERS Pius: Van horen en verstaan; verklaring en gebruik van de Schrift, EBellemakers S., al. Hilversum 1987, Gooi & S. 160 p. Fb 550. – RCollatVL 18 (1988) 125s (P. Kevers).

37 DUBARLE Dominique, †25.IV.1987: Recueil ~ = RICathP 26 (1988): témoignages; 161-185 bibliog. (P. Colin, al.).

38 DUMÉZIL Georges 1898-1986: Hommage à ~ = RÉtGC 3 (1987) [= Bedi Kartlisa 46] xv-262 p.; portr.; biog. ix-xv (G. Charachidzé). 13 art.; 2 infra.

39 DUNAYEVSKY Immanuel 1906-1968, ❿ Ha-adrikalūt ... The architecture of ancient Israel from the prehistoric to the Persian period, in memory of ~, EKatzenstein Hannah, al. J 1987, Israel Exploration Soc. 284 p.; 300 fig. $25. 27 art. – RIsrEJ 38 (1988) 103s (I. G.: English version awaited).

40 Ebrach Abteikirche, Fs. 700 Jahre 1285-1985, EWiemer Wolfgang, Zimmermann Gerd. Ebrach 1985, Vier-Türme. 355 p. – RCîteaux 39 (1988) 367-9 (K. Wollenberg, auch über Fs-PIELENHOFEN 1987).

41 EDWARDS I. E. S.: Pyramid studies and other essays, EBaines John, al.: Occas. Publ. 7. L 1988, Egypt Exploration Society. x-288 p.; portr.; 44 pl. bibliog. p. 1-4 (A. Leahy). 0-85698-106-0. 33 art.; 16 infra.

42 EGGERMONT P. H. L.: India and the ancient world history; trade and culture before A.D. 650, 70th b., EPollet Gilbert, OrLovAnal 25, 1987 → 3,50: 90-70192-15-1; 17 art.; 2 infra. – ROrLovPer 19 (1988) 244s (G. Van Damme).

42* EHRMAN Albert [1933-1981]: Fucus; a Semitic/Afrasian gathering in remembrance of ~, EArbeitman Yoel L. [p. vii gives no indication that 'gathering' means 'meeting' rather than 'compilation']: Current Issues in Linguistic Theory 58. Amst 1988, Benjamins. xvi-530 p.; portrait; bibliog. p. xv-xvi [p. 522-7 give 3 reprints of Ehrman on saqor 'fucus, red lichen', also as root of Iscariot]. 90-272-3552-X. 28 art., 21 infra.

43 ELITZUR Yehuda: ❿ Iyyûnê Miqrā' ... Studies in Bible and Exegesis 2, ESimon Uriel. Ramat-Gan 1986, Bar-Ilan Univ. 282 p.; biog. 9-19 (S. Vargon), bibliog. 21-28 (A. Frisch). [CBQ 51,182]. 12 art., infra.

44 ERON Dov mem., Studies in Hebrew and Arabic, EDotan Aron: Teʿuda 6. TA 1988, Univ. Eng. XXV + ❿ 225 p.; portr.; biobibliog. p. 9-14 [BO 45,476]. 16 art.; 5 infra. – RSefarad 48 (1988) 430-2 (María T. Ortega Monasterio).

45 ÉTIENNE Robert: Hommage au prof. ~ EMayet Françoise = RÉtAnc 88 (1986). 414 p.; portr.; bibliog. p. 9-18. 9 art. Aquitaine; 12 art. péninsule ibérique.

46 FAGGIN Giuseppe: Ars majeutica; scritti in onore di ∼, EVolpi E. Vicenza 1985, Neri Pozza. – RStPatav 34 (1987) 166-173 (A. *Jori*).

47 FENSHAM Frank C.: Text and context; Old Testament and Semitic studies, EClaassen W.: JStOT Sup 48. Sheffield 1988, Academic. 321 p.; portr.; biobibliog. p. 301-310. £25. 1-85075-040-8. 22 art.; infra. [BL 89,12 titles sans pp.; JStJud 20,118; TR 85,74, tit. pp.]. – RHenoch 10 (1988) 391s (P. G. *Borbone*).

FERNÁNDEZ-SEVILLA J., → 102, MARIN N.

48 FISCHER Robert H.: = CurrTM 15,6 (1988); 488-496 biobibliog. (R. W. *Dishno*).

49 FLETCHER VALLS Domingo [II-III]: Archivio de Prehistoria Levantina 18s. Valencia 1988s, Diputación. 439 p.; 453 p. 19 + 24 art., 1 infra.

50 [FONTINOY Charles, discreetly and apparently only for Part I., L'Humour, one article by him and 9 others], EThéodoridès Aristide, *Naster* P., *Ries* J., Humour, Travail et Science en Orient: Acta Orientalia Belgica 5. Lv 1988, Peeters. 364 p.; 3 maps [p. 4-8 phot. biobibliog. Fontinoy]. 38 art., 20 infra.

51 FRANKE Peter R. = Jahrbuch für Numismatik und Geldgeschichte 36 (1986). München [1989], Staatliche Münzsammlung. 183 p.; portr.; 21 pl.; bibliog. p. 9-12.

52 FREI Hans W.: Scriptural authority and narrative interpretation, 65th b., EGreen Garrett. Ph 1987, Fortress. xiii-208 p.; bibliog. 199-201 (by and about Frei). $25. 0-8006-0839-9 [TDig 36,82]. 10 art., infra [< TR 85,73]. – RHorBT 9,2 (1987) 113s (P. D. *Miscall*).

53 GANOCZY Alexandre: Creatio ex amore; Beiträge zu einer Theologie der Liebe, ∼ 60. Gb., EFranke Thomas, *al*. Wü 1988, Echter. 362 p.; portr.; bibliog. p. 353-362. 3-429-01203-1. 23 art.; 19 infra [< ZIT 89,355].

53* GARCÍA LAHIGUERA mons.: Ministerio y carisma; homenaje a ∼. Valencia 1975. → g8.

54 GIMBUTAS Marija: Proto-Indo-European; the archaeology of a linguistic problem, ESkomal Susan N., *Polomé* Edgar C. Wsh 1987, Institute for the study of man. 396 p.; 18 fig.; 12 pl.; 7 maps. $65. 0-941694-29-1. – RAntiquity 62 (1988) 177s (J. *Mallory*).

54* GJERSTAD Einar & Antiquities Dept. 50th anniversary: Archaeologia Cypria 1. Nicosia 1985, Assoc. Cypriot Archaeologists. 137 p.; 24 pl. [< AnPg 58 (1987) 813: dépouillé].

55 GRELOT Pierre, La vie de la parole; de l'Ancien Testament au Nouveau Testament 1987 → 3,63: RJStJud 19 (1988) 266-8 (A. S. van der *Woude*).

56 GRIBOMONT Jean: Mémorial Dom ∼ (1920-1986): StEph AugR 27. R 1988, Inst. Patristicum Augustinianum. 642 p.; portr.; biobibliog. 5-58 (J. *Mallet*, A. *Thibaut*). 35 art.; 10 infra.

57 GRUIJS A.; Codex in context; Studies over codicologie, kartuizergeschiedenis en laatmiddeleeuws geestesleven, EBacker C. de, *al*.: Nijmeegse codicologische cahiers 4-6. Nijmegen-Grave 1985, Alfa. 365 p. – RBTAM 14 (1988) 534-6 (G. *Hendrix*).

GONZÁLEZ P. → 102, MARIN N.

58 GRZYBEK Stanisław: RuBi 41,4 (1988) 273[-360].

59 GUILLAUMONT Antoine: Mélanges ∼, contributions à l'étude des christianismes orientaux, présent. *Lucchesi* E., *Troupeau* G. (p. 307): CahOrientalisme 20. Genève 1988, Cramer. xi-311 p.; portr.; bibliog. p. vii-xi (*Coquin* R. G.) 29 art.; 6 infra. – RPrOrChr 38 (1988) 402s (M. P. *Martin*).

60 HANSON Richard P. C.: Scripture, tradition and reason; a study in the criteria of Christian doctrine, essays in honour of ∼, EBauckham Richard,

Drewery Benjamin. E 1988, Clark. viii-297 p.; portr.; biobibliog. 3-13-32 (A. T. *Hanson*). 0-567-09482-0. 9 art.; 8 infra [NRT 111,954, L.-J. *Renard*].

61 HEINSMANN Heribert; Ministerium iustitiae, 60 Gb., ᴱ**Gabriels** André, *Reinhardt* Heinrich J. E. Essen 1985, Ludgerus. 428 p. 3-97497-174-0. Most but not all on canon law. – ᴿBijdragen 49 (1988) 108 (R. G. W. *Huysmans*).

HEUSS Alfred, Symposion → 684*.

62 HILLER Friedrich: Studien zur klassischen Archäologie, 60 Gb., ᴱ**Braun** Karin, *Furtwängler* Andreas, 1986 → 3,79; DM 120: ᴿEirene 25 (1988) 171s (J. *Bažant*).

63 HIRUDAYAM Ignatius, S.J.; In Spirit and in truth, essays dedicated to ~, the founder of Aikiya Alayam, ᴱ**Viyagappa** Ignatius. Madras 1985, Aikiya Alayam. 247 p. $4. – ᴿJEcuSt 24 (1987) 465s (S. E. *Fittipaldi*).

64 HOFFMANN J. G. H.: Esprit révolutionnaire et foi chrétienne, hommage à ~ = RRéf 39,3 (1988), c. 80 p. [< ZIT 88,528].

65 HOFFMANN Karl, MüStuSprW [→ 1,65], 44ss. Mü 1985, Kitzinger. 812 p. (3 vol.) DM 40 + 33 + 33: ᴿKratylos 33 (1988) 67-71 (H.-P. *Schmidt*).

66 HOLMER Paul: The grammar of the heart; new essays in moral philosophy and theology. SF 1988, Harper & R. 259 p. $25. – ᴿParadigms 4 (1988s) 170s (R. J. *Ray*).

67 HOLWERDA D.: Scholia, Studia ... textuum 1985 → 2,46*: ᴿZSav-R 105 (1988) 976-8 (J. *Konidoris*).

68 HOWE John: Authority in the Anglican communion; essays presented to Bishop ~, ᴱ**Sykes** Stephen W., Toronto 1987, Anglican. 286 p. C$19. – ᴿTLond 91 (1988) 334s (J. H. *Davies*); TorJT 4 (1988) 297-9 (D. *Thompson*).

69 HYMAN Arthur: A straight path; studies in medieval philosophy and culture; essays in honor of ~, ᴱ**Link-Salinger** Ruth, *al.* Wsh 1988, Catholic Univ. of America. xiv-310 p. $35. 24 art. [JQR 77 (1986s!) 340; RÉJ 148,143: both sans pp.].

JOLY Robert 1988 → 585.

70 JORDÁ CERDÁ Francisco, 70 años: Zephyrus 37s. Salamanca 1984s, Univ. 412 p. 32 art. 2 infra.

71 JWAIDEH Wadie: Islamic and Middle Eastern societies; ᴱ**Olson** Robert, *Ani* Salman al-. Brattleboro VT 1987, Amana. 217 p. $17.50; pa. $10 [JNES 47,78].

72 KÁDÁR Zoltan: Acta Classica Univ. Debrecen 22 (1986) 103 p.; biobibliog. 7-11-20 (L. *Havas*; Marta *Nagy*). 10 art.; 2 infra.

73 KANIA Wojciech: Miscellanea patristica = Vox Patrum, Antyk Chrześcijański 12s (1987). Lublin 1988, KUL. 570 p.; portr.; biobibliog. p. 9-37 (S. *Longosz*). zł. 800. 83-228-0123-8. 31 art., 8 infra.

74 KASKE Robert E.: Magister Regis, Studies in honor of, ᴱ**Groos** Arthur, *al.* NY 1986, Fordham Univ. vii-292; front.; p. 18, biog. $50. 19 art., 1 infra. – ᴿSpeculum 63 (1988) 1026 (tit. pp.).

75 KAUFMANN Hans B.: Glaube im Dialog; 30 Jahre religionspädagogische Reform, ~ 60. Gb., ᴱ**Gossmann** K. Gü 1987, Mohn. 308 p. DM 58. 3-579-00219-8 [TsTNijm 28, 203, L. van der *Tuin*; TLZ 114,178s, E. *Winkler*, tit. pp.].

76 KAUFMANN Ludwig, Biotope der Hoffnung, zu Christentum und Kirche heute, ~ zu Ehren, ᴱ**Klein** Nikolaus, *al.*, Olten 1988, Walter. 404 p.; 4 fig. Fs 36. [Orientierung 52, 221 adv.; ZIT 89,68, tit. pp.]. 3-530-07751-8. 30 Art. (meist Befreiung); 4 infra.

77 KEE Howard C.: The social world of formative Christianity and Judaism ['New Perspectives on Ancient Judaism' vol. 1 (also 2: NTAbs 32,171; TDig 37,175)], ᴱNeusner Jacob, *al.* Ph 1988, Fortress. xii-367 p.; bibliog. p. 342-356 (M. *Greenwald*, D. *Edwards*). 0-8006-0875-5. 19 art., infra.

78 KIEFER G.: Contemplata aliis tradere; zum Gedenken an ∼, ᴱFox H., *Mereker* H. Landau 1987, Hochschule Sem. Kath. Theol. ➔ 2278.

79 KIEVIT L.: Verbi Divini Minister, 65 verjaardag, ᴱOort J. van, *al.* Amst 1983, Ten Bolland. 267 p. 90-700-5783-2. – ᴿBijdragen 49 (1988) 345 (J. *Besemer*).

80 KILGORE William J.; Contemporary essays on Greek ideas, ᴱBaird Robert M., *al.* Waco 1987, Baylor Univ. xxii-306 p.; biog. vii-xx (W. F. *Cooper*), bibliog. 295-303. 0-918954-46-0. 18 art.; 3 infra.

81 KIM David S. C.: How can the religions of the world be unified? Interdisciplinary researches in honor of ∼, ᴱWilson Andrew: Symposium series 21. Lewiston NY 1987, Mellen. xv-147 p. [TDig 35,273].

82 KINGDON Robert M.: Regnum, religio et ratio, essays presented to ∼ [ed. SixtC; 60th b.]: SixtC Essays & Studies 8. Kirksville MO 1987, SixtC. 186 p. $25. 15 art. [TDig 35,284].

83 KIRKWOOD Gordon M.: Language and the tragic hero; essays on Greek tragedy, ᴱPucci Pietro, (*Rogers* Stephen B.): Homage Series. Atlanta 1988, Scholars. xv-191 p.; portr.; biobibliogr. p. ix-xv. 1-55540-268-2. 10 art.; 2 infra.

84 KLEINHEYER Bruno: Lebt unser Gottesdienst? Die bleibende Aufgabe der Liturgiereform; 65. Gb., ᴱMaas-Ewerd Theodor. FrB 1988, Herder. 350 p. DM 25. – ᴿTR 84 (1988) 316-320 (K. *Richter*).

85 KLIJN A. F. J.; Text and testimony; essays on New Testament and apocryphal literature, ᴱBaarda T., *al.* Kampen 1988, Kok. 286 p.; portr.; bibliog. p. 276-285 [NRT 111,432, X. *Jacques*]. 90-242-3404-2. 25 art., infra.

86 KOLB Albert: Beiträge zur Geographie der Kulturerdteile: Berliner geographische Studien 20. B 1986, Technische Univ. viii-348 p. DM 34. [*Hassenpflug* W., on Remote Sensing by satellite pictures]. – ᴿMundus 24 (1988) 55 (J. *Hohnholz*: Kolb coined the term for 'cultivated parts of the world').

87 KORHERR Edgar J.: Treue zu Gott — Treue zum Menschen; diakonia liturgia martyria, Fs. 60. Gb. ∼, ᴱSchnider Andreas, *Renhart* Erich. Graz 1988, Styria. 446 p.; ill.; Bibliog. p. 427-436. Sch 298. – ᴿZkT 110 (1988) 499-502 (H. *Pissarek-Hudelist*).

88 KRÄNZLEIN Arnold, Beiträge zur antiken Rechtsgeschichte, ᴱWesener G., *al.*, 1986 ➔ 3,93: ᴿKlio 70 (1988) 230-2 (K. *Treu*).

89 KRISTELLER Paul O.: Supplementum festivum, ᴱHankins James: MedRenTSt 49. Binghamton NY 1987, Medieval & Renaissance Texts and Studies. xxxvii-630 p.; bibliog. p. xvii-xxxvii. $50 [TR 84,515].

90 KÜNG Hans: Gegenentwürfe; 24 Lebensläufe für eine andere Theologie, 60. Gb., ᴱHäring Hermann, *Kuschel* Karl-Josef. Mü 1988, Piper. 378 p. 3-492-03188-9. – ᴿActuBbg 25 (1988) 238 (J. *Boada*); HerdKorr 42 (1988) 254 (U. *Ruh*).

90* KULLMANN Wolfgang: Festgabe 60. Gb., ᴱDoering Klaus, *al.*: Wü Jb Altertumswissenschaft 13. Wü 1987, Schöningh. 271 p.; 3 pl. [< AnPg 58,814: dépouillé].

91 LABARBE Jules; Stemmata; mélanges de philologie, d'histoire et d'archéologie grecques, ᴱServais Jean †, *Hackens* Tony, *Servais-Soyez* Brigitte: AntClas Sup. Liège 1987. xvi-464 p.; portr.; biobibliog. p. v-xvi. 37 art., 4 infra.

92 LABROUSSE Michel = Pallas 1986. Toulouse 1987, Univ. ⟶ 3,98:
ᴿRÉLat 65 (1987) 421s (tit. pp.).

93 LADIKA Josip: Bogoslovska Smotra 58,4 (Zagreb 1988). 176 p.; biog. 3-
13 (J. *Baloban*, A. *Hoblaj*).

94 LAUSBERG Heinrich: Text-Etymologie; Untersuchungen zu Textkörper
und Textinhalt, Fs. für ∼ 75 Gb., ᴱArens Arnold. Wsb 1987, Steiner.
434 p. DM 120 [Hermes 116/2 adv., authors only].

95 LE BONNIEC Henri: Res Sacrae, hommages à ∼, ᴱPorte Danielle, *Ne-
raudau* J.-P. [Sorbonne et] Coll. Latomus 201. Bru 1988. xiii-466 p.; phot.;
bibliog. p. xiii-xvi. 2-87031-141-9. 41 art.; 4 infra.

96 LECHNER Odilo, Abt: Weite des Herzens, Weite des Lebens. Rg c. 1988,
Pustet [TPhil 63,60].

97 LINDARS Barnabas [= Frederick C.]: It is written; Scripture citing
Scripture; ᴱCarson D. A., *Williamson* H. G. M. C 1988, Univ. xx-381 p.;
portr.; bibliog. p. xiii-xvi. £37.50. 0-521-32347-9. 10 art. on OT; 9 on
citations in the separate NT areas; infra. – ᴿTrinJ 9 (1988) 223-231 (C. A.
Evans: very detailed analyses).

97* LØNNING Inge: 50 år: NorTTs 89,1 (1988).

LOHSE Bernhard, 60. Gb. ᴱGrane L. 1988 ⟶ 224.

98 (I) LORETZ Oswald: Cananea selecta, Fs. 60. Gb., present. *Xella* P. =
StEpLing 5 (1988). 229 p.; phot.; bibliog. p. 1-12. 17 art., infra.

99 (II) LORETZ Oswald: = UF 20 (1988). 418 p.; portr.

100 MADER Johann: Verantwortung; Beiträge zur praktischen Philosophie,
ᴱVetter Helmuth, *al*. W 1987, Univ. 225 p. – ᴿTPhil 63 (1988) 467-9
(M. *Brasser*: ... Semantik, HEIDEGGER).

101 MARÇAIS Philippe: Mélanges à la mémoire de ∼ [† 1980], ᴱMartin
Aubert. P 1985, A. Maisonneuve. xvi-199 p.; portr.; bibliog. p. xiii-xv.
2-7200-1032-4. 13 art.; 4 infra.

102 MARIN N., FERNÁNDEZ-SEVILLA J., GONZÁLEZ P.:   Studia litteraria
atqve lingvistica ∼ oblata. Granada 1988, Univ.

103 MARTYN J. Louis: Apocalyptic and the New Testament, ᴱMarcus Joel,
Soards Marcus L.: JStOT Sup. 24. Sheffield 1988, Academic. c. 225 p.
£25; sb. £18.50. 1-85075-175-7 [JPseud 2,126 adv.].

104 MAYRHOFER Manfred: Festgabe 60. Gb. = Die Sprache 32,1 (1986)
245 p. [⟶ 3,113] + Fasz. 2, p. 247-756. 22 art.

105 MEISEZAHL Richard O., Vicitrakusumāñjali, ᴱEimer Helmut: Indica et
Tibetica 11. Bonn 1986, Indica et Tibetica. xiv-146 p. DM 36. [Some on
Sanskrit or missionary scholarship: Mundus 24,99].

106 METZ Johann B.: Mystik und Politik; Theologie im Ringen um
Geschichte und Gesellschaft, ∼ 60. Gb., ᴱSchillebeeckx Edward. Mainz
1988, Grünewald. 413 p.; Bibliog. p. 407-411 [NRT 111,449, R. *Escol*].
3-7867-1372-3. 35 art., 13 infra. – ᴿHerdKorr 42 (1988) 541s (U. *Ruh*);
Orientierung 52 (1988) 205-9 (W. *Dirks*).

107 MEYER Robert T.,   Diakonia, Studies in honor of ∼, ᴱHalton Thomas
P., *Williman* Joseph P. 1986 ⟶ 2,73: ᴿSpeculum 63 (1988) 742 (tit. pp.).

108 MITCHELL Basil: The rationality of religious belief; essays in honour of
∼, ᴱAbraham William J., *Holtzer* Steven W. Ox 1987, Clarendon.
viii-269 p. $52. 13 art. [TDig 35,83].

109 MONNERET DE VILLARD Ugo (1881-1954): Studi in onore di ∼ III.
India, Iran, Asia centrale e rapporti tra oriente e occidente, ᴱBussagli
Mario, *al*. = RSO 60 (1986) [1988]. 243 p. 13 art.; 2 infra.

110 MUTH Robert: Mythos, Deutung und Bedeutung [70. Gb., Vorträge
von:] *Kullman* W., *Flashar* H., *Hampl* F.: BeiKulturW 5. Innsbruck 1987,
Univ. 67 p.; 18 fig.; 4 color. pl..

111 MYLONAS George E.,   Ⓖ *Philia epē* (60th year of excavating) I, ᴱ**Bonis**
K.G., 1986 ⇢ 3,121*a*; xv-347 p.; 58 pl.; biobibliog. 1-16. 20 art.+11 Ⓖ. –
II, 1988; 419 p.; 69 pl.; 19 art.+17 Ⓖ. – Infra 9 art.
NAGEL Wolfram, Altvorderasien 1988 ⇢ 234; ᶠNASTER Paul, 1988 ⇢ 763.

111* ORLANDIS ROVIRA José: Hispania christiana, ᴱ**Saranyana** J.I., *Tejero*
E.: HistIgl 14.   Pamplona 1988, Eunsa.   799 p.; ill.; bibliog. 27-47 [AnnTh
3,415-9, A. *Chacon*].

112 OSBORN Eric: In honour of ∼, = Australian Biblical Review 35 (1987).
c. 120 p.; 1-5 biobibliog., *Breward* Ian.   14 art.; some infra, many 1987.

112* OTTEN Heinrich: Documentum Asiae Minoris antiquae, 75. Gb., ᴱ**Neu**
Erich, *Rüster* Christel.   Wsb 1988, Harrassowitz.   x-420 p.; portr.; bibliog.
p. 371-7 (Jana *Siegelová*). 3-447-02866-1.   27 art., 15 infra.

113 PALAZZINI Pietro, card.:   Studi in onore di ∼, ᴱ**Leoni** Francesco, *Lanzi*
Nicola.   Pisa 1987, Giardini.   239 p. – ᴿDocCom 40 (1987) 291-5 (D.
Composta).

114 PANNENBERG Wolfhart: Vernunft des Glaubens; wissenschaftliche Theologie und kirchliche Lehre, Fs. 60. Gb., ᴱ**Rohls** Jan, *Wenz* Gunther. Gö
1988, Vandenhoeck & R.   734 p.; portr.; Bibliog. p. 689-718, *Burkhardt*
Berndt, 438 items; 719-731, mit. *Dunkel* Achim, Sekundärliteratur deutsch,
77 items; Eng. 78-235. 3-525-58152-1.   30 art., 20 infra.

115 PESCH Wilhelm: Studien zum Matthäusevangelium, Fs. für ∼, 65. Gb.,
ᴱ**Schenke** Ludger: SBS.   Stu 1988, KBW.   317 p. DM 39 [CBQ 51,190]
3-460-32721-9.   15 art., infra.

116 PETERS Eugene H. 1929-1983,   Faith and creativity, essays in honor of
∼, ᴱ**Nordgulen** George, *Shields* George W.   St. Louis 1987, 'CBP'. -
237 p. $13 [CBQ 50,560; TDig 35,58]. 10 art., largely on process theology.

117 PIFFL-PERČEVIĆ Theodor: Am Beginn des theologischen Dialogs; Dokumentation des römischen, des Wiener und des Salzburger Ökumenismus;
zehn Pro-Oriente-Symposien 1982-5, ᴱ**Stirnemann** Alfred: Pro Oriente 10.
Innsbruck 1987, Tyrolia.   420 p. DM 64. – ᴿZkT 110 (1988) 225 (L. *Lies*).

118 PINTORE Franco mem.:   Studi Orientalistici, ᴱ**Carruba** O. *al.* 1983
⇢ 64,94:   ᴿBO 45 (1988) 289-291 (B. *Halpern*: high praise).
ᶠPOLOTSKY H.J., I. Essays on Egyptian 1985-6 ⇢ 711; Lingua Sapientissima 1984/7 ⇢ 712.

119 POSENER Georges, mém.: RÉgp 39 (1988).   227 p.   2-252-02201-9.

119* PUGLIESE CARRATELLI Giovanni: 75º compleanno: Studi classici e
orientali 37.   Pisa 1987, Giardini.   594 p. [< AnPg 58,815: dépouillé].
QUACQUARELLI Antonio, Sapientia et eloquentia 1988 ⇢ 246.

120 RAAB Heribert: Staat und katholische Wissenschaft in der Neuzeit [p.
209-217, *Studer* Eduard, Reformation kein Thema? ... Goethezeit].

121 RADICE Betty: The translator's art, essays in honour of ∼, ᴱ**Radice**
William, *Reynolds* Barbara. Hw 1987, Penguin.   281 p. £7. – ᴿClasR 102
(1988) 386s (R. *Stoneman*).

122 RADKE Gerhard: Beiträge zur altitalischen Geschichte, ᴱ**Altheim-Stiehl**
Ruth, *Rosenbach* Manfred.   Münster 1986, Aschendorff.   376 p.; 15 pl.
[RÉLat 65,424].

122* REPGEN Konrad: Politik und Konfession, 60. Gb., ᴱ**Albrecht** Dieter, *al.*
B 1983, Duncker & H.   591 p.; portr. DM 178. – ᴿZkT 110 (1988) 248.
Revista Bíblica (Buenos Aires) Jubileo 1939-1988: RBíbArg 50,2s (1988).

123 RIBUOLI Riccardo: (I) Commemoratio, Studi di filologia in ricordo di ∼,
ᴱ**Prete** S.: Didascalie. 2. Sassoferrato 1986, Ist. Studi Piceni. 135 p. – (II)
Studi per ∼, filologia, musicologia, storia, ᴱ**Piperno** F.   R 1986, Storia e
Letteratura.   175 p. – ᴿBStLat 17 (1987) 188-190 (C. *Salemme*).

124 [ROBINSON J. A. T.:], God's Truth; essays to celebrate the 25th anniversary of Honest to God, ᴱJames Eric. L 1988, SCM. £9.50 [TLond
91,566]. – ᴿNBlackf 69 (1988) 297s (M. *Wiles*).

124* RODRÍGUEZ ADRADOS Francisco: Athlon, satura grammatica II. ᴱBa-
deñas de la Peña P., *al.* M 1987, Gredos. 899 p. [I. 1984, 540 p.: AnPg 55,
Nᵒ 13442].

125 ROSE D. Glenn mem. [aet. 53, † 1982]: Archaeology and biblical interpretation, ᴱPerdue Leo G., *Toombs* Lawrence E., *Johnson* Gary L.
Atlanta 1987, Knox. xiii-365 p.; 42 fig. $25 [TDig 35,258]. 11 art. –
ᴿNESTR 9,2 (1988) 48-50 (L. E. *Siverns*).

126 RUSSELL George H.: Medieval English religious and ethical literature;
essays in honour of ∼, ᴱKratzmann Gregory, *Simpson* James. C 1986,
Brewer. vi-250 p.; portr.; biog. p. 1-18. $37.50. 17 art. – ᴿRelStR 14
(1988) 258 (E. U. *Crosby*: for a New Zealander who after Cambridge
taught in Australia); Speculum 63 (1988) 1027 (tit. pp.).

127 ṢALEḤ ʿAbdel-ʿAziz: ASAE 71 (1987). xiv-264 p.; résumés ❹ 1-7; portr.;
biobibliog. vii-xiv. 25 art.; 16 infra.

128 SARKADY János: Acta Classica Univ. Debrecen 23 (1987). 105 p.; bibliog.
p. 97-101 (Z. *Nemes*). 11 art.

129 SCHEELE Paul-Werner: *a*) Communio sanctorum; Einheit der Christen —
Einheit der Kirche, ᴱSchreiner Josef. Wü 1988, Echter. 637 p.; bibliog.
p. 625-633. DM 68 [TR 84,249; ZkT 111,380-2, L. *Lies*]. – *b*) Bischof und
Dom, Fs 60. Gb., & 800. Wiederkehr der Würzburger Domweihe: Wü
Diözesangeschichtsblätter 50 (1988). c. 800 p. [< ZIT 88,549].

130 SCHEIBER Alexander: Occident and Orient; a tribute to the memory of
∼, ᴱDán Robert. Budapest/Leiden 1988, Akadémiai/Brill. 419 p.; portr.
963-05-4024-X / 90-04-08169-0. 37 art.; 5 infra.

131 SCHILLING Hans: Den Menschen nachgehen; offene Seelsorge als Diakonie in der Gesellschaft, 60. Gb., ᴱSchulz Ehrenfried, *al.* Sankt Ottilien
1987, EOS. xiii-363 p.; portr. 3-88096-023-2. 18 art.; 1 infra [< ZIT 88,655].

132 SCHIRMANN Hayyim (= Jefim): Jubilee Volume, ᴱAbramson Shraga,
Mirsky Aaron. J 1970, Schocken Inst. (x-) 430 p.; portr.; bibliog.
p. 413-427 (*Pages* D., *Fleischer* E.). 23 art., meist neoheb. Lit.; 4 infra.

132* SCHNEIDER Ulrich: Hinduismus und Buddhismus, ᴱFalk Harry. Fr 1987,
Hedwig Falk. 414 p.; 9 pl. DM 84. – ᴿJRAS (1988) 424s (K. *Werner*).

133 Schweiz.-KBW, 50-Jahr.: Egger Rita, *al.*, Die Bibel lebt; 21 Er-
fahrungsberichte. Z 1986 (FrS, Imba). 133 p. – ᴿNZMissW 43 (1987) 226s
(G. *Schelbert*).

133* SCHWENDENWEIN Hugo: Recht im Dienste des Menschen, eine
Festgabe ∼ 60. Gb., ᴱLüdicke Klaus, *al.* Graz 1986, Styria. 671 p.;
Biobibliog. 19-25 (G. *Wieser*) 27-30. DM 100. 40 art. – ᴿTR 84 (1988)
494-7 (Ursula *Beykirch*).

134 SEVČENKO Ihor: Okeanos, ᴱMango Cyril, *al.* 1983 ➤ 3,149; biog. p. 1-4
(O. *Pritsak*); bibliog. 5-26 (M. *Labunka*); 0363-5570; 48 art., 3 infra.

135 SIMON Heinrich: Der Vordere Orient in Antike und Mittelalter, Festgabe
für ∼, 65. Gb. B 1987, Humboldt-Univ. 63 p.; phot. – ᴿOLZ 83 (1988)
267s (D. *Sturm*).
ᶠSIRET Luis 1984/6 ➤ 772.

136 SPAEMANN Robert: *Oikeiōsis*, Fs. für ∼, ᴱLöw Reinhard. Weinheim
1987, Acta Humaniora. x-339. DM 68. 3-527-17588-1. – ᴿGregorianum
69 (1988) 804s (X. *Tilliette*).

137 STACHEL Günter: Glauben ermöglichen; zum gegenwärtigen Stand der
Religionspädagogik, Fs für ∼, ᴱPaul Eugen, *Stock* Alex. Mainz 1987,

Grünewald. 386 p. DM 48. – ᴿForumKT 3 (1987) 318s (H.-A. *Klein*); ZkT 110 (1988) 496-9 (H. *Pissarek-Hudelist*).

138 Starr Chester G.: The craft of the ancient historian, ᴱEadie John W., *Ober* Josiah. Lanham MD 1985, UPA. x-458 p.; 1-20, Starr as historian (E. *Badian*). $34.25. 0-8191-4787-3; 20 art., 3 infra. – ᴿLatomus 47 (1988) 476s (J. A. *Straus*: haute qualité).

139 Stevenson R. B. K.: From the Stone Age to the 'Forty-Five, ᴱO'Connor Anne, *Clarke* D. V. E 1983, Donald. xiii-621 p.; portr.; bibliog. p. 616-621. 37 art., mostly Scots archeology.

140 Stoodt Dieter, Unterwegs für die Volkskirche, 60. Gb., ᴱFederlin Wilhelm-Ludwig. Fra 1987, Lang. 707 p.; ill.; Biobibliog. p. 679-787. 3-8204-9846-X. 50 art.; 11 infra.

141 Stuhlmueller Carroll: Scripture and prayer, a celebration for ~, ᴱOsiek Carolyn, *Senior* Donald. Wilmington 1988, Glazier. [vi-] 184 p.; portr.; bibliog. p. 158-178 (K. G. *O'Malley*). [NewTR 3/4,93, L. *Boadt*]. 11 art., infra.

141* Tandoi Vincenzo: Studi Classici e Orientali 26. Pisa 1986, Giardini. 328 p. [< AnPg 58,816: dépouillé].

142 Tena Pere: La celebración posconciliar de la Eucaristía, homenaje a Mons. ~ = Phase 28,165s (1988) 177-367. 19 art.; 1 infra.
ᶠThomsen Christian J., [b. 29.XII.1788] 1987/8 → 777.

142* Thomsen Rudi: Studies in ancient history and numismatics, 70 b. ᴱDamsgaard-Madsen Aksel, *al.* Aarhus 1988, Univ. 270 p.; portr.; bibliog. 243s (S. E. *Mathiassen*). 24 art.; 6 infra.

143 Tietjen John H.: For the sake of the Gospel; essays in honor of ~ = CurrTM 15,1 (1988). 136 p.; portr.; bibliog. 10-15 (H. Lucille *Hager*). 8 art. infra + songs etc.

143* Tietze Andreas: Fs 70. Gb. = WZKM 26 (W 1986). 328 p. 39 art. on Turcology, also Ottoman [JRAS 88,188].
Tréheux Jacques: Colloque en l'honneur de ~ 1988 → 698.

144 Tucci Giuseppe: Orientalia ~ memoriae dicata, ᴱGnoli Gherardo, *Lanciotti* Lionello: Serie Orientale Roma 56. R 1985/7/8 Ist. Italiano per il Medio ed Estremo Oriente. xx-455 p.; p. 459-1004; p. 1007-1570. 100 art.; 3 infra.

144* Uleyn Arnold: Rond godsdienst en psychoanalyse, essays voor dr. ~; ᴱBelzen J. A. Van, *Lans* J. M. Van der, Kampen c. 1987, Kok. 224 p. – ᴿCollatVL 18 (1988) 124 (E. Vanden *Berghe*).

145 Veen J. M. van: Terugblik voor de toekomst, 80e verjaardag, ᴱOosterzee Klaas van, *Zunneberg* Herman. Kampen 1986, Kok. 128 p. ƒ 32,50. 90-242-0774-6 [NedTTs 42,169].
Verbeke W. 1988 → a67.

146 Vergote A.: Over de grens, de religieuze 'behoefte' kritisch onderzoekt, ᴱHutsebaut J., *Corveleyn* J., Lv 1987, Univ./Peeters. x-276 p. Fb 750. 90-6186-240.X. – ᴿTsTNijm 28 (1988) 106 (D. *Loose*).

146* Vernant Jean-Pierre: Poikilia, présent. Detienne Marcel, *al.*: RHScSoc 26. P 1987, ÉPHÉS. 464 p. [< AnPg 58,816: dépouillé].

147 Wallace Pat: Religious education and the future, ᴱLane Dermot A. Dublin c. 1986, Columba.

147* Walser Gerold: Labor omnibus unus, 70 Gb., ᴱHerzig Heinz E., *Frei-Stolba* Regula. Hist-Einz. 60. Wsb 1988, Steiner. 368 p. DM 90 [Hermes 116/4 adv.].

148 Weingreen Jacob: 80th b., ᴱBeattie D. R. G., *Russell* E. A. = Irish Biblical Studies 10,1 + 4 (1988). 60 p.; bibliog. p. 4-11 (*McCann* E.); p. 166-224.
ᶠWendorf Fred 1987 → g445.

149 WERBLOWSKY R.J. Zwi, Gilgūl; essays on transformation, revolution
and permanence in the history of religions; EShaked S.: Numen Sup 50.
Leiden 1987, Brill. viii-326 p.; bibliog. p. 1-10. 22 art.; 10 infra.
150 WIDMER Gabriel-P.: BCentProt 40,5s (1988). 62 p.; bibliog. p. 55-62.
F 10.
151 WINDER Richard B.: A way prepared; essays on Islamic culture,
EKazemi Farhad, McChesney R.D. NY 1988, NY Univ. xxiii-299 p.
$45 [JNES 47,238].
152 WORMELL D.E.W.: Hermathena 143 (1987) 120 p.; front. [JTS 18,676].
153 ZAW 100. Band (1988) Supplement. 280 p., infra; p. 2-21, Smend Rudolf,
Die älteren Herausgeber der Zeitschrift für die alttestamentliche Wissenschaft.
154 ZEDDA Silverio: RivB 36,3 (1988) 285-375; portr.; bibliog. p. 285s [fasc. 3;
ma anche fasc. 4 p. 425-437 e 439-461; inoltre p. 540-2, apprezzamento di
Canfora Giovanni, specie per la difesa dell'Associazione Biblica Italiana
da parte di Zedda come presidente].

A1.2   **Miscellanea** unius auctoris.

155 **Aalen** Sverre, Gud i Kristus; nytestamentlige studier. Oslo 1986, Univ.
128 p. 82-00-18360-2. 6 art., 1952-71 [NTAbs 32,361]. – RTsTKi 58
(1987) 71s (R. Hvalvik).
156 **Adams** Daniel J., Cross-cultural theology; Western reflections in Asia
[articles 1974-84]. Atlanta 1988, Knox. vi-124 p. $20 [TDig 35,339].
157 **Adams** James L., a) The prophethood of all believers, EBeach George K.,
1986 ► 3,175; – b) Voluntary associations, EEngel J. Ronald. 1986,
Exploration. – RTTod 45 (1988s) 79-83 (W.J. Everett).
158 **Adams** Robert M., The virtue of faith and other essays in philosophical
theology. NY 1987, Oxford-UP. xi-270 p. £22.50; pa. £9. – RTLond 91
(1988) 522s (B. Mitchell).
159 **Alföldy** Géza, Römische Herresgeschichte, Beiträge 1962-1985: Mavors
Roman Army Researches 3. Amst 1987, Gieben. xii-575 p. ill. DM 150. –
RClasR 102 (1988) 335-7 (T. Wiedemann); Gymnasium 95 (1988) 452s (P.
Herz).
160 **Arzi** Meir, Ⓗ Qobeṣ ma'amarim [collection of essays in biblical research].
TA 1988, Meir Fund. [OIAc D88].
161 **Aubineau** Michel, CHRYSOSTOME... et alii; patristique et hagiographie
grecques; inventaires de manuscrits, textes inédits, traductions, études:
Collected Studies 276. L 1988, Variorum. xvi-366 p. £34. – RRHE 83
(1988) 687-690 (A. de Halleux).
162 **Baum** Gregory, Theology and society [< The Ecumenist etc.]. NY 1987,
Paulist. vi-298 p. $13 [TDig 35,340; NRT 111,105, L. Volpe].
163 **Becatti** Giovanni [† 1973], Kosmos, studi sul mondo classico: StArch 37.
R 1987, Bretschneider. xv-765; (color.) ill. [Athenaeum 67, 316-8, C.
Saletti]. – RAJA 92 (1988) 447s (Brunilde S. Ridgway).
164 **Bethge** Eberhard, Bekennen und Widerstehen. Mü 1984, Kaiser. 247 p.
– RRelStR 14 (1988) 143 (Martha J. Reineke).
165 **Biffi** I., Esistenza cristiana, principi e prassi. Casale Monferrato 1987,
Piemme. 72 p. – RRivScR 2 (1988) 416-8 (E. Juliá).
166 **Boff** Leonardo, Zeugen Gottes in der Welt; Ordensleben heute [Aufsätze
1971-6]. Z 1985, Benziger. 344 p. – RTPhil 63 (1988) 305s (M. Sievernich).
167 **Borgen** P., Philo, John and Paul; new perspectives on Judaism and early
Christianity: BrownJudSt 13. Atlanta 1987, Scholars. 324 p. $42. 1-
55540-183-0 [NTAbs 32,230].

168 **Braulik** Georg, Studien zur Theologie des Deuteronomiums: SBAufs 2. Stu 1988, KBW. 342 p. DM 39 pa. [CBQ 51,186]. 3-460-06021-2. 10 art., ➤ 7705.

169 **Brunner** Hellmut, Das hörende Herz; Kleine Schriften zur Religions- und Geistesgeschichte Ägyptens, ᴱ*Röllig* Wolfgang: OBO 80. FrS/Gö 1988, Univ./VR. x-433 p. Fs 98/DM 145. 3-7278-0567-6 / 3-525-53709-3 [BL 89,121, K. A. *Kitchen*; ZAW 10,310, tit. pp.].

170 **Calmel** R. T. [o.p. † 1975], Brève apologie pour l'Église de toujours [réimprimés < Itinéraires]; postface *Mardiran* Jean, 'L'Église de France était occupée et tenue par une gauche maçonnique et moderniste que couronnait le trio cardinalice Liénart-Feltin-Gerlier' p. 149. Orleans 1987, Difralivre. 152 p. – ᴿEsprVie 98 (1988) 87s (P. *Jay*: contre PAUL VI).

171 **Cassin** Elena, Le semblable et le différent; symbolismes du pouvoir dans le Proche-Orient ancien [11 reprints + ineditum added to 'Le droit et le tordu']: Textes à l'appui. P 1987, Découverte. 374 p. F 225. 2-7071-1656-4. – ᴿBO 45 (1988) 81-84 (M. *Stol*: tit. pp. analyses).

172 **Clarke** Thomas E., Playing in the Gospel; spiritual and pastoral models. KC 1986, Sheed & W. 192 p. $9. – ᴿRExp 85 (1988) 159 (E. G. *Hinson*: despite title, serious essays).

173 **Congar** Yves, *a)* Called to life [... spirituality, 13 published articles], ᵀ*Burridge* William. NY 1988, Crossroad. vii-148 p. $13 [TDig 35,159]. – ᴿHomP 88,12 (1987s) 84 (J. R. *Sheets*). – *b)* Llamados a la vida [< Vie Spir], ᵀ*Kirchner* Montserrat. Barc 1988, Herder. 190 p. pt. 950. 88-254-1584-5. – ᴿActuBbg 25 (1988) 262s (I. *Riudor*).

174 **Cothenet** Éd., Exégèse et liturgie [conférences 1972-87]: LDiv 133. P 1988, Cerf. 356 p. F 200. 3-204-02931-9 [ÉTRel 64,630, M. *Bouttier*; NRT 111,290, A. *Harvengt*].

175 **Curran** Charles E., Tensions in moral theology [10 reprints]. ND 1988, Univ. vii-214 p. $20. 0-268-01866-9 [TDig 36,152].

176 **Deku** Henry, Wahrheit und Unwahrheit der Tradition; metaphysische Reflexionen [22 Aufsätze 1953-82], ᴱ*Bierwaltes* Werner. St. Ottilien 1986, EOS. 490 p. – ᴿTPhil 63 (1988) 442-4 (J. *Splett*).

177 **Delp** A., Der Herrgott (Ges. Schr.), ᴱ*Bleistein* R., I-IV, Fra 1985, Knecht [TPQ 136,267].

178 **De Mesa** José M., In solidarity with the culture; studies in theological re-rooting [10 art.]: Maryhill Studies 4. Quezon City 1987, Mary Hill School of Theology [TKontext 10,129, G. *Evers*].

179 **Dietzfelbinger** Hermann, 'Überfluss haben am Wort der Wahrheit', LUTHERs erste Sorge. Fürth 1984, Flacius. 112 p. [< LuJb 55 (1988) 139; 5 dort zitierte Art.].

180 **DIMIER** Anselme: Mélanges à la mémoire du Père ~, présent. **Chauvin** Benoît; 1. L'homme, l'œuvre; 2. travaux inédits et rééditions. Arbois 1987, Chauvin. 861 p.; ill. [TR 84,515].

181 **Dover** Kenneth J., Greek and the Greeks; collected papers I. Ox 1987, Blackwell. viii-318 p. £32.50. – ᴿClasR 102 (1988) 377s (H. *Lloyd-Jones*: excellent).

182 **Dubourg** B., L'invention de Jésus, I. L'Hébreu [langue originale] du NT [8 art., some reprinted]: L'Infini. P 1987, Gallimard. 283 p. F 95. 2-07-071093-9 [NTAbs 32,370].

183 **Dulles** Avery, The reshaping of Catholicism; current challenges in the theology of Church. SF 1988, Harper & R. xii-276 p. $20 [CBQ 51,187]. 0-06-254856-5. 12 art., infra.

184 **Dunn** J. D. G.,   The living word [4 Oxford lectures + 2 Churchman articles; on NT authority...]. L/Ph 1987, SCM/Fortress.   ix-196 p.   £7 pa. /0-8006-2097-6. – ᴿTLond 91 (1988) 524s (F. *Watson*).

185 **Dupront** Alphonse,   Du sacré; croisades et pèlerinages, images et langages [art. 1958-1986]: Bibliothèque des histoires.   P 1987, Gallimard.   544 p. – ᴿRThom 88 (1988) 674 (B. *Montagnes*).

186 **Efron** J.,   Studies on the Hasmonean period [< 1980 ❺ reprints, Ḥiqrê ha-Teqûpâ...]: StJudLA 39.   Leiden 1987, Brill.   xvi-442 p. *f* 144.   90-04-07609-3.   7 art. [JPseud 2,120].

187 **Eminjan** Maurice,   Signs of the times.   Malta 1987, Jesuit Publications. vi-106 p. – ᴿMeliT 39 (1988) 74-76 (J. *Cassar Pullicino*).

188 **Fackenheim** Emil L.,   The Jewish thought of ∼; a reader [40 selections] ᴱ*Morgan* Michael L.   Detroit 1987, Wayne State Univ.   394 p. $40; pa. $16 [TDig 35,356].

189 **Fichter** Joseph H.,   A sociologist looks at religion: Theology and Life 23. Wilmington 1988, Glazier.   256 p. $16 pa.   0-89453-637-0 [TDig 36,158].

190 **Flusser** David, ᴱ*Young* Brad,   Judaism and the origins of Christianity.   J 1988, Magnes.   xxviii-725 p.; 13 phot.   965-233-627-6.   32 reprints + 13 inedita; 20 infra.

191 **Flusser** D.,   Entdeckungen im NT I. Jesusworte und ihre Überlieferung [18 art., jetzt alle deutsch]. Neuk 1987, Neuk-V.   viii-260 p. DM 58 pa. 3-7887-0793-3 [NTAbs 32,363]; ÉTRel 64,117, M. *Bouttier*].

192 **Flusser** David,   Tussen oorsprong en schisma; artikelen over Jezus, het jodendom en het vroege christendom, ᵀ*Bruin* T. de, *al.*: Informatie Jodendom 2.   Hilversum 1984, Folkertsma.   360 p. [KirSef 61,397].

193 **Forte** Bruno, *a*) Laïcat et laïcité, essais ecclésiologiques.   P/Montréal 1987, Médiaspaul/Paulines.   122 p. F 57. – ᴿEsprVie 98 (1988) 397s (P. *Jay*). – *b*) Laie sein; Beiträge zu einem ganzheitlichen Kirchenverständnis [5 Aufsätze]. Mü 1987, Neue Stadt.   118 p. DM 14,80. – ᴿTGL 78 (1988) 175s (W. *Beinert*).

194 **Fries** Heinrich,   'Damit die Welt glaube'; Gefährdung, Ermutigung, Erneuerung 1987 → 3,220: ᴿNorTTs 89 (1988) 206-8 (Ola *Tjørhom*).

195 **Galot** Jean,   Vivere con Maria nella vita consacrata [< VitaCons 1983-6]. Mi 1987, Àncora.   204 p. [Salesianum 50,603].

196 **Gaston** Lloyd,   Paul and the Torah (7 reprints + 3 inedita].   Vancouver 1987, Univ. British Columbia.   262 p.   0-7748-0284-7. – ᴿJStNT 33 (1988) 117s (D. *Hill*: tour de force claiming no anti-Judaism or criticism of Torah in Paul); SWJT 31,2 (1988s) 56s (E. E. *Ellis*); TTod 45 (1988s) 501-3 (V. L. *Wimbush*).

197 **Gelpi** Donald L., [→ 9683] Grace as transmuted experience and social process, and other essays in North American theology.   Lanham ᴍᴅ 1988, UPA.   202 p. $26.25; pa. $12.75 [TDig 35,360].

198 **Gleason** Philip,   Keeping the faith; American Catholicism past and present (1969-1985, + some inedita). ND 1987, Univ.   vii-285 p. $25. – ᴿCCurr 23 (1988s) 106-8 (R. *Van Allen*); TS 49 (1988) 568s (Patricia *Byrne*).

199 **Goldin** Judah,   Studies in Midrash and related literature, ᴱ*Eichler* Barry L., *Tigay* Jeffrey H.: Scholar of Distinction Series.   Ph 1988, Jewish Publication.   xx-419 p.; bibliog. p. 401-5.   0-8276-0277-4.   26 art.; 3 infra; several others on r. Nathan.

200 **Grant** George,   Technology and justice.   Toronto 1986, Anansi.   138 p. – ᴿSR 17 (1988) 117s (L. *Schmidt*).

201 **Grant** Sara, Lord of the dance and other papers [14 from her ashram life in India]. Bangalore 1987, Asian TC. 197 p. r 25 [TDig 35,66].

202 **Grimal** Pierre, Rome, la littérature et l'histoire [98 scripta minora 1938-1984]: Coll.ÉcFrR 93. R 1986, École française. viii-728 p.; p. 729-1299; 18 fig. 2-7283-0126-3. - ᴿAntClas 57 (1988) 380 (M. *Dubuisson*); ClasR 102 (1988) 379s (Miriam *Griffin*); RFgIC 116 (1988) 485-8 (J. H. *Waszink*); RPLH 61 (1987) 324s (P. *Flobert*).

203 **Gutiérrez** Gustavo, La Verdad los harà libres. Lima 1986, Confrontaciones. 3 art. [TKontext 10,128, M. *Sievernich*].

204 **Heller** Jan, An der Quelle des Lebens; Aufsätze zum Alten Testament: BeiATJ 10. Fra 1988, Lang. 287 p.; portr.; bibliog. p. 265-287. 3-8204-9856-7. 7 inedita (vel čeh. edita), infra; + 17 ex VT, CommViat ...

205 **Hennis** Wilhelm, Max WEBERS Fragestellung; Studien zur Biographie des Werks [+ 1 ineditum]. Tü 1987, Mohr. iv-242 p. DM 34. - ᴿDLZ 109 (1988) 430-2 (F. *Hauer*).

206 **Heurgon** Jacques, Scripta varia; préf. *Renard* M.: Coll. Latomus 191. Bru 1986. x-490 p.; XLI pl. Fb 2400. - ᴿGymnasium 95 (1988) 467s (K.-J. *Hölkeskamp*); RÉLat 65 (1987) 417-420 (J.-C. *Richard*); RPLH 61 (1987) 334s (P. *Flobert*).

206* **Heusch** Luc de, Écrits sur le royauté sacré. Bru 1987, Univ. 320 p. Fb 1200: 2-8004-0928-2. - ᴿJRelAf 18 (1988) 267-271 (R. P. *Werbner*).

207 **Horst** Pieter W. van der, Der onbekende God; essays over de joodse en hellenistische achtergrond van het vroege Christendom: Utrechtse Theologische Reeks 2. Franeker 1988, Wever. 386 p. *f* 30 [TLZ 114,281, W. *Popkes*]. 90-72235-02-9. 15 reprints + 2 inedita; 8 infra. - ᴿJStJud 19 (1988) 251s (F. *García Martínez*).

208 **Isachsen** Karsten, Før vi går fra hverandre; essays og prekener. Oslo 1987, Gyldendal. 119 p. Nk 138. - ᴿNorTTs 89 (1988) 114 (K. M. *Hansen*).

209 **Jaki** Stanley J., Chance or reality and other essays [13, 1967-85]. Lanham MD 1986, UPA. viii-249 p. $13.75 pa. 0-8191-5657-4. - ᴿGregorianum 69 (1988) 596-8 (P. *Haffner*).

210 **Jonas** Hans, Wissenschaft als persönliches Erlebnis. Gö 1987, Vandenhoeck & R. 77 p. DM 9,80. 3 art. - ᴿNorTTs 89 (1988) 236 (S. A. *Christoffersen*).

211 **Ker** Neil R. [1908-1982], Books, collectors and libraries; studies in the medieval heritage [28 art. 1937-1981], ᴱ*Watson* Andrew G. L 1985, Hambledon. xiv-528 p.; portr.; 33 fig.; p. 371-9 bibliog. since ᶠKer 1976 (*Gibbs* Joan). - ᴿRHE 83 (1988) 824 (H. *Silvestre*).

211* **Kitagawa** Joseph, Understanding Japanese religions [reprints]. Princeton 1987, Univ. xxxi-343 p. £31.40; pa. £10. - ᴿJRAS (1988) 477s (Joy *Hendry*).

212 KOCH Klaus [zum 60. Gb.; seine] Studien zur alttestamentlichen und altorientalischen Religionsgeschichte, ᴱ*Otto* E., Gö 1988, Vandenhoeck & R. 254 p. DM 68. 3-525-53579-1. 8 art. 1962-84 + ineditum, 'Die Götter, denen die Väter dienten' 9-31 [ZAW 100,319 tit. pp.], infra.

213 **Küng** Hans, Theologie im Aufbruch; eine ökumenische Grundlegung. Mü 1987, Piper. 320 p. DM 40. - ᴿJEcu St 25 (1988) 475 (Joyce *Irwin*).

214 KUTSCH Ernst, Kleine Schriften zum AT, zum 65. Gb., ᴱ*Schmidt* L., ...: BZAW 168, 1986 ➤ 2,183: ᴿBO 44 (1988) 512-4 (H. *Haag*).

215 **Lapide** Pinchas, Het leerhuis van de hoop; Joodse geloofservaringen voor christenen van vandaag. Baarn 1986, Ten Have. 103 p. *f* 15. 90-259-4301-2 [NedTTs 42,161].

216 **Leclercq** Jean, Recueil d'études sur saint BERNARD et ses écrits [I. ...; II. 1966; III. 1969] IV: Storia e letteratura 167. R 1987, Storia e Lett. 435 p. Lit. 70.000.

217 **Légaut** Marcel, *a)* Croire à l'Église de l'avenir. P 1985, Aubier. 189 p.; – *b)* Creer en la Iglesia del futuro, ᵀ*Melero* Domingo: Presencia teológica⸴ 43. Santander 1988, Sal Terrae. 205 p. 84-293-0794-X. – ᴿActuBbg 25 (1988) 239 (I. *Riudor*: de hace 20 años pero que hoy siguen siendo actuales).

218 **Leslau** Wolf, Fifty years of research; selection of articles on Semitic, Ethiopian Semitic and Cushitic. Wsb 1988, Harrassowitz. 3-447-02829-7 [OIAc D88].

218* **LEVI DELLA VIDA** Giorgio, Visita a Tamerlano; saggi di storia e letteratura, ᴱ**Amadasi Guzzo** M. G., *Michelini Tocci* F.: Collana di storia 1. N 1988, Morano. 246 p. Lit. 25.000. 33 art.

219 **Lochman** Jan M., Christ and Prometheus? A quest for theological identity [< Birmingham & Princeton lectures]. Geneva 1988, WCC (Kutztown PA). ix-105 p. $8.50. 2-8254-0931-6 [TDig 36,171].

220 **Løgstrup** K. E., Solidaritet og kærlighed og andre essays. K 1987, Gyldendal. 180 p. Dk 180 [TsTKi 58,321].

221 **Lövestam** Evald, Axplock; nytestamentliga studier: Religio 26. Lund 1987, Univ. Reprocentralen. 124 p. [SvTKv 65,36, S. *Svensson*; TLZ 114, 893, tit. pp.] 0280-5723. 10 art., infra.

222 **Lohfink** Gerhard, [reprints: not indicated] Wem gilt die Bergpredigt? Beiträge zu einer christlichen Ethik. FrB 1988, Herder. 238 p. DM 28. 3-451-20165-8. – ᴿTsTNijm 28 (1988) 308 (S. van *Tilborg*: 'De gebroeders Lohfink wedijveren met elkaar om onze kerkvoorstelling te reformeren').

223 **Lohfink** Norbert, Studien zum Pentateuch [ausser Dt]: Stuttgarter Biblische Aufsatzbände 4. Stu 1988, KBW. 324 p. 3-460-06041-7. 12 art.; infra.

224 **LOHSE** Bernhard: Evangelium in der Geschichte, Studien zu LUTHER und der Reformation, zum 60. Gb. des Autors, ᴱ**Grane** Leif, *al.* Gö 1988, Vandenhoeck & R. 442 p.; bibliog. p. 412-430 [TLZ 114,503]. 3-525-58151-3. 23 art.; 8 infra.

225 **Lonergan** Bernard J. F., A third collection, ᴱ*Crowe* Frederick 1985 ➜ 1,200: ᴿHeythJ 29 (1988) 477-9 (G. *Walmsley*).

226 **Machen** J. Gresham, Education, Christianity, and the State; essays [on 50th anniversary of his death], ᴱ*Robbins* John W. Jefferson MD 1987, Trinity Foundation. 179 p. $8 pa. – ᴿCalvinT 23 (1988) 299s (J. M. *Snapper*).

227 **Marchadour** A., Grands thèmes bibliques; naissance et affirmation de la foi [9 thèmes]: Petite encyclopédie moderne du christianisme. P 1987, Desclée-B. 48 p. F 36. 2-220-02670-1 [NTAbs 32,385].

228 **Marcovich** Miroslav, Studies in Graeco-Roman religions and Gnosticism: Studies in Greek and Roman Religion 4. Leiden 1988, Brill. ix-195 p. 90-04-08624-2. 10 reprints + 5 inedita.

229 **Margolin** Jean-Claude, ÉRASME, le prix des mots et de l'homme [12 reprints 1964-83]. L 1986, Variorum. 318 p. – ᴿBiblHumRen 49 (1987) 707-9 (H. *Vredeveld*).

230 **Marzotto** Damiano, Celibato sacerdotale e celibato di Gesù. CasM 1987, Piemme. 124 p. Lit. 12.000. – ᴿCC 139 (1988,3) 542s (G. *Ferraro*: dibattito attuale); RClerIt 69 (1988) 711s (G. *Marocco*); Teresianum 39 (1988) 224 (M. *Caprioli*).

231 **Merklein** H., Studien zu Jesus und Paulus [p. 1-106 ineditum]: WUNT 43. Tü 1987, Mohr. x-479 p. DM 74 pa. 3-16-145152-X; pa. 1-1 [NTAbs 32,364].

232 **Momigliano** Arnaldo, On pagans, Jews, and Christians [19 selections from Contributo; cfr. → 3,260]. Middletown CT 1987, Wesleyan Univ. xii-343 p. $30. 0-8195-5173-2 [NTAbs 32,393]. 19 art. → g7.

233 **Moscati** Sabatino, Scritti fenici minori. R 1988, Cons. Naz. Ricerche. 665 p.; ill.; bibliog. 9-17. 70 art.; → e945a.

234 **Nagel** Wolfram, Altvorderasien in [seinen] kleinen Schriften, Fs., ᴱJacobs Bruno. Wsb 1988, Reichert. xxii-425 p.; phot.; Bibliog. p. xiii-xxii. 3-88226-445-4. 21 art.; 3 infra.

235 **Neal** Marie Augusta, The just demands of the poor; essays in sociotheology. NY 1987, Paulist. v-142 p. $9 pa. – ᴿHorizons 15 (1988) 431 (S. *Casey*).

236 **Newbigin** Lesslie, Mission in Christ's way; Bible studies [lectures at 1986 Synod of South India]: Mission Series 8. Geneva 1987, WCC. vii-40 p. $3 pa. [TDig 35,382].

237 **Newman** Richard, Black power and black religion; essays and reviews. West Cornwall CT 1987, Locust. xix-237 p. $25 [TDig 35,80].

238 **Oberman** Heiko A., The dawn of reformation; essays in late medieval and early reformation thought [12 reprints 1963-79; related to → 3,268a?]. E 1986, Clark. ix-309 p. £15. – ᴿJTS 39 (1988) 297 (A. *McGrath*); RefTR 46 (1987) 89s (R. C. *Doyle*).

239 **Patzer** Harald, Gesammelte Schriften, ᴱ*Leimbach* Rüdiger, *Seidel* Gabriele. Wsb 1985, Steiner. xii-515 p. DM 78. 3-7705-0191-8. – ᴿGymnasium 95 (1988) 468-470 (H. *Bannert*).

240 **Pesch** Otto H., Dogmatik im Fragment; Gesammelte Studien [13, 1967-86]. Mainz 1987, Grünewald. 442 p. DM 48 pa. – ᴿRHPR 68 (1988) 481 (A. *Birmelé*); TGL 78 (1988) 283 (W. *Beinert*); TLZ 113 (1988) 846-8 (K. *Raiser*).

241 **Pezzella** Sosio, Momenti e problemi di storia del Cristianesimo dall'antico al contemporaneo, ᴱ*Bronzini* Giovanni B., *Colajanni* Antonino. Galatina LE 1986, Congedo. 270 p. – ᴿCC 139 (1988,1) 305 (C. *Capizzi*).

242 **Pixley** Jorge V., Biblia y liberación; [5] ensayos de Teología Bíblica Latinoamericana. México 1986, Centro Montesinos [TKontext 10,132, M. *Sievernich*].

243 **Pollard** W. G., Transcendence and providence; reflections of a physicist [executive director for 27 years at Oak Ridge] and priest ['Anglican communion', ordained 1952; collected papers]: Theology and Science at the Frontiers of Knowledge 6. E 1987, Scottish Academic. xi-269 p. £12.50. – ᴿJTS 39 (1988) 652s (A. *Peacocke*).

244 **Pouilloux** Jean, D'Archiloque à Plutarque, littérature et réalité [c. 40 art. 1950-84]: Coll. Épigraphique 16/1. Lyon 1986, Maison de l'Orient. 663 p.; ill. 2-903264-08-2. – ᴿAntClas 57 (1988) 450s (A. *Martin*).

245 **Preston** Ronald H., The future of Christian ethics [reprints and inedita]. L 1987, SCM. viii-280 p. – ᴿSalesianum 50 (1988) 240 (G. *Abbà*).

246 **Quacquarelli** Antonio: *a*) Sapientia et eloquentia, studi per il 70 genetliaco di ∼ [17 reprints by him, 13 art. by others = VetChr 25 (1988)]: Univ. Bari, Ist. Lett. Cr. Ant. Bari 1988, Edipuglia. xiii-705 p.; ill. – *b*) Cinquant'anni di ricerca; bilancio e prospettive: VetChr 25 (1988) ix-xxx (-xlii, bibliog.). Il fascicolo I intero è ristampa di alcuni suoi articoli.

247 **RATSCHOW** Carl Heinz, Von der Gestaltwerdung des Menschen, Beiträge zu Anthropologie und Ethik, [E]*Keller-Wentorf* Christel, *Repp* Martini. B 1987, de Gruyter. viii-398 p. DM 178. 3-11-010912-3 [NSys 30,130 adv.].

248 **RATSCHOW** Carl Heinz, Von den Wandlungen Gottes, Beiträge zur systematischen Theologie [zum 75. Geb.], [E]*Keller-Wentorf* Christel, *Repp* Martin. B 1986, de Gruyter. viii-405 p. DM 162. 3-11-010911-5 [NSys 30,130 adv.].

250 **Reumann** J. H. P., Ministries examined; laity, clergy, women, and bishops in a time of change [updated reprints]. Minneapolis 1987, Augsburg. 271 p. $13. 0-8066-2296-2 [NTAbs 32,386].

251 **RIGGI** Calogero, Epistrophe, tensione verso la divina armonia; [suoi] scritti di filologia patristica, LXX Genetliaco, [E]**Amata** Biagio, 1985 ➤ 1,234; 88-213-0118-4; 39 art.; 5 infra.

252 **Roberts** J. Deotis, Black theology in dialogue [eleven revised publications]. Ph 1987, Westminster. 132 p. $13 [TDig 35,84].

253 **Rosenzweig** Franz, Zweistromland [title from a published work, 'chosen to show that he lived on several horizons'; not related to Mesopotamia], kleinere Schriften zu Glauben und Denken, [E]*Mayer* R. & A.: Ges. Schr. 3. Dordrecht 1984, Nijhoff. xxii-884 p. *f*285. – [R]TLZ 113 (1988) 892s (P. *Heidrich*).

Ruckstuhl Eugen 1988 ➤ 4203.

254 **Runcie** Robert [Archbishop of Canterbury], One light for one world. L 1988, SPCK. viii-198 p. £7 pa. – [R]TLond 91 (1988) 341s (T. G. A. *Baker*).

255 **Samartha** Stanley J., Ganges en Galilea, een keuze uit het werk van ~, [E]*Jongeneel* J. A. B. Kampen 1986, Kok. 147 p. *f*24,50. 90-242-308-10. – [R]NedTTs 42 (1988) 270s (H. H. *Burggraaff*).

256 **Schillebeeckx** Edward, Revelation and theology. L 1987=1967, Sheed & W. I. xiv-298 p.; II. x-212 p. 0-7220-7398-4; 9-2.

257 **Schlesinger** Walter, Ausgewählte Aufsätze, 1965-1979, [E]*Patze* Hans, *Schwind* Fred: Konstanzer Arbeitskreis für mittelalterliche Geschichte 34. Sigmaringen 1987, Thorbecke. xxviii-696 p. – [R]GGA 240 (1988) 263-282 (J. *Ehlers*).

258 **Schmid** Wolfgang, Ausgewählte philologische Schriften, [E]*Erbse* Hartmut, *Küppers* Jochem. B 1984, de Gruyter. 756 p. – [R]RPLH 61 (1987) 325s (Antoinette *Novara*).

259 **Schniewind** Julius (1883-1948), Nachgelassene Reden und Aufsätze, [E]*Kraus* Hans-J. Giessen 1987=1951 ([E]*Kähler* E.), Brunnen. viii-207 p. DM 29. – [R]SNTU-A 13 (1988) 228 (A. *Fuchs*).

260 **Segal** A. F., The other Judaisms of late antiquity [7 reprints, modified]: BrownJudSt 127. Atlanta 1987, Scholars. xvii-213 p. $36. 1-555-4-0178-3 [NTAbs 32,278; BL 89,145, F. W. *Coxon*].

261 **SEVERUS** Emmanuel von: [same title as [F]1984 ➤ 65,131] Itinera Domini, Gesammelte Aufsätze aus Liturgie und Mönchtum, 80 Gb., [E]*Rosenthal* Anselm. Münster 1988, Aschendorff. 370 p. DM 68 [TGL 78,460].

262 **Shear-Yashuv** Aharon, Religion, philosophy and Judaism, I. From Christianity to Judaism, theological and philosophical articles. J 1987, Mass. 328 + 16 p. 39 art.; 4 infra.

263 **Siri** Giuseppe, card., Il sacerdozio cattolico I: Opera 5. Pisa 1986, Giardini. xv-329 p. – [R]Divinitas 32 (1988) 609s (D. *Venturini*).

264 **Smalley** Beryl, Medieval exegesis of wisdom literature [< Dominican Studies & Archives d'histoire doctrinale et littéraire du Moyen Âge 1949s], [E]*Murphy* Roland E., Atlanta 1986, Scholars. x-142 p. $14. – [R]RelStR 14 (1988) 152 (J. L. *Crenshaw*).

265 **Smend** R., Zur ältesten Geschichte Israels, Gesammelte Studien 2 [meist zwei Monographien 1959 und 1963; Band 3 über die Geschichte der kritischen Schriftauslegung angekündigt]: BeiEvT 100. Mü 1987, Kaiser. 258 p. DM 48. – RZAW 100 (1988) 324s (H.-C. *Schmitt*: tit. pp.).

266 **Sobrino** Jon, Liberación con espíritu; apuntes para una nueva espiritualidad [12 art. desde 1980]: Presencia Teológica 23. Santander 1985, Sal Terrae. 219 p. – RTPhil 63 (1988) 317 (M. *Sievernich*).

267 **Sölle** Dorothee, Das Fenster der Verwundbarkeit; theologisch-politische Texte. Stu 1987, Kreuz. 347 p. 3-7831-0843-8. – RActuBbg 25 (1988) 232 (J. *Boada*).

268 **Stuhlmacher** P., Jesus von Nazareth — Christus des Glaubens [first essay, plus two reprints]. Stu 1988, Calwer. 107 p. DM 16,80. 3-7668-0869-9 [NTAbs 32,376].

269 **Syme** Ronald, Roman papers [Antiquity 62,657 indicates *two* volumes as IV], E*Birley* Anthony R. Ox 1988, Clarendon. viii-430 p., £45 / vi-402 p.; £35 [EchMClas 33, 333-340, K. R. *Bradley*].

270 **Täubler** Eugen (1879-1953), Ausgewählte Schriften zur Alten Geschichte: Heid Althist. Beit. 3. Stu 1987, Steiner. 343 p. portr.; bibliog. p. 326-332 (J. *Hahn*) [RÉLat 65,425]. 3-515-04780-8. 24 art., 3 infra [JStJud 20,116, A. van der *Woude*].

271 **Talmon** S., Gesellschaft und Literatur in der hebräischen Bibel: Gesammelte Aufsätze 1 [6 art. already in Eng. in King, Cult 1986 ➤ 2,227; plus others]: Information Judentum 8. Neuk-V 1988. 234 p. DM 62. 3-7887-0794-1 [BL 89,23]. – RProtestantesimo 43 (1988) 215s (J. A. *Soggin*); ZAW 100 (1988) 466 (tit. pp.).

272 **Thils** Gustave, Les laïcs et l'enjeu des temps 'post-modernes': RTLv Cah. 20. P 1988, Procure. 120 p. Fb 400. – REsprVie 98 (1988) 512 (H. *Wattiaux*: 4 exposés distincts, de haute qualité littéraire); RTLv 19 (1988) 487-9 (A. de *Halleux*).

273 **Tinsley** John [bp. Bristol], Tragedy, irony and faith [four Exeter Prideaux lectures 1982]. Bristol IN 1985, Wyndham Hall. 57 p. $7. – RRelStR 14 (1988) 148 (K. *Lewis*: stimulating after the pedestrian one on OT).

274 **Trevor-Roper** Hugh, Catholics, Anglicans and Puritans; seventeenth-century essays. Ch 1988, Univ. xiii-317 p. $27.50 [TDig 36,90].

275 **Trilling** Wolfgang, Studien zur Jesusüberlieferung: SB Aufsatzbände 1. Stu 1988, KBW. 368 p. DM 39. 3-460-06011-5 [CBQ 51,396, tit. pp. without source]. 15 art.; 13 infra.

276 **Tutu** Desmond Mpilo, Esperanza y sufrimiento; sermones y discursos, E*Mutloatse* Mothobi, *Webster* John. Buenos Aires / GR 1988, Nueva Creación / Eerdmans. 195 p. $8. 0-8028-0277-X. – RActuBbg 25 (1988) 271 (R. de *Sivatte*).

277 **Vauchez** André, Les laïcs au moyen âge; pratiques et expériences religieuses [articles déjà publiés pour la plupart]. P 1987, Cerf. 309 p. – RRHE 83 (1988) 693-6 (M. *Lauwers*).

278 **Vogel** Manfred H., A quest for a theology of Judaism; the divine, the human and the ethical dimensions in the structure-of-faith of Judaism; essays in constructive theology [14, during 20 years]: Studies in Judaism. Lanham MD 1987, UPA. xxxv-292 p. $28.50; pa. $15.75 [TDig 35,294].

279 **Wach** Joachim, *a*) Essays in the history of religions [8 essays, some inedita]. – *b*) Introduction to the history of religions [his 1924 Habilitation + 5 art. < RGG²], E*Kitagawa* Joseph M., *al.*, partlyT. NY 1988, Macmillan. xxi-202 p.; xxxiv-234 p. $30 each [TDig 35,294].

280 **Warren** Michael,   Youth, gospel, liberation [7 reprints + 5 inedita]. SF 1987, Harper & R.   xv-138 p. $14 [TDig 35,193].

281 **Westbrook** Raymond,   Studies in biblical and cuneiform law: CahRB 26. P 1988, Gabalda.   vii-150 p.

282 **White** Hayden,   The content of the form; narrative discourse and historical representation [8 reprints 1979-85]. Baltimore 1987, Johns Hopkins Univ.   xi-245 p. – ᴿHistTheor 27 (1988) 282-7 (W. H. *Dray*).

283 **White** Lynnᴶ,   Mediaeval religion and technology [UCLA 1978=] 1986. – ᴿChH 57 (1988) 84s (I. P. *Culianu*).

284 **Wiseman** T. P.,   Roman studies, literary and historical: Collected Classical Papers 1.   Liverpool 1987, Cairns.   x-419 p.; 4 pl. £40. – ᴿGymnasium 95 (1988) 470-2 (K.-J. *Hölkeskamp*); RÉLat 65 (1987) 425-7 (P. *Moreau*).

285 **Yassine Khair**,   Archaeology of Jordan, essays and reports [13 art., some in collaboration; ADAJ, BASOR, ZDPV etc. source not indicated]. Amman 1988, auct. (POB 410403). 273 p. $30 [BL 89,32, J. R. *Bartlett*]. – ᴿSBFLA 38 (1988) 469 (P. *Kaswalder*).

A1.3   *Plurium compilationes* **biblicae.**

286 ᴱ**Assmann** Aleida & J.,   Kanon und Zensur; Archäologie der literarischen Kommunikation.   Mü 1987, Fink. [ZAW 100,318] → 1435, *Crüsemann* F.

287 ᴱ**Aune** David E.,   Greco-Roman literature and the New Testament: SBL Sources 21.   Atlanta 1988, Scholars.   vii-146 p.   1-55540-231-3; 09-7 [ZNW 79,296]. 7 art., infra.

288 ᴱ**Barbero** G., *al.*,   Ebraismo e cristianesimo: Storia delle idee politiche, economiche e sociali 2/1.   T 1985, UTET.   678 p.; 18 pl. + 3 color. – ᴿHenoch 10 (1988) 393s (G. *Garbini*: virtualmente una monografia di Fausto PARENTE p. 1-478).

289 Bericht der H. Kunst Stiftung zur Förderung der nt-lichen Textforschung 1985-7. Mü 1988, Kunst-Stiftung.   122 p. [One article by *Kunst* himself, plus 6 others by B. & K. *Aland*, G. *Mink*, F. *Schmitz* ...]. – ᴿNT 30 (1988) 380-3 (G. D. *Kilpatrick*).

290 **Bloom** Harold, The Bible: Modern critical views. Edgemont PA 1987, Chelsea.   viii-150 p. $27.50. 15 art. OT, 5 NT [TDig 35,54].

291 *Bonora* A., *al.*, Fede VT → 8331; NT → 8710, ParSpV 17 [18 → 8431].

292 [*Dumais* Marcel, présent.; Groupe ASTER, ᴰ*Légaré* Clément] *Chené* Adèle, *al.*,   De Jésus et des femmes; lectures sémiotiques, suivies d'un entretien avec A. J. *Greimas*: Recherches NS 14.   Montréal/P 1987, Bellarmin/Cerf. 217 p. $18 [CBQ 50,558]. 2-89007-654-7 / 2-204-02551-8. 9 art., infra. – ᴿSémBib 52 (1988) 41-50 (J. *Delorme*).

293 ᴱ**Christensen** Duane L.,   Experiencing the Exodus from Egypt [originating as a study-guide to *Lohfink* N., Option for the poor 1987 → 3,h84]. Berkeley CA 1988, BIBAL (Berkeley Institute of Bible, Archeology, and Law).   v-95 p. $8 [TDig 35,375].

294 ᴱ**Cohen** Arthur A., *Mendes-Flohr* Paul, Contemporary Jewish religious thought. NY 1986, Scribner. $75. 0-684-18688-4. – ᴿAmerica 157 (1987) 163 (J. *Harris*).

295 ᴱ**Cooper** H.,   Soul searching; studies in Judaism and psychotherapy. L 1988, SCM.   240 p. £10. – ᴿMonth 249 (1988) 906s (L. *Marteau*).

297 ᴱ**Dundes** Alan,   The flood myth.   Berkeley 1988, Univ. California.   vi-452 p. $48; pa. $16 [JBL 107,786].

298 ᴱ**Eckardt** Alice L.,   Jerusalem, city of the ages [31 essays, some reprints; some on archeology, most on current striving for peace]: American

Academic Association for Peace in the Middle East. Lanham MD 1987, UPA. 407 p. $37.50; pa. $20 [TDig 35,71].

299 ᴱExum J. Cheryl, *Bos* Johanna W. H., Reasoning with the foxes; female wit in a world of male power [all the articles are about the Old Testament]: Semeia 42 (1988). 156 p.

300 ᴱFrerichs Ernest S., The Bible and Bibles in America: SBL centennial, The Bible in American Culture 1. Atlanta 1988, Scholars. ix-224 p. $19. 1-55540-096-5. 8 art.; 4 infra.

301 *a*) ᴱFriedman Mordechai A., *Gil* Moshe, Studies in Judaica: Teʻuda 4, 1986 → 2,246: ᴿZDMG 138 (1988) 420 (L. *Prijs*). – *b*) ᴱTsur Reuven, *al.*, Studies in [postbiblical] Hebrew literature: Teʻuda 5. TA 1986, Univ. xxv-326 p. ❹; Eng. summaries V-XXV. 15 art. on modern lit.

303 ᴱGarrett Duane A., *Melick* Richard R.ᴶ, Authority and interpretation; a Baptist perspective. GR 1987, Baker. 220 p. $11. 0-8010-3817-0. 9 contributors. – ᴿBS 145 (1988) 348s (R. P. *Lightner*); RExp 85 (1988) 154-8 (Bill J. *Leonard*).

304 ᴱGerhart Mary, *Williams* James G., Genre, narrativity, and theology: Semeia 43. Atlanta 1988, Scholars. ix-167 p. 5 art. + responses, infra.

305 ᴱGörres Albert, *Kasper* Walter, Tiefenpsychologische Deutung des Glaubens? Anfragen an Eugen DREWERMANN: QDisp 113. FrB 1988, Herder. 174 p. 3-451-02113-7. 8 art., infra.

306 ᴱGraetz Michael, *Gründer* Karlfried, Hebraische Beiträge zur Wissenschaft des Judentums deutsch angezeigt [ᵀ*Mach* Dafna], I/1s. Heid 1985, Schneider. xix-176 p. – ᴿZDMG 138 (1988) 184 (L. *Prijs*).

307 ᴱGreen Garrett, Scriptural authority and narrative interpretation [ten responses to H. *Frei*]. Ph 1987, Fortress. xiii-208 p. $25. 0-8006-0839-9. – ᴿRelStR 14 (1988) 367 (S. G. *Post*).

309 ᴱHedrick Charles W. ['The tyranny of the Synoptic Jesus' 1-8], The Historical Jesus and the rejected Gospels = Semeia 44 (1988). 140 p. 6 art.; infra.

310 ᴱHoffman Lawrence A., The land of Israel; Jewish perspectives: Studies in Judaism and Christianity in Antiquity 6. ND 1986, Univ. 352 p. $30. 0-268-02180-5. – ᴿAmerica 157 (1987) 163s (J. *Harris*).

311 ᴱHoffmann Paul (p. 15-67 and 416-452), Zur neutestamentlichen Überlieferung von der Auferstehung Jesu: WegFor 522. Da 1988, Wiss. vii-499 p. DM 74; sb. 59. p. 453-483, chronologische Bibliographie Seit 1770. 17 art., 12 infra. – ᴿBiKi 43 (1988) 179s (P.-G. *Müller*).

312 ᴱHoffmann R. J., *Larue* G. A., Biblical versus secular ethics; the conflict [15 art.]. Buffalo 1988, Prometheus. 191 p. $23. 0-87975-418-4 [NTAbs 32,383]. 15 art.

312* *Horst* Pieter W. van der, Corpus Hellenisticum Novi Testamenti, geschiedenis en doel van een project [ineditum]: → 207, De onbekende God 1988, 256-266.

313 ᴱJames Robinson B., The unfettered word; Southern Baptists confront the authority–inerrancy question. Waco 1987, Word. 190 p. $9. 12 art. – ᴿBS 145 (1988) 217s (E. H. *Merrill*: 'moderate' but distressingly non-evangelical resistance to current tidal wave of fundamentalism); PerspRelSt 15 (Baptist, 1988) 292s (J. *Barnhart*: mostly tightly-reasoned against).

314 Judendom och kristendom under de första århundradena: Nordiskt Patristikerprojekt 1982-5, 2. Oslo 1986, Univ. 304 p. Nk 240. 82-00-18152-9 [NTAbs 32,392].

315 ᴱ**Kaplan** Kalman J., *al.*, The family; biblical and psychological foundations: JPsy&Jud 8,2. NY 1984, Human Sciences. 132 p.; ill. [KirSef 61,394].

317 ᴱ**Mulder** Martin J. (*Sysling* Harry), Mikra; text, translation, reading and interpretation of the Hebrew Bible in ancient Judaism and early Christianity: Comp NT 2. Literature 1 (2 and 3/1 have already appeared; ➤ 3,a449). Assen/Ph 1988, Van Gorcum / Fortress. xxvi-929 p.; bibliog. p. 797-852. $70. 90-232-2363-5 / 0-8006-0604-3 [TDig 36,175]. 20 art., infra. – ᴿSBFLA 38 (1988) 516-520 (F. *Manns*); Streven 56 (1988s) 463s (P. *Beentjes*).

318 ᴱ**Neusner** Jacob, Struggle for the Jewish mind; debates and disputes on Judaism then and now [32 items on 'ethnic scholarship, avenging and celebratory' vs. 'disciplinary Jewish studies, applying university standards (and) skepticism']: Studies in Judaism. Lanham MD 1988, UPA. xv-193 p. $19 [TDig 35,381].

320 ᴱ**Plum** K. Friis (mme), *Hallbäck* G., Det gamle Testamente og den kristne fortolkning: Forum for bibelsk eksegese 1. K 1988, Museum Tusculanum. 137 p. 87-7289-034-7 [BL 89,113, K. *Jeppesen*; no tit. pp.].

321 ᴱ**Rapoport-Albert** Ada, Essays in Jewish historiography: History & Theory Beiheft 27. Middletown CT 1988, Wesleyan Univ. 175 p. 9 art., 5 infra.

322 ᴱ**Russell** Elizabeth, *Greenhalgh* John, 'If Christ be not risen...' Essays in resurrection and survival: Tracts for our Times 3. L 1986, St. Mary's. £2.50. – ᴿNBlackf 68 (1987) 364s (D. F. *Ford*).

323 ᴱ**Salas** A., Profetismo y sociedad ¿Por qué está hoy el mundo tan necesitado de profetas?: Biblia y Fe 14,4 (M 1988). 174 p. pt. 600. 0210-5209 [NTAbs 32,386].

323* ᴱ**Sanders** Wilm, Andreas — Apostel der Ökumene zwischen Ost und West. Köln 1985, Wienand. 288 p.; 109 fig. DM 44. – ᴿTrierTZ 97 (1988) 70s (E. *Sauser*).

324 ᴱ**Schmidt** E. R., *Korenhof* M., *Jost* R., Feministisch gelesen; 32 ausgewählte Bibeltexte für Gruppen, Gemeinden und Gottesdienste, I. Stu 1988, Kreuz. 296 p. DM 39,80. 3-7831-0909-4. 16 OT, 1 'Apocr', 15 NT [BL 89,92, R. *Hammer*].

325 ᴱ**Seitz** Christopher R., Reading and preaching the Book of Isaiah. Ph 1988, Fortress. 126 p. $7. 6 art. – ᴿNewTR 1,4 (1988) 78s (C. *Stuhlmueller*).

326 ᴱ**Shanks** Hershel, Ancient Israel; a short history from Abraham to the Roman destruction of the Temple [by 8 authors of separate chapters]. Wsh c. 1988, Biblical Archaeology Soc. $24.

327 ᴱ**Sitarz** E., Höre, Israel! Jahwe ist einzig; Bausteine für eine Theologie des Alten Testaments: BBasB 5. Stu/Kevelaer 1987, KBW/Butzon & B. 350 p. DM 34. 3-460-27051-9 / 3-7666-9231-3. 8 art. infra. – ᴿZAW 100 (1988) 317 (H.-C. *Schmitt*: noch 9 Bände).

328 ᴱ**Wallis** Gerhard, Zwischen Gericht und Heil; Studien zur alttestamentlichen Prophetie im 7. und 6. Jahrhundert vor Chr.: Atl. Arbeitsgemeinschaft DDR [8. Jahrh. 1984 ➤ 3640]. B 1987, Ev.VA. 120 p. 3-374-00045-2 [ZAW 101,480, tit. pp.]. 4 art., infra.

329 ᴱ**Wertheimer** Jack, The American synagogue, a sanctuary transformed [14 commissioned essays]: Jewish Theol. Sem. Centennial publ. C 1987, Univ. xviii-433 p. $34.50 [TDig 36,43].

330 ᴱ**White** H. C. (p. 1-24. 41-63), Speech act theory and biblical criticism [*Austin* J., *Searle* J.]: Semeia 41. Atlanta 1988, Scholars. vii-178 p. $15; sb. $10; discount for 4. 0095-571X [BL 89,97, R. P. *Carroll*].

331 ᴱWillis W., The Kingdom of God in 20th century interpretation [14 art.]. Peabody MA 1987, Hendrickson. xii-208 p. $13. 0-913573-82-5 [NTAbs 32,259: authors + subjects].

332 ᴱYedaya M., ⊕ *Qadmoniot ha-Galil ha-maʿaravi*, The western Galilee antiquities. Mateh Asher 1986, Ministry of Defence. 555 p. NŠ 37. 50 art. [IsrEJ 38,102].

333 ᴱZamagna D., A verdade da justiça = EstudosB 14. Petrópolis 1987, Vozes. 75 p. [NTAbs 32,260: 7 authors/subjects; *Siqueira* T. M. on Jer 22,13-19; *Zamagna* Wis 1,15; *Lockmann* T. Mt 5,17-20].

334 ᴱAntoniazzi A., Crises e saidas [7 art.; *Oliveira de Azevedo* W., Mc 6,37; *Messias de Oliveira* E., Rev 2,8-11; *Antoniazzi*, 1 Pt]: EstudosBíb 15. Petrópolis 1987, Vozes. 86 p. [NTAbs 32,253].

A1.4 *Plurium compilationes* **theologicae.**

335 ᴱAntoun Richard T., *Hegland* Mary E., Religious resurgence; contemporary cases in Islam, Christianity, and Judaism. Syracuse NY 1987, Univ. 269 p. $27.50. – ᴿJEcuSt 25 (1988) 457-9 (J. E. *Biechler*).

337 ᴱArokiasamy S., *Gispert-Sauch* G., Liberation in Asia; theological perspectives [on the 1984 and 1986 Vatican documents; mostly Vidyajyoti reprints]: Jesuit Theological Forum 1. Anand 1987, Gujarat-SP. 269 p. $9.50; pa. $8.50 [TDig 36,67]. 12 art.; 4 infra.

338 ᴱAvis Paul, The threshold of theology. Glasgow 1988, Marshall Pickering. viii-182 p. – ᴿTLond 91 (1988) 444.

339 ᴱBaumber Christof, *Mette* Norbert, Gemeindepraxis in Grundbegriffen; Ökumenische Orientierungen und Perspektiven. Mü/Dü 1987, Kaiser/ Patmos. 420 p. DM 58. – ᴿHerdKorr 42 (1988) 97s (K. *Nientiedt*).
   ᴱBecker Hansjakob, *al.*, Im Angesicht des Todes; ein inderdisziplinäres Kompendium: Pietas Liturgica 3s. 1987 ➤ 523.

340 ᴱBiemer Günter, Glaube zum Leben; die christliche Botschaft [La foi des catholiques; catéchèse fondamentale, ᴱ*Chenu* B., ... 1984 ➤ 1,7161]. FrB 1986, Herder. 840 p. DM 29,80. – ᴿTGL 78 (1988) 184 (G. *Ruppert*: 'deutlich, dass die deutsche Ausgabe nicht einfach eine Übersetzung sein kann; Biemer hat ... umfangreiche Bearbeitungen vorgenommen').

341 ᴱBowden Henry W., Centennial Issue: Church History 57-Supplement (Ch 1988). 138 p. 9 art., 7 infra.

342 ᴱBurnham Frederic B., *al.*, Love, the foundation of hope; the theology of Jürgen MOLTMANN and Elisabeth MOLTMANN-WENDEL. SF 1988, Harper & R. xvi-160 p. $17 [CBQ 51,399].

343 ᴱCampana Giuseppe, *al.*, Religione e linguaggio: Quad. S. Carlo 2. Modena 1986, Mucchi. 115 p. 6 art., 3 infra.

344 ᴱCaplan Lionel, Studies in religious fundamentalism. Albany 1987, SUNY. x-216 p. $39.50; pa. $15. – ᴿRelStR 14 (1988) 359s (J. L. *Price*: anthropological, building on James BARR but including Sikh, Tamil ...).

345 ᴱCarey Patrick, American Catholic religious thought. NY 1987, Paulist. iv-302 p. $11 [TDig 35,151].

346 ᴱChelini Jean, *Branthomme* Henry, Histoire des pèlerinages non chrétiens; entre le magique et le sacré, le chemin des dieux. P 1987, Hachette. F 158. [*Motte* A., Grèce; *Belayche* N., Rom]. – ᴿKernos 1 (1988) 255s (Vinciane *Pirenne-Delforge*).

347 ᴱCipriani R., La teoria critica della religione; il fenomeno religioso nell'analisi della Scuola di Francoforte. R 1986, Borla. – ᴿFilT 1,1 (1988) 177s (G. P. *Cammarota*).

348 ᴱ**Cohen** Richard A., Face to face with LEVINAS. Albany 1986, SUNY. xi-264 p. 0-88706-259-8. – ᴿBijdragen 49 (1988) 348-350 (H. de *Vries*).

349 Communio 13 (P 1988; Gent 1988; also Eng. ital.); deutsch = **IkaZ**.

350 Concilium-Paris [similar but not identical editions in English, German (= IZT), Spanish, etc.]: **215** (1988), ᴱ*Küng* H., *Moltmann* J., Œcuménisme; une assemblée pour la paix; 152 p. – **216** (1988), ᴱ*Duquoc* C., *Floristán* C., Spiritualité; l'identité chrétienne; 155 p. – **217** (1988), ᴱ*Provost* J., *Walf* K., Institutions ecclésiales; le pouvoir dans l'Église; 159 p. – **218** (1988), ᴱ*Greinacher* N., *Mette* N., Théologie pratique; la diaconie; 160 p. – **219** (1988), ᴱ*Elizondo* V., *Boff* L., Théologie du Tiers Monde; convergences et différences; 172 p. – **220** (1988), ᴱ*Beuken* W., *al.*, Écriture Sainte, Histoire de l'Église: La vérité et ses victimes; 180 p.

352 ᴱ**Cooey** Paula M., *al.*, Embodied love; sensuality and relationship as feminine values. SF 1988, Harper & R. viii-241 p. $25; pa. $15 [TDig 36,57]. 13 art.

353 Cristologia africana. Mi 1987, Paoline. 277 p. Lit. 18.000. – ᴿHumBr 43 (1988) 888s (R. *Monolo*).

354 ᴱ**Dijk-Hemmes** F. van [author of the chapter on Jewish-Christian position of women; others on Greek (*Sancisi-Weerdenburg* H.), Roman (*Hemelrijk* E. A.), *al.*], ''t Is kwaad gerucht als zij niet binnen blijft'; Vrouwen in oude culturen. Utrecht 1986, 'HES'. 157 p. ƒ19,50. 90-6194-475-9. – ᴿNedTTs 42 (1988) 346s (Japke *Huisman*).

355 ᴱ**Doré** Joseph, Le christianisme et la foi chrétienne; manuel de théologie. P 1985, Desclée. 12 vol. – ᴿRTLv 19 (1988) 71-77 (E. *Brito*).

356 ᴱ**Endelman** Todd M., Jewish apostasy in the modern world. NY 1987, Holmes & M. ix-344 p. [JQR 77 (1986s) 337, titles sans pp.] 12 art.; 1 infra.

358 ᴱ**Fredrich** Edward C., *al.*, LUTHER lives; essays ... 500th anniversary. Milwaukee 1983, Northwestern. 168 p. [< LuJb 54,144].

359 ᴱ**Fries** Paul, *Nersoyan* Tiran, Christ in East and West. Macon GA 1987, Mercer. xvi-223 p. $32; pa. $15 [CBQ 50,356].

360 ᴱ**Furlong** Monica, Mirror to the Church; reflexions on sexism. L 1988, SPCK. 135 p. £6. – ᴿTLond 91 (1988) 356s (Susan F. *Parsons*).

361 ᴱ**Gannon** Thomas M., World Catholicism in transition [22 experts' inedita]. NY 1988, Macmillan. xiv-402 p. $35. 0-02-911280-X [TDig 36,193].

362 **Garijo Guembe** Miquel M., *al.* Mahl des Herrn, ökumenische Studien. Fra/Pd 1988, Lembeck/Bonifatius. 340 p. DM 68. – ᴿÖkRu 37 (1988) 498s (G. *Schütz*).

363 ᴱ**Gill** Robin, Theology and sociology, a reader. L/NY 1987, Chapman/ Paulist. xii-424 p. £12 pa. [JTS 39,678].

364 ᴱ**Gramick** Jeannine, *Furey* Pat (pseudonym), The Vatican and homosexuality [the document, *Quinn* J. presentation, ten responses, and seven essays on what to expect]. NY 1988, Crossroad. xxi-226 p. $15. 0-8245-0864-5 [TDig 36,189].

365 **Hartt** Julian N., *Hart* Ray L., *Scharlemann* Robert P., The critique of modernity; theological reflections on contemporary culture. Charlottesville 1986, Univ. Virginia. xx-92 p. – ᴿRelStR 14 (1988) 141 (J. J. *DiCenso*).

366 ᴱ**Heine** Susanne, Europa in der Krise der Neuzeit; M. LUTHER, Wandel und Wirkung seines Bildes. Köln 1986, Böhlau. 187 p.; ill. [9 Art. in LuJb 55 (1988) 139 zitiert]. – ᴿTLZ 112 (1987) 282s (G. *Haendler*).

367 ᴱ**Henderson** Lisbeth, Konflikt i kirken; om befrielsesteologi og kirke i Latinamerika og Sydafrika. Århus 1988, ANIS. 160 p. Dk 138. – ᴿNorTTs 89 (1988) 271 (K. *Nordstokke*).

368 ᴱHerbstrith Waltraud, TERESA von Avila — Martin LUTHER; grosse Gestalten katholischer Reform: Edith-Stein-Carmel Tübingen 12. München 1983, Kaffke. 148 p. [< LuJb 54,144].

369 ᴱHeubach Joachim, Lutherische Kirche in der Welt = Jb des Martin-Luther-Bundes 14 (1987). 206 p. [< LuJb 55 (1988) 140]. → b387.

370 ᴱHoffmann Paul, Priesterkirche: Theologie zur Zeit 3. Dü 1987, Patmos. 368 p. DM 29,80. 3-491-77683-X. – ᴿTGL 78 (1988) 185-7 (W. Beinert); TsTNijm 28 (1988) 418 (A. Willems).

371 ᴱJardine Alice, Smith Paul, Men in feminism [Kamuf P. art.: 'femmeninism'; (P)MLA session]. NY 1987, Methuen. vii-288 p. $30; pa. $12. 24 art. – ᴿRelStR 14 (1988) 134 (Kathryn A. Rabuzzi calls R. SCHOLES, T. EAGLETON, Elaine SHOWALTER 'luminaries').

372 ᴱKhoury Adel T., Hünermann Peter, Wie sollen wir mit der Schöpfung umgehen? Die Antwort der Weltreligionen: Herderbücherei 1338. FrB 1987, Herder. 160 p. DM 9,80. – ᴿZkT 110 (1988) 112 (M. Hasitschka).

373 ᴱKing U., Women in the world's religions, past and present: God, the contemporary discussion. NY 1987, Paragon. x-261 p. $23; pa. $13. 0-913757-32-2; 0-3 [NTAbs 32,257].

374 ᴱKlemm David E., Hermeneutical inquiry [selection of texts]. Atlanta 1986, Scholars. 285 p.; 217 p. 1-555-40032-9; 4-5. – ᴿRExp 85 (1988) 360s (D. L. Mueller).

375 ᴱKuntz M. L. & P. G., Jacob's Ladder and the Tree of Life; concepts of hierarchy and the great chain of being: AmerUnivSt 5/14. NY 1987, Lang. 434 p. [RHE 83,423*].

376 ᴱLadrière P., Luneau R., Le retour des certitudes; événements et orthodoxie depuis Vatican II [17 articles on the problems and prospects of Asia, Africa, Latin America, Poland, USA, Netherlands ...]. P 1987, Centurion. 312 p. – ᴿRSPT 72 (1988) 188s (C. Boureux: 161-178, Blanquart P., Le pape en voyage; la géopolitique; 122-141, Laeyendecker L., Du cardinal ALFRINK au cardinal SIMONIS ...); RTLv 19 (1988) 197-9 (R. Guelluy: 'débats autour de la réception de Vatican II'); Spiritus 29 (1988) 218s (J.-M. Jolibois).

377 ᴱLaffin Arthur J., Montgomery Anne, Swords into plowshares; nonviolent direct action for disarmament. NY 1987, Harper & R. xxi-243 p. $9. – ᴿCurrTM 15 (1988) 454s (S. Schroeder).

378 I laici e la missione della Chiesa. Mi 1987, Istra. – ᴿRivScR 2 (1988) 423-9 (E. Juliá).

379 ᴱLatourelle René, Vatican II, bilan et perspectives vingt-cinq ans après (1962-87). Montréal/P 1988, Bellarmin/Cerf. 679 p.; 554 p.; 633 p. 2-89007-642-3; 3-1; 5-X / P 2-204-02552-6; 3-4; 4-2. Simul Eng., infra; español Salamanca, Sígueme; ital. → k608*: Assisi (1987) Cittadella. 65 art.; plures infra. – ᴿGregorianum 69 (1988) 741-761 & ScEspr 40 (1988) 227-237 (ipse).

380 ᴱLatourelle R., Vatican II, assessment and perspectives. NY 1988, Paulist. I, xix-710. [II-III 1989, xiii-528 p.; xiii-624 p.]. 0-8091-0412-1 [3-X; 4-8].

381 ᴱLicharz W. Nicht Du trägst die Wurzel — die Wurzel trägt Dich [Röm 11,18]; Hanna WOLFF und die Frage nach einer christlichen Identität: Arnoldshainer Texte 30. Fra 1985, Haag & H. vi-99 p.; DM 14,80 pa. 3-88129-880-0 [NTAbs 32,385: includes Lapide P./Georgi D. on unease with regard to the Jewish Jesus/Paul].

382 ᴱLink Hans-Georg [cf. → 9086], One God, one Lord, one Spirit; on the explication of the apostolic faith today. Faith & Order 139. Geneva 1988, WCC. 139 p. $10 pa. – ᴿJEcuSt 25 (1988) 609 (P. Cogan).

383 ᴱ**Lovin** Robin, Religion and American public life; interpretations and explorations. NY 1986, Paulist. 181 p. $9. – ᴿTTod 45 (1988s) 380.382 (J. E. *Gilman*).

384 ᴱ**Manno** A. G., L'origine dell'uomo. N 1987, Dehoniane. 340 p. Lit. 40.000. 13 inediti. – ᴿRasT 29 (1988) 108s (G. *Lauriola*).

384* [*Marinelli* Francesco, present.] La carità; teologia e pastorale alla luce del Dio-Agape: Pont. Ist. Pastorale, Univ. Lateranense, Fede e annuncio 15. Bo 1988, Dehoniane. 300 p.; p. 19-32, *Penna* R. su 1 Cor 13. 88-10-20315-1.

385 ᴱ**Meyer** H., *Gassmann* G., Rechtfertigung im Ökumenischen Dialog. Fra 1987, Lembeck/Knecht. 277 p. DM 36. – ᴿHerdKorr 42 (1988) 447 (U. *Ruh*).

385* ᴱ**Michaelson** Robert S., *Roof* Wade C., Liberal Protestantism; realities and possibilities. c. 1987, Pilgrim. 283 p. $12. – ᴿAmerica 157 (1987) 67-69 (J. *Gros*).

386 ᴱ**Milhaven** Annie L., The inside story; 13 valiant women challenging the Church. Mystic CT 1987, Twenty-third. xvii-269 p. $13. – ᴿTS 49 (1988) 587 (Bernadette *Topel*).

387 ᴱ**Mollenkott** Virginia R., Women of faith in dialogue. NY 1987, Crossroads. 195 p. $10. – ᴿRelStR 14 (1988) 358 (Frances B. *Sullivan*: 'abreast of feminist thought ... adds new dimensions').

388 ᴱ**Moltmann-Wendel** Elisabeth, *al.*, Was geht uns Maria an? Beiträge zur Auseinandersetzung in Theologie, Kirche und Frömmigkeit: Tb-Siebenstern 453. Gü 1988, Mohn. 208 p.; ill. 3-579-00493-X. Slightly revised reprint of IZK-Concilium 19,10 (1983). 13 art.; 6 infra.

388* ᴱ**Moore** Robert L., Carl Jᴜɴɢ and Christian spirituality. Mahwah NJ 1988, Paulist. xii-252 p. $15 pa. [TDig 36,51].

389 ᴱ**Morris** Thomas V., The concept of God: Oxford Readings in Philosophy. NY 1987, Oxford-UP. 276 p. 0-198-750-765. – ᴿRExp 85 (1988) 377s (D. L. *Mueller*).

390 ᴱ**Müller** Hans-P., Was ist Wahrheit? [... *Ratschow* C.-H., *Vorgrimler* H., *al.*]. Stu c. 1988, Kohlhammer. → 2046.

391 ᴱ**Mulder** D. C., De religieuze gezagsdrager: Vrije Univ. Instituut voor Godsdienstwetenschap Publ. 2. Amst 1984, VU. ƒ27,50. 90-6256-215-9. – ᴿNedTTs 42 (1988) 68 (P. F. *Goedendorp*).

392 Le mythe et le mythique: Cahiers de l'Hermétisme. P 1987, Michel. 224 p. – ᴿRHR 205 (1988) 309 (D. *Dubuisson*).

393 ᴱ**Nash** Ronald, Process theology [essays by 12 evangelical theologians and W. N. *Clark*]. GR 1987, Baker. 387 p. $18 [TDig 35,83].

394 ᴱ**Neuhaus** Richard J., *Cromartie* Michael, Piety and politics; evangelicals and fundamentalists confront the world. Wsh 1988, Ethics and Public Policy center. [Lanham MD, UPA] x-424 p. $24; pa. $13. 26 essays [TDig 36,75]. –ᴿTTod 45 (1988s) 374s (J. H. *Moorhead*: 16 assessments, 10 answers).

395 ᴱ**Neuhaus** Richard J., The preferential option for the poor: Encounter 8. GR 1988, Eerdmans. ix-116 p. 0-8028-0208-7. – *Stackhouse* M. L., Prot., p. 1-34; *McCann* Dennis P., Cath. p. 35-52.

396 ᴱ**Nicholas** John A., *Shank* Lillian T., Medieval religious women, I. Distant echoes: Cistercian Studies 71. Kalamazoo 1984, Cistercian. xi-299 p. $23; pa. $12. – ᴿCathHR 73 (1987) 260s (Mary M. *Mc-Laughlin*).

397 ᴱ**Niewiadomski** Józef, Eindeutige Antworten? Fundamentalistische Versuchung in Religion und Gesellschaft: Theologische Trends 1. Thaur

1988, Österreichischer Kulturverlag. 210 p. Sch 198 [CBQ 51,189]. –
ᴿBiKi 43 (1988) 129s (D. *Bauer*).

398 ᴱ**Packer** J. I., *Fromer* Paul, The best in theology [annual of articles
chosen by Christianity Today editors]. Waco 1987, Word. 429 p.
0-917-463-145. – ᴿRExp 85 (1988) 358s (D. L. *Mueller*).

399 ᴱ**Päschke** Bernd, Befreiung von unten lernen; zentralamerikanische
Herausforderung theologischer Praxis [Erlebnisberichte, Zeitungsarti-
kel ...], Vorw. *Richard* Pablo. Münster 1986, Liberación. 332 p. – ᴿTPhil
63 (1988) 312s (M. *Sievernich*).

400 ᴱ**Pavan** A., *Milano* A., Persona e personalismi. N 1987, Dehoniane.
xv-466 p. Lit. 34.000. – ᴿNRT 110 (1988) 755 (R. *Escol*).

401 ᴱ**Penaskovic** Richard, Theology and authority; maintaining a tradition of
tension [10 inedita]; pref. *Curran* Charles. Peabody MA 1987,
Henrickson. xvi-130 p. $10 pa. [TDig 36,88].

402 ᴱ**Plas** D. van der, Effigies Dei; essays on the history of religions: Numen
Sup 51. Leiden 1987, Brill. vii-170 p. *f* 75. 90-04-08655-2. 12 art. [BL
89,119, N. *Wyatt*: P. van der HORST on Shiur Qomah measurements of
the divine body; G. HAHN on celluloid iconology, Jesus in films].

403 ᴱ**Pobee** John B., *Hallencreutz* Carl F., Variations in Christian theology in
Africa. Nairobi c. 1987, Uzima [TKontext 10,126, N. B. *Abeng*].

404 ᴱ**Press** Margaret, *Brown* Neil, Bicentennial reflections: Faith and Culture
14. Sydney 1988, Catholic Institute. [viii-] 195 p.; ill. 0-908-22413-3
[Salesianum 51,386s, M. *Montani*]. 14 art.; 3 infra.

405 ᴱ**Prestwich** Menna, International Calvinism 1985 → 3,448.

406 ᴱ**Pye** Michael, *Stegerhoff* Renate, Religion in fremder Kultur; Religion
als Minderheit in Europa und Asien: Schriften der internationalen Kul-
tur- und Geisteswelt 2. Saarbrücken-Scheidt 1987, Dadder. 231 p. [Mun-
dus 24,312].

407 ᴱ**Rau** G., *al.*, Frieden in der Schöpfung; das Naturverständnis
protestantischer Theologie [Fak. Heid]. Gü 1987, Mohn. 271 p. DM 68.
3-579-00268-6. – ᴿTsTNijm 28 (1988) 192 (M. E. *Brinkman*).

408 ᴱ**Rodd** Cyril S., Foundation documents of the faith [brief essays on the
various Creeds, mostly from ExpTim]. E 1987, Clark. 0-567-29138-3. –
ᴿRExp 85 (1988) 383s (E. G. *Hinson*).

409 ᴱ**Rouner** Leroy S., Civil religion and political theology: Boston Univ. St.
Ph. & Religion 8. ND 1986, Univ. xv-228 p. $25. – ᴿScotJT 41 (1988)
431-3 (Gethin *Rhys*: Margaret MILES excellent on early North African
patriarchy).

410 ᴱ**Rovira** German, *Stöhr* Johannes, Totus tuus; theologische Kommentare
zur Mariologie JOHANNES PAULS II., Band I. Bamberg 1986, St. Otto. –
ᴿForumKT 3 (1987) 67s (G. *Söll*).

411 ᴱ**Schleip** H., Zurück zur Natur-Religion? Wege der Ehrfurcht vor dem
Leben [19 Antworten an Schleips 'Fragen eines Ungläubigen']. FrB 1986,
Bauer. 300 p. – ᴿZAW 100 (1988) 472 (O. *Kaiser*, ohne tit. pp.).

413 ᴱ**Schuon** Frithjof, Christianity/Islam; essays in esoteric ecumenicism,
ᵀ*Polit* Gustavo. 1985, World Wisdom. 270 p. $12. – ᴿJAAR 56 (1988)
355-7 (A. H. *Khan*).

414 ᴱ**Seidel** Walter, Kirche — Ort des Heils; Grundlagen — Fragen —
Perspektiven [Mainzer Dom Vorträge, *Lehmann* K., *Kasper* W., *al.*] Wü
1987, Echter. 154 p. – ᴿÖkRu 37 (1988) 379s (H. *Vorster*); TPhil 63
(1988) 295s (W. *Löser*).

415 ᴱ**Smedes** Louis D., Ministry and the miraculous; a case study [of
reactions to J. WIMBER 1982 course claiming that NT gifts of healing

have not ceased] at Fuller Theological Seminary.   Pasadena 1987, Fuller. 80 p. $7. – RBS 145 (1988) 221 (R. P. *Lightner*).

416 Sprekend kerkvolk [A people of the Church that has something to say]; naar een niet-klerikale visie [reaktie op de lineamenta van de romeinse bischoppensynode van 1987]: Theologie en samenleving 9.   Hilversum 1987, Gooi & S.   120 p. *f*17.50.   90-304-0394-2. – RTsTNijm 28 (1988) 320 (H. J. van *Hout*).

417 EStott John, *Greenacre* Roger,   Stepping stones; joint essays on Anglican Catholic and Evangelical unity.   L 1987, Hodder & S.   xiii-210 p. £8 pa. – RTLond 91 (1988) 345-7 (J. *Tinsley*).

418 ESutherland Stewart, *al.*,   The world's religions [58 essays].   Boston 1988, Hall.   xiv-995 p. $75 [TDig 35,296].

419 ESwidler Leonard, *O'Brien* Herbert,   A Catholic bill of rights [post-KÜNG 1980 Association for the Rights of Catholics in the Church, Delran NJ]. KC 1988, Sheed & W.   x-187 p. $9 [TDig 35,157].

420 ESykes Stephen, *Booty* John,   The study of Anglicanism [31 chapters by everybody who is anybody, including two women].   L/Ph 1988, SPCK/Fortress.   467 p. £17.50. – RTLond 91 (1988) 335-8 (R. *Holloway*: immensely stimulating).

421 ETaubes J.,   Theokratie: Religionstheorie und politische Theologie 3. Mü/Pd 1987, Vink/Schöningh.   327 p. DM 78.   3-506-77163-9. – RTsT-Nijm 28 (1988) 428 (P. A. van *Gennip*).

422 ETucker R. A., *Liefeld* W. L.,   Daughters of the Church; women and ministry from NT times to the present.   GR 1987, Zondervan.   552 p. $16 pa.   0-310-45741-6 [NTAbs 32,259].

423 ETurner Philip, *Sugeno* Frank,   Crossroads are for meeting; essays on the mission and common life of the Church in a global society [preparation for 1988 Lambeth Conference].   USA SPCK 1986.   xlv-288 p. £7 pa. – RTLond 91 (1988) 67s (C. *Elliott*).

424 EUllrich L.,   Kirche in nichtchristlicher Welt: Erfurter Theol. Schr. 15.   Lp 1986.   79 p. 4 art.; *Reindl* J., AT; *März* C., NT. – RForumKT 3 (1987) 250 (A. *Ziegenaus*).

426 EVerbeke W., *al.*,   The use and abuse of eschatology in the Middle Ages: Mediaevalia Lovaniensia 1/15.   Lv 1988, Univ.   ix-513 p.; 25 fig. [RHE 83,274*].

427 EWacker Marie-Therese,   Der Gott der Männer und der Frauen: Theol. z. Zeit 2.   Dü 1987, Patmos.   172 p. DM 22.   3-491-77677-5.

428 EWoodbridge John D.,   Great leaders of the Christian Church [Peter, Paul, John... earliest writers...].   Ch 1988, Moody.   384 p. $23 [TDig 36,61].

429 EZanotti Barbara,   A faith of one's own; explorations by Catholic Lesbians.   Trumansburg NY 1986, Crossing Press Feminist Series. xvii-202 p. $9. – RRelStR 14 (1988) 142 (Kathryn A. *Rabuzzi*).

430 EZiegler Josef G.,   'In Christus'; [3 kath., 3 ev.] Beiträge zum ökumenischen Gespräch: Moraltheologische Studien, Syst. 14.   St. Ottilien 1987, EOS.   168 p. DM 38. – RTGL 78 (1988) 445-7 (P. *Inhoffen*); TR 84 (1988) 497-500 (H. *Gleixner*).

431 EZinser Hartmud [Mundus 24,260],   Der Untergang von Religionen.   B 1986, Reimer.   324 p.; 20 fig.

A1.5   *Plurium compilationes* **philologicae** *vel* **archaeologicae**.

432 EAcquaro E., *Pernigotti* S.,   Studi di Egittologia e di antichità puniche 1. Bo 1987, Univ. – RArEspArq 61 (1988) 351 (M. *Fernández-Miranda*).

433 ᴱ**Affeldt** Werner, *Kuhn* Annette, Frauen in der Geschichte 7. Früh-mittelalter: Geschichtsdidaktik 39. Dü 1986, Schwann-Bagel. 296 p.; 13 fig. DM 54. – ᴿHZ 245 (1987) 694s (Edith *Ennen*).

434 ᴱ**Archer** Léonie J., Slavery and other forms of unfree labour. L 1988, Routledge. xii-307 p. $28; pa. £13. 0-415-00203-6; 4-4 [Antiquity 62,657].

435 ᴱ**Benedetti** Gaetano, *Rauchfleisch* Udo, Welt der Symbole; interdiszi-plinäre Aspekte des Symbolverständnisses [Vorlesungsreihe]. Gö 1988, Vandenhoeck & R. 253 p.; 52 (color.) fig. 3-525-01410-4. 17 art.; 1 infra.

436 ᴱ**Binder** G., Saeculum Augustum, [I. 1987 → 3,483] II. Religion und Literatur: WegFor 512. Da 1988, Wiss. ix-481 p. – ᴿArTGran 51 (1988) 385s (A. *Segovia*).

437 ᴱ**Blok** Josine, *Mason* Peter, Sexual asymmetry; studies in ancient society. Amst 1987, Gieben. ix-298 p. 90-70265-41-9. 9 art.; 3 infra.

438 ᴱ**Bremmer** Jan, Interpretations of Greek mythology. Totowa NJ 1986, Barnes & N. viii-294 p. $28.50. 0-389-20679-2. – ᴿClasW 82 (1988s) 127 (D. *Sider*).

439 ᴱ**Eggebrecht** Arne & Eva, *al.*, Ägyptens Aufstieg zur Weltmacht. Mainz 1987, von Zabern. 384 p. DM 50. 3-8053-0964-3 [BO 45,471].

440 ᴱ**French** Roger, *Greenaway* Frank, Science in the early Roman empire; PLINY the Elder, his sources and influence. Totowa NJ 1986, Barnes & N. 287 p. $28.50. – ᴿAmHR 93 (1988) 398 (J. M. *Riddle*).

442 ᴱ**Gaffney** Christopher F. & Vincent L., Pragmatic archaeology; theory in crisis?: BAR-Int. 167. Ox 1987. vii-119 p.

443 ᴱ**Gledhill** John, *al.*, State and society; the emergence and development of social hierarchy and political centralization: One World Archaeology 4. L 1988, Unwin Hyman. xx-347 p.; ill. 0-04-445023-0. p. 113-120, *Shay* Talin, Palestine Bronze Age.

444 ᴱ**Grant** Michael, *Kitzinger* Rachel, Civilization of the ancient Mediter-ranean, Greece and Rome. NY 1988, Scribner's. I. xxvi-719 p.; II. xiv + p. 722-1297; II. xiv + p. 1301-1880. 0-684-18864-5; 5-1; 6-X.

444* ᴱ**Hammond** Michael, *al.*, Studies in syntactic typology: Typological studies in language 17. Amst 1988, Benjamins. xiv-394 p.

445 ᴱ**Harrold** Francis B., *Eve* Raymond A., Cult archaeology and crea-tionism; understanding pseudoscientific beliefs about the past. Iowa City 1987, Univ. Iowa. xii-163 p. $20. 0-87745-176-1. – ᴿAntiquity 62 (1988) 611s (P. *Fowler*).

447 ᴱ**Hodder** Ian, Archaeology as long-term history: New Directions. C 1987, Univ. viii-145 p.; 44 fig. £25. 0-521-32923-X. – ᴿAntiquity 62 (1988) 392.394 (J. & M. *Megaw*).

448 ᴱ**Holdsworth** Christopher, *Wiseman* T. P., The inheritance of histo-riography, 350-900: Exeter Studies in History 12. Exeter 1986, Univ. vi-138 p. £7.50 pa. – ᴿClasR 102 (1988) 160s (J. M. *Alonso-Núñez*).

449 ᴱ**Hussain** Asaf, *al.*, Orientalism, Islam, and Islamists. Brattleboro VT 1985, Amana. 300 p. $17.50. – ᴿRelStR 14 (1988) 267 (H. *Algar*: weakest on critique of B. LEWIS).

450 ᴱ**Jacobsen** Jerome, Studies in the archaeology of India and Pakistan [Delhi...]. Wmr 1987, Aris & P. xx-327 p. ill. £16. – ᴿBInstArch 25 (1988) 126s (S. *Ratnagar*).

452 ᴱ**Kushner** David, Palestine in the Late Ottoman period; political, social and economic transformation: Yad Ben Zvi. J/Leiden 1986, BenZvi/Brill. xii-434 p. ƒ140. 965-217-027-5 / 90-04-07792-8. – ᴿBO 45 (1988) 214s (C. *Nuland*).

453 ᴱLyons John, al., New horizons in linguistics 2. L 1987, Penguin/Pelican. vi-465 p. 0-14-022612-5. 16 art.; Lyons on semantics, p. 1-29 and 152-178; *Gazdar* G., *Mellish* C., Computational linguistics, p. 225-248.
454 ᴱMacready Sarah, *Thompson* F. H., Roman architecture in the Greek world: Occas. Papers NS 10. L 1987, Soc. Antiquaries (Thames & H.). viii-124 p. 28 fig.; 11 pl. 0-500-99047-6. 10 art., 8 infra.
455 ᴱMura Sommella Anna, al., Lo sport nel mondo antico; 'athla' e atleti nella Grecia classica: Roma, Palazzo dei Conservatori, Ag.-Nov. 1987. R 1987, Min. Beni Culturali. 64 p.; ill. Exposition catalogue with many short general articles.
456 ᴱPatzer Andreas, Der historische Sokrates: WegFor 585. Da 1987, Wiss. vi-473 p. – ᴿGnomon 60 (1988) 147s (K. *Döring*).
456* Peredneaziatskij Sbornik IV: drevnjaja i sredievekovaja istorija i filologija. Moskva 1986, Nauka. 250 p.; ill.; Eng. summaries.
457 ᴱPotts D. T., Araby the blest; studies in Arabian archaeology: C. Niebuhr Publ. 7 [0902-5449]. K 1988, Univ. 264 p. 87-7289-051-7. 9 art.; 4 infra.
458 ᴱRaaflaub Kurt A., Social struggles in archaic Rome; new perspectives on the conflict of the orders. Berkeley 1986, Univ. California. xxv-464 p. $55. 0-520-05528-4. – ᴿClasW 82 (1988s) 318 (G. P. *Verbrugghe*); Gymnasium 95 (1988) 447-9 (A. *Poláček*); RelStR 14 (1988) 250 (R. J. *Penella* notes R. Mɪᴛᴄʜᴇʟʟ's 'improbable' thesis that the Roman senate was originally a priesthood).
459 ᴿRast Walter W. (*Zeiger* Marion), Preliminary reports of ASOR-sponsored excavations [1980-4 (1986) ⇒ 2,354], 1982-5: BASOR Sup 25. Baltimore 1988, Johns Hopkins Univ. 222 p.; ill. 0-8018-3697-2. 7 art., infra.
461 ᴱStuard M., Women in medieval history and historiography. Ph 1987, Univ. Pennsylvania. xvi-203 p. [RHE 83,442*].
462 ᴱStuip R. E. V., *Vellekoop* C., Visioenen: Utrechtse Bijdragen tot de Mediëvistiek 6. Utrecht 1986, Hes. 243 p. – ᴿJStJud 19 (1988) 129 (I. P. *Culianu*: largely a re-run, of slight interest outside Netherlands; something on Sanskrit and on the 1189 Jewish Gᴏᴛᴛꜱᴄʜᴀʟᴋ).
463 ᴱTaylor Mark C., Deconstruction in context; literature and philosophy [anthology]. Ch 1986, Univ. vii-446 p. $45; pa. $17. – ᴿRelStR 14 (1988) 137 (D. L. *Miller*).
464 ᴱVirgilio Biagio, Studi ellenistici [I. 1987 ⇒ 3,367], II. Pisa 1987, Giardini. 209 p. 11 art., 3 del Virgilio; 7 infra.
465 ᴱWegstaff M., Landscape and culture; geographical and archaeological perspectives. Ox 1987, Blackwell. 233 p.; 26 fig. £29.50; pa. £10. 0-631-13729-7; 5288-1. – ᴿAntiquity 62 (1988) 396 (M. *Jones*).
466 ᴱWaithe Mary Ellen, A history of women philosophers [title from 1984 Eng. of G. *Ménage*], I, 1987, Nijhoff. $67; pa. $20. 90-247-3448-0; 368-5. – ᴿClasR 102 (1988) 429s (Gillian *Clark* gives date of Ménage as 1690).
467 ᴱYoffee Norman, *Cowgill* George L., The collapse of ancient states and civilizations [Mesopotamia, Greece, Rome, China]. Tucson 1988, Univ. Arizona. 333 p.; ill. 0-8165-1049-0. – ᴿAntiquity 62 (1988) 800s (C. *Renfrew*: prolegomena).

A2 Acta *congressuum* .1 biblica [*Notitiae*, reports ⇒ Y7.2].

468 Annual meeting 1988, American Academy of Religion, Society of Biblical Literature & ASOR, 19-22 November 1988. Chicago. 304 p. [program only; for seminar summaries ⇒ 500].

469 ᴱ**Augustin** Matthias, *Schunck* Klaus-Dietrich, 'Wünschet Jerusalem Frieden', collected communications to the XIIth Congress of the International Organization for the Study of the OT, Jerusalem 1986 [short papers, supplementing ᴱ*Emerton* J. VTS 1988 ➤ 482]: Beiträge zur Erforschung des ATs und des Antiken Judentums 13. Fra 1988, Lang. xi-481 p.; 477-480, Bericht [< BZ 19 (1987) 159-161]. 3-8204-9887-7. 43 art.; infra.

470 [**Backus** Irena], Troisième colloque international d'histoire d'exégèse biblique au XVIᵉ siècle, Genève 31 août - 2 sept. 1988 [on attend les Actes ...]: RHE 83 (1988) 854 (J.-F. *Gilmont*); 6 items infra.

471 ᴱ**Bar-Asher** Moshe, ⊕ *Meḥqārîm ba-lāšōn* / Language studies I. [partly discussions 1981 and 1983]. J 1985, Hebrew Univ. x-161 p. + XLII Eng. summaries. 0334-6110. 18 art., infra.

471* *Bo* C., present., Fede e cultura dal Vangelo di Giovanni; ciclo S. Fedele, Milano: Teologia viva 4. Bo 1986, Dehoniane. 269 p.; ill. 88-10-40905-1.

472 ᴱ**Bori** Pier Cesare, Atti del 5º seminario di ricerca su 'Studi sulla letteratura esegetica cristiana e giudaica antica', Torino 14-16 ottobre 1987: AnStoEseg 5 (1988). 351 p. Lit. 35.000. 88-10-20255-4. 16 art.; infra.

473 ᴱ**Brooke** George J., Temple Scroll studies [Symposium Manchester Dec. 1987]: JPseud Sup 7. Sheffield 1988, Academic. c. 120 p. £26.50; sb. £20. 1-85075-200-1 [JPseud 2,20 adv.].

474 ᴱ**Chiesa** B., Correnti culturali e movimenti religiosi del giudaismo; Associazione italiana per lo studio del giudaismo, V Congresso internazionale 12-15 nov. 1984: Testi e Studi 5. R 1987, Carucci. 336 p. Lit. 40.000. – ᴿJStJud 19 (1988) 98s (F. *García Martínez*: tit. pp.; analyses).

475 ᴱ**Chmiel** Jerzy, ⊕ Materiały z sympozjum biblistów — Częstochowa 1987: RuBi 41 (1988) 2-84; 84-86, relatio, *Matras* Tadeusz; 57s, nomina 81 participantium (addresses, residence).

476 Conference on Biblical Inerrancy (Ridgecrest NC, 1987), Proceedings. Nv 1987, Broadman. 554 p. $13 pa. 12 [each with 2 responses] + 17 art. [TDig 36,55].

477 ᴱ**Corona** Raimondo, Il Vangelo secondo Luca, lettura esegetico esistenziale; Atti della Prima Settimana Biblica Abruzzese O.F.M. 24-29.VI.1985 [brani d'esegesi di *Adinolfi* Marco (*Bottini* Claudio)]. Tocca Casauria 1988, Convento S. Bernardino. 263 p. [Marco, 1984/7 ➤ 3,531, 'seconda'].

478 ᴱ**Cox** C. E., Sixth Congress Septuagint/Cognate 1986/7 ➤ 3,533; 19 art., infra < CBQ 51,390.

479 ᴱ**Dan** Joseph, Early Jewish mysticism; proceedings of the first international conference on the history of Jewish mysticism [1984 ➤ 3,535]: Jerusalem Studies in Jewish Thought (0333-7081) 6,1s. J 1987, Hebrew Univ. Scholem Center. ⊕ 267 p.; 10 art.; Eng. 132 p.; 7 art. - 11 infra.

480 ᴱ**Dirksen** P. B., *Mulder* M. J., The Peshitta, its early text and history; symposium Leiden 30-31 August 1985: Peshiṭta Inst. Mg. 4. Leiden 1988, Brill. x-310 p. *f* 110. 90-04-08769-1 [BL 89,45, J. F. *Healey*, tit. pp.]. 10 art., infra.

482 ᴱ**Emerton** J. A., Congress volume [IOSOT Aug. 24-29], Jerusalem 1986: VTSup 40. Leiden 1988, Brill. vii-303 p. [TLZ 114,891, tit. pp.]. 90-04-08499-1. 25 art., infra; and ➤ 469.

483 ᴱ*Fernández Marcos* N., *al.*, Simposio bíblico [pre-IOSOT] español (Salamanca 1982) 1984 → 65,415; 1,469: ᴿJTS 39 (1988) 142-6 (A. *Chester* in great detail); Sefarad 48 (1988) 208-212 (M. J. de *Azcárraga*).

484 ᴱ**Garrigues** Jean Miguel, L'unique Israël de Dieu; approches chrétiennes du Mystère d'Israël. Limoges 1987, Criterion. 240 p. – ᴿRHPR 68 (1988) 258s (E. *Jacob*: dialogue entre chrétiens).

485 **Ghiberti** G., [introd., p. 9-23], La posizione del debole nella Bibbia: Associazione laica di cultura biblica, Atti del convegno nazionale [Casale Monferrato 16-17.V.1987]. Settimello-FI 1987, Biblia. 4 art., infra [< ᴢᴀᴡ 100,310].

486 ᴱ**Gibaud** Henri, Les problèmes d'expression dans la traduction biblique; traduction, interprétation, lectures; Actes du colloque des 7-8 novembre 1986 [anniv.: 450ᵉ, mort de Tyndale; 1600ᵉ, Vulgate]: Centre de Linguistique Religieuse, Cah. 1. Angers 1988, Univ. Institut de Perfectionnement en Langues Vivantes. 206 p. F 175 [CBQ 51,188]. 0987-7290. 20 art., 18 infra.

487 [*Gibert* P., Gn 1-11], Mémoire de l'humanité; du néolitique à la Bible [Colloque du Groupe interdisciplinaire de la faculté des sciences, Chantilly 4-5 janvier 1985]: Cah. Inst. Cath. Lyon 17. Lyon 1986. 110 p. – ᴿRThom 88 (1988) 149 (J.-M. *Maldamé*).

488 ᴱ**Ginzel** Günther B., Auschwitz als Herausforderung für Juden und Christen [Kolloquium Köln 1978 ... Juifs, Catholiques, Protestants sur la révision de l'exégèse et de la christologie]. Heid 1980, Schneider. 671 p. – ᴿRHPR 68 (1988) 260-2 (E. *Jacob*).

489 ᴱ**Hoffman** R. Joseph, *La Rue* Gerald A., Jesus in history and myth [AA symposium April 1985, Committee for the Scientific Examination of Religion]. c. 1987, Prometheus. 217 p. $22. 16 art. – ᴿAmerica 157 (1987) 338 (R. A. *Krieg*: in title as above; in text, title is 'Jesus: in Myth and History').

490 ᴱ**Iancu** Carol, *Lassère* Jean-M., Juifs et judaïsme en Afrique du Nord dans l'antiquité et le haut Moyen Âge: UER 4 [colloque 1983]. Montpellier 1985, Univ. P. Valéry. 117 p. – ᴿRÉAug 34 (1988) 203s (G. *Dahan*).

491 Jérusalem dans les traditions juives et chrétiennes; colloque des 11 et 12 nov. 1982: Publ. Institutum Judaicum Bru, 5. Bru 1987, Peeters. 127 p. Fb 800. – ᴿRTLv 19 (1988) 222s (P.-M. *Bogaert*).

491* ᴱ**Kertelge** Karl., Der Prozess gegen Jesus; historische Rückfrage und theologische Deutung [NT-Tagung Graz 6.-10.IV.1987]: QDisp 112. FrB 1988, Herder. 236 p. DM 39,50 pa. 3-451-02112-9 [NTAbs 32,372]. 8 art., infra.

492 ᴱ**Mandilaras** Basil G., Proceedings of the XVIII international congress of papyrology, Athens 25-31 May 1986. Athens 1988, Greek Papyrological Society. 491 p.; 523 p. 960-85019-1-1; 2-X. 108 art., 10 infra.

493 ᴱ**Mickelsen** Alvera, Women, authority and the Bible [Evangelical Colloquium, Oak Brook IL Oct. 9-11, 1984]. DG 1986, InterVarsity. 304 p. $10 pa. [TDig 35,94]. 14 art. + responses. – ᴿBS 145 (1988) 218s (H. W. *House*: 'the finest' but several philological weaknesses).

494 ᴱ**Neusner** Jacob, *al.*, Judaisms and their Messiahs at the turn of the Christian era [AAR sessions]. NY 1987, Cambridge Univ. xvi-299 p. $37.50; pa. $13 [TDig 35,369: authors; subjects).

495 ᴱ**Osborn** Eric, *McIntosh* Lawrence, The Bible and European literature; history and hermeneutics; Proceedings of a conference held at Queen's College, University of Melbourne, 15-18 May 1987. Melbourne 1987, Academia. vii-252 p. $30 [CBQ 51,402].

495* EPirola Giuseppe, Coppellotti Francesco, Il 'Gesù storico' problema della modernità [Centro Teologico di Torino, Seminario di Filosofia Politica 1985/6]. CasM 1988, Piemme. 219 p. Lit. 24.000. 88-384-1275-8. 10 art.; infra.

496 ERevuelta Sanudo M., Morón Arroyo C., El Erasmismo en España [Coloquio Menéndez Pelayo 10-14.VI.1985]. Santander 1986, Soc. M. Pelayo. xiii-523 p. – RSefarad 47 (1987) 413-6 (María V. Spottorno).

497 ERothschild Jean-Pierre, Sixdenier Guy D., Études samaritaines; Pentateuque et Targum, exégèse et philologie, chroniques; Table Ronde P 1985, Les manuscrits samaritains, problèmes et méthodes: RÉJ Coll. 6. Lv 1988, Peeters. 315 p. Fb 1200. 90-6831-112-3. 23 art., 14 infra.

498 ESchluchter W., Max WEBERS Sicht des antiken Christentums [einschliesslich 6 Art. AT, infra; Reiner-Stiftung-Konferenz]: Tb-Wissenschaft 548. Fra 1985, Suhrkamp. 568 p. DM 24! [ZAW 100,328]. 3-518-28148-8.

499 ESharon Moshe, The Holy Land in history and thought; papers submitted to the international conference on the relations between the Holy Land and the world outside it, Johannesburg 1986 [South Africa title, Pillars of smoke and fire]: Eric Samson Chair in Jewish Civilization 1. Johannesburg/Leiden 1988, Southern/Brill. xiv-291 p. 1-86812-048-1 / 90-04-08855-5. 23 art.; 16 infra.

500 Society of Biblical Literature 1988 seminar papers [124th meeting, 19-22 Nov. 1988, Chicago → 468], ELull David J.: SBL Seminars 27. Atlanta 1988, Scholars. ix-644 p. 1-55540-297-6. 46 art.; infra.

500* Society for OT study, bulletin for 1988: a) Winter meeting, London 5-7 Jan. 1988: Nicholson E., (pres.); Desacralization in Dt.; Brooke G., Another 'Pentateuch' [Jub + Temple Scroll + TestMos]; Cathcart K. J., Targum Min. Proph. – b) Summer Meeting, Oxford 19-22 July 1988: McKane W., Jer 27,5-8; Gelston A., Is 53; Salters R. B., Ps 82; Dalley Stephanie, Yahweh in Hamath [name not confirmed at Ebla, Mari, Rimah, Alalakh, Ugarit, Amarna]; Mason R. A., Chronistic themes in Ezr/Neh; Beattie D., Yemenite Targum Ruth; Aitken K., Is 41-44; Haran M., Psalms, 4 Doxologies / 5 'Books' (unacceptable).

501 EStammen T., Vertreibung und Exil; Lebensformen — Lebenserfahrungen [Tagung Fr 1986]. Mü 1987, Schnell & S. 143 p.

502 EStine Philip C., Issues in Bible translation [UBS workshop May 1987, Harpers Ferry WV]: UBS Mon 3. L 1988, United Bible Societies. viii-296 p. 0-8267-0453-0. 15 art.; infra.

503 EStramare Tarcisio, La Bibbia 'Vulgata' dalle origini ai nostri giorni; Atti del Simposio 1985/7 → 3,566; 88-209-1562-6; 14 art., 11 infra.

504 La terminologia esegetica nell'antichità; Atti del primo seminario di antichità cristiane (Bari, 25 ottobre 1984). Bari 1987, Edipuglia. 178 p. Lit. 28.000. – RRasT 29 (1988) 308 (R. Maisano); StPatav 35 (1988) 718-722 (C. Corsato).

505 EUffenheimer Benjamin, Reventlow Henning, Creative biblical exegesis; Christian and Jewish hermeneutics through the centuries [conference TA Univ. 16-17 Dec. 1985, with Bochum kath./ev. Fak.]: JStOT Sup 59. Sheffield 1988, Univ. 225 p. £27.50 [ZAW 101,312, tit. pp.]. 1-85075-082-3. 18 art., infra.

506 EVermes Geza, Symposium on the manuscripts from the Judaean Desert, Warburg Institute, London University College June 11-12, 1987: JJS 39,1 (1988) 1-79 [4 of the 9 papers; others to follow in JJS (but none in 1988/2)].

507 EVilliers P.G.R. de,   Liberation theology and the Bible [symposium
     Pretoria 1986]: Miscellanea Congregalia 31.   Pretoria 1987, Univ. S.
     Africa.   76 p. R 13,65.   0-86981-528-8.   4 art.; de Villiers on Lk 4; J. *Le
     Roux* on Is 61 [NedTTs 42 (1988) 337].
508 EVilliers P.G.R. de,   Like a roaring lion... Essays on the Bible, the
     Church and demonic powers [Univ. S. Africa conference 1986].   Pretoria
     1987, Univ.   ii-205 p. R 17.   0-86981-473-7 [NTAbs 32,382].   15 art.
509 *Vorster* W. S., *al.*,   Hoe lees 'n mens die Bybel?   [Pretoria-Kaapstad
     Powell-Bybelsecentrum seminaar 1985]: Miscellanea Congregalia 33.
     Pretoria 1988, Univ.   134 p. R 18,90.   0-86981-539-3.   6 art., infra.
510 John WYCLIF e la tradizione degli studi biblici in Inghilterra [Atti Univ.
     Genova 1984].   Genova 1987, Melangolo.   155 p. [STEv NS 1,91, P.
     Bolognesi].

A2.3   **Acta congressuum theologica** [reports ➤ Y7.4].

511 EAbignente Donatella, *al.*,   La Donna nella Chiesa e nel mondo; studi
     promossi dalla Facoltà Teologica dell'Italia Meridionale e dalla Com-
     missione Diocesana Donna [Futuroggi].   N 1988, Dehoniane.   451 p.
     Lit. 28.000.   11 art. di donne, 11 di uomini. – RAsprenas 35 (1988) 287s
     (S. *Cipriani*); CC 139 (1988,3) 94s (M. *Simone*); RasT 29 (1988) 606s (V.
     Fusco); Teresianum 39 (1988) 539s (V. *Pasquetto*).
512 EAdler Gilbert,   Formation et Église, pratiques et réflexion [colloque
     Strasbourg 1985].   P 1987, Beauchesne.   140 p. F 75. – REsprVie 98 (1988)
     76 (L. *Debarge*).
512* EAlberigo Giuseppe,   Giovanni XXIII transizione del Papato e della
     Chiesa [colloquio Bergamo 1986 (➤ 3,577), Istituto Scienze Religiose di
     Bologna].   P 1988, Borla.   180 p. Lit. 16.000. – RRSPT 72 (1988) 668-670
     (J.-N. *Walty*).
513 The alliance of the hearts of Jesus and Mary (International theol-
     ogical/pastoral conference, Manila 30 Nov.-3 Dec. 1987).   Manila 1988,
     Development Foundation.
514 L'anima nell'antropologia di S. Tommaso d'Aquino [congresso Roma
     2-5.I.1986]: Univ. S. Thomae.   Mi 1987, Massimo.   645 p. Lit. 50.000. –
     RSacDoc 33 (1988) 228-231.
515 EAntoun Richard T., *Hegland* Mary E.,   Religious resurgence; con-
     temporary cases in Islam, Christianity, and Judaism [SUNY-Binghamton
     Asia and North Africa conference 1981/3].   Syracuse NY 1987, Univ.
     xiii-269 p. $27.50 [TDig 35,189].
516 AUGUSTINUS: EBoeft Jan den, *Oort* Johannes van,   Augustiniana Traiec-
     tina, communications présentées au Colloque international d'Utrecht,
     13-14 novembre 1986.   P 1987, Études Augustiniennes.   204 p. ➤ 3,591;
     2-85121-086-6; 10 art.; 3 infra.
517 *a)* Congresso internazionale su S. Agostino nel XVI centenario della
     conversione, Roma, 15-20 settembre 1986; Atti I-III: St. Eph. Aug. 24-26.
     R 1987, Inst. Patristicum 'Augustinianum'.   574 p.; 618 p.; 495 p., 24 fig. –
     RTPhil 63 (1988) 600-2 (H. J. *Sieben*). – *b)* Toulouse 30 jan. 1987: BLitEc
     88,3s (1987) 161-352 [NRT 110,934, D. *Dideberg* sans tit. pp.; TLZ 114,
     129, H.-J. *Diesner*].
518 *a)* ECaprioli A., *Vaccaro* L.,   Agostino e la conversione cristiana (prima
     sessione, Agostino nelle terre di Ambrogio): Augustiniana, Testi e Studi 1.
     Palermo 1987, Augustinus.   96 p. Lit. 20.000. – *b)* L'opera letteraria di
     Agostino tra Cassiciacum e Milano; Agostino nelle terre di Ambrogio

(seconda sessione, 1-4 ottobre 1986): Augustiniana, Testi e Studi 2. Palermo 1987, Augustinus. 221 p. Lit. 32.000. – RRasT 29 (1988) 603s (Teresa *Piscitelli Carpino*).

519 ECiolini Gino, AGOSTINO e LUTERO; il tormento dell'uomo: Convegni [del Convento] di S. Spirito 1. Palermo 1985, Augustinus. 124 p. 3 art. – RRTLv 19 (1988) 97s (J.-F. *Gilmont*).

520 Conversione e storia: Convegni S. Spirito-Firenze 3 [1986]. Palermo 1987, Augustinus. 88 p. Lit. 11.000 [*Grech* Prosper, La conversione nella S. Scrittura p. 25-55]. – RStPatav 35 (1988) 715-7 (C. *Corsato*).

521 EBattaglia Vincenzo, L'uomo e il mondo alla luce di Cristo; Atti del secondo Simposio Rieti 19-21 aprile 1985 [primo 1984/5 ➤ 2,407]: Studi e Testi Francescani NS 5. Vicenza 1986, L.I.E.F. 240 p. Lit. 15.000. – RGregorianum 69 (1988) 361 (J. *Galot*); Salesianum 50 (1988) 583 (S. *Felici*).

522 EBau Gerhard, *al.*, Frieden in der Schöpfung; das Naturverständnis protestantischer Theologie [Ringvorlesung Heid]. Gü 1987, Mohn. 271 p. DM 64. – RÖkRu 37 (1988) 392s (Christa *Springe*).

523 EBecker Hansjakob, *al.*, Im Angesicht des Todes, ein interdisziplinäres Kompendium [Tagung Mainz 1982]: Pietas Liturgica 3s. St. Ottilien 1987, EOS. xi-707 p.; xi-p. 709-1479; ill. DM je 148. – RTGL 78 (1988) 185 (W. *Beinert*); ZkT 110 (1988) 484-7 (H. B. *Meyer*).

524 EBeinert Wolfgang, *al.*, Maria — eine ökumenische Herausforderung [kath./ev. Tagung München 22.-24. April 1983]. Rg 1984, Pustet. 184 p. DM 22,80. 7 art.; 4 infra. – RZkT 110 (1988) 340-4 (L. *Lies*: tit. pp. Analyse).

525 EBekkenkamp J., *al.* (Interuniversitaire Werkgroep Feminisme en Theologie), Van zusters, meiden en vrouwen; tien jaar feminisme en theologie op fakulteiten en hogescholen in Nederland: IIMO 19. Leiden 1986, IIMO. 325 p. *f* 25. 90-71387-17-8. – RTsTNijm 28 (1988) 93s (Carla *Claassen*).

526 EBiffi Franco, La pace; sfida all'Università Cattolica; Atti del Simposio fra le Università Ecclesiastiche, Roma 3-6.XII.1986. R 1988, Herder. 914 p. 73 art.; 6 infra.

528 EBlock Walter, *Hexham* Irving, Religion, economics and social thought; proceedings of an international symposium [Vancouver Aug. 1982]. Vancouver BC 1986, Fraser Institute. xiv-574 p. – RSR 17 (1988) 120s (G. H. *Crowell*).

529 Bodel R., *al.*, Ernst BLOCH; teologia, utopia e coscienza anticipante [Seminario Ferrar 1985]. Bo 1985, Cappelli. 78 p. Lit. 5000. – RProtestantesimo 43 (1988) 110-2 (Elena *Bein Ricco*: fra l'altro PIROLA G., prospettiva cattolica).

530 EBourg Dominique, [CERIT, Colloque Strasbourg 1985] L'Être et Dieu: CogF 138. P 1986, Cerf. 252 p. – RRTLv 19 (1988) 485s (E. *Brito*).

532 EBraham Randolph L. The origins of the Holocaust; Christian anti-Semitism [March 1985 City Univ. NY conference on *Maccoby* H., The sacred executioner 1962]: Social Science Monographs. NY 1986 (Columbia Univ., distrib.). viii-85 p. – RRelStR 14 (1988) 264 (A. *Kamesar*).

533 EBrockway Allan R., *Rajashekar* J. Paul, New religious movements and the churches [Lutheran World Federation/WCC, Amsterdam Sept. 1986]. Geneva 1987, WCC. xix-200 p. $12.50 [TDig 35,281].

534 EBryant M. Darrol, *Mataragnon* Rita H., The many faces of religion and society [Unification Church meeting]: God, the contemporary discussion.

NY 1985, Paragon. xiii-200 p. $13. – ᴿRelStR 14 (1988) 360 (J. V. *Spickard*: of little value).

535 ᴱ**Bsteh** Andreas, Dialog aus der Mitte christlicher Theologie [Tagung Wien-Mödling 1.-4. April 1986]: Beiträge zur Religionstheologie 5. Wien-Mödling 1987, St. Gabriel. iv-245 p. DM 45. 8 art. – ᴿZkT 110 (1988) 352 (W. *Kern* gibt keine Seiten aber nennt 'Seilakt ohne Netz' seinen eigenen Artikel, 'Bekehrung der Kirche zum Kreuzesglauben; ein Beitrag zur Bekehrung der Religionen?').

536 ᴱ*Campogalliani* Paolo, *Sartori* Luigi, Nuove concezioni di spazio-tempo e immagine di Dio, contributo a un dibattito interdisciplinare [Convegni e simposi 15]: StPatav 34 (1987) 497-551.

537 ᴱ**Caplan** Lionel, Studies in religious fundamentalism [six from 1985, London BSOAS seminar, three others; 'predominantly anthropological, though several participants are sociologists', TDig 35,290]. Albany 1988, SUNY. x-216 p. $39.50; pa. $15.

538 ᴱ**Caplan** Pat, The cultural construction of sexuality [London Univ. seminars 1984]. L 1987, Tavistock. ix-304 p. £25. – ᴿAnthropos 83 (1988) 583-5 (T. O. *Beidelman*).

539 *Castiau* C. présent., Péché collectif et responsabilité [colloque 1985]: Publ. 40. Bru 1986, Fac. Univ. S. Louis. xiii-198 p. Fb 750. – ᴿRTLv 19 (1988) 386s (H. *Wattiaux*).

540 ᴱ**Coero-Borga** P., *Intrigillo* G., La Sindone; nuovi studi e ricerche; Atti del III Congresso Nazionale di Studi sulla Sindone, Trani. T 1986, Paoline. 438 p. Lit. 38.000. 88-215-1070-0 [NTAbs 32,369: *Ghiberti* G., NT].

541 Conciencia y libertad humana, Toledo 29.VI-3.VII.1987: Semana de Teología Espiritual 13. Toledo 1988, Cete. 421 p. 84-86103-17-7. 20 art.; → 5584.

542 ᴱ**Costa Ruy** O., One faith, many cultures; inculturation, indigenization, and contextualization [Boston Theological consortium March 1986]: Annual 2. Maryknoll / CM 1988, Orbis / Boston Theological Institute. xvii-162 p. $24; pa. $11 [TDig 35,384].

543 ᴱ**Couturier** Guy, *al.*, Essais sur la mort [Séminaire 1978-82, Univ. Montréal]: Héritage et projet 29. Montréal 1985, Fides. 517 p. $25. – ᴿÉglT 17 (1986) 246s (H. *Doucet*).

544 ᴱ**Crotty** Robert B., The Charles Strong lectures [on Australian and comparative religion], 1972-1984. Leiden 1987, Brill. xviii-206 p. $31 pa. 12 art. – ᴿRelStR 14 (1988) 133 (G. *Yocum*).

545 ᴱ**Crow** Paul A., *al.*, Papers and addresses from the International Dialogue between Disciples of Christ and the World Alliance of Reformed Churches, March 9-11, 1987, Birmingham, England = Mid-Stream 27,2 (1988) 87-219.

546 ᴱ**Daly** Robert J., Rising from history; U.S. Catholic theology looks to the future [Milwaukee meeting 1984]: AnCTSA. Lanham MD 1987, UPA. xi-221 p. $24.50; pa. $12.75 [TDig 35,285: ...Americanism, feminism, computers].

547 ᴱ**Dautzenberg** Gerhard, *al.*, Rechtfertigung, Ringvorlesung... Lutherjahr 1983: Schriften zur Theologie 3. Giessen 1984, Univ. 139 p. [< LuJb 55 (1988) 141].

548 ᴱ**Davis** Stephen T., Encountering Jesus; a debate on Christology [*Hick* J., *Cobb* J.; also → 8093, *Pentz* Rebecca T., *Robinson* James M.]. Louisville 1988, Knox. 200 p. $14. 0-8042-0537-X [TDig 36,157].

549 ᴱ**DeKlerk** Peter, CALVIN and Christian ethics [1985 meeting]. GR 1987, Calvin Studies. 148 p. – ᴿCalvinT 23 (1988) 97-100 (J. H. *Kromminga*).

550 Denaro e coscienza cristiana [Atti del convegno Bologna apr. 1987]. Bo 1987, Dehoniane. 298 p. Lit. 30.000. – ᴿViPe 71 (1988) 793-6 (Francesca *Duchini*).

551 El Dios cristiano y la realidad social; XXI Semana de Estudios Trinitarios. Salamanca 1987, Secretariado Trinitario. 166 p. – ᴱEstBíb 46 (1988) 556-8 (G. *Pérez*).

552 ᴱ**Distante** Giovanni, La legittimità del culto delle icone; Oriente e Occidente riaffermano insieme la fede cristiana; Atti del III Convegno Storico interecclesiale, 11/13 Maggio 1987, Bari = Nicolaus 15,1s (Bari 1988). 352 p. 15 art. (+13), 4 infra.

553 ᴱ**Dockrill** D. W., *Tanner* R. G., The concept of Spirit; papers from the conference held at St. Paul's College, University of Sydney, 21-24 May 1984: Prudentia Supp. Auckland 1985, Univ. 232 p. – ᴿRTLv 19 (1988) 90s (A. de *Halleux*: p. 5-25, J. Wʀɪɢʜᴛ on *rûaḥ*; 81-113, E. J. Sᴛᴏʀᴍᴏɴ, Procession).

554 ᴱ**Dockrill** D. W., *Tanner* R. G., The idea of salvation, sacred and secular; conference at St. Paul's College, Univ. Sydney 22-23 August 1986: Prudentia Sup. Auckland 1988. vi-258 p. 0110-487-X.

555 ᴱ**Eber** Irene, Confucianism; the dynamics of tradition [Jerusalem Hebrew University colloquium March 14-16, 1983]. NY 1986, Macmillan. xxii-234 p. $27.50 [TDig 35,60].

556 ᴱ**Eck** Diana L., *Jain* Devaki, Speaking of faith; cross-cultural perspectives on women, religion and social change [1983 Harvard conference]. L 1986, Women's. vi-288 p. £6. – ᴿScotJT 41 (1988) 439s (Henrietta *Hall*).

557 ᴱ**Eijl** Edmond J. M. van, L'image de C. Jᴀɴsᴇɴɪᴜs jusqu'à la fin du XVIIIᵉ siècle; Actes du colloque (Louvain, 7-9 nov. 1985): BiblETL 79. Lv 1987, Peeters. 264 p. – ᴿArTGran 51 (1988) 271s (A. *Segovia*); RThom 88 (1988) 672s (B. *Montagnes*).

558 ᴱ**Ellis** Kail C., The Vatican, Islam, and the Middle East [Villanova Univ. conference, Oct. 25-26, 1985]. Syracuse NY 1987, Univ. xviii-344 p. $40. [TDig 35,92] 15 art. – ᴿIslamochristiana 14 (1988) 369-371 (M. *Borrmans*).

559 ᴱ**Evans** Bernard F., *Cusack* Gregory D., Theology of the land [farm, not Israel; 1985 Collegeville conference]. Collegeville MN 1987, Liturgical. 126 p. $6 [TDig 35,291: 'Walter *Brueggemann* explores the biblical covenantal relationship as a way of speaking about land management']. – ᴿFurrow 39 (1988) 334s (sr. Margaret *Brennan*).

560 ᴱ**Falaturi** A., *al.*, Universale Vaterschaft Gottes; Begegnung der Religionen: Oratio Dominica 14. FrB 1987, Herder. 199 p. DM 46. 3-451-21098-3. – ᴿTsTNijm 28 (1988) 428s (A. van *Dijk*).

561 ᴱ**Feifel** Erich, *Kasper* Walter, Tradierungskrise des Glaubens [kath. Bischofskonferenz Kolloquium für Erziehung, Uni 1986] 1987 ⇒ 3,628: ᴿTLZ 113 (1988) 390 (G. *Adam*).

562 ᴱ**Felici** S., Crescita dell'uomo nella catechesi dei Padri (Età prenicena) [convegno 1986, Pont. Inst. Altioris Latinitatis]. R 1987, LAS(alesianum). 292 p. Lit. 35.000. – ᴿColcT 58,1 (1988) 131-3 (J. *Gliściński*); RasT 29 (1988) 100 (E. *Cattaneo*).

563 Foi chrétienne et pouvoirs des hommes: [Action des Chrétiens pour l'abolition de la torture; *Defois* Gérard présent.]: ACAT colloque de Lyon 22-23 mai 1987 [= SupVSp 162 (1987)]. P 1988, Cerf. 176 p. 9 art.; 2 infra.

564 [Fʀᴀɴᴢ von Assisi und die Armutsbewegung seiner Zeit] Auswirkungen von Lᴜᴛʜᴇʀs Thesen bis zum Augsburger Religionsfrieden und Kardinal

KLESL: Symposien für Vergleichende Kirchengeschichte, Österreich 1. W 1987, Dom. 96 p. [TLZ 113 (1988) 902].

565 ᴱFries Paul, *Nersoyan* Tiran, Christ in East and West [USA Faith and Order consultation]. Macon GA 1987, Mercer Univ. xvii-223 p. $32; pa. $15 [TDig 35,58].

566 [*Gibert* P., Bible; *Martelet* G., théologie] Évolution et création; du Big Bang à l'homme: Groupe interdisciplinaire de la faculté des sciences: Cah. Inst. Cath. Lyon 1987. 214 p. – ᴿRThom 88 (1988) 150 (J.-M. *Maldamé*: écarte tout risque de concordisme).

567 ᴱGillespie Thomas W., Creation: the second annual symposium, Princeton Theol. Sem. Oct. 16-19, 1987: ExAuditu 3 (1987). 147 p. 10 art.; infra.

568 **González Montes** Adolfo, present., Iglesia, teología y sociedad; veinte años después del Segundo Concilio del Vaticano; congreso Fac. Teol. de Wurtzburgo y Salamanca (del 26 al 29 de Mayo de 1987): Salmanticensis 35,1s (1988) 314 p. – ᴿCiTom 115 (1988) 591s (L. *Lago Alba*).

569 ᴱGriffin David R., Physics and the ultimate significance of time; BOHM [David], PRIGOGINE [Ilya] and process philosophy [Claremont Center for Process Studies March 1984 conference]. Albany 1986, SUNY. 322 p. $44.50. – ᴿRExp 85 (1988) 171s (D. *Stiver*).

570 ᴱGrossi Vittorino, Cristianesimo e giudaismo; eredità e confronti; XVI incontro di studiosi dell'antichità cristiana, Roma 7-9 maggio 1987: Augustinianum 28,1s (Roma 1988). 460 p. 26 art.; 25 infra.

571 ᴱGryson Roger, Nature et mission de l'université catholique [Actes Éméritat Mgr. *Massaux*] (LvN 25 avril 1986): RTLv Cah 17. LvN 1987, Univ. 100 p. Fb 200. – ᴿRTLv 19 (1988) 503 (J. *Ponthot*).

572 ᴱGuelt Jean, Sixième congrès orthodoxe en Europe occidentale (Walbourg 1-3 mai 1987): Contacts/Orthodoxe 39,139 (1987) 169-245.

573 ᴱGupta Bina, Sexual archetypes, east and west ⇒ 3,409: ['Is there a divine intention for male-female relationships?'; conference Seoul Aug. 9-15, 1984]: God, the contemporary discussion / New ERA. NY 1987, Paragon. xiv-133 p. $23; pa. $13 [TDig 35,86]. – ᴿCCurr 23 (1988s) 219s (Denise L. *Carmody*); RelStR 14 (1988) 357s (Martha J. *Reineke*).

574 ᴱHaines Byron L., *Cooley* Frank L., Christians and Muslims together; an exploration by Presbyterians [for their 199th General Assembly]. Ph 1987, Geneva [Westminster]. $8 [TDig 35,157].

575 ᴱHalman L., *al.*, Traditie, secularisatie en individualisering; een studie naar de waarden van de Nederlanders in een Europese context [enquête 1981 in 10 landen; symposium Kath. Univ. Brabant 21.X.1987]. Tilburg 1987, Univ. – ᴿTsTNijm 28 (1988) 73 (F. *Heunks*, 'De toekomst van de traditie').

576 ᴱHamon Léo (*Soisson* Jean-Pierre), Du jansénisme à la laïcité; le jansénisme et les origines de la déchristianisation: Entretiens d'Auxerre [c. 1985]. P 1987, Sciences de l'homme. 245 p. – ᴿEsprVie 98 (1988) 497s (R. *Epp* n'indique pas date et lieu de la rencontre).

577 ᴱHarrison Stanley M., *Taylor* Richard C., The life of religion; a Marquette University symposium on the nature of religious belief. Lanham MD 1986, UPA. xxxi-92 p. $22.50; pa. $8.75. – ᴿRelStR 14 (1988) 360 (J. A. *Stone*).

578 **Hernández** Ramón, Buena noticia para los pobres [coloquio Bogotá sept. 1986]: CiTom 114 (1987) 415-436 [-652, ponencias].

579 ᴱHick John, *Knitter* Paul F., The myth of Christian uniqueness; toward a pluralistic theology of religion [Claremont meeting, March 7-8, 1986]:

Faith meets faith. Maryknoll NY 1988, Orbis. xii-227 p. $25; pa. $13 [TDig 35,381].

580 ᴱHill Samuel S., Varieties of southern [USA] religious experience [lectures at Florida State University, Tallahassee, April 1981]. Baton Rouge LA 1988, Louisiana State Univ. vii-241 p. $25. 0-8071-1372-7 [TDig 31,189 indicates 'social gospel' (also 'Roman Catholics and slavery'), otherwise nothing noticeably biblical].

581 ᴱHillerbrand Hans J. Radical tendencies in the Reformation; divergent perspectives [Sixteenth Century Studies conference, St. Louis 1986]: SixtC Studies and Essays 9, Kirksville MO 1988, SixtC. 140 p. $30. – ᴿSixtC 19 (1988) 518-520 (T. A. *Brady*).

582 ᴱHoldsworth Christopher, *Wiseman* T.P., The inheritance of historiography, 3500-900 [mostly about clergy church historians; conference Exeter Jan. 1985]: Exeter Studies in History 12. Exeter 1986, Univ. 138 p. £7.50. – ᴿRelStR 14 (1988) 256 (T. F. X. *Noble*: 'not a weak paper in the volume; how often can one say that?').

583 ᴱHünermann Peter, *Schaeffler* Richard, Theorie der Sprachhandlungen und heutige Ekklesiologie; ein philosophisch-theologisches Gespräch [Eichstätt 20.-23. Nov. 1985]; QDisp 109, 1987 → 3,644; Einf. *Averkamp* Ludwig: ᴿZkT 110 (1988) 335-7 (E. *Runggaldier*).

584 ᴱHughes Richard T., The American quest for the primitive Church [Abilene Univ. conference 1985: American Puritan to Fundamentalist yearning for the less complex, happier, and more perfect order of yore narrated in the Protestant Scriptures]. Urbana 1988, Univ. Illinois. viii-257 p. $32.50; pa. $13. 18 art. [TDig 36,43].

585 JOLY Robert, Aspects de l'anticléricalisme du Moyen Âge à nos jours; hommage à ~ [Colloque de Bruxelles, Juin 1988 [= ProbHistChr 18 (1988) c. 200 p. < ZIT 89,183]. 11 art., aucun infra.

586 ᴱJunod É., La dispute de Lausanne (1536); la théologie réformée après Zwingli et avant Calvin; textes du Colloque international (29 sept.-1 oct. 1986): Bibliothèque historique Vaudoise 90. 232 p. [RHE 83,406*: plusieurs des art. *ibid.*; 1 infra].

587 Kačić: Acta symposii de provincia SS. Redemptoris in Croatia, occasione 250 anni a fundatione eiusdem provinciae, a die 5. ad diem 7. decembris 1985, Split. Split 1988. 559 p. [Antonianum 63,681].

588 ᴱKing Ursula, Women in the world's religions, past and present [Puerto Rico conference Jan. 1984]: God, the contemporary discussion / New ERA. NY 1987, Paragon. x-261 p. $23; pa. $13 [TDig 35,94]. 14 art.

589 Klapsis Emmanuel, *al.*, Le témoignage en son contexte; consultation interorthodoxe de Néapolis (Thessalonique) avril 1988: Contacts 40/144 (1988) 241-295.

590 ᴱKliever Lonnie D., The terrible meek; essays on religion and revolution [Washington D.C. symposium, 'Ideology, religion and revolution']: Washington Institute. NY 1987, Paragon. xvi-259 p. $23; pa. $13 [TDig 35,89].

591 ᴱKlinger Elmar, *Zerfass* Rolf, Die Kirche der Laien; eine Weichenstellung des Konzils [Symposion Würzburg]. Wü 1987, Echter. 174 p. – ᴿLebZeug 42,4 (1987) 91s (A. *Weiser*).

591* ᴱKöckert Heidelore, *Krötke* Wolf, Theologie als Christologie; zum Werk und Leben Karl BARTHS; ein Symposium [B 9.-11.V.1986]. B 1988, Ev.-V. 192 p. 3-374-00472-5. 11 art., 4 infra.

592 ᴱKrenn Kurt, *al.*, Jubiläumsband [zum Teil Regensburger Tagung 1984, mit Veränderung des Namens der Gesellschaft in 'Internationale Ges. für Religionspsychologie *und Religionswissenschaft*': ArchRelPs 17. Gö 1985, Vandenhoeck & R. 322 p. – ᴿTPhil 63 (1988) 144s (U. J. *Niemann*).

593 ᴱ**Kyle** John E., Urban mission; God's concern for the city [15th InterVarsity Missions conference, Urbana IL, Dec. 27-31, 1987]. DG 1988, InterVarsity. 192 p. $9 pa. 0-8308-1711-5 [TDig 36,189].

594 ᴱ**Lak Yeow Choo**, Doing theology and people's movements in Asia: Occas.P. 3. Singapore 1987, Atesea. [v-] 250 p. $7 [CBQ 51,189].

595 ᴱ**Limouris** Gennadios, Church — Kingdom — world; the Church as mystery and prophetic sign [Chantilly 1.I.1985]: Faith and Order 130. Geneva 1986, WCC. 209 p. Fs 20. – ᴿNorTTs 89 (1988) 272s (K. *Nordstokke*).

596 *Link* Christian, *al.* [kath.-prot. Bern/Fr], Sie aber hielten fest an der Gemeinschaft... Einheit der Kirche als Prozess im NT und heute. Z 1988, Benziger/Reinhardt. 275 p. DM 32. – ᴿHerdKorr 42 (1988) 494 (U. *Ruh*).

597 **Llamas** Enrique, present., La piedad mariana en España, siglos XIX y XX (1800-1960) [< X Congreso Mariológico Internacional, Kevelaer 11-18.IX.1987]: EstMar 53 (1988) 341 p.

598 ᴱ**Lobato** A., *Ols* D., Antropologia e Cristologia ieri e oggi; Atti del convegno di studio della S[ocietà] I[nternazionale] TA[quino, 3-4.IV.1987]. R 1987, Pont. Univ. S. Tommaso. 135 p. – ᴿAngelicum 65 (1988) 291-3 (P. *Montini*).

599 ᴱ**Locke** Hubert G., The Barmen confession; papers from the Seattle assembly [Univ. Washington, Apr. 1984]: Toronto Studies in Theology 26. Lewiston NY 1986, Mellen. xi-362 p. $60 [TDig 35,152].

600 ᴱ**Lopez** Donald S., jr., Buddhist hermeneutics [LA Kuroda Institute conference, 1984]: Studies in East Asian Buddhism. Honolulu 1988, Univ. Hawaii. viii-298 p. $35 [TDig 35,344].

601 *Lubac* H. de, *al.*, Alle sorgenti della cultura cristiana; omaggio a Sources Chrétiennes [conferenze alla Mostra apr.-maggio 1986]. N 1987, D'Auria. 104 p. – ᴿRasT 29 (1988) 100s (E. *Cattaneo*).

602 ᴱ**MacGregor** Geddes, Immortality and human destiny; a variety of views [New ERA conference, Puerto Rico, Feb. 8-12, 1986]. NY 1986, Paragon. xxi-235 p. $20; pa. $13. 17 art. [TDig 35,273].

603 ᴱ**Mannermaa** T., *al.*, Thesaurus Lutheri; auf der Suche nach neuen Paradigmen der Luther-Forschung; Referate des LUTHER-Symposiums in Finnland 11.-12. Nov. 1986: Publ. A 24. Helsinki 1987, Luther-Agricola. 327 p. 951-9111-65-4. – ᴿTsTNijm 28 (1988) 186 (T. *Bell*).

604 ᴱ**Manns** Peter, *Meyer* Harding, LUTHER's ecumenical significance, an interconfessional consultation [➤ 65,519, Ökumenische Erschliessung 1983], ᵀᴱ*Lindberg* Carter, *McSorley* Harry. Ph/Ramsey NJ 1984, Fortress/Paulist. xxiv-288 p. [< LuJb 54,144].

605 *María madre de la reconciliación* [Segovia 11-14 sept. 1984]: EstMar 50. Salamanca 1985, Kadmos. 323 p. – ᴿMarianum 50 (1988) 629-632 (A. *Molina Prieto*).

606 ᴱ**Mateo-Seco** Lucas F., *Bastero* Juan L., Coloquio, Gregorio de Nisa. 1988.

607 ᴱ**Matthews** Bruce, *Nagata* Judith, Religion, values and development in Southeast Asia [Singapore conference 1982]. Singapore 1986, Institute of Southeast Asian studies. viii-168 p. 10 art. – ᴿSR 17 (1988) 369-371 (T. P. *Day*).

608 *Médiations africaines du sacré*; [3ᵉ] colloque international de Kinshasa 16-22 février 1986. Kinshasa 1987, Fac. Théol. Catholique [TKontext 10,135, N. B. *Abeng*].

609 *Melsen* A. G. M., *al.*, Wetenschap en geloof; verslag van een studiedag, Katholiek Studiencentrum Nijmegen 30.III.1985. Nijmegen 1987. Kath-

SC. 112 p. ƒ12,50. 90-70713-13-6. – ᴿTsTNijm 28 (1988) 191 (Teije *Brattinga*).

610 ᴱ**Mette** N., *Blasberg-Kuhnke* M., Kirche auf dem Weg ins Jahr 2000; zur Situation und Zukunft der Pastoral [Tagung Wien 1983]. Dü 1986, Patmos. 198 p. DM 29,80. 3-491-776760-8. – ᴿTsTNijm 28 (1988) 102s (Geert van *Gerwen*).

611 ᴱ**Metz** Johann B., *Rottländer* Peter, Lateinamerika und Europa; Dialog der Theologen ['Theologists', Mundus 24,311]. Mainz 1988, Grünewald. 144 p.

612 ᴱ**Minkiel** Stephen J., Excellence in seminary education [Brighton MA conference Oct. 9-11, 1987]. Erie PA 1988, American Catholic Philosophical Association Committee on Priestly Formation [221 W. 6th, 16507]. vi-139 p. $10 [TDig 35,355].

613 ᴱ**Moltmann** Jürgen, Friedenstheologie-Befreiungstheologie [ev. Tagung 1987]. Mü 1988, Kaiser. 145 p. DM 14,80. – ᴿÖkRu 37 (1988) 504s (H. *Vorster*).

614 ᴱ**Moret** Giampiero, CEB, un nuovo modo di essere Chiesa (VI incontro interecclesiale delle comunità di base del Brasile luglio 1986). Bo 1987, EMI. 168 p. Lit. 12.000. – ᴿCC 139 (1988,3) 535-7 (G. *Cornado* non spiega come l'abbiamo in italiano).

615 [*Muñóz* Jesús, Our Lady in the NT, *al*. **Ⓖ**] A symposium on Mariology, Taipei 16-17 Aug. 1988, Fu-Jen Univ. = ColcFuJen 78 (1988) 459-587 [469-496; 598-588 (sic, Eng.) *Swanson* Allen J., The Protestant position].

616 ᴱ**Nicholls** Bruce J., The Church, God's agent for change [1983 Wheaton meeting on 1974 Lausanne congress agenda]: World Evangelical Fellowship Theological Commission. Exeter 1986, Paternoster. 299 p. £8. 0-85364-444-6. – ᴿScotBEv 6 (1988) 53s (C.A.M. *Sinclair*).

617 ᴱ**Novak** Michael, Liberation theology and the liberal society [1985 Warrenton ᴠᴀ conference]. Wsh 1987, American Enterprise Institute for Public Policy Research. xiv-238 p. $26.50; pa. $14.75 [TDig 36,67].

618 ᴱ**O'Brien** Denise, *Tiffany* Sharon W., Rethinking women's roles; perspectives from the Pacific [1979 and 1980 symposia in Clearwater FL and Galveston TX]. Berkeley 1984, Univ. California. xiii-237 p. $32.75. – ᴿAnthropos 83 (1988) 279s (T. *Bargatsky*).

619 ᴱ**Oliver Román** Miguel, El diaconado de la Iglesia en España; simposio Conf. Episcopal Española [abril 1986], pról. *Buxarrais Ventura* mons. Ramón. M 1987, Edice (Conf. Episc. Esp.) 220 p. 84-7141-185-7. – ᴿActuBbg 25 (1988) 235s (A. M. *Tortras*).

620 *Pantaloni* P., present. Congresso mondiale Abati O.S.B. 'E voi che dite che io sia?' Mc 8,29 [18-28 sett. 1984]. Parma 1986, Benedettina. 100 p. – ᴿSalesianum 50 (1988) 259s (E. *dal Covolo*, titoli senza pp.).

621 ᴱ**Pathil** Kuncheria, Mission in India today; the task of St. Thomas Christians [Dharmaram Vidya Kshetram seminar 4-7.VIII.1987]. Bangalore 1988, Dharmaram. xvi-366 p. – ᴿJeevadhara 13 (1988) 382-8 (J. B. *Chethimattam*).

622 ᴱ**Pavan** Antonio, *Milano* Andrea, Persona e personalismi [Ist. Internaz. J. Maritain]. N 1987, Dehoniane. 466 p. Lit. 34.000. 88-396-0016-7. – ᴿActuBbg 25 (1988) 199-201 (J. *Vives*).

623 Per una teologia della pace [seminario Roma 1986, Centro internazionale per la pace]. R 1987, Borla. 186 p. Lit. 14.000. – ᴿRasT 29 (1988) 115s (Lorena *Corradino*).

624 ᴱ**Peretto** Elio, Maria nell'Ebraismo e nell'Islam oggi, Atti del 6º Simposio Mariologico (Roma, 1-9 ott. 1986). R-Bo 1987, Ma-

rianum/Dehoniane.   190 p. – ᴿMarianum 50 (1988) 627s (Bruna *Costa-curta*).

625 ᴱ**Petuchowski** Jakob,   When Jews and Christians meet [Cincinnati HUC Bronstein conference].   Albany 1988, SUNY.   190 p. $34.50;   pa. $13.   0-88706-631-3;   3-X.   11 art., 3 infra. – ᴿJEcuSt 25 (1988) 629s (J. F. *Moore*).

626 ᴱ**Piffl-Perčević** Theodor, [➤ 117], *Stirnemann* Alfred, *a*) Ökumenische Hoffnungen;   neun Pro-Oriente-Symposien.   – *b*) Im Dialog der Liebe: neunzehn 1971-81: 1965-1970: Pro Oriente 9.   Innsbruck 1984/6, Tyrolia. 255 p., DM 48. / 360 p. DM 56. – ᴿZkT 110 (1988) 223s (L. *Lies*).

627 Popoli e spazio romano tra diritto e profezia [... Dan]: Séminaire 3, 'Da Roma alla Terza Roma' 21-23 apr. 1983.   N 1986, Scientifiche. xxxiii-680 p. – ᴿRHR 205 (1988) 311s (R. *Turcan*).

628 Presencia de San José en el Siglo XVII; Actas del Cuarto Simposion internacional (Kalisz, 22-29 septiembre 1985): EstJos 41 (1987). 828 p.; XII pl.   45 art., 3 infra.

629 **Pricoco** Salvatore,   Storia della Sicilia e tradizione agiografica nella tarda antichità; Atti del Convegno di Studi (Catania, 20-22 maggio 1986). Soveria Mannelli CZ 1988, Rubbettino.   233 p. Lit. 30.000.   4 art.; 1 infra.

630 La proclamación del mensaje cristiano; Actas del IV Simposio de Teología Histórica (28-30 abril 1986): Valentina 17.   Valencia 1986, Fac. Ferrer. 435 p. – ᴿTsTNijm 28 (1988) 426 (E. *Henau*).

631 IVᵃ consulta de la societas oecumenica europea, '¿Neutralidad eclesiológica en el Movimiento ecuménico?' (Erfurt, 1-6.IX.1986): DialEcum 23,77 (1988) 287-322 ... [ᴢɪᴛ 89,60].

632 **Ratzinger** Joseph présent.,   Commission théologique internationale, textes et documents (1969-1985).   P 1988, Cerf.   461 p.   2-204-02796-0. – ᴿGregorianum 69 (1988) 563s (J. *Dupuis*).

633 ᴱ**Rauch** Albert, *Imhof* Paul,   Das Priestertum in der einen Kirche; Diakonat, Presbyterat und Episkopat; Regensburger Ökumenisches Symposium 15.-21. Juli 1985: Koinonia 4.   Aschaffenburg 1987, Kaffke. 225 p. – ᴿZkT 110 (1988) 238s (K. H. *Neufeld*).

634 ᴱ**Rauscher** A.,   Katholizismus; Bildung und Wissenschaft im 19. und 20. Jahrhundert [16. Symposium Okt. 1985 (15.1984/6 ➤ 3,699)]: BeitKatholizismusforschung B.   223 p. DM 29,80.   3-506-70744-2. – ᴿTsTNijm 28 (1988) 412 (A. van *Harskamp*: zeer informatief).

635 ᴱ**Richard** Jean (dir.),   Religion et culture, Actes du colloque international du centenaire Paul TILLICH, Univ. Laval 18-22 août 1986.   Québec/P 1987, Univ. Laval / Cerf.   646 p. – ᴿRHPR 68 (1988) 480 (G. *Siegwalt*).

636 ᴱ**Rittner** Reinhard,   Apostolizität und Ökumene [Tagung 1986]: Fuldaer Hefte 30.   Hannover 1987, Lutherisches-Vh. 100 p. DM 16,80. – ᴿÖkRu 37 (1988) 376s (H. *Vorster*).

637 ᴱ**Rostagno** Sergio, [*Birkner* H.J., *al.*]   SCHLEIERMACHER e la modernità [convegno Roma 26-27.X.1984].   T 1986, Claudiana. – ᴿFilT 1,2 (1988) 177-180 (A. *Mastantuoni*); RasT 29 (1988) 109-111 (Giuseppina *De Simone*).

638 ᴱ**Rudin** A. James, *Wilson* Marvin R.,   A time to speak — the Evangelical-Jewish encounter [Gordon College conference].   GR/Austin 1987, Eerdmans / Center for Judaic-Christian Studies. xvi-202 p. $12 pa. – ᴿMissiology 16 (1988) 233s (L. R. *Ringenberg*).

639 ᴱ**Runzo** Joseph, *Ihara* Craig K.,   Religious experience and religious belief; essays in the epistemology of religion [California State Univ. philosophy symposium].   Lanham MD 1986, UPA.   xvii-141 p. $23.50;   pa. $10.75. – ᴿRelStR 14 (1988) 360 (J. A. *Stone*).

640 SAINT-SERGE: [ᴱPistoia A., *Triacca* A. M.,] Eschatologie et liturgie; XXXIᵉ Semaine d'Études liturgiques [Saint-Serge], 26-29 juin 1984. R 1985, Liturgiche. 384 p. Lit. 40.000. – ᴿEsprVie 98 (1988) 187s [P. *Rouillard*].

641 ᴱTriacca A. M., *Pistoia* A., La Mère de Jésus-Christ et la communion des Saints; conférences Saint-Serge 32, Paris 25-28 juin 1985: Bibl. EphLtg 37, 1986 → 3,733*: ᴿEsprVie 98 (1988) 188-191 (P. *Rouillard*); FoiTemps 19 (1987) 370-2 (A. *Haquin*); Marianum 39 (1987) 641-5 (aussi P. *Rouillard*).

642 Saints et sainteté dans la liturgie, XXXIIIᵉ Semaine d'Études liturgiques [S-Serge], 22-26 juin 1986. R 1987, Liturgiche. 372 p. Lit. 40.000. – ᴿEsprVie 98 (1988) 190s (P. *Rouillard*).

643 [ᴱTriacca A. M.] Les Bénédictions et les Sacramentaux dans la liturgie; Conférences Saint-Serge, XXXIV semaine. P/R 1988, 'CLV' / Liturgiche. 382 p. – *Cazelles* H., Les bénédictions des personnes et des choses dans l'AT. – ᴿMaisD 175 (1988) 97-100 (A. *Haquin*).

644 Salvezza cristiana e culture odierne II. Spiritualità, riconciliazione, escatologia; Atti del II Congresso Internazionale 'La Sapienza della Croce oggi', Roma 6-9 febbraio 1984. T-Leumann 1986, Elle Di Ci. 527 p. Lit. 26.000. 88-01-15802-5. – ᴿGregorianum 69 (1988) 396s (J. *Galot*).

645 ᴱSamuel Vinay, *Sugden* Christopher, The Church in response to human need. GR/Ox 1987, Eerdmans/Regnum. xii-268 p. [ZNW 79,298].

646 ᴱSchatz Oskar, *Spatzenegger* Hans, Wovon werden wir morgen geistig leben? Mythos, Religion und Wissenschaft in der 'Postmoderne' [Tagung Salzburg 1986]. Salzburg 1986, Pustet. 248 p. – ᴿBogSmot 58,4 (1988) 169 (M. *Valković*).

647 ᴱSchnaubelt Joseph C., *al.*, Proceedings of the fifth international St. Anselm conference; St. ANSELM and St. AUGUSTINE — episcopi ad saecula: Anselm Studies 2. White Plains NY 1988, Kraus. xii-634 p. $55. 0735-0864 [TDig 35,340].

648 ᴱSchneider Theodor, *Ullrich* Lothar, Vorsehung und Handeln Gottes [Arbeitsgemeinschaft katholischer Dogmatiker, Tagung 2.-6. Januar 1987]: QDisp 115. FrB 1988, Herder. 207 p. 3-451-02115-3 [= Erfurter Theologische Schriften 16; Lp 1988, St. Benno]. 8 art.; infra.

649 ᴱSchnucker Robert V., Calviniana; ideas and influence of Jean CALVIN [symposium... 16 art.]: Sixteenth Century Essays and Studies 10. Kirksville MO 1988, SixtC. 286 p. $30 [TDig 36,50].

650 Secularization and religion; the persisting tension [Acta, 19th International Conference, Sociology of Religion, Tü Aug. 1987]. Lausanne c. 1988, CISR. 270 p. Fs 35. – ᴿStPatav 35 (1988) 191 (E. *Pace*).

651 ᴱSheils W. J., The Church and healing [Eccl. Hist. Soc. 20/21]. Ox 1985, Blackwell. xxiv-440 p. $45. – ᴿChH 57 (1988) 261s (G. W. *Reid*).

652 ᴱSheils W. J., Monks, hermits and the ascetic tradition: StudChHist 22, 1985 → 2,502: ᴿCathHR 73 (1987) 97s (J. H. *Lynch*); Salesianum 50 (1988) 399s (P. T. *Stella*: tit. pp.).

653 ᴱShinn Larry D., In search of the divine; some unexpected consequences of interfaith dialogue [New Ecumenical Research 3d annual God Conference]. NY 1987, Paragon. xxix-146 p. $23; pa. $13. – ᴿJEcuSt 25 (1988) 457 (T. *Dean*); RelStR 14 (1988) 358 (F. X. *Clooney*: tantalizes).

654 ᴱSiriwardena R., Equality and the religious traditions of Asia [Sri Lanka International Centre for Ethnic Studies / UNESCO conference]. NY 1987, St. Martin's. 173 p. $30 [TDig 35,267].

654* ᴱSpera Salvatore,   Uomini e donne nella Chiesa; Atti della VII
Primavera di Santa Chiara 1987. R 1988, Vivere In. 283 p. Lit. 30.000.
15 art.; 4 infra.

655 ᴱStark Rodney, Religious movements; Genesis, Exodus, and Numbers
[New ERA conference, May 1982, Orcas Island WA]: Sociology of
religion. NY 1986, Paragon. 354 p. $20; pa. $12 [... astrology, gurus,
Paisleyism, not Gn-Ex-Nm: TDig 35,284]. – ᴿRelStR 14 (1988) 360 (J. V.
Spickard).

656 ᴱStrege Merle D.,   Baptism and Church; a Believers' Church vision [7th
conference, Anderson IN, June 1984]. GR 1986, Sagamore. 221 p. –
ᴿRelStR 14 (1988) 232 (J. F. *Puglisi*).

657 ᴱSwidler Leonard,   Breaking down the wall between Americans and East
Germans; Jews and Christians, through dialogue [Temple Univ. in Berlin
and Leipzig May 1984].   Lanham MD 1987, UPA. $23; pa. $11.75 [TDig
35,261].

658 'Teologi laici nelle Chiese cristiane', Colloquio . Palermo 24-26 aprile
1987: HoTheológos 5 (1987). 351 p.

659 ᴱTrentin Giuseppe,   Le Venezie e l'Oriente Cristiano [nel millennio
dell'evangelizzazione della Russia; convegno Padova 28.V.1987]: StPatav
35,2 (1988). 293 p. 12 art.; 1 infra.

661 ᴱVan Beek Walter E. A.,   The quest for purity; dynamics of Puritan
movements [Utrecht workshop]: Religion and Society 26.   B 1988,
Mouton de Gruyter. [viii-] 273 p. 0-89925-376-8. 11 art.

662 ᴱVilliers P. G. R. de,   Liberation theology and the Bible [4 papers for
1986 seminar, Univ. S. Africa]. Pretoria 1987, Univ. x-76 p. R 13.65.
0-86981-528-8 [NTAbs 32,382].

663 ᴱVisser Derk,   Controversy and conciliation; the Reformation and the
Palatinate, 1559-1583 [Ursinus College, Collegeville PA 1983 conference
on Zacharinus URSINUS, 1534-1583]: PittTheolMon 18.   Allison Park PA
1986, Pickwick.   ix-239 p. $20. – ᴿRelStR 14 (1988) 258 (R. *Kolb*).

664 ᴱVorster W. S.,   Church and industry [symposium]. Pretoria 1983, Univ.
S. Africa. viii-113 p. – ᴿCalvinT 23 (1988) 238-240 (J. H. *Boer*).

665 ᴱWainwright Geoffrey,   BEM, a liturgical appraisal [1985 Societas
Liturgica congress Rotterdam 1986. = StLtg 16,1s]. 128 p. $13.50. –
ᴿJEcuSt 24 (1987) 459s (J. L. *Empereur*).

666 ᴱWelker Michael,   Theologie und funktionale Systemtheorie; LUHMANNs
Religionssoziologie in theologischer Diskussion [8 art. < 'Arbeitsprozess
seit 1979']: Tb-Wissenschaft 495. Fra 1985, Suhrkamp. 144 p. – ᴿTLZ
113 (1988) 923-6 D. *Pollack*).

667 ᴱWillis Wendell,   The Kingdom of God in 20th century interpretation.
Peabody MA 1987, Hendrickson. xii-208 p. $13 [TDig 35,371: 14 essays, 7
from SBL central section meetings].

668 ᴱWood James E.ᴶ,   Ecumenical perspectives on Church and State;
Protestant, Catholic, and Jewish [1986 Dawson Institute conference].
Waco 1988, Baylor Univ. viii-175 p. $11; pa. $7 [TDig 36,57].

669 ᴱYarnold Edward,   Christian priesthood and ministry; papers given to the
Catholic Theological Association of Great Britain, Leeds 1987: NBlackf
68,810 (1987) 470-539.

A2.5   *Acta* philologica *et* historica [reports ➜ ʏ7.6].

670 ᴱBarnes Jonathan, *Mignucci* Mario, Matter and metaphysics; fourth
Symposium Hellenisticum [Pontignano-Siena 21-28 ag. 1986]: Elenchos 14.
N 1988, Bibliopolis. 596 p. 88-7088-187-3. 9 art., infra.

671 ᴱ**Bolognesi** G., *Pisani* V., Linguistica e Filologia, Atti del VII Convegno Milano 12-14 sett. 1984. Brescia 1987, Paideia. 573 p. Lit. 50.000. – ᴿKratylos 33 (1988) 33-36 (Rüdiger *Schmitt*).
ᴱ**Braund** David C., The administration of the Roman Empire 1986/8 → d573*.

672 **Cambiano** Giuseppe, Storiografia e dossografia nella filosofia antica [Colloquio internazionale Stres 27-28 sett. 1984, Univ. Torino]: Biblioteca storico-filosofica. T 1986, Tirrenia. vi-286 p. – ᴿGnomon 60 (1988) 675-680 (A. *Laks*).

673 ᴱ**Cassin** Barbara, Positions de la sophistique; colloque de Cerisy 7-17 sept. 1984: Bibliothèque d'Histoire de la Philosophie. P 1986, Vrin. 338 p. F 216. 3-7116-0918-9. 18 art.; 2 infra.

674 ᴱ**Castillo** Arcadio del, Ejército y sociedad [Seminario sobre Historia del Mundo Antiguo, Univ. León 15-17.V.1985]. León 1986, Univ. 133 p. 5 art. – ᴿClasR 102 (1988) 443 (N. *Mackie*).

674* ᴱ**Chevalier** Bernard, *Sauzet* Robert, Les Réformes, enracinement socio-culturel, XXVᵉ colloque international d'études humanistes, Tours 1-3.VII.1982. P 1985, Trédaniel. 451 p. – ᴿCahHist 30 (1985) 351-4 (G. A. *Pérouse*).

675 ᴄᴏᴡɢɪʟʟ Warren (1929-1985): Studies in memory of ∼; Papers from the Fourth East Coast Indo-European conference, Cornell Univ. [Ithaca NY], June 6-9, 1985, ᴱ**Watkins** Calvert. B/NY 1987, de Gruyter. x-327 p. DM 178. 3-11-011127-6 (vol. 3: Sprache 33 cover adv.).

676 ᴱ**Crevatin** Franco, Ricostruzione linguistica e ricostruzione culturale, Trieste 25-26 ottobre 1982: Mg 22. Trieste 1983, Univ. Scuola Superiore per Interpreti e Traduttori. 148 p. – ᴿSalesianum 50 (1988) 269 (R. *Bracchi*: otto domande; vivace dibattito).

677 ᴱ**Despotopoulos** K., Ⓖ (etc.), *Hē archaía sophistikē*, The sophistic movement; Acts of the first international symposium, Athena 27-29 Sept. 1982. Athena 1984, Greek Philosophical Society/Library. 343 p. – ᴿGnomon 60 (1988) 145s (Barbara *Cassin*: a useful venture despite polyglot errors).

679 ᴱ**Embleton** Sheila, Fourteenth ʟᴀᴄᴜs forum 1987. 1988, Linguistic Association of Canada and the United States. → 4770, *Levin* S.

680 ᴱ**Frezouls** E., Sociétés urbaines, sociétés rurales dans l'Asie Mineure et la Syrie hellénistiques et romaines: Actes du colloque de Strasbourg (nov. 1985): Univ. Inst. Hist. Rom. contrib. 4. Strasbourg 1987, AECR. 284 p.; 12 pl. – ᴿRÉLat 65 (1987) 428 (J. *Ferrary*, titres).

681 **Ganz** Peter, The role of the book in medieval culture 1982/6 → 3,756*: some infra.

682 ᴱ**Giardina** Andrea, Tradizione dei classici, trasformazioni della cultura [Roma/Napoli sem. Gramsci]: Società romana e impero tardoantico 4. R 1986, Laterza. 284 p.; 48 pl. Lit. 45.000. – ᴿClasR 102 (1988) 365-8 (H. D. *Jocelyn*).

683 ᴱ**Harmatta** J., Actes du VIIᵉ Congrès de la Fédération Internationale des Associations d'Études classiques, Budapest 1979. Budapest 1984, Akad. 464 p.; 612 p. – ᴿAcAntH 31 (1985-8) 171-5 (Zs. *Ritoók*).

684 ᴱ**Henrich** Dieter, *Iser* Wolfgang, Funktionen des Fiktiven [Kolloquium; wo? wann?]: Poetik und Hermeneutik 10. Mü 1983, Fink. 567 p. 3-7705-2056-4; pa. 5-6. 38 art.; 4 infra.

684* ʜᴇᴜss Alfred, Symposion für ∼ [Gö 30.VI.1984], ᴱ**Bleicken** Jochen: Frankfurter Althistorische Studien 12. Kallmünz 1986, Lassleben [→ 3,758]; 100 p.; phot.; bibliog. p. 93-100. 3-7847-7112-2. 7 art., 1 infra.

685 ᴱIllievski Petar H., *Crepajac* Ljiljana, Tractata Mycenaea; Proceedings of the Eighth Int. Coll. on Mycenaean studies, Ohrid 15-20 Sept. 1985. Skopje 1987, Macedonian Acad. 404 pl.; ill.

686 ᴱJanni Pietro, *al.*, Cultura classica e cultura germanica settentrionale: Atti del Convegno internazionale, Macerata 2-4.V.1985. Macerata 1988, Univ. xi-451 p. 88-85876-05-6. 16 art.

687 ᴱKloft Hans, Soziale Massnahmen und Fürsorge; zur Eigenart antiker Sozialpolitik [Tagungen Berlin 1984, Bremen 1985]: Graz 1988, Horn. vii-185 p. 10 art.; 2 infra.

688 ᴱKocka Jürgen, Max WEBER, der Historiker [XVI. Historiker-Kongress Stu 1985, Sektion Methodologie]: Kritische Studien zur Geschichtswissenschaft 73. Gö 1986, Vandenhoeck & R. 281 p. DM 48. – ᴿDLZ 109 (1988) 17-21 (H. *Schleier*); HZ 245 (1987) 115s (G. *Schöllgen*).

689 ᴱKrämer Sigrid, *Bernhard* Michael, Scire litteras; Forschungen zum mittelalterlichen Geistesleben [Symposion München 8.I.1987]: Abh ph/h 99. Mü 1988, Bayerische Akademie. 438 p.; ill. 3-7696-0094-0. 39 art.; p. 277-289, *Meyvaert* Paul, Fragments of a JEROME source.

689* ᴱLehmann Winfred P., Language typology 1985; papers from the linguistic typology symposium, Moscow, 9-13 December 1985: Current Issues in Linguistic Theory 47. Amst 1986, Benjamins. viii-209 p. 90-272-3541-4. 13 art.; 2 infra.

690 ᴱMarkovich Miroslav, *Brenk* Frederick E. *al.*, Athens 1987 Conference, International Plutarch Society = IʟCLSt 13,2 (1988), p. 219-529.

691 ᴱMeulenbeld G. Jan, *Wujastik* Dominik, Studies in Indian medical history, Wellcome Inst. 2-4.IX.1985: Groningen Oriental Studies 2. Groningen 1987, Forsten. vii-247 p. ƒ65. – ᴿJRAS (1988) 443-5 (S. S. *Strickland*).

692 *Olmo Lete* G. del [Ancient Near East; the other 9 articles are on Greece], La Dona en l'antiquitat [symposium Barc]: Orientalia Barcinonensia 1. Barc 1987, AUSA. 141 p. $12. 84-86329-11-6 [BL 89,123, N. *Wyatt*].

693 La pluridisciplinarité dans l'étude de la religion grecque antique, colloque Athènes 28-29 nov. 1987: Acta in Kernos 1 (1988) 93-233. 12 art., infra.

694 ᴱQuesta Cesare, *Raffaelli* Renato, Il libro e il testo, Atti del convegno internazionale (Urbino, 20-23 sett. 1982). Urbino 1984. xiii-445 p. – ᴿMaia 40 (1988) 81-84 (Emma *Condello*).

695 Religione e città nel mondo antico: Atti Bressanone ott. 1981, Univ. Padova. R 1984, Bretschneider. 496 p.; 46 pl. – ᴿKlio 70 (1988) 618 (R. *Günther*).

696 ᴱSilvestri D., Atti del convegno su 'Linee e momenti di preistoria linguistica dell'Eurasia ['proto-nostratic']' (Napoli, 16-17 maggio 1988): AION-Clas. 10 (1988) 339 p.

697 ᴱTannen Deborah, Linguistics in Context; connecting observation and understanding; lectures from the 1985 LSA/TESOL and NEH Institutes [Georgetown Univ. Wsh, July]: Advances in discourse processes 29. Norwood NJ 1988, Ablex. xviii-320 p. 0-89391-454-1; pa. 5-X. 13 art.

697* **Tomlin** Russell S., Coherence and grounding in discourse; symposium Eugene OR, June 1984: Typological studies in language 11. Amst 1987, Benjamins. 90-272-2882-5; pa. 1-7; US 0-915027-85-2; 6-0. 20 art.; 3 infra.

698 ᶠTRÉHEUX Jacques, Comptes et inventaires dans la Cité grecque; Actes du colloque international d'épigraphie tenu à Neuchâtel du 23 au 26 septembre 1986 en l'honneur de ~, ᴱKnoepfler Denis: Univ. Neuchâtel, Recueil 40. Genève 1988, Droz. xvi-392 p.; ill.; portr.; bibliog. p. 1-5; thèses dirigées p. 6s [*Quellet* Nicole]. 21 art.; 13 infra.

699 ᴱUglione R., Atti del Convegno nazionale di studi su La donna nel mondo antico, Torino 21-23 aprile 1986. T 1987. 303 p.; 10 pl. Lit. 20.000. 88-7678-036-X. – ᴿBStLat 18 (1988) 172-5 (Valeria *Viperelli*).

700 ᴱVérilhac Anne-Marie, La femme dans le monde méditerranéen, I. Antiquité [séminaire 1982s]: Travaux 10. Lyon 1985, Maison de l'Orient. 190 p.; 6 pl. F 125. 2-903264-39-2. 10 art.; 1 infra. – ᴿAntClas 57 (1988) 513s (G. *Raepsaet*: tit. pp.).

701 ᴱVitale-Brovarone A., *Mombello* G., Atti del V colloquio della International Beast Epic, Fable and Fabliau Society, Torino-St. Vincent, 5-9 sett. 1983. Alessandria, Italia 1987, Orso. 356 p.; 45 fig. Lit. 80.000 [RHE 83,424*].

702 ᴱYuge Toru, *Doi* Masaoki, Forms of control and subordination in antiquity: Int. Symposium for Studies on Ancient Worlds 1986. Leiden 1988, Brill. xi-625 p. 90-04-08349-9. 70 art., 3 infra.

A2.7 *Acta* **orientalistica**.

703 ᴱBarsanti Claudia, *al.*, Milion [scomparso monumento di Costantinopoli, centro di vie], studi e ricerche d'arte bizantina; Atti Giornata di Studio, CNR Roma 4.XII.1986. R 1988, Biblioteca di Storia Patria. 395 p. 14 art., 5 infra.

704 ᴱBorgeaud Philippe, *al.*, L'animal, l'homme, le Dieu dans le Proche-Orient ancien; Actes du Colloque de Cartigny 1981: CEPOA Cah. 2. Lv 1985, Peeters. 171 p.; ill. → 3,775; 90-6831-024-0. 13 art.; infra. – ᴿFaventia 9,1 (1987) 115-7 (Victória *Solanilla*).

705 ᴱEnglund Gertie, *Frandsen* Paul J., Crossroad, chaos or beginning of a new paradigm; papers from the conference on Egyptian grammar, Helsingør 28-30 May 1986: CNI 1. K 1986, Carsten Niebuhr Inst. 87-503-6303-4 [BO 45,269-289, W. *Schenkel*].

705* ᴱFronzaroli Pelio, Miscellanea eblaitica [Seminari Firenze], I: Quad-Semit 15. F 1988, Univ. ix-279 p. [BL 89,149, W. G. *Lambert*].

706 ᴱGatier Pierre-Louis, *al.*, Géographie historique au Proche-Orient (Syrie, Phénicie, Arabie, grecques, romaines, byzantines: Actes de la Table Ronde de Valbonne, 16-18 sept. 1985: Notes et Mg Techniques 23. P 1988, CNRS. 371 p.; ill. F 130. 2-222-04113-9. 21 art., infra.

707 ᴱHauptmann Harald, *Waetzoldt* Hartmut, Wirtschaft und Gesellschaft von Ebla, Akten der Internationalen Tagung Heidelberg 4.-7. November 1986: Heid Studien zum Alten Orient 2. Heid 1988, Orientverlag. xviii-390 p.; 15 pl. DM 148. 3-927552-00-3. → 718; 705*. 9 art. archaeol., 29 philolog.

708 ᴱJungraithmayr Herrmann, *Müller* Walter M., Proceedings of the 4th International Hamito-Semitic Congress, Marburg, 20-22 Sept. 1983: Current Issues Ling. Theory 44. Amst 1987, Benjamins. xiv-609 p. ƒ 200. 90-272-2538-4 [BO 44,837].

709 ᴱKhalidi Tarif, Land tenure and social transformation in the Middle East [conference Beirut 1983; i. Antiquity; ii-iv. up to now]. Beirut 1984. 531 p. – ᴿRSO 61 (1987) 218-222 (Ilaria *Alpi*).

710 ᴱKrupp F., *al.*, Proceedings of the symposium on the fauna and zoogeography of the Middle East [...]: TAVO A-28. Wsb 1987, Reichert [< Mundus 24,170]. → h75.

711 (I) Polotsky H. J., Essays on Egyptian grammar [for his visit Dec. 7, 1985], ᴱSimpson William K.: Eg. St. 1. NHv 1986, Yale Egyptological Sem. vi-42 p. $8.50. 0-912532-900. – ᴿJAmEg 24 (1987) 148-151 (E. S. *Meltzer*).

712 (II) POLOTSKY H.J., Lingua sapientissima; a seminar in honour of ~, with Fitzwilliam Museum, ᴱRay J.D. C 1987, Univ. Faculty of Oriental Studies. v-79 p. 1-870954-00-0. 6 art., infra [including Polotsky's Glanville Lecture].

713 ᴱSancisi-Weerdenburg Heleen, [2-3 with *Kuhrt* A.], Achaemenid History; 1. Sources, structures and synthesis [➜ 3,787]; 2. The Greek sources; 3. Method and theory [Proceedings of the Achaemenid History Workshop, Groningen 1983s, London 1985]. Leiden 1987/7/8, Nederlands Instituut N. Oosten. xiv-196 p.; xiii-175 p.; xv-228 p. *f*85; 80; 95 [sb. 75; 70; 85]. 90-6258-401-2; 2-0; 3-9 [BL 89,40, R.J. *Coggins*].

714 ᴱSchuler Einar von, XXIII. Deutscher Orientalistentag vom 16.-20. September 1985 in Würzburg; ausgewählte Vorträge: ZDMG Sup. 7. Stu 1988, Steiner. 688 p.; ill. [Mundus 24,227].

715 ᴱVleeming S.P., Aspects of demotic lexicography; Acts of the Second International Conference for Demotic Studies, Leiden, 19-21 September 1984: Studia Demotica 1. Lv 1986. xiii-162 p. – ᴿAegyptus 68 (1988) 271s (Lucia *Criscuolo*).

A2.9 *Acta* **archaeologica** [reports ➜ Y7.8].

716 ᴱAldenderfer Mark S., Quantitative research in archaeology; progress and prospects [Society for American Archaeology 50th meeting 1985, 20th anniversary of BINFORD's factor analysis]. Newbury Park CA 1988, Sage. 312 p.; 43 fig. £35. 12 art. – ᴿAntiquity 62 (1988) 597s (C. *Orton*).

717 Archaeological Institute of America, 89th general meeting [c. 300 word summaries of some 200 papers with author-index]: AJA 92 (1988) 229-284.

718 ᴱArchi Alfonso, Eblaite personal names and Semitic name-giving [Symposium Univ. Rome 15-17.VII. 1985]: ARE Studi 1. R 1988, Univ. xiii-306 p.; 1 pl. Lit. 70.000. [BL 89,120, A.R. *Millard*, no tit. pp.]. 14 art.; infra. Further ➜ 707.

719 ᴱAurenche Olivier, *al.*, Chronologies du Proche Orient... Relative chronologies and absolute chronology 16,000-4,000 B.P., C.N.R.S. int. symposium, Lyon (France) 24-28 Nov. 1986: BAR-379/1-2. Lyon/Oxford 1987. 398 p.; p. 401-744. ill. 0-86054-487-7. £45 [in $ plus 8]. 37 art., 13 infra. – ᴿRArchéom 12 (1988) 102 (L. *Langouet*).

720 ᴱBaratte Françoise, Argenterie romaine et byzantine, Actes de la Table Ronde, Paris 11-13.X.1983. P 1988, de Boccard. 231 p.; ill.

721 ᴱBarbet Alix, La peinture murale antique; restitution et iconographie; Actes du IXᵉ séminaire de l'Association Française pour la PMA, Paris 27-28 avril 1985: Documents d'Archéologie Française 10. P 1987, Sciences de l'Homme. 100 p.; (colour.) ill. F 158. 2-7351-0209-2. – ᴿAntiqJ 68,1 (1988) 133s (R. *Ling*).

722 ᴱBoardman John, *Vaphopoulou-Richardson* C.E., Chios, a conference at the Homereion in Chios, 1984. NY 1986, Oxford-UP. 361 p.; 227 fig. $74. 0-19-814864-X [AJA 92,625].

723 ᴱBodson L., L'animal dans l'alimentation humaine; les critères de choix, Actes du colloque international de Liège (26-29 nov. 1986): Anthropozoologica spec. 2 (1988). 249 p.; 26 fig. – ᴿRArchéom 12 (1988) 101 (J. *Desse*).

724 ᴱBrink Edwin C.M. van den, The archaeology of the Nile Delta, problems and priorities; Proceedings of the Seminar held in Cairo, Netherlands Institute 15th anniversary, 1986. Amst 1988, Netherlands

Foundation for Archaeological Research in Egypt. xv-325 p. 90-70556-30-8. 22 art.; infra.

725 **Buccellati** Giorgio, present., Ancient Syria [ASOR symposium 1985]: BASOR 270 (1988) 1s (-92); Buccellati 43-62, The kingdom and period of Khana.

726 ᴱ**Cadogan** Gerald, The end of the early bronze age in the Aegean [Cincinnati symposium 1979 to honor J. CASKEY († 1981)]: Cincinnati ClasSt 6. Leiden 1986, Brill. xiii-196 p.; 3 maps. ƒ90. – ᴿAJA 92 (1988) 294 (Karen P. *Foster*); GreeceR 34 (1987) 225 (B. A. *Sparkes*); MeditHistR-TA 3,2 (1988) 123-6 (J. D. *Muhly*).

727 CLARK J. Desmond: Papers in honour of ~ [Berkeley CA conference 1986], ᴱ**Phillipson** David W., *al.* = African Archaeological Review 5. C 1987, Univ. 207 p.; ill. £15. 0263-0338. 16 art. – ᴿAntiqJ 68,1 (1988) 131s (R. R. *Inskeep*).

728 ᴱ**Coulston** J. C., Military equipment and the identity of Roman soldiers; proceedings of the fourth Roman military equipment conference [Newcastle Univ. 12-13 April 1986]: BAR-Int 394. Ox 1988. xi-341 p. 7 art., 1 infra. ➤ 731.

729 ᴱ**Curtis** J., Bronze-working centres of Western Asia c. 1000-539 B.C. [British Museum colloquium 1986]. L 1988, Kegan Paul. 342 p.; 182 pl. £30. 0-7103-0274-6 [BL 89,25, J. F. *Healey*]. – ᴿBInstArch 25 (1988) 111s (Georgina *Herrmann*).

730 ᴱ**David** R. A., Science in Egyptology; proceedings of the symposia [Manchester 1979 & 1984]. Manchester 1986, Univ. vi-525 p.; ill. £14.70. 55 art. – ᴿDiscEg 12 (1988) 91-96 (J.-C. *Goyon*).

731 **Dawson** M., The accoutrements of war: Proceedings of the 3d Roman military equipment research seminar [1985]: BAR-Int. 336. Ox 1987. xi-178 p.; ill. 0-86054-430-3. 11 art.; 2 infra. ➤ 728.

732 ᴱ**Duval** Yvette, *Picard* Jean-Charles, L'inhumation privilégiée [chrétienne] du IVᵉ au VIIIᵉ siècle en Occident; Actes du colloque tenu à Créteil [= Univ. Paris XII] les 16-18 mars 1984. P 1986, De Boccard. 260 p. – ᴿAJA 92 (1988) 457s (P. J. *Geary*).

733 ᴱ**Fischer-Hansen** Tobias, East and west; cultural relations in the ancient world [seminar Univ. Copenhagen, 22-24 April 1987]: Acta Hyperborea [0904-2067] 1. K 1988, Museum Tusculanum. 167 p.; ill. 87-7289-061-4. 15 art.; 11 infra.

734 ᴱ**Fox** Michael V., Temple in society [Madison, Univ. Wisconsin symposium 1986]. Winona Lake IN 1988, Eisenbrauns. vi-138 p. 0-931464-38-2. 7 art.; infra.

735 ᴱ**French** E.B., *Wardle* K.A., Problems in Greek prehistory [centenary conference, Manchester, April 1986]. Bristol 1988, Classical. ix-609 p.; 30 pl.

736 ᴱ**Frézouls** E., Sociétés urbaines, sociétés rurales dans l'Asie Mineure et la Syrie hellénistiques et romaines; Actes du colloque de Strasbourg (1985). Strasbourg 1987, Univ. Inst. Hist. Romaine. 284 p. – ᴿRHist 280, 567 (1988) 240-4 (Sylvie et Yann *Le Bohec*).

737 ᴱ**Garrard** Andrew N., *Gebel* Hans G., The prehistory of Jordan; the state of research in 1986 [< Tü congress 1986 cf. ➤ 3,816]: BAR-Int. 396. Ox 1988. – ᴿPaléorient 14,1 (1988) 180s (Monique *Lechevallier*).

738 ᴱ**Gibson** McGuire, *Biggs* Robert D., The organization of power ... ANE 1983/7 ➤ 3,781 (Chicago symposium included also Medieval and Ottoman, April 16-17, 1983); 0-918986-51-6; 10 art.; 8 infra.

738* ᴱ**Gignoux** P., Transition periods in Iranian history; Actes du Symposium FrB 22-24.V.1985, Societas Iranologica Europea: StIran Cah

5.   Lv 1987, Peeters.   263 p.   Fb 2000. – ᴿJRAS (1988) 411-4 (F. de *Blois*: serious analyses, but without pp. or often titles).

739 ᴱHägg R., *Marinatos* N., The function of the Minoan palaces; Proceedings of the Fourth International Symposium at the Swedish Institute in Athens, 10-16 June, 1984: Acta Inst. Athen. Sueciae 35. Sto 1987. (Göteborg, Åström). 344 p.; 190 fig. Sk 400 [AnzAltW 41,253]. – ᴿAntiquity 62 (1988) 803-5 (J. F. *Cherry*).

740 ᴱHägg Thomas, Nubian culture past and present, Uppsala 11-16.VIII. 1986: Akad. Konferenser 12. Sto 1987, Almqvist & W. 438 p.; ill. Sk 185. [JNES 47,238]. – ᴿAntiquity 62 (1988) 382s (B. G. *Trigger*).

742 ᴱHeltzer Michael, *Lipiński* Edward, Society and economy in the eastern Mediterranean (c. 1500-1000 B.C.), Proceedings of the International Symposium held at the University of Haifa 28 April - 2 May 1985: OrLovAn 23. Lv 1988, Peeters. xiv-397 p. 90-6831-135-2. 24 art., infra.

743 ᴱHerrmann Bernd, Innovative Trends in der prähistorischen Anthropologie, Beiträge zu einem internationalen Symposion vom 26.2. bis 1.3.1986 in Berlin (West): Mitt. Anthrop. 7. B 1986, Spiess. 171 p. DM 48 [PraehZts 63, 184, R. *Knaussmann*].

744 ᴱHole Frank, The archaeology of Western Iran; settlement and society from prehistory to the Islamic conquest [< seminar 1977]: Smithsonian Series in Archaeological Inquiry. Wsh 1987. 332 p.; 90 fig. $50. – ᴿPaléorient 14,1 (1988) 177-9 (W. M. *Sumner*).

745 ᴱHornus Jean-Michel, Architecture of the Eastern churches [Acta ...]. Birmingham, England 1981, Eastern Churches group. 39 p. £1.30. 4 art.; 2 infra. – ᴿRelStR 14 (1988) 255 (R. *Ousterhout*).

746 Itinéraire d'Égérie: congrès international Arezzo 23-25 oct. [MondeB 52 (1988) 49].

747 ᴱKahil Lilly, *al.*, [LIMC colloque; 1. 1979/81 (? CNRS) ↠ 62,793]; 2., Iconographie classique et identités régionales, Paris 26 et 27 mai 1983: BCH Sup 14. P 1986, École Française d'Athènes (diff. de Boccard). xxiii-459 p.; ill. – ᴿAntClas 57 (1988) 557-561 (C. *Delvoye*).

748 ᴱKarageorghis V., Acts of the International Symposium, 'Cyprus between the Orient and the Occident'; colloquium Nicosia 1985. Nicosia 1986, Dept. Antiquities. xxx-333 p. 103 fig. ↠ 3,823; 9963-36-407-1. 37 art., 8 infra. – ᴿPEQ 120 (1988) 152s (V. *Hankey*); RArchéol (1988) 123s (M.-C. *Hellmann*).

749 ᴱKnell Heiner, *Wesenberg* Burkhardt, Vɪᴛʀᴜᴠ-Kolloquium Darmstadt 17.-18. Juni 1982. Da 1984. 281 p. 3-88607-031-X. 13 art.

750 ᴱKrause Martin, Nubische Studien; Tagungsakten der 5. Internationalen Konferenz der International Society for Nubian Studies, Heidelberg, 22,-25. September 1982. Mainz 1986, von Zabern. xlii-421 p.; ill. 3-8053-0878-7. 57 art.; 23 infra.

751 ᴱKyrieleis Helmut, *a)* Archaische [und klassische] griechische Plastik (Akten des internationalen Kolloquiums vom 22.-25. April 1985 in Athen): DAI-A. Mainz 1986, von Zabern. 225 p.; 81 pl.; 251 p., 156 pl. – ᴿAJA 92 (1988) 610s (A. *Stewart*). – *b)* Klassische griechische Plastik: DAI-A, Akten des internationalen Kolloquiums 'Archaische und klassische griechische Plastik' vom 22.-25. April 1985 in Athen, II. Mainz 1986, von Zabern. vi-254 p. 42 fig.; 75 pl.; 3 Beilagen. 3-8053-0902-3. 21 art.; 4 infra.

752 ᴱLaffineur Robert, Thanatos; les coutumes funéraires en Égée à l'Âge de Bronze; Actes du Colloque de Liège (21-23 avril 1986). Liège 1987, Univ. 245 p. 59 pl. – ᴿAJA 92 (1988) 604-6 (C. *Gates*).

753 ᴱLaperrousaz E.-M., Archéologie, art et histoire de la Palestine; Colloque du Centenaire de la Section des Sciences Religieuses, École Pratique des Hautes Études (sept. 1986). P 1988, Cerf. 215 p.; 53 pl. F 125 [BL 89,29, A. G. *Auld*]. – ᴿEsprVie 98 (1988) 259s (É. *Monloubou*: avec une importante délégation d'israéliens); MondeB 55 (1988) 61 (J. *Briend*).

754 **Lipinski** E., Carthago; ActaBru 2-3.V.1986.: StPhoen 6 / OrLovAnal 26. Lv 1988, Peeters. x-280 p.; p. 259-280. Index cumulativus St. Phoen. I-VI (*Debergh* J.). 90-6831-106-9 [BO 45,478]. 18 art., infra.

755 ᴱ**Liritzis** Yannis, *Hackens* Tony, First south European conference in archaeometry: PACT 15. Strasbourg 1986, Council of Europe. 216 p. Fb 2000. – ᴿAntiquity 62 (1988) 406s. 410 (I. *Freestone*: unfavoring).

756 ᴱ**McClendon** Charles B., Rome and the provinces; studies in the transformation of art and architecture in the Mediterranean world [symposium for 60th anniversary of starting Dura-Europos excavation]. NHv 1986, NHv Society, Archaeological Institute of America. 50 p.; 55 fig. – ᴿAJA 92 (1988) 454 (Susan B. *Downey*).

758 ᴱ*Mandolesi* Almarella, Seminario internazionale di studi su 'La Siria dal Tardoantico al Medioevo; aspetti e problemi di archeologia e storia d'arte' Ravenna 19-26 marzo 1988; Colloquio internazionale sul tema 'La Siria araba da Roma a Bisanzio', Ravenna 22-24 marzo 1988. Ravenna 1988, Girasole. xv-382 p. Lit. 55.000. 88-7567-183-4. 19 art.; 6 infra.

759 ᴱ**Manzanilla** Linda, Studies in the neolithic and urban revolutions; the V. Gordon Childe Colloquium, Mexico 1986: BAR-Int. 349. Ox 1987. 381 p.; 30 fig. £20 pa. 0-86054-449-4 [AJA 92,626]. – ᴿAntiquity 62 (1988) 175s (F. A. *Hassan*).

760 ᴱ**Mikasa** (H. I. H. Prince) Takahito, Essays on Anatolian studies in the second millennium B.C. [lecture series 1983]: Bulletin of the Middle Eastern Culture Center in Japan, 3. Wsb 1988, Harrassowitz. vii-85 p. 3-447-02781-9. 4 art., infra.

761 Modes de contacts et processus de transformation dans les sociétés anciennes; Actes du colloque de Cortone (24-30 mai 1981) Pisa/R 1983, Scuola Normale Superiore/Éc. Franç. iv-1164 p.; ill. – ᴿLatomus 47 (1988) 712s (Arlette *Roobaert*).

762 ᴱ**Nash** D. T., *Patraglia* M. D., Natural formation processes and the archaeological record [Society for American Archaeology 51st meeting, New Orleans April 1986]: BAR-Int 352. Ox 1987. $23. – ᴿAJA 92 (1988) 441s (T. H. van *Andel*).

763 [ᶠNASTER Paul, 'conformément aux normes en vigueur', 'fruit d'une session de nos Journées orientalistes' p. viii], ᴱ**Théodoridès** Aristide, *al.*, Archéologie et philologie dans l'étude des civilisations orientales: Acta Orientalia Belgica 4. Lv 1986, Peeters. viii-310 p., ill. 30 art.; 19 infra.

764 ᴱ**Olshausen** Eckart, Stuttgarter Kolloquium zur Historischen Geographie des Altertums, 1 [8.-9.XII.1980, Kɪʀsᴛᴇɴ Ernst mem.]: Geographica Historica 4. Bonn 1987, Habelt. vii-246 p.; 16 maps. 3-7749-2302-7. 6 art.; 3 infra.

765 **Perrot** Jean, présent., Actes du Séminaire CNRS/NSF de Bellevaux (24-29 juin 1985), L'évolution des sociétés complexes du sud-ouest de l'Iran: Paléorient 11,2 (1985) 1-129.

766 ᴱ**Postgate** Nicholas, *Powell* Marvin, Irrigation and cultivation in Mesopotamia, Sumerian Agriculture Group meeting, Leiden July 1987 = BSumAg 4 (1988) xii-221 p., 12 art.; infra [others to appear in vol. 5].

767 **Raschke** Wendy J., The archaeology of the Olympics; the Olympics and other festivals in antiquity [< UCLA symposium 5-6.IV.1984]. Ma-

dison 1988, Univ. Wisconsin. 297 p., 32 fig. 0-299-11334-5. 14 art., 10 infra.

768 Ricerche di pittura ellenistica; lettura e interpretazione della produzione pittorica dal IV secolo a.C. all'ellenismo [colloquio Acquasparta 8-10 aprile 1983, already published in Dialoghi di Archeologia 1983/2 and 1984/1s]: Quaderni di DialArch 1. R 1985, Quasar. 295 p. – ᴿGnomon 60 (1988) 467-9 (Berthild *Gossel-Raeck*).

769 **Schiering** Wolfgang, präsent., Kolloquium zur Ägäischen Vorgeschichte; Mannheim, 20.-22.II.1986: Schriften des Deutschen Archäologen-Verbandes 9 [➤ 773 infra]. Mannheim 1987, Univ. 209 p.; ill.

770 ᴱ**Schoske** Sylvia, Akten des vierten internationalen Ägyptologen-Kongresses, München 1985; Band I [aus 5]; Methoden und Geschichte der Ägyptologie — Informatik — Keramologie — Anthropologie: StAltägKu Beih 1. Ha 1988, Buske. x-358 p.; 18 pl. 3-87118-901-4. 41 art.; infra.

771 ᴱ**Sieveking** G., *al.*, Scientific Study / Human uses: of flint and chert: Proceeding of Brighton symposium 10-15 April 1983. C 1986s, Univ. xiii-290 p.; xiii-263 p. £60 each. – ᴿBInstArch 25 (1988) 170s (R. *Holgate*).

772 SIRET Luis (1934-1984): Homenaje a ~ [➤ 3,152], Actas del congreso, Cuevas del Almanzora, junio 1984, ᴱ**Arteaga** Oswaldo, *al.* Andalucía 1986, Junta. 637 p. 84-505-3511-5. 53 art.; 2 infra.

773 ᴱ**Steckner** Cornelius, Archäologie und neue Technologien: Deutscher Archäologen-Verband 10 [cf. 9 ➤ 769 supra]. 170 p. 12 art.

774 ᴱ**Steinsland** Gro, Words and objects; towards a dialogue between archaeology and history of religion [conference 1984]. Ox/Oslo Univ. 1987. 283 p. £32.50. 82-00-07751-9. – ᴿBInstArch 25 (1988) 172s (H. *Mytum*).

776 ᴱ**Thomas** Eberhard, Forschungen zur ägäischen Vorgeschichte; das Ende der mykenischen Welt; Akten des int. Kolloquiums, 7.-8. Juli 1984 in Köln. Köln 1987. xi-239 p.; ill. 17 art., 8 infra.

777 THOMSEN Christian Jürgensen: symposium 1987 for 200th birthday Dec. 29, 1988; present. *Olsen* Olaf: Aarbøger for Nordisk Oldkyndighed og Historie. K 1988, Oldskriftselskab. 225 p. 87-87483-11-4. 18 art., 3 infra ➤ d761.

778 Transition periods in Iranian history; Symposium FrS, 22-24.-V.1985. Lv 1987, Peeters. 264 p. Fb 2000 [BO 44,838].

779 TYLECOTE R. F. [Belfast symposium 1984, Comité pour la Sidérurgie ancienne], The crafts of the blacksmith; essays presented to ~, ᴱ**Scott** B. G., *Cleere* H. Belfast 1987, Ulster Museum. vi-180 p.; 251 fig. £31. 0-900761-202. – ᴿAntiquity 62 (1988) 818 (B. *Trinder*).

780 ᴱ**Vickers** M., Pots and pans; a colloquium on precious metals and ceramics in the Muslim, Chinese and Graeco-Roman worlds: Studies in Islamic art 3. Ox 1985. 223 p.; 120 pl. £15. – ᴿClasR 102 (1988) 179 (J. F. *Healy*: largely on the problem of to what extent ceramic imitated metal vessels).

781 ᴱ**Zivie** Alain-Pierre, Memphis et ses nécropoles au Nouvel Empire; nouvelles données, nouvelles questions: Actes du Colloque international CNRS, Paris 9-11 oct. 1986. P 1988, CNRS. 129 p.; 4 fig. (map); 16 pl. 2-222-041738. 14 art.; 8 infra.

A3   *Opera consultationis* – **Reference works**   .1 *plurium* **separately** *infra.*

782 **ANRW**: Aufstieg und Niedergang der römischen Welt II. Principat, ᴱ**Haase** W. [20,1 ... 36,1s 1987 ➤ 3,845] **10,1,1**, ᴱ*Temporini* Hildegard, Politische Geschichte (Provinzen und Randvölker; Afrika und Ägypten),

x-1064 p.   3-11-008843-6. – **11,1**, ^E*Temporini*... Sizilien und Sardinien, Italien und Rom, Allgemeines. viii-875 p.   3-11-010365-6. – **25,5**, ^E*Haase*, (Vorkonst. Christentum) Jac.-Jud., Apk., Apokrypha; p. 3621-4194. 3-11-011893-9. – **25,6**, Apokrypha, Nag' Hammadi, p. 4195-4794. 3-11-011894-7. B 1988, de Gruyter. – ^RAntClas 57 (1988) 411-4 (Marie-Thérèse *Raepsaet-Charlier*, 32/1-5); Athenaeum 66 (1988) 628-631 (B. *Chiesa*, 20/1); BL (1988) 133 (M. *Knibb*, 20/1); DLZ 109 (1988) 207-9 (W. *Schindler*, 12/3); Gymnasium 95 (1988) 82-84 (F. *Bömer*, 20/1-2; 32/5) & 563-6 (18; 25/4; 36/1); NRT 110 (1988) 595-7 (X. *Jacques*, 20/2; 25/4); ZSav-R 105 (1988) 932-8 (D. *Nörr*, 16/3; 18/1; 32/4s).

783 **AugL**: Augustinus-Lexikon, ^E**Mayer** Cornelius, *al.* [1/1s, 1986 ➤ 2,637*; 3,846], 1/3 Anima/us-Asinus. Ba 1988, Schwabe. col. 321-380. DM 39. 3-7965-0867-7. – ^RMusHelv 45 (1988) 262s (C. *Schäublin*); NRT 110 (1988) 931-3 (D. *Dideberg*); TZBas 44 (1988) 379s (R. *Brändle*). – 1,1s: ^RAntClas 57 (1988) 446-8 (H. *Savon*); DLZ 109 (1988) 369-371 (J. *Irmscher*); Gregorianum 69 (1988) 575s (F.-A. *Pastor*); IrTQ 54 (1988) 242-4 (G. *Watson*); JEH 39 (1988) 140 (H. *Chadwick*); RTPhil 120 (1988) 483 (E. *Junod*); TPhil 63 (1988) 267s (H. J. *Sieben*).

784 **BijH**: Bijbels Handboek, ^E**Woude** A. S. van der [I, 1981 ➤ 63,750; IIA, 1983 ➤ 64,741; IIB, 1983 ➤ 65,723]. III. Het Nieuwe Testament. Kampen 1987, Kok. 678 p. Fb 2500. – ^RCollatVL 18 (1988) 485s (A. *Denaux*); Streven 55 (1987s) 949s (P. *Beentjes*). – **Eng.** The world of the Bible I, 1986 ➤ 2,576; 3,847: ^RBA 51 (1988) 60s (J. J. M. *Roberts*).

785 **CAH**: Cambridge Ancient History, revised [= ? 2d] edition, 4. Persia, Greece and the Western Mediterranean c. 525 to 479 B.C., ^E**Boardman** J., *al.* C 1988, Univ. xxi-928 p. £60. – Plates, xi-248 p. £37.50. 0-521-22804-2; 30580-2 [BL 89,34, J. R. *Bartlett*].

786 Catholicisme, ^E**Mathon** G., *al.* [XI,52 ➤ 3,848*]; XI,53, -1278 + vi p. addenda. P 1988, Letouzey & A. – ^RGregorianum 69 (1988) 400 (J. *Wicki*, 50) & 790 (J. E. *Vercruysse*, 51); NRT 110 (1988) 155 (L. J. *Renard*, 51); PrOrChr 38 (1988) 206s (P. *Ternant*); RHPR 68 (1988) 347 (P. *Maraval*, 49-52).

787 **CGMG**, Christliche Glaube in moderner Gesellschaft, ^E**Böckle** F., *al.*, 1980s ➤ 62,852; 63,753: **Copray** Norbert, Werkbuch zur Enzyklopädischen Bibliothek 'Christlicher Glaube in moderner Gesellschaft'; ein didaktischer Schlüssel. FrB 1987, Herder. 175 p. – ^RBogSmot 58,4 (1988) 164s (M. *Valković*).

788 **CHIran**: The Cambridge History of Iran, 2. ^E**Gershevitch** I., 1985 ➤ 1,885 ... 3,849; — 3. ^E**Yarshater** E., 1983 ➤ 64,744; — 6. ^E**Jackson** P., *al.*, 1986 ➤ 3,849: ^RAmHR 92 (1987) 390-2 (J. *Buckler*, 2); Eirene 25 (1988) 132s (P. *Oliva*, 2); HZ 245 (1987) 674-6 (H. *Mejcher*, 6); WeltOr 19 (1988) 211-3 (H. *Gaube*, 3).

789 **CHJud**: The Cambridge History of Judaism, ^E**Davies** W., *al.*, I. Introduction; the Persian period 1984 ➤ 1,886 ... 3,850: ^RJStJud 19 (1988) 245-8 (A. S. van der *Woude*: bibliography reaches 1977).

790 **DHGE**: Dictionnaire d'Histoire et de Géographie Ecclésiastiques, ^E**Aubert** R. [XXI,124, 1986 ➤ 2,581; 3,851]: XXI.125. – XXII.126. Grégoire-Grimani, col. 1-256; 1987; 127. -Gualter, -512, 1988; 128. -Guibert, -768, 1988; 129s. -Guy, -1280, 1988; 131. -Haeglsperger, -1506 + Supp. 1507-1520: 1988. P, Letouzey. 2-7063-0138-4. – ^RNRT 110 (1988) 155s (N. *Plumat*, 126s); RHE 83 (1988) 801-3 (H. *Silvestre*, 128ss).

791 **DictSpir**: Dictionnaire de Spiritualité, ^E**Rayez** A., *al.* [XII,85 ➤ 2,582; 3,852] XII-2, 86ss. Piaristes-Quodvultdeus [+ Pélage] 1986. col. 1409-2942.

XIII,89s, Robert-Ryelandt, col. 705-1196 + listes d'auteurs et d'articles; 2-7010-1167-1. – XIV,91, Sabbatini-Savonarola, col. 1-384; 2-7010-1168-X. P. 1988, Beauchesne. – ᴿDivThom 89s (1986s) 518-525 (G. *Perini*, 83ss); Gregorianum 69 (1988) 578s (M. *Ruiz Jurado*, 86ss); Marianum 49 (1987) 638-640 & 50 (1988) 620-4 (L. *Gambero*, 80-84; 86-101); NRT 110 (1988) 626s (L.-J. *Renard*, 83-88); OrChrPer 54 (1988) 234-7 (V. *Poggi*, 86-88); RHE 83 (1988) 521 & 803s (R. *Aubert*, 86-88; 89-91); RHPR 68 (1988) 346s (M. *Chevallier*, 83-88); TEsp 31 (1987) 286s (V. T. *Gómez*, 78-85).

792 **DMA**: Dictionary of the Middle Ages, ᴱ**Strayer** J. R. [IX, 1987 and Interim Index 1-5, 1985, ➤ 3,853s]; X, Polemics-Scandinavia; xv-708 p. – XI. Scandinavian-Textiles. xiv-719 p. NY 1988, Scribner's. 0-684-18276-9; 7-7.

793 **DPA**: Dizionario patristico e di antichità cristiane, ᴱ**Di Berardino** Angelo [II, 1984 ➤ 1,889 ... 3,855]: III. Atlante patristico, Indici. R 1988, Marietti. viii-422 p. Lit. 100.000. – ᴿArTGran 51 (1988) 307 (A. *Segovia*); StPatav 35 (1988) 717s (C. *Corsato*); VoxP 15 (1988) 1105-9 (B. *Degórski*).

794 **EncIslam**: Encyclopédie de l'Islam² / Encyclopaedia of Islam², ᴱ**Bosworth** C. E., *al.* [VI,104 ➤ 3,856], VI,105s, Mandats-Marāsim. Leiden/P 1988, Brill/Maisonneuve & L. p. 385-512. 90-04-08826-1 [Eng. 5-3 (Mānd-Marʿāshis); N. B. *Mantik* col. 427 (Eng. 442) means 'logic'].

795 **EncRel**: Encyclopedia of Religion, ᴱ**Eliade** M. 1987 ➤ (2,585) 3,857; 16 vol. $1200: ᴿCouStR 17,2 (Macon GA 1988) 31.33 (W. *Harrelson*); RelStR 14 (1988) 193-9 (N. *Smart*: surpasses HASTINGS, though with less depth); ScripTPamp 20 (1988) 303-6 (M. *Guerra*).

796 **EncRel**: 7 critical comments: *a*) *Byrne* Peter, Theory of Religion and Method; – *b*) *Gunton* Colin, Christianity among the religions; – *c*) *Clarke* Peter B., Religions traditional and new; – *d*) *Hardy* Friedhelm, India and beyond; – *e*) *Ward* Keith, Philosophy and philosophy of religion; – *f*) *Baldick* Julian, Islam and the religions of Iran; – *g*) *Jantzen* Grace M., Christian spirituality and mysticism: RelSt 24,1 (C 1988) 3-10 / 11-18 / 19-27 / 29-37 / 39-46 / 47-56 / 57-64.

797 **EncTF**: Enciclopedia di teologia fondamentale; storia progetto autori categorie, I, ᴱ**Ruggieri** Giuseppe, 1987 ➤ 3,858: ᴿCC 139 (1988,4) 98 (Z. *Alszeghy*: non propone ma auspica la costruzione di una nuova teologia fondamentale); RasT 29 (1988) 203s (C. *Greco*); RClerIt 69 (1988) 145s (F. G. *Brambilla*); ViPe 71 (1988) 307-311 (G. *Cristaldi*).

798 **EvKL**: Evangelisches Kirchenlexikon, ᴱ**Fahlbusch** E., I, 1985 ➤ 1,893 ... 3,861: ᴿLutherJb 55 (1988) 125s (H. *Junghans*). – 2, Lfg. 3 (Gabun-Hellenismus) & 4 (Hellenistisch-römische Religion-Karman). Gö 1988, Vandenhoeck & R. col. 1-480; 481-479. 3-525-50129-3; 30-7.

799 **HbDTg**: Handbuch der Dogmen- und Theologiegeschichte, ᴱ**Andresen** C., *al.* [1s, 1980-2 ➤ 1,897; 3,1984 ➤ 2,589; 3,863]: ᴿTsTKi 58 (1987) 72s (O. *Skarsaune*, 1) & 314s (Å. *Holter*, 2s).

800 **HbFT**: Handbuch der Fundamentaltheologie, ᴱ**Kern** Walter, *Pottmeyer* Hermann J., *Seckler* Max [1ss, 1985s ➤ 1,898; 3,865]: 4. Traktat, Theologische Erkenntnislehre; Schlussteil, Reflexion auf Fundamentaltheologie. FrB 1988, Herder. 544 p. 3-451-20104-6. 9 art.; infra. – ᴿArTGran 51 (1988) 322s (A. S. *Muñoz*: authors, themes).

801 **ISBEnc**: The international standard Bible encyclopedia³ [¹1916; ²1929; III. ➤ 2,590; 3,865]: IV. Q-Z, ᴱ**Bromiley** Geoffrey W. GR/Exeter 1988, Eerdmans/Paternoster. 1211 p. $40 [all 4 vol. $160/ £115 [TDig 35,368]. 0-

8028-8162-9 (0-2, all 4). – ᴿCBQ 50 (1988) (M. D. *Futato*: brief praise);
RefTR 46 (1987) 19s (J. G. *Mason*); RRel 46 (1987) 633s (B. A. *Buby*).

802 **LexÄg**: Lexikon der Ägyptologie, ᴱ**Helck** W., *al.* [VI,49 ➔ 2,592] (VII,50
erst 1989): ᴿWZKM 78 (1986) 226-233 (E. *Winter*, IV-VI).

803 **LexMA**: Lexikon des Mittelalters, ᴱ**Avella-Widhalm** Gloria, *al.* [IV,3
➔ 3,867]; IV,4: Fosterage-Freiheit, col. 673-896; 5, -Gart, -1120; 6,
-Germanos, -1344; 7, -Goslar, -1568. Mü 1988, Artemis. 3-7608-8834-8;
5-6; 6-4; 7-2. – ᴿActuBbg 25 (1988) 288s (A. *Borràs*, IV,1-4); AnzAltW 41
(1988) 103-110 (W. *Trillitzsch*, III); ArHPont 26 (1988) 439s (P.
Rabikauskas, IV,1-4); ColcFr 56 (1986) 109; 57 (1987) 117 (T. *Jansen*,
III,4-10); DLZ 109 (1988) 690-2 (J. *Irmscher*); RHE 83 (1988) 480-2 (J.
Pycke: 4 fasc. Drack/Erz); RSPT 72 (1988) 178s (J.-N. *Walty*, III); TAth
54 (1988) 899-901 (K. G. *Bonis*, IV,1-4 ⊛).

804 **NBL**: Neues Bible-Lexikon [Nachfolger zu *Haag* H.], ᴱ**Görg** Manfred,
Lang Bernhard, Lfg 1. Aaron-Artemis; 2. Arwad-Bruderliebe.   Z 1988s,
Benziger.   176 col.; col. 177-336. [je] DM 23.   3-545-23039-2; 53-8.

805 [*Born* A. van den > *Haag*] ᴱ**Bogaert** P.-M., *al.*, Dictionnaire ency-
clopédique de la Bible: Maredsous Informatique et Bible 1987 ➔ 3,888:
ᴿBLitEc 89 (1988) 232s (A.-G. *Martimort*); FoiTemps 18 (1988) 184-6 (A.
Wénin); RThom 88 (1988) 646s (L. *Devillers*: 'revision' of van den Born
shunting off 365 of the articles to the Maredsous data-bank); SNTU-A 13
(1988) 205s (A. *Fuchs*: hart gegen Art. 'Kol' 'Eph'; ROLLANDS 'ex-
travagante und unhaltbare Hypothese').

806 **NDizTB**: Nuovo Dizionario di Teologia Biblica, ᴱ**Rossano** P., *Ravasi* G.,
Girlanda A.   CinB 1988, Paoline.   xxii-1739 p. Lit. 70.000. – c. 200 items
listed with author p. 1733-7; analytic index 1693-1732. – ᴿTItSett 13
(1988) 379-381 (P. *Grech*).

807 **RAC**: Reallexikon für Antike und Christentum, ᴱ**Dassmann** Ernst, *al.*
[➔ 3,870]: XIV,105-107, Heilig-Henoch, -480; 1987; 108-112, -Hexe, -1288:
1988. Stu, Hiersemann. 3-7772-8835-7. – ᴿJTS 39 (1988) 592-7 (C. P.
Hammond Bammel, 91-96); NRT 110 (1988) 156 (N. *Plumat*, 102-4); TLZ
113 (1988) 253-9 (H. *Seidel*, 81-96).

808 **RLA**: Reallexikon der Assyriologie, ᴱ**Edzard** D. O., 7,1s, 1987 ➔ 3,871:
ᴿOLZ 38 (1988) 414-6 (H. *Klengel*). – 7,3s, Luhuzattija - Maltai.   B 1988,
de Gruyter.   p. 161-320. DM 112.   3-11-010440-7.

809 **SDB**: Supplément au Dictionnaire de la Bible, ᴱ**Briend** Jacques, *Cothenet*
Édouard [XI,61, 1987 ➔ 3,872] XI,62, Salut-. P 1988, Letouzey & A. col.
513-740 [737-740 anticipées de fasc. 63]. F 200. – 2-7063-0016-3. – ᴿBL
(1988) 9 (R. N. *Whybray*, 61); NRT 110 (1988) 626 (J.-L. *Ska*, 60); RB 95
(1988) 429s (R. J. *Tournay*, 61).

810 **StSp**: Storia della Spiritualità [< ᴱ*Bouyer* L.; I. 1985; ➔ 2,614 *non*
'Borla'], II. ᴱ**Barbaglio** Giuseppe, La spiritualità del NT.   Bo 1988,
Dehoniane.   378 p. Lit. 38.000.   88-10-34012-8.

810* **StSp-G**: Storia della Spiritualità [collana con titolo identico al preceden-
te], ᴱ**Grossi** Vittorino, *al.*   R 1985s, Borla ➔ 8336*.

811 **TDNT**: Theological Dictionary of the NT, one-volume, ᴱ**Bromiley** G. W.
1985 ➔ 3,873: ᴿScotJT 41 (1988) 426s (I. R. *Torrance*).

812 **TDOT**: Theological Dictionary of the OT, ᴱ**Ringgren** Helmer [➔ 815 ᵀ]
5,1986 ➔ 3,873: ᴿSVlad 31 (1987) 259-261 (M. *Prokurat*, V).

813 **TRE**: Theologische Realenzyklopädie, ᴱ**Müller** Gerhard, *al.* [XVI. 1987
➔ 3,875]. XVII, Jesus-Katechismuspredigte. B 1987 [bis S. 310]-1988 [bis
Ende S. 814], de Gruyter. 3-11-011506-9. – ᴿBibHumRen 50 (1988) 222-4
(I. *Hazlett*, 15); BL (1988) 19 (R. N. *Whybray*, 16); DielBl 24 (1987) 746-8
(R. *Albertz*, 16, 'Israel' altertümlich); GGA 240 (1988) 1-19 (M. *Tro-*

witzsch, 1-15!); JEH 39 (1988) 157 (O. *Chadwick*, 15); NedTTs 42 (1988) 244-6 (A. van den *Beld*, 10-15); NorTTs 89 (1988) 145-9 (S.A. *Christoffersen*, 10s, along with Freud's Letters); NRT 110 (1988) 156s (R.E.) & 627 (V. *Roisel*, 16); Protestantesimo 43 (1988) 248 (J.A. *Soggin*, 16); RHPR 68 (1988) 345s (M.A. *Chevallier*, 15); TPQ 136 (1988) 90s (G. *Bachl*, 15); TR 84 (1988) 359-361 (R. *Bäumer*, 16); TZBas 44 (1988) 278s (W. *Rordorf*, 13ss).

814 **TUmAT**: Texte aus der Umwelt des Alten Testaments 2 [Lfg. 1s, 1986s ➔ 3,876]; Lfg. 3. *Butterweck* C., *al.*, Religiöse Texte (Rit. Beschw. II); 4, *Butterweck* C. + 13 *al.*, Grab-, Sarg-, Votiv- und Bauinschriften. Gü 1988, Mohn. p. 293-452 / 453-640. DM 138, sb. 118.   3-579-00068-3; 9-1 [BL 89,121, W.G. *Lambert*, 2/4]. – ᴿNorTTs 89 (1988) 278s (H.M. *Barstad*, 2/3); PhoenixEOL 33,2 (1987) 63s (K.R. *Veenhof*, 2/1); Streven 56 (1988s) 83s (P. *Beentjes*, 2/2s); ZAW 100 (1988) 467 (2/2, tit. pp.); ZkT 110 (1988) 346s (F. *Mohr*, 2/1s).

815 **TWAT**: Theologisches Wörterbuch zum Alten Testament, ᴱ**Ringgren** Helmer [VI,5, 1987 ➔ 3,877]; VI,6s, *pālal - ṣō'n*, col. 609-863.   Stu 1988, Kohlhammer. 3-17-009919-1. – ᴿBiblica 69 (1988) 129-131 (J.A. *Soggin*, 5); Bijdragen 49 (1988) 90 (W. *Beuken*, 5/9s); BL (1988) 8s (R.N. *Whybray*, 5/9s; 6/1); NRT 109 (1987) 126s; 110 (1988) 624-6 (J.-L. *Ska*, 4/3-5/4; 5/5-6/2); TR 84 (1988) 188s (W. *Kornfeld*, 6/1s) & 277-9 (6/3ss, Fehlzitationen).

A3.2   *Opera consultationis non separatim infra;* **not subindexed.**

816 ᴱ**Achtemeier** Paul J.,   Harper's Bible dictionary 1985 ➔ 1,913…3,878: ᴿCalvinT 23 (1988) 61-66 (J.H. *Stek*: holes, blunders, and inconsistencies); JTS 39 (1988) 213s (W.D. *Stacey*: dangerous for the non-specialist who may believe that there is such a thing as the claimed 'non-sectarian consensus view').

817 ᴱ**Alexander** Pat,   Die Welt der Bibel; Nachschlagewerk zur Bibel, Informationen in Wort und Bild [➔ 3,879s]; ᵀ*Schmidt* Reinhild, *Maikranz* Christiane.   Wu 1988, Brockhaus. 352 p.; ill.; maps. 3-417-24567-2.

818 ᴱ**Arnold** Pierre,   Traces; annuel des religions, Édition [1986, 22 auteurs] 1987 [35 auteurs, analyse de la presse courante]. Turnhout 1987, Brepols. 254 p. Fb 745. – ᴿRTLv 19 (1988) 396 (H. *Wattiaux*).

819 ᴱ**Bäumer** R., *Scheffczyk* L., Marienlexikon, I. AA - Chagall.   St. Ottilien 1988, Eos.

820 **Barthel** Manfred, (*Dopatka* Ulrich),   Lexikon der Pseudonyme; über 1000 Künstler-, Tarn- und Decknamen.   Dü 1986, Econ. 272 p. DM 30. – ᴿBiblos 36 (1987) 121s (W.G. *Wieser*).

821 ᴱ**Beinert** Wolfgang,   Lexikon der katholischen Dogmatik 1987 ➔ 3,884: ᴿHerdKorr 42 (1988) 50 (U. *Ruh*); StiZt 206 (1988) 646 (M. *Kehl*); TPhil 63 (1988) 615 (auch M. *Kehl*); TüTQ 168 (1988) 74s (W. *Kasper*).

822 **Blaiklock** E.M.,   Today's [= 1979¹] Handbook of Bible characters [740 short studies, e.g. 16 on Abraham].   Minneapolis 1987, Bethany. 639 p. $18. – ᴿBS 145 (1988) 225 (T.L. *Constable*).

823 **Blair** E.P.,   The illustrated Bible handbook.   Nv 1987, Abington. 538 p. $28.   0-687-18680-3 [NTAbs 32,230].

824 ᴱ**Boardman** J., *al.*,   The Oxford history of the classical world 1986 ➔ 2,603; 3,887: ᴿJHS 108 (1988) 216s (A.R. *Burn*).

825 **Bridgland** C. [OT 1982], *Foulks* F. [NT c.1978], Pocket guide to the Bible. Leicester/DG 1988, Inter-Varsity. 394 p.; 6 fig.; 6 maps. $13. 0-8308-1401-9 [NTAbs 32,361].

826 **Calvocoressi** Peter, Who's who in the Bible. L 1988, Penguin. xxxi-269 p.; 5 maps. £5. [JTS 39,678].

827 **Chevalier** Jean, *Gheerbrant* Alain, Diccionario de los símbolos [1969], ᵀ*Silvar* M., *al.* 1986 ➤ 3,891: ᴿBrotéria 125 (1987) 355 (I. *Ribeiro da Silva*).

828 ᴱ**Davies** J.G., New Westminster Dictionary of Liturgy² 1986 ➤ 2,609; 3,895: ᴿInterpretation·42 (1988) 88 (G. E. *Saint-Laurent*); ModT 4 (1987) 222-4 (K. *Flanagan*); NBlackfr 68 (1987) 50s (E. *Yarnold*).

829 ᴱ**Della Corte** Francesco, Dizionario degli scrittori greci e latini [fino al 600; in ordine alfabetico solo una sessantina più importante; gli altri radunati in gruppi omogenei]. Mi-Settimo 1988, Marzorati. 2433 p. (3 vol.) Lit. 255.000. – ᴿCC 139 (1988,4) 611 (A. *Ferrua*).

830 Dictionnaire de la Bible [➤ 805] et des trois religions du Livre [➤ 3,888]: L'Univers de la Bible 10 [➤ d9]. Turnhout 1985, Brepols. 454 p. Fb 2830. 2-503-52001-4. – ᴿBijdragen 49 (1988) 207 (F. *De Meyer*).

831 **Drehsen** Volker (*Baumotte* Manfred), Wörterbuch des Christentums. Gü 1988, Mohn. 1439 p. DM 196 [TR 84,515].

832 ᴱ**Easterling** P. E., *Knox* B. M. W., The Cambridge History of Classical Literature, I. Greek 1985 ➤ 1,928 ... 3,901: ᴿPhoenix 42,1 (Toronto 1988) 79-85 (J. *Herington*).

833 ᴱ**Eberhard** F., (*Taylor* Anne C. M.), World list of universities / Liste mondiale des universités¹⁷. P 1988, International Association of Universities. xxi-666 p. 0-333-37183-6.

834 ᴱ**Eicher** Peter, Dictionnaire de théologie. P 1988, Cerf. 838 p. F 650. – ᴿÉtudes 369 (1988) 710 (R. *Marlé*: remplace l'Encyclopédie de la foi postconciliaire).

835 **Erickson** Millard A., Concise dictionary of Christian theology 1986 ➤ 3,904: ᴿBS 145 (1988) 105 (R. P. *Lightner*: unfair to fundamentalists and HENRY J., YOUNG E.; prefers WCC).

836 ᴱ**Fahlbusch** E., Taschenlexikon Religion und Theologie⁴ʳᵉᵛ 1983 ➤ 1, 936*; 2,615: ᴿTRu 53 (1988) 417-423 (H. *Spieckermann*, auch über RICHARDSON-BOWDEN und EICHER-FISCHER).

837 ᴱ**Feiner** Johannes, *Löhrer* Magnus, Mysterium salutis, Grundriss heilsgeschichtlicher Dogmatik [I-V 1965-76 ➤ 51,4199 ... 55,5165] Ergänzungsband, ᴱ*Löhrer*, *al.* Z 1981, Benziger [6789 p. in all.]. – ᴿTsTKi 58 (1987) 307-9 (I. *Asheim*).

838 ᴱ**Ferguson** Sinclair B., *Wright* David F., New dictionary of theology: Master Reference. Nottingham/DG 1988, InterVarsity. xix-738 p. £19/ $25 [TDig 35,185]. 0-85110-636-6/. – ᴿFurrow 39 (1988) 676 (J. *Caffrey*); RefTR 47 (1988) 54s (R. *Swanton*).

839 **Grant** Michael, A guide to the ancient world; a dictionary of classical place names 1986 ➤ 2,621: ᴿGreeceR 34 (1987) 227 (P. *Walcot*: archeology aspects outdated).

840 **Grimal** P., Dizionario di mitologia greca e romana [1951; Eng. 1985 ➤ 2,622], ᵀᴱ*Cordié* C. Brescia 1987, Paideia. xxxviii-821 p. – ᴿBStLat 18 (1988) 158s (G. *Cupaiuolo*).

841 ᴱ**Härle** Wilfried, *Wagner* Harald, Theologenlexikon, [400] von den Kirchenvätern bis zur Gegenwart: B. Reihe 321, 1987; 3-406-31893-2: ᴿActuBbg 25 (1988) 227 (J. *Boada*); ForumKT 3 (1987) 325 (H.-A. *Klein*).

842 **Hanselmann** Johannes, *al.*, FachwörterbuchTheologie, Wu 1987, Brockhaus. 184 p. [ZNW 79,162].

843 ᴱ**Harrison** R. K., Encyclopedia of biblical and Christian ethics. Nv 1987, Nelson. 472 p. $25 [TDig 35,269].

Henze Dietmar, Enzyklopädie der Entdecker und Erforscher der Erde III, 1988 → d757.

844 Hilfe zum Verständnis der Bibel; Fakten über den historischen, geographischen, religiösen und kulturellen Hintergrund der Bibel und Einzelheiten über darin erwähnte Personen, Völker, Orte, Pflanzen, Tiere und Aktivitäten, IV. Griechenland - Jeremia. Wsb 1983, Wachtturm; p. 573-762; ill.; maps [KirSef 61,391].

845 **Kelly** John N. D., Reclams Lexikon der Päpste, ᵀ*Oeser* Hans-Christian. Stu 1988, Reclam. 375 p. – ᴿTPhil 63 (1988) 596-8 (K. *Schatz*: eine Reihe von Mängeln, besonders Gewichtung und historische Einordnung).

846 ᴱ**Khoury** Adel T., Lexikon religiöser Grundbegriffe; Judentum, Christentum, Islam 1987 → 3,920: ᴿTGL 78 (1988) 99s (W. *Beinert*); ZkT 110 (1988) 108s (W. *Kern*).

847 [*König* Franz] **Waldenfels** Hans, Lexikon der Religionen; Phänomene, Geschichte, Ideen. FrB 1988, Herder. xiv-729 p. – ᴿAnthropos 83 (1988) 653s (O. *Gächter*); TLZ 113 (1988) 881-3 (K.-W. *Tröger*); VerbumSVD 29 (1988) 201s (J. *Kuhl*).

849 ᴱ**Komonchak** J. A., *al.*, The new dictionary of theology 1987 → 3,923: ᴿFurrow 39 (1988) 735s (P. *Hannon*); Horizons 15 (1988) 399s (R. P. *McBrien*); NewTR 1,2 (1988) 105-7 (K. *O'Malley*: important); Tablet 242 (1988) 38s (R. *Butterworth*); TorJT 4 (1988) 286-8 (M. G. *Steinhauser*: commends without reservation); TS 49 (1988) 756-8 (W. V. *Dych*).

850 ᴱ**Krüger** Hanfried, *al.*, Ökumene-Lexikon; Kirchen — Religionen — Bewegungen² [¹1983 → 64,949]. Fra 1987, Lembeck-Knecht. 1346 col. DM 130. – ᴿZkT 110 (1988) 235s (L. *Lies*).

851 **Lass** Abraham H., *Kiremidjian* David, *Goldstein* Ruth M., The Facts on File dictionary of classical, biblical, and literary allusions. NY 1987, Facts on File. viii-240 p. $19 [TDig 35,276].

852 **LIMC**: Lexicon iconographicum mythologiae classicae, ᴱ**Kahil** Lilly [3, 1986 → 3,924]: IV/1, Eros-Heracles. Z 1988, Artemis. xxix-951 p. 3-7608-8751-1. – ᴿAJA 92 (1988) 138s (Brunilde S. *Ridgway*, 3); AntClas 57 (1988) 554-7 (C. *Delvoye*, 3); Eirene 25 (1988) 135s (J. *Bouzek*, 1); ParPass 237 (1987) 469-472 (P. Enrico *Arias*, 1-3); Phoenix 42 (1988) 358-370 (*Tran Tam Tink*, 2s franç.); RBgPg 66 (1988) 182-4 (R. *Lambrechts*).

853 ᴱ**Lippy** Charles H., *Williams* Peter W., Encyclopedia of the American religious experience; studies of traditions and movements. NY 1988, Scribner's. xvi-665 p.; -1265; -1872 p. – ᴿAndrUnS 26 (1988) 90-93 (G. R. *Knight*: Millennialism and Adventism p. 831-844, gives very broad context); ChH 57 (1988) 514-8 (W. S. *Hudson*).

854 ᴱ**Lissner** Anneliese, *al.*, Frauenlexikon; Traditionen, Fakten, Perspektiven. FrB 1988, Herder. vi-1245 col. (632 p.). DM 65, sb. 58. – ᴿTGL 78 (1988) 450 (W. *Beinert*).

855 ᴱ**Lockyer** Herbert, Illustrated Bible dictionary. L 1988, Hodder & Stoughton. 1130 p. £17 [PrPeo 2,202].

856 ᴱ**Lurker** Manfred, Wörterbuch der Symbolik⁴ʳᵉᵛ: Taschenausgabe 464. Stu 1988, Kröner. xvi-845 p. 3-520-46404-7.

857 **McFarlan** D. M., Concise Bible dictionary 1986 → 3,928: ᴿCBQ 50 (1988) 506s (R. L. *Hayden*).

858 ᴱ**Melton** J. Gordon, *a)* The encyclopedia of American religions; religious creeds [not = Encyclopedia of American Religions² 1986 (TDig 35,62; but cf. → 3,932 < TDig 34,370)]. Detroit 1988, Gale. xxiii-838 p. $125. – *b)* The encyclopedia of American religions². Detroit 1987, Gale. xv-899 p. $165. – ᴿRelStR 14 (1988) 175 (D. A. *Johnson*).

859 **Monloubou** L., *Du Buit* F. M., Dizionario biblico storico/critico, ᵀᴱ*Fabris*
R., 1987 ➤ 3,934: ᴿAntonianum 63 (1988) 432 (M. *Nobile*); CC 139
(1988,1) 298 (S. *Votto*).

860 ᴱ**Mostyn** Trevor, (*Hourani* Albert), The Cambridge Encyclopedia of the
Middle East and North Africa. C 1988, Univ. 504 p.; ill. (only p. 39-60
treats everything up to Islam). 0-521-32190-5.

861 **Müller** Karl, *Sundermeier* Theo, Lexikon missionstheologischer Grundbegriffe. B 1987, Reimer. 546 p. DM 48. – ᴿTPQ 136 (1988) 180 (F.
Schragl).

862 ᴱ**Myers** Allen C., The Eerdmans Bible dictionary. GR 1987. $23;
0-8028-2402-1. – ᴿBAR-W 14,4 (1988) 60 (W. *Harrelson*); BTrans 19
(1988) 345s (P. *Ellingworth* compares favorably with Harpers 1985, same
price, which has 100 more pages, is deeper but less broad, and is not
moderate-evangelically committed).

863 **Olderr** Steven, Symbolism; a comprehensive dictionary. Jefferson ᴺᶜ
1986, McFarland. vi-153 p. 0-89950-187-7.

864 a) *Pais* István, Ⓜ Szegény Biblia! [poor Bible!: Képes Bibliai Lexikon
(Budapest 1987, Minerva)]: Élet és Irodalom (1987) 37; – b) Ⓜ *Magassy*
Sándor, Ⓜ 'Abel-Zsuzsanna' in the pillory; observations on a strange
criticism: Theologiai Szemle 31 (1988) 112-6.

865 ᴱ**Poupard** Paul, a) Diccionario de las religiones [Dictionnaire des
religions, 1984 ➤ 65,788],ᵀ. Barc 1987, Herder. 1889 p. pt. 12.000. 84-
254-1547-0. – ᴿActuBbg 25 (1988) 283s (J. *Boada*); ComSev 21 (1988) 295
(J. *Duque*). – b) Grande dizionario delle Religioni, ᵀ*Corsani* Mirella, *al.*
Assisi/CasM 1988, Cittadella/Piemme. A-L p. xvii-1192; M-Z p. 1193-
2330.

866 Reallexikon der deutschen Kunstgeschichte [I-II being reprinted] Lfg.
95-97 Fingerzahlen-Fisch. Mü 1986s, Beck. VIII: viii p.; col. 1281-1520;
IX: col. 1-128. – ᴿNRT 110 (1988) 786 (Y. *Torly*).

866* **Room** Adrian, Dictionary of coin names. L 1987, Routledge-KP. £15.
– ᴿNumC 148 (1988) 215-220 (R. G. *Doty*).

867 ᴱ**Ruh** Ulrich, *al.*, Handwörterbuch religiöser Gegenwartsfragen 1986
➤ 2,648; 3,941: ᴿTGL 78 (1988) 97s (G. *Ruppert*); TR 84 (1988) 60s (D.
Emeis).

868 ᴱ**Sartore** Domenico, *Triacca* Achille M., Nuevo diccionario de liturgía,
ᵀᴱ*Canals* Juan M. M 1987, Paulinas. 2135 p. 84-285-1204-5. – ᴿActuBbg 25 (1988) 278s (A. *Borràs*).

869 ᴱ**Stöckle** Bernhard, Wörterbuch der ökologischen Ethik; die Verantwortung des Christen für den Bestand der Schöpfung: Herderbücherei
1262, 1986 ➤ 2,652: ᴿTR 84 (1988) 330 (P. *Schmitz*).

870 **Toon** Peter, *Schneider* Herbert, The compact Bible dictionary [to
(Catholic) NAB]. AA 1987, Servant. xii-158 p. $7 pa. 0-89283-321-1
[NTAbs 32,367].

871 ᴱ**Urban** Hans J., *Wagner* Harald, Handbuch der Ökumenik [I. 1985; II.
1986 ➤ 9137 infra] III,1 [➤ 3,7918]. Pd 1987, Bonifatius. 268 p. DM 36.
– ᴿÖkRu 37 (1988) 491-4 (H. *Gaese*); ZkT 110 (1988) 219 (L. *Lies*).

872 ᴱ**Voigt** E. M., Lexikon des frühgriechischen Epos, Lfg. 10 [II,1], *bádēn–
Diōnē*. Gö 1982, Vandenhoeck & R. xviii + 320 col. DM 168. – ᴿMnemosyne 40 (1987) 175-8 (W. J. *Verdenius*: puts in effect the drastic
compression needed to complete the work in 20 years).

873 ᴱ**Weger** K.-H., *Bossong* K., Argumente für Gott; Gott-Denker von der
Antike bis zur Gegenwart, ein Autorenlexikon: Herderbücherei 1393, 1987
➤ 3,1070; 3-451-08393-0. – ᴿTsTNijm 28 (1988) 87 (N. P. van *Beijnen*).

874 ^E**Yarshater** Ehsan, Encyclopaedia Iranica [I,1-9, 1985 ➤ 3,949; not = ➤ 788 supra], III. fasc. 7, Barian - Bardesanes. L 1988, Routledge-KP. 0-7100-9119-2 [OIAc D88]. – ^RJAOS 108 (1988) 169s (R. N. *Frye*); StIran 17 (1988) 106-110 (J. *Calmard*).

A4 **Bibliographiae** .1 **biblicae.**

875 **Azcárraga Servet** María J., *al.*, Sefarad, Volumen de Índices, años XVI-XXV (1956-1965). M 1988, Cons. Sup. Inst. Fg vi-187 p. 0037-0894.

876 **Belle** Gilbert van, Johannine bibliography 1966-1985; a cumulative bibliography on the Fourth Gospel: Coll. Bib. Rel. 1. Bru 1988, Kon. Acad. 563 p. Fb 2700.

877 **Charlesworth** James H., *al.*, The NT apocrypha and pseudepigrapha, a guide to publications 1987 ➤ 3,952: ^RCBQ 50 (1988) 713s (Janet *Timbie*); VigChr 42 (1988) 307s (A. F. J. *Klijn*).

878 *Claassen* Walter T., Computer-assisted methods and the text and language of the Old Testament — an overview: ➤ 47, ^FFENSHAM F., Text 1988, 283-299.

879 *Demsky* Rivka, *Zimmer* Ora, America and the Holy Land; a select bibliography of publications in Hebrew: CHistEI 50 (1988) 167-191 [paralleling 3 (1983) 327-356, publications in English]; 193, subdivisions in English.

880 **Dimant** Devorah, *Mor* Menaḥem, *Rappaport* Uriel, Bibliography for Jewish history in the Persian, Hellenistic and Roman periods 1981-5. J 1988, Shazar Center. 129 p. – ^RKirSef 61 (1986s) 451s (Bitya *Ben-Shammai*); Zion 53 (1988) 72-74 (D. *Schwartz*).

881 Dissertation Abstracts in biblical studies from DissA 47,1-6 (July-Dec. 1986 / 7-12 (Jan.-June 1987) / 48,1-6 (July-Dec. 1988) / 7-12 (Jan.-June 1988), with complete abstract in each case: StudiaBT 15 (1987) 94-132 / 254-284 / 16 (1988) 122-142 / 246-278 [N.B. without advance warning, pp. (15) 132s. 284-7 and (16) 142 give 'Other Fuller dissertations': StudiaBT is published at Fuller Sem., Pasadena].

882 ^E*Ernst* Juliette L., Auteurs et textes: Testamenta [under this rubric are contained 369 items, entirely from the *New* Testament]: AnPg 57 (1988 for 1986) 288-308; under other rubrics there are passing allusions to biblical archeology, epigraphy, grammar; and sections noted here under A1.1 and Y8.5.

883 *Gotenburg* Erwin, Bibelwissenschaft [Theologische Bibliographie]: TR 84 (1988) 73-5 [-88]. 161-3 [-176]. 249-251 [-264]. 337-9 [-352]. 425-7 [-440]. 515-7 [-528].

884 *a*) *Hang* Fred, *al.* Audio/Visuals in review; – *b*) *Stuhlmueller* Carroll, The OT in review; – *c*) *Senior* Donald, The NT in review: BToday 26 (1988) 123s . 382-5 / 116-122 . 184-192 . 374-381 / 249-255 . 311-7.

885 *Harrington* Daniel J., *a*) Second Testament [i.e. NT] exegesis and the social sciences; a bibliography: BibTB 18 (1988) 77-85; – *b*) [31] Books on the Bible: [150 words each]: America 157 (1987) 431-7.

886 *Hendrickx* F., Literatuuroverzicht 1987: OnsGErf 62 (1988) 1-164; 1274 items; 9 categories, of which the largest two are chronological (Middle Ages and 'since before Trent').

887 *Homan* M. J., Computer assisted biblical research: ConcordJ 14,2 (1988) 150-7 [< NTAbs 32,285].

Hughes John, Bits, bytes and biblical studies 1987 ➤ 1618.

889 *Hui* Timothy K. [and Dallas faculty], Periodical reviews: Bibliotheca
    Sacra 145 (1988) 98-101 . 211-6 . 343-5 . 452-5.
890 ᴱ**Hupper** William G., Index to English periodical literature on the OT
    and ANE studies [1. 1987 ➤ 3,966]; 2: ATLA Bibliog. 21/2. Metuchen NJ
    1988, Scarecrow. xxxviii-502 p. $45. 0-8108-[1984-8]-2126-5. – ᴿAustral-
    BR 36 (1988) 68-71 (J. *Wright*, 1: high praise, some flaws).
891 L'illustrazione di Terra Santa [opere stampate 1500-1941; i 26 volumi di
    GOLUBOVICH Girolamo disponibili $514]: TerraS 64 (1988) 320-5.
892 **IZBG**: Internationale Zeitschriftenschau für Bibelwissenschaft und
    Grenzgebiete, ᴱ**Lang** Bernhard, *al.* 35 (1987s); Dü, Patmos [1989].
893 JStNT 28-33 (1986-8) index: 33 (1988) 122-8; JStOT 36-41 (1986-8) index:
    41 (1988) 121-8.
894 *Jocque* Luc, Bibliographie canoniale, 1984s: RÉAug 34 (1988) 106-143.
895 *Kealy* Sean P., A Bible bookshelf: AfER 29 (1987) 227-235.
895* KirSef 61 (1986s) 599-625 (Bible), 728s (archeology) 755s (in mem.).
    N. B. The fourth fascicle (published 1989) does not contain an index,
    which presumably will appear as a separate fascicle.
896 **Langevin** Paul-Émile, Bibliographie biblique III, 1985 ➤ 1,1007 ... 3,972:
    ᴿBrotéria 125 (1987) 477s (I. *Ribeiro da Silva*); FoiTemps 19 (1987) 364s
    (C. *Focant*); ScotJT 39 (1988) 284s (I. R. *Torrance*: regrets not provided
    on computer-disk).
897 *Lust* J., Sacra Scriptura VT [*Neirynck* F., *Van Segbroeck* F., NT]:
    Elenchus Bibliographicus 1987: ETL 63 (1987) 117*-199* [-265*].
898 *Muñoz Abad* Carmen *al.*, Elenco de artículos de revistas: Sefarad 48
    (1988) 217-232.
899 *Murphy* Roland, Update on Scripture studies: RelEd 82 (Ch 1987) 624 ...
    [< ZIT].
900 *O'Grady* John F., New Testament books in their context: ChSt 26
    (1987) 87-99.
901 *Peitzner* V. C., New Testament reading for busy pastors; Lutheran
    Theological Journal 21,3 (1987) 133-141 [< NTAbs 32,294].
902 *Perani* Mauro, Frammenti di manoscritti ebraici nell'archivio storico
    comunale di Imola [... B. Bibbia; C. commenti biblici; D. dizionari e
    grammatiche ... T. talmud]: Henoch 10 (1988) 219-234.
903 *Piñero Sáenz* Antonio, Boletín de Filología Neotestamentaria: FgNt 1,1
    (1988) 119-136, 227-239.
904 [ᴱ*Poswick* R. F.] Bible et informatique 1985/6 ➤ 2,389: ᴿHenoch 10
    (1988) 389-391 (P. G. *Borbone*).
905 **Pruter** Karl, Jewish Christians in the United States; a bibliography:
    Bibliographies on Sects and Cults in America 7, Social Science 306. NY
    1987, Garland. xi-192 p. $38. – ᴿRelStR 14 (1988) 171 (J. D. *Sarna*:
    glaring omissions: Israel's Advocate; Jewish Chronicle; Israelite Indeed; L.
    Meyer, J. *Sarna*, *al.*).
    Purvis J. D., Jerusalem, the Holy City; a bibliography: ATLA 20, 1988
    ➤ e680.
    Radice Roberto, PHILO bibliography 1988 ➤ a993.
906 **RAMBI**: ᴱ*Ben-Shammai* Bitya, Index of articles on Jewish studies 28
    (1986). J 1988, Jewish National and University Library. xlv-463 [-vii] p.;
    Eng. index 463-433 (sic). 0073-5817.
907 *Ravera* Marco, Ermeneutica 1986/87: FilT 1,1 (N 1988) 158-167.
908 Record of work published or in progress: BSeptCog 21 (1988) 10-22.
909 **Ruud** Inger Marie, Women and Judaism, a select annotated bibliography:
    Ref. Libr. Soc. Sc. 316. NY 1988, Garland. xxiv-232 p. $34 [TDig 36,80].

910 **Scholar** David M., Bibliographia gnostica; Supplementum XVII; NT 30 (1988) 339-372 [continues the new numbering begun with XVI from the still not published NH Bibliog.].

911 **Spurgeon** Charles H., *al.*, A classic Bible study library for today. GR 1988, Kregel. 92 p. $4 pa. [JBL 107,790].

912 *Thiel* Winfried, Der Gottesdienst in der Geschichte der Kirche; altorientalische und israelitisch-jüdische Religion: JbLtgHymn 30 (1986) 133-156 [156-210, *Poscharsky* P., *al.*,... in der Gegenwart].

913 *Tosaus Abadía* J. P., Algunas publicaciones recientes sobre san Pedro: EstBíb 46 (1988) 375-398: CULLMANN 1952 siempre clásico.

914 *Vattioni* Francesco, Saggio di bibliografia semitica 1986-1987 / 1987-1988: AION 47 (1987) 441-499 / 48 (1988) 267-337.

915 **Wagner** Günter, Exegetical bibliography... Mt Mk 1983, Lk Acts 1985, John 1987 → 3,985: ᴿPerspRelSt 15 (1988) 182-4 (D. M. *Scholer*).

Wal Adri van der, Nahum, Habakkuk bibliography, with special section on Qumran 1988 → 4029.

916 *Wansbrough* Henry, New Testament chronicle [21 books]: PrPeo 2 (1988) 293-7.

917 *Watson* Duane F., The New Testament and Greco-Roman rhetoric; a bibliography: JEvTS 31 (1988) 465... [< ZIT 89,149].

918 **White** Leland J., Jesus the Christ, a bibliography: Theological and Biblical Resources 4. Wilmington 1988, Glazier. 157 p. $9. 0-89453-645-1 [NTAbs 32,387].

919 Zion index 41-50 (1976-1985): 53 (1988) ⊕ 83-128; Eng. 128-112.

A4.2 *Bibliographiae* **theologicae.**

920 *Arató* Pál, Bibliographia historiae pontificiae: ArchHPont 25 (1987) 461-736; 26 (1988) 457-725.

921 *Bächtold* Hans U., *a)* mit *Bührer* Georg, Literatur zur schweizerischen Reformgeschichte; – *b)* mit *Haag* Hans J., Literatur zur zwinglischen Reformation: Zwingliana 16 (1983-5) 546-570; 17 (1986-8) 140-168 / 17 (1986-8) 317-334. 513-534.

922 *Baer* Hans A., Bibliography of social science literature on Afro-American religion in the United States: RRelRes 29,4 ('Black American Religion in the twentieth century' 1988) 413-... [349-412: < ZIT 88,606].

923 ᴱ**Bass** Dorothy C., *Boyd* Sandra H., Women in American religious history; an annotated bibliography and guide to sources. Boston 1987, Hall. xiv-155 p. $30. – ᴿRelStR 14 (1988) 174 (D. A. *Johnson*).

924 BEINTKER Horst, Bibliographie zum 70. Gb.: TLZ [108 (1983) 144-152, *Friedrich* P.] 113 (1988) 75-77 (*Seils* M.).

925 *Belle* A. Van, (*Haverals* M.): Bibliographie: Revue d'histoire ecclésiastique 83 (1988) 1*-192*. 193*-344*. 345*-612* [7632 items plus some 2000 book-reviews].

926 *Berger* Teresa, Internationale Kongresse der Societas Liturgica; eine bibliographische Übersicht: ArLtgW 30 (1988) 38-40.

927 *a) Berger* W. J., *Lans* J. M. van der, Kroniek van godsdienstpsychologie en pastorale psychologie; – *b) Firet* J., Kroniek van de praktische theologie: PrakT 14 (1987) 286-296. ...

928 **Berkhout** Carl T., *Russell* Jeffrey B., Medieval heresies; a bibliography 1960-1979: Subsidia Mediaevalia 11, 1981 → 63,891: ᴿRelStR 14 (1988) 161s (G. A. *Zinn*).

929 *Bertuletti* Angelo, *al.*, I problemi metodologici della teologia sulle riviste del 1987: TItSett 13 (1988) 310-378 [326-334 ermeneutica e teologia biblica].

930 **Besutti** Giuseppe M., Bibliografia mariana 1978-1984, pref. *Söll* Georg: Scripta Mariana NS 11. R 1988, Marianum. xxxii-712 p. Lit. 150.000 [Greg 69,820]. – ᴿMarianum 50 (1988) 593s (R. *Farina*).

931 *Billet* Bernard, Notes mariales [... le Rosaire; plusieurs livres infra]: EsprVie 98 (1988) 537-542.

932 **Bjorling** Joel, The Churches of God, Seventh Day; a bibliography: Sects and cults 8. NY 1987, Garland. xix-296 p. $48 [TDig 35,153].

933 **Blasi** Anthony J., *Cuneo* Michael W. Issues in the sociology of religion: Bibliog. in Soc. 8 / Ref. Lib. Soc. Sc. 340. NY 1986, Garland. xxiii-363 p. $53 [TDig 35,154].

934 ᴱ**Borchardt** C. F. A., *Vorster* W. S., South African theological bibliography, 1. 1984; 2, 1983; 3, 1988: Studia Composita 1-3. Pretoria, Univ. 426 p.; 304 p.; 534 p. $15.30; $18.30; $33 surface mail. 0-86981-322-6; 300-5; 535-0.

935 *Bueno de la Fuente* Eloy, ¿Redescubrimiento de los laicos o de la Iglesia? Boletín bibliográfico 1985-1987: RET 48 (1988) 213-249.

936 Bulletin, Secretariatus pro Non-Christianis, Index = 22,2 (1987) 161-217.

937 **Buonocore** Marco, Bibliografia dei fondi manoscritti della Biblioteca Vaticana (1968-1980) 1986 → 2,702: ᴿGnomon 60 (1988) 540-3 (H. *Walter*: unverzichtbar).

938 CAMPBELL: *Roberts* R. L., Dissertations on Alexander Campbell: RestQ 30 (1988) 169 ... [+ 67-168, 9 articles on him: ZIT 88,672].

939 *Castillo Caballero* Dionisio, El tema del ateismo en los años [1950-1967] 1968-1987: NatGrac [15 (1968) 265-284; 16 (1969) 87-102] 35 (1988) 7-63.

940 ᴱ**Cohen** Susan S., Antisemitism, an annotated bibliography, I (1984-5): Social Science 366. NY 1987, Garland. xxix-392. $47 [TDig 35,52].

941 ᴱ**Cress** Elizabeth J. & Donald A., A guide to rare and out-of-print [15th-19th century] books in the [St. Louis university, 21 of its 101 microfilms] Vatican film library; an author list. Lanham MD 1986, UPA. viii-269 p. $26. – ᴿRelStR 14 (1988) 367 (S. H. *Hendrix*).

942 *DeKlerk* Peter, CALVIN bibliography 1988: CalvinT 23 (1988) 195-221.

943 Efemerides Mexicana, Indice 1,1-4,12: EfMex 5,13 (1987) 172-182; Indice 5,13-15: EfMex 5,15 (1987) 497s.

944 ᴱ*Evers* Georg, Informationen über theologische Beiträge aus Afrika, Asien, Ozeanien und Lateinamerika; Zeitschriftenschau, Zusammen-fassungen ausgewählter Beiträge, Berichte über theologische Konferenzen, Autoren- und Sachregister: Theologie im Kontext 9,1s (1988). 156 p. [je]. – Now available also in English, TContext 5,1s (1988).

945 FAEHN Helge, Bibliografi: NorTTs 89 (1988) 225-235 [221-4 present. *Bloch-Hoell* N. E.: 70 årsdag].

946 *Fares* D. J., *Albistur* F., Fichero de revistas latinoamericanas [... VII. Sagrada Escritura]: Stromata 44 (1988) 551-607 [563-7].

947 ᴱ**Fenton** Thomas P., *Heffron* Mary J., Women in the Third World; a directory of resources. Maryknoll 1987, Orbis. 143 p. – ᴿColcFuJen 75 (1988) 147-9 (L. *Gutheinz* ☯); TGL 78 (1988) 449 (K. J. *Tossou*).

947* ᴱ**Gaventa** Beverly R., Critical review of books in religion [1] 1988 ['expands and enhances the existing book review sections of JAAR and JBL', without indicating whether any or all the JAAR/JBL reviews are here included beside others]. No publisher indicated, but adv. at end suggests Atlanta, Scholars. $20, no ISBN. 476 p.

948 ^EGliściński Jan [Kalinkowski Stanisław], Biuletyn patrystyczny: ColcT 58 (1988) 2,143-152 . 4,137-145 [1,127-136].

948* Granado Carmelo, Boletín de lit. antigua cristiana: EstE 63 (1988) 351-366.

949 a) Gy Pierre-Marie, Bulletin de Liturgie; – b) Bériou Nicole, Bulletin d'histoire des doctrines médiévales; pastorale et spiritualité au Moyen Âge; – c) Durand G.-M. de, Bulletin de patrologie: RSPT 72 (1988) 313-324 / 443-463 / 605-629.

950 Habilitationen / Dissertationen im akademischen Jahr 1987/88: TR 84 (1988) 509s / 511-4.

951 Häussling Angelus A., Neunheuser Burkhard, Der Gottesdienst der Kirche; Texte, Quellen, Studien: ArLtgW 30 (1988) 49-147 (425-468) [148-187, Severus E. v., in Klöstern; 188-225, Küppers K., Volksfrömmigkeit; 303-410, Brakmann H., Ostkirche; 411-425, Wisse S., nichtchristlich].

952 **Haidinger** Alois, Katalog der Handschriften des Augustiner Chorherrenstiftes Klosterneuburg, I. Cod. 1-100: ph/h Denkschrift 168. W 1983, Österr. Akad. xxvi-234 p.; 63 pl. DM 70. – ^RRHE 83 (1988) 748-750 (J. Pycke: NICOLAS de Tournai, Expositio in Lucam; Leopoldsbibel; Klosterneuburger Bibel 1310/5; AUG., HIERON....).

953 Halleux A. de, al., Elenchus bibliographicus 1987: ETL 63 (1987) 1*-542*.

954 **Hanssens** S., Tables générales, Revue d'Histoire Ecclésiastique 56 (1961) -70 (1975). Lv 1988, RHE. Fb 3000.

955 HarvTR 81 (1988) 463-477, ten year index.

955* Heiser W. C., Book List: TDig 35 (1988) 51-95. 151-195. 256-296. 339-394.

956 ^EHohlweg A., Papademetriou H., Bibliographische Notizen und Mitteilungen: ByZ 81 (1988) 97-246. ...

957 Index international des dissertations doctorales en théologie et en droit canonique présentées en 1987 [... 1986 etc.]: RTLv 19 (1988) 515-586 [p. 532-541, AT-NT, 150 titres]; 517-527, index des dissertations par institutions.

958 **Jarboe** Betty M., John & Charles WESLEY; a bibliography [4723 items; topical index]. Menuchen NJ 1987, American Theological Library Asn / Scarecrow. xv-404 p. $39.50. – ^RRelStR 14 (1988) 386 (M. R. Fraser).

959 **Jones** Charles E., Black holiness; a guide to the study of black participation in Wesleyan Perfectionist and glossolalic Pentecost movements: ATLA bibliog. 18. Metuchen NJ 1987, Scarecrow. xxxi-388 p. $35 [TDig 35,71].

960 ^EJunghans Helmar, al., LUTHERbibliographie 1987/1988: LuJb 54 (1987) 139-226 / 55 (1988) 136-212.

961 Kaminski Richard, ℗ Religious sociology bibliography of the parish (1961-1986): ColcT 58,3 (1988) 127-145.

962 **Kapsner** Oliver L., A Benedictine bibliography [universal, first since BOUILLON 1778; 2 vol. 1950 ²1962] Supplement I, author and subject part 1982 → 63,932: ^RRTAM 55 (1988) 244s (H. Sonneville).

963 Lazcano Rafael, Información bibliográfica sobre san AGUSTÍN en castellano [263 items: i. general; ii. biography; iii. works; iv. philosophy; v. psychology; vi. Bible 10 items; vii. theology; viii. spirituality; ix. monasticism; x. pastoral; xi. art; xii. actuality]: RAg 29,88s (M 1988) 235-259.

964 **Lippy** Charles, Bibliography of religion in the South. Macon GA 1985, Mercer. 498 p. $50. – ^RRExp 85 (1988) 374s (B. J. Leonard: invaluable).

965 ᴱLippy Charles H., Religious periodicals of the United States; academic and scholarly journals. Westport c. 1987, Greenwood. xix-607 p. $65. – ᴿPerspRelSt 15 (1988) 297 (W. E. *Mills*).

966 *Madec* Goulven, *al.*, Bulletin Augustinien pour 1977/1988: RÉAug 34 (1988) 316-422.

967 Mémoires de licence 1986s [31; 2 de philologie biblique]: RTLv 19 (1988) 133-5.

968 ᴱ*Mišerda* Marko, *al.*, Bibliographia sacra croatica (1982-1984): Bog-Smot 58,2s (1988) 310 p.; 2231 items.

969 Moltmann Jürgen, Bibliographie, ᴱIsing Dieter, *al.* Mü 1987, Kaiser. 77 p. DM 18 [NorTTs 89,268].

970 *Motte* Mary, *Neely* Alan, *al.*, Selected annotated bibliography: Missiology 16 (1988) 115-126. 235-246. 367-382. 494-506 (248-255, American Society of Missiology, Directory of Members).

971 **Musto** Ronald G., The peace tradition in the Catholic Church; an annotated bibliography: Social Science 339. NY 1987, Garland. xxix-590 p. $67 [TDig 35,184]. – ᴿJRelEth 16 (1988) 363s (J. T. *Johnson*).

972 Pelas revistas: REB 48 (1988) 251-6. 520-8. 761-8. 1030-5.

973 *Pöhlmann* Horst G., Zeitschriftenschau: NSys 30 (1988) 117-130. 327-339.

973* **Raffelt** Albert, Proseminar Theologie; Einführung in das wissenschaftliche Arbeiten und die theologische Bücherkunde⁴ʳᵉᵛ. FrB 1985, Herder. 192 p. – ᴿAtKap 110 (1988) 335-7 (M. *Marczewski*; gives 'Albert' as surname).

974 Recension des revues: RSPT 72 (1988) 144-176. 337-368. 481-507. 630-666 [p. 677-9, index important des pages des revues dépouillées].

975 *a*) Recent dissertations in religion [no subdivision on 'Bible', only 'Ancient Near East', 'Christian Origins' (with some 30 titles) and several on 'Judaism' (with 1-3 titles each)]: RelStR 14 (1988) 185-191. – *b*) Dissertations in Progress, some 250, not noted infra: RelStR 14 (1988) 281-7; p. 285, some 10 on OT, i.e. 'Ancient Near East' and 20 on NT, i.e. 'Christian Origins'.

976 *Röhling* Horst, Zeitschriftenschau: OstkSt 37 (1988) 67-78. 218-230 [Bibliographie, nach Kategorien: 79-104. 231-280. 349-371].

977 Salesianum 50,4 (1988) 651-814: indici generali dei volumi I-L (1939-1988), cioè ristampa del 'Contenuto' delle singole annate, con un indice di rinvio agli Autori, altro alla Materie. — No advertence at all to the voluminous and valuable book-reviews.

978 ᴱSchadel E., Bibliotheca trinitariorum [I. 1984 ⇢ 65,929 … 3,7185]; II. Register und Ergänzungsliste. Mü 1988, Saur. xxxvii-594 p. [Ecclesia Orans 6,107, E. *Salmann*].

979 *Seveso* Bruno, Libri di testo e insegnamento della teologia pastorale: TItSett 13 (1988) 257-280.

980 *Siebenrock* Roman, Mitteilungen aus dem Karl-Rahner-Archiv: ZkT 110 (1988) 310-2.

981 ᴱSnyderwine L. Thomas, Researching the development of lay leadership in the Catholic Church since Vatican II; bibliographical abstracts: Roman Catholic Studies 1. Lewiston NY 1987, Mellen. 192 p. $50 [TDig 35,290: by year from 1957 to 1986; from Gannon Univ., Erie PA].

982 Tertullianea et Cyprianea, Chronica: RÉAug 34 (1988) 284-315 (R. *Braun*).

983 [175] Tesi di Laurea discusse nel Pontificio Istituto Liturgico (1962-1987): EcOrans 4 (1987) 71-83.

984 **Theodorou** Evangelos D., ⊙ Greek theological bibliography 5 for 1981 / 6 for 1982 (both ᴱ*Anestidis*, A. S.). Athenai 1985, Theologia. xxxix-692 p. / xxxix-854 p. – ᴿTAth 54 (1988) 404-6 (V. T. *Stavridis* ⊙); 205s (P. V. *Paschos* ⊙).

984* Thèses et mémoires soutenus à l'Institut Protestant de Théologie [Montpellier] d'octobre 1985 à décembre 87: ÉTRel 63 (1988) 335s.

985 *Trevijano Etcheverría* Ramón, Bibliografía patrística hispano-luso-americana V: Salmanticensis 35 (1988) 373-405.

986 Université catholique de Louvain, Travaux de doctorat en théologie et droit canonique, NS 9 (LvN 1987). 12 dissertations, résumé souvent reprint, pagination particulière à chacune.

986* *Vavřinek* Vladimir, Bibliographie: BySlav 40 (1988) 78-183 . 255-320.

987 **Wells** A. F., Bibliography on mission studies: IntRMiss 77 (1988) 146-166 . 285-306 . 460-480 . 571-590.

988 ᴱ**Welzig** Werner, Katalog gedruckter deutschsprachiger katholischer Predigtsammlungen II: Szb W 484*a*, 1987 ➤ 3,1071; 3. 7001-0642-4. – ᴿJEH 39 (1988) 488s (G. F. *Nuttall*); ZkT 110 (1988) 371s (H. B. *Meyer*).

989 *a*) ᴱ*Weron* Eugeniusz, ❷ Biuletyn teologii laikatu; – *b*) ᴱ*Marcol* Alojzy, ❷ Biuletyn teologicznomoralny; – *c*) ᴱ*Nadolski* Bogusław, ❷ Biuletyn liturgyczny; – *d*) ᴱ*Kubik* Władysław, ❷ Biuletyn katechetyczny; – *e*) ᴱ*Piwowarski* Władysław, ❷ Biuletyn socjologii religii: ColcT 58 (1988): 1,113-125; 2,107-120; 3,113-124 / 2,71-87; 3,95-111; 4,87-105 / 1,89-98; 2,51-70; 3,79-93 / 1,99-112; 2,89-106; 3,79-93; 4,107-121 [123-136] / 2, 121-142; 3,125-145.

990 ZINZENDORF: **Meyer** Dietrich, *al.*, Bibliographisches Handbuch zur Zin-zendorf-Forschung. Dü 1987. xvi-636 p. – ᴿTRu 53 (1988) 321-4 (J. *Wallmann*).

A4.3 *Bibliographiae* **philologicae** *et* **generales.**

991 **Beck** Frederick A. G., Bibliography of Greek education and related topics. Sydney 1986, auct. vii-333 p.

992 *Borgna* E., *al.*, Rassegna bibliografica di storia romana: Labeo 33 (1987) 112-125 . 225-237 . 342-363 [➤ 3,1077]; non continuata nel 34 (1988).

993 *Brisson* Luc, (*Ioannidi* Hélène), PLATON 1980-1985: Lustrum 30 (1988) 11-285 (-294).

994 CHOMSKY Noam, A personal bibliography 1951-1986, ᴱ**Koerner** E. F., *Tajima* Matsuji: Sources in Linguistics 11. Amst 1986, Benjamin. xii-217 p. 90-272-1000-4. – ᴿBSLP 83,2 (1988) 26s (G. *Rebuschi*).

995 Classical and medieval philology, classical archaeology and ancient history in Sweden in the years 1986-7: Eranos 86 (1988) 175-198.

996 *Cupaiuolo* Giovanni, Notiziario bibliografico 1985/6 - 1986/7 -1987/8, by classical authors in alphabetical order: BStLat 16 (1986) 270-234; 17 (1987) 355-428; 18 (1988) 281-350 (no index of modern authors); N.B. superb Rivista della Riviste, 16, 162-269; 17, 214-354; 18, 187-280.

997 *De Gregorio* Giuseppe, Indice delle testimonianze scritte citate nei volumi 1-10 di ScrCiv: ScrCiv 11 (1987) 270 p. [annata intera].

Gelfand E., *Hules* V., French feminist criticism ... literature ... bibliography 1985 ➤ 9973.

998 Gnomon: 1988 [... etc.] zu erwartende Neuerscheinungen des deutsch-sprachigen Verlagsbuchhandels: Gnomon 60 (1988) 84-94 [so jedes Jahr ...]; Bibliographische Beilage, 1, p. 1-32 nach Fasz. 1; p. 33-64 nach Fasz. 3; p. 65-96 nach Fasz. 5, p. 97-144 nach Fasz. 7.

999 KREISSIG Heinz, Bibliographie: Klio 70 (1988) 302-7.

1000 **Kren** George M., *Christakes* George, Scholars and personal computers; microcomputing in the humanities and social sciences. NY 1988, Human Sciences. 209 p. $30. – ᴿJEcuSt 25 (1988) 645 (R. *Wright*).

1001 **Lacharité** Normand, Introduction à la méthodologie de la pensée écrite. Québec 1987, Univ. xvi-235 p. $18 [TR 84,515].

1002 **La Rue** Rodrigue *al.*, Clavis/repertorium scriptorum graecorum et latinorum. Trois-Rivières 1985, Univ. Bibliothèque. LXIII-3493 p. (4 vol.). – ᴿBStLat 18 (1988) 152-8 (G. *Cupaiuolo*).

1003 *Modrzejewski* Joseph, Bibliographie de papyrologie juridique 1972-1982, IV: ArPapF 34 (1988) 79-136.

1004 Multi-Lingual Scholar (an English/Hebrew/Greek/Arabic/Russian word processor). Santa Monica CA c. 1987, Gamma. $350. – ᴿScotJT 41 (1988) 142 (Mrs. Jean *Miles*).

1004* *Packer* Margaret M., Research in Classical Studies for University degrees in Great Britain and Ireland: BInstClas 33 (1986) 143-178.

1005 *Pepe* L., *al.*, Indice generale degli anni 1948-1987: GitFg 39 (1987) 257-308.

1006 *Peters* Martin, Indogermanische Chronik 32/33: Sprache 32 (1986) 107-245 . 391-756 / 33 (1987) 125-488.

1007 *Pirenne-Delforge* Vinciane, Revue des revues [... à Liège 1986s]: Kernos 1 (1988) 265-271.

1008 Les provinces hellénophones de l'Empire romain, de Pompée au milieu du IIIᵉ siècle ap. J.-C.; Recueil bibliographique à partir des analyses du BAHR [Bullettin analytique de l'histoire romaine] (1962 à 1974). Strasbourg 1986, Univ. AECR. 515 p. 2-904337-16-4. – ᴿAntClas 57 (1988) 528; Gnomon 60 (1988) 369s (P. *Guyot*).

1009 Rassegna bibliografica [diritto romano]: Ivra 35 (1984) 251-408; indice 409-450 / 36 (1985) 239-411; indice 412-452.

1010 *Rudman* Joseph, Selected bibliography for computer courses in the humanities: CompHum 21 (1987) [235-] 245-254.

1011 **Sierra Bravo** Restituto, Tesis doctorales y trabajos de investigación científica; metodología general de su elaboración y documentación 1986 ➤ 2,799: ᴿLumenVr 37 (1988) 183s (U. *Gil Ortega*).

1012 [Software] ProDOS Gutenberg Senior Version 3.0. Scarborough ONT c. 1987, Gutenberg. $360. – ᴿJStOT 40 (1988) 118s (R. J. *Elford*: not for beginners) ➤ 4348.

1013 *Traufman* John C., 1987 survey of audio-visual materials in the classics: ClasW 80 (1986s) 245-309.

1014 **Weiss** Günter, Byzanz; kritischer Forschungs- und Literaturbericht 1963-1985: HZ Sonderheft 14. Mü 1986, Oldenburg. ix-351 p. DM 98. – ᴿMundus 24 (1988) 220-2 (A. *Böhlig*).

A4.4 *Bibliographiae* **orientalisticae.**

1015 *Balconi* Carla, *al.*, Bibliografia metodica degli studi di Egittologia e di Papirologia / Testi recentemente pubblicati: Aegyptus 68 (1988) 283-343 / 207-246.

1016 *Deller* Karlheinz, *Klengel* Horst, Keilschriftbibliographie *49.* 1987 (mit Nachträgen aus früheren Jahren): Orientalia 57,4 (1988) 1*-127*, 2000 items; 127*-135*, index nominum; 135*-143* index systematicus (by categories).

1017 **Elwell-Sutton** Lawrence P. †, Bibliographical guide to Iran. Suffolk/...
NJ 1983, Harvester/Barnes & N. xxv-462 p. $35. – ᴿJNES 47 (1988) 225
(J. R. *Perry*).

1017* **Fiey** J. M., MIDÉO, Mélanges de l'Institut Dominicain d'Études
Orientales du Caire, Tables générales 1-13 (1954-1977). Beyrouth 1980,
Librairie du Liban. – ᴿAcOrH 38 (1984) 431s (T. *Iványi*, adding contents
of 14,1980 and 15,1982).

1018 Göttinger Miszellen, Beiträge zur ägyptologischen Diskussion, Gesamt-
inhaltsverzeichnis 81-100: GöMiszÄg 104 (1988) 7-24, by authors only.

1019 ᴱ*Guzman* Diane, *Gow* Mary, Reviews of Egyptological literature, Sept.
1986-Sept. 1987 [by author's name, only of books reviewed; no key to
reviewers]: BEgSem 8 (1986s) 131-147.

1020 *Homès-Fredericq* Denyse, *Tanret* Michel, Conspectus librorum II/III/IV:
Akkadica 56 (1988) 42-46 / 57, 32-36 / 59, 30-36.

1021 *Huot* Jean-Louis, Maîtrises / Thèses soutenues récemment [1981-7, sous
sa direction], Centre d'Archéologie Orientale, Univ. Paris I: Akkadica 59
(1988) 37-39 / 39s.

1022 *Jacq* Christian, Index général de [*Zonhoven* L.] l'Annual Egyptological
Bibliography 1980. P 1987, Institut Ramsès [OIAc D88].

1023 *Loersch* Sigrid, Dokumentation über neu entdeckte Texte: ZAHeb 1,1
(1988) 138-145 [→ a217].

1023* *Martin* Geoffrey T., Current research for higher degrees in Egyptology, Coptic, and related studies in the United Kingdom, 6s [continuing
JEA]: DiscEg 2 (1985) 25s; 3 (1985) 29.

1024 *Oelsner* J., Afroasiatic linguistics, vol. 1,1-9,2, 1974-84, listing of all the
articles in 15 categories: OLZ 83 (1988) 437-9.

1025 **OIAc**: *a*) Oriental Institute Research Archives acquisitions list, ᴱ**Jones**
Charles E. Chicago 1988 (five times annually, some twenty columns of
some ten new books each, plus some ten columns of periodicals or
offprints); → 3,1107. – *b*) Dissertations on the Ancient Near East in
preparation; Dec. 13, 1988. – *c*) Chicago University Dissertations [not
listed in DissA nor available from AA Univ. Microfilms], Near Eastern
Studies (17 titles): OIAc (Dec. 1988-Jan. 1989) 16 / 22s.

1026 Oriento ❹ Index I-XXX: vol. XXX Supplement (1987) 1-32 . 40-94; N.B.
p. 33-40 contains by year the contents of Orient [-Japan] 1 (1960) - XXIII
(1987).

1027 Orientalistische Dissertationen: ZDMG 138 (1988) *27.

1028 *Thissen* Heinz-J., Demotistische Literaturübersicht XVI: Enchoria 16
(1988) 101-118.

A4.5 *Bibliographiae* **archaeologicae.**

1029 Bibliographie zu Ur- und Frühgeschichte 1987: AusgF 33 (1988)
277-313.

1030 *Calmeyer* Peter, Archäologische Bibliographie 1985/1986: ArchMIran
19 (1986) 339-353 / 20 (1987) 375-386.

1031 EILERS W. seit Fs 1967: ArchMIran 20 (1987) 11-16 (Erika *Eilers*).

1032 ᴱ*Feugère* Michel, Bibliographies thématiques en archéologie, 1-8,
Bibliographies sur l'Âge de Fer. Montagnac 1988, Mergoil [AJA 92,626].

1033 *Finney* Paul C., Early Christian art and archaeology I (A.D. 200-500); a
selected bibliography 1945-1985: SecC 6,1 (1987s) 203-238.

1034 **Hermann** Werner, *al.*, Archäologische Bibliographie 1986/1987: DAI. B
1987/8, de Gruyter. xxxvii-353 p. 0341-8308. / xxxix-451 p.

1035 *Heymann* F., *Dollfus* G., Bibliographie générale: Paléorient 11,2 (1985) 167-186; 12,2 (1986) 119-143.

1036 HINZ Walther, Bibliographie: ArchMIran 19 (1986) 9 [seit 9 (1976) 9-14] (Heidemarie *Koch*).

1037 *King* Monique, Bibliographie: Textiles anciens 66 (1988) 63-73.

1038 KIRCHNER Horst, Schriften zum 75. Gb.: PraehZts 63 (1988) 133s (H.-G. *Kohnke*).

1039 *Kümmel* Hans H., †, Kleinasien, Bibliographie: AfO 34 (1987) 336-360.

1040 *Mazza* F., *al.*, Bibliografia 16 (1.I.1987-31.XII.1987): RStFen 16 (1988) 269-287.

1041 *Müller* Walter W., Südarabien im Altertum; ausgewählte und kommentierte Bibliographie 1986: AfO 34 (1987) 361-5.

1042 EPiotrovskij B. B., Tesori d'Eurasia; 2000 anni di storia in 70 anni di Archaeologia Sovietica. Mi 1987, Mondadori. 88-04306-74-2 [OIAc D88].

1043 EPommerantz Inna, Excavations and surveys in Israel 6 (1987s) [< Hadashot Arkheologiyot, ESussman Ayala, *Greenberg* R.]. J 1987s. vii-120 p.; 49 fig.; 32 phot.; 2 maps.

1044 **Prodhomme** Jean, La préparation des publications archéologiques; réflexions, méthodes et conseils pratiques: Documents d'archéologie française 8. P 1987, Sciences de l'Homme. F 195. 2-7351-0187-8 [AJA 92,626].

1045 **Silberstein Trevisani** Susanna, Indici vol. 1-30 e supplementi: Annali dell'Istituto Italiano di Numismatica 31-35 (1988) ix + 185 (autori); 188 p. (soggetti).

1046 *Taracha* Piotr, ❷ Materials for the bibliography of classical archaeology in Poland for the years 1980-3: Archeologia 36 (Wrocław 1985) 133-170.

1047 **Willis** Lloyd A., Archaeology in Adventist literature: Diss. 7. Berrien Springs MI 1982, Andrews Univ. 0-943872-39-1 [OIAc D88].

1048 EZach Michael, Bibliographie 1985 (Nachtrag), 1986: BeiSudan 3 (1988) 167-170-221.

II. Introductio

B1   *Introductio* .1 *tota vel VT* – **Whole Bible or OT**

1049 **Anderson** B. W., Understanding the OT⁴ 1986 ⇒ 2,787; 3,1135: RHorizons 15 (1988) 379 (Rita J. *Burns*).

1050 **Augustin** Matthias, *Kegler* Jürgen, Bibelkunde des ATs, ein Arbeitsbuch 1987 ⇒ 3,1137: RErbAuf 64 (1988) 150 (L. *Opgen-Rhein*); TLZ 113 (1988) 18-20 (E.-J. *Waschke*).

1051 **Baldermann** I., Einführung in die Bibel [= ³revDie Bibel — Buch des Lernens, Uni 1946]. Gö 1988, Vandenhoeck & R. 291 p. DM 27,80. 3-525-03268-4 [BL 89,66, C. S. *Rodd*].

1052 **Barucq** A., *al.*, Scritti dell'Antico Vicino Oriente e fonti bibliche [⇒ 2,602*], TEBorgonovo Gianantonio: Piccola Enciclopedia Biblica. R 1988, Borla. 295 p. 88-263-0525-0.

1053 **Benware** P. N., Survey of the Old Testament: Everyman's Bible Commentary. Ch 1988, Moody. 267 p. $9. 0-8024-2091-5 [BL 89,7].

 Blair Edward P., The illustrated Bible handbook [= ²Abingdon Bible handbook] 1987 ⇒ 823.

1055 **Boadt** Lawrence, Reading the OT 1984 → 1,1172 ... 3,1139: ᴿHeythJ 29 (1988) 505s (G. G. *Nicol*: general level of debate inadequately represented).

1056 **Bridgland** Cyril, *Foulkes* Francis, Pocket guide to the Bible: Master Reference. DG 1987, InterVarsity. 394 p. $13 [GraceTJ 9,303].

1057 **Bruggen** J. van, Het lezen van de Bijbel; een inleiding². Kampen 1986, Kok. 174 p. – ᴿNedTTs 42 (1988) 261s (T. *Baarda*).

1058 **Buzzetti** Carlo, [→ 1110 infra] La Bibbia e la sua comunicazione 1987 → 3,1140; Lit. 9000: ᴿAsprenas 35 (1988) 178 (C. *Marcheselli-Casale*); Divinitas 32 (1988) 726s (T. *Stramare*).

1059 ᴱ**Cameron** Nigel, The challenge of evangelical theology 1987 → 3,598: ᴿThemelios 14 (1988s) 73s (T. *Baxter*).

1060 **Charpentier** E., Wegwijs in het Oude/Nieuwe Testament. Baarn 1987, Ten Have. – ᴿCollatVL 18 (1988) 118s (P. *Kevers*).

1061 **Childs** Brevard, Introduction to the OT as Scripture 1979 → 60,1279 ... 2,794: ᴿVerkF 31,1 (1986) 85s (H. *Seebass*).

1062 *Citrini* T. Scrittura: → 806, NDizTB (1988) 1447-1472.

1063 *Colpe* Carsten, Heilige Schriften: → 807, RAC 14,106 (1987) 184-223.

1064 **Craigie** Peter C. †, The Old Testament; its background, growth and content 1986 → 2,797; 3,1144: ᴿCBQ 50 (1988) 495-7 (Camilla *Burns*); Interpretation 42 (1988) 297-9 (W. E. *Lemke*).

1065 **Drane** J., Introducing the Old Testament. SF 1988, Harper & R. 352 p. $23. 0-06-062071-4 [NTAbs 32,400].

1066 **Elwell** W. A., Kleines Bibelhandbuch [Shaw pocket Bible handbook, Wheaton 1984], ᵀᴱ*Hartmann* H. Konstanz 1988, Bahn. 402 p.; (color.) ill.; maps. DM 29 [ZAW 101,456].

1067 **Fohrer** Georg, Erzähler und Propheten im Alten Testament; Geschichte der israelitischen und frühjüdischen Literatur: Spectrum. Heid 1988, Quelle & M. 332 p. DM 38. 3-494-01156-7 [BO 45,476].

1068 *a) Frerichs* Ernest S., The Jewish school of biblical studies: –*b) Yavin* H., Modern 'doxologies' in biblical research: → 3,355, ᴱ*Neusner* J., *Levine* B. A., *Frerichs* E. S., Judaic perspectives on ancient Israel 1987, 1-6 / 271-280 [+ 12 art., 9 infra (3 → 1989) < JBL 108,364].

1069 **Fuentes** Antonio, A guide to the Bible. Houston 1987, Lumen Christi. 262 p. $13. – ᴿHomP 88,12 (1987s) 84s (W. J. *Kaifer*: vade mecum for every priest).

1070 **Gillièron** Bernard, La Bible n'est pas tombée du ciel; l'étonnante histoire de sa naissance. Aubonne 1988, Moulin. 128 p. F 58.

1071 **Gottwald** Norman K., The Hebrew Bible, a socio-literary introduction 1985 → 1,1183 ... 3,1149: ᴿBA 51 (1988) 58s (G. *Herion*); Gregorianum 69 (1988) 766-770 (G. L. *Prato*); JAOS 108 (1988) 523-5 (J. A. *Soggin*); TorJT 4 (1988) 132-4 (I. *Friesen*); Vidyajyoti 52 (1988) 605s (P. M. *Meagher*).

1072 **Jacob** Edmond, L'Antico Testamento [Que sais-je? 1280, 1967], ᵀᴱ*Corsani* Bruno. Cosenza 1988, Giordano. 139 p.

1073 **Josipovici** Gabriel, The book of God; a response to the Bible. NHv 1988, Yale. xvi-350 p. $30. 0-300-04320-1 [BL 89,80, P. R. *Davies*: a literary critic well versed in exegetical writings and languages].

1074 **Kaiser** Otto, Einleitung in das AT*rev* 1984 → 65,1010; 1,1191: ᴿProtestantesimo 43 (1988) 43 (J. A. *Soggin*): ZkT 110 (1988) 91 (R. *Oberforcher*).

1075 **Laffey** Alice B., An introduction to the OT; a feminist perspective. Ph 1988, Fortress. xii-243 p. $13. 0-8006-2078-X. – ᴿTTod 45 (1988s) 506s (Carolyn J. *Pressler*: examples valuable, articulation not).

1076 **Lambiasi** Francesco, Breve introducción e la Sagrada Escritura [1985
➤ 3,1156], ᵀ*Arias* Isidro. Barc 1988, Herder. 139 p. pt. 750. 84-
254-1614-0. – ᴿActuBbg 25 (1988) 215 (R. de *Sivatte*); LumenVr 37 (1988)
442 (F. *Ortiz de Urtaran*).

1077 *a*) *Limbeck* Meinrad, Die Heilige Schrift; – *b*) *Pesch* Otto H., Das
Wort Gottes als objektives Prinzip der theologischen Erkenntnis: ➤ 800,
HbFT 4 (1988) 68-99 / 27-50.

1078 **Luke** K., TPI Companion to the Bible; I. Bible in general and Old
Testament. Bangalore 1987, Theological Publication in India. ii-228 p.
rs 28; $5. – ᴿVidyajyoti 52 (1988) 250 (P. M. *Meagher*: inexpensive
textbook of high standard).

1079 **Maillot** Alphonse, Gros plan sur l'AT — ses thèmes et ses défis.
Aubonne 1987, Moulin. 108 p. – ᴿRTPhil 120 (1988) 95 (M.-H. *La-
vanchy*).

1080 **Martins Terra** João E., Leitura da Biblia na Igreja. São Paulo 1988,
Loyola. 62 p.

1081 **Negenman** J., De wording van het Woord 1986 ➤ 3,1160: ᴿGerefTTs
88 (1988) 53s (J. *Helderman*); NedTTs 42 (1988) 247s (P. B. *Dirksen*).

1082 **Neusner** Jacob, The oral Torah; the sacred books of Judaism; an
introduction 1986 ➤ **2**,808: ᴿSalesianum 49 (1987) 551s (R. *Vicent*).

1083 *Noort* E., Een serie Exegese Oude Testament ter introductie; Omgaan
met koningen; tendenzen in de exegetische literatuur: GerefTTs [vervolg
op 79s (1979s) 'Methoden in de bijbelwetenschap'] 88 (1988) 65-81.

1084 **Ohler** Annemarie, Grundwissen Altes Testament [I. Pentateuch 1986
➤ 2,810]; [II. Dt.-Lit. 1987]; III. Propheten — Psalmen — Weisheit. Stu
1988, KBW. 152 p. DM 39. – ᴿBLtg 61 (1988) 76-78 (L. *Schwienhorst-
Schönberger*, 1); Streven 56 (1988s) 81 (P. *Beentjes*, 2); TLZ 113 (1988)
811s (V. *Hirt*, 3).

1085 **Ohler** Annemarie, Studying the OT – from tradition to canon [1972]
ᵀ*Cairns* David 1985 ➤ 1,1198 ... 3,1458: ᴿMonth 249 (1988) 776s
(Margaret *Eason*).

1085* *Petersen* David L., Hebrew Bible textbooks [introduction, not textual
criticism], a review article: ➤ 947* Critical Review 1 (1988) 1-18.

1086 *a*) [Ouvriers Jocistes, al.] Alla scoperta della Bibbia I-II, 1985 ➤ 3,558:
ᴿSalesianum 50 (1988) 415s (C. *Bissoli*). – *b*) Al soffio delle Scritture;
leggere il Vangelo con giovani studenti. T-Leumann 1987, Elle Di Ci.
160 p. Lit. 9500. – ᴿParVi 33 (1988) 73s (F. *Mosetto*).

1087 **Perkins** Pheme, Reading the New Testament; an introduction²ʳᵉᵛ
[¹c.1978]. NY 1988, Paulist. vii-350 p. $8. 0-8091-2939-6 [NTAbs 32,365].

1088 **Rendtorff** R., The OT, an introduction 1986 ➤ 1,1200 ... 3,1164 [³1988]:
ᴿComSev 21 (1988) 93 (M. de *Burgos*).

1089 *Sæbø* Magne, The history of Old Testament studies; problems of its
presentation [*Diestel* L.; *Kraus* H.-J.]: ➤ 469, Wünschet 1986/8, 3-14.

1090 *a*) *Sanders* James A., The strangeness of the Bible: – *b*) *Anderson*
Bernhard W., The dramatic movement of Scripture: UnSemQ 42,1s
(1988) 33-38 / 39-42 [< ZIT].

1091 **Schmidt** W. H., Old Testament Introduction 1984 ➤ 65,1024 ... 3,1166:
ᴿHeythJ 29 (1988) 99s (B. P. *Robinson*).

1092 **Schultz** Samuel J., The message of the Old Testament; [abridgment of]
the Old Testament speaks. SF 1986, Harper & R. 197 p.; ill. 0-06-
067135-1.

1093 **Soden** W. v., Bibel und Alter Orient: BZAW 162, 1985 ➤ 1,247; 3,1168:
ᴿJTS 39 (1988) 550-2 (J. A. *Emerton*).

1094 **Soggin** J. Alberto, Introduzione all'AT[4] 1987 [[3]1979] → 3,1169:   [R]Angelicum 65 (1988) 600s (B. G. *Boschi*); Antonianum 63 (1988) 172-4 (M. *Nobile*); BL (1988) 91 (P. R. *Davies*); CC 139 (1988,3) 96s (G. L. *Prato*); EstBíb 46 (1988) 412s (J. M. *Abrego*: overlooks Spanish works, but no more than Spanish periodicals overlooked his first edition); ParVi 33 (1988) 469s (Anna *Passoni Dell'Acqua*); RB 95 (1988) 614 (R. J. *Tournay*); Protestantesimo 43 (1988) 204s (D. *Garrone*); RivB 36 (1988) 411-414 (L. *Monari*: nessuna critica, solo allargamento degli obiettivi).

1095 [E]**Szlaga** Jan, ℗ Wstęp ogólny ... General introduction to Holy Scripture. Poznań 1986, Pallottinum.   332 p. – [R]ColcT 58,4 (1988) 167s (J. *Warzecha*).

1096 **Taylor** Justin, As it was written 1987 → 3,1171: [R]RB 95 (1988) 443 (J.-M. de *Tarragon*: traduire!).

1097 **Vischer** Wilhelm, L'Écriture et la Parole 1985 → 2,230: [R]CBQ 50 (1988) 161s (S. B. *Marrow*).

1098 [E]**Woude** A. S. van der, Inleiding tot de studie van het Oude Testament 1986 → 3,1163; *f* 35,50: [R]GerefTTs 88 (1988) 43-45 (C. *Houtman*).

1099 **Zeilinger** Albert, Das Alte Testament verstehen [I. 1986] II. Von Josua bis Maleachi; die Geschichte und Prophetie Israels; III. Der Psalter und die Weisheitsbücher Israels, mit grundsätzlichen systematischen Überlegungen und geschichtlichen Informationen, Einführung, Auslegung und Anleitung zur Praxis de Glaubens. Bibel-Kirche-Gemeinde 24s.   Konstanz 1987s, Christliche VA. 316 p.; 334 p. je DM 24,50 [TLZ 113,813].

B1.2   'Invitations' to Bible or OT.

1100 **Anderson** Bernhard W.,   The unfolding drama of the Bible[3] [[1]1952: [2]1971]. Ph 1988, Fortress.   93 p. $5 pa. [TDig 35,258].

1101 **Bagot** Jean-Pierre, *Dubs* Jean-Claude, Pour lire la Bible.[5] P 1988, Bergers/Mages. 205 p. F 50. 2-85304-061-5.

1102 **Bagot** J.-F., *Dubs* J. C., Para leer la Biblia, [T]*Darrícal* N. Estella 1987. V. Divino. 204 p. – [R]NatGrac 34 (1987) 427s (M. *González*).

1103 **Barbiero** Flavio, La Bibbia senza segreti: Orizzonti della Storia. Mi 1988, Rusconi. 467 p. 88-18-88005-3.

1104 *a) Barr* James, The theological case against biblical theology; – *b) Petersen* David L., Israel and monotheism; the unfinished agenda: → 25, [F]CHILDS B., Canon 1988, 3-19 / 92-107.

1105 **Beauchamp** Paul, Parler d'Écritures Saintes 1987 → 3,1177: [R]ArTGran 51 (1988) 284 (A. *Segovia*); RThom 88 (1988) 650s (L. *Devillers*: style plus facile); ScripTPamp 20 (1988) 913s (V. *Balaguer*); VieCons 60 (1988) 188s (J.-P. *Sonnet*).

1106 *a) Bergant* Dianne / *b) McIlhone* James P., Ten questions about the Bible / the NT: ChSt 25,3 ('100 questions', 10 each about Christology, Church history, canon law, etc., 1986) 313-320 / 321-9.

1107 **Boa** Kenneth, The Open Bible companion; a supplement for your Bible study. Nv 1986, Nelson. 93 p.; ill. [KirSef 61,393].

1108 **Bohlen** Reinhold, Geschichte vom Wort Gottes; Einführung in die hl. Schrift. Aschaffenburg 1985, Pattloch. 128 p.; ill. DM 34. – [R]ErbAuf 64 (1988) 68 (L. *Opgen-Rhein*).

1109 **Brisebois** M., Métodos para leer mejor la Biblia. M 1987, Paulinas. 108 p. – [R]BibFe 14 (1988) 322 (M. *Sáenz Galache*).

1110 **Buzzetti** Carlo, La Biblia y sus transformaciones, [T]*Ortiz García* A. Estella 1986, VDivino. 143 p. – [R]NatGrac 34 (1987) 429 (D. *Castillo*).

1111 **Daleau** C.,   La Bible, les livres en résumé. P 1988, Téqui.   88 p. F 33 [RThom 88,523].

1112 **Delhez** Charles,   Apprendre à lire la Bible.   Kinshasa 1986, St-Paul. 160 p. – ᴿTéléma 14,55s (1988) 91-94 (R. *Capoen*).

1113 *Donáth* László, Ⓜ It is not yet over (On the Alef books; Bible and Judaism for children and other Hungarians); Theologiai Szemle 31 (1988) 127s and back cover.

1114 **Duhaime** J.-L. [VT], *Couturier* G. [profetas], *Martucci* J. [sabios], *Guillemette* P. [evv.], *Genest* O. [Pablo], La Biblia, libro para hoy. M 1987, Paulinas.   156 p. – ᴿBibFe 14 (1988) 153s (M. *Sáenz Galache*).

1115 **Edwards** Paul,   People of the Book 1987 ➤ 3,1183:   ᴿMonth 249 (1988) 557s (Claire Jane *Elliot*: many chapters were Month articles).

1116 *Fang* Mark, Ⓒ Vatican II and the Bible reading movement: ColcFuJen 75 (1988) 35-44.

1117 **Hall** Thelma,   Too deep for words; rediscovering Lectio Divina.   NY 1988, Paulist.   v-110 p. $5.   0-8091-2959-0.

1118 **Kaiser** Walterᴶ,   Hard Sayings of the Old Testament. DG/Leicester 1988, Inter-Varsity.   259 p. [JBL 107,788].

1119 **Kaiser** Walter C.ᴶ,   Toward rediscovering the Old Testament 1987 ➤ 3,1187:   ᴿGraceTJ 9 (1988) 145-7 (R. E. *Averbeck*).

1120 ᴱ**Klopfenstein** M. A., *al.,*   Mitte der Schrift? 1985/7 ➤ 3,549:   ᴿProtestantesimo 43 (1988) 215 (J. A. *Soggin*).

1121 *Laurenzi* Maria Cristina,   Tempo discontinuo e fede biblica: HumBr 43 (1988) 744-754.

1122 *Livio* Jean-Bernard,   La Bible, un lieu de formation permanente: Tychique 66 (1987) 49-52.

1122* **Lohfink** Gerhard,   Enfin je comprends la Bible! Un livre sur la critique des formes [1973 ➤ 55,503, wrongly in 3,1157], ᵀ*Neipp* Bernadette: Essais Bibliques 14.   Genève 1987, Labor et Fides.   152 p. [RThom 89,477, L. *Devillers*].

1123 **Lys** Daniel,   Treize énigmes de l'Ancien Testament; le livre, le peuple, le message [l'espace et le temps; l'existence et le néant...]. Initiations. P 1988, Cerf.   261 p. F 138.   2-204-02891-6. – ᴿÉTRel 63 (1988) 630 (*ipse*); Protestantesimo 43 (1988) 205 (J. A. *Soggin*: anche i temi più soliti come Lega tribale, geografia, rivelazione ... a un livello assolutamente superiore).

1124 **Martin** George,   Leggere la Scrittura come parola di Dio; approcci e atteggiamenti pratici: Meditazioni bibliche 10.   Mi 1979, O. R.   175 p. – ᴿRivLtg 75 (1988) 143s (G. *Crocetti*).

1125 *Martin* Gerhard M.,   Mehrdimensionaler Umgang mit der Bibel in Handlungsfeldern der Praktischen Theologie: VerkF 31,2 (1986) 34-46.

1126 **Martini** Carlo M.,   Il pane per un popolo; meditazioni alla Scuola della Parola: Centro Ambrosiano.   CasM 1987, Piemme.   96 p. – ᴿDivinitas 32 (1988) 727 (T. *Stramare*).

1127 **Mattill** A. J.,   The art of reading the Bible.   Gordo AL 1988, Flatwoods.   41 p. $2 [NTAbs 32,364].

1128 **Mettinger** T. N. D.,   Namnet och Närvaron; Gudsnamn och Gudbild i Böckernas Bok [The name and the presence; names of God and ideas about God in the Book of Books; ➤ 2476s]. Örebro 1987, Libris.   222 p. Sk 260.   91-7194-497-4 [BL 89,110, B. *Albrektson*: admirable popularization].

1129 *Miller* Patrick D.ᴶ,   The way of Torah: PrincSemB 8,3 (1987) 17-32 [< ᴢɪᴛ].

1130 ᴱNeusner Jacob, *al.* [→ 1068; 3,355], Judaic perspectives on ancient Israel [14 essays such that no one would know came from a Jew]. Ph Fortress. $35. – ᴿCurrTL 15 (1988) 380 (R. W. *Klein*: ecumenically important, but also original: neglected passages; 'Why Jews are not interested in biblical theology').

1131 **Noakes** Susan, Timely reading; between exegesis and interpretation. Ithaca NY 1988, Cornell Univ. xvii-249 p.; front. 0-8014-2144-6.

1132 **Oden** Robert A., The Bible without theology; the theological tradition and alternatives to it 1987 → 3,269: ᴿBR 4,4 (1988) 8 (F. R. *Brandfon*); JAAR 56 (1988) 815s (S. *Niditch*).

1134 *O'Grady* J. F., The Bible as a classic [*Brueggemann* W. 1987; *Achtemeier* P. 1987; *Collins* R. 1986: will help persons of faith to return to an understanding of their own faith]: ChSt 27,1 (1988) 96-108 [NTAbs 32,294.

1135 *Premnath* D. N., The Old Testament against its cultural background, and its implications for theological education: AsiaJT 2,1 (1988) 98-105.

1136 *Ravasi* Gianfranco, L'esperienza religiosa nella Bibbia, I. Alla sorgente del fiume; II. Il fiume di Dio: RClerIt 63 (1987) 28-35 . 96-105.

1137 **Rohr** Richard, *Martos* Joseph, The great themes of Scripture [OT 1987 → 3,1200] New Testament. Cincinnati 1988, St. Anthony Messenger. xi-178 p. $7 [TDig 35,286].

1138 **Simone** R. T., *Sugarman* R. I., Reclaiming the humanities; the roots of self-knowledge in the Greek and biblical worlds. Lanham MD 1986, UPA. viii-214 p. $27.25; pa. $10.25. 0-8191-5093-2; 4-0 [NTAbs 32,398].

1139 **Storniolo** Ivo, *Balancin* Euclides M., Conozca la Biblia: Vida y Crecimiento 3. Florida ARG 1988, Paulinas. 207 p. 950-09-0706-2.

1140 **Stuart** Douglas, Favorite Old Testament passages, a popular commentary for today. Ph 1985, Westminster. 130 p. $9. – ᴿCBQ 50 (1988) 515s (R. L. *Hayden*).

1141 **Wypych** Stanisław, ❷ Wprowadzenie w myśl i wezwanie ... Introduction to the thought and appeal of the biblical books, I. Pentateuch. Wsz 1987, Akad. Teol. Kat. 212 p. zł 520. – ᴿAtKap 110 (1988) 332-5 (D. *Tomczyk*).

1142 **Zuidema** W., Op zoek naar Tora; verkenningen in de rabbijnse traditie. Baarn 1987, Ten Have. 139 p. Fb 450. – ᴿCollatVL 18 (1988) 115s (R. *Hoet*).

B1.3 *Paedagogia biblica* – **Bible-teaching techniques.**

1143 **Asheim** Ivar, *Mogstad* Sverre D., Religionspedagogikk; tolkning, undervisning, oppdragelse. Oslo 1987, Univ. 198 p. Nk 160. – ᴿNorTTs 89 (1988) 212-220 (Sigurd *Hjelde*).

1144 **Baudler** Georg, Kindern heute Gott erschliessen 1986 → 3,1206: ᴿLebZeug 42,1 (1987) 83-85 (B. *Neumann*).

1145 **Branham** Bill, Scripture memory [60 biblical verses in various English translations for mastering Navigator's Topical Memory System (computer)]. Dallas c.1987, MVP Software. $35. – ᴿRExp 85 (1988) 144 (J. E. *Dent*).

1146 **Bubolz** Georg, Wege zu Jesus – Sekundarstufe. Hirschgraben 1986, CVK. 136 p. DM 12,80. 3-454-14130-3. – ᴿBiKi 43 (1988) 88s (R. *Hoppe*).

1147 **Cowgill** Carol, *Campbell* James, Christ yesterday and today [workbook for adult learners]. Rockford IL 1986, TEL. 141 p. $10. – ᴿRRel 46 (1987) 150s (Fara *Impastato*).

1148 **Fuentes** Antonio, A guide to the Bible [for adult study groups]. Houston 1987, Lumen Christi.   262 p. $13 [BToday 26,184].

1149 **Glavich** sr. Mary Kathleen, Leading students into Scripture. Mystic CT 1987, Twenty-third.   xi-100 p. $10 [CBQ 50,165].

1150 **Gutsche** F., *al.,* Die Bibel kennen, 30 Arbeitsblätter. Gö 1986, VR. 136 p. DM 24. – ᴿPrakT 14 (1987) 107s (F. H. *Kuiper*).

1151 *Hafemann* Scott J., Seminary, subjectivity, and the centrality of Scripture; reflections on the current crisis in evangelical seminary education: JEvTS 31 (1988) 129-144 [< ᴢɪᴛ 88,588].

1152 **Kloos** Heribert, *al.,* The Youth Bible, ᵀ*Molestina* Teresa. Estella 1986, VDivino. 158 p. – ᴿScripB 19 (1988s) 20s (J. C. *Conroy*).

1153 **Krych** Margaret A., Teaching the Gospel today. Minneapolis 1987, Augsburg.   173 p. $11 pa. – ᴿCurrTM 15 (1988) 600 (R. *Conrad*).

1154 ᴱ**Langer** Wolfgang, Handbuch der Bibelarbeit 1987 ➤ 3,349: ᴿBiKi 43 (1988) 184s (E. *Bons*); TPQ 136 (1988) 289s (M. *Scharer*).

1155 **Martins Terra** J. E., A Biblia na evangelização do Brasil. São Paulo 1988, Loyola. 103 p.

1156 **Monschouwer** D., Gevierde Schrift [... 12 themas]; systematische leesoefeningen in een Amsterdams leerhuis. Kampen 1987, Kok. 173 p. ƒ 26,50. – ᴿCollatVʟ 18 (1988) 489 (R. *Hoet*); PrakT 14 (1987) 596 (A. van *Diemen*).

1157 **Morrison** Mary C., Approaching the Gospels together; a leader's guide for group Gospels study. Wallingford PA 1986, Pendle Hill. xiii-160 p. $11. – ᴿAnglTR 70 (1988) 103s (I. T. *Kaufman*).

1158 *Osmer* Richard R., The study of Scripture in the congregation; old problems and new programs: Interpretation 42 (1988) 254-267.

1159 *Pereira* Jude S., The Bible and the pastor of today: Word and Worship 21 (1988) 23-26 [< TKontext 10,53].

1160 **Prinz** J., Die Geschichten der Bibel [bis 1 Kön 11] für Kinder erzählt. Fra 1988 = 1934, Athenäum.   214 p.; ill. Wallenberg H. DM 38 [ZAW 100,464].

1161 *Ritter* Werner H., Auf dem Weg zu einer neuzeitlichen Religionspädagogik: TLZ 113 (1988) 785-800.

1162 **Romaniuk** Kazimierz, ❷ Biblia lepiej rozumiana ... The Bible better understood in pastoral transmission. Wsz 1988, Marki-Struga. 120 p.

1163 **Schoneveld** Jacobus, Die Bibel in der israelischen Erziehung 1987 ➤ 3,1231: ᴿÖkRu 37 (1988) 386-9 (L. *Klein*).

1164 **Standaert** B., De drie pijlers van de wereld; bijbels meedenken met de nieuwe evangelisering. Lannoo 1987, Tielt. 180 p. Fb 585. – ᴿCollatVʟ 18 (1988) 493s (J. De *Kesel*).

1165 *Talkenberger* Wolf-Dietrich, Bibelwoche und Gemeindeaufbau: Standpunkt 15 (B 1987) 289-292 [< ᴢɪᴛ].

1166 **Turrado** Lorenzo, Pequeña historia de un breve pasaje (nᵒ. 17) [(schema); displicet quia sub nomine NT tractat sola Evangelia] de la Constitución 'Dei Verbum' del Concilio Vaticano II: Salmanticensis 35 (1988) 369-372.

1167 **Untergassmair** Franz G., *Kappes* Michael, Zum Thema 'Wie wörtlich ist die Bibel zu verstehen?': 1987 ➤ 3,1234: ᴿBLtg 61 (1988) 139s (T. *Söding*); TGʟ 78 (1988) 92s (K. *Backhaus*: nach ᴄᴏɴᴢᴇʟᴍᴀɴɴ lebt die Kirche faktisch davon, dass die Ergebnisse der exegetischen Forschung in ihr nicht publik werden).

1168 *Vaggi* Giulia, Bibbia e catechesi: Humanitas 42 (Brescia 1987) 286-290.

1169 **Vogt** Theophil,   Bibelarbeit 1985 ➤ 2,870; 3,1235:   RLebZeug 42,3 (1987) 77s (A. *Weiser*); TR 84 (1988) 144s (E. *Sturm*).

1170 *Weinrich* M.,   Das Schriftprinzip und der Unterricht; systematisch-theologische Überlegungen zu einer didaktischen Verlegenheit: Pastoraltheologie 77 (Gö 1988) 292-305 [< ZIT 88,560].

1171 World Catholic Federation for the Biblical Apostolate criteria for the basis and direction of the biblical apostolate: Word and Worship 21 (Bangalore 1988) 51-64.

1172 *Yeatts* John R.,   Variables related to recall of the English Bible; comprehensibility, structural importance, meaningfulness, interest, specificity of denotation and abstractness-concreteness: JScStRel 27 (1988) 593-608 [< ZIT 89,282].

B2.1   **Hermeneutica.**

1173 *a) Abraham* William J.,   Intentions and the logic of interpretation; – *b) Gill* Jerry H.,   Mediated meaning; a contextualist approach to hermeneutical method: AsbTJ 43,1 (1988) 11-25 / 27-41.

1174 **Alonso Schökel** Luis,   Hermenéutica de la Palabra I. 1986 ➤ 2,874; II. Interpretación literaria de textos bíblicos [12 reprints 1964-86] 1987 ➤ 3,178:   RActuBbg 25 (1988) 57s (X. *Alegre* S., 1) 206 (R. de *Sivatte,* 2); BL (1988) 100 (P. R. *Ackroyd*, 1: sensitivity and poetic feeling); CiuD 201 (1988) 490 (J. *Gutiérrez,* 1); OTAbs 11 (1988) 192 (J. I. *Hunt,* 2: reprints, now all in Spanish; titles here all in English, with pp.).

1175 **Alonso Schökel** Luis,   La Palabra Inspirada³ 1986 ➤ 2,875; 3,1241: RCiuD 201 (1988) 489s (J. *Gutiérrez*).

1177 **Barr** James,   Sémantique du langage biblique [1961; T*Auscher* D., *Prignaud* J. ¹1971]²: Initiations.   P 1988, Cerf. viii-344 p. 2-204-02857-6. – RRÉJ 147 (1988) 444s (C. *Aslanoff*); RTLv 19 (1988) 495 (J. *Ponthot*).

1178 **Baxter** A.,   John CALVIN's use and hermeneutics of the OT: diss. Sheffield 1987. 459 p. British Library DX 82807. – DissA 49 (1988s) 1946-A.

1179 *a) Bergen* Robert D.,   Text as a guide to authorial intention; an introduction to discourse criticism: JEvTS 30 (1987) 327-336; – *b) Watson* Nigel,   Authorial intention — suspect concept for biblical scholars?: ➤ 112, FOSBORN E., AustralBR 35 (1987) 6-13 [< ZIT].

1180 **Betti** Emilio,   Zur Grundlegung einer allgemeinen Auslegungslehre [Teoria generale 1955 ➤ 3,1244]. Tü 1988 Mohr. 98p. 3-16-24350-X.

1181 *Brandmüller* Walter,   L'insegnamento dei concili sulla corretta interpretazione delle Sacre Scritture fino al Concilio Vaticano I: AnnTh 2 (R 1988) 207-259.

1182 ECarson J. A.,   *Woodbridge* John D., Hermeneutics, authority and canon 1986 ➤ 2,240:   RRB 95 (1988) 423 (F. *Langlamet*: tit. pp.); RefTR 46 (1987) 50s (P. *O'Brien*).

1183 ECasciaro J. M.,   Biblia y hermenéutica, VII simposio, Navarra [abril 1985] 1986 ➤ 2,366*: REstBib 46 (1988) 125-8 (J. M. *Sánchez Caro*).

1184 **Chmiel** Jerzy, ❷ De narrationibus biblicis *genologiczne* ('resp. ejdologiczne'; origo, non genealogia) et hermeneutice: ➤ 475, RuBi 41 (1988) 44-51.

1185 **Corrington** Robert S.,   The community of interpreters; on the hermeneutics of nature and the Bible in the American philosophical tradition [C. S. *Peirce*; J. *Royce*]: Studies in American Biblical

Hermeneutics 3. Macon GA 1987, Mercer Univ. xiii-109 p. $35 [RelStR 15,351, P. *Mullins*]. 0-86554-284-8.

1186 **Cowley** Roger W., Ethiopian biblical interpretation; a study in exegetical tradition and hermeneutics: Oriental Publ. 38. C 1988, Univ. xvi-490 p. 0-521-35219-3.

1187 **Croatto** J. Severino, Biblical hermeneutics; toward a theory of reading as the production of meaning 1987 → 3,1252: ᴿHorBT 10,2 (1988) 83-85 (R. *Polzin*); NewTR 1,3 (1988) 95s (D. *Bergant*); RExp 85 (1988) 730-2 (C.J *Scalise*: perpetuates the myth of Jamnia, downplays centrality of Christ).

1188 **Diel** Paul, ᴱ*Diel* Jane, The God-Symbol, its history and its significance [La divinité], ᵀ*Marans* Nelly. SF 1986, Harper & R. 194 p. 0-06-254805-0 [this ISBN and also the French title not identical with → 2,889; 3,1255].

1189 **Dunnett** Walter M., The interpretation of Holy Scripture; issues, principles, models 1984 → 1,1306; 2,889*: ᴿCalvinT 23 (1988) 118 (P.L. *Bremer*).

1190 *Elata-Alster* Gerda, *Salmon* Rachel. Vertical and horizontal readings of the biblical text; an application of JAKOBSON's metaphor-metonymy model: LingBib 60 (1988) 31-59.

1191 *Evdokimov* Paul, Principes de l'herméneutique orthodoxe: Contacts 38 (1986) 289-306 / 39 (1987) 61-67. 127-135 / 40 (1988) 69-72 ...

1192 **Ferguson** D.S., Biblical hermeneutics, an introduction 1987 → 2,891: ᴿBL (1988) 103s (F.F. *Bruce*).

1193 **Fishbane** Michael, Biblical interpretation in ancient Israel 1985 → 1,1308 ... 3,1359: ᴿBO 44 (1987) 752-7 (P. *Höffken*); Carthaginensia 4 (1988) 366 (R. *Sanz Valdivieso*); Henoch 10 (1988) 106s (E. *Jucci*); HeythJ 29 (1988) 504s (J. *Blenkinsopp*); SWJT 31,2 (1988s) 55s (E.E. *Ellis*).

1193* *Fowl* Stephen, The ethics of interpretation or What's left over after the elimination of meaning [*Hirsch* E. 1967; *Schüssler Fiorenza* Elisabeth 1988]: → 500, SBL Seminars 1988, 69-81.

Fraigneau-Julien B., Les sens spirituels ... SYMÉON 1985 → k40.

1194 **Froehlich** Karlfried, Biblical interpretation in the early Church [IRE-NAEUS, ORIGEN, DIODORE ... selections translated] 1984 → 65,1135: ᴿAsbTJ 43,2 (1988) 140s (D. *Bundy*).

Ganoczy A., *Scheld* S., Die Hermeneutik CALVINS 1983 → k145*.

1195 *Gerhart* Mary, Genric [sic, p. iii and 41 in footnote to p. 29; but title has Generic] competence in biblical hermeneutics: → 304, Semeia 43 (1988) 29-44; 45-51 response, *Detweiler* Robert, 'How to read a jaguar'.

1196 *Germain* Yves, Du symbolisme dans les Écritures: PenséeC 234 (1988) 67-69.

1197 *Gerstenberger* Erhard, Der Realitätsbezug alttestamentlicher Exegese: ZeichZt 42 (1988) 144-8 [< ZIT 88,612].

1198 *Gisel* Pierre, Esprit et Écriture, ou comment dépasser certains héritages protestants: Hokhma 37 (1988) 25-42; 43-50, réaction de *Kocher* Michel.

1199 *Givone* Sergio, Poesia e interpretazione della Bibbia: → 472, AnStEseg 5 (1988) 7-17; 19-37, discussione (*Bolgiani* Franco, *al.*).

1200 **Graham** William A., Beyond the written word; oral aspects of scripture in the history of religion. NY 1987, Cambridge-UP. xiv-406 p. $32.50 [TDig 35,168].

1201 **Grech** P., Ermeneutica e teologia biblica 1986 → 2,166: ᴿEuntDoc 41 (1988) 496-8 (P. *Miccoli*).

1202 **Groves** Joseph W., Actualization and interpretation in the OT ᴰ1987 ➤ 3,1263: ᴿETL 64 (1988) 455 (J. *Lust*).

1203 **Gunneweg** A. H. J., Comprendere l'Antico Testamento, un'ermeneutica 1986 ➤ 2,897; 3,1265: ᴿProtestantesimo 43 (1988) 203s (R. *Casonato*: scorrevole).

1204 *Hamilton* G. J., Divino afflante Spiritu; Catholic interpretation of Scripture: CanadCathR 6,5 (1988) 171-6 [< NTAbs 32,285].

1205 *Hart* Larry, Hermeneutics, theology and the Holy Spirit: PerspRelSt 14,4 (1987) 53-64 [< ZIT 88,447].

1206 *Jacobsen* Douglas, From truth to authority to responsibility; the shifting focus of evangelical hermeneutics, 1915-1986: TFS Bulletin 10 (March/May 1987) 8-15 / 10-14 [< BS 145 (1988) 215s (E. H. *Johnson*)].

1207 *Jeanrond* Werner G., Hermeneutics and Christian praxis; some reflections on the history of hermeneutics: Literature and Theology 2 (Ox 1988) 174-188 [< ZIT 88,741].

1208 **Kamin** Sarah, ❹ *Peśûtô* ... The literal sense of Scripture and scriptural midrash. J 1986, Hebrew Univ. 297 p. – ᴿBethM 32,111 (1986s) 387-9 (M. *Śaśar* ❹).

1209 **Keegan** T. J., Interpreting the Bible; a popular introduction to biblical hermeneutics 1985 ➤ 1,1319 ... 3,1268: ᴿRB 95 (1988) 126s (B. T. *Viviano*).

1210 *Klauck* H. J., Allegorese: ➤ 804, NBL Lfg 1 (1988) 75-77.

1211 ᴱ**Klemm** David E., Hermeneutical inquiry 1-2 [... *Bultmann*; *Perrin*] 1986 ➤ 3,348: ᴿTS 49 (1988) 158-160 (R. F. *Scuka*).

1212 *Kossen* P., Interpreting and applying Scriptures: VoxRef 50 (1988) 3-38 [39-47, *Gardner* G. G., Archaeology as a tool; < GerefTTs 88 (1988) 261].

1213 **Kugel** James L., *Greer* Rowan A., Early biblical interpretation: [ᴱ*Meeks* W.] Library of early Christianity 3, 1985 ➤ 2,905; 3,1270: ᴿJRel 67 (1987) 538s (Carol *Newsom*: Kugel is on Judaism but not fully enough).

1214 *La Fargue* Michael, Are texts determinate? DERRIDA, BARTH and the role of the biblical scholar: HarvTR 81 (1988) 341-357.

1215 *a*) *La Potterie* Ignace de, Interpretation of the Holy Scripture in the spirit in which it was written (Dei Verbum 12c), ᵀ*Wearne* Leslie; – *b*) *Vanni* Ugo, Exegesis and actualization in the light of *Dei Verbum*, ᵀ*Wearne*: ➤ 380, Vatican II Assessment 1 (1988) 220-266 / 344-363; français ➤ 379, Bilan 1,235-276 / 351-369.

1216 **Larkin** William J.ᴶ, Culture and biblical hermeneutics; interpreting and applying the authoritative Word in a relativistic age. GR 1988, Baker. 401 p. [JBL 108,568].

1217 **Laurant** J.-P., Symbolisme et Écriture; le cardinal PITRA et la 'Clef' de MÉLITON de Sardes; préf. *Poulat* E.: Patrimoines Christianisme 1. P 1988, Cerf. 368 p. – ᴿRBén 98 (1988) 410 (D. *Misonne*).

1218 *Lindhardt* Jan, Metaforens væsen: DanTTs 51 (1988) 112-125 [< ZIT 88,512].

1219 *a*) *Liwak* Rüdiger, Literary individuality as a problem of hermeneutics in the Hebrew Bible; – *b*) *Banitt* Menahem, Exegesis or metaphrasis; – *c*) *Hoffman* Yair, The technique of quotation and citation as an interpretive device: ➤ 505, Creative 1985/8, 89-101 / 13-29 / 71-79.

1220 *Long* B. O., Ätiologie: ➤ 804, NBL Lfg 1 (1988) 58s.

1221 *Long* Thomas G., Committing hermeneutical heresy: TTod 44 (1987s) 165-9.

1222 **McHann** James C.J, The three horizons; a study in biblical hermeneutics with special reference to W. PANNENBERG: diss. Aberdeen. 1987. 507 p. BRDX-84498. – DissA 49 (1988s) 3390-A.

1223 ᴱ**McKim** Donald K., A guide to contemporary hermeneutics 1986 ➤ 2,258; 3,1274: ᴿEvQ 60 (1988) 348s (C. *Brown*); Salesianum 50 (1988) 425s (R. *Vicent*).

1224 *Macky* Peter W., *a)* The multiple purposes of biblical speech acts: PrincSemB 8,2 (1987) 50 ... [< ZIT]; – *b)* Exploring the depths of artistic biblical metaphors [ch. 11 of his forthcoming Metaphor in the Bible]: ProcGLM 8 (1988) 167-176.

1225 *McNamara* Martin, Midrash, culture medium and development of doctrine; some facts in quest of a terminology: PrIrB 11 (1988) 67-87.

1226 *Macuch* Rudolf, Les bases philologiques de l'herméneutique et les bases herméneutiques de la philologie chez les Samaritains: ➤ 497, Samarit. 1985/8, 149-158.

1227 *a)* *Marrion* M., Biblical hermeneutics in the Regula Benedicti; – *b)* *Kardong* T.G., The devil in the rule of the Master: Studia Monastica 30,1 (Barc 1988) 17-40 / 41-62 [< ZIT 88,770].

1228 **Mayhue** Richard, How to interpret the Bible for yourself [... avoid 15 pitfalls: prooftexting, spiritualizing, overliteralizing ...]. Ch 1986, Moody. 183 p. $4. – ᴿBS 145 (1988) 224s (R. B. *Zuck*).

1229 **Milano** Andrea, Rivelazione e ermeneutica. Urbino 1988, Quattro Venti. 176 p. Lit. 20.000. – ᴿHumBr 43 (1988) 906s (F. *Bertoldi*).

1230 **Molina Palma** Mario A., La interpretación de la Escritura en el Espiritu [diss. ᴰ*La Potterie* I. de] 1987 ➤ 3,1277: ᴿAngelicum 65 (1988) 604-6 (J. *García Trapiello*); Gregorianum 69 (1988) 568s (M. *Ruiz Jurado*); RivB 36 (1988) 126 (A. *Bonora*).

1231 **Morgan** R. (*Barton* J.), Biblical interpretation: Oxford Bible Series. Ox 1988, UP. ix-342 p. £9. 0-19-213257-1 [BL 89,88, R. *Davidson*: mandatory; p. 296 wisely 'The risk of getting it wrong is a condition of all interpretation and all comunication'].

ᴱ**Mulder** Martin J., [*Sysling* H.], Mikra; text, translation, reading and interpretation of the Hebrew Bible in ancient Judaism and early Christianity: CompNT 2/1, 1988 ➤ 317.

1232 *Navone* John, The question-raising Word of God: Parabola 13,3 (NY 1988) 40-43.

1233 **Olthuis** J.H., *al.* A hermeneutics of ultimacy. Lanham MD 1987, UPA. 90 p. £9. – ᴿThemelios 14 (1988s) 32 (M. *Alsford*: read SHEPPARD's final response first, to get an idea of what it is all about; D. BLOESCH moderately and C. PINNOCK less fairly contest Olthuis' claim that hermeneutic should be less dependent on 'biblical authority' accepted by all but in very varying ways).

1234 **Oost** R., Omstreden Bijbeluitleg; aspecten ... ᴰ1986 ➤ 3,1280; *f* 19,50; 90-242-5486-8: ᴿBL (1988) 114 (J. *Barr*: Amsterdam anticipated the better-publicized American 'canonical criticism'); GerefTTs 88 (1988) 42s (C. *Houtman*); NedTTs 42 (1988) 331 (P. C. *Bentjes*).

1235 *Oshun* C.O., The Word of God as word; a Pentecostal viewpoint: AfJB 2 (1987) 106-112.

1236 *a)* *Oss* Douglas A., Canon as context; the function of *sensus plenior* in evangelical hermeneutics; – *b)* *Barentsen* Jack, The validity of human language; a vehicle for divine truth; – *c)* *Spencer* Stephen R., Is natural theology biblical?: GraceTJ 9 (1988) 105-127 / 21-43 / 59-72.

1237 *Ott* Heinrich, Die hermeneutische Problematik und das Entmythologisierungsprogramm: TZBas 44 (1988) 222-238.

1238 *Pépin* Jean (*Hoheisel* Karl) Hermeneutik, [T]*Kehl* Alois: ➤ 807, RAC 14,108s (1988) 722-771.

1239 **Piret** Pierre, L'Écriture et l'Esprit; une étude théologique sur l'exégèse et les philosophies 1987 ➤ 3,1283: [R]ArTGran 51 (1988) 298s (A. S. *Muñoz*); ÉTRel 63 (1988) 611s (J. *Ansaldi*); Irénikon 61 (1988) 433s (M. G.).

1240 **Poland** Lynn M., Literary criticism and biblical hermeneutics 1985 ➤ 1,1339: [R]ÉglT 18 (1987) 238-240 (W. *Vogels*).

1241 **Prickett** Stephen, Words and the Word; language, poetics and biblical interpretation 1986 ➤ 2,918; 3,f284: [R]JTS 39 (1988) 340-4 (M. *Warner*); NBlackf 69 (1988) 300s (R. *Strange*); TLond 91 (1988) 221s (J. *Drury*).

1242 [E]**Ravera** Marco, Il pensiero ermeneutico; testi e materiali. Genova 1986, Marietti. – [R]FilT 1,1 (1988) 181-3 (C. *Ciancio*).

1244 *Schenker* A., Anthropomorphismus: ➤ 804, NBL Lfg 1 (1988) 109-111.

1245 *Scholer* David M., Issues in Bible interpretation [... 'you professors can interpret if you want to, but I'm just going to accept what the Bible says']: EvQ 60 (1988) 5-22.

1246 *Schüssler Fiorenza* Elisabeth, The ethics of biblical interpretation; decentering biblical scholarship [SBL presidential address, Boston Dec. 5, 1987]: JBL 107 (1988) 3-17.

1247 *Schweizer* Harald, Biblische Texte verstehen; Arbeitsbuch zur Hermeneutik und Methodik der Bibelinterpretation 1986 ➤ 2,922: [R]ETL 64 (1988) 191s (J. *Lust*); FreibZ 35 (1988) 268 (A. *Schenker*); TLZ 113 (1988) 423s (J. *Rohde*).

1248 *Simian-Yofre* Horacio, Pragmalingüística; comunicación y exégesis [... 'comprensible' aquí significa 'relevante']: RBibArg 30s (año 50, 1988) 75-95.

1249 *Smend* Rudolf, Hermeneutik AT [*Stuhlmacher* Peter, NT]: ➤ 798, EvKL 2 (1988) 491-3 [494-6; *al.* -502].

1250 **Stadelmann** Helge, Grundlinien eines bibeltreuen Schriftverständnisses 1985 ➤ 1,1342: [R]Themelios 14 (1988s) 31s (I. H. *Marshall*: fine).

1251 **Stell** Stephen L., Hermeneutics and the Holy Spirit; Trinitarian insights into a hermeneutical impasse: diss. Princeton Theol. Sem. 1988. – RelStR 15,191.

1252 *Tábet Balady* M. A., La hermenéutica bíblica de san AGUSTÍN: AugM 33 (1988) 195-213.

1253 [E]**Tardieu** Michel, Les règles de l'interprétation 1982/7 ➤ 3,569: [R]JTS 39 (1988) 215s (N. *Lash*); RÉJ 146 (1987) 438s (M.-R. *Hayoun*); RTPhil 120 (1988) 376s (E. *Junod*); ScripTPamp 19 (1987) 677 (F. *Varo*); TLZ 113 (1988) 51s (H. *Reventlow*).

1254 *Thiselton* A. C., La nouvelle herméneutique [< [E]*Marshall* I., NT Interpretation 1977-85], [T]*Hickel* Pascal, *al.*: Hokhma 33 (1986) 1-35.

1255 [E]**Thoma** C., *Wyschograd* M., Understanding Scripture 1984/7 ➤ 3,570: [R]BL (1988) 116 (R. A. *Mason*); JEcuSt 25 (1988) 294s (G. S. *Sloyan*); NewTR 1,2 (1988) 122-4 (H. G. *Perelmuter*); Numen 35 (1988) 154-6 (M. *Greenberg*).

Tracy David, Plurality and ambiguity; hermeneutics 1987 ... ➤ a858.

Trigg Joseph W., Biblical interpretation: Message of the Fathers 9, 1988 ➤ h701.

1256 *Trilling* Wolfgang, 'Sola scriptura' und 'Selbstauslegung der Schrift' im Lichte der Exegese [< [F]*Kleineidam* E., Sapienter ordinare: ErfTSt 24 (1969) 49-72]: ➤ 275, Studien 1988, 247-275.

1257 *Tsippor* Moshe, ❸ Name-midrash in Scripture: BethM 34,116 (1988s) 81-96.

1258 *a) Uffenheimer* Benjamin, Some reflections on modern Jewish biblical research; – *b) Falk* Ze'ev W., Jewish and Christian understanding of the Bible; – *c) Dubois* Marcel, Roman Catholic undertanding...; – *d) Reventlow* Henning, Protestant understanding...: ➤ 505, Creative 1985/8, 161-174 (195s) / 197-201 / 203-211 / 213-5.

1259 *Visotzky* Burton L., Jots and tittles; on Scriptural interpretation in rabbinic and patristic literatures: Prooftexts 8 (1988) 257-269.

1260 **Whitman** Jon, Allegory; the dynamics of an ancient and medieval technique. CM 1987, Harvard. xiv-281 p. $25. – ᴿTS 49 (1988) 739s (T. W. *Tilley*).

1260* *a) Wood* Charles M., Hermeneutics and the authority of Scripture; – *b) Tanner* Kathryn E., Theology and the plain sense; – *c) Outka* Gene, Following at a distance; ethics and the identity of Jesus; – *d) Hauerwas* Stanley, The church as God's new language: ➤ 52, ᶠFʀᴇɪ H., Authority/narrative 1987, 3-20 / 59-78 / 144-160 / 179-198.

1261 *Youssif* Pierre, Exégèse et typologie bibliques chez S. Éᴘʜʀᴇᴍ de Nisibe et chez S. Thomas d'Aǫᴜɪɴ: ParOr 13 (1986) 31-50 [< ᴢɪᴛ].

1262 *Zimmermann* Gunter, Schrift und Geist: BTZ 5 (1988) 202-218.

B2.2 **Structuralismus biblicus** (generalior ➤ J9.4).

1263 **Greenwood** David [† 1984], Structuralism and the biblical text: Religion and Reason 32, 1985 ➤ 1,1358 ... 3,1298: ᴿJTS 39 (1988) 535s (I. H. *Jones*: a bit conservative); NedTTs 42 (1988) 256-8 (A. van der *Kooij*); Orpheus 9 (1988) 399-401 (A. *Di Marco*).

1264 **Milne** Pamela J., Vladimir Pʀᴏᴘᴘ and the study of structure in Hebrew biblical narrative [Morphology of the folktale 1928, Eng. 1968, Univ. ᴛx]. Sheffield 1987, JStOT ➤ 3,1309; Ithaca ɴʏ 1988, Cornell Univ. 325 p. $42.50 [TDig 35,379]. 1-85075-087-4; pa. 6-6.

B2.4 *Analysis* **narrationis** *biblicae* (generalior ➤ J9.6).

1265 *a) Arens* Edmund, 'Wer kann die grossen Taten des Herrn erzählen?': Die Erzählstruktur christlichen Glaubens in systematischer Perspektive; – *b) Müller* Karlheinz, Bedingungen einer Erzählkultur; Judaistische Anmerkungen zum Programm einer 'narrativen Theologie': – *c) Fuchs* Gotthard, 'Ein Abgrund ruft den anderen' (Ps 42,8); das eine Glaubens-Geheimnis und die vielen Dogmen-Geschichten; – *d) Zeller* Eva, Heilungsversuche durch Schreiben: ➤ 1284, Erzählter Glaube 1988, 13-27 / 28-51 / 52-86 / 186-197.

1266 **Berlin** Adle, Poetics and interpretation of biblical narrative 1983 ➤ 64,1166 ... 2,928: ᴿBO 44 (1987) 759s (J. P. *Fokkelman*).

1267 *a) Birch* Bruce C., Old Testament narrative and moral address; – *b) Hanson* Paul D., Biblical interpretation, meeting place of Jews and Christians: ➤ 25, ᶠCʜɪʟᴅs B., Canon 1988, 75-91 / 32-47.

1268 ᴱ**Coats** George W., Saga, legend ... narrative forms in OT literature: JStOT Sup 35, 1985 ➤ 1,274: ᴿBZ 32 (1988) 130-2 (H. *Engel*); OrAnt 27 (1988) 150-3 (M. *Liverani*).

Damrosch David, The narrative covenant; transformation of genre in the growth of biblical literature 1987 ➤ 8305.

1269 *Doderer* Klaus, Über das 'betriegen zur Wahrheit'; die Fabelarbeitungen M. LUTHERS: in ᴱ*Hasubek* Peter, Fabelforschung: WegFor 572. Da 1983, Wiss. p. 207-223 [< LuJb 55,164].

1270 *Doron* Pinchas, The art of biblical narrative: Dor 17 (1988s) 1-9. 91-96.

ᶠ**Frei** Hans, Scriptural authority and narrative interpretation 1987 ➤ 52.

1271 *Friedman* Richard E., The hiding of the face; an essay on the literary unity of biblical narrative: ➤ 1130, ᴱ*Neusner* J., Judaic perspectives 1987, 207-222.

1272 *a*) *Fuchs* Ottmar, Narrativität und Widerspenstigkeit; Strukturanalogien zwischen biblischen Geschichten und christlichen Handeln; – *b*) *Wachinger* Lorenz, 'Der Mensch ist ein Geschichtenerzähler' (S. MINOUCHIN); zur therapeutischen Funktion des Erzählens; – *c*) *Sill* Bernhard, 'Sinn für die mögliche Wirklichkeit' (R. *Musil*); ars narrandi und ethische Predigt; – *d*) *Siller* Hermann P., Das Evangelium in eigener Erfahrung sagen und in der Erfahrung anderer hören; zum biographischen Erzählen des Zeugen; – *e*) *Stock* Alex, Bilder-Geschichten ...: ➤ 1284, Erzählter Glaube 1986/8, 87-126 / 127-141 / 142-158 / 159-170 / 171-185.

1273 **Funk** Robert W., The poetics of biblical narrative: Foundations and facets, literary facets. Sonoma CA 1988, Polebridge. xv-318 p. $20. 0-944344-04-6.

1274 *Gordon* Robert P., Simplicity of the highest cunning; narrative art in the Old Testament [1986 Finlayson lecture]: ScotBEv 6 (1988) 69-80.

1275 **Gunkel** H., Das Märchen im AT [1921] 1987 ➤ 3,1301: ᴿRBgPg 66 (1988) 650s (H. W. am *Zehnhoff*).

1276 **Kort** Wesley A., Story, text, and Scripture; literary interests in biblical narative. University Park 1988, Penn State Univ. xii-159 p. $20 [TDig 36,66]. – ᴿTTod 45 (1988s) 460.462.464 (Mieke *Bal*).

1277 **McCarthy** Carmel, *Riley* William, [Ruth Esther Jonah Tobit Judith] The OT short story; explorations into narrative spirituality: Message Bib. Spirituality 7, 1986 ➤ 2,8022; 3,1305: ᴿAustralBR 36 (1988) 63s (J. J. *Scullion*: unencumbered by higher criticism).

1278 ᴱ**McConnell** Frank, The Bible and the narrative tradition 1986 ➤ 2,385; 3,1305*: ᴿThemelios 14 (1988s) 72 (S. E. *Porter*).

1279 *Macky* P., The multiple purposes of biblical speech acts: PrincSemB 8,2 (1987) 50-61 [NTAbs 32,143].

1280 *Moore* Stephen D., Narrative commentaries on the Bible; context, roots, and prospects: Forum 3,3 (Sonoma 1987) 29-63.

1281 **Robinson** Bernard P., Israel's mysterious God; an analysis of some OT narratives 1986 ➤ 3,705: ᴿCBQ 50 (1988) 513s (S. *Greenhalgh*).

1282 **Savran** George W., Telling and retelling; quotation in biblical narrative [Gen through 2 Kgs]: Indiana StBLit. Bloomington IN 1988, Indiana Univ. ix-161 p. $40. 0-253-35928-7 [TDig 36,182].

1283 **Sternberg** Meir, The poetics of biblical narrative 1985 ➤ 2,935; 3,1310: ᴿBZ 32 (1988) 128-130 (H. *Schweizer*); JAAR 56 (1988) 360-2 (F. *Landy*); TS 49 (1988) 151s (L. *Boadt*).

1283* *a*) *a*) *Thiemann* Ronald F., Radiance and obscurity in biblical narrative; – *b*) *Wiles* Maurice, Scriptural authority and theological construction; the limits of narrative interpretation; – *c*) *Green* Garrett, 'The Bible as ...'; fictional narrative and scriptural truth; – *d*) *Crites* Stephen, The spatial dimensions of narrative truthtelling; – *e*) *Kelsey* David H., Biblical narrative and theological anthropology; – *f*) *Lindbeck* George, The story-shaped Church; critical exegesis and theological interpretation: → 52, ᶠFREI H., Authority/narrative 1987, 21-41 / 42-58 / 79-96 / 97-118 / 121-143 / 161-176.

1284 ᴱZerfass Rolf, Erzählter Glaube, erzählende Kirche (Tagung Goslar 29.IX-4.X.1986): QDisp 116. FrB 1988, Herder. 203 p. 3-451-02116-1. 9 art. → 1265, 1272.

B2.6   *Critica reactionis lectoris* – **Reader-response criticism.**

1285 *Brown* Schuyler, Reader response; demythologizing the text: NTS 34 (1988) 232-7.

1286 *Combrink* H.J.B., Readings, readers and authors; an orientation: Neotestamentica 22,2 (1988) 189-203 [-484 *al.*: the rest of the (half-) fascicle contains 14 readings of Luke 12,35-48].

Kingsbury J.D., Reflections on 'the reader' of Mt 1988 → 4468.

1287 **McKnight** Edgar V., The Bible and the reader; an introduction to literary criticism 1985 → 1,1658; 3,1608: ᴿRelStR 14 (1988) 150 (W. Lee *Humphreys*).

1288 **McKnight** Edgar V., Post-modern use of the Bible; the emergence of reader-oriented criticism. Nv 1988, Abingdon. 288 p. $16 pa. [JBL 108,380]. 0-687-33178-1.

1288* *Moore* Stephen D., Stories of reading; doing gospel criticism as/with a 'reader' [since 1960 the reader has acceded to the role of protagonist in literary studies]: → 500, SBL Seminars 1988, 141-159.

B3   *Interpretatio ecclesiastica*   .1   **Bible and Church.**

1289 **Ammerman** Nancy T., Bible believers; fundamentalists in the modern world. New Brunswick NJ 1987, Rutgers Univ. 247 p. $12 pa. [GraceTJ 9,301]. – ᴿTTod 45 (1988s) 482. 484 (G.M. *Marsden*).

1290 **Annarelli** James J., Academic freedom and Catholic higher education: Contributions to the study of education 21. Westport CT 1987, Greenwood. xxi-236 p. $35 [TDig 35,52].

1290* *Auza* Bernardito, Dissent in the Church today; concern or rebellion?: PhilipSa 27 (1987) 175-241.

1291 **Baldwin** Louis, The Pope and the mavericks. Buffalo NY 1988, Prometheus. 217 p. $20 [GraceTJ 9,301].

1292 *Barkley* Roy, The fundamentalist threat; why are Catholics becoming fundamentalists?: HomPast 88,5 (1988) 45-53 [< ZIT].

1293 *Barr* J., Religious fundamentalism: St. Mark's Review 133 (Canberra 1988) 3-10 [< NTAbs 32,283].

1294 **Barton** J., People of the Book? The authority of the Bible in Christianity (Bampton lectures 1988) [against fundamentalism]. L 1988, SPCK. xi-96 p. £5. 0-281-04387-6 [BL 89,100, E.A. *Phillips*].

1295 *Bergant* Dianne, Fundamentalists and the Bible: New Theology Review 1,2 (1988) 36-50 [*al.* 3-35; 58-87].

1296 *Bjork* William G., A critique of Zane HODGES, The Gospel under siege; a review article: JEvTS 30 (1987) 457 ... [< ZIT].

1297 *Böckle* Franz, Le magistère de l'Église en matière morale [< rapport Barc 1986, Fédération Int. Univ. Catholiques]: RTLv 19 (1988) 3-16.

1298 **Breck** John, The power of the Word in the worshiping church 1986 → 3,1318: ᴿBogSmot 58 (1988) 159s (M. *Zovkić*).

1299 *a) Broucker* José de, L'information religieuse est d'abord une information; – *b)* Déclaration de Cologne [< DocCath 5.III.1989], ᵀ, avec appui francophone 20.II.1989: Masses Ouvrières 425 (1989) 38-48 / 50-57.

1300 **Brown** Raymond E., Biblical exegesis and Church doctrine 1985 → 1,159 ... 3,1319: RCommonweal 114 (1987) 22s (Pheme *Perkins*); Gregorianum 69 (1988) 147s (G. *O'Collins*); ModT 5 (1988s) 181s (C. *Rowland*); RRel 46 (1987) 147s (E. *Hensell*).

1301 *Brown* R. E., Scripture and dogma today: America 157 (1987) 286-9 [NTAbs 32,141].

1302 **Burke** Cormac, Authority and freedom in the Church. SF 1988, Ignatius. 235 p. $13 pa. [TDig 36,49].

1303 **Burke** Cormac, Autoridad y libertad en la Iglesia, T*Fernández Agudo* Francisco J. M 1988, Rialp. 331 p. – RCarthaginensia 4 (1988) 401 (F. *Martínez Fresneda*); CiuD 201 (1988) 689s (J. M. *Ozaeta*).

1304 **Camilleri** René, The 'sensus fidei' of the whole Church and the Magisterium, from the time of Vatican I to Vatican II: diss. Pont. Univ. Gregoriana, D*Sullivan* F. Rome 1987. 349 p.; extr. No 3450, 117 p. – RTLv 19,559.

1305 *a) Cimosa* Mario, La Bibbia nella vita della Chiesa dopo il Concilio; – *b) Pacomio* Luciano, Evento e profezia per la vita della Chiesa; – *c) Mannucci* Valerio, Rivelazione e Bibbia; – *d) Lambiasi* Francesco, La 'verità' della Bibbia; – *e) Della Torre* Luigi, La Lectio divina: ParVi 33,1 ('La Costituzione Dei Verbum' 1988) 11-17 / 7-10 / 18-22 / 23-34 / 36-44.

1306 *Clutter* Ronald T., A background history of Grace Theological seminary [Brethren church distancing from Fundamentalism ...]: GraceTJ 9 (1988) 205-232.

1307 *Corradino* Lorena, Il discernimento spirituale oggi [della comunità ecclesiale riguardo a problemi attuali]: RasT 29 (1988) 580-9.

1308 **Curran** C. E., Faithful dissent 1986 → 2,948; 3,1323: RAustralasCR 65 (1988) 120-2 (D. *Smith* 'fiddling while Rome burns'); Commonweal 114 (1987) 537-9 (R. G. *Hoyt*).

1309 *Dalferth* Ingolf U., Wissenschaftliche Theologie und kirchliche Lehre: ZTK 85 (1988) 98-128.

1310 *Díaz-Rodelas* Juan M., Exegesis al servicio de la fe; notas en torno al uso de la Sagrada Escritura en el Tercer Catecismo de la Comunidad Cristiana: Teología y Catequesis 25s (M 1988) 233-245.

1311 FDíez Alegría J. M., Gonzalez Ruiz J. M., Teología y Magisterio, EFloristán Casiano: Verdad y Vida 100, 1987 → 3,629: RRET 48 (1988) 112-4 (M. *Gesteira*).

1312 *Dulles* Avery, Lehramt und Unfehlbarkeit, T*Berchtold* C., *Kessler* M.: → 800, HbFT 4 (1988) 153-178.

1313 **Dybácz** Martin, Fundamentalism, a Catholic response [lesson-plans]. Villa Maria PA 1986, Center for Learning. 96 p. $13 [BToday 26,192].

1314 **Edwards** David L. (*Stott* John), Essentials — a liberal-evangelical [-fundamentalist] dialogue. L 1988, Hodder & S. 354 p. £6 pa. 0-340-42623-3. – RScotBEv 6 (1988) 123s (D. F. *Wright*); Themelios 14 (1988s) 3-5 (D. *Wenham*: 'The most significant division in Christendom today is not the division between Roman Catholicism and Protestantism' but between 'evangelical and liberal theology').

1315 *a) Faivre* Alexandre, Théologiens 'laïcs' et laïcs théologiens; position des problèmes à l'époque paléochrétienne; – *b) Grootaers* Jan, Les laïcs théologiens entre le moyen-âge et le début de ce siècle. Ho Theológos 5 (1987) 9-49 / 135-159.

1316 a) *Geffré* Claude, Raligion und Moderne; ein Weg aus dem Konflikt,
T*Himmelsbach* A.; – b) *Baum* Gregory, Bussfertigkeit im kirchlichen Lehramt; → 106, F METZ J.-B., Mystik 1988, 130-142 / 311-321.

1317 a) *Geldbach* Erich, Fundamentalismus; – b) *Kremer* Jacob, Wortgetreu
– nicht buchstäblich; Grenzen und Möglichkeiten einfachen Bibellesens; –
c) *Fuchs* Ottmar, Grundstrukturen des Fundamentalismus aus der
Perspektive des Erzengels Michael; – d) *Hottinger* Arnold, Die Versuchung des Gottesstaates; zum islamischen Fundamentalismus: BiKi 43
(1988) 97-102 / 103-108 / 109-114 / 114-118.

1318 *Habiger* Matthew, Is the Magisterium a reliable moral guide?:
HomPast 88 (1987s) 31-... [< ZIT].

1319 *Hafstad* Kjetil, Autoritet og forandring; fundamentalistisk ufeilbarhet
— i lys av den katolske: → 97*, F LØNNING I., NorTTs 89 (1988) 79-90.

1320 E**Hagen** Kenneth, *al.*, The Bible in the churches [Marquette Univ.
symposium 1982] 1985 → 1,473: R CalvinT 23 (1988) 67s (P. L. *Bremer*:
ecumenical, significant); IntRMiss 77 (1988) 563 (H. *Rowold*).

1321 *Hubbard* J. M., Is the ordinary magisterium infallible? HomP 88
(1987s) 28- ... [< ZIT 88,633].

1322 **Hunter** James D., American evangelism; conservative religion and the
quandary of modernity. New Brunswick NJ 1983, Rutgers Univ. –
R JPsy&T 15 (1987) 77-79 (F. H. *Touchet*: invaluable; from 1500 ques-
tionnaires).

1323 *Joest* Wilfried, Ⓜ Fundamentalizmus [< TRE 11 (1983) 733-7], T *Karasszon* I.: Theologiai Szemle 31 (1988) 116-9.

1324 *Johnson* H. Wayne, The 'analogy of faith' and exegetical methodology;
a preliminary discussion on relationships: JEvTS 31 (1988) 69-80 [< ZIT
88,515].

1325 E**Johnston** Robert K., The use of the Bible in theology; evangelical
options 1985 → 2,960; 3,1338: R GraceTJ 9 (1988) 287s (D. S. *Dockery*);
TTod 44 (1987s) 284s (R. A. *Muller*).

1326 **Keating** Karl, Catholicism and fundamentalism; the attack on
'Romanism' by 'Bible Christians'. SF 1988, Ignatius. 360 p. $20; pa. $13
[TDig 35,370: against SWAGGERT, GREEN, CHICK, RIVERA, ALAMO]. –
R HomP 89,4 (1988s) 77s (K. *Baker*); SpTod 40 (1988) 359s (P.
Hebblethwaite: anti-Catholicism and apostasy claimed to be on the
increase).

1327 *Kelly* Kevin T., Conformity and dissent in the Church: Way 28 (1988)
87-101 [-148, *al.*].

1328 *Kerkhofs* Jan, Le peuple de Dieu est-il infaillible? L'importance du
sensus fidelium dans l'Église postconciliaire: FreibZ 35 (1988) 3-19.

1329 a) *Kerkhofs* Jan, Between 'Christendom' and 'Christianity'; – b)
Zulehner Paul M., Ecclesiastical atheism: JEmpT 1,2 (1988) 88 ... / 5-20
[< ZIT 89,120].

1330 *Lathuilière* Pierre, Le fondamentalisme dans les traditions chrétiennes:
LumièreV 37,186 ('Le courant fondamentaliste chrétien — l'écriture
immobile' 1988) 69-85 [2-105 *al.*].

1331 *Kirchschläger* Walter, Bibel und Konzil; das Zweite Vatikanum aus der
Sicht des Exegeten (Gastvorlesung Linz 1985): TPQ 136 (1988) 65-74.

1332 *Kottukapally* Joseph, The Curran case; some theological considerations:
Jeevadhara 16,96 (1986) 482-8.

1333 *Laishley* F. J., Repression and liberation in the Church; an anatomy of
I. repression; II. ... liberation; III. Theological reflection: HeythJ 29
(1988) 157-174 / 329-342 / 450-460.

1334 **Laurentin** R., Come riconciliare l'esegesi e la fede? UnivT 16, 1986
→ 2,962*b*: RHumanitas 42 (Brescia 1987) 293s (M. *Orsatti*); StPatav 34
(1987) 431-3 (G. *Segalla*).

1335 *a*) *Lawler* Michael B., Freedom of inquiry, thought, and expression; the
theologian in the Catholic Church and University; – *b*) *Rigali* Norbert J.,
Moral theology and the Magisterium: Horizons 15 (1988) 109-115 /
116-123.

1336 **Lee** Philip J., Against the Protestant gnostics 1987 → 3,1342: RTTod
45 (1988s) 360. 362s (W. H. *Becker*: he means *all* American Protestants of
all periods).

1337 *a*) *Löhrer* Magnus, Dogmatische Erwägungen zur unterschiedlichen
Funktion und zum gegenseitigen Verhältnis von Lehramt und Theologie
in der katholischen Kirche; – *b*) *Fries* Heinrich, Sensus fidelium; der
Theologe zwischen dem Lehramt der Hierarchie und dem Lehramt der
Gläubigen; – *c*) *Müller* Alois, Ekklesiologische Erwägungen zum Thema
'Gehorsam'; – *d*) *Heinemann* Heribert, Lehrbeanstandungsverfahren —
ein Problem und seine Lösungsversuche: TBer 17 (Z 1988) 11-54 / 55-78
/ 111-144 / 145 ... [< ZIT 89,167].

Maggiolini Sandro, L'obbedienza nella Chiesa, attualità di una virtù difficile 1988 → 8949.

1338 **Marsden** George M., Reforming Fundamentalism 1987 → 3,1348:
RCalvaryB 4,1 (1988) 75s (E. R. *Jordan*: most important book pub-
lished in the Christian world in 1987); GraceTJ 9 (1988) 296s (R. T.
Clutter).

1339 EMay William W., Vatican authority and American Catholic dissent ...
CURRAN 1987 → 3,437: RCalvinT 23 (1988) 267-271 (J. H. *Kromminga*:
cites bottom-line from RAUSCH, 'The magisterium cannot safeguard its
credibility merely by appealing to its own authority ... must rely on
competence of careful but critical theologians'); JEcuSt 25 (1988) 618 (W.
Yates); NewTR 1,2 (1988) 100s (J. G. *Yockry*: HITCHCOCK superficial,
NOVAK weak).

1340 *Moingt* Joseph, Séductions fondamentalistes: Études 369 (1988) 667-
680.

1341 **Molnar** Thomas, The pagan temptation. GR 1987, Eerdmans. $12.
0-8028-0262-1. – RRHPR 68 (1988) 484s (G. *Vahanian*: intégriste plus
séduisant et plus dangereux que LEFEBVRE).

1342 *Mucci* Giandomenico, *a*) La competenza del magistero infallibile: CC
139 (1988,3) 17-25; – *b*) Infallibilità della Chiesa, magistero e 'autorità
dottrinale' dei fedeli: CC 139 (1988,1) 431-442.

1343 *Napiórkowski* Stanisław C., Wahrheit und Kirche [... Besitzer der
Wahrheit oder Pilger zur Wahrheit? ... Schädlichkeit des traditionellen
Schemas von der Wahrheit der Kirche ...]: ColcT Sp 58 (1988) 21-28.

1344 *O'Collins* Gerald, Note a proposito della consultazione dei fedeli
[NEWMAN J. H., On consulting the faithful in matter (sg., reso 'in tema
di') of doctrine]: CC 139 (1988,4) 40-45.

1345 *O'Donohue* John F., Fundamentalism; a psychological problem: AfER
29 (1987) 344-350.

1346 **Orsy** Ladislas, The Church learning and teaching; magisterium, assent,
dissent, academic freedom. Wilmington / Dublin / Leominster 1987,
Glazier / Dominican / Fowler Wright. 172 p. $15 [TDig 35,186]. –
0-89453-646-X/. – RBibTB 18 (1988) 151s (D. P. *Killen*: a gem, and of
practical usefulness, though for theologians 'dissent' often means
'pontificate'); Furrow 39 (1988) 194s (B. *Cosgrave*); LvSt 13 (1988)

389-391 (R. *Michiels*); NBlackf 69 (1988) 549 (R. *Ombres*); PrPeo 2 (1988) 300-2 (R. *Quan Yan Chui*).

1347 **Peshkin** A., God's choice ... a fundamentalist school 1986 ➤ 3,1357: R JAAR 56 (1988) 170-2 (Nancy T. *Ammerman*).

1348 *Roberge* René-Michel, La fonction magistérielle dans l'Église; à propos d'un ouvrage récent [*Naud* A., Le magistère incertain 1987]: LavalTP 44 (1988) 375-391.

1349 **Robinson** R. B., Roman Catholic exegesis since Divino Afflante Spiritu; hermeneutical implications [diss. Yale 1982, D*Childs* B.; treats chiefly R. E. BROWN, L. ALONSO-SCHÖKEL, N. LOHFINK]: SBL diss. 111. Atlanta 1988, Scholars. vii-183 p. $12 pa.; sb. $9 [ZAW 101,125, H.-C. *Schmitt*]. 1-55540-240-2; 1-0.

1350 *a*) *Sanders* James A., Fundamentalism and the Church; theological crisis for mainline Protestants; – *b*) *White* Leland J., Fundamentalism and the 'fullness of Christianity'; Catholicism's double challenge: BibTB 18 (1988) 43-49 / 50-59.

1351 **Silva** Moisés, Foundations of contemporary interpretation: Has the Church misread the Bible? 1987 ➤ 3,1365: R SWJT 31,2 (1988s) 66s (L. R. *Bush*).

1352 *Spencer* Robert B., Is biblical scholarship really objective? [... a myth of objectivity surrounds it]: HomP 89,7 (1988s) 52-58.

1353 **Stenhouse** Paul, Catholic answers to Bible Christians; a light on biblical fundamentalism. Kensington NSW 1988, Chevalier [AustralasCR 66,373, D. *Maguire*].

1354 *Stöhr* Martin, Denken in Beton; protestantischer Fundamentalismus in den USA, Südafrika und bei uns: Junge Kirche 48 (Bremen 1987) 692-6 [< ZIT].

1355 **Sullivan** F. A., Magisterium (Gill & M 1985) 1983 ➤ 64,1353 ... 3,1368: R Carmelus 35 (1988) 241-4 (M. V. *Attard*); ForumKT 3 (1987) 155s (L. *Scheffczyk*); LvSt 13 (1988) 180s (R. *Michiels*).

1356 **Sullivan** Francis A., Il magistero nella chiesa cattolica [1983 ➤ 64, 1353],T. Assisi 1986, Cittadella. 246 p. Lit. 18.000. – R CC 138 (1988,3) 429s (G. *Mucci*: libro di consultazione ineludibile, ma affine all'*antirö-mischer Affekt*).

1358 *Trollinger* William V., [Minneapolis 1936-47, W. B.] RILEY's empire; Northwestern Bible School and fundamentalism in the Upper Midwest: ChH 57 (1988) 197-212.

1359 *Ven* J. A. van der, Bischoppen en theologen in dialog; de pastoraal werk(st)er: PrakT 14 (1987) 481-490 [491-500, *Vossen* H.].

B3.2 *Homiletica* – The Bible in preaching.

1360 **Bailey** Ivor, Prate, prattle or preach. Melbourne 1987, Joint Board of Christian Education. 137 p. 0-85819-262-3. – R ExpTim 99,11 2d-top choice (1987s) 323s (C. S. *Rodd*).

1361 *Barié* Helmut, Juden aus der Sicht junger Prediger; Dokumentation einer nötigen und schon im Gang gekommenen homiletischen Umkehr: KIsr 3 (1988) 65-80.

1362 **Best** E., From text to sermon; responsible use of the New Testament in preaching. E 1988, Clark. £5 [TLond 91,446].

1363 *Bukowski* Peter, Die Bibel als Chance des Predigers: Deutsches Pfarrerblatt 88 (Essen 1988) 43-46 [< ZIT].

1364 **Burghardt** Walter J., Preaching; the art and the craft 1987 ➤ 3,1374: R SWJT 31,2 (1988s) 68s (J. L. *Heflin,* also on HOWARD J., WALKER A.,

STAPLETON J.); Tablet 242 (1988) 754s (V. *Felzmann*); TTod 45 (1988s) 241s (Joan *Delaplane*); Worship 62 (1988) 383s (J. A. *Melloh*).

1365 **Burke** John, *Doyle* Thomas P.,   The homilist's guide to Scripture, theology, and canon law.   NY 1987, Pueblo.   xiii-282 p. $13 pa. [TDig 36,49]. – ᴿHomP 88,10 (1987s) 76s (E. P. *Atzert*).

1366 **Buttrick** David,   Homiletic; moves and structures   1987   → 3,1367: ᴿTLond 91 (1988) 243-5 (S. *Platten*); TTod 45 (1988s) 108.   110-2 (T. G. *Long*).

1367 **Buttrick** David G.,   Preaching Jesus Christ; an exercise in homiletic theology.   Ph 1988, Fortress.   94 p. $6. – ᴿWorship 62 (1988) 475s (A. C. *Rueter*).

1368 **Byers** John B.,   A study of biblical interpretation in the Warrack Lectures on Preaching from 1940 to 1975: diss. St. Andrews, ᴰ*Whyte* J. 355 p. – RTLv 20,582 sans date.

1369 *Cañizares Llovera* Antonio,   Teología de la predicación en el s. XVI español, 'De sacra ratione concionandi':   RET 48 (1988) 15-51.

1370 **Coggan** Donald,   Preaching; the sacrament of the Word.   NY 1988, Crossroad.   170 p. $13 [TDig 36,54].

1371 ᴱ**Cox** James W.,   Best sermons I.   SF 1988, Harper & R.   x-387 p. $17 [CBQ 51,187].

1372 **Damblon** Albert,   Die Predigt, der Prediger und der Predigtort im Gottesdienst; Bemerkungen zum Predigtverständnis des II. Vatikanums, aufgezeigt an den liturgischen Predigtorten: Diss. ᴰ*Bartsch*.   Fra 1987s. – TR 84 (1988) 511.

1373 **Decker** Robert D.,   The preaching style of David M. LLOYD-JONES [not idolized]: diss. Calvin Sem., ᴰ*Kromminga* C.   GR 1988.   iv-95 p. + bibliog. – CalvinT 23 (1988) 301.

1374 *Denecke* A.,   Mythos, Märchen und die biblische Verkündigungs-situation: PastT 77 (Gö 1988) 254-271 [< ZIT 88,491].

1375 **Eslinger** Richard L.,   A new hearing; living options in homiletic method. Nv 1987, Abingdon.   191 p. $11 pa. [TDig 35,355]. – ᴿInterpretation 42 (1988) 438s (T. G. *Long*: his claimed via media buries prematurely the idea-centered sermon).

1376 **Frankl** Razelle,   Televangelism, the marketing of popular religion. Carbondale 1987, Southern Illinois Univ.   xviii-204 p.; ill. $20. – ᴿRelStR 14 (1988) 178 (L. E. *Schmidt*).

1377 **Gradwohl** Roland,   Bibelauslegungen aus jüdischen Quellen, Die alttestamentlichen Predigttexte: 1. (3. Jahrgangs) 1986; 2 (4. Jg.) 1987 → 3,1383:   ᴿBiKi 43 (1988) 84s (P. G. *Müller*); KIsr 3 (1987) 98 (Julie *Kirchberg*).

1378 *Heyer* C. J. den,   De Bijbel als verhalenboek; over de kloof tussen wetenschappelijke bijbelkommentaren enerzijds en de praktische preekvoorbereiding anderzijds: PrakT 15 (Zwolle 1988) 293-303 [-325, *al.*: < ZIT 88,637].

1379 **Hirschler** Horst,   Biblisch predigen.   Hannover 1988, Lutherisches VH. 592 p.   3-7859-0556-4 [Bijdragen 49,475]. – ᴿTLZ 113 (1988) 848-850 (E. *Winkler*).

1380 **Howard** J. Grant,   Creativity in preaching: Craft of Preaching series. GR 1987, Zondervan.   112 p. [GraceTJ 9,308].

1381 **Hoyer** George W.,   What happened next? Nine messages on some of Jesus' great acts and stories.   Minneapolis 1987, Augsburg.   108 p. 0-8066-2299-7. – ᴿRExp 85 (1988) 594s (L. J. *Thompson*: creative sermons).

1382 **Jensen** Richard A., Telling the story; variety and imagination in preaching. Minneapolis 1980, Augsburg. 189 p. 0-8066-1766-7. – RBijdragen 49 (1988) 342 (J. *Besemer*).

1383 *Kern* Brigitte, Fragen in der [rabbinischen] Homilie; ein Mittel der Text- oder der Formkonstitution: LingBib 61 (1988) 57-86; Eng. 86.

1384 **Marchesi** G., Il Vangelo della speranza; commento biblico e teologico alle letture delle domeniche e feste, [Anno A 1986 → 3,1391] Anno B. R 1987, Città Nuova 451 p. Lit. 28.000. – RRasT 29 (1988) 92s (G. *Manca*).

1385 *Melloh* John A., Publish or perish; a review of preaching literature, 1982-1986: Worship 62 (1988) 497-514.

1386 *a) Munroe* Brad, Appropriating BARTH for the task of preaching; – *b) Harrington* Thomas W., The persuasive elements of José MIGUEZ-BONINO's sermon 'Much will be required'; a rhetorical analysis; – *c) Waters* Mark, ARISTOTLE's classical canons and Jürgen MOLTMANN's sermon 'Revolutionary love of our enemies': Paradigms 4 (Louisville 1988) 5-21 / 22-41 / 42-69.

1387 **Nichols** J. Randall, Building the word; the dynamics of communication and preaching. SF 1980, Harper & R. 174 p. *f* 39,20 0-06-066109-7. – RBijdragen 49 (1988) 344s (J. *Besemer*).

1388 *Parmisano* Stan, Preaching and contemporary exegesis: HomP 89,3 (1988s) 21-25.

1389 **Pawlikowski** John T., *Wilde* James A., When Catholics speak about Jews; notes for homilists and catechists. Ch 1987, Liturgy Training. 80 p. $6 pa. – RJEcuSt 25 (1988) 288s (S. R. *Isenberg*).

1390 **Preuss** Horst D., Das Alte Testament in christlicher Predigt 1984 → 65,1227 ... 3,1393: RTR 84 (1988) 146s (P. *Deselaers*).

1391 **Schott** Christian-Erdmann, Predigtgeschichte als Zugang zur Predigt 1986 → 2,1002*: RTLZ 113 (1988) 59-61 (H. *Theurich*).

1392 **Smith** Christine M., Weaving; a metaphor and method for women's preaching: diss. Graduate Theological Union. Berkeley 1987. – RelStR 14,185.

1393 *Smith* Herbert F., Homilies as they should be: HomP 89,9 (1988s) 9-17.

1394 TESosland Henry A., ZAHALON Jacob, *Or ha-Darshanim*, a guide for preachers on composing and delivering sermons, a seventeenth century Italian preacher's manual [with historical and updating notes]. NY 1987, Jewish Theol. Sem. – RJudaism 37 (1988) 497-9 (M. M. *Fenster*).

1395 **Tooley** Anthony D., The Illusaurus [computer sermon-illustration treasury]. 1985, Computer Assistant. $199. – RRExp 85 (1988) 151s (J. E. *Dent*).

1396 **Toulouse** Teresa, The art of prophesying; New England sermons [J. COTTON ... R. W. EMERSON] and the shaping of belief. Athens 1987, Univ. Georgia. xii-211 p. $23. – RRelStR 14 (1988) 175 (D. M. *Greenshaw*: skilful analysis).

1397 **Vogels** Walter, Reading and preaching the Bible; a new semiotic approach [1985 → 3,1294] 1986 → 2,1005; 3,1402: RCBQ 50 (1988) 311-3 (S. *Doyle*: 'the reader gives the text its meaning'?); SpTod 40 (1988) 173-5 (E. M. *Ruane*).

1398 **Watson** Nigel, Striking home; interpreting and proclaiming the New Testament. L 1987, Epworth. 206 p. £7.50. 0-7162-0438-X. – RExpTim 99 (1987s) 350s (J. M. *Lieu*).

1399 *Wells* Paul, Comment interpréter et prêcher la Parole de Dieu: → 28*, FCOURTHIAL P., Dieu parle! 1984, 69-84.

[E]**Welzig** Werner, Katalog gedruckter deutschsprachiger katholischer Predigtsammlungen 2. [1770-1848]: Szb W 484, 1987 → 988.

B3.3 Inerrantia, inspiratio [Revelatio → H1.7].

1401 **Achtemeier** Paul J., L'inspiration de l'Écriture [1980 → 61,2018], [T]*Desjardins* Maurice, 1985 → 1,1438: [R]ÉglT 18 (1987) 360s (L. *Laberge*).

1402 **Bemmelen** Peter M. van, Issues in biblical inspiration; SANDAY and WARFIELD: Doctoral Diss. 13, [D]*Dederen* R. Berrien Springs MI 1988, Andrews Univ. vii-421 p. 0-943872-49-9.

1403 *a) Berthoud* Pierre, L'autorité et l'interprétation de l'AT; – *b) Blocher* Henri, Inerrance et herméneutique; – *c) Gonin* François, Essai sur l'humanité des Écritures: → 28*, [F]COURTHIAL P., Dieu parle 1984, 1-11 / 85-103 / 53-68.

1404 *Blandino* Giovanni, The inspiration and truth of Sacred Scripture: Teresianum 39 (1988) 465-477 ['more organic and simple' treatment of his Questioni dibattute I (R 1977, Pont. Univ. Lateranense) 11-44].

1405 **Burkhardt** Helmut, Die Inspiration heiliger Schrift bei PHILO von Alexandrien [Diss. Göttingen 1987s – RTLv 19,559]. Giessen 1988, Brunnen. xi-265 p. DM 39. 3-7655-9340-0 [BL 89,131, J. *Barton*].

1406 **Crutsinger** Gene C., The Bible as a moral authority; its use by contemporary American Evangelical theologians: diss. Fuller Theol Sem. Pasadena 1988. 308 p. 88-16094. – DissA 49 (1988s) 1847-A.

1407 *Dockery* D.S., *Wise* P.D., Biblical inerrancy: pro or con?: TEd 37 (1988) 15-44.

1408 **Dunn** James D.G., The living Word [on NT authority]. L 1987, SCM. 196 p. £7. – [R]Themelios 14 (1988s) 73 (D.F. *Wright*).

1409 **Fackre** Gabriel, The Christian story; authority; Scripture in the Church for the world; a pastoral systematics 2. GR 1987, Eerdmans. 366 p. $15 [GraceTJ 9,305 'Frackre'].

1410 *Forestell* J.T., Without error; fundamentalism and the interpretation of the Bible: CanadCathR 5,11 (Saskatoon 1987) 405-412 [NTAbs 32,142].

1411 **Gnuse** Robert, The authority of the Bible 1985 → 1,1450 ... 3,1414: [R]TLZ 113 (1988) 221s (H.-J. *Kühne*).

1412 **Goldingay** J., Theological diversity and the authority of the Old Testament [[D]1983] 1987 → 3,1415: [R]AndrUnS 26 (1988) 142-6 (G.F. *Hasel*); BL (1988) 105 (R.E. *Clements*); EvQ 60 (1988) 349-351 (M.J. *Selman*); HorBT 9,2 (1987) 109-112 (W.E. *Lemke*); TLond 91 (1988) 425s (R.P. *Carroll*: pushes coherence of the Bible's teaching as a single book).

1413 *Graham* R.W., *a)* The inspiration of Scripture ¿*Packer* J.; *Lampe* G.; *Smith* R.F.]: LexTQ 22,4 (1987) 97-105 [NTAbs 32,142]; – *b)* Scripture: → 795, EncRel 14 (1987) 133-145.

1414 *Grelot* Pierre, Diez proposiciones sobre la inspiración de la Escritura [< EsprV 96 (1986) 97-105], [TE]*Bernal* J.M.: SelT 26 (1987) 329-339.

1415 *Grossmann* Walter, GRUBER [Eberhard L., 1665-1728] on the discernment of true and false inspiration: HarvTR 81 (1988) 363-387.

1416 *Hempelmann* Heinzpeter, 'Gott ein Schriftsteller!' Die Schriftlehre Johann G. HAMANNS und ihre hermeneutischen Konsequenzen: TBei 19 (1988) 128-153 [< ZIT 88,463].

1417 **Holdrege** Barbara A., Veda and Torah; ontological conceptions of Scripture in the Brahmanical and Judaic traditions: diss. Harvard. CM 1987. 310 p. 88-06045. – DissA 49 (1988s) 525-A.

1418 **Huyssteen** Wentzel van, The realism of the text; a perspective on biblical authority: Miscellanea Congregalia 28. Pretoria 1987, Univ. 64 p. R 5,60. 0-86981-472-9.

1419 **Marshall** I. H., Biblische Inspiration [Vorlesungen Nov. 1981 Oxford],[T]. Giesen 1986, Brunnen. 141 p. DM 17,80. – [R]SNTU-A 13 (1988) 207-210 (U. *Borse*).

1420 **Murray** John, CALVIN on Scripture and divine sovereignty. GR 1978 = 1960, Baker. 71 p. – [R]Zwingliana 17 (1988) 77s (E. *Saxer*).

1421 **Ogden** S. M., On theology [... 2. Revelation; 3. Authority of Scripture ...] 1986 ➤ 2,198; 3,270: [R]Interpretation 42 (1988) 82-85 (R. *Grigg*).

1422 **Olthuis** James H., *al.*, A hermeneutics of ultimacy; peril or promise? [Scripture authority]. Lanham MD 1987, UPA. 90 p. $8.25. 0-8191-5801-1. – [R]RExp 85 (1988) 362s (C. J. *Scalise*).

1423 *a*) *Robinson* Bernard P., Biblical authority; is it time for another paradigm shift? – *b*) *Stewart* Alistair C., Scripture as process; a reply to B. P. Robinson: ScripB 18 (1987s) 38-41 / 19 (1988s) 12s.

1424 **Ruokanen** Miikka [not Mükka ➤ 2,1023*] Doctrina divinitus inspirata; Martin Luther's position in the ecumenical problem of biblical inspiration. Helsinki 1985, Luther Agricola Soc. 163 p. 951-9047-19-0. – [R]ÉTRel 63 (1988) 477s (J.-D. *Kraege*).

1425 *Ruokanen* Miikka, Does LUTHER have a theory of biblical inspiration?: ModT 4 (1987s) 1-16.

1426 **Trembath** Kern R., Evangelical theories of biblical inspiration; a review and proposal 1987 ➤ 3,1430; £22.50; 0-19-504911-X: [R]CBQ 50 (1988) 736-8 (S. *McKnight*: ecumenical near-Catholic soteriology; but changes all the rules by defining inspiration as the experience of the believer).

B3.4 **Traditio, canon.**

1427 *Auld* A. Graeme, Word of God and word of man; prophets and canon: ➤ 29, Mem. CRAIGIE P., Ascribe 1988, 237-251.

1428 **Barr** James, Holy Scripture; canon, authority, criticism 1983 ➤ 64,1464 ... 2,1030: [R]TZBas 44 (1988) 283s (K. *Seybold*).

1429 **Beckwith** Roger, The OT canon of the NT Church 1985 ➤ 1,1472 ... 3,1436: [R]AnglTR 70 (1988) 262-4 (D. F. *Morgan*); CBQ 50 (1988) 706s (G. W. E. *Nickelsburg*); Interpretation 42 (1988) 78-82 (A. C. *Sundberg*); JSS 33 (1988) 278s (J. *Day*); NedTTs 42 (1988) 154s (P. W. van der *Horst*); VT 38 (1988) 384 (R. P. *Gordon*).

1430 *a*) *Beckwith* Roger T., Formation of the Hebrew Bible; – *b*) *Ellis* E. Earle, The OT canon [/ interpretation] in the early Church: ➤ 317, Mikra 1988, 39-86 / 653-690 [691-725].

1431 *Berger* Herman, Tradition aus humanistischer und anti-humanistischer Sicht: Bijdragen 49 (1988) 175-187; franç. 187.

1432 *Brandmüller* W., 'Traditio Scripturae interpres'; La doctrina de los concilios sobre la recta interpretación de la Biblia hasta el Concilio de Trento: ➤ 111*, [F]ORLANDIS R., J., Hispania christiana 1988, 65-84.

1433 *a*) *Bruce* Frederick F., Scripture in relation to tradition and reason; – *b*) *Bauckham* Richard J., Tradition in relation to Scripture and reason; – *c*) *Pailin* David A., Reason in relation to Scripture and tradition; – *d*) *Kelly* Joseph F., Scripture and tradition in the early Irish church: ➤ 60, [F]HANSON R., Scripture 1988, 35-64 / 117-145 / 207-238 / 146-173.

1434 *a) Childs* Brevard S., Biblische Theologie und christlicher Kanon; – *b) Link* Hans-Georg, Der Kanon in ökumenischer Sicht; – *c) Baldermann* Ingo, Didaktischer und 'kanonischer' Zugang; der Religionsunterricht vor dem Problem des biblischen Kanons; – *d) Sæbø* Magne, Vom 'Zusammendenken' zum Kanon; Aspekte der traditionsgeschichtlichen Endstadien des ATs; – *e) Oeming* Manfred, Text — Kontext — Kanon; ein neuer Weg alttestamentlicher Theologie? ... Childs: JbBT 3 (1988) 13-28 / 83-96 / 97-114 / 115-134 / 241-252.

1435 *Crüsemann* P., Das 'portative Vaterland'; Struktur und Genese des alttestamentlichen Kanons [3. Teil]: ➤ 286, Kanon und Zensur 1987, 63-79.

1436 *a) Dassmann* Ernst, Wer schuf den Kanon des Neuen Testaments? Zum neuesten Buch von Bruce M. METZGER; – *b) Stemberger* Günter, Pseudonymität und Kanon; zum gleichnamigen Buch von David G. MEADE: JbBT 3 (1988) 275 ... / 267-274 [< ZIT 89,174].

1437 **Farmer** W. R., *Farkasfalvy* D. M., Formation of NT canon 1983 ➤ 64,1475 ... 2,1035: ᴿSecC 6 (1987) 247-9 (J. D. *Laurance*).

1438 **Fogarty** Gerald, Nova et vetera; the theology of tradition in American Catholicism: Père Marquette Theology lecture 1987 ➤ 3,1446: ᴿRelStR 14 (1988) 88 (K. *Osborne*).

1438* *Freedman* David N., The earliest Bible: ➤ 3,356, Backgrounds 1987, 29-37 [< JBL 108,174].

1439 **Gamble** Harry Y., The New Testament as canon; its making and meaning 1985 ➤ 1,1479 ... 3,1449: ᴿCurrTM 15 (1988) 446 (E. R. *Kalin*; ÉTRel 63 (1988) 588 (J. *Zumstein*); SecC 6 (1987s) 123-5 (W. R. *Farmer*).

1440 **Gisel** P., Croyance incarnée; tradition, Écriture, canon, dogme 1986 ➤ 3,1450: ᴿLavalTP 44 (1988) 417s (R. M. *Roberge*); Protestantesimo 43 (1988) 657s (F. *Ferrario*); RThom 88 (1988) 681s (G. *Narcisse*).

1441 *Grelot* Pierre, Qu'est-ce que la Tradition?: VChr Sup 327. P c.1988 [Masses Ouvrières 427,109].

1442 *a) Kessler* C., Apprendre à transmettre dans le Judaïsme; – *b) Dupuy* P., La transmission dans le Catholicisme; – *c) Ashkénazy* L., Souvenir et tradition juive: Sens 11 (P 1987) 295-300 / 301-5 / 12 (1988) 41-48 [< Judaica 44,127s].

1443 *Künneth* Walter, Kanon: ➤ 813, TRE 17 (1988) 562-570.

1444 *Liebing* Heinz, Sola Scriptura — die reformatorische Antwort auf das Problem der Tradition: ➤ 3,104, ꟳLIEBING 1986, 163-176 [< LuJb 55 (1988) 165].

1445 *Lohse* Bernhard, Die Entscheidung der lutherischen Reformation über den Umfang des alttestamentlichen Kanons [ineditum]: ➤ 224, Evangelium 1988, 211-236.

1446 **McDonald** L., The formation of the Christian biblical canon. Nv 1988, Abingdon. 205 p. [TS 50,411].

1447 *a) Maier* Johann, Zur Frage des biblischen Kanons im Frühjudentum im Licht der Qumranfunde; – *b) Stemberger* Günter, Jabne und der Kanon; – *c) Miller* Patrick D.ᴶ, Der Kanon in der gegenwärtigen amerikanischen Diskussion: JbBT 3 (1988) 135-146 / 163-174 / 217-240 [< ZIT 89,174].

1448 **Maldonado** Robert D., Canon and Christian scripture; toward a multi-level, contingent understanding of canonical value: diss. Graduate Theological Union, ᴰ*Morgan* Donn F. Berkeley 1988, 253 p. 89-06586 – DissA 49 (1988s) 3763-A.

1449 **Meade** David G., Pseudonymity and canon...: WUNT 39, 1986 ➤ 2,1040; 3,1455: ᴿBijdragen 49 (1988) 94s (P. C. *Beentjes*); CBQ 50

(1988) 143s (E. V. *Gallagher*); ÉTRel 63 (1988) 288s (J.-M. *Prieur*); JBL 107 (1988) 560-2 (H. *Gamble*); Salesianum 50 (1988) 427 (R. *Vicent*).

1450 **Metzger** Bruce M., The canon of the NT 1987 → 3,1456: ᴿAfJB 2 (1987) 113s (N. *Onwu*); AnglTR 70 (1988) 357-360 (F. W. *Hughes*); ChH 57 (1988) 522s (R. M. *Grant*); JTS 39 (1988) 585-8 (J. K. *Elliott*: only 60 of the 5000 Greek NT mss contain the whole NT, so few pre-print Christians ever saw a whole Greek NT); LvSt 13 (1988) 272s (J. *Delobel*); NedTTs 42 (1988) 456 (P. W. van der *Horst*); ScripTPamp 20 (1988) 832-6 (G. *Aranda*); SWJT 31,2 (1988s) 49 (J. A. *Brooks*); TS 49 (1988) 734s (Rowan A. *Greer*); TTod 45 (1988s) 496s (R. W. *Wall*).

1451 *Mucci* Giandomenico, Che cos'è la tradizione della Chiesa?: CC 139 (1988,4) 223-236.

1452 *Müller* Mogens, Jødedommens Bibel på nytestamentlig tid og den kristne Bibel: DanTTs 51 (1988) 220 ... [< ZIT 88,659].

1453 **Noll** Mark A., Between faith and criticism; evangelicals, scholarship ... 1986 → 3,1353: ᴿAndrUnS 26 (1988) 197-9 (G. R. *Knight*); AsbTJ 43,2 (1988) 137s (L. G. *Stone*); CurrTM 15 (1988) 204s (E. *Krentz*); RExp 85 (1988) 158s (B. J. *Leonard*); TTod 45 (1988s) 251s (G. T. *Sheppard*).

1454 *O'Malley* John W., Tradition and traditions; historical perspectives: Way 27 (1987) 163-173.

1455 **Robbins** Gregory A., *Perì tôn endiathēkōn graphôn*; EUSEBIUS and the formation of the Christian Bible: diss. Duke. Durham NC 1986. – RelStR 14,189.

1456 *a) Rüger* Hans Peter, Das Werden des christlichen Alten Testaments; – *b) Sieben* Hermann J., Die Kontroverse zwischen BOSSUET und LEIBNIZ über den alttestamentlichen Kanon des Konzils von Trient; – *c) Berndt* Rainer, Gehören die Kirchenväter zur heiligen Schrift? Zur Kanon-theorie des HUGO von St. Viktor; – *d) Hübner* Hans, Vetus Testamentum und Vetus Testamentum in Novo receptum; die Frage nach dem Kanon des ATs aus neutestamentlicher Sicht: JbBT 3 (1988) 175-190 / 201-216 / 191-200 / 147-162.

1457 **Sanders** James A., From sacred story to sacred text; canon as paradigm [essays 1975-85] 1987 → 3,1466: ᴿAnglTR 70 (1988) 264s (D. F. *Morgan*); BibTB 18 (1988) 37 (L. J. *White*); Interpretation 42 (1988) 89 (K. H. *Richards*).

1458 *Scanlin* Harold P., What is the canonical shape of the Old Testament text we translate?: → 502, Issues/Translation 1987/8, 207-220.

1459 *Schenk* Wolfgang, Code-Wandel und Christliche Identität; der Kanon des 'Neuen Testaments' als semiotisches Problem: LingBib 61 (1988) 87-113; Eng. 113s.

1460 *Steck* Odil H., Der Kanon des hebräischen Alten Testaments; historische Materialien für eine ökumenische Perspektive: → 114, ᶠPANNENBERG W., Vernunft 1988, 231-252.

1461 **Stuhlhofer** F., Der Gebrauch der Bibel von Jesus bis EUSEB; eine statistische Untersuchung zur Kanonsgeschichte, Vorw *Riesner* Rainer. Wu 1988, Brockhaus. 160 p. DM 28 [RHE 83,359*]. 3-417-29335-9.

1461* *Stuhlhofer* Franz, Der Ertrag von Bibelstellenregistern für die Kanonsgeschichte: ZAW 100 (1988) 244-260; Eng. 260s.

1462 *Valliere* Paul, Tradition: → 795, EncRel 15 (1987) 1-16.

1463 *Weissengruber* Franz, Zum Problem der Pseudepigraphie und des Kanons: SNTU-A 13 (1988) 179-192.

1464 *a) Wiederkehr* Dietrich, Das Prinzip der Überlieferung; – *b) Pottmeyer* Hermann J., Normen, Kriterien und Strukturen der Überlieferung: → 800, HbFT 4 (1988) 100-123 / 124-152.

1465 *Youngblood* R., *Gaffin* R. B., *al.,* The canon; how God gave his Word to the Church: ChrTod 32,2 (1988) 23-38 [NTAbs 32,140].

B4 *Interpretatio humanistica* – .1 **The Bible and man.**

1466 [E]**Dekker** G., *Veenhof* J., Werken; zin of geen zin; twaalf theologische visies op arbeid ['colleges' VU 1985] 1986 → 3,618: [R]NedTTs 42 (1988) 356-8 (R. van *Kessel).*

1467 **Derksen** N., *Andriessen* H., Bibliodrama en Pastoraat; de Schrift doen als weg tot dieper geloven: Pastorale Handreiking 46. Haag 1985, Voor-hoeve. 168 p. *f*29. 90-297-0823-9. – [R]NedTTs 42 (1988) 177 (J. *Visser).*

1468 **Dulin** Rachel Z., A crown of glory; a biblical view of aging. Mahwah NJ 1988, Paulist. vii-145 p. $9 [RB 96,140, R. J. *Tournay].*

1469 *a)* [E]**Fahlbusch** W., *al.,* Arbeit ist nicht alles; Versuche zu einer Ethik der Zukunft. – *b)* **Brakelmann** G., Der Arbeit geboren? Beiträge zu einer christlichen Arbeitsethik: SWI-Studien 6.11. Bochum 1987s, SWI. 130 p.; DM 14,50 / 212 p.; DM 16. 3-925895-10-8 / 1-6. – [R]TsTNijm 28 (1988) 423 (R. Van *Driessche).*

1470 **Fuller** Robert C., Religion and the life cycle [college course]. Ph 1988, Fortress. xi-157 p. $11 [TDig 36,160].

1471 **Harrington** Wilfrid, A cloud of witnesses; creative people of the Bible. Wilmington 1988, Glazier. 185 p. $13 [JBL 108,379].

1472 **Hooker** Roger, *Lamb* Christopher, Love the stranger (Christian ministry in multi-faith areas) ['the assumptions we bring to our reading of the Bible profoundly affect the message we think we take from it']. L 1986, SPCK. 160 p. £4.50. – [R]Themelios 14 (1988s) 33 (C. *Merchant*: reserves).

1473 **L'Heureux** Conrad, Life journey and the OT; an experiential approach to the Bible and personal transformation 1986 → 2,1062: [R]CBQ 50 (1988) 300s (W. *Wink*); Horizons 15 (1988) 380s (L. J. *Biallas*); IntRMiss 77 (1988) 563 (H. *Rowold*); IrTQ 54 (1988) 319s (Carmel *McCarthy);* ScripB 19 (1988s) 22 (A. *Jürgens).*

1474 *Schottroff* W. [AT], L. [NT]: Arbeit: → 804, NBL Lfg 1 (1988) 151-4.

1475 **Tidball** Derek, Skilful shepherds [Bible and history of exegesis on Belief, Forgiveness, Suffering, Unity, Ministry]. Leicester 1986, Inter-Varstty. 368 p. £9. – [R]Themelios 14 (1988s) 34s (P. *Manson).*

1476 **Vaux** Kenneth L., Health and medicine in the Reformed tradition; promise, providence and care. NY 1984, Crossroad. viii-149 p. $15. – [R]CalvinT 23 (1988) 241-4 (J. H. *Boer).*

1477 *Zerafa* P., The Old Testament life span: Angelicum 65 (1988) 99-116.

B4.2 *Femina, familia;* **Woman in the Bible** [→ H8.8s].

1478 *Amaru* Betsy H., Portraits of biblical women in JOSEPHUS' Antiquities: JJS 39 (1988) 143-170.

1479 **Aschkenasy** Nehama, Eve's journey; feminine images in Hebraic literary tradition. Ph 1986, Univ. Pennsylvania. xv-269 p. – [R]Prooftexts 8 (1988) 143-7 (Naomi B. *Sokoloff).*

1480 *Azria* Régine, Études juives au féminin [*Brenner* A. 1985; *Biale* R. 1984]: ArchScSocRel 65,2 (1988) 177-183.

1481 *Bélinki* K., Biblical women — Jewish literary and religious ideals: NordJud 7 (1986) 149-157 [< JStJud 19 (1988) 153].

1482 *Bonora* Adalberto, Ester e Susanna, Debora e la figlia di Iefte: / Sara, Rebecca, Rachele / Gezabele ed Erodiade / La donna nei libri sapienziali / Regina madre sposa / Maria e Marta: Presbyteri 22 (1988) 299-310 / 385-390 / 465-470 / 543-8 / 623-9 (779-784) / 703-8.

1483 **Brenner** Athalya, The Israelite woman; social role and literary type in biblical narrative: Biblical Seminar 2, Sheffield 1985 ➤ 1,1510 ... 3,1485: RTorJT 4 (1988) 136-8 (Gale A. *Yee*).

1484 *Brenner* A., Zelfverloochening als middel tot zelfbevestiging; sociaal gedrag van vrouwen in het oude Israël: Mara 1,2 (1988) 19-30 [< GerefTTs 88 (1988) 63].

1485 **Brooten** Bernadette J., Women leaders in the ancient Synagogue 1982 ➤ 64,1503 ... 3,1486: RBZ 32 (1988) 118s (J. *Maier*: nüchternes Urteilsvermögen); FraJudBei 15 (1987) 163-7 (Margaret *Schlüter*).

1486 **Callaway** Mary, Sing, O barren one 1986 ➤ 64,1503 ... 3,1486: RAustralBR (1988) 85 (Mary *Reaburn*: good but 1978 dissertation-sources not updated); VT 38 (1988) 498 (J. W. *Emerton*).

1487 **Carmody** Denise L., Biblical women; contemporary reflections on scriptural texts. NY 1988, Crossroad. xvi-168 p. $11 pa. [JBL 108,184].

1488 T**Caspi** Mishael M., Daughters of Yemen [Arabic Jewish poetry]. Berkeley 1985, Univ. California. xv-264 p. £23. – RJJS 39 (1988) 129s (D. *Wasserstein*).

1489 *Coggins* Richard, The contribution of women's studies to Old Testament studies; a male reaction: TLond 91 (1988) 5-16.

1490 **Deen** Edith, All of the women of the Bible. SF 1988 = 1955, Harper & R. xxii-409 p. 0-06-061852-3.

1491 **Detrick** R. Blaine, Favorite women of the Bible. Lima OH 1988, 'CSS'. 99 p. $6.50 [BToday 26,379].

1492 *Edwards* R. B., Woman: ➤ 801, ISBEnc³ 4 (1988) 1089-97 [in church leadership, *Hugenberger* G. P., 1098-1100].

1493 **Eider** Dorothy, Women of the Bible speak to women of today. Marina del Rey CA 1986, De Vorss. 247 p. – RRelStR 14 (1988) 238s (Frances B. *Sullivan*).

1494 E**Emdem** Rachel van, ... Die mij niet gemaakt heeft tot man; ... Joodse vrouwen 1986 ➤ 3,402: RBijdragen 49 (1988) 93s (Elly *Beurskens*).

1494* **Engelken** Karen, Die Frau — die Frauen; eine Begriffsgeschichtliche Untersuchung zum AT: ev. Diss. D*Seebass* H. Mainz 1988, 388 p. – RTLv 20,539.

1495 **Evans** Mary J., Women in the Bible 1983 ➤ 64,1510; 3,1493: RJEcuSt 22 (1985) 129s (Patricia A. *De Leeuw*).

1496 *a*) *Finkel* Asher, Women in the biblical tradition; – *b*) *Mackenzie* Caroline, A woman's experience of religious symbolism in a cross cultural setting; – *c*) *Ata* Abe W., Sexual inequality amongst Muslim Arabs: JDharma 13 (1988) 5-14 / 79-87 / 15-30.

1497 *Gablenz* Clara von, Frauengestalten im AT [6 Bücher]: EvKomm 21 (1988) 418.

1498 *a*) *Genest* Olivette, La sémiotique et les femmes du NT; – *b*) Entretien avec A. J. GREIMAS: ➤ 292, Jésus/Femmes 1982/7, 189-207 / 209-214.

1499 *Gerstenberger* Erhard S., Bibelexegese und biblische Theologie angesichts feministischer Kritik: Deutsches Pfarrerblatt 88,1 (Essen 1988) 6-9 [< ZIT].

1500 *a*) *Goitein* S. D., Women as creators of biblical genres; – *b*) *Steinmetz* Devora, A portrait of Miriam in rabbinic Midrash; – *c*) *Rosen* Tova, On tongues being bound and let loose; women in medieval Hebrew literature; – *d*) *Sokoloff* Naomi B., Feminist criticism and [modern] Hebrew literature [*Aschkcnasy* N. 1986; *Fuchs* E. 1987]: Prooftexts 8 (1988) 1-33 / 35-65 / 67-88 / 143-156.

1501 *Gruber* Mayer I., Women in the cult according to the Priestly Code: ➤ 3,355, E*Neusner* J., Judaic perspectives 1987, 35-48.

1502 **Heister** Maria-Sybilla,   Frauen in der biblischen Glaubensgeschichte. Gö 1984, Vandenhoeck & R.   226 p. DM 32 pa. – ᴿTLZ 113 (1988) 260-2 (Silvia *Schroer*).

1503 ᴱ**Keay** Kathy,   Men, women and God.   Basingstoke 1987, Marshall Pickering.   304 p. £6. – ᴿThemelios 14 (1988s) 23-26 (Sally *Alsford*: short chapters by a wide range of evangelical authors; the review treats also *Loades* A. 1987; *Heine* S. 1987).

1504 **Kirk** Martha Ann,   Celebrations of biblical women's stories; tears, milk and honey.   KC 1987, Sheed & W.   113 p. $10 [BToday 26,379].

1505 **Korczak** J.,   I bambini nella Bibbia.   R 1987, Carucci. [Henoch 10,255].

1506 **Langemeyer** Georg B.,   Als Mann und Frau leben; biblische Perspektive der Ehe 1984 → 1,1531:   ᴿWissWeish 50 (1987) 79s (M. *Gerwing*).

1507 *London* Gloria A.,   Pre-patriarchal society; homage to the elders: → 3,62*, ᶠGratz College 1987 ...

1508 *Maselli* D., La donna: → 485, La posizione del debole nella Bibbia 1987, 25-44.

1509 **Mayer** Günter,   Die jüdische Frau in der hellenistisch-römischen Antike 1987 → 3,1508:   ᴿBijdragen 49 (1988) 447s (P. C. *Beentjes*); BL (1988) 137 (L. *Grabbe*); TLZ 113 (1988) 25s (W. *Wiefel*); TsTNijm 28 (1988) 82 (E. van *Wolde*); Tyche 3 (1988) 293s (J. *Diethart*); ZkT 110 (1988) 192 (K. *Stock*).

1510 **Meyers** C.,   Discovering Eve; ancient Israelite women in context.   NY 1988, Oxford-UP.   0-19-504934-3 [BL 89,156].

1511 **Ohler** Annemarie,   Frauengestalten der Bibel.   Wü 1987, Echter. 228 p. DM 24,80. – ᴿZkT 110 (1988) 351 (R. *Frick-Pöder*).

1512 **Roith** Estelle,   The riddle of Fʀᴇᴜᴅ; Jewish influences on his theory of female sexuality.   L 1987, Tavistock New Library of Psychoanalysis. 199 p. – ᴿJJS 39 (1988) 120-2 (Naomi *Segal*).

1513 **Sölle** Dorothee, *Schottroff* Luise,   Mijn broeders hoedster; vrouwen lezen de bijbel [een aantal bijbelstudies = Die Erde gehört Gott 1985], ᵀ. Baarn 1986, Ten Have.   152 p. ƒ 19,50.   90-259-4298-9 [NedTTs 42,152].

1514 **Stanton** Elizabeth C.,   The woman's Bible; the original feminist attack on the Bible [1895-8], abridged; introd. *Spender* Dale.   E 1985, Polygon. v-152 + 187 p.; facsims. [KirSef 61 (1987s) 614].

1515 **Volger** Gisela, *Welck* Karin V.,   Die Braut; geliebt, verkauft, getauscht, geraubt — zur Rolle der Frau im Kulturvergleich [... OT, Egypt ...]. Köln 1985, Rautenstrauch-Joest-Museum.   896 p. (2 vol.) [RelStR 15,339, J. *Gutmann*].

1516 **Walter** K., *Bartolomei* M. C.,   Donne alla riscoperta della Bibbia. Brescia 1988, Queriniana.   207 p. Lit. 17.000.

1517 **Weems** Renita J.,   Just a sister away [... women's relationships in the Bible].   San Diego 1988, Lura Media.   xi-145 p. $10 [RelStR 15,346, J. H. *Evans*].

1518 *Wegner* Judith R.,   Tragelaphos [*koy* Bik. 2,8-11] revisited; the anomaly of woman in the Mishnah: Judaism 37 (1988) 160-172.

1519 **Williams** James G.,   Women recounted; narrative thinking and the God of Israel 1982 → 63,1579 ... 3,1519:   ᴿBO 45 (1988) 170s (E. *Talstra*).

B4.4   *Exegesis litteraria* – **The Bible itself as literature.**

1520 ᴱ**Alter** Robert, *Kermode* Frank,   The literary guide to the Bible 1987 → 3,324; also Collins, £30;   0-00-217439-1:   ᴿBL (1988) 69 (W. G. E. *Watson*); CalvinT 23 (1988) 259-261 (T. R. *Wolthuis*); CCurr 23 (1988s) 221-3 (P. *Grant* under title 'How to read the Bible, maybe'); ChrCent 105

(1988) 506-8 (G. *Gunn*: 'approach and avoidance'); ClasW 82 (1988s) 317 (W. S. *Anderson*: recommended); ExpTim 99,11 1st choice (1988s) 321-3 (C. S. *Rodd*); Horizons 15 (1988) 436s (L. S. *Cunningham*); New Yorker (Jan. 11,1988) 94-98 (G. *Steiner*); Tablet 242 (1988) 563s (J. *Coulson*); TLond 91 (1988) 421-4 (Meg *Davies*); TTod 45 (1988s) 348. 350 (J. A. *Darr*).

1521 **Alter** Robert, The invention of Hebrew prose; modern fiction and the language of realism. Seattle 1988, Univ. of Washington. xi-122 p. $15 [JBL 107,785].

1522 *Downing* F. Gerald, À bas les aristos; the relevance of higher literature for the understanding of the first Christian writings: NT 30 (1988) 212-230.

1523 *a)* *Fontinoy* Charles, La bible et l'humour; – *b)* *Destrée* Annette, Le comique et l'humour dans les sociétés orientales: → 50, [F]FONTINOY C. 1988, 73-81 / 9-14.

1524 **Frye** Northrop, Le grand code, [T]*Chalier* Catherine, 1984 [→ 3,1539 [T]*Malamoud* Catherine]: [R]RBgPg 66 (1988) 651-3 (J. *Chopineau*).

1525 **Frye** N., Il grande codice, la Bibbia e la letteratura, [T]*Rizzoni* Giovanni, 1986 → 3,1540: [R]Humanitas 42 (Brescia 1987) 476s (A. *Marchese*); ViPe 70 (1987) 238-240 (G. *Langella*).

1526 **Gabel** John B., *Wheeler* Charles B., The Bible as literature, an introduction 1986 → 2,1106; 3,1541: [R]BL (1988) 76 (J. C. L. *Gibson*: even the paper acid-free); LvSt 13 (1988) 82s (R. F. *Collins*); RelStR 14 (1988) 149s (D. *Jobling*: exegetical old stuff by two English professors who ignore current ferment over the Bible as literature).

1527 **Gottcent** John H., The Bible, a literary study: Masterwork 2. Boston 1986, Twayne. xxxiv-125 p. $18; pa. $7. – [R]RelStR 14 (1988) 149 (D. *Jobling*).

1528 *Kselman* John S., The literary study of the Bible: America 157 (1987) 297-9.310.

1529 **Longman** Tremper[III], Literary approaches to biblical interpretation: Foundations of contemporary interpretation 3. GR 1987, Zondervan. xi-164 p. $13. 0-310-40941-1 [BL 89,84, D. J. A. *Clines*].

1530 **Sternberg** Meir, The poetics of biblical narrative 1985 (pa. 1986) → 1,1617; 2,1120: [R]VT 38 (1988) 243-9 (Naomi *Segal*).

1531 **Walczak** B., ✪ Znaczenie Biblii w dziejach języków i językoznawstwa: Życie i Myśl 35,9s (Poznań 1987) 37-42 [The significance of the Bible 'in the history of languages and linguistics' (NTAbs 32,293 'in matters of language and learning languages')].

1532 **Wright** T. R., Theology and literature: Signposts in Theology. Ox 1988, Blackwell. 0-631-14848-5; pa. 9-3 [BL 89,157]. – [R]LvSt 13 (1988) 393s (H.-E. *Mertens*); RelSt 24 (1988) 534s (B. L. *Horne*).

B4.5 **Influxus biblicus in litteraturam profanam,** *generalia* → F1.7.

1533 *Arthur* Ross G., The day of judgment is now; a Johannine pattern in the Middle English *Pearl*: AmBenR 38 (1987) 227-242.

1534 *Colombo* U., Bibbia e letteratura: → 806, NDizTB (1988) 192-209.

1535 **Dabezies** André, *al.,* Jésus-Christ dans la littérature française, anthologie I-II: JJC, Résonances 2. P 1987, Desclée. 321 p.; 318 p. – [R]Espr Vie 98 (1988) 111s (E. *Vauthier*); RSPT 72 (1988) 326s (J.-P. *Jossua*).

1536 **Fowler** David C., The Bible in Middle English literature 1984 → 1,1589; 2,1104*: [R]Speculum 63 (1988) 659-661 (M. M. *Gatch*).

1537 ^E**Hartman** G.H., *Budick* S., Midrash and literature 1986 ➤ 2,249; 3,1544 (Hartmann): ^RFraJudBei 15 (1987) 155-8 (A. *Goldberg*); JTS 39 (1988) 216-9 (A. *Chester*).

1537* **Herr** M., Les tragédies bibliques au XVIIIe siècle. P/Genève 1988, Champion/Slatkine. 269 p.; 10 fig. [NRT 111,1070].

1538 **Holton** Frederick S., Exegesis and eschatology in Old English poetry: diss. Edinburgh 1979. 331 p. BRD-80106. – DissA 49 (1988s) 91-A.

1539 ^E**Jens** W., *Küng* H., Dichtung und Religion 1985 ➤ 3,1550: ^RRSPT 72 (1988) 328s (J.-P. *Jossua*).

1540 ^E**Jens** Walter, *Küng* Hans, *Kuschel* Karl-J., Theologie und Literatur; zum Stand des Dialogs 1986 ➤ 3,1550: ^RTLZ 113 (1988) 47-51 (P.P. *Sänger*). ➤ 1572.

1541 *Mirsky* Aharon, ❻ Rabbinical exposition in English biblical poetry: ➤ 132, ^FSCHIRMANN H., Jubilee 1970, 174-194.

1542 ^E**Preminger** A., *Greenstein* E. L., The Hebrew Bible in literary criticism 1986 ➤ 2,262; 3,1559: ^RBibTB 18 (1988) 36 (J.F. *Craghan*: their selection of modern Israeli authors greatly enhances the volume); Horizons 15 (1988) 154 (D.C. *Hopkins*); RRel 47 (1988) 156 (A. *Arkin*: not 'Hebrew *text*').

1543 ^E**Rosenberg** David, Congregation; contemporary writers read the Jewish Bible. NY 1987, Harcourt-BJ. 526 p. $28.50. – ^RTTod 45 (1988s) 468. 470.472.474 (W. *Brueggemann*, also on HARTMAN-BUDICK).

1544 *Schmidt-Sommer* Irmgard, Bibel und Gegenwartsliteratur: ErbAuf 63 (1987) 149s.

1545 **Schwartz** Howard, Lilith's cave; Jewish tales of the supernatural. SF 1988, Harper & R. xi-294 p. $22.50 [TDig 36,82].

1546 *Spicehandler* Ezra, The attitude towards the Land of Israel in Spanish Hebrew poetry: ➤ 499, Holy Land 1986/8, 117-140 [-172 *al.,* recent Jewish literature].

1547 **Wood** Ralph C., The comedy of redemption; Christian faith [NIEBUHR/ BARTH theologies] and comic vision in four American novelists. ND 1988, Univ. xii-310 p. $33. – ^RAnglTR 70 (1988) 372-5 (Barbara *Smith-Morgan*).

1548 *Wright* Charles D., Biblical influence on Old English poetic vocabulary: ➤ 74, ^FKASKE R. 1986, 9-21.

B4.6 *Singuli auctores* – **Bible-influence on individual authors.**

1549 BLAKE: *Billigheimer* Rachel V., Blake's 'Eyes of God' [Ex Ezek Zech Rev]; cycles to apocalypse and redemption: PgQ 66 (1987) 231-257.

1550 *Spector* Sheila A., Hebraic etymologies of proper names in Blake's Myth [*De Luca* V. 1978]: PgQ 67 (1988) 345-363.

1551 **Villalobos** John C., William Blake and biblical criticism: diss. Southern California, ^D*Schulz* M. 1987. – DissA 49 (1988s) 261-A.

1552 BOWMAN: *Jossua* Jean-Pierre, Bulletin de théologie littéraire [Bowman F., Le Christ des barricades 1987; POZZI Catherine 1987...]: RSPT 72 (1988) 325-336.

1553 BRINK: *Gibert* Pierre, Bible et anti-Bible chez André Brink [romancier sud-africain]: Études 368 (1988) 651-661.

1554 COLERIDGE Samuel T., Confessions of an inquiring spirit³ [1853]: Fortress Texts in Modern Theology. Ph 1988, Fortress. 104 p. [CBQ 50, 750].

1555 CONRAD: *a*) *Rousseau* Marie-Claude, La Bible, à plus d'un titre [quip for (mainly AngloAmerican) 'titles of books and films borrowed from the

Bible']; exemples d'intertextualité; – *b*) *Lombard* François, [Joseph] Conrad et la Bible: → 486, Traduction 1986/8, 125-136 / 163-8; Eng. 125.163.

1556 DANTE: **Charity** A.C., Events and their afterlife; the dialectics of Christian typology in the Bible and Dante. C c.1987, Univ. £13 [TLond 91,77].

1557 DOSTOIEVSKY: **Patterson** David, The affirming flame; religion, language, literature [he teaches Russian; treats John, Luke, Dostoievsky, BAKHTIN, WIESEL...]. Norman 1988, Univ. Oklahoma. x-175 p. $22.50 [TDig 36,74].

1558 GIDE: **Taylor** Donald R., André Gide's application of biblical parable to express a moral philosophy ['live as you please']: diss. Southern Mississippi 1987, ᴰ*Johnson* R. 114 p. 88-06639. – DissA 49 (1988s) 813s-A.

1559 GOETHE: *Mendes de Castro* Joaquim, Inspiração bíblica do Fausto: Brotéria 124 (1987) 287-298.

1560 HOPKINS: **Brittain** Clark M., Logos, creation and epiphany in the poetics of Gerard M. Hopkins: diss. Univ. Virginia. Charlottesville 1987. – RelStR 14,188.

1561 HUGO: *Malavié* Jean, Saint Jean et saint Paul dans l'œuvre de Victor Hugo: RThom 88 (1988) 620-635.

1562 MACDONALD: **Reed-Nancarrow** Paula E., Remythologizing the Bible; fantasy and the revelatory hermeneutic of George MacDonald: diss. Minnesota, ᴰ*Madden* W. Minneapolis 1988. 235 p. 88-15296. – DissA 49 (1988s) 1811-A.

1563 MILTON: **Bauman** Michael, Milton's Arianism. Fra 1987, Lang. xvi-378 p. – ᴿTrinJ 9,1 (1988) 105-110 (E. E. *Ericson*: continuation of a sizable controversy).

1564 *Berkeley* David S., The 'mysterious' marriage of Adam and Eve in Paradise Lost: PgQ 66 (1987) 195-205.

1565 **Honeygosky** Stephen R., Milton's House of God; Church, Scripture, sacrament: diss. Wisconsin, ᴰ*Chambers* A. Madison 1988. 644 p. 88-20050. – DissA 49 (1988s) 2667-A.

1566 **Lim Swee Huat** Walter, Biblical analogy and the heroic paradigm in 'Paradise Lost' and 'Paradise Regained': diss. Toronto 1988, ᴰ*MacCallum* H. R. – DissA 49 (1988s) 811-A.

1567 **MacCallum** Hugh, Milton and the Sons of God; the divine image in Milton's epic poetry. Toronto 1986, Univ. x-325 p. $35. – ᴿRelStR 14 (1988) 149 (Stella P. *Revard*).

1568 **Schwartz** Regina M., Remembering and repeating biblical creation in Paradise Lost. C 1988, Univ. ix-144 p.; front. £22.50. 0-521-34357-7.

1569 **Shoaf** R. A., Milton, poet of duality; a study of semiosis in the poetry and prose [... Adam and Eve; Samson]. NHv 1985, Yale Univ. xiv-225 p. $17. – ᴿRelStR 14 (1988) 148s (Stella P. *Revard*).

1570 **Wittreich** Joseph, Interpreting Samson Agonistes. Princeton 1987, Univ. xxx-394 p. $42.50. – ᴿPgQ 67 (1988) 389-393 (Wendy *Furman*).

1571 PASCAL: *Brun* Jean, Pascal et la Bible: → 28*, ᶠCOURTHIAL P., Dieu parle! 1984, 159-168.

1572 ᴱ**Küng** H., *Jens* W., Wereldliteratuur en religie; Pascal, Gryphius, Lessing, Hölderlin, Novalis, Kierkegaard, Dostojewski, Kafka. Hilversum 1986, Gooi & S. 288 p. ƒ49,50. 90-304-0367-5. – ᴿTsTNijm 28 (1988) 427 (H.-E. *Mertens*). → 1539s.

1573 QUINTUS: *García Romero* Francisco A., El Nuevo Testamento y los Post Homerica de Quinto de Esmirna: FgNt 1,1 (1988) 103-7; Eng. 107s: the author was not Christian.

1574 SHAKESPEARE: **Shaheen** Naseed, Biblical references in Shakespeare's tragedies. Newark NJ 1987, Univ. of Delaware. – ᴿSixtC 19 (1988) 719s (F. *Ardolino*).

1575 SHOLEM ALEICHEM: **Nave** Yudit, Biblical motifs representing the 'lyrical self' in the works of Sholem Aleichem, *al.*: diss. Brandeis. Boston 1987. 186 p. 88-19770. – DissA 49 (1988s) 1800-A.

1576 SINGER: **Reyer** William R., Biblical figures in selected short fiction of Isaac B. Singer: diss SUNY. Bowling Green 1988. 108 p. 88-24668. – DissA 49 (1988s) 2661-A.

1577 STRYJKOWSKI Julian, ✆ [Biblijne powieści tworzące trylogię] Odpo-wiedź / Król Dawid żyje / Juda Makabi. Poznań 1984/4/6, W drodze. 116 p.; 304 p.; 194 p. – ᴿRuBi 41 (1988) 361-5 (S. *Pisarek*).

1578 XENOPHON E.: *Bauer* Johannes B., [Parallelen Lk 1,80; 2,40.52; Gn 32,23-33 ...] In Xenophontis Ephesii quem vocant fabellam commenta-riola: GrazBei 14 (1987) 229-238.

B4.7 *Interpretatio* **athea, materialistica, psychiatrica.**

1579 *Albrecht* Clemens, *al.*, Fragen an Eugen DREWERMANN: EvKomm 21 (1988) 463-5 [< ZIT 88,589].

1580 *Barbaglio* G., Psicologia ➤ 806, NDizTB (1988) 1257-1271.

1581 *Barth* Hans-Martin, Gottes Wort ist dreifaltig; ein Beitrag zur Aus-einandersetzung mit der 'archetypischen Hermeneutik' Eugen DRE-WERMANNS [Gastvorlesung Greifswald 1987]: TLZ 113 (1988) 241-254.

1582 *Bechter* Hugo, Bibelauslegung — historisch-kritisch oder tiefenpsy-chologisch?: Katechetische Blätter 113,2 (Mü 1988) 112-8 (-126, *al.*).

1583 *Díaz Murugarren* José, Hermenéutica teológica y psicoanálisis: CiTom 115 (1988) 469-489.

1584 **Drewermann** E., [➤ 2170] Tiefenpsychologie und Exegese 1984s ➤ 65, 1386 ... 3,1570; jetzt I⁶ 575 p.; II⁶ 851 p.; 3-530-16855-6; 6-5: ᴿErbAuf 63 (1987) 237s (J. *Kaffanke*, 2); RHPR 68 (1988) 487s (B. *Kaempf*, 1s); WissWeis 49 (1986) 237s (H.-J. *Klauck*, 2).

1585 **Drewermann** E., 'An ihren Früchten sollt ihr sie erkennen'; Antwort auf R. PESCH und G. LOHFINKS 'Tiefenpsychologie und keine Exegese' ['typical device for a group-condemnation to bypass Church authority' mit Zustimmung *Schmitz* S. p. 177-202]. Olten 1988, Walter. 204 p. DM 22. – ᴿGeistL 61 (1988) 315s (J. *Sudbrack*); HerdKorr 42 (1988) 447 [zu Drewermann auch 114-8, A. A. *Bucher*]; TPQ 136 (1988) 288s (J. *Janda*).

1586 *Drewermann* E., Streit um Tiefenpsychologie und Exegese [answer to (excerpts from) LOHFINK G., PESCH R.]: Reformiertes Forum 2,9 (Ba 1988) 17s [< NTAbs 32,285].

1587 **Gay** Peter, A godless Jew; FREUD, atheism and the making of psy-choanalysis. NHv 1987, Yale Univ. xiii-182 p. $17.50. – ᴿJJS 39 (1988) 291 (L. *Kochan*); RelStR 14 (1988) 359 (D. *Merkur*: 'highly readable ... pretext for Gay's own atheistic polemic').

1588 **Glenny** James B., Biblical and psychological perspectives on family relationship: diss. ᴰ*Cooke* W. Belfast 1987. 329 p. – RTLv 19,582.

1589 **Hunt** David, *McMahon* T. J., The seduction of Christianity; spiritual discernment in the last days. Eugene OR 1985, Harvest. 249 p. $8. 0-89081-441-4. – ᴿJPsy&T 15 (1987) 168-170 (K. L. *Williams*: against

'New Age Movement'; 500,000 copies sold; but uses psychology dangerously).

1590 **Kandathil** Candida sr., Gospel communication in a new key; a psychotherapeutic approach to evangelization: diss. Roma, Urbaniana. 1988. xvi-381 p.

1591 **Kaplan** Kalman J., *al.,* The family; biblical and psychological foundations [special issue of JPsy&Jud]. NY 1984, Human Sciences. 132 p. – ᴿRExp 85 (1988) 185 (Diana R. R. *Garland*: contrasts Greek and Hebrew models).

1592 **Lohfink** G., *Pesch* R., Tiefenpsychologie und keine Exegese ... DREWERMANN 1987 ➤ 3,1571: ᴿBiKi 43 (1988) 33s (S. *Schmitz*); ErbAuf 64 (1988) 68s (B. *Schwank,* auch 233 zu D's Antwort); FreibZ 35 (1988) 269-271 (Marie-Louise *Gubler*); RuBi 41 (1988) 270s (J. *Łach*); Streven 55 (1987s) 570 (P. *Beentjes*).

1593 *Niehl* Franz W., Wie tiefenpsychologisch darf die Exegese sein?: KatBlätt 112 (Mü 1987) 971 ... [< ZIT].

1594 **Patten** Donald W., Catastrophism and the Old Testament; the Mars-Earth conflicts. Seattle 1988, Pacific Meridian. (xviii-)289 p. $15 [CBQ 51,403].

1595 **Propst** L. Rebecca, Psychotherapy in a religious framework; spirituality in the emotional healing process. NY 1987, Human Sciences. 209 p. $30 [TDig 36,76].

1596 *Rebell* Walter, Theologe oder Guru? [DREWERMANN E.]: EvKomm 21 (1988) 345-7: 'enorme Breitenwirkung' [463s, Fragen, *Albrecht* C. *al.].*

1597 **Rotenberg** Mordechai, Re-biographing and deviance; psychotherapeutic narrativism and the midrash. NY 1987, Praeger. 221 p. $40 [RelStR 15,366, S. *Kepnes*].

1598 *a)* **Schnackenburg** Rudolf, Exegese und Tiefenpsychologie [DREWERMANN E.]; – *b)* *Sudbrack* Josef, ... aus der Sicht geistlicher Exegese; – *c)* *Görres* Albert, Erneuerung durch Tiefenpsychologie?: ➤ 305, Tiefenpsychologische 1988, 26-48 / 98-114 / 133-174.

1599 **Stein** Dominique, Lectures psychanalytiques de la Bible 1985 ➤ 2,1131: ᴿBLitEc 89 (1988) 236s (Jacqueline Des *Rochettes*); FoiTemps 19 (1987) 284s (C. *Focant*).

1600 *Stein* Dominique [Lectures psychanalytiques de la Bible, Cerf 1985] Une lecture psychanalytique de la Bible; Le sacrifice interdit de Marie BALMARY [1986]: RSPT 72 (1988) 95-108.

1601 *Tam Siang-Yang,* Cognitive-behavior therapy; a biblical approach and critique: JPsy&T 15 (1987) 103-112.

1602 **Vitz** Paul C., Sigmund FREUD's Christian unconscious [neurotic response to his Catholic nanny...]. NY 1988, Guilford. xv-287 p. $20 [RelStR 15,55].

B5 Methodus exegetica.

1603 **Abercrombie** John R., Computer programs for literary analysis. Ph 1984, Univ. Pennsylvania. 203 p. – ᴿCompHum 20 (1986) 108-110 (Nancy M. *Ide*).

1604 *a)* *Alonso Schökel* Luis, Trends, plurality of methods, priority of issues; – *b)* *Rendtorff* Rolf, Between historical criticism and holistic interpretation; some trends in Old Testament exegesis: ➤ 482, VTS 40, Jerusalem congress 1986/8, 285-292 / 298-303.

1605 *Andrew* M.E., Old Testament studies; prevalent attitudes and contextual ministry: AsiaJT 1 (1987) 292-302.

1606 **Bader** Winfried, Der Einsatz der EDV [Elektronische Datenverarbeitung] bei der Analyse hebräischer Texte; Diskussionsbeitrag zu Wolfgang RICHTER: BibNot [37 (1987) 73-103] 43 (1988) 27-48.

1607 **Beattie** D.R.G., First steps in biblical criticism: Studies in Judaism. Lanham MD 1988, UPA. x-108 p. $14.50 [JBL 107,785].

1608 **Berger** Klaus, Exegese und Philosophie: SBS 123s, 1986 ➤ 2,1138; 3-460-04231-1: ᴿTLZ 112 (1987) 836-9 (M. *Petzoldt*); TR 84 (1988) 292-4 (G. *Dautzenberg*); WissWeis 50 (1987) 218-221 (N. *Hartmann*).

1609 **Brisebois** Mireille, Métodos para leer mejor la Biblia; exégesis histórico-crítica [Des méthodes], ᵀ*Martínez de Lapera* Victor A.: Estudios Bíblicos 1. M 1987, Paulinas. 108 p. 84-285-1183-7. – ᴿActuBbg 25 (1988) 207s (R. de *Sivatte*); NatGrac 34 (1987) 429 (D. *Castillo*).

1610 ᴱ**Dijk** Teun A. Van, Handbook of discourse analysis. L 1985, Academic. I. xvii-302 p.; II. xvii-279 p.; III. xviii-251 p.; IV. xvii-228 p. 0-12-712001-7; 2-5; 3-3; 4-1.

1611 **Dyk** P.J. van, How to analyse the Bible; discovering the context of Scripture by using the historical-critical method. Pretoria c. 1987, van Schaik. 84 p. r. 14. – ᴿOTEssays 1,1 (c. 1988) 73-75 [F.E. *Deist*].

1612 *Fohrer* Georg, Methoden und Moden in der alttestamentlichen Wissenschaft: ➤ 153, ZAW 100 Supp. (1988) 243-254.

1613 *Fowler* Robert M., Post-modern biblical criticism [presidential address, Cleveland 1988]: ProcGLM 8 (1988) 1-22.

1614 *Gilbert* Maurice, New horizons and present needs; exegesis since Vatican II: ➤ 380, Vatican II Assessment 1 (1988) 321-343, ᵀ*Wearne* Leslie; français ➤ 379, Bilan 1, 329-349.

1615 **Giroud** J.-C., *Panier* L., Semiótica, una práctica de lectura y análisis de los textos bíblicos. Estella 1988, VDivino. 67 p. – ᴿBibFe 14 (1988) 323 (M. *Sáenz Galache*).

1616 ᴱ**Gregor** Bernd, *Krifka* Manfred, Computerfibel für die Geisteswissenschaften, Einsatzmöglichkeiten des Personal Computers und Beispiele aus der Praxis. Mü 1987, Beck. 286 p. DM 34. 3-406-30876-7 [Bijdragen 49,358].

1617 **Guillemette** Pierre, *Brisebois* Mireille, Introduction aux méthodes historico-critiques 1987 ➤ 3,1596: ᴿCC 139 (1988,2) 504s (V. *Fusco*); NRT 110 (1988) 912s (X. *Jacques*); RivB 36 (1988) 420s (R. *Penna*).

1618 **Hughes** John J., Bits, bytes, and biblical studies 1987 ➤ 3,965 ['... and the Bible' from announced title]; xxxvii-643 p. $31. 0-310-28581-X. – – ᴿBR 4,4 (1988) 8s.44 (R.G. *Harder*); SWJT 31,1 (1988s) 48s (L.R. *Bush*).

1619 *Klein* Ralph W., WORDsearch; state of the art [computer] concordance: CurrTM 15 (1988) 194-6: *Within* a regular word-processing program, this concordance [BibleSoft, #3 Box 182, Monroe LA 71203; $250] can tell you where sin and grace occur in the same verse, or how many times Peter and Paul occur; but not where Peter-James-John occur in the same verse [11 times], nor that 'love' or 'friend' occur in only 192 of the 4906 in which God is 'Lord', 'mighty'.

1620 ᴱ**Knight** D.A., *Tucker* G.M., The Hebrew Bible and its modern interpreters 1985 ➤ 1,293 ... 3,1602: ᴿTRu 53 (1988) 223-5 (O. *Kaiser*).

1621 **Kren** George M., *Christakes* George, Scholars and personal computers; microcomputing in the humanities and social sciences. NY 1988, Human Sciences. 209 p. $30 [TDig 35,72].

1622 *Krentz* Edgar, The perfect WORD; software for Bible study and research: CurrTM 15 (1988) 444s.

1623 *Lohfink* Norbert, Zur Lage der alttestamentlichen Wissenschaft: EvKomm 21 (1988) 638-641.

1624 **Maas** Jacques, *Tromp* Nico, Constructief Bijbellezen; zelfstandig en actief in de Bijbel lezen, een semiotische methode. Hilversum 1987. 120 p. 90-304-0401-9. – ᴿSémBib 49 (1988) 36-39 (G. J. *Nijhoff*).

1625 *a*) *Melugin* Roy F., Canon and exegetical method; – *b*) *Gerstenberger* Erhard S., Canon criticism and the meaning of *Sitz im Leben*; – *c*) *Wilson* Robert R., Approaches to Old Testament ethics: → 25, ᶠCHILDS B., Canon 1988, 48-61 / 20-31 / 62-74.

1626 *a*) *Patte* Daniel, Speech act theory and biblical exegesis; – *b*) *Buss* Martin J., The contribution of speech act theory to biblical studies; – *c*) *White* Hugh C., The value of speech act theory for Old Testament hermeneutics [/ Speech act theory and literary criticsm]; – *d*) *Jarrett* Charles E., Philosophy of language in the service of religious studies [/ Two bibliographies]: Semeia 41 ('Speech act theory and biblical criticism' 1988) 85-102 / 125-134 / 41-66 [1-26] / 143-162 [163...173...]].

1627 *Patterson* P., *James* R., The historical-critical study of the Bible; dangerous or helpful?: TEd 37 (1988) 45-74 [< NTAbs 32,286].

1628 *Pelletier* Anne-Marie, Exégèse et histoire; tirer du nouveau de l'ancien: NRT 110 (1988) 641-665.

1629 *Pesce* Mauro, L'esegesi storica nella Chiesa oggi: RClerIt 69 (1988) 256-267.

1630 **Piret** Pierre, L'écriture et l'esprit; une étude théologique sur l'exégèse et les philosophies. Bru 1987, Inst.Ét.Théologiques. 300 p. – ᴿEsprVie 98 (1988) 261 (É. *Cothenet*: enseignement universitaire); Études 368 (1988) 567s (P. *Gibert*).

1631 ᴱ**Poswick** R.-F., *al.,* Actes du premier colloque international 'Bible et informatique' LvN 1985/6 → 2,389: ᴿRTLv 19 (1988) 494s (J.-C. *Haelewyck*: typographie détestable, innombrables coquilles ... témoignage convaincant de la qualité du travail informatique).

1632 **Ralph** Margaret N., And God said what? ... literary forms 1986 → 2,1152; 3,1613: ᴿEstBíb 46 (1988) 128s (J. M. *Sánchez Caro*); Vidyajyoti 52 (1988) 463 (P. M. *Meagher*).

1633 *Rast* W. E., ◉ Kyūyaku-seisho ... Tradition history and the OT [1972 → 54,536], ᵀ*Higuchi* S. Tokyo, Kyōbunkwan. Y 1500 [BL 89,91 without date or pp.].

1634 *Ratzinger* Joseph, Foundations and approaches of biblical exegesis: Origins 17 (Wsh 1988) 593-602 [NTAbs 32,144].

1635 *Raupp* Wolfgang, Die Bibel im Computer: Deutsches Pfarrerblatt 88 (Essen 1988) 311 ... [< ᴢɪᴛ 88,630].

1636 *Raurell* Frederic, Lettura plurale del testo; metodi biblici: Laurentianum 29 (1988) 251-286.

1637 *Ritt* Hubert, Gegen die verkopften Methoden der Bibelwissenschaft?: BLtg 61 (1988) 210-216.

1638 *Rose* Martin, Approches classiques de l'Ancien Testament; techniques exégétiques et implications théologiques: ÉTRel 63 (1988) 337-360.

1639 *Sánchez Mielgo* Gerardo, Métodos actuales en la exégesis; descripción y balance: EscrVedat 17 (1987) 7-60.

1640 *Schram* T., Developing an exegetical awareness [... like learning a new language]: Notes on Translation 121 (Dallas 1987) 31-39 [< NTAbs 32,288].

1641 *Schweizer* Harald, Hilfen für deskriptive Exegese [CATSS 1s; *Egger* W.; *Berger* K.]: TüTQ 168 (1988) 64-70.
1642 **Silvan** Arthur, New light on the origin of the Bible. Ba 1984, auct. 189 p. [KirSef 61,394: gematria].
1643 *Simian-Yofre* Horacio, Pragmalinguística; comunicación y exégesis: RBíbArg 50 (1988) 75-95.
1644 **Stendebach** F. J., *al.,* Come leggere la Bibbia: Capire la Bibbia 6. Bo 1980, Dehoniane. 156 p. – ᴿRivB 36 (1988) 531 (M. *Làconi*).
1645 **Stenger** Werner, Biblische Methodenlehre 1987 ⇒ 3,1617; 3-491-77681-3: ᴿLingBib 61 (1988) 115-123 (W. *Schenk*).
1646 *a) Stuhlmueller* Carroll, Studying the Bible canonically; – *b) Pilch* John J., Interpreting Scripture; the social science method; – *c) Fuerst* Wesley J., Literary, rhetorical criticism; – *d) Bertram* Michael, Semiotics, the structural approach; – *e) Scott* Bernard B., Lost junk, found treasure; – *f) Donahue* Felix, Modern or early Church interpretation?: BToday 26 (1988) 5-12 / 13-19 / 20-24 / 26-30 / 31-34 / 35-38.
1647 *Tov* Emanuel, Computers and the Bible; BR 4,1 (1988) 38-42.
1648 **Tucker** G. M., ❹ Form-criticism of the OT [1971], ᵀ*Ii* K. Tokyo 1988, Kyōbunkwan. 179 p. Y 1800 [BL 89,96].
1649 *Vedder* Ben, Kennistheoretische beschouwingen bij een interpretatie van teksten in het perspectief van 'wirkungsgeschichtliche' exegese: Bijdragen 49 (1988) 238-262; Eng. 262s.
1650 *Watson* D. F., Rhetorical criticism [name and proposal from J. MUILENBURG 1968]: ⇒ 801, ISBEnc³ 4 (1988) 181s.
1651 *Watson* Nigel, Reception theory and biblical exegesis: AustralBR 36 (1988) 45-56.
1652 *Weder* Hans, Zu neuen Ufern? Exegetische Vorstösse in methodisches Neuland: EvKomm 21 (1988) 141-4.
1653 *Wenham* Gordon J., The place of biblical criticism in theological study: Themelios 14 (1988s) 84-89.

III. Critica Textus, Versiones

D1   **Textual Criticism.**

1654 ᴱ**Barthélemy** Dominique, *al.,* Critique textuelle de l'AT, I. 1982 ⇒ 63, 720; II. 1986 ⇒ 2,1157; 3,1621: ᴿBO 44 (1987) 760-2 (P. B. *Dirksen*: indispensable tool); CBQ 50 (1988) 280-2 (L. *Laberge*: splendid); JBL 107 (1988) 737-9 (P. E. *Dion*: only half the emendations coincide with Stu BH); JNES 47 (1988) 153s (D. *Pardee*); JQR 78 (1987) 137-140 (M. *Greenberg,* 1); JTS 39 (1988) 169-172 (W. *McKane,* 2: too conservative and theological); VT 38 (1988) 382s (J. A. *Emerton,* 2).
1655 **Beit-Arié** M., *al.,* ❺ Specimens of mediaeval Hebrew scripts, I. Oriental and Yemenite script. J 1987, Israel Academy. vii-14 p.; 154 pl. 965-208-081-0 [BL 89,148, S.C. *Reif*].
1656 **Bérard** François, *al.,* Guide de l'épigraphiste; bibliographie choisie des épigraphies antiques et médiévales: Bibl. Éc. Normale Supérieure; guides 2. P 1986, Éc.N.Sup. 367 p. – ᴿRPLH 61 (1987) 317-320 (P.-L. *Gatier*).
1657 *Bogaert* P.-M., Polyglottes (Bibles): ⇒ 786, Catholicisme XI,51 (1987) 604s.
1658 *Borbone* Pier Giorgio, Un tentativo di 'critica della critica' testuale dell'Antico Testamento: Biblica 69 (1988) 422-9 [on BARTHÉLEMY

committee, vol. 2 (his comment on vol. 1 was in RivStoLR 20, 1984, 251-274): the commttee is determined to 'protect' the Masoretic text at the cost of sacrificing philological method].

1659 **Cavallo** Guglielmo *al.,* Libri, scritture, scribi a Ercolano; introduzione allo studio dei materiali greci: Cronache Ercolanesi 13, Sup. 1, 1983 ➤ 1,1675*: ᴿGnomon 60 (1988) 398-401 (Herwig *Maehler*).

1659* ᴱ**Chartier** Roger, Les usages de l'imprimé, XVᵉ-XIXᵉ s. P 1987, Fayard. 446 p. F 150 [RHE 84,230, J.-F. *Gilmont*].

1660 **Clark** Gordon H., Logical criticisms of textual criticism. Jefferson MD 1986, Trinity Fd. viii-49 p. $3. – ᴿBS 145 (1988) 469 (D. B. *Wallace*: illogical and full of blunders).

1661 *a) Cook* Johann, New horizons in textual criticism; – *b) Zijl* J. B. van, Structural linguistics and textual criticism: ➤ 47, ᶠFᴇɴsʜᴀᴍ F., Text 1988, 51-61 / 209-216.

1662 **Detienne** Marcel, (*Camasso* Georgio *al.*), Les savoirs de l'écriture en Grèce ancienne: CahPg 14, Apparat critique. Lille 1988, Presses Univ. 540 p. 2-85939-322-6.

1662* Fälschungen im Mittelalter, Internationaler Kongress München 16.-19. Sept. 1986: Monumenta Germaniae Historica, Schriften 33. Hannover 1988, Hahn. 5 vol., 780 + 748 + 726 + 724 + 752 p.; ill. je DM 98 [RHE 84,113*; TR 85,253 tit. pp.].

1663 *Fikhman* I. F., ⊕ Deux siècles d'existence de la papyrologie documentaire: VDI 187 (1988) 202-8.

1664 **Gallo** L., A handbook of Greek and Latin papyrology. L 1986, Inst. Clas. Studies. 153 p.; 17 pl. £9. – ᴿGymnasium 95 (1988) 462s (R. *Scholl*).

1665 *Gilissen* Léon, Codicologie; à propos de publications récentes [*Derolez* A. 1984, 1982]: ScrCiv 10 (1986) 289-302; 303-312, réponse; 313s, *Gumbert* J. P., note.

1666 ᴱ**Glenisson** Jean, Le livre au Moyen Âge. P 1988, CNRS. 248 p.; ill. 2-87682-015-3. 39 art.; *Estin* C., *Dukan* M., Les scribes hébreux, p. 57-64; *Fellows* S., Une Bible à la rencontre des cultures, p. 148-154. ➤ a878.

1667 *a) Grier* James, Lᴀᴄʜᴍᴀɴɴ, [Joseph] Bᴇ́ᴅɪᴇʀ and the bipartite stemma; towards a responsible application of the common-error method; – *b) Amphoux* Christian-B., Un indice de variation pour le classement des états d'un texte: RHText 18 (1988) 263-278 / 279-299.

1668 **Hamman** A.-G., L'épopée du livre; la transmission des textes anciens, du scribe à l'imprimerie 1985 ➤ 1,1682 ... 3,1626: ᴿTGL 78 (1988) 174s (H. *Drobner*).

1669 *Haran* Menahem, ⊕ The codex, the *pinax,* and the wooden slats: Tarbiz 57 (1987s) 151-164.

1670 *a) Haran* Menahem, On the diffusion of literacy and schools in ancient Israel; – *b) Puech* Émile, Les écoles dans l'Israël préexilique; données épigraphiques; – *c) Lipinski* E., Royal and state scribes in ancient Jerusalem: ➤ 482, VTS 40, Jerusalem congress 1986/8, 81-95 / 189-203 / 157-164.

1670* *Hendrix* D., À propos de manuscrits médiévaux: RTAM 55 (1988) 207-220.

1671 **Johnson** Richard R., The role of parchment in Greco-Roman antiquity: diss. LA 1968. x-141 p.

Kunst-Stiftung zur Förderung der neutestamentlichen Textforschung, Bericht für die Jahre 1985 bis 1987: 1988 ➤ 289.

1672 **Mazal** O., *a)* Lehrbuch der Handschriftenkunde: Elemente des Buch- und Bibliothekwesens, 10. Wsb 1986, Reichert. xvi-388 p.; ill. [RHE 84,15*];

– *b*) Paläographie und Paläotypie 1984 → 2,7884: ᴿDLZ 109 (1988) 737-740 (A. *Schmitt*).

1672* **Neske** L.,   Die Handschriften der Stadtbibliothek Nürnberg, II. Die lateinischen mittelalterlichen Handschriften, 2. Bibelhandschriften und Liturgica einschliesslich der griechischen Texte. Wsb 1987, Harrassowitz. xxi-192 p.; 32 pl. DM 112. – ᴿRTAM 55 (1988) 214s (G. *Hendrix*).

1673 **Pächt** Otto,   Book illumination in the Middle Ages; an introduction; ᵀ*Davenport* Kay; pref. *Alexander* J.J.G. NY 1986, Oxford-UP/Millar. 221 p.; 210 fig. + 132 color. $40. – ᴿManuscripta 32 (1988) 50s (M. *Camille*).

1674 ᴱ**Questa** C., *Raffaelli* R.,   Il libro e il testo, Urbino 1982/4 → 2,771; 3,1639: ᴿRPLH 61 (1987) 354s (P. *Flobert*: magnifique!; titres pp.).

1675 *Rabin* Chaim,   Lexical emendation in biblical research: → 42*, Eʜʀᴍᴀɴ A. mem., Fucus 1988, 379-413; bibliog. 413-8.

1676 *Sirat* Colette,   Les manuscrits en caractères hébraïques; réalités d'hier et histoire d'aujourd'hui: ScrCiv 10 (1986) 239-288; 5 fig.

1677 *Soderlund* S.K. [*Sitterly* C.F., *Greenlee* J.H.] Text and mss of the OT [NT]: → 801, ISBEnc³ 4 (1988) 78-814 [-822]; 969-983, Versions, *Vööbus* A.

1678 *Stringer* Gary A., *Vilberg* William R.,   The Donne Variorum textual collation program: CompHum 21 (1987) 83-89.

1679 *Tait* William J.,   Rush and reed; the pens of Egyptian and Greek scribes: → 492, XVIII. Papyrol. 2 (1986/8) 477-481.

1680 **Turner** E.G., ²ʳᵉᵛ*Parsons* P.J.,   Greek manuscripts of the ancient world: Bulletin Sup 46. L 1987, Univ. London Inst. Classical Studies. xvi-174 p. (88 photos, each with explanatory page opposite). 0-900587-48-2.

1681 *Wilson* Nigel,   Variant readings with poor support in the manuscript tradition: RHText 17 (1987) 1-13.

D2.1   *Biblia hebraica,*   **Hebrew text.**

1682 *a) Anderson* Robert T.,   Clustering Samaritan Hebrew Pentateuchal manuscripts; – *b) Sirat* Colette,   Paléographie hébraïque et paléographie samaritaine; – *c) Crown* Alan D.,   A chronological suvey of style and format in Samaritan binding: → 497, Samarit. 1985/8, 57-66 / 45-55 / 67-81.

1683 *Cohen* D.,   The 'Masoretic text' and the extent of its influence on the transmission of the biblical text in the Middle Ages: → 43, ᶠEʟɪᴛᴢᴜʀ Y., II (1986) 229-256.

1684 *Goldberg* Arnold,   Die Schrift der rabbinischen Ausleger: FraJudBei 15 (1987) 1-15.

1685 *Goshen-Gottstein* M.H.,   The Hebrew Bible in the light of the Qumran scrolls and the Hebrew University Bible: → 482, VTS 40, Jerusalem congress 1986/8, 42-53.

1686 **McCarter** P. Kyle,   Textual criticism; recovering the text of the Hebrew Bible: GuidesBS 1986 → 2,1192; 3,1650: ᴿCBQ 50 (1988) 690s (R. *Althann*: clear and attractive; some caveats).

1687 **McCarthy** Carmel,   The Tiqqune Sopherim ...: OBO 36, 1981 → 62, 1930 ... 64,1720: ᴿTsTKi 58 (1987) 312 (M. *Sæbø*).

1688 *Miletto* Gianfranco,   Quattro colophon inediti in manoscritti biblici ebraici della biblioteca palatina di Parma: Henoch 10 (1988) 377-383 + 4 foto.

1689 *a) Mulder* Martin J., The transmisson of the biblical texts; – *b) Perrot* Charles, The reading of the Bible in the ancient synagogue: → 317, Mikra 1988, 87-135 (136 photo)/ 137-159.

1690 *Pavoncello* Nello, Pergamene ebraiche negli Archivi di Stato e Comunali dell'Umbria [Perugia e 4 altre città; c. 15° sec.: Lv 2s; 4, 14; Dt 33; Is 5s; 14s; Ezech 48]: AION 47 (1987) 369-372; IV pl.

1691 *Rothschild* Jean-Pierre, Quelques listes de livres hébreux dans des manuscrits de la Bibliothèque nationale de Paris: RHText 17 (1987) 291-344.

1692 **Scott** William R., A simplified guide to BHS; critical apparatus, masora, accents, unusual letters and other markings: BIBAL. Berkeley CA 1987. iii-88 p. $6. 0-941037-04-5 [BL 89,49, P. W. *Coxon*].

1693 **Sed-Rajna** Gabrielle, The Hebrew Bible in medieval illuminated manuscripts. NY 1987, Rizzoli. 173 p.; 120 fig. + 60 color. $85. – ᴿRelStR 14 (1988) 366 (J. *Gutmann*).

1694 *Tishby* Peretz, ⊕ Hebrew incunabula — Spain and Portugal (Guadalajara): KirSef 61 (1986s) 521-9; 530-546 facsimiles.

1695 *Tov* Emanuel, Hebrew biblical manuscripts from the Judaean Desert; their contribution to textual criticism: → 506 = JJS 39 (1988) 5-37.

1696 **Wonneberger** R., Understanding BHS...: SubsBPont 8, 1984 → 65,1484; 2,1197: ᴿRHPR 68 (1988) 229s (J.-G. *Heintz*).

1697 **Würthwein** Ernst, Der Text des Alten Testaments; eine Einführung in die Biblia Hebraica⁵. Stu 1988 = ¹1952, Deutsche Bibelgesellschaft. 263 p.; 50 pl. 3-438-06006-X.

D2.2 Targum.

1698 **Amram** David W., The makers of Hebrew books in Italy; being chapters in the history of the Hebrew printing press. L 1988, Holland. xviii-417 p.; some facsimiles. 0-900470-46-1.

1699 **Chester** Andrew, Divine revelation and divine titles in the Pentateuchal Targumim 1986 → 2,1199; 3,1659: ᴿBL (1988) 130 (A. *Gelston*); ScripTPamp 19 (1987) 982 (S. *Ausín*).

1700 ᴱ**Diez Macho** Alejandro, Targum palaestinense in Pentateuchum; additur Targum Pseudojonatan ejusque hispanica versio, ed. critica: Biblia Polyglotta Matritensia 4/1 (Gn). M 1988. xxi-578 p. 84-00-06940-4.

1701 **Glessmer** Uwe, Entstehung und Entwicklung des Targum zum Pentateuch als literar-kritisches Problem, dargestellt am Beispiel der Zusatztargume: Diss. ᴰ*Koch* K. Hamburg 1988. 472 p. – RTLv 20,542.

1702 **Golomb** David M., A Grammar of Targum Neofiti [ᴰ1978] 1985 → 1,1733,8838 ... 3,1662: ᴿAulaO 6 (1988) 77-82 (J. *Ribera*); BO 45 (1988) 184-6 (B. *Grossfeld*); BZ 32 (1988) 122s (J. *Maier*); JNES 47 (1988) 285s (W. R. *Garr*: some minor blemishes); TLZ 113 (1988) 813s (Jutta *Körner*).

1703 **Grossfeld** Bernard, The Targum Onqelos to Genesis / Exodus / Leviticus and Numbers / Deuteronomy: Aramaic Bible 6-9. E/Wilmington 1988, Clark/Glazier. xiv-193 p.; xv-120 p.; xv-171 p.; 126 p. £35 (Gn); £30 each. 0-567-19463-4; 64-2; 65-0; 66-9 (77-4, series) [BL 89,46, P. W. *Coxon*; JBL 107,787].

1703* **Harrington** D., *Saldarini* A., Targum Jonathan of the Former Prophets 1987 → 3,1666: ᴿÉTRel 63 (1988) 456s (D. *Lys*); RB 95 (1988) 612-4 (G. J. *Norton*); TS 49 (1988) 735-9 (J. A. *Fitzmyer*).

1704 **Klein** Michael L., Genizah manuscripts of Palestinian Targum to the Pentateuch 1986 ➤ 2,1298; 3,1609: RIsrEJ 38 (1988) 100s (A. *Shinan*); JBL 107 (1988) 772-5 (B. *Chilton*); JSS 33 (1988) 279-281 (S. *Brock*); JTS 39 (1988) 187-190 (S. C. *Reif*); Tarbiz 57 (1987s) 451-460 (S. E. *Fassberg*).

1705 *a) Le Déaut* Roger, Manuscrits du targum samaritain et targums juifs; – *b) Margain* Jean, Targum samaritain; aspects de la langue du ms. J; – *c) Tal* Abraham, L'exégèse samaritaine à travers les manuscrits du targum; – *d) Girón-Blanc* Luis F., Un signo controvertido en la vocalización del Pentateuco hebréo-samaritano [*Ben-Hayyim* Zev, réponse]: ➤ 497, Samarit. 1985/8, 109-121 / 123-9 / 139-148 / 95-106[-8].

1706 **Levine** Etan, The Aramaic version of the Bible; contents and context: BZAW 174. B 1988, de Gruyter. xiv-258 p. DM 118. 3-11-011474-7 [BL 89,155].

1707 **Levy** B. Barry, Targum Neophyti 1; a textual study, I. Introduction, Genesis (p. 85-313), Exodus (p. 339-435). Lanham MD 1986, UPA. xix-450 p. $36.50; pa. $21.75. – RJBL 107 (1988) 568-570 (B. *Grossfeld*).

1708 **Ryder** David, ❂ Targum Jonathan ben Uzziel al ha-Tôrâ, British Museum Add. 127031. J 1984. I. (Gn-Ex) 169 + 146 p.; II. 161 p. + 146-309. – RKirSef 61 (1986) 602s (E. *Yiṣḥaqi*).

1709 *a) Tal* Abraham, The Samaritan Targum of the Pentateuch; – *b) Alexander* Philip S., Jewish Aramaic translations of Hebrew scriptures: ➤ 317, Mikra 1988, 189-216 / 217-253.

1710 *Verkindère* Gérard, Les Targoums; traduction et interprétation: ➤ 486, Traduction 1986/8, 181-190; Eng. 181.

D3.1   *Textus graecus* – **Greek NT.**

1711 **Aland** Kurt & Barbara, The text of the NT; an introduction to the critical editions and to the theory and practice of modern textual criticism [1982 ➤ 63,1795], TRhodes Erroll F., 1987 ➤ 3,1677: RBS 145 (1988) 467s (D. B. *Wallace*: does not replace METZGER, and is autocratic); BTrans 39 (1988) 338-342 (J. N. *Birdsall*); CBQ 50 (1988) 313-5 (L. W. *Hurtado*: some flaws, in general excellent); GraceTJ 9 (1988) 279-285 (D. B. *Wallace*); NT 30 (1988) 380s (G. D. *Kilpatrick*); PerspRelSt 15 (1988) 298s (W. T. *Sawyer*); RasT 29 (1988) 93s (R. *Maisano*).

1712 **Aland** K. & B., Il testo del Nuovo T., TTimparano S. Genova 1987, Marietti. 372 p. 88-211-6772-0. – RComSev 21 (1988) 98s (M. de *Burgos*).

1713 *Aland* Kurt, The [NT] text of the Church?: TrinJ 8 (1987) 131-144.

1714 **Duplacy** Jean, † 1983, Études de critique textuelle du NT, EDelobel J.: BiblETL 78, 1987 ➤ 3,215: RCiuD 201 (1988) 687 (J. *Gutiérrez*); NRT 110 (1988) 603-5 (X.*Jacques*); NT 30 (1988) 286 (J. K. *Elliott*); RThom 88 (1988) 477-481 (R. *Robert*).

1715 **Elliott** J. K., A survey of manuscripts used in editions of the Greek NT: NT Sup 57, 1987 ➤ 3,1682: RETL 64 (1988) 205s (F. *Neirynck*); JTS 39 (1988) 555 (J. N. *Birdsall*).

1716 *Elliott* J. K., Why the international Greek New Testament project is necessary: RestQ 30 (Abilene 1988) 195-206 [< ZIT 89,161].

1717 **Galavaris** G., The illustrations of the prefaces in Byzantine Gospels: Byz Vindob 11, 1979 ➤ 61,2360: RVizVrem 48 (1987) 204-8 (V. G. *Putsko*).

1718 *Hirunuma* Toshio, ❂ Studia textus Novi Testamenti [Shinyaku Kenkyu ➤ 64,3819: Nº 196 for 1982] continues regularly his 'one-man periodical'; Nº 275 (July 1989) treats Lk 7,24-27.

1718* ᴱHoleczek Heinz, ERASMUS, Novum Instrumentum 1516 Faksimile 1986 → 2,1216. – ᴿLutherJb 54 (1987) 129s (H. *Junghans*).
1719 **Hort** Fenton J. A., *Westcott* B. F., Introduction to the NT in the original Greek. Peabody MA 1988 = 1882, Hendrickson. xxxi-384 + 188 p. $20 [RelStR 15,262, B. D. *Ehrman*].
1720 *Kada* S. N., ⑥ Notations of the manuscripts of Mt. Athos, Xeropotamos monastery: Byzantina 14 (1988) 307-382.
1721 *Kim* Young Kyu, Palaeographical dating of P⁴⁶ to the later first century [not 3d as *Wilcken* U.]: Biblica 69 (1988) 248-257; 3 fig.
1722 ᴱ**Letis** Theodore P., The majority text; essays and reviews in the continuing debate [5 inedita by Letis, 5 others reprinted]. Fort Wayne 1987, Institute for Reformation Biblical Studies. xvi-210 p. $9. – ᴿBS 145 (1988) 469s (D. B. *Wallace*: loose reasoning).
1723 *Metzger* Bruce M., History of editing the Greek NT: PrincSemB 8,3 (1987) 33-45 = ProcAmPhilS 131,2 (Ph 1983) 148-158 [NTAbs 32, p. 9].
1724 **Nees** Laurence, The Gundohnius Gospels: Medieval Acad. 95. CM 1987. xiv-263 p.; 35 fig.
1725 *Sevrugian* Petra, Text und Bild im Rossano-Kodex und in den Sinope-Fragmenten: Diss. Heid. christlich-archäologisches Seminar 1987. – ArchAnz (1988) 104.
1726 [*Vaganay* L.] ²**Amphoux** C.-B., Initiation à la critique textuelle du NT 1986 → 2,1224; 3,1696: ᴿFoiTemps 19 (1987) 365s (C. *Focant*); RThom 88 (1988) 144s (L. *Devillers*); RTLv 19 (1988) 217-9 (J.-C. *Haelewyck*).

D3.2   *Versiones graecae* – **VT, Septuaginta etc.**

1727 *a*) *Bammel* C. P., Die Hexapla des ORIGENES; die Hebraica ueritas im Streit der Meinungen; – *b*) *Opelt* Ilona, San GIROLAMO e i suoi maestri ebrei: → 570, AugR 28 (1988) 125-149 / 327-338.
1728 *Briel* Steven C., The pastor and the Septuagint: ConcordiaTQ 51 (1987) 261-274 [NTAbs 32,216].
1729 ᴱ**Cox** Claude E., VI Congress Septuagint and Cognate 1986/7 → 3,533: ᴿJStJud 19 (1988) 243s (F. *García Martínez*).
1730 *Engberg* Sysse G., Sinai, TISCHENDORF, and the Greek manuscript fragment Cambridge University Library add. 1879. 1 [Gn 10,4-9; Prov 13,9-14,6.26; Is 27,33-28,8]: ClasMed 39 (1988) 253-8.
1731 *Hanhart* Robert, Die Bedeutung der Septuaginta für die Definition des 'hellenistischen Judentums': → 482, VTS 40, Jerusalem Congress 1986, 67-80.
1732 **Harl** Marguerite, *Dorival* Gilles, *Munnich* Olivier, La Bible grecque des Septante; du judaïsme hellénistique au christianisme ancien: Initiations au christianisme ancien. P 1988 Cerf/CNRS. 369 p. F 194. 2-204-02821-2 / CNRS 2-222-04155-4. – ᴿEsprVie 98 (1988) 383s (L. *Monloubou*); ÉTRel 63 (1988) 601s (C.-B. *Amphoux*); Études 369 (1988) 425s (P. *Gibert*); Sefarad 48 (1988) 432-5 (N. *Fernández Marcos,* también sobre Gen 1986).
1733 *Heller* Jan, *a*) Die Übersetzungsmethode der Septuaginta [< čeh. Studie a Texty 2 (1979) 7-53]; – *b*) Die Entstehung des Gesetzes und der Propheten [< čeh. Studie a Texty 7 (1984) 166-196]; – *c*) Bis an die Enden der Erde [< čeh. Studie a Texty 5 (1982) 5-27]; – *d*) Prager Forschung und Arbeit am Alten Testament: → 204, An der Quelle 1988, 185-224 / 241-8 / 225-240 / 159-173.
1734 *Kooi* A. van der, SYMMACHUS, 'de vertaler der Joden': NedTTs 42 (1988) 1-20; Eng. 67: not an Ebionite Christian, as in *Schürer-Vermes* 3/1, 493.

1735 **Lee** J. A. L., A lexical study of the Sept. Pentateuch 1983 → 64,1778 ... 2,1230: ᴿÉglT 18 (1987) 356s (L. *Laberge*); NT 30 (1988) 184s (G. D. *Kilpatrick*).

1736 *a) Murray* Oswyn, The letter of Aristeas [= RAC Sup 1 (1986) 573-87]; – *b) Troiani* Lucio, Il libro di Aristea e il giudaismo ellenistico (premesse per un'interpretazione); – *c) Harari* Maurizio, Un punto di vista archeologico sulla lettera di Aristea: → 464, St. Ellenistici II (1987) 15-29 / 31-61 / 91-106; 2 fig.

1737 *Pani* Giancarlo, L'edizione sistina dei Settanta, quattro secoli dopo: SMSR 54 (1988) 371-389; 1 facsimile.

1738 *Pietersma* A., New Greek fragments of biblical manuscripts in the Chester Beatty library [Gn 24,48-50. 60-61; Nm 5,19s.25s; 7,44-47.54s; Dt 2,35-37; Job 9,2s.12s; Ps 80,15-81,6; 82,17-83,4; Lk 14,7-14; also some Henoch and Phileas]: BASP 24 (1987) 37-49 + 12 pl.

1739 **Prijs** L., Jüdische Tradition in der Septuaginta; die grammatikalische Terminologie des Abraham ɪʙɴ Esʀᴀ [1948-50 + Bibliographie, *Prijs* Eva). Hildesheim 1987, Olms. xxvi-118 + 152 + 153* + 186* p. – ᴿArTGran 51 (1988) 394s (A. *Torres*).

1740 *Soderlund* Sven K., Septuagint: → 801, ISBEnc³ 4 (1988) 400-409.

1741 *a) Talshir* Zipora, Double translations in the Septuagint; – *b) Wright* Benjamin G., The quantitative representation of elements; evaluating 'literalism' in the LXX; – *c) Muraoka* Takamitsu, Towards a Septuagint Lexicon: → 3,533, ᴱCox C., 6th LXX 1986/7, 21-63 / 311-335 / 255-276.

1742 **Tov** E., A computerized data base for Septuagint studies; the parallel aligned text of the Greek and Hebrew Bible: CATSS 2 / JNWS sup. 1. Stellenbosch 1986, JNWS. xviii-144 p. [BL 89,50, D. G. *Deboys*: hardly 'aimed at all scholars who ... turn to the textual criticism of the Bible' (p. ii)].

1743 *Tov* Emanuel, The Septuagint: → 317, Mikra 1988, 161-188.

1744 *a) Tov* Emanuel, The nature and study of the translation technique of the LXX in the past and present; – *b) Aejmelaeus* Anneli, The significance of clause-connectors in the syntactical and translation-technical study of the Septuagint; – *c) Barr* James, Translators' handling of verb tense in semantically ambiguous contexts; – *d) Soisalon-Soininen* Ilmeri, Methodologische Fragen der Erforschung der Septuaginta-Syntax: → 3,533, ᴱCox C., 6th LXX 1986/7, 337-359 / 361-380 / 381-403 / 425-444.

1745 *Trebolle Barrera* Julio, Los Judíos de Alejandría y la versión de los Setenta: → 558*, ᴱPelaez del Rosal J., Para entender 1984, 85-98.

1746 *Wevers* John W., BarᴛʜÉʟᴇᴍʏ [Devanciers d'Aquila 1963] and ProtoSeptuagint studies: BSeptCog 21 (1988) 23-34.

1747 *Ziegler* Joseph, Die Wiedergabe der nota accusativi *'et, 'æt* mit *sýn*: → 153, ZAW 100 Supp. (1988) 222-233.

D4 Versiones orientales.

1748 *Dirksen* Peter B., The Old Testament Peshitta: → 317, Mikra 1988, 254-297.

1749 *a) Gelston* A., Dodekapropheton; – *b) Dirksen* P. B., Judges, 2 Samuel; – *c) Jenner* K., 1-2 Kgs Prov Eces Ct Dan: collations of Peshiṭta ms 9d2; 10c4; 10t6; 11d2; 12t9, available too late for inclusion in the corresponding Leiden Peshiṭta volumes: → 480, Peshitta 1985/8, 266-310.

1750 *a) Jenner* K. D.,   Some introductory remarks concerning the study of 8al; – *b) Weitzman* M. P.,   The originality of unique readings in Peshiṭta MS 9al: ➤ 480, Peshitta 1985/8, 200-224 / 225-258.

1751 *Kuntz* M. L.,   Guillaume POSTER and the Syriac Gospels of Athanasius KIRCHER: Renaissance Quarterly 40 (NY 1987) 465-484 [< RHE 83,359*].

1752 **Strothmann** W.,   Wörterverzeichnis der apokryphen-deuterokanonischen Schriften des ATs in der Peshitta: GöOrF 1/27.   Wsb 1988, Harrassowitz. xii-492 p. 3-447-02683-9 [BL 90,47, S. *Brock*].

1753 *Bouvarel-Boud'hors* Anne,   Fragments du NT fayoumique à la Bibliothèque Nationale: LOrA 1 (Lv 1988) 95-116.

1754 *Giversen* Søren,   The Manichaean papyri of the Chester Beatty library [over 1000 texts in Coptic]:   PrIrB 11 (1988) 1-22.

1755 **Schmitz** Franz-Jürgen, *Mink* Gerd,   Liste der koptischen Handschriften des NTs I, 1986 ➤ 1,1242; 3,1711:   ᴿBO 45 (1988) 596s (J. *Helderman*); NT 30 (1988) 185-7 (J. K. *Elliott*).

1756 **Zanetti** Ugo,   Les lectionnaires coptes 1985   ➤ 3,1712:   ᴿHeythJ 29 (1988) 521s (L. S. B. *MacCoull*).

1757 *Browne* Gerald M.,   Griffith's Old Nubian lectionary; the revision revised [i.e. text of his Papyrol.Castroct 8, Rome 1982, incorporating corrections published meanwhile]: BASP 24 (1987) 75-92.

1758 **Zuurmond** R.,   Research into the text of the synoptic gospels in Ge'ez; general introduction; edition of the gospel of Mark: diss. Utrecht 1988, ᴰ*Baarda* T.   288 p.; 401 p. – TsTNijm 28 (1988) 298.

1759 **Cox** Claude E.,   Hexaplaric materials preserved in the Armenian version 1986 ➤ 2,1253; 3,1722:   ᴿJBL 107 (1988) 353-5 (A. *Terian*).

1760 *Vinel* F.,   Tournures infinitives et antériorité; un hébraïsme dans la traduction arménienne du NT?:   RÉArmén 20 (1986s) 57s.

1761 *Outtier* Bernard,   Essai de répertoire des manuscrits des vieilles versions géorgiennes du NT: LOrA 1 (Lv 1988) 171-9.

1762 *a) Shehadeh* Haseeb,   The groups of the Samaritan manuscripts of the Arabic translation of the Pentateuch; – *b) Zafrani* Haïm,   Langues juives du Maroc et traductions judéo-arabes de la Bible: ➤ 497, Samarit. 1985/8, 205-218 / 219-234.

1763 *Asmussen* Jes P.,   Remarks on Judeo-Persian translations of some Aramaic passages in the Hebrew Bible [Gn 31,47; Jer 10,11; Dan 5,25; 6,8]: ArOr 56 (1988) 341-5.

1764 **Griepentrog** Wolfgang,   Synopse der gotischen Evangelientexte: Münchener Studien zur Sprachwissenschaft Beih NF 14.   Mü 1988, Kitzinger. 171 p.   3-920645-42-1.

D5   Versiones latinae.

1765 *Bogaert* Pierre-Maurice,   La Bible latine des origines au Moyen Âge; aperçu historique, état des questions: RTLv 19 (1988) 137-159.276-314; Eng. 268.

1766 *Bogaert* P.-M., *Gryson* R.,   Centre de recherches sur la Bible latine; rapport d'activités 1987 [i. l'édition d'Isaïe...]: RTLv 19 (1988) 126-131.

1767 **Buonocore** Marcus, Codices Vaticani Latini codices 9734-9782 (codices Amatiani). Vaticano 1988, Biblioteca. cii-173 p. 88-210-0612-3.
1768 *Eleen* Luba, New Testament manuscripts and their lay owners in Verona in the thirteenth century [< Scriptorium 41 (1987)]: BCanadMed 8,3 (1988) 1s.
Fischer Bonifatius, Die lateinischen Evangelien I. Varianten zu Matthäus 1988 → 4460.
1769 **García Moreno** A., La Neovulgata, precedentes y actualidad 1986 → 2,1274; 3,1743: ᴿDivThom 89s (1986s) 419-421 (B. *Estrada*).
1770 *Giraldo* Néstor, La Nueva Vulgata: Cuestiones Teológicas 14,1 (Medellín 1987) 7-24 [< RET 48,120].
1771 *Gribomont* Jean, *a*) Aux origines de la Vulgate; – *b*) La Bible de Saint-Paul [hors les murs, Rome]; – *c*) Critique des lettrés et des philologues: → 503, Vulgata/Sisto 1985/7, 11-20 / 30-39 / 137.
1772 *Haudebert* Pierre, La traduction du grec au latin peut devenir une interprétation [JÉRÔME, Metanoia; Jn 1,9; Act 2,42]: → 486, Traduction 1986/8, 119-123; Eng. 119.
1773 **Henry** Avril, Biblia pauperum. L 1987, Scolar/Gower. 178 p. £42. 0-85967-542-4 [different in → 3, 1746]: ᴿExpTim 99 (1987s) 346 (C. S. *Rodd*: magnificent; 41 woodcuts).
1774 **Hertz** Anselm [comm.], De boodschap van Jezus [Evangeliar Aachen]ᵀ. Haarlem 1984, Gottmer. 48 p.; ill. – ᴿPrakT 14 (1987) 104 (F. H. *Kuiper*).
1775 *Himmighöfer* Traudel, 400 Jahre Neustadter Bibel: Blätter für pfälzische Kirchengeschichte 55 (Grünstadt 1988) 7-20 [< ZIT 89,32].
1776 *Horst* Ulrich, Der Streit um die Autorität der Vulgata; zur Rezeption des Trienter Schriftdekrets in Spanien: Rev.Univ. Coimbra 29 (1983) 157-252 [ForumKT 2 (1986) 314s, P. *Schäfer*].
1777 *Jonge* Henk J. de, The relationship of ERASMUS' [Latin] translation of the New Testament to that [also Latin] of the Pauline Epistles by LEFÈVRE d'Étaples: Erasmus in English Newsletter 15 (1987s) 2-7; 3 fig. [25-27, *Rummel* Erika].
1778 *Kedar* Benjamin, The Latin translations: → 317, Mikra 1988, 299-338.
1779 *McNamara* Martin, Hiberno-Latin bulletin: PrIrB 11 (1988) 88-96.
1780 Nova Vulgata², Vaticano 1986 [= 1979 + praef., notae, modificationes versionis biblicae]. xxxi-2316 p. Fb 2491. – ᴿNRT 110 (1988) 911s (H. *Jacques*: éveillera les problèmes ... 'signification d'un text officiel').
1781 *Pagano* Sergio M., Nuove ricerche sul codice biblico latino purpureo di Sarezzano [→ 3,1744]: Benedictina 34 (1987) 25-165.
1782 *Palazzo* Éric, L'illustration de l'Évangéliaire au haut Moyen Âge: MaisD 176 (1988) 67-80; 7 fig.
1783 *Sainte-Marie* Henri de, *a*) Storia dell'edizione critica della Volgata; – *b*) Sisto V e la Volgata: → 503, Vulgata/Sisto 1985/7., 144-8 / 61-67.
1784 *a*) *Schick* Eduard, Il codice di Fulda; storia e significato di un manoscritto della Volgata del secolo VI; – *b*) *Pasqualetti* Olindo, Il latino nelle varianti sistine dei Sinottici; – *c*) *Balboni* Dante, L'edizione a stampa della 'Vulgata' di Sisto V: → 503, Vulgata/Sisto 1985/7, 21-29 / 98-106 / 107-117.
1785 **Stramare** Tarcisio, La Bibbia 'Vulgata' dalle origini ai nostri giorni, 1985-7 → 3,566: ᴿEstBíb 46 (1988) 130s (J. M. *Sánchez Caro*); ScripTPamp 19 (1987) 927-9 (F. *Varo*).
1786 *a*) *Stramare* Tarcisio, La Neo-vulgata; storia della revisione, sue finalità e caratteristiche; – *b*) *Mallet* Jean, La latinité de la Néo-Vulgate; –

c) Gribomont Jean, La révision conciliaire du Psautier de la Néo-Vulgate:
➤ 503, Vulgata/Sisto 1985/7, 149-175 / 176-191 / 192-7.

D5.5.   *Citationes apud Patres* – the Patristic Bible.

1787 Biblia patristica 4. EUSÈBE de Césarée, CYRILLE de Jérusalem, ÉPIPHANE
de Salamine. P 1987, CNRS. 330 p. F 180. – ᴿNRT 110 (1988) 931 (V.
Roisel: 41.000 références, 60% AT; contre la majorité NT dans les 107.000
précédentes, dont 57.000 ORIGÈNE).

1788 **Frede** Hermann J., Kirchenschriftsteller, Aktualisierungsheft 1988: Vetus Latina 1/1B. FrB 1988, Herder. 100 p.

1789 *a) Marin* Marcello, Citazioni bibliche e parabibliche nel De aleatoribus
pseudociprianeo; – *b) Girardi* Mario, Un *agraphon* nelle Omelie sui salmi
di BASILIO di Cesarea? [su Sal 28,2b: 'Dice: Non progettate per me luoghi
di culto e assemblee private']: ➤ 472, AnStoEseg 5 (1988) 169-184 /
185-199.

D6   **Versiones modernae**   .1   *romanicae,* **romance.**

1790 ᴱ**Casalis** G., *Roussel* R., *al.,* OLIVÉTAN, traducteur de la Bible 1985/7
➤ 3,527: ᴿEsprVie 98 (1988) 525s (L. *Walter*); RevSR 62 (1988) 189 (D.
Renaud); RThom 88 (1988) 510s (G.-T. *Bedouelle*); VSp 142 (1988) 139s
(D. *Barthélemy*).

1791 [Amari] **Perry** Anne J., La passion des jongleurs [ᴰ1978] 1981 ➤ 64,
1815: ᴿÉglT 17 (1986) 92-94 (L. *Laberge*).

1792 *Poswick* Ferdinand, Recouvrement lexical des traductions françaises et
la typologie qui s'en dégage: ➤ 486, Traduction 1986/8, 63-71, Eng. 63.

1793 **Quereuil** Michel, La Bible française du xiiiᵉ siècle; édition critique de la
Genèse: Publ. romaines et françaises 183. Genève 1988, Droz. 421 p. [JTS
40,744].

1794 **Szirmai** Julia C., La Bible anonyme du Ms. Paris B. N. f.fr. 763: Univ.
Leiden Altfranzösische Bibelübersetzungen in Versen. Amst 1985, Rodopi
[➤ 2,1278*]. 399 p. – ᴿZkT 110 (1988) 194 (K. *Stock*).

1795 **TOB**: Traduction œcuménique de la Bible: *a)* Bible en un seul volume ²ʳᵉᵛ.
P 1988, Bibliothèque Biblique. 3120 p. F 350. – *b)* Nouveau Testament
[déjà revue, surtout Jn]. F 140. – ᴿEsprVie 98 (1988) 631-3 (É. *Cothenet*:
F. *Refoulé* gives the history of the enterprise, since 1965, which A. BEA
did not favor).

1796 *Alonso Schökel* Luis, La traducción de la Biblia de LUTERO y las
traducciones españolas: ➤ 1,601*, ᴱ*Koniecki* D., *Almarza-Meñica* J., M.
Lutero 1983/4, 53-68 [< LuJb 55 (1988) 166].

1797 *Alonso* Vital, La Biblia en el nuevo mundo [...versión indígena?]:
RBíbArg 30s (1988) 125-133.

1798 *Burgués Dalmau* José P., La Biblia del P. Felipe SCIO primera edición
católica de la Biblia en España (1790-1793); AnCalas 29 (1987) 259-335
[-550, sobre Colegio Scio, Salamanca, 25 años].

1799 **Bover** José M., *O'Callaghan* José, Nuevo Testamento trilingüe²: BAC
400. M 1988, Católica. lviii-1380 p.

1800 **Reino** Casiodoro de, La Biblia del Oso [1569], ᴱ*Guillén Torralba* Juan,
al. M 1987, Aguilar. 554 p.; 960 p.; 1184 p.; 698 p. – ᴿBibFe 14 (1988)
480 (A. *Salas*).

1801 **Thompson** Colin P., The strife of tongues; Fray Luis de LEÓN and the

golden age of Spain [... vernacular Bible]: Iberian and Latin American
Studies.   C 1988, Univ.   xii-307 p. $54.50 [JBL 108, 571].

D6.2   *Versiones anglicae* – English Bible translations.

1802 **Backus** Irena D.,   The Reformed roots of the English NT ... BEZA ᴰ1980
→ 62,2057:   ᴿZwingliana 16 (1985) 178s (E. J. *Furcha*).

1803 Christian community Bible ... for the Christian communities of the Philippines and the Third World, and for those who seek God.   Manila 1988,
St. Paul / Divine Word [Bloomington IN, Meyer-Stone].   1147- 513 p.; ill.
2 maps [less-important parts of the OT in smaller print: TDig 35,342].

1804 *a) Crim* Keith R.,   Bible translation by committees; – *b) Scanlin* Harold
P.,   Bible translation by American individuals; – *c) Sarna* Jonathan D. &
Nahum M.,   Jewish Bible scholarship and translations in the U. S. – *d)*
Fogarty Gerald P.,   American Catholic translations of the Bible: → 300,
ᴱ*Frerichs* E., The Bible and Bibles in America 1988, 29-41 / 43-82 / 83-116
/ 117-143.

1805 *a) Dayras* Solange,   La KNOX Version; une traduction controversée; – *b)*
Gachelin Jean-Marc,   Traductions écossaises: → 486, Traduction 1986/8,
19-32 / 33-41; Eng. 19.33.

1806 **Gaus** Andy,   The unvarnished Gospels, translated from the original
Greek.   Brighton MA / Putney VT 1988, Threshold.   xvi-252 p. $12 pa.
[CBQ 50,751].   0-939660-25-3.

1807 *Ginsberg* David,   Ploughboys versus prelates; TYNDALE and MORE and
the politics of biblical translation: SixtC 19,1 (1988) 45-62 [< ZIT].

1808 *Greenspoon* Leonard J.,   A book 'without blemish'; the Jewish Publication Society's Bible translation of 1917:   JQR 79 (1988s) 1-21.

1809 **Levi** Peter,   The English Bible from WYCLIFF to William BARNES. West
Sussex 1985 = 1974, Churchman.   222 p. – ᴿChH 57 (1988) 398s (D. G.
Danner).

1810 *McDonnell* Jim,   Ronald KNOX; relevance and readability: PrPeo 2
(1988) 405-7 [400-428 *al.,* on Knox, born 1888; nothing really on his
translation of the whole Bible].

1811 **NAB**: New American Bible New Testament, revised edition.   Nv 1986,
Nelson.   640 p. $13; pa. $3. – ᴿBTrans 39 (1988) 144s (R. G. *Bratcher*:
'inclusive language' within limits; 'dynamic' abandoned for 'formal'
equivalence).

1812 **NIV**: ᶠPALMER Edwin H.,   The NIV; the making of a contemporary
translation, ᴱ**Barker** K. 1986 → 3,125:   ᴿEvQ 60 (1988) 265s (P. *Ellingworth*).

1813 **Purkis** R.,   The English Bible and its origins. 1988, Angel. £2 [TLond
91,567].

1814 **Sherry** Thomas E.,   Attitudes, practices and positions toward Joseph
SMITH's translation of the Bible; a historical analysis of publications,
1847-1987: diss. Brigham Young 1988, ᴰ*Gale* D. 273 p.   88-21909. –
DissA 49 (1988s) 2270-A.

1815 *Wolfers* David,   Modern biblical translations [... some deplorable
practices]:   Dor 17 (1988s) 141-152.

D6.3   *Versiones germanicae* – Deutsche Bibelübersetzungen.

1816 Biblia sacra, frühneuhochdeutsche Bibelübersetzung (Strassburg 1466,
Mentelin). B 1987, Berndt. – ᴿJudaica 44 (1988) 55s (D. *Flusser*).

1817 **Bluhm** Heinz, Martin Luther as a creative Bible translator: 'StL' (1965) [LutherJb 55,128; but 54 (1987) p.170, Nr. 607 seems to give source as [F]WALTHER D., A tribute to Martin Luther = AndrUnS 22 (1984) 35-44].

1818 a) *Brecht* Martin, Luthers Bibelübersetzung; – b) *Beintker* Horst, Schwierigkeiten im katholischen Lutherbild heute; – c) *Seils* Martin, Kontinuität und Wandel in Luthers Theologie: → 3,585, [E]*Bartel* H., ML Leistung und Erbe 1983/6, 118-125 / 402-407 / 139-141 [< LuJb 55 (1988) 163.170.156 (p.140, noch 54 Titel zitiert)].

1819 **Brügger** Samuel, Die deutschen Bibelübersetzungen des 20. Jahrhunderts im sprachwissenschaftlichen Vergleich; Studien zum Metapherngebrauch in den Verdeutschungen des NTs: EurHS 1/707. Bern 1983, Lang. 342 p. Fs 68. – [R]ZkT 110 (1988) 218s (J. *Schermann*).

1820 [E]**Deissler** A., *Vögtle* A., (*Nützel* J. M.), Neue Jerusalemer Bibel [1968[1-17]] 1985 → 1,1830: [R]ZkT 110 (1988) 89s (F. *Mohr*).

1821 *Dellsperger* Rudolf, 'Das Heilig wort Gottes in der Haubtstatt'; zum theologie- und kirchengeschichtlichen Hintergrund der Berner Piscatorbibel: Zwingliana 16 (1985) 500-516.

1822 **Dietzfelbinger** Ernst, Das Neue Testament, Interlinearübersetzung griechisch-deutsch. Stu-Neuhausen 1986 [2]1987, Hänssler. xxviii-1139 p. – [R]TPhil 63 (1988) 252 (N. *Baumert*).

1823 **Ebert** Helmut, Alltagssprache und religiöse Sprache in LUTHERS Briefen und in seiner Bibelübersetzung; eine satzsemantische Untersuchung am Beispiel von Aufforderungssätzen und Fragesätzen [Diss. Bonn 1985s]: EurHS 1,929. Fra 1986, Lang. 248 p. – LuJb 55 (1988) 164.

1824 **Frettlöh** Regina, Die Revisionen der LUTHERbibel in wortgeschichtlicher Sicht [Diss. Münster 1984]: Göppinger Arbeiten zur Germanistik 434. Göppingen 1986, Kümmerle. iii-610 p. – LuJb 55 (1988) 164.

1825 **Himmighöfer** Traudel, Die Neustadter Bibel von 1587/88, die erste reformierte Bibelausgabe Deutschlands. Speyer 1986, Ev. 248 p. – [R]LutherJb 54 (1987) 134s (H. *Junghans* zitiert A. ALT, Altes Testament und Neues Testament dürfen nie abegkürzt werden).

1826 *Knoch* Otto B., Die Katholiken und die Bibel [... Übersetzungen]; ein Gang durch die Geschichte: TPQ 136 (1988) 239-251.

1827 *Lippold* Ernst, Die alten Namensformen in der neuen LUTHERbibel; Entscheidungen im Spannungsfeld ökumenischer, sprachlicher und frömmigkeitsgeschichtlicher Verantwortung: MatKonfInst 37 (Bensheim 1986) 11s [< LuJb 54 (1987) 172].

1828 *Lohse* Bernhard, a) Die Aktualisierung der christlichen Botschaft in LUTHERS Bibelübersetzung [< Luther 51 (1980) 9-25]; – b) Entstehungsgeschichte und hermeneutische Prinzipien der Lutherbibel [< [E]*Gnilka* J., Übersetzung der Bibel 1984, 133-148]: → 224, Evangelium 1988, 177-193 / 194-210.

1829 a) *Meurer* Siegfried, Ist die Zeit schon reif für eine Einheitsbibel der deutschsprachigen Christenheit?; – b) *Lippold* Ernst, Die Revision des NTs der Lutherbibel von 1981 bis 1984: → 2,1305, Die neue Lutherbibel 1985, 91-102 / 13-30 [< LuJb 54,172].

1830 *Müller* P. G., Ein katholischer Versuch; die Bibelübersetzung Johannes ECKS: Klerusblatt 68,1 (Mü 1988) 15-17 [< ZIT].

1831 Münchener Neues Testament, [E]**Hainz** Josef: Studienübersetzung. Dü 1988, Patmos. xi-506 p. 3-491-71083-9.

1832 *Panning* Armin, Luther as Bible translator: → 358, [E]*Fredrich* E., Luther lives 1983, 69-84 [< LuJb 57,172].

1833 **Reinitzer** Heimo, Biblia deutsch, LUTHERs ... 1983 ➤ 64,1862 ... 3,1779: ᴿArKulturG 70 (1988) 262-4 (H.-J. *Köhler*).

D6.4   Versiones nordicae *et variae.*

1834 *a)* **Bielemans** J. A. A. M., [sic RHE 84,10* Nᵒ 88; ➤ 65,1610; 2,1306 Biemans] Codices manuscripti Sacrae Scripturae neerlandicae / Middelnederlandse Bijbelhandschriften. Leiden 1984, Brill. xii-337 p. – ᴿArchief voor de Geschiedenis van de Katholieke Kerk in Nederland 30 (Utrecht 1988) 137-9 (A. H. *Bredero*). – *b)* Willibrordvertaling; de Bijbel uit de grondtekst vertaald. Boxtel 1988, Kath./Vlaamse Bijbelstichting. xv-1587 p.; 6 maps. *f* 39.50. – ᴿStreven [43 (1975s) 135-142] 56 (1988s) 471s (P. *Beentjes*).

1834* **Kirby** Ian J., Bible translation in Old Norse: Univ. Lausanne 27. Genève 1986, Droz.

1835 *Sæbø* Magne, The Norwegian Bible translation of 1978/85 — what have we learned?: BTrans 39 (1988) 308-316.

1836 *Sæbø* Magne, *Sandvik* Bjørn, Norsk alternativ Bibeloversettelse av 1988 [ᴱ*Wisloff* C., *al.,* Oslo Norsk Bibel AS, 1286 p.]: TsTKi 59 (1988) 305-7/307s (NT).

1837 *Batalden* Stephen K., Gerasim PAVSKII's clandestine Old Testament; the politics of nineteenth-century Russian Bible translation: ChH 57 (1988) 486-498.

1838 *Coman* Constantin, ⑥ Three hundred years since the first translation of the Bible in Roumanian language (1688-1988): DeltioVM 17,2 (1988) 23-30.

1839 **Kartanos** Ioannikios, ⑥ Palaiá te kaì Néa Diathēkē [Venice 1536], I. Athēna 1988, Tinos, 280 p. – ᴿTAth 54 (1988) 605-8 (P. *Simotas* ⑥).

1840 *Wittig* A., Die Verurteilung der Bibelübersetzung des HILARION des Sinaiten durch die Patriarchalsynode von 1823: AnHistConc 18 (1986) 448-455.

1841 **Rijks** Piet, A guide to Catholic Bible translations, 1. The Pacific [largely Australia and New Zealand; excluding Philippines, Japan]. Stu c.1987, World Catholic Federation for the Biblical Apostolate. 147 p. [BToday 26,185].

1842 **Covell** Ralph R., Confucius, the Buddha, and Christ; a history of the Gospel in Chinese 1986 ➤ 2,1318; 3,1794: ᴿCalvinT 23 (1988) 77-79 (R. R. *DeRidder*); PhilipSa 23 (1988) 155s (R. *Carter*).

1843 *Harbsmeier* Christoph, Marginalia sino-theologica [in English: history and problems of Chinese Bible-translation]: SvEx 53 (1988) 69-84.

1844 **Strandenaes** Thor, Principles of Chinese Bible translation ... Mt 5,1-12; Col 1 [Diss. Uppsala 1987]: ConBib NT 19, 1987 ➤ 3,1795: ᴿTR 84 (1988) 500s (W. *Promper*).

1845 **Kimura** Naoji, Das Christentum als sprachliches Problem in Japan: Eichstätter Hochschulreden 51. Mü 1986, Minerva. 21 p. – ᴿTGL 78 (1988) 100s (H. *Waldenfels*).

1846 *a)* **Schneider** Bernardin, The new Japanese common Bible translation; – *b)* *Raymaker* John, The Bible and the Japanese apostolate: Japan Missionary Bulletin 41 (Tokyo 1987) 167-173 / 236-241 [< TKontext 9/2,50].

1847 Studium biblicum Franciscanum: The Holy Bible; ⑩ the books of Zephaniah, Haggai, Zechariah. Malachi, Lamantations, Baruch and the Letter of Jeremiah / the Books of Exra and Nehemiah. Tokyo 1987s, Chuo Shuppansha. 311 p.; 181 p.

1848 *Vraux* Sylvie, Histoire et difficultés des versions japonaises: ➤ 486, Traduction 1986/8, 73-77.
1849 Scriptures of the world[11] [1848 dialects in which at least one complete book of the Bible has appeared]. L 1986, United Bible Societies. 127 p.; maps [NTAbs 32,237].

D7   *Problemata vertentis* – **Bible translation techniques.**

1850 **Barnwell** Katharine, Bible translation, an introductory course in translation principles[3rev]. Dallas 1986, Summer Institute of Linguistics. 274 p. $6.65. 0-88312-651-6. (Teacher's Manual[3] 1987, 264 p. $6.25). [= Tradução bíblica 1979, $4]. – [R]BTrans 39 (1988) 347s (J. A. *Loewen*).
1851 *Bedouelle* Guy, Le débat catholique sur la traduction en langue vulgaire: ➤ 471, Exégèse XVIe s. 1988 ...
1852 *Brock* S. P., Translating the OT: ➤ 97, [F]LINDARS B. 1988, 87-98.
1853 **Buzzetti** Carlo, La Biblia y sus transformaciones; historia de las traducciones bíblicas y reflexiones hermenéuticas [1986], [T]*Ortiz García* Alfonso: Buena noticia 16. Estella 1986, TDivino. 143 p. 84-7151-471-0.
1854 *Evenou* Jean, Les traductions liturgiques; du centre à la périphérie: EsprVie 98 (1988) 385-392.
1855 *Fućak* M. Jerko, Quaedam problemata ad stilum pertinentia in traducendo NT (croat.): BogSmot 58 (1988) 110-122.
1856 **García Yebra** V., Teoría y práctica de la traducción. M 1985 [Biblica 69,447].
   [E]**Gibaud** Henri, Les problèmes d'expression dans la traduction biblique 1988 ➤ 486.
1857 **Hardesty** Nancy A., Inclusive language in the Church [... Bible translation]. Atlanta 1987, Knox. 114 p. $8. – [R]TTod 45 (1988s) 143 (Diane *Tennis*).
1858 *Hohulin* E. L., Concepts and categories; when is a tree not a tree?: Notes on Translation 122 (Dallas 1987) 1-25 (-43) [< NTAbs 32,292].
1859 **Holmes** James S., Translated! Papers on literary translation and translation studies; introd. *Broeck* Raymond van den: Approaches to Translation Studies 7. Amst 1988, Rodopi. 117 p. 90-6203-739-9.
1860 [E]**Jäger** Gert, *Neubert* Albrecht, Semantik, Kognition und Äquivalenz: Übersetzungswissenschaftliche Beiträge 11. Lp 1988, VEB-Enz. 192 p. 3-324-00300-8.
1861 *Kaczmarkowski* Michał, ⊕ Übersetzungstheorie (Gegenstand, Problematik, Platz unter den anderen Wissenschaften): ➤ 73, [F]KANIA W. = VoxPa 12s (1987s) 205-218; deutsch 218.
1862 **Lapide** Pinchas, Ist die Bibel richtig übersetzt?: Siebenstern 1415, 1986 ➤ 2,1329; 3,1804: [R]TLZ 113 (1988) 355-7 (J. *Rohde*).
1863 **Lapide** Pinchas, Is de Bijbel goed vertaald? [T]*Marel* M. P. van der. Kampen 1988, Kok. 147 p. *f*22,50. 90-242-5211-3 [Bijdragen 49,475].
1864 *a) Marchessou* Hélène, Est-il possible de traduire la Bible?; – *b) Marchadour* Germain, Phobie de la répétition chez S. JÉRÔME, ÉRASME et TYNDALE: ➤ 486, Traduction 1986/8, 57-61 / 43-56; Eng. 57.43.
1865 *Marín* Francisco, Revisionismo necesario; puntualización de textos bíblicos [Ex 19,5; Sal 41,5 ...]: Carthaginensia 4 (1988) 223-233.
1866 *Mikre-Sellassie* G. Ammanuel, Problems in translating pronouns from English versions: BTrans 39 (1988) 230-7 [Amharic; Mt 6,1s; 25,3-13; Ex 3,5] (p. 238-246, report of Swahili workshop.).

1867 *Minkoff* Harvey,   Problems of translations; concern for the text versus the common reader: BR 4,4 (1988) 34-40.

1868 *Nida* Eugene A.,   Intelligibility and acceptability in Bible translating: BTrans 39 (1988) 301-8.

1869 *a) Noss* Philip A.,   Quotation, direct, indirect and otherwise in translation; – *b) Marchese Zogbo* Lynell,   Advances in discourse study and their application to the field of translation: ➤ 508, Issues/Translation 1987/8, 129-145 / 1-29.

1870 **Olofsson** S.,   Guds Ord och människors språk; en bok om bibelöversättning 1986 ➤ 2,1134:   ᴿBL (1988) 63 (G. W. *Andersen*).

1871 *Scanlin* Harold P.,   Bible translation as a means of communicating NT textual criticism to the public: BTrans 39 (1988) 101-112; 113 chart [NAB has fewest (70) and JerB most (602) textual footnotes of seven major English translations].

1872 *Schwarz* Werner,   Schriften zur Bibelübersetzung und mittelalterlichen Übersetzungstheorie [< Eng. 1944-1974 + 2 inedita], ᴱ*Reinitzer* Heimo: Vestigia Bibliae, Jb. des deutschen Bibel-Archivs Hamburg 7 (1985) 9-139 . 199-202. – ᴿLutherJb 55 (1988) 119-121 (M. *Beyer*).

1873 *Schwarz* Werner, *a)* Prinzipien der Bibelübersetzung; – *b)* Proben von Luthers Bibelübersetzung: ➤ 2,1337* = Vestigia Bibliae 7 (Hamburg 1985) 36-41 / 119-126 [< LuJb 55 (1988) 166].

1874 *a) Stine* Philip C.,   Sociolinguistics and Bible translation; – *b) Ansre* Gilbert,   To unify or dialectize? Some sociolinguistic and psycholinguistic factors in language development for Bible translation: ➤ 502, Issues/ Translation 1987/8, 146-171 [172-186, *Hatton* H., Thai] / 197-206.

1875 *a) Truffaut* Louis,   Qu'est-ce donc que traduire?; – *b) Wyss* Simone, *Veyriras* Paul,   La traduction littéraire et ses problèmes; – *c) Urbain* Roland,   Traduction et religion; approches et problèmes contemporains: BICLyon 86 (1988) 7-22 / 23-29-33 / 35-43.

1876 *Ulrich* Eugene,   Double literary editions of biblical narratives and reflections on determining the form to be translated: PerspRelSt 15,4 (1988) 101-116 [unexplained why only this fascicle does not continue the page-numbering of the rest of the volume].

1877 **Waard** Jan de, *Nida* Eugene A.,   From one language to another; functional equivalence in Bible translating. Nv 1987, Nelson. 224 p. $16. 0-8407-7555-5 [BTrans 39,348]. – ᴿBiblica 69 (1988) 445-7 (L. *Alonso Schökel*).

1878 **Wendland** Ernst R.,   The cultural factor in Bible translation; a study of communicating the Word of God in central African cultural context 1987 ➤ 3,1825:   ᴿNT 38 (1988) 253 (J. A. *Emerton*).

D8   *Concordantiae, lexica specialia* – **Specialized dictionaries, synopses.**

1879 **Cochrane** J., *Chouinard* G.,   Concordance [à *Segond* L. 1910 ²1975] et index de la Bible, 2. Nouveau Testament.   Québec 1987, Distributions Évangéliques. xiii-425 p. C$35. 2-902147-04-8 [NTAbs 32,362].

1880 **Epps** Chris, CompuBIBLE [concordance to four English versions]. 1984, National Software Systems. $249. – ᴿRExp 85 (1988) 150s (J. E. *Dent*).

1881 *a)* **Maurer** H.,   Kleines Register zur Bibel; wo steht was — was steht wo; – *b)* ᴱ**Hartmann** H.,   Kleine Konkordanz zur Lutherbibel ... in der revidierten Fassung von 1984: Bibel-Kirche-Gemeinde 21s. Konstanz 1986, Chrístliche VA.   237 p.; 329 p., je DM 16,80. – ᴿSNTU-A 13 (1988) 214 (A. *Fuchs*).

1882 **Neirynck** F., *Segbroeck* F. van, NT vocabulary 1984 ➤ 65,1653 ...
    3,1828: ᴿSvEx 53 (1988) 121s (C. C. *Caragounis*).
1883 **Odelain** O., *Séguineau* R., Concordance thématique du Nouveau
    Testament [format de poche]. P c.1988, Cerf. 1088 p. F 249 [MaisD 176
    cover adv.].
1884 **Oetinger** Friedrich C. (1702-82), Biblisches und emblematisches Wör-
    terbuch (1776), ᴱ*Tschiżewski* Dmitrij: Emblematisches Cabinet 9. Hil-
    desheim 1987, Olms. xxiv-866 p. 3-487-02345-8.
1885 **Opálény** Mihály, *Balász* Károly, Ⓜ Újszövetségi szövegmutató szótar
    [NT contextual concordance]. Budapest 1988, Univ. 1372 p. (p. 1135-
    1171, Greek equivalents alphabetically).
1886 **Strong** James, Strong's exhaustive concordance [1890]. *a*) GR 1982,
    Baker. 132 + 128 + 79 p. [KirSef 61,393]. – *b*) Nv 1984, Nelson 'with main
    concordance and appendix'. 1260 + 85 + 243 p.; + 127 Ⓞ, 79 Ⓖ; finally
    15 p. of various tables. 0-8407-5360-8.
1887 **Strothmann** W., *al.,* Konkordanz zur syrischen Bibel; der Pentateuch:
    GöOrF 1/26, 1986 ➤ 3,1832*b*: ᴿBL (1988) 51 (M. P. *Weitzman*: con-
    tinues to ignore Leiden critical Peshitta: e.g. no indication that oldest ms.
    nearly always has *kespā* instead of *sēmā*); BO 45 (1988) 183s (M. J.
    Mulder); JSS 33 (1988) 133-9 (S. *Brock*); OLZ 83 (1988) 426s (P. *Kawerau,*
    Propheten).
1888 **Whitaker** Richard E., (*Goehring* James E.), The Eerdmans analytical
    concordance to RSV [with 'Ãpocrypha']. GR 1988, Eerdmans. xiv-
    1548 p. $50 [TDig 35,353]. 0-8028-2403-X.

IV. ➤ K 1	V. Exegesis generalis VT vel cum NT

D9   Commentaries on the whole Bible or OT.

1889 La Bibbia di Navarra [Vangeli] Mi 1988, Ares. 1120 p. – ᴿAvvenire (22.
    X. 1988 > ScuolC 12,888, G. *Biffi*); OssRom (22. X. 1988 > ScuolC
    22,899, P. *Rossano*).
1890 ᴱ**Bruce** F. F., The international Bible commentary with NIV [replacing
    RSV of 1979 Bible Commentary for today] 1986 ➤ 2,1351; 3,1836: ᴿCBQ
    50 (1988) 489-491 (K. M. *Craig*); Salesianum 50 (1988) 416s (R. *Vicent*:
    espléndido).
1891 *Chilton* B. D., Commenting on the OT: ➤ 97, ᶠLINDARS B. 1988,
    122-140.
1892 **Federici** Tommaso, Per conoscere Lui e la potenza della Resurrezione di
    Lui; per una lettura teologica del Lezionario [I. 1987 ➤ 3,216] II, III:
    Puteoli Resurgentes (1)3s. N 1988, Dehoniane. II, ciclo B, 1987; 586 p.;
    Lit. 38.000; – III, ciclo C, 1988; 827 p.; Lit. 40.000. 88-396-0019-4; 115-5.
    – ᴿAsprenas 35 (1988) 283-6 (P.*Giustiniani*); CC 139 (1988,2) 204 (C. *De
    Gennaro,* 2); ParVi 33 (1988) 308-310 (S. *Virgulin*: entusiasmo).
1893 **Friedman** Alexander Z., Wellsprings of Torah; an anthology of Biblical
    commentaries [< Yiddish 1969], ᵀ*Hirschler* Gertrude; ᴱ*Alper* Nison. NY
    1986, Judaica. xxiv-549 p. [KirSef 61,390].
1894 ᴱ**Gaebelein** Frank E., The Expositor's Bible commentary [➤ 64,1910 ...
    3,1840] with NIV, 4, 1 Kings – Job. GR 1988, Zondervan. xvi-1060 p.
    $30 [TDig 35,356]. – ᴿSWJT 31,1 (1988s) 46s (D. G. *Kent,* 6).

1894* **Gomá Civit** Isidro, Reflexiones en torno a los textos bíblicos dominicales; pról. **González de Cardedal** Olegario. Montserrat 1988, Abadia/Misioneras de Nazaret. 1033 p.; map.; p. 1029-33, índice de los domingos y solemnidades; ningun índice de los pasajes bíblicos. 84-7202-906-9.

1895 ᴱ**Mays** James L. [*al., SBL*] Harper's Bible commentary [including 'Apocrypha'; *Alonso-Schökel* Luis, Judith 804-814; *Reese* James M., Wisdom 820-835; *Crenshaw* James L, Sirach 836-854; *Schiffman* Lawrence H., 1-2 Mcb 875-915 (but also 3-4 Mcb 916-934; '2' Esdras 776-790)]. SF 1988, Harper & R. 1326 p.; ill. (credits p. 1320): 16 color. maps. $32.50. 0-06-06541-0. – ᴿBAR-W 14,6 (1988) 68-70 (G. *Shepherd*).

1896 *Moore* S. D., [Polebridge Press projected] Narrative commentaries on the Bible; context, roots, and prospects: Forum 3,3 (1987) 29-62 [NTAbs 32,143].

1897 **Parker** T. H. L., CALVIN's Old Testament commentaries [... their doctrine and principles of biblical interpretation] 1986 ➤ 2,1357; 3,1845: ᴿEvQ 60 (1988) 89-91 (N. *Cameron*); Interpretation 42 (1988) 198s (R. *Boyce*); JTS 39 (1988) 631-3 (M. *Sadgrove*); SixtC 19 (1988) 509 (D. K. *McKim*).

1898 ᴱ**Schoenhals** O. Roger, WESLEY's notes on the Bible. GR 1987, Zondervan/Asbury. 612 p. [abridged from the original 3682 p. in 2 vol. NT 1755, 3 vol. OT 1765s]. $28 [TDig 35,93].

1899 **Seethaler** Paula-Angelika, Register zum Stuttgarter Kleinen Kommentar Altes Testament: StuKK AT 25. Stu 1987, KBW. 144 p. 3-460-05251-1.

1900 ᵀ*Zotenberg* Hermann, Les prophètes et les rois; extrait de la chronique de Tabari, I. à David; II. aux Sassanides: Bibliothèque de l'Islam, Textes. P 1984, Sindbad. 364 p.; 398 p. [KirSef 61,394].

VI. Libri historici VT

E1 **Pentateuchus, Torah** .1 *Textus, commentarii.*

1901 ᵀᴱ**Baumgarten** Jean, Jacob BEN ISAAC Achkenazi de Janow, Le commentaire sur la Torah: [yidich]: Les Dix Paroles. Lagasse 1987, Verdier. 942 p. – ᴿÉtudes 368 (1988) 116s (J. *Rolland*).

1902 **Goulet** Richard, La philosophie de Moïse; ... commentaire préphilonien du Pentateuque 1987 ➤ 3,1849: ᴿElenchos 9 (1988) 186-190 (R. *Radice*); RivFgIC 116 (1988) 359-364 (M. *Simonetti*); RPLH 62,1 (1988) 153-5 (É. des *Places*: long, excès de richesse); RSPT 72 (1988) 605-7 (G.-M. de *Durand*).

1903 **Hertz** Joseph H., Pentateuch und Haftaroth — hebräischer Text und deutsche Übersetzung mit Kommentar [cf. ➤ 2,1378; Ⓜ ➤ 1,1908 = 2,1363*] Z 1984, Morescha. xvi-544 p.; xvi-611 p.; xv-478 p.; xv-482 p.; xv-620 p. – ᴿJudaica 44 (1988) 57s (S. *Schreiner*).

1904 **Lattes** Dante, Nuovo (1949) commento alla Torah. R 1986, Carucci. xv-749 p. Lit. 45.000. – ᴿAntonianum 63 (1988) 175s (M. *Nobile*: originale, ricco).

1905 ᵀᴱ**Pelcovitz** Raphael, Obadiah ben Jacob SFORNO (c.1470-c.1550), Ⓗ Commentary on the Torah I: Art Scroll Mesorah. Brooklyn 1987, Mesorah. xxiv-440 p. 0-89906-238-5; pa. 9-3.

1906 **Radice** Roberto, (*Reale* G.) FILONE di Alessandria, La filosofia mosaica; la creazione del mondo secondo Mosè [T*Kraus Reggiani* Clara ➤ 3,1914]; Le allegorie delle leggi: I classici del pensiero. Mi 1987, Rusconi. cxli-580 p. Lit. 34.000. 88-18-22009-8 [Bijdragen 49,234]. – RGregorianum 69 (1988) 790-2 (G. *Pelland*); OrChr 72 (1988) 235s (W. *Gessel*); RPLH 62,1 (1988) 152 (É. des *Places*: utile).

E1   *Pentateuchus*   .2   **Introductio; Fontes JEDP.**

1907 **Friedman** Richard E., Who wrote the Bible? 1987 ➤ 3,1857: RAmerica 157 (1987) 432 (D.J. *Harrington*: really on JEPD in Gn-Dt; his 'most original' ideas include 'Ezra was final redactor'); BL (1988) 75 (R.P. *Carroll*: absurd; American, of course, and in that brash, self-confident style so typical of American scholarship); CurrTM 15 (1988) 283s (R.W. *Klein*: exciting defense of JEPD, featured in U.S.News and Wall Street Journal, but defective); TS 49 (1988) 377 (J.C. *Endres*: reviewed in Wall Street Journal and US News).

1908 **Hurvitz** A., A linguistic study of the relationship between the priestly source and the book of Ezekiel: RB Cah 20, 1982➤ 63,1970; 65,1676: RLešonenu 51 (1986s) 235-9 (E. *Qimron*).

1909 *a) Hurvitz* Avi, Dating the priestly source in light of the historical study of biblical Hebrew; a century after Wellhausen; – *b) Perlitt* Lothar, Priesterschrift im Deuteronomium?: ➤ 153, ZAW 100 Supp. (1988) 88-100 / 65-88.

1910 **Kikawada** Isaac M., *Quinn* Arthur, Before Abraham was; a provocative challenge to the documentary hypothesis. Nv 1985, Abingdon. 144 p. $11. – RCurrTM 15 (1988) 373s (W.L. *Michel*: unfair); JAOS 108 (1988) 310s (E. *Yamauchi*: attack on JEPD at its strongest point, Gen 1-11).

1911 *McCarter* P. Kyle[J], A new challenge to the documentary hypothesis [*Kikawada* I., *Quinn* A. 1985]: BR 4,3 (1988) 34-39: no.

1912 **Paul** Mart-Jan, Het Archimedisch punt van de Pentateuchkritiek; een historisch en exegetisch onderzoek naar de verhouding van Deuteronomium en de reformatie van koning Josia (2 Kon 22-23): diss. Leiden,[D]*Mulder* M. 1988. Haag 1988, Boekencentrum. 391 p. – TsTNijm 28 (1988) 296; RTLv 20,541.

1913 *Schmidt* Werner H., Plädoyer für die Quellenscheidung: BZ 32 (1988) 1-14.

1914 **Terino** A., L'origine del Pentateuco [after scholarly rundown, defends Mosaic authorship]: Prospettive evangeliche. Fondi LT 1986, UCEB. 355 p. Lit. 19,500 [BL 89,95, C.J.A. *Hickling*].

1914* **Tengström** Sven, Die Toledotformel ... 1981 ➤ 63,1982 ... 2,1373: RTs-TKi 59 (1988) 309s (Dagfinn *Rian*).

1915 E**Tigay** Jeffrey H., Empirical models for biblical criticism 1985 ➤ 1,315; 3,1862. – RJTS 39 (1988) 532-5 (J.W. *Rogerson*: theme of the book is that ancient Middle East realities confirm JEPD); TüTQ 168 (1988) 163s (W. *Gross*).

1916 **Van Seters** John, Der Jahwist als Historiker [wrote during exile, largely 'facts' of his own invention, or mythologized back to an age of the gods...]: TStud 134. Z 1987, Theol.-V. 95 p. Fs 14. 3-290-17134-5 [BL 89,42, P.R. *Davies*].

1917 **Whybray** R.N., The making of the Pentateuch: JStOT Sup 53,1987 ➤ 3,1863: RBiblica 69 (1988) 270-3 (J.L. *Ska*); BL (1988) 97 (A.G. *Auld*: admittedly largely negative critique of the past century's efforts);

Carthaginensia 4 (1988) 362 (R. *Sanz Valdivieso*); CurrTM 15 (1988) 201s (R.W. *Klein*); Interpretation 42 (1988) 308. 310 (G.E. *Gerbrandt*); NBlackf 69 (1988) 50s (H. *Mowvley*); RB 95 (1988) 444-7 (F. *Langlamet*); RelStR 14 (1988) 64 (W.L. *Humphreys*); TLZ 113 (1988) 103-7 (E. *Blum*).

E1.3 *Pentateuchus,* **themata.**

1918 a) *Alexander* Philip S., Retelling the OT; – b) *Williamson* H.G.M., History [cited in NT]: ➤ 97, ᶠLINDARS B., It is written 1988, 99-121.

1919 **Andrade** Barbara, Encuentro con Dios en el Pentateuco 1985 ➤ 1,1932; 2,1375: ᴿRB 95 (1988) 617-9 (J. *Loza*).

1920 *Baillet* Maurice, Les divers états du Pentateuque Samaritain: ➤ 22, Mém. CARMIGNAC J., RQum 13 (1988) 531-545.

1921 *Böhl* Felix, Die Metaphorisierung (*metila*) in den Targumim zum Pentateuch: FraJudBei 15 (1987) 111-149.

1922 a) *Cook* J., The composition of the Peshiṭta version of the OT (Pentateuch); – b) *Kooij* A. van der, On the significance of MS 5b1 for Peshiṭta Genesis; – c) *Koster* M.D., Which came first, the chicken or the egg? The development of the text of the Peshiṭta of Genesis and Exodus in the light of recent studies: ➤ 480, Peshiṭta 1985/8, 147-168 / 183-199 / 147-168.

1923 *García Casar* María F., Los tropos metonómicos del Pentateuco hebreo: CiuD 201 (1988) 539-550.

1924 *Goudoever* Jan van, Celebration of Torah [... Torah dates relate not to history but to liturgical times]: Antonianum 63 (1988) 458-484; franç. 458.

1925 *Gross* Walter, [P-Grundschrift] Israel's hope for the renewal of the state [< ᴱ*Schreiner* J., Unterwegs zur Kirche 1987, 87-122]: JNWS 14 (1988) 101-133.

1926 *Lohfink* Norbert, a) Die Schichten des Pentateuch und der Krieg [< Gewalt, QDisp 96 (1983) 51-110] – b) Der Schöpfergott und der Bestand von Himmel und Erde; das Alte Testament zum Zusammenhang von Schöpfung und Heil [< Sind wir noch zu retten? (Pustet 1978) 15-39]; – c) Die Ursünden in der Priesterlichen Geschichtserzählung [< ᶠ*Schlier* H. 1970, 38-57]: ➤ 223, Studien zum Pentateuch 1988, 255-315 / 191-211 / 169-189.

1927 *Hossfeld* Frank-Lothar, Der Pentateuch [biblische Theologie]: ➤ 327, Höre 1987, 11-68.

1928 **Mann** Thomas W., The book of the Torah; the narrative integrity of the Pentateuch [Princeton lectures]. Atlanta 1988, Knox. 180p. $15 pa. 0-8042-0085-8 [TDig 36,174].

1929 *Moucarry* Georges C., The alien according to the Torah [< Ichthus 132 (1985) 3-10], ᵀ*Smith* Joyce: Themelios 14 (1988s) 17-20.

1930 *Nicholson* E.W., P as an originally independent source of the Pentateuch: ➤ 148, ᶠWEINGREEN J. = IrBSt 10 (1988) 192-206.

1931 *Pagan* Samuel, Sociology, theology, and hope; the priestly case [Pentateuch-P] in exile: BTrans 39 (1988) 317-329.

1932 *Savignac* Jean de, L'importance scientifique de la Thorah d'Israël: ➤ 50, ᶠFONTINOY C., Humour ... science 1988, 304-310.

1933 *Segal* Alan F., Torah and *nómos* in recent scholarly discussion [< SR 13 (1984) 19-28]: ➤ 260, Other Judaisms 1987, 131-145.

  Struppe Ursula, Die Herrlichkeit Jahwes in der Priesterschrift ᴰ1988 ➤ a270.

1935 *Urbach* E.E., Torah, ᵀ*Garber* A.: ➤ 795, EncRel 14 (1987) 556-565.

1936 *Wenham* Gordon,   *a)* The perplexing Pentateuch [morality, science, ritual...]: VoxEvca 17 (L 1987) 7-21; – *b)* Genesis; an authorship study and current pentateuchal criticism: JStOT 42 (1988) 3-18.

E1.4   **Genesis;** *textus, commentarii.*

1937 **Arenhoevel** Diego,   Ur-Geschichte; Genesis 1-11⁴ [ital. ↠ 3,1881]: StuKK AT 1.   Stu 1985 (¹1970), KBW.   88 p.   3-460-05011-X.
1937* *a)* **Behaghel** Otto,   Heliand und Genesis, ⁹*Taeger* Burkhard: Altdeutsche Textbibliothek 4.   Tü 1984, Niemeyer.   xxxi-294. – *b)* **Taeger** B.,   Der Heliand; Studien-Ausgabe in Auswahl: Altd. Textb. 95.   Tü 1984, Niemeyer.   xiv-86 p. – ᴿStudi Medievali 28 (1987) 263-281 (Ute *Schwab*).
1938 **Boice** James M.,   Genesis; an expositional commentary, II (12,1-36,43): Ministry resources library, 1985 ↠ 2,1381; – III (37-50).   GR 1987, Zondervan.   366 p. [JAOS 108,675].
Diez Macho A., Targum palaestinense in Gn 1988 ↠ 1700.
1939 **Gowan** D.E.,   From Eden to Babel; a commentary on the Book of Genesis I-II: Int. Theol. Comm.   E/GR 1988, Handsel/Eerdmans.   ix-125 p. $8 pa.   0-905312-85-6 / 0-8028-0337-7 [BL 89,155].
1940 ᵀ**Grosjean** Jean,   La Genèse.   P 1987, Gallimard.   154 p. – ᴿRHPR 68 (1988) 235s (P. de *Robert*: version de poète).
Grossfeld Bernard,   The Targum Onqelos to Genesis 1988 ↠ 1703.
1941 **Harbach** Robert C.,   Studies in the Book of Genesis.   Grandville MI 1986, Reformed Church.   938 p. $22. – ᴿBS 145 (1988) 463s (T. L. *Constable*: a thorough commentary; but nondispensationalist, 'double predestination').
1942 **Hargreaves** John,   A guide to the book of Genesis.   Delhi 1987 = 1969, ISPCK.   xix-180 p.; rs 25. – ᴿVidyaiyoti 52 (1988) 204-6 (P. M. *Meagher*, also on his Psalms and on 6 other 1987 reprints of this SPCK Study Guide series).
1943 **Harl** Marguerite,   La Genèse, traduction du texte grec de la Septante: Bible d'Alexandrie 1, 1986 ↠ 2,1384*; 3,1887:   ᴿBijdragen 49 (1988) 208 (M. *Parmentier*: exciting and helps to 'overlook' i.e. survey the area of research); BLitEc 89 (1988) 291s (H. *Crouzel*); Contacts/Orthodoxe 40 (1988) 132-4 (J. M.); ÉTRel 63 (1988) 284s (C.-B. *Amphoux*); Irénikon 61 (1988) 139 (E. L.); RÉAug 34 (1988) 198 (C. *Perrot*); RÉJ 146 (1987) 431s (H. *Savon*); RHE 83 (1988) 94-96 (P.M. *Bogaert*: avec sept chercheurs); RivB 36 (1988) 107s (Anna *Passoni Dell'Acqua*); RThom 88 (1988) 130 (H. *Ponsot*).
1944 **Isabelle de la Source** sr.,   La Genèse: Lire la Bible avec les Pères. P 1988, Paulines.   173 p. – ᴿContacts/Orthodoxe 40 (1988) 150s (Y. D.).
1945 **Kidner** Frank D.,   Génesis, introducción y comentario [1967]: Didaqué 1. BA 1985, Certeza.   258 p.
1946 *Lilla* Salvatore,   Alcuni frammenti delle omelie XV e XVI (sulla Genesi) di S. Giovanni CRISÓSTOMO nel codice Vat. gr. 2646: Lincei BClas 9 (1988) 89-99; IX pl.
1947 *Malet* André, *al.*,   Commentaires de Jean CALVIN sur l'Ancien Testament, I. Le livre de la Genèse.   Aix-en-Provence 1978, Kerygma. 686 p.
1948 **Neri** U.,   Biblia; i libri della Bibbia interpretati dalla grande Tradizione; AT 1, Genesi, 1986 ↠ 2,1386; 3,1891:   ᴿBL (1988) 62 (S.P. *Brock*); Carmelus 35 (1988) 237s (B. *Secondin*); CC 139 (1988,1) 87s (G. L. *Prato*); CrNSt 9 (1988) 168s (A. *Schenker*: ²1988); MeliT 39 (1988) 76-80 (A. *Abela*: 'elegant but expensive, encyclopedic but profound'); RClerIt 63

(1987) 317-320 (C. *Scaglioni*); RivScR 2 (1988) 167-9 (M. A. *Tábet*); SBFLA 38 (1988) 485-492 (L. *Cignelli*: cita la lode di 'Dain Cohenel' = Dolindo RUOTOLO, 'morto in concetto di santità nel 1970' senza menzione del documento ecclesiastico su di lui).

1949 **Neusner** J., Comparative midrash ... Gn/Lv Rabbah: BrownJudSt 111, 1986 ➤ 3,1892. – RJBL 107 (1988) 346-8 (Z. *Garber*).

1950 **Nielsen** Eduard, Første Mosebog fortolket 1987 ➤ 3,1894: RNorTTs 89 (1988) 151s (A. S. *Kapelrud*).

1951 **Peters** Melvin K. H., A critical edition of the Coptic (Bohairic) Pentateuch, 1-2 GnEx: SBL SeptCog 19.22, 1985s ➤ 63,1995; 2,1365*: RScotJT 41 (1988) 287s (D. C. *Parker*); TLZ 117 (1988) 421-4 (H.-M. *Schenke*).

1952 EPetit Françoise, Catenae graecae in GnEx 2, Coislin.Gn: CCG 15, 1986 ➤ 2,1388; 3,1896: RJTS 39 (1988) 263-5 (L. R. *Wickham*); TS 49 (1988) 381s (G. H. *Ettlinger*).

1952* **Ross** Allen P., Creation and blessing; a guide to the study and exposition of the book of Genesis. GR 1988, Baker. 744 p. [JBL 107,790].

1953 **Ruppert** L., Das Buch Genesis II (25,19-50,26): Geistliche SL 6/2, 1984 ➤ 65,1705 ... 3,1899: RRB 95 (1988) 128s (J. *Loza*).

1954 *Ventura Avanzinelli* Milka, Il 'luterano' BRUCIOLI e il suo commento al libro della Genesi: Bollettino Soc. Studi Valdesi 159 (1986) 19-33.

1955 **Weitzmann** K., *Kessler* H. L., The Cotton Genesis 1986 ➤ 2,1395: RSpeculum 63 (1988) 731-3 (Sharon E. *Gerstel*).

1956 **Wenham** Gordon J., Genesis 1-15: Word 1, 1987 ➤ 3,1903; LIII-352 p.: RHomP 88,10 (1987s) 77 (W. G. *Heidt*: merits recommendation); RefTR 47 (1988) 61s (M. *Harding*: will stimulate, reward and edify); Themelios 14 (1988s) 102 (R. S. *Hess*); TrinJ 9 (1988) 231-6 (J. H. *Sailhamer*).

1957 **Westermann** Claus, Genesis, TScullion J.: I. 1984 ➤ 65,1711; II. (ch. 12-36) 1985 ➤ 2,1397; III. 1986; ch. 37-50, not as ➤ 3,1904: RIrBSt 9 (1987) 89-92 (A. D. H. *Mayes*: significant contribution of the translator) & 10 (1988) 102s; IrTQ 54 (1988) 72s (M. *Drennan*, 2); JJS 39 (1988) 114-6 (J. *Hughes*, 2); ScotJT 41 (1988) 137s (J. D. *Martin*, 2), 138-140 (D. C. *Parker*, 3); VT 38 (1988) 252s (J. A. *Emerton*, 1) & 127s (H. G. M. *Williamson*, 2s). – RBTZ 4 (1987) 149-166 (P. *Welten*, 1).

1958 EZeytunyan A. S., Girk‛ Cnndoc‛ ... Critical text of the Book of Genesis: The Most Ancient Monuments of Translation into Armenian 1. Erevan 1985, Armenian SSR Academy of Sciences. r 4,70. – RJTS 39 (1988) 180-2 (S. Peter *Cowe*: not perfect but vastly better than earlier editions).

1959 EZucker Moshe, ❶ *Pîrûšê* ... SAADYA's commentary on Genesis. NY 1984, American Rabbinical College. xix-487 p.; 22 pl. – RKirSef 61 (1986s) 601s (H. *Ben-Shammai*).

E1.5 *Genesis*, **themata.**

1960 **Amadou** Robert, De la langue hébraïque restituée à l'ésotérisme de la Genèse: Gnostica. P 1987, Cariscript. 43 p.; ill. 2-87601-003-8.

1961 EBloom Harold, Genesis [9 authors as samples of literary criticism]: Modern critical interpretations. NY 1986, Chelsea. vii-144 p. $24.50 [TDig 35,166].

1962 *a) Cook* J., The exegesis of the Greek Genesis; – *b) Peters* M. K. H., The affinities of the Coptic (Bohairic) version of Genesis: ➤ 478, 6th SeptCog 1986/7, 91-125 / 233-254.

1963 **Ellison** H. L., Fathers of the covenant; studies in [→ 60,2895 'some great chapters in'] Genesis and Exodus. Exeter 1978, Paternoster. 122 p. £1.90. – ᴿScripB 19 (1988s) 44 (R. C. *Fuller*: fundamentalist).

1964 *Emerton* J. A., The priestly writer in Genesis [Israel symposium 1984]: JTS 39 (1988) 381-400.

1966 *Greenhalgh* Stephen, Genesis, the narratives and the book: ScripB 17,2 (1987s) 26-35.

1967 *Maggioni* Bruno, Gli itinerari educativi della Bibbia [Gn (1-3); Evv]: Ambrosius 64 (1988) 489-504.

1968 ᴱ**Maruani** Bernard [ᵀavec *Cohen-Arazi* Albert], Genèse Rabba: Midrach Rabba 1: Les Dix Paroles. Lagrasse 1987, Verdier. 554 p. F 198. 2-86432-058-4. – ᴿÉTRel 63 (1988) 457s (D. *Lys*); Études 368 (1988) 117 (J. *Rolland*).

1969 *Navarro Peiró* Ángeles, Las treinta y tres reglas de interpretación según el texto del Génesis ha-Gadol [ᴱ*Margulies* M. 1975, 23-29]: EstBíb 46 (1988) 79-96.

1970 **Radday** Yehuda T., *Shore* Haim, Genesis; an authorship study in computer-assisted statistical linguistics 1985 → 1,1982 .... 3,1913: ᴿBS 145 (1988) 111s (W. R. *Bodien*: those who object to this method as used against JEPD had nothing against it as used to defend several Isaiahs).

1971 **Rendsburg** Gary A., The redaction of Genesis 1986 → 2,1412; 3,1915: ᴿCBQ 50 (1988) 695s (D. L. *Christensen*); JQR 78 (1987) 113-9 (M. *Brettler*: in the tradition of FOKKELMAN; most of his claims not acceptable).

1972 a) *Simonetti* Manlio, Le Quaestiones di TEODORETO su Genesi e Esodo; – b) *Pollastri* Alessandra, Le Quaestiones di AGOSTINO su Genesi; struttura dell'opera e motivazioni storico-dottrinali; – c) *Cavalcanti* Elena, La Genesi alla lettera [Agostino] tra '800 e '900 [1825 e dopo]: → 472, AnStoEseg 5 (1988) 39-56 / 57-76 / 297-313.

1973 **Thompson** T. L., The origin tradition of ancient Israel; I. The literary formation of Genesis and Exodus 1-23: JStOT Sup 55, 1987 → 3,1917: ᴿBL (1988) 92 (R. N. *Whybray*: valuable).

1973* **Valentin** frère, La Genèse en re-création ['selon' *Guibert* J., al.]: Libre Parole 6. Bru 1988. 95 p.

1974 **Vos** Howard F., Genesis and archaeology. GR 1985, Zondervan Academie. 125 p. [KirSef 61 (1986s) 616].

E1.6 **Creatio,** *Genesis 1s.*

1975 *Agouridis* Savas, Ⓖ Mythos — history – theology [analysis of passages from Gn 1-11]: DeltioVM 17,1 (1988) 5-20.

1976 **Alexandre** Monique, Le commencement du livre, Genèse I-V; la version grecque de la Septante et sa réception: Christianisme antique 3. P 1988, Beauchesne. 408 p.; 23 pl. F 372 [TS 50,626]. 2-7010-1151-5.

1977 **Anderson** Bernhard W., Creation in the OT, reprints 1984 → 65,265; 1,1987: ᴿScripB 19 (1988s) 42 (R. C. *Fuller*).

1978 *Arranz* Rodrigo, Interpretación AGUSTINIANA del relato genesíaco de la creación: AugM 33 (1986) 47-56.

1979 *Belletti* Bruno, La creazione delle idee e dell'uomo nel trattato De opificio mundi di FILONE Alessandrino: Humanitas 42 (Brescia 1987) 273-9.

1980 **Brito** Emilio, La création selon SCHELLING; Universum. Lv 1987, Peeters. xxxv-646 p. Fb 3000 [TS 50,176-8, T. F. *O'Meara*].

1981 *Capponi* Filippo, Note ambrosiane (II) [Hexameron dies V, sermo VII]: LinceiBClas 7 (1986) 79-92.

1982 **Castel** François, *al.,* Los Comienzos, ᵀ*Ortiz García* Alfonso 1986 ➤ 3,1925: ᴿActuBbg 25 (1988) 208 (R. de *Sivatte*); BibFe 14 (1988) 156 (M. *Sáenz de Santamaría*); ScripTPamp 20 (1988) 335s (G. *Aranda*).

1983 **Cerbelaud** Dominique, Création et Trinité; les enjeux théologiques de l'interprétation 'trinitaire' de Gn 1:1-2 des origines à saint Augustin: cath. diss. ᴰ*Munier* C. Strasbourg 1987. 853 p. (3 vol.). – RTLv 19,542.

1984 *c) Costa Freitas* Manuel B., O criacionismo de Leonardo COIMBRA; trajectoria de uma ideia; – *b) Abranches de Soveral* Eduardo, Análise de 'O criacianismo' ...: Didaskalia 17 (1987) 5-26 / 27-40.

1985 ᴱ**Dales** Richard C., *Gieben* Servus, Robert GROSSETESTE, Hexaemeron: Auctores Britannici Medii Aevi 6, 1982 ➤ 65,1723 ... 2,1421: ᴿColcFr 56 (1986) 145s (B. de *Armellada*).

1986 *a) DeRoche* Michael, The *rûaḥ 'elōhîm* in Gen 1:2c; creation or chaos?; – *b) Combs* Eugene, Has YHWH cursed the ground? Perplexity of interpretation in Genesis 1-5 [5,29]: ➤ 29, Mem. CRAIGIE P., Ascribe 1988, 303-318 / 265-287.

1987 **Eberlein** Karl, Gott der Schöpfer — Israels Gott 1986 ➤ 2,1423: ᴿBL (1988) 102 (D. J. A. *Clines*); ExpTim 99 (1987s) 328 (R. J. *Coggins*); TZBas 44 (1988) 376s (H. *Reventlow*).

1988 *Frymer-Kensky* Tikva, Biblical cosmology: ➤ 3,356, ᴱO'Connor M., Backgrounds 1987, 231-240 [< JBL 108,174].

1989 *Gerbelaud* Dominique, Creation et trinité [Gn 1 ...; < diss. cath. Strasbourg 1987]: RSPT 72 (1988) 88-94.

1990 **Gisel** Pierre, La creazione. Genova 1987, Marietti. 235 p. Lit. 45.000. – ᴿParVi 33 (1988) 76s (L. *Melotti*).

1991 *Kowalski* Wojciech, The biblical account of creation ... The universe and man: Pastoral Orientation Service (Tanzania, 1988/1) 1-16 [< TKontext 10/1,22].

1992 *Kwasman* Tuviah, [Gn 1] Die ent- und angeeignete Bibel: KIsr 2 (1987) 102-8.

1993 *Lamberigts* M., JULIAN of Aeclanum, a plea for a good creator: AugLv 38 (1988) 5-24 [< ZIT 89,178].

1994 **Lee Young Za**, Il carattere sincronico dell'esegesi della creazione (Gen. 1,1 – 2,4a): diss. Pont. Univ. Urbaniana, Nº 3307. R 1988. 130 p.

Levenson Jon D., Creation and the persistence of evil; the Jewish drama of divine omnipotence 1988 ➤ 8026.

1996 *a) Lindsey* William D., Gerrard WINSTANLEY's theology of creation; an appraisal; – *b) Wiebe* Donald, An unholy alliance? The creationists' quest for scientific legitimation: TorJT 4 (1988) 178-190 / 162-177.

1997 *Mentré* M., Éléments bibliques et non bibliques dans l'iconographie de la création au XIᵉ s.: Bulletin de la Société des Antiquaires de France (1986) 125-134 [< RHE 83,429*].

1998 ᴱ**Muradyan** K. M., Barsel Kesarac'i, Yalags... BASILE de Césaree, Homélies sur l'Hexaémeron (édition critique de l'ancienne version arménienne). Erévan 1984, Maténadaran, xlii-379 p. – ᴿRÉArmén 20 (1986s) 585s (J.-P. *Mahé*).

1999 **Niditch** Susan, Chaos to cosmos 1985 ➤ 1,2017 ... 3,1938: ᴿÉglT 17 (1986) 85s (W. *Vogels*); JAAR 56 (1988) 347-9 (Katheryn P. *Dart*); RB 95 (1988) 129s (J. *Loza*).

2000 *Recchia* Vincenzo, Il commento allegorico di Genesi, 1-3 nelle opere esegetiche di GREGORIO Magno: ➤ 246, VetChr 25 (1988) 421-449.

2001 **Savasta** Carmelo, Forme e strutture in Gen 1-11: Ricerche e proposte. Messina c. 1987, Sfameni [BbbOr 30,186].

2002 *Scult* A., *al.*, Genesis and power; an analysis of the biblical story of creation: Quarterly Journal of Speech 72 (1986) 113-131 [< ZAW 101, 136].

2003 **Tasini** Giovanni P., In principio; interpretazioni ebraiche del racconto della creazione, I. Il midrash: Tradizioni d'Israele 3. R 1988, Città Nuova. 148 p. 88-311-4910-5.

2004 **Traudisch** François, Die Botschaft der Bibel I. Schöpfung ... 18 Farbtransparente, Textbuch. Offenbach 1986, Jünger. DM 130. – ᴿBiKi 43 (1988) 125 (D. *Bauer*).

2005 *Winden* Jacobus C. M. van, Hexaemeron: ➤ 807, RAC 14,111s (1988) 1250-69.

2006 *Schweizer* Harald, Sémiotique (française) contre exégèse historico-critique (allemande)?; remarques à partir de Genèse 1,1-10: SémBib 47 (1987) 1-17.

2007 *Naldini* Mario, Sull'interpretazone esamerale di Gen. 1,2, 'Spiritus Dei ferebatur super aquas': ➤ 56, Mém. GRIBOMONT J. 1988, 445-452.

2009 *Lambert* W. G., [Gn 1,2] A further note on *tōhū wābōhū*: UF [19 (1987) 309-315, *Tsumura* D. T.] 20 (1988) 135 only.

2010 *Hancher* Michael, Performative utterance [Fiat lux, Gn 1,3; BARTHES, DERRIDA...], the word of God, and the death of the author: Semeia 41 (1988) 27-40.

2011 *Duchesne-Guillemin* Jacques, Et Spiritus Dei ... (Gen 1,12): ➤ 109, ᶠMONNERET U. = RSO 60 (1986/8) 141-7.

2012 **Van Till** Howard J., [Gn 1,14s] The fourth day 1986 ➤ 2,1450; 3,1953: ᴿBS 145 (1988) 349s (F. R. *Howe*: exegetically second-hand defense of evolution); Zygon 23 (1988) 483s (W. B. *Drees*).

Imago Dei Gn 1,26:

2013 **Aguilar Schreiber** Milton, L'uomo immagine di Dio [diss. Teresianum]. R 1987, Teresianum. 174 p. – ᴿCC 139 (1988,3) 319s (G. *Blandino*); EuntDoc 41 (1988) 173-5 (anche G. *Blandino*).

2014 *Colella* Pasquale, Immagine e somiglianza nell'iscrizione di Tell Fekhriyeh e nella Genesi: Lateranum 54 (1988) 34-57.

2015 **Hall** Douglas J., Imaging God; [first of three about] dominion as stewardship 1986 ➤ 2,1456; 3,1959: ᴿTTod 45 (1988s) 101s. 104 (Elizabeth D. *Gray*).

2016 **Hoekema** Anthony A., Created in God's image 1986 ➤ 2,1456; 3,1960: ᴿRefTR 46 (1987) 53s (P. F. *Jensen*).

2017 **Jónsson** Gunnlaugur A., The image of God; Genesis 1: 26-28 in a century of OT research: [Diss. Lund, ᴰ*Mettinger* T.]: ConBib OT 26. Lund 1988, Almqvist & W. xvi-253 p. 91-22-01215-X. – ᴿTüTQ 168 (1988) 241 (W. *Gross*).

2018 **Ockinga** Boyo, Die Gottebenbildlichkeit im Alten Ägypten und im AT [Diss. Tübingen]: ÄgAT 7, 1984 ➤ 65,1765; 1,2039: ᴿBZ 32 (1988) 119-121 (C. *Dohmen*).

2020 **Ross** Ellen M., Humans' creation in God's image; RICHARD of St. Victor, Walter HILTON, and contemporary theology: diss. Ch. Divinity Sch. Ch 1987, – RelStR 14,189; RTLv 20,550.

2021 *Rue Zang-Sun,* ◐ Der Mensch als Ebenbild Gottes: Samok 116 (Seoul 1988) 105-118; 117 (1988) 68-82 [< TKontext 10/1,66s].

2022 *Testa* Emmanuele, Lo sviluppo teologico della 'immagine e somiglianza di Dio' secondo la Sinagoga; la filosofia e la fede cristiana: EuntDoc 41 (1988) 33-80.

2023 *Thompson* John L., Creata ad imaginem Dei, licet secundo gradu; woman as the image of God according to John CALVIN: HarvTR 81 (1988) 125-141.

2024 ᴱUthemann Karl-Heinz, ANASTASII Sinaitae Sermones duo in constitutionem hominis secundum imaginem Dei...: CCG 12, 1985 ➤ 1,2042* ... 3,1967: ᴿOrChrPer 54 (1988) 253-5 (J. D. *Baggarly*).

2025 *Werther* David, Animal reason and the [only human] *imago Dei*: RelSt 24 (C 1988) 325-335.

2026 *Angelini* Giuseppe, Il 'dominio' della terra; Genesi 1,28 e la questione ambientale: RClerIt 69 (1988) 407-418.

2027 *Piselli* Francesco, [Gn 1,31] Cuncta erant valde bona; postille estetologiche alla Sacra Bibbia [Salmi; Ct...]: BbbOr 30 (1988) 65-70.

2027* *Nodes* Daniel J., The seventh day of creation in *Alethia* of Claudius Marius Victor: VigChr 42 (1988) 59-74.

2028 *Wallace* Howard N., Genesis 2:1-2 — creation and sabbath: Pacifica 1,3 (1988) 235-250 [< ZIT 89,159].

E1.7   *Genesis 1s*:   **Bible and myth** [➤ M3.5].

2029 **Anderson** Bernhard, Creation versus chaos ... mythic symbolism [1967 + *al.*] 1987 ➤ 3,1973; $8: ᴿCurrTM 15 (1988) 455s (R. D. *Haak*).
    Brunner-Traut Emma, Gelebte Mythen³ 1988 ➤ b894.

2030 *Chomarat* Jacques, La création du monde selon le poète PALINGÈNE [1535 Zodiacus vitae; mis sur l'Index]: BBudé (1988) 352-364.

2031 **Day** John, God's conflict with the dragon and the sea [ᴰ1977] 1985 ➤ 1,2051 ... 3,1975: ᴿHeythJ 29 (1988) 507s (W. *Watson*); JAOS 108 (1988) 152s (S. B. *Parker*); ScripB 19 (1988s) 43s (S. *Greenhalgh*).

2032 ᴱ*Derousseaux* L. (*Blanquart* F.) La création ... ACFEB 1985/7 ➤ 3,521: ᴿEstBíb 46 (1988) 399-401 (M. *García Cordero*); FoiTemps 19 (1987) 470s (A. *Wénin*); Gregorianum 69 (1988) 156s (L. F. *Ladaria*); RTLv 19 (1988) 214s (J. *Ponthot*).

2033 *Fontaine* Carol, The deceptive goddess in Ancient Near Eastern myth: Semeia 42 (1988) 84-102.

2034 **Frazer** James G., ◐ Folklore in the Old Testament², ᴱ*Tokaryeva* S. A., ᵀ*Volpina* D.: Biblioteka ateistíčeskoy literaturi. Moskva 1985, Polit.-Lit. Ed. 510 p; ill. [KirSef 61,393].

2035 **Furley** David, The Greek cosmologists, 1. The formation of the atomic theory and its earliest critics. C 1987, Univ. viii-220 p. – ᴿRPLH 62,1 (1988) 137s (É. des *Places*).

2036 **Gibert** Pierre, Bible, mythes et récits de commencement 1986 ➤ 2,1468*; 3,1976: ᴿBL (1988) 76 (P. R. *Davies*); CahÉv 62 (1987) 73 (A. *Marchadour*); Divinitas 32 (1988) 666-691 (P.-L. *Carle*: brillant, vicié); RThom 88 (1988) 146-9 (J.-M. *Maldamé*).

2036* **Granger** James R.ᴶ, Adam, the Altaic ring and 'the children of the sun'. Wsh 1987, Uraeus. vi-213 p. [CBQ 50,751].

2037 **Graves** Robert, *Patai* Raphaël, Les mythes hébreux, ᵀ*Landais* J.-P. P 1987, Fayard. – ᴿÉtudes 368 (1988) 710 (P. *Gibert*).

2038 **Haas** Volkert, Vorzeitmythen und Götterberge in altorientalischer und griechischer Überlieferung; Vergleiche und Lokalisation: Univ.-Reden 145, 1983 ➤ 3,1977; DM 14,80: ᴿEirene 25 (1988) 157s (R. *Hošek*).

2038* *Huffmon* Herbert B., *Babel und Bibel*; the encounter between Babylon and the Bible: ➤ 3,356, ᴱ**O'Connor** M., Backgrounds 1987, 125-136 [< JBL 108,174].

2039 **Kirkpatrick** Patricia G., The Old Testament and folklore study [GUNKEL...: diss. Oxford, ᴰ*Nicholson* E.]: JStOT Sup 63. Sheffield 1988. 152 p. £35. (Ithaca NY, Cornell Univ.) [TDig 35,372]. 1-85075-114-5; pa. 3-7. – ᴿBiblica 69 (1988) 574-6 (J.L. *Ska*).

2040 *Koch* Klaus, Qädäm; Heilsgeschichte als mythische Urzeit im Alten (und Neuen) Testament: ➤ 114, ᶠPANNENBERG W., Vernunft 1988, 253-288.

2041 *a*) *Lambert* W.G., Old Testament mythology in its ancient Near Eastern context; – *b*) *Ottosson* Magnus, Eden and the land of promise: ➤ 482, VTS 40, Jerusalem congress 1986/8, 124-143 / 177-188.

2042 **Lara Peinado** F., Mitos sumerios y acádicos. M 1984, Nacional. 548 p. – ᴿBAsEspOr 22 (1986) 418-420 (G. *Carrasco Serrano*).

2043 **Lincoln** Bruce, Myth, cosmos, and society; Indo-European themes [➤ 2,1477] of creation and destruction. CM 1986, Harvard Univ. xvi-278 p. $22.50. – ᴿRelStR 14 (1988) 20 (C. *Hallisey*); RHR 205 (1988) 205s (D. *Bouvier*).

2044 *McCurley* Foster R., American myths and the Bible [Adam, Abraham, Moses...]: WWorld 8 (1988) 226-233 [< OTAbs 11,294].

2045 *Miller* Patrick D., Cosmology and world order in the Old Testament; the divine council [from Near East mythology p. 71] as cosmic-political symbol: HorBT 9,2 (1987) 53-78.

2046 *Müller* Hans-Peter, Mythos — Kerygma — Wahrheit; zur Hermeneutik einer biblischen Theologie: ➤ 390, Was ist Wahrheit? c. 1988, 53-67.

2047 *a*) *Müller* Hans-Peter, Babylonischer und biblischer Mythos der Menschenschöpfung und Sintflut; ein Paradigma zur Frage nach dem Recht mythischer Rede; – *b*) *Neumann* Gerhard, [Adam-Ursprungs-mythos] Heilsgeschichte und Literatur; die Entstehung des Subjekts aus dem Geist der Eucharistie: ➤ 3,567, ᴱ**Strolz** W., Vom alten zum neuen Adam 1985/6, 43-68 / 94-150.

2048 *a*) *Müller* Hans-Peter, Mythos in der biblischen Urgeschichte (Gen 1-11); – *b*) *Schröer* Henning, Vom Logos zum Mythos und zurück?; – *c*) *Lenzen* Dieter, Ent- oder Remythisierung der Kultur? Anmerkungen zu einer falschen Entgegensetzung: EvErz 40,1 ('Mythos' 1988) 6-18 / 19-36 / 50-58 [-110 *al.*, < ZIT].

2049 *Parker* Richard A., *Lesko* Leonard H., The Khonsu cosmogony: ➤ 41, ᶠEDWARDS I., Pyramid studies 1988, 168-175.
   Petersen Claus, Mythos im AT ... BZAW 157, 1982 ➤ 3192.

2050 **Sterckx** Claude, Éléments de cosmogonie celtique: Fac. Lett. 97. Bru 1986, Univ. 127 p. Fb 525. – ᴿRHR 205 (1988) 82-85 (B. *Sergent*).

2051 *Van Seters* John, The primeval histories of Greece and Israel compared: ZAW 100 (1988) 1-22 [Gn form due much more to Greece than to Mesopotamia].

2052 **von Franz** Marie-Louise, Patterns of creativity mirrored in creation myths: Seminar Series 6. Dallas 1986=1972, Spring. 250 p. 0-88214-106-6.

2053 **Wolkstein** Diane, *Kramer* S. N., Inanna 1983 ⇢ 1,2067 ... 3,1993: ᴿAr-Or 56 (1988) 95-97 (B. *Hruška*).

E1.8   **Genesis 1s: The Bible, the Church, and Science.**

2054 ᴱ**Aichelburg** Peter C., *Kögeler* Reinhard, Evolution; Entwicklungs-prinzipien und menschliches Selbstverständnis in einer sich wandelnden Welt: Forum St. Stephan 3. W-St. Pölten 1987, NÖ. 124 p. Sch. 128. – ᴿTPQ 136 (1988) 280 (J. *Janda*).

2055 **Augros** Robert, *Stanciu* George, The new biology; discovering the wisdom in nature 1987 ⇢ 3,1999: ᴿHomP 88,2 (1987s) 76.78 (J. D. *Meehan*).

2056 **Banner** Michael C., The justification of science and the rationality of religious belief [... *Kuhn*]: diss. Oxford 1986. 313 p.   BRD-83138. – DissA 49 (1988s) 2250-A.

2057 **Bartholomew** David J., God of chance 1984 ⇢ 65,1805 ... 3,2003: ᴿHeythJ 29 (1988) 397 (Eileen *Barker*).

2058 **Becker** Thomas, Geist und Materie in den ersten Schriften P. TEILHARD de Chardins: FreibTSt 134. FrB 1987, Herder. 240 p. DM 48 pa. – ᴿZkT 110 (1988) 471s (K. H. *Neufeld*).

2059 **Bein Ricco** E., *Pons* G., Conoscenza scientifica e fede; incontri e scontri fra saperi del nostro tempo. T 1988, Claudiana. 226 p. – [STEv 1/2, 214-7, P. *Bolognesi*].

2060 **Bergold** Ralph, Der Glaube vor dem Anspruch der Wissenschaft; der Dialog zwischen Naturwissenschaft und Theologie am Beispiel von Schöpfungsglaube und Evolutionstheorie: Diss. Münster 1988, ᴰ*Vor-grimler* H. – TR 84 (1988) 512.

2061 **Berry** R. J., God and evolution; creation, evolution and the Bible [= ²Adam and the ape]. L 1988, Hodder & S. 189 p. £7.   0-340-34249-8. – ᴿExpTim 2d-top choice 99,9 (1987s) 258 (C. S. *Rodd*).

2062 ᴱ**Birtel** Frank T., Religion, science, and public policy [mostly Tulane Univ. lectures]: Tulane Judeo-Christian studies. NY 1987, Crossroad. xiii-152 p. $17 [TDig 35,284: titles sans pp.] 8 art.

2063 *a)* *Blandino* Giovanni, Il caso e l'anti-caso, l'errore del Darwinismo [*Eigen* M., *al.*]; – *b)* *Marchesi* Giovanni, La Pontificia Accademia delle Scienze, luogo d'incontro tra ragione e fede: CC 139 (1988,3) 256-268 / 235-246.

2064 **Bosshard** Stefan N., Erschafft die Welt sich selbst? 1985 ⇢ 1,2081* ... 3,2006; ²1987: ᴿSalmanticensis 35 (1988) 423-5 (J. L. *Ruiz de la Peña*); ZkT 110 (1988) 459-463 (K.-H. *Nusser*).

2065 *Bube* R. H., Science and Christianity: ⇢ 801, ISBEnc³ 4 (1988) 351.

2066 *a)* *Caldecott* Stratford, Cosmology, eschatology, ecology; – *b)* *Balthasar* Hans U. von, Creation and Trinity, ᵀ*Arndt* S. W.; – *c)* *Kasper* Walter, The Logos character of reality, ᵀ*Arndt*; – *d)* *Schmitz* Kenneth L., Traces of eternity; – *e)* *Pannenberg* Wolfhart, Theological questions to scientists [< ᴱ*Peacocke* A., Sciences 1981]: Comm-ND 15 (1988) 305-318 / 285-293 / 274-284 / 295-304 / 319-333.

2067 **Carvin** W. P., Creation and scientific explanation. E 1988, Scottish Academic. £10.50 [TLond 91,570].

2068 **Coppens** Yves, La scimmia, l'Africa e l'uomo 1985 ⇢ 1,2095b: ᴿSt-Patav 34 (1987) 230 (P. *Pampaloni*).

2069 **Cornélius** J.-B. [... officier de marine], La Genèse et la préhistoire; préf. *Bruckberger* R.-L. P 1986, Lanore & S. 192 p. – ᴿRThom 88 (1988) 149 (J.-M. *Maldamé*: décevant).

2070 **Corsi** Pietro, Science and religion; BADEN POWELL and the Anglican debate, 1800-1860. C 1988, Univ. x-346 p. £32.50. 0-521-24245-2. – RIrénikon 61 (1988) 307 (E. *Lanne*).

2071 *Dallaporta* Nicola, L'immagine di Dio di fronte all'evoluzione scientifica del mondo secondo il volume di P. DAVIES, 'Dio e la nuova fisica': ➤ 536, ECampogalliani P., Spazio-tempo: StPatav 34 (1987) 509-514.

2072 **Davies** Paul, Gott und die moderne Physik [1983 ➤ 65,1821], T*Klewer* W. A. [ital. 1983 ➤ 2,1498]. Mü 1986, Bertelsmann. 319 p.; DM 40. 23 fig. 3-570-04906-X. – RActuBbg 25 (1988) 225s (J. *Boada*); TLZ 113 (1988) 878s (H. H. *Jenssen*).

2073 **Denton** Michael, Evolution, a theory in crisis. Bethesda MD 1986, Adler. 368 p. $20. – RSWJT 31,2 (1988s) 50s (E. E. *Ellis*).

2074 **Dolch** Heimo, Grenzgänge zwischen Naturwissenschaft und Theologie: [25] Gesammelte Aufsätze 1986 ➤ 2,151: RTPhil 63 (1988) 463s (R. *Koltermann*).

2075 **Dória** [➤ 2,1499 Dóriga] Enrique L., El universo de Newton y de Einstein. Barc 1985, Herder. 278 p. – RBrotéria 124 (1987) 114 (I. *Ribeiro*).

2076 EDorst Jean, Histoire des êtres vivants [... l'homme; l'évolution]. P 1985, Hachette. 536 p. – RRThom 88 (1988) 150 (J.-M. *Maldamé*: passionnant).

2077 E**Durant** John, Darwinism and divinity 1982/5 ➤ 2,426; 3,2018*: RZygon 23 (1988) 486-8 (C. *Welch*).

2078 **Eastham** S., Nucleus 1987 ➤ 3,2020: RHorizons 18 (1988) 195s (J. M. *Thompson*).

2079 E**Ferembach** Denise, *al.,* L'homme, son évolution, sa diversité. P 1986, CNRS/Doin. 574 p. – RRThom 88 (1988) 150 (J.-M. *Maldamé*).

2080 **Fiddes** V. H., Science and the Gospel: Theology and Science at the Frontiers of Knowledge 7. E 1987, Scottish Academic. xii-113 p. £10.50. – RThemelios 14 (1988s) 115 (E. C. *Lucas*).

2081 **Foley** Robert, Another unique species; patterns in human evolutionary ecology. L/NY 1987, Longman/Wiley. xxii-313 p.; 112 fig. £13 pa. 0-582-44690-2 / 0-470-20728-9. – RAntiquity 62 (1988) 599s (R. *Crompton*).

2082 **Ford** Adam, Universe; God, science and the human person. Mystic CT 1987, Twenty-Third. 228 p. $10 pa. [TDig 35,165]. – RSpTod 40 (1988) 276-9 (D. R. *Zusy*).

2083 *Galli* G. Mario, La svolta culturale del secolo XIII e la nascita della scienza moderna [... Rapporti tra scienza e religione]: Angelicum 65 (1988) 3-43.

2084 **Gange** Robert, Origins and destiny; a scientist examines God's handiwork. Waco 1986, Word. 193 p. $13. – RBS 145 (1988) 460s (F. R. *Howe*).

2085 **Gargantini** Mario, I Papi e la scienza; antologia del magistero della Chiesa sulla questione scientifica da Leone XIII a Giovanni Paolo II. Mi 1985, Jaca. 272 p. – RDivinitas 32 (1988) 627s (D. *Composta*).

2086 **Geisler** Norman L., *Anderson* J. Kerby, Origin Science. GR 1987, Baker. 198 p. $9. – RBS 145 (1988) 456 (F. R. *Howe*).

2087 **Gilkey** Langdon, Creationism on trial 1985 ➤ 2,1505; 3,3027*: RZygon 23 (1988) 481s (M. D. *Guinan*).

2088 **Gowlett** John A., Auf Adams Spuren; die Archäologie des frühen Menschen [Ascent to Civilization 1984], T*Becker* A. 1985 ➤ 2,1508: RPraehZts 63 (1988) 186s (K. J. *Narr*).

2089 **Ham** Ken, The lie: evolution. El Cajon 1987, Master. 168 p. – RSWJT 31,2 (1988s) 61s (L. R. *Bush*).

2090 *Hefner* Philip, The evolution of the created co-creator [*Darwin*; *Teilhard, Peacocke ...*]: CurrTM 15 (1988) 512-525.

2091 *a*) *Heller* Michał, ☉ How to rescue evolution; – *b*) *Kunicki-Goldfinger* W., ☉ Evolutionary epistemology: Przegląd Powszechny 258 (1988) 350-5 / 356-364.

2092 **Henderson** Charles P.J, God and science; the death and rebirth of theism 1986 → 2,1512: RScotBEv 6 (1988) 64s (J. C. *Sharp*) [unaccountably reprinted 125s].

2093 EHübner J., Der Dialog zwischen Theologie und Naturwissenschaft; ein bibliographischer Bericht: ForBerEvStGem 41, 1987 → 3,1036: RArT-Gran 51 (1988) 324s (A. S. *Muñoz*); NorTTs 89 (1988) 149s (K. M. *Hansen*).

2094 **Hummel** Charles E., The GALILEO connection; resolving conflicts between science and the Bible 1986 → 2,1514; 3,2036: RBS 145 (1988) 222 (F. R. *Howe*); JPsy&T 15 (1987) 90 (R. E. *Larzelere*).

2095 **Hyers** C., Meaning of creation 1984 → 1,2125 ... 3,2037: RTTod 44 (1987s) 264-6 (H. P. *Nebelsich*).

2096 **Jackson** Wes, Altars of unhewn stone; science and the earth. SF 1987, North Point. x-158 p. $20. – RAnglTR 70 (1988) 91s (M. C. *Engle*).

2097 *Jaki* Stanley L., *a*) Language, logic, logos [< symposium on 'The human dimension in artificial intelligence' 1988]: AsbTJ 43,2 (1988) 95-136; – *b*) The Universe in the Bible and in modern science: → 567, ExAud 3 (1987) 137-147.

2098 *Jordana* Rafael, El origen del hombre; estado actual de la investigación paleoantropológica: ScripTPamp 20 (1988) 65-98; lat. Eng. 99.

2099 *a*) *Kaiser* Christopher B., The early Christian belief in creation; background for the origins and assessment of modern Western science; – *b*) *Nebelsick* Harold P., God, creation, salvation and modern science: HorBT 9,2 (1987) 1-30 / 79-103.

2100 **Kealy** Seán P., Science and the Bible. Dublin 1987, Columba. 96 p. £5. – RDocLife 37 (1987) 436s (N. *Porter*); Furrow 38 (1987) 479s (P. *Briscoe*).

2101 *Kozhamthadam* Job, Science and religion; contenders or collaborators?: Vidyajyoti 52 (1988) 362-377 [506, reaction of *Monteiro* Hurbert A.].

2102 **Kropp** Richard W., Evil and evolution; a theodicy 1984 → 1,2143; 2,1522: RÉglT 17 (1986) 104-6 (J. *Pambrun*).

2103 *a*) *Kümmel* Reiner, Physik und Schöpfungsglaube; – *b*) *Maiwald* Lucius, Natur als Schöpfung — eine unverzichtbare Dimension des menschlichen Handelns: → 53, FGANOCZY A., Creatio 1988, 264-274 / 247-263.

2104 **Kummer** Christian, Evolution als Höherentwicklung des Bewusstseins; über die intentionalen Voraussetzungen der materiellen Selbstorganisation: Symposion 80 [monograph, not symposium]. FrB 1987, Alber. 325 p. DM 78 pa. – RZkT 110 (1988) 474s (B. *Braun*).

2105 *a*) *Lejeune* Jérôme, La science seule ne peut pas sauver le monde; – *b*) *Le Tourneau* Philippe, Maîtrise de la vie ou domination par la science?: PenséeC 233 (1988) 31-38 / 39-69 + 3 fig.

   Lindberg D., *Numbers* R., God and nature ... Christianity and science 1986 → 8275.

2106 **Livingstone** David N., DARWIN's forgotten defenders 1987 → 3,2047: RChH 57 (1988) 558s (G. M. *Marsden*).

2107 ᴱMcMullin Ernan, Evolution and creation 1983/5 ⮞ 2,464: ᴿThomist 52 (1988) 556-562 (R. *Dennehy*).
2108 *Maldamé* Jean-Michel, L'itinéraire de Maurice BELLET [*L'immense* 1987; Le Dieu pervers 1979 ²1987; Naissance de Dieu 1975 ...]; une phénoménologie de la création: RThom 88 (1988) 299-314.
2109 *Malu wa Kalenga*, Science et foi; un débat archaïque?; RAfT 11 (1987) 221-6.
2110 **Mitchell** Ralph G., EINSTEIN and Christ; a new approach to the defence of the Christian religion. E 1987, Scottish Academic. 231 p. £13.50. – ᴿAustralasCR 65 (1988) 498-500 (G. *Gleeson*: 'personal, even eccentric' study by a Queensland priest); Tablet 242 (1988) 753s (F. *Copleston*); TLond 91 (1988) 220s (J. *Polkinghorne*: Catholic priest, chatty more about SCHRÖDINGER 1944 and SHERRINGTON, POPPER, ECCLES, SHELDRAKE than about Einstein).
2111 *Moore* James R., Interpreting the new creationism: ⮞ 3,356, ᴱO'Connor M., Backrounds 1987, 111-124 [< JBL 108,174].
2112 **Morris** Henry M., Science and the Bible [= ²ʳᵉᵛThe Bible and ('biblical basis for' 1984 ⮞ 2,1531) modern science 1951]. Ch 1986, Moody. 154 p. $6. – ᴿBS 145 (1988) 108s (F. R. *Howe*).
2112* **Munitz** Milton K., Cosmic understanding; philosophy and science of the universe. Princeton 1986, Univ. 298 p. $25 [JAAR 57,206-9, K. J. *Sharpe*].
2113 *Newbigin* Lesslie, Religion, science and truth in the school curriculum: TLond 91 (1988) 186-193 [In some US area schools, 'the introduction of ice-hockey is a significant event which earns a place in history; the fact that missionaries from the US were working in every part of the world is not'].
2114 *a)* **Oates** David, Social Darwinism and natural theodicy; – *b)* *Williams* George C., HUXLEY's Evolution and Ethics in sociobiological perspective: Zygon 23 (1988) 439-454 / 383-407.
2115 *a)* *Pambrun* James R., Philosophical foundations of theological attitudes toward science; – *b)* *Van den Hengel* John, Technology and Christian faith; – *c)* *O'Grady* Paul, *al.,* An inquiry into the religion of scientists and eminent scientists: ÉglT 18 (1987) 29-53 / 55-78 / 101-124.
2116 *a)* *Pannenberg* Wolfhart, The doctrine of creation and modern science [rejoinder *Russell* Robert J., Contingency in physics and cosmology]; – *b)* *Wicken* Jeffrey S., Theology and science in the evolving cosmos; a need for dialogue; – *c)* *Griffin* David R, On Ian BARBOUR's Issues in science and religion [Barbour, response]: Zygon 23 (1988) 3-22 [23-44] / 45-56 / 57-82 [83 ...; < ZIT].
2117 **Paul** Iain, Knowledge of God — CALVIN, EINSTEIN and POLANYI. E 1988, Scottish Academic. 155 p. £10.50. 0-7073-0537-3. – ᴿExpTim 99 (1987s) 314s (J. *Polkinghorne*: 'Torrance-country' lingo).
2118 **Paul** Iain, Science and theology in EINSTEIN's perspective 1986 ⮞ 3,2058: ᴿModT 4 (1987s) 219 (J. *Polkinghorne*).
2119 **Peacocke** Arthur, God and the new biology 1986 ⮞ 2,1540; 3,2059: ᴿAnglTR 70 (1988) 190-3 (J. H. *Snow*); HomP 89,6 (1988s) 76-79 (O. *Bennett*: no); RExp 85 (1988) 167s (D. *Stiver*); SpTod 40 (1988) 83-85 (D. R. *Zusy*); Tablet 242 (1988) 904 (Monica *Lawlor*); TS 49 (1988) 370s (F. R. *Haig*).
2120 **Peterson** Roland, Everyone is right; a new look at comparative religion and its relation to science. Marina del Rey CA 1986, DeVorss. 304 p. $13 pa. – ᴿJEcuSt 24 (1987) 657 (J. R. *Nelson*: spurious).

2121 E*Piperno* Marcello, Le origini dell'uomo: Archeo 43 (1988) 46-102, color ill.; 70-73, *Leakey* Mary.

2122 **Piveteau** Jean, [? = ➤ 3,2060] Image de l'homme dans la pensée scientifique; science et métaphysique. P 1986, OEIL. 172 p. – RRThom 88 (1988) 149s (J.-M. *Maldamé*: résultats de la paléontologie).

2123 **Polkinghorne** John, One world; the interaction of science and theology 1986 ➤ 2,1544: RBijdragen 49 (1988) 216 (J.-J. *Suurmond*).

2124 **Polkinghorne** J., Scienza e fede. Mi 1987, Mondadori. 160 p. Lit. 16.000. – RProtestantesimo 43 (1988) 238s (S. *Brofferio*).

2125 **Poole** M. W., *Wenham* G. J., Creation or evolution; a false antithesis? (Latimer Studies 23s). Ox 1987, Latimer. 84 p. £3. – RRefTR 47 (1988) 27 (P. *Jensen*).

2126 E**Poupard** P., GALILEO Galilei; toward a resolution of 350 years of debate, 1633-1983 [1983 ➤ 65,1864; 1,2170*a*], T. Pittsburgh 1987, Duquesne Univ. xxiii-208 p. $28. – RCathHR 74 (1988) 623s (W. E. *Carroll*); Isis 78 (1987) 634s (M. A. *Finocchiaro*) [< RHE 83 (1988) 423*].

2127 E**Poupard** Paul, Scienza e fede 1986 ➤ 2,1544*: RViPe 71 (1988) 312-4 (B. *Belletti*).

2128 **Poythress** V. S., Science and hermeneutics [applying *Kuhn* T. S., The structure of scientific revolutions]: Foundations of contemporary interpretation 6. GR 1988, Zondervan. 184 p. 0-310-40971-3 [BL 89,114, L. L. *Grabbe*: severe; D. STANESBY much better].

2129 **Ratzsch** Del, Philosophy of science; the natural sciences in Christian perspective 1986 ➤ 3,2063: RIrBSt 9 (1987) 50-52 (J. T. *MacCormack*).

2130 **Redondi** Pietro, GALILEO eretico 1983 ➤ 64,2144; Galilée hérétique 1985: RStreven 55 (1987s) 454-8 (G. *Groot*: awaited in Dutch, 1988 Agon). – GALILEO heretic, TRosenthal Raymond. Princeton 1987, Univ. x-356 p. $30 [TDig 35,83].

2131 **Richards** Robert J., DARWIN and the emergence of evolutionary theories of mind and behavior. Ch 1988, Univ. xviii-700 p. $30 [TS 50,801, B. J. *Verkamp*].

2132 *a*) *Robbins* J. Wesley, Seriously, but not literally; pragmatism and realism in religion and science; – *b*) *Huyssteen* Wentzel van, Experience and explanation; the justification of cognitive claims in theology; – *c*) *Hefner* Philip, Theology's truth and scientific formulation: Zygon 23 (1988) 229-245 / 247-261 / 263-279 [281-290, responses, *Gerhart* Mary, *Murphy* Nancey C.].

2133 **Roberts** Jon H., Darwinism and the divine in America; Protestant intellectuals and organic evolution, 1859-1900. Madison 1988, Univ. Wisconsin. xviii-339 p. $26.75 [RelStR 14,319 adv.].

2134 **Rolston** Holmes III, Science and religion, a critical survey 1987 ➤ 3,2067; NY, Random: RZygon 23 (1988) 203-5 (J. *Pickle*).

2135 *Rottschaefer* William A., The new interactionism between science and religion [20 authors]: RelStR 14 (1988) 218-224.

2136 **Santmire** H. Paul, The travail of nature. Ph 1985, Fortress. 288 p. $16. – RZygon 23 (1988) 484-6 (J. S. *Nelson*).

2137 *Sarasohn* Lisa T., French reaction to the condemnation of GALILEO, 1632-1642: CathHR 74 (1988) 34-54.

2138 *Schröder* Richard, Bemerkungen zur copernicanischen Reform: BTZ 5 (1988) 48-67.

2139 **Sherrard** Philip, The rape of man and nature; an enquiry into the origins and consequences of modern science. 1987, Golgonooza. 124 p. £12.50. – RTLond 91 (1988) 521s (J. *Lambert*).

2140 **Smith** Wolfgang, TEILHARD and the new religion [evolution, founded on sand]. Rockford IL 1988, Tan. 232 p. $8 pa. – ᴿHomP 89,8 (1988s) 77-79 (V. P. *Miceli*).

2141 ᴱ**Spaemann** Robert *al.,* Evolutionismus und Christentum [Symposium Rom]: Civitas Resultate 9, 1985/6 ➤ 3,722 (2,1550*): ᴿMüTZ 39 (1988) 145s (A. *Kreiner*);TPhil 63 (1988) 148s (R. *Koltermann*); TüTQ 168 (1988) 244-7 (W. *Kasper*); ZkT 110 (1988) 475-7 (B. *Braun*).

2142 **Spanner** Douglas, Biblical creation and the theory of evolution 1987 ➤ 3,2073: ᴿBL (1988) 116 (J. *Gibson*: more eirenic to DARWIN than to those who have reserves about historicity of Genesis); RefTR 47 (1988) 58s (J. A. *Friend*); Themelios 14 (1988s) 77s (N. *Cameron*).

2143 *a*) *Stoeger* William R., What does science say about creation?; – *b*) *Barnes* Michael, Gods of creation – a Hindu view of the universe; – *c*) *Turner* Frank, In the beginning was...; in what sense are myths of creation 'true'?: Month 249 (1988) 805-811 / 813-7 / 826-831.

2144 **Tattersall** Ian, *al.,* Encyclopedia of human evolution and prehistory. NY 1988, Garland. xxxvi-603 p.; ill. $87.50 [Antiquity 63,173, J. *Wymer*: fully up to date].

2145 *[Testa] Bappenheim* Italo, Vita e natura: BbbOr 30 (1988) 39-47 [111-6, antropologia e santità; 163-8; 223-230].

2146 *Thigpen* Thomas P., On the origin of theses; an exploration of Horace BUSHNELL's rejection of Darwinism: ChH 57 (1988) 499-513.

2147 *Thomas Vadaya* D., The emergence of holographic perspective; towards a convergence of scientific and religious world views: JDharma 12 (1987) 261-5.

2148 *a*) **Thomson** Alexander, Tradition and authority in science and theology. 116 p.; *b*) **Pollard** W. G., Transcendence and providence; reflections of a physicist and priest. 269 p. –: Theology and Science at the frontiers of knowledge. E 1987, Scottish Academic. – ᴿRHPR 68 (1988) 485s (G. *Siegwalt*: d'intérêt réel).

2149 **Torrance** Thomas F., Reality and scientific theology [1970 Dundee Harris lectures] 1985 ➤ 2,1558; 3,2077; 0-7073-0429-6: ᴿScotBEv 6 (1988) 50s (J. C. *Sharp*); ScotJT 41 (1988) 273-280 (D. F. *Ford*).

2150 *Torrance* Thomas F., *[al.]*, Realism and openness in scientific inquiry: Zygon 23,2 ('The credibility of religion in a scientific age' 1988) [115-] 159-169.

2151 *Trundle* Robert C., Religious belief and scientific Weltanschauungen: JDharma 13 (1988) 116-140.

2152 **Wallace** William A., Galileo and his sources 1984 ➤ 1,2186; 2,1650: ᴿHeythJ 29 (1988) 370s (J. L. *Russell*).

2153 **Wells** Jonathan, Charles HODGE's critique of Darwinism; an historical-critical analysis of concepts basic to the 19th century debate. Lewiston NY 1988, Mellen. x-242 p. $50 [RelStR 15,182, W. R. *Garrett*].

2154 *Wiebe* Don, Postulations for safeguarding preconceptions; the case of the scientific religionist: Religion 18,1 (L 1988) 11-20 [< ZIT].

2155 **Wilkins** Walter J., Science and religious thought; a Darwinism case study ᴰ1987 ➤ 3,2078: ᴿJAAR 56 (1988) 599-602 (D. W. *Rutledge*); Zygon 23 (1988) 207-9 (Nancey *Murphy*).

2155* *Winkler* Gerhard B., GALILEI und die Kirche: TPQ 136 (1988) 231-8.

2156 ^E**Wood** Bernard, *al.,* Major topics in primate and human evolution. NY 1986, Cambridge-UP. 364 p.; ill. £19.50. – ^RPraehZts 63 (1988) 185s (C. *Niemitz*).

E1.9   *Peccatum originale,*   **The Sin of Eden,** *Genesis 2-3.*

2157 *Andersen* Francis I.,   On reading Genesis 1-3: ➤ 3,356, ^E*O'Connor* M., Backgrounds 1987, 137-150 [< JBL 108,174].

2158 **Ayán Calvo** Juan J.,   Antropología de San JUSTINO; exégesis del mártir a Gén. I-III: Collectanea scientífica 4. Santiago 1988. 264 p.   84-7009-272-3. – ^RCompostellanum 33 (1988) 307-9 (J. L. *Montanet*).

2159 *Barr* James,   The authority of Scripture, the book of Genesis and the origin of evil in Jewish and Christian tradition: ➤ 23, ^FCHADWICK H., Christian authority 1988, 59-75.

2160 *Bird* Phyllis,   Genesis 1-3 as a source for a contemporary theology of sexuality: ➤ 567, ExAud 3 (1987) 31-44.

2160* *a) Breitbart* Sidney,   Adam I and Adam II; – *b) Liptzin* Sol; Adam's missing years; evolution of a legend [a person could give part of his allotted life to another in Jewish folklore]: Dor 16 (1987s) 192-6 / 149-57.

2161 **Bur** Jacques,   Le péché originel; ce que l'Église a vraiment dit: Théologies. P 1988, Cerf.   131 p. F 75.   2-204-01722-7. – ^RActuBbg 25 (1988) 243 (R. de *Sivatte*); Angelicum 65 (1988) 613s (M. F. *Manzanedo*); EsprVie 98 (1988) 267s (P. *Jay*); ETL 64 (1988) 490s (E. *Brito*); Gregorianum 69 (1988) 783 (J. M. *McDermott*); RSPT 72 (1988) 515s (A. M. *Dubarle*); VSp 142 (1988) 599s (aussi A. M. *Dubarle*).

2162 *Canivet* Pierre,   Le bestiaire adamique dans les mosaïques de Hūarte (Syrie, fin Ve s.); le symbolisme du Griffon: ➤ 704, ^E*Borgeaud* P., L'animal 1981/5, 145-154; 4 fig.

2162* **Chauvin** J.,   Dieu a-t-il vraiment dit? (ou le risque de devenir adulte, selon Genèse 3). Aubonne 1988, Moulin.   81 p. [RHPR 69,88].

2163 *Citati* Pietro [< Corriere della Sera 10.XI.87], Sull'albero del peccato sbocciò la civiltà: BbbOr 30 (1988) 49-55.

2164 **Cottiaux** Jean,   La sacralisation du mariage; de la Genèse ... 1982 ➤ 63,7235 ... 2,1572: ^RGregorianum 69 (1988) 159s (J. M. *Millás*: claims to clarify, with dubious distinction between 'fixist' and 'evolutionist').

2165 *Daniel* Robert W.,   It started with Eve [read Eve ('a Christian name in the Greek East' despite her dubious biblical standing) as mother of the girl on a love-charm]: ZPapEp 74 (1988) 249-251.

2166 *Davidson* Richard M.,   The theology of sexuality; In the beginning, Genesis 1-2/3: AndrUnS 26 (1988) 5-24 / 121-132.

2167 **Day** Peggy L.,   An adversary in heaven; Satan in the Hebrew Bible: HarvSemMg 43. Atlanta 1988, Scholars.   xi-177 p. $18 [CBQ 51,399]. 1-55540-248-8.

2168 *Derby* Josiah,   Adam's sin: Dor 17 (1988s) 71-82.

2169 **Dohmen** Christoph,   Schöpfung und Tod; die Entfaltung theologischer und anthropologischer Konzeptionen in Gen 2/3: SBB 17.   Stu 1988, KBW.   331 p.   3-460-00171-2.

2170 **Drewermann** Eugen [➤ 1584-6], Strukturen des Bösen; die jahwistische Urgeschichte in exegetischer, psychoanalytischer und philosophischer Sicht; 1. Die jahwistische Urgeschichte in exegetischer Sicht ⁵1984; 2... in psychoanalytischer ...⁵1985; 3. in philosophischer ... ⁴1983: PdTheolSt 4-6. Pd ¹1977s, Schöningh; ➤ 60,2724. DM 58 + 68 + 68.   3-506-76254-0; 5-9;

6-7. – ᴿRB 95 (1988) 106-113 (J. *Loza*: entreprise interdisciplinaire réussie).

2171 *Irrgang* Bernhard, Das Ethische als blosse Funktion des Religiösen? Eine Auseinandersetzung mit E. DREWERMANNS Interpretation der J-Urgeschichte: MüTZ 39 (1988) 138-143.

2172 *Duffy* Stephen J., Our hearts of darkness; original sin revisited: TS 49 (1988) 597-622.

2173 **Elasky-Fleming** Joy, A rhetorical analysis of Genesis 2-3 with implications for a theology of man and woman: Prot. diss. ᴰ*Heintz* J. Strasbourg 1987. 407 p. – RTLv 19,533.

2174 *Feuillet* André, La connexion de la révélation divine avec l'histoire du salut dans l'annonce prophétique du Sauveur messianique et de sa Mère; le Protévangile, les oracles messianiques d'Isaïe [7,14;9-11] et de Michée [5,1s]: Divinitas 32 (1988) 543-564. 643-665.

2175 **Forsyth** Neil, The old enemy; Satan and the combat myth 1987 ➤ 3,2095: ᴿJournal of American Folklore 102 (1989) 107-110 [reply 103,73-84]; JStOT 42 (1988) 122 (R. P. *Carroll*: a beautiful book, beautifully produced).

2176 *Fuller* D. P., Satan: ➤ 801, ISBEnc³ 4 (1988) 340-4.

2178 *Görg* Manfred, Adam: ➤ 804, NBL Lfg. 1 (1988) 29-32.

2179 *Goldin* David, The metaphor of original sin; a key to [1883-96, Emilia] PARDO BAZAN's Catholic naturalism: PgQ 64 (1985) 38-49.

2180 **Heaney Hunter** Jo Ann C., The links between sexuality and original sin in the writings of John CHRYSOSTOM and AUGUSTINE: diss. Fordham, ᴰ*Ettlinger* G. NY 1988. 304 p. 89-04648. – DissA 49 (1988s) 3762s-A.

2181 *Hermansen* Marcia K., Pattern and meaning in the Qur'ānic Adam narratives: SR 17 (1988) 41-52.

2182 *Hess* Richard S., 'Ādām as 'skin' and 'earth'; an examination of some proposed meanings in biblical Hebrew: TyndaleB 39 (1988) 141-9.

2183 **Hong Beom-Kee** Peter, 'Sünde der Welt' und 'Erbsünde'; eine Untersuchung zur Erbsündenlehre Piet SCHOONENBERGS: Diss. FrB 1987s, ᴰ*Lehmann*. – TR 84 (1988) 511; RTLv 20,568.

2184 *Hutter* M., Dämonen und Zauberzungen; Aspekte der magie im Alten Vorderasien: Grenzgebiete der Wissenschaft 37 (1988) 215-230 [< ZAW 101,298].

2185 *Hyman* Ronald T., [Gn 3,1-5; Nm 22,28-30] Questions by the serpent and the ass; analysis and parallels with classroom teaching: Dor 16 (1987s) 18-28 . 104-111.

2186 **Jobling** David, [Gn 2,4-3,24; Dt ...] The sense of biblical narrative, structural analyses 2 [1, 1978 ➤ 60,3607]: JStOT Sup 39, 1986 ➤ 2,176: ᴿBiblica 69 (1988) 122-6 (R. *Polzin*); CBQ 50 (1988) 687s (C. H. *Miller*: is structuralism like the emperor's new clothes?); Interpretation 42 (1988) 199s (R. G. *Bowman*); DTAbs 11 (1988) 89s (W. J. *Urbrock*).

2187 **Kasujja** Augustine, Polygenism and the theology of original sin ['today' or? 'East African contribution to the solution of the scientific problem'; diss. 1979, 'The impact of evolutionism in modern theology']: Collectio Nᵒ3268. R 1986, Pont. Univ. Urbaniana. 204 p. Lit. 18.000 ➤ 2,1581: ᴿAfER 29 (1987) 380s (P. *Vonck*); DivThom 91 (1988) 254s (L. J. *Elders*: conservative but declares 'origin of a species from only two individuals is not possible').

2188 *a) Lanser* Susan S., (Faminist) Criticism in the Garden; inferring Genesis 2-3; – *b) Detweiler* Robert, Speaking of believing in Gen. 2-3; –

c) Grimes Ronald L., Infelicitous performances and ritual criticism: Semeia 41 (1988) 67-84 / 135-142 / 103-124.

2189 *Lapide* Pinchas, Was Eva overal de schuld van? Gesprekken over de schepping ᵀ*Stolk* L. F. Kampen 1986, Kok. 74 p. *f*12.90. 90-242-5314-4 – ᴿBijdragen 49 (1988) 94 (F. *Droës*).

2190 *Lapide* Pinchas, Touching the forbidden fruit [God said 'don't eat'; Eve cited 'don't touch' < source not indicated], ᵀ*Swidler* Arlene: BR 4,4 (1988) 42s.

2191 *LaPorte* J., Models from PHILO in ORIGEN's teaching on original sin: LavalTP 44 (1988) 191-203.

2192 **Levison** J. R., Portraits of Adam in early Judaism, from Sirach to 2 Baruch: JPseud Sup 1. Sheffield 1988, Academic. 254 p. £30. 1-85075-062-9 [BL 89,155].

2193 *Lohfink* Norbert, *a*) 'Macht euch die Erde untertan'? [< Orientierung 38 (1974) 137-142]; – *b*) Genesis 2f als 'geschichtliche Ätiologie'; Gedanken zu einem neuen hermeneutischen Begriff [< Scholastik 38 (1963) 321-334]; – *c*) Gn 3,15, 'weil du ihm nach der Ferse schnappst [mit *Haspecker* J., < Scholastik 36 (1961) 357-372]: → 223, Studien 1988, 11-28 / 29-45 / 47-66.

2194 **Martelet** Gustave, Libre réponse à un scandale 1986 → 2,1585; 3,2108: ᴿBLitEc 89 (1988) 153s (H. *Crouzel*); CiTom 114 (1987) 173s (E. *García*); ÉglT 18 (1987) 382s (A. *Peelman*); Gregorianum 69 (1988) 191 (*ipse*); Téléma 13,1 (1987) 89-91 (M. *Lafue-Veron*).

2195 **Martelet** G., Libera risposta ad uno scandalo; la colpa originale, la sofferenza e la morte: GdT 177. Brescia 1987, Queriniana. 210 p. Lit. 16.000. – ᴿRasT 29 (1988) 312 (Daniela *Lucarelli*: efficace).

2196 *Masset* Pierre, Réflexion philosophique [...mais sur Adam et Rom] sur le péché original: NRT 110 (1988) 879-902.

2197 **Mattioli** Anselmo, Le realtà sessuali nella Bibbia; storia e dottrina. Casale Monferrato 1988, Piemme. 262 p. Lit. 35.000. – ᴿCC 139 (1988,3) 320 (C. *Di Sante*).

2198 *Milne* Pamela J., Eve and Adam; is a feminist reading possible?: BR 4,2 (1988) 12-21.39.

2199 *Molina* Mario A., Génesis 2-3; el hombre, su mundo y su pecado: CiuD 201 (1988) 98-111.

2200 *Moor* Johannes C. de, [Gn 2s; Ug.KTU 1.100,107] East of Eden: ZAW 100 (1988) 105-111.

2201 **Nelson** James B., Between two gardens [Eden and Ct]; reflections on sexuality and religious experience 1983 → 1,2232: ᴿRelStR 14 (1988) 126 (Christine E. *Gudorf*) & 127s (R. W. *Blaney*).

2202 *Och* Bernard, The garden of Eden; from creation to covenant, from re-creation to reconciliation: Judaism 37 (1988) 143-156 . 340-351.

2203 **Pagels** Elaine, Adam, Eve, and the serpent. NY 1988, Random. xxviii-191 p. $18 [CBQ 51,189].

2204 **Phillips** John A., Eva – von der Göttin zur Dämonin. Stu 1987, Kreuz. 192 p. – ᴿNatGrac 34 (1987) 434 (A. *Villalmonte*).

2205 *Phipps* William E., Eve and Pandora contrasted: TTod 45 (1988s) 34-48.

2206 *a) Riedlinger* Helmut, Der Übergang von der Unschuld zur Sünde; zur geschichtlichen und geistlichen Auslegung des Mythos von Adam, Eva und der Schlange; – *b) Schäfer* Peter, Adam in der jüdischen Über-lieferung; – *c) Strubel* Robert, Zur tiefenpsychologischen Auslegung der Adam-Christus-Typologie; – *d) Brandenburger* Egon, Adam und neuer

Mensch, erster und letzter Adam-Anthropos: → 3,567, ᴱStrolz W., Vom alten zum neuen Adam 1985/6, 11-42 / 69-93 / 151-181 / 182-223.

2207 **Rigby** P., Original sin in AUGUSTINE's Confessions. Ottawa 1987, Univ. x-142 p. C$ 18 [RThom 88,176].

2208 *Ruiz* Guillermo, L'enfance d'Adam selon saint IRÉNÉE de Lyon: BLit-Ec 89 (1988) 97-115; Eng. 82.

2209 **Russell** Jeffrey B., Lucifer 1984 → 1,2236 ... 3,2116: ᴿCathHR 73 (1987) 266s (R. K. *Emmerson*); ChH 57 (1988) 85s (D. *Bornstein*); JEH 39 (1988) 240-5 (P. *Biller*).

2210 **Russell** Jeffrey B., Mephistopheles; the devil in the modern world 1986 → 3,2117: ᴿJAAR 56 (1988) 177-180 (A. M. *Olson*); TLZ 113 (1988) 54-6 (M. J. *Suda*).

2211 **Russell** Jeffrey B., The prince of darkness; radical evil and the power of good in history [a fifth volume about the devil, but leaving documentation to the other four]. Ithaca NY 1988, Cornell Univ. xii-288 p. $22 [TS 50,586, R. M. *Gula*].

2212 *Sayés* José A., Teología del pecado original: Burgense 29 (1989) 9-49.

2213 *Shinan* Avigdor, ◐ [Gn 2,21 Targ.] Note; the thirteenth rib: Tarbiz [54 (1984s) 269, *Beit Arié* M.] 57 (1987s) 119s, Eng. V.

2214 **Storms** C. Samuel, Tragedy in Eden; original sin in the theology of Jonathan EDWARDS. Lanham MD 1985, UPA. xii-316 p. $12.75 pa. – ᴿGraceTJ 9 (1988) 295s (D. S. *Dockery*).

2215 *Thorion-Vardi* Talia, [Gn 3,7] Remarks on Genesis Rabba 22,6: → 42*, EHRMAN A. mem., Fucus 1988, 463-9.

2216 *Tobin* Thomas H., The creation of man; PHILO...: CBQ Mg 14, 1983 → 64,2021 ... 1,2022: ᴿJQR 79 (1988s) 73-75 (D. M. *Hay*).

2217 **Toorn** Karel van der, Sin and sanction in Israel and Mesopotamia 1985 → 1,2242 ... 3,2122: ᴿAfO 34 (1987) 69-72 (W. von *Soden*); JNWS 14 (1988) 224 (F. C. *Fensham*); OLZ 83 (1988) 567-9 (W. *Herrmann*).

2218 *Torrance* Thomas F., The goodness and dignity of man in the Christian tradition [Hong Kong symposium 1986]: ModT 4 (1987s) 309-322.

2219 **Wallace** Howard N., The Eden narrative [Harvard diss. 1982, ᴰCross F. M.]: HarvSemMg 32, 1985 → 1,2243 ... 3,2125: ᴿCBQ 50 (1988) 703s (B. F. *Batto*); ÉglT 17 (1986) 233s (W. *Vogels*); RB 95 (1988) 130-133 (J. *Loza*); VT 38 (1988) 124 (J. A. *Emerton*).

2220 **Waschke** Ernst-J., Untersuchungen zum Menschenbild der Urge-schichte; ein Beitrag zur alttestamentlichen Theologie: TArb 42, 1984 → 65,1749: ᴿNedTTs 42 (1988) 150 (K. A. *Deurloo*).

2221 *Webster* John, The firmest grasp of the real; BARTH on original sin: TorJT 4 (1988) 19-29.

2222 *Young* John, Original sin; a controverted doctrine: HomP 89,3 (1988s) 9-16.

2223 *Zimmermann* Anthony, Adam and Eve; is original sin transmitted through the sex act?: HomPast 88,4 (1988) 58-62 [< ZIT].

2224 **Zumkeller** Adolar, Erbsünde, Gnade, Rechtfertigung und Verdienst 1984 → 1,7295; 3,7338: ᴿLutherJb 54 (1987) 123s (H. *Junghans*); TrierTZ 97 (1988) 68-70 (A. *Dahm*).

2225 *a) Dellazari* Romano, Gênesis 2,18-25; uma etiologia do matrimônio e da igualdade entre o homem e a mulher; – *b) Moesch* Olavo, A doutrina de Sto Agostinho sobre o matrimônio: Teocomunicação 16,74 (1986) 31-36 / 17-30 [< TKontext 9/2,74].

2226 *Wilfong* Marsha M., Genesis 2: 18-24 ['helpmate']: Interpretation 42 (1988) 58-63.

2227 *Kessler* Rainer, Die Frau als Gehilfin des Mannes? – Genesis 2,18.20 und das biblische Verständnis von 'Hilfe': DielBl 24 (1987) 120-126.

2228 *Uehlinger* Christoph, Eva als 'lebendiges Kunstwerk'; Traditions-geschichtliches zu Gen 2,21-22 (23.24) und 3,20: BibNot 43 (1988) 90-99.

2229 *Ramsey* George W., Is name-giving an act of domination in Genesis 2:23 and elsewhere?: CBQ 50 (1988) 24-35.

2230 *Lindner* Helgo, Spricht Gen. 2,24 von der Ehe?: TBei 19,1 (Wu 1988) 23-32 [< ZIT].

2231 *Moberly* R.W.L., [Gen 3,4s] Did the serpent get it right? [they did not in fact die, and their life was in fact enriched ... but look deeper]: JTS 39 (1988) 1-27.

2231* *Husson* Geneviève, Le paradis de délices (Genèse 3,23-24): RÉG 101 (1988) 64-73.

2232 *Wyatt* Nicholas, When Adam delved; the meaning of Genesis III, 23: VT 38 (1988) 117-122.

E2.1 **Cain et Abel;** *Gigantes, longaevi;   Genesis 4s.*

2233 **Alonso Schökel** Luis, ¿Dónde está tu hermano? Textos de fraternidad en el libro de Génesis 1985 ➤ 1,1969; 3,2133: RCBQ 50 (1988) 103s (R.H. *McGrath*).

2234 *Soleh* M.Z., **❶** Cain's sin and dwelling in tents: BethM 32,111 (1986s) 381s.

2235 **Eichhorn** David M., Cain, son of the serpent[2]. Chappaqua NY 1985, Rossel. 160 p. – RKirSef [53 p. 453 ed. 1] 61 (1986s) 409.

2236 **Fraade** Steven D., Enosh and his generation 1984 ➤ 65,1944; 2,1618: RJQR 78 (1987) 172s (J.C. *VanderKam*).

2237 *Golka* F.W., Cain and Abel; biblical or dogmatic interpretation ['Kein Gnade für Kain' < F*Westermann* C. 1980]: ScripB 19 (1988s) 29-34.

2238 *Neufeld* Ernest, Cain and Abel: Dor 17 (1988s) 40-43.

2239 *Young* Dwight W., On the application of numbers from Babylonian mathemetics to biblical life spans and epochs: ZAW 100 (1988) 331-361 [they still function symbolically].

2240 *Jay* Nancy, [Gn 4,1; 5,3 ...] Sacrifice, descent and the Patriarchs: VT 38 (1988) 52-70.

2241 *Wojciechowski* Michał, **❷** Ab mythis ad theologiam ('filii Dei' in Gen 6,1-4): RuBi 41 (1988) 340-7.

E2.2 *Diluvium,* **The Flood;** Gilgameš (Atraḥasis); **Genesis 6 ...**

2242 *Barré* Lloyd M., The riddle of the Flood chronology: JStOT 41 (1988) 3-20.

2243 **Caduff** Gian Andrea, Antike Sintflutsagen 1986 ➤ 2,1622; 3,2152: RGnomon 60 (1988) 531s (W. *Fauth*); RivStoLR 24 (1988) 347-350 (M.P. *Schmude*).

2244 **Cors i Meya** J., El viatge al món dels morts en l'Odissea [... iii. El viatge de Gilgameš]. Barc 1984, Universitat Autónoma. 524 p. – RAulaO 6 (1988) 109-111 (F.R. *Adrados*).

2245 *Dowell* Susan, Back to the Ark [biblically based anti-pacifism]: NBlackf [67 (1986) 204-215, R. *Ruston*] 69 (1988) 27-34.

2246 ᴱDundes Alan, The flood myth [25 selections]. Berkeley 1988, Univ. California. vi-452 p. $48; pa.$16 [TDig 35,357]. 0-520-06353-8.

2247 *Emerton* J. A., An examination of some attempts to defend the unity of the Flood narrative in Genesis, Part II: VT [I: 37 (1987) 401-420] 38 (1988) 1-21.

2248 **Ish-Horowicz** Moshe, Theodicy as evidenced by early rabbinic discussions of the Flood: diss. Victoria Univ. Manchester 1987. 420 p. BRD 80558. – DissA 49 (1988s) 100-A.

2249 *Lambert* Wilfred G., The Flood in Sumerian, Babylonian and biblical sources: CanadMesop 5 (1983) 27-40.

2250 *Newsom* Carol A., 4Q370; an admonition based on the Flood: ➤ 22, Mém. CARMIGNAC J., RQum 13 (1988) 23-43; 1 pl.

2251 **Seyersted** P., Gilsgamesj; han som så alt [free rendering into Norwegian, staged c.1967], pref. *Kapelrud* Arvid S. Oslo 1987, Cappelsen. 83 p. 82-02-04301-8 [BL 89,127, G. W. *Anderson*].

2252 **Stiebing** William H.ᴶ, Ancient astronauts, cosmic collisions and other popular theories about man's past [... Deluge]. Buffalo NY 1984, Prometheus. 217 p. $19; pa. $10. – ᴿAndrUnS 26 (1988) 99-102 (H. *Storck* doubts that the pyramids were tombs).

2253 **Tigay** Jeffrey H., The evolution of the Gilgamesh epic 1982 ➤ 63,2249 ... 3,2168: ᴿWZKM 77 (1987) 198-201 (L. M. *Young*).

2254 *Wilhelm* Gernot, Neue akkadische Gilgameš-Fragmente aus Ḫattusa: ZAss 78 (1988) 99-121.

2255 *Rüterswörden* Udo, Der Bogen in Genesis 9; militärhistorische und traditionsgeschichtliche Erwägungen zu einem biblischen Symbol: UF 20 (1988) 247-263.

2256 *Priest* James E., Gen 9:6; a comparative study of bloodshed in Bible and Talmud: JEvTS 31 (1988) 145-152 [< ZIT 88,588].

2257 Histoire de l'exégèse de Gn 9,20-28, ivresse de Noé [séminaire ...]: ➤ 471, Exégèse XVIᵉ s. 1988 ...

2258 *Steinmetz* David C., *a*) [Gn 9,20] LUTHER and the drunkenness of Noah; – *b*) Abraham and the Reformation: ➤ 2,d571, Luther in context 1986, 111-132 / 130-133 [< LuJb 55 (1988) 166].

2259 *Block* D. I., [Gn 10] Table of nations: ➤ 801, ISBEnc³ 4 (1988) 708-713.

2260 *Harrison* R. K., [Gn 10,14] Philistine origins; a reappraisal: ➤ 29, Mem. CRAIGIE P., Ascribe 1988, 11-19.

2261 **Bost** Hubert, Babel; du texte au symbole 1985 ➤ 1,2283; 2,1639: Genève 1985, Labor et fides. 268 p. – ᴿProtestantesimo 43 (1988) 206s (J. A. *Soggin*); RB 95 (1988) 133-5 (J. *Loza*).

2262 *Lardet* Pierre, [Gn 11] Peuples et langues de Calvin à Bodin; la référence à la Genèse: ➤ 471, Exégèse XVIᵉ s. 1988 ...

E2.3 Patriarchae, Abraham; *Genesis 12s.*

2263 *Abela* Antonio, 'Tutte le generazioni mi chiameranno padre' (Le valutazioni della figura di Abramo nelle tradizioni bilbiche): Nuova Umanità 57 (1988) 59-76; 58 (1988) 71-91.

2264 **Alexander** Thomas D., A literary analysis of the Abraham narrative in Genesis [11,27-25,11]: diss. Queen's. Belfast 1982. 280 p. BRDX 83414. – DissA 89 (1988s) 2690-A.

2265 **Arenhoevel** Diego, Erinnerung an die Väter; Genesis 12-50[2] ([1]1976): StuKK AT 2. Stu 1987, KBW. 191 p. 3-460-05021-7.

2266 **Baldwin** Joyce G., The message of Genesis 12-50: The Bible Speaks Today 1986 → 3,2180: [R]BL (1988) 54 (J.C.L. *Gibson*: sees as epitome of Christian gospel); EvQ 60 (1988) 63s (P.E. *Satterthwaite*); IrBSt 9 (1987) 46s (I. *Patterson*).

2267 *Conrad* Edgar W., Isaiah and the Abraham connection: AsiaJT 2,2 (1988) 382-393.

2268 **Forsberg** Juhani, Das Abrahambild in der Theologie LUTHERS 1984 → 1,2288; 3,2184: [R]LutherJb 54 (1987) 120s (H. *Junghans*); WissWeis 50 (1987) 227-9 (H.-M. *Stamm*).

2269 *Görg* Manfred, Abraham — historische Perspektiven: BibNot 41 (1988) 11-14.

2270 *Harris* George W., Socrates and Abraham: → 80, [F]KILGORE W.J. 1987, 55-74.

2272 *Koch* Klaus, Die Götter, denen die Väter dienten [ineditum]: → 212, Studien 1988, 9-31.

2273 *a)* *McCarter* P. Kyle[J], The historical Abraham; – *b)* *Anderson* Bernhard W., Abraham, the friend of God; – *c)* *Baird* William, Abraham in the New Testament; tradition and the new identity; – *d)* *Wharton* James A., On the road again; Abraham and contemporary preaching; – *e)* *Buttrick* David G., Genesis 15:1-18; – *f)* *Alston* Wallace M.[J], Genesis 18:1-11; – *g)* *Tietjen* John H., Hebrews 11:8-12; Interpretation 42,4 (1988) 341-352 / 352-366 / 367-379 / 381-392 / 393-7 / 397-402 / 403-7.

2274 *a)* *Marchadour* Alain, Le récit patriarcal et l'intrigue du Pentateuque; – *b)* *Pury* Albert de, La tradition patriarcale en Genèse 12-35; – *c)* *Gibert* Pierre, Pour un 'bon usage' de l'histoire des Patriarches; – *d)* *Cazeaux* Jacques, De la chênaie de Sichem au chêne de Mambré; les grands lieux de la Genèse; – *e)* *Lévy-Valensi* Éliane A., Les patriarches, ou de la transmission; une lecture juive; – *f)* *Arnaldez* Roger, Figures patriarcales et prophétiques dans le Coran; – *g)* *Collin* Mathieu, La tradition des 'pères' dans le NT: LumièreV 37,188 (1988) 7-19 / 21-34 / 35-42 / 43-68 / 69-79 / 81-95 / 101-111.

2275 *a)* *Muñoz Iglesias* S., La fe de María y la fe de Abraham; – *b)* *Serra* Aristide M., Maria, 'profondamente permeata dello spirito dei "poveri di Jahve"' (RM 37); testimonianze biblico-giudaiche sul trinomio 'fedeltà alla legge di Dio — preghiera — liberazione'; Marianum 50 (1988) 176-192 / 193-289.

2275* **Papus**, [on Abraham ...] Le Sepher Jesirah: Gnostica. P 1987, Cariscript. 30 p.

2276 *a)* *Pennacchini* Bruno, La promessa ad Abramo; – *b)* *Spreafico* Ambrogio, Esodo, memoria e promessa; – *c)* *Sacchi* Alessandro, Le promesse di Dio sono diventate 'sì'; – *d)* *Mosetto* Francesco, Figli della promessa; – *e)* *Hélewa* Giovanni, Una visione biblica della storia: ParVi 33,2 ('La promessa' 1988) 99-106 / 107-113 / 115-121 / 122-8 / 87-97.

2277 **Scheepers** Coenraad, Argeologie [RTLv 20,541] en die Abraham-tradisies; 'n Wetenskapsfilosofiese beoordeling van die metodologie van John VAN SETERS: diss. [D]Deist F. Pretoria c.1988. 154 p.

2278 *Schmid* H., Die Gestalt Abrahams: → 78, Mem. KIEFER G. 1987, 195-214 [< ZAW 100,313].

2279 *Scullion* John J., 'Die Genesis ist eine Sammlung von Sagen' (Hermann GUNKEL) — Independent stories and redactional unity in Genesis 12-36: → 469, Wünschet 1986/8, 243-7.

2280 *Soards* Marion L.,   The early Christian interpretation of Abraham and the place of James within that context: IrBSt 9 (1987) 18-26.
2281 **Vandergriff** Kenneth L.,   The Messianic significance of the 'Seed of Abraham' concept in pre-Christian Judaism: Diss. SW Baptist Theol. Sem. 1988. – RelStR 15,193.
2282 *Weimar* P.,   Abraham: ➤ 804, NBL Lfg. 1 (1988) 14-22.
2283 *a) Weinfeld* Moshe,   The promise to the Patriarchs and its realization; an analysis of foundation stories; – *b) Zertal* Adam,   The water factor during the Israelite settlement process in Canaan; – *c) Eitam* David,   The settlement of nomadic tribes in the Negeb highlands during the 11th century B.C.: ➤ 742, Society 1985/8, 353-369 / 341-352; 2 fig. / 313-340; 2 maps.
2283* **Wieser** Friedrich E.,   Die Abrahamvorstellungen im NT [Diss. Zürich 1986, ᴰ*Schweizer* E.]: EurHS 23/317. x-209 p. Fs 46,20 [TLZ 114,37s, G. *Haufe*].

2284 *Evans* Craig A., [Gn 12 ...] The Genesis Apocryphon and the rewritten Bible: ➤ 22, Mém. CARMIGNAC J., RQum 13 (1988) 153-165.
2285 *Jensen* H. J. Lundager, [Gn 12, not 1-11, is *the* myth of Israel's origins] De fremmede [främmande], Der gamle Testamente, vi: Religionsvidenskabeligt Tidsskrift 10 (1987) 27-52 [< ZAW 100,296].
2286 *Carrillo Alday* Salvador,   'Y serán bendecidas en tí todas las familias de la tierra' (Gn 12,1-3 en el diálogo judío-católico): Medellín 14,54 (1988) 231-242 [< TKontext 10,94].
2287 **Salanga** Victor, [Gn 12,10-20; 20,1-18; 26,1-11] Three stories of the endangered wife; a narrative and stylistic analysis: diss. Pont. Univ. Gregoriana, ᴰ*Ska* J. R 1988, 211 p. – RTLv 20,541.
2288 **Niditch** Susan, [Gn 12 ... 27] Underdogs and tricksters; a prelude to biblical folklore 1987 ➤ 3,2189: ᴿBS 145 (1988) 463 (E. H. *Merrill*: useful, even edifying).
2289 *Gordon* Cyrus H.,   Marriage in the guise of siblingship [RS 21,230]:   UF 20 (1988) 53-56 [Gn not mentioned].
2290 *Weimar* P.,   Ahnfraugeschichten [Gefährdung, Gn 12,10-20; 20; 26,1-13]: ➤ 804, NBL Lfg 1 (1988) 67s.
2291 *Jeansonne* Sharon Pace, [Gn 13,7] The characterization of Lot in Genesis: BibTB 18 (1988) 123-9.
2292 *Na'aman* Nadav, [Gn 13,7 ...] Canaanites and Perizzites: BibNot 45 (1988) 42-47.

E2.4   **Melchisedech, Sodoma;** *Genesis 14.*

2293 **Cabrejos-Vidarte** Miguel,   El capítulo XIV del Génesis; su lugar y su función en las redacciones patriarcales: diss. LvN 1986, ᴰ*Bogaert* P.-M.: ➤ 986, Travaux de doctorat en théologie 12 (1989) théol. 1; 30 p.
2294 **Gianotto** Claudio,   Melchisedek e la sua tipologia: RivB Sup 12, 1984 ➤ 65,1886 ... 3,2200: ᴿRB 95 (1988) 113s (É. *Puech*: important).
2295 *Mahé* Jean-Pierre,   La fête de Melkisédeq le huit août en Palestine d'après les Tropologia et les ménées géorgiens [sic; texte et traduction]: ➤ 38, Mém. DUMÉZIL G. = RÉtGC 3 (1987) 83-125.
2296 **(Mianbé) Bétoudji** Denis,   El, le Dieu suprême ... (Genesis 14,18-20) 1986 ➤ 2,1652; 3,2202: ᴿJTS 39 (1988) 539s (J. *Day*, very severe: ignores

CROSS, ALBRIGHT, ALT, THOMPSON, VAN SETERS...); ZkT 110 (1988) 105 (G. *Fischer*).

2297 **Mulder** M.J., Sodom en Gomorra, een verhaal van dode steden: Exegetische Studies 4. Kampen 1988, Kok. 93 p. *f* 18. 90-242-3083-7 [Bijdragen 49,359].

2298 **Smart** Jerry W., The Sodom tradition [no other event is mentioned so often in the Bible] and the hermeneutical task: diss. Southern Baptist Theol. Sem., ᴰ*Kelley* P. 1988. 219 p. 89-01502. – DissA 49 (1988s) 3055-A.

2299 *Staniek* Edward, ❷ Discussion sur Melchisédech (AMBROSIASTER - JÉRÔME): ➤ 73, ꟳKANIA W. = VoxPa 12s (1987s) 345-353; franç. 353.

2299* *a*) *Waldman* Nahum M., Genesis 14 — meaning and structure; – *b*) *Berg* Edmund, Who was Melchizedek?; – *c*) *Katzoff* Louis, Sodom; manners, morals, misdeeds: Dor 16 (1987s) 256-262 / 183-5 / 211-3.

2300 *Gnilka* Christian, [Gn 14,11.16] Eine Spur altlateinischer Bibelversion bei PRUDENTIUS: VigChr 42 (1988) 147-155.

E2.5 The Covenant (alliance, Bund); *Foedus, Genesis 15...*

2301 *Abela* Anthony, Genesis 15, a non-genetic approach: Melita Theologica 37,2 (1986) 9-40.

2302 **Barré** Michael L., The god-list in the treaty between Hannibal and Philip V, 1983 ➤ 64,2283 ... 3,2206: ᴿJCS 40 (1988) 129-2 (W. G. *Lambert*); JNES 47 (1988) 156s (J. *Teixidor*).

2303 *Caquot* André, Une homélie éthiopienne attribuée à Saint Mari Éphrem sur le séjour d'Abraham et Sara en Égypte: ➤ 59, ꟳGUILLAUMONT A., 1988, 173-185, avec texte éthiopien.

2304 *Klein* Ralph W., Call, covenant, and community; the story of Abraham and Sarah: ➤ 143, ꟳTIETJEN J. = CurrTM 15 (1988) 120-7.

2305 **McCarthy** Dennis J. †, Institution and narrative: AnBib 108, 1985 ➤ 1,204.2309; 3,2212: ᴿBL (1988) 109 (R. E. *Clements*); RivB 36 (1988) 271s (A. *Spreafico*).

2306 **Mathew** P. C., Berith, the Semitic concept of divine human relationship: Semitic Theological Series, 3. Kottayam 1987. xvi-263 p. $15 [JNES 47,77].

2307 **Méroz** Christianne, Des femmes libres: Sarah, Agar, Rébecca, Rachel, Léa. Aubonne 1988, Moulin. 92 p. – ᴿMondeB 54 (1988) 59 (P. I. *Fransen*: fantaisie; textes lus tels qu'on voudrait qu'ils soient); Protestantesimo 43 (1988) 208s (G. *Conte*).

2308 *Begg* Christopher T., Rereadings of the 'animal rite' of Genesis 15 in early Jewish narratives [Jub 14,9-19; Josephus Ant 1,183-5; Pseudo-Philo Bib. Ant. 23,6s; ApocAbr 9-32]: CBQ 50 (1988) 36-46.

2309 **Mölle** Herbert, Genesis 15; eine Erzählung von den Anfängen Israels: ForBi 62. Wü 1988, Echter. 412 p.

2310 *Samely* Alexander, [Gn 15,1; 36,1s; Lv 1,1; 9,7; Nm 7,3s] The background of speech; some observations on the representation of targumic exegesis [the Targum, while proceeding solely from the masoretic text, manages to give a quite different *story*]: JJS 39 (1988) 251-260.

2311 *Roldanus* J., [Gn 15,5] L'héritage d'Abraham d'après Irénée: ➤ 85, ꟳKLIJN A., Text 1988, 212-224.

2312 *Ciampa* Pio, [Gn 16] The best African girl in the Bible — Hagar, a teacher of biblical spirituality: Vidyajyoti 52 (1988) 269s. 275s. 284.

2313 *Gaffney* James, Hagar and her sisters, precedent for conduct; surrogate motherhood in the Bible: Commonweal 114 (1987) 240-2.

2314 *Fenton* P., Ismaël dans la tradition juive: Les nouveaux cahiers 91 (P 1987) 4-10 [< Judaica 44,127].

2315 *Koenen* Klaus, Wer sieht wen? Zur Textgeschichte von Genesis XVI,13: VT 38 (1988) 468-474.

2316 *Weimar* Peter, Gen 17 und die priesterschriftliche Abrahamgeschichte: ZAW 100 (1988) 22-60.

2317 *Lohfink* Norbert, Textkritisches zu Gn 17,5.13.16.17 [< Biblica 48 (1967) 439-442]: ➤ 223, Studien 1988, 67-70.

2318 **Miller** William T., [Gn 18,1-16; 32,22-33] Mysterious encounters at Mamre and Jabbok: BrownJudSt 50, 1984 ➤ 65,2002; 2,1668: ᴿAbrNahr 26 (1988) 121s (Anne E. *Gardner*); ÉglT 17 (1986) 234s (W. *Vogels*).

2319 *Brunner* Hellmut, Gen 19 und das 'Frauenverbrechen': BibNot 44 (1988) 21s.

E2.6   The 'Aqedâ;   *Isaac, Genesis 22...*

2319* **Agus** Aharon (Ronald E.), The binding of Isaac and Messiah; law, martyrdom and deliverance in early rabbinic religiosity: Judaica. Albany 1988, SUNY. xi-327 p. $54.50; pa. $20 [JBL 108,753].

2320 *Bar-David* Yoram, Autour du sacrifice d'Abraham; um commentateur chrétien [*Hebel* P., 1760-1826] et un commentateur juif [*Hirsch* S., 1808-1888] qui s'accordent à la lettre: ➤ 486, Traduction 1986/8, 139-149; Eng. 139.

2321 *Calder* Norman, From midrash to Scripture; the sacrifice of Abraham in early Islamic tradition: Muséon 101 (1988) 375-402.

2322 *a) Coffin* Edna A., The binding of Isaac in modern Israeli literature; – *b) Lehman* David, Fantasia on KIERKEGAARD and Sir Gawain and the Green Knight: ➤ 3,356, ᴱ*O'Connor* M., Backgrounds 1987, 293-308 / 309-319 [< JBL 108,174].

2323 *Edgerton* W. Dow, The binding of Isaac: TTod 44 (1987s) 207-221.

2324 *Frank* Évelyne, Isaac dans 'Jacob' de Pierre EMMANUEL [1970]: RThom 88 (1988) 288-298.

2325 *Kartun-Blum* Ruth, 'Where does this wood in my hand come from?'; the binding of Isaac in modern Hebrew poetry: Prooftexts 8 (1988) 293-310.

2326 *Kreuzer* Siegfried, Das Opfer des Vaters — die Gefährdung des Sohnes; Genesis 22: Amt und Gemeinde 37 (W 1986) 62-70 [< LuJb 55,165].

2327 **Martin-Achard** Robert, Abraham sacrifiant; de l'épreuve du Moriya à la nuit d'Auschwitz. Aubonne 1988, Moulin. 93 p. – ᴿÉTRel 63 (1988) 598 (D. *Lys*); Protestantesimo 43 (1988) 207s (G. *Conte*).

2328 *Mees* Michael, Isaaks Opferung in frühchristlicher Sicht, von CLEMENS Romanus bis CLEMENS Alexandrinus: ➤ 517, AugR 28 (1988) 259-272.

2329 **Milgrom** J., The binding of Isaac; the *Akedah,* a primary symbol of Jewish thought and art [diss. 1978]. Berkeley 1988, Bibal. xii-322 p. $17. 0-941037-05-3 [BL 89,86, L. L. *Grabbe*: omits important CBQ 1978,514].

2330 *Moberly* R. W. L., [Gn 22, 15-18] The earliest commentary on the Akedah: VT 38 (1988) 302-323.

2331 *Moskowitz* Moshe, Towards a rehumanization of the *Akedah* and other sacrifices: Judaism 37 (1988) 288-294.

2332 *Moster* Julius B., [Gn 22] The testing of Abraham: Dor 17 (1988s) 237-242.

2333 *Philippides* Dia M.L.,   Rhyming patterns in the Erotokritos and the Sacrifice of Abraham [both c. 1600 A.D.]; a preliminary investigation: Cretan 1 (1988) 205-216.

2334 *Segal* Alan F.,   The sacrifice of Isaac in early Judaism and Christianity [= 'He who did not spare his only son ...'; Jesus, Paul, and the Akedah < ᶠ*Beare* F. 1984 169-184]: ➤ 260, Other Judaisms 1987, 109-130.

2335 *Ska* Jean Louis,   Gn 22,1-19; essai sur les niveaux de lecture: Biblica 69 (1988) 324-339; Eng. 339.

2336 *Veijola* Timo,   Das Opfer des Abraham — Paradigma des Glaubens aus dem nachexilischen Zeitalter: ZTK 85 (1988) 129-164.

2337 *Turiot* Cécile,   Le mariage d'Isaac (Gen. 24); un texte à lire aujourd'hui: *a*) RICathP 27 (1988) 13-31; – *b*) SémBib 51 (1988) 22-34.

E2.7   **Jacob** and Esau; ladder-dream; *Jacob, somnium, Genesis 25 ...*

2338 **Ben Horin** Mirjam Viterbi,   Il sogno di Giacobbe, pref. *Sartori* Luigi.   R 1988, Borla.   155 p.   88-263-0476-9.

2339 **Blum** Erhard, [Gn 25-31] Die Komposition der Vätergeschichte [Diss. Heidelberg]: WMANT 57, 1984 ➤ 65,1970; 2,1686:   ᴿCBQ 50 (1988) 282-4 (W.H. *Irwin*: sober).

2340 **Hendel** Ronald S.,   The epic of the patriarch; the Jacob cycle and the narrative traditions of Canaan and Israel: HarvSemMon 42, 1987 ➤ 3,2237; Atlanta 1987, Scholars.   1-55540-184-9:   ᴿBiblica 69 (1988) 574-6 (J.L. *Ska*); Dor 17 (1988s) 261-4 (S. *Liptzin*).

2341 **Fokkelman** J.P.,   Oog in oog met Jakob 1981 ➤ 62,2503; 63,2332: ᴿHenoch 10 (1988) 102s (J.A. *Soggin*).

2342 *Kempinski* Aharon,   Jacob in history: BAR-W 14,1 (1988) 42-47 [< ᴱ*Israelit-Groll* S., Pharaonic Egypt 1985, 129-137].

2343 *Terino* Jonathan ('missonary in Italy'),   A text linguistic study of the Jacob narrative: VoxEvca 18 (L 1988) 45-62.

2344 *Yanîv* Iris, ❻ Words for offering ... of Jacob: BethM 34,116 (1988s) 68-75.

2345 *Luke* K., [Gn 26s] Esau's marriage: IndTSt 25 (1988) 171-190.

2346 *a*) *Martin-Achard* Robert,   Remarques sur Genèse 26; – *b*) *Cross* Frank M., Reuben, first-born of Jacob: ➤ 153, ZAW 100 Supp. (1988) 22-46 / 46-65.

2347 **Nicol** G.G.,   Studies in the interpretation of Genesis 26,1-33: diss. Oxford 1987. – RTLv 19,535.

2348 *Schmidt* Ludwig,   Jakob erschleicht sich den väterlichen Segen; Literarkritik und Redaktion von Genesis 27,1-45:   ZAW 100 (1988) 159-183: distinguishes (and maintains) J and E; von RAD's 'early little Credo' and NOTH's amphictyony have come and gone with scarcely any effect on JEPD-analyses.

2349 *Levin* S., [Gen 27,2] Isaac's blindness; a medical diagnosis [... assuming with ROSENZWEIG that patriarchs' ages were double, i.e. each winter and each summer counted as one year]: Judaism 37 (1988) 81-83.

2350 *Bulka* Reuven P., [Gn 27,35] Isaac's blessing; who was deceived?:   Dor 17 (1988s) 185-9.

2351 *Ḥemi'el* Ḥ.Y., [Gn 27,41] ❻ The mother of Jacob and Esau: BethM 32,111 (1987s) 332-344.

2352 *Guillaume* Paul-Marie, [Gn 29s] Rachel et Lia: ➤ 791, DictSpir XIII,86 (1987) 25-30.

2353 *Ventura* Milka,   Nella terra di Labano; una lettura di Genesi XXIX-XXX: Anima [psicologia/simboli; 'si pubblica una volta l'anno, all'inzio di primavera'] 1 (F 1988) 77-88.

E2.8   Jacob's wrestling; the Angels;   *lucta, Angelus/mal'ak Gn 31 ...*

2354 *Caquot* André, [DJD 7 (1982) 221] Le service des anges: ➤ 22, Mém. CARMIGNAC J., RQum 13 (1988) 421-9.

2355 **Fossum** Jarl E.,   The Name of God and the Angel of the Lord; Samaritan ... Gnosticism [ᴰ1982]: WUNT 36, 1985 ➤ 1,2344*b* ... 3,2245: ᴿGregorianum 69 (1988) 547-9 (G. L. *Prato*); JBL 107 (1988) 153-6 (M. A. *Williams*).

2356 *García Cordero* Maximiliano,   Los ángeles según las creencias judías del tiempo de Jesús: CiTom 115 (1988) 409-440.

2357 *Jacob* Edmond,   Variations et constantes dans la figure de l'ange de YHWH: RHPR 68 (1988) 405-414.

2358 **MacGregor** Geddes,   Angels, ministers of grace [... a well-established part of the folklore of the world, taken seriously in all the great religions]. NY 1988, Paragon.   xii-230 p. $26; pa. $13 [TDig 36,69].

2359 **Meier** Samuel A.,   The messenger in the ancient Semitic world: HarvSemMg 45. Atlanta 1988, Scholars.   xvii-269 p. $14; sb./pa. $10 [JBL 108,380].

2360 *Monloubou* L.,   Et si nous parlions des anges!: EsprVie 98 (1988) 225-9 . 247-255 [p. 255, 'le langage biblique n'est pas le nôtre'; p. 256, 'parler des Anges c'est parler de Dieu; simplement, d'une manière existentielle, qui dessine Dieu présent dans l'existence des hommes'].

2361 **Santangelo** Maria N.,   Le berceau des anges. Lv 1988, Peeters.   220 p. Fb 1200.   90-6831-119-0.

2362 **Schneiderman** Stuart,   An angel passes; how the sexes became undivided [Lacan-psychoanalytic: Christians set themselves the task of ridding the heavens of erotic desires; fate of the fallen angels; efforts to model human lives on the theologized existence of the angels ...]. NY 1988, NYU. 362 p. $28 [TDig 36,81].

2363 *Schwebel* Horst,   Die Wiederkehr der Engel: Religion heute (Hannover 1988,3) 178-183 [< ZIT 88,781].

2364 *Slager* Don, [Gn 16,7-14; 21,17-21; 22,9-19 ...] Who is the 'Angel of the Lord'?: BTrans 39 (1988) 436-8: God himself [in these passages; nothing said about elsewhere].

2365 **Vernier** J.-M.,   Les anges chez saint Thomas d'AQUIN; fondements historiques et principes philosophiques; préf. *Boutang* P., 1986 ➤ 3,2249: ᴿRHPR 68 (1988) 490s (G. *Siegwalt*).

2366 *Wels* Richard D.,   Lessons on wrestling with the unseen; Jacob at the Jabbok: RefR 42 (1988s) 96-112 [< ZIT 89,304].

2367 *Kogut* Simcha, **⊕** [Gn 31,29 + 4 + Sir 5,1] The biblical phrase (*yēš / eyn*) *lᵉēl yād* ['in power of' should be *lô lᵉyad, lô* as Ug./Akk. 'power']; on the interpretations and development of a mistake: Tarbiz 57 (1987s) 435-444; Eng. IIIs.

2368 *Steinberg* Naomi, [Gen 31,33] Israelite tricksters; their analogues and cross-cultural study: Semeia 42 (1988) 1-13; response 117-132, *Good* Edwin M.

2369 *Asmussen* Jes P.,   Remarks on Judeo-Persian translations of some Aramaic passages in the Hebrew Bible [Gn 31,47; Jer 10,11 ...]: ArOr 56 (1988) 341-5.

2370 *Anbar* Moshé,   La 'reprise' [originale: Gn 32,14/22; 2 Sam 14,24/28; 2 Kgs 8.29/9,15; Jer 37,21 / 38,13.28; Ruth 4,9/10; – secondaire, surtout Jos 2,22; 5,10; 6,20; 10,43; 13,33: VT 38 (1988) 385-398.

2371 *a) Utzschneider* Helmut,   Das hermeneutische Problem der Uneindeutigkeit biblischer Texte — dargestellt an Text und Rezeption der Erzählung von Jakob am Jabbok (Gen 32,23-33); – *b) Grözinger* Albrecht, Das 'Epische' als Aufgabe der Praktischen Theologie [... Gn 22]: EvT 48 (1988) 182-198 / 199-217.

2372 *Daverio* Annetta, [Gn 32,26-33; *Teilhard* ...] La lotta di Giacobbe con l'angelo: FutUomo 13,3 (1986) 4-11.

2373 *Fass* David E., [Gn 32,33] Jacob's limp: Dor 17 (1988s) 222-9.

2374 *Klein* Michael L.,   'Not to be translated in public' [Rabbinic lists including Gn 35,22; Ex 32,21-35 ...]: JJS 39 (1988) 80-91.

E2.9   **Joseph;** Tamar, Jacob's blessings; *Genesis 37* ...

2375 **Humphreys** W. Lee,   Joseph and his family; a literary study: Studies on the personalities of the OT.   Columbia 1988, Univ. S. Carolina.   xiv-230 p. $20 [TDig 36,64].

2376 **Knauf** Ernst A.,   Midian; Untersuchungen zur Geschichte Palästinas und Nordarabiens am Ende des 2. Jahrtausends v. Chr.: AbhDPV. Wsb 1988, Harrassowitz. xii-194 p. 3-447-02862-9.

2377 *Niehoff* Maren,   The figure of Joseph in the Targums: JJS 39 (1988) 234-250.

2378 **Osman** Ahmed,   Stranger in the Valley of the Kings; the identification of Yuya as the patriarch Joseph. SF 1988, Harper & R.   176 p. $18 [BAR-W 15/2,8, D. B. *Redford*: unfounded and full of errors; JBL 108,186 gives subtitle 'Solving the mystery of the ancient Egyptian mummy'].

2379 *Piredda* Anna Maria,   La tipologia sacerdotale del patriarca Giuseppe in AMBROGIO: Sandalion 10s (Sassari 1987s) 153-163 [BTAM 14, p. 585, H. *Bascour*].

2380 **Resenhöfft** Wilhelm,   Die Quellenberichte im Josef-Sinai-Komplex (Gn 27 ... Ex 34) 1983 ➤ 64,2356; 2,1712: ᴿTR 84 (1988) 190s (H. *Seebass*).

2381 **Scharbert** J.,   Ich bin Josef, euer Bruder; die Erzählung von Josef und seinen Brüdern, wie sie nicht in der Bibel steht [existing previously among Joseph tribes, incorporated by Yahwist in Solomon's court, written down by E in the north 722]. St. Ottilien 1988, EOS. 114 p. DM 14,80. 3-88096-703-2 [BL 89,92, J. W. *Rogerson*].

2382 *Schimmel* Sol,   Joseph and his brothers; a paradigm for repentance: Judaism 37 (1988) 60-65.

2383 *Schmidt* L.,   Literarische Studien zur Josephsgeschichte [bound with *Aejmelaeus* A. in BZAW 167] 1986 ➤ 2,1715; 3,2263 ᴿJBL 107 (1988) 519s (J. G. *Williams*: not undeservedly doomed by its BZAW second place); NedTTs 42 (1988) 338s (C. *Houtman*: pleidooi for the updated documentary theory); VT 38 (1988) 369s (J. A. *Emerton*).

2384 *Schmidt* Ludwig,   Josephnovelle: ➤ 813, TRE 17 (1987) 255-8.

2385 *Friedlander* Albert, [Gn 37,16] 'Ich suche meine Brüder': KIsr 2 (1987) 6-13.

2386 *Greger* Barbara, [Gn 37,26 ...] Ein Erklärungsversuch zu *şor(y)y*: Bib-Not 45 (1988) 28-39 ['Greger' S. 3 und 28 ohne Beobachtung; aber 'Gregor' in 41 (1988) S. 3 und S. 19].

2387 *a) Bos* Johanna W. H., Out of the shadows; Genesis 38; Judges 4,17-22; Ruth 3; – *b) Fuchs* Esther, 'For I have the way of women'; deception, gender and ideology in biblical narrative: Semeia 42 ('Reasoning with the foxes; female wit in a world of male power' 1988) 37-67; response 103-116, *Ashley* K. M. / 68-83; response 133-155, *Bal* Mieke.

2388 *Goldin* Judah, The youngest son; or Where does Genesis 38 belong? [< JBL 96 (1977) 27-44]: ➤ 199, Studies 1988, 121-139.

2389 *Ska* Jean Louis, L'ironie de Tamar (Gen 38) [*O'Callaghan* M. 1981]: ZAW 100 (1988) 261-3; Eng. 263.

2390 *Rendsburg* Gary A., [Gn 41,50-52] The Egyptian sun-god Ra in the Pentateuch: Henoch 10 (1988) 3-15; franç. 15.

2391 *Pautasso* Luigi G., Gen. 44:18 — a case for the textual relevance of the Targumic Tosefta: Henoch 10 (1988) 205-218; franç. 218.

2392 *Rogerson* John, [Gn 45,5 ...] Can a doctrine of Providence be based on the Old Testament?: ➤ 29, Mem. CRAIGIE P., Ascribe 1988, 529-543.

2393 *Baarda* T., [Gn 46,11 Kohath son of Levi] *a)* Qehath — 'what's in a name?'; concerning the interpretation of the name 'Qehath' in the Testament of Levi 11:4-6: JStJud 19 (1988) 215-229; – *b)* De namen van de kinderen van Levi: AmstCah 8 (1987) ...

2394 *Bartal* Arieh, ⊕ [Gen 46,14] The mystery of Sered and Jahleel: BethM 34,118 (1988s) 265-7.

2395 *Schweizer* Harald, [Gen 48,7-13] Literarkritik, 1. Theorie; 2. Bei-spielanalyse: TüTQ 168 (1988) 23-43.

2396 *Somekh* Alberto, *a)* Il Targūm Onqelōs di Genesi 49: AnStoEseg 5 (1988) 143-168; – *b)* Apologia messianica nel Targum Onqelos a Genesi 49: ➤ 570, AugR 28 (1988) 249-257.

2397 **Syrén** Roger, The blessings in the Targum ... Gn 49; Dt 33: 1986 ➤ 2,1722; 3,2268: ᴿNorJ 7 (1986) 37-49 (T. *Kronholm*); Salesianum 50 (1988) 436s (R. *Vicent*).

E3.1 **Exodus event and theme;** *textus, commentarii.*

2398 *Bimson* J., defense of his Exodus dating in reply to *Halpern* B.: BAR-W [1987 ➤ 3,2278] 14,4 (1988) 52-55.

2399 ᴱ**Bloom** Harold, Exodus [7 selections]: Modern critical interpretations. NHv 1987, Chelsea. viii-143 p. $20 [TDig 35,356].

2399* *a) Bohris* Walter, Konfirmandenunterricht als Exodus-Erfahrung; – *b)* *Elb* Marika, Konfirmanden entdecken die Bibel in ihrem Leben; biblische Symbolübungen im Konfirmandenunterricht: ➤ 140, ᶠSTOODT D. 1987, 51-62 / 123-132.

2400 ᴱ**Borret** Marcel, ORIGÈNE, Homélies sur l'Exode: SChr 321, 1985 ➤ 2,1725; 3,2279: ᴿRBgPg 66 (1988) 120s (J. *Schamp*).

2401 *a) Burns* R., El libro del Éxodo; – *b) Zenger* E., El Dios del Éxodo en el mensaje de los profetas; el ejemplo del libro de Isaías; – *c) Casey* J. S., El tema del éxodo en el Apocalipsis; – *d) Lapide* P., El Éxodo en la tradición judía; – *e) Kort* W. A., 'Éxodo' y su paradigma bíblico; – *f) Dussel* E., El paradigma del éxodo en la teología de la liberación; [... negra, *Young* J. / ... feminista, *Bergant* D.]: Concilium 23,209 (M 1987) 17-30 / 31-46 / 47-58 / 59-68 / 87-98 / 99-114 [115-124 / 125-134].

2402 **Cazelles** H., Autour de l'Exode 1987 ➤ 3,201: RAngelicum 65 (1988) 287-290 (B. G. *Boschi*); EsprVie 98 (1988) 109-111 (L. *Monloubou*).

2403 **Christensen** D.L., Experiencing the Exodus from Egypt [Jewish-Christian cooperative]. Berkeley c.1988, Bibal. v-95 p. $8. 0-941037-03-7 [BL 89,102, R. *Hammer*].

2404 *a*) *Cocchini* Francesca, Le Quaestiones di AGOSTINO sull'Esodo; osservazioni storiche, esegetiche, dottrinali [discussione]; – *b*) *Gaeta* Giancarlo, Il Liber regularum di TICONIO; studio sull'ermeneutica scritturistica; – *c*) *Bori* Pier C., La ricezione delle Regole di Ticonio, da Agostino a ERASMO: ➤ 472, AnStoEseg 5 (1988) 77-95 [-102] / 103-124 / 125-142.

2405 *Cohen* N.J., The Book of Exodus through a midrashic prism [on Psalms 19,2]: JRefJud 35,1 (1988) 27-32 [< NTAbs 32,351].

2406 **Costa** Michi, Fammi udire la tua voce; il racconto dell'Esodo per passare la fede ai figli, II. T-Leumann 1987, Elle Di Ci. 180 p. Lit. 14.000. – RParVi 33 (1988) 74 (F. *Mosetto*).

2407 **Croatto** J. Severino, Êxodo, uma hermenéutica da liberdade, TAmérico de Assis Coutinho J. São Paulo 1981, Paulinas. – REstudosB 16 (1988) 81-83 (L. *Garmus*).

2409 **Dunnam** Maxie D., Exodus. Communicator's comm. Waco 1987, Word. 395 p. $19 [BToday 26,117].

2410 **Durham** John I., Exodus: Word 3, 1987 ➤ 3,2284: RBiblica 69 (1988) 576-9 (J. L. *Ska*); BibTB 18 (1988) 34 (R. *Gnuse*); EvQ 60 (1988) 351-4 (W. *Johnstone*); Interpretation 42 (1988) 308 (D. T. *Olson*); JTS 39 (1988) 154 (E. W. *Nicholson*); RefTR 47 (1988) 53s (A. M. *Harman*).

2411 EGorgulho Gilberto, (*Garmus* L.), A memória popular do Êxodo: Estudos Bíblicos 16. Petrópolis 1988, Vozes. 84 p. 7 art., J. *Comblin* on Paul; J. S. *Croatto* and G. V. *Pixley* commentary-reviews; M. *Schwantes* ...
Grossfeld Bernard, The Targum Onqelos to Exodus 1988 ➤ 1703.

2412 *Hastoupis* Athanasios P., Ⓖ The book of Exodus: TAth 58 (1987) 748-779.

2413 **Horst** P. W. van der, Joods-hellenistische poëzie; de fragmenten der gedichten van EZECHIEL Tragicus, Philo Epicus en Theodotus, en de vervalste dichtercitaten. Kampen 1987, Kok. 90 p. *f* 19,25. – RPhoenEOL 34,2 (1988) 65-67 (M. L. *Fomer*); Streven 55 (1987s) 568s (P. *Beentjes*).

2414 **Houtman** C., Exodus vertaald en verklaard, I. 1,1-7,13: CommOT 1986 ➤ 3,2288: RBZ 32 (1988) 300s (J. *Scharbert*); CBQ 50 (1988) 684-6 (W. *Vogels*); RB 95 (1988) 621 (J. *Loza*).

2415 *Hyde* Clark, The remembrance of the Exodus in the Psalms; Worship 62 (1988) 404-414.

2416 *Josse* Robert, L'Exode, chemin de libération: VChrét 324 (1988) 16-22; 325 (1988) 14-19; 326 (1988) 13-20.

2417 **Khoudair** Anthony J., Doctrina del Éxodo en los Salmos: diss. DAusin Olmos S. Pamplona 1987. 207 p. – RTLv 19,534.

2418 EKnevel A. G., *al.*, Verkenningen in Exodus. Kampen 1986, Kok. 168 p. *f* 25,15. – RGerefTTs 88 (1988) 42 (C. *Houtman*).

2419 *Magonet* J., L'attitude envers l'Égypte dans le livre de l'Exode: ➤ 351, Concilium 219 (P 1988) 15-25.

2420 *Nagel* Peter, Papyrus Bodmer XVI und die achmimische Version des Buches Exodus: ➤ 16, FBÖHLIG A., Religion 1988, 94-152.

2421 **Pixley** George V., Êxodo [1983 ➤ 65,2057], TRezede Costa J.: Grande Comentário Bíblico. S. Paulo 1987, Paulinas. 247 p. – REstudosB 16 (1988) 83s (L. *Garmus*).

2422 **Pixley** George V., On Exodus; a liberation perspective, [T]*Barr* Robert R. Maryknoll NY 1987, Orbis. xx-236 p. $20 [TDig 35,283]. – [R]NewTR 1,4 (1988) 77s (Dianne *Bergant*).

2423 *Rizzi* Armido, Sull'Esodo come paradigma teologico-politico: FilT 1,3 (1988) 33-44.

2424 **Sabar** Y., **Ⓞ** The book of Exodus in Neo-Aramaic in the dialect of the Jewish community of Zakho, including selected texts in other Neo-Aramaic dialects and a glossary: Hebrew Traditions 12. J 1988, Magnes. 38+81 p.; Eng. summary. [ZAW 191,326, S. *Segert*].

2425 **Sandberg** Ruth N., The merit of Israel and the redemption from Egypt; a study of a rabbinic debate: diss. Pennsylvania, [D]*Goldin* J. Ph 1988, 279 p. 88-16227. – DissA 49 (1988s) 1482-A.

2426 **Sanderson** Judith E., An Exodus scroll from Qumran ... and the Samaritan tradition [diss. ND 1985, [D]*Ulbrich* E.] 1986 ⮞ 3,1737: [R]CurrTM 15 (1988) 449s (R. *Nelson*); JBL 107 (1988) 303-7 (K. A. *Mathews*: she is editing it with Ulrich for DJD); JSS 33 (1988) 132s (R. *Coggins*); JTS 39 (1988) 183-7 (G. J. *Brooke*).

2427 *Sanderson* Judith E., The contributions of 4QPaleoExod[m] to textual criticism: ⮞ 22, Mém. CARMIGNAC J., RQum 13 (1988) 547-560.

2428 **Sarna** Nahum M., Exploring Exodus 1986 ⮞ 2,1738; 3,2306: [R]Interpretation 42 (1988) 408-410 (W. E. *Rast*); SpLife 33 (1987) 109s (R. *Jordan*).

2429 **Schmidt** W. H., Exodus [I-II, 1977/83 ⮞ 3,2308] III. (5,1–6,30) BK AT 2/4, Neukirchen 1988. vii + p. 241-312. DM 26,80; sb. 19,80. 3-7887-0421-7 [BL 89,61, A. *Mayes*: new author announced for the volume Ex 25-40].

2430 *a) Schwantes* Milton, O êxodo como evento exemplar; – *b) Trein* Hans A., A situação histórica dos hebreus no Egito e no AT; – *c) Anderson* Ana F., *Gorgulho* Gilberto, A mulher na memória do êxodo; – *d) Dreher* Carlos A., As tradições do êxodo e do Sinai; – *e) Gallazzi* Sandro, Êxodo 3 e o profetismo camponés; – *f) Comblin* José, O êxodo na teologia paulina: Estudos Bíblicos 16 ('A memória popular do Êxodo' 1988) 9-18 (31-37) / 19-30 / 38-51 / 52-68 / 69-75 / 76-80.

2431 [E]**Shinan** Avigdor, **Ⓞ** Midrash Shemot Rabbah, chapters 1-XIV, a critical edition based on a Jerusalem manuscript 1984 ⮞ 65,2060; 1,2396: [R]JQR 79 (1988s) 79s (L. S. *Kravitz*).

2432 *Sixdenier* Guy D., Le targum samaritain du Pentateuque; examen comparé de quelques variantes à témoins rares des versions de l'Exode: ⮞ 497, Samarit. 1985/8, 131-7.

2433 **Spreafico** A., Exodo, memoria e promessa [D]1985 ⮞ 1,2397 ... 3,2309: [R]Carthaginensia 4 (1988) 176 (R. *Sanz Valdivieso*); EuntDoc 41 (1988) 155 (S. *Virgulin*).

2434 *Stadelmann* Luis G., La misión del Pueblo de Dios en el Éxodo [< PerspT 17 (1985) 343-368], [TE]*Rocafiguera* José M.: SelT 26 (1987) 95-107.

2435 *Sutton* Dana F., Ezechieliana [Exagōgē]: RheinMus 130 (1987) 34-39.

2436 *Vervenne* Marc, De uittocht uit Egypte; 'verdrijving' en 'vlucht'?: Bijdragen 49 (1988) 402-408; Eng. 409 [Ex 14,5 shows that there is no incompatibility between 'expulsion' and 'flight'].

2437 **Walzer** M., **Ⓞ** Exodus and revolution [1985 ⮞ 1,2401], [T]*Arai* S. Tokyo 1987, Shinkyō S. 234 p. Y 2200 [BL 89,119].

2438 **Wilson** Ian, Exodus, the true story 1985 ⮞ 2,1749; 3,2313: [R]BibTB 18 (1988) 39s (J. I. *Hunt*: Père VINCENT would have been surprised to learn that he was a Jesuit, p. 35).

2439 *a*) *Zenger* Erich, Der Gott des Exodus; – *b*) *Gross* Heinrich, Befreiung in den Psalmen; – *c*) *Hoffmann* Paul, Er ist unsere Freiheit; Aspekte einer konkreten Christologie: BiKi 42 (1987) 98-103 / 104-8 / 109-115.

E3.2   **Moyses**   – Pharaoh, Goshen – *Exodus 1 …*

2440 *Amado Lévy-Valensi* E., *Gross* B., Égypte et les Hébreux d'après la tradition juive: Études philosophiques 42 (1987) 127-138 [< RSPT 72,153].

2441 **Aurelius** Erik, Der Fürbitter Israels [Israel CBQ 51,186]; eine Studie zum Mosebild im AT [Diss. ᴰ*Mettinger* T.: RTLv 20,538]: ConBib OT 27. Sto 1988, Almqvist & W. viii-224 p. Sk 167. 91-22-00940-X. – ᴿNorTTs 89 (1988) 281s (A. S. *Kapelrud*).

2442 **Balout** L., *Roubet* R., La momie de Ramsès II [analyzed at Musée de l'Homme] 1985 ➤ 1,d275; F 379: ᴿBO 45 (1988) 134 (T. *Falke*). ➤ h214.

2443 *Pääbo* Svante, The mummy of Ramses II reconsidered [ᴱ*Balout* L., *Roubet* R. 1985]: OLZ 83 (1988) 389-394: severe.

2444 **Bock** Emil, Moses; from the mysteries of Egypt to the Judges of Israel. Edinburgh 1986, Floris. 224 p.; ill. [KirSef 61,389].

2445 *Casperson* Lee W., The lunar date of Ramesses II [accession likeliest 1279; next 1304]: JNES 47 (1988) 181-4.

2446 *Cazelles* Henri, Par ʿoh: ➤ 815, TWAT 6,6 (1988) 760-3.

2447 **Chan Tak-Kwong** Joseph, La vocation de Moïse (Ex 3 et 4); recherche sur la rédaction dite deutéronomique du Tétrateuque: diss. ᴰ*Bogaert* P. LvN 1988. 221 p. – RTLv 19,409 (résumé).

2448 **Coats** George W., Moses, heroic man, man of God: JStOT Sup 57. Sheffield 1988, JStOT. 250 p. $35. 1-85075-096-3; pa. 5-5. – ᴿETL 64 (1988) 457-9 (J. *Lust*); ÉTRel 63 (1988) 598s (D. *Lys*); VT 38 (1988) 506 (J. A. *Emerton*).

2449 *Coats* George W., Healing and the Moses traditions: ➤ 25, ᶠCHILDS B., Canon 1988, 131-146.

2450 *Daneri Rodrigo* Alicia, An enigmatic [Ramesses II] inscription at Aksha: JSStEg 15 (1985) 68-71.

2451 *Donohue* V. A., The vizier Paser [of Ramesses II; his titles refer to Ramesses-cult]: JEA 74 (1988) 103-123; pl. XVIII.

2452 *Harari* I., À propos d'une clause essentielle du traité entre Ramsès II et Hattušili: DiscEg 10 (1988) 89-94.

2453 **Freud** Sigmund, L'homme Moïse et la religion monothéiste, trois essais, ᵀ*Heim* Cornelius, préf. *Moscovici* Marie: Connaissance de l'inconscient/ Œuvres de Freud, traductions nouvelles. P 1986, Gallimard. 256 p. [Kir-Sef 61,394].

2454 *Frizzell* Lawrence E., Commitment in the Hebrew Bible; Moses, Elijah and Jeremiah: JDharma 12 (1987) 218-227.

2455 *a*) *Fuerst* Wesley J., Moses as intercessor; – *b*) *Perelmuter* Hayim G., When sacrifice became prayer: ➤ 141, ᶠSTUHLMUELLER C. Scripture and prayer 1988, 5-19 / 88-103.

2456 *Girón* Luis F., La crónica de Moisés [Nuestro maestro: sui generis midraš (menor), introducción/traducción]: Sefarad 48 (1988) 390-4 / 395-425.

2457 *Glassner* Jean-Jacques, Le récit autobiographique de Sargon [… exposé sur l'eau et adopté; *Lewis* B. 1980]: RAss 82 (1988) 1-11.

2458 **Kitchen** K. A., Pharaoh triumphant … Ramesses II, 1982 ➤ 64,2377 … 2,1754: ᴿAmHR 91 (1986) 1167s (R. J. *Leprohon*).

2459 *Marshall* Robert C., Moses, Oedipus, structuralism, and history: Hist-Rel 28 (1988s) 245-266.
2460 **Martini** Carlo M., Through Moses to Jesus; the way of the paschal mystery. ND 1988, Ave Maria. 123 p. $5 [BToday 26,380].
2461 *Newing* Edward G., The Moses-Yahweh dialogues and the Confucian loyal adviser: AsiaJT 2 (1988) 413-425.
2462 **Way** Thomas von der, Die Textüberlieferung Ramses' II zur Qades-Schlacht 1984→ 65,9677: ᴿJEA 74 (1988) 279-281 (K. A. *Kitchen*).
2463 **Wildavsky** A., The nursing father; Moses as a political leader 1984 → 65,2086 ... 2,1765: ᴿBL (1988) 117s (L. L. *Grabbe*: more homiletic than hermeneutic).

─────────

2464 *Holladay* John S.ᴶ, [Ex 1,11] A biblical/archaeological whodunit [Maskhuta was Pithom, but was uninhabited at the time the Bible says it was rebuilt]: BCanadMed 8,2 (1988) 6-8.
2465 *Pierce* R. W., Rameses [Gn 47,11], Raamses (Ex 1,11): → 801, ISBEnc³ 4 (1988) 39. [41-44, Ramses II & III, W. S. *LaSor*].
2466 *Kalimi* Isaac [Ex 2,15; Nm 19,29...] Three assumptions about the Kenites [contradicted rather than confirmed in the Bible]: ZAW 100 (1988) 386-392.
2467 *Sekine* Masao, [Ex 3,1s] Wort, Name und Geist im AT – in bezug auf die Frühzeit Israels dargestellt: AnJapB 14 (1988) 3-9.

E3.3 **Nomen divinum, Tetragrammaton;** *Exodus 3,14...*

2468 *Buchanan* George W., [Some unfinished business with the Dead Sea Scrolls, (1) The destruction of Qumran; (2)] The pronunciation of the tetragrammaton [Yahowah or Yahuwah, not Yahweh or Jahveh]: → 22, Mém. CARMIGNAC J., RQum. 13 (1988) (411-) 413-420.
2469 *Faraone* Christopher A., *Kotansky* Roy, An inscribed gold phylactery in Stamford CT: ZPapEp 75 (1988) 257-266; pl. IXa [*iao* and other vowel-sequences; Barûch apparently as name of a separate god; arbarbaphraraphrax rathrathax...; 4th Cent. C.E.].
2470 **Fischer** Georg, Jahwe unser Gott; Sprache, Aufbau und Erzähltechnik in der Berufung des Mose (Ex 3-4) [Diss. 1987s → 3,2340; Exzerpt]. Innsbruck 1988. xvii-33 p.
Gimaret Daniel, Les noms divins en Islam 1988 → b997.
2471 *Grözinger* Karl E., The names of God and the celestial powers; their function and meaning in the Hekhalot literature: → 479, Mysticism 1984/7, 53-69.
2472 **Kohata** Fujiko, Jahwist and Priesterschrift in Exodus 3-14: BZAW 166, 1986 → 2,1776; 3,2343: ᴿBO 45 (1988) 171-4 (M. J. *Mulder*); RTPhil 120 (1988) 369 (T. *Römer*); ZDMG 138 (1988) 182 (H. W. *Hoffmann*).
2473 *Levine* Etan, El simbolismo exegético de la zarza ardiente: Helmantica 37 (1986) 355-384.
3474 ᴱ**Libera** Alain de, *Zum Brunn* Émilie, Celui qui est; interprétations juives et chrétiennes d'Exode 3,14 [second cycle d'études]: Patrimoines, 1986 → 2,1778; 3,2344: ᴿGregorianum 69 (1988) 388s (P. *Gilbert*); RÉJ 147 (1988) 453-5 (J.-P. *Rothschild*).
2475 *Lohfink* Norbert, Die priesterschriftliche Abwertung der Tradition von der Offenbarung des Jahwenamens an Mose [< Biblica 49 (1968) 1-8]: → 223, Studien 1988, 71-78.

2476 **Mettinger** Tryggve N. D., The dethronement of Sabaoth: ConBibOT 18, 1982 ➤ 63,2427 ... 2,1780: ᴿJNES 47 (1988) 58-60 (J. *Day*).

2477 **Mettinger** Tryggve N. D., [➤ 1128] In search of God; the meaning and message of the everlasting names, ᵀ*Cryer* F. H. Ph 1988, Fortress. xiv-251 p.; ill. 0-8006-0892-5 [OIAc D88].

2478 **Norin** Stig I. L., Sein Name allein ist hoch 1986 ➤ 2,1783; 3,2347: ᴿJBL 107 (1988) 122s (E. D. *Mallon*).

2479 *Osborn* Noel, *a*) [Ex 3,14s] This is my name forever; 'I am' or 'Yahweh'?: BTrans 39 (1988) 410-5; – *b*) Circumspection about circumcision in Exodus 4,24-26; ➤ 502, Issues/Translation 1987/8, 247-264.

2480 *Neufeld* Ernest, [Ex 7s plagues] Residual magic in the Bible: Dor 17 (1988s) 255-9 + 229.

2481 *Rendsburg* Gary A., [Ex 10,10 ...] Bilingual wordplay in the Bible: VT 38 (1988) 354-7.

E3.4 *Pascha, sanguis, sacrificium:* **Passover, blood, sacrifice,** *Ex 11 ...*

2482 *Otto* Eckart, [Ex 12,13 ...] Zur Semantik von hebr. *psḥ/pisseᵃḥ* und akk. *pessû(m)/pessātu(m)*: BibNot 41 (1988) 31-35.

2483 *Delcor* Mathias, [Ex 12,46; 12,10G] L'interdiction de briser les os de la victime pascale d'après la tradition juive: ➤ 704, L'animal 1981/5, 71-81.

2484 *Görg* Manfred, Pæsaḥ (Pascha), Fest des 'schlagenden' Gottes?: Bib-Not 43 (1988) 7-11.

2485 *Otto* E., *Pesaḥ*: ➤ 815, TWAT 6,6s (1988) 659-682 [683-7, *pisseaḥ, Clements* R. E.].

2486 *Potocki* Stanisław, ❷ De mysterio paschatis Veteris Testamenti: RuBi 41 (1988) 274-286.

2487 *Hubbard* R. L.ᴶ, Red Sea: ➤ 801, ISBEnc³ 4 (1988) 58-61.

2488 *Kohata* Fujiko, [Ex 13,17-14,31] Die Endredaktion (ᴿᴾ) der Meerwundererzählung: AnJapB 14 (1988) 10-37.

2489 *Shear-Yashuv* Aharon, Exegese von Exodus 14; eine kritische Untersuchung der Auszugstradition auf dem Hintergrund ägyptischer Nachrichten [1984]: ➤ 262, Religion (1987) 252-271.

2490 **Ska** J.-L., Le passage de la mer, Ex 14,1-31: AnBib 109, ᴰ1986 ➤ 2,1803*; 3,2362: ᴿBL (1988) 91 (E. W. *Nicholson*: stimulating and rewarding); Carthaginensia 4 (1988) 381 (J. F. *Cuenca Molina*); CBQ 50 (1988) 123s (W. *Vogels*: studies the scenes synchronically, but themes and symbols diachronically; is this a surrender?); JBL 107 (1988) 509s (S. M. *Olyan*: concerned about vowel-transcriptions); LavalTP 44 (1988) 258s (M. *Girard*); Salesianum 50 (1988) 434s (R. *Vicent*); TPhil 63 (1988) 586s (H.-W. *Jüngling*).

2491 **Burns** Rita J., [... Ex 14,21] Has the Lord indeed spoken only through Moses? ... Miriam [ᴰ1980] 1987 ➤ 3,2367: ᴿJSS 33 (1988) 271s (R. E. *Clements*; model of clarity); VT 38 (1988) 497 (G. I. *Davies*).

2492 *Steinmetz* D., A portrait of Miriam in rabbinic midrash: Prooftexts 8,1 (1988) 35-65 [NTAbs 32,223].

2493 **Bertalot** Valdo, Le chant de la mer (Exode 15,1-18); une analyse 'textuelle': diss. prot. ᴰ*Heintz* J. Strasbourg 1987. – RTLv 19,532.

2494 **Turgman** Victor, De l'autorité de Moïse, Ex 15,22-27, 1987 ➤ 3,2370: ᴿTR 84 (1988) 106s (N. *Lohfink*).

2495 *Lohfink* Norbert, *a*) 'Ich bin Jahwe, dein Arzt' (Ex 15,26); Gott, Gesellschaft und menschliche Gesundheit in einer nachexilischen Pentateuchbearbeitung (Ex 15,25b.26) [< 'Ich will euer Gott werden', SBS 100 (1981) 11-73]; – *b*) De Moysis epinicio (Ex. 15,1-18 [< Verbum Domini 41 (1963) 277-289]: ➤ 223, Studien 1988, 91-155 / 79-89.

2496 *Beit-Arieh* Itzhaq, The route through Sinai; why the Israelites fleeing Egypt went south: BAR-W 14,3 (1988) 28-35; ill.

2497 *Marangon* Antonio, [Ex 17,7] Massa e Meriba; il tempo del deserto: RClerIt 69 (1988) 355-361.

2498 *Lee* Hindishe, [Ex 17,14s] In the shadow of Amalek: Dor 17 (1988s) 44-49.

2499 *Avishur* Y., Treaty terminology in the Moses-Jethro story (Exodus 18:1-12): AulaOr 6 (1988) 139-147.

2500 *Robinson* Bernard P., Acknowledging one'e dependence; the Jethro story of Exodus 18: NBlackf 69 (1988) 139-142.

2501 *Abe* Gabriel O., [Ex 19s] The religious value of the Sinai covenant: AfJB 2 (1987) 97-105.

2502 **Anati** Emmanuel, La montagne de Dieu Har Karkom; recherches archéologiques sur la route de l'Exode: Bibliothèque historique 1986 ➤ 3,2385*b*. – ᴿRTLv 19 (1988) 87 (P.-M. *Bogaert*).

2503 *Finkelstein* Israel, Raider of the lost mountain [*Anati* E., Mountain of God 1986]: BAR-W 14,4 (1988) 46-51: no.

2504 *Faiman* David, Where was the mountain of God?: Dor 17 (1988s) 211-219 + 2 fig. (map): Giddi Pass 70 k ENE of Suez.

2505 *Harrison* R. K., *Hoffmeier* J. K., Sinai: ➤ 801, ISBEnc³ 4 (1988) 525-8.

2506 *Weimar* Peter, Sinai und Schöpfung; Komposition und Theologie der priesterschriftlichen Sinaigeschichte [Ex 19,1 + 24,15s + 39,43 + 40,17.34]: RB 95 (1988) 337-385; Eng. 387s.

2507 **Maiberger** P., Topographische und historische Untersuchungen zum Sinaiproblem: OBO 54, 1984 ➤ 65,2128 ... 2,1814: ᴿBO 45 (1988) 697s (C. H. J. de *Geus*); OLZ 83 (1988) 571-3 (J. *Conrad*).

2508 *Van Seters* John, 'Comparing Scripture with Scripture'; some observations on the Sinai pericope of Exodus 19-24: ➤ 25, ᶠCHILDS B., Canon 1988, 111-130.

2509 **Ellis** Robert R., An examination of the covenant promises of Exodus 19:5-6 and their theological significance for Israel: diss. SW Baptist Theol. Sem. 1988, – RelStR 15,192.

E3.5 **Decalogus,** *Ex 20* = *Dt 5; Ex 21ss;* **Ancient Near East Law.**

2510 **Carmichael** Calum, Law and narrative in the Bible 1985 ➤ 1,2482; 3,2387: ᴿClasW 80 (1987s) 55 (M. *Gagarin* gives the author's first name as Calvin, and says the book is interesting but unconvincing).

2511 ᴱ**Cennamo** M., *Vaudo* F., Díez cardenales explican los diez mandamientos [1984 ➤ 1,2483],ᵀ. Barc 1986, Noguer. 256 p. 84-279-3891-8. – ᴿEstE 63 (1988) 509s (G. *Higuera*); Téléma 13,3 (1987) 97s (C. *Delhez*).

2512 **Cicchese** M., Le dieci parole. R 1987, GBU. 127 p. – ᴿSTEv 11,21 (1988) 156s (R. *Coletto*).

2513 **Hennig** Kurt, Das Grundgesetz Gottes, eine Auslegung der Zehn Gebote²ʳᵉᵛ. Stu 1982, Quell. 296 p. – ᴿSalesianum 50 (1988) 227s (G. *Abbà*: pastorale non accademico).

2514 *Johnstone* William, The Decalogue and the redaction of the Sinai pericope in Exodus: ZAW 100 (1988) 361-385.

2515 *Larrabe* José Luis, Los diez mandamientos (sentido y actualidad) (I): TEsp 31 (1987) 381-409; (II) 32 (1988) 107-129.

2516 **Lochman** Jan M., I comandamenti, segnali stradali verso la libertà [1979 (français 1981)], T*Benna* Luigi, 1986 ➤ 3,2396: RDivinitas 32 (1988) 631s (D. *Composta*); StMoralia 26 (1988) 309-311 (J. *Desclos*).

2517 E**Maren** J.W. van, MARQUARD von Lindau, Das Buch der Zehn Gebote (Venedig 1483): QForsch zur Erbauungsliteratur 7, 1984 ➤ 1,2489: ROnsGErf 62 (1988) 368s (J. *Andriessen*).

2518 **Meesters** Carlos, Los diez mandamientos: T*Castelli* César La buena noticia 6. Florida ARG 1988, Paulinas. 79 p.; cartoons.

2519 *Mikolašek* Adrian, La numérotation du Décalogue à la lumière de la tradition de l'Israël de la Loi: ➤ 497, Samarit. 1985/8, 85-93.

2520 **Rosales** Antonio M., A study of a 16th century Tagalog manuscript on the ten commandments... J. de OLIVER 1984 ➤ 1,2495: RCathHR 73 (1987) 134 (J. N. *Schumacher*).

2521 **Schreiner** J., Die Zehn Gebote im Leben des Gottesvolkes[2] [Dt form prior and normative; [1]1966]. Mü 1988, Kösel. 152 p. DM 29,80. 3-466-20297-3 [BL 89,93, A. G. *Auld*].

2522 *Tomić* Celestin, Deset zapovijedi-dekalog: ObnŽiv 43 (1988) 197-212 [48s, 279s, *Fuček* Ivan].

2523 *Tong Fung-Wan*, Ⓖ The ten commandments, model of Christian ethics according to Exodus 20,1-17: Taiwan Journal of Theology 9 (1987) 5-29 [< TKontext 10,39].

2524 *Wright* C. J. H., Ten Commandments: ➤ 801, ISBEnc[3] 4 (1988) 786-790.

Hamilton Gordon J., The first commandment; a theological reflection ➤ 2709.

2526 *Harvey* Warren Z., Ⓞ The first commandment and the God of history; HALEVY and Crescas vs. IBN EZRA and MAIMONIDES: Tarbiz 57 (1987s) 203-216; Eng. IIs.

2527 **Dohmen** C., Das Bilderverbot: BoBB 62, 1985 ➤ 1,1829; 3,2399: RTrierTZ 97 (1988) 159s (E. *Haag*).

2528 E**Dohmen** C., *Sternberg* T., ... Kein Bildnis machen 1987 ➤ 3,395: RTrierTZ 97 (1988) 78s (E. *Sauser*).

2529 *Dohmen* C., Hat das 2, Konzil von Nikaia 787 das Bilderverbot ausser Kraft gesetzt? [both the iconoclasts and their opponents could claim a certain line of development of OT traditions]: Zeitschrift für ostkirchliche Kunst, Hermeneia 3 (1987) 200-7 [< ZAW 100,305].

2530 **Grizzard** Carol S., The aniconic theology of the OT: diss. Southern Baptist Theol. Sem. DTate M. 1988. 320[9?]p. 89-01497. – DissA 49 (1988s) 3061s-A.

2531 *Hendel* Ronald S., a) Images of God in ancient Israel [lecture summary]: BAngIsr 8 (1988s) 81s; – b) The social origins of the aniconic tradition in early Israel: CBQ 50 (1988) 365-382.

2532 **Schroer** Silvia, In Israel gab es Bilder ...: OBO 74, 1987 ➤ 3,2404: RBL (1988) 89s (R. *Murray*; serene but a bit feminist); ExpTim 99 (1987s) 330s (R. J. *Coggins*); JBL 107 (1988) 747s (W. *Roth*); OTAbs 11 (1988) 195 (also W. *Roth*); TR 84 (1988) 103-6 (C. *Dohmen*).

2533 a) *Tsevat* Matitiahu, The prohibition of divine images according to the Old Testament; – b) *Jackson* Bernard S., Some literary features of the Mishpatim: ➤ 469, Wünschet 1986/8, 211-220 / 235-242.

2534 *Harman* Allan M., [Ex 20,7; Dt 5,11, name of God in vain] The interpretation of the Third Commandment: RefTR 47 (1988) 1-7.

2535 *Meinhold* Arndt, [Ex 20,7 nomen in vanum] Jüdische Stimmen zum Dritten Gebot: KIsr 2 (1987) 159-168.
2536 **Matysiak** Bogdan, [Ex 20,8] ❾ Przykazanie spoczynku sobotniego ... The commandment of sabbath rest in the light of the deuteronomic tradition: diss. ᴰ*Stachowiak* L. Lublin 1988. 147 p. – RTLv 20,540 [deuteronomicznej, 'Deuteronomistic'].
2537 *Reines* A., Two concepts of Shabbat and the seventh-day Shabbat: JRefJud 34,4 (1987) 13-28 [< Judaica 44,126].
2538 **Robinson** Gnana, The origin and development of the Old Testament sabbath; a comprehensive exegetical approach [< ev. Diss. Hamburg 1975, ᴰ*Koch* K.]: BeitBExT 21. Fra 1988, Lang. 442 p. Fs 75 [ZAW 101,32s, H.-C. *Schmitt*]. 3-8204-1373-1.
2539 *Scott* Marshall S., [Ex 20,12] Honor thy father and mother; Scriptural resources for victims of incest and parental abuse: JPastCare 42 (1988) 139-149 [< ZIT 88,634].
2540 **Gnuse** Robert, [Ex 20,15] You shall not steal 1985 ⇸ 1,7862 ... 3,2414: ᴿCBQ 50 (1988) 284-6 (A. J. *Petrotta*).
2541 **Gnuse** Robert, Comunidad y propiedad en la tradición bíblica [You shall not steal], ᵀ*Ruiz Garrido* Constantino: Buena noticia 16, 1987 ⇸ 3,2414c: ᴿActuBbg 25 (1988) 210 (R. de *Sivatte*).

2542 *Crüsemann* Frank, [Ex 21-23] Das Bundesbuch — historischer Ort und institutioneller Hintergrund: ⇸ 482, VTS 40, Jerusalem congress 1986/8, 27-41.
2543 **Otto** E., Wandel der Rechtsbegründungen in der Gesellschaftsgeschichte des Antiken Israel; eine Rechtsgeschichte des 'Bundesbuches' Ex XX 22 – XXIII 13: Studia Biblica 3. Brill 1988, Leiden. viii-107 p. ƒ40. 90-04-08346-4 [BL 89,112, A. D. H. *Mayes*].
2544 **Alonso Fontela** Carlos, [Ex 21,1-11] La esclavitud a través de la Biblia: Bibliotheca Hispana Biblica 9, 1986 ⇸ 3,2423: ᴿBAsEspOr 24 (1988) 493s (G. *Carrasco Serrano*).
2545 **Cardellini** Innocenzo, Die biblischen 'Sklaven-'Gesetze...: BoBB 55, 1981 ⇸ 62,2663 ... 2,1858: ᴿBO 45 (1988) 640-5 (C. *Zaccagnini*).
2546 *a) Dreher* Carlos A., Escravos no Antigo Testamento; – *b) Dobberahn* Friedrich E., O destino do escravo José — observações sobre a escravidão no Antigo Egipto; – *c) Tavares Zabatiero* Julio P., Servos do império — uma análise da servidão no Déutero-Isaías; – *d) Konzen* Leo Z., *Walker* Décio J., 'Noventa cabeças por um talento...' — sobre a escravidão no tempo dos Macabeus; – *e) Wegner* Uwe, Os evangelhos, Jesus, os escravos: EstudosB 18 (1988) 9-25 / 26-36 / 37-43 / 45-52 / 53-72.
2547 *Schenker* Adrian, Affranchissement d'une esclave selon Ex 21,7-11 [*Ognibene* B. 1988: lo'/lō]: Biblica 69 (1988) 547-556.
2548 *a) Stol* M., [Ex 21,22] Oog om oog, tand om tand; een barbaarse wet?; – *b) Deurloo* K. A., Recht in Israël: PhoenixEOL 33,2 (1987) 38-44 / 44-50.
2549 *Ahuviya* Abraham, ❾ [Ex 22,28] Mᵉla'ᵃtkâ...: BethM 34,116 (1988s) 24-26.
2550 *Fensham* F. C., Liability of animals in biblical and Ancient Near East law: JNWS 14 (1988) 85-90.

2551 **Barbiero** Gianni, L'asino del nemico; non violenza e amore del nemico nella legislazione dell'Antico Testamento (Ex 23,4-5; Dt 22,1-4; Lv 19,18): diss. ᴰ*Lohfink* N. Fra 1987s. – RTLv 20,539; TR 84 (1988) 511 [*anche* Fra St. Georgen col prenome Gianguerrino].

2552 *Knauf* Ernst A., [Ex 23,19 ...] Zur Herkunft und Sozialgeschichte Israels; 'das Böckchen in der Milch seiner Mutter': Biblica 69 (1988) 153-168; franç. 169.

2553 *Bascom* Robert A., [Ex 23,20; Mal 3,1.23; Mk 1,2s; Jn 14,2] Preparing the way; midrash in the Bible: → 502, Issues/Translation 1987/8, 221-246.

2554 *Álvarez Londoño* L.F., La legislación civil en el Antiguo Testamento: Universitas 74 (Bogotá 1988) 209-220 [< Stromata 44,564].

2555 *Belzer* J., Apodiktik/apodiktisch: → 804, NBL Lfg 1 (1988) 122-4.

2556 *Cohen* Shaye J., From the Bible to the Talmud; the prohibition of intermarriage: HebAnR 7 (1983) 23-29.

2557 **Cohn** Haim H., Human rights in Jewish Law 1984 → 65,2161; 1,2515: ᴿHeythJ 29 (1988) 365-7 (P. *Sieghart*).

2558 *Crüsemann* F., Recht und Theologie im AT: ᴱ**Schlaich** K., Studien zu Kirchenrecht und Theologie I [Texte und Materialien A 26 (Heid 1987) Ev. Studiengemeinschaft] 11-81 [ZAW 100,326].

2559 **Epsztein** Léon, Social justice 1986 → 2,1860; 3,3441: ᴿJTS 39 (1988) 139-141 (A. *Chester*: limitations in comparison with the splendid work of SICRE); OLZ 83 (1988) 173s (G. *Pfeifer*); PrzOr (1988,2) 181-3 (W. *Tyloch*).

2560 *Gladson* Jerry A., Grace in the Old Testament law codes: BToday 26 (1988) 366-371.

2561 *Hookerman* Jacob, ❶ The law of life (*nepeš*) in biblical tradition, 11: BethM 34,116 (1988s) 27-38.

2562 *a*) *Nobile* Marco, I codici legislativi dell'AT; – *b*) *Boschi* Bernardo G.L., Esperienza di salvezza e legge; – *c*) *Odasso* Giovanni, La Torah; significato e valore; – *d*) *Cimosa* Mario, Il salmo [119] della Legge; – *e*) *Ghidelli* Carlo, La legge di Cristo: ParVi 33,3 ('La Legge' 1988) 182-9 / 167-170 / 171-181 / 190-6 / 197-302.

2563 *Otto* E., Interdependenzen zwischen Geschichte und Rechtsgeschichte des antiken Israels: Rechtshistorisches Journal 7 (1988) 347-368 [< ZAW 101,303].

2564 **Patrick** Dale, OT law 1985 → 1,2523 ... 3,2433: ᴿBA 51 (1988) 59s (R. *Westbrook*: uneven style); Themelios 14 (1988s) 28 (D.G. *Deboys*); Vidyajyoti 52 (1988) 301s (P.M. *Meagher*).

2565 *Pons* Jacques, La référence au séjour en Égypte et à la sortie d'Égypte dans les codes de loi de l'AT: ÉTRel 63 (1988) 169-182.

2566 *Schwager* Raymund, Rache – Gerechtigkeit – Religion; Überlegungen zu einer interdisziplinären Forschungsarbeit: ZkT 110 (1988) 284-299.

2567 *a*) *Valacca-Pagella* V., Dio e gli stranieri; – *b*) *Artm* [sic ZAW 100,310 ? Artzi] E., Gli oppressi nella Bibbia; – *c*) *Bianchi* E., Poveri nella società regia biblica; i contadini: → 485, Debole nella Bibbia 1987, 45-74 / 75-89 / 91-122.

2568 **Westbrook** Raymond, Studies in biblical and cuneiform law [i. abuse of power; ii. revenge, ransom, talio; iii. slaves; iv. theft]: CahRB 26. P 1988, Gabalda. ix-150p. F 160 [CBQ 51,191]. 2-85021-034-X. – ᴿPhoenEOL 34,2 (1988) 61 (M. *Steiner*).

2569 *Würthwein* Ernst, AT [*Hübner* Hans, NT], Gesetz: ➤ 798, EvKL 2 (1988) [135-8] 138-143 [-154, al.].
2570 *Zemel* D., From code to guide; from theology to sociology [< Judaica 44,126]: JRefJud 35,1 (1988) 43-48.
2571 *Ziskind* Jonathan R., Legal rules on incest in the Ancient Near East: RIDA 35 (1988) 79-109.

———

2572 *Artzi* Pinhas, In search of just retribution in law; new data from Ancient Near Eastern sources: ➤ 130, Mem. SCHEIBER A. 1988, 13-20.
2573 *Bonneau* Danielle, Aspect juridique de l'asylie en Égypte d'après la documentation grecque: DiscEg 10 (1988) 77-86; map p. 87.
2574 **Dandamaev** Muhammad A., Slavery in Babylonia ... 626-331 B.C., ᵀ*Powell* Victoria A. 1984 ➤ 65,9687 ... 3,2439: ᴿJNES 47 (1988) 307s (Martha T. *Roth*); ZAss 78 (1988) 305-9 (J. *Oelsner*).
2575 *Grandet* Pierre, L'Égypte, comme institution, à l'époque ramesside: DiscEg 8 (1987) 77-92 [93-101, *Harari* Ibram. Les decrets royaux, source de droit].
2576 **Haase** Richard, Texte zum hethitischen Recht 1984 ➤ 65,2194 ... 2,1861: ᴿAfO 34 (1987) 75s (M. *Marazzi*).
2577 *Haase* Richard, Some problems of Hittite law and jurisdiction: ➤ 742, Society 1985/8, 69-77.
2578 *Harari* I, La publicité des dispositions législatives dans le Temple: DiscEg 11 (1988) 103-9.
2579 *a)* *Harari* Ibram, Les dispositions juridiques prises par Séti Ier à Kanais; – *b)* *Valbelle* Dominique, La notion de règlement dans les fondations royales d'époque pharaonique: DiscEg 7 (1987) 87-104 / 81-85.
2580 *Mauer* G., Die 'Gesetze' von Ešnunna — eine Schreiberübung: BibNot 42 (1988) 36-43.
2581 **Klíma** Josef, Zákony Asýrie a Chaldeje; pokračovatelé Chammurapiho (Les lois assyriennes et chaldéennes; les continuateurs de Hammourabi) ➤ 2,1862; Praha 1985, Česk. Akad. 334 p.; 16 pl. Kr 46. – ᴿOrLovPer 18 (1987) 239 (P. *Naster*); SborBrno 31 (1986) 197s (J. *Češka*).
2582 **Malul** Meir, Studies in Mesopotamian legal symbolism: AOAT 221. Neuk/Kevelaer 1988, Neuk-V./Butzon & B. xiii-512 p, 3-7887-1299-6 / Kev 3-7666-9418-9.
2583 *Menu* Bernadette, Quelles sources pour le droit égyptien ancien? [introduction a la Table Ronde, Sorbonne 7.XII.1985]: DiscEg 4 (1986) 77s.
2584 *Mirzojev* M. N., ⊕ L'esclavage en Babylonie kassite: VDI 187 (1988) 109-131; franç. 131.
2585 *a)* *Naster* Paul, Ambacht en ambachtslui in het Mesopotamisch Recht; – *b)* *Lerberghe* Karl Van, De slaven en hun werk in de Oud-Babylonische periode; – *c)* *Limet* Henri, La notion de travail chez les Sumeriens; – *d)* *Talon* Philippe, Le travail du métal à Mari: ➤ 50, ꟳFONTINOY C., Humour, travail 1988, 143-6; franç. 146 / 139-141 / 123-5 / 127s.
2586 *Otto* E., Depositrecht; ZSav-R 105 (1988) 1-31 [ZAW 101,146].
2587 *Roth* Martha T., 'She will die by the iron dagger'; adultery and Neo-Babylonian marriage: JESHO 31 (1988) 186-206.
2588 **Schild** Wolfgang, Alte Gerichtsbarkeit; vom Gottesurteil bis zum Beginn der modernen Rechtsprechung. Mü 1985, Callwey. 256 p.; ill. 3-7667-0782-5.

2589 **Sick** U.,   Die Tötung eines Menschen und ihre Ahndung in den keilschriftlichen Rechtssammlungen...: Diss. Tü 1984 ➤ 65,2207 ... 2,1869: ᴿIvra 35 (1984) 161-7 (G. *Gardascia*).

2590 *a) Veenhof* K. R., Rechtspraak bij de Oude Assyriërs; – *b) Houwing ten Cate* Philo H. J., De Hettitische wettenverzameling; – *c) Van den Boorn* G. P. F., De vizier en de rechtspraak in Egypte rond 1500 v. C.; – *d) McDowell* A., Een schijnproces in het Egyptische strafrecht?: PhoenixEOL 33,2 (1987) 23-37 / 50-59 / 10-17 / 17-22.

2591 **Wesel** Uwe,   Frühformen des Rechts in vorstaatlichen Gesellschaften; Umrisse einer Frühgeschichte des Rechts bei Sammlern und Jägern und akephalen Ackerbauern und Hirten. Fra 1985, Suhrkamp. 388 p. 3-518-57706-9; pa. 23-9.

2592 **Westbrook** Raymond,   Old Babylonian marriage law: AfO Beih 23. Horn 1988, Berger. 148 p.

2593 **Wright** D. P.,   The disposal of impurity; elimination rites in the Bible and in Hittite and Mesopotamian literature [Berkeley ᴰ1984] 1987 ➤ 3,2456; 1-55540-056-6; pa. 7-4: ᴿAustralBR 36 (1988) 61s (A. E. *Gardner*); BL (1988) 118s (J. F. *Healey*); VT 38 (1988) 255s (G. I. *Davies*).

E3.6 **Cultus,** *Exodus 25-40*.

2594 *Dall* M. A.,   The Temple; symbolic form in Scripture [mystical 'speakings' in Ex demystified in Rev]: Soundings 70,1s (1987) 145-154 [NTAbs 32,196].

2595 *Ellul* Jacques,   Dîmes et prémices: Tychique 70 (1987) 7-9.

2596 *Görg* Manfred, *a)* Aaron; – *b)* Altar: ➤ 804, NBL Lfg. 1 (1988) 1s/ 81s.

2597 *Haran* Menahem,   Priesthood, temple, divine service; some observations on institutions and practices of worship: HebAnR 7 (1983) 121-135.

2598 **Holder** Arthur G.,   Bᴇᴅᴇ's commentaries on the Tabernacle and the Temple: diss. Duke, ᴰ*Gregg* R. Durham NC 1987. 207 p. 88-10875. – DissA 49 (1988s) 846-A.

2599 *Monloubou* Louis,   Recherche sur la signification du culte selon l'Ancien Testament: EsprVie 98 (1988) 586-590.

2600 **Nielsen** Kjeld,   Incense in ancient Israel: VTSup 38, 1986 ➤ 2,1874; 3,2470: ᴿBL (1988) 112 (A. R. *Millard*: not definitive; overlooks CAD); TLZ 113 (1988) 339s (E.-J. *Waschke*).

2601 *Ravasi* Gianfranco,   Una comunità santa, sacerdotale, pura; la comunità 'ecclesiale' secondo la tradizione sacerdotale: RivB 36 (1988) 1-27; Eng. 27.

2602 **Revel-Neher** Elisabeth,   Le signe de la rencontre; l'Arche d'Alliance dans l'art juif et chrétien du second au dixième siècles [diss. J 1981] 1984 ➤ 1,2552 ... 3,2464. – ᴿJudaica 44 (1988) 247s (M. *Petit*).

2603 *Schultheis* Herbert,   Die Menora: ➤ 129, ꟳSᴄHᴇᴇʟᴇ P. = WüDiöz-Blätter 50 (1988) 781 ... [< ᴢɪᴛ 88,551].

2604 **Utzschneider** Helmut,   Das Heiligtum und das Gesetz; Studien zur Bedeutung der sinaitischen Heiligtumstexte Ex 25-40; Lev 8-9 [Hab.-Schr. Mü]: OBO 77. FrS/Gö 1988, Univ./VR. vi-320 p. DM 124 [TR 84,249]. 3-7228-0558-7; VR 3-525-53706-9.

2605 *Westerholm* S.,   Tabernacle: ➤ 801, ISBEnc³ 4 (1988) 698-706.

2606 **Zwickel** Wolfgang,   Räucherkult und Räuchergeräte; Studien zum Räucheropfer im Alten Testament und in seiner Umwelt: Diss. ᴰ*Donner* H. Kiel 1988. – RTLv 20,542.

2607 *Wilcox* Max, 'According to the pattern (*tbnyt*)...'; Exodus 25,40 in the New Testament and early Jewish thought: → 22, Mém. CARMIGNAC J., RQum 13 (1988) 647-657.

2608 *Goetschel* Roland, [Ex 32] La faute du Veau d'Or dans l'interprétation kabbalistique de la Bible: RHR 205 (1988) 267-286; Eng. 267.

2609 *Propp* William H., [Ex 34,29-35] Did Moses have horns? [no; *qāran* means '(his skin) was tough' and thus he could look on God unharmed]: BR 4,1 (1988) 30-37 . 44.

2610 *Gane* R., *al.*, [Ex 35,12 + 25-mal] Parokæt 'Vorhang': → 814, TWAT 6,6 (1988) 755-7.

E3.7 Leviticus.

2611 ᵀᴱ**Danieli** Maria Ignazia, ORIGENE, Omelie sul Levitico: Testi patristici 51, 1985 → 2,1879: ᴿSalesianum 50 (1988) 240 (S. *Felici*).

2612 **Freedman** D. N., *Mathews* K. A., Paleo-Hebrew Lev 1985 → 1,2873 ... 3,2481: ᴿCBQ 50 (1988) 114-6 (B. E. *Shafer*: high quality; holds for a complex system of paragraphing).

  Grossfeld Bernard, The Targum Onqelos to Leviticus and Numbers 1988 → 1703.

2613 **Harlé** Paul [with help from *Harl* M.], *Pralon* Didier, Le Lévitique ... Septante: La Bible d'Alexandrie 3. P 1988, Cerf. 224 p. F 125. 2-204-02972-6 [BL 89,47].

2614 *Hastoupis* Athanasios, ⊙ The book of Leviticus: TAth 59 (1988) 121-136.

2615 **Kadushin** M. [1895-1980], A conceptual commentary on Midrash Leviticus Rabbah; value concepts in Jewish thought: BrownJudSt 126. Atlanta 1987, Scholars. xiii-252 p. $37. 1-55540-175-9 [NTAbs 32,265].

2616 **Keil** C. F., Leviticus, Numeri und Deuteronomium³ [1870]. Giessen 1987, Brunnen. 610 p. [ZAW 101,157].

2617 *Neusner* Jacob, Appropriation and imitation; the priority of Leviticus Rabbah over Pesiqta deRab KAHANA: PAAR 54 (1987) 141-168 [< NTAbs 32,354]; – *b*) Studying Synoptic texts synoptically; the case of Leviticus Rabbah: PAAR 52 (1985) 111-145 [< JStJud 19 (1988) 291].

2618 *Owens* R. J., APHRAHAT as a witness to the early Syriac text of Leviticus; → 480, Peshiṭta 1985/8, 1-48.

2618* ᵀ**Shachter** Jay F., The commentary of Abraham IBN EZRA on the Pentateuch, 3. Leviticus. Hoboken NJ 1986, KTAV. 191 p. 0-88125-109-7.

2619 **Wevers** J. W., Leviticus: Gö Septuagint 2/2, 1986 → 2,1884*a*: ᴿTAth 54 (1988) 904-7 (P. *Simotas*).

2620 **Wevers** John W., Text history of the Greek Leviticus 1986 → 2,1884*b*; 3,2489: ᴿBijdragen 49 (1988) 331s (Tamis *Wever*); BL (1988) 52 (S. *Brock*); JBL 107 (1988) 510s (R. W. *Klein*); NT 30 (1988) 379s (G. D. *Kilpatrick*); TR 84 (1988) 366s (A. *Schenker*: Titel mag täuschen: Einführung in Lv-LXX).

2622 **Anderson** G. A., [Lv 1s...] Sacrifice 1987 → 3,2476: ᴿVT 38 (1988) 377s (J. A. *Emerton*).

2623 *Carpenter* E. E. [*Schreiner* T. R.] Sacrifices and offerings in the OT [NT]: → 801, ISBEnc³ 4 (1988) 260-273 [-277].

2624 **Kiuchi** N., [Lv 4-8; 10; 16 *ḥaṭṭa't*] The purification offering in the priestly literature; its meaning and function [diss. British Council, [D]*Wenham* G. 1986]: JStOT Sup 56. Sheffield 1987, Academic. 204 p. £25. – [R]Themelios 14 (1988s) 102s (P. *Jenson*).

2625 *Marx* Alfred, [Lv 5,14-16 *āšām*] Sacrifice de réparation et rites de levée de sanction: ZAW 100 (1988) 183-198.

2626 *Leeuwen* J. H. van, The meaning of *tuppîn* in Lev 6,14: ZAW 100 (1988) 268; Eng. 269, the 'folded', not cut, parts of the flat meal-offering.

2627 **Seidl** Theodor, Tora für den 'Aussatz'-Fall ... Lev 13s: AOtt 18, 1982 ➤ 1,2588; 3,2498: [R]JNES 47 (1988) 287 (D. *Pardee*).

2628 *Azuwo Onibere* S. G., Old Testament sacrifice in African tradition; a case of scapegoatism: ➤ 469, Wünschet 1986/8, 193-203.

2629 *Deiana* Giovanni, Azazel in Lv 16: Lateranum 54 (1988) 16-33.

2630 *Guinot* J.-N., [Lv 16] L'exégèse du bouc émissaire chez CYRILLE d'Alexandrie et THÉODORET de Cyr: AugR 28 (1988) 603-630.

2631 **Schwartz** Baruch J. ✪ Selected chapters of the Holiness Code – a literary study of Leviticus 17-19: diss. Hebrew Univ. J 1988. 358 p. 88-15183. – DissA 49 (1988s) 2278-A.

2632 *Levine* Baruch A., [Lv 17s] The language of holiness; perceptions of the sacred in the Hebrew Bible: ➤ 3,356, [E]*O'Connor* M., Backgrounds 1987, 241-255 [< JBL 108,174].

2633 *Zohar* Noam, [Lev 17,11; *Milgrom* J.] Repentance and purification; the significance and semantics of *ḥaṭṭa't* in the Pentateuch: JBL 107 (1988) 609-618.

2634 *Magonet* Jonathan, The structure and meaning of Leviticus 19: HebAnR 7 (1983) 151-167 [< OTAbs 11,262].

2635 *Koch* R., [NTAbs 32,362; on the call to holiness in Lv 19,2; Mt 5,48; Lk 6,36]: ➤ 21, [F]CAPONE D., Coscienza 1987 ...

2636 **Mathys** Hans-Peter, Liebe deinen Nächsten wie dich selbst ... Lev 19,18 [Diss. [D]*Klopfenstein* M.]: OBO 71, 1986 ➤ 2,1895; 3,2507: [R]BO 45 (1988) 173-6 (P. *Höffken*); RivB 36 (1988) 125s (A. *Bonora*: 'deine nächsten'); RTPhil 120 (1988) 371s (G. *Lasserre*); TüTQ 168 (1988) 336s (W. *Gross*).

2636* **Becker** Henri, Qui est mon prochain? (Luc 10,29); 'réà' dans Lévitique 19,18 et son interprétation dans la littérature biblique et dans la pensée juive: diss. prot. [D]*Robert* P. Strasbourg 1987. 260 p. – RTLv 19,532.

2637 *Quitslund* Sonya A., [Lv 19,33; Dt 10,18 ...] The alien among you: BToday 26 (1988) 80-86.

2638 *Alt* Jörg, 'Der Fremde, der sich bei euch aufhält, soll euch wie ein Einheimischer gelten ...' (Lev 19,34): BLtg 61 (1988) 171-4.

2639 *Gottesman* Abraham H., [Lv 23,15] Reflections on Shavuoth: Dor 17 (1988s) 250-254.

2640 *Avishur* Yiṣḥaq, ✪ 'The fruit of goodly trees' (Lv 23,40): BethM 34,117 (1988s) 135-140.

2641 *Bruinier* Thomas, Ein Jahr der Befreiung — das Shabbatjahr: Forum Religion (Stu 1988,1) 15-23 [< ZIT].

2642 *Meinhold* Arndt, Jubeljahr: ➤ 813, TRE 17 (1987) 280s (-285 Neuzeit, *Smolinsky* H.).

2643 *Kallani* Joe, [Lv 25,10] A theology of *deror*: Vidyajyoti 52 (1988) 191-7.

2644 *Olivier* Hannes, [Lv 25; *dᵉrôr/yôbēl*; *šemiṭṭâ*] The periodicity of the *mēšarum* again: ➤ 47, [F]FENSHAM F., Text 1988, 227-235.

2645 *Levy-Feldblum* A., The prohibition of interest in relation to the laws of redemption and jubilee: ➤ 43, [F]ELITZUR Y., II (1986) 29-44 [< diss. Jewish Theol. Sem].

2646 *Lohfink* Norbert, *a*) Die Abänderung der Theologie des priesterlichen Geschichtswerks im Segen des Heiligkeitsgesetzes; zu Lev. 26,9.11-13 [< ᶠ*Elliger* K. 1973, 129-136]; − *b*) Die Priesterschrift und die Geschichte [< IOSOT Gö 1977, VTSup 29 (1978) 189-225]: ➤ 223, Studien 1988, 157-168 / 213-253.

2647 *Drijvers* Han J. W., [Lv 26,30] Aramaic *ḥmn'* and Hebrew *ḥmn*; their meaning and root [not 'incense-stand' but 'sheltered divine presence' √ *ḥmb* 'protect']: JSS 33 (1988) 165-179 + 4 fig.

2648 *Levine* Baruch E., [Lv 26,45] The epilogue to the Holiness Code; a priestly statement on the destiny of Israel: ➤ 3,355, ᴱ*Neusner* J., *Levine* B., *al.,* Judaic Perspectives on Ancient Israel 1987, 9-34.

E3.8   *Numeri*;   Numbers, Balaam.

2649 ᵀᴱ**Danieli** Maria Ignazia, ORIGENE, Omelie sui Numeri: Testi patristici 76. R 1988, Città Nuova. 439 p. 88-311-3076-5.

2650 *Hastoupis* Athanasios P., Ⓖ The book of Numbers: TAth 59 (1988) 278-295.

2651 **Jagersma** H., Numeri [I. 1-15, 1983 ➤ 64,2557] II. 16-24: PredikOT. Nijkerk 1988, Callenbach. 198 p. ƒ69.50; sb. 62.50. 90-266-0733-4 [ZAW 101,463].

2652 **Philip** James, Numbers: Communicator's comm. Waco 1987, Word. 364 p. $19 [BToday 26,117]. − ᴿSWJT 31,1 (1988s) 46 (D. G. *Kent*).

2653 *Greenstein* Edward L., [Num 6,24-26 'deciphered' on *Barkay-Yardeni* silver strips] Theory and argument in biblical criticism: HebAnR 10 (1986) 77-93.

2654 **Jobsen** Aarnoud, Krisis en hoop; een exegetisch-theologisch onderzoek naar de achtergronden en tendensen van de rebelliecyclus in Numeri 11:1-20:13: diss. ᴰ*Jagersma* H. Bru 1987. RTLv 19,533.

2655 **Rotman Garrido** Pablo, Moïse, le leader face aux murmures du peuple d'Israël, du Sinaï aux plaines de Moab (Nombres 11 à 21:9); diss. prot. ᴰ*Robert* P. Strasbourg 1987. 338 p. − RTLv 19,535.

2656 **Fisch** H., 'Eldad and Medad are prophesying in the camp' — structuralist analysis of Numbers XI [charismatic is related to institutionalized leadership as quail to manna and camp to tent]: ➤ 43, ᶠELITZUR Y. II (1986) 45-55.

2657 *Brisco* T. V., Wanderings of Israel: ➤ 801, ISBEnc³ 4 (1988) 1005-13.

2658 *Milgrom* Jacob, The structures of Numbers: Chapters 11-12 and 13-14 and their redaction; preliminary gropings: ➤ 3,355, ᴱ*Neusner* J., Judaic perspectives 1987, 49-61.

2659 *Ahuviya* Abraham, Ⓗ And Moses said to him *'ha-mqn' 'th ly?'* [Num 11 (sic)]: BethM 34 (not 33 as Heb. cover),118 (not 108 as Eng. cover) (1988s) 231-5.

2660 *a*) *Milgrom* Jacob, The rebellion of Korah, Numbers 16-18; a study in tradition history; − *b*) *Rivkin* Ellis, The story of Korah's rebellion, key to the formation of the Pentateuch: ➤ 500, SBL Seminars 1988, 570-3 / 574-581.

2661 *Propp* William H., [Num 20,1-13] The rod of Aaron and the sin of Moses: JBL 107 (1988) 19-26.

2662 *Asurmendi* Jesús, [Nm 21,4-9] En torno a la serpiente de bronce: EstBíb 46 (1988) 283-294; Eng. 283.

2663 *Garbini* Giovanni, [Nm 21,4-9; 2 Reg 18,4] Le serpent d'airain et Moïse, ᵀ*Durand* Olivier: ZAW 100 (1988) 264-267; Eng. 267: the real Moses was a Qenite smith.

2664 **Maneschg** Hans, Die Erzählung von der ehernen Schlange (Num 21,4-9) ... 1981 ➤ 62,2752 ... 1,2622: ᴿRuBi 41 (1988) 267s (B. *Poniży*: 'Meneschg'),

2665 *Poniży* Bogdan, ❷ Narratio de serpente aeneo (Num 21,4-9) pro signo salutis in traditionibus biblicis: ➤ 475, RuBi 41 (1988) 14-25.

2666 *Schmitt* Hans-Christoph, Das Hesbonlied Num. 21,27a*b*b-30 und die Geschichte der Stadt Hesbon: ZDPV 104 (1988) 26-43.

2667 *Cohen* Jeffrey M., [Nm 22-24] Balaam's misson — failure or success?: Dor 17 (1988s) 112-6.

2668 **Hackett** Jo Ann, The Balaam text from Deir'alla 1984 ➤ 65,2375 ... 3,2533: ᴿRSO 61 (1987) 238s (G. *Garbini*).

2669 *Wesselius* J.W., Thoughts about Balaam; the historical background of the Deir Alla inscription on plaster [*Hackett* J. 1984]: BO 44 (1987) 589-599.

2670 *Koenig* Jean, L'inscription de Deir Alla; Balaam et le prophétisme: ➤ 763, Archéologie 1986, 195-206.

2671 **Moore** Michael S., The Balaam traditions; their character and development: diss. Drew. Madison ɴᴊ 1988. 271 p. 88-17637. – DissA 49 (1988s) 1853-A; RelStR 15,193.

2672 **Rouillard** Hedwige, La péricope de Balaam (Nombres 22-24) 1985 ➤ 1,2627 ... 3,2537: ᴿBiblica 69 (1988) 273-7 (H. *Simian-Yofre*); Muséon 101 (1988) 217-9 (P.-M. *Bogaert*); RHR 205 (1988) 299-301 (É. *Puech*).

2673 *a) Betz* Otto, Die Bileamtradition und die biblische Lehre von der Inspiration; – *b) Timm* Stefan, Der heilige Mose bei den Christen in Ägypten; eine Skizze zur Nachgeschichte alttestamentlicher Texte; – *c) Beltz* Walter, Biblische und ägyptische Religionsgeschichte; Prämissen und Prädispositionen: ➤ 16, ᶠBÖHLIG A., Religion 1988, 18-53 / 197-220 / 11-17.

2674 *Safren* Jonathan D., [Nm 22,22-35] Balaam and Abraham: VT 38 (1988) 105-113.

2675 *Schlossberg* Eliezer, ❹ [Nm 24,6] 'Like aloes Y' has planted': BethM 34,119 (1988s) 328-340.

2676 *Sakenfeld* Katharine D., *a)* In the wilderness, awaiting the Lord; the daughters of Zelophehad and feminist interpretation: PrincSemB 9 (1988) 179-196 [< ᴢɪᴛ 89,230]; – *b)* [Nm 27; 36] Zelophehad's daughters: PerspRelSt 15,4 (1988) 37-47.

2677 *Ben-Barak* Zafrira, The legal status of the daughter as heir in Nuzi and Emar: ➤ 742, Society 1985/8, 87-97.

2678 *Bernhardt* Karl-Heinz, Kadesch [Barnea Nm 32,8]: ➤ 813, TRE 17 (1988) 509s.

E3.9 Liber Deuteronomii.

2679 **Braulik** G., Deuteronomium: NEchter 15, 1986 ➤ 2,1922; 3,2544: ᴿZAW 100 (1988) 450 (H.-C. *Schmitt*).

2680 *Braulik* Georg [➤ 168], Die gesellschaftliche Innenseite der Kirche; das Deuteronomium: BiKi 43 (1988) 134-9.

2681 **Buchholz** Joachim, Die Ältesten Israels im Deuteronomium [Diss. ᴰ*Perlitt* L., 1987 ➤ RTLv 19,533]: GöTheolArb 36. Gö 1988, Vandenhoeck

& R.   140 p.   DM 28.   3-525-87389-1. – RZAW 100 (1988) 451 (H.-C.
Schmitt).
2682 **Ginsberg** H. Louis,   The Israelian heritage of Judaism 1982 ➤ 63,2622 ...
1,2640:   ROLZ 83 (1988) 174-6 (R. *Stahl*).
2683 *Gross* Walter,   Der Einfluss der Pronominalisierung auf die Syn-
tagmen-Folge im hebräischen Verbalsatz, untersucht an Dtn 1-25:   Bib-
Not 43 (1988) 49-69.
Grossfeld Bernard,   The Targum Onqelos to Deuteronomy 1988 ➤ 1703.
2684 TEHammer Reuven,   Sifre, a tannaitic commentary on the Book of
Deuteronomy: Yale Judaica 24, 1986 ➤ 3,2549:   RJBL 107 (1988) 152s
(H. W. *Basser*).
2685 *Hastoupis* Athanasios, ⊕ Deuteronomy: TAth 54 (1988) 712-746.
2686 **Herbrechtsmeier** William E.,   The biblical legacy of religious violence;
the evolution of Deuteronomic law and Israelite religious culture: diss.
Columbia. NY 1987. 451 p.   88-09364. – DissA 49 (1988s) 525-A.
2687 *Jacob* Edmond,   L'Expérience spirituelle d'Israël dans le livre du
Deutéronome: Tychique 76 (1988) 6-9.
2688 *Kahana* Menahem, ⊕ Pages of the Deuteronomy *Mekhilta* on *Ha'azinu*
and *We-Zot ha-berakha*: Tarbiz 57 (1987s) 165-201.
2689 **Labuschagne** C. J.,   Deuteronomium I B: PredikOT.   Nijkerk 1987,
Callenbach.   299 + 45 p. ƒ87,50 [CBQ 50,752]. – RTsTNijm 28 (1988) 404
(A. *Schoors*).
2690 ELohfink Norbert,   Das Deuteronomium 1983/5 ➤ 1,481 ... 3,2553:
RAntonianum 63 (1988) 433 (M. *Nobile*); TLZ 113 (1988) 175-7 (O.
Kaiser).
2691 *Miller* Patrick D.ᴶ,   The many faces of Moses; a Deuteronomic portrait:
BR 4,5 (1988) 30-35.
2692 **Neusner** J.,   Sifre to Dt, an analytical translation I-II: Brown JudSt
98; 101.   Atlanta 1987, Scholars.   xiii-347 p.;   xix-467 p. $30; $40.
1-55540-145-7 [NTAbs 32,271].
2693 **Neusner** Jacob,   Sifre to Dt, an introduction to the rhetorical, logical,
and topical program: BrownJudSt 124. Atlanta 1987, Scholars.   xii-187 p.
$25.   1-55540-168-6 [NTAbs 32,271].
2694 TNielsen E., *Ejrnaes* B.,   Femte Mosebog, Josva & Dommerbogen: Det
gamle Testamente i ny oversættelse.   K 1988, Dansk. Bibelselskab. 258 p.
Dk 80.   87-7523-205-7 [BL 89,53].
2695 **Payne** David F.,   Deuteronomy: Daily Study Bible 1985 ➤ 1,2646*:
RCBQ 50 (1988) 675s (F. C. *Holmgren*).
2696 **Regt** L. J. de,   A parametric model for syntactic studies of a textual
corpus demonstrated on the Hebrew of Deuteronomy 1-30 [diss. Leiden
1988, DHoftijzer J. – PhoenEOL 34,2 (1988) 5-7]: StSemNeer 24.   Assen
1988, Van Gorcum.   ix-138 p.; Sup. 91 p. ƒ45.
2697 **Rofé** A., ⊕ Introduction to Deuteronomy; Part I and further chapters.
J 1988, Akademon.   xvii-325 p. [ZAW 101,326, J. *Maier,* titles and texts
of the 24 chapters, loosely corresponding to the chapters of Dt]. –
Reference is given to where 12 chapters had been published in English. –
RBethM 34,118 (1988s) 255-260 (M. *Anbar*).
2698 *Rofé* Alexander,   The arrangement of the laws in Deuteronomy: ETL
64 (1988) 265-287.
2699 **Suzuki** Y., ❹ Shinmeiki no Bunken-gaku-teki Kenkyū (A science-
of-literature study in Deuteronomy) [basic: laws in 3d person or 2d sg.;
two 2d sg. then two 2d pl. editings]. Tokyo 1987, Nihon Krisutokyō S.
698 p. Y 7400 [BL 89,94, K. K. *Sacon*].

2700 **Tchape** Jean-Bosco, La terre promise dans le Deutéronome; signification juridique et religieuse: cath. diss. D*Renaud* B. Strasbourg 1987. 249 p. – RTLv 19,535.

2701 **White** Sidney A., A critical edition of seven [4Q] manuscripts of Deuteronomy: diss. Harvard. CM 1988, 339 p. 89-01693. – DissA 49 (1988s) 3055-A; HarvTR 81 (1988) 455s ('Sidnie').

2702 *Veijola* Timo, Principal observations on the basic story in Deuteronomy 1-3: ➤ 469, Wünschet 1986/8, 249-259.

2703 *Millard* A. R., [Dt 3,11] King Og's bed and other ancient ironmongery: ➤ 29, Mem. CRAIGIE P., Ascribe 1988, 481-492.

2704 **Knapp** Dietrich, Deuteronomium 4; literarische Analyse und theologische Interpretation [ev. Diss. 1986]: GöTheolArb 35, 1987 ➤ 3,2564: RBL (1988) 81 (A. G. *Auld*); TLZ 113 (1988) 884 (F.-L. *Hossfeld*); TR 84 (1988) 279-281 (N. *Lohfink*); TsTNijm 28 (1988) 305 (A. *Schoors*).

2705 *Braulik* Georg, a) Weisheit, Gottesnahe und Gesetz — Zum Kerygma von Deuteronomium 4,5-8 [< F*Kornfeld* W. 1977, 165-195]; – b) Die Freude des Festes; das Kultverständnis des Deuteronomium — die älteste biblische Festtheorie: ➤ 168, Studien 1988, 53-93 / 161-218 [+ 8 art. über Dt < Biblica etc.].

2706 *Martin-Achard* Robert, [Dt 4,9.23 + 10 fois] La mémoire de Dieu, devoir et grâce, selon l'AT: ÉTRel 63 (1988) 183-197.

2707 *McNutt* Paula M., [Dt 4,20; 1 Kgs 8,51; Jer 11,4] Egypt as an 'iron furnace', a metaphor of transformation — a writer's perspective: ➤ 500, SBL Seminars 1988, 293-301.

2708 **Benjamin** D. C., [Dt 4,41-26,19] Deuteronomy and city life 1983 ➤ 64,2596 ... 1,2657: RVT 38 (1988) 488 (G. I. *Davies*).

2709 *Hamilton* G. J., [Dt 6,5] The first commandment; a theological reflection: NBlackf 69 (1988) 174-181 [< NTAbs 32,308].

2710 *Vassiliadis* Petros, God's will for his people; Dt 6: 20-25: IntRMiss 77 (1988) 179-184.

2711 *Margalith* Othniel, [Dt 7,1] The Hivites: ZAW 100 (1988) 60-70: *aḥivi = Achaeans.

2712 *Lamblin* Jacques-Paul, [Dt 10,19] La rencontre des autres selon l'Ancien Testament: ÉglRur 485 (1987) 119-128.

2713 *Nicol* George G., Watering Egypt (Deuteronomy XI, 10-11) again: VT 38 (1988) 347s.

2714 **Langer** Gerhard, Von Gott erwählt — Jerusalem; die Rezeption von Dtn 12 im früheren Judentum: Diss. D*Füglister* N. Salzburg 1987s. – TR 84 (1988) 514.

2715 *Stricker* B. H., Deuteronomy [12,2: to eliminate Shechem]: DiscEg 3 (1985) 57-59.

2716 **Morrow** William S., The composition of Deuteronomy 14:1-17:1: diss. D*Dion* P. E. Toronto 1988. – DissA 49 (1988s) 2645-A.

2717 **Elliott** John H., [Dt 15,9, let your eye not be evil against your brother ...] The fear of the leer; the Evil Eye from the Bible to Li'l Abner [mostly in reverse order; after a fairly modern rundown largely on indecent gestures, p. 54 enumerates 16 mentions of 'the Evil Eye' in 11 texts, and p. 57s analyzes a few]: Forum 4,4 (1988) 42-71.

2718 *Braulik* Georg, Zur Abfolge der Gesetze in Deuteronomium 16,18-21,23; weitere Beobachtungen: Biblica 69 (1988) 63-91; franç. 92.

2719 *Foresti* Fabrizio †,   Storia della redazione di Dtn. 16,18-18,22 e le sue connessioni con l'opera storica deuteronomistica [prima delle tre parti della dissertazione dottorale lasciata incompiuta]: Teresianum 39 (1988) (3-)5-189; 191-9 bibliog.

2720 **Rüterswörden** Udo, Von der politischen Gesellschaft zur Gemeinde... Dt 16,18-18,22: BoBB 65, 1987 ➤ 3,2557; 3-610-09101-0: ᴿJBL 107 (1988) 514s (L. J. *Hoppe*); TPQ 136 (1988) 281s (G. *Braulik*); ZAW 100 (1988) 321 (H.-C. *Schmitt*).

2721 *Weinfeld* Moshe, ❺ [Dt 20,16 more ruthless than JE Ex 23(-34) or P Nm 33,52] The ban of the Canaanites and its development in Israelite law: Zion 53 (1988) 135-147; Eng. v.

2722 **Locher** Clemens, Die Ehre einer Frau in Israel... Dt 22,13-21: OBO 70, 1986 ➤ 2,1938; 3,2582: ᴿJBL 107 (1988) 511-4 (Tova *Meltzer*); JSS 33 (1988) 118s (L. L. *Grabbe*); OLZ 83 (1988) 428-430 (W. *Thiel*); Orientalia 57 (1988) 96-99 (M. *Malul*); RB 95 (1988) 302 (R. *Westbrook*).

2723 *Grillot* Françoise, [Dt 25,5] À propos d'un cas de 'lévirat' élamite: JAs 276 (1988) 61-69; Eng. 70.

2724 *Huld* Martin E.,   Homeric *dāēr* [= Latin levir; Dt 25,5s]: AmJPg 109 (1988) 424-430.

2725 *Revell* E. J., 'Obed (Deut 26:5) and the function of the participle in MT: Sefarad 48 (1988) 197-205; español 205.

2726 *Hill* Andrew E., [Dt 27] The Ebal ceremony as Hebrew land grant?: JEvTS 31 (1988) 399-406 [< ᴢɪᴛ 89,148].

2727 *Rooy* H. F. van,   Deuteronomy 28,69 — superscript or subscript?: JNWS 14 (1988) 215-222.

2728 **Axelsson** Lars E., [Dt 33,2] The Lord rose up from Seir; studies...: ConBib OT 25, 1987 ➤ 3,2592: ᴿVT 38 (1988) 379 (G. I. *Davies*).

2729 **Schulz** H., [Dt 33,8-11; Gn 49,5s; Ex 32,29] Leviten im vorstaatlichen Israel und im Mittleren Osten. Mü 1987, Kaiser. 203 p. DM 45. – ᴿZAW 100 (1988) 323s (H.-C. *Schmitt*).

2730 *Goldin* Judah, [Dt 34,8] The death of Moses; an exercise in rabbinic transposition [< ᶠ*Pope* M. 1987]: ➤ 199, Studies 1988, 175-186.

E4.1   *Deuteronomista, XII Tribus, Amphictyonia;* **Liber Josue.**

2731 *Arata Mantovani* Piera, La 'conquista' di Israele: RivB 36 (1988) 47-60; Eng. 60.

2732 **Coote** Robert B., *Whitelam* Keith W., The emergence of early Israel in historical perspective: Social World of Biblical Antiquity 5, 1987 ➤ 3,2595: ᴿBiblica 69 (1988) 581-4 (N. P. *Lemche*). BL (1988) 36 (J. R. *Bartlett*: archeology and social theory more reliable than Pentateuch and Deuteronomist history); JBL 107 (1988) 731-3 (A. C. *Hauser*); VT 38 (1988) 509s (J. A. *Emerton*); ZAW 100 (1988) 313 (H.-C. *Schmitt*).

2733 **Finkelstein** Israel, The archaeology of the Israelite settlement, ᵀ*Saltz* D. J 1988, Israel Expl. Soc. 384 p.; 107 fig. $36. 965-221-007-2. – ᴿBAR-W 14,5 (1988) 34-45. 58s (his own adaptation, 'Searching for Israelite origins') & 6.8.10.12 (D. *Esse*); BL 89, 26s (A. G. *Auld*: original heartland first Manasseh before 1200, then Ephraim-Benjamin.

2734 *Finkelstein* I., The Israelite settlement — the sociological school in the light of archaeological evidence [does not support *Mendenhall* G.; *Gottwald* N.]: ➤ 43, ᶠEʟɪᴛᴢᴜʀ Y., II (1986) 175-186.

2735 **Frick** Frank S., The formation of the state in ancient Israel; a survey of models and theories [*Evans-Pritchard* E.; *Renfrew* C....]: Social World of

Biblical Antiquity 4, 1985 ➤ 1,2799*; 3,2596: ᴿCBQ 50 (1988) 499-501 (W. R. *Wifall*); JBL 107 (1988) 729-731 (R. *Gnuse*); OrAnt 27 (1988) 148-150 (M. *Liverani*: parochial).

2737 *Gottwald* Norman K., Religious conversion and the societal origins of ancient Israel [defense against J. *Milgrom*]: PerspRelSt 15,4 (1988) 49-65.

2738 **Halpern** Baruch, The emergence of Israel in Canaan 1983 ➤ 65,2337 ... 3,2598: ᴿÉglT 18 (1987) 125-8 (L. *Laberge*); IsrEJ 38 (1988) 200-2 (A. *Hurowitz*: with MENDENHALL and GOTTWALD in the front line); OLZ 83 (1988) 170-3 (J. *Conrad*).

2739 *Kaswalder* Pietro, I nuovi dati archeologici [e (piuttosto) le teorie di LEMCHE, COOTE-WHITELAM e FINKELSTEIN] e le origini di Israele: SBFLA 38 (1988) 211-226.

2740 **Lemche** Niels P., [➤ d98] Early Israel, ᵀ*Cryer* F. H. 1985 ➤ 2,1955; 3,2602: ᴿÉTRel 63 (1988) 279s (D. *Lys*).

2741 *Sicre* José Luis, Los origenes de Israel; cinco respuestas a un enigma histórico [... tradicional, *Kaufmann*; asentamiento pacífico, *Alt, Noth*; conquista, *Albright*; revolución campesina, *Mendenhall, Gottwald*; simbiosis, *Fritz*; revolución progresiva, *Lemche*]: EstBib 46 (1988) 421-456; Eng 421: archeology will tell!

2742 *Thiel* Winfried, Vom revolutionären zum evolutionären Israel? Zu einem neuen Modell der Entstehung Israels [*Lemche* Niels P. 1985]: TLZ 113 (1988) 401-410.

2743 *Weinfeld* Moshe, Historical facts behind the Israelite settlement pattern: [VT Sup 40 (1988) 270-283] VT 38 (1988) 324-332.

2744 **Bruce** Barbara J., ORIGEN's homilies on Joshua, an annotated translation: diss. Southern Baptist Theol. Sem., ᴰ*Hinson* E., 1988. 313 p. 89-01057. – DissA 49 (1988s) 2695-A.

2745 **Butterworth** M., Understanding Old Testament history today (Joshua-Esther); eight Bible studies for students and young adult groups. L. c.1987, Bible Society. £1.75 [TLond 91,78].

2746 **Davis** Dale R., No falling words; expositions of the Book of Joshua: Expositor's Guide to the Historical Books. GR 1988, Baker. 204 p. [GraceTJ 9,305].

2747 **Goslinga** C. J., Joshua, Judges, Ruth, ᵀ*Togtman* R.: Bible Student's Comm. 1986 ➤ 3,2615; $30. 0-319-45280-5; ᴿBL (1988) 67 (J. G. *Snaith*).

2748 **Gray** J., Joshua, Judges, Ruth: NCent 1986 [¹1967 ²1977] ➤ 2,1960: ᴿNedTTs 42 (1988) 151s (P. B. *Dirksen*: the book nowhere says it is a reprint of 1967).

Harrington D. J., **Saldarini** A., Targum Jonathan of the Former Prophets 1987 ➤ 1703*

2749 *Kellermann* Diether, Das Buch Josua und das Buch der Richter: ➤ 327, Höre ... Theologie des ATes 1987, 69-87.

2750 **Martínez Borobio** Emiliano, Targum Jonatán de los Profetas Primeros en tradición babilónica I. 1986, Josue-Jueces; II. 1987 [➤ 2814] 2 Sam: TEstCisn 46.38: ᴿMuséon 101 (1988) 423 (P.-M. *Bogaert*).

2751 **Noth** M., ❶ Kyūyaku-seisho ... [Überlieferungsgeschichtliche Studien³ 1967], ᵀ*Yamaga* T. with 44-p. appendix on study of deuteronomist. Tokyo Nihon Krisuto Kyōdan S. 494 p. Y 6500 [BL 89,89 without date].

2752 *Niehaus* Jeffrey J., Joshua and Ancient Near Eastern warfare: JEvTs 31 (1988) 37-50 [< ZIT 88,515].
2753 **Soggin** J. Alberto, Joshua, a commentary: OTLibrary. Ph/L 1988, Westminster/SCM. xvii-245 p. 0-334-00812-3.
2754 *Zobel* Hans-Jürgen, Josua [/-buch]: ➤ 813, TRE 17 (1987) 269-278.

_____

2755 EFischer Danielle, Jean CALVIN, Congrégation sur Josué 1,1-5 (4 juin 1563), première édition du manuscrit original: FreibZ 35 (1988) 201-221.
2756 *Baudry* G.-H., [Jos 2 (Job 9,13)] Rahab: ➤ 786, Catholicisme 12,55 (1988) 442s.
2757 **Floss** Johannes P., Kunder oder Kundschafter? Jos 2.1: AOtt 16, 1982 ➤ 63,2687 ... 2,1965: RJNES 47 (1988) 286 (D. *Pardee*).
2758 *Luria* Ben-Zion, *a*) ✝ [Jos 7s] The location of Ai Adar/Eder: Dor 17 (1988s) 153-162; – *b*) ✝ The *qᵉduššâ* of Migdal [referred to: Jos 10??]: BethM 34,118 (1988s) 198-201.
2759 *Arndt* Marian B., [Jos 13,18; Jer 48,21...] ✝ Lokalizacja biblijnego Mefaat: ➤ 475, RuBi 41 (1988) 59-74.
2760 *Noort* Edward, Transjordan in Joshua 13; some aspects: ➤ e824, Jordan III 1986/7, 125-130.
2761 *Galil* Gershon, ✝ [on Jos 15,21-62 ➤ 3,2628, defends his Zion 52 (1987) 495-509 against *Eph'al* I., *Naveh* J.]: Zion 53 (1988) [211-3] 214-6.

E4.2   *Liber Judicum:* **Richter, Judges.**

2762 *Dirksen* P. B., The ancient Peshiṭta MSS of Judges and their variant readings: ➤ 480, Peshiṭta 1985/8, 127-146.
2763 **Klein** Lillian R., The triumph of irony in the Book of Judges: JStOT Sup 88. Bible & Lit 14. Sheffield 1988, Almond (Ithaca NY, Cornell Univ.) 260 p. £25 1-85075-100-5 [TDig 36,168].
2764 *Lindars* Barnabas, A commentary on the Greek Judges?: ➤ 478, ECox C., 6th LXX 1986/7, 167-200.
2765 *Moyer* James, Weapons and warfare in the Book of Judges: ➤ d633, Discovering 1986, 42-50.
2766 *O'Connor* M., The women in the Book of Judges: HebAnR 10 (1986) 277-293.
2767 **Soggin** J. Alberto, Le livre des Juges 1987 ➤ 3,2636: RAntonianum 63 (1988) 441s (M. *Nobile*); ComSev 21 (1988) 252s (M. de *Burgos*); NRT 110 (1988) 106s (J.-L. *Ska*); RTLv 19 (1988) 217 (P.-M. *Bogaert*: fait honneur à la collection); RTPhil 120 (1988) 369s (G. *Lasserre*); TLZ 113 (1988) 107s (G. *Sauer*); TR 84 (1988) 189s (T. *Römer*).
2768 **Stone** Lawson G., From tribal confederation to monarchic state; the editorial perspective of the Book of Judges: diss. Yale. NHv 1988. – RelStR 15,193; RTLv 20,541.
2769 **Webb** Barry G., The book of Judges, an integrated reading [D1985]: JStOT Sup 46, 1987 ➤ 3,2638: RBiblica 69 (1988) 579-581 (A. *Wénin*); BL (1988) 92, (A. *Auld*: fails to note Jg 6,7-10, important for him, is absent im a Qumran text); JTS 39 (1988) 540-4 (A. D. H. *Mayes*: fruitful insights); RefTR 47 (1988) 59s (A. E. *Cundall*: some blemishes); Themelios 14 (1988s) 28s (D. F. *Pennant* 'Theme in the Book of Judges; a literary study of the book in its finished form').

_____

2770 *Gilead* Ḥayyim, ✝ The story of the war of Deborah and Baraq [Jg 4-8]: BethM 34,119 (1988s) 292-301.

2771 *Neef* Heinz-Dieter, Der Sieg Deboras und Baraks über Sisera; exegetische Beobachtungen zum Aufbau und Werden von Jdc 4,1-24: ZAW 51 (1989) 28-49.

2772 **Bal** Mieke, Murder and difference; gender, genre, and scholarship on Sisera's death, ᵀ*Gumpert* M.: Indiana Studies in Biblical Literature. Bloomington 1988, Indiana Univ. x-150 p. $35. 0-235-33905-7 [OIAc D88].

2773 **Bechmann** Ulrike, Das Deboralied zwischen Geschichte und Fiktion; eine exegetische Untersuchung zu Ri 5: Diss. ᴰ*Görg* M. Bamberg 1988. – RTLv 20,539.

2774 *a)* *Gray* J., Israel in the Song of Deborah; – *b)* *Hobbs* T. R., An experiment in militarism [... emergence of Israel in Canaan]: ➤ 29, Mem. CRAIGIE P., Ascribe 1988, 421-455 / 457-480.

2775 **Lepre** Cesare, Il canto di Debhorah: Storie e Testi 6. N 1987, D'Auria. 210 p. 1987 ➤ 3,2695: ᴿAsprenas 35 (1988) 399s (A. *Rolla*); Koinonia 12 (1988) 71s (R. *Maisano*); RasT 29 (1988) 96s (anche R. *Maisano*).

2776 *a)* *Stager* L. E., Archaeology, ecology, and social history; background themes to the Song of Deborah; – *b)* *Weinfeld* Moshe, The pattern of the Israelite settlement in Canaan: ➤ 482, VTS 40, Jerusalem congress 1986/8, 221-234 / 270-283.

2777 **Lo Pa-Huen** William, Conversion and salvation; a narrative and stylistic analysis of Judges 5-7: diss. Pont. Ist. Biblico, ᴰ*Ska* J. L. R 1989. Extr. 65 p. – AcPIB 9,5 (1988s) 384.424s.

2778 *Delorme* Jean, VIIIème rencontre nationale des groupes 'Sémiotique et Bible'; Bayonne du 29 août au 2 septembre 1988; la geste de Gédéon, Juges 6-8, analyse discursive: SémBib 52 (1988) 34-40.

2779 **Gibert** Pierre, De l'élaboration historiographique; le cas du cycle de Gédéon (Judes 6-8): diss. État, Sorbonne, ᴰ*Caquot*. A. P 1988, – RTLv 20,540.

2780 *a)* *Soggin* J. Alberto, The Migdal temple, Migdal Šᵉkem Judg 9 and the artifact on Mount Ebal; – *b)* *Zertal* Adam, A cultic center with a burnt-offering altar from early Iron Age I period at Mt. Ebal; – *c)* *Rösel* Hartmut N., [Ri 1] Das 'negative Besitzverzeichnis' — traditions-geschichtliche und historische Überlegungen; – *d)* *Amit* Yairah, The use of analogy in the study of the Book of Judges: ➤ 469, Wünschet 1986/8, 115-9 / 137-147; 148-153, 9 phot. / 121-135 / 387-394.

2781 *Vanstiphout* H. L. J., [Jg 9,8-15] Fabels uit Mesopotamië: PhoenEOL 34,2 (1988) 15-28.

2782 **Marcus** David, [Jg 11,29-40] Jephthah and his vow 1986 ➤ 2,1993; 3,2650: ᴿCBQ 50 (1988) 302s (L. J. *Hoppe*); Dor 16 (1987s) 201 + 196 (C. *Abramowitz*); JAOS 108 (1988) 312-4 (S. B. *Parker*); JBL 107 (1988) 515-7 (J. Cheryl *Exum*).

2783 *Trible* Phyllis, A daughter's death; feminism, literary criticism, and the Bible: ➤ 3,356, Backgrounds 1987, 1-14 [< JBL 108,174].

2784 **Trible** P., Texts of terror 1984 ➤ 65,1331* ... 3,2649: ᴿCrNSt 9 (1988) 617s (Esther *Fuchs*).

2785 **Trible** Phyllis, Mein Gott, warum hast du mich vergessen! Frauen-schicksale im AT: Siebenstern 491. Gü 1987, Mohn. 176 p. DM 19,80. – ᴿZAW 100 (1988) 468 (E. S. *Gerstenberger*).

2786 *Rendsburg* Gary A., [Jg 12,6] More on Hebrew *šibbōlet*: JSS 33 (1988) 255-8; 259-261, *Beeston* A.F.L.

2787 *Sasson* Jack M., Who cut Samson's hair? (and other trifling issues raised by Judges 16): Prooftexts 8 (1988) 333-9.

2788 *Feldman* L. H., JOSEPHUS' version of Samson: JStJud 19 (1988) 171-214.
2789 **Organ** Barbara, Judges 17-21 and the composition of the Book of Judges: diss. St. Michael, ᴰ*Peckham* B. Toronto 1987. 261 p. – RTLv 19,535.

E4.3 **Liber Ruth,** *'V Rotuli',* the Five Scrolls.

2790 **Abercrombie** J. R., Ruth [...computer MT-LXX]: SBL SeptCog 20. Atlanta 1986, Scholars. vii-325 p. – ᴿVT 38 (1988) 368 (G. I. *Davies*).
2791 *Beattie* D. R. G., The textual tradition of Targum Ruth; some preliminary observations: ⇥ 148, ᶠWEINGREEN J., IrBSt 10 (1988) 12-23.
2792 *Beck* Eleonore, Die vier Novellen; Rut, Tobit, Judit, Ester: ⇥ 327, Höre ... Theologie des ATes 1987, 143-166 (239-243, Das Hohelied).
2792* **Dürst** Fritz, Dein Gott ist mein Gott; Predigten über das Buch Ruth. 2 1988, Theol.-V. 109 p. DM 22 [TLZ 114,311, H.-D. *Preuss*].
2793 *Fewell* Danna N., *Gunn* David M., 'A son is born to Naomi!'; literary allusions and interpretation in the book of Ruth: JStOT 40 (1988) 99-108.
2793* **Hubbard** Robert L., The book of Ruth: NICOT. GR 1988, Eerdmans. xiv-317 p. [TR 85,162]. 0-8028-2358-0.
2794 **Joüon** P., Ruth² [= ¹1953 with list of corrigenda] 1986 ⇥ 2,2002*: ᴿBL (1988) 79s (D. J. A. *Clines*); RB 95 (1988) 302s (J. *Loza*: still dissociates the Biblical Institute from the postexilic dating).
2795 **Kraft** Robert A., *Tov* E., Ruth: CATSS 1, 1986 ⇥ 2,2003; 3,2658: ᴿCBQ 50 (1988) 298-300 (L. J. *Greenspoon*: Margolis for Joshua wrote and classified by hand 25,000 slips) [Each volume of this Elenchus still contains 25,000 typed or handwritten slips, plus 50,000 index: all classified by hand by the same person before going to the computerized printer — while awaiting the promised-messiah program to do it]; JBL 107 (1988) 360-2 (K. G. *O'Connell*).
2796 *Langerak de Garcia* Ana, Bible study notes on the Book of Ruth [Nicaragua]: Latin American Pastoral Issues 14,2 (Costa Rica 1987) 25-29 [< TKontext 10,91].
2797 **Martin** R. A., *Scorza* Sylvio, Syntactical concordance to the correlated Greek and Hebrew text of Ruth; the Septuagint series: Computer Bible 30. Wooster OH 1988, Biblical Res. Assoc. xxi-279 p. $45 [JBL 108,186].
2798 **Mesters** Carlos, *a)* Rute: Comentário Bíblico AT. Petrópolis 1986, Vozes. 67 p. – *b)* Rut, ᵀ*Pistocchi* Bruno. R 1987, Borla. 93 p. 88-263-0591-9.
2799 ᵀᴱ**Mopsik** Charles, Le Zohar; le livre de Ruth: les dix paroles. Lagrasse 1987, Verdier. 217 p. F 98. 2-86432-064-9. – ᴿÉTRel 63 (1988) 458 (D. *Lys*).
2800 *a) Saltman* A., Nicholas de LYRA's commentary on the Book of Ruth; – *b) Cohen* G. H., Name-giving in the Book of Ruth: ⇥ 43, ᶠELITZUR Y., II (1986) 257-282 / 151-160.
2801 *a) Schmidt* H., ⊖ The five scrolls; – *b) Hsieh* Theresia, ⊖ The faithful follower — Ruth: ColcFuJen 77 (1988) 321-8 / 329-334.
2802 *Vuilleumier* René, Stellung und Bedeutung des Buches Ruth im alttestamentlichen Kanon [Gastvorlesung Bern]: TZBas 44 (1988) 193-310.
2803 *Wendland* Ernst R., Structural symmetry and its significance in the Book of Ruth: ⇥ 502, Issues/Translation 1987/8, 30-63.

2804 **Zenger** Erich, Das Buch Ruth 1986 → 3,2664: [R]TLZ 113 (1988) 21s (A. *Meinhold*); TR 84 (1988) 191s (H. *Engel*).

2805 *Hubbard* Robert L., Ruth IV,17; a new solution [(*qara'*) *šem* = '(his) importance']: VT 38 (1988) 293-301.

E4.4 1-2 Samuel.

2806 **Baldwin** Joyce G., 1 and 2 Samuel, an introduction and commentary: Tyndale OT. Leicester 1988, Inter-Varsity. 299 p.; maps. £6.25. 0-85111-640-X; pa. 842-9.

2807 **Campbell** Anthony F., Of prophets and kings; a late ninth-century document (1 Samuel 1 – 2 Kings 10): CBQ Mon 17, 1986 → 2,2012; 3,2667: [R]BZ 32 (1988) 302-4 (W. *Thiel*); JQR 78 (1987s) 326-8 (R. *Polzin*); JTS 39 (1988) 155-9 (H. G. M. *Williamson*: basis slender, developments suggestive).

2808 **Crocetti** G., 1-2 Samuele, 1-2 Re: LoB 1/8. Brescia 1987, Queriniana. 158 p. Lit. 15.000 [BL 89,71, F. F. *Bruce*].

2809 **Fernández Marcos** N., *Busto Saiz* R., THEODORETUS, Quaestiones in Reges et Par.: TEstCisn 32, 1984 → 65,2396 ... 2,2013: [R]Sefarad 48 (1988) 207s (Maria V. *Spottorno*).

2810 **Gordon** Robert P., 1 & 2 Samuel, comm. 1986 → 2,2016; 3,2672: [R]CBQ 50 (1988) 681s (P. D. *Miscall*: linked to his OTGuide); JTS 39 (1988) 544-6 (P. A. *Ackroyd*: does not probe the extent to which Samuel like Chronicles is itself a reworking of earlier material); RefTR 47 (1988) 22s (J. *Woodhouse*: excellent).

2811 **Gordon** R. P., 1 & 2 Samuel: OTGuides 1984 → 65,2400 ... 3,2671: [R]ScripTPamp 20 (1988) 537 (G. *Aranda*).

2812 *Klein* R. W., Samuel (and) books of: → 801, ISBEnc³ 4 (1988) 311-320.

2813 **McCarter** P. Kyle, II Samuel: AnchorB 9, 1984 → 65,2402 ... 2,2019: [R]Gregorianum 69 (1988) 345-9 (G. L. *Prato*); HeythJ 29 (1988) 100s (R. *Coggins*); ZkT 110 (1988) 101s (J. M. *Oesch*).

2814 **Martínez Borobio** Emiliano, Targum Jonatán de los Profetas Primeros en tradición babilónica, [I → 2750] 2, I-II Samuel: TEstCisn 38, 1987 → 3,1672.2674: [R]AulaO 6 (1988) 120s (J. *Ribera*); ComSev 21 (1988) 95s (M. de *Burgos*); JBL 107 (1988) 570s (D. J. *Harrington*); JQR 78 (1987s) 329-331 (E. J. *Revell*); ScripTPamp 19 (1987) 982s (G. *Aranda*).

2815 **Miscall** Peter D., 1 Samuel; a literary reading 1986 → 2,2021: [R]CBQ 50 (1988) 510s (J. D. *Newsome*).

2816 [E]**Nautin** P. & M.-T., ORIGÈNE, Homélies sur Samuel: SChr 328, 1986 → 3,2676: [R]Bijdragen 49 (1988) 213 (J. *Declerck*); RHPR 68 (1988) 357s (D. A. *Bertrand*).

2817 **Newsome** James D.[J], A synoptic harmony of Samuel, Kings, and Chronicles 1986 → 2,2023; 3,2677: [R]BS 145 (1988) 358 (T. L. *Constable*); BTrans 39 (1988) 342s (L. O. *Dorn*); CBQ 50 (1988) 119s (R. *Gnuse*).

2818 **Pisano** Stephen, Additions or omissions in the books of Samuel[D]: OBO 57, 1984 → 65,2409 ... 3,2678: [R]BO 45 (1988) 393-5 (J. A. *Soggin*: konservative Bevorzugung des MTs); JQR 79 (1988s) 83-85 (F. H. *Polak*); TLZ 113 (1988) 20s (T. *Novotný*).

2819 *Saviv* Aaron, ⊕ On narrative artistry according to the system of J. P. FOKKELMAN vol. II: BethM 33 (1987s) 111s.

2820 *Sijpesteijn* Pieter J., [1-4 Règnes] Stichométrie biblique dans une inscription des Kellia; CdÉ [62 (1987) 277-280 *Partyka* J.] 63 (1988) 191s.

2821 *a)* *Spottorno* Victoria, Some remarks on JOSEPHUS' biblical text for 1-2 Kings [= H 1-2 Sam]; – *b)* *Fernándes Marcos* Natalio, Literary and editorial fcatures of the Antiochian text in Kings; – *c)* *Busto Saiz* José R., On the Lucianic manuscripts in 1-2 Kings: ➤ 478, *Cox* C., 6th LXX 1986/7, 277-285 / 287-304 / 305-310.
2822 *Wahl* Otto, Die Bücher Samuel und Könige: ➤ 327, Höre ... Theologie des ATes 1987, 89-119.
2823 **Zijl** A.H. Van, I Samuel: PredikOT. Nijkerk 1988, Callenbach. 90-266-0739-3 [BL 89,157].

2824 *Silber* D., [1 Sam 1] Kingship, Samuel and the story of Hanna: Tradition 23,2 (NY 1988) 64-75 [< Judaica 44,191].
2825 *Simon* Uriel, The story of Samuel's birth — structure, genre, and meaning [1 Sam 1,1-2,21]: ➤ 43, FELITZUR Y., II (1986) 57-110.
2826 *Kasper* Clemens M., Erat vir unus (1 Sam 1,1) in der Auslegung der Väter [einzigartige Übersetzung des ORIGENES inspirierte GREGORIUS, BEDA, *al.* mit der Idee, hier sei] eine Kurzformel zu Weg und Ziel asketischen Strebens: TPhil 63 (1988) 230-241.
2827 *Walters* Stanley D., Hannah and Anna; the Greek and Hebrew texts of Samuel 1: JBL 107 (1988) 385-412.
2828 *a)* *Boogaert* Thomas A., Narrative theology in the story of the capture of the Ark; – *b)* *Coughenour* R., Hearing and heeding; tasks for OT interpretation; – *c)* *Hesselink* I. John, The providence and the power of God: RefR 41 (Holland MI 1988) 139 .../ 117-138 / 97-116 [< ZIT].
2829 *Kalluveettil* Paul, [1 Sam 2,4-8] La dialéctica marginadora de la Biblia [< Bible Bhashyam 11 (1985) 201-214], TEMessa Josep: SelT 26 (1987) 265-272.

E4.5   *1 Sam 7 ... Initia potestatis regiae,* **Origins of kingship.**

Barker Margaret, The older Testament ... ancient royal cult 1987 ➤ b836.
2830 *Ben-Barak* Zafrira, The appeal to the king as the highest authority for justice: ➤ 469, Wünschet 1986/8, 169-177.
2831 **Camponovo** O., Königtum 1983 ➤ 64,2733 ... 3,2685: RVT 38 (1988) 499 (W. *Horbury*).
2832 **Chan Cheng-Yi** Silas, The prophetic concept of kingship in First Samuel and its influence on the Lukan depiction of Jesus of Nazareth: diss. Fuller Theol. Sem. Pasadena 1987. 371 p. 88-06518. – DissA 49 (1988s) 527-A.
2832* *Eaton* John H., Kingship and the Psalms[2] [[1]1976 ➤ 58,3539]: Biblical Seminar. Sheffield 1986, JStOT. xii-247 p. £7. – RTLZ 113 (1988) 807-810 (O. *Kaiser*).
2833 *Finkelstein* Israel, ❶ The emergence of the monarchy in Israel; environmental and socio-political aspects: CHistEI 50 (1988) 3-26; Eng. 195.
2834 **Gerbrandt** Gerald E., Kingship according to the Deuteronomistic history 1986 ➤ 2,2033; 3,2687: RAustralBR 36 (1988) 64s (Anne E. *Gardner*); IrBSt 9 (1987) 87-89 (A.D.H. *Mayes*); JSS 33 (1988) 119-121 (R.E. *Clements*).
2835 *Howard* David M.[J], The case for kingship in the Old Testament narrative books and the Psalms: TrinJ 9,1 (1988) 19-35.
2836 *Miller* David H., Sacral kingship, biblical kingship, and the elevation of Pippin the Short: ➤ 3,154, FSULLIVAN R., Religion 1987, 131-154.

2837 **Rosenberg** Joel, [Gn (2s; 12-25) 'companion work to 2 Sam'] King and kin; political allegory in the Hebrew Bible 1986 ➤ 3,2692: ᴿThemelios 14 (1988s) 29 (K. M. *Craig*).

2838 **Eslinger** Lyle M., Kingship of God in crisis; a close reading of 1 Samuel 1-12: 1985 ➤ 1,2808*; 3,2698: ᴿCBQ 50 (1988) 497s (R. D. *Nelson*).

2839 **Wénin** André, Samuel et l'instauration de la monarchie (1 S 1-12); une recherche littéraire sur le personnage [diss. Rome, Inst. Biblique Pontifical 1987, ᴰ*McCarthy* D. – AcPIB 9,5 (1988s) 383]: EurHS 23/342. Fra 1988, Lang. 490 p. Fs 76 [ZAW 101,330, H.-C. *Schmitt*]. 3-631-40384-4.

2840 *Rofé-Roifer* A., Gli albori delle sette nel Giudaismo postesilico [1 Sam 7,6 LXX attesta già le divergenze fra Sadducei e Farisei; ugualmente 3Is, Sir, Mal]: ➤ 474, Correnti 1984/7, 25-35.

2841 **Weber-Möckl** Annette, 'Das Recht des Königs, der über euch herrschen soll'; Studien zu 1 Sam 8,11 ff. in der Literatur der frühen Neuzeit Historische Forschungen 27. B 1986, Duncker & H. 214 p. DM 88. 3-428-05963-8. – ᴿBL (1988) 95 (R. P. *Carroll*: largely post-biblical).

2842 *Edelman* Diana, Saul's journey through Mt. Ephraim and Samuel's Ramah (1 Sam. 9:4-5; 10:2-5): ZDPV 104 (1988) 44-58; 2 maps.

2843 *Ben-Naḥum* Jonathan, ✪ [1 Sam 10,10; 19,24] What happened to the son of Kish?: BethM 34,118 (1988s) 236-240.

2844 *Catastini* Alessandro, [1 Sam 11,1] 4 Q Samᵃ: II. Nahash il 'serpente': Henoch 10 (1988) 17-46; franç. 46-49.

2845 **Fokkelman** J.P., The crossing fates (I Sam. 13-31 and II Sam. 1): Narrative art 2, 1986 ➤ 2,2042; 3,2701: ᴿCBQ 50 (1988) 295s (P. D. *Miscall*).

2845* *Fokkelman* J.P., Structural reading on the fracture between synchrony and diachrony: JbEOL 30 (1987s) 123-136.

2846 *Luria* Ben-Zion, ✪ [1 Sam 13,9...] Why Saul had no right to worship: BethM 34,119 (1988s) 289-291.

2847 *Sijpesteijn* P.J., A new reading in Regnorum I 13,21 [*theristēr* for *trygētós*]: StClasOr 38 (1988) 309 sola.

2848 **Foresti** F., [1 Sam 15] The rejection of Saul ᴰ1984 ➤ 65,2434 ... 3,2705: ᴿAION 48 (1988) 159-161 (Cecilia *Carniti*).

2849 **Berges** Ulrich, Die Verwerfung Sauls; eine thematische Untersuchung: Diss. Pont. Univ. Gregoriana, ᴰ*Conroy* C. R 1988. – RTLv 20,539.

E4.6   *1 Sam 16 ... 2 Sam*:   *Accessio Davidis*.   **David's Rise.**

2850 **Brueggemann** Walter, [1 Sm 16s] David's truth 1985 ➤ 1,2814 ... 3,2707: ᴿBibTB 18 (1988) 32 (M. D. *Guinan*: not one of his more successful efforts).

2851 **Cazeaux** Jacques, L'impossible David; critique de la royauté dans Samuel et Rois. L'Arbresle 1988, Centre T. More. 92 p. 2-905600-06-3.

2852 *a*) *Deeley* Mary Katharine, The rhetoric of memory in the stories of Saul and David; a prospective study; – *b*) *Alles* Gregory D., Wrath and persuasion; the Iliad and its context: ➤ 500, SBL Seminars 1988, 285-292 / 263-272.

2853 **Dietrich** Walter, David, Saul und die Propheten ... BWANT 122, 1987 ➤ 2,3709: ᴿBL (1988) 73 (A. *Auld*); RHPR 68 (1988) 236 (P. de *Robert*: important même si les critères ne son pas pleinement convaincants).

2854 *Edelman* Diana, Tel Masos, Geshur, and David: JNES 47 (1988) 253-8 [continuing 241-252, *Finkelstein* I. ➤ h462].

2855 **Flanagan** James W., David's social drama; a hologram of Israel's early Iron Age [... compared with rise of Ibn Saud]: JStOT Sup 73 / Social World 7. Sheffield 1988, Almond. 373 p. £24. 1-85075-291-X; pa. 2-8 [BL 89,154] – ᴿBAngIsr 8 (1988s) 68s (B. *Isserlin*).

2856 *Garrett* James D., The Davidic-Zion movement in ancient Israel; a study of the literary exaltation of Yahweh and its historical correlation: diss. Louisville 1983. 438 p. – KirSef 61,390.

2857 **Heike** Friis, Die Bedingungen des davidischen Reichs in Israel und seiner Umwelt [K 1968 =] DielBl Beih 6. Heid 1986. 250 p. – ᴿEfMex 4,12 (1986) 162-5 (R. *Duarte Castillo*).

2858 ᴱ**Ishida** Tomoo, Studies in the period of David and Solomon 1979/82 ➤ 63,434 ... 2,2049: ᴿJNES 47 (1988) 150s (D. *Pardee*).

2859 **Kausemann** Josef, *a)* Ein Mann nach Gottes Herz; – *b)* Der König, den Gott wählte: Die Lebensgeschichte des Königs David 1s. Dillenburg 1988, Christliche VG. 241 p.; 208 p. 3-921-29258-1; 67-0.

2860 **Mills** C. Michael, David, lion and lamb. Lima OH 1988, 'CSS'. 105 p. $6.75 [BToday 26,381: for high school].

2861 **Ollenburger** Ben C., Zion 1987 ➤ 3,2718: ᴿBL (1988) 113s (J. R. *Porter*); ETL 64 (1988) 192s (J. *Lust*); ÉTRel 63 (1988) 100s (D. *Lys*).

2862 *Polan* Gregory J., Biblical portraits of David: BToday 26 (1988) 215-9.

2863 *Kruger* Paul A., The symbolic significance of the hem (*kānāf*) in 1 Samuel 15.27: ➤ 47, ᶠFENSHAM F., Text 1988, 105-116.

2864 *a) Eslinger* Lyle, 'A change of heart', 1 Samuel 16; – *b) Walters* S. D., [1 Sam 16] The light and the dark; – *c) Polzin* Robert, On taking renewal seriously; 1 Sam 11:1-15: ➤ 29, Mem. CRAIGIE P., Ascribe 1988, 341-361 / 567-589 / 493-507.

2865 **Barthélemy** D. *al.*, The story of David and Goliath [1 Sam 17]: OBO 73, 1986 ➤ 2,2060-2062; 3,2720: ᴿCarthaginensia 4 (1988) 361 (R. *Sanz Valdivieso*); JJS 39 (1988) 294s (A. *Salvesen*: 'symposium by correspondence'); JTS 39 (1988) 546-8 (H. *Mowvley*: fascinating, though no sign that any of the four learned anything from the others as claimed); Themelios 14 (1988s) 103s (H. G. M. *Williamson*: favors GOODING).

2866 *Nagasawa* Takashi, Notes sur l'évolution de l'iconographie du 'Combat de David contre Goliath' des origines au Xᵉ s.: Byzantion 58 (1988) 123-139.

2867 *Rofé* Alexander, The battle of David and Goliath; folklore, theology, eschatology: ➤ 3,355, Judaic perspectives 1987, 117-151.

2868 *Grottanelli* Cristiano, [1 Sam 25 ...] Storie di Giuda: EgVO 11 (1988) 167-183.

2869 *Klauss* Nathan, [1 Sam 25,24s] ✪ The oracle of Abigail: BethM 32,111 (1986s) 320-331.

2870 *Schwienhorst-Schönberger* Ludger, Saul bei der Totenbeschwörerin von En Dor (1 Sam 28): BLtg 61 (1988) 264-7.

2871 *Simon* Uriel, *a)* 1 Samuel 28:3-25; the stern prophet and the kind witch: ➤ 469, Wünschet 1986/8, 281-7; – *b)* [1 Sam 28,8-25] A balanced story; the stern prophet and the kind witch: Prooftexts 8 (1988) 159-171.

2872 *Kelly* Douglas F., CALVIN's teaching on guidance as expressed in his sermons on II Samuel: RefTR 46 (1987) 33-42.

2873 *Yee* Gale A.,   The anatomy of biblical parody; the dirge form in 2 Samuel 1 and Isaiah 14: CBQ 50 (1988) 565-586.

2874 *Whedbee* J. William, [2 Sam 5-8] On divine and human bonds; the tragedy of the House of David: ➤ 25, FCHILDS B., Canon 1988, 147-165.

2875 *Rosen* Baruch, [2 Sam 6,2 Baal-Judah]   Early Israelite cultic centres in the hill country: VT 38 (1988) 114-7.

2876 *Begg* Christopher,   The reading in 2 Sam 7,7; some remarks: RB [94 (1987) 389-396, *Murray* D.] 95 (1988) 551-8; franç. 551.

2877 *Jüngling* H.-W., [2 Sm 11s; Is 7], Die religiöse Doppeldeutigkeit des davidisch-salomonischen Staates: 1ZT 24 (1988) 446-454 = L'ambiguité religieuse de l'État davidique et salomonienne: Concilium 220 (P 1988) 27-41.

2878 *Nicol* Geroge G.,   [2 Sam 11; not 1 Sam as often on p. 360] Bathsheba, a clever woman? [not 'stupid' as *Whybray* N.]: ExpTim 99 (1987s) 360-3.

2879 *Yee* Gale A.,   'Fraught with background'; literary ambiguity in II Samuel 11:   Interpretation 42 (1988) 240-253.

2880 *Fischer* Alexander,   David und Batseba; ein literarkritischer und motivgeschichtlicher Beitrag zu II Sam 11: ZAW 101 (1989) 50-59; Eng. 59.

2881 **Lategan** B.C., *Vorster* W.S., [2 Sam 12; Mk 4] Text and reality 1985 ➤ 1,1323 ... 3,2746: RÉglT 18 (1987) 237s (W. *Vogels*).

2881* *Jongeling* K. [2 Sam 13,39] Joab and the Tekoite woman: JbEOL 30 (1987s) 116-122.

2882 *Rottzoll* Dirk U.,   II Sam 14,5 — eine Parallele zu Am 7,14f: ZAW 100 (1988) 413-5.

2883 *Brin* Gershon, ❸ Working methods of biblical translators [i.e. translation within the biblical text itself; 2 Sam 14,7; Jer 36,25; 47,5...] and their relevance in establishing the text: Tarbiz 57 (1987s) 445-449; Eng. IV.

2884 **Fokkelman** M.P., Narrative art ... I: 2 Sam 9-20; 1 Kgs 1-2, 1981 ➤ 63,2962a ... 1,2815: RJNES 47 (1988) 61-62 (D. *Pardee*: history ignored).

2885 **Blum** Erhard,   Der Anfang der Geschichtsschreibung im Alten Israel? Anmerkungen zur sog. 'Thronfolgegeschichte' und zum Umgang mit geschichtlicher Wirklichkeit im Alten Israel: Diss. RRendtorff R. Heidelberg 1988. – RTLv 20,539.

2886 *Bartal* Arieh, ❸ [2 Sam 18,18] Absalom in the King's Valley: BethM 34,116 (1988s) 59-61.

2887 *Chang* Wilson,   Pathos of a father; reading the Davidic court history and William FAULKNER's Absalom, Absalom from a reader response perspective: ➤ 469, Wünschet 1986/8, 409-413.

2888 **Gregory** Mark W.,   Narrative time in the Keret Epic and the Succession Narrative: diss. Southern Baptist Theol. Sem., DSmothers T. 1988.   244 p. 89-01496. – DissA 49 (1988s) 3020-A.

2889 *Hill* Andrew E.,   A Jonadab connection in the Absalom conspiracy?: JEvTS 30 (1987) 387-390 [< ZIT].

2890 **Ishida** Tomoo,   Royal succession in the kingdoms of Israel and Judah with special reference to the people under arms as a determining factor in the struggles for the throne: ➤ 482, VTS 40, Jerusalem congress 1986/8, 96-106.

2891 *Kaiser* Otto,   Beobachtungen zur sogenannten Thronnachfolgeerzählung Davids: ETL 64 (1988) 5-20.

2892 *Keys* Gillian,   The so-called succession narrative; a reappraisal of ROST's approach to theme in II Samuel 9-20 and I Kings 1-2: IrBSt 10 (Belfast 1988) 140-155 [< ZIT 88,538].

2893 *Brueggemann* Walter, 2 Samuel 21-24; an appendix of deconstrucion?
[i.e. carefully composed to combat the established royal ideology]: CBQ 50
(1988) 382-397.
2894 *Geyer* Marcia L., Stopping the juggernaut; a close reading of 2 Samuel
20:13-22: UnSemQ 41,1 (1986s) 33-42 [< ZIT].
2895 **Schnabl** Heinrich, [2 Sam 21,1-14; 9-20; 1 Kön 1-2] Untersuchungen zur
literarischen Eigenständigkeit, literarkritischen Abgrenzung und Intention
der Thronfolgeerzählung Davids: Diss. ᴰ*Gross*: Theorie und Forschung
55. Regensburg 1987s, Roderer. xxvii-223 p. 3-89073-405-7. – TR 84
(1988) 512.
2896 *Na'aman* Nadav, [2 Sam 23] The list of David's officers (*šālîsîm*): VT 38
(1988) 71-80.
2897 *Rendsburg* Gary A., The northern origin of 'The last words of David' (2
Sam 23,1-7): Biblica 69 (1988) 113-121.
2898 [Ben-Gurion circle, notes on Samuel] (II 24, 18) ◑ The threshing-floor
of Araunah and David's vision on the building of the Temple: BethM
34,118 (1988s) 268-288.

E4.7 *Libri Regum;* **Solomon, Temple: 1 Kings...**

2900 **Dilday** Russell H., 1,2 Kings: Communicator's Comm. Waco 1987,
Word. 512 p. – ᴿSWJT 31,1 (1988s) 44s (D. G. *Kent*).
2901 **Keil** C.F., Die Bücher der Könige [1876], ᴱ*Siemens* Peter: TVG
Kommentare. Giessen 1988, Brunnen. x-430 p. DM 68. 3-7655-9207-2
[BL 89,56, G. H. *Jones*].
2902 *Matthews* Victor H., Kings of Israel; a question of crime and
punishment: → 500, SBL Seminars 1988, 517-526.
2903 *Meyers* Carol, The Israelite empire; in defense of King Solomon:
→ 3,356, ᴱ*O'Connor* M., Backgrounds 1987, 181-197 [< JBL 108,174].
2904 **Mulder** M.J., Koningen deel I (1-7): CommOT. Kampen 1987, Kok.
306 p. *f* 67,50. 90-242-0784-3 [BL 89,59, F. F. *Bruce*].
2905 **Nelson** Richard D., First and Second Kings: Interpretation Comm.
Atlanta 1988, Knox. viii-273 p. $20 [TDig 35,368]. 0-8042-3109-5.
2906 *Nelson* Richard D., The anatomy of the book of Kings: JStOT 40
(1988) 39-48.
2907 *Runia* K., Preken over 1 en 2 Koningen: GerefTTs 88 (1988) 193-307.

2908 **Parker** Kim, Narrative tensions in 1 Kings 1-11; a study of the
structural and thematic unity of the Solomonic narrative, ᴰ*Coombs*: diss.
McMaster. Hamilton 1988. – DissA 49 (1988s) 2290-A; RelStR 15,193.
2909 *Parker* Kim I., Repetition as a structuring device in 1 Kings 1-11:
JStOT 42 (1988) 19-27.
2910 *Wittenberg* Günther, King Solomon and the theologians: JTSAf 63
(1988) 16-29 [< ZIT 88,595].
2911 *Vogüé* A. de, Une citation remarquable de GRÉGOIRE le Grand (In I
Reg 1,5) dans la 'Vie de Jean de Cantimpré': RBén 98 (1988) 327s.
2912 *Rogers* Jeffrey S., Narrative stock and deuteronomistic elaboration in 1
Kings 2: CBQ 50 (1988) 398-413.
2913 **Carr** David M., Royal ideology and the technology of faith; a comparative midrash study of 1 Kings 3:2-15: diss. ᴰ*Sanders* J. Claremont
1988. 360 p. 89-00968. – DissA 49 (1988s) 3388-A; RelStR 15,192.

2914 **Kenik** Helen A., Design for kingship ... 1 Kgs 3,4-15: SBL diss. 69, 1983 ➤ 64,2803 ... 2,2088: ᴿJQR 78 (1987) 148-150 (R. *Polzin*).

2915 *Jonker* Louis C., *hyh mwšl*; an exegetical note on the use of the participle active in 1 Kings 5:1 (MT): JNWS 14 (1988) 135-141.

2916 *Millard* A.R., King Solomon's gold; biblical records in the light of antiquity: CanadMesop 15 (1988) 5-11.

2917 *Muhly* James D., Solomon, the copper king; a twentieth century myth [*Glueck* N., Kheleifeh] Expedition 29,2 (Ph 1987) 38-47; 11 fig.

Templum:

2918 *Doll* M., The Temple; symbolic form in Scripture: Soundings 70 (1987) 145-154 [< ZAW 100,298].

2919 **Endres** John, Temple, monarchy and word of God: Message of Biblical Spirituality 2. Wilmington 1988, Glazier. 247 p. $13; pa. $10 [TDig 36,58].

2920 *a) Haran* Menahem, Temple and community in ancient Israel; – *b) Kramer* Samuel S., The Temple in Sumerian literature; – *c) Burkert* Walter, The meaning and function of the temple in classical Greece: ➤ 734, ᴱ*Fox* M., Temple 1986/8, 17-25 / 1-16 / 27-47 [-138, *al.*, India, Japan, Mesoamerica].

2921 *Laffey* Alice L., A theological construction of Israel's Temple [Chr]: BToday 26 (1988) 209-214.

2922 *a) Mink* Hans-Aage, Tempel und Hofanlagen in der Tempelrolle; – *b) Delcor* Mathias, La description du Temple de Salomon selon Eu-POLÉMOS et le problème de ses sources: ➤ 22, Mém. CARMIGNAC J., RQum 13 (1988) 273-285 / 251-271.

2923 *Patrich* Joseph, *a)* ✪ The structure of the Second Temple — a new reconstruction: Qadmoniot 21 (1988) 32-40; ill. [The alternative double-height façade is made a pylon engulfing the real entry-gate, and continuing as a kind of superstructure]. – *b)* ✪ The Mesibah of the Temple according to the Mishna Middot: CHistEI 42 (1987) 39-53.

2924 *Gupta* R.C., [1 Kgs 7,23; 2 Chr 4,2] On the values of π [3.1416] from the Bible [an interesting survey of various mathematicians' hypotheses: Ganita Bhāratī [0970-0307; Birla Institute of Technology, Mesra-Ranchi] 10 (1988) 51-58.

2925 *Westerholm* S., Temple: ➤ 801, ISBEnc³ 4 (1988) 759-776 (-783, Temples, *Pratico* G.).

2926 **Talstra** R., Het gebed van Salomo; synchronie en diachronie in de kompositie van 1 Kon. 8,14-61: diss. ᴰ*Mulder* M. Leiden 1987. 264 p. – RTLv 19,535; TsTNijm 28 (1988) 77. – ᴿETL 64 (1988) 460 (E. *Eynikel*).

2927 **Beyer** Rolf, Die Königin von Saba; Engel und Dämonen; der Mythos einer Frau. Bergisch Gladbach 1987, Lübbe. 304 p. – ᴿJudaica 44 (1988) 184s (S. *Hurwitz*).

2928 *Hubbard* D.A., [1 Kgs 10,1-10] Queen of Sheba: ➤ 801, ISBEnc³ 4 (1988) 8-11.

2929 *Lemaire* André, [1 Rois 11,14 + 3 fois] Hadad l'Édomite ou Hadad l'Araméen?: BibNot 43 (1988) 14-18.

2930 *Frisch* Amos, Shemaiah the prophet versus King Rehoboam; two opposed interpretations of the schism (1 Kings XII, 21-24): VT 38 (1988) 466-8.

2931 **Hayes** John H., *Hooker* Paul K., A new chronology for the kings of Israel and Judah and its implications for biblical history and literature [rejecting co-regencies; often preferring OT numbers]. Atlanta 1988, Knox. 112 p. 0-8042-0152-8 [BL 89,37, G. H. *Jones*].

2932 **Thiele** Edwin R., The mysterious numbers of the Hebrew Kings[3rev]. [¹1951] 1983 ► 64,2828: ᴿJNES 47 (1988) 54-56 (A. *Lemaire*: discutable).

2933 *Holder* John The presuppositions, accusations, and threats of 1 Kings 14: 1-18; JBL 107 (1988) 27-38.

2935 *Gordon* Cyrus H., Ugaritic *rbt / rabītu* [real 'queen' was not wife but mother of king, as *gᵉbîrâ* 1 Kgs 15,1.13]: ► 29, Mem. CRAIGIE P., Ascribe 1988, 129-132.

2936 *Arbeli* Shoshana, [1 K 15,9-13] The removal of the Tawananna [queen(-mother)] from her position: ► 742, Society 1985/8, 79-85.

E4.8 *1 Regum 17-22: Elias,* **Elijah.**

Bowman John Elijah and the Pauline Jesus Christ 1988 ► 5864.

2937 Elia ed Eliseo (52 titoli recenti): Carmelus 35 (1988) 309-313.

2938 *Ginn* Roman, Elijah, model of Christian behavior: SpLife 32 (1986) 3-8.

2939 *Kasher* R., Patterns of activity of the miracle-workers in the Bible: ► 43, ᶠELITZUR Y., II (1986) 161-174.

2940 *Margalit* Shlomoh, ❂ The *nābî'* of Tišba of Gilead: Scripture, midrash, haggada: BethM 34,118 (1988s) 216-222.

2941 *Timm* S., Ahab: ► 804, NBL Lfg 1 (1988) 65.

2943 *Rendsburg* Gary A., The mock of Baal in 1 Kings 18:27: CBQ 50 (1988) 414-7.

2944 *Schmoldt* Hans, Elijas Begegnung mit Jahwä (1 Kön 19,9-14): BibNot 43 (1988) 19-26.

2945 *Maller* Allen S., Elijah's recovery from depression: Dor 17 (1988s) 34-36.

2946 *Moreno Hernández* Antonio, Glosas inéditas de Vetus Latina en manuscritos españoles; aportaciones para la reconstrucción de 1 Re 20: Sefarad 48 (1988) 343-356.

2947 *Rofé* Alexander, [1 Kgs 21] The vineyard of Naboth; the origin and message of the story: VT 38 (1988) 89-104.

2948 *Ahlström* G. W., The battle at Ramoth-Gilead in 841 BC: ► 469, Wünschet 1986/8, 157-166.

2949 *Hirth* Volkmar, 'Der Geist' in 1 Reg 22: ZAW 101 (1989) 113s.

2950 *Weippert* Helga, Ahab el campeador? Redaktionsgeschichtliche Untersuchungen zu 1 Kön 22: Biblica 69 (1988) 457-479; franç. 479.

2951 *Welten* Peter, [1 K 22] Josaphat: ► 813, TRE 17 (1987) 242s.

E4.9 *2 Reg 1 ... Elisaeus,* **Elisha.**

2952 **Cogan** Mordechai, *Tadmor* Hayim, II Kings: AnchorB 11. GCNY 1988, Doubleday, xxxv-371 p. $20 [TDig 35,347]. – ᴿZAW 100 (1988) 452 (H.-C. *Schmitt*).

2952* **Hobbs** T. R., 2 Kings: Word 13, 1985 ► 2,2116; 3,2805: ᴿGraceTJ 9 (1988) 142-5 (R. *Patterson* prefers to DEVRIES 1 Kings); RefTR 46 (1987) 52s (J. W. *Woodhouse*).

2953 *Begg* Christopher, The Chronicler's non-mention of Elisha: BibNot 44 (1988) 7-11.

2954 *a) Conrad* Joachim, 2 Kön 2,1-18 als Elija-Geschichte; – *b) Schäfer-Lichtenberger* Christa, Joschua und Elischa — Ideal-Typen von Führerschaft in Israel: ► 469, Wünschet 1986/8, 263-271 / 273-280.

2955 *a) Spronk* K., 2 Koningen 2, een onderzoek naar ontstaan en opbouw van de tekst en naar de achtergrond van de daarin vermelde tradities; – *b) Smelik* K. A. D., De betekenis van 2 Koningen 5, een 'Amsterdamse' benadering: GerefTTs 88 (1988) 82-97 / 98-115.

2956 *Long* Burke O., [2 Kgs 4,8-37] A figure at the gate; readers, reading, and biblical theologians: ⇥ 25, ᶠCHILDS B., Canon 1988, 166-186.

2957 **Moore** Rick D., Didactic salvation stories in the Elisha cycle; an analysis of 2 Kings 5; 6:9-23; and 6:24-7:20: diss. Vanderbilt. Nv 1988. 88-15736. – DissA 49 (1988s) 1174-A; RelStR 15,193.

2958 *Trebolle* Julio, Le texte de 2 Rois 7,20-8,5 à la lumière des découvertes de Qumrän (6Q4 15): ⇥ 22, Mém. CARMIGNAC J., RQum 13 (1988) 561-8.

2959 **Barré** Lloyd M., The rhetoric of political persuasion; the narrative artistry and political intentions of 2 Kings 9-11 [diss. 1986: RTLv 19,532]: CBQ Mg 20. Wsh 1988, Catholic Biblical Association of America. ix-161 p. $5; sb. $4. 0-915170-19-1.

2960 *Mullen* E. Theodoreᴶ, [2 Kgs 10,28-31] The royal dynastic grant to Jehu and the structure of the books of Kings: JBL 107 (1988) 193-206.

2961 *Handy* Lowell K., [2 Kgs 11,1-3] Speaking of babies in the Temple: ProcGLM 8 (1988) 155-165.

2962 *Reviv* Hanoch, [2 Kgs 12] The priesthood as a political pressure-group in Judah: ⇥ 469, Wünschet 1986/8, 205-210.

2963 *Bakon* Shimon, The fall of Samaria; biblical historiosophy on trial: Dor 17 (1988s) 26-33.

2964 *Horst* P. W. van der, De Samaritaanse diaspora in de oudheid [721 ...]: NedTTS 42 (1988) 134-144; Eng. 146.

2965 *Na'aman* Nadav, *Zadok* Ran, Sargon II's deportations to Israel and Philistia (716-708 B.C.): JCS 40 (1988) 36-46.

2966 *Steinmann* Andrew E., The chronology of 2 Kings 15-18: JEvTS 30 (1987) 391-8 [< ZIT].

2966* *Nelson* Richard D., [2 Kgs 16] The altar of Ahaz; a revisionist view: HebAnR 10 (1986) 267-276.

2967 *Cogan* Mordechai, [2 Kgs 17,24-33] For we, like you, worship your God; three biblical portrayals of Samaritan origins: VT 38 (1988) 286-292.

2968 **Becking** B., De ondergang van Samaria ... II Kon 17, 1985 ⇥ 3,2819: ᴿETL 64 (1988) 195s (E. *Eynikel*).

2969 *Becking* Bob, Theologie na de ondergang; enkele opmerkingen bij 2 Koningen 17 [,7-23]: Bijdragen 49 (1988) 150-172; Eng. 173s, reproaching the whole people of God.

2970 *Galil* Gershon, ⊕ [1 Kgs 18,13-19,37 two traditions but not two campaigns] Sennacherib versus Hezekiah; a new look at the Assyrian campaign to the west in 701 B.C.E.: Zion 53 (1988) 1-12; Eng. i.

2971 **Gonçalves** Francolino J., [2 Rois 18,17] L'expédition de Sennachérib ... [diss. J, 1971]: EtBN 7, 1986 ⇥ 2,2131; 3,2822: ᴿBZ 32 (1988) 295-8 (W. *Thiel*); CBQ 50 (1988) 679-681 (B. D. *Chilton*: a stunning contribution, recommended without reservation); Henoch 10 (1988) 395-7 (J. A. *Soggin*: tensione critica/conservatrice); JBL 107 (1988) 117-9 (W. H. *Shea*: updated by a decade); NRT 110 (1988) 110s (J.-L. *Ska*); TR 84 (1988) 449s (O. *Loretz*: convincing).

2972 *Görg* Manfred, *a)* Ein weiteres Fragment der Palästina-Annalen Sanheribs aus Assur: BibNot 44 (1988) 27-29; I pl.; – *b)* Nachtrag zu den Annalenduplikaten Sanheribs aus Assur: BibNot 45 (1988) 26s.

2973 *Shea* William H., Sennacherib's description of Lachish and of its conquest: AndrUnS 26 (1988) 171-180.

2974 **Hardmeier** Christoph, Die Polemik gegen Ezechiel und Jeremia in den Hiskija-Jesaja-Erzählungen; diss. ᴰ*Crüsemann* F. Bielefeld-Bethel 1987s. – RTLv 19,533.

2975 **Spieckermann** Hermann, Juda unter Assur in der Sargonidenzeit: FRLANT 129, 1982 ⮕ 64,2861 ... 2,2137: ᴿTrierTZ 97 (1988) 163s (E. Haag).

2976 *Boncquet* Jan, De koningin-moeder in de neo-assyrische periode: ⮕ 763, Archéologie 1986, 183-194.

2977 *Begg* Christopher, [2 Kgs 20,12-19] Hezekiah's display; another parallel: BibNot [38s (1987) 14-17] 41 (1988) 7s.

2979 **Provan** Iain W., Hezekiah and the books of Kings [< diss. Cambridge 1986]: BZAW 172. B 1988, de Gruyter. xiii-218 p. DM 90. 3-11-011557-3 [BL 89,90, A. G. *Auld*]. – ᴿETL 64 (1988) 459s (E. *Eynikel*).

2980 **Vera Chamaza** Galo W., Hizkijjahû rey de Judá; interpretación y reconstrucción de las narraciones de Ezequías [kath. Diss. ᴰ*Gross* W. Tü 1986 ⮕ 2,2135*; RTLv 20,542]: Inst.S.Jerónimo 20. Valencia 1988, Soler. 468 p. 84-86067-19-7.

2981 **Vogt** Ernst †, Der Aufstand Hiskias...: AnBib 106, 1986 ⮕ 2,2136; 3,2824: ᴿBL (1988) 94s (R. E. *Clements*: admirable clarity); BO 45 (1988) 648-650 (H. *Spieckermann*: würdiger Abschluss seines Lebenswerkes); CBQ 50 (1988) 519s (W. W. *Frerichs*); NRT 110 (1988) 111s (J.-L. *Ska*); RelStR 14 (1988) 68 (M. A. *Sweeney*).

2982 **Tatum** Lynn W., From text to tell; King Manasseh in the biblical and archaeological record: diss. Duke, ᴰ*Meyers* E. Durham NC 1988. 561 p. 88-22039. – DissA 49 (1988s) 2271-A.

2983 *Eslinger* Lyle, Josiah and the Torah book; comparison of 2 Kgs 22:1-23:28 and 2 Chr 34:1-35:19: HebAnR 10 (1986) 37-62.

2984 **Tagliacarne** Pierfelice, 'Keiner war wie er'; Untersuchung zur Struktur von 2 Könige 22-23: Diss. ᴰ*Seidl*. München 1987s. – TR 84 (1988) 512.

2985 *Lurja* Ben-Zion, ✪ [2 Kgs 22,8] Shafan, the king's scribe: BethM 34,118 (1988s) 261-4.

2986 **Zawadzki** Stefan, The fall of Assyria and Median-Babylonian relations in light of the Nabupolassar Chronicle: Historia 149. Poznań/Delft 1988, Univ. Mickiewicza/Eburon. 83-232-0122-6 / 90-5166-034-0 [OIAc D88].

2987 *Bakon* Shimon, Josiah, the impact of his life and death: Dor 17 (1988s) 163-9.

2988 *Spieckermann* Hermann, Josia: ⮕ 813, TRE 17 (1987) 264-7.

2989 *a)* *Talstra* E., De hervorming van Josia, of de kunst van het beeldenstormen; – *b)* *Spronk* K., Aanhangsel of uitvloeisel? over het slot van het deuteronomistische geschiedeniswerk (2 Koningen 25:27-30): GerefTTs 88 (1988) 143-161 / 162-170.

2990 *Malamat* A., The kingdom of Judah between Egypt and Babylon; a small state within a great power confrontation: ⮕ 47, ᶠFENSHAM F., Text 1988, 117-129.

2991 *Green* Alberto R., [2 Kgs 23,29] Ashur-Uballit II and the inscription 88 from Arad; an observation [on *Aharoni* Y. and *Yadin* Y.; the last Assyrian king told Josiah to allow passage to Necho]: ZAW 100 (1988) 277-280; deutsch 281.

2992 **Visaticki** Karlo, Die Reform des Josija und die religiöse Heterodoxie in Israel: diss. Pont. Univ. Gregoriana, ᴰ*Prato* G. Roma 1987. xii-335 p.; publ. N° 3428, 329 p. – RTLv 19,535.

2993 **Wiseman** D. J., Nebuchadrezzar and Babylon (Schweich Lectures 1983) 1985 ⮞ 1,2908 ... 3,2836: ᴿBSOAS 51 (1988) 121s (J. F. *Healey*); PhoenixEOL 33,2 (1987) 62s (K. R. *Veenhof*).

2994 *Kegler* Jürgen, Die Verarbeitung der Zerstörung Jerusalems 587/6 in der prophetischen Überlieferung Jeremias und Ezechiels: ⮞ 469, Wünschet 1986/8, 303-312.

2995 *Ben-Yashar* M., The last kings of Judah [Johanan of 1 Chr 3,15 is Joahaz...]: ⮞ 43, ᶠEʟɪᴛᴢᴜʀ Y., II (1986) 111-133.

2996 *Wanke* Gunther, Jojachin/Jojakim: ⮞ 813, TRE 17 (1987) 225-7 / 227-9.

E5.1 *Chronicorum libri* – The Chronicler.

2997 *Allen* Leslie C., Kerygmatic units in 1&2 Chron.: JStOT 41 (1988) 21-36.

2998 **Becker** J., 1 Chronik I: NEchter 18, 1986 ⮞ 3,2840: ᴿBL (1988) 55 (H. G. M. *Williamson*: sparse, eclectic); BLtg 61 (1988) 142-4 (G. *Steins*). – II. Lfg 20. Wü 1988, Echter. 133 p. [JBL 107,785].

2999 *Begg* Christopher T., *a*) The classical prophets in the Chronistic history: BZ 32 (1988) 100-7; – *b*) Babylon and Judah in Chronicles [... Jᴏsᴇᴘʜᴜs]: ETL 64 (1988) 142-163.

3000 **Braun** Roddy L., 1 Chronicles: Word Comm. 14, 1986 ⮞ 2,2144; 3,2841: ᴿBL (1988) 56 (R. J. *Coggins*: defense of Solomon unexpected since 2 Chron will have a different author); EvQ 60 (1988) 354s (W. *Johnstone*); GraceTJ 9 (1988) 288s (D. G. *Barker*); Interpretation 42 (1988) 92s (J. C. *McCann*); RefTR (1987) 83 (A. M. *Harman*); TLZ 113 (1988) 431-3 (K.-D. *Schunck*: holds 1-9 post-'Chronicler').

3001 *De Vries* Simon J., *a*) The forms of prophetic address in Chronicles: HebAnR 10 (1986) 15-36; – *b*) Moses and David as cult founders in Chronicles: JBL 107 (1988) 619-639.

3002 **Dillard** Raymond B., 2 Chronicles: Word comm 15, 1987 ⮞ 3,2485; xxiv-323 p. $25 [GraceTJ 9,305]. 0-8499-0214-2.

3003 **Duke** Rodney K., A rhetorical analysis of the Books of Chronicles; the Chronicler's art of persuasion: diss. Emory, ᴰ*Hayes* J. Atlanta 1988. 252 p. 88-16937. – DissA 49 (1988s) 1481-A; RTLv 20,539.

3004 **Im Tae-Soo**, Das Davidbild in den Chronikbüchern; David als Idealbild des theokratischen Messianismus für den Chronisten: EurHS 23/263, 1985 ⮞ 2,2145: ᴿNedTTs 42 (1988) 250s (P. B. *Dirksen*).

3005 **Johnson** Fred H., Twice told tales; ... David in Chronicles: diss. Drew 1947. 344 p. 88-07380. DissA 49 (1988s) 100-A.

3006 **Kegler** J., *Augustin* M., Synopse zum chronistischen Geschichtswerk 1984 ⮞ 65,2539 ... 3,2843: ᴿNedTTs 42 (1988) 255s (K. A. D. *Smelik*).

3007 *Kellermann* Ulrich, Anmerkungen zum Verständnis der Tora in den chronistischen Schriften: BibNot 42 (1988) 49-92.

3008 **McConville** J.G., I&II Chronicles: Daily Study Bible 1984 ⮞ 65,2540... 2, 2149: ᴿCBQ 50 (1988) 301s (S.B. *Reid*, also on his Ezra, rather severely).

3009 **McKenzie** Steven L., The Chronicler's use of the Deuteronomistic history: HarvSemMon 33, 1984 ⮞ 1,2913 ... 3,2846: ᴿBZ 32 (1988) 135-7 (Helga *Weippert*).

3010 *Mendels* D., [Chron] 'Creative history' in the Hellenistic Near East in the third and second centuries B.C.; the Jewish case: JPseud 2 (1988) 13-20.

3011 **Noth** Martin, The Chronicler's history [1943] 1987 ⮞ 3,2847: ᴿThemelios 14 (1988s) 66 (G. *McConville*).

3012 **Pratt** Richard L., Royal prayer and the Chronicler's program: diss. Harvard. CM 1988. – HarvTR 81 (1988) 453s; RelStR 15,193.

3013 *Simon* Rashi, The book of Chronicles, its history and purpose: Dor 17 (1988s) 190-6.
3014 **Throntveit** Mark A., When kings speak ... Chr ᴰ1987 ➤ 3,2849; 0-89130-998-5; pa. 9-3: ᴿETL 64 (1988) 196s (J. *Lust*); JBL 107 (1988) 517s (R. L. *Braun*).
3015 *a*) *Wahl* Thomas P., Chronicles; the rewriting of history; – *b*) *Boadt* Lawrence, Chronicles and genealogies: BToday 26 (1988) 197-202 / 203-8.
3016 *a*) *Weinberg* Joel P., Gott im Weltbild des Chronisten; die vom Chronisten verschwiegenen Gottesnamen; – *b*) *Ackroyd* Peter R., Chronicle-Ezra-Nehemiah; the concept of unity: ➤ 153, ZAW 100 Supp. (1988) 170-189 / 189-201.
3017 *Weinberg* J. P. ❻ Man in the world-picture of the Chronist; his mentality: ➤ 456*, Peredneaz. IV (1986) 91-104.
3018 **Wilcock** Michael, The message of Chronicles 1987 ➤ 3,2852: ᴿBL (1988) 97 (H. *Williamson*); BS 145 (1988) 465s (T. L. *Constable*); EvQ 60 (1988) 362s (J. *Job*: very distinguished); RefTR 47 (1988) 26 (A. M. *Harman*).
3019 *Wypych* Stanisław, Das Werk des Chronisten: ➤ 327, Höre ... Theologie des ATes 1987, 121-141.

3020 *Aufrecht* Walter E., Genealogy and history in ancient Israel: ➤ 29, Mem. CRAIGIE P., Ascribe 1988, 205-235.
3021 *Bar Magen* M., ❻ *Îšîm wᵉ-yuḥusîm*... Men and (genealogical) relationships in the Bible: BethM 34,117 (1988s) 149-152.
3022 **Johnson** Marshall D., The purpose of the biblical genealogies with special reference to the setting of the genealogies of Jesus² [¹1969 ➤ 51,2298]: SNTS Mg 8. C 1988, Univ. xxxiv-310 p. 0-521-35644-X.
3023 *Ben Zvi* Ehud, The authority of 1-2 Chronicles in the late Second Temple period: JPseud 3 (1988) 59-88.
3024 *Schneider* Tsvi, [1 Chr 5,29-41; 9,10s; Ezra 7,1] Azariahu son of Hilkiahu (high priest?) on a City of David bulla [= ❻ Qadmoniot 81s (1988) 56]: IsrEJ 38 (1988) 139-141; 1 fig.
3025 *Edelman* Diana, The Asherite genealogy in 1 Chronicles 7:3-40: BiRes 33 (Ch 1988) 13-23.
3026 *Hausmann* Jutta, Gottesdienst als Gotteslob; Erwägungen zu 1 Chr 16,8-36: in, ᴱ**Wagner** H., Spiritualität (Stu 1987) 83-92 [< ZAW 101.327].
3027 *Garfinkel* Yosef, 2 Chr 11:5-10 fortified cities list and the *Lmlk* stamps — reply to Nadav NAʼAMAN: BASOR [261 (1986) 5-21] 271 (1988) 69-73; 74-77 rejoinder.
3028 *Handy* Lowell K., [2 Chr 29-31] Hezekiah's unlikely reform [depends on influence of ALBRIGHT and ROWLEY, and on Chr reliability]: ZAW 100 (1988) 111-5.
3029 *Throntveit* Mark A., [2 Chr 29-32] Hezekiah in the Books of Chronicles: ➤ 500, SBL Seminars 1988, 302-311.
3030 *Begg* Christopher, The fate of Judah's four last kings in the book of Chronicles [II 36: does not indicate]: OrLovPer 18 (1987) 79-85.

E5.4   *Esdrae libri*, **Ezra-Nehemiah.**

3031 *Begg* Christopher, Ben-Sirach's non-mention of Ezra: BibNot 42 (1988) 14-18.

3032 **Blenkinsopp** Joseph, Ezra-Nehemiah, a commentary. Ph 1988, Westminster. 366 p. $30 [JBL 108,153].

3033 *Burggraf* Wayne A., Ezra, an example of leadership: CalvaryB 4,1 (1988) 43-60.

3034 *a) Crüsemann* F., Israel in der Perserzeit; eine Skizze in Auseinandersetzung mit Max WEBER; – *b) Talmon* Shemaryahu, Jüdische Sektenbildung in der Frühzeit der Periode des Zweiten Tempels; ein Nachtrag zu Max Webers Studie über das antike Judentum; – *c) Wasserstein* A., Die Hellenisierung des Frühjudentums; die Rabbinen und die griechische Philosophie: ⇒ 498, ^E*Schluchter* W., Max Webers Sicht 1985, 205-232 / 233-280 / 281-316.

3035 *Boschi* B. G., Alle radici del Giudaismo [Babilonia (Persia); Ezra, contro *Koch* K.]: ⇒ 474, Correnti 1984/7, 9-23.

3036 **Eskenazi** Tamara C., In an age of prose; a literary approach to Ezra-Nehemiah: SBL Mg 36. Atlanta 1988, Scholars. viii-211 p. [JBL 108,184]. 1-55540-260-7; pa. 1-5.

3037 *Eskenazi* Tamara C., The structure of Ezra-Nehemiah and the integrity of the book: JBL 107 (1988) 641-656: analysis of the many lists proves that Ez-Neh is not continuation of Chr.

Ezra-Nehemiah ❶ 1987 ⇒ 1847.

3038 *Fang* Mark, ❻ History and theology of Esdras I, II: ColcFuJen 77 (1988) 399-410.

3039 **Hausmann** Jutta, Israels Rest ^D1987 ⇒ 3,2869: ^RProtestantesimo 43 (1988) 213 (J. A. *Soggin*: di altissimo valore); TüTQ 168 (1988) 339s (W. *Gross*); ZAW 100 (1988) 317 (H.-C. *Schmitt*).

3040 **Holmgren** F. C., Israel alive again: comm Ezra-N. 1987 ⇒ 3,2870: ^RThemelios 14 (1988s) 104 (M. J. *Selman*).

3041 **Koch** Heidemarie, Persien zur Zeit des Dareios; das Achaemenidenreich im Lichte neuer Quellen: Univ. Marburg vorgesch. Seminar 25. Marburg 1988, Elwert. 40 p.; 30 fig. – ^RZAW 100 (1988) 459 (O. *Kaiser*).

3042 **Lightstone** J. N., Society, the sacred, and Scripture in ancient Judaism; a sociology of knowledge: Studies in Christianity and Judaism 3. Waterloo ON 1988, W. Laurier Univ. xiii-126 p. $17.50. [ZAW 101,467, H.-C. *Schmitt*].

3043 *Rofé* Alexander, ❾ Promise and desertion — Eretz Israel and the beginning of the Second Commonwealth: CHistEI 41 (1986) 3-10.

3044 *Talshir* David, A reinvestigation of the linguistic relationship between Chronicles and Ezra-Nehemiah: VT 38 (1988) 165-193 [against H. *Williamson* concludes that the burden of proof is rather on those who deny identical authorship; confirmed p. 358s].

3045 **Williamnson** H. G. M., Ezra-N., Word 16, 1985 ⇒ 2,2176; 3,2880: ^RÉgl-T 18 (1987) 358-360 (W. *Vogels*); VT 38 (1988) 253 (G. W. *Anderson*).

3046 **Williamson** H. G. M., Ezra and Nehemiah: OTGuides 1987 ⇒ 3,2881: ^RJStJud 19 (1988) 96-98 (E. *Tigchelaar,* also on COGGINS R., Hag-Mal); ScripB 19 (1988s) 22 (J. E. *Rybolt*); VT 38 (1988) 128 (J. A. *Emerton*).

3047 *Williamson* H. G. M., The governors of Judah under the Persians [Tyndale biblical Archaeology Lecture 1987]: TyndaleB 39 (1988) 59-82.

––––

3048 *Krüger* Thomas, Esra 1-6; Struktur und Konzept: BibNot 41 (1988) 65-75.

3049 *Williamson* H. G. M., [Ezra 2,2; 3,2 ...] Zerubbabel: ⇒ 801, ISBEnc³ 4 (1988) 1191s.

3050 *Zadok* R., A note on *sn'h* [Ezra 2,35]: VT 38 (1988) 483-6.
3051 *H.-Mallau* Hans, The redaction of Ezra 4-6; a plea for a theology of scribes: PerspRelSt 15,4 (1988) 67-80.
3052 **Getz** Gene A., Nehemia. Haag 1986, Voorhoeve. *f*24,50 [KerkT 39,354].
3053 **Gunneweg** A.H.J., Nehemia [with introd. & chronology reprinted from 1986 Esra]: KAT 19/2. Gü 1988, Mohn. 216p. DM68; sb.60. 3-579-04281-5 [BL 89,77 G.H. *Jones*].
3054 *Holmgren* Frederick C., [Neh 5,19; 13,14; 6,14; 13,29] Remember me, remember them: ➤ 141, ᶠSTUHLMUELLER C., Scripture and prayer 1988, 33-45.
3055 *Bliese* Loren F., Chiastic structures, peaks and cohesion in Nehemiah 9.6-37: BTrans 39 (1988) 208-215.
3056 *Spaer* Arnold, [Neh 12,11] Jaddua the High Priest?: IsrNumJ 9 (1986s) 1-3.

3057 **Cousin** H., *al.,* Quatrième livre d'Esdras, traduction française, présentation et index. Lyon 1987, Fac. Théologie. 81p. 2-85317-037-3. [NTAbs 32,289].
3058 *Cook* Joan E. [4 Esdras 8,20-36] Ezra's confession; appeal to a merciful God: JPseud 3 (1988) 89-100.
3059 *Stone* Michael E., The question of the Messiah in IV Ezra: ➤ 494, Judaisms/Messiahs 1987, 209-224.

E5.5 **Libri Tobiae, Judith, Esther.**

3060 *Bertrand* Daniel A., [Tob 2,13] Le chevreau d'Anna; la signification de l'anecdotique dans le livre de Tobit: RHPR 68 (1988) 269-274.
3061 **Gross** Heinrich, Tobit/Judit: NEchter 19, 1987 ➤ 3,2900: ᴿOTAbs 11 (1988) 198 (R.D. *Gehrke*).
3062 **Marinoni** M.C., La versione valdese del libro di Tobia: Traduttologia 2. Bari 1986, Schena. 106p. – ᴿAevum 62 (1988) 402-8 (E. *Barbieri*).
3063 *a) Nowell* Irene, The narrator in the book of Tobit; – *b) Soll* William, Tobit and folklore studies, with emphasis on PROPP's Morphology; – *c) Nickelsburg* George W.E., Tobit and Enoch; distant cousins with a recognizable resemblance: ➤ 500, SBL Seminars 1988, 27-38 / 39-53 / 54-68.

3064 *Alonso Schökel* Luis, Judith, ᵀ*González* Justo L. ➤ 1985, ᴱ**Mays** J., Harper's Bible Commentary (1988) 804-814.
3065 **Grintz** Y.M. ✪ Sefer Yehudith, 2d printing. J 1986, Bialik. 244p.; 22 fig.; maps. [KirSef 61,395].
3066 **Moore** Carey A., Judith: AnchorB 40, 1985 ➤ 1,2948*; 2,2190: ᴿCBQ 50 (1988) 305s (J.F. *Craghan*: his Tobit awaited).
3067 **Straten** Adelheid, Das Judith-Thema in Deutschland im 16. Jahrhundert [Diss. München 1983]: Studien zur Ikonographie. München 1983, Minerva. 301p.; ill. – LuJb 55 (1988) 166.
3068 *Zenger* Erich, Judith [/buch]: ➤ 813, TRE 17 (1988) 404-8.
3069 *Gardner* Anne E., The song of praise in Judith 16: 2-17 (LXX 16:1-17): HeythJ 29 (1988) 413-422.

3070 *Bergey* Ronald L., Post-exilic Hebrew linguistic developments in Esther; a diachronic approach: JEvTS 31 (1988) 161-8 [< ZIT 88,588].

3071 *Costas* Orlando E., The subversiveness of faith; Esther as a paradigm for a liberating theology: EcuR 40 (1988) 66-78.

3072 *Dionisotti* A.C., The letter of Mardochaeus the Jew to Alexander the Great [5-page Latin text, probably of Jewish origin and possibly from 2-4 century C.E.]: JWarbC 51 (1988) 1-13.

3073 **Gallazzi** Sandro, Ester, a mulher que enfrentou o palácio: Comentário bíblico ecuménico. Petrópolis 1987, Vozes/Metodista/Sinodal. 185 p. – ᴿREB 48 (1988) 498-500 (J.P.T. *Zabatiero*).

3074 **Gallazzi** S., Ester, ᵀ*Pistocchi* Bruno. R 1987, Borla. 236 p. Lit. 15000 [CC 139/2 dopo p. 208]. 88-263-0539-0.

3074* *Greenstein* Edward L., A Jewish reading of Esther: ⇥ 3,355, ᴱ*Neusner* J., Judaic perspectives 1987, 225-243.

3075 **Herrmann** W., Ester im Streit der Meinungen 1986 ⇥ 2,2195; 3,2910: ᴿBL (1988) 78 (D.J.A. *Clines*).

3076 *Jackowski* Karol, Holy disobedience in Esther: TTod 45 (1988s) 403-414.

3077 *Lazarus-Yafeh* Haya, [Esth 2,10 Meg.] ✪ Queen Esther — [described as] one of the Marranos?: Tarbiz 57 (1987s) 121s; Eng. V.

3078 **Lemosín Martal** Rogelio, El libro de Ester y el Irán antiguo; estudio filológico-derásico de vocablos aramoelamitas persas: Bibl. Hispana Bíblica 10. M 1983, Inst. Suárez. 215 p.; ill. – KirSef 61 (1986s) p. 391.

3079 *Margaliot* Meshullam, The hidden strife between the God of Israel and Haman; mantic aspects in the Esther scroll: ⇥ 3,62*, ᶠGratz College 1987...

3080 *Moore* Carey A., Esther revisited again; a further examination of certain Esther studies of the past ten years: HebAnR 7 (1983) 169-186 [< OTAbs 11,270].

3081 **Musaph-Andriesse** R., Ester, het oude verhaal opnieuw vertaald en ingeleid. Baarn 1987, Ten Have. 79 p. ƒ15. ᴿStreven 55 (1987s) 948s (P. *Beentjes*).

3082 *Hutter* Manfred, [Esther 7,8...] Iranische Neujahrsfestmythologie und der Traum des Mordechai: BibNot 44 (1988) 39-45.

3083 *Uchelen* N.A. Van, [Esther/Purim] Tosephta Megillah III, 28; a tannaitic text with a mystic connotation?: ⇥ 479, Mysticism 1984/7, 87-94.

3084 *Waegeman* Maryse, Motifs and structure in the Book of Esther: ⇥ 469, Wünschet 1986/8, 371-384.

E5.8 *Machabaeorum libri,* 1-2 [-4] Maccabees.

3085 **Baronowski** Donald W., Treaties of military alliance between Rome and Hellenistic states in the last three centuries B.C.: diss. Toronto 1982. Available from National Library in 5 microfiches, Ottawa. 0-315-14277-4 [OIAc N88].

3086 **Bickerman** Elias J., The Jews in the Greek age [completed just before his death in 1981; 'stability and change in Jewish society 330-175 B.C.E.'].ᴱ*Baumgarten* Albert. CM 1988, Harvard Univ. xii-338 p. $30 [TDig 36,46]. – ᴿTS 49 (1988) 731s (D.J. *Harrington*).

3087 *Dimant* Devorah, [Mcb Wis] The problem of non-translated biblical Greek: ⇥ 478, ᴱ*Cox* C., 6th LXX 1986/7, 1-19.

3087* *Eisen* Arnold, Self and other, self as other; teaching the history of Judaism: ⇥ 947*, Critical Review 1 (1988) 43-60.

3088 **Efron** Joshua, Studies on the Hasmonean period: StJudLA 39, Leiden 1987, Brill. xvi-442 p. ƒ144 [JBL 108,184].

3089 **Enermalm-Ogawa** Agneta, Un langage de prière juif en grec ... 1-2 Mcb [diss. 1986]: ConBib NT 17, 1987 ➤ 3,2918: RBibTB 18 (1988) 149 (L. E. *Frizzell*); CBQ 50 (1988) 676s (D. J. *Harrington*); RTPhil 120 (1988) 373s (T. *Römer*); SvEx 53 (1988) 116-8 (C. *Cavallin*).

3090 **Goldstein** Jonathan A., II Maccabees: AnchorB 41A, 1983 ➤ 64,2931 ... 3,2920: RJTS 39 (1988) 119s (M. *Goodman*); ZkT 110 (1988) 102-4 (J. M. *Oesch*).

3091 *a) Goldstein* Jonathan A., How the authors of 1 and 2 Maccabees treated the 'messianic' promises; – *b) Collins* John J., Messianism in the Maccabean period: ➤ 494, Judaisms/Messiahs 1987, 69-96 / 97-109.

3092 **Harrington** Daniel J., The Maccabean revolt; anatomy of a biblical revolution: OT Studies 1. Wilmington 1988, Glazier. 143 p. $10 [Rel-StR 15,273, R. D. *Chesnutt*].

3093 **Kampen** John, The Hasideans and the origins of Pharisaism; a study in 1 and 2 Maccabees [diss. HUC, DWacholder B.]: SBL SeptCog 24. Atlanta 1988, Scholars. x-241 p. $18; sb./pa. $12 [JBL 108,185].

3094 *Kellermann* Diether, Die Bücher der Makkabäer: ➤ 327, Höre ... Theologie des ATes 1987, 167-182.

3095 *Laperrousaz* E.-M., Une analyse ethnologique de la révolte machabéenne [*Will* E., *Orrieux* C. 1986]: RÉAnc 90 (1988) 183-6.

Mendels D., The land of Israel as a political concept in Hasmonean literature [1 Mcb, Dan 7-12, Sirach, Judith, 1 Henoch, Jubilees...]: TStAntJud 15, 1987 ➤ h285.

3096 *VanderKam* James C., Hanukkah, its timing and significance according to 1 and 2 Maccabees: JPseud 1 (1987) 23-40.

3097 *Hall* Robert G., [1 Mcb 1,15] Epispasm [the unmaking of circumcision] and the dating of ancient Jewish writings: JPseud 2 (1988) 71-86.

3098 **Schmidt** W., Untersuchungen zur Fälschung historischer Dokumente bei Pseudo-Aristaios [und 2 Mcb 1,1-19...; Diss. DVogt E]: Diss.-Reihe Klas. Pg. 37. Bonn 1986, Habelt. x-165 p. DM 38 [ZAW 101,167, I. *Kottsieper*].

3099 **Henten** Jan Willem van, De joodse martelaren ... 2/4 Makk. D1986 ➤ 2,2211*: RNedTTs 42 (1988) 78s (A. C. *Kooyman*: overtuigend).

3100 *Jonge* M. de, Jesus, death for others and the death of the Maccabean martyrs [2 Mcb 6,18-31; 7; 4 Mcb 5-7; 8-18]: ➤ 85, FKLIJN A., Text 1988, 142-151.

3101 *Gardner* Anne E., ⊕ III and IV Maccabees; reflection on the Maccabean crisis [III (100 B.C.E.) and IV (18-54 C.E.) not misnamed because they adopt elements of II Mcb]: Zion 53 (1988) 291-301; Eng. xi.

3102 *Parente* Fausto, The third book of Maccabees as ideological document and historical source: Henoch 10 (1988) 143-181; franç. 181s.

Williams David S., Josephus and IV Maccabees D1988 ➤ d436*.

VII. Libri didactici VT

E6.1	*Poesis .1 metrica,* **Biblical versification.**

3103 **Alonso Schökel** Luis, A manual of Hebrew poetics: SubsBPont 11. R 1988, Pontificio Istituto Biblico. xi-228 p. Lit. 24.500. 88-7653-567-5.

3104 **Alonso Schökel** Luis, Manual de poética [< Hermenéutica de la palabra II]: Academia Christiana 41. M 1988, Cristiandad. 251 p. pt. 800. 84-7057-424-8.

3105 **Alter** Robert, The art of biblical poetry 1985 → 1,2978 ... 3,2930: ᴿCBQ 50 (1988) 673-5 (A. R. *Ceresko*: some of the analyses seem to be prior and contradictory to the overall program).

3106 *Alter* Robert, Structures of intensification in Hebrew poetry: → 3,355, ᴱ*Neusner* J., Judaic perspectives 1987, 189-206.

3107 **Angoujard** Jean-Pierre, Aspects d'une micro-prosodie (le modèle arabe): diss. d'État P VIII, ᴰ*Ruwet* N. – ᴿLOrA 1 (Lv 1988) 197-9 (G. *Bohas*).

3108 *Bar-Magen* M., ❼ *Hitqabbûlat* ... parallelism in the Bible: BethM 34,118 (1988s) 207-215.

3109 *Bazak* Jacob, a) Numerical devices in biblical poetry: VT 38 (1988) 332-7; – b) ❼ Unnoticed literary ornaments (arithmetical) in biblical poetry: BethM 34,116 (1988s) 39-49.

3110 **Berlin** Adele, The dynamics of biblical parallelism 1985 → 1,2983 ... 3,2933: ᴿAfO 34 (1987) 89-91 (S. *Segert*); BO 44 (1987) 757-9 (J. P. *Fokkelman*); CBQ 50 (1988) 107s (R. C. *Culley*: appealing); JBL 107 (1988) 734-6 (P. D. *Miller*); Themelios 14 (1988s) 29s (K. M. *Craig*).

3111 ᴱ**Carmi** T., The Penguin book of Hebrew verse 1981 → 63,2991; 64,2943: ᴿScripB 19 (1988s) 45s (W. G. E. *Watson*).

3112 **Cloete** W. T. W., Verse and prose; does the distinction apply to the Old Testament?: JNSW 14 (1988) 9-15.

3113 **Diakonov** I. M., ❼ Lyric poetry of the ancient East, ᵀ*Achmatovoy* A., al. Moskva 1984, Nauka. 230 p.; ill. [KirSef 61,393].

3114 **Dion** Paul E., Hebrew poetics; a student's guide. Mississauga ON 1988, Benben. v-44 p. $7 [JBL 108,184].

3115 **Fisch** Harold, Poetry with a purpose, biblical poetics and interpretation: Indiana Studies in Biblical Literature. Bloomington 1988, Indiana Univ. vii-205 p. $37.50 0-253-34557-X [NTAbs 32,400].

3116 ᴱ**Follis** Elaine R., Directions in biblical Hebrew poetry 1987 → 3,540: ᴿBL (1988) 73 (J. *Gibson*); ETL 64 (1988) 191 (J. *Lust*); ÉTRel 63 (1988) 452s (Françoise *Smyth*).

3117 **Gerstenberger** E. S., Psalms I [to Ps 60] with an Introduction to Cultic Poetry: FOTLit 14 [5th of the 24 to appear]. GR 1988, Eerdmans. xv-260. £16 (Exeter, Paternoster). 0-8028-0255-9. [BL 89,54, J. H. *Eaton*].

3118 **Grol** H. van, De versbouw in het klassieke Hebreeuws; fundamentele verkenningen: diss. Kath. Theol. Hoogschule, ᴰ*Beuken* W. Amst 1986, auct. xii-267 p. – ᴿBL (1988) 77 (W. *Watson*); RB 95 (1988) 447s (R. J. *Tournay*); ZAW 100 (1988) 316 (D. *Kinet*).

3119 **Krašovec** Jože, Antithetic structure in biblical Hebrew poetry: VTSup 35, 1984 → 65,2604 ... 3,2936: ᴿCBQ 50 (1988) 503-5 (W. G. E. *Watson* has found ten examples in Ugaritic though K. says there are none).

3120 *Mathieu* Bernard, Études de métrique égyptienne, I. Le distique heptamétrique dans les chants d'amour: → 119, Mém. POSENER G., RÉgp 39 (1988) 63-81; Eng. 82.

3121 **Meer** Willem van der, **Moor** Johannes C. de, The structural analysis of biblical and Canaanite poetry: JStOT Sup 74. Sheffield 1988, Academic. ix-423 p. $37.50. 1-85075-194-3 [BL 89,156].

3122 *Moor* Johannes C. de, Narrative poetry in Canaan [Mesha ...]: UF 20 (1988) 149-171.

3123 *Reed* W. L., A poetics of the Bible; problems and possibilities: JLit&T 1,2 (Ox 1987) 154-166 [NTAbs 32,144].

3124 *Reyburn* William D., Poetic parallelism; its structure, meaning and implication for translators: ➤ 502, Issues/Translation 1987/8, 81-112.
3125 *Soll* William M., [Ps 145; 25; Prov. 31, 10-31] Babylonian and biblical acrostics: Biblica 69 (1988) 305-322; franç. 323.
3126 **Watson** W. G. E., Classical Hebrew poetry 1984 ➤ 65,2607; 1,2231 (1986 ➤ 3,2945): ᴿAulaOr 6 (1988) 285-7 (H. *Simian-Yofre*); BO 45 (1988) 389-393 (T. *Booij*).
3127 *Watson* W. G. E., a) Delaying devices in Ugaritic verse: ➤ 98, ᶠLORETZ O., StEpL 5 (1988) 207-218; – b) Internal (half-line) parallelism in Ugaritic once more: UF 20 (1988) 365-374; – c) More on metathetic parallelism [*Bronznick* N. e.g. Ps 35,7]: WeltOr 19 (1988) 40-44.
3128 **Zurro** E., Procedimientos iterativos en la poesía ugarítica y hebrea: BibOrPont 43,1987 ➤ 3,2947: ᴿArTGran 51 (1988) 405s (A. *Torres*); BL (1988) 99 (W. *Watson*); Orientalia 57 (1988) 408-410 (also W. G. E. *Watson*); RB 95 (1988) 614s (R. J. *Tournay*).

E6.2   Psalmi, textus.

3129 **Ammassari** Antonio, Il Salterio latino di Pietro [terza delle quattro versioni nel codice Cassinese Latino 557, XII sec., con indizi di originale ebraico] 1987 ➤ 3,2949: ᴿBL (1989) 43s (R. *Murray*: claims modestly that the author wrote 'in persona Petri' but emphatically that he held a Jerusalem-Franciscan-style Judaeo-Christian theology); CC 139 (1988,3) 199-201 (G. L. *Prato*); ErbAuf 64 (1988) 232s (O. *Tramèr*).
3130 **Díez Macho** A, Biblia babilónica, fragmentos de Salmos, Job, y Proverbios, ᴱ*Navarro Peiro* Ángeles 1987 ➤ 3,2955: ᴿSefarad 48 (1988) 429s (María T. *Ortega Monasterio*).
3131 **Díez Merino** Luis, Targum de Salmos 1982 ➤ 64,2960 ... 3,2956: ᴿCBQ 50 (1988) 111-3 (Z. *Garber,* also on his Job and Prov).
3132 **Estin** Colette, Les Psautiers de JÉRÔME ᴰ1984 ➤ 65,2614 ... 3,2957: ᴿRivStoLR 24 (1988) 166 (B. *Chiesa*).
3133 **Giversen** Søren, Psalm Book I-II: Manichaean Coptic Papyri in the Chester Beatty Library, Facsimile Edition 3s/ Cahiers d'Orientalisme 16s. Geneva 1988, Cramer. xiv-344 pl.; xi-234 pl. [RelStR 15,264, B. A. *Pearson*].
3134 **Kahsnitz** Rainer, Der Werdener Psalter in Berlin. Dü 1979, Schwann. 488 p.; 411 fig.; 1 color. pl. DM 72. – ᴿTrierTZ 97 (1988) 76 (E. *Sauser*).
3135 *Kahsnitz* Rainer, Der christologische Zyklus im Odbert-Psalter: Zts Kunstgeschichte 51,1 (Mü 1988) 33-125; 72 fig.
3136 ᴱ*Mortari* Luciana, Il Salterio della tradizione ... LXX 1983 ➤ 64,2963a ... 2,2240: ᴿDivThom 89s (1986s) 525-9 (G. *Perini*).
3137 *Papazoglou* Georges K., Le Michel Cantacuzène du Codex Mavrocordatianus et le possesseur homonyme du Psautier de Harvard: RÉByz 46 (1988) 161-5.
3138 *Petraglio* Renzo, Le interpolazioni cristiane del Salterio greco: ➤ 570, AugR 28 (1988) 89-109.
3139 **Sàvoca** Gaetano, I canti di Sion; traduzione interlineare dei Salmi Ebraici² [¹1983]. Messina 1986, Quartiere. 260 p. – ᴿBbbOr 30 (1988) 185.
3140 **Wagenaar** Christofoor, Het boek der psalmen naar de Septuagint: Schrift en Liturgie 12. Bonheiden 1988, Abdij Bethlehem. 447 p. ƒ 66,25. 90-71837-11-4 [Bijdragen 49,360].

3141 **Wilson** Gerald H.,   The editing of the Hebrew Psalter 1985 → 1,3022 ...
3,2970:   ᴿBO 45 (1988) 178-183 (J. *Becker*); ÉglT 17 (1986) 387s (L.
Laberge); OLZ 83 (1988) 424s (G. *Pfeifer*); VT 38 (1988) 253s (H. G. M.
Williamson).

E6.3   **Psalmi, introductio.**

3142 **Allen** Leslie C.,   Psalms [Commentary (Word 21) 1985 → 3151]; Biblical
themes 1987 → 3,2971:   ᴿBibTB 18 (1988) 85 (T. A. *Hoffman*); EstBíb 46
(1988) 136s (V. *Morla*); VT 38 (1988) 374 (R. P. *Gordon*).
3143 *Gevaryahu* Haim,   Tehillim, the book of Psalms [lecture Princeton 1976]:
Dor 16 (1987s) 235-241; 17 (1988s) 83-90.
3144 **Longman** Tremperᴵᴵᴵ,   How to read the Psalms. DG/Leicester 1988,
Inter-Varsity. 106 p. [CBQ 51,402].
3145 **Miller** P. D.,   Interpreting the Psalms 1986 → 2,2256; 3,2975:   ᴿAnglTR
69 (1987) 86s (D. J. *Harrington*).
3146 **Ravasi** Gianfranco, [antologia per illustrare i metodi dei suoi tre volumi
→ 3161] 1985 → 2,3029:   ᴿSalesianum 50 (1988) 228s (M. *Cimosa*).
3147 *Rouillard* P.,   Psaumes: → 786, Catholicisme 12,54 (1988) 176-194 (-196,
Psautier).
3148 *Simonetti* Manlio,   I 'Salmi' nel Nuovo Testamento: Orpheus 9 (1988)
1-20.
3149 **Treves** M.,   The dates of the psalms [all but 45 and two others from
170-103 B.C.E.]; history and poetry in ancient Israel.   Pisa 1988, Giardini.
109 p. [BL 89,95, G. W. *Anderson*: fascinating, unconvincing].
3150 **Zenger** E., Mit meinem Gott überspringe ich Mauern ... Ps.Buch 1987
→ 3,2977:   ᴿErbAuf 64 (1988) 234 (E. *Tschacher*).

E6.4   **Psalmi, commentarii.**

3151 **Allen** Leslie C., Psalms 101-150: Word Comm. 21, 1983 → 64,2976;
1,3032; 2,2258:   ᴿSvEx 53 (1988) 112-4 (L. O. *Eriksson*).
3152 *Béné* Charles, *al.* ERASMUS D., Opera V-2s [les seuls textes de l'AT dont
il a traité, onze Psaumes: 1-4; 14; 22; 28; 33; 38; 83; 85]. Amst 1985,
North-Holland.   iv-400 p.; 7 pl.; iv-449 p.; 5 pl. – ᴿLatomus 47 (1988)
211s (R. *Crahay*).
3153 *Conley* Thomas M.,   Grammar and rhetoric in Euthymius ZIGABENUS'
commentary on Psalms 1-50:   ILCLSt 12,2 ('Byzantium and its legacy'
1987) 265-275.
3154 **Craigie** Pater C.,   Psalms 1-50, Word 19, 1983 → 64,2980 ... 3,2981:
ᴿSR 17 (1988) 371s (J. W. *Wevers*).
3155 **Dorival** Gilles,   Les chaînes exégétiques grecques sur les Psaumes 1986
→ 3,2984:   ᴿDivThom 91 (1988) 190s (G. *Testa*); NRT 110 (1988) 107s
(J.-L. *Ska*).
   Gerstenberger Erhard S., Psalms I [-50], with an introduction to cultic
poetry: FOTLit 14, 1988 → 3117.
3157 **Girard** Marc, Les Psaumes I (1-50) 1984 → 65,2642 ... 2,2265:   ᴿSR 17
(1988) 109s (J. *Duhaime*).
3158 **Kroll** W. M.,   Psalms; the poetry of Palestine. Lanham MD 1987, UPA.
ix-453 p. $37.50; pa. $24.75.   0-8191-5750-3; 1-1 [BL 89,83, J. H. *Eaton*:
pre-critical].
3159 **McNamara** Martin,   Glossa in Psalmos ... Hiberno-Latin ...: ST 310,
1986 → 2,2267:   ᴿGregorianum 69 (1988) 144s (E. *Farahian*); JTS 39

(1988) 172-4 (M. *Winterbottom*: the text demonstrates shortcomings of early Irish scholarship in comparison with more sophisticated BEDE and ALCUIN).

3160 **Prinzivalli** Emanuela, DIDIMO il Cieco e l'interpretazione dei Salmi: SMSR Quad NS 2. L'Aquila 1988, Japadre. 142 p. 88-7006-159-0.

3161 **Ravasi** Gianfranco, Il libro dei Salmi I-III, 1981-4 ➤ 62,3147 ... 3,2988: ᴿRB 95 (1988) 135s (R. J. *Tournay*).

3162 **Ravasi** G., I Salmi. BUR Poesia L 601. Mi 1986, Rizzoli. Lit 12.000. – ᴿPalCl 67 (1988) 784 (G. *Lavarda*); StPatav 35 (1988) 195s (M. *Milani*).

3163 **Ringgren** Helmer, Psaltaren 1-41: Komm.GamlaT. U 1987, EPS. 248 p.; ill. Sk 197. 91-7080-771-X [NTAbs 32,401]. – ᴿNorTTs 89 (1988) 280 (H. M. *Barstad*).

3164 **Rondeau** Marie-Josèphe, Les commentaires patristiques du Psautier II 1985 ➤ 1,3047; 3,2989: ᴿRPLH 61 (1987) 332s (J. *Irigoin*).

3165 **Sabourin** Léopold, Le livre des Psaumes, traduit et interprété: Recherches NS 18. Montréal 1988, Bellarmin. 631 p. 2-89007-670-9.

3166 ᵀ**Sulowski** J., ᴱ*Stanula* E., Św. AUGUSTYN, Objaśnienia Psalmów: Pisma Starochrześcijańskich Pisarzy 37-42, 1986 ➤ 3,2992: ᴿTLZ 113 (1988) 826 (J. *Rohde*).

3167 **Turoldo** Davide M., *Ravasi* Gianfranco, 'Lungo i fiumi'; i Salmi, traduzione poetica e commento. Mi – Ciniselli Balsamo 1987, Paoline. 524 p. Lit. 25.000. – ᴿCC 139 (1988,3) 320 (C. *Di Sante*); EphLtg 102 (1988) 481s (G. *Crocetti*).

3167* **Waaijman** Kees, [a-f ➤ 3,2993; g:] Psalmen vanuit de ballingschap: VBGed. Kampen 1986, Kok. – ᴿStreven 55 (1987s) 373s (P. *Beentjes*).

E6.5   Psalmi, themata.

3168 *Aeschbacher* Gerhard, Über den Zusammenhang von Versstruktur, Strophenform und rhythmischer Gestalt der Genfer Psalmlieder: Jb-LtgHymn 31 (1987s) 53-71; Eng. 71.

3169 *Alexander* T. D., The Psalms and the after life: IrBSt 9 (1987) 2-17.

3170 *Anderson* A. A., Psalms [cited in NT]: ➤ 97, ᶠLINDARS B., It is written 1988, 56-66.

3171 *Belkin* Ahuva, Suicide scenes in Latin Psalters of the thirteenth century as reflection of Jewish midrashic exposition: Manuscripta 32 (1988) 75-92.

3172 **Catalano** Rosann Marie, 'How long, O Lord?' A systematic study of the theology and practice of the biblical lament: diss. St. Michael, ᴰ*Donovan* D. Toronto 1988. 442 p. – RTLv 20,581.

3173 **Croft** Steven J. L., The identity of the individual in the Psalms 1987 ➤ 3,3003: ᴿBL (1988) 71 (J. *Gibson*); ÉTRel 63 (1988) 454s (D. *Lys*); RB 95 (1988) 623 (R. J. *Tournay*); VT 38 (1988) 511s (J. A. *Emerton*).

3174 **Curti** Carmelo, Eusebiana I. Commentarii in Psalmos [12 reprints]. Catania 1987, Univ. x-266 p. – ᴿCivClCr 9 (1988) 241 (P. *Frassinetti*).

3175 *Fretheim* Terrence E., Creation's praise of God in the Psalms: ➤ 567, ExAud 3 (1987) 16-30.

3175* *Füglister* Notker, Die Verwendung und das Verständnis der Psalmen und des Psalters um die Zeitwende: ➤ 3226, Beiträge zur Psalmenforschung 1987/8, 319-384.

3176 *Gonnelli* Fabrizio, Parole 'callimachee' nella parafrasi del Salterio: StItFgC 81 (1988) 91-104.

3177 ᶠGROSS H., Freude an... Psalmen, ᴱ*Haag* E., 1986 ➤ 2,41; ²ʳᵉᵛ1987: ᴿTrierTZ 97 (1988) 64-66 (R. *Mosis*).

3178 *Hernando* Eusebio, Experiencia de Dios y testimonio en los salmos sapienciales [no 'penitenciales' como p. 419]: TEsp 31 (1987) 203-222.

3179 *Hughes* Andrew, Psalter: ➤ 792, DMA 10 (1988) 200-2 [202, *Kessler* H., Illumination].

3180 *Hurvitz* Avi, Wisdom vocabulary in the Hebrew Psalter; a contribution to the study of 'Wisdom Psalms': VT 38 (1988) 41-51.

3181 *Iserloh* Erwin, 'Existentiale Interpretation' in LUTHERS erster Psalmvorlesung?: ➤ 2,175, Kirche-Ereignis 1985, II, 209-221.

3182 **Jauss** Hannelore, Tor der Hoffnung; Vergleichsformen und ihre Funktion in der Sprache der Psalmen: ev. Diss. Tübingen 1988, ᴰ*Rüger* H. 330 p. – RTLv 20,540; TLZ 114,398.

3183 **Jeremias** Jörg, Das Königtum Gottes in den Psalmen ... kanaan. Mythos...: FRLANT 141, 1987 ➤ 3,3009: ᴿÉTRel 63 (1988) 109s (T. *Römer*); ExpTim 99 (1987s) 328s (R. J. *Coggins*); VT 38 (1988) 237-9 (T.N.D. *Mettinger*).

3185 **Keel** Othmar, Der wereld van de oud-oosterse beeldsymboliek en het Oude Testament, toegelicht aan de hand van de Psalmen [1977 ➤ 58,3554],ᵀ. Kampen 1984, Kok. 370 p.; ill. + booklet of 24 pl. [KirSef 61,391].

Khoudair Anthony J., Doctrina del Éxodo en los Salmos, ᴰ1987 ➤ 2417.

3186 **Kraus** H. J., Theology of the Psalms, ᵀ*Crim* Keith 1986 ➤ 2,2288; 3,3012: ᴿInterpretation 42 (1988) 90. 92 (J. L. *Mays*).

3187 *a*) *Lelièvre* A., Qui parle dans les Psaumes?; – *b*) *Trublet* J., Le motif de la création dans les Psaumes: FoiVie 87,5 (CahB 27), 1988) 3-13 / 23-48.

3188 *Maiberger* Paul, Zur Problematik und Herkunft der sogenannten Fluchpsalmen: TrierTZ 97 (1988) 183-214.

3189 **Moore** Ralph K., An investigation of the motif of suffering in the psalms of lamentation: diss. Baptist Theol. Sem., ᴰ*Bailey* D. New Orleans 1988. 164 p. 88-20028. – DissA 49 (1988s) 2277-A.

3190 *Murray* Robert, The Psalms in their original world and in tradition [Upholland College Worden lecture]: PrPeo 2 (1988) 274-280.

3191 **Nasuti** Harry P., Tradition history and the Psalms of Asaph: SBL diss. 88 [Yale 1983, ᴰ*Wilson* R.]. Atlanta 1988, Scholars. vii-204 p. $21; sb./pa $14. 0-89130-971-3 [OIAc D88].

3191* *Otto* Eckart, Mythos und Geschichte im AT — zur Diskussion einer neuen Arbeit von Jörg JEREMIAS [Königtum Gottes in den Psalmen 1987]: BibNot 42 (1988) 93-102.

3192 **Petersen** Claus, Mythos im AT ... Psalmen: BZAW 157, 1982 ➤ 63,3146 ... 3,3020: ᴿNumen 35 (1988) 139s (R. J. Z. *Werblowski*).

3193 *Quacquarelli* Antonio, Riflessioni di CASSIODORO sugli schemi della retorica attraverso i Salmi [< ?] ➤ 246, VetChr 25 (1988) 67-93.

3194 *a*) *Raja* Rao T. J., Agony and anguish; the psalmist in his sufferings; – *b*) *Onunwa* Udobata, Individual laments in Hebrew poetry; a positive response to the problem of suffering: Jeevadhara 13 (1988) 94-100 / 101-111.

3195 *Reinelt* Heinz, Theologie der Psalmen: ➤ 327, Höre 1987, 183-219.

3196 *Schuller* Eileen, [English] Inclusive-Language psalters: BToday 26 (1988) 173-9.

3197 *Smith* Mark S., 'Seeing God' in the Psalms; the background to the beatific vision in the Hebrew Bible: CBQ 50 (1988) 171-183 [*Dahood* M. on Ps 11; 17; 27; 42s; 63].

3198 **Smith** William H., Theological interpretation of the Book of Psalms; a model developed from the work of the Puritan, Francis ROBERTS, and

modern exegesis: diss. Golden Gate Baptist Theol. Sem. ᴰ*Eakins* J.   SF
1988. 108 p. – 88-15838. – DissA 49 (1988s) 1483-A.

3199 *a) Sundén* Hjalmar,   Saint AUGUSTINE and the Psalter in the light of
role-psychology; – *b*) reactions (*Holm* N., *Wikstrom* O., *Lans* J. van der):
JScStR 26 (1987) 375-382 (-432).

3200 *Tronina* Antoni, ⊕ De psalmis 'eucharisticis' seu todah: RuBi 41 (1988)
286-299.

3201 *Velema* W.H.,   Depressiviteit in het licht van de psalmen: TRef 31
(Woerden 1988) 360-9 [< ZIT 89,92].

3202 *Zevit* Ziony,   Psalms at the poetic precipice: HebAnR 10 (1986)
351-366.

E6.6   *Psalmi: oratio, liturgia;* **Psalms as prayer.**

3203 **Aejmelaeus** Anneli,   The traditional prayer in the Psalms: BZAW 167a,
1986 ➤ 2,2295; 3,3027:   ᴿJBL 107 (1988) 518-520 (J. G. *Williams*); RB 95
(1988) 307 (R. J. *Tournay*); RivB 36 (1988) 121s (A. *Bonora*).

3204 *a) Bjornard* R. B.,   The faith of the Psalmists; – *b*) *Hoppe* Leslie J.,
Prayer and mission; the Hodayot of Qumran: ➤ 141, ᶠSTUHLMUELLER
C., Scripture and prayer 1988, 46-61 / 76-87.

3205 **Brueggemann** Walter,   Israel's praise; doxology against idolatry and
ideology [Richmond Union Sem. Sprunt lectures]. Ph 1988, Fortress.
xii-196 p. $10 pa. [TDig 36,48]. 0-8006-2044-5. – ᴿRExp 85 (1988) 559s
(T. G. *Smothers*); TTod 45 (1988s) 506 (T. R. *Fretheim*).

3206 **Carrarini** Sergio,   Salmi d'oggi; condivisione e contemplazione diventano
preghiera di un credente: Solco 1.   Verona 1988 = 1985, Mazziana.
158 p.; ill.   88-85073-05-0.

3207 *Davril* Anselme,   La psalmodie chez les Pères du Désert: ColcCist 49
(1987) 132-9.

3208 **Del Colle** Beppe, introd., I salmi pregati da S. AGOSTINO. R 1986,
Paoline.   336 p. Lit. 12.000. – ᴿRivAscM 12,1 (1987) 91s (G. *Podio*).

3209 *Fiedler* Peter,   Zur Herkunft des gottesdienstlichen Gebrauchs von
Psalmen aus dem Frühjudentum: ArLtgW 30 (1988) 229-237.

3210 **George** A., ⊕ Prier les Psaumes, ᵀ*Fang* M., *Yu* P. c.1987 = c.1977,
Kuangchi. – ᴿColcFuJen 77 (1988) 451-5 (Magdalena *Wang*).

3211 *Gilbert* Maurice,   I salmi: ➤ 810*, StSpG 1 (1988) 540-580.

3212 **Gillingham** S. E.,   Personal piety in the study of the Psalms; a
reassessment: diss. Oxford 1987. – RTLv 20,540.

3213 **Hollmann** K.,   Verbirg nicht Dein Gesicht vor mir; mit 20 Psalmen in
Gespräch [1; ... 150]: Pd 1986, Bonifatius.   242 p. DM 24.   3-87088-488-6.
– ᴿTsTNijm 28 (1988) 81 (P. *Kevers*).

3214 **Montorsi** Giambattista,   I Salmi,   preghiere di ogni giorno³ 1987
➤ 3,3036;   88-7026-669-9:   ᴿCC 139 (1988,1) 204 (G. *Caprile*: edizione
aggiornata ma più concisa).

3215 **Neveu** Louis,   Au pas des Psaumes; lecture organique à trois voix, I:
Centre de Linguistique Religieuse, Cah 2.   Angers 1988, Univ. Cath. de
l'Ouest, Inst. Langues Vivantes.   199 p. F 115. 0987-7290.

3216 Psalms and Canticles,   prepared by a Sister of St. Mary's Abbey,
Glencairn [entirely hand-lettered in semi-Gothic style]. Blackrock, Dublin
1988, Conference Book Service.   624 p. 1-871337-00-3.

3217 **Ravasi** Gianfranco,   I canti di Israele; preghiera e storia di un popolo.   Bo 1986, Dehoniane.   299 p. – ᴿTeresianum 39 (1988) 215s (V.
Pasquetto).

3218 **Shaw** Graham, God in our hands [... Psalter]. L 1987, SCM. 255 p. £10. – ᴿNBlackf 69 (1988) 352 (H. P. *Owen*).
3219 **Smith** Mark S., Psalms, the divine journey 1987 ⇥ 3,2039: ᴿLvSt 13 (1988) 387s (J. *Luyten*); PrPeo 2 (1988) 303s (R. *Murray*).
3220 **Strauss** Hans, Gott preisen heisst vor ihm leben; exegetische Studien zum Verständnis von acht ausgewählten Psalmen Israels: BibTSt 12. Neuk 1988. 106 p. 3-7887-1279-1.
3221 ᴱ**Suffi** Nicolò, Salterio corale; salmi e canti biblici, traduzione interconfessionale in lingua corrente. T-Leumann 1987, Elle Di Ci. 367 p. – ᴿEphLtg 102 (1988) 477-481 (G. *Crocetti*).
3222 **Tournay** R. J., Voir et entendre Dieu avec les psaumes, ou: La liturgie prophétique du Second Temple à Jérusalem [mostly of Chronicler date c.300]: CahRB 24. P 1988, Gabalda. ix-221 p. F 302. 2-85021-031-5 [BL 89,95, J. H. *Eaton*]. – ᴿPrOrChr 38 (1988) 408s (P. *Ternant*).
3223 *Vincent* Monique, La prière selon saint AUGUSTIN d'après les 'Enarrationes in Psalmos': NRT 110 (1988) 371-402.
3224 **Zim** Rivkah, English metrical psalms; poetry as praise and prayer, 1535-1601: 1987 ⇥ 3,3044: ᴿRHE 83 (1988) 242 (F. *Hockey*: not clear whether they are actual psalms or poems under influence of the psalms, or both).

E6.7 *Psalmi:* **verse-numbers.**

3225 *Mattioli* Anselmo, [Ps 1 ...] Identità letteraria e dottrinale delle beatitudini della Bibbia ebraica — classificazione tematica: Antonianum 63 (1988) 189-226; Eng. 189.
3226 ᴱ**Schreiner** Josef, Beiträge zur Psalmenforschung; Psalm 2 und 22 [Tagung Salzburg 25.-29.VIII.1987]: ForBi 60. Wü 1988, Echter. 384 p. DM 68. 3-429-01174-4 [TR 85,73]. – *Loretz* O., Eine kolometrische Analyse von Ps. 2, 9-26; – *Deissler* A., Die Stellung von Ps. 2 im Psalter; Folgen für die Auslegung 27-71; – *Maiberger* Paul, Das Verständnis von Ps. 2 in der Septuaginta, im Targum, in Qumran, im frühen Judentum und im NT, 73-83.
3227 *Rinsveld* Bernard van, Deux allusions littéraires au rituel de la destruction des pots (P. Beatty III pl. 8 Rᵒ, 10,9 et Psaume 2:9): ⇥ 763, Archéologie 1986, 207-212.
3228 *Auffret* Pierre, Note complémentaire sur la structure littéraire du Psaume 6 [OBO 49, 1982]: BibNot 42 (1988) 7-13.
3229 *Lohfink* Norbert, Was wird anders bei kanonischer Schriftauslegung? Beobachtungen am Beispiel von Psalm 6: JbBT 3 (1988) 29-54 [< ZIT 89,174].
3230 *Smit Sibinga* J., Gedicht en getal; over de compositie van Psalm 6: NedTTs 42 (1988) 185-207; Eng. 243, 'Poem and number'.
3231 *Hardmeier* Christof, 'Denn im Tod ist kein Gedenken an dich...', (Psalm 6,6); der Tod des Menschen — Gottes Tod?: EvT 48 (1988) 292-311.
3232 *Hutton* Rodney R., [Ps 7 ...] Cush the Benjaminite and Psalm midrash: HebAnR 10 (1986) 123-137.
3233 *Stanula* Emil, ℗ 'La table de la Parole de Dieu' d'après le traité (commentaire) sur le 13ème Psaume de saint HILAIRE de Poitiers: ⇥ 73, ᶠKANIA W. = VoxPa 12s (1987s) 355-370; franç. 370.
3234 **Steingrimsson** Sigurdur Ö., Tor der Gerechtigkeit ... Einzugsliturgien im AT: Ps 15 ... 1984 ⇥ 65,2724 ... 2,2321: ᴿOLZ 83 (1988) 681-3 (L. *Wächter*); RÉJ 146 (1987) 427s (Hedwige *Rouillard*).

3235 *Daniel* Robert W., *Maltomini* Franco,   From the African Psalter [Ps 15,10; 20,2-7] and liturgy: ZPapEp 74 (1988) 253-265.

3236 *Tournay* R. J.,   Le psaume 16,1-3:   RB 95 (1988) 332-6; Eng. 332.

3237 *Toorn* R. van den, [Ps 17,3.15 ...] Ordeal procedures in the Psalms and the Passover meal: VT 38 (1988) 427-445.

3238 **Loretz** Oswald,   Die Königspsalmen; die altorientalisch-kanaanäische Königstradition in jüdischer Sicht, I: Ps 20,21,72, 101 und 144; Beitrag zu Papyrus Amherst, Kottsieper I: UgBLit 6.   Münster 1988, Ugarit-V. vii-261 p.   DM 78; sb 70.   3-917120-01-4 [ZAW 101,320, H.-C. *Schmitt*].

3239 *Kottsieper* Ingo,   Anmerkungen zu Pap. Amherst 63; I. 12,11-19 — eine aramäische Version von Ps 20:   ZAW 100 (1988) 217-244.

3240 *Kuntz* J. Kenneth,   King triumphant; a rhetorical study of Psalms 20 and 21:   HebAnR 10 (1986) 157-176.

3241 *Magee* John, [Ps 21,19; Mt 27,25; Jn 19,23] Note on BOETHIUS, Consolatio I, 1,5; 3,7; a new biblical parallel: VigChr 42 (1988) 79-82.

3242 **Becker-Ebel** Jochen,   Psalm 22, Rettungs- und Loblied eines 'Gottverlassenen': Diss. FrB 1989. 295 + 44 p.; (color.) ill.

3243 *Hogg* William R.,   Psalm 22 and Christian mission; a reflection: IntRMiss 77 (1988) 238-246.

3244 *Zwanepol* K.,   'Ziet, hoe tere is de here'; de zondeloosheid van Christus in LUTHERS uitleg van Psalm 22; een dogmatische verkenning in theologiehistorisch perpectief: GerefTTs 88 (1988) 1-19.

3245 *a) Vanoni* Gottfried,   Psalm 22, Literarkritik; – *b) Irsigler* Hubert, Psalm 22, Endgestalt, Bedeutung und Funktion; – *c) Schreiner* Josef,   Zur Stellung des Psalms 22 im Psalter; Folgen für die Auslegung; – *d) Fabry* Heinz-Josef,   Die Wirkungsgeschichte des Psalms 22: ➤ 3226, Beiträge zur Psalmenforschung 1987/8, 153-192 / 193-239 / 241-277 / 279-317.

3246 *Foley* C. M.,   Pursuit of the inscrutable; a literary analysis of Psalm 23: ➤ 29, Mem. CRAIGIE P., Ascribe 1988, 363-383.

3246* *McCarthy* David P.,   A not-so-bad DERRIDEAN approach to Psalm 23 [... deconstruction]: ProcGLM 8 (1988) 177-191.

3247 *Mazor* Yair,   Psalm 23; the Lord is my shepherd — or is he my host?: ZAW 100 (1988) 416-420.

3248 *Smith* Mark S.,   Setting and rhetoric in Psalm 23:   JStOT 41 (1988) 61-66.

3249 *Sung* Ludovicus, Ⓔ The most beautiful prayer, Ps. 23:   ColcFuJen 77 (1988) 301-8.

3250 *Maier* Johann,   Salmo 24,1; interpretazione rabbinica, berakah giudaica e benedizione cristiana, ᵀ*Vivian* Angelo: ➤ 570, AugR 28 (1988) 285-300.

3251 *Barré* Michael L., [Ps 27,13 ...] *'rṣ (h)ḥyym* — 'the land of the living'? [implications of *eternal* life somewhat as in *Dahood* M., but with reserves]: JStOT 41 (1988) 37-59.

3252 *Auffret* Pierre,   'Il jubile, mon cœur'; étude structurelle du psaume 28: EstBíb 46 (1988) 187-216; español, Eng. 187.

3253 **Kloos** Carola, [Ps 29; Ex 15] Yhwh's combat with the sea 1986 ➤ 2,2333; 3,3071: ᴿBO 45 (1988) 645-7 (O. *Loretz*); JTS 39 (1988) 151-4 (J. *Day*: enjoyable but extreme); NedTTs 42 (1988) 331-3 (J. A. *Wagenaar*); RB 95 (1988) 136-8 (R. J. *Tournay*).

3254 **Loretz** O.,   Psalm 29, 1984 ➤ 65,2315 ... 3,3072:   ᴿCBQ 50 (1988) 689s (M. L. *Barré*: important, but heavy-handed in 'colometry').

3255 *Malamat* A.,   The Amorite background of Psalm 29: ➤ 153, ZAW 100 Supp. (1988) 156-160.

3256 *Neveu* Louis,   Lecture du Psaume 29: ➤ 486, Traduction 1986/8, 191-8.

3257 *Tsumura* D.T., 'The deluge' (*mabbûl*) in Psalm 29:10:   UF 20 (1988) 351-5.

3258 *a) Auffret* Pierre, 'Tu as entendu'; étude structurelle du psaume 31; – *b) Dion* Paul E., Strophic boundaries and rhetorical structure in Psalm 31: ÉglT 18 (1987) 147-181 / 183-192.

3259 *Auffret* Pierre, Essai sur la structure littéraire du psaume xxxii: VT 38 (1988) 257-285.

3260 **Park Sang Hoon**, An exegetical study of Psalm 33: diss. Calvin Sem., ᴰ*Stek* J.   GR 1988.   v-130 p. + bibliog. – CalvinT 23 (1988) 307s.

3261 *Wéber* Edith, Les aventures sémantiques du Psaume XXXIII: FoiVie 87,1 (1988) 57-65.

3262 *Andia* Ysabel de, In lumine tuo videbimus lumen (Ps. 35,10); l'illumination par l'Esprit dans le De Spiritu Sancto de Saint BASILE: ➤ 56, Mém. GRIBOMONT J. 1988, 59-74.

3262* *Auffret* Pierre, 'Yahve, qu'('elle nous est) chère, ta loyauté!'; étude structurelle du Ps 36: ScEsp 40 (1988) 57-73.

3263 *Riess* Hermann, Predigt über Psalm 36,6-10: EvDiaspora 57 (1988) 37-44.

3264 *Maier* Johann, Auslegungsgeschichtliche Beobachtungen zu Ps 37,1.7.8: ➤ 22, Mém. CARMIGNAC J., RQum 13 (1988) 465-479.

3265 *Riggi* Calogero, L'"auxesis' del salmo XXXVIII nel 'De officiis' di S. AMBROGIO [< Salesianum 29 (1967) 623-668]: ➤ 251, Epistrophe 1985, 234-279.

3265* *Auffret* Pierre, 'Toi, tu répondras'; étude structurelle du Psaume 38: ScEspr 40 (1988) 295-314.

3266 *Alonso Schökel* Luis, Todo Adán es Abel; Salmo 39: EstBíb 46 (1988) 269-282; Eng. 269.

3267 *Semiryon* Ṣemaḥ, ⊕ Ps 42s: BethM 12,111 (1986s) 296-8.

3268 *Coetzee* J.H., The functioning of elements of tension in Psalm 44: TEvca 21 (Pretoria 1988) 2-5 [< OTAbs 11,274].

3269 *a) Pavan* Vincenzo, GIROLAMO e l'interpretazione antica di 'circumdata varietate' (Sal 44,10.14): la diversità dei carismi; – *b) Siniscalco* Paolo, La teoria e la tecnica del commentario biblico secondo GIROLAMO: ➤ 472, AnStoEseg 5 (1988) 239-252 / 225-238.

3270 *Caquot* André, Cinq observations sur le Psaume 45: ➤ 29, Mem. CRAIGIE P., Ascribe 1988, 253-264.

3271 *Loader* J.A., "n Tyd vir alles', Psalm 46: ➤ 509, Hoe lees 1985/8 ...

3272 *Smit Sibinga* Joost, Some observations on the composition of Psalm XLVII: VT 38 (1988) 474-480.

3273 *Barré* Michael L., The seven epithets of Zion in Ps 48,2-3:   Biblica 69 (1988) 557-563.

3274 *Bordreuil* Pierre, *Mizzebul lô*; à propos de Psaume 49:15: ➤ 29, Mem. CRAIGIE P., Ascribe 1988, 93-98.

3275 *Almeida* Ivàn, Le devenir discursif du sujet; remarques sur le traitement sémiotique d'un psaume [51 Miserere]: BibSém 50 (1988) 2-26.

3276 *Hernando* Eusebio, Lectura cristiana del Salmo 51 (Miserere): TEsp 32 (1988) 131-147.

3277 *Renaud* B., Purification et recréation; le 'miserere' (Ps. 51): RevSR 62 (1988) 201-217.

3278 *Begg* Christopher, *a)* 'Dove' and 'God(s)' in Ps 56,1:   ETL 64 (1988) 393-6: – *b)* Ps 58,2a; a Forschungsbericht and a proposal: ETL 64 (1988) 397-404.

3279 **Carniti** Cecilia, Il salmo 68, studio letterario [diss. 1984] BibSR 68, 1985 ➤ 1,3146 ... 3,3083: ᴿAsprenas 35 (1988) 181 (C. *Marcheselli-Casale*);

EstBíb 46 (1988) 266s (V. *Morla Asensio*); RB 95 (1988) 138 (R. J. *Tournay*); RivB 36 (1988) 109s (F. *Festorazzi*); VT 38 (1988) 502 (W. *Horbury*).

3280 *Cassou* Françoise, En quête de Dieu: Psaume 69, proposition de structure: FoiVie 87,5 (CahB 27, 1988) 49-56.

3281 *Lohse* Bernhard, LUTHERS Auslegung von Psalm 71 (72), 1 und 2 in der ersten Psalmenvorlesung [< ᶠ*Lau* F. 1967, 191-203]: ➤ 224, Evangelium 1988, 31-43.

3282 *Dietrich* M., *Loretz* O., Von hebräisch '*m/lpny* (Ps 72:5) zu ugaritisch '*m* 'vor': ➤ 29, Mem. CRAIGIE P., Ascribe 1988, 109-116.

3283 *Caquot* André, Psaume LXXII, 16 [not 'may there be abundance of grain' but 'may he (the king) be a lively wild plant ...']: VT 38 (1988) 214-220.

3284 *Michel* D., [Ps 73; Qoh] Ich aber bin immer bei dir; von der Unsterblichkeit der Gottesbeziehung: Pietas Liturgica 3 (1987) 637-658 [< ZAW 101,136].

3285 *Koopmans* William T., Psalm 78, Canto D — a response: UF [18 (1986) 208-212, *Korpel* M., *Moor* J. de] 20 (1988) 121-3.

3286 *Tromp* Nicholas J., La métaphore engloutie; le langage métaphorique du Psaume 80: SémBib 47 (1987) 30-43.

3287 *Layton* Scott C., Jehoseph in Ps 81,6: Biblica 69 (1988) 406-411.

3288 *Smith* Mark S., The structure of Psalm LXXXVII: VT 38 (1988) 357s.

3289 *Culley* Robert C., Psalm 88 among the complaints: ➤ 29, Mem. CRAIGIE P., Ascribe 1988, 289-301.

3290 *Veijola* Timo, The witness in the clouds; Ps 89:38: JBL 107 (1988) 413-7.

3291 *Bouchard* Marie-Noël, Une lecture monastique du Psaume 90; les sermons de saint BERNARD sur le Psaume 'Qui habitat': ColcCist 49 (1987) 156-172.

3292 *Ozaeta* José M., Salmos [Vlg. 90; 103; 71; 61; 44; 8; 63]: CiuD 201 (1988) 57-77.

3293 *Lohse* Bernhard, Gesetz, Tod und Sünde in LUTHERS Auslegung des 90. Psalms [< ᶠ*Thielicke* H. 1968, 139-155]: ➤ 224, Evangelium 1988, 379-394.

3294 *Booij* T., The Hebrew text of Psalm XCII,11: VT 38 (1988) 210-214.

3295 **Jeremias** J., [Ps 93; 97; 99 ...] Das Königtum Gottes in den Psalmen; Israels Begegnung mit dem kanaanäischen Mythos in den Jahwe-König-Psalmen: FRLANT 141, 1987 ➤ 3,3099; 3-525-53820-0. – ᴿBL (1988) 79 (J. H. *Eaton*); TsTNijm 28 (1988) 180 (P. *Kevers*).

3296 *Pardee* Dennis, The poetic structure of Psalm 93: ➤ 98, ᶠLORETZ O., StEpL 5 (1988) 163-170.

3297 *Balancín* E. Martins, A fonte da corrupção e da injustiça (Salmo 94): Vida Pastoral (São Paulo 1988) 7-10 [< Stromata 44,564].

3298 *Friedland* Eric L., [Ps 94,1] O God of vengeance, appear!: Judaism 37 (1988) 73-80.

3299 *Herman* Wayne R., [Ps 97; 29; 50; and 8 passages outside the psalms] The kingship of Yahweh in the hymnic theophanies of the Old Testament: StudiaBT 16 (1988) 169-211.

3300 *Weisblit* Shlomoh, ⊕ Ps 97 – cry of the return to Zion: BethM 34,117 (1988s) 185-190.

3301 *Gollwitzer* Helmut, 'Singt dem Herrn einen neuen Gesang, denn Wunderbares hat er getan'; Predigt über Psalm 98,1: EvT 48 (1988) 489-491.

3302 *Booij* T., Psalm CI,2 – 'When wilt thou come to me?': VT 38 (1988) 458-462.

3303 *Olivier* Jean-Marie, Un fragment palimpseste du Commentaire de DIODORE de Tarse sur les Psaumes [104 et 118] (Vindob. Theol. Gr. 177, Xe s.): RHText 18 (1988) 233-241.

3304 *Bazak* Yaʿaqob, ❶ Ps 107: BethM 32,111 (1986s) 301-319.

3305 *Lim* Agnes, ❷ To interpret Ps 114 by a deleite Chinese poetry: ColcFuJen 75 (1988) 7-15.

3306 *Wernberg-Møller* P.C.H., The old accusative case-ending in biblical Hebrew; observations on *ha-maw^etah* in Ps. 116:15: JSS 33 (1988) 155-164.

3307 *Mays* James L., Psalm 118 in the light of canonical analysis: ➤ 25, ^FCHILDS B., Canon 1988, 299-311.

3308 **Demarolle** Pierre, Le Psautier glosé et exposé de LUDOLPHE le Chartreux (Psaume 119, extrait d'une traduction médiévale): Le Psautier glosé et exposé 'CRAL' 4,1988 ➤ 3,3113: ^RBTAM 14 (1988) 545s (G. *Hendrix*).

3309 **Milhau** Marc, [Ps 119H] HILAIRE de Poitiers, Commentaire sur le Psaume 118: SChr 344.347. P 1988, Cerf. 283 p.; 336 p. F 164/205. 2-204-02982-3; 3052-6. – ^RRÉAug 34 (1988) 99-101 (J. *Doignon*).

3310 *Lerner* M.B., [Ps 121,1; Dan 12,3...] ❶ Novel explanations to some enigmatic passages in Sifre and Mekhilta 'Eqev: Tarbiz 57 (1987s) 599-607; Eng. III.

3311 *Donner* Herbert, Psalm 122: ➤ 47, ^FFENSHAM F., Text 1988, 81-91.

3312 **Beyerlin** Walter, Weisheitliche Vergewisserung mit Bezug auf dem Zionskult... 125. Psalm: OBO 68, 1985 ➤ 1,3171 ... 3,3120: ^RBO 45 (1988) 395-7 (T. *Booij*); BZ 32 (1988) 137s (H. *Niehr*).

3313 *Wal* A.J.O. van der, The structure of Psalm CXXIX: VT 38 (1988) 364-7.

3314 *Marrs* Rick R., A cry from the depths (Ps 130): ZAW 100 (1988) 81-90.

3315 *Shoemaker* H. Stephen, Psalm 131; theology as lullaby: RExp 85 (1988) 89-93.

3316 **McIver** Ian, An interpretation of Psalm 132: diss. Calvin Sem., ^D*Stek* J. GR 1988. vi-152 p. + bibliog. – CalvinT 23 (1988) 306.

3317 *Nel* Philip, Psalm 132 and covenant theology: ➤ 47, ^FFENSHAM F., Text 1988, 183-191.

3318 *Bazak* Jacob, ❶ [Ps 136] 'For his mercy is forever' — the 'Great Hillel': BethM 34,119 (1988s) 341-354.

3319 **Hartberger** Birgit, 'An den Wässern von Babylon...'; Psalm 137 auf dem Hintergrund von Jeremia 51 ... [Diss. 1985]: BoBB 63, 1986 ➤ 3,3128: ^RJBL 107 (1988) 307-9 (M.H. *Floyd*: non sequitur); RB 95 (1988) 306 (R.J. *Tournay*).

3320 *Renfroe* F., Persiflage in Psalm 137: ➤ 29, Mem. CRAIGIE P., Ascribe 1988, 509-527.

3321 *Kselman* John S., Psalm 146 in its context: CBQ 50 (1988) 587-599.

3322 *Haran* Menahem, The two text-forms of Psalm 151: JJS 39 (1988) 171-181.

E7.1 **Job,** *Textus, commentarii.*

3323 **Alonso Schökel** L., *Sicre Díaz* J.L., Job 1983 ➤ 64,3149 ... 3,3135: ^RJTS 39 (1988) 165-8 (A. *Chester*: indubitably major).

3324 *Bánescu* Marcu, Randbemerkungen zum Buch Hiob (rum.): Mitropolia Banatului 37,1 (1987) 13-21 [TLZ 114,636].

Díez Macho Alejandro, Biblia babilónica, fragmentos de Salmos, Job y Proverbios 1987 → 3130.

3325 **Habel** Norman C., The book of Job, a commentary 1985 → 1,3195 ... 3,3141: ᴿBS 145 (1988) 113s (R. B. *Zuck*: outstanding); CurrTM 15 (1988) 376s (W. L. *Michel*); Interpretation 42 (1988) 189-191 (J. M. *Lindenberger*: a mature reading).

3326 ᴱ**Hagedorn** Ursula & Dieter, OLYMPIODOR, Diakon von Alexandria, Kommentar zu Hiob: PatrTSt 24, 1984 → 65,2788 ... 2,2393: ᴿOrChrPer 54 (1988) 257-9 (J. D. *Baggarly*); SecC 6,1 (1987s) 62s (R. P. *Vaggione*).

3327 **Hartley** John E., The book of Job: NICOT. GR/Exeter 1987, Eerdmans/Paternoster. 545 p. £19.50. 0-8028-2362-7. – ᴿRExp 85 (1988) 559 (J. D. W. *Watts*).

3328 **Heinen** Karl, Der unverfügbare Gott; das Buch Ijob: Kl.Komm. 18. Stu 1988, KBW. 100 p. 3-460-05181-7.

3329 **Janzen** J. Gerald, Job 1985 → 2,2395: ᴿBS 145 (1988) 228s (R. B. *Zuck*: excellent; some weaknesses); CBQ 50 (1988) 686s (M. B. *Dick*: convoluted); CurrTM 15 (1988) 377s (W. L. *Michel*); Interpretation 42 (1988) 76-78 (Dianne *Bergant*).

3330 *Levinger* Jacob, MAIMONIDES' exegesis of the book of Job: → 505, Creative 1985/8, 81-88.

3331 **Mitchell** Stephen, The book of Job. SF 1987, North Point. – ᴿDor 17 (1988s) 53-56 (D. *Wolfers*: free but incomplete translation, as lively as HABEL is unoriginal).

3332 **Morgan** Campbell, The analyzed Bible; Job [1909]. GR 1983, Baker. xi-235 p. [KirSef 61,394].

3333 **Nicole** J. M., Le livre de Job, II (ch.20-) 1987 → 3,3145; 2-904407-06-5: ᴿÉTRel 63 (1988) 455 (J. *Rennes*: due light on masoretic text from all ancient and modern versions; but no higher criticism; Job is a premosaic patriarch).

3334 **Schroten** H., Het boek Job voor de gemeente verklaard. Haag 1986, Boekencentrum. ƒ39,90. – ᴿKerkT 39 (1988) 353s (B. *Maarsingh*).

3335 **Selms** A. van, Job, a practical comm. 1985 → (65,2797) 2,2399; 3,3148: ᴿCurrTM 15 (1988) 378s (W. L. *Michel*).

3336 **Simundson** Daniel J., The message of Job; a theological commentary 1986 → 2,2400; 3,3149: ᴿCurrTM 15 (1988) 379 (W. L. *Michel*).

3337 ᵀᴱ**Sorlin** Henri, (*Neyrand* Louis), CHRYSOSTOME, Commentaire sur Job, I (i-xiv)-II (xv-xlii): SChr 346.348. P 1988, Cerf. 366 p.; 312 p. F 332; F 190. 2-204-03007-4; 50-3.

3338 *Zuckerman* Bruce, The date of 11Q Targum Job; a paleographic consideration of its Vorlage: JPseud 1 (1987) 57-78.

E7.2   *Job: themata,* **Topics** ... *Versiculi,* **Verse-numbers.**

3339 *Alonso Schökel* Luis, *a*) Pedro LÓPEZ DE AYALA y el libro de Job; – *b*) Las Epístolas de Job de Antonio ENRÍQUEZ GÓMEZ; – *c*) La traducción de Job del Conde DE REBOLLEDO: Cuadernos Bíblicos 13 (1988) 1-24 / 25-38 / 39-63.

3340 *Alvarado* Napoleón, Y Dios se hizo Job en Jesús; entrevista con el autor del libro de Job [< Diakonia 45 (1986)]: Christus 53, 620 (Méx 1988) 60-66.

3341 *Cavallero* P., La adaptación poética de los Moralia in Job de San GREGORIO en el Rimado de Palacio del Canciller [LÓPEZ DE] AYALA: Hispania Sacra 38,77s (1986) 401-518: he adapted the text of Job *and* the text of the Moralia [< RSPT 72,490].

3342 *Cox* Claude E., Methodological issues in the exegesis of LXX Job: ➤ 478, 6th LXX 1986/7, 79-89.

3343 *Dassmann* Ernst, Akzente frühchristlicher Hiobdeutung: JbAC 31 (1988) 40-56.

3344 *Davis* Patricia E., Revelation in BLAKE's Job [engravings 1823-6; four shown here]: PgQ 65 (1986) 447-477.

3345 *Freedman* David N., Is it possible to understand the book of Job?: BR 4,3 (1988) 26-33 . 44.

3346 *Feuer* Lewis S., The book of Job; the wisdom of Hebrew stoicism: ➤ 9386, ᴱ*Larue* G., Biblical versus secular ethics 1986/8, 79-97.

3347 *Gaulmyn* Maiou de, Dialogue avec Job: SémBib 52 (1988) 1-14.

3348 **Girard** René, De aloude weg der boosdoener [1985 ➤ 3,3161],ᵀ. Kampen/ Kapellen 1985, Kok/Agora. 201 p. Fb 525. – ᴿCollatVL 18 (1988) 120s (R. *Hoet*).

3349 **Gutiérrez** G., Hablar de Dios ... Job 1986 ➤ 2,2409; 3,3163: ᴿEfMex 5,14 (1987) 305-313 (V. *Girardi*).

3350 **Gutiérrez** G., [Giobbe] Parlare di Dio 1986 ➤ 3,3164: ᴿHumanitas 42 (Brescia 1987) 461 (F. *Montagnini*).

3351 **Gutiérrez** Gustavo, On Job; God-talk and the suffering of the innocent 1987 ➤ 3,3165: ᴿExpTim 99,12 first choice (1987s) 353s (C. S. *Rodd*: a profound contribution, also bibliographically); NewTR 1,3 (1988) 96s (S. *Bevans*); SpTod 40 (1988) 360-3 (J. *Risley*); TLond 91 (1988) 224s (U. *Simon*); TS 49 (1988) 776s (A. J. *Tambasco*); ZMissRW 72 (1988) 314s (E. *Zeitler*).

3352 **Gutiérrez** G., Job; parler de Dieu à partir de la souffrance de l'innocent: Théologies P 1987, Cerf. 174 p. F 98. 2-204-02680-8. – ᴿBL (1988) 58 (R. J. *Hammer*); FoiTemps 18 (1988) 608 (H. *Thomas*); Téléma 14,55s (1988) 101s (C. *Delhez*).

3353 **Gutiérrez** G., Gerechtigheid om niet, reflecties op het boek Job, ᵀ*Schuurman* B. Baarn 1987, Ten Have. 90-259-4339-X. – ᴿCollatVL 18 (1988) 395s (J. De *Kesel*); TsTNijm 28 (1988) 198 (L. Van *Nieuwenhove*).

3354 *Häring* Hermann, Ijob in unserer Zeit; zum Problem des Leidens in der Welt: ➤ 648, Vorsehung 1987/8, 168-191.

3355 **Hainthaler** Barbara T., 'Von der Ausdauer Ijobs habt ihr gehört' (Jak. 5,11); zur Bedeutung des Buches Ijobs im Neuen Testament: Diss. St. Georgen, ᴰ*Beutler* J. Fra 1987s. – TR 84 (1988) 511.

3356 **Huber** Paul, Hiob – Dulder oder Rebell? Byzantinische Miniaturen zum Buch Hiob in Patmos, Rom, Venedig, Sinai, Jerusalem und Athos, 1986 ➤ 2,2411; DM 120: ᴿEvKomm 21 (1988) 115s (Renate *Fechner*); Leb-Zeug 41,4 (1986) 81-83 (Verena *Lenzen*).

3357 *Jeremias* Jörg, Hiob der Rebell und Hiob der Gehaltene: KatBlätt 113 (Mü 1988) 592-8 [-606, *Hochstaffl* J.: < ZIT 88,635].

3358 *Knauf* Ernst A., Hiobs Heimat ['Rand der Ökumene']: WeltOr 19 (1988) 65-83.

3359 *Ko* Agnes, ⊜ An overview on the book of Job: ColcFuJen 77 (1988) 309-320.

3360 *Koops* Robert, Rhetorical questions and implied meaning in the book of Job: BTrans 39 (1988) 415-423.

3361 *Kutsch* Ernst, Hiob: ➤ 798, EvKL 2 (1988) 531-4.

3362 *Lasine* Stuart, Bird's-eye and worm's-eye views of justice in the book of Job: JStOT 42 (1988) 29-53.

3363 *Legrain* Jean-François, Variations musulmanes sur le thème de Job: BÉtOr 37s (1985) 51-114.

3364 **Loades** A.L., KANT and Job's comforters 1985 ➤ 2,2415; 3,3172: ᴿIrTQ 54 (1988) 77 (D. *O'Connor*: only a few lines on Job).

3365 **Maag** Victor, Hiob, Wandlung...: FRLANT 128, 1982 ➤ 63,3258 ... 1,3218: ᴿZkT 110 (1988) 93-95 (R. *Oberforcher*).

3366 *Miller* Ward S., Job, creator's apprentice: ChSt 26 (1987) 166-177.

3367 *O'Connor* D., Theodicy in the whirlwind: IrTQ 54 (1988) 161-174.

3368 **Penchansky** David, Dissonance in Job; the weight of literary and theological conflict: diss. Vanderbilt. Nv 1988. 88-15378. – DissA 49 (1988s) 1174-A; RelStR 15,193.

3369 *Ravasi* Gianfranco, 'Ora i miei occhi ti vedono'; l'itinerario spirituale di Giobbe: ➤ 810, StSp 1 (1988) 604-626.

3370 *Schenker* Adrian, Hiob; gibt es Trost im Leid?: WAntw 29 (Mainz 1988) 161-4 [148-183 ... < ZIT 89,20].

3371 *Schreiner* Susan E., 'Where shall wisdom be found?' GREGORY's interpretaton of Job: AmBenR 39 (1988) 321-342 [261-276, *Clark* Francis, on Gregory].

3372 **Scott** John M., Without thorns, it's not a rose [... Job-like approach]. Huntington IN 1988, Our Sunday Visitor. 176 p. $5 [TDig 36,82].

3373 **Susman** Margarete, Het boek Job en de lijdensweg van het joodse volk, ᵀ*Spek-Begeman* Trudie van der. Kampen 1987, Kok. 127 p. ƒ22,50.

3374 *Tsemudi* Joseph, ❶ God's answer to Job: BethM 34,119 (1988s) 302-311.

3375 **Unen** Chaim van, Job, dwarsligger of verbondgenoot? Een nieuwe kijk op een oud boek. Kampen 1987, Kok. 111 p. ƒ17,50. 90-242-0898-X. – ᴿNedTTs 42 (1988) 335s (P.B. *Dirksen*); Streven 55 (1987s) 755s (P. *Beentjes*).

3376 *Van Praag* Herman M., Job's agony, a biblical evocation of bereavement and grief: Judaism 37 (1988) 175-187.

3377 **Vermeylen** J., Job, ses amis et son Dieu 1986 ➤ 2,2418; 3,3179: ᴿBL (1988) 93s (J.H. *Eaton*: somewhat forced); CBQ 50 (1988) 702s (J.A. *Gladson*).

3378 *Vivian* Angelo, Il targum di Giobbe; analisi concettuale contrastiva di TgGb 1-4: Henoch 10 (1988) 293-333; franç. 333s.

3379 *Weinfeld* Moshe, Job and its Mesopotamian parallels — a typological analysis: ➤ 47, ᶠFENSHAM F., Text 1988, 217-226.

3380 *Wolfers* David, Jot, tittle and waw (Job 19:25) [Mt 5,18]: Dor 17 (1988s) 230-6.

3381 *a) Wolfers* David, Job ... the third cycle; dissipating a mirage II; – *b) Corey* Lawrence, The paradigm of Job; suffering and the redemptive destiny of Israel; – *c) Heckelman* Joseph, The liberation of Job: Dor 17 (1988s) 19-25 / 121-8 / 128-132.

3382 **Michel** Walter L., [Job 1,1-14,22] Job in the light of NW Semitic I, 1987 ➤ 3,3174: ᴿBO 45 (1988) 649-652 (P. *Höffken*: wichtig wenn auch nicht überzeugend); CurrTM 15 (1988) 448s (R.W. *Klein*); JNWS 14 (1988)

229s (F.C. *Fensham*); JTS 39 (1988) 168s (J. *Job*: convincingly *lō* 'the Victor', not 'not'; *ken* 'the Honest One' not 'thus' and many other divine names: as DAHOOD, but 'judicious enough to step back from some of Dahood's more outlandish suggestions'); OTAbs 11 (1988) 318s (W.J. *Urbrock*); RB 95 (1988) 448s (R.J. *Tournay*).

3383 *Long* Thomas G., Job; second thoughts in the land of Uz: TTod 45 (1988s) 5-20.

Day Peggy L., Satan, an adversary in Heaven 1988 → 2167.

3384 *Janzen* J. Gerald, Creation and the human predicament in Job 1:9-11 and 38-41: → 567, ExAud 3 (1987) 45-53.

3385 *Lugt* Pieter van der, Stanza-structure and word-repetition in Job 3-14: JStOT 40 (1988) 3-38.

3386 *Perdue* Leo G., [Job 3] Job's assault on creation: HebAnR 10 (1986) 295-315.

3387 **Waddle** Sharon H., Dubious praise; the form and context of the participial hymns in Job 4-14: diss. Vanderbilt. Nv 1987. – RelStR 15,193.

3388 *Clines* David J.A., Belief, desire and wish in Job 19:23-27 — clues for the identity of Job's 'Redeemer': → 469, Wünschet 1986/8, 363-370.

3389 *a)* *Geller* Stephen A., Where is wisdom?; a literary study of Job 28 in its settings; – *b)* *Silberman* Lou H., The question of Job's generation [*dōrō*]; BUBER's Job: → 3,355, ᴱ*Neusner* J., Judaic perspectives 1987, 155-188 / 261-9.

3390 *Curtis* John B., [Job 32s] Why were the Elihu speeches added to the Book of Job?: ProcGLM 8 (1988) 93-99.

3391 *Ḥaggai* Yiśrael, ✡ Job 35,10: BethM 32,111 (1986s) 373-380.

3392 *Oorschot* Jürgen van, Gott als Grenze ... Hiob 38-42: BZAW 170, 1987 → 3,3175: ᴿBO 45 (1988) 397-400 (P. *Höffken*); RB 95 (1988) 449 (R.J. *Tournay*); TR 84 (1988) 281s (H. *Gross*); ZkT 110 (1988) 107s (G. *Fischer*).

3393 **Keel** Othmar, Jahwes Entgegnung an Ijob ... 38-41/zeitgenössische Bildkunst: FRLANT 121, 1978 → 60,4341 ... 64,3212: ᴿZkT 110 (1988) 95s (R. *Oberforcher*).

3394 **Han Jin Hee**, [Job 38,1-40,2; 40,6-41,26] Yahweh replies to Job; Yahweh's speeches in the book of Job, a case of resumptive rhetoric: diss. ᴰ*Roberts* J., Princeton Theol. Sem. 1988. 143 p. 88-18497. – DissA 49 (1988s) 3040s-A.

3395 *Müller* Hans-Peter, [Ijob 38,2 ...] Gottes Antwort an Ijob und das Recht religiöser Wahrheit: BZ 32 (1988) 210-231.

3396 *Begg* Christopher T., [Job 38,22; Bar 3,15] Access to heavenly treasuries; the Traditionsgeschichte of a motif: BibNot 44 (1988) 15-20.

3397 *Müller* Hans-Peter, [Hi 39,13-18] Die sog. Straussenperikope in den Gottesreden des Hiobbuches: ZAW 100 (1988) 90-105.

3398 *a)* *Watson* Wilfred G.E., [Job 41,20 arrow ‖ slingstone; ... Gn 29,14 bone ‖ flesh ...] Some additional word pairs; – *b)* *Forrest* R.W.E., The two faces of Job; imagery and integrity in the prologue; – *c)* *Gibson* J.C.L., On evil in the book of Job: → 29, Mem. CRAIGIE P., Ascribe 1988, 179-201 / 385-398 / 399-419.

3399 *Bergant* Dianne, 'Things too wonderful for me' (Job 42:3): → 141, ᶠSTUHLMUELLER C., Scripture and Prayer 1988, 62-75.

3400 *a)* *Margain* Jean, [Job H42,10 ...] 11QtgJob et la langue targumique; à propos de la particule *bdyl*; – *b)* *Lübbe* John C., Describing the translation process of 11QtgJob; a question of method: ➤ 22, Mém. CARMIGNAC J., RQum 13 (1988) 525-8 / 583-593.

E7.3 *Canticum canticorum,* **Song of Solomon** – *textus, commentarii.*

3400* ᵀ**Aranguren** J., introd. *Torre* J. M. de la, S. BERNARDO, Sermones sobre el Cantar de los Cantares: Obras 5/ BAC 491. M 1987, Católica. xviii-1070 p. [RThom 88,173].

3401 **Arminjon** Blaise, La cantate de l'Amour 1983 ➤ 64,3215 ... 2,2427: ᴿÉglT 17 (1986) 90s (L. *Laberge*).

3402 **Bélanger** Rodrigue, GRÉGOIRE sur le Cantique: SChr 314, 1984 ➤ 65,2840 ... 2,2429: ᴿRÉAnc 90 (1988) 237s (M. *Dulaey*); RPLH 62,1 (1988) 168s (M. *Reydellet*).

3403 **Bloom** Harold, The Song of Songs: Modern critical interpretations. NY 1988, Chelsea. vii-174 p. $20 [TDig 36,84].

3404 **Curtis** Edward M., Song of Songs: Bible Study comm. GR 1988, Zondervan. 120 p. [GraceTJ 9,304].

3405 **Knight** George A. F. [*Golka* Friedemann W.], Revelation of God; a commentary on the books of The Song of Songs [and Jonah]: International Theological Commentary. E/GR 1988, Handsel/Eerdmans. ix-136 p. £5. 0-905312-74-0 / 0-8028-0336-9 [BL 89,57, R. B. *Salters*].

3406 ᵀᴱ**McCambley** Casimir, GREGORY of Nyssa, Commentary on the Song of Songs: Iakovos Library 12. Brookline MA 1987, Hellenic College. 295 p. $15 pa. [TDig 35,168].

3407 **Neri** U., Il Cantico dei Cantici; Targum e antiche interpretazioni ebraiche²ʳᵉᵛ [Italian translation of *Sperber* A. 1968]: Tradizione d'Israele 1. R 1987, Città Nuova. 212 p. Lit. 18.000. 88-311-4908-3 [NTAbs 32,394]. – ᴿRasT 29 (1988) 206s (R. *Maisano*).

3408 *Santis* P. De, ABELARDO interprete del Cantico dei Cantici per il Paracleto: ➤ 64,112,ᶠSMET J. M. de, Pascua mediaevalia, ᴱ**Lievens** R. (Lv 1983) 284-294 [RHE 83 (1988) 773: 'l'allusion qu'il fait dans son sermon XXIX à un commentaire qu'il aurait fait du Cantique vise sans doute un écrit perdu'].

3409 **Thompson** Yaakov, The commentary of Samuel BEN MEIR on the Song of Songs: diss. Jewish Theol. Sem. NY 1988. 437 p. 88-16917. – DissA 49 (1988s) 2261-A.

3411 **Tournay** Raymond J., Word of God, song of love; a commentary on the Song of Songs [Quand Dieu parle 1982 ➤ 63,3305 ... 2,2444], ᵀ*Crowley* J. Edward. NY 1988, Paulist. vi-194 p. $12. 0-8091-3007-6.

3412 **Vregille** B.De, *Neyrand* L., APPONIUS: In Cantica Canticorum expositio: CCLat 19 [+ 13 microfiches lexicologica A-36] 1986 ➤ 2,2445: ᴿJTS 39 (1988) 273-6 (M. *Winterbottom* found he was not iron-stomached enough for what follows Book 5); NRT 110 (1988) 114 (V. *Roisel*); RÉLat 65 (1987) 314-6 (J. *Fontaine*).

E7.4 **Canticum,** *themata, versiculi.*

3413 *Augustin* Matthias, Schönheit und Liebe im Hohenlied und dessen jüdische Auslegung im 1./2. Jahrhundert: ➤ 469, Wünschet 1986/8, 395-408.

3413* *Bogaard* L. van den, Vertalen van metaforen en vergelijkingen, met name in Hooglied: AmstCah 9 (1988) 117-135 [TR 85,425].

3414 *Casuscelli* P., Sul Cantico esposto nella sua nudità da CERONETTI: Aquinas 31 (R 1988) 355-376 [< ZIT 89,259].

3415 *Ch'en* Luke, ☉ The [Canticle of] Canticles, a song of vocation: ColcFuJen 373-384 [335-372 *al.*].

3416 *Consolino* F. E., 'Veni huc a Libano'; la 'sponsa' del Cantico dei Cantici come modello per le vergini negli scritti esortatori di AMBROGIO: Athenaeum NS 62 (1984) 399-415 [< BTAM 14,427].

3417 *Delesalle* Jacques, Amour et connaissance; 'Super Cantica Canticorum' de GUILLAUME de Saint-Thierry: ColcCist 49 (1987) 339-346.

3418 *a) Fernández Tejero* Emilia, Fray Luis DE LEÓN, hebraísta; el Cantar de los Cantares; – *b) Fernández Marcos* N., De los nombres de Cristo de Fray Luis de León y De arcano sermone de ARIAS MONTANO [no hay dependencia, pero sí de la Cabala cristiana]: Sefarad 48 (1988) 271-292; Eng. 292 / 245-269; Eng. 270.

3419 **Elliott** sr. M. Timothea, The literary unity of the Canticle: diss. Pontifical Biblical Institute, ᴰ*Gilbert* M. R 1988. – Acta PIB 9,5 (1988s) 384.422; Biblica 70,146; RTLv 20,539.

3420 *a) Feuillet* André, Le drame d'amour du Cantique des Cantiques remis en son contexte prophétique; – *b) Huguet* Marie-Thérèse, La Bien-Aimée du Cantique; défigurations et occultations: NVFr 62 (1987) 81-127 / 128-147. 179-217.

3421 *Finkel* Irving L., A fragmentary catalogue of lovesongs: AcSum 10 (1988) 17s; 1 fig.

3422 **Fox** Michael V., The Song of Songs and ancient Egyptian love songs 1985 ⇢ 1,3271 ... 3,3215; ᴿBL (1988) 74 (K. A. *Kitchen*); BS 145 (1988) 115 (W. R. *Bodine*: good except for his conclusions regarding premarital sex in Israel); CBQ 50 (1988) 677-9 (W. J. *Urbrock*).

3423 **Heinevetter** Hans-Josef, 'Komm nun, mein Liebster! Dein Garten ruft dich!' Das Hohelied als programmatische Komposition [Diss. ᴰ*Zenger*. Münster 1987s. – TR 84 (1988) 512]: BoBB 69. Fra 1988, Athenaeum. 242 p. DM 68 [JBL 108,568].

3424 **Landy** Francis, Paradoxes of paradise; identity and difference in the Song of Songs 1983 ⇢ 64,3239 ... 2,2456: ᴿBO 44 (1987) 762-4 (J. P. *Fokkelman*).

3425 **Mariaselvam** Abraham, The Song of Songs and ancient Tamil love poems; poetry and symbolism [diss. Pontifical Biblical Institute 1987 ⇢ 3,3200]: AnBib 118. R 1988, Pont. Ist. Biblico. 336 p. Lit. 46.000. 88-7653-118-1.

3426 *Meyers* Carol, Gender imagery in the Song of Songs: HebAnR 10 (1986) 209-223.

3427 **Müller** H.-P., Vergleich und Metapher im Hohenlied: OBO 56, 1984 ⇢ 65,2868 ... 3,3222: ᴿRHPR 68 (1988) 238s (J.-G. *Heintz*).

3428 *Pope* Marvin H., Metastases in canonical shapes of the super song: ⇢ 25, ᶠCHILDS B, Canon 1988, 312-328.

3429 *Salgado* Jean-Marie, Les considérations mariales de RUPERT de Deutz († 1129 ... 1135) dans ses 'Commentaria in Canticum Canticorum': Divinitas 32 (1988) 692-709.

3430 *Segal* Benjamin J., Four repetitions / Literary patterns in the Song of Songs: Dor 16 (1987s) 32-39 / 17 (1988s) 179-184.

3431 **Villiers** Dawid W. de, [Ct 2,7; 3,5; 8,4] Die funksie van die 'besweringsrefrein' in Hooglied: diss. ᴰ*Burden* J. Pretoria 1988. 164 p. – RTLv 20,539; Eng. title in OTEssays 2/2, 75.

3432 *Feuillet* André, [Ct 5,2; Apc 3,20] La mystique nuptiale et la réponse de l'homme à l'amour divin: Carmel 41 (1986) 2-14.

3433 *Luciani* Ferdinando, L'ultima parola di Ct 5,1la nei LXX e nelle versioni derivate: RivB 36 (1988) 73-78.

3434 *Müller* Hans-Peter, Begriffe menschlicher Theomorphie; zu einigen cruces interpretum in Hld [Ct] 6,10: ZAHeb 1,1 (1988) 112-121.

E7.5   *Libri sapientiales* – **Wisdom literature.**

3435 **Abela** F.-J., Proverbes populaires du Liban sud, Saïda et ses environs: Les littératures populaires de toutes les nations NS 28.32. P 1981/5, Maisonneuve & L. I. 481 p.; II. 304 p. + ❹ 70. 2-7068-0827-6; 908-6.

3436 *a) Albertz* Rainer, Ludlul bēl nēmeqi — eine Lehrdichtung zur Ausbreitung und Vertiefung der persönlichen Mardukfrömmigkeit; – *b) Livingstone* Alasdair, 'At the cleaners' and notes on humorous literature: → 32, ᶠDELLER K., AOAT 220 (1988) 25-53 / 175-187.

3437 *Alonso Schökel* Luis, Proverbi biblici e cultura populare cristiana: CC 139 (1988,3) 345-353.

3438 *Boeder* Winfried, La structure du proverbe géorgien: RÉtGC 1 (= Bedi Kartlisa 44, 1985) 97-115.

3439 **Brunner** Helmut, Altägyptische Weisheit; Lehren für das Leben: Bibliothek der Alten Welt. Z 1988, Artemis. 528 p. 3-7608-3683-6 [OIAc D88].

3440 *Burkard* Günter, Ptahhotep und das Alter [... um einen Nachfolger zu bitten]: ZägSpr 115 (1988) 19-30.

3441 *Clements* R. E., *a)* Wisdom [books cited in NT]: → 97, ᶠLINDARS B., 1988, 67-83; – *b)* Solomon and the origins of wisdom in Israel: PerpRelSt 15,4 (1988) 23-35.

3442 *Cottini* Valentino, Autorità e società nei sapienziali: ParVi 32 (1987) 39-46.

3443 *a) Cottini* Valentino, La sapienza nella storia di Israele; – *b) Milani* Marcello, Metodi e forme espressive della Sapienza; – *c) Cirignano* Giulio, I grandi interrogativi; – *d) Infante* Renzo, Gesù sapienza e maestro di sapienza: ParVi 33,5 ('La sapienza' 1988) 326-333 (356-361) / 334-344 / 345-355 / 362-370.

3444 *Cox* Dermot, Learning and the way to God; the spiritual master in the wisdom literature of Israel: StMiss 36 (1987) 1-23.

3445 **Crenshaw** J. L., ❶ Chie no Maneki [OT wisdom, an introduction 1981], ᵀ*Nakamura* K. Tokyo 1987, Shinkyō Suppan-sha. 350 p. Y2800 [BL 89,71]. – ᴿKatKenk 27 (1988) 327-338 (H. *Kruse*).

3446 *Crenshaw* James L. [*Brown* Alexandra R.], Wisdom literature [theoretical perspectives]: → 795, EncRel 15 (1987) 401-9 [-412].

3447 ᴱ**Fanuli** A., Sapienza e Torah 1986/7 → 3,539: ᴿRivB 36 (1988) 414-7 (C. *Ginami*).

3448 *Fischer-Elfert* Hans W., Zum bisherigen Textbestand der 'Lehre eines Mannes an seinen Sohn'; eine Zwischenbilanz: OrAnt 27 (1988) 173-209.

3449 *Gilbert* Maurice, *a)* Sagesse, AT: → 791, DictSpir XIV,91 (1988) 72-81; – *b)* Sapienza; → 806, NDizTB (1988) 1427-1442.

3450 **Goedicke** Hans, Studies in 'The Instructions of King Amenemhet I for his son': VAeg Sup 2. San Antonio 1988, Van Siclen. 2 fasc. 0-933175-15-9 [OIAc N88].

3451 *Görg* Manfred, Weisheit in Israel — Wurzeln, Wege, Wirkungen: KatBlätt 113 (Mü 1988) 544-9 [< ZIT 88,634].

3452 **Goldsworthy** Graeme, Gospel and wisdom; Israel's wisdom literature in the Christian life 1987 → 3,2326: ᴿSalesianum 50 (1988) 421 (G. *Abbà*);

Themelios 14 (1988s) 30 (D. *Kidner*: to remedy the scarcity of books treating the relationship of OT wisdom to NT and Christ).

3453 **Jasnow** Richard L., A late period hieratic wisdom text (P. Brooklyn 47.218.135): diss. ᴰ*Johnson* Janet. Ch 1988. – OIAc D88.

3454 *Koyama* Masato, ❶ Text and interpretation of the Instruction of Hardjedef: Orient 30,2 (1987) 61-68.

3455 *Lang* Bernhard, Theologie der Weisheitsliteratur: → 327, Höre 1987, 221-238.

3456 **Lichtheim** Miriam, Late Egyptian wisdom ... OBO 52, 1983 → 64,3267 ... 3,3240: ᴿArOr 56 (1988) 288s (B. *Vachala*).

3457 *Luke* K., The wisdom of Canaan: LivWord 94 (1988) 131-148 [< TKontext 10 / 1,48].

3458 *Mack* Burton I., Wisdom makes a difference; alternatives to 'messianic' configurations: → 494, Judaisms/Messiahs 1987, 15-48.

3459 **O'Connor** Kathleen M., The wisdom literature: Message of Biblical Spirituality 5. Wilmington 1988, Glazier. 199 p. $13; pa. $10 [CBQ 51,402].

3460 *Packer* J.I., Wisdom along the way: Eternity (April 1986) 19-23 (May p. 32-37; June 36-39) [< BS 144 (1987) 107, S.S. *Cook*].

3461 *Pedersen* Jørgen, Prior omnium sapientia: DanTTs 51 (1988) 263-274 [< ZIT 89,5].

3462 **Perepelkin** Y.Y., ❷ Perevorot Amen-hotpa IV. Moskva 1967/84, Nauka. I. 296 p.; II. 287 p.

3463 **Preuss** Horst D., Einführung in die alttestamentliche Weisheitsliteratur: Urban-Tb 383, 1987 → 3,3244: ᴿBL (1988) 86 (J. *Snaith*); TLZ 113 (1988) 265s (R. *Lux*); TPhil 63 (1988) 587-590 (H. *Engel*).

3464 **Rad** G. von, ❶ Isuraeru no Chie ... [Weisheit in Israel 1970], ᵀ*Katsumura* H. Tokyo 1988, Nihon Kirisuto Kyōdan S. 537 p. Y 7800 [BL 89,91].

3465 **Rad** G. von, Sabiduria en Israel [1970 → 52,1859], ᵀ*Mínguez Fernández* D. 1985 = 1973 → (1,3324*) 2,2487: ᴿCiTom 115 (1988) 397s (J.L. *Espinel*).

3466 *Ravasi* Gianfranco, present., I Proverbi nella Bibbia; 3000 anni di saggezza antica e sempre nuova. Mi 1988, Paoline. I: 84 color. fot.; II: 84 color. fot.

3467 *Renaud* Odette, Ipouer le mal-aimé: BSocÉg 12 (Genève 1988) 71-75.

3468 **Roos** Paolo, Sentenza e proverbio nell'antichità e i 'Distici di Catone'; il testo latino e i volgarizzamenti italiani; con una scelta e traduzione delle massime e delle frasi proverbiali latine classiche più importanti o ancora vive oggi nel mondo neolatino. Brescia 1984, Morcelliana. 254 p. Lit. 30.000. – ᴿGnomon 60 (1988) 116-9 (W. *Bühler*).

3469 **Sandelin** Karl-Gustav, Wisdom as nourisher [Prov 9,1-6; Sir 14,20-15,10 ...] 1986 → 2,2488*: ᴿCBQ 50 (1988) 514s (J.M. *Reese*); JBL 107 (1988) 750-2 (D. *Winston*); JStJud 19 (1988) 123s (R.E. *Murphy*); SvEx 53 (1988) 118s (J. *Bergman*).

3470 *Savignac* Jean de, Le travail dans la littérature sapientiale d'Israël: → 50, ᶠFONTINOY C., 1988, 169-175.

Smalley Beryl, Medieval exegesis of wisdom literature, ᴱ*Murphy* Roland E. 1986 → 264.

3471 **Thissen** Heinz J., Die Lehre des Anchscheschonqi 1984 → 65,2908; 3,3247: ᴿBO 44 (1987) 641-6 (R.K. *Ritner*); CdÉ 63 (1988) 276-8 (M. *Chauveau*); OLZ 83 (1988) 148-150 (S.P. *Vleeming*).

3472 *Vanstiphout* Herman,   The importance of 'the tale of the fox' [Akkadian; *Smith* G. 1876]: AcSum 10 (1988) 191-227.

E7.6   **Proverbiorum liber,** *themata, versiculi.*

3473 **Aitken** Kenneth T.,   Proverbs: Daily Study Bible 1986 → 2,2496; 3,3249: ᴿBS 145 (1988) 230 (R. B. *Zuck*: one of the best); CBQ 50 (1988) 672s (J. C. *Kesterson*); EvQ 60 (1988) 355s (D. G. *Deboys*).

3474 **Alonso Schökel** L., *al.,*   Proverbios: Sapienciales I, 1984 → 65,2915 ... 2,2498: ᴿGregorianum 69 (1988) 349-351 (G. L. *Prato*).

3475 **Alonso Schökel** Luis, *Vílchez Líndez* J.,   I Proverbi, traduzione e commento [1984], ᵀ*Tosatti* Teodora, *Brugnoli* Pietro: Commenti Biblici. R 1988, Borla. 638 p. Lit. 60.000. 88-263-0568-2. – ᴿRClerIt 69 (1988) 710s (A. *Bonora*).

3476 **Camp** Claudia V.,   Wisdom and the feminine in the Book of Proverbs 1985 → 1,3335*; 3,3250:   ᴿVT 38 (1988) 498s (R. P. *Gordon*).

3477 *a) Camp* Claudia V.,   Wise and strange; an interpretation of the female imagery of Proverbs in light of trickster mythology; – *b) Steinberg* Naomi, Israelite tricksters; their analogues and cross-cultural study; – *c) Ashley* Kathleen M.,   Interrogating biblical deception and trickster theories; narratives of patriarchy or possibility?: Semeia 42 (1988) 14-36 / 1-13 / 103-114.

3478 *Clincke* M.,   Livres des Proverbes: → 786, Catholicisme 12,54 (1988) 116-121.

3479 *Engelken* Karen,   Erziehungsziel Gewaltlosigkeit? Überlegungen zum Thema 'physische Gewalt' im Buch Proverbien: BibNot 44 (1988) 12-18.

3480 **Géhin** Paul,   ÉVAGRE le Pontique, Scholies aux Proverbes: SChr 340, 1987 → 3,3254: ᴿNRT 110 (1988) 761 (V. *Roisel*); RTPhil 120 (1988) 484s (J. *Borel*).

3481 *Jenkins* R. G.,   The [Proverbs] text of P Antinoopolis 8/210 [*Roberts* C. 1950]: → 478, ᴱ*Cox* C., 6th LXX, 1986/7, 65-77.

3482 **Krispenz-Pichler** Jutta,   Spruchkompositionen im Buch Proverbia; die Sammlungen II und V.: ev. Diss. ᴰ*Jeremias* J. München 1987. 262 p. – RTLv 19,534.

3483 **Sæbø** Magne,   Fortolkning til Salomos ordspråk ... Prov Qoh Ct Lam 1986 → 2,2507: ᴿSvEx 53 (1988) 114-6 (L. O. *Eriksson*).

3484 **Sell** Charles,   The house on the rock; wisdom from Proverbs for today's families. Wheaton ᴵᴸ 1987, Victor. 168 p. $6. – ᴿBS 145 (1988) 466 (R. B. *Zuck*).

3485 **Harris** Scott L.,   A study of inner-biblical interpretation within Proverbs 1-9: diss. Union Theol. Sem., ᴰ*Greenstein* E. NY 1988. 322 p. 88-22287. – DissA 49 (1988s) 2276-A; RelStR 15,191.

3486 *Meinhold* A.,   Der Gewaltmensch als abschreckendes Beispiel in Proverbien 1-9: ᶠHɪɴᴢ C., '... und Friede' 1988, 82-97 [< ᴢᴀᴡ 101,329].

3487 *Murphy* Roland E.,   Wisdom and eros in Proverbs 1-9: CBQ 50 (1988) 600-3.

3488 **Overland** Paul B.,   Literary structure in Proverbs 1-9: diss. Brandeis. Boston 1988. 447 p. 88-19772. – DissA 49 (1988s) 1792-A.

3489 **Lang** Bernhard, Wisdom and Prov [1,20-38] 1986 → 2,2510: 3,3260: ᴿRB 95 (1988) 138s (R.J. *Tournay*); TR 84 (1988) 192-4 (R. *Albertz*).

3490 **Pardee** Dennis, Ugaritic and Hebrew poetic parallelism; a trial cut ['nt I and Proverbs 2]: VT Sup [0083-5889] 39. Leiden 1988, Brill. xvi-201 p. *f*136 [TR 84,249]. 90-04-08368-5.

3491 **Clayton** Allen L., The orthodox recovery of a heretical proof-text; ATHANASIUS of Alexandria's interpretation of Proverbs 8:22-30 in conflict with the Arians: diss. Southern Methodist. 1988. – RelStR 15,193.

3492 *Auwers* Jean-Marie, TERTULLIEN et les Proverbes; une approche philologique à partir de Prov. 8,22-31; → 56, Mém. GRIBOMONT J. 1988, 75-83.

3493 *Dellazari* Romano, Provérbios 8,22 e Colossenses 1,15b; a exegese de Ario e Atanásio; proposta para uma crítica: Teocomunicação 17,75s (Porto Alegre 1987) 34-44. 61-69; 17,77 (1987) 97-106 / 17,78 (1987) 53-68 [< TKontext 10/1,84].

3494 *Matlack* Hugh, [Prov 8,22-31] The play of wisdom: CurrTM 15 (1988) 425-430.

3495 *Cavedo* Romeo, Guardare il mondo per essere saggi (Proverbi 10-31; Cantico) / Il sapiente educato dalla fede (da Siracide a Sapienza): → 810*, StSpG 1 (1988) 582-602 / 628-648.

3496 *Hildebrandt* Ted, Proverbial pairs; compositional units in Proverbs 10-29: JBL 107 (1988) 207-224.

3497 **Cottini** Valentino, La vita futura nel libro dei Proverbi [12,28...] 1984 → 65,2930: 2,2513: ᴿÉglT 17 (1986) 87-90 (L. *Laberge*).

3498 *Bonora* Antonio, L'enigmatico proverbio di Pr 14,9: RivB 36 (1988) 61-66.

3499 *Vanoni* G., Volkssprichwort und YHWH-Ethos; Beobachtungen zu Spr 15,16: BibNot 35 (1986) 73-108.

3500 *Emerton* J.A., The interpretation of Proverbs 21,28: → 153, ZAW 100 Supp. (1988) 161-170.

3501 *Hildebrandt* Ted, Proverbs 22:6a; train up a child?: GraceTJ 9 (1988) 3-19.

3502 **Römheld** Diethard, Wege der Weisheit; die Lehren Amenemopes und Proverbien 22,17 – 24,22: Diss. ᴰ*Kaiser* O. Marburg 1988. 442 p. – RTLv 20,541.

3503 *Feiertag* Jean-Louis, Quelques commentaires patristiques de Proverbe 22,2; pour une nouvelle approche du problème richesses et pauvreté dans l'Église des premiers siècles: VigChr 42 (1988) 156-178.

3504 **Naré** L., Proverbes salomoniens et proverbes mossi ... Pr 25-29, ᴰ1986 → 2,2516; 3,3274: ᴿRB 95 (1988) 624s (R.J. *Tournay*).

3505 **Van Leeuwen** Raymond C., Context and meaning in Proverbs 25-27 [diss. St. Michael's 1984, ᴰ*Dion* P.]: SBL diss. 96. Atlanta 1988, Scholars. xi-171 p. $15; pa. $11 [CBQ 50,754]. 0-55540-004-3; 5-1.

3506 *Dressler* Harold H.P., The lesson of Proverbs 26:23: → 29, Mem. CRAIGIE P., Ascribe 1988, 117-125.

3507 *Brunsch* Wolfgang, 'Tria sunt insaturabilia ... et os vulvae ...' (Proverbia 30,15-16) und Setne, V, 29-30: EgVO 11 (1988) 51-53.

3508 *Crenshaw* James L., A mother's instruction to her son (Proverbs 31:1-9): PerspRelSt 15,4 (1988) 9-22.

3509 *Wolters* Al, Proverbs XXXI, 10-31 as heroic hymn; a form-critical analysis: VT 38 (1988) 446-457.

3510 *Bonora* Antonio, La donna eccellente, la sapienza, il sapiente (Pr 31,10-31): RivB 36 (1988) 137-163; Eng. 163s.

E7.7   *Ecclesiastes* – **Qohelet,** *themata, versiculi.*

3511 **Anderson** Don, Ecclesiastes; the mid-life crisis. Neptune NJ 1987, Loizeaux. 267 p. $8 pa. [GraceTJ 8,309].

3512 **Crenshaw** James L., Ecclesiastes, a commentary: OT Library 1987 ➤ 3,3282; also L 1988, SCM; £10.50; 0-334-00361-X: ᴿTrinJ 9,1 (1988) 170-3 (T. *Longman*); TS 49 (1988) 572s (L. *Boadt*: technically excellent).

3513 *Crenshaw* James L., *a)* Qoheleth in current research: HebAnR 7 (1983) 41-56 [< OTAbs 11,277]; – *b)* Youth and old age in Qoheleth: HebAnR 10 (1986) 1-13.

3514 **Davidson** Robert, Ecclesiastes and the Song of Solomon: Daily Study Bible 1986 ➤ 2,2523; 3,3283: ᴿCBQ 50 (1988) 673 (J. C. *Kesterson*).

3515 **De Gregorio** Domenico, Gli insegnamenti teologici di S. GREGORIO di Agrigento nel suo Commento all'Ecclesiaste: diss. Pont. Athenaeum Antonianum, ᴰ*Adinolfi* M. Roma 1988. 374 p. – RTLv 20,586.

3516 **Díez Merino** L., Targum de Qohelet 1987 ➤ 3,3284: ᴿEstBíb 46 (1988) 267s (A. *Rodríguez Carmona*).

3517 *Dillmann* Rainer, Hat Leben Sinn? Exegetische Überlegungen zu Kohelet — Aktualisierungsmöglichkeiten: KatBlätt 113 (Mü 1988) 561-9 [-575, *Peek-Horn* Margret: < ZIT 88,635].

3518 *Festorazzi* Franco, In margine a un libro su Qohelet [*Bonora* A., 1987 ➤ 3,3281]: RivB 36 (1988) 67-72.

3519 *Fox* Michael V., Qohelet's epistemology: HUCA 58 (1987) 137-155.

3520 **Fredericks** Daniel C., Qoheleth's language; re-evaluating its nature and date: Ancient NE TSt V/3. Lewiston NY 1988, Mellen. 301 p. $60 [RelStR 15,258, J. L. *Crenshaw*]. 0-88946-088-4.

3521 *Garrett* Duane A., Qoheleth on the use and abuse of political power: TrinJ 8 (1987) 159-177.

3522 **Isaksson** Bo, Studies in the language of Qoheleth, with special emphasis on the verbal system [diss. Uppsala]: StudSemUps 10, 1987 ➤ 3,3288: ᴿNorTTs 89 (1988) 132 (A. S. *Kapelrud*); TüTQ 168 (1988) 242-4 (W. *Gross*).

3523 *Laato* Antti, Predikaren och Salomo: SvEx 53 (1988) 14-25.

3524 **Loader** J. A., Ecclesiastes 1986 ➤ 2,2531; 3,3293: ᴿBS 145 (1988) 231s (R. B. *Zuck*: food for thought, though claims written not by Solomon, indeed 250 B.C.).

3525 *Margalit* Shlomoh, ⓂQohelet: BethM 34,117 (1988s) 176-184.

3526 **Michaud** Robert, Qohélet et l'hellénisme: Lire la Bible 77, 1987 ➤ 3,3295: ᴿAngelicum 65 (1988) 466s (J. *Garcia Trapiello*); Bijdragen 49 (1988) 332 (P. C. *Bentjes*); BL (1988) 84 (R. B. *Salters*: strong on history, shallow on theology); EstBib 46 (1988) 134s (V. *Morla*); VSp 142 (1988) 291 (T. *Chary*).

3527 **Michel** Diethelm, Qohelet: ErtFor 258. Da 1988, Wiss. vi-180 p. [TR 84,426]. 3-534-08317-2. – ᴿArTGran 51 (1988) 295s (J. *Vílchez*).

3528 **Ogden** Graham, Qoheleth [excursus on Chinese wisdom]: Readings, a new biblical commentary. Sheffield 1987, JStOT. 236 p. $45 [TDig 35,384]. – ᴿExpTim 99 (1987s) 375s (C. S. *Rodd*); OTAbs 11 (1988) 200 (R. E. *Murphy*: format confusing).

3529 *Pazera* Wojciech, ❷ De timore Domini et cultu in Qohelet: RuBi 41 (1988) 307-313.

3530 **Ravasi** Gianfranco, Il libro di Qohelet; ciclo di conferenze, Centro culturale S. Fedele Milano: Conversazioni bibliche. Bo 1988, Dehoniane. 120 p. 88-10-70905-5.

3531 **Ravasi** Gianfranco, Qohelet: La parola di Dio. CinB 1988, Paoline. 474 p.

3532 *Salters* Robert B., Exegetical problems in Qoheleth: ➤ 148, FWEIN-GREEN J. = IrBSt 10,1 (1988) 44-59.

3533 *Schoors* Antoon, The use of vowel letters in Qoheleth: UF 20 (1988) 277-286.

3534 **Shaw** Jean, The better half of life; meditations from Ecclesiastes. GR 1983, Zondervan. 183 p. [GraceTJ 9,315: '1983'].

3535 E**Strothmann** Werner, Der Kohelet-Kommentar des JOHANNES von Apamea; syrischer Text mit vollständigem Wörterverzeichnis: GöOrF 1/30. Wsb 1988, Harrassowitz. 283 p. [Mundus 24,228]. 3-447-02854-8.

3536 E**Strothmann** Werner, Kohelet-Kommentar des DIONYSIUS bar Ṣalibi; Auslegung des Septuaginta-Textes: GöOrF 1/31. Wsb 1988, Harrassowitz. xiii-116 p. 3-447-02855-6.

3537 E**Strothmann** Werner, Syrische Katenen aus dem Ecclesiastes-Kommentar des THEODOR von Mopsuestia; syrischer Text mit vollständigem Wörterverzeichnis: GöOrF 1/29. Wsb 1988, Harrassowitz. xxxiii-133 p. 3-447-02853-X.

3538 *Strothmann* Werner, Der Kohelet-Kommentar des THEODOR von Mopsuestia: ➤ 16, FBÖHLIG A., Religion 1988, 186-196.

3539 **Tylor** Louis R., The language of Ecclesiastes as a criterion for dating: diss. Texas, DBar-Adon A. Austin 1988. 332 p. 88-16594. – DissA 49 (1988s) 1785-A.

3540 *Fox* Michael V., Qohelet 1.4: JStOT [34 (1986) 91, *Ogden* G.] 40 (1988) 109 only.

3541 *Whybray* R. N., Ecclesiastes 1.5-7 and the wonders of nature: JStOT 41 (1988) 105-112.

3542 *Deist* F. E., 'God met ons?' Prediker 3,1-9: ➤ 509, Hoe lees 1985/8, ...

3543 *Gelio* Roberto, Osservazioni critiche sul *māšāl* di Qoh, 7,5-7: Lateranum 54 (1988) 1-15.

3544 *Ogden* Graham S., Translation problems in Ecclesiastes 5. 13-17: BTrans 39 (1988) 423-8.

3545 *D'Alario* Vittoria, Qo 7,26-28; un testo antifemminista?: ➤ 511, EAbignente Donatella, al., La Donna nella Chiesa e nel mondo: Fac. Teol. It. Merid. (1988) 225-234.

3546 *Fox* Michael V., Aging and death in Qohelet 12: JStOT 42 (1988) 55-77.

3547 *Uricchio* F., Vanità delle vanità e tutto è vanita (Eccle 12,8) nella lettura evangelica di S. FRANCESCO (1 Reg 8,7): ➤ 351, FDI FONZO L. 1985, 150-203.

3548 *Goldin* Judah, [Qoh 12,14] The end of Ecclesiastes; literal exegesis and its transformation [< EAltmann A., Biblical Motifs (1966) 135-156]: ➤ 199, Studies 1988, 3-25.

E7.8 *Liber Sapientiae* - **Wisdom of Solomon.**

3549 TE**Albert** Karl, Meister ECKHART, Kommentar zum Buch der Weisheit: Texte zur Philosophie 7. St. Augustin 1988, Academia. 167 p. DM 29,50 pa. [JBL 108,567]. 3-88345-431-1.

3550 **Beentjes** Panc, Wijsheid van Salomo: Belichting. Boxtel 1987, Kath. Bijbelstichting. 160 p. *f* 19,50. 90-6173-431-2 [Bijdragen 49,234].

3551 *Gilbert* Maurice, 'Sagesse de Salomon': ➤ 791, DictSp XIV,91 (1988) 57-72.

3552 *Monti* Dominic V., A reconsideration of the authorship of the commentary on the Book of Wisdom attributed to St. BONAVENTURE: ArFranH 79 (1986) 359-391.

3553 **Poniży** Bogdan, ✪ Reinterpretacja wyjścia Izraelitów z Egiptu w ujęciu Księgi Mądrości, De reinterpretatione Exodi in libro Sapientiae: Pont. Fac. Theologica Posnaniae, Studia et Textus 8. Poznań 1988, Św. Wojciecha. 155 p.; Eng. p. 147-9. 83-7015-120-5.

3554 **Schmitt** Armin, Das Buch der Weisheit: NEchter 1986 ➤ 2,2547: ᴿBijdragen 49 (1988) 333 (P. C. *Beentjes*); TR 84 (1988) 107s (H. D. *Preuss*).

3555 *Sheppard* G. T. [*Morgan* D. F.], Wisdom [of Solomon]: ➤ 801, ISBEnc³ 4 (1988) 1074-82 [-84].

3556 *Seeley* David, Transumptive narration and the structure of Wisdom 1-5: ➤ 500, SBL Seminars 1988, 245-8.

3557 *Scarpat* Giuseppe, *a*) Una speranza piena di immortalità (Sap 3,4): RivB 36 (1988) 487-494; – *b*) Ancora sulla data di composizione della Sapientia Salomonis; il termine *diágnōsis* (Sap 3,18; At 25,21): ➤ 154, ᶠZEDDA S., RivB 36 (1988) 363-375; Eng. 375 [after 30 B.C.].

3558 *Poniży* Bogdan, Gotteserkenntnis nach dem Buch der Weisheit 13,1-9: ➤ 469, Wünschet 1986/8, 465-474.

E7.9   *Ecclesiasticus, Siracides;* **Wisdom of Jesus Sirach.**

3559 *Beentjes* Pancratius C., Hermeneutics in the book of Ben Sira; some observations on the Hebrew Ms. C: EstBíb 46 (1988) 45-59; castellano 45.

3560 *a*) *Brasil Pereira* Ney, A mulher no Sirácide; – *b*) *Meyers* Carol L., As raízes da restrição — as mulheres no Antigo Israel [< Bible & Liberation, ᴱGottwald N. (1984) 289-306], ᵀ; – *c*) *Trible* Phyllis, [Juízes 19,1-30] Uma concubina anônima — o cúmulo da violência [< Texts of terror 1984, ch. 3], ᵀ: EstudosB 20 (1988) 9-25 / 26-45 / 46-58.

3561 *Di Lella* Alexander A., The newly discovered sixth [not 4th as claimed by *Scheiber* A. in publishing it] manuscript of Ben Sira from the Cairo Geniza: Biblica 69 (1988) 226-238; 4 pl.

3561* *Gilbert* Maurice, GRÉGOIRE de Nazianze et le Siracide: ➤ 56, Mém. GRIBOMONT J. 1988, 307-314.

3562 **Michaud** R., Ben Sira et le judaïsme; la littérature de sagesse, histoire et théologie 3 / Lire la Bible 82. P 1988, Cerf. 216 p. F 90 [NRT 111,930, J.-L. *Ska*].

3563 **Minissale** Antonio, Siracide; le radici nella tradizione: LoB 1/17. Brescia c.1987, Queriniana. 104 p. Lit. 9500. 88-399-1567-2. – ᴿBbbOr 30 (1988) 124s.

3564 **Nelson** Milward D., The Syriac version of the Wisdom of Ben Sira compared to the Greek and Hebrew materials: SBL diss. 107. Atlanta 1988, Scholars. viii-142 p. 1-55540-193-7; pa. 4-5 [BL 89,156].

3565 **Sanders** Jack T., Ben Sira and demotic wisdom: SBL Mg 28, 1983 ➤ 2,2561; 3,3327; ᴿCdÉ 63 (1988) 281-3 (M. *Pezin*: déplorable qu'il n'ait pas utilisé ... HELCK); OLZ 83 (1988) 317-9 (H.-F. *Weiss*).

3566 **Schnabel** Eckhard J., Law and wisdom from Ben Sira to Paul ... [diss. Aberdeen 1983; BRDX-84502; DissA 49 (1988s) 3760-A]: WUNT 2/16, 1985 ➤ 1,3396 ... 3,3328: ᴿHeythJ 29 (1988) 509s (R. N. *Whybray*); JBL 107 (1988) 319s (B. L. *Mack*); NedTTs 42 (1988) 74s (P. W. van der *Horst*).

3567 **Skehan** Patrick W. †, ᴱ*Di Lella* Alexander A., The wisdom of Ben Sira: AnchorB 39, 1987 ➤ 3,3329: ᴿETL 64 (1988) 463s (J. *Lust*: 'palliates a lacuna'); JStJud 19 (1988) 268-271 (P. C. *Beentjes*); Paradigms 4 (1988) 93s (M. *Jolley*); RB 95 (1988) 623s (R. J. *Tournay*).

3568 **Thiele** Walter, Sirach I: Vetus Latina 11/2, [Lfg 1, 1987 ➤ 3,3330] Lfg. 2 (Einleitung, Schluss). FrB 1988, Herder. 79 p. – ᴿZkT 110 (1988) 192s (K. *Stock*: auch über 11/1; 11/2/1; 12/1; 25/2-4.

3569 *Van Leeuwen* R. C., Sirach: ➤ 801, ISBEnc³ 4 (1988) 529-533.

3570 **Wright** Benjamin G.ᴵᴵᴵ, New perspectives on biblical vocabulary and translation technique; Sirach in relation to its presumed Hebrew 'Vorlage': diss. Pennsylvania, ᴰ*Kraft* R. Ph 1988. 395 p. 88-16255. – DissA 49 (1988s) 1483-A.

3571 *Morla* Victor, Un extraño uso de *b'r* en Eclo 8,10b: EstBíb 46 (1988) 250s.

3572 *Beentjes* P. C., The reliability of text-editions in Ben Sira 41.14-16; a case study in repercussions on structure and interpretation: Bijdragen 49 (1988) 188-194.

3573 **Lee** Thomas R., Studies in the form of Sirach 44-50: SBL diss 75, 1986 ➤ 2,2565; 3,3336: ᴿAustralBR 36 (1988) 67s (Anne E. *Gardner*); CBQ 50 (1988) 505s (R. R. *Hann*); JStJud 19 (1988) 110-2 (J. *Duhaime*); TLZ 113 (1988) 433-5 (G. *Sauer*).

3574 **Mack** Burton L., [Sir 44,1-50,24] Wisdom and the Hebrew epic 1985 ➤ 1,3403; 3,3337: ᴿBibTB 18 (1988) 117 (Betty Jane *Lillie*); TorJT 4 (1988) 134-6 (W. H. *Irwin*).

3575 *Lim* Timothy H., 'Nevertheless these were men of piety' (Ben Sira XLIV,10): VT 38 (1988) 338-341.

3576 *Peterca* Vladimir, Das Porträt Salomos bei Ben Sirach (47,12-22); ein Beitrag zu der Midraschexegese: ➤ 469, Wünschet 1986/8, 457-463.

VIII. Libri prophetici VT

E8.1 **Prophetismus.**

3577 *Alonso Fontela* Carlos, Anotaciones de Alfonso de ZAMORA en un comentario a los Profetas Posteriores de Don Isaac ABRAVANEL: Sefarad 47 (1987) 227-243.

3578 *Amsler* S., *al.*, I profeti e i libri profetici, ᵀ*Godio* Virgilio, ᴱ*Borgonovo* Gianantonio: Piccola Enciclopedia Biblica 4. R 1987, Borla. 400 p. Lit. 30.000. 88-263-0607-9.

3579 **Asurmendi** Jesús, El profetismo desde sus orígenes a la época moderna [Le prophétisme 1985 ➤ 1,3409], ᵀ*Bernal* José M.: Cristianismo y Sociedad 15. Bilbao 1987, Desclée-B. 123 p. 84-330-0708-4. – ᴿActuBbg 25 (1988) 207 (R. de *Sivatte*); LumenVr 37 (1988) 440s (M. A. *de Paz*).

3580 *Auneau* J., Prophètes et prohétisme: ➤ 786, Catholicisme 11,53 (1988) 1261-1273 (-1278 iconographie, *David-Danel* M.-L.).

3581 **Barton** J.,   Oracles of God 1986 ➤ 2,2577; 3,3346:   ᴿEstE 63 (1988) 344s (J. *Alonso Díaz*); NBlackf 68 (1987) 416s (H. *Mowvley*); Salesianum 50 (1988) 416 (R. *Vicent*); ScotJT 41 (1988) 543-5 (R. P. *Carroll*); ScripB 19 (1988s) 23s (P. *Robson*); VT 38 (1988) 486-8 (R. P. *Gordon*).

3582 **Beaucamp** Évode,   Les prophètes d'Israël, ou le drame d'une alliance [= 1968 = Sous la main de Dieu 1956]: Lire la Bible 75 [0588-2257].   P 1987, Cerf.   364 p. F 99.   2-204-02640-9 [BL 88,70]. – ᴿVSp 141 (1987) 488 (T. *Chary*).

3583 *Begg* Christopher T.,   The 'classical prophets' in JOSEPHUS' Antiquities: LvSt 13 (1988) 341-357.

3584 *a*) *Borbone* Pier Giorgio,   La profezia nell'antico Israele; – *b*) *Marconcini* Benito,   L'esperienza di Dio alla radice della profezia; – *c*) *Nobile* Marco, Il linguaggio dei profeti; – *d*) *Borgonovo* Gianantonio,   Profetismo e messianismo; – *e*) *Loss* Nicolò M.,   Chi è il profeta?:   ParVi 33,4 ('La Profezia' 1988) 247-257 / 258-265 / 266-271 / 272-286 / 287-294.

3585 **Brueggemann** Walter, [Jer Ezek 2-Is] Hopeful imagination; prophetic voices in exile.   Ph 1986, Fortress.   160 p. $8.   0-8006-1925-0. – ᴿCBQ 50 (1988) 104s (J. E. *Rybolt,* also on AULD A., Amos guide).

3586 **Buber** M.,   La fede dei profeti 1985 ➤ 1,3614*b* ... 3,3351:   ᴿProtestantesimo 43 (1988) 44s (M. *Grube*).

3587 **Carroll** R. P.,   When prophecy failed 1979 ➤ 60,4642 ... 64,3369:   ᴿProtestantesimo 43 (1988) 116s (J. A. *Soggin*).

3588 *Carroll* Robert P.,   Inventing the prophets [as biographical figures]: ➤ 148, ꜰWEINGREEN J. = IrBSt 10 (1988) 24-36.

3589 *a)* *Casas* Victoriano,   El compromiso profético; reflexiones desde la revelación bíblica; – *b*) *Cañellas* Gabriel,   Los profetas de Israel; incidencia religiosa y socio-política: BibFe 14 (1988) 157-181 / 182-207.

3590 *a)* *Chmiel* Jerzy,   The paradigms of inculturation in the prophetic literature; – *b*) *Petersen* David L.,   Rethinking the end of prophecy; – *c*) *Hasel* Gerhard F.,   'New moon and sabbath' in eighth century Israelite prophetic writings (Isa 1:13; Hos 2:13; Amos 8:5); – *d*) *Bosman* Hendrik, Adultery, prophetic tradition and the Decalogue: ➤ 469, Wünschet 1986/8, 31-36 / 65-71 / 37-64 / 21-30.

3591 *a)* *Clements* Ronald E.,   Patterns in the prophetic canon; healing the blind and the lame; – *b*) *Tucker* Gene M.,   The Law in the eighth-century prophets; – *c*) *Sheppard* Gerald T.,   True and false prophecy within Scripture: ➤ 25, ꜰCHILDS B., Canon 1988, 189-200 / 201-216 / 262-282.

3592 *Conrad* Joachim,   Überlegungen zu Bedeutung und Aktualität der Unheilsbotschaft der vorexilischen Schriftpropheten: ➤ 328, Gericht/Heil 1987, 91-120.

3593 **Crenshaw** J.l.,   Los falsos profetas 1986 ➤ 2,2586; 3,3357:   ᴿCompostellanum 33 (1988) 306s (J. *Precedo*).

3594 *Day* John,   Prophecy [OT cited in NT]: ➤ 97, ꜰLINDARS B., It is written 1988, 39-55.

3595 **Dearman** J. A.,   Property rights in the eighth-century prophets; the conflict and its background: SBL diss. 106 [Emory 1981]. Atlanta 1988, Scholars.   x-171 p. $11; sb./ pa. $8 [ZAW 101,313, G. *Wanke*].

3595* **Deissler** Alfons,   Dann wirst du Gott erkennen [Os 2,22]; die Grundbotschaft der Propheten 1987 ➤ 3,3359:   ᴿColcT 58,2 (1988) 130-3 (J. W. *Roslon*).

3596 *Dionisio* Francesco,   Profeti, profetismo e profeti da ... 'Quattro versicoli' nell'A.T.:   BbbOr 30 (1988) 145-161 . 193-222.

3597 **Dobberahn** Friedrich E., Verkündigung und Sprachdisintegration; Aspekte der Schriftlichkeit der vorexilischen Gerichtsprophetie des ATs (D1980) 1984 ➤ 65,3003; 1,3417: ᴿOLZ 83 (1988) 565-7 (R. *Stahl*).

3598 **Fahd** Toufic, La divination arabe: La bibliothèque arabe. P 1987, Sindbad. xii-564 p. – ᴿRThom 88 (1988) 505s (J. *Jomier*).

3599 *Fang* Mark, ☉ The Prophets in the Old Testament: ColcFuJen 76 (1988) 157-160.

3600 *a) Feldman* Louis H., Prophets and prophecy in JOSEPHUS; – *b) Winston* David J., Two types of Mosaic prophecy according to PHILO: – *c) Berchman* Robert M., Arcana mundi; prophecy and divination in the Vita Mosis of Philo of Alexandria: ➤ 500, SBL Seminars 1988, 424-441 / 442-455 / 385-423.

3601 *Gilead* Ḥayyim, ❶ M*e*sibbeh n*e*bû'ît ... the prophetic circle ...: BethM 34,116 (1988s) 62-67.

3602 *a) Goldstein* Jonathan A., The historical setting of the Uruk prophecy: JNES 47 (1988) 43-46; – *b) Kaufman* Stephen A., Prediction, prophecy, and apocalypse in the light of new Akkadian texts: ➤ 60,629, Jerusalem sixth congress 1973/7, I.223-7 [JAOS 95 (1975) 371-5].

3603 **Graffy** Adrian, A prophet confronts his people...: AnBib 104, 1984 ➤ 65,3006 ... 2,2588: ᴿRelStR 13 (1987) 67 (D. L. *Petersen*).

3604 **Green** Joel B., How to read prophecy 1986 ➤ 2,2589; 3,3364: ᴿEvQ 60 (1988) 266s (S. H. *Travis*); Vidyajyoti 52 (1982) 250 (P. M. *Meagher*: eschews fundamentalism).

3605 **Hagemann** Ludwig, Propheten — Zeugen des Glaubens; koranische und biblische Deutungen 1985 ➤ 1,3421; 3,3366: ᴿDivThom 89s (1986s) 421s (G. *Testa*); ÉglT 18 (1987) 364 (L. *Laberge*).

3605* **Henbrechtsmeier** William, False prophecy and canonical thinking, 'GSAS' Columbia Univ. diss. NY 1986. – RelStR 14,188; RTLv 20,540.

3606 **Hungs** Franz-Josef, Die Propheten der Bibel; ein Arbeitsbuch für Schule, Erwachsenenbildung und Katechese. Fra 1986, Knecht. 192 p. DM 22 pa. – ᴿÉtClas 56 (1988) 194s (X. *Jacques*); TPQ 135 (1987) 178 (F. *Hubmann*).

3607 *Kida* K., ❹ What is a prophet?: Kirisutokyo Gaku (Christian Studies NS) 29 (1987) ... [BL 89,19; that issue contains 159 p.].

3608 **Koch** K., Die Propheten I²: Urban-Tb 280, 1987 ➤ 3,3372: ᴿTPQ 136 (1988) 282 (B. *Baldauf*).

3609 **LaRondelle** Hans K., The Israel of God in prophecy; principles of prophetic interpretation 1983 ➤ 64,3392; 2,2598*: ᴿAustralBR 36 (1988) 65s (M. *O'Brien*).

3610 *Leaman* Oliver, MAIMONIDES, imagination and the objectivity of prophecy: Religion 18,1 (L 1988) 69-80 [< ZIT].

3611 *Légasse* Simon, Prophétisme; ➤ 791, DictSpir 12 (1986) 2410-2434 (-2446, *Vallin* P., dans l'Église).

3612 *Le Roux* J. H., Eschatology and the prophets (a survey of the research): OTEssays 1,1 (Pretoria 1988) 1-26.

3613 **Lowden** John, Illuminated prophet books; a study of Byzantine manuscripts of the major and minor prophets. University Park 1988, Pennsylvania State Univ. 128 p.; 134 fig. + 8 color. $50 [RelStR 15,350, J. *Gutmann*]. 0-271-00604-8.

3614 ᴱ**Mays** J. *Achtemeier* P., Interpreting the prophets [21 articles on prophets from Interpretation 1978-85] 1987 ➤ 3,352: ᴿExpTim 99 (1987s) 341 (H. *Mowvley*).

Meier Samuel A., The messenger in the ancient Semitic world: HarvSemMg 45, 1988 → 2359.

3615 **Miller** John W., Meet the prophets 1987 → 3,378; $12: ᴿPrPeo 2 (1988) 437s (B. *Robinson*); TS 49 (1988) 573 (M. D. *Guinan*).

3616 **Monloubou** Louis, Les prophètes de l'Ancien Testament: CahÉv 43. P 1987, Cerf. 63 p. F 17. – ᴿMondeB 54 (1988) 59 (J. *Asurmendi*).

3617 *a) Murray* Robert, From biblical roots; – *b) Byrne* Brendan, Prophecy now; the tug into the future: Way 27,2 ('Sustaining the prophets' 1987) 79-88 / 106-116.

3618 *Onunwa* Udobata, The nature and development of early Israelite prophecy; an historical prolegomenon: Bible Bhashyam 13 (1987) 79-88.

3619 **Overholt** Thomas W., Prophecy in cross-cultural perspective; a sourcebook for biblical researchers 1986 → 2,2603; 3,3382: ᴿAustralBR 36 (1988) 66s (M. *O'Brien*); IrBSt 9 (1987) 49s (J. R. *Boyd*).

3620 *Overholt* Thomas W., The end of prophecy; no players without a program: JStOT 42 (1988) 103-115.

3621 ᴱ**Petersen** David L., Prophecy in Israel; search for an identity 1987 → 3,358: ᴿPrPeo 2 (1988) 438s (A. *Graffy*); TLond 91 (1988) 223s (R. *Coggins*: does not achieve the aim as well as other books in the Issues series).

3622 **Ravasi** Gianfranco, I profeti. Mi 1987, Àncora. 295 p. – ᴿTeresianum 39 (1988) 216 (V. *Pasquetto*).

3623 *Reiterer* Friedrich V., Der Prophet als Verkünder und Fürbitter für die Bedrohten: Diakonia Christi 23 (1988) 12-18.21-30.

3624 *Renaud* B., La critique prophétique de l'attitude d'Israël face aux nations [Am Is; Jon; Is 19,16-25]: Concilium 220 (P 1988) 43-53.

3625 *Reventlow* Henning Graf, Die Prophetie im Urteil Bernhard DUHMS: ZTK 85 (1988) 259-274.

3626 **Richards** Larry, Tomorrow today [what some OT and NT prophecies meant to their recipients and how they relate to believers today]. Wheaton IL 1986, Victor. 129 p. $5. – ᴿBS 145 (1988) 108 (R. P. *Lightner*).

3627 *Ricœur* Paul, Le sujet convoqué; à l'école des récits de vocation prophétique: RICathP 28 (1988) 83-99.

3628 *a) Ringgren* Helmer, Israelite prophecy; fact or fiction?; – *b) Roberts* J. J. M., Does God lie? Divine deceit as a theological problem in Israelite prophetic literature; – *c) Uffenheimer* Benjamin, Prophecy, ecstasy, and sympathy: → 482, VTS 40, Jerusalem congress 1986/8, 204-210 / 211-220 / 257-269.

3629 **Rofé** Alexander, The prophetical stories; the narratives about the prophets in the Hebrew Bible, their literary types and history [1982 → 63,3496], ᵀ*Levy* D. J 1988, Hebrew University. 218 p. $22. 965-223-685-3.

3630 **Sawyer** John F. A., Prophecy 1987 → 3,3387: ᴿBL (1988) 89 (A. *Auld*); JStJud 19 (1988) 96s (E. *Tigchelaar*: too little attention to almost-contemporary pseudepigrapha); NBlackf 69 (1988) 550 (D. *Sanders*); RHR 205 (1988) 92s (A. *Caquot*).

3631 *Schenker* Adrian, Anuncio de juicio y ofuscación en los profetas preexílicas [< RB 93 (1986) 563-580], ᵀᴱ*Priego* Juan J.: SelT 27 (1988) 335-343.

3632 *Seybold* Klaus, Die symbolischen Handlungen der alttestamentlichen Propheten: → 435, ᴱ*Benedetti* G., ..., Welt der Symbole 1988, 101-111.

3633 **Sicre** José L., 'Con los pobres de la tierra'; la justicia social en los profetas de Israel 1984 → 65,3034 ... 3,3388: ᴿJTS 39 (1988) 159-162 (A.

Chester: impressive and moving; free from dogmatic presuppositions and exegesis; lets the prophets speak for themselves).

3634 **Sicre** J.L., Los profetas ... antologia 1986 ➤ 2,2610; 3,3389: ᴿBL (1988) 90 (J.R. *Porter*: 'An English translation could have a wide appeal'); EstE 63 (1988) 507 (J. *Vílchez*).

3635 *Sicre-Díaz* José L., La spiritualità dei profeti: ➤ 810, StSp 1 (1988) 334-538.

3636 *Stendebach* Franz-Josef, Theologie der Propheten: ➤ 327, Höre 1987, 245-301.

3637 **Tångberg** K.A., Die prophetische Mahnrede; form- und traditions-geschichtliche Studien zum prophetischen Umkehrruf [Hab.-Diss. Oslo]: FRLANT 143, 1987 ➤ 3,3393: ᴿBL (1988) 91 (P.R. *Ackroyd*).

3638 **Then** Reinhold, Schriftprophetie in frühjüdischer Zeit unter besonderer Berücksichtigung der Chronik: Diss. ᴰ*Schmitt*. Rg 1987s. – TR 84 (1988) 512.

3639 *Trublet* Jacques, Prophètes AT: Où est la volonté de Dieu?: VChr 313 (1987) 13-16 [314, 15-20; 315, 5-12; 316 (1988) 13-20 (Amos); 317, 16-21; 318, 2-8 (Michée, Isaïe); 319, 17-22; 320, 13-18; 321, 8-13; 322, 9-14; 323, 15-21 (Jean-Baptiste)].

3640 ᴱ**Wallis** Gerhard [atl. Arbeitsgemeinschaft DDR], Von Bileam bis Jesaja; Studien zur alttestamentlichen Prophetie von ihren Anfängen bis zum 8, Jahrhundert v.Chr. 1984 ➤ 65,314: ᴿColcT 58,2 (1988) 183s (J.W. *Roslon*).

3641 *Wallis* Gerhard, Prophet und Ämter im AT: ➤ 328, Gericht/Heil 1987, 11-34.

3642 *Ward* James M., The eclipse of the prophet in contemporary prophetic studies: UnSemQ 42,1 (1988) 97-104 [< ᴢɪᴛ].

3643 **Weippert** Helga, *al.*, Beiträge zur prophetischen Bildsprache in Israel und Assyrien: OBO 64, 1985 ➤ 1,3458 ... 3,3397*: ᴿArOr 56 (1988) 372 (O. *Klíma*); Protestantesimo 43 (1988) 211s (J.A. *Soggin*); VT 38 (1988) 127 (G.I. *Davies*).

3644 *Weippert* Manfred, Aspekte israelitischer Prophetie im Lichte ver-wandter Erscheinungen des Alten Orients: ➤ 32, ᶠDELLER K., AOAT 220 (1988) 287-319.

3645 **Westermann** Claus, Prophetische Heilsworte im AT: FRLANT 145, 1987 ➤ 3,3398: ᴿBL (1988) 96 (A. *Gelston*); Carthaginensia 4 (1988) 174 (F. *Marín*: intended as completion of his 1964 Grundformen); ExpTim 99 (1987s) 329s (R.J. *Coggins*).

3646 *Westermann* Claus, Las 'palabras de salvación' en los profetas [< ZAW 98 (1986) 1-13], ᵀᴱ*Aleu* José: SelT 27 (1988) 344-352.

3647 **Wolff** Hans W., Studien zur Prophetie [10 art. 1977-86] 1987 ➤ 3,320: ᴿRTPhil 120 (1988) 371 (T. *Römer*).

E8.2 **Proto-Isaias,** *textus, commentarii.*

3648 **Alonso Schökel** Luis, Sicre Díaz José Luis, Profetas I. Isaias, Jeremias [1980 ➤ 61,4515], ᵀ*Álvarez* Anacleto: Grande Comentário bíblico. São Paulo 1988, Paulinas. 680 p. 85-05-00699-2 [8-4 obra completa].

3649 ᴱ**Brock** S.P., Isaiah: OT in Syriac 3/1, 1987 ➤ 3,3399: ᴿÉTRel 63 (1988) 602s (A.G. *Martin*).

3650 *Brock* S.P., Text history and text division in Peshiṭta Isaiah: ➤ 480, Peshiṭta 1985/8, 49-80.

3651 **Chilton** B. D., The Isaiah Targum 1987 ➤ 3,3400: ᴿVT 38 (1988) 504s (H. G. M. *Williamson*).

3652 *Conrad* Edgar W., The royal narratives and the structure of the book of Isaiah: JStOT 41 (1988) 67-81.

3653 *Evans* Craig A., On the unity and parallel structure of Isaiah: VT 38 (1988) 129-147.

3654 **Gryson** Roger, Esaias (Lfg. 1s 1987 ➤ 3,3401) [1,22-5,7] ; 3 Lfg. [5,8-7,14]: Vetus Latina Beuron 12. FrB 1987s, Herder. P. 81-160; 161-240. je DM 81,50, sb. 72. 3-451-00441-0; 2-9 [BL 89,50].

3655 ᴱ**Guinot** Jean-Noel, THÉODORET de Cyr, Commentaire sur Isaïe: I, SChr 276, 1980 ➤ 61,4606; II. SChr 295, 1982 ➤ 63,3527 (wrongly in 2,2622); III. (44,23-66,24); SChr 315, P 1984, Cerf. 403 p. – ᴿBijdragen 49 (1988) 212 (J. *Declerck*).

3656 **Hayes** J. H., *Irvine* S. A., Isaiah the eighth-century prophet; his times and his preaching. Nv 1987, Abingdon. 416 p.

3657 **Jacob** Edmond, Ésaïe 1-12, 1987 ➤ 3,3403: ᴿBL (1988) 59 (P. R. *Ackroyd*); ÉTRel 63 (1988) 105s (D. *Lys*); MondeB 52 (1988) 59 (J. *Asurmendi*); RevSR 62 (1988) 186s (B. *Renaud*); RivB 36 (1988) 122s (A. *Bonora*); RTPhil 120 (1988) 370s (G. *Lasserre*).

3658 **Jay** Pierre, L'exégèse de JÉROME, Isaïe 1985 ➤ 1,3467 ... 3,3404: ᴿBTAM 14, (1988) 429s (P. *Hamblenne*); RÉLat 65 (1987) 387-9 (H. *Savon*); Salesianum 50 (1988) 423s (M. *Cimosa*).

3659 **Kilian** Rudolf, Jesaja 1-12: NEchter 1986 ➤ 2,2627; 3,3408: ᴿBL (1988) 60 (P. R. *Ackroyd*).

3660 *Myers* Edith, The authorship of Isaiah [... really predicted Cyrus]: HomP 89,5 (1988s) 53-57.

3661 **Oswalt** John N., The book of Isaiah, chapters 1-39: NICOT, 1986 ➤ 2,2628; 3,3410: ᴿBiblica 69 (1988) 277-280 (R. E. *Clements*: much worth pondering, but methodology arbitrary); BTrans 39 (1988) 142s (J. G. *Snaith*); CBQ 50 (1988) 120s (G. M. *Tucker*); NedTTs 42 (1988) 249s (L. A. *Snijders*); RExp 85 (1988) 131 (J. D. W. *Watts*); TLZ 113 (1988) 885-8 (E.-J. *Waschke*).

3662 *Ratzaby* Y., Additional fragments of SAʿADIAH Gaon's commentary on Isaiah: ➤ 43, ꜰELITZUR Y., II (1986) 175-186.

3663 ᴱ**Ribera Florit** Josep, El Targum de Isaias; la versión aramea del profeta Isaias: Biblioteca Midrásica 6. Valencia 1988, Inst. S. Jerónimo. 277 p. 84-86067-32-4.

3664 **Ridderbos** J., Isaiah [Korte Verklaring 1922 p. 67, despite title-page '1951'], ᵀ*Vriend* John: Bible Student's commentary, 1985 ➤ 1,3473 ... 3,3413: ᴿCBQ 50 (1988) 697s (J. *Limburg*: smooth and learned, for 60 years ago).

3665 **Roth** Wolfgang, Isaiah. Atlanta 1988, Knox. 181 p. $10 [BToday 26,375].

3666 **Sawyer** John F. A., Isaiah vol. II: Daily Study Bible 1986 ➤ 2,2685: ᴿCBQ 50 (1988) 696s (J. *Limburg*).

3667 **Sawyer** J. F. A., Izaya-sho I [Daily Study Bible Isaiah I, 1984 ➤ 65, 3066], ᵀ*Higuchi* S. Tokyo 1988, Shinkyō Shuppan-sha. 519 p. Y 3800 [BL 89,61].

3667* **Schneider** Dieter, Der Prophet Jesaja 1 Teil, Kapitel 1 bis 39: Studienbibel AT. Wu 1988, Brockhaus. 496 p. 3-417-25316-0; pa. 216-4.

3668 **Watts** John D. W., Isaiah 34-66: Word 25,1987 ➤ 3,3417: ᴿAndrUnS 26 (1988) 104s (N.-E. *Andreasen*); BibTB 18 (1988) 154 (Chris *Franke*); BL (1988) 67 (W. J. *Houston*: apotheosis or reductio ad absurdum of 'final

form' approach: Is 1-66 a single drama in twelve acts; factual errors);
CBQ 50 (1988) 127-9 (C. *Stuhlmueller*, 1); EstBíb 46 (1988) 263s (J. M.
Abrego); EvQ 60 (1988) 356-9 (R. P. *Gordon*); JTS 39 (1988) 162-4 (R. E.
Clements: 'not a scholar to take fresh insights and approaches lightly' so
dates the whole of Isaiah around 435 but embodying materials from 735
on; sometimes 'so arbitrary and idiosyncratic as to leave the reader
gasping'); RefTR 46 (1987) 26s (J. *Woodhouse*); RExp 85 (1988) 715-7
(W. *Brueggemann*: idiosyncratic but justifiably); SWJT 31,1 (1988s) 47s
(L. R. *Bush*); VT 38 (1988) 124s (J. A. *Emerton*).

3670 **Wildberger** Hans, Jesaja [BK] I (1-12) 1978 ²1980 ➤ 61,4615; II (13-27)
1978 ➤ 61,4615*b*; III (28-39) 1982 ➤ 65,3070: ᴿZkT 110 (1988) 92s (R.
Oberforcher).

E8.3 [Proto-] **Isaias 1-39**, *themata, versiculi.*

3671 *Daoust* J. [< *Asurmendi* J. MondeB 49, 1987] Isaïe dans son temps:
EsprVie 98 (1988) 183-5.

3672 *Dietrich* Walter, Jesaja: ➤ 798, EvKL 2 (1988) 813-8.

3673 **Høgenhaven** Jesper, Gott und Volk bei Jesaja; eine Untersuchung zur
biblischen Theologie [Diss. K 1988, ᴰ*Nielsen* E.]: Acta Theologica Danica
24. Leiden 1988, Brill. ix-271 p. 90-04-08863-6.

3674 **Koenig** Jean, L'herméneutique ... d'après les témoins textuels d'Isaïe:
VTSup 33, 1982 ➤ 65,3531 ... 1,3477: ᴿOLZ 83 (1988) 313-5 (G. *Mayer*).

3675 *Ollenburger* Bennie C., [also First-] Isaiah's creation theology: ➤ 567,
ExAud 3 (1987) 54-71.

3676 **Schmitt** John J., Isaiah and his interpreters 1986 ➤ 2,2644; 3,3427:
ᴿBibTB 18 (1988) 33s (Chris *Franke*: fills its stated purposes admirably);
Gregorianum 69 (1988) 552s (C. *Conroy*); LvSt 13 (1988) 179 (A.
Schoors).

3677 *Seidel* M., ❿ Internal parallels in the book of Isaiah and the book of
Jeremiah: ➤ 132, ꟳSCHIRMANN H., Jubilee 1970, 149-158.

3678 *Theunis* Guy, Isaïe, prophète des temps difficiles: Select 20s (Kinshasa
1988) 48-69 [< TKontext 10,30].

3679 **Sweeney** Marvín A., Isaiah 1-4 and the post-exilic understanding of the
Isaianic tradition [diss. 1983, ᴰ*Knierim* R.]: BZAW 171. B 1988, de
Gruyter. x-211 p. DM 98. [TDig 36,87] 3-11-01-1034-2 / US 0-89925-
403-9.

3680 *Gevaryahu* Haim, Isaiah-Hezekiah: Dor 16 (1987s) 78-85.

3681 *Lohfink* Gerhard, 'Forjarán de sus espadas azadones' [Is 2,1-5; Mi 4,1-5
< TüTQ 166 (1986) 184-207], ᵀᴱ*Giménez* Josep: SelT 27 (1988) 91-101.

3682 *Anderson* Bernhard W., 'God with us' — in judgment and in mercy; the
editorial structure of Isaiah 5-10 (11): ➤ 25, ꟳCHILDS B., Canon 1988,
230-247.

3683 *Köberle* Adolf, Das Lied vom Weinberg (Jes. 5,1-7): TBei 19 (1988)
113-6 [< ZIT 88,463].

3684 *Premnath* D. N. Latifundialization and Isaiah 5.8-10: JStOT 40 (1988)
49-60.

3685 *Geerlings* Wilhelm, Jesaja 7,9b bei AUGUSTINUS: die Geschichte eines
fruchtbaren Missverständnisses: WissWeis 50 (1987) 5-12.

3686 *Croatto* J. Severino, El 'Enmanuel' (-nm- muchas veces en el texto] de Isaías 7.14 como signo de juicio; análisis de Isaías 7,1-25: RBíbArg 30s (1988) 135-142.

3687 **Laato** Antti, Who is Immanuel? The rise and the foundering of Isaiah's messianic expectations [diss. – TR 84,426]. Åbo 1988, Akademi. 394 p. Fm 135. 951-9498-22-2. – RNorTTs 89 (1988) 280s (H. M. *Barstad*).

3688 *a) Laato* Antti, [Is 7,14] Immanuel — who is with us? Hezekiah or Messiah?; – *b) Wodecki* Bernard, Synonymous designations of Jerusalem in Isa 1-39; – *c) Nielsen* Kirsten, Reinterpretation of metaphors — tree metaphors in Isa 1-39: → 469, Wünschet 1986/8, 313-322 / 345-360 / 425-9.

3689 *Schoors* A, The Immanuel of Isaiah 7,14 ['almâ is Ahaz's wife; birth not miraculous]: OrLovPer 18 (1987) 67-77.

3690 *Kooij* Arie van der, 1QIsaᵃ col. VIII,4-11 (Isa 8,11-18); a contextual approach of its variants: → 22, Mém. CARMIGNAC J., RQum 13 (1988) 569-581.

3691 **Gosse** Bernard, Isaïe 13,1-14,23 dans la tradition littéraire du livre d'Isaïe et dans la tradition des oracles contre les nations: OBO 78. FrS/Gö 1988, Univ. / Vandenhoeck & R. 300 p. 3-7278-0559-5 / 3-525-53707-7. – RNorTTS 89 (1988) 282-4 (H. M. *Barstad*).

3692 *O'Connell* Robert H., Isaiah XIV, 4b-23; ironic reversal through concentric structure and mythic allusion: VT 38 (1988) 407-418.

3693 *Taylor* J. Glen, [Is 14,9] A first and last thing to do in mourning; KTU 1.161 and some parallels: → 29, Mem. CRAIGIE P., Ascribe 1988, 151-177.

3694 *Kooij* Arie van der, The Old Greek of Isaiah 19:16-25; translation and interpretation: → 478, ᴱCox C., 6th LXX 1986/7, 127-166.

3695 *Flint* Peter W., *a)* The Septuagint version of Isaiah 23:1-14 and the Massoretic text: BSeptCog 21 (1988) 35-54; – *b)* [Is 23,1.6.10.14] From Tarshish to Carthage; the Septuagint translation of *taršîš* in Isaiah 23: ProcGLM 8 (1988) 127-133.

3696 **Johnson** Dan G., From chaos to restoration; an integrative reading of Isaiah 24-27 [diss. 1985 → 3,3458; ᴰ*Roberts* J.]: JStOT Sup 61. Sheffield 1988, Univ. 150 p. £25. 1-85075-112-9; pa. 061-0.

3697 *a) Redditt* Paul L., Once again, the city in Isaiah 24-27 [9 candidates; concludes only 'foil to Jerusalem']; – *b) Halpern* Baruch, 'The excremental vision'; the doomed priests of doom in Isaiah 28: HebAnR 10 (1986) 317-335 / 109-121.

3698 *Sweeney* Marvin A., Textual citations in Isaiah 24-27; toward an understanding of the redactional function of chapters 24-27 in the book of Isaiah: JBL 107 (1988) 39-52.

3699 *Toorn* K. van der, Echoes of Judaean necromancy in Isaiah 28,7-22: ZAW 100 (1988) 199-216; franç. 216s.

3700 *Neri* Paolo, [Is 29,1] 'Guai ad Ariel': BbbOr 30 (1988) 38.

3701 **Steck** Odil H., Bereitete Heimkehr; Jesaja 35 als redaktionelle Brücke zwischen dem ersten und dem zweiten Jesaja: SBS 121. Stu 1987, KBW. 113 p. [RelStR 15,257, M. A. *Sweeney*).

3702 *Brueggemann* Walter, Isaiah 37:21-29; the transformative potential of a public metaphor; HorBT 10,1 (1988) 1-32.

E8.4 **Deutero-Isaias 40-52:** *commentarii, themata, versiculi.*

3703 *Blenkinsopp* J., Second Isaiah — prophet of universalism: JStOT 41 (1988) 83-103.

3704 **Bonora** Antonio, Isaia 40-66; Israele; servo di Dio, popolo liberato: LoB 1/19. Brescia 1988, Queriniana. 157 p. Lit. 15.000. 88-399-1569-9. – RRivB 36 (1988) 523-5 (**B.** *Marconcini*).

Carena Omar, Il resto di Israele 1985 ➤ a322; **Haussmann** J., Israels Rest 1987 ➤ 3039.

3705 **Harner** Philip B., Grace and law in Second Isaiah; 'I am the Lord': Ancient Near Eastern Texts and Studies 2. Lewiston NY 1988, Mellen viii-193 p. 0-88946-087-6.

3706 *Hermisson* Hans-J., Deuterojesaja-Probleme: VerkF 31,1 (1986) 53-84.

3707 **Jerger** Günter, 'Evangelium des Alten Testaments'; die Grundbotschaft des Propheten Deuterojesaja in ihrer Bedeutung für den Religions-unterricht: SBB 14, 1986 ➤ 2,2681; 3,3469: RBZ 32 (1988) 301s (F. *Schicklberger*); CBQ 50 (1988) 501s (C. *Stuhlmueller*); ZkT 110 (1988) 105s (G. *Fischer*; jetzt SIMIAN-YOFRE H. TWAT '*ebed*).

3708 **Lichosyt** Jan, ❷ Znaczenie 'dābār' u Deutero-Izajasza: diss. D*Mu-szyński* H. Wsz 1987. – RTLv 19,534.

3708* *Lichtenstein* Aaron, The Cyrus cylinder and Isaiah 40-50: Dor 16 (1987) 164-9.

3709 **Matheus** Frank, Form und Funktion der Hymnen in Jesaja 40-55: diss. D*Rendtorff* R. Heidelberg 1987. – RTLv 19,534.

3710 *Nápole* Gabriel M., 'Mi salvación por siempre será y mi justicia no caerá'; salvación en Is. 40-55: RBíbArg 30s (1988) 143-164.

Sawyer J. F. A., Isaiah vol. 2, 1986 ➤ 3666.

3711 *Watts* James W., The remnant theme; a survey of New Testament research, 1921-1987: PerspRelSt 15 (1988) 109-130 [< ZIT 88,601].

3712 *Beaucamp* E., Le IIe Isaïe (Is XL,1 - XLIX,13) — problème de l'unitè du livre: RevSR 62 (1988) 218-226.

3713 **Koenig** Jean, [Is. 40; 53; '*ebed* Y. = groupe de la synagogue exilique] Oracles et liturgies de l'exil babylonien: ÉtHPR 69. P 1988, PUF. 210 p. F 225. 2-13-041688-8 [ZAW 101,465, H.-C. *Schmitt*].

3714 *Tsumura* David T., *Tōhū* in Isaiah XLV, 19: VT 38 (1988) 361-4.

3715 *Steck* Odil H., Zur literarischen Schichtung in Jesaja 51: BibNot 44 (1988) 74-86.

3716 *Janzen* J. Gerald, Rivers in the desert of Abraham and Sarah and Zion (Isaiah 51:1-13): HebAnR 10 (1986) 139-155.

3717 *Freund* Joseph, ❹ [Is 52,11 depart, depart]: BethM 34,116 (1988s) 50-58.

3718 *Rofé* Alexander, How is the word fulfilled? Isaiah 55:6-11 within the theological debate of its time: ➤ 25, FCHILDS B., Canon 1988, 246-261.

E8.5 *Isaiae 53ss, Carmina Servi YHWH:* **Servant-Songs.**

3719 *Dion* Paul E., [Is 42,1-9] Institutional model and poetic creation; the first song of the Servant of the Lord and appointment ceremonies: ➤ 29, Mem. CRAIGIE P., Ascribe 1988, 319-339.

3720 **Ekofo** Bonyeku, 'Iesoûs païs theoû'; l'interprétation d'Ésaïe 53 par Jésus et par l'Église primitive: prot. diss. DTrocmé E., Strasbourg 1987. 305 p. – RTLv 19,537.

3721 **Goldingay** John, God's prophet, God's servant, Jer/Is 40-55 ➤ 65,3146 ... 3,3495: RHeythJ 29 (1988) 345s (R. N. *Whybray*).

3722 **Haag** Herbert, Der Gottesknecht bei Deuterojesaja: ErtFor 233, 1985
➤ 1,3537; 3,3496: ᴿJSS 33 (1988) 121s (R. N. *Whybray*); ZkT 110 (1988)
99s (M. *Hasitschka*).

3723 **Kleinknecht** K. T., Der leidende Gerechtfertigte ... und Paulus: WUNT
2/13, 1984 ➤ 1,3339 ... 3,3498: ᴿHeythJ 29 (1988) 352s (F. F. *Bruce*);
SNTU-A 13 (1988) 237-9 (R. *Oberforcher*).

3724 *Maurer* Ernstpeter, Der leidende Prophet; Meditation zu Jesaja 52,13 -
53,12: Glaube und Lernen 3,1 (Gö 1988) 16-21 [< ZIT 88,487].

3725 *Merendino* Rosario P., I canti del Servo di Dio; una rilettura del
Deuteroisaia [franç./Eng. Sidic 19 (1986) 11-15]: Humanitas 42 (Brescia
1987) 22-32.

3726 *Pezhumkattil* Abraham, The mission of the 'Ebed Yahweh and his
vicarious suffering: Jeevadhara 13 (1988) 81-93.

3727 *Razhabi* Yehuda, ⊕ The commentary of R. SAADIA Gaon on the 'my
servant' section in Isaiah: Tarbiz 57 (1987s) 327-347; Eng. I.

3729 *Wilcox* Peter, *Paton-Williams* David, The servant songs in
Deutero-Isaiah: JStOT 42 (1988) 79-102.

E8.6 [Trito-] Isaias 56-66.

3730 *a) Anderson* Bernhard W., The apocalyptic rendering of the Isaiah
tradition; – *b) Rofé* Alexander, The onset of sects in postexilic Judaism;
neglected evidence from the Septuagint, Trito-Isaiah, Ben Sira, and
Malachi: ➤ 77, ᶠKEE H., Social world 1988, 17-38 / 39-49.

3731 *Begg* Christopher T., The absence of YHWH ṣᵉbā'ôt in Isaiah 56-66:
BibNot 44 (1988) 7-14.

3732 **Koenen** Klaus, Ethik und Eschatologie im Tritojesajabuch, eine
literarische und redaktionsgeschichtliche Studie; ev. Diss. Tü 1987,
ᴰ*Hermisson* H. 305 p. – TLZ 114,154s, längeres Kompendium; RTLv
19,534.

3733 **Polan** Gregory J., In the ways of justice ... Is 56-59, 1986 ➤ 2,2709;
3,3506: ᴿCBQ 50 (1988) 512s (Elizabeth *Achtemeier*); ÉglT 18 (1987)
128-130 (M. *Girard*); Gregorianum 69 (1988) 145-7 (C. *Conroy*); NedTTs
42 (1988) 334s (N. J. *Tromp*); RB 95 (1988) 303s (R. J. *Tournay*).

3734 *Koenen* Klaus, Sexuelle Zweideutigkeiten und Euphemismen in Jes 57,8:
BibNot 44 (1988) 46-53.

3735 *Braulik* Georg, Fasten, das Gott gefällt; eine Betrachtung zu Jesaja 58,
1-12: GeistL 61 (1988) 108-112.

3736 *Dickson* Kwesi E., He is God because he cares: Is 58:1-12: IntRMiss 77
(1988) 229-237.

3737 *Koenen* Klaus, [Is 58,11; 59,10; 61,2s.6.7; 66,2.3] Textkritische Anmerkungen zu schwierigen Stellen im Tritojesajabuch: Biblica 69 (1988)
564-573.

3739 **Fischer** Irmtraud, Wo ist JHWH, unser Vater? Das Volksklagelied Jes
63,7-64,11 als Ausdruck des Ringens um eine gebrochene Beziehung: Diss.
ᴰ*Marböck* J. Graz 1988. 300 p. – RTLv 20,540.

3740 *Koenen* Klaus, Zum Text von Jes 63,18: ZAW 100 (1988) 406-9; Eng.
409 'To littleness they threshed your holy people'.

E8.7 Jeremias.

3741 **Ash** Anthony L., Jeremiah and Lamentations: Living Word Comm.
Abilene 1987, Christian Univ. 370 p. $17 [TDig 36,45].

3742 **Bak Dong Hyun,** Klagender Gott, klagende Menschen; das Klage-Phänomen im Jeremiabuch: Diss. ᴰ*Hentschke.* B 1988s. – RTLv 20,539.

3742* **Baumgartner** Walter, [not Lam but *Book* of] Jeremiah's poems of lament [Klagedichte 1917], ᵀ*Orton* D.E.: Historic Texts and Interpretations in Biblical Scholarship. Sheffield 1987, Almond. 115 p. £17.50; pa. £7. 1-85075-116-1; 5-3 [BL 89,67, G.I. *Emmerson*].

3743 **Blanchet** René, *al.,* Jeremia, Prophet in einer Zeit der Krise [1985 ➤ 1,3564], ᵀ*Kaufmann* J., *Stotzer-Klos* H.: Bibelarbeit in der Gemeinde 6. Z 1986, Benziger. 209 p.; 3 fig. DM 32 [TLZ 114,63s, D. *Mendt*].

3744 ᴱ**Bogaert** P.-M., Le livre de Jérémie 1980/1 ➤ 62,509 ... 1,3566: ᴿJQR 79 (1988s) 71s (M. *Greenberg*).

3745 **Bourguet** Daniel, Des métaphores de Jérémie: EtBN 9, 1987 ➤ 3,3512: ᴿEsprVie 98 (1988) 590s (L. *Monloubou* 'ne saisit pas bien quel en est le fruit').

3745* *Bovati* Pietro, Geremia: StSp 1 (1987) 376-381 ➤ 3,3513, ma si tratta della serie Dehoniane (qui ➤ 810) non StSpG (ᴱ*Grossi* V., Roma/Borla ➤ 810*).

3746 **Brueggemann** Walter, To pluck up. to tear down; a commentary on the Book of Jeremiah 1-25: Internat. Theol. Comm. GR 1988, Eerdmans. 222 p. $11 [TS 50,627]. 0-8028-0112-9.

3747 *Brueggemann* Walter, Jeremiah; intense criticism/thin interpretation [*Carroll* R., *McKane* W., *Holladay* W.: all 1986]: Interpretation 42 (1988) 268-280.

3748 **Carroll** R., Jeremiah 1986 ➤2,2718; 3,3516: ᴿBijdragen 49 (1988) 92 (P.C. *Beentjes*); BS 145 (1988) 115s (E.H. *Merrill*: 'perhaps definitive' but very unsatisfactory); RelStR 14 (1988) 331-4 (T.W. *Overholt*); ScotJT 41 (1988) 415-7 (G. *Auld*); TrinJ 8 (1987) 242-8 (A.R. *Diamond*: redaction criticism 'quixotic'); VT 38 (1988) 502s (H.G.M. *Williamson*).

3749 **Clements** R.E., Jeremiah: Interpretation Comm. Atlanta 1988, Knox. xi-276 p. $18 [JBL 108,566].

3750 **Cruells** [➤ 3,3517!] i **Viñas** Antoni, El *dābār* en Jeremías (Jer 1-45) 1986 ➤ 2,2718: ᴿRCatalT 12 (1987) 451-4 (R. *Sivatte*).

3751 **Davidson** Robert, Jeremiah II and Lamentations: Daily Study Bible 1985 ➤ 2,2721*b*: ᴿCBQ 50 (1988) 675s (F.C. *Holmgren*).

3752 *Davis* L.D., Jeremiah; prophet doomed to strife: BToday 26 (1988) 104-112.

3753 ᵀᴱ**Hayward** Robert, The Targum of Jeremiah: Aramaic Bible 12, 1987 ➤ 3,3522: ᴿJJS 39 (1988) 299 (S. *Brock*).

3754 **Herrmann** Siegfried, Jeremia, 1. Lfg: BK AT. Neuk 1986. 80 p. – ᴿRHPR 68 (1988) 241-3 (P. de *Robert,* aussi sur CARROLL, MCKANE, HOLLADAY, tous 1986).

3755 **Holladay** W.J., Jeremiah I [ch. 1-25]: Hermeneia 1986 ➤ 2,3725; 3,3524: ᴿBiblica 69 (1988) 430-4 (P. *Bovati,* Eng.); BibTB 18 (1988) 35 (L. *Boadt*: the Hermeneia commentaries are not for beginners); CBQ 50 (1988) 682-4 (J.R. *Lundbom*: erudite but the poetry is wooden and some schemes too grandiose); CurrTM 15 (1988) 284-6 (R.W. *Klein,* also on CARROLL and MCKANE; prefers THIEL); ETL 64 (1988) 197s (J. *Lust*); Gregorianum 69 (1988) 351-4 (C. *Conroy*); JBL 107 (1988) 739-742 (T. *Polk*); RelStR 14 (1988) 330s.333s (T.W. *Overholt*).

3756 *Ibañez Arana* Andrés, Jeremías y 'los profetas': ScriptV 35 (1988) 5-56. 233-319.

3757 *Kaufman* Stephen A., Rhetoric, redaction, and message in Jeremiah: ➤ 3,355, Judaic perspectives 1987, 63-74.

3758 **Kidner** Derek, The message of Jeremiah: The Bible Speaks Today. Nottingham/DG 1987, Inter-Varsity. 176 p. £4.50. 0-85110-779-6 / 0-8308-1225-3 [BL 89,56, R. *Hammer*].

3759 **Kilpp** Nelson, Niederreissen und Aufbauen; das Verhältnis von Heils-
verheissung und Unheilverkündigung bei Jeremia, Diss. Marburg 1987,
D*Schmidt-Bonn* W. – RTLv 19,534.

3760 **Liwak** Rüdiger, Der Prophet und die Geschichte; eine literarhistorische
Untersuchung zum Jeremiabuch [Hab. Bochum 1984]: BWANT 121, 1987
➤ 3,3828: RBL (1988) 82 (W. *McKane*: 'history invoked to concretize
theological convictions' dubious); Protestantesimo 43 (1988) 211 (J. A.
Soggin: rilegato 'all'americana': si sfascia rapidamente e non può più
essere rilegato); TR 84 (1988) 450-4 (Helga *Weippert*); TüTQ 168 (1988)
337s (W. *Gross*).

3761 **McKane** W., ICC Jeremiah I (1-25) 1986 ➤ 2,2728; 3,3530: RAnglTR
70 (1988) 95s (D. F. *Morgan*); BibTB 18 (1988) 87 (J. I. *Hunt*); CBQ 50
(1988) 692s (J. M. *Berridge*: describes as 'a rolling *corpus*' against THIEL
W., WEIPPERT H.); JBL 107 (1988) 124s (T. W. *Overholt*: completed
1981); JRAS (1988) 165s (E. *Ullendorff*); RelStR 14 (1988) 332-4 (T. W.
Overholt); ScotJT 41 (1988) 285-7 (J. *Eaton*); TorJT 4 (1988) 272-5
(Marion *Taylor*: diverges on fundamentals from HOLLADAY and
CARROLL); TTod 45 (1988s) 510s (J. J. M. *Roberts,* also on HOLLADAY).

3762 *McKane* William, Jeremia, T*Hoffmann* H.: ➤ 798, EvKL 2 (1988) 806-9.

3763 *Margalith* Othniel, Religious life in Jerusalem on the eve of the fall of
the First Temple: ➤ 42*, EHRMAN A.Mem., Fucus 1988, 335-351.

3764 **Martens** Elmer A., Jeremiah: Believers Church Bible Comm., 1986
➤ 2,2729; 3,3531: RCBQ 50 (1988) 693-5 (J. E. *Huesman*: a masterful
pedagogue, with simplified goals); GraceTJ 9 (1988) 290s (R. *Patterson*:
clear, simple).

3765 **Oosterhoff** B. J., Jeremia en het Woord van God: Apeldoornse Studies
24. Kampen 1987, Kok. 38 p. ƒ 11,90. 90-242-4248-7 [NedTTs 42,335].

3766 **Polk** Timothy, The prophetic persona 1984 ➤ 65,3185 ... 3,3534:
RHeythJ 29 (1988) 144s (R. *Carroll*); TLZ 113 (1988) 262s (S. *Herrmann*).

3768 **Soderlund** Sven, The Greek text of Jeremiah; a revised hypothesis:
JStOT Sup 47, 1985 ➤ 2,2741; 3,3539: RCBQ 50 (1988) 124-7 (J. W.
Olley, also on STULMAN L. 1985); JBL 107 (1988) 126s (L. *Greenspoon*).

3769 **Stulman** L., The other text of Jeremiah 1985 ➤ 2,2743; 3,3540:
RSalesianum 50 (1988) 436 (M. *Cimosa*: molto utile).

3770 **Stulman** Louis, The prose sermons of the Book of Jeremiah; a
redescription of the correspondences with deuteronomistic literature ...
[diss. Drew]: SBL diss. 83, 1986 ➤ 2,2742; 3,3541: RCBQ 50 (1988) 699s
(G. H. *Matties*); JBL 107 (1988) 520s (C. R. *Seitz*).

3771 *Thiel* Winfried, Jeremia: ➤ 329, Gericht/Heil 1987, 35-57.

3772 **Unterman** Jeremiah, From repentance to redemption; Jeremiah's thought
in transition: JStOT sup. 54, 1988 ➤ 3,3543: RBL (1988) 93 (R. P.
Carroll); ETL 64 (1988) 200s (J. *Lust*); ExpTim 99 (1987s) 341s (R.
Carroll).

3773 **Variyamattom** Mathew, The language of suffering in the Book of
Jeremiah; a semantico-theological study: diss. Pont. Univ. Gregoriana,
D*Conroy* C., No 3494. R 1988. ix-470 p. – RTLv 20,542.

3774 **Vieweger** Dieter, Die Spezifik der Berufungsberichte Jeremias und
Ezekiels im Umfeld ähnlicher Einheiten des ATs: Diss. Leipzig 1985.
177 p. – TLZ 112 (1987) 860-2. [Fra 1986 ➤ 2,2748*b*]. – RBL (1988) 94
(R. P. *Carroll*).

3775 *Vieweger* Dieter, Die Arbeit des jeremianischen Schulkreises am
Jeremiabuch und deren Rezeption in der literarischen Überlieferung der
Prophetenschrift Ezechiels: BZ 32 (1988) 15-34.

3776 *Smothers* Thomas G., A lawsuit against the nations; reflections on the Oracles against the Nations in Jeremiah: RExp 85 (1988) 545-554.

3777 *Nasuti* Harry P., A prophet to the nations; diachronic and synchronic readings of Jeremiah 1: HebAnR 10 (1986) 249-266.

3778 *a) Ngoy* M. K. [Jér 1,4-19]...; – *b) Bulkeley* B. & T., [Jer 31,15-22, 'la consécration des femmes,' lecture féministe; – *c) Deer* D. S. [unité et diversité dans le NT]: Revue Zaïroise de Théologie Protestante 1 (1986) ... [RHPR 68 (1988) 517 J.-F. *Collange*].

3779 *Jenni* Ernst, Jer 3,17 'nach Jerusalem'; ein Aramaismus: ZAHeb 1,1 (1988) 107-111.

3780 *Álvarez Barredo* Miguel, [Jer 7,1-8,3] Discurso de Jeremías sobre el Templo; crítica de la praxis religiosa: Carthaginensia 4 (1988) 3-20.

3781 *Gregor* Barbara, 'Gold aus Ofir'?: Jer 10,9 und eine minäische Inschrift: BibNot 41 (1988) 19-22 ['Gregor' S. 3 und 19; cf. 'Greger B.', 45 (1988) S. 3 und 28].

3782 *Reimer* David J., A problem in the Hebrew text of Jeremiah X,13; LI,16: VT 38 (1988) 348-354.

3783 **Diamond** A. R., [Jer 11 ...] The Confessions of Jeremiah in context ... 1987 ➤ 3,3521: ᴿETL 64 (1988) 199s (J. *Lust*).

3784 **O'Connor** Kathleen M., The confessions of Jeremiah; their interpretation and role in chapters 1-25: diss. [Princeton] SBL 94. Atlanta 1988, Scholars. xv-183 p. $15; pa. $11 [TDig 36,73].

3785 **Mottu** Henry, [Jér 11-20] Les 'Confessions' de Jérémie; une protestation contre la souffrance 1985 ➤ 1,3603; 3,3553: ᴿEstBíb 46 (1988) 264-6 (J. M. *Abrego*).

3786 *Seybold* Klaus, [Jer 15,11] Der Schutzpanzer des Propheten; Re-staurationsarbeiten an Jer 15,11-12: BZ 32 (1988) 265-273.

3787 *Shear-Yashuv* Aharon, Exegese von Jeremia 17,5-11 [1964]: ➤ 262, Religion 1987, 24-36.

3788 *Parker* Simon B., [Jer 20,15] The birth announcement: ➤ 29, Mem. CRAIGIE P., Ascribe 1988, 133-149.

3789 **Franzkowiak** Johannes, Der Königszyklus Jer 21,1-23,8; das vor-deuteronomische Traditionsgut und seine redaktionelle Bearbeitung: Diss. ᴰ*Schreiner* J. Wü 1987s. – TR 84 (1988) 513 ['Jes 21 ...'].

3790 *Wiebe* John M., The form of the 'announcement of a royal savior' and the interpretation of Jeremiah 23:5-6: StudiaBT 15 (1987) 3-22.

3791 *Althann* Robert, *bĕrē'šît* in Jer 26:1; 27:1; 28:1; 49:34: JNWS 14 (1988) 1-7.

3792 *Schmitt* H.-C., Exil als Heimat und Ort des neuen Exodus; zur Bewältigung der Exilserfahrung Israels in der alttestamentlichen Prophetie [Jer 29,5-7; 1 Reg 8,46-50; 2 Reg 25,27-30]: ➤ 501, Vertreibung 1986/7, 110-128.

3793 *Morla* Victor, Ironía de Jr 29,22: EstBib 46 (1988) 249s.

3794 **Burke** Donald E., Hope for your future; the composition and coherence of Jeremiah 30-33: diss. St. Michael, ᴰ*Peckham* B. Toronto 1988. – RTLv 20,539.

3795 **Bozak** Barbara A., Life 'anew'; a literary-theological study of Jer 30-31: diss. Pont. Univ. Gregoriana, ᴰ*Conroy* C. R 1988. – RTLv 20,539.

3796 *Biddle* Mark, The literary frame surrounding Jeremiah 30,1 — 33,26: ZAW 100 (1988) 409-413.

3797 *Wiebe* John M., The Jeremian core of the Book of Consolation and the redaction of the poetic oracles in Jeremiah 30-31 [generally admitted to be the earliest layer of the Book of Consolation]: StudiaBT 15 (1987) 137-161.

3798 *Rogers* John B.ᴶ, Jeremiah 31: 7-14 [God's compassion]: Interpretation 42 (1988) 281-5.

3799 *a) Mendecki* Norbert, Jer 31,7-9 — Berührungen mit der Botschaft Deuterojesajas?: – *b) Carroll* Robert P., Dismantling the Book of Jeremiah and deconstructing the prophet: ➤ 469, Wünschet 1986/8, 323-336.

3800 *Focant* Camille, *Wénin* André, [Jer 31] L'Alliance ancienne et nouvelle: NRT 110 (1988) 850-866.

3801 **Levin** Christoph, Die Verheissung des neuen Bundes...: FRLANT 137, 1985 ➤ 1,3616 ... 3,3566: ᴿSNTU-A 13 (1988) 210-2 (R. *Oberforcher*).

3802 *a) Hals* Ronald M., Some aspects of the exegesis of Jeremiah 31; 31-34; – *b) Sarason* Richard S., The interpretation of Jeremiah 31: 31-34 in Judaism: ➤ 635, When Jews 1986/8, 87-97 / 99-123.

3803 *a) McKane* William, [Jer 35] Jeremiah and the Rechabites; – *b) Stamm* Johann J., Der Name Jeremia: ➤ 153, ZAW 100 Supp. (1988) 106-123 / 100-106.

3804 **Abrego** José M., Jeremías y el final del reino ... Jer 36-45: Jerón AT 3, 1983 ➤ 64,3599 ... 2,2763: ᴿRTLv 19 (1988) 216 (J. *Vermeylen*).

3805 *Schulte* Hannelis, [Jer 36; 38,7s] Baruch und Ebedmelech — persönliche Heilsorakel im Jeremiabuche? [Antrittsvorlesung Heidelberg 1982]: BZ 32 (1988) 257-265.

3806 *Dicou* A., Geen wijsheid meer in Edom; Jeremia 49,7 en Obadja 7-8: AmstCah 9 (1988) 90-96 [TR 85,425].

E8.8 **Lamentationes,** *Threni;* **Baruch.**

3807 **Bishop** Ronald E., An investigation of the Jeremianic authorship of Lamentations: diss. Baptist Theol. Sem., ᴰ*Bailey* D., New Orleans 1988. 171 p. 88-20023. – DissA 49 (1988s) 2257-A.

3808 **Brandscheidt** Renate, Das Buch der Klagelieder: Geistliche Schriftlesung AT 10. Dü 1988, Patmos. 168 p. DM 29,80; sb. 26. 3-491-77166-8 [BL 89,51].

3809 **Cohen** Mark E., The canonical lamentations of ancient Mesopotamia. Potomac MD 1988, Capital Decisions. I. 417 p.; II. p. 419-798 + 799-843 facsimiles. 0-9620013-0-9; 1-7.

3810 **Gous** Ignatius G. P., Die herkoms van Klaagliedere: diss. ᴰ*Loader* J. Pretoria 1988. 229 p. – RTLv 20,51; OTEssays 2/2,76 (Eng. title).

3811 **Marcus** David, Non-recurring doublets in the Book of Lamentations: HebAnR 10 (1986) 177-195.

3812 **Maul** Stefan M., 'Herzberuhigungsklagen'; die sumerisch-akkadischen Eršahunga-Gebete. Wsb 1988, Harrassowitz. 3-447-02833-5 [OIAc D88].

3813 ᴱ**Paulus** P., Pascasii RADBERTI Expositio in Lamentationes Hieremiae, libri quinque: CCMed 85. Turnhout 1988, Brepols. xx-375 p.; color. front. Fb 4150 [NRT 111, 967s, V. *Roisel*].

3814 *Cavalcanti* Elena, Osservazioni sull'uso patristico di Baruch 3, 36-38 [... (Dio ha fatto dono della sapienza a Giacobbe) 'Poi è stato visto sulla terra e si è aggirato fra gli uomini']: ➤ 56, Mém. GRIBOMONT J. 1988, 145-165.

3815 **Murphy** Frederick J., The structure and meaning of Second Baruch: SBL diss. 78, 1985 ➤ 1,3629 ... 3,3583: ᴿJBL 107 (1988) 149s (G. B. *Sayler*).

E8.9   **Ezechiel:** *textus, commentarii; themata, versiculi.*

3816 **Bodi** Daniel, Terminological and thematic comparisons between the Book of Ezekiel and Assyro-Babylonian literature with special reference to the Poem of Erra: diss. Union Theol. Sem. NY 1987. 420 p. 88-22281. – DissA 49 (1988s) 3019-A; RelStR 15,191.

3817 **Brownlee** William H., Ezekiel 1-12, ᴱ*Allen* L.: Word 28, 1986 ➤ 2,2777; 3,3587: ᴿBS 145 (1988) 232s (E. H. *Merrill*: manipulations); CBQ 50 (1988) 108-110 (Hemchand *Gossai*); ÉglT 18 (1987) 357s (W. *Vogels*); GraceTJ 9 (1988) 289s (R. *Patterson*); RefTR 46 (1987) 84s (J. *Woodhouse*); VT 38 (1988) 496s (J. A. *Emerton*).

3818 **Brun** Miguel, Une théologie de l'exil: prot. diss. ᴰ*Mahl* R. Strasbourg 1987. 694 p. – RTLv 19,560.

3819 *a) Cothenet* E., Influence d'Ézéchiel sur la spiritualité de Qumrân; – *b) García Martínez* F., L'interprétation de la Torah d'Ézéchiel dans les mss. de Qumran: ➤ 22, Mém. CARMIGNAC J., RQum 13 (1988) 431-9 / 441-452.

3820 *Dassmann* Ernst, Hesekiel: ➤ 807, RAC 14,111s (1988) 1132-1191.

3821 **Davis** Ellen, Swallowing the scroll; textuality and the dynamics of discourse in Ezechiel's prophecy: diss. Yale. NHv 1987, 241 p. – RTLv 20,539.

3822 **Dijkstra** M., Ezechiël I: Tekst en toelichting. Kampen 1986, Kok. *f* 37,50. – ᴿGerefTTs 88 (1988) 50s (A.J.O. van der *Wal*); Streven 55 (1987s) 663s (P. *Beentjes*).

3823 **Durlesser** James A., The rhetoric of allegory in the Book of Ezekiel: diss. ᴰ*Gowan* D. Pittsburgh 1988. 420 p. 88-16993. – DissA 49 (1988s) 1829s-A.

3824 **Fuchs** Hans F., Ezechiel [I, 1986 ➤ 3,3589] II 25-48: NEchter 22. Wü 1988, Echter. p. 135-275. DM 28; sb. 24. 3-429-01137-X [vol. I -0873-5]. [BL 89,53s, R. E. *Clements*].

3825 **Halperin** David J., The faces of the chariot; early Jewish responses to Ezekiel's vision: TStAntJud 16. Tü 1988, Mohr. xx-610 p. DM 178 [TDig 35,363: hekhalot merkabah midrash]. 3-16-145115-5.

3826 **Greenberg** Moshe, Ezekiel 1-20: AnchorB 22, 1983 ➤ 64,3618 ... 2,2781; ᴿJNES 47 (1988) 288s (D. *Pardee*: brilliant).

3827 *Knibb* Michael A., Hebrew and Syriac elements in the Ethiopic version of Ezekiel?: JSS 33 (1988) 11-35.

3828 **Kollmitz** Reinhold, Das Land; eine Studie am Ezechielbuch: Diss. ᴰ*Rendtorff* R. Heidelberg 1987. – RTLv 19,534.

3829 ᴱLevey S. H., The Targum of Ezekiel: Aramaic Bible 13, 1987 ➤ 3,3596: ᴿBL (1988) 48 (P. *Wernberg-Møller*).

3830 *Lurja* Ben-Zion, ✡ In the Babylonian exile: BethM 34,116 (1988s) 4-23.

3831 ᴱ**Lust** J., Ezekiel and his book 1985/6 ➤ 2,384; 3,3597: ᴿBijdragen 49 (1988) 92s (P. C. *Beentjes*); ETL 64 (1988) 461-3 (A. *Schoors*); ÉTRel 63 (1988) 107s (D. *Lys*); TR 84 (1988) 454-8 (R. *Mosis*).

3832 **Maarsingh** B., Ezechiël [I. 1985 → 1,3646] diel II: PredikOT. Nijkerk 1988, Callenbach. 303 p. *f* 82.50 [JBL 108,380]. – ᴿNedTTs 42 (1988) 333s (M. *Dijkstra,* 1).

3833 **McGregor** Leslie J., The Greek text of Ezekiel; an examination of its homogeneity: SBL SeptCog 18, 1985 → 1,3647 ... 3,3599: ᴿJBL 107 (1988) 126s (L. *Greenspoon*).

3834 **Monari** Luciano, Ezechiele, un sacerdote-profeta: LoB 1.21. Brescia 1988, Queriniana. 143 p. Lit. 13.000. 88-399-1571-0 [Asprenas 36,108, A. *Rolla*].

3835 ᴱ**Morel** Charles, Gʀᴇ́ɢᴏɪʀᴇ, Homélies sur Ézéchiel I: SChr 327 → 2,2789*a*; 3,3601: ᴿRÉLat 66 (1988) 282-5 (M. *Banniard*); RHE 83 (1988) 217 (P.-I. *Fransen*).

3836 **Mulder** M.J., Ezekiel: OTSyriac 3/3, 1985 → 1,3649; 3,3602: ᴿBO 45 (1988) (J.W. *Wevers*); OrLovPer 19 (1988) 243 (L. *Van Rompay*).

3837 *Mulder* M.J., Some remarks on the Peshiṭta translation of the Book of Ezekiel: → 480, Peshiṭta 1985/8, 169-182.

3838 *Nobile* Marco, *a)* Apporto del libro di Ezechiele alla conoscenza dell'Israele veterotestamentario: Antonianum 63 (1988) 3-25; – *b)* Influssi iranici nel libro di Ezechiele?: Antonianum 63 (1988) 449-457; Eng. 449.

3839 *Reindl* Joseph †, Zwischen Gericht und Heil; zum Verständnis der Prophetie Ezechiels: → 328, Gericht/Heil 1987, 58 ...

3840 **Rooker** Mark F., Biblical Hebrew in transition; the language of the Book of Ezekiel: diss. Brandeis. Boston 1988, 286 p. 88-19773. – DissA 49 (1988s) 1789-A.

3841 **Smith** Jonathan Z., To take place; toward a theory in ritual [... aborigines; Ezekiel] → 3,f799; Ch 1987, Univ. xvii-183 p. $27.50. – ᴿRRelRes 30 (1988s) 207s (R.A. *Littlewood*).

3842 *Stol* M., Nieuw licht op de babylonische ballingschap: PhoenEOL 34,2 (1988) 36-38.

3843 *Strugnell* John, *Dimant* Devorah, 4Q Second Ezekiel: → 22, Mém. Cᴀʀᴍɪɢɴᴀᴄ J., RQum 13 (1988) 45-58; pl. II.

3844 **Tidiman** Brian, Le livre d'Ézéchiel I (1985) II 1987 → 3,8604; 2-904407-03-0; 5-7. ᴿÉTRel 63 (1988) 108 (J. *Pons*); NRT 110 (1988) 108 (J.-L. *Ska*).

_____

3845 *Block* Daniel I., Text and emotion; a study in the 'corruptions' in Ezekiel's inaugural vision (Ezekiel 1:4-28): CBQ 50 (1988) 418-442.

3846 *Pacheco* José A., [Ezeq 3,1-3; Apc 10,8-11] La ingestión del libro: RBíbArg 30s (1988) 165-9.

3847 *Miccoli* G., The exegesis of Ezekiel 3:18 in Fʀᴀɴᴄɪs of Assisi: CrNSt 9 (Bo 1988) 23-56.

3848 *Uehlinger* C., 'Zeichne eine Stadt ... und belagere sie!'; Bild und Word in einer Zeichenhandlung Ezechiels gegen Jerusalem (Ez 4f.): → 3,e48, ꟳKᴇᴇʟ-Lᴇᴜ 100. Gb. 1987, 111-200.

3849 *Malul* Meir, [Ezek 16,1-7...] ❺ Foundlings and adoption in the Bible and Mesopotamian sources: Tarbiz 57 (1987s) 461-482; Eng. I.

3850 *Heider* George C., A further turn on Ezekiel's baroque twist in Ezek 20:25-26: JBL 107 (1988) 721-8.

3851 *Gosse* Bernard, Ézéchiel 28,11-19 et les détournements de malédictions: BibNot 44 (1988) 30-38.

3852 *Koch* Robert, Il dono messianico del cuore nuovo (Ez. 36,25-27): StMoralia 26 (1988) 3-14; franç. 13.

3853 *Matheny* James F., Is there a Russian connection? An exposition of Ezekiel 37-39. Enid OK 1987, Jay. 77 p. [GraceTJ 9,311]. $4. 0-939422-01-8.

3854 *a) Lust* Johan, Exegesis and theology in the Septuagint of Ezekiel; the longer 'pluses' and Ezek. 43:1-9; – *b) Marquis* Galen, Consistency of lexical equivalents as a criterion for the evaluation of translation technique as exemplified in the LXX of Ezekiel: ➤ 478, ᴱ*Cox* C., 6th LXX 1986/7, 201-232 / 405-424.

3855 *Fishbane* Michael, Through the looking glass; reflections on Ezek 43:3, Num 12:8 and 1 Cor 13:8: HebAnR 10 (1986) 63-78.

3856 *Brzegowy* Tadeusz, ❷ [Ez 43,2...] De theophania eschatologica in Sion: RuBi 41 (1988) 299-306.

3857 *Duke* Rodney K., Punishment or restoration? Another look at the Levites of Ezekiel 44.6-16: JStOT 40 (1988) 61-81.

E9.1   Apocalyptica VT.

3858 **Alexander** Paul J. † 1977, ᴱ*Abrahamse* Dorothy F., The Byzantine apocalyptic tradition 1985 ➤ 1,3666*; 3,3620: ᴿHeythJ 29 (1988) 362 (J. A. *Munitiz*); RÉByz 45 (1987) 241s (Marie-Hélène *Congourdeau*).

3859 **Bäumlin** Klaus, Der Himmel und die Erde werden vergehen; Beobachtungen zum Thema Apokalyptik: Reformatio 37 (1988) 119-131 > 'Heaven and earth will pass away'; thoughts on apocalyptic, TDig 36,141-5, ᵀᴱ*Asen* B.

3860 **Collins** John J., The apocalyptic imagination 1984 ➤ 65,3262 ... 3,3621: ᴿJEcuSt 25 (1988) 108s (L. *Dean*: not much on Christianity-Judaism).

3861 **Crown** Ronald W., The nonliteral use of eschatological language in Jewish Apocalyptic and the New Testament: diss. ᴰ*Sanders* E. Oxford 1987. – RTLv 19,536s.

3862 **Delcor** Mathias, Studi sull'apocalittica, [1986] ᵀ*Zani* A., 1987 ➤ 3,3622: ᴿCC 139 (1988,3) 306s (G. L. *Prato*); Henoch 10 (1988) 110-2 (P. *Sacchi*); Protestantesimo 43 (1988) 213s (D. *Bouchard*); StPatav 35 (1988) 196s (M. *Milani*).

3863 *Gignoux* P., L'apocalyptique iranienne est-elle vraiment la source d'autres apocalypses?: AcAntH 31 (1985-8) 67-78.

3864 *Halperin* David J., Ascension or invasion; implications of the heavenly journey in ancient Judaism: Religion 18,1 (1988) 47-68 [< ZIT].

3865 ᴱ**Hellholm** David, Apocalypticism in the Mediterranean world and the Near East 1979/83 ➤ 64,274 ... 3,3624: ᴿGregorianum 69 (1988) 174-7 (U. *Vanni*); OLZ 83 (1988) 526-8 (H. F. *Weiss*).

3866 **Kappler** Claude, Apocalypses et voyages dans l'au-delà 1987 ➤ 3,3625: ᴿArTGran 51 (1988) 326s (A. S. *Muñoz*); JStJud 19 (1988) 129-134 (I. P. *Culianu*); SMSR 54 (1988) 394-8 (Liliana *Rosso Ubigli*).

3867 **Körtner** U. H. J., Weltangst und Weltende; eine theologische Interpretation der Apokalyptik [Hab.-Diss. ev. Kirchliche Hochschule Bethel 1987]. Gö 1988, Vandenhoeck & R. 428 p. DM 58. 3-525-56178-4 [NTAbs 32,384]. – ᴿHerdKorr 42 (1988) 542 (W. S.).

3868 *Müller* K., Apokalyptik: ➤ 804, NBL Lfg 1 (1988) 124-132.

3869 *Pöhlmann* Wolfgang, Apokalyptische Geschichtsdeutung und geistiger Widerstand: KerDo 34 (1988) 60-75; Eng. 75.

3870 *Rowland* Christopher, Apocalyptic literature [Daniel and pseudepigrapha cited in NT]: ➤ 97, ᶠLINDARS B. 1988, 170-189.
3871 *Rubinkiewicz* Ryszard, ❷ De apocalyptica ab initio aerae christianae: ➤ 475, RuBi 41 (1988) 51-59.
3872 *Schlageter* Johannes, Apokalyptisches Denken bei Petrus Johannes OLIVI: WissWeis 50 (1987) 13-27 [... und FIORE, 150-163].

E9.2 **Daniel:** *textus, commentarii; themata, versiculi.*

3873 *Asen* Ben, Reflections on Daniel and apocalyptic [coping with parishioners' enthusiasm for FALWELL-style interpretations about Russia]: CurrTM 15 (1988) 263-6.
3874 *Bauer* Dieter, Das Buch Daniel: ➤ 327, Höre ... Theologie des ATes 1987, 303-315.
3875 **Beale** G. K., Use of Daniel in ... Rev [ᴰ1980] 1984 ➤ 65,3276 ... 3,3633: ᴿJTS 39 (1988) 207-9 (P. M. *Casey*: erudition vitiated by slyly-concealed fundamentalism).
3876 **Bodenmann** Reinhard, Naissance d'une exégèse; Daniel...: BeiGBEx 28, 1986 ➤ 2,2823; 3,3636: ᴿCiuD 201 (1988) 487s (J. *Gutierrez*); RSPT 72 (1988) 613s (G.-M. de *Durand*).
3877 **Davies** Philip R., Daniel: OT Guides, 1985 ➤ 1,3692 ... 3,3639: ᴿCBQ 50 (1988) 294s (J. G. *Gammie*).
3878 *Fang* Mark, ❸ Characteristics of the Book of Daniel: ColcFuJen 77 (1988) 385-398.
3879 **Faulstich** E. W., History, harmony, and Daniel; a new computerized evaluation. Spencer IA 1988, Chronology Books. vi-181 p. [JBL 108, 567].
3880 **Goldingay** John E., Daniel: Word Comm. 30. Dallas 1988, Word. liii-351 p. $25 [JBL 108,754].
3881 *Homerski* Józef, ❷ De versione graeca Libri Danielis in testimoniis Patrum: ➤ 73, ᶠKania W. = VoxPa 12s (1987s) 175-187; lat. 188.
3882 **Koch** K., Daniel (1,1-21) BK 1986 ➤ 2,2831: ᴿBL (1988) 60 (P. R. *Davies*).
3883 **Koch** Klaus, Deuterokanonische Zusätze zum Danielbuch I-II: AOAT 38, 1987 ➤ 3,3645: ᴿZAW 100 (1988) 459 (H.-C. *Schmitt*).
3884 **LaCocque** André, Daniel in his times [1983 ➤ 64,3668], ᵀ*Cochrane* Lydia: Studies on Personalities of the OT. Columbia 1988, Univ. S. Carolina. xvii-240 p. $20 [RelStR 15,70, W. Lee *Humphreys*].
3885 *Mason* Rex A., The treatment of earlier biblical themes in the book of Daniel: PerspRelSt 15,4 (1988) 81-100.
3886 *Scarcia Amoretti* Biancamaria, A proposito della mediazone giudaica nell'Islam; il caso di Daniele: ➤ 109, ᶠMONNERET U. = RSO 60 (1986/8) 205-211.

3887 **Fewell** Danna N., Circle of sovereignty; a story of stories in Daniel 1-6 [= diss. Sages and sovereigns, ᴰ*Newsom* Carol A., 1987 ➤ 3,3653]: JStOT Sup 72, B&Lit 20. Sheffield 1988, Almond. 207 p. £25. 1-85075-158-7.
3888 *Towner* W. Sibley, Daniel 1 in the context of the canon: ➤ 25, ᶠCHILDS B., Canon 1988, 285-298.
3889 **Cook** E. M., [Dan 2,4-7,28] Word order in the Aramaic of Daniel: AfrAsLing 9/3, 1986 ➤ 3, 3656: ᴿBL (1988) 147 (A. *Hayman*).

3890 *Margain* Jean, Le livre de Daniel; commentaire philologique du texte araméen: LOrA 1 (Lv 1988) 73-93.

3891 *Wesselius* J.W., Language and style in biblical Aramaic; observations on the unity of Daniel II-VI: VT 38 (1988) 194-209.

3892 **Mastin** B.A., The reading of 1QDan[a] at Daniel II,4: VT 38 (1988) 341-6.

3893 *Giannarelli* Elena, Daniele [2,34s.45], la montagna e Maria; contributo alla storia di un simbolo cristiano: ➤ 492, AnStoEseg 5 (1988) 253-9.

3894 **Albertz** R., Der Gott des Daniel [4-6 LXX; *Bludau* A. 1897 (sic)] sowie die Komposition und Theologie des aramäischen Danielbuches: SBS 131. Stu 1988, KBW.   239 p.   DM 42 [ZAW 101,307, H.-C. *Schmitt*]. 3-460-04311-3.

3895 *Grabbe* Lester L., Another look at the Gestalt of 'Darius the Mede' [still likeliest a composite character created by the author of Daniel; despite *Whitcomb* J. 1959; *Wiseman* D. (= Cyrus 'not impossible') 1965; and the carefully-studied *Shea* W. 1971; 1982]: CBQ 50 (1988) 198-213.

3896 *Flusser* David, a) The four empires in the Fourth Sibyl and in the Book of Daniel [< IsrOrSt 2 (1972) 148-187]; – b) The fourth empire — an Indian rhinoceros? [ineditum]: ➤ 190, JudOrChr 1988, 317-344 / 345-354.

3897 *Shea* William H., Bel(te)shazzar meets Belshazzar: AndrUnS [20 (1982) 133-149] 26 (1988) 67-81, reply to *Grabbe* L., 59-66, The Belshazzar of Daniel and the Belshazzar of history.

3898 **Soesilo** Daud H., Balancing Belshazzar's scales; toward achieving parity between faithfulness and readability in translating Daniel 5: diss. Union Theol. Sem.   Richmond 1988, 138 p.   88-20006. – DissA 49 (1988s) 2261-A.

3899 *Wiig* Arne, [Dan 5,25] Mene, mene, tekel u-farsin: SvEx 53 (1988) 26-35.

3900 **Jeansonne [Pace]** Sharon J., The Old Greek translation of Daniel 7-12 [diss. [D]*Ulrich* E.]: CBQ Mg 19. Wsh 1988, CBQ. viii-147 p. $5 0-915170-18-3. – [R]SBFLA 38 (1988) 483-5 (G. *Bissoli*).

3901 *Sheriffs* Deryck C.T., [Dan 7-11; Is 40-55] 'A tale of two cities' — nationalism in Zion and Babylon [Tyndale OT lecture 1986]: TyndaleB 39 (1988) 19-57.

3902 *Worschech* Udo, Der assyrisch-babylonische Löwenmensch und der 'menschliche' Löwe aus Daniel 7,4: ➤ 32, [F]DELLER K., AOAT 220 (1988) 321-332; 2 fig.

3903 a) *Weimar* Peter, 'Seine Macht ist eine ewige Macht, die nicht vergeht' (Dan 7,14); Perspektiven und Strukturen apokalyptischen Denkens in Dan 7; – b) *Kellner* Wendelin, Die politisch-theologische Botschaft der Apokalyptik; zu Daniel 7 und äthiopischem Henoch VI-X: RUntHö 31 (Dü 1988) 362-373 / 386-393 [< ZIT 89,126].

3904 *Goldingay* John, 'Holy ones on high' in Daniel 7:18: JBL 107 (1988) 495-7.

3905 **Kalafian** Michael, [Dan 9,2] The impact of the Book of Daniel on Christology; a critical review of the prophecy of the 'seventy weeks' of the Book of Daniel as viewed by three major theological interpretations [premillennialist, amillennialist, 'higher critics']: diss NYU 1988, [D]*Thompson* Norma.   361 p.   89-01455. – DissA 49 (1988s) 3763-A.

3906 *Catastini* Alessandro, [Dan 13] Il racconto di Susanna; riconsiderazioni di ipotesi vecchie e nuove: EgVO 11 (1988) 195-204.

3907 *Halleux* A. de,   Une version syriaque revisée du commentaire d'HIP-
POLYTE sur *Suzanne*:   Muséon 101 (1988) 297-341.

E9.3   *Prophetae minores,* **Dodekapropheton ... Hosea, Joel.**

3908 ᴱ**Azcarraga Servert** M. J. de,   Minhat Šay de Y. S. de NORZI, Profetas
menores (traducción y anotación crítica): TEstCisn 40, 1987 ➤ 3,3671:
ᴿBL (1988) 44 (P. *Wernberg-Møller*); JStJud 19 (1988) 91s (J. *Maier*);
Sefarad 48 (1988) 429 (E. *Fernández Tejero*).

3909 **Fuller** Russell E.,   The minor prophets manuscripts from Qumrân Cave
IV: diss. Harvard.   CM 1988.   219 p.   89-01676. – DissA 49 (1988s)
3012-A.

3910 **Gelston** A.,   The Peshiṭta of the Twelve Prophets 1987 ➤ 3,3674:   ᴿJBL
107 (1988) 744-6 (B. *Chilton*); JSS 33 (1988) 281-5 (M. D. *Koster*).

3911 *Gelston* A.,   Some readings in the Peshiṭta of the Dodekapropheton:
➤ 480, Peshiṭta 1985/8, 81-98 (266-9).

3912 ᴱ**Sainte-Marie** H. de, *Gribomont* J. †, *Mallet* J.,   Liber duodecim pro-
phetarum ex interpretatione S. Hieronymi: Vulgata Benedictina 17
(➤ 3,3675). R 1987, Vaticano.   xlvii-290 p. – ᴿBiblica 69 (1988) 434-6 (S.
Pisano); Gnomon 60 (1988) 716-720 (W. *Thiele* furnishes the names of the
responsible editors, who presuppose here some of their convictions gained
from editing also the major prophets Is Jer Ezek Dan); JTS 39 (1988) 176s
(G. D. *Kilpatrick*); RÉLat 66 (1988) 278-281 (J. *Fontaine*).

3913 **Tov** Emanuel,   The Seiyâl collection I. the Greek minor prophets scroll
from Naḥal Ḥever (8 Ḥev XII gr): DJD.   Ox 1988, Clarendon.   192 p.
£50. 0-19-826327-9 [Antiquity 62,401 adv.].

3914 **Anderson** F., *Freedman* D., Hosea: AnchorB 24; 1953 = 1980 ➤ 61,4919
... 1,3732: ᴿJSS 33 (1988) 272-4 (P. R. *Ackroyd*: unsatisfactory).

3915 *Boling* Robert G.,   Repenting, praying and knowledge of God according
to Hosea: ➤ 141, ᶠSTUHLMUELLER C., Scripture and prayer 1988, 20-32.

3916 **Borbone** P. G., *Mandracci* F.,   Concordanze del testo siriaco di Osea
1987 ➤ 3,3677:   ᴿHenoch 10 (1988) 104-6 (A. *Vivian*); OrChrPer 54
(1988) 255s (R. *Lavenant*).

3917 **Bucher** Christina,   The origin and meaning of ᴢɴʜ terminology in the
Book of Hosea: diss. Claremont 1987. – RelStR 15,192.

3918 **Catlett** Michael L.,   Reversals in Hosea; a literary analysis: diss. Emory,
ᴰ*Tucker* G.   Atlanta 1988. 308 p.   88-16934. – DissA 49 (1988s) 1484-A;
RTLv 20,539.

3919 **Daniels** Dwight R.,   Hosea and salvation history; the early traditions of
Israel in the prophecy of Hosea: diss. ᴰ*Koch* K.   Hamburg 1987. – RTLv
19,533.

3920 *Köckert* Matthias,   *a*) Prophetie und Geschichte im Hoseabuch: ZTK 85
(1988) 3-30; – *b*) Verbindliches Reden von Gott in der Verkündigung des
Propheten Hosea: Glaube und Lernen 3 (1988) 105-119 [< ZAW 101,441].

3921 *Kruger* P. A.,   Prophetic imagery; on metaphors and similes in the book
Hosea [sic]: JNWS 14 (1988) 143-151.

3922 **Limburg** James,   Hosea-Micah: Interpretation Comm.   Atlanta 1988,
Knox.   viii-201 p. $18 [TDig 35,368].

3923 ᵀᴱ**Lipshitz** Abe,   The commentary of Rabbi Abraham IBN EZRA on
Hosea, edited from six manuscripts and translated with an introduction

and notes. NY 1988, Sepher-Hermon. 148 p. + ❻ 38; 3 pl. $20 [JBL 108,379] 0-87203-127-6.

3924 **Mba-Abessole** Paul, La traduction du prophète Osée de l'hébreu en fang; les problèmes de linguistique et d'exégèse: diss. Inst. Cath. & Sorbonne, ᴰ*Levêque* J.... P 1988. 946 p. – RICathP 29,113s; RTLv 20,540.

3925 **Neef** Heînz-Dieter, Heilstraditionen ... Hosea [Diss. Tü]: BZAW 169, 1987 ➤ 3,3683: ᴿJBL 109 (1988) 742-4 (G. M. *Tucker*); RB 95 (1988) 621s (J. *Loza*); RHPR 68 (1988) 239-241 (J. G. *Heintz*); TR 84 (1988) 365s (H. *Utzschneider*).

3926 **Stuart** D., Hosea-Jonah: Word Comm. 31. Waco 1987, Word. xlv-537 p. $25. 0-8499-0235-5 [BL 89,62, G. I. *Emmerson,* severe].

3927 *Thiel* Winfried, Hosea: ➤ 798, EvKL 2 (1988) 567s.

3928 **Tucker** G., [Hosea diss.] 308 p. 88-16934. – DissA 49 (1988s) 1484-A.

3929 *Wacker* M. T., Frau — Sexus — Macht; eine feministisch-theologische Relecture des Hoseabuches: ➤ 427, Gott/Frauen 1987, 101-125.

3930 **Wolff** H. W., Oseas hoy; las bodas de la ramera 1984 ➤ 65,3324: ᴿBurgense 29 (1988) 581s (P. *Arenillas,* también su Amós).

3931 **Yee** Gale A., Composition and tradition in the book of Hosea: SBL diss. 102, 1987 ➤ 3,3684: ᴿBL (1988) 98s (G. I. *Emmerson*); JBL 107 (1988) 521-3 (W. *Vogels*).

────────

3932 *Cathcart* Kevin J., Targum Jonathan to Hosea 1-3: ➤ 148, ᶠWEIN-GREEN J., IrBSt 10,1 (1988) 37-43.

3933 *Anderlini* Giampaolo, 'Ešet zᵉnuim (Os.1,2): BbbOr 30 (1988) 169-182.

3934 *Borbone* Pier Giorgio, 'Comprensione' o 'speranza'? Osea 2,17 nella Pešitta: Henoch 10 (1988) 277-281; franç. 282.

3935 *Vogels* Walter, Hosea's gift to Gomer (Hos 3,2): Biblica 69 (1988) 412-421.

3936 *Bakon* Shimon, For I am God and not man [1 Sam 15,29, God 'is not human, that he should change his mind'; but Hos 11,9, 'I have had a change of heart ... for I am God and not man']: Dor 17 (1988s) 243-9.

3937 *Kruger* P. A., Yahweh's generous love; eschatological expectations in Hosea 14: 2-9: OTEssays 1,1 (c.1988) 27-48.

────────

3938 **Bergler** Siegfried, Joel als Schriftinterpret [Diss. München, ᴰ*Jeremias* J.]: BeitErfAntJud 16. Fra 1988, Lang. Fs 74. – RTLv 19,532; TR 84,426. 3-8204-0289-6.

3939 *Deist* Ferdinand E., Parallels and reinterpretation in the Book of Joel; a theology of the Yom Yahweh?: ➤ 47, ᶠFENSHAM F., Text 1988, 63-79.

3940 *Jeremias* Jörg, Joel [/buch]: ➤ 813, TRE 17 (1987) 91-97.

3941 *Loretz* Oswald, Regenritual und Jahwetag im Joelbuch [kanaanäischer Hintergrund, Kolometrie, Aufbau und Symbolik eines Prophetenbuches]: Ugaritisch-biblische Literatur 5. Altenberge 1986, CIS. 189 p.; bibliog. p. 170-181 [KirSef 61,392].

3942 **Ogden** G. S., *Deutsch* R. R., Joel/Mal comm. 1987 ➤ 3,3691: ᴿThemelios 14 (1988s) 104s (M. J. *Selman*).

3943 **Prinsloo** Willem S., The theology of the book of Joel: BZAW 163, 1985 ➤ 1,3757 ... 3,3693: ᴿCBQ 50 (1988) 122 (C. R. *Seitz*).

3944 **Romerowski** S., Les livres de Joël et d'Abdias: Comm. Év. 9. Vaux 1989, Édifac. 302 p. F 120 [NRT 111,933, J-L. *Ska*].

3945 *Leeuwen* C. van, Tekst, structuur en betekenis van Joël 2: 1-11: NedTTs 42 (1988) 89-98, Eng. 145.

3946 *Luria* B. Z., ❶ Date of Joel 4: BethM 32,111 (1986s) 345-9.

E9.4 Amos.

3947 **Bjørndalen** Anders J., Untersuchungen zur allegorischen Rede der Propheten Amos und Jesaja: BZAW 165, 1986 ➤ 2,2886; 3,3698: ᴿBijdragen 49 (1988) 91s (W. *Beuken*); BO 45 (1988) 176-8 (A. *Gelston*); NedTTs 42 (1988) 150s (C. van *Leeuwen*); TR 84 (1988) 20-22 (H.-P. *Müller*).

3948 **Clements** R., When God's patience runs out; the truth of Amos for today: Living Word. Nottingham 1988, Living Word. 192 p. £4. 0-85110-496-7 [BL 89,102, R. *Hammer*: anecdotal].

3949 *Crocker* Piers, History and archaeology in the oracles of Amos: BurH 23 (1987) 7-15 [< OTAbs 11,284].

3950 *Diebner* Bernd J., 'Sozialgeschichtliche Auslegung' des Alten Testaments als Erbe der 'Offenbarungs-Archäologie': ... W. SCHOTTROFF 'Amos': DielB 24 (1987) 127-145.

3951 *Giles* Terry, An introductory investigation of Amos by means of the model of the voluntary social movement: ProcGLM 8 (1988) 135-153.

3952 *Ginat* Lifa, ❶ Order of the Gentile prophecies in Amos: BethM 34,118 (1988s) 250-4.

3953 *Gosse* Bernard, Le recueil d'oracles contre les nations du livre d'Amos et l''histoire deutéronomique': VT 38 (1988) 22-40.

3954 **Hayes** John H., Amos the eighth-century prophet; his times and his preaching. Nv 1988, Abingdon. 256 p. $14 [JBL 108,379].

3955 **Keddie** Gordon J., [Amos] The Lord is his name: Welwyn comm. Welwyn 1986, Evangelical. 137 p. [KirSef 61,391].

3956 **King** Philip J., Amos, Hosea, Micah — an archaeological commentary. Ph 1988, Westminster. 292 p. $21; pa. $16. 0-664-21876-8; pa. 4077-1. – ᴿBAR-W 14,4 (1988) 6.60 (P. D. *Hanson*); SWJT 31,2 (1988s) 51 (F. B. *Huey*: fascinating).

3957 **Martin-Achard** R., *al.,* Amos[-Lam] 1984 ➤ 65,3343 ... 3,3708: ᴿScEspr 40 (1988) 115-8 (G. *Couturier*); StPatav 34 (1987) 415s (A. *Moda*).

3958 **Mbelé** Philémon, La justice sociale ou l'ultime possibilité de salut pour Israël selon le prophète Amos: diss. Montpellier 1988. – RTLv 20,540.

3959 *Pfeifer* G., Die Fremdvölkersprüche des Amos — spätere vaticinia ex eventu?: VT 38 (1988) 230-3.

3960 **Ruiz González** G. [➤ 3,3711], ᴱ*Ortega Monasterio* M. T., Comentarios hebreos medievales al libro de Amós: Comillas 1/31/1/20, 1987: ᴿAulaOr 6 (1988) 282s (J. *Ribera*); JStJud 19 (1988) 257s (A. van der *Heide*); ZkT 110 (1988) 104s (J. M. *Oesch*).

3961 **Soggin** J. Alberto, The prophet Amos 1987 ➤ 3,3712; Ph $16; 0-334-00053-X. – ᴿBL (1988) 65 (J. M. *Dines*); RExp 85 (1988) 557s (P. H. *Kelley*: one of the best); Themelios 14 (1988s) 65s (Å. *Viberg*).

3962 **VanHorn** William W., An investigation of *yom YHWH* as it relates to the message of Amos: diss. New Orleans Baptist Theol. Sem. 1987, ᴰ*Smith* B. K. – 207 p. 88-10260. – DissA 49 (1988s) 854-A.

3963 **Walzer** Michael, [Amos:] Interpretation and social criticism. CM 1987, Harvard. 96 p. $12.50. – ᴿInterpretation 42 (1988) 310s (R. S. *Dietrich*).

3964 *Weippert* H., Amos [-buch]: ➤ 804, NBL Lfg 1 (1988) 92-95.
3965 *Zenger* Erich, Die eigentliche Botschaft des Amos; von der Relevanz der Politischen Theologie in einer exegetischen Kontroverse: ➤ 106, FMETZ J.-B., Mystik 1988, 394-406.

3966 *Tsumura* D. T., 'Inserted bicolon'; the AXYB pattern, in Amos I,5 and Psalm IX,7: VT 38 (1988) 234-6.
3967 *Jeremias* Jörg, a) Amos 3-6; Beobachtungen zur Entstehungsgeschichte eines Prophetenbuches: ➤ 153, ZAW 100 Supp. (1988) 123-138 – b) Amos 3-6; from the oral word to the text, TIrvine Stuart A.: ➤ 25, FCHILDS B., Canon 1988, 217-229.
3968 a) *Bosman* H. L., Does disaster strike only when the Lord sends it? Prophetic eschatology and the origin of evil in Amos 3,6; – b) *Helberg* J. L., Disillusionment on the day of Yahweh with special reference to the land (Amos 5); – c) *Williams* D. T., The sword, famine and pestilence; expectation of health and prosperity in the prophets: OTEssays 1,2 (c. 1988) 21-30 / 31-45 / 1-19.
3969 *Pfeifer* Gerhard, 'Rettung' als Beweis der Vernichtung (Amos 3,12): ZAW 100 (1988) 269-277.
3970 *Smith* Gary V., Amos 5:13; the deadly silence of the prosperous: JBL 107 (1988) 289-291.
3971 *Hirth* Volkmar, [Am 5,18-27; Dt 4,28] Der Dienst fremder Götter als Gericht Jahwes: BibNot 45 (1988) 40s.
3972 *Borger* R., Amos 5,26, Apg 7,43 und Šurpu II, 180: ZAW 100 (1988) 70-81: Amos reading *sakkut* not confirmed by Šurpu.
3973 *King* Philip J., [Am 6,4s] The *marzeaḥ* Amos denounces: BAR-W 14,4 (1988) 14-44.
3974 *Cooper* Alan, The absurdity of Amos 6:12a: JBL 107 (1988) 725-7.
3975 **Beyerlin** Walter, [Am 7,7s] Bleilot, Brecheisen oder was sonst? Revision einer Amos-Vision: OBO 81. FrS/Gö 1988, Univ./VR. 61 p. DM 28 [TR 84,426]. 3-7278-0579-X / VR 3-525-53710-7.
3976 *Utzschneider* Helmut, Die Amazjaerzählung (Am 7,10-17) zwischen Literatur und Historie: BibNot 41 (1988) 76-101.
3977 *Wolters* Al, Wordplay and dialect in Amos 8:1-2: JEvTS 31 (1988) 407-410 [< ZIT 89,148].
3978 *Kobayashi* S., ❶ Amos 9,1-4.5-6: Kirisutokyo Gaku 28 (Tokyo St. Paul's Univ. Association of Christian Studies 1986) ... [BL 89,19: 121 p. in that issue]. In fasc. 29 (1987) he relates Amos 1,14s to Jer 49,2s.

E9.5 Jonas.

Alexander T. Desmond, Jonah 1988 ➤ 4019.
3979 **Almbladh** Karin, Studies in the Book of Jonah 1986 ➤ 2,2912: RBO 45 (1988) 395 (A. *LaCocque*).
3980 **Barnard** Will J., *Riet* Peter van 't, Als een duif naar het land van Assur; het boek Jona verklaard vanuit Tenach en rabbijnse traditie tegen de achtergrond van de tijd. Kampen 1988, Kok. 286 p. *f* 75. 90-242-4810-8 [Bijdragen 49,357].
3981 *Chmiel* H.Y., ❶ God's answer to Jonah: BethM 34,117 (1988s) 121-134.
3982 *Combet* L., al., Jonas ou 'il y a toujours plus à l'Est que soi': SémBib 49 (1988) 1-14.

3983 **Durussel** André, Jonas retranché. Genève 1987, Eliane Vernay. 66 p. Fs 18. – ᴿÉTRel 63 (1988) 326 (R. *Chapal*).
3984 ᴱ**Duval** Yves-Marie, JÉROME ... sur Jonas: SChr 323, 1985 ⇒ 1,3784 ... 3,3728: ᴿAntClas 57 (1988) 441-4 (H. *Savon*); Gregorianum 69 (1988) 167 (A. *Orbe*); RB 95 (1988) 104-8 (G. G. *Stroumsa*); RÉAug 34 (1988) 202s (P. *Jay*); VigChr 42 (1988) 92-94 (G. J. M. *Bartelink*).
3985 *Eagleton* Terry, J. L. AUSTIN [How to do things with words] and the Book of Jonah: NBlackf 69 (1988) 164-8.
3986 **Ebach** Jürgen, Kassandra und Jona; gegen die Macht des Schicksals 1987 ⇒ 3,3729: ᴿExpTim 99 (1987s) 376 (R. *Coggins*); GrazBei 15 (1988) 237-241 (Barbara *Feichtinger*).
3987 **Eubanks** Larry L., The cathartic effects of irony in Jonah: diss. Southern Baptist Theol. Sem. ᴰWatts J. 1988. 213 p. 89-01495. – DissA 49 (1988s) 3052-A.
3988 *Golka* Friedemann W., Jonaexegese und Antijudaismus: KIsr 1 (1986) 51-61.
3989 **Heerden** Willem Schalk van, Die interpretasie van die Boek Jona in die Nederduitse Gereformeerde Kerk: diss. Unisa, ᴰDeist F. Pretoria 1988. 199 p. – RTLv 20,538; OTEssays 2/2,79 (Eng.).
3990 *Hope* E. R., [Jonah] Pragmatics, exegesis and translation: ⇒ 502, Issues/Translation 1987/8, 113-128.
3991 *McCann* Joseph F., Jonah; Doctor Strangelove: BToday 26 (1988) 298-303.
3992 *Ratner* Robert J., Jonah; toward the re-educaton of the prophets: Dor 17 (1988s) 10-18.
3993 *Roffey* John W., God's truth, Jonah's fish; structure and existence in the book of Jonah: AustralBR 36 (1988) 1-18.
3994 **Zandbelt** André, Jona: Belichting. Boxtel 1987, Kath.Bijbel. 54 p. ƒ15. 90-6175-398-7 [Bijdragen 49,235].
3995 *Zobel* Hans-Jürgen, Jona [/buch]: ⇒ 813, TRE 17 (1987) 229-234.

3996 *Golka* Friedemann W., [Jonas 1...] Die Figura etymologica im Alten Testament: ⇒ 469, Wünschet 1986/8, 415-424.
3997 *Harviainen* Tapani, Why were the sailors not afraid of the Lord before [sic] verse Jonah 1,10?: StOrFin 64 (1988) 78-81.
3998 **Steffen** Uwe, Jona und der Fisch; der Mythos von Tod und Wiedergeburt: Symbole. Stu c. 1988, Kreuz. 189 p. DM 29,80 [ErbAuf 64,494].
3999 *Lubeck* R. J., Prophetic sabotage; a look at Jonah 3:2-4: TrinJ 9 (1988) 37-46.

E9.6   *Michaeas,* **Micah.**

4000 **Brisson** Ervin C.ᴶ, Hans DENCK's Der Micha-Kommentar [16th cent. Anabaptist], an annotated translation: diss. Southern Baptist Sem., ᴰGeorge T., 1987. 88-00343. – DissA 49 (1988s) 103-A.
4001 **Cuffey** Kenneth, The coherence of Micah; a review of the proposals and a new interpretation: diss. Drew. Durham NC 1987. – RTLv 20,539; RelStR 14,188.
4002 **Hagstrom** David G., The coherence of the book of Micah [diss. Union Theol. Sem. ᴰMays J. L., Richmond 1982]: SBL Diss. 89. Atlanta 1988, Scholars. 152 p. $17; sb./pa. $8 [ZAW 101,461, H. C. *Schmitt*].

4003 **Hillers** D. R., Micah 1984 → 65,3380 ... 2,2926: ᴿTLZ 113 (1988) 810s (J. *Conrad*).

4004 **Jeppesen** Knud, Græder ikke saa saare [tears are not wounds; diss.]: Studier i Mikabogens sigte, B1-2. Aarhus 1987, Univ. 603 p. Dk 288. 87-7288-078-3. – ᴿBL (1988) 78 (G. W. *Anderson*); NorTTs 89 (1988) 152s (H. M. *Barstad*).

4005 *Luria* Ben-Zion, ❻ Micha on the end of days: BethM 34,119 (1988s) 362-6.

4006 *Marrs* Rick, Micah and the task of ministry: RestQ 30,1 (Abilene 1988) 1-16 [< ZIT].

4007 *Nielsen* Eduard, Mika-bogen — et trøsteskrift fra eksilet?: DanTTs 51 (1988) 204-219 [< ZIT 88,659].

4008 *Otzen* Benedikt, Eksilsituation og profettradition, Mika: [*Jeppesen* K. 1987]: Religionsvidenskabeligt Tidsskrift 12 (1988) 25-38 [< ZAW 101,137].

4009 **Renaud** B., Michée, Sophonie, Nahum: Sources Bibliques 1987 → 3, 3740: ᴿMondeB 54 (1988) 59 (J. *Asurmendi*).

4010 **Stansell** Gary, Micah and Isaiah; a form and tradition historical comparison: SBL diss. 85. Atlanta 1988, Scholars. vii-165 p. $17. 0-89130-962-4; pa. 3-2.

4011 **Strydom** Johannes G., Micah, Anti-Micah and Deutero-Micah; a critical discussion with A. S. van der WOUDE: diss. ᴰ*Loader* J. Pretoria 1988. 239 p. – RTLv 20,541; OTEssays 2/2,78.

Waltke Bruce K., Micah 1988 → 4019.

4012 *Cathcart* Kevin J., Micah 2:4 and Nahum 3:16-17 in the light of Akkadian: → 42*, EHRMAN A. mem., Fucus 1988, 191-200.

4014 *Koyama* Kosuke, The mountain of the Lord; Micah 4:1-7: IntRMiss 77 (1988) 194-200.

4015 *Pannell* Randall J., The politics of the Messiah; a new reading of Micah 4:14-5:5: PerspRelSt 15 (1988) 131-143 [< ZIT 88,602].

4016 *Dawes* S., Walking humbly; Micah 6.8 revisited: ScotJT 41 (1988) 331-9.

4017 *Werner* Wolfgang, Micha 6,8 — eine alttestamentliche Kurzformel des Glaubens? Zum theologischen Verständnis von Mi 6,8 [Hab. Vorlesung Augsburg]: BZ 32 (1988) 232-248.

4018 *Vargon* S., Micah 7:8-10 — message of encouragement: → 43, ꟳELITZUR Y., II (1986) 135-150.

E9.7 *Abdias, Sophonias ...* **Obadiah, Zephaniah, Nahum.**

4019 **Baker** David W., Obadiah [*Alexander* T., Jonah; *Waltke* B. Micah]: Tyndale OT comm. Leicester 1988, Inter-Varsity. 207 p. £5.50.

4020 *Hastoupis* Athanasios P., ❺ The book of Obadiah: TAth 54 (1988) 466-475.

4021 *Robinson* Robert B., Levels of naturalization in Obadiah: JStOT 40 (1988) 83-97.

4023 **Wehrle** Josef, Prophetie und Textanalyse; die Komposition Obadja 1-21 interpretiert auf der Basis textlinguistischer und semiotischer Konzeptionen: Mü Univ AOtt 28, 1987 → 3,3750: ᴿBL (1988) 96 (G. I. *Davies*).

4024 **Ball** I. J.ᴶ, Zephaniah, a rhetorical study [diss. 1983 not updated]. Berkeley 1988, Bibal. iv-308 p. $17. 0-941037-02-9 [BL 89,66, J. A. *Emerton*].

4025 **Deissler** A., Zwölfpropheten III; Zefanja, Haggai, Sacharja, Maleachi: NEchter 21. Wü 1988, Echter. p. 235-342. DM 28; sb. 24. 3-429-01138-8 [BL 89,52, A. *Gelston*].

4026 **House** Paul R., Zephaniah, a prophetic drama: Bible & Lit 16 / JStOT Sup 69. Sheffield 1988, Almond. 146 p. £22. 1-85075-075-0. [ZAW 101,462].

4027 **Achtemeier** Elizabeth, Nahum [to] Malachi 1986 → 3,3761: [R]Interpretation 42 (1988) 191-3 (D. A. *Farmer*); TTod 44 (1987s) 288.290 (S. *Terrien*).

4028 **Baker** David W., Nahum, Habakkuk and Zephaniah, an introduction and commentary: Tyndale OT Comm. Leicester 1988, Inter-Varsity. 121 p. £3.75. 0-85111-644-2; pa. 845-3. Habakkuk p. 43-77.

4029 **Wal** Adri van der, Nahum, Habakkuk, a classified bibliography [with Qumran section...]. Amst 1988, Free Univ. xiii-208 p. *f* 70. 90-6256-662-6 [Bl 89,97, A. *Gelston*]. – [R]Henoch 10 (1988) 397s (P. G. *Borbone*).

4030 *Schneider* Thomas, Nahum und Theben; zum topographisch-historischen Hintergrund von Nah 3,8f: BibNot 44 (1988) 63-73.

4031 *Christensen* Duane L., The book of Nahum; the question of authorship within the caonical process: JEvTS 31 (1988) 51-58 [< ZIT 88,514].

4032 **Coggins** R. J., [Nah Ob], *Re'emi* S. P. [Esther], Israel among the nations: IntTheolC 1985 → 1,3822 ... 3,3763: [R]CBQ 50 (1988) 122s (C. R. *Seitz*).

4033 *Harrison* C. Robert[J], The unity of the Minor Prophets in the LXX; a reexamination of the question [Nahum, Joel]: BSeptCog 21 (1988) 55-72.

4034 **Lee** Hyung Won, The function of figurative language in the Book of Nahum: diss. Southern Baptist Theol. Sem., [D]*Kelley* P. 1988. 252 p. 89-01499. – DissA 49 (1988s) 3063-A.

4035 *Patterson* Richard D., *Travers* Michael E., Literary analysis and the unity of Nahum: GraceTJ 9 (1988) 45-58.

E9.8 *Habacuc,* **Habakkuk.**

Baker David W., Habakkuk 1988 → 4028: p. 43-77.

Feltes H., Die Gattung des Hab.-Kommentars 1986 → b41.

4036 **Nitzan** Bilha, ⊕ Pesher Habakkuk 1986 → 2,2941; 3,3771: [R]JBL 107 (1988) 528-530 (F. E. *Greenspahn*).

4037 **Szeles** Maria E., Wrath and mercy; a commentary on the books of Habakkuk and Zephaniah: International Theological Comm. GR 1987, Eerdmans. 118 p. $8 pa. [GraceTJ 9,316].

4038 *Haak* Robert D., 'Poetry' in Habakkuk 1:1-2:4?: JAOS 108 (1988) 437-444.

4039 *Wal* A. J. O. van der, *Lō' nāmūt* in Habakkuk I,12; a suggestion: VT 38 (1988) 480-3.

4040 **Hiebert** Theodore, God of my victory ... Hab 3 [Diss. [D]*Cross* F.]: HarvSemMon 38, 1986 → 2,2945: [R]CBQ 50 (1988) 492s (W. *Brueggemann*: threadbare 'significance' categories); JBL 107 (1988) 309-311 (M. A. *Sweeney*); Orientalia 57 (1988) 235-7 (W. G. E. *Watson*); RB 95 (1988) 304s (R. J. *Tournay*).

4041 *Barré* Michael L., Habakkuk 3:2; translation in context: CBQ 50 (1988) 184-197.

4042 *Mello* Alberto, In Deo Jesu meo; Abacuc 3,18 e il Magnificat: SBFLA
38 (1988) 17-38.

E9.9. *Aggaeus*, **Haggai** – *Zacharias*, **Zechariah** – *Malachias*, **Malachi.**

4043 **Schuller** Eileen, sr., Post-exilic prophets: Message of Biblical Spirituality
4. Wilmington 1988, Glazier. 192 p. $13; pa. $10 [CBQ 51,403].

4044 **Meyers** Carol L. & Eric M., Haggai, Zech 1-8: AnchorB 25B, 1987
➤ 3,3781: ᴿAndrUnS 26 (1988) 193-5 (J. *Dyrdahl*); ETL 64 (1988) 465-7
(J. *Lust*); Gregorianum 69 (1988) 770-2 (C. *Conroy*); Interpretation 42
(1988) 311. 314 (J. D. *Newsome*); JBL 107 (1988) 523-6 (D. L. *Petersen*);
MeliT 39 (1988) 69-74 (A. *Abela*: fascinating); NRT 110 (1988) 109 (J.-L.
Ska).

4045 **Prokurat** Michael, Haggai and Zechariah 1-8; a form critical analysis:
diss. Graduate Theological Union, ᴰ*Gold* V. Berkeley 1988. 526 p.
89-06588. – DissA 49 (1988s) 3699-A.

4046 *a) Rooy* H. F. van, Eschatology and audience; the eschatology of
Haggai; – *b) Althann* R., The destination of the white horses in
Zechariah 6:6: OTEssays 1,1 (S.Afr. c. 1988) 49-63 / 65-71.

4047 **Schwantes** Milton, *a)* Ageu: Comentário bíblico AT. Petrópolis 1986,
Vozes. 75 p. – *b)* Aggeo, ᵀ*Pistocchi* Bruno. R 1987, Borla. 107 p. Lit.
8000 [CC 139/2 dopo 208]. 88-263-0610-9.

4048 **Stuhlmueller** Carroll, Rebuilding with hope; a commentary on the books
of Haggai and Zechariah: International Theological Commentary. E/GR
1988, Handsel/Eerdmans. xv-165 p. £5. 0-905312-75-9 / 0-8028-2374-2
[BL 89,62, R. A. *Mason*: pungency and perceptiveness].

4049 **Verhoef** Pieter A., The books of Haggai and Malachi: NICOT 1987
➤ 3,3783: GR 1987, Eerdmans. xxv-364 p. $22. – ᴿBL (1988) 66 (R. A.
Mason); CBQ 50 (1988) 700-2 (H. *Gossai*: van der WOUDE and J.
BALDWIN can do no wrong); VT 38 (1988) 123 (J. A. *Emerton*).

4050 *Verhoef* P. A., Notes on the dates in the Book of Haggai: ➤ 47,
ᶠFENSHAM F., Text 1988, 259-267.

4051 *a) Wessels* W. J., Haggai from a historian's point of view; – *b) Snyman*
S. D., Eschatology in the book of Malachi: OTEssays 1,2 (c. 1988)
47-61 / 63-77.

4052 **Wolff** H. W., Dodekapropheton 6. Haggai 1986 ➤ 2,2954; 3,3784:
ᴿTLZ 113 (1988) 264 (A. H. J. *Gunneweg*).

4053 *Prinsloo* W. S., The cohesion of Haggai 1:4-11: ➤ 469, Wünschet
1986/8, 337-343.

4054 ᵀᴱ**Cataldo** Antonio. CIRILLO di Alessandria, Commento ai profeti
minori Zaccaria e Malachia: Collana di Testi Patristici 60. R 1986, Città
Nuova. 376 p. – ᴿStRicOrCr 10 (1987) 59s (F. *Carcione*); Teresianum 39
(1988) 201-5 (M. *Diego Sánchez*, también sobre 9 otros títulos de esta
Collana).

4055 *Fensham* F. C., Zechariah: ➤ 801, ISBEnc³ 4 (1988) [1182-] 1183-6
[1189-91, Zephaniah, *Schneider* D. A.].

4056 **Gorgulho** G., Zaccaria [3,3786],ᵀ. R 1987, Borla. 184 p. Lit. 13.000
[CC 139/2 dopo 208]. 88-263-0609-5.

4057 **Heater** Homerᴶ, Zechariah: Bible Study Comm. GR 1987, Zondervan.
122 p. [GraceTJ 9,307].

4058 *Lurja* B. Z., ❶ The vision of Zechariah 2,1-9:   BethM 34,117 (1988s) 191s.
4059 *Finley* T. J.,   'The apple of his eye' (*bābat 'ênô*) in Zechariah II, 12:   VT 38 (1988) 337s.
4060 *Woude* Adam S. van der,   *a*) Zion as primeval stone in Zechariah 3 and 4: ↠ 47, ᶠFENSHAM F., Text 1988, 237-248; – *b*) Serubbabel und die messianischen Erwartungen des Propheten Sacharja: ↠ 153, ZAW 100 Supp. (1988) 138-156.
4061 *Mittmann* Siegfried,   Die Einheit von Sacharja 8,1-8: ↠ 47, ᶠFENSHAM F., Text 1988, 269-282.
4062 *Clark* David J.,   Discourse structure in Zechariah 9-14; skeleton or phantom?: ↠ 502, Issues/Translation 1987/8, 64-80.

4063 **Barsotti** D.,   Le prophète Malachie, ᵀ*Solms* E. de.   P 1988, Téqui.   25 p. F 33.   2-85244-866-1 [BL 89,67, R. A. *Mason*].
4064 **Blake** Richard D.,   The rhetoric of Malachi: diss. Union Theol. Sem. NY 1988. 402 p. 88-22280. – DissA 49 (1988s) 3395-A; RelStR 15,191.
4065 *Gorgulho* G.,   Malaquias e o discernimento da justiça: EstudosB 15 (1987) 18-31.
4066 *Meyers* Eric M.,   Priestly language in the book of Malachi: HebAnR 10 (1986) 225-347.
4067 **O'Brien** Julia M.,   Priest and Levite in Malachi: diss. Duke, ᴰ*Meyers* E. Durham NC 1988. 325 p. 88-22031. – DissA 49 (1988s) 2270-A.
4068 *Gray* S. W.,   Fuegos fatuos; la adoración en los tiempos de Malaquías: Diálogo Teol. 30 (Calí 1988) 47-65 [*al*. 6-17; 32-46; 80-107; 108-118 < Stromata 44,564].
4069 *Ogden* Graham S.,   The use of figurative language in Malachi 2.10-16: *a*) ↠ 502, Issues/Translation 1987/8, 265-273. – *b*) BTrans 39 (1988) 223-230.

IX. NT Exegesis generalis

F1.   **New Testament Introduction.**

4070 *Aletti* Jean-Noël,   Sagesse — Nouveau Testament: ↠ 791, DictSpir XIV,91 (1988) 92-96 [-132, Pères etc., *al*.].
4071 **Aune** David E., [↠ 287] The New Testament in its literary environment. Library of Early Christianity 8, 1987 ↠ 3,3801;   0-664-21912-8: ᴿAsbTJ 43,1 (1988) 93-95 (M. R. *Mulholland*); CBQ 50 (1988) 522-4 (J. H. *Elliott*: indispensable); JAAR 56 (1988) 559-562 (J. P. *Meier*); RB 95 (1988) 473s (J. *Murphy-O'Connor*: an astounding achievement).
4072 **Bammel** Ernst,   Jesu Nachfolger; Nachfolgeüberlieferungen in der Zeit des frühen Christentums: Studia Delitzschiana 3/1.   Heid 1988, Schneider. 99 p. DM 48 [CBQ 51,186]. 3-7953-0852-6.
4073 **Barr** David L.,   NT story, an introduction 1987 ↠ 3,3803. – ᴿInterpretation 42 (1988) 439 (J. D. *Kingsbury*).
Baxter Margaret,   New Testament Introduction 1988, I ↠ 4283; II ↠ 4120.
4075 **Berger** Klaus, *Colpe* Carsten,   Religionsgeschichtliches Textbuch zum NT: NTD Texte 1, 1987 ↠ 3,3805: ᴿBZ 32 (1988) 142s (H.-J. *Klauck*); NRT 110 (1988) 602 (X. *Jacques*); SNTU-A 13 (1988) 213 (A. *Fuchs*); TLZ 113 (1988) 268s (E. *Reinmuth*).

4076 **Berger** Klaus, Hermeneutik des Neuen Testaments. Gü 1988, Mohn. 456 p. 3-579-00088-8.

4077 **Brown** Schuyler, The origins of Christianity; a historical introduction to the NT 1984 ➤ 54,3433 ... 2,2972: RJEH 39 (1988) 233s (D. *Nineham*).

4078 **Childs** B. S. The NT as canon 1984 ➤ 65,3446 ... 3,3810: RHeythJ 29 (1988) 347-350 (J. *Blenkinsopp*); ZkT 110 (1988) 217s (R. *Oberforcher*).

4079 **Chilton** Bruce, Beginning NT study 1986 ➤ 3,3811: REvQ 60 (1988) 78s (S. H. *Travis*); ModT 4 (1987s) 291s (Deborah F. *Middleton*); ScotJT 41 (1988) 289s (J. A. *Ziesler*).

4080 *Craddock* F. B., The Gospels as literature: Encounter 49,1 (1988) 19-35 [NTAbs 32,149].

4081 **Davies** Stevan L., The New Testament, a contemporary introduction. SF 1988, Harper & R. xi-207 p. $19 [JBL 108,378].

4082 ᵀᴱ**Derron** Pascale, Pseudo-Phocylide Sentences: Coll. Budé, 1986 ➤ 2, 2981: RAntClas 57 (1988) 365s (D. *Donnet*).

4083 **Downing** F. Gerald, Strangely familiar [extracts paralleling NT; layout so unusual that no publisher would take it, the author rather contentedly admits] 1985 ➤ 2,f67: RAustralBR 36 (1988) 86s (N. M. *Watson*: recommends proffered student edition).

4084 **Drane** John, Introducing the New Testament [= Paul 1976, Jesus 1979, Early Christians 1982; expanded] 1986 ➤ 3,3814: RGraceTJ 9 (1988) 147s (D. B. *Sandy*); TS 49 (1988) 199 (D. J. *Harrington*).

4085 *Fang* Mark, ☉ Historico-geographic background of the NT: ColcFuJen 73 (1987) 351-362.

4086 **Ferguson** Everett, Backgrounds of early Christianity 1987 ➤ 3,3817: RRelStR 14 (1988) 383 (Elizabeth A. *Clark*).

4087 **Ford** J. Massyngbaerde, Bonded with the immortal; a pastoral introduction to the NT [with Covenant as leitmotif] 1987 ➤ 3,3818; RCBQ 50 (1988) 316s (J. M. *Reese*); NewTR 1,4 (1988) 79s (Marie-Eloise *Rosenblatt*).

4088 **Freed** Edwin D., The NT, a critical introduction 1986 ➤ 2,2984: RInterpretation 42 (1988) 437 (J. D. *Kingsbury*).

4089 **Graff** F. de, Jezus de Verborgene, een voorbereiding tot inwijding in de mysteriën van het Evangelie. Kampen 1987, Kok. 567 p. ƒ79,50. – RKerkT 39 (1988) 244-8 (H. *Vreekamp*).

4090 *Gratseas* Georgias, ☉ The problem of PLUTARCH's Symposiaca IV,5 in connection with New Testament times: DeltioVM 17,1 (1988) 21-47.

4091 *Guijarro Oporto* Santiago, La buena noticia de Jesús 1987 ➤ 3,3823: REstBíb 46 (1988) 261 (L. F. *García-Viana*).

4092 **Hill** Gary, *Archer* Gleason L., The discovery Bible, New American Standard NT [with]: H.E.L.P.S. ['emphatic' words in color; tense-force indicated by symbols; homophones (e.g. 'might') distinguished by exponents]. Ch 1987, Moody. xxxi-591 p.; 15 maps. $18 (leather $28) [TDig 35,153].

4093 *Hyslop* H., La interpretación de los Evangelios: TBraga 20 (1985) 187-195.

4094 **Johnson** Luke T., The writings of the NT 1986 ➤ 3,3828: RHorizons 15 (1988) 156 (Pheme *Perkins*).

4095 **Koester** Helmut, Introducción al Nuevo Testamento [➤ 64,3828b], ᵀ*Lacarra* J., *Pifiero* A., Salamanca 1988, Sigueme. 905 p. [NatGrac 36,176, F. F. *Ramos*].

4096 *Lemcio* Eugene E., The unifying kerygma of the New Testament: JStNT 33 (1988) 3-17.

4097 *Lövestam* Evald, *a*) Begreppet 'Guds Ord' i Nya testamentet; – *b*) Urkyrkans skriftförståelse [< SvTKv 48 (1972) 112-8 = Judendom/patristikerprojekt 1986, 259-267]: ↠ 221, Axplock 1987, 7-15 / 17-25.

4098 **Manaranche** André, Rue de l'Évangile [livre de poche pour des jeunes]: Lumière Vérité. P 1987, Fayard. 320 p. – ᴿEsprVie 98 (1988) 393-5 (P. *Jay*: défense de ce manuel pour des groupes pas parfaits, contre la conjuration du silence ou les chuchotements qui l'entourent).

4099 *Marcel* Pierre, L'autorité du Nouveau Testament [... du rejet à l'échec]: ↠ 28*, ᶠCOURTHIAL P., Dieu parle! 1984, 39-52 [169-187].

Martin Francis, Narrative parallels to the NT 1988 ↠ 4379.

4101 **Moloney** Francis J., The living voice of the Gospel; the gospels today 1987 ↠ 3,3839: ᴿLvSt 13 (1988) 274s (P. J. *Judge*); NBlackf 69 (1988) 249s (R. J. *Taylor*); ScripTPamp 20 (1988) 916 (J. M. *Casciaro*); Vidyajyoti 52 (1988) 609s (P. M. *Meagher*).

4102 *Navone* John, The dynamic of the question in the Gospel narrative: MilltSt 17 (1986) 75-111: 109 questions of Jesus plus 47 to or about him listed, then analyzed in tabular form.

4103 **Neill** Stephen, The interpretation of the New Testament 1861-1961, ²*Wright* Tom, updated to 1986. Ox 1988, UP. x-464 p. [TLond 91,446]. 0-19-283057-0.

4104 **Perkins** Pheme, Reading the New Testament² [¹1978 ↠ 60,5307]. NY 1988, Paulist. vii-350 p. $8. 0-8091-2939-6.

4105 **Plessis** Isak du, Nazareth or Egypt; who was right? A historical perspective on the New Testament, ᵀ*Emslie* B. L. Pretoria 1985, van Schaik. xi-160 p. [CBQ 50,355].

4106 **Price** James L., The NT, its history and theology³ ↠ 3,3843: ᴿInterpretation 42 (1988) 438 (J. D. *Kingsbury*).

4107 **Punt** Neal, What's good about the Good News? Ch 1988, Northland. 142 p. $8 [GraceTJ 9,314].

4108 **Roetzel** Calvin J., The world that shaped the NT 1987 ↠ 2,3007; 3,3846: ᴿVidyajyoti 52 (1988) 608s (P. M. *Meagher*).

4109 **Ryken** Leland, Words of life; a literary introduction to the NT. GR 1987, Baker. 182 p. – ᴿSWJT 312 (1988s) 56 (L. R. *Bush*: companion to his Words of delight—OT, also Baker 1987).

4111 ᴱ**Segovia** Fernando F., Discipleship in the NT 1982/5 ↠ 1,491 ... 3,3853: ᴿRExp 85 (1988) 149s (M. C. *Parsons*).

4112 **Tarjányi** Béla, Ⓜ Újszövetségi alapismeretek ... Basic information about the NT. Budapest 1988s, Pázmány Akadémia. I. The Church's life; Paul's letters 1988, 188 p. – II. Jesus' good news; the Church teaching 1989, 129 p.

4113 **Tuckett** C., Reading the NT 1987 ↠ 3,3858: ᴿAnglTR 70 (1988) 355-7 (C. C. *Black*).

4114 **Watson** Nigel M., Striking home; interpreting and proclaiming the New Testament. L 1987, Epworth. ix-206 p. $13. 0-7162-0438-X [NTAbs 32,239]. – ᴿAustralBR 36 (1988) 79s (J. W. *Roffey*).

4115 **Weiser** Alfons, Miteinander Gemeinde werden; Sachbuch zum NT und zum kirchlichen Leben 1987 ↠ 3,3862: ᴿBiKi 43 (1988) 127s (R. *Hoppe*).

4116 *Williams* Raymond, New Testament ['introduction'] textbooks; a review article: ↠ 947*, Critical Review 1 (1988) 19-41.

4117 *Witherington* B., Principles for interpreting the Gospels and Acts; Ashland Theological Journal 19,1 (Ohio 1987) 35-70 [< NTAbs 32,296].

4118 *Wolter* Michael,   Die anonymen Schriften des Neuen Testaments; Annäherungsversuch an ein literarisches Phänomen [MtMk Jn Lk Apg 1 Jn]: ZNW 79 (1988) 1-16.

F1.2   *Origo Evangeliorum;* **the Origin of the Gospels** [➤ F2.7].

4119 *Amphoux* Christian-B.,   Le style oral dans le Nouveau Testament: ÉTRel 63 (1988) 379-384.

4120 **Baxter** Margaret,   The formation of the Christian Scriptures: NT Introd. 2 [1. ➤ 4283]. L 1988, SPCK. 146 p. £5 [PrPeo 2,388].

4121 *Collins* Adela Y.,   Narrative, history and gospel; a general response: ➤ 304, Semeia 43 ('Genre, narrativity and theology' 1988) 145-154.

4122 *Culpepper* R. Alan, ['Gospel' genre; 'Atonement and the American psyche'] Lincoln: an American Gospel: Forum 4,2 (1988) 33-46.

4123 *a) Fabris* Rinaldo,   Vangelo / Gesú Cristo; – *b) Fusco* V.,   Vangeli: ➤ 806, NDizTB (1988) 1620-1639. 595-620 / 1610-1620.

4124 **Flusser** D.,   Ontdekkingen in het Nieuwe Testament; woorden van Jezus en hun overlevering. Baarn 1988, Ten Have, 168 p. Fb 498 [CollatVL 18,506].

4125 **Frankemölle** Hubert,   Evangelium — Begriff und Gattung; ein Forschungsbericht: SBB 15. Stu 1988, KBW. vi-255 p. DM 39. 3-460-00151-8.

4126 **Fredriksen** Paula,   From Jesus to Christ; the origins of the New Testament images of Jesus. NHv 1988, Yale Univ. xii-256 p. $22.50. 0-300-04018-0 [TDig 36,160].

4127 **Gerhardsson** Birger,   The Gospel tradition: ConBib NT 15, 1986 ➤ 2,3027; 3,3868:   ᴿCBQ 50 (1988) 136 (B. F. *Meyer*: redimensions W. KELBER); Interpretation 42 (1988) 94. 96 (M. L. *Soards*); TR 84 (1988) 25s (R. *Kampling*).

4128 **Goldsworthy** Graeme,   Gospel and Wisdom [< diss.]. Exeter 1987, Paternoster. 202 p.£5. – ᴿScripB 19 (1988s) 47 (R. C. *Fuller*).

4129 **Grelot** Pierre,   L'origine des évangiles 1986 ➤ 2,3029; 3,3869:   ᴿIndTSt 25 (1988) 105-7 (L. *Legrand*); JBL 107 (1988) 754s (R. H. *Fuller*: worth translating); JTS 39 (1988) 196s (C. M. *Tuckett*); RICathP 25 (1988) 79-81 (M. *Trimaille*); ScEspr 40 (1988) 244-6 (G. *Rochais*).

4130 **Kelly** Joseph F.,   Why is there a New Testament? 1986 ➤ 2,3032; 3,3871 ('Kelley'):   ᴿIrBSt 9 (1987) 92s (A. W. C. *Brown*).

4131 **Meagher** J. C.,   Five Gospels 1983 ➤ 64,3880 ... 2,3033:   ᴿÉglT 17 (1986) 238-240 (W. *Vogels*).

4131* *O'Callaghan* José,   Verso le origini del Nuovo Testamento: CC 139 (1988,4) 269-272.

4132 *a) Orsatti* Mauro,   Il genere letterario 'vangelo'; – *b) Maggioni* Bruno, Il cristianesimo è ancora 'vangelo'?; – *c) Bianchi* Mansueto,   'Mi ha mandato per annunziare un lieto messaggio'; – *d) Ravasi* Gianfranco,   La dimensione estetica dell'Evangelo: ParVi 33,6 ('Evangelo' 1988) 424-430 / 406-412 / 413-423 / 431-8.

4133 **Perrier** [➤ 3,3876!] Pierre,   Karozoutha; annonce orale de la Bonne Nouvelle en araméen et Évangiles gréco-latines 1986 ➤ 2,2034:   ᴿOrChr 72 (1988) 221s (M. van *Esbroeck*); RevSR 62 (1988) 77s (C. *Munier*: guère recevable); RTLv 19 (1988) 496s (A. de *Halleux*: innombrables erreurs, érudition mal digérée).

4134 **Quesnel** M.,   L'histoire des Évangiles: Bref 1, 1987 ➤ 3,3877:   ᴿEsprVie 98 (1988) 204s (L. *Walter*); RICathP 28 (1988) 146-8 (J. *Doré*).

4135 **Rolland** Philippe, Les premiers Évangiles 1984 ⇥ 65,3781 ... 3,4188: ᴿColcT 58,1 (1988) 173-7 (R. *Bartnicki*).

4136 *Rossé* Gérard, La formazione dei Vangeli; a proposito di una questione dibattuta [*Tresmontant* C., *Carmignac* J., *Grelot* P.]: NuovaUm 10,56 (1988) 105-117.

4137 **Schwarz** Günther, 'Und Jesus sprach'...; zur aramäischen Urgestalt: BWANT 118, 1985 ⇥ 1,3919 ... 3,3881: ᴿErbAuf 63 (1987) 477s (E. *Tschacher*); NedTTs 76s (P. W. van der *Horst*).

4138 *a) Talbert* Charles H., Once again; Gospel genre; – *b) Williams* James G., Parable and chreia; from Q to narrative Gospel: ⇥ 304, Semeia 43 (1988) 53-73 (75-84, *Moessner* David P., response, 'What sort of "essence"?') / 85-114 (115-9, *Buss* Martin J., response).

F1.3 **Historicitas,** *chronologia* **Evangeliorum.**

4139 **Blomberg** Craig, The historical reliability of the Gospels 1987 ⇥ 3,3886: ᴿEvQ 60 (1988) 267-9 (J. W. *Drane*); RefTR 47 (1988) 18s (P. *O'Brien*); RExp 85 (1988) 351 (S. M. *Sheeley*).

4140 *Caba* José, Historicity of the Gospels (Dei Verbum 19); genesis and fruits of the conciliar text: ⇥ 380, Vatican II Assessment 1 (1988) 299-320; français, ᵀ*Raymond* L.-B. ⇥ 379, Bilan 1,307-327.

4141 *Carmignac* Jean, La datation des Évangiles; état actuel de la recherche: ⇥ 28*, ꟳCOURTHIAL P., Dieu parle! 1984, 12-22.

4142 *Diprose* Rinaldo, Il quadrivangelo; la questione della sua storicità [ᴱ*Wenham* D., *al.*, Gospel perspectives, 6 vol. 1980-6]: STEv 11,21 (1988) 145-153.

4143 **Dunn** James D. G., The evidence for Jesus 1985 ⇥ 1,3925; 3,3889: ᴿRB 95 (1988) 146s (J. *Murphy-O'Connor*).

4144 *Focant* Camille, La chute de Jérusalem et la datation des évangiles: RTLv 19 (1988) 17-37.

4145 **France** R. T., The evidence for Jesus 1986 ⇥ 3,3926: ᴿGraceTJ 9 (1988) 148s (J. E. *McGoldrick*).

4146 **Grelot** P., Évangiles et histoire 1986 ⇥ 2,3046; 3,3890: ᴿÉTRel 63 (1988) 586s (J. *Zumstein*).

4147 **Grelot** Pierre, Los Evangelios y la historia, ᵀ*Arias* Isidro: Biblioteca Herder, Sagr. Escr. 179. Barc 1987, Herder. 327 p. pt. 1800. 84-254-1567-5. – ᴿActuBbg 25 (1988) 210s (X. *Alegre S.*).

4148 **Grelot** Pierre, Les paroles de Jésus: Intr 3/7, 1986 ⇥ 2,3046; 3,3890: ᴿCBQ 50 (1988) 319-321 (J. S. *Kloppenborg*).

4149 **Grelot** Pierre, Las palabras de Jesucristo, ᵀ*Martínez de Lapera* A. Barc 1988, Herder. 386 p. – ᴿNatGrac 35 (1988) 437s (F. F. *Ramos*).

4150 **Robinson** John A. T., Wann entstand das NT? 1986 ⇥ 2,3051; 3,3897: ᴿColcT 58,4 (1988) 162s (R. *Bartnicki*); ZkT 110 (1988) 205 (K. *Stock*).

4151 **Robinson** John A. T., Re-dater le NT [1976] 1987 ⇥ 3,3898: ᴿActu-Bbg 25 (1988) 217s (X. *Alegre S.*); RTPhil 120 (1988) 96-98 (C. *Riniker*); Téléma 14,55s (1988) 96s (M. *Lafue-Veron*).

F1.4 *Jesus historicus* – **The human Jesus.**

4152 **Artieri** G., *Lombardo* E., Cena con Gesù (Fede e ragione) [72 chapters on the life of Jesus]. Mi 1985, Mondadori. x-389 p.; ill. Lit. 26.500. 88-0025242--9 [NTAbs 32,368].

4153 **Badia** Leonard F., Jesus; introducing his life and teaching 1985
→ 1,3934 ... 3,3903: ᴿCiTom 114 (1987) 371 (J. L. *Espimel*).

4154 **Barbaglio** Giuseppe, Il vissuto spirituale di Gesù di Nazaret: → 810,
StoSp 2 NT (1988) 63-97.

4155 **Borg** M. J., Jesus, a new vision; spirit, culture, and the life of
discipleship. SF 1987, Harper & R. viii-216 p. $17. 0-06-060914-1
[NTAbs 32,368].

4156 *Borg* Marcus J., A renaissance in Jesus studies: TTod 45 (1988) 280-292.

4157 **Bowden** John, Jesus, the unanswered questions. L 1988, SCM. xxi-
259 p. [NBlackf 70,154, J. *Galot*]. 0-334-02099-9.

4158 **Braun** Herbert, Jesus — der Mann aus Nazareth und seine Zeit²
[= ¹1984 → 2,3062 + 12 Kapitel]: Siebenstern 1422. Gü 1988, Mohn.
268 p. 3-579-01422-6.

4159 **Bruce** Frederick F., Gesù visto dai contemporanei: Piccola Biblioteca
Teologica 19. T 1988, Claudiana. viii-204 p. Lit. 18.000.

4160 **Bruggen** J. van, Christus op aarde; zijn levensbeschrijving door
leerlingen en tijdgenoten: CommNT 3/1. Kampen 1987, Kok. 287 p.
90-242-0877-7 [NTAbs 32,247].

4161 *a) Burchard* Christoph, Jesus von Nazareth; – *b) Riches* John K., Die
Synoptiker und ihre Gemeinden: → 3,326, ᴱ**Becker** J., Anfänge 1987,
12-58 / 160-184.

4162 *Carrington* Don, Some NT stories about Jesus which point to a new
style of ministry: Melanesian Journal of Theology 2 (Papua-NG 1986)
125-144 [< TKontext 9/2, 69].

4163 **Coulot** Claude, Jésus et le disciple; étude sur l'autorité messianique de
Jésusᴰ: ÉtBN 8, 1987 → 3,3917: ᴿSBFLA 38 (1988) 493-5 (T. *Chary*).

4164 *Crossan* John Dominic, Materials and methods in historical Jesus
research: Forum 4,34 (1988) 3-24.

4165 *Culpepper* R. H., The humanity of Jesus the Christ; an overview: Faith
& Mission 5,2 (Wake Forest NC 1988) 14-27 [< NTAbs 32,337].

4166 **Cunningham** Philip, Jesus and the evangelists; the ministry of Jesus and
its portrayal in the Synoptic Gospels. NY 1988, Paulist. 240 p. $12 [JBL
108,184]. 0-8091-2928-5.

4167 **Doré** Joseph, Jésus-Christ: Première bibliothèque de connaissances
religieuses. P 1987, Mame. 79 p. – ᴿRICathP 25 (1988) 74 (C. *Perrot*).

4168 **Dumbauld** E., Sayings of Jesus [RSV, under 141 captions alpha-
betically]. Lanham MD 1988 = 1967, UPA. 196 p. $10.75. 0-8191-
6753-3 [NTAbs 32,371].

4169 *Evans* Craig A., *a*) The historical Jesus and Christian faith; a critical
assessment of a scholarly problem: ChrSchR 18,1 (1988) 48-64 [< ZIT
89,72]; – *b*) Jesus of Nazareth; who do scholars say that he is? A review
article [10 books]: Crux 23,4 (1987) 15-19 [NTAbs 32,151].

4170 **Fallon** Michael, Who is Jesus? 1987 → 3,3924: ᴿAustralasCR 65
(1988) 243s (B. *Lucas*).

4171 **Floris** Ennio, Sous le Christ, Jésus; méthode d'analyse référentielle
appliquée aux évangiles. P 1987, Flammarion. 321 p. F 120. 2-08-
064865-9. – ᴿArchScSocRel 65 (1988) 264s (J.-D. *Dubois*) [RHE 83, 380*];
ÉTRel 63 (1988) 119-121 (M. *Carrez*).

4172 **Goergen** Donald J., The mission and ministry / death and resurrection
of Jesus: A theology of Jesus 1s, 1986s → 3,3078; also Dublin, Gill &
M., £10 each: ᴿEvQ 60 (1988) 84s (J. B. *Green*); Furrow 39 (1988) 805s
(G. *Daly*); SpTod 40 (1988) 181s (D. A. *Helminiak,* 1).

4173 *González* Faus J.I., La 'filosofía de la vida' de Jesús de Nazaret: RLatAmT 5,13 (1988) 33-44 [< NTAbs 32,296].

4174 *Grad* Hermann J., The humanity of Christ as seen by Indian theologians: Diwa (Philippines 1987) 119-155 [< TKontext 9/2,58].

4175 **Hamaide** Jacques, Jésus de Nazareth, que dis-tu de toi-même?: Maranatha 13. P/Montréal 1988, Médiaspaul/Paulines. 188 p. F 69. – REsprVie 98 (1988) 675 (P. *Jay*).

4176 EHarrell Irene B., *Benson* Alie Harrell, This man Jesus. GR 1988, Zondervan. 215 p. [GraceTJ 9,307].

4177 **Igartua** José M., El Mesías, Jesús de Nazaret 1986 → 3,3931: REstE 63 (1988) 511s (G. *Higuera*).

4178 *Kocher* Michel, Jésus communicateur; essai sur la figure du communicateur chrétien: Hokhma 33 (1986) 63-80.

4179 **Kroll** Gerhard, Auf den Spuren Jesu[10] [[1]1964; [8]1980 → 61,t804]. Lp 1988, St. Benno. 470 p.; ill.; maps. 3-7462-0050-4.

4180 **Kudasiewicz** Józef, ☉ Jezus historii a Chrystus wiary [→ 3,3936]: Jak rozumiec Pismo święte 3. Lublin 1987, KUL. 184 p. – RTR 84 (1988) 204s (S. *Rabiej*).

4181 **Kümmel** W. G., Jesusforschung seit 1981; 1. Forschungsgeschichte, Methodenfragen: TRu 53 (1988) 229-249.

4182 **Leivestad** Ragnar, Jesus in his own perspective; an examination of his sayings, actions, and eschatological titles 1987 → 3,3938: RAnglTR 70 (1988) 270-2 (R. B. *Richard*); JPseud 2 (1988) 122s (J. *VanderKam*: p. 162 Son of Man 'is an expression that Jesus did not regard himself to be a person of any importance').

4183 **McGrath** Alister E., Understanding Jesus; who Jesus Christ is and why he matters. GR 1987, Zondervan. 184 p. $13 [TDig 35,76].

4184 *McGuckin* John A., Jesus' self-designation as a prophet: ScripB 19,1 (1988s) 2-11.

4185 *Malina* Bruce J., Patron and client; the analogy behind synoptic theology [as commonly presented, in terms of the Mediterranean world of that time; the big Patron allows lower-level groups to act as mediator with him; Jesus sets up such a group (for God the Father), and thus enters into conflict with rivals in the same profession; after he dies, his person-centered faction is transformed into a group-centered faction with features of its own]: Forum 4,1 (1988) 2-32.

4186 **Marcel** Pierre, Face à la critique, Jésus et les apôtres 1986 → 3,3941: RÉTRel 63 (1988) 144s (J. *Ansaldi*).

4187 **Martín Descalzo** José Luis, Vida y mistério de Jesús de Nazaret [1.1986 → 2,3088; 2. 1987 → 3,3942] 3. La cruz y la gloria: Nueva Alianza 105. Salamanca 1987, Sígueme. 449 p. – RBibFe 14 (1988) 325; LumenVr 37 (1988) 187s (F. *Ortiz de Urtaran*); ScripTPamp 19 (1987) 984s (L. F. *Mateo Seco,* 1).

4188 **Mataji** Vandana, Jesus the Christ; who is he? What was his message? Anand 1987, Gujarat-SP. xv-60 p. $3.50. – RIndTSt 25 (1988) 393 (L. *Legrand*).

4189 **Mendelssohn** Harald von, Jesus — Rebell oder Erlöser? Die Geschichte des frühen Christentums: dtv-Tb 10722. Mü 1987=1981 (→ 62,4162). 319 p. DM 12,80. – RBiKi 42 (1987) 189s (P.-G. *Müller*).

4190 *Moloney* Francis J., Jesus Christ; the question to cultures: Pacifica 1,1 (Melbourne 1988) 15-43 [< ZIT 89,309].

4191 *Navone* John, Communicating Christ as a friend; the Church's laws express the demands of friendship: HomP 88,1 (1987s) 48-54.

4192 **O'Collins** Gerald, Para interpretar a Jesús [1983 ➤ 64,3949], ᵀ*Santidrián* Pedro R.: Teología y Pastoral B. M 1986, Paulinas. 261 p. 84-285-1086-5. – ᴿActuBbg 25 (1988) 97 (X. *Alegre* S.); SalT 75 (1987) 416s (J. A. *Garcia*).

4193 *a*) O'Grady John F., Jesus and history; the virginal conception and Resurrection; – *b*) *Kodell* Jerome, The Gospels as theological reflection: ChSt 26 (1987) 259-271 / 243-258.

4194 **Palucki** Jerzy, ❷ Chrystus boski lekarz ... Christ divine doctor, educator and teacher in the writings of CLEMENT of Alexandria: diss. ᴰ*Drączkowski* F. Lublin 1988. xxii-268 p. – RTLv 20,548.

4195 **Pelikan** J., Jesus through the centuries 1985 ➤ 1,3975...3,3950: ᴿJAAR 56 (1988) 349s (J. W. *O'Malley*).

4196 **Pelikan** Jaroslav, Gesù nella storia, pref. *Quinzio* Sergio. R 1987, Laterza. xix-306 p. Lit. 36.000. – ᴿCC 139 (1988,3) 436s (C. *Capizzi*: ignora 7 cattolici; incertezze teologiche); HumBr 43 (1988) 867-875 (B. *Bertoli*).

4197 **Pelikan** Jaroslav, Jezus door de eeuwen heen; zijn plats in de cultuurgeschiedenis. Kampen/Kapellen 1987, Kok/DNB-Pelckmans. 286 p. Fb 795. 90-242-7571-7 / 90-289-1194-4. – ᴿCollatVL 18 (1988) 122 (E. Vanden *Berghe*); Streven 55 (1987s) 858s (P. *Beentjes*); TsTNijm 28 (1988) 312 (L. *Goosen*).

4198 *Pesce* M., Some aspects of the prophetic role of Jesus: Sidic 20,3 (R 1987) 5-12.

4199 **Riesner** Rainer, Jesus als Lehrer² 1984 ➤ (62,4080) ... 2,3037: ᴿSBFLA 38 (1988) 498-503 (F. *Manns*).

4200 **Rovella** Giuseppe, Vita di Gesù; pref. *Ronfani* Ugo. Mi 1987, Prospettive d'Arte. 194 p. Lit. 15.000. – ᴿCC 139 (1988,2) 98s (G. *Giachi*: riflessioni di un filosofo); Orpheus 9 (1988) 384s (Amalia *Tuccillo*: scritta 30 anni fa).

4203 **Ruckstuhl** Eugen, Jesus im Horizont der Evangelien: Biblische Aufsatzbände 3. Stu 1988, KBW. 410 p. 3-460-06031-X. 12 art.; 3 infra.

4204 *Sabourin* Léopold, Il enseignait avec autorité: StMiss 36 ('Spiritual masters; Christianity and other religions' 1987) 25-63.

4205 **Schillebeeckx** Edward, Jesus in our western culture (1986 Amsterdam Free Univ. lectures) 1987 ➤ 3,3959: ᴿDoctLife 37 (1987) 486-8 (D. *Carroll*).

4206 **Schillebeeckx** Edward, Jesús en nuestra cultura; mística, ética y política [Amst 1986], ᵀ*López* Ambrosio: Pedal 191. Salamanca 1987, Sígueme. 105 p. – ᴿLumenVr 37 (1988) 337 (F. *Ortiz de Urtaran*).

4207 *a*) *Schmithals* Walter, Il Gesù storico, l'apocalittica e gli inizi della Cristologia, ᵀ*Coppellotti* F.; – *b*) *Jüngel* Eberhard, La rilevanza dogmatica del problema del Gesù storico, ᵀ*Russo* Giovanni; – *c*) *Grässer* Erich, Il problema del Gesù storico nella ricerca odierna in Germania, ᵀ*Russo*: ➤ 495*, Gesù storico 1985/8, 37-64 / 161-185 / 187-204.

4208 **Schweitzer** A., Storia della ricerca della vita di Gesù 1986 ➤ 2,3103; 3,3960: ᴿAsprenas 35 (1988) 273-6 (A. *Rolla*); Humanitas 42 (1987) 615s (U. *Regina*); Protestantesimo 43 (1988) 118s (V. *Subilia*); StPatav 35 (1988) 705-7 (G. *Leonardi*).

Schweizer Eduard, Jesus Christ the man from Nazareth and the exalted Lord 1986 ➤ 8544.

4210 **Segundo** Juan Luis, Jésus devant la conscience moderne, l'histoire perdue, ᵀ*Guibal* Francis (abrégée): CogF 148. P c. 1988, Cerf. 400 p. F 239. – ᴿÉtudes 369 (1988) 427s (R. *Marlé*).

Segundo J. L., The historical Jesus of the Synoptics 1985 ➤ 8563.

4211 **Séverin** Gérard & Marie, Le Christ en direct; les quatre évangiles: Origines. P 1987, Ouvrières. 656 p. – [R]EsprVie 98 (1988) 526 (L. *Walter*: pas des meilleurs dans son genre).

4212 **Shea** John, The spirit master. Ch 1987, T. More. 249 p. $15. [R]NewTR 1,2 (1988) 97s (F. G. *Hang*).

4213 **Sloyan** Gerard S., The Jesus tradition; images of Jesus in the West 1986 → 2,3106; 3,3965: [R]AnglTR 69 (1987) 89-91 (D. F. *Winslow*); RRel 46 (1987) 305 (J. P. *Gaffney*).

4214 **Stuhlmacher** Peter, Jesus von Nazareth — Christus des Glaubens. Stu 1988, Calwer. 107 p. DM 16,80. 3-7668-0869-9. – [R]ActuBbg 25 (1988) 233 (J. *Boada*); TLZ 113 (1988) 821-3 (E. *Schweizer*).

4214* *Teklak* Czesław, ❷ Do contemporary Russian religious sciences accept the historical existence of Jesus of Nazareth? [yes, cautiously, since 1980]: ZeKUL 30,1 (1987) 3-27; Eng. 27.

4215 **Theissen** Gerd, Der Schatten des Galiläers 1986 → 2,3109; 3,3968: [R]ActuBbg 25 (1988) 76 (X. *Alegre S.*); BiKi 43 (1988) 87s (M. *Helsper*: gelungenes Beispiel narrativer Theologie); KIsr 3 (1988) 212 (Julie *Kirchberg*).

4216 **Theissen** Gerd, The shadow of the Galilean 1987 → 3,3969: [R]CBQ 50 (1988) 548s (J. H. *Neyrey*: culturally misleading); ComSev 21 (1988) 255 (M. de *Burgos*); NBlackf 69 (1988) 410-2 (R. J. *Taylor*); Streven 56 (1988s) 82 (J. Van *Gerwen*); TLond 91 (1988) 146-8 (C. J. A. *Hickling*: 'quest of the historical Jesus' is only a part).

4217 **Theissen** Gerd, La sombra del Galileo; las investigaciones históricas sobre Jesús traducidas a un relato, [T]*Ruiz Garrido* Constantino. Salamanca 1988, Sígueme. 272 p. 84-301-1061-5 [Carthaginensia 5,336, R. *Sanz Valdivieso*].

4218 **Thompson** W. M., The Jesus debate 1985 → 1,3989* ... 3,3970: [R]CiTom 114 (1987) 383s (J. L. *Espinel*).

4219 **Toy** John, Jesus, man for God. Ox 1988, Mowbray. viii-144 p. £5 [JTS 40,365].

F1.5 *Jesus et Israel* - **Jesus the Jew.**

4220 **Aus** Roger D., [Mt 1s] Weihnachtsgeschichte — [Lk 10,33] Barmherziger Samariter — [Lk 15,11s] Verlorener Sohn: Studien zu ihrem jüdischen Hintergrund: ArbNTZ 2. B 1988, Inst. Kirche und Judentum. 189 p. DM 19,80 [JBL 108,377].

4221 [E]**Berg** M. Van den, *al.*, Uit de sjoel geklapt; christelijke belangstelling voor de joodse traditie: Excelsior Deo Iuvante 23e lustrum. Hilversum 1986, Gooi & S. 222 p. 90-304-0354-3. – [R]Bijdragen 49 (1988) 446 (T. C. de *Kruijf*).

4222 *Berger* Klaus, Jesus als Pharisäer und frühe Christen als Pharisäer: NT 30 (1988) 231-262.

4223 *Brockway* Allan R., Learning Christology through dialogue with Jews: JEcuSt 25 (1988) 347-357.

4224 **Callan** Terrence, Forgetting the root 1986 → 2,3124; 3,3978: [R]JEcuSt 25 (1988) 107 (S. N. *Rosenbaum*); JStJud 19 (1988) 95s (F. *García Martínez*); RÉJ 146 (1987) 170-2 (Madeleine *Petit*); Vidyajyoti 52 (1988) 608 (P. *Meagher*).

4225 **Charlesworth** James H., Jesus within Judaism (Edinburgh 1985 Gunning Lecture): new light from exciting archaeological discoveries: Anchor Bible

Reference Library. NY 1988, Doubleday. xvi-265 p.; 21 fig.; 3 maps. [JBL 108,182 adv.]. 0-385-23610-7.

4226 **Charlier** Jean-Pierre, Jésus au milieu de son peuple: Lire la Bible 78, 1987 → 3,3979]: ᴿEsprVie 98 (1988) 205 (L. *Walter*).

4227 **Chilton** Bruce, A Galilaean rabbi ... Isaiah 1984 → 65,3597 ... 3,3980: ᴿHeythJ 20 (1988) 247s (J. D. M. *Derrett*).

4228 *Chilton* Bruce D., Jesus and the repentance [both attributed and experienced, with deliberate Pauline ambiguity] of E. P. SANDERS [Jesus and Judaism 1985 ...]: TyndaleB 39 (1988) 1-18.

4229 **Chouraqui** André, Jésus et Paul, fils d'Israël. Aubonne 1988, Moulin. 92 p. – ᴿProtestantesimo 43 (1988) 222s (G. *Conte*).

4230 *Daoust* J., Jésus et les synagogues de Galilée [< MondeB 50 (1987)]: EsprVie 98 (1988) 114-6.

4231 **Dommershausen** Werner, Die Umwelt Jesu; Politik und Kultur in neutestamentlicher Zeit; Theol. Sem. FrB 1987, Herder. 136 p. – ᴿColcT 58,2 (1988) 179 (J. W. *Rosłon*).

4232 **Dubourg** Bernard, L'invention de Jésus, I. L'hébreu du NT: L'infini 1987 → 3,3985: ᴿÉtudes 368 (1988) 113-6 (J.-L. *Schlegel*: hallucinations exégétiques).

4233 **Duvernoy** Claude, Scandaleux Jésus. Maurepas 1984, Action Chrétienne pour Israël. 144 p. [KirSef 61,397].

4234 *Ehrlich* Ernst L., Jesus in der Sicht des Judentums: BiKi 43 (1988) 38-40.

4235 *Feneberg* Rupert, Abba – Vater; eine notwendige Besinnung: KIsr 3 (1988) 41-52.

4236 *Flusser* David, (57) Thesen zur Entstehung des Christentums aus dem Judaismus: KIsr 1 (1986) 62-70 [3 (1988) 179-189, *Theissen* Gerd, Reaktion].

4237 **Flusser** David, [→ 190-192] Jewish sources in early Christianity. NY 1987, Adama. 89 p.; ill. $20 [RelStR 15,365, R. B. *Vinson*: misrepresents his opinions as scholarly consensus].

4238 **Freyne** Sean, Galilee, Jesus and the Gospels; literary approaches and historical investigations. Dublin 1988, Gill & M. viii-311 p.; map. £11. 0-7171-1601-8.

4239 *Galot* Jean, Révélation du Christ et liturgie juive: EsprVie 98 (1988) 145-152.

4240 **Guevara Castillo** Hernando, El ambiente político del pueblo judío en tiempos de Jesús: Academia Christiana 30, 1985 → 2,9564; 84-7057-384-5: ᴿActuBbg 25 (1988) 211s (X. *Alegre S.*).

4241 **Hagner** Donald A., The Jewish reclamation of Jesus 1984 → 65,3605 ... 3,3991: ᴿJudaica 44 (1988) 56s (S. *Schreiner*).

4242 *Hahn* Ferdinand, Die Verwürzelung des Christentums im Judentum: KerDo 34 (1988) 193-208; Eng. 209.

4243 **Hilton** Michael, (*Marshall* Gordian), The Gospels and rabbinic Judaism; a study guide. Hoboken/L 1988, KTAV/SCM. 169 p. $10 [TS 50,411]. 0-334-02021-2. – ᴿFurrow 39 (1988) 737s (P. *Briscoe*); Month 249 (1988) 1021s (N. *King*).

4244 **Horsley** Richard A., Jesus and the spiral of violence; popular Jewish resistance in Roman Palestine 1987 → 3,3995: ᴿAnglTR 69 (1987) 392-4 (D. J. *Harrington*); BibTB 18 (1988) 114.116 (K. C. *Hanson*); BR 4,3 (1988) 4 (D. *Rhoads*); TS 49 (1988) 732-4 (J. *Topel*: 'burkes' Jesus' question); TTod 45 (1988s) 499-501 (B. G. *Wright*).

4245 *a)* **Horsley** Richard, [→ d478] Bandits, Messiahs, and longshoremen; popular unrest in Galilee around the time of Jesus; – *b)* *Saldarini* Anthony J., Political and social roles of the Pharisees and Scribes in Galilee; – c) *Edwards* Douglas R., First century urban/rural relations in lower Galilee; exploring the archaeological and literary evidence; – d) *Overman* J. Andrew, Who were the first urban Christians? Urbanization in Galilee in the first century; – e) *Wink* Walter, Neither passivity nor violence; Jesus' third way: ➤ 500, SBL Seminars 1988, 183-199 / 200-9 / 169-182 / 160-8 / 210-224.

4246 *Hyldahl* Niels, E.P. SANDERS' Jesusbog: DanTTs 51 (1988) 104-111 [< ZIT 88,512].

4247 *Imbach* Joseph, A chi appartiene Gesù? L'uomo di Nazaret nell'ebraismo contemporaneo: MiscFranc 88 (1988) 265-276.

4248 **Kippenberg** Hans G., *Wewers* Gerd A., Testi giudaici per lo studio del Nuovo Testamento [1979 ➤ 61,b472], TE *Firpo* G. NT sup 8. Brescia 1987, Paideia. 343 p. Lit. 30.000. 88-394-0400-7. – RAntonianum 63 (1988) 608s (M. *Nobile*); ParVi 33 (1988) 234s (Anna *Passoni dell'Acqua*).

4249 *Krotz* Fritz, Die Juden im Neuen Testament: Forum Religion (Stu 1988,1) 24-30 [< ZIT].

4249* **Lapide** Pinchas, Warum kommt er nicht? Jüdische Evangelienauslegung: Siebenstern 1421. Gü 1988, Mohn. 122 p. 3-579-01421-8.

4250 **Lee** Bernard J., The Galilean Jewishness of Jesus; retrieving the Jewish origins of Christianity: Conversation on the road not taken 1; StJudChr. NY 1988, Paulist. vi-158 p. $8 pa. 0-8091-3021-1 [RelStR 15,263, P.J. *Hass*].

4251 *Lentzen-Deis* Fritzleo, Esegesi della Bibbia oggi [sviluppo sul metodo esegetico]: RivScRel 1 (Molfetta 1987) 347-359 [➤ 3,1604; 'eredità giudaica di Gesù': *Sardini* F., BbbOr 30 (1988) 127s].

4252 **Lohfink** Norbert, Das Jüdische am Christentum 1987 ➤ 3,4003: RBiKi 42 (1987) 137s (M. *Helsper*); BL (1988) 137 (J. *Ashton*: title misleading); Carthaginensia 4 (1988) 372 (R. *Sanz Valdivieso*); CBQ 50 (1988) 537s (J.T. *Pawlikowski*); ColcT 58,4 (1988) 170-4 (J.W. *Roston*); EvKomm 21 (1988) 479s (Carola *Enke*); FreibZ 35 (1988) 266s (A. *Schenker*); TPQ 136 (1988) 284s (H. *Wurz*); TR 84 (1988) 187s (C. *Thoma*); TsTNijm 28 (1988) 181 (W. *Weren*); ZkT 110 (1988) 347s (M. *Hasitschka*).

4253 **Mateos** Juan, *Camacho* Fernando, El horizonte humano; la propuesta de Jesús: En torno al Nuevo Testamento 2. Córdoba 1988, Almendro. 200 p. 84-86077-61-3.

4254 **Mussner** Franz, Die Kraft der Wurzel 1987 ➤ 3,4010; 3-451-20954-3: RColcT 58,4 (1988) 174-7 (J.W. *Roston*); ErbAuf 64 (1988) 487s (J. *Kaffanke*); Judaica 44 (1988) 60s (T. *Willi*); SNTU-A 13 (1988) 223-7 (L. *Oberlinner*); StiZt 206 (1988) 213 (W. *Feneberg*); TsTNijm 28 (1988) 82 (W. *Weren*); ZkT 110 (1988) 213s (M. *Hasitschka*); ZMissRW 72 (1988) 315s (J. *Kuhl*).

4255 **Neusner** Jacob, Christian faith and the Bible of Judaism; the Judaic encounter with Scripture. GR 1987, Eerdmans. xviii-205 p. $13. 0-8028-0278-8. – RVidyajyoti 52 (1988) 607 (P.M. *Meagher*).

4256 **Neusner** J., Judaism in the beginning of Christianity 1984 ➤ 65,3615 ... 3,4012: RHeythJ 29 (1988) 243s (Margaret *Barker*).

4257 **Neusner** Jacob, Le judaïsme à l'aube du christianisme 1986 ➤ 2,3145; 3,4013: RBLitEc 89 (1988) 292s (S. *Légasse*); CC 130 (1988,4) 610s (S. *Katunarich*); FoiTemps 19 (1987) 364 (C. *Focant*); ScEspr 40 (1988) 124s (R. *David*).

4258 **Neusner** J., Judentum in frühchristlicher Zeit, T. Stu 1988, Calwer, 119 p. DM 24,80 [RHE 83,446*]. 3-7668-0775-7.

4259 **Neusner** Jacob, De joodse wieg van het christendom [Judaism in the beginning of Christianity 1984], [T]. Haag 1987, Boekencentrum. 119 p. f 19,80. 90-242-0791-6. – [R]NedTTs 42 (1988) 263s (P. W. van der *Horst*); TsTNijm 28 (1988) 181 (W. *Weren*).

4260 **Neusner** Jacob, Judaism and Christianity in the age of Constantine; history, Messiah, Israel and the initial confrontation 1987 → 3,4011: [R]ChH 57 (1988) 520-2 (G. T. *Armstrong*); Horizons 15 (1988) 388s (J. S. *Siker*); JAAR 56 (1988) 810-2 (C. T. Mc *Cullough*); JStJud 19 (1988) 252s (G. *Stemberger*); TS 49 (1988) 576s (R. A. *Wild*).

4261 *a*) *Pesce* Mauro, Un convegno sulla permanente eredità giudaica nel cristianesimo; temi, problemi e limiti; – *b*) *Sacchi* Paolo, L'eredità giudaica nel cristianesimo: → 570, Cristianesimo e giudaismo 1987 = AugR 28 (1988) 7-21 / 23-50.

4262 *a*) *Pesce* M., Le prophétisme de Jésus; – *b*) *Stawsky* D., La prophétie avant et après le Second Temple: Sidic 30,3 (R 1987) 5-13 / 14-21.

4263 **Robillard** Edmond, Nos racines chrétiennes dans l'historie d'Israël et du monde méditerranéen 1985 → 1,b330: [R]ÉglT 18 (1987) 355s (L. *Laberge*).

4264 **Ronai** Alexander, *Wahle* Hedwig, Das Evangelium — ein jüdisches Buch? 1986 → 2,3147; 3,4016: [R]JEcuSt 25 (1988) 630s (F. L. *Horton*).

4265 **Rosenberg** R. A., rabbi, Who was Jesus? Lanham MD 1986, UPA. 123 p. – [R]EstBíb 46 (1988) 409s (R. *Aguirre*).

4265* **Rowland** Christopher, Christian origins; from messianic movement to Christian religion 1985 → 2,3148; 3,4017: [R]BR 4,1 (1988) 7s (J. J. *Collins*); PerspRelSt 15 (1988) 283-6 (D. B. *Gowler*).

4266 **Russell** D. S., From early Judasim to early Church 1986 → 2,3149 ... 3,4018: [R]JEcuSt 25 (1988) 628s (R. S. *Kraemer*).

 Saldarini Anthony J., Pharisees, scribes and Sadducees in Palestinian society; a sociological approach 1988 → h410*.

4267 **Sanders** E. P., Jesus and Judaism 1985 → 1,4028 ... 3,4019: [R]AmHR 92 (1987) 935s (H. C. *Kee*).

4268 **Schelkle** Karl H., Israel im NT 1985 → 1,4029: [R]Judaica 43 (1987) 59s (S. *Schreiner*).

4269 *Schnelle* Udo, Jesus, ein Jude aus Galiläa: BZ 32 (1988) 107-113.

4270 *Schwartz* G. David, Is there a Jewish reclamation of Jesus?: JEcuSt 24 (1987) 104-8.

4271 **Spong** J. S. (episcopal bishop), The Hebrew Lord[2rev] [... personal struggle to translate the power of Jesus into categories of our day]. SF 1988, Harper & R. xvi-192 p.; 9 fig. $9 pa. 0-06-254806-9 [NTAbs 32,387].

4272 *Stegner* William R., The ancient Jewish synagogue homily: → 287, [E]*Aune* D., Greco-Roman 1988, 51-69.

4273 **Swidler** L., Yeshua, a model for moderns. KC 1988, Sheed & W. 134 p. $9 [TS 49,793].

4274 *Ullendorff* Edward, Jesus in the Hebrew Bible? [or rather in a Jewish calendar for 1987/8 with Ethiopian biblical drawings, English and Hebrew captions in sharp contrast with the Amharic text and the actual picture; *distinct* from this is a 90-page booklet in Hebrew and Amharic called 'The Messiah of Israel']: JJS 39 (1988) 269-272.

 Van Buren Paul M., Christ in context 1988 → 8555; in, A theology of the Jewish-Christian reality [I-II, 1980/3 → 8436].

4275 *Vermes* Geza, Jesus the Jew; Christian and Jewish reactions: TorJT 4 (1988) 112-123.

4276 *Vermes* Geza, La religione di Gesù l'Ebreo, [T]*Costa* Eugenio: → 495*, Gesù storico 1985/8, 19-35.

4277 **Winogradsky** Alexandre A., Paroles d'Évangile, mémorial d'Israël, préf. *Dubois* Marcel-J.: Radio Notre-âme. P 1987, Fayard. 233 p. F 85. – REsprVie 98 (1988) 256 (L. *Monloubou*: fantaisiste).

4278 **Zeitlin** Irving M., Jesus and the Judaism of his time. C/NY 1988, Polity/Blackwell. viii-204 p. $25. 0-7456-0448-X [TDig 36,194].

4279 **Delitzsch** Franz, Die vier Evangelien ins Hebräische übersetzt (1877-1890-1902) [E*Carmignac* J. 1-3 → 63,4086 ... 2,3159]: Traductions hébraïques des Évangiles 4. Turnhout 1984, Brepols. lxiv-206/206 p. Fb 1400. – RRB 95 (1988) 145 (É. *Puech*).

4280 The New Covenant, commonly called the New Testament; Peshitta Aramaic text with a Hebrew translation: Aramaic Scriptures Research Society in Israel. J 1986, The Bible Society. v-383 p.

F1.6   *Jesus in Ecclesia* – **The Church Jesus.**

4281 **Barron** Bruce, The health and wealth gospel [... also called 'the Faith Teaching Movement': Oral *Roberts* ...]; what's going on today in a movement that has shaped the faith of millions? DG c. 1987, InterVarsity. 204 p. $7. – RThemelios 14 (1988s) 79 (A. *Barbosa da Silva*: very significant).

4283 **Baxter** Margaret, [→ 4120] New Testament introduction, I. Jesus Christ, his life and his Church: TEF Study Guide 24. L 1987, SPCK. x-144 p.; ill.; 2 maps. 0-381-04315-9 [NTAbs 32,230].

4284 **Betz** Georg, *a)* Verehren wir den falschen Gott? Einspruch gegen die Verharmlosung der Sache Jesu. – *b)* Klartext; zur Sache Jesu ohne Wenn und Aber. FrB 1987, Christophorus. je 160 p. DM 19,80. – RBiKi 43 (1988) 32s (F. *Porsche*).

4285 **Durrleman** Freddy [1881-1944, fondateur de La Cause, mort en prison], Jésus et le Christianisme, E*Bauberot* J. Carrières-sous-Poissy 1987, La Cause. iii-449 p. – RÉTRel 63 (1988) 140s (A. *Gounelle*); RHPR 68 (1988) 495s (E. *Frank*); RTPhil 120 (1988) 489 (B. *Reymond*).

4286 **Ellul** Jacques, The subversion of Christianity 1986 → 3,4032: RGraceTJ 9 (1988) 152s (R. M. *Rogers*).

4287 **Ellul** J., Subversief christendom. Kampen/Kapellen 1987, Kok/Pelckmans. 251 p. – RCollatVL 18 (1988) 394 (E. Vanden *Berghe*).

4288 *Holtz* Traugott, Jesus: → 798, EvKL 2 (1988) 824-831.

4289 **Lohaus** Gerd, Die Geheimnisse des Lebens・Jesu in der Summa (AQUINAS D1984) 1985 → 1,4048*; 3,4033: RTPQ 136 (1988) 92 (R. *Schulte*).

4290 **Manaranche** A., Un amour nommé Jesus: Lumière Vérité 1986 → 3,4035: RNRT 110 (1988) 443 (A. *Toubeau*).

4291 **Marzola** O., Gesù Cristo centro vivo della fede — dall'esperienza religiosa all'annunzio cristiano [diss.]. R 1986, Pont. Univ. Lateranense. xvi-388 p. – RDivThom 91 (1988) 201-6 (L. *Iammarrone*).

4292 **Moreland** J. P., Scaling the secular city; a defense of Christianity. GR 1987, Baker. 267 p. $13 pa. – RCalvinT 23 (1988) 273-7 (J. W. *Cooper*).

4293 **Nolan** Albert, Jesus before Christianity. Maryknoll NY 1985 = 1978 (→ 58,6039; franç 1,4050), Orbis. 156 p. $9. 0-88344-230-2. – RVidyajyoti 52 (1988) 610s (P. M. *Meagher*).

4294 **Segundo** J. L., The Christ of the Ignatian Exercises 1987 → 3,4039: RTS 49 (1988) 578s (A. T. *Hennelly*).

4295 **Sesboüé** Bernard,   Gesù Cristo nella tradizione della Chiesa.   Alba 1987, Paoline.   343 p. Lit. 16.000. – RHumBr 43 (1988) 136 (G. *Cittadini*).

4296 **Thurmer** John,   The Son in the Bible and the Church.   Exeter 1987, Paternoster.   103 p. £5.   0-855364-449-7. – RVidyajyoti 52 (1988) 612 (P. M. *Meagher*).

F1.7   *Jesus 'anormalis':* to atheists, psychoanalysts, romance ...

4297 *Albert* John,   The Christ of Oscar WILDE: AmBenR 39 (1988) 372-403.

4298 **Arnaldez** Roger,   Jésus dans la pensée musulmane: JJC 32,   P 1988, Desclée.   281 p. – RIslamochristiana 14 (1988) 315-7 (M. *Borrmans*).

4299 **Buddhadasa** V.,   Un bouddhiste dit le christianisme aux bouddhistes... thaï: JJC 31.   P 1987, Desclée.   214 p. – RBSecrNChr 23 (1988) 178-181 (F. *Tollu*).

4300 **Castelli** Ferdinando,   Volti di Gesù nella letteratura moderna 1987 → 3,4048:   RHumBr 43 (1988) 153s (G. *Penati*).

4301 **Chalfoun** Khalil,   La figure de Jésus-Christ dans la vie et l'œuvre de Khalil GIBRAN (1883-1931): diss. Inst. Cath. & Sorbonne, DHayek M.   P 1987. 792 p. – RTLv 19,546.

4302 **Chenu** Bruno,   Le Christ noir américain: JJC 21,   1984 → 1,4067: RÉTRel 63 (1988) 307s (H. *Mottu*).

4303 **Cragg** Kenneth,   Jesus and the Muslim 1985 → 2,3812; 3,4051:   RJAAR 56 (1988) 138s (F. M. *Denny*); JEcuSt 24 (1987) 449 (M. M. *Ayoub*).

4304 *Crossan* John D.,   The hermeneutical Jesus: → 3,356, Backgrounds 1987, 15-27 [< JBL 108,174].

4305 **Dart** John,   The Jesus of heresy and history; the discovery and meaning of the Nag Hammadi Gnostic library.   SF 1988, Harper & R.   xx-204 p. $19; pa. $11 [CBQ 51,399; TTod 45,504 adv. '512 p.'].

4306 **Downing** F. Gerald,   Christ and the Cynics; Jesus and other radical preachers in first-century tradition: JStOT Manuals 4.   Sheffield 1988, Univ. xiii-232 p.   1-85075-150-1.

4307 **Ellul** Jacques,   Jesus and Marx, from gospel to ideology, THanks Joyce M.   GR 1988, Eerdmans.   xvi-187 p. $13 pa. [CBQ 51,400].

4308 **Epalza** Mikel de,   Jésus otage 1987 → 3,4055: RBAsEspOr 24 (1988) 482s (F. *Valderrama Martínez*); Islamochristiana 14 (1988) 327s (J. M. *Gaudeul*).

4309 **Füssel** Kuno,   Drei Tage mit Jesus im Tempel; Einführung in die materialistische Lektüre der Bibel für Religionsunterricht ...   Münster 1987, Liberación. DM 34,80. – RBiKi 43 (1988) 183s (M. *Helsper*).

4310 **Grönbold** Günter,   Jesus in Indien; das Ende einer Legende 1985 → 1,4080; 2,3186:   ROLZ 83 (1988) 714-6 (N. *Klatt*).

4311 **Hassnain** Fida, *Levi* Dahan,   The fifth gospel. Srinagar 1988, Dastqir. xvi-320 p.; ill.

4312 **Helms** Randel,   Gospel fictions.   Buffalo 1988, Prometheus.   154 p. $22 [TS 50,411].

4314 **Jaschke** Helmut,   Psychotherapie aus dem Neuen Testament; heilende Begegnungen mit Jesus: Bücherei 1347.   FrB 1987, Herder.   160 p. DM 9,80. – RTPQ 136 (1988) 289 (O. B. *Knoch*); ZkT 110 (1988) 210 (M. *Hasitschka*).

4315 *Joos* André,   Il Cristo di DOSTOEVSKIJ nell'esperienza cristiana russa: RasT 29 (1988) 539-557.

4316 *a) Kasper* Walter, Tiefenpsychologische Umdeutung des Christentums?: – *b) Furger* Franz, Psychoanalyse und christliche Ethik; zur Auseinandersetzung mit Eugen DREWERMANN aus moraltheologischer Sicht; – *c) Bürkle* Horst, Das Christentum — eine missverstandene Religion?: ➤ 305, Tiefenpsychologische 1988, 9-25 / 67-80 / 115-132.

4317 **Kelsey** Morton, Christianity as psychology; the healing power of the Christian message 1986 ➤ 3,4060; 0-8066-2194-X: ᴿCurrTM 15 (1988) 279s (P. R. *Swanson*); JPsy&T 15 (1987) 82 (C. R. *Wells*).

4318 **Kreeft** Peter, Socrates meets Jesus; history's great questioner confronts the claims of Christ. DG 1987, InterVarsity. 182 p. $7. 0-87784-999-4. – ᴿRExp 85 (1988) 734s (D. R. *Stiver*: witty, though Socrates often confronts rather a modern liberal divinity school).

4319 *Lermen* Birgit, Das Bild Jesu in der Gegenwartsliteratur: TGegw 30 (1987) 73-88.

4320 **McCarthy** Vincent A., Quest for a philosophical Jesus 1986 ➤ 2,3192; 3,4066: ᴿETL 64 (1988) 216s (E. *Brito*); JAAR 56 (1988) 595-7 (G. E. *Michalson*),

4321 **McGloin** Joseph T., The way *I* see him; a writer's look at Jesus. NY 1986, Alba. xiv-212 p. $7. 0-8189-0498-4. – ᴿVidyajyoti 52 (1988) 611s (R. J. *Raja*: US journalese).

4322 *Meyer* William E. H.ᴶ, Jesus in hypervisual American literature: Listening 23,1 (Oak Park 1988) 25-48 [< ZIT].

4323 *Miller* J. W., Jesus' 'Age Thirty Transition'; a psychological probe: JPsy&Chr 6,1 (GR 1987) 40-51 [NTAbs 32,152].

4324 **Panas** H., Il Vangelo secondo Giuda ('apocrifo') [romanzo moderno]. R 1981, 'e/o'. 247 p. Lit. 14.000. – ᴿProtestantesimo 43 (1988) 223s (P. *de Petris*: stimolante).

4325 *Paraplackal* Mathew, Jesus in the Qur'an: Jeevadhara 13 (1988) 167-178.

4326 *Piemontese* A. M., Storie di Maria, Gesù e Paolo nel commento coranico persiano di Sûrâbâdî: ➤ 144, Mem. TUCCI G. 3 (1988) 1101-1118.

4327 *Riloba* Fortunato, Gesù confermato dallo Spirito Santo secondo il Corano: TerraS 64 (1988) 18-24 (98-101, L'Annunciazione; 163-5, Ascensione; 206-210, miracoli; 254-8, Presentazione di Maria; 302-8, Ultimo Giudizio).

4328 **Scharrer** E., Jesus im Gespräch; Therapie und Seelsorge in den Dialogreden Jesu: ABCteam 389. Wu 1987, Brockhaus. 176 p. DM 19,80 [TLZ 114,71, C. *Möller*].

4329 **Stein** Murray, JUNG's treatment of Christianity; the psychotherapy of a religious tradition 1985 ➤ 3,4085: ᴿZygon 23 (1988) 209-212 (W. B. *Clift*).

4330 **Vander Berg** Edward, A study of Quranic Jesus texts and their missionary implications [... example better than conversion-efforts]: diss. Calvin Sem., ᴰ*Recker* R. GR 1988. iii-118 p. + bibliog. – CalvinT 23 (1988) 310.

4331 **Verkuyl** J., Antroposofie en het Evangelie van Jezus Christus 1986 ➤ 3,4086; 90-242-4638-5: ᴿBijdragen 49 (1988) 221s (L. *Groen*).

4332 **Vernette** J., Jésus dans la nouvelle religiosité; ésotérismes, gnoses et sectes d'aujourd'hui: JJC 29, 1987 ➤ 3,4087: 2-7189-0320-1: ᴿÉTRel 63 (1988) 623 (J. *Ansaldi*); NRT 110 (1988) 137-9 (L. *Volpe*).

4333 **Wolff** Hanna, Jesus the therapist [Jesus als Psychotherapeut 1978 → 60,5638; ⁶1985] ᵀ*Barr* R. R. Oak Park IL 1987, Meyer-Stone. xiii-178 p. $30; pa. $13. 0-940989-11-5; pa. 10-7 [NTAbs 32,248].

F2.1 *Exegesis creativa* – **innovative methods.**

4334 **Agua Pérez** A. del, El método midrásico 1985 → 1,4112; 3,4091: ᴿHelmantica 37 (1986) 423 (C. *Carrete Parrondo*).

4335 *Black* C. Clifton, Rhetorical criticism and the New Testament: Proc-GLM 8 (1988) 72-85; bibliog. 85-92.

4336 **Bultmann** R., NT and mythology, ᴱ*Ogden* S. 1984 → 1,g75; 2,3211: ᴿRRel 46 (1987) 148 (V. P. *Branick*).

4337 **Chevallier** Max-Alain, L'exégèse du NT, initiation à la méthode 1984 → 65,3707 ... 2,3512: ᴿRThom 88 (1988) 143s (L. *Devillers*).

4338 **Egger** Wilhelm, Methodenlehre zum Neuen Testament; Einführung in in linguistische und historisch-kritische Methoden 1987 → 3,4096: ᴿSNTU-A 13 (1988) 206s (A. *Fuchs*); TLZ 113 (1988) 442s (U. *Schnelle*); TR 84 (1988) 289-291 (T. *Söding*); TüTQ 168 (1988) 65-69 (H. *Schweizer*); ZkT 110 (1988) 212s (M. *Hasitschka*).

4340 *Fuller* R. H., Trends in New Testament studies: St. Mark's Review 131 (Canberra 1987) 16-20 [< NTAbs 32,281].

4341 ᴱ**Geest** D. de, *Bulckens* J., De verborgen rijkdom van bijbelverhalen; theorie en praktijk van de structurele bijbellezing: Niké 14, 1986 → 3,4099; ƒ37,50. 90-334-1425-2: ᴿTsTNijm 28 (1988) 104 (F. *Peerlinck*).

4342 *Hekman* D., Some comparisons between Old and New Testament exegesis: Notes on Translation 121 (Dallas 1987) 15-31 [< NTAbs 32,285].

4343 **Jasper** David, The New Testament and the literary imagination 1987 → 3,4103: ᴿTLond 91 (1988) 145s (U. *Simon*).

4344 *Kelber* Werner H., Gospel narrative and critical theory: BibTB 18 (1988) 130-6.

4345 **Kenny** Anthony, A stylometric study of the NT 1986 → 2,3222; 3,4105: ᴿJTS 39 (1988) 194-6 (D. L. *Mealand*); NT 30 (1988) 373-5 (G. D. *Kilpatrick*); ScripTPamp 20 (1988) 339-341 (J. *Chapa*).

4346 *Lombard* H., Anonimiteit en pseudonimiteit van Bybelse geskrifte: HervTS 42 (1986) 705-728 [< NTAbs 32,281].

4347 **Lührmann** Dieter, Auslegung des NTs 1984 → 65,3717; 3,4106; ²1987: ᴿÉTRel 63 (1988) 587s (J. *Zumstein*); RHPR 68 (1988) 245 (M.-A. *Chevallier*: approche insolite de l'exégèse allemande protestante traditionnelle).

4348 *Mealand* David, [→ 887s] Computers in New Testament research, an interim report: JStNT 33 (1988) 97-115.

4349 **Mercer** Calvin R., Norman PERRIN's interpretation of the NT; from 'exegetical method' to 'hermeneutical process': Studies in American Biblical Hermeneutics 2, 1986 → 3,g837: ᴿCBQ 50 (1988) 725s (K. A. *Barta*: fine, despite Mark/Son of Man lacuna).

4349* **Munoz León** Domingo, Deras I. targúmico y NT 1987 → 3,1610: ᴿDivinitas 32 (1988) 725s (T. *Stramare*); EstBíb 46 (1988) 303-314 (S. *Muñoz Iglesias*).

4350 **Nida** E. A., *al.*, Style and discourse ... Greek NT 1982/3 → 64, 1982.3855 ... 2,3226: ᴿFgNt 1,1 (1988) 112s (D. A. *Black*).

4351 *Niebuhr* K.-W., Einige Tendenzen und Probleme neutestamentlicher Forschung der Gegenwart: ZeichZt 41,12 (B 1987) 293-303 [< NTAbs 32,282].

4352 **Painter** John, Theology as hermeneutics; R. BULTMANN's interpretation of the history of Jesus: Historic Texts and Interpreters, 1987 ➤ 3,4113: ᴿAustralBR 36 (1988) 81-83 (N. *Young*); Biblica 69 (1988) 588-591 (M. *Waldstein*); CBQ 50 (1988) 541s (G. S. *Sloyan*: too-sympathetic defense against R. JOHNSON 1974, R. ROBERTS 1977, A. THISELTON 1980, overlooking K. JASPERS, C. COLPE); EvQ 60 (1988) 279s (A. C. *Thiselton*); JTS 39 (1988) 644 (R. *Morgan*); TLond 91 (1988) 46-48 (F. *Watson*).

4353 ᴱ**Pfammatter** Josef, *Furger* Franz, Methoden der Evangelien-Exegese: TBer 3. Z 1985, Benziger. 187 p. – ᴿTPhil 63 (1988) 252s (H. *Engel*: tit. pp. analys.: 11-39, *Schelbert* G., Wo steht die Formgeschichte?; 41-86, *Marguerat* D., Strukturale Textlektüren des Evangelium; 87-121, *Venetz* H.-J., Beitrag der Soziologie; 123-163, *Füssel* K., Materialistische Lektüre der Bibel; 165-182, *Mussner* F., Rückfrage nach Jesus; Bericht über neue Wege und Methoden).

4354 *Rollman* Hans, From Baur to Wrede; the quest for a historical method: SR 17 (1988) 443-454.

4355 *Schnelle* Udo, Sachgemässe Schriftauslegung: NT 30 (1988) 115-131.

4356 *Smith* M. W. A., The revenger's tragedy; the derivation and interpretation of statistical results for resolving disputed authorship: CompHum 21 (1987) 21-55.

4357 *Snyman* Andreas H., On studying the figures (*schēmata*) in the New Testament [*Perelman* C.]: Biblica 69 (1988) 93-107.

4358 **Tuckett** Christopher, Reading the NT; methods of interpretation [... Mk 3,1-6] 1987 ➤ 3,4117; also Ph 1987, Fortress: 0-8006-2058-5: ᴿEvQ 60 (1988) 77s (I. H. *Marshall*); NBlackf 69 (1988) 193 (C. C. *Rowland*); RExp 85 (1988) 722s (Linda M. *Bridges*: 'adeptly summarizes massive mountains of literature'); TLond 91 (1988) 57-59 (W. R. *Telford*).

4359 *Weder* H., Zu neuen Ufern? Exegetische Vorstösse in methodisches Neuland: EvKomm 21 (1988) 141-4 [NTAbs 32,290: feminism-psychology-linguistics perspectives risk concealing the strangeness of NT faith].

4360 *Vorster* W. S., Op weg na 'n post-kritiese Nuwe-Testamentiese wetenskap: HervTS 43 (Pretoria 1987) 374-394 [< NTAbs 32,290].

F2.2 *Unitas VT-NT:* The Unity of the Two Testaments.

4362 *Beale* G. K., Did Jesus and his followers preach the right doctrine from the wrong texts? [... non-contextual OT exegesis]; an examination of the presuppositions of Jesus' and the apostles' exegetical method: Themelios 14 (1988s) 89-96.

4363 **Broadhurst** Donna & Mal. Passover, before Messiah and after. Carol Stream IL 1988, Shofar. 238 p. [JBL 108,183].

4364 ᴱ**de Gennaro** G., L'AT interpretato dal Nuovo; il Messia 1982/5 ➤ 1,464 ... 3,4128: ᴿAsprenas 35 (1988) 167s (A. *Rolla*); BL (1988) 104s (J. R. *Porter*).

4365 *De Martino* Umberto, Il compimento delle profezie messianiche: StCattMi 32 (1988) 304-7.

4366 *Di Sante* Carmine, L'Antica e la Nuova Alleanza; il rapporto tra i due Testamenti: RasT 29 (1988) 419-430.

4367 *Ellis* E.E., [OT and other] Quotations in the NT: ➤ 801, ISBEnc³ 4 (1988) 18-25.

4368 *Engelbrecht* B., The ultimate significance of the Torah [... Jesus]: JTSAf 61 (1987) 45-58 [NTAbs 32,340].

4369 *Gossai* Hemchand, The Old Testament; a heresy continued: WWorld 8 (1988) 150-7 [< OTAbs 11,289].

4370 **Grollenberg** L., Onverwachte Messias; de Bijbel kan ook misleidend zijn [especially Mt uses OT as a prophecy of what Jesus did]. Baarn 1987, Ten Have. 224 p. ƒ30. 90-259-4313-6. – ᴿTsTNijm 28 (1988) 311 (A. van *Schaik*: some of the 'questions' border on the sensational: p. 77, 'is no wife of Jesus mentioned in the tradition because she died young?'); Streven 55 (1987s) 858 (P. *Beentjes*).

4371 *Halsema* J.H. van, De Torah en het Woord: KerkT 39 (1988) 110-6.

4372 **Hanson** A.T., The living utterances of God; the NT exegesis of the Old 1983 ➤ 64,4119 ... 2,3240: ᴿStPatav 35 (1988) 707s (G. *Segalla*).

4373 **Hanson** Paul D., L'Écriture une et diverse 1985 ➤ 1,4159 ... 3,4149: ᴿRThom 88 (1988) 517 (H.-D. de S.); ScEspr 40 (1988) 246-9 (G. *Rochais*).

4374 *Jensen* Joseph, Prediction-fulfillment in Bible and liturgy [against *Pawlikowski* J., al., When Catholics speak about Jews; notes for homilists and catechists 1987]: CBQ 50 (1988) 646-662.

4375 **Juel** Donald, Messianic exegesis; Christological interpretation of the OT in early Christianity 1987 ➤ 3,4136; 0-8006-0840-2: ᴿAnglTR 70 (1988) 362-4 (J.W. *Trigg*); Biblica 69 (1988) 439-441 (J. *Swetnam*); ExpTim 99 (1987s) 342s (A. *Hanson*); RelStR 14 (1988) 379 (R. *Fuller*: with DAHL he holds that Christianity originated in the crucifixion of Jesus as a messianic pretender; but Juel's own data show rather Jesus' prior self-understanding as eschatological prophet); RExp 85 (1988) 568s (C.J. *Scalise*).

4376 **Kronholm** Tryggve, Texter och tolkningar; en studie om gammalte-stamentliga texter och nyatestamentliga tolkningar. Sto 1985, EFS. 206 p. – ᴿSvTEv 63 (1987) 129s (R. *Söderlund*).

4377 **Lohfink** Norbert, Das Alte Testament christlich ausgelegt; eine Reflexion im Anschluss an die Osternacht: *a*) Meitinger Kleine Bücherei 114. Meitingen-Friesing 1988, Kyrios. 40 p. DM 4,40. 3-7838-2114-2 [NTAbs 32,385]. – *b*) GeistL 61 (1988) 98-107.

4378 *a*) *Marshall* I. Howard, [OT in NT] An assessment of recent developments; – *b*) *Chester* Andrew, Citing the OT; – *c*) *Wilcox* Max, Text form: ➤ 97, ᶠLINDARS B., It is written 1988, 1-21 / 141-169 / 193-204.

4379 **Martin** Francis, Narrative [... O.T.] parallels to the New Testament: SBL Resources 22. Atlanta 1988, Scholars. xxv-266 p. 1-55540-255-5; pa. 9-3.

4380 **Martins Terra** J.E., Releitura judaica e cristã da Bíblia. São Paulo 1988, Loyola. 87 p.

4380* *Neaga* Nicolae, Jesus Christus im AT (rum.): Mitropolia Banatului 37,5 (1987) 23-30 [TLZ 114,637].

4381 *a*) *Simian-Yofre* Horacio, Old and New Testament; participation and analogy; – *b*) *Lyonnet* Stanislas, A word on Chapters IV and VI of *Dei Verbum* [OT and New]; the amazing journey involved in the process of drafting the conciliar text; – *c*) *Swetnam* James, The Word of God and pastoral theology in the contemporary Church: ➤ 380, Vatican II Assessment 1 (1988) 267-298 / 157-207 / 364-381; – français ➤ 379, Bilan 1, 277-305 / 171-221 / 371-388.

4382 *Slenczka* Reinhard, Was heisst und was ist schriftgemäss?: KerDo 34 (1988) 304-320; Eng. 320: Scripture points to Jesus.

Van Roo William A., Telling about God, I. Promise and fulfilment 1986 → 8447.

4383 **Villegas** Guillermo V., The Old Testament as a Christian book; a study of three Catholic biblical scholars, Pierre GRELOT, John L. MCKENZIE, Luis ALONSO SCHÖKEL [diss. Pont. Univ. Gregoriana, ᴰ*Latourelle* R.]: Tagaytay Studies 6. Manila 1988, Divine Word. ix-250 p. 971-510-027-9.

4384 *Wong* Teresa, ☉ Relationship between the Old Testament and the New Testament: ColcFuJen 77 (1988) 411-9.

F2.5 *Commentarii* – **Commentaries on the whole NT.**

4385 *Auneau* J., al., Vangeli sinottici e Atti degli apostoli, ᵀ*Mariotti* Piergiorgio: Piccola enciclopedia biblica 9. R 1983, Borla. 329 p. Lit. 14.000.

4386 **Coffey** Jeremiah, GREGORY the Great ad Populum; a reading of XI. Homiliarum in Evangelia Libri: diss. Fordham. – Bronx NY 1987. – RelStR 15,191.

4387 **Jeanne** d'Arc sr., Évangile selon Matthieu / Marc / Luc [translations with their pagination as in prior edition 1986s → 3,4216. 4746. 4946; notes adapted]. P 1988, de Brouwer. xiii-203 p.; viii-141 p.; x-233 p. F 56; 49; 59. 2-220-02699-X; 694-9; 700-7 [NTAbs 32,370].

4388 **Lachs** Samuel T., A rabbinic commentary on the NT; Mt Mk Lk 1987 → 3,4156: ᴿCBQ 50 (1988) 331s (D.J. *Harrington*: learned but uncritical); JJS 39 (1988) 123s (G. *Vermes*: unsatisfying); JEcuSt 25 (1988) 460s (F.L. *Horton*); JQR 78 (1987s) 340-3 (B.L. *Visotsky*); JStJud 19 (1988) 108s (J.D.M. *Derrett*: 'overtakes' BILLERBECK/BONSIRVEN); TLZ 113 (1988) 266-8 (W. *Wiefel*).

4389 **Reeve** Anne, ERASMUS NT, Gospels (1535) 1986 → 3,4158: ᴿBibl-HumRen 49 (1987) 222-4 (G. *Bedouelle*); cf. 50 (1988) 803s on *Rummel* E.

4390 **Schlatter** A., Erläuterungen zum Neuen Testament [revision of 1961-5, 10 vols. paperback]. Stu 1987, Calwer. 3440 p. DM 98. 3-7668-0843-5 [NTAbs 32,366].

4391 **Smeets** J.R., La Bible de MACÉ de la Charité VI. Évangiles, Actes 1986 → 3,4160: ᴿRBgPg 66 (1988) 682-4 (H.R. *Runte*).

X. Evangelia

F2.6 **Evangelia Synoptica;** *textus, commentarii.*

4392 **Aland** Kurt, Synopsis quattuor evangeliorum 1986¹³ʳᵉᵛ (¹1963) → 3, 4163: ᴿTR 84 (1988) 367s (G.D. *Kilpatrick*: since ed. 9, H for Hesychius replaced by sigla for the single manuscripts; why M replaced K, read the introduction).

4393 **Boismard** M.-E., *Lamouille* A., Synopsis graeca quattuor Evangeliorum 1986 → 2,3253; 3,4164: ᴿBZ 32 (1988) 140-2 (R. *Schnackenburg*); CBQ 50 (1988) 707-9 (J.S. *Kloppenborg*); ComSev 21 (1988) 96-98 (M. de *Burgos*); RTLv 19 (1988) 219s (J. *Ponthot*); TR 84 (1988) 285-7 (T. *Söding*); ZkT 110 (1988) 208s (M. *Hasitschka*: als Arbeitsinstrument kann sich nicht messen mit Aland¹³).

4394 **Denaux** Adelbert, *Vervenne* Marc, Synopsis van de eerste drie evangeliën 1986 ➤ 2,3253*; 3,4165: ᴿRTLv 19 (1988) 220s (J. *Ponthot*).

4395 **Kloppenborg** John S., Q parallels; synopsis, critical notes and concordance: Foundations and Facets. Sonoma CA 1988, Polebridge. xxxv-249 p.; maps. 0-944344-00-3; pa. 1-1.

4396 **Knoch** Otto, (*Sitarz* Eugen), Vollständige Synopse der Evangelien, nach dem Text der Einheitsübersetzung, mit wichtigen ausserbiblischen Parallelen. Stu 1988, KBW. xxiv-325 p. 3-920609-28-X.

4397 **Neirynck** Frans, Q-synopsis; the double tradition passages in Greek [in the order of Luke]: StNT Auxilia 13. Lv 1988, Univ./Peeters. 63 p. Fb 240 [JTS 40,742]. 90-6186-284-1.

4398 *Neirynck* F., A synopsis of Q [his own 1988, and more extensive *Kloppenborg* J. 1988]: ETL 64 (1988) 441-9.

4399 **Pesch** Rudolf, *al.*, Synoptisches Arbeitsbuch zu den Evangelien I-III, 1980s ➤ 61,5518 ... 63,4286; IV. Auswahlkonkordanz, 1980; 28 p.; V. Synopse nach Johannes 1981; 88 p.; Benziger 3-545-23034-1; 6-8; Gü 3-579-04886-4; 1781-0.

4400 **Poppi** Angelico, Sinossi dei quattro vangeli [I. testo⁶ 1983 ➤ 64,4156] II. (1987? ➤ 3,4171) 1988; 88-7026-801-2: ᴿCiVit 43 (1988) 302 (B. *Farnetani*); HumBr 43 (1988) 893s (M. *Orsatti*); MiscFranc 88 (1988) 223-8 (F. *Uricchio*); ParVi 33 (1988) 318s (F. *Mosetto*).

4401 **Schmithals** Walter, Einleitung in die drei ersten Evangelien 1985 ➤ 1,4177 ... 3,4173: ᴿÉTRel 63 (1988) 80s (F. *Vouga*); ScotJT 419-421 (J. N. *Birdsall*: 'Schmidthals' some six times).

F2.7 *Problema synopticum:* **The Synoptic problem.**

4402 *Bigg* Howard C., The present state of the Q hypothesis: VoxEvca 18 (L 1988) 63-73.

4403 **Carmignac** J., *a*) La naissance des évangiles synoptiques² 1984 ➤ 65,3769; 3,4177; – *b*) Nascita dei Vangeli sinottici 1986 ➤ 2,3264. – ᴿAsprenas 35 (1988) 168-170 (C. *Marcheselli-Casale*).

4404 **Crossan** J. D., Sayings parallels 1986 ➤ 2,3255; 3,4179: ᴿRExp 85 (1988) 144s (M. C. *Parsons*); ScotJT 41 (1988) 547-9 (C. M. *Tuckett*).

4405 *Downing* F. Gerald, *a*) Compositional conventions and the synoptic problem: JBL 107 (1988) 69-85; – *b*) Quite like Q; a genre for 'Q'; the 'lives' of Cynic philosophers: Biblica 69 (1988) 196-224; franç. 225.

4406 **Havener** Ivan, Q, the sayings of Jesus 1987 ➤ 3,4182: ᴿBibTB 18 (1988) 34s (H. *Fleddermann*); RelStR 14 (1988) 252 (L. *Cope*).

4407 **Kloppenborg** John S., The formation of Q; trajectories in ancient Wisdom collections 1987 ➤ 3,4184: ᴿCBQ 50 (1988) 720-2 (Adela Y. *Collins*); SR 17 (1988) 227s (T. *Prendergast*); TLZ 113 (1988) 435-7 (D. *Lührmann*); TorJT 4 (1988) 308s (A. M. *Osiander*).

4408 **Longstaff** T. *al.*, The Synoptic problem, a bibliography 1716-1988: New Gospel Studies 4. Macon GA 1988, Mercer Univ. xxviii-235 p. $35 [JBL 108,380].

4409 *Martin* R. P., Q: ➤ 801, ISBEnc³ 4 (1988) 1-4.

4410 *Orchard* B., The formation of the Synoptic Gospels: DowR 106 (1988) 1-16 [NTAbs 32,299].

4411 **Rolland** P., Les premiers évangiles ... problème synoptique: LDiv 116, 1984 ➤ 65,3781 ... 3,4188: ᴿÉglT 17 (1986) 388-390 (M. *Dumais*); RB 95 (1988) 97-101 (M.-É. *Bosimard*).

4412 **Sato** Migaku, Q und Prophetie; Studien zur Gattungs- und Traditionsgeschichte der Quelle Q: WUNT 2/29. Tü 1988, Mohr. xiii-437 p. DM 89 pa. [CBQ 50,753]. 3-16-144974-6. – ᴿArTGran 51 (1988) 299 (A. *Segovia*: define Q 'libro profético del AT' *sic*! ii. 'cotejo del microgénero de la fuente Q con los Libros proféticos del AT').

4413 *a) Scholer* David M., Q bibliography 1981-1988; – *b) Fleddermann* Harry, The Cross and discipleship in Q; – *c) Boring* M. Eugene, A proposed reconstruction of Q 10; 23-24 [= Mt 13,16s; Lk 10,23s]: ➤ 500, SBL Seminars 1988, 483-495 / 472-482 / 456-471.

4414 *Smith* Morton, The Synoptic problem in rabbinic literature, a correction: JBL [105 (1986) 499-507, *Neusner* J.] 107 (1988) 111s.

4415 **Stein** Robert H., The Synoptic problem; an introduction 1987 ➤ 3, 4189; also Nottingham 1988, Inter-Varsity: 0-85110-665-X: ᴿPerspRelSt 15 (1988) 180-2 (R. B. *Vinson*); RExp 85 (1988) 353s (S. M. *Sheeley*); Themelios 14 (1988s) 70s (D. R. *de Lacey*).

4416 **Vaage** Leif E., Q; the ethos and ethics of an itinerant intelligence: diss. Claremont 1984. – RelStR 14,188; RTLv 20,546.

4417 *a) Vaage* Leif E., The woes in Q (and Matthew and Luke); deciphering the rhetoric of criticism; *–b) Mack* Burton L., The kingdom that didn't come; a social history of the Q tradents; – *c) Tashjian* Jirair S., The social setting of the Q mission; three dissertations: ➤ 500, SBL Seminars 1988, 582-607 / 608-635 / 636-644.

F2.8   *Synoptica:* **themata.**

4418 *Abogunrin* S. O., The Synoptic gospel debate; a re-examination in the African context: AfJB 2 (1987) 25-51.

4419 **Banks** Robert, Jesus and the law in the synoptic tradition 1975 ➤ 57,3481; 58,4440 ...: ᴿÉTRel 63 (1988) 121 (J.-D. *Dubois*: no comment on why now).

4420 **Bauer** Ulrich, 'Rechtssätze' im neuen Testament? Eine form- und gattungsgeschichtliche Untersuchung zu den Synoptikern: Diss. Bamberg 1987s, ᴰ*Hoffmann*. – TR 84 (1988) 511; RTLv 20,543.

4420* **Bayer** Hans F., Jesus' predictions of vindication and resurrection; the provenance, meaning and correlation of the Synoptic predictions: WUNT 2/20, 1986 ➤ 2,3277; 3,4697: ᴿGregorianum 69 (1988) 148 (G. *O'Collins*); TLZ 113 (1988) 113s (K. T. *Kleinknecht*).

4421 *Bovon* François, The Synoptic Gospels and the noncanonical Acts of the Apostles: HarvTR 81 (1988) 19-36.

4422 **Čabraja** Ilija, Der Gedanke der Umkehr bei den Synoptikern; eine exegetisch-religionsgeschichtliche Untersuchung: Diss. Theol. (Mü, ᴰ*Gnilka* J. ➤ 1,4198) 10. St. Ottilien 1985, EOS. 265 p. – ᴿBogSmot 58 (1988) 157s (M. *Zovkić*).

4423 *Estrada* Bernardo, Il binomio 'kalein-akolouthein' nei Vangeli sinottici; la vocazione al ministero gerarchico e alla santità nel proprio stato: DivThom 91 (1988) 72-91.

4424 *Hooker* Morna D., Traditions about the Temple in the sayings of Jesus: BJRyL 70,1 (1988) 7-19.

4425 **Hübner** Hans, Das Gesetz in der synoptischen Tradition; Studien zur These einer progressiven Qumranisierung und Judaisierung innerhalb der synoptischen Tradition[2] [= [1]1971/3 Hab.-Diss. + brief updatings]. Gö 1986, Vandenhoeck & R. 277 p. DM 68. – ᴿJTS 39 (1988) 555-7 (R. *Morgan*: vexed).

4426 **Kosch** Daniel,   Die eschatologische Tora des Menschensohnes;   Untersuchungen zur Rezeption der Stellung Jesu zur Tora in Q: Diss. ᴰ*Venetz*.   FrS 1987s. 510 p. – TR 84 (1988) 514; RTLv 20,544.

4427 ᴰ**Martin** Raymond A.,   Syntax criticism of the synoptic gospels: Studies in the Bible and Early Christianity 10, 1987 ↠ 5,4197: $50 not £:   ᴿJTS 39 (1988) 568-571 (E.J. *Pryke*: massive statistical research).

4428 *Miller* Robert J.,   The rejection of the prophets in Q [Luke 11:47-51; 13-34-35]: JBL 107 (1988) 225-240.

4429 **Orchard** Bernard, *Riley* Harold,   The order of the synoptics; why three synoptic gospels? 1987 ↠ 3,4198:   ᴿCBQ 50 (1988) 539s (F.J. *Matera*: fanciful, but so are defenses of Marcan priority); DowR 106 (1988) 67-77 (A.G. *Murray*); HeythJ 29 (1988) 510s (P. *Fitzgerald-Lombard*); SNTU-A 13 (1988) 214s (A. *Fuchs*).

4430 **Reicke** Bo [† 17.V.1987] The roots of the Synoptic Gospels 1986 ↠ 2,3290*; 3,4201:   ᴿTR 84 (1988) 194s (T. *Söding*).

4431 **Schilling** A.,   Geschichten Jesu — weitererzählt [art of 20 Synoptic texts]: Tb 1513.   FrB 1988, Herder.   158 p. DM 10.   3-451-08513-5 [NTAbs 32,246].

4432 **Schmidt** Thomas E.,   Hostility to wealth in the Synoptic Gospels [diss. Cambridge 1985] 1987 ↠ 3,4204:   ᴿRExp 85 (1988) 718s (S. *Sheeley*); TTod 45 (1988s) 382s (R.D. *Witherup*: technical).

4433 *Segalla* Giuseppe,   Spiritualità dei Vangeli sinottici: ↠ 810, StSp 2 NT (1988) 177-218.

4434 **Tuckett** C.M.,   Nag Hammadi and the Synoptic tradition 1986 ↠ 2,8609; 3,4205:   ᴿJSS 33 (1988) 139-141 (K.H. *Kuhn*).

4435 *Tyson* Joseph B., *Dewey* Joanna, *Walker* William O.ᴶ, *Fuller* Reginald H.,   Order in the Synoptic Gospels; patterns of agreement within pericopes [*Longstaff* T.]:   SecC 6 (1987s) 65-67 / 68-82 / 83-98 / 107-9; Longstaff response, 98-106.

F3.1   **Matthaei evangelium:**   *textus, commentarii.*

4436 *Aranda* Pérez Gonzalo,   La versión sahídica de san Mateo en Bodmer XIX y Morgan 569:   EstBíb 46 (1988) 217-230; Eng. 217.

4437 *Brown* V.,   A new commentary on Matthew in Beneventan script at Venosa: Mediaeval Studies 49 (1987) 443-465 [< RSPT 72,157].

4438 **Bruner** Frederick D.,   The Christbook ... Mt 1-12, 1987 ↠ 3,4209: ᴿAndrUnS 26 (1988) 87s (R.K. *McIver*); EvQ 60 (1988) 360-2 (D. *France*); RefTR 47 (1988) 19s (T.L. *Wilkinson*).

4439 **Davies** W.D., *Allison* Dale C.,   The gospel according to St. Matthew, I-VII; a critical and exegetical commentary: ICC.   E 1988, Clark.   788 p. £27.50   0-567-09481-2.

4440 **Gnilka** Joachim,   Das Matthäusevangelium [I 1986 ↠ 2,3304; 3,4212], II: TheolKomm 1/2.   FrB 1988, Herder.   viii-552 p. DM 118. – ᴿActuBbg 25 (1988) 63 (X. *Alegre S.*, 1); BiKi 43 (1988) 178s (P.-G. *Müller*, 2); EstE 63 (1988) 371s (A. *Vargas-Machuca*, 1); TPhil 63 (1988) 255s (J. *Beutler*, 1); TrierTZ 97 (1988) 66s (G. *Schmahl*, 1).

4442 **Howard** George,   The Gospel of Matthew according to a primitive Hebrew text [Even Bohan 14th cent.] 1987 ↠ 3,4215:   ᴿCBQ 50 (1988) 717s (D.J. *Harrington*).

4443 *Howard* George,   A primitive Hebrew gospel of Matthew [< Even Bohan 1380] and the Tol'dot Yeshu: NTS 34 (1988) 60-70.

4444 **Jeanne d'Arc** sr., [➤ 4387], Év. selon Matthieu 1987 ➤ 3,4216: ᴿÉtudes 368 (1988) 136 (Nicole *Gueunier*); RThom 88 (1988) 131-3 (M.-É. *Lauzière*).

4445 **Limbeck** Meinrad, Mt.-Ev: Kl. Komm NT 1, 1986 ➤ 2,3306; 3,4218: ᴿTR 84 (1988) 23s (A. *Sand*).

4446 ᴱ**Longobardo** Luigi, ILARIO di Poitiers, Commentario a Matteo: Testi Patristici 74. R 1988, Città Nuova. 326 p. Lit. 24.000. 88-311-3074-9.

4447 The Navarre Bible, Matthew. Dublin 1988 Four Courts. 236 p. $20; pa. $12.50. – ᴿHomP 89,7 (1988s) 75s (W. G. *Most*).

4448 **Nolli** Gianfranco, Evangelo secondo Matteo; testo greco, neovolgata latina, analisi filologica, traduzione italiana. Vaticano 1988, Editrice. xxxxvi (i.e.46)-958 p. 88-209-1597-9. – ᴿScuolC 22 (1988) 821 (G. P. *Colò*).

4449 ᴱ**Ossola** Carlo, (*Cavallarin* Anna Maria), Juan de VALDÉS, Lo Evangelio di San Matteo 1985 ➤ 3,4221: ᴿBibHumRen 50 (1988) 798-801 (J. C. *Nieto*); SixtC 19 (1988) 515s (Elisabeth L. *Gleason*).

4450 **Patte** Daniel, The Gospel according to Matthew, a structural commentary on Matthew's faith, I. 1987 ➤ 3,4222 (+ faith!): ᴿCBQ 50 (1988) 144s (F. W. *Burnett*); JBL 107 (1988) 756-8 (J. D. *Kingsbury*); RExp 85 (1988) 135 (D. E. *Garland*); RHPR 68 (1988) 248s (M. *Carrez*).

4451 **Sand** Alexander, Das Evangelium nach Matthäus: Rg NT, 1986 ➤ 3,4224: ᴿActuBbg 25 (1988) 73s (X. *Alegre S.*); Carthaginensia 4 (1988) 178s (F. *Marín*); CBQ 50 (1988) 543-5 (C. E. *Carlston*: no clear locus of the final author vis-à-vis Mk/Q); CiuD 201 (1988) 485 (A. *Salas*); Claretianum 27 (1987) 420s (B. *Proietti*); Gregorianum 69 (1988) 772s (R. *Penna*); JBL 107 (1988) 538-540 (J. D. *Kingsbury*); TLZ 113 (1988) 110-3 (W. *Wiefel*); TPhil 63 (1988) 253-5 (J. *Beutler*); ZkT 110 (1988) 194s (K. *Stock*).

4452 *Schlatter* Fredric W., The author of the Opus Imperfectum in Matthaeum: VigChr 42 (1988) 364-375.

F3.2 **Themata** de Matthaeo.

4453 *Allison* Dale C.ᴶ, The son of God in Israel; a note on Matthaean Christology: IrBSt 9 (1987) 74-81.

4454 *a) Anderson* James C., Matthew; sermon and story; – *b) Via* Dan O.ᴶ, The Gospel of Matthew; hypocrisy as self-deception; – *c) Barta* Karen A., Mission in Matthew; the second discourse as narrative; – *d) Snodgrass* Klyne, Matthew and the law: ➤ 500, SBL Seminars 1988, 496-507 / 508-516 / 527-535 / 536-554.

4455 *Aprea* Mariano, Tre visioni profetiche dell'Antico Testamento nel frontespizio al Vangelo di San Matteo nel codice Parisinus graecus 74 / Il frontespizio del Vangelo di San Matteo dell'Evangeliario di Ottone III: StRicOrCr 10 (1987) 63-78; 4 fig. / 79-92; 6 fig.

4456 **Bauer** David R., The structure of Matthew's Gospel, a study in literary design: JStNT Sup 31, B&Lit 15. Sheffield 1988, Almond. 182 p. £25 [TR 85,163]. 1-85075-105-6.

4457 *a) Böcher* Otto, Matthäus und die Magie; – *b) Knoch* Otto, Kenntnis und Verwendung des Matthäus-Evangeliums bei den Apostolischen Vätern; – *c) Mussner* Franz, Die Stellung zum Judentum in der 'Redequelle' und in ihrer Verarbeitung bei Matthäus; – *d) Schneider* Gerhard, 'Im Himmel — auf Erden'; eine Perspektive matthäischer Theologie: ➤ 115, ᶠPESCH W., Studien Mt. 1988, 11-24 / 157-177 / 209-225 / 283-297.

4458 **Crosby** Michael H., House of disciples; Church, economics, and justice in Matthew. Maryknoll NY 1988, Orbis. $24; pa. $12 [Interp 42,439].

4459 *Doyle* R. Rod, Matthew's intention as discerned by his structure: RB 95 (1988) 34-54; franç. 34.

4460 **Fischer** Bonifatius, Die lateinischen Evangelien bis zum 10. Jahrhundert, I. Varianten zu Matthäus: Vetus Latina 13. FrB 1988, Herder. 48*-496 p. 3-451-00497-6.

4461 *France* Dick, Matthew's Gospel in recent study: Themelios 14 (1988s) 41-46.

4462 *Freyne* S., Oppression from the Jews; Matthew's Gospel as an early Christian response: Concilium 200 (E 1988) 47-54 = L'oppression de la part des juifs; l'évangile de Matthieu, réaction chrétienne des origines: Concilium 220 (P 1988) 57-65.

Geist Heinz, Menschensohn und Gemeinde ... im Matthäusevangelium 1986 → 8653.

4463 **Gench** Frances T., Wisdom in the Christology of Matthew: diss. Union Theol. Sem. Richmond 1988. 375 p. 88-22338. – DissA 49 (1988s) 2276-A.

4464 *Giesen* Heinz, Matthäus und seine Gemeinde; neue Kommentare zum Mt-Ev [Themen aus *Sand* A., *Luz* U., *Gnilka* J., *al.*]: TGegw 30 (1987) 257-266.

4465 **Howell** D. B., Matthew's inclusive story; a study in the narrative rhetoric of the gospel and the contribution [of] redaction criticism [to] literary studies: diss. Oxford 1988. – RTLv 20,544: 'of ... of'.

4466 **Jefford** Clayton N., An analysis of the sayings of Jesus in the teaching of the twelve apostles; the role of the Matthean community: diss. Claremont 1988. 279 p. 89-01010. – DissA 49 (1988s) 3393-A (Didaché); RelStR 15,193.

4467 **Kingsbury** Jack Dean, Matthew as story[2rev] [[1]1986 → 2,3325; 3,4239]. Ph 1988, Fortress. x-181 p. 0-8006-2099-2.

4468 *Kingsbury* Jack D., Reflections on 'the reader' of Matthew's Gospel: NTS 34 (1988) 442-460.

4469 **Kwon** Sung-Soo, 'Your reward in heaven is great'; a study on gradation of reward in Matthew: diss. Westminster Theol. Sem. 1988, [D]*Gaffin* R. 283 p. 88-13322. – DissA 49 (1988s) 1843-A.

4470 *Limbeck* Meinrad, Die nichts bewegen wollen! Zum Gesetzes-verständnis des Evangelisten Matthäus: TüTQ 168 (1988) 299-320.

4471 **Malina** Bruce J., *Neyrey* Jerome H., [Mt 12 & 26s], Calling Jesus names; the social value of labels in Matthew. Sonoma CA 1988, Polebridge. xviii-174 p. [Paradigms 5/1, 73-75, R. *Webber*].

4472 *Martin* François, Parole écriture accomplissement dans l'Évangile de Matthieu: SémBib 50 (1988) 27-51; 51 (1988) 8-21 [Mt 2, 'Naître entre juifs et païens']: 52 (1988) 17-33 [Mt 13, 'Parler'].

4473 **Massaux** É., Influence de l'Évangile de saint Matthieu sur la littérature chrétienne avant Irénée 1950 = 1986 → 2,3327; 3,4247: [R]TR 84 (1988) 116s (I. *Borer*).

4474 *a) Meyer* Paul, Context as a bearer of meaning in Matthew; – *b) Farmer* William R., Source criticism; some comments on the present situation: UnSemQ 42,1 (1988) 69-72 / 49-58.

4475 *Mowery* Robert L., God, Lord and Father; the theology of the Gospel of Matthew: BiRes 33 (Ch 1988) 24-36.

4476 *Neirynck* Frans, *Apò tóte ḗrxato* and the structure of Matthew: ETL 64 (1988) 21-59.

4477 **Newman** Barclay M., *Stine* Philip C., A translator's handbook on the Gospel of Matthew: Helps for Translators. L 1988, United Bible Societies. x-939 p.; maps. $13. 0-8267-0134-5.

4478 *Onwu* Nlenanya, Righteousness and eschatology in Matthew's Gospel; a critical reflection: IndTSt 25 (1988) 213-235.

4479 **Schenk** Wolfgang, Die Sprache des Matthäus 1987 → 3,4253: ᴿActuBbg 25 (1988) 218s (X. *Álegre S.*); RHR 205 (1988) 313s (A. *Méhat*); TR 84 (1988) 22s (F. *Mussner*).

4480 **Schweizer** Eduard, Matteo e la sua comunità [1974 → 56,2819], ᵀ*Delvai Golino* Graziella: StBPaid 81. Brescia 1987, Paideia. 220 p. 88-394-0405-8.

4481 **Sigal** Phillip, The Halakhah of Jesus according to the Gospel of Matthew 1986 → 2,3338; 3,4255: ᴿJQR 79 (1988s) 88s (A. J. *Saldarini*); Judaism 37 (1988) 122-4 (G. S. *Sloyan*).

4482 **Spila** Arnaldo, Apollo di Corinto, autore del I Vangelo. R 1988, Istituto Salesiano Pio XI. 103 p.

4483 *Stanton* Graham, Matthew [citing OT]: → 97, ᴱLINDARS B. 1988, 205-219.

4484 **Stock** Klemens, ❸ Jesus — Künder der Seligkeit; Betrachtungen zum Matthäusevangelium [1986 → 2,3340], ᵀ*Bang Sang-man*. Seoul 1988, Catholic publ. 207 p. 2500 won. [AcPIB 9/5, 363].

4485 **Wilkins** Michael M., The concept of disciple in Matthew's Gospel as reflected in the use of the term *mathētēs*: NTSup 59. Leiden 1988, Brill. xi-261 p. *f*90; sb. 74 [JBL 108,572].

4486 **Wolthuis** Thomas R., Experiencing the Kingdom; reading the Gospel of Matthew: diss. Duke, ᴰ*Via* D. Durham NC 1987. 88-13569. – DissA 49 (1988s) 1483-A.

4487 **Zumstein** Jean, Mateo el teólogo [1986 → 2,3340] ᵀ*Darrical* Nicolau: CuadBib 58. Estella 1987, VDivino. 62 p. 84-7151-537-7. – ᴿActuBbg 25 (1988) 224 (R. de *Sivatte*).

F3.3 **Mt 1s** (Lc 1s → F7.5) *Infantia Jesu* – **Infancy Gospels.**

Aus Roger D., Weihnachtsgeschichte — jüd. Hintergrund 1988 → 4220.

4488 *Barrett* J. Edward, Can scholars take the Virgin Birth seriously?: BR 4,5 (1988) 10-15. 29 [Isaiah is simply not talking about what Matthew says Isaiah is talking about ... Maybe the virgin conception stories are poetic symbols, not biology reports].

4489 *Bergamelli* Ferdinando, 'La verginità di Maria' nelle lettere di IGNAZIO di Antiochia [Patristic Conference 10, Oxford Aug. 1987]: Salesianum 50 (1988) 307-320.

4490 ᴱ**Bonaccorsi** G., I vangeli dell'Infanzia dai Vangeli Apocrifi. F 1987, LEF. 143 p. [CC 139/2 dopo 208].

4491 **Boulton** Maureen, The Old French Évangile de l'Enfance 1984 → 3, 4262: ᴿEstJos 42 (1988) 136 (J. A. *Carrasco*).

4492 ᴱ**Boulton** Maureen, Les enfaunces de Jesu Crist [= ? 1984 → 3,4262]: Anglo-Norman texts 43. L 1986, (Birkbeck College). vii-119 p.; front. £15. – ᴿSpeculum 63 (1988) 906s (Jeanette *Beer*).

4493 *a) Bovon* François, Die Geburt und die Kindheit Jesu; kanonische und apokryphe Evangelien; – *b) Bauer* Johannes B., Jesusüberlieferungen in den Apokryphen: BiKi 42 (1987) 162-170 / 158-161 [145-157, *al.*].

4494 **Brown** Raymond E., A coming Christ in Advent; essays on the gospel narratives preparing for the birth of Jesus, Matthew 1 and Luke 1. Collegeville MN 1988, Liturgical. 71 p. $4 [TDig 36,149]. 0-8146-1587-2.

4495 *Cranfield* C. E. B., Some reflections on the subject of the Virgin Birth: ScotJT 41 (1988) 177-189.

4496 ᵀᴱ**Danieli** Maria Ignazia, Girolamo, La perenne verginità di Maria (Contro Elvidio). R 1988, Città Nuova. 82 p. Lit. 7000. 88-311-3070-6. – ᴿCC 139 (1988,4) 406 (E. *Cattaneo*).

4497 *Delaney* Carol, The meaning of paternity and the Virgin Birth debate: Man 21 (1986) 494-513 [< BibTB 18,119].

4498 *Dorman* T. M., Virgin birth of Jesus: → 801, ISBEnc³ 4 (1988) 990-3.

4499 **Harrington** W., The drama of Christ's coming [infancy narratives Christology]. Wilmington 1988, Glazier. 117 p. $8. 0-89453-649-4 [NTAbs 32,242].

4500 **Horsley** Richard A., The liberation of Christmas; the infancy narratives in social context. NY 1988, Crossroad. xiv-201 p. $19 [TS 50,820, A.J. *Tambasco*].

4501 *Kasper* Walter, Brief zum Thema 'Jungfrauengeburt': IkaZ 16 (1987) 531-5.

4502 *Łach* Jan, ❷ Jesus natus ex Maria Virgine: RuBi 41 (1988) 242-252.

4503 **Laurentin** R., I Vangeli del Natale. Casale Monferrato 1987, Piemme. 268 p. Lit. 12.000 [CC 139/2 dopo 208].

4504 **Paul** André, Il vangelo dell'infanzia secondo san Matteo [1968], ᵀ· R 1986, Borla. 186 p. Lit. 12.000. – ᴿParVi 33 (1988) 158s (M. *Orsatti*: difetti di traduzione, 'Culman anziché Culmann').

4505 *Quacquarelli* A., La conoscenza della natività dalla iconografia dei primi secoli attraverso gli Apocrifi: → 3,527*, Sponsa, mater, uirgo 1985, 41-67.

4506 *Quin* J. Cosslett, The infancy narratives with special reference to Matthew 1 and 2: IrBSt 9 (1987) 63-69.

4507 *Robinson* Neal, Fakhr al-Din al-Râzî and the virginal conception: Islamochristiana 14 (1988) 1-16.

4508 **Schaberg** Jane, The illegitimacy of Jesus; a feminist theological interpretation of the Infancy Narratives 1987 → 3,4273: ᴿBibTB 18 (1988) 118s (B. *Malina* seems to have nothing against this 'excellent historical-critical book' except the ignoring of some better approaches).

4509 **Segalla** Giuseppe, Una storia annunziata; i racconti dell'infanzia di Matteo. Brescia 1987, Morcelliana. 160 p. Lit. 15.000. 88-372-2307-7. – ᴿHumanitas 42 (Brescia 1987) 616 (M. *Orsatti*); RivB 36 (1988) 110-2 (anche M. *Orsatti*); RivScR 2 (1988) 223 (A. *Pitta*).

4510 *Silvestre* H., Le jour et l'heure de la Nativité et de la Résurrection pour Rupert de Deutz [suivant Jérôme: un dimanche minuit / minuit entre samedi et dimanche]: → 64,112, ᶠSmet J.M. de, Pascua mediaevalia, ᴱ**Lievens** R. (Lv 1983) 619-630 [< RHE 83 (1988) 774].

4511 *Welburn* A.J., Iranian prophetology and the birth of the Messiah; the Apocalypse of Adam: → 782, ANRW 2,25,6 (1988) 4752-4794.

4512 *Williams* Rowan D., Jungfrauengeburt, ᵀ*Hoffmann* H.: → 798, EvKL 2 (1988) 907-910.

4513 *Feuillet* André, Observations sur les deux généalogies de Jésus-Christ de saint Matthieu (1,1-17) et de saint Luc (3,23-38): EsprVie 98 (1988) 605-8; continued on the separately numbered yellow sheets of the cover, page 294, but erroneously under title of Babinet R., Icône.

Johnson M., The purpose of the biblical genealogies ... of Jesus ²1988 → 3022.

4514 *Nettelhorst* R. P., The genealogy of Jesus: JEvTS 31 (1988) 169-172 [< ZIT 88,588].

4515 *a) Stramare* Tarcisio, Significato della genealogia di Gesù in S. Matteo; – *b) Brändle* Francisco, La historia de José y su influjo en la teología de San José según San Mateo; – *c) Bartina* Sebastián, Doctrina de S. Ioseph secundum Ioannis DA SYLVEYRA carmelitani in textum evangelicum commentarios: ➤ 628, Acta 4, EstJos 41 (1987) 33-58 / 59-68 / 777-808.

4516 *Plümacher* Eckhard, [Mt 1,16] Joseph: ➤ 813, TRE 17 (1987) 245s (-249, Aseneth; Joseph-'Novelle' Gn ➤ 2558).

4517 *Calkins* A. B., [Mt 1,18-25] The justice of Joseph revisited: HomPast 88,9 (1988) 8-19.

4518 *Bartina* Sebastián, Sentido de la palabra justo (*dikaios*) en Mateo 1,19: EstJos 42 (1988) 197-204.

4519 *a) Balembo* Buetubela, The father of Jesus Christ; – *b) Naré* Laurent, Bible and evangelization; – *c) Hevi* Jacob K., New Testament ethics [3, continuing TKont 9 (1988) 1,47 & 2,27]: Biblical Pastoral Bulletin 1 (Nairobi 1988) 16-24 / 1-15 / 25-47.

4520 *Galot* Jean, *a)* Giuseppe 'il Giusto' e la vita consacrata; – *b)* L'istituzione della maternità spirituale di Maria: ViConsacr 24 (1988) 177-190 / 3-15. 85-95 [... 295-307. 379-392. 445-459. 526-537. 619-632. 705-718. 785-793].

4521 **Stramare** Tarcisio, San Giuseppe virgulto rigoglioso; rassegna storico-dottrinale. Casale Monferrato 1987, Piemme. 151 p. Lit. 16.000. [CC 139 (1988,1) 619].

4522 *Mussies* Gerard, Joseph's dream (Matt. 1,18-23) and comparable stories: ➤ 85, ᶠKLIJN A., Text 1988, 177-186.

4523 *Vicent Cernuda* Antonio, [Mt 1,19: Bethlehem] El domicilio de José y la fama de María: EstBíb 46 (1988) 5-25; Eng. 5.

4524 *Martin* François (CADIR), [Mt 2 à la GREIMAS ➤ 4472] Naître entre juifs et païens: FgNt 1,1 (1988) 77-90; Eng. 91-93.

4525 *Charbel* Antonio, I Magi nell'ambiente nabateo: TerraS 64 (1988) 4-12.

4526 *Wojciechowski* Michał, Mt 2,20; Herod and Antipater? A supplementary clue to dating the birth of Jesus [8-7 B.C.]: BibNot 44 (1988) 61s.

4527 *Skey* M., The death of Herod in the Cursor Mundi: Medium Aevum 57 (1988) 74-80 [RHE 84,50*].

4528 *Merkel* Helmut, [*Korol* Dieter], Herodes der Grosse: ➤ 807, RAC 14, 110 (1988) 815-830 [-Ikonographie].

4529 *Graves* T. H., A story ignored; an exegesis of Matthew 2:13-23: Faith & Mission 5,1 (Wake Forest NC 1987) 66-75 [NTAbs 32,156: three scenes, each with a different geographical location (Egypt, Bethlehem, Nazareth) and each with a quotation from earlier Jewish stories tied to the same locale (Hos 11,1; Jer 31,15; less-clear for Nazareth text)].

4530 ᴱ**Hoste** Anselme, *Dubois* J., RIEVAULX Aelred de, 'Quand Jésus eut douze ans' ...: SChr 60, 1987 = 1958 ➤ 3. 5002: ᴿBTAM 14 (1988) 504s (G. *Hendrix*).

4531 *Léthel* François-M., Vie cachée de Jésus, vie cachée de l'homme [interview]: Carmel 45 (1987) 2-12.

F3.4 **Mt 3 ...** *Baptismus Jesu,* **Beginning of the Public Life.**

4532 *Samuel* S. Johnson, Communalism or commonalism; a study of Matthew's account of Jesus' baptism (3: 13-17): IndTSt 25 (1988) 334-347.

4533 *Böcher* Otto, Johannes der Täufer: ➤ 813, TRE 17 (1987) 172-181.

4534 *Cleary* Michael, The Baptist of history and kerygma: IrTQ 54 (1988) 211-227.

4535 **Garside** Dale C., 'The Legend of St. John the Baptist'; a translation and critical edition of the fourteenth-century French manuscript [compiled from various Greek and Latin sources]: diss. Cincinnati 1988. 397 p. 88-22790. – DissA 49 (1988s) 3021s-A.

4536 **Lupieri** Edmondo, Giovanni Battista nelle tradizioni sinottiche: StBPaid 82. Brescia 1988, Paideia. 126 p. Lit. 13.000. 88-394-0409-0. – RAntonianum 63 (1988) 611s (M. *Nobile*: presagio di una più ampia monografia); Henoch 10 (1988) 404-8 (P. *Sacchi*); ParVi 33 (1988) 471s (R. *Infante*).

4537 **Lupieri** Edmondo, Giovanni Battista fra storia e leggenda: Bibl. Cultura Religiosa 53. Brescia 1988, Paideia. 476 p. Lit. 45.000. 88-394-0414-7.

4538 *Merklein* Helmut, a) Die Umkehrpredigt bei Johannes dem Täufer und Jesus von Nazaret [< BZ 25 (1981) 29-46]; – b) Jesus, Kunder des Reiches Gottes [< HbFundT 2 (1985) 145-174]: ➤ 231, Studien 1987, 109-126 / 127-156.

4539 a) *Witherington* Ben, Jesus and the Baptist — two of a kind?; – b) *Stegner* William R., Narrative Christology in early Jewish Christianity: ➤ 500, SBL Seminars 1988, 225-244 / 249-262.

4540 *Futterlieb* Hartmut, Die Götzen des Verwirrers; eine Unterrichtsskizze zur Versuchserzählung (Mt 4,1-11): Schönberger Hefte 18,2 (Fra 1988) 1-29 [< ZIT 88,491].

4541 *Bruckner* E., ☉ The temptation of Jesus: ColcFuJen 75 (1988) 17-26.

4542 *Hemelsoet* B. P. M., De verzoeking van Jesus in de woestijn: AmstCah 9 (1988) 97-116 [< TR 85,425].

4543 a) *Geftman* Rina, Le désert dans la tradition d'Israël; – b) *Rey* Bernard, Jésus et le désert; – c) *Derousseaux* Louis, Élie...; – d) *Bourguet* Daniel, Osée...: Tychique 72 (1988) 3-7 / 33-36 / 11-14 / 15-19.

4544 **Neugebauer** Fritz, Jesu Versuchung [hat wirklich stattgefunden, wie in Mt]; Wegentscheidung am Anfang 1986 ➤ 2,3379; 3,4311: RProtestantesimo 43 (1988) 217s (V. *Subilia*); TLZ 113 (1988) 437s (W. *Vogler*).

4545 *Okeke* George E., The temptations of Jesus Christ: LivWord 93 (Kerala 1987) 395-407 [< TKontext 9/2,38].

4546 *Delhez* Charles, La tentation de Jésus et la vie religieuse: VieCons 60 (1988) 107-121.

F3.5 *Sermo montanus,* Mt 5 ... Sermon on the Mount [... plain, Lk 6,17].

4547 **Alt** F., Liebe ist möglich; die Bergpredigt im Atomzeitalter[2]: Serie Piper 429. Mü 1985, Piper. 220 p. DM 9.80. [Frieden ist möglich 1983 ➤ 65,3907]. – RSNTU-A 13 (1988) 218s (A. *Fuchs*).

4548 **Betz** Hans D., Studien zur Bergpredigt 1985 ➤ 1,4322 ... 3,4321a: RSvEx 53 (1988) 123s (T. *Fornberg*); Protestantesimo 43 (1988) 218s (V. *Subilia*).

4549 **Betz** H. D., Essays on the Sermon on the Mount 1985 ➤ 1,4323 ... 3,4321: RETL 64 (1988) 405-414 (D. C. *Allison*); JEcuSt 25 (1988) 462s (D. P. *Efroymson*).

4550 *Carlston* Charles E., BETZ [H. D.] on the Sermon on the Mount [document existing in a strict Jewish-Christian community, taken over unchanged into Matthew's gospel] — a critique: CBQ 50 (1988) 47-57.

4551 **Blank** J., *Käsemann* E., *Moltmann* J., al., Il discorso della Montagna (Mt 5-7) una provocazione per la coscienza moderna [Provokation

Bergpredigt, Stu 1982]. R 1986, Città Nuova. 166 p. – [R]Teresianum 39 (1988) 336s (V. *Pasquetto*).

4552 *Bornkamm* Karin, Umstrittener 'spiegel eines Christlichen lebens'; LUTHERS Auslegung der Bergpredigt in seinen Wochenpredigten von 1530 bis 1532: ZTK 85 (1988) 409-454.

4553 **Bouterse** J., De boom en zijin vruchten; Bergrede en Berg-redechristendom bij Reformatoren, Anabaptisten en Spiritualisten in de zestiende eeuw; diss. Leiden 1986 → 3,4324: [R]NedTTs 42 (1988) 347-9 (W. *Nijenhuis*).

4554 **Carson** D.A., The Sermon on the Mount 1986 (= ? 1978 → 60,5952; 3,4327): [R]Salesianum 50 (1988) 225s (G. *Abbà*).

4554* **Davenport** Gene L., Into the darkness; discipleship in the Sermon on the Mount. Nv 1988, Abingdon. 302 p. $16 [JBL 108,566].

4555 *Flusser* David, *a*) A rabbinic parallel to the Sermon on the Mount [ineditum]; – *b*) Matthew's 'Verus Israel'; – *c*) A lost Jewish benediction in Matthew 9,8; – *d*) The Didache and the Noachic commandments; – *e*) 'I am in the midst of them' (Mt 18,20); – *f*) Jesus and the sign of the Son of Man [inedita]: → 190, JudOrChr 1988, 494-508 / 561-574 / 535-542 / 508 / 515-525 / 526-534.

4556 **Ginzel** Günter B., Die Bergpredigt, jüdisches und christliches Glaubensdokument 1985 → 1,4331; 2,3399: [R]JEcuSt 25 (1988) 106s (M. *Wyschogrod*: helpful but not nuanced).

4557 *Hauerwas* Stanley, Le sermon sur la montagne, guerre juste et recherche de la paix: Concilium 215 (P 1988) 51-59.

4558 **Hendrickx** H., El sermón de la montaña 1986 → 3,4342: [R]BibFe 14 (1988) 149 (A. *Salas*).

4559 **Lambrecht** Jan, 'Eh bien! Moi je vous dis'; le discours-programme de Jésus: LDiv 125, 1986 → 2,3402; 3,4347: [R]FoiTemps 19 (1987) 285 (C. *Focant*).

4560 **Lapide** P., The Sermon on the Mount 1986 → 2,3405; 3,4349: [R]JEcuSt 24 (1987) 127 (J.T. *Pawlikowski*); ScripTPamp 19 (1987) 937-941 (J.M. *Casciaro*: 'non es longe a Regno Dei').

4561 *Lapide* Pinchas, Come amare i propri nemici? Leggere il Discorso della montagna con un ebreo [conferenza Trento]: Humanitas 42 (Brescia 1987) 167-185.

4562 [E]*Leloir* L., S. EPHREM, le texte de son commentaire du Sermon de la Montagne: → 56, Mém. GRIBOMONT J. 1988, 361-391 [Syriac-Latin on facing pages].

4563 *Löfstedt* Bengt, Zu AUGUSTINS Schrift 'De sermone Domini in monte' [addenda zu *Mutzenbecher* A. 1967]: Orpheus 9 (1988) 96s.

4564 **Lohfink** Gerhard, Wem gilt die Bergpredigt? Beiträge zu einer christlichen Ethik. FrB 1988, Herder. 238 p. DM 28. – [R]BiKi 43 (1988) 125s (M. *Helsper*); TLZ 113 (1988) 897-9 (E. *Lohse*).

4565 *Mounce* R.H., Sermon on the Mount: → 801, ISBEnc[3] 4 (1988) 411-6 (-7, on the plain, *Danker* F.W.).

4566 *Müller* Burkhard, Politik der Bergpredigt?: Wege zum Menschen 40 (1988) 142-156.

4567 **Panimolle** S.A., Il discorso della montagna, esegesi e vita: Fame e sete della Parola 5. T 1986, Paoline. 230 p. – [R]RivB 36 (1988) 113-5 (V. *Fusco*).

4568 **Prabhavananda** Swami, Il Discorso della Montagna secondo il Vedanta, [T]*Guarnero* Levi & Elsa. T 1988, Gribaudi. 151 p. Lit. 12.000.

4569 **Stock** Klemens, Discorso della Montagna Mt 5-7; le beatitudini. R 1988, Pontificio Istituto Biblico. iv-134 p.

4570 **Stoll** Brigitta, 'De virtute in virtutem'; zur Auslegungs- und Wirkungsgeschichte der Bergpredigt in Kommentaren, Predigten und hagiographischer Literatur: *a)* zwischen 800 und 1200: Diss. D*Schindler* A. Bern 1987. 340 p. – RTLv 19,543. – *b)* ... von der Merowingerzeit bis um 1200: BeiGBEx 30. Tü 1988, Mohr. xviii-351 p. 3-16-145351-4.

4571 **Strecker** Georg, The Sermon on the Mount, an exegetical commentary [²1985 → 65,3929], T*Dean* O. C. E 1988, Clark. 223 p. 0-567-29152-9.

4572 **Syreeni** Kari, The making of the Sermon on the Mount I, 1987 → 3,4360: RBibTB 18 (1988) 119s (L. J. *White*).

4573 **Vaught** Carl G., The Sermon on the Mount; a theological interpretation 1986 → 3,4362: RSWJT 31,2 (1988s) 54 (W. M. *Tillman*: philosophy teacher's Sunday school presentation); TS 49 (1988) 200 (C. *Bernas*).

4574 **Venetz** Hermann J., Die Bergpredigt: biblische Anstösse. Dü/Fr 1987, Patmos/Kanisius. 128 p. 3-491-72190-3. – RBiKi 43 (1988) 88 (M. *Helsper*).

4575 **Vouga** François, Jésus et la Loi selon la tradition synoptique; préf., *Schweizer* E.: Le Monde de la Bible. Genève 1988, Labor et Fides. 331 p. 2-8309-0102-9. – RÉTRel 63 (1988) 608 (J. *Ansaldi*).

F3.6 Mt 5,3-11 (Lc 6,20-22) Beatitudines.

4576 **Borao** Jesús, El camino de las bienaventuranzas. Estella 1987, VDivino. 227 p. – RNatGrac 34 (1987) 282 (D. *Castillo*).

4577 *Boring* M. Eugene, The historical-critical method's 'criteria of authenticity'; the beatitudes in Q and Thomas as a test case: → 309, Semeia 44 (1988) 9-44.

4578 **Broer** Ingo, Die Seligpreisungen der Bergpredigt...: BoBB 61, 1986 → 2,3415; 3,4366: RBiKi 42 (1987) 84s (R. *Baumann*); TPhil 63 (1988) 256s (J. *Beutler*).

4579 *a) Brooke* George J., The wisdom of Matthew's Beatitudes (4QBeat and Mat. 5:3-12): ScripB 19 (1988s) 35-41; – *b) Puech* Émile, Un hymne essénien en partie retrouvé et les Béatitudes; 1QH V 12 – VI 18 (= col. XIII-XIV 7) et 4QBéat: → 22, Mém. CARMIGNAC J., RQum 13 (1988) 59-88; 2 fig.; pl. III.

4580 **Camacho** Fernando, La proclama del reino; análisis semántico y comentario exegético de las Bienaventuranzas de Mateo (5,3-10) 1986 → 3,4367: RFgNt 1 (1988) 224s (J. *Peláez*); también 2,1 (1989) 99s (D. A. *Black*).

4581 **Coste** René, Le grand secret des Béatitudes 1985 → 1,4352*; 2,3418: RFoiTemps 19 (1987) 285s (P. *Wéber*).

4582 **Lambert** Bernard, Las Bienaventuranzas y la cultura hoy: Nueva Alianza 106, 1987 → 3,4368 ['de' hoy]: RCiTom 115 (1988) 577 (J. L. *Espinel*); NatGrac 34 (1987) 282 (D. *Castillo*).

4583 **López-Melús** Francisco M. Las bienaventuranzas, ley fundamental de la vida cristiana; pref. *Díez Macho* Alejandro: Nueva alianza 109 [no 106 como cobierta]. Salamanca 1988, Sígueme. 588 p. pt 2000. 84-301-1058-5. – RCiTom 115 (1988) 577s (J. L. *Espinel*); NatGrac 35 (1988) 438s (F. F. *Ramos*).

4584 **Plackal** Antony O., Tradition and redaction in the Matthean Beatitudes: diss. D*Getty* M. Wsh 1988. – RTLv 20,545.

4585 **Pobee** John,   Who are the poor 1987 → 3,4369:   ᴿAnglTR 70 (1988) 285s (T. *Presler*).

4586 *Boxel* P.W. van,   You have heard that it was said [Mt 5,21(-48)]: Bijdragen 49 (1988) 362-377.

4587 *Black* David A.,   Jesus on anger; the text of Matthew 5: 22a revisited: NT 30 (1988) 1-8.

4588 *Wolbert* Erner [Mt 5,22] 'Wer seinem Bruder ohne Grund zürnt'; zu einer Lesart der 1. Antithese: TGL 78 (1988) 160-170.

4589 *Vijver* E., [Mt 5,31 ...] El uso de la Biblia en cuestiones éticas; el caso del divorcio: Cuadernos de Teología 8,1 (BA 1987) 17-33 [NTAbs 32,206].

4589* *Ruckstuhl* Eugen, [Mt 5,31 ...] Hat Jesus die Unauflöslichkeit der Ehe gelehrt? [< Jésus a-t-il enseigné ... YbTantur 1973s, 79-96]: → 4203, Jesus im Horizont der Evangelien 1988, 49-66; Nachtrag 66-69.

4590 *Crouzel* Henri,   Le sens de 'porneia' dans les incises matthéennes [5,32; 19,9; *Cottiaux* J. 1982 overlooked his 1972 proof that ancient citations show Mt 19,9 in the form of 5,32, without mention of remarriage]: NRT 110 (1988) 903-910.

4591 *Venetz* Hermann-J.,   [Mt 5,31s] Die Ehe unter dem Anspruch der Bergpredigt; neue Kommentare zum Matthäusevangelium: Orientierung 52 (1988) 229-233.

4591* *Donelson* Lewis R., [Mt 5,39] 'Do not resist evil' and the question of biblical authority: HorBT 10,1 (1988) 33-46.

4592 **Mollenkott** Virginia R., [Mt 5,43] Godding 1987 → 3,4393: 0-8245-0824-6:   ᴿHorizons 15 (1988) 421 (Georgia M. *Keightley*); RExp 85 (1988) 172s (Molly *Marshall-Green*: awkward neologism 'godding' means incarnation for cocreating a just and loving society); TTod 45 (1988s) 363.366.368 (Renita J. *Weems*).

4593 *Ulonska* H.,   Glück den Unglücklichen; Zu den Makarismen des Neuen Testaments: EvErz 39 (Fra 1987) 530-547 [NTAbs 32,206].

4594 *a) Zeller* Dieter,   Jesus als vollmächtiger Lehrer (Mt 5-7) und der hellenistische Gesetzgeber; – *b) Dautzenberg* Gerhard,   Mt 5,43c und die antike Tradition von der jüdischen Misanthropie; – *c) Hoffmann* Paul, Der Q-Text der Sprüche vom Sorgen; Mt 6,25-33/Lk 12,22-31, ein Rekonstruktionsversuch: → 115, ᶠPESCH W., Studien Mt 1988, 299-317 / 47-77 / 127-155.

F3.7   **Mt 6,9-13** (Lc 11,2-4) *Oratio Jesu,* Pater Noster, **Lord's Prayer** [→ H1.4].

4595 *Aland* Kurt,   Noch einmal; der ROTAS/SATOR-Rebus [= Paternoster + AÖ, *Grosser* F. 1926; PR Supp 15 (1978) 477-565; *Baines* W. NTS 33 (1987) 469-476]: → 85, ᶠKLIJN A., Text 1988, 9-23.

4597 *Apecechea Perurena* Juan,   Comentario del Padrenuestro de Joaquín LIZARRAGA, el Vicario de Elcana (las dos primeras peticiones):   ScripV 35 (1988) 413-432.

4598 **Boff** Léonardo,   Le Notre Père, une prière de libération intégrale, ᵀ*Durban* Christine & Luc: Théologies.   P/Montréal 1988, Cerf/Bellarmin. 168 p.   F 89. – ᴿEsprVie 98 (1988) 351 [repété sans explication p.447s: G.-M. *Oury* n'approuve pas p.153, 'Le Malin représenterait simplement l'organisation de l'injustice ...'].

4599 *Chernoff* Robert,   Jewish origins of the Lord's Prayer: Dor 17 (1988s) 37-39.

4600 **Coenen** Gertrud, Das Gebet des Herrn als katechetische Hilfe: Diss. DEmeis. Münster 1987s. – TR 84 (1988) 512.

4601 *Cunningham* Laurence S., We dare to say 'Our Father': Commonweal 114 (1987) 291s.

4602 *Gil* Luis, Versiones del Pater noster al castellano en el Siglo de Oro: FgNT 1 (1988) 175-191; Eng. 191.

4603 **Gillet** Lev, The Jesus prayer[2] [[1]1974 < French], EWare Kallistos, bp. Crestwood NY 1987, St. Vladimir. 120 p. $6 [TDig 35,65].

4604 *Gispert-Sauch* George, La 'preghiera del Signore' in sanscrito, TPoli Flavio: StRicOrCr 9 (1986) 209-215.

4605 *LaVerdiere* Eugene, The Lord's Prayer in literary context: → 141, FSTUHLMUELLER C., Scripture and prayer 1988, 104-116.

4606 **Lustiger**, Jean-Marie, card., The Lord's prayer, TBalinski Rebecca H. Huntington IN 1988, Our Sunday Visitor. 159 p. $10; pa. $4 [TDig 35,375].

4607 *Magne* Jean, La variante du Pater de Lc 11,2: LavalTP 44 (1988) 369-374 [< ZIT 89,12].

4608 EPetuchowski Jacob J., *Brocke* Michael, The Lord's prayer and Jewish liturgy 1976 → 60,6016...: RIndTSt 25 (1988) 110s (M.D. *Ambrose*).

4609 **Rondyang** Yakobo, 'Your kingdom come' in the traditional religion of the Bari (Sudan) and in the Lord's Prayer; a comparative study: diss. Angelicum, DBorriello L. Rome 1987. – RTLv 19,554.

4610 **Sabugal** Santos, Il Padrenostro nella catechesi antica e moderna [cf. 1985 → 2,3440]: TENicolosi Mauro: Cristianismo 2. Palermo 1988 = 1985, Augustinus. 412 p. Lit. 22.000.

4611 **Sandstrom** Philip J., Bishop Lancelot ANDREWES, a man of his times, and his nineteen sermons upon prayer in general and the Lord's Prayer in particular [c.1585]: diss. Inst. Cath. DGy P.; P 1987. 218 p. – RICathP 25 (1988) 97.

4612 *Sinkewicz* R.E., An early Byzantine commentary on the Jesus prayer; introduction and edition [Eng. with reconstituted Greek text]: Mediaeval Studies 49 (1987) 208-220 [< RSPT 72,157].

4613 **Stritzky** Maria-Barbara von, Studien zur Überlieferung und Interpretation des Vaterunsers in der frühchristlichen Literatur: Diss. DCramer. Münster 1987s. – TR 84 (1988) 512.

4614 *Taussig* Hal, The Lord's prayer: Forum 4,4 (1988) 25-41.

4615 *Davidson* J.A., [Mt 6,25-34] Living one day at a time: ExpTim 99 (1987s) 367-9.

4616 *Wang* Weifent, [Mt 6,28] Lilies of the field: Chinese Theological Review (Holland MI 1987) 125-138 [< TKontext 10/1,35].

4617 *Derrett* J.D.M., Christ and reproof (Matthew 7.1-5 / Luke 6,37-42): NTS 34 (1988) 271-281.

4618 *Lips* Hermann von, Schweine füttert man, Hunde nicht — ein Versuch, das Rätsel von Matthäus 7,6 zu lösen: ZNW 79 (1988) 165-186.

4619 *Crossan* John D., [Mt 7,7; 21,22...] Aphorism in discourse and narrative [p. 121 and iii; but page-headings have 'in disclosure and narrative']: → 404, Semeia 43 (1988) 121-140 (141-4, *Tannehill* Robert C., response).

4620 *Łach* Jan, ● De relatione 'principii aurei agendi' in Mt 7,12 ad praeceptum inimicos diligendi in Mt 5,43-48: RuBi 41 (1988) 457-465.

4621 **MacDougall** Daniel W., [Mt 7,16; 21,18-22; 24,32-34] The fig and fig tree imagery in the Gospel of Matthew: diss. Calvin Sem. ᴰ*Van Elderen* B. GR 1988. iii-159 p. + bibliog. – CalvinT 23 (1988) 305s.

4622 **Wegner** Uwe, Der Hauptmann von Kafarnaum (Mt 7,28s...): WUNT 2/14, 1985 → 1,4401 ... 3,4411: ᴿRTLv 19 (1988) 497-9 (Alice *Dermience*: pas convaincant).

4623 *Kingsbury* Jack D., On following Jesus; the 'eager' scribe and the 'reluctant' disciple (Matthew 8. 18-22): NTS 34 (1988) 45-59.

4624 *Smith* Mahlon H. [Mt 8,20 = Thomas Gospel 86, 'foxes have holes...'] No place for a Son of Man: Forum 4,4 (1988) 83-107.

4625 **Carson** D. A., When Jesus confronts the world; an exposition of Matthew 8-10. GR 1987, Baker. 154 p. $8 pa. 0-8010-2522-2 [NTAbs 32,240]. – ᴿRExp 85 (1988) 562 (J. E. *Jones*: reworked sermons).

F4.1   **Mt 9-12;**   *Miracula Jesu* – **The Gospel Miracles.**

4626 *a) Abecassis* A., Le miracle juif; – *b) Hruby* K., Le miracle dans la tradition hassidique: Sidic 21,2 (R 1988) 5-9 / 15-17.

4627 **Achterberg** Jeanne, Imagery in healing; shamanism and modern medicine [which harmfully ignores effect of mind on body]. Boston 1985, New Science. 253 p. $10. – ᴿCurrTM 15 (1988) 214 (P. R. *Swanson*).

4628 **Beck** Daniel A., Miracle and mechanical philosophy; the theology of Robert BOYLE in its historical context: diss. ND 1986. – RelStR 14,186.

4629 **Blue** Ken, Authority to heal. DG 1987, InterVarsity. 268 p. $12 pa. [GraceTJ 9,302].

4630 **Brown** Colin, That you may believe; miracles then and now, GR 1985, Paternoster 1986 → 1,4414; 2,3454: ᴿEvQ 60 (1988) 79s (S. H. *Travis*).

4631 *a) Cavill* Paul, 'Signs and wonders' and the Venerable BEDE [*Bridge* D. 1985]; – *b) Gardner* Rex, Miracles of healing in Anglo-Celtic Northumbria as recorded by the venerable Bede and his contemporaries; a reappraisal in the light of twentieth century experience: British Medical Journal 287 (1983) p. 1927-1933.

4632 **Charlier** Jean-Pierre, Signes et prodiges; les miracles dans l'Évangile 1987 → 3,4418: ᴿEstBíb 46 (1988) 133s (F. *González García*); Études 368 (1988) 566s (P. *Gibert*); MondeB 53 (1988) 59; RThom 88 (1988) 648-50 (L. *Devillers*: ressuscite une exégèse ultra-libérale); VSp 142 (1988) 292s (H. *Cousin*).

4633 **Coates** G., He gives us signs; understanding miracles. L c.1987, Hodder & S. £10 [TLond 91,77].

4634 **Dzielska** M., APOLLONIUS of Tyana in legend and history [1983 → 3,4421], ᵀ*Pieńkowski* Piotr: Problemi e Ricerche di Storia Antica 10. R 1986, Bretschneider. 229 p. 88-7062-599-0 [NTAbs 32,262]. – ᴿAthenaeum 66 (1988) 643-5 (G. *Salmeri*).

4635 *Engelbrecht* J., Trends in miracle research: Neotestamentica 22,1 (1988) 139-161.

4636 **Fiederlein** Friedrich M., Die Wunder Jesu und die Wundererzählungen der Urkirche. Mü 1988, Don Bosco. 264 p. DM 24,80 pa. – ᴿBiKi 43 (1988) 180s (P. G. *Müller*).

4637 *Fuhrmann* Manfred, Wunder und Wirklichkeit; zur Siebenschläferlegende und anderen Texten aus christlicher Tradition: → 684, Fiktiv 1983, 209-224 [393-5, *Kulenkampff* Jens].

4638 **Gardner** Rex, Healing miracles; a doctor investigates 1986 → 2,3461; 3,4423: ScotBEv 6 (1988) 128s (J. *Wilkinson*).

4639 *Giesen* Heinz, Jesu Krankenheilungen im Verständnis des Matthäus-evangeliums: → 115, FPESCH W., Studien Mt 1988, 79-106.

4640 **Glavich** sr. M. Kathleen, Acting out the miracles and parables; 52 five-minute plays for education and worship. Mystic CT 1988, Twenty-Third. 129 p. $13 pa. [TDig 36,61].

4641 *Gousmett* Chris, Creation order and miracle according to AUGUSTINE: EvQ 60 (1988) 217-240.

4642 **Harper** Michael, The healings of Jesus [... same kind as today] 1986 → 2,3446; 3,4426: RBS 145 (1988) 233 (R. P. *Lightner*).

4643 *Hellwig* Monika K., The miracles of Jesus: ChSt 26 (1987) 272-283.

4644 **Hendrickx** H., The miracle stories in the Synoptic Gospels. NY/L 1987, Harper & R. / Chapman. x-310 p. $17 pa. 0-06-254851-4/L 0-225-66487-0 [NTAbs 32,371].

4645 **Jenkins** David, God, miracle and the Church of England 1987 → 3,4429: RNBlackf 69 (1988) 304 (N. P. *Harvey*); Themelios 14 (1988s) 74s (R. *Sturch*); TLond 91 (1988) 331-3 (K. W. *Clements*: not chiefly a defence of his stance in the controversies generated by the author as Bishop of Durham).

4646 **Kee** Howard C., Medicine, miracle and magic in NT times: SNTS Mg 55, 1986 → 2,3468 ... 3,4430: RCBQ 50 (1988) 330s (B. J. *Malina*: uses discarded 4Q Therapeia, and no general views like MURDOCK G. P., Theories of illness, a world survey, Univ. Pittsburg 1980; YOUNG A., The anthropologies of illness, & WORSLEY P., Non-western medical systems, Annual Review of Anthropology 11 (1982) 257-285 / 315-348); Interpretation 42 (1988) 106 (J. D. *Kingsbury*); JAAR 56 (1988) 585-7 (S. N. *Olson*); JHS 108 (1988) 248s (Helen *King*); PerspRelSt 15 (1988) 179s (Sharyn E. *Dowd*); RExp 85 (1988) 137s (D. E. *Garland*).

4647 **Knoch** Otto, Dem, der glaubt, ist alles möglich; die Botschaft der Wundererzählungen der Evangelien; ein Werkbuch zur Bibel. Stu 1986, KBW. 584 p.; 37 fig. (Anna Braungart). DM 48. 3-460-32491-0. – RTR 84 (1988) 201-4 (A. *Kolping*); ZkT 110 (1988) 199 (K. *Stock*).

4648 **Larmer** Robert A. H., Water into wine? An investigation of the concept of miracle. Kingston/Montreal 1987, McGill-Queen's Univ. xi-155 p. $22.50 [TDig 35,276].

4649 *Larson* E. L. & S. M., A philosophy of healing from the ministry of Jesus: Faith & Thought 112,1 (Exter 1986) 63-75 [NTAbs 32,203].

4650 **Latourelle** René, Miracles de Jésus et théologie du miracle 1986 → 2,3471; 3,4423: RBLitEc 89 (1988) 152 (H. de *Gensac*); RTPhil 120 (1988) 375 (Aline *Lasserre*).

4651 **Latourelle** René, Miracoli di Gesù e teologia del miracolo [1986 → 2,3471],T. Assisi 1987, Cittadella. 464 p. Lit. 26.000. – RCC 189 (1988,4) 199 (V. *Fusco*); HumBr 43 (1988) 887s (R. *Tononi*); ScripTPamp 20 (1988) 948 (C. *Izquierdo*); ScuolC 32 (1988) 157 (U. *De Martino*).

4652 **Latourelle** R., The miracles of Jesus and the theology of miracles, TO'Connell M. J. NY 1988, Paulist. vi-371 p. $15 [NRT 111, 752, X. *Jacques*]. 0-8091-2997-3.

4653 *Levoratti* Armando J., Milagros de Jesús y teología del milagro: RBibArg 29 (1988) 1-32.

4654 **McCaslin** Keith, What the Bible says about miracles. Joplin MO 1988, College. 425 p. $14 [JBL 108,380].

4655 **McGarey** William A., Healing miracles; using your body energies, SF 1988, Harper & R. 189 p. $8.45 [JAAR 57,455].

4656 a) *Maier* Gerhard, L'esegesi dei miracoli neotestamentari nel corso degli ultimi due secoli; [T]*Grosso* S.; – b) *Yamauchi* Edwin, Magia o miracolo? Malattie, demoni ed esorcismi [< Gospel Perspective(s)], [T]*Terino* J.: STEv 11,21 (1988) 9-51 / 53-144.

4657 **Maillot** A.,   Ces miracles qui nous dérangent 1986 → 3,4439:   [R]Protestantesimo 43 (1988) 119s (G. *Conte*).

4658 **Manigne** Jean-Pierre, Le maître des signes. P 1987, Cerf. 179 p. – [R]CiTom 115 (1988) 397 (J. L. *Espinel*); VSp 142 (1988) 140s (D. *Cerbelaud*).

4659 **Martins Terra** J. E., O milagre; filosofia-história-linguagem-Bíblia-teologia. São Paulo 1981, Loyola. 253 p. – [R]Gregorianum 69 (1988) 186 (E. *Farahian*).

4660 **Mosetto** F., I miracoli ... ORIGENE 1986 → 2,3474; 3,4442: [R]Asprenas 35 (1988) 406-8 (L. *Fatica*); Claretianum 28 (1988) 403s (B. *Proietti*); CrNSt 9 (1988) 181-3 (M. *Fédou*); JTS 39 (1988) 246s (R. M. *Grant*: fine, but 'Origen did not always tell Celsus just what he told fellow-Christians'; 'each accepted only the miracles of his own "faith", though it would appear both had questions about some of them'); RivB 36 (1988) 117-9 (M. *Làconi*); SBFLA 38 (1988) 512-6 (L. *Cignelli*); StPatav 35 (1988) 725s (C. *Corsato*).

4661 **Nichols** Terence I., Miracles as a sign of the good creation: diss. Marquette. Milwaukee 1988. 368 p. 89-04277. – DissA 49 (1988s) 3764-A.

4662 **Nielsen** Helge K., Heilung und Verkündigung 1987 → 3,4443: [R]BiKi 43 (1988) 126s (W. *Stenger*).

4663 *Olu Igenoza* A., Medicine and healing in African Christianity; a biblical critique: AfER 30,1 (1988) 12-25 [< NTAbs 32,343].

4664 *Pearl* Leon, Miracles and theism: RelSt 24 (C 1988) 483-495.

4665 **Penndu** Théophile, Les miracles de Jésus, signes du monde nouveau. Montréal 1985, Levain. 352 p. F 96. – [R]DivThom 89s (1986s) 490s (Y. *Poutet*).

4666 **Perrin** Louis, Guérir et sauver; entendre la parole des malades: Recherches Morales. P 1987, Cerf. 248 p. – [R]SémBib 49 (1988) 35s (L. *Panier*).

4667 *Pilch* John J., Understanding biblical healing; selecting the appropriate model: BibTB 18 (1988) 60-66.

4668 **Remus** Harold, Pagan-Christian conflict over miracle 1983 → 64,4376 ... 3,4450: [R]Bijdragen 49 (1988) 334s (M. *Parmentier*).

4669 *Rusecki* Marian, ❷ La dimension sotérique du miracle: ColcT 58,1 (1988) 71-86; franç. 87.

4670 *Sharp* John C., Miracles and the 'Laws of Nature': ScotBEv 6 (1988) 1-19.

4671 **Shorter** Aylward, Jesus and the witchdoctor 1985 → 1,4442: [R]Vidyajyoti 52 (1988) 118s (J. *Antony*).

4672 **Sigal** P.-A., L'homme et le miracle dans la France médiévale 1985 → 3,4445: [R]SR 17 (1988) 374s (P. *Boglioni*).

4673 **Torell** Jean-Pierre, *Bouthillier* Denise, PIERRE le Vénérable et sa vision du monde; sa vie, son œuvre, l'homme et le démon: Spicilegium Sacrum 42. Lv 1986. XL-454 p. – [R]Gregorianum 69 (1988) 149-151 (R. *Latourelle*: 'ouvrage axé sur le De miraculis').

4674 *Uricchio* F., Miracolo: → 806, NDizTB (1988) 954-978.

4675 a) *Weiser* Alfons, 'Die Gabe, Krankheiten zu heilen'; Jesus und die Kranken; – b) *Richter* Klemens, 'Ist einer von euch krank ...'; Krankensalbungen in der frühen Kirche: BiKi 43 (1988) 2-7 / 13-16.

4676 ᴱ**Wenham** David, *Blomberg* Craig, The miracles of Jesus: Gospel Perspectives 6, 1986 → 2,271: ᴿBZ 32 (1988) 145s (I. *Broer*).

4677 **Wiles** Maurice, God's action in the world [Bampton Lectures] 1986 → 3,4461; 0-334-62028-X: ᴿModT 5 (1988s) 187-190 (B. *Hebblethwaite*); ScotBEv 6 (1988) 67s (R. *Kearsley*) unaccountably reprinted 129s.

4678 *Young* William, Miracles in Church History: Churchman 102 (L 1988) 102-121 [< ZIT 88,585].

4679 *Sauget* Joseph-Marie († 6.IV.1988), [Mt 9,9-13] Une homélie syriaque sur la vocation de Matthieu attribuée à Jean CHRYSOSTOME: → 59, ᶠGUILLAUMONT A. 1988, 187-199.

4680 *Kalin* Everett R., Matthew 9:18-26, an exercise in redaction criticism: → 143, ᶠTIETJEN J. = CurrTM 15 (1988) 39-47.

4681 *Bartnicki* Roman, Die Jünger Jesu in Mt 9,35 – 11,1: ColcT 58 sp (1988) 39-54.

4682 **Levine** Amy-Jill, The social and ethnic dimensions of Matthean salvation history, 'Go nowhere among the Gentiles ...' (Matt. 10:5b): StBEC 14. Lewiston NY 1988, Mellen. xii-319 p. 0-88946-614-9.

4683 *O'Callaghan* José, Probabile armonizzazione in Mt 10,14: RivB 36 (1988) 79s.

4684 *Giesen* Heinz, [Mt 10,23] Naherwartung im Neuen Testament?: TGegw 30 (1988) 151-164.

4685 *Cook* John G., The sparrow's fall in Mt 10,29b: ZNW 79 (1988) 138-144.

4686 *O'Callaghan* José, Armonizaciones en Mt 11,18; 10,8: Emerita 18 (1988) 117-120.

4687 *Allison* Dale C.ᴶ, Two notes on a key text, Matthew 11:25-30 ['perhaps the most important verses in the Synoptic Gospels', *Hunter* A.]: JTS 39 (1988) 477-485.

4688 **Deutsch** Celia, Hidden wisdom and the easy yoke ... Mt 11,25-30: JStNT Sup 18, ᴰ1987 → 3,4488: ᴿBiblica 69 (1988) 587s (T. *Prendergast*); CBQ 50 (1988) 526s (D. J. *Harrington*); Themelios 14 (1988s) 66 (D. *France*).

4689 *Lods* Marc, Jésus et les petits enfants (note exégétique); PosLuth 36 (1988) 75-80 [< ZIT 88,524].

4690 **Mulloor** Augustine, Jesus' prayer of praise; a study of the meaning and function of Mt 11,25-30 in the First Gospel: diss. Pont. Ist. Biblico, ᴰ*Lentzen-Deis* F. 223 p. – AcPIB 9,5 (1988s) 384; 425s; Biblica 70,443.

4691 *Robbins* Vernon K., [Mt 12,22-37 ...] Pronouncement stories from a rhetorical [*chreia*] perspective: Forum 4,2 (1988) 3-28; imposing bibliography 28-32.

4692 **Gilles** Jean, [Mt 12,46; 13,55; Mc 3,31 ...] I 'fratelli e sorelle' di Gesù 1985 → 1,4512; 2,3534: ᴿSalesianum 50 (1988) 420s (C. *Bissoli*: 'si dichiara cattolico').

F4.3 **Mt 13** ... *Parabolae Jesu* – **the Parables.**

4693 **Arens** Edmund, Kommunikative Handlungen ... Gleichnisse Jesu 1982 → 63,4539 ... 1,4470: ᴿZkT 110 (1988) 216s (R. *Oberforcher*).

4694 *Arens* Edmund,   Metaphorische Erzählungen und kommunikative Handlungen Jesu; zum Ansatz einer Gleichnistheorie [*Harnisch* W. 1985]: BZ 32 (1988) 52-71 ['Theo-Psychologen wie E. *Drewermann* und Theo-Poeten wie Amos N. *Wilder*' ...].

4695 *Bacq* Philippe, *Mourlon Beernaert* Pierre,   Paraboles de l'Évangile et communication: LVitae 42 (1987) 281-290.

4696 **Baudler** Georg,   Jesus im Spiegel seiner Gleichnisse; das erzählerische Lebenswerk Jesu, ein Zugang zum Glauben 1986 ➤ 2,3504; 3,4497: ᴿDocCom 40 (1987) 307-9 (G. zu *Forst*); LebZeug 42,2 (1987) 81-83 (B. *Sill*); SNTU-A 13 (1988) 221s (A. *Fuchs*); TGegw 30 (1987) 275 (H. *Giesen*); TR 84 (1988) 110-2 (E. *Arens*).

4697 **Borsch** F.H.,   Many things in parables; extravagant stories of new community. Ph 1988, Fortress. x-167 p. $13 pa. 0-8006-2042-9 [NTAbs 32,240].

4698 *a*) *Culbertson* P.,   Einführung in die Gleichnisse Jesu in ihrem jüdischen Kontext; – *b*) *Kremers* H.,   Beitrag des NT zu einer Christologie im Dialog zwischen Juden und Christen: Gespräche in Israel 6,1 (Nes Ammim 1988) 21-38 / 3-20 [< Judaica 44,188].

4699 *Davis* Christian R.,   Structural analysis of Jesus' narrative parables; a conservative approach: GraceTJ 9 (1988) 191-204.

4700 **Donahue** John R.,   The Gospel in parable; metaphor, narrative, and theology in the Synoptic Gospels. Ph 1988, Fortress. xi-354 p. $30 [TDig 35,351]. 0-8006-0852-6.

4701 **Drury** John,   The parables in the Gospels; history and allegory 1985 ➤ 1,4478; 2,3510:   ᴿSvEx 53 (1988) 122 (A. *Ekenberg*).

4702 **Dschulnigg** Peter,   Rabbinische Gleichnisse und das NT; die Gleichnisse der PesK im Vergleich mit den Gleichnissen Jesu und dem NT [Hab.-Diss. Luzern 1988, ᴰ*Kirchschläger*. – TR 84 (1988) 510]: Judaica et Christiana 12. Bern 1988, Lang. xvii-654 p. [TR 85,251]. 3-261-03912-4.

4703 **Dutzmann** Martin,   Gleichniserzählungen Jesu als Texte evangelischer Predigt: Diss. ᴰ*Wintzer* G.   Bonn 1988. – RTLv 19,537.

4704 **Erlemann** Kurt,   Das Bild Gottes in den synoptischen Gleichnissen [Diss. Heidelberg, ᴰ*Berger* K.]: BWANT 126. Stu 1988, Kohlhammer. 308 p. DM 78. 3-17-010089-0. – ᴿÉTRel 63 (1988) 609s (E. *Cuvillier*); TsTNijm 28 (1988) 308 (J. *Smit*).

4705 **Espinel** J.L.,   La poesía de Jesús 1986 ➤ 2,3512; 3,4499:   ᴿClaretianum 27 (1987) 396s (B. *Proietti*); DivThom 91 (1988) 191s (G. *Testa*); Salesianum 50 (1988) 418s (C. *Bissoli*); Salmanticensis 35 (1988) 411s (G. *Pérez*).

4707 *Gerhardsson* Birger,   *a*) The narrative meshalim in the Synoptic Gospels; a comparison with the narrative meshalim in the Old Testament: NTS 34 (1988) 339-363; – *b*) De berättande maschalerna i de synoptiska evangelierna; en jamförelse med samma textsort i Gamla testamentet: SvEx 53 (1988) 36-62.

4708 **Glavich** Mary Kathleen sr.,   Voices; messages in Gospel symbols [meditations on: manger, gold, turtledoves, wine, nets, perfume, fringe, leftovers, sycamore, water jar, coin, fish, towel, thorns, stone]. Mystic CT 1988, Twenty-Third. 96 p. $6 pa. [TDig 35,361].

4709 *Granado* Carmelo,   Las parábolas de misericordia en PACIANO de Barcelona: EstE 63 (1988) 435-454.

4710 **Harnisch** Wolfgang,   Die Gleichniserzählungen Jesu; eine hermeneutische Einführung 1985 ➤ 1,4485; 2,3514:   ᴿTGL 78 (1988) 430s (E. *Spiegel*).

4711 **Hendrickx** H., The parables of Jesus 1986 → 2,3514*: ᴿNBlackf 68 (1987) 415s (M. *Davies*).

4712 *Hermans* C. A. M., Understanding parables and similes qua metaphors: JEmpT 1,2 (Kampen 1988) 21-50 [< ᴢɪᴛ 89,120].

4713 *Hoover* Roy W., Sayings from Q; parables round two: Forum 4,4 (1988) 109-128.

4714 **Martini** Carlo M., Der Acker ist die Welt; was uns Jesus in Gleichnissen sagt 1986 → 3,4508: ᴿTLZ 113 (1988) 471s (E. *Spiegel*).

4715 *O'Neill* J. C., The source of the parables of the bridegroom and the wicked husbandmen [Mt 9,14s; 21,33-46: the only parables in which Jesus seems to refer to himself by telling stories about figures who could well be taken as allegorical representations of the Messiah]: JTS 39 (1988) 485-9.

4716 **Praeder** Susan M., [Mt 13,33; 25,1-13; Lk 15,8-10; 18,1-8] The world in women's worlds; four parables: Zacchaeus Studies [ᴱ*Getty* Mary Ann]. Wilmington 1988, Glazier. 120 p. $7. 0-89453-667-2 [TDig 36,194].

4717 *a*) *Riches* John, Parables and the search for a new community; – *b*) *Anderson* Hugh, Jesus; aspects of the question of his authority; – *c*) *Dunn* James D. G., Pharisees, sinners, and Jesus: → 77, ᶠKᴇᴇ H., Social world 1988, 235-263 / 290-310 / 264-289.

4718 **Schramm** Tim, *Löwenstein* Kathrin, [Mt 13,44...] Unmoralische Helden — anstössige Gleichnisse Jesu 1986 → 2,3525; DM 28; 3-525-53575-9: ᴿSalesianum 50 (1988) 231 (G. *Abbà*); TsTNijm 28 (1988) 85 (L. *Grollenberg*).

4719 *Siverns* L. E., A definition of parable: NESTR 9,1 (1988) 60-75.

4720 *a*) *Stroker* William D., Extracanonical parables and the historical Jesus; – *b*) *Crossan* John D., Divine immediacy and human immediacy; towards a new first principle in historical Jesus research: → 309, Semeia 44 (1988) 95-120 / 121-140.

4721 **Thoma** Clemens, *Lauer* Simon, Die Gleichnisse der Rabbinen, I. Pesiqta de Rav Kahana 1986 → 2,3529; 3,4514: ᴿTR 84 (1988) 283-5 (A. *Goldberg*).

4722 **Trigo** Helenice B., O discurso parabólico: diss. ᴰ*Lopes* E. Araraquara, Brésil, 1986. – SémBib 52,52.

4723 **Wailes** Stephen L., Medieval allegories of Jesus' parables: UCLA Center for Medieval and Renaissance Studies 23. Berkeley 1988, Univ. California. x-270 p. $35 [TDig 36,93].

4724 *Wailes* Stephen L., Why did Jesus use parables? The medieval discussion: MedHum NS 13 (1985) 43-64 [BTAM 14 (1988) 460].

4725 **Westermann** Claus, Vergleiche und Gleichnisse ANT 1984 → 65,4071 ... 2,3531: ᴿRHPR 68 (1988) 237s (J. G. *Heintz*).

4726 *a*) *Williams* James G., Parable and chreia; from Q to narrative Gospel [response, *Buss* Martin J.]; – *b*) *Crossan* John D., Aphorism in discourse and narrative [response, *Tannehill* Robert C.]: → 304, Semeia 43 (1988) 85-114 [-120] / 121-140 [-144].

4727 **Wojciechowski** Michał, Les actions symboliques de Jésus à la lumière de l'AT: diss. Wsz 1986. – BInfWsz (1988,3) 24-27.

4728 *Burchard* Christoph, Senfkorn, Sauerteig, Schatz und Perle in Matthäus 13: SNTU-A 13 (1988) 5-36.

4729 *Kamugisha* Joseph, The mission of the Church in the light of the parable of the sower: Pastoral Orientation Service (Tanzania 1987/3) 26-30 [< TKontext 10/1,20].

4730 *Schaup* Klemens, 'Un sembrador salió al campo a sembrar... [<... Zur Frage der Integration von psychologischer Hilfestellung und geistlicher Begleitung: GeistL 59 (1986) 269-275], ᵀᴱ*Font* Jordi: SelT 27 (1988) 332-4.

4731 *Scorza Barcellona* Francesco, [Mt 13] La parabola della zizzania in AGOSTINO; a proposit[i]o di Quaestiones in Matthaeum 11: ➤ 472, AnStoEseg 5 (1988) 215-223.

4731* *Ramaroson* Léonard, [Mt 13,3-9] 'Parole-semence' ou 'peuple-semence' dans la parabole du semeur?: ScEspr 40 (1988) 91-101.

4732 *Gryson* Roger, La vieille-latine, témoin privilégié du texte du Nouveau Testament; l'exemple de Matthieu 13,13-15: RTLv 19 (1988) 413-432.

4733 **Kogler** Franz, Die Entwicklung der jesuanischen Vorstellung vom Reich Gottes, dargestellt am traditions- und redaktionsgeschichtlichen Wachstumsprozess des synoptischen Doppelgleichnisses vom Senfkorn und vom Sauerteig (Mk 4,30-32 par. Mt 13,31-33 par. Lk 13,18f.20f) [Diss. ᴰ*Fuchs*. Linz 1987s. – TR 84 (1988) 514]: ForBi 59. Wü 1988, Echter. 292 p. DM 39. 3-429-01166-3.

4734 *Ricca* Paolo, Predigt über Matthäus 13,44: EvDiaspora 57 (Kassel 1988) 59-66 [< ZIT].

4735 **Martini** Carlo M., [Mt 14,13-21...] Il pane per un popolo; meditazioni alla scuola della Parola. Casale Monferrato / Mi 1987, Piemme / Centro Ambrosiano. 96 p. Lit. 8000. 88-384-2027-X [NTAbs 32,244].

4736 *Thériault* Jean-Yves, Le maître maîtrisé! Matthieu 15,21-28: ➤ 292*, Jésus/Femmes 1982/7, 19-34.

4737 *Magne* Jean, [Mt 15,32-39] Le processus de judaïsation au témoignage des réécritures du récit de la multiplication des pains: ➤ 570, AugR 28 (1988) 273-283.

4738 *Stoevesandt* Hinrich, Das Wort vom Kreuz; theologische Überlegungen zu Matthäus 16,13-28: Glaube und Lernen 3,1 (Gö 1988) 22-33 [< ZIT 88,488].

F4.5 **Mt 16** ... *Primatus promissus* – **The promise to Peter.**

4739 **Brown** Catherine A., The primacy of Rome; a study of its origin and development: diss. ᴰ*Drewery* B. Manchester 1987. 391 p. BRD-83931. – DissA 49 (1988s) 3057-A; RTLv 20,547.

4740 *Chilton* Bruce, Shebna, Eliakim, and the promise to Peter: ➤ 77, ꜰKᴇᴇ H., Social world 1988, 311-326.

4741 **Claudel** Gérard, La confession de Pierre; trajectoire d'une péricope évangélique [diss. ᴰ*Schlosser* J. Strasbourg 1986 ➤ 2,3546]: ÉtBN 10. P 1988, Gabalda. 544 p. F 545.

4742* *Derrett* J. D. M., [Mt 16,16-20] 'Thou art the stone, and upon this stone...' [*Pesch* R. double entendre 'precious stone' 'bed-rock' hardly adequate; rather foundation-stone of a new building]: DowR 106 (1988) 276-285.

4742 *D'Cruz* Peter, 'The Rock' in the New Testament: Vidyajyoti 52 (1988) 285-292.

4743 *Duling* Dennis C., Binding and loosing; Matthew 16:19, 18:18; John 20-23: Forum 3,4 (1987) 3-32 [< ZIT 88,537].

4744 *Galot* Jean, Le pouvoir donné à Pierre: EsprVie 98 (1988) 33-40.

4745 **Gill** David W., Peter the Rock; extraordinary insights from an ordinary man. DG 1986, InterVarsity. 206 p. $7 [RelStR 15,159, J. T. *Ford*].
Granfield Patrick, The limits of the Papacy 1987 → 9162.
4746 *Marcus* Joel, The gates of Hades and the keys of the Kingdom (Matt 16: 18-19): CBQ 50 (1988) 443-455.
4747 *Porter* Stanley E., Vague verbs, periphrastics, and Matt 16:19: FgNT 1 (1988) 155-172; castellano 172s.
4748 **Smith** Terence V., Petrine controversies 1985 → 1,4538... 3,4544: ᴿJBL 107 (1988) 337-9 (P. J. *Achtemeier*); CrNSt 9 (1988) 177-181 (E. *Norelli*).
4749 **Thiede** C.P., Simon Peter, from Galilee to Rome 1986 → 2,3557; 3,4547: ᴿEstBíb 46 (1988) 397s (J. P. *Tosaus Abadía*: 'ejemplo de lo que nunca debería escribir un exegeta'); ScotBEv 6 (1988) 41-43 (R. *Bauckham*); Vidyajyoti 52 (1988) 62 (R. *Lewicki*).
4750 **Tillard** J.-M. R., Il vescovo di Roma 1985 → 3,4548: ᴿCC 139 (1988,3) 502-7 (M. *Fois*).
4751 **Tillard** J.-M. R., El obispo de Roma, estudio sobre el papado [1982 → 63,903],ᵀ Santander 1986, Sal Terrae. 224 p. – ᴿChristus 53,620 (Méx 1988) 57-59 [C. *Bravo*]; Stromata 44 (1988) 537 (E. *Laje*).

4752 *Bouttier* Michel, Fêter la transfiguration du Christ: ÉTRel 63 (1988) 233-6.
4753 **Hall** S., [Mt 17,1-9...] Synoptic transfigurations; Mark 9,2-10 and partners: KingsTR 10,2 (1987) 41-44 [NTAbs 32,164].
4754 **McGuckin** John A., The Transfiguration 1986 → 2,3563: ᴿHeythJ 29 (1988) 249-251 (D. V. *Way*).
4755 **Niemand** Christoph, Studien zu den Minor Agreements der synoptischen Verklärungsperikopen; eine Untersuchung der literarkritischen Relevanz der gemeinsamen Abweichungen des Matthäus und Lukas von Markus 9,2-10 für die synoptische Frage: Diss. ᴰ*Fuchs*. Linz 1987s. – TR 84 (1988) 514.
Reid Barbara E., Transfiguration Lk 9,28-36, ᴰ*Meier* J. 1988 → 5182*.
4756 **Sachot** M., Les homélies grecques sur la Transfiguration; tradition manuscrite. P 1987, CNRS. 136 p. F 100 [NRT 111, 966s, V. *Roisel*].
4757 **Wild** Robert, His face shone like the sun 1986 → 3,4555: ᴿVidyajyoti 52 (1988) 515s (R. J. *Raja*).
4758 **Derrett** J. D. M., Moving mountains and uprooting trees (Mk 11:22; Mt 17:20, 21:21; Lk 17:6): BbbOr 30 (1988) 231-244.
4759 *Baarda* T., [Mt 17,26] Geven als vreemdeling; over de herkomst van een merkwaardige variant van Ms. 713 in Mattheus 17,26; NedTTs 42 (1988) 99-113; Eng. 145.
4760 **Rossé** Gérard, L'ecclesiologia di Matteo; interpretazione di Mt. 18,20: Contributi di Teologia 6. R 1987, Città Nuova. 116 p. Lit. 9000 [TR 84,427].
4761 *Rossé* Gérard, *a*) Il 'discorso comunitario' di Mt 18; – *b*) Il 'Dio-con-noi' nell'ecclesiologia matteana: NuovaUm 9,54 (1987) 13-24 / 52s (1987) 13-22.
4762 *Sievers* J., 'Where two or three...' the rabbinic concept of Shekhinah [2 Mcb 14,35] and Matthew 18:20: SIDIC 17,1 (Rome 1984) 4-10 [< NTAbs 32,303].
4763 *a*) *Schnackenburg* Rudolf, Grosssein im Gottesreich; zu Mt 18,1-5; – *b*) *Pesch* Rudolf, 'Wo zwei oder drei versammelt sind auf meinen Namen

hin ...' (Mt 18,20); zur Ekklesiologie eines Wortes Jesu; – *c*) *Merklein* Helmut, Der Prozess der Barmherzigkeit; Predigtmeditation zu Mt 18,21-35: ➤ 115, FPESCH W., Studien Mt. 1988, 269-282 / 227-243 / 201-7.

4764 **Jeschke** Marlin, [Mt 18,15-18] Discipling in the Church; recovering a ministry of the Gospel*Brev*; foreword *Lapp* James M. Scottdale PA 1988, Herald. 202 p. $10. 0-8361-3480-X.

4765 *Burggraf* David L., Principles of discipline in Matthew 18:15-17; Part I, a contextual study: CalvaryB 4,2 (1988) 1-23.

4766 *Lafont* Ghislain, Fraternal correction in the Augustinian community; a confrontation between the Praeceptum IV, 6-9 and Matthew 18:15-17, T*Nelson* D.: WSpirit 9 (1987) 87-91.

4767 *De Boer* Martinus C., Ten thousand talents? Matthew's interpretation and redaction of the parable of the unforgiving servant (Matt 18:23-35): CBQ 50 (1988) 214-232.

4768 *Candelier* Gaston, Mariage et divorce; problèmes actuels: RTLv 19 (1988) 433-458 [seule p. 453, très peu sur Mt 19,9; 1 Cor 7,12-16].

4769 E**Pizzolato** Luigi F., [Mt 19,16-22] Per foramen acus 1986 ➤ 2,3572; 3,4566: RGregorianum 69 (1988) 165s (M. *Ruiz Jurado*); Orpheus 9 (1988) 154-7 (Teresa P. *Carpino*); RasT 29 (1988) 608s (G. *Mattai*); RHE 83 (1988) 248-250 (A. de *Halleux*: 'EMaggioni B.'); RivStoLR 24 (1988) 366-375 (Rossana *Stanchi*); StPatav 35 (1988) 651-4 (G. *Leonardi*).

4770 *Levin* Saul, [Mt 19,24] A camel or a cable [*kámēlon* 'anchor rope' preferred by CYRIL A. but not by ORIGEN] through a needle's eye?: ➤ 679, Lacus Forum 1987/8, 406-415.

4771 *O'Callaghan* José, Examen crítico de Mt 19,24: Biblica 69 (1988) 401-5.

4772 **Pausch** Alfons & Jutta, [Mt 19,24] Steuern in der Bibel 1986 ➤ 2,3572*: RTRu 53 (1988) 112 (W. *Pöhlmann*).

F4.8 **Mt 20** ... *Regnum eschatologicum* – **Kingdom eschatology.**

4773 *a*) *Schenke* Ludger, Die Interpretation der Parabel von den 'Arbeitern im Weinberg' (Mt 20,1-15) durch Matthäus; – *b*) *Lohfink* Norbert, Der Messiaskönig und seine Armen kommen zum Zion; Beobachtungen zu Mt 21,1-17: ➤ 115, FPESCH W., Studien Mt 1988, 245-268 / 179-200.

4774 *Rodríguez* José D., The parable of the affirmative action employer [Mt 20,1-16: 'The God Movement is like a farmer ... ten dollars a day ... others just hanging around ... they raised a squawk ... pick up your pay and run along; are you bellyaching simply because I've been generous?']: CurrTM 15 (1988) 418-424.

4775 *Trilling* Wolfgang, *a*) Der Einzug in Jerusalem Mt 21,1-17 [< F*Schmid* J. 1963, 303-9]; – *b*) Die Täufertradition bei Matthäus [< BZ 3 (1959) 271-289]; – *c*) Matthäus, das kirchliche Evangelium; Überlieferungsgeschichte und Theologie [< E*Schreiner* J., Gestalt/NT 1969, 186-199]; – *d*) Geschichte und Ergebnisse der historisch-kritischen Jesusforschung [< E*Schierse* F., Jesus 1977, 187-213]: ➤ 275, Studien 1988, 67-75 / 45-65 / 93-108 / 13-41.

4776 *Amphoux* Christian, [Mt 21,28-32] La parabole matthéenne du Fils prodigue; la version du Codex Bezae (D05 du NT): LOrA 1 (Lv 1988) 167-171.

4777 *Giuliano,* Raffaele, 'Perché sarà tolto il regno di Dio a voi'; il dramma d'Israele in Mt 21,33-46: RivScR 2 (Molfetta 1988) 13-27.

4778 *Manns* Frédéric, Une tradition rabbinique réinterprétée dans l'Évangile de Mt 22,1-10 et en Rm 11,30-32: Antonianum 63 (1988) 416-426.

4779 **Schwankl** O., [Mt 22,23-33] Die Sadduzäerfrage (Mk 12,18-27 parr.)...: BoBB 66, 1987 ➤ 3,4578: ᴿSNTU-A 13 (1988) 229s (A. *Fuchs*).

4780 *Bockmuehl* K. [Mt 22,34-40] The great commandment: Crux 23,3 (1987) 10-20 [NTAbs 32,160].

4781 *Lemcio* Eugene E., [Mt 22,38], Pirke 'Abot 1:2(3) and the synoptic redactions of the commands to love God and neighbor: AsbTJ 43,1 (1988) 43-53.

4782 **Becker** Hans-Jürgen, Auf der Kathedra des Mose; Mt. 23,1-12 als Beispiel für die Verbindung rabbinisch-theologischen Denkens und antirabbinischer Polemik bei Matthäus: Diss. ᴰ*Osten-Sacken* P. v. der. Berlin 1988. 387 p. – RTLv 20,543.

4783 **Kühschelm** Roman, [Mt 23,29-36; Mk 13,9-13] Jüngerverfolgung und Geschick Jesu ...: ÖstBSt 5, 1983 ➤ 64,4517 ... 2,3588: ᴿZkT 110 (1988) 200 (K. *Stock*: gegen solche, die Kampf und Veränderung in den Evangelien zu viel betonen).

4784 *Ross* J. M., [Mt 23,34-36] Which Zachariah?: IrBSt 9 (1987) 70-73.

4785 **Agbanou** Victor Kossi, Le discours eschatologique de Mt 24s [diss. München, ᴰ*Gnilka* J]: ÉtBN 2, 1983 ➤ 65,4125 ... 2,3590: ᴿRB 95 (1988) 280-4 (V. *Mora* a lu avec joie malgré les nombreuses fautes et l' 'ostracisme' de BOISMARD-LAMOUILLE).

4786 **Dupont** J., [Mt 24s] Le tre apocalissi sinottiche 1987 ➤ 1,4572 ... 3,4582: ᴿRivB 36 (1988) 112s (V. *Fusco*: complemento ai suoi 5 studi su Mc 13, ital. 1979).

4787 *Muñoz León* Domingo, Jesús y la apocalíptica pesimista (a propósito de Lc 18,8b y Mt 24,12): EstBíb 46 (1988) 457-496; Eng. 457.

4788 **Wenham** David, [Mt 24,1-36] The rediscovery of Jesus' eschatological discourse: GospPersp 4, 1986 (1984 ➤ 65,4126) ... 3,4584. – ᴿActuBbg 25 (1988) 76s (X. *Alegre* S.).

4788* *Lövestam* Evald, [Mt 24,34] This 'generation' will not pass away before all these things take place [< ᴱ*Lambrecht* J., Apocalypse 1980, 403-413]: ➤ 221, Axplock 1987, 91-101.

4789 **Martini** Carlo M., [Mt 25,14-30] La scuola fra efficienza e solidarietà: ViPe 70 (1987) 562-571.

4790 *England* James, Matthew 25:31-46 ['done also to me']: RExp 85 (1988) 317-320.

4791 **Gray** Sherman W.ᴶ, Matthew 25:31-46 ['I was hungry and you gave me to eat']; a history of interpretation: diss. Catholic Univ., ᴰ*Fitzmyer* J. Wsh 1987. – RTLv 19,538.

4792 Séminaire sur l'histoire de l'exégèse de Mt 26,6-13, l'onction de Béthanie: ➤ 471, Exégèse XVIᵉ s., 1988 ...

4793 *Thiemann* Ronald F., [Mt 26,6] The unnamed woman at Bethany: TTod 44 (1987s) 179-188.

F5.1   *Redemptio; Mt 26, Ultima coena;* **The Eucharist** ➤ H7.4.

4794 **Abi Acar** Antoine, ... manger cette pâque; entretiens avec le prêtre YOUNANE. P 1988, Cariscript. 212 p.

4795 *Alluntis* Félix, Reflexiones teológicas sobre la Eucaristía de Xavier ZUBIRI: EstE [56 (1981) 41-59, inaugural Deusto] 63 (1988) 285-312.

4796 **Alonso Schökel** Luis, Celebrating the Eucharist; biblical meditations [Meditaciones 1987], ᵀ*Sedlmeier* Franz. Slough/NY 1988, St.Paul/ Crossroad [1989]. 159 p. [AcPIB 9/5,357]. 3-87996-231-6.

4797 *Alonso Schökel* Luis, Eucharystia... : Współczesna Ambona [15,4 (1987) 125-130 → 3,4597] 16,2 (1988) 136-148; 16,3 (1988) 153-164.

4798 **Alonso Schökel** Luis, Meditações bíblicas sobre a Eucaristia. São Paulo 1988, Paulinas. 130 p. [AcPIB 9/5,356].

4799 *Alonso Schökel* Luis, Meditações bíblicas sobre a Eucaristia [I-X, num. 132-7, 1987] XI. Comunhão: Vida Pastoral 29,138 (São Paulo 1988) 33-37.

4800 **Barth** Markus, Das Mahl des Herrn; Gemeinschaft mit Israel, mit Christus und unter den Gästen 1987 → 3,4598. 3-7887-0796-8: RBij-dragen 49 (1988) 340s (A. van *Eijk*); ZkT 110 (1988) 337-340 (L. *Lies*).

4801 **Barth** Markus, Rediscovering the Lord's Supper; communion with Israel, with Christ, and among the guests. Atlanta 1988, Knox. iv-113 p. $12 pa. [JBL 107,785].

4802 **Bermejo** Luis M., Body broken and blood shed 1986 → 3,4600: RFurrow 38 (1987) 789s (P. *McGoldrich*; TS 49 (1988) 551-3 (J. H. *McKenna*).

4803 *Böcher* O., Abendmahl: → 804, NBL Lfg. 1 (1988) 4-7.

4804 **Bürki** Bruno, Cène du Seigneur — Eucharistie de l'Église 1985 → 3,4604: RTR 84 (1988) 485s (T. A. *Schnitker*).

4805 **Cabié** Robert, The Eucharist: The Church at prayer, an introduction to the liturgy[4] [[1]1961, EMartimort G.; [3]1965; ital. 1985 → 3,4605], TO'Connell Matthew J. L 1986, Chapman. xvii-270 p. £12.50. – RJTS 39 (1988) 657s (B. D. *Spinks*).

4806 *Cesana* Felice, La testimonianza eucaristica dei Padri: ViPe 70 (1987) 206-221; 4 pl.

4807 *Colombo* Giuseppe, Per il trattato sull'Eucaristia, I: TItSett 13 (1988) 95-130; Eng. 131.

4808 **Cuccaro** Elio, Monument to memorialism; John HOOPER's Defense of the Lord's Supper: diss. Drew. Madison NJ 1987. – RelStR 14,186.

4809 *Dąbek* Tomasz M., ℗ De Eucharistia praeparanda in Vetere Testamento utpote cibo spirituali: RuBi 41 (1988) 313-9.

4810 *Decyk* Jan, ℗ Réconciliation avec Dieu et les frères — condition pour prendre dignement part à l'Eucharistie: ColcT 58,4 (1988) 17-24; 24s franç.

4811 *Della Torre* Luigi, Il vino nei pasti religiosi ebraici [e altri articoletti]: RivPastLtg 22,123 inserto (1984) 15-18.

4812 *Dietzfelbinger* Hermann, Das Heilige Abendmahl in LUTHERS Glaubenswelt: → 179. Überfluss 1984, 71-90.

4813 *Douglas* Elizabeth A., LEONARDO's Last Supper; some issues of interpretation: ChrSchR 18 (1988) 65 ... [< ZIT 89,72].

4814 *Duchesne-Guillemin* Jacques, Agnus Dei [Mt 26,27, the bread and wine really are the body and blood of Jesus, the Paschal Lamb]: → 149, FWERBLOWSKY R., Gilgul 1987, 69s.

4815 *Dura* Ion, L'Eucharistie dans l'Église orthodoxe: FoiTemps 19 (1987) 195-214.

4816 *Eicher* Peter, 'Leben, um zu essen'; zu einer biblischen Erneuerung der Eucharistie: Katechetische Blätter 113,1 (1988) 38-43 [< ZIT].

4817 **Galbiati** Enrico, L'Eucaristia nella Bibbia. Mi 1982 = 1966, IPL. 256 p. Lit 7.000. – RRivPastLtg 22,123 (1984) 56 (R. *Falsini*).

4818 **Gamber** Klaus, Beracha; Eucharistiegebet und Eucharistiefeier in der Urkirche: StudPatrLtg 16. Rg 1986, Pustet. 124 p. – ROstKSt 36 (1987) 336 (B. *Plank*).

4819 *Geense* A., Avondmaals-vernieuwing, kerkvernieuwing en vernieuwing van de gemeenschap der mensen: KerkT 39 (1988) 4-22.

4820 *Giavini* Giovanni, L'eucaristia nelle comunità del NT: RivPastLtg 22,123 (1984) 9-15.

4821 *Giraudo* Cesare, A proposito della comunione di Gesù nel cenacolo [opinio communis fino a 1500 malgrado il silenzio della tradizione biblica]: CC 139 (1988,1) 31-42.

4822 **Gollwitzer** Helmut, Coena Domini; die altlutherische Abendmahlslehre in ihrer Auseinandersetzung mit dem Kalvinismus, dargestellt an der lutherischen Frühorthodoxie [1937], ²*Braun* D.: TBü syst. 79, Mü 1988, Kaiser. 328 p. DM 89. [TLZ 114,756-9, G. *Wenz*].

4823 **Jones** Paul H., The mode of Christ's Eucharistic presence; an historical archaeology and ecumenical proposal: diss. Vanderbilt. Nv 1988. – RelStR 15,191.

4824 **Léon-Dufour** Xavier, Le partage du pain eucharistique selon le NT 1982 ↦ 63,4689 ... 2,3628: ᴿTLZ 113 (1988) 117-120 (H.C.C. *Cavallin*: mit aller gallischen Klarheit und Eleganz).

4825 **Léon-Dufour** X., Sharing the Eucharistic bread 1987 ↦ 3,4620: Furrow 39 (1988) 739-741 (sr. Carmel *McCarthy*); HomP 88,10 (1987s) 70-72 (R.W. *Gilsdorf*: makes problems); MilltSt 22 (1988) 118-125 (R. *Moloney*, also on POWER D., BERMEJO L.); NRT 110 (1988) 429 (S.B. *Marrow*); TS 49 (1988) 336s (J.D. *Laurance*); Worship 62 (1988) 280s (E.J. *Cutrone*).

4826 **Lies** Lothar, ORIGENES' Eucharistielehre 1985 ↦ 1,4624 ... 3,4621: ᴿHeythJ 29 (1988) 515s (J.A. *McGuckin*); JEcuSt 24 (1987) 121s (S. *Grenz*).

4827 **Lies** Lothar, Wort und Eucharistie bei Origenes; zur Spiritualisierungstendenz des Eucharistieverständnisses: InnsbTSt 1. Innsbruck 1982, Tyrolia. 364 p. – ᴿSalesianum 49 (1987) 188s (A.M. *Triacca*).

4828 **Lo Kuo-Hwei**, ☺ Passover; history and meaning of Lent and Holy Week. Hong Kong 1987. – ᴿColcFuJen 73 (1987) 487-492 (M. *Fang* ☺).

4829 *Martuccelli* Paolo, L'eucaristia e la Chiesa; unità e santità della Chiesa in prospettiva eucaristica: RasT 29 (1988) 20-36.

4830 *Merklein* Helmut, *a*) Erwägungen zur Überlieferungsgeschichte der neutestamentlichen Abendmahlstraditionen [< BZ 21 (1977) 88-101 . 235-244]; – *b*) Der Tod Jesu als stellvertretender Sühnetod; Entwicklung und Gehalt einer zentralen neutestamentlichen Aussage [< Pastoralblatt Aachen usw. 37 (1985) 63-73]: ↦ 231, Studien 1987, 157-180 / 181-191.

4831 *Meyer* Ben F., The expiation motif in the Eucharistic words; a key to the history of Jesus?: Gregorianum 69 (1988) 461-486; franç. 487: favors R. *Pesch* 1978 over G. *Friedrich* and X. *Léon-Dufour* 1988.

4831* *a*) *Muszyński* H. Interprétation biblique de [Jn 13,1] 'Il les a aimés jusqu'à la fin'; – *b*) *Bartnicki* Roman, La pâque juive et le repas eucharistique chrétien; – *c*) *Czajkowski* Michał, Les descriptions néotestamentaires de l'institution de l'Eucharistie; – *d*) *Frankowski* Janusz, L'Eucharistie dans la spiritualité de saint Paul; BInfWsz (1987,6) 30s / 31s / 32s / 33s (résumés *Chrostowski* W.).

4832 **O'Carroll** Michael, Corpus Christi, an encyclopedia of the Eucharist. Wilmington 1988, Glazier. x-220 p. $42 [TDig 35,383].

4833 *Onwu* Nienanya, The Eucharist as covenant in the African context: AfTJ 16 (1987) 145-158 [< TKontext 10/1,17].

4834 *Pasquato* Ottorino, Eucaristia e Chiesa in AGOSTINO / nel CRISOSTOMO: EphLtg 102 (1988) 46-63; lat. 46 / 240-252.

4835 *Pérès* Jacques-Noël, La Cène est-elle la vraie icône du Christ? (Aux origines du dogme eucharistique) [réactions à l'iconoclasme...]: ÉTRel 63 (1988) 529-545.

4836 **Pahl** Irmgard, Cena Domini I, 1983 ➤ 65,4176; 1,4633: RZwingliana 16 (1985) 577-9 (F. *Büsser*).

4837 **Power** D. N., The sacrifice we offer 1987 ➤ 3,4625: RCathHR 74 (1988) 504-6 (J. *Wicks*); Divinitas 32 (1988) 735s (R. M. *Schmitz*, sfavorevole); Interpretation 42 (1988) 332 (G. E. *Saint-Laurent*); JEcuSt 25 (1988) 127s (C. *Lindberg*); NewTR 1,2 (1988) 113-5 (G. *Ostdiek*); Themelios 14 (1988s) 76s (R. *Beckwith*); TS 49 (1988) 343-5 (E. J. *Kilmartin*); Worship 62 (1988) 189s (also E. J. *Kilmartin*).

4838 **Reumann** John, The supper of the Lord 1985 ➤ 1,4639 ... 3,4626: RJEcuSt 22 (1985) 548s (G. *Sloyan*); RelStR 14 (1988) 231s (J. F. *Puglisi*).

4839 **Sayés** José Antonio, El misterio eucarístico: BAC 482, 1986 ➤ 2,3639; 3,4629: RGregorianum 69 (1988) 565s (J. *Galot*); ScripTPamp 20 (1988) 324-7 (J. *Sancho*).

4840 *Schwarz* Reinhard, Das Abendmahl — die Testamenthandlung Jesu: Luther 19 (1988) 13-25.

4841 **Spinks** Bryan, From the Lord and the best Reformed churches [Puritan Eucharist; Durham diss.]: EphLtg Subsidia 33. R 1984, Liturgiche. 212 p. Lit. 28.000. – RJTS 39 (1988) 312-4 (K. *Stevenson*).

4842 **Stevenson** Kenneth W., Eucharist and offering 1986 ➤ 3,4637: RWorship 62 (1988) 557s (R. J. *Daly*).

4843 **Stuhlhofer** Franz, Symbol oder Realität? — Taufe und Abendmahl. Berneck 1988, Schwengler. 109 p. DM 8.

4844 *Thurston* Bonnie B., 'DO THIS'; a study on the institution of the Lord's Supper: RestQ 30 (1988) 207-218 [< ZIT 89,161].

4845 **Tonzig** Luisa C., The teaching of St. AMBROSE on real presence; its misunderstanding in later tradition and the significance of its recovery for contemporary Eucharistic theology: diss. Duquesne. Pittsburgh 1988. – RelStR 15,193.

Wehr Lothar, Arznei der Unsterblichkeit; die Eucharistie ... Jn 6: 1987 ➤ 5574.

4846 *White* John L., Beware of leavened bread; Markan imagery in the Last Supper: Forum 3,4 (Sonoma 1987) 49 ... [< ZIT 88,537].

F5.3   **Mt 26,30** ‖ ...: *Passio Christi*; **Passion-Narrative.**

4847 **Allison** Dale C.J, The end of the ages has come ... Passion, Resurrection 1987 ➤ 2,3648; 3,4642: RJTS 39 (1988) 561s (I. H. *Jones*: profitable); TLond 91 (1988) 60s (J. *Muddiman*); TLZ 113 (1988) 438-440 (G. *Haufe*).

4847* **Bader** Günter, Symbolik des Todes Jesu: HermUnT 25. Tü 1988, Mohr. x-258 p. DM 89. 3-16-145363-8. – RErbAuf 64 (1988) 486s (B. *Schwank*).

4848 **Blumenberg** Hans, Matthäuspassion: Bibliothek 998. Fra 1988, Suhrkamp. 311 p.

4849 *Broer* Ingo, Bemerkungen zur Redaktion der Passionsgeschichte durch Matthäus: ➤ 115, FPESCH W., Studien Mt 1988, 25-46.

4850 **Brown** Raymond E., A crucified Christ in Holy Week; essays on the four Gospel Passion narratives 1986 ➤ 2,3652; 0-8146-1444-2: RVidyajyoti 52 (1988) 59s (P. M. *Meagher*).

4851 **Fricke** W., Standrecht gekreuzigt ... Prozess 1986 ➤ 2,3658: RProtestantesimo 43 (1988) 27-29 (J. A. *Soggin*).

4852 **Friedrich** G., De verkondiging van Jezus' dood in het Nieuwe Testament [1982], ᵀ*Poll* E. W. van der 1986 ⇢ 3,4651; *f*29,50: ᴿNedTTs 32 (1988) 340 (J. W. van *Henten*).

4853 ᵀ**Garzón Bosque** Isabel, ᴱ*Trisoglio* Francisco, GREGORIO Nacianceno, La pasión de Cristo: Biblioteca de Patristica 4. M 1988, Ciudad Nueva. 160 p. 88-85159-95-0. – ᴿActuBbg 25 (1988) 281 (J. *Vives*).

4854 *Gnilka* Joachim, Iesu ipsissima mors ℗ ᵀ*Ordon* H.: ⇢ 475, RuBi 41 (1988) 2-13.

4855 **Goergen** Donald, The death and resurrection of Christ: A theology of Jesus 2. Wilmington 1988, Glazier. 287 p. $13. 0-89453-604-4 [TDig 35,361; vol. 1 was The mission and ministry]. – ᴿSpTod 40 (1988) 181-3 (D. A. *Helminiak*).

4856 **Green** Joel B., The death of Jesus; tradition and interpretation in the Passion narrative: WUNT 2/33. Tü 1988, Mohr. xvi-351 p. DM 98 [JBL 108,754].

4857 **Hendrickx** H., Los relatos de la pasión, estudio sobre los evangelios sinópticos 1986 ⇢ 3,4656: ᴿBibFe 14 (1988) 148s (A. *Salas*).

4858 **Houlden** J. L., Backward into light 1987 ⇢ 3,4657: ᴿNBlackf 68 (1987) 576s (K. *Grayston*); ScripTPamp 20 (1988) 916s (J. M. *Casciaro*); Vidyajyoti 52 (1988) 303 (R. J. *Raja*).

4859 *Kapkin* D., Cuestiones en torno a la pasión, muerte y resurrección de Jesús: Cuestiones Teológicas 14,1 (Medellín 1987) 25-55 [< RET 48,120].

4860 **Kremer** Jacob, Das Evangelium von Jesu Tod und Auferstehung [Fernkurs]: Kleine Reihe zur Bibel 26. Stu 1988, KBW. 95 p. 3-460-10261-2.

4861 **Leenhardt** F.-J., Mort et testament de Jésus 1983 ⇢ 64,4610 ... 2,3665: ᴿStPatav 34 (1987) 426-8 (A. *Moda*).

4862 **Léon-Dufour** Xavier, Life and death in the NT 1986 ⇢ 2,3666; 3,4662: ᴿBibTB 18 (1988) 117 (E. L. *Bode*); HomP 88,7 (1987s) 74-76 (J. R. *Sheets*: historical-critical method has to 'bracket out' the Holy Spirit); Horizons 15 (1988) 382s (Mary Rose *D'Angelo*); RRel 47 (1988) 305s (C. *Bernas*); SpTod 40 (1988) 177s (B. T. *Viviano*: some methodological pretenses).

4863 *Livrea* Enrico, *Accorinti* Domenico, NONNO [di Panopoli, vescovo di Edessa] e la Crocifissione: StItFgCL 81 (3/6, 1988) 262-278.

4864 **Martin** Ernest L., Secrets of Golgotha; the forgotten history of Christ's Crucifixion. Alhambra CA 1988, LSK. 279 p. [CBQ 50,752].

4865 **Matera** Frank J., Passion narratives and Gospel theologies 1986 ⇢ 2,3669; 3,4664: ᴿBiblica 69 (1988) 441-4 (D. *Hamm*); Carthaginensia 4 (1988) 369 (R. *Sanz Valdivieso*); EstBíb 46 (1988) 407s (S. *Guijarro*); EvQ 60 (1988) 365 (J. B. *Green*); Horizons 15 (1988) 157 (D. *Senior*); RRel 47 (1988) 306s (E. *Hensell*); TLond 91 (1988) 63-65 (S. *Barton*); TorJT 4 (1988) 309-311 (M. G. *Steinhauser*: a success); TS 49 (1988) 378s (E. R. *Martinez*).

4866 *Mazzarollo* Isidoro, O processo de Jesus: Teocomunicação 17,77 (Porto Alegre 1987) 88-96 [< TKontext 10/1,84].

4867 *Moberly* W., Proclaiming Christ crucified; some reflections on the use and abuse of the Gospels [... which differ in their portrayals of the Crucifixion]: Anvil 5,1 (1988) 31-52 [< NTAbs 32,297].

4868 *Morín* Alfredo, Los Zelotas y la muerte de Jesús: Medellín 14,54 (1988) 243-252 [< TKontext 10/1,94].

4869 *Orbe* Antonio, Doctrina de Marción en torno a la pasión y muerte de Jesús: Compostellanum 32 (1987) 7-24.

4870 **Rivkin** Ellis, What crucified Jesus? 1986 → 2,3676; 3,4671: ᴿVidyajyoti 52 (1988) 613s (P. M. *Meagher*).

4871 *Robbins* Vernon K., The crucifixion and the speech of Jesus [the five extant versions of the Passion are identical really only on seven points (including minor ones like the vinegar and divided garments) but *all* also feature Pilate asking Jesus 'Are you King of the Jews?' and the answer 'You say']: Forum 4,1 (1988) 33-46.

4871* *Ruckstuhl* Eugen, Zur Chronologie der Leidensgeschichte Jesu I-II [< SNTU 10 (1985) 27-61; 11 (1986) 97-129]: → 4203, Jesus im Horizont der Evangelien (1988) 101-140.141-176; Nachtrag 177-184.

4872 **Schürmann** Heinz, Gottes Reich — Jesu Geschick; Jesu ureigener Tod ... 1985 → 1,4690; 2,3679: ᴿRuBi 41 (1988) 268s (D. *Tomczyk*).

4873 **Senior** D., [→ 5067 Mk; 5216* Luke] Passion in Mt 1985 → 1,4693 ... 3,4672: ᴿAustralBR 36 (1988) 72 (B. R. *Doyle*).

4874 *a) Sorger* Karlheinz, Die Passion Jesu in den Evangelien; Sachinformation zur Kreuzigung; – *b) Dross* Reinhard, Was bedeutet uns Jesu Leidensgeschichte? Orientierung zum Verstand des Todes Jesu bei Leonardo BOFF; – *c) Krah* Willi, Wege nach Golgatha; Beispiele für existentielle und kreative Zugänge zur Passion: ZPraxRU 18,1 (Stu 1988) 2-6 / 7-11 / 18-22.

4875 *Spiazzi* Raimondo, Le reazioni psicosomatiche del 'Christus patiens': SacDoc 33 (1988) 566-577.

4876 *Tremblay* Réal, La mort du Christ, une naissance filiale; exposé et évaluation de la pensée de F.-X. DURRWELL: StMoralia 26 (1988) 231-242; Eng. 241.

4877 **Villey** Lucile, 'Il a subi pour nous'; fonction de la préposition 'hypó' dans le langage chrétien de saint CLÉMENT de Rome à JUSTIN Martyr: diss. Inst. Cath., ᴰ*Kannengiesser* C. P 1988. 197 p.; 266 p.; 196 p. – RICathP 28 (1988) 161s; RTLv 20,546.

4878 *Visonà* Giuseppe, Pasqua quartodecimana e cronologia evangelica della Passione: EphLtg 102 (1988) 259-315.

4879 *Vögtle* Anton, Das heilseffiziente Todesverständnis Jesu; echte Frage oder Scheinproblem?: Jb. Heid. Akad (1987) 28s.

4880 **Zugibe** F. T., The Cross and the Shroud; a medical examination of the Crucifixion² [¹1982]. NY 1988, Paragon. x-214 p.; ill. $22; pa. $10. 0-913729-75-2; 46-9 [NTAbs 32,248].

4881 *Beck* B. [Mt 26,36-46 Gethsemani in the four gospels: EpworthR 15,1 (1988) 57-65 [NTAbs 32,152].

4882 **Feldmeier** Reinhard, Die Krisis des Gottessohnes; die Gethsemaneerzählung ... Mk [14,34-42]: WUNT 2/21. Tü 1987, Mohr. XII-299 p. DM 78. 3-16-144972-X. – ᴿGregorianum 69 (1988) 355s (G. *Ferraro*).

4883 *Bartnik* Czesław, Judas l'Iscariote, histoire et théologie: ColcT 58 sp. [1,5-18] (1988) 57-69.

4884 **Klauck** Hans-Josef, Judas — ein Jünger des Herrn: QDisp 111, 1987 → 3,4683: ᴿTR 84 (1988) 458-461 (T. *Söding,* auch über VOGLER W. ²1985); ZkT 110 (1988) 210 (M. *Hasitschka*).

4885 **Schwarz** Günther, Jesus und Judas; aramaistische Untersuchungen zur Jesus-Judas-Überlieferung der Evangelien und der Apostelgeschichte: BWANT 123. Stu 1988, Kohlhammer. x-308 p. DM 69. 3-17-009663-X.

- ᴿErbAuf 64 (1988) 234 (J. *Kaffanke*); Protestantesimo 43 (1988) 218 (V. *Subilia*); TsTNijm 28 (1988) 405s (W. H. *Berflo*).

4886 *Suggit* John, Comrade Judas, Mt 26:50: JTSAf 63 (1988) 56 ... [< ZIT 88,595].

4887 *Lüthi* Kurt, Judas: → 813, TRE 17 (1987) 296-304 (-307, eine jüdische Stellungnahme, *Goldschmidt* H. L.).

4889 **Zullino** Pietro, Giuda. Mi 1988, Rizzoli. 192 p. Lit. 22.000. – ᴿHum-Br 43 (1988) 612 (Giulia *Carazzali*: romanzo non senza base esegetica).

4890 **Pesch** R., Der Prozess Jesu geht weiter: Bücherei 1507. FrB 1988, Herder. 126 p. DM 8. – ᴿNRT 110 (1988) 585s (L. *Renwart*).

4891 *Mussner* Franz, Der Prozess gegen Jesus von Nazareth [ᴱ*Kertelge* K. 1985; *Pesch* R. 1988]: TR 84 (1988) 353-360.

4892 *a) Gnilka* Joachim, Der Prozess Jesu nach den Berichten des Markus und Matthäus mit einer Rekonstruktion des historischen Verlaufs; – *b) Broer* Ingo, Der Prozess gegen Jesus nach Matthäus; – *c) Müller* Karlheinz, Möglichkeit und Vollzug jüdischer Kapitalgerichtsbarkeit im Prozess gegen Jesus von Nazaret; – *d) Lentzen-Deis* Fritzleo, Passionsbericht als Handlungsmodell? Überlegungen zu Anstössen ans der 'pragmatischen' Sprachwissenschaft für die exegetischen Methoden: → 491*, *Kertelge* K., Prozess 1987/8, 11-40 / 84-110 / 41-83 / 191-232.

4893 **Romaniuk** Kazimierz, ⊕ *Sprawa* ... The trial of Jesus of Nazareth. Wroclaw 1988, Archidiecezja. 197 p.

4893* *Bănescu* Marcu, Pilatus; Zweideutigkeit einer Haltung (rum.): Mitropolia Banatului 37,2 (1987) 15-23 [TLZ 114,637].

4894 **Kampling** Rainer, Das Blut Christi und die Juden Mt 27,25, 1984 → 65,4237 ... 3,4688: ᴿBijdragen 49 (1988) 450-2 (M. *Parmentier*); JJS 39 (1988) 300s (W. *Horbury*); TR 84 (1988) 369s (E. *Bammel*).

4895 **Mora** Vincent, Le refus d'Israël, Mt. 27,25: LDiv 124, 1986 → 2,3692; 3,4691: ᴿBLitEc 89 (1988) 296s (S. *Légasse*); EstE 63 (1988) 249s (A. *Tornos*); RÉJ 146 (1987) 168-170 (Madeleine *Petit*: n'utilise pas de sources non-bibliques); RThom 88 (1988) 481-4 (L. *Devillers*: ignore D. MARGUERAT).

4896 *Jordan* William C., [Mt 27,48] The last tormentor of Christ; an image of the Jew in ancient and medieval exegesis, art, and drama: JQR 78 (1987) 21-47; 3 fig.

4897 *Ceresa-Gastaldo* Aldo, 'Dio mio, Dio mio, perché mi hai abbandonato?' (Matteo 27,46 e Marco 15,34): Renovatio 23 (1988) 101-6 [278-80].

4898 **Rossé** Gerard, [Mc 15,34] Grido di Gesù in croce. R 1984, Città Nuova. 168 p. Lit. 19.000. 88-311-3611-5. Cf. → 63,4755; Jésus abandonné 1983 → 65,4421 ... 3,4483.

4899 **Rossé** Gérard, The cry of Jesus on the Cross, a biblical and theological study. NY 1987, Paulist. x-145 p. $9. – ᴿLvSt 13 (1988) 391s (H.-E. *Mertens*); NRT 110 (1988) 583 (L. *Renwart*); PrPeo 2 (1988) 436 (F. J. *Selman*); TS 49 (1988) 777s (H. *Fleddermann*).

4900 *Yates* John, 'He descended into Hell'; creed, article and Scripture: Churchman 102 (1988) 240-250. 303-315.

F5.6 Mt 28 ‖ : Resurrectio.

4901 **Andronikov** Constantin, Il senso della Pasqua nella liturgia bizantina, I. I giorni della preparazione e della Passione; II. I cinquanta giorni della festa 1986 → 2,3694; Lit. 22.000; 15.000: ᴿCC 139 (1988,1) 88-90 (C. *Capizzi*).

4902 **Baader** Franz H.,   Die Auferstehung Jesu in der theologischen Diskussion seit dem 19. Jahrhundert: Diss. ᴰ*Track* J.   Erlangen-Nürnberg 1987.   339-xii p. – RTLv 19,560.

4903 ᴱ**Broer** Ingo (p. 29-61),   *Werbick* Jürgen (p. 81-131),   'Der Herr ist wahrhaft auferstanden' (Lk 24,34); biblische und systematische Beiträge zur Entstehung des Osterglaubens: SBS 134.   Stu 1988, KBW.   157 p. DM 31,80.   3-460-04341-5. – *Fiedler* P., p. 9-28; *Verweyen* H. 63-80; *Wenz* G. 133-157.

4904 *Broer* Ingo,   'Der Herr ist dem Simon erschienen' (Lk 24,34); zur Entstehung des Osterglaubens: SNTU-A 13 (1988) 81-100.

4905 **Caba** José,   Resucitó Cristo, mi esperanza 1986 → 2,3698; 3,4701:   ᴿBiblica 69 (1988) 131-5 (S. B. *Marrow*); CiuD 201 (1988) 175 (J. *Gutiérrez*); EstE 63 (1988) 234s (A. *Vargas-Machuca*); Teresianum 39 (1988) 218 (V. *Pasquetto*).

4906 **Caba** José,   Cristo, mia speranza, è risorto; studio esegetico dei 'vangeli' pasquali, ᵀ*Sanguineti Ferrero* Grazia: Parola di Dio 2/8.   CinB 1988, Paoline.   436 p.   88-215-1507-9.

4907 *Cantalamessa* Raniero,   'È stato risuscitato per la nostra giustificazione' [< La vita nella signoria di Cristo (Mi 1988, Ancora) 101-122]: ViConsacr 24 (1988) 277-294.

4908 *Carnley* Peter,   The structure of resurrection belief 1987 → 3,4702: ᴿHeythJ 29 (1988) 233-5 (F. J. van *Beeck*); TTod 45 (1988s) 497-9 (Pheme *Perkins*: 'Angelican Archbishop of Perth').

4909 *Christensen* Jens,   Opstanden på den tredje dag efter skrifterne: DanTTs 51 (1988) 91-103 [< ZIT 88,512].

4910 **Cleverley Ford** D. W.,   Preaching the risen Christ [24 sermons]. L 1988, Mowbray.   128 p. £5.   0-264-67081-7. – ᴿExpTim 99 (1987s) 343 (G. *Patrich*).

4911 *Collin* Louis,   Résurrection [de Jésus, Jn 10,17s]; vie reçue ou vie reprise?: → 486, Traduction 1986/8, 87-96; Eng. 87.

4912 **Craig** William L.,   The historical argument for the resurrection of Jesus during the Deist controversy [diss. 1982]: TextsStRel 23, 1985 → 1,4715: $70; sb. $40:   ᴿChH 57 (1988) 379s (R. A. *Muller*); RelSt 24 (1988) 395s (P. *Byrne*).

4913 *Craig* William L.,   Pannenbergs Beweis für die Auferstehung Jesu, ᵀ*Slenczka* R. [< Diss. ᴰ*Pannenberg*]:   KerDo 34 (1988) 78-104; Eng. 104.

4914 *Drobner* Hubertus R.,   SEVERIAN von Gabala; die Berechnung der Auferweckung des Herrn nach drei Tagen (CPG 4295/15); Edition, Übersetzung, Kommentar: TGL 78 (1988) 305-317 [3 p. Greek text with facing translation].

4915 *Galvin* John P.,   The origin of faith in the resurrection of Jesus; two recent perspectives [*Pesch* R. 1973; *Verweyen* H. 1981]: TS 49 (1988) 25-44.

4916 *Grødal* Thor S., [Norw.] The resurrection — and theory of historical science [*Lakatos* I. ...]: TsTKi 59 (1988) 15-26.

   Habermas Gary, *Flew* Antony,   Did Jesus rise from the dead? 1987 → 4923.

4917 **Harries** Richard,   Christ is risen.   L / Wilton CT 1988, Mowbray / Morehouse-Barlow.   ix-131 p.   £2.50 / $8 pa.   0-264-67107-4 /0-8192-1473-6 [NTAbs 32,371]. – ᴿExpTim 99 (1987s) 343 (G. *Patrich*).

4918 **Hendrickx** Herman,   Los relatos de la resurrección; estudio sobre los evangelios sinópticos, ᵀ*Requena Calvo* Eloy: Palabra de Dios-A.   M 1987, Paulinas.   181 p.   84-285-1158-6. – ᴿActuBbg 25 (1988) 212 (X. *Alegre* S.); BibFe 14 (1988) 149s (A. *Salas*).

ᴱHoffmann Paul, Zur neutestamentlichen Überlieferung von der Auferstehung Jesu: WegFor 522, 1988 ➤ 311.

4920 Hryniewicz W., ❷ Nasza Pascha z Chrystusem ... sketch of Christian
Paschal theology, II. Lublin 1987, KUL. 547 p. - ᴿAtKap 110 (1988)
162s (J. Królikowski).

4921 Kartsonis Anna D., Anastasis; the making of an image. Princeton
1986, Univ. $57.50. - ᴿJAAR 56 (1988) 583-5 (Diane Apostolos-Cappa-
dona).

4922 Kessler H., Sucht den Lebenden nicht bei den Toten; die Auferstehung
Jesu Christi 1985 ➤ 1,4727 ... 3,4713: ᴿArTGran 51 (1988) 327s (E.
Barón).

4922* a) Leipoldt Johannes, Zu den Auferstehungs-Geschichten [< TLZ 73
(1948) 737-742]; – b) Bickermann Elias, Das leere Grab [< ZNW 23
(1924) 281-292; – c) Gilmour S. MacLean, Die Christophanie vor mehr
als fünfhundert Brudern [< JBL 80 (1961) 248-252; ᵀZwosta Franz]; – d)
Becker Jürgen, Das Gottesbild Jesu und die älteste Auslegung von
Ostern [< ᶠConzelmann H. (1975) 105-126]; – e) Dodd Charles H., Die
Erscheinungen des auferstandenen Christus; ein Essay zur Formkritik der
Evangelien [< Mem. Lightfoot R. 1957, 9-35, ᵀZwosta]: ➤ 311, Hoffmann
P., WegF 522 (1988) 285-296 / 271-284 / 133-8 / 203-227 / 297-330.

4923 ᴱMiethe Terry L., Did Jesus rise from the dead? [debate in which Gary
R. Habermas handily beat Antony Flew, with comments by Pannenberg
W., Hartshorne C., Packer J.] 1987 ➤ 3,4710: ᴿBibTB 18 (1988) 114
(E. L. Bode); TS 49 (1988) 203s (P. E. Devenish); Zygon 23 (1988) 371-3
(T. Peters).

4924 Milet Jean, La résurrection du Christ ou le duel entre la vie et la mort
[i. données de l'Écriture; ii. signification; iii. ... psychologique; iv. le duel;
v. sens de la victoire; vi. une spiritualité]: EsprVie 98 (1988) 97-104.
121-124. 133-9.

4925 Muller R.A. [Morris L.], Resurrection [of Jesus]: ➤ 801, ISBEnc³ 4
(1988) 145-150 [-154].

4927 Neyrey Jerome H., The resurrection stories: Zacchaeus Studies.
Wilmington 1988, Glazier. 109 p. $7. 9-89453-664-8 [TDig 36,194].

4928 Nicolas Marie-Joseph, Théologie de la Résurrection 1982 ➤ 65,4260:
ᴿBLitEc 89 (1988) 62-66 (S. Méringnhac).

4929 O'Collins Gerald, Interpreting the Resurrection. NY 1988, Paulist.
88 p. $9 [TS 50,411].

4930 O'Collins Gerald, Jesus risen [Darton-LT subtitle:] What actually
happened and what does it mean?➤ 3,4718; [also NY 1987, Paulist, with
subtitle:] an historical, fundamental and systematic examination of
Christ's Resurrection. vi-233 p. 0-8091-0393-1. - ᴿHeythJ 29 (1988) 233-
5 (F.J. van Beeck); HomP 88,6 (1987s) 76s (J.R. Sheets: accurate exc.
p. 189 on BALTHASAR); Horizons 15 (1988) 402s (F.X. Murphy); JStNT
33 (1988) 119 (A.T. Lincoln: not exactly what he prefaces); LvSt 13 (1988)
275s (H.-E. Mertens); NewTR 1,3 (1988) 101s (D.W. Buggert); NRT 110
(1988) 586s (L. Renwart); RExp 85 (1988) 577s (D.L. Mueller: deserves
our thanks); ScripTPamp 20 (1988) 954s (C. Izquierdo); TLond 91 (1988)
143-5 (F. Watson: best on early debates, weak on historicity in the current
outlook; travesties HUME); TS 49 (1988) 758-760 (J. L. Heft).

4931 O'Collins Gerald, Jesús resucitado; estudio histórico, fundamental y
sistemático. Barc 1988, Herder. 332 p. [Carthaginensia 5,285, F. Martínez Fresneda].

4932 **Perkins** Pheme, Resurrection 1985 ➤ 65, 4265 ... 2,3720: ᴿHeythJ 29 (1988) 350s (J. *Murphy-O'Connor*); IrBSt 9 (1987) 47s (J. *Brennan*).

4933 **Perry** Charles A., The Resurrection promise 1986 ➤ 3,4724: ᴿAnglTR 70 (1988) 105-7 (R. R. C. *Grigg*).

4934 **Puente Santidrián** Pablo, La terminología de la Resurrección en TERTULIANO: PubFacTNEspaña 54. Burgos 1987, Aldecoa. 392 p. – ᴿETL 64 (1988) 473s (A. de *Halleux*).

4935 **Reeves** Keith H., The resurrection narrative in Matthew; a literary-critical examination: diss. Union Theol. Sem. Richmond 1988, 195 p. 88-19785. – DissA 49 (1988s) 1832-A.

4936 **Rodríguez** Isidoro, La resurrección de Jesucristo; estudio filológico de algunos textos neotestamentarios [< Helmantica 118s (1988) 5-109]. Salamanca 1988, Univ. Pont. 111 p. – ᴿCarthaginensia 4 (1988) 371s (P. *Marin*).

4937 *Schmied* Augustin, Fragen um die Auferstehung Jesu; zu beachtenswerten Veröffentlichungen [*Kessler* H. 1985; *Perkins* P. 1984]: TGegw 30 (1987) 58-64.

4938 **Schottroff** Luise & Willy, Die Macht der Auferstehung; sozialgeschichtliche Bibelauslegung. Mü 1988, Kaiser. 132 p. DM 12,80. ᴿBiKi 43 (1988) 182s (M. *Helsper*).

4939 *Schützeichel* Heribert, The meaning of Christ's resurrection [< TrierTZ 95 (1986) 98-114], ᵀᴱ*Asen* B. A.: TDig 35 (1988) 245-9.

4940 *Smit* D. J., The resurrection of Jesus — what was it? Plurality and ambiguity in the Christian resurrection hope [*Tracy* D., 'ambiguity of history'; the question cannot be answered fully but must continue to be asked]: Neotestamentica 22,1 (1988) 163-178.

4941 *Tran Van Toan*, Saint AMBROISE de Milan et la foi en la Résurrection: MélSR 45 (1988) 131-150; Eng. 150.

4942 **Vincent** Louis-Marie, Peut-on croire à la résurrection?. 1988, Dervy. 344 p. F 130. – ᴿÉtudes 369 (1988) 281s (J.-M. *Moretti*).

4943 ᶠVÖGTLE A., Auferstehung Jesu — Auferstehung der Christen, ᴱ**Oberlinner** Lorenz: QDisp 105, 1985 ➤ 2,120; 3,4730: ᴿColcT 58,2 (1988) 184s (S. *Mędala*).

4944 *Wilkins* Stephen R., The Resurrection appearances as objective visions; a critical appraisal: StudiaBT 15 (1987) 79-91.

4945 *Winling* R., La résurrection du Christ dans les traités pseudo-athanasiens 'Contra Apollinarium': RevSR 62 (1988) 27-41 . 101-110.

4946 *Jarvis* Cynthia A., Matthew 28: 1-10 ['How do people come to belief?']: Interpretation 42 (1988) 63-68.

4947 *Engemann* J., [Mt 28,1-8] Frauen am Grabe: ➤ 803, LexMA IV,4 (1988) 874s.

4948 *Reicke* Bo, Das leere Grab (Mt 28,1-8): TBei 19 (Wu 1988) 58-60 [< ZIT].

4949 *Petersen* William L., [Mt 28,2] An important unnoticed diatessaronic reading in Turfan fragment M-18: ➤ 85, ᶠKLIJN A., Text 1988, 187-192.

4950 *Bolognesi* Pietro, Matteo 28,16-20 e la sua struttura: BbbOr 30 (1988) 129-137.

4951 *Howard* George, A note on the short ending of Matthew [28,19s in *Eusebius,* without baptismal formula]: HarvTR 81 (1988) 117-120.

4952 *Ker* Donald,   Jesus and the mission to the Gentiles: IrBSt 10 (1988) 89-101.

F6.1   **Evangelium Marci** – *Textus, commentarii.*

4953 **Achtemeier** Paul J.,   Mark²ʳᵉᵛ [¹1975]: Proclamation Comm. 1986 ➤ 2,3730:   ᴿThemelios 14 (1988s) 66 (D. *Wenham*: not a commentary but a series of studies).

4954 **Aranda Pérez** Gonzalo,   El Evangelio de San Marcos en copto sahídico (Texto de M 569 y aparato crítico): TEstCisn 45.   M 1988, Cons.Inv.Ci. 150 p.   84-00-06474-7.

4955 ᴱ**Corona** R.,   Il vangelo secondo Marco; lettura esegetico-esistenziale, L'Aquila 1987 ➤ 3,531:   ᴿCiuD 201 (1988) 491 (J. *Gutiérrez*).

4956 **Drewermann** Eugen,   Das Markusevangelium I (Mk 1,1-9,13); Bilder von Erlösung.   Olten 1987, ²1988, Walter. 656 p. (43 p. Bibliog.)   3-530-16871-8. [TR 85,271-8, J. *Goldbrunner*].

4957 **Gnilka** Joachim,   Marco: Commenti e Studi biblici 1987 ➤ 3,4744: ᴿParVi 33 (1988) 395-7 (M. *Làconi*).

4957* **Iersel** B. van,   Marcus.   Boxtel/Brugge 1986, Kath.-BS/Tabor. 270 p. *f* 24,75. – ᴿStreven 55 (1987s) 82s (P. *Beentjes*).

4958 **Lührmann** Dieter, Das Markusevangelium 1987 ➤ 3,4749:   ᴿActuBbg 25 (1988) 216 (X. *Alegre* S.); BZ 32 (1988) 278s (R. *Schnackenburg*); EstE 63 (1988) 374-6 (A. *Vargas-Machuca*); TLZ 113 (1988) 816 (D.-A. *Koch*).

4959 **Mann** C. S.,   Mark: AnchorB 27, 1986 ➤ 2,3736; 3,4750:   ᴿAsbTJ 43,1 (1988) 89-91 (D. R. *Bauer*: flawed by same favor for Matthean priority as his Anchor Mt); CBQ 50 (1988) 141-3 (Elizabeth S. *Malbon*: gained worldwide publicity by claiming Mark used Mt-Lk); Horizons 15 (1988) 155 (J. P. *Meier*: bad every way); Interpretation 42 (1988) 193-6 (F. J. *Matera*); TS 49 (1988) 154-7 (J. R. *Donahue*: idiosyncratic).

4960 Navarre Bible: St.Mark. Dublin c.1987, Four Courts. – ᴿFurrow 38 (1987) 795s (N. *Drennan*: uncritical).

4960* **Schenke** Ludger,   Das Markusevangelium: Urban-Tb 405.   Stu 1988, Kohlhammer. 188 p. DM 24 pa. [JBL 108,187].

4961 ᵀᴱ**Stébé** Hélène, *Goudet* Marie-Odile, Marc commenté par Jérôme et Jean Chrysostome, homélies: Les Pères dans la foi 1986 ➤ 2,3743; 3,4756:   ᴿBLitEc 89 (1988) 308s (H. *Crouzel*).

4962 ᵀ**Torro** J. Pascual; introd. *Guerrero Martínez* J., Jerónimo, Comentario al evangelio de San Marcos (10 homilías). M 1988, Ciudad Nueva. 104 p. [NatGrac 36,177, G. *Rodríguez*].

Zuurmond R.,   Gospel of Mark in Ge'ez ᴰ1988 ➤ 1758.

F6.2   *Evangelium Marci,* **Themata.**

4963 **Barta** Karen A.,   The Gospel of Mark: Message of Biblical Spirituality 9.   Wilmington 1988, Glazier. 136 p. 0-89453-559-5; pa. 75-7.

4964 **Best** Ernest,   Disciples and discipleship; studies in the Gospel according to Mark 1986 ➤ 2,132*; 3,4758:   ᴿBibTB 18 (1988) 114 (M. *McVann*: essays about redaction-criticism, not about discipleship, even 'The role of the disciples'); Interpretation 42 (1988) 201s (Bonnie B. *Thurston*); IrBSt 10 (1988) 103-5 (V. *Parkin*); ScotJT 41 (1988) 545-7 (J. K. *Elliott*).

4965 **Biguzzi** Giancarlo,   'Io distruggerò questo tempio'; il tempio e il giudaismo nel vangelo di Marco 1987 ➤ 3,4759:   ᴿAngelicum 65 (1988)

290 (G. *Grasso*); CBQ 50 (1988) 524s (J.P. *Heil*); ParVi 33 (1988) 399s (M. *Cimosa*); RasT 29 (1988) 101-3 (V. *Fusco*: ponderato, scorrevole); Teresianum 39 (1988) 537s (V. *Pasquetto*); ZkT 110 (1988) 196s (K. *Stock*).

4966 *Black* C. Clifton[II], The quest of Mark the redactor; why has it been pursued, and what has it taught us?: JStNT 33 (1988) 19-39.

4967 *Black* David A., Some dissenting notes on R. STEIN'S The synoptic problem and Markan 'errors' [10,20 *ephylaxámēn*; 2,4 *krábattos*; 1,12 *ekbállei*...]: FgNt 1,1 (1988) 95-100; español 100s.

4968 [E]**Cancik** H., Markus-Philologie: WUNT 33, 1984 ↠ 65,273.4321 ... 3,4765: [R]SvEx 53 (1988) 124-6 (L. *Hartman*).

4969 **Cárdenas Pallares** José, A poor man called Jesus ... Mark 1986 ↠ 2,3753; 3,4766: [R]Themelios 14 (1988s) 67 (H. *Kvalbein*).

4970 *a)* **Carlson** Richard P., The main street in Mark [Passion narrative]; – *b)* **Hinlicky** Paul R., Conformity to Christ in the Gospel of Mark: CurrTM 15 (1988) 356-363 / 364-8.

4971 *Cook* D. E., A Marcan portrait of Jesus: Faith and Mission 5,2, (Wake Forest NC 1988) 58-63.

4972 *Crockett* Bennie R.[J], The function of mathetological prayer in Mark: IrBSt 10 (1988) 123-139 [< ZIT 88,538].

4973 **Derrett** J. D. M., The making of Mark 1985 ↠ 1,4774 ... 3,4769: [R]HeythJ 29 (1988) 511s (Marion *Smith*).

4974 **Dols** William L.[J], Toward a field critical hermeneutic of the phrase *ho huios tou anthropou* in the narrative world of Mark; interreadings from literary criticism, analytical psychology and cultural anthropology: diss. Graduate Theological Union. Berkeley 1987. – RelStR 15,189.

4975 *Doohan* Leonard, Mark's portrait of Jesus: MilltSt 21 (1988) 62-86.

4976 **Ernst** Josef, Markus, ein theologisches Portrait. Dü 1987, Patmos. 144 p. 3-491-71684-8.

4977 *Fusco* Vittorio, Marco; il vangelo difficile?: RClerIt 63 (1987) 754-761.

4978 *a)* *Grassi* Joseph A., The secret heroine of Mark's drama [an ideal disciple (apparently not precisely Magdalene) up to the Cross]; – *b)* *Beavis* Mary Ann, Women as models of fatih in Mark [four *chreia*-form anecdotes, Mk 5,24-34; 7,25-30; 12,41-44; 14,3-9]: BibTB 18 (1988) 10-15 / 3-9.

4979 [E]**Hahn** Ferdinand, Der Erzähler des Evangeliums; methodische Neuansätze in der Markusforschung: SBS 118s. 1985 ↠ 2,246* (3,4778): [R]ÉTRel 63 (1988) 81-83 (F. *Vouga*).

4980 *Harris* Michael A., Structuralism, hermeneutics, and the Gospel of Mark; a review article [of? ZIT 88,449]: PerspRelSt 15,1 (1988) 61 ...

4981 *Hooker* Morna D., Mark [citing OT]: ↠ 97, [F]LINDARS B. 1988, 220-230.

4982 *Hurtado* L. W., The Gospel of Mark in recent study: Themelios 14 (1988s) 47-52.

4983 **Kanjirakompil** Cherian, Proclamation in Mark; an exegetical study of the kerygmatic terminology in the Second Gospel: diss. Rome 1988, Pontifical Biblical Institute, [D]*Stock* K. – Biblica 69 (1988) 448.

4984 *a)* *Kee* Howard C., Christology in Mark's Gospel; – *b)* *MacRae* George, Messiah and Gospel; – *c)* *Charlesworth* J. H., From Jewish Messianology to Christian Christology; some caveats and perspectives: ↠ 494, Judaisms/Messiahs 1987, 187-208 / 169-185 / 225-264.

4985 *Kelber* Werner H., [Mark] Narrative and disclosure; mechanisms of concealing, revealing, and reveiling [sic]: → 304, Semeia 43 (1988) 1-20; 21-29, response, *Via* Dan O., Irony as hope in Mark's gospel; – general responses to the volume, 145-153, *Collins* Adela Y.: 155-167, *Kermode* Frank.

4986 **Klosinski** Lee E., The meals in Mark: diss. Claremont 1988. 252 p. 89-00990. – DissA 49 (1988s) 3389-A; RelStR 15,193.

4987 *Kudasiewicz* Józef, Teologia Ewangelii według św. Marka: Współczesna Ambona 16,1 (Kielce 1988) 3-11.

4987* **Maas** W. J., Volmacht als predikaat van het Heil; een exegetisch-hermeneutisch onderzoek in het Markusevangelie [Proefschrift Bru]. Voorburg Prot. Stichting. 157 p. *f*25. – RStreven 56 (1988s) 82s (P. *Beentjes*).

4988 **Mack** Burton L., A myth of innocence; Mark and Christian origins. Ph 1988, Fortress. xii-432 p. $30. 0-8006-2113-1 [NTAbs 32,243].

4989 *McVann* Mark, Markan ecclesiology; an anthropological experiment: Listening 32,2 (Glenview IL 1988) 95-105 [< NTAbs 32,307].

4990 **Malbon** Elisabeth S., Narrative space and mythic meaning in Mark 1986 → 2,3769: RBibTB (1988) 86s (D. L. *Barr*); CurrTM 15 (1988) 212 (R. W. *Roschke*); EvQ 60 (1988) 269s (J. B. *Green*); Horizons 15 (1988) 383s (Joanna *Dewey*); JBL 107 (1988) 540-2 (Jouette M. *Bassler*).

4991 **Matera** Frank J., What are they saying about Mark? 1987 → 3,4795: RAsbTJ 43,1 (1988) 87-89 (D. L. *Thompson*); EstBib 46 (1988) 259 (A. *Rodríguez Carmona*); GraceTJ 9 (1988) 294s (D. R. *Wallace*); Interpretation 42 (1988) 314-6 (M. *Powell*); TS 49 (1988) 378 (Elizabeth S. *Malbon*).

4992 **May** David M., The role of house and household language in the Markan social world: diss. Southern Baptist, D*Borchert* G. 1987. 229 p. 88-05803. – DissA 49 (1988s) 279s-A.

4993 **Monshouwer** Dirk, Markus en de Torah; een onderzoek naar de relatie tussen het evangelie en de synagogale lezingen in de eerste eeuw: diss. D*Hemelsoet* B. Amst 1987. 224 p. [Kampen → 3,4797]; RCollatVL 18 (1988) 489s (R. *Hoet*); Streven 55 (1987s) 374 (P. *Beentjes*).

4994 **Myers** Ched, Binding the strong man; a political reading of Mark's story of Jesus. Maryknoll NY c.1988, Orbis. $30; pa. $17 [Interp 42,439 adv.].

4995 **Neirynck** Frans, Duality in Mark²*rev* [¹1972]: BiblETL 31. Lv 1988, Univ. 252 p. Fb 1200. 90-6186-279-5 / Peeters 90-6831-128-X [RTLv 20,371, C.*Focant*].

4996 *Oberlinner* Lorenz, Die Botschaft vom Kreuz als die Botschaft vom Heil nach Markus: BLtg 61 (1988) 56-65.

4997 *O'Day* Gail R., Hope beyond brokenness; a Markan reflection on the gift of life: CurrTM 15 (1988) 244-251.

4998 *a) Ong* Walter J., Text as interpretation; Mark and after; – *b) Renoir* Alain, Oral formulaic poetry and the interpretation of written texts; – *c) Lord* Albert P., The merging of two worlds; oral and written poetry as carriers of ancient values: → 3,756, E*Foley* J., Oral tradition 1986, 147-169 / 103-135 / 19-64.

4999 *O'Reilly* L., The Gospel of St Mark — good news for bad disciples: Furrow 39 (1988) 78-85.

5000 **París** Ghislain, Jesús, Marcos y nosotros; guía de trabajo para una lectura. M 1987, Paulinas. 115 p. – RBibFe 14 (1988) 325 (M. *Sáenz Galache*).

5001 **Peabody** David B.,   Mark as composer [... recurrent phraseology; diss. Southern Methodist, ^D*Farmer* W.]: New Gospel Studies 1, 1987 ➤ 3,4801: ^RCBQ 50 (1988) 334s (J. T. *Fleddermann*); NT 30 (1988) 377-9 (J. K. *Elliott*).

5002 *a*) *Pudussery* Paul S.,   Discipleship and suffering in the Gospel of Mark; – *b*) *Kallikuzhuppil* John,   The attitude of Jesus towards suffering: Jeevadhara 13 (1988) 121-139 / 112-120 [229-230 comment, *Chethimattam* John B.].

5003 **Reiser** Marius,   Syntax und Stil .. Mk: WUNT 2/11, 1984 ➤ 65,4353 .. 3,4805: ^RTLZ 113 (1988) 893-5 (P. *Pokorný*).

5004 **Richards** Clare,   A close look at Mark — a guide for discussion groups. – 1988, McCrimmons.   75 p. £3.50 [PrPeo 2,202].

5005 **Robbins** Vernon K., Jesus the teacher ... Mark 1984 ➤ 65,4355 ... 3,4806: ^RÉTRel 63 (1988) 84s (F'. *Vouga*).

5006 *Rodríguez Carmona* Antonio, La Iglesia en Marcos: EstE 63 (1988) 129-163.

5007 **Roth** Wolfgang,   Hebrew Gospel; cracking the code of Mark.   Oak Park IL 1988, Meyer Stone.   xii-148 p. $35; pa $17 [JTS 40,729, Morna D. *Hooker*].

5008 ^E**Sabbe** M.,   L'Évangile selon Marc, tradition et rédaction [*Aland* K., *al.*]^{2rev} [¹1971/4 ➤ 56,2950]: BiblETL 34.   Lv 1988, Univ.   601 p. Fb 2400. 90-6186-280-9 / Peeters 90-6831-129-8.

5009 *Saldarini* Anthony J.,   The social class of the Pharisees in Mark: ➤ 77, ^FKEE H., Social world 1988, 69-77.

5010 **Schüling** Joachim,   Studien zum Verhältnis von Logienquelle und Markusevangelium: Diss. Giessen 1988, ^D*Dautzenberg* G.   221 p. – RTLv 20,546.

5011 **Sergeant** John,   Lion let loose; the structure and meaning of St. Mark's Gospel.   Exeter 1988, Paternoster.   95 p. £5.   0-85364-475-6.

5012 *Stenger* Werner,   'Die Grundlegung des Evangeliums von Jesus Christus'; zur kompositionellen Struktur des Markusevangeliums: LingBib 61 (1988) 7-55; Eng 55s.

5013 **Swartz** Herbert L.,   Fear and amazement responses; a key to the concept of faith in the Gospel of Mark, a redactional/literary study: diss. Victoria/Emmanuel.   Toronto 1988, 334 p. 88-17218. – DissA 49 (1988s) 1845-A.

5014 **Sweetland** Dennis M.,   Our journey with Jesus; discipleship according to Mark: Good News Studies 22, 1987 ➤ 3,4814:   ^RBibTB 18 (1988) 152s (H. *Humphrey*).

5015 *Theobald* Michael,   Gottessohn und Menschensohn; zur polaren Struktur der Christologie im Markusevangelium: SNTU-A 13 (1988) 37-80.

5016 **Thiede** Carsten P.,   Il più antico manoscritto dei Vangeli? Il frammento di Marco di Qumran e gli inizi della tradizione scritta del Nuovo Testamento: SubsBPont 10. R 1987, Pontifical Biblical Institute.   64 p. Lit. 11.000. – ^RCC 139 (1988,2) 205s (C. *Carniti*).

5017 **Thompson** Mary R.,   Negation as a level of meaning in Mark's Gospel: diss. McMaster, ^D*Sanders* E.   Hamilton 1987. – DissA 49 (1988s) 272-A; RelStR 14,189; RTLv 20,546.

5018 *Thompson* William G.,   Mark's Gospel and faith development: ChSt 26 (1987) 139-154.

5019 **Turlington** Darla D.,   Views of the Spirit of God in Mark and 'Q'; a tradition-historical study: diss. Columbia.   NY 1988. 308 p. 88-15706 – DissA 49 (1988s) 1495-A.

5020 **Via** Dan O., The ethics of Mark's Gospel — in the middle of time 1985
→ 1,4808 ... 3,4816: ᴿÉTRel 63 (1988) 83s (F. *Vouga*); JBL 107 (1988)
139-141 (V. K. *Robbins*); Salesianum 50 (1988) 437s (G. *Abbà*: metodo
insufficiente).

5021 **Williams** James G., Gospel against [the background of] parable; Mark's
language of mystery 1985 → 2,3789; 3,4819: ᴿÉTRel 63 (1988) 465s (E.
Cuvillier); JBL 107 (1988) 324s (M. E. *Boring*).

5022 *Wink* Walter, The education of the apostles; Mark's view of human
transformation: RelEd 83 (Ch 1988) 277-290 [< ᴢɪᴛ 88,564].

5023 **Zwick** Reinhold, Montage im Markusevangelium; Studien zur narrativen Organisation der ältesten Jesuserzählung: Diss. ᴰ*Schmuttermayr*.
Rg 1987s. – TR 84 (1988) 512.

F6.3 Evangelii Marci versiculi 1,1 ...

5024 *LaVerdiere* E., *a*) [Mk 1s...] Jesus and the call of the first disciples:
Emmanuel 94 (1988) 154-9 . 190-7 . 264-273 [< NTAbs 32,306]; – *b*) [Mk
1,1] Looking ahead to the year of Mark: Emmanuel 93 (1987) 494-501
(546-553 ...); [NTAbs 32,162]; – *c*) [Mk 1,9-14...] The Baptism of the Lord
/ Jesus the Christ: Emmanuel 94 (1988) 6-13.21 / 74-81.

5025 **Barber** Raymond C., Mark as narrative; a case for chapter one: diss.
Graduate Theological Union. Berkeley 1988. 88-02868. – DissA 49
(1988s) 277-A; RelStR 15,192.

5026 *Matera* Frank J., The prologue as the interpretative key to Mark's
Gospel: JStNT 34 (1988) 3-20.

5027 *Iersel* B. M. F. van, He will baptize you with the Holy Spirit (Mark 1,
8); the time perspective of *baptisei*: → 85, ꜰKʟɪᴊɴ A., Text 1988, 132-141.

5028 *Marín Heredia* Francisco, Nueva perspectiva para Mc 1,12-13: Carthaginensia 4 (1988) 97-105.

5029 **Oyen** G. Van, De summaria in Marcus en de compositie van Mc
1,14-8,26: Studiorum NT Auxilia 12, 1987 → 3,4824: ᴿRHE 83 (1988)
758s (J. *Dupont*: élève de Nᴇɪʀʏɴᴄᴋ F., reprenant Eɢɢᴇʀ W. 1976).

5030 *Alfaro* Juan I., Exegesis pastoral; Mc 1,16-2,17, un desafío para hoy:
RBíbArg 30s (1988) 171-182.

5031 **De Santis** Luca, Mc 1,16-21a [chiamata di Pietro ... Giovanni]; esegesi e
teologia: diss. Angelicum, ᴰ*Salguero* J. Roma 1988. 358 p. – RTLv
20,544.

5032 *Garland* David E., 'I am the Lord your healer'; Mark 1:21-2:12: RExp
85 (1988) 327-343.

5033 *Verheyden* Jozef, Mark 1,32-34 and 6,53-56 [*Oyen* G. van 1987; *Egger*
W. 1976]: ETL 64 (1988) 415-428.

5034 *Casey* Maurice, Culture and historicity; the plucking of the grain (Mark
2.23-28): NTS 34 (1988) 1-23, based on reconstructed Aramaic.

5035 *Bartelmus* Rüdiger, Mk 2,27 und die ältesten Fassungen des Ar-
beitsruhegebotes im AT; Biblisch-theologische Beobachtungen zur Sab-
batfrage: BibNot 41 (1988) 41-64.

5036 *a*) *Sellew* Philip, Beelzebul in Mark 3; dialogue, story, or sayings
cluster?; – *b*) *Oakman* Douglas E., Rulers' houses, thieves, and usurpers;
the Beelzebul pericope; – *c*) *Funk* Robert W., Gospel of Mark parables
and aphorisms: Forum 4,3 (1988) 93-108 / 109-123 / 124-143.

5037 **Kirschner** Estevan F., The place of the exorcism motif in Mark's
Christology with special reference to Mark 3: 22-50: diss. UK Council for
Academic Awards. 295 p. BRDX-83957. – DissA 49 (1988s) 3053-A.

5038 *Lövestam* Evald, Logiet om hädelse mot den helige Ande (sin against the Holy Spirit, Mark 3;28 f par.; Matt 12:31 f; Luk 12:10) [< SvEx 33 (1968) 101-117]: → 221, Axplock 1987, 39-50.

5039 **Lategan** Bernard C., *Vorster* William S., [Mk 4...] Text and reality 1985 → 1,1323 ... 3,4832: ᴿBO 45 (1988) 240-2 (N. J. *Tromp*).

5040 **Marcus** Joel, [Mk 4] The mystery of the Kingdom of God ᴰ1986 → 2,3797*; 3,4833*: ᴿJBL 107 (1988) 542-5 (C. C. *Black*); RelStR 14 (1988) 253 (L. *Cope*: fine).

5041 *Tuckett* C. M., Mark's concerns in the parables chapter (Mark 4,1-34): Biblica 69 (1988) 1-26, franç, 26.

5042 *Mateos* Juan, Terminos relacionados con 'legión' en Mc 5,2-20: FgNT 1 (1988) 211-5.

5043 *Delorme* Jean, [Mc 5,25] Jésus et l'hémorroïsse ou le choc de la rencontre: SémBib 44 (1986) 1-17.

5044 *Black* David A., The text of Mark 6.20: NTS 34 (1988) 141-5.

5046 *Wink* W., [Mk 6,30-8,26] The education of the Apostles; Mark's view of human transformation: RelEd 83,2 (NHv 1988) 177-290.

5047 **Booth** Roger P., Jesus and the laws of purity; tradition and legal history in Mark 7: JStNT Sup 13, 1986 → 2,3809; 3,4838:   ᴿJBL 107 (1988) 325-7 (R. H. *Gundry*); JTS 39 (1988) 197s (M. D. *Hooker*).

5048 *a) Malina* Bruce J., A conflict approach to Mark 7; – *b) Pilch* John J., A structural functional analysis of Mark 7; – *c) Neyrey* Jerome H., A symbolic approach to Mark 7: Forum 4,3 (1988) 3-30 / 31-62 / 63-91.

5049 *FitzPatrick* M., From ritual observance to ethics; the argument of Mark 7,1-23: AustralBR 35 (1987) 22-27 [< NTAbs 32,307].

5050 *Michaud* Jean-Paul, *Daviau* Pierrette T., Jésus au-delà des frontières de Tyr, Marc 7,24-31: → 292, Jésus/Femmes 1982/7, 35-57.

5051 *Andersen* Ernst, Antinomien i Markusevangeliets kapitel 8: DanTTs 81 (1988) 81-90 [< zIT 88,512].

5052 *Raja* R. J., The possibility of the Eucharist being open-ended — a comparative study of Mk 8: 1-10 with 6:15-44: Word and Worship 21 (Bangalore 1988) 83-99.111 [< TKontext 10/1,54].

5053 *Cuvillier* Elian, 'Il proclamait ouvertement la Parole', notule sur la traduction de Marc 8/32a: ÉTRel 63 (1988) 427s.

5054 *Léon-Dufour* Xavier, [Mk 8,36] To lose one's life: CCurr 38 (1988s) 340-.

5055 **Chu Wong-Wah** Samuel, The healing of the epileptic boy in Mark 9:14-29; its structure and its theological implications: diss. Vanderbilt. Nv 1988. 276 p. 88-28131. – DissA 49 (1988s) 3060-A; RelStR 15,193.

5056 *Eckel* Paul T., Mark 10:1-6 [Mt 5,31s: he asked his congregation 'If divorce has touched personally ... any member of your immediate family, please raise your hand'. Every hand went up!]: Interpretation 42 (1988) 285-291.

5057 *Jüngel* Eberhard, Predigt zu Markus 10,17-22 [unum tibi deest]: → 53, ᶠGANOCZY A., Creatio 1988, 125-133.

5058 *Neusner* Jacob, Penningväxlarna i templet (Mark 11:15-19); Mishnas förklaring [... *Sanders* E. P.]: SvEx 53 (1988) 63-68.

5059 **Dowd** Sharyn E., Prayer, power, and the problem of suffering; Mark 11,22-25 in the context of Markan theology: SBL diss. 105. Atlanta 1988, Scholars. x-186 p. $12 [TR 85,163].

5060 *Brocke* Edna, *Bauer* Gerhard, Dialog-Bibelarbeit zu Markus 12,1-12: KIsr 2 (1987) 69-79.

5060* *Viviano* Benedict T., [Mk 12,13-17] Render unto Caesar [... four approaches]: BToday 26 (1988) 272-6 [< NTAbs 33,28].

5061 **Schwankl** O.,   Die Sadduzäerfrage (Mk 12,18-27 parr.): BoBB 66, 1987
➤ 3,4864:   ᴿCrNSt 9 (1988) 622-4 (J. *Dupont*: d'un intérêt exceptionnel).

5062 *Schwankl* Otto,   Die Sadduzäerfrage (Mk 12,18-27) und die Aufer-
stehungserwartung Jesu: WissWeis 50 (1987) 81-92.

5063 **McIlhone** James P.,   'The Lord your God is one'; a redaction-critical
analysis of Mark 12: 28-34: diss. Marquette. Milwaukee 1987. 312 p.
88-11063. – DissA 49 (1988s) 1179-A.

5064 **Mateos** Juan, Marcos 13; el grupo cristiano en la historia: LecturaNT 3.
M 1987, Cristiandad. 570 p. pt. 7000. [TR 84,517].

F6.8   **Passio secundum Marcum**, 14,1 ... [➤ F5.3].

5065 *Fusco* Vittorio, La Passione secondo Marco: RClerIt 69 (1988) 176-185
[419-425, Il discepolo in Mc].

5066 *McVann* Mark, The Passion in Mark; transformation ritual: BibTB 18
(1988) 96-101.

5067 **Senior** Donald, La Passione di Gesù nel vangelo di Marco [1984
➤ 1,4879],ᵀ. Mi 1988, Àncora. 174 p. Lit. 18.000. – ᴿRClerIt 69 (1988)
544 (B. *Maggioni*); RivAscM 13 (1988) 377s (P. *Mori*).

5068 *Navone* John, [Mk 14,17 ...] *a*) The last day and the last supper in Mark's
Gospel: TLond 91 (1988) 38-43. – *b*) L'ultimo giorno e l'ultima cena nel
Vangelo di Marco: CC 139 (1988,2) 20-29.

5069 **Feldmeier** Reinhard,   Die Krisis des Gottessohnes; die Gethsemaneerzählung als Schlüssel der Markuspassion [Diss. Tü]: WUNT 2/21,
1987 ➤ 3,4873:   ᴿCBQ 50 (1988) 315s (F. J. *Matera*: it is God who
delivers his own Son into the hands of sinners).

5070 *Bratcher* Robert G., [Mk 14,41] Unusual sinners [here (Son of Man is
handed over to) 'those who do not take God into account' (though
GOODSPEED's 'godless' is 'too extreme'); but in passages like Lk 6,32s
rather 'nonconformists; people who do not keep the Jewish dietary laws']:
BTrans 39 (1988) 335-7.

5071 *Frassinetti* Paolo, Le negazioni di Pietro nel Vangelo secondo Marco:
CivClCr 9 (1988) 351-375.

5072 **Ruhland** Maria, [Mk 14,66-72] Die Markuspassion aus der Sicht der
Verleugnung 1987 ➤ 3,4872:   ᴿZkT 110 (1988) 196 (K. *Stock*).

5074 **Schreiber** Johannes, Der Kreuzigungsbericht des Markusevangeliums:
Mk 15,20b-41; eine traditionsgeschichtliche und methodenkritische Untersuchung nach William WREDE (1859-1906) [Diss. 1959, vollständiger
als in Theologie des Vertrauens 1967 und mit Updating]: BZNW 48, 1986
➤ 2,3852; 3,4880: xvi-517 p. DM 176. – ᴿCBQ 50 (1988) 547 (R. *Scroggs*:
defense of his 1959 thesis, here in phototype, misunderstood from his 1967
summary 'Theologie des Vertrauens'); RHPR 68 (1988) 249s (M. *Carrez*);
TR 84 (1988) 198 (R. *Pesch*: wertlos).

5075 *Guichard* Daniel, La reprise du Psaume 22 dans le récit de la mort de
Jésus (Marc 15,21-41): FoiVie 87,5 (CahB 27, 1988) 59-64 [67-80, *Cottin*
Bettina, Seigneur, attaque ceux qui m'attaquent).

5076 *Brown* Raymond E., The burial of Jesus (Mark 15:42-47): CBQ 50
(1988) 233-245.

5076* *Paulsen* Henning, Mk XVI 1-8 [< NT 22 (1980) 138-175, gekürzt]:
➤ 311, ᴱ*Hoffmann* P., WegF 522 (1988) 376-415.

5077 *O'Collins* Gerald, The fearful silence of three women (Mark 16:8c):
Gregorianum 69 (1988) 489-503; franç. 503.

5077* *Kendall* Daniel, [Mk 16,7s] Why disobedient silence ?: PrPeo 2 (1988) 91-96.
5078 **Magness** J. Lee, Sense and absence; structure and suspension in the ending of Mark's Gospel 1986 → 2,3858; 3,4891: ᴿJBL 107 (1988) 327-9 (Elizabeth S. *Malbon*).

XII. Opus Lucanum

F7.1   *Opus Lucanum* – **Luke-Acts.**

5079 *Allison* Dale C.ᴶ, Was there a 'Lukan community'?: IrBSt 10 (1988) 62-70.
5080 *Barrett* C. K., Luke-Acts [citing OT]: → 97, ꟳLINDARS B. 1988, 231-244.
5081 **Bock** Darrell L., Proclamation from prophecy and pattern; Lucan OT theology [diss. Aberdeen 1982, ᴰ*Marshall* I. H.] 1987 → 3,4898: ᴿBiblica 69 (1988) 284-6 (J. *Swetnam*: vigorously written); ExpTim 99 (1987s) 54s (A. *Hanson*: too confident of Jesus' ipsissima verba); EvQ 60 (1988) 270-273 (D. A. *Carson*); JTS 39 (1988) 562-4 (D. *Catchpole*: some direct hits on Raymond BROWN).
5082 **Bovon** F., L'œuvre de Luc [13 art. 1967-1984], études d'exégèse et de théologie: LDiv 130, 1987 → 3,195: ᴿCahÉv 61 (1987) 73 (H. *Cousin*); ComSev 21 (1988) 257s (M. de *Burgos*); EsprVie 98 (1988) 523s (L. *Walter*).
5082* **Bovon** François, Luc le théologien; vingt-cinq ans de recherches (1950-1975)²ʳᵉᵛ [still '25 years' though the English 'translation' of the first edition is entitled '33 years', 1987 → 3,4899]: Le Monde de la Bible. Genève 1988, Labor et Fides. 496 p. Fs 38,40. 0-915138-93-X. – ᴿSBFLA 38 (1988) 503-6 (G. C. *Bottini*, anche su Lukas in neuer Sicht 1985).
5083 **Bovon** François, Lukas in neuer Sicht 1985 → 1,157; 3,4900: ᴿTZBas 44 (1988) 86-89 (W. *Bieder*).
5084 **Brawley** Robert L., Luke-Acts and the Jews: SBL Mg 33, 1987 → 3,4902: ᴿJEcuSt 25 (1988) 461s (R. R. *Hann*: ghost of BAUR, also behind SANDERS).
5085 **Carroll** John T., Response to the end of history; eschatology and situation in Luke-Acts [diss. Princeton]: SBL diss. 92. Atlanta 1988, Scholars. vii-208 p. $20; pa. $13 [TDig 36,52]. 1-55540-148-1; 9-X.
5086 *Carroll* John T., Luke's portrayal of the Pharisees: CBQ 50 (1988) 604-621.
5087 **Chance** J. Bradley, Jerusalem, the Temple, and the new age in Luke-Acts [< diss. Duke]. Macon GA 1988, Mercer Univ. xii-168 p. $25 [TDig 36,52].
5088 **Colmeiro Vega** Alejandro, La oración en los Hechos de los Apóstoles; relación entre oración y evangelización en los escritos lucanos: diss. Pamplona 1988, ᴰ*García-Moreno* A. – RTLv 20,544.
5089 **Ernst** Josef, Luca, un ritratto teologico [1985 → 3,4907], ᵀ. Brescia 1988, Morcelliana. 256 p. Lit. 24.000. – ᴿCC 139 (1988,3) 304s (P. *Vanzan*); HumBr 43 (1988) 892s (M. *Orsatti*).
5090 **Esler** Philip F., Community and Gospel in Luke-Acts; the social and political motivations of Lucan theology: SNTS Mon 57, 1987 → 3,4908:

RJTS 39 (1988) 564-6 (H. *Marshall*); Studium 28 (M 1988) 520 (P. *Blázquez*); TsTNijm 28 (1988) 407 (W. *Weren*).

5091 **Garrett** Susan R., Magic and miracle in Luke-Acts: diss. Yale. 1988. – RelStR 15,193; RTLv 20,544.

5092 *Haacker* Klaus, Verwendung und Vermeidung des Apostelbegriffs im lukanischen Werk: NT 30 (1988) 9-38.

5093 *Heard* Warren, Luke's attitude toward the rich and the poor: TrinJ 9,1 (1988) 47-80.

5094 **Hoffmann** Michael, Das eschatologische Heil Israels nach den lukanischen Schriften: Diss. DBurchard C. Heidelberg 1988. – RTLv 20,544.

5095 *Hosaka* Takaya, Lukas und das Imperium Romanum, unter besonderer Berücksichtigung der literarischen Funktion des Furchtmotives: AnJapB 14 (1988) 82-134.

5096 *Igenoza* Andrew O., Luke the Gentile theologian; a challenge to the African theologian: AfTJ 16 (1987) 231-241 [< TKontext 10/1,17].

5097 *Jenny* Markus, Lukas der Liturgiker: JbLtgHymn 30 (1986) 66-72 (only Luke quotes expressly from the psalter of the OT).

5098 **Klinghardt** Matthias, Gesetz und Volk Gottes; das lukanische Verständnis des Gesetzes nach Herkunft, Funktion und seinem Ort in der Geschichte des Urchristentums; WUNT 2/32. Tü 1988, Mohr. viii-371 p. 3-16-145298-4 [JTS 40,563-5, F. F. *Bruce*].

5100 **Lindeboom** G. A., Dokter Lukas. Amst 1988, Rodopi, 123 p.; 10 fig. f19,50 [NRT 111,319].

5101 *Marshall* I. Howard, The present state of Lucan studies: Themelios 14 (1988s) 52-57.

5102 *Mosetto* Francesco, Perché Luca-Atti?: RClerIt 69 (1988) 765-772.

5103 **Murphy** Larry E., The concept of the Twelve in Luke-Acts as a key to the Lukan perspective on the restoration of Israel: diss. Southern Baptist Theol. Sem. 1988, DSonger H. 272 p. 88-18526. – DissA 49 (1988s) 1854-A.

5104 *Ó Fearghail* Fearghus, Israel in Luke-Acts: PrIrB 11 (1988) 23-43.

5105 **Prete** Benedetto, L'opera di Luca; contenuti e prospettive 1986 → 2,206; 3,4928; 88-01-14421-0: RSalesianum 50 (1988) 423 (C. *Bissoli*).

5106 **Sanders** Jack T., The Jews in Luke-Acts 1987 → 3,4930: RCBQ 50 (1988) 729s (Susan M. *Praeder*); Interpretation 42 (1988) 316.318 (D. L. *Barr*: 'inditement,' if valid, warrants excluding Lk-Acts from the canon); JTS 39 (1988) 566-8 (C. K. *Barrett*); NBlackf 69 (1988) 461; Themelios 14 (1988s) 67s (I. H. *Marshall*); TLond 91 (1988) 61-63 (F. *Watson*).

5107 *Sheeley* Steven M., Narrative asides and narrative authority in Luke-Acts: BibTB 18 (1988) 102-7.

5108 **Squires** John T., The plan of God in Luke-Acts: diss. Yale. NHv 1988. – RelStR 15,193; RTLv 20,546.

5109 ETalbert Charles H., Luke-Acts, new perspectives 1984 → 65,440 ... 2,3900: RBibTB 18 (1988) 37-39 (E. Jane *Via*, detailed analyses); RRel 46 (1987) 314s (R. F. *O'Toole*).

5110 **Tannehill** Robert C., The narrative unity of Luke-Acts I, 1986 → 2,3901; 3,4935: RBiblica 69 (1988) 135-8 (C. H. *Talbert*); BibTB 18 (1988) 39 (J. H. *Neyrey*: lucid); CBQ 50 (1988) 734s (W. S. *Kurz*: 'ex-demoniacs would likely not be married'); CurrTM 15 (1988) 201 (F. W. *Danker*).

5111 *Tiede* David L., 'Glory to thy people, Israel'; Luke-Acts and the Jews: → 77, FKEE H., Social world 1988, 327-341. → 5112.

5112 **Tyson** Joseph B., Luke-Acts and the Jewish people; eight critical perspectives. Minneapolis 1988, Augsburg. 157 p. $16; 124-137, The problem of Jewish rejection in Acts (Tyson); 21-34, *Tiede* David L., 'Glory to thy people Israel'; Luke-Acts and the Jews; 51-75, *Sanders* Jack T., The Jewish people in Luke-Acts; 35-50, *Moessner* David P., The ironic fulfillment of Israel's glory; 76-82, *Salmon* Marilyn, Outsider or insider? Luke's relationship with Judaism [TR 85,251]. ➤ 5360.

5113 **Van Linden** Philip, The Gospel of Luke and Acts: Message of Biblical Spirituality 10, 1986 ➤ 2,3902; 3,4937: ᴿVidyajyoti 52 (1988) 513 (R.J. *Raja*).

5114 **Wagner** Günter, An exegetical bibliography of the NT; Luke and Acts 1985 ➤ 2,3903: ᴿJBL 107 (1988) 165-7 (E.J. *Epp*).

5115 **Walaskay** Paul W., And so we came to Rome; the political perspective of St. Luke 1984 ➤ 64,4863 ... 2,3904: ᴿCurrTM 15 (1988) 207s (R.H. *Smith*).

5116 *Willert* N., Apologetiske og indignatoriske tendenser i Lukasskrifterne: DanTTs 50 (1987) 221-236.

F7.3 **Evangelium Lucae** – *Textus, commentarii.*

5117 **Benetti** Santos, Una alegre noticia; comentario del Evangelio de Lucas. M 1984, Paulinas. 379 p. – ᴿStudium 28 (M 1988) 151 (M.F. de *Villacorta*).

5118 **Bonsen** J.; Verlaat het vaderhuis! Een materialistische exegese van het Lucasevangelie: Eltheto, 1986 ➤ 3,4939; 90-6184-288-3: ᴿTsTNijm 28 (1988) 309 (H. *Welzen*).

5119 *Breen* Anthony, A fragment of the Sahidic version of Luke [21, 36-22,10]: Muséon 101 (1988) 291-6; 2 pl.

5120 **Butin** Jacques D., *al.*, L'Évangile selon Luc commenté par les Pères: Les Pères dans la foi. P 1987, Desclée-B. 174 p. F 87. – ᴿEsprVie 98 (1988) 260s (É. *Cothenet*).

5121 **Elliott** J.K., The NT in Greek, Lk 1-2, 1984-7 ➤ 58,5032; 3,4941: ᴿETL 64 (1988) 207 (F. *Neirynck,* 2); JBL 107 (1988) 758-762 (W.L. *Petersen*: was it worth $225 and the 60-year wait? 'Like rearranging deck chairs on the Titanic, there is something tragic about [similar efforts]').

5122 **Fitzmyer** Joseph A., The Gospel according to Luke I-II: AnchorB 28.28A, 1981/5 ➤ 62,9051 ... 3,4943: ᴿEvQ 60 (1988) 76s (I.H. *Marshall*: the definitive commentary in English; IsrEJ 38 (1988) 93s (G. *Stroumsa,* 1); TLZ 113 (1988) 183-5 (C. *Burchard*: only SCHÜRMANN is ampler, but at what cost!).

5123 **Fitzmyer** Joseph A., El evangelio según Lucas, I. Introducción general, ᵀ*Mínguez* Dionisio. M 1986, Cristiandad. 84-7057-396-9. – ᴿActuBbg 25 (1988) 61s (X. *Alegre S.*); CiuD 201 (1988) 488s (J. *Gutiérrez*).

5124 **Kilgallen** John J., A brief commentary on the Gospel of Luke. Mahwah NJ 1988, Paulist. vi-233 p. $12.50. 0-8091-2928-0.

5125 **Masini** Mario, Luca, il vangelo del discepolo: LoB 2.3. Brescia 1988, Queriniana. 201 p. Lit 18.000. 88-399-1579-6.

5126 **Meynet** Roland, L'Évangile selon saint Luc, analyse rhétorique, I. planches; II. commentaire. P 1988, Cerf. 258 p.; 277 p. F 350 [TR 85,163].

5127 **Quecke** Hans, Das Lukasevangelium, saïdisch 1977 ➤ 58,1362 ... 62, 5059: ᴿOLZ 83 (1988) 569-571 (H.-F. *Weiss*).

5128 **Radl** Walter, Das Lukas-Evangelium: ErtFor 261. Da 1988, Wiss. xviii-170 p. 3-534-03213-6.

5129 **Sabourin** L., L'évangile de Luc 1985 → 1,4946 ... 3,4958: REglT 18 (1987) 240s (M. *Dumais,* unoriginal).
5130 **Tiede** David L., Luke: CommNT. Minneapolis 1988, Augsburg. 457 p. $20 [TR 85,163].
5131 **Vesco** Jean-Luc, Jérusalem et son prophète; une lecture de l'évangile selon saint Luc. P 1988, Cerf. 132 p. F 80. 2-204-02882-7. − REsprVie 98 (1988) 524s (L. *Walter*); MondeB 54 (1988) 60 (F. *Brossier*); RThom 88 (1988) 649s (L. *Devillers*: bref commentaire).
5132 **Voetz** Lothar, Die St. Pauler Lukasglossen; Untersuchungen, Edition, Faksimile; Studien zu den Anfängen althochdeutscher Textglossierung: St. Althochd. 7. Gö 1985, Vandenhoeck & R. 271 p.; 4 (color.) pl. [BeiNam 24,404 A. *Masser*].
5133 **Weifel** Wolfgang, Das Evangelium nach Lukas: THandK NT 3. B 1988, Ev.-V. xviii-418 p. 3-374-00040-1.
5134 **Zahn** T., Das Evangelium des Lucas (1920), Vorw. *Hengel* M.: TVG Reprint. Wu 1988, Brockhaus. xiv-774 p. DM 78. 3-417-29213-1 [NTAbs 32,377].

F7.4 *Lucae themata* − **Luke's Gospel, topics.**

5135 *Abraham* M. V., Good news to the poor in Luke's gospel: BangalTF 19,1 (1987) 1-13 [NTAbs 32,166].
    Adinolfi M., brani d'esegesi di Luca 1985/8 → 477.
5135* **Baergen** Rudy E., The identity of Jesus in the Galilean ministry of Luke: diss. Union. Richmond 1987. − RelStR 14,188.
    Chan Cheng-Yi S., Kingship in 1 Sam and ... Luke D1987 → 2832.
5136 *Cope* O. Lamar, On the history of criticism of the Gospel of Luke: UnSemQ 42,1s (1988) 59-62 [< ZIT].
5136* **Dawsey** J., Lukan Voice 1986 → 2,3921: RJBL 107 (1988) 545s (J. B. *Tyson*).
5137 **Derrett** J. D. M., New resolutions ... Luke 1987 → 2,3923: REvQ 60 (1988) 273-5 (J. *Nolland*: alienated from professional exegetes).
5137* *D'Sa* Thomas, The salvation of the rich in the Gospel of Luke: Vidyajyoti 52 (1988) 170-180.
5138 *Farmer* William R., Luke's use of Matthew; a literary inquiry: AfJB 2 (1987) 7-24.
5138* **Grassi** Joseph A., God makes me laugh; a new approach to Luke: Good News Studies 17, 1986 → 2,3924: RAustralBR 36 (1988) 72s (B. R. *Doyle*; claims of 'comedy' altogether forced, especially 'everyone who exalts himself will be humbled' is a 'comic punchline').
5139 **Gueuret** Agnès, La mise en discours; recherches sémiotiques à propos de l'Évangile de Luc D1987 → 3,4967: RAntonianum 83 (1988) 610s (M. *Nobile*); Biblica 69 (1988) 286-9 (J.-N. *Aletti*).
5139* **Iersel** B. van, *al.*, Parabelverhalen in Lukas; van semiotiek naar pragmatiek: TFT 8, 1987 → 3,4868: RTsTNijm 28 (1988) 406s (P. J. *Farla*: 9 passages between Luke 8 and 20); SémBib 49 (1988) 39s (unsigned).
5140 **McMahan** Craig T., Meals as type-scenes in the Gospel of Luke: diss. Southern Baptist 1987, DCulpepper R. 340 p. 88-05804. − DissA 49 (1988s) 280-A.
5140* *Menken* M. J. J., The position of *splanchnizesthai* and *splánchna* in the Gospel of Luke: NT 30 (1988) 107-114 [114 response, *Smit Sibinga* J.].
5141 *Miller* Robert J., Elijah, John, and Jesus in the Gospel of Luke: NTS 34 (1988) 611-622.

5141* **Moxnes** Halvor, The economy of the Kingdom; social conflict and economic relations in Luke's Gospel: OvBT 23. Ph 1988, Fortress. 205 p. [JAAR 57, 695]. 0-8006-1548-4.

5142 **Ravasi** Gian Franco, Il vangelo di Luca: conferenze S. Fedele Milano. Bo 1988, Dehoniane. 134 p. 88-10-70904-7.

F7.5   *Infantia, cantica* – **Magnificat, Benedictus: Luc. 1-3.**

5142* **Drewermann** Eugen, Dein Name ist wie der Geschmack des Lebens; Tiefenpsychologische Deutung der Kindheitsgeschichte nach dem Lukasevangelium 1986 → 3,4975: ᴿLebZeug 42,2 (1987) 80s (H. *Geist*); TLZ 113 (1988) 226-8 (G. *Baudler*: Lukas 'nach- und mitzuträumen'); TPhil 63 (1988) 257-9 (H. *Engel*).

5143 *Itumeleng* Mosala, Black Theology versus the social morality of settler colonialism; hermeneutical reflections on Luke 1 and 2: JBlackT 1,1 (1987) 26-42 [< TKontext 10/1,23].

5144 *Stenger* Hermann, Die Wiederentdeckung der Bilder; Überlegungen zu Eugen DREWERMANNS Deutung der lukanischen Kindheitsgeschichte: TGegw 30 (1987) 232-241.

5144* *Buit* M. Du, [Lc 1,5] Quirinius: → 786, Catholicisme 12,55 (1988) 402s.

5145 *Brown* Raymond E., *a)* The annunciation to Mary, the Visitation, and the Magnificat (Luke 1:26-56); – *b)* The annunciation to Zechariah, the birth of the Baptist, and the Benedictus (Luke 1: 5-25, 57-80): Worship 62 (1988) 249-259; p. 367, correction / 482-496.

5145* *Kronbauer* L. G., A relação plena entre a história e a graça em Maria (Lc.1,26-38): Teocomunicação 76 (1987) 8-15 [< Stromata 44,565].

5146 *Gubler* Marie-Louise, Selig, die geglaubt hat — Das Marienbild des Lukas: TPQ 136 (1988) 130-9 [> TDig 36,19-24, 'Luke's portrait of Mary'].

5147 **López Melús** Francisco M., María de Nazareth, la Virgen del Magníficat: Pastoral aplicada 146. M 1988, PPC. 120 p. – ᴿProyección 35 (1988) 240 (B.A.O.).

5148 *Rossé* Gérard, Maria nel Vangelo di Luca: NuovaUm 10,60 (1988) 9-18.

5149 *Jankowski* Augustyn, ❷ De principiis mariologiae lucanae: RuBi 41 (1988) 320-9.

5150 *Nelson* Richard D., David; a model for Mary in Luke?: BibTB 18 (1988) 138-142.

5151 **Muñoz Iglesias** Salvador, Los Evangelios de la Infancia, II. Los anuncios angélicos previos en el Evangelio lucano 1986 → 3,4981: III. Nacimiento e infancia de Juan y de Jesús en Lucas 1-2: BAC 488. M 1987, Católica. xiv-353 p. 84-220-1286-3. – ᴿAngelicum 65 (1988) 601-4 (J. *Salguero,* 3); Biblica 69 (1988) 290-2 (K. *Stock*); DivThom 91 (1988) 192-4 (B. *Estrada,* 3); RB 95 (1988) 629s (J. *Loza,* 2); EstBib 46 (1988) 260s (E. *Tourón*); EstJos 42 (1988) 138s (J.A. *Carrasco*); Salmanticensis 35 (1988) 407-410 (G. *Pérez*); ScripTPamp 19 (1987) 932-5 (J.M. *Casciaro,* 2).

5152 *a) Masini* Mario, Il saluto di Elisabetta a Maria (Lc 1,42); – *b) Ravasi* Gianfranco, 'Beata colei che ha creduto!' (Lc 1,45); l'esclamazione di Elisabetta chiave di lettura de la enciclica [Redemptoris Mater]; – *c) Valentini* Alberto, Il secondo annuncio a Maria (RM 16): Marianum 50 (1988) 138-158 / 159-175 / 290-322.

5153 **Bemile** Paul, The Magnificat [Cath. diss. Rg 1983, ᴰ*Mussner* F.] 1986 → 2,3945: ᴿCBQ 50 (1988) 129s (M.L. *Soards*: relates stimulatingly but not always adequately to Third World social theology); TsTNijm 28 (1988) 84 (F. van *Helmond*).

5154 **Coste** René, Le Magnificat, ou la révolution de Dieu 1987 ➤ 3,4984: ᴿGregorianum 69 (1988) 160s (C.I. *González*); Marianum 39 (1987) 611-3 (A. *Bossard*).

5155 **Coste** René, The Magnificat, the revolution of God, ᵀ*Golob* L., *Plescia* L. Quezon City 1988, Claretian. vi-168 p. $10. 971-501-259-0 [TDig 36,151].

5156 **Farris** Stephen, The hymns of Luke's infancy narratives 1985 ➤ 1,4990 ... 3,4996: ᴿVidyajyoti 52 (1988) 60 (P.M. *Meagher*).

5157 *Flusser* David, The Magnificat, the Benedictus and the War Scroll: ➤ 190, JudOrChr 1988, 126-149, ineditum.

5158 **González Novalín** J.L., El comentario al 'Magnificat' de LUTERO en los albores de la Reforma: DialEcum 23 (Salamanca 1988) 249-285 [< ZIT 89,60].

5159 **Lentini** S., Il Magnificat. Palermo 1988, Fiamma Serafica. 154 p. [CC 139/3 dopo 104].

5160 **Reiterer** F.V., [Lk 1,46-55] Die Funktion des alttestamentlichen Hintergrundes für das Verständnis der Theologie des Magnifikat: HDienst 41,4 (Salzburg 1987) 129-154 [< NTAbs 32,310].

5161 *Schützeichel* Heribert, 'Das berühmte und denkwürdige Lied der heiligen Jungfrau'; CALVINS Auslegung des Magnificat: ➤ 53, ᶠGANOCZY A., Creatio 1988, 300-311.

5162 **Valentini** Alberto, Il Magnificat; genere letterario, struttura, esegesi [diss.]: RivB Sup 16, 1987 ➤ 3,4993: ᴿParVi 33 (1988) 394s (M. *Zappella*); RivB (1988) 525-8 (M. *Làconi*).

5163 *Mussies* Gerard, Vernoemen in de antieke wereld; de historische achtergrond van Luk. 1,59-63: NedTTs 42 (1988) 114-125; Eng. 145: the naming of children after (grand-) parents is found in Egypt and Phoenicia, but not among the Jews before Elephantine; in Palestine not before Alexander.

5164 *Carter* Warren, Zechariah and the Benedictus (Luke 1,68-79); practicing what he preaches: Biblica 69 (1988) 239-247.

5165 *Leaney* A.R.C., The virgin birth in Lucan theology and in the classical creeds: ➤ 60, ᶠHANSON R., Scripture 1988, 65-100.

5165* *Heck* Erich, Krippenkind-Schmerzensmann; eine bibeltheologische Betrachtung zu Lukas 2,1-20: GeistL 61 (1988) 451-9.

5166 *a) Serra* Aristide, '...e lo avvolse in fasce...' (Lc 2,7b); un segno da decodificare: – *b) Köhler* Théodore, 'Pour le présenter au Temple' (Lc 2,22), Exégèse moderne: ➤ 13, ᶠBERTETTO D., Virgo fidelis 1988, 81-134 / 513-522.

5166* *Smyth* Kevin, 'Peace on earth to men...' (Lk 2.14): IrBSt 9 (1987) 27-34.

5167 *Kilpatrick* Ross S., The Greek syntax of Luke 2.14: NTS 34 (1988) 472-5.

5167* *Renoux* Charles, Une homélie [en arménien] sur Luc 2,21 attribué à JEAN de Jérusalem: Muséon 101 (1988) 77-95.

5168 *Simón Muñoz* Alfonso, Cristo, luz de los Gentiles; puntualizaciones sobre Lc 2,32 [< diss. El Mesías y la Hija de Sion... Lc 2,29-35, Roma 1986, Angelicum]: EstBíb 46 (1988) 27-44; Eng. 27.

5168* *Elliott* J.K., Anna's age (Luke 2:36-37) [over 100]: NT 30 (1988) 100-2.

5169 *D'Urso* G., [Lc 2,50] Le prime parole di Gesù: RivAscM 12,3 (1987) 195-202.

5169* *Ćurić* Josip, [in Croatian] Progress in age, wisdom and grace [Lk 2,52]: ObnŽiv 43,6 (17th Summer School, 'Christian and human maturity', 1988) 479-495; Eng. 495.

F7.6   Evangelium Lucae 4,1 ...

5170 **Meynet** R., Initiation à la rhétorique biblique [Lc 4,14-30...] 1982 ➤ 63,1254 ... 2,3959:   ᴿBL (1988) 83s (J. *Barr*: wrathfully demands the impossible of modern translations).

5171 *Finkel* A.,   Jesus. preaching in the synagogue on the sabbath (Luke 4,16-28): SIDIC 17,3 (R 1984) 4-10 [< NTAbs 32,311].

5172 *Kavunkal* Jacob, [Lk 4,16-20] Jubilee the framework of evangelization: Vidyajyoti 52 (1988) 181-190.

5173 *Walker* T. Vaughn,   Luke 4:16-30 [in Nazareth synagogue, whether Jesus chose this passage or not]: RExp 85 (1988) 321-4.

5174 **Allegro** John M.,   [Lk 4,23] Physician, heal thyself [Essene theology] 1985 ➤ 2,3964:   ᴿHorizons 15 (1988) 161s (L. F. *Badia*).

5175 *Osborn* Noel D., *al.*,   Lk 5,8 [insoluble whether Jesus got out of the boat before commanding Peter]: BTrans 39 (1988) 439-441.

5176 *Skeat* T.C.,   The 'second-first' sabbath (Luke 6:1); the final solution: NT 30 (1988) 103-6 [no such word].

5177 *Williams* David T., [Codex D Bezae Lk 6,4 (even if not authentic) Jesus saw a man working on the sabbath and said, 'Man, if indeed you know what you are doing, you are blessed; but if you do not know, you are a transgressor'] The Sabbath, mark of distinction: Themelios 14 (1988s) 96-101: for the clergy anyway Sunday is perforce the hardest work-day of the week.

5178 *Ravens* D.A.S.,   The setting of Luke's account of the anointing; Luke 7,2-8,3:   NTS 34 (1988) 282-292.

5179 *Pelaez del Rosal* J., [Lc 7,12...] 'La reanimación de un cadáver'; un problema de fuentes y géneros: Alfinge 1 (Córdoba 1983) 151-173 [NTAbs 32,167].

5180 *a)* *Legaré* Clément,   Jésus et la pécheresse, Luc 7,36-50; – *b)* *Genest* Olivette,   De la fille à la femme à la fille: ➤ 292, Jésus/Femmes 1982/7, 59-104 / 105-120.

5181 *Manns* Frédéric,   Luc 7,47 et les traditions juives sur Rahab [Jos 2]: RevSR 61 (1987) 1-18.

F7.7   Iter hierosolymitanum – Lc 9 ...

5182 *Roquet* Gérard,   L'esprit de géométrie; le jeu et son empreinte culturelle dans l'Égypte dynastique et copte; de *znt* a CHNE; à propos de Luc 9:14): LOrA 1 (Lv 1988) 157-165.

5182* **Reid** Barbara E.,   The transfiguration; an exegetical study of Luke 9:28-36: diss. Catholic Univ., ᴰ*Meier* J.P. Wsh 1988.   266p. 88-14959. – DissA 49 (1988s) 1494s-A; RTLv 20,545.

5183 *Vollenweider* Samuel,   'Ich sah den Satan wie einen Blitz vom Himmel fallen' (Lk 10,18): ZNW 79 (1988) 187-203.

5184 *Boers* Hendrikus, [Lc 10] Traduction sémantique transculturelle de la parabole du bon Samaritain, ᵀavec *Sebbe* Helen: SémBib 47 (1987) 18-29.

Becker Henri, Qui est mon prochain? (Luc 10,29, ᴰ1987 ➤ 2636, Lev. 19,18.

5184* **Parsons** Mikeal C., 'Allegorizing allegory'; narrative analysis and parable interpretation: PerspRelSt 147-164, taking off from AUGUSTINE QEv 2,19 [Lk 10,30-35] 'A certain man' = Adam; 'Jericho' = our mortality; 'innkeeper' = Paul ...

Aus Roger D., Lk 10,33; 15, 11s, jüdisch. Hintergrund 1988 ➤ 4220.

5185 *Oakman* Douglas E., The buying power of two denarii; a comment on Luke 10:35: Forum 3,4 (Sonoma 1987) 33-38 [< ZIT 88,537].

5186 **Brutscheck** Jutta, Die Maria-Marta-Erzählung ... Lk 10,38-42: BoBB 64, 1986 ➤ 2,3977 ... 3,5027: ᴿCBQ 50 (1988) 130s (F. W. *Danker*: challenges customary 'active vs. contemplative' portrayal); TLZ 113 (1988) 269s (G. *Sellin*); TR 84 (1988) 23s (D. *Dormeyer*).

5187 *Canopi* Anna M. sr., Maria ... ascoltava (Luca 10,38-42); Gesù e gli amici di Betania: ParVi 33 (1988) 296-301 (e altre meditazioni negli altri fascicoli).

5188 *Magne* Jean, La réception de la variante 'vienne ton Esprit Saint sur nous et qu'il nous purifie' (Lc 11,2) et l'origine des épiclèses, du baptême et du 'Nôtre Père': EphLtg 102 (1988) 81-106; lat. 81.

5189 *Philonenko* Marc, La parabole sur la lampe (Luc 11,33-36) et les horoscopes qoumrâniens: ZNW 79 (1988) 145-151.

5190 *Moessner* David P., [Lk 12,1 ...] The 'leaven of the Pharisees' and 'this generation': Israel's rejection of Jesus according to Luke: JStNT 34 (1988) 21-46.

5191 *a*) *Sebothoma* W. [Luke 12,35-40 (distillation of Mt 25,1-13 ten virgins, 'I know you not') + 12,41-48 conscientious stewardship] A reading by a black South African; – *b*) *Staden* P. van, A sociological reading ...; – *c*) *Scheffler* E., A psychological reading ...; – *d*) *Plessis* I. J. du, Reading Luke 12:35-48 as part of the travel narrative: Neotestamentica 22,2 (1988) 325-335 / 337-353 / 355-371 / 217-234.

5192 *a*) *Tilborg* S. van, [Lk 12,35-48] An interpretation from the ideology of the text; – *b*) *Aarde* A. G. van, Narrative point of view; an ideological reading of Luke 12:35-48; – *c*) *Botha* J., [1970s W.] ISER's wandering viewpoint; a reception-analytical ideological reading ...; – *d*) *Wuellner* W., The rhetorical structure of Luke 12 in its wider context; – *e*) *Rensburg* J. J. J. van, A syntactical reading ...; – *f*) *Smit* D. J., Responsible hermeneutics; a systematic theologian's response to the readings and readers of Luke 12:25-48: Neotestamentica 22,2 (1988) 205-215 / 235-252 / 253-268 / 283-310 / 415-439 / 441-484.

5193 *a*) *Plessis* J. G. du, [Lk 12,41, 'Be ready ... I know you not' for us or for all?] Why did Peter ask his question and how did Jesus answer him? or, Implicature [sic, explained p. 311] in Luke 12:35-48; – *b*) *Schnell* C. W., Historical context in parable interpretation; a criticism of current tradition-historical interpretations of Luke 12:35-48; – *c*) *Hartin* P. J., Angst in the household; a deconstructive reading of the parable of the Supervising Servant (Lk 12:41-48); – *d*) *Lategan* B. C., *Rousseau* J., Reading Luke 12:35-48; an empirical [reader-reaction] study: Neotestamentica 22,2 (1988) 311-324 / 269-282 / 373-390 / 391-413.

5194 *Milot* Louise, Guérison d'une femme infirme un jour de sabbat; Luc 13,10-17: ➤ 292, Jésus/Femmes 1982/7, 121-133.

5195 **Janiszeski** Timothy A., [Lk 14,15-24] The parable of the great banquet in its Lukan thematic and contextual framework: diss. Calvin Sem., ᴰVanderHoek G. GR 1988. iv-125 p. + bibliog. – CalvinT 23 (1988) 304.

5196 *Billy* Dennis J., [Lk 15,11-32] Conversion and the Franciscan preacher; BONAVENTURE'S commentary on the Prodigal Son: ColcFr 58 (1988) 259-275; ital. 275.

5197 ᴱGalli G., Interpretazione ... Figliol Prodigo 1986/7 ➤ 3,543:   ᴿStPatav 35 (1988) 708-710 (C. *Corsato*).

5198 *Jones* Peter, La parabole du fils prodigue; deux méthodes d'interprétation: ➤ 28*, ᶠCOURTHIAL P., Dieu parle 1984, 23-38.

5199 *Plessis* I. J. du, Die gelykenis van die verlore seun, Lukas 15:11-32: ➤ 509, Hoe lees 1985/8 ...

5200 *Scobel* Gert, Das Gleichnis vom verlorenen Sohn als metakommunikativer Text; Überlegungen zur Verständigungsproblematik in Lukas 15: FreibZ 35 (1988) 21-67.

5201 *Burgos Núñez* Miguel de, El escándalo de la justicia del Reino en Lucas XVI: ComSev 21 (1988) 167-190.

5202 *Byrne* Brendan, Forceful stewardship and neglectful wealth; a contemporary reading of Luke 16: Pacifica 1,1 (1988) 1-14 [< ZIT 88,309].

5203 *Steinhauser* M. G., Noah in his generation; an allusion in Luke 16,8b 'eis tēn geneàn tēn heautôn': ZNW 79 (1988) 152-7.

5204 **Westra** Abe, De gelijkenis van de rijke man en de arme Lazarus (Lukas 16,19-31) in de werken van de Grieks vroeg-christelijke schrijvers tot en met J. CHRYSOSTOMUS: diss. ᴰJonge M. de. Leiden 1987. xxv-174 p. – TsTNijm 28,77; RTLv 19,541.

5205 *Dagron* Alain, [Luc 17...] De la lecture ou propos sur le texte en quête de lecteur: SémBib 51 (1988) 35-40.

5206 *Sacchi* Alessandro, Pazienza di Dio e ritardo della parusia (Lc 18,7): ➤ 154, ᶠZEDDA S., RivB 36 (1988) 299-326; Eng. 327.

5207 **Reist** Thomas, Saint BONAVENTURE as a biblical commentator; a translation and analysis of his commentary on Luke, XVIII,34 – XIX,42. Lanham MD 1985, UPA. xx-263 p. $12.50. – ᴿColcFr 56 (1986) 146s (C. *Bérubé*); ZkT 110 (1988) 194 (K. *Stock*).

5208 *Contreras Molina* Francisco, [Lc 19,1-10] El relato de Zaqueo en el Evangelio de Lucas: ComSev 21 (1988) 3-47.

5209 **Kariamadam** Paul, The Zacchaeus story (Lk. 19,1-10) [< The end of the travel narrative, diss. Rome, Biblical Institute, ᴰLa Potterie I. de] 1985 ➤ 1,5046 ... 3,5057: ᴿCBQ 50 (1988) 138s (D. *Hamm*: solid); IndTSt 25 (1988) 391s (L. *Legrand*); Vidyajyoti 52 (1988) 61 (R. J. *Raja* feels that the requirement of dissertation-publication could have been attained by stressing the main lines and omitting 'sundry details' and foreign-language notes).

5210 *Vitório* Jaldemar, 'E procurava ver quem era Jesus...' Análise do sentido teológico de 'ver' en Lc 19,1-10: PerspT 19,1 (1987) 9-26 [< RET 48,258].

5211 ᴱWatkins Owen C., BUNYAN John [1628-1688], Seasonable counsel [and (Lk 18,10)] A discourse upon the Pharisee and the Publican: Miscellaneous Works of Bunyan 10. Ox 1988, Clarendon. xxxviii-260 p. $79 [TDig 36,49].

5212 *Haudebert* P., [Lc 19,1; 18,9] Publicain: ➤ 786, Catholicisme 12,55 (1988) 269-272.

5213 *Hamm* Dennis, Luke 19:8 once again; does Zacchaeus defend or resolve?: JBL 107 (1988) 431-7.

5214 **Giblin** Charles H., The destruction of Jerusalem ... Luke: AnBib 107, 1985 ➤ 1,5952 ... 3,5061: ᴿAustralBR 36 (1988) 73s (B. R. *Doyle*);

JBL 107 (1988) 329-331 (E. *Richard*); Vidyajyoti 52 (1988) 61 (R. J. *Raja*).

F7.8   **Passio** – *Lc 22*...

5215 *Macina* Menahem,   Fonction liturgique et eschatologique de l'anamnèse eucharistique (Lc 22,19; 1 Cor 11,24.25); réexamen de la question à la lumière des Écritures et des sources juives: EphLtg 102 (1988) 3-25; lat. 3: contra communem sententiam, nullo modo VTi instituta radicitus abolet [thema plus minus continuatur p. 145s(-233)].

5216 **Soards** Marion L.,   The Passion according to Luke [diss. 1984] 1987 ► 3,5063:   RRelStR 14 (1988) 253 (L. *Cope*); RExp 85 (1988) 352s (S. M. *Sheeley*).

5216* *Senior* Donald,   The passion of Jesus in the Gospel of Luke: Passion 3. Wilmington 1989, Glazier.   192 p. $11 pa.   0-89453-46-0 [TDig 36,389].

5217 *Baarda* T.,   Luke 22:42-47a; the emperor Julian as a witness to the text of Luke: NT 30 (1988) 289-296.

5218 *a) Schneider* Gerhard,   Das Verfahren gegen Jesus in der Sicht des dritten Evangeliums (Lk 22,54-23,25); Redaktionskritik und historische Rückfrage; – *b) Radl* Walter,   Sonderüberlieferungen bei Lukas? Traditionsgeschichtliche Fragen zu Lk 22,67f; 23,2 und 23,6-12: ► 491*, Prozess 1987/8, 111-130 / 131-147.

5219 *Manus* Chris U.,   The universalism of Luke and the motif of reconciliation in Luke 23:6-12:   AfTJ 16 (1987) 121-135 [< TKontext 10/1,17].

5220 **Grandez** Rufino,   Las tinieblas en la muerte de Jesús; estudio sobre Luc 23,44-45: diss. Antonianum, DBottini C.   Roma 1987.   264 p.; 105 p. – RTLv 19,537.

5221 *Schubert* Paul,   Struktur und Bedeutung von Lukas 24 [< FBultmann, BZNW 21 (1954) 166-186], TZwosta Franz: ► 311, EHoffmann P., WegF 522 (1988) 331-359.

5222 *Kremer* Jacob,   Die Bezeugung der Auferstehung Christi in Form von Geschichten; zu Schwierigkeiten und Chancen heutigen Verstehens von Lk 24,13-53:   GeistL 61 (1988) 172-187.

5223 *O'Collins* Gerald,   Did Jesus eat fish? (Luke 24:42-43):   Gregorianum 69 (1988) 65-76; franç. 76.

XII. Actus Apostolorum

F8.1   **Acts** – *text, commentary, topics.*

5224 **Bassey** Michael E.,   Witnessing in the Acts of the Apostles; a study of the communicational strategies and their relevance to the evangelization of the Africans today: diss. Pont. Univ. Urbaniana, DVirgulin S.   R 1988. xx-477 p.; ill.

5225 *a) Birdsall* J. Neville,   The Georgian versions of the Acts of the Apostles; – *b) Bouwman* Gijs,   Der Anfang der Apostelgeschichte und der 'westliche' Text: ► 85, FKLIJN A., Text 1988, 39-45 / 46-56.

5226 **Boismard** M. E., *Lamouille* A.,   Le texte occidental des Actes 1984 65,4597* ... 3,5086:   RCBQ 50 (1988) 709-711 (G. *Vall*); EstBíb 46 (1988) 401-6 (J. *Trebolle Barrera*); JTS 39 (1988) 571-7 (J. N. *Birdsall*: serious and challenging; but the incidence of the misleading and the inaccurate is high).

5227 **Bruce** Frederick F.,   The book of the Acts²ʳᵉᵛ: NICOT.   GR 1988, Eerdmans. xxiii-541 p. $19.50.   0-8028-2418-8.

5228 **Cassidy** Richard J.,   Society and politics in the Acts of the Apostles 1987 → 3,5088:   ᴿAnglTR 70 (1988) 360-2 (R. S. *Richard*); ExpTim 99 (1987s) 377s (Ruth B. *Edwards*); NewTR 1,3 (1988) 98s (M. *Trainor*); RExp 85 (1988) 727s (S. *Scheeley*: some reserves); TS 50 (1989) 199 (A. J. *Tambasco*); Vidyajyoti 52 (1988) 303s (R. J. *Raja*: continues 1978 Jesus, politics and society ... Luke's Gospel).

5229 **Conzelmann** Hans,   Acts of the Apostles [¹1972] ᵀ*Limburg* J., *al.*; Hermeneia, 1987 → 3,5089:   ᴿRExp 85 (1988) 352 (S. M. *Sheeley*); Themelios 14 (1988s) 30s (W. W. *Gasque*); TS 49 (1988) 530s (R. E. *Brown*: the word 'probably' should have been used oftener); Vidyajyoti 52 (1988) 614 (R. J. *Raja*).

5230 **Delebecque** É.   Les deux Actes des Apôtres: ÉtBN 6, 1986 → 2,4028; 3,5090:   ᴿRTLv 19 (1988) 367-9 (J.-C. *Haelewyck*).

5231 *Elliott* J. K.,   The text of Acts in the light of two recent studies [*Sturz* H., *Boismard* M.]: NTS 34 (1988) 250-8.

5232 *Gasque* W. Ward,   Recent commentaries on the Acts of the Apostles: Themelios 14 (1988s) 21-23.

5233 *a) Gasque* Ward W.,   A fruitful field; recent study of the Acts of the Apostles; – *b) Tyson* Joseph B.,   The emerging Church and the problem of authority in Acts; – *c) Gaventa* Beverly R.,   Toward a theology of Acts; reading and rereading; – *d) Willimon* William H.,   'Eyewitnesses and ministers of the Word'; preaching in Acts: Interpretation 42 (1988) 117-131 / 132-145 / 146-157 / 158-170.

5234 *Geer* Thomas C.,   Codex 1739 in Acts and its relationship to manuscripts 945 and 1891:   Biblica 69 (1988) 27-46; franç. 42 (sic).

5235 **Gourgues** M.,   Misión y comunidad (Hch 1-12). Estella 1988, VDivino. 62 p. – ᴿBibFe 14 (1988) 323s (M. *Sáenz Galache*).

5236 *Haelewyck* Jean-Claude,   Le texte occidental des Actes des Apôtres, à propos de la reconstitution de M.-É. *Bosimard* et A. *Lamouille*:   RTLv 19 (1988) 342-353; Eng. 412.

5237 **Hengel** Martin,   La storiografia protocristiana [1979 → 60,6613], ᵀ*Cessi* Viviana, ᴱ*Soffritti* Omero. Brescia 1985, Paideia.   191 p. Lit. 16.000. – ᴿHelmantica 118s (1988) 243 (L. *Amigo*).

5238 **Kilgallen** John J.,   A brief commentary on the Acts of the Apostles.   NY 1988, Paulist.   vi-232 p. $12.50.   0-8091-2977-9.

5239 **Krodel** G. A.,   Acts: Augsburg Comm. 1986 → 3,5100:   ᴿInterpretation 42 (1988) 302-5 (R. H. *Smith*: 'exciting events in the amazing panorama of the ancient world', GOODSPEED E. J.).

5240 **LaHurd** Carol J. S.,   The author's call to the audience in the Acts of the Apostles; a literary-critical anthropological reading: diss. Pittsburgh 1987. 286 p. 88-08329. – DissA 49 (1988s) 842-A.

5241 **Larsson** E.,   Apostlagärningarna 13-20: KNyaT 5B.   U 1987, EFS. v-187 p.; 3 maps.   Sk 197.   91-7080-770-1 [NTAbs 32,373].

5242 **L'Éplattenier** Charles,   Les Actes des Apôtres 1987 → 3,5101:   ᴿÉTRel 63 (1988) 122s (J.-P. *Gardelle*); Protestantesimo 43 (1988) 120s (P. *Tognina*).

5243 [Hugo] **Lopes** Eliseo,   El camino recorrido por la Palabra; ayuda para la lectura de los Hechos de los Apóstoles [O caminho], ᵀ*Castelli* César:

La Buena Noticia 7. Buenos Aires–Florida 1988, Paulinas. 48 p. 950-09-0768-2.

5244 **Lüdemann** Gerd, Das frühe Christentum nach den Traditionen der Apostelgeschichte; ein Kommentar 1987 ➤ 3,5103: ᴿBZ 32 (1988) 291-3 (F. *Mussner*); CBQ 50 (1988) 722-4 (R. F. *O'Toole*: 'Kommentar'? study of the historical value of what is found in Acts); NRT 110 (1988) 922s (X. *Jacques*); RivStoLR 24 (1988) 584-6 (V. *Fusco*); SNTU-A 13 (1987) 232s (A. *Fuchs*).

5245 *Luedemann* Gerd, Acts of the Apostles as a historical source: ➤ 77, ᶠKᴇᴇ H., Social world 1988, 109-125.

5245* **Maloney** Linda, All that God had done with them; the narration of the works of God in the early Christian community as described in the Acts of the Apostles: kath. Diss. ᴰ*Lohfink* G. Tübingen 1988s. – TR 85,519.

5246 *Okeke* George E., The death-resurrection of Jesus Christ in the kerygma of the early Church; evidence from the Acts of the Apostles: LivWord 94,1 (1988) 3-21 [< TKontext 10/1,47].

5247 **O'Reilly** Leo, Word and sign in the Acts of the Apostles; a study in Lucan theology ᴰ1987 ➤ 3,5106: ᴿBibTB 18 (1988) 152 (L. E. *Frizzel*: on p. 149 Frizzell); Furrow 39 (1988) 61s (J. *McPolin*).

5248 **Pervo** Richard I., Profit with delight; the literary genre of the Acts of the Apostles [ᴰ1979] 1987 ➤ 3,5108: ᴿAnglTR 70 (1988) 186-8 (H. *Graham*); ExpTim 99 (1987s) 378 (Ruth B. *Edwards*: will have lasting influence); RExp 85 (1988) 564s (S. *Sheeley*); TS 49 (1988) 779s (L. T. *Johnson*; VigChr 42 (1988) 306 (A. F. J. *Klijn*).

5249 **Pesch** Rudolf, Die Apostelgeschichte I (1-12) 1986 ➤ 2,4037; 3,5109: ᴿActuBbg 25 (1988) 70s (X. *Alegre S.*); RHPR 68 (1988) 250s (M. *Carrez*); SNTU-A 13 (1988) 231s (A. *Fuchs*); Streven 55 (1987s) 280s (P. *Beentjes*).

5250 **Scaglioni** Angelo, I racconti dei miracoli negli Atti degli Apostoli e loro significato teologico: diss. Angelicum, ᴰ*Boschi* B. R. 1987. 303 p. – RTLv 19,540.

5251 **Schneider** Gerhard, Gli Atti degli Apostoli: CommNT 5/1s, 1985s ➤ 2,4040; 3,5113: ᴿAntonianum 63 (1988) 176s (M. *Nobile,* 2); StPatav 35 (1988) 645-9 (G. *Leonardi*).

5252 *Schneider* G., Apostelgeschichte: ➤ 804, NBL Lfg 1 (1988) 138-141.

5253 *Schrader* Richard J., Notes on the text, interpretation, and sources of ARATOR [Acts; Bible-Epic 544 A.D., *McKinlay* 1951]: VigChr 42 (1988) 75-78.

5254 *Slingerland* Dixon, The composition of Acts; some redaction–critical observations: JAAR 56 (1988) 99-113.

5255 **Taylor** James P., Christianity is born; a creative approach to the Acts of the Apostles. Slough 1988, St. Paul. 128 p. £5.50. 0-85439-275-0.

5256 *Toubert* H., Un nouveau témoin de la tradition illustrée des Actes des Apôtres; les fresques romanes découvertes à l'abbaye de Nonantola: CahCivMéd 30 (1987) 227-244 + 4 pl. [< RSPT 72,146].

5257 *Tremolada* Pierantonio, L'azione contro Gesù e le sue implicazioni nel libro degli Atti degli Apostoli: ScuolC 116 (1988) 609-670.

5258 *Troiani* Lucio, Per una riconsiderazione degli *Héllēnes* nel NT: Athenaeum 66 (1988) 179-190.

5259 *Wall* Robert W., The Acts of the Apostles in canonical context: BibTB 18 (1988) 16-24.

5260 **Weiser** Alfons, Die Apostelgeschichte Kap. 13-28: ÖkTb NT 5,2 / Siebenstern 508, 1985 ➤ 1,5097: ᴿTLZ 113 (1988) 440s (N. *Walter*).

5261 **Wildhaber** Bruno,   Paganisme populaire et prédication apostolique,
d'après l'exégèse de quelques séquences des Actes; éléments pour une
théologie lucanienne de la mission [diss. FrS, ^D*Trémel* B.] 1987 ➤ 3,5120:
^RCBQ 50 (1988) 340s (K. E. *Brower*: on Simon Magus, death of Herod,
Cyprus conflict, Lystra, Philippi, Ephesus exorcists and Artemis, Malta
miracles); RThom 88 (1988) 135 (H. *Ponsot*: un peu grandiloquent).
5262 **Willimon** W. H.,   Acts: Interpretation Comm.   Atlanta 1988, Knox.
xi-197 p. $17.   0-8042-3119-2 [NTAbs 32,377].

F8.3   *Ecclesia primaeva Actuum:*   **Die Urgemeinde.**

5263 *Aarde* A. G. van,   Gedagtes oor die begin van die Kerk — 'n
geschiedenis van versoenende verskeidenheid [... reconciliation-producing
diversity]: HervTS 43,3 (Pretoria 1987) 325-351 [< NTAbs 32,339].
5264 **Achtemeier** Paul J.,   The quest for unity in the NT church; a study in
Paul and Acts [< CBQ 48 (1986) 1-26], 1987 ➤ 3,5121:   ^RAsbTJ 43,1
(1988) 91s (J. S. *Wang*); CBQ 50 (1988) 704s (L. T. *Johnson*: severe);
JEcuSt 25 (1988) 462 (J. C. *Cooper*); TS 49 (1988) 778s (D. *Hamm*).
5265 *a)* **Aguirre** Rafael,   La iglesia de Antioquía de Siria; la apertura
universalista y las dificultades de la comunión; – *b)* **Goitía** José de, La
iglesia de Roma; origen, naturaleza y preeminencia: Iglesias del NT (1-2).
Bilbao 1988, Desclée-B. 66 p.; 49 p. [NatGrac 35,437].
5266 **Aguirre** Rafael,   Del movimiento de Jesús a la Iglesia cristiana 1987
➤ 3,3122:   ^RCiuD 201 (1988) 491s (J. *Gutiérrez*); NatGrac 34 (1987) 109
(R. *Robles*).
5267 *Aguirre* Rafael,   Identitad y función del laico a partir de las primeras
comunidades cristianas: LumenVr 37 (1988) 328-336.
5268 *Amewowo* Wynnand,   The Christian community and Acts of the
Apostles: BPast 6 (Nairobi 1987) 31-38 [< TKontext 9/2,17].
5269 *Balembo* Buetubela,   L'autonomie des jeunes Églises et les Actes: RAfrT
11,21 (1987) 5-22 [< NTAbs 32,316].
5270 *Beeck* Franz J. Van,   The worship of Christians in PLINY'S letter: StLtg
18 (Rotterdam 1988) 121-131 [< ZIT 89,56].
5271 *Betori* Giuseppe,   Chiesa e Israele nel libro degli Atti [*Dupont* J. 1984;
Lohfink G. 1976, ital. 1983 ...]: RivB 36 (1988) 61-97.
5272 **Brown** R. E.,   L'Église héritée des apôtres 1987 ➤ 3,5127:   ^RBrotéria
126 (1988) 96 (I. *Ribeiro da Silva*); CahÉv 62 (1987) 74 (M. *Quesnel*);
EsprVie 98 (1988) 94s (L. *Walter*: séduit et irrite); FoiTemps 18 (1988) 403
(C. *Focant*); MondeB 53 (1988) 60 (F. *Brossier*: 'fautes énormes' tra-
duction/typo); ScEspr 40 (1988) 171-4 (M. *Gourgues*: badly proofread);
VSp 142 (1988) 462 (H. *Cousin*).
5273 **Brown** Raymond E.,   Las Iglesias que los Apóstoles nos dejaron, ^T*Pérez*
Gemma: Cristianismo y Sociedad 13, 1986 ➤ 3,5128: ^RCiTom 114 (1987)
375s (A. *Bandera*); CiuD 201 (1988) 485s (A. *Salas*); ScripTPamp 20
(1988) 344s (F. *Varo*).
5274 **Brown** R. E., *Meier* J. P.,   Antioche et Rome, berceaux du christianisme
[1983 ➤ 64,5048],^T: LDiv 131.   P 1988, Cerf.   230 p.   F 195.   2-204-
02843-6. – ^REsprVie 98 (1988) 564-9 (É. *Cothenet*); Études 369 (1988) 426
(P. *Gibert*); RThom 88 (1988) 651-3 (M.-É. *Lauzière*).
5275 **Brown** R. E., *Meier* J. P., Antiochia e Roma 1987 ➤ 3,5131:   ^RAsprenas
35 (1988) 526-8 (A. *Rolla*).
5276 **Clévenot** Michel,   Von Jerusalem nach Rom; Geschichte des Christentums im 1. Jahrhundert, ^T*Füssel* Kuno. 1987, Exodus-Verlag. c. DM 35. –
^RBiKi 42 (1987) 90-2 (Silvia *Schroer*).

5277 *Coleman* R. E., The fellowship of the Church in the Book of Acts: EvRT 12,1 (Exeter 1988) 17-28 [< NTAbs 32,317].

5278 *a) Colpe* Carsten, Die älteste judenchristliche Gemeinde; – *b) Becker* Jürgen, Paulus und seine Gemeinden; – *c) Löning* Karl, [Stephanuskreis ...]; – *d) Lampe* Peter, *Luz* Ulrich, Nachpaulinisches Christentum und pagane Gesellschaft: ➤ 3,326, Anfänge 1987, 59-79 / 102-159 / ... / 185-216.

5279 **Cwiekowski** Frederick J., The beginnings of the Church; pref. *Brown* R. E. NY 1988, Paulist. viii-222 p.; map. $10 pa. 0-89091-2926-4 [NTAbs 32,381]; also Dublin, Gill & M. £9. – [R]ETL 64 (1988) 469-471 (A. de *Halleux*); RivB 36 (1988) 531s (V.*Fusco*).

5280 **Faivre** Alexandre, I laici alle origini della Chiesa [1984 ➤ 65,4635],[T]: Problemi e dibattiti 3. R 1986, Paoline. 274 p. – [R]Salesianum 50 (1988) 234 (G. *Groppo*: riserve).

5281 *Fitzmyer* Joseph A., Jesus in the Early Church through the eyes of Luke-Acts: ScripB 17 (1986) 26-35.

5282 **Goppelt** Leonhard, L'età apostolica e subapostolica: NT Sup 5. Brescia 1986, Paideia. 318 p.

5283 **Grossi** Vittorino, *Siniscalco* Paolo, La vita cristiana nei primi secoli [testi biblici e patristici]. R 1988, Studium. 315 p. Lit. 23.000. – [R]CC 139 (1988,4) 407 (C. *Capizzi*).

5284 **Guillet** Jacques, Entre Jésus et l'Église: Parole de Dieu 24, 1985 ➤ 1,5109; 2,4056: [R]ZkT 110 (1988) 205s (K. *Stock*).

5285 **Hadot** J. ['agnostique' p. 5]. Les origines du christianisme: FORel Cah 2. Charleroi 1988, Fac. Univ. Religions et laïcité. 131 p. [NRT 111,435, X. *Jacques*].

5286 *Hann* Robert W., Judaism and Jewish Christianity in Antioch; charisma and conflict in the first century: JRelHist 14 (1986s) 341-360.

5287 **Hengel** Martin, Acts and the history of earliest Christianity 1979 ➤ 60,6912*b* (1986 ➤ 2,4059): [R]DeltioVM 17,1 (1988) 61-65 (S. *Agouridis*, **G**).

5288 **Hooker** Morna D., Continuity and discontinuity; early Christianity in its Jewish setting [Melbourne Sanderson lectures]. L 1986, Epworth. iv-76 p. £4. – [R]NBlackf 68 (1987) 315 (A. R. C. *Leaney*).

5289 **Hoornaert** Eduardo, Die Anfänge der Kirche in der Erinnerung des christlichen Volkes, [T]*Kuhlmann* Jürgen: Bibliothek Theologie der Befreiung. Dü 1987, Patmos. 239 p. [TR 85,291-5, H. R. *Seeliger*].

5290 **Iori** Renato, La solidarietà cristiana nelle comunità primitive: diss. Pont. Univ. Gregoriana, [D]*Rasco* E. Roma 1987. 320 p. – RTLv 19,538.

5291 *Jáuregui* Jose A., Función de los 'doce' en la Iglesia de Jerusalén; estudio histórico-exegético sobre el estado de la discusión: EstE 63 (1988) 257-284.

5292 *a) Jones* Peter, La croissance de l'Église dans le NT; – *b) Daumas* Jean-Marc, Des principaux facteurs de renouveau dans l'histoire de l'Église: RRéf 39,2 (1988) 1-11 / 12-21 [< ZIT].

5293 *Kretschmar* Georg, Anspruch auf Universalität in der Alten Kirche und Praxis ihrer Mission: Saeculum 38 (1987) 150-177.

5294 **Làconi** Mauro, San Lucas y su Iglesia [1986 ➤ 2,3884], [T]*Jáuregui* José A. Estella 1987, VDivino. 140 p. pt. 635. 84-7151-521-9. – [R]ActuBbg 25 (1988) 214s (R. de *Sivatte*).

5295 **Lütgert** W., Die Liebe im NT, ein Beitrag zur Geschichte des Urchristentums. Giessen 1986 = 1905, Brunnen. 275 p. DM 34 pa. – [R]SNTU-A 13 (1988) 219 (A. *Fuchs*: 'Das Vorwort des [nicht genannten] Herausgebers hebt hervor, dass das Thema des Buches in der prote-

stantischen Exegese, zum Unterschied von der katholischen, jahr-
zehntelang keine besondere Aufmerksamkeit gefunden hat...' Glaube viel
öfter).

5296 **MacDonald** Margaret Y., The Pauline churches; a socio-historical study
of institutionalization in the Pauline and Deutero-Pauline writings [diss.
Oxford]: SNTS Mg 60. C 1988, Univ. xii-286 p. $44.50. 0-521-35337-8.

5297 **Meyer** Ben F., The early Christians 1986 → 2,4066; 3,5151: ᴿInterpretation 42 (1988) 96s (J. B. *Tyson*).

5298 **Moda** Aldo, Il cristianesimo nel primo secolo; un itinerario e un dossier
[... ii. diaspora; iii. Romani]. Bari 1986, Ecumenica. 128 p. – ᴿAevum 62
(1988) 146s (A. *Barzanò*).

5299 *a*) *Moxnes* Halvor, Hva slags religion var urkristendommen?: – *b*) *Seim*
Turid K., I asketisk frihet? Urkirkens enker i nytt lys glimt fra en
forskningssituasjon: → 97*, ᶠLØNNING I., NorTTs 89 (1988) 47-66 /
27-45.

5300 **Neal** Randall S., Synagogue and church; the model of the Jewish
synagogue in the formation of first-century Chritianity: diss. SW Baptist
Theol. Sem. 1988. 244 p. 88-27977. – DissA 49 (1988s) 3058-A; RelStR
15,193.

5301 *Nechutová* Jana, Ecclesia primitiva in der hussitischen Lehre: SborBrno
33 (1988) 87-93; deutsch 93.

5302 *Neufeld* Karl H., Cattolicesimo nascente, proposta di un termine [invece
del 'protocattolicesimo' dell'italiano 1985 (e francese 1972) di KÄSE-
MANN]: RivB 36 (1988) 255-8.

5303 *Orioli* G., Le origini della Chiesa di Antiochia e la sua fondazione
petrina nella documentazione fino al sec. v.: Apollinaris 60 (1987) 645-9.

5304 *Raja* R.J., Communal conflicts in the nascent Church: Word and
Worship 21 (Bangalore 1988) 163-170 [< TKontext 10,54].

5305 *Ritt* Hubert, Gemeindemodelle im NT: BLtg 61 (1988) 133-140.

5306 *Roloff* Jürgen [NT], *al*., Gemeinde: → 798, EvKL 2 (1988) [46-48]-77.

5307 *Sabourin* Leopold, 'Early Catholicism' in the New Testament [< ScEspr
38 (1986) 301-315], ᵀᴱ*Jermann* Rosemary: TDig 35 (1988) 239-243.

5308 *Schöllgen* Georg, Hausgemeinden, Oikos-Ekklesiologie und monar-
chischer Episkopat: JbAC 31 (1988) 74-90.

5309 **Storm** Melvin R., Excommunication in the theology and the life of the
primitive Christian communities: diss. Baylor. Waco ... – RelStR 14,189.

5310 *Strecker* Georg, Judenchristentum: → 813, TRE 17 (1988) 310-325.

5311 **Tigcheler** J., Gemeenschappen in het Nieuwe Testament 1987 → 3,5158;
90-242-4848-0: ᴿKerkT 39 (1988) 355s (M. H. *Bolkestein*); TsTNijm 28
(1988) 311 (A. van *Diemen*).

5312 *Ukpong* Justin S., Mission in the Acts of the Apostles, from the perspective of the evangelized: AfTJ 17 (1988) 72-88 [< TKontext 10/1,18].

5313 *Trites* Allison A., Church growth in the book of Acts: Bibliotheca
Sacra 145 (1988) 162-173.

5314 **Venetz** Hermann-J., C'est ainsi que l'Église a commencé 1986 → 2,4072;
3,5160: ᴿBLitEc 89 (1988) 299s (S. *Légasse*); RTLv 19 (1988) 226s (C.
Focant).

5315 **Vögtle** Anton, Die Dynamik des Anfanges; Leben und Fragen der
jungen Kirche [Vortrag 1987]. FrB 1988, Herder. 206 p. DM 19,80.
3-451-21191-2. – ᴿBiKi 43 (1988) 128s (R. *Hoppe*); TsTNijm 28 (1988) 405
(L. *Grollenberg*).

5316 **Vouga** François, A l'aube du christianisme; une surprenante diversité
1986 → 2,4073; Fs 12,80: ᴿProtestantesimo 43 (1988) 216s (V. *Subilia*).

5317 *Werners* Hans, Was haben heutige Gemeinden von der Gemeinde Jesu zu lernen?: Diakonia 19,1 (Mainz 1988) 6-14 [< ZIT].

F8.5 Ascensio, Pentecostes; ministerium Petri − *Act 1* ...

5318 **Marlow** John T.A., A narrative analysis of Acts 1-2: diss. Golden Gate Baptist Theol. Sem. *DHarrop* C. SF 1988. 106 p. − 88-15837. − DissA 49 (1988s) 1481s-A.

5319 *Gagnebin* Laurent, L'Ascension; une fête antiprotestante?: ÉTRel 63 (1988) 415-9.

5320 *Madec* Goulven, Ascensio, ascensus: ➤ 783, AugL 1,3 (1988) 465-475 [-9, *Geerlings* Wilhelm, ascensio Christi].

5321 **Parsons** Mikeal C., The departure of Jesus in Luke-Acts; the ascension narratives in context: JStOT Sup 21. Sheffield 1988, Academic. 301 p. $37 [TDig 36,74].

5322 **Weinert** Franz-Rudolf, Christi Himmelfahrt; neutestamentliches Fest im Spiegel alttestamentlicher Psalmen; zur Entstehung des römischen Himmelfahrtsoffiziums: kath. Diss. *DBecker* H. Mainz 1987. 361 p. − RTLv 19,553; TR 84,511.

5323 *Parsons* Mikeal C., The text of Acts 1:2 reconsidered [*Fitzmyer* J.,...]: CBQ 50 (1988) 58-71.

5324 *McConaughy* Daniel L., An Old Syriac reading of Acts 1:4 and more light on Jesus' last meal before his Ascension: OrChr 72 (1988) 63-67.

5325 *Fabris* Rinaldo, La presenza della Vergine nel Cenacolo (At 1,14); l'interpretazione di GIOVANNI PAOLO II: Marianum 50 (1988) 397-407.

5326 *Miller* Donald G., [Acts 1,21...] Some observations on the New Testament concept of 'witness': AsbTJ 43,1 (1988) 55-71.

5327 *Bauer* Johannes B., *Kardiognōstēs,* ein unbeachteter Aspekt (Apg 1,24; 15,8): BZ 32 (198) 114-7.

5328 **O'Reilly** Leo, Word and sign in the Acts of the Apostles [2-4 chiefly]; a study in Lucan theology: AnGreg 243. R 1987, Gregorian Univ. 242 p.; 2 foldouts. Lit. 37.000 pa. − R JBL 107 (1988) 762s (R.C. *Tannehill*: helpful, but takes 'rhetorical criticism' in a rather narrow sense; and too many typos).

5329 *Rius-Camps* Josep, Pentecostés versus Babel; estudio crítico de Hch 2: FgNt 1,1 (1988) 235-59; Eng. 60s.

5330 *Ouspensky* Leonard, Iconography of the descent of the Holy Spirit, T*Dvorkin* A., *Rodger* C.: SVlad 31 (1987) 309-347.

5331 *Harm* F.R., [Acts 2,10] Structural elements related to the gift of the Holy Spirit in Acts: ConcordiaJ 14,1 (1988) 28-41 [NTAbs 32,177].

5332 *Du Buit* M., [Act 2,11] Prosélytes: ➤ 786, Catholicisme 12,54 (1988) 34-38.

5333 *Andersen* T. David, The meaning of *échontes chárin pròs* in Acts 2.47: NTS 34 (1988) 604-610.

5333* *Balthasar* Hans Urs von († 26.VI.1988), [Act 3,21] Apokatastasis: TrierTZ 97 (1988) 169-182.

5334 *a*) *Bottino* Adriana, La figura di Pietro quale esponente della fede cristiana negli Atti degli Apostoli; − *b*) *Kilgallen* John J., Paul, theologian and teacher; − *c*) *Ferraro* Giuseppe, Gli autori divini dell'insegnamento nel quarto Vangelo; Dio Padre, Gesù Cristo, lo Spirito: StMiss 37 ('Teachers of Religion; Christianity and other religions' 1988) 1-25 / 27-51 / 53-76.

5335 *Walaskay* Paul W., Acts 3:1-10 ['Beyond belief': first post-Ascension healing]: Interpretation 42 (1988) 171-5.

5336 *Schlosser* Jacques, Moïse, serviteur du kérygme apostolique d'après Ac 3,22-26: RevSR 61 (1987) 17-31.

5337 *Cantamessa* Bruno, La comunione dei beni nella comunità gerosolimitana di Atti degli Apostoli: NuovaUm 9,49 (1987) 33-49.

5338 *Prete* Benedetto, Anania e Saffira (At 5,1-11); componenti letterarie e dottrinali: RivB 36 (1988) 463-486; Eng. 486.

5339 **Hanssen** Ove C., [Act 6,5; 8,17...] Handspåleggelsens funksjon ved kristen initiasjon i Apostlenes Gärningar (Laying on of hands in Christian initiation in the Acts of the Apostles): diss. ᴰ*Gerhardsson* B. Lund 1987. 214 p. – RTLv 19,538 ['Gjerninger'].

5340 *Dschulnigg* Peter, Die Rede des Stephanus im Rahmen des Berichtes über sein Martyrium (Apg 6,8-8,3): Judaica 24 (1988) 195-213.

5341 *Arai* Sasagu, Zum 'Tempelwort' Jesu in Apostelgeschichte 6,14: NTS 34 (1988) 397-410.

5342 **Szymik** Stefan, ✆ Interpretacja historii zbawienia ... Interpretation of history of salvation in the speech of St. Stephen (Acts 7,2-53): diss. ᴰ*Szlaga* J. Lublin 1988. xxxvi-332 p. – RTLv 20,546.

5343 *Derrett* J. D. M., The Son of Man standing (Acts 7,55-56) [elsewhere usually 'sitting' as Ps 110, 1]: BbbOr 30 (1988) 71-84.

5344 **Wildhaber** Bruno, [Act 8,4-25...] Paganisme populaire et prédication apostolique, d'après l'exégèse de quelques séquences des Actes; éléments pour une théologie lucanienne de la mission: Monde de la Bible. Genève 1987, Labor et Fides. 226 p.; front. 2-8309-0045-6 [AntClas 58, 355, R. *Joly*].

5345 *Hofmann* Inge, Der Wirklichkeitsgehalt von Apg 8,26-39: BeiSudan 3 (1988) 39-48.

5346 *Heimerdinger* Jenny, La foi de l'eunuque éthiopien; le problème textuel d'Actes 8/37: ÉTRel 63 (1988) 521-8.

5347 *Mann* C. S. [Acts 9,2] Saul in Damascus ['How much did Luke know about the situation of the Christian community in Jerusalem?']: Exp-Tim 99 (1987s) 331-4.

5348 *a*) *Townsend* John T., Acts 9:1-29 and early Church tradition; – *b*) *Fitzmyer* Joseph A., The Pauline letters and the Lucan account of Paul's missionary journeys; – *c*) *Brawley* Robert L., Paul in Acts; aspects of structure and characterization; – *d*) *Carroll* John T., Literary and social dimensions of Luke's apology for Paul: ➤ 500, SBL Seminars 1988, 119-131 / 82-89 / 90-105 / 106-118.

5349 *Rouillard* Philippe, [Act 9,3-8; 26,12-18...; français 1886-1965]. Peut-on croire aux récits de conversion?: EsprVie 98 (1988) 353-361.

5350 *Neri* Paolo, La visione di Gesù da parte di Paolo sulla via di Damasco: BbbOr 30 (1988) 121s.

5351 *Bechtler* Steven R., The meaning of Paul's call and commissioning in Luke's story; an exegetical study of Acts 9, 22, and 26: StudiaBT 15 (1987) 53-77.

5352 *Smit Sibinga* J., Acts 9,37 and other cases of ellipsis obiecti: ➤ 85, ᶠKʟɪᴊɴ A., Text 1988, 242-6.

5353 *Derrett* J. D. M., Clean and unclean animals (Acts 10:15; 11:9); Peter's pronouncing power observed: HeythJ 29 (1988) 205-221.

5354 **Jung Tae-Hyun** Callistus, [S. Korea], Peter's speech at Caesarea (Acts 10,34-43]; the problem of tradition and redaction: diss. Leuven 1988, ᴰ*Delobel* J. xv-436 p. – TsTNijm 28,396; RTLv 20,544; LvSt 13,369s.

5355 *Hull* Robert F., [Acts 10; 13; 17; *MacKenzie* R. S.] 'Lucanisms' in the western text of Acts? a reappraisal: JBL [104 (1985) 637-650] 107 (1988) 695-707.

5356 *Overman* J. Andrew, [Acts 10,1 ... 18,7] The God-fearers; some neglected features: JStNT 32 (1988) 17-26.

5357 *a) Lotz* Dunton, Peter's wider understanding of God's will, Acts 10: 34-48; – *b) Wainwright* Elaine, God wills to invite all to the banquet, Mt 22,1-10: IntRMiss 7 (1988) 201-207 / 185-193.

5358 *Davies* [cover Davis] Glenn N., [Acts 10,35; Rom 2,7] When was Cornelius saved?: RefTR 46 (1987) 43-49.

5359 *Tiede* David L., Acts 11:1-18 [Peter and Cornelius; yet Gal 1:8 denounces 'another Gospel' even if from 'an angel']: Interpretation 42 (1988) 175-180.

F8.7   **Act 13 ...** *Itinera Pauli,* **Paul's Journeys.**

5360 *a) Cook* Michael J., The mission to the Jews in Acts; unraveling Luke's 'myth of the "myriads"'; – *b) Tannehill* Robert C., Rejection by Jews and turning to Gentiles; the pattern of Paul's mission in Acts; – *c) Jervell* Jacob, The Church of Jews and God-fearers: ➤ 5112, [E]*Tyson* J., Luke-Acts and the Jewish people 1988, 102-123 / 83-101 / 11-20.

5361 **Keeney** Donald E., Paul's opponents in Acts in light of Gentile descriptions of Jews: diss. Southern Baptist Sem., [D]*Songer* H. 1987. 218 p. 88-05802. – DissA 49 (1988s) 279-A.

5362 *Moessner* David P., Paul in Acts; preacher of eschatological repentance to Israel: NTS 34 (1988) 96-104.

5363 **Rosenblatt** Marie-Eloise M., Under interrogation: Paul as witness in juridical contexts in Acts and the implied spirituality for Luke's community: diss. Graduate Theological Union. Berkeley 1987. 88-02863. – DissA 49 (1988s) 104-A; RelStR 14,187; RTLv 20,545.

5364 *a) Scheld* Stefan, Die missionarische Verkündigung des Paulus in CALVINS Kommentar der Apostelgeschichte; – *b) Fatio* Olivier, Bemerkungen zu Zeit und Ewigkeit bei Calvin: ➤ 53, [F]GANOCZY A., Creatio 1988, 312-328 / 338-351.

5365 **Rius-Camps** Josep, El camino de Pablo a la misión de los paganos ... Hch 13-28, 1984 ➤ 1,5151 ... 2,4114: [R]ActuBbg 25 (1988) 217 (X. *Alegre* S.).

5366 *Ferrando Lada* José L., Hechos 13,1-3; relectura teológica: EscrVedat 18 (1988) 7-32.

5367 *Black* C. Clifton II, [Act 13,15 ...] The rhetorical form of the Hellenistic Jewish and early Christian sermon; a response to Lawrence WILLS: HarvTR [77 (1984) 277-299] 81 (1988) 1-18.

5368 *Kilgallen* John J., Acts 13,38-39; culmination of Paul's speech in Pisidia: Biblica 69 (1988) 480-506; franç. 506.

5369 *Haacker* Klaus, Vollmacht und Ohnmacht — Charisma und Kerygma; Bibelarbeit über Apg 14,8-20: TBei 19 (Wu 1988) 317-324 [< ZIT 89,19].

5370 *Boismard* Marie-Émile, Le 'Concile' de Jérusalem (Act 15,1-33), essai de critique littéraire) [conférence pour son doctorat h.c. 1988]: ETL 64 (1988) 433-440 [501-4, *Neirynck* F. de caerimonia collationis].

5370* *Villiers* P. G. R. de, Die eenheid van die kerk, Handelinge 15: ➤ 509, Hoe lees 1985/8 ...

5371 *Bryan* Christopher, A further look at Acts 16:1-3 [Paul circumcised Timothy]: JBL 107 (1987) 292-4.

5372 *Neidhart* Walter, Was Menschen mit Paulus in Philippi erlebt haben; eine Geschichte zu Apg 16,11-40 und Phil 4,2-3: CLehre 41 (1988) U81-86 [< ZIT 88,486].

5373 **Elliger** Winfried, [Apg 16,11 ...] Paulus in Griechenland; Philippi, Thessaloniki, Athen, Korinth² 1987 → 3,5209: RTLZ 113 (1988) 441s (K. *Matthiae*).

5374 *Zweck* D. W., The Areopagus speech of Acts 17: LuthTJ 21,3 (Adelaide 1987) 111-122 [< NTAbs 32,320].

5375 *Míguez* Néstor O., Lectura socio-política de Hechos 17,1-10: RBíbArg 30s (1988) 183-206.

5376 *Marcus* Joel, [Acts 17,16-34] Paul at the Areopagus, window on the Hellenistic world: BibTB 39 (1988) 143-8.

5377 *Torrance* T. F., [Acts 17,16-31] Phusikos kai theologikos logos, St Paul and Athenagoras at Athens: ScotJT 41 (1988) 11-26.

5378 *Horst* Pieter W. van der, De onbekende god; de inscriptie op het altaar in Athene (Handelingen 17:23) in het licht van de antieke gods-dienstgeschiedenis [ineditum]: → 207, De onbekende God 1988, 9-36.

5378* *Cole* Dan P., [Acts 18,11; 19] Corinth and Ephesus — why did Paul spend half his journeys in these cities?: BR 4,6 (1988) 20-30.

5379 **Wehnert** Jürgen, Die Wir-passagen der Apostelgeschichte: ein lukanisches Stilmittel aus jüdischer Tradition: Diss. ᴰ*Lüdemann* G. Gö 1987s. – RTLv 19,541.

5380 *Deer* Donald F., Getting the 'stor[e]y' straight in Acts 20.9 [feels absolutely certain (without proof) that Greek *tristegon* means 'third storey' in the American sense (counting the ground floor as first), rather than in the sense of Britain and all Europe, where therefore it ought to be translated 'second storey']: BTrans 39 (1988) 246s.

5381 **Aejmelaeus** Lars, Die Rezeption der Paulusbriefe in der Miletrede (Apg 20,18-35) 1987 → 3,5217: RBZ 32 (1988) 289-291 (F. *Mussner*).

5382 *Lövestam* Evald, En gammaltestamentlig nyckel [OT clue] till Paulus-talet i Miletos (Apg 20:18-35) [< SvEx 51s (1986s) 137-147]: → 221, Axplock 1987, 81-90.

5383 *Harrisville* Roy A., Acts 22:6-21 [Luke's second account of Paul's calling]: Interpretation 42 (1988) 181-5.

5384 *Kilgallen* John J., Paul before Agrippa (Acts 26,2-23); some considerations: Biblica 69 (1988) 170-194; franç. 195.

5385 *Warnecke* Heinz, [Act 27s] Die tatsächliche Romfahrt des Apostels Paulus 1987 → 3,5226: RIndTSt 25 (1988) 107s (L. *Legrand*); OstkSt 36 (1987) 335s (O. F. A. *Meinardus*); SNTU-A 13 (1988) 233s (A. *Fuchs*).

5386 *Oberweis* Michael, Ps. 23 als Interpretationsmodell für Act 27: NT 30 (1988) 169-183.

5387 *Flusser* David [Act 28,1-6; Nm 21,8] 'It is not a serpent that kills' [ineditum]: → 190, JudOrChr 1988, 543-551.

5388 *Metallenos* George D. ⑤ [Acts 28,1 Melitē, KJV Melita, RSV Malta] Cephalonia, the Melitus of the Acts of the Apostles: TAth 54 (1988) 507-529.

XIV. Johannes

G1 *Corpus Johanneum* .1 **John and his community.**

5389 *Barrett* C. Kingsley, Johanneisches Christentum: → 3,326, Anfänge 1987, 255-278.

5390 **Berg** Robert A., Pneumatology and the history of the Johannine community; insights from the farewell discourses and the first epistle: diss. Drew. Madison NJ 1988. 324 p. 88-17625. – DissA 49 (1988s) 1846-A; RelStR 15,192.

5391 **Brown** Raymond E., La communauté du disciple bien-aimé 1983 ↠ 65,4732 ... 2,4129: ᴿRThom 88 (1988) 137s (L. *Devillers*).

5392 **Burge** Gary M., The anointed community; the Holy Spirit in the Johannine tradition [diss. Aberdeen, ᴰ*Marshall* I.] 1987 ↠ 3,5230: ᴿCBQ 50 (1988) 711s (F. F. *Segovia*); Themelios 14 (1988s) 69 (C. *Jack*).

5393 *Carson* D.A., John and the Johannine epistles [citing OT]: ↠ 97, ꟳLINDARS B. 1988, 245-264.

5394 **Eller** Vernard, The beloved disciple — his name, his story, his thought; two studies from the Gospel of John. GR 1987, Eerdmans. xi-124 p. [TR 84,427].

5395 **Hemleben** Johannes, Johannes der Evangelist, mit Selbstzeugnissen und Bilddokumenten: Mg 194. Ha-Reinbek 1988, Rowohlt. 158 p.; ill. 3-499-50194-3.

5396 *a) Lombard* H.A., John's Gospel and the Johannine church; a mirror of events within a text or/and a window on events within a church; – *b) Kotzé* P.P.A., Ironie in die Johannesevangelie: HervTS 43 (Pretoria 1987) 395-413 / 431-447 [NTAbs 32,313].

5397 *Pryor* J.W., Covenant and community in John's gospel: RefTR 47 (1988) 44-51.

5398 **Rebell** Walter, Gemeinde als Gegenwelt; zur soziologischen und didaktischen Funktion des Joh.-ev.: BeiBExT 20, 1987 ↠ 3,5234: ᴿTPhil 63 (1988) 260s (J. *Beutler*).

5399 *Reim* Günter, Zur Lokalisierung der johanneischen Gemeinde: BZ 32 (1988) 72-86.

5400 **Rensberger** David, Johannine faith and liberating community. Ph 1988, Westminster. 168 p. $15 [TS 50,791, F. J. *Matera*].

5401 **Schnelle** *Udo,* Antidoketische Christologie im Johannesevangelium; eine Untersuchung zur Stellung des vierten Evangeliums in der johanneischen Schule: FRLANT 144, 1987 ↠ 3,5237: ᴿTLZ 113 (1988) 818-20 (C. *Wolff*); TR 84 (1988) 370-2 (J. *Becker*).

5402 *Thyen* Hartwig, Johannesbriefe/-evangelium: ↠ 813, TRE 17 (1987) 186-200/-225.

5403 **Tuní Vancells** Josep O., Jesús y el evangelio en la comunidad juánica; introducción a la lectura cristiana del evangelio de Juan: Biblia y Catequesis 13. Salamanca 1987, Sígueme. 183 p. 84-301-1035-6. – ᴿActuBbg 25 (1988) 221s (X. *Alegre* S.); BibFe 14 (1988) 326 (A. *Salas*); CiTom 115 (1988) 580s (J. L. *Espinel*); Gregorianum 69 (1988) 775s (M. *Ruiz Jurado*); LumenVr 37 (1988) 191s (F. *Ortiz de Urtaran*).

5404 **Tuñi** J.O., Las comunidades joánicas; particularidades y evolución de una tradición cristiana muy especial: Iglesias del NT (3). Bilbao 1988, Desclée-B. 41 p. – ᴿNatGrac 35 (1988) 437 (R. *Robles*).

5405 **Vander Hoek** [? Heok: RelStR 15,192] Gerald W., The function of Ps 82 in the Fourth Gospel and history of the Johannine community; a comparative midrash study: diss. Claremont 1987. 88-20117. – DissA 49 (1988s) 1833-A.

5406 *Vouga* François, The Johannine school; a Gnostic tradition in primitive Christianity?: Biblica 69 (1988) 371-385.

5407 **Wengst** Klaus, Interpretación del evangelio de Juan [Bedrängte Gemeinde 1981 ²1983 ↠ 1,5186], ᵀ*Olasagasti* Manuel: Biblia y Catequesis 11. Salamanca 1988, Sígueme. 146 p. 84-301-1045-3. – ᴿActuBbg 25

(1988) 223s (X. *Alegre S.*); BibFe 14 (1988) 484 (A. *Salas*: ... ubicar a la comunidad); NatGrac 35 (1988) 498 (D. *Montero*); QVidCr 142 (1988) 124 (P.-R. *Tragan*).

5408 **Witkamp** L. T., Jezus van Nazareth in de gemeente van Johannes; over de interaktie van traditie en ervaring. Kampen 1986, van den Berg. xii-451 p. ƒ45 pa. 90-6651-049-8 [NTAbs 32,247].

5409 *Zevini* Giorgio, La spiritualità nella tradizione giovannea: → 810, StoSpir 2 NT (1988) 219-252.

G1.2 **Evangelium Johannis:** *textus, commentarii.*

5410 ᴱ**Backus** I., Martini BUCERI, Enarratio in Evangelium Iohannis (1528, 1530, 1536): Studies in Medieval and Reformation Thought 40. Leiden 1988, Brill. lxxxv-619 p.; 3 fig. ƒ216. [NRT 111, 976s, R. *Escol*]. 90-04-07876-2.

5411 **Beasley-Murray** George R., John: Word Comm. 36, 1987 → 3,5243: ᴿBibTB 18 (1988) 85s (U. C. von *Wahlde*); PerspRelSt 15 (1988) 177s (C. H. *Talbert*); RefTR 47 (1988) 17s (D. *Peterson*); RExp 85 (1988) 566s (R. A. *Culpepper*); SWJT 31 (1988s) 45s (G. L. *Munn*); Vidyajyoti 52 (1988) 513s (G. *Mlakuzhyil*).

5411* ᴱ**Berrouard** M.-F., AUGUSTIN, Homélies sur l'Évangile de saint Jean XXXIV-XLIII. P 1988, Ét.Aug. 539 p. [NRT 111,318].

5412 ᴱ**Betori** G., Come leggere [e attualizzare] un testo biblico [Gv: 1,1-18; 2,1-11; 6,35-58; 9,1-41; 11,1-54; 17,1-26]. Bo 1987, Dehoniane. 159 p. Lit. 10.000. 88-10-10711-X [NTAbs 32,368].

5413 **Brown** Raymond E., The Gospel and Epistles of John; a concise commentary. Collegeville MN 1988, Liturgical. 136 p. 0-8146-1283-0.

5414 **Comfort** Philip W., A study guide to translating the Gospel of John, with the Greek text ... compiled from the earliest papyrus manuscripts: Studies in the Greek NT for English Readers 1. [GR 1986, Baker] Wheaton IL 1987, Tyndale. 345 p. $16. – ᴿBTrans 39 (1988) 146s (R. G. *Bratcher*: some flaws); NT 30 (1988) 375-7 (J. K. *Elliott*).

5414* **Cothenet** E., *al.*, Gli scritti di San Giovanni e la lettera agli Ebrei [1984 → 5448], ᵀ*Brugnoli* Piero; ᴱ*Valentino* Carlo: Piccola Enciclopedia Biblica 10. R 1985, Borla. 377 p. Lit. 22.000. 88-263-0439-4.

5415 *Delebecque* Édouard, Évangile de Jean, texte traduit et annoté: CahRB 23, 1987 → 3,5250: ᴿBBudé (1988) 270-2 (J. *Irigoin*: 'on n'épiloguera pas ici sur les circonstances fâcheuses ... publicité maladroite parue dans le BBudé').

5416 **Doohan** Leonard, John, Gospel for a new age. Santa Fe 1988, Bear. xi-222 p. $11. 0-939680-52-1.

5417 **Ellis** Peter F., The genius of John; a composition-critical commentary 1984 → 65,4756 ... 2,4144: ᴿRExp 85 (1988) 349-351 (R. A. *Culpepper*).

5418 **Fatica** Luigi, I commentari a Giovanni di TEODORO di Mopsuestia e di CIRILLO di Alessandria; confronto fra metodi esegetici e teologici: StEphAug 29. R 1988, Inst. Patristicum Augustinianum. 332 p.

5419 *Funk* Wolf-Peter, Der Anfang des Johannesevangeliums auf Faijumisch: ArPapF 34 (1988) 33-42.

5420 ᴱ**Goggin** Thomas A., John CHRYSOSTOM, Commentary on Saint John the Apostle and Evangelist, [I. (1-47) 1969 = 1957], II [ch. 48-88]: Fathers of the Church [33] 41. Wsh 1988 = 1984, Catholic University of America. [xx-492 p.] xii-495 p. 0-8132-00 [33-4;] 41-5.

5421 **Gruenler** Royce C., The Trinity in the Gospel of John; a thematic commentary 1986 ➤ 1,4147; 3,5255: RScotJT 41 (1988) 288s (Ruth B. *Edwards*: meditation rather than commentary, but to be taken seriously).

5421* **Haenchen** Ernst, EBusse U. John I-II TFunk R., Hermeneia comm. 1984 ➤ 61,6619 ... 2,4148: RAnglTR 69 (1987) 300s (R. I. *Pervo*).

5422 **Heer** Josef, *al.*, Das grössere Leben; Johannes-Evangelium: BAusPrax 19. Stu 1988, KBW. 159 p. 3-460-25191-3.

5423 **Kysar** Robert, John: Augsburg Comm. 1986 ➤ 2,4150; 3,5258: RCurrTM 15 (1988) 457 (R. H. *Smith*); Interpretation 42 (1988) 202.204 (T. F. *Johnson*).

5424 **Landier** Jean, *al.*, Avec Jean; pour accompagner une lecture de l'Évangile de Jean, chapitres 1 à 12. P 1988, Ouvrières. 298 p. F 98. – REsprVie 98 (1988) 258 (É. *Cothenet*). FoiTemps 18 (1988) 404 (C. *Focant*).

5425 **Léon-Dufour** Xavier, Lecture de l'Évangile selon Jean, I (chapitres 1-4) 1987 ➤ 3,5259: RArTGran 51 (1988) 292 (A. *Segovia*); Études 369 (1988) 409s (P. *Gibert*, 1986); TLZ 113 (1988) 816-8 (W. *Wiefel*, 1988).

5426 **Libermann** François, Commentaire de saint Jean [1-12, 1840], ENoël Bernard. P 1988, Nouvelle Cité. 746 p. F 198. – REsprVie 98 (1988) 350s (G.-M. *Oury*).

5427 *Livrea* Enrico, Towards a new edition of NONNUS' paraphrase of St. John's Gospel: Mnemosyne 41 (1988) 318-324.

5428 **Losacco** Luigi, La lettura biblica di ROSMINI ne 'L'Introduzione del Vangelo secondo Giovanni commentata'. Stresa NO 1986, Sodalitas. 48 p. Lit. 10.000. – RCC 139 (1988,2) 408s (F. *Evain*).

5429 TEMcCarthy Brian, The Navarre Bible, St. John, texts and commentaries. 1987, Four Courts. 247 p. $13. – RHomP 88,12 (1987s) 86-88 (W. G. *Most*).

5430 *Metzger* Bruce M., Greek manuscripts of John's Gospel with 'hermeneiai': ➤ 85, FKLIJN A., Text 1988, 162-9.

5431 **Muñoz León** Domingo, Predicación del Evangelio de San Juan; guía para la lectura y predicación: Formación permanente, Comisión episcopal del clero. M 1988, Edice. 426 p. 84-7141-210-1.

5431* **Nieuwenhuis** Jan, Groeten van Johannes; Berichten uit het vierde evangelie. Delft 1987, Meinema. 144 p. ƒ23.50. – RStreven 55 (1987s) 1037s (P. *Beentjes*).

5432 *Phillips* Jane E., ERASMUS, CYRIL, and the Annotationes on John: BiblHumRen 50 (1988) 381-4.

5433 **Porsch** Felix, Johannes-Evangelium: SKK NT 4. Stu 1988, KBW. 231 p. DM 22,80 pa. [CBQ 51,189]. 3-460-15341-5.

5434 **Quecke** Hans, Das Johannesevangelium saïdisch 1984 ➤ 65,4769; 2, 4156: REnchoria 16 (1988) 155-8 (A. *Biedenkopf-Ziehner*); NT 30 (1988) 91 (G. D. *Kilpatrick*); SecC 6 (1987s) 251-3 (O. *Wintermute*).

5435 **Quéré** France, Une lecture de l'évangile de Jean 1987 ➤ 3,5261: RRThom 88 (1988) 143 (L. *Devillers*).

5436 **Rettig** J. W., St. AUGUSTINE; Tractates on the Gospel of John I-10 / 11-27: Fathers of the Church 78s. Wsh 1988, Catholic Univ. xiii-236 p.; xiv-306 p. $30 each. [RHE 83,362*]. 0-8132-0078-4; 9-2.

5437 **Ridderbos** Herman N., Het Evangelie naar Johannes, proeve van een theologische exegese I. Kampen 1987, Kok. 439 p. – RGerefTTs 88 (1988) 51s (J. *Helderman*), repeated p. 439; KerkT 39 (1988) 158-160 (G. de *Ru*); Streven 55 (1987s) 755 (P. *Beentjes*).

5438 **Sloyan** G. S., John: Interpretation comm. Atlanta 1988, Knox. xxiii-239 p. $19. 0-8042-3125-7 [NTAbs 32,246].

5439 **Tresmontant** C., Évangile de Jean 1984 → 65,4777 ... 3,5265: ᴿScrip-TPamp 20 (1988) 836-9 (A. *Garcia-Moreno*).

5440 **Turoldo** David M., Il Vangelo di Giovanni; Nessuno ha mai visto Dio: Problemi attuali. Mi 1988, Rusconi. 192 p. Lit. 22.000. 88-18-01029-8. − ᴿCiVit 43 (1988) 568 (B. *Farnetani*).

5441 **Wengert** Timothy J., Philip MELANCHTHON's 'Annotationes in Johannem' in relation to its predecessors and contemporaries: TravHum Ren 220, 1987 → 3,5267: ᴿBibHumRen 50 (1988) 804-6 (Irena *Backus*).

5442 **Zevini** Giorgio, Vangelo secondo Giovanni [I: 1984 → 65,4782 ... 3,5629]; II. cap. 11-21. R 1987, Città Nuova. 331 p. Lit. 20.000. 88-311-3707-7. − ᴿAsprenas 35 (1988) 170-3 (S. *Cipriani*; vol. 1 in Oss Rom 3.XII.1984 p. 3); BLitEc 89 (1988) 235 (S. *Légasse*); Gregorianum 69 (1988) 555s (G. *Ferraro*, 2); ParVi 33 (1988) 237s (A. *Casalegno*); StPatav 34 (1987) 421s (A. *Moda*, 1).

G1.3 **Introductio** *in Evangelium Johannis.*

5443 ᴱ**Ashton** John, The interpretation of John 1986 → 2,235; 3,5273: ᴿÉTRel 63 (1988) 589s (J. *Zumstein*); HeythJ 29 (1988) 248s (A. *Parish*); Themelios 14 (1988s) 68s (R. *Porter*).

Belle Gilbert Van, Johannine bibliography [gospel] 1966-1985 → 876.

5444 **Bittner** [-*Schwob*, RTLv 19,536] Wolfgang J., Jesu Zeichen im Johannesevangelium; die Messias-Erkenntnis im Joh.-Ev. vor ihrem jüdischen Hintergrund: WUNT 2/26, 1987 → 3,5274: ᴿJTS 39 (1988) 199s (B. *Lindars*: persuasive); RivB 36 (1988) 528-530 (R. *Fabris*); TsTNijm 28 (1988) 407s (A. van *Diemen*).

5445 **Bjerkelund** Carl J., Tauta egeneto ; die Präzisierungssätze im Joh.-Ev. 1987 → 3,5275: ᴿTGegw 30 (1987) 278s (H. *Giesen*); TLZ 113 (1988) 185 (U. *Schnelle*).

5446 **Calloud** J., *Genuyt* F., L'évangile de Jean II (lecture sémiotique ch. 7-12) 1987 → 3,5396: ᴿVSp 142 (1988) 595s (A. *Lion*).

5447 *Carson* D. A., Selected recent studies of the Fourth Gospel: Themelios 14 (1988s) 57-64.

5448 **Cothenet** Édouard, *al.*, Les écrits de saint Jean et l'Épître aux Hébreux 1984 → 65,4754; 1,5194: ᴿÉTRel 63 (1988) 585s (J. *Zumstein*). → 5414*.

5450 *Cothenet* Édouard, L'évangile de Jean rythmé par les fêtes [< MondeB 53, 1988]: EsprVie 98 (1988) 584-6 (J. *Daoust*).

5451 **Countryman** L. William, The mystical way in the Fourth Gospel 1987 → 3,5276: ᴿAnglTR 70 (1988) 265-7 (A. K. M. *Adam*); Interpretation 42 (1988) 432.434 (Karen A. *Barta*).

5452 **Culpepper** R. A., Anatomy of the Fourth Gospel 1983 → 64,5199 ... 2,4165: ᴿTPhil 63 (1988) 259s (J. *Beutler*).

5453 **Dodd** C. H., La tradition historique du Quatrième Évangile [1953]: LDiv 128, 1987 → 3,5277: ᴿEsprVie 98 (1988) 93s (L. *Walter*).

5454 **Fortna** Robert T., The Fourth Gospel and its predecessor; from narrative source to present gospel. Ph 1988, Fortress. 348 p. [JAAR 57,684].

5455 **Grob** F., Faire l'œuvre de Dieu; Christologie et éthique dans l'évangile de Jean [diss. Strasbourg, ᴰ*Trocmé* E.]: ÉtHPR 68, 1986 → 3,5280: ᴿStPatav 35 (1988) 167-9 (G. *Segalla*: sconcertante).

5456 **Hinrichs** Boy, 'Ich bin'; die Konsistenz des Johannes-Evangeliums in der Konzentration auf das Wort Jesu: SBS 133. Stu 1988, KBW. 96 p. DM 26,80. 3-460-04331-8.

5457 *Kiley* Mark, The exegesis of God; Jesus' signs in John 1-11: ➤ 500, SBL Seminars 1988, 555-569.

5458 **Kittlaus** Lloyd R., The author of John and the Gospel of Mark: diss. Divinity School. Ch 1988. – OIAc D88.

5459 *Koester* Helmut, Johannesevangelium: ➤ 798, EvKL 2 (1988) 840-3 [835-7, Apk., *Karrer* Martin; 838-840, Briefe, *Strecker* Georg].

5460 **Kügler** Joachim, Der Jünger, den Jesus liebte [Diss. Bamberg 1986, *DHoffmann* ➤ 3,5282]: SBB 16. Stu 1988, KBW. 518 p. 3-460-00161-5.

5461 **McGann** Diarmuid, Journeying within transcendence; a Jungian perspective on the Gospel of John. NY 1988, Paulist. iv-217 p. $9. 0-8091-2952-3.

5462 **Mlakuzhyil** George, The Christocentric literary structure of the Fourth Gospel [D1987]: AnBib 117, 1987 ➤ 3,5286: RExpTim 99 (1987s) 377 (Judith *Lieu*); JStNT 33 (1988) 116 (D. *Hill*: a major contribution); TLZ 113 (1988) 895s (J. *Becker*); Vidyajyoti 52 (1988) 154-9 (P. M. *Meagher*).

5463 **Moore** T., His witness is true; John and his interpreters. NY 1988, Lang. 242 p. $43.50 [TS 50,627].

5464 *a) Munn* G. Lacoste, An introduction to the Gospel of John; – *b) Ellis* E. Earle, Background and Christology ... selected motifs; – *c) Lea* Thomas D., Exegesis of crucial texts [1,1-5.14; 3,5; 8,58; 9,3s; 10,27s; 15,1-6; 20,30s...]: SWJT 31,1 (1988s) (5-)7-11 / 24-31 / 14-23 [32-41, *al.*].

5465 *a) Ravasi* Gianfranco, Principi di esegesi; introduzione al Vangelo di Giovanni; – *b) Colzani* Gianni, 'Se tu conoscessi il dono di Dio'; – *c) Angelini* Giuseppe, Morale e civiltà alla luce del Vangelo di Giovanni; – *d) Grampa* Giuseppe, Il libro dei simboli; – *e) Boracco* Pierluigi, Il Vangelo di Giovanni nella storia della spiritualità; – *f) Pozzoli* Luigi, La letteratura contemporanea interroga il Vangelo di Giovanni; – *g) Santucci* Luigi, Il Vangelo di Giovanni per un narratore cristiano; – *h) Ferrari* Curzia, Giovanni il 'divino' e il suo vangelo; iconografia dei contenuti: Fede e cultura dal Vangelo di Giovanni [ciclo di conversazioni, Centro Culturale S. Fedele, Milano; present. *Bo* Carlo: Teologia Viva [Bo 1986, Dehoniane. 269 p. Lit. 22.000. 88-10-40905-1] 5-79 / 81-109 / 111-139 / 141-167 / 169-193 / 195-209 / 223-247 / 249-267, 16 color. fot.

5466 **Robinson** J. A. T., The priority of John 1985 ➤ 1,5234 ... 3,5291: RJTS 39 (1988) 200-4 (E. *Bammel*).

5467 **Ruckstuhl** Eugen, Die literarische Einheit des Jo.-Evs. 1987 ➤ 3,5292: RErbAuf 64 (1988) 401s (V. A.).

5468 **Smith** D. Moody, Johannine Christianity 1987 ➤ (65,4745) 3,303.5238: RJTS 39 (1988) 204s (S. S. *Smalley*); TLond 91 (1988) 532-4 (J. *Riches*: splendid).

5469 *a) Smith* D. Moody, The life setting of the Gospel of John; – *b) Culpepper* R. Alan, The theology of the Gospel of John: RExp 85 (1988) 433-444 / 417-432.

5470 **Staley** Jeffrey L., The print's first kiss; a rhetorical investigation of the implied reader in the Fourth Gospel [D1985, Berkeley GTU ➤ 1,5238]: SBL diss. 82. Atlanta 1988, Scholars. viii-138 p. $17. 0-89130-946-2; pa. 7-0.

G1.4 *Johannis themata,* topics.

5471 *a)* **Asensio** Manuel, María Magdalena. – *b)* **Hereza** Rafael, El desvelamiento de la revelación; María Magdalena y el discípulo amado [both hold John Mark was her son by Jesus]. M 1984/1, Rama Dorada. 111 p.; 286 p. 84-85381-25-4; 30065-49-0. – ᴿEstBíb 46 (1988) 118-120 (Carmen *Bernabé Ubieta*).

5472 *Bekken* Per J., [Norw.] On the variety of Judaism in the first century A.D.; Jewish cult in PHILO, Acts and the Gospel of John: TsTKi 59 (1988) 161-173.

5473 **Belle** Gilbert van,   Les parenthèses dans l'Évangile de Jean 1985 ➤ 1,5243 ... 3,5299. – ᴿScotJT 41 (1988) 417-9 (J. N. *Birdsall*: in the loose card provided to facilitate reference, P for *paroles* is importantly misprinted as V); TLZ 113 (1988) 115s (H. *Weder*).

5474 **Boismard** M.-É.,   Moïse ou Jésus; essai de christologie johannique: BiblETL 84. Lv 1988, Univ./Peeters [ETL 64,428]. – ᴿPrOrChr 38 (1988) 410s (P. *Ternant*); SBFLA 38 (1988) 508-512 (V. *Mora*).

5475 **Borgen** Peder,   PHILO, John and Paul; new perspectives on Judaism and early Christianity: BrownJudSt 131. Atlanta 1987, Scholars: ➤ 3,a267; 324 p.; 1-55540-183-0. – P. 75-101, Jn 1; p. 103-120, Jn 3,13s; p. 121-144, Jn 6; p. 185-204, Jn 12 ...

5476 *Braine* David D. C.,   The inner Jewishness of St. John's Gospel as the clue to the inner Jewishness of Jesus: SNTU-A 13 (1988) 101-156.

5477 *Brownson* James,   The odes of Solomon and the Johannine tradition: JPseud 2 (1988) 49-69.

5477* *a) Burns* J. A.,   Commenting on commentaries on the Book of John; – *b) Cook* W. R.,   Eschatology in John's Gospel; – *c) Lea* T. D., Preaching from John; – *d) Parker* J.,   The incarnational Christology of John; – *e) Morris* L.,   The atonement in John's Gospel: CriswellT 3,1 (Dallas 1988) 185-197 / 79-99 / 161-184 / 31-48 / 49-64 [< NTAbs 33,168s].

5478 **Caron** Gérald,   Les 'iudaioi' dans l'Évangile de Jean: diss. Ottawa 1988, ᴰ*Michaud* J. 451 p. – RTLv 20,543.

5479 **Cirillo** Antonio,   Cristo rivelatore del Padre nel Vangelo di S. Giovanni secondo il commento di S. Tommaso d'AQUINO: diss. Pont. Univ. S. Thomae (Angelicum), ᴰ*Duroux* Benoît. R 1988. xii-369 p.

5480 *Colombo* Dalmazio,   Il Gesù di Giovanni: PalCl 66 (1987) 153-162.

5481 *Conrad* Donald L.,   Why not also a series on John? [the new lectionary has a three-year cycle, one year each for Mt Mk Lk]: CurrTM 15 (1988) 349-355.

5482 *Cothenet* Édouard, *al.,*   L'évangile de Jean [14 snippets]: MondeB 53 (1988) 3-40; ill.

5483 **Duke** Paul D.,   Irony in the Fourth Gospel 1985 ➤ 1,5250 ... 3,5308: ᴿJBL 107 (1988) 141s (M. L. *Soards*).

5484 **Ecclestone** Alan,   The scaffolding of spirit; reflections on the Gospel of St. John [as a dramatic religious poem]. L 1987, Darton-LT. 137 p. £5 pa. – ᴿTLond 91 (1988) 555 (S. S. *Smalley*: unusual).

5485 *Edanad* Antony,   Interiorized Word and transforming Spirit; Johannine model of spirituality: JDharma 13 (1988) 238-247.

5486 **Engelbrecht** E.,   'Ken' as deel van die spraakpatroon van die verteller in die Johannesevangelie ['To know' as part of the pattern of speech of the narrator in John's Gospel, NTAbs 32,313]: HervTS 43 (Pretoria 1987) 414-430.

5487 *Fernández Ramos* F.,   Los signos en los Tractatus in Ioannem: AugM 33 (1988) 57-76.

5488 **Ferraro** Giuseppe,   La gioia di Cristo nel quarto vangelo: StBPaid 83. Brescia 1988, Paideia. 309 p. Lit. 32.000. 88-394-0424-4.

5489 **Ferraro** Giuseppe, Lo Spirito e Cristo nel vangelo di Giovanni: StBPaid 70, 1984 → 65,4809 ... 3,5310: [R]EstTrin 20 (1986) 410s (X. *Pikaza*).

5490 **Ford** Carey A.[III], The implications of the Johannine concept of history for understanding the eternality of Jesus Christ: diss. SW Baptist Theol. Sem. 1988. – RelStR 15,193.

5490* **Groot** Maria de, Messiaanse ikonen; een vrouwenstudie van het evangelie naar Johannes. Kampen 1988, Kok. 353 p. *f* 50. – [R]Streven 56 (1988s) 468s (P. *Beentjes*).

5491 [E]**Hartman** L., *Olsson* B., Aspects on the Johannine literature 1986/7 → 3,546: [R]TsTKi 59 (1988) 311s (E. *Larsson*).

5492 *Heine* Ronald E., The role of the Gospel of John in the Montanist controversy: SecC 6,1 (1987s) 1-19.

5493 *Iacopino* Giuliana, Iesus incomprehensus; Gesù frainteso nell'Evangelo di Giovanni: RivB 36 (1988) 165-196; Eng. 197.

5494 *Ibuki* Yu, Die Doxa des Gesandten — Studie zur johanneischen Christologie: AnJapB 14 (1988) 38-81.

5495 *Klaiber* Walter, Tareas de una interpretación teológica del cuarto evangelio [< ZTK 82 (1985) 300-324],[TE]*Castanye* José: SelT 26 (1987) 243-255.

5496 **Kotila** Markku, Umstrittener Zeuge; Studien zur Stellung des Gesetzes in der johanneischen Theologiegeschichte [diss. Helsinki 1987: RTLv 20,545]: AnAcScFenn, Diss. 48. Helsinki 1988, Suomalainen Tiedeakatemia. vi-239 p. 951-41-0564-8. [i. Das Gesetz als Argument für die Orthopraxie und die Orthodoxie; ii. Die himmlische Herkunft des Gesandten als Argument gegen das Gesetz; iii. Der Gesandte als Geber eines neuen Gesetzes].

5497 *Kurichianil* John, La glorificación de Jesús en el evangelio de Juan [< Bible Bhashyam 12 (1986) 42-58], [TE]*Pericas* Rafael M.: SelT 27 (1988) 303-8.

5498 **Lauzeral** Paul [trois étudiants de Salamanque dialogant en Terre Sainte], En route avec saint Jean; croquis johanniques. P 1988, Téqui, 176 p. F 72. – [R]EsprVie 98 (1988) 239 (J. *Daoust*).

5499 *Lieu* J. M., Blindness in the Johannine tradition: NTS 34 (1988) 83-95.

5500 **Lill** M., Zeitlichkeit und Offenbarung; ein Vergleich von M. HEIDEGGERS 'Sein und Zeit' mit R. BULTMANNS 'Ev. des Johannes': EurUnivSt 23/313. Fra 1987, Lang. x-370 p. $55.40. 3-8204-1055-4 [NTAbs 32,373].

5501 **Lovette** Roger, Questions Jesus raised; 21 answers from the Gospel of John. Nv 1986, Broadman. 128 p. 0-8054-2259-5. – [R]RExp 85 (1988) 181s (R. *Bailey*).

5502 **Maloney** George A., Entering into the Heart of Jesus; meditations on the indwelling Trinity in St. John's gospel. Staten Island NY 1988, Alba. xx-170 p. $9 [TDig 36,70].

5503 **Manns** F., John and Jamnia; how the break occurred between Jews and Christians c. 80-199 A.D. [... John's Christian answer to Jamnia], [T]*Duel* Mildred, *Riadi* Marina J 1988, Franciscan. 74 p.; ill. $5 [BL 89,156].

5504 *Manns* Frédéric, Les mots à double entente; antécédents et fonction herméneutique d'un procédé johannique: SBFLA 38 (1988) 39-57.

5505 *Matera* Frank J., 'On behalf of others', 'cleansing' and 'return'; Johannine images for Jesus' death: LvSt 13 (1988) 161-178.

5506 **Menken** M. J. J., Numerical literary techniques in John 1985 → 2,4200; 3,5323: [R]SvEx 53 (1988) 136s (L. *Hartman*).

5507 *Morgen* Michèle, Devenir disciple, d'après S. Jean; Après la rencontre. le temps de la décision: VChrét 305 (1987) 6-13 [306, 18-22; 307, 14-19; 308, 19-22, 309, 12-15; 310, 14-18; 311, 18-21].

5508 **Morujão** Geraldo D., Relações Pai-Filho em S. João; subsidos para a teologia trinitária a partir do estudo de correspondentes sintagmas verbais: diss. ᴰ*Casciaro* R. Pamplona 1987. 543 p. – RTLv 19,539 ['Gasciaro'].

5509 **Neyrey** Jerome H., An ideology of revolt; John's Christology in social-science perspective. Ph 1988, Fortress. xii-260. $25 [TS 50,792, F. J. *Matera*: relation to DOUGLAS model not clear].

5510 **Nieuwenhuis** J., Groeten van Johannes; berichten uit het vierde evangelie. Delft 1987, Meinema. – ᴿCollatVL 18 (1988) 400s (R. *Hoet*).

5511 **O'Day** Gail R., Revelation in the Fourth Gospel; narrative mode and theological claim ᴰ1986 → 2,4203: ᴿRelStR 14 (1988) 159 (D. M. *Smith*).

5512 *Paciorek* Antoni, ⊕ De exegesi IV Evangelii in scriptis Patrum Apostolicorum: → 73, ᶠKANIA W. = VoxPa 12s (1987s) 326-335.

5513 *Prete* B., I giudei nei dati del quarto vangelo: → 474, Correnti 1984/7, 79-104.

5514 *Ravindra* Ravi, The Gospel [John] as Yoga: Parabola 13,2 (1988) 39-47.

5515 **Rodríguez Ruiz** Miguel, Der Missionsgedanke des Johannesevangeliums; ein Beitrag zur johanneischen Soteriologie und Ekklesiologie [Diss. ᴱ*Schnackenburg* R.]: ForBi 55, 1987 → 3,5329: ᴿBurgense 29 (1988) 297-9 (E. *Bueno*); CBQ 50 (1988) 727-9 (J. T. *Forestell*); EstBíb 46 (1988) 551-6 (D. *Muñoz León*); Gregorianum 69 (1988) 773-5 (G. *Ferraro*); VerbumSVD 29 (1988) 445-450 (J. *Kuhl*).

5516 **Rutumbu** Juvénal, Le 'Monde' dans le quatrième évangile: diss. ᴰ*Sevrin* J. LvN 1987. – RTLv 19, 260s (résumé) & 540; Travaux de doctorat 12,5. – Extr. La portée historique et théologique du 'Monde' dans le quatrième évangile: Nouvelles Rationalités Africaines 3 (1988) 189-221.

5517 *Schenke* Ludger, Der 'Dialog mit den Juden' im Johannesevangelium; ein Rekonstruktionsversuch: NTS 34 (1988) 573-603.

5518 *Schnackenburg* Rudolf, Die Agape Gottes nach Johannes: → 53, ᶠGANOCZY A., Creatio 1988, 36-47.

Scroggs R., The reality and revelation of God; Christology in Paul and John 1988 → 8461.

5518* *a*) *Silva* M., Approaching the Fourth Gospel; – *b*) *Mathews* K. A. John, Jesus and the Essenes; trouble at the Temple: CriswellT 3,1 (Dallas 1988) 17-29 / 101-126 [< NTAbs 33,170s].

5519 *Smith* Robert H., 'Seeking Jesus' in the Gospel of John: → 143, ᶠTIETJEN J. = CurrTM 15 (1988) 48-55.

5520 *Stefano* Frances, Lordship over weakness; Christ's graced humanity as locus of divine power in AUGUSTINE's tractates on the Gospel of John: AugSt 16 (Villanova 1985) 1-19.

5521 **Stimpfle** Alois, Blinde sehen; die Eschatologie des Johannesevangeliums im traditionsgeschichtlichen Prozess: Diss. Augsburg 1987s, ᴰ*Leroy*. – TR 84 (1988) 511.

5522 **Stones** Alan G., Lord of the feasts; Johannine metaphors of Christ in connection with Tabernacles and Dedication: diss. Basel 1988, ᴰ*Stegemann* E. – RTLv 20,546.

5523 **Thompson** Marianne Meye, The humanity of Jesus in the fourth gospel [... *Käsemann* E., *Bultmann* R.; diss. Duke, ᴰ*Smith* D. M.]. Ph 1988, Fortress. viii-168 p. $12. 0-8006-2075-5 [TDig 36,187].

5524 *Thurston* Bonnie B.,   The Gospel of John and Japanese Buddhism: Japanese Religions 15,2 (Kyoto 1988) 57-68.

5525 *Trilling* Wolfgang, *a*) Gegner Jesu ... Joh-Ev und die Juden [< TJb 1980, 222-238]; – *b*) Die Wahrheit von Jesus-Worten in der Interpretation neutestamentlicher Autoren [< KerDo 23 (1977) 93-112]: → 275, Studien 1988, 209-231 / 141-164.

5526 **Whitacre** Rodney,   Johannine polemic ᴰ1982 → 63,5372 ... 2,4210*: ᴿDeltioVM 17,1 (1988) 65-68 (S. *Agouridis* ●).

5527 **Wijngaards** John,   The Spirit in John: Zacchaeus Studies.   Wilmington 1988, Glazier.   99 p. $7.   0-89453-666-4 [TDig 36,194].

5528 *Wilson* M.P.,   St John, the Trinity, and the language of the Spirit: ScotJT 41 (1988) 471-483.

G1.5   Johannis Prologus 1,1 ...

5529 *Bandera* A.,   Una eclesiología trinitaria y sapiencial; el prólogo de San Juan, I: Vida y Espiritualidad 9 (Lima 1988) 9-29 [< Stromata 44,565].

5530 **Barth** Karl,   Witness to the word [1925s lectures on John 1(-8)], ᵀ*Fürst* W. 1986 → 2,4224 ... 3,5353:   ᴿCurrTM 15 (1988) 213 (J.C. *Rochelle*); RefTR 46 (1987) 17 (M. *Harding*).

5531 ᵀᴱ**Cristiani** Marta,   Giovanni Scoto [ERIUGENA], Omelia sul prologo di Giovanni → 3,5344: Vicenza/Verona 1987, Valla/Mondadori.   lxviii-146 p. Lit. 30.000:   ᴿRasT 29 (1988) 305 (R. *Maisano*); RivStoLR 24 (1988) 595-8 (A. *Bodrato*); StCattMi 32 (1988) 347 (A. *Zaccuri*).

5532 *Gibaud* Henri,   In principio erat sermo (ÉRASME) [we should now say 'logos', valid in all modern languages]: → 486, Traduction 1986/8, 97-106; Eng. 97.

5533 *Genuyt* François,   Le prologue de Jean (1,1-18):   SémBib 49 (1988) 15-34.

5534 **Hofrichter** P.,   Im Anfang war der 'Johannesprolog' 1986 → 2,4217; 3,5345:   ᴿBLitEc 89 (1988) 296-8 (H. *Hauser*); ErbAuf 63 (1987) 312s (E. *Tschacher*); JBL 107 (1988) 546-8 (J. *Goss*); OrChrPer 54 (1988) 242-4 (E.G. *Farrugia*); StPatav 35 (1988) 649-651 (G. *Segalla*).

5535 **Mortley** Raoul,   From word to silence, I. The rise and fall of logos; II. The way of negation, Christian and Greek: Theophaneia.   Bonn 1986, Hanstein.   168 p.; 292 p. → 2,d339; DM 78 + 128:   ᴿJTS 39 (1988) 260-3 (A. *Louth*).

5536 **Theobald** Michael,   Die Fleischwerdung des Logos; Studien sum Verhältnis des Johannesprologs zum Corpus des Evangeliums und zu 1 Joh: NTAbh NF 20.   Münster 1988, Aschendorff.   ix-537 p.   3-402-03642-8.

5537 **Waesberghe** Henri van,   De Proloog [... in de liturgie].   1988.   66 p.

5538 *Weder* H.,   Der Mythos vom Logos; Überlegungen zum Problem der Entmythologisierung: EvKomm 20 (Stu 1987) 627-631.

5539 **Luther** Martin,   Explication du premier et du deuxième chapitre de Jean dans la prédication de 1537 et 1538: Œuvres 13.   Genève 1987, Labor et Fides.   334 p. – ᴿActuBbg 25 (1988) 216s (A. *Borràs*: 'la prédications').

5540 *Toit* A.B. du,   Marturía in Johannes 1:   SkrifKerk 6,2 (1985) 113-124 [NTAbs 32,174].

5541 *Galot* Jean,   [Gv 1,13 emendato] Maternità virginale di Maria e paternità divina: CC 139 (1988,3) 209-222.

5542 *Edwards* Ruth B.,   *Chárin antì cháritos* (John 1.16); grace and the law in the Johannine prologue: JStNT 32 (1988) 3-15.

5543 *Borgen* Peder,   Creation, Logos and the Son; observations on John 1:18 and 5: 17-18: ➤ 567, ExAud 3 (1987) 88-97.

5544 *La Potterie* Ignace de,   'C'est lui qui a ouvert la voie'; la finale du prologue johannique: Biblica 69 (1988) 340-369; Eng. 370.

5545 **Pinet** A.,   Het Lam Gods.   Antwerpen 1987, Unistad.   64 p. Fb 995. – RCollatVL 18 (1988) 122s (P. *Schmidt*).

5546 *Grütters* F.,   [Jn 1,29] Agnus Dei; archaische Worte und Zeichen und eine theologische Betrachtung: Renovatio 43,3 (Köln 1987) 129-137 [NTAbs 32,197].

5547 **Kuhn** Hans-J.,   Christologie und Wunder; Untersuchungen zu Joh 1,35-51: BibUnt 18.   Rg 1988, Pustet.   679 p.; bibliog. p. 559-615. DM 48. 3-7917-1141-5. – RActuBbg 25 (1988) 213s (X. *Alegre* S.).

5547* **Lütgehetmann** Walter,   Die Hochzeit von Kana (Joh. 2,1-11); zu Ursprung und Deutung einer Wundererzählung im Rahmen johanneischer Redaktionsgeschichte: kath. Dis. Fra 1988s, DHainz. – TR 85,515.

5548 **Moreira Azevedo** C. A.,   O milagre de Cana na iconografia paleocristiana: I. – Catálogo de monumentos; II. – Estudo interdisciplinar. Porto 1986. – RRivArCr 62 (1988) 452-6 (A. *Recio Veganzones*).

5549 *Moreira Azevedo* Carlos A.,   História e sentido do milagre de Caná na liturgia antica: Didaskalia 15 (1985) 267-304.

5550 *Owings* Timothy L.,   John 2:1-11 [Cana]: RExp 85 (1988) 533-7.

5551 *Riesner* Rainer,   Fragen um 'Kana in Galiläa':   BiKi 43 (1988) 69-71.

5552 *a) Zevini* Giorgio,   Presenza e ruolo di Maria alle nozze messianiche di Cana (Gv 2,1-12) nella lettura di Giovanni Paolo II; – *b) Díez Merino* Luis,   María junta a la Cruz (Jn 19,25-27), relectura evangélica de Juan Pablo II en la 'Redemptoris Mater':   Marianum 50 (1988) 347-365 / 366-396.

5553 *Mees* Michael,   [Jn 2,12-19] Die Tempelreinigung nach der Darlegung des ORIGENES: ➤ 56, Mém. GRIBOMONT J. 1988, 433-444.

G1.6   Jn 3ss ... Nicodemus, Samaritana.

5554 *Grese* William C.,   'Unless one is born again'; the use of a heavenly journey in John 3: JBL 107 (1988) 677-693.

5555 *O'Day* G. R.,   [Jn 3,1-15] New birth as a new people; spirituality and community in the Fourth Gospel: WWorld 8,1 (1988) 53-61 [NTAbs 32,174].

5556 *Schneiders* Sandra M.,   [Jn 3,1-15] Born anew: TTod 44 (1987s) 189-196.

5557 *Greiner* Albert,   [Jn 3,14] Le serpent d'airain et le Crucifié; quelques réflexions relatives à deux textes bibliques conjoints: PosLuth 34 (1986) 22-27 [< LuJb 55,164].

5558 *Eslinger* L.,   [Jn 4,1-42] The wooing of the woman at the well; Jesus, the reader and reader-response criticism: LitTOx 1,2 (1987) 167-183 [NTAbs 32,175].

5559 *Francis* M.,   The Samaritan woman: AsiaJT 2,1 (1988) 147s [< NTAbs 32,315].

5560 **Boers** Hendrikus,   Neither on this mountain nor in Jerusalem; a study of John 4: SBL Mg 35.   Atlanta 1988, Scholars.   xvii-230 p. 1-555-40220-8; pa. 1-6.

5560* *Dockery* D. S.,   Reading John 4:1-45; some diverse hermeneutical perspectives: CriswellT 3,1 (Dallas 1988) 127-140 [< NTAbs 33,171].

5561 **Leidig** Edeltraud,   Jesu Gespräch mit der Samaritanerin und weitere Gespräche im Joh.-ev.: TDiss 1979 ➤ 60,7280:   RÉTRel 63 (1988) 592 (J. *Zumstein*).

5562 *Nemeshegy* Pierre, [Jn 4] Un passage du Tract. in Ev. Joh. 15,10: RÉAug 34 (1988) 78s.

5563 **Poffet** Jean-Michel, La méthode exégétique d'HÉRACLÉON et d'ORIGÈNE ... Jean 4, 1985 ➤ 1,5308 ... 3,5376: ᴿRThom 88 (1988) 135 (A. *Schenker*).

5564 **Okure** Teresa, The Johannine approach to mission; a contextual study of John 4,1-42 [diss 1984 ➤ 1,5307]: WUNT 2/31. Tü 1988, Mohr. x-342 p. DM 89. [TPQ 136/1 adv.]. 3-16-145049-3.

5565 *Vorster* W. S., Oor lees, lesers en Johannes 4: ➤ 509, Hoe lees 1985/8, ...

5566 *Derrett* J. D. M., The Samaritan woman's purity (John 4:4-52): EvQ 60 (1988) 291-8.

5567 *Manus* Chris U., The Samaritan woman (Jn. 4:7ff); reflection on female leadership and its implication towards national building in modern Africa: AfJB 2 (1987) 52-63.

5568 *Samuel* S. [Jn 4,19-24] 'Neither on this mountain nor in Jerusalem'; the Johannine understanding of worship: Bangal Theological Forum 19,2 (1987) 121-9 [NTAbs 32,175].

5569 *Menken* Maarten, De genezing van de lamme en de omstreden christologie in Joh. 5: CollatVL 118 (1988) 418-435.

5570 *Duke* Paul D., John 5:1-15 [Bethesda pool]: RExp 85 (1988) 539-542 [myth charmingly played out in the movie Cocoon].

5571 *a) Polhill* John B., John 1-4: the revelation of true life; – *b) Songer* Harold S., John 5-12; opposition to the giving of true life: RExp 85 (1988) 445-457 / 459-471.

G1.7 **Panis Vitae** – *Jn 6 ...*

5572 *Bailey* Raymond, John 6: RExp 85 (1988) 95-98.

5573 *Federlin* Wilhelm-Ludwig, Kritisches zur Aufklärungspredigt; Anmerkungen HERDERS zu einem Predigtentwurf J. Georg MÜLLERS zu Johannes 6,1ff; Pilotstudie für eine neue Herderpredigtenedition: ➤ 140, ᶠSTOODT D., Unterwegs 1987, 133-154.

5574 **Wehr** Lothar, Arznei der Unsterblichkeit; die Eucharistie bei IGNATIUS A. und im Joh.-Ev.: NTAbh NF 18, 1987 ➤ 3,5393. – ᴿBiblica 69 (1988) 292-7 (W. R. *Sch[r]oedel*); BZ 32 (1988) 156-9 (R. *Schnackenburg*); JTS 39 (1988) 597-9 (S. G. *Hall*: 'proficient'); NRT 110 (1988) 921s (X. *Jacques*); RHR 205 (1988) 314-6 (M. *Carrez*); TR 84 (1988) 26-8 (J. A. *Fischer*).

5575 **Kuzenzama** K. P. M., La structure bipartite de Jn 6,26-71; nouvelle approche: Recherches Africaines de Théologie 9. Kinshasa 1987, Fac. Théologie Catholique. 124 p. [NRT 111,950s, Y. *Simoens*].

5576 *Brändle* Francisco, [Jn 6,42 ...] ¿San José en el Evangelio de San Juan?: EstJos 42 (1988) 205-213.

5577 *Menken* M. J. J. *a)* The provenance and meaning of the Old Testament quotation in John 6:31: NT 30 (1988) 39-56 [Ps 78,24]; – *b)* The OT quotation in John 6:45; source and redaction: ETL 64 (1988) 164-172.

5578 *Rabiej* Stanisław, [Jn 6,35 + 23 fois] ❷ *Egō eimi* dans l'Évangile de saint Jean comme le signe de la dignité divine de Jésus: ColcT 58,2 (1988) 19-27; franç. 27.

5579 *Ehrman* Bart D., Jesus and the adulteress [John 7,53-8,12; DIDYMUS interpretation in the midst of Eces 7,21s]: NTS 34 (1988) 24-44.

5580 *Moir* Ian A., Fam. 272 – a new family of manuscripts in the 'pericope adulterae' (John 7,53-8,11)?: ➤ 85, ᶠKLIJN A., Text 1988, 170-6.

5581 *Rivard* Richard, Loi ancienne et écriture nouvelle, Jean 8,2-11: ➤ 292, Jésus/Femmes 1982/7, 135-156.
5582 *Robert* René, [Jn 8,24.28] Le malentendu sur le Nom divin au chapitre VIII du quatrième évangile: RThom 88 (1988) 278-287.
5583 **Muñoz Bolívar** Ovidio A., '*Mathētēs*', estudio exegético-teológico del término en el cuarto evangelio a la luz de Jn 8,31-32: diss. Pont. Univ. Gregoriana, ᴰ*Caba* J. R 1988. 147 p. – RTLv 20,545.
5584 *La Potterie* Ignacio de, [Jn 8,32] Verdad, Espíritu y libertad: ➤ 541, Conciencia 1987/8, 87-99.
5585 *Grelot* Pierre, Jean 8,56 et Jubilés 16,16-29: ➤ 22, Mém. CARMIGNAC J., RQum 13 (1988) 621-8.
5586 *O'Flaherty* Wendy D., [Veda; Christ Jn 10,11; not on Zech 10s] The good and evil shepherd: ➤ 149, ᶠWERBLOWSKY R., Gilgul 1987, 169-191.
5587 *Wyller* Egil A., [Jn 10,23] In Solomon's porch; a henological [structural-pattern] analysis of the architectonic of the Fourth Gospel: ST 42 (1988) 151-167.
5588 **Wagner** Josef, *a*) Das Lazarusthema im Spiegel johanneischer Redaktions- und Theologiegeschichte; eine Untersuchung zu Joh. 11,1-12,19: Diss. ᴰ*Hainz*. Fra 1987s. – TR 84 (1988) 511; – *b*) Auferstehung und Leben; Joh 11,1 – 12,19 als Spiegel johanneischer Redaktions- und Theologiegeschichte: BibUnt 19. Rg 1988, Pustet. 501 p. 3-7917- 1173-3.
5589 **Bridges** James J., Structure and history in John 11; a methodological study comparing structural and historical critical approaches: diss. Graduate Theological Union, ᴰ*Boyle* J. Berkeley 1988. 88-16905. – DissA 49 (1988s) 1828-A; RelStR 15,192.
5590 *Genuyt* F., La résurrection de Lazare; Évangile de Jean, analyse sémiotique du chapitre 11: SémBib 44 (1986) 18-37.
5591 **Kremer** J., Lazarus 1985 ➤ 1,5340 ... 3,5407: ᴿFreibZ 35 (1988) 261-6 (Marie-Louise *Gubler*); StPatav 35 (1988) 165-7 (G. *Segalla*); SvEx 53 (1988) 127-9 (L. *Hartman*); TLZ 113 (1988) 28-30 (W. *Vogler*).
5592 **Marchadour** Alain, Lazare; histoire d'un récit, récits d'une histoire: LDiv 132. P 1988, Cerf. 290 p. F 165. 2-204-02853-3. – ᴿEsprVie 98 (1988) 522s (L. *Walter*); ÉTRel 63 (1988) 467s (E. *Cuvillier*); Études 369 (1988) 426 (R. *Marlé*).
5593 *Neri* Paolo, [Gv 11,33 *embrimaíomai*] 'Gesù allora ... si sdegnò nel proprio intimo': BbbOr 30 (1988) 48.
5594 *Robert* René, Du suaire de Lazare à celui de Jésus; Jean XI,44 et XX,7: RThom 88 (1988) 410-420.
5595 *Vogels* Walter, De la mort à la vie vers la mort; Jean 12,1-11: ➤ 292, Jésus/Femmes 1982/7, 157-172.
5596 *Coakley* J. F., [Jn 12,1-8] The anointing at Bethany and the priority of John: JBL 107 (1988) 241-256.
5597 *Menken* M.J.J., Die Form des Zitates aus Jes 6,10 in Joh 12,40; ein Beitrag zum Schriftgebrauch des vierten Evangelisten: BZ 32 (1988) 189-209.

G1.8   Jn 13 ... Sermo sacerdotalis et Passio.

5598 *Wojciechowski* Michał, La source de Jean 13,1-20: NTS 34 (1988) 135-141.
5599 *a*) *Beasley-Murray* George R., John 13-17; the community of true life; – *b*) *Garland* David E., John 18-19; life through Jesus' death; – *c*) *Borchert* Gerald L., The resurrection perspective in John; an evangelical summons: RExp 85 (1988) 472-483 / 485-499 / 501-513.

5600 **Speyr** Adrienne von, The farewell discourses; meditations on John 13-17, ᵀ*Nelson* E. A. [one of four volumes on John's Gospel]. SF 1987, Ignatius. 377 p. $20 [TDig 35,290].

5601 *Noordegraaf* A., Johannes 13 en het diakonaat: TRef 31,1 (1988) 6-25 [< GerefTTs 88,124].

5602 *Muszyński* Henryk, [Jn 13,1-3] L'interprétation biblique de la devise du Congrès Eucharistique [national, juin 1987; symposium 4 mai], Il les aima jusqu'à l'extrême: BInfWsz (1988,2) 15s.

5603 **Martini** Carlo M., [Joh 13,6] Du, Herr, willst uns die Füsse waschen? Meditationsgedanken zum Evangelium der Fusswaschung. Mü 1988, Neue Stadt. 80 p. DM 9,80 [TGL 78,460].

5604 *Mazzola* Antonio, Note sul commento AGOSTINIANO a Io 13, 26-27; la *buccella* e il traditore svelato: → 246, VetChr 25 (1988) 557-566.

5605 **Carson** D. A., Jesus and his friends ... Jn 14-17: Living Word, 1986 → 3,5429: ᴿIrBSt 10 (1988) 108s (I. *Hull*).

5606 **McCaffrey** James, The house with many rooms; the Temple theme in Jn. 14,2-3 [diss. Pont.Ist.Biblico 1981, ᴰ*Vanhoye* A.]: AnBib 114. R 1988, Pont. Ist. Biblico. 293 p. 88-7653-114-9.

5607 **Kwong** Magdalena, Ⓒ 'The Spirit will remind you' (John 14:26): ColcFuJen 75 (1988) 27-34.

5608 *Ferraro* Giuseppe, La rivelazione sul 'Paraclito' nel quarto vangelo: CC 139 (1988,3) 26-39.

5609 **Franck** Eskil, Revelation taught; the Paraclete in the Gospel of John: ConBib NT 14, 1985 → 1,5363; 2,4294: ᴿNedTTS 42 (1988) 70-72 (L. T. *Witkamp*).

5609* *Black* D. A., On the style and significance of John 17: CriswellT 3,1 (Dallas 1988) 141-159 [< NTAbs 33,173].

5610 a) *Rosenblatt* Marie-Eloise, The voice of the one who prays in John 17;
– b) *Senior* Donald, Jesus in crisis: → 141, ᶠSTUHLMUELLER C., Scripture and prayer 1988, 131-144 / 117-130.

5611 **Diouf** Jean-Noël, Gloire et glorification du Christ en S. Jean; le Jom, sens de l'homme et de la dignité chez les Seereer du Sénégal; étude comparative en regard de l'inculturation: diss. Pont. Univ. Gregoriana, ᴰ*La Potterie* I. de. R 1987. xvi-907 p. – RTLv 19,537.

5612 *Beutler* Johannes, [Jn 17,11.16] In der Welt, nicht von der Welt; zum Ort der Christen nach dem NT: StiZt 206 (1988) 37-46.

5613 **Orbe** A., Padre, è giunta l'ora. R 1987, Città Nuova. 338 p. Lit. 22.000. – ᴿRasT 29 (1988) 408 (L. *Borriello*).

5614 a) *Blank* Josef, Die Johannespassion, Intention und Hintergründe; – b) *Ritt* Hubert, Plädoyer für Methodentreue; Thesen zur Topographie und Chronologie der Johannespassion: → 491*, Prozess 1987/8, 148-182 / 183-190.

5415 **Cobo Franco** Calixto, El sacrificio de Cristo en San Juan: diss. ᴰ*García-Moreno* A. Pamplona 1987. – RTLv 19,537.

5616 *La Potterie* I. de, La Passion de Jésus selon l'Év. de Jean; Texte et Esprit [Het Passieverhaal 1983] 1986 → 2,4290; 3,5434: ᴿBijdragen 49 (1988) 96 (M. J. J. *Menken*); ÉTRel 63 (1988) 590s (J. *Zumstein*); IndTSt 25 (1988) 104s (L. *Legrand*); RevSR 62 (1988) 75 (C. *Coulot*); ScEspr 40 (1988) 118-121 (G. *Rochais*); VSp 142 (1988) 293 (C. *Coulot*).

5617 **La Potterie** Ignace de, La Passione di Gesù secondo il vangelo di Giovanni; Testo e Spirito [dal francese], ᵀ*de Rosa* Elena. CinB 1988, Paoline. 172 p. Lit. 10.000. 88-215-1620-2.

5618 *Hill* David, 'My kingdom is not of this world' (Jn 18,36): IrBSt 9 (1987) 54-62.

5619 **Osiander** Alfons M., The theme of the 'Jewish Trial' of Jesus in the Gospel of John; a study of Johannine sources: diss. St. Michael, ᴰ*Peckham* B. Toronto 1987. 238 p. – RTLv 19,539.

5620 *Stendahl* Krister, Predigt über Johannes 19,1-6: KIsr 2 (1987) 99-101 [109-124, Podiumsgespräch mit *Wyschogrod* M., *Rendtorff* R., al.].

5621 **Panackel** Charles, 'Idou ho anthropos'; an exegetical-theological study of John 19,5ᵇ in light of the use of the term 'anthropos' designating Jesus in the Fourth Gospel: diss. Pont. Univ. Gregoriana, ᴰ*Caba* J. [extr. N°3401: 142 p. – RTLv 19,539]: AnGreg 251. R 1987, Gregoriana. xviii-554 p. Lit. 50.000. 88-7652-581-5.

5622 *Culpepper* R.A., The death of Jesus; an exegesis of John 19,18-37: Faith and Mission 5,2 (Wake Forest NC 1988) 64-70 [< NTAbs 32,315].

5623 *Bergmeier* Roland, *Tetélestai* Joh 19,30: ZNW 79 (1988) 282-290.

5624 *More* Thomas M., John 19:32-35 and 1 John 5:6-8; a study in the history of interpretation: diss. Drew. Madison NJ 1985. – RTLv 19,539.

5625 *Brock* S.P., 'One of the soldiers pierced ...' — the mysteries [of Eastern Churches ecclesiology] hidden in the side of Christ: Christian Orient 9 (Kerala 1988) 51-59 [< TKontext 10/1,51-59].

5626 *Sylva* Dennis D., Nicodemus and his spices (John 19.39): NTS 34 (1988) 148-151.

5627 *Benoit* Pierre, Maria Magdalena und die Jünger am Grabe nach Joh 20,1-18 [< ᶠ*Jeremias* J., BZNW 26 (1960) 143-152, ᵀ*Bouillon* Irene]: → 311, ᴱ*Hoffmann* P., WegF 522 (1988) 360-376.

5628 *Chené* Adèle, Marie de Magdala au tombeau; Jean 20,1-18: → 292, Jésus/Femmes 1982/7, 173-187.

5629 *Winandy* Jacques, Les vestiges laissés dans le tombeau et la foi du disciple (Jn 20,1-9): NRT 110 (1988) 212-9.

5630 *Babinet* Robert, Le Sindon et la découverte du tombeau vide en Jean 20,3-10: EsprVie 98 (1988) 330-6.

5631 *Greinacher* Norbert, Maria Magdalena, die erste Apostolin; Bibelarbeit zu Johannes 20,11-16: Diakonia 19 (Mainz 1988) 204 ... [< ZIT].

5632 *Baarda* T., 'She recognized him'; concerning the origin of a peculiar textual variation in John 20,16 Syˢ: → 85, ᶠKʟɪᴊɴ A., Text 1988, 24-38.

5633 *Lyon* Robert W., John 20: 22, once more: AsbTJ 43,1 (1988) 73-85.

5634 *Cameron* Ron, [Jn 20,29] Seeing is not believing; the history of a beatitude in the Jesus tradition: Forum 4,1 (1988) 47-57.

5635 *Trudinger* Paul, Joh 21 revisited once again: DowR 106 (1988) 145-8.

5636 *Neirynck* F., Note sur Jn 21,14: ETL 64 (1988) 429-432.

G2.1   **Epistulae Johannis.**

5637 *a*) *Beutler* Johannes, Die Johannesbriefe in der neuesten Literatur (1978-1985); – *b*) *Wengst* Klaus, Probleme der Johannesbriefe: → 782, ANRW 2,25,5 (1988) 3773-90 / 3753-72.

5638 **Bonnard** Pierre, Les Épîtres johanniques 1983 → 64,5381 ... 3,5448: ᴿRThom 88 (1988) 142s (L. *Devillers*).

5639 **Brown** Raymond E., The epistles of John: AnchorB 30, 1982 → 63,5472 ... 2,4310: ᴿRThom 88 (1988) 140-2 (L. *Devillers*); SecC 6 (1987s) 244-7 (R.A. *Culpepper*).

5640 **Delebecque** Édouard, Épîtres de Jean, texte traduit et annoté; préf. *Spicq* C.: RB Cah 25. P 1988, Gabalda. viii-48 p. 2-85021-033-1 [RThom 89,478, L. *Devillers*].

5641 *Ferraro* Giuseppe, Il tema della gioia nelle lettere giovannee: [➤ 154, FZEDDA S.] RivB 36 (1988) 439-461; Eng. 461.

5642 **Jackman** David, The message of John's letters; living in the love of God: The Bible Speaks Today. DG/Leicester 1988, Inter [-] Varsity. 202 p. [JBL 107,788].

Kistemaker Simon J., ... Epistles of John 1986 ➤ 6401.

5643 **Kysar** Robert, I,II,III John. Minneapolis 1986, Augsburg. 159 p., $10. 0-8066-8862-9. – RCurrTM 15 (1988) 457 (R. H. *Smith*); Interpretation 42 (1988) 98.100 (C. C. *Black*).

5644 **Morgen** Michèle, Les épîtres de Jean: CahÉv 62. P 1987, Cerf. 74 p. F 24.

5645 **Morgen** Michèle, Las cartas de Juan: CuadB 62. Estella 1988, VDivino. 74 p. [EfMex 7,298, E. *Serraima Cirici*].

5646 *Antoniotti* sr. Louise-Marie, Structure littéraire et sens de la Première Épître de Jean: RThom 88 (1988) 5-35.

5647 TEBiedermann Hermenegild M., Unteilbar ist die Liebe; Predigten des hl. AUGUSTINUS über den ersten Johannesbrief: Augustinus — heute 5, 1986 ➤ 3,5457: RTPhil 63 (1988) 268s (H. J. *Sieben*).

5648 **Dalbesio** Anselmo, Elementi di esperienza cristiana nella Prima Lettera di san Giovanni; studio di teologia biblica: diss. SBF 296, DManns F. J 1987. xvii-300 p. – SBFLA 38 (1988) 539s.

5649 *Dalbesio* Anselmo, Alcuni aspetti esperienziali della *pistis* e dell'*agápē* in 1 Gv: Laurentianum 29 (1988) 3-34.

5650 **Edanad** Antony, [1Jn] Christian existence and the New Covenant. Bangalore 1987, Dharmaram. xiii-342 p. – RJDharma 12 (1987) 432s (J. *Kallikuzhuppil*).

5651 *Klauck* H.-J., Gegner von innen; der Umgang mit den Sezessionisten im ersten Johannesbrief: IZT 24 (1988) 467-473; = Adversaires à l'intérieur; les rapports avec les sécessionistes dans la première lettre de Jean: ➤ 351, Concilium 200 (P 1988) 67-77.

5652 *Kügler* Joachim, Die Belehrung der Unbelehrbaren; zur Funktion des Traditionsarguments in 1 Joh: BZ 32 1988) 249-254.

5653 **Sharma** H., *Hemraj* S., ➤ 3,5461: Kauṇakarīyam upadeśāmritam; the First Letter of John in Sanskrit. Ranchi 1987, Satya Bharati. 128 + 30 p. – RLvSt 13 (1988) 383s (W. M. *Callewaert*).

5654 *Mian* Franca, Due note alla prima epistola di Giovanni [1,1-5; 3,19-24]: BbbOr 30 (1988) 35-37.

5655 *Hiebert* D. Edmond, An exposition of 1 John 1:1-4 / 1:5-2:6 / 2:7-17 / 2:18-28 plus 6 other parts to come]: Bibliotheca Sacra 145 (1988) 197-210 / 329-342 / 420-435 [146 ...].

5656 *Strecker* Georg, Der Antichrist; zum religionsgeschichtlichen Hintergrund von 1 Joh 2,18-22; 4,3 und 2 Joh 7: ➤ 85, FKLIJN A., Text 1988, 247-254.

5657 *Vázquez Janeiro* Isaac, [1 Jn 2,18...] Anticristo 'mixto', Anticristo 'místico'; varia fortuna de dos expresiones escatológicas medievales: Antonianum 63 (1988) 522-550; Eng. 522.

5657* *Manns* Frédéric, 'Le péché, c'est Bélial'; 1 Jn: 3,4 à la lumière du Judaïsme: RevSR 62 (1988) 1-9.

5658 *Ehrman* Bart D., 1 Joh 4,3 and the orthodox corruption of Scripture: ZNW 79 (1988) 221-243.

5659 *Infante* Lorenzo, Una catechesi sull'*agápē*; 1 Gv 4,7-12: RivScR 2 (Molfetta 1988) 247-264.
5660 **Spaemann** Heinrich, [1 Jn 4,8.16] Il principio amore [Das Prinzip Liebe, FrB 1986, Herder], ᵀ*Bressani* Clara: Pellicano. Brescia 1988, Morcelliana. 150 p. 88-372-1342-5.
5661 *De Boer* Martinus C., Jesus the baptizer; 1 John 5:5-8 and the Gospel of John: JBL 107 (1988) 87-106.

5662 **Lieu** Judith, The second and third epistles of John; history and background: StudNT&W 1986 ➤ 3,5468: ᴿCBQ 50 (1988) 332-4 (J. E. *Bruns*: exciting); Interpretation 42 (1988) 208.210 (R. *Kysar*); ScotJT 41 (1988) 423s (Ruth B. *Edwards*).
5663 *Bonsack* Bernhard, Der Presbyteros des dritten Briefs und der geliebte Jünger des Evangeliums nach Johannes: ZNW 79 (1988) 45-62.

G2.3   *Apocalypsis Johannis* – **Revelation: text, introduction.**

5664 ᴱ**Burger** Edward K., JOACHIM of Fiore, Enchiridion super Apocalypsim: ST 78, 1986 ➤ 3,5476: ᴿAevum 62 (1988) 417s (G. L. *Potestà*); ColcFr 57 (1987) 136 (G. *Zamora*).
5665 **Collins** Adela Y., The Apocalypse: NTMessage 22. Wilmington 1988 = 1979, Glazier. xiv-155 p. 0-89453-145-X.
5666 **Corsini** Eugenio, L'Apocalypse maintenant, ᵀ*Arrighi* R., 1984 ➤ 65, 4984 ... 3,5477: ᴿTLZ 113 (1988) 31s (O. *Böcher*).
5667 **González Ruiz** José M., Apocalipsis de Juan; el libro del testimonio cristiano: Biblia y lenguaje 9. M 1987, Cristiandad. 227 p. [TR 84,517]. 84-7057-412-4. – ᴿCiTom 115 (1988) 396 (J. L. *Espinel*); QVidCr 140 (1988) 113-5 (G. *Camps*).
5668 **Jens** Walter, Das A und das O; die Offenbarung des Johannes 1987 ➤ 3,5480: ᴿTRu 53 (1988) 426-8 (T. *Holts*).
5669 **Kealy** Seán P., The Apocalypse of John: Message of Biblical Spirituality 15, 1987 ➤ 3,5481: ᴿCBQ 50 (1988) 327s (P. *Zilonka*).
5670 **Lohse** Eduard, Die Offenbarung des Johannes⁷ʳᵉᵛ [¹1935]: NTD 11. Gö 1988, Vandenhoeck & R. 127 p. 3-525-51369-0.
5671 **Prevost** J. P., Para terminar con el miedo; el Apocalipsis. M 1987, Paulinas. 115 p. – ᴿBibFe 14 (1988) 483 (M. *Sáenz Galache*).
5672 **Prigent** Pierre, L'Apocalypse de saint Jean² [¹1981 ➤ 62,6202]: Comm NT 14. Genève 1988, Labor et Fides. 383 p. 2-8309-0114-2. – ᴿÉTRel 63 (1988) 469 (E. *Cuvillier*: 2 ed. corrigée, non révisée).
5673 **Roloff** Jürgen, Die Offenbarung des Johannes 1984 ➤ 65,4999; 1,5426: ᴿTLZ 113 (1988) 275-7 (H.-F. *Weiss*).
5674 *Romero Pose* Eugenio, La importancia de los 'Comentarios de Beato' en la historia de la literatura cristiana: Compostellanum 33 (1988) 53-91.
5675 **Steinhauser** Kenneth B., The Apocalypse commentary of TYCONIUS; a history of its reception and influence [diss. FrB, ᴰ*Frank* K. S.]: EurHS 23/301. Fra 1987, Lang. xvi-430 p. Fs 25. – ᴿTS 49 (1988) 162s (J. T. *Lienhard*).
5676 **Vanni** Ugo, L'Apocalisse; ermeneutica, esegesi, teologia: RivB Sup 17. Bo 1988, Dehoniane. 432 p. Lit. 50.000. 88-10-30205-2 [Asprenas 36, 111s, C. *Marcheselli-Casale*].

5677 **Vuyst** J. De, De Openbaring van Johannes. Kampen 1987, Kok. 142 p. Fb 450. – ᴿCollatVL 18 (1988) 393s (R. *Hoet*).

G2.4 *Apocalypsis,* Revelation, topics.

5678 **Alexander** Paul J., The Byzantine apocalyptic tradition, ᴱ*Abrahamse* D. 1985 → 1,5434; 3,5491: ᴿCathHR 73 (1987) 271s (Emily A. *Hanawalt*).

5679 **Beagley** Alan J., The 'Sitz im Leben' of the Apocalypse: BZNW 50, 1987 → 3,5494: ᴿÉTRel 63 (1988) 293s (E. *Cuvillier*); Salmanticensis 35 (1988) 420-3 (R. *Trevijano*).

5680 *Beale* G. K., Revelation [citing OT]: → 97, ᶠLINDARS B. 1988, 318-336.

5681 *Berrigan* Daniel, [Rev] War in heaven, peace on earth: SpTod 40 (1988) 36-51.

5682 ᴱ**Bloom** Harold, The Revelation of St. John the Divine: Modern Critical Interpretations. NY 1988, Chelsea. viii-150 p. $20 [TDig 36,78].

5683 *Böcher* Otto, Die Johannes-Apokalypse in der neueren Forschung [... und Qumran]: → 782, ANRW 2,25,5 (1988) 3850-93 [-98].

5684 **Boesak** Allan A., Comfort and protest; reflections on the Apocalypse of John of Patmos [compared with an angelic revelation to the author in prison for opposing apartheid] 1987 → 3,5497: ᴿBS 145 (1988) 117 (J. F. *Walvoord*: his liberal interpretation of Rev as non-prophecy political pamphlet won't help his cause).

5685 *Browne* Gerald M., [Apc 1,4s.8s; 2,5s] An Old Nubian version of Ps.-CHRYSOSTOM, In quattuor animalia: AltOrF 15 (1988) 215-9.

5686 *Collins* Adela Y., Oppression from without; symbolisation of Rome as evil in early Christianity: Concilium 200 (E 1988) 66-74 = L'oppression du dehors; Rome symbole du Mal dans le christianisme primitif [... Apc]: → 351, Concilium 220 (P 1988) 79-88.

5687 *Cothenet* Édouard, 'Révélation'-Apocalypse: → 791, DictSpir XIII,86s (1987) 453-482.

5688 **Cowley** Roger W., The traditional interpretation of Apc. ... Ethiopian 1983 → 64,5414 ... 2,4342: ᴿOstkSt 36 (1987) 340-2 (S. *Uhlig*).

5689 **Cuvillier** Elian, L'apocalypse ... c'était demain; les apocalypses du NT, un manifeste pour l'espérance 1987 → 3,5506: ᴿÉTRel 63 (1988) 162s (*ipse*).

5690 **Czajkowski** Michał, ❷ → 3,5507: L'Apocalypse comme livre du message prophétique de l'admonestation, de la consolation et de l'espérance: Hab.-Diss. 1987. – BInfWsz (1988,3) 15s.

5691 *Downing* F. Gerald, PLINY's prosecutuon of Christians; Revelation and 1 Peter: JStNT 34 (1988) 105-123.

5692 *Emmerson* R. K., *Lewis* S., Census and bibliography of medieval manuscripts containing Apocalypse illustrations, ca. 800-1500: Traditio ... 43 (1986) 443-472, last page.

Gaines Elizabeth A., The eschatological Jerusalem; the function of the image in the literature of the biblical period: diss. Princeton Theol. Sem. 1987 → a72.

5693 *Giesen* H., Der Christ und das Gericht – Heilsaussagen in der Johannes-Apokalypse: TGegw 30 (1987) 27-37.

5694 **Guthrie** Donáld, The relevance of John's Apocalypse [1985 Nazarene College Didsbury Lectures]. Exeter 1987, Paternoster. 128 p. £4. 0-85364-460-8 [EvQ 60,140 adv.]. – RefTR 47 (1988) 63 (M. *Harding*).

5695 **Hocking** David, The coming world leader; understanding the Book of Revelation. Portland OR 1988, Multnomah. 319 p. $13 pa. [GraceTJ 9,308].

5696 *Jeske* Richard L.,   The study of the Apocalypse today: RelStR 14 (1988) 337-340 [the impetus came from *Feuillet* A. 1963].

Kappler Claude, Apocalypses et voyages dans l'au-delà 1987 ➤ 3866.

5697 **Karrer** Martin,   Die Johannesoffenbarung als Brief; Studien zu ihrem literarischen, historischen und theologischen Ort [Diss. Erlangen]: FRLANT 140, 1986 ➤ 2,4354; 3,5515:   ᴿSalmanticensis 35 (1988) 417-420 (R. *Trevijano*); SNTU-A 13 (1988) 245-7 (H. *Giesen*); TLZ 113 (1988) 348s (M. *Rissi*).

5698 *Kimpel* Harald,   Die Apokalypse-Industrie; zur Beschwichtigungs-ikonographie der Science Fiction: UnSa 43 (1988) 120-8.

5699 **Kretschmar** Georg,   Die Offenbarung des Johannes; die Geschichte ihrer Auslegung im 1. Jahrtausend 1985 ➤ 1,5418; 3,5518:   ᴿNedTTs 42 (1988) 157s (J. W. van *Henten*).

5700 *Ladd* G. E.,   Revelation, book of: ➤ 801, ISBEnc³ 4 (1988) 171-7 [161-170, Reveal, revelation, *Bromiley* G. W.].

5701 **Laws** Sophie, In the light of the Lamb; imagery, parody, and theology in the Apocalypse of John: Good News Studies 31.   Wilmington 1988, Glazier. 98 p. $10 pa. [JBL 108,379]. 0-89453-639-7.

5702 *Lempa* Henryk, ❷ De symbolismo ecclesiali in Apocalypsi: ➤ 475, RuBi 41 (1988) 25-40.

5703 *Lewis* S.,   Tractatus adversus Judaeos in the Gulbenkian-Apocalypse: Art Bulletin 68 (NY 1986) 543-566; 26 fig. [< RHE 83,437*].

5704 *Lobrichon* Guy,   Conserver, réformer, transormer le monde? les manipulations de l'Apocalypse au moyen âge central: ➤ 681, Book 1983/6, II, 75-94 [BTAM 14 (1988) 489s (H. *Silvestre*)].

5705 **Lohse** [Dr.] E.,   Wie christlich ist die Offenbarung des Johannes? [presidential address SNTS Göttingen, August 1987]: NTS 34 (1988) 321-338.

5706 *a*) *McGinn* Bernard,   Symbols of the Apocalypse in medieval culture; – *b*) *Collins* John J.,   The apocalyptic context of Christian origins: ➤ 3,356, ᴱO'Connor M., Backgrounds 1987, 273-291 / 257-271 [< JBL 108,174].

5707 **McIlraith** Donal,   The reciprocal love between Christ and the Church in the Apocalypse: diss. Pont. Univ. Gregoriana, Nᵒ 3547, ᴰ*Vanni* U.   Roma 1988. xiv-246 p. – RTLv 20,545.

5708 **Maggioni** Bruno,   L'Apocalisse; per una lettura profetica del tempo presente³ [¹1981 ➤ 62,6190]: Bibbia per tutti.   Assisi 1988, Cittadella. 247 p. Lit. 12.000.

5709 *Martin* Gerhard M.,   Wie die Offenbarung des Johannes in apokalyptischen Zeiten zu leben und zu lesen ist: UnSa 43 (1988) 139-145. 155.

5710 *Müller* Ulrich B.,   Apokalyptische Strömungen [auch Mk 13 und 2 Thess]: ➤ 3,326, Anfänge 1987, 217-254.

5711 *Newport* Kenneth G. C.,   Some Greek words [ónoma, skēnē...] with Hebrew meanings in the book of Revelation: AndrUnS 26 (1988) 25-31.

5712 *Paulien* Jon, *a*) Elusive allusions; the problematic use of the OT in Revelation: BiRes 33 (Ch 1988) 37-53; – *b*) Recent developments in the study of the Book of Revelation: AndrUnS 26 (1988) 159-170.

5713 **Peterson** Eugene H.,   Reversed thunder; the Revelation of John and the praying imagination.   SF 1988, Harper & R.   194 p. $16.   0-06-066500-9. – ᴿRExp 85 (1988) 718 (J. L. *Blevins*).

5714 **Pippin** T.,   Political reality and the liberating vision; the context of the Book of Revelation: diss. So. Baptist. Sem. 1987, ᴰ*Blevins* J. 219 p. 88-05806. – DissA 49 (1988s) 280-A.

5715 **Poucouta** Paulin,   La perspective missionnaire de l'Apocalypse johannique: diss. Inst. Cath. & Sorbonne, ᴰ*Cothenet* E.   P 1987. 317 p. – RICathP 23 (1987) 151-3; RTLv 19,540.

5716 *Poucouta* Paulin, La mission prophétique de l'Église dans L'Apocalypse johannique: NRT 110 (1988) 38-57.

5717 *Reddish* Mitchell G., Martyr Christology in the Apocalypse: JStNT 33 (1988) 85-95.

5718 *Rowland* Christopher, Keeping alive the dangerous vision of a world of peace and justice: Concilium 200 (E 1988) 75-86 = Garder vivante la dangereuse vision d'un monde de justice et de paix [... Apc]: Concilium 220 (P 1988) 89-101.

5719 **Schüssler Fiorenza** Elisabeth, The book of Revelation; justice and judgment 1985 ➤ 1,5466 ... 3,5529: ᴿAndrUnS 26 (1988) 159-165 (J. *Paulien* compares with Adela COLLINS, both important); RelStR 14 (1988) 340-4 (D. L. *Barr,* also comparing Adela COLLINS).

5720 *a) Seebass* Gottfried, Die Bedeutung der Apokalyptik für die Geschichte des Protestantismus; – *b) Voss* Gerhard, Die Johannes-Apokalypse in der römischen Liturgie: UnSa 43 (1988) 101-111 / 146-9.

5721 *Skiadaressis* John, ☉ Genesis and Apocalypse: DeltioVM 17,1s (1988) 48-60. 68-86.

5722 **Spivey** Steven W., Karl BARTH's book of Revelation: diss. Baylor. Waco ... – RelStR 14,187.

5723 **Swain** Lionel, The people of the resurrection, 1. the Apostolic Letters [i.e. eschatology in the NT, not Apostolic Fathers] 1986 ➤ 2,4483: ᴿAustralBR 36 (1988) 78s (C. G. *Kruse*).

5723* **Thompson** Stephen The Apocalypse and Semitic syntax: SNTS Mg 52, ᴰ1985 ➤ 1,5469 ... 3,5532: ᴿEvQ 60 (1988) 67-69 (J. N. *Birdsall*); ScripB 19 (1988s) 47s (Jennifer *Dynes*).

5724 **Timm** Gottfried, Die Heilsgemeinde in der Welt; zur Ekklesiologie der Johannesapokalypse: Diss. Rostock 1986. 254 p. – TLZ 11,156.

5724* *a) Vanni* Ugo, L'Apocalisse nel NT; – *b) Grossi* Vittorino, A proposito dell'apocalittica cristiana antica: FutUomo 13,2 (1986) 6-15 / 16-24.

5725 *Vetrali* Tecle, Il messaggio spirituale dell'Apocalisse: ➤ 810, StoSpir 2 NT (1988) 319-343.

5726 *a) Vorster* W. S., 'Genre' and the Revelation of John; a study in text, context and intertext; – *b) Botha* P. J. J., God, emperor worship and society; contemporary experiences and the Book of Revelation: Neotestamentica 22,1 (1988) 103-123 / 87-102.

5727 *a) Webber* Randall C., Group solidarity in the Revelation of John; – *b) Jeffers* James S., The influence of the Roman family and social structures on early Christianity in Rome: ➤ 500, SBL Seminars 1988, 132-140 / 370-384.

5728 *Wessel* Hugh, Le livre de l'Apocalypse et la fin des temps: RRéf 39,4 (1988) 1-8 [< ZIT 88,748].

5729 **Zager** Werner, Begriff und Wertung der Apokalyptik in der neutestamentlichen Forschung: ev. Diss. ᴰ*Brandenburg* E. Mainz 1987. – ᴿTLv 20,547.

G2.5 *Apocalypsis,* **Revelation** 1,1 ...

5730 *Kirby* John T., The rhetorical situations of Revelation 1-3: NTS 34 (1988) 197-207.

5731 **Woschitz** Karl M., [Apk 1-3] Erneuerung aus dem Ewigen; Denkweisen— Glaubensweisen in Antike und Christentum nach Offb 1-3, 1987 ➤ 3,5538; Sch 340 ᴿZkT 110 (1988) 211s (M. *Hasitschka*).

5732 *Barr* David L., [Apc 1,2] How were the hearers blessed? Literary reflections on the social impact of John's Apocalypse: ProcGLM 8 (1988) 49-59.

5733 *Wojciechowski* Michał, Seven churches and seven celestial bodies (Rev 1,16; Rev 2-3): BibNot 45 (1988) 48-50.

5734 **Sieg** Franciszek, ❷ Listy do siedmiu Kościołów, Apk 1-3: Bobolanum 12. Wsz 1985, Jezuitów. – RColcT 58,1 (1988) 177-9 (R. *Bartnicki*).

5735 *Contreras Molina* Francisco, [Apc 2s] Las cartas a las siete iglesias: EstBíb 46 (1988) 141-172; Eng. 141.

5736 **Hemer** Colin J., The letters to the seven churches...: JStNT Sup 11, 1986 → 2,4378; 3,5540: RInterpretation 42 (1988) 210.212 (J. E. *Stanley*); JBL 107 (1988) 766-8 (W. W. *Gasque*); TLZ 113 (1988) 354s (G. *Maier*).

5737 *[Calloud]* J., Note sur la lettre à l'église d'Éphèse, Apocalypse 2,1-7: SémBib 44 (1986) 38-51.

5738 *Schrage* Wolfgang, Meditation zu Offenbarung 2,8-11 [... Schuld der Nazizeit-Kirchen]: EvT 48 (1988) 388-403.

5739 *Wilkinson* Richard H., The *stylos* of Revelation 3:12 and ancient coronation rites: JBL 107 (1988) 498-501.

5741 *Gangemi* Attilio, La struttura liturgica dei capitoli 4 e 5 dell'Apocalisse di S. Giovanni: EcOrans 4 (1987) 301-358.

5742 **Musvosvi** Joel N., [Rev 6,9-11; 19,2] The concept of vengeance in the Book of Revelation in its Old Testament and Near Eastern context: diss. Andrews, DStrand K. Berrien Springs MI 1987. – AndrUnS 28 (1988) 83s.

5743 *Beneitez* Manuel, Algunas reflexiones en torno al 'séptimo sello' del Apocalipsis (Apc 8,1): EstE 63 (1988) 29-62.

5744 **Paulien** Jon, Decoding Revelation's trumpets; literary allusions and interpretation of Revelation 8: 7-12: Doctoral Diss. 11. Berrien Springs MI 1988, Andrews Univ. Seminary. xii-497 p. 0-943872-44-8.

5745 *a) Villiers* P. G. R. de, [Apc 11,8] The Lord was crucified in Sodom and Egypt; symbols in the Apocalypse of John; – *b) Rand* J. A. du, The imagery of the heavenly Jerusalem (Revelation 21:9-22:5): Neotestamentica 22,1 (1988) 125-138 / 65-86.

5746 *Delebecque* Édouard, [Apc 11,11s] 'Je vis' dans l'Apocalypse: RThom 88 (1988) 460-6.

5747 *Robinson* Bernard P., The two persecuted prophet-witnesses of Rev 11: ScripB 19 (1988s) 14-19.

5748 *Vanni* Ugo, La Donna della Genesi (3,15) e la Donna dell'Apocalisse (12,1) nella 'Redemptoris Mater': Marianum 50 (1988) 422-435.

5749 *Bergmeier* R., Die Erzhure und das Tier; Apk 12,18-13,18 und 17f; eine quellen- und redaktionskritische Analyse: → 782, ANRW 2,25,5 (1988) 3899-3916.

5750 *Kreitzer* Larry, Hadrian and the Nero redivivus myth ['standard interpretative feature in most commentaries on Rev (13,3; 17,8-11)']: ZNW 79 (1988) 92-115.

5751 *Trudinger* P., [Rev 17,10s] The 'Nero redivivus' rumour and the date of the Apocalypse of John: St Mark's Review 131 (Canberra 1987) 43s [< NTAbs 32,336].

5752 *Mazzaferri* Fred, [Rev 19,10] *Martyría Iēsoû* revisited: BTrans [36 (1985) 129-134, *Vassiliadis* P.] 39 (1988) 114-122.

G2.7 **Millenniarismus,** *Apc 21* ...

5753 *Blandre* Bernard, [... Apc] Le Christ de retour en 1873; à propos d'un ouvrage de Nelson H. *Barbour* [Evidences/Midnight Cry NY 1871]: RHR 205 (1988) 287-297; Eng. 287.

5754 *Boesak* Craig A.,   Development of dispensationalism ... 1. [within orthodoxy (founded by J. N. DARBY around 1830; high-point the C. I. SCOFIELD Reference Bible 1909)]; 2. [within dispensationalism, grappling with the identity of the system]: BS 145 (1988) 133-140 . 254-280 [281-300, *Ice* Thomas D., An evaluation of theonomic postmillennialism].

5755 *Buss* Dietrich G.,   Meeting of heaven and earth; a survey and analysis of the literature on millennialism in America, 1965-1985:   FidH 20,1 (Longview TX 1988) 5-28 [< ZIT 88,620].

5756 **Crenshaw** Curtis I.,   *Gunn* Grover E.[III],   Dispensationalism today, yesterday, and tomorrow.   Memphis 1985, Footstool.   431 p. $10. – [R]BS 145 (1988) 104s (C. A. *Blaising*: unscholarly attack by two former dispensationalists).

5757 *a) Crutchfield* Larry V.,   The Apostle John and Asia Minor as a source of premillennialism in the early Church Fathers; – *b) Patterson* James A., Changing images of the beast; apocalyptic conspiracy theories in American history: JEvTS 31 (1988) 411-428 / 443-452 [< ZIT 89,148s].

5758 **Joanta** Romul,   Roumanie, tradition et culture hésychastes; préf. *Clément* Olivier: Spiritualité orientale 46.   Bellefontaine 1987, Abbaye. 314 p. – [R]EsprVie 98 (1988) 265s (P. *Jay*).

5759 [E]**Popkin** Richard H.,   Millenarianism and Messianism in English literature and thought 1650-1800: Clark Library 10. Leiden 1988, Brill. vii-210 p. *f* 68 [JBL 108,756].

5760 *a) Schmidt-Biggemann* Wilhelm,   Apokalyptische Universalwissenschaft; Johan H. ALSTEDS 'Diatribe de mille annis apocalypticis'; – *b) Katz* David S.,   Millenarianism, the Jews, and biblical criticism in seventeenth-century England: Pietismus und Neuzeit 14 ('Chiliasmus in Deutschland und England im 17. Jahrhundert' Gö 1988) 50-71/166-184 [< ZIT 89,253].

5761 **Poythress** Vern S.,   Understanding dispensationalists.   GR 1987, Zondervan.   137 p. [GraceTJ 9.314].

5762 *Böcher* Otto, ❷ [Apc 21s] Caelestis urbs Jerusalem; animadversiones de ecclesiologia et eschatologia in Apocalypsi: RuBi 41 (1988) 330-7.

5763 **Dumbrell** William J.,   The end of the beginning; Revelation 21-22 and the OT 1985 → 2,4403:   [R]SR 17 (1988) 379s (D. *MacLachlan*).

5764 *Christe* Y.,   La cité de la sagesse [Apc 21,14s. l'ange mesurant le Jérusalem céleste est représenté sous les traits du Christ, comme aussi la Sagesse édifiant sa maison Prov 9,1 dans l'enluminure Nat.Bibl.Wien cod. 1179]: CahCivMéd 31 (1988) 29-35 [< RSPT 72,634].

5765 *Flusser* David, *a)* [Rev 21,22] No temple in the city [ineditum]; – *b)* Hystaspes and John of Patmos [< [E]*Shaked* S., Irano-Judaica 1982, 12-75]: → 190, JudOrChr 1988, 454-465 / 390-453.

5766 *Delebecque* Édouard,   Où situer l'Arbre de vie dans la Jérusalem céleste? Note sur Apocalypse XXII,2: RThom 88 (1988) 124-130.

XIII. Paulus

G3.1   **Pauli vita, stylus, chronologia.**

5767 *Banks* R.,   Paul — the experience within the theology: EvRT 12,2 (Exeter 1988) 116-128 [< NTAbs 32,321].

5768 **Bea** Fernando,   Saulo, Saulo ... un testimone di Cristo.   R 1988, Città Nuova.   248 p. Lit. 17.000. – [R]CC 139 (1988,3) 307s (G. *Giachi*: 'Come mai Bea non ha pensato a un incontro di Saulo con Maria?').

5769 **Bertrand** P., À la découverte des lettres de saint Paul. P 1987, Téqui. 95 p. F 33. 2-85244-843-2 [NTAbs 32,378].

5770 **Best** Ernest, Paul and his converts [1985 Sprunt Lectures]. E 1988, Clark. viii-175 p. $25 [JAAR 57,682]. 0-567-09147-3; pa. 2.

5771 **Biser** E., *al.*, Paulus 1985 ➤ 1,5517: ᴿJEcuSt 24 (1987) 131 (M. *Wyschogrod*).

5772 *Boers* Hendrikus W., The foundations of Paul's thought, a methodological investigation; the problem of the coherent center of Paul's thought: ST 42 (1988) 55-68.

5773 **Breton** Stanislas, Saint Paul: Philosophies 18. P 1988, PUF. 126 p. F 28. – ᴿRICathP 28 (1988) 156-8 (M. *Quesnel*).

5774 *Bruce* F. F., The enigma of Paul; why did the early Church's great liberator get a reputation as an authoritarian?: BR 4,4 (1988) 32s.

5775 **Cartigny** Charles, Le carré magique [sator arepo ➤ 4595], testament de Saint Paul 1984 ➤ 65,5154 ... 2,4508: ᴿLatomus 47 (1988) 200s (P. *Salmon*).

5776 **Cunningham** Philip A., Jewish apostle to the Gentiles; Paul as he saw himself 1986 ➤ 2,4417; 3,5577: ᴿFurrow 39 (1988) 482s (M. *Neary*).

5777 *De Lorenzi* Lorenzo, La vita spirituale di S. Paolo: ➤ 810, StoSpir 2 NT (1988) 99-175.

5778 **Dietzfelbinger** Christian, Die Berufung des Paulus als Ursprung seiner Theologie [Hab. 1982]: WMANT 58, 1985 ➤ 2,4418; 3,5578: ᴿJBL 107 (1988) 142-4 (Beverly R. *Gaventa*).

5779 *Feldmann* Erich, Apostolus (apostolatus): ➤ 783, AugL 1,3 (1988) 395-406.

5780 **Flanagan** Neal, Friend Paul 1986 ➤ 3,5580; also L, Chapman: ᴿAustralBR 36 (1988) 77s (B. *Byrne*); IrBSt 9 (1987) 97-99 (K. *Condon*).

5781 **Flemming** Dean E., Essence and adaptation; contextualisation and the heart of Paul's Gospel: diss. Aberdeen 1987, ᴰOrs. – RTLv 20,544 'adaption'.

5782 *Haacker* Klaus, Urchristliche Mission und kulturelle Identität; Beobachtungen zu Strategie und Homiletik des Apostels Paulus: TBei 19 (1988) 61-72 [< ᴢɪᴛ].

5783 *Harrington* D. J., A new paradigm for Paul: America 157 (NY 1987) 290-3 [NTAbs 32,181].

5784 **Harrington** Wilfrid, Jesus and Paul; signs of contradiction 1987 ➤ 2, 4423; 3,5585: ᴿInterpretation 42 (1988) 97s (J. W. *Aageson*).

5785 **Hyldahl** Niels, Die paulinische Chronologie 1986 ➤ 2,4427; 3,5587: ᴿJBL 107 (1988) 549s (R. *Jewett*: too audacious spirit unleashed by Kɴᴏx); RB 95 (1988) 309s (J. *Murphy-O'Connor*); TLZ 113 (1988) 186-191 (A. *Suhl*: aggressive, negative, wrong).

5786 **Johnson** Sherman E., Paul the Apostle and his cities; Good News Studies 21, 1987 ➤ 3,5589: ᴿCBQ 50 (1988) 533 (D. M. *Stanley*).

5787 **Knox** John, Chapters in a life of Paul (1950), ²*Hare* D. 1987 ➤ 3,5591; $35; pa. $14: ᴿRExp 85 (1988) 565 (Molly *Marshall-Green*).

5788 **Lüdemann** G., Paul ... chronology 1984 ➤ 1,5541 ... 3,5594: ᴿHeythJ 29 (1988) 534s (F. F. *Bruce*).

5789 *Martyn* J. L., Paul and his Jewish-Christian interpreters: UnSemQ 42,1s (1988) 1-15.

5790 *Meeks* Wayne A., St. Paul of the cities: ➤ 3,640, Civitas 1982/6, 15-23.

5791 *Merk* Otto, Paulus-Forschung 1936-1985: TRu 53 (1988) 1-81.

5792 *Mesters* Carlos, Una entrevista con el Apóstol Pablo, ᵀ*Cervantes* Carlos: Christus 53,616 (Méx 1987s) 45-52; 617s, 77-89.

5793 **Morstad** Erik, Ich verfolgte die Kirche Gottes ...; Schuldbekenntnis und personale Gemeinschaft als tragende Elemente in der Ekklesiologie des Apostels Paulus. Oslo 1988. I. 203 p.; II. p. 204-374.

5794 *Obijole* O., The influence of the conversion of St. Paul on his theology of the Cross: EAfJEvT 6,2 (1987) 27-36 [< NTAbs 32,322].

5795 *Osiek* Carolyn, Paul's prayer: ➤ 141, FSTUHLMUELLER C., Scripture and prayer 1988, 145-157.

5796 *a) Pathrapankal* Joseph, Conviction, conversion, commitment; a study on the religious personality of St. Paul; – *b) Navone* John [Acts 22,8.10], The dynamics of the question in the quest for God: JDharma 12 (1987) 289-301 / 228-246.

5797 **Plevnik** Joseph, What are they saying about Paul?. 1986 ➤ 2,4445; 3,5599: REstBíb 46 (1988) 137 (F. *Pastor Ramos*).

5798 **Rebell** W., Gehorsam und Unabhängigkeit; eine sozialpsychologische Studie zu Paulus 1986 ➤ 2,4448; 3,5600: RSNTU-A 13 (1988) 236s (F. *Weissengruber*).

5799 **Romaniuk** Kazimierz, Ⓟ Święty Paweł, życie i dzieło² [life and work, ¹1981]. Katowice 1988. S. Jacek. 151 p. 83-7030-019-7.

5800 *Rossano* Pietro, Paolo: ➤ 806, NDizTB 1988, 1064-1081.

5801 *Saffrey* H. D., Sur les pas de saint Paul: MondeB 52 (1988) 41-48 / 53,43-49 / 54, aussi 43-49 / 55,43-48 / 56 (1988) 43-49 ...; ill.

5802 **Sanders** E. P., Paulus and das palästinensische Judentum 1985 ➤ 1,5552 ... 3,5602: RErbAuf 63 (1987) 398 (J. *Kaffanke*).

5803 **Sanders** Ed P., Paolo e il giudaismo palestinese; studio comparativo su modelli di religione [1977 ²1984], TE*Pesce* Mauro, 1986 ➤ 2,4451; 3,5603: RAsprenas 35 (1988) 173s (A. *Rolla*); CC 139 (1988,2) 206 (C. *Di Sante*); StPatav 35 (1988) 159-165 (G. *Segalla*: Paolo, un quarto, alla fine; affascina[n]te e noioso).

5804 **Sandnes** Karl Olav, Paul, one of the prophets? A contribution to the Apostle's self-understanding: diss. Oslo 1988. 367 p. – RTLv 20,545; ST 43,233s.

5805 *Scaltriti* Giacinto A., L'imitazione di San Paolo: Renovatio 23 (1988) 404-424. 578-607.

5806 **Senft** Christophe, Jésus de Nazareth et Paul de Tarse 1985 ➤ 1,5555 ... 3,5605: RCiTom 114 (1987) 167s (J. *Huarte*).

5807 **Templeton** D. A. [a man], Reexploring Paul's imagination; a cynical laywoman's guide to Paul of Tarsus. Eilsbrunn 1988, Ko'amar. x-129 p. DM 32. 3-927136-02-6 [TsTNijm 28,331].

5808 **Thomé** Maria, Paulus, Weltmissionar — auf [400] Briefmarken: Gabriel-Bildhefte 6. Rommerskirchen c. 1987, Schönen, 83 p. [ZNW 79,164].

5809 **Trilling** Wolfgang, A conversation with Paul 1986 ➤ 2,4458; 3,5608: RAnglTR 70 (1988) 272s (S. B. *Marrow*); SpTod 40 (1988) 171-3 (R. F. *O'Toole*: some reserves).

5810 EVanhoye A., L'Apôtre Paul 1984/6 ➤ 2,398; 3,5611: RActuBbg 25 (1988) 222s (X. *Alegre S.*); BZ 32 (1988) 283-5 (M. *Theobald*); Carthaginensia 4 (1988) 181 (J. D. *Cuenca Molina*); CiuD 201 (1988) 177 (J. *Gutiérrez*); JBL 107 (1988) 782s (E. J. *Epp*: tit. pp.); RHPR 68 (1988) 251-3 (M. *Schoeni*); RThom 88 (1988) 133 (H. *Ponsot*, cité 'N. Ponsot' p. 487); ScripTPamp 20 (1988) 920s (J. *Chapa*).

5811 **Weiss** Herold, Paul of Tarsus, his gospel and life 1986 ➤ 3,5612; 0-943872-27-8: RAndrUnS 26 (1988) 207-9 (J. C. *Brunt*).

5812 *Wolff* Christian, Niedrigkeit und Verzicht in Wort und Weg Jesu und in der apostolischen Existenz des Paulus: NTS 34 (1988) 183-196.
5813 *Yagi* Selichi, Paulus und Shinran: EvT 48 (1988) 36-46.

G3.2 **Corpus paulinum;** *introductio, commentarii.*

5813* ᴱ*Betz* Hans D., *al.*, The editors' bookshelf; new literature on the authentic letters of the Apostle Paul: JRel 68 (1988) 186-203 (titles only).
5814 **Cugusi** Paolo, Evoluzione ... dell'epistolografia latina 1983 ➤ 2,4466: ᴿOrpheus 7 (1987) 206-8 (Maria Laura *Astarita*).
5815 *Fauconnet* Jean-Jacques, Confrontation des vices et des vertus dans les Épîtres du Nouveau Testament: BLitEc 89 (1988) 83-96; Eng. 82.
5816 **Johnson** David W., The revision of PELAGIUS' Pauline commentaries by CASSIODORUS and his students: diss. Princeton Theol. Sem. 1988. – RelStR 15,193.
5817 **Jonge** Henk J. de, Strong, coherent reasonings; John LOCKE's interpretatie van Paulus' brieven: Inaug.-Rede Leiden. Leiden 1988, Brill. 25 p.
5818 **Keck** Leander E., Paul and his letters² ^{rev} [¹1979 ➤ 60,7601 (not = The Pauline Letters, with *Furnish* V. 1984 ➤ 65,5114)]: Proclamation Comm. Ph 1988, Fortress. x-164 p. 0-8006-2340-1.
5819 **Keck** L. E., Paolo e le sue lettere 1987 ➤ 3,5621: ᴿRivB 36 (1988) 115-7 (R. *Fabris*); Teresianum 39 (1988) 538s (V. *Pasquetto*); StPatav 35 (1988) 198s (G. *Segalla*).
5820 **Malherbe** Abraham J., Ancient epistolary theorists [selections translated]: SRL Sources 19. Atlanta 1988, Scholars. x-88 p. $17; sb./pa. $11 [RB 96,293]. 0-89130-900-4; pa. 1-2.
5821 **Marrow** Stanley B., Paul, his letters and his theology 1986 ➤ 2,4473; 3,5623: ᴿAnglTR 69 (1987) 187-9 (E. C. *Hobbs*: excellent); BR 4,3 (1988) 10 (R. J. *Karris*); EstBíb 46 (1988) 261s (N. *Fernández*); Horizons 15 (1988) 158s (J. A. *Grassi*); RB 95 (1988) 147s (J. *Murphy-O'Connor*).
5822 *Parsons* Michael, Being precedes act; indicative and imperative in Paul's writing: EvQ 60 (1988) 99-127.
5823 **Richards** E. Randolph, The role of the secretary in Greco-Roman antiquity and its implication for the letters of Paul: diss. SW Baptist Theol. Sem. 1988. 410 p. 88-27436. – DissA 49 (1988s) 2698-A; RelStR 15,193.
5824 **Schmeller** Thomas, Paulus und die 'Diatribe' ...: NTAbh 19, 1987 ➤ 3,5628: ᴿBZ 32 (1988) 288s (R. *Schnackenburg*); NRT 110 (1988) 929s (X. *Jacques*).
5825 **Schnider** Franz, *Stenger* Werner, Studien zum neutestamentlichen Briefformular: NT Tools & Studies 1987 ➤ 3,5629: ᴿBiKi 43 (1988) 180s (D. *Zeller*).
5826 *Smith* D. Moody, The Pauline literature [citing OT]: ➤ 97, ᶠLINDARS B. 1988, 265-291.
5827 **Soards** Marion L., The Apostle Paul; an introduction to his writings and teaching 1987 ➤ 3,5630: ᴿInterpretation 42 (1988) 320.322 (W. *Baird*); ScripTPamp 20 (1988) 917s (J. *Chapa*); TS 49 (1988) 200 (A. *Tambasco*).
5828 **Stein** Robert H., Difficult passages in the Epistles. GR 1988, Baker. 162 p. [FgNt 2,212, D. A. *Black*].
5829 **Stowers** S. K., Letter writing in Greco-Roman antiquity: Library of Early Christianity 5, 1986 ➤ 2,4482; 3,5633: ᴿRB 95 (1988) 454s (J. *Murphy-O'Connor*: amply delivers what it promises).

5830 *Stowers* Stanley K., Social typification and the classification of ancient letters: → 77, [F]KEE H., Social world 1988, 78-90.

5831 **Thekkekara** Mathew, The face of early Christianity; a study of the Pauline letters. Bangalore 1988, KJC. xviii-259 p.

5832 *Walker* William O.[J], Text-critical evidence for interpolations in the letters of Paul: CBQ 50 (1988) 622-631.

5833 **White** John L., Light from ancient letters 1986 → 2,4486; 3,5637: [R]Gregorianum 69 (1988) 356s (J. *Janssens*); RB 95 (1988) 453s (J. *Murphy-O'Connor*: no usefulness for NT); RExp 85 (1988) 136 (D. E. *Garland*); TLZ 113 (1988) 358 (T. *Holtz*).

5834 *a) White* John L., Ancient Greek letters; – *b) Robbins* Vernon K., The chreia; – *c) Stowers* Stanley K., The diatribe: → 287, Greco-Roman 1988, 85-105 / 1-23 / 71-83 [107-126, *Aune* D., biography; 127-146, *Hock* R., novel].

Wouters Alfons, The Chester Beatty codex AC 1499, a Graeco-Latin lexicon on the Pauline epistles 1988 → a647.

G3.3 **Pauli theologia.**

5835 *Agnew* Francis H., Paul's theological adversary in the doctrine of justification by faith; a contribution to Jewish-Christian dialogue: JEcuSt 25 (1988) 538-554.

5836 *Barbaglio* Giuseppe, *a)* La 'soteria' in Paolo: RasT 29 (1988) 338-360 [con *sōzō* e *sōtēr* 34 volte sulle 200 del NT]; – *b)* Sul salvifico cristiano; la soteriologia paolina: Religioni e società 3,5 ('Salvezza e salvezze' 1988) 14-36 [< ZIT 89,141].

5837 *Beker* J. C., Paul's theology; consistent or inconsistent?: NTS 34 (1988) 364-377.

5838 *Bonge* Gloria van, In what way is Paul's Gospel (euangelion) of freedom theology of the Cross (theologia crucis)?: Colloquium 21,1 (1988) 19 ... [< ZIT 89,146].

5839 *Bossman* David M., Images of God in the letters of Paul [a father to his family, as in Pharisaism; role in Mediterranean culture markedly different from contemporary American experience]: BibTB 18 (1988) 67-76.

5840 **Dobbeler** Axel von, Glaube als Teilhabe ... der paulinischen Theologie: WUNT 2/22, 1987 → 3,5641: [R]BZ 32 (1988) 146-9 (M. *Theobald*); TGegw 30 (1987) 277s (H. *Giesen*); TR 84 (1988) 372-4 (D. *Zeller*); TsTNijm 28 (1988) 182s (A. *Brants*).

5841 *Ejenobo* David T., The meaning and significance of the death of Christ in the theology of St. Paul: AfJB 2 (1987) 64-76.

5842 **Fitzmyer** J., Paul and his theology [< Jerome comm. updated]. ENJ 1988, Prentice-Hall. 119 p. – [R]HomP 89,7 (1988s) 77-79 (W. G. *Most*: some defects, more good things).

5843 *Fryer* N. S. L., The intermediate state in Paul: HervTS 43,3 (Pretoria 1987) 448-484 [< NTAbs 32,322].

5844 **Greene** Michael D., Cult sacrifice and the death of Christ; a study in Pauline theology. diss. Virginia. Charlottesville 1987. 260 p. 89-01243. – DissA 49 (1988s) 3398-A; RelStR 14,189; RTLv 20,544.

5845 **Harper** George, Repentance in Pauline theology: diss. McGill, [D]*Johnston* G. Montreal 1988. – RTLv 20,544; RelStR 15,193.

5846 **Huarte Osacar** Juan, Evangelio y comunidad; estudio de teología paulina 1983 → 64,5576 ... 1,5594: [R]DivThom 89s (1986s) 492 (A. *Zürich*).

5847 **Kreitzer** L. Joseph,   Jesus and God in Paul's eschatology [diss. London King's College, ᴰ*Stanton* G.] 1987 ➤ 3,5648 ['Larry J. Kreitzer']: Sheffield 1987, JStOT.   293 p. £12.50.   1-85075-066-1 – ᴿRExp 85 (1988) 719s (G. *Sheeley*); Themelios 14 (1988s) 106s (S. *Travis*: significant).

5848 **Lincoln** Andrew T.,   Paradiso ora e non ancora; cielo e prospettiva escatologica nel pensiero di Paolo [1981], ᵀᴱ*Zani* Antonio: BiblCuRel 48, 1985 ➤ 1,5598; 3,5649:   ᴿRTPhil 120 (1988) 99s (A. *Moda*).

5849 **Lubomirski** Mieczysław,   Il ruolo dello Spirito Santo nel passaggio dell'uomo vecchio all'uomo nuovo secondo San Paolo: diss. Pont. Univ. Gregoriana, Nº 3501, ᴰ*Vanni* U.   Roma 1988.   xiii-408 p. – RTLv 20,545.

5850 *Merklein* Helmut, *a*) Die Bedeutung des Kreuzestodes Christi für die paulinische Gerechtigkeits- und Gesetzesthematik [ineditum]; – *b*) Entstehung und Gestalt des paulinischen Leib-Christi-Gedankens [< ᶠ*Breuning* W. 1985, 115-140]; – *c*) Die Ekklesia Gottes; der Kirchenbegriff bei Paulus und in Jerusalem [< BZ 23 (1979) 48-70]; – *d*) Zum Verständnis des paulinischen Begriffs 'Evangelium': ➤ 231, Studien 1987, 1-106 / 319-344 / 296-318 / 279-295.

5851 *Monte* William D.,   The place of Jesus' death and resurrection in Pauline soteriology: StudiaBT 16 (1988) 39-98.

5852 *Müller* Paul-Gerhard,   Die Fortschreibung der Christologie durch Paulus: BiKi 43 (1988) 54-65.

5853 **Pobee** John S.,   Persecution and Martyrdom in the theology of Paul 1985 ➤ 1,5604 ... 3,5654:   ᴿScripB 19 (1988s) 25s (J. *Dines*).

5854 **Scaturchio** Vincenzo,   Tempio e corporeità; il significato del corpo del cristiano come tempio dello Spirito Santo in S. Paolo: diss. Pont. Univ. Gregoriana, ᴰ*Vanni* U.   R 1988. – RTLv 20,546.

5855 **Schlier** H.,   Linee fondamentali di una teologia paolina 1985 ➤ 3,5656: ᴿProtestantesimo 43 (1988) 219s (V. *Subilia*).

5856 **Theissen** Gerd,   Psychological aspects of Pauline theology [1983] 1987 ➤ 3,5658:   ᴿAnglTR 70 (1988) 99-101 (J. A. *Davis*); Interpretation 42 (1988) 318.320 (M. L. *Hoops*); RelStR 15 (1989) 38-40-42 (J. D. *Tabor*; W. *Wink*); TLond 91 (1988) 529s (C. J. A. *Hickling*); TS 49 (1988) 337-9 (R. J. *Karris*).

5857 **Thüsing** Wilhelm,   Gott und Christus in der paulinischen Soteriologie I³ʳᵉᵛ: NTAbh NF 1, 1986 ➤ 3,5659:   ᴿRThom 88 (1988) 133s (H. *Ponsot*); TLZ 113 (1988) 820s (H. *Hübner*).

5859 **Way** D. V.,   The Lordship of Christ; a critical analysis of Ernst KÄSEMANN's interpretation of Pauline theology: diss. Oxford 1987. – RTLv 20,554.

5860 **Wedderburn** A. J. M.,   Baptism and Resurrection; studies in Pauline theology against its Graeco-Roman background: WUNT 44, 1987 ➤ 3,5661:   ᴿArTGran 51 (1988) 302 (A. *Segovia*); TsTNijm 28 (1988) 408s (L. *Visschers*).

G3.4   **Themata paulina**   [Israel et Lex ➤ G4.6].

5861 *Ballard* Paul H.,   Pastoral theology as theology of reconciliation [... Paul]: TLond 91 (1988) 375-380.

5862 *Becquet* Gilles,   Laïcs [le mot n'est pas dans le NT] collaborateurs de Saint Paul: Sève 498 (1988) 310-4.

5863 **Beker** Johan C.,   Der Sieg Gottes; eine Untersuchung zur Struktur des paulinischen Denkens: SBS 132. Stu 1988, KBW.   108 p. [TR 85,251].

5864 *Bowman* John, Elijah and the Pauline Jesus Christ: Abr Nahrain 26 (1988) 1-18.

5865 *Breytenbach* C., Probleme rondom die interpretasie van die 'versoeningsuitsprake' [reconciliation-dictums, *pace* NTAbs 32,321] bij Paulus: HervTS 42,4 (Pretoria 1986) 696-704.

Bristow John T., What Paul really said about women 1988 ➤ 9889.

5866 *Büchsel* Elfriede, Paulinische Denkfiguren in HAMANNS Aufklärungskritik; hermeneutische Beobachtungen zu exemplarischen Texten und Problemstellungen: NSys 30 (1988) 269-285 [209-326, Themenheft J. G. Hamann † 1788].

5867 *Comblin* J., *a*) O êxodo na teologia paulina; – *b*) Paulo e a mensagem de liberdade: EstudosB 16 (1987) 76-80 / 14 (1987) 64-70.

5868 *Danken* Frederick W., Bridging St. Paul and the Apostolic Fathers; a study in reciprocity: ➤ 143, FTIETJEN J. = CurrTM 15 (1988) 84-94.

5869 *Deidun* Thomas, Beyond dualisms; Paul on sex, *sarx,* and *sōma*: Way 28 (1988) 195-205.

5870 **Dennison** William D., Paul's two-age construction and apologetics [D1980] 1985 ➤ 1,5626 ... 3,5672: RScripTPamp 20 (1988) 919s (J. *Chapa*).

5871 *Eckert* Jost, 'Dreimal habe ich den Herrn angefleht ...'; Krankheit in der Sicht des Apostels Paulus: BiKi 43 (1988) 8-12.

5872 *Fowl* Stephen, Some uses of story in moral discourse; reflections on Paul's moral discourse and our own: ModT 4 (1987s) 293-308.

5873 **Franco** E., Comunione ... nell'epistolario paolino [D1983] 1986 ➤ 2, 4516; 3,5676: RAngelicum 65 (1988) 308-310 (A. *Borriello*).

5874 [**Gundry**] **Volf** Judith, Perseverance and falling away in Paul's thought: ev. Diss. Tübingen 1988, DHofius O. 349 p. – RTLv 20,544.

5875 **Hanson** Anthony T., The paradox of the Cross in the thought of St. Paul: JStNT Sup 17, 1987 ➤ 3,5681: RInterpretation 42 (1988) 434 (D. L. *Bartlett*); RB 95 (1988) 463s (J. *Murphy-O'Connor*).

5876 **Hoffmann** R. J., MARCION ... radical Paulinist theology 1984 ➤ 65,5131 ... 2,4491: RJTS 39 (1988) 227-232 (C. P. *Bammel*: wholly incompetent).

5877 *Kraftchick* Steven J., Creation themes in Pauline literature: ➤ 567, ExAud 3 (1987) 72-87.

5878 **Jones** F. Stanley, 'Freiheit' in den Briefen des Apostels Paulus; eine historische, exegetische und religionsgeschichtliche Studie (Diss. Gö, DStrecker G.]. GöTheolArb 34, 1987 ➤ 3,5688: RNRT 110 (1988) 928s (X. *Jacques*: 'in den Briefe', dormitat Homerus); TsTNijm 28 (1988) 408 (H. van de *Sandt*).

  Kitzberger Ingrid, Bau der Gemeinde; das paulinische Wortfeld 1986 ➤ a628.

5879 *a*) *Klein* Günter, Ein Sturmzentrum der Paulusforschung [das Gesetz]; – *b*) *Weder* Hans, Exegese und Psychologie; zu Gerd THEISSENS Analyse paulinischer Theologie: VerkF 33,1 (1988) 40-56 / 57-63.

5880 **Koch** Dietrich A., Die Schrift als Zeuge des Evangeliums ... bei Paulus: BeiHistT 69, 1986 ➤ 2,4525; 3,5690: RActuBbg 25 (1988) 212s (X. *Alegre* S.); ÉTRel 63 (1988) 92s (F. *Vouga*: exhaustif, systématique et méticuleux); JBL 107 (1988) 331-3 (R. B. *Hays*); Salmanticensis 35 (1988) 415-7 (R. *Trevijano*); TLZ 113 (1988) 349-352 (H. *Hübner*: unverzichtbar).

5881 *Kroeger* C., Paul, sex, and the immoral majority: Daughters of Sarah 14,3 (Ch 1988) 26-28.

  Leonarda Salvatore, La gioia nelle lettere di S. Paolo 1988 ➤ 6241.

5883 **Meeks** Wayne A., The first urban Christians ... Paul 1983 ➤ 64,5641 ...
3,5696: ᴿAntonianum 63 (1988) 178-181 (Z. I. *Herman*).

5884 **Meeks** Wayne A., Los primeros cristianos urbanos; el mundo social del
apóstol Pablo, ᵀ*Olasagasti* M. Salamanca 1988, Sígueme. 376 p. –
ᴿNatGrac 35 (1988) 439-441 (F. F. *Ramos*); QVidCr 143 (1988) 129 (P.-R.
Tragan).

5885 **Ménard** Camille, L'Esprit de la nouvelle alliance chez S. Paul [diss.
1983]: Recherches NS 10, 1987 ➤ 3,5697: ᴿDivinitas 32 (1988) 724s (T.
Stramare); Études 368 (1988) 858 (R. *Marlé*); TLZ 113 (1988) 896s (W.
Schenk).

5886 *Moore* Hamilton, Paul and Apocalyptic: IrBSt 9 (1987) 35-46.

5887 **Myre** André, Un souffle subversif; l'Esprit dans les lettres pauliniennes:
Recherches NS 12. Montréal/P 1987, Bellarmin/Cerf. 160 p. – ᴿÉglT 19
(1988) 428-430 (N. *Bonneau*); VieCons 60 (1988) 378s (A. *Faucher*).

5888 *Ortkemper* Franz-J., Vivir como cristiano; reflexiones a partir de la ética
de Pablo [1 Cor 6,12-20; 7,1-7; Rom 12,14-21; < BiKi 40 (1985) 125-132];
ᵀᴱ*Priego* Juan J.: SelT 27 (1988) 125-130.

5889 **Park Heon-Wook,** Die Vorstellung vom Leib Christi bei Paulus: ev.
Diss. ᴰ*Betz* O. Tübingen 1988. 359 p. – RTLv 20,545; TR 85,518.

5890 *Parsons* Michael, 'In Christ' in Paul: VoxEvca 18 (L 1988) 25-44.

5891 *a) Prior* Michael, Paul on 'power and weakness'; – *b) Soskice* Janet M.
[some say it is wrong to speak of] God of power and might: Month 249
(1988) 939-944 / 934-8.

5892 **Reinmuth** Eckart, Geist und Gesetz; Studien zu Voraussetzungen und
Inhalt der paulinischen Paränese: TArb 44, 1985 ➤ 2,4538: ᴿBZ 32
(1988) 149-151 (M. *Theobald*).

5893 **Renwick** David A., Paul, the Temple, and the presence of God: diss.
Union. Richmond 1988. 354 p. 88-27020. – DissA 49 (1988s) 2693-A.

5894 *Sawatzky* Sheldon, Sources for Paul's conception of *sōma*: Taiwan
JTheol 9 (1987) 199-220 [< TKontext 10/1,39].

5894* *Schöllgen* G., Was wissen wir über die Sozialstruktur der paulinischen
Gemeinden? Kritische Anmerkungen zu einem neuen Buch von W. A.
MEEKS [1983]: NTS 34 (1988) 71-82.

5895 **Schoon** Johannes, Umstrittene 'Apologien' in Paulusbriefen: ev. Diss.
Gö 1988s, ᴰ*Strecker*. – TR 85,516.

5896 **Seeley** David, The concept of noble death in Paul; Greco-Roman
martyrological backgrounds to Pauline soteriology: diss. Claremont 1984.
– RelStR 14,188.

5897 *Spicq* C., La joie selon saint Paul: Carmel 44 (1986) 242-7.

5898 **Tobin** Thomas H., The spirituality of Paul 1987 ➤ 3,5713: ᴿCBQ 50
(1988) 735s (P. *Zilonka*); SpTod 40 (1988) 184s (Pheme *Perkins*);
Vidyajyoti 52 (1988) 514s (R. J. *Raja*).

5899 *Vollenweider* Samuel, Zeit und Gesetz; Erwägungen zur Bedeutung
apokalyptischer Denkformen bei Paulus: TZBas 44 (1988) 97-116.

5900 *a) Wagner* Guy, La mort et la vie selon l'apôtre Paul; – *b) Grelot* Pierre,
La Bible et l'expérience de la mort: Tychique 74 (1988) 30-33 / 22-25.

5901 *Wedderburn* A. J. M., Paul and Jesus; similarity and continuity: NTS
34 (1988) 161-182.

G4 **Ad Romanos** .1 *Textus, commentarii.*

5902 **Barth** Karl, Breve commentario all'Epistola ai Romani [1940=1956],
ᵀ*Laurenzi* Maria C.: GdT 138, 1982 ➤ 63,5763 ... 65,5205: ᴿStPatav 35
(1988) 221 (A. *Moda*).

5903 ᴱCocchini Francesca, ORIGENE, Commento alla Lettera ai Romani, Libri VII-X, vol. II, 1986 → 3,5724: ᴿSMSR 54 (1988) 193s (L. *Navarra*).

5904 **Dunn** James D. G., Romans: Word Comm. 38AB. Dallas 1988, Word.

5905 ᶠ**Fraenkel** P., *Perrotet* L., Théodore de BÈZE, Cours sur les Épîtres aux Romains et aux Hébreux, 1564-66. TravHumRen 226. [STEv NS 1,88, G. *Emetti*].

5906 **Heil** John P., Paul's letter to the Romans; a reader-response commentary 1987 → 3,5729: ᴿFgNT 1 (1988) 220 (D. A. *Black*: disappointingly superficial); TorJT 4 (1988) 303-5 (J. *Plevnik*).

5907 **Heil** John P., Romans — Paul's letter of hope: AnBib 112, 1987 → 3,5730; Lit. 30.000: ᴿArTGran 51 (1988) 289s (A. *Segovia*); NRT 110 (1988) 607 (X. *Jacques*).

5908 **Ince** Gwenda, Creation, justification, resurrection; an exposition and critique of KÄSEMANN's Romans: diss. Edinburgh 1986. 410 p. BRD-81005. – DissA 49 (1988s) 527-A.

5909 **Kruijf** T. C. de, De brief van Paulus aan de Romeinen: Het NT 1986 → 2,4559; ƒ75: ᴿStreven 56 (1988s) 81 (P. *Beentjes*); TsTNijm 28 (1988) 85 (L. *Visschers*).

5910 **Landes** Paula F., AUGUSTINE on Romans 1982 → 65,5772 ... 1,5675: RB 95 (1988) 633s (B. T. *Viviano*).

5910* **Lloyd Jones** David M., Romans, an exposition of ch. 1: the Gospel of God. GR 1986, Zondervan. xii-394 p. $17 [TDig 34,368].

5911 **Morris** Leon, The Epistle to the Romans. GR/Leicester 1988, Eerdmans/Inter-Varsity. xii-578 p. $28. 0-8028-3636-4 / 0-85111-747-3 [NTAbs 32,380]. – ᴿRExp 85 (1988) 736s (S. *Sheeley*).

5912 **Parker** T. H. L., [6 Catholic, 5 Protestant] Commentaries on the Epistle to the Romans 1532-1542: 1986 → 2,4564; 3,5734: ᴿEvQ 60 (1988) 91 (A. S. *Wood*); RB 95 (1988) 313s (J. *Murphy-O'Connor*: important).

5913 **Schmithals** Walter, Der Römerbrief, ein Kommentar. Gö 1988, Mohn. 583 p. 3-579-00087-X.

5914 ᴱ**Strohm** Stefan, Johannes BRENZ, Explicatio epistolae Pauli ad · Romanos I, 1986 → 2,4567; 3,5738: ᴿGregorianum 69 (1988) 556s (J. *Wicks*).

5915 **Zeller** Dieter von, Der Brief an die Römer: Rg NT 1985 → 2,4570; 3,5740: ᴿActuBbg 25 (1988) 77s (X. *Alegre S.*); JTS 39 (1988) 577s (J. D. G. *Dunn*); TLZ 113 (1988) 30s (H.-F. *Weiss*).

G4.2 *Ad Romanos: themata*, topics.

5916 *Bielecki* Stanisław, ❷ Salvation-history in St. Paul's letter to the Romans: Współczesna Ambona 16,2 (1988) 130-6.

5917 **Bluhm** Heinz, Luther translator of Paul; studies in Romans and Galatians 1984 → 1,5664: ᴿLutherJb 55 (1988) 127-9 (H. *Junghans*: 30 art.].

5918 **Byrne** Brendan, Reckoning with Romans 1986 → 2,4551; 3,5723: ᴿRB 95 (1988) 460s (J. *Murphy-O'Connor*).

5919 **Cantalamessa** R., La vita nella signoria di Cristo. Mi 1986, Milano. 281 p. – ᴿClaretianum 28 (1988) 382s (R. M. *Serra*).

5920 *Lowe* W., BARTH as critic of dualism; re-reading the Römerbrief ['regarded by many as the very paradigm of theological dualism'...]: ScotJT 41 (1988) 377-395.

5921 *Miller* D. G., Romans: → 801, ISBEnc³ 4 (1988) 222-8 [-236 Rome, *Vos* H. F.].

5922 *Moxnes* Halvor,   Honour and righteousness in Romans: JStNT 32 (1988) 61-77.
5923 *Penna* Romano,   Aspetti narrativi della lettera di S. Paolo ai Romani: RivB 36 (1988) 29-45; Eng. 45.
5924 **Ponsot** Hervé,   Une introduction à la lettre aux Romains: Initiations. P 1988, Cerf. 218 p. F 125 [TR 85,427]. 2-204-02981-5.
5925 **Randt** Cornelis du,   *Elpis* in Romans: diss. Pretoria 1988. – DissA 49 (1988s) 3396-A.
5926 **Wedderburn** A.,   The reasons for Romans: StNT&W [ᴱ*Riches* J.].   E 1988, Clark. 184 p. $22 [TS 50,835]. 0-567-09499-5.

G4.3   *Naturalis cognitio Dei* ... **Rom 1-4.**

5927 *DeYoung* James B.,   The meaning of 'nature' in Romans 1 and its implications for biblical proscriptions of homosexual behavior: JEvTS 31 (1988) 429-442 [< ZIT 89,149].
5928 **Garlington** Don B., [Rom 1,5; 16,26] The obedience of faith; a Pauline phrase in historical context: diss. ᴰ*Dunn* J.   Durham 1987. BRD-80336. – DissA 49 (1988s) 103-A; RTLv 19,537.
5929 *Segalla* Giuseppe, L''obbedienza di fede' (Rm 1,5; 16,26) tema della lettera ai Romani?: ➤ 154, ꟳZEDDA S., RivB 36 (1988) 329-342; Eng. 342.
5930 *Rossi* Benedetto,   Struttura letteraria e articolazione teologica di Rom 1,11-11,36: SBFLA 38 (1988) 59-133.
5931 *Cocchini* Francesca,   L'esegesi ORIGENIANA di Rom 1,14; aspetti di una situazione ecclesiale: SMSR 54,3 (1988) 71-80.
5932 *Lafontaine* René,   Hacia una nueva evangelización ... Rom 1,18-2,29 [< NRT 108 (1986) 641-665], ᵀᴱ*Giménez* Josep: SelT 27 (1988) 11-24.
5933 *Aletti* Jean-Noël,   Rm 1,18-3,20; incohérence ou cohérence de l'argumentation paulinienne?: Biblica 69 (1988) 47-62; Eng. 62.
5934 *Billy* Dennis J.,   Grace and the natural law in ... THOMAS' commentary on Romans 2:14-16: Studia Moralia 26 (1988) 15-36; Eng. 36.
5935 *Löfstedt* Bengt,   Notes on St. Paul's letter to the Romans [3,4; 4,15.22; 9,17]: FgNT 1 (1988) 209s.
5936 *Penna* Romano,   La funzione strutturale di 3,1-8 nella lettera ai Romani: Biblica 69 (1988) 507-542; Eng. 542.
5937 *Lafon* Guy,   Une loi de foi; la pensée de la loi en Romains 3,19-31: RevSR 61 (1987) 32-53.
5938 *Thompson* Richard W.,   The inclusion of the Gentiles in Rom 3,27-30: Biblica 69 (1988) 543-546.
5939 *Guerra* Anthony J.,   Romans 4 as apologetic theology: HarvTR 81 (1988) 251-270.
5940 *Steinmetz* David,   CALVIN and Abraham; the interpretation of Rm. 4 in the 16th century: *a*) ➤ 471, Exégèse XVIᴱ siècle 1988 ...; – *b*) ChH 57 (1988) 443-455.
5941 *Moore* Richard K.,   Romans 4.5 in TEV [Today's English version: world's-record 50 million paperbacks sold in its first ten years]; a plea for consistency: BTrans 39 (1988) 126-9.

G4.4   *Peccatum originale; redemptio cosmica:* **Rom 5-8.**

5942 *Rolland* Philippe,   L'antithèse de Rm 5-8: Biblica 69 (1988) 396-400.
5943 *De Bruyn* Theodore S.,   PELAGIUS's interpretation of Rom. 5: 12-21; exegesis within the limits of polemic: TorJT 4 (1988) 30-43.

5944 *a*) *Byrne* Brendan,   'The type of the one to come' (Rom 5:14); fate and responsibility in Romans 5:12-21; – *b*) *Stuhlmacher* Peter,   The theme of Romans: AustralBR 36 (1988) 31-44.

5945 *Marcus* Joel, [Rom 6,12] 'Let God arise and end the reign of sin!'; a contribution to the study of Pauline parenesis: Biblica 69 (1988) 386-395.

5946 *Morrison* Bruce, *Woodhouse* John,   The coherence of Romans 7:1-8:8: RefTR 47 (1988) 8-16.

5947 *Dautzenberg* Gerhard,   Simul iustus et peccator; zur Auslegung von Röm 7: ➤ 547, Rechtfertigung 1983/4, 85-104 [< LuJB 55,163].

5948 *Segal* Alan F.,   Romans 7 and Jewish dietary laws [< SR 15 (1986) 361-374]: ➤ 260, Other Judaisms 1987, 167-194.

5949 *Ziesler* J. A.,   The role of the tenth commandment in Romans 7: JStNT 33 (1988) 41-56.

5950 **Oh Woo Sung,**   A history of interpretation of Romans 7:14-25; converted or unconverted, or tertium quid?: diss. Drew. Madison NJ 1987. – RelStR 15,192.

5951 *Nicol* W.,   Hoe direk lei die Gees? 'n Dogmatiese en eksegetiese onder-soek rondom Romeine 8:14: SkrifKerk 7 (1986) 173-197 [NTAbs 32,184].

5952 *Obeng* E. A., [Rom 8,15f; Gal 4,6] Abba, Father; the prayer of the sons of God: ExpTim 99 (1987s) 363-6.

5953 **Scott** James M., [Rom 8,15.23 + 3 times] *Hyiothesia*; an exegetical investigation into the background of divine 'adoption as sons' in the corpus paulinum: ev. Diss. [D]STUHLMACHER P. Tübingen 1988s. 411 p. – RTLv 20,546; TR 85,518.

5954 *Helewa* Giovanni,   'Sofferenza' e 'speranza della gloria' in Rom 8,17: Teresianum 39 (1988) 233-273.

5955 *Tremblay* R. [Rom 8,21 ...]: ➤ 21, [F]CAPONE D., Coscienza 1987 ...

5956 *O'Brien* Peter,   Romans 8:26,27; a revolutionary approach to prayer?: RefTR 46 (1987) 65-73.

5957 *Snyman* A. H.,   Style and the rhetorical situation of Romans 8: 31-39: NTS 34 (1988) 218-231.

5958 *Tisdale* Leonora T.,   Romans 8:31-39 ['a loving God and human suf-fering']: Interpretation 42 (1988) 68-72.

G4.6 *Israel et Lex,*   **The Law and the Jews,** *Rom 9-11.*

5959 **Cassirer** Heinz W.,   Grace and law; St. Paul, KANT, and the Hebrew Prophets. GR 1988, Eerdmans. 176 p. $13 [TS 50,627].

5960 *a*) *Fiore* Benjamin,   Romans 9-11 and classical forensic rhetoric; – *b*) *Dewey* Arthur J., Outlaw/In-law [Rom 9,3]; social-historical observations on Romans 9-11: ProcGLM 8 (1988) 117-126 / 101-115.

5961 **Fuchs-Kreimer** Nancy,   The essential heresy; Paul's new law according to Jewish writers, 1886-1986: diss. Temple. Ph 1988. – RelStR 15,189.
   Gaston Lloyd,   Paul and the Torah 1987 ➤ 196.

5962 *Getty* Mary Ann,   Paul and the salvation of Israel; a perspective on Romans 9-11: CBQ 50 (1988) 456-469.

5963 **Gorday** Peter, Principles of patristic exegesis; Romans 9-11 in ORIGEN, John CHRYSOSTOM, and AUGUSTINE 1983 ➤ 65,5256 ... 2,4617: [R]Bijdra-gen 49 (1988) 452 (M. *Parmentier*); RExp 85 (1988) 732s (E. G. *Hinson*).

5964 *Harrington* Daniel J.,   Israel's salvation according to Paul: BToday 26 (1988) 304-8.

5965 **Hübner** Hans, Law in Paul's thought [²1980 (¹1978)], [T]*Greig* J.: StNTW 1984 ➤ 63,5257 ... 3,5798: [R]CBQ 50 (1988) 324s (J. L. *Gillman*).

5966 ᴱ**Kertelge** K.,   Das Gesetz im NT: QDisp 108, 1986 ➤ 2,382; 3,5800:
ᴿTPQ 136 (1988) 286 (K. M. *Woschitz*).

5967 **Lübking** Hans-M.,   Paulus und Israel im Römerbrief ... 9-11 [ᴰ1984]:
EurHS 23/260, 1986 ➤ 2,4622: ᴿÉTRel 63 (1988) 92 (F. *Vouga*); TR 84
(1988) 294-7 (F. *Mussner*).

5968 **Marino** Joseph S.,   Saint Paul and the Law; toward a doctrine of Church
law: diss. Pont. Univ. Gregoriana, ᴰ*Ghirlanda* G. R 1988. xx-411 p.

5969 *a) Meyer* Ben F.,   Election-historical thinking in Romans 9-11 and
ourselves; – *b) Chilton* Bruce,   Romans 9-11 as Scriptural interpretation
and dialogue with Judaism; - *c) Hesselink* I. John, CALVIN's
understanding of the relation of the Church and Israel based largely on
his interpretation of Romans 9-11; – *d) Miller* Donald G., Can Romans
9-11 be used in the pulpit?; – *e) Buttrick* David G., On preaching from
Romans 9-11: ExAud 4 (1988) 1-7 / 27-37 / 59-69 / 95-112 / 113-122.

5970 **Osten-Sacken** Peter von der, Evangelium und Tora; Aufsätze zu Paulus:
TBüch 77, 1987 ➤ 3,372: ᴿNRT 110 (1988) 609 (X. *Jacques*).

5971 **Räisänen** Heikki, Paul and the law: WUNT 29, 1983 ➤ 64,5532; 3,5805:
ᴿZkT 110 (1988) 214s (R. *Oberforcher*).

5972 **Räisänen** Heikki, The Torah and Christ, essays 1986 ➤ 2,209; 3,5806:
ᴿBZ 32 (1988) 151-3 (K. *Müller*); ScotJT 41 (1988) 421-3 (I. H. *Marshall*).

5973 *Räisänen* Heikki, Paul, God, and Israel; Romans 9-11 in recent
research: ➤ 77, ᶠKᴇᴇ H., Social world 1988, 178-206.

5974 **Roukema** Riemer, The diversity of laws in ORIGEN's commentary on
Romans: diss. ᴰ*Datema* C., Vrije Univ. Amst 1988. 117 p. 90-6256-
667-7. – TsTNijm 28 (1988) 294.

5975 **Schmitt** Rainer, Gottesgerechtigkeit — Heilsgeschichte — Israel in der
Theologie des Paulus: EurHS 13/240, 1984 ➤ 65,5265: ᴿÉTRel 63 (1988)
90s (F. *Vouga*: 'pamphlet' contre Günter KLEIN).

5976 *a) Schümmer* L., Le mystère d'Israël et de l'Église, postérité d'Abraham;
– *b) Siegwalt* Gérard, L'élection éternelle de l'Église en Christ et l'élection d'Israël; la dialectique biblique de l'élection et du rejet dans l'histoire:
Irénikon 61 (1988) 207-241; Eng. 241s / 5-27; Eng. 27.

5977 **Siegert** Folker, [Rom 9-11 ...] Argumentation bei Paulus: WUNT 34,
1985 ➤ 1,5766; 3,5809: ᴿHeythJ 29 (1988) 512s (F. F. *Bruce*); NedTTs 42
(1988) 72s (J. S. *Vos*: eenzijdig apologetisch).

5978 **Simpson** John W., The future of non-Christian Jews: 1 Thess 2,15-16
and Rom 9-11: diss. Fuller Theol. Sem. Pasadena 1988. 362 p. 88-16095. –
DissA 49 (1988s) 1855-A.

5979 *Snodgrass* Klyne, Spheres of influence; a possible solution to the
problem of Paul and the Law: JStNT 32 (1988) 93-113.

5980 **Watson** Francis, Paul, Judaism and the Gentiles; a sociological approach [ᴰ1984] 1986 ➤ 2,4634*; 3,5814: ᴿBZ 32 (1988) 285-7 (M. *Theobald*); EvQ 60 (1988) 86-88 (D. J. *Graham*); JEcuSt 25 (1988) 107s (Sue
Frank); JJS 39 (1988) 296-9 (E. P. *Sanders*: 'not successful' though 'one of
the most interesting books on Paul to appear in recent years'); ModT 4
(1987s) 217s (S. *Fowl*); RB 95 (1988) 461-3 (J. *Murphy-O'Connor*); RTLv
19 (1988) 200-4 (C. *Focant*); ScripTPam 19 (1987) 985s (F. *Varo*).

5981 **Westerholm** Stephen, Israel's Law and the Church's faith; Paul and
his recent interpreters. GR 1988, Eerdmans. viii-238 p. $15. 0-8028-
0288-5. – ᴿTrinJ 9.1 (1988) 123-5 (T. R. *Schreiner*).

5982 *Rese* Martin, Israel und Kirche in Römer 9: NTS 34 (1988) 208-217.

5983 **Piper** John, The justification of God ... Rom 9,1-23: 1983. – ᴿEvQ 60 (1988) 80-84 (N. T. *Wright*: deep-seated objections).

5984 *Flusser* David, *a*) From the Essenes to Romans 9: 24-33; – *b*) Jesus' opinion about the Essenes [inedita]: → 190, JudOrChr 1988, 75-87 [cf. Sifriat Poalim 1982, 397-401 ⊕] / 150-169.

5985 *Watts* James W., [Rom 9,27; 11,5] The remnant theme; a survey of New Testament research, 1921-1987: PerspRelSt 15 (1988) 109-129.

5986 *Baarda* T., Het einde van de wet is Christus; Rom. 10:4-15 een Midrasj van Paulus over Deut 30:11-14: GerefTTs 88 (1988) 208-248.

5987 **Badenas** Robert, Christ the end of the law; Rom 10,4 [diss. Andrews, ᴰ*Terian* A.] 1985 → 1,5775 ... 3,5822: ᴿAndrUnS (1988) 181-4 (H. *Weiss*); JBL 107 (1988) 145-7 (F. *Thielman*); RB 95 (1988) 153s (J. *Murphy-O'Connor*); RHPR 68 (1988) 253s (M. *Schoeni*).

5988 *Linss* Wilhelm C., Exegesis of *télos* in Romans 10:4: BiRes 33 (Ch 1988) 5-12.

5989 *Eckstein* Hans-Joachim, 'Nahe ist dir das Wort'; exegetische Erwägungen zu Röm 10,8: ZNW 79 (1988) 204-220.

5990 *a*) *Hafemann* Scott, The salvaton of Israel in Romans 11:25-32; a response to Krister STENDAHL; – *b*) *Haynes* Stephen R., 'Recovering the real Paul'; theology and exegesis in Romans 9-11; – *c*) *Rumscheidt* H. Martin, 'Do not live in fear, little flock!' The interpretation of Romans 9-11 of Georg EICHHOLZ; – *d*) *Barth* Markus, One God, one Christ, one people: ExAud 4 (1988) 38-58 / 70-84 / 85-94 / 8-26.

5991 **Refoulé** François, '... et ainsi tout Israël sera sauvé', Romains 11,25-32: LDiv 117, 1984 → 65,5281 (non 5821 comme:) ... 3,5825: ᴿÉglT 17 (1986) 391-5 (L. *Laberge*); SNTU-A 13 (1988) 241-3 (H. *Hübner*); SvEx 53 (1988) 129-131 (R. *Kieffer*).

5992 *Osborne* William L., The OT background of Paul's 'all Israel' in Romans 11:26s: AsiaJT 2 (1988) 282-293.

G4.8 Rom 12 ...

5993 *Voss* Gerhard, In Christus Gemeinschaft bilden; eine Auslegung des 12. Kapitels des Römerbriefs: UnSa 43 (1988) 277-283.342.

5994 *Betz* Hans D., Das Problem der Grundlagen der paulinischen Ethik (Röm 12,1-2) [... an mehreren amerikanischen und europäischen Universitäten vorgetragen]: ZTK 85 (1988) 199-218.

5995 *Gubler* M.-L., 'Passt euch nicht den Massstäben dieser Welt an!' (Röm 12,2); von der Zivilcourage biblischer Frauen: Diakonia 18 (1987) 305-316 [NTAbs 32,185].

5996 *McKee* Elsie Anne, CALVIN's exegesis of Romans 12:8 — social, accidental, or theological?: CalvinT 23 (1988) 6-18.

5997 *Nürnberger* K., Theses on Romans 13: Scriptura 22 (1987) 40-47 [NTAbs 32,186: legitimizes the overthrow of an illegitimate government, subject to the other criteria of the 'just war' theory].

5998 **Pohle** Lutz, Die Christen und der Staat nach Römer 13, 1984 → 65,5285 ... 3,5832: ᴿTPhil 63 (1988) 261s (P. *Schmitz*).

5999 *Venetz* Hermann-Josef, Zwischen Unterwerfung und Verweigerung; Widersprüchliches im Neuen Testament? Zu Röm 13 und Offb 13: BiKi 43 (1988) 153-163.

6000 *Boyer* S., Exegesis of Romans 13:1-7: Brethren Life and Thought 32 (Oak Brook IL 1987) 208-216 [NTAbs 32,185].

6001 *Draper* Jonathan, 'Humble submission to Almighty God' and its biblical foundation; contextual exegesis of Romans 13:1-7: JTSAf 63 (1988) 30-38 [< ZIT 88,595].

6002 *Shear-Yashuv* Aharon, Römer 13,1-7 und Offenbarung 13 [1966]; ➤ 262, Religion 1987, 91-115.

6003 *Winter* Bruce W., The public honouring of Christian benefactors; Romans 13.3-4 and 1 Peter 2.14-15: JStNT 34 (1988) 87-103.

6004 **Schneider** Nelio, Die Starken und die Schwachen in der römischen Gemeinde – Röm 14-15: Diss. Kirchliche Hochschule Wuppertal 1988s. – TR 85,519.

6005 *a*) *Jewett* Robert, [Rom 15,24; 16,1] Paul. Phoebe, and the Spanish mission; – *b*) *Moxnes* Halvor, Honor, shame, and the outside world in Paul's letter to the Romans: ➤ 77, ᶠKEE H., Social world 1988, 142-161 / 207-218.

6006 *Arichea* Daniel C.ᴶ, Who was Phoebe? Translating *diakonos* in Romans 16.1: BTrans 39 (1988) 401-9.

6007 *Finger* R.H., [Rom 16,1s] Phoebe, role model for leaders: Daughters of Sarah 14,2 (Ch 1988) 5-7 [< NTAbs 32,227].

6008 *Walkenhorst* Karl-Heinz, ❶ [Rom 16,27] The concluding doxology of the Letter to the Romans and its theology: KatKenk 53,1 (1988) 99-132.

G5.1   **Epistulae ad Corinthios** (I vel I-II) – *textus, commentarii.*

6009 **Borchert** Gerald L., [1 Cor, Jn, Heb] Assurance and warning. Nv 1987, Broadman. 214 p. $6 [TDig 35,261].

6010 **Fee** Gordon D., The First Epistle to the Corinthians 1987 ➤ 3,5842: ᴿBTrans 39 (1988) 344s (P. *Ellingworth*: high praise, though 'massive'); CBQ 50 (1988) 715-7 (J. *Plevnik*: 'of slightly evangelical flavor'); EvQ 60 (1988) 363-5 (S.H. *Travis*: superb).

6011 **Heim** Karl [1874-1958], Die Gemeinde des Auferstandenen; Tübinger Vorlesungen über den ersten Korintherbrief, ²*Melzer* F. [¹1949; Vorlesungen 1932]: TVG Mg. & Studienbücher 239. Giessen 1987, Brunnen. viii-264 p. 3-7655-9239-0 [NTAbs 32,251].

6012 **Kilgallen** John, First Corinthians 1986 ➤ 3,5845: ᴿEstBíb 46 (1988) 410s (F. *Pastor-Ramos*); RB 95 (1988) 458s (J. *Murphy-O'Connor*: style limpid, pedagogy careful; exegesis questionable); ScripTPamp 20 (1988) 921s (J. *Chapa*).

6013 **Lang** Friedrich, Die Briefe an die Korinther: NTD 7, 1986 ➤ 2,4661; 3,5846: ᴿÉTRel 63 (1988) 88 (F. *Vouga*); RB 95 (1988) 312 (J. *Murphy-O'Connor*); SvEx 53 (1988) 131-3 (C. *Cavallin*).

6014 ᴱ**O'Kelly** Bernard, *Jarrott* Catherine A.L., John COLET's Commentary on First Corinthians: Latin text, tr. ...: MedRenTSt 21, 1985 ➤ 1,5809: ᴿRHE 83 (1988) 132-7 (G. *Marc'hadour*).

6015 **Pesch** Rudolf, Paulus ringt um die Lebensform der Kirche; vier Briefe [alle = 1Kor] an die Gemeinde Gottes in Korinth: Herderbücherei 1291, 1986 ➤ 2,4666; 3,5848: ᴿColcT 58,1 (1988) 184s (R. *Bartnicki*); RB 95 (1988) 148s (J. *Murphy-O'Connor*); TLZ 113 (1988) 33s (T. *Holtz*).

6016 **Talbert** Charles H., Reading Corinthians; a literary and theological commentary on 1 and 2 Cor 1987 ➤ 3,5851: ᴿCBQ 50 (1988) 733s (Mary Ann *Getty*); ÉTRel 63 (1988) 88s (F. *Vouga*: 'inoffensive self-

praise'); RB 95 (1988) 311s (J. *Murphy-O'Connor*); TS 49 (1988) 157s
(A.C. *Mitchell*).

G5.2   *1 & 1-2 Ad Corinthios   –   themata,* **topics.**

6017 *Adamo* David,   Wisdom and its importance to Paul's Christology in 1
   Corinthians: DeltioVM 17,2 (1988) 31-42; **G** 42s.
6018 *Davis* James A.,   The interaction between individual ethical consciousness and community ethical consciousness in 1 Corinthians: HorBT
   10,2 (1988) 1-18 [51-66, *Stone* Ronald H.].
6019 **Fitzgerald** John T.,   Cracks in an earthen vessel; an examination of the
   catalogues of hardships in the Corinthian correspondence [diss. Yale 1984,
   ᴰ*Malherbe* A.]: SBL diss. 99. Atlanta 1988, Scholars.   vii-289 p. $18.
   1-55540-087-6; pa. 8-4.
6020 *Furnish* Victor P.,   Corinth in Paul's time — what can archaeology tell
   us?: BAR-W 14 [mistakenly XV], 3 (1988) 14-27; ill.
6021 *Genest* Olivette,   L'interprétation de la mort de Jésus en situation
   discursive; un cas-type, l'articulation de figures de cette mort en 1-2
   Corinthiens: NTS 34 (1988) 506-535.
6022 *Gilchrist* J.M.,   Paul and the Corinthians — the sequence of letters and
   visits: JStNT 34 (1988) 47-69.
6022* **Gooch** Paul W.,   Partial knowledge ... in Paul 1987 ➔ 3,5857: ᴿSR 17
   (1988) 491s (Ben F. *Meyer*); TorJT 4 (1988) 305-7 (B.W. *Henaut*).
6023 **Green** Michael,   To Corinth with love. Waco 1988, Word.   189 p.
   [GraceTJ 9,306].
6024 **Hurd** John C.,   The origin of 1 Corinthians 1983 [= 1965 + pref.]
   ➔ 64,5749; 65,5305:   ᴿBR 4,2 (1988) 9-11.44 (B.A. *Pearson,* also on
   Furnish V., 2 Cor.).
6025 **Marshall** Peter,   Enmity in Corinth [diss.]: WUNT 2/23, 1987 ➔ 3,5860:
   ᴿSalmanticensis 35 (1988) 413-5 (R. *Trevijano*).
6026 **Meili** Josef,   The ministry of Paul in the community of Corinth [in] 1
   Cor: diss. Ateneo di Manila. Taiwan 1982, Catholic Mission. xiii-607 p.
   ᴿNZMissW 43 (1987) 148s (F. *Annen*).
6027 **Murphy-O'Connor** Jérôme,   Corinthe au temps de saint Paul [1983] 1986
   ➔ 2,4663; 3,5863:   ᴿBLitEc 89 (1988) 294 (S. *Légasse*); ÉglT 19 (1988)
   261s (N. *Bonneau*); RTLv 19 (1988) 223s (J. *Ponthot*); ScEspr 40 (1988)
   381s (J.-Y. *Thériault*); TLZ 113 (1988) 209s (C. *Wolff*); TR 84 (1988)
   461-3 (G. *Dautzenberg*); TZBas 44 (1988) 80 (R. *Brändle*).
6028 **Schuurman** L.,   De 'zwakheid' van God; bespreking van gedeelten uit de
   eerste brief aan de Corinthiërs voor gebruik in gespreksgroepen.
   Driebergen 1988, N.H. Kerk Centre Educ.   68 p. *f*7 [TsTNijm 28,431].
6029 *Shanor* Jay,   Paul as master builder; construction terms in First
   Corinthians: NTS 34 (1988) 461-471.
6030 *Templeton* Douglas, ⓦ Celtic and Pannonian aspects of interpretation:
   Paul and Corinth, ᵀ*Szücs* Ferenc: Theologiai Szemle 31 (1988) 91-94.
6031 **Tomson** Peter,   Jewish law in First Corinthians: diss. ᴰ*Aschkenasy* Y.
   Amst KU 1988.   346 p. – RTLv 20,543; TsTNijm 29,57.
6032 **Verbrugge** Verlyn D.,   The collection and Paul's leadership in the church
   of Corinth: diss. ᴰ*Collins* Adela Y. ND 1988.   88-16741. – DissA 49
   (1988s) 1833-A; RTLv 20,546; RelStR 15,193.

G5,3   **1 Cor 1-7:** *Sapientia crucis ... abusus matrimonii ...*

6033 *Jacobs* L.D.,   Die makro-gesprekstrategie in 1 Korintiërs 1-4: SkrifKerk 7,2
   (1986) 140-9 [NTAbs 32,186: series of speech acts instead of sharp rebuke].

6034 *Eichler* Johannes, Nicht über das Wort vom Kreuz hinaus (1. Kor 1 und 2): TBei 19 (Wu 1988) 281-6 [< ZIT 89,18].

6035 **Hendrickx** Marie, Sagesse de la parole (1 Co 1,17) selon saint Thomas d'AQUIN; le commentaire de saint Thomas et la 'Grande Glose' de Pierre LOMBARD [diss. LvN, ᴰ*Étienne* J.]: NRT 110 (1988) 336-350 [= Travaux de Doctorat LvN 9/8].

6036 *Marshall-Green* Molly, 1 Corinthians 1:18-31 [God/world wisdom]: RExp 85 (1988) 683-6.

6037 *Cipriani* Settimio, [1 Cor 1,20; 2,5...] 'Sapientia crucis' e sapienza 'umana' in Paolo: → 154, ᶠZEDDA S., RivB 36 (1988) 343-361; Eng. 361.

6038 *Merklein* Helmut, *a)* Die Weisheit Gottes und die Weisheit der Welt (1 Kor 1,21) [< ᶠ*Boeckle* 1986, 391-403]; – *b)* 'Es ist gut für den Menschen, eine Frau nicht anzufassen'; Paulus und die Sexualität nach 1Kor 7 [< ᴱ*Dautzenberg* G., Frau 1983, 225-253]; – *c)* Die Einheitlichkeit des ersten Korintherbriefs [< ZNW 75 (1984) 153-183]; – *d)* Paulinische Theologie in der Rezeption des Kolosser- und Epheserbriefes [< ᴱ*Kertelge* K., Paulusrezeption 1981, 25-69]: → 231, Studien 1987, 376-384 / 384-408 / 345-375 / 409-453.

6039 *Reiling* J., Wisdom and the Spirit; an exegesis of 1 Corinthians 2,6-16: → 85, ᶠKLIJN A., Text 1988, 200-211.

6040 *Shear-Yashuv* Aharon, Exegese von 1. Korinther 2,6-9 [1964]: → 262, Religion 1987, 37-47.

6041 *Haykin* M. G. A., A sense of awe in the presence of the ineffable; 1 Cor. 2.11-12 in the pneumatomachian controversy of the fourth century [< diss. ᴰ*Egan* J.]: ScotJT 41 (1988) 341-357.

6042 **Bidaut** Bernard, Fonction apostolique de la prédication et unité dans la communauté de Corinthe en 1 Co 3: diss. Nº 3510, Pont. Univ. Gregoriana, ᴰ*Vanni* U. Roma 1988. 157 p. – RTLv 20,543.

6043 **Plank** Karl A., [1 Cor 4,9-13] Paul and the irony of affliction [ᴰ1983] 1987 → 3,5887: ᴿAustralBR 36 (1988) 74s (J. *Painter*); CBQ 50 (1988) 726s (Moisés *Silva*); RB 95 (1988) 464s (J. *Murphy-O'Connor*).

6044 *Zaas* Peter S., Catalogues and context; 1 Corinthians 5 and 6: NTS 34 (1988) 622-9.

6045 *Joy* N. George, Is the body really to be destroyed? (1 Corinthians 5.5): BTrans 39 (1988) 429-436.

6046 *West* A., Sex and salvation; a Christian feminist study of 1 Corinthians 6.12-7.39: ModChm 29,3 (1986s) 17-24 [NTAbs 32,187].

6047 **Plunkett** Mark A., Sexual ethics and the Christian life; a study of I Corinthians 6:12-7:7: diss. Princeton Sem. 1988. 88-18493. – DissA 49 (1988s) 2260-A; RelStR 15,193.

6048 *Orge* Manuel, El propósito temático de 1 Corintios 7; un discernimiento sobre la puesta en prática del ideal de la continencia sexual y del celibato Claretianum 27 (1987) 5-125; 28 (1988) 5-114...

6049 **Wimbush** Vincent L., Paul, the worldly ascetic ... 1 Cor 7 [ᴰ1983] 1987 → 3,5894: ᴿCBQ 50 (1988) 549s (Carolyn *Osiek*); TS 49 (1988) 575 (A. C. *Mitchell*).

6050 *Ward* Roy B., [1 Cor 7,8...] Paul; how he radically redefined marriage: BR 4,4 (1988) 26-31.

6051 *Baasland* Ernst, [1 Cor 7,25 + 10-mal] Die *perí*-Formel und die Argumentation(ssituation) des Paulus: ST 42 (1988) 69-87.

6052 *Botman* Russell, *Smit* Dirkie, 1 Corinthians 7:29-31, 'To live ... as if it were not!': JTSAf 65 (1988) 73 ... [< ZIT 89,153].

6053 *Gramaglia* P. A.,   Le fonti del linguaggio paolino in 1 Cor. 7,35 e 7,1: AugR 28 (1988) 461-502.
6054 *Marrow* Stanley B., [1 Cor 7,39 ...] Marriage and divorce in the New Testament: AnglTR 70 (1988) 3-15.

G5.4   *Idolothyta ... Eucharistia:*   **1 Cor 8-11.**

6055 **Gooch** Peter,   Food and the limits of community; 1 Corinthians 8:1 to 11:1: diss. Toronto 1988, ᴰ*Richardson* G. – DissA 49 (1988s) 2691-A; RelStR 15,193.
6056 **Rainbow** P. A.,   Monotheism and Christology in 1 Corinthians 8:4-6: diss. Oxford 1988. – RTLv 20,545.
6057 **Martin** Dale R.,   Slave of Christ, slave of all; Paul's metaphor of slavery and 1 Corinthians 9: diss. Yale. NHv 1988. 90-09412. – DissA 50 (1989s) 3026-A; RelStR 15,193; RTLv 20,545.
6058 *a) Nasuti* Harry P.,   The woes of the prophets and the rights of the Apostle; the internal dynamics of 1 Corinthians 9; – *b) Murphy-O'Connor* Jerome, 1 Corinthians 11:2-16 once agains [*Delobel* J. 1986]:   CBQ 50 (1988) 246-264 / 265-274.
6059 *Álvarez-Verdes* L., [1 Cor 9,19-23]: → 21, ꜰCAPONE D., Coscienza 1987, ...
6060 *Badke* William B., [1 Cor 10,2] Baptised into Moses — baptised into Christ; a study in doctrinal development: EvQ 60 (1988) 23-29.
6061 *Dąbek Tomasz M.,* ❷ Eucharistia ut esca spiritalis in 1 Cor 10,3: RuBi 41 (1988) 465-470.
6062 *Pérez Gordo* Ángel,   ¿Es el velo en 1 Co 11,2-16 símbolo de libertad o de sumisión?:   Burgense 29 (1988) 337-366.
6063 *Thompson* Cynthia L., [1 Cor 11,2-16] Hairstyles, head-coverings and St. Paul; portraits from Roman Corinth: BA 51 (1988) 99-115; ill.
6064 *Sandt* Huub van de,   1 Kor. 11,2-16 als een retorische eenheid: Bijdragen 49 (1988) 410-424; Eng. 425 'as a rhetorical unit[y?]'.
6065 **Oster** Richard,   When men wore veils to worship; the historical context of 1 Corinthians 11.4:   NTS 34 (1988) 481-505.
6066 *Visotzky* B. L. [1 Cor 11,3-12] Trinitarian testimonies: UnSemQ 42,1s (1988) 73-85 [< NTAbs 32,328].
6068 **Schari** Kurt,   Das theologische Problem der Tradition; eine Untersuchung zum Traditionsproblem mit Hilfe linguistischer Kriterien anhand der Abendmahlsperikope 1 Kor 11,17-34: ev. Diss. Bern, ᴰ*Wegenast.* – TR 85,513.
6069 *Hofius* Otfried,   Herrenmahl und Herrenmahlsparadosis; Erwägungen zu 1 Kor 11,23b-25:   ZTK 85 (1988) 371-408.
6070 *Bogunyowski* Józef, [1 Cor 11,20; 14,23] '*Epì tò autó*', die älteste christliche Bezeichnung des liturgischen Raumes: EphLtg 102 (1988) 446-455.

G5.5   **1 Cor 12 ... Glossolalia, charismata.**

6071 *Baumert* Norbert,   Zur Semantik von *chárisma* bei den frühen Vätern: TPhil 63 (1988) 60-78.
6072 **Birnstein** Uwe,   Neuer Geist in alter Kirche? Die charismatische Bewegung in der Offensive 1987 → 3,5915: ꞎTLZ 113 (1988) 384 (D. Mendt).
6073 *a) Bundy* David,   L'émergence d'un théologien pentecôtisant; les écrits de Louis DALLIÈRE de 1922 à 1932; – *b) Carrel* Serge,   Essai sur le corps à

partir du vécu de la mouvance pentecôtiste: Hokhma 38 (1988) 23-51 / 37 (1988) 50-63; 38 (1988) 52-82.

6074 **Burgess** Stanley M., The Spirit and the Church; Antiquity, 1984 ➤ 1,5847: ᴿSecC 6,1 (1987s) 60s (Rebecca H. *Weaver*).

6075 *Bussmann* Magdalene, 'Man muss Gott mehr gehorchen als den Menschen!' Der Konflikt um Amt und Charisma in der mittelalterlichen Kirche: Diakonia 19 (1988) 245-250.

6076 **Carson** D. A., Showing the Spirit; a theological exposition of 1 Corinthians 12-14 [1985 Sydney Moore College lectures] 1987 ➤ 3,5921: ᴿAndrUnS 26 (1988) 184-6 (W. E. *Richardson*); RExp 85 (1988) 726s (S. *Sheeley*).

6077 **Dayton** Donald W., Theological roots of Pentecostalism 1987 ➤ 3,5923; 0-310-39371-X: ᴿAsbTJ 43,2 (1988) 141-4 (M. E. *Dieter*).

6078 *Edgar* Thomas R., The cessation of the sign gifts: Bibliotheca Sacra 145 (1988) 371-386.

6079 **Foster** Kenneth N., Discernment, the powers and spirit-speaking: diss. Fuller Theol. Sem., ᴰ*Gilliland* D. Pasadena 1988. 271 p. 88-18724. – DissA 49 (1988s) 1848s-A.

6080 *a*) *Gallego* Epifanio, La misión profética de Jesús, reto a una sociedad con ansias de ser feliz; – *b*) *Folgado Flórez* Segundo, La misión profética, hoy; hacia una eclesiología encarnada en el hombre; – *c*) *Keller* Miguel Ángel, Profetismo y proyecto evangelizadora; el carisma profético en la sociedad contemporanea; – *d*) *Salas* Antonio, Denuncia profética y praxis de liberación: BibFe 14,41 ('Profetismo y sociedad' 1988) 208-231 / 232-259 / 260-287 / 288-317.

6081 **Gerosa** Libero, Charisma und Recht; Kirchenrechtliche Überlegungen zum Urcharisma der Vereinigungsformen in der Kirche: kath. Diss. Eichstätt, ᴰ*Krämer*. – TR 85,511.

6082 **Grudem** Wayne, The gift of prophecy in the New Testament and today. Eastbourne, E. Sussex 1988, Kingsway. 315 p. £8. 0-86065-508-3.

6083 *Harper* George W., Renewal and causality; some thoughts on a conceptual framework for a charismatic theology: JEcuSt 24 (1987) 93-103.

6084 **Hemphill** Kenneth S., Spiritual gifts empowering the New Testament Church. Nv 1988, Broadman. 212 p. (audiocassette form also available) [JBL 107,788].

6085 ᴱ**Hinnebusch** Paul, Contemplation and the charismatic renewal 1986 ➤ 2,443; 3,5929: ᴿSpTod 40 (1988) 89s (Amata *Fabbro*).

6086 *Huarte* Juan, Reflexiones bíblicas en torno a una práctica teológica ➤ 3,8554 [... práctica social de inspiración bíblica ... Iglesia más evangélica]: CiTom 114 (1987) 477-501.

6087 **Lambourne** R. A., Community, Church and healing [1963]. L 1987, James. 181 p. £4 pa. – ᴿRefTR 47 (1988) 64 (M. *Hill*).

6088 **Lewis** I. M., Religion in context; cults and charisma 1986 ➤ 2,4719: ᴿRHR 205 (1988) 195-7 (J.-P. *Roux*: trop court).

6089 *Lohfink* Norbert, *a*) Wo sind heute die Propheten?:   StiZt 206 (1988) 183-192; – *b*) Waar zijn er vandaag nog profeten?   Streven 55 (1987s) 771-780.

6090 **Malony** H. Newton, *Lovekin* A. Adams, Glossolalia; behavioral science perspectives on speaking in tongues 1985 ➤ 2,4720; 3,5937: ᴿJScStR 26 (1987) 267s (Margaret M. *Paloma*).

6091 ᴱ**Martin** David, *Mullen* Peter, Strange gifts? 1984 ➤ 1,378; 2,4722: ᴿHeythJ 29 (1988) 273 (F. A. *Sullivan*).

6092 ᴱ**Mills** Watson E.,   Speaking in tongues 1986 ➤ 2,683; 3,5940:   ᴿJTS 39 (1988) 658-661 (J. D. G. *Dunn*); ScotBEv 6 (1988) 48s (M. *Turner*).

6093 **Neitz** Mary Jo,   Charisma and community; a study of religious commitment within the charismatic renewal. New Brunswick NJ 1987, Transaction. xii-294 p. $35 [TDig 36,72].

6094 *Perrot* Charles, Les charismes de l'Esprit dans les Églises pauliniennes: Christus 33 (P 1986) 281-293 [> SelT 27 (1988) 309-316, ᵀᴱ*Ribas* Manuel].

6095 *a) Reimer* H.-D.,   Die charismatische Bewegung; – *b) Hale* J. R.,   Die Zähmung der Charismatiker: Pastoraltheologie 77 (Gö 1988) 509-517 [< ZIT 89,123].

6096 *Robeck* C. M.ᴶ,   Tongues, gift of: ➤ 801, ISBEnc³ 4 (1988) 871-4.

6097 *Sarles* Ken L.,   An appraisal of the Signs and Wonders movement [believe that gifts of the Spirit have not ceased, but do not wish to be called charismatic]: BS 145 (1988) 57-82.

6098 **Secondin** Bruno,   Segni di profezia nella Chiesa; comunità gruppi movimenti: Teol. Spir. 3, 1987 ➤ 3,5953:   ᴿETL 64 (1988) 210s (A. de *Halleux*); RivScR 2 (1988) 179-185 (E. *Juliá*); Salesianum 50 (1988) 608s (A. *Favale*).

6099 **Sullivan** Francis A.,   Charismes et renouveau charismatique, une étude biblique et théologique [1982 ➤ 63,5942], préf. *Suenens* Léon-J.,ᵀ: Chemin neuf, Pneumathèque. P 1988, Desclée de Brouwer. 284 p. F 50. – ᴿÉtudes 369 (1988) 282s (J. *Thomas*); Spiritus 29 (1988) 442 (H. *Frévin*).

6100 *Sullivan* Francis A.,   La conversion, une 'expérience charismatique', ᵀ*Henry* Colette: Tychique 76 (1988) 41-43.

6101 **Talbot** John M.,   The fire of God. NY 1986, Crossroad. 158 p. $8. – ᴿRExp 85 (1988) 163s (E. G. *Hinson*).

6102 *Vanhoye* Albert,   The biblical question of 'charisms' after Vatican II: ➤ 380, Vatican II Assessment 1 (1988) 439-467, ᵀ*Wearne* L.; français ➤ 379, Bilan 1,441-467.

6103 **Wimber** John, *Springer* Kevin,   Power healing [... a normal part of the Christian life: Vineyard Christian Fellowship]. SF 1987, Harper & R. 293 p. $15. – ᴿBS 145 (1988) 102-4 (R. B. *Zuck*); Missiology 16 (1988) 106s (R. K. *Smith* gives title as 'Power evangelism').

6104 *Güting* Eberhard, [1Kor 12,2-3.6-13; 14,20-29] Neuedition der Pergamentfragment London Brit. Libr. Pap. 2240 aus dem Wasi Sarga mit neutestamentlichem Text [*Crum* W., *Bell* H. 1922]: ZPapEp 75 (1988) 97-114.

6105 *Brunner-Traut* Emma, [1 Kor. 12,12] Der menschliche Körper — eine Gliederpuppe: ZägSpr 115 (1988) 8-14.

6106 *Louw* Johannes P.,   The function of discourse in a sociosemiotic theory of translation, illustrated by the translation of *zēloûte* in 1 Corinthians 12.31: BTrans 39 (1988) 329-335.

6107 *Rebell* Walter,   Gemeinde als Missionsfaktor im Urchristentum; 1 Kor 14,24f. als Schlüsselsituation: TZBas 44 (1988) 117-134.

6108 *Munro* Winsome,   Women, text and the canon; the strange case of 1 Corinthians 14:33-35: BibTB 18 (1988) 26-31.

6109 **Hauke** Manfred, [1 Cor 14,33-40] Women in the priesthood? A systematic analysis in the light of the order of creation and redemption [< Diss. ᴰ*Scheffczyk* L., called by BALTHASAR 'the definitive work available'], ᵀ*Kipp* David. SF 1988, Ignatius. 498 p. $20 [TS 50,813-5, D. *Donovan*].

6110 *Allison* Robert W.,   Let women be silent in the churches (1 Cor. 14.33b-36); what did Paul really say, and what did it mean?:   JStNT 32 (1988) 27-60.

6111 *Flood* Edmund, [1 Cor 14,35] Was Paul a male chauvinist? [no, because he held racial equality]: Tablet 242 (1988) 84 only.

G5.6   **Resurrectio;** *1 Cor 15 ...*

6112 **Barth** Karl, La resurrezione dei morti [lezioni universitarie su 1 Cor 15, Gö 1923], ᵀᴱ*Gallas* A.: Dabar 7.   Casale Monferrato 1984, Marietti. XXVI-144 p. − ᴿStPatav 35 (1988) 221s (A. *Moda*).

6113 ᴱ**De Lorenzi** Lorenzo, Résurrection du Christ et des chrétiens (1 Co 15) 1983/5 ➤ 1,466 ... 3,5973:   ᴿClaretianum 27 (1987) 376-8 (B. *Proietti*).

6114 **Sellin** Gerhard,   Der Streit um die Auferstehung der Toten; eine religionsgeschichtliche und exegetische Untersuchung von 1 Kor 15: FRLANT 138, 1986 ➤ 3,5975:   ᴿActuBbg 25 (1988) 74s (X. *Alegre S.*); Protestantesimo 43 (1988) 220s (U. *Eckert*); TLZ 113 (1988) 352-4 (C. *Wolff*).

6115 **De Boer** Martinus C.,   The defeat of death; apocalyptic eschatology in 1 Corinthians 15 and Romans 5: JStNT Sup 22.   Sheffield 1988, Academic. 278 p. £25.   1-85075-089-0.

6116 *a) Metzger* Bruce M.,   Ein Vorschlag zur Bedeutung von 1 Kor 15,4b [< JTS 8 (1957) 118-123, ᵀ*Zwosta* F.]; − *b) Wilckens* Ulrich,   Der Ursprung der Überlieferung der Erscheinungen des Auferstandenen; zur traditionsgeschichtlichen Analyse von 1. Kor. 15,1-11 [< ᶠ*Schlink* E. 1963, 56-95]; − *c) McArthur* Harvey K.,   'Am dritten Tag', I Kor 15,4b und die rabbinische Interpretation von Hosea 6,2 [< NTS 18 (1971s) 81-86, ᵀ*Zwosta*]; − *d) Harnack* Adolf von,   Die Verklärungsgeschichte Jesu, der Bericht des Paulus (1. Kor. 15, 3ff.) und die beiden Christusvisionen des Petrus [< Szb B 1922, 62-80 = KᴸS 1980, 600-618]: ➤ 311, ᴱ*Hoffmann* P., WegF 522 (1988) 126-132 / 139-193 / 194-202 / 89-117.

6117 *Plevnik* Joseph,   Paul's appeals to his Damascus experience and 1 Cor. 15:5-7 [9,1; Gal 1,11s]; are they legitimations?:   TorJT 4 (1988) 101-111.

6118 *Jones* Peter,   Paul le dernier apôtre; 1 Corinthiens 15,8 [< TyndB 36 (1985)], ᵀ*Nzinga* Dika, *al.*: Hokhma 33 (1986) 36-62.

6119 *Hill* C. E.,   Paul's understanding of Christ's kingdom in 1 Corinthians 15:20-28:   NT 30 (1988) 297-320.

6120 *Gillman* John,   A thematic comparison; 1 Cor 15:50-57 and 2 Cor 5:1-5: JBL 107 (1988) 439-454.

6121 *Moor* Johannes C. De, [1 Cor 15,55] 'O death, where is thy sting?': ➤ 29, Mem. CRAIGIE P., Ascribe 1988, 99-107.

G5.9   **Secunda epistula ad Corinthios.**

6122 **Aejmelaeus** Lars,   Streit und Versöhnung; das Problem der Zusammensetzung des 2. Korintherbriefes [Riidan ja sovun dokumentti 1983], ᵀ*Trabant* K.-J.: Schriften 46, 1987 ➤ 3,5985; 951-9217-01-9;   ᴿRB 95 (1988) 459s (J. *Murphy-O'Connor*).

6123 **Best** Ernest,   Second Corinthians: Interpretation Comm.   Atlanta 1987, Knox.   x-142 p. 0-8042-3135-4. − ᴿRB 95 (1988) 459 (J. *Murphy-O'Connor*).

6124 **Carrez** Maurice,   La deuxième épître de saint Paul aux Corinthiens: CommNT NS 8, 1986 ➤ 3,5988:   ᴿBiblica 69 (1988) 444s (R. *Penna*); BZ

32 (1988) 153s (H.-J. *Klauck*); CBQ 50 (1988) 525s (J. *Plevnik*: recommended despite weaknesses); CiTom 115 (1988) 575 (J. *Huarte*); ÉglT 19 (1988) 259-261 (M. *Dumais*); JTS 39 (1988) 206s (Margaret E. *Thrall*); NRT 110 (1988) 923-5 (X. *Jacques*); Protestantesimo 43 (1988) 48s (F. *Ferrario*); RB 95 (1988) 313 (J. *Murphy-O'Connor*); RICathP 25 (1988) 75-78 (C. *Tassin*).

6125 **Furnish** Victor P.,   II Corinthians: AnchorB 32A, 1984 → 65,5416 ... 3,5991:   RGregorianum 69 (1988) 186s (E. *Farahian*); HeythJ 29 (1988) 351s (F. F. *Bruce*); IsrEJ 38 (1988) 99s (G. *Stroumsa*); ScotJT 41 (1988) 549-553 (Frances *Young*, D. *Ford*).

6126 **Georgi** Dieter,   The opponents of Paul in Second Corinthians [1964 revised + 120-p. epilogue] T, 1986 →2,4763; 3,5992:   RAnglTR 70 (1988) 101-3 (R. L. *Pervo*); CBQ 50 (1988) 317-9 (T. H. *Tobin*: very important); RB 95 (1988) 151 (J. *Murphy-O'Connor*).

6127 **Klauck** H.-J.   2 Korintherbrief 1986 → 2,4763*:   RRB 95 (1988) 150s (J. *Murphy-O'Connor*).

6128 **Kruse** Colin, 2 Corinthians: Tyndale NT Comm. 1987 → 3,5993:   RRefTR 47 (1988) 56s (P. *Barnett*: worthy successor to TASKER R.).

6129 **Maillot** Alphonse,   (*Olombel* A.),   Deuxième épître de Paul aux Corinthiens ou l'Église sous la croix 1985 → 2,4765;   2-85-369-050-4: RÉTRel 63 (1988) 468 (E. *Cuvillier*).

6130 **Martin** Ralph P.,   2 Corinthians: Word 40, 1986 → 2,4767; 3,5994: RGraceTJ 9 (1988) 292s (D. C. *Baker*); JBL 107 (1988) 550-3 (F. W. *Danker*); RB 95 (1988) 149s (J. *Murphy-O'Connor*); RefTR 46 (1987) 54s (J. G. *Mason*).

6131 **Pesch** Rudolf,   Paulus kämpft um sein Apostolat; drei weitere Briefe [= 2 Kor] an die Gemeinde Gottes in Korinth, Paulus neu gesehen: Herderbücherei 1382, 1987:   → 3,5996:   RColcT 58,4 (1988) 161s (R. *Bartnicki*); TPhil 63 (1988) 594-6 (A. *Brendle,* auch über 'Paulus ringt', 1Kor).

6132 *Segalla* Giuseppe,   Coerenza linguistica e unita letteraria della 2 Corinzi: TIt Sett 13 (1988) 149-166. 189-219; Eng. 166.219.

6133 **Young** Frances, *Ford* David F.   Meaning and truth in 2 Corinthians 1987 → 3,5999:   RTLond 91 (1988) 530-2 (C. J. A. *Hickling*).

6134 *Kruse* Colin G.,   The offender and the offence in 2 Corinthians 2:5 and 7:12:   EvQ 60 (1988) 129-139.

6135 **Duff** Paul B.,   Honor or shame; the language of processions and perception in 2 Cor 2,14-6,13; 7,2-4: diss. Divinity School. Ch 1988. – OIAc D88.

6136 Ede **Lorenzi** Lorenzo,   Paolo, ministro del NT (2 Cor 2,14-4,6) 1985/7 → 3,538:   RClaretianum 28 (1988) 370-2 (B. *Proietti*); DivThom 89s (1986s) 410-4 (G. *Testa*); Gregorianum 69 (1988) 558 (J. *Galot*); NRT 110 (1988) 608 (X. *Jacques*); RTLv 19 (1988) 225s (J. *Dupont*).

6137 **Oliveira** Anacleto de,   Die Diakonie der Gerechtigkeit und der Versöhnung in der Apologie des 2. Korintherbriefes; Analyse und Auslegung von 2 Kor 2,14-4,6; 5,11-6,10: Diss. DKertelge K.   Münster 1987s. – TR 84 (1988) 512.

6138 **Hafemann** S.,   Suffering and the Spirit, 2 Cor 2,14-3,3 WUNT 2/19, 1986 → 2,4775; 3,6008:   RCBQ 50 (1988) 137s (Carolyn A. *Osiek,* new CBQ NT book review editor); JBL 107 (1988) 553-5 (D. A. *Black*); RB 95 (1988) 152s (J. *Murphy-O'Connor*).

6139 *Pikaza* Xabier, Culto a la forma; libertad realizante 'versus' coacción esclavizante (2 Cor 3): BibFe 14 (1988) 341-374.

6140 *a*) *Cook* Michael J. The ties that blind; an exposition of II Corinthians 3:12 – 4:6 and Romans 11:7-10; – *b*) *Buchanan* George W., [*ibid* (2 Cor 3:4...)] Paul and the Jews: ➔ 625, When Jews 1986/8, 125-139 / 141-162.

6141 **Pate** Charles M., Adam Christology as the exegetical and theological substructure of II Corinthians 4:7-5:21: diss. Marquette. Milwaukee 1988. 90 p. 89-04278. – DissA 49 (1988s) 3765-A.

6142 *Carrez* Maurice, [2 Cor 4,10s] Que représente la vie de Jésus pour l'apôtre Paul?: RHPR 68 (1988) 155-161.

6143 *Murphy-O'Connor* Jerome, *a*) Faith and resurrection in 2 Cor 4: 13-14: RB 95 (1988) 543-550; – *b*) PHILO and 2 Cor 6:14-7:1: RB 95 (1988) 55-69; franç. 55; – *c*) Pneumatikoi in 2 Corinthians: PrIrB 11 (1988) 59-66.

6144 *Craig* W. L., Paul's dilemma in 2 Corinthians 5.1-10: a 'Catch-22'? [i.e. a subordinate comment making inapplicable what precedes]: NTS 34 (1988) 145-7.

6145 *Yates* J., [2 Cor 5,1-10] Immediate or intermediate? The state of the believer upon death: Churchman 101 (1987) 310-322 [NTAbs 32,188].

6147 *Jezierska* sr. Ewa Józefa, ❷ De praeexsistentia biblica christiana secundum 2 Cor 5,15: ➔ 475, RuBi 41 (1988) 40-43.

6148 *Fatula* Mary Ann, [2 Cor 5,18] The ministry of reconciliation: SpTod 40 (1988) 157-164.

6149 **Betz** H. D., 2 Corinthians 8 and 9: 1985 ➔ 1,5922; 3,6023: ᴿÉTRel 63 (1988) 86s (F. *Vouga*); RB 95 (1988) 456-8 (J. *Murphy-O'Connor*: based on entirely mistaken assumptions).

6150 *Schoenborn* Ulrich, La inversión de la gracia; apuntes sobre 2 Corintios 8,9: RBíbArg 30s (1988) 207-218.

6151 *Iori* Renato, Uso e significato di *isótēs* in 2 Cor 8,13-14: [➔ 154, ᶠZEDDA S.] RivB 36 (1988) 425-437; Eng. 438.

6152 **Wong Ho-Yee** Kasper, Boasting and foolishness; a study of 2 Cor 10,12-18 and 11,1a: diss. ᴰ*Lambrecht* J., Leuven 1988. xxxviii-255 p. – LvSt 13 (1988) 372s; RTLv 20,547.

6153 *Marguerat* Daniel, 2 Corinthiens 10-13; Paul et l'expérience de Dieu: ÉTRel 63 (1988) 407-519.

6154 *Sampley* J. Paul, Paul, his opponents in 2 Corinthians 10-13, and the rhetorical handbooks: ➔ 77, ᶠKEE H., Social world 1988, 162-177.

6155 **Spencer** Aida B., Paul's literary style ... 2 Cor 11:16-12:13, Rom 8:9-39; Phlp 3:2-4:13: 1984 ➔ 65,5433 ... 2,4790. – ᴿThemelios 14 (1988s) 31 (P. *Trebilco*).

6156 *Müller* K., [2 Kor 11,32] Aretas: ➔ 804, NBL Lfg 1 (1988) 165-7.

6157 *Young* Brad H., The Ascension motif of 2 Corinthians 12 in Jewish, Christian and Gnostic texts: GraceTJ 9 (1988) 73-103.

6158 **Tabor** James D., [2 Cor 12,2-4] Things unutterable; Paul's ascent to Paradise ... [< diss. Chicago 1981, ᴰ*Smith* J. Z.] 1986 ➔ 2,4791; 3,6029: ᴿCBQ 50 (1988) 149s (T. M. *Finn*: clear, refreshing); JBL 107 (1988) 555-8 (V. P. *Furnish*).

6159 *Dwyer* M. E., [2 Cor 12,2] An unstudied redaction of the Visio Pauli: Manuscripta 32 (1988) 121-138.

6160 *McCant* Jerry W., [2 Cor 12,7] Paul's thorn of rejected apostleship: NTS 34 (1988) 550-572.

6161 *Pathrapankal* J. M., 'When 1 am weak, then 1 am strong' (2 Cor 12:10); Pauline understanding of apostolic sufferings: Jeevadhara 13 (1988) 140-151.

6162 **North** R., [not this Elenchus editor; – ? 2 Cor 12,11] Fools for God. L c1988, Collins. £11 [TLond 91,165].

6163 *Di Marco* Angelino-S., *Koinōnía pneúmatos* (2 Cor 13,13; Flp 2,1) — *pneûma koinōnías*; circolarità e ambivalenza linguistica e filologica: FgNt 1,1 (1988) 63-73; Eng. 73-75.

G6.1 Ad Galatas.

6164 **Allaz** J., *Bovon* F., *al.*, Chrétiens en conflit; l'Épître de Paul aux Galates [séminaire de Suisse romande]: Essais Bibliques 13, 1987 ➤ 3,6030: RRTPhil 120 (1988) 98s (Aline *Lasserre*).

6165 **Barclay** John M.G., Obeying the truth; a study of Paul's ethics in Galatians [diss. C 1986]: StNT&W [ERiches J.]. E 1988, Clark. xv-298 p. £17. 0-567-09493-6.

6166 **Betz** H.D., Der Galaterbrief, ein Kommentar zum Brief des Apostels Paulus an die Gemeinde in Galatien [1979 Hermeneia ➤ 60,8047], TAnn Sibylle. Mü 1988, Kaiser. vi-596 p. DM 198. 3-459-01705-8. – RArT-Gran 51 (1988) 284s (A. *Segovia*); BiKi 43 (1988) 178s (P.-G. *Müller*).

6167 **Brandenburg** Hans, Der Brief des Paulus an die Galater: Studienbibel NT. Wu 1986 = 1961, Brockhaus. 148 p. 3-417-25110-9; pa. 010-2.

6168 **Buscemi** Alfio M., L'uso delle preposizioni nella Lettera ai Galati: SBF Anal 17, 1987 ➤ 3,6033: RCBQ 50 (1988) 712s (J.J. O'*Rourke*); CiuD 201 (1988) 490s (J. *Gutiérrez*); [TüTQ 168,346 'Mauscemi'].

6169 *Buscemi* A.M., I casi nella lettera ai Galati: SBFLA 38 (1988) 135-171.

6170 **Cosgrove** Charles H., The Cross and the Spirit; a study in the argument and theology of Galatians. Macon GA 1988, Mercer Univ. xv-216 p. [JBL 108,566]. 0-86554-347-1.

6171 *a) Dunn* James D.B., The theology of Galatians; – *b) Gaventa* Beverly R., The singularity of the Gospel; a reading of Galatians: ➤ 500, SBL Sem. 1988, 1-16 / 17-26.

6172 **Ebeling** Gerhard, Die Wahrheit des Evangeliums; eine Lesehilfe zum Galaterbrief 1981 ➤ 62,6629 ... 65,5444: RIstina 33 (1987) 320-2 (B. *Dupuy*).

6173 **Fung** Ronald Y.K., The Epistle to the Galatians: NICNT. GR 1988, Eerdmans. xxxiii-342 p. £17.25. 0-8028-2175-X.

6174 **Herman** Zvonimir I., Liberi in Cristo ... Galati: Spicilegium Antonianum 27, 1986 ➤ 2,4803 ... 3,6042: RCBQ 50 (1988) 322-4 (S.B. *Marrow*: amounts to a commentary, even theological); Salesianum 50 (1988) 422s (J. *Heriban*).

6174* **Heyer** C.J. den, Galaten: Tekst en toelichting. Kampen 1987, Kok. 145 p. ƒ22,50. – RStreven 55 (1987s) 754s (P. *Beentjes*).

6175 **Jegher-Bucher** Verena, Der Galaterbrief auf dem Hintergrund antiker Epistolographie und Rhetorik: Diss. Basel 1988s, DStegemann. – TR 85,513.

6176 **Krentz** Edgar, Galatians [... *al.* ➤ 6226] 1985 ➤ 3,6045: RCurrTM 15 (1988) 457s (R.H. *Smith*).

6177 *Lührmann* Dieter, Galaterbrief: ➤ 798, EvKL 2 (Lfg. 4, 1988) 4s.

6178 *Martyn* J. Louis, A law-observant mission to Gentiles; the background of Galatians: ➤ 3,356, EO'Connor M., Backgrounds 1987, 199-214 [< JBL 108,174].

6179 **Mussner** F., La lettera ai Galati 1987 ➤ 3,6047: RComSev 21 (1988) 258 (M. de *Burgos*); StPatav 35 (1988) 710-2 (G. *Leonardi*).

6180 *Pastor-Ramos* Federico, La Cristología de Galatas; síntesis y observaciones: EstBíb 46 (1988) 315-324; Eng. 315.

6181 *Refoulé* François, Date de l'Épître aux Galates [juillet-août 56]: RB 95 (1988) 161-183; Eng. 161.

6182 *Vouga* François, Zur rhetorischen Gattung des Galaterbriefs: ZNW 79 (1988) 291s.

6183 *William* Sam K., [*epangelía*] Promise in Galatians; a reading of Paul's reading of Scripture: JBL 107 (1988) 709-720.

6184 *Omanson* Roger L., [Gal 1s, Acts 15] A Gentile palaver: → 502, Issues/Translation 1987/8, 274-286.

6185 *Baarda* T., MARCION's text of Gal 1:1; concerning the reconstruction of the first verse of the Marcionite Corpus Paulinum: VigChr 42 (1988) 236-256.

6186 *Lategan* Bernard, Is Paul defending his apostleship in Galatians? The function of Galatians 1.11-12 and 2.19-20 in the development of Paul's argument: NTS 34 (1988) 411-430.

6187 *Borgen* Peder, [Gal 2,1-10] Catalogues of vices, the Apostolic Decree, and the Jerusalem meeting: → 77, FKEE H., Social world 1988, 126-141.

6188 **Bartolomé** Juan J., El evangelio y su verdad; la justificación por fe y su vivencia en común; un estudio exegético de Gal 2,5.14 [diss. Pont. Ist. Biblico, Roma, magna cum laude: AcPIB 9,5 (1988s) 383; no como 9,2 (1985s) 115]: BiblScRel 82. R 1988, LAS. 170 p. Lit. 20.000. 88-213-0170-2. – [NatGrac 36,378, F. F. *Ramos*].

6189 *Dietzfelbinger* Hermann, Der 'erste und Hauptartikel'; Bibelarbeit über Galater 2,11-21: → 179, Überfluss 1984, 31-49.

6190 *Kieffer* René [Gal 2,14-21] Foi et justification à Antioche ...: LDiv 111, 1982 → 63,6013 ... 1,5963: RSvEx 53 (1988) 134 (T. *Fornberg*).

6191 **Farahian** Edmond, Le 'je' paulinien; étude pour mieux comprendre Gal. 2,19-21: AnGreg 253. R 1988, Pont. Univ. Gregoriana. 305 p. Lit. 47.000. 88-7652-591-2.

6192 *Neyrey* Jerome H., [Gal 3,1] Bewitched in Galatia; Paul and cultural anthropology: CBQ 50 (1988) 73-100.

6193 *Johnson* H. Wayne, The paradigm of Abraham in Galatians 3:6-9: TrinJ 8 (1987) 179-199.

6194 **Buckel** John, 'The curse of the law'; an exegetical investigation of Galatians 3,10-14: diss. Leuven 1988, DLambrecht J. lxxxv-389 p. – RTLv 20,543.

6195 *Alszeghy* Zoltán, ◑ Christ has redeemed us (Gal 3:13): KatKenk 27,54 (1988) 125-139 = 311-325; Eng. xviii-xx.

6196 *Cosgrove* Charles H., Arguing like a mere human being; Galatians 3.15-18 in rhetorical perspective: NTS 34 (1988) 536-549.

6197 *Lührmann* Dieter, Die 430 Jahre zwischen den Verheissungen und dem Gesetz (Gal 3,17): ZAW 100 (1988) 420-3.

6198 *Hanson* A. T., [Gal 3,24] The origin of Paul's use of *paidagōgós* for the Law: JStNT 34 (1988) 71-76.

6199 **MacDonald** Dennis R., [Gal 3,28; 1 Cor 11,2] There is no male and female; the fate of a dominical saying in Paul and Gnosticism [diss. Harvard 1978, DMacRae G.] → 2,4818; HarvDissRel 20. Ph 1987, Fortress. xxiii-132 p. 0-8006-7076-0. – RAnglTR 70 (1988) 267-270 (S. M. *Pogoloff*); Interpretation 42 (1988) 322 (R. F. *Hock*).

6200 *Helminiak* Daniel A., [Gal 3,28] Human solidarity and collective union in Christ: AnglTR 70 (1988) 34-59.

6200* *Schweizer* Eduard, Slaves of the elements and worshipers of Angels; Gal 4:3,9 and Col 2:8,18,20: JBL 107 (1988) 455-468.

6201 *Aletti* Jean-Noël, Une lecture de Ga 4,4-6; Marie et la plénitude du temps: Marianum 50 (1988) 408-421.

6202 *Drijvers* J.W., MARCION's reading of Gal 4,8; philosophical background and influence of Manichaeism: → 6, ᶠASMUSSEN J. 1988, 339-348.

6202* *Jewett* Paul K., [Gal 4,21-31] Children of grace: TTod 44 (1987s) 170-8.

6203 *Matera* Frank J., The culmination of Paul's argument to the Galatians: Gal. 5.1-6.17: JStNT 32 (1988) 79-91.

G6.2 Ad Ephesios.

6204 **Comblin** José, Epístola aos Efésios: Comentário bíblico NT. Petrópolis 1987, Vozes / Metodista / Sinodal. 111 p.

6205 **Lemmer** Hermanus R., Pneumatology and eschatology in Ephesians; the role of the eschatological Spirit in the Church: diss. ᴰ*Roberts* J. Pretoria. 598 p. RTLv 20,545, sans date.

6206 **Penna** Romano, La lettera agli Efesini; intr. versione commento: Scritti delle origini cristiane 10. Bo 1988, Dehoniane. 277 p. [TR 85,163]. 88-10-20601-0.

6207 a) *Pedersen* Michael B., Jøde eller hedning? — Efeserbrevets forfatter: – b) *Tronier* Henrik, Den paulinske typologi og historieforståelse: DanTTs 51 (1988) 277-288 / 289 ... [< ᴢIT 89,5].

6208 **Pfammatter** Josef, Epheserbrief, Kolosserbrief: NEchter 10.12, 1987 → 3,6080: ᴿActuBbg 25 (1988) 71s (X. *Alegre S.*).

6209 San Pablo, Epístolas de la cautividad: Sagrada Biblia 8. Pamplona 1986, Univ. Navarra. 310 p. 84-313-0934-2 [EstE 64,564].

6210 *Schneider* Alfred, Mysterium Ecclesiae in epistola ad Ephesios (en croate): BogSmot 58 (1988) 61-84; deutsch 84s.

6211 **Speyr** Adrienne von, L'Épître aux Éphésiens, ᵀ*Catry* Patrick, *Delattre* Bertrand: Le Sycomore. P 1987, Lethielleux. 223 p. F 110. 2-283-61154-7. – ᴿActuBbg 25 (1988) 269s.

6212 **Wharton** Carolyn J., A study of the function of *chara* and *chairo* in Paul's epistle to the Ephesians: diss. Calvin Sem., ᴰ*Bandstra* A. GR 1988. iv-130 p. + bibliog. – CalvinT 23 (1988) 311.

6213 *Steinmetz* Franz-Josef, Beyond walls and fences; somatic unity in Ephesians [against current view that 'we' means former Jews and 'you' Gentile Christians, especially Eph 1,3-12: < GeistL 59 (1986) 202-214], ᵀᴱ*Asen* B. A.: TDig 35 (1988) 227-232.

6214 *Melano Couch* Beatriz, Blessed be he who has blessed; Eph 1:3-14: IntRMiss 77 (1988) 213-220.

6215 **Cunningham** Mary K., Karl BARTH's interpretation and use of Ephesians 1:4 in his doctrine of election; an essay in the relation of Scripture and theology: diss. Yale 1988. – DissA 50,3623-A; RTLv 20,537.

6216 **Kitchen** Martin, [Eph 1,10] The 'anakephalaiosis' of all things in Christ; theology and purpose in the epistle to the Ephesians: diss. Manchester 1988. 377 p. – RTLv 20,544: dir. 'Lindaer B.'

6217 *Loscalzo* Craig, Ephesians 4:1-16 [unity in diversity]: RExp 85 (1988) 687-691.

6218 **Moronta Rodríguez** Mario, Ser luz en el Señor (Ef. 5,8); el símbolo de la luz en Pablo y su significación teológico-bíblica. Caracas 1986, Trípode. xxviii-196 p. – ᴿAngelicum 65 (1988) 137s (M. F. *Manzanedo*).

6219 *Roberts* J. H., Die huwelik 'n krisis; is daar raad? Efesiërs 5:18-33: ➤ 509, Hoe lees 1985/8 ...

6220 *Vanhoye* Albert, Il 'grande mistero'; la lettura di Ef 5,21-33 nel nuovo documento pontificio: OssRom (28.X.1988) 1.4.

6221 **Miletic** Stephen F., 'One flesh'; Eph 5,22-24; 5,31; Marriage and the New Creation [diss. Marquette 1985 ➤ 2,4838]: AnBib 115. R 1988, Pontificio Istituto Biblico. 136 p. Lit. 30.000. 88-7653-115-7. – ᴿArTGran 51 (1988) 296s (A. *Segovia*).

6222 *Berkhof* Hendrikus, Widerstand in der Gottesfinsternis (Eph 6,13): TBei 19 (1988) 169-174 [< ᴢɪᴛ 88,609].

G6.3   Ad Philippenses.

6223 *Bercovitz* J. Peter, Paul at Ephesus and the composition of Philippians: ProcGLM 8 (1988) 61-76.

6224 **Ernst** Josef, Le lettere ai Filippesi, a Filemone, ai Colossesi, agli Efesini 1986 ➤ 2,4842 ... 3,6098: ᴿDivThom 91 (1988) 194-6 (G. *Testa*).

6225 **Hawthorne** Gerald F., Philippians: Word Themes 1987 ➤ 3,6100: ᴿRefTR 47 (1988) 63 (P. *O'Brien*); SvEx 53 (1988) 135-8 (L. O. *Eriksson*).

6226 **Koenig** John, Philippians and Philemon 1985 [➤ 6176, *Krentz* E. Gal.] ➤ 3,6100*: ᴿCurrTM 15 (1988) 458 (R. H. *Smith*).

6227 **Masini** Mario, Filippesi — Colossesi — Efesini — Filemone; le lettere della prigionia 1987 ➤ 3,6102: ᴿNRT 110 (1988) 925 (X. *Jacques*); ParVi 33 (1988) 393s (Emanuela *Ghini*).

6228 **Portefaix** Lilian, Sisters rejoice; Paul's letter to the Philippians and Luke-Acts as seen by first-century Philippian women: ConBib NT 20. Sto 1988, Almqvist & W. xix-260 p.; ill.; maps. Sk 167.

6229 **Schenk** Wolfgang, Die Philipperbriefe des Paulus 1984 ➤ 65,5504 ... 2,4844: ᴿTR 84 (1988) 198-201 (N. *Walter*).

6230 **Silva** Moisés, Philippians: Wycliffe Exegetical Comm. Ch 1988, Moody. xxiii-255 p. $24 [JBL 108,381].

6231 *Watson* Duane F., A rhetorical analysis of Philippians and its implications for the unity question: NT 30 (1988) 57-88.

6232 *Droge* Arthur J., [Phlp 1,21-26] Mori lucrum, Paul and ancient theories of suicide: NT 30 (1988) 263-286.

6233 **Verwilghen** A., Christologie ... Phlp 2,5-11, 1985 ➤ 1,6015; 2,4849: ᴿNRT 110 (1988) 935 (D. *Dideberg*).

6234 **Robuck** Thomas D., The Christ-hymn in Philippians; a rhetorical analysis of its function in the letter: diss. SW Baptist Theol. Sem. 1987. 247 p. 88-06941. – DissA 49 (1988s) 528-A.

6235 *Rousseau* François, Une disposition des versets de Philippiens 2,5-11: SR 17 (1988) 191-8.

6236 *Trudinger* P., [Phlp 2,5-11] Making sense of the Ascension; the Cross as glorification: St. Mark's Review 133 (Canberra 1988) 11-13 [< NTAbs 32,231].

6237 *Fitzmyer* Joseph A., The Aramaic background of Philippians 2:6-11: CBQ 50 (1988) 470-483.

6238 *Müller* Ulrich B., Der Christushymnus Phil 2,6-11: ZNW 79 (1988) 17-44.

6239 *Steenburg* Dave, [Phlp 2,6-11] The case against the synonymity of *morphē* and *eikōn*: JStNT 34 (1988) 77-86.

6240 *O'Neill* J.C., HOOVER on *Harpagmos* reviewed, with a modest proposal concerning Philippians 2:6: HarvTR [64 (1971) 95-119] 81 (1988) 445-9.

6241 **Leonarda** Salvatore, 'Mia gioia e mia corona' (Fil 4,1); ricerca biblico-teologica, La gioia nelle lettere di S. Paolo [diss. R, Pont. Univ. Urbaniana]: Theologia 1. Palermo 1988, Augustinus. 198 p. Lit. 28.000.

G6.4   **Ad Colossenses.**

6242 *Cipriani* Settimio, [Col-Ef ... Tim 1Pt] *a*) L'esperienza spirituale negli scritti di tradizione paolina e giudeo-cristiana: → 810, StoSpir 2 NT (1988) 253-298; – *b*) [sapienza e legge in Colossesi/Efesini] → 21, FCAPONE D., Coscienza 1987 ...

6243 **Comblin** 'Joseph', Lettera ai Colossesi, lettera a Filemone [1986 → 3,6125]. R 1987, Borla. 151 p. Lit. 10.000. 88-263-0590-0.

6244 **Hartman** Lars, Kolosserbrevet: KommNyaT 12. U 1985, 'EFS'. 208 p. – RSvEx 53 (1988) 138-141 (N.A. *Dahl*); RB 95 (1988) 455s (J. *Murphy-O'Connor*).

6245 **Kiley** Mark, Colossians as pseudepigraphy 1986 → 2,4857; 3,6127: RCBQ 50 (1988) 534s (Beverly R. *Gaventa*: confirmed by lack of reference to Paul's financial arrangements); EvQ 60 (1988) 69-71 (C.E. *Arnold*, not convinced); JBL 107 (1988) 334s (L.R. *Donelson*).

6246 **Pokorný** Petr, Der Brief des Paulus an die Kolosser: THK NT 10/1, 1987 → 3,6132: RTLZ 113 (1988) 270-3 (E. *Schweizer*).

6247 **Schweizer** Eduard, La carta a los Colosenses, TOlasagasti Manuel: BiblEstB 58. Salamanca 1987, Sígueme. 266 p. 84-301-1024-0. – RAc-tuBbg 25 (1988) 220 (X. *Alegre S.*); BibFe 14 (1988) 483 (A. *Salas*); CiTom 115 (1988) 192 (J. *Huarte*); LumenVr 37 (1988) 532-4 (J.M. *Arróniz*).

6248 **Van Broekhoven** HaroldJ, Wisdom and world; the functions of wisdom imagery in Sirach, pseudo-Solomon and Colossians [Christology]: diss. Boston Univ. 1988, DKee H. 247 p. 87-24733. – DissA 48 (1987s) 2084-A.

6249 **Wright** N.T., The Epistles of Paul to the Colossians and Philemon: NTyndale NT 1986 → 3,6135: REvQ 60 (1988) 275s (J. *Barclay*); IrBSt 10 (1988) 107s (I. *Hull*).

___

6250 *Shogren* Gary S., Presently entering the Kingdom of Christ; the background and purpose of Col 1:12-14: JEvTS 31 (1988) 173-180 [< ZIT 88,588].

6251 *Helyer* Larry R., Arius revisited; the firstborn over all creation (Col 1:15): JEvTS 31 (1988) 59-68.

6252 **Wink** Walter, [Col 1,16] Unmasking the powers [II] 1986 → 2,4869: RRelStR 14 (1988) 236 (J.J. *Shea*: projected vol. 3, 'Engaging the powers').

6253 *Ferguson* Everett. [Col 2,11 ...] Spiritual circumcision in early Christianity: ScotJT 41 (1988) 485-497.

6254 *Owanikin* Rebecca M., Colossians 2:18, a challenge to some doctrines of certain Aladura churches in Nigeria [Pentecostals ... worship of angels; visions for choice of marriage-partners]: AfJB 2 (1987) 89-95.

6255 *Balch* David L., [Col 3,18...] Household codes: ➤ 287, Greco-Roman 1988, 25-50.

6256 **Gielen** Marlis, Tradition und Theologie der neutestamentlichen Haustafelethik; ein Beitrag zur Frage einer christlichen Auseinandersetzung mit gesellschaftlichen Normen: kath. Diss. Bonn 1988s, ᴰ*Merklein*. – TR 85,514.

6257 *Harman* L., [Col 3,18-4,1] Some unorthodox thoughts on the 'household-code' form: ➤ 77, ᶠKᴇᴇ H., Social world 1988, 219-232.

6258 *Bockmuehl* Markus, A note on the text of Colossians 4:3: JTS 39 (1988) 489-494.

G6.5   *Ad Philemonem*   **Slavery in NT background.**

6259 *Bartchy* S.S., Slavery: ➤ 801, ISBEnc³ 4 (1988) 539-546.

6260 **Bradley** K.R., Slaves and masters in the Roman Empire 1984 ➤ 65,5534 ... 3,6146: ᴿAmHR 91 (1986) 88 (W.D. *Phillips*); Gymnasium 94 (1987) 88s (L. *Schumacher*); RBgPg 66 (1988) 174s (J.A. *Straus*); RPLH 61 (1987) 337-9 (J.-C. *Dumont*).

6261 **Collange** Jean-François, L'Épître de S. Paul à Philémon 1987 ➤ 3,6147: ᴿEsprVie 98 (1988) 261s (É. *Cothenet*); ÉTRel 63 (1988) 292s (E. *Cuvillier*); NRT 110 (1988) 926s (X. *Jacques*); Protestantesimo 43 (1988) 49s (P. *Tognina*); TS 39 (1988) 580s (C.F.D. *Moule*: rich, repaying study).

6262 *a*) *Comblin* José, Os escravos e o evangelho de Paulo / O batismo do ministro da rainha da Etiópia; – *b*) *Hoornaert* Eduardo, A leitura da Bíblia em relação à escravidão negra no Brasil-colônia (um inventário); – *c*) *Gamaleira Soares* Sebastião A.G., 'Porventura não valeis para mim tanto quanto os negros?' (cf. Am 9,7); – *d*) (com *Vieira de Mello* Agostinha), Protesto e resistência (leitura do Salmo 137): EstudosB 17 (1988) 69-76 e 63-68 / 11-29 / 31-46 e 47-61.

6263 *Coulton* J.J., *al.*, Balboura survey: Onesimos ['the city-slave', builder of Exedra and Nemesis-temple c. 150 A.D.; no link with Philemon suggested] and Meleager, I: AnSt 38 (1988) 121-165; 8 fig.; pl. IX-XII.

6264 *Derrett* J.D.M., The functions of the epistle to Philemon: ZNW 79 (1988) 63-91 [91: ancient Judaism was recruited by means of slave-girls: Gn 16,2 cf. Mt 16,18; Act 9,31; Rom 15,20].

6265 *Dumont* Jean Christian, Quelques aspects de l'esclavage et de l'économie agraire chez PLINE: Helmantica 37 (1986) 293-306.

6266 **Garlan** Yvon, Slavery in ancient Greece. Ithaca NY 1988, Cornell Univ. xi-216 p. $13. 0-8014-9504-0 [Antiquity 62,420].

6267 **Guenther** Rosemarie, Frauenarbeit – Frauenbindung; Untersuchungen zu unfreien und freigelassenen Frauen in den stadtrömischen Inschriften: Univ. Mannheim Hist. Inst. 9. Mü 1987, Fink. 375 p.

6268 **Jones** Lawrence P., A case study in Gnosticism; religious responses to slavery in the second century C.E.: diss. Columbia. NY 1988. 256 p. 89-06038. – DissA 49 (1988s) 3759-A; RelStR 15,193.

6269 **Klein** R., Die Sklaverei in der Sicht der Bischöfe AMBROSIUS und AUGUSTINUS: Forschungen zur antiken Sklaverei 20. Stu 1988, Steiner. 264 p. DM 63 [RHE 84,97*].

6270 ^E**Kreissig** Heinz, *Kühnert* Friedmar, Antike Abhängigkeitsformen ... Actes du colloque sur l'esclavage, Iéna 1981/5 → 2,536; M 40: ^RHZ 244 (1987) 663s (F. *Gschnitzer*).

6271 *Kudlien* Fridolf, Zur sozialen Situation des flüchtigen Sklaven in der Antike: Hermes 116 (1988) 232-252.

6272 *MacMullen* Ramsay, Late Roman slavery: Historia 36 (1987) 359-382.

6273 *Parsons* Michael, Slavery and the New Testament; equality and submissiveness: VoxEvca 18 (1988) 90-96.

6274 **Petersen** Norman R., Rediscovering Paul; Philemon and the sociology of Paul's narrative world 1985 → 1,6057 ... 3,6159: ^RJStNT 32 (1988) 114-7 (S. E. *Porter*); RelStR 14 (1988) 118-121 (J. A. *Darr*) & 121-4 (V. L. *Wimbush*).

6275 **Phan** Peter C., Social thought [... slavery in the early Church]: Message of the Fathers 20, 1984 → 65,d135: ^RSecC 6,1 (1987s) 52s (P. M. *O'Cleirigh*).

6275* *Schenk* Wolfgang, Philemon in der neueren Forschung (1945-1985): ANRW 2/25/4 (1987) 3439-3495 [→ 3,6114*b*].

6276 *Straus* J. A., L'esclavage dans L'Égypte romaine: → 782, ANRW 2,10,1 (1988) 841-911.

6277 **Vernant** Jean-Pierre, *Vidal-Naquet* Pierre, Travail et esclavage en Grèce ancienne: Historiques. Bru 1988, Complexe. x-176 p. 2-87027-246-4.

6278 **Watson** Alan, Roman slave law 1987 → 3,6164: ^RAmHR 93 (1988) 1026s (B. W. *Frier*); ÉchMClas 32 (1988) 434-6 (S. *Treggiari*); Phoenix 42 (Toronto 1988) 274-6 (K. R. *Bradley*); RelStR 14 (1988) 155s (J. S. *Ruebel*).

6279 **Wiedemann** T. E. J., Slavery: New Surveys in the Classics 19. Ox 1987, Clarendon. 51 p.; 8 fig. 0-903035-48-0.

G6.6 Ad Thessalonicenses.

6280 *Agouridis* Savas, Ⓖ The intense expectation of the eschata; how it was dealt with by 1 and 2 Thessalonians: DeltioVM 17,2 (1988) 5-22.

6281 **Boor** Werner de, Die Briefe des Paulus an die Thessalonicher⁷ [¹1959]: Studienbibel NT. Wu 1982, Brockhaus. 168 p. 3-417-25013-7.

6282 **Collins** Raymond F., Studies on 1 Thess: BiblETL 66, 1984 → 65,556 ... 3,6169: ^RRTLv 19 (1988) 224s (J. *Ponthot*); TLZ 113 (1988) 31s (T. *Holtz*).

6283 **Frede** Hermann J., Einleitung Thes Tim: Vetus Latina 25/1, 1975-82 → 58,1293 ... 1,6096: ^RCBQ 50 (1988) 527-530 (A. *Cody*).

6284 *a) Havener* Ivan †, First and Second Thessalonians, an introduction; – *b) Krentz* Edgar, Roman Hellenism and Paul's Gospel; – *c) Collins* Raymond F., 'The Lord Jesus Christ'; – *d) Hodgson* Robert^J, Gospel and ethics in First Thessalonians; – *e) Giblin* Charles H., The heartening apocalyptic of Second Thessalonians: BToday 26,6 (1988) 324-7 / 328-337 / 338-343 / 344-9 / 350-354.

6285 *a) Hays* Richard B., Crucified with Christ; a synthesis of 1 and 2 Thessalonians, Philemon, Philippians and Galatians; – *b) Segal* Alan F., The costs of proselytism and conversion: → 500, SBL Seminars 1988, 318-335 / 336-369.

6287 **Holtz** Traugott, Der erste Brief an die Thessalonicher: EvKK NT 13, 1986 → 2,4894; 3,6172: ^RActuBbg 25 (1988) 67 (X. *Alegre S.*); CiTom 115 (1988) 187s (J. *Huarte*).

6288 **Jewett** Robert, The Thessalonian correspondence 1986 → 2,4895;

3,6173: ᴿCBQ 50 (1988) 325s (J. L. *Gillman*); Horizons 15 (1988) 384s (Rea *McDonnell*); Interpretation 42 (1988) 410-2 (S. *Kraftchick*); JBL 107 (1988) 763-6 (H. *Hendrix*: compelling thesis); RB 95 (1988) 311 (J. *Murphy-O'Connor*: Betz-style rhetorical analysis weak); RExp 85 (1988) 132-5 (D. E. *Garland*); RHPR 68 (1988) 254s (M. *Schoeni*); Themelios 14 (1988s) 71s (M. *Bockmuehl*).

6289 **Johanson** Bruce C., To all the brethren ... 1 Thes: ConBib NT 16, 1987 ➤ 3,6174: ᴿCBQ (1988) 531-3 (C. H. *Talbert*); ÉTRel 63 (1988) 90 (F. *Vouga*); JTS 39 (1988) 578s (E. *Best*: breaks new ground, but whether it was worth breaking is another matter); NRT 110 (1988) 927s (X. *Jacques*); SvEx 53 (1988) 142-4 (B. *Holmberg*); TR 84 (1988) 113-5 (T. *Söding*).

6290 *Lacan* Marc-François, La première lettre de Paul: Tychique (1988) 71,36-40; 73,26-31; 75,42-48.

6291 *Lambrecht* Jan, De apostolische inzet van de eerste christenen; een actualiserende lezing van 1 Tessalonicenzen: CollatVL 18 (1988) 403-417.

6292 **Malherbe** Abraham J., Paul and the Thessalonians 1987 ➤ 3,6178: ᴿCBQ 50 (1988) 538s (V. P. *Branick*: successful).

6293 **Marxsen** Willi, La prima lettera ai Tessalonicesi; guida alla lettura del primo scritto del Nuovo Testamento [1979 ➤ 60,8232], ᵀ*Abate Leibbrandt* Mirella: Parola per l'uomo di oggi 6. T 1988, Claudiana. 109 p.; map. Lit. 10.500. 88-7016-069-6.

6294 **Morris** Leon, The epistles of Paul to the Thessalonians, an introduction and commentary²ʳᵉᵛ [¹1956]: Tyndale NT Comm. Leicester/GR 1984, Inter-Varsity/Eerdmans. 152 p. 0-85111-882-8 / 0-8028-0034-3.

6295 **Pesch** Rudolf, La scoperta della più antica lettera di Paolo; Paolo rivisitato = Le lettere alla comunità dei Tessalonicesi [1984 ➤ 65,5565], ᵀ*Panini* Marisa A.: StBPaid 80. Brescia 1987, Paideia. 136 p. Lit. 25.000. 88-394-0403-1.

6296 **Spross** Daniel B., Sanctification in the Thessalonian epistles in a canonical context: diss. Southern Baptist Theol. Sem. 1988, ᴰ*Ward* W. 289 p. 88-10923. – DissA 49 (1988s) 854-A.

6297 *Tenney* M. C., Thessalonians 1-2: ➤ 801, ISBEnc³ 4 (1988) 832-6 (-8, Thessalonica, *Madvig* D.ʹH.).

6298 **Ubieta** José Angel, La iglesia de Tesalónica; una iglesia en proceso de evangelización: IglNT. Bilbao 1988, Desclée-B. 61 p. [NatGrac 35,437].

6299 *Okeke* George E., The context and function of 1 Thess. 2:1-12 and its significance for African Christianity: AfJB 2 (1987) 77-88.

6299* **Yarbrough** O. Larry, [1 Thes 4,5 ...] Not like the Gentiles; marriage rules in the letters of Paul [diss. Yale 1984, ᴰ*Meeks* W.]: SBL diss. 80, 1985 ➤ 1,5660; 3,6191: ᴿJBL 107 (1988) 147-9 (R. F. *Hock*).

6300 *Howard* Tracy L., The literary unity of 1 Thessalonians 4:13-5:11: GraceTJ 9 (1988) 163-190.

6301 *Reicke* Bo †, Paulus über den Tag des Herrn; homiletisch orientierte Auslegung von 1 Thess 5,1-11: TZBas 44 (1988) 91-96.

6302 **Holland** Glenn S., The tradition that you received from us; 2 Thessalonians in the Pauline tradition [diss. Ch, ᴰ*Betz* H.]: HermUnT 24. Tü 1988, Mohr. 172 p. DM 96, [TR 84,251]. 3-16-145203-8. – ᴿEstE 64 (1988) 570s (A. *Rodriguez Carmona*); TsTNijm 28 (1988) 310 (J. *Smit*).

6303 **Weima** Jeffrey A. D., 'The man of lawlessness'; a critical examination of 2 Thessalonians 2:1-12: diss. Calvin Sem., ᴰ*Holwerda* D. GR 1988. ii-136 p. + bibliog. – CalvinT 23 (1988) 310s.

6304 *Trilling* Wolfgang, *a*) Antichrist und Papsttum; Reflexionen zur Wirkungsgeschichte von 2 Thes 2,1-10a [< TJb 1980, 363-380]; – *b*) Literarische Paulusimitation im 2. Thessalonicherbrief [< ᴱ*Kertelge* K., Paulus: QDisp 89 (1981) 146-156]: → 275, Studien 1988, 277-301 / 233-243.

6305 *Russell* R., The idle in 2 Thess 3.6-12; an eschatological or a social problem?: NTS 34 (1988) 105-119.

6306 *Quacquarelli* Antonio, Nota sull'esegesi di 2 Th. 3,10 [Chi non vuol lavorare non deve mangiare] nella letteratura monastica antica: → 56, Mém. GRIBOMONT J. 1988, 503-519.

G7 **Epistulae pastorales.**

6307 **Donelson** Lewis R., Pseudepigraphy and ethical argument in the Pastoral Letters: HermUnT 22, 1986 → 2,4909; 3,6202: ᴿCBQ 50 (1988) 131-3 (L. T. *Johnson*: dissertation jargon); JBL 107 (1988) 558-560 (R. J. *Karris*); Salesianum 50 (1988) 227 (G. *Abbà*).

6308 *Donelson* Lewis R., The structure of ethical argument in the Pastorals: BibTB 18 (1988) 108-113.

6309 *Feuillet* André, Le dialogue avec le monde non-chrétien dans les épîtres pastorales et l'épître aux Hébreux: EsprVie 98 (1988) 125-8. 152-9.

6310 **Fiore** Benjamin, The function of personal example in the Socratic and Pastoral epistles [diss. Yale 1982, ᴰ*Malherbe* A.]: AnBib 105, 1986 → 2,4913: ᴿCBQ 50 (1988) 134s (R. J. *Karris*: impressive parallels need charts); JBL 107 (1988) 335-7 (H. D. *Betz*).

6311 **Knoch** Otto, 1. und 2. Timotheusbrief; Titusbrief: NEchter. Wü 1988, Echter. 87 p. 3-429-01139-6. – ᴿArTGran 51 (1988) 291 (A. *Segovia*).

6312 *Lohfink* Gerhard, Die Vermittlung des Paulinismus zu den Pastoralbriefen: BZ 32 (1988) 169-188.

6313 *Marshall* I. Howard, The Christology of the Pastoral Epistles: SNTU-A 13 (1988) 157-178.

6314 **Miller** James D., The pastoral letters as composite documents: diss. ᴰ*O'Neill* J. Edinburgh 1988. 325 p. – RTLv 20,545.

6315 **Okorie** Andrew M., Marriage in the Pastoral Epistles: diss. Southern Baptist 1988, ᴰ*Polhill* J. 206 p. 88-18527. – DissA 49 (1988s) 1854-A.

6316 **Wolter** M., Die Pastoralbriefe als Paulustradition [ev. Hab. Mainz 1986]: FRLANT 146. Gö 1988, Vandenhoeck & R. 322 p. DM 98. 3-525-53827-8 [NTAbs 32,381].

G7.2 **1-2 ad Timotheum.**

6317 *Marshall* I. Howard, The Christian life in 1 Timothy: Taiwan Journal of Theology 9 (1987) 151-164 [< TKontext 10/1,39].

6318 **Roloff** Jürgen, Der erste Brief an Timotheus: EvKK NT 15. Z/Neuk 1988, Benziger/Neuk. 395 p. [TR 85,163]. 3-545-23116-X / Neuk 3-7887-1292-1.

6319 *Stitzinger* Michael F., Cultural confusion and the role of women in the Church; a study of 1 Timothy 2: CalvaryB 4,2 (1988) 24-42.

6320 **Küchler** Max, Schweigen, Schmuck und Schleier; drei neutestamentliche Vorschriften [1 Tim 2,8-15; 1 Cor 14,33-36; 11,3-16; 1 Pt 3,1-6] zur Verdrängung der Frauen auf dem Hintergrund einer frauenfeindlichen Exegese des ATs im antiken Judentum: NTOrbAnt 1, 1986 → 2,4924: ᴿBiKi 42 (1987) 44-46 (Helen *Schüngel-Straumann*); JBL 107 (1988) 563-5 (Adela Y. *Collins*); RB 95 (1988) 466-8 (J. *Murphy-O'Connor*); TGʟ 78

(1988) 91s (W. *Beinert*); TR 84 (1988) 463-6 (H. *Frankemölle*; aus dem Vorwort 'heute die drei K: Kinder, Köchin, Komputer').

6321 *Jagt* Krijn van der,   Women are saved through bearing children; a sociological approach to the interpretation of 1 Timothy 2.15: *a*) ➤ 502, Issues/Translation 1987/8, 287-295; – *b*) BTrans 39 (1988) 201-8.

6322 *Sandnes* Karl O., [Norw.] Shame and honour in 1 Tim 2:11-15: TsTKi 59 (1988) 97-108; Eng. 108.

6323 *Wilshire* Leland E.,   The T(hesaurus) L(inguae) G(raecae) computer and further reference to *authenteō* in 1 Timothy 2.12:   NTS 34 (1988) 120-134.

6324 **Stenger** Werner,   Der Christushymnus 1 Tim 3,16 ... [D1973] 1977 ➤ 58,7396:   RLingBib 61 (1988) 124-9 (W. *Schenk*).

6325 *Winter* B.W.,   Providentia for the widows of 1 Timothy 5:1-16 [... Acts 6,1-5]: TyndaleB 39 (1988) 83-99.

6326 *McKee* Elsie,   Les anciens et l'interprétation de 1 Tm 5,17 [l'ouvrier est digne de son salaire] chez CALVIN; une curiosité dans l'histoire de l'exégèse: RTPhil 120 (1988) 411-7.

6327 *Stöger* Alois,   Die Wurzel priesterlichen Lebens; 2 Tim 1,6-14: TPQ 136 (1988) 252-7.

6328 *Piñero* Antonio,   Sobre el sentido de *theópneustos*; 2 Tim 3,16: FgNT 1 (1988) 143-152; Eng. 152s.

G8   Epistula ad Hebraeos.

6329 **Allen** David L.,   An argument for the Lukan authorship of Hebrews: diss. Univ. Texas, DLongacre R.   Arlington 1987. 230 p. 88-12833. – DissA 49 (1988s) 1492-A.

6330 **Braun** Herbert, An die Hebräer 1984 ➤ 65,5609 ... 3,6225:   RCurrTM 15 (1988) 206s (E. *Krentz*: Callimachus' *Mega biblion mega kakon* partly true here).

6331 **Collins** Raymond F.,   Letters that Paul did not write; the Epistle to the Hebrews and the Pauline Pseudepigrapha: Good News Studies 28. Wilmington 1988, Glazier. 327 p. $18 pa. [CBQ 51,187]. 0-89453-652-4.

Dussaut L., Épître aux Hébreux 1984 ➤ 5414*.

6332 *Ellingworth* Paul, *a*) Hebrews and the anticipation of completion: Themelios 14 (1988s) 6-11; – *b*) Hebrews in the eighties [review of 8 commentaries]: BTrans 39 (1988) 131-8.

6333 **Evans** Louis H.J,   Hebrews: Communicator's Comm. 10, 1985 ➤ 1,6125; 2,4934:   RAndrUnS 26 (1988) 88-90 (R.K. *McIver*).

6334 *Fabris* Rinaldo,   La spiritualità della lettera agli Ebrei: ➤ 810, StoSpir 2 NT (1988) 299-318.

6335 EFeld Helmut,   Wendelini STEINBACH Commentarii in epistolam ad Hebraeos pars altera: Opera 3. Wsb 1987, Steiner. lxxiii-486 p. – RBTAM 14 (1988) 559s (G. *Michiels*).

6336 *Flusser* David, *a*) Messianology and Christology in the Epistle to the Hebrews [ineditum]; – *b*) [with *Young* Brad], Messianic blessings in Jewish and Christian texts: ➤ 190, JudOrChr 1988, 246-279 / 280-300.

Fraenkel P., *Perrotet* L., BÈZE, Hébr (1564-6) 1988 ➤ 5905.

6337 EFrede Hermann J.,   Vetus Latina 25/2 Epistulae ad Thessalonicenses ... Hebraeos [Lfg. 3s, 1987 ➤ 3,6232] Lfg. 5, Hbr 2,16-5,8. FrB 1988, Herder. pp. 1157-1236. 3-451-00466-6.

6338 *Galley* Hans-D., Der Hebräebrief und der christliche Gottesdienst: JbLtgHymm 31 (1987s) 72-83.

6339 *Hanson* A. T., Hebrews [citing OT]: ➤ 97, [F]LINDARS B. 1988, 292-302.

6340 **Hegermann** Harald, Der Brief an die Hebräer: THandK NT 16. B 1988, Ev.V. xvi-303 p. 3-374-00042-8.

6341 **Käsemann** E., The wandering people of God [1939] 1984 ➤ 65,5636 ... 2,4941: [R]RB 95 (1988) 630 (B. T. *Viviano*).

6342 **Laub** Franz, Hebräerbrief: Kl.Kommentar NT 14. Stu 1988, KBW. 190 p. 3-460-15441-5.

6343 **Mondet** Jean-Pierre, Le sacerdoce dans le 'Commentaire sur l'Épître aux Hébreux' de saint Jean CHRYSOSTOME: diss. [D]*Houssiau* A. LvN 1986. xx-277 p. – RTLv 18,552. FoiTemps 18 (1988) 259-286: Clarté sur le sacerdoce ministériel; le témoignage de saint Jean Chrysostome dans son 'Commentaire sur l'épître aux Hébreux' ➤ 986, Travaux de doctorat 12, Théologie 7.

6344 *Parsons* Mikeal C., Son and High Priest, a study in the Christology of Hebrews: EvQ 60 (1988) 195-216.

6345 *a) Radcliffe* Timothy, Christ in Hebrews; cultic irony; – *b) Harbert* Bruce, The quest for Melchisedek: ➤ 669, Christian Priesthood = NBlackf 68 (1987) 494-504 / 529-539.

6346 **Riggenbach** Eduard, Der Brief an die Hebräer [³1922 + pref. *Hofius* O.]. Wu 1987, Brockhaus. lxi-464 p. DM 58. 3-417-29216-6 [NTAbs 32,252]. – [R]KerkT 39 (1988) 156s (G. de *Ru*).

6347 **Rissi** Mathias, Die Theologie des Hebräerbriefs; ihre Verankerung in der Situation des Verfassers und seiner Leser: WUNT 41, 1987 ➤ 3,6242: [R]BZ 32 (1988) 159-161 (H. *Merklein*); TGegw 30 (1987) 276s (H. *Giesen*); TLZ 113 (1988) 273s (C.-P. *März*).

6348 **Schlossnikel** Reinhard, Der Brief an die Hebräer und das Corpus Paulinum; eine linguistische 'Bruchstelle' im Codex Claromontanus (Paris, Bib. Nat. grec 107 + 107A + 107B) und ihre Bedeutung im Rahmen von Text- und Kanongeschichte: kath. Diss. Tübingen 1988s, [D]*Frede*. – TR 85,519.

6349 **Scholer** John M., Proleptic priests; an investigation of the priesthood in the Epistle to the Hebrews: diss. Union Theol. Sem. Richmond 1988. 376 p. 88-14647. – DissA 49 (1988s) 1490s-A.

6350 **Sigeneger** Roswitha, Evangelium als Verheissung; eine Untersuchung zum Zusammenhang von Verheissung und Christologie im Hebräerbrief: Diss. Rostock 1988s, [D]*Weiss*. – TR 85,520.

6351 *Spadafora* Francesco, La lettera agli Ebrei: Renovatio 23 (1988) 263-277.

6352 **Tetley** Joy D., The priesthood of Christ as the controlling theme of the Epistle to the Hebrews: diss. Durham UK, 1987. 344 p. BRD-81352. – DissA 49 (1988s) 528-A.

6353 *Tetley* Joy, The priesthood of Christ in Hebrews: Anvil 5,3 (1988) 195-206 [< ZIT 89,71].

6354 *Weiss* Hans-F., Hebraerbrief: ➤ 798, EvKL 2 (1988) 395s.

6355 *Oberholtzer* Thomas K., *a)* The eschatological salvation of Hebrews 1:5-2:5: – *b)* The Kingdom rest in Hebrews 3:1-4:13; – *c)* The thorn-infested ground in Hebrews 6:4-12; – *d)* The danger of willful sin in Hebrews 10:26-39 [*e*] The failure to heed his speaking in Hebrews

12:25-29 ...]: BS 145 (1988) 83-97 / 185-196 / 319-328 / 410-9 [to continue in vol. 146].

6356 *Mugridge* Alan, [Heb 2,1-4 ...] 'Warnings in the Epistle to the Hebrews'; an exegetical and theological study: RefTR 46 (1987) 74-82.

6357 *Flusser* David, 'Today if you will listen to his [not 'this' as p. 5] voice'; creative 'Jewish' [omitted p. 5] exegesis in Hebrews 3-4: → 505, Creative 1985/8, 55-62.

6358 *Wood* Charles M., [Heb 4,12s] On being known: TTod 44 (1987s) 197-206.

6359 **Vilar Hueso** Vicente, Notas marginales de S. Juan de RIBERA a Hebreos 4,16 a 5,10: → 53*, FGARCÍA LAHIGUERA 1975, 69-76.

6360 *Jacob* René, Devenir parfaits par l'obéissance (Hé 5,9): Tychique 76 (1988) 59-63.

6361 *Berényi* Gabriella, La portée de *dià toûto* en Hé 9,15: Biblica 69 (1988) 108-112.

6362 **Cosby** Michael R., The rhetorical composition and function of Hebrews 11 in light of example lists in antiquity. Macon GA 1988, Mercer Univ. 143 p. [JAAR 57,683]. 0-86554-320-8.

6363 *Cosby* Michael R., The rhetorical composition of Hebrews 11: JBL 107 (1988) 257-273.

6364 *Durand* G. M. de, [... Heb 11,1] Études sur Marc le moine IV, une double définition de la foi: BLitEc 89 (1988) 23-40; Eng. 4.

G9.1 **1 Petri.**

6365 **Adinolfi** Marco, La prima lettera di Pietro nel mondo greco-romano: Bibl.Pont.Ath. Antonianum 21. R 1987, Antonianum. 223 p. Lit. 25.000 [TR 84,427]. – RAntonianum 63 (1988) 428s (*ipse*); Asprenas 35 (1988) 525s (A. *Rolla*); Gregorianum 69 (1988) 776 (E. *Rasco*).

6366 EAland K., *al.*, Text und Textwert ... NT I. Die katholischen Briefe I-III 1987 → 3,6264: RETL 64 (1988) 203-5 (F. *Neirynck*); Muséon 101 (1988) 424-7 (P.-M. *Bogaert*); NT 30 (1988) 187-9 (J. K. *Elliott*); RHE 83 (1988) 671-3 (C. R. *Amphoux*); TR 84 (1988) 368 (O. B. *Knoch*).

6367 *Antoniazzi* A., A saída é ... ficar — o conflito dos cristãos com a sociedade segundo a primeira epístola de Pedro: EstudosB 15 (1987) 57-68.

6368 **Frankemölle** Hubert, 1 Petr., 2 Petr., Judas: NEchter 1987 → 3,6269: RArTGran 51 (1988) 288 (A. *Segovia*); ColcT 58,4 (1988) 180-2 (J. W. *Roslon*).

6369 **Grudem** Wayne A., The First Epistle of Peter; an introduction and commentary: Tyndale NT Comm. 17. Leicester/GR 1988, Inter-Varsity/Eerdmans. 239 p. $6 pa. [CBQ 51,400].

6370 TEHurst David, BEDE the Venerable, The commentary on the seven catholic epistles: CistSt 82,1985 → 1,6167 ... 3,6272: REglT 17 (1986) 244s (K. C. *Russell*).

6371 **Junack** K., *Grunewald* W., Das NT auf Papyrus, I. die katholischen Briefe 1986 → 2,4972; 3,6271: RNT 30 (1988) 92s (J. K. *Elliott*); RHE 83 (1988) 737s (P.-M. *Bogaert*). → 6396.

6372 **Kistemaker** Simon J., Peter and Jude: NT Comm. GR 1987, Baker. 451 p. 0-8010-5484-2. – RRExp 85 (1988) 721 (S.*Sheeley*: good, but used the wrong book of ELLIOTT).

6373 **Koger** A. Dennis, The question of a Petrine theology; a critical examination: diss. Baylor. Waco ... – RelStR 14,189; RTLv 20,544 'of a distinctive Petrine'.

6374 **Lamau** Marie-Louise, Des chrétiens dans le monde; communautés pétriniennes au Ier siècle: LDiv 134. P 1988, Cerf. 379 p. F 150. 2-204-02958-0.

6375 **Michaels** J. Ramsey, 1 Peter: Word Comm 49. Waco 1988, Word. LXXV-337 p. 0-8499-0248-7 [JTS 40,586-8, C. E. B. *Cranfield*].

6376 **Prostmeier** Ferdinand, Handlungsmodelle im ersten Petrusbrief: kath. Diss. Regensburg. – TR 85,518.

6377 **Reichert** Angelika, Eine urchristliche 'praeparatio ad martyrium'; Studien zur Komposition, Traditionsgeschichte und Theologie des 1. Petrusbriefes: kath. Diss. ^D*Klein* G. Münster/Wf 1988. 624 p. – RTLv 20,545; TR 85,517.

Smith T. V., Petrine controversies in early Christianity 1985 → 4748.

6379 ^E**Talbert** Charles H., Perspectives on First Peter 1986 → 2,4980: ^RPerspRelSt 15 (1988) 286-9 (J. R. *Michaels*).

6380 *Voorwinde* S., Old Testament quotations in Peter's Epistles: VoxRef 49 (1987) 3-16 [< GerefTTs 88 (1988) 63].

6381 **Young** Robert G., Was there a Petrine community? An examination of first and second century documents ascribed to Simon Peter: diss. Southern Baptist Sem., ^D*Blevins* J. 1987. 278 p. 88-05807. – DissA 49 (1988s) 272-A.

6382 *a*) *Cothenet* Édouard, La Première de Pierre; bilan de 35 ans de recherches; – *b*) *Bauckham* Richard J., 2 Peter [Jude], an account of research; – *c*) *Soards,* M. L., *al.,* 1Pt-2Pt-Jud as evidence for a Petrine school: → 782, ANRW 2,25,5 (1988) 3685-3712 / 3713-3752 [3791-3826] / 3827-49.

6383 *Stevick* Daniel B., A matter of taste; 1 Peter 2:3: RRel 47 (1988) 707-717.

6384 *Frankemölle* Hubert, 'All our fathers have passed through the sea' [1 Cor 10,1; but really about Ex 19,6 and 1 Pt 2,9, 'kingdom of priests']; an example of Christian-Jewish Bible interpretation [< Orientierung 51 (1987) 41-43. 57-60], ^{TE}*Asen* B.: TDig 35 (1988) 143-9.

6385 *Légasse* S., La soumission aux autorités d'après 1 Pierre 2,13-17; version spécifique d'une parénèse traditionnelle: NTS 34 (1988) 378-396.

6386 **Bosetti** Elena, 'Poimèn kai épiskopos' [accenti di RTLv 20,543]; la figura del pastore nella Prima Lettera di Pietro (2,18-25; 5,1-4): diss. Pont. Univ. Gregoriana, ^D*Vanni* U. Roma 1988. 441 p.; 126 p.

6387 **Haldeman** Madelynn, The function of Christ's suffering in 1 Peter 2:18-25: diss. Andrews 1988, ^D*Johnston* R. 331 p. – RTLv 20,544.

6388 *Ghiberti* Giuseppe, Le 'sante donne' di una volta (1 Pt 3,5): → 154, ^FZEDDA S., RivB 36 (1988) 287-297; Eng. 297.

6389 ... [? *Baumert* Norbert, TPhil 63,60n: 1 Pt 4,7-11] Geistliche Gastfreundschaft: → 96, ^FLECHNER O. ...

G9.2 **2 Petri.**

6390 *Bauckham* Richard, [at least 2 Pt] Pseudo-apostolic letters: JBL 107 (1988) 469-494.

6391 **Breese** David, Living for eternity; eight imperatives from Second Peter. Ch 1988, Moody. 143 p. $7 pa. [GraceTJ 9,303].

6392 *Cavazza* Franco, Sempronius Asellio fr. 2 Peter [sic]: Orpheus 9 (1988) 21-37.

6393 **Houwelingen** Pieter H. R. van, De tweede trompet; de authenticiteit van de tweede brief van Pieter: diss. ᴰ*Bruggen* J. van. Kampen 1988. 318 p. – RTLv 20,546.

6394 *Picirilli* Robert E., Allusions to 2 Peter in the Apostolic Fathers: JStNT 33 (1988) 57-83.

6395 *Meier* Sam, 2 Peter 3:3-7 — an early Jewish and Christian response to eschatological skepticism: BZ 32 (1988) 255-7.

G9.4   **Epistula Jacobi.**

6396 **Aland** Barbara (*Juckel* A.) Die grossen katholischen Briefe: Das NT in syrischer Überlieferung 1 / ArbNTF 7, 1986 ➤ 2,1246; 3,6293: ᴿJBL 107 (1988) 351-3 (W. L. *Petersen*); NT 30 (1988) 93-95 (J. K. *Elliott*); TZBas 44 (1988) 377 (G. D. *Kilpatrick,* Eng.); ZDMG 138 (1988) 185 (M. *Krause*). ➤ 6371.

6397 *Bauckham* Richard, James, 1 and 2 Peter, Jude [citing OT]: ➤ 97, ᶠLɪɴᴅᴀʀs B. 1988, 303-317.

6397* **Becquet** Gilles, al., La carta de Santiago: CuadB 61. Estella 1988, VDivino. 74 p. [EfMex 7,299, E. *Serraima Cirici*].

6398 *a) Davids* P. H., The epistle of James in modern discussion; – *b) Baasland* Ernst, Literarische Form, Thematik und geschichtliche Einordnung des Jakobusbriefes: ➤ 782, ANRW 2,25,5 (1988) 3621-3645 / 3646-3684.

6399 **Gruson** Philippe présente, La lettre de Jacques; lectures socio-linguistiques [11 auteurs nommés sans rapport aux textes]: CahÉv 61. P 1987, Cerf. 74 p. 0222-9714.

6400 **Hartin** Patrick, James; a New Testament wisdom writing and its relationship to Q: diss. Pretoria, ᴰ*Plessis* I. J. du. 437 p. – RTLv 20,544 sans date.

6401 **Kistemaker** Simon J., Exposition of the Epistle of James and the Epistles of John 1986 ➤ 3,6302: ᴿGraceTJ 9 (1988) 149-151 (R. V. *Rakestraw*).

6402 *Kotzé* P. P. A. 'n Brief van strooi? Die Evangelie in Jakobus: Skrif-Kerk 6,2 (1985) 137-146 [NTAbs 32,194].

6403 **Loo** Hans van de, De Brief van Jacobus 1986 ➤ 3,6297: ᴿStreven 55 (1987s) 181 (P. *Beentjes*).

6404 **Martin** Ralph P., James: Word Comm. 48. Waco 1988, Word. lix-240 p. 0-8499-0247-9.

6405 **Maynard-Reid** Pedrito U., Poverty and wealth in James 1987 ➤ 3,6303: ᴿAndrUnS 26 (1988) 93-95 (J. C. *Brunt*); IndThSt 25 (1988) 192-4 (L. *Legrand*); Vidyajyoti 52 (1988) 304s (R. J. *Raja*).

6406 **Popkes** Wiard, Adressaten, Situation und Form des Jakobusbriefes 1986 ➤ 2,4999: ᴿBogSmot 58 (1988) 158s (M. *Zovkić*).

6407 **Schnider** Franz, Der Jakobusbrief: RgNT 1987 ➤ 3,6309: ᴿActuBbg 25 (1988) 219s (X. *Alegre S.*); ArTGran 51 (1988) 290 (A. *Segovia*); Claretianum 28 (1988) 406-8 (B. *Proietti*); TsTNijm 28 (1988) 310 (L. *Visschers,* also on Pʀᴀᴛscʜᴇʀ).

6408 *Strecker* Georg, Jakobusbrief: ➤ 798, EvKL 2 (1988) 794s.

6409 **Vouga** F., L'épître de saint Jacques 1984 ➤ 65,5700; 2,5002: ᴿTLZ 113 (1988) 274s (C. *Burchard*).

Soards Marion L., [Abraham in James] 1987 ➤ 2280.

6410 **Marconi** Gilberto, 'Sia ognuno restio a parlare ...' Gc 1,19-27; 3,1-12: ᴰ1985 → 1,6208: ᴿSalesianum 50 (1988) 426 (C. *Bissoli*).
6411 *Manns* F., Une tradition liturgique juive sousjacente à Jacques 1,21b: RevSR 62 (1988) 85-89.
6412 *Johnson* Luke T., The mirror of remembrance (James 1: 22-25): CBQ 50 (1988) 632-645.
6413 *Marconi* Gilberto, La 'sapienza' nell'esegesi di Gc 3,13-18: RivB 36 (1988) 239-254.
6414 *Peck* George, James 5:1-6 [forces us to take an active stand on today's crippling inequities]: Interpretation 42 (1988) 291-6.
6415 **Hainthaler** Theresia, 'Von der Ausdauer Ijobs habt ihr gehört' (Jak. 5,11); zur Bedeutung des Buches Ijob im NT [Diss. ph./th. Hochschule Frankfurt]: EurHS 23/337. Fra 1988, Lang. 465 p. Fs 75 [TR 84,251].

G9.6 Epistula Judae.

6416 *Paulsen* Henning, Judasbrief: → 813, TRE 17 (1987) 307-310.
6417 **Watson** Duane F., Invention, arrangement, and style; rhetorical criticism of Jude and 2 Peter [diss. Duke, ᴰ*Young* F., 1986]: SBL diss 104. Atlanta 1988, Scholars. xii-214 p. [TR 85,251]. $21. 1-55540-155-4; pa. 6-2.
6418 *Whallon* William, Should we keep, omit, or alter the *hoi* in Jude 12?: NTS 34 (1988) 156-9 [with the reading *achatais* for *agapais* (→ 64,6159*) *hai ... tois* should be read for *hoi ... tais*].

Desunt hoc anno – Nᵒ 6419-7999 – **not used this year.**

XV. Theologia Biblica

H1 **Biblical Theology** .1 [OT] **God**

8000 *Axelsson* Lars E., God still dwells in the desert — a conception characteristic for North-Israelite Yahwism: → 469, Wünschet 1986/8, 17-20.
8001 *Bailey* Lee W., Religious projection; a new European tour [Simon Vᴇsᴛᴅɪᴊᴋ 1898-1971; De Toekomst der Religie 1947 carried forward Fᴇᴜᴇʀʙᴀᴄʜ und Fʀᴇᴜᴅ on religious projection, 'unmasking God'; Fokke Sɪᴇʀᴋsᴍᴀ 1917-77, De religieuze projectie 1956, added phenomenological psychology; Han Fᴏʀᴛᴍᴀɴɴ 1912-70, Als ziende de onzienlijke 1964-8, more moderate on projection, 'not a fact of experience but a hypothesis']: RelStR 14 (1988) 207-211.
8002 **Baker** Don, A fresh new look at God [... the persons of the Trinity through the eyes of Moses]. Portland OR 1986, Multnomah. 153 p. $9. – ᴿBS 145 (1988) 105 (R. P. *Lightner*: admittedly somewhat fictional).
8003 *Barr* James, Mᴏᴡɪɴᴄᴋᴇʟ, the Old Testament, and the question of natural theology [Oslo 2d Mowinckel lecture 27.XI.1987]: ST 42 (1988) 21-38.
8004 *Barstad* Hans, Da 'Gud' ble til; noen gammeltestamentlige perspektiver: → 97*, ꜰLøɴɴɪɴɢ I. NorTTs 89 (1988) 19-26.
8005 *Becquet* Gilles, Dieu, partenaire des hommes dans l'histoire de son peuple: Sève 501 (1988) 504-510 [497 (1988) 235s, Serviteur, Is 42ss].

8006 *a*) **Beek** A. van der, Waarom? Over lijden, schuld en God. – *b*) Nogmaals, waarom? Artikelen over en reacties op het boek. Nijkerk 1986, Callenbach. 126 p. – ᴿNedTTs 42 (1988) 354s (R. *Hensen*).

8007 **Béguerie** Philippe, Dieu de la Bible: Aux sources de la foi 1. P 1987, Cerf. 88 p. F 37. – ᴿEsprVie 98 (1988) 58s (L. *Barbey*).

8007* *Boisvert* Léandre, Les images bibliques de Dieu dans l'œuvre de Gustavo GUTIÉRREZ: ÉglT 19 (1988) 307-321.

8008 *Bonhoeffer* Thomas, Gotteslehre, eine pastoralpsychologische Zuspitzung: TLZ 113 (1988) 865-872.

Bottéro J., Naissance de Dieu 1986 → b945.

8009 **Boyce** Richard N., The cry to God in the Old Testament [*z'q; ş'q*]: SBL diss. 103. Atlanta 1988, Scholars. ix-93 p. $17. 1-55540-229-1; 30-5..

8010 **Buckley** Michael J., At the origins of modern atheism. NHv 1987, Yale Univ. viii-445 p. $38. – ᴿJTS 39 (1988) 638-640 (D. *Brown*: a quite outstanding achievement; 'Micheal'); TTod 45 (1988s) 219s. 222 (L. S. *Cunningham*: brilliant).

8011 *Buit* M. du, Puissance de Dieu: → 706, Catholicisme 12,55 (1988) 288-293.

8012 **Burrell** David B., Knowing the unknowable God: IBN-SINA, MAI-MONIDES, AQUINAS 1986 → 2,5017; 3,6331; 0-268-01225-3; ᴿBijdragen 49 (1988) 87-89 (F. De *Grijs*: not boring); Horizons 15 (1988) 170s (J. *Renard*); NBlackf 69 (1988) 45s (M. *Dodds*); RelSt 24 (1988) 541s (A. *Broadie*); Thomist 51 (1987) 699-709 (W. J. *Hill*).

8013 *Carella* Michael J., *Sheres* Ita, Hebraic monotheism; the enduring attitude: Judaism 37 (1988) 229-239.

8014 *a*) *Cazelles* Henri, Quand la Bible dit 'Dieu'; – *b*) *Marlé* René, Qui est Dieu? [*Duquoc* C. 1978; *Jüngel* E.]: Masses Ouvrières 419 (1988) 9-21 / 39-53.

8015 *Clark* R. L., CUPITT and divine imagining: ModT 5 (1988s) 45-60.

8015* **Cupitt** Don, Only human 1985 → 1,6225... 3,6334: ᴿHeythJ 29 (1988) 486-8 (B. R. *Brinkman*).

8016 **Finance** Joseph de, Le sensible et Dieu; en marge de mon vieux catéchisme [... s'il est 'esprit pur', comment peut-il connaître le sensible en tant que sensible?]. R/P 1988, Pont. Univ. Gregoriana / Beauchesne. 344 p. Lit. 42.000. 2-7010-1172-8.

8017 *Gregersen* Niels H., Forsynstankens mulighed og umulighed: DanTTs 51 (1988) 241-262 [< ZIT 89,5].

8017* **Gross** Karl, Menschenhand und Gotteshand 1985 → 1,6232... 3,6338: ᴿGregorianum 69 (1988) 169 (J. *Janssens*); RB 95 (1988) 123s (R. J. *Tournay*); TRu 53 (1988) 424-6 (E. *Dassmann*).

8018 ᴱ**Haag** Ernst, Gott, der einzige [gegen *Lang* B.] 1984/5 → 1,288; 3,6340: ᴿNedTTs 42 (1988) 255 (K. A. D. *Smelik*).

8019 **Hall** D. J., God and human suffering; an exercise in the theology of the Cross 1986 → 2,5032; 3,6341: ᴿAnglTR 70 (1988) 107-9 (S. *Pepper*); NRT 110 (1988) 425 (L. *Renwart*).

8020 **Hebblethwaite** Brian, The ocean of truth; a defense of objective theism [against Don CUPITT]. C 1988, Univ. x-165 p. $34.50; pa. $12. 0-521-35182-0; 975-9 [TDig 36,162].

8020* *Heller* Jan, *a*) Das AT als Niederschlag des Ringens mit den Göttern um den einzigen Gott [Gastvorlesung Marburg 1986]; – *b*) Anthropomorphismen und Chrematomorphismen im AT [Gastvorlesung Berlin 1967; ᶠ*Pakozdy*]; – *c*) Das Ringen um Leben und das Ringen gegen den Tod in den Religionen des fruchtbaren Halbmondes und im AT

[Gastvorlesung Mainz 1986]: ➤ 204, An der Quelle 1988, 257-263 / 129-148 / 249-255.

8021 **Hurtado** Larry W., One God, one Lord [... despite preexisting Wisdom etc.]. Ph 1988, Fortress. 192 p. $13 [BToday 26,376].

8022 **Jüngel** Eberhard, Dios como misterio del mundo. – ᵀ*Vevia* Fernando C. 1984 ➤ 65,5725 ... 2,5036: ScripTPamp 20 (1988) 316-324 (J. L. *Illanes*).

8023 **Köckert** Matthias, Vätergott und Väterverheissungen; eine Auseinandersetzung mit Albrecht ALT und seinen Erben: FRLANT 142. Gö 1988, Vandenhoeck & R. 387 p. DM 98. 3-625-53821-9. – ᴿTLZ 113 (1988) 806s (A. H. *Gunneweg*).

8023* **Kreuzer** Siegfried, Der lebendige Gott: BWANT 116, 1983 ➤ 64,6184: ᴿRB 95 (1988) 309s (J. M. de *Tarragon*).

8024 **Lang** Bernhard, Monotheism and the prophetic minority 1983 ➤ 64, 191.6188 ... 3,6349: ᴿNedTTs 42 (1988) 254s (K. A. D. *Smelik*).

8024* **Langer** Birgit, Sonne der Gerechtigkeit; eine Studie zu Gott als 'Licht' in Israel und Mesopotamien: Diss. ᴰ*Braulik* G. W 1987s. – TR 84 (1988) 514; RTLv 20.540.

8025 **Leroy** Gérard, Dieu est un droit de l'homme; préf. *Geffré* C.: Parole présente. P 1988, Cerf. 135 p. F 75. – ᴿEsprVie 98 (1988) 267 (P. *Jay*: plus de vivacité que de clarté).

8026 **Levenson** John D., Creation and the persistence of evil; the Jewish drama of divine omnipotence. SF 1988, Harper & R. xvi-182 p. 0-06-254845-X.

8027 **McCabe** Herbert, God matters 1987 ➤ 3,249: ᴿFurrow 39 (1988) 267s (sr. Margaret *Brennan*); HeythJ 29 (1988) 468-470 (B. *Hebblethwaite*: forfeits our sympathy at once with the categorical claim that 'there is no significant world religion except Christianity'); Month 249 (1988) 555 (N. D. *O'Donoghue*).

8028 **McFague** Sallie, Models of God ... for an ecological nuclear age 1987 ➤ 3,6354; [experiments with metaphors and 'nonsense to see if it can make a claim to truth' p. 69]: ᴿAnglTR 70 (1988) 85-90 (O. C. *Thomas*); CurrTMiss 15 (1988) 208s (R. *Busse*); ExpTim 99 (1987s) 222s (J. *Polkinghorne*: 'traditional Christianity abandoned'); JTS 39 (1988) 647-9 (Ruth *Page*: 'What should we be doing for our time that would be comparable to what Paul and John did for theirs?' p. 30); Horizons 15 (1988) 401s (Catherine M. *LaCugna*); NewTR 1,2 (1988) 103-5 (S. *Bevans*); RExp 85 (1988) 359s (D. *Stiver*); TLond 91 (1988) 420s (M. *Wiles*: excellent); TTod 45 (1988s) 95s. 98-101 (G. D. *Kaufman*); TS 49 (1988) 550s (R. *Schreiter*).

8029 *McKelway* Alexander J., The freedom of God and human liberation; the structure of divine freedom: PrincSemB 9 (1988) 197-210 [< ZIT 89,230].

8030 **Macquarrie** John, In search of deity (1983s Gifford Lectures) 1984 ➤ 1,6247: ᴿHeythJ 29 (1988) 101s (J. *O'Donnell*).

8031 *Metz* Johann B., Theologie gegen Mythologie; kleine Apologie des biblischen Monotheismus [< Giessen, 14. Philosophie-Kongress]: Herd-Korr 42 (1988) 187-193.

8032 ᴱ**Morris** Thomas V., The concept of God: Oxford readings in philosophy. Ox 1987, UP. vi-276 p. 0-19-875077-3; 076-5. 12 art.

8033 *Neusner* Jacob, Is the God of Judaism incarnate?: RelSt 24 (1988) 213-238.

8034 *Nicolas* Jean-Hervé, Miséricorde et sévérité de Dieu: RThom 88 (1988) 181-214. 533-555.

8035 *Osiek* Carolyn,   Images of God; breaking boundaries: SpTod 40 (1988) 333-344.

8036 *Plathow* Michael, El sufrimiento humano como sentimiento de la ausencia de Dios [Menschenleid als Leiden an Gottes Verborgenheit: TZBas 40 (1984) 275-295], ᵀᴱ*Puig Massana* Ramón: SelT 26 (1987) 3-13.

8037 **Sambonet** Giorgio,   Dio l'Ebreo; Ebreo d'amore [poetry-style reflections briefly on unnumbered pages]. Genova 1987, Marietti.   88-211-9991-6.

8038 **Scarry** Elaine,   The body in pain; the making and unmaking of the world. NY 1985/7, Oxford-UP.   v-385 p. $25/pa. $9. – ᴿRelStR 14 (1988) 311-6 (Jorunn J. *Buckley*: high quality interdisciplinary on the Bible, creation, pain, war, Marx; 'the immorality of God; his unpredictable willfulness is projected onto his people as *their* disobedience' p. 278).

8039 *a) Schreiner* Josef,   Gott liebt sein Volk — eine Botschaft des Alten Testaments; – *b) Simonis* Walter,   Gottesliebe — Nächstenliebe; Überlegungen zum sogenannten Doppelgebot im Lichte des biblischen Schöpfungs- und Bundesglaubens: ➤ 53, ᶠGANOCZY A., Creatio 1988. 17-35 / 60-83.

8040 *Scullion* John J.,   The God of the Patriarchs: Pacifica 1 (Melbourne 1988) 141-156 [< ZIT 88,445].

8041 **Sponheim** Paul R.,   God; the question and the quest; toward a conversation concerning Christian faith 1985 ➤ 2,2058; 3,6374: ᴿRExp 85 (1988) 170s (D. *Stiver*).

8042 **Surin** Kenneth,   Theology and the problem of evil 1986 ➤ 2,5060; 3,6376: ᴿModT 4 (1987s) 408s (D. Z. *Phillips*); NBlackf 69 (1988) 251 (P. *Smyth*); ScotJT 41 (1988) 539-41 (Grace M. *Jantzen*).

8043 **Varone** François,   El Dios ausente; reacciones religiosa, atea y creyente [Ce Dieu absent qui fait problème 1984 ➤ 3,6381], ᵀ*García Valenceja* J. J.: Presencia Teológica 35. Santander 1987, Sal Terrae. 230 p. 84-293-0964-8. – ᴿActuBbg 25 (1988) 233s (J. *Giménez Meliá*).

H1.2 *Immutabilitas* – **God's suffering; process theology.**

8044 **Basinger** David,   Divine power in process theism: a philosophical critique. Albany 1988, SUNY series in philosophy.   viii-135 p. $34.50; pa. $11 [TDig 35,259].

8045 *a) Bracken* Joseph A.,   The divine pleroma; – *b) Hallman* Joseph M.,   The presence of the risen Lord, a Whiteheadian approach: ChSt 26,1 ('Process theology' 1987) 25-36 / 51-61.

8046 *Brito* E.,   Dieu en mouvement? Thomas d'AQUIN et HEGEL: RevSR 62 (1988) 111-135.

8047 *Clark* W. N. *al.*, in ᴱ**Nash** R., Process theology 1987 ➤ 393.

8048 **Creel** Richard E.,   Divine impassibility 1986 ➤ 2,5072;   3,6390: ᴿCurrTM 15 (1988) 290s (M. *Root*); ModT 5 (1988s) 182-4 (S. *Sia*); NBlackfr 68 (1987) 48s (D. A. *Pailin*).

8048* **Daane** J.,   Unchangeability of God: ➤ 801, ISBEnc³ 4 (1988) 942-4.

8049 **Dodds** M. J.,   The unchanging God of love 1986 ➤ 2,5074; 3,6392: ᴿAngelicum 65 (1988) 134-7 (A. *Wilder*: a distinguished accomplishment).

8050 *Elmore* Floyd S.,   An evangelical analysis of process pneumatology: Bibliotheca Sacra 145 (1988) 15-29.

8051 **Fiddes** Paul S.,   The creative suffering of God. Ox 1988, Clarendon. x-281 p. $59 [TDig 35,357]. – ᴿETL 64 (1988) 485-8 (M. *Steen*, Eng.); TTod 45 (1988s) 488. 490 (M. D. *Meeks*).

8052 **Fretheim** Terence E., Il Dio compromesso; una meditazione sull'AT [The suffering of God 1984 → 65,5752], ᵀ. Mi 1987, Paoline. 227 p. Lit. 14.000. – ᴿHumBr 43 (1988) 446s (A. *Bonora*).

8053 *Fretheim* Terence E., The repentance of God; a key to evaluating Old Testament God-talk: HorBT 10,1 (1988) 47-70.

8054 **Frohnhofen** Herbert, Apatheia tou theou 1987 → 3,6394: ᴿArBegG 30 (1986s) 234-6 (*ipse*); RÉAnc90 (1988) 255s (A. Le *Boulluec*).

8055 *Grant* Colin, Possibilities for divine passibility: TorJT 4 (1988) 3-18.

8056 *Hay* Eldon, God, creativity and the world; a process typology of religions?: SR 17 (1988) 131-142.

8057 **Jüngel** Eberhard, L'essere di Dio è nel divenire; due studi [1965] sulla teologia di Karl BARTH. CasM 1986, Marietti. 181 p. Lit. 26.000. – ᴿProtestantesimo 43 (1988) 227s (V. *Subilia*).

8058 **Kowalczyk** Stanisław, Centuries about God, from the pre-Socratic period to process theology. Wrocław 1986, Archdiocese. 426 p. (also ❷ Wieki o Bogu, 472 p.). – ᴿDivThom 89s (1986s) 468-470 (E. *Wallewander*).

8059 *Lochman* Jan M., Von der Mitleidenschaft Gottes; was hat uns das Kreuz Christi zu sagen?: EvKomm 20 (1987) 506-9 [> NSys 30 (1988) 122s].

8059* **Lodahl** Michael E., Shekhinah/Spirit; a process pneumatology founded on Jewish-Christian conversation: diss. Emory, ᴰ*Boozer* J. Atlanta 1988. 336 p. 88-27902. – DissA 49 (1988s) 3063-A; RelStR 15,189; RTLv 20,387.

8060 **Meesen** Frank, Unveränderlichkeit und Menschwerdung Gottes; eine theologiegeschichtlich-systematische Untersuchung: Diss. ᴰ*Lehmann* K. FrB 1988. 555 p. – RTLv 20,569.

8060* *Nicholls* David, Federal politics and finite God; images of God in United States theology [*Whitehead* A. N.: Psalms worship of glory arising from power is barbaric and dangerous]: ModT 4 (1987s) 373-400.

8061 *Orlando* Pasquale, L'immutabilità di Dio; il pensiero di S. TOMMASO di fronte ad HEGEL e a KIERKEGAARD: DocCom 40 (1987) 278-284.

8062 *Paton* Margaret, Can God forgive?: ModT 4 (1987s) 225-233.

8063 **Pittenger** Norman, The pilgrim church and the Easter people [... process theology; 1983 lectures at John Carroll Univ., Cleveland]: Theology and Life. Wilmington 1987, Glazier. 112 p. $9 [TDig 35,282].

8064 *Post* Stephen G., The inadequacy of selflessness; God's suffering and the theory of love: JAAR 56 (1988) 213-228.

8065 *Regan* Thomas J., La 'process theology', ᵀ*Farnham* Dana: Études 368 (1988) 81-92.

8065* *Reymond* Bernard, Théologie systématique et prédication; exemple, la 'Process Theology': ÉTRel 63 (1988) 251-262.

8066 **Rovira Bellosa** J. M., La humanidad de Dios 1986 → 3,6415: ᴿTEsp 31 (1987) 280s (S. *Fuster*).

8067 *a)* *Rowland* Christopher, Change and the God of the Bible; – *b)* Sia Santiago, The doctrine of God's immutability; introducing the modern debate: NBlackfr 68 (1987) 212-9 / 220-232.

8068 *Russell* John M., Impassibility and pathos in BARTH's idea of God: AnglTR 70 (1988) 221-232.

8069 ᴱ**Sia** S., Process theology and the Christian doctrine of God: World & Spirit sup. 1986 → 3,6418: ᴿHorizons 15 (1988) 171-3 (L. S. *Ford*).

8070 *a)* *Sia* Santiago, A changing God?; – *b)* *Trethowan* Illtyd, God's changelessness; – *c)* *Bracken* Joseph A., Process perspectives and

Trinitarian theology; – *d*) *O'Donnell* John, God's historicity; Trinitarian perspectives: WSpirit 8 (1986) 13-30 / 31-43 / 51-64 / 65-79.

8071 **Smith** Huston, Has Process Theology dismantled classical theism? [no, because it restricts our immortality to God's memory of us: 32d Bellarmine lecture, St. Louis Univ. 1988, unabridged]: TDig 35 (1988) 303-318.

8072 **Trethowan** Illtyd, Process theology and the Christian tradition; an essay in post Vatican II thinking 1985 ➤ 1,6310; 3,6421:   ᴿRExp 85 (1988) 168-170 (D. *Stiver*).

8072* *Veken* J. van der, Process theology: ➤ 186, Catholicisme 11 (1988) 1103-1111.

8073 *Vorgrimler* Herbert, Das Leiden Gottes: TGegw 30 (1987) 20-26.

8074 **Weinandy** Thomas G., Does God change? 1985 ➤ 1,6993... 3,6422: ᴿNBlackf 68 (1987) 581s (D. L. *Burrell*, also on TRETHOWAN I.).

8075 **Williams** Trevor. Form and vitality in the world and God; a Christian perspective 1985 ➤ 2,5097; 3,6423: ᴿModT 4 (1987s) 102s (A. E. *Harvey*).

H1.4   *Femininum in Deo*   –   **God as father and as mother.**

8076 *Beilner* Wolfgang, 'Einer ist euer Vater' (Mt 23,9) — neutestamentliches zum Titel Abt: Sancta Crux 49,106 (1988) 20-32.

8077 **Bloesch** D. G., The battle for the Trinity; the debate over inclusive God-language 1985 ➤ 1,6316; 2,5100; 0-89283-230-4. – ᴿJPsy&T 15 (1987) 258 (C. J. *Barber*).

8078 **Boff** Leonardo, The maternal face of God; the feminine and its religious expressions 1987 ➤ 3,6430:   ᴿHorizons 15 (1988) 416s (Marie Anne *Mayeski*); NewTR 1,3 (1988) 103s (W. *Brennan*); RelStR 14 (1988) 142 (Kathryn A. *Rabuzzi*: irritating; e.g. 'we' as if women did not exist 'cannot know what the feminine is in its objectivity' p. 26); Tablet 242 (1988) 343 (Elizabeth *Meakins*).

8079 *Corrington* Gail P., The 'divine woman'?: AnglTR 70 (1988) 207-220.

8080 **Daly** Mary, Beyond God the Father. L 1986 = 1973, Women's Press. xxxiv-225 p. £5. – ᴿModT 4 (1987s) 289-291 (Ann *Loades*).

8081 **Durrwell** François-X., Le Père; Dieu en son mystère 1987 ➤ 3,6436: ᴿÉglT 19 (1988) 104-6 (A. *Perlman*); ETL 64 (1988) 212s (A, de *Halleux*); NBlackf 69 (1988) 302 (I. *Trethowan*); RHPR 68 (1988) 488s (G. *Siegwalt*); ScEspr 40 (1988) 387s (L. *Sabourin*).

8082 *Frye* Roland M., Language for God and feminist language; problems and principles: ScotJT 41 (1988) 441-469.

8083 *Fuster* Sebastián, ¿Un Dios varón? Sobre la maternidad divina: EscrVedat 17 (1987) 75-125.

8083* **Gelpi** Donald L., The divine mother... Holy Spirit ➤ 1,6322; 2,5113. – ᴿHeythJ 29 (1988) 399s (J. *O'Donnell*: does not focus 'feminity' of God).

8084 **Gerstenberger** E. S., Jahwe — ein patriarchaler Gott? Traditionelles Gottesbild und feministische Theologie: Urban-Tb 391. Stu 1988, Kohlhammer. 171 p. DM 20. 3-17-009947-7 [BL 89,105, C. S. *Rodd*: starting with a four-year-old girl's question, 'Does God have a penis?', claims monotheism developed only after the Exile]. – ᴿProtestantesimo 43 (1988) 206s (J. A. *Soggin*).

8085 *Grünfelder* Anne-Marie, Theologica feministica velut mors Dei patriarchalis? (en croate): BogSm 58 (1988) 29-58; deutsch 59s.

8086 **Hosmer** Rachel, Gender and God; love and desire in Christian spirituality. CM 1986, Cowley. 142 p. $8. 0-936384-39-5. – ᴿHorizons 15 (1988) 422s (M. *Downey*, also on Sophia).

8087 *Llewellyn* Patrick, 'Passing the love of women' [... Yahweh as womanlike]: Month 249 (1988) 1024-7.

8088 *a*) *Lurker* Manfred, Vatergott — Schöpfergott — Himmelsgott; Manifestationen des Väterlichen in Mythos und religiöser Überlieferung; – *b*) *Schwarzenau* Paul, Symbolik des göttlichen Kindes: Symbolon 9 (Köln 1988) 38-51 / 52-62 [< NTAbs 33,57].

8089 *Mawhinney* Allen, God as Father; two popular theories reconsidered [i. Jesus' use of *abba* was unique (wrong); ii. comforting for Christians (must be reconsidered)]: JEvTS 31 (1988) 181-190 [< ZIT 88,588].

8090 *Montero* A., El rostro femenino y materno de Dios: Studium 28 (M 1988) 217-233.

8091 *Mulack* Christa, Maria und die Weiblichkeit Gottes: ➤ 584, Maria ökumenisch 1983/4, 143-170.

8092 **Oddie** William, What will happen to God? 1984 ➤ 65,7541; 1,8600: ᴿScotJT 41 (1988) 117-124 (Elaine *Storkey*: few books have polarised so effectively).

8093 *a*) *Pentz* Rebecca T., Can Jesus save women?: – *b*) *Robinson* James M., Very goddess and very man: Jesus' better self ➤ 548, Encountering 1988.

8094 *Reynolds* Lyndon, BONAVENTURE on gender and godlikeness: DowR 106 (1988) 171-194 [< ZIT 88,660].

8095 **Ruether** Rosemary R., Sexism and God-talk 1983 ➤ 64,7678 ... 3,6459: ᴿTEdn 24 (1987s) 147-9 (Ellen *Leonard*).

8095* *Rupprecht* Friederike, 'Den Felsen, der dich gebar, täuschtest du ...' Gott als gebärende Frau in Dtn 32,18 und anderen Texten der Hebräischen Bibel: KIsr 3 (1988) 53-61.

8096 **Schneiders** Sandra M., Woman and the Word; the gender of God ... 1986 ➤ 2,5123; 3,6460: ᴿRRel 47 (1988) 310s (D. L. *Fleming*).

8097 *Thistlethwaite* Susan B., God and her survival in a nuclear age: JFemStRel 4 (1988) 73-92 [< ZIT 88,574].

8098 *Timm* Hermann, Gottes Vater- und Sohnschaft im Christentum: TPrac 23 (Mü 1988) 161-173.

8099 **Torres Queiruga** A., Creo en Dios Padre 1986 ➤ 3,6463: ᴿTEsp 31 (1987) 279s (S. *Fuster*).

8099* **Winter** Urs, Frau und Göttin; exegetische und ikonographische Studien zum weiblichen Gottesbild im alten Israel und in dessen Umwelt [I. OBO 53, 1983 ➤ 64,1534] II: Hab. Diss. FrS 1988, ᴰ*Keel* O. – TR 84 (1988) 510.

H1.7 **Revelatio.**

8100 **Artola** Antonio M., [*Lessius* L.] De la revelación a la inspiración 1983 ➤ 64,1425 ... 3,6469: ᴿActuBbg 25 (1988) 78s (F. de P. *Solà*); RHE 83 (1988) 790s (R. *Aubert*).

8100* **Carnicella** Maria Cristina, La scienza della comunicazione, la rivelazione divina e la teologia: diss. Pont. Univ. Gregoriana, Extr. Nº 3484, ᴰ*O'Collins* G. R 1988. 104 p. – RTLv 20,537.

8101 *Costa* Filippo, *Bof* Giampiero, Rivelazione ['Dizionario']: FilT 1,2 (1988) 119-132 / 133-142.

8102 **Dartigues** A., La Révélation; du sens au salut: [ᴱ*Doré* J.] Le christianisme et la foi chrétienne 6. P 1985, Desclée. 288 p. [RTLv 19,73, E. *Brito*]. – ᴿLavalTP 44 (1988) 124s (R.-M. *Roberge*).

8103 **Dartigues** André, La Rivelazione; dal senso alla salvezza [... la salvezza non può essere fondata sulla conoscenza]. Brescia 1988, Queriniana. 333 p. Lit. 32.000. – ᴿCC 139 (1988,4) 608-610 (J. *O'Donnell*).

8104 *a) Dassmann* Ernst, Geschichtlichkeit der Offenbarung und gnostische Bedrohung; – *b) Splett* Jörg, Wahrheit und Geschichte, Mythos und Person; religionsphilosophische Anmerkungen: ➤ 305, Tiefenpsychologische 1988, 49-66 / 81-97.

8105 **Dulles** Avery, Models of revelation 1983 ➤ 64,1379 ... 2,5159: ᴿTR 84 (1988) 220-2 (H. *Waldenfels*).

8106 **Fisichella** Rino, La rivelazione; evento e credibilità: Corso Teol. Sist. 2, 1985 ➤ 2,5162; 3,6475: ᴿNRT 110 (1988) 423s (L. *Renwart*).

8107 **Haught** John F., The revelation of God in history: Zacchaeus Studies. Wilmington 1988, Glazier. 104 p. $6 [TDig 35,394].

8107* *Hughson* Thomas, DULLES and AQUINAS on revelation: Thomist 52 (1988) 445-471.

8108 **Kessler** Michael, FICHTE, Kritik aller Offenbarung 1986 ➤ 2,5184; 3,6482: ᴿTPQ 136 (1988) 291s (H. *Petri*).

8108* *Koch* Günter, Der geschaffene Mensch — offen für Gottes Offenbarung? Zur Entwicklung der Korrelationsproblematik: ➤ 53, ᶠGANOCZY A., Creatio 1988, 112-124.

8109 *Lafont* Ghislain, La Constitution 'Dei Verbum' et ses précédents conciliaires: NRT 110 (1988) 58-73.

8110 *Lubac* Henri de, *Cattaneo* Enrico, La constitución 'Dei Verbum' veinte años después [< RasT 26 (1985) 385-400], ᵀᴱ*Persia* Daniella: SalT 26 (1987) 340-5.

8110* **Madigan** Patrick, Christian revelation and the completion of the Aristotelian revolution. Lanham MD 1988, UPA. 128 p. $19.75; pa. $10.25. 0-8191-7090-9; 1-7.

8111 *a) O'Collins* Gerald, Revelation past and present; – *b) Alszeghy* Zoltan, The Sensus Fidei and the development of dogma: ➤ 380, Vatican II Assessment 1 (1988) 125-137 / 138-156; – français ➤ 379, Bilan 1, 141-152 / 153-170.

8111* *Pannenberg* Wolfhart, Revelation in early Christianity: ➤ 23, ᶠCHADWICK H. 1988, 76-86.

8112 *Patterson* Bob E., Revelation and the Bible: PerspRelSt 14,4 (1987) 19-30 [< ZIT 88,447].

8113 **Price** Theron D., Revelation and faith; theological reflections on the knowing and doing of truth. Macon GA 1987, Mercer Univ. 188 p. $15. 0-86554-260-0. – ᴿRExp 85 (1988) 164-6 (D. *Stiver*: also on world religions).

8114 *Russell* John F., The theology of revelation [*Dulles* A.; *Moran* G.]: IrTQ 54 (1988) 21-40.

8115 **Ruiz Arenas** Octavio, Jesús, epifanía del amor del Padre; teología de la Revelación: Coll. Seminarios Latinoam. 2/1. Bogotá 1987, Consejo Episcopal CELAM. 543 p. 958-625-074-1. – ᴿGregorianum 69 (1988) 357s (C. I. *González*).

8116 **Schmitz** Josef, Offenbarung: Leitfaden Theologie 19. Dü 1988, Patmos. 225 p. DM 24,80. – ᴿTGL 78 (1988) 438 (W. *Beinert*).

8116* **Schwarz** Hans, Divine communication; word and sacrament in biblical, historical and contemporary perspective [? 1984 ➤ 2,5215] 1985 ➤ 1, 6435; 0-8006-1846-7: ᴿScotBEv 6 (1988) 49s (D. F. *Wright*).

8117 *Seckler* Max, *a)* Was heisst Offenbarungsreligion? Eine semantische Orientierung: ➤ 114, ᶠPANNENBERG W., Vernunft 1988, 157-175. – *b)*

Interdependencia entre ilustración [Aufklärung] y revelación [< TüTQ 165 (1985) 161-173], ᵀᴱTorres María José de: SelT 27 (1988) 68-74.

8118 Sesboüé Bernard, Le Christ illuminateur; le salut par révélation [< J.C. l'unique Médiateur, à paraître]: NRT 110 (1988) 351-370.

8119 **Terry** Milton S., Biblical apocalyptics; a study of the most notable revelations of God and of Christ. GR 1988, Baker. 512 p. [GraceTJ 9,316].

8120 **Thiemann** Ronald E., Revelation and theology; the Gospel as narrated promise 1985 ➤ 1,6442... 3,6496: ᴿAnglTR 69 (1987) 107-9 (O. C. *Thomas*); CBQ 50 (1988) 151 (J. G. *Lodge*); CurrTM 15 (1988) 438-443 (P. *Keifert*).

8121 **Vögtle** Anton, Offenbarungsgeschehen... 1985 ➤ 1,259: ᴿColcT 58,1 (1988) 179-182 (R. *Bartnicki*).

8122 *Wallace* Mark I., Theology without revelation?: TTod 45 (1988s) 208-213.

H1.8 Theologia fundamentalis.

8123 **Adriaanse** H. J., *al.*, Het verschijnsel theologie; over de wetenschappelijke status van de theologie. Meppel 1987, Boom. 138 p. ƒ28. 90-6009-789-0. – ᴿTsTNijm 28 (1988) 190 (N. *Schreurs*).

8124 **Albert** Hans, La miseria della teologia, ᵀFabbio A. R 1985, Borla. – ᴿFilT 1,2 (1988) 183-5 (G. P. *Cammarota*).

8125 *Ancona* Giovanni, Sulla teologia fondamentale: RivScR (Molfetta 1988) 451-9.

8126 *Angelini* Giuseppe, Serve la teologia alla Chiesa?: RClerIt 63 (1987) 806-817.

8127 **Avis** Paul, The methods of modern theology 1986 ➤ 3,6503: ᴿScotJT 41 (1988) 536-9 (P. *Forster*).

8128 *Bayer* Oswald, *a*) Oratio, meditatio, tentatio [a try]: eine Besinnung auf LUTHERs Theologieverständnis: LutherJb 55 (1988) 7-59; – *b*) Unangepasste Wissenschaft; zum Verhältnis von Glauben und Wissen: EvKomm 20 (1987) 384-9 [> NSys 30 (1988) 117s].

8129 *Benvenuto* Edoardo, Attuali statuti epistemologici e filosofici della verità [i. Prologo agostiniano... v. 'verità-coerenza' al servizio della teologia... vii. disvelamento]: RasT 29 (1988) 37-62.

8130 *Bertuletti* Angelo, La teologia tra la fondazione ermeneutica e la fondazione metafisica; riflessioni intorno al Seminario di studio su 'Teologia e cultura': TItSett 13 (1988) 232-248; Eng. 249.

8131 *a*) *Bie* H. J. de, Geen dogmatiek zonder aandacht voor de Judaïstiek; – *b*) *Geertsema* H. G., Relationele waarheidsopvatting en Schriftgezag: TRef 31 (Woerden 1988) 116-129 / 130... [< ZIT 88,460].

8132 *a*) *Biser* Eugen, Der Spiegel des Glaubens; zum Prozess der theologischen Selbstkorrektur; – *b*) *Hoffmann* Fritz, Macht und Grenze der Sprache in der theologischen Reflexion: MüTZ 39 (1988) 229-240 / 249-258.

8133 *Borgman* Erik, Gefundeerd, maar niet te funderen [1 Kor 3,11]; theologie als bevrijdende hermeneutiek: TsTNijm 28 (1988) 113-134; 134, 'Well-founded, but not to be grounded'.

8134 **Bucher** Rainer, NIETZSCHEs Mensch und Nietzsches Gott; das Spätwerk als philosophisch-theologisches Programm: Würzburger Studien zur Fundamentaltheologie 1. Fra 1986, Lang. 407 p. – ᴿTGL 78 (1988) 96s (B. *Fraling*).

8134* **Castelein** John D., Standing on the promises of God; the contribution of fundamental theology to Peter BERGER's quest for non-projected transcendence: diss. Chicago 1988. – RelStR 15,191.

8135 FCOPLESTON F. C., The philosophical assessment of theology, EHughes Gerard J. 1987 ➤ 3,41: RTLond 91 (1988) 503 (P. *Sherry*).

8136 **Dalferth** Ingolf U., Theology and philosophy: Signposts in Theology. NY 1988, Blackwell. x-236 p. $40. 0-631-15354-3 [TDig 36,153].

8137 *Decleve* Henri, Sur le statut scientifique de la théologie: CahSPR 3 (Bru 1988) 69-105.

8138 *a)* *Díaz Murugarren* José, Teología fundamental y 'signos de los tiempos'; – *b)* *Lago Alba* Luis, Jornadas de Teología Fundamental (Pamplona, junio 1987): CiTom 115 (1988) 5-27 / 141-7 [(161-) 165-181, libros sobre TF].

8139 *Di Noia* J. A., Philosophical theology in the perspective of religious diversity: TS 49 (1988) 401-416.

8139* *a)* *Dubied* Pierre-Luigi, La place d'une faculté de théologie dans l'universitè d'aujourd'hui; – *b)* *Paroz* Pierre, La foi au risque de la réflexion scientifique: RTPhil 120 (1988) 21-28 / 29-39.

8140 **Evans** Gillian R., *McGrath* Alister E., *Galloway* Allan D., The science of theology: History of Christian Theology 1, 1986 ➤ 3,6520: RTLond 91 (1988) 507s (Frances *Young*: really just a history of the three periods; and only the middle one, on Reformation, touches on theology as science).

8141 *Fantino* Jacques, L'art de la théologie et l'attitude du théologien selon saint IRÉNÉE de Lyon: RThom 88 (1988) 65-86 / 229-255.

8141* **Fischer** Johannes, Die Theologie und die Wissenschaften; untheologische Betrachtungen zum Ort der Theologie: ev. Hab.-Diss., DJüngel E. Tü 1988. – RTLv 20,537.

8142 **Forte** Bruno, La teologia come compagnia, memoria e profezia 1987 ➤ 3,6525: RAsprenas 35 (1988) 242-252 (T. *Stancati*); RClerIt 63 (1987) 630-3 (F. G. *Brambilla*).

8143 **Fries** Heinrich, Fundamentaltheologie 1985 ➤ 1,6379; 2,5164: RWissWeis 49 (1986) 238 (W. *Dettloff*).

8144 **Fries** H., Teologia fondamentale: BiblTeolContemp 55: Brescia 1987, Queriniana. 756 p. Lit. 65.000. – RStPatav 35 (1988) 683-6 (E. R. *Tura*).

8145 **Graf** Friedrich W., Theonomie; Fallstudien zum Integrationsanspruch neuzeitlicher Theologie. Gü 1987, Mohn. 246 p. DM 64 pa. – RTR 84 (1988) 480-2 (G. *Wenz*: TILLICHs Begriff).

8146 *a)* *Greinacher* Norbert, Praktische Theologie als kritische Theorie kirchlicher Praxis in der Gesellschaft: TüTQ 168 (1988) 283-299. – *b)* *Gräb* Wilhelm, Dogmatik als Stück der Praktischen Theologie; das normative Grundproblem in der praktisch-theologischen Theoriebildung: ZTK 85 (1988) 474-492.

8147 *a)* *Gustafson* James M., Reflections on the literature on theological education published between 1955-1985; – *b)* *Fiorenza* Francis S., Thinking theologically about theological education: TEdn Sup. 2 (1988) 9-86 / 89-119.

8147* **Hofmann** Peter, Glaubensbegründung; neuere Entwürfe der Fundamentaltheologie bei J. B. METZ, W. PANNENBERG und C. BOFF: Karl APELs 'Transformation' der (Fundamental-)Philosophie und das Programm einer 'transformierten' Fundamentaltheologie: Diss. DSplett. Fra 1987s. – TR 84 (1988) 511.

8148 *Izquierdo* César, *Odero* José-Miguel, Manuales de teología fundamental II: ScripTPamp 20 (1988) 223-268.

8149 *a) Kasper* Walter, Die Wissenschaftspraxis der Theologie; – *b) Kern* Walter, Der Beitrag des Christentums zu einer menschlicheren Welt: ➤ 800, HbFT 4 (1988) 242-277 / 278-314.

8150 **Kenny** Anthony. Reason and religion 1987 ➤ 3,241: ᴿMonth 249 (1988) 731s (P. *Burns*).

8151 **Kraus** Georg, Gotteserkenntnis ohne Offenbarung und Glaube? Natürliche Theologie als ökumenisches Problem [Hab.-Diss.]: KkKSt 50, 1987 ➤ 3,6553; 3-87058-480-0: ᴿActuBbg 25 (1988) 228s (J. *Boada*); ETL 64 (1988) 215s (É. *Brito*); TGL 78 (1988) 176s (A. *Klein*); TPQ 136 (1988) 96s (S. *Birngruber*); TR 84 (1988) 135-7 (G.-L. *Müller*).

8151* **Kuld** Lothar, Lerntheorie des Glaubens; religiöse Lehren und Lernen nach J. H. NEWMANs Phänomenologie des Glaubensaktes: Diss. FrB 1987s, ᴰ*Biemer*. – TR 84 (1988) 511.

8152 ᴱ**Latourelle** R., *O'Collins* G., Problèmes et perspectives TFund 1982 ➤ 65,5837: ᴿMaisD 173 (1988) 153-6 (R. *Le Gall*).

8152* *Latourelle* René, Absence et présence de la Fondamentale à Vatican II: ➤ 379, Vatican II Bilan 3 (1988) 371-403; Eng. ➤ 380, Assessment 3,378-415.

8153 ᴱ**Lauret** B., *Réfoulé* F., Initiation à la pratique de la théologie I-V, 1982s ➤ 64,335... 2,5189: ᴿCiTom 114 (1987) 176-8 (P. *Fernández*, français; 384-6 español, M 1986 ➤ 1,6406).

8154 **Lerle** Ernst, Moderne Theologie unter der Lupe: Tagesfragen 38. Nauhäusen 1987, Hänssler. 111 p. DM 14,80 [TüTQ 168,346 unter Exegetica].

8155 *Llanes Maestre* José Luis, La teología como saber de totalidad: RET 48 (1988) 149-192.

8156 **McIntyre** John, Faith, theology and imagination. E 1987, Handsel. 176 p. 0-905-31265-1. – ᴿScotBEv 6 (1988) 63s (J. *Wilson*) unaccountably reprinted p. 124s.

8157 **Mackey** J. P., Modern theology; a sense of direction: Opus, 1987 ➤ 3,6560: ᴿNRT 110 (1988) 580 (L. *Renwart*).

8158 *Milbank* John, Theology without substance; Christianity, signs, origins, II: Literature and Theology 2 (Ox 1988) 131-152 [< ZIT 88,741].

5159 *Moloney* Raymond, The notion of fundamental theology after RAHNER and LONERGAN: MilltSt 17 (1986) 65-74.

8160 **Moltmann** Jürgen, Was ist heute Theologie? Zwei Beiträge zu ihrer Vergegenwärtigung [für die italienische Enciclopedia del novecento geschrieben]: QDisp 114. FrB 1988, Herder. 102 p. DM 19,80. 3-451-02114-5. – ᴿActuBbg 25 (1988) 229s (J. *Boada*); TsTNijm 28 (1988) 316 (E. *Borgman*).

8161 **Moltmann** Jürgen, Theology today; two contributions towards making theology present. L 1988, SCM. x-99 p. 0-334-02359-9.

8162 **Mueller** J. J., What is theology? [Was ist heute Theologie? QDisp 114, 1988], ᵀ*Bowden* J.: Zacchaeus studies. Wilmington 1988, Glazier. 103 p. $6 [TDig 35,394].

8163 **Muller** Richard A., Post-Reformation Reformed dogmatics, I. Prolegomena to theology. GR 1987, Baker. 365 p. $7. – ᴿScotBEv 6 (1988) 112-122 (D. F. *Kelly*: 'a rehabilitation of scholasticism?').

8164 *Murphy* Nancey C., Theology; an experimental science?: PerspRelSt 15 (1988) 219-234.

8165 **Neufeld** Karl Heinz, Probleme und Prospektiven dogmatischer Theologie [ital 1983 ➤ 1,387] ➤ 3,6564; ᵀᴱ*Ullrich* Lothar; also Lp 1986,

St. Benno. 557 p. – ᴿTPQ 136 (1988) 177 (A. *Seigfried*: Planungstätigkeit Neufelds).

8166 **Neufeld** K. H., Problemas y prospectivas de teología dogmática. Salamanca 1987. Sígueme. 527 p. – ᴿRET 48 (1988) 253-7 (G. *Flórez*).

8166* **Nielsen** Bent F., Die Rationalität der Offenbarungstheologie; die Struktur des Theologieverständnisses von Karl BARTH: Diss. Asrhus 1988. 238 p. – RTLv 20,538.

8167 **Ogden** Schubert M., On theology. SF 1986, Harper & R. 180 p. $19.50. 0-86683-529-6. – ᴿCurrTM 15 (1988) 215s (T. *Peters*).

8168 **O'Leary** Joseph S., Questioning back 1985 → 1,6423 ... 3,6566: ᴿN-Blackf 69 (1988) 196s (D. *Brown*: good on HEIDEGGER and DERRIDA).

8169 *O'Meara* Thomas F., Between idealism and neo-scholasticism; the fundamental and apologetic theology of Alois SCHMID (1825-1910): ÉglT 17 (1986) 335-354.

8169* **Peukert** Helmut, Science, action, and fundamental theology: toward a theology of communicating action [1976 → 58,870]: Studies in Contemporary German Social Thought. CM 1984, MIT. xxvii-330 p. £36. – ᴿHeythJ 29 (1988) 109-111 (G. *Daly*: top-heavy FT ecclesiastical edifice has disintegrated despite hasty repairs by Y. CONGAR on the foundation).

8170 **Poythress** Vern S., Symphonic theology; the validity of multiple perspectives in theology. GR 1987, Zondervan. 128 p. [GraceTJ 9,314].

8171 *a)* *Puntel* Lorenz B., Das Verhältnis von Philosophie und Theologie; Versuch einer grundsätzlichen Klärung; – *b)* *Rendtorff* Trutz, Theologiestudium — Ausbildung durch Wissenschaft?: → 114, ᶠPANNENBERG W., Vernunft 1988, 11-41 / 210-228.

8172 **Raschke** Carl A., Theological thinking; an in-quiry. Ithaca NY (POB 6525) 1988, Scholars. $20; pa. $13. 1-55540-187-2; 8-0 [TDig 35,244 adv.].

8173 **Ratzinger** J., Principles of Catholic theology 1987 → 3,281: ᴿAmerica 157 (1987) 483-5 (J. B. *Benestad*); HomP 89,10 (1988s) 71s (J. R. *Sheets*).

8174 **Ratzinger** J., Teoría de los principios teológicos; materiales para una teología fundamental 1985 → 2,5208: ᴿTEsp 31 (1987) 284s (M. *Gelabert*).

8175 **Ritschl** Dietrich, The logic of theology 1986 → 3,6575; ᵀ*Bowden* John: ᴿScotJT 41 (1988) 407s (A. E. *Lewis*); Themelios 14 (1988s) 35 (G. *Lewis*: not about God but about his own insights concerning some Jews and Christians; 'the term revelation should be avoided').

8176 *Sanchis Quevedo* Antonio, Magisterio y teólogos ante el reto de la nueva cultura: EscrVedat 17 (1987) 127-142.

8177 *a)* *Schumacher* Joseph, Apologetik und Fundamentaltheologie bei M. J. SCHEEBEN; – *b)* *Piolanti* Antonio, Ragione e fede in M. J. Scheeben: → k289, Divinitas 32 (1988) 63-87; ital. 88 / 41-61.

8178 *Seckler* Max, *a)* Enzyklopädische Fundamentaltheologie; zu einer Neuerscheinung [ᴱ*Ruggieri* G. 1987]: TüTQ 168 (1988) 321-337; – *b)* Die theologische Prinzipien- und Erkenntnislehre als fundamentaltheologische Aufgabe: TüTQ 168 (1988) 182-193.

8179 *a)* *Seckler* Max, Fundamentaltheologie; Aufgaben und Aufbau, Begriff und Namen; – *b)* *Reikerstorfer* Johann, Fundamentaltheologische Modelle der Neuzeit; – *c)* *Pottmeyer* Hermann J., Zeichen und Kriterien der Glaubwürdigkeit des Christentums; – *d)* *Kunz* Erhard, Glaubwürdigkeitserkenntnis und Glaube (analysis fidei) [→ 8706 *Neuner*]: → 800, HbFT 4 (1988) 451-519 / 347-372 / 373-413 / 414-449.

8180 ᴱ**Seidel** Walter, Offenbarung durch Bücher?; Impulse zu einer 'Theologie des Lesens'. FrB 1987, Herder. 160 p. DM 10. – ᴿTPQ 136 (1988) 302 (J. *Hörmandinger*).

8181 *Sequeri* Pierangelo, La ragione teologica e la cultura della modernità: TItSett 13 (1988) 219-231; Eng. 231.

8182 *Shriver* Donald W., What can liberals and evangelicals teach each other?: ChrCent (Aug. 12/19, 1987) 687-690 [< BS 145 (1988) 100].

8183 *Slenczka* Reinhard, Fundamentaltheologie nach Vaticanum I und II: TRu 53 (1988) 277-291.

8184 *Stock* Konrad, [*al.*,] Theologische Gegenwartsdeutung: Marburger Jb Theologie 2 (1988) 69-83 [3-111 ...: < ZIT 89,157].

8185 **Strotmann** Norberto, La situación de la teología. Lima 1985, Criterion. 180 p. – ᴿDocCom 40 (1987) 310-2 (C. *Petino*).

8186 *Verkamp* Bernard J., On doing the truth; orthopraxis and the theologian [... division of labor leaves him room for a certain neutrality]: TS 49 (1988) 3-24.

8187 *Vicente Burgoa* Lorenzo, Evidencia y credibilidad; razonamiento y juicio de credentidad: Studium 28 (M 1988) 459-474.

8188 **Viladesau** Richard, Answering for faith; Christ and the human search for salvation. NY 1987, Paulist. xii-312 p. $13. – ᴿCalvinT 23 (1988) 285-9 (J. W. *Cooper*).

8189 *Vries* H. de, Theologie en moderniteit, rationaliteit en skepsis: NedTTs 42 (1988) 21-41; Eng. 67.

8190 **Waldenfels** H., Kontextuelle Fundamentaltheologie 1985 ➤ 1,6448 ... 3,6590: ᴿNRT 110 (1988) 422 (L. *Renwart*).

8191 *Wilden* Matthias, Zur Bedeutung der Wort-Gottes-Theologie für die Ansätze gegenwärtiger Theologie: WissWeish 49 (1986) 98-133 [50 (1987) 28-54, in T. SOIRON und K. BARTH].

8192 *Wyschogrod* Edith, Theology in the wake of the other [*Taylor* Mark C., Altarity (sic), Univ. Ch 1987; 371 p. $42.50; pa. $16]: JAAR 56 (1988) 115-130.

8192* **Yee** M. M., The validity of theology as an academic discipline; a study in the light of the history and philosophy of science and with special reference to ... Austin FARRER: diss. Oxford 1988. – RTLv 20,538.

H2.1   **Anthropologia theologica – VT & NT.**

8193 **Alfaro** Juan, De la cuestión del hombre a la cuestión de Dios: Verdad e imagen 103. Salamanca 1988. Sígueme. 286 p. 84-301-1049-6. – ᴿGregorianum 69 (1988) 811s (*ipse*); LumenVr 37 (1988) 535s (U. *Gil Ortega*).

8194 **Amata** Biagio, Problemi di antropologia arnobiana 1984 ➤ 1,6452; 2,5234: ᴿRÉLat 65 (1987) 394s (J. *Fontaine*).

8195 **Andia** Y. [González] de, Homo vivens ... IRÉNÉE 1986 ➤ 2,5248; 3,6595: ᴿChH 57 (1988) 217s (A. A. *Bell*); CrNSt 9 (1988) 625-7 (R. *Tremblay*); NRT 110 (1988) 266s (D. *Dideberg*); ScEspr 40 (1988) 127s (G. *Pelland*); StMoralia 26 (1988) 302-4 (R. *Tremblay*).

8196 **Avelino de la Pienda** J., [autor de Antropología transcendental de K. RAHNER, ᴰ1982] El sobrenatural de los cristianos: Verdad e Imagen 91. Salamanca 1985, Sígueme. 219 p. – ᴿDivThom 89s (1986s) 422-6 (L. *Iammarrone*).

8196* *Bauer* Johannes B., *al.*, Herz: ➤ 807, RAC 14,111s (1988) 1093-1131.

8197 *Bavel* Tarcisius J. van, The anthropology of AUGUSTINE: MilltSt 19s (1987) 25-39 (41-47. 49-53, *Mathews* W., *Boyd* R., responses).

8198 **Ben-Chorin** Schalom, Was ist der Mensch? Anthropologie des Judentums 1986 ➤ 3,6600: ᴿGregorianum 69 (1988) 763-5 (D. *Cox*).

8199 **Bianchi** G.,   Dalla parte di Marta; una teologia del lavoro 1986
➤ 3,6601: ᴿStudium 83 (R 1987) 462 (B. *Belletti*).

8200 **Biffi** Inos,   Identità cristiana; essere uomini in Gesù Cristo: Sacra
Doctrina 5.   CasM 1988, Piemme.   38 p. Lit. 3500. – ᴿViPe 71 (1988)
553-5 (F. *Botturi*).

8201 **Blattner** Jürgen,   Toleranz als Strukturprinzip; ethische und psy-
chologische Studien zu einer christlichen Kultur der Beziehung [kath. Diss.
FrS, ᴰ*Stoeckle* B.]: Freib[B]TSt 129, 1985 ➤ 3,6603: ᴿTLZ 113 (1988)
372-4 (K. *Lüthi*).

8202 *Bonner* Gerald, Aᴜɢᴜsᴛɪɴᴇ's doctrine of man: LvSt 13 (1988) 41-57.

8203 *Brotzman* Ellis R.,   Man and the meaning of *nepeš* [Gn 2,7 + 750 times]:
Bibliotheca Sacra 145 (1988) 400-409.

8204 *Caporale* Vincenzo,   Antropologia e cristologia nella 'Gaudium et spes':
RasT 29 (1988) 142-165. ➤ 8497.

8205 *Coda* Piero,   L'antropologia trinitaria; una chiave di lettura della
'Gaudium et Spes':   NuovaUm 10,56 (1988) 17-47.

8205* *Coffey* David,   Christian anthropology ➤ 404, *Press* M., Bicentennial
1988, 130-141.

8206 **Comblin** José,   Das Bild vom Menschen [1985 ➤ 3,6614], ᵀ: Bibliothek
Theologie der Befreiung.   Dü 1987, Patmos.   246 p. – ᴿTPhil 63 (1988)
307s (M. *Sievernich*).

8207 *Cooper* John W.,   The identity of resurrected persons; fatal flaw of
monistic anthropology [now that body-soul dualism has faded]: CalvinT
23 (1988) 19-36.

8208 **Deissler** Alfons,   Wer bist du, Mensch? Die Antwort der Bibel 1985
➤ 1,6472; 2,5241: ᴿZkT 110 (1988) 90s (F. *Mohr*).

8208* **Despland** Michael,   Christianisme, dossier corps [Christian attitudes
toward the body ... formed by the clergy's grasping for power]. P 1987,
Cerf.   139 p. [RelStR 15,75, C. *Eire*: simplistic, homiletical, unconvincing;
but useful].

8209 *Donovan* Mary Ann,   Alive to the glory of God; a key insight in St.
Iʀᴇɴᴀᴇᴜs: TS 49 (1988) 283-297.

8210 **Engel** Mary P.,   John Cᴀʟᴠɪɴ's perspectival anthropology: [J]AAR 52.
Atlanta 1988, Scholars. $27; pa. $18 [TDig 35,354].

8211 *Figueiras* F. J.,   Dimensión antropológica de la moral cristiana:
Compostellanum 32 (1987) 93-120.

8212 *Fredriksen* Paula,   Beyond the body/soul dichotomy; Aᴜɢᴜsᴛɪɴᴇ on
Paul against the Manichees and the Pelagians: RechAug 23 (1988) 87-114.

8213 *Galot* Jean,   Cristo verità dell'uomo: CC 139 (1988,3) 115-127.

8214 **Gollnick** James,   'Flesh' as transformation symbol in the theology of
Aɴsᴇʟᴍ of Canterbury; historical and transpersonal perspectives 1985
➤ 3,6633: ᴿÉglT 18 (1987) 371-3 (A. *Guindon*); SR 17 (1988) 373 (C.
Davis).

8215 **González Faus** José I.,   Proyecto de hermano; visión creyente del
hombre: Presencia Teológica 40.   Santander 1987, Sal Terrae.   751 p.
84-293-0785-0. – ᴿActuBbg 25 (1988) 189-193 (F. J. *Vitoria*); Carthaginensia 4 (1988) 105s (F. *Martínez Fresneda*); LumenVr 37 (1988) 189-191
(F. *Ortiz de Urtaran*); RET 48 (1988) 110s (L. F. *García-Viana*).

8216 *Grom* Bernhard,   Anthroposophie und Christentum; *a*) Erkenntnisweg
und Menschenbild; – *b*) Das Weltbild: StiZt 206 (1988) 297-317 /
377-394.

8217 *Hallet* C.,   Temas antropológicos y vida espiritual según Balduino de
Fᴏʀᴅ: Studia Monastica 29 (1987) 225-250 [< RSPT 72,501].

8218 **Hamman** A. G., L'homme image de Dieu; essai d'une anthropologie chrétienne dans l'Église des cinq premiers siècles: Relais/Études 2, 1987 → 3,6629: ᴿEsprVie 98 (1988) 511 (J. *Pintard*); RevSR 61 (1987) 244 (R. *Winling*).

8219 *Helling* Barbara, *Mertin* Andreas, Ecce homo; vom Christusbild zum Menschenbild; Anregungen für den Religionsunterricht: Forum Religion (Stu 1988,3) 2-13 [< ZIT 88,708].

8220 *Hernando* Eusebio, Imagen del hombre según el Antiguo Testamento, luces y sombras: TEsp 32 (1988) 201-225.

8221 *Jüngel* Eberhard, Humanización del hombre [Menschwerdung des Menschen: EvKomm 12 (1984) 446-8], ᵀᴱ*Castanyé* Josep: SelT 26 (1987) 15-17.

8221* **Kangundi** Stanislas K. W., La théologie comme herméneutique; anthropologie africaine: diss. ᴰ*Gesché* A. LvN 1987. ix-332 p. – ETL 64,230.

8222 *Kühn* Rolf, Le corps retrouvé; une phénoménologie subjective radicale appliquée à une investigation sur la corporéité [*Henry* M., 1963-88]: RSPT 72 (1988) 557-567; Eng. 568.

8223 **Ladaria** L. F., Antropología teológica 1983 → 64,6252 ... 1,6487: ᴿCarthaginensia 4 (1988) 373s (F. *Martínez Fresneda*).

8224 **Langemeyer** Georg, Menschsein im Wendekreis des Nichts; Entwurf einer theologischen Anthropologie auf der Basis des alltäglichen Bewusstseins. Münster 1988, Aschendorff. iv-116 p. DM 19,80. 3-402-03349-6 [Bijdragen 49,475].

8225 *Laudazi* Carlo, L'uomo nel progetto di Dio: Teresianum 39 (1988) 339-373.

8226 *Lotz* Johannes B., 'Magis anima continet corpus ... quam e converso' (STh 1, q 76, a 3); zum Verhältnis von Seele und Leib nach Thomas von AQUIN: ZkT 110 (1988) 300-9.

8227 **Maggioni** B., Uomo e società nella Bibbia. Mi 1987, Jaca. – ᴿFilT 1,3 (1988) 207s (A. *Isola*).

8228 *Mantzaridis* Georges I., La déification de l'homme: Contacts/Orthodoxe 40 (1988) 6-18.

8229 *Martikainen* Eeva, Die Distinktion von Natur und Person in der lutherischen Ethik von Paul ALTHAUS: KerDo 34 (1988) 2-10; Eng. 10.

Moltmann Jürgen, On human dignity 1984 → 9487.

8230 **Nellas** Panayotis [1936-1986], Deification in Christ; Orthodox perspectives on the nature of the human person, ᵀ*Russell* Norman: Contemporary Greek theologians 5. Crestwood NY 1987, St. Vladimir. 254 p. $13 [TDig 35,381].

8231 *Neufeld* Karl H., Zum Menschenbild des Zweiten Vatikanischen Konzils: TPQ 136 (1988) 150-8.

8232 **O'Connell** Robert J., The origin of the soul in St. AUGUSTINE's later works [revising some conclusions of O'Connell's five earlier relevant writings]. NY 1987, Fordham Univ. xiii-363 p. $37 [TDig 35,383].

8233 *Orbe* Antonio, Deus facit, homo fit; un axioma de san IRENEO: Gregorianum 69 (1988) 629-661; Eng. 662: in Ireneus' context refers to the body, which man is per se, not *noûs* as in Neoplatonism.

8234 **Pannenberg** W., Anthropologie 1983 → 64,6259 ... 2,5273: ᴿKerkT 39 (1988) 356-8 (H. W. de *Knijff*); TPhil 63 (1988) 139-144 (J. *Schmidt*).

8235 **Pannenberg** W., Anthropology 1985 → 1,6499 ... 3,6648: ᴿHeythJ 29 (1988) 497s (J. *O'Donnell*); ScotJT 41 (1988) 409-411 (C. *Gunton*).

8236 **Pannenberg** Wolfhart, Antropologia in prospettiva teologica [1983
➤ 64,6259], ᵀ: BiblTeolContemporan. 11. Brescia 1987, Queriniana.
638 p. Lit. 60.000. – ᴿCC 139 (1988,3) 305s (G. O'Collins); StPatav 35
(1988) 216-8 (A. Moda).

8237 **Paulos** Mar Gregorios, Cosmic man, the divine presence; the theology
of GREGORY of Nyssa (ca. 330 to 395 A.D.): New ERA. NY 1988 =
1980, Paragon. xxviii-274 p. $9 [TDig 35,385].

8237* **Peralta Ansorena** Pablo, El hombre y su apertura al misterio en un
mundo secularizado; una interpretación de la obra de Bernhard WELTE:
Diss. ᴰHünermann. Tü 1987s. – TR 84 (1988) 513.

8238 **Pesch** Otto H., Liberi per grazia; antropologia teologica [1983
➤ 65,5909], ᵀ. Brescia 1988, Queriniana. 609 p. Lit. 55.000. – ᴿCC 139
(1988,3) 430s (J. O'Donnell); RivScR 2 (1988) 467-471 (G. Ancona).

8239 *Pury* Albert de, Animalité de l'homme et humanité de l'animal dans la
pensée israélite; comment l'homme se définit-il par rapport à l'animal:
➤ 704, ᴱBorgeaud P., L'animal 1981/5, 47-70.

8240 **Raurell** F., Lineamenti di antropologia biblica 1986 ➤ 2,5282; 3,6652:
ᴿBiKi 42 (1987) 41-43 (Helene Schüngel-Straumann); DivThom 89s
(1986s) 418s (M. A. Tábet); RivScR 2 (1988) 169-175 (anche M. A.
Tábet).

8241 *Rindone* E., L'antropologia tomista è unitaria o dualistica?: Aquinas 31
(1988) 477-500.

8242 *Rizzerio* Laura, Note di antropologia in CLEMENTE di Alessandria; il
problema della divisione dell'anima e dell'animazione dell'uomo: Sandalion 10s (Sassari 1987s) 115-143.

8243 **Ruiz de la Peña** J. L., Imagen de Dio; antropología fundamental.
Santander 1988, Sal Terrae. 286 p. – ᴿCarthaginensia 4 (1988) 373 (F.
Martínez Fresneda).

8244 **Rulla** Luigi M., Anthropology of the Christian vocation I, 1986
➤ 3,6655: ᴿTPhil 63 (1988) 617-620 (H. Goller).

8245 **Sahagun Lucas** Juan de, El hombre, ¿quién es? Antropología cristiana:
Biblioteca básica del creyente. M 1988, Atenas. 243 p. – ᴿLumenVr 37
(1988) 532 (F. Ortiz de Urtaran).

8246 *a) Schmidt* Werner H., 'Was ist der Mensch?' / Anthropologische
Einsichten des ATs; – b) *Stendebach* Franz-J., ... des Jahwisten; – c) *Görg*
Manfred, ... der Priesterschrift: BiKi 42 (1987) 2-15 / 15-20 / 21-29.

8247 *Seils* Martin, LUTHER's significance for contemporary theological
anthropology: ➤ 604, Luther's ecumenical significance 1983/4, 183-202
[< LuJb 54,161].

8248 **Splett** Jörg, Freiheits-Erfahrung; Vergegenwärtigungen christlicher An-
thropo-theologie 1986 ➤ 3,6658: ᴿTPhil 63 (1988) 456-9 (N. Stroescu);
TR 84 (1988) 421s (H. Verweyen); ZkT 110 (1988) 109s (W. Kern).

8249 **Swinburne** Richard, The evolution of the soul 1986 ➤ 3,6663: ᴿJAAR
56 (1988) 363s (J. R. Sibley); JTS 39 (1988) 344-6 (B. Hebblethwaite).

8250 *Toro Jaramillo* I. D., Consideraciones en torno a la antropología de
JUAN PABLO II: Cuestiones Teológicas 14,2 (Medellín 1987) 83-100
[< RET 48,120].

8251 *Victoria Hernández* L., La llamada de Dios en la Biblia; vocación a ser
radicalmente hombre: Cuestiones Teológicas 14,1 (Medellín 1987) 57-80
[< RET 48,120].

8252 *Vilar* Johannes, Das Menschenbild der Wissenschaft [... der Offen-
barung]; zur Anthropologie der technischen Forschung: RivScR 2 (R
1988) 369-400.

8253 *a) Zavalloni* Roberto, Esigenze e prospettive di rinnovamento nella concezione dell'uomo; – *b) Giordani* Bruno, La psicologia umanistico-esistenziale e il concetto di persona umana: Antonianum 63 (1988) 356-389; Eng. 356 / 390-415; Eng. 390.

8253* *Zumkeller* Adolar, AUGUSTINUS, De anima et eius origine: → 783, AugL 1,3 (1988) 340-350 [-356, *Lütcke* K.-H., ... quantitate; ... 321-340, *O'Daly* G. J. P., Anima, animus].

H2.8 Œcologia VT & NT – saecularitas.

8254 **Altner** G., Die Überlebungskrise in der Gegenwart; Ansätze zum Dialog mit der Natur in Naturwissenschaft und Theologie: WB-Forum 10. Da 1988, Wiss. x-234 p. DM 19,80. 5-534-80019-2 [TsTNijm 28,329].

8255 *Ambroise* Yvon [*al.*], The ecological problem in India and its consequences: Jeevadhara 13,103 (1988) 5-75.

8256 **Auer** Alfons, Etica dell'ambiente; un contributo teologico al dibattito ecologico: [Umweltethik² 1985 → 3,6672]: BiblTeolContemp 56. Brescia 1988, Queriniana. 324 p. Lit. 30.000. 88-399-0356-9 [Greg 69, 819].

8257 **Austin** Richard C., Beauty of the Lord; awakening the senses: Environmental theology 2 [1. Baptized into Wilderness; 3-4 awaited]. Atlanta 1988, Knox. xi-225 p. $11 pa. [TDig 35,259].

8258 *Borg* M. B. ter, Over de secularisering van het heilige: NedTTs 42 (1988) 317-327; Eng. 330.

8259 **Carroll** Denis, Towards a story of the earth; essays in the theology of creation. Dublin 1987, Dominican. 224 p. £7. – RDoctLife 37 (1987) 379 (G. *Daly*); PrPeo 2 (1988) 339s (E. P. *Echlin*: good).

8260 *Carroll* Denis, Towards a just and sustainable society; a challenge to creation theology: MilltSt 18 (1986) 19-30.

8261 *a) Clifford* Richard J., Genesis 1-3, permission to exploit nature?: – *b) Regensburger* Nancy, Shepherding God's creatures; – *c) Senior* Donald, The Gospels and the earth; – *d) Wild* Robert A., Creation in the teaching of Paul; – *e) Collins* Adela Y., The physical world in the book of Revelation: BToday 26,3 (1988) 133-7 / 138-140 / 141-5 / 150-5 / 156-9.

8262 **Duchrow** U., *Liedke* G. Schalom, der Schöpfung Befreiung... Frieden 1987 → 3,6821: RÖkRu 37 (1988) 393s (G. *Fritz*).

8263 *Esquiza* Jesús, Teología de la liberación y secularización: LumenVr 37 (1988) 97-113.

8264 *Frey* Christofer, Theologie und Ethik der Schöpfung; ein Überblick: ZevEth 32 (1988) 47-59 [> NSys 30 (1988) 327s].

8265 *Frisch* Heinz, Die Sorge um die Umwelt als Aufgabe christlicher Gemeinden: StiZt 206 (1988) 112-124.

8266 *Girardi* S. Victorino, Entre secularidad y secularismo: EfMex 5,15 (1987) 373-397.

8267 *Grumelli* Antonio, Secolarizzazione e modernizzazione: Studium 84 (R 1988) 93-107.

8268 *Hanssens* Jo, Conciliair proces rond vrede, gerechtigheid en heelheid van de schepping: CollatVL 18 (1988) 454-466.

8269 *Herrero* Javier, Cristianismo y modernidad, a propósito de un libro de Henrique C. DE LIMA VAZ [Problemas de fronteira 1986]: EstE 63 (1988) 227-233.

8270 *Hervieu-Léger* Danièle, Sécularisation et modernité religieuse: Esprit 106 (1985) 50-62 [> SelT 26 (1987) 217-227, TEBistué Javier de].

8271 *Kahl* Brigitte. Zwischen Exodus und Harmagedon (II), Bibelauslegung... Bewahrung der Schöpfung: Standpunkt 16 (B 1988) 301s
[< ZIT 89,89]; III in 17,8-12.

8272 *Koch* Kurt, Der Mensch und seine Mit-Welt als Schöpfungs-Ebenbild
Gottes — Schöpfungstheologische Aspekte der menschlichen Verantwortung für die Natur: Catholica 42 (1988) 28-55.

8273 *a*) *Kretschmar* Georg, Wie heilig ist die Natur?; – *b*) *Lübbe* Hermann,
Wider der Moralisierung der Ökologie; zur Kulturgeschichte unseres
Naturverhältnisses; – *c*) *Mohr* Hans, Vom Kampf des Menschen um sein
Dasein; Überlegungen eines Biologen zum Naturbegriff: Zeitwende 51,1
(1988) 27-43 / 1-8 / 9-26.

8274 *Lejeune* C., Écologie et foi chrétienne: FoiTemps 18 (1988) 43-62.

8275 E*Lindberg* D., *Numbers* R. God and nature... Christianity and science
1986 ⟶ 2,461: R*ChH* 57 (1988) 119s (W. M. *Stevens*); Thomist 52 (1988)
562-8 (W. H. *Austin*).

8276 *Linzey* Andrew, Christianity and the rights of animals 1987 ⟶ 3,6692:
R*TLond* 91 (1988) 549s (R. *Attfield*: some good counsels questionably
based); TS 49 (1988) 586 (J. L. *Hooper*).

8277 E*Linzey* Andrew, *Regan* Tom, Animals and Christianity, a book of
readings. NY 1988, Crossroad. xvii-210 p. $15 [TDig 36,44].

8278 *Lippert* Peter, Aspekte der Säkularisierung; eine bleibende pastorale und
geistliche Herausforderung: TGegw 30 (1987) 109-113. 165-170.

8278* *Lobato Casado* Abelardo, Fray Luis de GRANADA [† 1588] profeta del
ecologismo: ComSev 21 (1988) 435-444 [387-414, sobre hermenéutica de
la predicación, *Burgos Núñez* M. de].

8279 *McDonagh* Enda, Between chaos and new creation [essays, half inedita,
since 1982] 1987 ⟶ 3,251; also Wilmington 1987, Glazier: R*Month* 249
(1988) 554s (K. T. *Kelly*); NBlackf 68 (1987) 413 (M. *Wiles*); SpTod 40
(1988) 354-6 (D. P. *Killen*).

8280 *Mattai* Giuseppe, Un problema morale nuovo, l'ecologia: Credere Oggi
6,33 (1986) 88-99 [> SelT 27 (1988) 102-8, TE*Messa* Josep].

8281 *Moltmann* Jürgen, God in creation [Gifford Lectures 1984s] 1985
⟶ 2,5315; 3,6702: R*ÉglT* 17 (1986) 412-5 (J. *Pambrun*); ScotJT 41 (1988)
267-273 (J. *McIntyre*); Horizons 15 (1988) 173s (Elizabeth A. *Johnson*);
ScripTPamp 20 (1988) 372 (J. *Morales*).

8282 *Moltmann* Jürgen, Dieu dans la création; traité écologique de la
création, T*Kleiber* Morand: CogF 146. P 1988, Cerf. 419 p. F 238.
2-204-02799-5. – R*ArTGran* 51 (1988) 334s (J. *Vílchez*); Études 368 (1988)
566s (R. *Marlé*); RThom 88 (1988) 467-472 (J.-M. *Maldamé*).

8283 *Moltmann* Jürgen, Dios en la creación; doctrina ecológica de la
creación, T*Martínez de Lapera* Víctor A.: Verdad e Imagen 102. Salamanca 1987, Sígueme. 339 p. 84-301-1034-8. – R*ActuBbg* 25 (1988)
249 (J. *Boada*); LumenVr 37 (1988) 338s (U. *Gil Ortega*); NatGrac 35
(1988) 235s (M. *González del Blanco*); RET 48 (1988) 251s (G. *Flórez*).

8284 *Moltmann* Jürgen, The ecological crisis; peace with nature?: *a*) ScotR
9,1 (Stirling 1988) 5-18 [< ZIT]; – *b*) Colloquium 20,2 (Sydney 1988) 1-11
[< ZIT 88,659].

8285 *Moltmann* Jürgen, Für eine ökologische Reformation: EvKom 21
(1988) 35-38 [TLZ 113,376].

8286 *Moran* Gabriel, Dominion over the earth; does ethics include all
creatures?: Commonweal 114 (1987) 697-701.

8287 *a*) *Murray* Robert, The Bible on God's world and our place in it; – *b*)
Echlin Edward P., The geo-theology of Thomas BERRY: Month 249

(1988) 798-803 (804 poem, by Murray 'Over the face of the waters') / 822-5.

8288 EPanikkar R., *Strolz* W., Die Verantwortung des Menschen für eine bewohnbare Welt im Christentum, Hinduismus und Buddhismus [Symposium Schwarzwald 1984]: Oratio Dominica 12, 1985 → 2,480*: RJEcuSt 25 (1988) 111s (C. *MacCormick*).

8289 *Ricci Sindoni* Paola, L'idea di natura nell'ebraismo contemporaneo: Studium 83 (R 1987) 759-763.

8290 **Rock** Martin, Die Umwelt ist uns anvertraut: Sachbücher zu Fragen des christlichen Glaubens 1987 → 3,6713; 3-7867-1278-6: RBijdragen 49 (1988) 460 (T. *Brattinga*).

8291 *Rodríguez F.* Jaime, ¿Hacia el eclipse de la 'secularización?: Salesianum 50 (1988) 539-563.

8292 *Ruether* Rosemary R., Ökologie und menschliche Befreiung, T*Hunnenbart-Schmitz* Angelika: BLtg 61 (1988) 217-226.

8293 *Schaeffer-Guignier* Otto, Éthique de la création et diaconie écologique: FoiVie 87,3s (1988) 3-30.

8294 *Schröfner* Erich, Säkularisierung, eine Herausforderung für die katholische Theologie?: GeistL 61 (1988) 35-44.

8295 *Stuhlmacher* Peter, *a*) The challenge of the ecological crisis to biblical theology: → 567, ExAud 3 (1987) 1-15; – *b*) Die ökologische Krise als Herausforderung an die Biblische Theologie: EvT 48 (1988) 311-329.

8296 **Tanner** Kathryn E., God and creation in Christian theology; tyranny or empowerment? NY 1988, Blackwell. $40. 0-631-15994-0 [TDig 36,186: has '1986 p.'].

8297 ETeutsch Gotthard M., Da Tiere eine Seele haben; Stimmen aus zwei Jahrtausenden. Stu 1987, Kreuz. 286 p. DM 29,80. – RRHPR 68 (1988) 493 (G. *Siegwalt*); Universitas 43 (Stu 1988) 383s (H. *Barth*).

8298 *Tillard* Jean-Marie R., La justice, la paix, le respect de la création; quel engagement pour l'Église catholique?: Irénikon 60 (1987) 5-15 [< SelT 27 (1988) 208-212, *Pou* Edward, '... para las iglesias'; además Tillard p. 269-281].

8299 *Tilley* W. Clyde, World-affirmation and the resurrection of Jesus Christ; a review article: PerspRelSt 15 (1988) 165 ... [< ZIT 88,602].

8300 *Tokar* Brien, The green alternative; creating an ecological future. San Pedro 1987, Miles. 174 p. $8 pa. – RAnglTR 70 (1988) 91-93 (M. C. *Engle*).

8301 *Van Dyke* Fred G., Planetary economies and ecologies; the Christian world view and recent literature: Journal of the American Scientific Affiliation 40,2 (1988) 66-71.

H3.1 *Foedus* – **the Covenant;** the Chosen People.

8302 **Beaucamp** É., Les grands thèmes de l'Alliance: Lire la Bible 81. P 1988, Cerf. 265 p. F 88. 2-204-02926-2 [BL 89,100, B. P. *Robinson*: from 18-month stay in a Muslim country where he found the covenant-idea ignored, and also underrated in Christianity; but none of the essays is on covenant itself].

8303 *Collin* L., Providence: → 786, Catholicisme 12,55 (1988) 122-133.

8304 **Coppedge** Allan, John WESLEY in theological debate [with CALVIN, on predestination]. Wilmore KY 1988, Wesley Heritage. 289 p. $18. 0-915143-03-8 [TDig 36,151].

8305 **Damrosch** David, The narrative covenant; transformations of genre in the growth of biblical literature 1987 → 3,6734: RInterpretation 42 (1988) 426.428 (P. L. *Redditt*); NorTTs 89 (1988) 268-271 (A. S. *Kapelrud*); Prooftexte 8 (1988) 347-354 (E. L. *Greenstein*); TS 49 (1988) 529s (F. L. *Moriarty*).

8305* **Dekker** Pieter W., The role of the covenant in the Kingdom of God: diss. Calvin Sem., DKlooster F. GR 1988. v-118 p. + bibliog. – CalvinT 23 (1988) 302s.

8306 *De Petris* Paolo, Teologi a confronto sulla dottrina della predestinazione; Walter KRECK e Giovanni CALVINO: Protestantesimo 43 (1988) 164-174.

8307 *Dockrill* D. W., 'No other name'; the problem of the salvation of pagans in mid-seventeenth century Cambridge: → 554, Salvation 1986/8, 117-151.

8308 **Dumbrell** W. J., Covenant and creation 1984 → 65,5966... 3,6735: RScripB 19 (1988s) 42s (J. R. *Duckworth*).

8308* *Ferrier* F., Prédestination: → 786, Catholicisme 11 (1987s) 764-781.

8309 **Guillén Torralba** Juan, La fuerza oculta de Dios; la Elección en el AT: EstJerón 15, 1983 → 64,6320... 3,6741: RRTLv 19 (1988) 215s (J. *Vermeylen*).

8310 **Hodges** Z. C., The Gospel under siege 1981 → 64,4018; 65,6500: RJEvTS 30 (1987) 457-467 [W. G. *Bjork*; wrongly holds that people can be saved — and really know it — yet not manifest good works in their lives as a result [NTAbs 32,202].

8311 *a) Hossfeld* Frank-Lothar, Wie sprechen die Heiligen Schriften, insbesondere das Alte Testament, von der Vorsehung Gottes?; – *b) Schulte* Raphael, Wie ist Gottes Wirken in Welt und Geschichte theologisch zu verstehen?; – *c) Studer* Basil, Zur frühchristlichen Lehre über die Vorsehung und das Wirken Gottes in der Welt; ein Diskussionsbeitrag; – *d) Weimer* Ludwig, Wodurch kam das Sprechen von Vorsehung und Handeln Gottes in die Krise? Analyse und Deutung des Problemstandes seit der Aufklärung: → 648, Vorsehung 1987/8, 72-93 / 116-167 / 109-115 / 17-71.

8312 **Jewett** Paul K., Election and predestination, pref. *Grounds* Vernon, 1985 → 3,6744*: RGraceTJ 9 (1988) 153s (D. S. *Dockery*); RefTR 46 (1987) 23 (R. *Swanton*).

8313 **Kaufmann** Yehezkel, Christianity and Judaism; two covenants [1930 Golah ve-Nekhar ch. 7-9], T Efroymson C. W. J 1988, Magnes. xi-230 p. $20. 965-223-694-2 [BL 89,107, R. B. *Salters*].

8314 *Knox* R. Buick, The Covenant in the Bible and in history; the Scottish National Covenant, 1638: IrBSt 10 (1988) 71-88.

8315 **Krötke** Wolf, Die Universalität des offenbaren Gottes, Ges. Aufs.: BEvTh 94, 1985 → 1,192b: RTRu 53 (1988) 324-7 (E. *Thaidigsmann*).

8316 **McComiskey** Thomas E., The covenants of promise 1985 → 1,6578... 3,6747: RIrBSt 9 (1987) 82-84 (T. D. *Alexander*: unsatisfactory on Abraham); RefTR 46 (1987) 86s (B. *Webb*).

8317 *McGiffert* Michael, From Moses to Adam; the making of the covenant of works [English Puritans c. 1600]: SixtC 19 (1988) 131-155.

8318 **Nicholson** Ernest W., God and his people; covenant theology in the OT 1986 → 2,5342; 3,6749; RAnglTR 69 (1987) 83-86 (I. T. *Kaufman*); CBQ 50 (1988) 306-8 (J. D. *Levenson*); CurrTM 15 (1988) 459 (R. W. *Klein*); JBL 107 (1988) 119s (J. L. *Mays*); JTS 39 (1988) 137-9 (G. W. *Anderson*: magisterial); TTod 44 (1987s) 271s (D. R. *Hillers*).

8319 *Olu Igenoza* Andrew, Universalism and New Testament Christianity: Evangelical Review of Theology 12 (1988) 261-275.

8320 *Panikkar* Raimundo, Chosenness and universality; can Christians claim both?: CCurr 38 (1988s) 309-324.

8321 **Punt** Neal, What's good about the Good News? The plan of salvation in a new light [minority view: all are elect except those the Bible declares not]. Ch 1988, Northland. 142 p. $8 pa. – [R]CalvinT 23 (1988) 290-4 (C. P. *Venema*).

8322 *Roehrs* W. R., Divine covenants; their structure and function: CordJ 14,1 (1988) 7-27 [NTAbs 32,204].

8322* **Schenker** Adrien, L'origine de l'idée d'une alliance entre Dieu et Israël dans l'AT: RB 95 (1988) 184-194; Eng. 184.

8323 **Sellers** C. Norman, Election and perseverance. Miami Springs FL 1987, Schoettle. 210 p. $13. – [R]BS 145 (1988) 349 (R. P. *Lightner*: courteous dispensational-Calvinistic rejection of R. SHANKS).

8324 **Storms** C. Samuel, Chosen for life; an introductory guide to the doctrine of divine election. GR 1987, Baker. 142 p. $7 pa. – [R]CalvaryB 4,1 (1988) 78 (E. R. *Jordan*); GraceTJ 9 (1988) 154s (G. *Zemek*).

8324* **Sugarman** Alvin M., God and finitude; toward a covenant of mutual affirmation: diss. Emory, [D]*Blumenthal* D. Atlanta 1988. – RTLv 20,541.

8325 **Vermeylen** J., Le Dieu de la promesse...: LDiv 126, 1986 → 2,5344; 3,6757: [R]Carthaginensia 4 (1988) 173 (J. F. *Cuenca Molina*); CBQ 50 (1988) 518s (C. *Bernas*); EstE 63 (1988) 245-7 (J. *Alonso Díaz*: estructuración perfecta); JTS 39 (1988) 536-8 (R. E. *Clements*: four levels of Dt composition labeled by their dates: Dtr585, Dtr575, Dtr560, Dtr525); RevSR 61 (1987) 236s (B. *Renaud*).

H3.3 *Fides in VT* – **Old Testament faith.**

8326 *Alonso Díaz* José, Religión 'versus' fe; Antiguo Testamento; proyecto desde la praxis histórica de Israel: BibFe 14 (1988) 25-50.

8326* **Ben-Chorin** Schalom, Als Gott schwieg; ein jüdisches Credo. Mainz 1986, Grünewald. 95 p. DM 14,80. – [R]GeistL 61 (1988) 239s (J. *Schreiner*).

8327 **Drane** John, El Antiguo Testamento; la fe [OT faith 1986 → 2,5347], [T]*Olasagasti* Manuel. Estella 1987, VDivino. 156 p.; ill. pt 1000. 84-7151-525-3. – [R]ActuBbg 25 (1988) 209s (J. M. *Rocafiguera*); BibFe 14 (1988) 147 (M. *Sáenz de Santamaría*).

8328 **Dumbrell** William J., The faith of Israel; its expression in the books of the Old Testament. GR 1988, Baker. 286 p. $13. 0-8010-2976-7 [TDig 36,156].

8329 **Fabris** Rinaldo, L'esperienza di fede nella Bibbia. R 1987, Paoline. 231 p. Lit. 18.000. – [R]CC 139 (1988,1) 99 (U. *De Mielesi*).

8329* **Kaiser** Otto, Ideologie und Glaube; eine Gefährdung christlichen Glaubens, am alttestamentlichen Beispiel aufgezeigt 1984 → 65,5984: [R]RB 95 (1988) 139s (F. *Langlamet*); ZkT 110 (1988) 110 (W. *Kern*: Gottesrechtfertigung).

8330 *Lapide* Pinchas, Wie man den Glauben erzählt: → 106, [F]METZ J. B., Mystik 1988, 364-373.

8330* **Pawlowski** Zdzisław, ❷ Wiara i przymierze... Faith and covenant in the oldest tradition of the Pentateuch: diss. [D]*Stachowiak* L. Lublin 1988. xvi-250 p. – RTLv 20,541 [tradycji 'traduction'].

8331 *Soggin* J. A., La fede nell'AT: Abramo, p. 7-16; Gn 22,1-19, *Bonora* A., p. 17-28; Esodo, *Virgulin* S., 29-41; Abacuc 2,4, *Cimosa* M., 42-51; Salmo 27,14, *Marin* M.; 52-59; Giobbe, *Ravasi* G. F., 69-80; *Emunah, Rochettes* J. des, 81-88: ParSpV 17 ('Credete al Vangelo' 1988).

H3.5   *Liturgia, spiritualitas VT* — **OT prayer.**

8332 **Ben-Chorin** S.,   Le Judaïsme en prière 1984 → 65,5988b ... 3,6766:   RCi-Tom 114 (1987) 186s (P. *Fernández*).

8333 **Blumenthal** David R.,   God as the center; meditations on Jewish spirituality. SF 1988, Harper & R. xxxii-246 p. $21 [JNES 47,237].

8334 *Cavalletti* Sofia,   Le correnti spirituali del mondo giudaico: → 810, StoSpir 2 NT (1988) 21-40.

8335 **Di Sante** Carmine,   La preghiera di Israele 1985 → 2,5358; 3,6771: RAsprenas 35 (1988) 271-3 (A. *Rolla*).

8336 **Estin** Colette,   Contes et fêtes juives: Le Conte et la Fête 1, 1987 → 3,6774:   RNRT 110 (1988) 763s (Y. *Simoens*).

8336* *Fanuli* Antonio, La spiritualità della Tôrāh / deuteronomista / Abramo, Giacobbe, Mosé e Giosuè: → 810, StSp [Dehoniane] 1987, 49-106 / 109-142 / 333-348 [già citato → 3,1868], in parte parallelo o identico al suo contributo a → 810*, StSpG [Borla] 1988.

8337 *Fishbane* Simcha,   Back to the Yeshiva; the social dynamics of an orthodox sabbath prayer service: Paradigms 4 (1988s) 134-151.

8338 EGreen Arthur,   Jewish spirituality: EWSp 13, 1986 → 2,5361; 3,6777: RJudaism 37 (1988) 121s (H. A. *Addison*).

8339 *Katz* Jacob, ❶ The Orthodox defence of the second day of the festivals: Tarbiz 57 (1987s) 385-434; Eng. IIs.

8340 **Kirchberg** Julie,   Theo-logie in der Anrede; Jüdische Gebetssprache und christliches Offenbarungsverständnis; zur theologischen Verständigung zwischen Juden und Christen nach dem Zweiten Vaticanum: Diss. DPott-meyer. Bochum 1987s. – TR 84 (1988) 511.

Koenig Jean, Oracles et liturgies de l'exil babylonien 1988 → 3713.

8341 ELicht Jacob S.,   Time and holy days in the biblical and second commonwealth periods: Biblical Encyclopaedia Library 3. J 1988, Mosad Bialik. 227 p.; ill. 965-342-515-3.

8342 **Manns** F.,   La prière d'Israël à l'heure de Jésus 1986 → 2,5370; 3,6783: RHenoch 10 (1988) 113s (G. *Boccaccini*: valido come inizio).

8342* *Martin* R. P., Worship (also NT): → 801, ISBEnc³ 4 (1988) 1117-33.

8343 *Mendecki* Norbert, ❷ De oratione 'Alenu': RuBi 41 (1988) 226-9.

8344 **Petuchowski** Jacob J.,   Aan Uw erbarmen is geen einde; joodse gebeden. Baarn 1987, Ten Have. 128 p. ƒ390. – RCollatVL 18 (1988) 492 (R. *Hoet*).

8345 EPetuchowski Jakob J., 'Dass wir Dir in Wahrheit dienen'; ein jüdischer Gottesdienst für den Sabbatmorgen. Aachen 1988, Einhard. 36 p. DM 7,80. 3-920284-40-2.

8346 **Reventlow** Henning, Gebet im AT 1986 → 2,5374; 3,6791;   RErbAuf 63 (1987) 70s (L. *Opgen-Rhein*); JBL 107 (1988) 299-301 (S. E. *Balentine*); KerkT 39 (1988) 152s (H. *Vreekamp*); TPQ 136 (1988) 284 (J. *Marböck*).

8347 *Ricci Sindoni* Paola,   Ascoltare il segreto di Dio; la spiritualità ebraica: Studium 83 (R 1987) 857-868.

8348 **Safran** Alexandre,   Israël dans le temps et dans l'espace; thèmes fondamentaux de la spiritualité juive 1980 → 61,b630:   RRHPR 68 (1988) 257s (E. *Jacob*: pas trop tard pour un livre qui restera longtemps apprécié).

8349 *Selles* Jean-Marie, Bénédiction synagogale et doxologie; la doxologie est-elle propre à la prière chrétienne?: MaisD 175 (1988) 7-25.

8350 **Sestieri** Lea, La spiritualità ebraica 1987 → 3,6782: ᴿAsprenas 35 (1988) 401 (A. *Rolla*); CC 139 (1988,1) 512s (S.M. *Katunarich*); Gregorianum 69 (1988) 551s (J. *Janssens*); HumBr 43 (1988) 298 (G. *Romano*); RClerIt 69 (1988) 222-4 (P. *De Benedetti*); RivB 36 (1988) 277s (Sofia *Cavalletti*).

8350* **Trolin** Clifford F., Prayer and the imagination; a study of the Shemoneh Esreh, the eighteen benedictions of the daily Jewish service: diss. GTU. Berkeley 1986. – RTLv 20,543.

8351 *Truijen* V., La lecture de l'Ancien Testament dans la liturgie rénovée: QLtg 68 (Lv 1987) 135-156.

8351* *Weinfeld* M., The morning prayers (Birkhoth hashachar) in Qumran and in the conventional Jewish liturgy: → 22, Mém. CARMIGNAC J., RQum 13 (1988) 481-494.

H3.7 *Theologia moralis VT* – **OT moral theology.**

8352 **Baloian** Bruce E., The aspect of anger in the Old Testament: diss. Claremont 1987. – RelStR 15,192.

8352* **Birch** Bruce C., What does the Lord require? [Micah 6,8] The OT call to social witness 1985 → 1,6630*; 2,5381*: ᴿCurrTM 15 (1988) 370s (W.L. *Michel*).

8353 **Bloch** Abraham P., A book of Jewish ethical concepts, biblical and post-biblical. NY 1984, KTAV. viii-294 p. $20. – ᴿHeythJ 29 (1988) 244s (L. *Jacobs*).

8354 **Herring** Basil F., Jewish ethics and halakhah for our time. NY 1984, KTAV. xii-243 p. $15; pa. $10. – ᴿHeythJ 29 (1985) 244s (L. *Jacobs*).

8354* ᴱ**Meier** Levi, Jewish values in bioethics. NY 1986, Human Sciences. 195 p. $27. – ᴿJRel 68 (1988) 136s (D. *Novak*).

8355 *Rossé* Gérard, L'esperienza di Israele con Dio alla luce dell'alleanza sinaitica (La relazione tra la presenza di JHWH e il comportamento etico): NuovaUm 9,51 (1987) 9-22.

8356 **Soete** Annette, Ethos der Rettung — Ethos der Gerechtigkeit; Studien zur Struktur von Normbegründung und Urteilsfindung im AT und ihrer Relevanz für die ethische Diskussion der Gegenwart 1987 → 3,6806: ᴿArTGran 51 (1988) 301 (A. *Segovia*); BL (1988) 115 (G.H. *Jones*); Salesianum 50 (1988) 435s (G. *Abbà*).

8357 *Stahl* Samuel M., Biblical and talmudic attitudes toward intermarriage: Dor 17 (1988s) 107-111. 170-8.184.

H3.8 *Bellum et pax VT-NT* – **War and peace in the whole Bible.**

8357* *Aboagye-Mensah* Robert, Karl BARTH's attitude to war in the context of World War II: EvQ 60 (1988) 43-59.

ᴱ**Biffi** F., La pace sfida 1986/8 → 526.

8358 *Botermann* Helga, CICEROs Gedanken zum 'gerechten Krieg' in *de officiis* 1, 34-40: ArKulturG 69 (1987) 1-29.

8359 **Brown** Robert M., Religion and violence² [= ¹1973 + introduction and bibliography supplement]. Ph 1987, Westminster. xxix-114 p. $9. – ᴿRelStR 14 (1988) 365 (J.A. *Keller*) → 8782, Girard.

8360 **Brueggemann** Walter, Revelation and violence; a study in contextualization [Père Marquette lecture, Milwaukee 1986] 1986 → 2,5398; 3,6815: ᴿCBQ 50 (1988) 284-6 (A.J. *Petrotta*).

8361 **Carmody** Denise L. & John T.,   Peace and justice in the Scriptures of the world religions; reflections on non-Christian Scriptures.   NY 1988, Paulist.   191 p. $10.

8362 *Coste* R.,   *a*) La communion ecclésiale comme service de la paix: NRT 110 (1988) 710-728. – *b*) Paix entre les hommes: → 791, DictSp 14 (1986) 40-56 (-73, intérieure, *Sieben* H.).

8363 ᴱ**Curry** Dean C.,   The Evangelicals and the [U.S. Catholic] bishops' pastoral letter [Challenge of peace 1983].   GR/Exeter 1984, Eerdmans/ Paternoster.   XVII-254 p.   £9.75. – ᴿHeythJ 29 (1988) 241s (J. *Ferguson*: BERNBAUM's final essay is worth all of J. DOUGHERTY put together).

8363* ᴱ**Daly** R.J.,   Christians and the military 1985 → 1,559 [= *Helgeland* J. → 8367]:   ᴿHeythJ 29 (1988) 513s (J. *Ferguson*: disappoints, pontificates).

8364 *Domeris* W.R.,   Biblical perspectives on the use of force: JTSAf 62 (1988) 68-72 [< NTAbs 32,340].

8365 **Friesen** Duane K.,   Christian peacemaking and international conflict 1986 → 2,5401*; 3,6825:   ᴿRExp 85 (1988) 372-4 (W.C. *Tilley*).

8366 **Häring** Bernard,   The healing power of peace and nonviolence 1986 → 2,5405:   ᴿLvSt 13 (1988) 87-89 (E.J. *Cooper*).

8367 **Helgeland** John, *al.*,   Christians and the military; the early experience [→ 8363] 1987 → 1,6677; 3,6833*:   ᴿTLond 91 (1988) 148s (A. *Louth*: never discusses HORNUS J.-M. 1960).

8368 *Herzog* Kristin,   La mujer, la guerra y la paz [< EvT 47 (1987) 60-82], ᵀᴱ*Puig* Ramón: SelT 27 (1988) 317-331.

8369 **Hoppe** Thomas,   Friedenspolitik mit militärischen Mitteln; eine ethische Analyse strategischer Ansätze [... Bewertung des Krieges seit AUGUSTINUS]: Theologie und Frieden 1, 1986 → 2,5410; 3,6836:   ᴿTüTQ 168 (1988) 249-251 (S. *Ernst*).

8369* *Horst* Pieter W. van der,   Het oorlogsvraagstuk in het christendom van de erste drie eeuwen [< Lampas 19 (1986) 405-420]: → 207, De onbekende God 1988, 210-228.

8370 **Jegen** Carol F.,   Jesus the peacemaker 1987 → 3,6837:   ᴿHorizons 15 (1988) 175 (D.F. *Gray*).

8371 **Johnson** James T.,   The quest for peace; three moral traditions in western culture.   Princeton 1987, Univ.   xx-300 p. $30. – ᴿRelStR 14 (1988) 240 [P. *Nelson*: 'our foremost historian of just war tradition'].

8371* **Johnson** James T.,   Can modern war be just? 1984 → 1,6681... 3,6838:   ᴿHeythJ 29 (1988) 384-6 (G. *Schedler*).

8372 **Kaufman** Gordon D.,   Una teologia per l'era nucleare [relazione ai 'simboli Dio/Cristo']: GdT 179.   Brescia 1988, Queriniana.   112 p. Lit. 11.000. – ᴿAsprenas 35 (1988) 293 (P. *Pifano*).

8373 **Kenny** Anthony,   The logic of deterrence.   Ch 1985, Univ.   104 p. $20; pa. $7.   0-226-43154-1; 6-8. – ᴿÉglT 17 (1986) 415-8 (G.J. *Walters*).

8374 **Klassen** William,   Love of enemies, the way to peace 1984 → 65,6070... 3,6839:   ᴿTZBas 44 (1988) 279s (G. *Müller*).

8375 **Langendörfer** Hans,   Atomare Abschreckung und kirchliche Friedensethik; eine Untersuchung zu neuesten katholischen Friedensverlautbarungen und zur ethischen Problematik heutiger Sicherheitspolitik.   Mainz/Mü 1987, Grünewald/Kaiser.   234 p. – ᴿCC 139 (1988,1) 91s (A. *Autiero*).

8376 **Lewy** Guenter,   Peace and revolution; the moral crisis of American pacifism.   GR 1988, Eerdmans.   283 p. $20 [GraceTJ 9,309].

8377 *Moltmann* Jürgen, Gerechtigkeit schafft Frieden: IZT 24 (1988) 75-82 = La justice crée la paix: Concilium 215 (P 1988) 139-152.

8378 **Musto** Ronald G.,   The Catholic peace tradition 1986 ➤ 3,6850:
ᴿDoctLife 37 (1987) 547s (A. *Draper*).

8379 *O'Connell* James,   Love, force and violence; a theological [biblical...]
note on peace: Month 249 (1988) 951-960.

8380 *Ott* Hervé,   Principles of nonviolent action [... resistance to land-ex-
propriation by army: VSp Sup 154 (1985) 41-56], ᵀᴱ*Jermann* Rosemary:
TDig 35 (1988) 213-7.

8381 *Papagiannopoulos* Ioannis G., **Ⓖ** Old Testament information about the
slaughter of men: TAth 54 (1988) 580-7.

8382 **Petraglio** R.,   Obiezione di coscienza; il NT provoca i cristiani: Etica
teologica oggi 1. Bo 1984, Dehoniane. 224 p. Lit. 8000. – ᴿAsprenas 35
(1988) 425 (R. *Russo*).

8383 **Por una paz sin armas**: Ariadna 4, 1984. – ᴿDivThom 89s (1986s) 461-4
(J. R. *Areitio*).

8384 **Pucciarelli** Enrico,   I Cristiani e il servizio militare; testimonianze dei
primi tre secoli: BiblPatr 9, 1987 ➤ 3,6854: ᴿClasR 102 (1988) 440 (E. D.
Hunt: nothing new, much misleading, but useful); VigChr 42 (1988) 406-8
(J. den *Boeft*).

8385 *Ruether* Rosemary R.,   War and peace in the Christian tradition =
Guerre et paix dans la tradition chrétienne: Concilium 195 (E 1988) 17-24
/ 215 (P 1988) 27-35.

8386 **Schenker** Adrian,   Chemins bibliques de la non-violence 1987 ➤ 3,6856:
ᴿNRT 110 (1988) 105s (J.-L. *Ska*: pas de dialogue avec GIRARD); RB 95
(1988) 309 (R. J. *Tournay*).

8386* *Schoville* K. N. [*Craigie* P. C.], War [idea of]: ➤ 801, ISBEnc³ 4 (1988)
1013-8 [-21].

8387 **Spiegel** Egon,   Gewaltverzicht; Grundlagen einer biblischen Frie-
denstheologie 1987 ➤ 3,6859; 3-88713-013-8: ᴿSNTU-A 13 (1988) 252s
(F. *Reisinger*: Lob); TsTNijm 28 (1988) 323s (A. van *Iersel*).

8388 *Steenkamp* A. W.,   Eskatologiese radikaliteit; enkele nuwe-testamentiese
perspectiewe op geweld en vrede: Scriptura 22 (1987) 18-39 [NTAbs
32,205].

8389 *Swan* Bernard,   Christ, servant of Yahweh; discovering the Prince of
Peace, in the nuclear age: PrPeo 2 (1988) 106-110.

8390 *Synan* E. A.,   St. Thomas AQUINAS and the profession of arms: MedSt
50 (1988) 404-437 [< RSPT 72,647].

8391 *Verkamp* Bernard J.,   Moral treatment of returning warriors in the
early Middle Ages [.... a penance was imposed]: JRelEth 16 (1988)
223-249.

8392 **Weigel** George,   Tranquillitas ordinis; the present failure and future
promise of American Catholic thought on war and peace 1987 ➤ 3,6866:
ᴿHomP 88,3 (1987s) 76-79 (Sharon D. *Rives*); Horizons 15 (1988) 429-431
(W. L. *Portier*); JRelEth 16 (1988) 191s (J. T. *Johnson*); RelStR 14 (1988)
59 (M. *Duffey*).

8393 *Weissengruber* Franz,   Pax romana und pax christiana: SNTU-A 13
(1988) 193-204.

8394 **Wengst** Klaus,   Pax romana; Anspruch und Wirklichkeit 1986 ➤ 2,5441;
3,6868:   ᴿBijdragen 49 (1988) 448s (H. W. *Woorts*); BTZ 4 (1987) 95-106
(U. *Visser* [➤ 3,6868 !]: peace is too important to pass over the way it is
here treated); NedTTs 32 (1988) 340s (J. N. *Sevenster*); SNTU-A 13 (1988)
253s (F. *Weissengruber*); TRu 53 (1988) 388-398 (G. *Lüdemann*, Helga
Botermann).

8395 **Wengst** Klaus, Pax romana and the peace of Jesus Christ 1987
➤ 3,6869; also L 1987, SCM: ᴿClasR 102 (1988) 441 (R. P. C. *Hanson*: 'a
thesis so crudely presented scarcely deserves refutation'); ComSev 21
(1988) 102 (M. de *Burgos*: obra excelente y práctica); TLond 91 (1988)
533-5 (J. *Richardson*: comic-strip history; infuriating ignorance and
erudition).

H4.1 Messianismus.

8396 *Becquet* Gilles, Noël avant Noël; comment un juif pieux attendait-il le
Messie?: Sève 493 (1987) 640-2.

8397 *Cazelles* Henri, *a*) Le Règne de Dieu dans l'AT; – *b*) La sainteté, les
saints et le culte vétérotestamentaire: ➤ 640, S-Serge 31 (1984-5)...;
➤ 642: 33 (1986-7) ... [EsprVie 98,187.190].

8398 *Cimosa* M., Messianismo: ➤ 806, NDizTB (1988) 937-953.

8398* *a*) *Green* William S., Messiah in Judaism; rethinking the question; – *b*)
Neusner Jacob, Mishnah and Messiah; – *c*) *Talmon* Shemaryahu, Waiting
for the Messiah; the spiritual universe of the Qumran covenanters; – *d*)
Nickelsburg George W. E., Salvation without a Messiah; developing
beliefs in writings ascribed to Enoch; – *e*) *Hecht* Richard D., Philo and
the Messiah: ➤ 494, Judaisms/Messiahs 1987, 1-13 / 265-282 / 111-137 /
49-68 / 139-168.

8399 **Grollenberg** Luc, Unexpected Messiah, or How the Bible can be
misleading, ᵀ*Bowden* J. L 1988, SCM. viii-199 p. £7. 0-334-02402-1 [BL
89,105, J. F. *Ashton*: competent on e.g. Ps 22, Wis 1s, but offers no new
insight into early Christian presenting of faith as fulfilment of prophecy];
Furrow 39 (1988) 738s (P. *Briscoe*).

8400 *Isser* Stanley, Studies of ancient Jewish messianism; scholarship and
apologetics: JEcuSt 25 (1988) 56-73.

Laato Antti, Who is Immanuel? The rise and the foundering of Isaiah's
messianic expectation 1988 ➤ 3687.

8401 **Landman** A., Messias-interpreties in de Targumim 1986 ➤ 3,6878:
ᴿNedTTs 42 (1988) 262s (H. *Sysling*).

8402 **Meldau** F. J., Der Messias in beiden Testamenten: Telos 7. Stu-Neuhausen 1988, Hänssler. 166 p. 3-7751-0073-3.

8403 *Moenikes* Ansgar, Messianismus im Alten Testament (vorapoka-
lyptische Zeit) [i. kulturelle Rahmenbedingungen; ii. Propaganda für das
Königtum; iii. Erwartung]: ZRGg 40 (1988) 290-306.

ᴱ**Neusner** Jacob, Judaisms and their Messiahs 1987 ➤ 494 [8398*
above].

8403* **Patai** Raphael, The Messiah texts. Detroit 1988, Wayne State Univ.
liii-373 p. [pa. = 1979]. 0-8143-1850-9.

8404 **Rizzi** Armido, El mesianismo en la vida cotidiana 1986 ➤ 2,5447:
ᴿScripTPamp 20 (1988) 915 (A. *García-Moreno*).

8405 **Schimanowski** Gottfried, Weisheit und Messias; die jüdischen Voraussetzungen der christlichen Präexistenzchristologie. Diss. Tü 1981:
WUNT 2/17, 1985 ➤ 1,6739 ... 3,6887: ᴿJBL 107 (1988) 137-9 (J. J.
Collins); JStJud 19 (1988) 259-263 (A. S. van der *Woude*); NedTTs 42
(1988) 75s (P. W. van der *Horst*).

8405* *Strauss* Hans, Messianisch ohne Messias... EurHS 23/252, 1984
➤ 65,6117 ... 3, 6888: ᴿErbAuf 63 (1987) 478 (J. *Kaffanke*).

8406 *Waschke* Ernst-Joachim, Die Frage nach dem Messias im Alten Testament als Problem alttestamentlicher Theologie und biblischer Hermeneutik: TLZ 113 (1988) 321-332.

H4.3   Eschatologia VT – OT hope of future life.

8407 *Buss* Martin J., Selfhood and biblical eschatology: ➤ 153, ZAW 100 Sup. (1988) 214-222.

8408 **Clarkson** George E., Grounds for belief in life after death [... Bible]: 'Symposium' series, 24, but not a symposium. Lewiston NY 1987, Mellen. 140 + 10 p. $40 [TDig 35,346].

8408* *Cornelius* Izak, Paradise motifs in the 'eschatology' of the Minor Prophets and the iconography of the Ancient Near East; the concepts of fertility, water, trees and 'Tierfrieden' and Gen 2-3 [< research project, 'The garden in ANE art']: JNWS 14 (1988) 41-64 + 20 fig.; bibliog. 76-83.

8409 **Gowan** Donald E., Eschatology in the OT 1986 ➤ 2,5445; 3,6897: ᴿCBQ 50 (1988) 296-8 (J. C. *Kesterson*); Dor 17 (1988s) 197s (S. *Liptzin*); IrBSt 9 (1987) 84s (T. D. *Alexander*); TLZ 113 (1988) 888s (K.-D. *Schunck*).

8410 *Harrelson* Walter, Eschatology and ethics in the Hebrew Bible: UnSemQ 42,1s (1988) 43-48 [< ZIT].

8410* **Himmelfarb** Martha, Tours of Hell 1985 ➤ 64,6474 ... 2,5458: ᴿClasW 82 (1988s) 204 (Colleen *McDannell*).

8411 **Krieg** Matthias, Todesbilder im Alten Testament oder 'Wie die Alten den Tod gebildet' [Diss. Z]: ATANT 63. Z 1988, Theol.V. 695 p. DM 80.

8412 *Lang* Bernhard, a) Afterlife; ancient Israel's changing vision of the world beyond: BR 4,1 (1988) 12-23; ill.; – b) Life after death in the prophetic promise: ➤ 482, VTS 40, Jerusalem congress 1986/8, 144-156; 2 fig.

8413 *Logister* Wiel, Het terughoudend spreken over verrijzenis in het Oude Testament; de betekenis van Israël's omgang met de dood: TsTNijm 28 (1988) 3-24; 25s, The hesitant references to resurrection in the OT.

8414 **Martin-Achard** M. R., La mort en face selon la Bible hébraïque: Essais Bibliques. Genève 1988, Labor et Fides. 136 p. Fs 24. 2-8309-0128-2 [BL 89,110, N. *Wyatt*: too briefly counters the rather strange views of DAHOOD and SPRONK].

8414* **Mindling** Joseph A., Conceptions of a felicitous afterlife in the Hebrew Old Testament: diss. Pont. Ist. Biblico, ᴰ*Gilbert* M. R 1989. – AcPIB 9,5 (1988s) 384.425.

8415 *Ribera* Josep, La exégesis judeo-targúmica sobre la resurrección: Est-Bíb 46 (1988) 295-302; Eng. 295.

8415* **Simon** Ulrich, Atonement; from holocaust to Paradise. C 1987, Clarke. IV-138 p. £6 [JTS 39,673].

8416 **Spronk** K., Beatific afterlife in ancient Israel and the ancient Near East: AOAT 319, 1986 ➤ 2,5463; 3,6902: ᴿAsprenas 35 (1988) 402-6 (C. *Marcheselli-Casale*).

8416* *Smith* Mark S., *Bloch-Smith* Elizabeth M., Death and afterlife in Ugarit and Israel [*Spronk* K. 1986]: JAOS 108 (1988) 277-284.

8417 ᴱ**Xella** Paolo, Archeologia dell'Inferno 1987 ➤ 3,844: ᴿBO 45 (1988) 523-5 (M. *Stol*); RivB 36 (1988) 99-106 (G. L. *Prato*).

H4.5   Theologia totius VT – General Old Testament theology.

8418 **Bächli** O., Das Alte Testament in der Kirchlichen Dogmatik von Karl BARTH. Neuk 1987. xii-368 p. DM 68. 3-7887-0792-5 [BL 89,99, R. E. *Clements*).

8419 **Childs** B.S., OT theology in a canonical context 1985 → 1,6759...
3,6906: RBR 4,2 (1988) 44 (D.M. *Howard*); CBQ 50 (1988) 491-3 (Ziony
Zevit); Interpretation 42 (1988) 186-8 (D.L. *Petersen*; title 'Construing the
OT as Christian Scripture'); Thomist 51 (1987) 714-6 (L. *Boadt*).

8420 *Hasel* Gerhard F., Old Testament theology from 1978-1987: AndrUnS
26 (1988) 133-158; p. 139, VRIEZEN rewrote his ³1966 (Eng.² 1970) entirely
in order to counter von RAD's 'disparate traditions'.

8421 **Hayes** J., *Prussner* F., OT theology 1985 → 1,6767; 3,6911: RHeythJ 29
(1988) 506s (L. *Swain*); HorBT 9,2 (1987) 105-7 (W. *Harrelson*).

8422 *Holter* K., Missiology and the Old Testament theology of religions:
Missionalia 16 (1988) 4-12.

8423 *Jacob* Edmond, L'Ancien Testament et la théologie: → 153, ZAW 100
Supp. (1988) 268-278.

8424 *Klopfenstein* Martin A., Alttestamentliche Themen [grossenteils Wörter:
'am, mal'ak, špt; Segen, Tafeln...] in der neueren Forschung: TRu 53
(1988) 331-353.

8425 *a) Kraus* Hans-Joachim, Das Telos der Tora; biblische-theologische
Meditationen; – *b) Weinrich* Michael, Vom Charisma biblischer Provo-
kationen; systematische Theologie im Horizont biblischer Theologie bei
Hans-Joachim Kraus: JbBT 3 (1988) 55-82 / 253-266.

8426 *LaFargue* Michael, Sociohistorical research and the contextualization of
biblical theology: → 77, FKEE H., Social world 1988, 3-16.

8427 **Legrand** Lucien, Le Dieu qui vient; la mission dans la Bible. P 1988,
Desclée. – 235 p. F 128. 2-7189-0374-0. – REsprVie 98 (1988) 561-5 [E.
Cothenet: not about the divine mission (of the Holy Spirit) nor the In-
carnation, but the viewpoint of a missioner in India on how God himself
comes, in the action of biblical personages, to constitute his people];
Études 369 (1988) 570s (R. *Marlé*); Spiritus 29 (1988) 406-411 (C. *Tassin*).

Maillot A., Gros plan sur l'Ancien Testament; ses thèmes et ses défis 1987
→ 1079.

8428 **Mayers** Ronald B., Evangelical perspectives; toward a biblical balance
[...evangelical differences on key issues: election, OT-NT, inspiration...].
Lanham MD 1987, UPA. 193 p. $12.75. – RBS 145 (1988) 457 (R.P.
Lightner: fills a need).

8429 *Metz* Johann B., Kampf um jüdische Traditionen in der christlichen
Gottesrede: KIsr 2 (1987) 14-23.

8429* **Murrell** Nathaniel S., A critical appraisal of the significance of James
BARR's critique of biblical theology: diss. Drew. Madison NJ 1988. –
RelStR 15,191.

8430 **Oeming** Manfred, Gesamtbiblische Theologien der Gegenwart... AT/
NT seit von Rad [Diss. DGunneweg A. 1984] 1985 → 1,6777; 2,5477:
RKerkT 39 (1988) 151s (H.W. de *Knijff*); TR 84 (1988) 185-7 (K.
Löning); ZkT 110 (1988) 68-73 (R. *Oberforcher*).

8431 *Ravasi* G.-F., La conoscenza religiosa nell'AT e nell'ebraismo; Osea;
ParSpV 18 (1988) 9-20; Dt, *Bonora* A., 21-34; Geremia, *Bovati* P., 35-48;
Ezech 16, *Virgulin* S., 49-62; Is 45,3, *Merendino* R.P., 63-74; La non
conoscenza di Dio nella tradizione ebraica, *Rochettes* J. des, 75-90.

8432 **Ringgren** Helmer, Israelitische Religion²ᵉᵛ.: Religionen der Menschheit
26, 1982 → 63,6483; 1,6782: RZkT 110 (1988) 97s (R. *Oberforcher*).

8433 **Schmidt** J.H., Biblische Theologie in der Sicht heutiger Alttesta-
mentler². Giessen 1988, Brunnen. vi-250 p. DM 38. 3-7655-9326-5 [BL
89,115, R.A. *Mason*: ultimately forces the OT into a doctrinal framework
alien to its writers].

8434 *Segalla* G., *Bonora* A., Teologia biblica: → 806, NDizTB (1988) 1533-1552.

ᴱ**Sitarz** E., Höre Israel! Jahwe ist einzig; Bausteine für eine Theologie des ATs 1987 → 327.

8435 **Stuhlmacher** Peter, Reconciliation, law, and righteousness; essays in biblical theology [1981 → 62, 297], ᵀ*Kalin* Everett R., 1986 → 2,226: ᴿCurrTM 15 (1988) 210 (E. *Krentz*: excellent translator slighted; sources not indicated).

8436 **Van Buren** Paul M., A theology of the Jewish-Christian reality I-II 1987 = 1980 → 61,k176; 1983 → 65,6165 [III → 8555]: ᴿRExp 85 (1988) 570-2 (E. G. *Hinson*).

8436* **Van Buren** Paul M., Eine Theologie des jüdisch-christlichen Diskurses; Darstellung der Arbeiten und Möglichkeiten I (aus 4), ᵀᴱ *Sacksofsky* Eva. Mü 1988, Kaiser. 220 p. DM 48 [KIsr 89,182, A. *Funke*].

8437 **Vogel** Manfred H., A quest for a theology of Judaism. Lanham MD 1987, UPA. xxxv-292 p. $28.50; pa. $15.75. − ᴿJJS 39 (1988) 278s (L. *Jacobs*).

8438 *Wagner* Siegfried, Zur Frage nach der Möglichkeit einer Biblischen Theologie: TLZ 113 (1988) 161-170.

H5.1 *Deus* − NT − God [as Father → H1.4]

8440 **Beilner** Wolfgang, Massstab Evangelium. Graz 1987, Styria. 211 p. DM 29,80 pa. − ᴿTPQ 136 (1988) 193s (O. B. *Knoch*).

8440* *a*) *Biser* Eugen, Jesus und sein Gott; − *b*) *Geffré* Claude, Die Gottesfrage heute: → 53, ᶠGANOCZY A., Creatio 1988, 100-111 / 84-99.

8441 *Guillet* Jacques, Sainteté de Dieu: → 791, DictSpir XIV,91 (1988) 184-192 (-4, de l'homme, *Solignac* Aimé).

8442 **Hurtado** Larry W., One God, one Lord; early Christian devotion and ancient Jewish monotheism [... how the risen Christ came to share in the cult normally reserved for God]. Ph 1988, Fortress. xiv-178 p. $13 pa. 0-8006-2076-3 [NTAbs 32,384]. − ᴿHorBT 10,1 (1988) 71-74 (U. W. *Mauser*).

8443 **Kasper** W., *a*) Le Dieu des Chrétiens 1985 → 1,6797... 3,6945: ᴿIstina 33 (1988) 88-90 (B. *Dupuy*). − *b*) El Dios de J. C. 1985 → 1,6798... 3,6944: ᴿScripTPamp 20 (1988) 308-316 (J. *Morales*).

8444 *Lago Alba* Luis, Libros sobre Dios [II: 11 libros]: CiTom 114 (1987) 311-340; 115 (1988) 555-574.

8445 **Muñoz** Ronaldo, *a*) El Dios de los Cristianos 1986 → 3,6950: ᴿCarthaginensia 4 (1988) 188s (J. M. *Roncero Moreno*). − *b*) Der Gott der Christen: Bibliothek Theologie der Befreiung. Dü 1987, Patmos. 231 p. − ᴿTKontext 9,2 (1988) 107 (M. *Sievernich*).

8446 **Schlosser** J., Le Dieu de Jésus: LDiv 129, 1987 → 3,6952: ᴿBZ 32 (1988) 276s (G. *Schneider*); Carthaginensia 4 (1988) 180 (J. F. *Cuenca Molina*); CBQ 50 (1988) 545s (S. P. *Kealy*); EstBíb 46 (1988) 131-3 (F. *González García*); IndTSt 25 (1988) 99-101 (L. *Legrand*); NRT 110 (1988) 920s (X. *Jacques*); RHPR 68 (1988) 247s (M. *Carrez*); RThom 88 (1988) 484s (L. *Devillers* dirait 'confiance filiale' plutôt que 'foi' de Jésus; et hésite à croire p. 129 'La conviction que le Règne va venir sans tarder... fut probablement celle de Jésus'); VSp 142 (1988) 462 (H. *Cousin*).

8447 **Van Roo** William A., Telling about God, I. Promise and fulfilment, 1986 → 2,3248; 3,4146; II. Experience, 1987 → 3,6378: ᴿBibTB 18 (1988) 153s (J. F. *Craghan*, I: exegetical sources rather limited; but, with vol. II, helpful for those seeking a more enriching experience of God); BLitEc 89 (1988) 149s (H. *Crouzel*, 1); IrTQ 54 (1988) 317s (B. *Kelly*); RRel 47 (1988) 944s (F.G. *McLeod*, 2).

8448 **Van Roo** W.A., Telling about God III. Understanding. R 1987, Pont. Univ. Gregoriana. xiii-351 p. Lit. 45.000. 88-7652-576-9. – ᴿGregorianum 69 (1988) 191-3 (*ipse*: not just De Deo uno); TR 84 (1988) 183-5 O.B. *Knoch*: ganzheitlicher Zugang zur biblischen Botschaft, 1-3).

H5.2 Christologia ipsius NT.

8449 *Berry* Donald L., Revisioning Christology; the logic of messianic ascription: AnglTR 70 (1988) 129-143.

8450 [*Cazelles* H.] *a*) Papieska komisja biblijna, Biblia i Chrystologia ❷: RuBi 41 (1988) 185-226. – *b*) ᴱ*Sanz Valdivieso* Rafael, Pontificia comisión bíblica, documento Biblia y Cristología: Carthaginensia 4 (1988) 113-162.

8450* **Dreyfus** F., Jésus savait-il qu'il était Dieu? 1984 ➤ 65,6193 ... 2,5514): ᴿÉglT 18 (1987) 130s (L. *Laberge*).

8451 **Fitzmyer** Joseph A., Scripture and Christology ... with commentary 1986: ➤ 2,5518: ᴿFurrow 38 (1987) 547 (M. *Drennan*); HomP 88,1 (1987s) 78s (J.R. *Sheets*).

8452 [ᴱ*Fitzmyer* J.A.] ᵀᴱ**Müller** Paul-G., Bibel und Christologie 1987 ➤ 3,6961: ᴿTLZ 113 (1988) 293-5 (W *Trilling*: Müllers Kommentar ist umfassender).

8453 **Guardini** Romano, Das Christusbild der paulinischen und johanneischen Schriften: Werke [ᴱ*Henrich* Franz]. Mainz/Pd 1987, Grünewald/ Schöningh. 230 p. – ᴿColcT 58,4 (1988) 165 (R. *Bartnicki*).

8454 **Habermann** Jürgen, Präexistenzaussagen im NT: ev. Diss. München 1988, ᴰ*Hahn* F. 944 p. – RTLv 20,544.

8454* *Harrington* Wilfrid, Christology and Scripture [... *Fitzmyer* J.]: DocLife 37 (1987) 63-73.

8455 *Hoffmann* Paul, Er ist unsere Freiheit; Aspekte einer konkreten Christologie im NT: ➤ 76, ᶠKAUFMANN L., Biotope 1988, 47-60.

8455* **Jonge** M. de, Christology in context; the earliest Christian response to Jesus; pref. *Meeks* W.A. Ph 1988, Westminster. 276 p. $16. 0-664-25010-6 [NTAbs 32,382]. – ᴿTTod 45 (1988s) 512 (J.K. *Robbins*).

8456 **Krieg** Robert A., Story-shared Christology; the roles of narratives in identifying Jesus Christ: Theological Inquiries. NY 1988, Paulist. 170 p. $9 pa. [BibTB 18/3 cover]. 0-8091-2941-8. – ᴿLvSt 13 (1988) 373s (H.-E. *Mertens*); TorJT 4 (1988) 290-2 (J.P. *Galvin*); TTod 45 (1988s) 384 (M.A. *Powell*: on others' Christologies).

8456* *Lövestam* Evald, Davids-son-kristologin hos synoptikerna [< SvEx 37s (1972s) 196-210]: ➤ 221, Axplock 1987, 27-38.

8457 **O'Connor** James T., The Father's Son 1984 ➤ 65,6210; 1,6846: ᴿScripTPamp 19 (1987) 935-7 (T.J. *McGovern*).

8458 **Pokorný** Petr, The genesis of Christology; foundations for a theology of the New Testament [1985 ➤ 1,6898], ᵀ*Lefebure* Marcus. E 1987, Clark ➤ 3,6973 [McLean ᴠᴀ, Books-Int. $34]. 0-567-09450-2; pa. 29144-8.

8459 **Richard** Earl, Jesus, one and many; the Christological concept of New Testament authors. Wilmington 1988, Glazier. 546 p. $30. 0-89453-641-9 [TDig 36,180].

8460 **Sabourin** L., *a*) La christologie à partir de textes clés 1986 ➤ 2,5537; 3,6975: ᴿBLitEc 89 (1988) 298s (S. *Légasse*); EstE 63 (1988) 252s (J.R.

García-Murga). – *b*) Christology; basic texts in focus 1984 ➤ 65,6214 ...
3,6974: ᴿHeythJ 29 (1988) 398s (J. P. *Galvin*: weaknesses).

8461 **Scroggs** Robin, The reality and revelation of God; Christology in Paul
and John: Proclamation Comm. Ph 1988, Fortress. x-129 p. 0-8006-
0599-3. – ᴿRExp 85 (1988) 721s (Molly *Marshall-Green*).

8462 **Segalla** G., La cristologia del Nuovo Testamento 1985 ➤ 1,6854 ...
3,6978: ᴿEstTrin 20 (1986) 201s (J. L. *Aurrecoechea*); Protestantesimo 43
(1988) 199-201 (M. F. *Berutti*); TR 84 (1988) 466 (J. *Galot*).

8563 **Segundo** J. L., *a*) The historical Jesus of the synoptics: Jesus 2, 1985
➤ 1,6855*; 2,5541: ᴿNBlackfr 68 (1987) 201s (T. *Williams*). – *b*) Jesus ...
3. The humanist Christology of Paul 1986 ➤ 2,5542; 3,6980: ᴿCBQ 50
(1988) 146s (J. C. *Turro*).

8463* ᴱ**Welte** B., La storia della cristologia primitiva; gli inizi biblici e la
formula di Nicea [1970] 1986 ➤ 2,5545*: ᴿComSev 21 (1988) 130 (M. de
Burgos).

H5.3   *Christologia praemoderna* – **patristic through Reformation.**

8464 *Adams* Marilyn M., The metaphysics of the Incarnation in some
fourteenth-century manuscripts ➤ 2,125*, ᶠWOLTER Allan B., ᴱ**Frank**
W., 1985, 21-57.

8465 *Basevi* Claudio, El cristocentrismo en [Luis de LEÓN] De los nombres de
Cristo y en [AGUSTÍN] La ciudad de Dios: CiuD 201 (1988) 113-132.

8465* **Bruns** Peter, Christologie nach syrischer Sprachstruktur — ein Beitrag
zum Christusbild APHRAHATS des Persischen Weisen: Diss. ᴰ*Geerlings*.
Bochum 1987s. – TR 84 (1988) 511.

8466 **Carol** Juniper B., Why Jesus Christ? Thomistic, Scotistic and concilia-
tory perspectives. Manassas VA 1986, Trinity Communications. xvi-
531 p. 0-937495-03-4. – ᴿColcFr 58 (1988) 382s (B. de *Armellada*); Gregorianum 69 (1988) 724-6 (J. *Dupuis*); TS 49 (1988) 742s (G. M. *Fagin*).

8466* **Cavadini** John C., The last Christology of the west; adoptionism in
Spain and Gaul, AD 785-817; diss. Yale. NHv 1988. 337 p. 89-17154. –
DissA 50, 1328-A; RelStR 15,194.

8467 ᵀᴱ**Corbin** Michel, *Galonnier* Alain, S. ANSELME de Cantorbéry 3. Lettre
sur l'incarnation du Verbe; pourquoi un Dieu-homme: Œuvres 3. P 1988,
Cerf. 495 p. – ᴿÉtudes 368 (1988) 711 (R. *Marlé*); RHPR 68 (1988) 494s
(G. *Siegwalt*).

8468 *Daley* Brian E., A humble mediator; the distinctive elements in St.
AUGUSTINE's Christology: WSpirit 9 (1987) 100-117.

8469 **Denis** Philippe, Le Christ étendard; l'Homme-Dieu au temps des
Réformes (1500-1565): Jésus depuis Jésus. P 1987, Cerf. 221 p. – ᴿBibl-
HumRen 50 (1988) 807s (M. *Engammare*).

8470 **Drobner** Hubertus R., Person-Exegese und Christologie bei AUGU-
STINUS: zur Herkunft der Formel una persona: Philosophia Patrum 8,
ᴰ1984/6 ➤ 3,6992; $47.25: ᴿCiuD 201 (1988) 492 (J. *Gutiérrez*); ZkT 110
(1988) 463-5 (K. H. *Neufeld*).

8471 ᵀᴱ**Durán** Manuel, *Kluback* William, Luis de LEÓN, The names of
Christ: Classics of Western Spirituality 1984 ➤ 1.6937*: ᴿHeythJ 29
(1988) 147s [Agnes *Heller*].

8472 ᵀᴱ**Ettlinger** Gerard H., Jesus, Christ and Savior: Message of the Fathers
2, 1987 ➤ 3,6994: ᴿRExp 85 (1988) 159s (E. G. *Hinson*).

8473 **Grillmeier** Alois, Jesus der Christus im Glauben der Kirche 2/1, 1986
➤ 2,5557; 3,7000: ᴿRHR 205 (1988) 101s (P. *Nautin*); RTLv 19 (1988)

80-83 (A. de *Halleux*); StiZt 206 (1988) 716s (B. *Kriegbaum*); TGegw 30 (1987) 143s (A. *Schmied*); TPQ 136 (1988) 91s (R. *Schulte*).

8474 **Grillmeier** Alois, Christ in Christian tradition. II. From the council of Chalcedon (451) to Gregory the Great, 1. Reception and contradiction; the development of the discussion about Chalcedon from 451 to the beginning of the reign of Justinian, 1987 → 3,7001; [T]*Allen* Pauline, *Cawte* John: [R]JTS 39 (1988) 618s (A. *Louth*); RÉByz 46 (1988) 255 (J. *Wolinksi*: 'Aloys'); ScotJT 41 (1988) 557s (L. R. *Wickham*).

8475 **Hanson** R. P. C., The search for the Christian doctrine of God; the Arian controversy 318-381. E 1988, Clark. xxi-931 p. 0-567-09485-5.

8476 *Henne* Philippe, À propos de la Christologie du Pasteur d'HERMAS; la cohérence interne des niveaux d'explication dans la Cinquième Similitude: RSPT 72 (1988) 569-578; Eng. 578.

8477 *House* Dennis K., The relation of TERTULLIAN's Christology to pagan philosophy: Dionysius 12 (Halifax 1988) 29-36.

8478 *Iammarrone* Giovanni, Attualità e limiti della Cristologia di G. Duns SCOTO per l'elaborazione del discorso cristologico oggi: MiscFranc 88 (1988) 277-299.

8479 **Lohaus** Gerd, Die Geheimnisse des Lebens Jesu in der Summa theologiae des heiligen Thomas von AQUIN [Diss. Bonn → 1,1048] 1984/5: [R]TLZ 113 (1988) 41-43 (P. *Heidrich*: Christologie 'Diss. Bochum'); TPQ 136 (1988) 92 (R. *Schulte*).

8480 [E]**Mahlmann** T., BRENZ J., Die christologischen Schriften I, 1981 → 63,6530: [R]Zwingliana 16 (1985) 171-3 (H. *Stucki*).

8480* *Malherbe* Abraham J., Herakles... christlich: Leben Jesu, Christologie; Paulus; Kirchenväter; [T]*Maiburg* Ursula: → 807, RAC 14,108s (1988) 559-583.

8481 *Martínez Fresneda* Francisco, La plenitud de gracia en Jesucristo según Odón RIGALDO [Sentencias 1243-5] / en san BUENAVENTURA: Carthaginensia 4 (1988) 45-77 / 235-266.

8482 [TE]**Mauro** Letterio, S. BONAVENTURA, La conoscenza in Cristo: Testi Bonaventuriani 3. Vicenza 1987, L.I.E.F. 287 p. Lit. 20.000. – [R]ColcFr 57 (1987) 360 (B. de *Armellada*).

8483 *Meyendorff* John, Christ's humanity; the paschal mystery: SVlad 31 (1987) 5-40.

8484 **Norris** Richard A., The Christological controversy [selections translated]: Sources of early Christian thought. Ph 1988, Fortress. viii-162 p. 0-8006-1411-9.

8485 **Posset** Franz, LUTHER's Catholic Christology according to his Johannine Lectures of 1527: diss. Milwaukee 1988, Northwestern. 267 p. – [R]Cîteaux 39 (1988) 391s (D. *Heller*).

8485* **Riestra** J. A., Cristo y la plenitud del corpo místico — estudio sobre la cristología de Santo Tomás de AQUINO 1985 → 2,5570; 3,7012: [R]DivThom 91 (1988) 206-211 (L. *Iammarrone*).

8486 **Ruello** Francis, La Christologie de Thomas d'AQUIN: THist 76, 1987 → 3,7013: [R]ComSev 21 (1988) 110s (A. *Lobato*); ScEspr 40 (1988) 390s (G. *Langevin*); TR 84 (1988) 127 (H. *Vorgrimler*); TS 49 (1988) 740-2 (R. *Cessario*); TsTNijm 28 (1988) 185 (P. *Valkenberg*).

8486* *Sanders* J., Le traité [arabe] 'de l'Incarnation' du ms. Paris B.N. syr. 371, F 107o-125r: Muséon 101 (1988) 343-373. ...

8487 **Seguenny** André, The Christology of Caspar SCHWENCKFELD [1489-1561]; spirit and flesh in the process of life transformation [Homme charnel 1975], [T]*Erb* Peter C., *Nieuwold* Simone. Lewiston NY 1987,

Mellen. 142 p. $40 [RelStR 15,171, Mary P. *Engel*]. – RSixtC 19 (1988) 695s (R. E. *McLaughlin*).

8488 *a*) *Simonetti* Manlio, Cristologia giudeocristiana; caratteri e limiti; – *b*) *Horbury* William, Messianism among Jews and Christians in the second century: → 570, AugR 28 (1988) 51-69 / 71-88.

8489 *Stăniloae* Dumitru, La Christologie de saint MAXIME le Confesseur: Contacts 40 (1988) 112-120.

8490 *a*) *Thetford* Gregory, The Christological council of 1166 and 1170 in Constantinople; – *b*) *Boojamra* John L., The transformation of conciliar theory in the last century of Byzantium: SVlad 31 (1987) 143-161 / 215-235.

8490* **Torrance** Iain R., Christology after Chalcedon; SEVERUS of Antioch and SERGIUS the Monophysite. Norwich 1988, Canterbury. xii-266 p. 0-907547-97-4.

8491 *Vycichl* Werner, Ptah-hotep, the father as sole author of procreation, a possible origin of Monophysitism: DiscEg 3 (1985) 61-63.

8491* *Wright* J. Robert, The authority of Chalcedon for Anglicans: → 23, FCHADWICK H. 1988, 224-251.

8492 *Zizioulas* Jean, Christologie et existence; la dialectique créé-incréé et le dogme de Chalcedoine: Contacts 36 (1984) 153-172 [> SelT 26 (1987) 51-58, EVillanova Gabriel].

H5.4   (*Commentationes de*) *Christologia* moderna.

8492* **Auer** Johann, Jesus Christus — Gottes und Mariä 'Sohn' 1986 → 2,5582; 3,7025: RTR 84 (1988) 484s (J. *Galot*).

8493 *Bartnik* Czesław, ❷ Bóg człowiekiem: ColcT 58,4 (1988) 5-16; franç. 16, Dieu homme: Cur Deus homo? propter structuram personalisticam.

8494 *Blandino* G., Recent hypotheses about the ontological constitution of Christ: EuntDoc 41 (1988) 117-152.

8495 **Bordoni** Marcello, Gesù di Nazaret, Signore e Cristo; saggio di cristologia sistematica, I. Problemi di metodo; II. Gesù al fondamento della cristologia 1982, ²1985; III. Il Cristo annunciato dalla Chiesa 1986 → 3,7027: RGregorianum 69 (1988) 362-6 (R. *Fisichella*); RasT 29 (1988) 88-90 (V. *Caporale*).

8496 *Brambilla* Franco G., Ancora su alcune cristologie italiane [*Bordoni* M., *Contri* A., *Lavatori* R.]: ScuolC 116 (1988) 3-29.

8497 *Caporale* Vincenzo, [→ 8204] Cristologia e società nella 'Gaudium et spes': RasT 29 (1988) 431-444.

8497* **Casas** Victoriano, Cristo al encuentro del hombre. M 1988, Claretianas. 343 p. – RBibFe 14 (1988) 479 (A. *Salas*).

8498 *Cavalcoli* G., La cristologia di E. SCHILLEBEECKX [condivide il giudizio di *Iammarrone* L. 1985]: DivThom 89s (1986s) 401-9.

8498* **Chesnut** Glen F., Images of Christ... Christology 1984 → HeythJ 29 (1988) 398 (J. P. *Galvin*).

8499 **Ciola** N., Introduzione alla Cristologia 1986 → 2,5597; 3,7033: RRivScR 2 (1988) 224s (V. *Angiuli*).

8500 *Cobb* John B., Christology in 'process-relational' perspective: WSpirit 8 (1986) 79-94.

8501 **Contri** Antonio, Gesù Cristo. Figlio di Dio e Salvatore 1985 → 2,5552; 3,6991: RCC 139 (1988,4) 413 (G. *Blandino*).

8501* **Corrington** G., The 'divine man' 1986 → 2,5599; 3,7035: RClasW 82 (1988s) 125s (R. J. *Penella*).

8502 **Crawford** Robert G., The saga of God incarnate 1985 → 2,5600; $16.25; 0-86981-485-0: RRefTR 46 (1987) 21 (P. F. *Jensen*: concedes too much to historical criticism).

8503 *Deneken* M., Pour une christologie de la pro-existence: RevSR 62 (1988) 265-290.

8504 *De Rosa* Giuseppe, Un singolare saggio di Cristologia [*Forte* B. 1981]: DivThom 89s (1986s) 3-133: severo.

8505 *de Souza* Archie, Towards a new Christology [centered on the Kingdom of God]: Focus 7 (Multan, Pakistan 1987) 87-93 [< TKontext 10/1,69].

8506 **Doyon** Jacques, L'option fondamentale de Jésus: Notre temps 28. 1984 → 1,6937; 2,5602: RÉglT 17 (1986) 240s (N. *Provencher*).

8507 *Dupuis* Jacques, On some recent Christological literature [*Juel* D.; *Hultgren* A., *Schlosser* J.; *Grillmeier* A.; *Serenthà* M. ...]: Gregorianum 69 (1988) 713-740.

8508 *Durrant* Michael, The logic of God incarnate — two recent metaphysical principles examined [*Morris* T. 1986]: RelSt 24 (1988) 121-7.

8509 *Espeja* Jesús, Hacia una cristología fundamental: CiTom 115 (1988) 77-106.

8510 **Fox** Michael, The coming of the cosmic Christ; the healing of Mother Earth and the birth of a global renaissance. SF 1988, Harper & R. 278 p. $15 pa. – RHomP 89,9 (1988s) 74-77 (J. R. *Sheets*: Dominican province theologians panel: 'nothing to condemn' true in a sense, but ...).

8511 *a) Gebara* Ivone, Cristologia fundamental; – *b) Ferraro* Benedito, Cristologia a partir de América Latina — pressupostos: REB 48 (1988) 259-272 / 283-309.

8512 **Gertler** T., J. C. ... Menschsein 1986 → 2,5611: RAngelicum 65 (1988) 300s (A. *Lobato*); TGegw 30 (1987) 144s (H. *Moll*); TR 84 (1988) 482s (G. L. *Müller*).

8513 *Gillis* Chester, John HICK's Christology: Bijdragen 49 (1988) 41-57.
      Goergen Donald J., A theology of Jesus 1986-8 → 4172.4855.

8514 *Guerrero* Jesús A., Jesucristo, salvador y liberador (La cristología de Jon SOBRINO): NatGrac 34 (1987) 27-96.

8515 *Gunton* Colin, Two dogmas revisited; Edward IRVING's Christology [c. 1830]: ScotJT 41 (1988) 359-376.

8516 **Hebblethwaite** Brian, The Incarnation; collected essays in Christology 1987 → 3,235: RRelSt 24 (1988) 539-541 (C. *Schwoebel*).

8517 **Heim** S. Mark, Is Christ the only way? Christian faith in a pluralistic world. Valley Forge PA 1985, Judson. 145 p. – RJEcuSt 24 (1987) 116 (T. *Dean*: mainline Protestant defense).

8518 *Heim* S. Mark, Thinking about theocentric Christology: JEcuSt 24,1 (1987) 1-16 (-52, responses by *Braaten* C., *Cobb* J., *Dean* T., *Fraser* Elouise, *Koyama* K., *Knitter* P.).

8519 **Helminiak** Daniel A., The same Jesus; a contemporary Christology 1986 → 2,5619; 3,7054: RAmerica 157 (1987) 339s (R. A. *Krieg*); Horizons 18 (1988) 174s (Mary T. *Rattigan*); TTod 44 (1987s) 301s (D. G. *Dawe*).

8520 **Herbst** K., Der wirkliche Jesus; das total andere Gottesbild. Olten 1988, Walter. 245 p. DM 33. 3-530-34551-2 [TsTNijm 28,431].

8521* **Kaiser** Alfred, Der christologische Neuansatz 'von unten' bei Piet SCHOONENBERG [... und] Nikolaus von KUES: Diss. DHaubst R. Trier 1988. – RTLv 20,568.

8521 *a) Kertelge* Karl, Irdischer Jesus und verkündigter Christus; woher diese Unterscheidung?; – *b) Limbeck* Meinrad, Der Weltenrichter als Freudenbote; von der Möglichkeit und den Grenzen einer alttestamentlichen Christologie: BiKi 43 (1988) 48-53 / 41-47.

8521* *Krasevac* Edward L., 'Christology from above' and 'Christology from below': Thomist 51 (1987) 298-306.

8522 **Küng** Hans, The incarnation of God ... HEGEL [1970], [T]*Stephenson* J. R. 1987 → 3,7061: [r]Gregorianum 69 (1988) 728-731 (J. *Dupuis*); TTod 45 (1988s) 375-7 (P. *Lakeland*).

8522* *Lakeland* Paul, A new pietism; Hegel and recent Christology [*Brito* E., *Jüngel* E.]: JRel 68 (Ch 1988) 57-71.

8523 **Lambiasi** F., Credo in Gesù Cristo; Cristologia. R 1988, Paoline. 165 p. Lit. 16.000 [CC 139/4 dopo 312].

8524 *Leuze* Reinhard, Homo factus est; zur wiedererwachten Aktualität des Mythosbegriffs und ihrer Bedeutung für die Christologie: → 114, [F]PANNENBERG W., Vernunft 1988, 525-539.

8525 *Loewe* W. P., The new Christologies; the recovery of Jesus' full humanity: Church 3,4 (1987) 19-25 [NTAbs 32,198].

8526 **Logister** Wiel, Een mensenleven door God getekend; inleiding in de christologie: CahLV 52, 1987 → 3,7064: [R]Bijdragen 49 (1988) 323-330 (P. *Valkenberg*; Eng. 330); Streven 55 (1987s) 753s (P. *Beentjes*).

McCready Douglas, The Christology of the Catholic Tübingen school, from DREY to KASPER: diss. Temple, 1987 → k270.

8528 *McDonald* H. D., The symbolic Christology of Paul TILLICH: VoxEvca 18 (1988) 75-88.

8529 **McGrath** Alister E., The making of modern German Christology 1986 → 2,5626; 3,7067: [R]AnglTR 69 (1987) 399s (J. W. *McClendon*); Interpretation 42 (1988) 200s (W. S. *Johnson*); JRel 68 (1988) 114s (Dawn *De Vries*); NBlackfr 68 (1987) 159 (C. *Gunton*); ScotJT 41 (1988) 125-8 (A. *Heron*).

McGrath Alister E., Understanding Jesus; who Jesus Christ is and why he matters 1987 → 4183.

8531 *Mateo García* Juan Antonio, Persona Christi; reflexión teológica en torno a la interpretación de E. SCHILLEBEECKX: Burgense 29 (1985) 51-91.

8532 [E]**Miguez Bonino** José, Faces of Jesus; Latin American Christologies 1984 → 3,7070: [R]HeythJ 29 (1988) 103-5 (J. P. *Galvin*).

8532* *Momose* Fumiaki, ◉ Validity and problems of a 'Christology from below': KatKenk 27,54 (1988) 77-107 = 263-293.

8533 **Morrone** Fortunato, Cristo il Figlio di Dio fatto uomo; l'incarnazione del Verbo nel pensiero cristologico di J. H. NEWMAN: diss. Pont. Univ. Gregoriana, [D]*González* C. R 1988. 408 p. – RTLv 20,569.

8533* **Museka Ntumba** Lambert, La nomination africaine de Jésus-Christ; quelle christologie?: diss. [D]*Gesché* A., LvN 1988. 497 p. – RTLv 19 (1988) 411.

8534 **Ohlig** Karl-Heinz, Fundamentalchristologie im Spannungsfeld von Christentum und Kultur 1986 → 2,5639; 3,7075; 3-466-20284-1: [R]ActuBbg 25 (1988) 46-50 (J. *Boada*); BiKi 43 (1988) 66-68 (W. *Stenger*); Carthaginensia 4 (1988) 186 (R. *Sanz Valdivieso*); TGL 78 (1988) 277s (W. *Beinert*); ZkT 110 (1988) 329-333 (H. *Verweyen*).

8535 *a*) *Ouwerkerk* C. A. J. van, Christus' uniciteit; een beschouwing op afstand; Eng. The unicity of Christ; an approach from a distance; – *b*) *Denaux* Adelbert, Bij niemand anders is er redding (Hand. 4,12); Eng. The unicity of JC in the NT; – *c*) *Logister* Wiel, Het unieke van Jezus — een systematische vingeroefening; – *d*) *Rossum* Rogier van, Jezus' uni-

citeit in missionair perspectief: TsTNijm 28 (1988) 213-226; Eng. 226s /
228-246; Eng. 246 / 247-271; Eng. 271 / 272-287; Eng. 287s.

8536 **Ramm** B., An evangelical Christology 1985 ➤ 3,7078: ᴿJPsy&T 15
(1987) 173s (G. R. *Lewis*: 'partially historic').

8536* **Potworowski** Christophe F., The Incarnation in the theology of
Marie-Dominique CHENU: diss. St. Michael, ᴰ*Donovan* D. Toronto 1988.
219 p. – RTLv 20,570.

8537 *Renwart* León, 'Pour nous, les hommes, et pour notre salut'; chronique de christologie [20 livres: *Grillmeier* A., *Studer* B., *Orazzo* A., *Gertler*
T., *Sobrino* J., *Fitzmyer* J., *Sabourin* L. ... *al.* infra]: NRT 110 (1988)
571-590.

8538 **Rey** Bernard, Jésus le Christ: Parcours / Bibliothèque de formation
chrétienne. 118 p. F 59. – ᴿEsprVie 98 (1988) 396s (P. *Jay*); Études 368
(1988) 857 (R. *Marlé*).

8539 *Richard* Lucien, The possibility of the Incarnation according to
Emmanuel LEVINAS: SR 17 (1988) 391-405.

8540 *Riestra* José A., La scienza di Cristo nel Concilio Vaticano II: AnnTh 2
(R 1988) 99-120.

8540* *Ritt* Paul E., The lordship of Jesus Christ; BALTHASAR and SOBRINO:
TS 49 (1988) 709-729.

8541 *Rössler* Andreas, Der ewige Christus und der Mensch Jesus: Leben
und Glauben 30 (1987) 24-26 [> 30 (1988) 330s].

8542 **Scheld** S., Die Christologie E. BRUNNERs 1981 ➤ 63,6657: ᴿZwingliana
16 (1985) 87-91 (W. J. *Hollenweger*).

8543 *Schottroff* Willy, Thesen zur Aktualität und theologischen Bedeutung
sozialgeschichtlicher Bibelauslegung im Kontext christlicher Sozialethik:
➤ 140, ᶠSTOODT D., Unterwegs 1987, 485-8.

8544 **Schweizer** Eduard, Jesus Christ, the man from Nazareth and the exalted
Lord 1986 ➤ 3,3962: ᴿCurrTM 15 (1988) 211s (E. *Krentz*); RExp 85
(1988) 140s (E. K. *Broadhead*).

8545 **Serenthà** Mario, Gesù Cristo ieri, oggi e sempre; saggio di cristologia³
[¹1982 ➤ 63,6668]. T 1988, Elle Di Ci. Lit. 25.000. – ᴿRClerIt 69 (1988)
472s (F. G. *Brambilla*).

8546 *a) Sesboüé* Bernard, Dall'affermazione patristica dell'unione ipostatica
al problema della coscienza di sé in Gesù, ᵀ*Costa* Eugenio; – *b) Duquoc*
Christian, Per una cristologia, ᵀ*Costa*: ➤ 495*, Gesù storico 1985/8,
65-94 / 205-215.

8547 *Sheridan* Daniel P., Stations keeping; Christ and Krishna as embodied:
CCurr 38 (1988s) 325-339.

8548 **Snook** Lee E., The anonymous Christ; Jesus as savior in modern
theology 1986 ➤ 3,7089; $11: ᴿCurrTM 15 (1988) 217s (F. *Reklau*:
'saves' from the sense of lostness).

8548* [*Sparn* Walter], *Macquarrie* John, Jesus Christus [V.] VI-VII Neuzeit,
ᵀ*Muhlenberg* Marianne: ➤ 813, TRE 17 (1987) [...-1-16] 16-64 (-76,
VIII-X, *al.*).

   Stuhlmacher Peter, Jesus von Nazareth — Christus des Glaubens 1988
➤ 4214.

8549 *Stuhlmann* Rainer, Tastende Schritte ins christologische Neuland —
Fortschritte im christlich-jüdischen Dialog [ᴱ*Brocke-Seim* 1986 ²1988]:
EvT 48 (1988) 474-9.

8550 **Tézé** Jean-Marie, Théophanies du Christ: JJC Résonances 4. P 1988,
Desclée. 204 p.; color. ill. – ᴿMaisD 176 (1988) 149, Anne de *Grunne*:
Christologie par images).

8551 **Theobald** Michael, Die Fleischwerdung des Logos: NTAbh NF 20. Mü 1988, Aschendorff. ix-537 p. DM 148.

8552 *a) Thompson* William, Christologies from above and below; – *b) Peter* Carl, Jesus Christ and dogma; Karl RAHNER on [p. 315; 'and' p. 241] Chalcedon: ChSt 26 (1987) 300-314 / 315-329.

8553 **Thurmer** J., The Son in the Bible and the Church [... Jesus thought of himself as the second person of the Trinity ... minus the terminology]. Exeter 1987, Paternoster. 102 p. £5. 0-85364-449-7 [NTAbs 32,259].

8554 *Tilliette* Xavier, De la 'philosophia Christi' à la christologie philosophique: RICathP 25 (1988) 21-35.

8555 **Van Buren** Paul M., [→ 8436] Christ in context: A theology of the Jewish-Christian reality 3. SF 1988, Harper & R. xix-312 p. $30 [JNES 47,240] 0-06-068823-8. – RTTod 45 (1988s) 478 . 480 (C. M. *Williamson*).

8556 **Webster** Douglas, A passion for Christ; an evangelical Christology 1987 → 3,7093: RSR 17 (1987) 508 (J. *Franklin*).

8557 *a)* **Wong** J. H. P., Logos-symbol ... Rahner 1984 → 1,6997 ... 3,7096: RÉglT 17 (1986) 108-111 (J. *Pambrun*); – *b) Young* Pamela D., RAHNER's searching Christology: NBlackf 68 (1987) 437-443.

H5.5 *Spiritus Sanctus; pneumatologia* – The Holy Spirit.

8557* **Akinjo** Adedayo, The role of the Holy Spirit in the renewal of the Church in the ecclesiology of Karl BARTH: diss. DDulles A. Wsh 1988. 88-14932. – DissA 49 (1988s) 1845-A; RTLv 20,563.

8558 **Anderson** James B., A Vatican II pneumatology of the paschal mystery; the historical-doctrinal genesis of Ad gentes 1,2-5 [diss. Pont. Gregorian Univ.] AnGreg 250. R 1988, Gregoriana. xix-335 p. Lit. 48.500 [TDig 36,44]. 88-7652-577-7.

8559 *Angiolini* Giuseppe, A proposito dell'Enciclica sullo Spirito Santo: Pal-Cl 66 (1987) 423-6.

8560 *Bartnicki* Roman, Les dons du Saint-Esprit à la lumière des textes du NT [symposium]: BInfWsz (1988,3) 8s.

8561 **Bermejo** Luis M., The Spirit of life; the Holy Spirit in the life of the Christian: Pastoral 23. Anand 1987, Gujarat Sahitya Prakash. 388 p. $10.50; pa. $8.50 [TDig 35,341].

8562 **Bernd** Jochen H., Heiliger Geist — heilender Geist. Mainz 1988, Grünewald-Reihe. 120 p. DM 16,80 pa. – RTGL 78 (1988) 444 (W. *Beinert*).

8563 **Boespflug** F., Dieu [Esprit-Saint] dans l'art ... BENOIT XIV/CRESCENCE 1984 → 65,6357 ... 2,5681: RNRT 110 (1988) 784s (M.-L. *Lievens-de Waegh*).

8564 *Coda* Piero, Lo Spirito Santo come 'in-mezzo-persona' che compie l'unità nella teologia di S. BULGAKOV: NuovaUm 9,52s (1987) 23-46.

8565 **Congar** Yves, Spirito dell'uomo, Spirito di Dio: GdT 170. Brescia 1987, Queriniana. 56 p. – RHumBr 43 (1988) 297s (G. *Colombi*).

8566 **Durrwell** François-X., Holy Spirit of God 1986 → 2,5694: RGregorianum 69 (1988) 153s (J. *Dupuis*); HomP 89,4 (1988s) 75s (J. R. *Sheets*: fine); IrBSt 9 (1987) 99s (K. *Condon*: spiritual reflection, not biblical theology).

8567 **Ferraro** Giuseppe, Lo Spirito Santo nel 'De Trinitate' di Sant'AGO-STINO; meditazioni. CasM 1987, Piemme. 142 p. Lit. 14.000. – RCC 139 (1988,2) 401s (D. *Marafioti*); Gregorianum 69 (1988) 403s (*ipse*); RasT 29 (1988) 506s (anche D. *Marafioti*); StPatav 35 (1988) 735s (C. *Corsato*).

8568 *Filarska* B., ❷ Iconography of the Holy Spirit in ancient Christian art: → 73, ᶠKANIA W. = VoxPa 12s (1987s) 155-164; Eng. 164.

8569 *Fredricks* Gary, Rethinking the role of the Holy Spirit in the lives of Old Testament believers [... *Wood* L., The Holy Spirit in the OT 1976]: TrinJ 9,1 (1988) 81-104.

8570 **Gelpi** Donald L., [→ 8083*] God breathes; the Spirit in the world: Zacchaeus Studies. Wilmington 1988, Glazier. 127 p. $6 [TDig 35, 394].

8571 **Granado** Carmelo, El Espíritu Santo en la teología patrística: Ichthys 4, 1987 → 3,7112: ᴿGregorianum 69 (1988) 604 (L. *Ladaria*); ScripTPamp 20 (1988) 348s (L. F. *Mateo-Seco*).

8572 **Gresham** John L., Charles G. FINNEY's doctrine of the baptism of the Holy Spirit. Peabody MA 1987, Hendrickson. 106 p. [GraceTJ 9,306].

8573 *a*) *Hsieh* Teresa, ❷ The Holy Spirit in St. Paul and the Christian life; – *b*) *Pan* Philip, ❷ The Holy Spirit and the New Creation; – *c*) *Clary* Lily T., ❷ The Eucharist and the Holy Spirit: ColcFuJen 76 (1988) 161-4 / 165-174 / 175-181.

8574 **Lambiasi** Francesco, Lo Spirito Santo, mistero e presenza; per una sintesi di pneumatologia: TeolSist 2. Bo 1987, Dehoniane. 376 p. Lit. 25.000. 80-10-50305-8. – ᴿCC 139 (1988,4) 607s (R. *Latourelle*); EuntDoc 41 (1988) 172s (G. *Blandino*); Gregorianum 69 (1988) 606s (*ipse*); RasT 29 (1988) 595-9 (P. *Giustiniani*); RivB 36 (1988) 532s (R. *Penna*).

8575 *Lim* Agnes, ❷ Kairos and the Spirit in St. John and St. Luke: ColcFuJen 73 (1987) 385-8.

8575* *McDonnell* Kilian, Communion ecclesiology and baptism in the Spirit; TERTULLIAN and the early Church: TS 49 (1988) 671-694.

8576 **Mühlen** Heribert, Der Heilige Geist als Person. Münster 1988, Aschendorff [TGL 78,141].

8577 *Mühlen* Heribert, Das Herz Gottes; neue Aspekte der Trinitätslehre [i. Der Schmerz Gottes über die Zurückweisung seines Heiligen Geistes; ... (b) Der Heilige Geist als der Schmerz Gottes in Person; ii. Der Heilige Geist und die Inkarnation (Trinitarische Inversion)]: TGL 78 (1988) 141-159.

8578 *Noble* T. A., GREGORY Nazianzen's use of Scripture in defence of the deity of the Spirit [Tyndale Christian Doctrine Lecture 1987]: TyndaleB 39 (1988) 101-123.

8579 *Paprocki* Henryk, Les fondements bibliques de la pneumatologie: Istina 33 (1988) 7-21.

8580 *Penna* R., Spirito Santo: → 806, NDizTB (1988) 1498-1518.

8581 *Rebel* J.J., 'Inspreekpunt' en pneumatologie: TRef 31 (Woerden 1988) 370-394 [< ZIT 89,92].

8581* **Schweizer** Eduard, Spirito Santo [1978 → 58,8398], ᵀCorsani Ezio: Piccola Biblioteca Teologica 18. T 1988, Claudiana. 151 p. Lit. 15.000. 88-7016-063-7.

8582 **Siebel** Wigand, Der Heilige Geist als Relation; eine soziale Trinitätslehre 1986 → 3,7129; DM 28: ᴿTR 84 (1988) 394s (J. *Werbick*).

8583 *Stock* Konrad, Pneumatologie und ethische Theorie: NSys 30 (1988) 163-178; Eng. 178.

8584 **Taylor** John V., The Go-between God; the Holy Spirit and the Christian mission. L 1987, SCM. ix-246 p.; ill. £7.50. 0-334-00565-1.

8585 **Wells** David F., God the Evangelist; how the Holy Spirit works to bring men and women to faith. GR/Exeter 1987, Eerdmans/Paternoster. x-128 p. £5/$7 pa. – RRefTR 47 (1988) 60s (G. N. *Davies*).

H5.6 *Spiritus et Filius*; 'Spirit-Christology'.

8586 **Congar** Yves J.-M., The Word and the Spirit 1986 → 2,5726; 3,7138; T*Smith* D.; £10: RGregorianum 69 (1988) 152s (J. *Dupuis*); ScotJT 41 (1988) 411 (A. E. *Lewis*).

8587 **Dupuy** Michel, L'Esprit, souffle du Seigneur: JJC Résonances. P 1988, Desclée. 287 p. F 165. – REsprVie 98 (1988) 349 (E. *Vauthier*).

8588 *Kamp* G. C. van de, *a)* Sporen van pneuma-christologie in de vroege Syrische traditie: NedTTs 42 (1988) 208-219; Eng. 243. – *b)* Pneuma-christologie; een oud antwoord op een actuele vraag?... HARNACK, SEEBERG, LOOFS: diss. Amst 1983, D*Veenhof* J.

8589 **Newman** Paul W., A Spirit Christology; recovering the biblical paradigm of Christian faith 1987 → 3,7141: RSR 17 (1988) 374s (J. *Webster*).

8590 *Pikaza* Xabier, Hijo eterno y Espíritu de Dios; preexistencia de Jesús, concepción virginal, persona del Espíritu: EstTrin 20 (1986) 227-311.

8591 *Rhodes* J. Stephen, Christ and the Spirit; 'Filioque' reconsidered: BibTB 18 (1988) 91-95 ['Filioque' unduly subordinates the Spirit to Christ].

8592 **Riaud** A., L'Esprit du Père et du Fils 1984 → 65,6392; 2,5728: REstTrin 20 (1986) 191s (N. *Silanes*).

8594 **Talatinian** Basilio, Spirito di Dio Padre e Figlio. J 1986, Franciscan. 129 p. [CBQ 50,359]. – ROrChrPer 54 (1988) 232-4 (E. G. *Farrugia* comincia 'Nell'ecumenismo è diventato usuale distinguere tra il "dialogo della carità" e quello "della verità"', e finisce 'Nell'incontro a Roma tra il Papa e il Patriarca Demetrios il credo fu recitato senza il Filioque').

8595 *Thornhill* John, Christ's prophetic anointing by the Spirit: Pacifica 1,1 (Melbourne 1988) 68-84 [< NTAbs 32,338].

8596 *Watson* Gordon, The Filioque — opportunity for debate?: ScotJT (1988) 313-330.

H5.7 *Ssma Trinitas* – The Holy Trinity.

8597 *a) Aranda* Antonio, Revelación trinitaria y misión de la Iglesia; – *b) Aranda Pérez* Gonzalo, Utilización del patrimonio bíblico en la trilogía trinitaria: ScripTPamp 20,2s ('Las Encíclicas trinitarias de JUAN PABLO II' 1988) 439-456 / 457-489 [-821, *al.*].

8598 *Bartel* Timothy W., The plight of the relative Trinitarian: RelSt 24 (C 1988) 129-155.

8598* **Bobrinskoy** Boris, Le mystère de la Trinité; cours de théologie orthodoxe 1986 → 3,7150: REvT 48 (1988) 370-4 (A. *Schloz*); RTPhil 120 (1988) 110s (J. *Borel*).

8599 **Boff** Leonardo, La Trinidad, la sociedad y la liberación 1987 → 3,7151: RCarthaginensia 4 (1988) 187 (J. M. *Roncero Moreno*); TEspr 31 (1987) 281-3 (S. *Fuster*).

8600 *Bucci* Onorato, La formazione del concetto di persona nel cristianesimo delle origini; 'avventura semantica' e itinerario storico: Lateranum 54 (1988) 383-450.

8601 *Cattazzo* Sergio, Dalle triadi divine alla Trinità cristiana: Credere Oggi 6,34 (1986) 5-15 [> SelT 27 (1988) 224-8, ᵀᴱ*Cerda* Jaume].

8602 **Cipollone** P., Studio sulla spiritualità trinitaria nei capitoli I-VII della 'Lumen gentium'; present. card. P. *Palazzini*. R 1986, Pro Sanctitate. 866 p. Lit. 50.000. − ᴿAsprenas 35 (1988) 297s (A. *Terracciano*).

8603 *Cizewski* Wanda, A theological feast; the commentary by RUPERT of Deutz on Trinity Sunday: RTAM 55 (1988) 41-52.

8604 **Coda** Piero, Il negativo e la Trinità; ipotesi su HEGEL. R 1987, Città Nuova. 456 p. Lit. 18.000. − ᴿCC 139 (1988,1) 193s (P. *Vanzan*).

8605 **Courth** Franz, Trinität in der Schrift und Patristik: HbDG 2 [,1b in der Scholastik 1985 ➤ 1,7058... 3,7157], 1a. FrB 1988, Herder. 216 p. 3-451-00745-2.

8606 *Engelhardt* Paulus, Von der Spekulation zur Bibel: WortAnt 29,2 ('Zugänge zur Dreifaltigkeit' 1988) 56 [52-88].

8607 **Ferlay** Philippe, L'homme face à Dieu; Trinité divine et mystère de l'homme: Racines. P 1988, Nouvelle Cité. 165 p. F 79. − ᴿEsprVie 98 (1988) 676 (P. *Jay*).

8608 **Forte** B., Trinità come storia 1985 ➤ 1,7061... 3,7160: ᴿEstTrin 20 (1986) 192-6 (N. *Silanes*).

8609 **Forte** Bruno, Trinidad como historia; ensayo sobre el Dios cristiano, ᵀ*Ortiz García* Alfonso: Verdad e Imagen 101. Salamanca 1988, Sígueme. 220 p. 84-301-1044-5. − ᴿActuBbg 25 (1988) 244s (R. de *Sivatte*); Carthaginensia 4 (1988) 379 (P. *Ruiz Verdú*); LumenVr 37 (1988) 348s (F. *Ortiz de Urtaran*); TEsp 32 (1988) 354s (S. *Fuster*).

8610 *Fuchs* Eric, Pour une réinterprétation éthique du dogme trinitaire: ÉTRel 61 (1986) 533-540 [> SelT 27 (1988) 213-8, ᵀᴱ*Villanova* Gabriel].

8611 *Goffi* Tullo, La fondazione trinitaria della vita morale e spirituale: Credere Oggi 6,34 (1986) 82-93 [> SelT 27 (1988) 219-223, ᵀᴱ*Messa* José].

8612 **Gunton** Colin, Enlightenment and alienation... Trinitarian theology 1985 ➤ 1,7065... 3,7162: ᴿHeythJ 29 (1988) 485s (J. *O'Donnell*).

8613 *Haight* Roger, The point of trinitarian theology: TorJT 4 (1988) 191-204.

8614 **Heinz** Hanspeter, Trinitarische Begegnungen bei BONAVENTURA 1985 ➤ 2,5752; 3,7164: ᴿGregorianum 69 (1988) 155 (J. *O'Donnell*).

8615 **Hilberath** Bernd J., Der Personbegriff der Trinitätstheologie... RAHNER/TERTULLIAN [ᴰ1985] 1986 ➤ 2,5753; 3,7165: ᴿColcT 58,2 (1988) 187s (L. *Balter*); JTS 39 (1988) 645-7 (E. J. *Yarnold*); NRT 110 (1988) 748s (L. *Renwart*); TLZ 113 (1988) 222-5 (R. *Slenczka*); TPhil 63 (1988) 293-5 (J. *Splett*); TS 49 (1988) 172-4 (R. *Kress*); ZkT 110 (1988) 313-8 + 321s (K. H. *Neufeld*); 318-320, Hilberaths Antwort.

8616 *Hilberath* Bernd J., Das ATHANASIANISCHE Glaubensbekenntnis in der Auslegung HILDEGARDS von Bingen; Bemerkungen zur Trinitätslehre: TPhil 63 (1988) 321-341.

8617 **Hill** Edmund, The mystery of the Trinity 1985 ➤ 2,5754: ᴿNBlackfr 68 (1987) 156s (J. P. *Mackey*).

8618 **Labbé** Y., Essai sur le monothéisme trinitaire: CogF 145. P 1987, Cerf. 210 p. F 125. 2-204-02751-0. − ᴿArTGran 51 (1988) 330 (R. *Franco*).

8619 *LaCugna* C. M., *McDonnell* K., Returning from 'the far country'; theses for a contemporary Trinitarian theology: ScotJT 41 (1988) 191-215.

8620 ᴱ**Ladaria** Luis, San HILARIO de Poitiers, La Trinidad: BAC 481, 1986 ➤ 2,5759; 3,7171: ᴿActuBbg 25 (1988) 123 (J. *Vives*).

8621 *McDade* John, The Trinity and the paschal mystery: HeythJ 29 (1988) 175-191.

8622 **MacKenzie** Charles S., The Trinity and culture: AmerUnivStud 7/34. NY 1987, P. Lang. ix-150 p. $26 [TDig 36,69].

8623 **Milano** Andrea, Persona in teologia 1984 → 1,1079 ... 3,7173: RBTAM 14 (1988) 412s (G. *Mathon*); Latomus 47 (1988) 235 (M. *Simon* †).

8624 **Milano** Andrea, La Trinità dei teologi e dei filosofi; l'intelligenza della Persona in Dio. N 1987, Dehoniane. xv-323 p. – RArTGran 51 (1988) 333s (A. *Segovia*).

8624* **Moltmann** J., Trinité et royaume de Dieu...: CogF 123, 1984 → 65,6426 ... 2,5767: RÉglT 18 (1987) 376-9 (J. R. *Pambrun*).

8625 *Nyamiti* C., The naming ceremony in the Trinity; an African onomastic approach: Chiea AfChrSt 4,1 (1988) 41-73 [< TKontext 10/1,19].

8626 **O'Donnell** John J., The mystery of the triune God: Heythrop Mg. L 1988, Sheed & W. viii-184 p. £8.50. 0-7220-5760-1. – RGregorianum 69 · (1988) 815s (*ipse*).

8627 *O'Donnell* John, The Trinity as divine community; a critical reflection upon recent theological developments: Gregorianum 69 (1988) 5-34; franç. 34.

8628 *Pardyová* Marie, À propos de la Trinité dans l'art chrétien: Eirene 25 (Praha 1988) 25-44; VIII pl.

8629 *Plantinga* Cornelius J, The threeness/oneness problem of the Trinity: CalvinT 23 (1988) 37-53.

8630 **Radlbeck** Regina, Der Personbegriff in der Trinitätstheologie der Gegenwart; eine Untersuchung der Entwürfe Jürgen MOLTMANNs und Walter KASPERS: Diss. DBeinert. Rg 1987s. – TR 84 (1988) 513.

8631 *Rohls* Jan, Subjekt, Trinität und Persönlichkeit Gottes; von der Reformation zur Weimarer Klassik: NSys 30 (1988) 40-71; Eng. 71.

8632 **Rusch** William G., The Trinitarian controversy [selections T]: Sources of Early Christian Thought. Ph 1987, Fortress. viii-182 p. 0-8006-1410-0.

8633 *Salmann* Elmar, Neuzeit und Offenbarung; Studien zur trinitarischen Analogik des Christentums: StAnselm 94. R 1986, Pont. Ateneo S. Anselmo. 392 p. – RTPhil 63 (1988) 289-293 (J. *Splett*).

8634 *a) Sartori* Luigi, Trinità e coscienza storica; un itinerario di pensiero; – *b) Bof* Giampiero, Trinità e storia in HEGEL; – *c) Ruggieri* Giuseppe, Lo spazio politico del Dio trinitario: Asprenas 35,4 (1988; Atti inediti del congresso ATI, S. Giovanni in Fiore 1983) 435-457 / 458-476 / 477-484.

8635 ESchadel Erwin, al., Bibliotheca trinitariorum I, 1984 → 65,929 ... 3,7184 [II → 979 supra]: RCCurr 23 (1988s) 119s (R. *Panikkar*); Gnomon 60 (1988) 159-161 (H. *Kraft*).

8636 *Schwarz* Hans, Die Aktualität des Trinitarischen im christlichen Gottesglauben: TZBas 44 (1988) 211-221.

8637 **Silberer** Michael, Die Trinitätsidee im Werk von Pavel A. FLORENSKIJ; Versuch einer systematischen Darstellung in Begegnung mit Thomas von AQUIN; Das östliche Christentum NF 36. Wü 1984, Augustinus. xliii-303 p. – RSVlad 31 (1987) 388-391 (J. van *Rossum*).

8638 *Slusser* Michael, The exegetical roots of trinitarian theology: TS 49 (1988) 461-476.

8639 **Smalbrugge** M. A., La nature trinitaire de l'intelligence augustinienne de la foi [... belief in the Trinity], Diss. DBeker E. Amst 1988. 211 p. – TsTNijm 28,395.

8640 **Torrance** T. F., The trinitarian faith; the evangelical theology of the ancient Catholic Church. E 1988, Clark. 345 p.; 2 color. front. 0-567-09483-9. – RRHPR 68 (1988) 489s (G. *Siegwalt*).

8641 a) *Torrance* Thomas F., Ⓜ The trinity of God; – b) *Sztojkov* Vaszilij bp.,
The Holy Trinity and creation; – c) *Oszipow* Alexij / *Willis* David,
Creation and human creativity: Theologiai Szemle 31 (1988) 14-25 /
26-30 / 37-41. 42-48 (all ᵀ*Kalos Foris* Éva).

8642 *Wehrli* E. S.,   Biblical dimensions of the Trinity: Prism 2.2 (1987) 4-15
[NTAbs 32,206].

8643 *Wendebourg* Dorothea,   Person und Hypostase; zur Trinitätslehre in der
neueren orthodoxen Theologie: ➤ 114, ᶠPANNENBERG W., Vernunft 1988,
502-524.

8644 *Wohlmuth* Josef,   Zum Verhältnis von ökonomischer und immanenter
Trinität — eine These [Antrittsvorlesung Bonn 1987]:   ZkT 110 (1988)
139-162.

H5.8   *Regnum messianicum, Filius hominis* – **Messianic kingdom, Son of Man.**

8645 *Agua Pérez* Agustín del,   El deras del 'reino de Dios' en la tradición
sinóptica; sugerencias tras la lectura de O. CAMPONOVO [Königtum 1984]:
EstBíb 46 (1988) 173-186; Eng. 173.

8645* *Aune* D. E.,   Son of man: ➤ 801, ISBEnc³ 4 (1988) 574-581 [571-4, Son
of God, *Anderson* R. S.].

8646 **Beasley-Murray** G. R.,   Jesus and the Kingdom of God 1986 ➤ 2,5782;
3,7194:   ᴿJBL 107 (1988) 320-2 (J. R. *Michaels*); JRel 68 (1988) 95s (N. T.
Wright); NedTTs 42 (1988) 258-260 (C. J. den *Heyer*); RefTR 46 (1987)
17s (D. *Peterson*); Themelios 14 (1988s) 69s (C. C. *Caragounis*).

8647 *Beasley-Murray* G. R.,   Jesus and the Kingdom of God: BapQ 32,3 (L
1987) 141-6 [NTAbs 32,151].

8648 **Buchanan** G. W.,   Jesus, the King and his kingdom 1984 ➤ 65,6440;
1,7096:   ᴿBR 4,2 (1988) 9 (J. D. M. *Derrett*).

8649 **Caragounis** Chrys C.,   The Son of Man; vision and interpretation:
WUNT 38, 1986 ➤ 2,5786; 3,7199:   ᴿCarthaginensia 4 (1988) 368 (R.
Sanz Valdivieso); JBL 107 (1988) 752-4 (Adela Y. *Collins*); Salesianum 50
(1988) 417s (R. *Vicent*); ScripTPamp 19 (1987) 984 (G. *Aranda*); TsTNijm
28 (1988) 84s (F. van *Helmond*); VT 38 (1988) 501 (J. *Day*: despite
weaknesses, convincingly shows Daniel-citation rather than pronoun).

8650 *dal Covolo* Enrico,   'Regno di Dio' nel dialogo di Giustino con Trifone
Giudeo: ➤ 570, AugR 28 (1988) 111-123.

8651 *De Martino* Umberto,   Nuovo nel Regno di Dio: StCattMi 32 (1988)
492-4.

8652 **Ehler** Bernhard,   Die Herrschaft des Gekreuzigten... KÄSEMANN:
BZNW 46,1986 ➤ 2,5790; 3,7205:   ᴿAntonianum 63 (1988) 182-4 (Z. I.
Herman).

8653 **Geist** Heinz,   Menschensohn und Gemeinde... [kath. Diss. Würzburg
1985, ᴰ*Schnackenburg* R.]: ForBi 57, 1986 ➤ 3,7209:   ᴿCBQ 50 (1988)
530s (R. D. *Witherup*); ColcT 58,4 (1988) 166s (R. *Bartnicki*); TsTNijm 28
(1988) 83 (P. J. *Farla*).

8654 **Gerleman** G.,   Der Menschensohn 1983 ➤ 64,6843... 3,7210:   ᴿSvEx 53
(1988) 119s (C. C. *Caragounis*).

8655 **Heyer** C. J. den,   De messiaanse weg 2. Jezus van Nazareth 1986
➤ 2,3137; 3,7215: ᴿBijdragen 49 (1988) 95s (W. *Weren*).

8656 **Kearns** Rollin,   Das Traditionsgefüge um den Menschensohn 1986
➤ 2,5796; 3,7218:   ᴿCBQ 50 (1988) 328-330 (M. E. *Boring*: quadriliteral
barnaš 'one who holds land as a vassal' applied to eschatologized

Haddad ...); Gregorianum 69 (1988) 142-4 (G. L. *Prato*); JBL 107 (1988) 536-8 (J. J. *Collins*: Hellenistic Egypt eschatology, dubiously relevant).

8657 **Kearns** Rollin, Die Entchristologisierung des Menschensohnes; die Übertragung des Traditionsgefüges um den Menschensohn auf Jesus. Tü 1988, Mohr. v-209 p. 3-16-145419-9.

8658 **Kellner** Wendelin, Der Traum vom Menschensohn 1985 ⇒ 1,7114; 3,7219: ᴿSNTU-A 13 (1988) 220 (A. *Fuchs*).

8659 **Lindars** Barnabas, Credi tu nel Figlio dell'uomo? I testi evangelici su Gesù Figlio dell'uomo alla luce delle ultime ricerche. Mi 1987, Paoline. 269 p. Lit. 16.000. – ᴿHumBr 43 (1988) 593s (G. *Segalla*: vivacità, humour).

8660 *Lohfink* Gerhard, Die Not der Exegese mit der Reich-Gottes-Ver-kündigung Jesu [Abschiedsvorlesung 1987; 'ich habe meine Professur in Tübingen aufgegeben, um ganz in der "integrierten Gemeinde" leben und arbeiten zu können']: TüTQ 168 (1988) 1-15 [> Eng. TDig 36, 103-111. ᵀᴱ*Asen* B.].

8661 *Marcus* Joel, Entering into the kingly power of God: JBL 107 (1988) 663-675.

8662 **Margerie** Bertrand de, Liberté religieuse et Règne du Christ [... con-tinuité de l'enseignement du Magistère dans le document du Concile, Dignitatis humanae 7.XII.1965]; préf. *Eyt* Pierre: Apologique. P 1988, Cerf. 134 p. – ᴿEsprVie 98 (1988) 346 (J. *Pintard*).

8663 *Moltmann* Jürgen, El cristiano, el hombre y el reino de Dios [< StiZt 203 (1985) 619-631], ᵀᴱ*Puig Massana* Ramón: SelT 26 (1987) 176-182.

8664 *Perkins* Pheme, The rejected Jesus and the Kingdom sayings: ⇒ 309, Semeia 44 (1988) 79-94.

8665 *Saucy* Robert L., The presence of the Kingdom and the life of the Church: Bibliotheca Sacra 145 (1988) 30-46.

8665* *a) Schlitt* Dale M., Hᴇɢᴇʟ on the Kingdom of God; – *b) McDermott* John M., Jesus and the Kingdom of God in the Synoptics, Paul, and John: ÉglT 19 (1988) 33-68 / 69-91.

8666 **Schwarz** Günther, Jesus 'der Menschensohn'; aramaistische Unter-suchungen zu den synoptischen Menschensohnworten Jesu: BWANT 119, 1986 ⇒ 2,3808; 3,7235: ᴿBiKi 42 (1987) 85s (P. *Baumann*); JBL 107 (1988) 535s (R. *Kearns*); TLZ 113 (1988) 26s (C. C. *Caragounis*).

9667 *Seckler* Max, Das Reich-Gottes-Motiv in den Anfängen der Katholischen Tübinger Schule (J. S. Dʀᴇʏ und J. B. Hɪʀsᴄʜᴇʀ); zugleich ein Beitrag zur Theorie des Christentums: TüTQ 168 (1988) 257-282.

8668 **Sheehan** Thomas, The first coming; how the Kingdom of God became Christianity 1986 ⇒ 2,3172; 3,7236: ᴿCBQ 50 (1988) 732s (C. *Kazmierski*); Gregorianum 69 (1988) 731-4 (J. *Dupuis*: his thoroughly dubious starting-point 'agreed by Protestant and Catholic theologians and exegetes ... Jesus did not think he was divine'); JRel 68 (1988) 127-9 (J. P. *Meier*); NRT 110 (1988) 587s (L. *Renwart*: triste); RTLv 19 (1988) 370s (C. *Focant*: guère compatible avec les Évangiles); Tablet 242 (1988) 753 (F. *Kerr*: the wrong key).

8669 **Sullivan** Clayton, Rethinking realized [Kingdom of God] eschatology. Macon GA 1988, Mercer. viii-152 p. $20. 0-86554-302-X [TDig 36,186].

8670 **Vanhoye** Albert, La Nuova Alleanza nel Nuovo Testamento. R 1988, Pont. Istituto Biblico. 183 p.

8671 **Viviano** Benedict T., The Kingdom of God in history: Good News Studies 27. Wilmington 1988, Glazier. 168 p. $9. 0-89453-600-1.

8671* **Wiebe** Ben,   Messianic ethics; Jesus' Kingdom-of-God proclamation and appropriate response: diss. McMaster. Hamilton 1988. – RelStR 15,193.

E**Willis** W.,   The Kingdom of God in 20th century interpretation 1987 → 331.

H6.1   *Creatio, sabbatum NT* [→ E3.5]; **The Creation** [→ E1.6; H2.8].

8672 *Ayán Calvo* J.J.,   La creación del cosmos en S. JUSTINO: Compostellanum 32 (1987) 25-64.

8673 **Bacchiocchi** S.,   Du sabbat au dimanche 1984 → 1,7135... 3,7240:   REst-Trin 20 (1986) 205-7 (J. *López Martín*).

8674 **Bayer** Oswald,   Schöpfung als Anrede 1986 → 2,5816: 3,7242:   RBTZ 5 (1988) 137-142 (C. *Gestrich*: 'Sinn und Geschmack fürs Endliche'); Gregorianum 69 (1988) 155s (L. F. *Ladaria*); LutherJb 55 (1988) 126s (H. *Junghans*); ScripTPamp 20 (1988) 956s (J. *Morales*).

8675 *a) Bellavista* Joan,   El domingo; valores e interrogantes: – *b) Maldonado* Luis,   El cristiano en busca de un significado para el sábado: Phase 28/164 (1988) 107-123 / 125-136.

8676 *Cesarini* D., *al.*,   Il giorno del Signore. Assisi 1988, Cittadella.   184 p.; p. 21-75, *Pennacchini* Bruno, VT; p. 76-88, *Calabrese* Vincenzo, NT; 5 *al.* – RHumBr 43 (1988) 897s (O. *Vezzoli*).

8677 *Cole* Graham,   Discovering God's will; [1743-1805 William] PALEY's problem with special reference to 'the Christian Sabbath'.   TyndaleB 39 (1988) 125-139.

8678 *Duquoc* Christian,   Procréation et dogme de la création ['Des déclarations récentes de personnalités ecclésiastiques tendent à remettre en honneur le soupçon contre la raison qui, aveuglée par la technique, serait devenue incapable de lire ce que Dieu a inscrit dans sa création']: LumièreV 37,187 ('Procréation et acte créateur' 1988) 51-65.

8679 **Engelbrecht** J., *Wyk* P. J. van,   On creation and re-creation. Pretoria 1987, van Schaik. 145 p. – ROTEssays 1,2 (1988) 79-82 [W. J. *Wessels*].

8680 **König** Adrio,   New and greater things; re-evaluating the biblical message on creation [Jn 1,1-18; 1 Cor 8,6; Col 1,15-20; Heb 1,1-14; Rev 3,14]: Studia Originalia 1. Pretoria 1988, Univ. 196 p. $23.40. 0-86981-483-4.

8681 *Laumann* Maryta,   ☉ Confucian spirituality from a creation perspective: ColcFuJen 76 (1988) 229-256.

Moltmann Jürgen,   God in creation 1985 → 8281s.

8681* *a) Moltmann* Jürgen,   Schöpfung, Bund und Herrlichkeit; zur Diskussion über Karl BARTHs Schöpfungslehre; – *b) Zimmermann* Gunter,   Geschöpflichkeit und Selbsterkenntnis nach Johannes CALVIN: EvT 48 (1988) 108-127 / 127-145.

8682 *a) Nadolski* Bogusław,   ℗ Dies dominica sacramentum Paschatis; – *b) Strycharz* Edward,   ℗ De theologicis et liturgicis aspectibus sabbati: Ru-Bi 41 (1988) 407-415 / 394-407 [415-426, *Rojewski* Andrzej].

8682* *Nethöfel* Wolfgang,   Creatio, creatura, creativitas: BTZ 5 (1988) 68-84.

8683 *Ramirez* A.,   Las posibilidades y los limites de la responsabilidad humana en la creación: Cuestiones Teológicas 14,2 (Medellín 1987) 41-60 [< RET 48,120].

8684 **Ratzinger** J.,   Creazione e peccato [omelie Münchener-Dom]. CinB 1986, Paoline.   59 p. Lit. 5000. – RAsprenas 35 (1988) 294s (P. *Pifano*).

8685 *Richard* Lucien, Toward a renewed theology of creation; implications for the question of human rights: ÉglT 17 (1986) 149-170.

8686 *Satelmajer* Nikolaus, Theophilus BRABOURNE and the Sabbath [1628 advocating Saturday observance]: AndrUnS 26 (1988) 43-56.

8687 *a) Schmid* Johannes, Creatio ex amore; zum dogmatischen Ort der Schöpfungslehre; – *b) Scheele* Paul-Werner, Geschöpflichkeit als radikales und totales Verdanktsein; Anmerkungen zu einer Grundkategorie der Agape-Theologie; – *c) Fraling* Bernhard, Schöpfungsgedanke und Grundlegung des Ethos; zum Gespräch zwischen Dogmatik und Ethik: ➤ 53, [F]GANOCZY A., Creatio 1988, 179-192 / 218-232.

8687* **Schuurman** Douglas J., Creation, eschaton, and ethics; the ethical significance of the creation-eschaton relation in the thought of Emil BRUNNER and Jürgen MOLTMANN: diss. Chicago 1988. – RelStR 15,192.

8688 **Sölle** D., Lieben und Arbeiten; eine Theologie der Schöpfung 1985 ➤ 2,5822; 3,7257: [R]Salmanticensis 35 (1988) 435s (J. L. *Ruiz de la Peña*).

8688* *Sullivan* John W., Matter for heaven; BLONDEL, Christ and creation ETL 64 (1988) 60-83.

8689 *Zimmermann* Gunter, Die Allmacht des Schöpfers: Zwingliana 17 (1988) 457-476.

H6.3 *Fides, veritas in NT* – **Faith and truth.**

8690 **Anderfuhren** J., À l'ombre du doute la foi; commentaire du Symbole des Apôtres. Genève 1984, Labor et Fides. 268 p. xv-25 p. – [R]Protestantesimo 43 (1988) 50s (Maria *Bonafede*).

8690* **Boice** James M., Foundations of the Christian faith [4 vols. 1978-81 ➤ 62,a452; now in one]. Leicester 1986, Inter-Varsity. 740 p. £17. – [R]EvQ 60 (1988) 190-2 (A. S. *Wood*).

8691 *Brandenburger* Egon, Pistis und Soteria; zum Verstehenshorizont von 'Glaube' im Urchristentum: ZTK 85 (1988) 165-198.

8692 **Bryan** D. B., From Bible to Creed; a new approach to the Sunday creed [backwards, from Church, Spirit ...]. Wilmington 1988, Glazier. 255 p. $9 pa. 0-89453-584-6 [NTAbs 32,381].

8693 **Certeau** Michel de (1925-1986), La faiblesse de croire, [E]*Giard* Luce: Esprit. P 1987, Seuil. xix-330 p. – [R]FoiTemps 18 (1988) 180-2 (P. *Hennequin*).

8694 **Congar** Yves, Im Geist und im Feuer; Glaubensperspektiven, [T]*Müller* Werner. FrB 1987, Herder. 160 p. – [R]ColcT 58,3 (1988) 187-9 (S. *Urbański*).

8694* **Cook** David, Thinking about faith; a beginner's guide. Leicester c. 1987, Inter-Varsity. 220 p. £5. – [R]EvQ 60 (1988) 344s (J. *Wood*).

8695 **Cunningham** Lawrence, Faith rediscovered; coming [back] home to Catholicism. Mahwah NJ 1987, Paulist. v-99 p. $4 pa. [TDig 36,55].

8696 *Fischer* Johannes, Über die Beziehung von Glaube und Mythos; Gedanken im Anschluss an Kurt HÜBNERs 'Die Wahrheit des Mythos' [1985 ➤ 1,a412]: ZTK 85 (1988) 303-328.

8697 *Freyburger* Gérard, Fides 1986 ➤ 3,7221: [R]Gnomon 60 (1988) 18-21 (J. *Ramminger*); RÉLat 65 (1987) 368-370 (J.-C. *Richard*).

8698 **Groos** Helmut, Christlicher Glaube und intellektuelles Gewissen, Christentumskritik am Ende des zweiten Jahrtausends. Tü 1987, Mohr. xvi-448 p. DM 78. 3-16-145245-3 [Bijdragen 49,474].

8699 **Kasper** Walter, Was alles Erkennen übersteigt; Besinnung auf den christlichen Glauben. FrB 1987, Herder. 112 p. – RColcT 58,4 (1988) 186s (S. *Moysa*, Ⓟ also on Kasper's Theologie und Kirche 1987); ScripTPamp 20 (1988) 866-871 (J. M. *Odero*).

8699* [*Kasper* W. *al.*, German bishops' conference], The Church's confession of faith, a Catholic catechism for adults, TWentworth Stephen, EJordan Mark. SF 1987, Ignatius. 378 p. $15. – RTS 49 (1988) 783s (R. W. *Chilson*).

8700 **Keil** Günther, Glaubenslehre; Grundzüge christlicher Dogmatik [reformatorisch; Rechtfertigung-Mitte]. Stu 1986, Kohlhammer. 212 p. DM 38. – RZkT 110 (1988) 229s (L. *Lies*).

ELink Hans-Georg, Apostolic faith today 1985 / Gemeinsam glauben und bekennen 1987 → 9086.

8701 **Lochman** J. M., The faith we confess [→ 2,5842!] 1984 → 1,7178; 3,7283: RJEcuSt 23 (1986) 609 (L. J. *Biallas*).

8702 **Lohff** Wenzel, Fundus des Glaubens; Zugänge zur Begründung elementaren Glaubenswissens 1986 → 2,186: RZkT 110 (1988) 232 (L. *Lies*).

8702* **McIntyre** John, Faith, theology and imagination. E 1987, Handsel. vii-176 p. £9.50 pa. – RTLond 91 (1988) 138-140 (B. L. *Horne*).

8703 **Marlé** René, Peut-on savoir ce qu'il faut croire? 1987 → 3,7286: RRICathP 26 (1988) 203; RTPhil 120 (1988) 489 (J.-D. *Kraege*); ScEspr 40 (1988) 388s (R. *Morency*: artîcles de revue revus).

8704 *Marlé* René, Religion et foi: → 791, DictSpir XIII, 86s (1987) 321-335.

8705 **Marthaler** Berard L., The creed. Mystic CT 1987, Twenty-Third. xviii-439 p. $8 pa. – RHorizons 15 (1988) 396-8 (W. P. *Roberts*, also on KEMMER A. 1986 → 3,7278).

8706 *a*) *Neuner* Peter, Der Glaube als subjektives Prinzip der theologischen Erkenntnis; – *b*) *Seckler* Max, Theologie als Glaubenswissenschaft: → 800, HbFT 4 (1988) 51-67 / 180-241 [→ 8179*d*].

8707 *Pannenberg* Wolfhart, *a*) Das Irreale des Glaubens; – *b*) Verdinglichung und Transfiguration: → 684, Fiktiv ...

8708 **Riess** Wolfgang, Glaube als Konsens; über die Pluralität im Glauben [Kath. Diss. Wien 1978]. Mü 1979, Kösel. 287 p. DM 38 pa. – RZkT 110 (1988) 117 (L. *Lies*).

8709 **Sabugal** Santos, Credo; la fe de la Iglesia 1986 → 2,5852: RBibFe 14 (1988) 152 (A. *Salas*); Carthaginensia 4 (1988) 374s (F. *Martínez Fresneda*).

8709* *a*) *Salas* Antonio, Fe 'versus' Religión, Nuevo Testamento; proyecto desde la praxis histórica de Jesús; – *b*) *Orcasitas* Miguel Ángel, Fe y religión en la Iglesia, ayer: BibFe 14 (1988) 51-79 / 80-99 [bibliog. 142-4].

8710 *Serra* A., La fede nel NT: Maria, p.91-103; Marco, *Maggioni* B., 104-117; Matteo, *Fusco* V., 118-142; Lc 7,36-50, *Laconi* M., 143-155; Giovanni, *La Potterie* I. de, 156-171; Gal 2,16, *De Lorenzi* L., 172-191; Paolo, *Pesce* M., 193-219; Ebrei, *Vanhoye* A., 220-240; nei Padri della Chiesa, *Panimolle* S. A., *al.*, 243-318: ParSpV 17 ('Credete al Vangelo' 1988).

8711 *Servais* Jacques, L'Atto di Fede del credente secondo J. H. NEWMAN: CC 139 (1988,1) 550-563.

8712 *Solignac* Aimé, Les excès de l''intellectus fidei' dans la doctrine d'AUGUSTIN sur la grâce: NRT 110 (1988) 825-849.

8713 *Steel* Carlos, The devils' faith; some considerations on the nature of faith in AUGUSTINE and AQUINAS: LvSt 13 (1988) 291-304.

8714 **Sutherland** Stewart R., God, Jesus and belief; the legacy of [untenable] theism 1984 ➤ 1,7194; 2,5855: ᴿHeythJ 29 (1988) 111s (R. G. *Swinburne*: a not-compelling revisionism).

H6.6 *Peccatum NT* – Sin, Evil [➤ E1.9].

8715 *Estrada* Juan A., Notas sobre una teología del pecado colectivo: Diakonia 11 (Managua 1987) 259-270.

8715* *Fuchs* Josef, Structuren der Sünde: StiZt 206 (1988) 613-622.

8716 **Kelly** Henry A., The devil at baptism 1985 ➤ 1,7208; 2,5870: ᴿOstkSt 37 (1988) 209 (B. *Plank*).

8717 *Marshall* I. Howard, The problem of apostasy in New Testament theology: PerspRelSt 14,4 (1987) 65-80 [< ZIT 88,447]; 15,1 (1988) 57-60, *Perkins* Robert L. ..., two notes.

8718 *Millás* José M., Pecado y existencia cristiana; la concepción del pecado en la teología de Rudolf BULTMANN: Gregorianum 69 (1988) 35-64; Eng. 64.

8718* **Munera Duque** Alberto, Pecado personal... original [ᴰ1973] 1983 ➤ 2,5873; 3,7327: ᴿÉglT 18 (1987) 380s (D. L. *Schlitt*).

8719 ᴱ**Parkin** David, The anthropology of evil [seminars and two 1983 symposia] 1985 ➤ 2,330: ᴿHeythJ 29 (1988) 501s (M. F. C. *Bourdillon*).

8719* *Scheffczyk* Leo, Colpa e riconciliazione nell'orizzonte umano e cristiano: RivScR 2 (R 1988) 343-356.

8720 *Schepers* Gerhard, SHINRAN's view of the human predicament and the Christian concept of sin: Japanese Religions 13,2 (Kyoto 1988) 1-17 [< TKontext 10/1,62].

8721 *Schoonenberg* Piet, Auf Gott hin denken; deutschsprachige Schriften zur Theologie [Erbsünde als 'Sünde der Welt'; jede Sünde hinterlässt 'Erbsünde'] 1986 ➤ 2,218; 3,293: ᴿZkT 110 (1988) 112s (W. *Kern*).

8722 **Sievernich** Michael, Schuld und Sünde; theologisch-praktische Untersuchungen zur Hamartologie im theologischen Denken der Gegenwart und in neueren Glaubensbüchern: Hab.-Diss. Fra St. Georgen 1987, ᴰ*Bertsch*. – TR 84 (1988) 509 ['Harmatologie'].

8723 *Sobrino* Jon, Pecado personal, perdón y liberación: RLatAmT 5,13 (1988) 13-31.

8724 **Surin** Kenneth, Theology and the problem of evil 1986 ➤ 3,7336: ᴿTLZ 113 (1988) 374s (M. J. *Suda*).

8725 *Tábet* Miguel Angel, La distinzione dei peccati secondo la loro gravità nell'insegnamento di Gesù: AnnTh 2 (R 1988) 3-34 [35-52, *Schumacher* J.; 53-82, *Tettamanzi* D.].

8726 *Tabet* Miguel Ángel, La graduazione dei peccati nella dottrina di Gesù: ScuolC 22 (1988) 99-108.

8727 *a*) *Virgulin* S., Peccato; – *b*) *Bonora* A., Male, dolore: NDizTB (1988) 1122-1140 / 870-887.

H7 Soteriologia NT.

8728 *Allison* C. Fitzsimons, The pastoral and political implications of Trent on justification; a response to the ARCIC Agreed Statement, Salvation and the Church: StLuke 31 (1988) 204-222.

8729 *Astorga* Christina A., A critique of LUTHER's theology of justification based on Catholic teaching: Landas 1 (Manila 1987) 206-227 [< TKontext 10/1,72].

8730 *a) Beaucamp* E., Le salut selon la Bible dans l'AT: – *b) Delorme* J., La théologie du salut dans le NT; Evv Act; – *c) Carrez* M.,... Paul; – *d) Cothenet* E.,... Ép. catholiques; – *e) Morgen* M., Jean: ➤ 809, SDB 11,62 (1988) 516-553 / 584-689 / 689-713 / 713-720 / 720-740.

8731 **Bezançon** Jean-Noël, Dieu sauve: Croire aujourd'hui. P/Montréal 1985, Desclée-B/Bellarmin. 132 p. $12. – ᴱEglT 17 (1986) 242 (N. *Provencher*).

8732 *Bienentreu* Maria-Sybille, Heil und Kirche; zum neuesten Dokument des anglikanisch/römisch-katholischen Dialogs: Catholica 42 (1988) 76-82.

8733 ᴱ**Broer** Ingo, *Werbick* Jürgen, 'Auf Hoffnung hin sind wir erlöst' (Röm 8,24)... Erlösungsverständnis heute: SBS 128, 1987 ➤ 3,7344: ᴿTGL 78 (1988) 102s (W. *Beinert*).

8734 *Carlos Otto* Federico de, La salvación en la predicación de P. TILLICH: RET 48 (1988) 53-100.

8735 *Cattazzo* Sergio, Il mondo tra creazione e salvezza (una rassegna dalla storia delle religioni): Credere Oggi 6,33 (1986) 18-28 [> SelT 27 (1988) 158-160, ᵀᴱ*Melloni* J.].

8736 *Daurio* Janice, Toward a theology of desire; the existential hermeneutic in the soteriology of Sebastian MOORE: DowR 106 (1988) 195... [< ZIT 88,660].

8737 *Dola* Tadeusz, ❷ Christologischer Ansatz der Heilsvermittlung: ColcT 58,1 (1988) 25-39: deutsch 40.

8738 **Driver** John, Understanding the Atonement for the mission of the Church 1986 ➤ 3,7347: ᴿBS 145 (1988) 196s (R. P. *Lightner*); CurrTM 15 (1988) 371 (J. C. *Rochelle*).

8739 *Drysdale* Derek, Justification by grace through faith: IrBSt 10 (Belfast 1988) 114-122 [< ZIT 88,538].

8740 *Ellacuria* Ignacio †, La historicidad de la salvación cristiana: RLAmT 1 (1984) 5-45 [> SelT 26 (1987) 59-80, ᴱ*Miralles* Josep].

8741 **Fitzgerald** Allan, Conversion through penance in the Italian church of the fourth and fifth centuries; new approaches to the experience of conversion from sin: Studies in the Bible and Early Christianity 15. Lewiston NY 1988, Mellen. xi-565 p. 0-88946-615-7.

8742 *Franke* Thomas, Salus ex amore; Erwägungen zu einer trinitarischen Soteriologie: ➤ 53, ꜰGANOCZY A., Creatio 1988, 48-59.

8743 **Gäde** Gerhard, 'Eine andere Barmherzigkeit'; zum Verständnis der Erlösungslehre ANSELMs von Canterbury: Diss. ᴰ*Knauer*. Fra 1987s. – TR 84 (1988) 511.

8744 *González de Cardedal* Olegario, Jesucristo redentor del hombre; esbozo de una soteriología crítica: EstTrin 20 (1986) 313-396.

8745 **Hallonsten** Gösta, Meritum bei TERTULLIAN 1985 ➤ 3,7357: ᴿChH 56 (1987) 103 (R. B. *Eno*); Gnomon 60 (1988) 258s (J.-C. *Fredouille*); RHE 82 (1988) 482 (A. de *Halleux*); ScripTPamp 19 (1987) 988 (A. *Viciano*).

8746 **Hallonsten** Gösta, Satisfactio bei TERTULLIAN 1984 ➤ 65,6546... 3,7356: ᴿSecC 6,1 (1987s) 49-52 (C. *Cox*).

8746* *Harding* Leander J., A unique and final work; the atonement as a saving act of transformative obedience: JEcuSt 24 (1987) 80-92,

8747 **Helm** Paul, The beginnings; Word and Spirit in conversion 1986 ➤ 3,7360; 0-85151-470-7: ᴿScotBEv 6 (1988) 47s (A. J. *Macleod*).

8748 **Hultgren** Arland J., Christ and his benefits; Christology and Redemption in the NT 1987 ➤ 3,7364: ᴿCBQ 50 (1988) 718-720 (B. F. *Meyer*); Interpretation 42 (1988) 430.432 (V. *Howard*); TS 49 (1988) 531s (S. B. *Marrow*); TTod 45 (1988s) 259-261 (G. S. *Sloyan*).

8748* **Jensen** Paul T., CALVIN and TURRETIN; a comparison of their soteriologies: diss. Virginia. 1988. – RelStR 15,193.

8749 **Johnson** Bo, Rättfärdigheten i Bibeln 1985 ➤ 1,7257; 3,7366: ᴿSvEx 53 (1988) 111 (H. *Ringgren*).

8750 *Langkammer* Hugolinus, Sein in Christus als soteriologisches Endstadium paulinischer Präpositionssprache: ➤ 430, In Christus 1987, 15-26.

8751 *McCullagh* C. Behan, Theology of atonement: TLond 91 (1988) 392-9 [... CALVIN's inconsistencies].

8752 **McDonald** H. D., The atonement of the death of Christ 1985 ➤ 1,7263; 3,7372: ᴿScotJT 41 (1988) 535s (D. *Macleod*).

8753 **McGrath** Alister E., Iustitia Dei; a history of the Christian doctrine of justification I.-II. 1986 ➤ 3,7373: ᴿHorizons 15 (1988) 387s (Ellen M. *Ross*); JTS 39 (1988) 295-7 (G. *Newlands*); NRT 110 (1988) 430 (B. *Pottier* cites II,97, 'the Catholic Church stopped talking about it in 1713'); RelStR 14 (1988) 254 (Mary P. *Engel*); RHE 83 (1988) 407s (F. *Hockey* †); ScotJT 41 (1988) 429-431 (J. *Atkinson*); TS 49 (1988) 160s (G. *Mansini*); ZKG 99 (1988) 402-4 (F. *Mildenberger*).

8754 **McGrath** A., Justification by faith; what it means for us today. GR 1987, Zondervan [= ➤ 8753]. $12. 0-310-21140-9 [TDig 36,173].

8755 *Montefiore* Hugh, Salvation and the Church [ARCIC misses the force of *dikaioûn/iustificare* as rendering the Hebrew for 'put in the right']: TLond 91 (1988) 43-46.

8756 **Muller** Richard A., Christ and the decree. GR 1988 [= 1986 ➤ 3, 7378 + index & bibliog.], Baker. $13. – ᴿÉTRel 63 (1988) 137s (A. *Gounelle*); SixtC 19 (1988) 510 (W. S. *Reid*); TrinJ 8 (1987) 233-5 (M. I. *Klauber*).

8756* **Naduvilekut** James, Christus der Heilsweg... BALTHASAR, ᴰ1986 ➤ 2,5914; 3,7379; ᴿETL 64 (1988) 491s (E. *Brito*); TR 84 (1988) 140-2 (M. *Tiator*).

8757 *Navone* John, Salvation without God? Christ is the hero of the melodrama of salvation: HomP 89,1 (1988s) 64-68.

8758 *Nossol* Alfons, Ort der Familie im Mysterium Salutis: ColcT 58 sp. (1988) 5-19.

8759 *Oftstad* Bernt T., 'Det avgjørende frelsesvalg' [the decisive choice of salvation, till S. MOES diss. 1988]: NorTTs 89 (1988) 249-266.

8760 *Olivieri Pennesi* Alessandro, NEWMAN e la giustificazione: PalCl 66 (1987) 927-943.

8761 *Ormerod* Neil, The soteriology of Sebastian MOORE; ANSELM revisited: ➤ 554, Salvation 1986/8, 174-183.

8762 *a) O'Sullivan* Moira, Salvation is a chameleon; – *b) Nobbs* Alanna, The idea of salvation; the transition to Christianity as seen in some early papyri: ➤ 554, Salvation 1986/8, 43-58 / 59-63.

8762* *Redman* Robert R.ᴶ, H. R. MACKINTOSH's contribution to Christology and soteriology in the twentieth century: ScotJT 41 (1988) 517-534.

8763 ᴱ**Reumann** J., *Fitzmyer* J., *Quinn* J., Righteousness 1982 ➤ 63,559... 1,7280: ᴿRB 95 (1988) 631-3 (B. T. *Viviano*).

8763* *Sanders* John E., Is belief in Christ necessary for salvation?: EvQ 60 (1988) 241-259.

8764 **Schwager** Raymund, Der wunderbare Tausch... Erlösungslehre 1985 ➤ 2,219; 3,7390: ᴿTPQ 136 (1988) 293s (W. *Gruber*); ZkT 110 (1988) 66-68 (L. *Lies*).

8765 **Sesboüé** Bernard, Jésus-Christ, l'unique médiateur; essai sur la rédemption et le salut, I. Problématique et relecture doctrinale: JJC 33. P 1988, Desclée. 400 p. F 165. – ᴿAntonianum 63 (1988) 613-6 (V. *Bat-*

taglia); EsprVie 98 (1988) 671-3 (P. *Jay*); Études 369 (1988) 709 (J. *Thomas*).

8766* *Sesboüé* Bernard, Salut: ➤ 791, DictSpir XIV,91 (1988) 251-283.

8767 **Steindl** Helmut, Genugtuung, biblisches Versöhnungsdenken — eine Quelle für ANSELMs Satisfaktionstheorie?: Diss. ᴰ*Brantschen*. FrS 1988. TR 84 (1988) 514.

8768 **Studer** Basil, Gott und unsere Erlösung im Glauben der Alten Kirche 1985 ➤ 1,7290... 3,7397: ᴿChH 57 (1988) 356s (R. *Ferguson*: high praise); RTLv 19 (1988) 83-86 (A. de *Halleux*); ZkT 110 (1988) 77-79 (R. *Schwager*).

8769 **Studer** B., Dio Salvatore nei Padri della Chiesa; Trinità – cristologia – soteriologia [Gott und unsere Erlösung 1985], ᵀ: Cultura Cristiana Antica. R 1986, Borla. 374 p. Lit. 26.000. – ᴿStPatav 35 (1988) 201s (O. *Pasquato*).

8770 *Taliaferro* Charles, A Narnian theory of the atonement [C. S. LEWIS parable]: ScotJT 41 (1988) 75-92.

8771 **Tuttle** George M., So rich a soil; J. M. CAMPBELL [1800-1872] on Christian atonement... 1986 ➤ 2,5929; 3,7401: ᴿChH 57 (1988) 391s (J. C. *Goodloe*); EvQ 60 (1988) 95s (P. *Toon*: Campbell was condemned as heretical but now favoured in Church of Scotland).

8772 **Viciano** Alberto, Cristo salvador y liberador del hombre; estudio sobre la soteriología de TERTULIANO 1986 ➤ 3,7404: ᴿRÉLat 65 (1987) 391-4 (J. *Fontaine*); TGL 78 (1988) 93s (H. R. *Drobner*).

8773 *Volk* Ernst, Verlorenes Evangelium [justification by faith alone in 'complementarity' of Lehrverurteilungen – kirchentrennend? 1986]: Ker-Do 34 (1988) 122-165; Eng. 165.

8774 *Wainwright* Geoffrey, Perfect salvation in the teaching of WESLEY and CALVIN: RefW 40 (Geneva 1988) 898-909 [< ZIT 88,717].

8775 *Walker* Michael, The atonement and justice: TLond 91 (1988) 180-6.

8776 *Wells* David F., Aftermath and hindsight of the [19th-century USA] atonement debate [➤ 3,2410]: Bibliotheca Sacra 145 (1988) 3-14.

8777 **Yule** George, LUTHER's understanding of justification by grace alone in terms of Catholic Christology: ➤ 1,413, Luther, theologian for Catholics and Protestants (E. Clark; xi-217 p.) 1985, 87-112 [< LuJb 54,167].

H7.2 *Crux, sacrificium* – **The Cross.**

8778 **Balmary** Marie, Le sacrifice interdit; FREUD et la Bible 1987 ➤ 3,7413: ᴿCahÉv 61 (1987) 74 (G. *Joly*).

8779 *Baudler* Georg, Jesus ist kein Opferlamm; zur 'nicht-sakrifiziellen' Evangelieninterpretation René GIRARDs: ZPraxRU 18,1 (Stu 1988) 28-30 [< ZIT].

8780 *Bourassa* F., Le sacrifice: ➤ 379, Vatican II Bilan 2 (1988) 121-192; Eng. ➤ 380, Assessment 2 (1988) 121-159.

8781 **Deneken** M., Le salut par la croix dans la théologie catholique contemporaine (1930-1985): Thèses. P 1988, Cerf. 419 p. F 158. – ᴿNRT 110 (1988) 584s (L. *Renwart*).

8782 **Girard** René, Das Heilige und das Gewalt [La violence et le sacré 1972; Eng. 1977 ➤ 58,7916], ᵀ*Maiberger-Ruh* Elisabeth. Z 1987, Benziger. 494 p. – ᴿErbAuf 64 (1988) 237 (E. *Tschacher*); LíngBib 61 (1988) 130s (W. *Magass*).

8783 *Grégoire* Réginald, Sang: ➤ 791, DictSpir XIV,91 (1988) 319-333.

8784 ᴱHamerton-Kelly R.G., Violent origins 1987 ➤ 3,639: ᴿJAAR 56 (1988) 788-790 (E. V. *Gallagher*).

8785 *Hanaway* W.L., Blood and wine; sacrifice and celebration in Manūchihrī's wine poetry: Iran 26 (1988) 69-80.

8785* **Hengel** Martin, Crocifissione ed espiazione [1980], ᵀ*Zani* Antonio: BiblCuRel 52. Brescia 1988, Paideia. 238 p. 88-394-0407-4.

8786 **Heusch** Luc de, Sacrifice in Africa; a structuralist approach; Themes in Social Anthropology 1 ➤ 2,5945 [franç. 1986 ➤ 3,7427]; Manchester/ Bloomington 1985, Univ./IndianaUniv. 320 p. £25. 0-7190-1715-5. – ᴿJRelAf 17 (1987) 172-6 (R. P. *Werbner*).

8786* *Jobling* W.J., Salvation and sacrifice in the Shara' mountains of southern Jordan [Gn 22; 2 Sam 15,32; and inscriptions]: ➤ 554, Salvation 1986/8, 1-12.

8787 *Jiménez-S.* J.D., Salvados en la vida crucificada de Dios (sentido soteriológico de la cruz y actualidad de la estaurología: Religión y cultura 34,1 (M 1988) 39-60 [< NTAbs 32,337].

8788 *Kente* Maria G., Sacrifice is the highest form of worship: Pastoral Orientation Service (Tabora, Tanzania 1987/3) 15-25 [< TKontext 10/1,20].

8789 *Lacourse* J., Réciprocité positive et réciprocité négative; de Marcel MAUSS à René GIRARD [*Clastres* P....]: Cahiers Internationaux de Sociologie 83 (1987) 291-305 [< RSPT 72,342].

8790 *Lamarche* Paul, Sacrifice: ➤ 791, DictSpir XIV,91 (1988) 51-56.

8791 **Lascaris** A., Advocaat van de zondebok... GIRARD en evangelie 1987 ➤ 3,7430*: ᴿTsTNijm 28 (1988) 414 (F. de *Lange*).

8792 *Lascaris* A.F., De verzoeningsleer en het offerchristendom; ANSELMUS, CALVIJN en GIRARD [eredoctoraat Amst VU 1985]: NedTTs 42 (1988) 220-242; Eng. 243: Anselm and Calvin do indeed presuppose that salvation is not possible without violence; Calvin moreover identifies 'satisfaction' with 'punishment'.

8793 *Lascaris* Andrew, GIRARD against fragmentation: NBlackf 69 (1988) 156-163 [continuing 66 (1985) 517-524; 68 (1987) 115-124].

8794 **McGrath** Alister E., LUTHER's theology of the Cross 1985 ➤ 1,7323; 2,5947: ᴿCurrTM 15 (1988) 293 (G.C. *Carter*).

8795 **McGrath** Alister E., The mystery of the Cross: Academie. GR 1988, Zondervan [= The enigma of... 1987 ➤ 3,7431].

8796 **Modalsli** Ole, Korsets gåte [the riddle of the Cross]; om Jesu døds betydning. Oslo 1987, Verbum. 237 p. Nk 225. – ᴿNorTTs 89 (1988) 205s (K. *Nordstokke*).

8797 **Morris** Leon, The Cross of Jesus [1988 Louisville So. Bapt. Gheens lectures]. GR/Exeter 1988, Eerdmans/Paternoster. x-118 p. $8. 0-8028-0344-X / 0-85364-434-9 [NTAbs 32,385].

8798 *Reynolds* Roger E., Stations of the Cross: ➤ 792, DMA 11 (1988) 467s.

8799 **Schwager** Raymund, Must there be scapegoats? 1987 ➤ 3,7442: ᴿTTod 45 (1988s) 351.354 (B. *Ollenburger*).

8800 **Stott** John R.W., The Cross of Christ 1986 ➤ 2,5957: ᴿBS 145 (1988) 220s (R.P. *Lightner*); EvQ 60 (1988) 277s (A.S. *Wood*); IrBSt 9 (1987) 86 (I. *Hull*).

8801 *Sundermeier* Theo, The cross in African interpretation: AfTJ 16 (1987) 136-144 [< TKontext 10/1,17].

8802 **Thaidigsmann** Edgar, Identitätsverlangen und Widerspruch; Kreuzes-theologie bei LUTHER, HEGEL und BARTH: FundTSt 8, 1983 ➤ 1,7334: ᴿTLZ 113 (1988) 136-141 (O. *Bayer*).

8803 *Tremblay* R., La mort du Christ, une naissance filiale; exposé et évaluation de la pensée de F.-X. DURRWELL: Studia Moralia 26 (R 1988) 231-242.

8804 **Valeri** Valerio, Kingship and sacrifice; ritual and society in ancient Hawaii [1969-81], ᵀ*Wissing* Paula. Ch 1985, Univ. xxiii-446 p. $22.50. – ᴿAnthropos 83 (1988) 650-2 (M. *Mersch*).

8805 *Williams* James G., The innocent victim; René GIRARD on violence, sacrifice, and the sacred: RelStR 14 (1988) 320-6.

H7.4 **Sacramenta,** *Gratia.*

8806 *Armellada* Bernardino de, La gracia, misterio de libertad; el sobrenatural en los primeros teólogos capuchinos: ColcFr 58 (1988) 277-304; Eng. 304.

8807 **Barrett** C. K., Church, ministry, and sacraments in the New Testament 1985 ➤ 1,7343; 3,7447: ᴿGraceTJ 9 (1988) 158s (D. L. *Turner*); TLZ 113 (1988) 823-5 (J. *Roloff*).

8808 **Barth** Gerhard, *a)* Il battesimo in epoca protocristiana [1981], ᵀ*Panini* Marisa A.: StBPaid 79. Brescia 1987, Paideia. 194 p. 88-394-0398-1; – *b)* El Bautismo... primitivo 1986 ➤ 2,5967; 3,7448; 84-301-1008-9: ᴿActuBbg 25 (1988) 58 (X. *Alegre* S.).

8809 *a) Barth* Gerhard, Taufe auf dem Namen Jesu; Kurzbericht über den Stand neutestamentlicher Arbeiten zum Verständnis der Taufe im Urchristentum; – *b) Track* Joachim, Kinder- oder Erwachsenentaufe? Zur Auseinandersetzung mit Karl BARTHs Taufverständnis: EvErz 40 (1988) 124-135 / 136-154 [< ZIT].

8810 *Baudry* Gérard-Henry, La réforme de la confirmation, de Vatican II à PAUL VI: MélSR 45 (1988) 83-101; Eng. 101.

8810* **Baumann** Urs, Ehe — ein Sakrament?: Hab.-Diss. Tübingen 1987, ᴰ*Kasper* W. – TR 84 (1988) 510.

8811 **Borobio** Dionisio, Reconciliación penitencial; tratado actual sobre el Sacramento de la Penitencia. Bilbao 1988, Desclée-B. 226 p. – ᴿLumenVr 37 (1988) 531 (F. *Ortiz de Urtaran*).

8812 *Bruns* B., Das Ehe-*sacramentum* bei AUGUSTINUS: AugLv 38 (1988) 205-226.

8813 **Chauvet** Louis-Marie, Symbole et sacrement; une relecture sacramentelle de l'existence chrétienne: CogF 144. P 1987, Cerf. 582 p. F 175. – ᴿETL 64 (1988) 213-5 (A. de *Halleux*); EcOrans 3 (1988) 231-5 (G. *Lafont*); RHPR 68 (1988) 500-2 (G. *Siegwalt*).

8814 *Chethimattam* John B., Grace in Christian religious tradition: JDharma 12 (1987) 330-353 [-431 *al.*, Hinduism].

8815 *Dalmais* Irénée-H., Sacrements: ➤ 791, DictSpir XIV,91 (1988) 45-51.

8815* **Ferraro** Giuseppe, I sacramenti e l'identità cristiana 1986 ➤ 3,7468: ᴿScEspr 40 (1988) 130s (L. *Sabourin*).

8816 *Franco* Ricardo, La penitencia actual y los 'modelos' de penitencia [... Mt; otros NT]: EstE 63 (1988) 189-204.

8816* **Gaboriau** Florent, Chrétiens 'confirmés'; le sacrement de la croissance: TNouv 8. P 1987, FAC. 253 p. F 100. – ᴿETL 64 (1988) 497s (A. de *Halleux*).

8817 **Ganoczy** Alexandre, La doctrine catholique des sacrements [1979], ᵀ*Burckel* J.: Relais-Études 4. P 1988, Desclée. 184 p. F 145. – ᴿEsprVie 98 (1988) 489s (P. *Rouillard*); Études 369 (1988) 280 (R. *Marlé*).

8818 **Ganoczy** A., An introduction to Catholic sacramental theology 1984 ➤ 1,7362: HeythJ 29 (1988) 251s (Mary C. *Grey*).

8819 **Green** Michael, Baptism; its purpose, practice and power. DG 1987, Inter-Varsity. 141 p. $7 pa. [GraceTJ 9,306]. – RCalvinT 23 (1988) 265-7 (W. M. *VanDyk*).

8820 *Greiner* Albert, Baptêmes d'enfants — baptêmes d'adultes: PosLuth 36 (1988) 81-90 [< ZIT 88,524].

8820* **Guillet** Jacques, De Jesús a los sacramentos: CuadBib 57, 1987 ➤ 3,7474: RBibFe 14 (1988) 148 (M. *Sáenz de Santamaría*).

8821 *Guy* J. *al.*, Pratiques de la confession 1983 ➤ 2,440: RCathHR 73 (1987) 93-95 (T. *Tentler*).

8822 **Hotz** R., Los sacramentos en nuevas perspectivas; la riqueza sacramental de Oriente y Occidente [1979 ➤ 61,8624], TGirbau B.: Lux Mundi 56. Salamanca 1986, Sígueme. 408 p. – RCiTom 114 (1987) 188 (D. S.); Salmanticensis 35 (1988) 426-9 (D. *Borobio*).

8823 **Jungkuntz** Richard, The gospel of baptism. 1968 reprinted, Pacific Lutheran Univ. $5. – RCurrTM 15 (1988) 221 (R. W. *Klein*).

8824 *Kasper* Walter, Il ruolo soteriologico della Chiesa e i sacramenti della salvezza: EuntDoc 41 (1988) 397-420.

8825 **Kavanagh** Aidan, Confirmation; origins and reform. NY 1988, Pueblo. xiii-173 p. $13 pa. [TDig 36,66: promoting G. AUSTIN, Anointing with the Spirit; the rise of Confirmation, the use of oil and chrism 1985]. – RETL 64 (1988) 495-7 (A. de *Halleux*).

8826 *Larrabe* José Luis, *a*) Panorama actual del bautismo: Studium 28 (M 1988) 107-133; – *b*) Sacramentalidad y espiritualidad del matrimonio (según el Concilio de Trento): NatGrac 35 (1988) 423-433.

8827 *Law* David, KIERKEGAARD on [infant] baptism: TLond 91 (1988) 114-122.

8827* **Lawler** Michael G., Symbol and sacrament; a contemporary sacramental theology. NY 1987, Paulist. VI-290 p. $12. – RETL 64 (1988) 492-5 (A. de *Halleux*).

8828 **Lorenzato** Bertrand, *Pety* Olivier, Sacrements du chrétien. P 1987, Desclée. 120 p. – REsprVie 98 (1988) 192 (P. *Rouillard*).

8829 *Lupi* Joseph, The development of the rite of baptism: MeliT 39,1 (1988) 1-31.

8830 **Maldonado** Luis, Sacramentalidad evangélica; signos de la Presencia para el camino: Presencia Teológica 41. Santander 1987, Sal Terrae. 238 p. 84-293-0789-3. – RActuBbg 25 (1988) 247s (I. *Riudor*).

8831 *Maldonado Arenas* Luis, Hacia la superación de una noción solamente 'regional' [sc. vitae, non geographiae] de la sacramentalidad: RET 48 (1988) 5-13.

8832 **Naglee** David I., From font to faith; John WESLEY on infant baptism and the nurture of children: AmerUnivStud 7/24. NY 1987, P. Lang. x-262 p. $34.50 [TDig 36,71].

8833 **Nettles** Thomas J., By his grace ... 1986 ➤ 3,7493: RBS 145 (1988) 219s (R. P. *Lightner*: south-oriented).

8834 **Neunheuser** Burkhard, Taufe und Firmung² [¹1956]: HbDG 4,2, 1983 ➤ 64,7032: RTLZ 113 (1988) 452-5 (K.-H. *Kandler*).

8835 *O'Donnell* John J., H. U. von BALTHASAR sulla teologia del matrimonio: CC 139 (1988,3) 483-8.

8836 **Osborne** Kenan B., The Christian sacraments of initiation; baptism, confirmation, Eucharist 1987 ➤ 3,7496: RAntonianum 63 (1988) 428 (*ipse*); CalvinT 23 (1988) 279-283 (P. G. *Schrotenboer*: not all Catholics are ready to accept his position).

8837 **Osborne** Kenan B., Sacramental theology; a general introduction. NY 1988, Paulist. 114 p. $8. – RAntonianum 63 (1988) 428 (*ipse*).

8838 **Perrin** Joseph-Marie, Le laïc, un baptisé [plutôt méditation et évolution des figures illustres comme Simone *Weil* que ce dominicain a connues]. P 1987, Nouvelle Cité. 157 p. – REsprVie 98 (1988) 63s (P. *Barbarin*).

8838* **Phan** Peter C., Grace and the human condition: Message of the Fathers 15. Wilmington 1988, Glazier. 317 p.

8839 **Quesnel** Michel, Petite bible du Baptême. P 1987, Nouvelle Cité. 139 p. F 60 [CBQ 50,358]. – RRICathP 28 (1988) 149-151 (J. *Doré*).

8840 *Quinn* Frank C., Confirmation, does it make sense?; EcOrans 3 (1988) 321-340.

8841 **Rahner** Karl, Les sacrements de l'Église [7 homélies publiées 1985], TDegacker Marc. P 1987, Nouvelle Cité. 136 p. F 80. – REsprVie 98 (1988) 191s (P. *Rouillard*: ne pas confondre avec l'important Église et sacrements 1960 T1970).

8842 **Ruster** Thomas, Sakramentales Verstehen... E. *Biser*, E. *Fuchs*: DispT 14, 1983 → 1,7386: RZkT 110 (1988) 230s (L. *Lies*).

8843 *a) Sadek* A. I., Les rites baptismaux dans l'Égypte ancienne; préfiguration du Baptême chrétien?; – *b) Coquin* René-Georges, L'usage de l'eau chez les coptes autrefois et de nos jours; – *c) Rassart-Debergh* Marguerite, Le baptême du Christ dans l'art: Monde Copte 13 (1988) 4-11 / 12-16 / 17-22; ill.

8843* **Schmitt** Émile, Le mariage chrétien dans l'œuvre de saint AUGUSTIN; une théologie baptismale de la vie conjugale 1983 → 65,6670; 2,6003: RÉglT 17 (1986) 94-96 (É. *Lamirande*).

8844 *Siebel* Wigand, Die Stellung der Firmung unter den Initiationssakramenten: TGL 78 (1988) 223-241.

8845 *Siret* Vincent, Les fondements bibliques de l'obligation de la confession des péchés pour les Pères du concile de Trente: RThom 88 (1988) 421-439.

8846 *Slenczka* Reinhard, Taufe – Tauferneuerung – Wiedertaufe: KerDo 34 (1988) 105-120; Eng. 121.

8847 **Stuhlhofer** Franz, Symbol oder Realität; Taufe und Abendmahl: Telos. Berneck 1988, Schwengeler. 110 p. 3-85-666-033X.

8848 **Taborda** Francisco, Sacramentos, praxis y fiesta; para una teología latinoamericana de los sacramentos, TOrtiz García Alfonso: Cristianismo y Sociedad 10. M 1987, Paulinas. 204 p. 84-285-1207-8. – RActuBbg 25 (1988) 251 (I. *Riudor*).

8849 *Taft* Robert F. [*al.*], Penance in contemporary scholarship [... anthropology; Anglican, Luth., Orthodox, Ev.]: StLtg 18,1 (1988) 2-21 [-115 < ZIT 88,565].

8850 **Tura** Ermanno R., Il Signore cammina con noi; introduzione ai sacramenti. Padova 1987, Gregoriana. 326 p. Lit. 19.500. – RCC 139 (1988,1) 90s (P. *Vanzan*).

8851 *Vandervelde* George, The grammar of grace; Karl RAHNER as a watershed in contemporary theology: TS 49 (1988) 445-459.

8852 *Vogt* Hermann J., Die Ehe ein Sakrament? Hinweise für eine Antwort aus der frühen Kirche: TüTQ 168 (1988) 16-23.

8853 **Vorgrimler** Herbert, Sakramententheologie: Leitfaden Theologie 17, 1987 → 3,7509: RSalmanticensis 35 (1988) 429s (D. *Borobio*); TGL 78 (1988) 103 (W. *Beinert*).

8854 *Wright* David F.,   One baptism or two? Reflections on the history of Christian baptism: VoxEvca 18 (1988) 7-23.

8855 **Zweck** Heinrich,   Osterlobpreis und Taufmotive; Studien zu Struktur und Theologie des Exultet und anderer Osterpraeconien unter besonderer Berücksichtigung der Taufmotive: RgStT 32. Fra 1986, Lang.   390 p. Fs 43.   3-8204-8216-4. – ᴿBijdragen 49 (1988) 98 (G. *Rouwhorst*).

H7.6   *Ecclesiologia, theologia missionis, laici* – **The Church.**

8856 **Adinolfi** Marco,   Il sacerdozio comune dei fedeli 1983 ➔ 64,7049 ... 2,7153:   ᴿGregorianum 69 (1988) 157s (E. *Rasco*).

8857 *Almeida* Antônio J. de,   Modelos eclesiológicos e ministérios eclesiais: REB 48 (1988) 310-352.

   Anderson James B.,   A Vatican II pneumatology of the paschal mystery [Church's missionary activity]; the historical-doctrinal genesis of Ad Gentes I,2-5: AnGreg 250, 1988 ➔ 8558.

8859 **Antón** Ángel,   El misterio de la Iglesia I. En busca de una eclesiología y de la reforma de la Iglesia: BAC 26 [I. 1986 ➔ 3,7517] II. R 1987, Pont. Univ. Gregoriana. – ᴿBurgense 29 (1988) 293-5 (N. *López Martínez*); CiTom 114 (1987) 374s; 115 (1988) 194-6 (A. *Bandera*); Compostellanum 33 (1988) 310-2 (J. A. *Gil Sousa*, 1); EstE 63 (1988) 112 (J. A. *Estrada*, 1); Gregorianum 69 (1988) 812s (*ipse*, 1s); NatGrac 35 (1988) 226s (A. *Villalmonte*, 2); NRT 110 (1988) 428s (R. *Escol*, 1).

8860 **Archer** Anthony,   The two Catholic Churches [power-struggle within Roman Catholicism]. L 1986, SCM. 273 p. £9.50. – ᴿNBlackfr 68,2 (1987) 56-63 (-107, whole fascicle: W. S. F. *Pickering*, al.).

8861 **Arnau-García** Ramón,   San Vicente FERRER y las eclesiologías del cisma 1987 ➔ 3,7519:   ᴿTS 49 (1988) 577 (L. D. *Davis*).

8862 *Aumann* Jordan,   The role of the laity in the Church and in the world: Angelicum 65 (1988) 157-169.

8863 *Barbour* Claude-Marie,   Jesus, Shalom, and rites of passage; a journey toward global mission and spirituality: Missiology 15 (1987) 299-313.

8864 [*Bennett* Gareth, preface 18 p.] Crockford's clerical directory 1987/8.   L 1987, Church House.   917 p. £27,50. – ᴿTLond 91 (1988) 155-7 (P. *Baelz*: entirely on the Preface — 'the Church of England is adrift' — with no mention of any author or relation to the 900 remaining pages) & 266-273 (George *Carey*, bishop of Bath: Bennett's suicide proved he was author of the preface, considered a savage attack on the Archbishop but really a balanced critique of his leadership of 'Parties in the Church of England').

8865 *Beyer* J.,   Subsidiarity in the Church [< NRT 108 (1986) 801-822], ᵀᴱ*Jermann* Rosemary: TDig 35 (1988) 233-8.

8866 *Biagi* Ruggero,   La Chiesa continuazione dell'opera salvifica di Cristo: SacDoc 33 (1988) 627-655.

8866* *Bieritz* Karl-Heinrich,   Literatur zum Gemeindeaufbau [*Herbst* M., *Sorg* T., *Möller* C., alle 1987]: BTZ 5 (1988) 288-296.

8867 *a) Blank* J.,   Zum Begriff der 'Macht in der Kirche'; neutestamentliche Perspektiven: IZT 24 (1988) 172-8; – *b) Lynch* J., Power in the Church: Concilium 197 (E 1988) 13-22 = L'exercice du pouvoir dans l'Église: Concilium 217 (P 1988) 13-24 / 25-35.

8868 *Boff* Clodovis,   La iglesia europea vista por un latinoamericano [< REB 45 (1985) 152-160], ᵀᴱ*Suñol* Miquel: SelT 26 (1987) 322-6.

8869 **Boff** Leonardo, Ecclesiogenesis; the base communities reinvent the church 1986 ⇒ 2,6030; 3,7537: ᴿLvSt 13 (1988) 279s (R. *Michiels*); Missiology 16 (1988) 91s (E. T. *Bachmann*); RelStR 14 (1988) 53 (J. T. *Ford*).

8870 *Bojorge* Horacio, El fiel laico en el horizonte de su pertenencia; aspectos bíblicos de la teología del laicado: Stromata 44 (1988) 423-474.

8871 *Bopp* Karl, Jugendpastoral und Ekklesiologie: ⇒ 131, ᶠSCHILLING H., Den Menschen nachgehen 1987, 137-152.

8872 *Borras* Alphonse, Appartenance à l'Église, communion ecclésiale et excommunication; réflexions d'un canoniste: NRT 110 (1988) 801-824.

8873 *Brambilla* Franco G., La parrocchia nella Chiesa; riflessione fondamentale: TItSett 13 (1988) 18-44; Eng. 44.

8874 **Bressolette** Claude, Le pouvoir dans la société et dans l'Église ... MARET 1984 ⇒ 3,7456: ᴿÉglT 17 (1986) 401s (A. *Peelman*).

8875 *a*) *Büsser* Fritz, ZWINGLI und die Kirche; Überlegungen zur Aktualität von Zwinglis Ekklesiologie; – *b*) *Pollet* J. V., Zwingli und die Kirche; Scholastik und Humanismus im Kirchenbegriff Zwinglis: Zwingliana 16 (1985) 186-200. 489-499.

8876 *Caillot* Joseph, L'Église et la tentation du pouvoir: Tychique 71 (1988) 41-49.

8877 *Calvez* Jean Y., La funzione diaconale della Chiesa: RasT 29 (1988) 217-234.

8878 **Carmody** Denise L. & John T., Bonded in Christ's love; an introduction to ecclesiology 1986 ⇒ 3,7554: ᴿHorizons 15 (1988) 177s (Susan *Wood*).

8879 **Chantraine** Georges, Les laïcs, chrétiens dans le monde 1987 ⇒ 3,7556: ᴿEsprVie 98 (1988) 61-63 (P. *Barbarin*) & 72 (L. *Debarge*); RivScR 2 (1988) 175-9 (E. *Juliá*); ScripTPamp 20 (1988) 882-6 (J. L. *Illanes*).

8880 *Chethimattam* John B., Theology of mission today: Jeevadhara 13 (1988) 350-361.

8881 [Fac. Lyon] Chrétiens en mouvement. Lyon 1987, Profac. 172 p. F 55. – ᴿEsprVie 98 (1988) 60s (L. *Barbey*: n'approuve pas p. 162, on ne peut parler d'un véritable rapport entre théologie et pratique en Europe; p. 164, l'hiérarchie tient 'deux discours', pratiquant une complicité de fait avec des 'statu quo' conservateurs).

8882 **Ciola** Nicola, Il dibattito ecclesiologico in Italia; uno studio bibliografico (1963-1984) 1986 ⇒ 2,6035; 3,7558: ᴿGregorianum 69 (1988) 561 (R. *Fisichella*).

8883 *Citrini* Tullio, Per una ecclesiologia postsinodale: RClerIt 69 (1988) 18-27.

8884 *Clément* Olivier, Quelques approches pneumatologiques de l'Église: Contacts/Orthodoxe 39 (1987) 17-30.

8885 *Collins* Raymond F., Small groups; an experience of Church [... house-church in Mk]: LvSt 13 (1988) 109-136.

8886 *Congar* Yves, Bulletin d'ecclésiologie: RSPT 72 (1988) 109-119 [*Schillebeeckx*, Plaidoyer 1987; *Dulles*, Catholicity 1987, *al*., infra]: RSPT 72 (1988) 109-119.

8887 *Conill* Jesús, Una Iglesia que acompaña el nacimiento y crecimiento de la fe: Iglesia Viva 118 (1985) 347-361 [> SelT 26 (1987) 183-9, ᵀᴱ*Fernández* Montserrat].

8888 *Conzemius* Victor, Legittimità della critica alla Chiesa, ᵀ*Colombi* G.: HumBr 43 (1988) 165-176.

8889 *Coste* René, Vers une élucidation du développement de la doctrine de l'Église catholique concernant la liberté religieuse [J. C. MURRAY peut-être minimise la portée de la déclaration du Concile]: EsprVie 98 (1988) 465-477.

8890 *Crouan* Denis, La notion de liberté ['l'Église doit défendre la liberté de foi: il y a liberté de religion ... l'Église elle-même doit avoir le droit de vivre ...']: EsprVie 98 (1988) 461-4.

8891 *Dagens* Claude, Situation actuelle de la foi et responsabilités de l'Église: NRT 110 (1988) 503-513.

8892 *Dahm* Karl-Wilhelm, Identität und Realität der Kirche; zum Gespräch mit Karl BARTH: → 140, FSTOODT D., Unterwegs 1987, 71-86.

8893 **da Spinetoli** O., Chiesa delle origini, chiesa del futuro. R 1986, Borla. 219 p. Lit. 15.000. – RAsprenas 35 (1988) 297 (L. *Longobardo*).

8894 **Dattrino** Lorenzo, Ottato di Milevi [OPTATUS Milevitanus], La vera chiesa: Testi Patristici 721. R 1988, Città Nuova. 272 p. 88-311-3071-4.

8895 **Descamps** Albert, Jésus et l'église 1987 → 3,213: RLvSt 13 (1988) 83s (R. F. *Collins*).

8896 **Dianich** Severino, Chiesa estroversa; una ricerca sulla svolta dell'ecclesiologia contemporanea: Problemi e dibattiti 8. CinB 1987, Paoline. 124 p. Lit. 9000. – RAsprenas 35 (1988) 295s (A. *Terracciano*: parte già edita Congresso ATI 1977).

8897 **Dianich** S., La Chiesa mistero di comunione: Teologia attualizzata 6. T 1987 = 1975, Marietti. – RRivScR 2 (R 1988) 409-415 (E. *Juliá*).

8898 **Dianich** Severino, Iglesia en misión; hacia una eclesiología dinámica [1985 → 2,6044], TOrtiz García A.: Verdad e Imagen 108. Salamanca 1988, Sígueme. 287 p. – RLumenVr 37 (1988) 534s (J. I. *Calleja*).

8899 **Diez** Karlheinz, Christus und seine Kirche; zum Kirchenverständnis des Petrus CANISIUS: KkKSt 51, 1987 → 3,7575; DM 48: RTPQ 136 (1988) 184s (G. B. *Winkler*).

8900 **Donovan** Daniel, The Church as idea and fact: Zacchaeus Studies. Wilmington 1988, Glazier. 95 p. $6 [TDig 35,394].

8901 **Dulles** Avery R., [→ 183] Models of the Church[2rev]. [[1]1974 → 56,5585; now added, 'disciples model']: Image. GCNY 1987, Doubleday. 256 p. $5 pa. [TDig 35,266].

8902 **Espeja** Jesús, L'Église, mémoire et prophétie [1983 → 64,2076], TEBrauns Eric: Théologies 1987 → 3,7585: RRSPT 72 (1988) 114 (Y. *Congar*: 'Théologie' sans -s; p. 116 série Cerf 'Théologies').

8903 **Estrada** Juan A., Del misterio de la Iglesia al pueblo de Dios; sobre las ambigüedades de una eclesiología mistérica: Verdad e Imagen 104. Salamanca 1988, Sígueme. 255 p. 84-301-1042-9 [Greg 69,822]. – RActuBbg 25 (1988) 236s (J. I. *González Faus*: del 'arbitrariamente destituido profesor de Granada' como aquí profetizado p. 32 'cuestionables medidas ... turbios asuntos financieros, compromisos con dictaduras'); ComSev 21 (1988) 262s (J. *Duque*).

8904 **Faivre** Alexandre, Les laïcs aux origines de l'Église 1984 → 65, 4635.6725 ... 3,7589: RÉglT 17 (1986) 242-4 (J. K. *Coyle*); RTLv 19 (1988) 379s (M. *Simon*).

8905 *Ferraro* Giuseppe, Il tema della Chiesa nella [JOHANNES PAULUS II] Dominum et vivificantem: PresPast 57,1 (1987) 159-169.

8906 **Flichy** Marc, Sur l'intégrisme, lettre à Mgr Jean-Charles THOMAS [sur le cas *Lefebvre*]. Versailles 1988, L'Évêché. 60 p. F 20. – REsprVie 98 *jaune* (1988) 115s (R. *Desvoyes*).

8907 **Flood** Edmund, The laity today and tomorrow; a report on the new consciousness of lay Catholics and how it might change the face of tomorrow's church 1987 → 3,7594: RLvSt 13 (1988) 376-8 (E. *Eynikel*).

8908 *a) Ford* J. M.,   The Holy Spirit and mission in the NT [... in China, *Woo* J. & F.]; – *b) Dayton* Donald H.,   The Holy Spirit and Christian expansion in the twentieth century [*al.* Pentecostals, Assemblies of God]; – *c) Lang* Joseph R.,   The specific missionary vocation in the post Vatican II period: Missiology 16 (1988) 439-453 [455-476] / 397-407 [409-437] / 387-396.

8909 **Forte** Bruno,   L'Église, icône de la Trinité 1985 → 2,6055; F 54:   ᴿSpiritus 29 (1988) 109 (E. *Desmarescaux*).

8910 **Forte** Bruno,   Laicado y laicidad, ensayos eclesiológicos, ᵀ*González Domingo* Germán: Pedal 192, 1987 → 3,7596:   ᴿCiTom 115 (1988) 587s (L. *Lago Alba*); LumenVr 37 (1988) 89 (F. *Ortiz de Urtaran*).

8911 *Galeota* Gustavo, *Mancia* Anita,   La chiesa locale nei Padri e nei primi concili: Asprenas 35 (1988) 195-214.

8911* *a) Galot* Jean,   Christ; revealer, founder of the Church, and source of ecclesial life; ᵀ*Wearne* L.; – *b) Antón* Ángel,   Postconciliar ecclesiology; expectations, results, and prospects for the future, ᵀ*Raymond* L.-B., *Hughes* E.: → 380, Vatican II Assessment 1 (1988) 385-406 / 407-438; français → 379, Bilan 1, 391-410 / 411-440.

8912 *a) Ganoczy* Alexander,   El apostolado de los laicos después del Concilio; – *b) Zerfass* Rolf,   ¿Es la diaconía un asunto del laicado?: → 568, Iglesia 1987, Salmanticensis 35 (1988) 103-117; Eng. 118 / 179-200; Eng. 200.

8913 **Gherardini** Brunero,   La Chiesa, ministero e servizio: Ut unum sint. R 1988, Pont. Univ. Lateranense. 281 p. – ᴿDivinitas 32 (1988) 719-722 (A. *Contat*).

8914 *Gherardini* Brunero,   La santità della Chiesa nella catechesi di Paolo VI: DocCom 40 (1987) 29-42.

8915 *Ghiberti* Giuseppe,   Il problema biblico della missione [ᴱ*Kertelge* K. 1982; *Senior* D., *Stuhlmueller* C. ital. 1985; *Rodríguez Ruiz* M. 1987; ParSpV 16, 1987]: RivB 36 (1988) 259-265.

8916 *González Faus* J. I.,   Para una reforma evangélica de la Iglesia: IglV 127 (1987) 89-99.

8916* *Gounelle* André,   *a)* Définition de l'Église; – *b)* Le sacerdoce universel: – *c)* Le ministre et la communauté: ÉTRel 63 (1988) 67-73 / 429-434 / 243-9.

8917 **Grelot** Pierre, [contre deux textes de *Lefebvre* M. 1985s] Libres dans la foi; liberté civique et liberté spirituelle: Spiritualité d'aujourd'hui. P 1987, Desclée. 237 p. F 125. – ᴿNRT 110 (1988) 794 (A. *Toubeau*: non sans indignation).

8918 **Guillet** Charles-M.,   L'Église communauté de témoins dans l'histoire: Parcours. P/Québec 1988, Centurion/Paulines. 111 p. F 59. – ᴿEsprVie 98 (1988) 395s (P. *Jay*: militant, risque de dater bien vite).

8919 *Haight* Roger,   The mission of the Church in the theology of the social gospel: TS 49 (1988) 477-497.

8920 **Hanson** Paul D.,   The people called 1986 → 2,6072; 3,7610:   ᴿAnglTR 70 (1988) 97-99 (J. I. *Hunt*); Interpretation 42 (1988) 299-302 (T. E. *Fretheim*); JBL 107 (1988) 503-6 (D. A. *Knight*); JEcuSt 24 (1987) 450s (M. *Wyschogrod*); JPsy&T 15 (1987) 75-77 (C. R. *Wells*); NewTR 1,3 (1988) 94s (C. *Stuhlmueller*); TrinJ 8 (1987) 239-242 (J. B. *Green*).

8921 *Harskamp* Anton van,   Kerkelijk gezag; vluchtoord voor de moderniteit; een interpretatie van J. A. Möhler's denken over de kerk: TsTNijm 28 (1988) 135-154; 154, Ecclesiastical authority; asylum in the face of modernity?

8922 ^{TE}**Hinson** E. Glenn, Understandings of the Church: Sources of Early Christian Thought. Ph 1986, Fortress. 116 p. 0-8006-1415-1. — ^RRExp 85 (1988) 713s (C. *Davis*).

8923 *a*) *Holter* Knut, Missiology and the Old Testament theology of religions; – *b*) *Fensham* Charles J., An evaluation of the nature of mission and the gospel of salvation in the 'Evangelical-Roman Catholic dialogue on mission': Missionalia 16,1 (Pretoria 1988) 4-12 / 25-39 [< TKontext 10/1,26].

8924 **Huguet** Marie-Thérèse, Miryam et Israël, le mystère de l'Épouse. Nouan-le-Fuzelier 1988, Lion de Juda. 203 p. – ^RMarianum 50 (1988) 609s (J. *Stern*).

8925 *Hunter* William F., *Mayers* Marvin K. [*Hesselgrave* David J., *al.*], Psychology and missions: JPsy&T 15 (1987) 269-273 [274-280-349].

8926 **Hutchison** William R., Errand to the world; American Protestant thought and foreign mission. Ch 1987, Univ. 227 p. $25. – ^RTTod 45 (1988s) 230.232.234 (J. A. *Scherer*).

8926* **Izco** J. A., ¿Qué misión quiere la Biblia? Raices bíblicas de la misión. M 1987, Misiones Extranjeras. 141 p. – ^RBibFe 14 (1988) 150 (M. *Sáenz Galache*).

8927 *Jiménez Ortiz* Antonio, La credibilidad de la Iglesia y el futuro de la fe en el pensamiento de Heinrich FRIES: EstE 63 (1988) 205-226.

8928 **Jongeneel** J. A. B., *a*) Missiologie, I. Zendingswetenschap. – *b*) Het christendom als wereldzendingsgodsdienst. Haag 1986, Boekencentrum. 208 p.; ƒ39,50 / 17 p.; ƒ9,50. 90-239-0635-7; 4-9. – ^RNedTTs 42 (1988) 168s (M. R. *Spindler*).

8929 *Jongeneel* J. A. B., *a*) Het christendom en de -ismen; een beschrijving, analyse en bijstelling van [H.] KRAEMERs zendingstheologie: KerkT 39 (1988) 92-109; – *b*) Christianity and the -isms; a description, analysis and rethinking of [H.] Kraemer's theology of missions: Bangalore Theological Forum 20,1s (1988) 17-41 [< TKontext 10/1,40].

8930 **Journet** Charles, Théologie de l'Église² [¹1957 = abrégé de L'Église du Verbe incarné]. P 1987, Desclée. 494 p. – ^REsprVie 98 (1988) 85s (P. *Jay*).

8931 **Kasper** Walter, Theologie und Kirche [14 art. 1980-5] 1987 → 3,240.7622: ^RÖkRu 37 (1988) 378s (R. *Schäfer*); RTLv 19 (1988) 499s (A. de *Halleux*); TS 49 (1988) 353 (R. *Kress*).

8932 *Kasper* Walter, The mission of the laity [< StiZt 112 (1987) 579-593], ^{TE}*Asen* B. A.: TDig 35 (1988) 133-8.

8933 *Kuttner* Stephan, The Church in the world [^FKEMPF F., Aus Kirche und Reich 1983 → 64,61]: CathHR 73 (1987) 576-584.

8933* **Kent** John, The unacceptable face; the modern Church in the eyes of the historian 1987 → 3,7628: ^RÉTRel 63 (1988) 133s (M. *Spindler*).

8934 ^E**Kern** W. *al.*, Traktat Kirche: HbFT 3,1986 → 800 [2,590; 3,864.7629]: ^RGregorianum 69 (1988) 315-323 (R. *Fisichella*: comincia: trattato che rinasce come la mitica 'Fenicia' ? per 'Fenice'); ZkT 110 (1988) 180-5 (W. *Klausnitzer*).

8935 *Kessler* Michael, Das synodale Prinzip; Bemerkungen zu seiner Entwicklung und Bedeutung: TüTQ 168 (1988) 43-60.

8936 *Kiwiet* John J., The Baptist view of the Church, a personal account: SWJT 31,2 (1988s) 13-21 [22-33, *Hendricks* William L., baptism; 34-41, *Carter* James E., Lord's Supper].

8936* *Kobler* John F., A phenomenological hermeneutics of the people of God; theoretical and practical dimensions: ETL 64 (1988) 84-105.

8937 **Koffeman** I. J.,   Kerk als sacramentum; de rol van de sacramentele ecclesiologie tijdens Vaticanum II; Proefschrift 1986 ➤ 3,7631;   90-6651-058-7:   ᴿBijdragen 49 (1988) 195-206 (A. van *Eijk*).

8938 **Kreck** Walter,   Grundfragen der Ekklesiologie 1981 ➤ 63,7027; 64,7098: ᴿZkT 110 (1988) 73-77 (L. *Lies*).

8939 ᶠKRETSCHMAR Georg: Kirchengemeinschaft — Anspruch und Wirklichkeit, ᴱ**Hauschild** W.-D., *al.* 1986: ➤ 2,56:   ᴿTR 84 (1988) 401-4 (W. *Ullmann*).

8940 **Lachner** Raimund,   Das ekklesiologische Denken J. S. DREYS 1986 ➤ 3,7634:   ᴿTR 84 (1988) 39-44 (K.-H. *Menke*); ZkT 110 (1988) 333-5 (W. *Füssl*)

8941 *a) Lea* Thomas D.,   The priesthood of all Christians according to the NT; – *b) Garrett* James L.ᴶ,   ... from CYPRIAN to John CHRYSOSTOM; – *c) Mikolaski* Samuel J.,   Contemporary relevance of...: SWJT 30,2 (1988) 15-21 / 22-23 / 6-14 [< ZIT].

8942 *a) Legrand* Lucien,   Vocation à la mission dans la NT; – *b) Buetubela* Balembo,   La mission selon les synoptiques et Paul; – *c) Rolland* Philippe, 'Je vous envoie'; – *d) Tassin* Claude,   La mission selon Mt 28,16-20; – *e) Pathrapankal* Joseph,   L'homme de la Pentecôte; Actes 1-15; – *f) Poucouta* Paulin,   Témoignage dans l'Apocalypse: Spiritus 29,113 ('Vous serez mes témoins' 1988) 339-352 / 353-8 / 359-365 / 366-385 / 386-396 / 397-405.

8943 **Leith** John H.,   The Reformed imperative; what the Church has to say that no one else can say. Ph 1988, Westminster. 152 p. $13. – ᴿTTod 45 (1988s) 503-5 (A. J. *McKelway*).

8944 *a) Leonard* Bill,   The Church and the laity; – *b) Diehl* William E., Ecumenism and the laity: RExp 85 (1988) 625-635 / 637-644 [-679, *al.*].

8945 *Limouris* Gennadios,   The Church, a mystery of unity in diversity: SVlad 31 (1987) 123-142.

8946 **Lohfink** G.,   Wie hat Jesus Gemeinde gewollt?⁵ [1982 ➤ 63,5118] 1984 ➤ 3,7369: ᴿVoxPa 12s (1987s) 465-9 (M. *Marczewski*).

8947 **Lohfink** Gerhard,   La Iglesia que Jesús quería 1986 ➤ 2,6092; 3,7640: ᴿChristus 53,619 (Méx 1988) 57-59 (J. *Jiménez Limón*); CiTom 114 (1987) 379s (A. *Bandera*); CiuD 201 (1988) 486 (A. *Salas*); ScripTPamp 19 (1987) 941-4 (F. *Varo*).

8948 **Macquarrie** John,   Theology, Church and ministry 1986 ➤ 2,189: ᴿLvSt 13 (1988) 177-9 (R. *Michiels*).

8949 **Maggiolini** Sandro,   L'obbedienza nella Chiesa; attualità di una virtù difficile. Mi 1988, Ares. 117 p. Lit. 10.000. – ᴿCiVit 43 (1988) 417 (A. *Pellegrini*); ViPe 71 (1988) 550-3 (F. *Botturi*).

8950 **Margerie** Bertrand de,   Écône [séminaire LEFEBVRE], comment dénouer la tragédie? P 1988, Téqui. 110 p. F 55. – ᴿEsprVie 98 (1988) *jaune* 300 (E. *Vauthier*).

8951 *Martin* Dennis D.,   MENNO and AUGUSTINE on the Body of Christ: Fides et Historia 20,3 (1988) 41-66 [< ZIT 89,181].

8952 **Martín Velasco** Juan,   Increencia y evangelización; del diálogo al testimonio ['nueva forma de presencia pública de la Iglesia en la sociedad']: Presencia Teológica 45. Santander 1988, Sal Terrae. 252 p. 84-293-0801-6. – ᴿActuBbg 25 (1988) 229 (J. I. *González Faus*).

8953 **Martini** Carlo M.,   Leben wir, was wir verkünden? Eine Selbstbestimmung für Menschen, die mit der Weitergabe des Wortes Gottes beauftragt sind. Mü 1988, Neue Stadt. 136 p. DM 17,80 [TGL 78,460].

8954 **Martini** Carlo M., Palabras sobre la Iglesia; pueblo de Dios para la vida del mundo [Parole sulla Chiesa], ᵀ*García Valenceja* J.J.: Servidores y Testigos 35. Santander 1988, Sal Terrae. 160 p. 84-293-0799-0. – ᴿActuBbg 25 (1988) 239s (I. *Riudor*).

8955 *Meini* Mario, La Chiesa come mistero complesso [*Congar* Y.]: RivAscM 12 (1987) 129-145. 203-221. 338-346.

8956 *Michiels* Robrecht, Kerk van Jezus Christus; een exegetisch-ecclesiologische bijdrage: CollatVL 18 (1988) 287-314 [258-361, *al.* (sociologisch/psych./hist.) 'Kerk als minderheid' i.e. more than half the citizens don't belong/practise].

8957 **Miller** Edward J., John Henry NEWMAN on the idea of the Church 1987 ➤ 3,7653: ᴿCathHR 74 (1988) 635-7 (Mary K. *Tillman*); Thomist 52 (1988) 760-3 (T. *Heath*).

8958 *Mobbs* Frank, L''unica vera Chiesa' secondo il Concilio Vaticano II: DocCom 41 (1988) 61-75.

8959 **Mondin** Giovanni B., La Chiesa, primizia del Regno: Corso di teologia sistematica 7, 1986 ➤ 2,6102; 3,7655: ᴿGregorianum 69 (1988) 189s (M. *Zalba*).

8960 **Monsegú** C.P. Berbado, La Iglesia que Cristo quiso 1986 ➤ 3,7657: ᴿBurgense 29 (1988) 295-7 (N. *López Martínez*); Studium 28 (M 1988) 155 (P. *Blázquez*).

8961 *Moritz* Frederick J., Church as body: CalvaryB 4,1 (1988) 1-24.

8962 *Mourlon Beernaert* P., Converting to the Gospel: LVitae 42,4 (1987) 369-379 [< NTAbs 32,295].

8963 *Mraida* C., Re-interpretación de la misión a la luz de la hermenéutica: Diálogo Teol. 31 (Calí, Colombia 1988) 62-76 [< Stromata 44,564].

8964 *Müller* Karl, Mission in der Weise Jesu [= Mission in Christ's way, IntRM 75 (1986) 366-375]: VerbumSVD 29 (1988) 415-428.

8965 **Neuner** Peter, Der Laie und das Gottesvolk. Fra 1988, Knecht. 236 p. – ᴿTGL 78 (1988) 442s (W. *Beinert*).

8966 *Neuner* Peter, Aspekte einer Theologie des Laien: UnSa 43 (1988) 316-324; > Eng. TDig 36,121-5, ᵀᴱ*Asen* B.

8967 *O'Callaghan* Paul, The holiness of the Church in early Christian creeds: IrTQ 54 (1988) 59-65.

8968 *Orsy* Ladislas, Participation and the nature of the Church: PrPeo 2 (1988) 356-362.

8969 *Osborne* Kenan B., The meaning of lay, laity, and lay ministry in the Christian theology of the Church [p. 253: Not all Christians are either lay or cleric...]: Antonianum 63 (1988) 227-258; Eng. 227. [> TDig 36,113-9; further there p. 120 < Asprenas 34,132, *Longobardo* L.; 121-5 < UnSa 43,316-324, *Neuner* P.; 127-131 < TPQ 135,205-212, *Zauner* W.].

8970 *Page* Ruth, Divine grace and Church establishment ['whether the legal establishment... affects doctrine in any way']: TLond 91 (1988) 284-297.

8971 **Pannenberg** Wolfhart, Etica y eclesiología 1985 ➤ 2,6115; Verdad e Imagen 71: ᴿLumenVr 37 (1988) 185s (U. *Gil Ortega*: 'eclesiología' en texto, 'sociología' en título).

8972 **Paul** William D., The role of conscience in the collective community of Christ: diss. Fuller, ᴰ*Anderson* R. Pasadena 1987. 428 p. – StudiaBT 15 (1987) 285s with summary.

8973 *Plaisted* Robert L., The homogeneous unit debate; its value orientations and changes: EvQ 87 (1987) 215-233 [< BS 145 (1988) 101 (M. *Pocock*); the summary does not define 'homogeneous unit (missionary theology)', nor really make clear on which side it is of the debate as to whether new converts should be sought as individuals or in their groups].

8974 *a) Popkes* Wiard, Das allgemeine Priestertum der Gläubigen; – *b) Barth* Hans-M., 'Allgemeines Priestertum der Gläubigen' nach M. LUTHER; – *c) Neuner* Peter, Aspekte einer Theologie des Laien: UnSa 43 (1988) 325-330 / 331-342 / 316-324.

8975 **Poulat** É., L'Église c'est un monde 1986 → 2,6124: ᴿRTLv 19 (1988) 92s (R. *Guelluy*: he means not a pluralist but a uniformist world, really only France; and the continuity from Pius IX through John Paul II overlooks the originality of John XXIII).

8976 *Preston* Geoffrey [†c.1977], The Church of the Trinity, I. of the Spirit; II. of the Son; III. of the Father: NBlackf 68 (1987) 270-7 / 339-346 / 393-9.

8977 *Quilotti* Raffaele, L'ecclesiologia del Messale Romano – IV-[V.] conclusioni: SacDoc 33 (1988) 119-187. 513-9.

8978 ᴱ**Rendtorff** T., Charisma und Institution 1984/5 → 2,391*; 3,7678: ᴿTRu 53 (1988) 226-8 (K. *Raiser*).

8979 **Ries** Julien, Les Chrétiens parmi les religions; des Actes des Apôtres à Vatican II: Le Christianisme et la foi chrétienne 5, 1987 → 3,a977; 2-7189-0356-2: ᴿEsprVie 98 (1988) 494s (L. *Nefontaine*); FoiTemps 18 (1988) 593-9 (G. *Harpigny*).

8980 *Ries* Jules [sic, mais professeur de l'Univ. Cath. Lv], L'Église conciliaire, le mouvement traditionaliste d'Écône [séminaire de Mgr. Marcel *Lefebvre*, où l'auteur a résidé quelques jours en 1975] et les religions non chrétiennes: EsprVie 98 (1988) 481-6.

8981 **Rowthorn** Anne, The liberation of the laity. Wilton CT 1986, Morehouse-Barlow. 141 p. $10 pa. – ᴿAnglTR 70 (1988) 117s (V. Nelle *Bellamy*: divisive tirade).

8982 *Schatz* Klaus, Die Missionen auf dem 1. Vatikanum: TPhil 63 (1988) 342-369.

8983 **Scherer** James A., Gospel, Church, and Kingdom [...where do various Christian groups stand in relation to mission?] 1987 → 3,7691: ᴿJEcuSt 25 (1988) 469s (R. B. *Norris*); Missiology 16 (1988) 479s (A. *Sovik*); NewTR 1,2 (1988) 111-3 (W. *McConville*); RelStR 14 (1988) 239 (B. *Fargher*).

8984 *Schillebeeckx* Edward, Tú, vosotros, yo; todos pertenecemos a la Iglesia [< Orientierung 49 (1985) 150-3], ᵀᴱ*Giménez* Josep: SelT 26 (1987) 190-4.

8985 **Schinella** I., Figli della Chiesa; saggio per una teologia del laicato. Tropea 1987, Parva Favilla. 194 p. – ᴿRasT 29 (1988) 214 (A. *Barruffo*).

8986 **Schmied** Gerhard, Kirche oder Sekte? Entwicklungen und Perspektiven des Katholizismus in der westlichen Welt: Piper 910. Mü 1988, Piper. 138 p. DM 14,80 pa. – ᴿTGL 78 (1988) 437 (W. *Beinert*).

8987 ᴱ**Schreiner** Josef, Unterwegs zur Kirche; Alttestamentliche Konzeptionen: QDisp 110, 1985/7 → 3,563: ᴿLebZeug 42,2 (1987) 71s (K. *Heinen*); NRT 110 (1988) 101-3 (J.-L. *Ska*); ÖkRu 37 (1988) 375s (F. *Crüsemann*); TPQ 136 (1988) 282s (W. *Berg*); TR 84 (1988) 102s (W. H. *Schmidt*); TsTNijm 28 (1988) 180s (A. *Schoors*).

8988 **Schwarz** Hans, Kurs [i.e. The Christian Church 1982 → 64,7127 organized for classroom instruction] Die Christliche Kirche; I. Die Entstehung der Kirche [→ 3,7694]; II. Die grossen Veränderungen; III. Die Verheissung für die Zukunft. Gö 1986, Vandenhoeck & R. 135 p.;

140 p.; 131 p. – ᴿRelStR 14 (1988) 255 (R. *Kolb*: no indication of translator or 'organizer').

8989 *Semeraro* Marcello, Popolo di Dio; una nozione ecclesiologica, al Concilio e vent'anni dopo: RivScR 2 (Molfetta 1988) 29-67.

8990 *Sieben* Hermann J., *a*) Concilium perfectum; zur Idee der sogenannten Partikularsynode in der Alten Kirche; – *b*) Die katholische Konzilsidee vor der Herausforderung durch die Demokratie: TPhil 63 (1988) 203-229 / 537-568.

8991 *Siegele-Wenschkewitz* L., Das Priestertum aller Gläubigen: EvKomm 21 (1988) 380-3 [< ZIT 88,515].

8992 **Siniscalco** Paolo, Laici e laicità, un profilo storico. R 1986, AVE. – ᴿStRicOrCr 10 (1987) 187s (Mariam de *Ghantuz Cubbe*).

8993 *Siniscalco* Paolo, Laicato e laicità: NuovaUm 9,50 (1987) 85-106.

8994 **Stötzel** Arnold, Kirche als 'neue Gesellschaft'; die humanisierende Wirkung des Christentums nach J. CHRYSOSTOMUS: Münsterische BeiTh. 51, 1984 ➤ 1,7566; 2,6139: ᴿTR 84 (1988) 31-33 (A. M. *Ritter*).

8995 **Teissier** Henri, La mission de l'Église 1985 ➤ 2,6141: ᴿÉglT 17 (1986) 100-103 (M. *Zago*).

8996 *Tepe* Valfredo, Jesus Cristo – a Igreja – o Homem: REB 48 (1988) 5-39.

8997 *Thils* Gustave, Les laïcs; à la recherche d'une définition: RTLv 19 (1988) 191-6.

8998 **Thomas** Pascal [pseudonyme d'auteur collectif], Ces chrétiens que l'on appelle laïcs après le synode sur les laïcs: Théologie/Repères. P 1988, Ouvrières. 244 p. – ᴿEsprVie 98 (1988) 399s (P. *Jay*).

8999 *a*) *Thomsen* Mark W., Jesus crucified and the mission of the Church; – *b*) *Allmen* Daniel von, The treasure in clay pots: IntRMiss 77 (1988) 247-264 / 265-271.

9000 *Tigges* Marianne, New spiritual movements ['the Church in movement' < Neue geistliche Bewegungen: Zts für Fragen des Ordenslebens 28 (1987) 289-299], ᵀᴱ*Asen* B. A.: TDig 35 (1988) 209-212.

9001 *Tillard* Jean-Marie R., Sacerdoce [baptismal, non-ministériel]: ➤ 791, DictSpir XIV,91 (1988) 1-37.

9002 **Valadier** René, L'Église en procès; catholicisme et société moderne 1987 ➤ 3,7713: ᴿEsprVie 98 (1988) 504s (R. *Epp*: ton violent, BALTHASAR et mère TÉRÉSA n'y échappent pas); LumièreV 37,186 (1988) 106-8 (L. *Panier*, F. *Martin*: 'dans le contexte actuel du catholicisme français, ce livre est plus qu'important, il est nécessaire' — rapport Église-société); RHPR 68 (1988) 481s (A. *Birmelé*: réaliste, mais ne connaît pas d'autre expression de la foi chrétienne que celle de son Église); TPhil 63 (1988) 622-4 (M. *Maier*); TR 84 (1988) 389s (K. *Müller*).

9003 ᴱ**Vanzan** P., Il laicato nella Bibbia e nella storia 1987 ➤ 3,572: ᴿHum-Br 43 (1988) 891 (B. *Belletti*).

9004 *Vanzan* Piersandro, Il Sinodo sui laici [R ott. 1987]; breve contestualizzazione e primo bilancio: RasT 29 (1988) 1-19.

9005 **Walker** Peter [bishop of Ely], Rediscovering the Middle Way: the Anglican Church Today. L 1988, Mowbray. 164 p. £7 pa. – ᴿTLond 91 (1988) 342-4 (L. *Houlden*).

9005* *Walls* Andrew F., Missionary societies and the fortunate subversion of the Church: EvQ 60 (1988) 141-155.

9006 **Webber** Robert E., *Clapp* Rodney, People of the truth; the power of the worshiping community in the modern world. SF 1988, Harper & R. viii-136 p. $15 [CBQ 51,404].

9007 *Wohlrabe* John C.[J], The Americanization of WALTHER's doctrine of the Church: ConcordTQ 52,1 (1988) 1-28 [< ZIT 88,587].

9007* **Woolever** James J., A critical evaluation of the appropriateness of Karl RAHNER's ecclesial model for the Catholic Church of the future: diss. Syracuse 1987. – RTLv 20,565.

9008 **Zirker** Hans, Ecclesiologia, [TE]*Falchetti* Maurizio: GdT 172, 1987 ➤ 3,7730: [R]Asprenas 35 (1988) 296s (A. *Terracciano*); CC 139 (1988,2) 609s (G. *Mucci*: tutto sembra provvisorio e difficilmente accostabile); ETL 64 (1988) 209s (A. de *Halleux*).

9009 **Zizioulas** J. D., Being as communion 1985 ➤ 1,7585... 3,7731: [R]TR 84 (1988) 53 (W. *Beinert*).

H7.7 *Œcumenismus* – **The ecumenical movement.**

9010 *Amaladoss* Michael, Diálogo y misión; ¿ realidades en pugna o convergentes? [< IntRMiss 75 (1986) 222-4], [TE]*Messa* Josep: SelT 27 (1988) 243-258.

9010* *Amiet* Peter, Der altkatholisch-orthodoxe theologische Dialog ist abgeschlossen: IkiZ 78 (1988) 42-50; 51-62, Beschlusstexte [79-89, *Papandreou* Damaskinos].

9011 *Arinze* Francis card., Interreligious dialogue; problems, prospects and possibilities: BSecrNC 22 (1987) 247-265.

9012 **Avis** Paul, Ecumenical theology and the elusivenese of doctrine 1986 ➤ 1,7404... 3,7740: [R]NBlackfr 68 (1987) 203s (J. *Lipner*).

9013 **Beck** Nestor, The doctrine of faith; a study of the Augsburg confession and contemporary ecumenical documents 1987 ➤ 3,7744: [R]CurrTM 15 (1988) 374s (G. C. *Carter*); JEcuSt 25 (1988) 616s (W. J. *Sullivan*).

9014 **Békés** Gerard J., Eucaristia e Chiesa; ricerca dell'unità nel dialogo ecumenico: Liturgia fonte e culmine 2, 1985 ➤ 3,7746; Lit. 16.000: [R]TR 84 (1988) 314-6 (A. *Klein*).

9015 [E]**Bent** Ans J. van der, Vital ecumenical concerns [➤ 3,7748]; sixteen documentary surveys. Geneva 1986, WCC. 333 p. Fs 25. 2-8254-0873-5. – [R]NedTTs 42 (1988) 167s (M. R. *Spindler*).

9016 *Biedermann* Hermenegild L., Apostolizität als Gottes Gabe im Leben der Kirche ['Apostolicity as God's gift in the life of the Church', Nov. 1, 1986, Boston declaration of joint Catholic/Orthodox bishops' commission]: OstkSt 37 (1988) 38-54 [328-338, 26.VI.1988 Valamo declaration on priesthood, deutsch].

9017 **Birmelé** André, Le salut en Jésus-Christ dans les dialogues œcuméniques 1986 ➤ 2,6163; 3,7752: [R]Gregorianum 69 (1988) 380-3 (J. *Wicks*); RTPhil 120 (1988) 114s (J.-E. *Bertholet*).

9018 [E]**Birmelé** André, *Ruster* Thomas, Vereint im Glauben – getrennt am Tisch des Herrn: Arbeitsbuch Ökumene 3. Gö 1987, Vandenhoeck & R. 107 p. DM 14,80 pa. – [R]JEcuSt 25 (1988) 119s (B. A. *Asen*); ZkT 110 (1988) 237 (L. *Lies*).

9019 *Bockmann* Peter, Justification by faith, Lutheran and Roman Catholic: Dialogue and Alliance 2,2 (1988) 9-17.

9020 **Borrély** André, *Eutizi* Max, L'Œcuménisme spirituel: Perspective orthodoxe. Genève 1988, Labor et Fides. 250 p. – [R]Contacts 40 (1988) 304-311 (Y. D.).

9021 *Bosch* David J., *a*) The Church in dialogue; from self-delusion to vulnerability: Missiology 16 (1988) 131-147; – *b*) 'Ecumenicals' and 'Evangelicals'; a growing relationship?: EcuR 40 (1988) 458-472.

9021* *Bouwen* Frans, Ussi Valamo [Finlande 19-27.VI] 1988, Cinquième session de la Commission internationale pour le dialogue théologique entre l'Église catholique et l'Église orthodoxe: PrOrChr 38 (1988) 281-296 [297-307, document, Le sacrement de l'Ordre].

9022 **Brandt** Hermann, Kirchliches Leben in ökumenischer Verpflichtung.. Rezeption ök. Documente ➤ 3,7758: ᴿTR 84 (1988) 399-401 (A. *Klein*).

9023 *Brosseder* Johannes, Papal infallibility; some ecumenical considerations: Dialogue and Alliance 2,2 (1988) 18-25.

9024 **Burrows** William R., The Roman Catholic magisterium on other religious ways; analysis and critique from a post-modern perspective: diss. Ch. Divinity 1987. – RelStR 14,186.

9025 **Carey** George, The meeting of the waters; a balanced contribution to the ecumenical debate [= ? ➤ 1,7432]. L 1985, Hodder & S 188 p. £5 pa. 0-340-37379-6. – ᴿScotBEv 6 (1988) 43s (C. M. *Cameron*).

9026 **Celier** G., La dimension œcuménique de la Réforme liturgique. Lyon-Ste.Foy 1987, Fideliter. 112 p. F 65. – ᴿEsprVie 98 (1988) 223s (G.-M. *Oury*).

9027 *Clarkson* Shannon, Steps toward unity – a mutual recognition of ordained minstries: JEcuSt 28 (1986) 479-491 (-503, *Martyn* W. J.).

9028 *a*) *Constable* John W., In search of a confessional ecumenism; – *b*) *Graesser* Carlᴶ, Biblical roots of our diversity [J (the Yahwist) the first Lutheran; P. the first Roman Catholic; D the first Reformed]; – *c*) *Krentz* Edgar, Historical criticism and confessional commitment: ➤ 143, ᶠTɪᴇᴛᴊᴇɴ J. = CurrTM 15 (1988) 21-26 / 27-33 / 128-136.

9029 *Craddock* F. B., Christian unity and the New Testament — a conversation between Luke and John: Mid-Stream 27,1 (Indianapolis 1988) 1-12 [< NTAbs 32,309].

9030 **Congar** Y., Diversità e comunione, ᵀ*Comba Corsani* Mirella, 1984 ➤ 65,6707: ᴿProtestantesimo 43 (1988) 61s (V. *Subilia*).

9031 *a*) *Congar* Yves, Thomismus und Ökumenismus; – *b*) *Fries* H., Fundamentaltheologie und ökumenische Theologie; – *c*) *Jüngel* E. / *Dulles* A., Meine Theologie: TJb (Lp 1988) 30-27 / 40-51 / 98-113 . 52-66 [< ᴢɪᴛ 89,385].

9032 *a*) *Crow* Paul A.ᴶ, Reflections on models of Christian unity; – *b*) *Heron* Alisdair I. C., Our common doctrinal roots; – *c*) *Harrison* Richard L.ᴶ, Sacraments in the life, thought, and practice of the Disciples; – *d*) *Duke* James O., *Lancaster* Lewis H., Ministry in the Disciples-Reformed dialogue: ➤ 545, Mid-Stream 27,2 (1987 Birmingham conference, 1988) 116-134 / 89-93 / 94-108 / 109-115.

9033 **Cullmann** O., Einheit durch Vielfalt 1986 ➤ 2,6177; 3,7767: ᴿProtestantesimo 43 (1988) 24-27 (V. *Subilia*); StPatav 35 (1988) 218s (A. *Moda*).

9034 **Cullmann** Oscar, L'unité par la diversité 1986 ➤ 2,6177*b*; 3,7768: ᴿContacts/Orthodoxe 40 (1988) 139-142 [Elisabeth *Behr-Sigel*]; Gregorianum 69 (1988) 588-590 (J. *Dupuis*); JEcuSt 24 (1987) 456 (Sonya A. *Quitslund*); VSp 142 (1988) 301s (J. *Hoffmann*).

9035 **Cullmann** O., L'unità attraverso la diversità; il suo fondamento e il problema della sua realizzazione: GdT 178, 1987 ➤ 3,7769; Lit. 13.000: ᴿAsprenas 35 (1988) 300s (D. *Pacelli*).

9036 **Cullmann** Oscar, Unity through diversity; its foundation, and a contribution to the discussion concerning the possibility of its actualization, ᵀ*Boring* M. Eugene. Ph 1988, Fortress. 109 p. $7. – ᴿCalvinT 23 (1988) 289s (R. C. *Gamble*); RelStR 14 (1988) 362 (J. T. *Ford*).

9037 *a*) *Curry* George,   Lambeth '88 and A.R.C.I.C. I: – *b*) *Baker* Tony, Evangelical approaches to theological dialogue: Churchman 102,1 (L 1988) 17-29 / 44-53 [< ZIT 88,433].

9038 **Derrick** Christopher,   Words and the word; notes on our Catholic vocabulary [40 in-words like 'collegiality'. 'relevance', 'encounter' open to ambiguity]. SF 1987, Ignatius.   134 p. $7 [TDig 35, 265].

9039 *Derrick* Christopher,   Ecumensim, a sacred cow?:   HomP 89,9 (1988) 50-56.

9040 *Desmet* Willy,   NEWMAN's oecumenische problematiek; actueel of voorbij?:   CollatVL 18 (1988) 86-102.

9041 *Dingemans* G.D.J.,   Eenheid en verscheidenheid in de nieuwe 'SOW' [Samen op Weg] – Kerk; op zoek naar een nieuw paradigma, dat Hervormden en Gereformeerden samen kan inspireren om kerk te zijn in de geseculariseerde wereld van de een-en-twintigste eeuw: GerefTTs 88 (1988) 129-142: exiel-model.

9042 **Dionne** J. Robert,   The Papacy and the Church; a study of praxis and reception in ecumenical perspective 1987 → 3,7776:   ᴿAmerica 157 (1987) 483s (J. B. *Benestad*); AustralasCR 65 (1988) 111 (J. *Thornhill*); ChH 57 (1988) 575s (R. F. *Costigan*: massive, useful); MilltSt 21 (1988) 124s (E. N. *Thiernaigh*); RSPT 72 (1988) 109-111 (Y. *Congar*); TR 84 (1988) 483s (W. *Beinert*: 7 interventions 1846-1965; concluding chapter, 'The head cannot say to the feet, I don't need you', 1 Cor 12,21); TS 49 (1988) 351-3 (T. P. *Rausch*); ZkT 110 (1988) 354-6 (R. *Schwager*).

9043 *Döring* Heinrich,   Taufe, Eucharistie und Amt im Kontext des Communio-Ekklesiologie; Analysen zur offiziellen römischen Antwort auf das Lima-Dokument [< HerdKorr 42 (1988) 27-43]:   Catholica 42 (1988) 170-194.

9044 **Dulles** Avery,   The catholicity of the Church 1985 → 1,7443 ... 3,7778: ᴿNBlackf 68 (1987) 46s (M. Cecily *Boulding*); ScotJT 41 (1988) 128-130 (D.W.D. *Shaw*).

9045 *Dulles* Avery, *a*) The emerging world church and the pluralism of cultures [< ProcCTSA 39 (1984) 1-12]; – *b*) The meaning of Catholicism; adventures of an idea [< ᶠ*Congar* Y., Thomist 48 (1984) 607-633]; – *c*) Vatican II and the purpose of the Church [< TDig 32 (1985) 341-352]: → 183, Reshaping 1988, 34-50 / 51-74 / 132-153; – *d*) Caminos hacia un acuerdo doctrinal; diez tesis [< TS 47 (1986) 32-47], ᵀᴱ*Torello* Josep M.: SelT 27 (1988) 281-8.

9045* *a*) *Dupuis* Jacques,   Dialogue interreligieux dans la mission évangélatrice de l'Église, ᵀ*Blanchette* Claude; – b) *Dhavamony* Mariasusai, Évangélisation et dialogue à Vatican II et au Synode de 1974, ᵀ*Chalon* Colette: → 379, Vatican II Bilan 3 (1988) 237-262 / 263-280.

9046 **Duquoc** C.,   Des églises provisoires 1985 → 1,7446 ... 3,7881:   ᴿFoi-Temps 18 (1988) 294-306 (G. *Fourrez*, aussi sur SCHILLEBEECKX).

9047 **Eham** Markus,   Gemeinschaft im Sakrament? Die Frage nach der Möglichkeit sakramentaler Gemeinschaft zwischen katholischen und nichtkatholischen Christen; zur ekklesiologischen Dimension der ökumenischen Frage [Diss. München]: EurHS 23/293, 1986 → 2,6191:   ᴿTGL 78 (1988) 188s (W. *Beinert*); TLZ 113 (1988) 155-8 (M. *Plathow*).

9048 *Eijk* A.H.C. van,   De sacramentaliteit van de kerk in het oecumenisch gesprek [*Koffeman* L., *Birmelé* A.]: Bijdragen 49 (1988) 195-206.

9049 *Estrada* Juan A.,   La configuración monárquica del primado papal: EstE 63 (1988) 165-188.

9050 *Famerée* Joseph,   'Chrétiens désunis' du P. CONGAR; 50 ans après: NRT 110 (1988) 666-686.

9050* **Fellows** Ward J., The dilemma of universalism and particularism in four Christian theological views of the relation of Christianity to other religions: diss. Union Theol. Sem. NY 1988. – RelStR 15,191.

9051 *Fleischer* Manfred, Lutheran and Catholic reunionists in the age of Bismarck: ChH Centennial Sup (1988) 89-107.

9052 *Floristán* C., La tensión unidad-pluralismo: IglV 127 (1987) 7-18.

9053 *Fortino* Eleuterio F., I dialoghi ecumenici come espressione di testimonianza comune: NuovaUm 9,50 (1987) 63-84.

9054 **Fries** Heinrich, *Pesch* Otto H., Streiten für die eine Kirche: Evangelium konkret 1987 → 3,7794: ᴿActuBbg 25 (1988) 82s (J. *Boada*); HerdKorr 42 (1988) 98 (U. *Ruh*); JEcuSt 25 (1988) 475s (A. *Turfa*); ÖkRu 37 (1988) 242-4 (K. *Raiser*); TGL 78 (1988) 189s (W. *Beinert*); TPhil 63 (1988) 296s (W. *Löser*).

9055 **Fries** H., *Rahner* K., a) Einigung der Kirchen 1983 → 64,7081 ... 2,6195: ᴿRTPhil 120 (1988) 113s (J.-E. *Bertholet*). – b) Unione delle chiese, possibilità reale 1986 → 2,6197; 3,7796: ᴿEstBib 46 (1988) 417-9 (J. L. *Larrabe*). – c) La unión de las iglesias, una posibilidad real 1987 → 3,7797: ᴿComSev 21 (1988) 107s (V. J. *Ansede Alonso*).

9056 **Garcías Palou** Sebastián, Ramón LLULL en la historia del ecumenismo. Barc 1986, Herder. 403 p. – ᴿLumenVr 37 (1988) 180 (U. *Gil Ortega*).

9057 a) *Gassmann* Günther, Baptism, Eucharist and Ministry; preliminary results and perspectives of an ecumenical process; – b) *Shannon* David, ... a personal reflection; – c) *Gros* Jeffrey, ... reception of the ecumenical movement in the Roman Catholic Church: AmBapQ 7,1 (1988) 25-37 / 15-24 / 38-49 [< ZIT].

9058 ᴱ**Gatwa** Tharcisse, *Buss* Théo, Culture et communication œcuménique; compte rendu d'un séminaire international Rwanda/Kigali 13-21 janv. 1986/7 → 3,631: ᴿRTLv 19 (1988) 230-3 (A. de *Halleux*, also on five cognate WCC pamphlets).

9059 *Geisen* Richard, Anthroposophie und Christentum; Anmerkungen zu einer Einladung [*Schröder* H., al., Christentum, Anthroposophie, Waldorfschule ... 1987]: TGL 78 (1988) 266-276.

9060 **Girault** René, *Nicolas* Albert, Sans tricher ni trahir 1985 → 2,6203: ᴿJEcuSt 25 (1987) 458 (G. *MacGregor*).

9061 ᴱ**Glass** Horst, *Bieger* Eckhard, Das Kirchen- und Religionsverständnis von Katholiken und Protestanten [zu *Köcher* Renate, Befragung im Vorfeld des Katholikentags Aachen 1986]. Mü 1988, Allgemein Gemeinnützige Programmges. 99 p. DM 8,20. – ᴿTGL 78 (1988) 447s (T. *Herr*).

9062 **Guthrie** Shirley C.ᴶ, Diversity in faith – unity in Christ 1986 → 2,6204*: ᴿInterpretation 42 (1988) 100 (R. D. *Zimany*).

9063 *Halleux* André de, a) Le décret chalcédonien sur les prérogatives de la nouvelle Rome: ETL 64 (1988) 288-323. – b) Une nouvelle étape du dialogue catholique-orthodoxe; le texte de Valamo: RTLv 19 (1988) 459-473.

9064 *Hamann* H. P., The Smalcald Articles as a systematic theology; a comparison with the Augsburg Confession: ConcordTQ 52,1 (1988) 29-40 [< ZIT 88,587].

9065 *Hambye* E. R., Problems and prospects of ecumenism in the Eastern Catholic churches: Christian Orient 9,1 (1988) 34-38.

9066 *Haugaard* William P., Richard HOOKER; evidences of an ecumenical vision from a twentieth-century perspective: JEcuSt 24 (1987) 427-439.

9067 *Held* Heinz J., Forderungen des Evangeliums; neutestamentliche Gedanken zum Thema der Gerechtigkeit in der ökumenischen Debatte: ÖkRu 37 (1988) 164-176.

9068 **Helleman** Adrian A., One flock, one shepherd [Jn 10,16 applies only to Christ; its preemption by Roman authority is a stumbling block to relations with other churches]; a study of the relationship of ecumenism and the mission of the contemporary Roman Catholic Church; diss. Calvin Sem., ᴰ*Recker* R. GR 1988. ix-155 p. + bibliog. – CalvinT 23 (1988) 303s.

9069 *Hengsbach* Friedhelm, Verdirbt politische Pluralität den Katholizismus? Anmerkungen zu einem wenig diskutierten Thema: HerdKorr 42 (1988) 335-340.

9070 *Herms* Eilert, Einigkeit in Fundamentalen; Probleme einer ökumenischen Programmformel: ÖkRu 37 (1988) 46-66.

9070* *a*) *Hintzen* Georg, Wo liegt die evangelisch-katholische Grunddifferenz?; – *b*) *Hardt* Michael, Papsttum und Ökumene; über die Möglichkeiten eines universalen Petrusdienstes: Catholica 42 (1988) 274-303 / 304-321.

9071 **Huwyler** Christoph, Das Problem der Interkommunion, dargestellt anhand kirchlicher Verlautbarungen, ökumenischer Dokumente und der theologischen Diskussion. Bad Honef 1984, Boek & H. 899 p. [2 vol.] DM 98. 3-88347-127-5. – ᴿTGʟ 78 (1988) 453s (W. *Beinert*).

9072 **Jacobs** J., Met het oog op een andere kerk 1986 → 3,7823: ᴿNedTTs 42 (1988) 264 (W. *Nijenhuis*); RHE 83 (1988) 850 (C. *Soetens*).

9073 **Jurich** James P., The ecumenical relations of Victor de BUCK S.J., with Anglican leaders on the eve of Vatican I: diss. ᴰ*Aubert* R. LvN 1988. ix-823 p. (3 vol.) – RTLv 19,410 (résumé).

9074 *Karmiris* Ioannis N., Ⓖ Orthodox-Protestant dialogue: TAth... 59 (1988) 7-47 . 209-229 . 409-437 . 609-659 [Eng. 919].

9074* ᴱ**Kertelge** Karl, Die Autorität der Schrift in der ökumenischen Gespräch: ÖkRu Beih 50, 1982/5 → 2,381: ᴿÉTRel 63 (1988) 153 (M. *Spindler*).

9075 **Kinnamon** Michael, Truth and community; diversity and its limits in the ecumenical movement. GR 1988, Eerdmans. 117 p. $9. – ᴿTS 49 (1988) 584s (J. *Gros*).

9076 *Klauck* H.-J., Eucharist and church community in Paul [< WissWeis 49,1 (1986) 1-14], ᵀᴱ*Asen* B.A.: TDig 35 (1988) 19-24.

9077 **Klausnitzer** Wolfgang, Das Papstamt im Disput zwischen Lutheranern und Katholiken; Schwerpunkte von der Reformation bis zur Gegenwart [→ 3,7831, Hab.-Diss. Innsbruck, ᴰ*Kern* W.]: InnsbrTSt 20, 1987: ᴱETL 64 (1988) 482-4 (A. de *Halleux*); JEcuSt 25 (1988) 299s (E. W. *Gritsch*); TGʟ 78 (1988) 281-3 (W. *Beinert*: PAUL VI 1967 hatte Recht; das Papsttum ist schwerstes Hindernis auf dem Weg zur Einheit); TrierTZ 97 (1988) 248 (H. *Schützeichel*).

9078 **Kraan** J. D., Bijbel en andersgelovigen; naar een bijbelse basis voor de ontmoeting met andersgelovigen. Kampen 1987, Kok. 217 p. ƒ34,50. 90-242-5341-3 – ᴿTsTNijm 28 (1988) 429 (R. *Bakker*).

9079 ᶠKRETSCHMAR Georg, Kirchengemeinschaft, Anspruch und Wirklichkeit, ᴱHauschild W.-D., *al.* 1986 → 2,56: ᴿOrChrPer 54 (1988) 246-8 (W. de *Vries*).

9080 **Krieger** David J., Das interreligiöse Gespräch; methodologische Grundlagen der Theologie der Religionen. Z 1986, Theol.-V. 183 p. – ᴿZMiss-RW 72 (1988) 78s (H. *Waldenfels*).

9081 *Kuncheria* Pathil, Unity and diversity; the Christian model of unity [*al.*, diversity in Islam, Buddhism, Sikhs etc.]; JDharma 12 (1987) 36-56 [6-35].

9082 ᴱLegrand Hervé, *Meyer* Harding, Face à l'unité; l'ensemble des textes adoptés (1972-1985) 1986 ⇒ 2,6218; 3,660*: ᴿGregorianum 69 (1988) 173s (J. *Wicks*).

9083 ᴱLehmann K., *Pannenberg* W., Lehrverurteilungen — kirchentrennend? 1986 ⇒ 3,661: ᴿJEcuSt 25 (1988) 300s (G. H. *Tavard*); MüTZ 39 (1988) 215s (G. *Schütz*).

9084 **Lin** J. van., Jezus Christus en andersgelovigen in Nederland; tussen praktijk en theologie in school en plaatselijke kerk. Kampen 1988, Kok. 142 p. ƒ24,75. 90-242-5171-0. – ᴿTsTNijm 28 (1988) 429 (R. *Bakker*).

9085 *Link* Christian, *al.* Sie aber hielten fest an der Gemeinschaft ...; Einheit der Kirche als Prozess im NT und heute. Z 1988, Benziger / Reinhardt. 275 p. 3-545-24071-1 / 3-7245-0612-0.

9086 ᴱLink Hans-Georg, *a*) Apostolic faith today, a handbook for study: Faith and Order 124, 1985 ⇒ 2,5841, cf. supra ⇒ 382 [=] *b*) Gemeinsam glauben und bekennen, Handbuch zum apostolischen Glauben. Pd/Neuk 1987, Bonifatius/Neuk.-V. 363 p. 3-87088-521-1 / 3-7887-1250-3. – ᴿBijdragen 49 (1988) 455-7 (M. *Parmentier*).

9087 *Löser* Werner, Das erste und das dritte Rom [Moskau] – Annäherungen im Dialog: Catholica 42 (1988) 195-208.

9088 **McGrath** Alister, ARCIC II and justification; an evangelical Anglican assessment of 'Salvation and the Church': Latimer Studies 26. Ox 1987, Latimer. 56 p. £1,50. 0-946307-25-3. – ᴿJEH 39 (1988) 641s (H. *Chadwick*).

9089 **Maddox** Randy, Toward an ecumenical foundational theology ᴰ1982/4 ⇒ 1,6411: ᴿJEcuSt 24 (1987) 118 (L. L. *Bundy*).

9090 *a*) *Marty* Martin E., Do Catholics take too much for granted ? – *b*) *Shinn* Roger L., Great expectations and some apprehensions: America 157 (1987) 406-8 / 399-402.

9091 **Mascall** E. L., The triune God; an ecumenical study. Worting 1986, Churchman. 86 p. £3 pa. – ᴿJEcuSt 25 (1988) 301s (R. *Penaskovic*).

9092 *May* John D., Integral ecumenism: JEcuSt 25 (1988) 573-591.

9093 ᴱMeeking Basil, *Stott* John, The Evangelical-Roman Catholic dialogue on mission, 1977-1984; a report 1986 ⇒ 2,468; 3,7851: ᴿRTLv 19 (1988) 234 (A. de *Halleux*); ScotBEv 6 (1988) 126s (C. M. *Cameron*).

9094 *Meyer* Harding, L'apostolicité de la foi et de la doctrine: PosLuth 36 (1988) 241-257 [< ZIT 89,230].

9095 *a*) *Meyer* Harding, Consensus et communion ecclésiale; – *b*) *Fleinert-Jensen* Flemming, Église universelle et identité confessionnelle: PosLuth 36 (1988) 91-122 / 123 ... [< ZIT 88,524].

9096 ᴱMiller John W., Interfaith dialogue, four approaches 1986 ⇒ 2,471*; 3,7853: – ᴿJEcuSt 24 (1987) 653 (J. D. *May*).

9097 *Moingt* Joseph, Diálogo de religiones [Rencontre des religions: Études 366 (1987) 97-110 ⇒ 3,a954], ᵀᴱ*Anglés* Jaime: SelT 27 (1988) 151-7.

9098 **Molendijk** Arie L., Getuigen ... 1986 ⇒ 2,6232; 3,7856: ᴿNedTTs 42 (1988) 271s (H. *Berkhof*); RAfT 11 (1987) 288s (R. de *Haes*).

9099 **Montefiore** (bp.) Hugh, So near and yet so far; Rome, Canterbury and ARCIC 1986 ⇒ 2,6234; 3,7857: ᴿNBlackf 68 (1987) 311-3 (A. *Stacpoole*).

9100 **Moran** Bob, A closer look at Catholicism; a guide for Protestants. Waco 1986, Word. 259 p. – ᴿRExp 85 (1988) 376s (B. J. *Leonard*).

9101 *Neufeld* Karl H., Œcuménisme et histoire: NRT 110 (1988) 403-421.

9102 *Neuhaus* Richard J., Ecumenism against itself [Rossner lecture, KC Rockhurst College 1988, unabridged]: TDig 35 (1988) 327-337.

9103 **Neuner** P., Breve manuale dell'Ecumene [1984] 1986 → 3,7866: ᴿAsprenas 35 (1988) 298 (B. *Forte*).

9104 *a*) *Neuner* Peter, Dialog als Methode der Ökumene; – *b*) *Döring* Heinrich, Müssen Spaltungen wirklich sein? – *c*) *Löwe* Hartmut, Die Kirchen vor der Aufgabe der Rezeption von Ergebnissen ökumenischer Gespräche und Verhandlungen; – *d*) *Kühn* Ulrich, Evangelische Rezeption altkirchlicher Bekenntnisse: → 114, ᶠPANNENBERG, Vernunft 1988, 670-687 / 611-636 / 637-651 / 652-669.

9105 *Nossol* Alfons, ℗ Einer ekklesialen eucharistischen Gemeinschaft entgegen: ColcT 58,1 (1988) 5-23; deutsch 23.

9106 *a*) *Onibere* Azuwou, Christian-traditionalist dialogue in Nigeria; – *b*) *Ejizu* Christopher I., Liminality in the contemporary Nigerian experience: AfTJ 16 (1987) 173-189 / 159-172 [< TKontext 10/1,17].

9107 *a*) *Ottlyk* Ernö, ⓜ Millennium of the Russian Orthodox church, I; – *b*) *Vischer* Lukas, ⓜ Kyrill LOUKARIS' heritage; contribution to the Orthodox-Reformed dialogue, ᵀ*Karasszon* I.: Theologiai Szemle 31 (1988) 67-72 ... / 78-85.

9108 **Papandreou** Damaskinos, ⓖ Dialoghi teologici; una prospettiva ortodoxa. Thessaloniki 1986, Kyriakidis. 356 p. – ᴿOrChrPer 54 (1988) 249-251 (J. *Spiteris*).

9109 *Ramón Villar* José, Ecumenismo e Iglesia particular; la teología de lengua francesa (1945-1959); ScripTPamp 20 (1988) 11-61; lat. 61s; Eng. 62s.

9110 **Rausch** Thomas P., The roots of the Catholic tradition [primacy, Mary, Eucharist, sacramentality: origins have to be reassessed also by Protestants] 1986 → 3,1462: ᴿBibTB 18 (1988) 118 (D. P. *Killen*).

9111 *Rausch* Thomas P., Unity and diversity in New Testament ecclesiology; twenty-five years after KÄSEMANN and BROWN [1963 Faith and Order conference: is ecumenism really so important?]: IrTQ 54 (1988) 131-9.

9112 **Robb** Edmund W. & Julia, The betrayal of the Church [... leftist ecumenism]. Westchester IL 1986, Crossway. 296 p. $9 pa. – ᴿCalvaryB 4,1 (1988) 79s (A. *Counterman*).

9113 *Ruggieri* G., Il vicolo cieco dell'ecumenismo: CrNSt 9 (1988) 563-615.

9114 **Saayman** W.A., Unity and mission: Manualia 28. Pretoria 1984 = 1988, Univ. 146 p. $8.80. 0-86981-313-7. – ᴿJEcuSt 23 (1986) 297s (M.A. *Werner*).

9115 **Sabra** George, Thomas AQUINAS' vision of the Church; fundamentals of an ecumenical ecclesiology [ᴰ1986]: TüTSt 27, 1987 → 3,7885: ᴿColcT 58,4 (1988) 184 (T. *Ludwisiak*). TsTNijm 28 (1988) 410s (H. *Rikhof*).

9116 *Sabra* George, Proselytism, evangelisation and ecumenism: NESTR 9,2 (1988) 23-36.

9117 *Samuel* David, The A.R.C.I.C. agreed statements are not agreeable to Scripture and ... the Church of England: Churchman 102 (L 1988) 151ss [rebuttal *Carey* G.: < ZIT 88,585].

9117* *Sanks* T. Howland, Forms of ecclesiality; the analogical Church: TS 49 (1988) 695-708.

9118 *Sanneh* Lamin, Pluralism and Christian commitment: TTod 45 (1988s) 21-33.

9119 **Santa Ana** Julio de, Ecumenismo y liberación 1987 → 3,7889: ᴿCarthaginensia 4 (1988) 198 (P. *Martínez Fresneda*).

9120 **Sartori** Luigi, Teologia ecumenica; saggi 1987 → 3,288: ᴿAsprenas 35 (1988) 299s (D. *Pacelli*).

9121 **Sawyer** Mary Ruth, Black ecumenism; cooperative social change movements in the Black Church: diss. Duke. Durham NC 1987. – RelStR 14 (1988) 185.

9122 **Schlink** Edmund, Ökumenische Dogmatik 1983 ➤ 65,6793 ... 3,7890*: ᴿActuBbg 25 (1988) 201-3 (J. *Boada*).

9123 *Schlüter* Richard, Zur Didaktik der Ökumene im konfessionellen Religionsunterricht – Versuch eines Zugangs: Catholica 42 (1988) 224-240.

9124 *a*) *Schmidt-Leukel* Perry, Die Suche nach einer Hermeneutik interreligiösen Dialogs; Phasen der ökumenischen Diskussion; – *b*) *Eck* Diana J., Interreligiöser Dialog; was ist damit gemeint?: UnSa 43 (1988) 178-188 / 189-200.

9125 *Schulz* Winfried, Nichtkatholische Christen als Mitglieder in katholischen Vereinigungen?: TGL 78 (1988) 334-351.

9126 *Scott* David A., Salvation and the Church [ARCIC II 1987] and theological truth-claims: JEcuSt 25 (1988) 428-436 (437-444, *Wright* J. R., response).

9127 **Sheard** Robert B., Interreligious dialogue in the Catholic Church since Vatican II; a historical and theological study: Toronto Studies in Theology 31. Lewiston NY 1987, Mellen. x-419 p. $70 [TDig 36,83].

9127* ᴱ**Sheils** W. J., Persecution and toleration [22-23 Meeting, Eccl. Hist. Soc]: Studies in Church History 21, 1984 ➤ 1,646: ᴿHeythJ 29 (1988) 252s (M. J. *Walsh*: one of the best meetings).

9128 **Sheppard** David, *Worlock* Derek [Roman Catholic and Anglican (arch-)bishops of Liverpool], Better together; Christian partnership in a hurt city. L 1988, Hodder & S. XII-292 p. £13. – ᴿTLond 91 (1988) 347-9 (E. S. *Heffer*: includes efforts at reconciliation after Heysel Stadium tragedy).

9128* *Spuler* Bertold, Die Orthodoxen Kirchen 97 / 98: IkiZ 78 (1988) 1-41 / 133-168.

9129 *Stacpoole* Alberic, Early ecumenism, early Yves CONGAR 1904-40; commemoration of the half-century of the beginnings of the World Council of Churches: Month 249 (1988) 502-510. 623-631 [p. 485 of Jan. issue wrongly numbers 1988 volume as 259].

9130 *Sullivan* Francis A., *a*) Il significato dell'affermazione del Vaticano II; la Chiesa di Cristo non 'è' ma 'sussiste' nella Chiesa Cattolica Romana: RasT 29 (1988) 527-538; – *b*) The significance of the Vatican II declaration that the Church of Christ 'subsists in' the Roman Catholic Church: ➤ 380, Vatican II Assessment 2 (1988) 272-287; français ᵀ*Pelchat* Marc ➤ 379, Bilan 2 (1988) 288-314.

9131 **Thomas** M. M., Risking Christ for Christ's sake 1987 ➤ 3,7906: ᴿRTPhil 120 (1988) 244 (K. *Blaser*); TTod 45 (1988s) 248. 250s (D. G. *Dawe,* also on D'COSTA).

9132 ᴱ**Thurian** Max, Churches respond to BEM [I-III, 1986s ➤ 3,472] IV, xii-257 p. $17.50; – V, 190 p.; $12.90; – VI, 141 p. $10.40: Faith & Order 137; 143; 144. Geneva 1987s, WCC. [TDig 35.264]. – ᴿEcuR 40 (1988) 543-5 (P. A. *Crow*: 1-6); ExpTim 99 (1987s) 248s (P. *Badham,* 3); JEcuSt 25 (1988) 303s (J. P. *Gaffney,* 4); RTPhil 120 (1988) 115s (J.-E. *Bertholet,* 1); SVlad 30 (1986) 360-4; 31 (1987) 184-9 (and 162-9, J. *Jorgenson,* 1s).

9133 **Tillard** Jean-Marie R., Église d'églises; l'ecclésiologie de communion 1987 ➤ 3,7911: ᴿBijdragen 49 (1988) 339s (A. van *Eijk*); CC 139 (1988, 3) 95s (G. *Mucci*); EsprVie 98 (1988) 296-9 (P. *Jay*); FoiTemps 19 (1987) 471s (G. *Harpigny*); JEcuSt 25 (1988) 122s (H. *Hatt*); JTS 39 (1988) 649-651 (E. J. *Yarnold*); MélSR 45 (1988) 46s (D. *Baudry*); NRT 110

(1988) 426-8 (A. *Toubeau*); RTLv 19 (1988) 354-9 (A. de *Halleux*: grand et beau); TS 49 (1988) 348-351 (G. H. *Tavard*).

9134 *a*) *Tillard* J.-M.R., The ecclesiological implications of bilateral dialogue; – *b*) *Davis* Kortright, Bilateral dialogue and contextualization; – *c*) *Gassmann* Günther, The relation between bilateral and multilateral dialogues: JEcuSt 28 (1986) 412-423 / 386-399 / 365-372.

9135 *a*) *Tillard* J.-M. R., La réception de Vatican II par les non-Catholiques; – *b*) *Greenacre* Roger, Two aspects of reception; – *c*) *Duprey* Pierre, A Catholic perspective on ecclesial communion; – *d*) *Chadwick* Owen, DÖLLINGER and reunion: ➤ 23, ᶠCHADWICK H., Christian authority 1988, 20-39 / 40-58 / 7-19 / 296-334.

9136 ᴱ**Torrance** Thomas F., Theological dialogue between Orthodox and Reformed Churches ➤ 2,511: [İstanbul 1979, Geneva 1981/3]. E 1985, Scottish Academic. 158 p. £10.50. 0-7073-0436-9. – ᴿScotBEv 6 (1988) 40s (D. F. *Wright*).

9137 **Urban** Hans-Jörg, *Wagner* Harald, Handbuch der Ökumenik I-II, 1985s ➤ 2,654; 3,7918: ᴿJEcuSt 24 (1987) 661-3 (J. T. *Ford*, 1s); PrOrChr 38 (1988) 404s (F. *Gruber*); RelStR 14 (1988) 236 (J. F. *Puglisi*, 1s). – III/1 ➤ 871 supra.

9138 *Vandervelde* George, BEM and the 'hierarchy of truths'; a Vatican contribution to the reception process: JEcuSt 25 (1988) 74-84.

9139 *Vanzan* Piersandro, Un'altra importante tappa nel cammino ecumenico; la risposta cattolica al 'BEM' [Lima 1982]: CC 139 (1988,1) 236-248.

9140 *a*) *Vercruysse* Jos E., A Catholic response [Churches Respond VI, 1988, 1-40; DocCath 85 (1988) 102-119: official but not intended to overrule other Catholic responses, p. 665] to the Faith and Order document on 'Baptism, Eucharist and Ministry': – *b*) *Vandervelde* George, Vatican ecumenism at the crossroads? The Vatican approach to differences with BEM: Gregorianum 69 (1988) 663-687; franç. 688 / 689-710; franç. 711.

9141 ᴱ**Vischer** Lukas, *Karrer* Andreas, Reformed and Roman Catholic in dialogue; a survey of the dialogues at national level. Geneva 1988, World Alliance of Reformed Churches. 112 p. Fs 10. – ᴿJEcuSt 25 (1988) 472s (R. M. *Healey*).

9141* *Vischer* Lukas, [ᴱ*Saxer* Ernst], Que disent aujourd'hui les Églises réformées à propos des condamnations des Anabaptistes dans les confessions de foi réformées?: ÉTRel 63 (1988) 385-401.

9142 *Wainwright* Geoffrey, *al.*, Ecumenical dimensions of George LINDBECK's 'Nature of Doctrine' [and 5 other essays on it]: ModT 4,2 (1988) 121-132 [107-120. 133-209].

9143 *a*) *Wentz* Frederick K., Samuel Simon SCHMUCKER and Philip SCHAFF; nineteenth century ecumenical pioneers; – *b*) *Wicks* Jared, Reform of the Church; a Roman proposal of 1522: CurrTM 15 (1988) 574-588 / 589-596.

9144 *Wiles* Maurice, Christianity and other faiths: some theological reflections: TLond 91 (1988) 302-8.

9144* *Willebrands* Johannes card., Le mystère de la Trinité Sainte et celui de l'Église une et diverse: PrOrChr 38 (1988) 272-280.

9145 **Witte** Henk, 'Alnaargelang hun band met het fundament van het christelijk geloof verschillend is'; Wording en verwerking van de uitspraak over de 'hiërarchie' van waarheden van Vaticanum II 1986 ➤ 3,7927; *f*76,50: ᴿBijdragen 49 (1988) 454s (A. van *Eijk*).

9145* **Wolff** Monika-Maria, Gott und Mensch; Yves CONGARS Beitrag zum ökumenischen Dialog: diss. Pont. Univ. Gregoriana, ᴰ*Neufeld* K. Roma 1988. 424 p. – RTLv 20,554.

9146 **Yarnold** Edward, Can the Roman Catholic and Anglican Churches be reconciled? A short enquiry course. L 1987. SPCK / Catholic Truth Soc. ii-17 p. £0.65. – ᴿTLond 91 (1988) 50-52 (P. *Avis*).

9147 *Ziegler* Albert, ZWINGLI – eine katholische Aufgabe, ein ökumenisches Anliegen: Zwingliana 16 (1985) 201-216.

9148 **Zoghby** Elias, Den zerrissenen Rock flicken... Wie lange wollen Katoliken und Orthodoxen noch warten? 1984 ➤ 65,d378 ᴿZkT 110 (1988) 222 (L. *Lies*).

H7.8 **Amt** – *Ministerium ecclesiasticum.*

9149 *a) Amjad-Ali* Christine M., Ministry in the New Testament; – *b) McVey* Chrys, The concept of ministry: Focus 8 (Multan, Pakistan 1988) 21-27 / 6-20 [< TKontext 10/1,69].

9149* **Areeplackal** Joseph, The pneumatological dimension of ordained ministry as presented by Yves CONGAR and John ZIZIOULAS: diss. Pont. Univ. Gregoriana, ᴰ*Rosato* J.; Extr. Nº 3506. R 1988. xviii-302 p. – RTLv 20,567.

9150 *Barrett* Richard J., Re-discovering the diaconate: PrPeo 2 (1988) 348-355.

9151 *Beyer* Jean, Le principe de subsidiarité; son application en Église: Gregorianum 69 (1988) 435-459 [413-433, in der Soziallehre, *Schasching* Johannes N.].

9152 *Bradshaw* Paul F., Lay people in the Church; some models of ministry: DocLife 37 (1987) 386-399.

9152* **Bressolette** Claude, Le pouvoir dans la société et dans l'Église... MARET 1984 ➤ 1,7597 ... 3,7546: ᴿCahHist 31 (1986) 81s (X. de *Montclos*).

9153 *Cantoni* Piero, Il sacerdozio in SCHEEBEN: Renovatio 23 (1988) 65-95.

9154 **Card** Terence, Priesthood and ministry in crisis [... *Moberly* R., *Congar* Y., *Schillebeeckx* E.]. L 1988, SCM. xi-128 p. £7 pa. – ᴿTLond 91 (1988) 354-6 (B. A. *Smith*).

9155 *Decker* Rodney J., Polity and the Elder issue: GraceTJ 9 (1988) 257-277.

9156 **De Rosa** Peter, Vicars of Christ; the dark side of the papacy. NY 1988, Crown. 484 p. $20. – ᴿHomP 89,10 (1988s) 75-77 (G. W. *Rutler*: 'the Pharisaism of pseudo-intellectuals').

9157 *Eijsink* A. H., Een staaltje van macht? kerkrechtelijke reflectie op de positie van leken in kerkelijke dienst: TsTNijm 28 (1988) 155-172; 172, A question of power; the position of the laity in ecclesiastical functions.

9157* *Fichter* Joseph H., The ordination of episcopal priests [as Roman Catholics]: America 159 (1988) 157-161.

9158 **Fischer** James A., Priests; images, ideals and changing roles. NY 1987, Dodd Mead. xx-100 p. $18 [TDig 35,357].

9159 *Frankemölle* H., Amt NT [AT *Scharbert* J.]: ➤ 804, NBL Lfg 1 (1988) 96-99 [96].

9160 *Fuller* Reginald H., Scripture, tradition and priesthood: ➤ 60, ᶠ*Hanson* R., Scripture 1988, 101-114.

9161 **Gallagher** Charles A., *Vandenberg* Thomas L., The celibacy myth; loving for life 1987 ➤ 3,7965: ᴿSpTod 40 (1988) 168-170 (J. J. *Hughes*: the author disagrees with Cardinal ODDI's 'the priest does not need a personal relationship with any other human being' because he has one with Christ').

9162 **Granfield** Patrick, The limits of the papacy; authority and autonomy in the Church 1987 ➤ 3,4537; also L, Darton-LT, £10: ᴿAmerica 157 (1987) 460-2 (L. *Orsy*); Furrow 39 (1988) 802-5 (P. *Connolly*: well-written); Horizons 15 (1988) 405s (D. J. *Grimes*); Month 249 (1988) 735-745 (B. R. *Brinkman*); Paradigms 4 (1988s) 174s (B. W. *Burton*); PrPeo 2 (1988) 114s (Mary E. *Mills*); RExp 85 (1988) 370s (E. G. *Hinson*); RSPT 72 (1988) 369s (Y. *Congar*: not as its title suggests a restriction of papal authority); Tablet 242 (1988) 173s (G. *Daly*).

9163 *a) Granfield* P., Légitimation et bureaucratisation du pouvoir dans l'Église [= Legitimation and bureaucratisation of ecclesiastical power, Concilium 197 (E 1988) 86-93]; – *b) Torfs* Rik, Auctoritas, potestas, iurisdictio, facultas, officium, munus [eine Begriffsanalyse; IZT 24 (1988) 209-215]; une analyse de concepts: Concilium 217 (P 1988) 109-117 / 81-93.

9164 **Grelot** Pierre, Les ministères dans le peuple de Dieu; lettre à un théologien: Apologique. P 1988, Cerf. 170 p. F 82. 2-204-02894-0. – ᴿÉtudes 369 (1988) 280s (J. *Thomas*); RICathP 28 (1988) 136-8 (F. *Brossier*).

9165 **Grootaers** Jan, Primauté ... PHILIPS 1986 ➤ 3,7969: ᴿBijdragen 49 (1988) 338s (J. *Jacobs*); CC 139 (1988,2) 403s (G. *Mucci*); Gregorianum 69 (1988) 324-331 (G. *Ghirlanda*).

9166 **Gunzel** Raymond J., Celibacy; renewing the gift, releasing the power. KC 1988, Sheed & W. xi-119 p. $9. 1-55612-197-0 [TDig 36,161].

9167 **Halliburton** John, The authority of a bishop [Anglican] 1987 ➤ 3,7971*: ᴿTLond 91 (1988) 52-54 (P. *Coleman*).

9168 **Heimerl** Hans, Der Zölibat; Recht und Gerechtigkeit 1985 ➤ 3,7927: ᴿTLZ 113 (1988) 284s (A. *Stein*).

9169 *Henau* Ernest, De dienst van de liefde in de christelijke geloofsgemeenschap: CollatVL 18 (1988) 5-23.

9170 *Herranz* Julián, Sacerdote ministeriale e legge del celibato: ScuolC 22 (1988) 367-379.

9171 **Hill** Edmund, Ministry and authority in the Catholic Chruch ['a book of advocacy'; favors papal but not 'magisterial papalist' authority, too concentrated; he focuses the results in history]. L 1988, Chapman [Bloomington IN, Meyer-Stone]. $15. 0-225-66527-1 [TDig 36,163, no pp.].

9172 **Hoge** Dean R., The future of Catholic leadership; responses to the priest shortage. KC 1987, Sheed & W. 270 p. $13. – ᴿTTod 45 (1988s) 130. 132 (A. M. *Greeley*: excludes relevance of celibacy).

9173 **Jeschke** Marlin Disciplining in the Church; recovering a ministry of the Gospel. Scottdale PA 1988, Herald. 202 p. 0-8361-3480-X.

9174 *Kasper* Walter, Nochmals; der theologische Status der Bischofskonferenzen: TüTQ 168 (1988) 237-240.

9175 *Kruse* Colin G., NT models for ministry; Jesus and Paul 1983 ➤ 1,7636; 2,6310: ᴿBibTB 18 (1988) 116 (J. *Keating*).

9176 *Lamarche* Paul, Presbytérat NT: ➤ 791, DictSp 12 (1986) 2069-2077 (-2107 *al.*).

9177 *Lawler* Michael, Christian marriage and Christian ministry: SpTod 40 (1988) 135-144.

9178 *Liedke* Gerhard, 'So ist es nicht unter euch' – Herrschaft und Gewalt in der Gemeinde – eine Problemanzeige: TPrac 23,1 ('Aspekte des Gemeindeaufbaus in der Volkskirche' 1988) 49-58 [< ZIT 88,492].

9179 *Lim* David, The development of the monepiscopate in the early Church: StudiaBT 15 (1987) 163-195.
9180 **Lingenfelter** Shirwood, *Mayers* Marvin, Ministering cross-culturally. GR 1986, Baker. 125 p. – ᴿCalvaryB 4,2 (1988) 86s (W. L. *Snyder*).
9181 **McBrien** Richard, Ministry 1987 ➤ 3,7979: ᴿHomP 88,12 (1987s) 85s (J. R. *Sheets*: thin and pretentious); TS 49 (1988) 582 (R. *Kress*: the old clericalism).
9182 **McKee** Elsie A., Elders and the plural ministry; the role of exegetical history in illuminating John CALVINS's theology: TravHumRen 223. Geneva 1988, Droz. 237 p. – ᴿTLZ 113 (1988) 904s (Irena *Backus*).
9183 **Macquarrie** John, Theology, church and ministry 1986 ➤ 2,189; 3,7983: ᴿModT 4 (1987s) 105 (P. *Avis*).
9183* **Maier** H. O., The social setting of the ministry as reflected in the writings of HERMAS, CLEMENT and IGNATIUS: diss. Oxford 1987. – RTLv 20,548.
9184 **Martini** Carlo M., Tun, was Er will; christliches Sendungsbewusstsein nach dem NT. FrB 1987, Herder. 144 p. DM 12,80 [Erb Auf 64,317].
9184* *Martini* Carlo M., Ministero e santità sacerdotale: Ambrosius 64 (1988) 389-399.
Marzotto Damiano, Celibato sacerdotale e celibato di Gesù 1987 ➤ 230.
9185 *Mayer* Bernhard, *Seybold* Michael, Die Kirche als Mysterium in ihren Ämtern und Diensten. Eichstätt 1987. – ᴿTGL 78 (1988) 441s (W. *Knoch*).
9186 *Menking* S., Jesus, the pioneer and perfecter of ministry: PerkinsJ 41,2 (1988) 1-23 [< NTAbs 32,328].
9187 *Mondet* J.-P., Clartés sur le sacerdoce ministériel [CHRYSOSTOME, Héb.]: FoiTemps 18 (1988) 259-286.
9188 **Nicolas** M.-J., La grâce d'être prêtre 1986 ➤ 2,6323; 3,7991: ᴿDocCom 40 (1987) 299s (C. *Petino*); ÉglT 18 (1987) 399s (R. *Quesnel*).
9189 *Nilsen* Else-Brit, Le ministère ordonné dans la tradition catholique et luthérienne: Thèses. 1987 ➤ 3,7992: ᴿNorTTs 89 (1988) 208-211 (Øyvind *Norderval*).
9190 *O'Donnell* Christopher, Does a Eucharistic ecclesiology [cover: theology] involve a married clergy? [*Hickey* R., A case for an auxiliary priesthood 1982]: MilltSt 21 (1988) 117-123.
9191 *O'Malley* John W., Priesthood, ministry, and religious life; some historical and historiographical considerations: TS 49 (1988) 223-257.
9192 *Pottmeyer* Hermann J., Was ist eine Bischofskonferenz?; zur Diskussion um den theologischen Status...: StiZt 206 (1988) 435-446.
9193 *Provost* James H., Ministry; reflections on some canonical issues: HeythJ 29 (1988) 285-299.
9194 **Reumann** John P., Ministries examined; laity, clergy, women and bishops in a time of change. Minneapolis 1987, Augsburg. 272 p. $13. 0-8066-2296-2. – ᴿJEcuSt 25 (1988) 469 (Mosella G. *Mitchell*).
9195 **Runcie** Robert, [Archbishop of Canterbury] Authority in crisis? An Anglican response [US discourses]. L 1988, SCM. ix-52 p. £3 pa. – ᴿTablet 242 (1988) 874s (E. *Yarnold*); TLond 91 (1988) 436s (P. *Coleman*).
9196 *Rutler* George W., A consistent theology of clerical celibacy; new research questions the consistency of a married diaconate: HomP 89,5 (1988s) 9-13.
9197 **Saenz** Alfredo, In persona Christi; la fisionomía espiritual del sacerdote de Cristo. Paraná ARG 1985, Mikael. 471 p. – ᴿGregorianum 69 (1988) 188 (J. *Galot*).

9197* *Schick* Ludwig, Ehe und Ehelosigkeit um des Himmelreiches willen: Ordenskorrespondenz 29,1 (1988) 31-39 > Eng.TDig 36,135-140, ᵀᴱ*Asen* B.

9198 **Schillebeeckx** Edward, *a* Plaidoyer... ministères 1987 ⇥ 3,8008: ᴿRT-Phil 129 (1988) 242 (L. *Rumpf*). – *b*) The Church with a human face 1985 ⇥ 1,7682; 2,6331: ᴿThomist 52 (1988) 158-165 (Joyce A. *Little*).

9199 *Schultze* Harald, 'Das [Bischofs]Amt der Einheit'; praktisch-theologische Reflexionen zum leitenden geistlichen Dienst: TLZ 113 (1988) 81-96.

9200 *Sedgwick* Peter, Recent criticisms of the concept of authority in the Church of England: TLond 91 (1988) 258-266.

9201 *Sobrino* Jon, Hacia una determinación de la realidad sacerdotal; el servicio al acercamiento salvífico de Dios a los hombres: RLAmT 1 (1984) 47-81 [> SelT 26 (1987) 35-50, ᴱ*Farràs* Josep].

9202 **Steele** David A., Images of leadership and authority for the Church; biblical principles and secular models. Lanham MD 1986, UPA. xvii-187 p. $23.50; pa. $13.25 [CBQ 51,190].

9203 *Stott* John R. W., Christian ministry in the 21st century, 1. The world's challenge to the Church; 2. The Church's mission in the world; 3. Christian preaching in the contemporary world [4. ideals of pastoral ministry]: Bibliotheca Sacra 145 (1988) 123-132 / 243-253 / 363-370 [vol. 146...]

9204 *a*) *Sykes* Stephen, Episcopacy, communion and collegiality; – *b*) *Nazir-Ali* Michael, Episcopacy and communion; Church, culture and change: Anvil 5 (1988) 101-112 / 119-132 [< ZIT 88,508].

9204* *Tourneux* André, L'évêque, l'eucharistie et l'église locale: ETL 64 (1988) 106-141.

9205 *Trilling* Wolfgang, *a*) Zum 'Amt' im NT; eine methodologische Besinnung [< TJb 1984, 453-475]; – *b*) Zum Petrusamt im NT [< TüTQ 151 (1971) 110-133]; – *c*) Zur Entstehung des Zwölferkreises; eine geschichtskritische Überlegung [< ᶠ*Schürmann* H. 1977, 201-222]; – *d*) Amt und Amtsverständnis bei Matthäus [< ᶠ*Rigaux* B. 170 = WegFo 439 (1977) 524-542]: ⇥ 275, Studien 1988, 333-364 / 111-139 / 185-208 / 77-92.

9206 *Valdrine* P., Prêtre: ⇥ 786, Catholicisme 11 (1988) 873-894.

9207 **Vanhoye** A., OT priests and the new Priest according to the NT 1986 ⇥ 2,6343; 3,8024: ᴿHomP 88,4 (1987s) 73s (J. R. *Sheets*: adapts scholarship to a current need).

9208 *Vanhoye* H., Sacerdozio / Ebrei / Carisma: ⇥ 806, NDizTB (1988) 1387-1398 / 430-7 / 245-250.

9209 *Vercruysse* Jos, Il ministero ordinato nel dialogo ecumenico: RasT 29 (1988) 445-459.

9210 *Wasser* Greg, Pastor-elder-overseer [James 5,13-16; Acts 11,27-30; 14,21-23; 15,1-23; 20,17-38; Eph 4,11-16; Phlp 1,1; 1 Tim 3,1-7; 5,17-19; 1 Pt 5,1-4]: CalvaryB 4,1 (1988) 61-75.

9211 ᴱ**Witte** H.P.J., *Geurts* T.M.J. Erkenning zonder vernieuwing? Een kritische doorlichting van de luthers/rooms-katholieke dialoog over het ambt in de kerk. Haag 1988, Sint Willibrord. 208 p. *f* 25. 90-7036550-2. – ᴿTsTNijm 28 (1988) 321 (W. *Boelens*).

H8   *Liturgia; oratio, vita spiritualis – NT –* **Prayer.**

9212 *Agresi* Giuliano, L'originale preghiera cristiana: Magistero salvifico. CasM 1986, Piemme. 88 p. – ᴿSalesianum 50 (1988) 255s (A. M. *Triacca*).

9213 *Alonso Schökel* Luis, → 4796-9 ℗ Liturgia aktu pokuty i pojednania [< Meditaciones bíblicas sobre la Eucaristia, parte 2 (1986)], ᵀ*Witczyk* Henryk: Współczesna ambona 16,1 (Kielce 1988) 123-8.

9214 ᴱ**Ancilli** Ermanno, La preghiera; Bibbia, teologia, esperienze storiche. R 1988, Città Nuova. I, 514 p. [Bibbia: *Garofalo* S., 41-72; NT *Helewa* G., 73-106]; II. 471 p. [237-386, prassi meditative asiatiche; Yoga, Zen...]. 88-311-9220-5.

9215 *Angelini* Giuseppe, La devozione al Sacro Cuore; saggio di riflessione teologico-pratica: TItSett 13 (1988) 45-64; Eng. 64: efforts of theologians like RAHNER ignored the 'historical-practical quality', here developed around themes of 'apostasy' 'pain and sorrow' 'feeling or sentiment'.

9216 *Arts* Herwig, À la recherche d'une nouvelle spiritualité: FoiTemps 18 (1988) 63-77 = Naar een nieuwe spiritualiteit?: CollatVL 17 (1987) 166-177.

9217 *Bachl* Gottfried, Thesen zum Bittgebet: → 648, Vorsehung 1987/8, 192-207.

9217* **Baldovin** John F., The urban character of Christian worship 1987 → 3,8037: ᴿPrOrChr 38 (1988) 401 (F. *Gruber*).

9218 *Banks* Robert, Meditation in Reformed perspective [*Baxter* R. 1650]: RefTR 46 (1987) 10-16.

9219 **Bernard** Charles A., Traité de théologie spirituelle 1986 → 3,8043: ᴿTS 49 (1988) 184s (W. C. *Marceau*).

9220 *Biedermann* H. M. [*Mutius* H. G. v.], Gebet: → 803, LexMA 4,6 (1988) 1155-8 [-9, Judentum].

9221 **Boever** Richard A., Finding God in everyday life. Liguori MO Publications 1988. 63 p. $2 pa. [TDig 36,47].

9222 **Boguniowski** Józef, 'Domus Ecclesiae'; der Ort der Eucharistiefeier in den ersten Jahrhunderten: Diss. Pont. Ist. Liturgico, ᴰ*Neunheuser* B. R 1986s. – EcOrans 4 (1987) 83.

9223 **Booty** John E., The Christ we know [Anglican and all-Christian spirituality]. CM 1987, Cowley. vii-174 p. $10 [TDig 35,342]. 0-936384-48-4. – ᴿRExp 85 (1988) 366 (E. G. *Hinson*).

9224 **Brock** Sebastian, The Syriac Fathers on prayer and the spiritual life: Cistercian Studies 101, 1987 → 3,8047: ᴿRHE 83 (1988) 794 (A. de *Halleux*).

9225 *Budzin* Allan J., JOVINIAN's four theses on the Christian life; an alternative patristic spirituality: TorJT 4 (1988) 44-59.

9226 **Burini** Clara, *Cavalcanti* Elena, La spiritualità della vita quotidiana negli scritti dei Padri. Bo 1988, Dehoniane. 304 p. – ᴿGitFg 40 (1988) 155s (Germana *Eichberg*).

9227 **Carretto** Carlo, Né pour l'éternité [en italien 'Un chemin sans fin']: Maranatha 15. P/Montréal 1987, Médiaspaul/Paulines. 158 p. F 66. – ᴿEsprVie 98 (1988) 673 [P. *Jay*: fervent, pastoral; 'l'auteur ne veut pas être théologien; mais cela donne trop d'assurance à la théologie qu'il fait quand même).

9228 **Carroll** Thomas K., *Halton* Thomas, Liturgical practice in the Fathers: Message of the Fathers of the Church 21. Wilmington 1988, Glazier. 342 p. 0-89453-324-X; pa. 61-4.

9229 **Casas García** V., Cristo al encuentro del hombre; hacia una espiritualidad cristiano-evangélica. M 1988, Clarentianas [sic, Antonianum 63, 617]. 344 p.

9230 **Castillo** J. M., El seguimiento de Jesús 1986 → 3,8050: ᴿCiuD 201 (1988) 191s (S. *Folgado Flórez*).

9231 *Chadwick* G., Praying the Scriptures: Search 10,2 (1987) 83-88 [NTAbs 32,141].
9232 **Corbon** Jean, The wellspring of worship, ᵀ*O'Connell* Matthew J. NY 1988, Paulist. vi-200 p. $13 pa. [TDig 36,55].
9233 **Cothenet** Édouard, Exégèse et liturgie; pref. *Gy* P.-M.: LDiv 133. P 1988, Cerf. 356 p. F 200. 2-204-02931-9.
9234 **Crichton** J. D., The living Christ; 'in Christ' through Scripture and liturgy. L 1988, Collins. 113 p. £2.50. – ᴿNBlackf 69 (1988) 555 (Mary *Neave*).
9235 **Cusson** Gilles, Biblical theology and the [Loyola I.] Spiritual Exercises; a method toward a personal experience of God as accomplishing within us his plan of salvation [³Pédagogie 1968], ᵀ*Roduit* Mary A., *Ganss* George E. St. Louis 1988, Institute of Jesuit Sources. xv-185 p. $24; pa. $19.50 [TDig 35,160] 0-912422-01-7; pa. 0-9. – ᴿSpTod 40 (1988) 369-371 (M. *Cooper*).
9236 **Dal Covolo** Enrico, Letture bibliche per la preghiera e per la vita; passi scelti e commentati AT-NT; pref. *Saldarini* G.; appendice *Cimosa* M. T 1987, Elle Di Ci. 167 p. – ᴿPalCler 67 (1988) 206 (G. *Lavarda*); Salesianum 50 (1988) 297.
9237 **Dezza** Paolo, Esercizi ignaziani. R/Mi 1987, CC/San Fedele. 320 p. Lit. 10.000. – ᴿCC 138 (1988,1) 409 (G. *Caprile*: ha preferito non seguire alla lettera lo schema ignaziano).
9238 **Dieter** Melvin E., and representatives of four other 'schools', Five views on sanctification. GR 1987, Zondervan. 254 p. $8. – ᴿBS 145 (1988) 107 (K. L. *Sarles*: superb).
9239 **Diletto** Lorenzo, Cronache del Monte Athos [ricordi di soggiorno ott. 1982 – magg. 1983], pref. *Povero* Orfeo. Valleripa Linato FO, Risurrezione. xii-270 p. Lit. 20.000. – ᴿCC 139 (1988,2) 408 (T. *Špidlík*).
9240 *a) Dunnett* Walter M., Scholarship and spirituality; – *b) Waltke* Bruce, Evangelical spirituality; a biblical scholar's perspective: JEvTS 31 (1988) 1-8 / 9-24 [< ZIT 88,514].
9241 **Dwyer** Vincent [Cistercian founder of Center for Human Development, ND 1975, Wsh since 1980], Lift your sails, the challenge of being a Christian. GCNY 1987, Doubleday. xxiii-189 p. $15 [TDig 35,266].
9242 **Eisenbach** Franziskus, Die Gegenwart Jesu Christi im Gottesdienst; systematische Studien zur Liturgiekonstitution des II. Vatikanischen Konzils [Diss. Fr ᴰ*Lehmann* K. 1981] 1982 → 65,6962; 1,7739: ᴿRTLv 19 (1988) 359-362 (A. *Tourneux*).
9243 *Evenepoel* Willy, La délimitation de 'l'année liturgique' dans les premiers siècles de la chrétienté occidentale; caput anni liturgici [not always/only March (1 or 25), as A. *Chavasse* 1952]: RHE 83 (1988) 601-616.
9244 *Faricy* Robert, The heart of Christ in the spirituality of TEILHARD de Chardin: Gregorianum 69 (1988) 261-276; franç. 277.
  Federici Tommaso, Per conoscere Lui e la potenza della resurrezione di lui; per una lettura teologica del lezionario 1987 → 1892.
9246 *Ferrando* M. A., La religiosidad popular en la perspectiva del Nuevo Testamento [... patrística, *Meis* A.]: TVida 28 (1987) 7-22 [23-40].
9247 *Flanagan* Kieran, Liturgy as play; a hermeneutics of ritual re-presentation: ModT 4 (1987s) 345-372.
9247* **Gibson** James E., Mimetic action; hermeneutic and therapeutic applications of mystical re-enactment: diss Temple. Ph 1988. – RelStR 15,189.

9248 ^E**Goffi** Tullo, *Piana* Giannino, Corso di Morale, 5. Liturgia: Etica della religiosità. Brescia 1986, Queriniana. 549 p. – ^REcOrans 4 (1987) 122s (A. *Nocent*).

9249 **Green** Thomas H., Come down Zacchaeus; spirituality and the laity. ND 1988, Ave Maria. 171 p. $6 [TDig 35,168].

9250 *Grelot* Pierre, La prière dans la Bible: → 791, DictSpir XII (1986) 2217-2247 [-2347 *al.*; 2196-2217, milieu].

9251 *Guillet* Jacques, Recherche de Dieu: → 791, DictSpir XIII,86 (1987) 211-7.

9252 **Guilbert** P., Il ressuscite le troisième jour [= l'existence chrétienne dans son ensemble]: Racines. P 1987, Nouvelle Cité. 256 p. F 116. 2-85313-18-5. – ^REsprVie 98 (1988) 84s (P. *Jay*).

9253 **Hall** Thelma sr., Too deep for words; rediscovering lectio divina with 500 Scripture texts for prayer. NY 1988, Paulist. vi-110 p. $5 pa. [BibTB 18/3 cover].

9254 *Henry* A.-M. †, Prière: → 786, Catholicisme 11 (1988) 909-971.

9255 **Jálics** Francisco, El encuentro con Dios²: Construir 23. Florida BA 1988, Paulinas. 157 p. 950-09-0764-X.

9256 *Janssens* Jos, Martirio ed esperienza spirituale nella Chiesa Antica: RasT 29 (1988) 361-381.

9257 *Jantzen* Grace M., Review article; recent writing in spirituality: TLond 91 (1988) 405-412.

9258 ^E**Jones** C. al., The study of spirituality 1986 → 3,420: ^RNBlackf 69 (1988) 47s (J. *Aumann*).

9259 **Kilmartin** E. J., Christian liturgy..., 1. Systematic theology of liturgy. KC 1988, Sheed & W. XI-405 p. $ 17. – ^RTS 49 (1988) 760-2 (C. W. *Gusmer*).

9259* *Klein* Christoph, Das Gebet in der Begegnung zwischen westlicher und ostkirchlicher Theologie und Frömmigkeit: KerDo 34 (1988) 232-249; Eng. 250.

9260 **Kolvenbach** Peter Hans, In cammino verso la Pasqua [Esercizi dati al Papa e alla Curia romana, Quaresima 1987]. R 1988, Civiltà Cattolica. 240 p. Lit. 20.000 [CC 139/4 cover].

9261 *Kurek* Ryszard, ❷ Biblica orientazione della meditazione pacomiana: → 73, ^FKANIA W. = VoxPa 12s (1987s) 247-259; ital. 259.

9262 **Kurichianil** John, Before thee face to face; a study on prayer in the Bible. Bangalore 1987, Asian TC. xiii-204 p. rs 30 [TDig 35,275].

9263 **La Potterie** Ignace de, Il mistero del cuore trafitto; fondamenti biblici della spiritualità del Cuore di Gesù: StBDeh 15. Bo 1988, Dehoniane. 183 p. 88-10-40716-4.

9264 **Leuenberger** Samuel, Cultus ancilla Scripturae; das Book of Common Prayer als erweckliche Liturgie – ein Vermächtnis des Puritanismus [Diss. Stellenbosch 1984]: Theol. Diss. 17. Ba 1986, Reinhardt. 404 p. DM 38. – ^RTLZ 113 (1988) 61-63 (H.-C. *Schmidt-Lauber*).

9265 ^E**McGinn** B., *Meyendorff* J., Christian spirituality; origins to the twelfth century: EWSp 16, 1985 → 1,371*; 3,8087: ^RChH 57 (1988) 528-530 (F. W. *Norris*); RelStR 14 (1988) 25-27 (C.M.N. *Eire*); RRel 46 (1987) 791s (F. G. *McLeod*).

9266 *Maggioni* B., Preghiera: → 806, NDizTB (1988) 1216-1231.

9267 *Marchesi* Giovanni, Il Cuore di Cristo, centro dell'incarnazione di Dio e della redenzione dell'uomo: CC 139 (1988,2) 440-452.

9268 **Martini** Carlo M., Hombres de paz y de reconciliación [Uomini di pace, esercizi per seminaristi di Saronno 1984 ^T*Ferrero* de G. V. Grazia &

Luigi: Servidores y Testigos 36. Santander 1988, Sal Terrae. 144 p. 84-293-0802-4 – ᴿActuBbg 25 (1988) 267s (I. *Riudor*).

9269 **Martini** Carlo M., Through Moses to Jesus; the way of the paschal mystery, ᵀ*Skerry* sr. M. Theresilide. ND 1988, Ave Maria. 123 p. $5 [TDig 35,378].

9270 *Mauri* Margarita, Recientes aportaciones al tema de la virtud: Actu-Bbg 25 (1988) 1-29.

9271 **Miles** Margaret R., Practicing Christianity; critical perspectives for an embodied spirituality. NY 1988, Crossroad. xi-207 p. $20. 0-8245-0904-8 [TDig 36,175].

9272 **Navone** John, Teologia del fallimento ²ʳᵉᵛ. R 1988, Gregoriana. 245 p. Lit. 17.000. – ᴿCC 139 (1988,3) 541 (G. *Ferraro*: si può dire 'teologia della Croce' in rapporto con la comunicazione odierna).

9273 *Navone* John, Tre interpretazioni della vita; bucolica, tragica e melodrammatica [... per conoscere meglio la Scrittura]: CC 139 (1988,4) 545-558.

9274 *Navone* John, The real self in communion (*koinōnía*): PrPeo 2 (1988) 285-290.

9275 **Old** Hughes O., Worship (guides to the Reformed tradition). Atlanta 1986, Knox. 202 p. £6.50 pa. 0-8042-3252-0. – ᴿScotBEv 6 (1988) 51-53 (J. *Stein*).

9276 *Olfors* Stephen F., The place of Scripture in Baptist worship: RExp 85 (1988) 19-31 [-85, *al.*].

9277 **Pable** Martin W., A man and his God; contemporary male spirituality. ND 1988, Ave Maria. 143 p. $6. 0-87793-380-4 [TDig 36,177]. → 9884.

9277* **Pannenberg** Wolfhart, Christliche Spiritualität; theologische Aspekte [Eng. 1983 → 1,7793]. Gö 1986, Vandenhoeck & R. 102 p. – ᴿRTPhil 120 (1988) 242s (D. *Müller*).

9278 *Parinthirickal* Mathew, Christian asceticism; imitation of Christ: Jeevadhara 13 (1988) 415-427.

9278* **Ratzinger** Joseph card., The feast of faith; approaches to a theology of the liturgy [1981, mostly reprints] ᵀ*Harrison* G. SF 1986, Ignatius. 153 p. – ᴿTLZ 113 (1988) 285s (H. *Kirchner*: wozu?).

9279 *Richard* Pablo, El fundamento material de la espiritualidad [< Estudos B 7, ᵀ*Cervantes* Carlos:] Christus 53, 613s (Méx 1988) 88-95.

9280 **Richards** Lawrence O., A practical theology of spirituality, 1987 → 3,8106: ᴿGraceTJ 9 (1988) 159s (G. T. *Meadors*).

9281 **Ruffini** Eliseo mons., Commento alle letture patristiche della Liturgia delle Ore. CinB 1986, Paoline. 664 p. – ᴿSalesianum 50 (1988) 263s (A. *Cuva*).

9282 *Schick* Ludwig, Ehe und Ehelosigkeit um des Himmelreiches willen: Ordenskorrespondenz 29 (Köln 1988) 31-39 [> TDig 36,135].

9283 *Schwager* Raymond, Imiter et suivre: Christus 34 (P 1987) 5-18 [> SelT 27 (1988) 173-8, ᵀᴱ*Muñoz* Maxim].

9284 **Shaw** Graham, God in our hands. L 1987, SCM. xvi-256 p. £10 pa. – ᴿTLond 91 (1988) 499s (D. *Nineham*: a book on prayer for an age in which 'the objective existence of God is no longer credible' but this by no means implies the end of religion).

9285 **Sion** Victor, Réalisme de l'Incarnation; Dieu est à nous. P 1987, Lethielleux. 189 p. – ᴿEsprVie 98 (1988) 266s (P. *Jay*: spiritualité).

9286 *Smolarski* Dennis C., The spirituality of computers [... somewhat on 'Ptolomy', *logos* ...]: SpTod 40 (1988) 292-307.

9286* **Sobrino** Jon, Liberación con espíritu, apuntes para una nueva espiritualidad: Presencia teológica 23, 1985 ➤ 2,6439; 3,8115: ᴿTKontext 9,2 (1988) 111 (M. *Sievernich*).

9287 **Špidlík** Tomáš, La spiritualità dell'Oriente cristiano 1985 ➤ 2,6440: ᴿSalesianum 50 (1988) 241s (O. *Pasquato*).

9288 **Špidlík** Tomáš, La spiritualité de l'Orient chrétien [I.] II. La prière: OrChrAn 230. R 1988, Pont. Inst. Stud. Orientalium. 459 p.

9289 **Špidlík** Tomáš, The spirituality of the Christian East 1986 ➤ 2,6441: ᴿAnglTR 69 (1987) 95-97 (A. *Jones*); Speculum 63 (1988) 476-8 (D. J. *Constantelos*).

9290 **Taft** Robert, The liturgy of the hours in East and West 1986 ➤ 2,6444; 3,8119: ᴿCathHR 74 (1988) 297s (G. *Austin*); CurrTM 15 (1988) 216s (M. B. *Aune*: challenges the current criterion, 'Will I get anything out of it?'); DocLife 37 (1987) 381s (P. *Gleeson*); PrPeo 2 (1988) 38s (G. *Steel*); Speculum 63 (1988) 478 (R. W. *Pratt*).

9291 **Thils** Gustave, Existencia y santidad en Jesucristo [1982],ᵀ: Lux Mundi 61. Salamanca 1987, Sígueme. 475 p. – ᴿLumenVr 37 (1988) 85s (U. *Gil Ortega*).

9292 *Tornos* Andrés, Fundamentos bíblico-teológicos del discernimiento: Manresa 60 (1988) 319-329.

9293 **Vanhoye** Alberto, Per progredire nell'amore [corso di esercizi]: Biblia e preghiera 1. R 1988, Apostolato della Preghiera. 214 p. Lit. 12.000. – ᴿCC 139 (1988,4) 404 (G. *Ferraro*); PalCl 67 (1988) 1408 (A. *Pedrini*).

9294 *Vilanova* Evangelista, Palabra de Dios y reforma litúrgica: ➤ 142, ᶠTENA P. = Phase 28 (1988) 203-210.

9295 *Waltke* Bruce K., Hermeneutics and the spiritual life: Crux 23 (March 1987) 5-10 [< BS 145 (1988) 211s (D. L. *Bock*)].

9296 *Wehrle* J., Anbetung: ➤ 804, NBL Lfg 1 (1988) 102s.

9297 *Willis* Robert E., Why Christian liturgy needs an enduring Jewish presence: JEcuSt 25 (1988) 22-38 (39-55, *Adams* William S.).

9298 *Wilson* Anne, Holistic spirituality [Jesus' holism vs. post-DESCARTES dualism]: SpTod 40 (1988) 208-219.

9299 **Woods** Richard, Another kind of love; homosexuality and spirituality³ʳᵉᵛ. Fort Wayne IN c.1987, Knoll. 192 p. $7. 0-940267-06-3 [SpTod (of which Woods is editor) 40, 144 adv.].

9300 *Zizioulas* J. D., Primitive Christianity; the original spirituality: Church 3,4 (1987) 10-14 [NTAbs 32,206].

H8.1 **Vocatio,** *vita religiosa communitatis* – *Sancti*; **the Saints.**

9300* **Arbuckle** Gerard A., Strategies for growth in religious life. Homebush NSW 1987, St. Paul. xix-240 p. – ᴿAustralasCR 65 (1988) 118s (K. *O'Shea*).

9301 *Berzal* Teodoro, El misterio de Nazaret en la vida religiosa; estudio en las Constituciones de un grupo de Congregaciones: EstJos 42 (1988) 147-195.

9302 *a*) *Beyer* J., La vie consacrée par les conseils évangéliques; – *b*) *Versaldi* Giuseppe, Le célibat sacerdotal du point de vue canonique et psychologique: ➤ 379, Vatican II Bilan 3 (1988) 81-103 / 141-164; Eng. ➤ 380, Assessment 3, 64-89 / 131-157.

9302* ᴱ**Bianchi** U., La tradizione dell'enkrateia 1982/5 ➤ 1,542...3,8126: ᴿBO 45 (1988) 236-8 (K.-H. *Uthemann*); JTS 39 (1988) 234-6 (A. *Louth*); TR 84 (1988) 205s (K. S. *Frank*).

9303 **Boff** Leonardo, Zeugen Gottes in der Welt; Ordensleben heute 1985
→ 1,7719: ᴿÖkRu 37 (1988) 383s (L. *Klein*).

9304 *a*) *Bonato* Antonio, L'idea di 'vita comunitaria' nelle opere ascetiche di
BASILIO; – *b*) *Tramontin* Silvio, Movimento cattolico e devozione al
cuore di Cristo: StPatav 35 (1988) 15-35; Eng. 35 / 17-50; Eng. 50.

9305 **Bondi** Roberta C., To love as God loves; conversations with the early
Church. Ph 1987, Fortress. 111 p. $6 [TDig 35,261]. 0-8006-2041-0. –
ᴿRExp 85 (1988) 728 (E.G. *Hinson*: on why monasticism is attracting
attention even among Protestants).

9306 **Brown** Peter, The body and society; men, women and sexual re-
nunciation in early Christianity. NY 1988, Columbia Univ. xx-504 p.;
map. 0-231-06100-5.

9307 **Brown** Peter, Le culte des saints; son essor et sa fonction dans la
chrétienté latine 1984 → 65,b685: ᴿPhase 28 (1988) 455s (L. *Prat*).

9308 *Demeerseman* Gérard, Dimension prophétique de la vie religieuse en
contexte musulman: BSecr NChr 23 (1988) 142-9.

9309 *Dihle* Albrecht [*Baumeister* T. *al.*] Heilig [-enverehrung]: → 807, RAC
14,105 (1987) 1-63 [96-150 (-184)].

9310 *Drijvers* Jan W., Virginity and asceticism in Late Roman western élites:
→ 437, Asymmetry 1987, 241-273.

9311 *Forman* Mary, Scripture and RB [Rule] as sources of Benedictine
spirituality: AmBenR 39 (1988) 85-112.

9312 *Fraternità* monastiche di Gerusalemme, monaci nelle città; una regola di
vita, ᵀ. CasM 1987, Piemme. 172 p. Lit. 16.000. – ᴿRasT 29 (1988) 211s
(M. *Salerno*).

9313 *García Paredes* J.C.R., Aportaciones de la 'teología política' a la
'teología de la vida religiosa': Claretianum 27 (1987) 127-148.

9314 **García Trapiello** J., Servir a la mejor causa; llamada divina y respuesta
humana según el pensamiento bíblico. M 1987, Atenas. 286 p. – ᴿAngelicum 65 (1988) 468 (A. *Huerga*).

9315 *Green* Thomas, Returning religious life to its biblical roots: Landas 2
(Manila 1988) 133-6 [< TKontext 10/1,73].

9315* *Kanichai* Cyriac, Towards an Indian understanding of the religious
vows: Word and Worship 20 (1987) 203-212 + 202 [deutsch TKontext
9/2,98].

9316 **Kieckhefer** Richard, *Bond* George D., Sainthood, its manifestation in
world religions. Berkeley 1988, Univ. California. xii-263 p. $38.50
(Kieckhefer on Christians; M. *Cohn* on Jews). [RelStR 15,236].

9316* *a*) *Kretschmar* Georg, Gemeinschaft der Heiligen im Neuen Testament
und in der frühen Kirche; – *b*) *Planer-Friedrich* Götz, Die Funktion der
Heiligen in einer ökumenischen Ekklesiologie: UnSa 43 (1988) 266-276 /
299-308.

9317 *Larentzakis* Grigorios, Heiligenverehrung in der Orthodoxen Kirche:
Catholica 42 (1988) 56-75.

9317* *Leplay* Michel, La Toussaint: ÉTRel 63 (1988) 227-241.

9318 **Levi** Peter, The frontiers of Paradise; a study of monks and monasteries. L 1987, Collins Harvill. 224 p. £12. – ᴿTLond 91 (1988) 227-9
(G. *Irvine*: witty).

9319 *Libânio* João B., O papel profético da vida religiosa: Convergência 21
(1986) 331-345 [> SelT 27 (1988) 179-187, ᵀᴱ*Suñol* Miguel].

9320 *Lohfink* Norbert, Ordenes religiosas; terapía de Dios para la Iglesia
[TDig 33 (1986) 203-212], ᵀᴱ*Sánchez i Vaque* Victor: SelT 27 (1988)
188-192.

9321 **López Amat** Alfredo, El seguimiento radical de Cristo; historia de la vida consagrada. M 1987, Encuentro. 350 p.; 75 p. – ᴿRHE 83 (1988) 784s (T. *Moral*: premier essai de ce genre).

9321* **Maldari** Donald C., The identity of religious life in the theology of Jean-Marie R. TILLARD: diss. ᴰ*Bavel* T. van. Lv 1987. 490 p. – ETL 64 (1988) 230.

9322 **Parenteau** André, Le charisme de la vie consacrée; La vie religieuse chrétienne [1. 1982 ➤ 1,7995; 2, 1984 ➤ 1,7996] 3: Hier-aujourd'hui 24. Montréal/P 1985, Bellarmin/Cerf. – ᴿÉglT 18 (1987) 400s (L. *Laberge*).

9322* *Prete* Benedetto, La Bibbia nella vita di S. DOMENICO di Guzmán e nella sua istituzione [< Parole di Vita]: SacDoc 33 (1988) 656-678.

9323 *Sabugal* S., El 'servicio' de la vida consagrada; sus raíces bíblicas y su fundamento eclesiológico: NVZam 12 (1987) 65-70 [< RET 48,127].

9324 *Schneider* Albert, The ecclesiological importance of religious life in German publications after Vatican II; survey and evaluation: Claretianum 28 (1988) 277-320; bibliog. 321-7.

9325 **Schneiders** Sandra, New wineskins 1986 ➤ 3,8150: ᴿHomP 88,2 (1987s) 78s (sr. M. Terese *Donze*: no).

9326 *Selge* Kurt-Victor, I movimenti religiosi laici del XII sec., in particolare i Valdesi, quale sfondo e premessa del movimento francescano: Protestantesimo 43 (1988) 71-92 [cf. 124s, ᴿ*Gonnet* G: **Dal Pino** F., Il laicato italiano tra eresia e proposta pauperistico-evangelica nei secoli XIIs (Univ. Padova 1984) 92 p.].

9327 **Sfameni Gasparro** Giulia, Enkrateia e antropologia 1984 ➤ 65,7022 ... 3,8151: ᴿRHR 205 (1988) 210s (J. *Doignon*).

9328 *Sfameni Gasparro* Giulia, L'epistula Titi discipuli Pauli de dispositione sanctimonii e la tradizione dell'enkrateia: ➤ 782, ANRW 2,25,6 (1988) 4551-4664.

9329 *Špidlík* Thomas, Saints, égl. byz./russe: ➤ 791, DictSpir XIV,91 (1988) 196-202 (-230 lat., *al*).

9330 *Stéphanos* mgr., Les origines de la vie cénobitique: ColcCist 49 (1987) 20-37.

9331 **Veraja** Fabijan, La Beatificazione; storia, problemi, prospettive: Sussidi per lo studio delle cause dei santi 2. R 1983, S. Congregazione per la Causa dei Santi. 206 p. – ᴿGregorianum 69 (1988) 133-8 (P. *Molinari*, P. *Gumpel*).

H8.2 Theologia moralis NT.

9332 *Allen* Joseph L., Catholic and Protestant theories of human rights [some 50 writings]: RelStR 14 (1988) 347-353.

9333 **Amstutz** Mark R., Christian ethics [... biblical foundations] and U.S. foreign policy. GR 1987, Zondervan Academie. 192 p. $13 pa. [TDig 35,258].

9334 *Asheim* Ivar, Hva annet enn etisk subjektivisme?: NorTTs [defense of his 87 (1986) 147 against *Christoffersen* S. 88 (1987) 17.145 ➤ 3,8160] 89 (1988) 157-171; Christoffersen 173-8.

9335 *Ashley* B.M., Scriptural grounds for concrete moral norms: Thomist 52 (1988) 1-22.

9336 *Asurmendi* Jesús M., Réfugiés, la Bible et les chrétiens: Spiritus 29 (1988) 59-67.

9337 **d'Aviau de Ternay** H., Traces bibliques dans la loi morale chez KANT 1986 ➤ 2,6460: ᴿCrNSt 9 (1988) 457 (D. *Bourel*); NRT 110 (1988) 124s

(J. *Javaux*†); RB 95 (1988) 285-8 (G. *Berceville*); TPhil 63 (1988) 410-2 (H. *Schöndorf*).

9338 a) *Barilier* Roger, L'Écriture et la discipline des mœurs; – b) *Edgar* William, L'hérésie de l'amour et la discipline biblique: → 28*, ᶠCOUR-THIAL P., Dieu parle! 1984, 104-114 / 115-126.

9339 *Barth* Hans-Martin, Die ekklesiologische Dimension der Ethik: KerDo 34 (1988) 42-59; Eng. 59.

9340 *Basevi* Claudio, [Bioetica] La cultura della vita nella Bibbia: StCattMi 32 (1988) 265-9.

9341 **Berlendis** A., La gioia sessuale... Bibbia, Chiesa e società 1985 → 2,6462: ᴿProtestantesimo 43 (1988) 233s (B. *Costabel*).

9342 **Blasi** Anthony J., Moral conflict and Christian religion: AmerUnivStud 7/35. NY 1988, P. Lang. x-180 p. $33.50 [TDig 36,47].

9343 *Bockmühl* Klaus, Gesetz und Geist; eine Anfrage an das Erbe protestantischer Ethik: TBei 19,1 (Wu 1988) 5-22 [< ZIT].

9344 *Bovon* François, Variété et autorité des premières éthiques chrétiennes: → 150, ᶠWIDMER G.-P. = BCentProt 40 (1988) 6-20.

9345 ᴱ**Bresciani** Carlo, Morale; ᴱ**Costa** Eugenioᴶ, Pratica: [**Lauret-Refoulé** → 9392] Iniziazione alla pratica della teologia. Brescia 1986s, Queriniana. 747 p.; 420 p.; Lit. 50.000; 35.000. – ᴿCC 139 (1988,2) 302s (F. *Cultrera*).

9346 *Brundage* James A., 'Allas...' sex and canon law [CathHR 72 (1986) 1-13]: BTAM 14 (1988) 452.

9347 *Burkhardt* Helmut, Neutestamentliche Ethik als Entwicklungsgeschichte ethischer Ideen im Urchristentum: TBei 19 (1988) 90... [< ZIT].

9348 **Cahill** Lisa S., Between the sexes... ethics 1985 → 1,7838 ... 3,8172: ᴿRelStR 14 (1988) 125s (Christine E. *Gudorf*) & 128s (R. W. *Blaney*).

9349 a) *Cahill* Lisa S., Divorced from experience; rethinking the theology of marriage; – b) *Cooke* Bernard, What God has joined together; reflections on indissolubility: Commonweal 114 (1987) 171-6 / 178-182.

9350 **Campbell** Alastair P., The Gospel of Anger 1986 → 2,6471: ᴿScotJT 41 (1988) 567s (N. P. *Harvey*).

9351 *Carmody* Denise L., [*al.*] Marriage in Roman Catholicism [... other world-religions]: JEcuSt 22 (1985) 28-40 [1-119].

9352 **Chilton** Bruce, *McDonald* J. I. H., Jesus and the ethics of the kingdom: Biblical Foundations in Theology 1987 → 3,8176: ᴿJTS 39 (1988) 559-561 (J. L. *Houlden*: series aimed to set in collaboration an exegete and a theologian).

9353 **Church** F. Forrester, Entertaining angels; a guide to heaven for atheists and true believers [not about heaven but about living rightly; quips]. SF 1987, Harper & R. 116 p. $14. 0-06-061372-6. – ᴿRExp 85 (1988) 385s (Melody *Mazuk*).

9354 ᴱ**Collins** Gary R., The secrets of our sexuality; role liberation for the Christian. Waco 1976 [AndrUnS 26,5: *Kinlaw* Dennis F., A biblical view of homosexuality... 105...].

9355 **Collins** Raymond F., Christian morality; biblical foundations 1986 → 2,6474; 3,8179: ᴿCalvinT 23 (1988) 76s (A. *Verhey*: Catholic but ecumenical and helpful); HomP 88,2 (1987s) 74-76 (R. *Zylla*); Salesianum 50 (1988) 226s (G. *Abbà*).

9356 **Countryman** L. William, Dirt, greed, and sex, sexual ethics in the NT and their implication for today. Ph 1988, Fortress. $20 [Interp 42,417 adv.].

9357 ᴱ**Curran** C., *McCormick* R., Official Catholic social teaching 1986 → 2,291; 3,8181: ᴿTLZ 113 (1988) 213s (H. *Kirchner*).

9358 **Curran** Charles E., Toward an American Catholic moral theology 1987
→ 3,210: ᴿJAAR 56 (1988) 325-8 (L. *Griffin*); RelStR 14 (1988) 144 (A. *Battaglia*).

9359 **Danesi** G., *Garofalo* S., Migrazioni e accoglienza nella Sacra Scrittura 1987 → 3,8185: ᴿHumBr 43 (1988) 137 (A. *Bonora*).

9360 **Davis** John J., Evangelical ethics. Philipsburg 1985, Presbyterian & R. 299 p. $15. – ᴿTrinJ 8 (1987) 247-9 (J. *Guimont*: fine book, despite some untenable positions).

9361 **Dominian** Jack, Sexual integrity; the answer to AIDS. L 1987, Darton-LT. vii-149 p. £5. – ᴿTLond 91 (1988) 439 (J. *Woodward*: Roman Catholic psychiatrist stresses that the *struggle* for integrity has no simple solutions).

9361* **Duff** Nancy J., Humanization and the politics of God; the *koinonia* ethics of Paul LEHMANN: diss. Union Theol. Sem. – NY 1987. – RelStR 15,191.

9362 **Dwyer** John C., Foundations of Christian ethics 1987 → 3,8195: ᴿRTLv 19 (1988) 386s (J. *Étienne*).

9363 Éthique, religion et foi ... U.E.R.: PoinT 43, 1985 → 2,280; 3,8199: ᴿTR 84 (1988) 412-4 (K.-W. *Merks*).

9364 **Farley** Margaret A., Personal commitments; beginning, keeping, changing. SF 1986, Harper & R. xi-148 p. $14. – ᴿHorizons 15 (1988) 124-133 (Anne E. *Patrick,* Susan A. *Ross,* J.P. *Hanigan,* Lisa S. *Cahill*; 133-149, Farley's response).

9365 *Ford* Norman, When does human life begin? Science, government, church: Pacifica 1 (1988) 298-327 [< ZIT 89,159].

9366 **Fowler** Paul B., Abortion; toward an evangelical consensus. Portland OR 1987, Multnomah. 225 p. $12. – ᴿCalvaryB 4,2 (1988) 83 (S. *Harbin*: sound Scriptural exegesis).

9367 *a) Frey* Christopher, The function of the Bible in recent Protestant ethics; – *b) Reventlow* Henning, Protestant understanding of the Bible: → 505, Creative 1985/8, 63-69 [N. B. new p. 69 supplied to replace notes p. 69-70] / 213-5.

9368 **Fuchs** E., La morale selon CALVIN 1986 → 3,8201: ᴿProtestantesimo 43 (1988) 122s (V. *Subilia*); SupVSp 164 (1988) 123-133 (R. *Simon*).

9368* *Fuchs* Eric, Entre raison et conviction; la place de l'éthique dans la société moderne: RTPhil 120 (1988) 453-463.

9369 **Fuchs** Josef, Christian morality; the Word becomes flesh, ᵀ*McNeil* Brian. Dublin [→ 3,221 =] / Wsh 1987, Gill & M. / Georgetown Univ. 212 p. $20; pa. $12. – ᴿHorizons 15 (1988) 425s (N. J. *Rigali*); Month 249 (1988) 730s (K. T. *Kelly*); RelStR 14 (1988) 363s (B. *Brady*); TS 49 (1988) 585s (P. S. *Keane*).

9370 *Fuchs* Josef, Diritto naturale o fallacia naturalistica?: RasT 29 (1988) 313-337.

9371 *Fuchs* Josef, Is there a Catholic medical moral? [< StiZt 113 (1988) 103-111], ᵀᴱ*Asen* B. A.: TDig 35 (1988) 203-8.

9372 **Gaudemet** Jean, Le mariage en Occident 1987 → 3,8206: ᴿAevum 62 (1988) 426s (G. *Picasso*); RevSR 61 (1987) 239s (C. *Munier*); ScripTPamp 20 (1988) 843s (D. *Ramos-Lissón*).

9373 *Genovesi* Vincent J., In pursuit of love; Catholic morality and human sexuality 1987 → 3,8202: ᴿHorizons 18 (1988) 191s (Christine E. *Gudorf*); TS 49 (1988) 181s (P. S. *Keane*).

9374 *Glebe-Møller* Jens, A modern American theology; James M. GUSTAFSON's ethics from a theocentric perspective: ST 42 (1988) 89-112.

9375 *Gleixner* Hans, Ethik unter dem Anspruch der biblisch-christlichen Freiheit: ZkT 110 (1988) 414-442.
9376 *Greinacher* Norbert, The problem of divorce and remarriage [< TüTQ 167 (1987) 106-115], ᵀᴱ*Asen* B. A.: TDig 35 (1988) 221-5.
9377 **Grimm** R., L'institution du mariage, essai d'éthique fondamentale 1984 ➤ 3,8212: ᴿProtestantesimo 43 (1988) 240s (G. *Conte*) [42 (1987) 123-5, recensione di Grimm, Les couples non mariés].
9378 *Grisez* Germain, The duty and right to follow one's own judgment of conscience: HomP 89,7 (1988s) 10-21.
9379 *Gudorf* Christine E., *Blaney* Robert W., Recent works on Christian sexual ethics: RelStR 14 (1988) 125-127-131.
9380 **Guindon** André, The sexual creators; an ethical proposal for concerned Christians 1986 ➤ 2,6501: ᴿRelStR 14 (1988) 129-131 (R. W. *Blaney*).
9381 **Haag** H., *Elliger* K., 'Stört nicht die Liebe' 1986 ➤ 3,8216: ᴿZkT 110 (1988) 367s (H. *Rotter*).
9382 *Hallett* Garth L., Infallibility and contraception; the debate continues: TS [43 (1982) 629-650; 47 (1986) 134-145, *Grisez* G.] 49 (1988) 517-528.
9383 **Hanigan** James P., Homosexuality; the test case for Christian sexual ethics; the place of sexuality and sexual behavior in the Christian life. NY 1988, Paulist. v-193 p. $10. – ᴿTS 49 (1988) 787s (Lisa S. *Cahill*).
9383* **Hatem** Jad, Éthique chrétienne et révélation; la spiritualité de l'Église d'Antioche 1987 ➤ 3,8221: ᴿETL 64 (1988) 473s (A. de *Halleux*).
9384 *a) Henrix* H. H., Geisel sein für den Anderen; eine Brüderlichkeit 'jenseits des Bürgerlichen' [... Gefahr der Instrumentalisierung des biblischen Wortes]; – *b) Häring* Bernhard, Das natürliche Sittengesetz im Lichte des Gesetzes Christi: TGegw 30 (1987) 89-98 / 99-108.
9385 *Hoekstra* Wim, Migrants, the Church and the Bible: ➤ 404, ᴱ*Press* M., Bicentennial 1988, 114-128.
9386 ᴱ**Hoffmann** R. Joseph, *Larue* Gerald A., Biblical versus secular ethics; the conflict. [Richmond VA Univ. meeting 1986]. Buffalo 1988, Prometheus. 191 p. 0-87975-418-4. – Larue, Biblical ethics and continuing interpretation, p. 17-27; – *Gaster* Theodor H., Secular humanism and the Bible, 29-36; – *Hoffmann* R. Joseph, The moral rhetoric of the Gospels, 57-68; – *Smith* Morton, On slavery; biblical teachings vs. modern morality, 69-78; *Rivkin* Ellis, Biblical foundation, 99-105; *Barnhart* Joe E., Relativity, 109-116.
9386* *a) Jacob* K., New Testament ethics; – *b) Sarah* Robert, The Christian family and the sacraments of the New Covenant: BPast 6 (Nairobi 1987) 1-17 / 19-30 [< TKontext 9/2,16].
9387 **Kelly** Kevin T., Life and love; towards a Christian dialogue on bioethical questions. L. 1987, Collins. 170 p. £5 pa. – ᴿTLond 91 (1988) 237s (S. *Platten*).
9388 *Kirchschläger* Walter, Ehe und Ehescheidung – Rückfragen an Bibel und Kirche: Diakonia 19 (Mainz 1988) 305-317 [293-348 *al.*, Für eine Neuorientierung der katholischen Ehelehre: ᴢɪᴛ 88,707].
9389 **Kötting** Bernhard, Die Bewertung der Wiederverheiratung (der zweiten Ehe) in der Antike und in der frühen Kirche: Rh/Wf Akad. Vorträge G 292. Opladen 1988, Westdeutscher. 43 p. [ZNW 79,297].
9390 *Langan* John, The Christian difference in ethics: TS 49 (1988) 131-150.
9391 *Larrabe* José Luis, Sobre los pecados de sexualidad ¿que dice la Biblia?: LumenVr 37 (1988) 249-275.
9392 **Lauret** B., *Refoulé* F., Iniciación I-V [➤ 8153] 1984s; IV 462 p.; V 494 p.: ᴿScripTPamp 20 (1988) 858-866 (C. *Izquierdo*, 4s).

9392* *Liébaert* Jacques †, Ancienneté et nouveauté de l'amour chrétien du prochain selon les Pères de l'Église: MélSR 45 (1988) 59-82.

9393 *Lövestam* Evald, *a*) Divorce and remarriage in the NT [< Jewish Law Annual 4 (1981) 47-65]; – *b*) Kärlek och äktenskap; vad säger Nya Testamentet [< Tro och Liv 1984, 9-16]: → 221, Axplock 1987, 61-79 / 51-59.

9394 **Lohse** Eduard, Theologische Ethik des Neuen Testaments: Theol. Wissenschaft 5/2. Stu 1988, Kohlhammer. 145 p. 3-17-010060-2.

9395 **McClendon** James W., Ethics: Systematic Theology 1, 1986 → 3,8242: ᴿTTod 45 (1988s) 114. 116 (Mary Ellen *Ross*).

9396 **McGrath** Aidan, A controversy concerning male impotence [differences between 1587 and 1977 Roman documents]: AnGreg 247. R 1988, Pont. Univ. Gregoriana. 328 p. Lit. 48,500. 88-7652-580-7.

9397 **MacNamara** Vincent, Faith and ethics; recent Roman Catholicism 1985 → 2,6524; 3,8245: ᴿIrTQ 54 (1988) 244-6 (R. *Preston*); NBlackf 69 (1988) 44s (B. *Soane*: good).

9398 **MacNamara** Vincent, The truth in love; reflections on Christian morality. Dublin 1988, Gill & M. 195 p. £8. – ᴿFurrow 39 (1988) 800-2 (S. *Ryan*).

9399 **Maguire** Daniel C., The moral revolution; a Christian humanist vision 1986 → 3,254: ᴿRExp 85 (1988) 579s (P. D. *Simmons*: his unorthodox wit has a better reception at Marquette than at Catholic U.); Salesianum 50 (1988) 448s (G. *Abbà*: affermazioni poco accurate, ambigue, affrettate).

9400 **Mahoney** John, The making of moral theology; a study of the Roman Catholic tradition 1987 → 3,8247: ᴿJEH 39 (1988) 573s (G. R. *Dunstan*); JTS 39 (1988) 348-350 (O. *O'Donovan*: reserves as to the history); Month 249 (1988) 683-5 (P. *Endean*); RelSt 24 (1988) 543s (P. *Byrne*); RHE 83 (1988) 411s (F. *Hockey* †); Salesianum 50 (1988) 449s (G. *Abbà*: parziale, fazioso); StMoralia 26 (1988) 313s (T. *Kennedy*); TLond 91 (1988) 368s (P. *Baelz*: limpid, enlightening); TS 49 (1988) 762s (J. R. *Pollock*).

9401 **Malherbe** Abraham J., Moral exhortation; a Greco-Roman sourcebook: Library of Early Christianity 4, 1986 → 2,6525; 3,8248: ᴿInterpretation 42 (1988) 206-8 (C. H. *Talbert*); RB 95 (1988) 472 (J. *Murphy-O'Connor*).

9402 *Marrow* Stanley B., Marriage and divorce in the New Testament: AnglTR 70 (1988) 3-15.

9403 **Meeks** Wayne A., The moral world of the first Christians 1986 → 2,6531; 3,8251: ᴿCBQ 50 (1988) 139-141 (H. W. *Attridge,* also on MALHERBE A. and STOWERS S. in Meeks' series); Horizons 15 (1988) 159s (Mary Rose *d'Angelo*); Month 249 (1988) 525s (J. *Ashton*: much better than STAMBAUGH-BALCH); RB 95 (1988) 472s (J. *Murphy-O'Connor*); TLond 91 (1988) 225-7 (L. *Houlden*).

9404 **Müller** Wunibald, Homosexualität, eine Herausforderung für Theologie und Seelsorge 1986 → 3,8255; 3-7867-1245-X: ᴿBijdragen 49 (1988) 459 (J. van *Hooydonk*).

9405 **Munier** Charles, Ehe und Ehelosigkeit in der alten Kirche (1.-3. Jahrhundert): Traditio Christiana 6. Bern 1987, P. Lang. lxxi-333 p. Fs 138. – ᴿTGL 78 (1988) 443s (W. *Beinert*).

9406 *Neckebrouck* V., Literary arguments on African polygamy [pro and con drawn from African oral literature; < RAfT 10 (1986) 15-30], ᴱ*Jermann* Rosemary: TDig 35 (1988) 119-122.

9407 *Nelson* James B. / *McNeill* John J. / *Lebacqz* Karen, After the revolution; the Church and sexual ethics: new series in Christian Century 104 (1987) 187-190 / 242-6 / 435-448 [RelStR 14 (1988) 127].

Nelson Paul, Narrative and morality; a theological inquiry 1987 → a928.

9408 [**Niebergall** Alfred Nachlass] ᴱ*Ritter* A. M. Ehe und Eheschliessung in der Bibel und in der Geschichte der Alten Kirche 1985 ➤ 2,6539: ᴿJBL 107 (1988) 150-2 (D. R. *Cartlidge*).

9409 *a) Ocáriz* F., La nota teologica dell'insegnamento dell'"Humanae vitae' sulla contracezione ['*de fide divina* or at least *Catholica* – anyway, it must be accepted with an unconditioned, final and total assent' p. 3]; – *b) Caffarra* C., La competenza del Magistero nell'insegnamento di norme morali determinate: Anthropotes, rivista di studi sulla persona e la famiglia (1988,1) 25-43 / 7-23.

9410 **O'Donovan** Oliver, Resurrection and the moral order; an outline for evangelical ethics 1986 ➤ 2,6540; 3,8259: ᴿCalvinT 23 (1988) 254-8 (D. J. *Schuurman*); JRel 68 (1988) 131-3 (J. M. *Gustafson*); PerspRelSt 15 (1988) 165-176 (W. C. *Tilley*); TTod 45 (1988s) 116-8 (D. P. *Hansen*).

9411 **Ogletree** T. W., The use of the Bible in Christian ethics 1983 ➤ 64,7354 ... 3,8261: ᴿHeythJ 29 (1988) 245s (J. *Barton*); ScotJT 41 (1988) 397-405 (P. *Sedgwick,* also on PANNENBERG and C. BRAATEN).

9412 **Panimolle** Salvatore A., La libertà cristiana; la libertà dalla legge nel Nuovo Testamento e nei primi Padri della Chiesa: Teologia sapienziale 8. Vaticano 1988, Editrice. 227 p. 86-209-1653-3.

9412* *Pawlikowski* John T., Christian ethics and the holocaust; a dialogue with post-Auschwitz Judaism: TS 49 (1988) 649-670.

9413 **Pinckaers** Servais, Ce qu'on ne peut jamais faire; la question des actes intrinsèquement mauvais; histoire et discussion: Études d'Éthique Chrétienne. FrS/P 1986, Univ./Cerf. 139 p. – ᴿDivThom 91 (1988) 231-3 (L. *Ciccone*); EsprVie 98 (1988) 77s (L. *Barbey* donne nombre de pages '14', mais cite p. 71, 84 ...); ETL 64 (1988) 219s (J. *Étienne*).

9414 **Pinckaers** Servais, Les sources de la morale chrétienne 1985 ➤ 2,6548; 3,8268: ᴿGregorianum 69 (1988) 162s (K. *Demmer*); SupVSp 164 (1988) 133-141 (R. *Simon*).

9415 **Plé** Albert, Duty or pleasure; a new appraisal of Christian ethics 1987 ➤ 3,8270: ᴿCCurr 23 (1988s) 228-230 (V. *Rush*).

9416 **Poupard** P., La morale cristiana nel mondo; indagine del Segretariato per i non credenti 1987 ➤ 3,8272: ᴿRasT 29 (1988) 214s (G. *Mattai*).

9417 **Powers** B. Ward, Marriage and divorce; the New Testament teaching 1987 ➤ 3,8273: ᴿRefTR 46 (1987) 91 (D. *Petersen*).

9418 *Ramsey* Paul, Human sexuality in the history of redemption: JRelEth 16 (1988) 56-86 [3-108, others on AUGUSTINE].

9419 *Ruggieri* G., Ecclesiology and ethics: CrNSt 9 (1988) 1-22.

9420 **Scanzoni** Letha D., Sexuality: Choices; guides for today's woman [1 of 12 books]. Ph 1984, Westminster. 113 p. $7. – ᴿRelStR 14 (1988) 125 (Christine E. *Gudorf*).

9421 **Schnackenburg** R., Die sittliche Botschaft des NTs I, 1986 ➤ 2,6553; 3,8287: ᴿArTGran 51 (1988) 300s (A. *Segovia*); BogSmot 58,4 (1988) 162s (M. *Valković*); ColcT 58,1 (1988) 182-4 (R. *Bartnicki*); ErbAuf 64 (1988) 233s (E. *Tschacher*); EstE 63 (1988) 372s (A. V. *Gutiérrez*); Salesianum 50 (1988) 229s (G. *Abbà*); StPatav 35 (1988) 170-4 (G. *Segalla*: classico, malgrado limiti ermeneutici); TLZ 113 (1988) 901s (G. *Strecker*); TR 84 (1988) 195-8 (H. *Frankemölle*).

9422 **Schnackenburg** Rudolf, Die sittliche Botschaft des neuen Testaments [I. 1954; ²1986 ➤ 2,6553] II. Die urchristlichen Verkündiger²ʳᵉᵛ. [I. 1954]: HerdTK NT Sup 2. FrB 1988, Herder. 285 p. 3-451-20690-0.

9423 **Schrage** Wolfgang, The ethics of the New Testament [1987 ➤ 3,8289], ᵀGreen David E. Ph 1988, Fortress. xiv-369 p. $30 [NTAbs 32,258].

0-8006-0835-6. – ᴿSWJT 31,1 (1988s) 54 (E. E. *Ellis*); TTod 45 (1988s) 355s (S. H. *Ringe*).

9424 **Schrage** W.,   Ética del NT, ᵀ*Lacarra* Javier: BiblEstBib 57. Salamanca 1987, Sígueme.   443 p. – ᴿCiTom 115 (1988) 579s (J. L. *Espinel*).

9424* *Schrage* Wolfgang, Zum Komparativ in der urchristlichen Ethik: EvT 48 (1988) 330-345.

9425 **Schüller** Bruno, L'uomo veramente uomo; la dimensione teologica dell'etica nella dimensione etica dell'uomo. Palermo 1987, Edi-Oftes. 270 p. Lit. 25.000. – ᴿRasT 29 (1988) 91s (G. *Mattai*).

9426 **Schulz** Siegfried, Neutestamentliche Ethik: Grundrisse zur Bibel 1987 → 3,8289; Fs 56: ᴿTLZ 113 (1988) 899-901 (G. *Strecker*).

9427 *Schuurman* Douglas J., [*Verhey* A.] The great reversal; ethics and the NT; a critical reassessment: CalvinT 23 (1988) 222-231; 231-7, Verhey response.

9428 **Sernau** Scott, Please don't squeeze the Christian into the world's mold. DG 1987, InterVarsity. 141 p. $6 [GraceTJ 9,315].

9429 **Spicq** Ceslas, Connaissance et morale dans la Bible 1985 → 1,7938 ... 3,8294: ᴿRTLv 19 (1988) 474-484 (H. *Wattiaux*, aussi sur *Pinckaers* T., *Demmer* K).

9430 **Spohn** William C., What are they saying about Scripture and ethics? 1984 → 65,7116 ... 3,8295: ᴿHeythJ 29 (1988) 246s (J. *Barton*).

9431 *Thornton* Larry R., A biblical approach to establishing marital intimacy, part I: intimacy and the Trinity: CalvaryB 4,2 (1988) 43-72.

9432 *Tuttle* Jeffrey P., Biblical principles for compensation [p. 73; contents 'Bible principles of compensation']: CalvaryB 4,2 (1988) 73-82.

9433 *Wackenheim* C., Réflexions théologiques sur un principe de droit et son évolution [les paroles du Christ sur l'indissolubilité du mariage pourraient être prophétiques, visant le Royaume]: Revue de Droit Canonique 38,1 (1988) 180-7 [3-179, *al.*, sur la législation de l'indissolubilité aux époques successives].

9434 ᵀᴱ**Womer** Jan L., Morality and ethics in early Christianity: Sources of Early Christian Thought. Ph 1987, Fortress. viii-135 p.

H8.4   *NT ipsum de reformatione sociali* – **Political action in Scripture.**

9435 *a*) *Barbero* Giorgio, Alle origini della teologia politica cristiana; religione politica e cultura nel quarto secolo; – *b*) *Zarone* Giuseppe, Redenzione ed eticità; per la critica del concetto di teologia politica: FilT 1,3 (1988) 45-69 / 3-32.

9436 **Bazarra** Carlos, Sí al hombre; el misterio de los pobres. Florida ARG 1988, Paulinas. 183 p. 950-09-0734-8.

9437 *Berinyuu* Abraham A., Poverty and hunger and the Churches' responses as model of redemption: Month 249 (1988) 912-917.

9438 **Boff** Leonardo, Passion of Christ, passion of the world, ᵀ*Barr* Robert R. Maryknoll NY 1988, Orbis. 141 p. 0-88344-563-8. – ᴿRExp 85 (1988) 729s (Molly *Marshall-Green*).

9438* **Bosowski** Andrzej, ℗ *Nauka* ... Doctrine de Jésus-Christ sur les biens matériels dans l'interprétation de la communauté chrétienne primitive: diss. ᴰ*Łach* J. Warszawa 1988. – RTLv 20,543.

9439 *Braaten* Carl E., The doctrine of the two kingdoms re-examined: CurrTM 15 (1988) 497-500.

9440 **Brown** Robert M., Religion and violence² [the hidden violence in our society ...]. Ph 1987, ¹1973, Westminster. xxix-114 p. $9 pa. [TDig 35,262].

9440* *Brox* Norbert, Die reichen und die armen Christen; eine Parabel aus der altrömischen Kirche: ➤ 76, F KAUFMANN L., Biotope 1988, 224-9.

9441 **Brummel** B. Lee, LUTHER on poverty and the poor; a study of Luther's exegetical understanding and use of the biblical language of poverty and the poor, 1513-1525: diss. Columbia. NY 1979. 278 p. – DissA 42 (1981s) 4040-A; LuJb 54 (1987) 167.

9442 **Büchele** H., Christlicher Glaube und politische Vernunft; für eine Neukonzeption der katholischen Soziallehre: Soziale Brennpunkte 12. W/Dü 1987, Europa/Patmos. 254 p. DM 28. 2-203-50999-7 / 3-491-77675-9. – R TsTNijm 28 (1988) 422 (A. *Rabau*).

9443 *Calvez* Jean-Yves, L'option préférentielle pour les pauvres, dans l'Église, récemment: VieCons 59 (1987) 269-284.

9444 *Clowney* Edmund P., Le Royaume de Dieu et la politique révolutionnaire: ➤ 64, F HOFFMANN J., RRéf 39,3 (1988) 61-70.

9445 **Comblin** José, Cry of the oppressed, cry of Jesus; meditations on Scripture and contemporary struggle, T *Barr* Robert. Maryknoll NY 1988, Orbis. V-90 p. $5. – R Furrow 39 (1988) 610s (J. *McPolin*).

9446 **Cort** John C., Christian socialism, an informal history. Maryknoll NY 1987, Orbis. $25; pa. $13. – R CCurr 23 (1988s) 226s (A. W. *Godfrey*: principles of the Gospels have economic applications).

9446* **Coulie** Bernard, Les richesses dans l'œuvre de S. Grégoire de Nazianze; étude littéraire et historique [diss. LvN 1985]: Publ. 32 1985 ➤ 3,8325: R Muséon 100 (1987) 441-3 (M. *Sicherl*, deutsch); RHE 82 (1987) 63-67 (A. de *Halleux*).

9447 **Defois** Gérard, Les Chrétiens dans la société; le mystère du salut dans sa traduction sociale. P 1986, Desclée. 278 p. F 120. – R EsprVie 98 (1988) 71s (L. *Debarge*).

9448 *Dulles* Avery, *a*) The Church, society, and politics [< Origins 16 (1987) 637-646 = Different Gospels (1988) ...]; – *b*) The basic teaching of Vatican II [< Church 1 (1985) 3-10]; – *c*) Authority and conscience; two needed voices [< Church 2 (1986) 8-15]: ➤ 183, Reshaping 1988, 154-183 / 19-33 / 93-109.

9449 *Eckert* Jost, 'Dein Reich komme!' Zum problematischen Verhältnis 'Kirche und Gesellschaft' in der Schriften des Neuen Testaments: BiKi 43 (1988) 147-153.

9450 *Eicher* Peter, The Church as contrast society? [< Orientierung 21 (1987) 230-2, on *Büchele* Herwig, ... kath. Soziallehre 1987], TE *Asen* B.: TDig 35 (1988) 139-142.

9451 **Eller** Vernard, Christian anarchy [... Anabaptist rediscovery of NT politics of faith]. 1987 ➤ 3,8332; $16: R RelStR 14 (1988) 240s (D. G. *Lasky*).

9452 **Elliott** Charles, Comfortable compassion? NY 1987, Paulist. 194 p. $8 [TDig 35,267].

9453 **Elliott** Charles, Praying the Kingdom; toward a political spirituality ➤ 2,6591; also NY 1985, Paulist. 150 p. $7 pa. – R SpTod 40 (1988) 165s (Gertrude *Foley*).

9454 **Ellul** Jacques, Jesus and Marx; from Gospel to ideology. GR 1988, Eerdmans. xvi-187 p. 0-8028-0297-4.

9455 *Ellul* Jacques, Les Chrétiens et l'État [1966; 'L'ordre de l'État n'est pas celui de la vérité'...]: LumièreV 37,190 ('Églises et État dans la société laïque' 1988) 77-87.

9456 **Farina** Marcella, Chiesa di poveri e Chiesa dei poveri [I. la fondazione biblica di un tema conciliare 1986 ➤ 2,6593; 3,8333]; II. La memoria della

Chiesa. R 1988, LASalesiano. 470 p. – ᴿAsprenas 35 (1988) 545s (A. *Di Donna*); Carthaginensia 4 (1988) 383s (F. *Martínez Fresneda*); Claretianum 27 (1987) 397s (B. *Proietti,*1); MiscFranc 88 (1988) 228-233 (A. *Pompei*).

9457 *Festa* F. Saverio, L'inconciliabile dialettica tra Cristianesimo e ordine politico in K. BARTH: FilT 1,3 (1988) 90-115.

Freeman Gordon M., The heavenly kingdom; aspects of political thought in the Talmud and the Midrash 1986 → b184.

9459 *Gay* Paolo, I credenti in Gesù Cristo e lo Stato: Protestantesimo 43 (1988) 153-163.

9460 *Geddert* T., Jesus and ethnicity: Direction 17,1 (1988) 73-77 [< NTAbs 32,296].

9461 **Glebe-Möller** Jens, A political dogmatic, ᵀ*Hall* Thor [with introduction on the theological situation in Denmark]. Ph 1987, Fortress. xxv-147 p. $11 pa. [TDig 36,61].

9462 *Griffin* Keith, The Christian nation debate in historical perspective: StudiaBT 16 (1988) 213-244.

9463 *Guerra* Augusto, Amor político; ante la inocencia y la posibilidad: REspir 44 (1985) 413-437 [> SelT 26 (1987) 108-116, ᵀ*Muñoz* Maxim].

9464 *Hendricks* William L., A theological basis for Christian social ministries: RExp 85,2 ['Church Social Work' 1988] 221-231.

9465 *a) Hollinger* Dennis, Enjoying God forever; an historical/sociological profile of the health and wealth gospel; – *b) Kaiser* Walter C.ᴶ. The OT case for material blessings and the contemporary believer; – *c) Schmidt* Thomas E., Burden, barrier, blasphemy; wealth in Matt 6:33, Luke 14:33, and Luke 16:15; – *d) Moo* Douglas, Divine healing in the health and wealth gospel; – *e) Larsen* David L., The gospel of greed versus the gospel of the grace of God: TrinJ 9 (1988) 131-149 / 151-170 / 171-189 / 191-209 / 211-220.

9466 **Holloway** Richard, The sidelong glance; L 1985 → 2,5833; now with subtitle, 'politics, conflict and the Church'. CM 1986, Cowley. 86 p. $7. – ᴿRelStR 14 (1988) 241 (T. F. *Sedgwick*: vignettes of bishop of Edinburgh for other Anglicans).

9467 **Hood** Robert E., Contemporary political orders and Christ; Karl BARTH's Christology and political praxis 1985 → 2,6608; 3,8337: ᴿTTod 44 (1987s) 302s (D. L. *Migliore*).

9468 **Hoppe** L. J., Being poor; a biblical study 1987 → 3,8338: ᴿBibTB 18 (1988) 149s (T. R. *Hobbs*); NewTR 1,3 (1988) 93s (L. *Boadt*); SpTod 40 (1988) 274-6 (R. *Keller*); TS 49 (1988) 377s (A. J. *Tambasco*).

9469 *a) Johnson* sr. Elizabeth, Christology and social justice; JOHN PAUL II and the American bishops; – *b) Pawlikowski* John, Christology as liberation from social sin: ChSt 26 (1987) 155-165 / 284-299.

9470 *a) Jossa* G., Politica; – *b) Panimolle* S. A., Povertà; – *c) Bonora* A., Liberazione: → 806, NDizTB (1988) 1171-1189 / 1202-1216 / 823-835.

9471 **Kammer** Charles L.ᴵᴵᴵ, Ethics and liberation, an introduction. Maryknoll NY 1988, Orbis. xi-243 p. $12 [TDig 36,65].

9472 *Kniazeff* Alexis, Le royaume de César et le Règne du Christ: Contacts/Orthodoxe 39 (1987) 265-278; 40 (1988) 19-36.

9473 *a) Kühschelm* R., Armenfürsorge; – *b) Schottroff* W. & L., Armut; – *c) Berger* K., Almosen: → 804, NBL Lfg 1 (1988) 170 / 171-4 / 78s.

9474 **Kuitert** H. M., Everything is politics, but politics is not everything → 2,6613; a theological perspective on faith and politics 1986: ᴿSalesianum 50 (1988) 237 (G. *Abbà*).

9475 *a*) *Langlois* Claude, Religions et révolution; présentation [fasc. sur la révolution française]; – *b*) *Caffiero* Marina, Prophétie, millénium et révolution; pour une étude du millénarisme en Italie a l'époque de la Révolution française: ArchScSocRel 66,1 (1988) 5-8 [-182] / 66,1 (1988) 187-199.

9476 *Lango* Pedro, Reflexiones agustinianas sobre la riqueza: AugSt 17 (Villanova 1986) 85-108.

9477 **Legido** Marcelino, Misericordia entrañable; historia de la salvación anunciada a los pobres. Salamanca 1986, Sígueme, 486 p. – ᴿNatGrac 34 (1987) 109s (R. *Robles*).

9478 **Lehmann** Paul, Christologie und Politik; eine theologische Hermeneutik des Politischen [The transfiguration of politics], ᵀ*Löhr* G., *Maurer* P.; Einf. *Sauter* G., 1987 ➤ 3,8345: ᴿEvT 48 (1988) 483-5 (E. *Bethge*); TR 84 (1988) 52s (E. *Arens*).

9479 *a*) *Lémonon* J.-P., Jésus et les pouvoirs [de Rome; des grands-prêtres; des groupes de pression...]; – *b*) *Chappuis* J.-M., L'invocation du Seigneur J.-C. comme limitation des pouvoirs humains; – *c*) *Jourjon* M., Le chrétien devant le pouvoir dans l'Église ancienne; – *d*) *Fuchs* E., Le pouvoir; un problème théologique et éthique... réformé; – *e*) *Duquoc* C., La complicité de l'Église et des pouvoirs: SuppVS 162 (1987) 43-55 / 35-42 / 57-66 / 67-84 / 85-95 [< RSPT 72,169].

9480 **Lohfink** Norbert F., Option for the poor; the basic principles of liberation theology in the light of the Bible [American Baptist Sem. West, Bailey Lectures] 1987 ➤ 3,8348: ᴿAustralBR 36 (1988) 59s (B. R. *Doyle*); Bijdragen 49 (1988) 444 (H. van *Grol*); BL (1988) 108 (C. S. *Rodd*); JStOT 42 (1988) 121 (M. D. *Carroll*: no concrete proposals); RB 95 (1988) 616s (R. J. *Tournay*); RivB 36 (1988) 123s (A. *Bonora*).

9481 *Lohfink* Norbert, Biblia y opción por los pobres [< StiZt 203, 449-64], ᵀᴱ*Giménez* Josep: SelT 26 (1987) 273-284.

9482 **McBrien** Richard P., Caesar's coin; religion and politics in America 1987 ➤ 3,8351: ᴿCommonweal 114 (1987) 567s (D. O'*Brien*); TorJT 4 (1988) 288-290 (R. *Haight*).

9483 *McDaniel* Jay, Christianity and the pursuit of wealth: Angl TR 69 (1987) 349-361.

9484 *Machovec* Milan, Über die Tragweite des marxistisch-christlichen Dialogs: EvT 48 (1988) 280-291 [< Vortrag für Doktorat h.c. Bern 1987].

9485 **Marshall** Paul, Thine is the kingdom; a biblical perspective on the nature of government and politics today 1986 ➤ 2,6619: ᴿCalvinT 23 (1988) 83-85 (S. V. *Monsma*).

9486 **Minnerath** Roland, Jésus et le pouvoir: PoinT 46, 1987 ➤ 3,8362: ᴿÉtudes 368 (1988) 566 (P. *Gibert*); TsTNijm 28 (1988) 183 (M. *Van Tente*).

9486* **Moioli** Giovanni, Beati i poveri. Viboldone 1987, ed. 157 p. Lit. 12.000. – ᴿRClerIt 69 (1988) 302s (Dora *Castenetto*).

9487 **Moltmann** Jürgen, On human dignity; political theology and ethics 1984 ➤ 65,7263 ... 3,8364, ᵀ*Meeks* M. Douglas: ᴿModT 4 (1987s) 401-3 (R. *Bauckham*).

9488 **Moltmann** Jürgen, Teología política, ética política, ᵀ*Martínez de Lapera* Victor A.: Verdad e Imagen 99, ➤ 65,5903: ᴿLumenVr 37 (1988) 186s (U. *Gil Ortega*).

9489 *a*) *Moltmann* Jürgen, Die Politik der Nachfolge Christi gegen christliche Millenniumspolitik; – *b*) *Sölle* Dorothee, Eine Erinnerung um der Zukunft willen; – c) *Fiorenza* Francis S., Politische Theologie und liberale Gerechtigkeits-Konzeptionen, ᵀ*Berz* A.; – d) *Lamb* Matthew L., Politische Theologie jenseits von Restauration und Liberalismus, ᵀ*Berz*: ➔ 106, ᶠMETZ J. B., Mystik 1988, 13-19 / 19-31 / 105-117 / 95-105.

9490 **Mullin** Redmond, The wealth of Christians 1984 ➔ 65,7267.d130; 1, f109 [not 'Christianity' or '1981']: ᴿHeythJ 29 (1988) 502s (W. *Slavin*).

9491 **Nash** Ronald H., Poverty and wealth; the Christian debate over capitalism. Westchester IL 1986, Crossway. 216 p. $9 pa. – ᴿAndrUnS 26 (1988) 95-97 (G. R. *Knight*).

9492 *Neff* R. W., The biblical basis for political advocacy [avoided by neither Jesus nor Paul]: Brethren Life and Thought 32,4 (1987) 201-7 [NTAbs 32,203].

9493 *Nell-Breuning* Oswald von, El cristiano y el poder [Macht – für den Christen ein Problem?: StiZt 203 (1985) 374-388], ᵀᴱ*Alemany* Alvaro: SelT 26 (1987) 83-94.

9494 **Oakman** Douglas E., Jesus and the economic questions of his day ᴰ1986 ➔ 2,6627: ᴿBibTB 18 (1988) 35s (J. J. *Pilch*); JEcuSt 24 (1987) 445s (Pheme *Perkins*); JTS 39 (1988) 557s (D. *Mealand*: some insights); TS 49 (1988) 777 (J. R. *Donahue*).

9495 ᴱ**Obelkevich** Jim, *al.,* Disciplines of faith; studies in religion, politics and patriarchy [< 1983 Oxford history workshop Religion & Society]. 1987 ➔ 3,684: ᴿRelStR 14 (1988) 46 (J. L. *Price*).

9496 a) *Pinchon* Michel, Le procès entre Jésus et le monde; – b) *Fitterer* Rémi, Dans les traces des prophètes, pour libérer l'homme de ses esclavages: Sève 495 (1988) 110-6 / 494 (1988) 40-48.

9497 **Prior** David, Jesus and power: Jesus Library. DG 1987, InterVarsity. 192 p. $9 [GraceTJ 9,314].

9498 ᴱ**Prodi** Paolo, *Sartori* Luigi, Cristianesimo e potere 1985/6 ➔ 2,489: ᴿFilT 1,3 (1988) 209-213 (F. S. *Festa*).

9499 ... Raices bíblicas de la Opción por los pobres: Revista de Vida Espiritual 2 (1988) 9-47.

9500 **Ratzinger** Joseph, Iglesia, ecumenismo y politica [Kirche, Ökumene 1987 ➔ 3,280*]: BAC 494. M 1987, Católica. 304 p. – ᴿArTGran 51 (1988) 343-5 (J. A. *Estrada*).

9501 **Ratzinger** Joseph, Chiesa, ecumenismo e politica; nuovi saggi di ecclesiologia [1987 ➔ 3,280*],ᵀ. Mi 1987, Paoline. 266 p. Lit. 18.000. – ᴿHumBr 43 (1988) 135 (R. *Tononi*); ViPe 71 (1988) 396-9 (F. *Botturi*).

9502 **Ratzinger** J., Église, œcuménisme et politique. – ᴿPenséeC 233 (1988) 89-96 (Y. *Daoudal*).

9503 **Ritter** Adolf M., Zwischen 'Gottesherrschaft' und 'einfachem Leben'; DIO Chrysostomus, Johannes CHRYSOSTOMUS und das Problem einer Humanisierung der Gesellschaft [Konsens der Neutestamentler gegen sozialrevolutionäre Armenfrömmigkeit im NT]: JbAC 31 (1988) 127-143.

9504 *Ronan* Marian, Teaching a political/social reading of the Hebrew Bible in the adult religious education setting: Paradigms 4 (1988s) 112-128.

9505 *Rotzetter* Antón, Por una espiritualidad profético-político [GeistL 59 (1986) 6-19], ᵀᴱ*Torres* María José de: SelT 27 (1988) 163-9.

9506 **Rumpf** L., Chrétiens devant l'injustice; question œcuménique et responsabilité personnelle. Genève 1985, Labor et Fides. 120 p. – ᴿProtestantesimo 43 (1988) 237s (P. *Ribet*).

9507 *Ruokanen* Miikka, AUGUSTIN und LUTHER über die Theologie der Politik: KerDo 34 (1988) 22-40; Eng. 40s.

9508 *Russo* Raffaele, L'impegno storico [= nella storia; lotta sociale] del cristiano; per una fondazione teologica: Asprenas 35 (1988) 307-334.

9509 **Schillebeeckx** E., Als politiek niet alles is... Jezus in de westerse cultuur: Kuyper-Lezingen 1986. Baarn 1986, Ten Have. 80 p. Fb. 298 [deutsch ital. 1987 → 3,8379s]. – ᴿCollatVL 18 (1988) 124s (K. *Vanlanduyt*).

9510 **Schillebeeckx** E., Perché la politica non è tutto; parlare di Dio in un mondo minacciato; GdT 175. Brescia 1987, Queriniana. 114 p. Lit. 10.000. – ᴿStPatav 35 (1988) 749-751 (E. R. *Tura*).

9511 **Schillebeeckx** Edward, *a)* Jesús en nuestra cultura; mística, ética y política [Als politiek niet alles ist] ᵀ*López* Ambrosio: Pedal 191, 1987 → 3,8380; 84-301-1038-0: ᴿActuBbg 25 (1988) (50-53) 231. – *b)* Jesus in our western culture; mysticism, ethics and politics [1986], ᵀ*Bowden* J. L 1987, SCM. vii-84 p. 0-334-02098-0.

9512 **Schmidt** Thomas E., Hostility to wealth in the Synoptic Gospels 1987 → 3,8383: ᴿBiblica 69 (1988) 585s (T. *Prendergast*).

9513 **Schottroff** Luisa, *Stegemann* Willi, Gesù di Nazareth speranza dei poveri [1978], ᵀ*Fiorillo* Michele: Piccola Collana Moderna, Biblica 53. T 1988, Claudiana. 216 p. Lit. 15.500. 88-7016-065-3. – ᴿHumBr 43 (1988) 894s (M. *Orsatti*).

9514 **Schottroff** Luise, *Stegemaun* Wolfgang, Jesus and the hope of the poor 1986 → 2,6636: ᴿMonth 249 (1988) 644s (J. A. *Crampsey*: all very fine but suggests a 'canon within the canon' and 'forget the historical Jesus'); NBlackf 68 (1987) 583 (Margaret *Davies*: 'Schottroft' 'Stegmann').

9515 **Shin Won Ha,** Christian ethical responsibility in resisting evil in government: diss. Calvin Sem., ᴰ*Minnema* T. GR 1988. vi-164 p. + bibliog. – CalvinT 23 (1988) 309.

9516 *Sittser* Gerald L.ᴶ, Christianity in public life; the Bible and the American experience: RefR 42,1 (1988s) 3-30.

9517 *a) Skotte* Phil, The problem of poverty and the OT; – *b) Graham* Helen R., 'Once there was a rich man...': BToday 26 (1988) 87-93 / 98-103.

9518 *Soares-Prabhu* George, *a)* Class in the Bible; the biblical poor a social class?: → 337, Liberation in Asia 1987, 65-92; – *b)* Clase en la Biblia; los pobres bíblicos ¿una clase social? [< Vidyajyoti]: RLatAmT 4 (1987) 217-239 [< NTAbs 32,345].

9519 **Stackhouse** Max L., Public theology and political economy; Christian stewardship in modern society 1987 → 3,8389: ᴿTTod 45 (1988s) 372-4 (J. P. *Wogaman*).

9520 *Stockmeier* Peter, Herrschaft: → 807, RAC 14,110 (1988) 877-936 [-1093, *al.,* -szeichen; Herrscherbild, -kult].

9521 *Templin* J. Alton, The individual and society in the thought of CALVIN: CalvinT 23 (1988) 161-177.

9522 **Ter Schegget** G. H., Volmacht in onmacht; over de roeping van de christelijke gemeente in de politiek. Baarn 1988, Ten Have. 348 p. ƒ45. 90-259-4274-1. – ᴿTsTNijm 28 (1988) 422 (A. van *Iersel*).

9523 *a) Viviano* Benedict T., Render unto Caesar; – *b) Reid* Barbara, The trial of Jesus – or Pilate?; – *c) Hoppe* Leslie J., Deuteronomy on political power; – *d) Dulin* Rachel, Anti-Davidic voices: BToday 26,5 ('Political power in the Bible' 1988) 272-6 / 277-282 / 261-6 / 267-271 [283-7, *Roseblatt* Marie-Eloise].

9524 **Walsh** J. P. M., The mighty from their thrones; power [*mišpaṭ*] in the biblical tradition: OvBT 21, 1987 → 3,2608: ᴿBibTB 18 (1988) (A. J. *Tambasco*: highly successful); CBQ 50 (1988) 521s (R. *Gnuse*: religion and

politics do mix); HorBT 10,1 (1988) 75s (M. E. *Polley*); RB 95 (1988) 616 (J.-M. de *Tarragon*); TS 49 (1988) 199 (R. J. *Clifford*).
Wengst Klaus, Humility, solidarity of the humiliated 1988 → b428.

H8.5   Theologia liberationis latino-americana.

9526 *Abesamis* C. H.,   The mission of Jesus and good news to the poor; exegetic-pastoral considerations for a Church in the Third World: AsiaJT 1,2 (1987) 429-460 [< NTAbs 32,150].

9527 **Aguilar Romero** Rodrigo,   Experiencia cristiana en el horizonte del reino de Dios; sobre carácter ecuménico de la Iglesia de los pobres en América Central 1973-1985: diss. ᴰ*Metz* J. Münster 1987s. – TR 84 (1988) 512.

9528 *Alemany* José J., *Barbero* José L.,   Teología de la liberación – bibliografia de revistas 1970-1988: MiscCom 46 (1988) 489-584 [7-487, all the articles are on 'human rights' and other religious issues in the history of Latin-American colonization].

9529 *a) Arana Quiroz* Pedro,   Towards a Reformed Christology in Latin America; – *b) Gouvêa Mendonça* António,   Christology and ecclesiology in a world of oppression: RefW 40,1 (Geneva 1988) 858-866 / 867-883 [< ZIT].

9530 *Augel* Johannes, *Hillen* Peter, *Ramalho* Lutz,   Die verplante Wohn-misere; urbane Entwicklung und 'armutsorientierter' Wohnungsbau in Afrika und Lateinamerika. Saarbrücken 1986, Brietenbach. 334 p. [Mundus 23,131: 'planned wretched housing conditions'].

9530* **Banga Bane** Joseph,   La perpective historique de la théologie de la libération: diss. Pont. Univ. Gregoriana, ᴰ*González* C.; Extr. Nº 3520. R 1988. 315 p. – RTLv 20,567.

9531 *a) Beozzo* José O. / *Comblin* José,   Medellín; vinte anos depois (1968-1988); – *b) Díaz Mateos* Manuel,   A voz profética de Medellín: REB 48 (1988) 771-805/ 806-829 / 842-859.

9532 **Berryman** Phillip,   Liberation theology; essential facts ... 1987 → 3,8406: ᴿCCurr 23 (1988s) 93-98 (H. *Lacey,* also on CHOPP R. 1986).

9533 **Biancucci** Duilio,   Dritte Welt – unsere Welt; Beispiel Lateinamerika 1985 → 3,8408; DM 28: ᴿTLZ 113 (1988) 73 (S. *Krügel*).

9534 **Biancucci** Duilio,   Einführung in die Theologie der Befreiung. Mü 1987, Kösel. 160 p. – ᴿComSev 21 (1988) 131 (M. de *Burgos*); NorTTs 89 (1988) 155 (K. *Nordstokke,* also on BERRYMAN P. 1987).

9535 **Boff** C.,   Mit den Füssen am Boden 1986 → 2,6662: ᴿTPhil 63 (1988) 304s (M. *Sievernich*).

9536 **Boff** Clodovis,   Feet-on-the-ground theology 1987 → 3,8409: ᴿFurrow 39 (1988) 127s (P. *Kirby*).

9537 **Boff** Clodovis,   Theology and praxis [ᴰ1976], ᵀ*Barr* R. 1987 → 3,8410: ᴿHorizons 15 (1988) 415s (J. V. *Apczynski*).

9538 *Boff* Clodovis,   Retrato de 15 años de Teología de la Liberación [< REB 46 (1986) 263-321]. ᵀᴱ*Comas de Mendoza* Enric: SelT 27 (1988) 298-302.

9539 **Boff** Leonardo,   Jesus Christus, der Befreier 1986 → 3,8413: ᴿMüTZ 39 (1988) 79-81 (E. *Feil*).

9540 **Boff** Leonardo,   When theology listens to the poor, ᵀ*Barr* Robert R. SF 1988, Harper & R. xi-147 p. $19 [CBQ 51,186].

9541 *Boff* Leonardo,   A originalidade da teologia da libertação em G. GUTIÉRREZ: REB 48,3 ('G. Gutiérrez: teologia a partir da tribulação', 1988) 531-543 (-564 *al.*).

9542 *Boff* Leonardo, Trinitarian community and social liberation: CCurr 38 (1988s) 289-308.

9543 **Boff** L. & C., Wie treibt man die Theologie der Befreiung? [Como fazer 1986 ➤ 2,6668] 1986 ➤ 3,8421: ᴿTPhil 63 (1988) 303s (M. *Sievernich*).

9544 **Boff** L. & C., Introducing liberation theology 1987 ➤ 3,8424: ᴿNewTR 1,2 (1988) 95-97 (J. T. *Pawlikowski*, also on BERRYMAN P. 1987).

9545 **Boff** L. & C., Salvation and liberation; in search of a balance between faith and politics 1984 ➤ 65,7208 ... 3,8426: ᴿÉglT 18 (1987) 272s (K. R. *Melchin*); HeythJ 29 (1988) 264s (Elizabeth *Lord*).

9546 *Brakemeier* Gottfried, Justification by grace and liberation theology; a comparision: EcuR 40 (1988) 215-222.

9547 ᴱ**Branson** Mark L., *Padilla* C. René, Conflict and context; Hermeneutics in the Americas [Tlayacapan Méx. 24-29.XI.1983] 1986 ➤ 2,7959; 3,522*: ᴿTLZ 113 (1988) 462s (J. *Langer*).

9548 **Brown** Robert M., Spirituality and liberation; overcoming the great fallacy. Ph 1988, Westminster. 158 p. $10 pa. [TDig 35,343].

9549 **Bussmann** Claus, Who do you say? Jesus Christ in Latin American theology 1985 ➤ 2,6671: ᴿColcFuJen 73 (1987) 483-6 (L. *Gutheinz* ©).

9550 *Cambón* Enrique, Dio in America latina: NuovaUm 9,54 (1987) 93-104.

9551 **Carroll** Denis, What is liberation theology? Dublin c.1986, Mercier. £5. – ᴿDoctLife 37 (1987) 382s (P. *Kirby*).

9552 **Castillo-Cardenas** Gonzalo, Liberation theology from below; the life and thought of Manuel QUINTIN LANE. Maryknoll NY c.1987, Orbis. 200 p. $17. – ᴿAmerica 157 (1987) 171s (A. T. *Hennelly*); JRel 68 (1988) 604-6 (T. D. *Swanson*).

9553 **Chopp** Rebecca S., The praxis of suffering 1986 ➤ 2,6674; 3,8437: ᴿHorizons 18 (1988) 198s (M. *Downey*); Missiology 16 (1988) 99s (W. *McConville*).

9554 *Clement* Olivier, Teología de la liberación y teología ortodoxa [= Le virus du 'Magnificat': Contacts 37 (1985) 285-299], ᵀᴱ*Suñol* Miquel: SelT 26 (1987) 210-6.

9555 **Codina** Víctor, Seguir a Jesús hoy; de la modernidad a la solidaridad: Pedal 187. Salamanca 1988, Sígueme. 291 p. – 84-301-1047-X. – ᴿActuBbg 25 (1988) 261 (J. *Vives*).

9556 **Cohn-Sherbok** Dan, On earth as it is in heaven; Jews, Christians, and liberation theology 1987 ➤ 3,8440: ᴿJEcuSt 24 (1987) 673 (J. F. *Moore*); NBlackf 69 (1988) 246s (A. *Kee*); TGL 78 (1988) 440s (K. J. *Tossou*); TLond 91 (1988) 509s (C. C. *Rowland*).

9557 *Colombo* Giuseppe, La teologia della liberazione, la questione del metodo; rilievi critici III: TItSett 13 (1988) 1-16; Eng. 17: 'C. BOFF has wholly given up his preceding positions under the guide of the theoretical plan of L. ALTHUSSER'.

9559 **Comblin** José, [➤ 9445 supra; 2,5688*] El Espíritu Santo y la liberación, ᵀ*Ortiz Garcia* Alfonso: Cristianismo y Sociedad 7. M 1987, Paulinas. 247 p. – ᴿCarthaginensia 4 (1988) 377 (F. *Martínez Fresneda*); CiTom 115 (1988) 584s (J. L. *Espinel*); ComSev 21 (1988) 405 (J. F. *Martínez Lahoz*); LumenVr 37 (1988) 345s (F. *Ortiz de Urtaran*).

9559* **Cook** Guillermo, The expectation of the poor; Latin American base ecclesial communities in Protestant perspective: Amer. Soc. Missiology 9, 1985 ➤ 3,8444: ᴿÉglT 18 (1987) 276s (R. P. *Hardy*).

9560 **Dixon** David C., A critical analysis of liberationist Christology in the writings of G. GUTIÉRREZ, L. BOFF, and J. SOBRINO: diss. SW Baptist 1988 – RelStR 15,191.

9560* *a*) *Dodd* Kevin, The triumph of grace; an investigation of J. L. SEGUNDO's 'A theology for artisans of a new humanity'; – *b*) *Short* Margaret I., Religion and the ideological foundations of Marxism-Leninism: StudiaBT 16 (1988) 99-120 / 3-37.

9561 **Donders** Joseph G., Liberation, the Jesus mode [B-cycle Gospels]. Maryknoll NY 1987, Orbis. xi-275 p. $11 [BToday 26,250].

9562 **Durán Flórez** Ricardo, La utopía de la liberación ¿teología de los pobres? Callao, Perú 1988. 335 p. – ᴿCarthaginensia 4 (1988) 401 (F. *Martínez Fresneda*).

9563 [Terán] *Dutari* Julio, Acercamiento a la Teología de la Liberación: Yachay 4,7 (Cochabama, Bolivia 1987) 39-62 [< TKontext 10/1,81].

9564 *Espeja* Jesús, Cómo llegó la salvación (diálogo entre las teologías europea y latino-americana): CiTom 115 (1988) 441-467.

9565 **Ferm** Deane W., Profiles in liberation; 36 portraits of Third World theologians. Mystic CT 1988, Twenty-Third. 193 p. $10 pa. 0-89622-377-9 [TDig 36,158].

9566 **Ferm** Deane W., Third world liberation theologies 1986 ⇥ 2,6687; 3,8457: ᴿEglT 18 (1987) 273-5 (R. P. *Hardy*); LvSt 13 (1988) 84s (Diana L. *Hayes*).

9567 **Fernando Castillo** L., Iglesia liberadora y política. Santiago, Chile 1986, ECO. 201 p. – ᴿChristus 53,620 (Méx 1988) 55s (J. *Jiménez Limón*).

9568 **Fischer** Klaus P., Gotteserfahrung; Mystagogie... RAHNER/Theologie der Befreiung 1986 ⇥ 2,6689; 3,8458: ᴿNRT 110 (1988) 424s (L. *Renwart*); TPhil 63 (1988) 285s (R. *Sebott*); ZkT 110 (1988) 115-7 (L. *Lies*).

9569 **Fogel** Daniel, Junipero SERRA, the Vatican and enslavement theology. SF 1988, Ism. 219 p. $9 [TDig 35,358: Serra, Franciscan, 1712-1784, was too harsh and chauvinist for canonization: anyway no God exists...].

9570 *Frostin* Per, La hermenéutica de los pobres; la ruptura epistemológica en las teologías del tercer mundo [< ST 39 (1985) 127-150], ᵀᴱ*Boix* Aureli: SelT 27 (1988) 43-56.

9571 ᴱ**Galilea** Segundo, Liberation theology and the Vatican document, ᵀ*Prendergast* Olga, *Rossa* Alberto: 1. General survey; 2. A Philippine perspective; 3. Perspectives from the Third World. Quezon City 1987, Claretian [Bloomington IN, Meyer-Stone]. vii-110 p.; viii-170 p.; ix-159 p. $10 each [TDig 35,374].

9572 **García** Ismael, Justice in Latin American theology of liberation ᴰ1987 ⇥ 3,8468: ᴿMissiology 16 (1988) 490s (sr. T. *O'Reilly*).

9573 **Gibellini** Rosino, The liberation theology debate [Il dibattito 1986 ⇥ 2,6693] 1987 ⇥ 3,8470: also Maryknoll NY, Orbis; $10 pa. – ᴿCC 139 (1988,3) 432s (P. *Vanzan*: riserve).

9574 **Goizueta** Roberto S., Liberation, method and dialogue; Enrique DUSSEL and North American theological discourse: [J]AAR 58. Atlanta 1988, Scholars. xxiv-174 p. $21; pa. $14 [TDig 35,361].

9574* *Goldstein* Horst, 'Reiche Gesellschaften können sich eine solche Theologie nicht leisten'; Ernüchternde Überlegungen zur Rezeption der latein-amerikanischen Befreiungstheologie im deutschsprachigen Raum: ⇥ 76, ᶠKAUFMANN L., Biotope 1988, 341-350.

9575 ᴱ**Greinacher** Norbert, Konflikt um die Theologie der Befreiung; Diskussion und Dokumentation 1985 ⇥ 1,8097; DM 34 pa.: ᴿTLZ 113 (1988) 309s (G. *Gassmann*).

9576 **Guillaumin** Armand, 'La séduction marxiste'; un prêtre médite MARX. Boulogne 1987, Sermis. 351 p. F 60. – ᴿSpiritus 29 (1988) 105 (J. *Sommet*).

9577 **Gutiérrez** Gustavo,   A theology of liberation; history, politics, and salvation; 15th anniversary edition [with new 30-p. essay], ᵀ*Inda* sr. Caridad, *Eagleson* John.   Maryknoll NY 1988, Orbis.   xlvi-264 p. $30; pa. $12. 0-88344-543-3; 2-3 [TDig 36,161].

9578 **Gutierrez** G.,   Aus der eigenen Quelle trinken 1986 ⇥ 2,6704; 3,8477: ᴿÖkRu 37 (1988) 124-6 (Reinhild *Traitler*).

9579 **Gutiérrez** G.,   La force historique des pauvres 1986 ⇥ 2.6706; 3,8482: ᴿBLitEc 89 (1988) 148 (H. de *Gensac*: ch. 5s, 8s du livre de 1982).

9580 *Gutiérrez* G. [interview < DIAL VII.1988],   L'affaire LEFEBVRE et la Théologie de la Libération: Sève 501 (1988) 465-470.

9581 *a*) *Gutiérrez* Gustavo,   Wenn wir Indianer wären, ᵀ*Goldstein* H.; – *b*) *Boff* Leonardo, Die Theologie der Befreiung post BATZINGER locutum, ᵀ*Flohr* F., – *c*) *Rottländer* Peter,   Option für die Armen; Erneuerung der Weltkirche und Umbruch der Theologie; – *d*) *Schillebeeckx* Edward, Befreiende Theologie, ᵀ*Zulauf* H.; – *e*) *Castillo* Fernando,   Theologie der Befreiung und Sozialwissenschaften ... Dependenztheorie, ᵀ*Zamora* J.A.: ⇥ 106, ᶠMETZ J.B., Mystik 1988, 32-44 / 287-311 /72-88 / 56-71 / 143-151.

9582 **Haight** Roger,   An alternative vision 1985 ⇥ 1,8107 ... 3,8487: ᴿNor-TTs 89 (1988) 141-3 (K. *Nordstokke,* also on CHOPP R., NÚÑEZ E.).

9583 **Hasenhüttl** Gotthold,   Freiheit in Fesseln; die Chance der Befreiungs-theologie; ein Erfahrungsbericht 1985 ⇥ 1,8111; 3,8489: ᴿIrTQ 54 (1988) 247s (S. *Murphy*).

9584 **Hayes** Diana L.,   Tracings of an American theology of liberation: from political theology to a theology of the two-thirds world: diss. ᴰ*Schrijver* G. De.   Lv 1988.   lxiv-560 p. – LvSt 13 (1988) 371s.

9585 *Herr* Theodor,   Theologie der Versöhnung in Cuba: TGL 78 (1988) 115-133.

9586 *Herzog* Frederick,   New Christology; core of new ecclesiology? [despite title, reviews six Liberation Theology books, BOFF's Ecclesiogenesis and others without Christology in title]: RelStR 14 (1988) 214-6.

9587 *a*) *Houtart* François,   Leuven en de bevrijdingstheologie; – *b*) *Damen* Frans,   De christelijke kerken en het fenomeen van de sekten in Latijns-Amerika: Wereld en Zending 17 (Amst 1988) 142-157 / 158-164 [< ZIT 88,572].

9588 **Hundley** Raymond C.,   Radical liberation theology; an evangelical response.   Wilmore KY 1987, Bristol.   141 p. [GraceTJ 9,308].

9589 **Imboden** Roberta,   From the Cross to the Kingdom; Sartrean dialectics and liberation theology; 1987 ⇥ 3,8492; pref. *Baum* Gregory: ᴿCCurr 23 (1988s) 245s (R. *Aronson*); SR 17 (1987) 499 (R. *Haight*).

9590 **Interdonato** Francisco,   Ser o no ser de la teología en Latinoamérica; a propósito de la Instrucción sobre algunos aspectos de la 'Teología de la Liberación'.   Lima 1985, Fac. Teología.   269 p. – ᴿActuBbg 25 (1988) 93 (F. de P. *Solà*).

9591 *Jelonek* Tomasz, ℗ De notione biblica libertatis [... Instructio 6.VIII.1984]: RuBi 41 (1988) 347-353.

9592 *Judd* Stephen M.,   The seamy side of charity [*Illich* I., 1967] revisited; American Catholic contributions to renewal in the Latin-American church: Missiology 15,2 (1987) 3-14.

9593 *Knapp* Markus, Die Option für die Armen als theologische Kategorie; Überlegungen zum Verhältnis von Erlösung und Befreiung: ➤ 53, FGA-NOCZY A., Creatio 1988, 134-153.

9594 *Kruip* Gerhard, Theologie der Befreiung und katholische Soziallehre [Tagung Essen 1.-3. Dez. 1985]; neue Ansätze im Dialog: ZMissRW 72 (1988) 55-64.

9595 *Kuczyńsky* Janusz, Christianity and Marxism; confrontation, dialogue, universalism: JEcuSt 25 (1988) 85-102.

9596 *Kuitert* H. M., Theologie van de bevrijding en bevrijding van de theologie [... Wat is theologie?]: GerefTTs 88 (1988) 20-31.

9597 *Lafontaine* René, 'La liberté chrétienne et la libération': réflexions sur l'instruction romaine: NRT 110 (1988) 181-211.

9598 **Libânio** João B., Teologia da libertação, roteiro didático para um estudo: Fé e Realidade 22. São Paulo 1988, Loyola. 300 p. – RREB 48 (1988) 1015s (C. M. *Boff*).

9599 *Libânio* João B., Comunidades eclesiales de base; ¿Qué se quiere decir con el término 'base'? [< PerspT 18 (1986) 63-76], TECulebras Antonio M.: SelT 27 (1988) 289-297.

9600 *Liszka* Piotr, ❷ W kręgu... The theological thought of Leonard BOFF: ZesKUL 29,2 (1986) 47-61; Eng. 61.

9601 *Lobo* George V., Rome accepts liberation theology: ➤ 337, Liberation in Asia 1987, 211-223 (189-209, *Kunnumpuram* Kurian).

9601* *McGovern* Arthur F., *Schubeck* Thomas L., Updating liberation theology: America 159 (1988) 32-35.47.

9602 **McLellan** David, Marxism and religion; a description and assessment of the Marxist critique of Christianity. L 1987, Macmillan. ix-209 p. £27.50; pa. £8. – RMonth 249 (1988) 598s (F. *Copleston*).

9603 **Marlé** R., Introduction à la théologie de la libération. P 1988, D-Brouwer. 172 p. 2-220-02692-2. – RTéléma 14,55s (1988) 100s (C. *Delhez*).

9604 *Martins Terra* J. E., Como se lê a Biblia na América Latina: RCuBib 45s (1988) 3-112 [-183]; 47s (1988) 3-10 [25-156].157-254 [255-9, *Martins Terra* nomeado bispo auxiliar de Recife].

9605 a) *Mette* Norbert, Europäische Christen vor der Befreiungstheologie; – b) *Bruhin* Josef, Schweiz: Dritte Welt; Prüfstand: Orientierung 52 (1988) 157-160 / 190-2.

9606 **Morello** Raúl, Rezar hasta la libertad. Florida BA 1988, Paulinas. 116 p. 950-09-0769-0.

9606* **Mulholland-Wozniak** Ann, Dangerous stories; the subversive ethnic [sic RelStR 15,192] in Latin American liberation theology: diss. Univ. S. California 1988.

9607 **Muñoz** Ronaldo, Dios de los cristianos: Cristianismo y Sociedad 4. M 1987, Paulinas. 252 p. 84-285-1153-5. – RActuBbg 25 (1988) 230s (J. *Giménez Melià*: perspectiva teol. lib.).

9607* **Nealen** Mary Kaye, The poor in the ecclesiology of Juan Luis SEGUNDO: diss. DGranfield P. Washington 1988. – RTLv 20,564.

9608 *Nessan* Craig L., Basic Christian community; liberation theology in praxis: CurrTM 15 (1988) 336-341.

9609 ENieuwenhove Jacques Van, Jésus et la libération en Amérique latine: JJC 26, 1986 ➤ 2,6747; 3,8516: RZMissRW 72 (1988) 85 (H. *Waldenfels*).

9610 *Nordstokke* Kjell, Frigjøringskristologi [*Sobrino* J. 1987; *Boff* L. 1986]: NorTTs 89 (1988) 133-140.

9611 **Novak** Michael, Will it liberate? 1986 → 2,6749; 3,8517: ᴿCalvinT 23 (1988) 88-91 (J. W. *Cooper*); Horizons 15 (1988) 199s (L. J. *Biallas*); RRelRes 30 (1988s) 85s (R. A. *Hoehn*); Thomist 52 (1988) 362-4 (M. J. *Kerlin*); TTod 45 (1988s) 369s. 372 (L. *Cormie*).

9612 **Núñez-C.** Emilio A., Liberation theology, ᵀ*Sywalka* Paul E, 1985 → 1,8155; 2,6750: ᴿMissiology 15,1 (1987) 125s (E. J. *Dunn*).

9612* **Parra** Alberto, De la Iglesia misterio a la Iglesia de los pobres: Cuad. Teol. 7, 1984 → 3,8521: ᴿDivThom 91 (1988) 211-3 (C.*Riccardi*).

9613 **Pasquetto** Virgilio, Mai più schiavi; aspetti religiosi e sociali del concetto biblico di liberazione. N 1988, Dehoniane. 528 p. Lit. 30.000. 88-396-0162-7.

9614 **Piepke** Joachim G., Die Kirche auf dem Weg zum Menschen; die Volk-Gottes-Ekklesiologie in der Kirche Brasiliens 1985 → 1,8166; 3,8525: ᴿMissiology 16 (1988) 92 (E. T. *Bachmann*).

9615 *Pregeant* Russell, Christological groundings for liberation praxis [*Sobrino* J.]: ModT 5 (1988s) 113-132.

9616 *Principe* Walter H., Catholicity, inculturation and liberation theology; do they mix?: FrancStAn 25 (1987) 24-43.

9617 *Raiser* Konrad, A new reading of the Bible? Ecumenical perspectives from Latin America and Asia: → 505, Creative 1985/8, 103-113.

9618 **Reinders** J. S., Violence, victims and rights; a reappraisal of the argument from institutionalized violence with special reference to Latin American liberation theology: diss. Amst Vrije Univ. ᴰ*Kuitert* H. 1988. 250 p. – TsTNijm 28, 294.

9619 **Richard** Pablo, La fuerza espiritual de la Iglesia de los pobres; pról. *Boff* L. San José CR 1987, Dep. Ecum. Inv. 187 p. 9977-904-55-3. – ᴿActuBbg 25 (1988) 240s (R. de *Sivatte*).

9620 ᴱ**Richard** Pablo, Raices de la teología latinoamericana; nuevos materiales... 1985 → 2,6762: ᴿTPhil 63 (1988) 315-7 (M. *Sievernich*).

9621 *Rizzi* Armido, Elementi di una teologia della liberazione per l'Occidente: RasT [28 (1987) 557-577] 29 (1988) 63-77.

9622 **Roos** Lothar, Befreiungstheologien und katholische Soziallehre: Kirche und Gesellschaft 119s. Köln 1985, Bachem. 3-7616-0811-X; 6-0. – ᴿWiss-Weis 50 (1987) 77-79 (M. *Lohmann*).

9623 ᴱ**Rottländer** Peter, Theologie der Befreiung und Marxismus 1986 → 3,455: ᴿTPhil 63 (1988) 310-2 (N. *Brieskorn*).

9624 *Ruiz* Octavio, La teología de la liberación y su método: Medellín 14,53 (1988) 41-64 [< TKontext 10/1,93].

9625 **Santa Ana** Julio de, Ecumenismo y liberación: Cristianismo y Sociedad. M 1987, Paulinas. 323 p. – ᴿChristus 53,620 (Méx 1988) 56s (J. *Jiménez Limón*).

9626 **Schottroff** Luise & Willy, Wer ist unser Gott? Beiträge zu einer Befreiungstheologie im Kontext der 'ersten' Welt 1986 → 3,8537: ᴿTPhil 63 (1988) 313-5 (M. *Sievernich*).

9626* *Schottroff* Luise, How my mind has changed; oder, Neutestamentliche Wissenschaft im Dienste von Befreiung: EvT 48 (1988) 247-261.

9627 **Segundo** J. L., Theology and church... response to RATZINGER [²ʳᵉᵛ 1985 → 1,8184... 3,8541]. 1987. – ᴿHomP 88,9 (1987s) 77-79 (J. V. *Schall*; belabored).

9628 ᴱ**Seibel** W., Dass Gott den Schrei seines Volkes hört; die Herausforderung der lateinamerikanischen Befreiungstheologie [6 Autoren < StiZt 1985s] 1987 → 3,462: ᴿTPhil 63 (1988) 309s (M. *Sievernich*).

9629 **Serrano Ursua** Félix, Puebla, balance de un debate teológico-pastoral sobre la misión de la Iglesia. Guatemala 1987, Inst. Teol. Salesiano 382 p. – ᴿActuBbg 25 (1988) 241 (I. *Riudor*).

9630 *Sievernich* Michael, Mysterium Liberationis, Enzyklopädie der Befreiungstheologie [53 Bände, 6 in 1987]: StiZt 206 (1988) 498-501.

9631 **Silva Moreira** Alberto da, '... doch die Armen werden das Land bekommen' (Ps 37,11); eine theologische Lektüre der Landkonflikte in Brasilien: Diss. ᴰ*Metz.* Münster 1987s. – TR 84 (1988) 512.

9632 **Silva Soler** Joaquín, El significado eclesiológico de la solidaridad de la Iglesia con los pobres; una sistematización a partir de le reflexión eclesiológica latinoamericana: diss. ᴰ*Hünermann.* Tü 1987s. – TR 84 (1988) 514.

9633 **Sobrino** Jon, Jésus en Amérique Latine, sa signification pour la foi et la christologie 1986 → 3,8544: ᴿDocCom 41 (1988) 184-8 (B. de *Margerie*).

9634 **Sobrino** Jon, Jesus in Latin America 1987 → 3,8546: ᴿMonth 249 (1988) 644s (Helen *Tomnay*).

9635 *Sölle* Dorothee, Unterwegs zu einer befreienden Theologie: Universitas 43 (Stu 1988) 49-52.

9635* **Stenger** Barry J., The option for the poor in Latin American liberation theology: diss. Chicago 1987. – RelStR 15,192.

9636 **Thuruthiyil** Scaria, Towards an anthropology of liberation; an approach proposed by Jiddu KRISHNAMURTI: Diss. Pont. Univ. Salesiana, ᴰ*Cantone* C. R 1987. – Salesianum 50 (1988) 473.

9637 *Tortolone* Gian Michele, Evento e kerygma; linee di sviluppo della teologia della liberazione latinoamericana nell'ultimo decennio (1978-1987): FilT 1,3 (1988) 141-159.

9638 *Ullrich* Lothar, Theologie aus der Perspektive der Armen; ein Versuch zum Verständnis der lateinamerikanischen Theologie der Befreiung: CLehre 41 (B 1988) 196-211 [< ZIT 88,629].

9639 *a) Vela* Jesús Andrés, Elementos metodológicos en la Teología de la Liberación: TXav 38,86s (1988) 105-133 [< TKontext 10/1,95]; – *b) Vizcaya* Manuel T., El método en la teología de la liberación: CiTom 114 (1987) 521-546.

9639* *a) Williams* David T., The heresy of prosperity teaching; a message for the Church in its approach to need: JTSAf 61 (1987) 33-44; – *b) Anderson* Allan, The prosperity message in the eschatology of some new charismatic churches: Missionalia 15.2 (1987) 72-83; response *Mofokeng* T. 84-86 [< TKontext 9/2,20s].

9640 *Witvliet* T., A place in the sun [Een plats onder de zon; Bevrijdingstheologie in de derde wereld. Baarn 1984, Ten Have] 1985 → 1, 8209 ... 3,8559: ᴿÉglT 17 (1986) 404-6 (R. P. *Hardy*).

9641 *Wolterstorff* N., Can a Calvinist be progressive? [... hear the cries of the world's oppressed; article in English 'by way of experiment']: GerefTTs 88 (1988) 249-258.

H8.6 *Theologiae emergentes* – '**Theologies of' emergent groups.**

9641* **Abeyasingha** Nihal, The radical tradition; the changing shape of theological reflection in Sri Lanka. Colombo 1985, Ecumenical Institute. 232 p. – ᴿTKontext 9,2 (1988) 106 (G. *Evers*).

9642 ᴱ**Ahn Byung-Mu,** *Glüer* Winfried, Draussen vor dem Tor; Kirche und Minjung in Korea. Gö 1986, Vandenhoeck & R. 156 p. [Mundus 23,131].

9643 ᴱ**Amato** A., *Strus* A., Inculturazione e formazione salesiana 1983/4 ➤ 65,474: ᴿNZMissW 43 (1987) 72s (J. *Baumgartner*).

9644 *Amjad-Ali* Christine M., The Bible and contextual theology, a review article [three books of exegesis]: Al-Mushir 29 (Rawalpindi 1987) 81-88 [< TKontext 10/1,68].

9645 *a) Arevalo* Catalino G., After Vatican II; theological reflection in the church in the Philippines: Landas 2,1 (Manila 1988) 11-24; – *b) Mesa* José M. de, Re-thinking the faith with indigenous categories: Inter Religio 13 (Nagoya 1988) 18-29 [TKontext 10/1,118 deutsch].

9646 *Arulsamy* S., La teología de la liberación en la India [< IndTSt 22 (1985) 266-288], ᵀᴱ*Cabié* Maite: SelT 27 (1988) 57-67.

9647 *a) Avi* Dick, Contextualization in Melanesia: Melanesian Journal of Theology 4,1 (1988) 7-22; – *b) Batumalai* S., The task of Malaysian theology: Inter Religio 13 (Nagoya Nanzan Univ., Japan 1988) 2-17 [TKontext 10/1,117 deutsch].

9648 ᴱ**Bartnik** Czesław S., ☉ Polska teologia Narodu (la teologia polacca della Nazione) [seminario]: Rozprawy Teol.-Kanon. 73. Lublin 1986, KUL. 347 p. – ᴿTeresianum 39 (1988) 226-8 (S. T. *Praskiewicz*).

9649 *Berger* Reingard, The Catholic Church in Zimbabwe [< Einheit und Vielheit in der Weltkirche; ein Zeugnis aus Afrika: Ordens-Korrespondenz 28,1 (1987) 6-16], ᵀᴱ*Asen* B. A.: TDig 35 (1988) 128s.

9649* *a) Bevans* Stephen, A local theology in a world Church; some U.S. contributions to systematic theology; – *b) Duffy* Regis [*Himes* Kenneth]... moral theology: NewTR 1,1 (1988) 72ss / 30ss [53ss].

9650 *Bilezikian* G., Hierarchist and egalitarian inculturations: JEvTS 30 (1987) 421-6 [NTAbs 32,201].

9651 *Botha* J., A critical view of the use of Scriptures in the Kairos Document: Orientation 48 (Pontchefstroom 1988) 87-95 [< TKontext 10/1,26].

9651* **Brown** Kelly D., 'Who do they say that I am?'; A critical examination of the Black Christ: Diss. Union Theol. Sem. NY 1988. – RelStR 15,191.

9652 **Bujo** Bénézet, Afrikanische Theologie 1986 ➤ 3,8587: ᴿZMissRW 72 (1988) 78 (H. *Janssen*).

9653 *Bujo* Bénézet, Can morality be Christian in Africa?: Chiea AfSt 4,1 (1988) 5-39 [TKontext 10/1,115 deutsch].

9654 *Burleson* Blake W., John Mʙɪᴛɪ as anti-historian of theology: AfTJ 16 (1987) 104-120 [< TKontext 10/1,17].

9655 *Caldwell* L. W., Third horizon ethnohermeneutics; re-evaluating NT hermeneutical models for intercultural Bible interpreters today: AsiaJT 1,2 (1987) 314-333 [NTAbs 32,141].

9656 *Cardot* Daniel, *Chataigné* Paul, Cheminement d'un groupe de missionnaires [6-années plan d'action de la Société des Missions Africaines] dans leur engagement envers les pauvres: Spiritus 29 (1988) 122-140.

9657 **Chan** Kim-Kwong, Towards a contextual ecclesiology; the Catholic Church in the People's Republic of China (1979-1983); its life and theological implications. Pasadena 1987, China Ministries. xxxvii-465 p. $12.50. [NewTR 2/2, 109, P. *Fleming*].

9658 ᴱ**Chenu** Bruno, Théologies chrétiennes [➤ 3,8594] des tiers mondes, présent. *Chenu* M.-D. P 1987, Centurion. 213 p. – ᴿArTGran 51 (1988) 316 (J. A. *Estrada*); Spiritus 29 (1988) 110 (G. *Meyer*); Téléma 14,55s (1988) 94-96 (M. *Duclaux*)

9659 ᴱ**Chenu** B., Teologie cristiane dei Terzi Mondi; present. *Chenu* M.-D.: GdT 181. Brescia 1988, Queriniana. 312 p. Lit. 22.000. – ᴿAsprenas 35 (1988) 294 (A. *Terracciano*).

9660 *Chow* Joseph, ☉ About 'elevation' in the process of indigenizing theology: ColcFuJen 76 (1988) 203-228.

9661 **Clark** Donald N., Christianity in modern Korea. Lanham MD 1986, UPA. xiii-55 p. $4.75. – ᴿMissiology 16 (1988) 354s (H. M. *Conn*).

9662 **Cone** James H., A black theology of liberation 1986 = 1970 ➤ 3,8601: ᴿModT 4 (1987s) 406 (D. *Cohn-Sherbok*: stimulating, but his own preface points out what changes should have been made).

9663 **Cone** James H., For my people 1984 ➤ 65,7320... 3,8603: ᴿJEcuSt 24 (1987) 124 (J. H. *Moorhead*).

9664 *a) Cone* J., Theologies of liberation among U.S. racial-ethnic minorities [Concilium 199 (E 1988) 54-64] = Théologies de la libération chez les minorités ethniques ou raciales des États-Unis; – *b) Mveng* E., La théologie africaine de la libération; – *c) Balasuriya* T., Apparition de théologies de libération asiatiques: ➤ 350, Concilium 219 (P 1988) 77-89 / 31-51 / 53-64.

9665 **Conn** Harvie M., Eternal Word and changing worlds; theology, anthropology, and mission in trialogue 1984 ➤ 2,6828: ᴿCalvinT 23 (1988) 117s (J. A. *DeJong*).

9665* *Corbon* Jean, L'inculturation de la foi chrétienne au Moyen-Orient; eléments de problématique ecclésiologique: PrOrChr 38 (1988) 255-271.

9666 *Czajkowski* Michał, Die Inkulturation des Evangeliums Jesu im Neuen Testament und heute: ColcT 58 sp. (1988) 29-38.

9667 *Danker* William J., Yardsticks for Japanese Christianity: ➤ 143, ᶠTIETJEN J. = CurrTM 15 (1988) 95-101.

9668 *Davis* Kortright, Prioridades teológicas en el tercer mundo [< ScotJT 40 (1987) 85-105], ᵀᴱ*Messa* Josep: SelT 27 (1988) 259-268.

9669 **De Gruchy** John, Theology and ministry in context and crisis; a South African perspective. L 1987, Collins. 183 p. £8 pa. – ᴿTLond 91 (1988) 362s (P. H. *Smith*).

9670 *Delhaye* Philippe, Études sur l'inculturation de la foi chrétienne d'après certains documents récents du Magistère: EsprVie 98 (1988) 1-11. 23-32. 40-45.

9671 **Diaz** Hector, A Korean theology,... CHONG YAK-JONG A. 1986 ➤ 3,8610: ᴿMissiology 16 (1988) 96 (*Wi Jo Kang*).

9672 **Dickson** Kwesi A., Theology in Africa 1984 ➤ 65,7325... 3,8610*: ᴿModT 5 (1988s) 83s (W. D. *Robinson*).

9673 **Dierks** Friedrich, Evangelium im afrikanischen Kontext; interkulturelle Kommunikation bei den Tswana [Diss. 1982] MissWissFor 19, 1986 ➤ 3,8611; DM 32: ᴿTLZ 113 (1988) 70 (J. *Schlegel*).

9674 **Dornberg** Ulrich, Kontextuelle Theologie in Sri Lanka; Neuere kirchliche und theologische Entwicklungen in einem asiatischen Land in ihrer exemplarischen theologischen Relevanz für die Weltkirche: Diss. ᴰ*Metz* J. Münster 1987s. – TKontext 10/1,130; TR 84 (1988) 512.

9675 *Edwards* Adrian, God above and God below [**Kirby** Jon P., God, shrines and problem-solving among the Anufo of northern Ghana. Coll. Anthropos (B 1986, Reimer) 368 p. DM 85; **Fernández** James W., Bwiti (among the Fang of Gabon; Princeton 1981, Univ.) xxiv-731 p.,£19]: NBlackf 69 (1988) 19-27.

9676 **Ela** Jean-Marc, Mein Glaube als Afrikaner; das Evangelium in schwarzafrikanischer Lebenswirklichkeit: Theologie der Dritten Welt 10, 1987 ➤ 3,8619: ᴿTPhil 63 (1988) 625s (J. *Kristöfl*).

9677 *Evers* Georg, Erste Schritte zu einer indischen Christologie; Seminar indischer Theologen in Madras, 15.-21. III. 1988: ZMissRW 72 (1988) 249s.

9678 *a) Felder* Cain H., Biblical hermeneutics and the Black Church tradition; – *b) Hamlin* E. John, Interpreting the Bible in Southeast Asia: UnSemQ 42,1s (1988) 63-68 / 105 ... [< ZIT].

9679 **Filbeck** David, Social context and proclamation ... cross-culturally 1985 ➤ 2,6844; 3,8624: ᴿMissiology 15,1 (1987) 126s (Marguerite G. *Kraft*).

9680 **Francisco** Jose M.C., A theoretical program for interpreting religious narrative [by] listening to the Philippine Payson tradition: diss. Graduate Theological Union. Berkeley 1986. – RelStR 14,185.

9680* ᴱ**Fugmann** Gernot, The birth of an indigenous church; letters, reports and documents of Lutheran Christians of Papua New Guinea: Point 10. Goroka 1986, Melanesian Institute for Pastoral. 276 p. – ᴿTKontext 9,2 (1988) 110 (H. *Janssen*).

9681 *a) Gächter* Othmar, The Church in India [< StiZt 112 (1987) 829-842]; ᵀᴱ*Asen* B.A.; – *b) Ambroise* Yvon, Sociological reflections on Indian liberation theology [< IndTSt 24 (1987) 103-142]. ᴱ*Jermann* Rosemary; – *c) Kolencherry* Antony, Caste in renascent India [< IndTSt 24 (1987) 301-320], ᴱ*Asen*: TDig 35 (1988) 107-111 / 112-4 / 115-9.

9682 *Galot* Jean, Christ, notre Ancêtre?: Téléma 14,53 (1988) 31-34.

9683 **Gelpi** Donald J., [➤ 197] Inculturating North American theology; an experiment in foundational method. Ithaca NY (POB 6525) 1988, Scholars. $20; pa. $13. 1-55540-210-0; 1-9.

9683* **Glélé** Maurice Ahanhanzo [Benin Catholic political scientist], Religion, culture et politique en Afrique noire. P 1981, Economica/Présence Africaine. 206 p. 2-7178-0291-6. – ᴿJRelAf 17 (1987) 93-96 (Å. *Hultekrantz*).

9684 *a) Gräf* H.J., Die Menschheit Jesu in der Sicht asiatischer Theologen dargestellt am Beispiel Indien; – *b) Waldenfels* H., Modelle christlicher Soteriologie in aussereuropäischem Kontext; – *c) Ullrich* L., Soteriologische Modelle in der Dogmengeschichte; eine Skizze als Orientierungshilfe; – *d) Beinert* W., 'Wesensgleich auch uns'; kontextuelle Modelle für eine Fundamentalaussage des christlichen Glaubens: TJb (Lp 1988) 207-233 / 153-275 / 234-254 /184-206 [< ZIT 89,386].

9685 *Gutheinz* Luis, Langsames Wachstum der Kirche Taiwans; missionstheologische Reflexionen: NZMissW 43 (1987) 1-16.

9686 *Harvey* Louis-Charles, From rejection to liberation; the development of the Black Church in Great Britain and the United States: IstRMiss 77 (1988) 67-77.

9687 **Hayes** D.L., Tracings of an American theology of liberation; from political theology to a theology of the two-thirds world: diss. ᴰ*Schrijver* G. de. Leuven 1988. lxiv-155 p. – TsTNijm 28,397.

9688 *Healey* Joseph G., *a)* Constructing a mission theology using African proverbs and sayings: Chiea AfChrSt 4,2 (1988) 71-85; – *b)* Proverbs and sayings, a window into the African Christian world view: Pastoral Orientation Service (Tanzania 1988,3) 1-15 [TKontext 10/1,19.22].

9689 *Hickey* Raymond, Slow progress towards an African Christianity: DoctLife 37 (1987) 183-190.

9690 **Hutchison** William R., Errand to the world; American Protestant thought and foreign missions. Ch 1987, Univ. xii-227 p.; 26 fig. $25. – ᴿRelStR 14 (1988) 175 (W. R. *Garrett*: mostly not just culture-imperialists or 'evangelizing sinners' [far from clear that sinners is objective case]).

9691 **[Ikenga] Metuh** Emefie, African religions in western conceptual schemes. Ibadan 1985, Pastoral Institute. xiv-176 p. – [R]HeythJ 29 (1988) 491 (G. *Parrinder*).

9692 *a) Ikenga-Metuh* E., African world-views as 'praeparatio evangelica'; – *b) Onwu* Nienanya, A divine commonwealth in Paul's thought; a critical reflection in an African context; – *c) Gbuji* Anthony, A review of the African response to Christian morality: Nigerian Journal of Theology 1,3 (1987) 46-60 / 61-72 / 5-23 [< TKontext 10/1,27].

9693 **Jesudasan** I., La teologia della liberazione in GANDHI [1984 ➤ 65,7339]. Assisi 1982, Cittadella. 243 p. – [R]Laurentianum 29 (1988) 171 (E. *Covi* 'Jesudan', '1982').

9694 *John* T.K., Theology of liberation and GANDHIAN praxis; a social spirituality for India: ➤ 337, Liberation in Asia 1987, 115-142.

9695 **Jongeneel** J.A.B., *Kniff* H.W., Een keuze uit het werk van Stanley J. SAMARTHA [honorary doctor Utrecht 11.VI. 1986]. Kampen 1986, Kok. 147 p. *f* 25,50. – [R]JEcuSt 25 (1988) 449 (M. *Bohen*).

9696 *a) Kabamba* Dianda, À la recherche d'une ecclésiologie Africaine; – *b) Mayamba Mbuya* Nianda, Rite Zarois ou rite romain...?: Select 20s (Kinshasa 1988) 71-97 / 98-111 [< TKontext 10/1,30].

9697 **Kabaséle** François, *al.*, Cristologia africana [*Doré* J., *al.* Chemins de la christologie africaine 1986 ➤ 3,8615],[T]. CinB 1987, Paoline. 283 p. Lit. 18.000. 88-215-1341-6. – [R]CC 139 (1988,4) 98 (Z. *Alszeghy*: continuità sì, ma anche rottura con la cultura previa); Gregorianum 69 (1988) 587s (A. *Wolanin*).

9698 *a) Kamuyu-wa-kang Ethe*, African response to Christianity; a case study of the Agikuyu of Central Kenya; – *b) Butselaar* G. Jan van. Gospel and culture in 19th century Mozambique: Missionalia 16 (1988) 23-44 / 45-56.

9699 **Khawam** René R., L'univers culturel des chrétiens d'Orient; pref. *Dalmais* Henri-I. P 1987 Cerf. 236 p. F 98. – [R]Spiritus 29 (1988) 441 (P. *Ternant*).

9700 **Kim Ee Kon,** 'Outcry' [Korean *minjung* '(downtrodden) people']; its context in biblical theology: Interpretation 42 (1988) 229-239.

9700* *Kim Sung-hae* sr., Liberation and inculturation; two streams of doing theology with Asian resources; the Catholic experience in Korea: EAPast 24 (1987) 379-391 [Interrreligio 12 (1987) 67-83; deutsch TKontext 9/2 (1988) 94].

9701 **Kirwen** Michael C., The missionary and the diviner 1987 ➤ 3,8652: [R]JEcuSt 25 (1988) 275s (N.E. *Thomas*); NewTR 1,3 (1988) 117s (A.J. *Gittins*).

9702 **Kochumuttom** Thomas, Comparative theology; Christian thinking and spirituality in Indian perspective. Bangalore 1985, Dharmaram. x-160 p. $5. – [R]LvSt 13 (1988) 182s (Catherine *Cornille*).

9703 **Kochupurackal** Cherian, India awaiting the Good News, Ernakulam 1988, CMI Mission Secretariat. 142 p. – [R]Jeevadhara 13 (1988) 389-392 (K. *Pathil*).

9704 *Kröger* Wolfgang, *a)* Grundlinien der Minjungtheologie; Theologie der Befreiung im koreanischen Kontext: EvT 48 (1988) 360-9; – *b)* 'Erfahrung' – ein Streitpunkt im ökumenischen Gespräch; Reflexion auf das Programm einer Befreiungstheologie im Kontext der Ersten Welt, ausgehend von Erfahrungen in Südkorea: ÖkRu 37 (1988) 185-199.

9705 *Lee* Peter K.H., Some critical issues in Asian theological thinking: Ching Feng 31 (Hong Kong 1988) 124-152 [TKontext 10/1,115 deutsch].

9706 *Leers* Bernardino, Contradições na Igreja inculturada no Brasil: Convergência 23 (1988) 288-304.

9707 *Lentzen-Deis* Fritzleo, Application de la Bible aux differentes cultures, ᵀ*Guillou* Delphine: ➤ 379, Vatican II Bilan 3 (1988) 407-429; Eng. ➤ 380 Assessment 3, 419-441.

9708 **Loth** Heinrich, Vom Schlangenkult zur Christuskirche; Religion und Messianismus in Afrika; Fischer Tb. Allg. 4372. Fra 1987, Fischer. 3-596-24372-6. – ᴿÖkRu 37 (1988) 385s (H.-J. *Becken*).

9709 **Luneau** René, 'Laisse aller mon peuple'; églises africaines au-delà des modèles. Karthala 1987. 180 p. F 80. – ᴿTéléma 13,1 (1987) 79-84 (Londi *Boka di Mpasi*).

9710 *McConnell* William T., The twentieth century reformation; Protestant involvement in the indiginization [sic] of theology in Latin America: FidH 20,1 (1988) 51- ... [< ZIT 88,620].

9711 *McConville* William M., Local theologies in a world church; Aloysius PIERIS and the epiphany of Asian Christianity: NewTR 1,3 (1988) 73-87.

9712 **Masson** Joseph, Père de nos pères [... prière africaine]: Documenta missionalia 21. R 1988, Pont. Univ. Gregoriana. 288 p. Lit. 38.500. 88-7652-579-3.

9713 ᴱ**May** John D., Living theology in Melanesia, a reader; POINT sup. 8. Goroka, Papua-NG 1985, Melanesian Institute. 310 p. – ᴿIntRMiss 77 (1988) 139-141 (H.-R. *Weber*).

9714 *May* John D., Contextual theology in Melanesia [< ZMissRW 71 (1987) 279-291], ᴱ*Asen* B. A.: TDig 35 (1988) 25-29.

9715 **Mbembe** Achille, Afriques indociles; christianisme, pouvoir et état en société post-coloniale. P 1988, Karthala. 222 p. F 85. – ᴿSpiritus 29 (1988) 327 (H. *Maurier*).

9716 **Mbiti** John S., Bible and theology in African Christianity 1986 ➤ 3,8663: ᴿJEH 39 (1988) 324s (A. *Hastings*); IntRMiss 77 (1988) 282-4 (H.-R. *Weber*).

9717 **Mbiti** John S., Bibel und Theologie im afrikanischen Christentum 1987 ➤ 3,8664: ᴿErbAuf 64 (1988) 235 (A. *Neumann*); ÖkRu 37 (1988) 506-8 (E. *Kamphausen*).

9717* **Menacherry** Cheriyan, An Indian philosophical approach to the personality of Jesus ... Surjit Singh, 'preface to personality; Christology in relation to Radhakrishnan's philosophy' [1952] 1986 ➤ 2,6868; 3,8665: ᴿTKontext 9,2 (1988) 115 (G. *Evers*).

9718 **Miranda** Dionisio M., Pagkamakatao; reflections on the theological virtues in the Philippine context. Manila 1987, Divine Word. 102 p. – ᴿVerbumSVD 29 (1988) 111s (F.-J. *Eilers*).

9719 *Mofokeng* G. A., A black Christology; a new beginning: JBlackT 1,1 (1987) 1-17 [TKontext 10/1,114 deutsch].

9720 *a) Mofokeng* Takatso, Black Christians, the Bible and liberation; – *b) Maimela* Simon S., Theological dilemmas and options for the Black Church; – *c) Lamola* J. M., Towards a Black Church; a historical investigation of the African Independent Churches as a model: JBlackT 2,1 (1988) 34-42 / 15-25 / 5-14 [< TKontext 10/1,24].

Moloney F. J.. Jesus Christ; the question to cultures: Pacifica 1,1 (1988) 15-43 ➤ 4190.

9722 ᴱ**Mulago gwa Cikale** V. M., Afrikanische Spiritualität ... 1986 ➤ 3,8677: ᴿNZMissW 43 (1987) 152 (W. *Bühlmann*).

9723 **Neckebrouck** Valeer, La Tierce Église devant le problème de la culture. Immensee 1987, NZMissW. 164 p. Fs 24. – ᴿETL 64 (1988) 218s (R. *Boudens*); Spiritus 29 (1988) 326s (H. *Maurier*).

9724 **Neill** Stephen, A history of Christianity in India I-II, 1984s → 65, 7353 ... 3,6888s: ᴿHeythJ 29 (1988) 133s (J. *Lipner,* 1s); ᴿNZMissW 43 (1987) 156-8 (J. *Wicki,* 2).

9725 **Newbigin** Lesslie, Foolishness to the Greeks; the Gospel and Western culture 1986 → 2,6890; 3,8684: ᴿScotJT 41 (1988) 541-3 (A. *Thomson*).

9726 *Ngindu Mushete* A., La figure de Jésus dans la théologie africaine: Concilium 216 (P 1988) 91-99.

9727 **Njoroge** Lawrence, African Christianity, a portrait: ChSt 26 (1987) 105-121.

9728 **Nyamiti** Charles, Christ as our ancestor 1984 → 3,8689: ᴿMilltSt 17 (1986) 113-7 (R. *Moloney,* with 17 titles on African Christology).

9729 *O'Hanlon* Gerard, An image of God for Ireland today: MilltSt 21 (1988) 13-27.

9730 **Okorocha** Cyris C., The meaning of religious conversion in Africa; the case of the Igbo in Nigeria. [diss. Univ. Aberdeen]. Brookfield VT 1987, Gower. xv-352 p. $105 [TDig 35,384].

9731 *Onwurah* Emeka, ◑ Is African culture anti-Christian? – A historical and factual reflection on aspects of Nigerian culture against Christian background, aspiration and hope: KatKenk 27,54 (1988) 109-123 = 295-300; Eng. xvi-xvii.

9732 **Paikada** Mathew, Characteristics of an Indian liberation theology as an authentic Christian theology; a study based on the analysis of the Indian situation and the documents of the CBCI and the FABC: diss. ᴰ*Metz* J. Münster 1987s. – TR 84 (1988) 512; TKontext 10/1,127.

9733 *Pang* Paul P., The encounter of Christianity with Chinese culture: EuntDoc 41 (1988) 439-460.

9734 **Park Il-Young,** Minjung, Schamanismus und Inkulturation; schamanistische Religiosität und christliche Praxis in Korea: Diss. ᴰ*Friedli.* FrS 1987s. – TR 84 (1988) 514.

9735 ᴱ**Parratt** John, A reader in African theology.TEF Study Guide. L 1987, SPCK. xi-178 p. [JTS 39,673].

9735* *Patience* Allan, Towards a theology of the Australian multicultural experience: AustralasCR 65 (1988) 423-440.

9736 **Pieris** Aloysius, Theologie der Befreiung in Asien 1986 → 2,6901; 3,8704: ᴿÖkRu 37 (1988) 505s (Takeshi *Yasui*); TPQ 136 (1988) 277s (J. *Janda*).

9737 *a*) *Pieris* Aloysius, A theology of liberation in Asian churches?: → 337, Liberation in Asia 1987, 17-38; – *b*) [Pieris A.] A truly Asian theology: Tablet 242 (1988) 668.670 (D. *Nicholl*).

9738 *Piryns* Ernest D., Japanese theology and inculturation: JEcuSt 24 (1987) 535-556 [TKontext 10/1,116 deutsch].

9739 *Pobee* John S., Ahnen und Heilige und die Kirche in Afrika,ᵀ: UnSa 43 (1988) 309-315.

9740 *a*) *Pomykol* Jan, The inculturation of the Church in Japan in and by means of the community; – *b*) *Evers* Georg, Die theologische Problematik der katholischen Kirche in China; – *c*) *Kirby* Jon P., Anthropology and mission in Ghana; the first 50 years: VerbumSVD 29 (1988) 355-370 / 327-354 / 371-385.

9741 *Poupard* Paul card., Évangile et cultures: Carmel 48 (1987) 280-304.

9742 *a*) *Reedijk* Piet, Geen andere Naam, maar hoe spreken wij die uit; – *b*) *Ariarajah* S. Wesley, Een christelijke minderheid in een niet-christelijke culturele en religieuze omgeving, vooral in de Derde Wereld: Wereld en Zending 17 (Amst 1988) 189-193 / 239-246 [-258 *al*.: < ZIT 88,719].

9743 **Roberts** J. Deotis, Black theology in dialogue 1987 → 3,8710: ᴿTS 49 (1988) 564 (J. P. *Hogan*).

9744 **Rücker** Heribert, 'Afrikanische' Theologie; Darstellung und Dialog: InnsbTSt 14, 1985 → 1,8342 ... 3,8712; 3-7022-15484: ᴿGregorianum 69 (1988) 377s (A. *Wolanin*); HeythJ 29 (1988) 490s (J. *Wijngaards*); NZMissW 43 (1987) 230 (*Clerici*).

9745 *Ruiz de Medina* Juan G., Sobre los origenes de la Iglesia Católica Coreana: → 111*, Hispania Sacra 40 (1988) 541- ... [< ZIT 89,398].

9745* **Sahi** Jyoti, Stepping stones; reflections on the theology of Indian Christian culture. Bangalore 1986, Asian TC. 226 p. – ᴿTKontext 9,2 (1988) 115 (G. *Evers*).

9746 **Sanon** Anselme Titianma, Das Evangelium verwurzeln; Glaubenserschliessung im Raum afrikanischer Stammesinitiation; intr. *Luneau* René: Theologie der Dritten Welt 7, 1985 → 3,8715: ᴿTR 84 (1988) 154-6 (K. J. *Tossou*).

9746* *Sanon* Anselme T., L'interculturation de l'évangile, un défi lancé à la mission d'évangélisation: Journal des Missions Évangéliques 162,4 (1987) 147-158 [< TKontext 9/2,91].

9747 *Sarpong* Peter K., Growth or decay; can Christianity dialogue with African traditional religion?: BSecrNChr 23 (1988) 189-106 (107-214, *Kayitakibiga* Mérard).

9748 *Schoffeleers* Matthew, Black and African theology in southern Africa; a controversy re-examined: JRelAf 18 (1988) 99-124.

9748* *Shaw* Rosalind, Agency, meaning and structure in African religion: JRelAf 18 (1988) 255-266.

9749 **Shorter** Aylward, Toward a theology of inculturation. L 1988, Chapman. xii-291 p. 0-225-66502-6.

9750 *Sievernich* Michael, Konturen einer interkulturellen Theologie: ZkT 110 (1988) 257-283.

9751 *Smit* D. J., Christologie uit 'n derde wereld-perspektief; 'n literatuur-ondersoek: Scriptura 21 (1987) 1-49 [NTAbs 32,198].

9752 *a*) *Smith* F. C., Espiritualidade; ponto de vista de um negro norte-americano; – *b*) *Silva* A. A. da, Espiritualidade e Negritude; – *c*) *Beozzo* J. O., As Américas Negras e a historia da Igreja: Grande Sinal 42,1 (1988) 9-12 / 13-31 / 59-72.

9753 **Stackhouse** Max L., Apologia; contextualization, globalization, and mission in theological education. GR 1988, Eerdmans. 237 p. $15 [GraceTJ 9,316].

9754 **Staffner** Hans, The significance of Jesus Christ in Asia. Anand 1985, Gujarat-SP. 264 p. – ᴿHeythJ 29 (1988) 533s (M. A. *Barnes*); TKontext 9,2 (1988) 119 (G. *Evers*).

9755 *Standaert* Nicolas, L'histoire d'un néologisme; le terme 'inculturation' dans les documents romains: NRT 110 (1988) 555-570.

9756 *Swetnam* James, Zimbabwean Catholics and the Bible: BToday 26 (1988) 168-172 [362-5: with this ends, or rather is left incomplete, the series of 14 articles].

9756* **Takenaka** Masao, God is rice; Asian culture and Christian faith [4 conferences]: Risk 30. Geneva 1986. 83 p. – ᴿTKontext 9, 2 (1988) 109 (G. *Evers*).

9757 *Thomas* Norman E., Liberation for life; a Hindu liberation theology: Missiology 16 (1988) 149-162.

9758 *a)* *Toit* Brian L. du, Theology, Kairos and the Church in South Africa; – *b)* *Oosthuizen* George C., Interpretation of demonic powers in Southern African Independent Churches; – *c)* *Hill* Bradley N., An African ecclesiology in process: Missionalia 16 (Scottdale 1988) 57-72 / 3-22 / 73-87.

9759 *Tossou* Kossi J., Welche Geister rufen wir? Voraussetzungen und Möglichkeiten einer Theologie des Heiligen Geistes aus afrikanischer Sicht: TGL 78 (1988) 242-260.

9760 ᴱ**Trompf** Garry W., The Gospel is not western 1987 ⇢ 3,734: ᴿMissiology 16 (1988) 129s (H. G. *Buehler*); ZMissRW 72 (1988) 84s (H. *Janssen*).

9761 *a)* *Ukpong* Justin S., Contextualization; concept and history; – *b)* *Boné* Édouard, Pour une théologie du développement: AfJT 11 (1987) 149-163 / 179-201.

9762 *Utuk* Efiong S., A missiological conspectus of emergent themes in African Christian ethics: AfTJ 17 (1988) 48-71 [< TKontext 10/1,18].

9763 *Wilfred* Felix, World religions and Christian inculturation: IndTSt 25 (1988) 5-26.

9764 **Witvliet** Theo, The way of the black Messiah 1987 ⇢ 3,8748: ᴿHorizons 15 (1988) 411s (D. A. *Brown*); TS 49 (1988) 565 (J. P. *Hogan*).

9765 **Yewangoe** A. A., Theologia crucis in Asia; Asian Christian views on suffering in the face of overwhelming poverty and multifaceted religiosity in Asia: Amst St. Theol. 6, 1987 ⇢ 3,8753; *f*70: ᴿTLZ 113 (1988) 860 (T. *Sundermeier*).

H8.7 *Mariologia* – The mother of Jesus in the NT.

9766 **Ackermann** R., Sainte Marie, mère de Dieu, modèle de l'Église; textes du Magistère catholique et des théologiens: Les Dossiers de la Documentation Catholique. P 1987, Centurion. 267 p. – ᴿRHPR 68 (1988) 497 (G. *Siegwalt*: pas facile mais utile pour un protestant).

9767 *Allchin* A. M., Mary, an Anglican approach: IrTQ 54 (1988) 120-130.

9768 *Ambrosio* Gianni, Il fenomeno delle apparizioni di Maria nell'attuale contesto socio-religioso: TltSett 13 (1988) 291-309.

9769 *Aranda Pérez* Gonzalo, Perspectivas bíblicas sobre la cooperación de María a la salvación: TBraga 20 (1985) 13-38.

9770 **Balthasar** Hans Urs von, Komm., JOHANNES PAULUS II, Enzyklika 'Mutter des Erlösers'; Maria – Gottes Ja zum Menschen; intr. *Ratzinger* Joseph, 1987 ⇢ 3,8760: ᴿTR 84 (1988) 222. (F. *Courth*).

9771 **Balthasar** Hans Urs von, Marie pour aujourd'hui [1987], ᵀ*Ouillet* Florence: Racines. P 1988, Nouvelle Cité. 88 p. – ᴿEsprVie 98 (1988) 539s (B. *Billet*).

9772 **Balthasar** Hans Urs von, Mary for today, [Apc 12, how the 'woman's children wage war' in 'giving birth to heaven'...], ᵀ*Nowell* Robert. SF 1988, Ignatius. 75 p.; ill. (Virginia Broderick). $6 pa. [TDig 36,45].

9773 **Beinert** W., *Petri* Heinrich, Handbuch der Marienkunde 1984 ⇢ 1,919 ... 3,8763: ᴿTRu 53 (1988) 312-320 (H. *Düfel*, 'De Maria numquam satis').

9774 *Beinert* Wolfgang, Maria in der feministischen Theologie: Catholica 42 (1988) 1-25; bibliog. 25-27.

9774* **Berger** Pamela, The goddess obscured 1985 ⇢ 2,6944; 3,8764*: ᴿSpeculum 63 (1988) 119-121 (Judith S. *Neaman*).

9775 **Bertetto** Domenico, Maria la serva del Signore; trattato di mariologia: Teologia a confronto 7. N 1988, Dehoniane. 640 p. – ᴿMarianum 50 (1988) 601-4 (M. *Semeraro*).

9776 *Bertetto* Domenico, *a*) Il contenuto e le caratteristiche dell'Enciclica 'Redemptoris Mater': PalCl 66 (1987) 1374-1389; – *b*) Le linee-madri dell'enciclica Redemptoris Mater: PresPast 57,4s (1987) 164-180.

Besutti Giuseppe M., Bibliografia mariana 1978-84: ➤ 930.

9777 **Boff** Leonardo, Je vous salue Marie; l'Esprit et le féminin, ᵀ*Durban* Christine & Luc: Théologies. P 1986, Cerf. 92 p. F 64. – ᴿRTLv 19 (1988) 244s (Alice *Dermience*).

9778 *Bolewski* Jacek, Das Assumptio-Dogma und seine Bedeutung für die Eschatologie nach Karl RAHNER: ColcT 58 sp (1988) 89-152.

9780 **Brennan** Walter T., The sacred memory of Mary. Mahwah NJ 1988, Paulist. 97 p. $6 pa. 0-8091-2955-8 [TDig 36,149]. – ᴿMarianum 50 (1988) 613-5 (L. M. *Choate*).

9781 **Campi** E., Via antiqua, umanesimo e Riforma; ZWINGLI e la Vergine Maria: Il tempo delle riforme religiose 1, 1986 ➤ 3,8774: ᴿNRT 110 (1988) 146 (R. E.); Protestantesimo 43 (1988) 54s (G. *Gonnet*).

9782 **Carroll** Michael P., The cult of the Virgin Mary, psychological origins 1986 ➤ 2,6953; 3,8777: ᴿChH 57 (1988) 581-3 (D. *Bornstein*: 'Princeton University Press should be ashamed of itself'); Commonweal 114 (1987) 569s (L. E. *Cunningham*).

9782* *Byrnes* Joseph F., Explaining the Mary cult; a hypothesis and its problems [*Carroll* M. 1986]: JRel 68 (1988) 277-285.

9783 *Castellano Cervera* Jesús, La Vergine Maria nella tradizione della Chiesa orientale: RivVSp 42 (1988) 223-239 [371-387, *Toniolo* E. M.].

9784 *Coffey* David, Mary, prototype of salvation: ➤ 554, Salvation 1986/8, 95-104.

9785 *Cole* John J., Recent directions in Marian studies: StudiaBT 15 (1987) 237-251.

9786 **Coleman** William E., Philippe de MÉZIÈRES' campaign for the feast of Mary's Presentation, edited from Bibliothèque Nationale mss. Latin 17330 and 14454: Toronto Medieval Latin Texts. Toronto 1981, Pontifical Institute of Mediaeval Studies. 120 p. – ᴿMarianum 39 (1987) 619s (D. M. *Montagna*).

9787 **Corlay** Loïc, Marie de Cana. P/Montréal 1988, Médiaspaul/Paulines. 128 p. – ᴿEsprVie 98 (1988) 537s (B. *Billet*).

9788 *a*) *Courth* Franz, Mariologie im Umfeld von Ökumene und Feminismus; – *b*) *Gubler* Marie-Louise, Selig, die geglaubt hat – das Marienbild des Lukas; Überlegungen aus der Perspektive einer Frau: TPQ 136 (1988), 140-9 / 130-9.

9789 *a*) *Cousin* Hugues, Marie dans le NT; – *b*) *Birmelé* André, La mère du Seigneur dans la théologie protestante; – *c*) *Sesboüé* Bernard, Théologie catholique de Marie et dialogue œcuménique; – *d*) *Godin* André, Une madone en danger d'idéalisation: LumièreV 37,189 (1988) 5-17 / 33-48 / 49-63 / 77-93.

9790 **Cunningham** Agnes, The significance of Mary. Ch 1988, T. More. 138 p. $10. – ᴿHomP 89,4 (1988s) 73s (Mary M. *Bolan*: orthodox, creative, disturbing).

ᵀᴱ**Danieli** Maria Ignazia, GIROLAMO, La perenne verginità di Maria 1988 ➤ 4496.

9792 *Daoust* J., Le culte de Marie en Orient [< *Nasrallah* Joseph, Œuvres d'Orient (659, févr. 1988)]: EsprVie 98 (1988) 519-521.

9793 **Da Spinetoli** Ortensio, Maria nella Bibbia. Bo 1988, Dehoniane. 235 p. Lit. 18.000. – ᴿSac Doc 33 (1988) 612-621 (B. *Prete*).

9794 **De Fiores** Stefano, Maria nella teologia contemporanea²ʳᵉᵛ [¹1985]: Pastorale/Studio 6. R 1987, Mater Ecclesiae. 587 p. Lit. 20.000. – ᴿHumBr 43 (1988) 450s (A. *Biazzi*); Marianum 50 (1988) 595-8 (X. *Pikaza*).

9795 **De Fiores** S., *Meo* S., Nuevo diccionario de Mariología [1985 ↠ 2,609*],ᵀ. M 1988, Paulinas, 2127 p. – ᴿCarthaginensia 4 (1988) 380 (F. *Martínez Fresneda*).

9796 *De Fiores* Stefano, Mary in postconciliar theology, ᵀ*Wearne* L.: ↠ 380, Vatican II Assessment 1 (1988) 469-539 [the page-headings have 'Mary in postconciliar theory']; français ᵀ*Blanc* Philippe ↠ 379, Bilan 1, 469-533.

9797 *Denaux* Adelbert, Maria en de œcumene: CollatVL 18 (1988) 59-85.

9798 *Esbroeck* Michel van, Le culte de la Vierge de Jérusalem à Constantinople aux 6ᵉ-7ᵉ siècles: RÉByz 46 (1988) 181-190.

9799 **Esquerda Bifet** Juan, Mariología per una Chiesa missionaria. R 1988, Urbaniana. 221 p. – ᴿVerbumSVD 29 (1988) 318-320 (E. *Zeitler*).

9800 ᵀᴱ**Fazzo** Vittorio, *a*) GERMANO di Costantinopoli, Omelie mariologiche; – *b*) ANDREA di Creta, Omelie mariane: Testi Patristici 49; 63. R 1985/7, Città Nuova. 203 p.; 202 p. Lit. 10.000/14.000. – ᴿRasT 29 (1988) 98s (R. *Maisano*).

9801 **Ferlay** Philippe, Maria madre degli uomini [1985 ↠ 1,8401],ᵀ. Padova 1986, Messaggero. 190 p. – ᴿSalesianum 50 (1988) 234s (D. *Bertetto*: riserve).

9801* **Flusser** D., *Pelikan* J., *al.,* Maria, die Gestalt der Mutter Jesu in jüdischer und christlicher Sicht 1985 ↠ 1,8405: ᴿErbAuf 64 (1988) 155s (J. *Kaffanke*).

9802 **Galot** Jean, Vivere con Maria nella vita communitaria. Mi 1987, Àncora. 204 p. Lit. 13.000. – ᴿCC 139 (1988,4) 409 (U. *De Mielesi*).

9803 **Galot** Jean, Vivre avec Marie; présence de Marie dans la vie consacrée. Lv 1988, Sintal. 141 p. – ᴿGregorianum 69 (1988) 814s (*ipse*).

9804 *Galot* Jean, *a*) Marie et l'unité de l'Église: EsprVie 98 (1988) 687-694; – *b*) Maria e l'unità della Chiesa: CC 139 (1988,1) 131-142.

9805 *Gerl* Hanna-Barbara, Maria come figura biblica e simbolica [< UnSa (1987,3) 251-261], ᵀ*Colombi* Giulio: HumBr 43 (1988) 328-347.

9806 ᵀᴱ**Gharib** Georges, Testi mariani del primo millennio, I. Padri e altri autori greci. R 1988, Città Nuova. 988 p. 88-311-9215-9; (9-1 set of 4 vol.).

9807 **Gherardini** B., LUTERO - Maria ... 1985 ↠ 1,2960; 3,8788: ᴿCiuD 201 (1988) 694 (S. *Folgado Flórez*).

9808 **Gironés** Gonzalo, La humanidad salvada y salvadora; tratado dogmático de la Madre de Cristo²: Series Academica 9. Valencia 1987, Fac. Teol. Ferrer. 186 p. 84-600-5289-3. – ᴿGregorianum 69 (1988) 784s (C. I. *González*).

9809 **González** Carlos I., Mariologia; Maria madre e discepola [Bogotá 1988],ᵀ. CasM 1988, Piemme. 344 p. Lit. 39.000. – ᴿCC 139 (1988,3) 443s (L. *Ladaria*); Marianum 50 (1988) 604-8 (M. *Semeraro*).

9810 **González Dorado** Antonio, De María conquistadora a María liberadora; mariología popular latinoamericana: Presencia Teológica 44. Santander 1988, Sal Terrae. 142 p. 84-293-0797-4. – ᴿActuBbg 25 (1988) 245 (R. de *Sivatte*).

9811 **Gorski** Helmut, Die Niedrigkeit seiner Magd; Darstellung und theologische Analyse der Mariologie M. LUTHERS als Beitrag zum gegenwärtigen lutherisch/römisch-katholischen Gespräch [Diss. Hamburg 1986, ᴰ*Pesch* O.]: EurHS 23/311. Fra 1987, Lang. 297 p. Fs 65. – ᴿTGL 78 (1988) 187s (W. *Beinert*).

9812 **Grassi** J. A., [& Carolyn], Mary, mother and disciple; from the Scriptures to the Council of Ephesus. Wilmington 1988, Glazier. 166 p. $9 pa. 0-89453-640-0 [NTAbs 32,383].

9813 *Greiner* Albert, Luther, commentateur de l'Ave Maria: PosLuth 36,1 (1988) 33-41 [< zit].

9814 *Grote* Heiner, Heilige Schrift und heilige Überlieferung am Beispiel der Enzyklika 'Redemptoris mater': KkMat 39 (1988) 43-48 [< zit 88,569].

9815 *Guella* Eloy, Princípios mariológicos de Lutero: Teocomunicação 16,4 (1986) 37-46.

9816 **Hamel** Édouard, Marie au cœur de nos vies. Montréal/P 1981, Paulines/Apostolat Éd. 95 p.. – ᴿMarianum 39 (1987) 660s (A. *Rum*: 'mariologia integrata nelle grandi questioni' contemporanee).

9817 *Heintze* Bischof, Maria im Urteil Luthers und in evangelischen Äusserungen der Gegenwart: → 524, Maria ökumenisch 1983/4, 57-74.

9818 *Heinz* Hanspeter, Maria als Ort der Begegnung von Gott und Mensch; die unersetzbare Funktion der Mariologie für die Theologie: WissWeis 49 (1986) 134-159.

9819 **Heister** Maria-Sybilla, Maria aus Nazareth. Gö 1987, Vandenhoeck & R. 113 p. – ᴿTGL 78 (1988) 188s (W. *Beinert*: inadequate to its ecumenical aim).

9819* *Hernando* Eusebio, La fe de María [... Enciclica de Juan Pablo II]: TEsp 31 (1987) 319-341.

9820 *Horst* Alvin H., Mary in current theology; a Lutheran view: CurrTM 15 (1988) 412-7.

9821 **Ibáñez** Javier, *Mendoza* Fernando, La madre del Redentor²ʳᵉᵛ [¹1980]. M 1988, Palabra. 399 p. – ᴿMarianum 50 (1988) 598-601 (C. I. *González*).

9822 **Iwashita** Kuniharu, Maria no contexto da religiosidade popular brasileira; uma análise religiosa e psicológica do sincretismo entre Iemanjá e a Virgem Maria: diss. ᴰ*Oliveira*. FrS 1987s. – TR 84 (1988) 514.

9823 **Jenny-Kappers** T., Muttergöttin und Gottesmutter in Ephesos; von Artemis zu Maria. Z 1986, Daimon. 199 p. Fs 29,80. 3-85630-027-9 [NTAbs 32,265].

9824 *Jobert* P., Marie, mère de l'Église, notre mère: EsprVie 98 (1988) 81-83.

9825 *Johnson* Elizabeth A., El carácter simbólico de las afirmaciones teológicas sobre María [< JEcuSt 22 (1985) 312-320], ᵀᴱ*Balle* Teodoro de: SelT 26 (1987) 256-264.

9826 *Jourjon* Maurice, La Vierge Marie dans l'œcuménisme: Études 368 (1988) 683-690.

9827 *Kertelge* K., Maria im Neuen Testament; Schriftgebrauch und Schriftauslegung in [Johannes Paul II] 'Redemptoris Mater': Klerusblatt 68 (Mü 1988) 87s.

9829 *Koch* Kurt, *Voss* Gerhard (Catholic), *Papandreou* Damaskinos (Orthodox), *Wilckens* Ulrich (Lutheran), Reactions to Redemptor Mater [< Origins 16,43 (1987) 746-766 < Una Sancta 42 (1987) 223-238], ᴱ*Asen* B. A.: TDig 35 (1988) 9-15.

9830 *Kowalski* Wojciech, Mary the mother of Jesus in the early Church according to Luke and John: Pastoral Orientation Service (Tanzania 1987/3) 1-12 [< TKontext 10/1,21].

9831 *Landazuri Ricketts* Juan, María y eucaristía: RTLim 22,1 (1988) 9-28 (-122, todo sobre María).

9832 *Langkammer* Hugolin, a) ❷ De S. Scriptura in encyclicis IOANNIS PAULI II 'Redemptoris Mater': RuBi 41 (1988) 252-267; – b) ❷ Virgo Mater – realitas an ideologia?: RuBi 41 (1988) 471-486.

9833 **La Potterie** Ignace de, Marie dans le mystère de l'Alliance: JJC 34. P 1988, Desclée. 293 p. [AcPIB 9/5, 360]. 2-7189-0395-3.

9834 **La Potterie** Ignace de, Maria nel mistero dell'Alleanza [Het Mariamysterie 1985 ➤ 1,8424], ᵀ*Tosolini* Fabrizio: Dabar giud. 6. Genova 1988, Marietti. 281 p. Lit. 35,000. 88-211-6799-2. – ᴿSacDoc 33 (1988) 601-9 (B. *Prete*).

9835 *La Potterie* Ignace de, La Figlia di Sion; lo sfondo biblico della mariologia dopo il Concilio: CC 139 (1988,1) 535-549.

9836 a) *La Potterie* Ignace de, La Figlia di Sion; lo sfondo biblico della mariologia dopo il Concilio Vaticano II; – b) *Margerie* B. de, 'Expleto terrestris vitae cursu'; l'Assomption, prix remporté par la course spirituelle de Marie, sans cesser d'être son privilège gratuit; – c) *Salgado* J.-M., Les appropriations trinitaires et la théologie mariale: Marianum 49 (1987) 356-376 / 296-355 / 377-448.

9837 a) *La Potterie* I. de, Maria, 'piena di grazia' (RM 7-11); – b) *McHugh* J., Mary's Fiat as the commencement of the New Covenant; – c) *Pikaza* Xabier, María, la 'primera de los pequeños' que conocen a Dios (RM 17): Marianum 50 (Enc. 'Redemptoris mater' 1988) 111-132 / 133-7 / 323-346.

9838 a) *McKenzie* John, Die Mutter Jesu im NT; – b) *Maron* Gottfried, Die Protestanten und Maria; – c) *Ben-Chorin* Schalom, Die Mutter Jesu in jüdischer Sicht; – d) *Moltmann* Jürgen, Gibt es eine ökumenische Mariologie? – e) *Moltmann-Wendel* Elisabeth, Maria oder Magdalena – Mutterschaft oder Freundschaft? – f) *Kassel* Maria, Maria, Urbild des Weiblichen im Christentum? Tiefenpsychologisch-feministische Perspektiven: ➤ 388, Was geht uns Maria an? 1983/8, 23-40 / 60-71 / 40-50 / 15-22 / 51-59 / 72-87.

9839 **Magli** Ida, La Madonna. Mi 1987, Rizzoli. 176 p. Lit. 22.500. – ᴿCC 139 (1988,1) 43-48 (G. *Marchesi*: lontano da ciò che i cristiani credono); RasT 29 (1988) 281-292 (C. *Marucci*: severità per un libro 'nemmeno discutibile'). ➤ 9855.

9840 **Manelli** Stefano, Mariologia biblica, I. Antico Testamento. Frigento 1987, Casa Mariana. – ᴿMiscFranc 88 (1988) 236-8 (M. *Wszolek*: 'pp. 3').

9840* *Mangan* Céline, Mary in Scripture: MilltSt 22 ('Mary, the woman for today' 1988) 41-44 [1-110].

9841 **Martini** Carlo M., La donna nel suo popolo. Mi 1984, Àncora. 144 p. Lit 5500. – ᴿPalCl 66 (1987) 319 (N. *Lamberti*).

9842 **Martini** Carlo M., Seht die Frau; Lebenswege mit Maria [La Donna nel suo popolo], 1987 ➤ 3,8809: ᴿTGL 78 (1988) 108s (W. *Beinert*).

9843 **Martini** Carlo M., La Femme dans son peuple; le cheminement de Marie avec les hommes et les femmes de tous les temps [retraite pour les religieuses de Milan], ᵀ*Lemoine* Jo: Maranatha 12. P/Montréal 1987, Médiaspaul/Paulines. 160 p. F 66. – ᴿÉtudes 368 (1988) 140 (J. *Thomas*); RThom 88 (1988) 351 (M.-E. L).

9844 **Martini** Carlo M., María la mujer de la reconciliación [1985]: ST breve 19. Santander 1987, Sal Terrae. 79 p. 84-293-0786-9. – ᴿActuBbg 25 (1988) 275 (I. *Riudor*).

9845 **Menvielle** Louis, Marie mère de vie... IRÉNÉE 1986 ➤ 2,6972; 3,8811: ᴿRAfT 11 (1987) 285s (R. de *Haes*).

9845* **Meo** Salvatore M., present., Maria e la chiesa oggi 1984/5 ➤ 1,615. – ᴿDivThom 91 (1988) 214-6 (B. *Ardura*).

9846 **Mori** Elios G., Figlia di Sion e serva del Signore nella Bibbia, nel Vaticano II, nel Postconcilio. Bo 1988, Dehoniane. 392 p. Lit. 25.000. – ᴿSacDoc 33 (1988) 609-612 (B. *Prete*).

9847 **Müller** A., Reflexiones teológicas sobre María, madre de Jesús; la mariología en perspectiva actual: Academia Christiana 16, 1985 ➤ 1,8430; 2,6973: ᴿRET 48 (1988) 111s (E. *Tourón*).

9848 **Mulack** Christa, Maria, die geheime Göttin im Christentum 1985 ➤ 1,8431... 3,8812: ᴿMarianum 39 (1987) 634-7 (R. F. *Esposito*).

9849 **Monni** Pietro, Maria, una riscoperta dell'uomo d'oggi. R 1987, Corso. 268 p. – ᴿSalesianum 50 (1988) 605s (D. *Bertetto*).

9850 *Mussner* F., Die Mutter Jesu im NT: ➤ 524, Maria ökumenisch 1983/4, 9-30.

9851 **Napiórkowski** Stanisław C., ❷ *Spór o Matkę* ... Le débat sur la Mère; la Mariologie comme problème œcuménique: Teologia w dialogu 3. Lublin 1988, KUL. 188 p. zl 320. – ᴿRTLv 19 (1988) 384s (Z. *Kijas*).

9852 **Obregón Barreda** Luis, María en los Padres de la Iglesia; antología de textos patrísticos: Los Padres hoy. M 1988, Ciudad Nueva. 256 p. pt 1300. 84-85159-97-7. – ᴿActuBbg 25 (1988) 268 (J. *Vives*).

9853 **Ossanna** Tullio. Il ruolo profetico di Maria: Nuovi sentieri di Emmaus, 1981 ➤ 63,7596: ᴿMarianum 39 (1987) 161s (Adriana *Bottino*).

9854 **Paltro** Piera, Maria; la vita della Madonna nel racconto dei Vangeli. T 1983, Paoline. 153 p. – ᴿMarianum 39 (1987) 683s (Maddalena *Santoro*).

9855 *Pifano* Paolo, La Madonna di Ida MAGLI [Mi 1987, Rizzoli: ➤ 9839]: Asprenas 35 (1988) 385-398.

9856 **Pinkus** Lucio, El mito de María, aproximación simbólica; materiales para la comprensión del psicodinamismo de lo femenino en la experiencia cristiana [ital.], ᵀ*Ruberte* Manuel: Cristianismo y sociedad 16. Bilbao 1987, Desclée-B. 140 p. – ᴿCiuD 201 (1988) 692s (S. *Folgado Flórez*: positivo; lo femenino religioso); LumenVr 37 (1988) 343s (F. *Ortiz de Urtaran*).

9857 **Prévost** Jean-Pierre, La Mère de Jésus; 10 questions sur Marie. Ottawa/P 1988, Novalis/Cerf. 128 p. – ᴿEsprVie 98 (1988) 538s (B. *Billet*).

9858 *Ranke-Heinemann* Uta, Maria und die zölibatären Männer: Zeit 31 (24.VII.1987) 29s [> NSys 30 (1988) 124s: Incarnation required genuine human father...].

9859 **Ricca** P., *Tourn* G., Gli Evangelici e Maria; le ragioni del no degli Evangelici all'anno mariano. T 1987, Claudiana 55 p. Lit. 5000. – ᴿAsprenas 35 (1988) 302s (P. *Pifano*).

9860 **Ricci** Carla, *al.* Se a parlare di Maria sono le donne. Mi 1988, Cooperativa in Dialogo. 5-22 [-59] p. Lit. 6000.

9861 *Romero* A., La presencia de María en la celebración de la Eucaristia: Cistercium 39 (1987) 9-25 [< RET 48,117].

9862 **Rostagno** Sergio, *al.*, Maria nostra sorella: Federazione Chiese Evangeliche. R 1988, Nuovi Tempi. 127 p. Lit. 15.000.

9863 *Rouiller* Grégoire, Une réponse et une question dans les yeux; en lisant 'Mulieris dignitatem': ÉchSMaur 18 (1988) 254-262.

9864 *Sauser* Ekkart La signification des icônes mariales pour le chrétien d'Occident: NRT 110 (1988) 321-335.

9865 *Schinella* Ignazio, La presenza 'tipica' di Maria nel mistero di Cristo: RasT 29 (1988) 460-473.

9866 *Schöndorf* Harald, Jungfrau und Mutter: ZkT 110 (1988) 385-413.

9867 *Schütte* H., Maria und die Einheit der Christen; Thesen zu einer ökumenischen Verständigung: ⇒ 524, Maria ökumenisch 1983/4, 117-141.

9868 **Scott** M. Philip, A virgin called woman; essays on N.T. Marian texts 1986 ⇒ 3,8829: ᴿPrPeo 2 (1988) 298-300 (T. *Cooper*).

9869 **Serra** Arístide, María según el evangelio [1987 ⇒ 3,8831],ᵀ: Biblia y Catequesis 10. Salamanca 1988, Sígueme. 160 p. 84-301-1051-8. – ᴿActuBbg 25 (1988) 221 (I. *Riudor*); LumenVr 37 (1988) 536s (U. *Gil Ortega*); Marianum 49 (1987) 613-6 (D. *Marzotto*).

9870 *Serra* A., *La Potterie* I. de, Maria: ⇒ 806, NDízTB (1988) 895-920.

9871 *a*) *Spiazzi* Raimondo, Novità tematiche nella enciclica 'Redemptoris Mater'; – *b*) *Ols* Daniel, La presenza di Maria nella fede della Chiesa: SacDoc 33 (1988) 6-33 / 34-52 [-91 *al.*].

9872 *Stock* Klemens, Berufung Marias: ⇒ 819, ᴱ*Bäumer* R., *al.*, Marienlexikon 1 (1988) 460-2.

9873 *a*) *Testa* Emmanuele, Maria, terra vergine, icona della Chiesa e socia della Trinità; – *b*) *Pikaza* X., María, la persona humana (relaciones entre mariología, antropología y misterio trinitario); – *c*) *T'Joen* Michel, Marie et l'Esprit dans la théologie de Hans Urs von BALTHASAR; – *d*) *Johnson* Cuthbert, *Ward* Anthony, The figure of Mary in the worship of the Church of England: Marianum 49 (1987) 87-106 / 107-161 / 162-195 / 254-295.

9874 **Treanor** Oliver, Mother of the Redeemer, mother of the redeemed; pref. *Magee* John. Dublin/Westminster MD 1988, Four Courts / Christian Classics. 84 p. 1-85182-034-5 [Greg 69,827].

9875 ᴱ**Triacca** Achille, Maria esule, itinerante, pia pellegrina; figura della Chiesa in cammino [13 saggi]. Padova 1988, Messaggero. 317 p. Lit. 22.000. – ᴿCC 139 (1988,4) 407s (C. I. *González*).

9876 *Vanzan* Piersandro, [Johannes Paulus II] 'Mulieris dignitatem'; reazioni, contenuti e prospettive: CC 138 (1988,4) 250-260.

9877 *Vincent* David, Mary, a Protestant perspective: Catalyst 18 (Papua NG 1988) 55-68 [< TKontext 10/1,78].

9878 *a*) *Wahl* Otto, Zum biblischen Hintergrund des marianischen Ehrentitels 'Virgo Fidelis' in der Lauretanischen Litanei; – *b*) *Bergamelli* Ferdinando, Maria nelle lettere di IGNAZIO di Antiochia: ⇒ 12, ᶠBERTETTO D., Virgo fidelis 1988, 135-144 / 145-174.

9879 ᵀᴱ**Wolter** Allan B., John Duns SCOTUS, four questions on Mary [Latin text on facing pages]. Santa Barbara 1988, Old Mission. $8.50. [TDig 36,156].

9880 ᴱ**Zavalloni** Roberto, *Mariani* Eliodoro, La dottrina mariologica di Giovanni Duns SCOTO; Spicilegium 28. R 1987, Antonianum. 256 p. – ᴿCiuD 201 (1988) 694s (S. *Folgado Flórez*); Marianum 49 (1987) 623s (D. M. *Montagna*).

H8.8 *Feminae NT* – **Women in the NT and early Church.**

9881 *Abrahamsen* V., Women at Philippi; the pagan and Christian evidence: JFemR 3,2 (1987) 17-30 [NTAbs 32,206].

9882 *Albrecht* Ruth, Erinnern, was vergessen ist; Frauen und der Begriff des Weiblichen in der Zeit der Kirchenväter: StiZt 113 (1988) 326-333 [> TDig 36,3-7 'Women in the time of the Church Fathers'].

9883 **Allen** sr. Prudence, The concept of woman; the Aristotelian revolution (750 B.C. - A.D. 1250). Montreal 1985, Eden. viii-577 p. – RÉglT 18 (1987) 251-3 (Maureen *Slattery*); SR 17 (1988) 226s (Dominique *Deslandres*).

9884 *Arnold* P.M., Masculine identity and biblical literature: Listening 23 (Glenville IL 1988) 106-114 [< NTAbs 32,283: small but growing body of works on a balanced picture of male spirituality]. → 9277.

9885 **Aubert** Jean-Marie, L'exil féminin; antiféminisme et christianisme. P 1988, Cerf. 274 p. F 125. – REsprVie 98 (1988) 478s (L. *Debarge*).

9886 *Basinger* D., Gender roles, Scripture, and science; some clarifications: ChrSchR 17,3 (GR 1988) 241-253 [< NTAbs 32,239].

9887 *Bernabé Ubieta* Carmen, Biblia y feminismo [14 (mostly) books]: EstBíb 46 (1988) 97-120.

9888 *Bernard* Felix, Ist die Frau in der katholischen Kirche rechtlos?: TrierTZ 97 (1988) 150-8 [> TDig 36,15-18, 'Do women lack rights in the Catholic Church?': The 1983 canon law rejects statements of 1917 code that on the basis of the creation and fall narratives women are subordinate to men and that they are temptresses].

9889 **Bristow** John T., What Paul really said about women. SF 1988, Harper & R. xiv-129 p. $13 [TDig 36,48]. 0-06-061059-4.

9890 *Brock* Sebastian P. [→ h926], The sinful woman [Mt 26,6-13...] and Satan; two Syriac dialogue poems: OrChr 72 (1988) 21-62.

9891 **Capelle** Catherine, Thomas d'AQUIN féministe?; préf. *Aubert* J.-M.: BiblThomiste 43. P 1982, Vrin. iv-180 p. – RRThom 88 (1988) 171s (Simonne *Nicolas*: érudit, remarquable; mais sacrifie trop à un a priori inconséquent).

9892 **Carmody** Denise, Biblical women; contemporary reflections on scriptural texts. NY 1988, Crossroad. xvi-168 p. $11 [CBQ 51,399].

9893 **Clark** Elizabeth., Ascetic piety and women's faith; essays on late ancient Christianity [13, half reprints]: Studies in Women and Religion 20, 1986 → 3,204: RTS 49 (1988) 380s (D. G. *Hunter*).

9894 *Conde Guerri* Elena, La mujer ideal en el 'Pedagogo' de CLEMENTE Alejandrino: Helmantica 37 (1986) 337-354.

9895 **Daichman** Graciela S., Wayward nuns in medieval [largely Spanish] literature. Syracuse 1986, Univ. 223 p. $15. – RRelStR 14 (1988) 256s (Lynda L. *Coon*).

9895* **Défossez** Marie-Paule, La parole ensevelie ou l'évangile des femmes: LDiv 128. P 1987, Cerf. 211 p. – RSR 17 (1988) 380 (E. *Lamirande*).

9896 **Deventer** Louis F. Van, Skrifbekouing en skrifgebruik... [The approach to and use of Scripture; changes as reflected in the discussion of the place of women in Reformed churches]: diss. Pretoria, DKönig A. – RTLv 20,571, sans date.

9896* Las mujeres en la Biblia; experiencias e interpelaciones. M 1987, Paulinas. 125 p. – RBibFe 14 (1988) 480 (M. *Sáenz Galache*).
  Dumais Marcel présent. [*Greimas* Algird J., 'entretien'; *Chené Adèle, al.*], De Jésus et des femmes; lectures sémiotiques: Recherche NS 14, 1987 → 292.

9897 **Fabris** Rinaldo, La femme dans l'Église primitive, TGaroche Sylvie; préf. *Hébrard* Monique: Racines. P 1987, Nouvelle Cité. 160 p. – REsprVie 98 (1988) 87 (P. *Jay*: F 160); Études 368 (1988) 711 (P. *Gibert*: F 67).

9898 *Foulkes* I.W. de, De Galilea a Roma; el camino de las mujeres en el NT: Senderos 32 (San Pedro, Costa Rica 1988) 21-28.

9898* *Gatier* P.-L., Aspects de la vie religieuse des femmes dans l'Orient paléochrétien; ascétisme et monachisme → 700, Fémme Médit. 1982/5, 165-183.

9899 *Grün* Anselm, Der Weg der Selbstwerdung der Frau nach den Dialogen GREGORS: ErbAuf 64 (1988) 97-106.

9900 **Hartel** Joseph F., 'Femina ut imago Dei' in the integral feminism of St. Thomas AQUINAS: diss. Pont. Univ. Gregoriana, ^D*Sprokel* N. Roma 1988. 671 p. – RTLv 20,550.

9901 **Hayter** Mary, The new Eve in Christ; use and abuse of the Bible ... 1987 ⇒ 3,8865: ^RAnglTR 70 (1988) 115-7 (Frances M. *Young*); BL (1988) 107 (J. *Gibson*); ScotJT 41 (1988) 145-7 (Mary I. *Levison*); TLond 91 (1988) 65s (S. *Barton*); TS 49 (1988) 780s (Joan *Gormley*).

9902 **Heine** Susanne, [⇒ 9991] Frauen der frühen Christenheit; zur historischen Kritik einer feministischen Theologie 1986 ⇒ 2,7007; 3,8866: ^RCBQ 50 (1988) 321s (L. J. *Topel*: very important, somewhat weak in hermeneutic).

9902* **Heine** S., Women and early Christianity; are the feminist scholars right? ^T*Bowden* J. Minneapolis/L 1988, Augsburg/SCM. vi-182 p. £7. 0-8066-2359-4 [NTAbs 32,383]. – ^RFurrow 39 (1988) 195-7 (Linda *Hogan*); ModT 4 (1987s) 288s (Elizabeth A. *Clark*: anti-feminist); NBlackf 69 (1988) 195 (Cecily *Boulding*); PrPeo 2 (1988) 387s (Anne *Inman*); TLond 91 (1988) 361s (Janet *Morley*: she dissociates herself from fringe-heresy, but of whom?).

9903 a) *Heine* Susanne, Diakoninnen – Frauen und Ämter in den ersten christlichen Jahrhunderten [< Cyprian-Symposion Wien 17.IX.1988]; – b) *Dunde* Siegfried R., Sexismus in der Kirche: IkiZ 78 (1988) 213-227 / 228-240; Bibliog. 241s.

9903* **Honoré-Lainé** Geneviève, La donna nel mistero dell'alleanza; pref. *La Potterie* I de. T-Leumann 1987, Elle Di Ci. 127 p. – ^RMarianum 50 (1988) 618s (P. *Sartor*).

9904 **Honoré-Lainé** Geneviève, Die Frau im Geheimnis des Bundes. Vallendar-Schönstatt 1987, Patris. 139 p. – ^RTGL 78 (1988) 191 (W. *Beinert*).

9904* **Hourcade** Janine, La femme dans l'Église [AT ... NT .. ministères ..; diss. Toulouse, Inst. Cath.]: Croire et Savoir, 1986 ⇒ 2,7069*b*; 3,8970: ^REsprVie 98 (1988) 112 (J. *Daoust*); RTLv 19 (1988) 245s (Alice *Dermience*).

9905 *Kähler* E., Zur 'Unterordnung' der Frau im NT: Reformiertes Forum 1,35 [sic NTAbs 32,203] (Z 1987) 11-14.

9906 a) *Keane* Marie-Henry, Woman in the theological anthropology of the early Fathers [ambivalent]; – b) *Ackermann* Denise, Feminist liberation theology, a contextual option: JTSAf 62 (1988) 3-13 / 14-28 [< TKontext 10/1,24].

9907 **La Porte** Jean, The role of women in early Christianity: Studies in women and religion 7, 1982 ⇒ 64,7595; 1,8473: ^RCurrTM 15 (1988) 292 (Terri *Driver-Bishop*); SpTod 40 (1988) 77s (Monika K. *Hellwig*).

9908 *Lindboe* Inger Marie, Hovedtrekk innen nytestamentlig forskning om kvinner [essentials of NT research on women] i perioden 1970-1987: NorTTs 89 (1988) 179-204.

9909 **McHaffie** Barbara J., Her Story 1986 ⇒ 2,7015; 3,8876: ^RChH 57 (1988) 260s (Sharon K. *Elkins*).

9910 *Martin* John H., The ordination of women and the theologians of the Middle Ages (II): EscrVedat 18 (1988) 87-143.

9911 a) *Moloney* Francis J., Jesus and woman; – b) *Charbel* Antonio, La fede pasquale nell'apparizione del Risorto a Maria di Magdala, Gv 20,1-8; ⇒ 13, ^FBERTETTO D., Virgo fidelis 1988, 53-80 / 43-46.

9912 *Mommaers* Paul, HADEWIJCH, a feminist in conflict [13 cent.]: LvSt 13 (1988) 58-81.

9913 **Mulack** Christa, Jesus – der Gesalbte der Frauen 1987 → 3,8885: RTs-TNijm 28 (1988) 421 (C. *Halkes*).

9914 *Nürnberg* Rosemarie, 'Non decet neque necessarium est, ut mulieres doceant'; Überlegungen zum altkirchlichen Lehrverbot für Frauen: JbAC 31 (1988) 57-73.

9914* *Obijole* Olubayo, St. Paul on the position of women in the Church; paradox or a change?: Orita 19,1 (Ibadan 1987) 57-69 [< TKontext 9/2,23].

9915 **Ohler** Annemarie, Frauengestalten der Bibel 1987 → 3,8887 ['in der']: RGeistL 61 (1988) 316s (C. *Brandl*); TGL 78 (1988) 90s (W. *Beinert,* auch über HEISTER M.; PFISTER H.).

9916 *O'Sullivan* Michael, The feminist hermeneutic of Eli[s]abeth Sc[HÜSS]LER FIORENZA [→ 3,8892; cf. infra → 9925]: MilltSt 21 (1988) 40-61.

9917 *Papademetriou* Nonna D., Ⓖ Woman in Byzantium and monasticism [Canadian Archaeological Institute conference, Athens 29 March 1988]: TAth 54 (1988) 595-600. → k702.

9918 **Peppe** Leo Posizione giuridica e ruolo sociale della donna romana in età repubblicana: Univ. Roma, Ist. Dir. Rom. Medit. 63. Mi 1984, Giuffrè. 182 p. – RIvra 35 (1984) 136-143 (E. *Cantarella*).

9919 *Perkins* Pheme, Biblical traditions and women's experience: America 157 (NY 1987) 294-6 [NTAbs 32,204: the Bible provides stories of faith that sustained our ancestors, not a social or ecclesial blueprint for feminists or antifeminists].

9920 *Rigato* Maria Luisa, Donne testimoni della Risurrezione: → 660, Uomini e donne 1987/8, 37-53.

9921 *a) Sakenfeld* Katharine D., Feminist perspectives on Bible and theology; *– b) Stroup* George W., Between Echo and Narcissus; the role of the Bible in feminist theology; *– c) Perkins* Pheme, Women in the Bible; *– d) Achtemeier* Elizabeth, The impossible possibility; evaluating the feminist approach to Bible and theology: Interpretation 42 (1988) 5-18 / 19-32 / 33-44 / 45-57.

9922 *a) Scharfenorth* Gerta, Martin LUTHER zur Rolle von Mann und Frau; *– b) Schmidt-Biesalski* Angelika, Frauen, Gottes mindere Geschöpfe? Rückfragen an M. Luther: → 2,d572, E(!) **Süssmuth** H., Das Luther-Erbe in Deutschland 1985, 111-129 / 226-231.

9923 ESchmidt Margot, *Bauer* Dieter R., 'Eine Höhe, über die nichts geht'; spezielle Glaubenserfahrung in der Frauenmystik? [Stuttgart diocesan conference 1984]: Mystik in Geschichte und Gegenwart 1/4, 1986 → 3,717*; DM 48. 3-7728-1152-3. – RGregorianum 69 (1988) 162s (J. *O'Donnell* can conclude only that men *emphasize* their experience less than women do); TLZ 113 (1988) 194 (P. *Heidrich*).

9924 *Scholer* David M., Participation in the issues of women and ministry in the New Testament: PerspRelSt 15 (1988) 101-8.

9925 **Schüssler Fiorenza** Elisabeth, En mémoire d'elle 1986 → 2,7025; 3,8893: RCiTom 115 (1988) 191s (E. *García*); Téléma 13,1 (1987) 88 (Maryvonne *Duclaux*).

9925* *Stahl* Janine, À propos d' 'En mémoire d'elle'; perspective et interprétations [*Schüssler Fiorenza* E., 'un des rare lives susceptibles de transformer des polémiques fondamentales']: RevSR 61 (1987) 225-235.

9926 *Serra* A., The beauty of Eve reflected on the people on Mt. Sinai [Jewish tradition], on the Church [2 Cor 11:3] and on Mary: Sidic 20,2 (R 1987) 15-21 [NTAbs 32,205].

9927 ^E**Sharma** Arvind, Women in world religions 1987 → 3,463: ^RHorizons 18 (1988) 212s (Arlene A. *Swidler*); JEcuSt 25 (1988) 455s (H.O. *Thompson*); SR 17 (1988) 123s (Marilyn F. *Nefsky*).

9927* *Skinner* M.B., Des bonnes dames et méchantes [on women in antiquity against T. *Fleming*, 'Des dames du temps jadis']: ClasJ 83,1 (1987) 69-74 [cf. NTAbs 32,209].

9928 *Soler* Josep M., Les Mères du désert et la maternité spirituelle: Studia Silensia 12 (1986) 45-62 = ColcCist 48 (1986) 235-250 [> TDig 36,31-35, 'The desert mothers and spiritual maternity'].

9928* **Starr** Lee Anna, [Methodist ordained 1880] The Bible status of women: Women in American Protestant Religion 1800-1930. NY 1987, Garland. 432 p. $62 [RelStR 15, 181, Frances B. *Sullivan*].

9929 *Storkey* Elaine, Nuns, witches and patriarchy: Anvil 5,3 (Bristol 1988) 207-214 [< ZIT 89,71].

9930 *Strahm* Doris [→ a40], 'Um unseres Heiles willen'; zur Funktion der Bibel im Befreiungsprozess von Frauen: Orientierung 52 (1988) 178-181.

9931 *Tepedino* Ana Maria, Jesus e a recuperação de ser humano mulher: REB 48 (1988) 273-282.

9932 ^E**Tolbert** Mary Ann, The Bible and feminist hermeneutics: Semeia 28, 1983 → 2,7030: ^RJEcuSt 23 (1986) 138s (Claudia V. *Camp*).

9933 **Tucker** Ruth A., *Liefeld* Walter, Daughters of the church; women and ministry from New Testament times to the present. GR 1987, Zondervan. 552 p. [GraceTJ 9,317]. $15. 0-310-45741-6. – ^RRelStR 14 (1988) 382 (Annabelle S. *Wenzke*: pre-feminist); RExp 85 (1988) 724-6 (Linda M. *Bridges*).

9934 *Ussia* Salvatore, Il tema letterario della Maddalena nel'età della Controriforma: RivStoLR 24 (1988) 385-424.

9935 **Walter** Karin, Frauen entdecken die Bibel: Frauenforum 1986 → 2,270; 3,8004: ^RZkT 110 (1988) 190-2 (M. *Heizer*).

9936 ^E**Walter** Karin, Donne alla riscoperta della Bibbia [Frauen entdecken die Bibel 1986 → 2,270], ^T*Bartolomei* Maria Cristina. Brescia 1988, Queriniana. 207 p.

9937 *Wilson* Anna M., AUGUSTINE on the status of women: MilltSt 19s (1987) 87-109 (111-5, response, *Watson* G., on JEROME and JOVINIANUS).

9938 **Witherington** Ben^{III}, Women in the ministry of Jesus [^D1981]: SNTS Mg 51, 1984 → 65,7469 ... 3,8906: ^RSecC 6 (1987s) 121s (R.S. *Kraemer*).

9939 **Witherington** Ben, Women in the earliest churches: SNTS Mg 59. C 1988, Univ. xiii-300 p. $39.50. 0-521-34648-7.

H8.9 *Theologia feminae* – **Feminist theology.**

9940 **Andolsen** Barbara H., Daughters of Jefferson, daughters of bootblacks; racism and American feminism 1986 → 2,7035; 3,8909: ^RTTod 45 (1988s) 368s (Jacquelyn *Grant*).

9941 ^E**Angenent-Vogt** M.J. ['Kaski'-enquête], Vrouw en Kerk; een onderzoek naar de relatie van Nederlandse katholieke vrouwen met de kerk 1987 → 3,374: ^RTsTNijm 28 (1988) 107 (B.L. de *Groot-Kopetzky*).

9942 *Antinucci* Lucia, I dialoghi ecumenici e la donna: Ho Theológos 5 (1987) 185-203.

9943 *Arnold* Patrick M., Masculine identity and biblical literature: Listening 23 (Oak Park 1988) 106-114 [< ZIT 88,444].

9944 **Astrachan** Anthony, How men feel; their response to women's demands for equality and power. GCNY 1986, Doubleday Anchor. xi-444 p. $20. – RRelStR 14 (1988) 134s (Kathryn A. *Rabuzzi*).

9945 E**Atkinson** Clarissa W., Immaculate and powerful 1985 → 1,536 ... 3,8910: RAmerica 157 (1987) 412 (Suzanne R. *Hiatt*).

9946 **Aubert** M.-J., Des femmes diacres; un nouveau chemin pour l'Église: PoinT 47. P 1987, Beauchesne. 216 p. F 120. – RNRT 110 (1988) 134 (A. *Toubeau*).

9947 **Behr-Sigel** Elisabeth, Le ministère de la femme dans l'Église; préf. Antoine de *Souroge* [évêque russ.-orth.]: Théologies. P 1987, Cerf. 239 p. F 39. – RContacts/Orthodoxe 40 (1988) 73-75 (Nicole *Maillard*); Études 368 (1988) 140 (J. *Thomas*); RSPT 72 (1988) 116 (Y. *Congar*).

9948 E**Beinert** Wolfgang, *al.* Frauenbefreiung und Kirche; Darstellung – Analyse – Dokumentation [1930-87]. Rg 1987, Pustet. 302 p. – RÖkRu 37 (1988) 391s (Hildburg *Wegener*); StiZt 206 (1988) 286s (W. *Seibel*).

9949 *Bendroth* Margaret L., Millennial themes and private visions; the problem of 'woman's place' in religious history: FidH 20,2 (1988) 24-... [< ZIT 88,620].

9950 [Lucchetti] *Bingemer* Maria C., Alegrai-vos (Lc 15,8-10) ou a mulher no futuro da teologia da libertação: REB 48 (1988) 565-587.

9951 E**Borreguero** C., La mujer española, de la tradición a la modernidad 1960-1980: Ciencias Sociales. M 1986, Tecnos. 142 p. – RComSev 21 (1988) 153s (J. *Duque*).

9952 *Boss* Sarah Jane, The 'weakness' of women: Month 249 (1988) 975-985.

9953 **Bouchier** David, The feminist challenge; the movement for women's liberation in Britain and the USA. NY 1984, Schocken. 252 p. $8. – RRelStR 14 (1988) 135 (Martha J. *Reineke*).

9954 *Bujo* Bénézet, Feministische Theologie in Africa: StiZt 113 (1988) 529-538 [> TDig 36,25-30].

9955 **Byrne** Lavinia, Women before God; our own spirituality. Mystic CT 1988, Twenty-Third. 140 p. $8 [TDig 36,50].

9956 **Cannon** Katie G., Black womanist ethics. Atlanta 1988, Scholars. 183 p. $24; pa. $16. – RTTod 45 (1988s) 484.486.488 (R. W. *Lovin*).

9956* **Carlson** Jeffrey D., Toward a post-inclusivist theology: diss. Chicago 1988. – RelStR 15,191.

9957 **Carr** Anne E., Transforming grace; Christian tradition and women's experience [partly already published]. SF 1988, Harper. ix-272 p. $17. 0-06-254824-7 [TDig 36,149]. – RHorizons 15 (1988) 365-7 (Mary Jo *Weaver*) & 367-370 (Constance F. *Parvey*) & 370-2 (W. M. *Thompson*) & 372-4 (Elizabeth A. *Johnson*); 375 author's response.

9958 **Chopp** Rebecca S., The power to speak; feminism, language, God, c.1988, Crossroad. $18 [TDig 36/1 cover adv.].

9959 **Christ** Carol P., Laughter of Aphrodite; reflections on a journey to the goddess. SF 1987, Harper & R. 238 p. $16 [GraceTJ 9,304].

9960 **Coakley** Mary L., Long liberated ladies [and some advantages which 'oppressed' women of the past enjoyed, 1300-1900]. SF 1988, Ignatius. 168 p. $9 pa. [TDig 36,54].

E**Cooey** Paula M., *al.*, Embodied love ... feminine values 1988 → 352.

9961 **Collins** A. Y., Feminist perspectives on biblical scholarship 1985 → 1,276 ... 3,8929: RÉglT 17 (1986) 235-7 (W. *Vogels*).

9962 *Coste* René, JEAN-PAUL II, Lettre apostolique 'Mulieris dignitatem' sur la dignité et la vocation de la femme: EsprVie 98 (1988) 609-624

[...*théotokos*; image de Dieu; Ève-Marie; attitude de Jésus par rapport aux femmes; maternité/virginité; Église épouse du Christ; la plus grande, c'est la charité].

9963 *Côté* Pauline, Socialisations sacrales, acteurs féminins, post-modernité; les femmes dans le Renouveau charismatique canadien francophone: SR 17 (1988) 329-346.

9964 *Craston* Colin, Development and reception; a key to disputes about the ordination of women: Anvil 5 (1988) 113-8 [< ZIT 88,508].

9965 **Cypser** Cora E., Taking off the patriarchal glasses. NY 1987, Vantage. xi-237 p. $15 [CBQ 50,355].

9966 *Dijk* Denise, The goddess movement in the U.S.A., a religion for women only: Archiv für Religionspsychologie 18 (Gö 1988) 258-266 [< ZIT 88,792].

9967 **Doane** Janice, *Hodges* Devon, Nostalgia and sexual difference; the resistance to contemporary feminism. NY 1987, Methuen. xiv-169 p. $25; pa. $10. – ᴿRelStR 14 (1988) 134 (Kathryn A. *Rabuzzi*: post-structuralist).

9968 *Doyle* Robert C., Women's ministry, social flexibility and the 16th century: RefTR 46 (1987) 1-9.

9969 *Edwards* Denis, The ordination of women and Anglican-Roman Catholic dialogue: Pacifica 1 (1988) 125-140 [< ZIT 88,445].

9969* *Estor* Marita, Frauenforderung — Weg und Instrument zur Chancengleichheit; Anmerkungen zur Institutionalisierung der Frauenpolitik: ➤ 76, ᶠKAUFMANN L., Biotope 1988, 245-254.

9970 **Esway** Judy, Womanprayer/Spiritjourney; 56 meditations on Scripture. Mystic CT 1987, Twenty-Third. x-70 p. $5. – ᴿNewTR 1,4 (1988) 91s (Ann O. *Graff*).

9971 *Ferreira* Cornelia R., The emerging feminist religion; feminism seeks to destroy the Church from within: HomP 89,8 (1988s) 10-21.

9972 ᴱ**Findeis** Hans-Jürgen, Die Frau in Religion und Gesellschaft; Hinduismus – Judentum – Christentum – Islam: Beit. Interkulturell. I. Bielefeld 1987, Lingua. 279 p. – ᴿZMissRW 72 (1988) 252-4 (Gudrun *Löwner*).

9973 **Gelfand** Elissa D., *Hules* Virginia T., French feminist criticism; women, language, and literature, an annotated bibliography. NY 1985, Garland. lii-318 p. $56. – ᴿRelStR 14 (1988) 148 (Kathryn A. *Rabuzzi*).

9974 **Gentili** Antonio, Se non diventerete come donne. Mi 1987, Àncora. Lit. 20.000. – ᴿCiVit 43 (1988) 198s (F. *Morandi*); ViPe 71 (1988) 555s (G. *Cristaldi*).

9975 **Gerber** Uwe, Die feministische Eroberung der Theologie: Beck'sche Reihe 335, 1987 ➤ 3,8950: ᴿTZBas 44 (1988) 285-7 (Elisabeth *Moltmann*).

9976 *Gironés* Gonzalo, La teología feminista: AnVal 14,27 (1988) 55-64.

9977 ᴱ**Gössmann** Elisabeth,... Eva, Gottes Meisterwerk: Archiv für Frauenforschung 2, 1985 ➤ 2,305: ᴿStiZt 204 (1986) 215s (E. von der *Lieth*).

9978 *Gössmann* Elisabeth, Alter Wein in neuen Schläuchen [*Gutting* E.; *Gerber* U., *Newman* B. 1987]: TR 84 (1988) 89-102.

9979 *a) Goldie* Rosemary, La donna nella Chiesa; – *b) Militello* Cettina, Teologia al femminile; – *c) Valerio* Adriana, Laici nella Chiesa; diritto di parola: ➤ 660, ᴱ*Spera* S., Uomini e donne 1987/8, 15-20 / 25-36 / 21-24.

9980 *Grampa* Giuseppe, La donna oggi, una sfida per la chiesa: Ambrosius 64 (1988) 238-259.

9981 ᴱ**Greenberg** Simon, The ordination of women as rabbis; studies and responsa: Moreshet 14. NY 1988, Jewish Theol. Sem. centennial (Ktav). viii-223 p. $20; pa. $12 [TDig 35,384].

9982 **Grey-Hughes** Mary, Towards a Christian feminist spirituality of redemption as mutuality in relation; 'a passion to make and make again where such un-making reigns': diss. ᴰ*Bavel* T. J. van. Leuven 1987. lxxv-533 p. – LvSt 13 (1988) 367s; RTLv 20,568.

9983 *Griffin* Leslie, Women in religious congregations and politics: TS 49 (1988) 417-444.

9984 *Guerra Gómez* Manuel, En torno a los términos femeninos correspondientes a las designaciones (sacerdos, episcopus, presbyter) de los sacerdotes cristianos: RivScR 2 (R 1988) 261-293.

9985 ᴱ**Haddad** Yvonne Y. ..., Women, religion and social change 1985 ➤ 1,581 ... 3,8958: ᴿJScStR 26 (1987) 268s (Dorothy P. *Ludlow*).

9986 *Halkes* Catherina, Feminism and spirituality [her discourse at retirement, ᵀ*Sman* Joan van der]: SpTod 40 (1988) 220-236.

9987 *Hampson* Daphne, *Ruether* Rosemary R., Is there a place for feminists in a Christian Church?: NBlackf 68 (1987) 7-24.

9988 *a) Hardesty* Nancy R., 'Whoever surely meaneth me'; inclusive language and the Gospel; – *b) Basinger* David, Gender roles, Scripture and science; some clarifications; – *c) Gallagher* Susan V., Feminist literary criticism; an ethical approach to literature; – *d) Wall* Robert, Wifely submission in the context of Ephesians; – *e) Erickson* Joyce Q., The feminist challenge to disciplinary tradition; an unsystematic review: ChrSchR 17,3 (1988) 231-240 / 241-253 / 254-271 / 272-285 / 294-306 [< ZIT 88,433].

9989 **Harrison** Beverly W., Making the connections 1985 ➤ 1,184 ... 3,8961: ᴿRelStR 14 (1988) 126 (Christine E. *Gudorf*).

9990 **Heine** S., [➤ 9902ss] Wiederbelebung der Göttinnen? Zur systematischen Kritik einer feministischen Theologie 1987 ➤ 2,2007; 3,8966: ᴿProtestantesimo 43 (1988) 125s (V. *Subilia*); RB 95 (1988) 465s (J. *Murphy-O'Connor*, also on Frauen 1986); TPQ 136 (1988) 295s (A. *Grabner-Haider*).

9991 **Heyward** Carter, 'Und sie rührte sein Kleid an'; eine feministische Theologie der Beziehung; Einl. *Sölle* Dorothee. Stu 1986, Kreuz. 218 p. – ᴿEvT 48 (1988) 80-82 (Evi *Krobath*: 'Am Anfang ist die Beziehung!').

9992 **Homans** Margaret, Bearing the word; language and female experience in nineteenth-century women's writing. Ch 1986, Univ. xiv-326 p. $22 [RelStR 15,154, D. *Jobling*: why no such superb methodology within our biblical field?].

9993 **Hosmer** Rachel, Gender and God; love and desire in Christian spirituality. C 1986, Cowley. 145 p. $8. – ᴿTTod 45 (1988s) 256.258s (C. *Keller*, also on CADY S.).

9994 *House* A. Wayne, Women in the ministry, 1. 'Neither male nor female in Christ Jesus'; – 2. Should a woman prophesy or preach before men?; – 3. The speaking of women and the prohibition of the law [1 Cor 14,33s] – 4. The ministry of women in the apostolic and postapostolic periods; [5. Distinctive roles for women in the second and third centuries]: Bibliotheca Sacra 145 (1988) 47-56 / 141-161 / 301-318 / 387-399 [vol. 146 ...].

9995 ᴱ**Hurcombe** Linda, Sex and God; some varieties of women's religious experience 1987 ➤ 3,417: ᴿCCurr 23 (1988s) 220 (Denise L. *Carmody*: 24 items, half by professed Lesbians).

9996 **Irigaray** Luce, Speculum of the other woman [1974], ᵀ*Gill* Gillian C. Ithaca NY 1985, Cornell Univ. 365 p. $42.50; pa. $17. – ᴿRelStR 14 (1988) 137 (Kathryn A. *Rabuzzi*: odd but indispensable).

9997 **Isasi-Diaz** Ada, *Tarango* Yolanda, Hispanic women; prophetic voice in the Church. SF 1988, Harper & R. xx-123 p. $9 pa. [BibTB 18/3 cover].

9997* *Janowski* J. Christine, Theologischer Feminismus; eine historisch-systematische Rekonstruktion seiner Grundprobleme: BTZ 5 (1988) 28-47. 146-177.

9998 *Jensen* Anne, Theologische Forschung von Frauen; eine 'europäische Gesellschaft' formiert sich [Lugano-Magliaso Juni 1986]: EvT 48 (1988) 76-79.

9999 JOHANNES PAUL II, Die Zeit der Frau, 'Mulieris dignitatem', Einl. *Ratzinger* J., Komm. *Gössmann* Elisabeth. FrB 1988, Herder. 152 p.; DM 16,80 pa. 3-451-21464-4 [Orientierung 52, 239 adv.].

a1 *a) Karrer* Leo, Stellen sich die Männer der Herausforderung durch die Frauen? [*Gubler* L.]; – *b) Heine* Susanne, Das 'Mannsbild' in der feministischen Theologie; – *c) Estor* Marita, Männer – auf dem Weg zur Partnerschaft: Diakonia 19,3 (1988) 145-9 / 162 / 168-172 [*al.*, 150-193].

a2 ᴱ**Kassel** Maria, Feministische Theologie; Perspektiven zur Orientierung. Stu 1988, Kreuz. 320 p. DM 29,80. – ᴿTGL 78 (1988) 436s (W. *Beinert*).

a2* *a) Keightley* Georgia M., Women's issues are laity issues; – *b) Shannon* William H., [also on] The bishops' pastoral letter on women: America 159 (1988) 77-83 / 84-86.

a3 **Keller** Catherine, From a broken web; separation, sexism, and self. Boston 1986, Beacon. xii-277 p. $22. – ᴿRelStR 14 (1988) 137 (Kathryn A. *Rabuzzi*: arachnean spirituality; critique of androcentric conceptions of selfhood).

a4 *Kimmerling* Ben, Women and the Church: DocLife 37 (1987) 272-286.

a5 ᴱ**King** Ursula, Women in the world's religions, past and present 1987 ➔ 3,422: ᴿJEcuSt 25 (1988) 456s (Adele B. *McCollum*).

a6 ᴱ**Kolbenschlag** Madonna, Authority, community and conflict [Agnes *Mansour*]. KC 1986, Sheed & W. 225 p. $18 pa. – ᴿCCurr 37 (1987s) 94s (Mary B. *Mahowald)*

a7 **Kramarae** Cheris, *Treichler* Paula A., A feminist dictionary [i.e. English not Manglish]. Boston 1986, Pandora. x-587 p. $29; pa. $13. – ᴿRelStR 14 (1988) 151 (Kathryn A. *Rabuzzi*).

a8 *Kroll* Una M., Beyond the issue of ordination [... women cannot ask to be ordained without questioning the whole tissue of clericalism]: EcuR 40 (1988) 57-65.

a9 ᴱ**Lacelle** E.J., La femme, son corps et la religion 1977/83 ➔ 64,507* ... 2,7076: ᴿDivinitas 32 (1988) 625s (D. *Composta*); ÉglT 17 (1986) 262-6 (Micheline *Lagué*).

a10 **Lakoff** George, Women, fire, and dangerous things; what categories reveal about the mind. Ch 1987, Univ. xvii-614 p. $30. – ᴿRelStR 14 (1988) 134 (Kathryn A. *Rabuzzi*: not about women's issues).

a11 **Langlois** Claude, Le catholicisme au féminin 1984 ➔ 65,7521; 1,8579: ᴿScripTPamp 20 (1988) 934s (A.M. *Pazos*).

a12 **Lehman** E., Women clergy 1985 [➔ 3,8983: 1987]: ᴿJScStR 26 (1987) 413 (Joy *Charlton*).

a13 **Loades** Ann, Searching for lost coins; explorations in Christianity and feminism. L 1987, SPCK. x-118 p. £5 pa. – ᴿFurrow 39 (1988) 341; PrPeo 2 (1988) 341 (Claire *Elliott*); TLond 91 (1988) 357-9 (Monica *Furlong*).

a14 *Lucarelli* Daniela, 'Mulieris dignitatem' [GIOVANNI PAOLO II, 15.VIII.1988]: RasT 29 (1988) 513-526 [i. donna, evento di salvezza; ii. uomo 'specchio' di Dio; iii. distribuzione dei ruoli; iv. uguaglianza evangelica; v. nuova umanità; vi. mistero sponsale; vi. 'genio' femminile; vii. interpretazione della Lettera USA ...].

a15 **Maitland** Sara, A map of the new country; women and Christianity 1983 → 64,7663; 65,7528:   ᴿJEcuSt 23 (1986) 141 (Catherine M. *Prelinger*).

a15* **Martin** Emily, The woman in the body; a cultural analysis of reproduction. Boston 1987, Beacon. xi-276 p.; ill. $22 [RelStR 15, 242, Kathryn A. *Rabuzzi*].

a16 ᴱ**Meadow** Mary Jo, *Rayburn* Carole A., A time to weep, a time to sing; faith journeys of [18] women scholars of religion 1985 → 2,327:   ᴿSpTod 39 (1987) 78s (Mary M. *Pazdan*).

a16* *Ngomanzungu* Joseph, L'ordination de la femme, sujet controverse et handicap œcuménique: Urunana 21,61 (Rwanda 1987) 22-35 [< TKontext 9/2,18].

a17 *Nilson* Jon, 'Let bishops give proof of the Church's motherly concern'; the prospect of women bishops in the light of Vatican II: JEcuSt 25 (1988) 511-523.

a18 *O'Connor* June, Dorothy Dᴀʏ and gender identity; the rhetoric and the reality: Horizons 15 (1988) 7-20.

a19 *O'Donovan* Theresa M., In persona Christi; a feminist response: Paradigms 4 (1988s) 152-169.

a20 **Oger** Jean, Homme ou femme; deux valeurs, virilité et féminité; préf. *Chauchard* Paul. Liège c.1988, Vaillant-Carmanne. 237 p. – ᴿEsprVie 98 (1988) 479 (E. *Vauthier*: courageux, complet, équilibré).

a21 **Osiek** Carolyn, Beyond anger; on being a feminist in the Church 1986 → 3,9003: ᴿIrTQ 54 (1988) 79s (sr. Aengus *O'Donovan*).

a22 *a) Parsons* Susan F., The intersection of feminism and theological ethics; a philosophical approach; – *b) Hampson* Daphne, On power and gender; – *c) Broughton* Lynne, Find the lady: ModT 4 (1987s) 251-266 / 234-250 / 267-281.

a23 *a) Pissarek-Hudelist* Herlinde, Die Herausforderung feministischer Theologie an den Fachbereich Katechetik-Religionspädagogik; – *b) Wuckelt* Agnes, Hinter dem Leben zurückbleiben? Gen 2 und 3 als Impuls einer feministischen Religionspädagogik: KatBlätt 113 (Mü 1988) 864-874 / 854-863 [-910, *al.*: < ᴢɪᴛ 89,50].

a24 **Prodolliet** Simone, Weder die Schamlosigkeit und das Elend der heidnischen Weiber. Z 1987, Limmat. – ᴿIntRMiss 77 (1988) 458s (Anne-Marie *Käppeli*).

a25 *Reed* John S., A 'female movement'; the feminization of nineteenth century Anglo-Catholicism: Anglican and Episcopal History 52 (1988) 199-238.

a26 *Round* W. D., Does the concept of priesthood exclude womanhood?: Churchman 102,1 (L 1988) 30-43 [< ᴢɪᴛ 88,433].

a27 **Ruether** Rosemary R., Contemporary Roman Catholicism; crises and challenges. KC 1987, Sheed & W. xvii-81 p. $6. – ᴿNewTR 1,3 (1988) 104-6 (Ann O. *Graff*).

a28 **Ruether** Rosemary R., Women-church 1985 → 2,7105; 3,9015:   ᴿCurrTM 15 (1988) 290 (Norma J. *Everist*).

a29 *a) Ruether* Rosemary R., Christian quest for redemptive community; – *b) Ronan* Marian, The liturgy of women's lives; a call to celebration: CCurr 23 (1988s) 3-16 / 17-31 [32-63, *al.*].

a30 *Ruh* Ulrich, 'Als Mann und Frau schuf er sie'; theologische Bemühungen um das Bild der Frau [Österr. St. Polten-Tagung]: HerdKorr 42 (1988) 574-8.

a31 **Russell** Letty M., Household of freedom; authority in feminist theology [1986 Princeton Warfield lectures] 1987 ➤ 3,9018; 0-664-24017-8: ᴿCurrTM 15 (1988) 450s (T. *Peters*); Horizons 15 (1988) 418s (Joan *Leonard*); RExp 85 (1988) 572 (Molly *Marshall-Green*).

a32 *Schilling* Hans, Frauen im Kirchen- und Gemeindedienst; Hilfskräfte oder Partnerinnen der Männer?: MüTZ 39 (1988) 93-107.

a33 *Scholer* David M., Participation in the issues of women and ministry in the New Testament: PerspRelSt 15 (1988) 101-8 [< ᴢɪᴛ 88,601].

a34 *Schottroff* Luise, Feministische Theologie und neutestamentliche Wissenschaft: Deutsches Pfarrerblatt 88 (Essen 1988) 263-6 [< ᴢɪᴛ 88,557].

a35 **Schüssler Fiorenza** Elisabeth, Geen stenen voor brood; de uitdaging van de feministische bijbelinterpretatie [1984 ➤ 1,8622],ᵀ. Hilversum 1986, Gooi & S. 191 p. ƒ35. 90-304-0369-1. – ᴿBijdragen 49 (1988) 445s (T. C. de *Kruijf*).

a36 *Schug* Walter, Die Rolle der afrikanischen Frau im Entwicklungsprozess: Universitas 43 (Stu 1988) 578-588.

a36* **Smith** Barbara D., Modern options in feminist Christology: diss. Boston Univ. 1987. – RelStR 15,191.

a37 **Soelle** Dorothee, The strength of the weak; toward a Christian feminist identity 1984 ➤ 65,7556... 2,7112: ᴿHeythJ 29 (1988) 253s (U. *King*); ModT 4 (1987s) 282-7 (Jane *Williams*).

a38 **Sorge** Elga, Religion und Frau; weibliche Spiritualität im Christentum: Tb 1038. Stu 1985, Kohlhammer. 144 p. DM 20. – ᴿTLZ 113 (1988) 52-4 (K. *Lüthi*).

a39 *Stackhouse* John G.ᴶ, Women in public ministry in 20th-century Canadian and American evangelicalism; five models: SR 17 (1988) 471-485.

a40 **Strahm** Doris [➤ 9930], Aufbruch zu neuen Räumen; eine Einführung in feministische Theologie: Theologie aktuell 7. FrS 1987, Exodus. 155 p. DM 18. – ᴿTGʟ 78 (1988) 173 (W. *Beinert*: Vorlesungen einer kath. Theologin an der Berner ev. Fakultät).

a41 *Suchocki* Marjorie H., Earthsong, Godsong; women's spirituality: TTod 45 (1988s) 392-402.

a42 *Ter Steeg-Van Wayenburg* Maria, God heeft mensen nodig; vrouwen en mannen zijn Gods Kerk: CollatVʟ 18 (1988) 177-188.

a43 *a) Throckmorton* Burton H.ᴶ, Some contributions of feminist biblical scholars; – *b) Bird* Phyllis A., Translating sexist language as a theological and cultural problem: UnSemQ 42, 1s (1988) 87s / 89-96 [< ᴢɪᴛ].

a45 *Vanzan* Piersandro, La donna 'partner' nel mistero della Redenzione; luci e ombre nella prima bozza della lettera dei vescovi statunitensi: CC 139 (1988,3) 379-391.

a46 *Vrebos-Delcourt* L., Pouvoir et solidarité dans les rapports entre hommes et femmes: FoiTemps 18 (1988) 438-456.

a47 **Wacker** Marie-Theres, Der Gott der Männer und die Frauen: Theologie zur Zeit 2. Dü 1987, Patmos. 172 p. DM 22 [TGʟ 78,459 'die F.'].

a48 **Wartenberg-Potter** Bärbel von, We will not hang our harps on the willows; global sisterhood and God's song, ᵀ*Kaan* Fred. Oak Park IL 1988, Meyer-Stone. xiv-126 p. $9. – ᴿTS 49 (1988) 586s (Mary Ellen *Ross*).

a49 *a) Wartenberg-Potter* Bärbel von, Community of women and men in the Church; – *b) Klein* Ingrid, Women in the Church – an Austrian model; – *c) Nayak* Jessie T., The women's movement and the Church in India: VerbumSVD 29 (1988) 145-155 / 117-127 / 129-144.

a50 **Weber** Christin L., WomanChrist 1987 → 3,9037: [R]Horizons 15 (1988) 419s (Demaris *Wehr*).

a51 *Wilkinson* Alan, Three sexual issues [i. the role of women in the government of Church and state]: TLond 91 (1988) 122-131.

a52 *Zelinsky* Anne, Le féminisme; l'histoire en marche: Sève [= ÉglRur] 492 ('Etre femme' 1987) 564-572 (*al.* 529-582; 583-590, *Quéré* F., Les femmes dans l'Évangile).

H9 Eschatologia NT, *spes, hope.*

a53 **Baarlink** Heinrich, Die Eschatologie der synoptischen Evangelien 1986 → 2,7141; 3,9049: [R]BiKi 42 (1987) 86s (R. *Baumann*); TLZ 113 (1988) 347s (P. *Pokorný*); TsTNijm 27 (1987) 106s (P. J. *Farla*).

a54 [E]**Badham** P. & L., Death and immortality 1987 → 3,377: [R]JEcuSt 25 (1988) 281s (H. *Obayashi*).

a55 **Balthasar** Hans Urs von, Espérer pour tous, [T]*Rochais* H., *Schlegel* J. L. P 1987, D-Brouwer. 152 p. F 74. – [R]Études 368 (1988) 137s (R. *Marlé*).

a56 **Balthasar** Hans Urs von, Kleiner Diskurs über die Hölle. Ostfildern 1987, Schwaben. 54 p. DM 9,80. – [R]TR 84 (1988) 396-8 (F.-J. *Nocke*).

a57 **Balthasar** H. v., Dare we hope 'that all men be saved'? with a short discourse on Hell [1986 + 1987]. SF 1988, Ignatius. 254 p. $10. – [R]HomP 89,8 (1988s) 74-76 (K. *Baker*); 89,90 (1988s) 10-21 (dissent, *O'Connor* James T).

a58 **Beck** Heinrich, Reinkarnation oder Auferstehung; ein Widerspruch?: Grenzfragen 14. Innsbruck 1988, Resch. 47 p. DM 10. – [R]TR 84 (1988) 398 (H. *Vorgrimler*).

a59 [E]**Becker** Hansjakob, *al.,* Im Angesicht des Todes; ein interdisziplinäres Kompendium I-II: Pietas Liturgica 3s. St. Ottilien 1987, Eos. xi (+ xi) – 1479 p., ill. je DM 148. 3-88096-283-9; 4-7 [Bijdragen 49,234].

a60 **Beker** J. Christiaan, Suffering and hope 1987 → 3,9054: [R]CurrTM 15 (1988) 291s (T. A. *Droege*); Interpretation 42 (1988) 436 (T. D. *Gordon*).

a61 **Bloch** Ernst, The principle of hope [T]*Plaice* Neville, *al.,* Ox 1986, Blackwell. xxiii-1420 p. (3 vol.) £120. – [R]NBlackf 68 (1987) 362 (F. *Kerr*).

a61* *a) Bonora* A., Morte; – *b) Fabris* R. Risurrezione [di Gesù; degli uomini]: → 806, NDizTB (1988) 1012-1025 / 1342-1361. (Per 'inferno' non c'è articolo o rinvio).

a62 **Bordoni** Marcello, *Ciola* Nicola, Gesù nostra speranza; saggio di escatologia. Bo 1988, Dehoniane. 270 p. Lit. 20.000 [CC 139/2 dopo 312]. – [R]RClerIt 69 (1988) 543 (G. *Colzani*).

a63 **Bougerol** Jacques-Guy, La théologie de l'espérance aux XIIe et XIIIe siècles; 1. Études; II. Textes; 1985 → 2,7146. – [R]RThom 88 (1988) 499-502 (T.-M. *Hamonic*).

a64 **Bourgeois** H., La speranza ora e sempre [1985 → 2,7147],[T]: Il cristianesimo e la fede cristiana. Brescia 1987, Queriniana. 370 p. Lit. 32.000. – [R]RasT 29 (1988) 205s (A. *Barruffo*).

a65 *Bourgeois* H., Purgatoire: → 786, Catholicisme 12,55 (1988) 304-313 (-314, *David-Danel* M., iconographie).

a66 **Brueggemann** Walter, Hope within history 1987 → 3,197: [R]RRel 47 (1988) 311s (P. M. *Jurkowitz*).

a67 *a) Bylina* S., Le problème du purgatoire en Europe centrale et orientale au bas moyen âge; – *b) Chocheyras* J., Fin des terres et fin des temps d'HÉSYCHIUS (Ve s.) à BÉATUS (VIIIe s.): → 145*, [F]VERBEKE W., The use and abuse of eschatology in the Middle Ages 1988, 473-480 / 72-81; 1 fig.

a68 *Cameron* Nigel M.,   Universalism [... universal salvation post mortem; *Hick* J.] and the logic of revelation: ScotBEv 6 (1988) 95-111.

a69 **Clapsis** Emmanuel G.,   Eschatology and the unity of the Church: diss. Union. [NY?] 1987 – RelStR 14,186.

a70 *Cole* G. A.,   Ethics and eschatology – [1743-1805 William] PALEY's system reconsidered: RefTR 47 (1988) 33-43.

a71 **Croce** Vittorio,   Quando Dio sarà tutto in tutti; escatologia.   CasM 1987, Piemme. 127 p. Lit. 12.000. – ᴿCC 139 (1988,1) 192s (G. *Mucci*); ScuolC 116 (1988) 672s (N. *Ciola*).

a72 *Decock* P. B.,   The eclipse and rediscovery of eschatology: Neotestamentica 22,1 (1988) 5-16.

a73 *Dewan* Lawrence,   Death in the setting of divine wisdom: Angelicum 65 (1988) 117-129.

a74 **Durst** Michael,   Die Eschatologie des HILARIUS 1987 ➤ 3,9069;   3-923946-08-2:   ᴿArTGran 51 (1988) 307s (A. *Segovia*); Bijdragen 49 (1988) 336 s (P. *Smulders*); Gregorianum 69 (1988) 573 (L. *Ladaria*); RÉAnc 90 (1988) 321s (J. *Fontaine*); ScripTPamp 20 (1988) 839-843 (A. *Viciano*); TGL 78 (1988) 94s (H. R. *Drobner*).

a75 *Eibach* Ulrich,   Unsterblichkeit der Seele, Reinkarnation und Erlösung im 'New Age' und in der christlichen Tradition: TBei 19 (1988) 191-214 [< ZIT 88,609].

a76 **Escribano-Alberca** Ignacio,   Eschatologie, von der Aufklärung bis zur Gegenwart: HbDG 4/7d, 1987 ➤ 3,9073:   ᴿScripTPamp 20 (1988) 369s (J. *Morales*); TLZ 113 (1988) 213-6 (K.-H. *Kandler*); ÉglT 18 (1987) 245-8 (Germain *Hudon*).

a76* ᴱ**Felici** Sergio,   Morte e immortalità 1984/5 ➤ 2,432:   ᴿClaretianum 27 (1987) 372s (B. *Proietti*).

a77 **Fontinell** Eugene,   Self, God. and immortality; a JAMESIAN investigation. Ph 1986, Temple Univ.   xvii-297 p. $35. – ᴿJTS 39 (1988) 347s (P. *Badham*).

a78 **Gaines** Elizabeth Ann,   The eschatological Jerusalem; the function of the image in the literature of the biblical period: diss. Princeton Sem. 1988. – RelStR 15,193.

a79 *García Cordero* Maximiliano,   La esperanza del más allá en el Nuevo Testamento: CiTom 78 (1987) 209-264.

a80 **Girard** Jean-Michel,   La mort chez saint AUGUSTIN; grandes lignes de l'évolution de sa pensée, telle qu'elle apparait dans ses traités: diss. ᴰ*Wermelinger*.   FrS 1987s. – TR 84 (1988) 514.

a81 *Glasson* T. Francis,   Theophany and parousia: NTS 34 (1988) 259-270.

a82 **Grelot** Pierre,   Nelle angosce la speranza [1983 ➤ 64,7718], ᵀ*Francini* L. Mi 1988, ViPe.   356 p. Lit. 29.000. 88-343-4803-6. – ᴿAsprenas 35 (1988) 276s (A. *Rolla*).

a83 **Gunton** Colin,   When the gates of hell fall down; towards a modern theology of the justice of God: NBlackf 69 (1988) 488-496 [497-503, Teresa *McLean*; 77-487, G. *Graham*].

a84 *Habachi* René,   Reincarnation ou immortalité?:   Études 369 (1988) 521-532.

a85 *Haes* René de,   La réincarnation: Téléma 14,55s (1988) 47-57.

a86 *Hahn* Ferdinand,   Heilsgewissheit angesichts irdischer Bedrohung; Endzeiterwartung im Neuen Testament: Zeitwende 59 (Karlsruhe 1988) 193-206 [< ZIT 89,315].

a87 *Hayes* Zachary,   Fundamentalist eschatology: New Theology Review 1,2 (1988) 21-35.

a88 **Hjelde** Sigurd, Das Eschaton und die Eschata; eine Studie über Sprachgebrauch und Sprachverwirrung in protestantischer Theologie von der Orthodoxie bis zur Gegenwart: BeiEvT 102. Mü 1987, Kaiser. 523 p. DM 110. 3-459-01702-3. – ᴿActuBbg 25 (1988) 245s (J. *Boada*); Gregorianum 69 (1988) 787 (L. F. *Ladaria*).

a89 *Hughes* Gerard J., Dead theories, live metaphors and the resurrection [of the dead]: HeythJ 29 (1988) 313-328.

a90 *a) Jones* Peter, Sauver et détruire; un aspect de l'enseignement biblique sur l'enfer et la vie éternelle; – *b) Rouvière* Christian, Réincarnation ou résurrection?: RRéf 39,4 (1988) 41-63 / 9-16 [< ᴢɪᴛ 88,748].

a91 **Karikampally** James, Immortality; a new understanding; a critical evaluation of I. T. ᴿᴀᴍsᴇʏ's approach to a perennial problem: diss. ᴰ*Mertens* H. Leuven 1988. xvii-357 p. – LvSt 13 (1988) 373s; TsTNijm 28,397.

a92 **Karpinski** Peter, Annua dies dormitionis; Untersuchungen zum christlichen Jahresgedächtnis der Toten auf dem Hintergrund antiken Brauchtums: EurHS 23/300. Fra 1987, Lang. 314 p. Fs 65. – ᴿTR 84 (1988) 376 (W. *Gessel*).

a93 **Kehl** Medard, Eschatologie 1986 ➤ 2,7179; 3,9098: ᴿActuBbg 25 (1988) 246s (J. *Boada*); Salesianum 50 (1988) 447 (G. *Abbà*); Salmanticensis 35 (1988) 432-4 (J. L. *Ruiz de la Peña*); TPhil 63 (1988) 299-302 (G. *Greshake*); TPQ 136 (1988) 294 (A. *Seigfried*); TR 84 (1988) 395s (H. *Vorgrimler*); TS 49 (1988) 553-5 (J. M. *Mc Dermott*).

a94 ᴱ**Keller** Carl-A., La Réincarnation; théories, raisonnements et appréciations; un symposium: 1986 ➤ 2,448: ᴿZMissRW 72 (1988) 89s (P. *Antes*).

a95 **Keller** Erwin, Eucharistie und Parusie; liturgie- und theologiegeschichtliche Untersuchungen zur eschatologischen Dimension der Eucharistie anhand ausgewählter Zeugnisse aus frühchristlicher und patristischer Zeit: Diss. ᴰ*Schönborn*. FrS 1987s. – TR 84 (1988) 514.

a96 *Kennedy* Leonard A., Early Jesuits [*Suárez, Lessius*: Platonist] and immortality of the soul: Gregorianum 69 (1988) 117-131.

a97 *King* J. Norman, *Whitney* Barry L., ᴿᴀʜɴᴇʀ and ʜᴀʀᴛsʜᴏʀɴᴇ on death and eternal life: Horizons 15 (1988) 239-261.

a98 *Kitagawa* Joseph M., Religious visions of the end of the world: ➤ 149, ᶠᴡᴇʀᴮʟᴏᴡsᴋʏ R., Gilgul 1987, 125-137.

a99 **Körtner** Ulrich H. J. Weltangst und Weltende; eine theologische Interpretation der Apokalyptik. Gö 1988, Vandenhoeck & R. 428 p. – ᴿTGʟ 78 (1988) 439 (W. *Beinert*).

a100 *Korošak* Bruno, L'eternità dell'inferno: EuntDoc 41 (1988) 483-494.

a101 **Krieg** Matthias, Todesbilder im Alten Testament, oder 'Wie die Alten den Tod gebildet': ATANT 73. Z 1988, Theol.-V. 658 p. Textheft, DM 86 [TGʟ 78,460].

a101* **Lanier** David E., The day of the Lord in the NT; a historical and exegetical analysis of its background and usage: diss. SW Baptist Theol. Sem. 1988, – RelStR 15,193.

a102 ᴱ**Lemieux** Raymond, *Richard* Réginald, Survivre... La religion et la mort 1983/5 ➤ 2,458: ᴿÉglT 17 (1986) 248-9 (H. *Doucet*).

a102* **Libânio** João B., *Bingemer* Maria C. L., *a)* Escatologia cristã. Petrópolis 1985, Vozes. – *b)* Christliche Eschatologie: Bibliothek Theologie der Befreiung. Dü 1987, Patmos. 283 p. – ᴿTKontext 9,2 (1988) 106 (M. *Sievernich*).

a103 *Lindner* Ruth, Hades: ➤ 852, LIMC 4,1 (1988) 367-394 (-406).

a104 **Lorizio** Giuseppe, Eschaton e storia nel pensiero di Antonio ROSMINI; genesi e analisi della teodicea in prospettiva teologica: Aloisiana 21. R/Brescia 1988, Pont. Univ. Gregoriana/Morcelliana 357 p. Lit. 42.000. 88-7652-595-5 / 88-372-1355-7.

a105 **Maas** Frans, De vluchtige tijd bijeenhouden in het moment van de ziel; de 'presentische' eschatologie van Meester ECKHART: TsTNijm 28 (1988) 26-49; 49, Eckhart's 'eschatology now',

a106 **McDannell** Colleen, *Lang* Bernhard, Heaven, a history. NHv 1988, Yale Univ. xiv-410 p. 0-300-04346-5.

a107 *McEniery* Peter, Pseudo-GREGORY and purgatory: Pacifica 1,3 (1988) 328 ... [< ZIT 89,159].

a108 **McGill** Arthur C. [† 1980; 1974 taped lectures] Death and life, an American theology, ᴱ*Wilson* Charles A., *Anderson* Per M. Ph 1987, Fortress. 108 p. $8 [TDig 36,69]. – ᴿCurrTM 15 (1988) 280s (M. *Root*).

a109 *Maier* Gerhard, Die aktuelle Bedeutung der Eschatologie J. A. BENGELS: TBei 19 (1988) 117-127 [< ZIT 88,463].

a110 **Marcheselli** Cesare, Risorgeremo, ma come? risurrezione dei corpi, degli spiriti o dell'uomo?: RivB Sup. Bo 1988, Dehoniane. 640 p. [RivB 36,298 adv.].

a111 **Marguerat** Daniel, Vivre avec la mort; le défi du NT. Aubonne 1987, Moulin. 91 p. – ᴿProtestantesimo 43 (1988) 221s (G. *Conte*).

a111* *Mauser* Ulrich, 'Heaven' in the world view of the New Testament: HorBT 9,2 (1987) 31-51.

a112 *Meier-Dörken* Christoph, 'Es gibt ein Leben vor dem Tod'; Religionsunterricht als Hilfe zur Lebensbewältigung am Beispiel einer Unterrichtseinheit zum Themenfeld 'Sterben – Tod – Auferstehung': → 140, ᶠSTOODT D., Unterwegs 1987, 329-342.

a113 **Milet** Jean, Le jugement de Dieu, mythe ou réalité?: EsprVie 98 (1988) 401-411 . 417-426.

a114 *Milikowski* Chaim, Which Gehenna? Retribution and eschatology in the Synoptic Gospels and in early Jewish texts: NTS 34 (1988) 238-249.

a115 *Miller-McLemore* Bonnie, The sting of death: TTod 45 (1988s) 415-426.

a116 *Miquel* Pierre, Purgatoire: → 791, DictSp 12 (1986) 2652-6 (-76 *al.*).

a117 *Moltmann* Jürgen, Der 'eschatologische Augenblick'; Gedanken zu Zeit und Ewigkeit in eschatologischer Hinsicht: → 114, ᶠPANNENBERG W., Vernunft 1988, 578-589.

a118 **Moraldi** Luigi, Nach dem Tode; Jenseitsvorstellungen von den Babyloniern bis zum Christentum, ᵀ*Haag* M. Z 1987, Benziger. 336 p. – ᴿTR 84 (1988) 398 (A. T. *Khoury*).

a119 **Müller** Denis, Réincarnation et foi chrétienne. Genève 1986, Labor et Fides. 152 p. Fs 59. 2-8309-0087-1. – ᴿActuBbg 25 (1988) 86 (J. *Boada*).

a120 **Mussner** Franz, Was lehrt Jesus über das Ende der Welt? 1987 → 3,9115: ᴿBiKi 43 (1988) 87 (M. *Helsper*); ColcT 58,4 (1988) 163s (R. *Bartnicki*); TPQ 136 (1988) 286s (S. *Stahr*).

a121 **Nachtwei** Gerhard, Dialogische Unsterblichkeit ... RATZINGERS Eschatologie 1986 → 3,9117: ᴿNRT 110 (1988) 753s (L. *Renwart*).

a122 *a) Noemi* J., Situación actual de la escatología; – *b) Moreno* C. A., Apóstoles y profetas: La Revista Católica (Chile) 87 (1987) 94-102 / 103-110 [< RET 48,260].

a123 **Oblau** Gotthard, Gotteszeit und Menschenzeit; Eschatologie in der Kirchlichen Dogmatik von Karl BARTH: Bei.Syst.Theol. 6. Neuk 1988. 319 p. DM 78. 3-7887-1234-1. – ᴿActuBbg 25 (1988) 250s (J. *Boada*).

a123* **Pajardi** P., Noi risorgeremo; riflessioni di un laico sulla vita dell'uomo nella risurrezione. Mi 1987, Rusconi. 150 p. Lit. 20.000. – RDivThom 91 (1988) 220-4 (G. *Perini*).

a124 *a*) **Palms** Roger C., Bible readings on hope. 111 p. – *b*) **Syverson** Betty G., Bible readings for caregivers. 108 p. Minneapolis 1987, Augsburg. $4 each [BToday 26 (1988) 121].

a125 **Pannenberg** W., Il destino dell'uomo, ᵀ*Dequal* M. Brescia 1984, Morcelliana. 160 p. Lit. 12.000. 88-372-1226-7. – RProtestantesimo 43 (1988) 60s (V. *Subilia*).

a126 *Panteghini* G., Il purgatorio; l'incontro purificator con Dio: Credere Oggi 8,3 (1988) 79-91.

a127 *Perrot* C., *al., Le retour du Christ: Théologie 31. Bru 1983, Fac. Univ. S. Louis. 191 p. – RRTPhil 120 (1988) 111s (H. *Mottu*).

a128 *Pesch* Otto H., Im Angesicht des barmherzigen Richters; Leben, Tod und Jüngster Tag in der Theologie Martin LUTHERS: Catholica 42 (1988) 245-273.

a129 **Pocock** Michael, The destiny of the world and the work of missions: Bibliotheca Sacra 145 (1988) 436-451 [< International Journal of Frontier Missions 1 (July 1984) 215-234].

a130 *Probst* Alain, Trois motifs eschatologiques de la 'théologie de la libération': RRéf 39,4 (1988) 64... [< ZIT 88,748].

a131 **Puente Santidrián** Pablo, La terminología de la resurrección en TERTULIANO, con un excursus comparativo [con] MINUCIUS Félix, [diss. Valladolid 1978]: Publ, Fac.T. NEspaña 54. Burgos 1987, Aldecoa. 392 p. – RScripTPamp 20 (1988) 280-4 (A. *Viciano*).

a132 **Ratzinger** Joseph, Eschatology; death and eternal life. Wsh 1988, Catholic Univ. xx-303 p. $30; pa. $15. – RHomP 89,11 (1988s) 83s (J. *Sheets*: rich).

a133 *Sauter* Gerhard, *a*) The concept and task of eschatology – theological and philosophical reflections [Durham/Oxford lecture 1986]: ScotJT 41 (1988) 499-515 [term stems from Abraham *Calov* 1677]; – *b*) Begriff und Aufgabe der Eschatologie; theologische und philosophische Überlegungen: NSys 30 (1988) 191-208; Eng. 208.

a134 *Scharr* Peter, Der Glaube an eine Reinigung nach dem Tod in der theologischen Fundierung durch AUGUSTINUS: WissWeis 49 (1986) 160-8.

a135 *Schmidt-Leukel* Perry, Sterblichkeit und ihre Überwindung; ein Beitrag zur Diskussion um Reinkarnationslehren aus der Perspektive des christlich-buddhistischen Dialogs: MüTZ 39 (1988) 281-304.

a136 *Schmied* Augustin, Neues Interesse an Jenseitsfragen: TGegw 30 (1987) 203-213.

a137 *Schmithals* Walter, Eschatologie und Apokalyptik: VerkF 33,1 (1988) 64-82.

a138 *Schoonenberg* Piet, Der Tod als Anfang: TPQ 136 (1988) 309-315 [316-325, *Reisinger* F., ... als Ende? Marxismus].

a139 **Steiner** Rudolf [1861-1925, Begründer der Anthroposophie], Das Leben nach dem Tod und sein Zusammenhang mit der Welt der Lebenden, ᴱ*Teichmann* F.: Themen aus dem Gesamtwerk 15. Stu 1987, Freies Geistesleben. 280 p. DM 14,80. – RTGL (1988) 279s cf. 266-276 (R. *Geisen*).

a140 *Stendahl* Krister, Immortality is too much and too little [1972]: → 65,256, Meanings 1984, 297s; RTR 84 (1988) 297s (Hans C. C. *Cavallin*, chiefly on the furore aroused in Sweden by this article).

a141 *Tavernier* Johan de, Sociale ethiek en eschatologie: Bijdragen 49 (1988) 378-401; Eng. 401.

a142 **Thomas** Pascal, ['nom' d'auteur collectif] La réincarnation, oui ou non? P 1987, Centurion. 142 p. F 72. – ᴿEsprVie 98 (1988) 398s (P. *Jay*: dialogue d'un groupe lyonnais avec des jeunes et des adultes parfois désireux de devenir chrétiens); Téléma 14,2 (1988) 77 (C. *Delhez*).

a143 **Travis** Stephen H., Christ and the judgement of God; divine retribution in the New Testament [diss.]. Basingstoke 1986, Marshall Pickering. 214 p. £10. 0-551-01358-3. – ᴿScotBEv 6 (1988) 45-47 (J. *Barclay*); ScotJT 41 (1988) 424-6 (R. T. *France*).

a144 **Valentine** Mary H., Words of comfort, consolation and hope in Scripture. Ch 1988, T. More. 191 p. $11 [BToday 26,189].

a145 *Veken* Jan Van der, Talking meaningfully about im-mortality: WSpirit 8 (1986) 95-108.

a146 **Vernette** Jean, Réincarnation, résurrection; communiquer avec l'au-delà; les mystères de la Vie après la vie. Mulhouse 1988, Salvator. 185 p. F 89 [EsprVie 98,701].

a147 *Vernette* Jean, La réincarnation; une croyance ancienne, répandue et séduisante: EsprVie 98 (1988) 655-662 . 677-683 . 694-700.

a148 *Wagner* Harald, Probleme der Eschatologie; Ökumenische Perspektiven: Catholica 42 (1988) 209-223.

a149 *Wiederkehr* Dietrich, Gestaltwandel katholischer Eschatologie; Desintegration – Integration – Brechungen: UnSa 43 (1988) 150-165.

a150 **Zaleski** Carol, Otherworld journeys... near-death experiences 1987 → 3,9157: ᴿCCurr 23 (1988s) 248-250 (P. *Giurlanda*); Horizons 18 (1988) 204s (J. J. *Heaney*); TLond 91 (1988) 236s (G. *Rowell*).

a151 *Žužek* Roman, L'escatologia di Pietro MOGHILA [c.1640]: OrChrPer 54 (1988) 353-385.

H9.5 *Theologia totius [V]NT* – **General [O]NT theology.**

a152 **Afflerbach** Horst, Die sanfte Umdeutung des Evangeliums; eine biblische Analyse des neuen Bewusstseins. Wu 1987, Brockhaus. 111 p. DM 14,80. – ᴿKerkT 39 (1988) 157s (G. de *Ru*).

a153 *Berger* Klaus, Neutestamentliche Theologien: TRu 53 (1988) 354-370.

a154 *Buess* Eduard, Theologie in der Krise der technischen Zivilisation [... Frage, in der Bibel überall gestellt]: TZBas 44 (1988) 168-187.

a155 **Demarest** Bruce, *Lewis* Gordon, Integrative theology I. GR 1987, Zondervan. 394 p. $18. – ᴿTrinJ 8 (1987) 235-9 (M. J. *Erickson*).

a156 **Dunn** James D. G., *Mackey* James P., New Testament theology in dialogue 1987 → 3,9161: ᴿTLond 91 (1988) 428s (S. W. *Need*).

a156* **Goppelt** L., Teologia del NT 1982 → 64,7791*b* ... 2,7228: ᴿRivPastLtg 22,122 (1984) 91 (T. *Colombetti*).

a157 *Kreck* W., Dogmatica evangelica; le questioni fondamentali: Sola Scriptura 11. T 1986, Claudiana. 372 p. Lit. 28.000. – ᴿStPatav 35 (1988) 686-9 (L. *Sartori*).

a157* **Lohse** Eduard, Grundriss der neutestamentlichen Theologie³ʳᵉᵛ: Theol. Wiss. 5. Stu 1984, Kohlhammer. 172 p. DM 24. 3-17-008614-6.

a158 **Lohse** E., Théologie du Nouveau Testament [Grundriss 1984], ᵀ*Jundt* P.: MondeB. Genève 1987, Labor et Fides. 285 p. 2-8309-0094-4 [NTAbs 32,385]. – ᴿMondeB 55 (1988) 59 (F. *Brossier*).

a159 **Lohse** Eduard,   Compendio di teologia del Nuovo Testamento, ᵀᴱ*Masini* Mario, intr. *Segalla* Giuseppe. Brescia 1987, Queriniana. 241 p. Lit. 28.000. – ᴿCC 189 (1988,4) 298s (V. *Fusco*: difetti di traduzione).

a160 *Luck* Ulrich,   Der Weg zu einer biblischen Theologie des Neuen Testaments: Deutsches Pfarrerblatt 88 (Essen 1988) 343-6.

a161 *Merk* Otto,   Gesamtbiblische Theologie; zum Fortgang der Diskussion in den 80er Jahren: VerkF 33,1 (NT 1986) 19-40.

a162 **Morris** Leon,   New Testament theology 1986 ➤ 2,7234:   ᴿAndrUnS 26 (1988) 195s (J. *Paulien*).

a163 *Müller* Norbert,   Das Denken Martin KÄHLERS [zum 150. Gb.] als Beitrag zur Diskussion um eine 'biblische Theologie':   EvT 48 (1988) 346-359.

a164 *Perkins* Pheme,   Theological implications of New Testament pluralism [CBA presidential address, Chicago Aug. 17, 1987: i. the challenge; (1 Peter) *Bauer* W., *Meeks* W., *Dunn* J., *Lindbeck* G.; ii. goals; theology as 'propositional' (*Brown* R. E.), 'experiential' (*Schillebeeckx* E.); liberation; iii. applicaton to Lk 1,26-56 (... *Callaway* M.); iv. its mythic transformation (Is 51,2; Rev. 12; Apc. Adam) ...]:   CBQ 50 (1988) 5-23.

a165 *Rasco* Emilio,   La théologie biblique; son renouveau et son influence sur la formation théologique, ᵀ*Raymond* Louis-B., ➤ 379, Vatican II Bilan 3 (1988) 333-354; Eng. ➤ 380, Assessment 3,337-360.

a166 *Scroggs* Robin,   Can New Testament theology be saved? The threat of contextualism: UnSemQ 42,1s (1988) 17-32 [< ZIT].

a167 **Segalla** Giuseppe,   Panorama teologico del NT: LoB 3/7, 1987 ➤ 3, 9178:   ᴿRasT 29 (1988) 204s (V. *Fusco*: anche su 'storico' e 'letterario'); RivB 36 (1988) 418-420 (R. *Penna*).

a168 **Siegwalt** Gérard,   Dogmatique pour la catholicité évangélique [I. Les fondements de la foi 1986] 2. Réalité et révélation. Genève/P 1987 ➤ 3,6581:   ᴿCarthaginensia 4 (1988) 375s (F. *Martínez Fresneda*); DivThom 91 (1988) 224-6 (Y. *Poutet*); ÉTRel 63 (1988) 145s (A. *Gounelle*); EvT 48 (1988) 176-180 (M. *Raden*); RTPhil 120 (1988) 239s (K. *Blaser*); TRu 53 (1988) 399-404 (A. *Peters* †, 'Recapitulatio in Christo?').

a169 **Stăniloae** Dumitru,   Orthodoxe Dogmatik, ᵀ*Pitters* Hermann; praef. *Moltmann* Jürgen: ÖkTheol 12, 1985 ➤ 1,8784; 2,7240; 3-545-24209-9 / Gü 3-579-00175-2:   ᴿActuBibg 25 (1988) 99 (J. *Boada*); ZkT 110 (1988) 221 (L. *Lies*).

a170 *Stock* Klemens,   La conoscenza religiosa nel NT (i demoni, Mc 1,34): ParSpV 18 (1988) 93-112; Lc 11,52, *Fabris* R., 113-126; 1 Cor 2,2, *Bianchi* E., 127-148; Ef 3,19, *Noyen* Carlos, 149-168; Giovanni, *La Potterie* I. de, 185-200 e *Zevini* G., 169-184; Padri, *Panimolle* S. A. (Gv 10,14s) *al*., 201-298.

a171 **Vos** Gerhardus,   Biblical theology, Old and New Testament. E 1985 = 1949, Banner of Truth. 425 p. £6. 0-85151-223-2. – ᴿScotBEv 6 (1988) 44s (G. W. *Grogan*).

XVI. Philologia biblica

J1 **Hebraica** .1 *grammatica*.

a172 **Andersen** Francis I., *Forbes* A. Dean,   Spelling in the Hebrew Bible: Dahood Memorial Lecture / BibOrPont 41, 1986 ➤ 2,7242; 3,9182:   ᴿBL (1988) 146 (J. A. *Emerton*: pioneering); CBQ 50 (1988) 267-280 (D.

Pardee); JBL 107 (1988) 128s (G. J. *Hamilton*: computer); JSS 33 (1988) 122-131 (J. *Barr*, whose Schweich Lectures 1986 on the same subject is in press); RelStR 14 (1988) 370s (S. D. *Sperling*: highly innovative); TüTQ 168 (1988) 161-3 (W. *Gross*); VT 38 (1988) 375-7 (G. I. *Davies*).

a172* *Ararat* Nissan, ➒ Dageš forte: BethM 34 (not 33 as Hebrew cover), 118 (not 108 as English cover; 1988s) 226-230.

a173 **Beall** T. S., *Banks* W. A., Old Testament parsing guide [I.] Genesis-Esther 1986 ➤ 3,9185: ᴿBL (1988) 147 (J. H. *Eaton*).

a174 **Bergsträsser** Gotthelf, ᴱ*Daniels* P. T., Introduction to the Semitic languages 1983 ➤ 64,7844 ... 3,9187: ᴿOLZ 83 (1988) 319-322 (J. *Oelsner*).

a175 *Blau* J., ➒ Notes on changes in accent in early Hebrew: ➤ 132, ᶠSCHIRMANN H., Jubilee 1970, 27-33.

a176 *Buccellati* Giorgio, The state of the 'stative': ➤ 42*, EHRMAN A. mem., Fucus 1988, 153-189.

a177 **Cheney** Michael S., The exegetical relevance of Ernst JENNI's theory of the Hebrew Piel [Grundbedeutung, somewhat as *Goetze* A. 1942 'factitive' as Akkadian D-stem; not intensive]; an examination from the point of view of linguistic and literary science: Master's thesis, Regent College, Vancouver; available in microfilm, Canadian University Microfilms 1988.

a178 *Chiera* Giovanna, Su alcuni aspetti dell'infinito assoluto ebraico: Henoch 10 (1988) 131-140; franç. 140s.

a178* ᴱ**Chiesa** B., Corso di ebraico biblico [1. Grammatica, di **Stähli** H.-P. (1984)ᵀ.], 2. Esercizi, crestomazia e glossario 1986 ➤ 2,7270; 3,9226: ᴿRB 95 (1988) 300s (J. *Loza*).

a179 **Cohen** D., La phrase nominale et l'évolution du système verbal en sémitique; études de syntaxe historique: Soc. Linguistique de Paris 72, 1984 ➤ 3,9192: ᴿArOr 56 (1988) 368s (L. *Drozdík*); BL (1988) 147 (J. *Barr*: formidably erudite).

a179* *Curtis* John B., On the Hifil infinitive absolute of *hālak*: ZAHeb 1,1 (1988) 22-31.

a180 **Döhmer** Klaus, Die Affixe des hebräischen in alphabetischer Darstellung. Passau 1988, Univ. 156 p. not numbered. 3-922016-77-4 [OIAc D88].

a181 **Drummond** Samuel J., A historical critique of the problem of conditional discourse in Hebrew: diss. Southern Baptist. Louisville 1986. 87-02211 [OIAc 88].

a183 *Fontinoy* C., Le duel verbal en hébreu biblique: ➤ 101, Mém. MARÇAIS P. 1985, 3-13.

a184 *Garbini* Giovanni, Qualche riflessione sui pronomi personali semitici: OrAnt 27 (1988) 105-113.

a185 **Garr** W. Randall, Dialect geography of Syria-Palestine, 1000-586 B.C.E. 1985 ➤ 1,8791*b* ... 3,9195: ᴿBASOR 270 (1988) 94-97 (S. *Izre'el*); BZ 32 (1988) 132-5 (W. *Gross*); CBQ 50 (1988) 116-8 (S. D. *Sperling*); OLZ 83 (1988) 577-580 (J. *Oelsner*); OrAnt 27 (1988) 143s (G. *Garbini*); PEQ 120 (1988) 72-74 (B. *Isserlin*).

a186 **Gross** Walter, Die Pendenskonstruktion ... I: AOtt 27, 1987 ➤ 3,9197: ᴿBiblica 69 (1988) (F. I. *Andersen*).

a187 *Gross* Walter, Satzgrenzen bei Pendenskonstruktionen — der Pendenssatz: ➤ 47, ᶠFENSHAM F., Text 1988, 249-257.

a188 *Guillaume* Gabriel, Regards sur le verbe hébreu d'après Gustave GUILLAUME [† 1960]: ➤ 486, Traduction 1986/8, 107-117; Eng. 107.

a189 **Hoftijzer** J., Function of... nun paragogicum 1985 ⇥ 1,8794 ... 3,9200: ᴿJAOS 108 (1988) 157s (S. *Segert*); OLZ 83 (1988) 54s (H. J. *Zobel*); RB 95 (1988) 611s (F. J. *Gonçalves*).

a189* **Hoftijzer** J. (*Laan* H. R. van der, *Koo* N. P. de), A search for method; a study in the syntactic use of the h-locale in classical Hebrew: StSemLLing 12, 1981 ⇥ 62,8704 ... 64,7819: ᴿRB 95 (1988) 608s (F. J. *Gonçalves*).

a190 **Hunter** A. Vanlier, Biblical Hebrew workbook; an inductive study for beginners. Lanham MD 1988, UPA. xii-234 p. $15.25 pa. [JBL 107,788].

a190* **Johnson** Bo, Hebraisches... mit Vorangehendem wᵉ 1979 ⇥ 60,a145; 61,a47: ᴿRB 95 (1988) 610s (F.-J. *Gonçalves*).

a191 *Kaddari* Menahem Z., On deontic modality in biblical and post-biblical Hebrew: ⇥ 130, Mem. SCHEIBER A., 1988, 251-260.

a192 **Köhn** R., Hebraisk grammatikk³ [less dependent on *Birkeland* H., than ¹1971, ²1972] Oslo 1988, Univ. 196 p. Nk 190. 82-00-02540-3 [BL 89,150, H. M. *Barstad*].

a192* **Kross** Kristiina, *Lᵉšon haqqodeš lᵉmathilim* [Hebrew for beginners, in Esthonian]. Tellinn 1985, Ev. Luth. Church. 111 p.; p. 112-125 + 71 + 56. – ᴿRB 95 (1988) 301s (M. *Heltzer*).

a193 **Levi** Jaakov, Die Inkongruenz im biblischen Hebräisch 1987 ⇥ 3,9209: ᴿSBFLA 38 (1988) 480-3 (A. *Niccacci*).

a193* *Levin* Saul, The Hebrew of the Pentateuch: ⇥ 42*, EHRMAN A. mem., Fucus 1988, 291-323.

a194 **McCarthy** John J., Formal problems in Semitic phonology and morphology [diss. MIT, CM 1979]: Outstanding Dissertations in Linguistics. NY 1985, Garland. 426 p. $53. 0-8240-5476-8.

a194* **McFall** Leslie, The enigma of the Hebrew verbal system 1982 ⇥ 62,8716 ... 3,9210: ᴿRB 95 (1988) 609s (F.-J. *Gonçalves*).

a195 **Mansoor** Menahem, [I.²] II.³ [readings from Genesis, ²1984 ⇥ 65,7694]. GR 1988, Baker.

a195* *Masson* Michel, *qaṭal / qaṭala* en hébreu biblique: GLECS 28,3 (1984) 493-505.

a196 *a)* *Morag* Shlomo, ❺ The beginnings of Hebrew; some semantic considerations; – *b)* *Kaddari* Menahem, ❺ The negative particle *'al* (a study in diachronic syntax); – *c)* *Azar* Moshe, ❺ The syntax and the unity of the Hebrew language; – *d)* *Bendavid* Abba, ❺ The historical division of Hebrew speech and Hebrew writing: ⇥ 471, Language 1985, 177-196; Eng. XXX / 197-210; Eng. XXXI / 157-161; Eng. XXVIII / 163-173; Eng. XXIX.

a197 **Muraoka** T., Emphatic words and structures in biblical Hebrew 1985 ⇥ 1,8804; 3,9212: ᴿJSS 33 (1988) 267-9 (P. *Wernberg-Møller*); NedTTs 42 (1988) 148s (L. J. de *Regt*).

a197* *Niccacci* Alviero, Basic principles of the biblical Hebrew verbal system in prose: SBFLA 38 (1988) 7-16.

a198 **Parker** Charles H., Biblical Hebrew, an exegetical approach [... Is 40; Ps 23; Job 1,1-3; Gn 1,1-8 ...]. Kingston ON 1987, Frye. xxiv-168 p. – ᴿSR 17 (1988) 379 (Eileen *Schuller*).

a199 *Pope* Marvin, Vestiges of vocative *lamedh* in the Bible: UF 20 (1988) 201-7.

a199* **Qimron** Elisha, The Hebrew of the Dead Sea Scrolls [Jerusalem diss. 1976, condensed/expanded]: HarvSemSt 29, 1986 ⇥ 2,7262; 3,9215: ᴿBZ 32 (1988) 305s (J. *Maier*); CBQ 50 (1988) 308s (S. *Segert*); JStJud 19 (1988) 115-7 (F. *García Martínez*); Orientalia 57 (1988) 101-3 (A. *Vivian*); PrzOr (1988,1) 75-77 (P. *Muchowski*).

a200 *Ratner* Robert, Does a *t*-preformative third person masculine plural verbal form exist in biblical Hebrew? [*Gordon* C., Dt 23,3; 5,20; Ezek 37,7; Job 19,15; + 6 *al.*; unconvincing; so W. *Moran*]: VT 38 (1988) 80-88.

a201 **Revell** E. J., Nesiga (retraction of word stress) in Tiberian Hebrew: TEstCisn 39. M 1987, Cons. Sup. Inv. 155 p. pt. 3500. 84-00-06476-3 [BL 89,152, J. *Barr*]. – ᴿSefarad 48 (1988) 435s (Maria T. *Ortega Monasterio*).

a202 *Revell* E. J., First person imperfect forms with *waw* consecutive: VT 38 (1988) 419-426.

a202* *Rooker* M. F., The diachronic study of biblical Hebrew: JNWS 14 (1988) 199-214.

a203 *a) Rosén* Haiim B., ❺ Outlines of a history of Hebrew verbal tenses; – *b) Goldenberg* Gideon, ❺ Verbal category and the Hebrew verb: → 471, Language 1985, 287-293; Eng. XXXVIII-XXXIX / 295-348; Eng. XL-XLII.

a204 **Sagarin** J. L., Hebrew noun patterns (Mishqalim); morphology, semantics, and lexicon. Atlanta 1987, Scholars. xiv-149 p. $27; sb./pa. $20. 1-55540-030-2; pa. 1-0 [BL 89,153, D. J. A. *Clines*].

a205 *Schoors* Antoon, A third masculine singular *taqtul* in biblical Hebrew [Qoh 10,15]?: → 47, ᶠFENSHAM F., Text 1988, 193-200.

a206 **Schweizer** H., Metaphorische Grammatik 1981 → 62,1424 ... 3,9223: ᴿAulaOr 6 (1988) 283s (G. del *Olmo Lete*).

a208 **Weingreen** J., Hébreu biblique; méthode élémentaire 1987 → 3,9229; ᵀ*Hébert* P.; ᴱ*Margain* J.: Religions 13: ᴿRThom 88 (1988) 647s (L. *Devillers*).

a209 **Zuber** Beat, Das Tempussystem: BZAW 164, 1985 → 1,8822 ... 3,9233: ᴿBO 45 (1988) 632-8 (C. van der *Merwe*); TR 84 (1988) 363-5 (H. *Schweizer*).

J1.2 **Lexica et inscriptiones hebraicae**; later Hebrew.

a210 *a) Abramson* Shraga, ❺ Biblical Hebrew in Mishnaic Hebrew; – *b) Rabin* Chaim, ❺ Biblical and Mishnaic elements in contemporary Hebrew; *c) Ornan* Uzzi, ❺ The last phase of the revival of Hebrew: → 471, Language 1985, 177-196; Eng. XXXII / 273-285; Eng. XXXVIs / 261-272; Eng. XXXV.

a211 ᴱ**Alonso Schökel** L., Materiales para un diccionario biblico hebreo + español I. Parte lexicográfica (alef, bet-hmt). R 1988, Biblical Institute. Lit. 6.000 + 13.000 [BL 89,148, D, *Clines*: refreshingly independent of German-English tradition; absence of dialogue with contemporary linguistic theory not felt].

a212 *Alonso* Schökel Luis, El diccionario bíblico hebreo-español: Sefarad 48 (1988) 373-389.

a213 **Aphek** Edna, **Tobin** Yishai, Word systems in modern Hebrew; implications and applications: Contributions to the Sociology of Jewish Languages 3. Leiden 1988, Brill. xv-143 p.; ill. 90-04-08258-1.

a214 *Ben-Ḥayyim* Ze'ev, [*Rabin* Chaim, *Sadan* Dov], ❺ The historical unity of the Hebrew language and its division into periods: → 471, Language 1985, 3-25. 45-53 [27-35; 37-43]: Eng. XI-XVII.

Bergey Ronald L., Post-exilic Hebrew 1988 → 3070.

a215 *a) Blau* Joshua, ❺ The influence of Middle Arabic on the Hebrew of Arabic speaking Jews; – *b) Sarfatti* Gad B., ❺ Loan translations from Arabic in Hebrew and in European languages [fraction and *šeber* < *kasr*;

root and *šoreš* < *jiḏr* ...]: → 471, Language 1985, 243-250; Eng. XXXIII / 251-260; Eng. XXXIV.

a215* **Brugnatelli** Vermondo, Questioni di morfologia e sintassi dei numeri cardinali semitici 1982 → 63,7828 ... 2,7285: ᴿGLECS 28 (1984) 576s (F. *Bron*).

a216 *Cross* Frank M., A report on the Samaria papyri: → 482, VTS 40, Jerusalem congress 1986/8, 17-26.

a217 *Doherty* Timothy, al., Bibliographische Dokumentation [etymological or other explanation of (some 150) Hebrew words, published since 1985]: ZAHeb 1 (1988) 122-137....

a218 *Dotan* Aron, ❻ The beginnings of Hebrew lexicography — a fragment of an ancient dictionary [36 *m*- items from Cairo Geniza]: → 44, ᴇʀᴏɴ D. Mem. 1988, 115-126; Eng. XIV-XV.

a219 *Drinkard* Joel E., [Hebrew, largely Arad] Epigraphy as a dating method: → 20, ᴱCᴀʟʟᴀᴡᴀʏ J., Benchmarks 1988, 417-439; 4 fig.

a220 *Eldar* Ilan, ❻ An ancient Genizah treatise on interchangeable letters in Hebrew: Tarbiz 57 (1987s) 483-510; Eng. Is.

a221 **Fowler** Jeaneane [SvTKv 65,32] D., Theophoric personal names in ancient Hebrew; a comparative study: JStOT Sup 49. Sheffield 1988, Academic. 321 p. £20.50. 1-85075-038-6; pa. 9-4. £20.50 [BL 89,149, H. G. M. *Williamson*: good though she is unduly hard on *Gray*].

a221* **Gluska** Isaac, ❻ The influences of Aramaic on Mishnaic Hebrew: diss. Bar-Ilan, ᴰ*Greenfield* J. TA 1988. - RTLv 20,542.

a222 a) *Goshen-Gottstein* Moshe, ❻ Corpus, genre and the unity of Hebrew; aspects of conceptualization and methodology; - b) *Bar-Asher* Moshe, ❻ The historical unity of Hebrew and Mishnaic Hebrew research; - c) *Tené* David, ❻ Historical identity and unity of Hebrew and the division of its history into periods: → 471, Language 1985, 57-73 / 75-99 / 101-155; Eng. XVIIIs / XX-XXII / XXIII-XXVII.

a222* *Hookerman* J., ❻ Biblical etymologies 12 (... *ahab, oyeb*); 13: BethM 34,118 (1988s) 223-6; 34,119 (1988s) 312-5.

a223 *Hospers* J. H., Das Problem der sogenannten semantischen Polarität im Althebräischen: ZAHeb 1,1 (1988) 32-39.

a224 **Jakerson** Semen M., ❻ Katalog inkunabulov 1985 → 3,969: ᴿOLZ 83 (1988) 427s (H. *Simon*).

a225 *Kaddari* Menahem Z., ❻ Pronominal 'copula' in Mishnaic Hebrew: → 44, ᴇʀᴏɴ D. Mem. 1988, 15-30; Eng. VII.

a226 *Kedar-Kopfstein* Benjamin, Synästhesien ['syntagmatische Verbindung(en) von zwei Lexemen ... unterscheidlicher Sinnesgebiete'] im biblischen Althebräisch in Übersetzung und Auslegung: ZAHeb 1 (1988) 47-60. ...

a227 *Kesterson* John C., The indication of the genitive relationship in 1QS: → 22, Mém. Cᴀʀᴍɪɢɴᴀᴄ J., RQum 13 (1988) 513-523.

a228 **Kirst** Nelson, al., Dicionário hebráico-português e aramaico-português. São Leopoldo/Petrópolis 1988, Sinodal/Vozes. x-305 p. 85-233-0130-5. - ᴿREB 48 (1988) 500s (L. *Garmus*).

a229 *Lipiński* Édouard, Emprunts suméro-akkadiens en hébreu biblique: ZAHeb 1,1 (1988) 61-73: some fifty.

a230 **Lüderitz** Gert, Corpus jüdischer Zeugnisse aus der Cyrenaika: TAVO B-53, 1983 → 64,7865; 1,8845: ᴿRB 95 (1988) 141s (É. *Puech*).

a231 **Masson** Michel, Langue et idéologie; les mots étrangers en hébreu moderne. P 1986, CNRS. 236 p. - ᴿBSLP 83,2 (1988) 288-291 (P. *Kirtchuk*).

a232 [*Gesenius* Wilhelm, ¹⁷*Buhl* Frants] ¹⁸**Meyer** R., *Donner* Herbert, Hebräisches und aramäisches Handwörterbuch über das Alte Testament, Lfg. 1, Alef-Gimel. B 1987, Springer. DM 248.

a233 *Morag* Shelomo, Qumran Hebrew; some typological observations: VT 38 (1988) 148-164.

a234 *Muraoka* Takamitsu, *Shavitsky* Ziva, Abraham IBN EZRA's biblical Hebrew lexicon; the five Megilloth, II: AbrNahr 26 (1988) 80-111.

a235 **Murtonen** A., Hebrew in its West Semitic [non-Masoretic] setting, I-A, Comparative lexicon, proper names: St. Sem. Lang. Linguistics 13, 1986 → 2,7306: ᴿAbrNahr 26 (1988) 122-6 (J. *Blau*: many addenda); BL (1988) 149 (J. C. L. *Gibson*); JSS 33 (1988) 264-7 (P. *Wernberg-Møller*).

a236 **Róth** Ernst, *Prijs* Leo, Hebräische Handschriften 1a, 1982 [Róth, *Striedel* Hans 1984 → 2,7313]: ᴿOLZ 83 (1988) 38.311s (G. *Pfeifer*).

Schmidt H. H., Semitismen bei PAPIAS 1988 → h746.

a236* **Silva** Moisés, Biblical words and their meaning; an introduction to lexical semantics 1983 → 64,7878 ... 1,8856: ᴿCBQ 50 (1988) 698s (C. H. *Miller*).

a237 **Sirat** Colette, *al.*, La Ketouba de Cologne, un contrat de mariage juif à Antinoopolis [417 C.E., in Aramaic and Greek] 1986 → 2,7316; 3,9286: ᴿBL (1988) 144 (S. C. *Reif*); JStJud 19 (1988) 127-9 (N. R. M. de *Lange*).

Smelik K. A. D., Historische Dokumente (= Behouden schrift 1984 → 1,8859) 1987 → d108.

a237* *Soden* Wolfram von, Bedeutungsgruppen unter den Substantiven nach der Nominalform *ma/iqtāl* mit Pluralformen nach *ma/iqtallîm/ôt* im Althebräischen: ZAHeb 1,1 (1988) 103-6.

a238 *Stone* Michael E., The months of the Hebrews [Armenian ms. 981 C.E.]: Muséon 101 (1988) 5-12.

a239 **Weinberg** W., The history of Hebrew plene spelling 1985 → 2,7323: ᴿVT 38 (1988) 125s (S. C. *Reif*).

a240 *Wittlieb* Marian, ❷ Quomodo polonice lexicon onomasticum biblicum ederetur?: RuBi 41 (1988) 229-231.

J1.3   **Voces** ordine alphabetico *consonantium* **hebraicarum**.

a241 *abbā':* *Barr* James, *a)* Abbā isn't 'daddy' [*Jeremias* J.]: JTS 39 (1988) 28-47; – *b)* 'Abba, Father' and the familiarity of Jesus' speech [variant presentation of JTS 39,28]: TLond 91 (1988) 173-9.

a242 *Van Gemeren* Willem A., *Abbā'* in the Old Testament?: JEvTS 31 (1988) 385-398 [< ZIT 89,148].

a243 *'ayin:* *Cohen* Chaim E., ❷ The declension of 'ayin in Tannaitic Hebrew: → 44, Mem. ERON D. 1988, 37-42; Eng. VIII.

a244 *amen:* → 804, NBL Lfg 1 (1988) 86s (K. *Berger*).

a245 *insān:* *Kahl* Oliver, IBN AL-HANBALI's Traktat über die Etymologie von arab. *insān*: OrLovPer 19 (1988) 197-9.

a246 *aqht:* *Margalit* Baruch, Ugaritic lexicography IV; the name Aqht: RB 95 (1988) 211-4; français 95: QHT, 'très obéissant'.

a247 *'rk:* **Richter** W., Untersuchungen I 1985 → 1,8957 ... 3,9302: ᴿJNWS 14 (1988) 227s (F. C. *Fensham*).

a248 *'rṣ:* *Tsumura* David T., A 'hyponymous' word pair; *'rṣ* and *thm(t)* in Hebrew and Ugaritic [like *yad / yemîn*, where the second parallel is really part of the first]: Biblica 69 (1988) 258-269.

a248* *Ararat* Nissan, ❷ An *'ôr'* not *'me'îr'* in biblical Hebrew: BethM 34,119 (1988s) 316-327.

a249 *'ēš:* **Morla Asensio** Víctor, El fuego en el Antiguo Testamento; estudio de semántica lingüística [diss. Pont. Inst. Bíblico 1988, ᴰ*Alonso Schökel* L.]: SJerónimo 21. Valencia/Bilbao 1988, Inst. S. Jerónimo / Inst. Dioc. Teología. 372 p. pt. 2500. 84-86076-27-8.

a250 *bdl* = *muškēnūtum*: UF 20 (1988) 221-6 (F. *Renfroe*).

a251 *bayit:* Cowling Geoffrey, The biblical household: ➤ 469, Wünschet 1986/8, 179-192.

a252 *Dziekan* Marek M., ❷ What is *bayt?* PrzOr (1987) 502-6.

a253 *brh:* UF 20 (1988) 226-232 (F. *Renfroe*).

a254 *bārak:* **Mitchell** Christopher W., The meaning of *brk* 'to bless' in the OT: SBL diss 95, 1987 ➤ 3,9307: ᴿAustralBR 36 (1988) 62s (J. J. *Scullion*: intrusive jargon); ETL 64 (1988) 193s (J. *Lust*); JBL 107 (1988) 507-9 (M. *Hillmer*).

a255 *Jongeling* Karel, The name element *brk* in Latin epigraphical sources: VO 7 (1988) 223-241.

a256 *Horst* P. W. van der, De birkat ha-minim in het recente onderzoek [*Minim* means always Jews; *noṣrim* not in earliest form; JEROME distinguishes *naṣrim* (Nazorites, Judeo-Christians) from *noṣrim* (Christians)]: Ter Herkenning 15,1 (1987) 38-45 [< JStJud 19,157].

a257 *gābāh...:* **Richter** Wolfgang, Untersuchungen zur Valenz althebräischer Verben 2. GBH, MQ, QSR: AOtt 25, 1986 ➤ 2,7336; 3,9310: ᴿZkT 110 (1988) 108 (G. *Fischer*).

a258 Hebrew *hēdād* 'thunder-storm': UF 20 (1988) 173-177 (J. C. de *Moor*).

a258* *hār / midbar:* Talmon S., ➤ a888, ᴱ*Mindlin* M. *al.*, Figurative language 1987, 117-142.

a259 *wāru:* Kienast Burkhard, *têrtum* [< *(w)āru(m)*] im Altassyrischen: ➤ 32, ꟻDELLER K., AOAT 220 (1988) 145-155: 'information'; 'assignment'.

a260 *zābaḥ:* Engammare Max, 'Mizbeaḥ' dans les polémiques sur 'Missa'; une référence étrange à l'hébreu dans la défense de la Messe comme sacrifice dans les premières années des Réformes: BiblHumRen 50 (1988) 661-9.

a260* *ḥᵃlôm:* **Robinson** Margaret, The dream in the OT: diss. Manchester 1988. – RTLv 20,541.

a261 *ḥanaka:* Gil'adi Avner, Some notes on *taḥnik* [rubbing a newborn child's palate with a date] in medieval Islam: JNES 47 (1988) 175-179.

a261* *Masson* Michel, La grâce et l'infamie; remarques sur les deux sens de l'hébreu *ḥesed:* GLECS 28,2 (1984) 341-357.

a262 *ṭôb:* Brin Gershon, The significance of the form *mah-ṭṭôb* [7 times, mostly in Wisdom-books]: VT 38 (1988) 462-5.

a263 *ṭrp* 'glow': HebSt 29 (1987) 75 ... (H. *Basser*).

a263* *ykḥ, môkîaḥ* (Middah 2,2): BethM 34,118 (1988s) 241-9 (Rivkah *Nega*).

a264 *yārā':* **Costacurta** Bruna, La vita minacciata; il tema della paura nella Bibbia Ebraica [diss. 1987 ➤ 3,9335]: AnBib 119. R 1988, Pont. Ist. Biblico. 360 p. Lit. 48.000. 88-7653-119-X.

a265 **Conrad** Edgar W., Fear not, warrior... al tirâ pericopes 1985 ➤ 1,8900 ... 3,9336: ᴿAbrNahr 26 (1988) 113-5 (J. J. *Scullion*); CBQ 50 (1988) 493-5 (W. *Brueggemann*: superb).

a266 *Zatelli* Ida, Yir'at Jhwh nella Bibbia, in Ben Sira e nei rotoli di Qumran; considerazioni sintattico-semantiche: RivB 36 (1988) 229-237.

a266* *Halpern* Marguerite, Les propositions avec *yeš* en hébreu biblique: GLECS 28 (1984) 535-560.

a267 *yāšen:* **Mc Alpine** T. H. Sleep, divine and human, in the OT: JStOT Sup 38, 1987 ➤ 3,9338*: RBL (1988) 99 (J. F. *Healey*); OTAbs 11 (1988) 204s (J. I. *Hunt*).

a268 *yaša':* *Pope* Marvin H., Hosanna; what it really means: BR 4,3 (1988) 16-25.

a269 *yat:* *Díez Merino* L., Diacronía de la partícula aramea *yât:* ➤ 22, Mém. CARMIGNAC J., RQum 13 (1988) 497-512.

a270 *kābôd:* **Struppe** Ursula, Die Herrlichkeit Jahwes in der Priesterschrift; eine semantische Studie zu kᵉbôd yhwh [kath. Diss. Wien 1984, DBraulik G.]: ÖsBibSt 9. Klosterneuburg 1988, Österr. KBW. v-258 p. DM 40. – RTüTQ 168 (1988) 241s (W. *Gross*); ZAW 100 (1988) 465s (H.-C. *Schmitt*).

a271 *kalama:* *Rubio* Luciano, Sentido del término árabe 'mutakallimun' ['teólogos especulativos'] traducido por los traductores medievales de textos árabes al Latín por 'loquentes': CiuD 201 (1988) 551-561.

a272 *l'm:* *Beyer* K., Akkadisches *līmu* und aramäisches *l'm* 'eponym': Orientalia 57 (1988) 82s.

a273 *lēb, nepeš, rûaḥ:* **Lauha** Risto, Psychophysische Sprachgebrauch im AT I. Emotionen 1983 ➤ 64,7953 ... 3,9347: RTZBas 44 (1988) 79s (M. *Dreytza*).

a274 *mgg:* 'Krieg führen, kämpfen'; eine bisher übersehene nordwestsemitische Wurzel: UF 20 (1988) 125-133 (I. *Kottsieper*).

a274* *maddua', lāmāh:* *Michel* D., 'Warum?' und 'wozu?'. Eine bisher übersehene Eigentümlichkeit des Hebräischen und ihre Konsequenzen für das alttestamentliche Geschichtsverständnis: Studien zur interkulturellen Geschichte des Christentums 48 (1988) 191-210 [< ZAW 101,139].

a275 *māgēn:* *O'Connor* M., Yahweh the donor [rather than 'shield', as already in his TWAT 4,646]: AulaO 6 (1988) 47-60.

a276 *mākar* 'buy' (Syriac): ➤ a316, *qasita* 329-331 (E. *Lipiński*).

a277 *mā'ad:* ➤ 44, ERON D. Mem. 1988, ❺ 31-35; Eng. VIII (A. *Tal*).

a278 *mašennu* 'steward': ➤ a316, *qaśita* 325-9 (E. *Lipiński*).

a279 *nau:* **Kunitsch** Paul, Über eine *anwā'*. Tradition mit bisher unbekannten Sternnamen: Szb, Bayerische Akad. p/h 1983,5. Mü 1983, Beck. 118 p. – ROLZ 83 (1988) 580-2 (G. *Strohmaier*).

a280 *Nouaeimith* (S.-Arab): ParPass 235 (1987) 290-2 (G. *Fiaccadori*).

a281 *nepeš:* **Rankin** John C., The corporeal reality of *nepeš* and the status of the unborn: JEvTS 31 (1988) 153-160 [< ZIT 88,588]. ➤ a234.

a283 *sōpēr:* *Arbeitman* Yoël L., [*soper,* (*Qiryat-)Seper*] Iranian 'scribe', Anatolian 'ruler' or neither; a city's rare chances for 'leadership' (reflections on recording and leading): ➤ 42*, EHRMAN A. mem., Fucus 1988, 1-95; bibliog. 96-101.

a284 *'ēber:* **Loretz** Oswald, Habiru-Hebräer ...: BZAW 160, 1984 ➤ 65, 7843 ... 3,9361: RCdÉ 63 (1988) 300s (E. *Lipiński*); JNES 47 (1988) 192-4 (N. *Na'aman*: some serious objections).

a284* *Na'aman* Nadav, Biryawaza of Damascus and the date of the Kāmid el-Lōz 'Apiru letters: UF 20 (1988) 179-193.

a285 *Ibrium:* *Michalowski* Piotr, Thoughts about Ibrium [name of a person at Ebla, but the article is about kingship in Mesopotamia]: ➤ 707, Wirtschaft 1986/8, 267-278.

a285* *'dy:* *Couroyer* B., 'Ēdût: stipulation de traité ou enseignement?: RB 95 (1988) 321-331; Eng. 321: Aram. *'dy*, Akkad. *adu*, not Heb. *'wd*.

a286 *phh:* *Petit* Thierry, L'évolution sémantique des termes hébreux et araméens *phh* et *sgn* et accadiens *paḥātu* et *šaknu*: JBL 107 (1988) 53-67.

a287 *panah* 'sich wenden' [*pinnah* 'Eck(stein)']: ⇒ 815, TWAT 6,6 (1988) 617-625 (J. *Schreiner*) [626-9, M. *Oeming*].

a288 *panim a*) 'Gesicht': ⇒ 815, TWAT 6,6 (1988) 629-658 (H. *Simian-Yofre*); – *b*) Angesicht: ⇒ 804, NBL Lfg 1 (1988) 104-7 (J. *Wehrle*).

a289 *pæsæl* '(Götter) Bild(-verbot)': ⇒ 815, TWAT 6,6 (1988) 688-697 (C. *Dohmen*).

a290 *pāʿal* 'machen': ⇒ 815, TWAT 6,6 (1988) 697-703 (K.-J. *Illman*).

a291 *paʿam* 'Mal': ⇒ 815, TWAT 6,6 (1988) 703-8 (M. *Sæbø*).

a292 *pāqad* 'beauftragen': ⇒ 815, TWAT 6,6 (1988) 708-723 (G. *André*).

a293 *pārad* 'trennen': ⇒ 815, TWAT 6,6 (1988) 735-8 (J. *Hausmann*).

a294 *pæraʿ* 'Haupthaar': ⇒ 815, TWAT 6,6s (1988) 757-760 (T. *Kronholm*).

a295 *pāraṣ* 'durchbrechen': ⇒ 815, TWAT 6,6s (1988) 763-770 (J. *Conrad*).

a296 *Zadka* Yitzhak, ❽ The Hebrew verb PRṢ and its meanings: ⇒ 44, ERON D. Mem. 1988, 91-108; Eng. XIIs.

a297 *pāraq* 'wegreissen': ⇒ 815, TWAT 6,6s (1988) 770-3 (F. *Reiterer*).

a298 *pārar*, '(Bund) brechen': ⇒ 815, TWAT 6,6s (1988) 773-780 (L. *Ruppert*).

a299 *pāraś*, 'ausbreiten': ⇒ 815, TWAT 6,6s (1988) 780-2 (H. *Ringgren*).

a300 *pāšaṭ*, 'ausziehen': ⇒ 815, TWAT 6,6s (1988) 787-791 (H. *Schmoldt*).

a301 *pæšaʿ*, 'Sünde': ⇒ 815, TWAT 6,6s (1988) 793-810 (H. *Seebass*; äg. H. *Ringgren*).

a302 *Basser* Herbert W., *Pesher hadavar*; the truth of the matter: ⇒ 22, Mém. CARMIGNAC J., RQum 13 (1988) 389-405.

a303 *pitô'm*, 'plötzlich': ⇒ 815, TWAT 6,6s (1988) 818-820 (W. *Thiel*).

a304 *pātaḥ* 'öffnen' [(Augen) *pāqaḥ*]: ⇒ 815, TWAT 6,6 (1988) 831-852 (R. *Bartelmus*) [723-5, J. *Hausmann*].

a305 *pātal*, 'verdrehen': ⇒ 815, TWAT 6,6s (1988) 852-5 (G. *Warmuth*).

a306 *ṣe'āh*, 'Schmutz': ⇒ 815, TWAT 6,6s (1988) 856-8 (K.-M. *Beyse*).

a307 *ṣdq*: **Krašovec** Joze, La justice (*ṣdq*) de Dieu dans la Bible hébraïque et l'interprétation juive et chrétienne [diss. 1986 ⇒ 2,7447]: OBO 76. FrS/ Gö 1988, Univ./Vandenhoeck & R. 452 p. Fs 110. 3-7278-0549-8 / 3-525-53705-0 [BL 89,109, J. R. *Porter* dubious about 452 p. on only 140 of the 523 occurrences]. – RETL 64 (1988) 456s (J. *Lust*).

a308 *Knight* G. A. F., Is 'righteous' right?: ScotJT 41 (1988) 1-10.

a308* *Freund* Joseph, ❽ *Zikkaron* and *ṣedāqâ*: BethM 34,118 (1988s) 202-5.

a309 **Weinfeld** M., Justice (*ṣedāqâ*) and righteousness in Israel and the nations 1985 ⇒ 1,8965: RVT 38 (1988) 126 (S. C. *Reif*).

a310 *Gossai* Hemchand, Ṣaddîq in theological and economic perspectives: SvEx 53 (1988) 7-13.

ṣaʿaq, qārā' ... **Boyce** Richard N., The cry to God in the OT 1988 ⇒ 8009.

a311 *ṣāpôn*: *Fass* David E., The symbolic uses of north [Ezek 1,4 and often]: Judaism 37 (1988) 465-473.

a312 *qdl*: *Blänsdorf* Jürgen, *Horst* Heribert, CODLIA — eine semitische Bezeichnung für garum [fish-product]?: ZDMG 138 (1988) 24-38.

a313 *qrsy*: *Garfinkel* Yosef, MLṢ HKRSYM in Phoenician inscriptions from Cyprus, the QRSY in Arad, HKRSYM in Egypt, and BNY QYRS in the Bible: JNES 47 (1988) 27-34; 2 fig.

a314 *'ntqysr* 'viceroy': HebSt 28 (1987) 72 ... (H. *Basser*, Word Studies in rabbinic Hebrew, 67-77) [NTAbs 32,215].

a315 *qṣṣ*: *McKane* William, *qṣwṣy p'h* and *p't mdbr*: ⇒ 47, FFENSHAM F., Text 1988, 131-8.

a315* **Raja** Rao T.J., 'Cry' in the OT (2), a study of *qārā'* with special reference to Isaiah: LivWord 93 (Kerala 1987) 151-175 [< TKontext 9/2,37].

a316 *qaṣiṭa* 'ewe': *Lipiński* Edward, In search of the etymology of some Semitic loan-words: → 42*, EHRMAN A. mem., Fucus 1988, [325-]331-3.

a316* *rab: Nibbi* Alessandra, The possible presence of the Semitic noun *rab/rabi* in some Egyptian texts: DiscEg 3 (1985) 43-48; 3 fig.

a317 *rîb:* **Bovati** Pietro, Ristabilire la giustizia; procedure, vocabolario, orientamenti [diss. R, ᴰ*Alonso Schökel* L.] 1986 → 2,7458; 3,9429: ᴿJBL 107 (1988) 302s (F. O. *Garcia-Treto*); TLZ 113 (1988) 339s (H. *Reventlow*: Lexikalisches zur Rechtspflege); VT 38 (1988) 495 (W. *Horbury* '44 p.').

a318 *repa'im: Dijkstra* Meindert, The legend of Danel and the Rephaim: UF 20 (1988) 35-52.

a318* *raqqâ: Rozelaar* Marc, An unrecognized part of the human anatomy ['open mouth' not 'temple' Ct 4,3; 6,7...]: Judaism 37 (1988) 97-101.

a319 *śyḥ: Rendsburg* Gary A., Hebrew *św/yḥ* and Arabic *šḫḫ*: → 42*, EHRMAN A. mem., Fucus 1988, 419-430.

a320 *Augusto Tavares* A., *śar, zāqēn, nāśî'*: Quelques termes bibliques relatifs à des institutions anciennes; problèmes de traduction et d'histoire: Didaskalia 15 (1986) 257-266.

a321 *śar:* **Rüterswörden** Udo, Die Beamten der israelitischen Königszeit [Diss. 1981]: BWANT 117, 1985 → 1,8983...3,9435: ᴿNedTTs 42 (1988) 69s (K. A. D. *Smelik*).

a322 *šeʾîrît:* **Carena** Omar, Il resto di Israele: RivB Sup 13, 1985 → 1,8977; 2,7464: ᴿCBQ 50 (1988) 286s (R. *Althann*); JBL 107 (1908) 121s (E. M. *Cook*: really on the origin of the concept of remnant); RB 95 (1988) 305 (R. J. *Tournay*); VT 38 (1988) 502 (W. *Horbury*).

a323 *šaknu: Stolper* Matthew W., The *šaknu* of Nippur: JCS 40 (1988) 127-155.

a324 *šālôm: Jenni* Ernst, 'Gehe hin in Frieden (*lšlwm / bšlwm*)!': ZAHeb 1,1 (1988) 40-46.

a325 *šāpaṭ:* **Niehr** Herbert, Herrschen und Richten... špṭ: ForBi 54, 1986 → 2,7471; 3,9445: ᴿBL (1988) 150 (A. D. H. *Mayes*); BO 45 (1988) 164-6 (W. *Richter*); NedTTs 42 (1988) 336s (P. B. *Dirksen*).

a326 *štwt* 'shame': HebSt 28 (1987) 67... (H. *Basser*).

a327 *mtwn* 'pious person': HebSt 28 (1987) 70... (H. *Basser*).

a328 *'ātnan: Soden* Wolfram von, Hurritisch *uatnannu* > mittelassyrisch *utnannu* und > ugaritisch *itnn* > hebräisch *'ātnan* 'ein Geschenk, Dirnenlohn': UF 20 (1988) 309-311.

a329 *t', t'y, t't* [Ug.]: nombre divino y acción cultual: UF 20 (1988) 27-33 (G. del *Olmo Lete*).

a330 *t'y:* UF [19 (1987) 33] 20 (1988) 313-321 'royal scribe, secretary of state' (W. H. van *Soldt*).

J1.5   *Phoenicia, Ugaritica* – **North-West Semitic** [→ T5.4].

a331 *a) Bordreuil* Pierre, Perspectives nouvelles de l'épigraphie sigillaire Ammonite et Moabite; – *b) Kooij* Gerrit van der, The identity of Trans-Jordanian alphabetic writing in the Iron Age: → e824, Jordan III 1986/7, 283-6 / 107-121.

a331* *Caquot* André, L'épigraphie sémitique: CRAI (1988) 612-617.

a332 *a) Caquot* A., Un recueil ougaritique de formules magiques; KTU 1.32; – *b) Cunchillos* J. I., Mes affaires sont terminées; traduction et commentaire de KTU 3.13: → 98, ꜰLORETZ O., StEpLing 5 (1988) 31-43 / 45-50.

a333 *Cooper* Alan, Two exegetical notes on Aqht [1-19.I.2-19 / 34-39]: UF 20 (1988) 19-26.

a334 *Cox* Michael G., AUGUSTINE, JEROME, TYCONIUS and the *lingua punica*: StOrFin 64 (1988) 83-105.

a335 **Gelb** Ignace J., Computer-aided analysis of Amorite 1980 ➤ 61, a341 ... 64,8037: ᴿOLZ 83 (1988) 31-35 (J. *Oelsner*).

a336 **Garbini** Giovanni, Venti anni di epigrafia punica nel Magreb (1965-1985) [= ➤ 3,9463]: RivStFen Sup 14. R 1986. 90 p. – ᴿBbbOr 30 (1988) 56-58 (A. van den *Branden*, franç.)

a337 **Garbini** Giovanni, Il semitico nordoccidentale; studi di storia linguistica: StSemit NS 5. R 1988, Univ. xiii-172 p.

a338 *Gordon* Cyrus H., West Semitic factors in Eblaite ['more or less intermediate between East and West Semitic']: ➤ 42*, EHRMAN A. mem., Fucus 1988, 261-6.

a339 *Healey* John F., Ugaritic lexicography and other Semitic languages: UF 20 (1988) 61-68.

a340 *Hoftijzer* J., Three unpublished Punic votive texts: OMRO 68 (1988) 41; 2 pl.

a341 *a) Hübner* Ulrich, Die ersten moabitischen Ostraka; – *b) Becking* Bob, Kann das Ostrakon ND 6231 von Nimrūd für ammonitisch gehalten werden?: ZDPV 104 (1988) 68-73 / 59-67.

a343 *Krahmalkov* C. R., Observations on the Punic monologues of Hanno in the Poenulus: Orientalia 57 (1988) 55-66.

a344 *Lemaire* André, Recherches actuelles sur les sceaux nord-ouest sémitiques: VT 38 (1988) 221-230.

a344* *Lemaire* André, La langue de l'inscription sur plâtre de DeirʿAlla: GLECS 28,2 (1984) 317-340.

a345 *a) Lipiński* E., L'aleph quiescent en ugaritique; – *b) Bordreuil* P., Variations vocaliques et notations sporadiques du génitif dans les textes alphabétiques de l'Ougarit; – *c) Sanmartín* J., Glossen zum ugaritischen Lexikon (V): ➤ 98, ᶠLORETZ O., StEpL 5 (1988) 113-119 / 25-30 / 171-180.

a346 *Margalit* B., Two Aqht passages; epigraphic restoration, prosodic reconstruction, and philological literary commentary: OrLovPer 19 (1988) 63-90.

a347 **Moor** J. C. De, *Spronk* K., A cuneiform anthology of religious texts from Ugarit: Semitic Study Series 6 [this self-styled 'translation series' has no translation or transliteration or table of signs in this volume 6, but gives a complete translation as volume 16] 1987 ➤ 3,b265a: ᴿBL (1988) 84 (W. G. E. *Watson*: with SEGERT's grammar the learner now has the basic tools).

a348 *Olmo Lete* G. del, *Sanmartín* J., A new Ugaritic dictionary [project]; its lexicographical and semantic structure: AulaOr 6 (1988) 255-274.

a349 **Pardee** Dennis, Les textes para-mythologiques de la 24e Campagne [de Ras Shamra] (1961): Mémoire 77. P 1988, RCiv. iv-333 p.; 20 fig. F 198. 2-86538-185-4.

a349* *Rendsburg* Gary A., The Ammonite phoneme /t/: BASOR 269 (1988) 73-79.

a350 ᴱRummel S., Ras Shamra parallels, III: AnOrPont 51, 1981 ➤ 62, 8873 ... 3,9485: ᴿIsrEJ 38 (1988) 94 (A. *Hurvitz*).

a351 *Sanmartín* J., Notas de lexicografía ugarítica [...*rpš, nsk/psl, bʾl aṭṭ/ššlmt, ḥmr kšmm, mšlḥ ḥdṭ, drt/drʿ*]: UF 20 (1988) 265-275.

a352 *Segert* Stanislas, The Ugaritic voiced postvelar in correspondence to the emphatic interdental: UF 20 (1988) 287-300.

a353 *Shea* William H., Protosinaitic inscription No. 357: UF 20 (1988) 301-8.

a354 **Siles** Jaime, Léxico de inscripciones ibéricas. M 1985, Ministerio de Cultura. 437 p. – ᴿFaventia 9,2 (1987) 142s (G. *Carrasco Serrano*).

a355 *a) Soden* W. von, Ebla, die früheste Schriftkultur Syriens; – *b) Fales* Mario F., Formations with *m*-prefix in the bilingual vocabularies; – *c) Müller* H.-P., Zur Bildung der Verbalwurzeln im Eblaitischen; – *d) Huÿssteen* P. van, Das Zeichen GÀM/KAM₄ in den eblaitischen Personennamen; – *e) Brugnatelli* Vermondo, Sprachwissenschaftliche Überlegungen zu einem literarischen Text aus Ebla: ↠ 707, Wirtschaft 1986/8, 325-332 / 205-9 / 279-292 / 225-230 / 173-8.

a355* *Sperling* S. David, KAI 24 re-examined [Kilamuwa, Zencirli 1902]: UF 20 (1988) 323-337.

a356 *Tropper* J., *Verreet* E., Ugaritisch *ndy, ydy, hdy, ndd* und *d(w)d*: UF 20 (1988) 339-350.

a357 **Verreet** E., Modi ugaritici; eine morpho-syntaktische Abhandlung über das Modalsystem im Ugaritischen: OrLovAn 27. Lv 1988, Univ. Dep. Orientalistiek. xxx-264 p. Fb 2950. 90-6831-116-6.

a358 *Xella* Paolo, L'elemento *'bn* nell'onomastica fenicio-punica: UF 20 (1988) 387-392.

a359 **Zuckerman** B., Puzzling out the past; making sense of ancient inscriptions from biblical times. Rancho Palos Verdes CA 1987, Maarav. 48 p. $10 [BL 89,33, A. R. *Millard*].

J1.6 **Aramaica**.

a360 *Andersen* Francis I., *Freedman* David N., The orthography of the Aramaic portion of the Tell Fekherye bilingual: ↠ 47, ᶠFENSHAM F., Text 1988, 9-49.

a360* ᶠAVIGAD Nahman = Erlsr 18 (1985) ↠ 1,12: ᴿBASOR 271 (1988) 85-87 (B. *Porten*, mostly on F. M. *Cross* Samaria papyrus 1 after 23 years).

a361 *Bar-Asher* Moshé, Le Syro-Palestinien [araméen] — études grammaticales: JAs 276 (1988) 27-59.

a362 *Ben-Hayyim* Z., ❸ Studies in Palestinian Aramaic and Samaritan poetry: ↠ 132, ᶠSCHIRMANN H., Jubilee 1970, 34-68.

a363 **Beyer** Klaus, The Aramaic language, ᵀ*Healey* J. F., 1986 ↠ 2,7506; 3,9502: ᴿJBL 107 (1988) 314s (E. M. *Cook*: idosyncratic).

a364 **Buth** Randall J., Word order in Aramaic from the perspectives of functional grammar and discourse analysis: diss. Univ. California. LA 1988. xxiv-522 p.

a364* *Cazelles* Henri, Observations sur la bilingue assyro-araméenne de Fekheryé (résumé): GLECS 28,2 (1984) 441s.

a365 *Daniels* Peter T., 'Shewing of hard sentences and dissolving of doubts' [Dan 5,12]; the first decipherment [of an ancient language, not Egyptian but Palmyrene, 1754 by J.-J. *Barthélemy*]: JAOS 108 (1988) 419-436.

a365* **Fales** Frederick M., Aramaic epigraphs on clay tablets of the Neo-Assyrian Period: Materiali per il lessico aramaico 1, 1986 ↠ 2,7512: ᴿBL (1988) 148 (A. R. *Millard*); BO 45 (1988) 510-7 (E. *Lipiński*).

a366 *Görg* M., Aramäisch; *Lipiński* E., Aramäer: ↠ 804, NBL Lfg 1 (1988) 148-150 / 146-8.

a367 *Hoftijzer* J., An unpublished Aramaic fragment from Elephantine: OMRO 68 (1988) 45-47; phot. 48.

a368 *Ibrahim* Jabir Kh., ❹ New Aramaic inscriptions from Hatra: Sumer 44 (1985s) 98-110; 22 fig.

a369 *Jastrow* Otto, Der neuaramäische Dialekt von Hertevin (Provinz Sûrt): Semitica Viva 3. Wsb 1988, Harrassowitz. 256 p. 3-447-02767-3 [BL 89,155].

a369* *Jones* Richard N., *al.*, A second Nabataean inscription from Tell esh-Shuqafiya, Egypt: BASOR 269 (1988) 47-64.

a370 *Kyrieleis* Helmut, [*Röllig* Wolfgang, aram. Inschrift], Ein altorientalischer Pferdeschmuck aus dem Heraion von Samos: MiDAI-A 103 (1988) 37-61 [62-75], pl. 9-15.

a370* *a) Layton* Scott C., ᴱ*Pardee* Dennis, Old Aramaic inscriptions: BA 51 (1988) 172-189; ill. – *b) Margain* Jean, Note sur la particule araméenne *lḥd'/h*: GLECS 28,2 (1984) 289-293.

a371 *Lewis* Naphtali, The papyri from Nahal Ḥever: → 492, XVIII Papyrol. 2 (1986/8) 127-132.

a371* **Maraqten** Mohammed, Die semitischen Personennamen in den alt- und reichsaramäischen Inschriften aus Vorderasien: Texte und Studien zur Orientalistik. Hildesheim 1988, Olms. vi-250 p. DM 39,80. 3-487-09042-2 [BO 45,758].

a372 **Naveh** Joseph, *Shaked* Saul, Amulets and magic bowls; Aramaic incantations of late antiquity 1985 → 1,9051 ... 3,9519: ᴿJNES 47 (1988) 152s (M. *Morony*); RB 95 (1988) 585-8 (É. *Puech*); StIran 17 (1988) 113 (Rika *Gyselen*).

a373 **Odisho** E.Y., The sound system of modern Assyrian (Neo-Aramaic): Semitica Viva 2. Wsb 1988, Harrassowitz. xvii-146 p. DM 64. 3-447-02744-4 [BL 89,152, J. *Barr*: the same word seems to be used for 'yesterday' and 'tomorrow'].

a374 *Otzen* Benedikt, Petitionary formulae in the Aramaic inscriptions from Hama: → 153, ZAW 100 Supp. (1988) 233-243.

a375 *Peñá* Ignacio, In Maalula si parla ancora la lingua di Gesù: TerraS 64 (1988) 156-162.

a376 **Porten** Bezalel, *Yardeni* Ada, Textbook of Aramaic documents from ancient Egypt, I. Letters [Appendix: Aramaic letters from the Bible] 1986 → 2,7529; 3,9523: ᴿJNES 47 (1988) 289s (S.A. *Kaufman*); Orientalia 57 (1988) 434-6 (E. *Lipiński*); RB 95 (1988) 294-9 (P. *Grelot*).

a377 *Porten* B., Aramaic papyrus fragments in the Egyptian museum of West Berlin: Orientalia 57 (1988) 14-54; → d996.

a378 *Porten* Bezalel, *Szubin* H.J., An Aramaic deed of bequest (Kraeling 9): → 3,62*, ᶠGratz College 1987 ...

Sabar Y., Exodus in Neo-Aramaic of Zakho 1988 → 2424.

Schwarz G., Jesus und Judas; aramaistische Untersuchungen 1987 → 4885.

a379 **Segal** J.B., Aramaic texts from North Saqqâra 1983 → 64,8092 ... 3,9529: ᴿCdÉ 63 (1988) 301-4 (E. *Lipiński*); JNES 47 (1988) 154-6 (D *Pardee*); JQR 78 (1987s) 308s (F.E. *Greenspahn*); OLZ 83 (1988) 180-3 (J. *Oelsner*).

a380 **SOISALON-SOININEN** Ilmari, (seine eigenen) Studien zur Septuaginta-Syntax, 70. Gb. ᴱ*Aejmelaeus* Anneli, *Sollamo* Raija: Ann. Ac. Fennicae 237. Helsinki 1987. 224 p. – ᴿNorTTs 89 (1988) 274s (H.M. *Barstad*).

a381 *a) Swiggers* P., Nombres et malédictions dans les inscriptions de Sefiré; – *b) Mawet* Francine, Cinq et sept en iranien ancien: → 50, ᶠFONTINOY C., Humour ... science 1988, 311-322 / 287-304.

a382 *a) Swiggers* P., Possessives with predicative function in official Aramaic; – *b) O'Connor* Michael P., The grammar of finding your way in Palmyrene Aramaic and the problem of diction in ancient West Semitic inscriptions: → 42*, EHRMAN A. mem., Fucus 1988, 449-461 / 353-369.

a383 *Szubin* H. Z., *Porten* Bezalel, A life estate of usufruct; a new interpretation of Kraeling 6: BASOR 269 (1988) 29-46.

a384 **Vleeming** S., *Wesselius* J., Studies in P. Amherst 63, 1985 → 1,9067; 3,9536: ᴿVT 38 (1988) 251s (J. A. *Emerton*).

J1.7 **Syriaca.**

a385 *Bohas* Georges, Quelques processus phonologiques en syriaque: LOrA 1 (Lv 1988) 17-31.

a386 *Féghali* J., †, L'influence du substrat syriaque dans la langue actuelle parlée au Liban: → 101, Mém. MARÇAIS P. 1985, 161-9.

a387 **Frey** Albert, Petite grammaire syriaque: OBO Subs. Didact. 3, 1984 → 65,7955; 3,9540: ᴿJNES 47 (1988) 235s (J. F. *Healey*).

a387* **Gignoux** P., Incantations magiques syriaques 1987 → 3,9543: ᴿAION 48 (1988) 251s (F. *Vattioni*); BSOAS 51 (1988) 619 (C. H. *Gordon*); ETL 64 (1988) 475s (A. de *Halleux*); RÉJ 146 (1987) 441s (Françoise *Briquel-Chatonnet*).

a388 **Kiraz** George A., Alaph Beth Font Kits [Syriac package, supplement to MLS (Multi-Lingual Scholar) package]. Los Angeles 1987, Alaph Beth. $195. – ᴿScotJT 41 (1988) 553-5 (I. R. *Torrance*: high praise).

a389 **Kiraz** G. A., The Syriac primer; reading, writing, vocabulary and grammar. Ox 1988, UP. 0-19-713607-9 [BL 89,155].

a390 *Moller* Garth I., Towards a new typology of the Syriac manuscript alphabet [Dura-Europos deed found 1933]: JNWS 14 (1988) 153-184; 185-197, photos and drawings.

a391 **Muraoka** T., Classical Syriac for Hebraists 1987 → 3,9550. xv-131 p. DM 58. – ᴿBL (1988) 149 (P. *Coxon*).

a391* *a) Puech* Émile, Une inscription syriaque sur mosaïque [New York; from a site not indicated but claimed to be also the source of three others]; – *b) Halloun* Moïn, Two Syriac inscriptions [USA]: SBFLA 38 (1988) 267-270; pl. 9-10 / 271-5: pl. 11-12.

a392 *Seidel* Ulrich, *a)* Möglichkeiten der syrischen (aramäischen) Lexikologie für die Sozial- und Wirtschaftsgeschichtsschreibung des Vorderen Orients: HalleB 10 (1986) 53-77. – *b)* Studien zum Vokabular der Landwirtschaft im Syrischen I: AltOrF 15 (1988) 133-173.

J2.1 **Akkadica** (sumerica).

a393 **Black** Jeremy A., Sumerian grammar in Babylonian theory: StPohl 12, 1984 → 65,7964 ... 3,9564: ᴿAulaO 6 (1988) 108s (G. *Gragg*); RelStR 14 (1988) 64 (J. M. *Sasson*); WZKM 78 (1986) 282-5 (M. *Krebernik*).

a394 *Brinkman* J. A., *Dalley* Stephanie, A royal *kudurru* from the reign of Aššur-nādin-šumi: ZAss 78 (1988) 76-98.

a395 **Caplice** Richard, Introduction to Akkadian ³ʳᵉᵛ (with *Snell* Daniel): StPohl 9. R 1988, Pontifical Biblical Institute. ix-106 p.; foldout. 88-7653-566-7.

a395* **Civil** Miguel, *al.*, The Sag-Tablet: MSL Sup. 1 1986 → 2,7543*: ᴿWZKM 78 (1986) 271-4 (J. A. *Black*).

a396 *D'Agostino* Franco, Die ersten 14 Zeilen des sog 'z à-m e'-Textes aus Abu Salabikh und die Bedeutung des Wortes z à-m e: OrAnt 27 (1988) 75-83.

a397 *Dombrowski* B. W. W., 'Eblaitic' = the earliest known dialect of Akkadian: ZDMG 138 (1988) 211-235.

a398 *Englund* R. K., Administrative timekeeping in ancient Mesopotamia [Sumerian 'sexagesimal system' divided work-day into 60 parts, with no relation to our 60 minutes/seconds]: JESHO 31 (1988) 121-182; 183-5, tables of signs.

a399 *Gomi* Tohru, Neue Kollationen zu den Texten PDT [Drehem], 1: Orient-J 24 (1988) 108-123.

a400 **Groneberg** Brigitte R. M., Syntax, Morphologie und Stil der jung-babylonischen 'hymnischen' Literatur. I. Grammatik; II. Belegsammlung und Textkatalog: FreibAltorSt 14. Wsb 1987, Steiner. x-212 p. (bibliog. 204-211); xvi-190 p. DM 70. 3-515-04859-6 [BO 45,474].

a401 *Hallo* William W., Sumerian literature, background to the Bible: BR 4,2 (1988) 28-38; ill.

a402 *Hess* Richard S., A preliminary list of the published Alalakh texts: UF 20 (1988) 69-87.

a403 *a) Jacobsen* Thorkild, The Sumerian verbal core; – *b) Wiggermann* F. A. M., An unrecognized synonym [SAL-HÚB] of Sumerian *sukkal* 'Vizier'; – *c) Krecher* Joachim, Der erste Band des Pennsylvania Sumerian Dictionary und der Stand der Sumerologie heute: ZAss 78 (1988) 161-220 / 225-240 / 241-275.

a404 *Kienast* Burkhart, KASKAL^{II} *ana GÌR^{II} ša PN šakānu* [... help for journey]: WeltOr 19 (1988) 5-34.

a404* *Malbran-Labat* Florence, L'expression du serment en akkadien: GLECS 28,2 (1984) 233-8.

a405 **Maul** Stefan M., 'Herzberuhigungsklagen'; die sumerisch-akkadischen Eršaḫunga-Gebete. Wsb 1988, Harrassowitz. xi-471 p.; Bibliog. p. 461-9. 3-447-02833-5.

a405* *Miller* Andrew, Pleiades perceived; MUL-MUL to subaru (Japanese for Pleiades): JAOS 108 (1988) 1-25; 8 fig.

a406 *Müller* Hans-Peter, Zur Bildung der Verbalwurzeln im Eblaitischen: → 707, E*Hauptmann* H., Wirtschaft/Ebla 1986/8, 279-289.

a407 *Neumann* Hans, Zum Stand der Forschung auf dem Gebiet der Sumerologie [*Sjöberg* dictionary, vol. 2]: OLZ 83 (1988) 5-13.

a408 *Pangas* J. C., Aspectos de la sexualidad en la antigua Mesopotamia [Šumma alu 104]: AulaOr 6 (1988) 211-226.

a408* *a) Parpola* Simo, Proto-Assyrian; – *b) Butz* K., *Wenning* W., ŠÀ und die 'eingefaltete Ordnung'; – *c) Davidović* Vesna, *Guruš* in the administrative texts from Ebla [spelled 'Elba' p. 199, and title given in Italian p. vii]; – *d) Lipiński* E., *Šu-bala-aka* und *badalum*: → 707, Wirtschaft 1986/8, 293-8 / 179s / 199-204 / 257-260.

a409 *Rainey* A. F., Some presentation particles in the Amarna letters from Canaan: UF 20 (1988) 209-220.

a410 *Römer* W. H. P., Aus einem Schulstreitgespräch in sumerischer Sprache: UF 20 (1988) 232-245.

a411 **Sachs** Abraham J., Astronomical diaries and related texts from Babylonia, I. Diaries from 652 B.C. to 262 B.C.: Denkschrift 195. W 1988. Österr. Akad. 377 p.; vol. of 69 pl. 3-7001-1227-0.

a411* *a) Scurlock* J. A., How to lock a gate; a new interpretation of CT 40 12; – *b) Volk* K., Eine bemerkenswerte nach-Fara-zeitliche Urkunde: Orientalia 57 (1988) 421-433 / 206-9.

a412 *Segert* Stanislav, Die Orthographie der alphabetischen Keilschrifttafeln in akkadischer Sprache aus Ugarit: → 98, F*LORETZ* O., StEpL 5 (1988) 189-205.

a413 **Soden** W. von, Einführung in die Altorientalistik 1985 ➤ 1,9116...
3,9598: ᴿOrientalia 57 (1988) 87s (W. G. *Lambert*).

a414 *Sollberger* Edmond, The cuneiform scripts [1983 AnRIM lecture]:
CanadMesop 7 (1984) 6-18.

a416 *Stieglitz* Robert R., The Chaldeo-Babylonian planet-names in
HESYCHIUS: ➤ 42*, EHRMAN A. mem., Fucus 1988, 443-7.

a417 **Thomsen** Marie-Louise, The Sumerian language 1984 ➤ 65,7992;
3,9600: ᴿBO 45 (1988) 499-509 (M. *Yoshikawa*); JAOS 108 (1988) 123-
133 (T. *Jacobsen*); JNES 47 (1988) 208-210 (G. *Gragg*); ZAss 78 (1988)
138-144 (D. Z. *Edzard*).

a418 **Vogelzang** M. E. (f.), Bin šar dadmē; edition and analysis of the
Akkadian Anu poem; diss. Groningen 1988, ᴰHospers J. – PhoenEOL
34,2 (1988) 5.

a419 **Walker** C. B. F., Cuneiform; reading the past 1987 ➤ 3,9602: ᴿBL
(1988) 128 (A. R. *Millard*).

J2.7 **Arabica.**

a420 *Abou Abdalla* Albert, Materiali per lo studio dell'antroponomia araba;
il Libano, zone di Nabaṭiyya e di Zghorta: OrMod 67 (1987) 147-180.

a421 **Allen** Roger, The Arabic novel; an historical and critical introduction.
Syracuse 1982, Univ. 181 p. $15. – ᴿJNES 47 (1988) 146-9 (Suzanne P.
Stetkevych: uncritical).

a422 *Antonini* Sabina, Nuovi incensieri iscritti yemeniti: OrAnt 27 (1988)
133-140; 1 fig.; pl. IV-VI.

a423 **Asbaghi** Asya, Die semantische Entwicklung arabischer Wörter im
Persischen [Diss. Berlin, ᴰ*Macuch*], 1987 ➤ 3,9603; DM 65. – ᴿMundus
24 (1988) 3s (H. *Müller*: 437 Arabic words).

a424 **Beeston** A. F., Sabaic grammar 1984 ➤ 65,8004...3,9608: ᴿArOr 56
(1988) 101s (K. *Petráček*); OLZ 83 (1988) 433-7 (H. *Preissler*).

a425 **Behnstedt** Peter, *Woidich* Manfred, Die ägyptisch-arabischen Dialekte
3/1, Delta-Dialekte: TAVO B-50/3, 1987 ➤ 2,7572; 3,9609; DM 140:
ᴿMundus 24 (1988) 95s (R. M. *Voigt*: documentation for already-pub-
lished parts 1-2 with 561 maps).

a426 *Behnstedt* Peter, Lexikalisches aus dem Jemen: WeltOr 19 (1988)
142-155.

a426* **Bohas** Georges, *Guillaume* Jean-Patrick, Étude des théories des
grammairiens arabes, I. Morphologie et phonologie: IFD 112. Damas
1984, Institut Français. xviii-501 p.

a427 **Borg** A., Cypriot Arabic 1985 ➤ 2,7574; 3,9613: ᴿStOrFin 64 (1988)
385-8 (H. *Palva*: abounds in diachronically intriguing linguistic material).

a428 ᵀᴱ**Bushnaq** Inea, Arab folktales. Hw 1987, Penguin. xxviii-386 p. 0-14-
059510-4.

a429 *Colin* Gérard, À propos des graffites sud-arabiques du ouādi Ham-
māmāt: BIFAO 88 (1988) 33-36; 2 fig.

a429* *Coquin* R.-G., Réflexions sur le lexique arabe biblique des Coptes
[*Graf* G. 1984, *Samir Khalil* 1967s]: PrOrChr 38 (1988) 229-237.

a430 *a) Doss* Madiha, Sur l'évolution de *qad* dans le système des particules
verbales de l'arabe; – *b) Taine-Cheikh* Catherine, Les altérations con-
ditionnées des chuintantes et des sifflantes dans les dialectes arabes:
GLECS 28,2 (1984) 359-364 / 413-435.

a430* ᴱ**Fleischhammer** Manfred, Altarabische Prosa: Universal Bibliothek
Belletristik. Lp 1988, Reclam. 352 p.

a431 ᴱGatje Helmut [† 1986], Grundriss der arabischen Philologie [I. 1982 ᴱFischer W.] II. Literaturwissenschaft. Wsb 1987, Reichert. xiv-560 p. DM 280. – ᴿMundus 24 (1988) 101s (H. Müller).

a432 Gilliot Claude, La formation intellectuelle de TABARI (224/5-310/839-923) [< diss. P 1987]: JAs 276 (1988) 203-241; index de noms 242-4.

a433 Goldenberg Gideon, Subject and predicate in Arab grammatical tradition: ZDMG 138 (1988) 39-73.

a433* Hary Benyamin H., Judeo-Arabic, written and spoken in Egypt in the sixteenth and seventeenth centuries: diss. California. Berkeley 1987. 450 p. 88-13894. – DissA 49 (1988s) 1443-A.

a434 Jamme Albert, Note on [three brief 'Safaitic' inscriptions from] Ǧebel Qurma: ZDPV [102 (1986) 110] 104 (1988) 125-7; 2 fig.

a434* Kanakri Mahmoud A., Style and style shifting in educated spoken Arabic of Jordan: diss. Wisconsin, ᴰZeps V. Madison 1988. 379 p. 88-17129. – DissA 49 (1988s) 2202-A.

a435 Kouloughli D. E., Renouvellement énonciatif et valeur aoristique; à propos de l'opposition mâ/lam en arabe: LOrA 1 (Lv 1988) 49-72.

a436 Lundin A. G., Sabaean dictionary, some lexical notes: → 10, ᶠBEESTON A., Ṣayhadica 1987, 49-56.

a437 Mansour Jacob, Texts in the Judaeo-Arabic dialect of Baghdad: AbrNahr 26 (1988) 68-79.

a438 Pabst Klaus-E., Die Wiedergabe griechischer und lateinischer Affixe bei der Bildung arabischer Wissenschaftlicher Termini: HalleB 10 (1986) 5-21.

a439 Pellat Charles, Cinq calendriers égyptiens: Textes Arabes 26. Cairo 1986, IFAO. – ᴿJAmEg 25 (1988) 257s (D. A. King).

a440 Reichmuth Stefan, Der arabische Dialekt der Šukriyya im Ostsudan: StudSprachW 2. Hildesheim 1983, Olms. x-309 p. DM 39,80. – ᴿJNES 47 (1988) 143-6 (D. O. Edzard).

a441 Roman André, Étude de la phonologie et de la morphologie de la koinè arabe: Univ. Provence 1983 → 2,7584: ᴿLOrA 1 (Lv 1988) 199-204 (D. E. Kouloughli).

a442 ᴱSamir Khalil, Actes du deuxième Congrès int. d'études arabes chrétiennes 1984/6 → 3,651: ᴿZDMG 138 (1988) 186s (A. Böhlig).

a443 Schall Anton, Elementa arabica; Einführung in die klassische arabische Sprache. Wsb 1988, Harrassowitz. viii-209 p. DM 48. 3-447-02433-X.

a444 Schregle Götz, al. Arabisch-deutsches Wörterbuch [Lfg. 5-8, 1983s → 2,7587], Lfg. 9-13. Wsb 1986, Steiner. – ᴿOLZ 83 (1988) 183s (G. Krahl).

a445 Shitomi Yūzō, La persécution [ḥimyarite] de Naǧrān; réexamen des dates figurant dans le Martyrium Arethae: Orient-J 24 (1988) 71-83.

a446 Talmon Rafael, al-kalam... al-ǧumla, a study in the history of sentence-concept and the Sībawaihian legacy in Arabic grammar: ZDMG 138 (1988) 74-98.

a447 Thalji Abdel-Majid I., Head-modifier agreement in case in Arabic. ArOr 56 (1988) 42-53.

a448 Voigt Rainer M., Die infirmen Verbaltypen des Arabischen und das Biradikalismusproblem [Hab. Tü 1983]: OrKomm Veröff 39. Stu 1987, Steiner. 192 p. [Mundus 24,257]. DM 98. – ᴿStOrFin 64 (1988) 381s (T. Harviainen: 'vol. XXXIXI').

a449 *Yrttiaho* Kaarlo, Texts from Arabia Petraea in the dialect of the semi-nomadic an-N^{e}māt tribe of the Shara mountains (Jordan): StOrFin 64 (1988) 145-168.

J3 Ægyptia.

a450 *Abdalla* A. M., Beginnings of insight into the possible meanings of certain Meroitic personal names; (1) non-verbal sentences: BeiSudan 3 (1988) 5-15.

a451 **Bakir** A. M., Notes on Middle Egyptian grammar[2] [[1]1954 ❹; 1978 Eng.] 1984 ➔ 65,8044; 3,9651: ᴿBO 45 (1988) 527s (M. *Malaise*).

a451* **Barguet** Paul, Les textes des sarcophages 1986 ➔ 3,9652: ᴿRB 95 (1988) 430-2 (R. *Beaud*).

a452 *Barta* Winfried, Zur Konstruktion der ägyptischen Königsnamen III-IV: ZäS 115 (1988) 1-8. 87-95 ...

a453 *a) Barta* Winfried, *Jn* als Pleneschreibung der Präposition *n*; – *b) Hannig* R., Überlegungen zum *sḏm.w*-Passiv; – *c) Kurth* Dieter, Die Lautwerte der Hieroglyphen in den Tempelinschriften der grie-chisch-römischen Zeit — zur Systematik ihrer Herleitungsprinzipien, ein Nachtrag (Prinzip XII): GöMiszÄg 103 (1988) 7-11; 1 fig. / 13-31 / 45-49; – *d) Barta,* Zum Verbaladjektiv sḏmtj.fj: GöMiszÄg 105 (1988) 7-9.

a454 **Beckerath** Jürgen von, Handbuch der ägyptischen Königsnamen 1984 ➔ 65,8046; 2,7594: ᴿCdÉ 63 (1988) 258-264 (Marie-Ange *Bonhème*).

a455 *Bresciani* Edda, Il papiro Dodgson [Elefantina; Ashmolean 1932-1159] e il *hp (n) wplt*: EgVO 11 (1988) 55-70.

a456 **Browne** Gerald M., Studies in Old Nubian: BeiSudan Beih 3. W-Mödling 1988, Univ. 63 p. Sch 350 [BO 45,472].

a457 *a) Browne* G. M., New light on Old Nubian; the Serra East codex; – *b) Abdalla* Abdelgadir M., Meroitic compound-verbs with 'ide' and its variants; – *c) Müller* Caspar D. G., Die Homilie über die zwei 'Canones von Nikaia'; Analyse und Einordnung eines altnubischen Textes; – *d) Hofmann* Inge, Nubische Sprachaufnahmen im 17. Jahrhundert; – *e) Hintze* Fritz, Beobachtungen zur altnubischen Grammatik, VI. Zur Morphophonologie; – *f) Smagina* Eugenia B., Einige Probleme der Morphologie des Altnubischen: ➔ 750, Nubian V, 1982/6, 219-222 / 3-18 / 341-6 / 295-7 / 287-293 / 391-7.

a458 **Buurman** Jan, *Grimal* N., Inventaire des signes hiéroglyphiques en vue de leur saisie informatique; manuel de codage des textes: Informatique et Égyptologie 2: AIBL Mémoire NS 8. P 1988, de Boccard. 215 p.

a459 **Cenival** Françoise de, Le mythe de l'œil du soleil: Demotische Studien 9. Sommerhausen D-8701 1988, Zauzich. x-116 p.; 23 pl. DM 96. 3-924151-02-4 [BO 45,755].

a460 **Cenival** Françoise de, Papyrus démotiques de Lille III: IFAO Mém 110. Le Caire 1984, IFAO. vi-126 p.; 17 pl. 2-7247-0009-0. – ᴿBO 45 (1988) 529-534 (Maria C. *Betrò*: title 'François', text 'Françoise'); CdÉ 63 (1988) 278-281 (R. K. *Ritner*).

a461 *Cesaretti* Maria P., Note prosopografiche... canopi Bologna: RStor-Ant 16 (1986) 189-200; 5 facsim.

a461* *Četveručin* A. S., ❺ Two approaches to the study of the Egyptian proposition: Istoriya/Filologiya Drevni. Vostoka (Moskva 1987) 64-83 (84-100 ... nominal proposition); – *b)* ❺ Logical-grammatical predicate in the ancient Egyptian nominal proposition and categories of case and determination in cognate languages: Drevni i Srednov. Vostok (Moskva 1983) 106-120 (88-105, ... logical stress).

a462 **Champollion** J. F., Dictionnaire égyptien en écriture hiéroglyphique. Starnberg 1988 = 1843, 'LTR'. 3-88706-258-2 [OIAc D88].

a463 *Chetveruchin* Alexander S., Unexpected linguistic interpretation of *jn* 'say(s), said': GöMiszÄg 104 (1988) 75-88.

a464 *Cipola* B., Ramses III and the Sea Peoples; a structural analysis of the Medinet Habu inscriptions: Orientalia 57 (1988) 275-306.

a465 **Clère** Jacques J., Le papyrus de Nesmin; un livre des morts hiéroglyphique de l'époque ptolémaïque: Bibliothèque Générale 10. Le Caire 1988, IFAO. 18 p.; 19 pl. 2-7247-0049-X [BO 45,472].

a466 *Crozier-Brelot* Claude, Indexes of citations from ancient Egypt literature: CompHum 20 (1986) 313-7.

a467 **Daumas** François, *al.*, Valeurs phonétiques des signes hiéroglyphiques d'époque gréco-romaine I-II [III awaited]. Montpellier 1988, Univ. Inst. Égyptologie. 2-905397-24-1; 5-X [OIAc N88].

a468 *Devauchelle* Didier, Naufragé 184-186: GöMiszÄg 101 (1988) 21-25.

a469 **Donadoni** Sergio, Appunti di grammatica egiziana, con un elenco di segni e di parole: Testi e documenti per lo studio dell'antichità 7. Mi 1983, Cisalpino. 127 p. 88-205-0457-X.

a470 **Doret** Eric, The narrative verbal system of Old and Middle Egyptian 1986 → 2,7603. – ᴿAulaO 6 (1988) 114-6 (J. *López*); DiscEg 9 (1987) 97-111 (P. *Vernus*); Muséon 101 (1988) 428s (C. *Vandersleyen*).

a471 **Englund** Gertie, Middle Egyptian, an introduction. U 1988, Balder. x-136 p.; 83 fig. 91-506-8660-3 [OIAc N88].

a471* **Eyre** C. J., Egyptian and Semitic conjugation systems in diachronic perspective [*Loprieno* A. 1986]: BO 45 (1988) 5-18.

a472 **Fischer-Elfert** Hans-Werner, Literarische Ostraka der Ramessidenzeit in Übersetzung 1986 → 3,9674; DM 36: ᴿBO 45 (1988) 305s (Virginia *Condon*); Mundus 24 (1988) 11-13 (K. *Jansen-Winkeln*); WeltOr 19 (1988) 161-3 (S. *Quirke*).

a473 *a) Foster* John, 'The shipwrecked sailor'; prose or verse? (postponing clauses and tense-neutral clauses); – *b) Bickel* Susanne, Furcht und Schrecken in den Sargtexten; – *c) Kessler* Dieter, Der satirisch-erotische Papyrus Turin 55001 und das 'Verbringen des schönen Tages'; – *d) Zibelius-Chen* Karola, Kategorien und Rolle des Traumes in Ägypten: StAltÄgK 15 (1988) 69-109 / 17-25 / 171-196 / 277-293.

a474 **Goedicke** Hans, Studies in the Hekanakhte papers. Baltimore 1984. – ᴿDiscEg 12 (1988) 97-102 (S. *Quirke*).

a474* *Goedicke* Hans, Papyrus Boulaq 8 reconsidered [neither about a sickness (Goedicke earlier) nor about a dowry (K. *Baer*) but about helping a young relative get a good job]: ZägSpr 115 (1988) 136-146; facsim.

a475 *Goedicke* Hans, Readings, III. Papyrus Ebers 25,3-8; IV. Urk VII 35,8-15; V. Sinuhe B 10: VarAeg 4 (1988) 33-42 / 201-6.

a476 *a) Hassan* Ali, Das Word *ḫ3*; – *b) Vandersleyen* Claude, Ouadi-Our ne signifie pas 'mer'; qu'on se le dise!: GöMiszÄg 103 (1988) 33-37 / 75-80.

a476* *Hennig* Rainer, Denkkategorien im Ägyptischen: GöMiszÄg 106 (1988) 29-45.

a477 *Herbin* François-René, Les premiers pages du Papyrus Salt 825: BIFAO 88 (1988) 95-112; long foldout.

a478 *a) Iversen* Erik, Reflections on some ancient Egyptian royal names; – *b) Caminos* Richard A., Mummy bandages inscribed with Book of the Dead spells: → 41, ᶠEDWARDS I., Pyramid studies 1988, 78-88 / 161-7.

a479 **Johnson** Janet H., Thus wrote 'Onchsheshonqy; an introductory grammar of demotic 1986 → 2,7615: ᴿOrientalia 57 (1988) 220-3 (H. *Quecke*).

a480 *Jürgens* Peter, Textkritische und Überlieferungsgeschichtliche Untersuchungen zu den Sargtexten: GöMiszÄg 105 (1988) 27-34 + 6 pl.

a481 *Kitchen* Kenneth A., The titularies of the Ramesside kings as expression of their ideal kingship: → 127, ꟲṢALEḤ A., ASAE 71 (1987) 131-141.

a481* **Korostovceva** M. A. ⊕ Journey of Wen-Amun, Papyrus Moscow 120. Moskva 1960, Izdatelstvo Vostočnoj Literatury. 135 p.; ill.

a482 *Kramer* Bärbel, Das Archiv des Nepheros und verwandte Texte I (mit *Shelton* John C.) - II: Aegyptiaca Treverensia 4. Mainz 1987, von Zabern. xii-162 p.; 31 pl. DM 155. 3-8053-0923-6 [BO 45,471].

a483 **Lalouette** Claire, Textes sacrés et textes profanes de l'ancienne Égypte, I. Des Pharaons et des hommes; II. Mythes, contes et poésie: Unesco. P 1987, Gallimard. 352 p.; 320 p. F 135; F 128 [BO 45,473]. 2-07-070142-5; 1176-5.

a484 **Loprieno** Antonio, Topos und Mimesis; zum Ausländer in der ägyptischen Literatur: ÄgAbh 48. Wsb 1988, Harrassowitz. viii-125 p. 3-447-02819-X.

a485 *a) Loprieno* Antonio, Verbal forms and verbal sentences in Old and Middle Egyptian; – *b) Kammerzell* Frank, Norm, Relikt oder Fiktion? Zweifel an der Existenz einer morphologisch-syntaktischen Kategorie 'indikativ-perfektivisches *sḏm=f*' im Mäg: GöMiszÄg 102 (1988) 59-72 / 41-57.

a486 ꟲLÜDDECKENS Erich: Grammata demotika, ᴱThissen Heinz J., *Zauzich* Karl-T., 1984 → 65,95: ᴿBO 45 (1988) 93-97 (Bernadette *Menu*); CdÉ 63 (1988) 244-6 (H. De *Meulenaere*); OLZ 83 (1988) 538-541 (R. S. *Bagnall*).

a487 **Lüscher** Barbara, Totenbuch, Spruch I, nach Quellen des Neuen Reiches: KLÄgT. Wsb 1986, Harrassowitz. ix-73 p. DM 32. – ᴿWeltOr 19 (1988) 160 (Malte *Römer*).

a488 **Magee** D. N. E., *Malek* J., A checklist of transcribed hieratic documents in the papers of the late Prof. Jaroslav ČERNÝ at the Griffith Institute. Oxford 1988, Ashmolean Museum. 39 p.

a488* **Majonica** Rudolf, Das Geheimnis der Hieroglyphen; die abenteuerliche Entschlüsselung der ägyptischen Schrift durch Jean François CHAMPOLLION. FrB 1986, Herder. 89 p.; ill. (H. *Seeber*).

a489 *Meltzer* Edmund S., The cuneiform list of Egyptian words from Amarna; how useful is it really for reconstituting the vocalization of Egyptian?: VarAeg 4 (1988) 55-62.

a490 *Mertens* Jan, *Tassier* Emmanuel, Proposal for a bibliography and description of demotic literary texts: GöMiszÄg 101 (1988) 49-55.

a491 *Meulenaere* Herman De, Le décret d'Osiris: CdÉ 63 (1988) 234-241.

a492 *Millet* N. B., Some canopic inscriptions of the reign of Amenhotep III [*Legrain* 1904; ... humour, irony?]: GöMiszÄg 104 (1988) 91-93.

a493 **Morschauser** Scott N., Threat formulae in ancient Egypt: diss. Johns Hopkins Univ. Baltimore 1987. 88-07453 [OIAc D88].

a494 *Morschauser* Scott N., The end of the Sḏf(3)-Tr(yt) 'oath' [... related to Megiddo and Qadeš]: JAmEg 25 (1988) 93-103.

a495 **Munro** Irmtraut, Untersuchungen zu den Totenbuch-Papyri der 18. Dynastie; Kriterien ihrer Datierung [Göttinger philosophische Diss.]: Studies in Egyptology. L 1988, Kegan Paul. xxi-369 p.; ill. £45. 0-7103-0288-6.

a496 *Nibbi* Alessandra, [? *rṯnw, ḫ3rw* ...] Some remarks on the lexikon entry 'Syrien, Syria': DiscEg 8 (1987) 33-47; 2 fig. [7 (1987) 13-27 on Zeder, Cedar].

a497 *Nur el-Din* Mohamed A.-H., Some demotic school exercises: ⇒ 127, ṢALEḤ A., ASAE 71 (1987) 199-204; 4 fig.

a498 *Ogdon* Jorge, On the name and the epithets of the beings called *mrwt.y* in the Coffin Texts: VarAeg 4 (1988) 221-232.

a498* *O'Mara* Patrick F., Is the Cairo stone a fake? An example of proof by default? [Alleged portion or cognate of Palermo Stone, offered for sale in 1910, was not drawn with ancient Egyptian cubit rod, and so could not be genuine]: DiscEg 4 (1986) 33-40.

a499 *Patanè* Massimo, *a*) À propos du 'carpe diem' dans la littérature égyptienne [chants d'Antef et Neferhotep]: DiscEg 12 (1988) 63-66; – *b*) Les traces de la construction ergative en égyptien: DiscEg 10 (1988) 69-72; – *c*) Le mutazioni consonantiche in egiziano: DiscEg 5 (1986) 55-58 [metatesi consonantica: 4 (1986) 67-72].

a500 **Pernigotti** Sergio, Leggere i geroglifici. Bo/Casalecchio 1988, Grafis. 87 p.; ill. Lit. 18.000.

a501 **Petráček** Karel †, Nochmals über die Struktur der Wurzeln mit den Pharyngalen im Altägyptischen und Semitischen und ihre Inkompatibilität: ⇒ 42*, EHRMAN A. mem., Fucus 1988, 371-7.

a502 **Plumley** J. Martin, *Browne* Gerald M., Old Nubian texts from Qasr Ibrim I: Texts from Excavations 9. L 1988, Egypt Explor. Soc. vi-80 p.; 11 pl. 0-85698-100-1 [BO 45,473].

a503 *a*) *Polotsky* H. J., Egyptology, Coptic studies, and the Egyptian language [1984 Glanville lecture, Cambridge]; – *b*) *Eyre* C. J., Speculations on the structure of Middle Egyptian; – *c*) *Junge* Friedrich, Morphology sentence forms, and language history: ⇒ 712, Lingua 1987, 5-21 / 22-46 / 47-56.

a504 **Quirke** [Quircke OIAc D88] Stephen, *Andrews* Carol, The Rosetta stone; facsimile drawing with intr.ᵀ. L 1988, British Museum. 0-7141-0948-7.

a505 *Roccati* Alessandro, La notazione vocalica nella scrittura geroglifica: OrAnt 27 (1988) 115-126.

a505* *Rousseau* Jean & Michel, Réhabilitation d'un célèbre scribe [alleged errors in 4th story of Cheops Westcar Papyrus]: DiscEg 5 (1986) 59-65.

a506 *a*) *Satzinger* Helmut, Towards reconstructing the tense system of Old Egyptian; – *b*) *Osing* Jürgen, New light on the vocalisation of Egyptian verbal forms; – *c*) *Leahy* M. Anthony, Multiple adverbial predicates in ancient Egyptian (the formula ír.n.f m mnw.f): ⇒ 712, Lingua 1988, 72-79 / 65-71 / 57-64.

a506* *Sayed* Ramadan el-, *a*) Mots et expressions évoquant l'idée de lumière: ⇒ 127, ᶠṢALEḤ A., ASAE 71 (1987) 61-86; – *b*) Quelques réflexions au sujet du titre *sḥnw 3ḥ*: BIFAO 88 (1988) 63-69.

a507 *Schenkel* Wolfgang, Aktuelle Perspektiven der ägyptischen Grammatik [ᴱ*Englund* G., *Frandsen* P. 1986 ⇒ 705]: BO 45 (1988) 269-289.

a508 **Schenkel** Wolfgang, Aus der Arbeit an einer Konkordanz zu den altägyptischen Sargtexten I-II: GöOrF 4/5/12, 1983 ⇒ 64,8219; 1,9220: ᴿBO 45 (1988) 105-7 (J. R. *Callender*).

a509 **Schenkel** Wolfgang, Zur Pluralbildung des Ägyptischen ... 1983 ⇒ 64, 8219, 1,9921: ᴿOLZ 83 (1988) 535-8 (J. *Hallof*).

a510 *Schenkel* Wolfgang, Erkundungen zur Reihenfolge der Zeichen im ägyptologischen Transkriptionsalphabet: CdÉ 63,125 (1988) 5-35.

a511 *Schulman* Alan R.,   The so-called Poem on the King's Chariot revisited: JSSEg 16 (1986) 19-35. 39-49.

a512 ᴱ*Simpson* William K.,   Personnel accounts of the early twelfth dynasty, papyrus Reisner IV.... Sections F-G by Peter **Der Manuelian**. Boston 1986, Museum of Fine Arts. 47 p.; 33 pl. $80 [JNES 46,78].

a513 **Smith** H. S., *Tait* W. J.,   Saqqâra demotic papyri I, 1983 ⇒ 65,8081: ᴿBO 45 (1988) 306-9 (M. *Smith*).

a514 *Spalinger* Anthony,   A sequence system: ⇒ 119, Mém. POSENER G., RÉgp 39 (1988) 107-129.

a514* **Sturtewagen** Christian, *al.*,   Geroglifici svelati 1987 ⇒ 3,9698:   ᴿOss-Rom 26.II.1988 p. 3 (G. *Nolli*).

a515 *Tobin* Vincent A.,   Ma'at and *dikē*; some comparative considerations on Egyptian and Greek thought: JAmEg 24 (1987) 113-121.

a515* [*Daumas* François †, *al.*] Valeurs phonétiques des signes hiéroglyphiques d'époque gréco-romaine. Montpellier 1988, Univ. 291 p.; p. 293-432.

a516 **Vernus** Pascal,   Le surnom au Moyen Empire: StPohl 13, 1986 ⇒ 2,7632: ᴿDiscEg 8 (1987) 107-110 (S. *Quirke*); JAmEg 25 (1988) 244s (R. J. *Leprohon*).

a517 *Vernus* Pascal,   La formule du bon comportement (bít nfrt): ⇒ 119, Mém. POSENER G., RÉgp 39 (1988) 147-154; Eng. 154.

a518 *Walle* B. van de,   Survivances de l'ancien égyptien dans la langue et la toponymie actuelle de l'Égypte: ⇒ 101, Mém. MARÇAIS P. 1985, 113-121.

a519 *Wallet-Lebrun* Christiane,   À propos de *rwt*, note lexicographique ['exit' rather than 'entrance' (-gate)]: VarAeg 4 (1988) 69-86.

a520 **Ward** William,   Essays on feminine titles of the Middle Kingdom 1986 ⇒ 2,7633: ᴿBO 45 (1988) 313-6 (Rosemarie *Drenkhann*, but col. 265 and 340 Drenkhahn).

a521 *Wilkinson* Richard H.,   The Horus name and the form and significance of the Serekh in the royal Egyptian titulary: JSStEg 15 (1985) 98-104; 6 fig.

J3.4   **Coptica.**

a522 **Biedenkopf-Ziehner** A.,   Untersuchungen zum koptischen Briefformular 1983 ⇒ 64,8229 ... 3,9702: ᴿWZKM 78 (1986) 211-8 (W. *Brunsch*).

a523 **Bourguet** Pierre du,   Les Coptes: Que sais-je? 2398. P 1988, PUF. 128 p. F 25. 2-13-041466-4 [BO 45,471]. – ᴿRICathP 28 (1988) 139 (I. H. *Dalmais*).

a524 **Bouvarel-Boud'hors** Anne, Catalogue des fragments coptes, I. Fragments bibliques nouvellement identifiés. P 1987, Bibl. Nat. 126 p.; 20 pl. F 300. – ᴿMuséon 101 (1988) 429-433 (E. *Lucchesi*).

a525 **Brunsch** Wolfgang,   Kleine Chrestomathie nichtliterarischer koptischer Texte 1987 ⇒ 3,9709: ᴿBO 45 (1988) 594-6 (L. S. B. *MacCoull*).

a526 *Cartreau* Frédéric,   Système 'codique' et système 'codé'; pertinence linguistique de la variante graphique en copte: LOrA 1 (Lv 1988) 33-47.

a527 **Cherix** Pierre,   Étude de lexicographie copte, Chenouté... CahRB 18, 1979 ⇒ 60,a545* ... 63,8221: ᴿJNES 47 (1988) 51-53 (M. *Smith*: nowhere in the book is any Coptic word actually studied).

a527* *Depuydt* Leo,   New horizons in Coptic and Egyptian linguistics: CdÉ 63 (1988) 391-406.

a528 *Frantz-Murphy* Gladys,   A comparison of Arabic and earlier Egyptian [Coptic, Greek...] contract formularies; III. The idiom of satisfaction;

IV. Quittance formulas: JNES [40 (1981) 203-235.355s; 44 (1985) 99-114]
47 (1988) 105-112 . 269-280.

a529 *Hannig* Rainer, Die Partikel *jw* und der Vorläufer des koptischen
Präsens 1 – Präformative: GöMiszÄg 105 (1988) 21-26.

a530 *Helderman* J., Von Jablonski / te Water tot Vycichl bij Jozef JANS-
SEN's pleidooi voor een nieuwe 'Wiedemann': PhoenEOL 34,2 (1988)
54-58.

a531 *Irmscher* Johannes, Berlin und die Koptologie: → 16, ᶠBÖHLIG A.,
Religion 1988, 83-93.

a532 *Kasser* Rodolphe, *a*) Nommer les principaux graphèmes vieux-coptes?:
BSocÉg 12 (Genève 1988) 53-57 [59s, 'Genève 1986' nouvelle série de
caractères typographiques coptes]; – *b*) Aleph initial ou final en copte:
Orientalia 57 (1988) 139-144.

a533 **Layton** Bentley, Catalogue of Coptic literary manuscripts in the British
Library acquired since the year 1906. L 1987, British Library. xlvii-
444 p.; 32 pl. £115. 0-7123-0003-1. – ᴿJTS 39 (1988) 608s (M. *Smith*:
splendid, continuing W. CRUM 1905); Orientalia 57 (1988) 237-9 (H.
Quecke).

a534 *Mikhail* Louis B., The second tenses in practice [Vie de Schnoudi, in
Boharic (sic) does not support *Polotsky*]: ZägSpr 115 (1988) 61-68.

a535 *Osing* Jürgen, Einige koptische Etymologien: → 127, ᶠṢALEḤ A.,
ASAE 71 (1987) 205-211.

a536 **Polotsky** H.J., Grundlagen des koptischen Satzbaus I.: American
Studies in Papyrology 27. Decatur GA 1987, Scholars. xi-168 p. $40.
1-55540-076-0 [NTAbs 32,365].

a537 *Satzinger* H., *Sijpesteijn* P.J., Koptisches Zauberpergament Moen III:
Muséon 101 (1988) 51-62 + 1 pl.

a538 **Shisha-Halevy** Ariel, Coptic grammatical categories: AnOrPont 53,
1986 → 2,7652; 3,9720: ᴿEnchoria 16 (1988) 159-168 (H. *Satzinger*: ein
Meilenstein); ZDMG 138 (1988) 180 (M. *Krause*).

a539 ᴱ**Shisha-Halevy** A., Coptic grammatical chrestomathy; a course for
academic and private study: OrLovAn 30. Lv 1988, Peeters. xix-277 p.
90-6831-139-5.

a540 **Vycichl** Werner, Dictionnaire étymologique... copte 1983 → 64,8250 ...
3,9722: ᴿJEA 74 (1988) 296-9 (K. H. *Kuhn*, W. J. *Tait*).

a541 *Vycichl* Werner, Étude sur la phonétique de la langue bohaïrique:
DiscEg 8 (1987) 67-76.

a542 **Zanetti** U., Les lectionnaires coptes annuels; Basse Égypte 1985
→ 2,7655; 3,9723: ᴿOrientalia 57 (1988) 103-5 (R.-G. *Coquin*).

a543 *Zanetti* Ugo, Un catalogue des Additions coptes de Londres: AnBoll
106 (1988) 171-181.

J3.8   Æthiopica.

a544 *Diem* Werner, Laryngalgesetze und Vokalismus; ein Beitrag zur Geschichte des Altäthiopischen: ZDMG 138 (1988) 236-262.

a545 *Görg* M., Äthiopien: → 804, NBL Lfg 1 (1988) 57s.

a546 **Leslau** Wolf, Comparative dictionary of Ge'ez 1987 → 3,9734; DM 248:
ᴿJSS 33 (1988) 346-9 (E. *Ullendorff*); Mundus 24 (1988) 293 (R. M.
Voigt).

a547 **Neugebauer** Otto, ABU SHAKER's 'Chronography'; a treatise of the 13th
century on chronological, calendrical, and astronomical matters, written

by a Christian Arab, preserved in Ethiopic: Szb ph./h. 498. W 1988, Akad. 199 p. 3-7001-1470-2.

a548 **Richter** Renate, Lehrbuch der amharischen Sprache 1987 ⇒ 3,9740: ROLZ 83 (1988) 690s (B. *Tafla*).

a548* *Schneider* Roger, La première attestation de l'alphabet éthiopien: GLECS 28,2 (1984) 239s; 2 fig.

a549 EUhlig Siegbert, *Tafla* Bairu, Collectanea aethiopica: ÄthFor 26. Stu 1988, Steiner. 233 p.; ill. [FHAMMERSCHMITT Ernest]. 3-515-04928-2.

a550 **Uhlig** Siegbert, Äthiopische Paläographie: ÄthFor 22. Stu 1988, Steiner. 834 p. 3-515-04562-7.

a551 **Ullendorff** E., A Tigrinya chrestomathy: ÄthFor 19, 1985 ⇒ 1, 9523 ... 3,9742: RBL (1987) 126 (M. *Knibb*: twin to Amharic 1965 ²1978); BO 45 (1988) 459-461 (Olga *Kapeliuk*).

a552 **Ullendorff** E., The two Zions; reminiscences of Jerusalem and Ethiopia. Ox 1988, UP. x-249. £19.50. 0-19-212275-4 [BL 89,23, data on *Polotsky* and other scholars].

J4 Anatolica.

a553 **Archi** A., Hethitische Briefe und Texte verschiedenen Inhalts, KUB 57, 1987 ⇒ 3,9743: ROrientalia 57 (1988) 88-92 (M. *Popko*; – Rituale, KUB 49.50.52 p. 234-5 ⇒ b809); ZAss 78 (1988) 309-314 (S. *Košak*); ZDMG 138 (1988) 376-8 (J. *Tischler*).

a554 *Beal* R. H., *Kule*- and related words: Orientalia 57 (1988) 165-180.

a555 *Boley* Jacqueline, The Hittite HARK-construction: Innsb. Bei. SprW 44, 1984 ⇒ 65,8116: RBO 45 (1988) 365-375 (Carol F. *Justus*).

a556 *Coindoz* Michel, D'où vient le nom Cappadoce? Les pièges de la toponymie: Archéologia 241 (Dijon 1988) 48-59, ramblings.

a557 *Coşkun* Yaşar, ● *Ḫupurnu*, a word of interest between Anatolia and Mesopotamia: Belleten 52,205 (1988) 1505-1507 [perfume-jar].

a557* *Faucounau* J., Les lettres sur plomb d'Assur, en écriture 'hittite hié-roglyphique': Belleten 202 (1988) 1-18; 4 fig.

a558 FGÜTERBOCK Hans G., Kaniššuwar, EHoffner H. A., *Beckman* G. M. 1986 ⇒ 3,42: RJNES 47 (1988) 215s (H. C. *Melchert*).

a559 **Güterbock** H., *Hoffner* H., Hittite Dictionary 3 [⇒ 2,7664] fasc. 3 (225-352) 1986: ROrAnt 27 (1988) 309-315 (Maria Stella *Raggi*).

a560 *Hawkins* J. D., The lower part of the Meharde stele: AnSt 38 (1988) 187-190; 2 fig.

a561 *Hoffner* Harry A.J, The song of Silver [hero's name] — a member of the Kumarbi cycle of 'songs': ⇒ 112*, FOTTEN H., Documentum 1988, 143-166.

a561* *Kossian* Aram V., The epithet 'celestial' [*tipasasi*] in the hieroglyphic Luwian inscriptions: AltOrF 15 (1988) 114-8.

a562 *Laroche* E., Luwier, Luwisch, Lu(w)iya [en français]: ⇒ 808, RLA 7,3s (1988) 181-4.

a562* *Mauer* Gerlinde, Zu einigen ideographischen Schreibungen im He-thitischen: ⇒ 32, FDELLER K., AOAT 220 (1988) 189-197.

a563 *a) Melchert* H. Craig, Luvian lexical notes; – *b) Gusmani* Roberto, Zur lydischen Betonung: HistSprF 101 (1988) 211-243 / 244-8.

a564 *Melchert* H. Craig, 'Thorn' and 'minus' in hieroglyphic Luvian orthography: AnSt 38 (1988) 29-42.

a564* *Neu* Erich, Zum hurritischen 'Essiv' in der hurritisch-hethitischen Bilingue aus Hattuša: Hethitica 9 (1988) 157-170.

a565 **Neu** Erich,   Das Hurritische; eine altorientalische Sprache in neuem Licht [Boğazköy Bilingue hurritisch-hethitisch]: AbhMainzAkad g/soz 1988/3. Wsb 1988, Steiner. 48 p.   3-515-05197-1.

a566 **Oettinger** Norbert,   'Indo-Hittite'-Hypothese und Wortbildung: Bei-SprW, kl 37.   Innsbruck 1986, Univ.   40 p.   3-85124-589-X.

a567 *Oshiro* Terumasa, *a*) *api* in hieroglyphic Luwian: ArOr 56 (1988) 246-252; – *b*) Some Luwian words of Indo-European origin: Orient-J 24 (1988) 47-54.

a567* *a*) *Poetto* Massimo,   Eteo... ᵘᶻᵘ*kudur* [termine sacrificale]; – *b*) *Luraghi* Silvia,   Der semantische und funktionelle Bau des althethitischen Kasussystems; – *c*) *Oettinger* Norbert,   Anatolische 'Kurzgeschichten': ZvgSprW 99 (1986) 220-2 / 23-42 / 43-53.

a568 *Soysal* Oğuz, Einige Überlegungen zu KBo III 60: VO 7 (1988) 107-128.

a569 **Starke** Frank,   Die keilschrift-luwischen Texte in Umschrift 1985 ⭢ 1,9277; 3,9762:   ᴿBO 45 (1988) 375-391 (Inge *Hoffmann*); JAOS 108 (1988) 525s (Gerlinde *Mauer*); WZKM 78 (1986) 274-280 (J. D. *Hawkins*).

a569* *Taracha* Piotr,   Zu den syntaktischen Verknüpfungen im Hattischen: AltOrF 15 (1988) 59-68.

a570 *Windekens* Albert-Joris Van,   Sur quelques mots hittites et louvites: MüStSprW 49 (1988) 149-164.

a571 *a*) *Yoshida* Kazuniho,   The present mediopassive endings -*tati* and -*yaštati* in Hittite; – *b*) *Lehrman* A.,   Anatolian cognates of the Proto-Indo-European word for 'wolf': Sprache 33 (1987) 29-33 / 13-18.

J4.4   Phrygia, Lydia, Lycia.

a572 *Bajun* L. S., *Orel* V. E., ⓔ La langue des inscriptions phrygiennes en tant que source historique, II: VDI 187 (1988) 132-167; franç. 167s.

a573 *Eichner* Heiner,   *a*) Die Akzentuation des Lydischen: ⭢ 104, ᶠMAYR-HOFER M. = Sprache 32 (1986) 7-21; – *b*) Neue Wege im Lydischen, I. Vokalnasalität vor Nasalkonsonanten: ZvgSprW 99 (1986) 203-219. ⭢ a563*b*.

a574 *Lubotsky* Alexander,   The Old Phrygian Areyastis inscription [from Yazılıkaya; out of 240, the only one with more than ten separate words]: Kadmos 27 (1988) 9-26.

a575 **Neumann** Günter,   Phrygisch und griechisch: Szb W 499. W 1988, Österr. Akad. 27 p. – ᴿAnzAltW 41 (1988) 245s (H. *Schmeja*).

J4.8   Armena, georgica.

a576 **Diakonoff** I. M., *Starostin* S. A.,   Hurro-Urartian as an Eastern Caucasian language: MüStSprW 12.   Mü 1986, Kitzinger.   x-103 p. – ᴿZAss 78 (1988) 314-6 (W. *Farber*).

a576* *Harouthyounyan* Nicolaï V.,   Nouveau lexique dans les tablettes cunéiformes ourartéennes: AltOrF 15 (1988) 119-123.

a577 **Kevorkian** R. H., ⓔ Catalogue des 'incunables' arméniens 1986 ⭢ 3,9774:   ᴿJAOS 108 (1988) 521s (J. A. C. *Greppin*); WeltOr 19 (1988) 213s (R. H. *Hewsen*).

a578 *Minassian* Martiros,   L'article du premier terme non substantivé d'une subordonnée en arménien classique: Muséon 101 (1988) 97-158.

J5   Graeca   .1 *grammatica, onomastica, inscriptiones.*

a579 [*Bauer* Walter] ⁶ʳᵉᵛ **Aland** K. & B.,   Griechisch-deutsches Wörterbuch zu den Schriften des NTs und der frühchristlichen Literatur.   B 1988, de

Gruyter. xxiv-1976 col. DM 148. 3-11-010647-7. – ᴿETL 64 (1988) 450-454 (F. *Neirynck*).

a579* **Adrados** F. R., Diccionario griego-español 2, 1986 → 2,7689; 3,9782: ᴿAntClas 57 (1988) 452s (M. *Leroy*); ScripTPamp 20 (1988) 825-7 (J. *Chapa*).

a580 **Archi** I. G., *Bartoletti Colombo* A. M., Novellae; legum Justiniani Imperatoris vocabularium, pars graeca IV: Univ. F. Mi 1988, Cisalpino. 494 p.

a581 **Bécares Botas** Vicente, Diccionario de terminología gramatical griega: Acta, Artes Dicendi 3. Salamanca 1985, Univ. xxvi-423 p. 84-7481-332-8. – ᴿAntClas 57 (1988) 453s (F. *Mawet*).

a581* **Becker-Bertau** Friedrich, Die Inschriften von Klaudiupolis; *Weiser* W., Münzen: Inschr. Kleinasien 31. Bonn 1986, Habelt. xvii-194 p.; 6 pl.; 2 maps. DM 135. – ᴿAntClas 57 (1988) 476s (J. *Bingen*: quoi faire de 180 inscriptions presque sans le moindre indice de date?).

a582 **Bernand** Étienne, Inscriptions grecques et latines d'Akoris: BiblÉt 103. Le Caire 1988, IFAO. xxxvi-175 p.; 64 pl. 2-7247-0058-9. – ᴿCdÉ 63 (1988) 165-172 (J. *Bingen*).

a583 **Betz** Hans D., The Greek magical papyri in translation I, 1986 → 2,7692; 3,9786: ᴿHistRel 28 (1988s) 182s (G. G. *Stroumsa*); JBL 107 (1988) 348-351 (F. W. *Danker*).

a583* **Biondi** Alessandro, Gli accenti nei papiri greci biblici 1983 → 63,8276 ... 3,9787: ᴿBASP 23,1s (1986) 65-67 (Kathleen *McNamee*: unsatisfactory).

a584 **Biville** Frédérique, Graphie et prononciation des mots grecs en latin: Bibliothèque de l'Information Grammaticale. Lv 1987, Peeters. 31 p.

a584* *Black* David A., New Testament Semitisms: BTrans 39 (1988) 215-223 [441, a reader-reaction].

a585 ᴱ**Boswinkel** E., *Pestman* P. W., Les archives privées de Dionysios, fils de Képhalos; textes grecs et démotiques: Papyrologica Lugduno-Batava 22A-B. Leiden 1982, Brill. x-342 p.; vol. of viii-44 pl. *f* 280. – ᴿGnomon 60 (1988) 128-131 (H. *Heinen*).

a585* *Boyer* James L., *a*) The classification of optatives; a statistical study: GraceTJ 9 (1988) 129-140; – *b*) Relative clauses in the Greek New Testament; a statistical study: GraceTJ 9 (1988) 233-256.

a586 **Browne** Dale R., Paradigms and principal parts for the Greek NT, 1987 → 3,9791: ᴿRB 95 (1988) 451s (V. *Pizzala*).

a587 *Brunner* Theodore F., P. Köln I.25 Frr, k-o; Iliad or not Iliad? [not]: CdÉ 63 (1988) 305-7.

a588 **Burton** Ernest D., Syntax of the moods and tenses in New Testament Greek³ [= ³1898; ¹1888]. E 1987, Clark. xxii-215 p. 0-567-01002-3.

a589 *Carson* D. A., Greek accents; a student's manual 1985 → 1,9305: ᴿEvQ 60 (1988) 74s (Ruth B. *Edwards*).

a590 *Clarke* Graeme W., Funerary inscriptions near Joussef Pasha, North Syria: AbrNahr 26 (1988) 19-29; pl. 1-7.

a591 ᴱ**Coles** R. A., *al.*, The Oxyrhynchus papyri **54**: Greco-Roman Memoires 74. L 1987, British Academy. x-271 p.; 16 pl.

a591* **Consani** Carlo, Persistenza dialettale e diffusione della *koinē* a Cipro; il caso di Kafizin. Pisa 1986, Giardini. 129 p. – ᴿMinos 23 (1988) 209s (M. *Negri*).

a592 **Corsani** Bruno, Guida allo studio del greco del NT 1987 → 3,9797; Lit. 22.500: ᴿStPatav 35 (1988) 713s (L. *Rebuli*).

a593 **Cunliffe** Richard J., A lexicon of the Homeric dialect. Norman 1986, Univ. Oklahoma. ix-445 p. 0-8061-1430-4.

a594 **Cuvigny** H., *Wagner* G., Les ostraca grecs de Douch I (1-57): DocFouilles 24, 1986 → 2,7705; 3,9798: ᴿEnchoria 16 (1988) 147-9 (W. *Clarysse*).

a595 **Cuvigny** H., *Wagner* C., Les ostraca grecs de Douch II (58-183). Le Caire 1988, IFAO. vi-89 p.; xxii pl. 2-7247-0057-0.

a596 **Delaunois** Marcel, Essai de syntaxe grecque classique; réflexions et recherches: Publ. 44. Bru 1988, Fac. Univ. S.-Louis. x-220 p. 2-8028-0056-6.

a597 *Delaunois* Marcel, Encore le temps-aspect en grec classique; essai limité de clarification: AntClas 57 (1988) 124-141.

a597* [Di Segni] *Campagnano* Lea, L'iscrizione metrica greca di Khirbet er Rajîb: SBFLA 38 (1988) 253-265; pl. 5-8.

a598 *Dobrov* Gregory, The syntax of coreference in Greek: CLPg 83 (1988) 275-288.

a599 **Dubois** Laurent, Recherches sur le dialecte arcadien: Inst. Ling. Cah 33-35. LvN 1986, Cabay. I, 236 p.; II. 324 p.; III. 134 p.

a600 *Ferrari* Franco, P. Berol. Inv. 13270; i canti di Elefantina: StClasOr 38 (1988) 181-227.

a601 **Finck** Gerhard, Die griechische Sprache, eine Einführung und eine kurze Grammatik des Griechischen. Mü 1986, Artemis. 384 p. [Salesianum 50,621].

a602 ᴱ**Fraser** P. M., *Matthews* E., A lexicon of Greek personal names, I. The Aegean islands, Cyprus, Cyrenaica 1987 → 3,9804: ᴿBeiNam 23 (1988) 277-280 (Rüdiger *Schmitt*).

a603 *Gallazzi* Claudio, *Sijpesteijn* Pieter J., Tebtynis; emendamenti a P. Mil. Vogl. III 129-182: CdÉ 63 (1988) 345-366.

a604 **Gigante** Marcello, La Germania e i papiri ercolanesi: Szb Heid ph/h 1988/1. Heid 1988, Winter. 56 p. 3-533-03969-2.

a605 **Greenlee** J. Harold, A New Testament Greek morpheme lexicon 1983 → 64,8330: ᴿFgNt 1,1 (1988) 113s (D. A. *Black*: not since X. JACQUES' List of NT words sharing common elements has a work had such potential for becoming the standard in its field).

a606 ᴱ**Gronewald** M. ... *Sijpesteijn* P. J., *al.*, Kölner Papyri 6: PapCol 7. Opladen 1987. x-289 p. 3-531-09923-X. – ᴿAegyptus 68 (1988) 269-271 (Lucia *Criscuolo*).

a607 **Guerra** Manuel, Diccionario morfológico del Nuevo Testamento² [¹1978]: FacTNEspaña 40. Burgos 1988, Aldecoa. 479 p. 84-7009-048-8.

a608 *Hägg* Thomas, 'Blemmyan Greek' and the letter of Phonen: → 750, Nubian V, 1982/6, 281-6.

a609 **Harrauer** H., *Sijpesteijn* P. J., Neue Texte aus dem antiken Unterricht: Mitteilungen Papyrussammlung Erzherzog Rainer 15. W 1985, Österr. Nat.-Bibliothek. 195 p. + vol. of 87 pl. 3-85119-217-6. – ᴿAegyptus 68 (1988) 261-3 (Carla *Salvaterra*); BO 45 (1988) 587-590 (A. *Wouters*).

a610 **Hasitzka** Monika, *al.*, Griechische Texte VII: Corpus Papyrorum Raineri 10. W 1986, Holinek. 182 p.; vol. of 60 pl. 3-85119-219-2. – ᴿBO 45 (1988) 584-7 (J. *Gascou*).

a611 *Hewett* James A., New Testament Greek; a beginning and intermediate grammar. Peabody MA 1986, Hendrickson. xv-234 p. $15. – ᴿRelStR 14 (1988) 157 (B. D. *Ehrman*).

a611* **Horsley** G. H. R., New documents illustrating early Christianity, vol. 4 for 1979: 1987 → 3,9818*: ᴿBiblica 69 (1988) 298s (J. *O'Callaghan*); NT 30 (1988) 89s (P. *Elbert*, 3); RB 95 (1988) 468s (J. *Taylor*).

a612 *Kasser* Rodolphe, Status quaestionis 1988 sulla presunta origine dei cosiddetti Papiri Bodmer [... testimonianze non più per ed-Debba 5k NE di Nag'-Ḥammadi, ma 22 km; o vicino a Assiut]: Aegyptus 68 (1988) 191-4.

a613 *Kortlandt* Frederik, The Greek 3d pl. endings: MüStSprW 49 (1988) 63-70.

a614 **Kramer** Bärbel, *al.*, Das Archiv des Nepheros und verwandte Texte I-II: Aeg. Treverensia 4. Mainz 1987, von Zabern. xii-162 p.; 31 pl. – ᴿCdÉ 63 (1988) 186-190 (M. *Blume*).

a615 **Kramer** Bärbel, *Hagedorn* Dieter, Griechische Papyri... Hamburg 1984 ➤ 3,9819: ᴿCdÉ 63 (1988) 177-182 (J. *Lenaerts*); Gnomon 60 (1988) 289-292 (H. *Maehler*).

a616 **Kramer** Johannes, Glossaria bilinguia 1983 ➤ 3,9821: ᴿAnzAltW 41 (1988) 176s (J. M. *Diethart*).

a616* *Kramer* Johannes, Xenophobie als Motiv für die Einführung der antikisierenden Aussprache des Griechischen im 16. Jahrhundert: AntAb 34 (1988) 79-88.

a617 *Lillo* Antonio, A propos de un nuevo libro sobre el arcadio [*Dubois* L. 1986]: Minos 23 (1988) 195-206.

a617* ᴱ**Louw** Johannes P., *Nida* Eugene A., Greek-English lexicon of the New Testament based on semantic domains, I. Introduction and domains; II. Indices. NY 1988, United Bible Societies. xxv-843 p.; iv-375 p. $20. – ᴿBibTB 18 (1988) 150s (J. M. *Reese*: an invaluable tool); FgNT 1 (1988) 217s (D. A. *Black*).

a618 **Marshall** M. H. B., Verbs, nouns, and postpositives in Attic prose: Scottish Classical Studies 3. E 1987, Scottish Academic. vi-178 p. – ᴿRPLH 62,1 (1988) 145s (P. *Monteil*).

a618* *Masson* Michel, À propos des critères permettant d'établir l'origine sémitique de certains mots grecs: GLECS 28,2 (1984) 199-231.

a619 a) *Masson* Olivier, Les anthroponymes grecs à Délos; – b) *Spoerri* Walter, Épigraphie et littérature; à propos de la liste des Pythioniques à Delphes: ➤ 698, Comptes 1986/8, 71-80 / 111-140.

a620 **Meiggs** Russell, *Lewis* David, A selection of Greek historical inscriptions to the end of the fifth century B.C.²ʳᵉᵛ (¹1969). Ox 1988, Clarendon. xx-317 p. 0-19-814266-8.

a621 **Meimaris** Yiannis E., Sacred names, saints, martyrs and church officials in the Greek inscriptions and papyri pertaining to the Christian Church of Palestine: Meletemata 2, 1986 ➤ 2,7731: ᴿGnomon 60 (1988) 664s (W. *Wischmeyer*); RB 95 (1988) 475 (J.-M. de *Tarragon*); RÉByz 46 (1988) 260-2 (B. *Flusin*).

a622 *Merkelbach* R., Ein Wort über griechische Epigraphik [... die Ausgräber sollten die neugefundenen Texte jüngeren Gelehrten zur Edition übergeben... schnell]: ZPapEp 71 (1988) 291-6.

a623 *Merkelbach* Reinhold, *Şahin* Sencer, Die publizierten Inschriften von Perge: EpAnat 11 (1988) 97-169 (map; the frontispiece is a color-photo of Plancia Magna of Perge); ❶ 170; corrigenda 12 (1988) 78.

a624 **Negev** A., The Greek inscriptions from the Negev: SBF min 25, 1981 ➤ 62,9051... 1,9334: ᴿMuséon 101 (1988) 223-6 (Pauline *Donceel-Voûte*).

a625 *O'Callaghan* José, Interpreting the Scriptures (Dei Verbum 12); affinities between the popular koine and the neotestamentary, ᵀ*Raymond* L.-B.: ➤ 380, Vatican II Assessment 1 (1988) 208-219; – français ➤ 379, Bilan 1, 223-234.

a626 **Orrieux** C., Les papyrus de Zénon; l'horizon d'un grec en Égypte ... 1983 ➤ 64,8351 ... 1,9336: ᴿBL (1988) 33 (T. *Rajak*: 'too Gallic and sketchy' on the 1200 documents of which 40 concern Zenon's year in Palestine).

a627 **Orrieux** Claude [< ᴰ1980 ➤ 1,f112], Zénon de Caunos, parépidémos, et le destin grec: Ann. Litt. Besançon 320. P 1985. 326 p. – ᴿAegyptus 68 (1988) 264-9 (Lucia *Criscuolo*); Gnomon 60 (1988) 457-9 (S. *Daris*, ital.).

a628 **Palmer** Leonard R., Die griechische Sprache, ᵀMeid W. 1986 ➤ 3,9839: ᴿAnzAltW 41 (1988) 1-3 (F. *Lochner von Hüttenbach*); BeiNam 23 (1988) 222-4 (Doris *Schawaller*).

a629 *Panayiotou* George, Addenda to the LSJ Greek-English lexicon; lexicographical notes on the vocabulary of the Oracula Sibyllina: Ellinika 38 (1987) 296-317.

a630 ᶠPapyrus Rainer 1983 ➤ 64,90: ᴿJEA 74 (1988) 293-6 (W. E. H. *Cockle*).

a631 *Piejko* Francis, The inscriptions of Icarus-Failaka: ClasMed 39 (1988) 89-116.

a632 **Pintaudi** Rosario, *al.*, Papyri graecae Wessely pragenses (PPrag I): PapFlorentina 16. F 1988, Gonnelli. 252 p.; XCIII pl. Lit. 250.000. – ᴿCdÉ 63 (1988) 379-389 (J. *Bingen*).

a633 ᴱ**Pleket** H. W., **Stroud** R. S., Supplementum epigraphicum graecum 31ss, 1984ss ➤ ... 3,9843: ᴿAntClas 57 (1988) 474s (A. *Martin*, 32s); Gnomon 60 (1988) 222-235 (D. *Knoepfler*).

a634 *Pouilloux* Jean, L'épigraphie grecque: CRAI (1988) 618-622 [623-8, latine, M. *Le Glay*; 629-634, chrétienne, C. *Piétri*].

a635 **Powell** Barry B., The dipylon oinochoe [oldest Greek alphabetic inscription] and the spread of literacy in eighth-century Athens: Kadmos 27 (1988) 65-86; 9 fig.; pl. I.

a636 *Rix* Helmut, The Proto-Indo-European middle; content, forms and origin: MüStSprW 49 (1988) 101-120.

a637 *Rosén* Haiim B., Der griechische 'dativus absolutus' und indogermanische 'unpersönliche' Partizipialkonstruktionen: HSprF 101 (1988) 92-103.

a638 **Scheelhaas** L. B., Wie 't kleine niet eert ... Het gebruik van het lidwoord bij persoonsnamen in het Nieuwe Testament: Kamper Cah. 60. Kampen 1987, Kok. 50 p. ƒ14. 90-242-4679-2 [KerkT 39,355].

a639 **Shelton** John C., Greek ostraca in the Ashmolean Museum from Oxyrhynchus and other sites: Papyrologica Florentina 17. F 1987, Gonnelli. 167 p.; LII pl.

a640 **Spicq** Ceslas, Note di lessicografia neotestamentaria I [1978 ➤ 60,368], ᵀBezza Giuseppe, *Viero* Franco L.: GLNT Sup 4. Brescia 1988, Paideia. 945 p. 88-394-0408-2.

a641 *Thorley* John, Subjunctive Aktionsart in New Testament Greek; a reassessment: NT 30 (1988) 193-211.

a642 **Turner** E. G., ²*Parsons* P. J., Greek manuscripts of the ancient world: Bulletin Sup 46. L 1987, Inst. Classical Studies. – ᴿAegyptus 68 (1988) 254s (S. *Daris*).

a643 *Urbán* Ángel, La coordinada modal en el Nuevo Testamento: FgNT 1 (1988) 193-207; Eng. 207s.

a644 **Varinlioğlu** Ender, Die Inschriften von Keramos [E Bodrum]: Österr./Rh.W.Akad., Inschriften griechischer Städte aus Kleinasien 30. Bonn 1986, Habelt. xv-109 p.; 14 pl., map. – ᴿGnomon 60 (1988) 603-9 (J. *Crampa*, Eng.).

a645 **Wehrli** C., Les papyrus de Genève 2, Nᵒˢ 82-117, 1986 → 3,9860: ᴿCdÉ 63 (1988) 182-6 (J. *Lenaerts*).

a646 **Windekens** A.J. Van, Dictionnaire étymologique 1986 → 3,9861: ᴿÉt-Clas 56 (1988) 116s (L. *Isebaert*).

a647 **Wouters** A., The Chester Beatty Codex Ac 1499; a Graeco-Latin lexicon on the Pauline epistles and a Greek grammar: C. Beatty Mon 12. Lv 1988, Peeters. xvi-193 p.; 25 facsimiles. Fb 2400 [RHE 83,350*].

———

a648 **Mackridge** P., The modern Greek language; a descriptive analysis of Standard Modern Greek. Ox 1985, Univ. xxiii-387. £30. – ᴿJHS 108 (1988) 275s (D. *Holton*).

J5.2 **Voces graecae** (ordine alphabetico graeco).

a649 *ágalma:* **Koonce** Kirsten, *ágalma* and *eikōn*: AmJPg 109 (1988) 108-110.

a650 *agapē, daímōn:* **Kahane** Henry & Renée, Religious key terms in Hellenism and Byzantium; three facets: ILCLSt 12 (1987) 243-263.

a651 *hágios:* **Beekes** R.S.P., P(roto-)I(ndo-)European *rhc-* in Greek [*lanthánō, lambánō, makrós, hágios*] and other languages: IndogF 93 (1988) 22-43.

a652 *Quacquarelli* Antonio, *Hagiophóros* in IGNAZIO di Antiochia [< ᶠ*Paratore* E. 1981, 819-825]: VetChr 25 (1988) 1-10.

a652* *adelphós:* **Camus** Jean, Sémantique du mot 'frère' dans le NT: Savanes-Forêts (Côte d'Ivoire 1987,3) 117-124 [< TKontext 9/2, 24].

a653 *aig-:* **Fowler** R.L., *aig-* in early Greek language and myth: Phoenix 42 (Toronto 1988) 95-113.

a654 *aiōn:* → 804, NBL Lfg 1 (1988) 52-54 (K. *Woschitz*).

a655 *anagénesis:* **Okeke** George E., *Anagenesis* (rebirth) in the New Testament: AfTJ 17 (1988) 89-99 [NTAbs 32,343].

a656 *anagignōskō:* **Nieddu** Gian Franco, Sulla nozione di 'leggere' in greco; decifrare [*ananémō, epilégomai, anagignōskō*]... percorrere [*diérchomai*]: GitFg 40 (1988) 17-37.

a656* *Rosén* Haiim B., *Ánthrōpos:* ZvgSprW 99 (1986) 243s.

a657 *apeithéō:* **Thibaut** André, L'infidélité du peuple élu; apeithô entre la Bible hébraïque et la Bible latine: Collectanea Biblica Latina 17. R 1988, San Girolamo. 336 p.

a658 *arrabōn:* **Kerr** A.J., Arrabōn [2 Cor 1,22; 5,5; Eph 1,14]: JTS 39 (1988) 92-97: 'a first instalment'.

a658* **Sikora** Ryszard, *'Archē'* w Nowym Testamencie; diss. ᴰ*Langkammer* H. Lublin 1988. xli-459 p. – RTLv 20,149.

a659 *átē:* **Doyle** Richard E., *Átē*, its use and meaning; a study in the Greek poetic tradition from Homer to Euripides 1984 → 1,9367: ᴿGnomon 60 (1988) 385-9 (J. *Gruber*).

a660 *auxō:* **Jacquinod** B., Étude de vocabulaire grec: *aúxō* et *áotos* [√ commun 'gonflement']: RÉAnc 90 (1988) 315-323.

a661 *baptízō:* **Augrain** Charles, Baptiser ou immerger? [Mc 7,4 'lavage'; *Chouraqui* 'Jean l'Immergeur']: → 486, Traduction 1986/8, 81-85; Eng. 81.

a662 *gnôsis:* **Bouyer** Louis, Gnosis; la connaissance de Dieu dans l'Écriture: Théologies. P 1988, Cerf. 189 p. 2-204-02903-3.

a662* *Roquet* Gérard, CHENOUTE critique d'une étymologie du Cratyle [*Platon* 398b], *daimónion:* ZägSpr 115 (1988) 153-6.

a663 *daímōn: Schenkeveld* D. M., Ancient views on the meaning of *daímōn* in 'Iliad' Θ 166: Hermes 116 (1988) 110-5. ➤ a650.

a663* *Macina* R., Pour éclairer le terme *dígamoi*: RevSR 61 (1987) 54-73.

a664 *didáskalos:* **Zimmermann** A. F., Die urchristlichen Lehrer, Studien zum Tradentenkreis der *didáskaloi* im frühen Urchristentum² [I, 1984 ➤ 65,8232]: WUNT 2/12. Tü 1988, Mohr. viii-258 p. DM 58. 3-16-145196-1 [NTAbs 32,388: 2-page preface on scholarly reactions to first edition].

a665 *diēnekēs: Meier-Brügger* Michael, Griech. *diēnekēs, diānekēs*: Sprache 33 (1987) 102-7.

a666 *Hebraistí* [= ? 'Aramaic']: BTrans [37 (1986)] 39 (1988) 130s (P. *Ellingworth*).

a667 *eirēnē: Lockwood* G., *Eirēnē* reaffirmed [... continuity and discontinuity with *šalôm*]: LuthTJ 21 (1987) 123-132 [< NTAbs 32,342].

a668 *ekklēsía: Hilhorst* A., Termes chrétiens issus du vocabulaire de la démocratie athénienne: FgNt 1,1 (1988) 27-32; Eng. 32-4 [*ekklēsía; leitourgía, chorēgía; theoría; parrhēsía*].

a669 *elegeîon: Lambin* Gérard, *élegos* et *elegeîon*: RPLH 62,1 (1988) 69-77.

a670 *en: Neuberger-Donath* Ruth, Zum Gebrauch von *en* und *eis* bei HOMER: GrazBei 15 (1988) 1-13.

a671 *embrúmion/embrímion*; à propos d'un objet mobilier égyptien [tabouret, non pas coussin]: CdÉ 63 (1988) 331-340; 2 fig. (G. *Husson*): 341-3 (M. *Pezin*, une étymologie égyptienne).

a672 *epithymía: Cerutti* Maria Vittoria, *Epithymía* e *phthorá* in testi tar-do-giudaici e gnostici (Apocalisse di Mosé e Apocalisse di Adamo): RivB 36 (1988) 199-226; Eng. 226s.

a673 *epō: Vine* Brent, Greek *épō* and Indo-European *sep*: IndogF 93 (1988) 52-61.

a674 *éschatos: Meier-Brügger* M., Zu griechisch *énkata* and *éschatos*: HistSprF 101 (1988) 289-295.

a674* *eulogía: Mateos* J., Análisis de un campo lexemático; *eulogía* en el Nuevo Testamento: FgNt 1,1 (1988) 5-24; Eng. 24s.

a675 *euchē:* **Dyrkiel** Zbigniew, Terminologia modlitwy [prayer] w Septua-gincie: diss. ᴰRubinkiewicz R. Lublin 1988. xxv-304 p. – RTLv 20,539.

a675* *hēlios: Huld* Martin E., Proto- and post-Indo-European designations for 'sun': ZvgSprW 99 (1986) 194-202.

a676 *itamos:* **Hunger** H., Graeculus perfidus, *italos ítamos*; il senso del-l'alterità nei rapporti greco-romani ed italo-bizantini, intr. *Kresten* G.: Conferenze 4. R 1987, Unioni Istituti Arte. 52 p. – ᴿAevum 62 (1988) 416 (C. M. *Mazzucchi*).

a676* *kairós: Guillamaud* Patrice, L'essence du kairos [mesure, médiation]: RÉAnt 90 (1988) 359-371; Eng. 359.

a677 *koinōnía: Ilski* Kazimierz, [*koinōnikón*] Communio während des ephesinischen Konzils: Eos 76 (1988) 345-352; deutsch 352.

a678 *makários: Pelsmaekers* J., Een korte bemerking bij de vertaling van de term *makários*: Bulletin Inst. Hist. Belge de Rome 58 (1988) 5-9.

a679 *metánoia:* **Gaventa** Beverly R., From darkness to light; aspects of conversion in the NT 1986 ➤ 2,7786; 3,9904: ᴿJBL 107 (1988) 322-4 (R. *Scroggs*).

a679* *nauteia* (in the papyri): ➤ 492, XVIII. Papyrol 2 (1986/8) 255-260 (D. *Gofas*).

a680 *Og-: Fauth* Wolfgang, Prähellenische Flutnamen Og(es)-Ogen(os)-Ogygos: BeiNam 23 (1988) 361-379.

a681 *oikía:* **Husson** Geneviève, Oikiá 1983 ➤ 64,8408...3,9909: ᴿJEA 74 (1988) 292s (J. D. *Thomas*).

a682 *oikodomē:* **Kitzberger** Ingrid R., Bau der Gemeinde; das paulinische Wortfeld *oikodomē/(ep)oikodomeín* [Diss. Salzburg]: ForBi 53. Wü 1987, Echter, x-357 p. [FgNt 2/1, 102-5, A. *Piñero*]. – ᴿCBQ 50 (1988) 535s (J. *Swetnam*: anti-coffee-table).

a682* *pneûma:* **Ruppe** David R., God, spirit, and human being; the reconfiguration of *pneuma*'s semantic field in the exchange between IRENAEUS of Lyons and the Valentinian gnosis: diss. Columbia. NY 1988. 206 p. 88-27639. – DissA 49 (1988s) 3058-A; RelStR 15,193.

a683 *sárkinos:* **Parsons** Mikeal C., *Sárkinos, sarkikós* in Codices F and G [Rom 7,14; 1 Cor 3,1; Heb 7,16; only 2 Cor 3,3 *sárkinos* without variant]: NTS 34 (1988) 151-5.

a684 *sidēraîos:* **Jördens** Andrea, *Sidēraîos = athánatos*?: ZPapEp 71 (1988) 99-104.

a685 *skándalon*, Ärgernis: ➤ 804, NBL Lfg 1 (1988) 54-57 (H. *Leroy*).

a685* *téknon, paîs* and related words in *koinē*: ➤ 492, XVIII Papyrol 1 (1986/8) 463-480 (G. *Stanton*).

a686 *hypakoúō:* **Chmiel** Jerzy, ❷ Ethos biblicum oboedientiae: RuBi 41 (1988) 353-360.

a687 *phaneróō:* **Bockmuehl** Markus N. A., Das verb phaneróō im Neuen Testament; Versuch einer Neuauswertung: BZ 32 (1988) 87-99.

a688 *-phernēs:* **Lecoq** Pierre, Le mot *farnah* et les Scythes: CRAI (1987) 671-682.

a689 *chaírō:* **O'Callaghan** José, Sobre BGU III 948,2-4 (IV-Vᴾ) [*chairin* for *chairein*, not *charin*]: Aegyptus 68 (1988) 99-101.

a690 *choîros:* **Golden** Mark, Male chauvinists and pigs [*choîros* means also vagina]: EchMClas 32 (1988) 1-12.

a691 *psychē:* **Sullivan** Shirley D., A multi-faceted term; *Psyche* in Homer, the Homeric Hymns, and Hesiod: StItFgCʟ 81 (3/6: 1988) 151-180.

J5.5   **Cypro-Minoa** [➤ T9.1-4].

a692 *Bartonek* Antonin, *a*) The substantives of the 1st declension in Mycenaean Greek: SborBrno 33 (1988) 21-32; Eng. 32: 130 words + possibly 120; half proper names. – *b*) Prospects and limitations of the dialectological study of ancient Greek: SborBrno 31 (1986) 139-157; Eng. 107. – *c*) The system of the Mycenaean cases: 32 (1987) 121-5; Eng. 126.

a693 **Baumbach** Lydia, Studies in Mycenaean inscriptions and dialect 1965-1978; a complete bibliography and index: Incunabula graeca 86. R 1986, Ateneo. 516 p.

a694 ᴱ**Best** Jan, *Woudhuizen* Fred, Ancient scripts from Crete and Cyprus: Frankfort Foundation 9. Leiden 1988, Brill. vii-131 p.; ill.; maps. 90-04-08431-2.

a695 **Chadwick** John, *al.*, Corpus of Mycenaean inscriptions from Knossos I: Incunabula graeca 88, 1986 ➤ 2,7813: ᴿAntClas 57 (1988) 473s (Y. *Duhoux*); Antiquity 62 (1988) 174 (Anna *Morpurgo Davies*); Kratylos 33 (1988) 99-102 (E. *Risch* †).

a696 **Chadwick** John, Linear B and related scripts 1987 ➤ 3,9943; £5: ᴿAntiquity 62 (1988) 404s (J. D. *Ray*: also on four similar-format booklets dated 1987).

a697 *Faucounau* J., Deux études sur des inscriptions chyprominoennes [Hala Sultan Tekke; Kalavassos]: → 42*, EHRMAN A. mem., Fucus 1988, 239-251.

a698 *Forssman* Bernhard, Mykenisch e-wi-ri-po und *eúripos* [Sund]: Mü-StSprW 49 (1988) 5-12.

a699 *Hooker* James, The great tablet of Knossos, KN As 1516 [list of men for/in service; not glamorous 'bodyguard']: Kadmos 27 (1988) 115-125; facsim.

a700 *a) Hooker* J.T., The varieties of Minoan writing; – *b) Duhoux* Yves, Les éléments grecs non doriens du crétois et la situation dialectale grecque au IIᵉ millénaire: Cretan 1 (1988) 169-189 / 57-72.

a701 *La Rosa* Vincenzo, *Pugliese Carratelli* Giovanni, Nuova rondella con iscrizione in lineare A dalla 'Villa Reale' di Haghia Triada: ParPass 237 (1987) 463-8.

a702 **Masson** Olivier, *Mitford* Terence B., Les inscriptions syllabiques de Kouklia-Paphos 1986 → 3,9950: ᴿClasR 102 (1988) 185 (J.T. *Hooker*); GGA 240 (1988) 58-61 (C. *Brixhe*); Gnomon 60 (1988) 65s (G. *Neumann*).

a703 *Masson* Emilia, Les écritures chyprominoennes; reflet fidèle du brassage des civilisations sur l'île pendant le Bronze Récent: → 748, Cyprus between, 1985/6, 180-200.

a704 ᴱ**Pini** Ingo (*Betts* John H., al.), Kleinere europäische Sammlungen: Corpus der minoischen und mykenischen Siegel 11. B 1988, Mann. xl-367 p. 3-7861-1522-2.

a705 *a) Popham* Mervyn, The historical implications of the Linear B archive at Knossos dating to either c. 1400 B.C. or 1200 B.C.; – *b) Hallager* Erik, Khania and Crete ca. 1375-1200 B.C.: Cretan 1 (1988) 217-227 / 115-124.

a706 *Risch* Ernst, Die mykenische Nominalflexion als Problem der indogermanischen und griechischen Sprachwissenschaft: → 104, ᶠMAYR-HOFER M. = Sprache 32 (1986) 63-77.

a707 **Trümpy** Catherine, Vergleich des Mykenischen mit der Sprache der Chorlyrik 1986 → 3,9954: ᴿSalesianum 50 (1988) 285s (R. *Gottlieb*).

J6 Indo-Iranica.

a708 **Alram** Michael, Nomina propria iranica in nummis; Materialgrundlagen zu den iranischen Personennamen auf antiken Münzen: IranPersNamBuch 4. W 1986, Österr. Akad. 347 p.; xxiii charts; vol. of 47 pl. DM 300. – ᴿJRAS (1988) 414s (A. D. H. *Bivar*).

a709 **Camps** Arnulf, *Muller* Jean-Claude, The Sanskrit Grammar and manuscripts of Father Heinrich ROTH S.J. (1620-1668), facsimile edition of Biblioteca Nazionale, Rome, MSS. OR. 171 and 172. Leiden 1988, Brill. 25 p. 90-04-08608-0.

a709* *Grillot* Françoise, Mécanismes de l'ancienne structure nominale en Élamite: StIran 16 (1987) 163-172 [173-6, *Herrenschmidt* Clarisse, note de vieux perse].

a710 *Huyse* Philip, Zum iranischen Namengut in Dura-Europos: Anzeiger Wien 125 (1988) 19-32.

a711 *Kasumova* S.Y., ☮ Nouvelles trouvailles d'inscriptions en iranien moyen à Derbent: VDI 184 (1988) 88-95; franç. 95.

a711* **Kellens** Jean, Le verbe avestique. Wsb 1984, Reichert. xxii-444 p. – ᴿZvgSprW 99 (1986) 310s (M. *Back*).

a712 **Macdonell** Arthur A., A Sanskrit grammar for students³. Ox 1986, Clarendon. – ᴿSalesianum 50 (1988) 274 (R. *Bracchi*: 'Macdonell'; ¹1901).

a712* ᴱ**Mayrhofer** Manfred, *al.*, Indogermanische Grammatik I, 1-2, 1986
➤ 3,9964: ᴿHistSprF 101 (1988) 302-312 (K. *Strunk*).

a713 **Pisowicz** Andrzej, Origins of the New and Middle Persian phonological
systems: Hab.-Diss. 101, Univ. Jagielloński. Kraków 1985. 190 p. zl 185.
– ᴿArOr 56 (1988) 86-89 (J. *Krámský*).

a714 *Schmitt* Rüdiger, Über fehlende Normierung im Achämenidisch-ela-
mischen: ArchMIran 19 (1986) 121-132.

a715 **Shahbazi** A. S., Old Persian inscriptions of the Persepolis platform 1985
➤ 3,9969: ᴿOLZ 83 (1988) 77-79 (W. *Sundermann*).

a716 ᴱ**Skalmowski** Wojciech, *Tongerloo* Alois van, Middle Iranian Studies
1982/4 ➤ 65,668 ... 3,9971: ᴿBO 45 (1988) 155-162 (S. *Shaked*).

a717 **Tikkanen** Bertil, The Sanskrit gerund; a synchronic, diachronic and
typological analysis: StOrFinn 62. Helsinki 1987, Finnish Oriental Soc.
vi-378 p. (inserted corrigenda). Fm 200. – ᴿJRAS (1988) 439s (Gillian R.
Hart).

a718 **Werner** Karel, The Indo-Europeans and the Indo-Aryans; the philological, archaeological and historical context: ➤ 14, ᶠBHANDARKAR R.
1987, 491-523.

a719 ᴱ**Yarshater** Ehsan, Persian literature: Columbia Lectures on Iranian
Studies 3. NY 1988, Persian Heritage Foundation. xi-562 p. 0-88706-
263-6.

J6.5 **Latina**

a720 **Béguelin-Reichler** Marie-José, Les noms latins du type *mēns*; étude
morphologique: Coll. Latomus 195, 1986. 271 p. – ᴿSalesianum 50 (1988)
279s (R. *Bracchi*: diss. prix Genève 1984).

a721 *Fleury* Philippe, Du texte latin à la concordance imprimée: CompHum
20 (1986) 239-246.

a722 **Hälvä-Nyberg** Ulla, Die Kontraktionen auf den lateinischen Inschriften
Roms und Afrikas, bis zum 8. Jahrh. nach Chr. Helsinki 1988, Acad.
Finnica. 270 p. – ᴿCC 139 (1988,3) 331s (A. *Ferrua*).

a723 **Hoffmann** Maria E., Negatio contrarii; a study of Latin litotes: Studies
in Greek and Latin linguistics. Assen 1987, Van Gorcum. xiv-290 p. –
ᴿGnomon 60 (1988) 362-4 (Iiro *Kajanto*: valuable for general linguistics
and rhetoric).

a724 *Keyser* Paul, The origin of the Latin numerals 1 to 1000: AJA 92
(1988) 529-546; 11 fig.

a725 **Odelman** Eva, Glossarium mediae latinitatis Sueciae [I. 1982] II. 1,
iustitia-metuendus; 2. micchi-officialitas: Acad. Sto. U 1982/7, Almqvist
& W. 73 p.; p. 75-142. – ᴿGnomon 60 (1988) 539s (P. *Dinter*).

a726 *Stickler* Alfonso, A 25 anni dalla Costituzione Apostolica 'Veterum
sapientia' [De Latinitatis studio provehendo] di Giovanni XXIII;
rievocazione storica e prospettive: Salesianum 50 (1988) 367-377.

a726* **Väänänen** Veikko, Introduzione al latino volgare³: Testi e manuali per
il latino 8. Bo 1988, Pàtron. 419 p.

a727 **Vercillo** Lunetto, I. Nuovo corso, l'etrusco sillabico; II. La stele di Roma
e la stele di Lemno. Rende, Cosenza 1986, auct. 204 p. Lit. 45.000. –
ᴿGnomon 60 (1988) 650s (G. *Radke*).

J8.1 **Philologia generalis.**

a728 *Alpers* K., Klassische Philologie in Byzanz: ClasPg 83 (1988) 342-
360.

Barr James, Sémantique du langage biblique [1961, ᵀ*Auscher* D., *Prignaud* J. 1971 + nouvelle préface] 1988 ➤ 1177.

a730 **Barz** Irmhild, Nomination durch Wortbildung: Linguistische Studien. Lp 1988, VEB-Enz. 233 p. 3-424-00371-7.

a731 **Boeckh** August, La filologia come scienza storica; enciclopedia e metodologia delle scienze filologiche [1877], ᵀ*Masullo* Rita; ᴱ*Garzya* Antonio: Micromegas 14. N 1987, Guida. 308 p. Lit. 26.000. – ᴿRasT 29 (1988) 95s (R. *Maisano*).

a732 **Brucker** Charles, L'étymologie: Que sais-je? P 1988, PUF. 125 p. 2-13-041972-0.

a733 **Buffa** Giovanni [esperto di spettroscopia molecolare], Fra numeri e dita; dal conteggio sulle dita alla nascita del numero. Bo 1986, Zanichelli. vii-174 p. – ᴿSalesianum 50 (1988) 215s (R. *Della Casa*).

a233* **Carrez** Maurice, *a)* Las lenguas de la Biblia 1984 ➤ 1,9455: ᴿVerVid 46 (1988) 496 (V. *Casas*). – *b)* Le lingue della Bibbia; dai papiri alle Bibbie a stampa [1983 ➤ 64,8495]. T 1987, Paoline. 122 p. – ᴿParVi 33 (1988) 397-9 (G. *Marocco*).

a734 *a) Ehret* Christopher, Language change and the material correlates of language and ethnic shift; – *b) Zvelebil* Marek & Kamil V., Agricultural transition and Indo-European dispersals; – *c) Sherratt* Andrew & Susan, The archaeology of Indo-European, an alternative view: Antiquity 62 (1988) 564-574 / 574-583 / 584-595.

a735 *García-Hernández* Benjamin, Lexematik und Grammatik, die Verbalklassen: IndogF 93 (1988) 1-21.

a736 ᴱ**Hartmann** R. R. K., The history of lexicography; papers from the Dictionary Research Centre seminar at Exeter, March 1986: Amst Ling 3/40. Amst 1986, Benjamins. viii-265 p. [Salesianum 50, 625].

a737 **Haugen** Einar, Blessings of Babel; bilingualism and language planning, problems and pleasures: Contributions to the sociology of language 46. Amst 1987, Mouton de Gruyter. xii-176 p. – ᴿBSLP 83,2 (1988) 52 (X. *Mignot*).

a737* **Holm** John A., Pidgins and Creoles: Language Surveys. C 1988s, Univ. I. 258 p. II. p. 259-704. 0-521-24980-5, pa. 7108-8; II. 0-521-35089-1; 940-6.

a738 *Horst* Pieter W. van der, *Mussies* Gerard, Subtractive versus additive composite numerals in antiquity [Latin, Greek]: ILCL 13,1 (1988) 183-202.

a739 *Müller* Hans-Peter, Das Bedeutungspotential der Afformativkonjugation; zum sprachgeschichtlichen Hintergrund des Althebräischen: ZAHeb 1,1 (1988) 74-98.

a740 ᶠOBERHUBER Karl, Im Bannkreis... Sprachgeschichte des AO, ᴱ**Meid** W. 1986 ➤ 2,81*. – ᴿBO 44 (1987) 394 (V. *Haas*).

a741 **Renfrew** Colin, Archaeology and language; the puzzle of Indo-European origins. L/NY 1987, Cape/Cambridge-UP. xiv-346 p.; 45 fig.; 14 pl. £16. 0-224-02495-7 / 0-521-35432-3. – ᴿAntiquity 62 (1988) 607-9 (J. *Mallory*).

a742 *Richter* H., Transliteration und Transkription 1983 ➤ 64,8516: ᴿWeltOr 19 (1988) 217-9 (H.-D. *Neef*).

a743 ᶠRISCH E.: ooperosi, ᴱ**Ester** A., 1986 ➤ 2,95: ᴿBSLP 83,2 (1988) 110-121 (C. de *Lamberterie*).

a744 *Rosén* Haiim, On the plausibility of ancient etymologies: HSprF 101 (1988) 116-126.

a745 **Seiler** Hansjakob, Possession as an operational dimension of language: Language Universals 2. Tü 1983, Narr. 91 p. DM 28. – ᴿIndogF 93 (1988) 260-7 (Anna *Orlandini*, Eng.).

a746 **Tomlin** Russell S., Basic word order; functional principles. L 1986, Croom Helm. 308 p.

J8.2 Grammatica comparata.

a746* **Anderson** Deborah W., Time in Indo-European; 'before' and 'after', 'past' and 'future'; a linguistic study of the spatio-temporal uses of PIE, *pro, *apo, *epi and opi: diss. UCLA 1988, ᴰPuhvel J. 156 p. 88-22145. – DissA 49 (1988s) 1785-A.

a747 a) *Argoujard* J. F., Gémination et redoublement; – b) *Elmedlaoui* Mohammed, De la gémination: LOrA 1 (Lv 1988) 1-15 / 117-156.

a748 *Bader* Françoise, Génitifs-adjectifs et dérivés d'appartenance d'origine pronominale: HistSprF 101 (1988) 171-210.

a749 *Beekes* Robert S. P., The P(roto) I(ndo) E(uropean) words for 'name' and 'me': Sprache 33 (1987) 1-12.

a750 *Bomhard* A. R., Toward Proto-Nostratic 1981 ²1984 → 1,9467; 3,9994: ᴿArOr 56 (1988) 65-69 (K. *Petráček*).

a751 *Delamare* X., Le vocabulaire indo-européen; lexique étymologique thématique. P 1984, Libr. d'Amérique et d'Orient. 331 p. – ᴿRÉAnc 90 (1988) 444 (J.-L. *Perpillou*).

a752 *Depuydt* L., Die 'Verben des Sehens'; semantische Grundzüge am Beispiel des Ägyptischen: Orientalia 57 (1988) 1-13.

a753 **Doerfer** Gerhard, Grundwort und Sprachmischung; eine Untersuchung an Hand von Körperteilbezeichnungen: MüOstasiastische Studien 47. Stu 1988, Steiner. viii-313 p. [Mundus 24,224 'Basic word and linguistic mixtures']. DM 45. – ᴿStOrFin 64 (1988) 410-5 (B. *Tikkanen*).

a754 *Dunast* Grégoire, New light on etymologies of Indo-European numerals: ArOr 56 (1988) 352-6.

a755 a) *Faber* Alice, Indefinite pronouns in early Semitic; – b) *Bomhard* Allan R., The reconstruction of the proto-Semitic consonant system; – c) *Vycichl* Werner, Arabisch nâq-a.t 'Kamelstute'; ein altes passives Partizip (ein Beitrag zur vergleichenden Hamitosemitistik): → 42*, EHRMAN A. mem., Fucus 1988, 221-238 / 113-134; Bibliog. 134-140 / 483-9.

a756 **Hohenberger** Johannes, Semitische und hamitische Wortstämme im Nilo-Hamitischen: Marburger Afrika 42. B 1988, Reimer. 310 p. [Mundus 24,225].

a757 **Khan** G., Studies in Semitic syntax: London Oriental Series 38. Oxford 1988, UP. 0-19-713607-9 [BL 89,155].

a757* **Knobloch** Johann, Sprache und Religion 3. Weihnachten und Ostern 1986 → 2,7840; ᴿSalesianum 50 (1988) 271 (R. *Bracchi*).

a758 **Loprieno** A., Das Verbalsystem im Ägyptischen und im Semitischen 1986 → 2,7842: ᴿBL (1988) 148s (J. *Barr*: powerfully thought out).

a759 **Mouton** Charles, Aspects grecs — aspects russes à la lumière des traductions modernes de textes anciens: Univ. Liège ph/lett 244. P 1986, BLettres. 193 + 14 p. – ᴿClasR 102 (1988) 299s (C. M. *Macrobert*); RBgPg 66 (1988) 106s (Isabelle *Forrest*); RÉLat 66 (1988) 245-252 (P. *Monteil*).

a760 **Olsen** Birgit A., The proto-Indo-European instrument noun suffix *-tlom and its variants: K. Danske Selskab Meddelelser h/fil [0106-0481] 55. K 1988, Munskgaard. 47 p. 87-7304-182-3.

a760* *Pezzi* Elena, Aportaciones para un estudio de lingüística ario-semitica; una hipótesis sobre el orígen del lenguaje: BAsEspOr 23 (1987) 289-303.

a761 *Sanmartín* J., Silabografías y segmentabilidad fonológica; travestidos gráficos en los silabarios antiguos: AulaO 6 (1988) 83-98: changes resulting in use of agglutinative syllabaries (Sumerian, Cypro-Minoan, Linear B) for inflected languages (Semitic, Indoeuropean).

a761* *a)* *Shields* Kenneth ʲ, Some remarks about the personal pronouns of Indo-European; – *b)* *Holland* Gary B., Nominal sentences and the origin of absolute constructions in Indo-European: ZvgSprW 99 (1986) 10-22 / 163-193.

a762 *Vázquez* Stella Maris, Lenguaje y libertad: DocCom 40 (1987) 181-6.

J8.3   Linguistica generalis.

a763 **Arrivé** Michel, Linguistique et psychanalyse; FREUD, SAUSSURE, HEJLMSLEV, LACAN et les autres; préf. *Coquet* Jean-Claude. P 1986, Klincksieck. – ᴿBSLP 83,2 (1988) 42-44 (S. *Auroux*: excellent).

a764 **Atkinson** Martin, *al.*, Foundations of general linguistics² [¹1982]. L 1988, Unwin Hyman. xv-437 p. 0-04-410005-1; 1-9.

a765 *Bergen* R. D., Text as a guide to authorial intention; an introduction to discourse criticism: JEvTS 30,3 (1987) 327-336 [< NTAbs 32,140].

a766 **Black** David A., Linguistics for students of New Testament Greek; a survey of basic concepts and applications. GR 1988, Baker. xvi-181 p.; 19 fig. $10 pa. 0-8010-0949-9 [NTAbs 32,361]. – ᴿFgNt 1 (1988) 223 (J. *Mateos*).

a767 **Brincat** Giuseppe, La linguistica prestrutturale: Biblioteca Linguistica 17. Bo 1986, Zanichelli. 259 p. – ᴿSalesianum 50 (1988) 259 (R. *Della Casa*).

a768 ᴱ**Buzzetti** Dino, *Ferriani* Maurizio, Speculative grammar, universal grammar and philosophical analysis of language: Amst St. Linguistic 42. Amst 1987, Benjamins. x-269 p. 90-272-4525-8.

a769 **Cardona** Giorgio R., Dizionario di linguistica. R 1988, Armando. 320 p.

a770 **Chomsky** Noam, Knowledge of language; its nature, origin, and use: Convergence. NY 1986, Praeger. xxix-311 p. 0-275-90025-8; pa. 1761-4.

a771 **D'Agostino** Fred, CHOMSKY's system of ideas. Ox 1988, Clarendon. xii-226 p. 0-19-824765-6; 465-7.

a771* **Droixhe** Daniel, [8 reprints sur les théories de ROUSSEAU et d'autres français] De l'origine du langage aux langages du monde: Lingua et traditio 9. Tü 1987, Narr. 132 p. – ᴿRBgPg 66 (1988) 662-5 (E. *Buyssens*).

a772 **Eco** Umberto, Semiotik und Philosophie der Sprache [ital./Eng. 1984], ᵀ*Tabant-Rommel* C., *Tabant* J.: Supplements 4. Mü 1985, Fink. 3-7705-2311-3. – ᴿLingBib 60 (1988) 119-122 (W. *Schenk*).

a773 ᶠFISIAK Jacek, Linguistics... I-II, ᴱKastovsky D., *Szwedek* A. 1986 ➔ 2,31: ᴿKratylos 33 (1988) 50-53 (H. B. *Rosén*).

a773* **Greimas** Algirdas J., *Courtès* Joseph, Sémiotique; dictionnaire raisonné de la théorie de langage, 2. (Langue, linguistique, communication). P 1986, Hachette. 270 p. 2-01-011363-2. – ᴿÉTRel 63 (1988) 159 (D. *Lys*).

a774 **Hattiangadi** J. N., How is language possible? Philosophical reflections on the evolution of language and knowledge. La Salle IL 1987, Open Court. xxi-224 p. $30; pa. $14. 0-8126-9044-3; 5-1.

a775 *Hendricks* William O., Discourse analysis as a semiotic endeavor [*Merrell* Floyd, A semiotic theory of texts 1985 ➔ a782*]: Semiotica 72 (1988) 97-124.

a776 **Horrocks** Geoffrey, Generative grammar: Linguistics library. L 1987, Longman. x-339 p. 0-582-01473-5; pa. 29131-3.

a777 **HSprF**: Historische Sprachforschung / Historical Linguistics [= ZvgSpr: 101 (1988) ss].

a778 *Huspek* Michael, Language analysis and power [*Mey* J., Whose language? 1985]: Semiotica 72 (1988) 341-359.

a779 **Jakobson** Roman, *Waugh* Linda R., The sound shape of language. B 1987, Mouton de Gruyter. xii-335 p.; ill. 0-89925-335-0.

a780 **Laneve** Cosimo, Lingua e persona. Brescia 1987. 172 p. Lit. 12.000. – ᴿStudium 84 (R 1988) 625s (M. *Baldini*).

a781 **Lindeman** Frederik O., Introduction to the 'laryngeal theory': Institute for Comparative Research/Sammlignende kulturforskning. Oslo/Oxford 1988. 156 p. £19.50; pa £9. 82-00-18459-5; 02628-0 [BO 45, 471].

a782 *Mayrhofer* Manfred, Zum Weiterwirken von SAUSSUREs 'Mémoire' [... voyelles indoeuropéennes, 1879 → a792]: Kratylos 33 (1988) 1-15.

a782* **Merrell** Floyd, A semiotic theory of texts: Approaches to Semiotics. B 1985, Mouton de Gruyter. 224 p. – ᴿRBgPg 66 (1988) 653s (R. *Tuffs*); → a775.

a783 *a)* *Mithun* Marianne, Is basic word order universal?; – *b)* *Thompson* Sandra A., 'Subordination' and narrative event structure; – *c)* *Tomlin* Russell S., Linguistic reflections of cognitive events: → 697*, Coherence 1984/7, 281-328 / 435-454 / 455-479.

a784 **Morgan** George A., Speech and society; the Christian linguistic social philosophy of Eugen ROSENSTOCK-HUESSY; bibliog. *Molen* Lise van der. Gainesville 1987, Univ. Florida. xii-209 p. [JTS 39,674].

a785 *a)* *Muñiz Rodríguez* Vicente, Problemas ontológicos del lenguaje; la concepción especular; – *b)* *Paredes Martín* Maria del Carmen, Percepción y lenguaje: NatGrac 35 (1988) 159-180 / 181-203.

a786 ᴱ**Newmeyer** Frederick J., *a)* Linguistic theory; foundations; – *b)* ... extensions and implications; – *c)* Language, psychological and biological aspects; – *d)* ... the socio-cultural context: Linguistics, the Cambridge Survey 1-4. C 1988, Univ. x-500 p.; viii-320 p.; ix-350 p.; x-294 p. 0-521-30832-1; 3-X; 5-6; 4-8.

a787 **Pedullà** Anna Maria, La seduzione del segno; cinque studi di semiotica: Poiesis 9. N 1984, Ed. Scientifiche. 93 p. + c. 50 pagine non numerate.

a788 ᴱ**Petőfi** János S., Text and discourse constitution; empirical aspects, theoretical approaches: Research in Text Theory 4. B 1988, de Gruyter. viii-516 p.; ill. 3-11-007566-0.

a789 *Raible* Wolfgang, Junktion; eine Dimension der Sprache und ihre Realisierungsformen zwischen Aggregation und Integration: Jb Heid Akad (1987) 56-58.

a790 **Rosén** Haiim B., East and west; selected writings on linguistics I-II, 1982/4 → 64,222; 65,245: ᴿOLZ 83 (1988) 51-53 (J. *Tischler*).

a791 *Saukkonen* Pauli, Die Perspektive als Quelle des Stils [Selbstanzeige seines 1984 Mistä tyyli syntyy?]: GGA 240 (1988) 156-172.

a792 **Saussure** Ferdinand de, Mémoire sur le système primitif de voyelles dans les langues indo-européennes [1879]. Hildesheim 1987, Olms. 303 p. 3-487-01833-0.

a792* *Schaller* Joseph J., Performative language theory; an exercise in the analysis of ritual: Worship 62 (1988) 415-432.

a793 *a)* *Timberlake* Alan, Metalanguage; – *b)* *Gamkrelidze* T. V., Lexico-semantic reconstruction and the linguistic paleontology of culture: → 689*. Typology 1985/6, 77-104 / 43-47.

a794 **Waldron** T.P., Principles of language and the mind. L 1985, Routledge-KP. xxiv-232 p. £15. – ᴿHeythJ 29 (1988) 480-2 (R. *Moloney* †).

a795 **Wells** G.A., The origin of language; aspects of the discussion from CONDILLAC to WUNDT. La Salle IL 1987, Open Court. viii-138 p. 0-8126-8029-X; pa. 30-3.

J8.4 *Origines artis scribendi* – The Origin of Writing.

a796 **Amadasi Guzzo** Maria Giulia, Scritture alfabetiche (Metodi). R 1987, V. Levi. 248 p.; 59 fig.; 22 fot. 16 pl.; 4 maps. Lit. 28.000 [BL 89, 148, W. G. E. *Watson*].

a796* [*Amiet* P. présent.] Naissance et évolution de l'écriture [exposition de 275 objets]. Bru 1984, Soc. Générale de Banque. xi-232 p. – ᴿRBgPg 66 (1988) 947s (L. *Gilissen*).

a797 *Bingen* Jean, Les 'Fayum Tablets', de prétendus abécédaires grecs archaïques: CdÉ 63 (1988) 315s.

a798 *Brovarski* Edward, Two Old Kingdom writing boards from Giza: → 127, ᶠSALEḤ A., ASAE 71 (1987) 27-52; 1 fig.; 2 pl.

a799 *Colless* Brian E., Recent discoveries illuminating the origin of the alphabet: AbrNahr 26 (1988) 30-67.

a800 *Demsky* Aaron, [*Bar-Ilan* Meir], Writing in ancient Israel [in early Judaism]: → 317, Mikra 1988, 1-20 [21-38].

a801 **Dietrich** M., *Loretz* O., Die Keilalphabete; die phönizisch-kanaanäischen und altarabischen Alphabete in Ugarit: ALASP 1 (Abh. Lit. Alt-Syrien-Palästinas). Münster 1988, Ugarit-Verlag [distr. Bielefeld, Cornelsen]. xiv-357 p.; map. DM 80. 3-917120-00-6 [BL 89, 122, A. R. *Millard*].

a802 *Dijkstra* M., De alfabetische inscripties van Serabit el-Khadim (Sinai); PhoenEOL 34,2 (1988) 39-53; 3 fig.

a803 **Février** James G., Histoire de l'écriture: Bibliothèque historique. P 1988 = ²1959, Payot. 616 p.; ill. F 187. 2-228-13470-8.

a804 ᶠHOSPERS J.H., Scripta signa vocis, ᴱ**Vanstiphout** H., 1986 → 2,47; ƒ65: ᴿBO 45 (1988) 162-4 (M.J. *Mulder*).

a805 *a) Irigoin* Jean, De l'alpha à l'oméga; quelques remarques sur l'évolution de l'écriture grecque; – *b) Musti* Domenico, Democrazia e scrittura [... greca]: ScrCiv 10 (1986) 7-19; 1 pl. / 21-48; 11 pl.

a806 **Kooij** Gerrit van der, Early North-West Semitic script traditions; an archaeological study of the linear alphabetic scripts up to c. 500 B.C.: Ink and Argillary. Leiden 1986, Rijksuniv. [OIAc D88].

a807 *Lejeune* Michel, De surprenants abécédaires [7 copper tablets (with 22 letters right to left repeated several times) known, 2 localizable in New York; only 1 published, in Würzburger JbAltW 12 (1986); structurally Semitic; traces of Greek and modern (falsification?)]: CRAI (1988) 144.

a808 *Lipiński* Edward, Les Phéniciens et l'alphabet: OrAnt 27 (1988) 231-260; 15 fig.; pl. VIII-IX.

a809 **Mendenhall** George F., The syllabic inscriptions from Byblos 1985 → 1,d728; 3,a54: ᴿCBQ 50 (1988) 508-510 (W. L. *Moran*: a failure); JAOS 108 (1988) 519s (S. *Izre'el*: far-fetched); OLZ 83 (1988) 573-6 (W. *Röllig*: bedauerlich schlechte wissenschaftliche Qualität); RStFen 16 (1988) 129-131 (G. *Garbini*); ZAW 100 (1988) 319s (O. *Rössler*: 'offenbar ohne Kenntnis seines Vorgängers', DHORME E. c. 1948).

a810 **Page** R.I., Runes: Reading the Past. L 1987, British Museum. 64 p. $19. 0-7141-8065-3 [AncHRes 19, 48, Ruth *Waterhouse*].

a811 **Rizkana** Ibrahim, *Seeher* Jürgen, Mâadi I. The pottery of the predynastic settlement 1987 ➤ 3,e846: [R]DiscEg 10 (1988) 73-5 (Rizkana with M. *El-Alfi*: the potmarks, here p. 76, anticipated hieroglyphs by several centuries.

a812 **Sass** Benjamin, The genesis of the [proto-Sinaitic] alphabet and its development in the second millenium B.C.: ÄgAT 13. Wsb 1988, Harrassowitz. xi-223 p.; 294 fig. DM 148. 3-447-02860-2 [BL 90,35, A. R. *Millard*].

a812* *Segert* Stanislav, Writing: ➤ 801, ISBEnc³ 4 (1988) 1136-1160.

a813 *Soravia* Giulio, La scrittura come fenomeno semiotico 'globale': SicGymn 11 (1987) 385-408.

a814 *Thompson* Claiborne W., Runes: ➤ 803, LexMA 10 (1988) 557-568.

a815 *a)* *Vanstiphout* H. L. J., *Miḫiltum*, or the image of cuneiform writing; – *b)* *Velde* H. te, Egyptian hieroglyphs as linguistic signs and metalinguistic informants: Visible Religion 6 (1988) 152-168 / 169-179 [< ZIT 88,576].

J9.1 *Analysis linguistica loquelae de Deo* – **God-talk.**

a816 *a)* *Baden* Matthias J., Hermeneutik der Entsprechung oder Hermeneutik der Nichtentsprechung; eine Gegenüberstellung der theologischen Hermeneutik von E. JÜNGEL und P. RICŒUR; – *b)* *Noller* Gerhard, Selbstverwirklichung oder Gottes Wirklichkeit? Anmerkungen zur Überwindung des Subjekt-Objektschemas: EvT 48 (1988) 217-232 / 233-246.

a817 *Baudler* Georg. Allah, Jahwe, Vishnu, Shiva; zur Eigenart der symbolischen Gottrede in den Weltreligionen: Bijdragen 49 (1988) 264-276.

a818 *Beauchesne* Richard J., Truth, mystery, and expression; theological perspectives revisited: JEcuSt 25 (1988) 555-572.

a819 *Brito* Emilio, Nommer Dieu; Thomas d'AQUIN et HEGEL: RTLv 19 (1988) 160-190; Eng. 268.

a820 *Cooper* Neil, The religious language-game: ScotR 9,1 (Stirling 1988) 29-39 [< ZIT].

a821 **Cupitt** Don, The long-legged fly [religious language à la DERRIDA, DELEUZE, R. RORTY]; a theology of language and desire. L 1987, SCM. vii-180 p. £7 pa. – [R]TLond 91 (1988) 137.

a822 **Derrick** Christopher, Words on the word; notes on our Catholic vocabulary. SF 1987, Ignatius. 134 p. $7. – [R]HomP 88,6 (1987s) 77s (R. J. *Fuhrman*: mania for accuracy).

a823 **Dillistone** F. W., The power of symbols in religion and culture 1986 ➤ 3,a77: [R]HomP 88,4 (1987s) 71 (J. R. *Sheets*: vague and generalizing); Interpretation 42 (1988) 101s (W. K. *Mahony*).

a824 *Forte* Bruno, La ricerca di un nuovo linguaggio su Dio: HumBr 43 (1988) 622-633.

a825 **Foucher** Daniel, Le langage, la grammaire et la foi. 1988, Montligeon. 462 p.

a826 **Geffré** Claude, The risk of interpretation; on being faithful to the Christian tradition in a non-Christian age, [T]*Smith* David, 1987 ➤ 3,a85; also L, Fowler Wright: [R]PrPeo 2 (1988) 435 (P. *Phillips*); TS 49 (1988) 206 (J. E. *Thiel*).

a827 **Gervasoni** Maurizio, La 'poetica' nell'ermeneutica teologica di Paul RICŒUR: R, Sem. Lombardo / Ric. Sc. Teol. 25, 1985 ➤ 1,9562... 3,a86: [R]CiTom 114 (1987) 377s (J. L. *Espinel*).

a828 **Guerra** Santiago, Símbolo y experiencia espiritual: REspir 44 (1985) 7-49 [> SelT 26 (1987) 117-132, [E]*Rocafiguera* José M.].

a829 *Hart* D.G., Poems, propositions, and dogma; the controversy over religious language and the demise of theology in American learning: ChH 57 (1988) 310-321.

a830 **Jager** O., De verbeelding aan het woord; pleidooi voor een dichterlijker en zakelijker spreken over God. Baarn 1988, Ten Have. 178 p. *f*25. 90-259-4379-9 [TsTNijm 28,431].

a831 *a) Jarrett* Charles E., Philosophy of language in the service of religious studies; – *b) Patte* Daniel, Speech act theory and biblical exegesis; – *c) Buss* Martin J., The contribution of speech act theory to biblical studies: Semeia 41 (1988) 143-159 / 85-102 / 125-134.

a832 **Jeanrond** Werner G., Text und Interpretation als Kategorien theologischen Denkens 1986 → 2,7910; 3,a92: ᴿArTGran 51 (1988) 326 (R. *Franco*).

a833 **Jeanrond** Werner G., Text and interpretation as categories of theological thinking [1986 → 2,7910], ᵀ*Wilson* Thomas J. NY 1988, Crossroad. xix-196 p. $20. 0-8245-0869-6 [TDig 36,166]. – ᴿAnglTR 70 (1988) 279-281 (D.S. *Cunningham*); JAAR 56 (1988) 797s (D.E. *Klemm*).

a834 **Jones** Hugh O. †, Die Logik theologischer Perspektiven; eine sprachanalytische Untersuchung (Hab. Mainz über J. *Wisdom*, R.M. *Hare*, J. *Hick*, I. *Barbour*): ForSysÖk 48, 1985 → 2,7912; 3,a94: ᴿRelStR 14 (1988) 238 (R.P. *Scharleman*: New Zealander settled in Mainz, died at 46).

a835 ᴱ**Kaempfert** M., Probleme der religiösen Sprache [13 reprints + 2 inedita]: WegFor 442, 1983 → 64,331.1213; 65,8426: ᴿNRT 110 (1988) 941.

a836 **Ladrière** J., L'articulation du sens... de la foi: CogF 124s, 1984 → 1,9587: ᴿRTLv 19 (1988) 391s (D. *Chavée*).

a837 *a) Lang* Harald, al., Von Gott in Bildern sprechen?; – *b) Bucher* Anton, Symboldidaktik: Katechetische Blätter 113,1 (Mü 1988) (4-) 16-22 / 23-27 [< ᴢɪᴛ].

a837* **Loehr** Davidson, The legitimate heir to theology; a study of Ludwig WITTGENSTEIN: diss. Ch 1988. – RelStR 15,189.

a838 **Long** Charles H., Significations; signs, symbols, and images in the interpretation of religion → 2,187; 3,a97: ᴿTLZ 113 (1988) 173s [N.-P. *Moritzen*: 'so fragte (BARTH) auch ein schwarzer theologischer Kollege (diesmal kein Katholik, sondern ein Kollege mit schwarzer Haut)...']; TTod 45 (1988s) 379 (J. *Buchanan*).

a839 *Loughlin* Gerard, See-Saying/Say-Seeing [*Crossan* J.D.: 'Reality is neither *in here* in the mind nor *out there* in the world; it is the interplay of both mind and world *in language*'; ... *Hick* J.]: TLond 91 (1988) 201-9.

a840 **Maas** Frans, God mee-maken in mensentaal; over de draagkracht van ervaring in geloof en theologie 1986 → 3,a99: ᴿTLZ 113 (1988) 376-381 (R. *Slenczka*); TsTNijm 28 (1988) 190s (F. *Jespers*).

a841 ᶠMᶜCᴀʙᴇ Herbert, Language, meaning and God, ᴱ**Davies** B., 1987 → 3,108: ᴿNBlackf 69 (1988) 457 (W.N. *Clarke*); TLond 91 (1988) 505 (G. *Loughlin*).

a842 **Macqueen** Kenneth, Speech act theory and the roles of religious language: diss. McGill. Montreal 1986. – RelStR 14,188.

a843 **Malherbe** J.F., Le langage théologique à l'âge de la science... J. LADRIÈRE 1985 → 1,9595... 3,a100: ᴿÉglT 17 (1986) 114-6 (B. *Garceau*).

a843* **Martz** John R., The implications for religious language in the thought of Herman DOOYEWEERD as contrasted with Thomas AQUINAS and Paul TILLICH: diss. Drew. Durham ɴᴄ 1988. – RelStR 15,189.

a844 *Milbank* John, Theology without substance; Christianity, signs, origins, part one: LitTOx 2,1 (1988) 1-17 [< ZIT].

a845 *a*) *Molari* Carlo, La teologia di fronte al problema del linguaggio religioso; – *b*) *Micheletti* Mario, Filosofia analitica e linguaggio religioso; – *c*) *Grampa* Giuseppe, La prospettiva ermeneutica da BULTMANN a RICŒUR: ➤ 344, Religione e linguaggio 1986, 9-19 / 21-41 / 43-60.

a846 *Moussé* Jean, Que signifie le mot 'Dieu'?: MélSR 45 (1988) 151-164; Eng. 164.

a847 *Murphy* George L., What can we learn from EINSTEIN about religious language?: CurrTM 15 (1988) 342-8.

a848 **Noppen** Jean-Pierre von, Erinnern, um Neues zu sagen; die Bedeutung der Metapher für die religiöse Sprache. Fra 1988, Athenäum. 319 p. [ZNW 79,297].

a849 **Patterson** David, The affirming flame; religion, language, literature [... Johannine logos]. Norman 1988, Univ. Oklahoma. x-175 p. 0-8061-2109-2.

a850 **Penati** Giancarlo, Verità, libertà, linguaggio; le vie postmoderne di religione e fede dopo HEIDEGGER e LÉVINAS. Brescia 1987, Morcelliana. 134 p. Lit. 12.000. – ᴿCC 139 (1988,2) 197 (P. *Vanzan*); StPatav 35 (1988) 190 (B. *Belletti*).

a851 *Placher* William C., Paul RICŒUR and postliberal theology; a conflict of interpretation?: ModT 4 (1987s) 35-52.

a851* **Prammer** Franz, Die philosophische Hermeneutik Paul RICŒURs in ihrer Bedeutung für eine theologische Sprachtheorie: InnsbTSt. Innsbruck 1988, Tyrolia. 237 p. 3-7022-1664-2.

a852 **Robinson** Edward, The language of mystery [... imagination; art; theology] 1987 ➤ 3,a111: ᴿTLond 91 (1988) 440-2 (T. D. *Jones*).

a853 *Saarinen* Risto, Metapher und biblische Redefiguren als Elemente der Sprachphilosophie LUTHERS: NSys 30 (1988) 18-38; Eng. 39.

a854 **Schermann** Josef, Die Sprache im Gottesdienst [Diss. Innsbruck 1984]: InnsbTSt 18, 1987 ➤ 3,a114: ᴿTLZ 113 (1988) 228s (M. *Josuttis*); TR 84 (1988) 488-491 (M. B. *Merz*).

a855 *Smalbrugge* M. A., Le langage et l'être; la question du Dieu personnel et la notion de similitude du langage dans la doctrine trinitaire de S. AUGUSTIN: RSPT 72 (1988) 541-555; Eng. 556.

a856 **Soskice** Janet M., Metaphor and religious language 1985 ➤ 1,9626 ... 3,a115: ᴿJAAR 56 (1988) 184s (Mary *Gerhart*).

a857 *Taillé* Michel, Y a-t-il une linguistique religieuse?: ➤ 486, Traduction 1986/8, 9-15; Eng. 9.

a857* **Tomkiss** William J., The problem of meaning in theological discourse with special reference to the work of Bernard LONERGAN: diss. Leeds 1987. 345 p. BRD-80065. – DissA 49 (1988s) 104s-A.

a858 **Tracy** David, Plurality and ambiguity; hermeneutics, religion, hope 1987 ➤ 3,a117: ᴿCalvinT 23 (1988) 110-6 (D. *McKim*); CurrTM 15 (1988) 453 (T. *Peters*).

a858* **Treitler** Wolfgang, Gotteswort im Menschenwort; das Problem theologisch-methodischen Redens nach Hans Urs von BALTHASAR: Diss. ᴰ*Reikerstorfer*. W 1988. – RTLv 20,538.

a859 *Trembath* Kern R., Evangelical subjectivism; E. J. CARNELL [1919-1967] and the logic of God: EvQ 60 (1988) 317-342.

a860 *Vardy* Peter, God of our fathers; do we know what we believe? 1987 ➤ 3,a121: ᴿHeythJ 29 (1988) 262s (H. *Meynell*); NBlackf 68 (1987) 577s

(M. *Durrant*); PrPeo 2 (1988) 263s (M. *Evans*); RelSt 24 (1988) 398-400
(P. *Avis*); TLond 91 (1988) 56s (I. *Markham*).

a861 **Watson** Walter, The architectonics of meaning; foundations of the new
pluralism ['the truth admits of more than one formulation'] 1985
→ 1,9636; $39.50; pa. $15:   ᴿRelStR 14 (1988) 136 (R. P. *Scharlemann*).

a862 *Winquist* Charles E., Analogy, apology, and the imaginative pluralism
of David TRACY [Plurality 1987 → a858]: JAAR 56 (1988) 307-319.

a864 **Wren** Brian [writer of hymns], What language shall I borrow? God-talk
in worship, a male response to feminist theology.   NY c. 1988, Crossroad.
$19 [TDig 36/1 cover adv.].

J9.2   *Hermeneutica paratheologica* – **wider linguistic analysis.**

a865 **Andrés** Mireille, LACAN et la question du métalangage.   P 1987, Point
Hors Ligne. 234 p. – ᴿBSLP 83,2 (1988) 44-46 (P. *Swiggers*).

a866 **Arrive** Michel, *Coquet* Jean-Claude, Sémiotique en jeu [*Greimas* A.-J.]:
Actes sémiotiques. 1987, ... Hadès-Benjamin [SémBib 49,41].

a867 **Barnes** Annette, On interpretation; a critical analysis.   Ox 1988,
Blackwell. vi-171 p. 0-631-15947-9; pa. 63-0.

a868 **Bori** P. C., L'interpretazione infinita.   Bo 1987, Mulino. 173 p. Lit.
18.000. – ᴿParVi 33 (1988) 389-392 (Maria Grazia *Mara*); StPatav 35
(1988) 712s (V. *Bortolin*).

a869 **Cloeren** Hermann J., Language and thought; German approaches to
analytic philosophy in the 18th and 19th centuries: Grundlagen der
Kommunikation. B 1988, de Gruyter. 267 p. 3-11-011301-5.

a870 **Coletti** Theresa, Naming the rose; ECO, medieval signs, and modern
theory.   Ithaca NY 1988, Cornell Univ. xi-212 p. 0-8014-2114-4.

a871 **Ellul** Jacques, Le bluff technologique.   P 1988, Hachette. – ᴿRHPR 68
(1988) 510s (G. *Vahanian*).

a872 *Farris* W. J. S., The hermeneutical arc [RICŒUR expression preferable to
GADAMER's fusion of two horizons]: TorJT 4 (1988) 86-100.

a873 **Fattal** Michel, Pour un nouveau langage de la raison; convergences
entre l'Orient et l'Occident: Archives de Philosophie, Bibliothèque NS 50.
P 1988, Beauchesne. 112 p. F120. 2-7010-1177-9.

a874 **Ferraris** Maurizio, Storia dell'ermeneutica.   Mi 1988, Bompiani. 484 p.
Lit. 45.000. – ᴿHumBr 43 (1988) 903s (G. *Sansonetti*).

a875 **Figl** Johann, Interpretation als philosophisches Prinzip; F. NIETZSCHES
universale Theorie der Auslegung im späten Nachlass: Mg. Texte
Nietzsche 7. B 1982, de Gruyter. xiv-223 p. DM 84. 3-11-008532-1. –
ᴿBijdragen 49 (1988) 465-7 (G. *Groot*).

a876 **Fontanille** Jacques, Le savoir partagé; sémiotique et théorie de la
connaissance chez Marcel PROUST: Actes Sémiotiques. ... 1987, Hadès-Benjamin [SémBib 49,41].

a877 **Gaier** Ulrich, HERDERs Sprachphilosophie und Erkenntniskritik.   Stu-
Bad Canstatt 1988, Frommann-Holzboog. 220 p. – ᴿNatGrac 35 (1988)
456s (E. *Rivera*).

a878 **Gellrich** Jesse M., The idea of the book in the Middle Ages; language
theory, mythology, and fiction.   Ithaca NY 1985, Cornell Univ. 292 p.; 9
fig. $27.50. – ᴿSpeculum 63 (1988) 664-7 (L. *Patterson*). → 1666.

a879 **Hallett** Garth L., Language and truth.   NHv 1988, Yale Univ. 227 p.
$21.50 [RelStR 15,137, J. *DiCenso*].

a879* **Heim** Michael, Electric language; a philosophical study of word
processing.   NHv 1987, Yale Univ. 305 p. $20 [RelStR 15,138, R. P.
Scharlemann].

a880 *Hettlage* Robert, Fremdheit und Fremdverstehen; Ansätze zu einer angewandten Hermeneutik: ArKulturG 70 (1988) 195-222.

a881 *Lentini* Claudio, GADAMER e i suoi critici italiani: StUrb B2 60 (1987) 79-121.

a882 **Madison** G. B., The hermeneutics of postmodernity; figures and themes: Studies in Phenomenology. Bloomington 1988, Indiana Univ. xvi-206 p. 0-253-32190-5.

a883 **Mainberger** Gonsalv K., Rhetorica I. Reden mit Vernunft; ARISTOTELES, CICERO, AUGUSTINUS: Problemata 116. Stu 1987, Frommann-Holzboog. 383 p. − ᴿLingBib 60 (1988) 106-9 (E. *Guttgemanns*).

a884 *Mainberger* Gonsalv K., Skeptische Aneignung des Fremden — rhetorische Verfremdung des Eigenen; Michel de MONTAIGNE auf dem geordneten Rückzug in die Welt: LingBib 60 (1988) 85-106.

a885 **Marchese** Angelo, Dizionario di retorica e di stilistica; arte e artificio nell'uso delle parole retorica, stilistica, metrica, teoria della letteratura. Mi 1987, Mondadori. 359 p. 88-04-14664-8.

a886 *Migliasso* Secondo, Per una teoria filosofico-teologica della metafora; libera coordinazione di recenti studi tedeschi [*Jüngel* E.; *Bühler* K., *Snell* B., *Löwith* K., *Allemann* B. van, *Blumenberg* H.; *Ricœur* P.]: StPatav 35 (1988) 95-120; Eng. 121.

a887 *Mignot* Xavier, Les mots ont-ils un sens?: BSLP 83,1 (1988) 21-39; Eng. 344s; español 345.

a888 ᴱ**Mindlin** M., *al.* Figurative language in the Ancient Near East. L 1987, Univ. [B]SOAS. xiii-155 p. 0-7286-0141-9: p. 41-75, *Veenhof* K. R., 'dying tablets', 'hungry silver'; 77-102, *Wilcke* C., 'a riding tooth'; 25-39, *Lambert* W. G., Religion and love; 13-24, *Edzard* D. O., architecture.

a889 *Niebuhr* Karl W., Keine Angst vor Linguistik: CLehre 41,1 (1988) 4-13 [< ZIT].

a890 *Pedersen* Sigfred, Lignelsen [comparison] som metafor: DanTTs 51 (1988) 1-11 [< ZIT].

a891 **Ricœur** Paul, La semantica dell'azione, ᵀᴱ*Pieretti* Antonio. Mi 1986, Jaca. 173 p. − ᴿDocCom 40 (1987) 216s (D. *Composta)*.

a892 *Russo* Francesco, Uomo, pensiero, linguaggio; l'ermeneutica di Hans-G. GADAMER: ScuolC 22 (1988) 205-9.

a892* *Scheffer* Pierre [continuateur du 'formalisme' du linguiste-anthropologiste jésuite] Marcel JOUSSE (1886-1961), ou le service de la parole, humaine et divine: ÉTRel 63 (1988) 367-378.

a893 *Segarelli* Gabriella, Paul RICŒUR tra concetto e kerygma; il 'kantismo post-hegeliano': FilT 1,2 (N 1988) 102-118.

a894 *Stambovsky* Phillip, Metaphor and historical understanding: HistTheory 27 (1988) 125-134.

a895 **Tejera** Victorino, Semitics from PEIRCE to BARTHES; a conceptual introduction to the study of communication, interpretation and expression. Leiden 1988, Brill. ix-201 p. 90-04085-97-1.

a896 *Vandevelde* P., Les mots à double voix; d'un usage HEIDEGGERIEN de la langue: RPhLv 85 (1987) 522-537 [< RSPT 72,49].

a897 **Weinsheimer** Joel, GADAMER's hermeneutics; a reading of Truth and method 1986 → 1,9637; 3,a165. − ᴿPgQ 67 (1988) 272-5 (H. *Rapaport*).

a898 **Wonneberger** R., *Hecht* H. P., Verheissung und Versprechen; eine theologische und sprachanalytische Klärung [Lehrveranstaltung Hamburg, 'Die Sprechakt-Theorie als Brücke zwischen Exegese und Ethik (p. 149-194 Bibel; Bund)]. 1986 → 3,a127: ᴿBL (1988) 118 (J. *Barr*); ZAW 100 (1988) 329 (H.-C. *Schmitt*).

a899 **Zilberberg** Claude, Raison et poétique du sens. P 1988, PUF. 227 p. [SémBib 51,41].

J9.3 *Critica reactionis lectoris* – **Reader-response criticism.**

a900 *Schenk* Wolfgang, Die Rollen der Leser oder der Mythos des Lesers?: LingBib 60 (1988) 61-84.

J9.4 **Structuralism; deconstruction.**

a901 ᴱ**Benjamin** Andrew, Post-structuralist classics: Warwick Studies. L 1988, Routledge. viii-273 p. 0-415-00922-7.

a902 **Burms** Arnold, *Dijn* Herman de, De nationaliteit en haar grenzen; kritiek en deconstructie. Lv/Assen 1986, Univ./Van Gorcum. vii-105 p. Fb 300. – ᴿLvSt 10 (1988) 287s (J. *Jans*).

a903 **Caputo** John D., Radical hermeneutics; repetition, deconstruction, and the hermeneutic project. Bloomington 1987, Indiana Univ. ix-319 p. $37.50; pa. $17.50 [JTS 39,675].

a904 *Jeffrey* David L., Caveat lector; structuralism, deconstructionism, and ideology: ChrSchR 17 (1988) 436-448 [< ZIT 88,584].

a905 **Merrell** Floyd, [author of Deconstruction reframed 1985], Semiotic foundations; steps toward an epistemology of written texts. Bloomington 1982, Indiana Univ. x-181 p. $25 [RelStR 15,66, D. *Jobling*].

a906 ᴱ**Silverman** Hugh J., *Ihde* Don, Hermeneutics and deconstruction [7 essays]. Albany 1985, SUNY. 304 p. $44.50; pa. $20 [RelStR 15,138, R. P. *Scharlemann*].

ᴱ**Taylor** Mark C., Deconstruction 1986 → 463.

a907 **Taylor** Mark C., Erring... DERRIDA 1984 1,g323; 2,e157: ᴿHeythJ 29 (1988) 395-7 (W. *Reiser*: an attempt to undo theology).

a908 **Wijzenbroek** Anita, De kunst van het begrijpen; een structuralistisch-hermeneutisch model voor de analyse van literair proza. Muiderberg 1987, Dick Coutinho. 140 p. – ᴿRBgPg 66 (1988) 654-6 (P. *Tasiaux*).

a909 **Winquist** Charles E., Epiphanies... deconstruction 1986 → 3,a172: ᴿJAAR 56 (1988) 373-6 (Edith *Wyschogrod*).

J9.6 *Analysis narrationis* – **Narrative-analysis.**

a909* **Adams** Jeff, The conspiracy of the text; the place of narrative in the development of thought: Social Worlds of Childhood. L 1986, Routledge-KP. vii-152 p. $35 [RelStR 15,154, D. *Jobling*].

a910 *Ankersmit* F. R., Twee vormen van narrativisme: Tijdschrift voor Filosofie 50 (1988) 40-81 [RSPT 72,661].

a911 ᴱ**Bühler** P., *Habermacher* J.-F., La narration; quand le récit devient communication: Lieux théologiques 12. Genève 1988, Labor et Fides. 310 p. [JBL 107,786].

a912 **Chatman** Seymour, *a)* Story and discourse; narrative structure in fiction and film. Ithaca NY 1988, Cornell Univ. 277 p. 0-8014-1131-9; pa. 9186-X. – *b)* Storia e discorso; la struttura narrativa nel romanzo e nel film: Nuovi Saggi. Parma 1987, Pratiche. 325 p. 88-7380-025-4.

a913 **Friemel** Franz Georg, *März* Claus-Peter, Geschichten, nicht nur biblische; Hilfen für eine narrative Praxis: Pastoral-Katechetische Hefte 66. Lp 1988, St. Benno. 303 p. 3-7462-0286-8.

a914 **Kort** Wesley A.,   Story, text, and Scripture; literary interests in biblical narrative: Univ. Park 1988, Pennsylvania State Univ.   xii-159 p. [RelStR 15, 66, W. Lee *Humphreys*].

a915 *McGaughey* Douglas R.,   RICŒUR's metaphor and narrative theories as a foundation for a theory of symbol: RelSt 24 (C 1988) 415-437.

a916 *Mahaney* Brian,   The affective narrative; a grammar of praxis: IrTQ 54 (1988) 50-58.

a917 **Ricœur** Paul,   Time and narrative [1,1986 → 3,2190] 3.   Ch 1988, Univ. 355 p.   0-226-71335-0 [1-8, I; 3-4, II]. – RÉglT 18 (1987) 401-5 (J. *Van den Hengel*, 2); HeythJ 29 (1988) 119s (W. *Reiser*, 1).

a918 **Ricœur** Paul,   Tempo e racconto I 1986 → 2,8016; 3,a189; Lit. 12.000: RCC 139 (1988,4) 197s (G. *Lorizio*); Salesianum 50 (1988) 595 (M. *Zanovello*).

a919 *Vincent* Gilbert,   Enjeux éthiques du concept d'identité narrative [*Ricœur* P., Temps et récit]: RHPR 68 (1988) 217-228.

J9.8   *Theologia narrativa* – Story-theology.

a920 **Crossan** J. D.,   The dark interval; towards a theology of story[2rev] [[1] c. 1977], pref. *Funk* R. W.   Sonoma CA 1988, Polebridge.   xiv-114 p.; 18 fig. $8 pa.   0-944344-06-2 [NTAbs 32,370].

a921 *Dijkman* J. H.,   Integratie van het verhaal in de ethiek ...:   TsTNijm 28 (1988) 50-72; 72, The possibilities and limits of narrative within a theological-ethical theory of action.

a922 **Ekpenyong** Michael O.,   The contribution of the theology of story to the emerging theologies of Africa: diss. Duquesne.   Pittsburgh 1988. – RelStR 15,191.

a923 *Hansen* Karstein M.,   Imøtegått transcendens; skapelsesteologisk kritikk av språkforståelsen i dansk narrativ teologi: NorTTs 89 (1988) 115-131.

a924 *Jones* L. Gregory,   Alasdair MACINTYRE on narrative, community and the moral life: ModT 4 (1987s) 53-69.

a925 *Kemp* P.,   Per un'etica narrativa; un ponte tra l'etica e la riflessione narrativa in RICŒUR: Aquinas 31 (1988) 435-458.

a926 *Kepnes* Steven D.,   A narrative Jewish theology: Judaism 37 (1988) 210-7.

a927 *Mertens* Herman-Emiel,   Making a long story short? A plea for narrative theology, T*Merrigan* Terrence: LvSt 13 (1988) 27-40.

a928 **Nelson** Paul,   Narrative and morality; a theological inquiry 1987 → 3,a204:   RJTS 39 (1988) 655-7 (J. L. *Houlden*); TS 49 (1988) 559-561 (T. W. *Tilley*).

a929 **Tilley** Terrence W.,   Story theology 1985 → 1,1369 ... 3,a206:   RRExp 85 (1988) 569 (W. L. *Hendricks*).

a930 EZerfass Rolf [*Arens* Edmund, *al.*],   Erzählter Glaube — erzählende Kirche: QDisp 116.   FrB 1988, Herder.   203 p.

(IV.) Postbiblica

K1   **Pseudepigrapha** [= catholicis 'Apocrypha'] .1 *VT, generalia.*

a931 EBarnstone Willis,   The other Bible 1984 → 65,8464; 2,8027*; RBR 4,1 (1988) 8s (G. *Howard*).

a931* *Bauer* J. B., Apokryphen [Pseudepigraphen]: → 804, NBL Lfg 1 (1988) 132-4.

a932 **Blail** Gerhard, Die Apokryphen; die Schriften zwischen Altem und Neuem Testament; eine Einführung und Orientierung. Stu 1988, Quell. 96 p. 3-7918-1900-3.

a933 Bibeln; tillägg till Gamla testamentet; de apokryfa: Bibelkommisjonens utgåva. Sto 1986, Liber. 530 p., maps. – ᴿRB 95 (1988) 102-4 (L.-M. *Dewailly*).

a934 *Buit* M. Du, Pseudépigraphes: → 786, Catholicisme 12,54 (1988) 197-201.

a935 *[Caquot* A.], La littérature intertestamentaire 1983/5 → 1,458... 3,a208: ᴿRÉAnc 90 (1988) 218s (Christiane *Ingremeau*); TLZ 113 (1988) 182s (tit. pp.).

a936 ᴱ**Charlesworth** James H., The OT Pseudepigrapha 1983/5 → 64,253... 3,a209: ᴿBA 51 (1988) 57s (L. H. *Silberman*: adds distaste for his NT volume); CBQ 50 (1988) 288-291 (G. W. E. *Nickelsburg* compares with SPARKS); Horizons 15 (1988) 381s (D. P. *McCarthy*); IrTQ 54 (1988) 73s (M. *McNamara*, 2); RÉJ 146 (1987) 147-150 (Madeleine *Petit*); RelStR 14 (1988) 111-3-7 (M. E. *Stone* & R. A. *Kraft*, both comparing with SPARKS H. 1984).

a937 **Charlesworth** J. H., The OT pseudepigrapha and the NT; prolegomena for the study of Christian origins 1985 → 1,9649... 3,a201: ᴿÉTRel 63 (1988) 113-5 (C. *Vallet*); JBL 107 (1988) 339-342 (F. J. *Murphy* finds no flaw); NedTTs 42 (1988) 73s (P. W. van der *Horst*).

a938 *a)* *Charlesworth* J. H., Biblical interpretation; the crucible of the pseudepigrapha; – *b)* *Hilhorst* A., [pseudep.] Biblical metaphors taken literally; – *c)* *Treu* Kurt, 'Apocryphe relatif à Jacob et Joseph' (van Haelst no. 571) und der Sitz im Leben von Apocrypha-Papyri; – *d)* *Vorster* Willem S., The Protevangelium of James and intertextuality: → 85, ᶠKLIJN A., Text 1988, 66-78 / 123-131 / 255-261 / 262-275.

a939 *Dimant* Devorah, Use and interpretation of Mikra in the Apocrypha and Pseudepigrapha: → 317, Mikra 1988, 379-419.

a940 ᴱ**Dupont-Sommer** André, *Philonenko* Marc, La Bible, écrits intertestamentaires 1987 → 3,a214: ᴿHenoch 10 (1988) 398-402 (Liliana *Rosso Ubigli*); JJS 39 (1988) 112-4 (S. *Brock*); JPseud 2 (1988) 113-5 [J. C. *VanderKam*]; NRT 110 (1988) 916s (X. *Jacques*); RB 95 (1988) 559-580 (P. *Grelot*); RHR 205 (1988) 69-78 (M. *Delcor*); RivB 36 (1988) 272s (A. *Bonora*); TLZ 113 (1988) 182 (W. *Wiefel*).

a941 *Horst* Pieter W. van der, Pseudo-Phocylides revisited: JPseud 3 (1988) 3-30.

a942 **Jonge** M. de, Outside the NT: CamCW 4,1988 → 2,254; 3,a216; $33.50 pa. 0-521-28554-2: ᴿAncSRes 17 (1987) 42s (F. I. *Andersen*); JAAR 56 (1988) 144-6 (J. R. *Mueller*).

a943 *Leloir* Louis, Utilité ou inutilité de l'étude des Apocryphes: RTLv 19 (1988) 38-70.

a944 **McNamara** Martin, Intertestamental literature: OT Message 23, 1983 → 64,6597... 3,a217: ᴿIrTQ 54 (1988) 75 (A. *O'Leary*).

a945 **Russell** D. S., The OT Pseudepigrapha; patriarchs and prophets in early Judaism 1987 → 3,a221: ᴿBL (1988) 143 (M. *Barker*); JPseud 1 (1987) 115s (J. C. *VanderKam*); TLond 91 (1988) 142s (G. *Lloyd Jones*: succeeds admirably in its aim).

a946 **Sparks** H. F. D., The apocryphal OT 1984 → 65,8477... 3,a223: ᴿBR

4,3 (1988) 7.9 (J. C. *VanderKam*); Henoch 10 (1988) 251-4 (Liliana *Rosso Ubigli*).

a946* *Wermelinger* Otto, Apocrypha: → 783, AugL 1,3 (1988) 385-391.

κ1.2   Henoch.

a947 **Barker** Margaret, The lost prophet; the book of Enoch and its influence on Christianity. L 1988 SPCK. xi-116 p. £5. 0-281-04381-7 [BL 89, 129, L. L. *Grabbe*: popularization of The Older Testament (1987 → 3,b237); annoyingly expresses irrelevant opinions].

a948 *Berger* Klaus, Henoch: → 807, RAC 14,107s (1987s) 473-545.

a949 **Black** M., The book of Enoch 1985 → 1,9865 ... 3,a227: ᴿHenoch 10 (1988) 107-110 (P. *Piovanelli*: testo eclettico); JBL 107 (1988) 342-4 (G. W. E. *Nickelsburg*: outdated).

a950 *Fröhlich* Ida, [1 Henoch 6-19] Les enseignements des veilleurs dans la tradition de Qumran: → 22, Mém. CARMIGNAC J., RQum 13 (1988) 177-187.

a951 **Hofmann** Helmut [*Odeberg* Hugo], Das sogenannte hebräische Henochbuch (3 Henoch)²: BoBB 58, 1984 → 65,8486 ... 2,8044: ᴿGregorianum 69 (1988) 549-551 (G. L. *Prato*).

a952 *Luke* K., Enoch's ascension; the apocalyptic tradition: IndTSt 25 (1988) 236-252.

a953 *Piovanelli* Pierluigi, Il testo e le traduzioni dell'Enoch etiopico 1976-1987: Henoch 10 (1988) 85-95.

a954 **Rubinkiewicz** R., [❷ Eschatologia 1984] Die Eschatologie von Hen 9-11 und das NT 1984 → 65,8491 ... 3,a236: ᴿRB 95 (1988) 628 (J. *Murphy-O'Connor*).

a955 **Sacchi** Paolo, L'apocalittica del I sec. [Ep/Parab Henoch; TestPatriarch]: → 474, Correnti 1984/7, 59-77.

a956 *Stone* Michael E., Enoch, Aramaic Levi and sectarian origins: JStJud 19 (1988) 159-170.

a957 **Uhlig** Siegbert, Das äthiopische Henochbuch: Apokalypsen, JSHZ 5s, 1984 → 65,8492 (p. 463-780.): ᴿRelStR 14 (1988) 262 (J. H. *Charlesworth*).

κ1.3   Testamenta.

a958 **Nordheim** Eckhard von, Das Testament als Literaturgattung im Judentum 1980 → 61,873 ... 64,8627 [II. 1985 → 2,8054]: ᴿJBL 107 (1988) 311-3 (R. E. *Murphy*, 2); OLZ 83 (1988) 38-40 (G. *Baumbach*); RB 95 (1988) 307s (J. M. de *Tarragon*, 2); TLZ 113 (1988) 109s (N. *Walter*, 2).

a959 **Schmidt** Francis, Le Testament grec d'Abraham 1986 → 2,8055; 3,a242: ᴿJBL 107 (1988) 345s (J. J. *Collins*); JStJud 19 (1988) 263-5 (F. *García Martínez*); RB 95 (1988) 626s (J. *Murphy-O'Connor*); ScripTPamp 19 (1987) 980 (G. *Aranda*).

a960 **Hollander** H. W., *Jonge* M. de, Testament of the Twelve 1985 → 1, 9679 ... 3,a240: ᴿJTS 39 (1988) 174-6 (J. C. *O'Neill*).

a961 *Jonge* M. de, The Testament of Levi and 'Aramaic Levi' [4Q not yet published in full]: → 22, Mém. CARMIGNAC J., RQum 13 (1988) 367-385.

a962 *Duling* Dennis C., The Testament of Solomon; retrospect and prospect: JPseud 2 (1988) 87-112.

a963 *Jackson* H. M.,   Notes on the Testament of Solomon [*Duling* D. in *Charlesworth* J. 1983, first complete translation from *McCown*'s definitive edition 1922]: JStJud 19 (1988) 19-60.

a964 *Horst* Pieter W. van der,   De rol van de vrouw in het Testament van Job [< Eng. NedTTs 40 (1986) 273-289]: ➤ 207, De onbekende God 1988, 189-209.

a964* *Troupeau* Gérard,   Une version arabe du 'Testament d'Adam': ➤ 59, ᶠGuillaumont A., 1988, 3-14.

3-4 Mcb ➤ E5.8 Mcb; 3-4 Esdras ➤ E5.4 Ezra; 2 Baruch ➤ E8.8 Baruch.

K1.5 Salomonis Psalmi (*et Odae epochae christianae*).

a965 *Hann* Robert R.,   The community of the pious; the social setting of the Psalms of Solomon: SR 17 (1988) 169-189.

a966 **Trafton** Joseph L.,   The Syriac version of the Psalms of Solomon; a critical evaluation 1985 ➤ 1,9694 ... 3,a249: ᴿJBL 107 (1988) 131-4 (R. B. *Wright*).

a967 **Blaszczak** Gerald R.,   A formcritical study of selected Odes of Solomon: HarvSemMon 36,1985 ➤ 1,9695; 3,a250: ᴿCBQ 50 (1988) 488s (Susan A. *Harvey*); JBL 107 (1988) 134s (J. H. *Charlesworth*); OLZ 83 (1988) 679-681 (R. *Stahl*).

Brownson James,   The Odes of Solomon and the Johannine tradition 1988 ➤ 5477.

a968 **Lattke** Michael,   Die Oden Salomos in ihrer Bedeutung für NT und Gnosis, III: OBO 25/3, 1986 ➤ 2,8069: ᴿActuBbg 25 (1988) 68 (X. *Alegre S.*); JSS 33 (1988) 285s (B. *McNeil*); NedTTs 42 (1988) 343 (P. W. van der *Horst*); OrChrPer 54 (1988) 265-7 (R. *Lavenant*); OrChr 72 (1988) 222s (M. van *Esbroeck*); RB 95 (1988) 626 (J. *Murphy-O'Connor*); VigChr 42 (1988) 97-99 (A. F. J. *Klijn*).

K1.6 Jubilaea, Adam, Aḥiqar, Asenet.

a969 **Endres** John C.,   Biblical interpretation in the Book of Jubilees [diss. Vanderbilt 1982, ᴰ*Harrelson* W.]: CBQ Mon 18, 1987 ➤ 3,a254: ᴿBL (1988) 131 (M. *Barker*); CBQ 50 (1988) 133s (D. J. *Harrington*: informative, challenging, and low-priced); JBL 107 (1988) 526-8 (M. *Fishbane*: seriously opens out non-legal interpretation).

a970 *a*) *Lignée* Hubert,   La place du livre des Jubilés et du Rouleau du Temple dans l'histoire du mouvement Essénien; ces deux ouvrages ont-ils été écrits par le Maître de Justice?; – *b*) *Tyloch* Witold,   Quelques remarques sur la provenance essénienne du Livre des Jubilés; – *c*) *VanderKam* James C.,   Jubilees and the priestly messiah of Qumran: ➤ 22, Mém. Carmignac J., RQum 13 (1988) 331-345 / 347-352 / 353-365.

a971 *Schelbert* Georg,   Jubiläenbuch: ➤ 813, TRE 17 (1987) 285-9.

a972 **Lindenberger** James M.,   The Aramaic proverbs of Ahiqar 1983 ➤ 64,8662 ... 3,a257: ᴿIsrEJ 38 (1988) 96s (A. R. *Millard*); RB 95 (1988) 588-592 (E. *Puech*: nombreuses corrections).

a973 *Chesnutt* Randall D.,   The social setting and purpose of Joseph and Aseneth: JPseud 2 (1988) 21-48.

a974 *Douglas* Rees C., Liminality and conversion in Joseph and Aseneth: JPseud 3 (1988) 31-42.

κ1.7   Apocalypses, ascensiones.

a975 *Hall* Robert G., The 'Christian interpolation' in the Apocalypse of Abraham: JBL 107 (1988) 107-110.

a976 **Bertrand** Daniel A., La Vie grecque d'Adam et Ève [= Apocalypse de Moïse] 1987 ➤ 3,a265: ᴿMuséon 101 (1988) 437s (J. *Mossay*); RB 95 (1988) 584s (É. *Puech*); RHPR 68 (1988) 262s (*ipse*); VT 38 (1988) 489 (W. *Horbury*).

κ2.1   Philo judaeus alexandrinus.

a977 *Amir* Yehoshua, Authority and interpretation of Scripture in the writings of Philo: ➤ 317, Mikra 1988, 421-453.

a978 **Berchman** Robert M., From Philo to ORIGEN; Middle Platonism in transition 1984 ➤ 65,8534; 2,8087: ᴿSecC 6 (1987s) 253s (T. H. *Tobin*).

Burkhardt H., Die Inspiration Heiliger Schrift bei Philo, ᴰ1988 ➤ 1405.

a979 *Carny* Pin'has, Philo's uniqueness and particularity: ➤ 505, Creative 1985/8, 31-38.

a980 *Cazeaux* Jacques, La sagesse selon Philon d'Alexandrie: ➤ 791, DictSpir XIV,91 (1988) 81-91.

Goulet R., La philosophie de Moïse... commentaire préphilonien [really about Philo] 1987 ➤ 1902.

a981 *Harrington* Daniel J., A decade of research on Pseudo-Philo's Biblical Antiquities: JPseud 2 (1988) 3-12.

a982 **Hoek** Annewies van den, CLEMENT of Alexandria and his use of Philo in the Stromateis; an early Christian reshaping of a Jewish model [Cath. diss. Nijmegen 1988, ᴰ*Davids* A.]: VetChr Sup 3. Leiden 1988, Brill. 261 p. 90-04-08756-7. – ᴿRSPT 72 (1988) 607-9 (G.-M. de *Durand*).

a983 *Horowitz* Michaël J., La philosophie judéo-hellénistique de Philon d'Alexandrie: NRT 110 (1988) 220-244.

a984 **Kraus Reggiani** C., Filone, l'uomo e Dio... sogni mandati da Dio [vol. 4 sul Pentateuco allegorizzato; ultime delle 19 opere]: I classici del pensiero 1/1. Mi 1986, Rusconi. 674 p. – ᴿClaretianum 27 (1987) 401-3 (B. *Proietti*).

a985 *Laporte* J., [*Poirier* P.-H.] La notion de salut dans l'œuvre de Philon d'Alexandrie [... JOSÈPHE; pseudépigraphes AT]: ➤ 809, SDB 11,62 (1988) 573-6 [559-573 / 576-584].

a986 **Martín** José P., Filón de Alejandría y la génesis de la cultura occidental: Oriente-Occidente 1986 ➤ 3,a276: ᴿActuBbg 25 (1988) 146 (F. de P. *Solà*); EstE 63 (1988) 508s (A. M. *Artola*); RThom 88 (1988) 339s (H. *Ponsot*); TLZ 113 (1988) 24s (W. *Wiefel*); ZKG 99 (1988) 407 (A. *García y García*, castellano).

a987 *Mazzanti* Angela M., L'uomo *methorios* da Filone all'*Asclepio*: SMSR 54 (1988) 61-69.

a988 *a) Mazzanti* Angela M., Antropologia e radici del male in Filone di Alessandria; due possibili opzioni; – *b) Cerutti* Maria Vittoria, Radici antropologiche del male in testi tardogiudaici; questioni storico-religiose; – *c) Michel* Alain, Judaïsme et Académie; Cicéron et Philon d'Alexandrie: ➤ 570, AugR 28 (1988) 187-201 / 203-217 / 219-236.

a989 **Méasson** Anita, Du char ailé de Zeus à l'Arche d'Alliance; ... Philon [diss. Lyon 1982, ᴰ*Pouilloux* J.] 1986 → 2,8095: ᴿSalesianum 50 (1988) 427s (R. *Vicent*); VigChr 42 (1988) 200-5 (D. T. *Runia*).

a990 **Ménard** Jacques, La gnose de Philon 1987 → 3,a277: ᴿGregorianum 69 (1988) 792s (G. *Pelland*); OrChr 72 (1988) 236 (W. *Gessel*).

a991 *Murphy* Frederick J., *a*) God in Pseudo-Philo [Biblical Antiquities]: JStJud 19 (1988) 1-18; – *b*) The eternal covenant in Pseudo-Philo: JPseud 3 (1988) 43-57; – *c*) Retelling the Bible; idolatry in Pseudo-Philo: JBL 107 (1988) 275-287.

a992 *Neary* Michael, Philo of Alexandria: IrTQ 54 (1988) 41-49.

a993 **Radice** Roberto (*Bitter* R. A., *al.*), Philo of Alexandria, an annotated bibliography 1937-1986 [< Filone 1983 → 64,852]: VigChr Sup 8. Leiden 1988, Brill. xii-469 p. 90-04-08986-1.

Radice R., Filone, la filosofia mosaica 1987 → 1906.

a994 **Riedweg** Christoph, Mysterienterminologie bei PLATON, Philon und KLEMENS A. 1987 → 3,a284: ᴿClasR 102 (1988) 164 (H. *Chadwick*); WissWeis 50 (1987) 217s (H.-J. *Klauck*).

a995 **Runia** David T., Philo of Alexandria and the Timaeus of PLATO: PhAnt 44, 1986 → 3,a285; 90-04-07477-5: ᴿAntClas 57 (1988) 364s (R. *Joly*); JStJud 19 (1988) 258s (A. *Hilhorst*).

a996 *Runia* D. T., God and man in Philo of Alexandria: JTS 39 (1988) 48-75.

a997 **Siegert** Folker, Philon von Alexandrien; über die Gottesbezeichnung 'wohltätig verzehrendes Feuer' (De Deo), Rückübersetzung des Fragments aus dem Armenischen, deutsche Übersetzung und Kommentar: WUNT 46. Tü 1988, Mohr. viii-190 p. 3-16-145234-8.

a998 **Sly** Dorothy, The perception of women in the writing of Philo of Alexandria: diss. McMaster. Hamilton 1987. – RelStR 15,194.

ᴱ**Terian** Abraham, Philon, Alexander... bruta animalia 1988 → h64.

Tobin Thomas H., The creation of man; Philo and the history of interpretation 1983 → 2216.

ĸ2.4   *Evangelia apocrypha* – **Apocryphal Gospels.**

a999 *a*) *Charlesworth* J. H., Research on the NT apocrypha and pseudepigrapha; – *b*) *Gero* Stephen, Apocryphal gospels; a survey of textual and literary problems: → 782, ANRW 2,25,5 (1988) 3919-68 / 3969-96.

b1 ᴱ**Schneemelcher** Wilhelm, Neutestamentliche Apokryphen⁵ 1987 → 3, a298*: ᴿBZ 32 (1988) 274-6 (R. *Schnackenburg*); VigChr 42 (1988) 304s (A. F. J. *Klijn*).

b2 *Kaestli* Jean-Daniel, Où en est l'étude de l' 'Évangile de Barthélemy'?: RB 95 (1988) 5-34; Eng. 5s.

b3 *a*) *Levin* Saul, The early history of Christianity, in light of the 'Secret Gospel' of Mark [*Smith* M. 1973]; – *b*) *Cothenet* Édouard, Le Protévangile de Jacques; origine, genre et signification d'un premier midrash chrétien sur la Nativité de Marie; – *c*) *Collins* Adela Y., Early Christian apocalyptic literature: → 782, ANRW 2,25,6 (1988) 4270-92 / 4252-69 / 4665-4711.

b4 *Junod* Éric, EUSÈBE de Césarée, SÉRAPION d'Antioche et l'Évangile de Pierre; d'un évangile à un pseudépigraphe: RivStoLR 24 (1988) 3-16.

b5 *Rodríguez Ruiz* Miguel, El Evangelio de Pedro; ¿un desafío a los evangelios canónicos?: EstBíb 46 (1988) 497-526; Eng. 497 [no; it is based on the canonical gospels].

b6 *a) Klijn* A. F. J., Das Hebräer- und das Nazoräerevangelium; – *b)*
Howard George, The Gospel of the Ebionites: ➤ 782, ANRW 2,25,5
(1988) 3997-4033 / 4034-53.

b7 *Lucchesi* Enzo, 'Martyre' de Zacharie et Protévangile de Jacques: Muséon 101 (1988) 65-76.

b8 *Lührmann* Dieter, Die griechischen Fragmente des Mariaevangeliums POx
3525 und PRyl 463: NT 30 (1988) 321-338.

b9 *Cignelli* Lino, La Sacra Famiglia nella 'Storia di Giuseppe il Falegname':
➤ 13, FBERTETTO D., Virgo fidelis 1988, 175-202.

b10 *Manns* Frédéric, Le récit de la Dormition de Marie (Vat. grec 1982),
contribution à l'étude des origines de l'exégèse chrétienne: Marianum 50
(1988) 439-555.

к2.6 Acta apocrypha apostolorum.

b11 **Leloir** Louis, Écrits apocryphes sur les apôtres [Venise arm. T: CCApocr
3, 1986 ➤ 2,8117; 3,a301: RBijdragen 49 (1988) 97s (M. *Parmentier*: a
critical Armenian text would be beyond the power of any scholar or
team); LavalTP 44 (1988) 121-3 (P.-H. *Poirier*); RSPT 72 (1988) 627s
(G.-M. de *Durand*); RTLv 19 (1988) 227s (A. de *Halleux*).

b12 *a) Bovon* F., Les Actes de Philippe; – *b) Junod* E., *Kaestli* J., ...de Jean; –
c) Poupon G., ...de Pierre; ... – *d) Prieur* J.-M., ...d'André: ➤ 782,
ANRW 2,25,6 (1988) 4431-4527 / 4293-4362 / 4363-83 / 4384-4414.

b13 **Junod** E., *Kaestli* J.-D., Acta Johannis: CCApocr 1, 1983 ➤ 64,8746...
2,8118: RSNTU-A 13 (1988) 248-251 (F. *Weissengruber*).

b14 **Sirker-Wicklaus** Gerlinde, Untersuchungen zur Struktur, zur
theologischen Tendenz und zum kirchengeschichtlichen Hintergrund der
Acta Johannis: Diss. DSchäferdiek K. Bonn 1988. – RTLv 20,549.

b14* *Rordorf* Willy, Les Actes de Paul sur papyrus; problèmes liés aux
PMich inv. 1317 et 3788: ➤ 492, XVIII Papyrol 1 (1986/8) 453-460 + 2 pl.

b15 **Poirier** Paul-H., La version copte de la prédication et du martyre
de Thomas 1984 ➤ 65,8579; 2,8120: ROLZ 83 (1988) 47-51 (H.-M.
Schenke).

к2.7 Alia pseudepigrapha NT.

b16 **Bocciolini Palagi** Laura, Epistolario apocrifo di Seneca e S. Paolo 1985
➤ 2,8107: RVigChr 42 (1988) 194s (J. den *Boeft*).

b17 *Cracco Ruggini* Lellia, La lettera di Anna a Seneca nella Roma pagana e
cristiana del IV secolo: ➤ 570, AugR 28 (1988) 301-328.

b18 *Beylot* Robert, Bref aperçu des principaux textes éthiopiens dérivés des
Acta Pilati: LOrA 1 (Lv 1988) 181-195.

b19 *Bauckham* Richard J., The Apocalypse of Peter, an account of research:
➤ 782, ANRW 2,25,6 (1988) 4712-50.

b20 **Buchholz** Dennis D., Your eyes will be opened; a study of the Greek
(Ethiopic) Apocalypse of Peter [c. 140 A.D.; diss. Claremont]: SBL diss. 97.
Atlanta 1988, Scholars. ix-482 p. $20; pa. $13 [TDig 36,49].

b21 EJeay Madeleine, Les évangiles des quenouilles 1985 ➤ 3,a306: Speculum 63 (1988) 943-5 (Roberta L. *Krueger*).

к3 Qumran .1 *generalia*.

b21* *Carmignac* J., Qumran, TLa Sor W.: ➤ 801, ISBEnc³ 4 (1988) 13-18.

b22 *Davies* Philip R., The Qumran texts, a new study edition [projected: an 'English Lohse' with Hebrew on facing pages; but also fascicles of individual texts for classroom use, ᴱ*Vermes* G. *al.*]: ➤ 506 = JJS 39 (1988) 74-79.

b22* *Davies* Philip R., How not to do archaeology; the story of Qumran: BA 51 (1988) 203-7 [favors LAPERROUSAZ summary over de VAUX].

b23 *Dionisio* Francesco, A Qumran con gli Esseni: BbbOr 30 (1988) 3.34. 85-110; ill.

b24 *Eshel* Ḥanan, ⊕ Finds and documents from a cave at Ketef-Yeriḥo: Qadmoniot 21 (1988) 18-23; ill.

b25 *Fitzmyer* J.A., The Dead Sea Scrolls and the Bible; after forty years: America 157 (NY 1987) 300-303 [NTAbs 32,214].

b25* **Fujita** Neil S., A crack in the jar 1986 ➤ 2,8128; 3,a311: ᴿRÉJ 146 (1987) 428s (A. *Lemaire*); Vidyajyoti 52 (1988) 302s (P. M. *Meagher*).

b26 *García Martínez* F., Estudios Qumránicos 1975-1985; Panorama crítico (III) (IV): EstBíb [45 (1987) 125-206. 361-402] 46 (1988) 325-374. 527-548 ...

b27 **Knibb** M. A., The Qumran community: CamCW 2, 1987 ➤ 3,a314: ᴿBL (1988) 136 (J. *Gibson*); JStJud 19 (1988) 105s (F. *García Martínez*); RB 95 (1988) 580-4 (J. *Murphy-O'Connor*); ScripB 19 (1988s) 46 (J. E. *Rybolt*).

b28 *Paul* A., Qumran: ➤ 786, Catholicisme 12,55 (1988) 404-410.

b29 **Soggin** J. Alberto, I manoscritti del Mar Marto; present. *Moscati* S.: Archeologia 10. La Spezia 1987 [reprint of 1978, though called 2d edition], Club del Libro. 207 p.; ill. Lit. 14.000.

b30 *Stegemann* Hartmut, How to connect Dead Sea Scroll fragments: BR 4,1 (1988) 24-29. 43.

b31 **Vermes** Geza, The Dead Sea Scrolls in English³ʳᵉᵛ [¹1962 = ²1975] 1987 ➤ 3,a318: ᴿJStJud 19 (1988) 265s (F. *García Martínez*).

ᴋ3.4 *Qumran*, **Libri biblici** et pseudo-biblici; **commentarii.**

b32 *Cook* J., The Qumran (biblical scrolls) data base [i.e. dictionary on disk; the other scrolls are being encoded in Jerusalem]: JNWS 14 (1988) 27-40.

b32* *Duhaime* Jean, Le dualisme de Qumrân et la littérature de sagesse vétérotestamentaire: ÉglT 19 (1988) 401-422.

b33 *Fishbane* Michael, Use, authority and interpretation of Mikra at Qumran: ➤ 317, Mikra 1988, 339-377.

Lignée H., *al.*, Qumran and Jubilees 1988 ➤ a970ac.

b34 *a) Puech* Émile, Quelques aspects de la restauration du Rouleau des Hymnes (1QH); – *b) Newsom* Carol, The 'Psalms of Joshua' from Qumran Cave 4: ➤ 506 = JJS 39 (1988) 38-55 / 56-73; 2 phot.

Sanderson Judith E., An Exodus scroll from Qumran ... Samaritan tradition 1986 ➤ 2426.

b35 *a) Allison* Dale C.ᴶ, The silence of angels; reflections on the songs of the sabbath sacrifice; – *b) Baumgarten* Joseph M., The Qumran Sabbath Shirot and rabbinic Merkabah traditions; – *c) Segert* Stanislav, Observations on poetic structures in the Songs of the Sabbath Sacrifice: ➤ 22, Mém. CARMIGNAC J., RQum 13 (1988) 189-197 / 199-213 / 215-223.

b36 **Newsom** Carol, Songs of the sabbath sacrifice 1985 ➤ 1,9793 ... 3,a326: ᴿBAR-W 14,2 (1988) 8 (R. S. *Hendel*); Biblica 69 (1988) 138-146 (F. *García Martínez*); BZ 32 (1988) 143s (K. *Müller*); EstBíb 45 (1939)

527-545 (F. *Garcia Martinez*); JBL 107 (1988) 315s (J. A. *Fitzmyer*: ten copies of this important text).

b37 **Schuller** Eileen M., Non-canonical psalms from Qumran; a pseudepigraphic collection [diss. ᴰ*Strugnell* J.]: HarvSemSt 28, 1986 → 2,8145; 3,a328: ᴿCBQ 50 (1988) 335s (J. C. *VanderKam*); JBL 107 (1988) 748-750 (J. M. *Baumgarten*: only a fraction of the Qumran non-canonical psalms awaiting publication); JSS 33 (1988) 274s (R. P. *Gordon*).

b38 **Brooke** George J., Exegesis at Qumran; 4QFlorilegium in its Jewish context: JStOT Sup 29, 1985 → 1,9789 ... 3,a320: ᴿBZ 32 (1988) 123-5 (J. *Maier*); JBL 107 (1988) 130s (J. A. *Fitzmyer*); JStJud 19 (1988) 92-95 (J. *Lübbe*).

b39 *Fabry* H. J., *Dahmen* U., *Pešær, pittārôn*: → 815, TWAT 6,6s (1988) 810-6.

b40 *Fröhlich* Ida, Caractères formels des Pesharim de Qumran et la littérature apocalyptique: → 469, Wünschet 1986/8, 449-456.

b41 **Feltes** Heinz, Die Gattung des Hab-Kom. [Diss. Bochum 1984, ᴰ*Ruppert* L.]: ForBi 58, 1986 → 2,8137: ᴿColcT 58,4 (1988) 177-180 (J. W. *Roslon*).

b42 *Sacchi* Paolo, Esquisse du développement du messianisme juif à la lumière du texte qumranien 11 Q Melch: → 153, ZAW 100 Sup. (1988) 202-214.

b42* *Šarbit* Baruch, ❿ The *perušim* according to a Judean Desert scroll: BethM 34,117 (1988s) 141-8.

K3.5 *Rotulus Templi* – The Temple Scroll, *al.*

b43 **Bean** Philip B., A theoretical construct for the Temple of the Temple Scroll: diss. Univ. Oregon. Eugene c. 1987. [OIAc D88 gives microfilm order No. 1332867, though most AA (printout) numbers begin with the last two digits of the year].

b44 *a*) **Brooke** George J., The Temple Scroll and the archaeology of Qumran, 'Ain Feshkha and Masada; – *b*) *Callaway* Phillip R., The Temple Scroll and the canonization of Jewish law: → 22, Mém. CARMIGNAC J., RQum 13 (1988) 225-237 / 239-250. → 2922*a*.

b45 *Qimron* Elisha, *a*) Column 14 of the Temple scroll: IsrEJ 38 (1988) 44-46; pl. 11; – *b*) The holiness of the Holy Land in the light of a new document from Qumran: → 499, Holy Land 1986/8, 9-13.

b46 *a*) *Schiffman* Lawrence H., The laws of war in the Temple Scroll; – *b*) *Reeves* John C., The meaning of *moreh ṣedeq* in the light of 11QTorah: – *c*) *Wacholder* Ben Zion, Does Qumran record the death of the *Moreh*? The meaning of *he'aseph* in Damascus Covenant XIX,35, XX, 14: → 22, Mém. CARMIGNAC J., RQum 13 (1988) 299-311 / 287-298 / 323-330.

b47 *Sweeney* Marvin A., Midrashic perspective in the Torat ham-Melek of the Temple scroll [against *Hengel* M., *Charlesworth* J., *Mendels* D.]: Hebrew Studies 28 (Madison 1987) 51-56 [NTAbs 32,215].

b48 **Wise** Michael O., The Temple scroll, its composition, date, purpose and provenance; diss. ᴰ*Golb* N. Ch 1988. – OIAc D88.

b49 *Wise* Michael O., A new manuscript join in the 'Festival of wood offering' (Temple scroll XXIII): JNES 47 (1988) 113-121; 1 fig.

b50 *Woude* A. S. van der, Ein bisher unveröffentlichtes Fragment der Tempelrolle: → 22, Mém. CARMIGNAC J., RQum 13 (1988) 89-92; pl. IV.

---

b51 *Stegemann* Hartmut [*al.*], Zu Textbestand und Grundgedanken von 1QS III,13-IV,26: → 22, Mém. CARMIGNAC J., RQum 13 (1988) 95-131.

b52 **Baillet** Maurice, Qumran Grotte 4, III: DJD 7, 1982 ➤ 63,8662: ᴿRB 95 (1988) 404-411 (É. *Puech*).

b53 *Duhaime* Jean, The War Scroll from Qumran and the Greco-Roman tactical treatises: ➤ 22, Mém. CARMIGNAC J., RQum 13 (1988) 133-151.

b54 *Wolters* Al, *a*) The fifth cache of the Copper Scroll, 'the plastered cistern of Manos': ➤ 22, Mém. CARMIGNAC J., RQum 13 (1988) 167-176; – *b*) The last treasures of the Copper Scroll: JBL 107 (1988) 419-429.

K3.6   Qumran et NT.

b55 *Betz* O., The Temple scroll and the trial of Jesus: SWJT 30,3 (1987s) 5-8 [NTAbs 32,297].

b56 *Betz* Otto, Los escritos de Qumran y los evangelios [< BiKi 40 (1985) 54-64], ᵀᴱ*Giménez* Josep: SelT 27 (1988) 3-10.

b57 *a*) *Draper* J. A., The twelve apostles as foundation stones of the heavenly Jerusalem and the foundation of the Qumran community; – *b*) *Bauckham* R., The Book of Revelation as a Christian War Scroll: Neotestamentica 2,1 (1968) 41-63 / 17-40.

b58 *a*) *Fitzmyer* Joseph A., The Qumran Scrolls and the New Testament after forty years; – *b*) *Derrett* J. D. M., New creation; Qumran, Paul, the Church, and Jesus; – *c*) *Nebe* G.-Wilhelm, 7Q4 — Möglichkeit und Grenze einer Identifikation; – *d*) *Schwartz* Daniel R., On Quirinius [p. vi Quirinus], John the Baptist, the Benedictus, Melchizedek, Qumran and Ephesus: ➤ 22, Mém. CARMIGNAC J., RQum 13 (1988) 609-620 / 597-608 / 629-633 / 635-646.

b59 *Flusser* David, *a*) Qumran und die Zwölf [< ᴱ*Bleeker* C., Initiation 1965, 134-146]; – *b*) The social message from Qumran [< Journal of World History 2 (1968) 107-115]; – *c*) The Last Supper and the Essenes [< Immanuel 2 (1973) 23-27]; – *d*) The hubris of the Antichrist in a fragment from Qumran: ➤ 190, JudOrChr 1988, 173-192 / 193-201 / 202-6 / 207-213.

b60 *García Martínez* F., Les limites de la communauté; pureté et impureté à Qumrân et dans le NT: ➤ 85, ᶠKLIJN A., Text 1988, 111-122.

b61 *Rohrhirsch* Ferdinand, Das Qumranfragment 7Q5 [ALAND nicht eigentlich gegen O'CALLAGHAN]: NT 30 (1988) 97-99.

K3.8   Historia et doctrinae Qumran.

b62 *Bardtke* Hans †, Einige Erwägungen zum Problem 'Qumran und Karaismus' [c. 1975]: Henoch 10 (1988) 259-274; franç. 274s.

b63 **Burgmann** Hans, Vorgeschichte und Frühgeschichte der essenischen Gemeinde von Qumran und Damaskus: ArbNTJud 7, 1987 ➤ 3,a363 [title somewhat different in TR 85,164]: ᴿBL (1988) 130 (P. R. *Davies*: uncritical, unwelcome).

b64 **Callaway** Phillip R., The history of the Qumran community, an investigation: JPseud Sup 3. Sheffield 1988, Academic. 272 p. £30; sb. £22.50. 1-85075-107-2 [JPseud 2,127 adv.].

b65 *Collins* J. J., Prophecy and fulfillment in the Qumran scrolls: JEvTS 30 (1987) 267-278 [NTAbs 32,214].

b65* **Davies** Philip R., Behind the Essenes; history and ideology in the Dead Sea Scrolls 1987 ➤ 3,a367: ᴿJStJud 19 (1988) 244s (F. *García Martínez*: essais indépendants à l'origine; âpre).

b66 *Delcor* Mathias, [in Slovene] Remembrance celebration in Qumran; historization of feasts: BogVest 47 (1987) 305-311; Eng. 311.

b66* **Grasham** William W., The priestly synagogue; a re-examination of the cult at Qumran: diss. Aberdeen 1988. 611 p. British Library DX-82638. − DissA 49 (1988s) 1838-A (no summary).

b67 *Kister* Menahem, ✪ Marginalia Qumranica [11Q TS 56:3-4; 51:16-18; 4Q 183; 164; and Flor: Serek 8,24-27]: Tarbiz 57 (1987s) 315-325.

b68 *Laperoussaz* E.-M., Critères internes de datation des MSS de la mer Morte; 'ordonnances premières' et 'ordonnances dernières': ➤ 22, Mém. CARMIGNAC J., RQum 13 (1988) 453-464.

b69 *Minde* Hans-Jürgen van der, Die Absonderung der Frommen; die Qumrangemeinschaft als Heiligtum Gottes: BLtg 61 (1988) 190-7.

b70 *Poirier* P.H., Le salut dans la littérature qumrânienne: ➤ 809, SDB 11,62 (1988) 553-9 [559-573, pseudépigraphes AT; 576-584, JOSÈPHE].

b71 **Weinfeld** Moshe, The organizational pattern and the penal code of the Qumran sect; a comparison with guilds and religious associations of the Hellenistic-Roman period 1986 ➤ 2,8188; 3,a383: ᴿBL (1988) 146 (P. *Davies*); JBL 107 (1988) 530s (Carol *Newsom*); Orientalia 57 (1988) 99-101 (J. *Maier*); RB 95 (1988) 627s (J. *Murphy-O'Connor*); VT 38 (1988) 126s (W.*Horbury*).

к4.1 **Esseni, Zelotae.**

Allegro John M., Physician, heal thyself [Essene theology] 1985 ➤ 5174.

b72 **Beall** Todd S., JOSEPHUS' description of the Essenes illustrated by the Dead Sea Scrolls: SNTS Mg 58. C 1988, Univ. vii-200 p. $37.50. 0-521-34524-3.

b73 ᵀᴱ**Chiesa** Bruno, *Lockwood* Wilfrid, Yaʿqūb al-QIRQISĀNĪ on Jewish sects and Christianity: JudUmw 10, 1984 ➤ 65,8793 ... 3,a384: ᴿRiv-StoLR 24 (1988) 168s (G. *Tamani*).

b73* *Donaldson* T.L., Zealot: ➤ 801, ISBEnc³ 4 (1988) 1175-9.

b74 *García Martínez* F., Essénisme Qumrânien; origines, caractéristiques, héritage [contre origine hasidéenne]: ➤ 474, Correnti 1984/7, 37-57.

b75 **Herman** Dov, Early Hasidim; the Hasidim and their school of thought in the Second Temple, Mishnaic and Talmud periods: diss. Bar-Ilan, ᴰ*Sperber* B. − RTLv 20,542 sans date.

b76 **Laperrousaz** Ernest-M., Gli Esseni secondo la loro testimonianza diretta [1982 ➤ 63,8716], ᵀ*Tosatti* Teodora: LoB 3.8. Brescia 1988, Queriniana. 115 p. Lit. 12.000. 88-399-1599-0.

b77 *Marcovich* Miroslav, The Essenes as Christians [ineditum]: ➤ 228, Studies 1988, 144-155.

b78 *Rofé* Alexander, ✪ The beginnings of sects in postexilic Judaism: CHist-EI 49 (1988) 13-22; Eng. 190.

b79 ᴱ**Vermes** Geza, *Goodman* Martin D., The Essenes according to the classical sources: Oxford Centre Textbooks 1. Sheffield c.1988, Academic. xi-103 p. £16.50.

b80 ᵀᴱ**Williams** Frank, The Panarion of EPIPHANIUS of Salamis, I (sects 1-46): NHS 35. Leiden 1987, Brill. xxvii-359 p. *f*180. 90-04-07926-2 [Bijdragen 49,116].

к4.3 **Samaritani.**

b80* *Anderson* R.T., Samaritans: ➤ 801, ISBEnc³ 4 (1988) 303-8 (295-3, Samaria, *Van Selms* A., *LaSor* W.).

b81 *Bóid* Ruairidh (*Saraf* M. N.),   Use, authority and exegesis of Mikra in the Samaritan tradition: ➤ 317, Mikra 1988, 505-633.
b82 **Crown** Alan D.,   Bibliography of the Samaritans 1984 ➤ 65,806 ... 3,a390: ᴿAbrNahr 26 (1988) 115-121 (Sylvia *Powels*; adds long list of misprints 'in no way affecting the value of the book'); BO 45 (1988) 653s (G. F. *Hasel* adds a dozen titles).
b83 ᴱ**Crown** A. D.,   The Samaritans. c. 1987. – ᴿBAngIsr 8 (1988s) 64s (Joan E. *Taylor*).
b85 **Egger** Rita,   JOSEPHUS Flavius und die Samaritaner: NTOrbAnt 4, 1986 ➤ 2,8195; 3,a392:   ᴿCBQ 50 (1988) 715 (D. E. *Aune*); JBL 107 (1988) 768-772 (R. *Pummer*: only in part right in absolving Josephus of hostility); RB 95 (1988) 288-294 (É. *Nodet*).
b86 *Macuch* Rudolf,   Der gegenwärtige Stand der Samaritanerforschung und ihre Aufgaben: ZDMG 138 (1988) *17-*25.
b87 a) *Noja* S.,   Gli ultimi dieci anni di studi sui Samaritani; – b) *Chiesa* B.,   Il Giudaismo caraita: ➤ 474, Correnti 1984/7, 139-149 / 151-173.
b88 **Pummer** R.,   The Samaritans: IconRel 23/5, 1987 ➤ 3,a399; *f*72:   ᴿNRT 110 (1988) 615 (X. *Jacques*).
b89 **Rabello** Alfredo M.,   Giustiniano, Ebrei e Samaritani; alla luce delle fonti storico-letterarie [I; II sarà giuridiche]: Monografie del Vocabolario di Giustiniano I.   Mi 1987, Giuffrè.   ix-491 p. Lit. 40.000. – ᴿJStJud 19 (1988) 254-6 (G. *Stemberger*).
b90 a) *Robert* Philippe de,   La naissance des études samaritaines en Europe aux XVIᵉ et XVIIᵉ siècles; – b) *Delcor* Mathias,   La correspondance des savants européens, en quête de manuscrits, avec les Samaritains du XVIᵉ au XIXᵉ siècle: ➤ 497, Samarit. 1985/8, 15-26 / 27-43.

κ4.5   *Ṣadoqitae, Qaraitae* – **Cairo Genizah; Zadokites, Karaites.**

b91 **Boyce** John M.,   The poetry of the Damascus Document: diss. ᴰ*Gibson* J. E 1988. 421 p. – RTLv 20,542.
b92 *Chiesa* Bruno,   A new fragment of al-QIRQISĀNĪ's *Kitāb al-Riyāḍ*:   JQR 78 (1987s) 175-185.
b93 a) *Chiesa* Bruno,   A note on early Karaite historiography; – b) *Chazan* Robert,   Representation of events in the Middle Ages: HistTheor Beih. 27 (1988) 56-65 / 40-55.
b94 **Friedman** Mordechai A.,   Jewish marriage in Palestine, a Cairo Geniza study I-II, 1980s ➤ 62,9473 ... 3,a404:   ᴿRB 95 (1988) 141s (E. *Puech*).
b95 **Goitein** S. D.,   The individual; portrait of a Mediterranean personality of the High Middle Ages as reflected in the Cairo Geniza: A Mediterranean Society 5.   Berkeley 1988, Univ. California.   xxxii-658 p.; map. $55. 0-520-05647-7 [BO 45,758].
b96 a) *Greenfield* Jonas C.,   The words of Levi son of Jacob in Damascus Document IV, 15-19; – b) *Davies* Philip R.,   [DamDoc VI,8-11] The Teacher of Righteousness and the 'end of days': ➤ 22, Mém. CARMIGNAC J., RQum 13 (1988) 319-322 / 313-7.
b97 *Kasher* Hana,   ❶ A Karaite (?) metaphysical work [proofs for the existence of God; 16th c. ms.]: Tarbiz 57 (1987s) 257-269; Eng. IV.
b98 **Kodsi** Mourad El-   The Karaite Jews of Egypt, 1882-1986.   Lyons NY 1987, Wilprint.   xiii-359. – ᴿJQR 79 (1988s) 81s (L. *Nemoy*).
b99 ᶠNEMOY Leon,   Studies in Judaica, Karaitica and Islamica 1982 ➤ 64,84: ᴿBO 45 (1988) 405 (J. P. M. van der *Ploeg*).

b100 *Nemoy* Leon, Israel AL-MAGHRIBĪ's Karaite Creed: Henoch 10 (1988) 335; franç. 341; texte arabe 354-342 (sic) [355-376, *Chiesa* Bruno, Due note di letteratura caraita].

b101 *Paul* A., Quaraïtes [sic]: → 786, Catholicisme 12,55 (1988) 340s.

b102 *Schenker* Adrian, Karäer: → 813, TRE 17 (1988) 625-8.

b103 *Zeldes* Nadia, ❹ A Geniza letter pertaining to the history of Sicilian Jewry in the Muslim period [c. 1040 C.E.] — a reevaluation: Zion 53 (1988) 57-64; Eng. iii: interprets as showing that Jews were being there/then persecuted, for which there is no other evidence.

K5 Judaismus prior vel totus.

b104 *Bammel* Ernst, Das Judentum als eine Religion Ägyptens: → 16, FBÖHLING A., Religion 1988, 1-10.

b105 *Bar Ilan* Meir, ❹ Magic seals on the body among Jews in the first centuries C.E.: Tarbiz 57 (1987s) 37-50; Eng. II.

b106 *Barth* Lewis M., Jochanan BEN ZAKKAJ, T*Wolter* Mariann: → 813, TRE 17 (1987) 89-91.

b107 **Boxel** Piet van, Sjabbatskind; vroeg-joodse tradities over leven en dood. Hilversum 1987, Gooi & S. 96 p. *f* 19,50. 90-304-0383-7. – RBijdragen 49 (1988) 446s (M. *Poorthuis*).

b108 *Boyarin* Daniel, Bilingualism and meaning in rabbinic literature; an example [Mekhilta Shirta 3]: → 42*, EHRMAN A. mem., Fucus 1988, 141-152.

b109 **Cohen** Shaye J.D., From the Maccabees to the Mishnah 1987 → 3,a413: RCBQ 50 (1988) 291s (D. J. *Harrington*); RExp 85 (1988) 561s (D. E. *Garland*).

b110 **Cohn-Sherbok** D., The Jewish heritage. Ox 1988, Blackwell. xiii-204 p. £25; pa. £8. 0-631-15413-2; 4-0 [BL 89,131, A. P. *Hayman*: out-of-date; theology in the guise of history, as exposed by GARBINI]. – RVT 38 (1988) 508 (W. *Horbury*).

b111 *a) Dexinger* Ferdinand, Judentum; – *b) Stemberger* Günter, Judaistik: → 813, TRE 17 (1988) 331-377 / 290-6.

Fishbane Michael A., Judaism; revelation and traditions 1987 → b281.

b113 EGarber Zev, Methodology in the academic teaching of Judaism 1986 → 3,342: RJEcuSt 25 (1988) 290s (W. H. *Becker*).

b114 *Hammer* R., A rabbinic response to the Bar Kochba era; the Sifre to Ha-azinu: PAAR 52 (1985) 37-53 [< JStJud 19 (1988) 291].

b115 **Katunarich** Sergio M., L'ebraismo da allora a oggi 1986 → 2,8226; 3,a424: RJEcuSt 25 (1988) 463s (M. P. *Roncaglia*).

b116 *Kooyman* A. C., Proselytisme in de tijd voor Bar Kochba: Ter Herkenning 15,4 (1987) 217-224 [< GerefTTs 88,62].

b117 EKraft Robert A., *Nickelsburg* G. W. E., Early Judaism and its modern interpreters 1986 → 2,255; 3,a425: RCBQ 51 (1989) 392-4 (Naomi *Janowitz*: tit. pp. analyses); Gregorianum 69 (1988) 342-5 (G. L. *Prato*); Interpretation 42 (1988) 197s (J. R. *Spencer*).

b118 *Lauer* S., Biblical wisdom in rabbinic garb [four parables of Pes. r. Kahana]: Christian Jewish Relations 20,1 (L 1987) 23-30 [NTAbs 32,220].

b119 **Lenhardt** Pierre, *Osten-Sacken* Peter von der, Rabbi AKIVA; Texte und Interpretationen zum rabbinischen Judentum und NT: ArbNtTheol 1. B 1987, Inst. Kirche und Judentum. 403 p. [JBL 107,788]. – RKIsr 3 (1988) 98s (Julie *Kirchberg*).

b120 *Lichtenberger* Hermann, Literatur zum antiken Judentum: VerkF 33,1 (1988) 2-19.

b121 **Limburg** J., Judaism, an introduction for Christians [Was jeder vom Judentum wissen muss³ 1985], ᵀadapted. Minneapolis 1987, Augsburg. 285 p. $6 pa. 0-8066-2263-6 [NTAbs 32,393].

b121* *Lurja* B. Z., ❶ And Apostomus burned the Torah [at TRLWSH, Luz (Bethel) rather than Talluza]: BethM 32 (1986s) 293-5 [< OTAbs 11,189].

b122 **Maccoby** Hyam, Early Rabbinic writings: CamCW 3 [not 2 as pre-title page]. C 1988, Univ. xxiv-245 p. 0-521-24248-7; pa. 8553-4. [RelStR 15, 273, M. S. *Jaffee*].

b123 *Milikowsky* Chaim, The status quaestionis of research in rabbinic literature [*Schäfer* P. ...]: JJS [37 (1986) 139-152] 39 (1988) 201-211.

b124 **Navarro Peiro** María A., Abot de Rabbi Natán 1987 ➤ 3,a432. – ᴿBibFe 14 (1988) 482 (A. *Salas*); FgNT 1 (1988) 219s (M. *Pérez*).

b125 **Neher** André, Chiavi per l'ebraismo; intr. *Federici* Tommaso: Radici 9. Genova 1988, Marietti. xxiv-125 p. 88-211-8360-2.

b126 **Neusner** Jacob, First principles of systemic analysis; the case of Judaism within the history of religion: Studies in Judaism. Lanham MD 1987, UPA. xiv-158 p. $17.50. 0-8191-6598-0 [NTAbs 32, 394].

b127 **Neusner** Jacob, From description to conviction; essays on the history and theology of Judaism: BrownJudSt 86. Atlanta 1987, Scholars. xviii-141 p. $30. 1-55540-118-X [NTAbs 32,394].

b128 **Neusner** Jacob, From Testament to Torah; an introduction to Judaism in its formative age. ENJ 1988, Prentice-Hall. xviii-187 p.; ill. 0-13-331620-3 [NTAbs 32,269].

b129 **Neusner** Jacob, The making of the mind of Judaism; the formative age: BrownJudSt 133. Atlanta 1987, Scholars. xii-172 p. $23. 1-55540-197-X [NTAbs 32,270].

b130 **Neusner** Jacob, The religious study of Judaism; description, analysis and interpretation I; II. The centrality of context: Studies in Judaism 1986 ➤ 2,8242; 3,a439: ᴿRelStR 14 (1988) 79 (Z. *Garber*).

b131 **Neusner** J., Scriptures of the oral Torah; sanctification and salvation in the sacred books of Judaism; anthology. SF 1987, Harper & R. 396 p. $25 [TDig 36,82].

b132 **Neusner** Jacob, The systemic analysis of Judaism: BrownJudSt 137. Atlanta 1988, Scholars. xii-131 p. $30. 1-55540-204-6 [NTAbs 32,395].

b133 **Neusner** Jacob, Vanquished nation, broken spirit; the virtues of the heart in formative Judaism 1987 ➤ 3,a442: ᴿBL (1988) 142 (A. *Hayman*); Month 249 (1988) 688s (N. *King*).

b134 *Neusner* J., Religiöse känslor under den formativa perioden av judendomens historia [summary of Vanquished Nation 1986]: NorJ 7 (1986) 47-52 [< JStJud 19,152].

b135 *Neusner* Jacob, Sage, story, and history; the medium and the message in the Fathers according to Rabbi Nathan: HebSt 28 (Madison WI 1987) 79-111 [NTAbs 32, 221].

b136 *Neusner* J., From [George F.] MOORE to URBACH and SANDERS [... they were all fundamentalists and felt sure that talmudic literature in itself could yield an accurate picture of early Judaism]; fifty years of 'Judaism'; the end of the line for a depleted category: RelStT 6,3 (1986) 7-26.

b137 *Neusner* Jacob, When intellectual paradigms shift; does the end of the old mark the beginning of the new?: HistTheor 27 (1988) 241-266.

b138 **Newby** Gordon D., A history of the Jews of Arabia; from ancient times to their eclipse under Islam: Studies in Comparative Religion. Columbia 1988, Univ. S. Carolina. xii-177 p. $35 [JBL 107,789].

b139 **Niebuhr** K.-W., Gesetz und Paränese; katechismusartige Weisungsreihen in der frühjüdischen Literatur [Diss. Halle 1986, ᴰ*Holtz* T.]: WUNT 2/28. Tü 1987, Mohr. ix-275 p. DM 98. 3-16-145232-1 [NTAbs 32,272]. – ᴿArTGran 51 (1988) 297s (A. *Segovia*).

b140 *Novak* David, The role of dogma in Judaism: TTod 45 (1988s) 49-61.

b141 **Pesce** Mauro, *al.*, L'Ebraismo: Quad. S. Carlo 4. Modena 1987, Mucchi. 125 p. Lit. 8000. P. 31-48, *Sacchi* Paolo, L'apocalittica giudaica.

b142 *Pesce* Mauro, L'importanza della tradizione rabbinica; l'opera di Jacob NEUSNER: RClerIt 69 (1988) 537-541.

b143 **Petuchowski** J.J., 'Zoals onze meesters leerden ...'; rabbijnse vertellingen [1982 → 65,8681],ᵀ. Baarn 1986 Ten Have. 128 p. ƒ17,50. 90-259-4307-1 [NedTTs 42,161].

b144 **Reeg** G., Die Geschichte von den zehn Märtyrern 1985 → 1,9892 ... 3,a447: ᴿNedTTs 42 (1988) 160s (P. W. van der *Horst*).

b145 *Rosenfeld* Ben-Zion, ❶ The crisis of the patriarchate in Eretz Israel in the fourth century [C.E.]: Zion 53 (1988) 239-257; Eng. ix.

b146 **Roth** Joel, The halakhic process 1986 → 2,8252; 3,a448: JQR 78 (1987s) 299-303 (G. J. *Blidstein*).

b147 *Sacchi* Paolo, Storicizzazione e rivelazione alle origini del giudaismo [*Kappler* C. 1987]: RivStoLR 24 (1988) 68-77.

b148 ᴱ**Safrai** Shmuel (*Tomson* Peter J.), The literature of the sages, I. Oral tora, halakha, Mishna, Tosefta, Talmud, external tractates: Compendium Rerum Iudaicarum ad NT 3/1, 1987 → 3,a449: ᴿCiuD 201 (1988) 685s (J. *Gutiérrez*); ÉTRel 63 (1988) 286s (Jeanne-Marie *Léonard*); JBL 107 (1988) 565-7 (J. *Neusner*); JStJud 19 (1988) 117-123 (G. *Stemberger*); Judaica 44 (1988) 48-50 (D. *Flusser*); NorTTs 89 (1988) 273s (H. M. *Barstad*); SBFLA 38 (1988) 520-4 (F. *Manns*); Streven 55 (1987s) 569s (P. *Beentjes*).

b149 **Scholem** G., Concetti fondamentali dell'ebraismo [1970] 1986 → 2,8255; Lit. 24.000: ᴿProtestantesimo 43 (1988) 45s (G. *Vetrano*).

b150 *Schwartz* Joshua, On priests and Jericho in the Second Temple period: JQR 79 (1988s) 21-48.

b151 *Schwartz* Seth, Judaism: → 444, Mediterranean 2 (1988) 1027-1045.

b152 **Segal** Alan F., The other Judaisms of late antiquity: BrownJudSt 127. Atlanta 1987, Scholars. xvii-213 p. 1-555-40178-3.

b153 **Sigal** Phillip, Judaism, the evolution of a faith [Judentum 1986 → 2,8256], ²ʳᵉᵛ *Sigal* Lillian. GR 1988, Eerdmans. xxii-326 p. 0-8028-0345-8.

b154 *Stawsky* D. B. R., Prophecy; crisis and change at end of Second Temple period: Sidic 20,3 (R 1987) 13-20 [NTAbs 32,223].

b155 *a) Stone* Michael E., The parabolic use of natural order in Judaism of the Second Temple age; – *b) Smart* Ninian, The importance of diasporas: → 149, ᶠWERBLOWSKY R., Gilgul 1987, 298-308 / 288-297.

b156 *Townsend* J.T., How can late rabbinic texts inform biblical and early Christian studies?: Shofar 6,1 (W. Lafayette IN 1987) 26-32 [NTAbs 32,223].

b157 **Tyloch** Witold, ❷ Judaizm. Wsz 1987, KAW. 345 p. – ᴿPrzOr (1988,1) 73-75 (P. *Muchowski*).

b158 *Weinberger* Theodore, Introduction to Judaism: Paradigms 4 (1988s) 129-133.

b159 *Yassif* Eli,   Traces of folk traditions of the second temple period in rabbinic literature: JJS 39 (1988) 212-233.

K6 **Mišna,** *tosepta; Tannaim.*

b160 *Bokser* Baruch M.,   Ritualizing the Seder: JAAR 56 (1988) 443-471.

b161 **Bunte** Wolfgang,   Seder Toharot 2, Traktat Ohalot-Zelte: Die Mischna 6. B 1988, de Gruyter.   ix-471 p. DM 298.   3-11-009808-3 [BL 89,131, P. S. *Alexander*].

b162 **Eilberg-Schwartz** Howard,   The human will in Judaism; the Mishnah's philosophy of intention: BrownJudSt 103, 1986 ➤ 2,8266; 3,6796*: ᴿJAAR 56 (1988) 152s (R. *Goldenberg*); JJS 39 (1988) 279-281 (L. *Jacobs*); JTS 39 (1988) 192-4 (D. M. *Lewis*).

b163 **Flesher** Paul,   Oxen, women, or citizens? Slaves in the system of the Mishnah: diss. Brown. Providence 1988. – RelStR 15,194.

b164 **Goldberg** Abraham, ❿ The Mishna treatise Eruvin. J 1986, Hebrew Univ. 99 + 322-xviii p. – ᴿJStJud 19 (1988) 112-5 (Margarete *Schlüter*).

b164* **Hagg** Gregory D.,   The relationship between the New Testament and Tannaitic [Mishnah] Judaism: diss. ᴰ*Gordon* C. NYU 1988. 346 p. 88-12631. – DissA 49 (1988s) 1176-A.

b165 **Halivni** David W.,   Midrash, mishnah, and gemara; the Jewish predilection for justified law 1986 ➤ 2,8269; 3,a456:   ᴿJudaism 37 (1988) 244-7 (L. *Jacobs*).

b166 *Kasher* Rimon,   The interpretation of Scripture in rabbinic literature: ➤ 317, Mikra 1988, 547-594.

b167 **Manns** Frédéric,   Pour lire la Mishna: SBF Anal. 21, 1984 ➤ 65,8690 ... 2,8271:   ᴿNRT 110 (1988) 765s (Y. *Simoens*).

b168 **Manns** Frédéric,   Leggere la Mishnah [SBF Anal 1984], ᵀ*Busi* G.: StBPaid 78, 1987 ➤ 3,a460; Lit. 22.000:   ᴿHenoch 10 (1988) 408s (P. *Capelli*: non menziona 'la scuola americana'); RivB 36 (1988) 275-7 (M. *Perani*).

b169 *Martola* N.,   Litterära former i Mishna: NorJ 7 (1986) 106-148 ➤ 3, a462: Utterances (some anonymous); Narratives (1. 'Precedence'; 2. Ordinances; 3. First person narratives; 4. Lists; 5. Illustrations, proofs); Interpretation of Scripture (1. Midrash; 2. Proof) [< JStJud 19 (1988) 153].

b170 **Neusner** Jacob,   Judaism, the evidence of the Mishnah²ʳᵉᵛ [but p. xix says 2d printing]: BrownJudSt 129. Atlanta 1988, Scholars. xxvii-497 p. 1-55540-181-3.

b171 **Neusner** J.,   The Mishnah, a new translation [showing *how* the Mishnah text got into its present form, better than Dᴀɴʙʏ's more literary translation]. NHv 1988, Yale Univ. xlv-1162 p. $55. 0-300-03065-7 [BL 89,141, A. P. *Hayman*].

b172 **Neusner** J.,   The Mishnah before 70 [= abridged Mishnaic Law of Purities 1974-7]: BrownJudSt 51. Atlanta 1987, Scholars. xiv-290 p. $40; sb. $27. 1-55540-106-6. – ᴿBL (1988) 141 (A. *Hayman*).

b173 **Neusner** Jacob,   Oral tradition in Judaism; the case of the Mishnah: Lord Studies in Oral Tradition 1. NY 1987, Garland. xv-167 p. $25. 0-8240-7849-7 [NTAbs 32,270].

b174 **Neusner** Jacob,   Scriptures of the oral torah [selections from Midrash and Talmud]; sanctification and salvation in the sacred books of Judaism. SF 1987, Harper & R. 896 p. $25 [Paradigms 5/1, 68s, J. W. *Watts*).

b175 **Rengstorf** K. H.,   Die Tosefta, Seder I. Zeraim 1983 ➤ 64,8905 ... 2,8278: ᴿOLZ 83 (1988) 40-42 (P. *Schäfer*).

b175* **Rengstorf** K. H., *Rost* L.,   Die Mischna, VI. Seder, Toharot; 2. Traktat, Ohalot-Zelte. B 1988, de Gruyter. ix-471 p. – ᴿArTGran 51 (1988) 394s (A. *Torres*).

b176 *Vivian* A.,   La crisi del sacerdozio aaronita [perdendo influsso al 'partito laico' tracciato in Heb e QumranRTempio] e l'origine della Mishna: ➤ 474, Correnti 1984/7, 105-120.

b177 **Wegner** Judith R.,   Chattel or person? The status of women in the Mishnah. NY 1988, Oxford-UP. xii-267 p. 0-19-505169-0.

к6.5   Talmud; midraš.

b179 **Aminoah** Noah, ❻ The redaction of the tractate Betza, Rosh-Hashana and Ta'anith in the Babilonian [sic] Talmud; compilation, redaction, textual readings, parallel sugyot. TA 1986, Univ. iv-352 p. – ᴿJJS 39 (1988) 124-6 (Y. *Elman*: continues and defends his 1979 volume).

b180 ᴱ**Bader** Gershom, The encyclopedia of Talmudic sages, ᵀ*Katz* Solomon. Northvale NJ 1988, Aronson. xii-876 p. $50 [TDig 35,340].

b181 *Banon* David, À la découverte du Talmud [*Strack-Stemberger* 1986]: RTPhil 120 (1988) 339-346.

b182 Bava Metzia I & II: Otzar mefarshei hatalmud [Bavli]. J 1983, Institute of Talmudic Research. 426 + 12 p.; 481 + 17 p. $15. – ᴿBO 45 (1988) 402-4 (J. *Neusner*: voluminous on separate phrases, but no continuity).

b183 **Chernick** Michael L. ❻ L*ᵉ-ḥeqer ha-middot 'Kᵉlal u-Pᵉraṭ we-kᵉlal' we 'Ribbui we-Meʽut'* ... Hermeneutical Studies in Talmudic and Midrashic literatures. TA 1984, Habermann. 175 p. – ᴿJQR 78 (1987s) 296-8 (H. W. *Basser*).

b184 **Freeman** Gordon M., The heavenly kingdom; aspects of political thought in the Talmud and Midrash 1986 ➤ 2,8285: ᴿCurrTM 15 (1988) 456 (H. G. *Perelmuter*); JAAR 56 (1988) 156s (A. J. *Saldarini*).

b185 *Friedman* Shamma, Literary development and historicity in the aggadic narrative of the Babylonian Talmud; a study based upon B. M. 83b-86a: ➤ 3,62, ᶠGratz College 1987 ...

b185* **Golinkin** David R., ❻ Rosh Hashanah: chapter IV of the Babylonian Talmud (part 2), a critical edition and commentary: diss. Jewish Theol. Sem. NY 1988. 487 p. 88-09459. – DissA 49 (1988s) 1175s-A.

b186 *Hobbel* A. J., Hva er midrasj?: NorJ 7 (1986) 57-70 [< JStJud 19,152].

b187 *Kraemer* David, Composition and meaning in the Bavli: Prooftexts 8 (1988) 271-291.

b188 **Melamed** E. Z., ❻ Halachic Midrashim of the Tannaim in the Babylonian Talmud. J 1988, Magnes. 614 p. 965-223-681-0.

b189 **Morag** S., Vocalised Talmudic manuscripts in the Cambridge Genizah collections, I. Taylor-Schechter Old Series: Genizah Series 4. C 1988, Univ. xii-56 p.; 8 pl. £30. 0-521-26863-X [BL 89, 151, P. S. *Alexander*].

b190 **Neusner** Jacob, The Bavli and its sources; the question of tradition in the case of Tractate Sukkah: BrownJudSt 85, 1987 ➤ 3,a494: ᴿBL (1988) 139 (P. *Alexander*).

b191 **Neusner** Jacob, Judaism, the classic statement ... Bavli, 1986 ➤ 2,8295: ᴿJAAR 56 (1988) 346s (J. *Zwelling*).

b192 **Neusner** Jacob, Judaism in society; the evidence of the Yerushalmi. Ch 1983, Univ. xxiv-270 p. – ᴿJQR 79 (1988s) 67-70 (E. A. *Goldman*).

b193 **Neusner** Jacob, What is midrash? 1987 ➤ 3,a500; 0-8006-0472-5: ᴿBibTB 18 (1988) 118 (J. I. *Hunt*); EstBíb 46 (1988) 549-551 (J. *Trebolle*).

b194 **Neusner** Jacob, Why no Gospels in Talmudic Judaism?: Brown JudSt 135. Atlanta 1988, Scholars. iii-85 p. 1-155-40198-8; pa. 9-6.

b195 **Neusner** Jacob, The wonder-working lawyers of Talmudic Babylonia; the theory and practice of Judaism in its formative age [from his History of the Jews in Babylonia 2-5, 1965-70]: Studies in Judaism. Lanham MD 1987, UPA. x-361 p. $28.50; pa. $16.75 [TDig 36,72].

b196 *Neusner* J., Toward a theory of comparison; the case of comparative midrash: Religion 16 (1986) 269-303 [< JStJud 19,154].

b196* *Neusner* Jacob, Talmud: → 801, ISBEnc³ 4 (1988) 717-724 [727-733, Targum, *Young* B. H.].

b197 *a) Neusner* Jacob, Judaic uses of history in Talmudic times; – b) *Jacobs* Louis, Historical thinking in the post-talmudic Halakah: → 321, HistTheor Beih, 27 (1988) 13-39 / 66-77.

b198 **Pacifici** Riccardo, Midrashim 1986 → 3,a503: ᴿStPatav 35 (1988) 197s (Teresa *Salzano*).

b199 Pe'ah: Talmud Yerušalmi. J 1987, Milta. 240 p.

b200 ᴱ**Rosenthal** E.S., Yerushalmi Neziqin... Escorial ms.; intr. *Liebermann* Saul 1983 → 64,8930: ᴿRelStR 14 (1988) 80 (A. J. *Avery-Peck*).

b201 *Rosenthal* E. S., *zal*, **Ⓗ** The history of the text and problems of redaction in the study of the Babylonian Talmud: Tarbiz 57 (1987s) 1-36; Eng. Is.

b202 ᵀ**Salzer** Israël, Le Talmud, traité Moed Katan: Les Dix Paroles. Lagrasse 1988, Verdier. 219 p. 2-86432-079-7.

b203 *Segal* Eliezer, Law as allegory? An unnoticed literary device in talmudic narratives: Prooftexts 8 (1988) 245-256.

b204 *Slomovic* E., Patterns of midrashic impact on the rabbinic midrashic tale: JStJud 19 (1988) 61-90.

b205 **Steinsaltz** Adin, Introduction au Talmud, ᵀ*Hanson* Nelly: Présence du Judaïsme. ... 1987, Michel. 326 p. F 140. – ᴿÉtudes 368 (1988) 858 (Dominique *Bourel*).

b206 *Stemberger* Günter, Midrasch in Babylonien, am Beispiel von Sota 9b-14a: Henoch 10 (1988) 183-202; franç. 202s.

b207 **Strack** H., *Stemberger* G., Introduction au Talmud et au Midras, ᵀᴱ*Hayoun* M. R. 1986 → 2,8306; 3,a509: ᴿComSev 21 (1988) 101 (M. de *Burgos*).

b208 **Tilly** Heinz-Peter, Moed Qatan – Halbfeiertage: Übersetzung des Talmud Yerushalmi 2/12. Tü 1988, Mohr. xvi-136 p. 3-16-745069-X.

b209 **Wewers** G. A., ᵀYerushalmi 2/11 Hagiga; 4/5s. Makkot, Shevuot 1983 → 65,8729: ᴿOLZ 83 (1988) 422-4 (L. *Wächter*).

b210 **Wewers** G. A. †, Pea-Ackerecke: Übers. TYer 1/2, 1986 → 2,8307; 3,a511: ᴿBL (1988) 144 (P. S. *Alexander*).

b211 **Wewers** Gerd A., Terumot-Priesterhebe: Übersetzung des Talmud Yerushalmi 1/2. Tü 1986, Mohr. xi-240 p. DM 122. 3-16-144987-8. – ᴿGregorianum 69 (1988) 765s (G. L. *Prato*).

K7.1 Judaismus mediaevalis, generalia.

b212 **Biale** David, Power and powerlessness in Jewish history 1986 → 3,a516: ᴿJudaism 37 (1988) 242-4 (M. B. *Schwartz*).

b213 **Bialik** H. N., *Rawnitzky* Y. H., Sefer ha-Aggadah [1910], selections ᵀ*Pearl* Chaim. TA 1988, Dvir. 302 p. š 32. – ᴿDor 17 (1988s) 260s (S. *Liptzin*: already surpassed in English by L. GINZBERG 1909-38, but this single volume of Jewish anecdotes meets a need).

b214 ^E**Brinner** W. M., *Ricks* S. D., Studies in Islamic and Jewish traditions 1982/6 → 3,523: ^RJTS 39 (1988) 219-223 (G. *Khan*).

b215 **Colafemmina** Cesare, Nozze nella Oria ebraica del secolo IX. Oria 1988, Comune. 69 p.

b216 **Grossman** Abraham, **O** The Babylonian exilarchate in the Geonic period: Jewish Historical Sources 1. J 1984, Shazar Center. 145 p. [RelStR 15, 82, B. M. *Bokser*].

b216* *Grossman* Avraham, **O** The relationship between the social structure and spiritual activity of Jewish communities in the geonic period: Zion 53 (1988) 259-272; Eng. ix.

b217 ^E**Iggers** W., Die Juden in Böhmen und Mähren; ein historisches Lesebuch. Mü 1986, Beck. 392 p. – ^RHenoch 10 (1988) 410 (J. *Maier*).

b217* *Kellner* Menachem, The conception of the Torah as a deductive science in medieval Jewish thought: RÉJ 146 (1987) 265-279.

b218 ^{TE}**Loewe** Raphael, The Rylands Haggadah [14th cent.]; a medieval Sephardi masterpiece in facsimile. L 1988, Thames & H. 76 p.; 114 full colour facsimiles. £48. 0-500-23519-8 [BL 89, 143, N. de *Lange*: monument of erudition and good taste].

b219 *Perez* M., 'Substitution' of one word for another as an exegetical method used by medieval scholars: → 43, ^FELITZUR Y., II (1986) 207-228.

b220 **Schwartz** Howard, Elijah's violin and other Jewish folktales collected and retold: Folklore Library. Hw 1987, Penguin. 249 p. 0-14-059502-3.

b221 *Schwarzfuchs* Simon, Rabbinate: → 792, DMA 10 (1988) 242-4.

b222 *a*) *Touitou* Elazar, Courants et contre-courants dans l'exégèse biblique juive en France au Moyen-Âge; – *b*) *Banitt* Menahem, Exegesis or metaphrasis [Old French Jewish Bible glosses]: → 505, Creative 1985/8, 131-147 / 13-29.

K7.2 **Maimonides.**

b223 *Dienstag* Jacob I., Maimonides' Guide for the perplexed; a bibliography of editions and translations: → 130, Mem. SCHEIBER A. 1988, 95-128.

b224 **Funkenstein** Amos, Maïmonide; nature, histoire et messianisme [**O** Radio Israël], ^T*Chalier* Catherine; préf. *Goetschel* Roland: La nuit surveillée. P 1988, Cerf. 124 p. – ^RÉTRel 63 (1988) 604s (Jeanne-Marie *Léonard*); RThom 88 (1988) 493-5 (S.-T. *Bonino*).

b225 ^{TE}**Geller** Anne-Marie, Moïse Maimonide, Le livre des commandements (Séfér hamitsvoth); préf. *Vadnai* Georges; introd. *Levinas* Emmanuel. Lausanne 1987, L'âge d'homme. 452 p. – ^RRThom 88 (1988) 495 (S.-T. *Bonino*).

b226 **Goldfeld** Lea N., M. Maimonides' treatise on Resurrection 1986 → 2,8326; 3,a453: ^RNRT 110 (1988) 270s (R. *Escol*).

b227 **Hayoun** Maurice-R., Maimonide: Que sais-je? 2378. P 1987, PUF. 128 p. – ^RRThom 88 (1988) 492s (S.-T. *Bonino*).

b228 *Ryan* W. F., Maimonides in Muscovy; medical texts and terminology: JWarb 51 (1988) 43-65.

b229 **Strauss** Leo, Maimonide; essais ^{TE}*Brague* Rémi: Épiméthée. P 1988, PUF. 376 p.; front. 2-13-041827-9.

K7.3 **Alii magistri Judaismi mediaevalis.**

b230 **Kamin** Sarah, RASHI... peshat/derash 1986 → 2,8337; 3,a557: ^REstBíb 46 (1988) 413-7 (J. *Ribera*).

b231 *Blau* Joshua, Some instances reflecting the influence of SAADYA Gaon's Bible translation on later Judeo-Arabic writings: ➤ 130, Mem. SCHEIBER A. 1988, 21-30.

b232 ᵀᴱ**Lambert** Mayer, SAADYA Gaon, Commentaire sur le Séfer Yesira ou Livre de la Création. P 1986, Bibliophane. xx-129 p. F 75. – ᴿRHR 205 (1988) 103s (J. P. *Rothschild*).

b233 *Jospe* Raphael, ❹ RAMBAN (Nahmanides) and Arabic: Tarbiz 57 (1987s); Eng. IIIs.

b234 ᵀᴱ**Feldman** Seymour, Levi ben Gershom (GERSONIDES), The wars of the Lord 1/1, Immortality of the soul 1984 ➤ 65,8741; 1,6744 [2,1987 ➤ 3,a564]: ᴿJJS 39 (1988) 277s (D. *Frank*).

b235 *Ta-Shema* Israel M., ❹ Questions and responses from heaven [r. JACOB of Marvège c.1200]: Tarbiz 57 (1987) 51-66.

b236 **Halevi** Jehudah, Liriche religiose e canti di Sion, ᴱ*Cattani* Luigi: Tradizione d'Israele 2. 192 p. 88-311-4909-1.

b236* **Silman** Yochanan, ❹ *Bêyn pilosop lᵉ-nabî'*... Yehuda HA-LEVI, Kuzari [1140]. Ramat Gan 1985, Bar-Ilan Univ. 325 p. – ᴿJQR 78 (1987s) 314s (D. J. *Lasker*).

b237 *Pines* Shlomo, ❹ On the term *ruḥaniyyot* [Arabic 'spiritual beings'] and its origin and on Judah HALEVI's doctrine: Tarbiz 57 (1987s) 511-540 [541-554, *Fleischer* Ezra, Halevi piyutim].

b238 ᴱ**Sáenz-Badillos** A., Menaḥem BEN SARUQ, Maḥberet, edición crítica e introducción. Granada 1986. 404-cxliii p. – ᴿTarbiz 57 (1987s) 309-311 (M. *Mishor*).

b239 **Cohen** Martin S., The Shi'ur Qomah 1983 ➤ 64,8941... 2,8341: ᴿGregorianum 69 (1988) 341s (G. L. *Prato*); JQR 79 (1988s) 90-92 (Margarete *Schlüter*); RHR 205 (1988) 217-9 (N. *Sed*); SecC 6,1 (1987s) 57s (R. *Brooks*).

b239* **Mustafa** Nurshîf A., IBN HAZM ['al-Fisal'] on Jews and Judaism: diss. Exeter 1988. 494 p. BRDX 82271. – DissA 49 (1988s) 2240-A.

b240 ᴱ**Perani** Mauro, Il midrash temurah; la dialettica degli opposti in un'interpretazione ebraica tardo-medievale 1986 ➤ 2,8346; 3,a575: ᴿHenoch 10 (1988) 117-9 (Elena *Loewenthal*: opera sec. XII pseudonimo di Aqiba/Išmael).

NORZI, Minhat Šay, Profetas menores 1987 ➤ 3908.

b240* **Samuelson** Norbert M., Abraham IBN DAUD (12 cent.), The exalted faith. Rutherford NJ 1986, F. Dickenson Univ. 406 p. [RelStR 15, 274, M. *Kellner*].

b241 *Yassif* Eli, ❹ The exemplary story in Sefer Hasidim [c.1200]: Tarbiz 57 (1987s) 217-255; Eng. III.

K7.4 *Qabbalâ, Zohar, Merkabâ* — **Jewish mysticism.**

b241* **Ariel** David S., The mystic quest; an introduction to Jewish mysticism. Northville NJ 1988, Aronson. xvii-237 p. $27.50 [RelStR 15, 274, E. K. *Ginsburg*].

b242 *a) Chernus* Ira, The pilgrimage to the Merkavah; an interpretation of early Jewish mysticism; – *b) Goldberg* Arnold, Quotations from Scripture in Hekhalot literature; – *c) Hayman* A. P., Sefer Yesira and the Hekhalot literature; – *d) Halperin* David J., A sexual image in Hekhalot Rabbati and its implications: ➤ 479, Mysticism 1984/7, 1-35 / 37-52 / 71-85 / 117-132.

b243 **Dan** Joseph, Jewish mysticism and Jewish ethics 1986 → 2,8352: [R]RelSt 24 (1988) 274s (D. *Cohn-Sherbok*).

b244 *Etkes* Immanuel, ⊕The question of the forerunners of the Haskala in Eastern Europe: Tarbiz 57 (1987s) 95-114; Eng. IV.

b245 **Fenton** Paul B., Deux traités de mystique juive. Lagrasse 1987, Verdier. 336 p. F 132 – [R]JJS 39 (1988) 273-6 (D. *Frank*).

b246 *Goetschel* Roland, Kabbala I [II. Christentum, *Betz* Otto]: → 813, TRE 17 (1988) 487-500 [501-9].

b247 [E]**Green** A., Jewish spirituality, from the sixteenth century revival to the present: EWSp 14, 1987 → 3,a585: [R]Parabola 13,3 (1988) 112-6 (J. *Omer-Man*); Worship 62 (1988) 467-9 (H. G. *Perelmuter*).

b248 **Idel** Moshe, Kabbalah, new perspectives. NHv 1988, Yale Univ. xx-419 p. $40. 0-300-03860-7 [TDig 36,165].

b248* **Idel** Moshe, Studies in ecstatic Kabbalah. Albany 1988, SUNY. $39.50; pa. $13 [RelStR 15, 274, E. K. *Ginsburg*].

b249 **Jellinek** Adolph, Kleine Schriften zur Geschichte der Kabbala [Lp 1851-4]. Hildesheim 1988, Olms. v-80 + viii-82-xviii* + xxiv*-76* + vi-35 + 52* + 53p. 3-487-09051-1.

b250 **Matt** Daniel C., The Zohar, the book of enlightenment 1984 → 2,8357: [R]HeythJ 29 (1988) 129 (L. *Jacobs*: only 2% of Zohar).

b251 [TE]**Mopsik** Charles, Lettre sur la sainteté; le secret de la relation entre l'homme et la femme dans la cabale (+ *Idel* Moché, Métaphores et pratiques sexuelles dans la cabale): Les Dix Paroles. Lagrasse 1986, Verdier. 364 p. 2-86432-051-7.

b252 **Schäfer** P., Geniza-Fragmente zur Hekhalot-L. 1984 → 65,8770... 2,8359: [R]OLZ 83 (1988) 564s (L. *Wächter*); RHR 205 (1988) 216s (N. *Sed*).

b253 **Schäfer** P. (*Reeg* G.) Konkordanz zur Hekhalot-Literatur [I. 1986 → 2,8361]; II. L-T: TStAJud 13. Tü 1988, Mohr. vi, p. 366-732; 3-16-145179-1 [BL 89, 144, A. P. *Hayman*].

b254 **Schäfer** Peter, *al.*, Übersetzung der Hekhalot-Literatur II, 81-334: TStAJud 17, 1987 → 3,a594 [DM 24?]: [R]JStJud 19 (1988) 124-7 (J. *Dan*: DM 98).

b255 **Schäfer** Peter, Hekhalot-Studien: TStAJud 19. Tü 1988, Mohr. 312 p. 3-16-145388-3.

b256 *a) Schäfer* Peter, ⊕ The problem of the redactionist identity of 'Hekhalot Rabbati'; – *b) Elior* Rachel, ⊕ The concept of God in Hekhalot mysticism; – *c) Schiffman* Lawrence, ⊕ Hekhalot mysticism and the Qumran literature; – *d) Idel* Moshe, ⊕ Enoch is Metatron; – *e) Bar Ilan* Meir, ⊕ The idea of crowning God in Hekhalot mysticism and the Karaitic polemic: → 479, Mysticism 1984/7, ⊕ 1-12 / 13-64 / 121-138 / 151-170 / 221-233.

b257 **Scholem** Gershom, Le grandi correnti della mistica ebraica [1985 → 1,a15],[T]. Genova 1986, Melangolo. 383 p. Lit. 50.000. 88-7018-058-1. – [R]Antonianum 63 (1988) 434s (M. *Nobile*).

b258 **Scholem** Gershom, Origins of the Kabbalah [1962] 1987 → 3,a596: [R]CCurr 23 (1988s) 236-9 (M. *Veiman*).

b259 **Swartz** Michael D., Liturgical elements in early Jewish mysticism; a literary analysis of *Ma'aseh Merkavah*: diss. NYU 1986. vii-330 p. AA 86-26916.

b260 **Swietlicki** Catherine, Spanish Christian Cabala [influences on TERESA, *al.*]. Columbia 1986, Univ. Missouri. xi-227 p. – [R]JQR 78 (1987s) 310-3 (M. *Idel*).

b261 **Wolfson** E. R., The Book of the Pomegranate, Moses de LEÓN's Sefer ha-Rimmon [< Zohar etc.; diss. Brandeis 1986, ᴰ*Fox* M., *Fishbane* M.]: BrownJudSt 144. Atlanta 1988, Scholars. xv-124+409 p. 1-55540-213-5 [NTAbs 32,400].

b262 *Wolfson* Elliot R., *a*) The hermeneutics of visionary experience; revelation and interpretation in the Zohar: Religion 18 (L 1988) 311-346 [*al.*, Iliad, Mormons, 'Coxey's Army': < ZIT 89,140]; – *b*) Light through darkness; the ideal of human perfection in the Zohar: HarvTR 81 (1988) 73-95.

K7.5   Judaismus saec. 14-18.

b262* *Domenichini* Daniele, Scienza biblica e curiosità filologiche in una lettera inedita di Benito ARIAS MONTANO [1588]: RaMIsr 52 (1986) 447-457.

b263 **Ben Israël** Menasseh (1604-1657) ᴱ*Méchoulan* Henri, *Nahon* Gérard, *a*) Espérance d'Israël. P 1979. – b) The hope of Israel [defective translation of Moses *Wall* 1652, with critical apparatus]: Littman Library. Ox 1987, Univ. [RHPR 68,258]. 0-19-710054-6. – ᴿÉTRel 63 (1988) 460s (Jeanne-M. *Léonard*).

b264 ᴱ**Bezalel** Safran, Hasidism, continuity or innovation?: JudTMg 5. CM 1988, Harvard. xvii-144 p. 0-674-38120-3.

b264* *Emanuel* Simcha, ❸ The responsa of R. MEIR of Rothenburg [c.1280] — Prague edition [1608]: Tarbiz 57 (1987s) 559-597; Eng. IIs.

b265 *Etkes* Emmanuel, ❸ Between Torah-scholarship and rabbinate in 19th century Lithuania: Zion 53 (1988) 385-403; Eng. xvi.

b266 *Grözinger* Karl E., Judentum-Chasidismus: ⇒ 813, TRE 17 (1988) 377-386.

b267* **Blumenthal** David R., God at the center; meditations on Jewish spirituality [of 18th cent. Hasidic Levi YITZHAK]. SF 1988, Harper & R. xxxii-246 p. $21 [RelStR 15, 276, M. *Verman*].

b267 **Israel** Jonathan I., European Jewry in the age of mercantilism, 1550-1750. Ox 1985. – ᴿZion 53 (1988) 65-71 (H. *Levine*).

b268 *Luke* K., *a*) Messianic movements in Judaism (circa A.D. 700-1800); – *b*) Hasidism, a mystical movement in modern Judaism: LivWord 93 (Kerala 1987) 211-224 / 305-324. [< TKontext 9/2,38].

b269 *Liebes* Yehuda, ❸ A crypto Judaeo-Christian sect of Sabbatean origin [letters before 1800]: Tarbiz 57 (1987s) 349-384; Eng. II.

K7.8   Judaismus contemporaneus.

b270 **Arendt** Hannah, Ebraismo e modernità [testi 1943-63]. Mi 1986, Unicopoli. 229 p. Lit. 24.000. – ᴿHumBr 43 (1988) 308 (G. *Sansonetti*).

b271 ᴱ**Cohen** Arthur A., *Mendes-Flohr* Paul, Contemporary Jewish religious thought 1986s ⇒ 2,242; 3,a615: ᴿJRel 68 (1988) 575-580 (M. L. *Morgan*) [< ZIT 89,65].

b272 *Cohen* Jonathan, 'If Rabbi Akiba were alive today...' or The authenticity argument [R. *Gordis* in claiming that Jewish law need not be immutable now *because* it was not so in the past, thereby admits that it must always be as it was]: Judaism 37 (1988) 136-142.

b273 **Cohon** Samuel S., Essays in Jewish theology, intr. *Petuchowski* Jakob J. 1987 ⇒ 3,206: ᴿJJS 39 (1988) 281s (L. *Jacobs*: immensely erudite Summa of Reform Jewish theology); JTS 39 (1988) 552-4 (S. C. *Reif*: mistaken piety to publish, so badly edited, essays which were up to date before his death in 1959).

b274 **Cuddihy** John M., The ordeal of civility [¹1974, Catholic study of Jewish intellectuals' resistance to modernization]; FREUD, MARX, LÉVI-STRAUSS, and the Jewish struggle with modernity[2], with new preface]. Boston 1987, Beacon, xx-272 p. – RJQR 78 (1987s) 305-7 (S. L. *Gilman*).

b274* XII Congresso dell'Unione delle comunità israelitiche italiane: RaMIsr 52,1 (1986) 314 p.

b275 **Ellis** Marc H., Toward a Jewish theology of liberation 1987 → 3,a620: RÉTRel 63 (1988) 116s (J. M. *Leonard*); ModT 4 (1987s) 103s (N. *Levine*); Month 249 (1988) 645s (J. *Rosen* admits irritation at title's use of buzz-word irrelevant to contents); but on p. 752-759 appears a lecture of Ellis with a similar title plus question-mark, and an answer p. 760-3 by N. *Solomon*); NBlackf 69 (1988) 246-8 (A. *Kee*); TLond 91 (1988) 509s (C. C. *Rowland*); TorJT 4 (1988) 301-3 (R. *O'Toole*); TZBas 44 (1988) 377s (R. R. *Deutsch*); Vidyajyoti 52 (1988) 516s (Marianne *Katoppo*).

b280 *Ellis* Marc H., Is there a Jewish theology of liberation?: Month 249 (1988) 752-9 [TKontext 10/1,116 deutsch].

b281 **Fishbane** M. A., Judaism, revelation and traditions: Religious Traditions of the World. SF 1987, Harper & R. x-149 p. $7. 0-06-062655-0 [NTAbs 32,263].

b281* *Freund* Wolfgang S., Jüdischer und islamischer Fundamentalismus: Universitas 42 (Stu 1987) 764-774.

b282 *Gordis* Robert, Process and pluralism in conservative Judaism: Judaism 37 (1988) 48-59.

b283 **Hirsch** Samson R., Dix-neuf épîtres sur le judaïsme [1836], THayoun M. R.; préf. *Eisenberg* Josy: Patrimoines, Judaïsme, 1987 → 3,a626; F 74: RRSPT 72 (1988) 513-5 (D. *Banon*: 'le judaïsme à l'épreuve de l'émancipation').

b284 **Kurzweil** Zvi, The modern impulse of traditional Judaism 1985 → 2, 8395; 3,a630: RJAAR 56 (1988) 341-3 (T. *Weinberger*).

b285 *Mendes-Flohr* Paul, Jewish continuity in an age of discontinuity; reflections from the perspective of intellectual history: JJS 39 (1988) 261-8.

b286 **Meyer** Michael A., Response to modernity; a history of the Reform movement in Judaism: Studies in Jewish History. NY 1988, Oxford-UP. xvi-494 p.; ill. 0-19-505167-X.

b287 **Neusner** Jacob, Death and birth of Judaism; the impact of Christianity, secularism and holocaust on Jewish faith 1987 → 3,a634: RRRelRes 30 (1988s) 107s (E. *Schoenfield*).

b288 **Neusner** Jacob, The enchantments of Judaism; rites of transformation from birth through death. NY 1987, Basic. 224 p. $16. – RRRelRes 30 (1988s) 295s (R. *Blumstock*); TTod 45 (1988s) 495 (Judith R. *Baskin*).

b289 **Neusner** Jacob, The way of Torah; an introduction to Judaism[4rev] [¹c.1975]. Belmont CA 1988, Wadsworth. xxv-194 p. 0-534-08040-5 [NTAbs 32,396].

b290 **Pavoncello** Nello, Le solennità e le ricorrenze ebraiche alla luce del Midrash. R 1988. 51 p.

b291 **Roth** Joel, The halakhic process, a systematic analysis 1986 → 2,8252 ['systemic']: RJAAR 56 (1988) 176s (J. *Neusner*).

b292 ESchwartz Howard, Lilith's cave; Jewish tales of the supernatural. NY 1988, Harper & R. 294 p. $23. – RParadigms 4 (1988s) 172-4 (D. *Cave*).

b293 **Shear-Yashuv** Aharon, The theology of Salomon L. *Steinheim* [1789-1866]: Studies in Judaism in modern times 7. Leiden 1986, Brill. x-115 p.; 6 pl. *f* 64. – ᴿRHR 205 (1988) 325s (J.-P. *Rothschild*).

b294 **Wine** Sherwin, Judaism beyond God. Farmington Hills MI 1985, Society for Humanistic Judaism. 286 p. $14. 0-912645-08-7. – ᴿJudaism 37 (1988) 499-502 (Ben *Halpern*: 'secularism as religion').

K8   *Philosemitismus* – **Judeo-Christian rapprochement.**

b295 **Angerstorfer** Ingeborg, MELITO und das Judentum: kath. Diss. ᴰ*Brox* N. Regensburg 1985. xxxv-301 p. – ᴿTR 84 (1988) 206s (B. *Lohse*).

b295* **Ankori** Zvi, ❻ Encounter in history; Jews and Christian Greeks 1984 ➤ 2,8409: ᴿSpeculum 63 (1988) 114s (S. *Bowman*).

b296 *Au* Joseph, ❻ On the responsibility of the Jews in killing Jesus and anti-Semitism: ColcFuJen 76 (1988) 257-268.

b297 *a) Baccarini* Emilio, Vita-Via-Verità; la riflessione ebraico-cristiana di F. ROSENZWEIG; – *b) Scalabrella* Silvano, Gesù di Nazareth e il dialogo ebraico-cristiano: Studium 83 (R 1987) 869-889 / 845-856.

b298 **Barbosa da Silva** António, Is there a new imbalance in the Jewish-Christian relation? 1983 ➤ 3,a733: ᴿRHPR 68 (1988) 259s (E. *Jacob*).

b299 *Ben-Chorin* S., *a)* Ist im Christentum etwas von Gott her geschehen? Aus jüdischer Sicht: IZT 24 (1988) 123-9. – *b)* Did God make anything happen in Christianity? An attempt at a Jewish theology of Christianity: Concilium 196 (E 1988) 61-70; *c)* Un essai de théologie juive du christianisme: Concilium 216 (P 1988) 77-88.

b300 **Berg** M. van den, *al.,* Uit de sjoel geklapt; Christelijke belangstelling voor joodse traditie. Hilversum 1986, Gooi & S. 222 p. – ᴿGerefTTs 88 (1988) 54 (J. *Helderman*).

b300* **Berg** J. Van den, *Wall* E.G.E. Van der, Jewish-Christian relations in the seventeenth century; studies and documents: Archives int.hist.idées 119. Dordrecht 1988, Kluwer. 210 p. *f* 77 [RelStR 15, 361, W. *Monter*: oddities].

b301 ᴱ**Berger** David, History and hate; the dimensions of anti-Semitism 1986 ➤ 3,a646: ᴿJEcuSt 25 (1988) 465s (H. *Coward*).

b302 *a) Berger* David, Mission to the Jews and Jewish-Christian contacts in the polemical literature of the High Middle Ages; – *b) Van Engen* John, The Christian Middle Ages as an historiographical problem: AmHR 91 (1986) 576-591 / 519-552.

b303 **Biemer** Günther, Freiburger Leitlinien... / (ᴱ) Was Juden und Judentum für Christen bedeuten² [¹1984 ➤ 65,8796]: Lernprozess Christen-Juden 2s, 2. Dü 1981 Patmos, 312 p. 3. FrB ²1986, Herder. 352 p., DM 42,50. – ᴿBiKi 43 (1988) 30s (W. *Baur*).

b304 *Boon* R., Goede Vrijdag en anti-joods sentiment: Ter Herkenning 16,1 (1988) 1-12 [< GerefTTs 88,123].

b305 ᴱ**Brocke** Edna, *Bauer* Gerhard, Nicht im Himmel — nicht überm Meer; jüdisch-christliche Dialoge zum Bibel 1973/85 ➤ 2.412: ᴿKIsr 2 (1987) 92-95 (F. *Crüsemann*).

b305* *Broer* I., Antijudaismus: ➤ 804, NBL Lfg 1 (1988) 113-5.

b306 ᴱ**Brooks** Roger, Unanswered questions; theological views of Jewish-Catholic relations. ND 1988, Univ. x-224 p. $20 [RelStR 15, 176, B. D. *Cytron*].

b307 *Brosseder* Johannes, Lutherbilder in der neuesten Literatur zu dem Thema M. LUTHER und die Juden: → 366, ᴱ*Heine* S., Europa 1986, 89-110.

b308 *Butselaar* Jan van, Israel in ecumenical thinking, an analysis: IntRMiss 78 (1988) 437-448 [< ZIT 88,571].

b309 **Cagiati** A., *Dani* G., Chi sono gli Ebrei? 1981 → 63,8877; 64,9004: ᴿJEcuSt 25 (1988) 295s (W. *Harrelson*).

b310 *Carmichael* J., Extracting anti-Semitism from Christianity: NY 34,3 (NY 1988) 3s [9 responses in fasc. 4: NTAbs 32,321].

b311 **Carpenter** Dwayne E., Alfonso X and the Jews; an edition of and commentary on 'Siete partidas' 7.24 'De los Judíos': Modern Philology 115. Berkeley 1986, Univ. California. xii-160 p.; front. $14. – ᴿSpeculum 63 (1988) 912-4 (B. R. *Gampel*).

b312 ᴱ**Chervin** Ronda, The ingrafting; the conversion-stories of ten Hebrew-Catholics. Petersham MA 1987, St. Bede's. 117 p. $7 [TDig 35,273].

b313 *Chrostowski* Waldemar, New Christian views of Judaism [= ❷ PrzPow 9 (1988) 263-278]: TDig 35 (1988) 319-325.

b314 *Cohen* Jeremy, Scholarship and intolerance in the medieval academy; the study and evaluation of Judaism in European Christendom: AmHR 91 (1986) 592-613 [BTAM 14 (1988) 486 (C. *Mews*)].

b315 *a*) *Colpe* Carsten, Das deutsche Wort 'Judenchristen' und ihm entsprechende historische Sachverhalte; – *b*) *Flusser* David, Paul's Jewish-Christian opponents in the Didache: → 149, ᶠWERBLOWSKY R., Gilgul 1987, 50-68 / 71-90.

b316 *Comen* A., Ritual murder accusations against the Jews during the days of Suleiman the Magnificent: Journal of Turkish Studies 10 (1986) 73-86 [< Belleten 52/205, 1761].

b317 ᴱ**Curtis** Michael, Antisemitism in the contemporary world [conference Rutgers 1983] 1986 → 2,423*: ᴿJScStR 26 (1987) 272 (D. A. *Gerber*).

b318 **Cutler** A. H. & H. E., The Jew as ally of the Muslim ... anti-Semitism 1986 → 2,8429; 3,a654: ᴿAmHR 92 (1987) 1188s (B. *Septimus*); CathHR 74 (1988) 334s (B. F. *Reilly*); JEcuSt 25 (1988) 104s (J. E. *Blechler*); Judaism 37 (1988) 240-2 (J. *Cohen*).

b319 *Dahan* Gilbert, Les 'figures' des Juifs et de la Synagogue; l'exemple de Dalila; fonctions et méthodes de la typologie dans l'exégèse médiévale: RechAug 23 (1988) 125-150.

b320 **Díez Antonanzas** Jesús R., Las polémicas antijudías en la época de transición (siglos VII-IX); EVANCIO de Toledo, ALVARO de Córdoba, Samuel EL MARROQUÍ: diss. ᴰ*Saranyana* J. Pamplona 1988. 264 p. – RTLv 20,542.

b321 **Dinnerstein** Leonard, Uneasy at home; anti-Semitism and the American Jewish experience [12 reprints]. NY 1987, Columbia Univ. xi-281 p. [RelStR 15, 84, J. D. *Sarna*].

b322 *Donnelly* John P., Antonio POSSEVINO and Jesuits of Jewish ancestry: ArchHistSI 55 (1986) 3-31.

b323 *Doucet* Louis, Un exemple de discours idéologique chrétien, l'antisé-mitisme: BICLyon 88 (1988) 9-22 (-76, *al.,* Idéologies et foi chrétienne).

b324 **Eckardt** A. R., Jews and Christians 1986 → 2,8437; 3,a660: ᴿHorizons 18 (1988) 208s (J. *Koenig*); TTod 44 (1987s) 294s (P. M. *Van Buren*).

b325 *a*) *Ehrlich* Ernst L., LUTHER und die Juden; – *b*) *Boendermaker* Johannes P., M. Luther — ein 'semi-iudaeus'?; der Einfluss des Alten Testaments und des jüdischen Glaubens auf Luther und seine Theologie:

➤ b355, ᴱKREMERS H., Die Juden und M. Luther 1985, 72-88 / 45-57 [< LuJb 54,190].

b326 Fifteen years of Catholic-Jewish dialogue 1970-1985; selected papers: Teologia e filosofia 11. Vaticano 1988, Libreria Pont. Univ. Lateranense. xxix-325 p. Lit. 35.000. 88-209-1587-1.

b327 *Fiedler* Peter, Zehn Thesen zur Behandlung des Judentums im Religionsunterricht: KIsr 2 (1987) 169-171.

b328 **Fornberg** Tord, Jewish-Christian dialogue and biblical exegesis [Mt 5,21-48; Mal 1,11]: Studia Missionalia Upsal. 47. U 1988. 74 p. 91-85424-14-5.

b329 **Friedman** Elias [Jewish Carmelite priest, in Israel since 1954], Jewish identity. Highland NY, Miriam. 231 p. $24; pa. $17 [TDig 36,589].

b330 *a) Friedman* Jerome, Jewish conversion, the Spanish pure blood laws and Reformation; a revisionist view of racial and religious antisemitism: SixtC 18 (1987) 3-29; – *b) Halpern Amaru* Betsy, Martin LUTHER and Jewish mirrors: Jewish Social Studies 46,2 (NY 1984) 95-102 [< LuJb 55,180].

b331 ᴱ**Friedman** Yvonne, PETRI Venerabilis, Adversus Iudaeorum inveteratam duritiem: CCMed 58, 1985 ➤ 1,a71; 3,a666: ᴿNRT 110 (1988) 117 (V. *Roisel*).

b332 *Friedmann* Friedrich G., Judentum, Christentum, Deutschtum; zur Aktualität Franz ROSENZWEIGS: StiZt 206 (1988) 193-206.

b333 **Gager** J., The origins of anti-Semitism 1985 ➤ 64,9022... 3,a668: ᴿSalesianum 50 (1988) 390s (E. *Fontana*).

b333* ᴱ**Garrigues** Jean-Miguel, L'unique Israël de Dieu; approches chrétiennes du Mystère d'Israël 1987 ➤ 3,a669: ᴿÉTRel 63 (1988) 461s (Jeanne-Marie *Léonard*).

b334 ᴱ**Geber** David A., Anti-semitism in American history. Urbana 1986, Univ. Illinois. 406 p. – ᴿJScStR 26 (1987) 270s (M. *Curtis*).

b335 **Geftman** Rina, Attendendo l'aurora; la testimonianza di una ebrea cristiana. CinB 1987, Paoline. 244 p. Lit. 12.000 – ᴿCC 139 (1988,1) 564-572 (F. *Castelli*).

b336 **Gerlach** Wolfgang, Als die Zeugen schwiegen; bekennende Kirche und die Juden: Studien zu Kirche und Israel 10. B 1987. 468 p. – ᴿEvT 48 (1988) 480-2 (D. *Koch*); Judaica 44 (1988) 115s (F. von *Hammerstein*).

b337 *Gollwitzer* Helmut, Kirchenkampf und 'Judenfrage' [*Herbert* K., 1985]: EvT 48 (1988) 273-7.

b338 **Gutwirth** Jacques, Les judéo-chrétiens d'aujourd'hui: Sciences humaines et religieuses. P 1987, Cerf. 295 p. – ᴿRHPR 68 (1988) 526s (J.-P. *Willaime*).

b339 *a) Haacker* Klaus, Elemente des heidnischen Antijudaismus im NT; – *b) Baumbach* Günther, Schriftbenutzung und Schriftauswahl im Rheinischen Synodalbeschluss ['Christen und Juden' 1980]; – *c) Michel* Otto, Hebräisches Denken [... zu *Schleiermacher* ... *Heschel*]; EvT 48 (1988) 404-418 / 419-431 [ähnliche Synode 1988: 463-7] / 431-446 [*Seim* J., 447-472; *Friedlander* Albert, 378-388]; 565-9 (*Kuppler* A. *al.*) Zehn Punkte zur Selbstkontrolle christlichen Redens mit und über Juden; 158, Sieben Feministen gegen Antijudaismus.

b340 **Harder** Günther , Kirche und Israel; Arbeiten zum christlich-jüdischen Verhältnis: St.jüd.Volk & chr. Gemeinde 7, 1986 ➤ 3,234; 3-923095-57-0: ᴿJEcuSt 24 (1987) 673s (M.P. *Miller*); TsTNijm 28 (1988) 322 (K. *Waaijman*).

b342 *Henrix* Hans H.,   Gesprächskreis 'Juden und Christen' beim Zentral-komitee der Deutschen Katholiken: KIsr 2 (1987) 185-7.

b343 **Henry** Marie-Louise,   Der jüdische Bruder und seine Hebräische Bibel. Ha 1988, Katholische Akademie. 118 p.

b344 *Heym* Stefan, Über Juden und Christen: KIsr 1 (1986) 16-25.

b345 **Heymann** F.,   Tod oder Taufe; die Vertreibung der Juden aus Spanien und Portugal im Zeitalter der Inquisition; Einl. *Schoeps* J. H.   Fra 1988, Athenäum.   180 p. DM 38 [RHE 83,446*].

b346 *Hilger* Georg,   Zur Behandlung des Judentums im Religionsunterricht: ZPraxRU 18 (1988) 46-48 [< ZIT].

b347 *Hinz* Christoph,   Entdeckung der Juden als Brüder und Zeugen: BTZ [4 (1987) 170-196] 5 (1988) 2-27.

b348 *Horst* Pieter W. van der,   *a*) Het heidense antisemitisme in de oudheid; – *b*) De *birkat ha-minim* in het recente onderzoek; – *c*) Een merkwaardige anti-joodse legende in een middeleeuws lexicon [< Ter Herkenning 13 (1985) 45-53; 15 (1987) 38-46.184-192]: ➤ 207, De onbekende God 1988, 137-147 / 229-239 / 247-255.

b349 **Hostens** Michiel, Anonymi [auct. Theognosiae c.900] contra Iudaeos: CCG 14, 1986 ➤ 2,8457; 3,a768:   ᴿGregorianum 69 (1988) 399 (J. *Wicki*); JTS 39 (1988) 278s (H. *Chadwick*); NRT 110 (1988) 115s (A. *Harvengt*); RivStoLR 24 (1988) 375-9 (Elena *Loewenthal*).

b350 *Johnson* E. Elizabeth,   Jews and Christians in the New Testament; John, Matthew, and Paul: RefR 42 (1988s) 113-128 [< ZIT 89,304].

b351 **Juden:** LuJb 54 (1987) 190s, Nr. 1172-1212; 55 (1988) 180, Nr. 960-971.

b352 **Katunarich** Sergio M.,   Breve storia dell'ebraismo e dei suoi rapporti con la cristianità   CasM 1987 ➤ 3,a679;   88-384-1199-9. – ᴿCC 139 (1988,4) 402s (C. *Capizzi*); EsprVie 98 (1988) 111 (L. *Monloubou*); NRT 110 (1988) 610 (V. *Roisel*); OrChrPer 54 (1988) 271s (V. *Poggi*).

b353 **Katz** J.,   Exclusion et tolérance; Chrétiens et Juifs du moyen âge à l'ère des Lumières.   P 1987, Lieu Commun.   284 p. – ᴿArchScSocRel 65 (1988) 281s (D. *Bensimon*).

b354 **Klenicki** L., *Wigoder* G.,   Piccolo dizionario del dialogo ebraico-cristiano [1984 ➤ 65,8831],ᵀ. Genova 1988, Marietti.   259 p. Lit. 22.000. – ᴿAsprenas 35 (1988) 304 (A. *Rolla*).

b355 ᴱ**Kremers** H.,   Die Juden und M. LUTHER [¹1985 ➤ 1,602*; 2,8473], ²1987: ᴿJEcuSt 25 (1988) 291s (R. *Modras*).

b356 ᴱ**Kremers** Heinz, *Schoeps* Julius H.,   Das jüdisch-christliche Religionsgespräch [Symposion Duisburg/Mülheim März 1986]: Studien zur Geistesgeschichte 9. 1988, Burg.   234 p. – ᴿKIsr 3 (1988) 105-8 (Julie *Kirchberg*).

b357 ᴱ**Kremers** Heinz, *Lubahn* Erich,   Mission an Israel in heilsgeschichtlicher Sicht.   Neuk 1985. 134 p. – ᴿKIsr 3 (19988) 96s (O. *Rodenberg*).

b358 **Lapide** Pinchas, *Rahner* Karl,   Encountering Jesus — encountering Judaism, a dialogue, ᵀ*Perkins* Davis.   NY 1988, Crossroad.   viii-111 p. $8 [TDig 35,176 puts under Lapide as author, though underneath indicating Rahner as first author; NTAbs 32,258 puts under Rahner].

b359 *Leist* Marielene,   Mein Antisemitismus, Spurensuche: StiZt 206 (1988) 629-637.

b360 *a*) *Licharz* Werner,   Umkehr — Dialog — Toleranz; Lernprozesse in der Begegnung mit dem Judentum; – *b*) *Schüssler* Roland,   Das Problem des Emotionalen im Religionsunterricht — umrissen am Beispiel der Darstellung des Judentums: ➤ 140, ᶠSTOODT D., Unterwegs 1987, 293-308 / 489-500.

b361 ᴱLimor Ora, ➍ The disputation of Majorca 1286, a critical edition and introduction. J 1985, Hebrew Univ. xviii-250 p.; xxvii-118 p. – ᴿSpeculum 63 (1988) 212-4 (J. *Cohen*).

b362 **Lindeskog** Gösta, Das jüdisch-christliche Problem 1986 ➤ 2,8481; 3,a693: ᴿTLZ 113 (1988) 191-3 (K.-W. *Niebuhr*).

b363 **Lubac** Henri de, Résistance chrétienne à l'antisémitisme; souvenirs 1940-1944. P 1988, Fayard. 270 p. F 89. – ᴿÉtudes 368 (1988) 696s (B. *Comte*).

b364 **Maccoby** Hyam, Judaism on trial 1982 ➤ 64,9054 ... 2,8484: ᴿHeythJ 29 (1988) 364s (A. *Hamilton*).

b365 **McGarry** M. B., The challenge of Jewish-Christian dialogue; a Roman Catholic perspective [... we need a new lectionary, not so 'typological']: Proceedings of the Center for Jewish Christian learning; inaugural lecture series. St Paul 1986, College of St. Thomas. [CBQ 50,647].

b366 ᴱMcInnes Val A., Renewing the Judeo-Christian wellsprings 1987 ➤ 3,553 [Index!]: ᴿJEcuSt 25 (1988) 294 (L. J. *Eron*); RExp 85 (1988) 363 (E. G. *Hinson*).

b367 **Markish** S., Erasmus and the Jews 1986 ➤ 2,8488; 3,a698: ᴿHorizons 15 (1988) 164s (J. E. *Biechler*); JAAR 56 (1988) 594s (J. B. *Payne*); JEcuSt 25 (1988) 292s (Mary S. *Laver*); JEH 39 (1988) 306s (A. H. T. *Levi*).

b368 **Marquardt** Friedrich-W., Die Gegenwart des Auferstandenen bei seinem Volk Israel 1983 ➤ 65,8844 ... 3,a699: ᴿTLZ 113 (1988) 55-59 (C. *Hinz*).

b369 *Mechtenberg* Theo, Zum jüdisch-polnischen Verhältnis; ist der Antisemitismus eine unüberwindbare Barriere? Orientierung 52 (1988) 117-9. 124-7. 140-2 [cf. 198-200, *Locher* Clemens).

b370 **Monti** J. E., Who do you say that I am? The Christian understanding of Christ and antisemitism 1984 ➤ 65,8847 ... 2,8491: ᴿJJS 39 (1988) 293 (W. *Horbury*).

b372 *Neudecker* Reinhard, L'Église catholique et le peuple juif, ᵀ*Gilles* Mireille, ➤ 379. Vatican II Bilan 3 (1988) 281-318; Eng. ➤ 380, Assessment 3,282-323.

b373 **Oesterreicher** John M., The new encounter between Christians and Jews 1986 ➤ 2,8498; 3,a711: ᴿCathHR 74 (1988) 311s (J. W. *Devlin*); JEcuSt 24 (1987) 452s (D. *Cohn-Sherbok*).

b374 *Parmentier* Martin, Five years of study in Canada on early Christian anti-Judaism [*Richardson* P.; *Wilson* S., 1986]: Bijdragen 49 (1988) 426-434.

b375 *a*) *Patte* D., Anti-Semitism in the NT; confronting the dark side of Paul's and Matthew's teaching; – *b*) *Cook* M. J., Confronting New Testament attitudes on Jews and Judaism; four Jewish perspectives: ChTSem 78,1 (1988) 31-52 / 3-30 [< NTAbs 32,284s].

b376 **Pawlikowski** J. T., *Wilde* J. A., *al.*, When Catholics speak about Jews; note for homilists and catechists. Ch 1987, Liturgy Training [CBQ 50,646]. – ᴿWorship 62 (1988) 92-94 (J. *Jensen*: some reserves).

b377 *Pawlikowski* John T., Judentum und Christentum, ᵀ*Schwöbel* C.: ➤ 813, TRE 17 (1988) 386-403.

b378 ᴱPopkin Richard H., *Signer* Michael A., Sᴘɪɴᴏᴢᴀ's earliest publication? The Hebrew translation of Margaret Fᴇʟʟ's A loving salutation to the seed of Abraham among the Jews. Assen / Wolfeboro NH 1987, Van Gorcum. x-106 p.; ill. – ᴿGerefTTs 88 (1988) 118s (A. van der *Heide*).

b379 *Pullan* Brian, The conversion of the Jews; the style of Italy: BJRyL 70,1 (1988) 53-70.

b380 *Reinhartz* Adele, The New Testament and anti-Semitism; a literary-critical approach: JEcuSt 25 (1988) 524-537.

b381 ᴱ**Rendtorff** Rolf, *Henrix* Hans H., Die Kirchen und das Judentum, Dokumente von 1945 bis 1985. Pd/Mü 1987, Bonifatius/Kaiser. 746 p. 3-87088-524-6 / Mü 3-459-01712-0. – ᴿBiKi 43 (1988) 185s (P. G. *Müller*); KIsr 3 (1988) 203-6 (E. *Zenger*).

b382 ᴱ**Richardson** P. (*Granskou* D.), Anti-Judaism in early Christianity, 1. Paul and the Gospels 1986 → 2,393; 3,a719: ᴿBZ 32 (1988) 154-6 (I. *Broer*); CBQ 50 (1988) 351-3 (A. T. *Kraabel*).

b383 **Rosenberg** Stuart E., The Christian problem; a Jewish view 1986 → 2,8513; 3,a723: ᴿHorizons 18 (1988) 209s (Ruth *Graf*); JEcuSt 24 (1987) 676 (J. T. *Pawlikowski*).

b384 *Sänger* Dieter, Neues Testament und Antijudaismus; Versuch einer exegetischen und hermeneutischen Vergewisserung im innerchristlichen Gspräch: KerDo 34 (1988) 210-231; Eng. 231.

b385 *Sarna* Jonathan D., The impact of nineteenth-century Christian missions on American Jews: → 356, ᴱ*Endelman* T., Jewish apostasy 1987...

b386 *Schafler* Samuel, Enemies or Jew-haters? Reflections on the history of anti-Semitism [... should be studied carefully, not left to mythmakers]: Judaism 37 (1988) 352-8.

b387 *Schendel* Eberhard, Martin LUTHER und die Juden, ein Plädoyer für Fairness: → 369, ᴱ*Heubach* J., Jb. M. Luther-Bundes 14 (1987) 183-194 [< LuJb 55 (1988) 180].

b388 **Schoonhoven** E. Jansen, Jodendom... HAMANN-MENDELSSOHN 1985 → 1,a128; 3,a728: ᴿJEcuSt 25 (1988) 289s (F. J. van *Beeck*).

b389 **Schreckenberg** Heinz, Die christlichen Adversus-Judaeos-Texte (11.-13. Jh.), mit einer Ikonographie des Judenthemas bis zum 4. Laterankonzil: EurHS 23/335. Fra 1988, Lang. 710 p.; front. 3-8204-1436-3.

b390 *Schreckenberg* Heinz, Die patristische Adversus-Judaeos-Thematik im Spiegel der karolingischen Kunst: Bijdragen 49 (1988) 119-138; 5 fig.

b391 *Seim* Jürgen, Auf einem gemeinsamen Weg zum Heil? Zum Verhältnis von Juden und Christen: BTZ 5 (1988) 265-279 [280-2, Antwort, *Brocke* Edna].

b392 **Simonsohn** Shlomo, The Apostolic See and the Jews; documents 492-1404. Toronto 1988, Pont. Inst. Medieval Studies. xv-549 p. 0-88844-094-4.

b393 *Soggin* J. Alberto, Ebrei e cristiani di fronte al nazionalsocialismo tedesco [*Kulka* O., *Mendes-Flohr* P. 1987]: Protestantesimo 43 (1988) 196-8.

b394 **Spatafora** F., Cristianesimo e Giudaismo. Caltanissetta 1987, Krinon. 127 p. – ᴿDivThom 91 (1988) 198s (M. *Tábet*).

b395 **Stow** K., The '1007 anon' 1984 → 1,a141 ... 3,a735: ᴿBTAM 14 (1988) 474-6 (G. *Dahan*).

b396 **Sweet-Laver** Mary, CALVIN, Jews and intra-Christian polemics: diss. Temple. Ph 1987. – RelStR 15,189.

b397 *Talmage* Frank, Polemics, Christian-Jewish: → 792, DMA 10 (1988) 1-7 [-9, *Perlmann* M., Islamic-Jewish].

b398 *Terracina* Fernando, Ebrei e non Ebrei, differenze psicologiche I-II: Nuova Um 9,50 (1987) 39-62; 51 (1987) 23-46.

b399 *Toaff* Elio (intervista di *Baggio* Antonio M.), Ebraismo; un compito per l'umanità: NuovaUm 10,56 (1988) 49-61.

b400 *Torell* Jean-Pierre, Les juifs dans l'œuvre de PIERRE le Vénérable [anti-sémite mais avec une connaissance rare du Talmud ...]: CahCivMéd 30 (1987) 331-346 [RSPT 72,342; BTAM 14 (1988) 503s (G. *Dahan*)].

b401 *Wallmann* Johannes, LUTHER on Jews and Islam: ↦ 505, Creative 1985/8, 149-160.

b402 *Willis* Robert E., BONHOEFFER and BARTH on Jewish suffering; reflections on the relationship between theology and moral sensibility: JEcuSt 24 (1987) 598-615.

b403 ᴱ**Wilson** Stephen G., Anti-Judaism in early Christianity [Canadian Society of Biblical Literature meeting]: Studies in Christianity and Judaism 2. Separation and Polemic 1986 ↦ 2,393; 3,a742: ᴿBZ 32 (1988) 280-3 (C. *Thoma*); RelStR 14 (1988) 157 (B. *Chilton*); TorJT 4 (1988) 138-140 (J. *Kozar*).

b404 **Yaseen** Leonard C., The Jesus connection; to triumph over anti-Semitism. NY 1986, Crossroad. 222 p. $10 pa. – ᴿJEcuSt 24 (1987) 454 (B. *Noone*).

b405 **Zuidema** Willem, God's partner; an encounter with Judaism, ᵀ*Bowden* J. 1987 ↦ 3,a745: ᴿDoctLife 37 (1987) 435s (J. *Paterson*); Furrow 39 (1988) 481s (J. D. *May*).

b406 **Zuidema** W., Partenaire de Dieu; à la rencontre du Judaïsme, ᵀ*Passelecq* G., 1987 ↦ 3,a746: ᴿCollatVL 18 (1988) 116 (A. *Denaux*).

XVII,3 Gnosis et religiones parabiblicae

M1.1   Gnosticismus classicus.

b407 *Broek* R. van den, Vrouwen en het vrouwelijke in de antieke gnosis: Mara 2,1 [?1988s; < GerefTTs 88,261] 5-17 [29-42, *Bekkenkamp* J.].

b408 **Buckley** Jorunn J., Female fault and fulfilment in Gnosticism 1986 ↦ 2,8545; 3,a749: ᴿJAAR 56 (1988) 767-770 (M. A. *Williams*).

b409 **Culianu** Ioan P., Gnosticismo e pensiero moderno; Hans JONAS 1985 ↦ 2,8546; 3,a751: ᴿBbbOr 30 (1988) 183-5 (E. *Jucci*); OrChrPer 54 (1988) 240-242 (E. G. *Farrugia*); RÉAnc 90 (1988) 259 (A. *Villey*).

b410 *Dehandschutter* Boudewijn, Gnosticisme vandaag; een probleemstelling: CollatVL 18 (1988) 131-152.

b411 *Duchesne-Guillemin* Jacques, On the origin of Gnosticism: ↦ 6, ᶠAS-MUSSEN J. 1988, 349-363.

b411* **Edwards** Mark J., PLOTINUS and the Gnostics: diss. Oxford 1987. 378 p. BRD-83186. – DissA 49 (1988s) 2268-A.

b412 *Forment* Eudaldo, El humanismo gnóstico: Studium 28 (M 1988) 485-510.

b413 *Frankemolle* Hubert, The world as prison; Gnosticism, human beings and the world [< Die Welt als Gefängnis: BiKi 41 (1986) 22-33], ᵀᴱ*Asen* B. A.: TDig 35 (1988) 218-220.

  Green Henry A., The economic and social origins of Gnosticism, ᴰ1985 ↦ b469.

b414 **Layton** B., The Gnostic scriptures 1987 ↦ 3,a759: ᴿRÉAug 34 (1988) 200s (A. *Le Boulluec*); VigChr 42 (1988) 199-201 (G. *Quispel*).

b415 *Luttikhuizen* Gerard P., *a*) The Jewish factor in the development of the Gnostic myth of origins; some observations: ↦ 85, ᶠKLIJN A., Text 1988,

152-161; – *b*) The evaluation of the teaching of Jesus in Christian Gnostic revelation dialogues;   NT 30 (1988) 158-168.

b416 **Moraldi** Luigi,   Le apocalissi gnostiche... Adamo, Pietro, Giacomo, Paolo: Adelphi 181, 1987 ➤ 3,a762:   ^RAntonianum 63 (1988) 609s (M. *Nobile*).

b417 *Oelmüller* Willi,   Hans JONAS; Mythos – Gnosis – Prinzip Verantwortung: StZt 206 (1988) 343-351.

b418 ^E**Pearson** Birger A., *Goehring* James E.,   The roots of Egyptian Christianity 1983/6 ➤ 2,484; 3,a763:   ^RBO 45 (1988) 597-9 (K. *Treu*); Gregorianum 69 (1988) 372 (E. *Farahian*); TLZ 112 (1987) 351-3 (W. *Löhr*).

b420 *Pearson* Birger A.,   Use, authority and exegesis of Mikra in Gnostic literature: ➤ 317, Mikra 1988, 635-652.

b421 **Pètrement** Simone,   Le Dieu séparé; les origines du gnosticisme 1984 ➤ 65,8001... 3,a766:   ^RRB 95 (1988) 154s (M.-J. *Pierre*).

b422 *Philonenko* Marc,   O uitae uera uita (Asclépius 41):   RHPR 68 (1988) 429-433.

b423 **Puech** H.-C.,   Sulle tracce della Gnosi 1985 ➤ 3,a767:   ^REuntDoc 41 (1988) 156 (P. *Miccoli*).

b424 *Rudolph* Kurt,   Gnosis; una concepción del mundo de la antigüedad tardía [< BiKi 41 (1986) 2-7], ^{TE}*Priego* Juan J.:   SelT 27 (1988) 138-142.

b425 *Stroumsa* Gedaliahu A.G.,   Another seed 1984 ➤ 65,8995 ... 3,a773: ^ROLZ 83 (1988) 199-204 (W. *Sundermann*); SecC 6 (1987s) 243s (B.A. *Pearson*).

b426 **Tardieu** M., *Dubois* J.,   Introduction à la littérature gnostique I, 1986 ➤ 2,8562; 3,a775:   ^RRÉAug 34 (1988) 199 (C. *Perrot*).

b427 *Tripp* D.H.,   'Gnostic worship'; the state of the question: StLtg 17 (1987) 210-222.

b428 **Valantasis** Richard,   Third century spiritual guides; a semiotic study of the guide-disciple relationship in Christianity, Neoplatonism, Hermetism and Gnosticism: diss. – HarvTR 81 (1988) 454s.

b429 **Williams** Jacqueline A.,   Biblical interpretation in the Gnostic Gospel of Truth from Nag Hammadi: [diss. Yale, ^D*Layton* B.]: SBL diss. 79. Atlanta 1988, Scholars.   vii-220 p. [RelStR 15,264, B.A. *Pearson*].

b430 **Williams** Michael A.,   The immovable race; a gnostic designation and the theme of stability in late antiquity [diss. Harvard 1977, ^D*MacRae* G.]: NHS 29, 1985 ➤ 1,a181... 3,a780:   ^RJBL 107 (1988) 161-4 (Ruth *Majercik*).

b431 *a*) *Wilson* R.M.,   Gnostic origins; an Egyptian connection?; – *b*) *Quispel* Gilles,   Anthropos and sophia; – *c*) *Zandee* Jan,   Der androgyne Gott in Ägypten; ein Erscheinungsbild des Weltschöpfers: ➤ 16, ^FBÖHLIG A., Religion 1988, 227-239 / 168-185 / 240-278.

M1.2 *Valentinus – Pistis sophia,* **Elchasai.**

b432 *Cirillo* Luigi,   Elchasai e la sua rivelazione [*Luttikhuizen* G. 1985]: RivStoLR 24 (1988) 311-330.

b433 **Frickel** Josef,   Hellenistische Erlösung in christlicher Deutung; die gnostische Naassenerschrift 1984 ➤ 65,8914; 3,a784:   ^ROLZ 83 (1988) 685-7 (H.-F. *Weiss*); SecC 6,1 (1987s) 53-55 (M. *Desjardins*).

b434 **Luttikhuizen** Gerard P.,   The revelation of Elchasai: TStAJ 8, 1985 ➤ 2,8572; 3,a786:   ^RSvEx 53 (1988) 144s (J.-E. *Eriksson*).

b435 *Mertens* Michèle, Une scène d'initiation alchimique, la 'Lettre d'Isis à Horus': RHR 205 (1988) 3-24; Eng. 3.

b436 *Orbe* Antonio, Trayectoria del Pneuma en la economía valentiniana de la salud: Compostellanum 33 (1988) 7-52.

b437 *Scholten* Clemens, Gibt es Quellen zur Sozialgeschichte der Valentinianer Roms?: ZNW 79 (1988) 244-261.

M1.3   **Corpus hermeticum; Orphismus.**

b438 **Büchli** Jörg, Der Poimandres; ein paganisiertes Evangelium [Diss. Zürich, ᴰ*Burkert* W.]: WUNT 2/27, 1987 → 3,a793: ᴿRelStR 14 (1988) 254s (B. A. *Pearson*).

b439 **Fowden** Garth, The Egyptian Hermes; a historical approach to the late pagan mind 1986 → 3,a797 ['to late paganism']: ᴿAegyptus 68 (1988) 275s (G. *Geraci*); ClasR 102 (1988) 293-5 (J. G. *Griffiths*); ClasW 82 (1988s) 205s (R. S. *Bianchi*); JTS 39 (1988) 232s (A. *Louth*); NedTTs 42 (1988) 147 (P. W. van der *Horst*); StPatav 35 (1988) 654-7 (D. M. *Cosi*).

b440 **Iversen** Erik, Egyptian and hermetic doctrine 1984 → 65,8924 ... 3,a799: ᴿAmJPg 109 (1988) 145-8 (D. *Lorton*).

b441 *Kehl* Alois, *al.,* Hermetik: → 807, RAC 14,109s (1988) 780-808.

b441* *Lambert* Jacques, Hermopolis, Memphis, Latopolis et les Dogon [petit peuple gnostique]: RHR 205 (1988) 133-149; Eng. 133.

b442 *McClintock* Giuliana Scalera, La Teogonia di Protogono nel Papiro Derveni; una interpretazione del Orfismo: FilT 1,1 (N 1988) 139-149.

b443 *a*) *Makris* N., Hermès Trismégiste et l'Égypte; – *b*) *Armstrong* A. H., Iamblichus and Egypt: Études philosophiques 42,2s ('L'Égypte et la philosophie' 1987) 169-178 / 179-188 [RSPT 72 (1988); *Armstrong*ᵀ; on attend un fasc. suivant].

b444 **Segal** R. A., Poimandres as myth 1986 → 2,8559; 3,a803: ᴿJAAR 56 (1988) 816-8 (L. H. *Martin*).

M1.5   **Mani,** *dualismus;* **Mandaei.**

b445 *Bianchi* Ugo, *a*) Dualism in religious ethnology: → 149, ᶠWERBLOWSKY R., Gilgul 1987, 45-49; – *b*) Omogeneità della luce e dualismo radicale nel Manicheismo: → 16, ᶠBÖHLIG A., Religion 1988, 54-64.

b446 *a*) *Bianchi* Ugo, Sur la question des deux âmes de l'homme dans le Manichéisme; – *b*) *Böhlig* Alexander, Zum Selbstverständnis des Manichäismus; – *c*) *Klimkeit* Hans-Joachim, Das Tor als Symbol im Manichäismus; – *d*) *Lieu* Samuel N. C., Sources on the diffusion of Manichaeism in the Roman Empire: → 6, ᶠASMUSSEN J., 1988, 311-316 / 317-338 / 365-381 / 383-399.

b447 **Bozóky** Edina, Le livre secret des Cathares, Interrogatio Iohannis, apocryphe d'origine bogomile, 1980 → 62,9789; 63,8980: ᴿJTS 39 (1988) 285s (M. D. *Lambert*: rare text directly from the Cathars).

b447* *Bryder* Peter, ... Where the faint traces of Manichaeism disappear: AltOrF 15 (1988) 201-8; 5 fig.

b448 **Fontaine** P. F. M., The light and the dark; a cultural history of dualism. Amst 1986/8, Gieben. I. Archaic Greece, xvi-293 p. – II. Greek history 5- 4 cent., xvi-295 p. – III. 1988, Greek literature 5-4 cent., xiii-227 p.   90-70265-40-0; 5063-004-9; 20-0. – ᴿClasR 102 (1988) 424 (R. W. *Jordan*, 1).

b449 **Hutter** Manfred, Mani und die Sasaniden; der iranisch-gnostische Synkretismus einer Weltreligion: Scientia 12. Innsbruck 1988. Sch 70. 1010-612X.

b450 ᴱ**Koenen** L., *Römer* C., Der Kölner Mani-Kodex 1985 ► 1,a204; 3,a813: ᴿBijdragen 49 (1988) 98s (M. *Parmentier*: the world's smallest manuscript, 3,8 × 4,5 cm., glued together into four lumps; separated by 'a scientist' 1969).

b451 **Lieu** Samuel N. C., Manichaeism in... China 1985 ► 1,a207 ... 3,a814: ᴿEWest 37 (1987) 473-5 (G. *Gnoli*); Speculum 63 (1988) 431s (G. *Bonner*).

b452 *Merkelbach* R., *a)* Manichaica (9), nochmals Beiträge zum Kölner Codex: ZPapEp 71 (1988) 51-54 [74 (1988) 84, E. *Maresch*; 229s, P. J. *Sijpesteijn*]. – *b)* Manichaica (10), Eine Fabel Manis: ZPapEp 75 (1988) 93s.

b453 *Oerter* Wolf B., Drei manichäisch-soghdische Parabeln im Lichte koptischer Manichaica [*Sundermann* W. 1985]: ArOr 56 (1988) 172-6.

b454 *Oort* Johannes van, Aᴜɢᴜsᴛɪɴᴇ and Mani on concupiscentia sexualis: ► 516, Aug. Traiectina 1986/7, 137-152.

b455 *Pennacchietti* Fabrizio A., Gli Acta Archelai e il viaggio di Mani nel Bēt 'Arbāyē: RivStoLR 24 (1988) 503-514.

b456 **Ries** Julien, Les études manichéennes; des controverses de la Réforme aux découvertes du XXᵉ Siècle: Coll. Cerfaux-Lefort 1. LvN 1988, Centre Hist. Rel. 271 p.; 2 pl. Fb 650.

b457 *Stroumsa* Sarah & Gedaliahu G., Aspects of anti-Manichaean polemics in late antiquity and under Islam: HarvTR 81 (1988) 37-58.

b458 **Tardieu** Michel, Il Manicheismo [Que sais-je Nᵒ 1940, 1981 ► 63,9002], ᵀᴱ*Sfameni Gasparro* Giulia. Cosenza 1988, Giordano. 187 p.

b459 *Tardieu* Michel, Sebastianus [comes de Julien contre les Perses] étiqueté comme manichéen: Klio 70 (1988) 494-500.

M2.1 Nagᶜ Ḥammadi, generalia.

b460 ᴱ**Robinson** James M., ³ʳᵉᵛ*Smith* Richard, The Nag Hammadi library in English, translated and introduced: Coptic Gnostic Library Project. Leiden 1988, Brill. xvi-549 p. 90-04-08856-3. – ᴿJEA 74 (1988) 299-301 (W. J. *Tait*, on Bᴀʀɴs J., Cartonnage 1981); ZDMG 138 (1985) 378s (M. *Krause* on 1984 introd.).

b460* ᴱ**Barc** B., Colloque NH 1978/81 ► 62,505 ... 65,8943: ᴿSecC 6 (1987s) 239-241 (M. W. *Meyer*).

b461 **Broek** R. van den, De taal van de Gnosis; gnostische teksten uit Nag Hammadi 1986 ► 3,a827; 90-263-0745-4: ᴿBijdragen 49 (1988) 209 (M. *Parmentier*).

Dart John, The Jesus of heresy and history; ... Nag Hammadi 1988 ► 4305.

b462 ᴱ**Hedrick** C., *Hodgson* R., Nag Hammadi, Gnosticism, and early Christianity 1986 ► 2,374; 3,a756: ᴿCBQ 50 (1988) 156s (J. A. *Timbie*: tit. pp. and some comments); CurrTM 15 (1988) 286s (P. *Rorem*); TS 49 (1988) 576 (D. W. *Johnson*); VigChr 42 (1988) 198s (G. *Quispel*).

b463 **Scholten** Clemens, Martyrium und Sophiamythos im Gnostizismus nach den Texten von NH [Diss. Bonn]: JbAC Egb 14. Münster 1987, Aschendorff. 316 p. DM 98. – ᴿVigChr 42 (1988) 197s (G. *Quispel*).

b464 *Scholten* Clemens, Die Nag-Hammadi-Texte als Buchbesitz der Pachomianer: JbAC 31 (1988) 144-172.

b465 **Tuckett** Christopher, Nag Hammadi and the Gospel tradition 1986 ► 3,4205: ᴿAustralBR 36 (1988) 76s (J. *Painter*); CBQ 50 (1988) 338-340

(Pheme *Perkins*: does not really refute claim of pre-Synoptic ApJas and DialSav); EvQ 60 (1988) 65-67 (J. N. *Birdsall*); TLZ 113 (1988) 27s (H.-M. *Schenke*).

M2.2.   *Evangelium etc. Thomae* – **The Gospel** (etc.) **of Thomas.**

b466 **Amersfoort** Jacobus van,   Het Evangelie van Thomas en de Pseu-do-Clementinen ᴰ1984 ⇒ 65,8958 ... 3,a831:   ᴿBO 45 (1988) 341s (B. *De-handschutter*).

b467 *a*) *Boring* M. Eugene,   The historical-critical method's 'criteria of authenticity'; the Beatitudes in Q and Thomas as a test-case; – *b*) *Robinson* James M.,   The study of the historical Jesus after Nag⸴ Hammadi; – *c*) *Koester* Helmut, The extracanonical sayings of the Lord as products of the Christian community [= ZNW 48 (1957) 220-237 + 75s]; – *d*) *Perkins* Pheme,   The rejected Jesus and the Kingdom sayings; – *e*) *Stroker* William D.,   Extracanonical parables and the historical Jesus; – *f*) *Crossan* John D.,   Divine immediacy and human immediacy; towards a new first principle in historical Jesus research: ⇒ 309, Semeia 44 (1988) 9-44 / 45-56 / 57-78 / 79-94 / 121-140.

b468 **Crossan** J. D.,   Four other Gospels 1985 ⇒ 1,a228 ... 3,a834:   ᴿÉglT 17 (1986) 237s (W. *Vogels*).

b469 *a*) *Fallon* Francis T., *Cameron* Ron,   The Gospel of Thomas; a Forschungsbericht and analysis; – *b*) *Tissot* Yves, L'encratisme des Actes de Thomas: ⇒ 782, ANRW 2,25,6 (1988) 4195-4251 / 4415-4430.

b470 **Jackson** Howard M.,   [Thomas Gospel logion 7] The lion becomes man; the gnostic leontomorphic creator and the Platonic tradition [diss. Claremont 1983, ᴰ*Robinson* J. M.]: SBL diss. 81, 1985 ⇒ 1,a162; 3,a837: ᴿAustralBR 36 (1988) 90s (D. *Minns*); JBL 107 (1988) 159-161 (M. W. *Meyer*); JSS 33 (1988) 288-290 (R. *Hayward*).

b471 **Kuntzmann** R., *Dubois* J. D.,   Nag Hammadi, evangelio según Tomás; textos gnósticos de los orígenes del cristianismo [1987 ⇒ 3,a840],ᵀ. Estella 1988, VDivino.   178 p. – ᴿBibFe 14 (1988) 481s (M. *Sáenz Galache*).

b472 **Lelyveld** Margaretha,   Les Logia de la Vie dans ÉvTh: NHS 34, 1987 ⇒ 3,a842:   ᴿVigChr 42 (1988) 99s (G. *Quispel*).

b473 *Marcovich* Miroslav,   *a*) The text of the Gospel of Thomas (Nag Hammadi II 2) [< JTS 20 (1969) 53-74]; – *b*) New Gnostic texts [ined.]; – *c*) The wedding hymn of Acta Thomae [< ILClasSt 6 (1981) 367-385]: ⇒ 228, Studies 1988, 55-79 / 129-133 / 156-173.

b474 **Patterson** Stephen J.,   The Gospel of Thomas within the development of early Christianity: diss. Claremont 1988. – RelStR 15,193.

b475 *a*) *Poirier* Paul-Hubert,   L'Évangile selon Thomas (log. 16 et 23) et Aphraate (Dem. XVIII,10-11); – *b*) *Troupeau* Gérard,   Une version arabe du 'Testament d'Adam': ⇒ 59, ᶠGUILLAUMONT A. 1988, 15-18 / 3-14.

b476 *a*) *Quispel* Gilles,   The Gospel of Thomas and the trial of Jesus; – *b*) *Drijvers* H. J. W., *Reinink* G. J.,   Taufe und Licht; TATIAN, Ebionäerevangelium und Thomasakten: ⇒ 85, ᶠKLIJN A., Text 1988, 193-9 / 91-110.

b477 **Ross** Hugh M.,   The Gospel of Thomas, newly presented.   NY 1987, Ebor.   v-112 p.   1-85072-019-3.

b478 **Strickert** Frederick M.,   The pronouncement sayings in the Gospel of Thomas and the Synoptics: diss. Iowa.   Iowa City 1988. – RelStR 15,193.

b479 *Tuckett* Christopher, Thomas and the Synoptics: NT 30 (1988) 132-157.

b480 **Kuntzmann** Raymond, Le livre de Thomas [l'Athlète] (NH II,7) 1986
➤ 2,8614; 3,a848: ᴿBZ 32 (1988) 139s (H. *Schnackenburg*); ETL 64
(1988) 208s (A. de *Halleux*); JTS 39 (1988) 223-7 (M. *Smith*: text
unsatisfactory).

b481 **Lipinski** Matthias, Konkordanz zu den Thomasakten: BoBB 67. Fra
1988, Athenäum. xiii-605 p. DM 128 [JBL 107,788].

b482 **Poirier** Paul-H., L'hymne de la perle des Actes de Thomas 1981
➤ 63,9037*; 64,9196: ᴿSecC 6 (1987s) 110-2 (Pheme *Perkins*).

b483 **Poirier** P.-H., *Lucchesi* E., La version copte de la prédication et du
martyre de Thomas 1984 ➤ 65,8579 ... 2,8120: ᴿOrChr 72 (1988) 234s
(Regine *Schulz*).

b484 *Rätsep* Kaide, The apostle Thomas in Christian tradition: StOrFin 64
(1988) 107-130.

M2.3   *Singula scripta* – **Nag° Hammadi, various titles.**

b485 *Dehandschutter* B., L'Epistula Jacobi apocrypha de Nag Hammadi (CG
1,2) comme apocryphe néotestamentaire: ➤ 782, ANRW 2,25,6 (1988)
4529-4550.

b486 **Rouleau** D., L'ép. apocryphe de Jacques [+ *Roy* L., L'acte de Pierre]
1987 ➤ 3,a855: ᴿRSPT 72 (1988) 616-9 (G.-M. de *Durand*, aussi sur
VEILLEUX A. 1986).

b487 **Veilleux** Armand, I-II apocalypse de Jacques NH V, 3s 1986s ➤ 3,a856:
ᴿETL 64 (1988) 467s (A. de *Halleux*).

b488 **Bream** Howard N. † ᴱ*Goedicke* Hans, The Apocryphon of John and
other Coptic translations. Baltimore 1987, Halgo. viii-250 p. – ᴿDiscEg
12 (1988) 81s (A. *Alcock*).

b489 *Myszor* Wincenty, ☉ Der Perlenverkäufer in den Petrusakten in Codex
VI von Nag Hammadi: ➤ 73, ᶠKANIA W. = VoxPa 12s (1987s) 303-5;
deutsch 305.

b490 **Schönborn** Ulrich, 'Diverbium salutis'; Studien zur Interdependenz von
literarischer Struktur und theologischer Intention des gnostischen Dialogs
ausgeführt an der koptischen 'Apokalypse des Petrus' aus Nag Hammadi
(NHC VII,3): Diss, Marburg 1988. 573 p. – RTLv 20,546.

b491 **Luttikhuizen** G.P., Gnostiche geschriften I. Het Evangelie naar Maria,
het Evangelie naar Filippus en de brief van Petrus aan Filippus: Na de
Schriften 2. Kampen 1986, Kok. 152 p.; ill. *f*32. 90-242-4133-2
[NedTTs 42,344]. – ᴿBijdragen 49 (1988) 209 (M. *Parmentier*).

b492 **Helderman** Jan, Die Anapausis im Evangelium Veritatis 1984 ➤ 65,
8972 ... 3,a851: ᴿBO 45 (1988) 599-602 (P.-H. *Poirier* adds some 60 to
the 110 corrigenda included with the book); OLZ 83 (1988) 178-180
(H.-M. *Schenke*).

b493 *a) Helderman* J., Das Evangelium Veritatis in der neueren Forschung; –
b) Sfameni Gasparro Giulia, Il 'Vangelo secondo Filippo'; rassegna degli
studi e proposte di interpretazione; – *c) Buckley* Jorunn J., Conceptual
models and polemical issues in the Gospel of Philip: ➤ 782, ANRW
2,25,5 (1988) 4054-4106 / 4107-66 / 4167-94.

b494 **Williams** J.A., Biblical interpretation in the Gospel of Truth from Nag
Hammadi [diss. Yale 1983, ᴰ*Layton* B.]: SBL diss. 79. Atlanta 1988,
Scholars. vii-220 p. $16. 0-89130-876-8; pa. 7-6 [NTAbs 32,400].

b495 **Morard** Françoise, L'Apocalypse d'Adam (NH V,5): BCNH-T 15, 1985 ➤ 1,a249; 3,a859: ᴿÉglT 18 (1987) 242s (J. K. *Coyle*); Gregorianum 69 (1988) 371 (A. *Orbe*).

b496 **Cherix** Pierre, Le concept de notre grande puissance (CG VI,4) 1982 ➤ 63,9045 ... 2,8622 [not IV,4]: ᴿOLZ 83 (1988) 315-7 (H.-G. *Bethge*).

b497 **Janssens** Yvonne, Leçons de Silvanos (NH VII,4) 1983 ➤ 64,2905 ... 2,8619: ᴿBO 45 (1988) 18-24 (W.-P. *Funk*); CdÉ 63 (1988) 198-201 (C. *Cannuyer*).

b498 *Broek* R. van den, Silvanus en de Griekse gnomische traditie: NedTTs 42 (1988) 126-133; Eng. 145.

b499 **Ménard** Jacques É., Le traité sur la Résurrection (NH 1,4): BCNH-T 12, 1983 ➤ 64,9206 ... 3,a864: ᴿCdÉ 63 (1988) 193-7 (C. *Cannuyer*).

b500 *Parrott* Douglas M., Eugnostos [NHC III and V] and 'all the philosophers': ➤ 16, ᶠBÖHLIG A., Religion 1988, 153-167.

b501 **Sevrin** Jean-Marie, Le dossier baptismal séthien; études sur le sacramentaire gnostique: BCNH-Ét 2, 1985 ➤ 1,a256 ... 3,a866: ᴿBO 45 (1988) 143-9 (H.-M. *Schenke*); Gregorianum 69 (1988) 370s (A. *Orbe*).

b502 **Scopello** Maddalena, L'exégèse de l'âme; NHC II,6: NHS 25, 1985 ➤ 1,a255 ... 3,a861: ᴿJBL 107 (1988) 164s (Deirdre *Good*).

M3   **Religiones comparatae** – *Historia religionum.*

b503 **Adriani** Maurilio, Lineamenti di storia delle religioni. F 1988, Nardini. 229 p. Lit. 28.000 [CC 139/3 dopo 208]. – ᴿCivClCr 9 (1988) 383 (G. *Puccioni*).

b504 *a) Ahlstrom* Sydney E., The problem of the history of religion in America; – *b) Mead* Sidney E., From coercion to persuasion; another look at the rise of religious liberty and the emergence of denom-inationalism: ChH Centennial Sup. (1988) 127-138 / 68-88.

b505 *Amaladoss* Michael, El cristiano y las escrituras no cristianas [< IndTSt 22 (1985) 62-78], ᵀᴱ*Pascual* Eduardo: SelT 26 (1987) 346-352.

b506 **Ariarajah** S. Wesley, The Bible and people of other faiths 1985 ➤ 1,a264 ... 3,a871: ᴿMissiology 15,1 (1987) 122s (G. R. *Hunsberger*).

b507 **Arthur** C. J., In the Hall of Mirrors; problems of commitment in a religiously plural world 1986 ➤ 2,8647: ᴿScotJT 41 (1988) 414s (G. *D'Costa*).

b508 **Becker** Gerhold, Die Ursymbole in den Religionen 1987 ➤ 3,a874: ᴿStiZt 206 (1988) 431s (P. *Neuner*); ZkT 110 (1988) 352s (W. *Kern*: Autor Baptist in Hongkong); ZMissRW 72 (1988) 85s (P. *Antes*).

b509 *Betz* Otto, Religion als Versuchung; Faszination des Irrationalen: TGegw 30 (1987) 114-123.

b510 **Bibby** Reginald W., Fragmented gods; the poverty and potential of religion in Canada. Toronto 1987, Irwin. xvi-320 p. – ᴿSR 17 (1988) 367s (W. C. *James*).

b511 **Bowker** John, Licensed insanities; religions and belief in God in the contemporary world 1987 ➤ 3,a879: ᴿTLond 91 (1988) 137s (R. *MacKenna*).

b512 **Brown** L. B., The psychology of religious belief. L 1987, Academic. xi-260 p. – ᴿArchScSocRel 65 (1988) 247s (J.-P. *Deconchy*).

b513 **Carmody** John & Denise L., Interpreting the religious experience; a worldview [... *Voegelin* E.]. ENJ 1987, Prentice-Hall. viii-215 p. $18 pa. [TDig 35,262].

b514 **Carrier** Hervé, Psico-sociologia dell'appartenenza religiosa[2rev]. T-Leumann 1988, Elle Di Ci. 286 p. Lit. 19.000. 88-01-14630-2. – RGregorianum 69 (1988) 813s (*ipse*).

b515 **Clark** Stephen R. L., The mysteries of religion. Ox 1986, Blackwell. x-277 p. £25; pa. £8. – RNBlackf 68 (1987) 206s (A. *O'Hear*).

b516 *Cohn-Sherbok* Dan, Ranking religions [not 'religion' as page-headings]: RelSt 22 (1986) 377-386.

b517 **Coward** Harold G., Sacred word and sacred text; Scripture in world religions. Maryknoll NY 1988, Orbis. x-222 p. $22; pa. $11 [TDig 35,348]. 0-88344-605-7; 4-9.

b518 **Cox** Harvey G., Many mansions; a Christian's encounter with other faiths. Boston 1988, Beacon. 216 p. $19. 0-8070-1208-4 [TDig 36,152].

b519 **Cragg** Kenneth, The Christ and the faiths 1986 → 2,8665; 3,a890: RJEcuSt 25 (1988) 278 (N. E. *Thomas*); ModT 4 (1987s) 220s (T. *Gabriel*); NBlackfr 68 (1987) 159s (G. *D'Costa*); TLond 91 (1988) 162s (K. *Cracknell*); TS 49 (1988) 774-6 (J. D. *Redington*).

b520 *Darrow* William R., The Harvard way in the study of religion: HarvTR 81 (1988) 215-234.

b521 **D'Costa** Gavin, Theology and religious pluralism 1986 → 2,8667; 3,a894: RComSev 21 (1988) 106s (V. J. *Ansede Alonso*); JAAR 56 (1988) 142-4 (P. F. *Knitter*); JEcuSt 25 (1988) 276-8 (Ellen T. *Charry*); Missiology 16 (1988) 228s (A. *Camps*); ModT 4 (1987s) 407 s (C. *Gillis*).

b522 **Dean** William, American religious empiricism 1986 → 3,a895: RJAAR 56 (1988) 545-551 (C. D. *Hardwick,* also on SHEA W. 1984).

b523 *Dhavamony* Mariasusai, Today's challenge; salvation offered by non-Christian religions: EuntDoc 41 (1988) 421-438.

b524 *Dupré La Tour* Augustin, Christology and non-Christian religions [< PrOrChr 36 (1986) 193-205]: TEJermann Rosemary; TDig 35 (1988) 103-6.

b525 **Edwards** Denis, Human experience of God. Dublin 1984, Gill & M. xiii-154 p. £6. – RHeythJ 29 (1988) 102s (J. *Sullivan*).

b526 **Eliade** M., A history of religious ideas 1-3, 1978-85 → 58,c695 ... 2,8673: RÉglT 18 (1987) 131-8 (L. *Laberge*).

b527 **Ellwood** Robert S., The history and future of faith; religion past, present, and to come. NY 1988, Crossroad. viii-194 p. $19. 0-8245-0879-3 [TDig 36,157].

b528 **Feil** Ernst, Religio; die Geschichte eines neuzeitlichen Grundbegriffs ... 1986 → 3,a904: RSR 17 (1988) 110s (G. *Vallée*).

b529 **Fenn** Richard, The dream of the perfect act; an inquiry into the fate of religion in a secular world. NY 1987, Tavistock. 166 p. $33. – RTTod 45 (1988s) 254s (Barbara *Hargrove*).

b530 **Fernando** A., Jesus and the world religions. ... c. 1988, Marc. £2.50 [TLond 91,570].

b531 **Ferrarotti** Franco, *a)* Il paradosso del sacro. R 1983, Laterza; – *b)* Le paradoxe du sacré, TJaveau G. Bru 1987, Éperonniers. – RFoiTemps 18 (1988) 193s (E. *Hribersek*).

b532 **Filoramo** G., *Prandi* C., Le scienze delle religioni. Brescia 1987, Morcelliana. 238 p. Lit 22.000. – RStPatav 35 (1988) 191 (E. *Pace*).

b533 **Frankenberry** Nancy, Religion and radical empiricism 1987 → 3,a906: RRelStR 14 (1988) 136 (Catherine *Keller*: tight and elegant).

b534 *Garcia Prada* José M., Competencia experiencial y construcción de la experiencia religiosa: CiTom 114 (1987) 3-36.

b535 *Gasbarro* Nicola,   *a*) La preghiera e la storia; – *b*) Religione e storia delle religioni in Angelo BRELICH: SMSR 54 (1988) 95-132 / 289-313 [227-276, *al.*].

b536 **Gaskin** J.C.A.,   The quest for eternity; an outline of the philosophy of religion 1984 ➤ 65,9023; 1,a297:   ᴿHeythJ 29 (1988) 265s (B. *Davies*).

b537 **Geisler** Norman, *Corduan* Winfried,   Philosophy of religion². GR 1988, Baker.   402 p. [GraceTJ 9,306].

b538 **Gesché** Adolphe,   Le christianisme et les autres religions: RTLv 19 (1988) 315-341; Eng. 412.

b539 **Graham** William A.,   Beyond the written word; oral aspects in the history of religion 1987 ➤ 3,a912:   ᴿParabola 13,3 (1988) 102.104.107 (F.M. *Denny*).

b540 **Grant** Robert,   Gods and the one God 1986 ➤ 2,8683; 3,a913:   ᴿChH 57 (1988) 519s (H. *Chadwick*); RB 95 (1988) 470s (J. *Murphy-O'Connor*); Thomist 51 (1987) 542-5 (W. *Placher*).

b541 *Greco* Carlo,   La deduzione del concetto di religione nelle 'Lezioni sulla filosofia della religione' d G.W.F. HEGEL: FilT 1,2 (N 1988) 67-85 [143-152, *Celano* Bruno].

b542 **Greschat** Hans-J.,   Was ist Religionswissenschaft?: Urban-Tb 390.   Stu 1988, Kohlhammer.   141 p. – ᴿZMissRW 72 (1988) 317s (F. *Usarski*).

b543 **Hegel** Georg W.F.,   Lectures on the philosophy of religion, [first] one-volume edition, ᵀ*Brown* R., ᴱ*Hodgson* Peter C., *al.*   Berkeley 1988, Univ. California.   xvii-552 p. $47.50; pa. $15 [RelStR 15,243, R.R. *Williams*].

b544 **Helm** S. Mark,   Is Christ the only way? 1985. – ᴿMissiology 15,1 (1987) 117s (D.J. *Adams*).

b545 **Hick** John,   Problems of religions pluralism 1985 ➤ 2,8688; 3,a920: ᴿJAAR 56 (1986) 162s (R.C. *Neville*).

b546 ᴱ**Hick** J., *Knitter* P.,   The myth of Christian uniqueness; toward a pluralistic theology of religions.   Maryknoll ɴʏ 1988, Orbis.   264 p. $25; pa. $13.   0-88344-603-0; 2-2. – ᴿTablet 242 (1988) 1431 (G. *D'Costa*); TTod 45 (1988s) 464-466 (Denise L. *Carmody*).

b547 **Jaeschke** Walter,   Die Vernunft in der Religion... HEGELS 1986 ➤ 3,a925:   ᴿBijdragen 49 (1988) 470s (H.J. *Adriaanse*); RelStR 14 (1988) 140 (P.C. *Hodgson*); RTLv 19 (1988) 207-212 (E. *Brito*).

b548 *a*) *Jockwig* Klemens,   Religion in unserer Gesellschaft;   – *b*) D'Costa Gavin,   Das Pluralismus–Paradigma in der christlichen Sicht der Religionen: TGegw 30 (1987) 171-180 / 221-231.

b549 *a*) *Keller* Carl-A.,   Religion et science des religions;   – *b*) *Blaser* Klauspeter,   Une approche théologique des religions;   – *c*) *Gerber* Francis, Des structures et des hommes; le courant néo-piagétien en psychologie religieuse: RTPhil 120 (1988) 147-160 / 179-194 / 195-216.

b550 **Knitter** Paul F.,   No other name? 1985 ➤ 1,a319 ... 3,a931:   ᴿHeythJ 29 (1988) 270s (G. *Parrinder*).

b551 **Knitter** Paul F.,   Ein Gott — viele Religionen; gegen den Absolutheitsanspruch des Christentums, ᵀ*Wimmer* J.   Mü 1988, Kösel.   219 p. DM 34.   3-466-20295-7. – ᴿActuBbg 25 (1988) 227s (J. *Boada*); MüTZ 39 (1988) 214s (P. *Schmidt-Leukel*); TLZ 113 (1988) 803-5 (W. *Pfüller*); VerbumSVD 29 (1988) 202-5 (H. *Dumont*).

b552 **Koyama** Kosuke,   Mount Fuji and Mount Sinai [L, SCM: 'a pilgrimage in theology' ➤ 65,9520; 1,a862]; a critique of idols.   Maryknoll ɴʏ 1984, Orbis.   278 p. $13 pa. – ᴿMid-Stream 27 (1988) 223s (R.L. *Brawley*).

b553 **Kramer** Kenneth, World scriptures; an introduction to comparative religions 1986 → 2,8704: [R]Gregorianum 69 (1988) 180 (J. *Dupuis*); LvSt 13 (1988) 286 (Catherine *Cornille*); Vidyajyoti 52 (1988) 206 (M. *Amaladoss*).

b554 **Krüger** J. S., Studying religion; a methodological introduction to science of religion: Studia Theologica 1. Pretoria 1988 (= 1982 → 63,9093), Univ. 92 p. $8.65.

b555 [E]**Küng** Hans, Christianity and the world religions, paths of dialogue with Islam, Hinduism, and Buddhism [1982/4 → 1,604], [T]*Heinegg* Peter 1986 → 3,a936: [R]JEcuSt 25 (1988) 454s (R. H. *Drummond*); Missiology 16 (1988) 353s (Virginia T. *Johnson*); TLond 91 (1988) 54-56 (G. *Loughlin*: Can Catholic Christianity recognize itself in Küng's book, as his own p. xv requires?).

b556 *Küng* Hans, Die Funktion der Religion zur Bewältigung der geistigen Situation; Versuch einer zeitgeschichtlichen Analyse: → 114, [F]PANNENBERG W., Vernunft 1988, 138-156.

b557 **Larner** Christina [† 1983], Witchcraft and religion; the politics of popular belief. Ox 1984, Blackwell. xi-172 p. £15. – [R]HeythJ 29 (1988) 257s (P. *Burke*).

b558 *Lasić* Hrvoje, 'Naravna' i 'nadnaravna' dimenzija ljudskug bića ['Natural' / 'supernatural'... human existence] u filozofiji religije: ObnŽiv 43 (1988) 366-380.

b559 **Lévi-Strauss** Claude, The way of the masks, [T]*Modelski* Sylvia. Seattle 1988, Univ. Washington. x-249 p.; (color.) ill. 0-295-96636-X.

b560 **Lott** Eric J., Vision, tradition, interpretation; theology, religion, and the study of religion: Religion and Reason 35. Hawthorne NY 1988, Mouton de Gruyter. viii-272 p. DM 118 [TDig 36,68: largely on India, where he is professor].

b561 *Lotz* Johannes B., Le christianisme et les religions non-chrétiennes en relation avec l'expérience religieuse, [T]*Chalon* Colette: → 379, Vatican II Bilan 3 (1988) 167-188; Eng. → 380, Assessment 3, 161-182.

b562 **Lübbe** Hermann, Religion nach der Aufklärung. Graz 1986, Styria. 336 p. DM 50. 3-222-11722-5. – [R]Bijdragen 49 (1988) 346s (H. J. *Adriaanse*: prolix, pedantic, but important); TRu 53 (1988) 327-330 (D. *Lange*).

b563 *a*) *Makrakis* Michael K., [G] Introduction to the philosophy of religion; – *b*) *Theodorou* Evangelos D., [G] The philosophy of religion of Johannes HESSEN: TAth 59 (1988) 164-186 . 323-345 / 296-304.

b564 [E]**Malamoud** Charles, *Vernant* Jean-Pierre, Corps des dieux. Le Temps de la Réflexion 7, 1986 → 2,464*. – [R]RHR 205 (1988) 89s (C. *Jacob*).

b564* **Manferdini** Tina, Il problema della religione; BARTH e SCHLEIERMACHER. Bo 1984, Clueb. – [R]FilT 1,1 (1988) 178-180 (C. *Ciancio*).

b565 *a*) *Marramao* Giacomo, Sacer/sanctus/sanctio; lo spazio del potere fra tempo della tradizione e tempo della secolarizzazione; – *b*) *Molari* Carlo, Dal tempo sacro al tempo salvifico; – *c*) *Mazzoleni* Gilberto, Ciclicità e linearità del tempo; un dibattito storico-religioso: RSocietà 2,3 (R 1987) 54-63 / 64-71 / 17-33 [< ZIT 88,574].

b566 **Meissner** W. W., Life and faith; psychological perspectives on religious experience 1987 → 3,a951; $25: [R]TS 49 (1988) 770s (M. J. *McGinniss*).

b567 *Mellor* Philip, The application of the theories of Michel FOUCAULT to problems in the study of religion: TLond 91 (1988) 484-493.

b570 **Meslin** Michel, *a*) l'expérience humain du divin. P 1988, Cerf. – *b*) [un chapître] L'analyse anthropologique du religieux: RICathP 25 (1988) 37-46.

b571 *Müller* Gerhard L.,   Le Sacré: ➤ 791, DictSpir XIV,91 (1988) 37-45.

b572 *Nabe* Clyde,   Mystery and religion; NEWMAN's epistemology of religion. Lanham MD 1988, UPA.   xi-64 p. $13.25; pa. $8 [TDig 36,71].

b573 ᴱNeusner J.,   Take Judaism, for example 1983 ➤ 65,298; 1,634:   ᴿOLZ 83 (1988) 176-8 (W. *Wiefel*).

b574 *Neusner* Jacob,   The theological enemies of religious studies; theology and secularism in the trivialization and personalization of religion in the west: Religion 18,1 (L 1988) 21-36 [< ZIT].

b575 **Nielsen** Niels C., *al.*,   Religions of the world²ʳᵉᵛ [50 chapters of 1982 (➤ 64,9301) reorganized into 26]. NY 1988, St. Martin's.   xxiv-679 p. [TDig 35,188].

b576 *Olson* Carl,   The concept of power in the works of ELIADE and van der LEEUW: ST 42 (1988) 39-53.

b577 **Oppenheim** Frank M.,   Josiah ROYCE's mature philosophy of religion 1987 ➤ 3,a960:   ᴿTS 49 (1988) 773s (R. J. *Roth*).

b578 **Pailin** David,   Attitudes to other religions; comparative religion in seventeenth- and eighteenth-century Britain 1984 ➤ 65,9057; 2,8726: ᴿHeythJ 29 (1988) 258s (F. J. *Hamilton*).

b579 **Parrinder** Geoffrey,   Encountering world religions. E 1987, Clark. vii-232 p. £7. – ᴿIndTSt 25 (1988) 395s (A. *Kolencherry*); RRel 47 (1988) 310s (R. L. *Schebera*); SpTod 40 (1988) 88s (Carla Mae *Streeter*).

b580 **Parrinder** Geoffrey,   De godsdiensten van de wereld, historisch en actueel. Utrecht 1986, Spectrum.   360 p. *f* 99.   90-274-9037-6. – ᴿBijdragen 49 (1988) 226 (J. G. *Hahn*).

b581 **Pettersson** Olof, *Åkerberg* Hans,   Interpreting religious phenomena; studies with reference to the phenomenology of religion: Acta Univ. Lund. 1/36. Sto 1981, Almqvist & W.   201 p.   91-22-00405-X.

b582 **Prades** José A.,   Persistance et métamorphose du sacré. P 1987, PUF. 336 p. F 160. – ᴿRHPR 68 (1988) 483s (G. *Vahanian*); StPatav 35 (1988) 191s (E. *Pace*).

b583 **Preus** J. Samuel,   Explaining religion; criticism and theory from Bodin to Freud 1987 ➤ 3,a971:   ᴿÉTRel 63 (1988) 619s (M. *Despland*); RHE 83 (1988) 712-5 (R. *Crahay*); TTod 45 (1988s) 222. 224. 226s. 230 (R. *Fenn*).

b584 **Proudfoot** Wayne,   Religious experience 1985 ➤ 2,8734; 3,a972:   ᴿRelSt 24 (1988) 396-8 (A. *Millar*).

b585 *a*) *Prozesky* Martin,   Explanations of religion as a part of and problem for religious studies; – *b*) *Wiebe* Donald,   'Why the academic study of religion?' Motive and method in the study of religion: RelSt 24 (C 1988) 303-310 / 403-413.

b585* **Reid** Patrick V.,   Readings in Western religious thought; the ancient world 1987 ➤ 3,a973;   0-8091-2850-9: ᴿVidyajyoti 52 (1988) 304s (P. M. *Meagher*).

b586 **Ricketts** Mac L.,   Mircea ELIADE, the Romanian roots, 1907-1945: Boulder East European Mg 248. NY 1988, Columbia.   iv-1453 p. $200 [RelStR 15,340, J. *Strong*].

 Ries Julien,   Les chrétiens parmi les religions; des Actes des Apôtres à Vatican II: Le christianisme et la foi chrétienne 5, 1987 ➤ 8979.

b588 **Ries** J. Les chemins du sacré dans l'histoire [1981], 1985 ➤ 1,a354... 3,a976:   ᴿÉglT 17 (1986) 411s (L. *Laberge*: synthesis of the topics of L'expression du sacré).

b589 ᴱ**Ries** J., L'expression du sacré 1-III 1978/86 ➤ 60,627... 3,2978:   ᴿÉglT 17 (1986) 407-411 (L. *Laberge,* 1s); FoiTemps 19 (1987) 368s (G.

Harpigny, 3); Gregorianum 69 (1988) 177s (J. *Dupuis*, 3); MélSR 45 (1988) 192s (L. *Debarge*, 3).

b590 ᴱRies J., *Limet* H., Les rites d'initiation: Homo Religiosus 13, 1984/6 → 2,494; 3,a979: ᴿEsprVie 98 (1988) 74s (L. *Debarge*); Gregorianum 69 (1988) 178s (J. *Dupuis*); RTLv 19 (1988) 78s (J. *Étienne*); ScripTPamp 20 (1988) 828-831 (M. *Guerra*); TR 84 (1988) 139 (A. T. *Khoury*).

b591 *Ries* Julien, Chronique d'histoire des religions; culture, religions et foi chrétienne; quelques jalons de la réflexion actuelle: EsprVie 90 (1988) 505-510.

b592 **Samuel** Albert, Les religions aujourd'hui. P/Lyon 1987, Ouvrières/ Chronique sociale. 304 p. F 105. – ᴿEsprVie 98 (1988) 75s (L. *Debarge*); MélSR 45 (1988) 42-44 (aussi L. *Debarge*).

b593 **Schaeffler** Richard, Religionsphilosophie, ᴱ*Ströker* Elisabeth, *Wieland* Wolfgang: Hb Philosophie 4, 1983 → 65,9075; 2,8753: ᴿTPhil 63 (1988) 445-7 (J. *Schmidt*).

b594 **Scharfenberg** Joachim, Sigmund FREUD and his critique of religion [1968], ᵀ*Dean* O.C. Ph 1988, Fortress [RelStR 15,240, Diane *Jonte-Pace*: poor translation retaining only a tenth of the footnotes].

b595 *Seidel* George J., Prolegomena to the study of religions: JDharma 12 (1987) 108-126.

b596 **Sell** Alan P.F., The philosophy of religion. L 1988, Croom Helm. x-252 p. [JTS 39,677].

b597 *a) Sharpe* Eric J., The secularization of the history of religions; – *b) Almagor* Uri, The structuration of meaning in a 'primitive religion': → 149, ꟳWERBLOWSKY R., Gilgul 1987, 257-269.

b598 **Shea** John J., Religious experiencing; William JAMES and Eugene GENDLIN. Lanham MD 1987, UPA. ix-145 p. $22.50; pa. $10.75 [TDig 35,389].

b599 **Siebert** Rudolf J., The critical theory of religion; the Frankfurt School, from universal pragmatic to political theology: Religion and Reason 29 1985 → 1,a370; 2,8758: ᴿBijdragen 49 (1988) 468-470 (H. de *Vries*).

b600 **Siebrand** H.J., SPINOZA and the Netherlands; an inquiry into the early reception of his philosophy of religion: diss. Groningen, ᴰ*Jong* A. de, 1988. Assen 1988, van Gorcum. xii-242 p. 90-232-2319-5. – TsTNijm 28 (1988) 296s.

b601 **Smart** Ninian, Religion and the western mind 1987 → 3,a991: ᴿRRel-Res 30 (1988s) 102s (M. L. *Stackhouse*: ill-edited).

b602 **Smith** Wilfred C., Towards a world theology 1981 → 61,k678 ... 1,a374: ᴿJEcuSt 24 (1987) 616-643 (S. R. *Isenberg*).

b603 **Stark** Rodney, *Bainbridge* William S., A theory of religion [... a set of axioms not reducing all religion to one metaphor like *Durkheim*'s 'society worshiping itself']: Toronto Studies in Religion 2. NY 1987, P. Lang. 386 p. $52.50 [TDig 36,85].

b604 *Stoesz* Donald B., Don WIEBE [The failure of nerve in the academic study of religion 1984]; a shift in his method?: TorJT 4 (1988) 71-85.

b605 **Stolz** Fritz, Grundzüge der Religionswissenschaft. Gö 1988, Vanden-hoeck & R. 260 p. DM 21,80. – ᴿRelStR 14 (1988) 358 (W. R. *Garrett*).

b606 **Strolz** W., Heilswege der Weltreligionen 1984-6 → 3,a993: ᴿKatKenk 53 (1988) 172-6 (S. *Takayanagi*).

b607 ᴱ**Swidler** Leonard, Toward a universal theology of religion 1987 → 3,a994: ᴿGregorianum 69 (1987) 590-2 (J. *Dupuis*); Irénikon 61 (1988) 590-2 (M. G.); PhilipSa 23 (1988) 473s (B. *Vargas*); REB 48 (1988) 501-7 (W. *Boff*).

b608 **Towler** Robert, The need for certainty; a sociological study of conventional religion. L 1984, Routledge-KP. vi-130 p. £13. – RHeythJ 29 (1988) 263s (Eileen *Barker*).

b609 *Vallet* Odon, Le sacré et le honteux : ÉTRel 63 (1988) 579-583.

b610 **Waardenburg** Jacques, Religion und Religionen; systematische Einführung in die Religionswissenschaft: Göschen 2228, 1986 → 2,8772; 3,b1; 3-11-010324-9: RBO 45 (1988) 465-470 (P. *Xella*).

b611 **Wach** Joachim, Introduction to the history of religions, EKitagawa J., al. NY 1988, Macmillan. xxxiv-234 p. 0-02-933530-2.

b612 **Wagner** Falk, Was ist Religion? Studien zu ihrem Begriff und Thema in Geschichte und Gegenwart 1986 → 2,8773; 3,b2: RActuBbg 25 (1988) 89 (J. *Boada*); Bijdragen 49 (1988) 225 (H. J. *Adriaanse*).

b613 **Ward** Keith, Images of eternity; concepts of God in five religious traditions 1987 → 3,b4: RTLond 91 (1988) 365-8 (W. C. *Smith*).

b614 **Wasson** R. G., al., Persephone's quest; entheogens [psychoactive mushrooms] and the origins of religion. NHv 1988, Yale. 257 p.; ill. $32.50 [RelStR 15,238, W. *Harman*: joyriding academic romp for undergraduates, will amuse most others].

b615 *Weier* Winfried, Existentieller Ursprung und psychologistische Deutung der Religion: ZkT 110 (1988) 1-23.

b616 *Welker* Michael, 'Einheit der Religionsgeschichte' und 'universales Selbstbewusstsein' — Zur gegenwärtigen Suche nach Leitbegriffen im Dialog zwischen Theologie und Religionswissenschaft: EvT 48 (1988) 3-18.

b617 **Westphal** Merold, God, guilt, and death; an existential phenomenology of religion 1984 → 65,9099; 1,a394: RRelStR 14 (1988) 139 (L. J. *Biallas*).

b618 **Whaling** Frank, Christian theology and world religions; a global approach: Contemporary Christian Studies 1986 → 3,b8: RGregorianum 69 (1988) 180s (J. *Dupuis*); JEcuSt 25 (1988) 112s (J. R. *Timm*); ScotJT 41 (1988) 280s (R. *Hooker*).

b619 EWhaling Frank, Contemporary approaches to the study of religion I-II, 1984s → 1,411... 3,b9: RGregorianum 69 (1988) 385s (M. *Dhavamony*); JTS 39 (1988) 350-3 (M. *Pye*, 1); RelSt 24 (1988) 400s (G. *Richards*, 1).

b620 EWhaling Frank, Religion in today's world [→ 3,479]; the religious situation of the world from 1945 to the present day 1987: RTLond 91 (1988) 558s (A. *Race*).

b620* *Wigen* Tore, [Norw.] Modern Jewish philosophy of religion [... *Buber*, *Heschel*, *Wiesel*]: TsTKi 59 (1988) 45-62.

b621 *Wilfred* Felix, Weltreligionen und christliche Inkulturation, TFaymonville Ursula: ZMissRW 72 (1988) 205-220; Eng. 218s.

M3.5 **Mythologia.**

b622 **Belmont** Nicole, Paroles païennes; mythe et folklore. P 1986, Imago. 176 p. – RArchScSocRel 65 (1988) 241 (Françoise *Lautman*).

b623 *Bianchi* Ugo, Mitologia orientale e mitologia greca: OrAnt 27 (1988) 261-9,

b624 **Birenbaum** Harvey, Myth and mind. Lanham MD 1988, UPA. xviii-271 p. $29; pa. $15.25 [TDig 35,342].

b625 *Boriaud* Jean-Yves, Les mythologies jésuites (fin du XVIIe siècle, début du XVIIIe) [pour dévoiler les origines de l'idolâtrie: AUBERY, GAUL-

TRUCHE, POMEY, de JOUVANCY, RIGORD]: RÉLat 65 (1987) 244-260; lat. 244.

b625* **Boswell** Fred & Jeanetta, What men or gods are these? A genealogical approach to classical mythology. Metuchen NJ 1980, Scarecrow. viii-315 p. 0-8108-1314-9.

b626 **Campbell** Joseph, [conversation with *Moyers* Bill], EFlowers Betty S., The power of myth. NY 1988, Doubleday, xix-231 p. $27.50; pa. $20 [RelStR 15,240, R. A. *Segal*].

b627 **Davidson** Hilda R. Ellis, Myths and symbols in pagan Europe; early Scandinavian and Celtic religions. Syracuse NY 1988, Univ. xii-268 p. $28; pa. $15. 0-8156-2438-7, 441-7. [TDig 36,153].

b628 **Detienne** Marcel, The creation of mythology, TCook Margaret 1986 → 3,b24: RJAAR 56 (1988) 147-9 (R. A. *Segal*).

b629 **Doty** W., Mythography 1986 → 2,8789; 3,b25: RJAAR 56 (1988) 149-152 (R. A. *Segal*).

b630 EDundes Alan, Sacred narrative; readings in the theory of myth [*Frazer, Malinowski, Eliade, Jung*...] 1984 → 1,e340; 3,b26: RJAAR 55 (1987) 829s (S. *Walens*).

b631 **Eisner** Robert, The road to Daulis; psychoanalysis, psychology, and [their misuse of] classical mythology. Syracuse NY 1987, Univ. xi-301 p. $32.50. 0-8156-0210-3. – RClasW 82 (1988s) 215 (Lois J. *Parker*).

b632 **Evers** John D., Myth as narrative; structure and meaning in some Ancient Near Eastern texts: diss. DGibson J. ... E 1988. – 215 p. [> AOAT]. – RTLv 20,537.

b633 **Gadamer** Hans-Georg, *Fries* Heinrich, Mythos und Wissenschaft [CGMG 2]: Enzyklopädische Bibliothek. FrB 1981, Herder. 136 p. 3-451-19202-0.

b634 **Gaskell** G. A., Dictionary of Scripture and myth. NY 1988, Dorset. 845 p. 0-88029-269-5.

b635 *Grabner-Haider* Anton, Probleme der Mythosforschung: TPQ 136 (1988) 362-7.

b636 *Heusch* Luc de, Myth as reality: JRelAf 18 (1988) 200-215.

b637 **Hübner** Kurt, Die Wahrheit des Mythos 1985 → 1,a412 ... 3,b34: RTPhil 63 (1988) 135 (H. *Watzka*).

b638 *Imhoof* Stefan, Le mythe contre la science [*Hübner* K., Die Wahrheit des Mythos 1985]: RTPhil 120 (1988) 217-224.

b639 **Jesi** Furio, Letteratura e mito: Piccola Biblioteca 421. T 1981, Einaudi. 245 p. Lit. 7000.

b640 *King* Thomas M., TEILHARD and the dimensions of myth: RRel 47 (1988) 868-872.

Kullman W. al., Mythos: FMUTH R. 1987 → 110.

b640* **Lévêque** Pierre, Colère, sexe, rire; le Japon des mythes anciens: Vérité des mythes. P 1988, Blettres. 110 p.; ill. 2-251-32410-0.

b641 **Lévi-Strauss** Claude, The jealous potter [Amerindian myths; introduction to structuralism and attack on FREUD], TChorier Bénédicte. Ch 1988, Univ. viii-250 p.; ill. $20 [RelStR 15,55, R. A. *Segal*].

b642 **Lindow** John, Scandinavian mythology, an annotated bibliography: Garland reference library of the humanities 394. NY 1988, Garland. xv-593 p. $43 [TDig 36,68].

b643 *Lindow* John, Scandinavian mythology: → 792, DMA 11 (1988) 22-34.

b644 *McCurley* Foster R., American myths and the Bible: Word + World 8,3 (1988) 226-233.

b645 *McGaughey* Douglas, Through myth to imagination: JAAR 56 (1988) 51-76.

b646 *MacQueen* Graeme, *Whose* sacred history? Reflections on myth and dominance: SR 17 (1988) 143-157.

b648 *Müller* H.-P., Pygmaion, Pygmalion und Pumaijaton; aus der Geschichte einer mythischen Gestalt: Orientalia 57 (1988) 192-205.

b649 **Puhvel** Jaan, Comparative mythology. Baltimore 1988, Johns Hopkins. x-302 p.; ill. 0-8018-3413-9.

b650 *Schjødt* Jens P., Recent scholarship in Old Norse mythology: RelStR 14 (1988) 104-110.

b651 **Strenski** Ivan, Four theories of myth in twentieth-century history; CASSIRER, ELIADE, LÉVI-SRAUSS and MALINOWSKI ['there is no such "thing" as myth ... manufactured by its "merchandisers" ']. Iowa City 1987, Univ. Iowa. viii-234 p. $22.50 [TDig 36,86].

b652 **Vidal-Naquet** Pierre, The black hunter; forms of thought and forms of society in the ancient world, ᵀ*Szegedy-Maszak* Andrew, 1986 ➤ 2,9979: ᴿAm-JPg 109 (1988) 282-5 (N. *Robertson*); ClasW 82 (1988s) 211s (D. *Sinos*).

b653 *Wolicka* Elżbieta, ❷ *Obecność mitu* ... The presence of [the] myth in the past and today: ZesKUL 29,2 (1986) 33-46; Eng. 46.

M4 **Religio romana.**

b653* *Arjava* Antti, Divorce in later Roman law: Artos 22 (1988) 5-21.

b654 **Baldassari** Mariano, La logica stoica 5b, 7b, 8 [testi con traduzione]. Como 1987, Noseda. 207; 112. 223 p. – ᴿClasR 102 (1988) 426s (J. *Barnes*: texts now complete, index awaited).

b655 **Barkan** Leonard, The gods made flesh; [OVID] Metamorphosis and the pursuit of paganism. NHv 1986, Yale. xvi-198 p.; 38 fig. – ᴿGnomon 60 (1988) 6s (Iiro *Kajanto,* Eng.).

b655* *Berczelly* László, The soul after death; a new interpretation of the Fortunati-Sarcophagus [Rome national museum]: AcANorv 6 (1987) 59-90; 17 fig.

b656 **Bettini** Maurizio, Antropologia [metafisica] e cultura romana; parentela, tempo, immagini dell'anima: Studi superiori NIS 19, Lettere. R 1986, La Nuova Italia Scientifica. 271 p. Lit. 32.000. – ᴿGnomon 60 (1988) 148-150 (V. *Pöschl*).

b657 ᴱ**Bianchi** Ugo, *Vermaseren* Maarten J., La soteriologia dei culti orientali nell'impero romano 1979/82 ➤ 63,691; 65,9128: ᴿBO 45 (1988) 462s (J. den *Boeft*).

b658 ᴱ**Bonfante** Larissa, Etruscan life and afterlife; a handbook of Etruscan studies [by experts in eight areas] 1986 ➤ 3,485: $45; pa. $15. 0-8143-1772-3; 813-4: ᴿClasW 82 (1988s) 60s (Helen *Nagy*).

b659 **Bremmer** J.N., *Horsfall* N.M., Roman myth and mythography 1987 ➤ 3,b48*: ᴿRÉLat 66 (1988) 354s (J.-C. *Richard*).

b660 *Cazanove* Olivier de, Jupiter, Liber et le vin latin: RHR 205 (1988) 245-265; Eng. 245.

b661 **Champeaux** Jacqueline, Fortuna ... culte: Coll. 64 [1982, 526 p. ➤ 65, 9131; 2,8811]. R 1987, École Française: ᴿRELat 66 (1988) 356-8 (H. *Le Bonniec*).

b662 *Classen* C. Joachim, Virtutes Romanorum; römische Tradition und griechischer Einfluss: Gymnasium 95 (1988) 289-302.

b663 **Colish** Marcia L., The Stoic tradition from antiquity to the early Middle Ages 1985 ➤ 3,b52: ᴿEirene 25 (1988) 160-2 (D. *Machovec*).

b664 *Curran* B.F.,   Soteriological themes and motifs in Roman religion:
➤ 554, Salvation 1986/8, 31-42.

b665 *Dumont* Jean-Paul,   L'idée de Dieu chez PLINE (HN 2,1-5, 1-27):
Helmantica 37 (1986) 219-237.

b666 *a) Ferguson* John,   Roman cults [Magic Divination]; – *b) Beard* Mary,
Roman priesthoods; – *c) North* John A.,   Sacrifice and Ritual / Afterlife:
➤ 444, Mediterranean ²(1988) 909-923 [881-6 / 951-8] / 933-9 / 981-6 /
997-1007.

b667 *Flobert* P.,   La relation de *sacrificare* et de *sacerdos*: ➤ 95, ᶠLE BON-
NIEC H. 1988, 171-6.

b668 *Georgi* Dieter,   Analyse des LIVIUSberichts über den Bakchanaliens-
kandal: ➤ 140, ᶠSTOODT D., Unterwegs 1987, 191-208.

b669 **Goulet-Cazé** Marie-Odile,   L'ascèse cynique; un commentaire de Dio-
gène LAËRCE, VI, 70-71: Histoire des doctrines de l'Antiquité classique
10.   P 1986, Vrin.   292 p.; front. F 267. – ᴿClasR 102 (1988) 162s (J.
Mansfeld).

b670 Les grandes figures religieuses; fonctionnement pratique et symbolique
dans l'Antiquité [colloque Besançon]: Centre Hist. Anc. Univ. Besançon
68.   P 1986.   607 p. 26 art. [RÉLat 65,429].

b671 **Hänlein-Schäfer** Heidi,   Veneratio Augusti; eine Studie zu den Tempeln
des ersten römischen Kaisers [Diss. Heid. 1982]: Archaeologica 39, 1985
➤ 1,a436; 3,b61:   ᴿHZ 247 (1988) 139-141 (P. *Zanker*); RPLH 62,1
(1988) 179-184 (A. *Vassileiou*).

b672 **Heck** Eberhard,   *Mē theomacheîn* oder: Die Bestrafung des Gottes-
verächters; Untersuchungen zu Bekämpfung und Aneignung römischer
Religio bei TERTULLIAN, CYPRIAN und LAKTANZ: StudKLPg 24.   Fra
1987, Lang. 257 p. Fs 56. – ᴿGnomon 60 (1988) 651-3 (Ilona *Opelt*).

b673 ᴱ**Henig** Martin, *King* Anthony,   Pagan gods and shrines of the Roman
Empire: Oxford Univ. Committee for Archaeology Mg 8, 1986 ➤ 2,8823;
£25:   ᴿAJA 92 (1988) 454s (R. *MacMullen*); BonnJbb 188 (1988) 582-4
(R. *Turcan*); ClasR 102 (1988) 296-8 (J. *Liebeschuetz*); RArchéol (1988)
426s (C. *Goudineau*).

b674 **Jaczynowska** Maria, ❷ *Religie świata rzymskiego* [of the Roman world].
Wsz 1987, PWN.   319 p. zł. 149. – ᴿEos 76 (1988) 383-6 (M. *Żyromski*);
VoxPa 12s (1987s) 478-486 (M. *Dzielska*).

b675 **Lane** E.N.,   The other monuments: Corpus cultus Iovis Sabazii II: ÉPR
100, 1985 ➤ 1,a442: ᴿSecC 6,1 (1987s) 58-60 (R.F. *Hock*).

b676 **Leclant** J., *Clerc* G.,   Inventaire bibliographique des Isiaca (IBIS);
répertoire analytique des travaux relatifs à la diffusion des cultes isiaques
1940-1969: ÉPR 18 [I. A-D, 1972 ➤ 53,7388; II. E-K, 1974 ➤ 56,7986],
III. L-Q, 1985 ➤ 3,1087:   ᴿAulaO 6 (1988) 118s (J. *Padró*); ClasR 102
(1988) 430 (J.G. *Griffiths*: the entries show that no one has enriched these
studies more than Leclant).

b678 *Lo Porto* Felice G.,   Testimonianze archeologiche di culti metapontini:
Xenia 16 (R 1988) 5-28; 20 fig.

b679 **Luck** George,   Arcana mundi; magic and the occult in the Greek and
Roman worlds; a collection of ancient texts.   Baltimore 1985, Johns
Hopkins Univ.   xv-395 p. $30; pa. $13. – ᴿAmJPg 109 (1988) 148-152
(Jean R. *Bram*).

b680 *McDonnell* M.,   Divorce initiated by women in Rome [PLAUTUS
evidence inconclusive]: AmJAncH 8,1 (CM 1983) 54-80 [NTAbs 32,225,
D.J. *Harrington*: 'a woman's freedom to divorce had to wait for a more
enlightened age'].

b681 **MacMullen** Ramsay, Le paganisme dans l'Empire romain [1981], ᵀ*Spiquel* A., *Rousselle* A.: Les chemins de l'histoire, 1987 → 3,b70: ᴿRÉLat 65 (1987) 359-362 (J.-L. *Fredouille*); RHist 280, 567 (1988) 248-252 (Élisabeth *Smadja*); RHR 205 (1988) 198-202 (R. *Turcan*).

b682 **Meer** L. B. van der, The bronze liver of Piacenza [c.100 a.C.]; analysis of a polytheistic structure: Dutch Mg. Anc. Hist. Arch. 2. Amst 1987, Gieben. 202 p.; 78 fig. – ᴿJRS 78 (1988) 208s (Larissa *Bonfante*); Salesianum 50 (1988) 582s (R. *Della Casa*).

b683 **Montanari** Enrico, Identità culturale e conflitti religiosi nella Roma repubblicana: Filologia e critica 54. R 1988, Ateneo. 178 p.

b684 *Negri* Angela M., Sunt lacrimae rerum et mentem mortalia tangunt: StItFgCl 81 (3/6, 1988) 240-258.

b685 **Parke** H. W., ᴱ*McGing* B. C., Sibyls and Sibylline prophecy in classical antiquity: Croom Helm Classical Studies. L 1988, Routledge. xii-236 p. £25. 0-415-00343-1 [Antiquity 62,657].

b686 **Price** S.R.F., Rituals and power 1984 → 65,9144 ... 3,b75: ᴿCurrTM 15 (1988) 208s (E. *Krentz*); Gymnasium 94 (1987) 462s (K. *Brodersen*); Latomus 47 (1988) 196-8 (M. *Le Glay*).

b686* [ᴱ**Puech** E.] *LeRoux* Françoise, [on Celts, p. 93-158; nothing on Romans] *al.*, Le religioni dell'Europa centrale precristiana: Bibl. Universale 220. R 1988, Laterza. 179 p.; map. Lit. 16.000. 88-420-3014-7. → b899.

b687 **Robert** Jean-Noël, Les plaisirs à Rome [... vs. 'bonheur']: Realia. P 1983, BLettres. 232 p. F 99. – ᴿGnomon 60 (1988) 172s (H. *Schneider*).

b688 **Sabbatucci** Dario, La religione di Roma antica, dal calendario festivo all'ordine cosmico: La Cultura 67. Mi 1988, Saggiatore. 372 p. 88-043-0954-7.

b689 **Schilling** Robert, Dans le sillage de Rome; religion, poésie, humanisme: Études et Commentaires 101. P 1988, Klincksieck. xii-283 p. 2-252-02611-1.

b690 **Schön** Dorit, Orientalische Kulte im römischen Österreich. Köln 1987, Böhlau. 262 p.; ill. [Mundus 24,174].

b690* **Schürmann** Wolfgang, Untersuchungen zu Typologie und Bedeutung der stadtrömischen Minerva-Kultbilder ᴰ1985 → 3,b78; 88-7689-089-0: ᴿBabesch 62 (1987) 179s (E. M. *Moormann*).

b691 **Selem** Petar, Les religions orientales dans la Pannonie romaine: ÉPR 85, 1980 → 61,m896; 64,9397: ᴿAntClas 57 (1988) 625s (J. C. *Balty*).

b692 ᴱ**Smith** R. C., *Lounibos* J., Pagan and Christian anxiety, a response to E. R. DODDS 1984 → 2,395: ᴿSecC 6 (1987s) 112s (Rebecca H. *Weaver*).

b693 ᴱ**Sordi** Marta, Santuari e politica nel mondo antico 1983 → 1,401*a*: ᴿKlio 70 (1988) 240-5 (Irina S. *Svencickaja*, F. A. *Michajlovskij*).

b694 **Turcan** Robert, Religion romaine: IconRel 17/1s. Leiden 1988, Brill. I. 49 p.; LII pl; II. 40 p.; aussi LII pl. 90-04-08799-0; 800-8. – ᴿRÉLat 66 (1988) 359s (Annie *Dubourdieu*).

b695 **Vaccai** G., Le feste di Roma antica; miti, riti, costumi. R 1986, Mediterranee. xxiv-277 p.

b695* **Vanggaard** Jens H., The Flamen; a study in the history and sociology of Roman religion. K 1988, Museum Tusculanum. 175 p. 87-7289-059-2.

b696 **Wrede** Henning, Consecratio in formam deorum [... private persons identified with a divinity] 1981 → 62,a38 ... 1,a455: ᴿAnzAltW 41 (1988) 202-5 (G. *Dobesch*).

b697 **York** Michael, The Roman festival calendar of Numa Pompilius: AmerUnivSt 2/. NY 1986, Lang. xiv-383 p. Fs 70,60. – ᴿGnomon 60 (1988) 14-17 (G. *Radke*).

M4.5 **Mithraismus.**

b698 **Beck** Roger, Planetary gods and planetary orders in the mysteries of Mithras: ÉPR 109. Leiden 1988, Brill. xiv-113 p.; VI pl. 90-04-08450-9.

b698* **Lissi-Caronna** Elisa, Il mitreo dei Castra Peregrinorum (S. Stefano Rotondo): ÉPR 104, 1986 → 2,8846: ᴿBonnJbb 188 (1988) 599s (R. *Turcan*).

b699 **Merkelbach** R., Mithras 1984 → 65,9155... 3,b85: ᴿRÉLat 65 (1987) 363-7 (J. *Beaujeu*).

b700 *Sandelin* Kurt-Gustav, Mithras = Auriga? [in English]: Arctos 22 (1988) 133-5.

b700* *a*) *Teeple* Howard M., How Mithra won the west; – *b*) *LiDonnici* Lynn R., Epidaurian miracle cures; – *c*) *Kessler* Gary B., Plato and the primal being: → 500, SBL Seminars 1988, 312-7 / 272-6 / 277-284.

b701 *Ziegle* Anne, Du culte de Mithra au couvent des Carmes [bordelais]: Archéologie 234 (Dijon 1988) 40-47.

M5 **Religio graeca.**

b702 **Ballabriga** Alain, Le Soleil et le Tartare; l'image mythique du monde en Grèce archaïque 1986 → 3,b91; F 230; 2-7132-0866-1: ᴿAntClas 57 (1988) 469s (Vinciane *Pirenne-Delforge*).

b703 *Baltes* Matthias, Die Todesproblematik in der griechischen Philosophie: Gymnasium 95 (1988) 97-128.

b704 *Bels* J., SOCRATE et la mort individuelle; sur la modification socratique de la perception traditionnelle de la mort dans la pensée grecque: RSPT 72 (1988) 437-442; Eng. 442.

b705 **Bernabò Brea** Luigi, Il tempio di Afrodite di Akrai [Siracusa]: Cah. J. Bérard 10/Recherches sur les cultes grecs d'occident 3. N 1986, Centre J. Bérard. 90 p.; 48 fig. – ᴿRArchéol (1988) 148s (G. *Vallet*).

b706 *Beschi* Luigi, Demeter: → 852, LIMC 4,1 (1988) 844-892 (-908, Ceres, *De Angeli* Stefano).

b707 *Bevan* Elinor, Ancient deities and tortoise-representations in sanctuaries: AnBritAth 83 (1988) 1-6.

b708 *Bianchi* Ugo, Il 'prima' e l''altrove'; variazioni sul tema del rapporto tra dèi e uomini nella religione greca antica: Kernos I (Liège 1988) 9-18.

b709 **Borgeaud** Philippe, The cult of Pan in ancient Greece [1979 → 61, k767.k920], ᵀ*Atass* Kathleen, *Redfield* James. Ch 1988, Univ. xi-273 p. 0-226-06595-2; pa. 6-0.

b710 *a*) *Bostock* David, Pleasure and activity in ARISTOTLE's Ethics; – *b*) *Heinaman* Robert, Eudaimonia and self-sufficiency in the Nicomachean Ethics: Phronesis 33 (1988) 251-272 / 31-53.

b711 **Brelich** A., I Greci e gli dèi. N 1985, Liguori. 141 p. – ᴿEuntDoc 41 (1988) 157 (P. *Miccoli*).

b712 **Broek** R. van den, *al.*, Knowledge of God in the Graeco-Roman world: ÉPR 112. Leiden 1988, Brill. ix-290 p.

b713 **Brulé** Pierre, La fille d'Athènes; la religion des filles à Athènes à l'époque classique; mythes, cultes et société: Centre de Recherches d'Histoire Ancienne 76. P 1988, BLettres. 455 p. 2-251-60363-8.

b714 *Brunschwig* Jacques, La théorie stoïcienne du genre suprême et l'ontologie platonicienne: ➤ 670, ᴱ*Barnes* J., IV Symposium Hellenisticum 1986/8, 19-127.

b715 **Burkert** Walter, Ancient mystery cults 1987 ➤ 3,b103: ᴿKernos 1 (1988) 249s (A. *Motte*); Parabola 13,3 (1988) 107-9 (Rachel *Fletcher*); Phoenix 42 (Toronto 1988) 266-270 (R. *Beck*).

b716 **Burkert** Walter, Greek religion 1985 ➤ 1,a464 ... 3,b104: ᴿClasW 80 (1986s) 58s (J. E. *Rexine*).

b717 **Burkert** Walter, Mito e rituale in Grecia 1987 ➤ 3,b105; ᵀ*Nuzzaco* Francesco: Coll. Storica. R 1987, Laterza. xiii-254 p. – ᴿOrpheus 9 (1988) 372-4 (Antonella *Borgo*).

b718 **Burkert** Walter, Die orientalisierende Epoche in der griechischen Religion und Literatur: Szb Heid 1984 ➤ 2,8864; 3,b102: ᴿOLZ 83 (1988) 14-18 (I. *Becher*).

b719 ᴱ**Calame** Claude, Métamorphoses du mythe en Grèce antique: Religions en perspective 4. Genève 1988, Labor et Fides. 247 p. 2-8309-0122-1. 14 art.; none infra.

b720 *Clauss* James J., Lies and allusions; the addressee and date of CALLIMACHUS' Hymn to Zeus: [Calif.] ClasAnt 5 (1986) 155-170.

b721 *Clinton* Kevin, The date of the classical telesterion at Eleusis: ➤ 111, ᶠMYLONAS G., *Phília épē* 2 (1987) 254-262.

b722 *a) Cole* Susan G., Greek cults; – *b) Turner* Judy A., Greek priesthoods; – *c) Pollard* John, Divination and oracles, Greece; – *d) Jameson,* Michael H., Sacrifice and ritual, Greece; – *e) Vermeule* Emily, The afterlife, Greece: ➤ 444, Mediterranean 1988, 887-908 / 925-931 / 941-950 / 959-979 / 987-996.

b723 *Connor* W. R., 'Sacred' and 'secular'; *hierà kaì hósia* and the classical Athenian concept of the state: AncS 19 (1988) 161-188.

b724 **Corsar** P. Kenneth, Discovering Greek mythology. L 1985, Arnold. 116 p. $17. 0-7131-0078-3. – ᴿAncHRes 18 (1988) 53s (A. & D. *Rontidis*: companion to his 1977 Discovering the ancient Greeks, here reviewed p. 51-53 by R. *McClure*).

b725 *Craighead* Houston A., Constructing the concept of God [Xenophanes ... *Kaufman* G.]: ➤ 80, ᶠKILGORE W. J. 1987, 247-268.

b725* **Dengate** Christina F., The sanctuaries of Apollo in the Peloponnesus: diss. Chicago 1988. – DissA 49 (1988s) 858-A.

b726 **Detienne** Marcel, Dioniso a cielo aperto, ᵀ*Garin* Maria. R 1987, Laterza. 112 p. Lit. 15.000. – ᴿSMSR 54 (1988) 393 (G. A. *Samonà*).

b727 **Diel** P., Symbolism [... dans la Bible 1975 ➤ 57,478] in Greek mythology; human desire and its transformations [1966], ᵀ*Stuart* Vincent, *al.* Boulder 1980, Shambhala. xx-218 p. 0-87773-178-0 / Random 0-394-51083-6.

b728 **Dietrich** Bernard C., Tradition in Greek religion 1986 ➤ 2,8872; 3,b115: ᴿAmJPg 109 (1988) 280s (J. D. *Mikalson*); AntClas 57 (1988) 468 (Vinciane *Pirenne-Delforge*); ClasW 82 (1988s) 57s (P. *Properzio*); HZ 247 (1988) 381s (F. *Graf*); RelStR 14 (1988) 153 (A. T. *Kraabel*).

b730 *Dietrich* Bernard C., Divine personality and personification: Kernos 1 (Liège 1988) 19-28.

b731 *a) Dietrich* Bernard C., A case for Minoan / Mycenaean religion; – *b) Corsten* Thomas, Zu den sogenannten schwebenden Gottheiten: ➤ 776, Ägäische Vorgeschichte 1984/7, 173-191 / 193-200.

b732 *Dorandi* Tiziano, Una 'ri-edizione' antica del Perì eusebeías di FILODEMO: ZPapEp 73 (1988) 25-29.

b733 **Döring** Klaus, Der Sokratesschüler Aristipp und die Kyrenaiker: Abh. g/soz 1988/1. Mainz 1988, Akad. Wiss. Lit. 71 p. 3-515-05139-2.

b734 **Dörrie** Heinrich, [E]*Dörrie* Annemarie, Der Platonismus in der Antike, I. Die geschichtlichen Wurzeln des Platonismus 1987 → 3,b117; DM 510: [R]ClasR 102 (1988) 69s (M. *Schofield*).

b735 **Erbse** Hartmut, Untersuchungen zur Funktion der Götter im homerischen Epos 1986 → 2,8875; 3,b121: [R]DLZ 109 (1988) 21-23 (F. *Jürss*).

b736 *a) Fauth* Wolfgang, Sakrale Prostitution im Vorderen Orient und im Mittelmeerraum; – *b) Kany* Roland, Dionysos Protrygaios; pagane und christliche Spuren eines antiken Weinfestes: JbAC 31 (1988) 24-39 / 5-23.

b737 **Ferber** Rafael, PLATOS Idee des Guten 1984 → 3,b123: [R]AnzAltW 41 (1988) 147-9 (H.-C. *Günther*).

b738 **Ferrari** Giovanni G. R. F., Listening to the cicadas; a study of PLATO's Phaedrus: ClasSt. C 1987, Univ. xiii-293 p. (not a translation) 0-521-26778-1.

b739 *a) Fontenrose* Joseph, The cult of Apollo and the games at Delphi; – *b) Harmon* Daniel P., The religious significance of games in the Roman age: → 767, Olympics 1984/8, 121-140 / 236-255.

b740 **Fortenbaugh** William W., Quellen zur Ethik THEOPHRASTS: Studien zur antiken Philosophie 12. Amst 1984, Grüner. x-380 p. – [R]AnzAltW 41 (1988) 156-8 (Waltraut *Desch*).

b741 **Freyburger-Galland** M. L., *al.*, Sectes religieuses en Grèce et à Rome dans l'antiquité païenne 1986 → 2,8877; 3,b124: [R]ClasR 102 (1988) 296-8 (J. *Liebeschuetz*); RÉLat 65 (1987) 367s (J.-C. *Richard*).

b742 *Furumark* Arne †, Linear A and Minoan religion: OpAth 17 (1988) 51-90.

b743 **Garland** Robert, The Greek way of death 1985 → 2,8880; 3,b127: [R]AmHR 91 (1986) 890s (J. D. *Mikalson*).

b744 *Gelinne* Michel, Les champs élysées et les îles des bienheureux chez HOMÈRE, HÉSIODE et PINDARE; essai de mise au point: ÉtClas 56 (1988) 225-240.

b745 [F]GIGANTE Marcello: Syzētēsis, Studi sull'epicureismo greco e romano: ParPass Biblioteca 16, 1983 → 64,403: [R]AnzAltW 41 (1988) 135-8 (K. *Kleve*).

b746 **Heitsch** Ernst, Überlegungen PLATONS im Theaetet: Abh g/soz 1988/9. Mainz 1988, Akad. Wiss. 205 p. 3-515-05301-8.

b747 **Herington** J., Aeschylus. NHv 1986, Yale Univ. ix-191 p. 0-300-03562-4.

b748 **Hopkinson** N., CALLIMACHUS, Hymn to Demeter 1984 → 1,a488: [R]JHS 108 (1988) 230-4 (A. *Griffiths,* also on MINEUR W. 'to Delos' 1984, BULLOCH A. 'fifth' 1985).

b749 *a) Irwin* T. H., Socrates and the tragic hero; – *b) North* Helen F., Socrates *deinòs légein*: → 83, [F]KIRKWOOD G., Language 1988, 55-83 / 121-130.

b750 *Isidori Frasca* Rosella, Educazione e libera espressione nel rito menadico: Stadion 14,1 (1988) 103-123.

b751 *Jordan* Borimir, Religion in THUCYDIDES: AmPgTr 116 (1986) 119-147.

b752 *Kahane* Henry & Renée, *a)* Linguistic aspects of sociopolitical keywords, Language Problems and Language Planning 8 (Austin 1984) 143-160; – *b)* Religious key terms in Hellenism and Byzantium; three facets [i. *agape*/caritas; ii. demon (Pachomius); iii. Paulician heresy]: ILCLSt 12,2 ('Byzantium and its Legacy' 1987) 243-263.

b753 *a) Keller* Mara Lynn,   The Eleusinian mysteries of Demeter and Persephone; fertility, sexuality, and rebirth; – *b) Jung* L. Shannon, Feminism and spatiality; ethics and the recovery of a hidden dimension: JFemRel 4 (1988) 27-54 / 55-72 [< ZIT 88,574].

b754 **Kerényi** Karl,   Hermes, guide of souls; the mythologem of the masculine source of life [1944], ᵀ*Stein* Murray: Dunquin 7. Dallas 1987, Spring. vi-104 p. 0-88214-207-0.

b755 *Korrés* Georgios,   Evidence for a Hellenistic chthonian cult in the prehistoric cemetery of Voïdokiliá in Pylos (Messenia): Klio 70 (1988) 311-328; 9 fig.

b756 *Lacroix* Léon,   PAUSANIAS, le coffre de Kypsélos et le problème de l'exégèse mythologique: RArchéol (1988) 243-261; 4 fig.

b757 **Lamberton** Robert,   HOMER the theologian; Neo-Platonist allegorical reading and the growth of the epic tradition: Transformation of the classical heritage 9, 1986 → 3,b140:   0-520-05437-7:   ᴿClasR 102 (1988) 288-290 (Anne *Sheppard*); JHS 108 (1988) 244s (J. *Dillon*).

b758 **Lefkowitz** Mary,   Women in Greek myth 1986 → 3,b141; $22.50: ᴿAmHR 93 (1988) 394s (Eva C. *Keuls*: amateurish); ClasW 81 (1987s) 56s (P. *Properzio*); RelStR 14 (1988) 153 (Susn G. *Cole*).

b759 **Long** A. A.,   *Sedley* D. N.,   The Hellenistic philosophers [I. 1987 → 3,b142]; II. Greek and Latin texts with notes and bibliography. C 1987, Univ. x-512 p.; $69.50. 0-521-25562-7 [NTAbs 32,267].

b760 *Lorenz* Günther,   Apollon – Asklepios – Hygieia; drei Typen von Heilgöttern in der Sicht der vergleichenden Religionsgeschichte: Saeculum 39 (1988) 1-11.

b761 **Magris** A.,   L'idea di destino nel pensiero antico 1-2, 1984s → 3,b145: ᴿJHS 108 (1988) 246 (R. W. *Sharples*).

b762 **Malkin** Irad,   Religion and colonization in ancient Greece [diss. Ph, Univ. Pennsylvania]: Studies in Greek and Roman religion 3. Leiden 1987, Brill. xv-297 p.; 13 fig.; 2 maps. 90-04-07119-9. [RelStR 15,70, R. E. *Bennett*].

b763 **Marinatos** Nanno,   Minoan sacrificial ritual; cult practice and symbolism: Svensk. Inst. Athen 9. Sto 1986, Åström. 79 p.; 78 fig. 91-85086-95-9. – ᴿClasR 102 (1988) 340-2 (B. C. *Dietrich*: her conjectures are reasonable).

b764 *Marinatos* Nanno,   Role and sex division in ritual scenes of Aegean art: JPrehRel 1 (1987) 23-34 [AnzAltW 41,247].

b765 **Martin** Luther H.,   Hellenistic religions 1987 → 3,b151:   ᴿRelStR 14 (1988) 377 (Antonia *Tripolitis*).

b766 **Melling** David J.,   Understanding PLATO. Ox 1988, Univ.-P. viii-178 p. 0-19-219129-2; pa. 6-2.

b767 ᴱ**Meyer** Marvin W.,   The ancient mysteries, a sourcebook 1987 → 3,b153:   ᴿCalvinT 23 (1988) 272s (A. J. *Bandstra*); ChH 57 (1988) 213 (C. L. *Hanson*).

b768 **Miller** Andrew M.,   From Delos to Delphi; a literary study of the Homeric Hymn to Apollo: Mnemosyne Sup 93. Leiden 1986, Brill. xii-130 p. *f*48. 90-04-07674-3. – ᴿAntClas 57 (1988) 321-3 (D. *Marcotte*); ClasR 102 = 38 (1988) 5s (N. J. *Richardson*).

b769 **Mora** F.,   Religione e religioni nelle Storie di ERODOTO. Mi 1986, Jaca. 270 p. Lit. 19.000. – ᴿStPatav 35 (1988) 187s (P. *Scarpi*).

b770 **Moret** Jean-Marc,   Oedipe, la sphinx et les Thébains; essai de mythologie iconographique: BiblHelvRom 23, 1984 → 3,b156:   ᴿRArchéol (1987) 391-3 (J. *Marcadé*).

b771 *a) Most* Glenn W., Sophistique et herméneutique (ᵀavec *Avni* Ora); – *b)* *Narcy* Michel, À qui la parole? Platon et Aristote face à Protagoras: ➤ 673, ᴱ*Cassin* B., Sophistique 1984/6, 233-245 / 75-90.

b772 *Motte* André, *Hágios* chez PLATON: ➤ 91, ᶠLABARBE J., Stemmata 1987, 135-152.

b773 *a) Moutsopoulos* Evanghélos A., Vers une approche pluridisciplinaire de la religion grecque antique; – *b) Couloubaritsis* Lambros, Mythe et religion; une alliance de raison; – *c) Motte* André, Philosophie et religion dans la Grèce antique; aperçu thématique et perspectives méthodologiques: ➤ 693, Actes = Kernos 1 (1988) 105-110 / 111-120 / 163-176.

b774 **Müller** Carl W., Erysichthon; der Mythos als narrative Metapher im Demeterhymnos des KALLIMACHOS: geist/soz Abh 1198.13. Mainz 1987, Akad. 104 p. – ᴿGGA 240 (1988) 173-183 (E.-R. *Schwinge*).

b775 *Mylonas* George E., Eleusis and the Eleusinian Mysteries: ArchEph 126 (1987) 383-396.

b776 **Navia** Luis E., Socratic testimonies [ᵀARISTOPHANES, XENOPHON, PLATO]. Lanham MD 1987, UPA. vii-370 p. $31; pa. $17 [RelStR 15,167, A. T. *Kraabel*].

b777 *Negbi* Ora, Levantine elements in the sacred architecture of the Aegean at the close of the Bronze Age: AnBritAth 83 (1988) 339-357; 10 fig.

b778 **Nill** Michael, Morality and self-interest in PROTAGORAS, ANTIPHON and DEMOCRITUS: Philosophia Antiqua 43. Leiden 1985, Brill. 123 p. *f* 42. – ᴿÉtClas 56 (1988) 391s (P.-P. *Druet*).

b779 **Nilsson** Martin P., Cults, myths, oracles, and politics in ancient Greece: SIMA pocket 44. Göteborg 1986 = 1951, Åström. 197 p. [AnzAltW 41 (1988) 250].

b780 **Ostenfeld** Erik, Ancient Greek psychology and the modern mind-body debate. Aarhus 1986, Univ. 109 p. Dk 79. – ᴿClasR 102 (1988) 427 (C. *Gill*).

b781 **Papachatzis** Nicolaos, ● *Hè thrēskeia...* Religion in ancient Greece. Athēnai 1987, Ekdotiki Athēnôn. 224 p., 148 fig. dr 3000. – ᴿKernos 1 (1988) 256s (I. *Loucas*).

b782 *Papachatzis* Nicolaos, Les origines de la déesse Athéna; un réexamen de l'évidence: Kernos 1 (Liège 1988) 79-92.

b783 **Paris** Ginette, Pagan meditations; the worlds of Aphrodite, Artemis, and Hestia, ᵀ*Moore* Gwendolyn. ... 1986, Spring 204 p. $13.50. – ᴿJAAR 56 (1988) 166-8 (D. L. *Miller*).

b784 **Parke** Herbert W., Athenische Feste [Festivals of the Athenians], ᵀᴱ*Hornbostel* Gertraut: KuGAW 38. Mainz 1987, von Zabern. 322 p.; 74 fig.

b785 ᴱ**Parker** W. H., Priapea; poems for a phallic god. L 1988, Croom Helm. viii-216 p.; 6 pl. £25. 0-7099-4099-8 [Antiquity 62,657].

b786 **Patzer** Harald, Die griechische Knabenliebe 1982 ➤ 64,9945... 1,a510: ᴿArchaiognōsía 3,1s (1982ss) 266s (A. D. *Skiadas*).

b787 *Peltenburg* E. J., A Cypriot model for prehistoric ritual: Antiquity 62 (1988) 289-293; 6 fig.

b788 *Penna* Romano, Componenti essenziali della spiritualità del mondo ellenistico: ➤ 810, StoSpir 2 NT (1988) 41-62.

b789 *Pirenne-Delforge* Vinciana, Epithètes cultuelles et interprétation philosophique à propos d'Aphrodite Ourania et Pandémos à Athènes: AntClas 57 (1988) 142-157.

b789* *Places* Édouard des, Chronique de la philosophie religieuse des Grecs (1986-1988): BBudé (1988) 379-393.

b790 **Reale** Giovanni, Per una nuova interpretazione di PLATONE; rilettura della metafisica dei grandi dialoghi alla luce delle 'Dottrine non scritte'[5] [[1]1984]: Centro Ricerche Metafisica 3. Mi 1987, ViPe. 720 p.; 1ll. 88-343-0252-4.

b791 *Riedweg* Christoph, Die Mysterien von Eleusis in rhetorisch geprägten Texten des 2./3. Jahrhunderts nach Christus: ILCL 13,1 (1988) 127-133.

b792 *Rist* John M., Pseudo-Ammonius and the soul/body problem in some Platonic texts of late antiquity: AmJPg 109 (1988) 402-415 [harmonizing of Moses and Jesus unusual].

b792* *Rochberg-Halton* F., Elements of the Babylonian contribution to Hellenistic astrology: JAOS 108 (1988) 51-62.

b793 *Rossi* Mary Ann, A survey of studies in CALLIMACHUS [Hymn to Zeus; to Delos...]: AntClas 57 (1988) 311-6.

b794 **Rousselle** Aline, Porneia; on desire and the body in antiquity. Ox 1988, Blackwell. x-213 p. £20. 0-631-13837-4 [Antiquity 62,641].

b795 **Setaioli** Aldo, SENECA e i greci; citazioni e traduzioni nelle opere filosofiche: Testi per il latino 26. Bo 1988, Pàtron. 545 p. Lit. 40.000.

b796 **Sfameni Gasparro** Giulia, Misteri e culti mistici di Demetra: Storia delle Religioni 3. R 1986. 371 p. – [R]RÉLat 65 (1987) 359 (J.-C. *Richard*).

b797 **Simon** Erika, Eirene und Pax; Friedensgöttinnen in der Antike: Szb Fra 24/3. Stu 1988, Steiner. 34 p.; 14 pl.

b798 *Smith* Warren, The disguises of the gods in the Iliad: Numen 35 (1988) 161-178.

b799 **Sophocleous** S., Atlas des représentations chypro-archaïques des divinités: SIMA 33, 1985 ➢ 1,a525; 3,b191: [R]Gnomon 60 (1988) 372s (R. *Senff*); MeditHistR-TA 3,2 (1988) 127-130 (Ora *Negbi*).

b800 *Sourvinou-Inwood* Christiane, Priestess in the text *Theano Menonos Agrylethen*: GreeceR 35 (1988) 29-39.

b801 **Stoneman** Richard, Land of lost gods; the search for classical Greece 1987 ➢ 3,b192: [R]ClasR 102 (1988) 387s (D. *Constantine*); JHS 108 (1988) 275s (A. R. *Burn*: skip ch. 1).

b802 *Tanner* R. G., 'The saviour with the sword' [Hellenistic/Roman military monarchy; *Toynbee* A.]: ➢ 554, Salvation 1986/8, 13-23.

b803 *a) Thissen* Heinz J., Aso und der König [... *Plutarchus,* Peri Isidos]; – *b) Dautzenberg* N., Ägyptologische Bemerkungen zu PLATONS Atlantis-Erzählung: GöMiszÄg 103 (1988) 71-74 / 102 (1988) 19-29.

b804 *Totti* Maria, *a)* Der griechisch-ägyptische Traumgott Apollon-Helios-Harpokrates-Tithoes in zwei Gebeten der griechischen magischen Papyri; – *b)* Karpokrates Astromantis und die Lychnomanteia: ZPapEp 73 (1988) 287-296 / 297-301.

b805 *Verbanck-Piérard* Annie, Images et piété en Grèce classique; la contribution de l'iconographie céramique à l'étude de la religion grecque: Kernos I (Liège 1988) 223-233.

b806 **Vernant** Jean-Pierre, Mythe et pensée chez les Grecs; études de psychologie historique[2rev] [= 1985?; [2]1971; [1]1965]. P 1988, Découverte. 432 p. 2-7071-1578-9.

b807 **Vernant** Jean-Pierre, *Vidal-Naquet* Pierre, Mythe et tragédie en Grèce ancienne II [I 1972]: Textes à l'appui 1986 ➢ 2,8936; F 180: [R]Gnomon 60 (1988) 577-583 (C. *Miralles,* franç.).

b807* *Vos* H. F., Religions of the biblical world; Greco-Roman: ➢ 801, ISBEnc[3] 4 (1988) 107-117.

b808 **White** Michael J., Agency and integrality; philosophical themes in the ancient discussions of determinism and responsibility: Philosophical

Studies 32. Dordrecht 1985, Reidel. xiii-285 p. £33.25. – ᴿClasR 102 (1988) 286-8 (Pamela M. *Huby*: clever and erudite but indigestible).

M5.5 Religiones anatolicae.

b809 **Archi** A., Hethitische Orakeltexte ... KUB 49.50.52. B 1979/83 Akademie. ix p., 50 pl.; x p., 50 pl.; viii p., 50 pl. M 48 + 48 + 78. – ᴿOrientalia 57 (1988) 234s (R. *Werner*).

b810 *a)* *Archi* Alfonso, Eine Anrufung der Sonnegöttin von Arinna; – *b)* *Houwink Ten Cate* P.H.J., Brief comments on the Hittite cult calendar ... nuntarriyašhaš; – *c)* *Haas* Volkert, Magie in hethitischen Gärten: ⇥ 112*, ᶠOᴛᴛᴇɴ H., Documentum 1988, 5-31 / 167-194 / 121-142.

b811 *a)* *Brandt* Hartwin, Kulte in Aspendos; – *b)* *Osten-Sacken* Elisabeth von der, Der kleinasiatische Gott der Wildflur: IstMitt 38 (1988) 237-250 / 63-81; 8 fig.; pl. 9-10.

b812 *Cornil* P., La fête de l'automne et du printemps de KUB LVII 106 – Bo 594: OrLovPer 19 (1988) 17-23.

b813 **Haas** Volkert, *Wegner* Ilse, Die Rituale der Beschwörerinnen ˢᴬᴸŠU.GI: Corpus der Hurritischen Sprachdenkmäler I. Boğazköy 5. R 1988, Multigrafica. I. Die Texte; II. Glossar.

b814 *Haas* Volkert, *a)* Betrachtungen zur Rekonstruktion des hethitischen Frühjahrsfestes (ᴇᴢᴇɴ purulliyaš): ZAss 78 (1988) 284-298; – *b)* Das Ritual gegen den Zugriff der Dämonin ᴰDìm.nun.me und die Sammeltafel KUB XLIII 55: OrAnt 27 (1988) 85-104.

b814* *Hoffner* H.A.ᴶ, Religions of Asia Minor (Hittite, Hurrian): ⇥ 801, ISBEnc³ 4 (1988) 79-85.

b815 **Hutter** Manfred, Behexung, Entsühnung und Heilung; das Ritual der Tunnawiya für ein Königspaar aus mittelhethitischer Zeit [KBo XXI 1 – KUB IX 34 – KBo XXI 6]: OBO 82. FrS/Gö 1988. 180 p. Fs 48 3-7278-0580-3 / VR 3-525-53712-3 [BO 45,757].

b816 **Klengel** H., *al.*, Hethitische Rituale ... KUB 54-56, 1984 ⇥ 65,9235 ... 3,b220: ᴿOrientalia 57 (1988) 88-92 (M. *Popko*).

b817 **Klengel** H., Hethitische · Gelübde- und Traumtexte: KaB 56, 1986 ⇥ 2,8944: ᴿOLZ 83 (1988) 286-290 (V. *Haas*, J. *Klinger*); ZAss 78 (1988) 145-9, 1 fig. (S. *Košak*); ZDMG 138 (1988) 375s (J. *Tischler*).

b818 *Laroche* E., La notion de 'salut, sauver' en Hittite: ⇥ 809, SDB 11,62 (1988) 514-6.

b818* *Lebrun* René, Divinités louvites et hourrites des rituels anatoliens en langue akkadienne provenant de Meskene: Hethitica 9 (1988) 147-155.

b819 *a)* *Lebrun* René, Temples et idoles hittites à la lumière des tablettes de Boğazköy; – *b)* *Kestemont* Guy, Les dieux néo-hittites: ⇥ 763, Archéologie 1986, 109s / 111-138.

b820 **McMahon** John G., The Hittite state cult of tutelary deities: diss. ᴰ*Hoffner* H. Ch 1988. – OIAc D88.

b821 *a)* *Mellaart* James, Animals in the neolithic art of Çatal Hüyük and Hacilar and their religious significance; – *b)* *Lebrun* René, Le zoomorphisme dans la religion hittite: ⇥ 704, ᴱ*Borgeaud* P., L'animal 1981/5, 39-42; 8 fig. / 95-103.

b822 ᶠNᴀsᴛᴇʀ Paul, Archéologie et religions de l'Anatolie ancienne, ᴱ**Donceel** R., *Lebrun* R. 1983 ⇥ 65,104: ᴿOLZ 83 (1988) 298-301 (G. *Neumann*).

b823 **Otten** H., *Rüster* C., Festbeschreibungen und Rituale: KUB 30, 1984 ⇥ 65,9240; 2,8947: ᴿOLZ 83 (1988) 290-4 (V. *Haas*, J. *Klinger*).

b824 **Popko** Maciej, Hethitische Rituale und Festbeschreibungen: KUB 58. B 1988, Akademie. x p.; 50 pl. 3-05-00709-5.

b824* *Popko* Maciej, *Taracha* Piotr, Der 28. und der 29. Tag des hethitischen AN.TAḪ.ŠUM-Festes: AltOrF 15 (1988) 82-113.

b825 *Sergent* Bernard, Les premiers cultes d'Anatolie: RÉAnc 90 (1988) 329-358; map; Eng. p. 329.

b826 *Ünal* Ahmet, a) Hittite architect and a rope-climbing ritual: Belleten 52,205 (1988) 1469-1503; – b) The role of magic in the ancient Anatolian religions according to the cuneiform texts from Boğazköy-Ḫattuša: ⇥ 760, Anatolian 1983/8, 52-85.

M6 Religio canaanaea, syra.

b827 **Ackerman** Susan, Syncretism in Israel as reflected in sixth-century prophetic texts: diss. Harvard. CM 1988. 88-06041. – OIAc D88.

b828 ᶠAHLSTRÖM Gösta W.: In the shelter of Elyon, ᴱ**Barrick** W., *Spencer* J., JStOT Sup 31, 1984 ⇥ 65,4; 1,5: ᴿJNES 47 (1988) 281-3 (J. F. *Healey*).

b829 **Amir** David, ⊕ Gods and heroes; Canaanite epics from Ugarit 1986 ⇥ 2,8953: ᴿKlio 70 (1988) 564s (J. P. *Weinberg*).

b830 *Archi* Alfonso, The cult of the ancestors and the tutelary god at Ebla: ⇥ 42*, EHRMAN A. mém., Fucus 1988, 103-112.

b834 *Baldus* Hans R., Eine 'hannibalische' Tanit?: Chiron 18 (1988) 1-14; 2 pl.

b836 **Barker** Margaret, The older Testament 1987 ⇥ 3,b237: ᴿBL (1988) 100 (J. R. *Porter*); HeythJ 29 (1988) 355s (J. F. A. *Sawyer*); JPseud 2 (1988) 115-7 (J. C. *VanderKam*); Month 249 (1988) 1018 (J. *Ashton*); TLond 91 (1988) 427s (R. *Coggins*); TS 49 (1988) 335 (J. J. *Collins*); VT 38 (1988) 380s (H. G. M. *Williamson*).

b838 *Bol* Peter C., Adonis-Tamuz [sic] als Verkörperung der Provinz Syrien?: DamszMit 3 (1988) 11-15; pl. 4-8.

b839 **Bonnet** Corinne, Melqart; cultes et mythes de l'Héraclès tyrien en Méditerranée: StPhoen 8. Lv/Namur 1988, Peeters/Univ. xi-491 p.; 36 fig.; 13 maps. 2-87037-116-0. – ᴿRStFen 16 (1988) 253-6 (S. *Moscati*).

b840 a) *Cagni* Luigi, Offerte sacrificali [sacrificiali in testatine] e votive ad Ebla; approccio metodologico e saggio-campione; – b) *Xella* Paolo, Tradition und Innovation; Bemerkungen zum Pantheon von Ebla: ⇥ 707, Wirtschaft 1986/8, 181-198 / 349-358.

b841 *Craigie* P. C., *Wilson* G. H., Religions of the biblical world; Canaanite (Syria and Palestine): ⇥ 801, ISBEnc³ 4 (1988) 95-101 (-107; 117-123 Egypt, Judaism, *LaSor* W.).

b842 ᶠCROSS F. M.; Ancient Israelite religion, ᴱ*Miller* P. D., *al.* 1987 ⇥ 3,42: ᴿRHPR 68 (1988) 230 (G. *Heintz*); TTod 45 (1988s) 112-4 (J. *Barr*).

b845 *Duarte Castillo* Raúl, ¿Fue 'Ashera esposa de Yhwh?: EfMex 5,13 (1987) 62-75.

b846 **Edzard** Dietz O., Hymnen, Beschwörungen und Verwandtes (aus dem Ebla-Archiv L. 2769): ARET 5. R 1984, Univ. 61 p.; 59 pl. – ᴿBO 45 (1988) 605-613 (B. *Kienast*).

b847 *Elayi* Josette, A Phoenician vase representing god Milqart?: BaghMit 19 (1988) 545-7; pl. 17-20.

b848 *Epstein* Claire, Basalt [fertility-cult] pillar figures from the Golan and the Ḥuleh regions: IsrEJ 38 (1988) 205-223; 7 fig.; pl. 29-33.

b849 *Falsone* Gioacchino, La statue de Motyé; aurige ou prêtre de Melqart?:
→ 91, ^FLabarbe J., Stemmata 1987, 407-427; 10 fig.

b850 *Fensham* F.C., Notes on Keret 194-206 (CTA 14:194B-206); the vow at
the sanctuary of Athirat: JNWS 14 (1988) 91-99.

b851 *Ferron* Jean, La religion punique de Carthage: Ibla 51,161 (1988) 3-25.

b852 *Fronzaroli* Pelio, Il culto dei re defunti in ARET 3,178: → 705*, Misc.
1987/8, 1-33.

b853 *Gatier* P.-L., Inscriptions religieuses de Gerasa (II): ADAJ 32 (1988)
151-5.

b854 *Grottanelli* Cristiano, *a)* Ancora sull'ebbrezza del dio El (KTU 1,114):
VO 7 (1988) 177-188; – *b)* La religione fenicio-punica; vecchi problemi e
studi recenti: SMSR 54 (1988) 171-184.

b854* **Gutmann** Joseph, The Jewish Life Cycle: IconRel 23/4, 1987 → 3,b252:
^RÉTRel 63 (1988) 459s (D. *Lys*).

b855 **Hajjar** Youssef, La triade d'Héliopolis-Baalbek; iconographie, théologie, culte et sanctuaires 1985 → 1,a570; 3,b253; C$80: ^RLatomus 47
(1988) 239-241 (M. *Malaise*: systématique et commode).

b855* *Handy* Lowell K., A solution for many *mlkm* [gods with title *mlk*
('ruler' not top 'king')]: UF 20 (1988) 57-59.

b856 *a) Healey* John F., The 'Pantheon' of Ugarit; further notes; – *b)*
Dietrich Manfried, Marduk in Ugarit; – *c) Xella* Paolo, 'I figli del re e le
figlie del re', culto dinastico e tradizioni amoree nei rituali ugaritici: → 98,
^FLoretz O., StEpL 5 (1988) 103-112 / 79-101 / 219-225.

b857 **Heider** G.C., The cult of Molek 1985 1,a572...3,b254: ^RAulaO 6
(1988) 116s (G. del *Olmo Lete*); BASOR 272 (1988) 90s (S. *Brown*); BZ 32
(1988) 125-7 (W. *Thiel*); JTS 39 (1988) 548-550 (H. *McKeating*); RStFen
16 (1988) 122-5 (S. *Ribichini*).

b858 *Hestrin* Ruth, A note on the 'lion bowls' and the Asherah: IsrMusJ 7
(1988) 115-8.

b859 *Hutter* Manfred, Der Gott Surmubel in Sanchunjatons Kosmogonie:
UF 20 (1988) 93-96.

b860 *Koch* K., Aschera als Himmelskönigin in Jerusalem: UF 20 (1988)
97-120.

b861 *Koch* Klaus, *a)* Der Tod des Religionsstifters, Erwägungen über das
Verhältnis Israels zur Geschichte der altorientalischen Religionen [< Ker-
Do 8 (1962) 100-123]; – *b)* Šaddaj [< VT 26 (1976) 299-332]; – *c)* Zur
Entstehung der Ba'al-Verehrung [< UF 11 (1979) 456-475]; – *d)* Paḥad
jiṣḥaq — eine Gottesbezeichnung [< ^F*Westermann* C., Werden 1980,
107-115]: → 212, Studien 1988, 32-61 / 118-152 / 189-205 / 206-214.

b862 *Lachs* S.T., Why was the 'amen' response interdicted in the Temple?
[Tosefta Ber. 6 (7) 22...]: JStJud 19 (1988) 230-240.

b863 *Lindner* Manfred, Eine al-'Uzzā-Isis-Stele und andere neu aufgefundene
Zeugnisse der al-'Uzzā-Verehrung in Petra (Jordanien): ZDPV 104 (1988)
84-91; 5 fig.; pl. 2-11.

b864 *Lipiński* E., Ea, Kothar et El: UF 20 (1988) 137-143.

b864* *a) Lipiński* E., Sacrifices d'enfants à Carthage et dans le monde
sémitique oriental [... Stèles]; – *b) Le Glay* Marcel, Nouveaux documents,
nouveaux points de vue sur Saturne africain: → 754, Carthago 1986/8,
151-162 [-185, 14 fig.] / 187-237; 18 fig..

b865 **Maier** Walter A.^{III}, 'Ašerah, extrabiblical evidence [diss. 1984, ^D*Cross*
F.]; HarvSemMg 37, 1986 → 2,8974: ^RBO 45 (1988) 388s (E. *Lipiński*:
distorted); BZ 32 (1988) 299s (H. *Niehr*); CBQ 50 (1988) 507s (H.O.

Thompson); JBL 107 (1988) 531s (D.R. *Hillers*: some forced identifications); JSS 33 (1988) 269-271 (J. *Day*).

b866 *Matthiae* Paolo, Sull'identità degli dèi titolari dei templi paleosiriani di Ebla: CMatArch 1 (R 1986) 335-358; bibliog. 358-362.

b867 *Mendecki* Norbert, ❷ Inscriptiones ex Kuntillet 'Aġrud et Hirbet el-Qom [...Jahwe eiusque Ašera]: RuBi 41 (1988) 337-9.

b868 **Alomia** Merling K., Lesser gods of the Ancient Near East and some comparisons with heavenly beings of the OT: diss. Andrews 1987. DissA 48 (1987s) 2084-A; AndrUnS 27,133; RTLv 19 (1988) 534.

b869 *Miller* Patrick D.ᴶ, Prayer and sacrifice in Ugarit and Israel: ➤ 47, ꟳFᴇɴsʜᴀᴍ F., Text 1988, 139-155.

b870 *Olmo Lete* G. del, *a*) Un ritual funerario de Ugarit (KTU 1.105); – *b*) El sacrificio de Sāpanu y otros sacrificios de Ugarit (KTU 1,148); – *c*) Posible ritual ugarítico de 'consulta' cúltica (KTU 1,104): AulaO 6 (1988) 189-194 / 11-17 / 99-101.

b871 **Olyan** Saul M.., Asherah and the cult of Yahweh in Israel: SBL Mg 34. Atlanta 1988, Scholars. xiv-100 p. 1-555-40254-2 [OIAc D88].

b872 *Ovadiah* Asher, *Roll* Israel, A Greek dedicatory inscription to 'Azizos [god attested in Hauran, by the stonecutter himself]: IsrEJ 38 (1988) 177-180; pl. 27.

b872* *Piccirillo* Michele, The Jerusalem-Esbus road and its sanctuaries in Transjordan: ➤ e824, Jordan III 1986/7, 165-172.

b873 **Ringgren** Helmer, Israele; i padri, l'epoca dei Re, il giudaismo [Israelitische Religion 1963 + bibliog. p. 389-410], ᵀLimiroli Maria Rosa; intr. *Ravasi* Gianfranco: Storia delle Religioni 11. Mi 1987, Jaca. viii-419 p. 88-16-32011-7. – ᴿFilT 1,3 (1988) 208 (A. *Isola*).

b874 *Shiffman* J.Š., ❻ The Phoenician cult of the male 'Aṭtar in Graeco-Roman historiography: ➤ 456*, Peredneaz. IV (1986) 80-82.

b875 *Smith* Mark S., Divine form and size in Ugaritic and pre-exilic Israelite religion: ZAW 100 (1988) 424-7.

b876 **Stähli** Hans-Peter, Solare Elemente im Jahweglauben des ATs: OBO 66, 1985 ➤ 1,6266; 3,b274: ᴿBO 45 (1988) 168s (M.J. *Mulder*).

b877 Studia Phoenicia III (ᴱ*Homès-Fredericq* Denyse, Neighbours) 1983/5 ➤ 1,852; IV (ᴱ*Bonnet* C. Religio) 1985/6 ➤ 2,551; 3,b238: ᴿArOr 56 (1988) 369s (Jana *Pečírková*); RHR 205 (1988) 331-3 (J. *Teixidor*).

b877* *a*) *Taylor* J. Glen, The two earliest known representations of Yahweh; – *b*) *Pardee* Dennis, A new datum for the meaning of the divine name Milkashtart: ➤ 29, Mem. Cʀᴀɪɢɪᴇ P., Ascribe 1988, 557-566 / 55-67.

b878 *a*) *Teixidor* Javier, Dieu de la tribu ou seigneur du lieu? Aspects de la divinité chez les Sémites de l'Ouest; – *b*) *Gonnet* Hatice, Dieux fugueurs, dieux captés chez les Hittites; – *c*) *Meeks* Dimitri, Notion de 'Dieu' et structure du panthéon dans l'Égypte ancienne: RHR 205 ('Qu'est ce qu'un dieu?' 1988) 415-424 / 385-398 / 425-446.

b879 **Tigay** Jeffrey H., You shall have no other gods; Israelite religion in the light of Hebrew inscriptions 1986 ➤ 3,b276: ᴿBO 45 (1988) 166-8 (M.J. *Mulder*); CBQ 50 (1988) 516-8 (J.W. *Betlyon*); JBL 107 (1988) 506s (S.A. *Kaufman*); RelStR 14 (1988) 151 (W.L. *Humphreys*).

b880 **Tubach** Jürgen, Im Schatten des Sonnengottes; der Sonnenkult in Edessa, Ḥarrān und Ḥaṭrā 1986 ➤ 2,8989; 3,b278: ᴿZDMG 138 (1988) 374s (E.A. *Knauf*).

b881 *Uehlinger* Christoph, Der Amun-Tempel Ramses' III. in *p3-Kn'n*, seine südpalästinischen Tempelgüter und der Übergang von der Ägypter- zur

Philisterherrschaft; ein Hinweis auf einige wenig beachtete Skarabäen: ZDPV 104 (1988) 6-25; 10 fig.; pl. 1.

b882 *Waterston* Alastair, The kingdom of 'Aṭtar and his role in the AB cycle: UF 20 (1988) 357-364.

b883 *Wyatt* N., The source of the Ugaritic myth of the conflict of Baʿal and Yam: UF 20 (1988) 375-385.

b884 [ᴱ*Xella* P.] Adonis 1981/4 → 65,670; 3,792: ᴿAulaO 6 (1988) 107 (G. del *Olmo Lete*); BO 45 (1988) 84s (M. *Stol*).

b885 *Xella* Paolo, *a*) Remarques sur le vocabulaire sacrificiel d'Ougarit: GLECS 28,3 (1984) 467-487; – *b*) D'Ugarit à la Phénicie; sur les traces de Rashap, Horon, Eshmun: WeltOr 19 (1988) 45-84.

M6.5   Religio aegyptia.

b886 **Abitz** F., König und Gott 1984 → 65,9284... 3,b283: ᴿCdÉ 63 (1988) 86-90 (D. *Lorton*).

b887 *Alfi* Mostafa El-, *a*) An altar from Athribis [in a Benha house]: DiscEg 10 (1988) 21-24 + 2 fig.; – *b*) Pathenfy — a priest from Heliopolis [adds to *Leahy* L. & A., JEA 72 (1986) 133, data from photos of a group-statuette in Vienna, hitherto published only as cover of *Steinbüchel* 1826]: DiscEg 11 (1988) 15-20; 3 fig.

b887* *a*) *Altenmüller* Hartwig, Die Vereinigung des Schu mit dem Urgott Atum; Bemerkungen zu CT I 385d – 393b; – *b*) *Delvaux* Luc, La statue Louvre A 134 du Premier Prophète d'Amon Hapouseneb: StAltÄgK 15 (1988) 1-16 / 53-67; pl. 1-3.

b888 ᴱ**Armstrong** A.H., Classical Mediterranean spirituality; Egyptian, Greek, Roman: EWSp 15, 1986 → 2,234; 3,375. – ᴿJTS 39 (1988) 233s (A. *Louth*); RelStR 14 (1988) 69 (R. *Wilken*); RRel 47 (1988) 945-7 (E.A. *Bourque*); SpTod 40 (1988) 175s (R. *Zawilla*); TLond 91 (1988) 74-76 (A. *Cameron*); TS 49 (1988) 186 (D.G. *Hunter*); Worship 62 (1988) 560-2 (W.E. *Klingshire*).

b889 **Baines** John, Fecundity figures [diss. Oxford 1975] 1985 → 2,a593 [3,d661 amid sculpture, but they are largely paintings]: ᴿJAmEg 25 (1988) 248s (E. *Cruz-Uribe*).

b889* *Begelsbacher-Fischer* B.L., Untersuchungen zur Götterwelt des Alten Reiches... Privatgräber IV.V.Dyn. OBO 37, 1981 → 62,a164... 1,a597: ᴿWZKM 77 (1987) 128-130 (S. *Allam*).

b890 **Beltz** Walter, Die Schiffe der Götter; ägyptische Mythologie. B 1987, Der Morgen. 255 p. [Mundus 24,308].

b891 *Blumenthal* Elke, Eine systematische Theologie der alten Ägypter [*Assmann* J. 1984]: OLZ 83 (1988) 133-140.

b892 *Bruneau* Philippe, Le sanctuaire et le culte des divinités égyptiennes à Érétrie: ÉPR 45, 1975 → 56,7943: ᴿOLZ 83 (1988) 403s (F. *Steinmann*).

b893 *Brunner* Hellmut [→ 169], Buchführung über Leben und Tod: ZägSpr 115 (1988) 14-19.

b894 **Brunner-Traut** Emma, Gelebte Mythen³ʳᵉᵛ. Da 1988, Wiss. x-128 p. DM 35. 3-534-08245-X [BO 45,472].

b895 *Brunsch* Wolfgang, Index to W. CLARYSSE, The demotic transcription of the Greek names of the eponymous priests: Enchoria 16 (1988) 119-128.

b896 *Cauville* Sylvie, Les mystères d'Osiris à Dendera; interprétation des chapelles osiriennes: BSocFrÉg 112 (1988) 23-36; 7 fig.

b897 *Cenival* Françoise de,   Papyrus Seymour de Ricci; le plus ancien des règlements d'association religieuse (4ème siècle av. J.-C.) (Pap. Bibl. Nationale E 241): ➤ 119, Mém. POSENER G., RÉgp 39 (1988) 37-46, facsimiles; pl. I.

b898 *Couroyer* B.,   'Le Dieu des sages' en Egypte, II-III: RB 95 (1988) 70-91. 195-211; Eng. 70.195.

b899 **Derchain** Philippe,   Le religioni in Egitto, ᵀ*Pierini* Maria N., p. 1-81; [p. 149-196, *Nougayrol* J.] Mesopotamia e [255-329, *Duchesne-Guillemin* J.] Persia: Universale 219.   R 1988, Laterza.   361 p.; map. [vol. 2 of ᴱ*Puech* E. ➤ b677]. Lit. 25.000.   88-420-2995-5.

b900 *Derchain* Philippe,   Encore le monothéisme [*Assmann* J. 1983]: CdÉ 63,125 (1988) 77-85.

b901 **Fazzini** Richard A.,   Egypt Dynasty XXII-XXV: Iconography of Religions 16/10.   Leiden 1988, Brill.   xii-36 p.; 48 pl. ƒ42.   90-04-07931-9 [BO 45,755].

b902 **Gitton** M.,   Les divines épouses de la 18ᵉ dynastie 1984 ➤ 3,b309: ᴿCdÉ 63 (1988) 96-98 (R. *Hari*†).

b902* **Goedicke** Hans,   Die Darstellung des Horus... Philae: WZKM Beih. 11, 1982 ➤ 63,9332... 2,9021: ᴿWZKM 77 (1987) 119-121 (P. *Derchain*).

b903 *Goedicke* Hans,   *a)* Coffin text spell 84 (CT II 49a-51c): BSocÉg 12 (Genève 1988) 39-52; – *b)* 'God' (*nṯr*): JSSEg 16 (1986) 57-62.

b904 *a) Görg* Manfred,   Neilos und Domitian; ein Beitrag zur spätantiken Nilgott-Ikonographie; – *b) Westendorf* Wolfhart,   Das leere Grab [LexÄg: Kenotaph] und der leere Stuhl: ➤ 16, ᶠBÖHLIG A., Religion 1988, 65-82 / 221-6.

b905 **Goyon** Jean-Claude,   Les dieux-gardiens et la genèse des temples... IFAO 627 = BiblÉt 93/1s, 1985 ➤ 1,a612:   ᴿBO 45 (1988) 535-540 (Heike *Sternberg el-Hotabi*); JAOS 108 (1988) 149 (Virginia *Condon*).

b906 *a) Griffiths* J. Gwyn,   Intimations in Egyptian non-royal biography of a belief in divine impact on human affairs; – *b) Baines* John,   An Abydos list of gods and an Old Kingdom use of texts; – *c) Malek* Jaromir,   The 'altar' in the pillared court of Teti's pyramid-temple at Saqqara: ➤ 41, ᶠEDWARDS I., Pyramid studies 1988, 92-102 / 124-133 / 23-34; 5 fig.

b907 **Hart** George,   A dictionary of Egyptian gods and goddesses 1986 ➤ 2,9024; 3,b312; 0-7102-0965-7; pa. 167-2:   ᴿBL (1988) 124 (K. A. *Kitchen*: enthusiastic).

b908 ᴱ**Helck** Wolfgang,   Tempel und Kult 1986/7 ➤ 3,818. b313:   ᴿMundus 24 (1988) 282-4 (B. *Ockinga*).

b909 **Hibbs** Vivian A.,   The Mendes maze; a libation table for the inundation of the Nile (2-3 cent A.D.): Outstanding dissertations of the fine arts [NYU 1979]. NY 1985, Garland.   241 p.; 170 pl. $40.   0-8240-6858-0. – ᴿBO 45 (1988) 556-562 (Danielle *Bonneau*); WZKM 78 (1986) 223s (G. *Vittmann*).

b910 **Hoffmeier** James K.,   Sacred ... Eg. dsr...: OBO 59, 1985 ➤ 1,a623... 3,b314:   ᴿJAOS 108 (1988) 159s (E. *Cruz-Uribe*); TLZ 113 (1988) 336s (U. *Luft*: beachtenswert).

b911 **Hornung** Erik, *al.*,   Der ägyptische Mythos von der Himmelskuh: OBO 46, 1982 ➤ 63,9342... 2,9027: ᴿJEA 74 (1988) 275-7 (J. G. *Griffiths*).

b912 **Hornung** Erik, *al.*,   Das Buch von den Pforten des Jenseits IIᵀᴱ 1984 ➤ 1,a625: ᴿBO 45 (1988) 309-311 (L. *Kákosy*).

b913 *Hornung* Erik,   Maat – Gerechtigkeit für alle? Zur altägyptischen Ethik: Eranos-Jb 56 (1987) 385-427.

b914 *a) Hornung* E., L'Égypte, la philosophie avant les grecs; – *b) Hani* J., Le temple égyptien [d'où jaillissent la pensée et la sagesse...]; – *c) Brisson* L., L'Égypte de PLATON; – *d) André* J.-M., Les Romains et l'Égypte [... échanges spirituels]: Études philosophiques 42,2s ('L'Égypte et la philosophie' 1987) 113-125 / 139-152 / 153-168 / 189-206 [< RSPT 72 (1988) 153].

b915 **Horst** P.W. van der, Chaeremon...: ÉPR 101, 1984 ➤ 65,9333...2,9028: ᴿSecC 6 (1987s) 119-121 (R. F. *Hock*).

b916 *Inconnu-Bocquillon* Danielle, Thot de Pnoubs (la ville) ou Thot du Nébès (l'arbre): ➤ 119, Mém. POSENER G., RÉgp 39 (1988) 47-61; Eng. 62.

b917 *Jacq* Christian, Le monde magique de l'Égypte ancienne: Gnose. Monaco 1988 [= 1983, Eng. 1985 ➤ 1,a628*ab*], Rocher 223 p.; ill. 2-268-00191-1.

b918 **Känel** F. von, Les prêtres-ouáb de Sekhmet ᴰ1978 [➤ 3,b321, non 1987] 1984: ᴿCdÉ 63 (1988) 90-96 (M. J. *Raven*).

b919 *Koch* Klaus, *a*) Wort und Einheit des Schöpfergottes in Memphis und Jerusalem; zur Einzigartigkeit Israels [< ZTK 62 (1965) 251-293]; – *b*) Erwägungen zu den Vorstellungen über Seelen und Geister in den Pyramidentexten [< ᶠ*Helck* W., StAltägK 1984, 425-454]: ➤ 212, Studien 1988, 32-60 / 215-242.

b920 **Kuhlmann** Klaus P., Das Ammoneion; Archäologie, Geschichte und Kultpraxis des Orakels von Siwa [Ost-Libyen Oasis]: ArchVeröff 75. Mainz 1988, von Zabern. 179 p.; 52 pl. + XII color. 3-8053-0819-1.

b921 *Labrique* Françoise, Le *sḏm.f* 'rituel' à Edfou; le sens est roi: Gö-MiszÄg 106 (1988) 53-63.

b922 **Lüscher** Barbara, Totenbuch Spruch I. 1988. DM 32. – ᴿMundus 24 (1988) 26s (K. *Jansen-Winkeln*).

b923 *a) Müller-Wollermann* Renate, Der Mythos vom Ritus 'Erschlagen der Feinde'; – *b) Kurth* Dieter, Zum Pfortenbuch, 12. Stunde, 90. Szene; – *c) Ziedler* Jürgen, Textkritik und Textgeschichte des Pfortenbuches: Gö-MiszÄg 105 (1988) 69-76 / 49-54 / 85-96.

b924 **Munro** Irmtraut, Das Zelt-Heiligtum des Min 1983 ➤ 64,9577; 65,9350: ᴿJAmEg 25 (1988) 249-251 (J. R. *Ogdon*).

b925 *Ogdon* Jorge R., Studies in ancient Egyptian magical thought, I. The hand and the seal; II. The 'Eye of Re'; – III. Knots and ties; notes on ancient ligatures: DiscEg 1 (1985) 27-34; 4 fig.; 2 (1985) 37-44; 3 fig.; 7 (1987) 29-36.

b926 *O'Mara* Patrick F., Was the *sed* festival periodic in early Egyptian history?: DiscEg 11 (1988) 21-30; 12 (1988) 55-62.

b927 *Perdu* Olivier, Sobekhotep, prêtre dans la région du Fayoum vers la XXVᵉ dynastie: GöMiszÄg 106 (1988) 75-81.

b928 **Plas** Dirk van der, L'hymne à la crue du Nil 1986 ➤ 2,9044; 3,b335: ᴿBO 45 (1988) 299-305 (H. W. *Fischer-Elfert*).

b929 *a) Quaegebeur* Jan, Divinités égyptiennes sur des animaux dangereux; – *b) Collon* Dominique, Les animaux attributs des divinités du Proche-Orient ancien; problèmes d'iconographie: ➤ 704, ᴱ*Borgeaud* P., L'animal 1981/5, 131-143; 19 fig. / 83-85.

b930 **Ryhiner** Marie-Louise, L'offrande du lotus: Rites égyptiens 6. Bru 1986, Fond. R. Élisabeth. x-281 p.; 5 pl. Fb 900. – ᴿRB 95 (1988) 432-4 (R. *Beaud*).

b931 **Sadek** Ashraf I., Popular religion in Egypt during the New Kingdom: Hildesheimer ÄgBeit 27. Hildesheim 1988, Gerstenberg. xxx-311 p.; XXVIII pl. 3-8067-8107-9.

b932 **Sauneron** Serge, Les prêtres de l'Ancienne Égypte^{2rev} [¹1957]. P 1988, Perséa. 207 p.; ill. 2-906427-02-0.

b932* **Schlögl** Hermann A., Der Gott Tatenen...: OBO 29, 1980 ➤ 61,m374 ... 65,9362: ᴿWZKM 77 (1987) 121-5 (J. *Assmann*).

b933 **Schumacher** Inke W., Der Gott Sopdu, der Herr der Fremdländer: OBO 79. FrS/Gö 1988, Univ./VR. xiv-352 p.; 6 pl. Fs 94. 3-7278-0566-8 / VR 3-525-53708-5 [BO 45,756].

b934 *Seguenny* Edwige, L'influence de l'Egypte gréco-romaine sur la religion méroïtique; témoignage des objets d'art mineur: ➤ 750, Nubian V, 1982/6, 171-5 + 7 fig.

b935 **Smith** M., The mortuary texts of Papyrus BM 10597. L 1987, British Museum. 191 p.; 11 pl. £95. – ᴿOrientalia 57 (1988) 218s (D. *Devauchelle*).

b936 *Tawfik* Sayed, Aton studies 7. Did any cult ritual exist in Aton temples at Thebes? An attempt to trace it: MiDAI-K 44 (1988) 275-281; 2 fig.; pl. 83-86.

b937 *Tobin* Vincent A., Mytho-theology in ancient Egypt: JAmEg 25 (1988) 169-183.

b938 **Vergote** Joseph, De godsdienst van het Oude Egypte: Inforïentreeks 7. Lv 1987, Peeters. ix-159 p.; 50 fig. 90-6831-093-3.

b939 *Wessetzky* Vilmos, Les symboles d'Égypte ancienne de la religion isiaque à l'époque romaine en Pannonie: ➤ 72, ᶠKÁDÁR Z., AcClas Debrecen 22 (1986) 21-23 [➤ 3,b150].

b940 **Zabkar** Louis V., Hymns to Isis in her temple at Philae. Hanover 1988, Univ. Press of New England. xviii-203 p.; ill. 0-87451-395-2.

M7   **Religio mesopotamica.**

b941 **Abusch** I. Tzvi, Babylonian witchcraft literature: BrownJudSt 132. Atlanta 1987, Scholars. xviii-154 p. + xii p. 1-555-40191-0 [BO 45,757].

b942 ᴱ**Alster** Bendt, Death in Mesopotamia 1979/80 ➤ 61,891: ᴿOLZ 83 (1988) 663-7 (H. *Neumann*).

b943 *Amiet* P., Le problème de l'iconographie divine en Mésopotamie dans la glyptique antérieure à l'époque d'Agadé: CMatArch 1 (R 1986) 1-69; 11(=98) fig.

b944 *Black* Jeremy, The slain heroes — some monsters of ancient Mesopotamia: CanadMesop 15 (1988) 19-25.

b945 **Bottéro** Jean, Naissance de Dieu; la Bible et l'histoire 1986 ➤ 2,136; 3,b357: ᴿDivThom 89s (1986s) 493s (Y. *Poutet*).

b945* *Bottéro* J., Magie [en français]: ➤ 808, RLA 7,3s (1988) 200-234 [-255, Hethiter, *Haas* V.].

b946 **Brockhoff** Victoria, Götter, Dämonen, Menschen; Mythen und Geschichten aus dem Zweistromland. Stu 1987, Freies Geistesleben. 298 p.; 18 fig. 3-7725-0918-5 [OIAc D88].

b947 **Charpin** Dominique, Le clergé d'Ur au siècle d'Hammurabi 1986 ➤ 2,9061; 3,b359: ᴿBO 45 (1988) 346-355 (D. R. *Frayne*); RB 95 (1988) 435-7 (M. *Sigrist*).

b948 **Downey** Susan B., Mesopotamian religious literature; Alexander through the Parthians. Princeton 1988, Univ. xix-197 p. $55 [RelStR 15,155, J. M. *Sasson*].

b949 *Fauth* Wolfgang, Diener der Götter — Liebling der Götter; der altorientalische Herrscher als Schützling höherer Mächte: Saeculum 39 (1988) 217-246.

b950 *Fontaine* Carole, The deceptive goddess in ancient Near Eastern myth; Inanna and Inaraš: Semeia 42 (1988) 84-102.

b951 *a) Foster* Benjamin R., When kingship went up to heaven; Sargon and Naram-Sin (c. 2300 BC); – *b) Michałowski* Piotr, Divine heroes and historical self-representation; from Gilgamesh to Shulgi: CanadMesop 16 (1988) 13-17 / 19-23.

b952 *Hallo* William W., Texts, statues and the cult of the divine king: → 482, VTS 40, Jerusalem congress 1986/8, 54-66.

b952* *Horsnell* M. J. A., Religions of Assyria and Babylonia: → 801, ISBEnc³ 4 (1988) 85-95.

b953 **Kinnier Wilson** J. V., The legend of Etana 1985 → 1,9103; 2,7553: ᴿClasW 82 (1988s) 123s (Julie *Williams*); OLZ 83 (1988) 544-6 (C. *Saporetti*).

b954 **Livingstone** A., Mystical and mythological... Babylonian 1987 → 3, b380: ᴿArOr 56 (1988) 270 (Jana *Pečírková*).

b955 *Loucas* Ioannis, La déesse de la prospérité dans les mythes mésopotamiens et égéens de la 'descente aux enfers': RHR 205 (1988) 227-244; Eng. 227s.

Mander P., Il pantheon di Abu-Salabikh; contributo allo studio del pantheon sumerico arcaico: Studi Asiatici min. 26, 1986 → g157*.

b956 *a) Matsushima* Eiko, Les rituels du mariage divin dans les documents accadiens; – *b) Watanabe* Kazuko, Ein neuer Beleg fur das 'Bett' des Gottes Šamaš: AcSum 10 (1988) 95-128 / 229s.

b957 *Mayer* W. R., Ein neues Königsritual gegen feindliche Bedrohung: Orientalia 57 (1988) 145-164.

b958 *Pardee* Dennis, Ṭukamuna wa Šunama [... dieux cassites, en français]: UF 20 (1988) 195-9.

b959 *Patzek* R., Die mesopotamische Dämonin Lamaštu im orientalisierenden griechisch-kolonialen Kulturkreis; ein Amulett aus Poggio Civitate und Ilias 21,479ff: OrAnt 27 (1988) 221-9 + 1 fig; pl. VII.

b960 *Sabbatucci* Dario, Inanna diventa dea: SMSR 54 (1988) 219-225.

b961 *a) Sauren* Herbert, Dieu rit; une interprétation du mythe d'Adapa; – *b) Naster* Paul, Sennacherib verrast door noodweer ['surprised by heavy weather'; p. 1 'moodweer']: → 50, ᶠFONTINOY c. 1988, 15-30 / 31-36; franç. 37.

b962 **Scurlock** Joann, *a)* Magical means of dealing with ghosts in ancient Mesopotamia: diss. ᴰ*Farber* W. Ch 1988. – OIAc D88; Mar Šipri 1,1 (1988) 3.5; – *b)* KAR 256 ‖ BMS 53; a ghostly light on *bīt rimki* [seven houses (BMS 53 missing 7th) of incantation transferring evils from the king]: JAOS 108 (1988) 203-9.

b963 *Sjöberg* Åke W., A hymn to Inanna and her self-praise: JCS 40 (1988) 165-178 + 8 pl.

b964 *Szaryńska* K., The Sumerian goddess Inana-kur: OrVars 1 (1987)... [< BO 45,526].

b965 *Talon* P., La mythe de la Descente d'Ištar aux Enfers: Akkadica 59 (1988) 15-25 (+ 3 p. inserts).

b966 **Thomsen** Marie-Louise, Zauberdiagnose und schwarze Magie in Mesopotamien: C. Niebuhr Publ. 2. K 1987, Mus. Tusc. 96 p. DM 42. – ᴿBO 45 (1988) 629-632 (M. J. *Geller*); WeltOr 19 (1988) 165-171 (S. M. *Maul*).

b967 *a) Thomsen* Marie-Louise, The wisdom of the Chaldaeans; Mesopotamian magic as conceived by classical authors; – *b) Andersen* Lene, Greek epic and Greek mythology and their links with the Near East: → 733, Acta Hyperborea 1987/8, 93-101 / 33-43.

b968 *Zettler* Richard L., Administration of the temple of Inanna at Nippur under the Third Dynasty of Ur; archaeological and documentary evidence: ➤ 738, Power 1983/7, 117-131.

M7.4 Religio persiana, *Iran*.

b969 **Boyce** Mary, ❷ Zaratusztrianie – wiara i życie, ᵀ*Józefowicz-Czabak* Zofia, *Korzeniowski* Bolesław J. Łódź 1988, Wyd. Łódź. 383 p. – ᴿPrzOr (1988,2) 373-5 (B. *Składanek*).

b970 *Darrow* William R., Keeping the waters dry; the semiotics of fire and water in the Zoroastrian *Yasna*: JAAR 56 (1988) 417-442.

b971 *Edwards* M.J., How many Zoroasters? ARNOBIUS, Adversus Gentes I 52: VigChr 42 (1988) 282-9.

b972 **Guest** John S., The Yezidis, a study in survival 1987 ➤ 3,b520: ᴿJRAS (1988) 190-2 (M.J.L. *Young*).

b973 *Herrenschmidt* Clarisse, Aspects universalistes de la religion et de l'idéologie de Darius Iᵉʳ: ➤ 144, Mem. TUCCI G. 2 (1987) 617-625.

b974 *Hultgård* Anders, Prêtres juifs et mages zoroastriens — influences religieuses à l'époque hellénistique: RHPR 68 (1988) 415-428.

b975 *Koch* Heidemarie, Zur Religion der Achämeniden: ZAW 100 (1988) 393-405; map.

b976 **Kreyenbroek** G., Sraoša in the Zoroastrian tradition: Or. Rheno-Traiectina 28. Leiden 1985, Brill. xii-200 p. ƒ68. – ᴿRHR 205 (1988) 79-82 (P. *Gignoux*).

b977 *Panaino* Antonio, Tištrya e Mithra: Acme 41 (1988) 229-242.

b978 *Pena* Ignacio, Les 'adorateurs de Satan': TerreS (sept. 1987) [> EsprVie 98 (1988) 118s, J. *Daoust*].

b979 **Russell** James R., Zoroastrianism in Armenia: Harvard Iranian 5. CM 1987, Harvard Univ. vi-578 p.; 5 pl., 2 foldout maps. $40 [TDig 36,79].

b979* *Yamauchi* E.M., Religions of Persia: ➤ 801, ISBEnc³ 4 (1988) 123-9.

M8 Religio islamica et proto-arabica.

b980 **Arkoun** Mohammed, L'Islam, morale et politique. P 1986, Unesco/ Desclée-B. 240 p. – ᴿRThom 88 (1988) 169s (J. *Jomier*).

b981 **Ayoub** Mahmoud M., The Qur'an and its interpreters I, 1984 ➤ 3,b409: ᴿSR 17 (1988) 121s (R. *Neufeldt*).

b982 **Basetti-Sani** Giulio, Louis MASSIGNON 1985 ➤ 2,9089: ᴿCiVit 43 (1988) 195s (M. *Adriani*); ColcFr 58 (1988) 369s (C. *Cargnoni*).

b983 *Basetti-Sani* Giulio, *a)* L. Massignon, un insigne promotore del pacifismo e del dialogo islamo-cristiano: StPatav 35 (1988) 617-621; – *b)* Sufi islamici condannati per l'esaltazione di Cristo sopra Maometto (Costantinopoli 1527-9) dalle relazioni dei legati della Repubblica Veneta: ➤ StPatav 35,2 (1988) 241-7; Eng. 248.

b984 **Biggar** Nigel, *al.*, Cities of God; faith, politics, and pluralism in Judaism, Christianity, and Islam: Contributions to the Study of Religion 16, 1986 ➤ 2,409: ᴿJEcuSt 25 (1988) 458s (J.E. *Biechler*).

b985 **Blichfeldt** Jan-Olaf, Early Mahdism; politics and religion in the formative period of Islam: StOrLund 2. Leiden 1985, Brill. xii-137 p. ƒ48. 90-07643-3. – ᴿBO 45 (1988) 440-5 (L.I. *Conrad*); BSOAS 51 (1988) 129s (W. *Madelung*).

b986 *Borrmans* Maurice, L'itinéraire spirituel du père Jean-Mohammed ABD-EL-JALIL [franciscain] (1904-1979): EsprVie 98 (1988) 321-9.

b987 **Boudiba** Abdelwahab, Sexuality in Islam, ᵀ*Sheridan* Alan, 1985 ➤ 2,9094; £27.50. 0-7100-9608-9: ᴿBO 45 (1988) 716-9 (L. I. *Conrad*: 'Bouhdiba', Sorbonne-trained sociologist; MERLEAU-PONTY influence).

b988 *Bouman* Johann, Der Islam als nachbiblische Religion: Renovatio 44 (Köln 1988) 82-87 [< ZIT 88,525].

b989 **Bürgel** Johann C., The feather of Simurgh; the 'licit magic' of the arts in medieval Islam. NYU 1988. xii-207 p.; ill. 0-8147-1102-2.

b990 **Cragg** Kenneth, The call of the minaret²ʳᵉᵛ [¹1956] 1986 ➤ 2,9099: ᴿScotJT 41 (1988) 281-3 (E. *Hulmes*).

b991 **Crone** P., *Hinds* M., God's Caliph 1986 ➤ 3,b418*: ᴿRHR 205 (1988) 215s (G. *Monnot*).

b992 **Danner** Victor, The Islamic tradition; an introduction. NY 1988, Amity. xi-255 p. $14. – ᴿParabola 13,3 (1988) 110-2 (C. W. *Ernst*).

b993 **Denny** Frederick M., Islam and the Muslim community: Religious Traditions of the World. SF 1987, Harper & R. xii-137 p. $8 pa. [TDig 36,56].

b994 **Endress** Gerhard, An introduction to Islam [1982 ➤ 64,9698], ᵀ*Hillenbrand* Carole. NY/E 1988, Columbia/Univ. ix-294 p. [bibliog. 70 p.]; 6 maps. $25; pa. $12 [TDig 35,354]. – ᴿJRAS (1988) 395s (D. O. *Morgan*).

b995 **Freitag** Rainer, Seelenwanderung in der islamischen Häresie: Islamkundliche Untersuchungen 110. B 1985, Schwarz. 389 p. DM 56. – ᴿMundus 24 (1988) 13-15 (T. *Nagel*: 'metempsychosis as a Muslim heresy').

b996 *Gilliot* Claude, Bulletin d'Islamologie et d'études arabes: RSPT 72 (1988) 121-143 [*Arkoun* M. 1986; ᴱ*Balta* P. 1986; *Rousseau* R. 1987 ...]. 465-480.

b997 **Gimaret** Daniel, Les noms divins en Islam: Patrimoines. P 1988, Cerf. 448 p. – ᴿIslamochristiana 14 (1988) 329-331 (M. *Borrmans*).

b998 ᴱ**Haarmann** Ulrich, Geschichte der arabischen Welt. Mü 1987, Beck. 720 p.; 124 maps. DM 128. – ᴿErbAuf 64 (1988) 242 (E. *Tschacher*); Mundus 24 (1988) 15s (H. *Müller*); PrzOr (1988,2) 186s (J. *Danecki*).

b999 ᴱ**Haines** B. L. Christians and Muslims ... Presbyterians 1987 ➤ 3,b433: ᴿMissiology 16 (1988) 219s (L. *Vander Werff*).

d1 *Halm* Heinz, Islam: ➤ 798, EvKL 2 (1988) 733-745 [-756, *al.*].

d1* *Harpigny* G., Qu'est-ce que l'intégrisme musulman?: FoiTemps 18 (1988) 344-372.

d2 *Heath* Michael J., Islamic themes in religious polemic: BibHumRen 50 (1988) 289-315.

d3 **Hock** Klaus, Der Islam im Spiegel westlicher Theologie: Kölner Veröff.RelG 8, 1986 ➤ 2,9112; 3,b437: ᴿZMissRW 72 (1988) 88s (H. *Vöcking*).

d3* *Isaiah* Emmanuel S., Muslim eschatology and its missiological implications; a thematic study: diss. Fuller Theol. Sem.; ᴰ*Woodberry* J. Pasadena 1988. 177 p. 88-19607. – DissA 49 (1988s) 2258-A.

d4 *Jourdan* François, La mort du Messie en croix dans les églises araméennes et sa relation à l'Islam jusqu'à l'arrivée des Mongols en 1258: diss Sorbonne/Inst. Cath., ᴰ*Meslin* M. P 1988 – 416 p.; 202 p. – RICathP 28 (1988) 163s.

d4* *Jung* Michael, The religious monuments of ancient southern Arabia; a preliminary typological classification: AION 48 (1988) 177-218; 20 fig.; XII pl.

d5 **Kedar** Benjamin Z., Crusade and mission 1984 ➤ 65,9464 ... 3,b441: ᴿHeythJ 29 (1988) 367s (J. *Muldoon*).

d6 **Keryell** Jacques, Louis MASSIGNON, L'hospitalité sacrée, textes inédits [sur le rapport-*badaliya* avec Mary *Kahil*]. P 1987, Nouvelle Cité. – [R]LumièreV 37,190 (1988) 104s (R. L. *Moreau*).

d7 **Khalidi** Tarif, Classical Arab Islam; the culture and heritage of the golden age 1985 → 1,a785; 3,b442: [R]WeltOr 19 (1988) 198-200 (R. *Eisener*).

d8 [T]**Khoury** Adel T. (*Abdullah* Muhammad S.), Der Koran. Gü 1987, Mohn. 578 p. DM 48. – [R]StiZt 206 (1988) 134-7 (H. *Zirker*).

d10 **Mason** Herbert, Memoir of a friend, Louis MASSIGNON [whose 4-volume Passion of al-Hallaj he translated]. ND 1988, Univ. 170 p. $19 [TDig 36,70].

d11 *Massignon* Daniel, Le voyage en Mésopotamie et la conversion de Louis MASSIGNON en 1908: Islamochristiana 14 (1988) 127-199.

d12 **Mernissi** Fatima, Beyond the veil; male-female dynamics in modern Muslim society[2rev] – [[1]1975]. Bloomington 1987, Indiana Univ. 200 p. $25; pa. $8. – [R]JEcuSt 25 (1988) 633s (Jane I. *Smith*).

d13 *a) Michel* Thomas, Christian-Muslim dialogue since Vatican II; – *b) Leveau* Remy, The Muslim community in France [< Études Mai 1986], [T]*Aufossy* Bridget: Month 249 (1988) 671-6 / 677-682.

d14 *a) Michel* Thomas, The theological situation now in Muslim-Christian dialogue; – *b) Borrmans* Maurice, Difficulties of the dialogue; – *c) Engineer* Asghar A., Muhammad as liberator; – *d) Ali* Zeenat S., Women in Islam; spirit and progress: Jeevadhara 13 (1988) 157-166 / 212-228 / 189-201 / 202-211.

d15 *a) Mitri* Tarek, Zukunftsaussichten für ein Zusammenleben von Muslimen und Christen in islamischen Ländern; – *b) Zirker* Hans, Die Hinwendung Gottes zu den Menschen in Bibel und Koran: UnSa 43 (1988) 220-8. 248 / 229-238.

d16 **Monteil** Vincent Mansour [disciple passé à l'Islam], 'Le linceul de feu', Louis MASSIGNON (1883-1962). 1987, Vegapress. 295 p. – [R]EsprVie 98 (1988) 105-8 (G. *Zananiri,* aussi sur HARPIGNY G. 1981).

d17 **Nasr** Seyyed H., Islamic art and spirituality 1987 → 3,b459: [R]JAAR 56 (1988) 165s (B. B. *Lawrence*).

d18 **Nasr** S., Islamic spirituality: EWSp 19, 1987 → 3,b460: [R]Horizons 18 (1988) 185s (J. *Carmody*).

d19 **Nasr** Seyyed H., Traditional Islam in the modern world. NY 1987, Kegan Paul. 335 p. $40. – [R]JAAR 56 (1988) 345s (R. C. *Martin*); JEcuSt 25 (1988) 103s (Jane I. *Smith,* also on TAHA M. 1987).

d20 *Nieuwenhuijze* C. A. O. van, Virtue and default of two-dimensional vision [Third World Quarterly (0143-6597) 10,2 ('Islam and politics' 1988) 473-1103; $9]: BO 45 (1988) 518-523.

d21 *Ohtsuka* Kazuo, Toward a typology of benefit-granting in Islam: Orient-J 24 (1988) 141-152 [< Oriento 29 (1986)].

d22 *O'Shaughnessy* Thomas J., The living God and living with God in the Qur'ān: Landas 2 (Manila 1988) 93-97 [< TKontext 10/1,73].

d23 *Palubicki* Władysław, ☻ The institution of harems in oriental tradition: PrzOr (1988,2) 123-134.

d24 *Rizzardi* Giuseppe, Islam, errore o eresia III-VI: Renovatio 23 (1988) 9-63 . 169-200 . 345-387 . 521-550.

d25 *Roest Crollius* Ary A., L'Église regarde les Musulmans, [T]*Chalon* Colette: → 379, Vatican II Bilan 3 (1988) 319-329; Eng. → 380, Assessment 3,324-334.

d26 *a) Rossing* D., De christelijke gemeenschappen en godsdienstige pluriformiteit in Israel; – *b) Heusden* P. van, De katholieke kerk en de staat Israel: Kosmos+Oekumene 22 (1988) 98-107 / 108-119.

d27 ᴱRousseau Richard W., Christianity and Islam 1985 ➤ 1,a808 ... 3,b472: ᴿHorizons 14 (1988) 417 (J. *Renard*); JEcuSt 24 (1987) 136s (M. K. *Masud*).

d28 *a) Schall* Anton, Gott, Welt und Mensch im Koran — Grundansichten des Islam; *–b) Radtke* Berndt, Die Stellung der islamischen Theologie und Philosophie zur Astrologie; – *c) Gramlich* Richard, Gottes Willen tun, ein Aspekt der islamischen Frömmigkeit: Saeculum 39 (1988) 247-258 / 259-267 / 268-276.

d29 **Schimmel** Annemarie, And Muhammad is his messenger; the veneration of the Prophet in Islamic piety [1981] 1985 ➤ 3,b477: ᴿJAAR 56 (1988) 180-2 (J. E. *Campo*).

d30 **Schwarzbaum** Haim, Biblical and extra-biblical legends in Islamic folk-literature 1982 ➤ 63,9501 ... 3,b479: ᴿJNES 47 (1988) 69-71 (J. R. *Perry*).

d31 *a) Sharon* Moshe, The birth of Islam in the Holy Land; – *b) Busse* Heribert, Jerusalem and Mecca, the Temple and the Kaaba; an account of their interrelation in Islamic times; – *c) Ayalon* David, Islam versus Christian Europe; the case of the Holy Land; – *d) Rosen-Ayalon* Myriam, New discoveries in Islamic archaeology in the Holy Land: ➤ 499, Holy Land 1986/8, 225-235 / 236-246 / 247-256 / 257-269.

d32 *Shepard* William, What is 'Islamic fundamentalism'?: SR 17 (1988) 5-26.

d33 **Smith** Peter, Babi and Baha'i religions; from messianic Shi'ism to a world religion. NY 1987, Cambridge-UP. xiv-242 p. $39.50. – ᴿRRel-Res 30 (1988s) 110s (Arfa *Aflatooni*).

d33* **Sourdel** D., *Bosch Vilá* J., Regierung und Verwaltung des Vorderen Orients in islamischer Zeit: HbOrientalistik 6/5/2: Leiden 1988, Brill. vi-152 p. 90-04-08550-5.

d34 *Talbi* Mohamed, Possibilities and conditions for a better understanding between Islam and the west: IEcuSt 25 (1988) 161-193.

d35 *Waardenburg* Jacques, Die Revitalisierung des Islam — religionswissenschaftlich gesehen: EvT 48 (1988) 46-64 [Fortsetzung von NSys 26 (1984) 238-255].

d36 *Watt* W. Montgomery, The study of Islam by orientalists: Islamo-christiana 14 (1988) 201-210.

d37 *Zaman* Muhammad Q., The relevance of religion and the response to it; a study of religious perceptions in early Islam: JRAS (1988) 265-287.

M8.5 **Religiones Indiae** *et variae*.

d38 **Arokiasamy** Soosai, Dharma, Hindu and Christian, according to Robert DE NOBILI; analysis of its meaning and its use in Hinduism and Christianity: Documenta Missionalia 19, 1986 ➤ 2,9152: ᴿZMissRW 72 (1988) 251s (H. *Waldenfels*).

d39 *Arthur* Chris J., West meets East [*Ariarajah* W. and 4 other recent books]: ScotJT 41 (1988) 253-265.

d40 **Bassuk** Daniel E., Incarnation in Hinduism and Christianity; the myth of the God-Man [also L, Macmillan] 1987 ➤ 3,b500: JEcuSt 25 (1988) 449s (E. *Brennan*); RelStR 14 (1988) 47 (R. B. *Williams*); TLond 91 (1988) 556s (J. *Lipner*).

d41 *Bechert* Heinz, Die Datierung des Buddha als Problem der Weltgeschichte: Saeculum 39 (1988) 24-34.

d42 *Bocchini* Sergio, Occidente cristiano e buddhismo, ieri e oggi: StPatav 35 (1988) 623-643; Eng. 644.

d43 ᴱ**Braun** Hans-Jürg, *Krieger* David J., Indische Religionen und das Christentum im Dialog. Z 1986, Theol.-V. 148 p. – ᴿZMissRW 72 (1988) 78s (H. *Waldenfels*).

d44 *Bulman* Raymond F., Buddha and Christ; changing models in times of oppression: JEcuSt 24 (1987) 53-79.

d45 **Chemperathy** George, God en het lijden; een indische theodicee [inaug. Utrecht]. Leiden 1986, Brill. 43 p. – ᴿNedTTs 42 (1988) 148 (L. P. van den *Bosch*).

d46 **Coomaraswamy** Ananda K. [1877-1947], Induismo e buddismo² 1987 → 3,b509: ᴿHumBr 43 (1988) 138s (Caterina *Conio*).

d47 **Coward** Harold, *al.*, Readings in Eastern religions. Waterloo ON 1988, Laurier Univ. viii-368 p. $30. 0-88920-955-3 [TDig 26,151].

d48 *Coward* Harold, The possibility of paradigm choice in Buddhist-Christian dialogue: JEcuSt 25 (1988) 370-382 (358-369, *Clooney* Francis X.).

d49 **Dammann** E., L'Africa; le religioni naturalistiche, ebraismo, cristianesimo e islamismo in Africa [Storia delle Religioni 10, 1985 → 2,9159; 3,b511*: ᴿStudium 83 (R 1987) 295 (A. *De Spirito*).

d50 **Dhavamony** Mariasusai, La luce di Dio nell'Induismo; preghiere, inni, cantici e meditazioni degli Indù: Preghiere di tutti i tempi 9. Mi 1987, Paoline. 221 p. Lit. 10.000. 88-315-0044-9. – ᴿGregorianum 69 (1988) 402s (*ipse*).

d51 **Dumoulin** Heinrich, Geschichte des Zen-Buddhismus I-II, 1985s → 3,b514: ᴿMüTZ 39 (1988) 212s (P. *Schmidt-Leukel*).

d52 **Fenton** John Y., *al*, Religions of Asia² [< *Nielsen* → b757]. NY 1988, St. Martin's. xii-320 p. [TDig 35,188].

d53 **Fernando** Antony, Zu den Quellen des Buddhismus; eine Einführung für Christen [1985 → 1,a848], ᵀ*Siepen* W.: Topos-Tb 169. Mainz 1987, Grünewald. 191 p. DM 12,80. – ᴿTPQ 136 (1988) 376s (J. *Janda*).

d54 *Fredericks* James, The Kyoto school; modern Buddhist philosophy and the search for a transcultural theology: Horizons 15 (1988) 299-315.

d55 **Gombrich** Richard F., Theravada Buddhism; a social history from ancient Benares to modern Colombo: Library of Religious Beliefs and Practices. NY 1988, Routledge-CH. x-237 p. $55; pa. $16 [TDig 36,61].

d56 **Griffiths** Bede, The cosmic revelation; the Hindu way to God. L 1987, Collins. 136 p. £4 pa. – ᴿTLond 91 (1988) 557s (J. *Lipner*).

d57 **Griffiths** Bede, River of compassion [Anglican priest's commentary on Bhagavad Gita]. Warwick NY 1987, Amity. 328 p. $12 [RelStR 15,92, R. N. *Minor*].

d57* **Hall** David L., *Ames* Roger T., Thinking through Confucius. Albany 1987, SUNY. xxii-394 p. – ᴿBSOAS 51 (1988) 591s (A. C. *Graham*).

d58 ᴱ**Heissig** Walter, *Klimkeit* Hans-Joachim, Synkretismus in den Religionen Zentralasiens [Bonn St. Augustin Kolloquium Mai, 1983]: Studies in Oriental Religions 13, 1987 → 3,642: ᴿMundus 24 (1988) 189-191 (H.-R. *Kämpfe*).

d59 **Jacobson** Nolan P. †, The heart of Buddhist philosophy. Carbondale 1988, Southern Illinois Univ. xiv-189 p. $17; pa. $10 [TDig 36,65].

d60 *King* Ursula, Women and spirituality; critical reflections on Christianity and Hinduism: Vidyajyoti 52 (1988) 225-233 . 258-269 . 327-339.

d61 **Kinsley** David, Hindu goddesses; visions of the divine feminine in the Hindu religious tradition. Berkeley 1986, Univ. California. viii-281 p.; ill. £29.75. – ᴿJRAS (1988) 212s (Karel *Werner*).

Kitagawa Joseph, Understanding Japanese religions 1987 → 211*.

d62 **Kochumuttom** Thomas A., Comparative theology; Christian thinking and spirituality in Indian perspective [1. Hindu; 2. Buddhist]. Bangalore 1985, Dharmaram. x-160 p. $5. – RGregorianum 69 (1988) 181s (J. *Dupuis*). *Kullman* W., *al.,* Vorträge für R. MUTH, Mythos 1987 → 110.

d63 **Lo Kuang** Stanislaus, Rapprochement between modernized Confucian thought and Christian belief: Ching Feng 31 (Hong Kong 1988) 153-165 [-191, *al.:* < TKontext 10/1,36].

d64 **MacInnes** sr. Elaine, Teaching Zen to Christians. Manila 1986, Zen Center. 110 p.; ill. [RelStR 15,237, D. J. *O'Hanlon*].

d65 **Martinson** Paul V., A theology of world religions; interpreting God, self, and world in Semitic, Indian, and Chinese thought 1987 → 3,h536: RRelStR 14 (1988) 141 (J. B. *Cobb*).

d66 **Matus** Thomas, Yoga and the Jesus prayer tradition 1984 → 1,a869: RBSecrNChr 23 (1988) 70-72 (B. de *Give*).

d67 **Mitra** Kana, Catholicism-Hinduism... PANIKKAR 1987 → 3,b538: RHorizons 15 (1988) 438s (D. P. *Sheridan*); JEcuSt 24 (1987) 651s (J. F. *Kane*).

d68 *a) Olson* Carl, TILLICH's dialogue with Buddhism; – *b) Tracy* David, The Christian understanding of salvation-liberation: Buddhist-Christian Studies 7 (1987) 183-198 / 129-138.

d69 *Pieris* Aloysius, East in the west; resolving a spiritual crisis: Horizons 15 (1988) 337-346 [347-364, symposium, *Knitter* Paul F., *Abe* Masao].

d70 **Ralston** Helen, Christian Ashrams, a new religious movement in contemporary India: Studies in Religion and Society 20. Lewiston NY 1987, Mellen. iv-154 p. 0-88946-854-0. – RVidyajyoti 52 (1988) 166s (P. *Mekkunnel*).

d71 *Riesenhuber* Klaus, ◐ Towards an understanding of Zen meditation: KatKenk 27,54 (1988) 1-22 = 187-208; Eng. i-iv.

d71* **Rule** Paul A., K'ung-tzu or Confucius? The Jesuit interpretation of Confucius. Sydney 1986, Allen & Unwin. xiii-303 p. £9.50. – RBSOAS 51 (1988) 593s (D. *Lancashire*).

d72 **Rwehumbiza** Philibert R. K., Patriarchal and Bantu cults compared: Spearhead 103. Eldoret, Kenya 1988, Amecea-Caba. 48 p.

d73 **Schayer** Stanisław, O filozofowaniu Hindusów, artykuły wybrane. Wsz 1988, Państwowe Wydawnictwo Naukowe. xxxii-539 p.; portr. 83-01-08657-2.

d74 **Schreiner** Peter, Begegnung mit dem Hinduismus: Bücherei 1143. FrB 1984, Herder. 128 p. DM 8. – ROLZ 83 (1988) 98s (M. *Thiel-Horstmann*).

d75 ESchumacher Stephan, *Woerner* Gert, Lexikon der östlichen Weisheitslehren, Buddhismus-Hinduismus-Taoismus-Zen. Mü 1986, Barth. xiv-497 p.; ill. DM 85. 3-502-67404-3. – RBijdragen 49 (1988) 226 (J. G. *Hahn*).

d76 **Singh** Harbans, *Delahoutre* Michel, Le Sikhisme, anthologie de la poésie religieuse...: Homo Religiosus 12. LvN 1985, Centre Hist. Rel. 260 p.; 105 fig. Fb 800. – RGregorianum 69 (1988) 387 (M. *Dhavamony*).

d77 **Snodgrass** Adrian, The symbolism of the [Buddhist] *stūpa*: Studies on Southeast Asia. Ithaca NY 1985, Cornell Univ. 407 p.; 286 fig. DM 42. – ROLZ 83 (1988) 517-525 (H. *Kottkamp*).

d78 **Stoltzmann** William, The pipe and Christ 1986 → 2,9191; 3,b548: RTR 84 (1988) 156s (N. M. *Borengässer*).

d79 *Sundermeier* Theo, Gott im Buddhismus?: EvT 48 (1988) 19-35.

d80 *Tanabe* Katsumi, The Iranian origin of the Buddhist *ûrṇâ* [tuft of hair on Buddha's head]: ArchMIran 20 (1987) 251-9; 7 fig.; pl. 22-23.

d81 **Teasdale** Wayne R.,   Toward a Christian vedanta; the encounter of Hinduism and Christianity according to Bede GRIFFITHS. Bangalore 1987, Asian-TC. vi-192 p. r 40 [TDig 36,87].

d82 *Thadathil* John, Christian ashrams and their significance: Claretianum 27 (1987) 149-199.

d83 *Vavroušková* Stanislava, Two recent Soviet studies of Hinduism [both ELitman A. D., *Rybakov* R. B., 1983 and 1985]: ArOr 56 (1988) 253-6.

d84 **Zago** Marcello, La spiritualità buddhista. R 1986, Studium. 256 p. Lit. 15.000. – RHumBr 43 (1988) 139 (Caterina *Conio*).

d85 **Zimmer** Heinrich, Maya, ou le rêve cosmique dans la mythologie hindoue [première partie de Māyā 1936], THulin Michèle, pref. *Biardeau* Madeleine: L'espace intérieur 34. P 1987, Fayard. 331 p.: RRHR 205 (1988) 98s (A. *Padoux*).

XVII,1. Historia Medii Orientis Biblici

Q1   *Syria, Canaan,*   **Israel Veteris Testamenti.**

d86 **Ahlström** Gösta W., Who were the Israelites? 1986 ↠ 2,9202.b811; 3,b557: RBiblica 69 (1988) 280-2 (H. *Engel*); CBQ 50 (1988) 485-7 (A. J. *Hauser*: rejects archeological evidence of Israel entry as in ALBRIGHT, but admits it for Sea-Peoples invasion); JNWS 14 (1988) 226 (F. C. *Fensham*: title echoes HALDAR A., Who were the Amorites?); TLZ 113 (1988) 22-24 (H. M. *Niemann*: a fresh approach); VT 38 (1988) 372s (J. A. *Emerton*).

d87 **Baumgarten** Albert J., The Phoenician History of PHILO of Byblos, a commentary: ÉPR 89, 1981 ↠ 62,a398 ... 1,a900: RJNES 47 (1988) 56-58 (D. *Pardee*, also on ATTRIDGE-ODEN 1981).

d88 EBautz F. J., Geschichte der Juden 1983 ↠ 64,245 ... 3,a901: ROLZ 83 (1988) 43 (G. *Pfeifer*).

d89 *Calderone* Philip J., Periods of biblical history: Landas 2 (Manila 1988) 98-103 [< TKontext 10/1,73].

d90 **Castel** F., History of Israel 1985 ↠ 1,a904; 3,b562: RBibTB 18 (1988) 32s (L. A. *Sinclair*: Ebla forbids us to say 'nomad' without qualification).

d91 **Castel** F., Storia di Israele [1983] it. ²1987 ↠ 2,9206; TZardi Leonardo; 88-215-1217-7: RRivB 36 (1988) 267-9 (F. *Festorazzi*).

d92 **Cazelles** Henri, Storia politica di Israele dalle origini ad Alessandro Magno [1981] 1985 ↠ 2,9209; 3,b564: RProtestantesimo 43 (1988) 44 (J. A. *Soggin*); RivB 36 (1988) 521s (B. *Boschi*: traduzione già datata come quasi-difesa della storicità pre-monarchica della Bibbia).

d93 **Clauss** Manfred, Geschichte Israels 1986 ↠ 2,9210; 3,b565: RBiblica 69 (1988) 282-4 (H. *Engel*: Enttäuschung der geweckten Erwartungen); RÉJ 146 (1987) 426 (A. *Caquot*); TR 84 (1988) 17-20 (D. *Conrad*).

d94 **Donner** Herbert, Geschichte des Volkes Israel I. 1984 ↠ 65,9546; II. 1986 ↠ 2,9211; 3,b568: RBiKi 42 (1987) 43s (F.-J. *Stendebach*); JNWS 14 (1988) 228s (F. C. *Fensham*, 2); OLZ 83 (1988) 168-170 (R. *Stahl*, 1).

d95 **Giardina** Andrea, *Liverani* Mario, *Scorcia* Biancamaria, La Palestina [↠ 3,b570] storia di una terra; l'età antica e cristiana, l'Islam, le questioni attuali: Libri di base 116. R 1987, Ed. Riuniti. 205 p.; maps. 88-359-3088-X. – RAegyptus 68 (1988) 258s (A. *Cristofori*); Henoch 10 (1988) 97-99 (G. *Garbini*: serve da correzione ai grossolani errori di Garribba N., Lo stato d'Israele 1983, n. 62 della stessa collana).

d96 *Hogendijk* Jan P., New light on the lunar crescent visibility table of Ya'qūb IBN TĀRIQ: JNES [27 (1968), *Kennedy* E. S.] 47 (1988) 95-104.

d97 **Knauf** Ernst A.,   Ismael 1985 ➤ 1,a924... 3,b578: ᴿBO 45 (1988) 425-7 (C. H. J. de *Geus*).

d97* *La Sor* W. S.,   Syria: ➤ 801, ISBEnc³ 4 (1988) 686-694.

d98 **Lemche** Niels P., [➤ 2740] Ancient Israel; a new history of Israelite society: Biblical Seminar.   Sheffield 1988, Academic. 276 p. £22.50; pa. £8. 1-85075-187-0; 017-3 [BL 89,37, A. *Mayes*].

d99 *a*) *Loon* Maurits Van, New evidence for North Syrian chronology from Hammam et-Turkman; – *b*) *Roaf* Michael, Problems in the chronology of Ninevite 5; – *c*) *Stomper* Matthew W., The [Babylon] Kasr archive; – *d*) *Kohl* Philip L., The northern 'frontier' of the Ancient Near East: AJA 92 1988) 580-5; 5 fig. / 589-591 / 587s / 591-6 [last installment of (E. *Porada* since 1966) Chronologies].

d100 **Mazar** Benjamin, The early biblical period, historical studies, ᴱ*Ahituv* S. ... 1986 ➤ 2,191; 3,b581: ᴿAJA 92 (1988) 288s (R. S. *Boraas*); BO 45 (1988) 693-7 (A. H. J. *Gunneweg*); JBL 107 (1988) 113s (W. R. *Wifall*).

d101 **Merrill** E. H.,   Kingdom of priests; a history of Old Testament Israel [... biblical witness inerrant]. GR 1987, Baker. 546 p. $25. 0-8010-6220-9 [BL 89,38, J. R. *Porter*]. – ᴿBS 145 (1988) 456s (C. H. *Dyer*: admirable success); SWJT 31,2 (1988s) 53 (F. B. *Huey*).

d103 **Miller** J. M., *Hayes* J. H. A history of ancient Israel and Judah 1986 ➤ 2,9232; 3,b583: ᴿAmerica 157 (1987) 306s (J. J. M. *Roberts*: crippling refusal to deal with what Israel considered its formative period); BS 145 (1988) 353s (E. H. *Merrill*: pre-monarchy too skeptical); CBQ 50 (1988) 303s (W. H. *Shea*); CiuD 201 (1988) 173s (J. *Gutiérrez*); Interpretation 42 (1988) 73-76 (W. *Brueggemann*); JAOS 108 (1988) 309s (J. *Van Seters*); JBL 107 (1988) 297-9 (J. W. *Flanagan*); ScripTPamp 19 (1987) 979 (S. *Ausin*: 'en ningún momento se aborda el contenido religioso'); Way 28 (1988) 69 (J. A. *Crampsey*).

d104 **Peláez del Rosal** Jesús, Los orígenes del pueblo hebreo: Estudios de cultura hebrea 1. Córdoba [1984 ➤ 65,9576; 3,558*] 1988, Almendro. 183 p. 84-86077-56-7.

d105 **Pikaza** Xabier, Para leer la historia del pueblo de Dios. Estella 1988, VDivino. 278 p. – ᴿBibFe 14 (1988) 482s (A. *Salas*); NatGrac 35 (1988) 441 (R. *Robles*).

d106 *Pitard* Wayne T. The identity of the Bir-Hadad of the Melqart stela [his Aram was not Damascus but in northern Syria]: BASOR 272 (1988) 3-21.

d107 **Scharbert** J.,   Zwangsumsiedlungen in Vorderasien zwischen dem 10. und dem 6. Jahrhundert v. Chr. nach altorientalischen und biblischen Quellen [... lessons regarding current Judaism]: Szb der Sudetendeutschen Akad. geistw. 1988/1. Mü 1988, Sudetenland. 39 p. 3-922423-30-2 [BL 89,41, G. H. *Jones*].

d108 **Smelik** Klaas A. D., Historische Dokumente aus dem alten Israel 1987 ➤ 3,b592: ᴿNorTTs 89 (1988) 275s (H. M. *Barstad*); ZDPV 104 (1988) 174-6 (E. A. *Knauf*).

d109 **Soggin** J. Alberto, A history of ancient Israel 1984 ➤ 65,9573 ... 3,b595: ᴿHeythJ 29 (1988) 346s (B. P. *Robinson*); JBL 107 (1988) 297-9 (J. W. *Flanagan*).

d110 **Soggin** J. A.,   Storia d'Israele 1984 ➤ 65,9574... 3,b594: ᴿColcT 58,4 (1988) 169s (J. *Warzecha*); RTLv 19 (1988) 87s (P.-M. *Bogaert*).

d112 [*Soggin* J. A., *al.*] Le origini di Israele 1987 ➤ 3,564: ᴿCC 139 (1988,4) 401s (G. L. *Prato*).

d113 *Soggin* J. Alberto, Probleme einer Vor- und Frühgeschichte Israels [< Henoch 8 (1986) 129-147]: ➤ 153, ZAW 100 Supp. (1988) 255-267.

d114 *Stolz* Fritz, Kanaan: ➤ 813, TRE 17 (1988) 539-556.

d115 *Täubler* Eugen, *a*) Chazor in den Briefen von Tell el-Amarna [< ᶠ*Baeck*
L. 1938, 9-30]; – *b*) The first mention of Israel [< PAAR 12 (1942)
115-120]; – *c*) Die weltpolitische Stellung des jüdischen Staates in der
hellenistisch-römischen Zeit [< Bericht der Lehranstalt Wiss. Judentums
30 (B 1912) 71-92]: ➤ 270, Schriften 1987, 17-38 / 39-44 / 173-192.

d116 *Tsau* Paul, ⊚ Contributions of the Semites to the Ancient Near East:
ColcFuJen 75 (1988) 45-51.

d117 **Van Seters** J., Der Jahwist als Historiker [Vorträge Schweiz/
Deutschland, Eng.], ᵀ*Schmid* H.: Theologische Studien 134. Z 1987,
Theol.-V. 95 p. – ᴿHenoch 10 (1988) 247-250 (P. *Sacchi*: tanto piccolo di
dimensioni, quanto importante).

d118 **Weiler** Gershon, Jewish theocracy. Leiden 1988, Brill. xiv-332 p. 90-
04-08630-7.

d119 *Wénin* A., Pouvoirs et solidarités dans l'AT; la monarchie en Israël et
Juda (1050 à 600 av. J.-C.): FoiTemps 18 (1988) 457-479.

d120 *Wright* Mary, ᴱ*Pardee* Dennis, Contacts between Egypt and Syro-
Palestine during the Old Kingdom: BA 51 (1988) 143-161; ill.

Q2 **Historiographia** – *theologia historiae.*

d121 **Altizer** Thomas J.J., History as apocalypse 1985 ➤ 1,a949; 2,9246:
ᴿChH 57 (1988) 120s (M. *Lieb*).

d122 *Ampio* Riccardo, La concezione Orosiana della storia, attraverso le
metafore del fuoco e del sangue: CivClCr 9 (1988) 217-236.

d123 *a*) *Ankersmit* F.R., Historical representation; – *b*) *Casement* William,
Husserl and the philosophy of history: HistTheor 27 (1988) 205-228 /
229-240.

d124 *Berthold* Werner, Zu den Weltgeschichtskonzeptionen Hegels und
Rankes: ZtsGeschW 36 (1988) 387-396.

d125 **Carr** David, Time, narrative, and history. Bloomington 1986, Indiana
Univ. 189 p. – ᴿHistTheor 27 (1988) 297-306 (N. *Carroll*).

d126 Christ Karl: Alte Geschichte und Wissenschaftsgeschichte, 65 Gb.,
ᴱ*Kneisel* P., *Losemann* V. Da 1988, Wiss. viii-537 p. – ᴿArTGran 51
(1988) 382s (A. *Segovia*).

d127 ᴱ**Croke** Brian, *Emmett* Alanna M., History and historians in late
antiquity [Macquarie Univ., Sydney 1981] 1983 ➤ 3,755: ᴿSecC 6 (1987s)
115-7 (T.R. *Martin*).

d128 *Dumais* Alfred, Ernst Troeltsch et la sécularisation de l'histoire:
LavalTP 44 (1988) 279-292 [< ZIT 89,11].

d129 **Finley** M.I. [† 1986], Ancient history; evidence and models 1986
➤ 2,9252; 0-6708-0970-5: ᴿClasW 82 (1988s) 63 (Jennifer T. *Roberts*;
words of wisdom far from compensating his death); HistTheor 27 (1988)
178-187 (D. *Konstan*).

d130 **Garbini** Giovanni, Storia e ideologia nell'Israele antico 1986 ➤ 2,9256;
3,b617: ᴿAthenaeum 66,1s (1988) 210-3 (E. *Jucci*); Biblica 69 (1988)
126-9 (H. *Engel*); CBQ 50 (1988) 743s (J.K. *Sullivan*: intriguing rather
than convincing); Claretianum 27 (1987) 407-412 (M. *Zappella*: ricco di
provocazioni); ÉTRel 63 (1988) 100 (J. *Pons*); JSS 33 (1988) 116s (N.
Faranda); KirSef 61 (1986s) 609 (A. *Rofé*); OrAnt 27 (1988) 303-9 (M.
Liverani: critica e laica); NRT 110 (1988) 613s (J.-L. *Ska*: que penser de
tout cela?); RB 95 (1988) 449s (J.-M. de *Tarragon*: presque provoquant);
RivStoLR 24 (1988) 130s (A.G. *Auld*).

d131 **Garbini** Giovanni, History and ideology in ancient Israel. L 1988, SCM. xvi-222 p. £10.50. 0-334-00621-X. – RBL (1988) 37 (J. R. *Bartlett*).

d132 **Gentili** Bruno, *Cerri* Giovanni, History and biography in ancient thought: London Studies in Classical Philology 20. Amst 1988, Gieben. 119 p. 90-70265-49-4.

d133 **Gillespie** Michael A., HEGEL, HEIDEGGER, and the ground of history 1984 → 1,a971: RRelStR 14 (1988) 141 (D. *Pellauer*).

d134 **Goetz** H.-W., Die Geschichtstheologie des OROSIUS: ImpulsFor 32, 1980 → 61,q75 ... 2,9259: RGrazBei 15 (1988) 302-6 (Henriette *Harich*).

d135 *González Blanco* Antonino, Teología y filosofía de la historia: Carthaginensia 4 (1988) 267-300.

d136 *Grafton* A. T., *Swerdlow* N. M., Calendar dates and ominous days in ancient historiography: JWarb 51 (1988) 14-42.

d137 **Gruner** Rolf, Philosophies of history; a critical essay. Aldershot 1985, Gower. 122 p. – RHeythJ 29 (1988) 471s (F. C. *Copleston*).

d138 **Hafstad** Kjetil, Wort und Geschichte; das Geschichtsverständnis Karl BARTHS: BeiEvG 98, 1985 → 3,b622: RTZBas 44 (1988) 282s (O. *Bächli*).

d139 **Halpern** Baruch, The first historians; the Hebrew Bible and history. SF 1988, Harper & R. xviii-285 p. $23 [CBQ 51,400].

d140 *a) Haug* Richard, BENGELS Theologie der Weltgeschichte; – *b) Brey-mayer* Reinhard, 'Gnomon typusque vitae Christianae'; zum emblematischen Hintergrund des 'Gnomon'-Begriffs bei Heinrich ORAEUS (1584-1646) und bei Johann A. Bengel (1687-1752): Blätter für württembergische Kirchengeschichte 88 (Stu 1988) 324-334 / 289-323 [< ZIT 89,248].

Haught John F., The revelation of God in history 1988 → 8107.

d141 *Herms* Eilert, Schuld in der Geschichte; zum 'Historikerstreit' [... biblisch; ... Nazi]: ZTK 85 (1988) 349-370.

d142 *Hurwitz* Ellen, *Ostrowski* Donald, The many varieties of historical writing; caterpillars and butterflies reexamined [factual vs. vivid]: → 134, FSEVČENKO I., Okeanos 1983, 296-308.

d143 EHoldsworth Christopher, *Wiseman* T. P., The inheritance of historiography 350-900: Exeter studies in history 12. Exeter 1986, Univ. 138 p. £7.50. [7-16 *Warmington* B. H., Did ATHANASIUS write history?; 45-52, *Harris* Jill, SOZOMEN and EUSEBIUS]. – RGnomon 60 (1988) 51-53 (H.-W. *Goetz*: good-sized summaries of the nine articles).

d144 **Jedin** H., Storia della mia vita, ERepgen K. [1984], TZanoni Zorzi C. Brescia 1987, Morcelliana. 452 p. Lit. 38.000. – RAevum 62 (1988) 681s (D. *Zardin*); NRT 110 (1988) 779s (N. *Plumat*); StPatav 35 (1988) 213s (S. *Tramontin*); ViPe 71 (1988) 315-7 (G. *Picasso*).

d145 *Karpov* G. M., *Solov'ev* A. K. Ⓖ Some hisorico-ethnographic motifs in the Bible: Istoriya Filologija Drevn. Vostoka (Moskva 1987) p. 192, but that page in the Table of Contents is missing at the end of the fascicle.

d146 *Lucas* Erhard, Geschichtsschreibung angesichts der Endlichkeit der Geschichte: Saeculum 38 (1987) 283-296.

d147 *Marchal* Luc, L'histoire pour CICÉRON: ÉtClas 55 (1987) 41-64; 56 (1988) 241-264.

d148 **Marchetta** A., OROSIO e Ataulfo nell'ideologia dei rapporti romano-barbarici. R 1987, Ist. storico Medio Evo. 420 p. – RBStLat 18 (1988) 146-9 (C. *Moreschini*).

d149 **Miller** J. Maxwell, The Old Testament and the historian: GuidesBS. Ph 1987 = 1976, Fortress. viii-87 p. 0-8006-0461-X.

d150 *Momigliano* A., Storia e storiografia antica: Storia. Bo 1987, Mulino. 396 p. Lit. 40.000. – ᴿRasT 29 (1988) 94s (R. *Maisano,* anche su 'Pagine ebraiche' 1987).

d151 ᴱ**Moxon** I., *al.,* Past perspectives 1983/6 ➤ 3,768: ᴿAntClas 57 (1988) 515s (D. *Viviers*).

d152 *Neusner* Jacob, Beyond myth, after apocalypse; the Mishnaic conception of history: ➤ 77, ᶠKᴇᴇ H., Social world 1988, 91-106.

d153 *Neusner* J., L'idea della storia nel periodo di formazione del Giudaismo (200-600 ca.): ➤ 474, Correnti 1984/7, 121-137.

d154 *Odero* José M., Cristo y la historia según Kᴀɴᴛ: CiTom 115 (1988) 149-152.

d155 *Razzino* Giuseppe, Sociologia della religione e filosofia della storia occidentale: FilT 1,2 (N 1988) 167-175.

d156 *Reinhold* Meyer, Human nature as cause in ancient historiography: ➤ 138, ᶠSᴛᴀʀʀ C., Craft 1985, 21-40.

d157 *Riggi* Calogero, Teologia della storia nel 'Simposio' di Mᴇᴛᴏᴅɪᴏ di Olimpo [< Augustinianum 16 (1976) 61-84]: ➤ 251, Epistrophe 1985, 481-504.

d158 *Rizzi* Armido, Cristianesimo e filosofia della storia; la secolarizzazione come categoria interpretativo del moderno: FilT 1,2 (N 1988) 40-65.

d158* **Rogan** Janet E., Across Lessing's ditch; Hᴇɢᴇʟ, Kɪᴇʀᴋᴇɢᴀᴀʀᴅ and historicality: diss. Essex 1987. 312 p. BRD-81066. – DissA 49 (1988s) 276s-A.

d159 *Rosowski* Martin, Geschichte — Hieroglyphe Gottes, II. Wem gehört die Geschichte?: Religion Heute (1988,2) 96-99 [< zɪᴛ 88,562].

d160 *a) Roth* Paul A., Narrative explanations: the case of history; – *b)* *Berthold-Bond* Daniel, Hᴇɢᴇʟ's eschatological vision; does history have a future?: HistTheory 27 (1988) 1-13 / 14-29.

d161 **Schlaudraff** Karl-Heinz, 'Heil als Geschichte'?; die Frage nach dem heilsgeschichtlichen Denken... O. Cᴜʟʟᴍᴀɴɴs [Vorwort]: BeiGBEx 29. Tü 1988, Mohr. xxi-282 p. 3-16-145387-5.

d162 **Schmale** Franz-Josef, Funktion und Formen mittelalterlicher Geschichtsschreibung. Da 1985, Wiss. x-223 p.; DM 59. – ᴿDLZ 109 (1988) 400-403 (W. *Eggert*).

d163 *Schulin* Ernst, Geschichtswissenschaft in unserem Jahrhundert; Probleme und Umrisse einer Geschichte der Historie: HZ 245 (1987) 1-30.

d164 *Sternberger* Dolf, Unzusammenhangende Notizen über Geschichte: Merkur 41 (1987) 733-748 [> NSys 30 (1988) 336s].

d165 *Sweet* Leonard I., Wise as serpents, innocent as doves; the new evangelical historiography [*Marsden* G. 1987; *Noll* M. 1986]: JAAR 56 (1988) 397-416.

d166 *Torres* Amadeu, Paulo Oʀᴏsɪᴏ, cidadão romano-bracarense, e a sua História contra os pagãos, à propósito da primeira versão portuguesa de José Cᴀʀᴅᴏsᴏ [1986, 580 p.]: TBraga 20 (1985) 317-322.

d167 **Uhlig** Christian, Funktion und Situation der Kirchengeschichte als theologischer Disziplin [ev. Diss. Münster 1976] 1985 ➤ 3,b646: ᴿTGʟ 78 (1988) 173s (G. *Ruppert*).

d168 **Van Seters** John, In search of history 1983 ➤ 64,9896... 3,b648: ᴿBR 4,3 (1988) 4-7 (G. W. *Ramsey*); HZ 245 (1987) 130s (W. *Helck*); JNES 47 (1988) 131-3 (W. J. *Murnane*); JStOT 40 (1988) 110-8 (L. *Younger*); OLZ 83 (1988) 677-9 (H. *Seidel*); TLZ 113 (1988) 177-180 (S. *Herrmann*); VT 38 (1988) 250s (J. A. *Emerton,* for the dropout reviewer).

d169 **Vercruysse** Marc, Het thema van de waarheidsverdraaiing in de Griekse geschiedenisschrijving; een onderzoek van POLYBIUS en zijn voorgangers: Verh. Ak. Belg. lett 46/115. 170 p. Fb 700. 90-6569-358-0. – ᴿAntClas 57 (1988) 363s (M. *Dubuisson*).

d170 **Voegelin** Eric., In search of order: Order and history 5. Baton Rouge 1987, Louisiana State Univ. xv-120 p. £14.20 [JTS 39,674].

d171 **Woodman** A. J., Rhetoric in classical historiography. L 1988, Croom Helm. xiv-236 p. £27.50. – ᴿClasR 102 (1988) 262-4 (T. P. *Wiseman*).

Q3 *Historia Ægypti* – **Egypt.**

d172 *Allam* Shafik, À propos de quelques décrets royaux de l'Ancien Empire: CdÉ 63,125 (1988) 36-41.

d173 *Ampolo* Carmine, *Bresciani* Edda, Psammetico re d'Egitto e il mercenario Pedon: EgVO 11 (1988) 237-244-252 + 3 fig.

d174 *Baráibar López* Juan, Significado y originalidad de la Historia de Egipto de MANETÓN: Sefarad 48 (1988) 3-17; Eng. 17.

d175 *Barta* Winfried, Das Kalendarium des Papyrus Ebers mit der Notiz eines Sothisaufgangs: GöMiszÄg 101 (1988) 7-12; 1 fig.

d176 **Bonhême** Marie-Ange, *Forgeau* Annie, Pharaon; les secrets du pouvoir. P 1988, Colin. 352 p. 2-200-37129-9 [BO 45,471].

d177 **Boorn** G. P. F. van den, The duties of the vizier; civil administration in the Early New Kingdom: Studies in Egyptology. L 1988, Kegan Paul. 0-7103-0330-0 [OIAc D88].

d178 *a)* *Bothmer* Bernard V., Amenhotep I in London and New York; an iconographical footnote; – *b)* *Lloyd* Alan B., MANETHO and the Thirty-First Dynasty: ➤ 41, ꟳEDWARDS I., Pyramid studies 1988, 89-91 / 154-160.

d179 **Bowman** A. K., Egypt after the Pharaohs; 332 B.C. – A.D. 642: 1986 ➤ 2,9302; 3,b661: ᴿAegyptus 68 (1988) 272-5 (G. *Geraci*); AntiqJ 68 (1988) 351s (D. M. *Bailey*); ClasW 82 (1988s) 310 (H. *Goedicke*: good).

d180 **Brugsch** Henri, Matériaux pour servir à la reconstruction du calendrier des anciens Égyptiens. Starnberg 1988 = 1864, LTR. 3-88706-255-8 [OIAc D88].

d181 **Burkhardt** Adelheid *al.*, Urkunden der 18. Dynastie [Sethe K., Urkunden 5-16] 1984 ➤ 2,9306: ᴿJEA 74 (1988) 274s (K. A. *Kitchen*); OLZ 83 (1988) 528-532 (also K. A. *Kitchen*).

d182 *Callender* Gael, A critical reexamination of the reign of Hatshepsut: AncHRes 18 (1988) 86-103.

d183 *Carney* Elizabeth D., The reappearance of royal sibling marriage in Ptolemaic Egypt: ParPass 237 (1987) 420-439.

d184 *Casanova* Gerardo, Una datazione tardiva di Tolomeo IV e il banchiere Protos di Crocodilopolis: Aegyptus 68 (1988) 13-18; fot.

d185 [*Helck* W.] ᵀCumming Barbara, Egyptian historical records 1-3, 1982-4 ➤ 65,9635; 3,b664: ᴿCdÉ 63 (1988) 246-8 (R. *Dauwe*).

d186 *Desanges* Jehan, Les sources de PLINE dans sa description de la Troglodytique et de l'Éthiopie (NH 6,163-97): Helmantica 37 (1986) 277-292.

d187 **Dorman** Peter F., The monuments of Senenmut; problems in historical methodology. L 1988, Kegan Paul. xvi-248 p., ill. 0-7103-0317-3.

d188 *Edakov* A. V., ⊕ Les réformes d'Amasis et leur destin à l'époque saïssien tardive: VDI 184 (1988) 112-124; franç. 125.

d189 *a)* *Foertmeyer* Victoria, The dating of the pompe of Ptolemy II Philadelphus; – *b)* *Hammond* N.G.L., Which Pompey gave troops and stood as protector of Pyrrhus' kingdom? [*Justin* 17.2.14s]: Historia 37 (1988) 90-104 / 405-413.

d190 **Franke** Detlef, Personendaten aus dem Mittleren Reich 1984 ➤ 2,9316: ᴿCdÉ 63 (1988) 264-7 (R.J. *Leprohon*: dating); OLZ 83 (1988) 396-8 (Elke *Blumenthal* does not make exactly clear that they are dates rather than data).

d191 *Franke* D., Zur Chronologie des Mittleren Reiches (12.-18. Dynastie, I. Die 12. Dynastie; II. Die sogenannte 'zweite Zwischenzeit' Altägyptens: Orientalia 57 (1988) 113-138 . 245-274.

d192 **Geraci** Giovanni, Genesi della Provincia Romana d'Egitto : Studi di Storia 9, 1983 ➤ 64,a10 ... 3,b674: ᴿArEspArq 61 (1988) 359s (Fabienne *Burkhalter*).

d193 **Gestermann** Louise, Kontinuität und Wandel ... des frühen Mittleren Reiches: GöOrF 4/18, 1987 ➤ 3,b675; DM 68: ᴿMundus 24 (1988) 276s (Renate *Müller-Wollermann*).

d194 *Görg* Manfred, Ägypten: ➤ 804, NBL Lfg. 1 (1988) 36-49; map.

d195 *Grenier* Jean-Claude, Notes sur l'Égypte romaine (1,1-7): CdÉ 63,125 (1988) 57-76; 2 fig.

d196 **Grimal** Nicolas-Christophe, Les termes de la propagande royale égyptienne (de la XIXe dynastie à la conquête d'Alexandre). P 1986. 764 p. – ᴿBO 45 (1988) 312s (A. *Spalinger*); DiscEg 12 (1988) 83-85 (S. *Allam*: avec 2933 notes, mais de consultation facile).

d197 **Helck** Wolfgang, *a)* Politische Gegensätze im Alten Ägypten: Hildesheimer äg. Beiträge 23, 1986 ➤ 2,9382; DM 28: ᴿMundus 24 (1988) 16-18 (Ingrid *Gamer-Wallert*). – *b)* Untersuchungen zur Thinitenzeit 1987 ➤ 3,b681: ᴿSBFLA 38 (1988) 471-4 (A. *Niccacci*).

d197* *a)* *Helck* Wolfgang, Erneut das angebliche Sothis-Datum des Pap. Ebers und die Chronologie des 18. Dynastie; – *b)* *Spalinger* Anthony, Dates in ancient Egypt; – *c)* *Morschauser* Scott N., Using history; some reflections on the Bentresh stela; – *d)* *Goedicke* Hans, Zum Königskonzept der Thinitenzeit: StAltÄgK 15 (1988) 149-164 [143-8 'Mehy'] / 255-276 / 203-223 / 123-141 [111-121, death of Pepi II – Neferkare].

d198 *Hobson* Deborah, Towards a broader context for the study of Greco-Roman Egypt: ÉchMClas 32 (1988) 353-363.

d199 *Hoffmeier* James K., A relief of a 'Chief of the Gang' from Deir el-Medineh [from the Chicago Univ. Oriental Institute, on loan] at Wheaton College, Illinois: JEA 74 (1988) 217-220.

d200 *Holm-Rasmussen* Torben, Collaboration in early Achaemenid Egypt: ➤ 142*, ᶠTHOMSEN R. 1988, 29-38.

d201 **James** T.G.H., Ancient Egypt; the land and its legacy. L 1988, British Museum. 224 p. £15. 0-7141-0945-2 [BO 45,473].

d202 *Jeffreys* D.G., *Smith* H.S., Memphis and the Nile in the New Kingdom; a preliminary attempt at a historical perspective: ➤ 781, Memphis 1986/8, 55-66; franç. 66.

d203 *Johnson* Janet H., Ptolemaic bureaucracy from an Egyptian point of view: ➤ 738, Power 1983/7, 141-9.

d204 **Kamil** Jill, Coptic Egypt; history and guide. Cairo 1988, American Univ. xiii-15 + 149 p.; maps (H. Ibrahim). 977-424-104-5.

d205 *Kitchen* K.A., Egypt and Israel during the first millennium B.C.: ➤ 482, VTS 40, Jerusalem congress 1986/8, 107-123.

d206 **Kitchen** K. A., Ramesside inscriptions VII, 6-8 [addenda to previously-published; → 3,b688*]. Ox 1987, Blackwell. 32 p.; £3.75 each. – ᴿBO 45 (1988) 528s (W. *Helck*, p. 102s, VII, 1-5).

d207 *Lanciers* E., Die Vergöttlichung und die Ehe des Ptolemaios IV. und der Arsinoe III.: ArPapF 34 (1988) 27-32.

d208 *Leahy* Anthony, The earliest dated monument of Amasis [570 B.C.] and the end of the reign of Apries [more than 8 months later]: JEA 74 (1988) 183-199; fig. 1; pl. XXV-XXVI.

d209 **Lewis** Naphtali, Greeks in Ptolemaic Egypt... social history 1986 → 3,b692: ᴿAmHR 93 (1988) 1302s (R. J. *Leprohon*); BO 45 (1988) 137-9 (C. *Orrieux*, aussi sur 'Yale Papyrology'); JHS 108 (1988) 253s (Dorothy J. *Thompson*).

d210 **Lewis** N., Life in Egypt under Roman rule 1983 → 64,a39... 3,b693: ᴿGymnasium 95 (1988) 460s (H. *Heinen*).

d210* **Lichtheim** Miriam, Ancient Egyptian autobiographies chiefly of the Middle Kingdom; a study and an anthology: OBO 84. FrS/Gö 1988, Univ./VR. 3-7278-0594-3 / 3-525-53713-1 [BL 89,155].

d211 *Lorton* David, The internal history of the Herakleopolitan period [Dyn. IX-X]: DiscEg 8 (1987) 21-28.

d211* **Manniche** Lise, Sexual life in ancient Egypt 1987 → 3,b697: ᴿDiscEg 11 (1988) 21-72 (G. *Robins*).

d212 **Manniche** Lise, Liebe und Sexualität im alten Ägypten; eine Text- und Bilddokumentation. Z 1988, Artemis. 194 p.; ill 3-7608-0994-4.

d212* *Masson* Olivier, *Yoyotte* Jean, Une inscription ionienne [clandestine, de Priène] mentionnant Psammétique Iᵉʳ: EpAnat 11 (1988) 171-9; pl. 25; ❶ 180.

d213 **Matzker** Ingo, Die letzten Könige der 12. Dynastie: EurHS 3/297, 1986 → 3,b698: ᴿBO 45 (1988) 111-6 (R. J. *Leprohon*).

d213* *Mélèze-Modrzejewski* J., Droits de l'individu et justice lagide: Revue historique de droit FÉ 85 (1987) 345-356 [< RSPT 72,359].

d214 *Menci* Giovanna, Numeri ordinali; giorni del mese [*Boyaval* B.] o indizioni: Aegyptus 68 (1988) 65-67.

d214* *Modrzejewski* Joseph, Nochmals zum Justizwesen der Ptolemäer: ZSav-R 105 (1988) 165-179.

d215 **Moftah** Ramses, Studien zum ägyptischen Königsdogma im Neuen Reich 1985 → 2,9346: ᴿBO 45 (1988) 540-5 (D. *Lorton*).

d215* **Moorey** P. R. S., Ancient Egypt ²ʳᵉᵛ (¹1970). Oxford 1988, Ashmolean Museum. 64 p.; 47 fig. 0-907849-76-8.

d216 **O'Mara** Patrick, *a*) Some indirect Sethic and lunar dates from the Late Middle Kingdom in Egypt; – *b*) Additional unlabeled lunar dates from the Old Kingdom in Egypt: Studies in the structural archaeology of ancient Egypt 3/2s. 1984s, Cambria. – ᴿDiscEg 6 (1986) 101-4 (S. *Quirke*).

d216* *O'Mara* Patrick F., Historiographies (ancient and modern) of the archaic period, I. Should we examine the foundations?; a revisionist approach; II. Resolving the Palermo Stone as a rational structure: DiscEg 6 (1986) 33-45; 3 fig.; 7 (1987) 37-49.

d217 *O'Mara* Patrick F., Probing for unlabeled astronomical datings in the Old and Middle Kingdoms, 1. Lunar materials in the Old Kingdom; 2. Sothic and Pseudo-Sothic materials: DiscEg 9 (1987) 45-54 / 10 (1988) 41-54.

d218 *Pavloskaja* A. I. ❶ La lutte socio-politique en Égypte de la fin du IIIᵉ. s. [A.D.], d'après des lettres et pétitions de l'époque: VDI 184 (1988) 43-55; franç. 55.

d218* **Pellat** Charles,   Cinq calendriers égyptiens: Textes arab. isl. 26.   Le Caire 1986, IFAO. xxviii-277 p.   2-7247-0034-1. – RZDMG 138 (1988) 192s (P. *Kunitzsch*).

d219 *a) Peltenburg* E. J.,   Ramesside Egypt and Cyprus;   – *b) Aupert* P., Amathonte, le Proche-Orient et l'Égypte: → 748, Cyprus between, 1985/6, 149-179 / 369-382.

d219* **Redford** Donald B.,   Pharaonic king-lists, annals and day-books; a contribution to the study of the Egyptian sense of history: SSEA [= JSStEg] 4. Mississauga 1986, Benben. xxi-353 p. 0-920168-07-8. – RBO 45 (1988) 107s (E. *Hornung*).

d220 **Rice** Ellen E.,   The [narrated] grand procession of Ptolemy Philadelphus 1983 → 65,9666 ... 2,9351: RJEA 74 (1988) 290-2 (H. *Maehler*).

d221 **Roccati** Alessandro,   La littérature historique sous l'Ancien Empire égyptien 1982 → 63,9699 ... 3,8710: RBO 45 (1988) 97s (H. *Goedicke*).

d221* **Schulze** Peter H.,   Frauen im alten Ägypten; Selbständigkeit und Gleichberechtigung im häuslichen und öffentlichen Leben.   Bergisch-Gladbach 1988, Lübbe. 312 p.; ill.

d222 *Šerkova* T. A.,   ☉ Contacts of Egypt with Kushan Bactria: Drevni i Srednev. Vostok (Moskva 1983) 121-138.   3-7857-0478-8.

d223 **Simpson** William K.,   EDer Manuelian P., Papyrus Reisner IV. Personnel accounts of the early twelfth dynasty, with indices to Papyrus Reisner I-IV, 1986 → 2,9235; 0-87-846261-9: RBO 45 (1988) 98-102 (D. *Franke*); VarAeg 4 (1988) 262-7 (S.*Quirke*).

d224 *Teixidor* Javier,   Ptolemaic chronology in the Phoenician inscriptions from Cyprus: ZPapEp 71 (1988) 188-190.

d225 *Topozada* Zekéya,   Les deux campagnes d'Amenhotep III en Nubie: BIFAO 88 (1988) 153-164; 3 fig.

d226 **Thomas** J. David,   The epistrategos in Ptolemaic and Roman Egypt 2, 1982 → 64,a65; 2,9357: RArKulturG 69 (1987) 473s (J. *Herrmann*).

d227 *Vandersleyen* Claude,   Les deux jeunesses d'Amenhotep III: BSocFrÉ 111 (1988) 9-30; 14 fig.

d228 **Vernus** Pascal, *Yoyotte* Jean, Les Pharaons. P 1988 'MA'. 184 p.; 44 pl. F 145. 2-86676-256-8 [BO 45,474].

d229 *Vycichl* Werner,   Ménès Thinites, réalité ou fiction?: BSocÉg 12 (Genève 1988) 77-82.

d229* **Way** Thomas von der,   Die Textüberlieferung Ramses' II zur Qades-Schlacht: HildÄgBeit 22, 1984 → 65,9677: RJAmEg 24 (1987) 153-6 (A. *Spalinger*).

d230 *Wipszycka* Ewa,   La christianisation de l'Égypte aux IVe-VIe siècles; aspects sociaux et ethniques: Aegyptus 68 (1988) 117-165.

Q4   Historia Mesopotamiae.

d231 *Barré* Michael L.,   A note on the Sin-Shumu-Lishir treaty: JCS [39 (1987) 150-4, *Grayson* A.] 40 (1988) 81-83.

d232 *Borger* Rykle,   König Sanheribs Eheglück: AnRIM 6 (1988) 5-11.

d232* **Brinkman** J. A.,   Prelude to empire; Babylonian society and politics, 747-626 B.C.: 1984 → 65,9683: RJAOS 108 (1988) 661-3 (B. T. *Arnold*).

d233 ECannadine David, *Price* Simon,   Rituals of royalty, power and ceremonial in traditional societies [→ 3,487]: Past and present. C 1987, Univ. xi-351 p., 6 maps. £25. 0-521-33513-2. 8 art. [Babylon, Rome ...]. – RAnt-Clas 57 (1988) 463-5 (M. *Graulich*).

d234 **Capomacchia** Anna Maria G., Semiramis, una femminilità ribaltata: Storia delle Religioni 4, 1986 ⇥ 2,9366: ᴿGregorianum 69 (1988) 793-6 (G. L. *Prato*).

d235 *a) Civil* Miguel, Ur III bureaucracy; quantitative aspects; – *b) Michałowski* Piotr, Charisma and control; on continuity and change in early Mesopotamian bureaucratic systems: ⇥ 738, Power 1983/7, 43-53 / 55-68.

d236 *Conradie* A. F., The fragmentary Ashurnaṣirpal II inscription in Detroit [transliteration and translation]: JNWS 14 (1988) 17-26.

d236* *Córdoba* J. M., Cambios y constantes en la historia de Asiria; una nueva imagen: BAsEspOr 22 (1986) 127-185.

d237 *Durand* Jean-Marie, Les anciens de Talhayûm [A. 2417 (à Zimri-Lim)]: RAss 82 (1988) 97-113; 6 phot.

d238 **Forbes** C., Documents of the Assyrian Empire (1115-612 B.C.); a collection of Assyrian sources on the imperialism of the Neo-Assyrian period, Tiglath-pileser I to the Babylonian conquest: Documents of the Ancient Near East for Secondary School 2, 1986 ⇥ 2,9371; vi-158 p. $13 pa.: ᴿAncHRes 18 (1988) 120-3 (P. R. *Bedford*).

d239 *Frame* G., *Grayson* A. Kirk, Marduk-zākir-šumi I and the 'exemption' of Borsippa; AnRIM 6 (1988) 15-21.

d240 *Glombiowski* Krzysztof, ❷ The sources of Assyrian and Median history by Dɪᴏᴅᴏʀᴜs (Bibl. II 1-34): Eos 76 (1988) 269-285; Eng. 286s.

d241 *Hall* J. D., The ideology of expansion in the Neo-Assyrian empire: AncSRes 17 (1987) 67-79; 11 fig.

d242 *Hallo* William W., Dating the Mesopotamian past; the concept of eras from Sargon to Nabonassar: CanadMesop 6 (1983) 7-18.

d243 **Harrak** Amir, Assyria and Hanigalbat; historical reconstruction of bilateral relations from the middle of the Fourteenth to the end of the Twelfth centuries B.C. [diss. Toronto 1987 ⇥ 3,b738]: TSt zur Orientalistik 4. Hildesheim 1987, Olms. xviii-315 p. DM 48. – ᴿWeltOr 19 (1988) 171s (W. von *Soden*).

d244 **Heinsohn** Gunnar, Die Sumerer gab es nicht; von den Phantom-Imperien der Lehrbücher zur wirklichen Epochenabfolge in der 'Zivilisationswiege' Südmesopotamien: Scarabäus. Fra 1988, von Eichborn. xiii-213 p. 3-8218-0410-8; 1-4.

d245 **Herzog** Roman, Staaten der Frühzeit; Ursprünge und Herrschaftsformen. Mü 1988, Beck. 3-406-33108-4 [OIAc D 88].

d246 **Huber** Peter J., *al.*, Astronomical dating of Babylon I and Ur III. Malibu 1982, Undena. 93 p. – ᴿOLZ 83 (1988) 554-8 (J. *Oelsner*).

d247 ᴱ**Kajanto** Iiro, Equality and inequality of man in ancient thought 1982/4 ⇥ 1,766: ᴿAnzAltW 41 (1988) 30-32 (E. *Stärk*).

d248 **Knapp** A. Bernard, The history of culture of Ancient Western Asia and Egypt. Ch 1988, Dorsey. xvi-284 p.; 20 pl. $30; pa. $15. 0-256-05698-6; 6217-X [BO 45,471].

d249 **Kromholz** Alfred H., Concordance of the Isin-Larsa year names: Assyriological Series 1. Berrien Springs MI 1986, Andrews Univ. 173 p. 0-943872-26-X.

d250 *McEwan* Gilbert, Babylonia in the Hellenistic period: Klio 70 (1988) 412-421.

d251 *MacGinnis* J. D. A., Cᴛᴇsɪᴀs and the fall of Nineveh: ILCL 13,1 (1988) 37-41.

d252 **Magen** Ursula, Assyrische Königsdarstellungen — Aspekte der Herrschaft 1986 ⇥ 3,b742; DM 140: Mundus 24 (1988) 29s (K. *Schippmann*).

d253 *Mayer* Walter,   *a)* Die Frühgeschichte der assyrisch-urartäischen Beziehungen vom 14. bis zur 2. Hälfte des 9. Jhd. v. Chr.: ⇒ 32, ᶠDELLER
K., AOAT 220 (1988) 199-245; map 246; – *b)* Der babylonische Feldzug
Tukulti-Ninurtas I. von Assyrien: ⇒ 99, ᶠLORETZ O., StEpL 5 (1988)
141-161.

d254 **Nissen** Hans J.,   Grundzüge einer Geschichte der Frühzeit des Vorderen
Orients 1983 ⇒ 64,a95; 65,9708:   ᴿRAss 82 (1988) 187 (P. *Amiet*).

d255 **Oelsner** Joachim,   Materialien zur babylonischen Gesellschaft und
Kultur in hellenistischer Zeit: Assyriologia 7, 1986 ⇒ 3,b745:   ᴿOLZ 83
(1988) 670-2 (T. *Fischer*).

d256 ᴱ**Parpola** Simo, *Watanabe* Kazuko,   Neo-Assyrian treaties and loyalty
oaths: State Archives of Assyria 2. Helsinki 1988, Univ. lxii-124 p.;
10 pl.; 1 microfiche. $45; pa. $29.50. 951-570-034-5; pa. 3-7.

d257 **Pettinato** G.,   Semiramide 1985 ⇒ 1,b114; 2,9381:   ᴿBL (1988) 126
(W. G. E. *Watson*).

d258 **Pettinato** Giovanni,   Semiramis, Herrin über Assur und Babylon. Z
1988, Artemis. 330 p. Fs 39,80. 3-7608-0748-8 [BO 45, 475].– ᴿPhoen-
EOL 34,2 (1988) 61s (M. *Steiner*).

d259 *Podany* Amanda H.,   The chronology and history of the Hana period:
diss. UCLA. – Mar Šipri 1,2 (1988) 3s.

d260 *Roth* Martha T.,   Women in transition and the bīt mār banî [25ᵉ
Rencontre]: RAss 82 (1988) 131-8; franc. 138.

d260* **Roux** Georges,   La Mésopotamie, préf. *Bóttero* J. 1985 ⇒ 1,b116;
2,9384:   ᴿRB 95 (1988) 434s (M. *Sigrist*: best-seller Ancient Iraq 1954
remanié).

d261 **Saggs** H. W. F.,   The greatness that was Babylon; a survey of the
ancient civilization of the Tigris-Euphrates Valley²ʳᵉᵛ (¹1962): Great
Civilizations. L 1988, Sidgwick & J. xxii-487 p.; ill. 0-283-99623-4
[...Assyria 1984 ⇒ 1,b117].

d262 *Salvini* Mirjo,   Un texte hourrite nommant Zimrilim: RAss 82 (1988)
59-69; facsim.; 3 phot.

d263 *a) Steiner* Gerd,   Der 'reale' Kern in den 'legendären' Zahlen von
Regierungsjahren der ältesten Herrscher Mesopotamiens; – *b) Maeda*
Tohru,   Two rulers by the name Ur-Ningirsu in pre-Ur III Lagash:
AcSum 10 (1988) 129-152 / 19-32 + 3 pl.

d264 *Steinkeller* Piotr,   The date of Gudea and his [2d Lagaš] dynasty: JCS
40 (1988) 47-53.

d265 *Williams* R. J.,   Relations between Egypt and Mesopotamia; Canad-
Mesop 10 (1985) 3-10.

d266 *Young* Dwight W.,   A mathematical approach to certain dynastic spans
in the Sumerian king list: JNES 47 (1988) 123-9.

Q4.5   *Historia Persiae,* **Iran.**

d266* *Alonso-Núñez* J.-M.,   The Roman universal historian Pompeius
TROGUS on India, Parthia, Bactria and Armenia: Persica 13 (1988s)
125-155.

d267 **Bailey** Harold W.,   The culture of the Sakas in ancient Iranian Khotan
[...to 1000 A.D.]: Columbia Lectures on Iranian Studies 1. Delmar NY
1982, Caravan. xii-109 p. 0-88206-053-8. – ᴿBO 45 (1988) 384 (K. W.
Bolle: awe-inspiring).

d268 **Balcer** Jack M.,   HERODOTUS and Bisitun; problems in ancient Persian
historiography: HistEinz 49, 1987 ⇒ 3,b765; DM 44:   ᴿClasR 102 (1988)
434s (Rosemary *Stevenson*).

d269 *Briant* P.,   Le nomadisme du grand roi [... multiplicité de ses résidences royales]: → 4, [F]AMIET P. = IrAnt 23 (1988) 253-273.

d270 *Carter* Elizabeth, *Stolper* Matthew W.,   Elam; surveys of political history and archaeology 1984 → 1,419 ... 3,b768:   [R]JNES 47 (1988) 135s (P. R. S. *Moorey*).

d271 **Chaumont** M.-L.,   La christianisation de l'Empire Iranien; des origines aux grandes persécutions du IVe siècle: CSCOr 499 / Subsidia 80. 0070-0444. Lv 1988, Peeters. XVI-198 p.

d272 *Chaumont* M. L.,   À propos des premières interventions parthes en Arménie et des circonstances de l'avènement de Tigrane le Grand: AcAntH 31 (1985-8) 13-25.

d272* **Cook** J. M., The Persian Empire 1983 → 65,9725 ... 3,b769:   [R]BA 51 (1988) 60 (G. H. *Oller*).

d273 **Frey** P., *Koch* K.,   Reichsidee/Perserreich: OBO 55, 1984 → 65,9730 ... 3,b772:   [R]Mundus 24 (1988) 275s (J. H. *Friedrich*).

d274 *Gschnitzer* Fritz,   Zur Stellung des persischen Stammlandes im Achaimenidenreich: – 32, [F]DELLER K., AOAT 220 (1988) 87-123.

d275 *Kettenhofen* Erich,   Das Staatsgefängnis der Sāsāniden: WeltOr 19 (1988) 96-101.

d276 **Koch** Heidemarie,   Persien zur Zeit des Dareios; das Achämenidenreich im Lichte neuer Quellen: Vorgesch. Sem. 25.   Marburg 1988, Univ. 40 p.; 30 fig.

d277 *Koch* Heidemarie,   *a*) Die Begegnung zwischen Persern und Griechen: OrAnt 27 (1988) 271-284 + 2 maps; pl. X-XVII; – *b*) Herrscher in der Persis unter Seleukiden und Parthern: WeltOr 19 (1988) 84-95; 4 fig.

d278 **Nagel** Wolfram,   Ninus und Semiramis in Sage und Geschichte; Iranische Staaten und Reiternomaden vor Darius: BBeiVorFrüh 2, 1982 → 63,9762; 65,9737:   [R]ArKulturG 70 (1988) 225-8 (J. *WieseHöfer*).

d279 **Neusner** Jacob,   Israel and Iran [< his History of the Jews in Babylonia 1965-70] 1986 → 3,b776:   [R]BL (1988) 140s (P. S. *Alexander*).

d280 *O'Neil* J. L.,   The life of Xerxes: [R]AncHRes 18 (1988) 6-15; 4 fig.

d281 *Petschow* H.,   Das Unterkönigtum des Cambyses als 'König von Babylon': RAss 82 (1988) 78-82.

d282 [E]**Sancisi-Weerdenburg** Heleen, Sources... Achaemenid history I 1983/7 → 3,787: [R]Persica 13 (1988s) 157-160 (R. *Descat*).

d282* *Sancisi-Weerdenburg* Heleen,   *Persikón* ... A typically Persian gift (Hdt IX 109):   Historia 37 (1988) 372-4.

d283 **Schippmann** K.,   Grundzüge der parthischen Geschichte 1980 → 61, q404 ... 3,b779:   [R]WZKM 78 (1986) 297-9 (B. G. *Fragner*).

d284 *Sekunda* Nicholas V.,   Some notes on the life of Datames [c. 400 B.C.]: Iran 26 (1988) 35; pl. II.

d284* **Staviskij** B. J.,   La Bactriane sous les Kushans; problèmes d'histoire et de culture[2rev]. [[1]1977], [T]*Bernard* P., *al.* P 1986, Libr. Amér. & Orient. 322 p.; XXVII pl. F 320. 2-7200-1945-6. – [R]AION 48 (1988) 72s (M. *Taddei*); Persica 13 (1988s) 161-6 (W. *Vogelsang*).

d285 **Walser** Gerold,   Hellas und Iran: ErtFor 209, 1984 → 65,9741 ... 3,b784: [R]SborBrno 31 (1986) 198-200 (J. *Češka*).

d286 *Wiesehöfer* Josef,   *a*) Iranische Ansprüche an Rom auf ehemals achämenidische Territorien: ArchMIran 19 (1986) 177-185; – *b*) Zur Frage der Echtheit des Dareios-Briefes an Gadatas: RheinMus 130 (1987) 396-8.

d287 **Winter** Engelbert,   Die Sāsānidisch-römischen Friedensverträge des 3. Jahrhunderts n.Chr.: EurHS 37. 344 p. Fs 68. 3-8204-1368-5 [BO 45,475].

d288 *Wolski* J.,   Alexandre le Grand et l'Iran; contribution à l'histoire de l'époque séleucide et arsacide: AcAntH 31 (1985-8) 3-11.

d289 *Yusifov* Yusif B., On the ancient population of the Urmia Lake region: ArchMIran 19 (1986) 87-93; map.

Q5 *Historia Anatoliae*: **Asia Minor, Hittites** [➤ T8.2], **Armenia** [➤ T8.9].

d290 **Allen** R. E., The Attalid kingdom 1983 ➤ 64,a117... 2,9408: ᴿVDI 185 (1988) 221-5 (A. O. *Klimov*).

d291 *Bryce* T. R., Tette and the rebellions in Nuhassi [against Hittite rule: KUB XIV 17]: AnSt 38 (1988) 21-28.

d292 *a*) *Carruba* Onofrio, Die Hajasa-Verträge Hattis; – *b*) *Wilhelm* Gernot, Zur ersten Zeile des Šunaššura-Vertrages: ➤ 112*, ᶠOTTEN H., Documentum 1988, 59-75 / 359-370.

d293 *Galter* Hannes D., 28,000 Hethiter: JCS 40 (1988) 217-235.

d294 *Glew* Dennis G., The Cappadocian expedition of Nicomedes III Euergetes, king of Bithynia: AmNumM 32 (1987) 23-55.

d294* *Grélois* Jean-Pierre, Les annales décennales de Mursili II (CTH 61,1): Hethitica 9 (1988) 17-144; map. 145.

d295 **Korošec** Viktor, *Pogodba*... Der Vertrag zwischen Šuppiluliuma I. und Šunaššura von Kizzuwatna (KBo 1,5); der Vertrag zwischen Narām-Sin und dem unbekannten elamischen Herrscher (MDP XI, 2-11). Ljubljana 1983, Slovenska Akad. x-80 p.; map. – ᴿOLZ 83 (1988) 36s (J. *Klíma*).

d296 ᶠLAROCHE E., Acta Anatolica = Hethitica 8, 1985/7 ➤ 3,824: ᴿOrAnt 27 (1988) 315-9 (G. F. *Del Monte*); WeltOr 19 (1988) 184-7 (M. *Popko*).

d297 **McGing** B. C., The foreign policy of Mithridates VI Eupator king of Pontus 1986 ➤ 3,b794; *f* 80: ᴿAntClas 57 (1988) 511s (J. A. *Straus*).

d298 **Macqueen** J. G., The Hittites and their contemporaries in Asia Minor²ʳᵉᵛ. (¹1975) 1986➤ 3,f688: ᴿAncHRes 18 (1988) 22-32 (T. R. *Bryce*).

d298* **Metaxiki-Mitrou** Fotini, The expedition of Philip V to Asia Minor in 201/0 B.C.: diss. Cincinnati 1988. 200 p. 88-22801. – DissA 49 (1988s) 2208-A.

d299 *Miller* Margaret C., Midas as the great king in Attic fifth-century vase-painting: AntKu 31,2 (1988) 79-89: pl. 18-19.

d300 *Mora* Clelia, 'Il paese di Ḫatti è pieno di discendenti della regalità' (KUB XXVI 1+I 10); ipotesi sull'ultimo periodo dell'impero ittita: Athenaeum 66 (Pavia 1988) 553-576 + 8 fig.

d301 **Otten** Heinrich, Das hethitische Königshaus im 15. Jahrhundert v. Chr. Zum Neufund einiger Landschenkurkunden in Boghazköy. – W 1987, Österr. Akad. 22-34 [Mundus 24,51].

d302 *Petit* Thierry, À propos des 'satrapies' ionienne et carienne: BCH 112 (1988) 307-322.

d303 **Remy** B., L'évolution administrative de l'Anatolie aux trois premiers siècles de notre ère: ÉtRomaines 5, 1986 ➤ 3,b798; 140 p.; 15 maps; 1 pl.: ᴿClasR 102 (1988) 437s S. *Mitchell*: first volume of three from a diss. *d'État*).

d304 *Savalli* Ivana, L'idéologie dynastique des poèmes grecs de Xanthos: AntClas 57 (1988) 103-123.

d305 **Smith** David N., HERODOTUS and the [? history OIAc D88; archeology DissA ➤ g503] of Asia Minor: diss. Univ. California. Berkeley 1987. 88-14072.

Q6 **Historia graeca et hellenistica incluso Alexandro.**

d306 *Alonso-Núñez* José M., HERODOTUS' ideas about world empires: AncS 19 (1988) 125-133.

d307 **Ameling** Walter, Herodes Atticus 1982 → 64,a140; 65,9759: ᴿAnzAltW 41 (1988) 193-5 (K. H. *Kinzl*).

d308 *Balcer* Jack M., Persian occupied Thrace (Skudra): Historia 37 (1988) 1-21.

d309 **Baldwin** Barry, [82] Studies on Greek and Roman history and literature 1985 → 2,192: ᴿAntClas 57 (1988) 433-7 (A. *Léonard*: titres sans pp.).

d310 *Barceló* Pedro, Aspekte der griechischen Präsenz im westlichen Mittelmeerraum: Tyche 3 (1988) 11-24.

d311 **Bengtson** Hermann, Die Diadochen, die Nachfolger Alexanders (323--281 v. Chr.). Mü 1987, Beck. 218 p. DM 38. – ᴿAmHR 93 (1988) 1303 (R. M. *Berthold*).

d312 **Bengtson** Hermann, Historia de Grecia [1950], ᵀ1986 [→ 3,b808] = 1965 = 1978: ᴿEmerita 18 (1988) 359s [A. *Alonso Troncoso*].

d313 **Bernal** Martin, Black Athena I, 1987 → 3,b809: ᴿJIntdis 19 (1988s) 400s (G. W. *Bowersock*: breathtaking).

d314 *Bernhardt* Rainer, *a*) Die Entstehung der Legende von der Tyrannenfeindlichen Aussenpolitik Spartas im sechsten und fünften Jahrhundert v. Chr.: Historia 36 (1987) 257-289; – *b*) Zu den Verhandlungen zwischen Dareios und Alexander nach der Schlacht bei Issos: Chiron 18 (1988) 181-198.

d315 **Bleicken** Jochen, Die athenische Demokratie 1985 → 3,b811: ᴿGGA 240 (1988) 20-49 (P. *Funke*).

d316 ᴱ**Boardman** John, *al.*, Greece and the Hellenistic world: Oxford History of the Classical World. Ox 1988, Univ. 446 p.; 142 fig. + 9 colour.; 6 maps. £10 pa. 0-19-282165-2 [Antiquity 63,26].

d316* *Boila* Emilia D., (Rum.) Auswärtige Beziehung von Kallatis in hellenistischer Zeit: Studii ... IsVArh 39 (1988) 243-9; map.

d317 **Braccesi** Lorenzo, Grecità adriatica; un capitolo della colonizzazione greca in Occidente²ʳᵉᵛ [= 1977; ¹1971]: Il mondo antico 7. Bo 1979, Pàtron. 450 p.; XXIV pl.; 6 maps.

d318 **Braccesi** Lorenzo, L'ultimo Alessandro (dagli antichi ai moderni) [late-legendary relations with the Romans]: Saggi/universitari 5/4, 1986 → 3,b813; Lit. 24.000; ᴿGnomon 60 (1988) 165-7 (J. R. *Hamilton*, Eng.: bold and stimulating).

d319 ᴱ**Brenk** Frederick E., *Gallo* Italo, Miscellanea Plutarchea 1985/6 → 2,521: ᴿAntClas 57 (1988) 367s (A. *Martin*).

d320 *Brown* Truesdell S., *a*) Early life of HERODOTUS; – *b*) Herodotus' travels [... Egypt]: AncW 17 (1988) 3-15 / 67-75 [-107].

d321 **Cantarella** Eva, Pandora's daughters; the role and status of women in Greek and Roman antiquity 1987 → 3,b815: ᴿAmHR 93 (1988) 674s (Sarah B. *Pomeroy*); Gnomon 60 (1988) 445-7 (W. *Schuller*); JHS 108 (1988) 248 (Helen *King*).

d322 **Carlier** Pierre, La royauté en Grèce avant Alexandre 1984 → 1,b167 ... 3,b816: ᴿGnomon 60 (1988) 413-7 (J. *Seibert*); Gymnasium 94 (1987) 457-9 (K.-W. *Welwei*); Phoenix 42 (Toronto 1988) 181-3 (A. J. *Podlecki*).

d323 **Carter** L. B., The quiet Athenian [who tried to mind his own business amid newfangled democratizing; diss. L 1982, ᴰ*Humphreys* S.] 1986 → 3,b817: ᴿAmHR 93 (1988) 125s (P. *Krentz*: reserves); ClasW 82 (1988s) 59s (J. M. *Hurwit*); LHS 108 (1988) 253 (D. *Whitehead*).

d324 ᴱ**Cataldi** Silvio, Symbolai e relazioni tra le città greche nel V secolo a. C. [Verträge]: Relazioni interstatali nel mondo antico 4. Pisa 1983, Scuola Normale. xxiv-463 p.; 12 pl. – ᴿHZ 244 (1987) 662s (F. *Gschnitzer*).

d325 **Chamoux** François, La civilisation grecque à l'époque archaïque et classique² [1963 text with updated bibliography but without the 250-some photos]. P 1983, Arthaud. F 55,50. 2-7003-0446-2. – ᴿÉchMClas 32 (1988) 413s (G. P. *Ouellette*).

d326 **Chamoux** François. La civilisation hellénistique: Les grandes civilisations. P 1988 [= 1981 sans fig. et index], Arthaud. 439 p. 2-7003-0544-2.

d327 **Connor** W. Robert, THUCYDIDES 1984 → 85,9768 ... 2,9427: ᴿAmJPg 109 (1988) 259-262 (C. W. *Kalkavage*).

d328 *Delvaux* G., Retour aux sources de PLUTARQUE: ÉtClas 56 (1988) 27-48.

d329 **Dover** K. J., Greek and the Greeks. Ox 1987, Blackwell. 318 p. £32.50. 0-631-15792-1 [Antiquity 62,420].

d330 **Drews** Robert, The coming of the Greeks; Indo-European conquests in the Aegean and the Near East. Princeton 1988, Univ. xviii-257 p. 0-691-03592-X [OIAc D87].

d331 **DuBois** Page, Sowing the body; psychoanalysis and ancient [... Greek] representations of women: Women in Culture and Society. Ch 1988, Univ. 227 p.; 13 fig. $30 [RelStR 15, 258, C. *Gallant*].

d332 *Ehrhardt* Christopher, HERODOT: → 807, RAC 14,110 (1988) 849-861.

d333 **Errington** Malcolm, Geschichte Makedoniens 1986 → 3,b820*: ᴿGnomon 60 (1988) 598-603 (M. B. *Hatzopoulos*: treats it as a new work, no hint of translation); Gymnasium 95 (1988) 77s (A. *Poláček*).

d335 **Flory** Stewart, The archaic smile of HERODOTUS. Detroit 1987, Wayne State Univ. 204 p. $25. 0-8143-1827-4. – ᴿClasW 82 (1988s) 318s (T. J. *Luce*).

d336 **French** A., Sixth-century Athens; the sources: Sources in Ancient History. Sydney 1987, Univ. 92 p. A$10 pa. 0-424-00123-3 [AncHRes 19, 33, P. *Fleming*].

d337 **Garner** Richard, Law and society in classical Athens. L 1987, Croom Helm. viii-161 p. £20. – ᴿGnomon 60 (1988) 649s (J. M. *Rainer*: Rechtsgeschichte).

d338 **Gehrke** Hans-Joachim, Jenseits von Athen und Sparta; das dritte Griechenland und seine Staatenwelt 1986 → 2,9440; DM 32: ᴿAmHR 93 (1988) 126 (J. *Buckler*); ClasR 102 (1988) 87-89 (S. *Hornblower*); Gnomon 60 (1988) 366-8 (J. B. *Salmon*); HZ 245 (1987) 680s (P. *Herrmann*); Mnemosyne 41 (1988) 458-461 (G. J. D. *Aalders H. Wzn*).

d339 *Gehrke* Hans-J., Die Griechen und die Rache; ein Versuch in historischer Psychologie: Saeculum 38 (1987) 121-149.

d340 **Grant** Michael, The rise of the Greeks. L 1987, Weidenfeld & N. 391 p.; 41 fig.; 13 maps. £18. 0-297-79228-8 [Antiquity 62,420].

d341 **Gruen** Erich S., The Hellenistic world and the coming of Rome 1984 → 1,b178; 3,b824: ᴿClasPg 83 (1988) 245-8 (M. G. *Morgan*).

d342 ᴱ**Hägg** R., The Greek renaissance in the eighth century B.C. 1981/3 → 64,637: ᴿVDI 184 (1988) 230-245 (A. Y. *Sogomonov*).

d343 **Hammond** N. G. L., *Walbank* F. W., A history of Macedonia [II, 1978 → 61,q729] III, 336-167 B.C. Ox 1988, Clarendon. xxx-655 p. 0-19-814815-1 [-5294-3 announced for I].

d344 *Hammond* N. G. L., The king and the land in the Macedonian kingdom: ClasQ 82 (1988) 382-391.

d345 *a) Hammond* N. G. L., The royal journal of Alexander; – *b) Carney* Elizabeth, The sisters of Alexander the Great; royal reliefs: Historia 37 (1988) 129-150 / 385-404.

d346 **Hansen** Mogens H.,   The Athenian assembly in the age of Demosthenes [1984 ➤ 3,b827], ᵀ.   Ox 1987, Blackwell.   viii-249 p.; 5 fig. £25. – ᴿClasR 102 (1988) 310s (P. J. *Rhodes*).

d347 *Hansen* Mogens H.,   The organization of the Athenian assembly; a reply: GRByz [26 (1985) 247-250; 28 (1987) 51-92, *Stanton* G., *Bicknell* P.] 29 (1988) 51-58.

d348 ᴱ**Harding** P.,   From the end of the Peloponnesian War to the battle of Ipsus: Translated Documents of Greece and Rome 2, 1985 ➤ 1,b180: ᴿRStorAnt 16 (1986) 208s (Germana *Scuccimara*).

d349 *Harris* B. F.,   The Greek renaissance and its biographer [PHILOSTRATUS c. 200 A.D.: *Anderson* G. 1986]: AncHRes 18 (1988) 170-6.

d350 **Hirsch** Steven W.,   The friendship of the barbarians; XENOPHON and the Persian empire 1985 ➤ 1,b185:   ᴿAmHR 92 (1987) 107s (W. E. *Higgins*); AmJPg 109 (1988) 139-142 (Paula W. *Sage*).

d351 **Högemann** Peter,   Alexander der Grosse und Arabien: Zetemata 82, 1985 ➤ 2,9450; 3,b831:   ᴿBO 45 (1988) 705-710 (E. Van der *Vliet*); ClasR 102 (1988) 435 (S. *Hornblower*); Gymnasium 94 (1987) 459-462 (F. F. *Schwarz*); HZ 245 (1987) 413s (K. *Brodersen*).

d351* ᴱ**Hopkinson** Neil,   A Hellenistic anthology [Greek with commentary]: Greek and Latin Classics. C 1988, Univ. xiv-288 p. 0-521-31425-9.

d352 **Hornblower** Simon,   THUCYDIDES.   Baltimore 1987, Johns Hopkins Univ.   ix-230 p. $25.   0-8018-3529-1. – ᴿClasW 82 (1988s) 202 (A. L. *Boegehold*).

d353 *Jarry* Jacques, Datierungsprobleme in Nord-Syrien [*Tchalenko* G. 1983]: Tyche 3 (1988) 129-134.

d355 **Kagan** Donald,   The fall of the Athenian Empire.   Ithaca NY 1988, Cornell Univ.   xviii-455 p.   0-8014-1935-2.

d356 *Krischer* Tilman,   Dynamische Aspekte der griechischen Kultur: WienerSt 101 (1988) 7-40.

d357 *Kuhlmann* K. P.,   The oracle of Amun at Siwa [300 k S Marsa Matruh in Egypt] and the visit of Alexander the Great: AncHRes 18 (1988) 65-85; 3 fig.

d358 ᴱ**Kuhrt** A., *Sherwin-White* S.,   Hellenism in the East; the interaction of Greek and non-Greek civilisations from Syria to Central Asia after Alexander.   L 1987, Duckworth.   xv-192 p.   13 figs; 8 pl. £28.   0-7156-2125-4 [BL 89,37. L. L. *Grabbe*], *Salles* J.-F., the Arab-Persian gulf; *Colledge* M., art and architecture; *Spek* R. J. van der, the Babylonian city. – ᴿRB 95 (1988) 597-9 (F. *Langlamet*: tit. pp.).

d359 *Kulak* Mirosław, ❷ De proelio ab Alexandro Magno cum Poro Indorum rege ad flumen Hydaspem commisso;   Meander 43 (1988) 229-241 [231-8, de flumine ad oceanum].

d360 **Lane Fox** Robin, Alexander the Great.   Hmw 1986 = 1973, Penguin.   568 p.; 17 pl. $15.   0-14-008878-4. – ᴿAncHRes 18 (1988) 33-41 (R. D. *Milns*).

d361 **Leimbach** R.,   Militärische Musterrhetorik; eine Untersuchung zu den Feldherrnreden des THUKYDIDES 1985 ➤ 2,9459:   ᴿAthenaeum 66 (1988) 213-5 (Laura *Boffo*).

d362 **Lintott** Andrew,   Violence, civil strife and revolution in the classical city, 750-330 B.C., 1982 ➤ 65,9792. – ᴿAntClas 57 (1988) 495 (J.-M. *Hannick*).

d363 **Lloyd** Alan B.,   HERODOTUS Book II, commentary 99-182: ÉPR 43. Leiden 1988, Brill.   viii-330 p.   90-04-04179-6; 7737-5.

d364 *a) Lloyd* Alan B.,   HERODOTUS' account of pharaonic history; – *b) McNeal* Richard A.,   The brides of Babylon; Herodotus 1.196; –

c) Nakategawa Yoshio, Isegoria in Herodotus: Historia 37 (1988) 22-53 / 54-71 / 257-275.

d365 **Loraux** Nicole, Tragic ways of killing a woman [how represented in Greek tragedy], ᵀ*Forster* Anthony. CM 1987, Harvard. xi-100 p. [RelStR 15, 260, D. *Boedeker*].

d366 **McGregor** Malcolm F., The Athenians and their empire. Vancouver 1987, B.C. Univ. xxii-219 p.; 8 fig.; 8 maps. – ᴿPhoenix 42 (Toronto 1988) 179s (R. *Sealey*).

d367 **Malitz** Jürgen, Die Historien des POSEIDONIOS: Zetemata 79. Mü 1983, Beck. 486 p. – ᴿAnzAltW 41 (1988) 158-161 (G. *Schepens*).

d367* **Mehl** A., Seleukos Nikator und sein Reich, I. Seleukos' Leben und die Entwicklung seiner Machtposition: Studia Hellenistica 28. Lv 1986. xvi-351 p. Fb 1650 [JHS 109, 254, F. W. *Walbank*].

d368 ᴱ**Moxon** L. S., *al*. Past perspectives; studies in Greek and Roman historical writing 1983/6 ➤ 3,768 ['I.S.']: ᴿAmHR 92 (1987) 101s (C. M. *Paul*).

d369 *Nicolaidis* Anastasios G., Ⓖ The purpose of PLUTARCH's Lives and the various theories about it: Archaiognōsía 3,1s (1987 for 1982-4) 93-113; Eng. 114.

d369* **Oliva** P., Solon – Legende und Wirklichkeit. Konstanz 1987, Univ. 96 p. DM 29,80 [Gymnasium 96, 557, K.-W. *Welwei*].

d370 **Osborne** R., *Demos*, the discovery of classical Attica 1985 ➤ 2,9464: ᴿClasPg 83 (1988) 70-76 (J. *Ober*); Eirene 25 (1988) 116 (P. *Oliva*).

d371 **Ostwald** Martin, From popular sovereignty to the rule of law: Law, society, and politics in fifth-century Athens. Berkeley 1986, Univ. California. xxii-663 p. $75. – ᴿGreeceR 35 (1988) 97 (P. J. *Rhodes*: footnote-reference to series and publisher dubious).

d372 **Pearson** Lionel, The Greek historians of the west; Timaeus and his predecessors: AmPg Mg 35. Atlanta 1987, Scholars. xi-305 p. 1-55540-078-7; pa. 161-1.

d372* **Perysinakis** I. N., Ⓖ *Ennoia*... Attention to wealth [its use and especially misuse] in HERODOTUS' History: Dodone 31. Ioannina 1987, Univ. 279 p. [JHS 109, 218, J. T. *Hooker*].

d373 *Piejko* Francis, The treaty between Antiochus III and Lysimachia: Historia 37 (1988) 151-165.

d374 *Pope* Maurice, THUCYDIDES and democracy: Historia 37 (1988) 276-296.

d375 **Powell** Anton, Athens and Sparta; constructing Greek political and social history from 478 B.C.: Croom Helm Classical Studies. L / Portland OR 1988, Routledge / Areopagitica. 423 p. £39.50; pa. £13. 0-415-00337-7; 8-5 / 0-918400-09-0 [Antiquity 62,641].

d376 *Prandi* Luisa, STRABONE ed Eforo; un'ipotesi sugli Historikà hypomnēmata: Aevum 62 (1988) 50-60.

d377 *a)* ᴱ**Prontera** F., *b)* ᴱ**Maddoli** G., STRABONE; contributi allo studio della personalità e dell'opera 1/2. Perugia 1984/6, Univ. ➤ 2,9470: 262 p.; map. / 199 p. Lit. 45.000 + 27.000. – ᴿJHS 108 (1988) 235 (J. M. *Alonso-Núñez*).

d377* **Raaflaub** Kurt, Die Entdeckung der Freiheit; zur historischen Semantik und Gesellschaftsgeschichte eines politischen Grundbegriffes bei den Griechen: Vestigia 37, 1985 ➤ 3,b851*. – ᴿClasR 38 (1988) 82-85 (M. *Ostwald*); Gnomon 60 (1988) 163-5 (R. *Sealey*).

d378 **Ramírez Trejo** A., HERÓDOTO, padre y creador de la historia científica. Méjico 1984, UNAM. 192 p. – ᴿHelmantica 37 (1986) 389 (S. *Jiménez*).

d379 ᵀᴱ**Rhodes** P. J., [➤ h554] ARISTOTLE, The Athenian constitution. Hmw 1984, Penguin. $7. 0-14-044431-9. – ᴿAncSRes 17 (1987) 34-38 (A. *French*, also on his Commentary 1981).

d380 *Rhodes* P. J., What Alcibiades did or what happened to him: AncHRes 18 (1988) 134-150.

d381 **Roberts** J. W., City of Sokrates — an introduction to classical Athens 1984 ➤ 3,b852; $28. 0-7102-1102-3: ᴿAncHRes 18 (1988) 180-6 (K. *Hartman*); HeythJ 29 (1988) 113s (J. *Ferguson*: good).

d382 *Romane* Patrick, Alexander's siege on Tyre: AncW 16 (1987) 79-90.

d383 *Rühfel* Hilde, Ammen und Kinderfrauen im klassischen Athen: Ant-Welt 19,4 (1988) 43-57; 17 fig.

d384 **Samuel** Alan E., The promise of the west; the Greek world, Rome and Judaism. L 1988, Routledge. xvi-432 p. 0-415-00274-5.

d385 *Samuel* Alan E., Philip and Alexander as kings; Macedonian monarchy and Merovingian parallels: AmHR 93 (1988) 1270-1286.

d386 **Schachermeyr** Fritz, Griechische Frühgeschichte 1984 ➤ 65,9808 ... 3,b859: ᴿAnzAltW 41 (1988) 37-40 (N. *Schlager*).

d387 **Schalles** Hans-Joachim, Untersuchungen zur Kulturpolitik der pergamenischen Herrscher 1985 ➤ 3,b860: ᴿRArchéol (1988) 404-7 (F. *Queyrel*).

d388 **Schuller** Wolfgang, Frauen in der griechischen Geschichte 1985 ➤ 2,9478; 3,b863: ᴿHZ 247 (1988) 133-5 (Marieluise *Deissmann*).

d389 **Schwenk** Cynthia J., Athens in the age of Alexander; the dated laws and decrees of 'the Lykourgan era' 338-322 B.C., 1985 ➤ 1,b211: ᴿEirene 25 (1988) 122s (P. *Oliva*).

d390 **Sealey** Raphael, The Athenian republic; democracy or the rule of law. Univ. Park 1987, Penn State Univ. 192 p. $22.50. – ᴿClasR 102 (1988) 85s (P. J. *Rhodes*).

d391 **Schiffmann** I. S., Ⓡ Aleksandr Makedonskij: Vseobščaya Istoriya. Leningrad 1988, Nauka. 207 p. [➤ 2,9480 'Šifman'].

d392 **Smarczyk** Bernhard, Bündnerautonomie und athenische Seebundspolitik im Deleischen Krieg: BeitKlasPg 177. Fra 1986, Athenäum. 112 p. DM 34. 3-445-02494-4. – ᴿAntClas 57 (1988) 504-6 (D. *Viviers*).

d393 *Soraci* Rosario, La figura di Alessandro Magno nell'opera di AMMIANO Marcellino: QuadCatan 9,18 (1987) 297-312.

d394 *Špilevskij* A. V., Ⓡ [PTOLEMAEUS] L'Almageste et la chronologie: VDI 186 (1988) 134-159; franç. 160.

d395 *a) Starr* Chester G., Why we can write early Greek history; – *b) Mattingly* Harold B., Methodology in fifth-century Greek history; ÉchMClas 32 (1988) 285-8 / 321-8.

d396 **Stone** I. F., The trial of Socrates. Boston 1988, Little Brown. xi-282 p. $19 [RelStR 15, 260, A. T. *Kraabel*).

d397 **Strauss** B. S., Athens after the Peloponnesian war; class faction and policy 403-386 B.C. L 1986, Croom Helm. 191 p. A$70. 0-7099-4424-1 [AncHRes 19, 169-171, V. J. *Gray*].

d398 **Szarmach** Marian, MAXIMOS von Tyros; eine literarische Monographie. Toruń 1985, Univ. Kopernika. 133 p. – ᴿEos 76 (1988) 353-9 (K. *Korus*).

d399 *Thomas* Carol G., Between literacy and orality; HERODOTUS' historiography: MeditHistR-TA 3,2 (1988) 54-70.

d400 *Thornton* Larry R., Alexander the Great and Hellenization: CalvaryB 4,1 (1988) 25-42.

d401 **Traill** John S., Demos and trittys; epigraphical and topographical studies in the organization of Attica. Toronto 1986, Victoria College. viii-150 p.; 16 pl.; 5 maps. $36. – ᴿÉchMClas 32 (1988) 415-7 (M. F. *McGregor*).

d402 **Tullio** Raffaele, Storia dell'Antichità; pref. *Moscati* S. R 1988, Gremese. 608 p. – ᴿAtenRom 33 (1988) 192-4 (M. Grazia *Iodice Di Martino*).

d403 **Vatai** Frank L., Intellectuals in politics in the Greek world 1984 ➤ 1,b215; 2,9487: ᴿEirene 25 (1988) 119-121 (J. *Souček*).

d404 *a) Virgilio* Biagio, Conflittualità e coesistenza fra Greci e non-Greci, e il caso di Alicarnasso del V secolo a. C.; – *b) Ambaglio* Delfino, Tensioni etniche e sociali nella *chōra* tolemaica: ➤ 464, Stud. Ellenistici II (1987) 109-127; 2 pl. / 129-162.

d404* *Vofchuk* Rosalía C., Los informes de ONESICRITO, cronista de Alejandro Magno sobre la India: BAsEspOr 22 (1986) 187-202.

d405 **Waters** K. H., HERODOTOS the historian 1985 ➤ 1,b218 ... 3,b869*: ᴿAncSRes 17 (1987) 43-45 (V. J. *Gray*).

d407 **West** M. L., The Hesiodic catalogue of women; its nature, structure, and origins. Ox 1985, Clarendon. viii-193 p. 0-19-814034-7.

d408 **Will** Wolfgang, Alexander der Grosse: Geschichte Makedoniens 2. Stu 1986, Kohlhammer. 208 p. 3-1700-8939-0. – ᴿHZ 246 (1988) 123s (J. *Seibert*).

d409 **Will** Wolfgang, Athen und Alexander; Untersuchungen zur Geschichte der Stadt von 338 bis 322 v. Chr. [ᴰ1980]: Münchener BeiträgePapF 77, 1983 ➤ 65,9916 ... 3,b870: ᴿAnzAltW 41 (1988) 191-3 (A. *Jähne*).

d410 **Zaïtsev** A. I., ❻ *Kul'turnyi perevorot* ... The cultural upheaval in ancient Greece in the 8th-5th centuries B.C. Leningrad 1985, Univ. 207 p. – ᴿJHS 108 (1988) 250s (A. *Liberman*).

Q7 Josephus Flavius.

d411 *Allen* Pauline, An early epitomator of Josephus, EUSTATHIUS of Epiphaneia: ByZ 81 (1988) 1-11.

Amaru Betsy H., Portraits of biblical women in Ant. 1988 ➤ 1478.

Beall Todd S., Josephus' description of the Essenes 1988 ➤ b72.

d412 **Bilde** Per, Flavius Josephus, between Jerusalem and Rome; his life, his works, and their importance: JPseud Sup 2. Sheffield 1988, Academic. 272 p. £30; sb. £22.50. 1-85075-060-2 [JPseud 2,118 adv.].

d413 *Bilde* P., Main trends in modern Josephus research: NorJ 8 (1987) 73-105, to be ch. 4 of his 1988 Josephus between Jerusalem and Rome [JStJud 19,153; ZAW 100,295].

d414 *Boer* W. den, Flavius Josephus en de theoretische geschiedenis: Theoretische geschiedenis 15 (1988) 26-38 [< RHE 83,422*].

d415 *Cohen* Shaye J. D., History and historiography in the Against Apion of Josephus: ➤ HistTheor Beih. 27 (1988) 1-11.

d415* *Deutsch* N., Iconographie ... Josèphe/Fouquet 1986 ➤ 3,b881: KirSef 61 (1986s) 792s (G. J. *Ormann*).

d416 *Diamant* Betinio, Juridical aspects in Josephus Flavius' Bellum Judaicum [ᵀ*Williamson* G., ᴱ*Smallwood* E. Mary (Hmw 1981, Penguin) 511 p.]: ZSav-R 105 (1988) 720-5.

d417 *Emerton* J. A., A consideration of two recent theories [*Yadin* Y. 1972, *Pixner* B. 1976] about Bethso in Josephus's description of Jerusalem [W 5,145] and a passage in the Temple Scroll: ➤ 47, ᶠFENSHAM F., Text 1988, 93-104.

d418 **Feldman** Louis H., Josephus, a supplementary bibliography 1986
➤ 2,9504: [R]EvQ 60 (1988) 64s (J.N. *Birdsall*); TPhil 63 (1988) 592s
(K.-S. *Krieger*).

d419 *Feldman* Louis H., Pro-Jewish intimations in anti-Jewish remarks cited
in Josephus' Against Apion: JQR 78 (1987s) 187-251.

d420 *a) Feldman* Louis H., Use, authority and exegesis of Mikra in the
writings of Josephus; – *b) Horst* Pieter W. van der, Minor Hellenistic
Jewish authors: ➤ 317, Mikra 1988, 455-518 / 519-546.

d421 **Gallant** Robert P., Josephus' expositions of biblical law; an internal
analysis: diss. Yale. NHv c. 1988. – RTLv 20,540.

d422 *Kopidakis* M.Z., ⊖ *Iōsēpos homerízōn*... Josephus' many reminiscences
of HOMER add both liveliness and gravity to his narrative: Ellinika 37
(1986) 3-25 [< JStJud 19, 280].

d423 *Manns* Frédéric, [B 7,323-336.341-388] Masada, il mito del suicidio
collettivo: TerraS 64 (1988) 315-7.

d424 *Martin* T.R., Quintus Curtius' presentation of Philip Arrhidaeus and
Josephus' accounts of the accession of Claudius: AmJAncH 8,2 (CM
1983) 161-190 [NTAbs 32,224].

d425 *Mayer* Günter, Josephus Flavius: ➤ 813, TRE 17 (1987) 258-264 [268s,
JOSIPPON, *Vivian* Angelo, [T]*Wirsching* R.].

d426 *Mason* Steve, Josephus on the Pharisees reconsidered; a critique of
[Morton] SMITH/NEUSNER [view that before 70 C.E. the Pharisees as one
of many sects had limited influence]: SR 17 (1988) 455-469.

d427 *Mason* S.N., Priesthood in Josephus and the 'pharisaic revolution': JBL
107 (1988) 657-661.

d428 [E]**Melik'išvili** Nino, Ioseb P[e]LAVIOSI, Mot'hrobani... Antiquitates ju-
daicae [I (1-7) 1987 ➤ 3,b889] II (8-15) in Georgian. Tbilisi 1988,
Mec'niereba. 552 p.; Eng. 545-8 [denies that 'the' translator of books
1-15 (12 cent.) was Ioane PETRITSI (books 16-20 were done in the 19th
cent. by David INANISHVILI); does not say specifically that the translation
here given is the anonymous one of the 12th century].

d429 *Momigliano* A., What Josephus did not see [< C VII contributo 1984]:
➤ 232, On pagans 1987, 109-119.

d430 **Paul** André, Le judaïsme ancien et la Bible: Relais Études 3, 1987
➤ 3,b893; F 195: [R]Biblica 69 (1988) 591-3 (J. *Maier*); EsprVie 98 (1988)
257s (É. *Cothenet*: études pour ANRW et autres; pourquoi Quoumrân?);
MélSR 45 (1988) 113s (G.-H. *Baudry*); RevSR 62 (1988) 323 (B. *Renaud*);
RivB 36 (1988) 417s (R. *Penna*).

d431 **Rajak** Tessa, Josephus [< diss. Oxford] 1983 ➤ 64,a211 ... 3, b895:
[R]AncSRes 17 (1987) 53s (P.W. *Barnett*).

d432 *Rokéah* David, ⊕ Zechariah ben Avkules – humility or zealotry?
[differently portrayed in Jewish War 2,409 and Talmudic sources]: Zion 53
(1988) 53-56; Eng. ii; 317-322, answer to *Schwartz* D.R. 313-6.

d433 *Shutt* James H., Josephus [A 2,51-113] in Latin; a retroversion into
Greek and an English translation: JPseud 1 (1987) 79-93.

d434 [TE]**Spottorno Díaz-Caro** M. Victoria, Flavio Josefo, Autobiografia; *Busto
Saiz* J.R., Sobre la antigüedad de los judíos (Contra Apionem): Libros de
bolsillo 1273. M 1987, Alianza. 235 p. – [R]EstE 63 (1988) 235s (F.
Pastor-Ramos).

d435 *Vermes* Geza, Josephus' portrait of Jesus reconsidered: ➤ 130, Mem.
SCHEIBER A. 1988, 373-382.

d436 **Villalba i Varneda** Père, The historical method of Flavius Josephus
[diss. 1981] 1986 ➤ 3,b904: [R]AmHR 93 (1988) 1305 (M. *Smith*,

mordant); BL (1988) 145 (L.L. *Grabbe*; translation and conclusions inadequate); HZ 246 (1988) 654s (M. *Clauss*); VT 38 (1988) 123s (W. *Horbury*).

d436* **Williams** David S., Josephus and the authorship of IV Maccabees; a critical investigation: diss. HUC, [D]*Rivkin* E. Cincinnati 1988. 128 p. 88-18736. – DissA 49 (1988s) 2262-A.

d437 *Williams* Margaret H., [Ant 20,195] *Theosebēs gàr ên* — the Jewish tendencies of [Nero's] Poppaea Sabina: JTS 39 (1988) 97-111.

Q8   *Historia epochae NT* – **Seleucids to Bar-Kochba.**

d438 **Alföldi** A. † 1981, [➤ d569] Caesar in 44 v. Chr. I, 1985 ➤ 3,b907: [R]ClasR 102 (1988) 124s (Elizabeth *Rawson*, also on the volume Caesariana 1984 of his Nachlass).

d439 **Avi-Yonah** Michael, The Jews under Roman and Byzantine rule; a political history from the Bar Kokhba war to the Arab conquest 1984 = [T]1976 ➤ 2,9528: [R]JNES 47 (1988) 232s (W. E. *Kaegi*: irreplaceable).

d440 *Beer* Moshe, ⊕ On solidarity among the sages [in resisting power of rich Jews collaborating with Rome]: Zion 53 (1988) 149-166; Eng. v.

d441 **Belloni** Gian Guido, Le 'Res gestae divi Augusti'; Augusto, il nuovo regime e la nuova Urbe. Mi 1987, ViPe. 152 p. – [R]Orpheus 9 (1988) 351-4 (Antonella *Borgo*).

d442 **Benario** Herbert W., Recent work on TACITUS: 1974-1983: ClasW 80 (1987s) 73-147.

d443 **Benko** Stephen, Pagan Rome and the early Christians 1984 ➤ 1,b254 ... 3,b913: [R]AmHR 91 (1986) 639s (É. *Lamirande*); SecC 6 (1987s) 114s (E. N. *Lane*: he claims pagan criticisms were not unfounded).

d444 **Bickerman** E. J., The Jews in the Greek age, [E]*Baumgarten* A. CM 1988, Harvard Univ. xii-338 p. [NTAbs 32,388].

d445 [E]**Binder** G., Saeculum augustum I: WegFor 266, 1987 ➤ 3,483: [R]ClasR 102 (1988) 326s (R. *Seager*); Gymnasium 95 (1988) 381-3 (Ines *Stahlmann*).

d445* [E]**Boardman** John, *al.*, The Roman world: Oxford History of the Classical World. Ox 1988, Univ. 456 p.; 145 fig. + 11 colour.; 4 maps. £10 pa. 0-19-282166-0 [Antiquity 63,26].

d446 *Boatwright* M. T., The style of the 'Laudes Neronis', Chapter 4,1 of SENECA's Apocolocyntosis: ClasB 62 (1986) 10-14 [< BStLat 18,211].

d447 **Bonner** Stanley F., L'educazione nell'antica Roma; da Catone il Censore a Plinio il Giovane [Methuen 1977], [T]: Educazione comparata e pedagogie 88. R 1986, Armando. 439 p. – [R]Salesianum 50 (1988) 610 (P. *Braido*).

d448 *Borzsák* I., Zu TACITUS' hellenistisch-orientalischen Beziehungen: AcAntH 31 (1985-8) 27-34.

d449 *Bremmer* Jan, Modern ancient historians and the rise of early Christianity: ProcClasAs 35 (1988) 36s.

d450 *Briquel* Dominique, *a)* Claude, érudit et empereur: CRAI (1988) 217-232: – *b)* Que savons-nous des Tyrrhenika de l'empereur Claude?: RFgIC 116 (1988) 448-470.

d451 **Broughton** T. R. S., The magistrates of the Roman Republic 3, 1986 ➤ 3,b919: [R]AmJPg 109 (1988) 609-611 (R. E. A. *Palmer*); ClasR 102 (1988) 314s (T. J. *Cadoux*); RÉLat 65 (1987) 349 (J.-L. *Ferrary*).

d452 **Bruce** F. F., Zeitgeschichte des NTs I-II 1986 ➤ 2,9540: [R]SNTU-A 13 (1988) 212s (A. *Fuchs*).

d453 ^E**Burstein** Stanley M.,   The Hellenistic age ...: Translated Documents 3, 1985 ➔ 1,b261; 3,b921:   ^RClasW 80 (1986s) 384s (J. *Clack*); Eirene 25 (1988) 121s (P. *Oliva*); Mnemosyne 41 (1988) 452-4 (A. J. L. van *Hooff*).

d454 *Campbell* Duncan B.,   Dating the siege of Masada [epigraphy suggests 74 rather than 73]: ZPapEp 73 (1988) 156-8.

d455 *Chaumont* M.-L.,   Un document méconnu concernant l'envoi d'un ambassadeur parthe vers Septime Sévère (P. Dura 60 R):   Historia 36 (1987) 422-447.

d456 **Christ** Karl,   Geschichte der römischen Kaiserzeit, von Augustus bis zu Konstantin. Mü 1988, Beck.   ix-869 p.

d457 **Cizek** Eugen,   L'époque de Trajan; circonstances politiques et problèmes idéologiques [roum.] ^T*Franţescu* Caius: Coll. Ét. Anc.   P 1983, BLettres. 566 p.

d458 **Crawford** Michael,   Die römische Republik, ^T*Evers* Barbara & Silke. Mü 1984, dtv. 252 p.; 22 fig. DM 16,80. – ^RArKulturG 70 (1988) 513s (M. *Jehne*).

d458* **Delling** Gerhard,   Die Bewältigung der Diasporasituation durch das hellenistische Judentum 1987 ➔ 3,b928:   ^RÉTRel 63 (1988) 459 (J. *Rennes*: difficile d'utilisation).

d459 **Diderot** D.,   Saggio sui regni di Claudio e Nerone, e sui costumi e gli scritti di Seneca (prima in italiano) ^T*Carpanetto* S., *Guerci* I. Palermo 1987, Sellerio. 397 p. – ^RBStLat 18 (1988) 142-4 (Carmen *Ambriani*).

d460 **Dumortier** Francis,   La patrie des premiers chrétiens.   P 1988, Éd. ouvrières.   322 p. F 148. – ^REsprVie 98 (1988) 569s (É. *Cothenet* ne mentionne aucune 'patrie' sauf fugacement Syrie et Bithynie; Palestine nulle part; il semble s'agir du monde économique romain); Études 369 (1988) 279s (P. *Vallin*).

d461 *Durst* Michael,   Christen als römische Magistrate um 200; das Zeugnis des Kaisers Septimius Severus für Christen aus dem Senatorenstand (TERTULLIAN, Ad Scapulam 4,6):   JbAC 31 (1988) 91-126.

d462 *Ensminger* J. J.,   The Sadducean persecution of the Christians in Rome and Jerusalem, A.D. 58 to 65:   SWJT 30,3 (1988) 9-13 [< NTAbs 32,346].

d463 **Ferguson** Everett,   Backgrounds of early Christianity.   GR 1987, Eerdmans. 464 p. $23.   0-8028-0292-3. – ^RVidyajyoti 52 (1988) 460s (P. M. *Meagher*).

d464 ^E**Fisher** C. D.,   TACITUS Cornelius, Historiarum libri.   Ox 1985 = 1911, Clarendon. viii-262 p.   0-19-814634-5.

d465 **Flusser** David,   Jewish sources in early Christianity.   NY 1987, Adama. 89 p.; ill. $20.   1-55-774-009-7; pa. 0-915361-92-2.

d466 **Freis** Helmut,   Historische Inschriften ... Augustus bis Konstantin 1984 ➔ 3,b934:   ^RRBgPg 66 (1988) 153s (R. *Lambrechts*); SborBrno 33 (1988) 173s (Jarmila *Bednaříková*).

d467 **Freyne** Sean,   Galilee from Alexander to Hadrian 1980 ➔ 61,q927 ... 3,b935:   ^RFraJudBei 15 (1987) 151-4 (P. *Schäfer*).

Gardner Jane F.,   Women in Roman law and society 1986 ➔ h354.

d468 **Gascou** Jacques,   SUÉTONE historien 1984 ➔ 1,6279 ... 3,b939:   ^RAntClas 57 (1988) 428-430 (Marie-Thérèse *Raepsaet-Charlier*); Orpheus 7 (1987) 165-170 (G. *Polara*).

d469 *a)* **Gaudemet** J.,   La condition juridique des Juifs dans les trois premiers siècles de l'Empire; – *b)* *Irmscher* Johannes,   La legislazione di Giustiniano sugli Ebrei; – *c)* *Bammel* Ernst,   Die Anfänge der Kirchengeschichte im Spiegel der jüdischen Quellen: ➔ 570, AugR 28 (1988) 339-359 / 361-5 / 367-379.

d470 *Georgiadou* Aristoula, The Lives of the Caesars and PLUTARCH's other Lives: ➤ 690, ILCL 13,2 (1988) 349-356.

d471 *Golan* David, Iudaei in the Scriptores historiae Augustae: Latomus 47 (1988) 318-339.

d472 **Goodman** Martin, The ruling class of Judaism; the origins of the Jewish revolt against Rome 1987 ➤ 3,b942: ᴿBL (1988) 133 (L. *Grabbe*); JJS 39 (1988) 108-112 (S. *Mitchell*); RÉLat 66 (1988) 341s (F. *Bérard*).

d473 *a*) *Goodman* Martin, ❶ The origins of the great revolt; a conflict of status criteria; – *b*) *Kindler* Arie, ❶ City coins of Eretz Israel and the Bar-Kokhba war: CHistEI 49 (1988) 23-36 / 37-61; Eng. 189s.

d474 **Grant** Michael, The Roman emperors; a biographical guide to the rulers of imperial Rome 31 BC–AD 476: 1985 ➤ 1,b282. – ᴿRelStR 14 (1988) 155 (J. H. *Elliott*).

d475 **Griffin** Miriam T., Nero, the end of a dynasty 1984 ➤ 1,b284... 3,b946: ᴿGymnasium 94 (1987) 463s (J. *Burian*); Mnemosyne 41 (1988) 465-7 (G. *Aalders*).

Halfmann Helmut, Itinera principum; Geschichte und Typologie der Kaiserreisen im römischen Reich: Heidelberger Althistorische Beiträge 2, 1986 ➤ h307.

d477 **Harari** Ruth, Hérode le Grand, ou le refus d'un peuple 1986 ➤ 2,9565: ᴿRThom 88 (1988) 486s (L. *Devillers*).

Horsley G. H. R., New documents illustrating early Christianity [Greek inscriptions 1979] 1987 ➤ a611*.

d478 **Horsley** R. A., *Hanson* J. S., Bandits, prophets and Messiahs 1985 ➤ 1,b291... 3,b253: ᴿHorizons 15 (1988) 157s (F. J. *Murphy*); JAAR 56 (1988) 163-5 (D. *Rhoads*); JBL 107 (1988) 135-7 (M. J. *Borg*).

d479 *Horst* Pieter W. van der, Het christendom in het Romeinse rijk in de eerste eeuw [< Hermeneus 58 (1986) 58-67]: ➤ 207, De onbekende God 1988, 175-188.

d480 *a*) *Houby-Nielsen* Sanne, Augustus and the Hellenistic kings; a note on the Augustan propaganda; – *b*) *Nedergaard* Elisabeth, The four sons of Phraates IV in Rome [20 B.C.]: ➤ 733, Acta Hyperborea 1987/8, 116-128 / 102-115.

d481 *Houghton* Arthur, *Le Rider* Georges, Un premier règne d'Antiochos VIII Épiphane à Antioche en 128: BCH 112 (1988) 401-411.

d482 **Huzar** Eleanor G., Mark Antony. L 1986 = 1978, Croom Helm. ix-347 p. $33 pa. 0-7091-94719-4. – ᴿAncHRes 18 (1988) 123-9 (M. *Lennon*).

d483 *a*) *Huzar* Eleanor G., Augustus, heir of the Ptolemies; – *b*) *Montevecchi* Orsolina, L'amministrazione dell'Egitto sotto i Giulio-Claudi: ➤ 782, ANRW 2,10,1 (1988) 343-382 / 412-471.

d484 **Jacobs** M., Das Christentum in der antiken Welt; von der früh-katholischen Kirche bis zu Kaiser Konstantin: Zugänge zur Kirchengeschichte 2, 1987 ➤ 3,b955: ᴿTsTNijm 28 (1988) 184 (F. van de *Paverd*).

d485 *Jacobson* David M., King Herod's 'heroic' public image: RB 95 (1988) 386-403.

d486 **Jagersma** Henk, A history of Israel from Alexander 1986 ➤ 2,9576; 3,b957: ᴿBS 145 (1988) 356 (E. H. *Merrill*: BODEN choppy and repetitive — or is that Jagersma?); CBQ 50 (1988) 118s (W. H. *Irwin* cites underwhelming examples of 'bad writing'); Henoch 10 (1988) 100s (J. A. *Soggin*).

d487 **Jehne** Martin, Der Staat des Dictators Caesar: Passauer Hist. For. 3. Köln 1987. Böhlau. viii-496 p. – ᴿGnomon 60 (1988) 613-9 (H. *Botermann*: Meriten unzweifelhaft, These unannehmbar)

d488 **Jerphagnon** Lucien, Histoire de la Rome antique, les armes et les mots. P 1987, Taillandier. 559 p. F 119. 2-235-01742-8. – ᴿÉTRel 63 (1988) 606 (J.-F. *Gounelle*).

d489 *Johnson* Gary J., De conspiratione delatorum; PLINY and the Christians revisited: Latomus 47 (1988) 417-422.

d490 **Kasher** Aryeh, The Jews in Hellenistic and Roman Egypt; the struggle for equal rights [diss. 1972] 1985 → 1,b298... 3,b958: ᴿAmHR 92 (1987) 392s (Ann E. *Hanson*); SecC 6,1 (1987s) 55-57 (J. T. *Collins*).

d491 **Keaveney** Arthur, Rome and the unification of Italy [to 81 B.C.]. L 1987, Croom Helm. 231 p. A$88. 0-7099-3121-2 [AncHRes 19, 44-46, Louise *Bloomfield*].

d492 *Kellner* Wendelin, Bar Kochba und die Gemeinde der christlichen Juden: BiKi 43 (1988) 140-146.

d493 *Kennell* N. M., Nerōn periodonikēs [tour of Greece in 66/7 excluding Athens and Sparta]: AmJPg 109 (1988) 239-251.

d494 *Keppe* Lawrence J. F., ❶ The history and disappearance of the Legion XXII Deiotariana: CHistEI 50 (1988) 49-57; Eng. 195.

d495 *Kneppe* Alfred, Augustus, Nero und das Geschichtsbewusstsein: ArKulturG 69 (1987) 263-287.

d496 *Koester* Helmut, *Limberis* Vasiliki, Christianity: → 444, Mediterranean 2 (1988) 1047-1073.

d497 *Latta* Bernd, Der Wandel in SALLUSTs Geschichtsauffassung, vom Bellum Catilinae zum Bellum Iugurthinum: Maia 40 (1988) 271-288.

d498 **Leach** John, Pompey the great: Classical Lives 1986 = 1978 → 3,b968; $22; 0-7099-4127-7: ᴿAncSRes 17 (1987) 108-110 (T. *Stevenson*).

d499 **Le Gall** Joël, *Le Glay* Marcel, L'empire romain, I. 31 av. J.-C. – 235 ap. J.-C. P 1987, PUF. 673 p.; map. 2-13-040023-X.

d500 **Lesbaupin** Ivo, Blessed are the persecuted; Christian life in the Roman Empire, A.D. 64-313, ᵀ*Barr* Robert R. 1987 → 3,b972: ᴿVidyajyoti 52 (1988) 62s (G. *Lobo*).

d501 **Levi** Mario A., Augusto e il suo tempo 1985 → 2,9587; 3,b973: ᴿEos 76 (1988) 155-7 (S. *Mrozek*).

d502 **Levick** Barbara, The government of the Roman Empire; a sourcebook 1985 → 2,9588; 3, b974: ᴿAncSRes 17 (1988) 54-58 (P. R. C. *Weaver*: sources should predominate over explanatory matter and be in a differentiated type).

d503 **Lewis** Naphtali, The Ides of March [translated snippets]: Aspects of Antiquity. Toronto 1985, Stevens. xxvii-168 p.; 7 pl. $10 pa. – ᴿClasW 80 (1987s) 49s (R. L. *Bates*: lively; marred).

d504 **Linder** A., The Jews in Roman imperial legislation [1983 ❶], ᵀ. Detroit/J 1987, Wayne State Univ./Israel Acad. 436 p. 0-8143-1809-6 [NTAbs 32,287].

d505 **Loposzko** Tadeusz, ❷ Historia społeczna [generalis] republikańskiego Rzymu. 366 p. – ᴿEos 76 (1988) 386-8 (E. *Dulski*).

d506* *Milikowsky* C., Seder 'Olam and Jewish chronography in the Hellenistic and Roman periods: PAAR 52 (1985) 115-139 [< JStJud 19 (1988) 291].

d507 ᴱ**Millar** Fergus, *Segal* Erich, Caesar Augustus, seven aspects 1984 → 1,767; 3,b989: ᴿAnzAltW 41 (1988) 196-9 (G. *Dobesch*).

d508 **Moda** Aldo, Il cristianesimo nel primo secolo; un itinerario e un dossier. Bari 1986, Ecumenica. 128 p. Lit. 13.000. – ᴿStPatav 35 (1988) 722s (C. *Corsato*).

d509 *Müller* K., Archelaus, Herodes / Antipas, Herodes: ➤ 804, NBL Lfg 1 (1988) 161-3 / 117-120.

d510 ᴱ**Nicolet** Claude, *al.*, Rome et la conquête du monde méditerranéen 264-27 av. J.-C.: Nouvelle Clio 8, P 1987, PUF. vol. I, Les structures de l'Italie romaine, 460 p.; F 170; II. Genèse d'un empire, p. 469-938; F 176. 2-13-039891-2; 42465-1.

d511 NIKIPROWETZKY Valentin mém., Hellenica et Judaica 1986 ➤ 2,81: ᴿJStJud 19 (1988) 98-104 (A. S. van der *Woude*: detailed analyses with tit. pp.).

d512 *Nobbs* Alanna E., The career of Pompey [... adulescentulus carnifex]: AncHRes 18 (1988) 151-5.

d513 ᴱ**Oppenheimer** A., *Rappaport* U., ❸ The Bar-Kokhba revolt, a new approach. J 1984 [IsrNumJ 9,46].

d513* *Orrieux* Claude, Zénon de Caunos, 'parépidèmos' et le destin grec: Univ. Besançon Hist. Anc. 64. P 1985, BLettres. 326 p. – ᴿRB 95 (1988) 411-6 (X. *Durand*).

d514 *Parker* R. W., A Greek inscription from Lesbos honoring a Julio-Claudian [emperor's 'father, surely': can only have been Drusus]: ZPapEp 75 (1988) 175-8.

d515 **Penna** Romano, L'ambiente storico culturale delle origini cristiane²ʳᵉᵛ. [antologia ¹1984] 1986 ➤ 3,b998: ᴿRivB 36 (1988) 273-5 (G. *Segalla*).

d516 **Plümacher** Eckhard, Identitätsverlust und Identitätsgewinn; Studien zum Verhältnis von kaiserzeitlicher Stadt und frühem Christentum: BibTSt 11, 1987 ➤ 3,b999; DM 25: ᴿCBQ 50 (1988) 542s (H. W. *Attridge*: persuasive); TLZ 113 (1988) 116s (F. W. *Horn*); TR 84 (1988) 298-300 (G. *Schöllgen*).

d517 **Podes** Stephan. Die Dependenz des hellenistischen Ostens von Rom zur Zeit der römischen Weltreichsbildung; eine Erklärungsversuch zum römischen Imperialismus aus der Sicht der Geschichte als historischer Sozialwissenschaft: EurHS 3/310. Fra 1986, Lang. 413 p. Fs 71. 3-8204-9468-5. – ᴿAntClas 57 (1988) 529s (J. A. *Straus*).

Pritz Ray A., Nazarene Jewish Christianity; from the end of the New Testament period until its disappearance in the fourth century: StPostB 37, 1988 ➤ e781.

d519 **Ramage** Edwin S., The nature and purpose of Augustus' Res Gestae: HistEinz 54. Stu 1987, Steiner. 168 p. DM 48. – ᴿClasR 102 (1988) 436s (J. *Carter*); Gymnasium 95 (1988) 457-9 (H. *Sonnabend*); RÉLat 66 (1988) 331s (J.-P. *Callu*).

d520 *Ramage* Edwin S., The date of Augustus' Res Gestae: Chiron 18 (1988) 71-82.

d521 *Raphael* C., Pagans, Christians, Jews [*Lane Fox* R. 1987]: Commentary 84,4 (NY 1987) 39-44 [NTAbs 32,209].

d522 *Roberts* Michael, The revolt of Boudicca (TACITUS, Annals 14.29-39) and the assertion of *libertas* in Neronian Rome: AmJPg 109 (1988) 118-132.

d523 **Roddaz** Jean-Michel, Marcus Agrippa 1984 ➤ 1,b331... 3,d5: ᴿLatomus 47 (1988) 453s (A. *Pelletier*).

d524 **Rubinsohn** Wolfgang Z., Der Spartakus-Aufstand und die sowjetische Geschichtsschreibung: Xenia 7. Konstanz 1983, Univ. 62 p. – ᴿGnomon 60 (1988) 657s (H. *Heinen*).

d525 *Saddington* Denis,   The administration and the army in Judaea in the early Roman period (from Pompey to Vespasian, 63 BC−AD 79): ➤ 499, Holy Land 1986/8, 33-40.

d526 **Safrai** Shmuel,   Een volk met een land; het ontstaan van het jodendom [**❶** 1970; Das jüdische Volk im Zeitalter des zweiten Tempels 1978], ^{T.} Haag 1986, Boekencentrum.   164 p. *f* 24,90 [NedTTs 42,161].

d527 **Salles** Catherine,   Tibère, le second César 1985 ➤ 3,d9:   ^RRBgPg 66 (1988) 161s (L. *Jerphagnon*).

d528 **Samuel** Alan E.,   From Athens to Alexandria; Hellenism and social goals in Ptolemaic Egypt: Studia Hellenistica 26, 1983 ➤ 65,d734; 3,b858: ^RAegyptus 68 (1988) 263s (L. *Criscuolo*).

d530 **Saulnier** Christiane,   Histoire d'Israël III, 531 a.C.−135 a.D. 1985 ➤ 1,a940... 3,d10:   ^RBijdragen 49 (1988) 90s (J. van *Ruiten*); CiuD 201 (1988) 172s (J. *Gutiérrez*); ÉglT 18 (1987) 353-5 (L. *Laberge*); Gregorianum 69 (1988) 553-5 (G. L. *Prato*); RBgPg 66 (1988) 162-4 (P. *Salmon*); Sefarad 48 (1988) 212-4 (F. *Sen*).

d531 **Saulnier** Christiane,   Storia d'Israele III, Dalla conquista di Alessandro alla distruzione del tempio (331 a.C.−135 d.C.), collaborazione di *Perrot* Charles.   R 1988, Borla.   511 p. Lit. 40.000. − ^RCC 139 (1988,3) 534s (G. L. *Prato*); RasT 29 (1988) 609s (V. *Fusco*); RÉJ 146 (1987) 167s (Madeleine *Petit*).

d532 **Schrömbges** Paul,   Tiberius und die res publica romana; Untersuchungen zur Institutionalisierung des frühen römischen Principats: Diss. Alte Geschichte 22.   Bonn 1986, Habelt.   x-410 p. − ^RGnomon 60 (1988) 343-6 (M. *Pani*, ital.).

d533 **Schuller** Wolfgang,   Frauen in der römischen Geschichte 1987 ➤ 3,d16: ^RClasR (1988) 173s (Gillian *Clark*); ClasW 82 (1988s) 124s (Nynke *Smits*: they had more freedom than in his counterpart volume on Greece); Gnomon 60 (1988) 265s (Sarah B. *Pomeroy*, Eng.); Gymnasium 95 (1988) 449s (A. *Poláček*); HZ 247 (1988) 136s (Helga *Botermann*); ZKG 99 (1988) 404-6 (R. *Klein*).

d534 *Schürer* Emil, ^E**Vermes** Geza, *al.*,   History of the Jewish people in the age of Jesus Christ 3/1s ➤ 2,9611; 3,d13:   ^RCBQ 50 (1988) 336-8.730-2 (J. J. *Collins*, 3/1s); Gnomon 60 (1988) 167s (A. H. J. *Gunneweg*, 3/2); JRAS (1988) 166-8 (E. *Ullendorff*, 3/1s); JTS 39 (1988) 190-2 (D. M. *Lewis*: 3/1s); NedTTs 42 (1988) 158s (T. *Baarda*, 3/1); RB 95 (1988) 142s.625s (J. *Murphy-O'Connor*, 3/1s); ScripTPamp 20 (1988) 277-280 (G. *Aranda*, 3/1); VT 38 (1988) 239-243 (W. *Horbury*, 3/1); WestTJ 50 (1988) 192s (M. *Silva*, 3/1s).

d535 [*Schürer* E.,] ^E**Vermes** G.,   Storia del popolo giudaico al tempo di Gesù Cristo II: BiblStStoriog 6, 1987 ➤ 3,d15:   ^RAntonianum 63 (1988) 607s (M. *Nobile*); Asprenas 35 (1988) 268-270 (A. *Rolla*); ÉtClas 56 (1988) 113s (X. *Jacques*, 1); Orpheus 7 (1987) 162-4 (Maria Laura *Astarita*, 1); StPatav 35 (1988) 705 (G. *Leonardi*).

d537 **Schwartz** Daniel, **❶** Agrippas I, first king of Judah.   J 1988s, Shazar. − ^RZion 53 (1988) 217-223 (U. *Rappaport*).

d538 **Schwier** Helmut,   Theologische und ideologische Faktoren im ersten jüdisch-römischen Krieg (66-74 n. Chr.) im Zusammenhang mit der Zerstörung des Jerusalemer Tempels: Diss. ^D*Theissen* G.   Heidelberg 1988. − RTLv 20,543.

d539 **Segal** Alan F.,   Rebecca's children; Judaism and Christianity in the Roman world 1986 ➤ 2,9613; 3,d18:   ^RAmHR 93 (1988) 129s (M. A. *Cohen*); HistRel 28 (1988s) 183 (J. D. *Tabor*); JBL 107 (1988) 317-9 (H. C.

Kee); JEcuSt 25 (1988) 293s (W. *Adler*); JTS 39 (1988) 581-4 (E.P. *Sanders*: entirety of biblical history, inevitably too much for socio-economic accuracy); TTod 45 (1988s) 512s (J.A. *Overman*); VigChr 42 (1988) 100s (G. *Quispel*).

d540 **Seibert** Jakob, Das Zeitalter der Diadochen: ErtFor 185, 1983 ➤ 64,a306; 65,9917; ᴿSborBrno 31 (1986) 201s (J. *Češka*).

d541 ᴱ**Sherk** R.K., Rome and the Greek East to the death of Augustus: Translated Documents 4, 1984 ➤ 65,9918... 3,d22: ᴿClasR 102 (1988) 435s (M.H. *Crawford*).

d542 ᴱ**Sherk** Robert K., The Roman Empire; Augustus to Hadrian: Translated Documents of Greece and Rome 6. C 1988, Univ. xxii-302 p. [CBQ 51,403].

d543 **Sherwin-White** A.N., Roman foreign policy in the East, 168 B.C. to A.D. 1, 1984 ➤ 65,9919... 3,d23: ᴿGnomon 60 (1988) 36-41 (S. *Podes*).

d544 *Shotter* D.C.A., TACITUS and Tiberius: AncS 19 (1988) 225-236.

d545 **Shove** Justin (*Fletcher* Alan), Chronology of eclipses and comets A.D. 1-1000: Woodbridge, Suffolk / Dover NH 1984, Boydell. xxxv-356 p.; ill. − ᴿJNES 47 (1988) 195 (N.M. *Swerdlow*).

d546 **Simon** Erika, Augustus, Kunst und Leben in Rom um die Zeitenwende 1986 ➤ 3,d24: ᴿBabesch 63 (1988) 205s (Barbara *Heldring*); Gnomon 60 (1988) 76-78 (P. *Gros*, franç.); RArchéol (1988) 427-430 (G. *Sauron*).

d547 **Simon** Marcel, Verus Israel... in the Roman empire, ᵀ*McKeating* H. 1986 ➤ 2,9617; 3, d24*: ᴿCurrTM 15 (1988) 209s (E. *Krentz*: 1948 but still unsurpassed, and translation excellent).

d547* *Sirianni* Frank A., Some lost authors of the late Roman Republic: AncSRes 17 (1987) 83-93.

d548 **Sordi** Marta, The Christians and the Roman Empire [1983 ➤ 65,9921] ᵀ*Bedini* Annabel, 1986 ➤ 2,9621; 3,d26: ᴿAmHR 93 (1988) 130 (S. *Benko*); ClasW 82 (1988s) 217 (R.L. *Bates*: old-hat); Gnomon 60 (1988) 245-9 (J. *Molthagen*); RÉAnc 90 (1988) 242s (M. *Perrin*); RRelRes 30 (1988s) 87-89 (J.M. *Bryant*).

d549 **Stemberger** Günter, Die römische Herrschaft im Urteil der Juden: ErtFor 195. Da 1983, Wiss. xii-183 p. − ᴿRHE 83 (1988) 738 (J.-M. *Hannick*).

d550 ᴱ**Stern** Menahem, Greek and Latin authors on Jews and Judaism 3, 1984 ➤ 65,9934... 3,d28: ᴿCBQ 50 (1988) 311 (N.J. *McEleney*).

d551 **[Storoni] Mazzolani** Lidia, Tibère ou la spirale du pouvoir; la force irrésistible du despotisme, ᵀ*Margueron* A.-E.; préf. *Heurgon* Jacques: Coll. ÉtAnc 1986 ➤ 3d29: ᴿAntClas 57 (1988) 524-6 (J. *Wankenne*); Gnomon 60 (1988) 173s (P. *Schrömbges*).

d552 *Syme* Ronald, Journeys of Hadrian: ZPapEp 73 (1988) 159-170.

d553 *Tucker* Robert A., What actually happened at the Rubicon?: Historia 37 (1988) 245-8.

d554 **Valenti Pagnini** R., Il potere e la sua immagine; semantica di 'species' in TACITO: Studi e Testi dell'Antichità 19. N 1987, SEN. 144 p. Lit. 20.000. − ᴿRasT 29 (1988) 213 (B. *Marra*).

d555 **Vanderbroeck** Paul J.J., Popular leadership and collective behavior in the Late Roman Republic (ca. 80-50 B.C.): Dutch Mg Anc. Hist 3. Amst 1987, Gieben. 281 p. *f*90. − ᴿGnomon 60 (1988) 609-612 (L. *Thommen*).

d556 **Wacher** John, The Roman Empire [not 'World' ➤ d557]. L 1987, Dent. x-314 p.; 28 fig.; 10 maps. £16. 0-460-04331-5. − ᴿAntiquity 62 (1988) 405s (R.J.A. *Wilson*).

d557 ^E**Wacher** John. The Roman world 1987 ⇸ 3,d36: ^RClasR 102 (1988) 92-94 (M. *Grant*); GreeceR 35 (1988) 86 (P. *Walcot*); JRS 78 (1988) 225s (G. *Woolf*).

d558 **Wallace-Hadrill** A., SUETONIUS, the scholar and his Caesars 1984 ⇸ 65,9931 ... 3,d37: ^REmerita 18 (1988) 155s (V. *Picón*).

d559 **Walsh** Michael, The triumph of the meek; why early Christianity succeeded. SF 1986, Harper & R. 256 p.; ill. $18. 0-06-069254-5. – ^RBibTB 18 (1988) 120 (A. J. *Tambasco*: pleasant elegant prose); ChH 57 (1988) 214s (J. W. *Trigg*); Interpretation 42 (1988) 214.216 (Rebecca H. *Weaver*).

d560 **Wendland** Paul, La cultura ellenistico-romana nei suoi rapporti con giudaismo e cristianesimo [1907 ('1912' ⇸ 3,d39), ^E*Dörrie* Heinrich 1972], ^{TE}*Firpo* G.: BStoriogB 2, 1986 ⇸ 2,9635: ^RAsprenas 35 (1988) 528s (L. *Longobardo*); RasT 29 (1988) 99s (S. *Tanzarella*); RTPhil 120 (1988) 96 (A. *Moda*).

d561 *White* Peter, Julius Caesar in Augustan Rome: Phoenix 42 (Toronto 1988) 334-356.

d562 **Whittaker** Molly, Jews and Christians, Graeco-Roman Views: CamCW 6, 1984 ⇸ 65,9932 ... 3,d40: ^RHeythJ 29 (1988) 357s (S. *Freyne*: fulfils the stated purpose better than LEANEY's 7).

d563 **Will** E., *Orrieux* C., Ioudaïsmos — Hellénismos 1986 ⇸ 2,9639; 3,d43: ^RClasPg 83 (1988) 248-251 (A. *Momigliano* †); RÉJ 146 (1987) 432-4 (Madeleine *Petit*); Salesianum 50 (1988) 439s (R. *Vicent*).

d563* **Wolf** Sonja, Die Augustusrede in Senecas Apocolocyntosis; ein Beitrag zum Augustusbild der frühen Kaiserzeit: BeiKlasPg 170. Königstein 1986, Hain. 219 p. DM 48. 3-445-02357-3. – ^RAntClas 57 (1988) 420s (J. *Wankenne*); Gnomon 60 (1988) 202-9 (R. *Jakobi*).

d564 **Wood** Leon J.†, ^{2rev}*O'Brien* David [¹1970], A survey of Israel's history. GR 1986, Zondervan. xv-416. $20. – ^RBS 145 (1988) 354s (E. H. *Merrill*: even better form of the textbook most acceptable to evangelicals, though GOTTWALD and NOTH are unduly bypassed).

d565 *Wolters* Reinhard, Zum Anhang der Res gestae divi Augusti: ZPapEp 75 (1988) 197-206.

d566 ^{TE}**Wuilleumier** Pierre, *Le Bonniec* Henri, TACITE, Histoires, Livre I.; notes *Hellegouarc'h* Joseph: Coll. Budé. P 1987, BLettres. lxvii-251 (doubles) p. – ^RGnomon 60 (1988) 712-5 (H. *Heubner*).

d568 *Zahrnt* Michael, Vermeintliche Kolonien des Kaisers Hadrian: ZPapEp 71 (1988) 229-248; 249 map, Thrakische Chersonese.

Q9 *Historia imperii romani* – **Roman-Byzantine Empire**

d569 **Alföldy** Géza, [⇸ d438] The social history of Rome [not exactly = German ²1979 ¹1975], ^T*Braund* David, *Pollock* Frank. L 1988 = 1985, Routledge. 251 p. £10 pa. 0-415-00805-0 [Antiquity 63,12].

d570 **André** Jacques, *Filliozat* Jean, L'Inde vue de Rome: Coll. Ét. Anc. P 1986, BLettres. 463 p. – ^RRPLH 61 (1987) 339s (P. *Flobert*).

d570* *Angus* S., *Renwick* A. M., Roman empire and Christianity: ⇸ 801, ISBEnc³ 4 (1988) 207-221 [-222, Roman Law, *Allen* G.].

d571 ^E**Bagnall** Roger S., *al.*, Consuls of the Later Roman Empire 1987 ⇸ 3,d49: ^RCC 139 (1988,1) 94s (A. *Ferrua*).

d572 **Barnes** Timothy D., Constantine and EUSEBIUS 1984 ⇸ 65,9943 ... 3,9646: ^RGnomon 60 (1988) 45-50 (F. *Kolb*, also on his New Empire 1982).

d573 ᵀᴱBloch R., *Guittard* C., [➤ d596] ᵀᴱGouillart Christian, TITE-LIVE,
Histoire romaine VIII / [XXX (livre XL)]: Coll. Budé. P 1987/6, BLettres. cxxx-132 (d.)p.; 8 fig.; 2 maps. / cxxxvi-146 (d.)p., map, F 130. 2-
251-01335-2 / 3-4. – ᴿAntClas 57 (1988) 406-8.411 (J. *Wankenne*); Gnomon 60 (1988) 323-333 (E. *Burck*, VIII; auch über FRIES J.; BRISCOE J.).

d573* ᴱBraund David C., The administration of the Roman empire
[conference Exeter Dec. 1986]. Exeter 1988, Univ. iv-111 p.; 3 fig. £2.25
[GreeceR 36, 245, T. *Wiedemann*].

d574 Brind'Amour Pierre, Le calendrier romain; recherches chronologiques:
ÉtAnc Ottawa 2, 1983 ➤ 1,b366; 2,9650: ᴿAntClas 57 (1988) 519s (A.
Martin: bibliog. p. 337-365 parfois mordant).

d575 *Burian* Jan, Konstantin — ein ungetaufter Christ: SborBrno 33 (1988)
63-68; deutsch 88.

d576 Cary Earnest (*Foster* Herbert B.), [Cassius] DIO's Roman history: Loeb
Greek. L/NY 1914-27, Heinemann/Putnam. 9 vol.; I. reprint 1972:
0-674-99036-6; IX. 1972: -196-6 [L 0-434-99032-9; 177-5].

d577 Češka Josef, Římský stát a katolická cirkev ve IV. stoleti. Brno 1983,
Univ. 164 p.; 16 pl. – ᴿSborBrno 31 (1986) 195s (J. *Kudrna*).

d578 Christ Karl, Römische Geschichte und Wissenschaftsgeschichte 1982
➤ 3,d60: ᴿKlio 70 (1988) 562-4 (K.-P. *Johne*); SborBrno 31 (1986) 202s
(J. *Češka*).

d578* Cosi D. M., Casta mater Idaea; GIULIANO l'apostata e l'etica della
sessualità 1986 ➤ 3,d63: ᴿJHS 108 (1988) 247s (Polymnia *Athanassiadi*).

d579 *Courtney* Edward, The Roman months in art and literature; MusHelv
45 (1988) 33-57.

d580 Cunliffe Barry, Greeks, Romans and barbarians; spheres of interaction.
L 1988, Batsford. 243 p.; 76 fig. £20. 0-7134-5273-0. – ᴿAntiquity 62
(1988) 805 (J. *Collins*: 'Totally to ignore one's colleagues' work is the
greatest academic insult possible').

d581 *Dal Covolo* Enrico, Fonti epigrafiche del secondo-terzo secolo per uno
studio dei rapporti tra gli imperatori Severi e il cristianesimo: StPatav 35
(1988) 123-132; Eng. 132.

d582 *Daoust* J., Naufrage de l'Église d'Afrique du Nord [*Mandouze* André,
Notre histoire 14 (avril 1988)]: EsprVie 98 (1988) 518s.

d583 DIO C.: Brancacci Aldo, Rhētorikē philosophousa; DIONE Crisostomo
nella cultura antica e bizantina. R 1985, Bibliopolis. 352 p. Lit. 35.000.
– ᴿRBgPg 66 (1988) 119s (M. *Delaunois*).

d584 Demandt Alexander, Der Fall Roms 1984 ➤ 65,9953... 2,9656: ᴿOrpheus 7 (1987) 172-4 (S. *D'Elia*); RÉAnc 90 (1988) 423-435 (Émilienne
Demougeot).

d585 Develin R., The practice of politics at Rome 366-167 B.C.: Coll.
Latomus 188, 1985 ➤ 3,d66; Fb 1575: ᴿGnomon 60 (1988) 422-5 (H.
Kloft).

d586 *Dovere* Elio, Tradizione e storia sulle origini di Roma [*Poucet* J. 1985]:
Labeo 33 (1987) 91-97.

d587 Ducellier Alain, *al.*, Byzance et le monde orthodoxe. P 1986, A. Colin.
504 p.; ill. (32 color. pl.); maps. F 375. 2-200-37105-5. – ᴿAntClas 57
(1988) 533s (C. *Delvoye*).

d588 *Ducos* Michèle, Les passions, les hommes et l'histoire dans l'œuvre de
TITE-LIVE: RÉLat 65 (1987) 132-147; lat. 132.

d589 Dyson Stephen L., The creation of the Roman frontier 1985 ➤ 2,9657:
ᴿAmHR 91 (1986) 366s (E. *Luttwar*); ClasW 81 (1987s) 233 (R. B.
Hitchner); RArchéol (1988) 423s (R. *Rebuffat*).

d590 *Errington* R. Malcolm,   Constantine and the pagans: GRByz 29 (1988) 309-318.

d591 ᵀᴱ**Evelyn White** Hugh G.,   AUSONIUS: Loeb.   CM/L 1985-8 = 1919-21, Harvard/Heinemann.   I. xliv-396 p.; II. 367 p.   0-874-99102-9; 27-3 / L 0-424-99096-5; 115-5.

d592 *García Matarranz* Félix,   'Juliano el Apóstata', de Gore VIDAL ¿una interpelación o una provocación?:   LumenVr 37 (1988) 145-178.

d593 *Gaudemet* Jean,   Des 'droits de l'homme' ont-ils été reconnus dans l'empire romain?: Labeo 33 (1987) 7-23.

d594 ᴱ**Gentili** Bruno,   Giuliano 1984/6 ➤ 3,757:   ᴿRBgPg 66 (1988) 165s (Pascale *Lambrechts*); Sandalion 10s (1987s) 185s (Giovanna M. *Pintus*).

d595 ᴱ**Golubtsov** E. C. ✪ Culture of ancient Rome.   Moskva 1985, Nauka. 429 p.; 396 p. ill.   r 2,30. – ᴿEirene 25 (1988) 165-7 (J. *Burian*).

d596 ᵀᴱ**Gouillart** Christian,   Tite-Live, Histoire romaine; tome XXX; livre XL: Coll. Budé 1986 ➤ 3,d76:   ᴿGnomon 60 (1988) 119-123 (E. *Burck*); RÉLat 65 (1987) 302-4 (J.-L. *Ferrary*).

Grimal Pierre, Rome, la littérature et l'histoire (98 scripta 1938-1984) 1986 ➤ 202.

d597 ᵀ**Hamilton** Walter,   AMMIANUS Marcellinus [selections],   The later Roman Empire (A.D. 354-378), ᴱ*Wallace-Hadrill* A.   Hmw 1986, Penguin. 506 p. $11.   0-14-044406-8. – ᴿAncHRes 18 (1988) 114-9 (Alanna *Nobbs*).

d598 **Hussey** J. M.,   The Orthodox Church in the Byzantine empire: Oxford History of the Christian Church 1986 ➤ 2,9668; 3,d82:   ᴿJTS 39 (1988) 279-81 (D. *Obolenski*); Speculum 63 (1988) 172-4 (M. *Philippides*).

d598* ᵀᴱ**Jeffreys** Elizabeth & Michael,,   The chronicle of John MALALAS: Byzantina Australiensia 4.   Sydney/Melbourne 1986, Asn. Byz. St./Univ. xli-371 p. A$27. – ᴿJHS 108 (1988) 270s (M. *Whitby*).

d599 **Jerphagnon** Lucien, Julien 1986 ➤ 2,9669; 3,d83:   ᴿRBgPg 66 (1988) 166 (P. *Salmon*).

d600 *Johne* Klaus-Peter,   Colonus, colonia, colonatus: Philologus 132 (1988) 308-321.

d601 *Kolb* Frank,   Zu chronologischen Problemen der ersten Tetrarchie [Diocletians Christenverfolgung c. 300]: Eos 76 (1988) 105-125, deutsch.

d602 **Lane Fox** Robin,   Pagans and Christians 1986 ➤ 3,d87:   ᴿNYRevBooks (Mar. 12, 1987) 24-27 (P. *Brown*: 'Brave old world'; quantum jump in quality of scholarship, embodying L. ROBERT's lifelong researches) [NTAbs 32,346].

d604 ᴱ**Lieu** Samuel N. C.,   The emperor Julian; panegyric and polemic: Translated texts for historians, Greek 1, 1986 ➤ 2,9673; 0-85323-335-7. – ᴿByZ 81 (1988) 51s (G. *Fatouros*); ClasW 82 (1988s) 205 (M. *Di Maio*); JEH 39 (1988) 139s (J. A. *Crook*); RHE 83 (1988) 104-7 (P. A. *Deproost*).

d605 *Lightfoot* C. S.,   Facts and fiction — the third siege of Nisibis (AD 350): Historia 37 (1988) 105-125.

d606 **Loverance** Rowena,   Byzantium.   L 1988, British Museum.   72 p. 50 fig. + 40 colour. A$19 pa.   0-7141-1687-4 [AncHRes 19, 176, Lena *Cansdale*]; also Harvard 1988 [RelStR 15,267, Susan A. *Harvey*].

d607 **MacMullen** Ramsay,   Christianizing the Roman Empire 1984 ➤ 65,9961 ... 3,d93:   ᴿBijdragen 49 (1988) 333s (M. *Parmentier*); Latomus 47 (1988) 237s (M. *Simon* †).

d608 **MacMullen** Ramsay,   Constantine: Classical Lives [= Dial 1969]. L 1987, Croom Helm.   236 p.; 16 pl. A$33 pa.   0-7099-4685-6 [AncHRes 19, 173-6, B. H. *Warmington*]. – ᴿRÉAnc 90 (1988) 243s (J. *Fontaine*); RÉLat 66 (1988) 347s (J.-P. *Callu*); RPLH 62,1 (1988) 175s (R. *Braun*).

d609 **MacMullen** Ramsay, Corruption and the decline of Rome. NHv 1988, Yale Univ. xii-319 p. 0-300-04313-9.

d610 *Mayerson* Philip, A note on the Roman limes: 'inner' versus 'outer': IsrEJ 38 (1988) 181-3.

d610* ᴱ**Morrison** Karl F., The Church in the Roman Empire 1986 ⇥ 2,9679: ᴿClasW 81 (1987s) 238 (Gail P. *Corrington*).

d611 **Pack** Edgar, Städte und Steuern in der Politik Julians; Untersuchungen zu den Quellen eines Kaiserbildes: Coll. Latomus 194, 1986 ⇥ 2,9685; Fb 1900: ᴿAntClas 57 (1988) 531-3 (Janine *Balty*).

d612 **Poucet** Jacques, Les origines de Rome; tradition et histoire 1985 ⇥ 1,b390 ... 3,d101: ᴿAmHR 93 (1988) 127s (L. *Richardson*); GitFg 40 (1988) 164s (Anna *Pasqualini*).

d613 **Rawson** Elizabeth, Intellectual life in the Late Roman Republic 1985 ⇥ 2,9691; 3,d103: ᴿPhoenix 42 (Toronto 1988) 272-4 (G. W. *Bowersock*).

d614 **Richardson** J. S., Hispaniae; Spain and the development of Roman imperialism 218-82 B.C. C 1986, Univ. xi-218 p. £25. 0-521-32183-2. – ᴿÉchMClas 32 (1988) 430-2 (L. A. *Curchin*); JRS 78 (1988) 212-4 (J. W. *Rich*: outstanding).

d615 *Rogers* G. M., The crisis of the third century A.D.: Belleten 52,205 (1988) 1509-26.

d616 *Rousselle* R., The emperer Piso; ClasB 62 (1986) 5-7 [< BStLat 18,211].

d617 **Shahid** Irfan, Rome/Byzantium and the Arabs 1984 ⇥ 65,9974 ... 3,d107: ᴿJNES 47 (1988) 221-5 (F. M. *Donner*).

d617* **Shelton** Jo-Ann, As the Romans did; a sourcebook in Roman social history. Ox 1988, UP. xx-492 p.; 5 fig.; 5 maps. £13 pa. [GreeceR 36, 245, T. *Wiedemann*].

d618 **Siniscalco** Paolo, Il cammino di Cristo nell'impero romano 1984/7 ⇥ 64,a366 ... 3,d108: ᴿAsprenas 35 (1988) 175.

d619 **Solin** Heikki, *Salomies* Olli, Repertorium nominum gentilium et cognominum latinorum: Alpha-Omega A-80. Hildesheim 1988, Olms. x-474 p. [Also in alphabetical order of the *endings*.] 3-487-07986-0.

d620 **Stemberger** Günter, Juden und Christen im Heiligen Land; Palästina unter Konstantin und Theodosius 1987 ⇥ 3,d110; DM 45: ᴿMüTZ 39 (1988) 209s (P. *Stockmeier*).

d621 **Teitler** H. C., 'Notarii' and 'exceptores' 1985 ⇥ 3,d111: ᴿBTAM 14 (1988) 409s (P. *Hamblenne*).

d621* ᴱ**Vavřínek** Vladimír, From late antiquity to early Byzantium 1982/5 ⇥ 3,791: ᴿEirene 25 (1988) 134s (J. *Burian*).

d622 ᴱ**Veyne** Paul, A history of private life, I. From pagan Rome to Byzantium [1985] ᵀ*Goldhammer* A. 1987 ⇥ 3,d113; 0-674-39975-7: ᴿClasR 102 (1988) 339s (S. C. *Humphreys*); JRS 78 (1988) 224s (Catharine *Edwards*).

d622* **Virlouvet** Catherine, Famines et émeutes à Rome 1985 ⇥ 2,9632; 3,d35*: ᴿClasR 102 (1988) 171s (A. *Lintott*).

d623 ᴱ**Watt** W. S., Velleius PATERCULUS, Historiarum libri duo. Lp 1988, Teubner. xv-103 p. 3-322-00451-1.

d624 **Wells** Colin, The Roman Empire: Fontana history of the Ancient World 1984 ⇥ 65,9981 ... 2,9696; 0-00-635704-0. – ᴿAncHRes 18 (1988) 186-8 (C. E. V. *Nixon*).

d625 **Wieacker** Franz, Römische Rechtsgeschichte; Quellenkunde, Rechtsbildung, Jurisprudenz und Rechtsliteratur: HbAltW 10/3/1/1. Mü 1988, Beck. I/1, Einleitung ... ix-724 p. 3-406-32987-X.

d626 **Winkelmann** Friedhelm, Papst Leo I. und die sog. Apostasia Palästinas: Klio 70 (1988) 167-175.

XVIII. Archaeologia terrae biblicae

T1 **General biblical-area archeologies.**

d627 *Adams* William Y., Archeological classification; theory versus practice: Antiquity 62 (1988) 40-56.

d627* [40] Archäologische Dissertationen: ArchAnz (1988) 101-4; 2 infra.

d628 **Barker** Philip, Understanding archaeological excavation 1986 → 3,d119: ᴿAJA 92 (1988) 285 (Martha S. *Joukowsky*).

d629 **Binford** Lewis R., Die Vorzeit war ganz anders; Methoden und Ergebnisse der Neuen Archäologie [1983 ᴱ*Cherry* J., *Torrence* R.] Mü 1984, Harnack. 280 p.; 147 fig. – ᴿBonnerJbb 188 (1988) 533-5 (M. K. H. *Eggert*).

d629* **Binks** Gillian, *al.*, Visitors welcome; a manual on the presentation and interpretation of archaeological excavations. L 1988, Stationery Office for English Heritage. x-162 p.; ill. £25 pa. 0-11-701210-6 [Antiquity 63, 174, D. *Fowler*].

d630 ᴱ*Biran* A., Biblical Archaeology today 1984/5 → 3,902: ᴿBO 45 (1988) 413-8 (Hanna *Blok*, also on ᴱ*Lipiński* E., Land of Israel 1984/5); OLZ 83 (1988) 558-562 (G. *Pfeifer*).

d631 ᴱ**Clayton** Peter A., *Price* Martin J., The seven wonders of the ancient world. L 1988, Routledge. xvi-176 p. £18. 0-415-00279-6 [JRS 78,474].

d632 *Daoust* J., Archéologie et évangile [< *Piccirillo* M., TerreS (mai 1987)]: EsprVie 98 (1988) 307-9.

d633 ᴱ**Dowley** Tim, Discovering the Bible; archeologists look at Scripture 1986 → 2,9711; 3,336.d129: ᴿBTrans 39 (1988) 141s (D. J. *Wiseman*); CBQ 50 (1988) 293s (H. O. *Thompson*, with tit. pp.: not to prove the Bible but to illustrate it); ClasW 82 (1988s) 66 (J. *Russell*).

d634 *a)* **Eakins** J. Kenneth, The future of 'biblical archaeology'; – *b)* *Dever* William G., Impact of the 'new archaeology': → 20, ᶠCALLAWAY J., Benchmarks 1988, 441-454 / 337-368.

d634* *a)* *Epstein* Stephen M., 'Scholars will call it nonsense'; the structure of Erich von DÄNIKEN's argument [extraterrestrials 1968, Erinnerungen an die Zukunft = Chariots of the gods; 7 million copies sold, plus 18 million of his other books]; – *b)* *Hartmann* Nicholas, Atlantis lost and found; the ancient Aegean from politics to volcanoes: Expedition 29,2 (Ph 1987) 12-18 / 19-26; ill.

d635 **Erdélyi** I., *Sugár* L., Embert keresünk (In search of mankind). Budapest 1985, Magvető. 256 p.; 16 fig. – ᴿAcArchH 40 (1988) 423 (Z. *Kádár*: vivid).

d636 *a)* Excavation opportunities; prize find [Sepphoris mosaic]: BAR-W 14,1 (1988) 18-33.40s [*Logan* Nicole P. 35-37] ill.; – *b)* 2000 places de fouilleurs pour l'été; où ferez-vous des fouilles cet été? [la plupart en France; pays bibliques seul Acco-Hayonim p. 84]: Archéologia 235 (Dijon 1988) 78-86; 236 (1988) 64-66 ['2500 places'].

d637 **Fagan** Brian, Quest for the past; great discoveries in archaeology. Prospect Heights ɪʟ 1988 = 1978, Waveland. 0-88133-344-1 [OIAc D88].

d638 **Fleury** Michel,   Point d'archéologie sans histoire [Zaharoff Lecture 1986s]. Ox 1988, Clarendon. 32 p. £3. 0-19-951555-7 [Antiquity 62,401 adv.].

d639 **Fritz** Volkmar,   Kleines Lexikon der Biblischen Archäologie: Bibel-Kirche-Gemeinde 26. Konstanz 1987, Christliche VA. 202 p. DM 24,50 [ZAW 101, 315, H.-C. *Schmitt*].

d639* *Fritz* V.,   Archäologie, biblische: → 804, NBL Lfg 1 (1988) 154-160.

d640 **Gallay** Alain,   L'archéologie demain 1986 → 2,9715; 3,d135:   ᴿRArchéol (1988) 381-5 (P. *Courbin*, peu favorable; auteur ethnologue de l'Afrique; protohistoire).

d641 **Gening** V. F.,   ⊕ Objekt i predmet... The object and subject-matter of archaeology. Kiev 1983, Nauk. 224 p. – ᴿSovArch (1987,2) 273-280 (M. I. *Gladkikh*).

d642 ᴱ**Hodder** Ian,   The archaeology of contextual meanings: New Directions in Archaeology 1987 → 3,499:   ᴿAntiqJ 68,1 (1988) 128s (R. *Chapman*).

d643 *a) Homès-Fredericq* Denyse,   Archéologie et philologie; étude de leurs rapports; – *b) Tunca* Ö.,   Constructions philologiques et archéologiques; confrontation des schémas théoriques; – *c) Gubel* Eric,   Enkele uitzonderingsgevallen in de verhouding tussen tekst en monument in de fenicische beschaving; – *d) Missir* Livio,   Archéologie et philologie chez les Latins d'Orient aux XVIIᵉ et XVIIIᵉ siècles: → 763, Archéologie 1986, 1-11 / 21-31 / 45-57 / 247-258.

d644 **Jackson** Bruce,   Fieldwork. Champaign 1987, Univ. Illinois. xiii-311 p. $40; pa. $14.   0-252-01370-0; 2-7 [Antiquity 62,39].

d645 **Kenyon** Kathleen M., ⁴*Moorey* P.,   The Bible and recent archaeology 1987 → 3,d143:   ᴿArOr 56 (1988) 371s (B. *Hruška*); BInstArch 25 (1988) 130 (B. *Isserlin*); BL (1988) 31 (A. R. *Millard*); PrPeo 2 (1988) 197s (T. *Axe*); Themelios 14 (1988s) 108 (H. G. M. *Williamson*); ZDMG 138 (1988) 156s (G. R. H. *Wright*).

d646 **Klejn** Leo S.,   Archaeological typology [⊕], ᵀ*Dole* Penelope: BAR-Int 153, 1982 → 64,a404:   ᴿBInstArch sup 24 (1987) 48s (C. *Orton*).

d647 **Lance** H. D.,   The OT and the archaeologist [Ph 1981 = 1986 → 3,d145]. L 1983, Holy Trinity Church. xii-98 p.; 12 fig.; 2 pl. £5. – ᴿPEQ 120 (1988) 68s (R. *Chapman*).

d648 **McIntosh** Jane, *a)* The archaeologist's handbook. L 1986, Bell & H. [= ? The practical archaeologist 1986 → 2,9727; 3,d147]. – *b)* Guía práctica de arqueología. M 1987, Blume. 192 p. – ᴿBSAA 54 (1988) 533 (A. *Balil*).

d649 *a) McRay* John,   The Bible and archaeology; – *b) Wilson* John,   Archaeology and the New Testament ['What did Jesus look like?'; 'Where are the lake cities of Galilee?'; 'Tombs and bone-boxes'; Temple; 'Where was Jesus buried?']; – *c) DeVries* LaMoine, Household altars: → d633, Discovering 1986, 7-26 / 67-140 / 51-55.

d650 **Magall** Miriam, Archäologie und Bibel; wissenschaftliche Wege zur Welt des ATs 1986 → 2,9728; 3,d148:   ᴿBL (1988) 32 (a. G. *Auld*].

d651 **Manzella** Ivan D.,   Mestiere di epigrafista; guida alla schedatura del materiale epigrafico lapideo. R 1987, Quasar. 315 p.; 218 fig. Lit. 70.000. – ᴿCC 139 (1988,3) 203s (A. *Ferrua*: frutto del suo riordinamento del Lapidario del Museo Vaticano).

d652 *Masson* V. M.,   The rise of civilisation; general traits and local variations [Gordon Childe lecture May 1988], ᵀ*Judelson* K., *Steele* J.: BInstArch 25 (1988) 1-7.

d653 **Meyers** E.-M., *Strange* J. F., Les Rabbins et les premiers chrétiens; archéologie et histoire 1984 ➤ 65,a17*b* ... 2,9731: ᴿOrAnt 27 (1988) 155 (J. A. *Soggin*).

d654 **Millard** Alan,   Archeologia e Bibbia [Treasures 1985 ➤ 1,b433; 3,d150], ᵀ*Mariani* Giuseppe. CinB 1988, Paoline.   192 p.

d655 **Mitchell** T. C.,   [➤ d696] Biblical archaeology; documents from the British Museum.   NY 1988, Cambridge Univ. Press.   112 p. $34.50; pa. $13 [TDig 35,380]. 0-7141-1608-X.

d656 *Oesch* Josef M.,   Die fundamentalistische Versuchung im Spannungsfeld von Bibel und Archäologie; die biblische Welt als Kulisse für das Gotteswort [... W. F. ALBRIGHTs Programm]: BiKi 43 (1988) 119-122.

d657 *Rachet* Guy,   Dictionnaire de l'archéologie 1983 ➤ 64,806; 1,b443: ᴿLatomus 47 (1988) 701s (Arlette *Roobaert*).

d658 ᴱ**Rowlands** Michael, *al.*, Centre and periphery in the ancient world 1980/7 ➤ 3,836: ᴿBInstArch 25 (1988) 158-160 (T. *Watkins*).

d659 **Sabins** Walter E.,   With Bible and spade [drawings to enliven Bible verses]. Lima 1987, 'C.S.S.'   60 p. $4.50 [BToday 26,185].

d660 **Shanks** Michael, *Tilley* Christopher, *a*) Reconstructing archaeology; theory   and   practice.   C   1987,   Univ.   xvi-267 p.;   53   fig. £27.50. 0-521-30141-6. – ᴿAntiqJ 68 (1988) 335s (T. C. *Champion*); Arctos 22 (1988) 243-5 (C. *Bruun*). – *b*) Social theory and archaeology. C/Albuquerque 1987, Polity/Univ. New Mexico.   vii-243 p.; 10 fig. £25; pa. £9. 0-7456-0183-9; 4-7 / $16.   0-8263-1064-8; 5-6. – ᴿAntiquity 62 (1988) 473-482 (K. *Kristiansen*).

d661 **Snyder** G. F.,   Ante pacem; archaeological ... before Constantine 1985 ➤ 2,9740; 3,d166. – ᴿCrNSt 9 (1988) 430-4 (P. *Testini*); SecC 6,1 (1987s) 44-46 (A. T. *Kraabel*).

d662 **Soden** Wolfram von,   Bibel und Alter Orient, ᴱ*Müller* H.: BZAW 162, 1985 ➤ 1,247: ᴿBO 45 (1988) 638-646 (J. P. J. *Olivier*).

d663 ᴱ**Spriggs** Matthew,   Marxist   perspectives   in   archaeology   1984 ➤ 65,398 ... 2,9742: ᴿBInstArch 25 (1988) 171s (J. *Chapman*).

d664 *Tsetlin* Y. B., ⊕ On the reconstruction of archaeological stratification of neolithic sites: SovArch (1988,1) 5-16; Eng. 16; cf. 208-217, *Boryaz* V. N.; 218-224, *Anikovich* M. V.

d665 *a*) *Van Beek* Gus W.,   Excavation of tells; – *b*) *McRay* John,   Excavation of low-level settlement sites; – *c*) *Kautz* James R.ᴵᴵᴵ,   Archaeological surveys; – *d*) *Boraas* Roger S.,   Publication of archaeological reports: ➤ 20, ꟳCALLAWAY J., Benchmarks 1988, 131-167 / 169-177 / 209-222 / 325-333.

T1.2   **Musea, organismi, expositiones.**

d666 *Allam* S.,   Zur Stellung der Frau im Altägypten (Zum Katalog einer Ausstellung in Hildesheim) [Nofret die Schöne 1984s]: DiscEg 5 (1986) 7-15.

d667 *Amandry* Pierre,   Rapport sur l'état et l'activité de l'École française d'Athènes 1987: CRAI (1988) 643-657 [658-670, de Rome, *Richard* Jean].

d668 **Arnst** Caris-Beatrice, *Müller* Wolfgang,   Adolf ERMAN, ein grosser Berliner Gelehrter, 1854-1937, Gedenkausstellung 1987.   B 1987, Staatliche Museen.   24 p.; ill.

d669 Athens in prehistory and antiquity; exhibition on architecture and city planning, 15th century B.C.-6th century A.D.; Stoa of Attalus June-Sept. 1985. Athenai 1985, Ministry of Culture.   72 p.; ill.

d670 Autun Bibliothèque Municipale, Les collections égyptiennes dans les Musées de Saône-et-Loire, 27 mai-3 octobre 1988. Macon 1988, Maison des Ursulines. 388 p.

d671 **Bianchi** Robert S., *al.*, Cleopatra's Egypt; age of the Ptolemies; catalog of exhibition, Brooklyn Museum Oct. 7,1988...; Detroit Institute of Arts, Feb. 14, 1989...; München Kunsthalle, 8.VI... Brooklyn 1988, Museum. 0-87273-113-8 [OIAc N88].

d672 *Bianchi* Robert S., Ptolemaic art under glass [exhibition Brooklyn etc. 1989]: Archaeology 41,5 (1988) 56-59.

d673 **Bol** P. C., Liebighaus-Museum alter Plastik; Antike Bildwerke I., Bildwerke aus Stein und Stück von archaischer Zeit bis zur Spätantike. Melsungen 1983, Gutenberg. 347 p.; 393 fig. – ᴿAJA 92 (1988) 609s (S. *Lattimore*).

d674 **Bothmer** Bernard V. (*Hall* Emma S.), Antiquities from the collection of Christos G. Bastis: NY exposition. Mainz 1987, von Zabern. xii-340 p. 3-8053-00951-1.

Bourriau Janine, Pharaohs and mortals; Egyptian art in the Middle Kingdom: exposition 1988 → e177.

d676 **Braccesi** Lorenzo, *al.*, Veder greco; le necropoli di Agrigento; mostra internazionale, Agrigento, 2 maggio-31 luglio 1988. R 1988, Bretschneider. xxvi-397 p.; (color.) ill. 88-7062-646-6.

d677 Bulletin de la Société Française d'Archéologie Classique 20 (1986-7): RArchéol (1988) 199-220.

d678 Célébration du Centenaire (1890-1990) de l'École Biblique et Archéologique Française de Jérusalem [Lyon 20-22 nov.]: Biblica 70,576.

d679 **Coulson** W. D. E., Palestinian objects at the University of Minnesota, 1986 → 3,d183: ᴿMesop-T 23 (1988) 190s (P. *Arata Mantovani*).

d680 *D'Andria* Francesco, Civiltà d'Anatolia [mostra Milano-Roma-Calabria]: Archeo 28 (1987) 28-33; color. ill.

d681 ᴱ**Dahm** Werner, Jemen, 3000 Jahre Kunst und Kultur des Glücklichen Arabiens: Katalog Mü 1987. Innsbruck c. 1987, Pinguin. 490 p.; ill. 45 art. – ᴿJRAS (1988) 160-4 (A. F. L. *Beeston*: on the 14 pre-Islamic items).

d682 ᴱ**Delivorrias** Angelos, Greece and the sea, catalogue of the exhibition... Amst 1987. Athenai 1987, Benaki Mus. 397 p.; 308 fig. – ᴿAntClas 57 (1988) 541-3 (C. *Delvoye*).

d683 **Donadoni** Anna Maria, Il Museo Egizio di Torino; guida alla lettura di una civiltà. Novara 1988, de Agostini. 239 p.; color. ill. 88-402-0040-1.

d683* **Droste zu Hülshoff** Vera von, *Schlick-Nolte* Birgit, Aegyptiaca Diversa: Corpus Antiquitatum Aegyptiacarum, Museen der Rhein-Main-Region 1. Mainz 1984, von Zabern. 24-147 loose pages. – ᴿJAmEg 24 (1987) 157-9 (C. C. *Van Siclen*).

d684 *Gardin* Jean-Claude [*al.*], De l'Euphrate à l'Indus, les fouilles françaises; hommage à Philippe GUILLEMIN [directeur depuis 1971, 'des Relations culturelles' depuis 1980]: DossHA 122 (1987) 8s [-94; 95-98 English summaries; 15-20, Mari, *Margueron* J.-C.; 35s, Larsa etc., *Huot* J.; 63-66 Suse, *Perrot* J.; 86s, Aï Khanoum, *Grenet* F.].

d685 *González Echegaray* Joaquín, La labor arqueológica del Instituto Español bíblico y arqueológico de Jerusalén (1956-1988): EstBíb 46 (1988) 231-247 [... Dalal, Medeineh; Hawam, Khiam].

d686 **Goring** Elizabeth, A mischievous pastime, digging in Cyprus in the nineteenth century: exhibition Aphrodite's Island, Edinburgh Royal Museum 14.IV-4.IX.1988. E 1988, National Museums of Scotland. 0-948636-11-4 [OIAc D88].

d687 *Heim* Suzanne, From Ebla to Damascus; art and archaeology of ancient Syria [exposition touring US]: CanadMesop 14 (1987) 31-38.

d688 *Hellmann* Marie-Christine, Vrais ou faux? De l'original à la falsification; les multiples facettes de la copie [exposition Cabinet des Médailles]: Archéologia 236 (1988) 40-47; ill.

d689 **Hölbl** Günther, Le stele funerarie della collezione egizia, Museo archeologico nazionale di Napoli. R 1985, Ist. Poligrafico. Lit. 5000 [BO 45,755].

d690 **Ibrahim** Moawiye, The museum of Jordan heritage. Irbid 1988, Univ. Institute of archaeology and anthropology. 92 p.; ill.; ❹ 104-94.

d691 *Jaeger* Bertrand, [16] Expositions relatives à l'Égypte: GöMiszÄg 101 (1988) 91-93 [encore 7, p. 95s; encore 6: 103 (1988) 93s; et 4, 104 (1988) 95s].

d691* Jahresbericht 1987 des Deutschen Archäologischen Instituts: ArchAnz (1988) 701-772.

d692 *Khalbhol* Alex, Le chalcolithique au Musée d'Israël: MondeB 55 (1988) 54-56; ill. [56 (1988) 52-54, *Maoz* Rivka, Codex d'Alep].

d693 *Kim Jae-Kwan*, ❺ The foundation and the activities of the Korean Society for Ancient Near Eastern Studies: Orient 30,2 (1987) 69-74.

d694 *Lombardo* Giovanna, Bronzi iranici del Museo Nazionale d'Arte Orientale di Roma; nuove acquisizioni: VO 7 (1988) 189-200 [201-215, *D'Amore* Paola, altri oggetti].

d695 **Lo Porto** Felice G., La collezione cipriota del museo di Antichità di Torino: Archaeologica 64. R 1986, Bretschneider. 239 p.; 70 pl.

d696 **Mitchell** T. C., The Bible in the British Museum; interpreting the evidence. L 1988, British Museum. 112 p. ➤ (= ?) d655.

d697 **Moorey** P. R. S., The Ancient Near East. Oxford 1987, Ashmolean Museum. 56 p.; ill. £5. [JNES 47,78].

d698 **Needler** Winifred, Predynastic Egypt and archaic Egypt in the Brooklyn Museum [Henri de MORGAN 1906-8]: Wilbour Mg 9, 1984 ➤ 65,a61: ᴿJNES 47 (1988) 206-8 (B. *Williams*).

d698* **Nemet-Nejat** Karen R., Late Babylonian field plans in the British Museum [70 tablets; ➤ 63,d290]: StPohl 11, 1982 ➤ 63,a321 ... 1,b496: ᴿWeltOr 19 (1988) 173s (K. *Kessler*).

d699 *O'Connor* David, The earliest Pharaohs ˉand the [Philadelphia] University Museum; old and new excavations 1900-1987: Expedition 29,1 (Ph 1987) 27-39; 19 fig.

d700 *Petrakou* Vasileios C., ❻ *Ideographía* of the Archeological Society in Athens: ArchEph 126 (1987) 23-197.

d701 *Posener-Kriéger* Paule, Travaux de l'IFAO au cours de l'année 1987-1988: BIFAO 88 (1988) 181-233; pl. XVIII-XXIV [... Balat; Douch].

d702 ᴱ*Rassart-Debergh* Marguerite, Arts tardifs et chrétiens d'Égypte, Exposition Louvain-la-Neuve 6.IX – 23.X.1988, catalogue = Monde Copte 14s (1988) 108 p.

d702* **Roberts** D. Andrew, Planning the documentation of museum collections. C 1985, Museum Documentation. vi-568 p. £35. – ᴿComp Hum 21 (1987) 193-6 (C. S. *Peebles*).

d703 ᴱ**Siliotti** Alberto, Padova e l'Egitto [mostra 'Viaggiatori veneti alla scoperta dell'Egitto' 1987]. F 1987, Arte e Natura. 130 p.; ill.

d704 **Spanel** Donald, Through ancient eyes; Egyptian portraiture [exhibition April-July 1988]. Birmingham AL 1988, Museum of Art. xiii-159 p.; 48 fig.

d705 *Trümpelmann* Leo, Persepolis, ein Weltwunder der Antike, Ausstellung München Staatssammlung 1989: AntWelt 19,4 (1988) 60s; 1 fig.

d706 **Ucko** Peter, Academic freedom and apartheid; the story of the World Archaeological congress [Southampton-London Sept. 1986, though 400 delegates withdrew when Ucko decided to ban South Africans (including some who had conspicuously opposed apartheid) because the situation there is so unique as to take precedence over academic freedom]; pref. *Ascherson* Neal. L 1987, Duckworth. xiii-305 p.; 16 pl. £10. 0-7156-2180-7; pa. 91-2. – ᴿAJA 92 (1988) 441 (Pam J. *Crabtree*: so should Israel be excluded if Arabs threaten to withdraw?); Antiquity 62 (1988) 202-4 (P. V. *Tobias*).

d707 *Vesco* P. [*Will* E.], Rapport sur l'état et les activités de l'École Biblique et Archéologique Française de Jérusalem pendant l'année 1986-7/1987-8: CRAI (1988) 31-36/562-5.

d707* ᴱ**Völger** Gisela, *al*., Pracht und Geheimnis; Kleidung und Schmuck aus Palästina und Jordanien [Ausstellung Sammlung W. Kawar]. 1988, Joest-Museum [ZAW 101,323].

d708 La voie royale; 9000 ans d'art au Royaume de Jordanie; Exposition, Musée de Luxembourg déc. 1986. Paris 1986, Association française d'action artistique. 304 p. (color.) ill. – ᴿBL (1988) 35 (A. R. *Millard*).

d709 **Waterhouse** Helen, The British School at Athens; the first hundred years 1986 → 3,d213: ᴿClasR 102 (1988) 138s (D. *Hunt*).

d710 *Whitehouse* Helen, A forgery exposed [Oxford Ashmolean Canopic jar]: DiscEg 9 (1987) 63-67; 2 fig.; p. 68 phot. [Whitehouse sic].

ᴛ1.3   *Methodi*, **Science in archeology.**

d711 *Ahmed* Tariq S., *Majeed* Balsem S., Application of electrical resistivity method in Ctesiphon archeological site: Sumer 43 (1984) 237s, ❹ 245-257.

d712 *a) Aurenche* Olivier, *al*., Une séquence chronologique dans le Proche Orient de 12 000 à 3 700 ʙᴄ et sa relation avec les données du radiocarbon; – *b) Waterbolk* H. T., Working with radiocarbon dates in southwestern Asia; – *c) Damon* Paul E., The history of the calibration of radiocarbon dates by dendrochronology; – *d) Aitken* M. J., Potential for luminescence dating in the Near East: → 719, Chronologies 1986/7, 21-37 [683-7] / 39-59 / 61-104 / 183-7 [*al*.] ill.

d712* ᴱ**Bonnin** J. *al*., La protezione e conservazione del patrimonio culturale nelle zone a rischio sismico: Atti del corso europeo di formazione, Ravello 2-13.XII.1985 = PACT 18. Lv 1987. xvi-274 p. Fb. 3000.

d713 *a) Bourriau* Janine, Processing finds from excavations; what does the future offer us?; – *b) Guksch* Christian E., Ethnoarchaeology in Egyptology — a view from anthropology; – *c) Hintze* Fritz, Die Anwendung numerisch-taxonomischer Verfahren in der Ägyptologie; – *d) Riederer* Josef, The microscopic analysis of Egyptian pottery from the Old Kingdom: → 770, Äg. Kong. IV-1 1985/8, 11-18 / 41-51 / 101-122 / 221-230.

d715 *a) Clark* P. A., *Templer* R. H., Thermoluminescence dating of materials which exhibit anomalous fading; – *b) Croudace* I. W., *Williams-Thorpe* O., A low dilution, wavelength-dispersive X-ray fluorescence procedure for the analysis of archaeological rock artefacts: Archaeometry 30 (1988) 19-36 / 227-236.

d716 *Cole* Dan P.,   Ground penetrating radar — new technology won't make the pick and trowel obsolete: BAR-W 14,1 (1988) 38-40.

d717 *Dibble* Harold L., *McPherron* Shannon P.,   On the computerization of archaeological projects: JField 15 (1988) 431-440.

d718 *Eggert* Manfred K. H.,   Die fremdbestimmte Zeit; Überlegungen zu einigen Aspekten von Archäologie und Naturwissenschaft [... Radiocarbon]: Hephaistos 9 (1988) 43-59.

d718* *Gratien* Brigitte,   Premières constatations sur les empreintes de sceaux de la forteresse de Mirgissa: → 750, Nubian V, 1982/6, 89s + 2 fig.

d719 *Guibert* P., *al.*,   Datation par thermoluminescence...: RArchéom 12 (1988) 17-27.

d720 *Hedges* R. E. M., *Housley* R. A.,   Radiocarbon accelerator dating: RivArch 12 (1988) 91-95.

d721 **Kelley** Jane H., *Hanen* Marsha P.,   [The Americas] Archaeology and the methodology of science. Albuquerque 1988, Univ. New Mexico. 437-xiii p. $30.   0-8263-1030-3. – ᴿAntiquity 62 (1988) 824s (Alice B. *Kehoe*).

d722 *Kreindler* Herbert,   The application of SEM [scanning electron microscope] for authentication of an important find of Year Five shekels of the Jewish War: IsrNumJ 15 (1986s) 38-45; 1 fig.; pl. 12-13.

d723 *Le Gorgeu* Jean-P., *al.*,   Les images SPOT; une révolution dans la photo aérienne: Archéologia 237 (Dijon 1988) 26-37; (color.) ill.

d724 **Leute** Ulrich,   Archaeometry, an introduction to physical methods in archaeology and history of art. Weinheim 1987, VCH. 176 p. DM 38. – ᴿRArchéom 12 (1988) 101s (L. *Langouet*).

d725 **Lock** Gary, *Wilcock* John,   Computer archaeology: Shire Archaeology. Aylesbury, Bucks 1987, Shire.   64 p.   0-85263-879-9.

d726 *Lynn* Thomas C.,   Dating papyrus manuscripts by the AMS Carbon-14 method: BA 51 (1988) 141s; ill.

d727 *a) McGeehan-Liritzis* V., *Gale* N. H.,   Chemical and lead isotope analysis of Greek Late Neolithic and Early Bronze Age metals; – *b) Beauchesme* F., *al.*,   Ion beam analysis of copper and copper alloy coins: Archaeometry 30 (1988) 199-225 / 187-197.

d728 **Møller** Jens T., *al.*, Arkaeologi og geofysiske sporingsmetoder: Working Papers 14. K 1984, National Museum. 215 p., 77 fig. 87-480-0574-6. – ᴿFornvännen 83 (1988) 132-4 (M. *Östergren*).

d729 **Mommsen** Hans,   Archäometrie; neuere naturwissenschaftliche Methoden und Erfolge in der Archäologie 1986 → 3,d239: ᴿAJA 92 (1988) 600 (J. A. *Brongers*); BonnerJbb 188 (1988) 531-3 (G. *Eggert*); PraehZts 63 (1988) 381-4 (G. *Schneider*).

d730 *a) Müller* Maya,   Informatik und Ägyptologie; – *b) Keith-Bennett* Jean L.,   Canopics on Computer I; a proposed program; – *c) Grimal* Nicolas, *Hainsworth* Michael,   Recueil informatisé de textes égyptiens; – *d) Crozier-Brelot* Claude,   How to use the Pyramid Texts data bank; – *e) Stief* Norbert,   Hieroglyphen, Koptisch und andere Schriften; Textausgabe über Computer; – *f) Strudwick* Nigel,   The sharing of data in Egyptology: → 770, Äg. Kong. IV-1, 1985/8, 167-173 / 145-158 / 139-143 / 133-7 / 187-196 / 197-204.

d731 **Parkes** Penelope A.,   Current scientific techniques in archaeology 1986 → 2,9821; 3,d241: ᴿAJA 92 (1988) 285s (P. E. *McGovern*).

d732 **Piccareta** Fabio,   Manuale di fotografia aerea; uso archeologico: Stud. Arch. 42, 1987 → 3,d241*: ᴿAevum 62 (1988) 124-6 (Chiara *Tarditi*); Salesianum 50 (1988) 578 (B. *Amata*).

d733 *Porat* Naomi, *Seeher* Jürgen, Petrographic analyses of pottery from predynastic Maadi: MiDAI-K 44 (1988) 215-228; pl. 46-47.

d734 *Prince* Gene, Photography for discovery and scale by superimposing old photographs on the present-day scene: Antiquity 62 (1988) 112-6; 4 fig.

d735 **Riederer** Josef, Archäologie und Chemie; Einblicke in die Vergangenheit: Ausstellung Rathgen-Forschungslabors 1987s. B 1987, SMPK. 276 p.

d736 **Riley** Derrick N., Air photography and archaeology. L 1987, Duckworth. 151 p.; 102 fig. £20. 0-7156-2101-7. − RAntiqJ 68,1 (1988) 130s (D. R. *Wilson*); Antiquity 62 (1988) 384s (R. *Bewley*).

d737 *Scheel* Bernd, Infrarot- und Ultraviolettfotografie in der Dokumentation: DiscEg 12 (1988) 67-73.

d738 *Sheets* Payson, *Sever* Tom, High-tech wizardry [remote sensing]: Archaeology 41,6 (1988) 28-35; color. ill.

d739 **Shennan** Stephen, Quantifying archaeology. E/San Diego 1988, Univ./Academic. x-364 p.; 109 fig. £35; $34.85. 0-85224-460-6 / 0-12- 639860-7. − RAntiquity 62 (1988) 598s (R. *Whallon*); BInstArch 25 (1988) 167-9 (P. L. *Main*).

d740 *Tabbagh* Jeanne [*al.*], Traitement des données et élimination des valeurs erronées en prospection électrique en continu: RArchéom 12 (1988) 1-9 [11-16].

d741 **Taylor** R. E., Radiocarbon dating; an archaeological perspective. Orlando FL 1987, Academic. xii-212 p.; 54 fig. $39.50. 0-12-684860-2. − RAntiquity 62 (1988) 620-2 (H. T. *Waterbolk*); AntiqJ 68 (1988) 334s (N. D. *Balaam*: unsatisfactory); Radiocarbon 30 (1988) 131s (F. *Hole*).

d742 *Wærn-Sperber* Anna, Mössbauer spectroscopy and quantitative chemical analyses of early Cypriote black-topped pottery: OpAth 17 (1988) 191-7; 5 fig.

d743 *a)* **Weinstein** James M., Radiocarbon dating; − *b)* *Sever* Thomas L., Remote sensing; − *c)* *Strange* James F., Computers and archaeological research; − *d)* *Horowitz* Avraham, Palynology: → 20, FCALLAWAY J., Benchmarks 1988, 235-259 / 279-304; 4 fig. / 307-324 / 261-278; 2 fig.

d744 *Xenophontos* C. [there are two other authors indicated, but the first note begins 'I am grateful...'], Major and trace-element geochemistry used in tracing the provenance of Late Bronze Age and Roman basalt artefacts from Cyprus: Levant 20 (1988) 169-183; 5 fig. (maps).

d745 **Yoshimura** Sakuji, *al.*, Non-destructive pyramid investigation; (1) by electromagnetic wave method: Studies in Egyptian Culture 6 [0912-2206]. Tokyo 1987, Washeda Univ. 98 p.; 74 fig. $50.

T1.4 *Exploratores* − **Excavators, pioneers.**

d746 **Benvenuti** Gino & Gianfranco, Vita di Ippolito ROSELLINI padre dell'Egittologia italiana. Pisa 1987, Giardini. 129 p.; 9 fig. − RDiscEg 11 (1988) 43-51 (S. *Pernigotti*).

d747 *Bloedow* Edmund F., SCHLIEMANN on his accusers, II. A study in the reuse of sources: AntClas 57 (1988) 5-30.

d748 ECalder William M.III, *Traill* David A., Myth, scandal, and history... SCHLIEMANN 1986 → 2,9850*b*; 3,d279: RClasW 81 (1987s) 411s (A. A. *Donohue*); DLZ 109 (1988) 572-7 (K. *Zimmermann* curiously concludes that *without* defending Schliemann one must uphold the maxim *in dubio pro reo*); JHS 108 (1988) 259s (J. T. *Hooker*: his baseness was accompanied by merits wholly lacking in his attackers).

d749 **Carbonell** Charles-Olivier, L'autre Champollion: Jacques-Joseph CHAM-POLLION-FIGEAC (1778-1867): Champollion et son temps 3. Toulouse 1984, Inst. Politiques/Asiathèque. xiii-333 p. 2-903847-07-X.

d750 *Cannuyer* Christian, Les Aegyptiaca dans le Specimen litterarum de Jean-Baptiste GRAMAYE (1622): DiscEg 11 (1988) 7-13.

d751 **Dewachter** Michel, Un avesnois, l'Égyptologue [Achille C. T. É.] PRISSE D'AVENNES (1807-1879) (Études et documents inédits): Soc. Archéologique et Historique, Mémoires 30. Avesnes 1988, L'Observateur. 211 p.; 31 fig.

d752 *Dewachter* Michel, Nouveaux documents relatifs à l'expédition franco-toscane en Égypte et en Nubie (1828-1829): BSocFrÉg 111 (1988) 31-73; 27 fig.

d753 *Dewachter* Michel, Le paradoxe des 'papiers Salvolini' [plagiaire] de la Bibliothèque Nationale (MSS NAF 20450-20454) et la question des manuscrits des frères Champollion: RÉgp 39 (1988) 215-227.

d754 **Eccles** Robert S., E. R. GOODENOUGH 1985 ➤ 1,b565 ... 3,d264: ᴿAustralBR 36 (1988) 89 (N. M. *Watson*).

d755 *Fales* Frederick F., The two lions; LAYARD between Assyria and Venice: CanadMesop 16 (1988) 7-11.

d756 *Gran-Aymerich* Évelyne et Jean, Les grands archéologues: Archéologia 1988, p. 70-77 environ de chaque numéro: **231**, René CAGNAT; **233**, Fernand BENOIT; **235**, Michel CLERC; **240**, changement d'approche, 'Les Phéniciens et la recherche archéologique française', C. CLERMONT-GANNEAU, M. de VOGÜÉ, M. DUNAND ... A. POIDEBARD; finalement **241**, *Verbanck-Pierard* [p. 3; Verbank p. 74] Annie, Les grands collectionneurs 74-78.

d757 **Henze** Dietmar, Enzyklopädie der Entdecker und Erforscher der Erde [II. 1985 ➤ 2,9838*]; III Lfg, 12 La Ro-Low. Graz 1988, Ak. V. 135 p. Sch 650 [DLZ 110,237, K. *Biermann*].

d758 **Hodgkin** Thomas, Letters from Palestine 1932-6 [assistant to J. GARSTANG], ᴱ*Hodgkin* Edward C. [his brother]. L 1986, Quarter. xx-202 p. £12. – ᴿPEQ 120 (1988) 68 (P. *Bienkowski*).

d759 *a)* **Horn** Siegfried H., Promise deferred. Wsh 1987, Review & H. 95 p. $7 pa. – *b)* **Rochat** Joyce, Survivor [HORN biography]. Berrien Springs MI 1986, Andrews Univ. xii-332 p. $10. – ᴿAndrUnS 26 (1988) 204s (L. T. *Geraty*).

d760 **Jacq** Christian, Sur les pas de CHAMPOLLION; l'Égypte des hiéroglyphes. 1988, Trinckvel. 189 p.; color. ill. 2-9075-7300-4.

d761 *a)* *Jensen* Jørgen, C. J. THOMSEN og treperiodesystemet [inventor of the Stone Age, Bronze Age, Iron Age terminology 1824]; – *b)* *Street-Jensen* Jørn, Thomsen og tredelingen – endnu engang; – *c)* *Kromann* Anne, *Jensen* Jørgen S., C. J. Thomsen som numismatiker: ➤ 777, ᶠTHOMSEN C. 1988, 11-18 / 19-27 / 97-110 (110-2 bibliog.); Eng. 18 / 28 / 112.

d762 **Käfer** Markus, WINCKELMANNs hermeneutische Prinzipien: HeidFor 27. Heid 1986, Winter. 188 p. DM 76; pa. 52. – ᴿAntClas 57 (1988) 547s (Didier *Martens*).

d763 **Kramer** Samuel N., In the world of Sumer; an autobiography 1986 ➤ 2,9839: ᴿBAR-W 14,1 (1988) 10s (W. W. *Hallo*); CBQ 50 (1988) 688s (A. *Fitzgerald*); Salesianum 50 (1988) 395s (R. *Vicent*).

d764 ᴱ**Kurtz** Donna, [1885-1970, J. D.] BEAZLEY and Oxford [Wolfson College Lectures]: Committee for Archaeology Mg 10. Ox 1985. 71 p. – ᴿAntClas 57 (1988) 571s (D. *Martens*).

d765 *Laurens* Henry, Le concept de race dans le Journal Asiatique du XIXᵉ siècle: JAs 276 (1988) 371-380; Eng. 381, 'the concepts created by that little group of scholars have become tools in political struggles for millions of persons in Europe and outside Europe'.

d766 *Le Calloc'h* Bernard, La littérature orientaliste de langue française et Alexandre CSOMA de Kőrös [fondateur des études tibétaines]; essai de bibliographie: JAs 276 (1988) 189-200.

d767 *Leclant* Jean, La modification d'un regard (1787-1826); du Voyage en Syrie et en Égypte de [C.-F.] VOLNEY au Louvre de CHAMPOLLION: CRAI (1987) 709-729.

d768 **Levine** Philippa, The amateur and the professional; antiquarians, historians and archaeologists in Victorian England, 1838-1886. C 1986, Univ. x-210 p. £25. – ᴿBInstArch 25 (1988) 135s (W. D. *Cocroft*).

d769 *Lewis* Jack P., James Turner BARCLAY, explorer of nineteenth-century Jerusalem: BA 51 (1988) 163-170; ill.

d770 *Lipman* V. D., The origins of the Palestine Exploration Fund: PEQ 120 (1988) 45-54.

d771 *Marquet* J.-F., La quête isiaque d'Athanase KIRCHER: Études philosophiques 42 (1987) 243-254 [207-226, *Matton* S.; < RSPT 72,153].

d772 *a*) *Miller* J. Maxwell, Antecedents to modern archaeology; – *b*) *King* Philip J., American archaeologists; – *c*) *Davies* Graham I., British...; – *d*) *Benoit* Pierre, French...; – *e*) *Weippert* Manfred & Helga, German...; – *f*) *Mazar* Amihai, Israeli archaeologists: → 20, ᶠCALLAWAY J., Benchmarks 1988, 3-14 / 15-35 / 37-62 / 63-86 / 87-108 / 109-128; 5 fig.

d773 *Montagnes* Bernard, Le rétablissement de l'Ordre des Prêcheurs à Jérusalem; du Couvent Saint-Étienne à l'École Biblique: ArFrPraed 58 (1988) 361-422.

   Trent'anni archeologia OFM in Terra Santa → e638; k718.

d774 **Olmo Lete** Gregorio del, Semitistas catalanes del siglo XVIII: Orientalia Barcinonensia 5. Barc-Sabadell 1988, AUSA. 276 p. 84-86329-29-9.

d775 *Padró* Josep, Eduard TODA, diplomate espagnol, érudit catalan et égyptologue du XIXᵉ siècle: BSocFrÉg 113 (1988) 32-41 + 4 fig.

d776 *Patanè* Massimo, *a*) G. VICO [1668-1774] et l'Égypte: DiscEg 7 (1987) 51-58; – *b*) Trois orientalistes suisses méconnus [NINET John 1815-1895; BERTONI Moise 1857-1929; GENTIZON Paul 1885-1955]: GöMiszÄg 105 (1988) 83 seule.

d777 *Pernigotti* Sergio, Una Vita di Ippolito ROSELLINI [*Benvenuti* Gino & Gianfranco, Pisa 1987]: DiscEg 11 (1988) 43-51.

d778 *Piggott* Stuart, Sir Thomas BROWNE [c. 1624] and antiquity: OxJArch 7 (1988) 257-269.

d779 **Rogers** J. M., *Ward* R. M., Suleyman the Magnificent [creator of Jerusalem's present wall; but the book does not mention that this is a catalogue of exposition from Topkapı]. L 1985, British Museum. xiv-225; 164 fig.; map. £13. – ᴿJRAS (1988) 404s (G. *Goodwin*).

d780 **Seton-Williams** M. V., The road to El-Aquzein [biog.]. L 1988, Kegan Paul. 160 p.; map. 0-7103-0286-X.

d781 *Siliotti* Alberto, Sulle antiche piste d'Egitto [... pionieri; BELZONI]: ArchViva 7,1 (1988) 12-25; (color.) ill.

d782 **Simon** Robert, Ignác GOLDZIHER, his life and scholarship as reflected in his works and correspondence: Budapest/Leiden 1986, Hungarian Academy/Brill. 457 p.; 8 pl. *f*180. 963-7301-57-7 / 90-04-07561-5. – ᴿBO 45 (1988) 435-9 (J. van *Ess*).

d783 **Smits** Jan,   De Verenigde Nederlanden op zoek naar het Oude Egypte (1580-1780); De traditie gevolgd en gewogen.   Culemborg 1988, auct. 312 p.   90-9002156-6 [BO 45,474].

d784 *Stern* Shimon, ⊕ Titus TOBLER, 19th century researcher of Eretz Israel: CHistEI 48 (1988) 30-45 (-48 bibliog., with *Goren* Chaim); Eng. 193: a Swiss doctor (1806-77), he visited the Holy Land in 1835, 1845s, 1857, and 1865.

d785 **Thesiger** Wilfred,   The life of my choice [... Ethiopia, Sudan, Arabia]. L 1987, Collins.   459 p.; 30 pl.; 12 maps. £15. – ᴿJRAS (1988) 478s (C. F. *Beckingham*).

d786 *Traill* David A.,   How SCHLIEMANN smuggled 'Priam's treasure' from the Troad to Athens: Hesperia 57 (1988) 273-7.

d787 **Tranié** Jean, *Carmigniani* J.-C.,   Bonaparte, la campagne d'Égypte.   P 1988, Pygmalion.   315 p.; (color.) ill.   2-85704-278-7.

d787* *Vajda* L.,   LUSCHAN, Felix von, 11.VIII.1854-7.II.1924; Ausgrabung Zencirli: → 808, RLA 7,3s (1988) 179.

d788 *Voltolina* Piero,   Matthias Johann SCHULENBERG (1661-1747): RitNum 90 (Centenario 1988) 561-581.

d789 *Wertime* Richard A., The ingenious Homer THOMPSON: Archaeology 41,6 (1988) 36-43; ill.

d789* **Whitteridge** Gordon,   Charles MASSON of Afghanistan; explorer, archaeologist, numismatist and intelligence agent.   Wmr 1986, Aris & P. x-181 p. £18. – ᴿBSOAS 51 (1988) 574s (A. D. H. *Bivar*).

d790 [*Winnett* F. V., *al.*] *a*) Theophile James MEEK; – *b*) Jacob Meier HIRSCHFELDER d. 1902: CanadMesop 13 (1987) 30 / 15 (1988) 27.

d791 *Zorn* Jeffrey,   William F. BADÉ: BA 51 (1988) 28-35; 36-44, The Badé Institute, Berkeley.

T1.5   *Materiae primae* – **metals, glass.**

d792 *Argentum*, SILVER: ᴱBlair Claude [*Painter* Kenneth, ancient world] The history of silver.   L 1987, Macdonald.   256 p.; (colour.) ill. £30. 0-356-14067-9. – ᴿAntiqJ 68,1 (1988) 132s (A. *Grimwade*).

d792* *Giorgadze* Gregor G.,   On the word for 'silver' with reference to Hittite cuneiform texts: AltOrF 15 (1988) 77-82.

d793 *Nibbi* Alessandra,   Some oxhide-shaped ingots [two representing silver, three copper] from Theban tomb 80 [*Shedid* A. 1988]: DiscEg 12 (1988) 49-54; 1 fig.

d794 *Aurum*, GOLD: *Bosse-Griffiths* Kate, [spectroscopy analysis of] Gold-leaf from the shrine of Queen Tiye: DiscEg 6 (1986) 7-10; 1 fig.

d795 *Moorey* P. R. S.,   The technique of gold-figure decoration on Achaemenid silver vessels and its antecedents: → 4, ᶠAMIET P. = IrAnt 23 (1988) 231-246 + 5 fig.

d796 **Dörig** José,   Les trésors d'orfèvrerie thrace.   R 1987, Bretschneider. 32 p.; 14 fig.; 12 pl. – ᴿRArchéol (1988) 391 (C. *Rolley*).

d797 *Cuprum*, COPPER: *Nibbi* Alessandra,   Some Middle-Kingdom oxhide-shaped ingots in the Egyptian iconography and their name *nms* and Ashmolean ingot 1892-919 [a small ingot of bronze; *nms* is used (also) for ingots of electrum or lead]:   DiscEg 4 (1986) 41-65; 10 fig., III pl.

d797* *a*) *Knauf* Ernst A., *Lenzen* C. J.,   Edomite copper industry: → e824, Jordan III 1986/7, 83-88; – *b*) *Weisberger* G., Malachit: → 808, RLA 7,3s (1988) 273-5.

d798 *a*) *Lerberghe* Karel van, Copper and bronze in Ebla and in Mesopotamia; – *b*) *Zaccagnini* Carlo, Terms for copper and bronze at Ebla; – *c*) *Amadasi Guzzo* Maria Giulia, Remboursement et passage de propriété d'objets en métal précieux à Ébla: → 707, Wirtschaft 1986/8, 253-5 / 359s / 121-4.

d798* *a*) ᴱ**Maddin** Robert, The beginning of the use of metals and alloys. CM 1988, MIT. 393 p.; 300 fig. 0-262-13232-X [Antiquity 63,294]. – *b*) *Trejster* M. Y., ⊕ Le rôle des métaux à l'époque de la grande colonisation grecque: VDI 184 (1988) 17-42; franç. 42.

d799 EMERY: *Heimpel* W., [*al.*] Philological [and archaeological] evidence for the use of emery in the Bronze Age Near East: JCS 40 (1988) 195-201 [-210].

d800 *Ferrum*, IRON: (*Stos-*) *Gale*, N. & Z., The 'finger-printing' of metals by lead isotopes and ancient iron production at Timna: DiscEg 1 (1985) 7-13 + 2 fig.

d801 *a*) *Cleuziou* Serge, *Berthoud* Thierry, Early tin in the Near East [Afghanistan]; – *b*) *Pigott* Vincent C., The innovation of iron; – *c*) *Horne* Lee, Fuel for the metal worker [charcoal: Iran]: Expedition 25,1 (1982s) 14-19 / 20-25 / 6-13.

d801* ᴱ**Sperl** Gerhard, The first iron in the Mediterranean; Proceedings of the Populonia/Piombino Symposium 15-22.X.1983: PACT 21. Strasbourg 1988. 199 p. Fb. 2000. 0257-8727. – P. 39-45, *Piaskowski* Jerzy, The earliest iron in the world [N. Turkey before 2000; smelted, not meteorite].

d802 GRANITE: *Wilson-Yang* K. M., *al.*, The degradation of Egyptian 'black granite': JSStEg 15 (1985) 52-54.

d802* *Bullard* R. G., Stones, precious: → 801, ISBEnc³ 4 (1988) 623-630.

d803 *Lignum*, WOOD: **Radkau** Joachim, Holz; ein Naturstoff in der Technikgeschichte. Ha 1987, Rowohlt. 312 p. [Mundus 24,85].

d803* **Noël** Michel, *Bocquet* Aimé, Les hommes et le bois; histoire et technologie du bois de la préhistoire à nos jours. P 1987, Hachette. 347 p.; 41 fig.; 37 pl. F 218. 2-01-011502-8 [Antiquity 63,177, Maisie *Taylor*].

d804 *Raven* Maarten J., Magic and symbolic aspects of certain materials [wood, lead, dough] in ancient Egypt: VarAeg 4 (1988) 237-242.

d805 OBSIDIAN: *Hammo* Nimat B., Characterization of some Iraqi obsidian archaeological samples; Sumer 43 (1984) 239-242.

d806 *Yellin* Joseph, *Garfinkel* Yosef, The source of archaeological obsidian from a pre-pottery Neolithic B site at Yiftahel, Israel [from Göllü Dağ near Konya]: Paléorient 12,2 (1986) 99-104; 2 fig.

d807 *Vitrum*, GLASS: **Barag** Dan, Catalogue of Western Asiatic glass in the British Museum I, 1985 → 1,b607 ... 3,d293: ᴿOLZ 83 (1988) 551-4 (R.-B. *Wartke*); RAss 82 (1988) 83s (Annie *Caubet*).

d808 ᴱ**Bimson** M., *Freestone* I.C., Early vitreous materials: Occasional Paper 56. L 1987, British Museum → 3,d294; 191 p.; 63 fig. £10 pa. 0-86159-056-2. – ᴿAntiquity 62 (1988) 613s (J. *Henderson*).

d809 *Bimson* M., *Freestone* J.C., Some Egyptian glasses dated by royal inscriptions: JGlass 30 (1988) 11-15.

d810 **Harden** Donald B., *al.*, Glass of the Caesars 1987 → 3,d297: ᴿAntiquity 62 (1988) 400.402 (G.C. *Boon*).

d811 **Kaczmarczyk** Alexander, *Hedges* Robert E.M., Ancient Egyptian faience 1983 → 64,a586 ... 3,d299: ᴿJNES 47 (1988) 138-140 (E. *Guralnick*).

d812 [Scatozza] **Höricht** Lucia Amalia, I vetri romani di Ercolano: Soprintendenza Catalogo 1. R 1986, Bretschneider. 119 p.; 40 pl. – ᴿGnomon 60 (1988) 745-8 (Karin *Goethert-Polaschek*).

T1.6   *Silex, os*: **'Prehistory' flint and bone industries.**

d813 *Amirkhanov* Kh. A., ⊕ The Acheulian of southern Arabia: SovArch (1987,4) 11-23; 10 fig.; Eng. p. 23.

d814 **Breunig** Peter, 14 C-Chronologie des vorderasiatischen, südost- und mitteleuropäischen Neolithikums: Fundamenta 13. Köln 1987, Böhlau. 408 p.; 48 fig. [Mundus 24,46]. 3-412-04187-4.

d815 ᴱ**Cauvin** M.-C., Traces d'utilisation sur les outils néolithiques du Proche Orient [symposium Lyon 1982] 1983 ➤ 64,709... 2,9878: ᴿAJA 92 (1988) 443s (A. *Moore*).

d816 **Daniel** Glyn [lectures 1955-7, published 1962], ²*Renfrew* Colin, The idea of prehistory. E 1988, Univ. viii-221 p.; 37 portraits. £19.50. 0-85224-532-7. – ᴿAntiquity 62 (1988) 394s (C. *Chippindale*: unrevised; added chapters also unsatisfactory; the reviewer refers his own awaited The invention of words for the idea of prehistory).

d816* **Delporte** H., Fiches typologiques de l'industrie osseuse préhistorique, I. Sagaies. Aix-en-Provence 1988, Univ. 37 loose pages. F 120. 2-85399-193-8 [Antiquity 63,294].

d817 *Dennell* R. W., *al.*, Early tool-making in Asia; two-million-year-old artefacts in Pakistan [Riwat and Dina SE of Rawalpindi]: Antiquity 62 (1988) 98-106; 4 fig.

d818 *Eichmann* Ricardo, Die Steingeräte aus dem 'Riemchen-Gebäude' in Uruk-Warka: BaghMit 17 (1986) 97-130; 24 fig.

d819 *Epstein* Claire. *Noy* Tamar, Observations concerning perforated flint tools from chalcolithic Palestine: Paléorient 14,1 (1988) 133-141; 5 fig.; II pl.

d820 *Fletcher* Roland, Stone tools, space and hominid evolution: Antiquity 62 (1988) 532-5.

d821 ᴱ**Garrard** Andrew N., *Gebel* Hans G., The prehistory of Jordan; the state of research in 1986: BAR-Int 396. Oxford 1988. 2 vol. £36. 0-86054-511-3. – ᴿAntiquity 62 (1988) 814-6 (A. E. *Marks*).

d822 **Gebel** Hans G., Das akeramische Neolithikum [nicht nur Türkei; bis Pakistan!] Vorderasiens; Subsistenzformen and Siedlungsweisen: TAVO B-52. Wsb 1984, Reichert. 521 p. DM 110. – ᴿBASOR 271 (1988) 87s (G. *Rollefson*).

d823 **Goring-Morris** A. N., At the edge; terminal pleistocene hunter-gatherers in the Negev and Sinai [survey 1979ss]: BAR-Int 361, 1987 ➤ 3,d313; £30: ᴿIsrEJ 38 (1988) 285s (I. *Gilead*).

d824 *Kaufman* D., New radiocarbon dates for the geometric Kebaran [Mt. Carmel]: Paléorient 14,1 (1988) 107-9.

d825 *Köhler-Rollefson* I., The aftermath of the Levantine neolithic revolution in the light of ecological and ethnographic evidence: Paléorient 14,1 (1988) 87-93; franç. 87.

d826 **Leroi-Gourhan** André †, ᴱ*Garanger* José, Dictionnaire de la préhistoire. P 1988, PUF. 1222 p.; ill.; maps. 2-13-041459-1.

d827 **Lewin** Roger, Bones of contention; controversies in the search for human origins. NY 1987, Simon & S. 348 p.; ill. £15. 0-671-52688-X [Antiquity 62,420].

d828 *Lindman* Gundela,   Power and influence in the Late Stone Age; a discussion of the interpretation of the flint dagger material: OxJArch 7 (1988) 121-138; 11 fig.

d829 **Miller** Robert,   Flintknapping and arrowhead manufacture at Tell Hadidi, Syria.   Milwaukee 1985, Museum. – [R]PEQ 120 (1988) 71s (C. *Bergman*: 'no price'; and no pages).

d830 **Muhesen** Sultan,   L'Acheuléen récent évolué de Syrie: BAR-Int 248, 1985 ► 1,b629;   £15:   [R]BInstArch sup 24 (1987) 31s (L. *Copeland*).

d831 *Olszewski* Deborah I.,   *a*) The North Syrian late epipaleolithic and its relationship to the Natufian complex: Levant 20 (1988) 127-137; 5 fig.; – *b*) A reassessment of average lunate length as a chronological marker: Paléorient 12,1 (1986) 39-44.

d832 *Plisson* Hugues, *Mauger* Manuelle,   Chemical and mechanical alteration of [flint] microwear polishes; an experimental approach: Helinium 28 (Wetteren 1988) 3-16.

d833 *Ronen* Avraham,   Modern-type, intelligent behaviour prior to 70 000 years ago: ► 499, Holy Land 1986/8, 3-8.

d834 [E]**Roodenberg** J.,   Aceramic Neolithic in S. E. Turkey, Round Table, Istanbul Netherlands Institute 2-4.VI.1986 = Anatolica 15 (1988). vii-232 p.; ill.; p. 1-24, *Aurenche* O., *Calley* Sylvie, L'architecture; 37-48, *Helmer* D., Animaux de Cafer; 49-67, plants, W. van *Zeist*.

d835 *Rosen* Steven A.,   A preliminary note on the Egyptian component of the chipped stone assemblage from Tel 'Erani: IsrEJ 38 (1988) 105-116; 6 fig.

d836 *Shackley* Myra,   Hot springs and 'glazed' flints; a controversial phenomenon observed on spring-mound artefacts in the Near East: Levant 20 (1988) 119-126; 4 fig. [8 sites, 5 in NW Africa].

d837 *Shea* John J., Spear points from the Middle Paleolithic of the Levant [Kebara]: JField 15 (1988) 441-7; 7 fig.

d838 *Simmons* A. H., *al*., Abu Suwwan [flints, near Jarash]... neolithic: ADAJ 32 (1988) 15-25; 5 pl.

d839 **Vaughan** P. C.,   Use-wear analysis of flaked stone tools.   Tucson 1985, Univ. Arizona.   204 p.; ill. $49.50. – [R]BInstArch 25 (1988) 182s (Kathryn *Ataman*).

d839* **Whittle** Alasdair,   Problems in Neolithic archaeology.   C 1988, Univ. xiv-232 p.; 74 fig. £27.50.   0-521-35121-9 [Antiquity 63,634, A. J. *Ammerman*].

T1.7 **Technologia antiqua.**

d840 *Bonnet* Charles,   Un atelier de bronziers à Kerma: ► 750, Nubian V, 1982/6, 19-22; 3 fig.

d841 *Castel* Georges, *Soukiassian* Georges,   Les mines de galène pharaoniques du Gebel el-Zeit [mer Rouge entre Hourghada et Ras Gharib] (Égypte): BSocFrÉg 112 (1988) 37-53; 5 fig.

d842 [E]**Curtis** John E.,   Bronzeworking centres of Western Asia c. 1000 – 539 B.C. [British Museum Colloquium 1986].   L 1988, Kegan Paul. 362 p.; 183 fig. 0-7103-0274-6. – Phoenicia 227-250, *Falsone* G.; Palestine 251-270, *Tubb* J. N.; West Semitic texts 271-284, *Mitchell* T. C.; Egypt 297-309, *Leahy* M. A.; N. Syria 193-225, *Winter* I. J.; *al*. Assyria.

d843 **Drenkhahn** Rosemarie,   Die Handwerker und ihre Tätigkeit im alten Ägypten: ÄgAbh 31.   Wsb 1976, Harrassowitz.   xii-170 p.; 59 fig. 3-447-01745-7. – [R]OLZ 83 (1988) 156s (F. *Steinmann*).

d844 *Gwinnett* A. John, *Gorelick* Leonard, The change from stone drills to copper drills in Mesopotamia; an experimental perspective: Expedition 29,3 (1987) 15-23; ill. [25,3 (1982s) 40-47].

d845 *Kaplan* G. M., ❷ L'invention des tours antiques pour le travail de la pierre, des métaux non-ferreux et des alliages: VDI 186 (1988) 94-118; franç. 115.

d846 *Kingery* W. David, *al.*, The beginnings of pyrotechnology, II. Production and use of lime and gypsum plaster in the pre-pottery neolithic Near East: JField 15 (1988) 219-244; 14 fig.

d847 *Knauf* Ernst A., Mirrors as mining tools: Levant [17 (1985) 106, *Beit-Arieh* I.] 20 (1988) 244.

d848 *Levy* Thomas E., *Shalev* Sariel, Prehistoric metalworking in the southern Levant; archaeometallurgical and social perspectives: World-Arch 20 (1988s) 352-367; 5 fig.; bibliog. p. 367-372.

d849 **Maréchal** Jean-René, La préhistoire de la métallurgie et ses prolongements. Avignon 1983, RArchéol. 413 p.; 8 fig. F 98,50. – ᴿBInst-Arch 25 (1985) 138-140 (P. T. *Craddock*).

d850 **Neumann** Hans, Handwerk in Mesopotamien 1987 ⇒ 3,d330: ᴿOLZ 83 (1988) 667-9 (H. *Limet*).

d851 **Nibbi** Alessandra, Ancient Egyptian pot bellows and oxhide ingot shape. Ox 1987. – ᴿDiscEg 10 (1988) 95-97 (Rosemarie *Drenkhahn*).

d852 *Paszthory* Emmerich, Laboratorien in ptolemäischen Tempelanlagen; eine naturwissenschaftliche Analyse: AntWelt 19,2 (1988) 2-20; 21 (color.) fig.

d853 **Pickles** Sydney, Metallurgical changes in Late Bronze Age Cyprus: Occasional Papers 17. E 1988, Univ. Dept. Archaeology. 0144-3313 [OIAc D88].

d854 *Preti* Alberto, L'estrazione degli obelischi egizi: Strenne. T 1988, SEI. 93 p.; 35 pl. Lit. 18.000. 88-05-05051-2.

d855 *Rankin* David I., The mining lobby at Athens: AncS 19 (1988) 189-205.

d856 *Scheel* Bernd, Anmerkungen zur Kupferverhüttung und Kupferraffination im alten Ägypten: DiscEg 11 (1988) 87-97; 1 fig.

d856* ᴱ**Wagner** Günther A., *Weisgerber* Gerd, Antike Edel- und Buntmetallgewinnung auf Thasos: Der Anschnitt, Zts für Kunst und Kultur im Bergbau 6. Bochum 1988, Deutsches Bergbau-Museum. 279 p.; 291 fig.; 8 foldout plans. 3-921533-40-6 [Antiquity 63,470].

d857 **White** Kenneth D., Greek and Roman technology: Aspects of Greek and Roman life, 1984 ⇒ 65,a198 ... 1,b660: ᴿAncSRes 17 (1987) 112-4 (B. *Croke*); Latomus 47 (1988) 720s (J. *Debergh*).

T1.8 **Architectura.**

d858 **Boysan-Dietrich** Nilüfer, Das hethitische Lehmhaus 1987 ⇒ 3,d339: ᴿWeltOr 19 (1988) 181-4 (V. *Haas*).

d859 **Braemer** Frank, L'architecture domestique du Levant à l'âge du Fer: RCiv Cah 8, 1982 ⇒ 63,a253 ... 2,9912: ᴿZDPV 104 (1988) 171-4 (Helga *Weippert*).

d860 *Byrd* B. F., *Banning* E. B., Southern Levantine pier houses; intersite architectural patterning during the Pre-Pottery Neolithic B: Paléorient 14,1 (1988) 65-72.

d861 ᴱ**Callebat** L., *Fleury* P., Vɪᴛʀᴜᴠᴇ X, 1986 ⇒ 2,9913; 3,d341: ᴿRÉLat 65 (1987) 304s (J. *Beaujeu*).

d862 **Chitham** Robert, Die Säulenordnungen der Antike und ihre Anwendung in der Architektur. Stu 1987, Dt. Verl. Anst. 159 p.; 50 fig.

d863 *a*) *Coulton* J.J., Greek architecture [building techniques]; – *b*) *Ling* Roger, Roman architecture; – *c*) *Packer* James E., Roman building techniques; – *d*) *Landels* John G., Engineering; ➤ 444, Mediterranean. 1988, 1653-1670 [277-297] / 1671-1690 / 299-321 / 323-352.

d864 **Damerji** Muzayad S. B., The development of the architecture of doors and gates in ancient Mesopotamia [Die Entwicklung: diss. Mü 1972], ᵀ*Takase* Tomio, *Okada* Yasuyoshi. Tokyo 1987, Kokushikan Univ. 4-930821-89-4 [OIAc D88].

d865 *Dodge* Hazel, Decorative stones for architecture in the Roman Empire: OxJArch 7 (1988) 65-80; 8 fig.

d866 **Downey** Susan, Mesopotamian religious architecture. Princeton 1988, Univ. xviii-198 p. 0-691-03589-X [BO 45,478].

d867 *Ellis* Simon P., The end of the Roman house [and the way of life of the ancient world: 550 A.D.]: AJA 92 (1988) 565-576; 5 fig.

d868 **Fagerström** Kåre, Greek Iron Age architecture; development through changing times: SIMA 81. Göteborg 1988, Åström. 172 p.; 125 + 101 fig. 91-86098-78-0.

d869 *Finney* Paul C., Early Christian architecture; the beginning (a review article) [*Deichmann* F. in Fs. KLAUSER 1964; *Rordorf* W. 1964; *Krautheimer* R. 1975; ... *White* M., diss. 1982]: HarvTR 81 (1988) 319-339.

d870 **Franz** Heinrich G., Palast, Moschee und Wüstenschloss 1984: I. ➤ 65,a217; II. ➤ 1,b680: [nicht *Heinrich* Gerhard F. wie ➤ 2,9922]: ᴿOLZ 83 (1988) 590-2 (E. *Baer*).

d871 **Ginouvès** René, *Martin* Roland, Dictionnaire méthodique de l'architecture grecque et romaine, I. Matériaux... 1986 ➤ 2,9915; 3,d346: ᴿLatomus 47 (1988) 242 (J. *Debergh*); RArchéol (1988) 128-130 (J.-F. *Bommelaer*); RBgPg 66 (1988) 204s (R. *Lambrechts*); RÉLat 65 (1987) 377s (G. *Sauron*).

d872 *a*) *Gye* D. H., Arches and domes in Iranian Islamic building; an engineer's perspective; – *b*) *Hillenbrand* Robert, Political symbolism in early Indo-Islamic mosque architecture; the case of Ajmīr: Iran 26 (1988) 129-144; 16 fig. / 105-117; 7 fig.; XII pl.

d873 ᴱ**Hägg** Robin, *Konsola* Dora, Early Helladic architecture and urbanization: SIMA 76, 1985/6 ➤ 3,817: ᴿBO 45 (1988) 661-8 (J. B. *Rutter*).

d874 **Hajnóczi** Julius Gy., Ursprünge der europäischen Architektur; Geschichte von Bautätigkeit und Baukunst im Altertum, I. Alter Orient und Randkulturen. oB 1986, VEB-Bauwesen. 263 p.; 422 fig. M56. – ᴿOLZ 83 (1988) 16-18 (C. *Tietze*).

d875 *Hamiaux* Marianne, Les éléments d'architecture de Magnésie du Méandre conservés au Musée du Louvre: RArchéol (1988) 83-108; 31 fig.

d876 **Heinrich** Ernst, Die Paläste im alten Mesopotamien: DAI Denkmäler antiker Architektur 15, 1984 ➤ 65,a222; 2,9921: ᴿJNES 47 (1988) 210-4 (Sally *Dunham*: companion to his book on Temples); ZAss 78 (1988) 151-4 (W. *Schirmer*).

d877 *Hellmann* Marie-Christine, À propos d'un lexique des termes d'architecture grecque: ➤ 698, Comptes 1986/8, 239-261.

d878 *Herr* Larry G., Tripartite pillared buildings and the market place in Iron Age Palestine: BASOR 272 (1988) 47-65; 4 fig.

d879 **Herzog** I., Stadttor 1986 ➤ 2,9923: 3,d349: ᴿMesop-T 23 (1988) 189s (P. *Arata Mantovani*); RStFen 16 (1988) 257s (anche Piera *Arata*

Mantovani); ZAss 78 (1988) 154-6 (G. R. H. *Wright*); ZDMG 138 (1988) 373s (R. *Hachmann*).

d880 *Holloway* R. Ross, Early Greek architectural decoration as functional art: AJA 92 (1988) 177-183; 4 fig.

d881 **Hult** G., Bronze Age ashlar...: SIMA 66, 1983 → 64,a640 ... 3,d352: ^RAulaOr 6 (1988) 278s (M. *Molist Montaña*); Babesch 62 (1987) 168s (T. L. *Heres*).

d882 *Kleiss* W., Aspekte urartäischer Architektur: → 4, ^FAMIET P. = IrAnt 33 (1988) 181-191; 27 fig.

d883 *Klemm* Rosemarie, Vom Steinbruch zum Tempel; Beobachtungen zur Baustruktur einiger Felstempel der 18. und 19. Dynastie im ägyptischen Mutterland: ZägSpr 115 (1988) 41-51; 8 fig.

d884 *Koščurnikov* S. G., Types of construction and prices for them in deeds of the Old Babylonian city Dilbata: Istorija e Filologija Drevnego i Srednevekova Vostoka (Moskva 1987) 12-18.

d885 **Lauter** Hans, Die Architektur des Hellenismus. Da 1986, Wiss. xii-329 p.; 80 fig.; 48 pl. – ^RBonnJbb 188 (1988) 562-6 (J. *Ganzert*); Gnomon 60 (1988) 279-281 (P. *Gros*).

d886 **Lauter-Bufe** Heide, Die Geschichte des sikeliotisch-korinthischen Kapitells; der sogenannte italisch-republikanische Typus. Mainz 1987. 105 p.; 48 pl. – ^RBSAA 54 (1988) 537-540 (M.ª Angeles *Gutierrez Behemerid*).

d887 **Leick** Gwendolyn, A dictionary of ancient Near Eastern architecture. L 1988, Routledge. xx-261 p.; 175 fig. £35. 0-415-00240-0 [Antiquity 62,689].

d888 ^E**Lévy** E., Le système palatial en Orient 1985/7 → 3,825: ^RClasR 102 (1988) 108 (N. *Marinatos*).

d889 *Lohuizen-Mulder* Mab van, Early Christian lotus-panel capitals and other so-called impost capitals: Babesch 62 (1987) 131-151; 13 fig.

d890 **MacDonald** William L., The architecture of the Roman Empire [1. 1965 ²1982 → 64,a646]; 2, An urban appraisal: Yale Publ. Hist. Art 35, 1986 → 2,9989; 3,d356: ^RAJA 92 (1988) 147-9 (J. E. *Packer*); Archaeology 41,4 (1988) 70-72 (W. E. *Mierse*); ClasR 102 (1988) 121s (G. B. *Waywell*); ClasW 81 (1987s) 60s (H. V. *Bender*); RArchéol (1988) 420-2 (P. *Gros*).

d891 *Macdonald* Colin F., *Driessen* Jan M., The drainage system of the domestic quarter in the palace of Knossos: AnBritAth 83 (1988) 235-258; 7 fig.; pl. 31-40.

d892 *Mango* M. M., The architecture of the Syriac churches: → 745, Architecture of the Eastern Churches 1981 ...

d892* *Margueron* Jean-Claude, Évolution de la structure des murs en Syrie: → 707, Wirtschaft 1986/8, 47-61 + 4 maps.

d893 *a) Margueron* Jean-Claude, Quelques principes méthodologiques pour une approche analytique de l'architecture de l'Orient Antique; – *b) Gregori* Barbara, Sullo sviluppo delle fortificazioni a casematte in Anatolia e Siria–Palestina: CMatArch 1 (R 1986) 261-285; fig. 46-53 / 213-260; fig. 39-46.

d893* **Merten** Elke W., Bäder und Badegepflogenheiten in der Darstellung der Historia Augusta 1983 → 3,d359: ^RAnzAltW 41 (1988) 64-66 (O. *Hiltbrunner*); Latomus 47 (1988) 707 (P. *Salmon*).

d894 **Pesando** Fabrizio, Oikos e ktesis; la casa greca in età classica. Perugia 1987, Quasar. 206 p.; ill.

d895 *Raeder* Joachim, VITRUV, de arch. VI 7 (aedificia Graecorum) und die hellenistische Wohnhaus- und Palastarchitektur: Gymnasium 95 (1988) 316-368.

d895* *Reber* K., Aedificia graecorum; zu VITRUVS Beschreibung des griechischen Hauses: ArchAnz (1988) 653-666.

d896 *Reich* Ronny, The hot bath-house (balneum), the Miqweh and the Jewish community in the Second Temple period: JJS 39 (1988) 102-7.

d896* **Richardson** Lawrence, Pompeii, an architectural history. Baltimore 1988, Johns Hopkins Univ. xxxviii-445 p.; 53 fig. £32 [GreeceR 36,246, B.A. *Sparkes*].

d897 *Richardson* Peter, Religion, architecture and ethics; some first century case studies: HorBT 10,2 (1988) 19-49.

d898 *Roaf* Michael, 'Ubaid houses and temples: Sumer 43 (1984) 80-90; 25 fig.

d899 **Roik** Elke, Das altägyptische Wohnhaus und seine Darstellung im Flachbild: EurHS 38/15. Bern 1988, Lang. vi-220 p.; vol. of 256 pl. Fs 88. 3-8024-0163-6 [BO 45,473].

d900 **Romano** Elisa, La capanna e il tempio, VITRUVIO o della architettura: Lett. clas. 15. Palermo 1987, Palumbo. 233 p. – ᴿBStLat 18 (N 1988) 134s (Maria Nicla *Diaferio*); Orpheus 9 (1988) 354-8 (G. *Polara*).

d901 **Romaniuk** Kazimierz, ❷ O budowaniu w Biblii. Wsz 1988, Rada Prymasowska Budowy Kościołów.

d902 **Seiler** Florian, Die griechische Tholos. Mainz 1986, von Zabern. vi-168 p.; 80 fig. DM 98. – ᴿClasR 102 (1988) 350-2 (R.A. *Tomlinson*).

d903 *Strocka* Volker M., Wechselwirkungen der stadtrömischen und kleinasiatischen Architektur unter Trajan und Hadrian: IstMitt 38 (1988) 291-307; pl. 38-47.

d904 **Tigerman** Stanley, The architecture of exile. NY 1988, Rizzoli. 192 p.; ill.; p. 162-181, various reconstructions of Herod's Temple. 0-8478-0902-1.

d905 *Tunca* Önhan, Remarques sur l'architecture des téménos d'Uruk et d'Ur à la période de la IIIᵉ dynastie d'Ur: BaghMit 17 (1986) 255-292; 7 fig.

d906 *Ünal* Ahmet, 'You should build for eternity' [KuB 31.100 obv. 10]; new light on the Hittite architects and their work: JCS 40 (1988) 97-106.

d907 *Vérité* Jacques, Restauration d'un arc romain en Tunisie: Archéologia 240 (1988) 52-61.

d908 *a)* *Waelkens* Marc [→ g505], The adoption of Roman building techniques in the architecture of Asia Minor; – *b)* *Dodge* Hazel, Brick construction in Roman Greece and Asia Minor: → 454, Roman architecture 1987, 94-105 / 106-116.

d909 **Wikander** Charlotte, Sicilian architectural terracottas, a reappraisal: ActaRom 8/15. Sto 1986, Åström. 51 p.; 14 fig. Sk 90. 91-7042-118-8. – ᴿBO 45 (1988) 657-9 (R.R. *Knoop*).

d910 *Wikander* Örjan, Ancient roof-tiles — use and function: OpAth 17 (1988) 203-216; 7 fig.

T1.9 *Supellex*; **furniture**; **objects of daily life.**

d911 **Allam** S., Some pages from... everyday life in ancient Egypt; Prism 1. Cairo 1985, Ministry of Culture. 132 p.; 71 fig. – ᴿDiscEg 6 (1986) 87s (A. *Dodson*: not about domestic and social life, but about the legal system; i. status of women ...).

d912 **Bühlmann** Walter, Wie Jesus lebte; vor 2000 Jahren in Palästina; Wohnen, Essen, Arbeiten, Reisen. Stu 1987, Rex. 139 p.; 173 fig. DM 32. – ᴿErbAuf 64 (1988) 484 (B. *Schwank*).

d913 **Dowley** Tim, Voyage dans la vie quotidienne aux temps bibliques, ᵀ. Guebwiller 1987, Ligue pour la lecture de la Bible. 44 p.; ill. R. Scott. F 59. 2-85031-129-4. – ᴿÉTRel 63 (1988) 448s (D. *Lys*).

d914 **Gower** Ralph, The new [*Wright* F.²ʳᵉᵛ.] Manners and customs of biblical times. Ch/Amersham 1987, Moody/Scripture. 393 p. [EvQ 60 (1988) 267].

d915 **Gubel** E., Phoenician furniture; a typology based on Iron Age representations, with reference to the iconographical context: StPhoen 7. Lv 1987, Peeters. viii-328 p.; XLIX pl. 90-6831-110-7.

d916 **James** T.G.H., Pharaos Volk; Leben im alten Ägypten. Z 1988, Artemis. 312 p. Fs. 36.80 3-7608-0745-3 [BO 45,473].

d917 **Jenkins** Ian, Greek and Roman life [British Museum exhibition]. L/CM 1986, Br. Museum/Harvard Univ. 70 p.; 60 fig.; 36 pl. 0-7141-2041-3 [RelStR 15,70, C.F. *Aling*].

d918 *Matthews* Victor, a) Meeting at the well; – b) Signed and sealed; – c) What happened at the city gate?: – d) Keep the lamps burning; – e) The farmer and his implements: → d633, Discovering the Bible 1986, 28-31 / 32-35 / 36-41 / 56-60 / 61-66.

d919 **Metzger** Martin, Königsthron: AOAT 15 1985 → 1,b720 ... 3,d377: ᴿRelStR 14 (1988) 151 (P.D. *Miller*).

d920 *Simpson* Elizabeth, Reconstructing an ancient table [Gordion tumulus MM]: Expedition 25,4 (1982s) 11-26; 25 fig.

d921 *Stampolidis* Nikos, ⑥ Altar-thrones: Archaiologika Analekta/Athens Annals of Archaeology 18 (1985) 231-245; 22 fig.; Eng. 245.

d922 **Teringo** J. Robert, The land and people Jesus knew 1985 → 1,b726: ᴿRExp 84 (1987) 124s (D. *Garland*: wide variety of aspects of daily life then).

d923 **Turcan** Robert, Vivre à la cour des Césars d'Auguste à Dioclétien: Coll. Ét. Anc. 57. P 1987, BLettres. 321 p.; 4 fig.

d924 **Willetts** R.F., Everyday life in ancient Crete. Amst 1988, Hakkert. 191 p.; 104 fig. 90-256-0900-7.

T2.1 *Res militaris*; **weapons.**

d925 ᴱ**Bishop** M.C., The production and distribution of Roman military equipment: 2d Seminar/BAR-Int 275, 1985 → 2,549: ᴿBonnJbb 188 (1988) 580s (J.K. *Haalebos*).

d926 *Bishop* M.C., Cavalry equipment of the Roman army in the first century A.D.: → 728, Military equipment 1986/8, 67-195.

d927 **Bittner** Stefan, Tracht und Bewaffnung des persischen Heeres 1985 → 2,9957; 3,d385: ᴿGymnasium 94 (1987) 451-3 (B. *Jacobs*).

d928 *Connor* W.R., Early Greek land warfare as symbolic expression: Past and Present 119 (Ox 1988) 3-29.

d929 **Dack** E. van 't, Ptolemaica selecta; études sur l'armée et l'administration lagides: Studia Hellenistica 29. Lv 1988, Orientaliste. xxvii-409 p.; portr. Articles by him from 1948 to 1985.

d930 **Davison** D.P., The barracks of the Roman army from the 1st to 3rd centuries A.D.: diss. Oxford 1987. 1175 p. (3 vol.) BRD-83178. – DissA 49 (1988s) 2351-A.

d931 **Devijver** H., Prosopographia militiarum equestrium quae fuerunt ab Augusto ad Gallienum IV, sup. 1. Lv 1987. – ᴿAegyptus 68 (1988) 255-7 (S. *Daris*).

d933 **Dintsis** Petros, Hellenistische Helme [Diss. W. 1982]: Archaeologica 43, 1986 ➤ 2,9959: ᴿKlio 70 (1988) 587-595 (T.-M. *Schmidt*); RÉLat 65 (1987) 371-3 (R. *Adam*).

d934 **Ducrey** Pierre, Guerre et guerriers dans la Grèce antique 1985 ➤ 3, d389; Fs 85: ᴿGnomon 60 (1988) 219-222 (H.-J. *Gehrke*); Mnemosyne 41 (1988) 454-8 (G. *Schepens*).

d935 **Ferrill** Arther [sic], The origins of war; from the Stone Age to Alexander the Great 1985 ➤ 1,b737; 3,d389*: ᴿAmHR 92 (1987) 100s (C. D. *Hamilton*).

d936 ᴱ**Freeman** Philip, *Kennedy* David, The defence of the Roman and Byzantine East; proceedings of a colloquium held at the University of Sheffield in April 1986: British Inst. Ankara Mg 8 / BAR-Int 297, 1986 ➤ 3,813: ᴿBInstArch 25 (1988) 118s (R. L. *Story*).

d937 *French* Eve, Nabataean warrior saddles: PEQ 120 (1988) 64-68; 6 fig.

d938 **Gerolymatos** André, Espionage and treason ... proxenia 1986 ➤ 3,d390: ᴿGnomon 60 (1988) 594-8 (C. *Marek*).

d939 **Gilliam** J. F., Roman army papers 1986 ➤ 2,9962: ᴿEirene 25 (1988) 131 (J. *Kepartová*).

d940 *a*) *Gröschel* Sepp-Gustav, Der goldene Helm der Athena (Ilias 5,743/44); – *b*) *Calmeyer* Peter, Zu einem ziselierten Bronzehelm des 8. Jahrhunderts: ArchMIran 19 (1986) 43-78; 5 fig.; pl. 13-15 / 79-86; 4 (foldout) fig.; pl. 15-20.

d941 *Hoffmeier* J. E., Weapons of war: ➤ 801, ISBEnc³ 4 (1988) 1033-43.

d942 *James* Simon, Dura-Europos and the introduction of the 'Mongolian [arrow-]release': ➤ 731, 3d military equipment 1985/7, 77-83; 4 fig.

d944 *Morschauser* Scott N., 'The mighty sword of Pharaoh': VarAeg 4 (1988) 151-164.

d945 *Pattenden* Philip, When did guard duty end? The regulation of the night watch in ancient armies: RheinMus 130 (1987) 164-174.

d946 *Rutkowski* Bogdan, Minoan double axe stands: Archeologia 36 (Wrocław 1985) 7-14.

d947 **Saddington** D. B., The development of the Roman auxiliary forces 1982 ➤ 2,9973; 3,d404: ᴿLatomus 47 (1988) 227s (B. *Dobson*).

d948 **Sekunda** Nick, Armies of classical Greece, 5th and 4th centuries B.C.: Elite 7. L 1986, Osprey. 64 p.; ill. (colour. pl., Angus McBride).

d949 *Shalev* Sariel, Redating the 'Philistine sword' at the British Museum; a case study in typology and technology [really MBI]: OxJArch 7 (1988) 303-311; 2 fig.

d950 *Tuplin* Christopher, XENOPHON and the garrisons of the Achaemenid Empire: ArchMIran 20 (1987) 167-241 + 6 maps.

 Vidal-Naquet Pierre, The black hunter; forms of thought and forms of society in the Greek world [essays] 1986 ➤ b652.

d952 *Whitehead* David, *Klopē polémou*; 'theft' in ancient Greek warfare: ClasMed 39 (1988) 43-53.

d953 *Wilkinson* Richard H., The turned bow in Egyptian iconography: VarAeg 4 (1988) 181-7; 4 fig.

d954 *Young* T. Cuyler ᴶ, The Assyrian army on the Middle Euphrates; evidence from current excavations: CanadMesop 6 (1983) 19-32.

T2.2 **Vehicula.**

d955 **Azzaroli** A., An early history of horsemanship 1985 ➤ 1,b760; *f* 68: ᴿRBgPg 66 (1988) 180-2 (Liliane *Bodson*).

d956 *Connolly* Peter, The Roman saddle: → 731, Military equipment 1985/7, 7-19; 4 fig. + 8 pl.

d957 **Green** Miranda J., The wheel as a cult-symbol 1984 → 2,9982; 3,d413: ᴿÉtClas 56 (1988) 217s (Berthe *Rantz*).

d958 *Kossack* Georg, Fremdlinge in Fars [Pasargadae Tierkopfringe, bits]: ArchMIran 20 (1987) 107-127; 9 fig.

d959 **Littauer** M., *Crouwel* J. H., Chariots and related equipment from the tomb of Tut'ankhamun: T. Tomb 8, 1985 → 1,b764; 3,d415: ᴿBO 45 (1988) 128-134 (W. *Decker*).

d960 *Littauer* M. A., *Crouwel* J. H., *a*) A pair of horse bits of the second millennium в.c. from Iraq: Iraq 50 (1988) 169-171; 2 fig.; pl. XII; – *b*) A new type of bit from Iran?: → 4, ᶠAmiet P. = IrAnt 33 (1988) 323-7; 3 fig.; 2 pl.

d961 *Maass* Michael, Helme, Zubehör von Wagen und Pferdegeschirr aus Urartu: ArchMIran 20 (1987) 65-92; pl. 1-10.

d962 *McNeill* William H., The eccentricity of wheels, or Eurasian transportation in historical perspective [... camel caravans]: AmHR 92 (1987) 1111-1126.

d963 *Pare* Christopher, Wheels with thickened spokes, and the problem of cultural contact between the Aegean world and Europe in the Late Bronze Age: OxJArch 6 (1987) 43-61; 14 fig.

d964 **Piggott** Stuart, The earliest wheeled transport 1983 → 64,a699 ... 1,b766: ᴿBASOR 272 (1988) 87-90 (J. D. *Muhly*).

d965 *Raepsaet* Georges, Charettes en terre cuite de l'époque archaïque à Corinthe: AntClas 57 (1988) 56-88.

d966 *Shramko* B. A., ❸ Specific types of harness in Scythia: SovArch (1988,2) 233-7; 3 fig.

d966* *Uchitel* Alexander, Charioteers of Knossos: Minos 23 (1988) 47-58.

т2.3 Nautica.

d967 **Basch** Lucien, Le musée imaginaire de la marine antique. Athenai 1987, Institut Hellénique pour la préservation de la tradition nautique. 525 p.; 1136 fig. – ᴿGnomon 60 (1988) 759-761 (A. *Göttlicher*).

d968 *Basch* Lucien, The Eleusis museum trireme and the Greek trireme: Mariner's Mirror 74 (1988) 163-197; 29 fig.

d968* ᴱ**Bass** George F., *Van Doorninck* Frederick H.ᴶ, Yassi Ada I., a seventh century Byzantine shipwreck: Nautical Archaeology 1. College Station 1982, Texas A & M Univ. xvi-349 p. – ᴿAJA 92 (1988) 459s (S. E. *Sidebotham*).

d969 *Bietak* Manfred, Zur Marine des Alten Reiches: → 41, ᶠEdwards I., Pyramid Studies 1988, 35-40; pl. 3-9.

d969* **Casson** Lionel, Ships and seamanship in the ancient world. Princeton 1986, Univ. xxviii-451 p.; ill. 0-691-00215-0.

d970 *Casson* Lionel, Transportation/Piracy: → 444, Mediterranean 1988, 353-365 / 837-844.

d971 **Eiseman** Cynthia J., *Ridgway* Brunhilde S., The Porticello shipwreck 1987 → 3,d430*: ᴿAntiquity 62 (1988) 388s (J. *Boardman*).

d972 **Ericsson** C. H., Navis oneraria 1984 → 65,a297 ... 2,a1: ᴿMusHelv 45 (1988) 267 (A. *Bielman*).

d973 **Garland** Robert, The Piraeus, from the fifth to rhe first century в.c. Ithaca NY 1988, Cornell Univ. 280 p.; 33 fig. $44.50. 0-8014-2041-5 [AJA 92,626].

d974 *Gianfrotta* Piero A.,   La resurrezione della Kyrenia [mercantile nau-
fragata 2000 anni fa]: Archeo 39 (1988) 122s; ill.

d975 **Göttlicher** Arvid,   Die Schiffe der Antike; eine Einführung in die
Archäologie der Wasserfahrzeuge. B 1985, Mann. 3-7861-1419-6. –
ᴿMünstHand 6,2 (1987) 124-130 (P. *Kracht*).

d976 *Hardie* Philip, Ships and ship-names in the Aeneid: ⇥ 17, ᶠBRAMBLE J.
1987, 163-171.

d977 *Hauben* Hans, The barges of the Komanos family [Egypt 187 B.C.]:
AncS 19 (1988) 207-211.

d977* *Hilgert* E., Ships, boats: ⇥ 801, ISBEnc³ 4 (1988) 482-9; 8 vivid fig.

d978 **Höckmann** Olaf, Antike Seefahrt 1985 ⇥ 1,b795... 3,d437: ᴿGymnasium 94 (1987) 373s (H.-W. *Keweloh*); Salesianum 50 (1988) 393s (G.
Gentileschi).

d979 *Houston* George W., Ports in perspective; some comparative materials
on Roman ships and ports: AJA 92 (1988) 553-564; 2 fig.

d980 **Ingelman-Sundberg** Catharina, Marinarkeologi; dykaren – arkeologen –
fynden. Höganäs 1985, Wikens. 206 p.; ill. 91-7024-235-6. – ᴿFornvännen 83 (1988) 142-4 (C. O. *Cederlund*).

d981 **Jones** Dilwyn, A glossary of ancient Egyptian nautical titles and terms:
Studies in Egyptology. L 1988, Kegan Paul. 0-7103-0284-3 [OIAc D88].

d982 [Strömberg] **Krantz** Eva S., Des Schiffes Weg mitten im Meer: ConBib
OT 19, 1982 ⇥ 63,a338... 1,b814: ᴿIsrEJ 38 (1988) 94-96 (S. *Ahituv*:
detailed; but the series is Coniectanea, not Coniecta, Biblica); JNES 47
(1988) 287s (D. *Pardee*: Ezek 27, not Prov 30,19 or seafaring in Israel).

d983 *Kreutz* Barbara M., Ships and shipbuilding, Mediterranean: ⇥ 792,
DMA 11 (1988) 229-238 [245-9, *Arenson* Sarah, Red Sea].

d984 *Laronde* André, Le port de Lepcis Magna [Libye]: CRAI (1988) 337-
353; 11 fig.

d985 *Laronde* André, Recherches sous-marines dans le port d'Apollonia de
Cyrénaïque: Bulletin des Antiquaires (1987) 322-330 (-332).

d986 *Lipke* Paul, Trials of the trireme [120-ft. Olympias]: Archaeology 41,2
(1988) 22-29; ill.

d987 **McGrail** Seán, Ancient boats in NW Europe 1987 ⇥ 3,d443; 0-582-
49267-X: ᴿAntiqJ 68 (1988) 337s (Margaret *Rule*); BInstArch 25 (1988)
137 (A. J. *Parker*).

d988 *McGrail* Seán, Assessing the performance of an ancient boat — the
Hasholme logboat [c. 300 B.C.]: OxJArch 7 (1988) 35-45; 6 fig.

d989 *a) Marazzi* Massimiliano, La più antica marineria micenea in occidente;
– *b) Bietti Sestieri* Anna Maria, The 'Mycenaean connection' and its
impact on the central Mediterranean societies: DialArch (1988,1) 5-22; 6
fig. / 23-51; 36 fig.

d990 **Meijer** Fik, A history of seafaring in the classical [? 'ancient' ⇥ 3,d444
(2,a17), Croom Helm] world. NY 1986, St. Martin's. 256 p. $32.50.
0-312-00075-8. – ᴿGnomon 60 (1988) 162s (L. *Casson*, Eng.: egregious
blunders, minimal competence); JHS 108 (1988) 249s (J. F. *Lazenby*:
disappointing).

d991 *Meijer* F.,   *a)* THUCYDIDES 1.13.2-4 and the changes in Greek
shipbuilding: Historia 37 (1988) 461-3; – *b)* Types of ship in the regatta
in Vergil's Aeneid (5,114-243): Latomus 47 (1988) 94-97.

d992 **Morrison** J. S., *Coates* J. F.,   The Athenian trireme [full-scale replica
launched 1987] 1986 ⇥ 2,a18; 3,d446: ᴿClasW 82 (1988s) 215s (H. *Williams*); ÉchMClas 32 (1988) 424-430 (P. D. *Emanuele*); JHS 108 (1988) 250
(J. F. *Lazenby*).

d993 *Morrison* John, The second British sea trials of the reconstructed trireme, 20 July–5 August 1988: Antiquity 62 (1988) 713s.

d994 ᴱ**Müller-Karpe** Hermann, Zur geschichtlichen Bedeutung der frühen Seefahrt: Kolloquien vergl. Arch. 2, 1981/2 ➤ 1,861: ᴿBO 45 (1988) 656s (H. T. *Wallinga*).

d995 ᴱ**Pearson** Colin, Conservation of marine archaeological objects. L 1987, Butterworth. 297 p.; ill. £55. 0-408-10668-9 [Antiquity 62,420].

d996 *Porten* B. [➤ a3766ss] The Aramaic boat papyrus (P.Ber. 23000), a new collation: Orientalia 57 (1988) 76-81.

d997 *Pulak* Cemal, The Bronze Age [? 1400 B.C.] shipwreck at Ulu Burun [Kaş near Xanthos E of Antalya], Turkey; 1984 campaign: AJA 92 (1988) 1-37; 41 fig. [also p. 244s].

d998 *Queyrel* François, Le motif des quatre osselets figuré sur des jas d'ancre: Archaeonautica 7 (1987) 207-212; 3 fig.

d999 *Rankov* N. B., The trireme project; achievement to date and aims for the future: AncHRes 18 (1988) 104-113.

d999* ᴱ**Runyan** Timothy J., Ships, seafaring and society; essays in maritime history: Great Lakes Historical Soc. Detroit 1987, Wayne State Univ. xiv-366 p. $13.50 [JAOS 108,678].

e1 *Sharawi* Galal, *Harpur* Yvonne, The identity and positions of relief fragments in museums and private collections; reliefs from various tombs at Saqqâra [a sailing boat, Cairo JE40049+Brooklyn 35.640; ...farm scenes]: JEA 74 (1988) 57-67; 6 fig.; pl. VI-IX.

e1* **Sperber** Daniel, Nautica talmudica: Stud NELangCul. RamatGan/ Leiden 1986, Bar-Ilan Univ./Brill. 180 p.; ill. *f* 85 [JAOS 108,360].

e2 **Throckmorton** Peter, The sea remembers. NY 1987, Weidenfeld & N. 240 p. $30 [JAOS 108,678].

e2* **Ucelli** Guido, Le navi di Nemi. R 1983 [= ²1950; ¹1940], Ist. Poligrafico dello Stato. xii-474 p.; 353 fig.+6 color.; 10 foldouts. – ᴿLatomus 47 (1988) 721 (J. *Debergh*).

e3 *Vagnetti* Lucia, Armi per i Micenei; da Micene alla Sardegna le prime navigazioni greche nell'occidente mediterraneo: Archeo 36 (1988) 22-27.

e4 *Wachsmann* Shelley, *a)* The [Sea of] Galilee boat; 2000-year-old hull recovered intact: BAR-W 14,5 (1988) 18-33; – *b)* The boat in the lake... fascinating find in Israel: ILN 276/7075 (Feb. 1988) 53.

e5 **Welsh** Frank, Building the trireme. L 1988, Constable. 232 p.; 76 fig. $13. 0-09-486880-9 [Antiquity 62,420]. – ᴿBInstArch 25 (1988) 149-151 (P. de *Souza*).

e6 *Wilkinson* Richard H., The coronational circuit of the wall, the circuit of the *ḥnw* barque and the heb-sed 'race' in Egyptian kingship ideology: JSStEg 15 (1985) 46-51.

T2.4 *Athletica,* **sport, games.**

e7 *Aigner* Heribert, Sport im römischen Heer [ganz wenig!]: Proceed. 'HISPA' Internat. Congr., 1-5 July 1985, Glasgow, p. 258-264 [< AnPg 58,804].

e8 *Beaujeu* J., Jeux latins et jeux grecs (à propos de Cɪᴄ., Fam. 1 et Att. XVI,5): ➤ 95, ᶠLᴇ Bonniec H. 1988, 10-18.

e9 [ᴱ**Bernhard** Günter] Zuschauer, Schiedsrichter, Veranstalter; ihr Einfluss auf Gestaltung und Ausgang von Wettkämpfen im Altertum: Sport in unserer Zeit, Arbeitstexte zum Verständnis der Olympischen Spiele, IV. W 1988, Min. Unterricht, Kunst, Sport. viii-103 p. [< AnPg 58,804].

e9* **Bugh** Glenn R., The horsemen of Athens. Princeton 1988, Univ. xvii-271 p.; 12 fig. $32.50 [GreeceR 36, 243, P. J. *Rhodes*].

e10 *Carter* Charles, Athletic contests in Hittite religious festivals: JNES 47 (1988) 185-7.

e11 *Chamoux* François, Celetizontes pueri [jockeys]: ➤ 91, FLABARBE J., Stemmata 1987, 443-450; 3 fig.

e12 *Crowther* N. B., Elis and the games: AntClas 57 (1988) 301-310.

e13 *Crowther* Nigel B., The age-category of boys at Olympia [? 17-19 as Anth 12,255, thus older than Pythia; but some as young as twelve]: Phoenix 42 (1988) 304-8.

e14 *Damiani Indelicato* Silvia, Were Cretan girls playing at bull-leaping? [no]: Cretan 1 (1988) 39-47; pl. XLI-XLIX.

e15 *Daris* Sergio, Lo spettacolo nei papiri greci: AevA 1 (Mi 1988) 77-93.

e16 **Decker** Wolfgang, Sport und Spiel im Alten Ägypten 1987 ➤ 3,d463; DM 38: RMundus 24 (1988) 7s (Ingrid *Gamer-Wallert*).

e17 *Decker* Wolfgang. Die mykenische Herkunft des griechischen Toten-agons: ➤ 776, Ägäische Vorg. 1984/7, 201-230.

e18 *Drew-Bear* Marie, Les athlètes d'Hermopolis Magna et leur ville au 3e siècle: ➤ 492, XVIII Papyrol. 2 (1986/8) 229-235.

e19 *a) Evjen* Harold D., Competitive athletics in ancient Greece; the search for origins and influences; – *b) Rystedt* Eva, The foot-race and other athletic contests in the Mycenaean world; the evidence of the pictorial vases: OpAth 16 (1986) 51-56 / 103-116; 25 fig.

e20 *Fielder* Wilfried, Sexuelle Enthaltsamkeit griechischer Athleten und ihre medizinische Begründung: Stadion 11,2 (1985) 137-175; Eng. 307.

e21 *Fitta* Marco, Dedicato a Olimpia; uomini e sport: ArchViva 7/1 (1988) 40s + inserto; ill.

e22 **Frisch** Peter, Zehn agonistische Papyri: Papyrologica Coloniensia 13, 1986 ➤ 3,d466: RClasR 102 (1988) 453s (J. D. *Thomas*); Gnomon 60 (1988) 42-45 (R. S. *Bagnall*: useful despite defects and unclarity of purpose).

e23 *Frisch* Peter, Die Klassifikation der paîdes bei den griechischen Agonen: ZPapEp 75 (1988) 179-185.

e24 *a) Glass* Stephen L., The Greek gymnasium; some problems; – *b) Young* David C., How the amateurs won the Olympics; – *c) Raschke* Wendy S., Images of victory; some new considerations of athletic monuments; – *d) Mallwitz* Alfred, Cult and competition locations at Olympia: ➤ 767, Olympics 1984/8, 155-173 / 55-75 / 38-64 / 79-109; II fig.

e25 *Gogos* Savas, Das antike Theater in der Periegese des PAUSANIAS: Klio 70 (1988) 329-339.

e26 *Hodge* Trevor A., What's that in dollars? [Panathenaic 200-meter footrace winner won prize worth (US 1980) $120,000]: BCanadMed 8,2 (1988) 11.

e27 **Humphrey** John H., Roman circuses, arenas for chariot racing 1986 ➤ 2,a44; 3,d469: RClasW 81 (1987s) 59s (A. *Cutler*); RArchéol (1988) 184-6 (P. *Gros*).

e28 *Khanoussi* Mustapha, Spectaculum pugilum et gymnasium; compte rendu d'un spectacle de jeux athlétiques et de pugilat, figuré sur une mosaïque de la région de Gafsa (Tunisie): CRAI (1988) 543-561; 13 fig.

e29 **Kolb** Franz, Agora und Theater, Volks- und Festversammlung: DAI-ArchFor 9, 1981 ➤ 65,a225: RAnzAltW 41 (1988) 75-78 (Veronika *Mitsopoulos-Leon*).

e30 **Kyle** Donald G., Athletics in ancient Athens: Mnemosyne Sup 85, 1987
→ 3,d471: ᴿClasW 82 (1988s) 72s (T. F. *Scanlon*); GreeceR 35 (1988) 107
(P. *Walcot*).

e31 *a*) *Loeben* Christian E., A throwstick of princess Nfr-nfrw-rʻ, with
additional notes on throwsticks of faience; – *b*) *Martin* Geoffrey T., A
throwstick of Nefertiti in Manchester: → 127, ᶠṢALEḤ A., ASAE 71
(1987) 143-9; 4 fig.; 1 pl. / 151s; 1 pl.

e32 *Longo* Oddone, Le regole della caccia nel mondo greco-romano: Aufidus
1 (Foggia 1987) 59-92 [< AnPg 58,804].

e33 *Loulloupis* M. C., Mosaic representations with gladiatorial games from
Kourion: → 749, Cyprus between, 1985/6, 471s.

e34 *Meulenaere* Herman De, Prophètes et danseurs panopolitains à la basse
époque: BIFAO 88 (1988) 41-49; pl. IV.

e35 *Meyer* Werner, Wettkampf und Spiel in den Miniaturen der Manes-
sischen Liederhandschrift: Stadion 14,1 (1988) 1-48; 16 pl.: Wettkampf,
Jagd; Brettspiele; Tanz, Turniere...

e36 *Nagy* Gregory, PINDAR's Olympian I and the aetiology of the Olympic
Games: AmPgTr 116 (1986) 71-88.

e37 **Olivová** Věra, Sports and games in the ancient world[3]. L 1986,
Bloomsbury. 207 p.; 244 fig. – ᴿEirene 25 (1988) 167s (B. *Hošek*).

e38 **Poliakoff** Michael B., Combat sports in the ancient world; competition, violence, and culture: Sport and History, 1987 → 3,d477; $22.50:
ᴿÉchMClas 32 (1988) 420-423 (F. A. *Beck*); Phoenix 42 (Toronto 1988)
270-2 (V. J. *Matthews*).

e39 *a*) *Puhvel* Jaan, Hittite athletics as prefigurations of the ancient Greek
games; – *b*) *Renfrew* Colin, The Minoan-Mycenaean origins of the
Panhellenic games; – *c*) *Raubitschek* A. E., The Panhellenic idea and the
Olympic games: → 767, Olympics 1984/8, 26-31 / 13-25 / 35-37.

e40 **Sansone** David, Greek athletics and the genesis of sport. Berkeley c.
1988, Univ. California. $20 [ClasPg 83/2 adv.].

e41 *Seiterle* Gérard, Maske, Ziegenbock und Satyr; Ursprung und Wesen der
griechischen Maske: AntWelt 19,1 (1988) 2-14; 23 (color.) fig.

e42 *a*) *Sjöberg* Åke W., 'Trials of strength'; athletics in Mesopotamia; – *b*)
Romano David G., Boycotts, bribes and fines; the ancient Olympic
Games; – *c*) *White* Donald, Roman athletics; classical antecedents to the
national mania: Expedition 27,2 (1985) 7-9; 5 fig. / 10-21; 21 fig. / 30-40;
18 fig.

e43 Lo sport nel mondo antico; ludi, munera, certamina a Roma, mostra
1987, Museo della Civiltà Romana. R 1987, Quasar. 132 p.; ill.; Eng.
summary.

e44 **Thuillier** Jean-Paul, Les jeux athlétiques dans la civilisation étrusque:
BEFAR 256, 1985 → 2,a59; 3,d485: ᴿRArchéol (1988) 155-7 (J.-R.
Jannot); RBgPg 66 (1988) 175-7 (R. *Lambrechts*).

e45 *Thuillier* J.-P., Le programme hippique des jeux romains; une curieuse
absence ['simplorum equorum certamen' in Latin summary = 'simples
courses de chevaux montés']: RÉLat 65 (1987) 53-73.

e46 **Veuve** Serge, Le Gymnase; architecture, céramique, sculpture: Fouilles
d'Aï-Khanoum 6. P 1987, de Boccard. xv-127 p.; 53 pl.; 13 foldouts.

e47 **Weiler** Ingomar, Der Sport bei den Völkern der Alten Welt 1981
→ 62,b194... 3,d487: ᴿArchaiognōsía 3.1s (1982ss) 267s (A. D. *Skiadas*).

e48 **Wörrle** Michael, Stadt und Fest im kaiserzeitlichen Kleinasien; Studien
zu einer agonistischen Stiftung aus Oinoanda: Vestigia 39. Mü 1988,
Beck. x-268 p.; 6 pl.

e49 *a) Young* David C., Athletics; – *b) Garland* Robert, Greek spectacles and festivals; – *c) Humphreys* John H., Roman games; – *d) Borthwick* Edward K., Music and dance: ➤ 444, Mediterranean 1988, 1131-1142 / 1143-1152 / 1153-1165 / 1505-1514.

e50 **Ziegler** Ruprecht, Städtisches Prestige und kaiserliche Politik; Studien zum Festwesen [Spiele...] in Ostkilikien im 2. und 3. Jahrhundert n. Chr. Dü 1985, Schwann. 168 p.; 14 pl. DM 48. – ᴿGnomon 60 (1988) 520-3 (H. *Halfmann*); Latomus 47 (1988) 455s (J. P. *Callu*).

T2.5 **Musica.**

e51 *Bélis* Annie, [hollow perforated bone cylinders] Charnières ou auloi? ['flûtes' inexact]: RArchéol (1988) 109-118; 13 fig.

e52 *Boehmer* Rainer M., Früheste Abbildungen von Lautenspielern [lute-...] in der althethitischen Glyptik: ➤ 112*, ᶠOᴛᴛᴇɴ H., Documentum 1988, 51-57; 9 fig.

e53 *Brennan* Brian, Aᴜɢᴜsᴛɪɴᴇ's De musica: VigChr 42 (1988) 262-281.

e54 **Camilleri** Charles, Mediterranean music. Malta 1988, Univ. Foundation for International Studies. 70 p.

e55 *Caubet* Annie, La musique à Ougarit: CRAI (1987) 731-754; 8 fig.

e56 **Corbin** Solange, La musica cristiana, dalle origini a Gregorio Magno [L'Église et la conquête de la musique 1960],ᵀ: Di fronte e attraverso 179. Mi 1987, Jaca. – ᴿSMSR 54 (1988) 194s (Elena *Zocca*).

e57 *Delattre* Daniel, À propos des livres II et III du *Perì mousikès* de Philodème; essai de 'reconstruction' de colonnes mutilées: ➤ 492, XVIII Papyrol. 1 (1986/8) 193-208.

e58 *a) de Martino* Stefano, Il lessico musicale ittita; usi e valori di alcuni verbi; – *b) Polvani* A. M., Appunti per una storia della musica cultuale ittita; lo strumento *huhupal* [?cembalo]: Hethitica 9 (1988) 5-16 / 171-9.

e59 *Deproost* Paul-Augustin, La polyphonie au temps de saint Aᴜɢᴜsᴛɪɴ? Position du problème et réflexions autour de quelques textes: ÉtClas 56 (1988) 145-154.

e60 *Dobosi* Viola T., [*Soproni* Ildikó], Jewelry, musical instruments and exotic objects from the Hungarian Paleolithic [The reconstruction of the Istál-lóskő flute]: Folia Archaeologica 36 (Budapest 1985) 7-32 [33-36].

e61 *Duchesne-Guillemin* Marcelle, Réfutation de l'interprétation Kɪʟᴍᴇʀ [Anne, Congrès des orientalistes, Paris 1973; disque 'Sounds from Silence' 1976] du chant hourrite [idée fausse de la musique babylonienne et de son utilisation par les Hourrites à Ras-Shamra]: ➤ 50, ᶠFᴏɴᴛɪɴᴏʏ C., 1988, 269-276.

e62 *a) Fischer* Henry G., The trumpet in ancient Egypt; – *b) Leclant* Jean, Un manche de sistre au nom de Shabataka: ➤ 41, ᶠEᴅᴡᴀʀᴅs I., Pyramid studies 1988, 103-110; 5 fig. / 152s; 2 fig.

e63 *Fridh* Åke, Cᴀssɪᴏᴅᴏʀᴜs' digression on music, Var. II 40: Eranos 86 (1988) 43-51.

e63* **Grözinger** Karl-E., Musik in der Theologie der frühen jüdischen Literatur 1982 ➤ 63,3079 ... 2,a67: ᴿRÉJ 146 (1987) 437s (M.-R. *Hayoun*).

e64 **Haïk Vantoura** Suzanne, [Les 150 Psaumes] La musique de la Bible révélée; une notation millénaire décryptée²ʳᵉᵛ [¹1978], 1985 ➤ 2,a68; ᴿRTLv 19 (1988) 212 (P. J. van *Tiggelen*).

e65 *Hoffmann-Erbrecht* Lothar, Die Musik im Grabkult der klassischen Antike; Bemerkungen zu einer neu aufgefundenen weissgrundigen Lekythos des Malers von Athen 1826 aus Privatbesitz: → 122*, ᶠRAHN H., Ainigma 1987, 15-22 [= → 3,134.d498].

e66 *Jannot* Jean-René, Musiques et musiciens étrusques: CRAI (1988) 311-334; 10 fig.

e67 *Lawergren* Bo, The origin of musical instruments and sounds: Anthropos 83 (1988) 31-45.

e68 **McKinnon** James, Music in early Christian literature [398 snippets] 1987 → 3,d501: ᴿJTS 39 (1988) 365 (H. *Chadwick*: does not replace QUASTEN J.); Salesianum 50 (1988) 574s (Kakesa *Makoko*).

e68* *Mazuela Coll* Rosario, El laud [árabe] sultan de los instrumentos musicales: BAsEspOr 23 (1987) 134-151.

e69 ᵀᴱ**Neubecker** Annemarie J., PHILODEMUS, Über die Musik IV. N 1986, Bibliopolis. 234 p. – ᴿClasR 102 (1988) 145s (E. K. *Borthwick*).

e70 *Polvani* Anna Maria, Osservazioni sul termine ittita ⁽ᵍⁱˢ⁾*arkammi* [tamburo ≅ BALAG. DI]*: OrAnt 27 (1988) 211-9.

e71 **Rashid** Subhi A., Mesopotamien: Musikgeschichte in Bildern 1984 → 2,a77: ᴿOLZ 83 (1988) 418-422 (J. *Elsner*).

e72 *Richter* Erich, Die georgische Musikbibliographie ... in Tiflis: Biblos 36 (1987) 10-23.

e73 *Roszkowska* K., Musical terminology in Hittite cuneiform texts: OrVars 1 (1987) ... [< BO 45,526].

e74 **Shelemay** Kay K., Music, ritual and Falasha history: Ethiopian Series Mg 17. East Lansing MI 1986. c.344 p. – ᴿJQR 79 (1988s) 49-65 (S. *Kaplan*: 'Falasha' religion).

e75 **Wegner** Ulrich, Afrikanische Saiteninstrumente. B c.1987, Museum für Völkerkunde. 305 p. DM 48. – ᴿMundus 24 (1988) 304-6 (J.-B. *Condat*).

e75* *Wrede* Henning, Die tanzenden Musikanten von Mahdia und der alexandrinische Götter- und Herrscherkult: MiDAI-R 95 (1988) 97-114; 1 fig.; pl. 40-47.

T2.6 **Textilia,** *vestis,* clothing.

e76 **Archi** A, Testi amministrativi; assegnazioni di tessuti (Archivio Ebla L. 2769): ARET 1, 1985 → 1,b873: ᴿBO 45 (1988) 613-9 (H. *Waetzoldt*).

e77 **Archi** Alfonso, Testi amministrativi; registrazioni di metalli e tessuti (Archivio L.2769): ARET 7. R 1988, Univ. Missione Archeologica in Siria. xxiv-251 p.; 46 pl.

e78 **Becker** John, Pattern and loom; a practical study of the development of weaving techniques in China, Western Asia and Europe. K 1988, Rhodos. 2 vol. Dk 298 pa. 87-7245-151-3; 204-8. – ᴿAntiquity 62 (1988) 816.818 (J. P. *Wild*).

e79 *Bogoslovskaja* I. V., ❻ Le costume des peuples nomades et migrateurs du Chanaan selon les images égyptiennes anciennes des XIVᵉ-XIIᵉ ss.av.n.è.; essai d'ethnologie historique: VDI 184 (1988) 126-138; franç. 138s.

e80 *Bonfante* Larissa, *Jaunzems* Eva, Clothing and ornament: → 444, Mediterranean 3 (1988) 1385-1416.

e81 **Browning** Daniel C.ᴶ, The textile industry of Iron Age Timnah and its regional and socioeconomic contexts; a literary and artifactual analysis: diss. SW Baptist. 1988. – RelStR 15,192.

e82 **Cauderlier** Patrice, Les tissus coptes, catalogue raisonné du Musée des Beaux-Arts. Dijon 1985s, Exposition. 125 p.; ill.

e83 *Cooke* W. D., *Tullo* A., The conservation of a collection of Coptic sprang hats in the Whitworth Gallery, Manchester: Textiles anciens 66 (1988) 5-14; 4 fig.

e84 *Fredricksmeyer* E. A., Alexander the Great and the Macedonian *Kausia*: AmPgTr 116 (1986) 215-227.

e85 **Gaitzsch** Wolfgang, Antike Korb- und Seilerwaren: Limesmuseum Aalen 38. Stu 1986, Ges. V₍ Frühgeschichte. 100 p.; 46 fig.

e86 *Giesecke* Heinz-Eberhard, Kretische Schurze [loin-cloths, Eng. p. 91]: OpAth 17 (1988) 91-98; 12 fig.

e87 **Hall** Rosalind, Egyptian textiles 1986 → 2,a94: ᴿVarAeg 4 (1988) 261 (D. P. *Ryan*).

e88 *Hall* Rosalind M., 'Crimpled' garments; a mode of dinner dress: DiscEg 5 (1986) 37-45; 3 fig.

e88* *Kitchen* K. A., Of bedspreads and hibernation; from Rio de Janeiro to the Middle Euphrates: → 29, Mem. CRAIGIE P., Ascribe 1988, 21-27.

e89 *Kokavkin* A. ❻ Two Coptic textiles with patriarch Joseph: SGErm 50 (1985) 43s, 4 fig.

e90 *Lafontaine-Dosogne* Jacqueline, *Jonghe* Daniël de, Les textiles coptes: → d702, Monde Copte 14s (1988) 31-49, ill.

e90* *Lane* Eugene N., *Pastós* [a textile, not a room; as only New English Bible 'which, however, I find to be dreadfully inaccurate for the NT']: Glotta 66 (1988) 100-123.

e91 **Martiniani-Reber**, Lyon, Musée historique des tissus; soieries sassanides, coptes et byzantines, Vᵉ-XIᵉ siècles: Inventaire coll. franç. 30, 1986 → 3,d515: ᴿRArchéol (1988) 437s (F. *Baratte*).

e92 **Petzel** Florence E., Textiles of ancient Mesopotamia, Persia and Egypt. Corvallis OR 1987, auct. 0-9618476-0-3 [OIAc D88].

e93 *Pleket* H. W., Greek epigraphy and comparative ancient history: two case studies [of (unavailable) data on textile-production]: EpAnat 12 (1988) 25-37; ❶ 38.

e94 **Ribichini** Sergio, *Xella* Paolo, La terminologia dei tessili di Ugarit 1985 → 3,d521: ᴿJNWS 14 (1988) 227 (F. C. *Fensham*); RStFen 16 (1988) 121 (D. *Pardee*).

e95 *Robins* Gay, The slope of the front of the royal apron: DiscEg 3 (1985) 49-56 [2 (1985) 51-56, slope of Amon-Re feathers].

e96 *Rutschmann* Hansuli † 1988, Webgewichte als Bildträger: AntWelt 19,2 (1988) 46-55; 3 fig.; 6 pl.

e97 *Ryder* M. L., *Gabra-Sanders* Thea, A microspopic study of remains of textiles made from plant fibres: OxJArch 6 (1988) 91-108; 20 fig.

e98 *Schick* Tamar, A neolithic cult headdress from the Nahal Hemar cave: IsrMusJ 7 (1988) 25-33; 10 fig.

e99 *Simpson* William H., A protocol of dress; the royal and private fold of the kilt [in opposite directions on Old Kingdom statues]: JEA 74 (1988) 203-5.

e100 *Szarzyńska* Krystyna, Records of garments and cloths in archaic Uruk/Warka: AltOrF 15 (1988) 220-230.

e101 **Thurman** Christa C. M., *Williams* Bruce, Ancient textiles from Nubia; Meroitic, X-group, and Christian fabrics from Ballana and Qustul: an exhibit. Ch 1979, Art Institute. 148 p.; 188 fig. 0-918986-25-7.

e102 **Tölle-Kastenbein** Renate, Frühklassische Peplosfiguren, Typen und Repliken: Antike Plastik 20, 1986 → 2,a106: ᴿAcArchH 40 (1988) 335-7 (M. *Szabó*); Gnomon 60 (1988) 523-7 (B. S. *Ridgway*).

e103 **Watson** Philip J.,   Costume of ancient Egypt. L 1987, Batsford. 64 p.;
132 fig. (Cassin-Scott J.).

e103* *Weippert* Helga,   Textilproduktion und Kleidung im vorhellenistischen
Palästina: → 707*, Pracht 1988, 136-142. 421s.

T2.7 *Ornamenta corporis,* jewelry, mirrors.

e104 *Brentjes* Burchard,   Vorislamische Kronen Mittelasiens: ArchMIran 20
(1987) 261-279; 17 fig.; pl. 24-26.

e105 *Cannuyer* Christian,   Les cognates sémitiques de *śrw*, 'périscélide'
[bracelet de jambes]: DiscEg 9 (1987) 21-24.

e106 *Chidašeli* Manana,   Die Gürtelbleche der älteren Eisenzeit in Georgien:
BeiVgArch 8 (1986) 7-72; 14 fig.

e107 **Content** Derek J.,   Glyptic art — ancient jewelry; an annotated
bibliography. Houlton 1985, auct. 158 p.

e108 *Culican* William †, *Zimmer* Jenny,   Decorated belts from Iran and the
Caucasus: IrAnt 22 (1987) 159-199; 22 fig.

e108* **D'Ambrosio** A.,   Gli ori di Oplontis; gioielli romani dal suburbio
pompeiano; mostra Roma apr. 1987. N 1987, Bibliopolis. 75 p.; 27 pl.
Lit. 30.000 [Gymnasium 96, 167, Lucia A. *Scatozza Höricht*].

e109 **Fellmann** Berthold,   Frühe olympische Gürtelschmuckscheiben aus
Bronze 1984 → 2,a115: ᴿArcheologia 36 (Wrocław 1985) 174s (J. *Wielowiejski*).

e110 *Gorelick* Leonard, *Gwinnett* A. John,   Diamonds from India to Rome
and beyond: AJA 92 (1988) 547-552; 3 fig.

e111 **Guillaumet** Jean Paul,   Les fibules de Bibracte, technique et typologie.
Dijon 1984, Univ. 83 p. – ᴿArcheologia 36 (Wrocław 1985) 188s (J.
Wielowiejski).

e112 *Jamzadeh* P.,   The function of girdle on Achaemenid costume in combat:
IrAnt 22 (1987) 267-273, II pl.

e113 **Kilian** Imma,   Nadeln der frühhelladischen bis archaischen Zeit von der
Peloponnes: PrBronz 13/8. Mü 1984, Beck. 325 p.; 116 pl. – ᴿEirene 25
(1988) 136s (J. *Bouzek*).

e114 *Kuhnen* Hans-Peter,   Zwiebelknopffibeln aus Palästina und Arabia;
Überelegungen zur Interpretation einer spätrömischen Fibelform: ZDPV
104 (1988) 92-124; 7 fig. (map); pl. 12.

e115 **Liepmann** Ursula, (*Riederer* Josef),   Corpus speculorum etruscorum,
Bundesrepublik Deutschland 2. Mü 1988, Hirmer. 189 p.; 34 plates with
drawing opposite. 3-7774-4640-8.

e116 **McGovern** P. E.,   Late Bronze Palestinian pendants 1985 → 2,a116;
3,d538: ᴿBL (1988) 32 (A. R. *Millard*).

e117 **Moscati** Sabatino,   I gioelli di Tharros; origini, caratteri, confronti:
StFenici 26. R 1988, Cons. Naz. Ric. 59 p.; 25 fig.; XXXII pl.

e118 *Müller-Karpe* Andreas,   Neue galatische Funde aus Anatolien [... Fibeln,
safety-pins]: IstMitt 38 (1988) 189-199; 4 fig.; foldout.

e119 **Oberleitner** Wolfgang, ᴱ*Langthaler* Gerhart,   Geschnittene Steine; die
Prunkkameen der Wiener Antikensammlung. Wien 1985, Böhlau. 77 p.;
69 fig. – ᴿGnomon 60 (1988) 469s (E. *Zwierlein-Diehl*).

e120 *Pedrini* Lidia,   On the possible function of the ribbons hanging behind
the royal heads: DiscEg 7 (1987) 59-65 + 7 fig.

e121 **Philipp** Hanna,   Mira et magica, Gemmen im Ägyptischen Museum...
Berlin-Charlottenburg 1986 → 3,d539; DM 158; 3-8053-0568-0: ᴿAntiqJ
68,1 (1988) 147 (G. *Lloyd-Morgan*: largely showing divinities; very little

magical material has survived other than on gems); ClasR 102 (1988) 450s
(M. *Henig*).

e121* **Pisano** Giovanna, I gioelli fenici e punici in Italia: Itinerari 2. R 1988,
Libreria dello Stato. 89 p.; 54 color. fot.

e122 *Raven* Maarten J., The Antef diadem reconsidered: OMRO 68 (1988)
77-86; 87-90 phot.

e122* *Ritter* H. W., Die Bedeutung des Diadems: Historia 36 (1987) 290-301.

e123 *Spaer* Maud, The pre-Islamic glass bracelets of Palestine: JGlass 30
(1988) 51-61.

e124 *Thomas* Angela P., Grave H45 at El Mahasna [ivory, combs...]: DiscEg
9 (1987) 55-61; phot. p. 62, bone comb.

Völger Gisela, *al.*, Pracht... Kleidung und Schmuck aus Palästina und
Jordanien 1988 → 707*

e125 *Wolinski* Arelene, Ancient Egyptian ceremonial masks: DiscEg 6 (1986)
47-52; 2 fig.

e126 **Younger** J. G., The iconography of Late Minoan and Mycenaean sealstones and finger rings. Bristol 1988, Classical. XXIX-432 p., 152 fig.

e127 **Zazoff** Peter, Die antiken Gemmen: HbArch. Mü 1983, Beck.
LI-446 p.; 132 pl. – ᴿBonnJbb 188 (1988) 597s (Marianne *Maaskant-
Kleibrink*).

T2.8 **Utensilia.**

e128 *Alden* John R., Ceramic ring scrapers; an Uruk period pottery
production tool: Paléorient 14,1 (1988) 143-150; 2 fig. (map); 1 pl.

e129 **Cain** Hans U., Römische Marmorkandelaber 1985 → 1,b926 ... 3,d549:
ᴿBabesch 62 (1987) 178s (E. M. *Moormann*); Latomus 47 (1988) 256 (R.
Chevallier).

e130 *Castel* C., *al.*, Masse d'arme ou support de vase [Larsa 1985]: Akkadica 60 (1988) 1-9 + 19 fig.

e131 *Cherf* William J., Some forked staves in the Tut'ankhamūn collection:
ZägSpr 115 (1988) 107-110.

e132 *Cliante* Traian, *Radulescu* Adrian, Le trésor de Sucidava [Roumanie,
près du Delta du Danube] en Mésie seconde [coupes, bols, cuillers en
métal...]: RArchéol (1988) 357-380; 14 fig. (map).

e133 *Costa* Barbara, [Headrests] Preparazione per un corpus dei poggiatesta
nell'antico Egitto; classificazione tipologica: EgVO 11 (1988) 39-50.

e134 *Couchoud* Sylvia, Calcul d'une horloge à eau: BSocÉg 12 (Genève 1988)
25-34; 3 fig.

e135 *Dembska* Albertyna, **℗** A discovery of a new Egyptological relic
[zabytku]: PrzOr (1987) 345-350, phot.

e136 *Doetsch-Amberger* Ellen, Klapper mit Hahn: GöMiszÄg 101 (1988)
27-29; phot. p. 30.

e137 *Goedicke* Hans, The scribal palette of Athu (Berlin Inv. Nr. 7798): CdÉ
63,125 (1988) 42-56.

e138 **Hall** Rosalind M., *Janssen* J. J., A priest's walking-stick: GöMiszÄg
105 (1988) 15-19 + phot. (top forked like snake-stopper).

e139 **Hengel** M., Achilleus in Jerusalem 1982 → 63,a467 ... 2,a131: ᴿGymnasium 95 (1988) 273s (Beat *Brenk*).

e140 *a*) *Hurschmann* Rolf, Zu ägyptischen Mehrzweckgeräten; – *b*) *Scheel*
Bernd, Fundobjekte einer ptolemäerzeitlichen Metallverarbeitungsstät-
te in Theben und Vergleichsfunde anderer vorderorientalischer Ausgra-
bungsplätze: StAltÄgK 15 (1988) 165-9; pl. 4 / 243-254; 6 fig.

e141 *Karageorghis* V., Torch-holders [*Schliemann* H.; from Tiryns] or bellows?: → 111, ᶠMYLONAS G., *Philia épē* 2 (1987) 22-26; 2 fig.

e142 *Lacroix* Léon, PAUSANIAS, le coffre de Kypsélos et le problème de l'exégèse mythologique: RArchéol (1988) 245-261; 4 fig.

e143 **La Rocca** E., L'età d'oro di Cleopatra; indagine sulla Tazza Farnese 1984 → 1,d96; 3,d557: ᴿAegyptus 68 (1988) 247-9 (G. G. *Belloni*); ArchClasR 38ss (1986ss) 284-6 (P. E. *Arias*).

e144 *Lazzari* Alessandra, Per una classificazione tipologica degli spilloni (pins) dell'Anatolia nell'Età di Bronzo: CMatArch 1 (R 1986) 67-211; fig. 12-38; maps.

e145 **Manning** W. H., Catalogue of the Romano-British iron tools, fittings and weapons in the British Museum. L 1985, BM. xviii-197 p.; 35 fig.; 85+25 pl. £45. – ᴿBInst Arch 25 (1988) 137 (L. *Keppie*).

e146 **Markoe** Glenn, Phoenician bronze and silver bowls from Cyprus and the Mediterranean: ClasSt 26. Berkeley 1985, Univ. California. XIII-379 p.; ill. – ᴿÉtClas 56 (1988) 211s (Corinne *Bonnet*).

e147 **Matthäus** H., Metallgefässe und Gefässuntersätze der Bronzezeit, der geometrischen und archaischen Periode auf Zypern: Praeh. Bronzef. 48, 1985 → 1,b943: ᴿAcArchH 40 (1988) 326s (M. *Szabó*).

e148 *Millard* A. R., The [Uruk-period 'bread mould'] bevelled-rim bowls, their purpose and significance: Iraq 50 (1988) 49-57; 5 fig.

e149 *Moorey* P. R. S., *al.*, New analyses of Old Babylonian metalwork from Tell Sifr: Iraq 50 (1988) 39-48; 4 fig.

e149* *Pérez Largacha* Antonio, Las paletas egipcias predinásticas; algunos aspectos y significados: BAsEspOr 22 (1986) 203-217.

e150 *Rahmani* L. Y., Chip-carving [Kerbschnitt, encoche] in Palestine: IsrEJ 38 (1988) 59-75; 4 fig.; pl. 12-19. Fig. 1 shows 8 carpenter's tools and 7 stonemason's tools on two respective tombstones.

e151 *Schultheis* H., Die Menora: Würzburger Diözesangeschichtsblätter 50 (1988) 781-8 [< RHE 83,438*].

e152 **Sinn** Friederike, Stadtrömische Marmorurnen: Beiträge Skulp.-Architektur 8. Mainz 1987, von Zabern. 315 p.; 104 pl. DM 198. – ᴿArctos 22 (1988) 256-9 (A. *Tammisto*).

e153 *Turcan* Robert, Jetons romains en plomb; problèmes de datation et d'utilisation: Latomus 47 (1988) 626-634; pl. XI-XII.

e153* *Vuk* Tomislas, Ein Granatapfel aus Elfenbein; weitere Überlegungen: SBFLA 38 (1988) 423-448.

e154 **Weber** Thomas, Bronzekannen ... Fra 1983, Lang. xxiv-502 p.; XXVII pl., 7 maps. – ᴿAthenaeum 66,1s (1988) 207s (M. *Harari*); Gnomon 60 (1988) 555 (Gisela *Zahlhaas*).

T2.9 *Pondera;* Weights and Measures.

e155 **Connor** R. D., The weights and measures of England [Roman ...]. L 1987, Stationery Office for Science Museum. xxvi-422 p.; 58 fig. £30. 0-11-290435-1. – ᴿAntiqJ 68,1 (1988) 134s (F. *Greenaway*).

e156 *Cook* E. M., Weights and measures: → 801, ISBEnc³ 4 (1988) 1046-55.

e157 *Geertman* Herman, Le capacità di metretae, amae e scyphi nel Liber Pontificalis: RivArCr 62 (1988) 193-201.

e158 *Kloner* Amos, *a)* ❹ A lead plaque weight of the Bar-Kokhba administration: Qadmoniot 21 (1988) 44-48; ill., also Eng. color-cover; – *b)* [Šimᶜon Ben Kosba], Name of ancient Israel's last president discovered on lead weight [Ḥorvat Alim, 8 k NW Marisa]: BAR-W 14,4 (1988) 12-17; ill.

e159 *Mayer* W. R., Ergänzendes zur Unterteilung des Sekels im spätzeitlichen Babylonien: Orientalia 57 (1988) 70-75.

e160 *Mulder* M. J., *Pa'am* as a measure of length in 1 Kings 7.4 and KAI 80.1: ➤ 47, [F]FENSHAM F., Text 1988, 177-181.

e161 *Qedar* Shraga, Two lead weights of Herod Antipas and Agrippa II and the early history of Tiberias: IsrNumJ 9 (1986s) 29-35; 2 fig.; pl. 4-5.

e162 *Reeves* C. Nicholas, Notes on an inscribed measure of Tuthmosis III: DiscEg 8 (1987) 49-51.

e163 *Siegelová* Jana, Ein Adlergewicht in den Sammlungen des Britischen Museums: ➤ 112*, [F]OTTEN H., Documentum 1988, 317-325 + 2 fig.

e164 *Wilhelm* G., Zu den Wollmassen in Nuzi: ZAss 78 (1988) 276-283.

T3.1 Ars, *motiva, pictura.*

e165 **Akurgal** Ekrem, Griechische und römische Kunst in der Türkei 1987 ➤ 3,d579: [R]Mundus 24 (1988) 263s (K. *Schippmann*).

e166 **Alok** Ersin, ❶ Anadolu'da kayaüstü resimleri [drawings on rock]. İstanbul 1988, Akbank. 975-7630-04-7 [OIAc D88].

e167 *Amato* Angelo, Nicea II (787); difesa delle immagini come affermazione del realismo dell'Incarnazione: Salesianum 50 (1988) 321-344.

e168 *Azarpay* G., The Roman twins in Near Eastern art: ➤ 4, [F]AMIET P. = IrAnt 23 (1988) 349-360 + IV pl.

e169 **Baggley** John, Doors of perception; icons and their spiritual significance. L 1987, Mowbray. xii-160 p. £10 pa. – [R]TLond 91 (1988) 72-74 (H. *Wybrew*).

e170 **Bahnassi** Afif, Die Kunst des Alten Syrien 1987 ➤ 3,d583; DM 79: [R]BiKi 43 (1988) 89s (P.-G. *Müller*).

e171 **Barbet** Alix, La peinture murale romaine; les styles décoratifs pompéiens 1985 ➤ 1,b971 ... 3,d584: [R]AntClas 57 (1988) 601-3 (Janine *Balty*); Babesch 62 (1987) 153-165 (Eric M. *Moormann,* in italiano).

e172 *a) Bisconti* Fabrizio, Un fenomeno di continuità iconografica; Orfeo citaredo, Davide salmista, Cristo pastore, Adamo e gli animali; – *b) Dequeker* Luc, L'iconographie de l'Arche de la Torah dans les catacombes juives de Rome: ➤ 570, AugR 28 (1988) 429-436; 5 pl. / 437-460.

e173 *Blankoff* Jean, L'art des Scythes; originalité, convergences et divergences: ➤ 763, Archéologie 1986, 139-147; 149-151, 7 fig.

e174 *Boardman* John, *al.,* Herakles: ➤ 852, LIMC 4,1 (1988) 728-838.

e175 [R]**Boespflug** F., *Lossky* N., Nicée II, 787-1987; douze siècles d'images religieuses 1986/7 ➤ 3,592: [R]RThom 88 (1988) 637-643 (D. *Cerbelaud*).

e176 [E]**Boulter** C. G., Greek art; archaic into classical; a symposium held at the University of Cincinnati April 2-3, 1982: Cincinnati ClasSt 5, 1985 ➤ 1,754; *f*80. 90-04-07079-6. – [R]ClasAnt 57 (1988) 550-2 (D. *Viviers*).

e177 **Bourriau** Janine, Pharaohs and mortals; Egyptian art in the Middle Kingdom [Fitzwilliam Museum exhibition]. C 1988, Univ. iv-168 p.; 199 fig. £27.50; pa. £10. 0-521-35319-X; 846-9 [BO 45,472].

e178 **Carpenter** T. H., Dionysian imagery in archaic Greek art; its development in black-figure vase painting. Oxford 1986, UP. 143 p.; 32 pl. – [R]AJA 92 (1988) 139s (Sheila *McNally*).

e179 *Chamoux* François, De l'art grec à l'art byzantin: CahArch 36 (1988) 5-12; 6 fig.

e180 *Cherpion* Nadine, Note sur l'emploi des fonds jaunes dans la peinture thébaine: GöMiszÄg 101 (1988) 19s.

e181 **Delporte** Henri, L'image de la femme dans l'art préhistorique. P 1979, Picard. 230 p.; 137 fig. [→ 61,b340]. Out of print; being reprinted. – RPraehZts 63 (1988) 189s (K. J. *Narr*).

e181* **Dierichs** Angelika,   Erotik in der Kunst Griechenlands: AntWelt Sondernummer 1, 1988. 85 p.; 122 (color.) fig.

e182 **Dillenberger** John,   A theology of artistic sensibilities; the visual arts and the Church 1987 → 3,d592; also L, SCM, £15:   RMonth 249 (1988) 549-551 (T.P.N. *Devonshire-Jones*); TLond 91 (1988) 240-2 (C. *Pickstone*).

e183 **Effenberger** Arne,   Frühchristliche Kunst und Kultur, von den Anfängen bis zum 7. Jahrhundert 1986 → 3,d595; DM 48:   RTrierTZ 97 (1988) 73s (E. *Sauser*).

e184 *Falkenburg* R. L.,   Bijbelse iconografie en spiritualiteit; enkele beschouwingen over de Nederlandse schilderkunst en grafiek in de XVIde eeuw: Theoretische geschiedenis 15 (1988) 5-15 [< RHE 83,437*].

e185 *Ferrari* Giuseppe,   La teologia dell'icona nei Padri del VII Concilio Ecumenico (Nicea 787): RivScR (Molfetta 1988) 265-273.

e186 *a)* *Froning* Heide,   Anfänge der kontinuierenden Bilderzählung in der griechischen Kunst; – *b)* *Hesberg* Henner von,   Bildsyntax und Erzählweise in der hellenistischen Flächenkust: JbDAI 103 (1988) 169-199; 29 fig. / 309-365; 30 fig.

e187 **Giraud** Marie-Françoise,   Approches des icônes, préf. *Garrigou-Titchenkova* Ludmilla. P 1987, Médiaspaul. 92 p. – ROrChrPer 54 (1988) 493-5 (E. G. *Farrugia*).

e188 **Giuliano** Antonio,   Arte greca; dall'età classica all'età ellenistica: La Cultura 38. Mi 1987, Saggiatore. p. 519-1108.

e189 **Gonzales Blanco** A.,   La Cueva Negra de Fortuna (Murcia) y sus Tituli Picti: Antigüedad y Cristianismo 4. Murcia 1987, Novograf. 374 p.

e190 **Grabar** André, Le vie della creazione nell'iconografia cristiana [= Christian Iconography + Antiquité et Moyen-Âge],T: Antichità e Medioevo. Mi 1983, Jaca. 292 p.; 246 fig. [meno dell'originale]. – ROrChrPer 54 (1988) 271 (P. *Stephanou*).

e191 *Green* Anthony R.,   The lion-demon in the art of Mesopotamia and neighbouring regions; Materials towards the encyclopaedia of Mesopotamian religious iconography 1/1: BaghMit 17 (1986) 141-232; bibliog. 232-254; 19 fig.; pl. 2-41.

e192 **Gross** Karl, Menschenhand und Gotteshand 1985 → 1,b997; 2,a178: RTLZ 113 (1988) 131s (H. G. *Thümmel*).

e193 **Hachlili** Rachel,   Ancient Jewish art and archaeology in the Land of Israel: HbOr. Leiden 1988, Brill. xxiv-427 p.; 109 pl. ƒ 220; sb. 192. 90-04-08115-1 [BL 89,28, S. C. *Reif*].

e194 *Halm-Tisserant* Monique, Sphinx; sur le fonctionnement d'une imagerie dans l'art grec [*Moret* J. Œdipe 1984]: RÉAnc 90 (1988) 419-422.

e195 **Hannestad** Niels,   Roman art and imperial policy 1986 → 2,a180: RAntClas 57 (1988) 599-601 (C. *Delvoye*); Gnomon 60 (1988) 438-444 (R. M. *Schneider*).

e196 **Haynes** D.,   Griechische Kunst und die Entdeckung der Freiheit [L 1981 < Tacoma 1977 lectures]: KultGAntW 13. Mainz 1982, von Zabern. 148 p.; 90 fig. DM 40. – RGymnasium 95 (1988) 173s (Gerda *Schwarz*).

e197 **Heinz-Mohr** G.,   Lessico di iconografia cristiana [1971 6 1981]: Il Sestante 3. Mi 1984, IPL. vii-363 p. – RStPatav 35 (1988) 228 (A. *Moda*).

e198 *Herding* Klaus,   Die Kritik der Moderne im Gewand der Antike; DAUMIERS 'Histoire ancienne' [c. 1850]: Hephaistos 9 (1988) 111-141; 22 fig., 2 pl. [from EDelteil L., 11 vol. 1925-30].

e199 *Hoffmann* Herbert, Why did the Greeks need imagery? An anthropological approach to the study of Greek vase painting: Hephaistos 9 (1988) 143-162; 24 fig.

e199* **James** T. G. H., Egyptian painting and drawing in the British Museum 1985 → 2,a187: ᴿBO 45 (1988) 336-8 (Cathleen A. *Keller*).

e200 *Kaissi* Bahira al-, Mural paintings and pigments in Iraq: Sumer 43 (1984) 168-174.

e201 **Kleemann** Ilse, Frühe Bewegung 1984 → 3,d616: ᴿGnomon 60 (1988) 463-5 (Eleanor *Guralnick,* Eng.: dense).

e202 **Koch** Guntram, Studien zur frühchristlichen Kunst II-III: GöOrF 2/9. Gö 1987, Harrassowitz. II. vii-159 p.; III. vii-105 p. DM 52. 3-447-02664-2. – ᴿBO 45 (1988) 603-5 (Jacqueline *Lafontaine-Dosogne*).

e203 *Kuzmina* E. E., The motif of the lion-bull combat in the art of Iran, Scythia, and Central Asia and its semantics: → 144, ᶠTUCCI G. 2 (1987) 729-745.

e204 **Lafontaine-Dosogne** Jacqueline, Histoire de l'art byzantin et chrétien d'Orient: Inst. Ét. Médiévales, Textes-Études-Congrès 7. Turnhout 1987, Brepols xxviii-288 p.; 48 pl. Fb 1500 [BO 45,473].

e205 **Lowry** Glenn D., (*Nemazee* Susan), A jeweler's eye; Islamic arts of the book from the Vever collection. Wsh 1988, Smithsonian, Sackler gallery. 240 p. 75 color pl. with description. 0-295-96676-9; pa. 7-7.

e206 *Lütcke* Karl-H., Ars: → 783, AugL L,3 (1988) 459-465.

e207 **Luzzatto** Lia, *Pompas* Renata, Il significato dei colori nelle civiltà antiche. Mi 1988, Rusconi. 264 p.; ill. 88-18-12072-7.

e208 **Maffre** Jean-Jacques, L'art grec: Que sais-je? 2278. P 1986, PUF. 128 p.; 14 fig. – ᴿAntClas 57 (1988) 548s (C. *Delvoye*).

e209 *Mazzoni* Stefania, La crisi dell'arte narrativa [art which narrates, not artfulness in narrative] neoassira; riflessioni in margine: EgVO 11 (1988) 111-6.

e210 *Meinardus* Otto F. A., A note on the conception *per oculum* in Coptic art: DiscEg 9 (1987) 37-43; 1 fig.

e211 *Mekhitarian* Arpag, Ouvriers au travail dans la peinture thébaine: → 50, ᶠFONTINOY C.,1988, 153-5.

e212 ᴱ**Metzger** Henri, Eidolopoiia; Actes du Colloque sur 'Les problèmes de l'image dans le monde méditerranéen classique, Lourmarin 2-3 sept. 1982. R 1985, Bretschneider. 198 p.; ill. – ᴿAntClas 57 (1988) 565-8 (D. *Martens*); Latomus 47 (1988) 491-3 (R. *Chevallier*).

e213 **Milburn** Robert, Early Christian art and architecture Aldershot 1988, Scolar. xviii-318 p.; 194 fig.; 4 maps. £35 [GreeceR 36, 249, B. A. *Sparkes*].

e214 **Milde** H., The vignettes in the Book of the Dead of Neferrenpet; a comparative iconographical study: diss. ᴰ*Heerma van Voss* M. Amst 1988. vii-204 p.; ill. – TsTNijm 28,395: PhoenEOL 34,2 (1988) 7s.

e215 **Nauerth** Claudia, Herakles; ikonographische Vorarbeiten zu mythologischen Themen der koptischen Kunst: DielB 24 (1987) 1-97 [= DielB Beih 8. Heid 1989. viii-86 p.; 12 pl.].

e216 *a*) **Ohly-Dumm** Martha, Bilder auf Krügen; – *b*) **Hamdorf** Friedrich W., Bilder auf Schalen: Attische Vasenbilder der Antikensammlungen in München nach Zeichnungen von Karl Reichhold [1856-1919], I-II. Mü 1975s, Beck. 72 p., 13 fig., 32 pl.; 72 p., 10 fig., 32 pl. – ᴿAntClas 57 (1988) 573s (D. *Martens*).

e217 *a*) *Ozolin* Nicholas, The theology of the icon; – *b*) *Bobrinskoy* Boris, The icon, sacrament of the Kingdom: SVlad 31 (1987) 297-308 / 287-296.

e218 *Ozols* Jakob T., Zur Ikonographie der eiszeitlichen Handdarstellungen: AntWelt 19,1 (1988) 46-52; 15 fig.

e219 **Pfeiffer** Heinrich, Gottes Wort im Bild; Christusdarstellungen 1986 → 2,a201; 3,d632: ᴿTPhil 63 (1988) 284 (G. *Schörghofer*).

e220 *Piščikova* E.V., ◐ On the question of ancient Egyptian traditions in Coptic art: Istoriya-Filologiya Drevn. Vostoka (Moskva 1987) 111-124.

e221 *Plazaola* Juan, El aniconismo del arte paleocristiano (En el duodécimo centenario del II Concilio de Nicea): EstE 63 (1988) 3-28.

e222 *Ploug* Gunhild, East Syrian art of Ist century B.C. − 2nd century A.D.: → 733, Acta Hyperborea 1987/8, 129-139.

e223 **Pollitt** J.J., Art in the Hellenistic age 1986 → 2,a204; 3,d635: ᴿAnc-HRes 18 (1988) 47-51 (P.J. *Connor*: comprehensive, judicious, stimulating); AntClas 57 (1988) 552-4 (C. *Delvoye*); AntiqJ 68,1 (1988) 146s (Susan E. *Alcock*).

e224 *Quacquarelli* Antonio, *Ut rhetorica pictura* nella sequenza degli schemi; una riflessione interdisciplinare fra letteratura cristiana antica e iconologia: VetChr 25 (1988) 343-358.

e225 *Ravasi* Gianfranco, Esegesi 'estetica' della Bibbia? Bibbia e arte: RClerIt 69 (1988) 655-666.

e226 **Riegl** Alois, Late Roman art industry, ᵀ*Winkes* Rolf: Archaeologica 36. R 1985, Bretschneider. xxxi-266 p.; 100 fig.; 23 pl. [RelStR 15,153, J.W. *Dixon*].

e227 *Rousseau* Jean, Les pseudo-canons égyptiens [proportions du corps humain]: DiscEg 8 (1987) 53-66; 9 quadrillages.

e228 **Schäfer** Heinrich [1919], ⁴*Brunner-Traut* Emma, Principles of Egyptian art [→ 3,d644*], ᵀ*Baines* John; pref. *Gombrich* E.H. Ox 1986, Griffith Inst. xxviii-470 p.; 330 fig.; 109 pl. − ᴿAJA 92 (1988) 446s (Karen P. *Foster*).

e229 ᶠSCHAUENBURG Konrad, Studien zur Mythologie und Vasenmalerei, ᴱBöhr Elke, *Martini* Wolfram 1986 → 2,100: ᴿAJA 92 (1988) 606-9 (Susan B. *Matheson*).

e230 *Schauenburg* Konrad, Der Raub des Kephalos auf unteritalischen Vasen: RArchéol (1988) 291-306; 11 fig.

e231 **Schefold** Karl, Die Bedeutung der griechischen Kunst für das Verständnis des Evangeliums: KultGAntW 16. Mainz 1983, von Zabern. 113 p.; 48 fig. DM 29,80. 3-8053-0639-3. − ᴿAnzAltW 41 (1988) 78-80 (K. *Stock*: einige Fragezeichen).

e232 **Schmidt** Heinrich & Margarethe, Il linguaggio delle immagini; iconografia cristiana. R 1988, Città Nuova. 319 p.; 83 fig.; 16 pl. 88-311-7008-2.

e233 **Schönborn** Christoph, L'icône du Christ; fondements théologiques³ 1986 → (2,a211) 3,d646: ᴿRÉByz 45 (1987) 257s (Marie-H. *Congourdeau*); Salesianum 50 (1988) 240s (A.M. *Triacca*: = ¹1976 revue avec nouvelle postface. Die Christus-Ikone 1984); Speculum 63 (1988) 994-6 (D.J. *Sahas*).

e234 **Schüssler** Karlheinz, Kleine Geschichte der ägyptischen Kunst: Tb 214. Köln 1988, DuMont. 352 p.; 170 fig. + 25 color. DM 24,80. 3-7701-1602-X [OIAc D88]. − ᴿAntWelt 19,4 (1988) 62.

e235 **Shedid** Abdel Ghaffar, Stil der Grabmalereien in der Zeit Amenophis' II untersucht an den thebanischen Gräbern Nr. 104 und Nr. 80: DAI-K ArchVeröff 66. Mainz 1988, von Zabern. 198 p.; 78 pl. DM 278. 3-8053-0931-7 [BO 45,756].

e236 *Simson* Otto von, Das Christusbild in der Kunst [J.C. XI]: → 813, TRE 17 (1987) 76-84.

e237 **Sourdive** Claude, La main dans l'Égypte pharaonique; recherches de morphologie structurale. Bern 1984, Lang. xiv-169 p. – ᴿJEA 74 (1988) 261-3 (G. *Robins*: mostly things *holdable* in the hand; spoons, unguent-horns ... headrests).

e237* *Spycket* Agnès, Malerei [en français]: → 808, RLA 7,3s (1988) 287-300; 5 fig.

e238 **Stawicki** Stanisław, Papirusy tebanskie; antyczne źródło wiedzy o technickach artystycznych [History of theory of art]: Teksty źródłowe do dziejów teorii sztuki 26. Wrocław 1987, Zakład Narodowy im. Ossolinskich. 83-04-02084-X [OIAc D88].

e239 *Stützer* H.A., Das Christusbild im antiken Rom: Das Münster 41 (1988) 93-98; 13 fig. [99-136, *al.*, bis zur Gegenwart].

e240 *a) Sullivan* R.W., Some Old Testament themes on the front predella of Duccio's Maestà; – *b) Hahn* C., 'Joseph-will-perfect, Mary-enlighten and Jesus-save-thee'; the Holy Family as marriage model in the Mérode triptych: Art Bulletin 68 (NY 1986) 597-609; 20 fig. / 54-66; 5 fig. [< RHE 83,429*].

e241 *a) Suttner* Ernst C., Die theologischen Motive im Bilderstreit; – *b) Phidas* Vlassios, Les causes de l'iconoclasme; – *c) Boespflug* François, Pour une nouvelle réception du décret de Nicée II: → 552, Icone 1987 = Nicolaus 8 (1988) 53-70 / 71-81 / 161-171.

e242 **Tissot** Francine, Les arts anciens du Pakistan et de l'Afghanistan: École du Louvre, les grandes étapes de l'art. P 1987, Desclée de Brouwer. 157 p.; 127 fig.; 5 maps. 2-220-02629-9.

e243 *Usherwood* Nicholas, present., The Bible in twentieth century art. 1987, Pagoda. 111 p. £16 [TLond 91,448]. – ᴿMonth 249 (1988) 688s (T.P.N. *Devonshire Jones*).

e244 *Velmans* Tania, Observations sur la peinture murale médiévale de Syrie et de Palestine; problèmes iconographiques: → 758, Ravenna 1988, 371-380.

e245 *a) Virgulín* Stefano, I fondamenti teologici dell'iconodulia; – *b) Miccoli* Paolo, Ermeneutica dell'icona: EuntDoc 41 (1988) 5-32 / 81-106.

e246 *Vulikh* N.V., *Neverov* O.Ye., Ⓡ Le rôle de l'art dans la propagande de l'idéologie officielle pendant le principat d'Auguste: VDI 184 (1988) 162-173; 10 fig.; 173 franç.

e247 *a) Walle* B. van de, L'emblème de la fonction figuré à l'appui du titre écrit sur les monuments privés de l'ancienne Égypte; – *b) Rammant-Peeters* Agnès, Een iconografische benadering van de gebedshouding in het antieke Egypte; – *c) Tefnin* Roland (résumé), Les méfaits de l'évidence; à propos de l'usage documentaire de l'image égyptienne: → 763, Archéologie 1986, 59-72 / 73-75 / 79s [< CdÉ 108, 218-244].

e247* *Walter* Christoph, 'Latter-day' saints [i.e. post-Apostolic, not Mormon] and the image of Christ in the ninth-century Byzantine marginal psalters: RÉByz 45 (1987) 205-222; 4 pl.

e248 **Wildung** Dietrich, Die Kunst des alten Ägypten. FrB 1988, Herder. 252 p.

e249 **Woodford** Susan, An introduction to Greek art [not 1982 'and Roman' → 63,a504]. L/Ithaca NY 1986, Duckworth/Cornell Univ. 251 p.; 3 colour. pl. £10/$39.50. 0-7156-2095-9 / 9-8014-1984-8. – ᴿAntClas 57 (1988) 549s (C. *Delvoye*); ClasW 82 (1988s) 212s (Beth *Cohen*).

e249* **Yalouris** N.,   Pegasus; ein Mythos in der Kunst [1975, Eng. 1977 Pegasus, the art of the legend'], ᵀ*Zigada* H. Mainz c.1988, von Zabern. 173 p.; 13 phot. + 134 color. DM 128 [Gymnasium 96, 256-8, W. *Ries*].

e250 *Zach* Michael, Das Herzblatt in der meroitischen Kunst: VarAeg 4 (1988) 99-108; 2 fig.

e251 **Zanker** Paul, Augustus und die Macht der Bilder. Mü 1987, Beck; Lp 1988, Koehler & A. 369 p.; 351 fig. DM 86. – ᴿDLZ 109 (1988) 966-8 (W. *Schindler* does not clarify whether chiefly statues are meant).

T3.2 Sculptura.

e252 *Abdalla* Aly, Wooden stelae from the late period in the Cairo Museum: VarAeg 4 (1986) 5-16; 7 fig.

e253 *Albertson* Fred C., A portrait of Marcus Aurelius from Syro-Palestine [marble head like Gerasa example]: DamaszMit 3 (1988) 1-9; pl. 1-3.

e254 '*Amr* Abdel-Jalil, *a*) Ten human clay figurines from Jerusalem: Levant 20 (1988) 185-196; 12 fig.; – *b*) Four unique double-faced female heads from the Amman citadel: PEQ 120 (1988) 55-63; 7 fig.

e254* **Andreae** Bernard, Laokoon und die Gründung Roms [Troy's death = Rome's birth]: KultGAntW 39. Mainz 1988, von Zabern. 220 p.; 36 fig. + 30 color. DM 50 [GreeceR 36,249, B. A. *Sparkes*].

e255 **Barnett** R. D., Ancient ivories in the Middle East...: Qedem 14, 1982 ➤ 63,a508 ... 3,d663: ᴿAulaOr 6 (1988) 275 (G. del *Olmo Lete*).

e256 *Bartman* Elizabeth, Decor et reduplicatio; pendants in Roman sculptural display ['pendant' is not defined in the article (nor in Webster's Collegiate) as a support *below* the statue or rather the statue itself so supported; though the article deals with such statues, they are 'pendants' in the sense (far down in Oxford Dictionary) of 'counterparts' to be seen simultaneously]: AJA 92 (1988) 211-225; 12 fig.

e257 *Belloni* Gian Guido, Momenti della comparsa e dell'evoluzione della figura umana e della figura divina nell'arte greca: AevA 1 (Mi 1988) 149-180.

e258 **Bersani** Leo, *Dutoit* Ulysse, The forms of violence; narrative in Assyrian art [palace reliefs] and modern culture 1985 ➤ 1,d75: ᴿAJA 92 (1988) 111-6 (W. *Davis*).

e259 **Besques** Simone, Musée du Louvre, catalogue raisonné des figurines et reliefs grecs... 4/1. P 1986, Réunion des Musées Nationaux. xvi-162 p.; vol. of 165 pl. – ᴿRArchéol (1988) 410-2 (C. *Rolley*).

e260 **Boardman** John, Greek sculpture 1985 ➤ 1,d76: ᴿAevum 62 (1988) 126-8 (Chiara *Tarditi*).

e261 **Boardman** John, Griechische Plastik; die klassische Zeit, ᵀ*Felten* Wassiliki & Florens: KultGAntW 35. Mainz 1987, von Zabern. 323 p., 246 fig.; 8 pl.

e262 **Bober** Phyllis P., *Rubinstein* Ruth, Renaissance artists and antique sculpture; a handbook of sources. Ox/L 1986, Univ./Miller. 522 p.; 526 fig. £45. – ᴿGnomon 60 (1988) 78-80 (R. *Harprath*).

e263 **Bol** Peter C., Antike Bronzetechnik; Kunst und Handwerk antiker Erzbildner 1985 ➤ 1,d78; 2,a229: ᴿGymnasium 94 (1987) 186-8 (U. *Jantzen*); Latomus 47 (1988) 460s (S. *Boucher*).

e264 *Brentjes* Burchard, Sibirische Tier-'Szepter' und verwandte Symbolgeräte: ArchMIran 20 (1987) 93-97; 5 fig.; pl. 11.

e264* *Bryan* Betsy M., Portrait sculpure of Thutmose IV: JAmEg 24 (1987) 3-20; 29 fig.

e265 *Cain* Hans-Ulrich, Chronologie, Ikonographie und Bedeutung der römischen Maskenreliefs: BonnJbb 188 (1988) 107-221; 57 fig.

e266 *Calcani* Giuliana, Galati modello: RINASA 10 (1987) 153-174; 25 fig.

e267 *Canby* Jeanny V., A monumental puzzle; reconstructing the Ur-Nammu stela: Expedition 29,1 (Ph 1987) 54-64; 20 fig.

e268 **Chadefaud** Catherine, Les statues porte-enseignes de l'Égypte ancienne... culte du Ka royal 1982 → 2,a231: ᴿAulaO 6 (1988) 111s (G. del *Olmo Lete*).

e269 **Chaisemartin** Nathalie de, Les sculptures romaines de Sousse et des sites environnants: Corpus/Tunisie 2/2, Collection 102. R 1987, Éc. Française. vi-170 p.; 215 fig.

e270 *Darga* A. Muhibbe, Les figurines en terre cuite de Şemsiyetepe: → 112*, ᶠOTTEN H., Documentum 1988, 77-81 + IV pl.

e271 *Deubner* Otfried, Die Statuen von Riace: JbDAI 103 (1988) 127-153; 14 fig.

e272 **Dörig** José, La frise est de l'Héphaisteion 1985 → 3,d676: ᴿGnomon 60 (1988) 253-6 (F. *Felten*).

e273 *Donderer* Michael, Nicht Praxiteles, sondern Pasiteles; eine signierte Statuenstütze in Verona: ZPapEp 73 (1988) 63-68.

e274 **Eaton-Krauss** Marianne, The representations of statuary in private tombs of the Old Kingdom: ÄgAbh 39, 1984 → 65,a461... 3,d677*: ᴿCdÉ 63 (1988) 295s (Nadine *Cherpion*).

e275 **Eschbach** Norbert, Statuen auf panathenäischen Preisamphoren des 4 Jhs. v. Chr. Mainz 1986, von Zabern. xxiv-182 p.; 99 fig.; 43 pl. DM 98. – ᴿDLZ 109 (1988) 963-6 (H. *Heres*); RArchéol (1988) 137s (H. *Metzger*). Figurines funéraires: **Bruns-Özgan** C. → e497; **Chappaz** J. → e499.

e276 **Fittschen** Klaus, *Zanker* Paul, Katalog der römischen Porträts in... Rom I 1985 → 1,d84... 3,d679: ᴿBabesch 62 (1987) 175s (R. de *Kind*).

e277 **Gabelmann** Hanns, Antike Audienz- und Tribunalszenen 1984 → 3, d680 ('Hans'): ᴿAnzAltW 41 (1988) 217-9 (F. *Felten*); BonnJbb 188 (1988) 584s (Diana E. E. *Kleiner*); HZ 247 (1988) 131s (F. *Kolb*).

e278 [ᴱ**Gaborit** Jean-René, *Ligot* Jack] *Colinart* Sylvie, *al.,* Sculptures en cire, de l'ancienne Égypte à l'art abstrait: Notes et documents 18. P 1987, Réunion Musées Nationaux. 465 p.; ill. 2-7118-2090-4.

e279 **Getz-Preziosi** Pat, Sculptors of the Cyclades; individual and tradition in the third millennium B.C. [< diss.]. AA 1987, Univ. Michigan. 254 p.; 53 fig.; 50 pl. + 11 color. £28. 0-472-10067-X. – ᴿAntiquity 62 (1988) 818-820 (C. *Renfrew*: handsome).

e280 **Giuliani** Luca, Bildnis und Botschaft; hermeneutische Untersuchungen zur Bildniskunst der römischen Republik. Fra 1986, Suhrkamp. 335 pl; 3 fig.; 66 pl. – ᴿBonnJbb 188 (1988) 588-597 (D. *Hertel*); Gnomon 60 (1988) 761-3 (R. R. R. *Smith*).

e281 **Grimal** N.C., La stèle triomphale de Pi (ʿankh)y 1981 → 63,9660.d459... 1,b41: ᴿOLZ 83 (1988) 20-22 (J. *Hallof*).

e282 **Higgins** Reynold, Tanagra [place in Boeotia] and the figurines [standing terracotta women in flowing cloaks]. Princeton 1987, Univ. 198 p.; 214 fig.; 10 color pl. $50. – ᴿAJA 92 (1988) 449-451 (Rebecca M. *Ammerman*).

e283 *Hofmann* Inge, Überlegungen zur 'Venus von Meroe' ÄS 1334: Bei-Sudan 3 (1988) 25-38; 4 fig. + color. cover.

e284 *Jenkins* I.D., *Middleton* A.P., Paint on the Parthenon sculptures: AnBritAth 83 (1988) 183-207.

e285 **Kiss** Zsolt, Études sur le portrait impérial romain en Égypte 1984 → 2, a242; 3,d685: ᴿArcheologia 36 (Wrocław 1985) 182-4 (N. *Bonacasa,* ital.).

e286 *Kobayashi* Toshiko, A study of the peg figurine with the inscription of Enannatum, I: Orient-J 24 (1988) 1-17; 5 fig.

e287 *Kozloff* Arielle P., The human form in classical bronze [exhibition]: Archaeology 41,6 (1988) 54-57; ill. ...

e288 ᴱ**Kyrieleis** H., Archaische und klassische griechische Plastik 1985/6 → 3,794: ᴿClasR 102 (1988) 345-7 (J. *Boardman*).

e289 **Lahusen** Götz, Untersuchungen zur Ehrenstatue in Rom 1983 → 1,d95: ᴿAnzAltW 41 (1988) 81-84 (H. *Gabelmann*).

e290 **Leander-Touati** Anne-Marie, The great Trajanic frieze; the study of a monument and of the mechanisms of message transmission in Roman art: Svenska Institutet i Rom 45. Sto 1987, Åström. 130 p.; 56 pl.

e291 *Loucas-Durie* Éveline, Simulacre humain et offrande rituelle: → 693, Actes = Kernos 1 (1988) 151-162.

e292 **Lunsingh Scheurleer** Robert A., Grieken in het klein; 100 antieke terracotta's. Amst 1986, A. Pierson Museum. 99 p.; 100 fig.

e293 **Lygkopoulos** Timotheos, Untersuchungen zur Chronologie der Plastik des 4. Jhs. v. Chr.: Diss. Bonn 1983, ᴰ*Himmelmann* N. 213 p.

e294 *Mačabeli* Kiti, Une sculpture géorgienne paléochrétienne; la stèle du village de Mamula: → 38, Mém. DUMÉZIL G. = RÉtGC 3 (1987) 133-140 + 7 fig.

e295 *Malaise* Michel, L'art du relief dans l'Égypte ancienne: → 101, Mém. MARÇAIS P. 1985, 91-102.

Martin Hans G., Römische Tempelkultbilder; eine archäologische Untersuchung zur späten Republik 1987 → e476.

e297 *a) Mayer-Opificius* Ruth, Gedanken zur Bedeutung frühdynastischer Rundbilder; – *b) Beran* Thomas, Leben und Tod der Bilder: → 32, ꟳDELLER K., AOAT 220 (1988) 247-268; pl. IV-XV / 55-60.

e298 *Moorey* P. R. S., The technique of gold-figure decoration on Achaemenid silver vessels and its antecedents: → 4, ꟳAMIET P. = IrAnt 33 (1988) 231-246; V pl.

e299 *Morandi* Daniele, Stele e statue reali assire; localizzazione, diffusione e implicazioni ideologiche: MesopT 23 (1988) 105-155.

e300 *a) Moursi* Mohamed, Two Ramesside stelae from Heliopolis; – *b) Ockinga* Boyo G., A First Intermediate Period stela at Nag el Mashayikh: GöMiszÄg 105 (1988) 59-61 + II pl. / 77-80 + 1 fig.

e301 **Müller-Karpe** Hermann, Frauen des 13. Jahrhunderts v. Chr. 1985 → 2,9733; 3,d696: ᴿBabesch 63 (1988) 189s (Maria *Stoof*).

e302 **Muscarella** Oscar W., Bronze and iron; Ancient Near Eastern artifacts in the Metropolitan Museum of Art. NY 1988, Museum. 501 p.; 609 phot.; index by object-type (not mostly sculpture). 0-87099-525-1.

e303 *a) Nachtergael* Georges, Le panthéon de terres cuites de l'Égypte hellénistique et romaine; – *b) Rassart-Debergh* Marguerite, Masques de momies, portraits et icônes: → d702, Monde Copte 14s (1988) 5-27 / 28-30 (50-57).

e304 **Niemeier** Jörg-Peter, Kopien und Nachahmungen im Hellenismus; ein Beitrag zum Klassizismus des 2. und frühen 1. Jahrhunderts vor Christus. Bonn 1985, Habelt. 246 p.; 38 fig. DM 45. – ᴿDLZ 109 (1988) 853-6 (W. *Schindler*).

e305 *Radwan* Ali, Six Ramesside stelae in the popular pyramidion-form [three from Zagazig, three from Ṣaqqâra]: → 127, ꟳṢALEH A., ASAE 71 (1987) 223-8; VI pl.

e306 *Rolley* Claude,   Les bronzes grecs; recherches récentes [VII]; RArchéol (1988) 341-355; 4 fig.

e307 *Russo* Eugenio,   La scultura del VI secolo in Palestina; considerazioni e proposte [*Bagatti* B., Dominus Flevit 1958 ...]: AcANorv 6 (1987) 113-248; 88 fig.

e308 *Salihi* Wathiq I. al-,   Mesene's bronze statue of 'Weary Hercules' [bearing Greek inscriptions]: Sumer 43 (1984) 219-229; 20 fig.; ❹ 136-145.

e309 **Schindler** Wolfgang,   Römische Kaiser; Herrscherbild und Imperium. W 1986, Böhlau. 220 p.; 43 fig.; 72 pl. Sch 348. 3-205-00563-5. – ᴿKlio 70 (1988) 295-307 (D. *Rössler*).

e310 **Schleiermacher** Mathilde,   Römische Reitergrabsteine; die kaiserzeitlichen Reliefs des triumphierenden Reiters: Abh. Kunst 338. Bonn 1984, Bouvier. 273 p.; ill.; map. DM 98. – ᴿEirene 25 (1988) 145-7 (Jana *Kepartová*).

e311 **Schneider** Rolf M.,   Bunte Barbaren; Orientalstatuen aus farbigem Marmor in der römischen Repräsentationskunst. Worms 1986, Werner. 301 p.; 50 pl. – ᴿBonnJbb 188 (1988) 587s (M. *Wissemann*).

e312 **Schulman** A. R.,   Ceremonial execution and public rewards; some historical scenes on New Kingdom private stelae: OBO 75. FrS/Gö 1988, Univ./VR. xxix-223 p.; 35 fig.; 6 pl. Fs 74. 3-7278-0548-X / VR 3-525-53704-2 [BL 89, 126s, K. A. *Kitchen*].

e313 *Shapiro* Kenneth D.,   The Berlin Dancer [1874, known in 7 marble replicas] completed; a bronze auletris in Santa Barbara: AJA 92 (1988) 509-527; 14 fig.

e314 *Skupinska-Løvset* Ilona, Funerary portraiture of Roman Palestine 1983 → 64,b158 ... 3,d706: ᴿRPLH 62,1 (1988) 184s (R. *Rebuffat*).

e315 **Smith** R.R.R.,   Hellenistic royal portraits: MgClasArch. Ox 1988, Univ. 0-19-813224-7 [OIAc D88].

e316 **Söldner** Magdalene,   Untersuchungen zu liegenden Eroten in der hellenistischen und römischen Kunst: EurHS 38/10. Fra 1986, Lang. xiii-379 p.; p. 380-788; 211 fig. Fs 149. – ᴿGnomon 60 (1988) 346-351 (B. *Schmaltz*).

e317 *a) Stross* F. H., *al.,* Sources of the quartzite of some ancient Egyptian sculptures; – *b) Mello* E., *al.,* Discriminating sources of Mediterranean marbles; a pattern recognition approach: Archaeometry 30 (1988) 109-119 / 102-108.

e318 *Stucky* Rolf, Kleinplastiken, Nachträge ...: ArchMIran 20 (1987) 161-5; 1 fig.; pl. 18-21.

e319 **Tripathi** Daya N.,   Bronzework of mainland Greece from c. 2600 B.C. to c. 1450 B.C.; diss. Southampton: SIMA pocket 69. Göteborg 1988, Åström. x-433 p., 154 pl. 91-86098-74-8.

e320 *Verlinden* Colette,   Réflexions sur la fonction et la production des figurines anthropomorphes minoennes en bronze: OpAth 17 (1988) 183-189; Eng. 183.

e321 **Vollkommer** Rainer,   Herakles in the art of classical Greece: Mg 25. Ox 1988, Univ. Committee for Archaeology. 124 p.: 103 fig.; 6 maps. 0-947816-25-9.

e322 *Vorster* Christiane,   Die Herme des fellbekleideten Herakles, Typenwandel und Typenwanderung in hellenistischer und römischer Zeit: KölnJbVFG 21 (1988) 7-34; 37 fig.; map.

e323 **Walter-Karydi** Elena,   Die äginetische Bildhauerschule; Werke und schriftliche Quellen: Alt-Ägina 2/2. Mainz 1987, von Zabern. 172 p.; 220 fig.; 66 pl.; foldout. – ᴿGnomon 60 (1988) 435-8 (P. E. *Arias*, ital.).

e324 **Warland** Rainer, Das Brustbild Christi, Studien zu spätantiken und frühbyzantinischen Bildgeschichte: RömQ Sup. 41. R 1986, Herder. 288 p.; 14 fig.; 139 pl. – ᴿRivArCr 62 (1988) 421-6 (V. *Saxer*).

e325 **Wood** Susan, Roman portrait sculpture 217-260 A.D. 1986 ⇥ 2,a261: ᴿAntClas 57 (1988) 604-8 (J. C. *Balty*); Babesch 63 (1988) 208s (R. de *Kind*); JRS 78 (1988) 257s (R. R. R. *Smith*).

e325* *Wood* Susan, Isis, eggheads and Roman portraiture: JAmEg 24 (1987) 123-141; 17 fig.

e326 **Wrede** Henning, Die antike Herme 1986 ⇥ 2,a262; 3,d720 [antike!]: ᴿBabesch 62 (1987) 176-8 (W. de *Beijer*); Gnomon 60 (1988) 75s (A. *Hermary*).

T3.3 *Glyptica*: **Stamp and cylinder seals,** scarabs, amulets.

e327 *Ahmad* Ali Y, Akkadian seals and seal impressions from Sippar: Sumer 45 (1987s) 61-69.

e328 *Alfi* Mostafa El-, A selection of scarabs [not on display] in the Musée d'Art et d'Histoire in Geneva: DiscEg 12 (1988) 11-18; 1 pl.

e329 **Avigad** Nahman, Hebrew bullae from the time of Jeremiah; remnants of a burnt archive, ᵀ*Grafman* R. 1986 ⇥ 2,a264; 3,d723: ᴿBijdragen 49 (1988) 443 (F. De *Meyer*); BSOAS 51 (1988) 542 (S. C. *Layton*); JAOS 108 (1988) 663 (G. A. *Rendsburg*: masterly); JQR 79 (1988s) 86s (E. J. *Revell*); MondeB 52 (1988) 55 (J. *Briend*); PEQ 120 (1988) 69-71 (A. R. *Millar*, also on BORDREUIL P.); RB 95 (1988) 592-4 (É. *Puech*: corrections); TLZ 113 (1988) 208 (K. *Jaroš*, Rubrik 'Christliche Archäologie'); VT 38 (1988) 378s (J. A. *Emerton*).

e330 *Avigad* Nahman, Hebrew seals and sealings and their significance for biblical research: ⇥ 482, VTS 40, Jerusalem congress 1986/8, 7-16.

e331 **Bailey** Virginia E. [HAMMERSLEY Katherine J. memorial], Minuscule monuments of ancient art; catalogue of Near Eastern stamp and cylinder seals [in] New Jersey museum of archaeology. Madison NJ 1988, Drew Univ. No pagination; 183 items with photos.

e332 *Becking* Bob, Kann das Ostrakon ND 6231 von Nimrūd für ammonitisch gehalten werden?: ZDPV 104 (1988) 59-67: rather a mixture of Ammonite and Israelite names.

e333 *Ben-Tor* Daphna, Scarabs bearing titles and private names of officials from the Middle Kingdom and the Second Intermediate period (c. 2050-1550 B.C.E.): IsrMusJ 7 (1988) 35-47; 20 fig.

e333* *Bergamini* Giovanni, Sigilli a stampo e a cilindro mesopotamici di collezione privata: MesopT 23 (1988) 63-90; fig. 33-36.

e334 *Blocher* Felix, Einige altbabylonische Siegelabrollungen aus Kiš im Louvre: RAss 82 (1988) 33-45; 23 fig.; franç. 46.

e335 *Boehmer* Rainer M., Einflüsse der Golfglyptik auf die anatolische Stempelglyptik zur Zeit der assurischen Handelsniederlassungen: Bagh-Mit 17 (1986) 293-8; map; pl. 42-44.

e336 *Bol'šakov* A. I., *Il'jina* Ju. I., ❻ Les scarabées égyptiens de l'île de Berezan: VDI 186 (1988) 51-66; franç. 66s; 5 fig.; 9 phot.

e337 **Bordreuil** P., Catalogue des sceaux ouest-sémitiques inscrits... 1986 ⇥ 3,d730: ᴿJSS 33 (1988) 115s (J. *Naveh*); Orientalia 57 (1988) 93-96 (F. *Israel*); RAss 82 (1988) 177s (P. *Amiet*); RHPR 68 (1988) 231s (E. *Jacob*); WeltOr 19 (1988) 194-7 (W. *Röllig*).

e338 *Boussac* Marie-Françoise, Sceaux déliens: RArchéol (1988) 307-340; 69 fig.

e339 **Boysan** Nilüfer, *al.*, Sammlung [luwisch-] hieroglyphischer Siegel I + Sup. 1983/5 → 64,a948 ... 3,d731: ᴿKratylos 33 (1988) 178s (N. *Oettinger*).

e340 *Bystrikova* M., ❷ Two Coptic bone amulets: SGErm 61 (1986) 48s; 3 fig.

e341 *Charvat* P., Archaeology and social history; the Susa sealings, ca. 4000-2340 B.C.: Paléorient 14,1 (1988) 57-63, franç. 57.

e342 **Collon** Dominique, *al.* Catalogue of the Western Asiatic seals in the British Museum, Cylinder seals II, Akkadian – Post-Akkadian Ur III periods 1982 → 63,a559 ... 3,d737: ᴿBO 45 (1988) 191-203 (Edith *Porada*).

e343 **Collon** D., Cylinder seals IV, Isin-Larsa, OB 1986 → 2,a276; 3,d738: ᴿBSOAS 51 (1988) 120s (Eva *Møller*); OLZ 83 (1988) 672-5 (Evelyn *Klengel-Brandt*); RAss 82 (1988) 89s (D. *Charpin*); ZAss 78 (1988) 158s (U. *Seidl*).

e344 **Collon** D., First impressions 1987 → 3,d739: ᴿAJA 92 (1988) 602-4 (Edith *Porada*); Antiquity 62 (1988) 402s (R. M. *Boehmer*); AntiqJ 68,1 (1988) 141s (P. R. S. *Moorey*); RAss 82 (1988) 186s (D. *Charpin*).

e345 *Collon* Dominique, Some cylinder seals from Tell Mohammed Arab: Iraq 50 (1988) 59-77; 10 fig.; pl. [? I-] VI-VII.

e346 **Courtois** J.-C., *Webb* Jennifer M., Les cylindres-sceaux d'Enkomi 1987 → 3,d741: ᴿBInstArch 25 (1988) 110 (Dominique *Collon*).

e347 *D'Angelo* M. Carmela, Analisi morfologica di un motivo araldico vicino-orientale [carvings of two horizontal figures flanking a vertical one, e.g. two animals and a tree]: EgVO 11 (1988) 155-164; 13 fig. + 15 on 2 pl. p. 165s.

e348 **Devauchelle** Didier, Ostraca démotiques au Musée du Louvre 1983 → 2,a280: ᴿOLZ 83 (1988) 657s (B. *Menu*).

e349 *Dinçol* Ali M. & Belkis, Hieroglyphische Siegel und Siegelabdrücke aus Eskiyapar: → 112*, ᶠOTTEN H., Documentum 1988, 87-97; V pl.

e350 *Fazzini* R. A., *Jasnow* R., Demotic ostraca from the Mut precinct in Karnak: Enchoria 16 (1988) 23-48; pl. 4-21.

e351 **Fernández** Jorge H., *Padró* Josep, Amuletos de tipo egipcio de Museo Arqueológico de Ibiza: Trabajos 16. Ibiza 1986, Conselleria d'Educació. 109 p.: 7 fig.; 17 pl. 84-505-4410-6. – ᴿBO 45 (1988) 338-340 (J. *Śliwa*).

e352 **Gasse** Annie, Catalogue des ostraca figurés de Deir el-Médineh Nos. 3100-3372 (5ᵉ fasc.) 1986 → 3,d744: ᴿJAmEg 25 (1988) 251s (C. A. *Keller*).

e353 **Gignoux** Philippe, *Gyselen* Rika, Bulles et sceaux sassanides de diverses collections: StIran Cah 4, 1987 → 3,d745: ᴿPersica 13 (1988s) 173-5 (Elisabeth C. L. *During Caspers*).

e354 **Giveon** Raphael, Egyptian scarabs ... OBO arch. 3, 1985 → 1,d140 ... 3,d746: ᴿOLZ 83 (1988) 285s (Magdalena *Stoof*); RStFen 16 (1988) 126s (Gabriella *Scandone Matthiae*).

e355 **Giveon** Raphael, *Kertesz* Trude, Egyptian scarabs and seals from Acco 1986 → 2,a286; Fs 19: ᴿBO 45 (1988) 567s (J. *Śliwa*).

e356 **Giveon** R., Scarabs from recent excavations in Israel, ᴱ*Warburton* D., *Uehlinger* C. [Giveon biobibliog., *Keel* O.]: OBO 83. FrS/Gö 1988, Univ./VR. vii-114 p.; 9 pl. Fs 36; DM 52. 3-7278-0581-1 / 3-525-53712-3 [BL 89,27 K. A. *Kitchen*].

e357 *Gosline* Sheldon L., Egyptian deity pendants [amulets, not 'correspondents']; defining a type of late dynastic religious artifacts: DiscEg 12 (1988) 19-26.

e358 *Gubel* E., Phoenician seals in the Allard Pierson museum, Amsterdam (CGPH 3): RStFen 16 (1988) 145-163.

e359 *Henrickson* E.F., Chalcolithic seals and sealings from Šeh Gabi, Western Iran: ➤ 4, ᶠAMIET P., IrAnt 23 (1988) 1-19; 3 pl.

e360 *Herr* L.G., Seal: ➤ 801, ISBEnc³ 4 (1988) 369-375; 20 fig.

e361 *Hübner* Ulrich, *a)* Die ersten moabitischen Ostraka [Diban samples unavailable]: ZDPV 104 (1988) 68-71; – *b)* Ein nordsyrisches Stempelsiegel aus Galiläa ['Orēme]: UF 20 (1988) 89-92; 2 fig.

e361* **Jaeger** Bertrand, Essai de classification et datation des scarabées Menkhéperré: OBO arch 2, 1982 ➤ 63,a568 ... 3,d756: ᴿWZKM 77 (1987) 131-6 (H. *Satzinger*).

e362 **Keel** Othmar, *Schroer* Sylvia, Studien zu den Stempelsiegeln aus Palästina/Israel, I: OBO 67, 1985 ➤ 1,d152 ... 3,d759: ᴿCBQ 50 (1988) 502s (G.J. *Hamilton*); WZKM 78 (1986) 281s (K. *Jaroš*).

e363 *Klengel-Brandt* E., Das Siegelbild als Widerspieglung gesellschaftlicher Verhältnisse des 3. Jahrtausend v. Chr. in Mesopotamien — Versuch einer Interpretation: Akkadica 59 (1988) 1-14.

e364 *Lambert* Wilfred G., Seals from West Central Asia and adjacent regions: ArchMIran 19 (1986) 34-40; 4 fig.; pl. 12.

e365 *Loon* Maurits N. van, Two Neo-Elamite cylinder seals with mounted huntsmen: ➤ 4, ᶠAMIET P. = IrAnt 33 (1988) 221-6; IV pl.

e365* *Lund* John [*Hvidberg-Hansen* F.O.], Two late Punic amphora stamps from the Danish excavations at Carthage: ➤ 754, Carthago 1986/8, 101-112 [-118, interpretation]; 5 + 2 fig. (map).

e366 **Marcus** Michelle Irene, The seals and sealings from Hasanlu IVB, Iran. Ph 1988, Univ. Pennsylvania. [OIAc D88; diss.] 88-16203.

e367 *Mayer-Opificius* R., Ein seltenes assyrisches Siegel: UF 20 (1988) 145-7 + 4 fig.

e368 ᴱ*Meekers-Ayat* Trokay M., Glyptica VI [bibliographie 1983-4]: Akkadica 60 (1988) 13-36.

e369 *Oates* David & Joan, An Urartian stamp cylinder from north-eastern Syria: ➤ 4, ᶠAMIET P. = IrAnt 33 (1988) 217s; pl. I.

e370 *O'Connor* David, The chronology of scarabs of the Middle Kingdom and the Second Intermediate Period: JSStEg 15 (1985) 1-41.

e371 *Özgüç* Nimet, Anatolian cylinder seals and impressions from Kültepe and Acemhöyük in the second millennium B.C.: ➤ 760, Anatolian 1983/8, 22-29 + 8 fig.

e372 **Pfrommer** Michael, Studien zu alexandrinischer und grossgriechischer Toreutik frühhellenistischer Zeit: DAI ArchForsch 16. B 1987, Mann. xv-312 p.; 62 pl. 3-7861-1433-1.

e373 **Platon** Nikolaos, *Pini* Ingo, Iraklion 3s, Corpus der minoischen und mykenischen Siegel II. B 1984s, Mann. lxxii-460 p., 390 fig.; lxxvi-305 p., 239 fig. – ᴿGnomon 60 (1988) 430-5 (W. *Schiering*).

e374 *Podzorski* Patricia V., Predynastic Egyptian seals of known provenience in the [Berkeley] R.H. Lowie Museum of Anthropology: JNES 47 (1988) 259-268; 6 fig.

e375 *Porada* Edith, *a)* Discussion of a cylinder seal, probably from Southeast Iran: ➤ 4, ᶠAMIET P., IrAnt 33 (1988) 139-143; 4 pl.; – *b)* Late Cypriote cylinder seals between East and West: ➤ 748, Cyprus between, 1985/6, 289-299; pl. XVII-XX.

e376 **Speck** Paul, *al.*, Byzantinische Bleisiegel in Berlin (West): Poikíla Vizantiná 5. Bonn 1986, Habelt. 261 p.; 15 pl. – ᴿEllinika 39 (1988) 185-9 (R. *Volk*).

e377 **Teissier** Beatrice, ANE cylinder seals ... Marcopoli 1984 ➤ 1,d170 ... 3,d777: ᴿBInstArch 25 (1988) 177s (Lamia *Werr*); OLZ 83 (1988) 549-551 (E. *Klengel-Brandt*).

e378 **Tufnell** Olga, Studies on scarab seals II, 1984 ➤ 65,a534 ... 3,d779: ᴿJAOS 108 (1988) 517s (J. M. *Weinstein*).

Uehlinger Christoph, Der Amun-Tempel Ramses' III. in p3-Knʿn ... ein Hinweis auf einige wenig beachtete Skarabäen 1988 ➤ b881.

e380 **Vollenweider** Marie-Louise, La collection V. Kenna et d'autres: Musée de Genève, Catalogue raisonné des sceaux 3. Mainz 1983, von Zabern. xx-244 p.; 245 fig. – ᴿRArchéol (1988) 387 (Evelyne *Veljović*); ZDPV 104 (1988) 162 (Hildi *Keel-Leu*).

e381 **Weingarten** Judith, The Zakro master 1983 ➤ 64,a998; 2,a321: ᴿRB 95 (1988) 124s (P. H. & R. S. *Merrillees*).

e382 *Weingarten* Judith, Seal-use at Late Minoan IB Ayia Triada; a Minoan élite in action; II. aesthetic considerations: Kadmos 27 (1988) 89-114; 2 fig.; pl. I-IV.

e383 [al-Gailani] **Werr** Lamia, Studies in the chronology and regional style of Old Babylonian cylinder seals: BibMesop 23. Malibu 1988, Undena. x-111 p.

e384 *Werr* Lamia al-Gailani, Cylinder seals made of clay: Iraq 50 (1988) 1-24; 17 fig.; pl. I-IV.

e385 *Winter* Irene J., Legitimation of authority through image and legend; seals belonging to officials in the administrative bureaucracy of the Ur III state: ➤ 738, Power 1983/7, 69-106 + 10 pl.

e385* **Younger** J. G., The iconography of Late Minoan and Mycenaean sealstones and finger rings. Bristol 1988, Classical. 432 p.; 152 fig. 0-906515-70-X [Antiquity 63,100].

e386 **Yule** Paul, Early Cretan seals 1981 ➤ 61,s433 ... 3,d783: ᴿGGA 240 (1988) 188-224 (J. G. *Younger*, Eng.; appendix of corrigenda and reviews).

T3.4 Mosaica.

e387 **Balmelle** Catherine, *al.*, Le décor géométrique de la mosaïque romaine; répertoire graphique et descriptif des compositions linéaires et isotropes 1985 ➤ 2,a325; 3,d785: ᴿRArchéol (1988) 416-420 (Suzanne *Goslan*).

e388 *Berczelly* Laszlo, The date and significance of the Menander mosaics at Mytilene [300 AD]: Bulletin Inst. Clas. Studies 35 (L 1988) 119-126; pl. 3-6.

e389 *Blanchard-Lemée* Michèle, À propos des mosaïques de Sidi Ghrib [Tunisie]; Vénus, le Gaurus et un poème de Symmaque: MÉF 100 (1988) 366-384; 7 fig.

e390 *Bruneau* Philippe, Philologie mosaïstique: JSav (1988) 3-73; 5 fig.

e391 **Daszewski** Wiktor A., Corpus of mosaics from Egypt I. Hellenistic and Early Roman period, 1985 ➤ 3,d788: ᴿAegyptus 68 (1988) 249-251 (G. G. *Belloni*); BO 45 (1988) 139-143 (C. H. *Ericsson*); BSAA 54 (1988) 543 (A. *Balil*: in press since 1979).

e392 **Donderer** Michael, Die Chronologie der römischen Mosaiken in Venetien und Istrien bis zur Zeit der Antonine: DAI-ArchF 15, 1986 ➤ 3,d789*; ᴿClasR 102 (1988) 360s (Katherine M. *Dunbabin*).

e393 **Lavagne** Henri, La mosaïque: Que sais-je? 2361. P 1987, PUF. 125 p.; 5 fig. – ᴿRÉLat 66 (1988) 366 (R. *Adam*).

e394 *Loos-Dietz* E. P. de, L'oiseau au ruban rouge autour du cou; la fonction apotropéique des motifs naturalistes et géométriques [mosaïques du couvent russe du Mont des Oliviers, Jérusalem; de Nébo; d'Antioche]: Babesch 63 (1988) 141-164; 17 fig.

e395 **Michaelidis** D., Cypriot mosaics: Picture Book 7, 1987 → 3,d794: ᴿRArchéol (1988) 389s (A.-M. *Guimier-Sorbets*).

e396 **Ovadiah** Ruth & Asher, Hellenistic, Roman and Early Byzantine mosaic pavements in Israel: Bibliotheca Archaeologica 6, R 1987, Bretschneider. 276 p.; 176 pl. + 16 color. – ᴿArctos 22 (1988) 261s (A. *Tammisto*); BonnJbb 188 (1988) 610s (Gisela H. *Salies*).

e397 *Piccirillo* Michele, The mosaics at Um er-Rasas in Jordan: BA 51 (1988) 208-213. 227-231; color. ill. and front cover.

e398 **Roussin** Lucille A., The iconography of the figural pavements of early Byzantine Palestine: diss. Columbia. NY 1985. 663 p. 88-09413. – DissA 49 (1988s) 534-A.

e399 **Russell** James, The mosaic inscriptions of Anemurium [S. Turkey]: ph/h Denkschrift 199; Tituli Asiae Minoris 13 Egbd. W 1987, Österr. Akad. 92 p.; 22 fig.; 27 pl. Sch 210. – ᴿGnomon 30 (1988) 662-4 (J. *Nolle*); JbAC 31 (1988) 232s (Katherine M. D. *Dunbabin*); OrChr 72 (1988) 238s (W. *Gessel*).

e400 *Salies* Gisela H. Die Mosaiken der Grossen Moschee von Damaskus: → 758, Ravenna 1988, 295-313.

T3.5 *Ceramica,* **pottery** [→ *singuli situs*].

e401 *Adams* William Y., *a)* Puzzle of the Nubian pots [creative eruption and decline c. 100-350 and 850-1550 A.D.]: Archaeology 41,2 (1988) 46-53; ill.; – *b)* Times, types, and sites; the interrelationship of ceramic chronology and typology: BEgSem 8 (NY 1986s) 7-46.

e402 *Arafat* K. W., Some more vases by the Ikaros painter: Bulletin of the Institute of Classical Studies 35 (L 1988) 111-7; 8 phot.

e403 *Ariel* Donald T., Two Rhodian amphoras [Bet-Šan 1951; with decipherment of fabricant stamps]: IsrEJ 38 (1988) 31-35; 1 fig.; pl. 8.

e404 **Arnold** Dean E., Ceramic theory and cultural process: New St. Arch., 1985 → 2,a334: ᴿBInstArch sup 24 (1987) 47s (Lea D. *Jones*).

e405 *Badenas* Pedro, *Olmos* Ricardo, La nomenclatura de los vasos griegos en castellano; propuestas de uso y normalización: ArEspArq 61 (1988) 61-75; p. 76-79 fig.

e406 ᴱ**Barrelet** M.-T., *Gardin* J.-C., À propos des interprétations archéologiques de la poterie; questions ouvertes 1986 → 2,a335: ᴿJSS 33 (1988) 263 (K. *Prag*); RAss 82 (1988) 187s (P. *Amiet*); WZKM 78 (1986) 290s (Jane *Moon*); ZAss 78 (1988) 149-151 (B. *Hrouda*).

e407 *Berg* Paul-Louis van, Les systèmes dans l'analyse du décor céramique; théorie et application au style de Hajji Firuz (Azerbaïdjan iranien): IrAnt 22 (1987) 1-23; 18 fig.; 1 pl.

e408 **Betancourt** Philip P. The history of Minoan pottery 1985 → 1,d202 ... 3,d815: ᴿClasR 102 (1988) 110s (S. *Hood*); JHS 108 (1988) 256s (K. *Branigan*).

e409 **Blomberg** Mary, Observations on the Dodwell painter: Memoir 4, 1983 → 1,b978: ᴿArchaiognosia 3,1s (1982ss) 276-9 (Nota *Kourou*).

e410 **Böhr** E., Der Schaukelmaler 1982 → 64,b25 ... 2,a340: ᴿAnzAltW 41 (1988) 73-75 (Gerda *Schwarz*).

e411 *Borowski* Oded, Ceramic dating: → 20, ᶠCALLAWAY J., Benchmarks 1988, 223-234; 4 fig.

e412 **Bothmer** D. von, The Amasis painter and his world 1985 → 2,a341; 3,d819: ᴿJHS 108 (1988) 269 (T. H. *Carpenter*).

e413 **Bourgeois** Brigitte, La conservation des céramiques archéologiques; étude comparée de trois sites chypriotes: Coll. 18, Archéol. 10. Lyon 1987, Maison de l'Orient. 100 p.; 43 fig.; maps. 2-903264-10-4.

e414 *Bourriau* Janine, Cemetery and settlement pottery of the Second Intermediate Period to Early New Kingdom: BEgSem 8 (NY 1986s) 47-57 + 2 fig.

e415 **Brijder** H. A. G., [Attic black-figure] Siana cups I and Komast cups. Amst 1983, Allard Pierson Museum. 316 p.; 82 fig.; vol. of 358 p., 104 pl. – ᴿRArchéol (1988) 132-6 (H. P. *Isler*).

e416 *Brugnone* Antonietta, Bolli anforari rodii dalla necropoli di Lilibeo [Marsala]: Kokalos 37 (Palermo 1986) 19-113; 3 fig.; XXV pl.

e417 **Burn** Lucilla, The Meidias painter [latest Athenian red-figure]. Ox 1988, Clarendon. 156 p. £40. 0-19-813221-2. – ᴿAntiquity 62 (1988) 610s (T. *Rasmussen*).

e418 **Cambitoglou** Alexandre, *al.*, Le peintre de Darius et son milieu; vases grecs d'Italie méridionale: Hellas et Roma 4. Genève 1986, Musée d'art et d'histoire. 285 p.; 138 fig.; 12 pl. – ᴿGnomon 60 (1988) 631-7 (P. E. *Arias*, ital.).

e419 *Caprariis* Francesca De, *al.*, Contenitori da trasporto dell'area siro-palestinese: MélÉcFrR-A 100 (1988) 305-320; 15 fig.

e420 *a*) *Chapman* J. C., Ceramic production and social differentiation; the Dalmatian neolithic and the Western Mediterranean; – *b*) *Frankel* David, Pottery production in prehistoric Bronze Age Cyprus; assessing the problem; – *c*) *Knapp* A. P., *al.*, Ceramic production and social change; archeometric analysis of Bronze Age pottery from Jordan: JMeditArch 1,2 (Sheffield 1988) 3-25 / 27-55 / 57-113.

e421 Corpus vasorum antiquorum, Deutschland: **48**: ᴱ**Kunze-Götte** Erika, München 9, 1982; 31 p.; 23 fig.; 62 pl., 13 foldouts. – **50**: ᴱ**Deppert** Kurt, Frankfurt am Main 3, 1982; 41 p.; 52 pl. – **51**: ᴱ**Wehgartner** Irma, Würzburg 3, 1983; 73 p.; 23 fig.; 52 pl. Mü, Beck; DM 94; 122; 122. – **52**, **54**, ᴱ**Böhr** Elke, ᴱ**Burow** Johannes, Tübingen 4s, 1984/6; 118 p., 40 fig., 52 pl.; 107 p., 36 fig., 48 pl. je DM 142. – ᴿDLZ 109 (1988) 99-104. 437-441 (E. *Paul*).

e422 **Cuomo di Caprio** Ninina, La ceramica in archeologia; antiche tecniche di lavorazione e moderni metodi d'indagine: La Fenice 6, 1985; 88-7062-565-6: ᴿDialArch (1988,2) 139-141 (M. *Vickers*).

e423 **Fukai** Shinji, Ceramics of ancient Persia, ᵀ*Crawford* Edna B. NY/ Tokyo 1981, Weatherhill/Tankosha. x-54 p.; 127 color. pl. [B. Takahashi photos]. $95. – ᴿBASOR 269 (1988) 91 (Gloria *London*).

e424 **Gabler** D., *Vaday* A. H., Terra sigillata im Barbaricum zwischen Pannonien und Dazien 1986 → 3,d827: ᴿStIsVArh 39 (1988) 79s (A. *Barnea*).

e425 *Goodside* Victor, Why is a bilbil called a bilbil?: BAR-W 14,1 (1988) 60 [it gurgles; YADIN thought perhaps named from narcotic content]; 14,3 (1988) 10, letters with other explanations.

e426 **Gunneweg** J., Provenience ... Eastern Terra Sigillata: Qedem 17, 1983 → 64,b37 ... 1,d214: ᴿOLZ 83 (1988) 433 (G. *Pfeifer*).

e427 ᴱ**Hackens** Tony, *Schvoerer* Max, Datation — caractérisation des céramiques anciennes [cours 6-18 avril 1981]: PACT 10, 1984 → 2,558; Fb 2800: ᴿAntClas 57 (1988) 541 (G. *Raepsaet*).

e428 **Haerinck** E., La céramique ... parthe ➤ 64,b37 ... 3,d831: ᴿPrzOr (1987) 243s (B. *Kaim*).

e429 *Hague* Rebecca, Marriage, Athenian style [in vase-paintings]: Archaeology 41,3 (1988) 32-36; ill.

e430 **Hemelrijk** J., Caretan hydriae [ᴰ1956], ᵀ1984 ➤ 1,d218 ... 3,d834: ᴿAcArchH 40 (1988) 337-9 (J. Gy. *Szilágyi*); Latomus 47 (1988) 702s (D. *Emmanuel-Rebuffat*).

e431 *Hofmann* Inge, Ein Gefässtyp der Endphase des meroitischen Reiches: VarAeg 4 (1988) 121-142; 34 fig. + map.

e431* **Jones** R. E., Greek and Cypriot pottery; a review of scientific studies: Fitch paper I, 1987 ➤ 3,d840; 0-904887-01-4: ᴿAntiqJ 68 (1988) 349s (M. J. *Hughes*).

e432 *a) Kafafi* Zeidan, The pottery neolithic in Jordan in connection with other Near Eastern regions; – *b) Schaub* R. Thomas, Ceramic vessels as evidence for trade communication during the Early Bronze Age in Jordan; – *c) Leonard* Albert, The significance of the Mycenaean pottery found east of the Jordan river: ➤ e824, Jordan III, 1986/7, 33-39 / 247-250 / 261-6.

e433 *Kanawati* Naguib, An elaborate blue-painted jar [Ṣaqqâra 1988]: Gö-MiszÄg 41-45 + 3 phot.

e434 *Kanowski* M. G., Greek pottery; right and wrong names, and a shattering of confidence: AncSRes 17,1 (1987) 5-15; 14 fig.

e435 *Kelemen* M., Italian amphorae, [➤ 3,d843] II. Roman amphorae in Pannonia: ActArchH 40 (1988) 111-150; 7 fig.

e436 *Kelley* Allyn L., The production of pottery in ancient Egypt; part II, the Middle Kingdom: ➤ 127, ᶠṢALEḤ A., ASAE 71 (1987) 127-9.

e437 **Kemp** Barry J., *Merrillees* Robert S., Minoan pottery in second millennium Egypt 1980 ➤ 62,b420 ... 65,a573: JNES 47 (1988) 304-7 (P. *Lacovara*).

e438 *Kepinski* Christine, Note d'anthropologie religieuse; à propos de différents types de supports en céramique [temple à Haradum, Iraq]: RAss 82 (1988) 47-57; II pl.

e438* *a) Knapp* A. B., *al.*, Ceramic production and social change; archeometric analysis of Bronze Age pottery from Jordan; – *b) Frankel* D., Pottery production in prehistoric Bronze-Age Cyprus; assessing the problem; – *c) Chapman* J. C., Ceramic production and social differentiation; the Dalmatian Neolithic and the western Mediterranean: JMeditArch 1,2 (1988) 57-113 / 27-55 / 3-25 [< BL 90,32].

e439 *Kühne* Hartmut, *Schneider* Gerwulf, *al.*, Neue Untersuchungen zur metallischen Ware [t. Šeḫ Ḥamad]: DamaszMit 3 (1988) 83-139; 14 fig. (map).

e440 **Kurtz** Donna C., The Berliner painter: Mg ClasArch 1983 ➤ 65,a420 ... 2, a357: ᴿAntClas 57 (1988) 572s (D. *Martens*).

e441 *a) La Genière* Juliette de, Les acheteurs des cratères corinthiens; – *b) Croissant* Francis, Tradition et innovation dans les ateliers corinthiens archaïques; matériaux pour l'histoire d'un style: BCH 112 (1988) 83-90; 7 fig. / 91-166; 103 fig.

e442 **Leeuw** S. E. van der, *al.*, The many dimensions of pottery 1984 ➤ 65,a575; 1,d223: ᴿBInstArch 25 (1988) 180-2 (J. *Chapman*).

e443 *Manacorda* Daniele, Anfore dai mille misteri: Archeo 24 (1987) 26-31; color. ill.

e444 *Martín de la Cruz* J. C., Mykenische Keramik aus bronzezeitlichen

Siedlungsschichten von Montoro am Guadalquivir: MadMit 29 (1988) 77-92; 5 fig.; pl. 9.

e445 *Le Mière* M., *Picon* M., Productions locales et circulation des céramiques au VIᵉ millénaire, au Proche-Orient: Paléorient 13,2 (1987) 133-147.

e446 **Lissarague** François, [vases d'Athènes] Un flot d'images; une esthétique du banquet grec. P 1987, A. Biro. 158 p., 111 fig. – ᴿRÉAnc 90 (1988) 456-8 (Marie-Christine *Villanueva-Puig*).

e447 *Mandel-Elzinga* Ursula, Ptolemäische Reliefkeramik: JbDAI 103 (1988) 247-307, 27 fig.

e448 *Mazar* Amihai, A note on Canaanite [12th century storage] jars from Enkomi: IsrEJ 38 (1988) 224-6; 3 fig.

e449 *Meyer* Marion, Männer mit Geld; zu einer rotfigurigen Vase mit 'Alltagsszene': JbDAI 103 (1988) 87-125; 33 fig.

e450 *Neely* James A., *Storch* Paul S., Friable pigments and ceramic surface; a case study from sw Iran: JField 15 (1988) 108-114; 4 fig.

e450* *Oakley* John H., Attic red-figured skyphoi of Corinthian shape: Hesperia 57 (1988) 165-174; 2 fig.; pl. 50-54; p. 175-192, catalog.

e451 ᴱ*Rice* Prudence M., Pots ... ceramic archaeology 1984 ⇒ 65,a582: ᴿRAss 82 (1988) 87s (P. *Amiet*, p. 192).

e452 *Schuring* Josine M., Terra sigillata africana from the San Sisto Vecchio in Rome: Babesch 63 (1988) 1-68; 42 fig.

e453 **Spivey** Nigel J., The Micali painter and his followers: Mg ClasArch. Ox 1987, Clarendon. xv-103 p.; 40 fig. 0-19-813225-5.

e454 *Stacey* David, Umayyad and Egyptian red-slip 'A' ware from Tiberias: BAnglsr (1988s) 21-33; ill.

e455 **Trendall** A.D., The red-figured vases of Paestum² [¹1936] R 1987, British School. xxxii-452 p.; 9 fig.; 242 pl. – ᴿRArchéol (1988) 152-5 (J.-M. *Moret*).

e456 **Vanderhoeven** Michel, La terre sigillée. Liège 1984, Inst. Archéologique. 32 p.; 28 pl. Fb 200. – ᴿLatomus 47 (1988) 490 (E. *Warmenbol*).

e457 **Venit** Marjorie S., Greek painted pottery from Naukratis in Egyptian museums: American Research Center in Egypt, Catalog 7. Winona Lake IN 1988, Eisenbruns. xiv-211 p.; 85 pl. 0-936770-19-8.

e458 **Vickers** Michael, *al.,* From silver to ceramic; the potter's debt to metalwork in the Graeco-Roman, Oriental and Islamic world. Ox 1986, Ashmolean.

e459 **Wehgartner** Irma, Ein Grabbild des Achilleusmalers [lécythe blanc]: Winckelmannsprogram 129. B 1985, de Gruyter. 52 p.; 31 fig. – ᴿRArchéol (1988) 397s (H. *Metzger*).

e460 **Williams** Bruce, Decorated pottery and the art of Naqada III, a documentary essay: MüÄgSt 45. Mü 1988, Deutscher Kunstv. xiii-93 p.; 36 fig. 3-422-00840-3.

т3.6 **Lampas.**

e461 **Amaré Tafalla** María Teresa, Lucernas romanas, generalidades y bibliografía. Zaragoza 1987, Univ. 123 p.; 2 fig.

e462 ῾*Amr* Abdel-Jalil, Two early Abbasid inscribed pottery lamps from Ǧeraš: ZDPV 104 (1988) 146-9; 1 fig.; pl. 13 [-151 *al.,* Name der Töpfer].

e463 **Bailey** Donald M., Roman provincial lamps: Catalogue of the lamps 3. L 1988, British Museum. xv-560 p.; 160 pl.

e464 **Engle** Anita, Light, lamps and windows in antiquity: Readings in Glass History 20. J 1987, Phoenix. 99 p.; 63 fig.

e465 **Hellmann** Marie-Christine, Lampes antiques de la Bibliothèque Nationale [I. Collection Froehner 1985] II, Fonds général; lampes préromaines et romaines, 1987 → 3,d876: ᴿAntClas 57 (1988) 575-7 (Francine *Blondé*, 1).

e465* *Krogulska* Maria, Une lampe à symboles juifs du temple d'Allat à Palmyre: → 12, ᶠBERNHARD M.-L. 1983, 209-214; 5 fig.

e466 *Naveh* Joseph, Lamp inscriptions and inverted writings: IsrEJ 38 (1988) 36-43; pl. 8-9.

e467 *Oikonomou* Anastasia, Lampes paléochrétiennes d'Argos: BCH 112 (1988) 481-502.

e468 **Sussman** Varda, Ornamented Jewish oil-lamps (1972) 1982 → 64,b68 ... 1,d246: ᴿBInstArch sup 24 (1987) 32s (B.S.J. *Isserlin*).

т3.7 Cultica.

e469 *Carroll* Michael P., DURKHEIM on the emergence of religion; reviewing the archaeological evidence (at last): StRel 17 (Toronto 1988) 291-302 [< ZIT 89,67].

e470 *Chen* Doron, The design of the ancient synagogues in Galilee, IV. Qasrin, Maoz Haim, Gush Halav: SBFLA 38 (1988) 247-252; pl. 1-4.

e470* **Gessler-Löhr** Beatrix, Die heiligen Seen ägyptischer Tempel 1983 → 64,b86: ᴿJEA 74 (1988) 256-8 (H. *Jaritz*); OLZ 83 (1988) 23-26 (Magdalena *Stoof*).

e471 *Grabbe* Lester L., Synagogues in pre-70 Palestine, a re-assessment: JTS 39 (1988) 401-410.

e472 *a) Laffineur* Robert, Archéologie et religion; problèmes et méthode; – *b) Donnay* Guy, L'étude monographique des sanctuaires grecs et la réalité vécue des cultes antiques; – *c) Vandenabeele* Frieda, The rediscovery of the Greek sanctuaries: → 693, Kernos 1 (1988) 129-140 / 121-7 / 215-222.

e473 *LaSor* W. S., *Eskenazi* T. C., Synagogue: → 801, ISBEnc³ 4 (1988) 676-684.

e474 *Lyttelton* Margaret, The design and planning of temples and sanctuaries in Asia Minor in the Roman imperial period: → 454, Roman architecture 1987, 38-49.

e475 *Ma'oz* Zvi U., Ancient synagogues of the Golan: BA 51 (1988) 116-128; ill.

e476 **Martin** Hans G., Römische Tempelkultbilder; eine archäologische Untersuchung zur Späten Republik: StMtMusCivRom 12, 1987 → 3,d889; 88-7062-579-6: ᴿAntiqJ 68 (1988) 350s (J. *Onians*); ArEspArq 61 (1988) 385s (Fabiola *Salcedo Garcés*).

e477 **Merrifield** Ralph, The archaeology of ritual and magic. L 1987, Batsford. 224 p.; 8 fig.; 58 pl. £15. 0-7134-4870-9. – ᴿAntiqJ 68,1 (1988) 129 (H. R. Ellis *Davidson*).

e478 *Olympiou* Nikolaos P., ⊚ *Hē thrēskeutikē architektonikē*... Religious architecture in the land of ancient Canaan: → 693, Actes = Kernos 1 (1988) 177-194; 12 fig.

e479 *Ottosson* M., Temples and cult places 1980 → 61,s602 ... 3,d881: ᴿRB 95 (1988) 121 (J.-M. de *Tarragon*).

e481 **Spencer** Patricia, The Egyptian temple, a lexicographical study 1984 → 65,8083; 1,d270: ᴿCdÉ 63 (1988) 252-8 (J.-C. *Goyon*); JNES 47 (1988) 195-9 (S. B. *Shubert*).

e482 **Stähli** H.-P., Antike Synagogenkunst. Stu 1988, Calwer. 112 p.
DM 29,80.   3-7668-0823-0 [NTAbs 32,398]. – ᴿBiKi 43 (1988) 88s (P.-G.
Müller).

e483 *Volkoff* Oleg V., Églises coptes du Caire; la Moallaqah: Monde Copte
12 (1987) 6-10; ill.

e484 **Wigoder** Geoffrey, The story of the synagogue 1986 → 3,d897:   ᴿSalesianum 50 (1988) 439 (R. *Vicent*: magníficamente presentado).

T3.8   **Funeraria;** *Sindon,* **the Shroud.**

e486 *Abdalla* Aly, A group of Osiris-cloths of the twenty-first dynasty in the
Cairo museum: JEA 74 (1988) 157-164; pl. XXI-XXIII.

e488 *Amand* Marcel, La réapparition de la sépulture sous tumulus dans
l'Empire Romain (II) Le bassin de la Mer Noire et les Balkans: AntClas
57 (1988) 176-203; 2 maps.

e489 **Babiker** Faisal S., Research into mortuary practices in Sudanese
prehistory and early history. Reading 1984, Univ. 3 vol. [British Library
Univ. Microfilms DX82346: OIAc D88].

e490 *Babinet* Robert, L'icône 'acheiropoïète' [not made by hands] du Sindon
est-elle un signe de foi en Christ ressuscité? [editor's note: new questions
about how the image got there, now that Carbon-14 tests have closed off
definitively the possibility of an earlier date than 1300]: EsprVie 98 (1988)
593-605.

e491 *Baffi Guardata* Francesca, Les sépultures d'Ébla à l'âge du Bronze
Moyen: → 707, Wirtschaft 1986/8, 3-21; pl. I-VI.

e492 *a) Ballestrero* Anastasio card., Sindone; quale futuro?; – *b) Baima
Bollone* Pierluigi, Un falso? Io non ci sto; – *c) Barberis* Bruno, Il
mistero rimane, anzi si è accentuato; – *d) Ghiberti* Giuseppe, Testimonianza che continua: Bollettino del Centro Internazionale di
Sindonologia, 'numero unico' (dic. 1988) 1s / 5.8 / 6.8 / 7s.

e492* **Baratte** François, *Metzger* Catherine, Musée du Louvre, catalogue des
sarcophages en pierre d'époque romaine et paléochrétienne 1985
→ 1,d276; 3,d899: ᴿRArchéol (1988) 190-3 (R. *Turcan*).

e493 *Bard* Kathryn, A quantitative analysis of the predynastic burials in
Armant cemetery [9 k SW Luxor] 1400-1500 [cemetery numbers, not date,
which was c. 3700-3400]: JEA 74 (1988) 39-55.

e494 *Barkay* Gabriel, Burial headrests as a return to the womb — a
reevaluation: BAR-W [13/4 (1987) *Keel* O.] 14,2 (1988) 48-50; ill.

e495 *Berghe* Louis Vanden, Les pratiques funéraires à l'âge du fer III au
Pusht-i Kūh, Luristan; les nécropoles 'genre War Kabūd': IrAnt 22
(1987) 201-246 + 20 fig. (map); XIV pl.

e496 **Boschung** Dietrich, Antike Grabaltäre aus den Nekropolen Roms:
Acta Bernensia 8. Bern 1987, Stämpfli. 136 p.; 61 pl.; 5 foldouts. –
ᴿAnzAltW 41 (1988) 249 (Elisabeth *Walde*).

e497 **Bruns-Özgan** Christine, Lykische Grabreliefs 1987 → 3,d903: ᴿGnomon 60 (1988) 556-8 (J. *Borchhardt*); RArchéol (1988) 393-5 (P. *De-
margne*).

e498 **Bulst** Werner, *Pfeiffer* Heinrich, Das Turiner Grabtuch und das Christusbild I. Das Grabtuch² [cf. → 62,b29]; Forschungsberichte und Untersuchungen. Fra 1987, Knecht. 188 p. DM 48. – ᴿTPQ 136 (1988)
405s (J. *Hörmandinger*); ZkT 110 (1988) 379s (K. *Stock*).

e499 **Chappaz** J.-L., Figurines funéraires égyptiennes 1984 → 65,a632 ...
2,a405: ᴿWZKM 78 (1986) 218-221 (E. *Haslauer*).

a500 *Chappaz* Jean-Luc, Répertoire annuel des figurines funéraires 2: BSocÉg 12 (Genève 1988) 83-96.

e501 *Conti* Hilary, The sacrifice of the Mass and the shroud of Turin: HomP 89,1 (1988s) 31s. 51-53 ['The author's position is that the Shroud is authentic, unless someone can prove it otherwise', p. 53].

e502 *Davis* John J., Excavation of burials: → 20, FCALLAWAY J., Benchmarks 1988, 179-208; 14 fig.

e503 *Demidčik* A. E., The term 3ḫ in the funeral ritual of Pharaoh Unas: Istoriya Filologiya Drev. Vostoka (Moskva 1987) 26-41.

e504 *Devauchelle* Didier, Une taxe funéraire sur un ostracon démotique: BSocÉg 12 (1988) 35s; 1 pl.

e505 **Dubarle** A.-M., Histoire ancienne du linceul 1985 → 1,d286 ... 3,d911: RBLitEc 89 (1988) 158s (H. *Crouzel*); RÉByz 45 (1987) 248s (Marie-Hélène *Congourdeau*).

e505* **Forest** Jean-Daniel, Les pratiques funéraires en Mésopotamie: RCiv Mém 19, 1983 → 64,b123 ... 3,d913*: RJAOS 108 (1988) 655-7 (S. *Dunham*).

e506 *Fossati* Luigi, Sindonologia; il volto di Cristo nelle copie [27 datate, 23 altre] della Sacra Sindone: ScuolC 22 (1988) 198-204 [862-7, Reliquia o icona?].

e506* *Gloer* T. H., Shroud (... of Turin): → 801, ISBEnc³ 4 (1988) 494-6.

e507 *Goedicke* Hans, The high price of burial: JAmEg 25 (1988) 195-9; 2 fig.

e508 *Gramaglia* Pier Angelo, La sindone di Torino; alcuni problemi storici [*Dubarle* A. 1986]: RivStoLR 24 (1988) 524-568.

e509 *Grothe-Paulin* Elina, Der ägyptische Sarg in Helsinki: StOrFin 64 (1988) 7-56; bibliog. 57-59; phot. p. 60-75.

e510 *Hershkovitz* Israel, Cremation, its practice and identification; a case study from the Roman period [Megiddo aqueduct]: TAJ 15s,1 (1988s) 98-100; pl. 16.

c511 **Hölbl** Günther, Museo Archeologico Nazionale di Napoli; le stele funerarie della collezione egizia. R 1985. xiv-73 p.; 14 pl. – ROrAnt 27 (1988) 155-7 (F. *de Salvia*).

e512 EJahnkuhn Herbert, Zum Grabfrevel in vor- und frühgeschichtlicher Zeit; Untersuchungen zu Grabraub und 'haugbrot' in Mittel- und Nordeuropa [Kolloquium Gö 14-16. Febr. 1977]: Abh Gö pg/h 113. Gö 1978, Vandenhoeck & R. 243 p. – RRHR 205 (1988) 329s (F.-X. *Dillmann*).

e513 **Joussaume** Roger, Dolmens for the dead; megalith-building throughout the world. Ithaca NY 1988, Cornell Univ. 320 p.; ill. 0-8014-2156-X.

e514 **Kleiner** Diana E. E., Roman imperial funerary altars with portraits: Archaeologica 62, 1987 → 3,d921; Lit. 65.000: RArctos 22 (1988) 248-256 (M. *Kajava*: 130 corrections, but 'Lit. 650.000'); ÉtClas 56 (1988) 407 (A. *Wankenne*).

e515 **Kranz** Peter, Jahreszeiten-Sarkophage: Die antiken Sarkophagreliefs 4. B 1984, Mann. 370 p. 3-7861-1379-3. – RArcheologia 36 (Wrocław 1985) 184-7 (Anna *Sadurska*).

e516 *Lindemeyer* Elke, Bemerkungen zu den Bestattungssitten des Vorderen Orients vom 10. bis 6. Jt. v.u.Z.: AltOrF 15 (1988) 367-373.

e517 *Marchesi* Giovanni, Il mistero della Sindone continua: CC 139 (1988,4) 261-8.

e518 *Morris* Ian, [→ h577] Tomb cult and the 'Greek renaissance'; the past in the present in the 8th century B.C.: Antiquity 62 (1988) 749-761; 2 maps.

e519 **Niwinski** Andrzej, 21st dynasty coffins from Thebes; chronological and typological studies: Theben 5. Mainz 1988, von Zabern. 3-8053-0926-0 [OIAc D88].

e520 *Ogdon* Jorge R., *dnit,* jar of embalming?: DiscEg 6 (1986) 21-32; 2 fig.

e521 **Parlasca** Klaus, Syrische Grabreliefs 1982 ⇒ 65,a659 ... 2,a430: ᴿArchClasR 38ss (1986ss) 242-4 (Eugenia *Equini Schneider*).

e522 *Pedaros* Georg, Homerische Begräbnisbräuche: ⇒ 693, Actes = Kernos 1 (1988) 195-206.

e523 *Pérez Die* M.C., Un sarcófago egipcio del Museo Arqueológico Nacional con el capítulo 72 del Libro de los Muertos: AulaO 6 (1988) 61-75; IV pl.

e524 **Prieur** J., La mort dans l'antiquité romaine 1986 ⇒ 2,a433: ᴿRÉLat 65 (1987) 370 (J.-C. *Fredouille*).

e525 *Rahmani* Levi Y., *a)* A Christian lead coffin from Caesarea: IsrEJ 38 (1988) 246-8; pl. 33-34; – *b)* Roman lead coffins in the Israel Museum collection: IsrMusJ 7 (1988) 47-55; 6 fig.; pl. I-V; – *c)* ⊕ Late second-temple period lead coffins in secondary use: Qadmoniot 21 (1988) 41-43; ill.

e526 **Rodante** S., La realtà della Sindone nelle riflessioni di un medico, Mi 1987, Massimo. vi-297 p. Lit. 30.000 [CC 139,2 dopo 104].

e527 *Roth* Ann M., The organization and functioning of the royal mortuary cults of the Old Kingdom in Egypt: ⇒ 738, Power 1983/7, 133-140.

e528 *Ryan* Donald P., The archaeological analysis of inscribed Egyptian funerary cones: VarAeg 4 (1988) 165-170.

e529 **Saleh** Mohamed, Das Totenbuch in den Beamtengräbern des Neuen Reiches [Diss. Heidelberg 1975] 1984 ⇒ 1,e126; 3,e745: ᴿJNES 47 (1988) 203-5 (P. A. *Piccione*).

e530 *Schmandt-Besserat* Denise, Tokens as funerary offerings: VO 7 (1988) 3-9; 1 fig.; pl. 1-5.

e531 **Siliato** Maria Gracia, El hombre de la Sábana Santa, ᵀ*Velasco* M.A. M 1987, Edica. 218 p. – ᴿNatGrac 35 (1988) 495 (C. *Compadre*).

e532 **Tsukimoto** Akio, Untersuchungen zur Totenpflege (kispum) 1985 ⇒ 1,d310; 3,d937: ᴿOrient 30,2 (1987) 90-96 (K. *Watanabe* ❶).

e533 **Voos** J., Studien zur Rolle von Statuen und Reliefs im syrohethitischen Totenkult während der frühen Eisenzeit (10.-7. Jh. v.u.Z.) [< Diss.]: Ethnographisch-archäologische Zts 29 (1988) 347-362 [< ZAW 101,297].

e534 **Wilson** Ian, The mysterious Shroud. NY 1988, Doubleday. xviii-189 p. $10 pa. [CBQ 51,404].

e535 **Zugibe** Frederick T., The Cross and the shroud; a medical inquiry into the Crucifixion²ʳᵉᵛ [¹1982]. NY 1988, Paragon. xii-236 p. $22 [TDig 36,95].

τ3.9 *Numismatica,* Coins.

e536 *Acquaro* E., Monete puniche e neopuniche del museo di Ippona: RStFen 16 (1988) 25-28; pl. V-X.

e537 **Amandry** Michel, Le monnayage des duovirs corinthiens: BCH Sup 15. P 1988, de Boccard. 269 p.; 18 pl. – ᴿRBgNum 134 (1988) 200-202 (Ghislaine *Moucharte*).

e538 *Amandry* Michel, *Callot* Olivier, Le trésor de Failaka 1984 (Koweit): RNum 30 (1988) 64-74; pl. XII-XIV.

e539 *a)* *Arnold-Biucchi* Carmen, *al.,* A Greek archaic silver hoard from Selinus; – *b)* *Kagan* Jonathan, Some archaic bovine curiosities; – *c)*

Houghton Arthur *al.*, Five Seleucid notes / A hoard of Aegean tetradrachms; – *d*) *Carter* Giles F., Zinc content of Neronian Semisses and Quadrantes and the relative value of zinc and copper in the coins of Nero: AmNumM 33 (1988) 1-35 / 37-44 / 55-69.71-89 / 91-106; ill.

e540 *Ashton* Richard, Rhodian coinage and the Colossus: RNum 30 (1988) 75-90; pl. XV-XVIII.

e541 *a*) *Augé* Christian, Sur le monnayage de Dion 'de Coelé-Syrie'; – *b*) *Sartre* Maurice, La Syrie Creuse n'existe pas: → 706, Géographie 1985/8, 325-341; 2 pl. / 15-40.

e542 **Aulock** Hans von †, Münzen und Städte Phrygiens [I. 1980] Tü 1987, Wasmuth. 148 p.; 48 pl.; foldout. DM 74. 3-8030-1726-2.

e543 *Barag* Dan, A silver coin of Yohanan the High Priest and the coinage of Judea in the fourth century B.C.: IsrNumJ 9 (1986s) 4-21; pl. 1.

e544 *Barkay* Rachel, A new variant of a coin of Alexander II Zebinas: IsrNumJ 9 (1986s) 26 only.

e545 **Betlyon** J.W., The coinage and mints of Phoenicia, [in] the pre-Alexandrine period 1982 → 2,a458; 3,d949: RIsrNumJ 9 (1986s) 92s (M. *Price*).

e546 *Bland* Roger, The last issue of Gallienus from the mint of Antioch: IsrNumJ 9 (1986s) 85-90; pl. 30-31.

e547 R**Burnett** A.M., *Crawford* M.H., The coinage of the Roman world in the late Republic [British Museum colloquium Sept. 1985]: BAR-Int. 326. Ox 1987. viii-185 p.; 12 pl.

e548 **Burnett** Andrew, Coinage in the Roman world. L 1987, Seaby. viii-168 p.; ill. – RRBgNum 134 (1988) 207s (J. van *Heesch*, vlaams).

e549 *Butcher* Kevin, *a*) The colonial coinage of Antioch-on-the-Orontes c. AD 218-253: NumC 148 (1988) 63-75; map; pl. 18-22; – *b*) Two related coinages of the third century A.D.; Philippopolis and Samosata: IsrNumJ 9 (1986s) 73-84; pl. 24-29.

e550 *Candilio* Daniela, Roma, monete dallo scavo della palestra nord-occidentale delle Terme di Diocleziano: BollNumism 10 (1988) 225-9, ill.

e551 **Carradice** Ian, *Price* Martin, Coinage in the Greek world. L 1988, Seaby. 154 p.; 302 fig. £13.50 [Antiquity 62,670 with 11-digit ISBN].

e552 *Carradice* Ian A., The Libyan War [241-238 B.C.] and coinage; a new hoard and the evidence of metal analysis: NumC 148 (1988) 33-52; pl. 7-12.

e553 **Casey** P.J., Understanding ancient coins 1986 → 3,d961: RRelStR 14 (1988) 153 (R.S. *Hanson*).

e554 **Christiansen** Erik, The Roman coins of Alexandria; quantitative studies. Aarhus 1988, Univ. 311 p. + vol. of 179 p. notes, 2 pl. 87-7228-158-5. – RAegyptus 68 (1988) 276-279 (A. *Savio*).

e555 **Cribb** J., The money fun book [... Mesopotamia, Egypt; mostly Britain]. L 1986, British Museum. 32 p. $5.50 pa. 0-7141-08669. – RAncHRes 18 (1988) 190 (R. *Thomson*).

e555* *Curiel* Raoul, *Gyselen* Rika, Monnaies des fouilles de Bīshāpūr: StIran 16 (1987) 7-43; pl. I-V.

e556 *Delamare* F., *al.*, Mécanique et frappe des monnaies ...: RArchéom 12 (1988) 81-99.

e557 *Depeyrot* Georges, Eumène, Épiphane et le système monétaire de Dioclétien: Mitt. Österr. Num. Ges. 28 (1988) 37-40.

e558 **Deppert-Lippitz** Barbara, Die Münzprägung Milets vom vierten bis ersten Jahrhundert v. Chr.: Typos 5, 1984 → 1,d339; 2,a464: RAnzAltW

41 (1988) 235-8 (W. *Szaivert*); Gymnasium 95 (1988) 176-8 (N. *Ehrhardt*); Mitt. Österr. Num. Ges 28 (1988) 20 (G. *Dembski*).

e559 *Deutsch* Robert, A portrait coin of Agrippa II reconsidered: IsrNumJ 9 (1986s) 36s.

e560 *D'jakonov* I.M., *Zejmal* Je. V., ❸ Le potentat parthe Andragore et ses monnaies: VDI 187 (1988) 4-18; franç. 18s.

e561 **Doyen** Jean-Marc, Les monnaies antiques da Tell Abou Danné et d'Oumm el Marra 1976-1985 (Aspects de la circulation monétaire en Syrie du nord sous les Séleucides). Bru 1987, Archaion. 178 p.; 14 pl. Fb 1680. – RNumC 148 (1988) 234s (K. *Butcher*); RBgNum 134 (1988) 196-8 (F. de *Callatay*).

e562 *Franke* Peter R., Zu den Homonoia-Münzen Kleinasiens: ➤ 764, Hist. Geographie 1980/7, 81-102.

e563 *Frolova* N.A., ❸ L'émission de monnaies du Bosphore aux VIe-IIe ss. avant n.è. [*Anokhin* V.A. 1986]: VDI 79,185 (1988) 122-142; franç. 142s.

e564 **Grunauer-von Hoerschelmann** Susanne, Griechische Münzen. Hannover 1988, Kestner-Museum. 90 p.; 262 x 2 fig. 3-924029-10-5.

e565 *a)* *Hoof* Christine van, Zur syrischen Tetradrachmenprägung der römischen Kaiserzeit; ein neuer Schatzfund; – *b)* *Klose* Dietrich O.A., As und Assarion – zu den Nominalsystemen der lokalen Bronzemünzen im Osten des römischen Reiches: JbNumG 36 (1986) 107-126; pl. 15-17 / 101-5.

e566 **Houghton** A., Coins of the Seleucid Empire 1983 ➤ 65,a698 ... 3,d966: RIsrNumJ 9 (1986s) 93s (A. *Kindler*); Mitt. Österr. Num. Ges. 28 (1988) 66 (G. *Dembski*).

e567 *Houghton* Arthur, A didrachm issue of Antiochus VI of Byblus: IsrNumJ 9 (1986s) 22-25; pl. 3.

e568 **Howgego** C.J., Greek imperial countermarks; studies in the provincial coinage of the Roman Empire 1985 ➤ 2,a471; 3,d967: RRBgNum 134 (1988) 202-4 (F. de *Callatay*).

e569 **Jidejian** Nina, Lebanon and the Greek world (333 to 64 B.C.); portraits of Alexander the Great, the Ptolemies, the Seleucid and Armenian kings, illustrated by coins in the Michel Eddé collection [avec Tfranç. *Jalabert* H.]. Beirut 1988, Dar el-Machreq. 144 p.; (color.) ill. – RBerytus 35 (1987!) 213s (Ḥ *Salamé-Sarkis*).

e570 **Jones** John M., A dictionary of ancient Greek coins 1986 ➤ 3,d969: RRNum 30 (1988) 290s (G. *Le Rider*).

e571 **Jurukova** J., Le monnayage des villes en Mésie Inférieure et en Thrace pendant le IIe-IIIe s., Hadrianopolis (en bulgare). Sofya 1987, Acad. Bulgare. 268 p.; LXVI pl. – RRitNum 90 (1988) 621s (G. *Gorini*).

e572 **Kaenel** Hans-Markus von, Münzprägung und Münzbildnis des Claudius: AMUGS 9, 1986 ➤ 3,d970; DM 96: RAJA 92 (1988) 146s (F. S. *Kleiner*); Gnomon 60 (1988) 174s (J.-B. *Giard*).

e573 **Kapossy** Balazs, Griechische Münzen – römisches Reich. Bern 1987, Stämpfli. 214 p. Fs 36. – RRBgNum 134 (1988) 199s (F. de *Callatay*).

e574 **Kindler** Arie, The coinage of Bostra 1983 ➤ 65,a702 ... 2,a473: RBO 45 (1988) 411s (J.P.A. van der *Vin*).

e575 **Kindler** Arie, *Stein* Alla, A bibliography of the city coinage of Palestine 200 BC – 300 AD: BAR 374. Ox 1987. VI-261 p.

e576 *a)* *Kindler* Arie, Coins and remains from a mobile mint of Bar Kokhba at Khirbet el-ʿAqd [2k E Amwas]; – *b)* *Eshel* Hanan, A coin of Bar Kokhba from a cave in Wadi el Māckūk [10 k W Jericho]: IsrNumJ 9 (1986s) 46-50; pl. 14-15 / 51s.

e577 **Klose** Dietrich O. A., Die Münzprägung von Smyrna in der römischen Kaiserzeit: DAI-Ant. Münzen 10. B 1987, de Gruyter. xxiv-359 p.; 63 pl. DM 198. – ᴿRÉLat 66 (1988) 375-7 (H. *Zehnacker*).

e578 *Kromann* Anne, *a*) Greek and Phoenician letters on Aradian tetradrachms: → 142*, ᶠTHOMSEN R., 1988, 104-113; – *b*) Western features in the Kushan coinage: → 733, Acta Hyperborea 1987/8, 151-8.

e579 *Kurz* Karel, Die Anfänge des Münzgeldes im Altertum (zum heutigen Erkenntnisstand): Eirene 25 (Praha 1988) 69-77.

e580 *Leisten* Thomas, Die Münzen von Uruk-Warka; Katalog der Münzfunde der Jahre 1913-1984: BaghMit 17 (1986) 309-367; 1 fig.; pl. 50-59.

e581 *Le Rider* Georges, *Olcay* Nekriman, Un trésor de tétradrachmes d'Alexandre trouvé à Akçakale en 1958: RNum 30 (1988) 42-54; pl. V-X [55-63, trésor de Haymana].

e582 *Leschhorn* Wolfgang, Zu den rhodischen Didrachmen des 4. und 3. Jh. v. Chr. – Der Schatzfund von Uşak (Coin Hoards II 68): JbNumG 36 (1986) 67-94; pl. 7-12.

e583 *Liampi* Katerini, Zur Chronologie der sogenannten 'anonymen' makedonischen Münzen des späten 4. Jhs. v. Chr.: JbNumG 36 (1986) 41-65; pl. 4-6.

e584 **MacIsaac** John D., The location of the Republican mint of Rome and the topography of the Arx of the Capitoline: diss. Johns Hopkins. Baltimore 1987. 271 p. 88-07449. – DissA 49 (1988s) 533-A.

e586 **Maltiel-Gerstenfeld** Jacob, New catalogue of ancient Jewish coins [rev. ed. of 1982, 260 years of ancient Jewish coins]. TA 1987, Minerva. 155 p.; ill. – ᴿNumC 148 (1988) 233 (A. *Burnett*: several new Herodian coins; irritating mistakes of spelling and sense).

e587 **Marek** V., Roman republican coins in the collection of the Charles University. Praha 1985, Univ. 112 p.; XLII pl. – ᴿEos 76 (1988) 388-394 (L. *Morawiecki*).

e588 **Martin** Thomas R., Sovereignty and coinage in classical Greece 1985 → 2,a479; 3,d976: ᴿAmHR 92 (1987) 103s (R. A. *Bauslaugh*); ClasPg 83 (1988) 237-245 (M. *Ostwald*); ÉchMClas 32 (1988) 417-420 (É. *Will*).

e589 *Masson* O., *Amandry* M., Notes de numismatique chypriote VI-VIII: RNum 30 (1988) 27-41; pl. I-IV [africaine III, 114-9 Amandry].

e590 *Meshorer* Ya'akov, The coins of Dora [Dor Jos 11,1]: IsrNumJ 9 (1986s) 59-72; pl. 18-23.

e591 *a*) *Meshorer* Yaakov, The mint of Pelusium; – *b*) *Acquaro* Enrico, Ricerche di numismatica punica; riletture e proposte: RitNum 90 (Centenario 1988) 57-62 / 51-55.

e592 *a*) *Metcalf* William E., The Michigan finds at Carthage, 1975-79; an analysis; – *b*) *Mørkholm* Otto, The date of the autonomous tetradrachms of Aegeae in Cilicia: AmNumM 32 (1987) 61-84 / 57-60.

e593 **Mildenberg** Leo, The coinage of the Bar Kokhba war 1984 → 1,d36 ... 3,d980: ᴿAnzAltW 41 (1988) 238s (W. *Szaivert*); BASOR 269 (1988) 92 (D. *Hendin*); ClasW 80 (1986s) 453s (S. E. *Sidebotham*); Gymnasium 95 (1988) 181-3 (D. *Mannsperger*); TR 84 (1988) 108-110 (R. *Wenning*).

e594 **Mildenberg** L., *Hurter* S., A.S. Dewing Greek coins 1985 → 3,d981: ᴿRNum 30 (1988) 276s (F. *Rebuffat*).

e595 ᶠMILDENBERG Leo, Numismatics... ᴱ**Houghton** A. *al.* 1984 → 65,102: ᴿRNum 30 (1988) 273-6 (D. *Gerin*).

e596 *Moore* Wayne, A bronze half-unit of Cleopatra Thea and Antiochus VIII from Akko-Ptolemais: IsrNumJ 9 (1986s) 27s; pl. II.

e597 *Morrisson* Cécile, *al.,* L'or monnayè, 1. Purification et altérations de Rome à Byzance: Cah. Babelon 2, 1985 → 2,a846: ᴿJRS 78 (1988) 256s (R. *Bland*); RÉByz 46 (1988) 262s (262s (J.-C. *Cheynet*: collaboration entre numismates et 'physiciens').

e598 *a) Naster* Paul, Toponymes en caractères araméens sur les monnaies anatoliennes (5ᵉ-4ᵉ s. av J.-C.); – *b) Destrooper-Georgiades* Anne, Two Cilician hoards of the fourth century [B.C.]: RBgNum 134 (1988) 5-17; pl. I / 19-39; pl. II-IV.

e599 **Nicolet** Hélène, *al.,* Collection J. & M. Delepierre, Bibliothèque Nationale, cabinet des médailles. P 1983, Bibl. Nat. 98 pl. – ᴿRArchéol (1988) 140 (M. *Amandry*).

e600 **Noe** S. P., The coinage of Metapontum. NY 1984 [= 1927+1931], American Numismatic Soc. x-120 p.; 44 pl. [IsrNumJ 9 (1986s) 94].

e601 *Nollé* Johannes, 'Oriens Augusti'; Kaiserpanegyrik und Perserkriegspropaganda auf Münzen der Stadt Side in Pamphylien unter Valerian und Gallienus (253-268): JbNumG 36 (1986) 127-143; pl. 18-19.

e602 Numismatic literature [NY 0029-6031]: 117 (1987) xv-166 p.; 923 items. – 118 (1987) xvi-176 p.; 931 items. 119 (1988) xiii-185 p.; 1023 items. – 120 (1988) lxii-168 p.; 951 items.

e603 (Panvini) *Rosati* Francesco, La moneta romana: Archeo 42 (1988) 46-97; color. ill.

e604 *Paz Garcia Bellido* M., Del origen de la moneda: → 70, ᶠJORDÁ F., Zephyrus 37s (1984s) 391-409; 9 fig.

e605 *a) Pera* Rossella, Commodo *Olympios* [p. 125; ma p. 5 'Thlympios'] su alcune monete della città di Efeso; – *b) Gaggero* Gianfranco, Testimonianze e problemi di numismatica nell'opera di Svetonio; – *c) Balil* Alberto, La prospettiva 'gerarchica' e altre prospettive nella monetazione romana del'età Giulio-Claudia: → 18, ᶠBREGLIA L., 1987, 125-132 / 107-123 / 101-5.

e606 **Pérez** Christine, Monnaie du pouvoir, pouvoir de la monnaie; une pratique discursive originale, le discours figuratif monétaire 1986 → 3,d987: ᴿRBgNm 134 (1988) 188s (T. *Vermeeren*); RÉLat 65 (1987) 385s (H. *Zehnacker*).

e606* *Philip* Graham, Hoards of the Early and Middle Bronze Ages in the Levant [Ugarit, Alalaḫ, Byblos, Israel...]: WorldArch 20 (1988s) 190-208; ill.

Room Adrian, Dictionary of coin names 1987 → 866*.

e607 *Root* Margaret C., Evidence from Persepolis for the dating of Persian and archaic Greek coinage: NumC 148 (1988) 1-12; pl. 1.

e608 *Rutter* N. K., HERODOTUS I, 94.1 and the 'first finders' of coinage: → 18, ᶠBREGLIA L., 1987, I, 59-62.

e609 **Ryan** N. S., Fourth-century coin finds from Roman Britain; a computer analysis: BAR-British 183. Ox 1988. 286 p. 0-86054-522-9.

e610 *Sari* Ṣaliḥ Kh., *a)* A note on al-Maqrīzī's remarks regarding the silver coinage of Baybars; – *b)* (with others) Contributions to the knowledge of the standard of fineness of silver coinage struck in Egypt and Syria during the period of the Crusades: JESHO 31 (1988) 298-301 / 301-3.

e611 *Schults* Sabine, Literaturüberblicke der griechischen Numismatik; Kilikien: Chiron 18 (1988) 91-164; Register 165-170.

e612 **Sear** David R., *al.,* Byzantine coins and their values². L 1987, Seaby. 526 p.; 600 fig.; maps. – ᴿRNum 30 (1988) 284s (C. *Morrisson*).

e613 **Sutherland** C. H. V., Roman history and coinage, 44 B.C. – A.D. 69 [→ 3,d995]; fifty points of relation from Julius Caesar to Vespasian 1987:

RClasW 82 (1988s) 219s (Catheryn *Cheal*); NumC 148 (1988) 254-6 (A. *Wallace-Hadrill*).

e614 a) *Sutherland* C.H.V., Variation of emphasis between the Res Gestae and the types of the imperial Augustus coinage; – b) *Macaluso* Rosalia, Contromarche con simboli su dipondi di Augusto; – c) *Alföldi* Maria R., Schildbilder der Römischen Kaiser auf Münzen und multipla: → 18, FBREGLIA L. 1987, II, 85-91 / 93-99 / 133-145.

e615 **Vacano** Otfried von, Typenkatalog der antiken Münzen Kleinasiens, E*Kienast* Dietmar, 1986 → 2,a496; DM 128: RJbNumG 36 (1986) 173s (D. O.A. *Klose*); Mundus 24 (1988) 218s (H.-W. *Ritter*: 'Ortfried'); NumC 148 (1988) 235-9 (T. V. *Buttrey*: should be in computer-disc form); RNum 30 (1988) 278 (F. *Rebuffat*).

T4 *Situs,* **excavation-sites** .1 *Chronica,* **bulletins.**

e616 Chronique archéologique [communications adaptées]: RB 95 (1988) 215-279 ...

e617 *González Echegaray* J., Investigaciónes arqueológicas en Levante, II: AulaO [I. 2 (1984) 207-223] 6 (1988) 19-46; 3 maps: Syria, Lebanon, Jordan, Israel, by archeological periods, with each excavation under the period to which it is particularly relevant.

e618 *Delvoye* C., Chronique archéologique: Byzantion 57 (1987) 491-505; 58 (1988) 256-293; 502-527; ill.

e619 Excavations [signed by the respective authors, infra]: IsrEJ 38 (1988) 76-92 . 187-199 . 273-281; 3 maps; ill.

e620 Excavations and surveys in Israel 1987/1988 [5 → 3,e6] 6; English edition of Hadashot Arkheologiyot. J 1988, Dept. Antiquities. 120 p.

e621 E*Piccirillo* Michele, Ricerca storico-archeologica in Giordania VIII: SBFLA 38 (1988) 449-470, pl. 67-72: indication of 37 sites, with signed accounts of six, and ten book-reviews.

e622 E**Rast** Walter E., Preliminary reports ASOR [1982-5: 1988 → 459] 1980-4: BASOR Sup 24, 1986 → 2,354: RAndrUnS 26 (1988) 202s (P. J. *Ray*).

T4.2 *Situs effossi,* **syntheses.**

e623 *Arata Mantovani* Piera, L'archeologia siro-palestinese e la storia di Israele; Rassegna di studi archeologici V: Henoch 10 (1988) 235-246 [... Cesarea].

e624 **Bagatti** Bellarmino, The Church from the Circumcision; history and archaeology of the Judaeo-Christians [= Alle origini; (franç. 1965) T*Hoade* E. 1971]: SBF min 2. J 1984, Franciscan. vii-326 p.

e625 *Barstad* Hans M., On the history and archaeology of Judah during the exilic period – a reminder: OrLovPer 19 (1988) 25-36.

e626 a) *Cauvin* J., Chronologie relative et chronologie absolue dans le néolithique du Levant nord et d'Anatolie entre 10.000 et 8.000 B. P.; – b) *Gebel* H. G. ... southern Levant; – c) *Hole* F., ... Iran: → 719, Chronologies 1986/7, 325-342. 395-8 / 343-351 / 353-379. 559-563.

e627 *Cohen* Rudolph, ✪ Settlement in the Negev highlands from the fourth millennium BCE to the fourth century BCE: Qadmoniot 21 (1988) 62-81.

e628 *Currid* John D., *Gregg* Jeffrey L., Why did the early Israelites dig all those pits?: BAR-W 14,5 (1988) 54-57; ill.

e629 **Finkelstein** Israel, The archaeology of the Israelite settlement [i. The results of excavations and surveys; ii. The regional study of the territory of Ephraim ... Shiloh excavations; iii. material culture; iv. process of settlement; < diss. TA 1983, 'Izbet Ṣartah excavations, ᴰ*Kochavi* M.; J 1986, Meuḥad]. J 1988, Israel Exploration Soc. 380 p.; 107 fig. $36. 965-221-007-2. – ᴿOrientalia 57 (1988) 410-2 (A. J. *Frendo*).

e630 **Finkelstein** I., ⊕ *Ha-Arkeologia šel ... ha-šopᵉtim,* The archeology of the period of settlement and Judges. TA/J 1986, Kibbutz Ha-Meuhad / Israel Expl. Soc. 358 p.; 107 fig. $16. – ᴿIsrEJ 37 (1987) 199 (Hannah *Katzenstein*).

e631 *Gal* Zvi, The Late Bronze Age in Galilee; a reassessment: BASOR 272 (1988) 79-84.

e632 *a) Meyers* Eric M., Early Judaism and Christianity in the light of archaeology [... tolerance till mid-4th century]; – *b) Groh* Dennis E., Jews and Christians in Late Roman Palestine; toward a new chronology: BA 51 (1988) 69-79 / 80-98; ill.

e633 **Kempinski** Aharon, Syrien und Palästina (Kanaan) in der letzten Phase der Mittelbronze–IIB–Zeit (1650-1570): v. Chr.: ÄgAT 4, 1983 ➤ 64,b253 ... 1,d406: ᴿBASOR 270 (1988) 93s (P. *Zimansky*).

e634 *Mazzoleni* Danilo, I luoghi del Nuovo Testamento: Archeo 38 (1988) 48-91; color ill.

e635 *Pérez Largacha* Antonio, Egipto y Sirio-Palestina en época de Tutmosis III: ➤ BAsEspOr 23 (1987) 317-332.

e636 *Portugali* Juval, Notes on socio-spatial change in the region of Israel, chalcolithic to iron age: Orient-J 24 (1988) 55-64 + 7 fig.

e637 **Stern** Ephraim, Material culture of the land of the Bible in the Persian period 1982 ➤ 63,a838 ... 2,a524: ᴿBInstArch 25 (1988) 173-6 (A. *Kuhrt*); JNES 47 (1988) 190s (D. *Esse*).

e638 La Terra Santa, studi di archeologia, R 1983, Antonianum = Trent'anni O.F.M. – ᴿRivB 35 (1987) 123s (A. *Rolla*). ➤ k718.

e639 **Weippert** Helga, Palästina in vorhellenistischer Zeit: HbArch/Vorderasien 2/1. Mü 1988, Beck. xxix-744 p.; 201 fig.; 23 pl. DM 338. 3-406-32198-4 [BL 89,31, A. G. *Auld*].

e640 *a) Wilken* Robert L., Byzantine Palestine; a Christian Holy Land; – *b) Schick* Robert, Christian life in Palestine during the Early Islamic period: BA 51 (1988) 214-218.233-7 / 218-221.239s; ill.

T4.3 **Jerusalem,** *archaeologia et historia.*

e641 **Abecassis** A. *al.,* Jérusalem dans les traditions juives et chrétiennes [colloque 11-12.XI.1982]. Bru c.1987, Inst. Judaicum. 127 p. Fb. 800. – ᴿRB 95 (1988) 422 (F. *Langlamet*: tit. pp.).

e642 *Abu Khalaf* Marwan, Three candlesticks from the Islamic museum of al-Haram al-Sharif, Jerusalem: Levant 20 (1988) 238-244; 10 phot.

e642* **Avigad** Nahman, Discovering Jerusalem 1983 ➤ 64,b265 ... 3,e17: ᴿRÉJ 146 (1987) 165s (E.-M. *Laperrousaz*).

e643 **Ben-Arieh** Yehoshua, Jerusalem in the 19th century; the Old City: 1984 ➤ 1,d418 ... 3,e22: ᴿJJS 39 (1988) 133s (S. *Kochav*).

e644 **Ben-Dov** Meir, In the shadow of the Temple; the discovery of ancient Jerusalem 1985 ➤ 2,a537; 3,e23: ᴿCurrTM 15 (1988) 205s (E. *Krentz*).

e645 *Berder* Michel, Itinéraire au Mont des Oliviers: MondeB 55 (1988) 11-31; ill. [6-40, *al.*].

e646 *Bieberstein* Klaus & Sabine, St. Thomas Alemannorum oder St. Peter ad Vincula? Zur historischen Identifizierung einer wiederentdeckten Kreuzfahrerkirche in der Altstadt Jerusalems: ZDPV 104 (1988) 152-161; 1 fig. [cf. same authors, St. Julian oder St. Joh. Ev., → 3,e24, ZDPV 103 (1987) 178-184].

e647 *Briend* Jacques, [télévision française 1987 sur résultats 1976 de *Mazar* A.] Une porte fortifiée à Jérusalem ['plus importante que la découverte des manuscrits de la mer Morte' ... 90 m E porte Hulda]: MondeB 52 (1988) 52.

e648 *Broshi* Magen, Jewish Jerusalem — a quarter of a century of archaeological research: IsrMusJ 7 (1988) 13-23; ill.

e649 **Burgoyne** Michael H., (*Richards* Donald S.), Mamluk Jerusalem, an architectural study: British School of Archaeology in Jerusalem. L 1987, World of Islam Festival Trust. xii-623 p. 250 fig.; 400 pl. + 32 colour. £115. – ᴿAntiquity 62 (1988) 527-532 (J. *Johns*); JRAS (1988) 175-7 (G.S.P. *Freeman-Grenville*); JSS 33 (1988) 349-351 (C. E. *Bosworth*); RB 95 (1988) 452s (J. *Murphy-O'Connor*).

e650 **Busse** Heribert, *Kretschmar* Georg, Jerusalemer Heiligtumstraditionen in altkirchlicher und frühislamischer Zeit 1987 → 3,e26; DM 52 pa: ᴿErbAuf 64 (1988) 484 (B. *Schwank*); MüTZ 39 (1988) 207-9 (R. *Kaczynski*).

e652 *Cohen* Amnon [→ h628], ❶ Arabic archival material as a source for Jewish history in Ottoman Jerusalem: CHistEI 50 (1988) 58-72; Eng. 195.

e653 **Cohn** Erich W., New ideas about Jerusalem's topography [mostly on watersources]. J 1987, Franciscan. 140 p.; maps. 965-322-087-6.

e654 *Corbo* Virgilio, Il Santo Sepolcro di Gerusalemme, nova et vetera [commento su reazioni di *Loffreda* S., *Nolli* G., OssRom 15.I.1983; 27.IV.1984 ed altri al suo Santo Sepolcro 1982]: SBFLA 38 (1988) 391-422; pl. 59-66.

e655 *Demirkent* Isın, Der Sieg von Hittin und die Eroberung Jerusalems durch die Moslems im Spiegel der westlichen Darstellung: Belleten 52,205 (1988) 1557-66; ❶ 1547-55.

e656 *Dequeker* Luc, The 'tomb of David' in the 'city of David'; a biblical tradition reconsidered: → 469, Wünschet 1986/8, 77-92.

e657 *Egender* Nikolaus, *a*) Die Liturgie Jerusalems und ihre Bedeutung für die Gesamtkirche; – *b*) Jüdisch-christliche Begegnung in Israel: ErbAuf 64 (1988) 117-127 / 333-340.

e658 *Figura* [Artur p. 496; Adam in Indice] ❷ De acropoli hierosolymitana a Davide usque ad 586 a.C.: RuBi 41 (1988) 487-496.

e659 *Gafni* Isaiah M., 'Pre-histories' of Jerusalem in Hellenistic, Jewish and Christian literature: JPseud 1 (1987) 5-22.

e660 *Garofalo* S., Gerusalemme, Sion: → 806, NDizTB (1988) 582-595.

e661 **Geirnaert** Noël, Het archief van de Familie Adornes en de Jeruzalemstichting te Brugge, I. Inventaris: Brugse Geschiedbronnen 19, 1987 → 3,e41: ᴿRHE 83 (1988) 757 (C. *Bruneel*).

e662 *Gibson* Shimon, Ras 'Amar 1987 (E.t.Ful, 1723.1365) burial caves: IsrEJ 38 (1988) 80-82.

e663 *Giese* Wolfgang, Untersuchungen zur Historia Hierosolymitana des Fulcher von Chartres: ArKultur G 69 (1987) 62-115.

e663* **Gockerell** Nina, *Neumeister* Werner, Ostern in Jerusalem; Karwoche und Auferstehungsfeiern der christlichen Kirchen 1987 → 3,e27; DM 59: ᴿIkiZ 78 (1988) 260 (B. *Spuler*).

e664 *a) Harper* Richard P., *Pringle* Denys, Belmont Castle [between Nebi Samwil and w. Soreq]: a historical notice and preliminary report of excavations in 1986: Levant 20 (1988) 101-118; 13 fig.; – *b*) RB 95 (1988) 277-9; fig. 26 (R. *Harper*).

e665 *Kaswalder* Pietro, Le lithostrotos et l'arc de l'Ecee Homo [TerreS mars 1988 ... ital. → 3,e47]: EsprVie 98 (1988) 516-8 (J. *Daoust*: choix ouvert entre porte de Jaffa, Lithostrotos des Franciscains, et vallon du Tyropoeon.

e666 **Konopnicki** Maurice, *Ben Rafael* Eliezer, Jérusalem [... histoire/archéologie sommairement; problèmes depuis 1967]: Que sais-je? P 1987, PUF. 128 p. – ᴿRHPR 68 (1988) 256s (E. *Jacob*).

e667 ᴱ**Küchler** M. *al.*, Jerusalem (ᶠKEEL-LEU H. & O.) 1987 → 3,e48: ᴿBTZ 5 (1988) 283-7 (P. *Welten*: 'Der Exeget als Fussgänger').

e668 *Laperrousaz* E.-M., *a*) La discontinuité (seam, straight joint) visible près de l'extrémité sud du mur oriental du Haram esh-Shérif marque-t-elle l'angle sud-est du 'Temple de Salomon'?: VT 38 (1988) 399-406; – *b*) Encore de nouveau sur les murailles antiques de Jérusalem: RÉJ 146 (1987) 205-213+4 plans, 10 phot. [147 (1988) 509-511, premier Temple?].

e669 *Magen* Menahem, Recovering Roman Jerusalem — the [Hadrian] entryway beneath Damascus Gate: BAR-W 14,3 (1988) 48-56; ill.

e670 *Manns* Frédéric, Tentativo di Giuliano [Apostata] di ricostruire il Tempio di Gerusalemme; un episodio tragico nella vita di S. CIRILLO di Gerusalemme: TerraS 64 (1988) 26-36; ill.

e671 **Mare** W. Harold, The archaeology of the Jerusalem area 1987 → 3,e59: ᴿAndrUnS 26 (1988) 192s (G. *Wheeler*); GraceTJ 9 (1988) 291s (R. *Ibach*); SWJT 31,2 (1988s) 49s (T. V. *Brisco*); WestTJ 50 (1988) 170-2 (A. *Wolters*: too many typos).

e672 *Mazar* Amihai, Jerusalem: Die Wasserversorgung antiker Städte [? 1982/7 → 3,e952] (3), 185-8.

e673 *Mazar* Benjamin, Jerusalem from Isaiah to Jeremiah: → 482, Jerusalem Congress VTS 40, 1986/8, 1-6.

e674 *Morgenstern* Matthias, Die Heilige — von der Bedeutung Jerusalems für Juden und Moslems: EvT 48 (1988) 65-75.

e675 *Murphy-O'Connor* Jérôme, Visite de la Cité de David: MondeB 55 (1988) 51-53; ill.

e676 **Nyssen** Wilhelm, Jerusalem — Ursprung der Bilder des Heils 1984 → 1,d459; DM 19,80: ᴿErbAuf 64 (1988) 318 (R. *Gordan*); OstkSt 37 (1988) 56s (H. M. *Biedermann*).

Ollenburger B. C., Zion 1987 → 2861.

e676* *Otto* Eckart, Jerusalem: → 798, EvKL 2 (1988) 809-813.

e677 *Patrich* Joseph, Reconstructing the magnificent Temple Herod built: BR 4,5 (1988) 16-29; drawings by Leen Ritmeyer.

e678 **Peters** F. E., Jerusalem 1986 → 2,a564; 3,e62: ᴿBAR-W 14,5 (1988) 12.62 (J. *Wilkinson*).

e679 **Price** Jonathan J., Jerusalem under siege; an internal history of the city during the Jewish Revolt, 66-70 C.E.: diss. Princeton 1987. 446 p. 88-04854. – DissA 49 (1988s) 588-A.

e680 **Purvis** James D., Jerusalem, the Holy City; a bibliography: ATLA 20. Metuchen NJ 1988, Scarecrow. xii-499 p. $42.50. 0-8108-1999-6 [NTAbs 32,397].

e681 **Rosenberg** A. W., *al.*, Jeruzalem (in jodendom, christendom en islam). Kampen 1986, Kok. 105 p. ƒ16,50. 90-242-4123-5. – ᴿKerkT 39 (1988) 155 (J.A.B. *Jongeneel*).

e682 *Shea* William H., Commemorating the final breakthrough of the Siloam tunnel [Siloam inscription]: ➤ 42*, EHRMAN A. Mem., Fucus 1988, 431-442.

e683 **Shiloh** Yigal, Excavations at the City of David I 1978-1982: Qedem 19, 1984 ➤ 65,a979 ... 3,e77: ᴿOLZ 83 (1988) 45-47 (K.-D. *Schunck*).

e684 *Shiloh* Yigal [died 14.XI.1987], Last thoughts [on his City of David excavations ...]: BAR-W 14,2 (1988) 14-27; 14,3 (1988) 38-46; ill.

e685 *Smith* Jonathan Z., Jerusalem; the city as place: ➤ 3,640, Civitas 1982/6, 25-38.

e686 *Stroumsa* Gedaliahu G., 'Vetus Israël'; les Juifs dans la littérature hiérosolymitaine d'époque byzantine: RHR 205 (1988) 115-31; Eng. 115.

e687 *Testa* Emmanuele, Le conseguenze della distruzione di Gerusalemme secondo la letteratura rabbinica e cristiana: SBFLA 38 (1988) 173-209.

e688 **Tushingham** A. D., *al.,* Excavations in Jerusalem 1961-1967: 1985 ➤ 1,d470; 3,e84: ᴿRelStR 14 (1988) 66s (W. T. *Pitard*).

e689 *Vilar Hueso* Vicente, El primer muro de Jerusalén antes del destierro: ➤ 49, ᶠFLETCHER VALLS D. III (1988s) 429-435.

e690 *Vuk* Tomislav, Neue Ausgrabungen in Jerusalem – Ketef Hinnom [Num 6,24-26 !]: BiKi 42 (1987) 30-36.

e691 *Waller* Elizabeth, Jerusalem in the time of Jesus; current archaeological contributions to an understanding of the Gospels: ProcGLM 8 (1988) 193-211.

e692 *Werblowsky* R. J. Zwi, Jerusalem, Holy City of three religions: ➤ 544, ᴱ*Crotty* R., Charles Strong Lectures 1972: 1987 ...

T4.4 *Situs alphabetice*: **Judaea, Negeb.**

e693 *Porat* Naomi, Local industry of Egyptian pottery in southern Palestine during the Early Bronze I period: BEgSem 8 (1986s) 109-119 + 17 fig. (map).

e693* **Schwartz** Joshua, ✪ Jewish settlement in Judea after the Bar-Kochba war until the Arab conquest 135 C.E. – 640 C.E.: 1986 ➤ 3,e90: ᴿJAOS 108 (1988) 311s (Shaye *Cohen*: 'thorough, competent, and — disappointing').

e694 *Shatzman* I., The beginning of the Roman defensive system in Judaea: AmJAncH 8,2 (CM 1983) 130-160 [NTAbs 32,213].

e695 *Singer* Hamar, Merneptah's campaign to Canaan and the Egyptian occupation of the southern coastal plain of Palestine in the Ramesside period: BASOR 269 (1988) 1-10.

e696 *Arad*: MondeB 54 (1988) 10-20 (R. *Amiran*) 22-39 (*al*).

e697 *Görg* M., Arad: ➤ 804, NBL Lfg 1 (1988) 145s.

e698 *Ussishkin* David, The date of the Judaean shrine at Arad: IsrEJ 38 (1988) 142-157; 7 fig.; pl. 24.

e699 *Artuf* 1985s, EB: RB 95 (1988) 215-7, fig. 1 (A. *Mazar*, P. de *Miroschedji*).

e700 *Ascalon*: 3d season 1986, 'erotic' disks in bathhouse (likelier than what headline says): BAR-W 14,2 (1988) 53 (L. *Stager*).

e701 *Bergoffen* Celia J., Some Cypriote pottery from Ashkelon: Levant 20 (1988) 161-8; 4 fig.

e702 *Avdat*: **Negev** Abraham, The Late Hellenistic and Early Roman pottery of Nabataean Oboda, final report: Qedem 22, 1986 ➤ 2,a620: ᴿJBL 107 (1988) 355s (P. C. *Hammond*).

e703 *Beersheba*: **Herzog** Ze'ev, Beer-Sheba II, 1984 ➤ 65,a812 ... 3,e100: ᴿBO 45 (1988) 422-5 (C.H.J. de *Geus*).

e704 **Schoors** A., Berseba 1986 → 3,e102: ᴿGerefTTs 88 (1988) 45 (C. *Houtman*).

e705 *Schoors* Antoon, Opgravingen in Beersheba: → 763, Archéologie 1986, 105-7.

e706 *Beit-Jimāl*: *Strus* Andrzej, La crypte de l'église byzantine à Beit-Jimal: SBFLA 38 (1988) 277-285; pl. 13-16.

e707 *Bet-Guvrin*: *Kloner* Amos, The Roman amphitheatre at Beth Guvrin; preliminary report: IsrEJ 38 (1988) 15-24; 7 fig.; pl. 4-5.

e708 *Bethlehem*: *Netzer* Ehud, [Herodium] Jewish rebels dig strategic tunnel system: BAR-W 14,4 (1988) 18-33; ill.

e709 Chariton, grotte (Bethlehem): RB 95 (1988) 270-2 (Y. *Hirschfeld*).

e710 *Erani* [120.110] 2d, 1987, EB I: IsrEJ 38 (1988) 88-90; plan (A. *Kempinski*, I. *Gilead*).

e711 *Gaza*: **Glucker** Carol A. M., The city of Gaza in the Roman and Byzantine periods: BAR-Int 325. Oxford 1987, vii-172 p.

e712 *Gezer*: **Dever** W. G., Gezer IV 1986 → 2,a598: ᴿRB 95 (1988) 122s (J.-M. de *Tarragon*).

e712* *a) Maeir* Aren M., Remarks on a supposed 'Egyptian Residency' at Gezer; – *b) Bunimovitz* Shlomo,... another suggestion: TAJ 15s,1 (1988s) 65-67 / 68-76.

e713 *Rosenfeld* Ben-Zion, The 'Boundary of Gezer' inscriptions and the history of Gezer at the end of the Second Temple period: IsrEJ 38 (1988) 235-245.

e714 *Gilgal*: *Noy* Tamar, Gilgal I – an early village [where?] in the lower Jordan valley; preliminary report of the 1987 winter season : IsrMusJ 7 (1988) 113s; 3 phot.

e715 *Ḥemar* 168.062, 25 k W Sedom: *Bar-Yosef* O., *Alon* D., *al.*, Naḥal Ḥemar Cave: Atiqot Eng. 18 (1988) 1-30 (-81) ill.; p. 59-63, *Yakar* R., *Hershkovitz* I., The modelled skulls.

e716 *Jericho*: **Bienkowski** Piotr, Jericho in the Late Bronze Age [ᴰ1984, Liverpool] 1986 → 2,a608; 3,e125: ᴿAJA 92 (1988) 444s (H. O. *Thompson*); BInstArch 25 (1988) 99-102 (S. *Bourke*); JBL 107 (1988) 115-7 (T. W. *Cartledge*); JNES 47 (1988) 189s (T. A. *Holland*); VT 38 (1988) 490-2 (Judith M. *Hadley*); ZDMG 138 (1988) 372s (R. *Hachmann*).

e717 *Palumbo* Gaetano, Per un'analisi delle sepolture contratte nel Bronzo Antico IV di Gerico: CMatArch 1 (R 1986) 287-306; fig. 54-58.

e718 *Gheva* David, *Louhivuori* Mikko, Typological proximity analysis of ceramic groups; a study of unpainted pottery from Jericho proto-urban tombs: BAngIsr 8 (1988s) 49-63.

e719 *Piattelli* D., Theodotos, apeleútheros dell'Imperatrice Agrippina nell'iscrizione di Gerico: Apollinaris 60 (1987) 657-666.

e720 *Ussishkin* David, The walls of Jericho [lecture summary]: BAngIsr 8 (1988s) 85-90; 4 fig.

e721 *Whitcomb* Donald, Khirbet al Mafjar reconsidered, the ceramic evidence: BASOR 271 (1988) 51-67; 2 fig.

e722 *Eshel* Hanan, *Misgav* Hagai, A fourth century B.C.E. [multiple payment] document from Ketef Yeriḥo: IsrEJ 38 (1988) 158-176; 8 fig.; pl. 25-26.

e723 *Eshel Ḥanan*, ⊖ Nailed sandals in Jewish sources [Mishna Shabbat 6,2 forbids on sabbath] and in the excavation of a cave at Ketef Jericho: Zion 53 (1988) 191-8; Eng. vii.

e724 *Karkom*: **Anati** Emmanuel, I siti a plaza di Har Karkom [→ ?2,1810s] Mg. Preistoria 9. Brescia 1987, Centro Camuno. 240 p. [RB 96,433, J.-M. de *Tarragon*].

e725 **Lachish**: *Ussishkin* David,   Restoring the Great Gate at Lachish: BAR-W 14,2 (1988) 42-47; ill.

e726 *Lahav/Ḥalif*, Chalco-EB 1987: IsrEJ 38 (1988) 278-281; pl. 36 (P. *Jacobs*, H. *Forshey*).

e727 *Borowski* Oded,   The biblical identity of Tel Halif [Rimmon likelier than Ziklag]: BA 51 (1988) 21-27; ill.

e728 **Makteš Gādôl**: *Maoz* Rivkah,   Une expédition dans le grand Maktesh [canyon]:   MondeB 56 (1988) 55-57; ill.

e729 **Mšaš**: **Fritz** V., *Kempinski* A., Ergebnisse ... Mšaš 1983 ➤ 64,b366 ... 3,e144:   RIsrEJ 38 (1988) 281s (E. *Stern*: some controversies); Qadmoniot 21 (1988) 117 (E. *Stern* ❻); ZDPV 104 (1988) 167-171 (C. H. J. de *Geus*).
  Tel Masos as major trade center: *Finkelstein* I. 1988 ➤ h462; *Edelman* D., 1988 ➤ 2854.

e730 **Mampsis**: **Negev** Avraham,   The architecture of Mampsis, final report, II. The Late Roman and Byzantine periods: Qedem 27. J 1988, Hebrew Univ. xviii-116 p.; 17 fig.; 144 phot.; 14 plans. 0333-5844.

e731 **Miqne** (Ekron) 1985s, Iron 1-II: RB 95 (1988) 228-239; pl. IV-VI; fig. 5-9 (... autels à cornes: T. *Dothan*, S. *Gittin*).

e732 **Mišmar**: *Moorey* P R.S.,   The chalcolithic hoard from Nahal Mishmar, Israel, in context: WorldArch 20 (1988) 171-189; 4 fig.; 6 pl. [209-228, *Rissman* Paul, Harappa].

e733 **Qaṣr**: *Hirschfeld* Yizhar, *Kloner* Amos,   Khirbet el-Qasr; a Byzantine fort in the Judaean Desert: BAngIsr 8 (1988s) 5-20; 12 fig.

e734 **Qiryat-Yearim**: *Buit* M. Du,   Qiriath-Yéarim: ➤ 786, Catholicisme 12,55 (1988) 327.

e735 *Qitmit*: *Beit-Arieh* Itzhaq   An Edomite shrine at Ḥorvat Qitmit in the biblical Negev: ➤ 469, Wünschet 1986/8, 75s.

e736 *Reḥovot*-in-the-Negev [kh. Ruḥeibeh], preliminary report, 1986: IsrEJ 38 (1988) 117-127; 6 fig.; pl. 21ss (Y. *Tsafrir*, K. G. *Holum*).

e737 **Tsafrir** Y., *al.*,   Excavations at Rehovot-in-the-Negev, I. The Northern Church: Qedem 25.   J 1988, Hebrew Univ.   209 p.; 75 fig.; 293 phot. + 2 color.; 14 pl. (drawings). $40. – RBAngIsr 8 (1988s) 65-68 (Claudine *Dauphin*); SBFLA 38 (1988) 530-2 (E. *Alliata*).

e738 *Sa'adon*, 40 k SW Beersheba: *Rubin* Rekav, *Scherschewsky* Yosef, ❻ Sa'adon — an urban settlement of the Byzantine period in the Negev: Qadmoniot 21 (1988) 49-54; ill.

e739 *Sekher*: *Gilead* Isaac, *Goren* Yuval,   Stations of the chalcolithic period in Nahal Sekher, northern Negev: Paléorient 12,1 (1986) 83-90; 6 fig.

e740 *Shiqmim* [Beersheba] 1987, chalcolithic: IsrEJ 38 (1988) 90-92 (T.E. *Levy*, D. *Alon*); Paléorient 13,2 (1987) 150-2 (Catherine *Commenge- Pellerin*).

e741 ELevy T.,   Shiqmim I; studies concerning chalcolithic societies in the northern Negev desert, Israel 1982-4: BAR-Int 356, 1987 ➤ 3,e148: RBAngIsr 8 (1988s) 71-76 (R. *Chapman*).

e742 **Timnah**: **Rothenberg** Benno,   The Egyptian mining temple at Timnah, researches in the Arabah 1959-84, 1: Metals in History 2.   L 1988, University College Institute for Archaeo-Metallurgical Studies.   317 p.; 92 fig.; 155 pl. + 29 colour. £75.   0-906183-02-2 [OIAc D88].

e743 *Urmeh*: *Eshel* Hanan, *Erlich* Zeev H., ❻ The fortress of Aqraba in Kh. Urmeh [= Aruman Jg 9,41; northernmost Judea capital, near Samaritan settlement]: CHistEI 47 (1988) 17-24; Eng. 194.

e744 *Yarmut* [Artuf/Beth Shemesh] 5th 1986, EB II ...: *a*) IsrEJ 38 (1988) 84-88; plan; 194-9; pl. 28 (P. de *Miroschedji*); – *b*) RB 95 (1988) 217-226; fig. 2-4; pl. II-III (P. de *Miroschedji*).

e744* **Miroschedji** Pierre de, Yarmouth I; rapport sur les trois premières campagnes de fouilles à Tel Yarmouth (Israël) (1980-1982): Mémoire 76. P 1988, RCiv. 281 p.: 53 + XXIX pl. F 131. 2-86538-186-2.

e745 *Miroschedji* Pierre de, Données nouvelles sur le Bronze Ancien de Palestine; les fouilles de Tel Yarmouth [depuis 1980]: CRAI (1988) 186-211; 13 pl. (map).

e746 *Zuweira* 1730.1717 (4 k SE Arad moderne) 1986, Rom. Byz.: RB 95 (1988) 267-269; fig. 24; pl. VIIb (R. P. *Harper*).

T4.5 **Samaria, Sharon.**

e747 *Bethel* location: BAR-W 14,5 (1988) 67s (A. F. *Rainey*).

e748 *Caesarea Maritima*: MondeB 56 (1988) 14-21 K. *Holum* & R. *Bull*, 'éclairage nouveau' sur 'points d'interrogation' laissés par la mission italienne des années 60) & 22-32 (A. *Raban*, port) [5-40, *al.*].

e749 *Gianfrotta* Piero A., Un porto per Erode: Archeo 23 (1987) 36-39; color. ill.

e750 Caesarea harbour and Hellenistic-Byzantine areas 1987: IsrEJ 38 (1988) 273-7; 2 plans; pl. 35 (A. *Raban*; R. R. *Stieglitz*).

e751 **Levine** Lee I., *Netzer* Ehud, Excavations at Caesarea Maritima 1975-6-9, final report: Qedem 21, 1986 ⇥ 2,a629: ᴿJBL 107 (1988) 356s (W. E. *Rast*).

e752 *Hohlfelder* Robert L., The 1984 explorations of the ancient harbors of Caesarea Maritima: ⇥ 459, ASOR 1982-5/8, 1-12; 17 fig.

e753 **Holum** K. G., (*Berman* A.), *al.*, King Herod's dream — Caesarea on the Sea. NY 1988. [IsrEJ 38,278].

e754 *Holum* Kenneth G., [Caesarea-M exhibition] Reliving King Herod's dream: Archaeology 41,3 (1988) 44-47; ill.

e755 *Colbi* S., ... histoire de Césarée Maritime: TerreS (janv. 1988) ... [EsprVie 98 (1988) 376-9 (J. *Daoust*)].

e756 *Carmel*: **Kuhnen** Hans-Peter, Nordwest-Palästina in hellenistisch-römischer Zeit; Bauten und Gräber im Karmelgebiet 1987 ⇥ 3,e160: RBInstArch 25 (1988) 132-4 (S. W. *Helms*); BonnJbb 188 (1988) 608s (A. *Schmidt-Colinet*); BSAA 54 (1988) 536 (A. *Balil*); ErbAuf 64 (1988) 485s (B. *Schwank*).

e757 *Segal* Arthur, *Naor* Yehuda, ◉ Four seasons of excavations at a Hellenistic site at Sha'ar ha-'Amaqim [2369.1609]: Qadmoniot 21 (1988) 24-30; ill.

e758 *Valla* F. R., *al.*, Un nouveau sondage sur la terrasse d'El-Ouad [Carmel], Israel: Paléorient 12,1 (1986) 21-38; 4 fig.; 1 pl.

e759 *Dawwar* (khirbat; Mukhmas 1778.1415) Iron Age walled city: IsrEJ 38 (1988) 79s (I. *Finkelstein*).

e760 *Finkelstein* Israel, ◉ Khirbet ed-Douwara — a fortified settlement of the early Israelite kingdom on the edge of the desert of Benjamin: Qadmoniot 21 (1988) 6-10; ill.

e761 *Dor*: **Stern** Ephraim, The walls of Dor: IsrEJ 38 (1988) 6-14; 3 fig.; pl. 1-3.

e762 *Far'a*: **Chambon** Alain, Tell el-Far'ah I. L'Âge du Fer 1984 ⇥ 65, a867 ... 3,e167: ᴿOLZ 83 (1988) 431s (W. *Kleiss*).

e763 **Mallet** Joël, Tell El-Fār'ah II, 1s, Le Bronze Moyen, stratigraphie des vestiges du Bronze moyen II (1re moitié du IIᵉ millénaire av. J. C.) dans les chantiers principaux II nord et IV: Mémoire 66. P 1987s, RCiv. 1. 153 p.; 2. 344 p.; 42 loose plans. 2-86538-154-4.

e764 *Ḥammah* 200.200, 1988; MB, Iron Age: IsrEJ 38 (1988) 191-4; plan; pl. 28A.

e765 *Jaffa-Tel Aviv*: **Mazar** Amihai, *al.*, Excavations at Tell Qasile II. The Philistine Sanctuary: Qedem 20, 1985 ➤ 1,d544: ᴿBASOR 271 (1988) 82-85 (W. R. *Kotter*).

e766 **Geva** Shulamit, Tell Jerishe: Qedem 15, 1982 ➤ 63,a985... 65,a874: ᴿOLZ 83 (1988) 167s (E. A. *Knauf*).

e766* *Izbet Ṣarṭa*: **Finkelstein** Israel, Izbet Sartah, an Early Iron Age site near Rosh Ha'ayin, Israel: BAR-Int 299. Ox 1986. xii-223 p. £15 pa [JAOS 108,676].

e767 *Lydda*: *Schwartz* Joshua, ✪ The history of Lod during the Persian period: CHistEI 49 (1988) 3-12; Eng. 190.

e768 *Ṣaf* [11 k SE Beth-Shan]: *Gophna* Ram, *Sadeh* Shelley, *al.*, Excavations at Tel Tsaf, an early chalcolithic site in the Jordan valley: TAJ 15s,1 (1988s) 3-36; 13 fig.; pl. 1-4 [37-46 flints, *Gopher* Avi; 47-51 fauna, *Hellwing* Salo; 52-55 flora, *Liphschitz* Nili, *Horowitz* Aharon].

e769 *Samaria*: *Rainey* Anson F., Toward a precise date for the Samaria ostraca [784s *Thiele*]: BASOR 272 (1988) 69-74.

e770 **Dar** Shimon, Landscape and pattern; an archaeological survey of Samaria, 800 B.C.E.-636 C.E.: BAR-Int 308, 1986 ➤ 3,e175: ᴿAJA 92 (1988) 445s (C. *Edens*); BInstArch 25 (1988) 112-4 (B. *Isserlin*).

e771 *Mazar* Amihai, answers Coogan on Samaria bull/Ebal sanctuary: BAR-W 14,4 (1988) 45.

e772 *Sharon*: *Borowski* Oded, The Sharon — symbol of God's abundance: BR 4,3 (1988) 40-43; ill.

e773 **Pringle** Denys, The red tower 1986 ➤ 2,a628, 3,a181*: ᴿAntiquity 62 (1988) 190s (J. *Jones*); AntiqJ 68,1 (1988) 160 (R. W. *Edwards*).

e774 *Singer* Itamar, *ʿĒmeq Šārōn* or *ʿĒmeq Śiryōn*?: ZDPV 104 (1988) 1-5.

e775 *Shechem*: **Cole** Dan P., Shechem I; the Middle Bronze IIB pottery 1984 ➤ 3,e177: ᴿJNES 47 (1988) 283-5 (D. L. *Esse*).

e776 *Wright* G. E., *Campbell* E. F., Shechem: ➤ 801, ISBEnc³ 4 (1988) 458-462.

e777 **Shiloh**: *Kaufman* Asher S., Fixing the site of the tabernacle at Shiloh: BAR-W 14,6 (1988) 46-52; ill.

e778 *Sumaqa* 1539.2308: *Dar* Shimon, Horvat Sumaqa — settlement from the Roman and Byzantine periods in the Carmel: BAngIsr 8 (1988s) 34-48; 13 fig.

T4.6 **Galilaea**; pro tempore *Golan*.

e779 *Gal* Zvi, The lower Galilee in the Iron Age II; analysis of survey material and its historical interpretation: TAJ 15s,1 (1988s) 56-64; 9 fig. (maps).

e780 *Na'aman* Yehuda, ✪ Misery in Galilee after the destruction of the Second Temple: BethM 34,119 (1988s) 366-380.

e781 **Pritz** Ray A., Nazarene Jewish Christianity, from the end of the New Testament period until its disappearance in the fourth century: Studia Post-Biblica 37. J/Leiden 1988, Magnes/Brill. 153 p. *f* 48. 90-04-08108-9 [Bijdragen 49,476].

e782 *Stadtler* David, Eine galiläische Mona Lisa: Das christliche Leben in Israel 27 (1988) > BiKi 43 (1988) 164; fig.

e783 *ʿAkko*: ➤ 804, NBL Lfg 1 (1988) 20s (M. *Görg*).

e784 *Rappaport* Uriel, ❸ Akko-Ptolemais and the Jews in the Hellenistic period: CHistEI 50 (1988) 31-48; Eng. 195.

e785 *Anafa*: **Berlin** Andrea Michelle, The Hellenistic and Early Roman common-ware pottery from Tel Anafa: diss. AA 1988. 88-12857 [OIAc D 88].

e786 *Araj* [and adjacent et-Tell, thought site of Bethsaida: 208.255] 1987, Hellenistic-Roman at et-Tell; only 4th-6th cent. at Araj: IsrEJ 38 (1988) 187s (R. *Arav*).

e787 *Belvoir* Castle, Kawkab al-Hawa, compared with Ajlun castle: ADAJ 32 (1988) 255-264; 5 fig. (Denise *Minnis*, Y. *Bader*).

e788 *Beth-Shan*: **Yadin** Y., *Geva* Shulamit, Investigations at Beth Shean; the early Iron Age strata: Qedem 23, 1986 → 2,a658; 3,e189: ᴿJBL 107 (1988) 357-9 (W. E. *Rast*).

e789 *Gergel* Richard A., The Beth Shean Hadrian [statue] reconsidered: → 717, AJA 92 (1988) 271.

e790 *Foerster* Gideon, *Tsafrir* Yoram, Nysa-Scythopolis — a new inscription and the titles of the city on its coins: IsrNumJ 9 (1986s) 53-58; pl. 16-17.

e791 *Koucky* Frank L., *Smith* Robert H., Lake Beisan and the prehistoric settlement of the northern Jordan Valley: Paléorient 12,2 (1986) 27-36; 7 fig.

e792 *Capharnaum*: **Bloedhorn** Hanswulf, Die Kapitelle der Synagoge von Kapernaum; ihre zeitliche und stilistische Einordnung im Rahmen der Kapitellentwicklung in der Dekapolis und in Palästina: AbhDPV. Wsb 1988, Harrassowitz. 148 p.; 40 pl. [Mundus 24,224: ʿAbh. 2787'].

e793 *Dan*: *Biran* Avraham, ❸ A mace-head and the office of Amadiyo at Dan: Qadmoniot 21 (1988) 11-17; ill., also Heb. color-cover.

e794 *Amir* D., ❸ More on the question of the 'identification' of the Golden Calf temple: Qadmoniot [20 (1987) 58] 21 (1988) 55.

e795 *Golan*: *Nemlich* Shlomit, *Killebrew* Ann, Rediscovering the ancient Golan; the Golan archaeological museum [Qatzrin]: BAR-W 14,6 (1988) 54-64; (color.) ill.

e796 **Urman** Dan, The Golan [diss. NYU 1979]: BAR-Int 269, 1985 → 1,d577; 3,e201: ᴿBInstArch 25 (1988) 179s (S. *Gibson*); JAOS 108 (1988) 162s (E. M. *Meyers*: outdated now).

e797 *Dar* Shimon, The history of the Hermon settlements: PEQ 120 (1988) 26-44; 14 fig. (map).

e798 *Haifa*: a) *Na'aman* Nadav, Pharaonic lands in the Jezreel valley in the Late Bronze Age; – b) *Dothan* Moshe, The significance of some artisans' workshops along the Canaanite coast; – c) *Balensi* J., Tell Abū Hawām; un cas exceptionnel?: → 742, Society 1985/8, 177-185 / 295-303 / 305-311; map.

e799 *Kursi*: *Provera* Mario, I resti del monastero di Gergesa-Kursi sulla riva orientale del Lago di Tiberiade: BbbOr 30 (1988) 139-144; ill.

e800 *Magdala*: *Riesner* Rainer, Neues vom See Gennesaret: BiKi 42 (1987) 171-3; phot., Schiffmosaik von Magdala.

e800* *Röllig* W., Magdala, Name verschiedener kanaanäischer Ortschaften [5; one near Lake Tiberias; three farther north; one in Nile Delta = Nm 33,7]: RLA 7,3s (1988) 200.

e801 *Megiddo*: *Singer* Itamar, Megiddo mentioned in a letter from Boğazköy: → 112*, ꜰOTTEN H., Documentum 1988, 327-332.

e802 **Davies** Graham I., Megiddo 1986 → 2,a680; 3,e214: ᴿCBQ 50 (1988) 292s (H. O. *Thompson*); PEQ 120 (1988) 150s (P. *Bienkowski*).

e803 *Milson* David, The design of the Early Bronze Age temples at Megiddo: BASOR 272 (1988) 75-78; 1 fig.

e804 *a) Singer* Itamar, The political status of Megiddo VIIA; – *b) Tsuk* Tsvika, The aqueduct to Legio and the location of the camp of the VIth Roman Legion: TAJ 15s,1 (1988s) 101-112 / 92-97; 4 fig.; pl. 14.

e805 **Nahariya**: **Dauphin** C., *Edelstein* G., L'Église byzantine de Nahariya 1984 ↝ 3,e218: ᴿBAngIsr 7 (1988) 50-53; 1 fig. (Y. *Hirschfeld*).

e806 **Nazareth**: **Folda** Jaroslav, The Nazareth capitals and the Crusader shrine of the Annunciation 1986 ↝ 2,a689: ᴿPEQ 120 (1988) 129s (D. *Pringle*); Speculum 63 (1988) 922-4 (A. *Borg*).

e807 Ya'ad burial cave [1735.2533 Nazareth]: IsrEJ 38 (1988) 76-78; 2 fig. (Nurit *Feig*).

e808 **Qaṣrin** 15k NW Capharnaum: *Ma'oz* Zvi U., *Killebrew* Ann, Ancient Qasrin, synagogue and village: BA 51 (1988) 5-21; 14 fig. + color front cover drawing of the reconstructed village in full activity.

e809 **Qiri**, SE Yoqneam: **Ben-Tor** A., *Portugali* Y., Tel Qiri, a village in the Jezreel valley: Qedem 24, J 1987, Univ. xix-298 p.; ill.; ᴿVT 38 (1988) 488s (Judith M. *Hadley*).

e810 **Šadûd**: **Braun** Eliot, En Shadud ... Jezreel valley: BAR-Int 249, 1985 ↝ 1,d573: ᴿOLZ 83 (1988) 43-45 (W. *Thiel*).

e811 **Šahal Taḥtit** 197.226 S Bet-Yeraḥ: *Gal* Zvi, Ḥ. Shaḥal Taḥtit and the 'early enclosures': IsrEJ 38 (1988) 1-5; 4 fig.; pl. 1.

e812 **Sepphoris** 1987, Roman-Byz.: IsrEJ 38 (1988) 188-190 (J. *Strange, al.*).

e813 *a) Meyers* E. & C., *Netzer* E., ❿ A mansion in the Sepphoris acropolis and its splendid mosaic; – *b) Talgam* Rina, *Weiss* Zev, 'The Dionysus cycle' in the Sepphoris mosaic: Qadmoniot 21 (1988) 87-92 / 93-99; color. ill., also Heb. cover.

e814 **Miller** Stuart S., Studies in the history and traditions of Sepphoris [diss. NYU]: StJLA 37, 1984 ↝ 65,a920 ... 3,e225: ᴿIsrEJ 38 (1988) 283s (D. R. *Schwartz*); OLZ 83 (1988) 312s (W. *Wiefel*).

e815 *Miller* S.S., Intercity relations in Roman Palestine; the case of Sepphoris and Tiberias: AJS Review 12,1 (CM 1987) 1-24 [< NTAbs 32,354].

e816 Sepphoris: ↝ 801, ISBEnc³ 4 (1988) 399s (Pauline *Viviano*; also 393, Seneh).

e817 **Šiqmona**: *Bondì* Sandro F., Shiqmona: Archeo 27 (1987) 24-29; color. ill.

e818 *Karmon* Nira, *Spanier* Ehud, Remains of a purple dye industry found at Tel Shiqmona: IsrEJ 38 (1988) 184-6; 1 fig.; pl. 27.

e819 *Peleg* Michal, A chapel with mosaic pavements near Tel Shiqmona (Tell es-Samak 1463.2477): IsrEJ 38 (1988) 25-30; 1 fig.; pl. 5-7.

e820 **Tiberias**: **Dothan** Moshe, Hammath Tiberias; early synagogues and the Hellenistic and Roman remains 1983 ↝ 64,8431 ... 1,d624: ᴿBO 45 (1988) 401s (J. *Wilkinson*).

e821 **Wawiyat** (178.244 Bet-Neṭofa valley) 1986s: *a)* ↝ 717, AJA 92 (1988) 244 (Beth A. *Nakhai, al.*); – *b)* 1986, LB-Iron I: RB 95 (1988) 247-251; fig. 12s (Beth *Nakhai, al.*).

e822 **Yiftaḥel**: *Hershkovitz* I., *al.*, Neolithic skeletal remains at Yiftahel, Area C (Israel): Paléorient 12,1 (1986) 73-81; 2 fig.; I pl.

e822* **Yiron**: **Ohel** Milla Y., The Acheulian of the Yiron plateau: BAR-Int 307. Ox 1986. – ᴿAJA 92 (1988) 443 (Pam J. *Crabtree*).

T4.8 *Transjordania*: **East-Jordan.**

e823 *Betts* Alison, *Helms* Svend, Rock art in eastern Jordan; 'kite' carvings?: Paléorient 12.1 (1986) 67-72; 3 fig.; 1 pl.

e823* **Boling** Robert G., The early biblical community in Transjordan [... archeological results up to 1984, Moses-to-Saul period]. Sheffield 1988, Almond [Ithaca NY, Cornell Univ.] 80 p. £16/$25 [TDig 36,47]. – RProtestantesimo 43 (1988) 209s (J. A. *Soggin*); SBFLA 38 (1988) 464s (P. *Kaswalder*).

e824 EHadidi Adnan, Studies in the history and archaeology of Jordan III, Tübingen 1986/Amman 1987 → 3,816: singula infra.

e825 *Henry* Donald O., The prehistory and environments of Jordan; an overview: Paléorient 12,2 (1986) 5-26; 6 fig.

e826 *a*) *Macadam* Henry I., PTOLEMY's geography and the Wadi Sirhan; – *b*) *Bowersock* G. W., The three Arabias in Ptolemy's Geography; – *c*) *Gatier* Pierre-Louis, Philadelphie et Gerasa du royaume nabatéen à la province d'Arabie; – *d*) *Graf* David F., Qura 'Arabiyya and Provincia Arabia; – *e*) *Villeneuve* François, Prospection archéologique et géographie historique; la région d'Iraq al-Amir (Jordanie): → 706, Géographie 1985/8, 55-75; 6 fig. / 47-53 / 159-170 / 171-191 (-203) + 12 pl. / 257-288; 14 fig.

e827 *McGovern* Patrick E., Central Transjordan in the Late Bronze and Early Iron ages; an alternative hypothesis of socio-economic transformation and collapse: → e824, Jordan III 1986/7, 267-273.

e828 *Parker* S. Thomas, Preliminary report on the 1985 season of the Limes Arabicus project: → 459, ASOR 1982-5/8, 131-174; 29 fig.

e829 EParker S. T., The Roman frontier in central Jordan: BAR-Int 340, 1987 → 3,506: RBInstArch 25 (1988) 152s (L. *Copeland*).

e830 *Parker* S. T., The Limes Arabicus project [E of Dead Sea] 1987: ADAJ 32 (1988) 171-187; 11 fig.

e831 **Stein** Aurel, Limes report EGregory S.: BAR-Int 272, 1985 → 1,d.641; 2,a910; 3,d267: RBInstArch sup 24 (1987) 33s (J. *Bowsher*).

---

e832 *Abata*: Deir 'Ain 'Abata 1988: SBFLA 38 (1988) 461s (C. *Politis*).

e833 *MacDonald* Burton, *Politis* Konstantinos D., Deir 'Ain 'Abata; a Byzantine church/monastery complex in the Ghor eş-Şafi: SBFLA 38 (1988) 287-296; pl. 17-20.

e834 *Abila*: 1988: SBFLA 38 (1988) 454-7 (W. H. *Mare*).

e835 **Fuller** Michael J., Abila of the Decapolis, a Roman-Byzantine city in Transjordan: diss. Washington Univ. St. Louis 1987. – 88-09597 [OIAc D88].

e836 *Abu Ḥamid*: *Dollfus* Geneviève, *Kafafi* Zeidan, Abu Hamid, Jordanie; premiers résultats: Paléorient 12,1 (1986) 91-100; 4 fig. (map); III pl.

e837 'Ammon / Amoriter: → 804, NBL Lfg 1 (1988) 88s / 90-92 (M. *Görg*).

e838 *Almagro Gorbea* A., Origins and repercussions of the architecture of the Umayyad Palace in Amman: → e824, Jordan III 1986/7, 181-192.

e839 **Olávarri Goicoechea** E., El palacio omeya de Amman, II. La arqueología 1985 → 1,d646: RAulaOr 6 (1988) 281s (H. *Kirchner*).

e839* **Moawiyah M. Ibrahim**, *Gordon* Robert L., *al.*, A cemetery at Queen Alia international airport: Yarmuk Univ. Publ. Arch/Anthrop 1. Wsb 1987, Harrassowitz. 98 p.; liv pl.; ◑ 5 p. DM 88 [JAOS 108,677].

e840 *Piccirillo* Michele, A chapel at Khirbet el-Kursi - Amman: SBFLA 38 (1988) 361-371; pl. 43-58 [372-382, pottery, 'Amr 'Abd el-Jalil; 383-9, inscriptions, *Puech* Émile].

e841 *Yassine* Khair, Ammonite fortresses; date and function: → 285, Archaeology of Jordan 1988, 11-24; fig. 1-9.

e842 Rabbah 1. = Ammon [2. in Judah Jos 15,60]: → 801, ISBEnc³ 4 (1988) 27-30 (A. F. *Rainey*).

e843 *'Amra*: *Grabar* Oleg, La place de Qusayr Amrah dans l'art profane du Haut Moyen Age: CahArch 36 (1988) 75-83; 13 fig.

e844 *Aqaba*: **Khouri Rami** G., *Whitcomb* Donald, Aqaba 'port of Palestine on the China Sea'. Amman 1988, Al Kutba. 36 p.; 35 fig. JD 0.900. – ᴿZDPV 104 (1988) 179-181 (E. A. *Knauf*, C. H. *Brooker*).

e845 *'Araba*: **Khoury Rami** G., The antiquities of the Jordan Rift valley, 1988. – ᴿSBFLA 38 (1988) 467s (M. *Piccirillo*).

e846 *MacDonald* Burton, *Clark* Geoffrey A., *Neeley* Michael, Southern Ghors and Northeast 'Araba archaeological survey 1985 and 1986, Jordan; a preliminary report: BASOR 272 (1988) 23-45; 10 fig.

e847 *Baq'a*: **McGovern** Patrick E., *al.*, LB/EI... Baq'ah 1977-81: 1986 → 3,e267: ᴿSBFLA 38 (1988) 462-4 (P. *Kaswalder*).

e848 *Bašan*: *Olmo Lete* G. del, Bašan o el 'infierno' cananeo: → 98, ᶠLORETZ O., StEpL 5 (1988) 51-60.

e849 *Ḍahr el-Medineh* 828-192 (7 k NW Jerash) MB-LB: RB 95 (1988) 226-8, pl. IVa (Z. *Kafafi*, E. A. *Knauf*).

e850 *Deir'Alla*: *a*) *Vilders* M., A technological study of the pottery from Deir'Alla phase M; – *b*) *Lagro* E., *Haes* H. de, Announcing a study of Islamic pottery from Tell Abu Sarbut (Jordan): Newsletter Pottery Technology 6 (Leiden 1988) 79-87 / 89-98.

e851 *Ḍarīh*: *Villeneuve* François, *Moheisen* Zeidoun al-, Fouilles à Khirbet-Edh-Dharīh (Jordanie) 1984-1987; un village, son sanctuaire et sa nécropole aux époques nabatéenne et romaine (Iᵉʳ-IVᵉ siècles ap. J.-C.): CRAI (1988) 458-479; 14 fig.

e851* *Dhuweila*: *Betts* Alison, 1986 excavations at Dhuweila, Eastern Jordan; a preliminary report: Levant 20 (1988) 7-21; 15 fig.

e852 *Gadara*: Umm Qeis, Gadara 1988: ADAJ 32 (1988) 349-352; 1 fig. (T. *Weber*).

e853 Umm Qeis: 1988: SBFLA 48 (1988) 452-4 (T. *Weber*).

e854 *Mershen* Birgit, *Knauf* Ernst A., From *Ǧadar* to *Umm Qais*: ZDPV 104 (1988) 128-145; 2 fig.; pl. 11B.

e855 *Ġazal*: *Rollefson* Gary O., *a*) Local and external relations in the Levantine Pre-Pottery Neolithic period; 'Ain Ghazal (Jordan) as a regional center: → e824, Jordan III 1986/7, 29-32; – *b*) Neolithic 'Ain Ghazal (Jordan); ritual and ceremony II: Paléorient 12,1 (1986) 45-52.

e856 *Gerasa*: ᴱ**Zayadine** Fawzi, Jerash archaeological project 1981-1983, I. Amman 1986, Dept. Antiq. 492 p.; 124 fig.; 142 pl. – ᴿZDPV 104 (1988) 182s (Cherie J. *Lenzen*).

e857 *Meyers* Carol, Glass from the [Jerash] North Theater Byzantine church and soundings 1982-3: → 459, ASOR 1982-5/8, 175-222; 13 fig.

e858 **Khouri** Rami G., Jerash / The Desert Castles: two 'Jordan Guides' of similar format. – ᴿZDPV 104 (1988) 179-181 (E. A. *Knauf*, C. H. *Brooker*).

e859 *Ġurâra*: *Hart* Stephen, Excavations at Ghrareh, 1986; preliminary report: Levant 20 (1988) 89-99; 9 fig.

e860 *Hallabât* 1984s, château omeyyade: RB 95 (1988) 272-7, fig. 25, pl. VIII-IX (G. *Bisheh*).

e861 *Hasa*: **MacDonald** Burton, The Wadi el Hasa archaeological survey 1979-1983, West-Central Jordan. Waterloo ON 1988, W. Laurier Univ. xvii-404 p.; ill. $45 0-88920-965-0 [OIAc D88].

e862 *Hauran*:   *King* Geoffrey R. D., *al.*,   Some churches of the Byzantine period in the Jordanian Ḥawrān: DamaszMit 3 (1988) 35-75; 14 fig., (map); pl. 16-23.

e863 *Hesban*:   **Ibach** Robert D.ᴶ,   Archaeological survey of the Hesban region; catalogue of sites and characterization of periods: Hesban 5. Berrien Springs MI 1987, Andrews Univ.   0-943872-16-2 [OIAc D88].

e864 *Ḥumayma*/Avara [15 k W of middle of Maʿan-ʿAqaba highway] 240 km² of aqueducts and cisterns: ADAJ 32 (1988) 157-169; map (J. P. *Oleson*).

e865 *Iktanu* 1987, EB-MB kilns: ADAJ 32 (1988) 59-73; 7 fig. (Kay *Prag*).

e866 *Irbid*, 1985 EB, LB, Iron: RB 95 (1988) 239-247, fig. 10s (C. J. *Lenzen*, E. A. *Knauf*).

e867 *Irbid*-Beit Ras survey 1984: ADAJ 32 (1988) 265-274; map (C. J. *Lenzen*, A. M. *McQuitty*).

e868 *Iskander* ḥ., 56 k S Amman: Expedition 28,1 (Ph 1986) 3-12; 13 fig.

e869 Iskander 1987: ➤ 717, AJA 92 (1988) 244 (Mary-Louise *Mussell*...).

e870 **Long** Jesse C.ᴶ,   Sedentary adaptations at the end of the third millennium B. C.; Khirbet Iskander and the excavated settlement sites of Early Bronze IV Palestine-Transjordan: diss. Drew.   Madison NJ 1988. – RelStR 15,192.

e871 Iskander 3d 1984, EB IV: ➤ 459, ASOR 1982-5/8, 107-130; 20 fig. (Suzanne *Richard*, R. *Boraas*).

e872 *Judayid* [wadi: S. Jordan Hisma], Thamudic inscriptions 1986s: ADAJ 32 (1988) 307-317; 5 fig. (Geraldine *King*).

e873 *Kharana*:   **Urice** Stephen K.,   Qasr Kharana in the Transjordan [excavations 1979-81],   1987 ➤ 3,e285 = Baltimore 1988, Johns Hopkins Univ. $28.50.   0-89757-206-6 [BASOR 271,68 adv.].

e874 *Lejjun* (Jordan) 1985, 1987, Rom. Byz.:   RB 95 (1988) 251-267, fig. 14-23 (S. T. *Parker*).

e875 *Madaba*:   **Médébielle** Pierre,   Madaba et son histoire chrétienne.   J 1987, Patriarcat Latin.   467 p. – ᴿSBFLA 38 (1988) 470 (M. *Piccirillo*).

e876 *Mazar*:   *Yassine Khair*,   Tell El Mazar field I ... *al.*: ➤ 459, Archaeology of Jordan 1988, 73-155, ill.

e877 *Mukawir*:   *Strobel* August,   Ein Grabstein aus römischer Zeit in Mukāwir [Machaerus]:   RB 95 (1988) 92-96; pl. I; franç. Eng. 92.

e878 *Nebo* - ʿAyûn Musa 1984-7: ADAJ 32 (1988) 195-205; 5 fig., mosaic inscriptions (M. *Piccirillo*).

e879 *Piccirillo* Michele,   La cappella del prete Giovanni di Khirbet el-Mukhayyat (villaggio di Nebo):   SBFLA 38 (1988) 297-315; pl. 21-38 [ceramica 317-360, pl. 39-42, *Alliata* Eugenio].

e880 Nebo, cappella del prete Giovanni: SBFLA 38 (1988) 457s (M. *Piccirillo*).

e881 *Piccirillo* Michele,   Une petite église [de Kaianos, au nord du Nébo] aux Sources de Moïse: MondeB 52 (1988) 49-51; ill.

e882 *Pella*/Faḥl 8th-9th, 1986s (Natufian EB-LB: ADAJ 32 (1988) 115-149; 15 fig. (T. F. *Potts*, *al.*).

e883 **McNicoll** Anthony, *al.*,   Pella in Jordan I, Sydney/Wooster 1979-81: 1982 ➤ 64,b486; 65,a987:   ᴿSBFLA 38 (1988) 465-7 (P. *Kaswalder*).

e884 *Wightman* G. J.,   An EB IV cemetery in the North Jordan valley: Levant 20 (1988) 139-159; 14 fig.

e885 *a*) *Smith* Robert H.,   Trade in the life of Pella of the Decapolis; – *b*) *Potts* T. F.,   A bronze age ivory-decorated box from Pella (Paḥel) and its foreign relations: ➤ e824, Jordan III 1986/7, 53-58 / 59-71.

e886 *Petra*, 1988: ADAJ 32 (1988) 189-194; 5 fig. (P. C. *Hammond*).

e887 **Lindner** M., Petra 1986 → 2,a746; 3,e308: ᴿPEQ 120 (1988) 153s (Eve *French*); RB 95 (1988) 441s (J.-M. de *Tarragon*). → b863.

e888 *Matthiae* Karl, Die Fassade des Bāb es-Sīq-Trikliniums in Petra; Bemerkungen zu ihrer Gestaltung: ZDPV 104 (1988) 74-83; 5 fig.

e889 *a*) *McKenzie* Judith, The dating of the principal monuments at Petra; a new approach; – *b*) *Zayadine* Fawzi, Decorative stucco at Petra and other Hellenistic sites; – *c*) *Schmidt-Colinet* Andreas, The mason's workshop of Hegra [Saudi Arabia], its relation to Petra, and the tomb of Syllaios; – *d*) *Lindner* Manfred, Archaeological explorations in the Petra region, 1980-4: → e824, Jordan III 1986/7, 295-305 / 131-142 / 143-150 / 291-4.

e890 *Wright* G. R. H., The noble head in Transjordan [Petra; severed; ? Celtic; ? John Baptist]: DamaszMit 3 (1988) 417-425; 3 fig.

e891 *Bartlett* J. R., The kingdom of Edom: → 148, ᶠWEINGREEN J. = IrBSt 10,4 (1988) 207-224.

e892 **Negev** Avraham, Nabatean archaeology today 1986 → 3,e316: ᴿAJA 92 (1988) 136s (D. W. *Roller*); BonnJbb 188 (1988) 606s (R. *Wenning*); BAR-W 14,6 (1988) 10 (P. C. *Hammond*); RB 95 (1988) 440s (J.-M. de *Tarragon*).

e893 *Negev* Avraham, Understanding the Nabateans: BAR-W 14,6 (1988) 26-45; (color.) ill.

e894 **Wenning** Robert, Die Nabatäer — Denkmäler und Geschichte: NTOrbAnt 3, 1987 → 3,e317: ᴿHZ 247 (1988) 388s (E. *Kettenhofen*); MusHelv 45 (1988) 189 (A. *Schmidt-Colinet*); NedTTs 42 (1988) 60-66 (P. W. van der *Horst*, also on the other three volumes of the series, 'met enthousiasme'); TR 84 (1988) 361-3 (E. *Otto*); ZDPV 104 (1988) 176-8 (E. A. *Knauf*).

e895 *a*) *Homès-Fredericq* Denyse, Prospection archéologique en Moab; – *b*) *Naster* Paul, De munten van Nabataea in de nabatese opschriften: → 763, Archéologie 1986, 81-100 / 101-4, franç. 104.

e896 *Sâdeh* [13 k S Petra-Harun] 1987, Edomite-Nabatean: ADAJ 32 (1988) 75-99; 11 fig. (M. *Lindner*, S. *Farajat*).

e897 *Safut*: *Wimmer* Donald H., The excavations at Tell Safut [10 k NW Amman]: → e824, Jordan III, 1986/7, 279-282.

e898 *Saḥab*: *Ibrahim* Moawiyah M., Saḥab [10 k SE Amman] and its foreign relations: → e824, Jordan III 1986/7, 73-81.

e899 *Sa'idiyeh* 3d 1987 (Iron I ...): ADAJ 32 (1988) 41-51; 2 fig. (J. N. *Tubb*); 52-58, list of graves (Dianne *Rowan*).

e899* **Pritchard** James B., Tell es-Sa'idiyeh, excavations on the tell 1964-1966: Museum Mg 66, 1985 → 1,d713: ᴿJAOS 108 (1988) 151s (S. M. *Paley*).

e900 *Tubb* Jonathan N., Tell es-Sa'idiyeh; preliminary report on the first three seasons of renewed excavations [1985-7]: Levant 20 (1988) 23-88; 52 fig.

e901 *Samra*: *Humbert* Jean-Baptiste, Khirbet es-Samra, la route et questions de chronologie: → e824, Jordan III 1986/7, 307-310.

e902 *Shobak* castle 1986, Late Islamic: ADAJ 32 (1988) 225-245; 14 fig. (R. M. *Brown*).

e903 *Šuna* N: 1984s: → e824, Jordan III 1986/7, 237-240 (Carrie *Gustavson-Gaube*).

e904 *Tor Ḥamar*: *Henry* Donald O., *Garrard* Andrew N., Tor Hamar, an epipaleolithic rockshelter in southern Jordan: PEQ 120 (1988) 1-25; 8 fig.

e905 **Uḏruḥ**: *Killick* Alistair, *a*) Udruh and the trade route through southern Jordan: → e824, Jordan III 1986/7, 173-9. – *b*) Udruh, exhibition catalogue [Bru etc.]. L 1987.

e905* '**Umeiri** [6 k NE Madaba]: AndrUnS 26 (1988) 217-252; 28 fig., map (L. T. *Geraty*, al.).

e906 **Umm Bighal** 1982 pottery: ADAJ 32 (1988) 319-347; 21 fig. (S. *Helms*, D. *McCreery*).

e907 **Umm Raṣaṣ**: 1988: SBFLA 38 (1988) 458s (M. *Piccirillo*) & 459s (C. *Bonnet*, *al.*, avec Umm Walid).

e908 Umm-Raṣaṣ, Umm-Walid [14 k SE Madaba] ADAJ 32 (1988) 101-113; 3 fig. (J. *Bujard*, *al.*).

e909 *Piccirillo* Michele, Le chiese e i mosaici di Um er-Rasas - Kastron Mefaa in Giordania: → 703, Milion 1986/8, 177-200 + XIII pl.

e910 **Yabis** (wadi, NW Ajlun) 1987 survey: ADAJ 32 (1988) 275-305; 14 fig. (J. *Mabry*, G. *Palumbo*).

T5.1   Phoenicia-*Libanus*, Lebanon.

e911 **Elayi** Josette, Pénétration grecque en Phénicie sous l'empire perse: Trav. Mém. Ét. Anc. 2. Nancy 1988, Presses Univ. 224 p.; 5 pl. F 76. 2-86480-296-1 [BO 45,475].

e912 *Elayi* Josette, Les sarcophages phéniciens d'époque perse: → 4, ᶠAMIET P. = IrAnt 23 (1988) 276-322; map.

e913 *Falsone* Gioacchino, La Fenicia come centro di lavorazione di bronzo nell'età del ferro: DialArch (1988,1) 79-110; 42 fig. [a parte: R 1988, Quasar].

e914 *Gillain* Bernadette, Restitution des pavements des églises byzantines de Syrie et du Liban [*Donceel-Voûte* Pauline]: DossHA 119 (1987) 52-57; ill.

e915 ᴱ**Gubel** E., *al.*, Studia Phoenicia I-III, 1983/5 → 65,814; 2,556: ᴿArOr 56 (1988) 369s (J. *Pečírková*, 3); IsrEJ 38 (1988) 98s (J. C. *Greenfield*, 1-3).

e916 **Hakimian** Suzy, Une archéologie parallèle; les découvertes clandestines et fortuites au Liban: Berytus 35 (1987) 199-209; 7 fig.

e917 **Hamdeh** Ahmad, Die sozialen Strukturen in Phönizien des ersten Jahrtausends vor Christus. Wü 1985, Universität. [OIAc N88].

e918 *Nibbi* Alessandra, The Lebanon (sic) [in title] and *Djahy* in the Egyptian texts: DiscEg 1 (1985) 17-26; 2 fig.

e919 **Šifman** I. S., ⊕ Recherches nouvelles sur l'histoire sociale et culturelle de la Phénicie: VDI 186 (1988) 188-201.

---

e920 **Ba'albek**: *Okamura* Lawrence, Western legions in Baalbek, Lebanon; colonial coins (A. D. 244-247) of the Philippi: Historia 37 (1988) 126-8.

e921 **Beirut**: *a*) *Davie* Michael F., Maps and the historical topography of Beirut; – *b*) *Davie* May, *Nordiguian* Lévon, L'habitat urbain de Bayrūt al-Qadīmat au 19ᵉ siècle: Berytus 35 (1987) 141-164; 8 fig. / 165-197; 16 fig.

e922 **Byblos**: **Saghieh** M., Byblos 1983 → 64,b514 ... 3,e334: ᴿBInstArch sup 24 (1987) 30s (T. *Watkins*); RArchéol (1988) 121s (J.-L. *Huot*).

e923 **Nibbi** Alessandra, Ancient Byblos reconsidered 1985 → 1,d729 ... 3,e340: ᴿJAmEg 24 (1987) 151-3 (E. S. *Meltzer*); JQR 78 (1987s) 323-5 (S. L. *Olson*: seeks facts, gives assumptions); Klio 70 (1988) 566-8 (J. *Hallof*).

e924 *Lorton* David, Where was ancient Egypt's *kpn(y)*? [*Nibbi* A. 1981; 1985]: DiscEg 6 (1986) 89-99: she should concentrate on disproving the intrenched views, instead of pursuing without solid evidence her new alternatives which have not gained scholarly approval.

e925 *Nibbi* Alessandra, Byblos (sic) [in title] and Wenamun; a reply to some recent unrealistic criticism [*Ray* J.; *Strange* J.]: DiscEg 11 (1988) 31-42; 2 fig. (map).

e926 **Nibbi** Alessandra, Wenamun and Alashiya reconsidered 1985 → 1,e388 ... 3,e340: ᴿJQR 79 (1988s) 76-78 (Janice *Kamrin*: unacceptable); Klio 70 (1988) 566-8 (J. *Hallof*); WZKM 78 (1986) 280s (K. *Jaroš*) & 224-6 (G. *Vittmann*).

e927 *Nibbi* Alessandra, Phoenician from 'carpenter' like *fnḫ(w)*? A new approach to an old problem [... all the forests along the borders of Egypt were in foreign hands]: DiscEg 6 (1986) 11-20; 3 fig.

e928 *Kāmid el-Lōz*: **Frish** Bertram *al.*, Kāmid el-Lōz 6. Die Werkstätten 1985 → 3,e346: ᴿOLZ 83 (1988) 162-6 (R.-B. *Wartke*).

e929 **Hachmann** Rolf, Bericht K/Loz 1971-4: 1982 → 1,d732 ... 3,e343: ᴿOLZ 83 (1988) 562-4 (G. *Pfeifer*); PhoenixEOL 33,2 (1987) 65-70 (W. H. van *Soldt*, E. J. van der *Steen*).

e930 *Ksar ʿAqil*: **Azoury** Ingrid, Ksar Akil I: BAR 289, 1986; ᴱ*Bergman* C., *Copeland* L.: → 3,e348: ᴿBInstArch 25 (1988) 97s (A. *Betts*).

e931 *Bergman* Christopher A., *Ohnuma* Katsuhiko, The Upper Palaeolithic sequence of Ksar ʿAkil, Lebanon: Berytus 35 (1987) 13-25 + 19 fig.

e932 *Marks* Anthony E., *Volkman* Philip, The Mousterian of Ksar Akil; levels XXVIA through XXVIIIB: Paléorient 12,1 (1986) 5-20.

e933 **Ohnuma** K., Ksar Akil Lebanon, a technological study of the earlier Upper Palaeolithic levels, III., Levels XXV-XIV: BAR-Int. 426. Ox 1988. 0-86054-551-2 [OIAc D88].

e934 *Sarafand*: *Anderson* William P., The kilns and workshops of Sarepta (Sarafand), Lebanon; remnants of a Phoenician ceramic industry: Berytus 35 (1987) 41-51 + 21 fig.

e935 *Sidon*: **Fleischer** Robert, Der Klagefrauensarkophag aus Sidon 1983 → 65,a643 ... 3,e351: ᴿZDMG 138 (1988) 370s (H.-G. *Buchholz*).

e936 *Salamé-Sarkis* Ḥassān, Un problème d'interpretatio phoenissa; la pseudo-tribune du temple d'Ešmun à Sidon: Berytus 35 (1987) 120-5 [126-139, Heliopolitana monumenta (Baalbek); 101—119, Baṭrūn].

e937 *Tyrus*: **Chéhab** Maurice H., Fouilles de Tyr; la nécropole: BMB 33-36. P 1983-6, R. Maisonneuve → 3,e354; 124 p., XVI pl.; 482 + 23 p., LXXXV pl.; p. 483-805, pl. LXXXVI-CLXV; 268 p., LXXIV pl. (monnaies). – ᴿRBgNum 134 (1988) 204 (P. *Naster*).

e938 **Karyszkowski** P. O., *Klejman* I. B., ❻ Drevni gorod Tira ... The ancient city Tyre; historico-archeological sketch. Moskva 1985. – ᴿVDI 184 (1988) 211-5 (M. V. *Agbunov*).

e939 **Linant de Bellefonds** P., Sarcophages attiques de la nécropole de Tyr; une étude iconographique: RCiv Mém. 52, 1985 → 3,e356: ᴿJHS 108 (1988) 270 (Glenys *Davies*).

e940 a) *Stewart* Andrew, Diodorus, Curtius, and Arrian on Alexander's mole at Tyre; – b) *Bikai* Patricia & Pierre, Tyre at the end of the twentieth century; – c) *Seeden* Helga, Lebanon's past today: Berytus 35 (1987) 97-99; 3 fig. / 67-83 + 12 pl. (map) / 5-8 + 15 fig.

e940* *Bordreuil* Pierre, *Ferjaoui* Ahmed, À propos des 'fils de Tyr' et des 'fils de Carthage': → 754, Carthago 1986/8, 137-142; 1 fig.

e941 ᴱ**Kortekaas** G. A. A., Historia Apollonii regis Tyri 1984 → 2,9582; 3,e358. – ᴿLatomus 47 (1988) 170s (R. *Verdière*); Speculum 63 (1988) 186-190 (R. *Hester*).

e942 ᴱSchmeling Gareth, Historia Apollonii regis Tyri: BiblSGRTeub. Lp 1988, Teubner. xxxi-143 p.

T5.2 *Situs mediterranei* **phoenicei et punici.**

e943 *Gran-Aymerich* Jean, Les Phéniciens: Archéologia 236 (Díjon 1988) 14-28; ill.

e944 ᴱLipiński E., Phoenicia and the East Mediterranean in the first millennium 1985/7 ⇥ 3,e826: ᴿBO 45 (1988) 690-2 (E. *Gubel*); DiscEg 10 (1988) 99-102 (Alessandra *Nibbi*).

e945 *Moscati* Sabatino, *a*) Baitylos; sulla cronologia delle più antiche stele puniche [< LinceiR 8/36 (1981) 101-5]: ⇥ 233, Scritti fenici minori 1988, 415-419 (420-427, 8 pl.); – *b*) Fenicio o punico o cartaginese?: RStFen 16 (1988) 3-13; – *c*) Dimensione tirrenica: RStFen 16 (1988) 133-144.

e946 *Niemeyer* Hans Georg, Les Phéniciens dans l'ouest; un modèle non grec d'expansion et de colonisation dans la Méditerranée [séance 13.XII.1986]: RArchéol (1988) 201-5.

e947 *a*) *Schubart* Hermanfrid, *Arteaga* Oswaldo, El mundo de las colonias fenicias occidentales; – *b*) *Padro i Parcerisa* Josep, Las importaciones egipcias en Almuñécar y los orígenes de la colonización fenicia en la península ibérica: ⇥ 772, ᶠSIRET L., 1984/6, 499-525 / 526-9.

---

e948 *Aspis*: *Fantar* Mahmed, Présence punique et libyque dans les environs d'Aspis au cap Bon: CRAI (1988) 502-518; 9 fig.

e949 *Cadiz*: *Schubart* Hermanfrid, Endbronzezeitliche und phönizische Siedlungsfunde von der Guadiaro-Mündung, Prov. Cádiz, Probegrabung 1986: MadMit 29 (1988) 132-165 + 13 fig.; pl. 10-11.

e950 *Cyprus*: **Bikai** Patricia M., The Phoenician pottery of Cyprus 1987 ⇥ 3,e370: 99-63560-05-9: ᴿAntiqJ 68,1 (1988) 142-4 (E. J. *Peltenburg*).

e950* **Markoe** Glenn, Phoenician bronze and silver bowls from Cyprus and the Mediterranean 1985 ⇥ 1,f755; 3,e368: ᴿJAOS 108 (1988) 657-9 (Jeanny V. *Canby*).

e951 *Markoe* G.E., A terracotta from Kazaphani, Cyprus, with stamped decoration in the Cypro-Phoenician tradition: RStFen 16 (1988) 15-23; pl. I-IV.

e952 *Bisi* Anna Maria, Le rôle de Chypre dans la civilisation phénicienne d'occident; état de la question et essai de synthèse ⇥ 748, Cyprus between, 1985/6, 341-350; pl. XXVI-XXIX.

e953 *Ebla*: *Bisi* Anna Maria, Antécédents Éblaïtes d'un apotropaïon phénico-punique: ⇥ 707, Wirtschaft 1986/8, 21-33; 10 fig.

e954 *Ibiza*: *Gòmez Bellard* Carlos, Novedades de arqueología fenicio-púnica en Ibiza: ArEspArq 61 (1988) 226-9; 3 fig.

e955 *Jordan*: *Homès-Fredericq* D., Possible Phoenician influences in Jordan in the Iron Age: ⇥ e824, Jordan III, 1986/7, 89-96, 6 fig.

e955* **Fantar** M., Kerkouane I, (Cap Bon, Tunisie) 1984 ⇥ 1,d765. – ᴿOLZ 83 (1988) 395s (B. *Brentjes*).

e956 *Mozia*: **Amadasi Guzzo** Maria Giulia, Scavi a Mozia — le iscrizioni 1986: StFenici 22. R 1986, Cons. Naz. Ric. 107 p.; 14 fig.; 15 pl. – ᴿJNWS 14 (1988) 230 (F. C. *Fensham*).

e957 *Falsone* Gioacchino, La scoperta, lo scavo, e il contesto archeologico: La statua marmorea di Mozia (Giornata di studio marsala 1.VI.1986): Studi e Materiali 8 [R 1988, Bretschneider] 9-28; ill.

e958 *Falsone* Gioacchino, The Bronze Age occupation and the Phoenician foundation at Motya: BInstArch 25 (1988) 31-49; 8 fig. + 4 pl.

e959 *Pyrgi*: *Hvidberg-Hansen* Finn O., The Pyrgi texts [one Phoenician, two Etruscan, on golden plates] seen in an East-West perspective: ➤ 733, Acta Hyperborea 1987/8, 58-68.

e960 **Sant'Antioco**: *Bernardini* P., S. Antioco 1983-6; l'insediamento fenicio: RStFen 16 (1988) 75-99; 11 fig.; pl. XIX-XXIV [p. 111-9, *Tronchetti* C., La fase romana].

e961 *Madau* M., Nota sui rapporti tra mondo nuragico e mondo fenicio e punico nella Sardegna nord-occidentale: RStFen 16 (1988) 181-190 + 3 fig.

e962 *Vagnetti* Lucia, Armi per i Micenei; da Micene alla Sardegna le prime navigazioni greche nell'occidente mediterraneo: Archeo Dossier 36 ('I Fenici' 1988) 22-27.

e963 *Moscati* Sabatino, Testimonianze fenicio-puniche a Oristano, catalogo *Uberti* Maria Luisa: Lincei Memorie 8/31/1. R 1988, Acc. Naz. Lincei. 63 p.; XXVI pl.

e964 **Bartoloni** P., Le anfore fenicie e puniche di Sardegna: Studia Punica 4. R 1988, Univ. 77 p.; 19 fig.

e965 **Hölbl** G., Ägyptisches Kulturgut im phönikischen und punischen Sardinien: ÉPR 102, 1986 ➤ 2,a793; ƒ320: RBO 45 (1988) 564-7 (E. *Gubel*).

e966 **Sulcis**: **Moscati** S., Le stele di Sulcis 1986 ➤ 3,a797: RJNWS 14 (1988) 225 (F. C. *Fensham*).

e967 **Moscati** Sabatino, Le officine di Sulcis: Studia Punica 3. R 1988, Univ. 130 p.; XXXII pl.

e968 **Taršiš**: **Koch** M., Tarschisch und Hispanien ... 1984 ➤ 65,b35; 3,e382: RRStFen 16 (1988) 128 (G. *Garbini*).

e968* **Harrison** Richard J., Spain at the dawn of history; Iberians, Phoenicians and Greeks: Ancient Peoples and Places, 105. L 1988, Thames & H. 176 p.; 13 fig. £17 [GreeceR 36,250, P. *Walcot*]. 0-500-02111-2.

e969 **Loman** Francisco J., *al.* [ch. 11-13 and 15-19 by *Blázquez* José-M. on Phoenicians], Historia de España I. Protohistoria² 1983 ➤ 3,e385: RJNES 47 (1988) 136-9 (Brigitte W. *Watkins*: 'little appeal for the discerning scholar').

e970 **Olmo Lete** Gregorio del, *Aubet Semmler* Maria Eugenia, Los Fenicios en la Península Ibérica, I. Arqueología, cerámica y plástica; II. Epigrafía y lengua; glíptica y numismática; expansión e interacción cultural 1986 ➤ 2,353: RÉtClas 55 (1987) 113s (Corinne *Bonnet*).

e971 *Tharros*: *Acquaro* E., Tharros [tofet], la campagna del 1987: RStFen 16 (1988) 207-219 pl. XXXV-XL [221-252, *Manfredi* L.-I.; *Madau* M.].

e972 **Barnett** R. D., *Mendleson* C., Catalogue of [Tharros] material in the British Museum 1987 ➤ 3,e391: RRAss 82 (1988) 190s (P. *Amiet*).

e973 **Moscati** S., *Uberti* M. L., Scavi al tofet di Tharros, i monumenti lapidei: StFen 21, 1985 ➤ 1,d776: RJNSW 14 (1988) 225 (F. C. *Fensham*).

e974 *Moscati* Sabatino, *Uberti* M. L., Le stele di Tharros e l'artigianato punico in Italia: Atti/Rendiconti Pont. Acc. Rom. Archeologia 57 (1986) 37-56.

e975 *Fedele* Francesco, *Foster* Giraud V., Tharros; ovicaprini sacrificali e rituale del Tofet: RStFen 16 (1988) 29-46; pl. XI-XV.

T5.3 Carthago.

e976 *Bénichou-Safar* Hélène, Sur l'incinération des enfants aux tophets de Carthage et de Sousse: RHR 205 (1988) 57-68; Eng. 57.

e977 *Ben Younes* Habib, Trente années d'archéologie et d'histoire ancienne en Tunisie 1956/1986; les faits – les idées: Ibla 50,159 (1987) 11-59.

e978 **Charles-Picard** Gilbert & Colette, Karthago, Leben und Kultur [La vie quotidienne 1958 ²1982], ᵀ*Miller* I. (1959). Stu 1983, Reclam. 295 p.; 26 fig.; 26 pl.; 5 maps. DM 30. – ᴿArKulturG 69 (1987) 474-6 (M. *Clauss*).

e979 *Clay* Diskin, The archaeology of the temple to Juno in Carthage (Aen, 1, 446-93): ClasPg 83 (1988) 195-205.

e979* *a) Fantar* M'hamed, L'impact de la présence phénicienne et de la fondation de Carthage en Méditerranée occidentale; – *b) Ennabli* Abdelmajid, Carthage, la campagne internationale; aspects puniques; – *c) Amadasi Guzzo* M. G., Dédicaces de femmes à Carthage: → 754, Carthago 1986/8, 3-14 / 51-59 / 143-9.

e980 *Gascou* Jacques, Y avait-il un pagus carthaginois à Thuburbo maius?: AntAfr 24 (1988) 67-80.

e981 **Gros** Pierre, Byrsa 3, 1985 → 2,b460; 3,e402: ᴿClasW 82 (1988s) 117 (S. R. *Wolff*); RÉAnc 90 (1988) 488s (L. *Maurin*).

e982 **Hans** Linda-Marie, Karthago und Sizilien; die Entstehung und Gestaltung der Epikratie auf dem Hintergrund der Beziehungen der Karthager zu den Griechen und den nichtgriechischen Völkern Siziliens (VI.-III. Jhd. v Chr.): HistTSt 7, 1983 → 1,d786; 2,a815: ᴿAntClas 57 (1988) 510s (T. Van *Compernolle*); ClasR 102 (1988) 89-91 (S. P. *Ellis*); JHS 108 (1988) 263s (R. J. A. *Talbert*).

e983 **Huss** W., Geschichte der Karthager 1985 → 1,d789; 2,a815: ᴿHZ 245 (1987) 414-7 (K.-W. *Welwei*).

e983* *a) Lancel* Serge, Les fouilles de la mission archéologique française à Carthage et le problème de Byrsa; – *b) Debergh* Jacques, Ombres et lumières sur la topographie de la Carthage punique; les errances de Byrsa; – *c) Picard* G. C., Le pouvoir suprême à Carthage: → 754, Carthago 1986/8, 61-89; 10 fig. / 91-99; map / 119-124.

e984 *Lipiński* E., [→ 754] Carthage et Tarshish: BO 45 (1988) 60-81.

e985 *Lund* John, Prolegomena to a study of the Phoenician/Punic colonization of Tunisia: → 733, Acta Hyperborea 1987/8, 44-57.

e986 *Sanders* Lionel J., Punic politics in the fifth century B.C.: Historia 37 (1988) 72-89.

e987 *Tsirkin* Yu. B., ❸ The historical development of Carthage: → 456*, Peredneaz. IV (1986) 83-90.

e988 *Warmington* R. H., The destruction of Carthage; a retractatio [his 'sown with salt' in Carthage (L 1960) was an invention of B. L. HALLWARD in CAH 8 (1930), as rightly R. T. *Ridley*]: ClasPg [81 (1986) 140-6, Ridley] 83 (1988) 308-310 [cf. 41s, *Visonà* Paolo, Passing the salt].

e989 *Xella* P., Una menzione del tempio di Eshmun a Cartagine (*CIS* I 2362,6): RStFen 16 (1988) 21-23.

e990 *Zahrnt* Michael, Die Verträge zwischen Dionysios I [Syrakus c.409] und den Karthagern: ZPapEp 71 (1988) 209-228.

T5.4 **Ugarit** – *Ras Šamra*.

e991 *a) Buit* M. Du, Ras Shamra, Ougarit: → 786, Catholicisme 12,55 (1988) 495-8; – *b) O'Connor* Michael P., Ugarit and the Bible: → 3,356, Backgrounds 1987, 151-164 [< JBL 108, 174].

e992 **Callot** O., Une maison à Ougarit: RCiv, Mém 28, 1983 → 64,b601 ... 3,e410: ᴿBabesch 62 (1987) 169 (T. L. *Heres*); BO 45 (1988) 688-690 (W. H. van *Soldt*).

e993 **Curtis** Adrian, Ugarit (Ras Shamra): Cities of the biblical world 1985
→ 1,d810; 3,e412: ᴿCBQ 50 (1988) 110s (P. M. *Bikai*).

e994 **Dietrich** M., *al.,* Ugarit-Bibliographie 1967-1971: 1973 → 55,6027;
2,666: ᴿOrientalia 57 (1988) 240 (W. G. E. *Watson*).

e995 *Dietrich* M., *Loretz* O., Die Alphabettafel aus Bet Šemeš und die
ursprüngliche Heimat der Ugariter: → 32, ꟳDELLER K., AOAT 220 (1988)
61-85; 3 fig.

e996 *Liverani* M., Ugarit, ᵀ*La Sor* W. S.: → 801, ISBEnc³ 4 (1988) 937-941.

e997 *a) Liverani* Mario, Il primo piano degli archivi di Ugarit; – *b) Moor*
J. C. de, The seasonal pattern in the legend of Aqhatu; – *c) Astour* M. C.,
Remarks on KTU 1.96; – *d) Sasson* J.-M., The numeric progression in
Keret 1: 15-20; yet another suggestion: → 98, ꟳLORETZ O., StEpL 5
(1988) 121-142 / 61-78 / 13-24 / 181-8.

e998 **Moran** William L., Les lettres d'El-Amarna: LAPO 13, 1987 → 3,e766:
ᴿJNWS 14 (1988) 223 (F. C. *Fensham*).

e998* *a) Saadé* Gabriel, La vie intellectuelle et l'enseignement à Ougarit; – *b)*
Kleven Terence, Kingship in Ugarit (KTU 1.16 I 1-23); – *c) Cunchillos*
J.-L., Que mère se réjouisse de père; traduction et commentaire de KTU
2.16: → 29, Mem. CRAIGIE P., Ascribe 1988, 69-90 / 29-53 / 3-10.

e999 *Sader* Helene, Ras Shamra-Ugarit and the Bible: NEStr 9,2 (1988)
37-46.

g1 **Stucky** R. A., Ras Shamra-Leukos Limen; die nachugaritische Besied-
lung 1983 → 64,b620 ... 2,a832: ᴿSovArch (1987,4) 291-4 (A. Yu. *So-*
gomonov).

g2 **Xella** Paolo, La terra di Baal (Ugarit e la sua civiltà): Bibliot. Archeol.
1984 → 1,d819; Lit. 35.000. 88-7555-011-5. – ᴿBL (1988) 129 (W.
Watson).

g3 ᴱ**Yon** M., Ras Shamra-Ougarit III. Le centre de la ville, 38ᵉ-44ᵉ campagnes (1978-1984): RCiv Mémoire 72, 1987 → 3,e420. – ᴿAulaO 6 (1988)
122-5 (J. *Sanmartín*); BL (1988) 35 (J. F. *Healey*).

T5.5   **Ebla.**

g4 *a) Arcari* Elena, The administrative organisation of the city of Ebla; – *b)*
Astour Michael C., The geographical and political structure of the Ebla
empire; – *c) Grégoire* Jean-Pierre, *Renger* Johannes, Die Interdependenz
der wirtschaftlichen und gesellschaftlich-politischen Strukturen von Ebla;
– *d) Mander* Pietro, The function of the Maliktum as based on the
documentation of the administrative texts of Ebla: → 707, Wirtschaft
1986/8, 125-9 / 139-158 / 211-224 / 261-6.

   Archi Alfonso, ARET 1.7, 1985/8 → e76, e77.

g5 *Archi* Alfonso, *a)* Position of the tablets of Ebla: Orientalia 57 (1988)
67-69; – *b)* Prices, workers' wages and maintenance at Ebla: AltOrF 15
(1988) 24-29.

g5* *Astour* Michael C., Toponymy of Ebla and ethonohistory of northern
Syria; a preliminary survey: JAOS 108 (1988) 545-555.

g6 **Colombo** Fausto, Gli archivi imperfetti; memoria sociale e cultura elet-
tronica. Mi 1986, ViPe. 112 p. Lit. 10.000. – ᴿBbbOr 30 (1988) 58-61
(D. *Sardini* vede qualche rapporto con 'il grande archivio di Ebla, la
biblioteca di Alessandria ...').

g7 *a) Dolce* Rita, Some aspects of the primary economic structures of Ebla in
the third and second milleniums B.C.; stores and workplaces; – *b) Steiner*
Gerd, Die Bezeichungen für den [politisch-geographischen] Begriff 'Land'

in den Texten aus Ebla: ➤ 707, Wirtschaft 1986/8, 35-45; plan; pl. VII-X / 333-343.

Dombrowski B., 'Eblaitic' 1988 ➤ a397.

g8 *a) Fronzaroli* P., [ritual for dead kings]; – *b) Tonietti* M. V. [professional 'singers' ➤ g22]; – *c) Bonechi* M. [verb-prefix *ti*]; – *d) Catagnoti* A. [kinship-term personal names]: ➤ 705*, Miscellanea eblaitica I (1988) 1-33 / 79-119 / 121-172 / 183-277 [< BL 89,149].

g9 *a) Fronzaroli* Pelio, Tre scongiuri eblaiti (ARET 5,1-3); – *b) Krebernik* Manfred, Ein neuer literarischer Text in semitischer Sprache aus Ebla: VO 7 (1988) 11-23 [243s, *Catagnoti* A.] / 25-33; pl. 6. [245-8 Ebla graphemics, *Platt* J.].

g10 ᴱGordon C. H., *al.,* Eblaitica 1987 ➤ 3,491: ᴿArOr 56 (1988) 370s (B. *Hruška*); BASOR 270 (1988) 100s (P. *Michalowski*); BL (1988) 123s (W. G. *Lambert*); JNWS 14 (1988) 230s (F. C. *Fensham*); WeltOr 19 (1988) 187-194 (P. J. J. van *Huyssteen*).

g11 *Gordon* Cyrus H., Ebla as backgound for the Old Testament: ➤ 482, VTS 40, Jerusalem congress 1986/8, 293-7.

g12 **Krebernik** Manfred, Die Beschwörungen aus Fara und Ebla 1984 ➤ 65,b82; 3,e437: ᴿBO 45 (1988) 384-7 (W. *Heimpel*).

g13 **Krebernik** Manfred, Die Personennamen der Ebla-Texte; eine Zwischenbilanz: BBeitVO 7. B 1988, Riemer. xvii-353 p. 3-496-00906-3.

g14 *La Sor* W. S., Tell Mardikh: ➤ 801, ISBEnc³ 4 (1988) 750-8.

g15 **Mander** Pietro, *a)* Sumerian personal names in Ebla: JAOS 108 (1988) 481-3; – *b)* Ebla's Palatine gynaiceum as documented in the administrative archives: OrAnt 27 (1988) 1-73.

g16 **Matthiae** Paolo, I tesori di Ebla 1985 ➤ 65,b87 ... 2,a838: ᴿJAOS 108 (1988) 518s (Marie-Henriette *Gates*).

g16* *Matthiae* Paolo, Le palais royal d'Ébla [nouveau, du IIᵉ millénaire; decouvert après 1987, dans la ville basse au nord de la colline des tablettes]: Archéologia 238 [Dijon 1988] 34-43; ill.

g17 *a) Matthiae* Paolo, On the economic foundations of the early Syrian culture of Ebla; – *b) Scandone Matthiae* Gabriella, Les relations entre Ébla et l'Égypte au IIIème et au IIème millénaire av. J.-C.; – *c) Mazzoni* Stefania, Economic features of the pottery equipment of Palace G: ➤ 707, Wirtschaft 1986/8, 75-80 / 67-73; pl. XI-XV / 81-105.

g18 *Muntingh* L. M., Second thoughts on Ebla and the Old Testament [... *Viganò* rightly, ʏʜᴡʜ reading not clear; and *Archi,* even if it were it did not correspond to what it meant for Israel]: ➤ 47, ᶠFᴇɴsʜᴀᴍ F., Text 1988, 157-171; bibliog. 171-5.

g19 **Pettinato** Giovanni, Ebla; nuovi orizzonti della storia 1986 ➤ 2,a841; Lit. 35.000: ᴿBL (1988) 126 (W. *Watson*); CC 139 (1988,1) 196-8 (G. L. *Prato*); ÉtClas 56 (1988) 210s (Corinne *Bonnet*); Salesianum 50 (1988) 224s (R. *Della Casa*).

g20 *a) Pettinato* Giovanni, Nascita, matrimonio, malattia e morte a Ebla; – *b) Weinfeld* Moshe, Initiation of political friendship at Ebla and its later developments: ➤ 707, Wirtschaft 1986/8, 299-316 / 345-8.

g21 *Pinnock* Frances, Trade at Ebla: CanadMesop 7 (1984) 19-36.

g22 *a) Tonietti* Maria Vittoria, La figura del n a r nei testi di Ebla; ipotesi per una cronologia delle liste di nomi presenti nei testi economici; – *b) Catagnoti* Amalia, I nomi di parentela nell'onomastica di Ebla; – *c) Conti* G. ... *ka*; ➤ 705*, Misc. 1987/8, 79-119 / 183-277 / 35-77.

g23 *Viganó* Lorenzo,   Enna-Dagan's letter to the e n of Ebla: SBFLA 38 (1988) 227-246.

T5.8   **Situs effossi Syriae** *in ordine alphabetico.*

g24 [Ajāja] *ʿAğāğa* - Šadikanni [Habur S Hassaka] 1982: DamaszMit 3 (1988) 141-185; 14 fig. (map); pl. 26-33 (Mahmud *As'ad, al.*).

g25 *Aleppo*:   **Gaube** H., *Wirth* E., Aleppo: TAVO-B 58, 1984 ➤ 65,b110 ... 3,e448:   ᴿOLZ 83 (1988) 592s (H. *Brentjes*).

g26 *Arslan Taš*:   *Albenda* Pauline,   The gateway and portal stone reliefs from Arslan Tash: BASOR 271 (1988) 5-30; 29 fig.

g27 *Baliḫ*: *Córdoba* J. M.,   Prospección en el valle de rio Baliḫ (Siria); informe provisional: AulaOr 6 (1988) 149-188; 6 fig.

g28 *Barîša*: **Peña** I., *al.,*   Inventaire du Jébel Baricha [74 siti archeologici + 63 altri toponimi]; SBF min. 33, 1987 ➤ 3,e445:   ᴿOrChrPer 54 (1988) 228s (V. *Poggi*); RB 95 (1988) 606s (J.-M. de *Tarragon*).

g29 *Barri*:   *Pecorella* Paolo E., Tell Barri, uno scavo italiano in Siria: ArchViva 7,3 (1988) 32-43; (color.) ill.

g30 *Bderi* (S. Hassaka) 1985, Early Dynastic-Akkad: DamaszMit 3 (1988) 223-386, 48 fig. (map); pl. 49-60 (*Pfälzner* Peter, *al.*).

g31 *Beth Zagba*: *Mango* Marlia M.,   Where was Beth Zagba [origin of Syriac Rabbula Gospels, in Mt. Riha (? Kafar Zbu) N Apameia, rather than in Mesopotamia]: ➤ 134, ᶠSEVČENKO I., Okeanos 1983, 405-430, 2 maps.

g32 *Brak*: **Meijer** Diederik J. W., A survey in northeastern Syria [Brak/Habur] 1986 ➤ 3,e445:   ᴿBO 45 (1988) 409-411 (G. M. *Schwartz*).

g33 *Buṣra* 2d, 1983-4: DamaszMit 3 (1988) 387-411; pl. 61-63 (Helga *Seeden*).

g34 *a) Farili Campanati* Raffaella,   Relazione sugli scavi e ricerche della missione Italo-Siriana a Bosra (1985, 1986, 1987); – *b) Dentzer* Jean-Marie,   Fouilles Franco-Syriennes à l'est de l'Arc Nabatéen (1985-1987); une nouvelle Cathédrale à Bosra? – *c) Zanardi* Bruno, Tecnica, successioni stratigrafiche e restauro nei dipinti murali della Chiesa di S. Sergio: ➤ 758, Ravenna 1988, 45-92 (121-132) / 13-34 / 225-232.

g35 *Freyberger* Klaus S.,   Zur Datierung des Theaters in Bosra: DamaszMit 3 (1988) 17-26; pl. 9-15.

g36 *Damascus*:   **Pitard** Wayne T.,   Ancient Damascus; a historical study of the Syrian city-state from earliest times until its fall to the Assyrians in 732 B.C.E. 1987 ➤ 3,e466:   ᴿBASOR 270 (1988) 97-100 (P. E. *Dion*); BSOAS 51 (1988) 543s (J. *Wansbrough*, also on SADER); JBL 107 (1988) 733s (J. M. *Miller*: some respectful dissents); RB 95 (1988) 607s (J.-M. de *Tarragon*).

g36* *Moaz* Abd al-Razzaq,   Note sur le mausolée de Saladin à Damas; son fondateur et les circonstances de son fondation: BÉtOr 39s (1987s) 183-9; pl. 1-4.

g37 **Pouzet** Louis,   Damas au VIIᵉ/XIIIᵉ siècle; vie et structures religieuses d'une métropole islamique: Recherches NS A-15.   Beyrouth 1988, Dar el-Machreq. 527 p.; maps.

g38 **Sader** Hélène S.,   Les états araméens 1987 ➤ 3,e467:   ᴿBerytus 35 (1987) 211s (J. N. *Postgate*: useful despite weaknesses; BL (1988) 127 (A. R. *Millard*); JRAS (1988) 394s (D. J. *Wiseman*).

g39 *Dara*: *Furlan* Halo,   Oikema katàgheion, una problematica struttura a Dara [NW Nisibis]: ➤ 703, Milion 1986/8, 105-118 + IX pl.

g40 *Emar*:   **Arnaud** Daniel,   Recherches au pays d'Aštata, Emar VI, 1-3 1985s ➤ 2,a870:   ᴿOLZ 83 (1988) 645-653 (H. *Klengel*).

g41 *Leemans* W. F., Aperçu sur les textes juridiques d'Émar: JESHO 31 (1988) 207-242.

g42 *Hadidi*: *a*) *Dornemann* Rudolph H., Tell Hadidi; one Bronze Age site among many in the Tabqa dam salvage area; – *b*) *Moore* Andrew, The prehistory of Syria; – *c*) *Gates* Marie-Henriette, Dialogues between ancient Near Eastern texts and the archaeological record; test cases from Bronze Age Syria: → 725, Ancient Syria 1985 = BASOR 270 (1988) 13-42 / 3-12 / 63-91.

g43 *Ḥalaf*: *Dolce* Rita, Per una riconsiderazione delle opere figurative di Gebelet el-Beyda [W Halaf]: CMatArch 1 (R 1986) 307-331 + fig. 59s.

g44 *Ḥama*: *Pentz* Peter, [Hama finds reexamined] A medieval workshop for producing 'Greek fire' grenades: Antiquity 62 (1988) 89-93; 5 fig.

g44* [Papanicolaou] *Christensen* A., *al.,* The Graeco-Roman objects of clay, the coins and the necropolis: Hama 1931-8, 3/3; Større Beretninger 10. K 1986, Nationalmuseet. 113 p.; 40 fig. [JHS 109,261, R. *Higgins*].

g45 **Ploug** Gunhild, The Graeco-Roman town: Hama fouilles 1931-8, 3/1 [the sixth]: Større Beretninger 9, 1985 → 1,d881: ᴿRArchéol (1988) 144-6 (P. *Leriche*).

g46 **Thuesen** I., Hama, fouilles et recherches 1931-1938, préf. *Riis* P. J.: Større Beretninger 11. K 1988, Nationalmuseet. (Vol. I) 279 p.; dont 213-279 pl.

g47 *Ḥamīdīya*, 30 k S Qamishli: **Eichler** Seyyare, **Haas** Volkert, *al.,* Tall al-Ḥamīdīya I, Vorbericht 1984: OBO Arch 4, 1985 → 1,d883; 2,a873: ᴿBO 45 (1988) 684-8 (H. H. *Curvers*); CBQ 50 (1988) 113s (J. D. *Seger*: no Kenyon-style section-drawings); JAOS 108 (1988) 304-6 (M. C. *Astour*).

g48 *Ḥammam Turkman*: *Akkermans* Peter M.M.G., An updated chronology for the northern Ubaid and late chalcolithic periods in Syria; new evidence from Tell Hammam et-Turkman: Iraq 50 (1988) 109-136; 137-145 = fig. 2-10.

g49 *Ḥuwayra*: **Moortgat-Correns** Ursula, *al.,* Tell Chuēra in Nordost-Syrien; vorläufiger Bericht über die neunte und zehnte Grabungskampagne 1982 und 1983 / elfte 1985. B 1988, Mann. 99 p.; 39 fig. / 68 p.; 28 fig.; VI plans. 3-7861-1451-X; 514-1.

g50 **Orthmann** Winfried, *al.,* Tell Chuēra ... 1982-3 ... 9.-10. Grabungs-kampagne: Oppenheim-Stiftung 12, 1986 → 3,e487: ᴿMundus 24 (1988) 211s (Eva A. *Braun-Holzinger*).

g51 *Kôm*: **Dornemann** R. H., A neolithic village at Tell el-Kowm 1986 → 2,a875; 3,e481: ᴿPaléorient 13,2 (1987) 149s (H. T. *Waterbolk*).

g52 *Mari*: ᴱ*Durand* J.-M., *Margueron* J.-C., Mari, bilan: Actes 1983/5 → 1,565 ... 3,e492: ᴿJCS 40 (1988) 245-250 (J. S. *Cooper,* also on ARM 25); OLZ 83 (1988) 542-4 (H. *Klengel*).

g53 **Talon** Philippe, Textes administratifs ... salles Y-Z: ARM 24, 1985 → 1,d896 ... 3,e501: ᴿWZKM 78 (1986) 285-290 (M. Van De *Mieroop,* auch über *Kupper* J., ARM 22); ZAss 78 (1988) 299-305 (J. *Oelsner,* auch über ARM 22s).

g54 *Finet* A., Les 'fantômes' à Mari: Akkadica 57 (1988) 1-7.

g55 **Durand** Jean-Marie, Archives épistolaires de Mari 1/1s: ARM 26. P 1988, RCiv. xi-639 p.; 589 p. 2-86538-189-7; 90-7.

g56 **Dalley** Stephanie, Mari and Karana 1984 → 1,d893 ... 3,e497: ᴿJNES 47 (1988) 214s (V. *Matthews*); PhoenixEOL 33,2 (1987) 61s (K. R. *Veenhof*).

g57 *Mozan* [central section of Ḥabur plain]: **Buccellati** Giorgio, *Kelly-Buccellati* Marilyn, Mozan 1, the soundings of the first two seasons:

BiblMesop 20. Malibu 1988, Undena. 158 p.; 50 fig.; XXV pl. 0-89003-195-9; pa. 4-0.

g58 **Palmyra**: **Assa'd** Khaled, *al.*, Palmyra; Geschichte, Kunst und Kultur der syrischen Oasenstadt; Katalog zur Ausstellung: Linzer archäologische Forschungen 16. Fra 1987, Liebighaus. 357 p.; ill. – RMundus 24 (1988) 316s (K.-H. *Golzio*).

g59 *Dodge* Hazel, Palmyra and the Roman marble trade; evidence from the baths of Diocletian: Levant 20 (1988) 215-230; 10 fig. (7 maps).

g60 Drevnosti Pal'miry, katalog vistavki ❽, Antiquities of Palmyra. Leningrad 1986, Ermitaž. 22 p.

g61 *Hoftijzer* J., A Palmyrene bas-relief with inscriptions: OMRO 68 (1988) 37; 38s phot.

g62 *Parlasca* Klaus, Ikonographische Probleme palmyrenischer Grabreliefs: DamaszMit 3 (1988) 215-221; pl. 45-48.

g63 *a) Parlasca* Klaus, Die Palmyrene, ihr geographischer Rahmen im Lichte der bildenden Kunst und Epigraphik; – *b) Dentzer-Feydy* Jacqueline, Frontières et matériel archéologique en Syrie du Sud; politique et culture du Ier siècle av. notre ère au IVe siècle de notre ère; – *c) Donceel-Voûte* Pauline, Provinces ecclésiastiques et provinces liturgiques en Syrie et Phénicie byzantines: → 706, Géographie 1985/8, 241-8; 2 pl. / 219-229 + 10 maps / 213-8; map 212.

g64 *Pucko* V. G., ❽ Deux portraits sculptés de Palmyre: VDI 186 (1988) 68-73; franç. 74.

g65 **Starcky** J., *Gawlikowski* M., Palmyre²rev 1985 → 3,e512: RBonnJbb 188 (1988) 612-4 (Ursula *Heimberg*).

g66 **Qudayr**: *Calley* Sylvie, L'atelier de Qdeir 1 en Syrie; exploitation des nucleus naviformes à la fin du PPNB, 6e millénaire; première approche: Paléorient 12,2 (1986) 49-68; 7 fig.

g67 **Quraya**: **Simpson** Kay, Qraya modular reports, 1. Early soundings: SyrMesSt 4/4. Malibu CA 1988, Undena. 44 p. 14 fig. 0-89003-050-2.

g68 **Resafa**: **Mackensen** Michael, Eine befestigte spätantike Anlage vor den Stadtmauern von Resafa ... Survey im Umland; DAI-Resafa 1, 1984 → 65,b159 ... 3,e518: RAnzAltW 41 (1988) 226-233 (T. *Weber*); Archeologia 36 (Wrocław 1985) 189 (T. *Scholl*); OLZ 83 (1988) 47s (P. *Kawerau*).

g69 **Ulbert** Thilo, Resafa II. Die Basilika des Heiligen Kreuzes 1986 → 2,a898; 3,e519: RGnomon 60 (1988) 281-3 (J. *Kramer*); JAOS 108 (1988) 659s (W. *Djobadze*); Latomus 47 (1988) 728 (R. *Chevallier*).

g70 **Sūkās**: **Lund** John, Sukas VIII. The habitation quarters 1986 → 3,e527: RRArchéol (1988) 392s (R. A. *Stucky*).

g71 **Terqa**: **Chavalas** Mark W., The house of Puzurum; a stratigraphic, distributional, and social analysis of domestic units from Tell Ashara/ Terqa, Syria, from the middle of the second millennium B.C.: diss UCLA 1988, DBuccellati G. 409 p. 88-13364. – DissA 49 (1988s) 1549s-A.

g72 **Yabrūd**: *Solecki* Ralph L. & Rose S., A reappraisal of Rust's cultural stratigraphy of Yabroud Shelter I: Paléorient 12,1 (1986) 53-59; 3 fig.

T6.1 **Mesopotamia**: *generalia*.

g73 **Abdul-Amir** Sabah J., Archaeological survey of ancient settlements and irrigation systems in the Middle Euphrates region of Mesopotamia: diss. Chicago 1988, – OIAc D88.

g74 **Asher-Greve** Julia M.,   Frauen in altsumerischer Zeit: BiblMesop 18, 1985
➤ 1,1502.b87 ... 3,e538: [R]JAOS 108 (1988) 158s (Tova *Meltzer*); JNES
47 (1988) 308-310 (Rivkah *Harris*); OLZ 83 (1988) 157-160 (J. *Bauer*);
Orientalia 57 (1988) 106 (U. *Seidl*).

g75 **Balkan** Kemal,   Studies in Babylonia feudalism of the Kassite period
(1943), [T]*Foster* B., *Gutas* D.: MANE 2/3. Malibu 1986. – [R]Mesop-T 23
(1988) 187-9 (C. *Paladini*).

g76 **Bergerhof** Kurt,   Mesopotamien und das Volk Gottes. Neuk 1983,
Neuk.-V.   129 p.; (color.) photos of 1978. – [R]CBQ 50 (1988) 106s (R. D.
Wells: beautifully produced, but also creative support to exegesis of F.
EISENSTADT and F. CRÜSEMANN).

g77 [F]BIROT Maurice: Miscellanea babylonica, [E]**Durand** J.-M., *Kupper* J.-R.
1985 ➤ 1,18*: [R]BO 45 (1988) 622-5 (H. *Klengel*).

g78 [F]BRAIDWOOD Robert J.,   The hilly flanks and beyond, [E]**Young** T. C., *al.*:
SAOC 36, 1983 ➤ 65,24: [R]JNES 47 (1988) 294-6 (Margaret C. *Brandt*);
Paléorient 12,1 (1986) 103-113 (Mary M. *Voigt*).

g79 **Charpin** Dominique,   Archives familiales et propriété privée en Babylonie
ancienne ... Tell Sifr 1980 ➤ 61,q387 ... 63,d271: [R]OLZ 83 (1988) 294-8
(J. *Oelsner*).

g80 *a) Copeland* L., *Hours* F.,   The Halafians, their predecessors and their
contemporaries in northern Syria and the Levant; relative and absolute
chronologies; – *b) Watkins* T., *Campbell* S.,   The chronology of the Halaf
culture; – *c) Oates* J., 'Ubaid chronology; – *d) Vértesalji* P. P.,   The
chronology of the chalcolithic in Mesopotamia (6200-3400 B.C.): ➤ 719,
Chronologies 1986/7, 401-425 / 427-464 / 473-482 / 483-523 [*al.*].

g81 **Debut** J.,   Continuité des méthodes d'enseignement mésopotamiennes du
troisième millénaire à l'époque byzantine: RÉAnc 90 (1988) 305-314;
Eng. 305.

g82 [E]**Finkbeiner** U., *Röllig* W.,   Ǧamdat Nasr, period or regional style?
[symposium Tübingen Nov. 1983]: TAVO-B 62, 1986 ➤ 3,812: [R]Me-
sop-T 23 (1988) 176-182 (P. *Fiorina*).

g83 *Liverani* Mario, The fire of Ḫaḫḫum: OrAnt 27 (1988) 165-171; 172 map.

g84 *Mazzoni* Stefania,   'Problèmes et questions ouvertes' nell'archeologia
orientale [[E]*Barrelet* M. T. 1984 e 1986]: VO 7 (1988) 59-69.

g85 *Saporetti* Claudio, Andare a scuola in Mesopotamia: Archeo 38 (1988)
124s.

g86 *Steele* F. R., Sumer: ➤ 801, ISBEnc[3] 4 (1988) 653-662.

g87 **Vértesalji** Peter P.,   Babylonien zur Kupfersteinzeit: TAVO-B 35, 1984
➤ 65,b176 ... 3,e548: [R]RAss 82 (1988) 90-92 (Catherine *Breniquet*).

g88 *a) Young* T. C.[J], Mesopotamia; perforce multicultural; – *b) Brown* S. C.,
Mesopotamia and South Asia (Indus Valley); reciprocal effects in the late
3d and early 2d millennia B.C.: CanadMesop 9 (1985) 5-13 / 15-24.

T6.3   *Mesopotamia,* **inscriptiones.**

g89 *Bonneterre* Daniel,   Pour une étude des dermatoglyphes digitaux sur des
tablettes cunéiformes: Akkadica 59 (1988) 26-29.

g90 *Cogan* Mordechai, *Tadmor* Hayim,   Ashurbanipal texts in the collection
of the Oriental Institute, University of Chicago: JCS 40 (1988) 84-96.

g91 **Cooper** Jerrold S.,   Presargonic inscriptions: Sumerian and Akkadian
Royal Inscriptions 1, 1986 ➤ 2,a914; 3,e551: [R]IsrEJ 38 (1988) 202s (R.
Kutscher); Orientalia 57 (1988) 223-230 (W. H. P. *Römer*); VT 38 (1988)
508s (J. N. *Postgate*).

g92 **Donbaz** Veysel, *Grayson* A. Kirk, Royal inscriptions on clay cones from Ashur now in Istanbul 1984 ➤ 65,b183 ... 2,a917: ᴿArOr 56 (1988) 197s (Jana *Pečírková*); BO 45 (1988) 627-9 (K. *Kessler*); JAOS 108 (1988) 516s (K. *Deller*); JNES 47 (1988) 218s (W. *Farber*); OLZ 83 (1988) 546-550 (O. *Pedersén*).

g93 *George* A. R., Babylonian texts from the folios of Sidney Sᴍɪᴛʜ [three of those more nearly fit for publication and not meanwhile published by others], part I: RAss 82 (1988) 139-162.

g94 **Gerardi** Pamela, A bibliography of the tablet collections of the [Pennsylvania] University Museum: Babylonian Fund Occas. Publ. 8, 1984 ➤ 65,b190: ᴿJAOS 108 (1988) 303s (H. *Neumann*).

g94* *Gerardi* Pamela, Epigraphs and Assyrian palace reliefs; the development of the epigraphic text [(and) wall reliefs, bull inscriptions, threshold slabs]: JCS 40 (1988) 1-35; 3 fig.

g95 **Greengus** Samuel, Studies in Ishchali documents: BibMesop 19. Malibu 1986, Undena. – ᴿRAss 82 (1988) 185s (D. *Charpin*).

g96 **Gross** Katarzyna, The archive of the Wullu Family: C. Niebuhr Publ. 5 [0902-5499]. K 1988, Museum Tusculanum. 87-7289-040-1 [OIAc D88].

g97 *Illingworth* N. J. J., Inscriptions from Tell Brak 1986: Iraq 50 (1988) 87-108 [83-86, *Finkel* Irving L., 1985].

g98 **Jakob-Rost** Liane, *Marzahn* Joachim, Assyrische Königsinschriften ... aus Assur 1985 ➤ 1,d962; 2,a931: ᴿBO 45 (1988) 625-7 (K. *Kessler*); OLZ 83 (1988) 35s (J. *Pečírková*).

g99 *Jankowska* N. B., Scribes and interpreters at Arrapḫa: ➤ 456*, Peredneaz. IV (1986) 37-64.

g100 **Kärki** Ilmari, Die Königsinschriften der Dritten Dynastie von Ur 1986 ➤ 3,e563: ᴿBO 45 (1988) 342s (M. *Stol*).

g101 **Kwasman** Theodore, Neo-Assyrian legal documents in the Kouyounjik collection of the British Museum: StPohl 14. R 1988, Pont. Ist. Biblico. lviii-526 p. Lit. 57.000. 88-7653-577-X.

g102 **Lafont** B., Documents ... de Tello 1985 ➤ 1,d965; 3,e567: ᴿBO 45 (1988) 619-622 (D. I. *Owen*); JAOS 108 (1988) 522s (Tohru *Gomi*).

g103 **Leichty** Erle, Tablets from Sippar [1. 1986 ➤ 2,a938; 2. 1987 ➤ 3, e568] 3: Catalogue of the Babylonian Tablets 8. L 1988, British Museum. xxxvii-442 p. 0-7141-1124-4. ᴿJAOS 108 (1988) 165s (M. A. *Dandamayev*, 1).

g104 **Livingstone** A., Mystical and mythological ... 1986 ➤ 2,a939: ᴿArOr 56 (1988) 276 (Jana *Pečírková*).

g105 **McEwan** Gilbert J. P., Late Babylonian texts in the Ashmolean Museum 1984 ➤ 2,a941; 3,e570: ᴿBO 45 (1988) 357-364 (F. *Joannès*).

g106 **Parpola** Simo, The correspondence of Sargon II, Part I, Letters from Assyria [170] and the West [68] 1987 ➤ 3,e574: ᴿBInstArch 25 (1988) 153-5 (A. *Kuhrt*); BL (1988) 33 (D. J. *Wiseman*); ZAW 100 (1988) 321 (O. *Kaiser*).

g107 **[Parpola** S. **53**, *Dietrich* M. **54]** *Pinches* T. G. **55-57**, Cuneiform Texts ... British Museum 1979/82 ➤ 63,d293; 3,e575: ᴿOLZ 83 (1988) 408-414 (J. *Oelsner*).

g108 *Rawi* Farouk N. H. al-, *Roaf* Michael, Ten Old Babylonian mathematical problems from Tell Haddad, Himrin: Sumer 43 (1984) 175-212; 213-6, facsimiles; 217s, 2 phot.

g109 *a) Römer* W. H. P., *a)* Addenda zu ... OMRO 36 (1986) 31ff, Ur-III-Texte; – *b)* Einige sumerische Texte ... Nimwegen: OMRO 68 (1988) 7; 8-11 phot. / 13-28; 29-36 phot.

g110 **Sachs** Abraham J., *Hunger* Hermann, Astronomical diaries and related texts from Babylonia, I. Diaries from 652 B.C. to 262 B.C.: Denkschr. p/h 195. W c.1987, Österr. Akad. 378 p.; vol of 69 pl. DM 130. – ᴿWeltOr 19 (1988) 174-9 (V. S. *Tuman*).

g111 ᴱ**Sigrist** Marcel, Textes économiques néo-sumériens de l'Université de Syracuse: Mém 29, RCiv 1983 ➤ 64,b733: ᴿBO 45 (1988) 344-6 (H. *Limet*); IsrEJ 38 (1988) 97s (R. *Kutscher*, also on his Andrews Univ. Texts 1, 1984 ➤ 3,a479).

g112 ᴱ**Spar** Ira, Tablets, cones, and bricks of the third and second millennia B.C.: Cuneiform Texts in the Met 1. NY 1988, Metropolitan Museum of Art. lii-194 p.; 156 pl. 0-87099-495-6.

g112* **Stol** M., [194] Letters from collections in Philadelphia, Chicago and Berkeley 1986 ➤ 2,a952; 3,e581: ᴿJAOS 108 (1988) 307-9 (W. L. *Moran*).

g113 *a*) *Tsukimoto* Akio, Sieben spätbronzezeitliche Urkunden aus Syrien [? Emar; in Hiroshima Museum]; – *b*) *Alster* Bendt, Sumerian literary texts in the National Museum, Copenhagen; – *c*) *Yoshikawa* Mamoru, Sumerian tablets in Japanese private collections (II): AcSum 10 (1988) 153-172; 173-8 facsimiles; 179-189, photos/ 1-10; 11-14 facsimiles; 15, photos / 243-256; 257-263, facsimiles.

g114 *Visicato* Giuseppe, Testi di Fara in parallelo: OrAnt 27 (1988) 159-163.

g115 *Walker* Christopher B. F., Halley's comet in cuneiform; the first recorded observation in Babylonia: CanadMesop 13 (1987) 1-11 + 20 fig.

g116 **Watson** P. J., Catalogue ... Neo-Sumerian / Drehem ... Birmingham 1986 ➤ 3,e584: ᴿArOr 56 (1988) 97-99 (B. *Hruška*); JAOS 108 (1988) 111-122 (D. L. *Owen*); OLZ 83 (1988) 28-31 (H. *Waetzoldt*).

g117 **Weiher** Egbert von, Spätbabylonische Texte aus Uruk [II. 1983 ➤ 2, a954] III. Ausgrabungen Uruk-Warka 12. B 1988, Mann. ix-341 p.; 120 facsim. 3-7861-1508-7.

g118 **Whiting** Robert M., Old Babylonian letters from Tell Asmar: Assyriological Studies 22. Ch 1987, Oriental Institute. xiii-177 p. $26. 0-918986-47-8 [BO 45,475].

g119 **Yıldız** Fatma, Die Puzriš-Dagan-Texte der Istanbuler Archäologischen Museen, II. 726-1379: FreibAltorSt 16. Stu 1988, Steiner. 280 p. 3-515-05228-3.

T6.5 **Situs effossi Iraq** *in ordine alphabetico.*

g120 *'Ana*: **Northedge** Alastair *al.*, Excavations at 'Āna, Qal'a Island: Iraq Archaeological Reports 1. xi-145 + 18 p.; XVI pl.; maps. 0-85668-425-2.

g121 *'Aqar*, tulul [Kar-Tukultī-Ninurta 3 k NE Aššur] 1986: MDOG 120 (1988) 97-138; 133 fig. (R. *Dittmann*, *al*.).

g122 *Aššur*: **Pedersén** Olof, Archives and libraries in the city of Assur 1985 ➤ 1,d981 ... 3,e590: ᴿArOr 56 (1988) 275s (Jana *Pečírková*); BO 45 (1988) 355-7 (J. N. *Postgate*); JNES 47 (1988) 217s (R. D. *Biggs*).

g123 *Stępniowski* Franciszek, Metrologische und geometrische Interpretationen der Grundrisse sakraler Bauwerke in Assur: MDOG 120 (1988) 173-188; 8 fig.

g124 *Kienast* Burkhart, Der Vertrag Ebla-Aššur in rechtshistorischer Sicht: ➤ 707, Wirtschaft 1986/8, 231-243.

g125 *Babylon*: **Oates** Joan, Babylon²ʳᵉᵛ 1986 ➤ 2,a960; 0-500-273847: ᴿAncSRes 17 (1987) 39-42 (J. D. *Hall*).

g126 *a*) *Lambert* Wilfred G., Esarhaddon's attempt to return Marduk to Babylon; – *b*) *Khoury* Raites G., Babylon in der ältesten Version über die

Geschichte der Propheten im Islam: → 32, FDELLER K., AOAT 220 (1988) 157-171; 172-4, facsimiles / 123-144.

g127 *Nagel* Wolfram, Wo lagen die 'Hängenden Gärten' in Babylon? [< MDOG 110 (1978) 19-28]: → 234, Altvorderasien 1988, 271-280.

g128 *Bergamini* Giovanni, Excavations in Shu Anna, Babylon 1987: MesopT 23 (1988) 5-17; 3 fig.; 10 phot.

g129 *George* Andrew, The topography of Babylon reconsidered: Sumer 44 (1985s) 7-23.

g130 *Baghdad*: **Strika** Vincenzo, *Khalīl* Jābir, The Islamic architecture of Baghdād; the results of a joint Italian-Iraqi survey: AION Sup. 47/3. N 1987, Ist. Univ. Orientale. xxiv-81 p.

g131 *Durdara*: *Spanos* Peter Z., Ausgrabungen in Tall Durdara (Eski-Mosul-Projekt) und Tall Ḥamad Aġa as-Ṣaġīr (Ǧazîra-Projekt), Nordirak, 1986: MDOG 120 (1988) 59-92; 22 fig. [p. 93-6, Bronzeherz aus Durdara, *Grimm* Alfred].

g132 *Eridu*: **Safar** Fuad, *al.*, Eridu 1981 → 63,d317 ... 1,d995: RRAss 82 (1988) 178-180 (P. *Amiet*).

g132* **Martin** Harriet P., Fara; a reconstruction of the ancient Meso-potamian city of Shuruppak. Birmingham 1988, C. Martin. 309 p.; ill; microfiche. 0-907695-02-7 [Antiquity 63,420].

g133 *Hatra*: *Abdulla* Muḥammad S., ❹ Excavation / Inscriptions at the twelfth temple (Temple of the god Nabu) in Hatra: Sumer 43 (1984) 100-109-118; ill.

g134 *Venco Ricciardi* Roberta, Preliminary report on the 1987 excavation at Hatra: MesopT 23 (1988) 31-42; fig. A-C; 23-32 [p. 43-61, epigrafia, *Pennacchietti* F. A.].

g135 *Imlihîya*: **Boehmer** R. M., *Dämmer* H.-W., Tell Imlihiye ... 1985 → 1,e1; 2,a967: RJESHO 31 (1988) 111s (W. F. *Leemans*); RAss 82 (1988) 183s (J.-L. *Huot*).

g136 *Isin* 1984/6: Sumer 45 (1987s) 8-39 (J. *Boessneck*, B. *Hrouda*).

g137 *Khorsabad*: **Albenda** Pauline, The palace of Sargon ... Wall Reliefs, (Botta -) Flandin drawings 1843s: 1986 → 2,a969: RAbrNahr 26 (1988) 112s (G. *Bunnens*); BL (1988) 28s (W. G. *Lambert*); Orientalia 57 (1988) 230-4 (U. *Seidl*).

g138 *Kîš*: *Reese* David S., A new engraved tridacna shell from Kish: JNES 47 (1988) 35-41; 1 fig.

g139 *Larsa*: **Huot** J.-L., Larsa (10ème campagne, 1983) et 'Oueili (4ème campagne 1983 → g164), Rapport préliminaire: DAF-Irak 4/Mém 73. P 1987, RCiv. 302 p., 54 pl., ❹ T*Hannouche* H. M., 85 p. 2-86538-174-9. – RMesop-T 23 (1988) 182-7 (A. *Invernizzi*, anche su 1978/81: 1983).

g140 *Huot* Jean-Louis, *al.*, Preliminary report on the 10th season at Larsa: Sumer 44 (1985s) 25-46 (47-54, texts, *Arnaud* D.).

g141 *Leilan*: **Schwartz** Glenn M., A ceramic chronology from Tell Leilan, operation 1: Tell Leilan Research 1. NHv 1988, Yale Univ. 0-300-04063-6 [OIAc D88].

g141* Lullu(bum) [Sulaymaniya region]: → 808, RLA 7,3s (1988) 164-8 (H. *Klengel*).

g142 *Maḏhur*: *Roaf* Michael, *al.*, Tell Madhhur, a summary report on ex-cavations: Sumer 43 (1984) 108-167; 26 fig.

g142* *Malyān* [tall; German Maljān (= ? Anšan); page-headings have Malijān but the article is in English]: → 808, RLA 7,3s (1988) 306-320 (W. M. *Sumner*).

g143 *Munbāqa* 1986: MDOG 120 (1988) 11-50; 31 fig. (D. *Machule*, *al.*).

g144 *Nimrud*: **Herrmann** Georgina, Ivories from Nimrud IV, 1986 → 2,a973; 3,e600: ᴿRAss 82 (1988) 188-190 (P. *Amiet*).

g145 *Paley* S.M., Reconstruction of an Assyrian palace: CanadMesop 10 (1985) 11-20 + 12 fig.

g146 *Nineveh*, 1987: MarŠipri 1/2 (1988) 1s (D. *Stronach*).

g147 *a*) *Reade* Julian, The discovery of Nineveh; – *b*) *Grayson* A. Kirk, Nineveh, capital of the world; Rome on the Tigris: CanadMesop 11 (1986) 11-17 / 12 (1986) 9-13.

g148 *Schwartz* G.M., The Ninevite V period and the development of complex society in northern Mesopotamia: Paléorient 13,2 (1987) 93-100.

g149 *Leichty* Erle, Ashurbanipal's library at Nineveh: CanadMesop 15 (1988) 13-18.

g150 *Nippur*: *Zettler* Richard L., Enlil's city, Nippur, at the end of the third millennium B.C.: CanadMesop 14 (1987) 7-19; 7 fig.

g151 *Nuzi*: *Maidman* M.P., Kassites among the Hurrians; a case study from Nuzi: CanadMesop 8 (1984) 15-21.

g152 *Rîma*: *Nashef* Khaled, [t. Rimah] Qattarā and Karanā: WeltOr 19 (1988) 35-39.

g153 *Salābîḫ* (Uruk-mound) 1987: Mar Šipri 1,1 (1988) 4 (Susan *Pollock*).

g154 **Postgate** J.N. *al.*, Abu Salabikh I. West Mound 1983 → 64,b767 ... 2,a976: ᴿJNES 47 (1988) 53s (Margaret C. *Brandt*).

g155 **Postgate** J.N., Abu Salabikh 2, graves 1 to 99, 1985 → 1,e18; vi-224 p.; 149 fig.; 32 pl.: ᴿBO 45 (1988) 700-5 (Pauline *Donceel-Voûte*).

g156 *Postgate* J.N., *Moon* J.A., Late third millennium pottery from Abu Essalabikh: Sumer 43 (1984) 69-79; 57 fig.

g157 *Postgate* J. Nicholas, *a*) Scratching the surface at Abu Salabikh; urban archaeology Sumerian style: CanadMesop 14 (1987) 21-29; 6 fig. (map); – *b*) A view from down the Euphrates [begins 'title of my talk "Ebla and Abu Salabikh" ']: → 707, Wirtschaft 1986/8, 111-4 + 3 plans.

g157* **Mander** Pietro, Il pantheon di Abu-Salabikh; contributo allo studio del pantheon sumerico arcaico: Studi Asiatici min. 26. N 1986, Ist. Univ. Orientale. 164 p.; 10 pl. [JAOS 108.677].

g158 *Seleucia*: *Valtz* Elisabetta, Trench on the east side of the Archives Square – Seleucia 13th season: MesopT 23 (1988) 19-29; fig. 11-22.

g159 *Sippar*: *Charpin* Dominique, Sippar; deux villes jumelles: RAss 82 (1988) 13-32; 1 facsim. [74-77, *Joannès* Francis].

g160 *Üç*: ᴱGibson M., Uch [Üç (3, really 9)] Tepe ... 1981 → 65,b249 ... 3,e619: ᴿRAss 82 (1988) 182s (P. *Amiet*).

g161 *Umma*: **Foster** Benjamin R., Umma in the Sargonic period 1982 → 63,d338 .. 2,e21: ᴿJESHO 31 (1988) 110s (W.F. *Leemans*); WZKM 77 (1987) 182-195 (P. *Steinkeller*).

g162 *Ur*: → 801, ISBEnc³ 4 (1988) 950-5 (W.S. *La Sor*).

g163 *Zettler* Richard L., From beneath the temple; inscribed objects from Ur: Expedition 28,3 (1986) 29-38; 15 fig.

g164 *Wali*: *Forès* J.-D., [*al.*], Tell el-ʿOueli preliminary report on the 4th season (1983), stratigraphy and architecture: Sumer 44 (1985s) 55-66 [-134]; ill.

g165 *Warka*: **Boehmer** Rainer M., *al.*, Uruk Kampagne 38, 1985; Grabungen in J-K/23 und H/24-25: Ausgrabungen in Uruk-Warka, Endberichte 1. Mainz 1987, von Zabern. xi-101 p.; 111 pl.; 2 plans + foldout. 2-8053-0965-1.

g166 *Boehmer* Rainer M., *Finkbeiner* Uwe, Uruk-Warka XXXVII, 1983/84; Survey des Stadtgebietes von Uruk: Sumer 43 (1984) 91-107; ill.

g167 **Funck** Bernd, Uruk zur Seleukidenzeit ... Pfründentexte/sozialökonomische Entwicklung 1984 → 1,e28: ᴿBO 45 (1988) 151-5 (F. *Joannès*); Eirene 25 (1988) 125s (P. *Musiolek*).

g168 *Sürenhagen* Dietrich, Archaische Keramik aus Uruk-Warka, I. Die Keramik der Schichten XVI-VI aus den Sondagen 'Tiefschnitt' und 'Sägegraben' in Eanna: BaghMit 17 (1986) 7-95; 209 fig.

g169 *Dolce* Rita, I rilievi decorativi a mattoni modanati [Warka, tempio di Inanna ...]; continuità o innovazione?: VO 7 (1988) 39-58; pl. VII-X.

g170 *a) Schmandt-Besserat* Denise, Tokens at Uruk; – *b) Pongratz-Leisten*, Keramik der frühdynastischen Zeit ...; – *c) Ess* Margarete van, Keramik von der Akkad bis altbab. Zeit [Ur III]; – *d) Boehmer* R. M., ... mittelbab. in Eanna: BaghMit 19 (1988) 1-175; pl. 1-12 / 177-319 / 321-442[-463] / 465-7.

g171 *Yarim*: *Merpert* N., *Menchaev* R. M., Soviet expedition's research at Yarim Tepe III settlement in northwestern Iraq, 1978-9: Sumer 43 (1984) 54-68, xvi fig.

g172 *Za'faran*: *Iacobini* Antonio, Un complesso monastico nella Mesopotamia bizantina, Deir Za'faran; l'architettura: → 703, Milion 1986/8, 129-160; 9 fig. + XV pl.

T6.7 **Arabia.**

g173 *Avanzini* Alessandra, Brevi osservazioni sui rapporti tra cultura sudarabica e le culture vicine: EgVO 11 (1988) 185-193.

g174 **Hallenberg** H., *Perho* I., Arabiaa Vasta-Alkajille — Seesam Aukene!: Uudistettu painos 2. Helsinki 1987, Yliopistopaino. 320 p.

g175 **MacAdam** Henry I., Studies in the history of the Roman province of Arabia, the northern sector [Northern East-Jordan]: BAR-Int 295, ᴰ1986 → 2,a986: ᴿClasR 102 (1988) 101-4 (G. W. *Bowersock*); JSS 33 (1988) 141-3 (F. *Millar*); RB 95 (1988) 634s (J. *Taylor*).

g176 *Müller* W. W., Araber: → 804, NBL Lfg 1 (1988) 143-5.

g177 **Parker** S. Thomas, Romans and Saracens; a history of the Arabian frontier 1986 → 2,a987; 3,e633: ᴿBASOR 269 (1988) 94 (J. W. *Eadie*); ClasPg 83 (1988) 173-6 (M. *Sartre,* franç.); JAOS 108 (1988) 317s (R. *Schick*); JRS 78 (1988) 240s (B. *Isaac*).

g178 *a) Parr* Peter J., Pottery of the Late Second Millennium B.C. from north west Arabia and its historical implications; – *b) Sauer* James A., *Blakely* Jeffrey A., *al.*, Archaeology along the spice route of Yemen; – *c) Potts* D. T., Arabia and the kingdom of Characene [Charax Spasinou, PLINY HN 6,31,138]; – *d) Robin* Christian, Two inscriptions from Qaryat al-Fâw mentioning women: → 457, ᴱ*Potts* D., Araby the Blest, studies in Arabian archaeology 1988, 73-90; map 72 / 91-111; 12 fig.; map p. 90; bibliog. p. 111-5 / 137-167; map p. 136; coins fig. p. 139 / 168-175; 2 fig.

g179 **Salibi** Kamal, The Bible came from Arabia 1985 → 1,e574 (2,b478 deutsch): ᴿJRAS (1988) 389-393 (A.F.L. *Beeston*: idée fixe does not deserve such a long though withering review; Cape showed 'well-nigh incredible irresponsibility' in publishing it; see T. *Parfitt* in Sunday Times, Oct. 25, 1985).

g180 ᴱ**Salles** Jean-François, L'Arabie et ses mers bordières, I. itinéraires et voisinages: Travaux de la Maison de l'Orient 16. P 1988, de Boccard. 2-903264-45-7 [OIAc D88].

g181 ᶠSHABAN M. A.: Arabia and the Gulf; from traditional society to modern states, ᴱ*Netton* Richard 1986 ⇒ 3,150: ᴿJRAS (1988) 179-182 (G. R. *Smith*).

g182 *Strobel* Karl, Zu Fragen der frühen Geschichte der römischen Provinz Arabia und zu einigen Problemen der Legionsdislokation im Osten des Imperium Romanum zu Beginn des 2. Jh. n. Chr.: ZPapEp 71 (1988) 251-280.

---

g183 *Bahrain*: *Konishi* Masatoshi A., *al.*, Archaeological researches in the Gulf... Bahrain, Qatar, 1987/8: Orient-J 24 (1988) 18-33 + 6 pl.; 7 fig. (2 maps).

g184 **Larsen** Curtis E., Life and land use on the Bahrain islands [diss. 1980]. Ch 1983, Univ. xx-339 p.; 70 fig. $9 pa. – ᴿBASOR 271 (1988) 79-82 (J.-F. *Salles*).

g185 *Dūr*: *Haerinck* E., *al.*, Archaeological reconnaissance at Ed-Dur, Umm al-Qaiwain, United Arab Emirates: Akkadica 58 (1988) 1-14 + 16 fig. (map); 3 pl.

g186 *Faylaka/Dilmun*: **Højlund** Flemming, Failaka/Dilmun, the Bronze Age Pottery: Jutland Archaeol. Soc. 17. Kuwait 1987, Nat. Mus. 195 p.; 725 fig. Dk 200. 87-7288-045-87. – ᴿBO 45 (1988) 427-433 (D. T. *Potts*); Mesop-T 23 (1988) 199-201 (E. *Valtz*).

g187 *Gaibov* V. A., *al.*, ❸ L'étude de sites de l'époque hellénistique dans l'île de Faylaka: VDI 79,185 (1988) 183-201.

g188 **Kjærum** Paul, Failaka/Dilmun VI Seals 1983 ⇒ 64,a973; 3,e638: ᴿZAss 78 (1988) 316-320 (Ursula *Seidl*).

g189 **Salles** J.-F., Failaka 1983; with *Calvet* Y. 1984-5: 1986s ⇒ 3,a639: ᴿBInstArch 25 (1988) 162s (D. *Collon*); Mesop-T 23 (1988) 191-5 (A. *Invernizzi*).

g190 **Hannestad** L., Ikaros 1983 ⇒ 3,e641: ᴿBInstArch 25 (1988) 122-4 (S. *Simpson*).

g190* *Magan* (? Bahrein; sometimes Prunkname for Egypt): ⇒ 808, RLA 7,3s (1988) 195-9 (W. *Heimpel*).

g191 *Saba*: *Pignères* Michel, Des momies au royaume de Saba [Yemen près de Sanaa]: Archéologia 235 (Dijon 1988) 26-31; ill.

g192 ᴱ**de Maigret** Alessandro, The Sabaean archaeological complex in the Wadi Yalā (eastern Ḥawlān aṭ-Ṭiyāl, Yemen Arab Republic), a preliminary report. Reports and Memoirs 21. R 1988, IsMEO. xvii-59 + 83 p.; 36 fig.; 56 pl. Lit. 100.000.

g193 *Tayma*: *Bawden* Garth, *Edens* Chirstopher, Tayma painted ware and the Hejaz Iron Age ceramic tradition: Levant 20 (1988) 197-213; 7 fig. (map).

g194 *Yemen*: *Hawass* Zahi, New archaeological sites in South Yemen: ⇒ 127, ᶠṢALEḤ A., ASAE 71 (1987) 107-118; III pl.

T6.9 **Iran,** *Persia*; Asia centralis.

g195 **Amiet** Pierre, L'âge des échanges inter-iraniens: 3700-1700 av. J.-C.: Notes et documents des Musées de France. P 1986, Musées nationaux. 332 p.; dont 100 d'ill. F 160 pa. 2-7118-0290-6. – ᴿAntiquity 62 (1988) 536-541; map (V. M. *Masson*: 'The Proto-Bactrian group of civilizations in the Ancient East'); RB 95 (1988) 437s (M. *Sigrist*).

g196 *Black* Jeremy, The history of Parthia and Characene in the second century A.D.: Sumer 43 (1984) 230-4.

g197 ᴱ**Hole** Frank, The archaeology of western Iran [7 experts]. Wsh 1987, Smithsonian. 332 p.; 90 fig. $50. 0-874774-526-8. – ᴿAntiquity 62 (1988) 195s (M. *Roaf*).

g198 *Mathiesen* Hans E., Late Parthian sculpture in Iran: → 142*, ᶠTHOM-SEN R., 1988, 204-213.

g199 ᶠSTÈVE M.-J., Fragmenta historiae elamicae; mélanges offerts à ~, ᴱ**Meyer** L. De, *al.*, 1986 → 3,153: ᴿBSOAS 51 (1988) 544-6 (Heidemarie *Koch*); JNES 47 (1988) 217 (R. D. *Biggs*).

g200 *Tadua* T. T., ❻ Les forteresses de Mithridate Eupator en Colchide: VDI 184 (1988) 139-147; franç. 147.

g201 **Yajima** Hikoichi *Kamioka* K., Iranian studies 1, Caravan routes across the Zagros mountains in Iran: Studia Culturae Islamicae 36. Tokyo 1988, Inst. Languages and Cultures of Asia and Africa. 199 p.; 74 phot.; maps.

---

g202 *Bardsir*: *Sahadi* S. Mansur S., Prehistoric settlements in the Bardsir plain, SE Iran: EWest 37 (1987) 11-55; 56-70, list of sites; 71-129, charts and pottery drawings.

g203 *Ecbatana*: *Dandamayev* Muhammad, Some Babylonians at Ecbatana [fisrt year of Darius I]: ArchMIran 19 (1986) 117-9.

g204 *Godin*: *Henrickson* Robert C., The [Tepe] Godin III chronology for central western Iran 2600-1400 B.C.: IrAnt 22 (1987) 33-82+34 fig. (map); addendum 118.

g205 *Hasanlu*: *Medvedskaya* Inna, Who destroyed Hasanlu IV? [Assyrians 714 B.C.; not Urartians before 800]: Iran 26 (1988) 1-15; 5 fig.

g205* *Luristan*: *Calmeyer* P., Luristan; Bronzen: → 808, RLA 7,3s (1988) 174-9; 57 fig.

g206 *Mālamir*: → 808, RLA 7,3s (1988) 275-287 (P. *Calmeyer*; philologisch M. W. *Stolper*, Eng.).

g206* *Naqš-i Rustam*: **Seidl** Ursula, Iranische Felsreliefs von Kūrāngūn und Naqš-e Rustam: Iranische Denkmäler 12, B 1986, Reimer. 25 p. 18 fig. ᴿMundus 24 (1988) 300-2 (W. *Eilers*; 'DM 145'); RAss 82 (1988) 180-2 (P. *Amiet*).

g207 *Pasargadae*: *Nagel* Wolfram, Pasargadae; ein Lagebericht zum Problem des Beginns achämenidischer Kunst und altpersischer Schrift [< MDOG 111 (1979) 75-88]: → 234, Altvorderasien 1988, 281-294; 6 fig.

g208 *Persepolis*: *Koch* Heidemarie, Einige Überlegungen zur Bauplanung in Persepolis: ArchMIran 20 (1987) 147-159; 4 fig.; pl. 14-17.

g209 *Schmitt* R., Persepolitanisches V: Historische Sprachforschung [= Zvgl-Spr] 101 (1988) 81-88.

g210 *Qaderabad*: *Kleiss* Wolfram, [Achämenidische] Staudämme bei Qaderabad (Fars) und südwestlich von Kashan: ArchMIran 20 (1987) 99-106; 8 fig.

g211 *Sarvistan*: **Bier** Lionel, Sarvistan; a study in early Iranian architecture: Mg. College Art Asn. 41 Univ Park 1986, Pennsylvania State Univ. 81 p.; 86 fig.

g212 *Shiraz*: **Whitcomb** D. S., Before the roses 1985 → 3,e672: ᴿMesop-T 23 (1988) 201-5 (Elisabetta *Valtz*); StIran 16 (1987) 139-142 (P. *Gignoux*).

g213 *Susa*: **Amiet** Pierre, Suse, 6000 ans d'histoire: Musées de France Mg. P 1988, Réunion Mus. Nat. 156 p. F 150 [RB 96,125, R. J. *Tournay*].

g214 *Berman* J.C., Ceramic production and its implications for the sociopolitical organization of the Suse phase Susiana: Paléorient 13,2 (1987) 47-60; franç. 47.

g215 *Dittmann* Reinhard, Bemerkungen zum Protoelamischen Horizont [Susa, Sialk...]: ArchMIran 20 (1987) 31-63; 12 fig.

g216 *Ghirshman* Roman, Susa, ᵀ*La Sor* W.: ➤ 801, ISBEnc³ 4 (1988) 667-9.

g217 *Kienast* Burkhart, A battle for Susa; the Gulf war in the ancient Near East: CanadMesop 13 (1987) 23-29.

g218 *a*) *Perrot* Jean, Suse à la période achéménide; – *b*) *Boucharlat* Rémy, Suse, marché agricole ou relais du grand commerce; Suse et la Susiane à l'époque des grands empires: ➤ 765, Suse = Paléorient 11,2 (1985) 67-69, 1 fig. / 71-81; 2 fig.

g219 *Spycket* Agnès, Lions en terre cuite de Suse: ➤ 4, ᶠAMIET P. = IrAnt 23 (1988) 149-156 + V pl.

g220 **Taq-i Bostân**: *Azarnoush* Massoud, Sâpûr II, Ardašîr II, and Šâpûr III; another perspective: ArchMIran 19 (1986) 219-247; 2 fig.

g221 **Tureng**: **Boucharlat** Rémy, **Lecomte** Olivier, Fouilles de Tureng Tepe (Jean DESHAYES), I. Les périodes sassanides et islamiques: Mém. 74. P 1987, RCiv. xi-236 p.; 32 fig.; 163 pl. F 237 [JNES 47,237].

g222 **Ziwiye**: **Boehmer** Rainer M., Ritzverzierte Keramik aus dem mannäischen (?) Bereich [Zendan, Ziwiye...]: ArchMIran 19 (1986) 95-115; 47 fig.

---

g223 *Amiet* Pierre, Au-delà d'Élam [... Iran SE, Afghanistan N]: ArchMIran 19 (1986) 11-20; 4 fig.; pl. 1-11.

g224 **Sarianidi** Viktor, Die Kunst des alten Afghanistan. Lp 1986, Seemann. 348 p.; 170 pl. – ᴿRAss 82 (1988) 84s (P. *Amiet*).

g225 *Aï-Khanoum*: Fouilles d'Aï Khanoum V. Les remparts: Mém DAFA 29. – ᴿRArchéol (1988) 146-8 (Y. *Garlan* given no editor or publication-data).

g226 **Bernard** Paul, Fouilles d'Aï Khanoum, IV. Les monnaies hors trésors 1985 ➤ 2,b24; 3,e681. – ᴿGnomon 60 (1988) 261-3 (T. *Fischer*).

g227 *Narain* A.K., On the foundation and chronology of Ai-Khanum, a Bactrian Greek city: ➤ 42, ᶠEGGERMONT P. 1987, 115-130.

g227* **Pottier** Marie-Hélène, Matériel funéraire de la Bactriane méridionale de l'âge du bronze: Mém. 36. P 1987, RCiv/ADPF. 232 p.; xlv pl. F 160 pa. [JAOS 108,678].

g228 *Serditykh* Z.V., *Koshelenko* G.A., ❷ Historical and cultural issues of Graeco-Bactria in recent publications: SovArch (1987,3) 237-251.

g229 **Bust**: *Allen* Terry, Notes on Bust [site in S. Afghanistan, E bank of Hilmand river]: Iran 26 (1988) 55-68; 8 fig.; pl. I-VIII.

g230 **Kavtaradze** G.L., ❷ On the chronology of the Georgian Eneolithic and Bronze Ages. Tbilisi 1983, Mečnereba. 153 p. – ᴿSovArch (1987,4) 273-283 (M.V. *Andreyeva*).

T7.1 **Aegyptus**, *generalia*.

g233 *Aguizy* Ola el-, Dwarfs and pygmies in Ancient Egypt: ➤ 127, ᶠṢALEḤ A., ASAE 71 (1987) 53-60.

g234 **Anderson** Robert, *Fawzy* Ibrahim, Egypt revealed [from Napoleon's Description]. Cairo 1987, American Univ. 196 p. $50. – ᴿArchaeology 41,6 (1988) 69-72 (Kathryn *Bard*).

g235 **Assmann** Jan, *al.*,   Problems and priorities 1985/7 ➤ 3,796:   ᴿBInstArch 25 (1988) 96s (H. M. *Stewart*).

g236 *Bard* Kathryn A.,   The geography of excavated predynastic sites and the rise of complex society: JAmEg 24 (1987) 81-93.

g237 ᶠBOTHMER B. V., Artibus Aegypti, ᴱ**Meulenaere** H. de 1983 ➤ 64,15*: ᴿJEA 74 (1988) 253s (C. *Vandersleyen*).

g237* Classement géographique/chronologique: BLCéramÉg 13 (1988) 1-50.

g238 ᴱ**Donadoni** Sergio, [➤ 3,e695] Égypte: Archéo [L'Encyclopédie de l'Archéologie] 1s.   P 1987, Atlas.   2-7312-0501-6; 2-4 [OIAc D88].

g239 ᴱ**Eggebrecht** A.,   Ägyptens Aufstieg zur Weltmacht (1550-1400 v.Chr.); Zeugnisse einer glanzvollen Epoche [Ausstellung Roemer/Pelizaeus Museum 1988]. Mainz 1987, Von Zabern.   384 p. DM 50.   3-8053-0964-3 [BL 89, 123, K. A. *Kitchen* calls Akhenaten 'notorious' but unnamed authors 'idiosyncratic'].

g239* **Fleming** Stuart, *al.*,   The Egyptian mummy; secrets and science.   Ph 1980, Masca and Univ. Museum.   x-93 p.; 17 + 116 fig.; 5 color. pl.; map. – ᴿJAmEg 24 (1987) 146-8 (W. B. *Harer*).

g240 *Fuchs* Gerald,   Die arabische Wüste [zwischen Nil und Rotem Meer] (Ägypten) und ihre historische Bedeutung von der Vorgeschichte bis in die Römerzeit: AntWelt 19,1 (1988) 15-30; 24 (color.) fig. (3 maps; fig. 20, p. 26, some 30 mines).

g241 *Haarlem* W. M. van,   Modern Egypt and [i.e. lack of interest in] its pharaonic heritage; a confrontation of two opinions [*Reid* D. traces to Islam's unconcern for paganism; *Bothmer* B. to (lack of) antiquities legislation]: DiscEg 11 (1988) 99-101.

g242 *a)* *Haas* H., *al.*,   Radiocarbon chronology and the historical calendar in Egypt; – *b)* *Nissen* H.-J., The chronology of the Proto- and Early historic periods in Mesopotamia and Susiana; – *c)* *Voigt* M.,   Relative and absolute chronologies for Iran between 6.500 and 3500 cal. ʙᴄ: ➤ 719, Chronologies 1986/7, 585-606 / 607-614 / 615-646.

g243 **Hobson** Christine,   Exploring the world of the Pharaohs 1987 ➤ 3,e703; £13.   0-500-05046-5:   ᴿAntiquity 62 (1988) 806 (J. *Baines*).

g244 *Hölbl* Günther,   Zur kulturellen Stellung der Aegyptiaca in der mykenischen und frühgriechischen Welt: ➤ 776, Ägäische Vorg. 1984/7, 123-145.

g245 ᴱ**James** T. G. H.,   Excavating in Egypt [1882-] 1982 ➤ 63,56; 64,a466: ᴿAncSRes 17 (1987) 98-104 (S. R. *Pickering*).

g246 *Leclant* J., *Clerc* G.,   Fouilles et travaux en Égypte et au Soudan, 1986-1987:   Orientalia 57 (1988) 307-404; pl. VI-LXXI.

g247 **Leprohon** Ronald J.,   Stelae I. The Early Dynastic period to the Late Middle Kingdom: Corpus Antiquitatum Aegyptiacarum, Boston Museum 2.   Mainz 1987, von Zabern.   218 loose sheets.   DM 78.   3-8053-0861-2. – ᴿBO 45 (1988) 562s (R. E. *Freed*).

g248 **Manniche** Lisa,   The ancient Egyptians: Activity book.   L 1985, British Museum.   17 p. $5.   0-7141-0941-X. – ᴿAncHRes 18 (1988) 177-180 (Esther N. *Kilkelly*, also on STEAD M.).

g249 *Martin* Geoffrey T.,   Theses in Egyptology and related fields in British universities, 1945-1963:   DiscEg 8 (1987) 29-31.

g249* **Meltzer** Edmund S.,   Ancient Egypt through three windows [*Lalouette* C. 1985; *James* T. 1984; *Redford* D. 1984]: JAOS 108 (1988) 285-290.

g250 ᶠMOKHTAR Gamal Eddin, Mélanges, IFAO Bib. Ét. 97, 1985 ➤ 2,77: ᴿBO 45 (1988) 291-9 (R. *Holthoer*).

g251 *Neumann* Claudio, *Ogdon* Jorge R.,   A new approach to ancient Egyptian objects, I. A preliminary report on statue Louvre E. 12627 [basic model of geometrical proportions (also among hieroglyphs) as applied to Cheops pyramid in their paper submitted to ASAE and circulated with permission at a Paris meeting: DiscEg 10 (1988) 55-68.

g252 *Pernigotti* Sergio, L'archeologia nell'antico Egitto: Archeo 40 (1988) 44-93; color. ill.

g253 **Quaegebeur** Jan, Egypte hertekend; het oude Egypte in de beeldverhalen. Lv 1988, Peeters. 127 p.; 34 fig.; mostly from cartoon-strips.

g254 *Rühlmann* Gerhard, Gedanken zu ERMANS [1885] Ägypten: ZägSpr 115 (1988) 157-160.

g255 FSÄVE-SÖDERBERGH T., Sundries: Boreas 13, 1984 → 65,126; 2,b40: RJEA 74 (1988) 254s (D. M. *Bailey*).

g256 **Sauneron** Serge, Villes et légendes d'Égypte² 1983 → 3,289: RCdÉ 63 (1988) 242s (K. M. *Pickavance*).

g257 **Seyfried** Karl-J., Beiträge zu den Expeditionen des Mittleren Reiches in die Ostwüste 1981 → 62,a557 ... 1, e 221: ROLZ 83 (1988) 274-282 (U. *Luft*).

g258 *Silverman* David, The curse of the curse of the Pharaohs: Expedition 29,2 (Ph 1987) 56-63; 10 fig.

g259 *Sourouzian* Hourig, Standing royal colossi [from Tanis, Bubastis, Memphis] of the Middle Kingdom reused by Ramesses II: MiDAI-K 44 (1988) 229-254; 8 fig. pl. 62-75.

g260 **Uphill** Eric P., Egyptian towns and cities. Aylesbury 1988, Shire. 72 p.; 36 fig. £2.50 pa. 0-85263-939-2 [Antiquity 62,641].

g261 **Vernus** Pascal, *Yoyotte* Jean, Les Pharaons. P 1988, MA. 2-86676-256-8 [OIAc D88].

g262 FWESTENDORF Wolfhart: Studien zu Sprache und Religion Ägyptens 1984 → 65,148: RCdÉ 63 (1988) 243s (H. De *Meulenaere*).

g263 *Westendorf* Wolfhart, Die Flügelsonne aus Ägypten: ArchMIran 19 (1986) 20-26; 7 fig.

T7.2 **Luxor**, *Karnak* [East Bank]; **Thebae** [West Bank].

g264 **Abd el-Raziq** [→ 3,e723] Mahmud, Die Darstellung und Texte des Sanktuars Alexanders des Grossen im Tempel von Luxor: Veröff.DAI-K 16, 1984: RJEA 74 (1988) 288s (E. *Winter*); OLZ 83 (1988) 146-8 (R. S. *Bianchi*).

g264* *Berg* David, The 29th Dynasty storehouse at Karnak: JAmEg 24 (1987) 47-52, 1 fig.

g265 *Golvin* Jean-Claude, Quelques travaux récents du centre franco-égyptien de Karnak, 1985-1988: CRAI (1988) 575-599; 7 fig.

g266 *a) Jacquet-Gordon* Helen, Graffiti at Khonsu [-temple, Karnak]; – *b) Roth* Ann M., The test of an epigraphic method: NewsAmEg 141 (1988) 5s / 7-13.

g267 *Leclant* J. *Clerc* G., Karnak; rive gauche thébaine: → g246, Orientalia 57 (1988) 345-361; pl. XXXVI-XLIII.

g267* *Schulman* Alan R., The great historical inscription of Merneptaḥ at Karnak; a partial reappraisal: JAmEg 24 (1987) 21-34.

g268 [**Weeks** K.] Battle reliefs of King Sety I: OIP 107, 1986 → 3,e719: RBO 45 (1988) 319-322 (K. A. *Kitchen*).

g269 **Parker** Richard A., *al.*, The edifice of Taharqa by the Sacred Lake of Karnak 1979 → 61,t368 ...: RJEA 74 (1988) 281-288 (M. *Smith*).

g270 **Saghir** Mohammed El-,   Le camp romain de Louqsor...: IFAO Mém. 83, 1986 ➤ 2,b52:   ᴿBO 45 (1988) 590-2 (H. *Devijver*).

---

g271 **Abitz** F.,   Ramses III. in den Gräbern seiner Söhne: OBO 72, 1986 ➤ 2,b59:   ᴿZAW 100 (1988) 306s (Brigitte *Michallik*).

g272 *Marciniak* Marek,   Les éléments nubiens du décor dans le tombeau de Ramsès III: ➤ 750, Nubian V, 1982/6, 151-4; 2 fig.

g273 *Ventura* Raphael,   The largest project for a royal tomb in the Valley of the Kings [Ramesses VI]:   JEA 74 (1988) 137-156.

g274 **Niwinski** Andrzej,   21st dynasty coffins from Thebes; chronological and typological studies: Theben 5.   Mainz 1988, von Zabern.   xxiv-208 p.; 24 pl.

g275 *Dodson* Aidan M.,   *a*) The tombs of the kings of the early Eighteenth Dynasty at Thebes; – *b*) The tombs of the queens of the Middle Kingdom: ZägSpr 115 (1988) 110-123 / 123-136.

g276 *Lipińska* Jadwiga,   The mysterious temple *ḏér-mnw* [prior or identical to *ḏér-3ḫt* between Deir el-Baḥri (Hatshepsut) and Mentuhotpe edifice]: VarAeg 4 (1988) 143-9; 3 fig.

g277 **Eigner** Diethelm,   Die monumentalen Grabbauten der Spätzeit in der thebanischen Nekropole [east of D. Bahri]: ÖsterrAI-K 6, Denkschrift 8; 1984 ➤ 65,b332; 1,e116:   ᴿJNES 47 (1988) 297-304 (P. *Der Manuelian*: important because unique).

g277* *a*) *Karkowski* Janusz,   The arrangement of the architraves in Hatshepsut's temple at Deir el Bahari; – *b*) *Marciniak* Marek,   Une liste de fugitifs à Deir el-Bahari: ➤ 12, ᶠBERNHARD M.-L. 1983, 139-153; 9 fig. / 249-255; 4 fig.

g278 **Manniche** Lise,   The wall decoration of three Theban tombs (TT 77, 175, and 249): C. Niebuhr Publ. 4.   K 1988, Museum Tusculanum.   65 p. 87-7289-036-3 [OIAc D88].

g279 **Manniche** Lise,   Lost tombs; a study of certain eighteenth dynasty monuments in the Theban necropolis: StEgyptology.   L 1988, Kegan Paul.   x-260 p.; 80 pl. £40.   0-7103-0200-2 [BO 45,756].

g280 **Hari** Robert,   La tombe thébaine du père divin Neferhotep (TT 50): Epigraphica 1985 ➤ 1,e119:   ᴿBO 45 (1988) 120-4 (Erika *Feucht*); OLZ 83 (1988) 398-402 (H. *Altenmüller*).

g280* *Bietak* Manfred, *al.*, Das Grab des 'Anch-Hor 1982 ➤ 65,b326 ... 2,b61: ᴿJAmEg 24 (1987) 160 (H. *Goedicke*).

g281 **Hegazy** Sayed A., *Tosi* M.,   A Theban private tomb, Nº 295: DAI-K Veröff 45, 1983 ➤ 2,b65; 3,e743:   ᴿJEA 74 (1988) 273s (N. *Strudwick*); JNES 47 (1988) 201 (C. F. *Nims*).

g282 **Jaroš-Deckert** Brigitte,   Grabung im Asasif 1963-1970, V. Das Grab des Jnj-jtj-f; die Wandmalereien der XI. Dynastie 1984 ➤ 65,b331:   ᴿCdÉ 63 (1988) 286-9 (Rita E. *Freed*); JEA 74 (1988) 269-273 (M. *Eaton-Krauss*).

g283 *Seyfried* Karl J.,   Bemerkungen zur Erweiterung der unterirdischen Anlagen einiger Gräber des Neuen Reiches in Theben — Versuch einer Deutung: ➤ 127, ᶠṢALEḤ A., ASAE 71 (1987) 229-249; VIII pl.

g284 **Ventura** Raphael,   'Living in a city of the dead' OBO 69, 1986 ➤ 3,e752: ᴿBO 45 (1988) 545-551 (J. *Lopez*).

g285 **Wachsmann** Shelley,   Aegeans in the Theban tombs 1987 ➤ 3,e746: ᴿBL (1988) 128 (K. A. *Kitchen*); BO 45 (1988) 551-6 (J. *Vercoutter*);

DiscEg 10 (1988) 102-6 (Alessandra *Nibbi* zeroes in on p. 50-54, ox-hide-shaped ingots); JHS 108 (1988) 260s (Vronwy *Hankey*).

---

g286 **Myśliwiec** Karol, Keramik und Kleinfunde aus der Grabung im Tempel Sethos' I. in Gurna: DAI-ArchVeröff 57, 1987 → 3,e748; DM 198: [R]Mundus 24 (1988) 115s (Ingrid *Gamer-Wallert*); PrzOr (1988,2) 179-181 (Albertyna *Dembska*).

g286* **Morimoto** Iwataro, Ancient human mummies from Qurna, Egypt II: Studies in Egyptian Culture 7 [0912-2206]. Tokyo 1988, Waseda Univ. 21 p.; 75 fig.

g287 *a) Nasr* Mohammed, The Theban tomb 261 of Kha'emwese in Dra' Abu el-Naga'; – *b) Moussa* Ahmed M., A Saite period anthropoid stone sarcophagus from the south-field at Giza; – *c) Lindblad* Ingegerd, An unidentified statue of Ahmose: StAltÄgK 15 (1988) 233-242; 4 fig.; pl. 12-16 / 225-231; 1 fig.; pl. 10-11 / 197-201; pl. 5-9.

g288 **Valbelle** Dominique, 'Les ouvriers de la tombe'; Deir el-Médineh à l'époque ramesside: IFAO BÉt 96, 1985 → 1,e131: [R]CdÉ 63 (1988) 267-276 (R. van *Walsem*); JAmEg 24 (1987) 156s (A. *Spalinger*).

g288* **Bogoslovskij** E. C., ⊕ Drevne-egipetskie mastera ... Der el-Medina 1983 → 2,9893: [R]OLZ 83 (1988) 660-2 (Magdalena *Stoof*).

g289 **Stadelmann** Rainer, (*Osing* Jürgen), Königliche Votivstelen aus dem Torraum des Totentempels Sethos' I, in Gurna: MiDAI-K 44 (1988) 254-274; 8 fig. pl. 76-82.

T7.3 Amarna.

g290 **Aldred** Cyril, Akhenaten, king of Egypt. L 1988, Thames & H. 320 p.; 30 fig.; 77 pl. £24. 0-500-05048-1 [Antiquity 63,12].

g290* *Allen* James P., Two altered inscriptions of the late Amarna period: JAmEg 25 (1988) 117-126; 3 fig.

g291 *Beinlich* Horst, Das Totenbuch bei Tutanchamun: GöMiszÄg 102 (1988) 7-18.

g292 *Boddens-Hosang* F. J. E., Akhenaten's year twelve reconsidered: DiscEg 12 (1988) 7-9.

g293 *Bongioanni* Alessandro, A proposito del 'prenomen' Aa-kheper-re della tomba di Anj ad El-Amarna: DiscEg 8 (1987) 7-13.

g294 **Borchardt** L., *Ricke* H., Die Wohnhäuser in Tell el-Amarna 1980 → 61,t314 ... 64,b849: [R]OLZ 83 (1988) 152-6 (M. *Mode*).

g295 **Cimmino** Franco, Akhenaton e Nefertiti, storia dell'eresia amarniana 1987 → 3,e757: [R]CC 139 (1988,2) 611s (F. *D'Adamo*); Letture 43 (1988) 463-5 (G. *Ravasi*).

g296 *Eaton-Krauss* Marianne, Tutankhamun at Karnak: MiDAI-K 44 (1988) 1-11; 3 fig.; pl. 16-17.

g297 *Edel* Elmar, Weitere Beiträge zum Verständnis der Geschenklisten des Amarnabriefes Nr. 14: → 112*, [F]OTTEN H., Documentum 1988, 99-114.

g298 *Fritz* Volkmar, Die Verbreitung des sog. Amarna-Wohnhauses in Kanaan: DamaszMit 3 (1988) 27-34; 6 fig.

g299 *Girbal* Christian, Der Paragraph 24 des [Amarna] Mitanni-Briefes: ZAss 78 (1988) 122-136.

g300 *Görg* M., Amarna: → 804, NBL Lfg 1 (1988) 83-85.

g301 **Hess** Richard S., Amarna proper names: diss. HUC/JIR. Cincinnati 1984. ix-557 p. AA 84-20005.

g302 *Holland* Gary B., *Stefanini* Ruggero,   A reverse word index to the
[Amarna 470-line Hurrian] Mitanni letter: VO 7 (1988) 71-106.

g303 **Kemp** Barry J., *al.*,   Amarna reports I, 1984 ➤ 65,b349:   ᴿCdÉ 63
(1988) 289-292 (R. *Hari* †); OLZ 83 (1988) 268-274 (M. *Mode*, auch über
MARTIN G., Royal tomb 1974).

g304 **Kemp** Barry J.,   Amarna reports II, 1985 ➤ 1,e144:   ᴿOLZ 83 (1988)
150-2 (M. *Mode*).

g305 **Kemp** Barry J.,   Amarna reports IV [III. 1986 ➤ 2,887; 3,e762]. L 1987,
Egypt Expl. Soc.   167 p.; 88 fig.   0-85698-102-8 [Antiquity 63,70].

g306 *Krauss* R., Drei Korrekturen und eine Ergänzung zu Ronald A. WELLS
[SAK 13 (1987) 313-333] 'Amarna Calendar Equivalent':   GöMiszÄg 103
(1988) 39-44.

g307 *McCafferty* Betty,   The Amarna letters: BToday 26 (1988) 232-9; ill.,
map.

g308 **Moran** W. L., *al.*,   Les lettres d'El-Amarna, ᵀ*Collon* D., *Cazelles* H.:
LAPO 13, 1987 ➤ 3,e766:   ᴿBL (1988) 125 (A. R. *Millard*: major,
standard).

g309 **Müller** Maya, Die Kunst Amenophis' III, und Echnatons. Ba 1988, Ver-
lag für Ägyptologie.   21 + 132 + 141 + 138 + 160 p.; 38 fig.   3-909083-01-3.

g310 **Redford** Donald B.,   Akhenaten, the heretic king 1984 ➤ 65,b351 ...
3,e768:   ᴿAmHR 92 (1987) 932 (J. *Baines*); JNES 47 (1988) 47s (W. J.
Murnane: some errors); WZKM 78 (1986) 233-5 (L. M. *Young*).

g311 **Redford** Donald, *al.*,   The [Karnak] Akhenaten Temple project 2.
Rwd-mnw, Foreigners and Inscriptions.   Toronto 1988, Univ.   xiv-118 p.;
16 fig.; 43 pl.   0-921428-00-6.

g312 *Reeves* C. Nicholas,   New light on Kiya [Akhenaten's lesser wife] from
texts in the British Museum: JEA 74 (1988) 91-101; 14 fig.; pl. XV-XVII.

g313 **Schlögl** H. [cf. Amenophis IV 1986 ➤ 3,e771] Echnaton-Tutanchamun
1983 ➤ 64,b862 ... 2,b97:   ᴿCdÉ 63 (1988) 98-102 (R. *Hari* †).

g314 *Tobin* Vincent A.,   Mythic symbolism in the Amarna system: JSSEg 16
(1986) 5-18.

T7.4   **Memphis,** *Saqqara*;   **Giza.**

g315 *a) Berlandini* Joselyne,   Contribution à l'étude du pilier-*djed* Memphite; –
b) Dijk Jacobus van,   The development of the Memphite necropolis in the
post-Amarna period; – *c) Labrousse* Audran,   Le temple funéraire de Pépi
I au Nouvel Empire; – *d) Graefe* Erhart,   Das Grab des Vorstehers der
Kunsthandwerker und Vorstehers der Goldschmiede, Aneneminet, in
Saqqara: ➤ 781, Memphis 1986/8, 23-33 / 37-46 / 67 / 49-53; 2 fig.

g316 ᴱ**Bresciani** Edda, *al.*,   Saqqâra IV; tomba di Bakenrenef (L. 24); attività del cantiere scuola 1985-1987.   Pisa 1988, Giardini.   90 p.; 14 fig.;
XXIV pl.

g317 **Davies** W. V., *al.*,   Saqqâra Tombs I., The Mastabas of Mereri and
Wernu 1984 ➤ 65,b359 ... 2,b103:   ᴿCdÉ 63 (1988) 283-6 (M. *Valloggia*);
JNES 47 (1988) 296s (D. P. *Silverman*); JSStEg 15 (1985) 42s (D. B.
Redford).

g318 *French* Peter,   Late dynastic pottery from the Berlin/Hannover excavations at Saqqâra, 1986:   MiDAI-K 44 (1988) 79-89; 21 fig.

g319 **Green** Christine I.,   The tomb furniture from the sacred animal
necropolis at North Saqqara: ExcMemoir 53, 1987 ➤ 3,e779:   ᴿJSSEg 16
(1986!) 36-38 (Sara E. *Orei*).

g320 **Jeffreys** D.G., *Smith* H.S., The Anubieion at Saqqâra, I. The settlement and the Temple precinct: Excavation Memoir 54. L 1988, Egypt Exploration Soc. xiii-115 p.; 79 fig.; 51 pl. 0-85698-103-6.

g321 *Jeffreys* D.G., *Malek* J., Memphis [Kôm Rabîʿa ...] 1986, 1987: JEA 74 (1988) 15-29; 10 fig.; pl. IV-V.

g322 **Jequier** Gustave, Tombeaux de particuliers contemporains de Pépi I: Saqqarah. Cairo 1983 = c. 1925, Service des Antiquités. iv-139 p.; 140 fig.; 17 pl. – ᴿOLZ 83 (1988) 532-4 (Eva *Martin-Pardey*).

g323 *Jones* Michael & Angela M., The Apis House project at Mit Rahinah; preliminary report of the sixth season, 1986: JAmEg 25 (1988) 105-116; 9 fig.

g324 *a*) *Lauer* Jean-Philippe, Sur certaines modifications et extensions apportées au complexe funéraire de Djoser au cours de son règne; – *b*) *Arnold* Dieter, Manoeuvering casing blocks of pyramids; – *c*) *Simpson* William K., Lepsius Pyramid LV at Dahshur; the mastaba of Si-Ese, vizier of Amenemhet II: ➤ 41, ᶠEDWARDS I., Pyramid studies 1988, 5-11; 1 fig. / 54-56; 2 fig. / 57-61.

g325 *Leclant* Jean, *a*) Découverte récent à Saqqarah (Égypte) de deux pyramides de reines: CRAI (1988) 262-5; – *b*) À la quête des Pyramides des Reines de Pépi Iᵉʳ [Saqqara]: BSocFrÉg 113 (1988) 20-26 + 7 fig.

g326 *Leclant* J., *Clerc* G., (Giza, Abousir) Saqqarah: ➤ g246, Orientalia 57 (1988) 324-334; pl. XXVI-XXXI.

g327 *Maehler* Herwig, Poésie alexandrine et art hellénistique à Memphis: CdÉ 63,125 (1988) 113-136; 4 fig.

g328 *Malek* Jaromir, The royal butler Hori at northern Saqqâra: JEA 74 (1988) 125-136; 3 fig.; pl. XIX-XX.

g329 **Martin** Geoffrey T., Corpus of reliefs of the New Kingdom from the Memphite necropolis and Lower Egypt: Studies in Egyptology. L 1987, Routledge-KP. xvi-64 p.; 56 pl. £45. 0-7103-0172-3 [BO 45,473]. – ᴿAntiqJ 68,1 (1988) 142 (M.L. *Bierbrier*).

g330 **Martin** Geoffrey T., *al.*, The tomb-chapels of Paser and Raʿia at Saqqara: Exc. Memoir 52, 1985 ➤ 1,e163: ᴿJSSEg 16 (1986) 63s (R.J. *Leprohon*).

g331 *Martin* G.T., The tomb of Maya, treasurer of Tutʿankhamūn [Saqqâra]; present knowledge and future prospects: ➤ 781, Memphis 1986/8, 69-71; franç. 72.

g332 *Martin* Geoffrey T., *al.*, The tomb of Maya and Meryt; preliminary report on the Saqqâra excavations 1987-8: JEA 74 (1988) 1-14; 3 fig.; pl. I-III.

g333 *Bosse-Griffiths* Kate, Some facts about Maya's tomb [Saqqara; Tutʿankhamun's treasurer]: DiscEg 4 (1986) 17-25; 1 fig.

g334 **Pernigotti** Sergio, Il libro dei morti su bende di mummia: Saqqara 2/1, Tomba di Boccori: EgVO Sup 4/3, 1985 ➤ 1,e164: ᴿDiscEg 8 (1987) 103-6 (Carol A.R. *Andrews*).

g335 *Moursi* Mohamed, Die Ausgrabungen in der Gegend um die Pyramide des Ḏd-k'-r' 'Issj' bei Saqqara; I: ➤ 127, ᶠSALEH A., ASAE 71 (1987) 187-193; 13 fig.; 2 pl. – II: GöMiszÄg 105 (1988) 65s + 2 phot.

g336 *Rizkana* Ibrahim, *Alfi* Mostafa El-, Maadi, Memphis and Heliopolis: DiscEg 11 (1988) 53-60.

g337 *Roth* Ann M., The organization of royal cemeteries at Saqqara in the Old Kingdom: JAmEg 25 (1988) 201-214; 13 fig.

g338 *Dodson* Aidan, Egypt's first antiquarians? [under the Step Pyramid, 12th Dynasty Sesostris III 1850 B.C.]: Antiquity 62 (1988) 513-7; 4 fig.

g339 *Rousseau* Jean, Les calendriers de Djoser [enceinte entre pyramide de 6 et de 4 degrés]: DiscEg 11 (1988) 73-86; 3 fig.
g340 **Thompson** Dorothy J., Memphis under the Ptolemies. Princeton 1988, Univ. 0-691-03593-8 [OIAc D88].

---

g341 **David** A. R., The pyramid builders of ancient Egypt 1986 → 2,b115; 3,e787: ᴿAmHR 92 (1987) 1184 (D. B. *Redford*).
g342 *Deaton* John C., The Old Kingdom evidence for the function of pyramids: VarAeg 4 (1988) 193-200.
g343 **Edwards** I. E. S., Pyramids 1985 → 2,b117; 3,e788: ᴿAncSRes 17 (1987) 95-98 (Lisa *Giddy*: bibliography not adequately updated).
ᶠEDWARDS I., Pyramid studies, ᴱBaines J. 1988 → 41.
g344 *Hatamori* Yasuko, ❶ The 'Pyramid city' in the Old Kingdom of Egypt: Orient 30,2 (1987) 14-27.
g345 *a)* *Hönig* Werner, Bauplan der Cheopspyramide mit ganzzahligem Ellenergebnis; – *b*) *Legon* John A. B., A ground-plan at Giza: DiscEg 10 (1988) 27-30 + 4 fig. / 33-40; 1 fig.
g345* Isler Martin, On pyramid building II: JAmEg 24 (1987) 95-112; 32 fig.
g346 *Kérisel* Jean, Le dossier scientifique sur la pyramide de Khéops: Archéologia 232 (Dijon 1988) 46-54; ill.
g347 *Legon* John A. B., The design of the pyramid of Khufu [(Cheops) Great Pyramid of Giza]: DiscEg 12 (1988) 41-48; 2 fig.
g348 *Stadelmann* Rainer, Königinnengrab und Pyramidenbezirk im Alten Reich: → 127, ᶠṢALEḤ A., ASAE 71 (1987) 251-260.
g349 *Trench* Jorge A., *a)* The concept of seked applied to the Great Pyramid: GöMiszÄg 101 (1988) 69s; 1 fig. – *b*) Geometrical model for the ascending and descending corridors of the Great Pyramid: GöMiszÄg 102 (1988) 85-94.
g350 *Wissa* Myriam, Sand beneath Giza; the karsts: GöMiszÄg 101 (1988) 75-88; 6 fig.
g351 **Swelim** Nabil, The brick pyramid at Abu Rowash; number '1' by Lepsius [1842s]: Publications, Arch. Soc. Alexandria 1987, Archaeological Society. – ᴿDiscEg 12 (1988) 87-89 (I. E. S. *Edwards* spells 'Rawash' but 'Rowash' in title; French 'Roach').
g352 **Arnold** Dieter, Der Pyramidenbezirk des Königs Amenemhet III in Dahschur, I. Die Pyramide: DAI-ArchVeröff 53. Mainz 1987, von Zabern. 105 p.; ill. – ᴿMundus 24 (1988) 91s (Ingrid *Gamer-Wallert*: German researches 1976-83).
g353 *a)* *Verner* Miroslav, Excavations at Abusir 1985/6; 1987; – *b*) *Preuss* Karel, Keramikfunde aus dem Pyramidentempel des Raneferef [Abusir]: ZägSpr 115 (1988) 77-85; 6 fig.; 163-172; 7 fig. / 69-76.
g354 **Debono** Fernand, *Mortensen* Bodil, The predynastic cemetery at Heliopolis 1950: DAI ArchVeröff 63. Mainz 1988, von Zabern. 59 p.; 20 pl., plan. DM 88. 3-8053-0945-7 [BO 45,755].

T7.5 **Delta Nili.**

g355 *Alexandria:* *Huzar* Eleanor G., Alexandria ad Aegyptum in the Julio-Claudian age: → 782, ANRW 2,10,1 (1988) 619-668.
g355* *a)* *Balty* Jean-C., Le 'bouleuterion' de l'Alexandrie sévérienne; – *b*) *Borkowski* Jan, Problèmes de conservation du théâtre, des thermes et des

citernes à Alexandrie; – c) *Daszewski* Wiktor A., Évolution de l''opus tessellatum' et le problème du chromatisme dans les mosaïques héllenistiques d'Alexandrie; – d) *Skowronek* Stefan, Observation concernant le sphinx composite sur les monnaies alexandrines; – e) *Tkaczow* Barbara, Le milieu artistique de l'antique Alexandrie: ➤ 12, ᶠBERNHARD M.-L. 1983, 7-12; 2 fig. / 31-38; 3 fig. / 53-62; 5 fig. / 329-333; 2 fig. / 393-403.

g356 *Venit* Marjorie S., The painted tomb from Wardian and the decoration of Alexandrian tombs: JAmEg 25 (1988) 71-91; 20 fig.

g357 *Bedon* Robert, [Alexandrie...] Les phares antiques: Archéologia 231 (Dijon 1988) 54-66; ill.

g358 **Atrib** 1985: ➤ 724, Delta 1986/8, 177-203 (K. *Myśliwiec*, T. *Herbich*).

g359 *Myśliwiec* Karol, *al.*, Remains of a Ptolemaic villa at Athribis [Benha]: MiDAI 44 (1988) 183-197; 6 fig. pl. 34-41.

g360 **Chemmis:** *Vycichl* Werner, L'île de Chemmis, 'qui flotte au gré des vents' [P. MÉLA; HÉRODOTE]: DiscEg 4 (1986) 73-76.

g361 **Kellia:** *a*) *Ballet* Pascale, La céramique des Kellia; nouvelles orientations et recherches; – *b*) *Bridel* Philippe, De la petite solitude des Kellia à la conquête de l'Ouest du Delta: ➤ 724, Delta 1986/8, 297-311 / 283-294.

g362 **Kasser** R., Le site monastique des Kellia 1984 [1984/6 ᴱ*Bridel* P. ➤ 3,e801]: ᴿBO 45 (1988) 150s (W. *Godlewski*).

g363 *Descœudres* Georges, L'architecture des Kellia: ➤ d702, Monde Copte 14s (1988) 75-96; ill.

g364 *a*) *Rassart-Debergh* M., Les fouilles aux Kellia; campagne 1981; – *b*) *Pelsmaekers* J., Het dodenverblijf op de Koptische dodenstèle in tekst en beeld: ➤ 763, Archéologie 1986, 227-238 / 239-245.

g365 *a*) *Rassart-Debergh* Marguerite, Le thème de la croix sur les peintures murales des Kellia, entre l'Égypte et la Nubie chrétiennes; – *b*) *Rodziewicz* Mieczysław, The Christian pottery in Nubia and Kharga Oasis: ➤ 750, Nubian V, 1982/6, 363s + 2 pl. / 367-9 + 8 fig.

g368 **Kom Abu Billu:** **Abd el-Hafeez** Abd el-Al, *Grenier* J.C., *Wagner* G., Stèles funéraires de Kom Abu Bellou: RCiv Mém 55, 1985 ➤ 2,b125; 3,e802 [both without the apparently correct 'surname' Abd-el-Hafeez]: ᴿBO 45 (1988) 592s (K. *Parlasca*); RHR 205 (1988) 310s (Gisèle *Clerc*).

g369 **Kom/Ḥiṣn:** *Wenke* Robert J., *al.*, Kom el-Hisn; excavation of an Old Kingdom settlement in the Egyptian Delta: JAmEg 25 (1988) 5-34; 15 fig.

g370 **Mashuṭa:** *Paice* Patricia, A preliminary analysis of some elements of the Saite and Persian period pottery at Tell el-Maskhuta: BEgSem 8 (NY 1986s) 95-103 + 8 fig.

g371 *Bagnall* Roger S., A second century Christian burial at Tell el-Maskhuta?: ZPapEp 74 (1988) 291s.

g372 **Mendes:** *Bothmer* Bernard V., The great naos at Mendes and its sculpture: ➤ 724, Delta 1986/8, 205-9 + 11 pl.

g373 **Minshat Abu Omar** [150 k NE Cairo] 1978-84: ➤ 724, Delta 1986/8, 11-52 + 8 pl. (Karla *Kroeper*).

g374 *Kroeper* Karla, The ceramic of the pre/early dynastic cemetery of Minshat Abu Omar: BEgSem 8 (NY 1986s) 73-82 + 90 fig.

g375 *Brink* Edwin C.M. van den, The Amsterdam University survey expedition to the northeastern Nile Delta (1984-6): ➤ 724, Delta 1986/8, 65-84 (+) 24 fig.; 8 pl.

g376 **Natrûn:** *Daoust* J., Chez les Coptes [visite au Wadi Natroun; *Asselbergs* W., Revue des Deux Mondes, oct. 1987]: EsprVie 98 (1988) 244-6.

g377 **Qantîr, Dab'a:** **Bietak** Manfred, Ein altägyptischer Weingarten in einem Tempelbezirk (Tell el-Dab'a 1. März-10. Juni 1985): Anz ÖstAkad ph/h 122 / 12. Wien 1985, Österr. Akad. 267-278; 13 (foldout) fig.; VIII pl.

g378 Dab'a: JhÖs 58B (1988) 1.1-5 (J. *Dorner*).

g379 *Tanis:* a) *Yoyotte* Jean, Tanis, les particularités d'un site protégé; – b) *Brissaud* Philippe, La nécropole royale de Tanis, état des recherches 1983-1986: ➤ 724, E*Brink* E.C.M. van den, The archaeology of the Nile Delta, problems and priorities [Cairo 19-22.X.1986] 1988, 151-7 / 159-163.

g380 E*Brissaud* Philippe, Cahiers de Tanis I: Mémoire 95. P 1987, RCiv. 188 p. F 187. 2-86538-180-3 [RB 96, 436, R. *Beaud*].

g381 *Dodson* Aidan, Some notes concerning the royal tombs at Tanis: CdÉ 63,126 (1988) 221-233.

g382 *Jansen-Winkeln* Karl, Weiteres zum Grab Osorkons II.: GöMiszÄg 102 (1988) 30-39.

g383 *Goyon* Georges, La découverte des trésors de Tanis 1987 ➤ 3,e807: R BO 45 (1988) 327-330 (A. *Dodson*).

g384 *DeVries* C.E., Zoan: ➤ 801, ISBEnc³ 4 (1988) 1201-3 ['Ramses II did much building at Ṣan ... YOYOTTE: claims (of Qantir and Ṣan as Raamses) about even; .. for ALT, PiRa'messe included both sites ..'].

g385 *Yahudîya: Alfi* Mostafa El-, Some recent discoveries from Tell el-Yahoudiyêh: [standing man in black sandstone with inscription]: DiscEg 9 (1987) 31s; 1 fig.

g386 *Zagazig:* **Snape** S.R., Six archaeological sites 1986 ➤ 3,e811: R VarAeg 4 (1988) 109s (C.C. *Van Siclen*).

T7.6 *Alii situs Aegypti* **alphabetice.**

g387 *Abydos: Munro* Irmtraut, Zum Kult des Ahmose in Abydos; ein weiterer Beleg aus der Ramessidenzeit: GöMiszÄg 101 (1988) 57-62; II pl.

g388 *Richards* Janet, Understanding the mortuary remains at Abydos: NewsAmEg 142 (1988) 5-8.

g389 *Aḥmim:* **Kuhlmann** Klaus P., Materialien ... von Achmim 1983 ➤ 64,b840 ... 3,e813: R BO 45 (1988) 322-5 (N. *Grimal*); JEA 74 (1988) 259-261 (N. *Kanawati*).

g390 **Kanawati** Naguib, The rock tombs of El-Hawawish, the cemetery of Akhmim, vol. 3s, 1982s ➤ 2,b157; 3,e814: R JNES 47 (1988) 201-3 (P. *Der Manuelian*).

g391 *Akoris:* 6th season, preliminary report (E**Kawanishi** H., *Tsujimura* S). Tokyo 1988.

g392 *Antinoopolis: Zahrnt* Michael, Antinoopolis in Ägypten; die hadrianische Gründung und ihre Privilegien in der neueren Forschung: ➤ 782, ANRW 2,10,1 (1988) 669-706.

g393 *Ašmunayn:* **Spencer** A.J., [cf. ➤ 3,816] Excavations at El-Ashmunein I. The topography 1983 ➤ 64,b867: R CdÉ 63 (1988) 292s (N. *Grimal*).

g394 *Aswan:* **Habachi** Labib, Elephantinc IV. The sanctuary of Heqaib 1985 ➤ 1,e208: R BO 45 (1988) 325-7 (H. De *Meulenaere*).

g395 **Dreyer** Günter, Elephantine VIII; der Tempel der Satet; die Funde der Frühzeit und des Alten Reiches: DAI-K Veröff. 19; 1986 ➤ 2,b148; DM 198: R BO 45 (1988) 116-8 (K. *Krömer*).

g396 **Junge** Friedrich, Elephantine XI. Funde und Bauteile, 1.-7. Kampagne 1969-1976: DAI-K/Schweiz. ArchVeröff 49. Mainz 1987, von Zabern. 92 p. 51 pl. DM 168. 3-8053-0604-0 [BO 45,472].

g397 *Kaiser* Werner, *al.*, Stadt und Tempel von Elephantine, 15./16. Grabungsbericht [1985-7]: MiDAI-K 44 (1988) 135-182; 15 fig.; pl. 48-59.

g398 **Badari:** *Holmes* D. L., The predynastic lithic industries of Badari, Middle Egypt; new perspectives and inter-regional relations: World Arch 20 (1988s) 70-86; 3 fig.

g399 **Bahria,** Oasis 300 k SW Cairo: *Gosline* Sheldon L., Reevaluation of the tomb of Amenhotep, governor of Bahria: DiscEg 8 (1987) 15-20; 3 fig. (vintage).

g400 **Cairo-**Fustat: *Cesaretti* Maria Pia, Babilonia d'Egitto; esegesi delle fonti: RStorAnt 16 (1986) 7-16.

g400* *Caselitz* Peter, Zur Klassifikation der prädynastischen Keramik von Heliopolis/Unterägypten: StAltÄgK 15 (1988) 27-52.

g401 **Dakhleh:** *Mills* A. J., *al.*, The Dakhleh Oasis project; an interim report on the 1984-1985 season: JSStEg 15 (1985) 44s, 105-114 [-129]; ill.

g402 **Dendera:** *Cauville* Sylvie, *a)* Le panthéon d'Edfou à Dendera; – *b)* avec *Gasse* Annie, Fouilles de Dendera, premiers résultats: BIFAO 88 (1988) 7-23; 1 pl. / 25-32; 3 fig.; pl. IIs.

g403 **Dûš** [230 k W Kom Ombo]: *Reddé* Michel, Une ville romaine dans le désert occidental d'Égypte, Douch: RArchéol (1988) 215-220; 2 plans.

g404 *Dunand* Françoise, *Lichtenberg* Roger, Les momies de la nécropole de Douch [S Kharga, W Aswan] et leurs rares tissus coptes: Archéologia 240 (Dijon 1988) 30-43.

g405 **Fayûm:** *Wenke* Robert J., *al.*, Epipaleolithic and neolithic subsistence and settlement in the Fayyum Oasis of Egypt: JField 15 (1988) 29-61; 11 fig.

g406 *Grossmann* Peter, Le chiese CH D 87, CH G 88 e CH H 88 di Medinet Madi: EgVO 11 (1988) 13-17 + 6 fig.

g407 *Lesko* Leonard H., Seila 1981 [small step-pyramid in Fayûm]: JAmEg 25 (1988) 215-235; 24 fig.

g408 **Heracleopolis,** Beni Sueif: *Carmen Pérez Die* María del, *a)* Excavaciones de la misión arqueológica española en Heracleópolis Magna: ArEspArq 61 (1988) 337-341; – *b)* Excavaciones en Heracleópolis Magna (Egipto), campaña de 1987: AulaO 6 (1988) 103s.

g409 **Mokhtar** Mohamed G., Ihnâsya el-Medina (Herakleopolis magna), its importance and its role in pharaonic history: BiblÉt 40, 1983 ➤ 54,b889 ... 3,e834: ᴿBO 45 (1988) 108-110 (F. *Gomaà*).

g410 **Hermopolis:** Snape Steven, *Bailey* Donald, The great portico at Hermopolis Magna; present state and past [sic, OIAc D88] prospects: Occas. Pap. 63. L 1988, British Museum. 0-86159-063-5.

g411 **Hibeh:** **Wenke** Robert J., Archaeological investigations at El-Hibeh 1980: 1984 ➤ 1,e218: ᴿCdÉ 63 (1988) 293-5 (Marie-Francine *Moens*).

g412 **Cruz-Uribe** Eugene, *Hibis* Temple project, I. Translations, commentary, discussions and sign-list. San Antonio 1988, Van Siclen. 0-933175-14-0 [OIAc N88].

g413 **Hierakonpolis:** Adams Barbara, The fort cemetery at Hierakonpolis I 1987 ➤ 3,e835: ᴿBInstArch 25 (1988) 93 (E. P. *Uphill*).

g414 **Hoffman** Michael A., *al.*, The predynastic of Hierakonpolis [cf. ➤ 64,b890]. Cairo/Macomb 1982, Univ./Western Illinois Univ. vii-154 p.; 8 pl. – ᴿJAmEg 24 (1987) 143s (L. *Krzyzaniak*); JEA 74 (1988) 265-8 (P. *Lacovara*).

g415 **Idfu:** Germond Philippe, Les invocations à la Bonne Année au temple d'Edfou 1986 ➤ 2,b155; 3,e838: ᴿJAOS 108 (1988) 151s (R. S. *Bianchi*).

g416 **Kâb:** *Meulenaere* Herman De, Deux personnages d'Elkab: CdÉ 63,126 (1988) 207-212.

g417 *Kôm al-Aḥmar* / Šarūna, 1988: GöMiszÄg 104 (1988) 53-64 + 7 (foldout) fig. (Louise *Gestermann, al.*).

g418 *Koptos* (40 k NW Luxor): *Cesaretti* Maria Pia, Nerone a Copto [Min-Isis temple rebuilt under Nero and his predecessors]: DiscEg 5 (1986) 17-26; IV pl.

g419 *Farid* Adel, Die Denkmäler des Parthenios, des Verwalters der Isis von Koptos: MiDAI-K 44 (1988) 13-65; 24 fig.; pl. 1-14.

g420 *Williams* Bruce, Narmer and the Coptos Colossi: JAmEg 25 (1988) 35-59; 10 fig.

g421 *Lišt:* **Arnold** Dieter, The pyramid of Senwosret I: South Cemeteries of Lisht 1. NY 1988, Metropolitan Museum of Art. 0-87099-506-5 [OIAc D88].

g422 *Maadi:* **Rizkana** Ibrahim, *Seeher* Jürgen, Maadi I. The pottery of the predynastic settlement: DAI-ArchVeröff 64, 1987 ➔ 3,e846; DM 168: ᴿMundus 24 (1988) 118s (Ingrid *Gamer-Wallert*); Starinar NS 38 (Beograd 1987) 139-142 (S. P. *Tutundžić*).

g423 **Rizkana** Ibrahim, *Seeher* Jürgen, Maadi II; the lithic industries of the predynastic settlement: DAI-ArchVeröff 65. Mainz 1988, von Zabern. 117 p.; 111 + XII pl. 3-8053-0980-5.

g424 *Merimde:* **Eiwanger** Josef, Merimde-Benisalâme II. Die Funde der Mittleren Merimdekultur: DAI ArchVeröff 51. Mainz 1988, von Zabern. 114 p.; 61 pl. DM 148. 3-8053-0606-7 [BO 45,755].

g425 **Eiwanger** Josef, Merimde-Benisalame I. die Funde der Urschicht: DAI-K Arch. Veröff. 47, 1984 ➔ 1,e227: ᴿJNES 47 (1988) 205s (B. *Williams*).

g426 *Maġara:* *Hendricks* S., *Midant-Reynes* B., Preliminary report on the predynastic living site Maghara 2 (Upper Egypt): OrLovPer 19 (1988) 5-16; VI fig.

g427 *Qobeba* (N. Esna), site copte, fouilles 1972: ➔ d702, Monde Copte 14s (1988) 98-103, ill. (A. I. *Sadek*).

g428 *Quṣayr/Qadīm,* Red Sea: *Bagnall* Roger S., Papyri and ostraka from Quseir al-Qadim: BASP 23,1s (1986) 1-60; pl. 1-27.

g429 *Šelwit: Zivie* Christiane M., Le temple de Deir Chelouit II 55-89, III 90-157, 1983/6 ➔ 64,b879; 2,b164: ᴿBO 45 (1988) 330-3 (L. *Kákosy*); JAOS 108 (1988) 149s (R. S. *Bianchi*).

g430 *Speos Artemidos,* missions épigraphiques: BSocÉg 12 (Genève 1988) 9-24; 4 pl. (S. *Bickel*, J.-J. *Chappaz*).

T7.7 **Situs Nubiae** *et alibi.*

g431 **Blackman** Aylward M., The temple of Dendûr [reassembled in NY]. Cairo 1911, photostatic reprint, Cairo Service des Antiquités. v-384 p.; 120 + 14 pl.; foldout. – ᴿOLZ 83 (1988) 18s (R. S. *Bianchi*).

g432 *Bongioanni* Alessandro, *Grazzi* Riccardo, Osservazioni sulla planimetria dell'Iseo di Industria [Monteu da Po (Torino)]: Aegyptus 68 (1988) 3-11; IV pl.

g433 *Bradbury* Louise, Reflections on traveling to 'God's Land' and Punt in the Middle Kingdom: JAmEg 25 (1988) 127-156; 11 fig.

g434 **Connah** Graham, African civilizations; precolonial cities and states in tropical Africa; an archaeological perspective. C 1987, Univ. xi-259 p.; 55 fig. £25; pa. £8. 0-521-31902-7. – ᴿAntiquity 62 (1988) 389s (J. *Alexander*).

g435 *a) Conwell* David, On ostrich eggs and Libyans; traces of a Bronze Age people from Bates' Island, Egypt; – *b) O'Connor* David, Egyptians and Libyans in the New Kingdom; an interpretation: Expedition 29,3 (Ph 1987) 25-34 / 35-37.

g436 **Curto** S., Le sculture egizie ed egittizzanti nelle [tre] Ville Torlonia: ÉPR 105, 1985 ➤ 1,e258; 3,e856: ᴿBO 45 (1988) 125-8 (M. *Budischovsky*); Latomus 47 (1988) 254s (M. *Malaise*).

g437 **Deichmann** Friedrich W., *Grossmann* Peter (*Feld* Otto), Nubische Forschungen: ArchForsch 17. B 1988, Mann. xiv-189 p.; ill. 3-7861-1512-5.

g438 **Fontana** Domenico, *a)* Della trasportatione dell'Obelisco Vaticano 1590, ᴱ*Carugo* Adriano, intr. *Portoghesi* Paolo: Libri rari 2. Mi 1979, Polifilo; – *b)* Die Art, wie der vatikanische Obelisk transportiert wurde [+ ital., 1590] ᴱ*Conrad* Dietrich. B 1987, VEB-Bauwesen. 2 vol.

g439 ᴱ**Geus** Francis, ANilM 1 (1986): ᴿBO 45 (1988) 135-7 (F. W. *Hinkel*).

g440 *Geus* Francis, *a)* Trois années d'activité de la Section Française de la Direction des Antiquités du Soudan (1979-1982); – *b)* Des tombes contemporaines du Néolithique de Khartoum à El Ghaba (Taragma): ➤ 750, Nubian V, 1982/6, 71-80 [-96, Shendi] / 67 + 6 fig.

g441 **Needler** Winifred, Predynastic and archaic Egypt in the Brooklyn Museum [H. de Morgan excavation; *Churcher* C. S. on Abu Zaidan fishtail knife]: Wilbour Mg 9, 1984 ➤ 65,a61: ᴿArOr 56 (1988) 289s (E. *Strouhal*); BO 45 (1988) 333-6 (L. *Krzyzaniak*).

g442 *Podvin* Jean-Louis, Aegyptiaca du nord de la Gaule: BSocÉg 12 (Genève 1988) 61-70; map.

g443 *Snitkuviené* A. P., ❸ Histoire de la collection d'antiquités égyptiennes en Lituanie: VDI 186 (1988) 75-92; franç. 93.

g444 *Vercoutter* Jean, L'obélisque de la Place de la Concorde: Archéologia 234 (1988) 36-39; ill.

g445 ᶠ**Wendorf** Fred, Prehistory of arid North Africa, ᴱ**Close** Angela E. Dallas 1987, Southern Methodist Univ. xvi-357 p.; 110 fig. $40; pa. $20. – ᴿAntiquity 62 (1988) 403s (R. *Solecki*).

g446 *Yoyotte* Jean, *Chuvin* Pierre, Le Zeus Casios de Péluse à Tivoli; une hypothèse: BIFAO 88 (1988) 165-180; 2 fig.; pl. XIV-XVII.

---

g447 ***Abri:*** *Fernández* Victor M. [Spanish archaeological mission 1981], *a)* A new Kerma site in Abri (Northern Prov. Sudan); – *b)* Early Meroitic in Northern Nubia: ➤ 750, Nubian V, 1982/6, 55-57 + 1 fig. / 59-63 + 4 fig.

g448 ***Akaša:*** **Maystre** Charles, al., Akasha [Sudanese Nubia], 1. Genève 1980, Univ. 246 p.; 51 fig.; 68 pl. – ᴿJNES 47 (1988) 48s (B. *Williams*).

g449 ***Cyrene:*** **Schaus** Gerald P., The extramural sanctuary of Demeter and Persephone at Cyrene, Libya; final reports, 2. The East Greek, island, and Lycaonian pottery: Museum Monographs 16. Ph/Tripoli 1985, Univ. Museum / Libya Antiquities Dept. xxii-140 p.; 10 fig.; 33 pl., 2 plans. – ᴿGnomon 60 (1988) 54-57 (H. P. *Isler*).

g450 *Marengo* Silvia M., L'agorà di Cirene in età romana alla luce delle testimonianze epigrafiche: MÉF 100 (1988) 87-101; plan.

g451 *Stucchi* Sandro, Missione a Cirene; trent'anni di scavi italiani nell'Atene d'Africa': Archeo 36 (1988) 14-21; ill.

g451* **Brogan** Olwen, *Smith* D. J., Ghirza, a Libyan settlement in the Roman period. Tripoli 1984, Dept. of Antiquities. 327 p.; 115 fig.; 172 pl. £55 [Antiquity 63, 173, R. J. A. *Wilson*].

g452 **Joly** Elda, *Tomasello* Francesco, Il tempio a divinità ignota di Sabratha. R 1984, Bretschneider. iii-196 p.; 56 fig.; 35 pl.; 14 foldouts. – ᴿLatomus 47 (1988) 253s (F. *Baratte*).

g453 *Dodekaschoinos:* **Burkhardt** Adelheid, Ägypter und Meroiten im Dodekaschoinos 1985 → 1,9188: ᴿOLZ 83 (1988) 26-28 (C. *Onasch*).

g454 *Faras:* a) *Martens-Czarnecka* Malgorzata, Observations on repainted murals from Faras; – b) *Karkowski* Janusz, A few remarks on stone used in Christian constructions at Faras; – c) *Zurawski* Bogdan, Bishops' tombs in Faras: → 750, Nubian V, 1982/6, 329-333 + 6 fig. / 311-5 + 7 fig. / 413-8 + 9 fig.

g455 *Kadada:* *Reinold* Jacques, La nécropole néolithique d'El Kadada au Soudan Central; quelques cas de sacrifices humains: → 750, Nubian V, 1982/6, 159-164 + 9 fig.

g456 *Kalabša:* **Strouhal** Eugen, Wadi Qitna and Kalabsha-South, I. Archaeology: Czech. Institute of Egyptology, 1984 → 65,b440; 2,b194: ᴿArOr 56 (1988) 287s (P. *Charvát*); CdÉ 63 (1988) 297-300 (A. *Vila*); JEA 74 (1988) 304s (A. J. *Mills*); JNES 47 (1988) 140s (W. Y. *Adams*); OrAnt 27 (1988) 157s (S. *Curto*); WZKM 77 (1987) 136-9 (I. *Hofmann*).

g457 *Kerma:* **Bonnet** Charles, *al.* Les fouilles archéologiques de Kerma (Soudan) 1986s, 1987s: Genava 34 (1986) 5-20; 36 (1988) 5-35; 26 fig.

g458 *Korosko:* **Curto** Silvio, *al.*, Korosko-Kasr Ibrim; incisioni rupestri nubiane. ·Mi 1987, Cisalpino. 83 p.; 82 fig.; 59 pl. (+) 28 fot. 88-205-0552-5. – ᴿBO 45 (1988) 579-581 (P. *Červiček*).

g459 *Leptis:* **Fant** J. C., IRT 794b and the building history of the Hadrianic Baths at Lepcis Magna: ZPapEp 75 (1988) 291-4.

g460 *Stucchi* Sandro, Intorno al 'motivo centrale' nelle absidi della basilica severiana di Leptis Magna: → 31, ᶠDE ANGELIS D'OSSAT G. 1987, 63-65; 3 fig.

g461 *Nag' eš Šeima* near Meroe: *Tomandi* Herbert, Bemerkungen zum Auftreten eines religiösen Motivs in der Wüstenkirche von Nagˁ eš Šeima und zu seiner Herkunft: VarAeg 4 (1988) 171-180; 5 fig.

g462 **Bietak** M., *Schwarz* M., Nagˁ el-Scheima; eine befestigte christliche Siedlung und andere christliche Denkmäler in Sayala-Nubien, I. Die österreichischen Grabungen 1963-1965: Denkschrift ph/h 191, 1987 → 3,e893: ᴿZAW 100 (1988) 449 (V. *Fritz*).

g463 *Meroë:* **Török** László, Der meroitische Staat 1: Meroitica 9. B 1986, Akademie. xx-391 p.; 4 maps. M 68. 3-05-000132-1. – ᴿBO 45 (1988) 581-3 (Inge *Hofmann*); WZKM 78 (1986) 221-2 (auch I. *Hofmann*).

g464 *Török* László, Geschichte Meroes; ein Beitrag über die Quellenlage und den Forschungsstand: → 782, ANRW 2,10,1 (1988) 107-341.

g465 **Scholz** Piotr, Kusch-Meroe-Nubien: AntW Sondernummer 1986 und 1987, je DM 15,80: ᴿBO 45 (1988) 569-571 (Inge *Hofmann*).

g466 *Böhm* Gerhard, Über den Namen Meroe: BeiSudan 3 (1988) 151-8.

g467 *Nubia:* **Török** László, Late antique Nubia; history and archaeology of the southern neighbour of Egypt in the 4th-6th c. A.D., pref. *Kirwan* L.: Antaeus 16. Budapest 1988, Acad. 279 p.; 189 pl. 0238-0218.

g468 *Grimm* Alfred, *T3-nbw* 'Goldland' und 'Nubien'; zu den Inschriften auf dem Listenfragment aus dem Totentempel des Djedkere: GöMiszÄg 106 (1988) 23-27; 28, 1 fig.

g469 **Grzymski** Krzysztof, *al.*, Archaeological reconnaissance in Upper Nubia. Toronto 1987, Benben 14. 58 p.; 6 fig.; 10 pl. 0-920168-09-4 [OIAc N88]. – ᴿBO 45 (1988) 571-3 (F. W. *Hinkel*).

g470 *Grzymski* K., Canadian expedition to Nubia: BCanadMed 8,2 (1988) 1-5; 8 fig.

ᴱHägg Thomas, Nubian culture past and present 1986/7 → 740.

g471 **Hein** Irmgard, Die ramessidische Bautätigkeit in Nubien; nach archäologischen Belegen südlich vom I. Nilkatarakte. W 1986, Univ. [OIAc N88].

g472 **Zibelius-Chen** Karola, Die ägyptische Expansion nach Nubien; eine Darlegung der Grundfaktoren: TAVO Beih B-78. Wsb 1988, Reichert. xxii-256 p.; map. 3-85226-421-7.

g473 *Qustul:* **Williams** B.B., Excavations between Abu Simbel and the Sudan frontier, I., The A-group royal cemetery at Qustul; cemetery L, 1985 → 3,e877; ᴿBO 45 (1988) 373-9 (A. *Vila*); Orientalia 57 (1988) 406-8 (J. *Vercoutter*).

g474 *Sahara: Baistrocchi* Massimo, Sahara; archeologia del deserto: Archeo 45 (1988) 49-93.

g475 ᴱ**Barich** Barbara E., Archaeology and environment in the Libyan Sahara; the excavations in the Tadrart Acacus, 1978-1983: BAR-Int 368. Ox 1987. xi-345 p.; ill.

g476 ᴱ**Vogg** Reiner, Forschungen in Sahara und Sahel I. Erste Ergebnisse der Stuttgarter geowissenschaftlichen Sahara-Expedition 1984: Stu Geog. Studien 106. Stu 1987, Univ. 260 p.; 103 fig.; 16 phot. – ᴿMundus 24 (1988) 338s (H. G. *Mensching*).

g477 *Yahky* Farid el-, The Sahara and predynastic Egypt, an overview: JSStEg 15 (1985) 81-85.

g478 *Tabo:* **Maystre** Charles, *al.*, Tabo I, statue en bronze d'un roi méroïtique (Mus. Khartoum Inv. 24705). Genève 1986. – ᴿBSocÉg 12 (Genève 1988) 98 (J.-L. *Chappaz*).

g479 *Vallis: Ferchiou* Naïdé, Le grand temple de Vallis [Tunisie] et sa place dans l'architecture de la province romaine d'Afrique: RArchéol (1988) 41-50; 10 fig.

T7.9 **Sinai.**

g480 *Anati* Emmanuel, [→ 2502] Har Karkom, la montagna di Dio? Scoperte nel biblico deserto Paran: Archeo 35 (1988) 24-31; ill.

g481 *Baruch* Uri, *Bar Yosef* Ofer, Upper paleolithic assemblages from Wadi Sudr, Western Sinai: Paléorient 12,2 (1986) 69-84; 10 fig.

g482 *Carrez-Maratray* Jean-Yves, *Abd el-Maksoud* Mohammed, Peluse ville oubliée du Sinaï nord: Archéologia 241 (1988) 60-66.

g483 *Digbassanis* Dimitrios, The Sinai papyri, ᵀ*Mandilaras* B.: → 492, XVIII Papyrol 1 (1986/8) 71-86 + VI pl.

g484 *Dijkstra* Meindert, The statue Sinai Nr. 348 and the tribe of the Kenites: → 469, Wünschet 1986/8, 93-102; 103, fig.

g485 **Stewart** Frank H., Bedouin boundaries in central Sinai and the southern Negev; a document from the Aḥaywāt tribe: MeditLangCulture Mg 2. Wsb 1986, Harrassowitz. 62 p.; 5 maps. – ᴿStOrFin 64 (1988) 395s (H. *Palva*).

g486 *Ventura* Raphael, Bent axis or wrong direction?; studies on the temple of Serabit el-Khadim: IsrEJ 38 (1988) 128-138; 3 fig.; pl. 23.

T8.1 **Anatolia,** *generalia.*

g487 **Akurgal** Ekrem, ⊕ Anadolu uygarlıkları [civilizations]. İstanbul 1988, Net Turistik. 975-479-031-0 [OIAc D88].

g488 *Ameling* Walter, Drei Studien zu den Gerichtsbezirken der Provinz Asia in republikanischer Zeit: EpAnat 12 (1988) 9-24; ❶ 24.

g489 *a) Coulton* J. J., Roman aqueducts in Asia Minor; – *b) Farrington* Andrew, Imperial bath buildings in South-West Asia Minor; – *c) Mitchell* Stephen, Imperial building in the eastern Roman provinces: ➤ 454, Roman architecture 1987, 72-84 / 50-59 / 18-25.

g490 *Cremer* Marie-Louise, *Nollé* Johannes, Lydische Steindenkmäler: Chiron 18 (1988) 199-212 + 4 pl.

g491 **Edwards** Robert W., The [Crusade] fortifications of Armenian Cilicia: Dumbarton Oaks Studies 23. Wsh 1987. xxxi-288 p.; 78 fig.; 254 pl. + 48 colour. $60. 0-88402-163-7. – RAntiqJ 68,1 (1988) 161 (D. *Pringle*).

g492 **Elsner** Jacques, Sites antiques du Sud-Est de l'Anatolie. Bodrum 1987, Yachting. 144 p.; ill. (*Binhas* Yuda).

g493 *Forlanini* Massimo, La regione del Tauro nei testi hittiti: VO 7 (1988) 129-169; map.

g494 **French** D. H., The year's work... Recent archaeological research: AnSt 38 (1988) 3-20 ... 191-208.

g495 **Greenhalgh** Jean, Roman Pisidia – a study of development and change: diss. Newcastle 1987. 713 p. BRDX-81343. – DissA 49 (1988s) 533-A.

g496 **Hellenkemper** Hansgerd, *Hild* Friedrich, Neue Forschungen in Kilikien: Tabula Imp. Byz. Veröff. 4, ph/h Denkschrift 186. W 1986, Österr. Akad. 144 p.; 24 + 201 fig. – RGnomon 60 (1988) 184-7 (M. *Waelkens*); OrChrPer 54 (1988) 227s (P. *Stephanou*).

g497 *Hill* S., Early church planning in Rough Cilicia: ➤ 745, Architecture of the Eastern Churches 1981 ...

g498 ELevick Barbara, *al.*, Monuments from the Aezanitis: Monumenta Asiae Minoris Antiquae 9. L 1988, Soc. Promotion Roman Studies. lxix-209 p.; XLVIII pl. 0-907764-10-X.

g499 FMELLINK Machteld J.: Ancient Anatolia; aspects of change and cultural development, ECanby Jeanny V., *al.* 1986: RBInstArch sup. 24 (1987) 24-26 (J. *Mellaart*); JNES 47 (1988) 290s (G. *Beckman*: fig. 4-le p. 49 is upside down and does not present the text cited p. 48).

g500 *Mellink* Machteld J., Archaeology in Anatolia [alphabetic order of sites within subdivision by periods]: AJA 92 (1988) 101-131; 36 fig.

g500* **Mutafian** Claude, La Cilicie au carrefour des empires I-II: Série grecque 113. P 1988, BLettres. 480 p.; 300 p., 150 fig. + 40 coul., 90 maps. F 380. 2-251-32630-8 [BBudé 88,99].

g501 **Neumann** G., Lydien/Lykien: ➤ 808, RLA 7,3s (1988) 184-6 / 189-191.

g501* **Rossner** Eberhard P., Die neuassyrischen Felsreliefs in der Türkei; ein archäologischer Führer: Felsdenkmäler in der Türkei 2. Mü 1987, auct. 108 p.; ill.

g502 **Sinclair** T. A., Eastern Turkey, an architectural and archaeological survey, I, 1987 ➤ 3,e920; xiii-454 p.; 64 pl.; 4 maps: RJRAS (1988) 407 (G. *Goodwin*: 'will form the scholarly source for any serious research').

g503 **Smith** David N., HERODOTOS and the archaeology [? history ➤ d305] of Asia Minor; a historiographic study: diss. California, DStroud R. Berkeley 1987. 313 p. 88-14072. – DissA 49 (1988s) 1245-A.

g504 **Trebilco** Paul R., Studies on Jewish communities in Asia Minor: diss. Durham UK 1987. BRD-80790. – DissA 49 (1988s) 321-A.

g505 **Waelkens** Marc, Die kleinasiatischen Türsteine 1986 ➤ 2,b207; 3,e921: RBonnJbb 188 (1988) 614-6 (Sylvia *Diebner*); ClasR 102 (1988) 349s (R. R. R. *Smith*).

g506 **Yakar** Jak, The later prehistory of Anatolia: BAR-Int 268, 1985
→ 1,e278: ᴿBInstArch sup 24 (1987) 26-28 (J. *Mellaart*).

g507 **Yardımcı** Nürettin, Treasures from Turkey [exposition Japan/Europe
1985; catalog in Dutch and Turkish only; all 376 objects in Japanese color
photo]. Leiden 1986, Rijksmuseum. 324 p. 90-71201-03-1. – ᴿBO 45
(1988) 406s (T. de *Feyter*).

T8.2 **Boğazköy,** *Hethaei* – **The Hittites.**

g508 **Bittel** Kurt, Denkmäler eines hethitischen Grosskönigs 1984 → 1,e281:
ᴿZAss 78 (1988) 159s (U. *Seidl*).

g509 **Kümmel** Hans M., Nichtliterarische Texte in akkadischer Sprache: KTB
28, 1985 → 1,e284: ᴿJAOS 108 (1988) 306s (G. F. *Del Monte*).

g510 **Macqueen** J. G., The Hittites and their contemporaries in Asia
Minor²ʳᵉᵛ (¹1975) 1986 → 3,f688: ᴿClasW 82 (1988s) 211 (A. *Ramage*);
JNES 47 (1988) 292-4 (R. H. *Beal*).

g511 ᴱ**Marazzi** Massimiliano, L'Anatolia hittita, I. I re: QuadGeogStorica 3.
R 1986, Univ. [OIAc D88].

g512 *a) Mellaart* James, Hatti, Arzawa and Ahhiyawa; a review of the
present stalemate in historical and geographical studies; – *b) Schachermeyr*
F., Der kleinasiatische Küstensaum zwischen Mykene und dem Hethiterreich: → 111, ᶠMʏʟᴏɴᴀs G., *Phília épē* 1 (1986) 74-84; 2 maps /
99-107.

g513 *Neve* Peter, Die Ausgrabungen in Boğazköy-Ḫattuša 1987: ArchAnz
(1988) 357-390; 42 fig.

g514 **Otten** Heinrich, Die Bronzetafel aus Boğazköy; ein Staatsvertrag
Tutḫalijas IV: Studien zu den Boğazköy-Texten, Beih 1. Wsb 1988,
Harrassowitz. xi-94 p.; 3 pl.; 4 foldout facsimiles. 3-447-02784-3.

g515 *Otten* Heinrich, Ebla in der hurritisch-hethitischen Bilingue aus
Boğazköy: → 707, Wirtschaft 1986/8, 291s.

g516 *Popko* Mathias, ⊕ The Hittites and Ahhiyawa; state of research:
Meander 43 (1988) 221-8.

T8.3 **Ephesus.**

g517 **Atalay** Erol, Weibliche Gewandstatuen im 2. Jahrhundert n. Chr. aus
ephesischen Werkstätten: Denkschrift ph/h. W 1988, Österr. Akad. 104 p.
40 pl. [Mundus 24,131].

g518 **Bammer** Anton, Das Heiligtum der Artemis von Ephesos: Welt der
Wunder, Wunder der Welt 1, 1984 → 65,b466; 2,b215; Sch 270;
3-201-01260-2: ᴿBO 45 (1988) 186-9 (J. M. *Hemelrijk*: badly organised, a
failure).

g519 *a) Bammer* Anton, Neue Grabungen an der Zentralbasis des Artemision
von Ephesos; – *b) Muss* Ulrike, *Büyükkolanci* Mustafa, Archaische
Freiplastik aus Ephesos: JhÖs 58B (1988) 2-31; 39 fig. / 36-46; 9 fig.

g520 **Elliger** W. Ephesos 1985 → 2,b217: ᴿHZ 245 (1987) 411s (Helga *Botermann*).
   Jenny-Kappers T., Muttergöttin und Gottesmutter in Ephesos; von Artemis
zu Maria 1986 → 9823.

g521 *Langmann* G., Grabungen 1987, Ephesos: JhÖs 58B (1988) 7-10.

g522 *a) Muss* Ulrike, Silen und Gigant auf dem ephesischen Simenfries; – *b)*
Bammer Anton, Ephesos in der Bronzezeit: JhÖsAk 57H (1986s) 29-38 /
57B (1986s) 1-40.

g523 *Öziyiğit* Ömer, Spätarchaische Funde im Museum von Ephesos und die Lage von Alt-Ephesos: IstMit 38 (1988) 83-96.

g524 *Runia* David T., Philosophical heresiography; evidence in two Ephesian inscriptions [*Horsley* G. 1979/87, 70-73]: ZPapEp 72 (1988) 241-3.

g525 **Thür** Hilke, Das Hadrianstor in Ephesos: Forschungen 11/1. Wien 1988, Österr. Akad. 128 p.; 179 fig.; 74 pl.; 16 plans [Mundus 24,134].

g526 *Vetters* Hermann, Ephesos, vorläufiger Grabungsbericht 1986/7: Anzeiger Wien 125 (1988) 85-98 (-126); 19 fig.; xxv pl. + 11 color.

T8.4 **Pergamum.**

g527 *a) Behr* Doris, Neue Ergebnisse zur pergamenischen Westabhang-keramik; – *b) Raeck* Wulf, Zur hellenistischen Bebauung der Akropolis von Pergamon: IstMitt 38 (1988) 97-178; 25 fig. / 201-236; 11 fig.

g527* *Chamoux* François, Pergame et les Galates: RÉG 101 (1988) 492-500.

g528 **Filgis** Meinrad N., *Radt* Wolfgang, *al.*, Die Stadtgrabung 1. Das Heroon: Altertümer von Pergamon 15, 1986 → 3,e951: RAJA 92 (1988) 299 (R. F. *Townsend*).

g529 *Kádár* Zoltan, L'importance religieuse et artistique du culte d'Asklé-pios-Aesculapius sur les médailles de l'époque de Caracalla à Pergamon: AcClasDebrecen 22 (1986) 31-35.

g530 *Karagöz* Şehrazad, *al.*, Ein römischer Grabbau auf dem Niyazitepe bei Pergamon: IstMitt 36 (1986) 99-160; 16 fig. pl. 28-49; foldouts 3-5.

g531 *Mellink* Machteld J., Pergamon: → g500, AJA 92 (1988) 126-8; fig. 29-35.

g532 *Radt* W., Pergamon 1987: AnSt 38 (1988) 202-5.

g533 *Radt* Wolfgang, Pergamon, Vorbericht über die Kampagne 1987: *a)* ArchAnz (1988) 461-485; 34 fig.; – *b)* TürkArk 27 (1988) 29-52; 53-67 = 37 fig.

g534 **Schalles** Hans-Joachim, Untersuchungen zur Kulturpolitik der perga-menischen Herrscher im dritten Jahrhundert vor Christus: IstFor 36, 1985 → 3,e960: RAJA 92 (1988) 142s (E. E. *Rice*).

g535 **Schalles** Hans-Joachim, Der Pergamonaltar zwischen Bewertung und Verwertbarkeit 1986 → 3,e959: REirene 25 (1988) 138-140 (M.*Kunze*).

g536 **Schultz** Sabine, Antike Münzen; griechische Prägung; Einführung in die Ausstellung im Pergamonmuseum I. oB 1984, Staatliche Museen. 70 p.; 46 fig.

T8.6 *Situs Anatoliae,* **Turkey sites** in alphabetical order.

g537 *Acem*: *Özten* Aliye, ❶ Les moulages en pierre à Acemhöyük; Belleten 203 (1988) 393-406 + 28 fig.

g538 *Alalach*: → 804, NBL Lfg 1 (1988) 71-73 (M. *Dietrich*, O. *Loretz*).

g539 *Alahan*: **Gough** Mary, Alahan 1985 → 2,b229; 3,e964: RStRicOrCr 9 (1986) 227-231 (Rossana *Avruscio*).

g540 *Amorium* [between Gordion and Yalvaç, near Sangarios source] 1987, a preliminary survey: AnSt 38 (1988) 175-184; 4 fig. (map); pl. XXI-XXIV (R. M. *Harrison*).

g541 *Andrinopolis*: Hadrianopolis (250 k NW Istanbul): → 790, DHGE 22,131 (1988) 1442-1466 (D. *Stiernon*).

g542 *Anemurium* 1987 [Roman]: AnSt 38 (1988) 191s (J. *Russell*).

g543 *Antalya*: *Grassi* Giulia, Precisazioni sulla Panaghia di Antalya: → 703, Milion 1986/8, 83-97 + VII pl.

g544 *Aphrodisias*: **Erim** Kenan T., Aphrodisias, city of Venus Aphrodite 1986 ➤ 3,e970; 33 fig. + 192 color. $45: ᴿAJA 92 (1988) 303s (F. K. *Yegul*); Archaeology 41,1 (1988) 72 (Nancy H. *Ramage*).

g545 *Erim* Kenan T., Recherches récentes et découvertes à Aphrodisias de Carie: CRAI (1988) 734-757; 17 fig.

g546 *Campbell* S. D., Armchair pilgrims; ampullae from Aphrodisias in Caria: MedSt 50 (1988) 539-545 [< RSPT 72,647].

g547 **Reynolds** Joyce, *Tannenbaum* Robert, Jews and Godfearers at Aphrodisias; Greek inscriptions with commentary: Pg Sup 12, ➤ 2,b236; 3,e974: ᴿRÉLat 66 (1988) 342-4 (O. *Munnich*).

g548 *Marinoni* Elio, Silla, Delfi e l'Afrodite di Afrodisia; per una interpretazione di APPIANO, B.C. I 97, 451-55: ➤ 3,57, Mem. GATTI C. 1987, 193-237.

g549 *Assos*: **Finster-Hotz** U., Der Bauschmuck des Athenatempels von Assos; Studien zur Ikonographie: Archaeologica 34. R 1984, Bretschneider. 164 p.; XXIII pl. – ᴿAcArchH 40 (1988) 334s (M. *Szabó*); AntClas 57 (1988) 578s (D. *Viviers*).

g551 *Johnston* Alan, *Wescoat* Bonna, An inscribed capital from the temple of Athena at Assos: EpAnat 11 (1988) 1-8; pl. 1-2.

g552 *Beşik*-Tepe 1985-6: ArchAnz (1988) 391-404 (M. *Korfmann*).

g553 *Cavi Tarlası 1983-4*: IstMitt 38 (1988) 1-35; 10 fig. (A. von *Wickede*, S. *Herbordt*); 37-62, Tierreste (J. *Schäffer*, J. *Boessneck*).

g554 *Carchemish*: *Hawkins* J. D., Kuzi-Tešub and the 'great kings' of Karkamiš: AnSt 38 (1988) 99-108.

g555 *Çatal*: **Caselli** Giovanni, The everyday life of a Stone Age trader [in Çatal Hüyük 6000 B.C., archaeologically-researched, largely in explanation of several reconstruction-paintings by G. Fornari]. L 1986, Macdonald. 28 p. £5. 0-536-13053-3. – ᴿAntiquity 62 (1988) 710-3 (N. *Merriman*).

g556 *Cayönü*: **Çambel** Halet, *al.*, The joint Istanbul-Chicago Universities' prehistoric research in southeastern Anatolia I. İstanbul 1980, Univ. Edebiyet Fak. 327 p.; 49 pl. – ᴿRArchéol (1988) 120 (J.-L.*Huot*: architecture spectaculaire).

g557 *Clazomenae* (40 k W Izmir): *Beek* R. van, *Beelen* J., Excavations in Klazomenai: Babesch 63 (1988) 138-140; 2 fig.

g558 *Commagene*: **Hoepfner** Wolfram, Das Hierothesion des Königs Mithradates I. Kallinikos von Kommagene nach den Ausgrabungen von 1963 bis 1967: IstFor 35, 1983 ➤ 1,e315: ᴿZDMG 138 (1988) 368-370 (H.-G. *Buchholz*).

g559 *Cremna*: *Mitchell* Stephen, *Waelkens* Marc, Cremna and Sagalassus 1987: AnSt 38 (1988) 53-65; 2 fig.; pl. I-VIII.

g560 *Demirci*: **Korfmann** Manfred, Demircihüyük I, 1983 ➤ 65,b490; 1,e325: ᴿBO 45 (1988) 680-4 (L. C. *Thissen*).

g561 *a*) **Kull** Brigitte, Die mittelbronzezeitliche Siedlung; – *b*) **Efe** Turan, Demircihüyük II/2, Die Keramik 2 C; die frühbronzezeitliche Keramik der jüngeren Phasen (ab Brandphase H). Mainz 1988, von Zabern. 350 p.; 300 fig.; 56 pl. / 200 p.; 100 fig.; 76 pl. [Mundus 24,131].

g562 **Seeher** [➤ 3,e981] Jürgen, Demircihüyük 3/1 Keramik 1987: ᴿMundus 24 (1988) 201s (K. *Schippmann* spells 'Seher').

g563 *Göreme*: **Ötüken** Yıldız, Göreme: Introducing Turkey 3. Ankara 1987, Başbakanlık. 63 p.; 27 fig.

g564 **Rodley** Lyn, Cave monasteries of Byzantine Cappadocia 1985 → 2,b248; 3,e985: [R]ByZ 81 (1988) 82-85 (Nicole *Thierry*); HeythJ 29 (1988) 517s (J. A. *Munitiz*); RÉByz 45 (1987) 268s (J. *Darrouzès*).

g565 *Jolivet-Lévy* Catherine, *Öztürk* Emre, Nouvelles découvertes en Cappadoce; les églises de Yükşekli: CahArch 35 (1987) 113-141; 25 fig.

g566 *Schiemenz* Günter P., Maria als Christusmutter in Güzelyurt: IstMitt 38 (1988) 315-342; 5 fig.

g567 *Thierry* Nicole, *a*) La nécropole de Göreme; – *b*) Avanos; – *c*) Nouvelles découvertes en Cappadoce: DossHA 121 (1987) 50-55 / 30-35 [26-29, 80-96 *al.*] / 22-25.

g568 *Fothergill* Dorothy, Pages from a Cappadocian diary: Month 249 (1988) 764-8; 2 phot.

g569 *Gordion*: **Young** Rodney S., *al.*, Three great early tumuli: Gordion Final Report 1 / Mus. Mg. 43, 1981 → 64,d54; 1,e332. – [R]BO 45 (1988) 190 (R. M. *Boehmer*).

g570 *Gritille* (Euphrates NE Carchemish) 1981-4: Expedition 27,1 (Ph 1985) 10-24; 22 fig. (Mary M. *Voigt*).

g571 *Halicarnassus*: [*Jeppesen* K.] **Luttrell** A., The Mausolleion at Halicarnassus II [1. The written sources] 2. The later history...: Jutland Archaeol. Soc. 15,2. Aarhus 1986, Univ. 222 p.; 16 fig.; 41 pl. – [R]ClasR 102 (1988) 175-7 (S. *Hornblower*, very severe and detailed on Jeppesen's part).

g572 *Ḥarran*: *Archi* Alfonso, Ḥarran in the III Millennium B.C.: UF 20 (1988) 1-8.

g573 *Esse* Douglas, Harran; city of Abraham and the moon god: CanadMesop 8 (1984) 5-13.

g574 *Laureano* Pietro, Harran; nel tempio dei sette pianeti: ArchViva 7,2 (1988) 52-57; color. ill.

g575 *Hierapolis*: *a*) 1987 (agora, theatre, N. necropolis): AnSt 38 (1988), 198 (Daria *de Barnardi Ferrero*); –*b*) theater cleared 1986 by Daria Ferraro: → g500, AJA 92 (1988) 130s, fig. 36 (M. *Mellink*).

g576 **Ritti** Tullia, Hierapolis, scavi e ricerche I. Fonti letterarie ed epigrafiche: Archaeologica 53, 1985 → 2,b252; 3,e992: [R]RPLH 62,1 (1988) 151s (C. *Dobias-Lalou*).

g577 **d'Andria** Francesco, *Ritti* Tullia, Hierapolis 2, Le sculture del teatro, 1985, Bretschneider: → 2,b252: [R]BonnJbb 188 (1988) 616-9 (G. *Koch*); RBgPg 66 (1988) 192-4 (F. *Baratte*).

g578 *İkiz*: **Alkim** U. Bahadir, *al.*, İkiztepe I, The first and second seasons excavations (1974-5) [also ❶]: Yayınları 5/39. Ankara 1988, Türk Tarih Kurumu. 975-16-0030-8.

g579 *İstanbul*: **Harrison** R. M., Excavations at Saraçhane in Istanbul I, 1986 → 3,e998; $90: [R]AJA 92 (1988) 458s (R. *Hodges*).

g579* **Mainstone** R. J., Hagia Sophia; architecture, structure and liturgy of Justinian's great church. L 1988, Thames & H. 288 p.; 305 fig. £35 [JHS 109, 273, Lyn *Rodley*].

g580 **Chaisemartin** Nathalie de, *Örgen* Emel, Les documents sculptés de Silahtarağa [W-bank Golden Horn; 400 A.D.]: Mémoires 46. P 1984, RCiv. 109 p.; 50 pl. F130. – [R]BonnJbb 188 (1988) 619s (Guntram *Koch*); Gnomon 60 (1988) 61-65 (R. *Fleischer*: invites to further study, along with Copenhagen group).

g581 *Roodenberg* J. J., İlipinar in the prehistory of Northwest Anatolia (Kadiköy): Palaeohistoria 29 (1987) 203-210; 4 fig.

g582 *Karatepe*: *Jasink* Anna M., [Karatepe] Danuna e Adana; alcune osservazioni sulla Cilicia: MesopT 23 (1988) 91-104.

g583 **Karatut** Mevkii [Euphrates 10 k N Samsat]: Excavations and perspectives on the Uruk/Jemdet Nasr expansion: Akkadica 56 (1988) 1-33 + 9 fig.; map (G. M. *Schwartz*).

g584 **Kültepe**: *Özgüç* Tahsin, Kültepe and Anatolian archaeology — relating to the Old Assyrian period: ➤ 760, Anatolian 1983/8, 1-9 + 13 fig.

g585 **Kurban** höyük excavations, 1984: TurkArk 27 (1988) 15-21; 22-27 = 8 fig. (L. *Marfoe*).

g586 **Limyra**: *Borchhardt* Jürgen, al., Die Felsgräber... von Limyra: JhÖs 58B (1988) 73-154; 46 fig.

g587 **Magnesia**: *Hamiaux* Marianne, Les éléments d'architecture de Magnésie du Méandre conservés au Musée du Louvre: RArchéol (1988) 83-108; 31 fig.

g588 **Miletus** 1987: IstMitt 38 (1988) 251-290; 22 fig.; pl. 24-37; foldouts 3-5 (W. *Müller-Wiener, al.*); 309-313, Senatsrede Marc Aurels (P. *Herrmann*).

g589 **Işık** Fahri, Ein wiedergefundener Girlandensarkophag in Milet: IstMitt 36 (1986) 161-181; pl. 50-54.

g590 ᴱ**Müller-Wiener** Wolfgang, Milet 1899-1980; IstMit Beih 31, 1980/6 ➤ 2,568*; 3,f8: ᴿBonnJbb 188 (1988) 556-9 (Doris *Pinkwart*).

g591 *Müller-Wiener* W., Milet 1976-1986; Ergebnisse aus 10 Jahren Ausgrabungstätigkeit: AntWelt 19,1 (1988) 31-42; 19 fig.

g592 **Mopsuestia**: *Dagron* G., Two documents concerning mid sixth-century Mopsuestia [< ᶠ*Charanis* P. 1980]: ➤ 175*, Romanité chrétienne 1984 VI, p. 19-30.

g593 **Oenoanda** Licinnii family: *Kearsley* R. A., A leading family of Cibyra and some Asiarchs of the first century: AnSt 38 (1988) 43-51.

g594 **Priene**: **Carter** Joseph C., The sculpture of the sanctuary of Athena Polias at Priene 1983 ➤ 1,e345: ᴿClasR 102 (1988) 347-9 (C. E. *Vafopoulou-Richardson*).

g595 *Jong* J. J. de, The temple of Athena Polias at Priene and the temple of Hemithea at Kastabos: Babesch 63 (1988) 129-137.

g596 **Sakçagözü**: *French* D. H., *Summers* G. D., Sakçagözü material [excavated 1908-11, *Garstang* J.; 1949, *Waechter* J.] in the Gaziantep museum: AnSt 38 (1988) 71-84; 8 fig.

g597 **Samosata**: *Özgüç* Nimet, ✪ Fouilles de Samosate en 1987: Belleten 202 (1988) 291-4; 3 color phot.; foldout.

g598 **Sardis** 1984/5: ➤ 459, ASOR 1982-5/8, 13-54; 33 fig. / 55-92; 32 fig. (C. H. *Greenewalt, al.*).

g599 Sardis: ➤ 801, ISBEnc³ 4 (1988s) 336s (R. *North*).

g600 **Brill** Robert H., **Cahill** Nicholas D., A red opaque glass from Sardis and some thoughts on red opaques in general: JGlass 30 (1988) 16-27.

g601 *Gusmani* Roberto, 'Steinmetzmarken' aus Sardis: Kadmos 27 (1988) 27-34; 2 fig.; II pl.

g602 **Balcer** Jack M., Sparda [... Sardis] by the Bitter Sea; imperial interaction in Western Anatolia: Brown JudSt 52, 1984 ➤ 65,b523; 1,e353: ᴿGnomon 60 (1988) 544-7 (J. *Wiesehöfer*).

g603 **Selge**: **Machatschek** Alois, *Schwarz* Mario, Bauforschungen in Selge [Pisidien]: Tituli Asiae Minoris Egbd 9 / Denkschrift ph/h 152, 1981 ➤ 65,b521; DM 77: ᴿAntClas 57 (1988) 579-583 (M. *Waelkens*).

g604 **Silifke**: *Eyice* Semavi, Ricerche e scoperte nella regione di Silifke nella Turchia meridionale: ➤ 703, Milion 1986/8, 15-33 + XXIII pl.

g605 **Smyrna**: ➤ 801, ISBEnc³ 4 (1988) 555s (R. *North*).

g606 **Akurgal** Ekrem, Alt-Smyrna I. Wohnschichten und Athenatempel: Yayınları 40, 1983 ➤ 64,d79; $20: ᴿGnomon 60 (1988) 249-253 (W. *Schiering*).

g607 **Strobilus**:   *Foss* Clive,   Strobilos [known only since 724 Willibald pilgrimage; site on coast east of Bodrum contains nothing assignable to 'the Dark Ages'] and related sites: AnSt 38 (1988) 147-174; map; pl. XIII-XX.

g608 *Tarsus*: ➤ 801, ISBEnc³ 4 (1988) 734-6 (C. J. *Hemer*).

g609 **Taş Kule**:   *Cahill* Nicholas,   Taş Kule; a Persian-period tomb near Phokaia [60 k S Bergama]: AJA 92 (1988) 481-501; 17 fig.

g610 **Taskun Kale**: **McNicoll** Anthony,   Taskun Kale, Keban rescue excavations, Eastern Anatolia: British Inst. Ankara Mg 6 / BAR-Inst 168. Ox 1983.   266 p.; 130 fig.; 40 pl. £15. – ᴿBInstArch sup 24 (1987) 28s (T. *Watkins*).

g611 **Thermos**:   *Stucky* Rolf A.,   Die Tonmetope mit den drei sitzenden Frauen von Thermos; ein Dokument hellenistischer Denkmalpflege: AntKu 31,2 (1988) 71-78; 2 fig. pl. 16-17.

g612 **Thyatira**:   ➤ 801. ISBEnc³ 4 (1988) 846 (R. *North*) [424-6, The Seven Churches, *Hemer* C. J.].

g613 **Tilki**: **Korfmann** Manfred, Tilkitepe 1982 ➤ 63,d576 ... 3,f35:   ᴿBO 45 (1988) 407-9 (P. *Akkermans*).

g614 **Troja**: **Séfériadès** Michael,   Troie I; matériaux pour l'étude des sociétés du Nord-Est égéen au début du Bronze Ancien: Cah 15, 1985 ➤ 1,e360; 3,f37; F 111. – ᴿPraehZts 63 (1988) 123-5 (P. Z. *Spanos*).

g615 ᴱ**Mellink** Machteld J.,   Troy and the Trojan War [Bryn Mawr symposium 1984] 1986 ➤ 3,837:   ᴿAJA 92 (1988) 295 (Karen P. *Foster*); BO 45 (1988) 668-680 (T. R. *Bryce*).

g616 **Wood** Michael,   In search of the Trojan War.   L 1987, BBC Books. 272 p.; 21 colour. pl. A$28.   0-563-20579-2 [AncHRes 19, 100-2, H. *Ackland*]. – ᴿAcAntH 31 (1985-8) 176-8 (L. M. *Young*).

g617 *Coindoz* Michel, Le cheval de Troie [analyse des bandes dessinés, 'petit Mickey', comic-book, de Jacques Martin chez Casterman; ... armements ... défensifs]: Archéologie 239 (Dijon 1988) 52-65.

g618 *Latacz* Joachim,   Neues von Troja: Gymnasium 95 (1988) 385-413; pl. XVII-XXIV.

g619 *Bloedow* Edmond F.,   The Trojan War and Late Helladic III C: PraehZts 63 (1988) 23-52; 8 fig.

g620 *Traill* David A.,   Hisarlik, 31 May, 1873, and the discovery of 'Priam's Treasure': Boreas 11 (Münster 1988) 227-234.

g621 *Cook* J. M.,   Cities in and around the Troad: AnBritAth 83 (1988) 8-19; pl. I; map.

g622 **Yalvaç**: *Saffrey* H. D.,   Un nouveau duovir à Antioche de Pisidie: AnSt 38 (1988) 67-69.

T8.9 **Armenia, Urarṭu.**

g623 *Blockley* Roger C.,   The division of Armenia between the Romans and the Persians at the end of the fourth century A.D.:   Historia 36 (1987) 222-234.

g624 **Chahin** M.,   The kingdom of Armenia [... Urartu]. L 1987, Croom Helm. xviii-332 p.; 16 pl.; 4 maps. £35. – ᴿBSOAS 51 (1988) 570s (A. E. *Redgate*: 2/3 on Urartu); JRAS (1988) 408s (T. A. *Sinclair*).

g625 **Chahin** M.,   Some legendary kings of Armenia [... Urarṭu]; can they be linked to authentic history?²: Occ.P.5.   CM 1986, Society for Armenian Studies.   47 + xx p. – ᴿJRAS (1988) 409s (T. A. *Sinclair*).

g626 *Drödemüller* Hans-Peter,   Der kurdisch-armenische Raum; eine Einführung: Gymnasium 84 (1987) 385-420; 6 maps; pl. IX-XVI.

g627 **Eichler** Seyyare, Götter, Genien und Mischwesen in der urartäischen Kunst 1984 ➤ 65,b536 ... 3,f46: ^RRAss 82 (1988) 92 (P. *Amiet*).

g627* ^E**Haas** Volkert, Das Reich Urartu 1984/6 ➤ 2,557; 3,f48: ^RAr-KulturG 70 (1988) 511-3 (H.-J. *Kellner*).

g628 **Kévorkian** R. H., *Mahé* J.-P., *al.*, Arménie; 3000 ans d'histoire. Marseille 1988, Maison Arménienne. 394 p.; 237 fig.

g629 **Kleiss** W., Bastam I, 1979 ➤ 61,y560 ... 1,e372: ^ROLZ 83 (1988) 597-9 ([G.] R. H. *Wright*).

g630 **Kleiss** Wolfram, *al.*, Bastam II; Ausgrabungen in den Urartäischen Anlagen 1977-1978: Teheraner Forschungen 5. 329 p. ill. 3-7861-1337-8.

g631 *Kleiss* W., Aspekte urartäischer Architektur: ➤ 4, ^FAMIET P. = IrAnt 23 (1988) 181-191 + 27 fig.

g632 **Slattery** David J., The northern frontier of Urartu; economic and administrative implications: diss. Victoria Univ. Manchester 1987. 230 p. BRD-80560. – DissA 49 (1988s) 131-A.

g633 **Zimansky** Paul E., Ecology and empire; the structure of the Urartian state: SAOC 41, 1985 ➤ 1,e371 ... 3,f51: ^RJAOS 108 (1988) 163-5 (M. N. van *Loon*); JNES 47 (1988) 219-221 (L. D. *Levine*); OLZ 83 (1988) 416-8 (R.-B. *Wartke*).

---

g634 *Poulter* Andrew, Nicopolis ad Istrum, Bulgaria; an interim report on the excavations 1985-7: AntiqJ 68,1 (1988) 69-89.

т9.1 **Cyprus.**

g635 *a) Baurain* Claude, Le rôle de Chypre dans la fondation de Carthage; – *b) Bisi* Anna M., Chypre et les premiers temps de Carthage: ➤ 754, Carthago 1986/8, 15-28 / 29-41.

g635* *Cook* Valerie, Cyprus and the outside world during the transition from the Bronze Age to the Iron Age: OpAth 17 (1988) 13-32; 7 fig.

g636 **Decaudin** Antoinette J., Les antiquités chypriotes dans les collections publiques françaises. Nicosie/Lyon 1987, Leventis/Maison de l'Orient. XX-265 p., XCIII pl. [RB 96, 443, J.-M. de *Tarragon*].

g637 **Iacovou** Maria, The pictorial pottery of eleventh century B.C. Cyprus [diss. 1984 ➤ 1,e375]: SIMA 79. Göteborg 1988, Åström. xii-90 p.; 92 fig. (map). 91-86098-59-4.

g638 **Karageorghis** V., *al.*, ⊖ Archaîa Kypriakē technē. Larnaca 1985, Pierides. 282 p.; ill. = L'art chypriote antique au Musée de la Fondation Piéridès, 1986. – ^RRArchéol (1988) 124s (A. *Hermary*).

g639 **Karageorghis** V., The archaeology of Cyprus; the ninety years after [J. L.] MYRES. L 1987, Leopard's Head. 15 p.; 25 pl. – ^RRÉAnc 90 (1988) 447s (J. *Pouilloux*).

g640 *Karageorghis* V., Chronique des fouilles et découvertes archéologiques en Chypre en 1987: BCH 112 (1988) 793-805.

g641 *Knapp* A. Bernard, Hoards D'Oeuvres; of metals and men on Bronze Age Cyprus: OxJArch 7 (1988) 147-177; 4 fig.

g642 *Meyer* Laure, L'art de Chypre dans l'antiquité [galérie rénovée du British Museum]: Archéologia 233 (Dijon 1985) 12-17; ill.

g643 *Sørensen* Lone W., Greek pottery from the geometric to the archaic period found on Cyprus: ➤ 733, Acta Hyperborea 1987/8, 12-32.

g644 **Stylianou** A. & J., The painted churches of Cyprus; treasures of Byzantine art ^{2rev}. L 1985, Trigraph/Leventis. 517 p.; 276 fig. + 20 color.; map. – ^RByzantion 58 (1988) 540-3 (Lydie *Hadermann-Misguich*).

g645 **Tatton-Brown** Victoria, Ancient Cyprus: British Museum. L/CM 1988, Museum/Harvard Univ. 72 p.; 83 fig. $9 pa. 0-7141-1686-6 / US 0-674-03307-8.

g646 *Alasia*: **Merrillees** R. S., Alashia revisited: CahRB 22, 1987 → 3,f64: ^RAegyptus 68 (1988) 280 (Anna *Passoni dell'Acqua*).

g647 *Nibbi* Alessandra, Hatiba of Alashiya and a correction to my proposed area for that country [Timsah-Suez canal, not Cyprus]: DiscEg 5 (1986) 47-54; 4 maps.

g648 *Amathous*: **Queyrel** Anne, Amathonte 4, Les figurines hellénistiques de terre cuite: Ét. Chyp. 10. P 1988, de Boccard. 155 p.; 85 pl.

g649 *Vandenabeele* Frieda, Amathonte; le chantier sous la porte de l'Acropole: BCH 112 (1988) 519-530; 29 fig.

g650 *Hala Sultan Tekke*: *Åström* Paul, Hala Sultan Tekke – an international harbour town of the Late Cypriote Bronze Age: OpAth 16 (1986) 7-17; 24 fig.

g651 *Kalavassos*: *Flourentzos* P., Tombs at Kalavassos; new cippi types and rare pottery forms: Levant 20 (1988) 235-8; 9 phot.

g652 *Kourion*: ^E**Soren** David, The sanctuary of Apollo Hylates at Kourion, Cyprus: Excavations at Kourion 1. Tucson 1987, Univ. Arizona. ix-340 p.; 195 pl. $35 [RelStR 15,72, D. E. *Smith*]. 0-8165-1041-5. – ^RClasR 102 (1988) 445s (E. J. *Peltenburg*); ClasW 82 (1988s) 214 (Ann O. *Koloski-Ostrow*: first of five projected reports).

g653 *Lemba*: 1986: Levant 20 (1988) 231-5; 3 fig. (E. J. *Peltenburg*).

g654 **Peltenburg** E. J., Excavations at Lemba I: SIMA 70/1, 1985 → 1,e398; 3,f75: ^RGnomon 60 (1988) 553s (H. *Matthäus*).

g655 *Paphos*: **Sztetyłło** Zofia, *a*) Nea Paphos, I. Les timbres céramiques (1965-1973). Wsz 1976. 111 p.; 393 fig. – ^RZDMG 138 (1988) 365-8 (H.-G. *Buchholz*); – *b*) Timbres céramiques des fouilles polonaises à Nea Paphos en 1978: → 12, ^FBERNHARD M.-L. 1983, 365-370.

g656 *Peltenburg* E. J., Prähistorische Religion in Zypern; der rituelle Hortfund von Kissonerga [12 k N Paphos]: AntWelt 19,3 (1988) 2-15; 23 (color.) fig.

g657 *a*) *Bikai* Patricia M., Trade networks in the Early Iron age; the Phoenicians at Palaepaphos; – *b*) *Rupp* David W., Vive le roi; the emergence of the state in Iron Age Cyprus; – *c*) *Fox* W. A., *al.*, Investigations of ancient metallurgical sites in the Paphos district, Cyprus: → 3,837, ^E*Rupp*, Western Cyprus 1986/7, 125-8 / 147-161 + 6 maps / 169-177; 2 maps, 4 fig.

g658 *Salamis*: *Rupp* David W., The 'royal' tombs at Salamis (Cyprus); ideological messages of power and authority: JMeditArch 1,1 (1988) 111-139.

T9.3   *Graecia*, **Greece** – mainland sites in alphabetical order.

g659 Archaiologikon Deltion 35 (1980) B-1, Chronika ⊙. Athena 1988. 345 p. 204 pl., 4 foldouts. – 36 (1981) B-2, Chronika ⊙. Athena 1988. 438 p.; 318 pl.

g660 *Catling* H. W., Archaeology in Greece, 1987-88; [JHS] Archaeological Reports 34 (1988) 3-85 [86-104, Knossos IV, 1978-82, *Warren* P. M.].

g661 *Papachatzis* Nicolaos, Chronique des fouilles: Kernos 1 (1988) 237-243.

g662 **Snodgrass** Anthony M., An archaeology of Greece; the present state and future scope of a discipline [Sather Classical Lectures 53] 1987 ➤ 3,f86: ᴿAntiquity 62 (1988) 795-7 (J. *Boardman*).

g663 **Thylander** Hilding, Den grekiska världen (Svenska Humanistiska förbundet 1985). Sto 1986, Almqvist & W. 546 p.; 312 pl.; 8 maps. 91-22-00795-4. – ᴿFornvännen 83 (1988) 117-120 (H. *Montgomery*).

g664 *Argos* 1987: BCH 112 (1988) 697-720; 29 fig. (Anne *Pariente, al.*).

g665 *Guggisberg* Martin, Terrakotten von Argos; ein Fundkomplex aus dem Theater: BCH 112 (1988) 167-234.

g666 *Asine*: **Nordquist** G.C., A Middle Helladic village, Asine ... 1987 ➤ 3,f91: ᴿJHS 108 (1988) 256 (S. *Dietz*).

g667 *Athenae*: **Brommer** Frank, Der Parthenonfries, Katalog und Untersuchung 1977 ➤ 64,a892: ᴿGnomon 60 (1988) 178-180 (Madeleine *Gisler*, franç.; justifiant la recension tardive).

g668 *Mantis* Alexandros, Neue Fragmente von Parthenonskulpturen: ➤ 751*b*, Klassische Plastik 1985/6, 71-76; pl. 102-6.

g669 **Berger** Ernst, Der Parthenon in Basel; Dokumentation zu den Metopen 1986 ➤ 3,f98: ᴿGnomon 60 (1988) 57-60 (G. B. *Waywell*, Eng.); RBgPg 66 (1988) 208-210 (P. *Gros*).

g670 ᴱ**Berger** Ernst, Parthenon-Kongress Basel, Referate und Berichte, 1982/4 ➤ 65,b587: ᴿGnomon 60 (1988) 625-631 (B. *Fehr*).

g671 *Tréheux* Jacques [*Peppas-Delmousou* Dina], Observations sur les inventaires du 'Brauronion' de l'Acropole d'Athènes: ➤ 698, ᶠTRÉHEUX J., Comptes 1986/8, 347-355 [323-346].

g672 *Harris* Diane, Nikokrates of Kolonos, metalworker to the Parthenon treasures: Hesperia 57 (1988) 329-337; pl. 88.

g673 **Hitchens** Christopher, *al.*, The Elgin marbles; should they be returned to Greece? L 1987, Chatto & W. 137 p.; 31 fig. £13. 0-7011-3163-2. – ᴿAntiquity 62 (1988) 181s (M. *Robertson*).

g674 *Shapiro* H.A., [PAUSANIAS 1,27,9s] The Marathonian bull on the Athenian akropolis [and efforts to recognize it in discovered fragments]: AJA 92 (1988) 373-382; 9 fig.

g675 **Muss** Ulrike, *Schubert* Charlotte, Die Akropolis von Athen. Graz 1988, Akademische-DV. 266 p.; 133 fig. 3-201-01390-0.

g676 **Camp** John M., The Athenian agora; excavations in the heart of classical Athens 1986 ➤ 2,b324; 3,f97; 0-500-39021-5. – ᴿClasW 82 (1988s) 128s (Susan I. *Rotroff*).

g677 *Harrison* Evelyn B., 'Theseum' east frieze; color traces and attachment cuttings: Hesperia 57 (1988) 339-349.

g678 *Mountjoy* Penelope A., (*Hankey* Vronwy), LH III C Late versus Submycenaean; the Kerameikos Pompeion cemetery reviewed: JbDAI 103 (1988) 1-33 (-37); 25 fig. (incl. map and 2 foldouts).

g679 *Hedrick* Charles W.ᴶ, The temple and cult of Apollo Patroos in Athens: AJA 92 (1988) 185-210; 7 fig.

g680 *Langdon* Merle K., Hymettiana II; [Athens, Zeze] An ancient quarry on Mt. Hymettos: AJA 92 (1988) 75-83; 9 fig.

g681 *Thompson* Homer A., The impact of Roman architects and architecture on Athens, 170 B.C. - A.D. 170: ➤ 454, Roman architecture 1987, 1-17.

g682 *Athos*: *Mylonas* Paul M., La trapeza de la Grande Lavra au Mont Athos: CahArch 35 (1987) 143-157; 15 fig.

g683 *Berbati*: **Homberg** Erik J., A Mycenean chamber tomb near Berbati in Argolis: Acta Soc. Sc. Lit. Gothob, humaniora 21. Göteborg 1983,

Univ.-Bibliothek. 54 p.; 29 fig.; 1 pl. – ᴿRArchéol (1988) 127 (P. *Darcque*: ignores SAFLUND G. 1965; ÅKERSTRÖM A. 1967).

g684 **Åkerström** Å., Berbati 2., The pictorial pottery: Svenska Institutet i Athen 36. Sto 1987, Åström. 140 pl.; 104 fig.; 53 pl.; plan. Sk 400. – ᴿClasR 102 (1988) 446s (R. L. N. *Barber*).

g685 *Corinthus*: **Biers** Jane C., The great bath on the Lechaion Road: Corinth excavations 17, 1985 ➤ 2,b337: ᴿClasR 102 (1988) 446 (A. *Farrington*).

g686 *Pfaff* Christopher A., A geometric well at Corinth; well 1981-6: Hesperia 57 (1988) 21-80; 39 fig.; pl. 27-32.

g687 **Salmon** J. B., Wealthy Corinth 1984 ➤ 1,5184... 3,f106: ᴿClasW 80 (1986s) 224s (J. G. *Pedley*); Mnemosyne 41 (1988) 223s (H. W. *Singer*).

g688 *McPhee* Ian, *Pemberton* Elizabeth, *Ou pantós esti Kórinthos* ['Corinth is not for everybody' wrongly deciphered on Attic red-figured skyphos]: ZPapEp 73 (1988) 89s.

g689 *Morgan* Catherine A., Corinth, the Corinthian Gulf and western Greece during the eighth century B.C.: AnBritAth 83 (1988) 313-338; 5 fig.

g690 *Williams* Charles K.ᴵᴵ, *Zervos* Orestes H., Corinth, 1987; south of Temple E and east of the theater: Hesperia 57 (1988) 95-146; 17 fig.; pl. 33-44.

g691 *Williams* C. K., The refounding of Corinth; some Roman religious attitudes: ➤ 454, Roman architecture 1987, 26-37.

g692 *Delphi*: *a*) *Bousquet* Jean, La reconstruction du temple d'Apollon à Delphes au IVᵉ siècle avant J.-C.; – *b*) *Picard* Olivier, Les monnaies des comptes de Delphes à 'apousia'; – *c*) *Marchetti* Patrick, Les cours de l'attique et de l'éginétique et les rapports or-argent dans les comptes de Delphes: ➤ 698, Comptes 1986/8, 13-25 / 91-100; 1 fig. / 103-110.

g693 **Daux** G., *Hansen* E., Topographie et architecture; le trésor de Siphnos: Fouilles de Delphes 2. P 1987, de Boccard. 253 p., 142 fig.; vol. of 108 pl. F 950 [JHS 109, 260, R. A. *Tomlinson*].

g694 **Kebric** Robert B., The paintings in the Cnidian Lesche at Delphi and their historical context: Mnemosyne Sup 80. Leiden 1983, Brill. ix-61 p. – ᴿGnomon 60 (1988) 465-7 (T. *Hölscher*).

g695 **Roux** Georges, Fouilles de Delphes II. Topographie et architecture; la terrasse d'Attale I [relevés *Callot* Olivier]: ÉcFrançAthènes. P 1987, de Boccard. viii-163 p.; 25 fig.; 67 pl.; 2 plans. – ᴿGnomon 60 (1988) 738-742 (H.-J. *Schalles*).

g696 *Roux* Georges, La tholos d'Athena Pronaia dans son sanctuaire de Delphes: CRAI (1988) 290-309; 12 fig.

g697 *a*) *Croissant* Francis, Les frontons du temple du IVᵉ siècle à Delphes; esquisse d'une restitution; – *b*) *Marcadé* Jean, Les sculptures décoratives de la Tholos de Marmaria à Delphes; état actuel du dossier: ➤ 751*b*, Klassische Plastik 1985/6, 187-197; 6 fig. pl. 154-6 / 169-173; pl. 145-8.

g698 *Dendra*: **Åström** Paul, The cuirass tomb... Dendra 2; SIMA 4, 1983 ➤ 64,d154: ᴿRBgPg 66 (1988) 184s (R. *Laffineur*).

g699 *Epidauros*: *Yalouris* Nikolaos, Die Skulpturen des Asklepiostempels von Epidauros: ➤ 751*b*, Klassische Plastik 1985/6, 175-186; 2 fig.; pl. 149-153.

g700 *Kastanas*: **Hochstetter** Alix, Kastanas; Ausgrabungen in einem Siedlungshügel der Bronze- und Eisenzeit Makedoniens 1975-1979; die handgemachte Keramik, Schichten 19 bis 1: Prähistorische Archäologie in Südosteuropa 3. B 1984, Spiess. 406 p.; 281 pl. DM 274. 3-88435-106-0. – ᴿFornvännen 83 (1988) 273-5 (P. *Hellström*).

g701 **Mycenae**:   *Crouwel* J.,   Mycenaean painted pottery from outside the citadel at Mycenae: AnBritAth 83 (1988) 25-36; 2 fig.; pl. 3-4.

g702 *Graziadio* Giampaolo,   The chronology of the graves of Circle B at Mycenae; a new hypothesis: AJA 92 (1988) 343-372; 5 fig.

g703 *Dietz* Søren,   On the origin of the Mycenaean civilization: ➤ 142*, FTHOMSEN R., 1988, 22-28.

g704 *a*) *Iakovidis* Sp. E.,   Destruction horizons at Late Bronze Age Mycenae; – *b*) *Shaw* Maria C.,   The Lion Gate relief of Mycenae reconsidered; – *c*) *Åström* Paul,   A dance scene from Mycenae; – *d*) *Amandry* P.,   Sièges mycéniens tripodes et trépied pythique: – 111, FMYLONAS G., *Philia épē* 1 (1986) 233-260; pl. 17-38 / 108-123; pl. 3-4 / 124s / 167-184; pl. 7-11.

g705 *Kilian* Klaus,   The emergence of *wanax* ideology in the Mycenaean palaces: OxJArch 7 (1988) 291-302; 3 fig.

g707 *Duhoux* Yves,   Les contacts entre Mycéniens et barbares d'après le vocabulaire du Linéaire B: Minos 23 (1988) 75-83.

g708 *a*) *Younger* John,   The end of Mycenaean art; – *b*) *Deger-Jalkotzy* Sigrid,   Zum Ende der mykenischen Zeit in Achaia: ➤ 776, Ägäische Vorgeschichte 1984/7, 63-72 / 1-5.

g709 **Schachermeyr** Fritz,   Mykene und das Hethiterreich: SzbW 472, 1986 ➤ 2,b347:   RClasR 102 (1988) 303-5 (D. F. *Easton*); Gnomon 60 (1988) 360s (H. G. *Güterbock*); JHS 108 (1988) 259s (also D. F. *Easton*).

g710 **Nemea**:   *Cherry* John F., *al.*,   Archaeological survey in an artifact-rich landscape; a Middle Neolithic example from Nemea, Greece: AJA 92 (1988) 159-176; 12 fig.

g711 *Miller* Stephen G.,   Excavations at Nemea, 1984-1986:   Hesperia 57 (1988) 1-20; pl. 1-26.

g712 **Olympia**:   *Belloni* Gian Guido,   Olimpia; considerazioni su alcune sculture del tempio di Zeus: QuadCatan 9,18 (1987) 263-285 + 19 fig.

g713 **Koenigs** Wolf,   Die Echohalle: Olympische Forschungen 14, 1984 ➤ 1,e444; 3,f120:   RRArchéol (1988) 138s (J. de *Courtils*).

g714 *Tersini* Nancy D.,   Unifying themes in the sculpture of the Temple of Zeus at Olympia: ClasAnt 6 (1987) 139-159; XII pl.

g715 *Mallwitz* Alfred [1919-1986],   Olympia und Rom: AntWelt 19,2 (1988) 21-45; 30 (color.) fig.

g716 *Herrmann* Hans-Volkmar,   Zum Problem des mykenischen Ursprungs griechischer Heiligtümer; Olympia und Delphi: ➤ 776, Ägäische Vorgeschichte 1984/7, 151-172.

g717 **Philippes**:   BCH 112 (1988) 725-7 (M. *Sève*).

g718 *Sève* Michel, *Weber* Patrick,   Un monument honorifique au forum de Philippes: BCH 112 (1988) 467-479.

g719 *Abrahamsen* Valerie,   Christianity and the rock reliefs at Philippi: BA 51 (1988) 46-56; ill.

g720 *Ducrey* Pierre,   Des dieux et des sanctuaires à Philippes de Macédoine: ➤ 698, Comptes 1986/8, 207-213; 1 fig.

g720* **Phocis**: **Fossey** John M.,   The ancient topography of eastern Phokis 1986 ➤ 2,b355; 3,f268:   RAntClas 57 (1988) 488-491 (D. *Marcotte*); AntiqJ 68,1 (1988) 139s (J. *Bintliff*: out of date).

g721 **Sparta**: **Christ** K.,   Sparta: WegFor 622, 1986 ➤ 2,347; 3,f127:   RHZ 245 (1987) 409 (M. *Clauss*).

g722 **Sunium**: *Lauter* Hans,   Das Teichos von Sunion: Marburger Winckelmann-Programm (1988) 11-33.

g722* **Thebae**: *Bartoněk* Antonín,   The names of [Boeotian] Thebes in the documents of the Mycenaean era: Minos 23 (1988) 39-46.

g723 **Tiryns**: *a*) *Kilian* Klaus,   Ausgrabungen in Tiryns 1982/83, Bericht zu den Grabungen; – *b*) *Schönfeld* Guntram,   Bericht zur bemalten my-kenischen Keramik; – *c*) *Podzuweit* Christian,   Keramik der Phase SH III C-Spät aus der Unterburg von Tiryns; – *d*) *Godart* Louis,   Autour des textes en linéaire B; – *e*) *Olivier* Jean-Pierre,   Tirynthian graffiti; – *f*) *Schwandner* Ernst-Ludwig,   Archaische Spolien aus Tiryns: ArchAnz (1988) 106-151; 46 fig. / 153-211; 13 fig. / 213-223 (-243, *Papademetriou* Alkestis) / 245-251; 5 fig. / 253-268; 5 fig. / 269-284; 14 fig.

g724 **Volimidia**: *Coulson* William D. E.,   Geometric pottery from Volimidia [20 k N Pylos, near Englianos, 'Nestor's Palace']: AJA 92 (1988) 53-74; 33 fig.

т9.4   Creta.

g725 *Adreyev* Y. V., ⊗ The palace and the 'town' on Crete in the second millennium B.C.: SovArch (1988,4) 37-51; Eng. 51.

g726 **Callender** Gae,   *a*) The Minoans; – *b*) Minoan civilisation – student workcards. Sydney 1987/6, Shakespeare Head. A$13/15. 0-7302-0816-8; 213-5 [AncHRes 19,30-32, Lynne *Allen*, Fiona *Stasivkynas*].

g727 *a*) *Damiani Indelicato* Silvia,   Plaidoyer pour un meilleur usage du mot palais en archéologie minoenne; – *b*) *Pelon* Olivier,   À propos d'un palais minoen: RÉAnc 90 (1988) 65-77 + 3 fig.; IV pl. / 85-87.

g728 *a*) *Effenterre* Henri van,   La Crète serait-elle une terre de colonisation?; – *b*) *Faure* Paul,   Cités antiques de la Crète de l'ouest: Cretan 1 (1988) 73-82 / 83-96.

g729 **Gesell** Geraldine C.,   Town, palace and house cult in Minoan Crete: SIMA 67, 1985 ➤ 1,e466; 3,f146: ᴿAJA 92 (1988) 137s (J. *Bennet*).

g730 *Gómez Fuentes* Alejandro,   El estado minoico y el modo de producción asiático: ➤ 70, ᶠJORDÁ F., Zephyrus 37s (1984s) 249-254.

g731 **Hallager** Erik,   *a*) Final palatial Crete; an essay in Minoan chronology: ➤ 142*, ᶠTHOMSEN R. 1988, 11-21; – *b*) The roundel [small inscribed clay disk] in the Minoan administrative system: ➤ 733, Acta Hyperborea 1987/8, 9-11.

g732 *Harrison* George W. M.,   Background to the first century of Roman rule in Crete: Cretan 1 (1988) 125-155.

g733 *Hayden* Barbara J.,   Fortifications of postpalatial and Early Iron Age Crete: ArchAnz (1988) 1-21; 21 fig.

g734 *Horst* Pieter W. van der,   The Jews of ancient Crete: JJS 39 (1988) 183-200.

g735 **Kanta** Athanasia, The Late Minoan III period in Crete ...: SIMA 58, 1980 ➤ 61,t642; 65,b628: ᴿArchClasR 38ss (1986ss) 204-8 (V. *Aravantinos*).

g736 ᴱ**Krzyszkowska** Olga, *Nixon* Lucia, Minoan Society, Proceedings of the Cambridge colloquium 1981/3 ➤ 65,709: ᴿKlio 70 (1988) 245-7 (R. *Witte*).

g737 *Marinatos* Nanno, *Hägg* Robin,   On the ceremonial function of the Minoan polythyron: OpAth 16 (1986) 57-73; 16 fig.

g738 **Preziosi** Donald,   Minoan architectural design; formation and sig-nification [diss. Harvard 1968]: Approaches to Semiotics 63. B 1983, Mouton. xxxi-522 p. £40. – ᴿBInstArch sup 24 (1987) 15-17 (S. *Hood*: maddening jargon but important).

g739 *Sakellarakis* J. A.,   The Idaean cave; Minoan and Greek worship: ➤ 693, Actes = Kernos 1 (1988) 207-214; 7 fig.

g740 **Sanders** Ian F.,   Roman Crete 1982 ➤ 64,d180; 65,b630:   ᴿHelmantica 37 (1986) 398s (E. R. *Panyagua*).

g741 *Sansone* David,   The survival of the Bronze-Age [Minoan-Mycenean] demon: ILCL 13,1 (1988) 1-17.

g742 *Spyridakis* Stylianos V.,   Notes on the Jews of Gortyna and Crete [2d cent. B.C.E.]: ZPapEp 73 (1988) 171-5.

g743 **Walberg** Gisela,   Tradition and innovation; essays in Minoan art. Mainz 1986, von Zabern.   x-162 p.; 156 fig.; front. DM 58. – ᴿAJA 92 (1988) 604s (Maria C. *Shaw*).

g744 *Weingarten* Judith,   The sealing structures of Minoan Crete; MM II Phaistos to the destruction of the palace of Knossos; part II, the evidence from Knossos until the destruction of the palace: OxJArch 7 (1988) 1-25; 6 fig.

g745 *Gortyna*:   *Allegro* Nunzio, *Ricciardi* Maria,   Le fortificazioni di Gortina in età ellenistica: Cretan 1 (1988) 1-16.

g746 *Kavousi*:   *Gesell* Geraldine C., *al.*,   Excavations at Kavousi, Crete, 1987: Hesperia 57 (1988) 279-302; 7 fig.; pl. 73-84.

g747 *Knossos*:   *Hägg* Robin,   The last ceremony in the throne-room at Knossos: OpAth 17 (1988) 99-105; 7 fig.

g748 *Malia*:   **Poursat** Jean-Claude,   La ville minoenne de Malia; recherches et publications récentes: RArchéol (1988) 61-82; 9 fig. (map, plan).

g749 *Phalasarna*: *Hadjidaki* Elpida,   Preliminary report of excavations at the harbor of Phalasarna in West Crete: AJA 92 (1988) 463-479; 21 fig.

g750 *Pseira*: *Betancourt* Philip P., *Davaris* Costis,   Excavations at Pseira [island 2 km NE of Crete], 1985 and 1986:   Hesperia 57 (1988) 207-226; 9 fig.; pl. 57-71.

g751 *Sphakia*:   *Nixon* Lucia, [Canadian Research Institute for the Advancement of Women] The Sphakia survey: BCanadMedit 8,2 (1988) 12.

T9.5   **Insulae graecae.**

g752 *Andel* Tjeerd H. van, *Runnels* Curtis N.,   An essay on the 'emergence of civilization' in the Aegean world: Antiquity 62 (1988) 234-247; 3 fig.

g753 **Effenterre** Henri van,   Les Égéens; aux origines de la Grèce, Chypre, Cyclades, Crète et Mycènes: Civilisations.   P 1986, Colin.   246 p.; ill.

g754 *Aegina*:   *Ohly-Dumm* Martha, *Robertson* Martin,   Aigina, Alphaia-Tempel XII. Archaic marble sculptures other than architectural: ArchAnz (1988) 405-421; 26 fig.

g755 *Cephallenia*:   **Brodbeck-Jucker** Sabina,   Mykenische Funde von Kephallenia im archäologischen Museum Neuchâtel: Archaeologica 42.   R 1986, Bretschneider.   140 p.; 15 fig.; 15 pl. – ᴿAntClas 57 (1988) 543-5 (R. *Laffineur*).

g756 *Chios*:   ᴱ*Boardman* J., *al.*, Chios 1984/7 ➤ 3,f154:   ᴿClasR 102 (1988) 305s (Chris *Emlyn-Jones*).

g757 *Délos*: BCH 112 (1988) 746-791 (A. *Farnoux, al.*).

g758 *a) Tréheux* Jacques,   Une nouvelle lecture des inventaires d'Apollon à Délos; – *b) Linders* Tullia,   The purpose of the inventories: ➤ 698. ᶠTRÉHEUX J., Comptes 1986/8, 29-35 / 37-47.

g759 **Vial** Claude,   Délos indépendante (314-167 avant J.-C.); Étude d'une communauté civique et de ses institutions: BCH Sup 10, 1984 ➤ 3,f157: ᴿGnomon 60 (1988) 516-9 (D. *Hennig*); RArchéol (1988) 400-4 (R. *Étienne*); VDI 187 (1988) 208-212 (G. B. *Lopukhova*).

g759* **Bruneau** Philippe, *Ducat* Jean, Guide de Délos[3rev] [[1]1965]: ÉcFrAth. P 1983, de Boccard. 280 p.; 106 fig. – [R]RÉG 101 (1988) 501-4 (C. *Le Roy*).

g760 *Dodecanesos*: *Melas* E. M., The Dodecanese and West Anatolia in prehistory; interrelationships, ethnicity and political geography: AnSt 38 (1988) 109-120; 3 fig. (map).

g761 *Keos*: *Caskey* M., ☉ The terracotta statues of Ayia Irini, Kea [sic; Bronze Age temple]: Archaiognōsía 3.1s (1987 for 1982-4) 81-91; Eng. 92.

g762 **Caskey** Miriam E., The temple at Ayia Irini, the statues: Keos 2/1, 1986 ➤ 3,f164: [R]MusHelv 45 (1988) 185 (D. *Willers*).

g763 **Georgiou** Hara S., Ayia Irini, specialized domestic and industrial pottery: Keos 6, 1986 ➤ 2,b395; 3,f163; [R]AntClas 57 (1988) 545-7 (R. *Laffineur*).

g764 **Bikaki** Aliki H., Ayia Irini; the potters' marks: Keos 4, 1984 ➤ 1,e496*b*: [R]Archeologia 36 (Wrocław 1985) 173 (J. *Ziomecki*).

g765 *Lemnos*: *Heurgon* Jacques, Homère et Lemnos: CRAI (1988) 12-30; 11 fig.

g766 *Lesbos*: *Pfrommer* Michael, Bemerkungen zum Tempel von Messa auf Lesbos: IstMitt 36 (1986) 77-94; 4 fig. pl. 23-27.

g767 **Melos**: **Renfrew** Colin, The archaeology of cult; the sanctuary at Phylakopi 1986 ➤ 2,b399; 3, f165: [R]AJA 92 (1988) 293s (Emily *Vermeule*: grandiose effort at generalization of shabby remains which may even have been workshop rather than shrine); BInstArch sup 24 (1987) 17-21 (B. *Dietrich*).

g768 **Barber** R. L. N., The Cyclades in the Bronze Age. L 1987, Duckworth. 283 p.; 168 fig. £28. 0-7156-2160-2. – [R]Antiquity 62 (1988) 820 (C. *Renfrew*: safe).

g769 **Getz-Preziosi** Pat, Early Cycladic art in North American collections: Virginia Museum of Fine Arts. Seattle 1988, Univ. Washington. 368 p.; 400 fig. $30 pa. 0-295-96553-3 [AJA 92,626].

g770 *Rhodus*: **Dietz** Søren, Excavations and surveys in southern Rhodes; the Mycenaean period 1984 ➤ 65,b658; 3,f167: [R]ArchClasR 38ss (1986ss) 282-4 (Lucia *Vagnetti*).

g771 **Mee** C., Rhodes in the Bronze Age 1982 ➤ 64,d194; 65,b660: [R]Helmantica 37 (1986) 402s (E. R. *Panyagua*); RArchéol (1988) 126 (P. *Darcque*).

g772 **Berthold** Richard M., Rhodes in the Hellenistic age 1984 ➤ 65,b657 ... 3,f168: [R]AmHR 93 (1988) 1302 (S. K. *Eddy*); ClasW 80 (1987s) 49 (J. E. *Coleman*).

g773 *Samos*: **Shipley** G., A history of Samos, 800-188 B.C. Ox 1987, Clarendon. xviii-352 p.; 24 fig.; 16 pl. £35. – [R]BInstArch 25 (1988) 169s (A. *Johnston*); GreeceR 35 (1988) 96 (P. J. *Rhodes*).

g774 *Samothrace*: **Ehrhardt** Hartmut, Samothrake; Heiligtümer in ihrer Landschaft und Geschichte als Zeugen antiken Geisteslebens 1985 ➤ 1,e505: [R]HZ 245 (1987) 132s (H.-J. *Gehrke*).

g775 *Tenos*: **Étienne** Roland, *Braun* Jean-Pierre, Ténos I., Le sanctuaire de Poséidon et d'Amphitrite: BÉFAR 263, 1986 ➤ 3,f171: [R]RArchéol (1988) 141-3 (Marie-Christine *Hellmann*); RÉAnc 90 (1988) 453-6 (J. *Marcadé*).

g776 *Thasos*: *Lianos* N., al., ☉ Thasos harbor survey and excavations 1987: Athens Annals of Archaeology 18 (1985!) 119-134; 135s; Eng./franç.

g777 **Weill** Nicole, La plastique archaïque de Thasos; figurines et statues de l'Artémision. I. Le haut archaïsme: Études Thasiennes 1, 1985 ➤ 3,f172: [R]RArchéol (1988) 130-2 (C. *Rolley*).

g778 **Thera**: **Aitken** M., *Michael* H. [... early], *Warren* P. [... late], The Thera eruption I-III: Archaeometry 30 (1988) 165-169-175-179.

g779 *Manning* Sturt, The Bronze Age eruption of Thera; absolute dating, Aegean chronology, and Mediterranean cultural interrelations: JMedit-Arch 1,1 (1988) 17-82

g780 *Marinatos* Nanno, The 'African' of Thera reconsidered: OpAth 17 (1988) 137-141; 7 fig.

T9.6 **Urbs Roma.**

g781 **Anderson** James C.[J], The historical topography of the imperial fora 1984 → 65,b665 ... 3,f176: [R]ArchClasR 38ss (1986ss) 275s (E. *Tortorici*); Gymnasium 95 (1988) 178s (H. *Bauer*).

g782 [E]**Avetta** Lucia, Roma Via Imperiale, scavi e scoperte (1937-1950) ...: Univ. R Tituli 3. R 1985, Storia e Letteratura. 300 p. 73 pl. – [R]CC 139 (1988,2) 305s (A. *Ferrua*); Phoenix 42 (Toronto 1988) 278-281 (M. *Janon*); RÉLat 66 (1988) 377 (A. *Chastagnol*).

g783 **Boatwright** Mary T., Hadrian and the city of Rome 1987 → 3,f178: [R]ClasR 102 (1988) 357s (T. P. *Wiseman*); Phoenix 42 (Toronto 1988) 276-8 (J. van der *Leest*); RArchéol (1988) 435-7 (P. *Gros*: he never liked it but enriched it architecturally).

g784 **Carettoni** Gianfilippo, Das Haus des Augustus auf dem Palatin, [T]*Feussner* S.: KultGAW Sonderband. Mainz 1983, von Zabern. 95 p. 19 fig., 22 pl. (Lohse H.), 2 plans. – [R]AnzAltW 41 (1988) 214-7 (Florens *Felten*); Gnomon 60 (1988) 640-9 (W. *Ehrhardt*).

g785 **Carpano** Claudio, Unter den Strassen von Rom... Führer, [T]*Callori-Gehlsen* Christina, *Raave* Andreas. FrB 1986, Herder. 180 p.; 24 fig. + 173 color. DM 68. – [R]TrierTZ 97 (1988) 77s (E. *Sauser*).

g786 **Chevallier** Raymond, Ostie antique, ville et port; préf. *Brouillet* René: Le monde romain 1986 → 3,f181: [R]Gnomon 60 (1988) 563s (L. *Vidman*).

g787 *D'Ambra* Eve, A myth for a smith; a Meleager sarcophagus from a tomb in Ostia: AJA 92 (1988) 85-100; 10 fig.

g788 *Daoust* J., Les communautés juives de Rome [onze synagogues anciennes: *Perrot* C., MondeB 51 (1987)]: EsprVie 98 (1988) 438-440.

g789 *Dillenberger* Jane and John, Michelangelo's Sistine ceiling; to clean or not to clean or not to clean: BR 4,4 (1988) 12-19 (-25); ill.

g790 *Esch* Arnold, Die Via Appia in der Landschaft; Hinweise zur Begehung im Gelände zwischen Genzano und Cisterna: AntWelt 19,1 (1988) 15-29; 17 (color.) fig.

g791 *Ganzert* Joachim, Der Mars-Ultor-Tempel auf dem Augustusforum in Rom: AntWelt 19,3 (1988) 36-59; 44 fig.

g792 *Ghedini* Francesca, Il foro: Archeo 38 (1988) 102-109; color. ill.

g793 *Hesberg* Henner von, *Pfanner* Michael, Ein augusteisches Columbarium im Park der Villa Borghese: JbDAI 103 (1988) 465-487; 18 fig. [491-513, *Brands* Gunnar, Augustusbogen von Fano].

g794 **Jonsson** Marita, La cura dei monumenti... Roma 1800-1830: 1986 → 3, f192 [Johnsson]: [R]Gnomon 60 (1988) 527-531 (C. *Gasparri*).

g795 *Kereszty* Roch, Peter and Paul and the founding of the Church of Rome; forgotten perspectives: Comm-ND 15 (1988) 215-223.

g796 **Kleiner** F. S., The arch of Nero in Rome 1985 → 1,e521*... 3,f194: [R]Athenaeum 66,1s (1988) 208-210 (S. *Maggi*); RBgPg 66 (1988) 207s (F. *Baratte*); RÉAnc 90 (1988) 468-470 (P. *Gros*).

g797 *Kleiner* Fred S., The arch in honor of C. Octavius and the fathers of Augustus: Historia 37 (1988) 347-357.

g798 *Koeppel* Gerhard M., Die historischen Reliefs der römischen Kaiserzeit V, Ara Pacis Augustae, Teil II: BonnJbb 188 (1988) 97-106.

g799 **Krautheimer** Richard, Rom; Schicksal einer Stadt 312-308 [Eng.], T*Kienlechner* T., *Hoffmann* U. Mü 1987, Beck. 424 p.; 420 fig. DM 98. – RMüTZ 39 (1988) 211s (P. *Stockmeier*).

g799* **Lepper** Frank, *Sheppard* Frere, Trajan's column. Gloucester 1988, Sutton. xviii-331 p.; 5 fig.; 108 pl.; 3 foldout maps. £25. 0-86299-467-5 [Antiquity 63, 627, Amanda *Claridge*].

g800 **Künzl** Ernst, Der römische Triumph; Siegesfeiern im antiken Rom. Mü 1988, Beck. 171 p.; 100 fig. – RRÉLat 66 (1988) 337 (R. *Adam*).

g801 **Rasch** Jürgen J., Das Maxentius-Mausoleum an der Via Appia in Rom: Spätantike Zentralbauten in Rom und Latium 1, 1984 ➤ 65,b674; 2,b427: RGnomon 60 (1988) 569-571 (K. D. *Licht*, T*Zanker* Dorothea).

g802 *Sauron* Gilles, Le message esthétique des rinceaux de l'Ara Pacis Augustae: RArchéol (1988) 3-40; 28 fig.

g802* **Settis** Salvator, *La Regina* Adriano, *al.*, La colonna traiana. T 1988, Einaudi. xix-597 p.; 92 fig.; 291 colour pl. Lit. 110.000. 88-06-59889-9 [Antiquity 63, 628, Amanda *Claridge*].

g803 **Sugano** Karin, Das Rombild des HIERONYMUS 1983 ➤ 65,d552... 2,b429: RLatomus 47 (1988) 217 (P. *Hamblenne*).

g804 **Townsend** G. B. The restoration of the Capitol in A.D. 70: Historia 36 (1987) 243-8.

g804* *Vismara* Cinzia, Ancora sugli Ebrei di Roma [... *Goodenough* E.]: ArchClasR 38ss (1986ss) 150-161.

g805 *Wood* Susan, Memoriae Agrippinae; Agrippina the Elder in Julio-Claudian art and propaganda: AJA 92 (1988) 409-426; 16 fig.

g806 *Zehnacker* Hubert, La description de Rome dans le livre 3 de la NH [de PLINE]: Helmantica 37 (1986) 307-320.

T9.7 *Roma,* Catacumbae.

g807 **Baruffa** Antonio, Le catacombe di San Callisto. T-Leumann 1988, Elle Di Ci. 190 p. [SMSR 55, 161, Myla *Perraymond*].

g808 **Deckers** Johannes G., *al.*, Die Katakombe 'Santi Marcellino e Pietro', Repertorium der Malereien: [mit Univ. FrB] Roma Sotterranea Cristiana 6, 1987 ➤ 3,f211: RJbAC 31 (1988) 226-230 (L. *Reekmans*, T*Rexin* G.); NRT 110 (1988) 781 (A. *Harvengt*); RHPR 88 (1988) 327-343 (P. *Prigent*); TLZ 113 (1988) 837-9 (H.-G. *Thümmel*).

g809 **Eisner** Michael, Zur Typologie der Grabbauten im Suburbium Roms [mostly surface]: MiDAI-R Erg.-H. 26, 1986 ➤ 3,f212: RClasR 102 (1988) 359s (G. *Davies*).

g810 *Fasola* U. M., La regione cimiteriale del II piano sotto la basilica costantiniana 'ad duas Lauros'; cronologia dell'origine e dello sviluppo: RivArCr 62 (1988) 7-20; 6 fig.

g811 **Ferrua** A., *Mazzoleni* D., Inscriptiones christianae Urbis Romae septimo saeculo antiquiores, 9. Viae Salariae coemeteria reliqua 1985 ➤ 3,f215: RRHE 83 (1988) 90-94 (L. *Reekmans*).

g812 *Ferrua* Antonio, Esedra sepolcrale nel sepolcreto vaticano: ➤ 31, FDE ANGELIS D'OSSAT G. 1987, 41s.

g813 **Fink** Josef †, Das Petrusgrab in Rom, E*Schmidinger* Heinrich M. Innsbruck 1988. 96 p.; 13 fig. – RTyche 3 (1988) 309s (R. *Pillinger*).

g814 **Guyon** Jean, Le cimetière aux deux Lauriers; recherches sur les catacombes romaines. Vaticano 1987, Pontificio Istituto di Archeologia Cristiana. 556 p.; 265 fig.; 14 pl. Lit. 150.000. – ᴿCC 139 (1988,4) 95s (A. *Ferrua*); RHE 83 (1988) 673-6 (L. *Reekmans*).

g815 **Konikoff** Adia, Sarcophagi from the Jewish catacombs 1986 → 2,b437; 3,f219: ᴿGnomon 60 (1988) 376-8 (L. H. *Kant*, L. V. *Rutgers*, Eng.); JbAC 31 (1988) 230-2 (P. C. *Finney*); JStJud 19 (1988) 106-8 (A. *Hilhorst*).

g816 **Mancinelli** Fabrizio, Katakumben und Basiliken; die ersten Christen in Rom². Firenze 1984, Scala. 64 p.; 120 color. fot. – ᴿSborBrno 33 (1988) 174-6 (Marie *Pardyová*).

g817 **Mielsch** H., *Hesberg* Henner von, *al.*, Die heidnische Nekropole unter St. Peter in Rom; die Mausoleen A-D: Atti Pont. Accad. Rom. di Arch. 3/16/1, 1986 → 2,b441; 3,f220: ᴿAnzAltW 41 (1988) 84s (W. K. *Kovacsovics*); Arctos 22 (1988) 259s (A. *Tammisto*); Gymnasium 94 (1987) 453-5 (V. *Kockel*); JRS 78 (1982) 252 (Glenys *Davies*).

g818 **Reekmans** Louis, Le complexe cémétérial du Pape Gaius dans la catacombe de Callixte: Roma sotterranea cristiana 8. R/Lv 1988, Pontificio Istituto di Archeologia Cristiana/Univ. xix-232 p.; 107 fig.; XXXIII (foldout) pl.

g819 **Stevenson** James, The Catacombs; life and death in early Christianity 1985 = 1978 → 2,b443: ᴿSecC 6,1 (1987s) 43 (G. F. *Snyder*).

g820 **Stutzinger** Dagmar, Die frühchristlichen Sarkophagreliefs aus Rom; Untersuchungen zur Formveränderung im 4. Jdt.: Diss. Klas. Arch. 16. Bonn 1982, Habelt. 191 p. 26 pl. 3-7749-1901-1. – ᴿAnzAltW 41 (1988) 85-87 (Guntram *Koch*); RivArCr 62 (1988) 448-462 (A. *Recio Veganzones*).

g821 *Willems* G. F., Een mysterieuze wandschildering in de Nieuwe Catacombe aan de Via Latina te Rome: Ter Herkenning 16,1 (1988) 31-43 [< GerefTTs 88,123].

T9.8 *Roma,* **Ars palaeochristiana.**

g822 **Arbeiter** Achim, Alt-St. Peter in Geschichte und Wissenschaft; Abfolge der Bauten – Rekonstruktion – Architekturprogramm. B 1988, Mann. 271 p.; 140 fig.; 3 foldouts. 3-7861-1410-2.

g823 **Buonocore** Marco, Le iscrizioni latine e greche dei Musei della Biblioteca Apostolica Vaticana. Vaticano 1987. 120 p. Lit. 20.000. – ᴿCC 139 (1988,3) 129s (A. *Ferrua*).

g824 ᴱ**Carletti** Carlo, Iscrizioni cristiane a Roma; testimonianze di vita cristiana (secoli III-VII): Bibliotheca Patristica 7, 1986 → 2,b445: ᴿSalesianum 50 (1988) 383s (O. *Pasquato*).

g824* *Dal Covolo* Enrico, Una 'domus ecclesiae' a Roma sotto l'impero di Alessandro Severo?: EphLtg 102 (1988) 64-71; lat. 64, non indicat auctoris responsum.

g825 **Duval** Yvette, Loca sanctorum Africae 1982 → 1,e543: ᴿCrNSt 9 (1988) 184-6 (V. *Saxer*); RÉLat 66 (1988) 391-4 (C. *Lepelley*).

g826 **Korol** Dieter, Die frühchristlichen Wandmalereien aus... Nola 1987 → 3,f227: ᴿCC 139 (1988,2) 414s (A. *Ferrua*).

g827 **Mazzucco** Ippolito, Iscrizioni della basilica e convento dei Santi Dodici Apostoli in Roma, con commento storico-religioso. R 1987, Apostoleion. 162 p. – ᴿCC 139 (1988,1) 196 (A. *Ferrua*).

g828 **Nauerth** Claudia, Vom Tod zum Leben; die christlichen Totenerweckungen in der spätantiken Kunst: Gö Univ. Orientalistik 2/1, 1980 → 62,b484: ᴿSborBrno 31 (1986) 211s (Marie *Pardyová*).

g829 [Fiocchi] **Nicolai** Vincenzo F.,   I cimiteri paleocristiani del Lazio, I. Etruria meridionale.   R 1988, Pontificio Istituto di Archeologia Cristiana. xviii-420 p.; 388 fig.; 5 pl.   Lit. 150.000. – ^RCC 139 (1988,3) 540s (A. *Ferrua*).

g830 **Ritz** Sándor,   Insurpassable création du passé, du présent et du futur; le Temple perpétuel de Saint Stefano Rotondo, à Rome, la nouvelle Jerusalem de l'Apocalypse; ^Tsr. *Dejean*. R 1988, auct. (v. Pilotta 25). 80 p.; ill.

т9.9   *(Roma) Imperium occidentale,* **Europa.**

g831 *Anderson* Maxwell L.,   Pompeian frescoes in the Metropolitan Museum of Art: Met. Bulletin 45,3 (1987s) 1-56.

g832 *Bergemann* Johannes,   Die Pferde von San Marco, Zeitstellung und Funktion: MiDAI-R 95 (1988) 115-128; pl. 48-55.

g833 ^E**Bonghi Jovino** Maria,   L'insula 5 della Regio VI: Ricerche a Pompei 5, 1984 → 3,f232:   ^RRArchéol (1988) 407s (Christiane *Delplace*).

g834 **Deichmann** Friedrich W.,   Rom, Ravenna, Konstantinopel, Naher Osten; gesammelte Studien zur spätantiken Architektur, Kunst und Geschichte [1938-82] 1982 → 65,181: ^RRelStR 14 (1988) 256 (R. *Ousterhout*).

g835 *Duval* Noël,   Études d'archéologie chrétienne nord-africaine, XVII. Une nouvelle cuve baptismale dans le centre de Carthage: RÉAug 34 (1988) 86-92 [247-266, XVIII-XIX].

g836 **Dwyer** Eugene J.,   Pompeian domestic sculpture... five houses 1982 → 63,a526 ... 65,b203: ^RAntClas 57 (1988) 609-611 (J. C. *Balty*).

g837 **Greco** Emanuele, *Theodorescu* Dinu, *al.,*   Poseidonia-Paestum III. Forum Nord: Coll.Éc.Fr.R 42, 1987 → 1,e550; 3,f236: ^RAJA 92 (1988) 452-4 (J. G. *Pedley*).

g838 *a) Greco* Emanuele,   Archeologia della colonia latina di Paestum; – *b) Pavolini* Carlo,   Ostia: DialArch (1988,2) 79-86; 4 fig. / 117-123; 2 fig.

g839 **Hälvä-Nyberg** Ulla,   Die Kontraktionen auf den lateinischen Inschriften Roms und Afrikas bis zum 8. Jh. n. Chr.:   Ann. Acad. Fennicae hum. 49. Helsinki 1988, Suomalainen Tiedeakatemia. 270 p. 951-41-0574-5.

g840 **Kaiser-Minn** Helga,   Die Erschaffung des Menschen auf den spätantiken Monumenten des 3. und 4. Jahrhunderts: JbAC Egbd 6, 1981 → 62, 2220 ... 2,1474: ^RSborBrno 32 (1987) 175-8 (Marie *Pardyová*).

g841 *Keys* David, The Roman postal service; greeting from AD 110 [letter found near Hadrian's Wall]: ILN 276 (Dec. 1988) 54.

g843 **Raeder** Joachim,   Die statuarische Ausstattung der Villa Hadriana bei Tivoli: EurHS 38/4. Fra 1983, Lang. 397 p.; 32 pl. – ^RBonnJbb 188 (1988) 600-602 (H. *Meyer*).

g844 **McIllwaine** I. C.,   Herculaneum; a guide to printed sources I-II. N 1988, Bibliopolis. 1029 p.; 7 fig. Lit. 200.000 [Gymnasium 96, 260, L. A. *Scatozza Höricht*).

g844* *Robotti* Ciro,   Pompei et Herculanum vus par les peintres de vues pittoresques aux 18e et 19e siècles: DossHA 119 (1987) 10-17; ill.

g845 *Rolley* Claude,   Paestum, la cité de Poséidon: Archéologia 233 (Dijon 1988) 18-25; ill. → e455.

g846 **Strocka** Volker M.,   Casa del Principe di Napoli: Häuser in Pompeji I, 1984 → 1,e558 ... 3,f246: ^RGGA 240 (1988) 96-103 (H. *Mielsch*).

g848 **Ueblacker** Mathias,   Das Teatro Marittimo in der Villa Hadriana: DAI Sonderschriften 5. Mainz 1985, von Zabern. x-102 p.; 99 fig.; 80 pl. + 1 color.; 30 foldouts. – ^RRArchéol (1988) 186-8 (P. *Gros*).

g849 **Wikander** Charlotte, Acquarossa I. The painted architectural terracottas, 2, Typological and decorative analysis: Rom Svenska Inst.
Skrifter 4⁰ 38,1/2. Sto 1988, Åström. 144 p.; 96 fig. 91-7042-080-7.

g850 **Wojcik** Maria R., La villa dei Papiri ad Ercolano; contributo alla
ricostruzione dell'ideologia della nobilitas tardorepubblicana: Soprint.
Pompei Mon 1, 1986 ➤ 2,b469: ᴿAJA 92 (1988) 145s (Eleanor W.
Leach).

XIX. Geographia biblica

U1 **Geographies.**

g851 **Aharoni** Yohanan, Das Land der Bibel, eine historische Geographie.
1984 ➤ 65,b711 ... 2,b471: ᴿMundus 24 (1988) 177s (J. H. *Friedrich* gives
no date, and twice in the title 'a historical biography'; cites 'Marten
Noth', 'M. Aviona'...); ZkT 110 (1988) 98s (R. *Oberforcher*).

g852 **Bakhuizen** S.C., Studies in the topography of Chalcis on Euboea (a
discussion of the sources): Studies of the Dutch Archaeological and
Historical Society 11. Leiden 1985, Brill. xviii-184 p.; 83 fig. – ᴿAntClas
57 (1988) 491-3 (D. *Marcotte*); RArchéol (1988) 398-400 (Antoinette
Charon).

g853 **Baly** Denis, Basic biblical geography 1987 ➤ 3,f247: ᴿCBQ 50 (1988)
487s (L. *Boadt*: not as successful as his longer works).

g854 *a) Baly* Denis, The pitfalls of biblical geography in relation to Jordan; –
b) Dornemann Rudolph H., Some observations on the geographical
extent of cultural areas in Syria and the Transjordan; – *c) Henry* Donald
O., Topographic influences on epipaleolithic land-use patterns in
southern Jordan: ➤ e824, Jordan III 1986/7, 123s / 275-8 / 275-8 / 21-27.

g855 *Caspers* N., *Herzhoff* B., Die Türkei – ein naturhistorischer und
biogeographischer Abriss: Natur und Museum 118 (Fra 1988) 23-28
[< Mundus 24,252].

g856 **Duerksen** Paul D., Canaan as a land of milk and honey; a study of the
evaluative descriptions of Israel's land: diss. Drew. Durham ɴᴊ 1988. –
288 p. 88-17627. DissA 49 (1988s) 1829-A; RelStR 15,193.

g857 *Fang* Mark, ☉ Historico-geographic background of the New Testament:
ColcFuJen 73 (1987) 351-361.

g858 *Grogan* G. W., Heilsgeographie; geography as a theological concept:
ScotBEv 6 (1988) 81-94.132.

g859 *Kirsten* Ernst [1911-1987; phot.], Möglichkeiten und Aufgaben der
historischen Geographie des Altertums in der Gegenwart: ➤ 764, Hist.
Geographie 1980/7, 1-50.

g860 **Kosack** Wolfgang, Historisches Kartenwerk Ägyptens; altägyptische
Fundstellen; mittelalterliches arabisches Ägypten; Koptische Kultur
(Delta; Mittelägypten; Oberägypten). Bonn 1971, Habert. 113 p.; folder of
9 loose maps. 3-7749-1126-6.

g860* **Lane** Belden C., Landscapes of the sacred geography and narrative in
American spirituality. NY 1988, Paulist. xii-237 p. $10 pa. [JTS 40,746].

g861 **Louis** Herbert, Landeskunde der Türkei, vernehmlich aufgrund eigener
Reisen: Erdkundliches Wissen 73 / GeogZts Beih. Stu c. 1987, Steiner.
xii-268 p.; 4 maps. DM 54. – ᴿMundus 24 (1988) 331s (K. *Kreiser* without
date).

g862 *Marcheselli Casale* Cesare, Luoghi e paesaggi della Bibbia; geografia, storia e itinerari della Terra Santa in una recente opera di grande interesse scientifico [*Keel* O. *al.* 1s, 1982-4]: Asprenas 35 (1988) 253-267.

g864 **Pritchett** W. K., Studies in ancient Greek topography [3s. 1980/2 ➤ 62,d58] 5. [... checkpoints; Thermopylae]: ClasSt. 31. Berkeley 1985, Univ. California. xii-221 p.; 91 pl. $38.50 pa. 0-5200-9698-3. – RClasW 82 (1988s) 63s (B. M. *Lavelle*).

g865 *Rainey* Anson F., Historical geography: ➤ 20, FCALLAWAY J., Benchmarks 1988, 353-368.

U1.2 **Historia geographiae.**

g866 **Arentzen** Jorg-Geerd, Imago mundi cartographica; Studien zur Bildlichkeit mittelalterlicher Welt- und Ökumenekarten unter besonderer Berücksichtigung des Zusammenwirkens von Text und Bild: Münstersche Mittelalter-Schriften 53, 1984 ➤ 3,f256: RArKulturG 70 (1988) 515s (O. G. *Oexle*); HZ 247 (1988) 149-151 (A. *Wolf*).

g867 *Arnaud* P., Observations sur l'original du fragment de carte [map of Pontus shore] du pseudo-bouclier de Doura-Europos: RÉAnc 90 (1988) 151-160; 2 fig.

g868 *Aujac* G., L'île de Thule, mythe ou réalité (Étude de géographie grecque): Athenaeum 66 (1988) 329-343.

g869 **Ballabriga** Alain, Le soleil et le tartare; l'image mythique du monde en Grèce archaïque: ÉPHÉS Rech. 20. P 1986. 298 p. – REllinika 38 (1987) 393-6 (F. *Lasserre*).

g870 *Bencheikh* Jamel-Eddine, L'espace de l'inintelligible; un ouvrage de cosmographie arabe au XIIIᵉ siècle: CRAI (1988) 149-161 (-164).

g870* *Brincken* A.-D. von den, Quod non vicietur pictura; die Sorge um das rechte Bild in der Kartographie: ➤ 1662*, Fälschungen im Mittelalter 1986/8, I, 587-599.

g871 *Calmeyer* Peter, Zur Genese altiranischer Motive, VIII. Die 'statistische Landcharte des Perserreiches', Nachträge und Korrekturen: ArchMIran 20 (1987) 129-146.

g872 Chartae latinae antiquiores P. 26: Italy VII. Z - Dietikon 1987, Urs Graf.

g873 **Dilke** O. A. W., Greek and Roman maps 1985 ➤ 1,e587 ... 3,f265: RAmHR 91 (1986) 891s (L. *Casson*); ClasW 80 (1986s) 319s (M. *Reinhold*); HZ 244 (1987) 665-9 (F. T. *Hinrichs*).

g874 *Dilke* O. A. W., Religion and ancient maps: ➤ 27, FCOLEIRO E., Laurea corona 1987, 1-6.

g875 *Donceel-Voûte* Pauline, La carte de Madaba; cosmographie, anachronisme et propagande: RB 95 (1988) 519-542; 3 fig.; Eng. 519.

g875* **Dunn** Ross E., The adventures of Ibn Battuta, a Muslim traveler of the fourteenth century. Berkeley 1986, Univ. California. $35. 0-520-05771-6. – RBSOAS 51 (1988) 191s (M. *Brett*).

g876 *Fischer* Karl A. F., *al.*, The Hebrew astronomical codex ms. Sassoon 823: JQR 78 (1987s) 253-292.

g876* *Garel* M., La première carte de Terre Sainte en hébreu (Amsterdam 1620/21): Studia Rosenthaliana 11 (Amst 1987) 131-9 [< Judaica 44,126].

g877 *Gazich* Roberto, Modello narrativo e moduli del racconto nella Naturalis Historia [PLINIO senior]: BStLat 18 (N 1988) 33-57.

g878 **Habicht** Christian, PAUSANIAS' Guide to Ancient Greece [German 1985 ➤ 3,f270]. Berkeley 1985, Univ. California. xvi-208 p.; 34 fig. £21.25.–

RAmJPg 109 (1988) 278-280 (S. V. *Tracy*); ClasR 102 (1988) 18s (D. *Fehling*); ÉtClas 56 (1988) 73-83 (D. *Marcotte*).

g879 EHarley J. B., Woodward David, The history of cartography, 1. Cartography in prehistoric, ancient, and medieval Europe and the Mediterranean. Ch 1987, Univ. [➤ 3,496]. xxii-599 p.; 344 fig.; 40 color. pl.; $120. 0-226-31633-5. – RAntiquity 62 (1988) 410 (C. *Chippindale*); AntiqJ 68,1 (1988) 132 (P. *Barber*).

g880 *Horowitz* Wayne, The Babylonian map of the world [a chapter from DMesopotamian Cosmic Geography, diss. Birmingham, DLambert W. G.]: Iraq 50 (1988) 147-165; 2 fig.; pl. X.

g881 *Huppertz* Josefine, Eine neue Weltkarte (... history of cartography): VerbumSVD 29 (1988) 207-237.

g882 *Karttunen* Klaus, Expedition to the end of the world; an ethnographic *tópos* in HERODOTUS: StOrFin 64 (1988) 177-181.

g883 EKretschmer Ingrid, al., Lexikon zur Geschichte der Kartographie 1986 ➤ 3,f273: RHZ 245 (1987) 122s (A. *Wolf*).

g884 EKunitzsch Paul, Claudius PTOLEMAEUS, Der Sternkatalog des Almagest; die arabisch-mittelalterliche Tradition, 1. Die arabischen Übersetzungen. Wsb 1986, Harrassowitz. 341 p. DM 298. – RMundus 24 (1988) 330s (G. *Grasshoff*).

g885 Le Bœuffle André, Astronomie, astrologie, lexique latin [< diss. 1970]. P 1987, Picard. 291 p.; 13 fig. F 250. – RGnomon 60 (1988) 509-516 (W. *Hübner*).

g886 *List* Franz K., al., Operational remote sensing for thematic mapping in Egypt and Sudan: Berliner Geowissenschaftliche Abhandlungen A-75,3 (1987) 873-906 [801-832, *Pohlmann* Gerhard: Mundus 24, 50s].

g886* a) *Marcotte* Didier, Origines puniques de la topographie romaine; – b) *Van Laer* Zacharias, La ville de Carthage dans les sources arabes des XIe-XIIIe siècles: ➤ 754, Carthago 1986/8, 239-244 / 245-258; 5 fig.

g887 *Mayerson* Philip, JUSTINIAN's novel[la (decree)] 103 and the reorganization of Palestine: BASOR 269 (1988) 65-71.

g888 MERCATOR [séminaire chaque après-midi du 31 août au 2. sept. 1988], ➤ 470, Exégèse XVIe s.

g889 *Mouraviev* S. N., ❾ Notes de géographie historique du Caucase; les peuples du Caucase selon PLINE l'Ancien: VDI 184 (1988) 156-161; map; franç. 161.

g890 Nenci G., *Vallet* G., Bibliografia topografica della colonizzazione greca in Italia e nelle Isole Tirreniche. Pisa / R 1977, Scuola Normale Superiore / École Française. xxxi-377 p. [2. Addenda, 1981: xiii-105 p.].

g891 *Netton* Richard, Arabia and the pilgrim paradigm of Ibn BAṬṬUṬA; a Braudelian approach: ➤ g181, FShaban M., Arabia 1986... [< JRAS 88,180].

g892 Nicolet Claude, L'inventaire du monde; géographie et politique aux origines de l'Empire romain. P 1988, Fayard. 345 p.; 54 fig.; 2 maps. – RRÉLat 66 (1988) 335-7 (P. *Moreau*); RHist 280,567 (1988) 244-8 (C. *Virlouvet*).

g893 *Nicolet* Claude, De Vérone au Champ de Mars; *chorographia* et carte d'AGRIPPA: MÉF 100 (1988) 127-138.

g894 Parroni Piergiorgio, POMPONII Melae De chorographia libri tres 1984 ➤ 1,e608 ... 3,f281: RBStLat 16 (1986) 123-6 (G. *Aricò*); Mnemosyne 41 (1988) 438-441 (E. Van der *Vliet*).

g895 *Peretti* Aurelio, Dati storici e distanze marine nel Periplo di SCYLACE: StClasOr 38 (1988) 13-137.

g896 *Piccirillo* Michele, *Briend* Jacques, La carte de Madaba: *a*) MondeB 53 (1988) 16-32 / 33-38; ill.; – *b*) EsprVie 98 (1988) 375s (J. *Daoust*).

g897 *Poignet* Jean-François, Visions médiévales de l'axe du monde: RHR 205 (1988) 25-56; Eng. 25.

g898 **Romm** James S., The edges of the earth in ancient thought; distance and the literary imagination: diss. Princeton 1987, 403 p. 88-04855. – DissA 49 (1988s) 249-A.

g899 *a*) *Sauren* Herbert, Les planètes et la cosmologie sumérienne; – *b*) *Eggermont* P. H. L., HIPPALUS and the discovery of the monsoons [followed by ERATOSTHENES and STRABO but unfortunately abandoned by PTOLEMAEUS]: ⇒ 50, FFONTINOY C., Humour... science 1988, 241-9 / 343-361; 3 maps.

g900 TESilberman A., POMPONIUS Mela. 2-251-01344-X. Choréographie: Coll. Budé. P 1988, BLettres. lxxiii-347 (doubles) p.

g901 *Stol* M., De babylonische wereldkaart: PhoenEOL 34,2 (1988) 29-35, 2 fig.

g902 *Sturm* Dieter, Die arabische geographische Literatur im Histori-kerkapitel des Kitāb al-Fihrist von IBN AN-NADĪM: HalleB 10 (1986) 23-36.

g903 *Tabacco* Raffaella, Itinerarium Alexandri; rassegna critica degli studi e prospettive di indagine: BStLat 17 (1987) 77-120.

g904 **Waerden** B. L. van der, Die Astronomie der Griechen; eine Einführung: AltW. Da 1988, Wiss. xi-315 p.; 53 fig. 3-534-03070-2.

g905 *Zubarev* V. G., *Maslennikov* A. A., ❻ Historical geography of European Bosporus according to Claudius PTOLEMY: SovArch (1987,3) 40-52; Eng. 52.

U1.4 Atlas – maps.

g906 **Aharoni** Yohanan, *Avi-Yonah* Michael, Atlante della Bibbia [1968 ²1977] 1987 ⇒ 3,f287: RCC 139 (1988,2) 505s (S. *Votto*); Divinitas 32 (1988) 723s (T. *Stramare*).

g907 **Aharoni** Y., *Avi-Yonah* M., ❺ Makumiran Seisho-Rekishi-Chizu [Macmillan Bible Atlas² 1977], TIkeda Y. Tokyo 1988, Hara-Shobo. 198 p. Y 15.000 [BL 89,33].

g908 **Beitzel** Barry J., The Moody Atlas of Bible lands 1985 ⇒ 1,e612... 3,f288: RGraceTJ 9 (1988) 141 (M. A. *Grisanti*: one of the best); VT 38 (1988) 488 (G. I. *Davies*: 'History of biblical map-making' its most distinctive and interesting part).

g909 EChadwick Henry, *Evans* Gillian, *a*) Atlas van het Christendom [1987 ⇒ 3,f291], TBooij P. Amst 1987, Agon. 240 p.; ill. 90-5157-015-5 [Bijdragen 49,357]. – *b*) Atlas du christianisme [1987], TCannuyer C., *Poswick* R. F. Turnhout 1988, Brepols. 240 p.; ill. Fb 1670 [NRT 111, 783s, A. *Toubeau*].

g910 *Foss* Clive, Classical atlases: ClasW 80 (1986s) 337-365.

g911 Gran Atlas de Arqueología, TBusquets M., *Angelo* R. de. Barc 1987, Ebrisa. 424 p. – RCiuD 201 (1988) 721 (F. *Díez*).

g912 Grande atlante di archeologia [EFlon Christine, (Encyclopaedia universalis) Le grand atlas de l'A. 1985, *Saletti* Cesare 'revis. scientifique'; préf. *Martin* Roland]. Novara 1988, de Agostini. 424 p.; ill. 88-402-0046-0.

g913 *a*) **Hirschfeld** Yizhar, ❻ Map of Herodium; – *b*) **Ronen** A., *Olamy* Y., ❻ Map of Haifa-East; – *c*) **Cohen** R., ❻ Map of Sede-Boker-West:

Archaeological Survey of Israel. J 1985/3/5. 128 p.; Eng. 66 p.; ill. / 65 p.; Eng. 21 p.; ill. / 93 p.; Eng. 35 p.; ill. – ᴿIsrEJ 38 (1988) 101s [Hanna *Katzenstein*].

g914 Illustrated wall maps of the Bible [with (ᴱ*Bruce* F. F.)] Students' Atlas of the Bible. Exeter c. 1987, Paternoster. £20 (atlas only, £3). – ᴿVidyajyoti 52 (1988) 515 (P. M. *Meagher*: 12 wall-maps 105 × 38 cm.; recommended).

g915 ᴱ**Jedin** H., *al*., Atlas zur Kirchengeschichte; die christlichen Kirchen in Geschichte und Gegenwart 1987 ➤ 3,f296: ᴿTsTNijm 28 (1988) 183 (C. *Brakkee*); TPQ 136 (1988) 296 (R. *Zinnhobler*).

g916 **Jenkins** S., Karten zur Bibel. Giessen 1986, Brunnen. 127 p. DM 17,80. – ᴿSNTU-A 13 (1988) 255s (A. *Fuchs*).

g917 ᴱ**Kopp** Horst ['coordinator', assistant to *Röllig* W.], Der Tübinger Atlas des Vorderen Orients. Wsb, Reichert. DM 225. – ᴿMundus 24 (1988) 66-68 [J. *Hohnholz* gives a price but no pages or date].

g918 **Laney** J. Carl, Baker's concise Bible atlas. GR 1988, Baker. 277 p. [GraceTJ 9,309].

g919 **Laor** Eran (*Klein* Shoshana), Maps of the Holy Land; cartobibliography of printed maps. NY 1986, Liss. 222 p.; 25 color pl. $77.50 [BAR-W 15/2,11, H. *Brodsky*]. – ᴿJNES 47 (1988) 194s (G. W. *Ahlström*).

g920 **Nebenzahl** Kenneth, Maps of the Holy Land 1986 ➤ 3,f280; $55: ᴿCurrTM 15 (1988) 447s (R. W. *Klein*).

g921 ᴱ**Pritchard** James B., The Harper [= The Times] atlas of the Bible 1987 ➤ 3,f305: ᴿCurrTM 15 (1988) 447s (R. W. *Klein*, also on ROGERSON); BL (1988) 40 (N. *Wyatt*); JRAS (1988) 388s (G. S. P. *Freeman-Grenville*).

g922 **Rhymer** Joseph, Atlante del mondo biblico 1986 ➤ 2,b522: ᴿSalesianum 50 (1988) 433 (B. *Amata*); StPatav 35 (1988) 194s (M. *Milani*).

g923 **Rogerson** John, Atlas of the Bible 1985 ➤ 1,e622... 3,f306: ᴿCBQ 50 (1988) 309-311 (D. *Baly*).

g924 **Rogerson** John, Nouvel atlas de la Bible 1985 ➤ 1,e623... 3,f307: ᴿBijdragen 49 (1988) 207s (F. De *Meyer*: inleiding meer dan atlas).

g925 **Rogerson** John, Land der Bibel; Geschichte – Kunst – Lebensformen: Weltatlas der alten Kulturen. Mü 1985, Christian. 240 p.; 350 fig. DM 88. – ᴿErbAuf 63 (1987) 314 (J. *Kaffanke*).

g926 **Rogerson** John, Atlante della Bibbia. Novara c. 1988, de Agostini. 240 p.; 352 color. ill. [Archeo 49 (1988) 129].

g926* ᴱ**Scarre** Chris, Past worlds; the Times atlas of archaeology. L 1988, Times Books. 319 p.; color. ill. 0-7230-0306-8 [Antiquity 63, 175, B. *Fagan*].

g927 **Strange** J., Bibelatlas [Danish, replacing *Bentzen* A.] K 1988, Det danske Bibelselskab. 64 p. Dk 150. 87-7523-215-4 [BL 89,42, K. *Jeppesen*).

g928 ᴱ**Vidal-Naquet** Pierre, Atlas historique, Histoire de l'humanité. P 1987, Hachette. 340 p. F195. – ᴿÉtudes 368 (1988) 131s (P. *Valadier*).

U1.5 **Photographiae.**

g929 **Alimenti** Dane, Al seguito di Gesù, pref. *Zeffirelli* Franco. Gorle BG 1987, Velar. 3 vol., 540 p.; fotografie di *Marzi* Franco. – ᴿCC 139 (1988,2) 100s (G. *Caprile*).

g930 [**Chuchra** U., *Lux* F. p. 8-38] Erez Israel; das Panorama des Heiligen Landes in Bild und Wort. Stu-Neuhausen 1987, Hänssler. 111 p. DM 50. – ^RTrierTZ 97 (1988) 160s (R. *Bohlen*).

g931 ^E**Cole** Dan P., NT archaeology slide set 1986 ➤ 2,b530: ^RJBL 107 (1988) 359s (V. P. *Furnish*).

g932 **Dowley** T., Biblische Stätten im Luftbild [High above 1986 ➤ 2,b531; *Halliday* S., *Lushington* L., Fotografinnen], Israel; Einf. *Bruce* F. F., Giessen 1986, Brunnen. 64 p. DM 38. – ^RSNTU-A 13 (1988) 256 (A. *Fuchs*).

g933 **Gavin** Carney E. S., The image of the east; 19th-century... BONFILS 1982 ➤ 1,e630: ^RBASOR 272 (1988) 85-87; 2 fig. (J. M. *Miller*).

g934 **Masom** C., *Alexander* P., Bijbels beeldarchief; *Millard* A., archeologisch. Haag/Kapellen 1987, Voorhoeve/Pelckmans. 192 p. Fb 990. – ^RCollatVL 18 (1988) 252s (F. *Lefevre*).

g935 ^E**Masom** Caroline, *Alexander* Pat., (*Millard* A., archäologisch). Grosser Bildführer zur Bibel. Giessen 1987, Brunnen. 192 p. DM 58. 3-7655-5737-4 [NTAbs 32,268]. – ^RTrierTZ 97 97 (1988) 161s (R. *Bohlen*).

g936 **Meyer-Ranke** Peter, Das Wunder Israel. Stu-Neuhausen 1988, Hänssler. 144 p.; 192 Fotos (H. & M. *Jacoby*). DM 60. – ^RGeistL 61 (1988) 471 (M. *Maier*).

g937 **Nash** Ernest, Pictorial dictionary of ancient Rome. NY 1981 = 1962, Hacker Art. 544 p.; pl. 1-674; II. 532 p.; pl. 675-1338.

g938 **Radovan** Zev, Land of the Bible photo archive. J c. 1988, POB 8441. The announcement offers further special photographic and computer services, also for 'the places mentioned in the book', but does not give pages or other data on 'the book' as such.

g939 **Stephens** William H., The New Testament world in pictures 1987 ➤ 3,f315: ^RBAR-W 14/6 (1988) 70 (J. R. *Teringo*).

g940 ^E**Weber** Hans, Die Türkei; Landschaften am Mittelmeer. Köln 1987, DuMont. 220 p.; ill.; maps. DM 86. – ^RMundus 24 (1988) 80 (J. H. *Hohnholz*).

Zink I., Tief ist der Brunnen der Vergangenheit; eine Reise durch die Ursprungsländer der Bibel 1988 ➤ h603.

U1.6 Guide books, *Führer*.

g943 **Bardorf** U. & W., Syrien – Jordanien, Reisehandbuch^{2rev}. Mü 1988, auct. (P. Lagarde-Str. 21). 416 p.; ill.; plans. DM 30,80. 3-925808-00-0.

g944 **Gonen** Rivka, Biblical holy places 1987 ➤ 3,f322: ^RBInstArch 25 (1988) 122 (A. *Pinhas*: including also Egypt, Turkey, Malta).

Kamil Jill, Coptic Egypt, history and guide 1988 ➤ d204.

g944* **Keel** O., *Küchler* M., Orte und Landschaften der Bibel 2, 1982 ➤ 63,d816... 3,f326: ^RRÉJ 146 (1987) 164s (A. *Lemaire*).

Khouri Rami G., A brief guide to the antiquities: *a*) Amman; – *b*) The desert castles; – *c*) Petra; – *d*) The antiquities of the Jordan Rift valley 1988 ➤ e844s; e858.

g945 **Koenigs** Wolf, Türkei, die Westküste von Troja bis Knidos^{4rev}.: Cicerone Kunst- und Reiseführer. Z 1988, Artemis. 244 p.; 149 fig. DM 34 [AntWelt 19/1 adv.].

g946 **Meyer** Marianne D., Richtig reisen; Ägypten. Köln 1987, DuMont. 353 p.; ill. DM 36. 3-7701-1753-0. – ^RWeltOr 19 (1988) 164s (Ingrid *Gamer-Wallert*).

g947 **Noort** Edward, Israel und das westliche Jordanufer; ein Reiseführer [1983 ➤ 65,b782], ᵀ*Bunte* Wolfgang. Neuk 1987, Neuk-V. 386 p. DM 39,80. – ᴿTrierTZ 97 (1988) 525s (R. *Bohlen*).

g948 **Scheck** Frank R., Jordanien, Völker und Kulturen zwischen Jordan und Roten Meer: Kunst-Reiseführer 1985 ➤ 2,b550; 3,f335: ᴿOLZ 83 (1988) 451-5 (H. *List*).

U1.7 **Onomastica.**

g949 **Aḥituv** Shmuel, Canaanite toponyms in ancient Egyptian documents 1984 ➤ 65,b786; 3,f336: ᴿCdÉ 63 (1988) 102-11 (K. A. *Kitchen* supplies missing Egyptian index); VT 38 (1988) 370-2 (J. D. *Ray*: cites 15 among many weaknesses).

g950 *Beinlich* Horst, Fragmente dreier geographischer Listen: ZägSpr 115 (1988) 96-107; 6 fig. [Korrektur p. 174].

g951 *a) Bordreuil* Pierre, Du Carmel à l'Amanus, notes de toponymie phénicienne [I. Toponymie, colloq. Strasbourg 1975/7, 177-184]; II; – *b) Riis* P. J., Quelques problèmes de la topographie phénicienne; Usnu, Paltos, Pelléta et les ports de la région: ➤ 706, Géographie 1985/8, 301-314 / 315-324; 3 maps.

g951* *Bordreuil* Pierre, Nouvelles restitutions de toponymes de l'Ougarit: UF 20 (1988) 9-18.

g952 **Calderini** Aristide, Dizionario dei nomi geografici e topografici dell'Egitto greco-romano [5, 1987 ➤ 3,f341], ᴱ*Daris* Sergio, Sup. 1, 1935-1986. Mi 1988, Cisalpino. 250 p. 88-205-0585-1.

g953 *Deroy* Louis, À propos du cadastre mycénien de Pylos; le mot *ra-ke* et la lagune d'Osmanaga: Minos 23 (1988) 59-74.

g954 *Edel* Elmar, Der Name *di-q3jˊ-j3-s* in der minoisch-mykenischen Liste *Enli* 8 gleich *Thebais*?: ZägSpr 115 (1988) 30-35.

g955 *Frankel* Rafael, Topographical notes on the territory of Acre in the Crusader period [improvements for Atlas of Israel Map 12/IX]: IsrEJ 38 (1988) 249-272.

g956 *Frei* Peter, Phrygische Toponyme: EpAnat 11 (1988) 9-32; pl. 3-9; ❶ 34.

g957 *Goedicke* Hans, Yam - More [Yam of Harkhuf's route is west of Abydos and Elephantine, southeast of Khargeh; not Butana as E. *Edel*]: GöMiszÄg 101 (1988) 35-41; map. 42.

g957* **Görg** Manfred, *a*) Kinza (Qadesch) in hieroglyphischen Namenlisten?: BibNot 44 (1988) 23-26; – *b*) Zu einer weiteren Afrikaliste Ramses' II; – *c*) Von 'Taḫši' nach 'Ḫatti'; – *d*) Toponymie und Soziographie; zur nichturbanen Bevölkerungsstruktur Nordpalästinas im 14. Jahrh. v. Chr.: BibNot 45 (1988) 19-21 / 22-25 / 51-61.

g958 *Horn* J., Das Gebiet des 12, Oberägyptischen Gaues; eine historisch-topographische Analyse II: OrLovPer 19 (1988) 37-61.

g959 **Na'aman** Nadav, Borders and districts in biblical historiography; seven studies in biblical geographical lists: Jerusalem Biblical Studies 4. J 1986, Simor. 284 p. $24 pa. – ᴿJBL 107 (1988) 114s (W. R. *Wifall*).

g960 *Radday* Yehuda T., Vom Humor in biblischen Ortsnamen: ➤ 469, Wünschet 1986/8, 431-446.

g961 *Segert* Stanislav. Diptotic geographical feminine names in the Hebrew Bible: ZAHeb 1,1 (1988) 99-102.

g961* *Steinkeller* Piotr, On the identity of the toponym LÚ.SU(.A) [= Šimaški (state)]: JAOS 108 (1988) 197-202.

g962 *Thirion* Michelle, Notes d'onomastique; contribution à une révision du RANKE PN [d'où le Fichier des anthroponymes théophores et to-pophores], sixième série: → 119, Mém. POSENER G., RÉgp 39 (1988) 131-146; Eng. 146.

g963 **Thompson** T.L., *Gonçalves* F.J., *Cangh* J.M. Van, Toponymie palestinienne [first on eleven northern and twenty southern regions, to preserve vanishing Arab traditions], Plaine de St. Jean d'Acre et corridor de Jérusalem: Inst. Orientaliste Publ. 37. Leuven 1988, Université Catholique (Peeters). 132 p. Fb 750. 0076-1265 [BL 89,42, A.G. *Auld*]. – ᴿPrOrChr 38 (1988) 413 (P. *Ternant*).

g964 *Weber* Dieter, Zu einigen iranischen Ortsnamen bei PTOLEMAIOS: → 6, ꜰASMUSSEN J. 1988, 493-5.

g965 *Yoshikawa* Mamoru, GABA-aš and GABA-ta in the Ur III Umma texts [GABA = 'the opposite side (of the Tigris)' i.e. Elam]: AcSum 10 (1988) 231-241.

g965* *Zadok* Ran, Notes on the prosopography of the Old Testament [...toponym Beth Hanan]: BibNot 42 (1988) 44-48.

g966 *Zevit* Ziony, Onomastic gleanings from recently published Judahite bullae: IsrEJ 38 (1988) 227-234; 5 fig.

u2.1   *Geologia;* soils, mountains, earthquakes.

g967 **Andel** Tjeerd H. van, *Runnels* Curtis, Beyond the Acropolis; a rural Greek past. Stanford 1987, Univ. xxii-221 p.; 34 fig.; 26 maps. $27.50. 0-8047-1389-8. – ᴿAntiquity 62 (1988) 390.392 (G. *Barker*); ClasW 82 (1988s) 131 (L.T. *Pearcy*: 50,000 years of soil erosion; but no reason to suppose that Bronze Age Greece had thicker soil or more lush forests).

g968 ᴱ**Baily** Geoff, *Parkington* John, The archaeology of prehistoric coastlines. C 1988, Univ. vi-154 p.; 60 fig. £25. 0-521-25036-6. – ᴿAntiquity 62 (1988) 812s (Bryony *Coles*).

g969 *Bernabé* A., Un mito etiológico anatólico sobre el Tauro (CTH 16) en Nonno (Dion. 1.408s): AulaO 6 (1988) 5-10: Mt. Taurus is named for Zeus in form of bull, taken from Hittite myth of the bull who lifted the mountain when the Hittite army was marching against Aleppo.

g970 **Eloni** S., (*Shachnai* A.), ❿ Geological survey of Israel 7. 9. Potential raw materials for building. J 1973. Includes three/two loose maps [OIAc D88]. (No. 2 by *Levi* Y., also 4 with *Shirav* M., 1974/2; No. 3 by *Minster* S., 1977).

g971 *Fowden* Garth, City and mountain in late Roman Attica: JHS 108 (1988) 48-59.

g972 *Goldberg* Paul, The archaeologist as viewed by the geologist: BA 51 (1988) 197-202; ill.

g973 *Hancock* R.G., al., Nile alluvium; soils and ceramics: BEgSem 8 (NY 1986s) 61-71; map.

g974 *Hughes* J. Donald, Land and sea [geology, hydrography]: → 444, Mediterranean 1 (1988) 89-133.

g975 ᴱ**Kempe** D.R.C., *Harvey* A.P., The petrology of archaeological artefacts 1983 → 65,b812: ᴿBInstArch 25 (1988) 127s (Caroline *Cartwright*).

g976 **Mann** Ulrich, Überall ist Sinai; die heiligen Berge der Menschheit. FrB 1988, Aurum. 245 p.; ill. 3-591-08273-2.

Aitken M.; *Manning* S.: Thera volcanic eruption 1988 → g778s.

g977 **Rosen** Lissie von, Lapis lazuli in geological contexts and in ancient written sources: SIMA pocket 65. Partille 1988, Åström. [OIAc D88].

U2.2   *Hydrographia:* **rivers, seas, salt.**

g978 **Armayor** G. Kimball, HERODOTUS' autopsy of the Fayoum; Lake Moeris... 1985 ➤ 1,e708; 3,f376: ᴿAmHR 92 (1987) 638s (J. A. S. *Evans*); DiscEg 12 (1988) 103-9 (Renate *Müller-Wollermann*).

g979 **Garbrecht** G., Die Wasserversorgung antiker Städte [1. Rom, 1982; 2. Pergamon, 1987 ➤ 3,e952] 3. Mensch und Wasser. Mainz 1988, von Zabern. 223 p.; (color.) ill. 3-8053-0984-8.

g980 *Gianotti* Gian Franco, Ordine e simmetria nella rappresentazione del mondo; ERODOTO e il paradosso del Nilo: QuadStor 14,27 (1988) 51-92.

g981 **Giddy** Lisa L., Egyptian oases; Bahariya, Dakhla, Farafra and Kharga during pharaonic times [diss. London 1984] 1987 ➤ 3,f389: ᴿBInstArch 25 (1988) 121 (H. M. *Stewart*); BL (1988) 122 (K. A. *Kitchen*).

g982 *Kadish* Gerald E., Seasonality and the name of the Nile [*itrw* 'the Recurrent']: JAmEg 25 (1988) 185-194.

g982* *Kunin* Robert, Water in biblical times: Dor 15 (1986s) 195-8 [< OTAbs 11,140].

g983 *Lindner* Manfred, Nabatäische Talsperren / *Hartung* Fritz, Historische Talsperren [dams] in Iran: in **Garbrecht** Günther, Historische Talsperren [Urartäer p. 140-5]. Stu 1987; p. 147-174 / 221-274 [< Mundus 24,83s].

g984 *Michalowski* Piotr, Magan and Meluḫḫa once again [... 'lower sea' area (Persian Gulf)]: JCS 40 (1988) 156-184.

g985 ᴱ**Quilici Gigli** S., Il Tevere e le altre vie d'acqua del Lazio antico [VII incontro CNR]. R 1986, Cons. Naz. Ricerche. 228 p. – ᴿAevum 62 (1988) 133-5 (V. *Manfredi*).

g986 **Ravasi** Gianfranco, Il Giordano, un fiume fra i due Testamenti. CinB 1988, Paoline. 256 p.; fotografie di *Meyer* F. Lit. 90.000. – ᴿCC 139 (1988,3) 544 (G. *Giachi*).

g987 *Shazly* E. M. el-, The Ostracinic branch; a proposed old branch of the river Nile: DiscEg 7 (1987) 69-78; 2 maps.

g988 *Shelton* John, Notes on the Ptolemaic salt tax under Ptolemy III: ZPapEp 71 (1988) 133-6.

g989 *Torres* Antonio, Sobre la etimología de Jordán: ➤ 102, ᶠMARIN/ FERNÁNDEZ-SEVILLA/GONZÁLEZ 1988, 251-7.

U2.3   **Clima,** *pluvia.*

g990 *Bottema* S., *Woldring* H., Late quaternary vegetation and climate of southwestern Turkey, I: Palaeohistoria 26 (1984) 123-149.

g991 *Gignoux* Philippe, Le mécanisme de la pluie entre le mythe et l'expérimentation (Dādestān ī dēnēg 92): ➤ 4, ᶠAMIET P. = IrAnt 33 (1988) 385-392.

g992 National Atlas of Jordan I., Climate and agroclimatology; II. Hydrology and agrohydrology. Amman 1986, National Geographic Centre [OIAc D88].

g993 ᴱ**Wigley** T. M. I., *al.*, Climate and history; studies in past climates and their impact on man. C 1983 'first paperback edition', Univ. xii-530 p. –

ᴿSalesianum 50 (1988) 384s (E. *Fontana*: titles and *first* pages; none on Levant).

U2.5   *Fauna;*   **Animals.**

g994 *Accattino* Paolo,   ALESSANDRO di Afrodisia e la trasmissione della forma nella riproduzione animale: AtTorino 122,2 (1988) 79-94.

g995 **André** Jacques,   ISIDORE de Séville, Étymologies XII, Des animaux 1986 ⇥ 3,f409:   ᴿClasR 102 (1988) 52-54 (Liliane *Bodson*); JRS 78 (1988) 265s (J. N. *Hillgarth*: also on 17, Agriculture).

g996 **Andreae** Bernard,   Die Symbolik der Löwenjagd.   Opladen 1985, Westdeutscher.   68 p.; 32 pl. DM 19,80. – ᴿClasR 102 (1988) 362s (R. R. R. *Smith*).

g997 *Balconi* Carla,   Bis gravidae pecudes; dichiarazioni di ovini demotiche con annotazione greca: Aegyptus 68 (1988) 47-50.

g998 *Beaux* Nathalie,   Étoile et étoile de mer [poisson Astérie]; une tentative d'identification du signe * : ⇥ 119, Mém. POSENER G., RÉgp 39 (1988) 197-204.

g999 *a) Beckman* Gary,   Herding and herdsmen in Hittite culture; – *b) Neve* Peter,   Ein hethitisches Stierrelief aus Derbent bei Boğazköy: ⇥ 112*, ᶠOTTEN H., Documentum 1988, 33-44 / 263-264 + 4 fig. (map).

h1 **Bevan** Elinor,   Representations of animals in sanctuaries of Artemis and other Olympian deities I-II: BAR-Int 315.   Oxford 1986.   ix-559 p.; ill.

h2 *a) Beyse* K.-M.,   Par 'Stier': – *b) Zobel* H.-J.,   *Pærœh*, 'Wildesel'; – *c) Maiberger* P., *Pærœd*, 'Maultier': ⇥ 815, TWAT 6,6 (1988) 725-731 / 731-5 / 738s.

h3 *Binyamini* N.,   Mycomycetes from Israel – II: Nova Hedwigia 44 (B 1987) 351-365 [< Mundus 24, 165].

h4 *Bodson* Liliane,   The welfare of livestock and work animals in ancient Greece and Rome: Medical Heritage 2 (Ph 1986) 244-249 [< AnPg 58,786].

h5 *a) Bodson* Liliane,   La zoologie romaine d'après la NH de PLINE; – *b) Byl* Simon,   Le stelio dans la NH de PLINE: Helmantica 37 (1986) 107-116 / 117-130.

h6 *a) Bodson* Liliane, Caractères et tendances de la zoologie romaine; – *b) Gourévitch* D., *Grmek* M.,   Medice, cura te ipsum; les maladies de GALIEN; – *c) Stückelberger* Alfred,   Die geographische Ortsbestimmung und das Problem der synchronen Zeitmessung: Revue Fac. Lettres Univ. Lausanne ('Sciences et techniques a Rome' 1986) [120 p.: RPLH 62, 1 (1988) 159].

h7 *Bökönyi* Sándor,   Subfossil elephant remains from Southwestern Asia [Malatya, Kamid el-Loz; not 'Syria' as p. 3]: Paléorient 11,2 (1985) 161-3; 4 fig.

h8 **Boessneck** Joachim,   Die Tierwelt des Alten Ägyptens.   Mü 1988, Beck. 197 p.; 252 fig.; DM 88. 3-406-333656 [OIAc D88].

h9 **Boessneck** J.,   Die Münchener Ochsenmumie 1987 ⇥ 3,f416:   ᴿJAmEg 25 (1988) 246s (A. *Gautier*).

h10 **Boessneck** J., Tuna el-Gebel I. Die Tiergalerien 1987 ⇥ 3,f417:   ᴿJAmEg 25 (1988) 247s (A. *Gautier*).

h11 *Boessneck* Joachim, *Driesch* Angela von den,   Tierknochenfunde vom Tell Ibrahim Awad im östlichen Nildelta: ⇥ 724, Delta 1986/8, 117-122 [111-4, *Zeist* Willen van, Plant remains].

h12 **Boessneck** J., *Driesch* A. von den, Studien an subfossilen Tierknochen aus Ägypten 1982 ➤ 63,d915; 65,b849; ᴿJAmEg 25 (1988) 245s (A. *Gautier*).

h13 *Boessneck* Joachim, *Peters* Joris, Tierknochen- und Molluskenfunde aus dem Grabungsbereich 'Kuppe' in Tall Munbāqa: MDOG 120 (1988) 51-58; 5 fig.

h14 *Bolomey* Alexandra (in Rumanian), Preliminary study of animal remains from the neo-aeneolithic site at Parţa: Studii... IsVArh 39 (Bucureşti 1988) 207-221.

h15 *Brewer* Douglas J., A faunal sample from El-Hibeh: JSStEg 15 (1985) 55-67, map.

h16 *Brice* William C., [Linear A] The 'livestock' tablet, Her. Mus. 1609: Kadmos 27 (1988) 155-161; 7 fig.

h17 **Capponi** F. *a*) Ornithologia latina. Genova 1979 ➤ 61,t991. – *b*) Le fonti del X libro della 'Naturalis historia' di PLINIO. Genova 1985, Univ. Fac. Lett. 342 p. – ᴿBStLat 17 (1987) 147s (C. *Salemme*).

h18 *Chaix* Louis, Quatrième note sur la faune de Kerma (Soudan), campagnes 1985 et 1986: Genava 34 (1986) 35-39.

h19 **Clutton-Brock** Juliet, A history of domesticated animals [pa.]. C c.1988, Univ./British Museum. 208 p.; ill. £10. 0-521-34697-5 [Antiquity 62,749].

h20 *Davies* Malcolm, *Kathirithamby* Jeyaraney. Greek insects 1986 ➤ 3,f430: ᴿAmHR 93 (1988) 1026 (T. W. *Africa*).

h21 **Davis** Simon, The archaeology of animals 1987 ➤ 3,f431; 0-7134-4572-6: ᴿAntiquity 62 (1988) 196s (A. J. *Legge*); BInstArch 25 (1988) 114s (S. W. *Hillson*).

h22 *Davis* S., *al.*, Quaternary extinctions and population increase in western Asia; the animal remains from Biq'at Quneitra: Paléorient 14,1 (1988) 95-105; 2 fig.; 2 pl.

h23 *Dayan* Tamar, *al.*, Animal exploitation in Ujrat el-Meked, a Neolithic site in southern Sinai: Paléorient 12,2 (1986) 105-116; 6 fig.

h24 *a*) *Derchain* Philippe, Des hirondelles et des étoiles; – *b*) *Roquet* Gérard, Migrateur et flamant rose dans l'Égypte dynastique et copte; milieu, image et signe: ➤ 704, ᴱ*Borgeaud* P., L'animal 1981/5, 105-110 / 111-126; 4 pl.

h25 *a*) *Cauvin* Jacques, Réflexion sur la signification des représentations animales dans le Proche-Orient préhistorique; – *b*) *Borgeaud* Philippe, L'animal comme opérateur symbolique; – *c*) *Chaix* Louis, Quelques réflexions sur le bucrâne: ➤ 704, L'animal 1981/5, 21-31 / 13-19 / 33-37.

h26 *De Salvia* Fulvio, Un nuovo esemplare di stele di 'Horo sui coccodrilli' rinvenuto in Italia [provenienza sconosciuta]: OrAnt 27 (1988) 127-131; pl. I-III.

h27 **Droste zu Hülshoff** Vera von, Der Igel im alten Ägypten: Hildesheimer ÄgBeiträge 11, 1980 ➤ 61,t996... 64,d450: ᴿJNES 47 (1988) 49s (B. *Williams*).

h28 *Figueras* P., Grafitos pisciformes en osarios y origen judío del *ichthús*: BAsEspOr 23 (1987) 119-134.

h29 *Fischer* Klaus D., Die Einleitung zum 1. Buch der Mulomedicina Chironis (Chiron 3): Philologus 132 (1988) 227-9.

h30 **Frayn** Joan M., Sheep-rearing and the wool trade in Italy during the Roman period 1984 ➤ 65,b866... 2,b630: ᴿBInstArch sup. 24 (1987) 21s (B. *Levitan*); ClasR 102 (1988) 96-99 (N. *Purcell*).

h31 *Garber* P. L., Sheep: ➤ 801, ISBEnc³ 4 (1988) 463-5.

h32 *Gilbert* Allan S., Zooarchaeological observations on the slaughterhouse of Meketre [Thebes, dated 2000 B.C., found 1920 A.D.]: JEA 74 (1988) 69-89; 6 fig.; pl. X-XIV.

h33 *Green* Anthony, A note on the 'lion-demon': Iraq 50 (1988) 167s: pl. XI.

h34 *Hallet* Charles, CLAUDIEN, poète animalier: ÉtClas 56 (1988) 49-66.

h35 *Handoussa* Tohfa, Fish offering in the Old Kingdom: MiDAI 44 (1988) 105-9; 1 fig.; pl. 15a.

h36 *Hawass* Zahi, *al.*, Chronology, sediments, and subsistence [cattle, sheep, goats, pigs, fish, hippopotamus; wheat, barley] at Merimda Beni Salama [60 k N Cairo]: JEA 74 (1988) 31-38.

h36* *Hepper* F. Nigel, The identity and origin of classical bitter aloes (aloe): PEQ 120 (1988) 146-8; 1 fig.

h37 **Hillson** Simon, Teeth. C 1986, Univ. 350 p. $47.50. 0-521-30405-9. – RBInstArch sup 24 (1987) 45 (K. M. *Dobney*).

h38 *Hoffmann* Herbert, The cicada on the omphalos [of Boston libation-bowl]; an iconological excursion: Antiquity 62 (1988) 744-9.

h39 **Hofmann** Inge, Hase, Perlhunen und Hyäne — Spuren meroitischer Oralliteratur: BeiSud Beih 41. W-Mödling 1988, Univ. Inst. Afrikanistik [OIAc D88].

h40 *Hofmann* Inge, *a*) Das Krokodil als Verschlinger; – *b*) Ein Gefässtyp mit plastisch aufgesetzten Tierfiguren: VarAeg 4 (1988) 43-53; 9 fig. / 215-220; 2 fig.

h41 **Houlihan** Patrick F., The birds of ancient Egypt 1986 → 2,b640; 3,f447: RBO 45 (1988) 318s (L. *Chaix*).

h42 **Johnson** Buffie, Lady of the beasts; ancient images of the goddess and her sacred animals. SF 1988, Harper & R. XII-386 p.; 332 fig.; 50 color pl. 0-06-250423-1.

h43 *Jones* Andrew K. G., *al.*, The worms of Roman horses and other finds of intestinal parasite eggs from unpromising deposits: Antiquity 62 (1988) 275s.

h44 *Kammenhuber* Annelies, On Hittites, Mitanni-Hurrians, Indo-Aryans and horse tablets in the IInd Millennium B.C.: → 760, Anatolian 1983/8, 35-51.

h45 **Kanowski** Maxwell, Old bones; unlocking archaeological secrets. Melbourne 1987, Longman Cheshire. 128 p. A$13. 0-582-71162-2 [AncHRes 19, 54, J. L. *Kohen*].

h46 *Kersten* A. M. P., Age and sex composition of epipalaeolithic fallow deer and wild goat from Ksar 'Akil: Palaeohistoria 29 (1987) 119-131; 6 fig.

h47 *Khazai* Khosrow, Les êtres hybrides et la cosmogonie orientale: → 763, Archéologie 1986, 13-19; 11 fig.

h48 *Kolska-Horowitz* Liura, *Tchernov* Eitan, ⊕ The relationship between man and beast in the Early Bronze Age: Qadmoniot 21 (1988) 2-5; ill.

h49 *Krzyszkowska* O. H., Ivory in the Aegean Bronze Age; elephant tusk or hippopotamus ivory?: AnBritAth 83 (1988) 209-233; 5 fig.; pl. 24-30.

h50 *Labarbe* Jules, Les mulets [*hēmíonoi* Iliade 24,277s] des Mysiens: AntClas 57 (1988) 40-55.

h51 *Lau* Dieter, Aquila / Aranea [Spinne, spider]: → 783, AugL 1,3 (1988) 429-431 / 432s.

h52 *Lau* Dieter, Animal, tierkundlich: → 783, AugL 1,3 (1988) 361-374 [356-361, *Baltes* Matthias].

h53 *Lambert* W. G., The history of the muš-ḫuš in ancient Mesopotamia: → 704, E*Borgeaud* P., L'animal 1981/5, 87-94: a lion with snake head and eagle talons; on enameled bricks of Babylon.

h54 **Leone** Aurora, Gli animali da trasporto nell'Egitto greco, romano e bizantino: PapyrolCastroctav 12. R 1988. Pont. Ist. Biblico. 102 p. Lit. 19.500. 88-7653-579-9.

h54* **Lincoln** Bruce, Priests, warriors, and cattle; a study in the ecology of religions 1981 ➤ 62,9931 ... 1,e792: ᴿRelStR 14 (1988) 16-22 (C. *Hallisey*, also on three more recent Lincoln books).

h55 *Livingstone* A., The Isin 'dog house' [Ninisina temple] revisited: JCS 40 (1988) 55-60.

h55* *Llagostera* Esteban, El gato, en el Egipto faraónico: BAsEspOr 22 (1986) 381-391; 2 fig.

h56 **Lortet** L. C., *Gaillard* C., La faune momifiée de l'ancienne Égypte: Archives Mus. Hist. Nat. 9/2. Lyon 1907 [OIAc D88], H. Georg.

h57 *McGovern* P. E., *Michel* R. H. [*Saltzman* M.], Has authentic *tēkēlet* been identified?: BASOR [265 (1987) 25-33, *Ziderman* I.] 269 (1988) 81-83 [83s]; 84-90, response and bibliog.

h57* *Morgan* J. R., Two giraffes emended [*aristerón* for *asteron* in Sylloge Constantini c. 950 A.D.]: ClasQ 38 = 81 (1988) 267-9.

h58 *Mudar* Karen M., The effects of context on bone assemblages; examples from the Uruk period in southwest Iran: Paléorient 14,1 (1988) 151-168; franç. 151.

h59 *Nagel* Wolfram, Frühe Tierwelt in Südwestasien I [< ᶠ*Gandert*, BBVFG 2 (1959) 106-118] – II [ZAss 55 (1963) 169-222]: ➤ 234, Altvorderasien 1988, 320-343, 29 pl. / 345-398 + XIV pl.

h60 *a*) *Naudts-Coppens* Marie-Anne, Die mesopotamische dierkapellen [... orchestras]; mythe of fantasie?; – *b*) *Walle* B. van de, La laborieuse abeille dans l'ancienne Égypte: ➤ 50, ᶠFONTINOY C. 1988, 129-138; 4 fig. / 147-151.

h61 *Niehr* H., *pārāš*, 'Pferd': ➤ 815, TWAT 6,6s (1988) 782-7.

h62 **Nikolaus** Gerhard, Distribution atlas of Sudan's birds with notes on habitat and status: Bonner Zoologische Monographien 25. Bonn 1987, Museum Koenig. 322 p. [Mundus 24,171].

h63 *Parker* A. J., The birds of Roman Britain: OxJArch 7 (1988) 197-226; 2 fig.

h64 ᵀᴱ**Terian** Abraham, PHILON d'Alexandrie, Alexander; vel de ratione quam habere etiam bruta animalia... (De animalibus) e versione armeniaca: Œuvres 36. P 1988, Cerf. 225 p. F 153. 2-204-03040-6.

h65 **Pilali-Papasteriou** A., Die bronzenen Tierfiguren aus Kreta: Präh. Bronzefunde 1/3, 1985 ➤ 2,b663; DM 138: ᴿPraehZts 63 (1988) 202 (H. *Matthäus*).

h66 *Reese* David S., Man meets hippo [pig-size; also pony-size elephant, from Cyprus about 8200 B.C. by Carbon-14 tests]: ASOR Newsletter (Fall 1989) 5; 2 fig.

h67 *Reiter* Karin, Falknerei im Alten Orient? Ein Beitrag zur Geschichte der Falknerei: MDOG 120 (1988) 189-206; 10 fig.

h68 *Renfroe* F., Diagnosing long-dead patients; the equine ailments in KTU 1.85: Orientalia 57 (1988) 181-191.

h69 *Rowley-Conwy* Peter, The camel in the Nile valley; new Radiocarbon Accelerator (AMS) dates from Qasr Ibrim: JEA 74 (1988) 245-8; pl. XXXV.

h70 *Säflund* Gösta, Girls and gazelles; reflections on Theran [sport] fresco imagery: ➤ 111, ᶠMYLONAS G., *Philia épē* 1 (1986) 185-190; 3 fig.; pl. 12-13.

h71 *Sanmartín* J., Textos hipiátricos de Ugarit y el discurso del método [*Cohen* 1983, *Pardee* 1985]: AulaOr 6 (1988) 227-235.

h72 *Schauenburg* Konrad, Eulen aus Athen und Unteritalien: JbDAI 103 (1988) 67-85; 31 fig.

h73 *Scheffer* Charlotte, Marine fauna – an unusual motif in Athenian black figure: OpAth 17 (1988) 231-4; 3 fig.

h74 *Schley* D. G., Wolf: → 801, ISBEnc³ 4 (1988) 1088s.

h75 *a) Schütt* H., The molluscs of the oasis Palmyra; – *b) Joger* U., An interpretation of reptile zoogeography in Arabia, with special reference to Arabian herpetofaunal relations with Africa; – *c) Krupp* F., Freshwater ichthyogeography of the Levant: → 710, Zoogeography 1987, 62-72 / 257-271 / 229-237 [< Mundus 24,168s].

h76 *Spycket* Agnès, Lions en terre cuite de Suse: → 4, ᶠAmiet P. = IrAnt 33 (1988) 149-156; 2 fig.; V pl.

h77 **Stein Gil** J., Pastoral production in complex societies; mid-late third millennium B.C. and medieval faunal remains from Gritille Höyük in the Karababa Basin, Southeast Turkey: diss. Pennsylvania. Ph 1988. – 88-16240 [OIAc D88].

h78 *Stein* Gil, Herding strategies at neolithic Gritille [NE Carchemish]; the use of animal bone remains to reconstruct ancient economic systems: Expedition 28,2 (Ph 1986) 35-42; 15 fig.

h79 *Tooley* Angela M. J., Coffin of a dog from Beni Hasan: JEA 74 (1988) 207-211; pl. XXVI-XXVII.

h79* *Toperoff* S. P., Fish / fox / goat / hart-hind in Bible and Midrash: Dor 16 (1987s) 46-50 . 112-5 . 196-200 . 271s + 216 (not 246 as indicated).

h80 *Vachon* M., *Kinzelbach* R., On the taxonomy and distribution of the scorpions of the Middle East: → 710, Zoogeography 1987, 91-103 [Mundus 24,257].

h81 *Wapnish* Paula, *Hesse* Brian, Urbanization and the organization of animal production at Tell Jemmeh in the Middle Bronze Age Levant: JNES 47 (1988) 81-94.

h82 *Waschke* O., ṣo'n, 'Kleinvieh': → 815, TWAT 6,6s.8 (1988) 858-868.

h83 *Weber* Manfred, Heuschrecke: → 807, RAC 14,111s (1988) 1231-50.

h88 *Westermann* James S., The fowling scenes in the Temple of Sety I — Abydos: GöMiszÄg 103 (1988) 81-91; 1 fig.

h89 *Wolff* R. J., Zoology: → 801, ISBEnc³ 4 (1988) 1204-10.

h90 *Yoyotte* Jean, Des lions et des chats; contribution à la prosopographie de l'époque libyenne: → 111, Mém. Posener G., RÉgp 39 (1988) 155-177; Eng. 178; pl. 2-6.

U2.7 **Flora;** *plantae biblicae et antiquae.*

h91 ᵀᴱ**Amigues** Suzanne, Théophraste, Recherches sur les plantes: Coll. Budé. P 1988s, BLettres. lvii + 66 (d.) + pp. 67-145; II. 118 + 119-305. 2-251-00403-7; 4-5.

h92 *Amigues* Suzanne, Le crocus et le safran sur une fresque de Théra: RArchéol (1988) 227-242; 4 fig.

h93 *Baruch* Uri, The Late Holocene vegetational history of Lake Kinneret (Sea of Galilee), Israel: Paléorient 12,2 (1986) 37-48; 4 fig.

h94 **Baudy** Gerhard J., Adonisgärten ... Samensymbolik 1986 → 3,f489: ᴿAnt-Clas 57 (1988) 471-3 (Brigitte *Servais-Soyez*: éphémère).

h95 **Baum** Nathalie, Arbres et arbustes de l'Égypte ancienne; la liste de la tombe thébaine d'Ineni (n. 81): OrLovAn 31. Lv 1988, Univ. xix-381 p.; 68 fig.

h96 *Baum* Nathalie, Essai d'identification de l'arbre ou arbuste *im3* des anciens Égyptiens: VarAeg 4 (1988) 17-31; 2 fig.: maerua crassifolia Forsk.

h97 *Beaux* Nathalie, The representation of Polygonum senegalense Meisn. in ancient Egyptian [... marsh-] reliefs and paintings: JEA 74 (1988) 248-252; 4 fig.; pl. XXXVI [author given as *Beaux* Nathalie, also in index]. ➤ h96.

h98 *Berg* Werner, Israels Land, der Garten Gottes; der Garten als Bild des Heils im Alten Testament [kath. Antrittsvorlesung Bochum 1985]: BZ 32 (1988) 35-51.

h99 *Betrò* M. Carmela, Erbari nell'antico Egitto [Tebtunis 20, *Tait* W. 1977]: EgVO 11 (1988) 71-110.

h100 *Chevallier* Raymond, Le bois, l'arbre et le forêt chez PLINE: Helmantica 37 (1986) 147-172.

h102 *Desautels* Jacques, La classification des végétaux dans la Recherche sur les plantes de THEOPHRASTE d'Érésos: Phoenix 42 (Toronto 1988) 219-243.

h103 *Diethart* Johannes, *Sijpesteijn* Pieter J., Gerste und Rizinus in Papyri aus Princeton: Tyche 3 (1988) 29-32; pl. 2-3.

h104 *Drège* Jean-Pierre, Les débuts du papier en Chine: CRAI (1987) 642-650 (-652).

h105 *Elayi* Josette, L'exploitation des cèdres du Mont-Liban par les rois assyriens et néo-babyloniens: JESHO 31 (1988) 14-41.

h106 *Eliner* Eliezer *zal.*, ☉ *Șîșîm û-pᵉraḥîm*. Blossoms and buds in the Bible: BethM 34,118 (1988s) 193-7. [This issue is numbered 108 on the English front cover, but rightly 118 on the Hebrew cover, where however the volume number is given as 33, though it comes after two issues of volume 34.]

h107 *Emery-Barbier* Aline, Analyses polliniques du quaternaire supérieur en Jordanie méridionale: Paléorient 14,1 (1988) 111-7; 1 pl.

h108 *Ferrari* L. C., The tree in the works of Saint AUGUSTINE: AugLv 38 (1988) 37-53.

h109 *Fischer* Henry G., [Perfume-flower bearers] The early publication of a relief in Turin: GöMiszÄg 101 (1988) 31s; 33, 2 phot.

h110 **Germer** Renate, Flora des pharaonischen Ägypten 1985 ➤ 1,e843 ... 3,f505: ᴿOLZ 83 (1988) 662s (W. *Barta*).

h111 **Germer** Renate, Katalog der altägyptischen Pflanzenreste der Berliner Museen ['Museum', Mundus 24,252]: ÄgAbh 47. Wsb 1988, Harrassowitz. ix-72 p.; 16 pl. 3-447-02788-6.

h112 ᵀᴱ**Goujard** Raoul, COLUMELLE, Les arbres 1986 ➤ 2,b696; 3,f508: ᴿAntClas 57 (1988) 427s (R. *Verdière*); ClasR 102 (1988) 154s (K. D. *White*); RÉLat 65 (1987) 305-7 (R. *Martin*).

h113 *Hansen* David H., Problems in identifying wood used in the manufacture of an Egyptian sarcophagus and coffin: DiscEg 12 (1988) 27-33 + 5 fig.; foldout.

h114 *Janssen* J. L., The price of papyrus [rejoinder to CAMINOS]: DiscEg 9 (1987) 33-35.

h115 **Kaempfer** Engelbert, Phoenix persicus; die Geschichte der Dattelpalme, ᵀ*Muntschick* Wolfgang. Marburg 1987, Basilisken. 227 p. 24 fig. DM 48. 3-925347-03-8. – ᴿJESHO 31 (1988) 326s (M. *Stol*).

h116 *a*) *Kedar-Kopfstein* B., *pᵉri* 'Frucht'; – *b*) *Kapelrud* A., *pærah* 'Spross': TWAT 6,6 (1988) 740-752 / 752-5.

h117 **Keimer** Ludwig, ᴱ*Germer* Renate, Die Gartenpflanzen im Alten Ägypten II, 1984 ➤ 1,e851; 3,f513: ᴿCdÉ 63 (1988) 249-252 (G. *Charpentier*: there are many more recent items).

h118 *Kinnier Wilson* J. V., Lines 40-52 of the banquet stele of Aššurnaṣirpal I [names of 41 kinds of trees]: Iraq 50 (1988) 79-82.

h119 [Montagno] *Leahy* Lise, The puzzling history of Turin 1673 [lily-pressing]: GöMiszÄg 105 (1988) 55-57.

h120 *Lüchtrath* Agnes, *tj-šps*, der Kampferbaum Ostafrikas: GöMiszÄg 101 (1988) 43-48.

h121 *Martínez F. F.* Javier, Cuatro himnos de S. EFRÉN sobre el aceite, el olivo y los misterios de Nuestro Señor (De Virginitate IV-VII): Compostellanum 32 (1987) 65-91.

h122 **Mayer** Hannes, *Aksöy* Hüseyin, Wälder der Türkei. Stu 1986, Fischer. xx-290 p.; 84 fig. DM 58. – RMundus 24 (1988) 152-4 (H. *Steinlin*).

h123 *Mazzini* Innocenzo, Présence de PLINE dans les herbiers de l'Antiquité et du haut Moyen-Âge: Helmantica 37 (1986) 83-94.

h124 **Meiggs** Russell, Trees and timber in the ancient Mediterranean world 1982 → 64,d499... 3,f518: RAmHR 91 (1986) 365s (H. C. *Boren*); JEA 74 (1988) 391-4 (R. *Burleigh*).

h125 *Nielsen* K., *pešæt*, 'Flachs': → 815, TWAT 6,6s (1988) 816-8.

h126 *Patella* Michael, Olives — Mediterranean treasure: BToday 26 (1988) 293-8.

h127 **Piperno** D. R., Phytolith analysis; an archaeological and geological perspective. L 1987, Academic. 280 p. £31. 0-12-557175-5 [Antiquity 62,391 adv.].

h128 *Rauschenbach* B., Apfel [-baum] *tappuaḥ*: → 804, NBL Lfg 1 (1988) 121 [notes that the Paradise fruit is not called apple, but says nothing about 'apricot', cf.*Stol* M., BO 45 (1988) 442].

h129 *Ryan* Donald P., Papyrus: BA 51 (1988) 132-140; ill.

h130 **Schahadat** Issa, Pflanzliche Kosmetika im Altertum; experimentelle Untersuchungen über ihre antimykotische und antibakterielle Wirkung: Diss. Düsseldorf 1979. 94 p.; ill. [< AnPg 58,797].

h131 ESchweizer Harald, ... Bäume braucht man doch! Das Symbol des Bäumes zwischen Hoffnung und Zerstörung 1986 → 2,338*; 247 p.; 40 fig. + 20 color. DM 32 pa.: RErbAuf 64 (1988) 328 (E. *Tschacher*).

h132 **Sjöquist** Karl-Erik, *Åström* Paul, Pylos, palmprints and palmleaves: SIMA pocket 31, 1985 → 2,b710: RBO 45 (1988) 659-661 (C. J. *Ruijgh*).

h133 *Stika* H.-P., Botanische Untersuchungen in der bronzezeitlichen Höhensiedlung Fuente Álamo: MadMit 29 (1988) 21-76; 38 fig.; 8 pl.; español 65, Eng. 65s.

h134 *Weische* Alfons, Arbor [... der Baum in wichtigen biblischen Texten]: → 783, AugL 1,3 (1988) 433-441.

h135 *a)* *Zeist* W. van, *Bakker-Heeres* J. A. H., Archaeobotanical studies in the Levant, 2. Neolithic/Halaf Ras Shamra; 3. Late-Paleolithic Mureybit; 4. Bronze Age sites on the North Syrian Euphrates: Palaeohistoria 26 (1984) 151-170 / 171-199 / 27 (1985) 247-316. – *b)* *Zeist, al.*, Ganj Dareh Tepe, Iran: Palaeohistoria 26 (1984) 201-224.

h136 *Zeist* W. van, *Waterbolk-van Rooijen* W., The paleobotany of Tell Bouqras, Eastern Syria: Paléorient 11,2 (1985) 131-147; 5 fig.

U2.8 Agricultura, alimentatio.

h137 *Abd-el-Ghany* Mohammed S., The problem of *ábrochos gê* in Roman Egypt: → 492, XVIII Papyrol 2 (1986/8) 295-299.

h138 *Adkin* N., Some notes on the content of JEROME's twenty-second letter [on food and drink ...]: GrazBei 15 (1988) 177-186.

h139 L'alimentazione nel mondo antico: i Romani, età imperiale (mostra Roma 1987); gli Egizi (mostra Torino 1987). R 1987, Ist. poligrafico.

h140 L'alimentazione nell'antichità; mostra Parma, 2-3.V.1985. Parma 1985, Archeoclub. 282 p.; ill.

h141 *Amedick* Rita, Zur Motivgeschichte eines Sarkophages [Cava dei Tirreni] mit ländlichem Mahl: MiDAI-R 95 (1988) 205-234; pl. 76-85.

h142 **Amouretti** Marie-Claire, Le pain et l'huile dans la Grèce antique, de l'araire au moulin 1986 ➤ 3,f530: ᴿAJA 92 (1988) 448s (V. *Hanson*).

h143 *a) Amouretti* M. C., La viticulture antique; contraintes et choix techniques; – *b) Villard* Pierre, Le mélange [du vin avec l'eau] et ses problèmes: RÉAnc 90,1s [réunion Bordeaux-Sophau 1986: 1988] 5-17, III fig. / 19-33.

h144 ᵀᴱ**André** Jacques, COLUMELLE, De l'agriculture XII (De l'intendante): Coll. Budé. P 1988, BLettres. 141 (doubles) p. 2-251-01342-3.

h145 *Bandstra* B. L., Wine (-press): ➤ 801, ISBEnc³ 4 (1988) 1069-72.

h146 *Beckwith* Roger T., The vegetarianism of the Therapeutae, and the motives for vegetarianism in early Jewish and Christian circles: ➤ 22, Mém. CARMIGNAC J., RQum 13 (1988) 407-410.

h147 *Bingen* Jean, HÈRONINOS, Théadelphie et son vin: CdÉ 63 (1988) 367-378.

h148 ᴱ**Blázquez Martínez** J.M., *Remesal Rodríguez* J., Producción y comercio del aceite [I 1980 ➤ 63,730] II 1982/3 ➤ 3,803: ᴿBInstArch sup 24 (1987) 22-24 (D. J. *Mattingly*); Klio 70 (1988) 238s (B. *Böttger*).

h149 **Borowski** Oded, Agriculture in Iron Age Israel [diss. Ann Arbor 1979, Nv 1983] 1987 ➤ 3,f535: ᴿBO 45 (1988) 419-422 (M. *Stol*: not sufficiently up-to-date); VT 38 (1988) 494s (Judith M. *Hadley*); ZDPV 104 (1988) 163-7 (H. & M. *Weippert*, auch über HOPKINS D. 1985).

h150 *Bouvier* Bertrand, *Wehrli* Claude, Lettre concernant les droits de fermage: Aegyptus 68 (1988) 19-26; 2 pl.

h151 *a) Braidwood* Robert J., The origin and growth of a research focus; agricultural beginnings; – *b) Sillen* Andrew, Dietary reconstruction and Near Eastern archaeology; – *c) Katz* Solomon H., *Voigt* Mary M., Bread and beer; the early use of cereals in the human diet: Expedition 28,2 (Ph 1986) 2-7 / 16-22 / 23-34; ill.

h152 *Cagiola* Lucia, Alcune note sui cereali dell'Antico Regno: DiscEg 9 (1987) 7-20.

h153 *Chaniotis* Angelos, Vinum creticum ęxcellens; zum Weinhandel Kretas: MünstHand 7,1 (1988) 62-87; Eng. 88s, franç. 89.

h154 *a) Charles* M.P., Irrigation in lowland Mesopotamia; – *b) Gasche* H., Le système fluviatile au sud-ouest de Baghdad; – *c) Hruška* B., Die Bewässerungsanlagen in den altsumerischen Königsinschriften von Lagaš; – *d) Steinkeller* P., Notes on the irrigation system in third millennium southern Babylonia; – *e) Soldt* W. van, Irrigation in Kassite Babylonia; – *f) Hunt* R.C., Hydraulic management in Southern Mesopotamia in Sumerian times: ➤ 766, BSumAgr 4 (1988) 1-39 / 41-48 / 61-72 / 73-92 / 104-120 / 189-206.

h155 **Cuvigny** Hélène, L'Arpentage par espèces 1985 ➤ 3,f542: ᴿAntClas 56 (1987) 440 lire 'arpentage-inspection' non 'vérification' [57 (1988) 639, correction, renvoi erroné 'AC 66 (1987)']; Gnomon 60 (1988) 236-9 (A. *Bülow-Jacobsen*); JHS 108 (1988) 255s (Dorothy J. *Thompson*).

h156 *Delia* Diana, Carrying dung in ancient Egypt; a contract to perform work for a vineyard: BASP 23,1s (1986) 61-64.

h157 *Donbaz* Veysel, Complementary data on some Assyrian terms [mostly relating to bread]: JCS 40 (1988) 69-76 + 4 facsimiles.

h158 **Dosi** A., *Schnell* F., I Romani in cucina: Vita e costumi dei Romani antichi 3. R 1986, Quasar. 127 p.; ill.

h159 *a) Driel* G. van, Neo-Babylonian agriculture; – *b) Stol* M., Old Babylonian fields; – *c) Kupper* J.-R., L'irrigation à Mari; – *d) Margueron* J.-C., Espace agricole et aménagement régional à Mari au début du IIIe millénaire; – *e) Powell* M. A., Evidence for agriculture and waterworks in Babylonian mathematical texts; – *f) Pemberton* W., *al.*, Canals and bunds, ancient and modern: → 766, BSumAgr 4 (1988) 121-159 / 173-188 / 93-103 / 49-60 / 161-172 / 207-221.

h160 *Erard-Cerceau* Isabelle, Documents sur l'agriculture mycénienne; peut-on concilier archéologie et épigraphie?: Minos 23 (1988) 183-190.

h161 **Frankel** Rafael, An oil press at Tel Safsafot [1869.2276 Tabor]: TAJ 15s,1 (1988s) 77-91; 7 fig.; pl. 5-12.

h162 *Gallant* Thomas W., [crop-] Crisis and response; risk-buffering behavior in Hellenistic Greek communities: JIntdis 19 (1988s) 393-414.

h163 **Gallo** Luigi, Alimentazione e demografia della Grecia antica 1984 → 1,f301 ... 3,f944: ^RRFgIC 116 (1988) 475-480 (M. *Faraguna*).

h164 **Garnsey** Peter, Famine and food supply in the Graeco-Roman world; responses to risk and crisis. C 1988, Univ. xix-303 p. ill. £25. 0-521-35198-7. – ^RArctos 22 (1988) 230-2 (C. *Bruun*).

h165 *Gauthier* Philippe, Sur le don de grain numide à Délos; un pseudo-Rhodien dans les comptes des hiéropes: → 698, Comptes 1986/8, 61-69.

h166 *Gingrich* André, *Iš wa milḥ*, Brot und Salz; vom Gastmahl bei den Ḥawlān bin 'Āmir im Jemen: MittAnthropGesWien 116 (1986) 41-69.

h167 *Glassner* J. J., [*Ünal* A., Hethiter], Mahlzeit: → 808, RLA 7,3s (1988) 259-267 [-270]; 270s, archäologisch, *Calmeyer* P.

h168 **Goins** Scott E., The agricultural life as a heroic ideal in HOMER and VIRGIL: diss. Florida State, ^DWhite W. 1988. 145 p. 88-22447. – DissA 49 (1988s) 2207-A.

h169 *Guillaumin* Jean-Yves, Les différents noms de l'angle chez les *agrimensores* latins: RÉAnc 90 (1988) 411-7.

h170 *Hansen* Julie M., Agriculture in the prehistoric Aegean; data versus speculation: AJA 92 (1988) 39-52; 3 fig.

h171 **Hanson** V. D., Warfare and agriculture in classical Greece 1983 → 64,d531 ... 2,b731: ^RRivFgIC 116 (1988) 81-84 (M. *Moggi*).

h172 *Hirschfeld* Yizhar, *Birger* Rebecca, ☉ Farm houses and winepresses at Ramat Ha-Nadiv [3 k S Zikhron Yaaqov]: Qadmoniot 21 (1988) 100-115.

h173 **Hopkins** David C., The highlands of Canaan; agricultural life in the Early Iron Age 1985 → 2,b773; 3,f550: ^RCBQ 50 (1988) 498s (W. R. *Wifall*); ÉTRel 63 (1988) 596s (Françoise *Smyth*); OrAnt 27 (1988) 145-7 (M. *Liverani*: of the 466-title bibliography, 95% is in English; 80% dated 1962-1982).

h174 *Hruška* Blahoslav, Überlegungen zum Pflug und Ackerbau in der altsumerischen Zeit: ArOr 56 (1988) 137-158; 9 fig.

h175 *Hunt* Robert C., The role of bureaucracy in the provisioning of cities; a framework for analysis of the Ancient Near East: → 738, Power 1983/7, 161-192.

h175* **Jongman** Willem, The economy and society of Pompeii [intensely agricultural and low-standard]: DutchMgAnc.Hist 4. Amst 1988, Gieben. 415 p.; 21 fig.; 32 pl.; plan. *f* 160 [GreeceR 36, 113, T. *Wiedemann*].

h176 **Kehoe** Dennis P., The economics of agriculture on Roman imperial estates in North Africa: Hypomnemata 89. Gö 1988, Vandenhoeck & R. xvii-281 p.

h177 *Kippenberg* H. G., Agrarverhältnisse im antiken Vorderasien und die mit ihnen verbundenen politischen Mentalitäten: ➤ 498, ᴱ*Schluchter* W., Max Webers Sicht 1985, 151-204.

h178 *Kloft* Hans, Das Problem der Getreideversorgung in den antiken Städten; das Beispiel Oxyrhynchos: ➤ 687, Soziale Massnahmen 1984/8, 123-154.

h179 *Lombardo* Mario, Pratiche di commensalità e forme di organizzazione sociale nel mondo greco; *symposia* e *syssitia*: AnPisa 18 (1988) 263-286.

h180 *a*) *Martin* René, Agriculture et religion; le témoignage des Agronomes latins; – *b*) *Dilke* O. A. W., Religious mystique in the training of Agrimensores: ➤ 95, ᶠLᴇBᴏɴɴɪᴇᴄ H. 1988, 294-305 / 158-162.

h181 *Masson* Michel, À propos de quelques mots grecs relatifs à l'alimentation [*chidron* Lv 2,14; 23,14; *alix*; *siphōn*]: RPLH 62,1 (1988) 25-39.

h182 *Mattingly* David J., Megalithic madness [T-shaped megaliths in ancient Libya once taken to be ritual monuments] and measurement; or, how many olives could an olive press press?: OxJArch 7 (1988) 177-195; 5 fig.

h183 *Moens* Marie-Francine, *Wetterstrom* Wilma, The agricultural economy of an Old Kingdom town in Egypt's West Delta [Kom el-Hisn]; insights from the plant remains: JNES 47 (1988) 159-173; 3 fig.

h184 **Mrozek** Stanisław, Les distributions d'argent et de nourriture dans les villes italiennes du Haut-Empire romain: Coll. 198. Bru 1987, Latomus. 115 p. – ᴿRÉLat 66 (1988) 338s (H. *Zehnacker*).

h185 *Nenci* Giuseppe, Pratiche alimentari e forme di definizione e distinzione sociale nella Grecia arcaica: AnPisa 18 (1988) 1-10.

h186 *Nesbitt* Mark, *Summers* G. D., Some recent discoveries of millet [definitely a crop] (Panicum miliaceum L. and Setaria italica L. P. Beauv.) at excavations in Turkey and Iran: AnSt 38 (1988) 85-97; 3 fig. (map).

h187 **Paroussis** M., Les listes de champs de Pylos et Hattuša et le régime foncier mycénien et hittite 1985 ➤ 3,f567: ᴿClasR 102 (1988) 451 (J. T. *Hooker*).

h188 *a*) *Ray* J. D., An agricultural dream; Ostracon BM 5671; – *b*) *Andrews* Carol A. R., The sale of a Pathyrite vineyard (P.BM 10071): ➤ 41, ᶠEᴅᴡᴀʀᴅꜱ I., Pyramid studies 1988, 176-183 / 193-9.

h189 *Renfrew* Jane M., Food for athletes and gods; a classical diet: ➤ 767, Olympics 1984/8, 174-181.

h190 *Richlin* Amy, Systems of food imagery in Cᴀᴛᴜʟʟᴜꜱ: ClasW 81 (1987s) 355-363.

h191 **Robert** Jean Noël, La vie à la campagne dans l'Antiquité romaine: Realia, 1985 ➤ 2,b746; F 150. 2-251-33807-1: ᴿAntClas 57 (1988) 522 (G. *Raepsaet*).

h192 *Runnels* Curtis, *Andel* Tjeerd H. Van, Trade and the origins of agriculture in the Eastern Mediterranean: JMeditArch 1,1 (1988) 83-109.

h193 (*Salza* Prina), *Ricotti* Eugenia, L'alimentazione nel mondo greco / Cibi e banchetti nell'antica Roma: Archeo 44 (1988) 49-91; 46 (1988) 52-97; color. ill.

h194 *Sanati-Müller* Shirin, Texte aus dem Sinkāšid-Palast [Warka], I. Gerstenwerkverträge und Mehllieferungsurkunden: BaghMit 19 (1988) 471-538.

h195 *Scaife* Allen R., Accounts for taxes on beer and natron; P. Austin inv. 34: ZPapEp 71 (1988) 105-9.

h196 *Schmid* Wolfgang P., Bier aus Olbia: ArchMIran 19 (1986) 187-190.

h197 **Spurr** M. S.,   Arable cultivation in Roman Italy c. 200 B.C.-A.D. 100: JRS Mg 3.   L 1986, Soc. Prom. RS. xiv-159 p.; 5 fig.; 4 pl. – [R]AntiqJ 68 (1988) 352 (J. R. *Patterson*); ClasR 102 (1988) 94-96 (K. D. *White*).

h198 **Tchernia** André,   Le vin de l'Italie romaine; essai d'histoire économique d'après les amphores: BÉF 261. 1986, 2,b754:   [R]AntClas 57 (1988) 612 (G. *Raepsaet*); ClasR 102 (1988) 99-101 (R. P. *Duncan-Jones*); Gnomon 60 (1988) 655-7 (J. *Paterson*, Eng.: superb); JRS 78 (1988) 194-8 (N. *Purcell*); RArchéol (1988) 182-4 (R. *Rebuffat*); RBgPg 66 (1988) 166s (J. *Mertens*); RÉLat 66 (1988) 443s (H. *Le Bonniec*).

h199 **Verhoeven** Ursula,   Grillen, Kochen, Backen im Alltag und im Ritual Altägyptens; ein lexikographischer Beitrag. Rites Ég. IV, 1984, → 1,e935; Fb 600:   [R]JEA 74 (1988) 263s (E. *Graefe*).

h200 **Weimert** Helmut,   Wirtschaft als landschaftsgebundenes Phänomen; die antike Landschaft Pontos, eine Fallstudie: EurHS 3/242. Fra 1984, Lang. 259 p. – [R]MünstHand 7,2 (1988) 92-94 (H. C. *Schneider*).

h201 *Wendorf* Fred and 8 others,   New radiocarbon dates and Late Palaeolithic diet at Wadi Kubbaniya [Aswan], Egypt: Antiquity 62 (1988) 279-283.

h202 *a) White* K. D.,   Farming and animal husbandry; – *b) Brothwell* Don R.,   Foodstuffs, cooking and drugs; – *c) Scarborough* John,   Medicine: → 444, Mediterranea 1988; 211-245 / 247-261 / 1227-1248.

h203 **Wilson** Hilary,   Egyptian food and drink: Shire Egyptology. Aylesbury, Bucks 1988. 64 p.   0-85263-972-4.

h203* *Wilson* Hilary,   Pot-baked bread in ancient Egypt: VarAeg 4 (1988) 87-97; 5 fig.

h204 **Zohary** Daniel, *Hopf* Maria,   Domestication of plants in the Old World. Ox 1988, Clarendon.   260 p.; 39 fig.; 25 maps £35.   0-19-854198-8 [Antiquity 62,401 adv.].

U2.9   **Medicina** *biblica et antiqua*.

h205 *Adamson* P. B.,   Some infective and allergic conditions in ancient Mesopotamia: RAss 82 (1988) 163-171.

h206 **André** Jacques,   Être médecin à Rome 1987 → 3,f587:   [R]RÉLat 66 (1988) 334 (Noëlle *Barbe-Banvard*).

h207 *André* Jean-Marie,   L'épidémiologie de PLINE: Helmantica 37 (1986) 45-52.

h208 *Arata Mantovani* Piera,   Circoncisi ed incirconcisi: Henoch 10 (1988) 51-67; franç. 68.

h209 *Barcia Goyanes* Juan José,   La anatomia en la Biblia: EscrVedat 17 (1987) 61-74; 18 (1988) 32-42.

h210 *Bardinet* Thierry,   Remarques sur les maladies de la peau, la lèpre, et le châtiment divin dans l'Égypte ancien: → 119, Mém. POSENER G., RÉgp 39 (1988) 3-36; Eng. 36.

h211 *Blickman* Daniel R.,   The role of the plague in the Iliad: [Calif.] ClasAnt 6 (1987) 1-10.

h212 **Bliquez** Lawrence J.,   Roman surgical instruments and minor objects in the University of Mississippi: SIMA pocket 58.   Gö 1988, Åström. vii-80 p.; 14 fig.

h213 **Brain** Peter,   GALEN on bloodletting; a study of the origins, development and validity of his opinions, with a translation of the three works [< diss. Natal 1978]. C 1986, Univ.   xiii-189 p. £25. – [R]ClasR 102 (1988) 19-21 (J. *Longrigg*).

h214 **Bucaille** Maurice, Les momies des pharaons et la médecine; Ramsès II à Paris, le pharaon et Moïse. P 1987, Séguier. 247 p.; 58 fig. F 140. – ᴿÉtudes 369 (1988) 705 (P. *Frison*). ⇒ 2442s.

h215 ᵀᴱ**Burguière** Paul, *al.*, Sᴏʀᴀɴᴏs d'Éphèse, Maladies des femmes I: Coll. Budé. P 1988, BLettres. ci-133 (doubles) p.; ill. 2-251-00402-9.

h216 *Byl* Simon, Rheumatism and gout in the Corpus Hippocraticum: AntClas 57 (1988) 89-102.

h217 *Casanova* Gerardo, Altre testimonianze sulla peste in Egitto; certezze ed ipotesi: Aegyptus [64 (1984) 163-201] 68 (1988) 93-97.

h218 *Cole* Dorothea, The role of women in the medical practice of ancient Egypt: DiscEg 9 (1987) 25-29.

h219 *Cole* Dorothea, Obstetrics for the women of ancient Egypt: DiscEg 5 (1986) 27-33; drawing from *Reeves* C., Illustration of medicine in Ancient Egypt: Journal of Audio Visual Media in Medicine 3,1 (1980) 4-13.

h220 *Dawson* Warren R., Hᴇʀᴏᴅᴏᴛᴜs as a medical writer: BInstClas 33 (1986) 87-95.

h221 Dᴇɪᴄʜɢʀᴀᴇʙᴇʀ Karl, Ausgewählte kleine Schriften [14, über Corpus Hippocraticum; 80 Gb.], ᴱ**Gärtner** Hans, *al.* Hildesheim 1984, Weidmann. 413 p. DM 74. – ᴿAntClas 57 (1988) 345 (R. *Joly*).

h222 **Di Benedetto** Vincenzo, Il medico e la malattia; la scienza di Iᴘᴘᴏᴄʀᴀᴛᴇ: Paperbacks 172, 1986 ⇒ 3,f596: ᴿAevum 62 (1988) 128-130 (Chiara *Faraggiana di Sarzana*); AntClas 57 (1988) 344s (R. *Joly*); Elenchos 9 (1988) 159-161 (F. *Minonzio*); Materiali e discussioni per l'analisi dei testi classici 20s (Pisa 1988) 203-250 (W. *Leszl*); RFgIC 116 (1988) 471-5 (G. *Cambiano*).

h223 ᵀᴱ**Dols** Michael W., Medieval Islamic medicine; Iʙɴ Rɪᴅᴡᴀɴ... [❶ ᴱ*Gamal* A. S.). Berkeley 1984, Univ. [3,f597]. xvi-186 p.; ❶ 63 p. – ᴿBSOAS 51 (1988) 132s (L. I. *Conrad*).

h224 **Duminil** Marie-Paule, Le sang, les vaisseaux, le cœur dans la collection hippocratique; anatomie et physiologie: Coll.ÉtAnc, 1983 ⇒ 1,e957... 3,f598: ᴿAnzAltW 41 (1988) 151-4 (C. *Mueller-Goldingen*).

h224* *Durling* Richard J., Some particles and particle clusters in Gᴀʟᴇɴ [... differing from his borrowings frm Hɪᴘᴘᴏᴄʀᴀᴛᴇs *al.*]: Glotta 66 (1988) 183-9.

h225 **Edelstein** Ludwig [† 1965], Ancient Medicine [17 essays c. 1940, reprinted from the 1967 edition minus three others], ᴱ*Temkin* Owsei & C. Lilian. Baltimore 1987, Johns Hopkins Univ. xvi-456 p. $15 [RelStR 15, 165, D. E. *Smith*].

h226 **Feldman** David M., Health and medicine in the Jewish tradition, 1986 ⇒ 2,b768; 3,f601: ᴿJEcuSt 24 (1987) 455 (Penelope *Johnstone*, also on Sᴍɪᴛʜ David H., 'in the Anglican tradition' 1986).

h227 *Fischer* Klaus-D., Arbeitskreis Alte Medizin [Univ. Mainz, Tagung 21.VI.1988; Notiz für 2.VII.1989]: Gnomon 60 (1988) 669s.

h228 **Fischer** Peter M., *al.*, Prehistoric Cypriot skulls; a medico-anthropological, archaeological and micro-analytical examination: SIMA 75, 1986 ⇒ 2,b770: ᴿRÉAnc 90 (1988) 449 (Anne *Pecontal-Lambert*).

h229 *Fortuna* Stefania, La definizione della medicina in Gᴀʟᴇɴᴏ: ParPass 234 (1987) 181-196.

h230 **Ghalioungui** Paul, The physicians of pharaonic Egypt: DAI-K Sonderheft 10, 1983 ⇒ 1,e960; 2,b773: ᴿJNES 47 (1988) 199-201 (R. K. *Ritner*).

h231 *Gibbins* David, Surgical instruments from a Roman shipwreck off Sicily [5 k S Siracusa]: Antiquity 62 (1988) 294-7; 3 fig.

h232 **Goerke** H., Arzt und Heilkunde; 3000 Jahre Medizin, vom Asklepios-priester zum Klinikarzt. Mü 1984, Callwey. 288 p.; ill. [RHE 83,422*].

h233 **Gourevitch** Danielle, Le triangle hippocratique 1985 → 1,e964; 2,b775: RClasW 81 (1987s) 409s (M. G. *Sollenberger*).

h234 **Greenblatt** Robert B., Search the Scriptures; modern medicine and biblical personages; pref. *Stanford* Henry K. (special illustrated ed.). Totowa NJ 1985, Barnes & N. xiv-223 p. [KirSef 61 (1986s) 609].

h235 **Grensemann** Hermann, Knidische Medizin II. [→ 3,f610] Versuch einer weiteren Analyse der Schicht A in den pseudohippokratischen Schriften De natura muliebri und De muliebribus I und II: Hermes Einz. 51. Stu 1987, Steiner. 91 p. DM 48. 3-515-04688-7. – RAntClas 57 (1988) 345-7 (R. *Joly*); ClasR 102 (1988) 454 (Vivian *Nutton*: 'De muliebribus').

h236 **Grmek** Mirko D., Diseases in the ancient Greek world [1983 → 65,b983], T*Meullner* Mirielle, *Muellner* L. [sic OIAC D88]. Baltimore 1988, Johns Hopkins Univ. 0-8018-2798-1.

h237 *Grmek* Mirko D., *Gourevitch* Danielle, Les expériences pharma-cologiques dans l'Antiquité: Archives Internationales d'Histoire des Sciences 35 (R 1985) 3-27 [< AnPg 58,794].

h238 **Hillert** Andreas, Antike Arztdarstellung; Diss. Mainz 1987. – ArchAnz (1988) 102.

h239 *Hohlweg* A., Medizinischer 'Enzyklopädismus' und das *Ponēma iatrikón* des Michael PSELLOS: ByZ 81 (1988) 39-49.

h240 TE**Ieraci** Anna Maria, GALENO, De bonis malisque sucis: Radici 8. N 1987, D'Auria. 143 p. [AnzAltW 41,243].

h241 E**Ihsanoğlu** Ekmeleddin, *Fihrist* ... Catalogue of Islamic medical manuscripts (in Arabic, Turkish and Persian) in the libraries of Turkey. İstanbul 1984, Research Centre for Islamic History. xxx-525 p. $30. – RBSOAS 51 (1988) 134 (L. I. *Conrad*).

h242 **Jackson** Ralph, Doctors and diseases in the Roman Empire. L c. 1988, British Museum. 208 p.; 50 fig.; bibliog. p. 196-202. £17.50. 0-7141-1390-5 [Antiquity 62,811 adv.].

h243 *Jacob* Walter, Drugs and Pharmaceuticals in the biblical world [notice of international symposium to be held Sept. 14-15, 1989, in Rodef Shalom Biblical Botanical Garden, Pittsburgh]: Dor 17 (1988s) 271.

h244 TE**Jones** W. H. S., *al.*, HIPPOCRATES: Loeb Classical Library. CM/L 1979- , Harvard Univ./Heinemann.

h245 *Jouanna* Jacques, IPPOCRATE e il sacro, T*Ieraci Bio* Anna M.: Koinonia 12 (1988) 91-113.

h246 E**Kaiser** Wolfram, *Völker* Arina, Medizin und Naturwissenschaft in der Wittenberger Reformationsära: Wiss. Beiträge zur Universitätsgeschichte 45. Halle 1982, Univ. 353 p. [< LuJb 54,144].

h247 **Krug** Antje, Heilkunst und Heilkult; Medizin in der Antike 1985 → 1,e978; 3,f619: REirene 25 (1988) 163s (R. *Hošek*); Gymnasium 94 (1987) 374s (Fridolf *Kudlien*); Salesianum 50 (1988) 296s (G. *Gentileschi*).

h248 **Kudlien** Fridolf, Die Stellung des Arztes in der römischen Gesellschaft 1986 → 2,b781: REirene 25 (1988) 164s (P. *Oliva*); Gregorianum 69 (1988) 167s (J. *Janssens*).

h249 *Kudlien* Fridolf, *a)* Heilkunde: → 807, RAC 14,106 (1987) 223-249 [-274, *Jüttner* Guido, Heilmittel]; – *b)* 'Krankensicherung' in der griechisch-römischen Antike: → 687, Soziale Massnahmen 1984/8, 75-102.

h250 E**Kuhn** J.-H., *Fleischer* U., Index Hippocraticus 1986-8 → 3,f621: RClasR 102 (1988) 143s (Helen *King*, Fasz. 1); GGA 240 (1988) 183-7 (R. *Renehan*).

h251 **Leca** Ange-Pierre, La medicina egizia al tempo dei Faraoni. 1986, Ciba-Geigy. 368 p., 108 fig.

h252 *Levine* Baruch A., *Tarragon* Jean-Michel de, 'Shapsu cries out in heaven'; dealing with snake-bites at Ugarit (KTU 1.100, 1.107): RB 95 (1988) 481-518; franç. 481.

h252* *Lincoln* Bruce, Physiological speculation [the four humors] and social patterning in a Pahlavi text [Zādspram 30,14-19]: JAOS 108 (1988) 135-140.

h253 *McEwan* G. J. P., Lunge [Lungs, Eng.] → 808, RLA 7,3s (1988) 170-2.

h254 ᴱ**Maloney** Gilles, *Frohn* Winnie, Concordance des œuvres hippocratiques. Montréal 1984, Sphinx / Hildesheim 1986, Olms. xxiii-4869 p. [3 vol.]. – ᴿGnomon 60 (1988) 4-14 (A. *Anastassiou*: very many emendation proposals).

h255 *Maloney* Gilles, À propos de l'exorde du traité hippocratique 'de la génération' ['La loi gouverne tout']: Hermes 116 (1988) 490-3; read *nomós* for *nómos*: 'Nourishment strengthens all; male seed weakens us'.

h255* *Marganne* Marie-Hélène, *a)* Une description des os du tarse; P. Lit. Lond 167: BASP 24 (1987) 23-34; – *b)* with *Mertens* P., Medici et medica; catalogue des papyrus littéraires grecs et latins: → 492, XVIII Papyrol. 1 (1986/8) 105-146.

Meer L. B. van der, The bronze liver of Piacenza; analysis of a polytheistic structure: Dutch Mon. Anc. Hist. 2, 1987 → b682.

ᴱ**Meulenbeld** G. Jan, *Wujastik* Dominik, Studies in Indian medical history 1985/7 → 691.

h257 *Mondrain* Brigitte, Un manuscrit d'Hippocrate; le Monacensis Graecus 71 et son histoire aux XVᵉ et XVIᵉ siècles: RHText 18 (1988) 201-214.

h258 **Moraux** Paul, GALIEN de Pergame, souvenirs d'un médecin 1985 → 1,a983; 3,f637: ᴿClasR 102 (1988) 149 (J. *Longrigg*).

h259 *Nielsen* Harald, Medicaments used in the treatment of eye diseases in Egypt, the countries of the Near East, India and China in antiquity: Odense Univ. Pr. 1987. 76 p.; ill. [Journal of the History of Medicine 42 (1987) 514s (Estes) < AnPg 58,796].

h260 ᴱ**Palmer** Bernard, Medicine and the Bible [→ 3,f840]. Exeter 1986, Paternoster (for Christian Medical Fellowship). 272 p. £8. – ᴿBTrans 39 (1988) 140s (D. & Glenys *Clark*); RefTR 46 (1987) 90 (D. *Kirkaldy*).

h261 *Perho* Irmeli, The use of the Koran and the Sunna in the medicine of the prophet: StOrFin 64 (1988) 131-143.

h262 **Pigeaud** J., Folie et cures de la folie chez les médecins de l'antiquité gréco-romaine; la manie: Coll.ÉtAnc 112. P 1987, BLettres. 266 p. – ᴿClasR 102 (1988) 375s (Vivian *Nutton*: Jackie Pigeaud extends his 1981 study); RPLH 62,1 (1988) 148s (J. *Boulogne*).

h263 *Pot* Tjeerd, Two Etruscan gold dental appliances, found in 19th century excavations at Satricum and Praeneste: Meded.Ned.Inst.Rome 47 (Haag 1987) 35-40.

h264 *Pouderon* Bernard, La chaîne alimentaire chez Athénagore; confrontation de sa théorie digestive avec la science médicale de son temps: Orpheus 9 (1988) 219-237.

h265 *Prosperi Valenti* Giuseppina, Medici e medicine per i soldati di Roma: AntRArch 12,1s (1987) 37-39; 2 fig.

h266 *a)* *Remy* Bernard, La médecine dans l'antiquité gréco-romaine [... Chypre, *Caubet* Annie]; – *b)* *Marganne* Marie-Hélène, Les papyrus de médecine grecs d'Égypte; – *c)* *Grmek* Mirko D., Les affections de la colonne vertébrale; – *d)* *Salles* Catherine, Les cachets d'oculistes; des ordonnances sur la pierre: DossHA 123 (1988) 6-15 [76-81] / 30-34 / 52-61 / 62-65; ill.

h267 **Riddle** John M., Dioscorides on pharmacy and medicine 1985 → 2,b799; 3,f644: RAmHR 92 (1987) 393 (V.J. *Bullough*); ClasW 80 (1986s) 317s (P. *De Lacy*).

h268 *Risel* Sara, [Bones and teeth of] The people of Herculaneum AD 79: Helmantica 27 (1986) 11-23; 8 phot.

h269 **Roccatagliata** Giuseppe, A history of ancient psychiatry: Contributions in Medical Studies 16. Westport CT 1986, Greenwood. viii-296 p. $45. – RAmHR 92 (1987) 102s (J. *Scarborough*).

h270 **Scarborough** John, Pharmacy's ancient heritage; Theophrastes, Nicander, and Dioscorides. Lexington 1984, Coll. Pharmacy. xii-93 p.

h271 *Scarborough* John, Criton, physician to Trajan; historian and pharmacist: → 138, FStarr C., Craft 1985, 387-405.

h272 **Schneble** Hansjörg, Krankheit der ungezählten Namen; ein Beitrag zur Sozial-, Kultur- und Medizingeschichte der Epilepsie anhand ihrer Benennungen vom Altertum bis zur Gegenwart; Vorw. *Matthes* A. Bern 1987, Huber. x-190 p.; 18 fig. Fs 58. – RGnomon 60 (1988) 361s (K. *Dieckhöfer*).

h273 *Stannard* Jerry, Herbal medicine and herbal magic in Pliny's time: Helmantica 37 (1986) 95-106.

h274 **Stjernberg** Magdalena, Farsoter under förhistorisk tid, I. Bakterier och rickettsier: Theses and papers im North-European Archaeology 10. Sto 1987, Interman. 91-7146-376-3. – RFornvännen 83 (1988) 125-7 (B. *Gräslund*).

h275 *Toombs* S. Kay, Medicine and the patient-physician relationship in ancient Greece: → 80, FKilgore W.J. 1987, 75-90.

h276 *Vegetti* Mario, Medicina e sport nell'antichità: → 455, Athla 1987, 46s.

h277 TE**Wasserstein** Abraham, Galen's commentary on the Hippocratic treatise Airs, waters, places, in the Hebrew translation of Solomon HA-MEATI: Proc. Israel Acad. 6/3, 1982 → 65,b968c: RAnzAltW 41 (1988) 6s (Jutta *Kollesch*).

U3 *Duodecim Tribus:* **Israel Tribes;** *Land-Ideology.*

h278 *Allan* Nigel, The religious and political significance of the early settlement of Levites in Judah: → 148, FWeingreen J. = IrBSt 10,4 (1988) 166-177.

h279 **Diamond** James S., Homeland or Holy Land? The 'Canaanite' critique of Israel. Bloomington 1986, Indiana Univ. – RJudaism 37 (1988) 364-375 (G. *Tucker*).

h280 *Gal* Zvi, ⊕ The valley of Iphtahel — the boundary between Asher and Zebulun [not Nahal Zippori, but Nahal Eblayim west of Bet Netofah valley]: CHistEI 50 (1988) 27-30; Eng. 195.

h281 *a) Helberg* Jacob, The significance of the capacity of God as Creator for his relationship to the Land in the Old Testament; – *b) Ashby* Godfrey, The contribution of the Holy Land to a theology of Church and State: → 499, Holy Land 1986/8, 48-62 / 43-47.

h282 *Hess* R.S., Tribes, territories of the: → 801, ISBEnc³ 4 (1988) 907-913.

h283 **Hocking** David, What the Bible says about Israel and its land. Portland OR 1987, Multnomah. 20 p. $2 [GraceTJ 9,308].

h284 **Kallai** Zecharia, Historical geography of the Bible; the tribal territories of Israel. J/Leiden 1986, Magnes/Brill. xii-543 p. – RBL (1988) 38s

(A. R. *Millard*); Henoch 10 (1988) 193 (J. A. *Soggin*); PEQ 120 (1988) 72 (A. G. *Auld*); RHPR 68 (1988) 232 (P. de *Robert*: second half of the title is correct).

h285 **Mendels** Doron,   The land of Israel as a political concept in Hasmonean literature; recourse to history in second century B.C. claims to the Holy Land: TStAJud 15, 1987 ➤ 3,f669:   ᴿBL (1988) 138 (P. *Alexander*); ÉTRel 13 (1988) 600s (T. *Römer*); Gregorianum 69 (1988) 139-142 (G. L. *Prato*); JJS 39 (1988) 120-2 (Tessa *Rajak*); NedTTs 42 (1988) 342 (P. W. van der *Horst*).

h286 *Parfitt* Tudor,   The connection between the Falashas and the Land of Israel: ➤ 499, Holy Land 1986/8, 105-113.

h286* **Richter** W.,   Israel und seine Nachbarräume; ländliche Siedlungen und Landnutzung seit dem 19. Jahrhundert: Erdwissenschaftliche Forschung 14, 1979 ➤ 60,u887: ᴿProtestantesimo 43 (1988) 202s (J. A. *Soggin*).

h287 **Varner** William,   Jacob's dozen; a prophetic look at the tribes of Israel. Bellmawr NJ 1987, Friends of Israel Gospel Ministry.   108 p. [GraceTJ 9,317].

h288 *Weinfeld* Moshe, ❻ The extent of the Promised Land; two points of view [Jg 20,1, Dan to Beer Sheba; Gn 15,18, Ariš to Euphrates]: CHistEI 47 (1988) 3-16; Eng. 194.

U4   *Limitrophi,* **adjacent lands.**

h289 **André** Jacques, *Filliozat* Jean,   L'Inde vue de Rome; textes latins de l'antiquité relatif à l'Inde. P 1986, BLettres. 182 p. – ᴿAntClas 57 (1988) 431-3 (J. *Wankenne*); Gnomon 60 (1988) 531-3 (W. *Schmitthenner*); JRAS (1988) 210s (A. D. H. *Bivar*).

h290 *Beit-Arieh* Itzhaq,   New light on the Edomites: BAR-W 14,2 (1988) 28-41; ill.

h291 *Bernard* Paul,   *a*) Les Indiens de la liste des tributs d'HÉRODOTE [3.94; mais en tête des pages: 'l'or du tribut indien']:   StIran 16 (1987) 177-190; pl. VI; Eng. 191; – *b*) Les nomades conquérants de l'empire gréco-bactrien; réflexions sur leur identité ethnique et culturelle: CRAI (1987) 758-768.

h292 **Bryce** T. R.,   The Lycians in literary and epigraphic sources: The Lycians 1, 1986 ➤ 2,b839 [not 6839 as] 3,f680:   ᴿBO 45 (1988) 381-3 (R. S. P. *Beekes*); Gnomon 60 (1988) 720-5 (P. *Frei*).

h293 **Eph'al** Israel,   The ancient Arabs 1982 ➤ 65,d35; 3,f682:   ᴿAmHR 93 (1988) 673s (G. *Buccellati*).

h294 **Haider** Peter W.,   Griechenland — Nordafrika; ihre Beziehungen zwischen 1500 und 600 v. Chr.: ImpFor 53. Da 1988, Wiss.   3-534-01862-1 [OIAc N88].

h295 **Kasher** Aryeh,   Jews, Idumaeans and ancient Arabs; relations of the Jews in Eretz-Israel with the nations of the frontier and the desert during the Hellenistic and Roman era (332 BC - 70 CE): TStAJ 18.   Tü 1988, Mohr.   xix-264 p.   3-16-145240-2 [OIAc D88].

h295* *Knauf* Ernst A.,   Edom und Arabien (Supplementa Ismaelitica 13): BibNot 45 (1988) 62-81. – his Midian ➤ 2376.

h296 **Margalith** O., ❻ The sea peoples in the Bible. TA 1988, Devir.   260 p. [ZAW 101, 320, J. *Maier*].

h297 *Redditt* Paul, The Midianites: BibIll 14 (1987) 56-59 [< OTAbs 11,143].

h298 *a*) *Singer* Itamar,   The origin of the Sea Peoples and their settlement on the coast of Canaan; – *b*) *Mazar* Amihai,   Some aspects of the 'Sea

Peoples'' settlement; – *c*) *Raban* Avner,   The constructive maritime role of the Sea Peoples in the Levant: → 742, Society 1985/8, 239-250 / 251-260 / 261-294; 14 fig.

h299 *Vandersleyen* C.,   Pount sur le Nil [quelque part; parce que *ouadj-our* ne désigne jamais la mer]: DiscEg 12 (1988) 75-80.

U4.5   *Viae* – **Routes, roads.**

h300 *Armstrong* A.   Hilary,   Itineraries in late antiquity: Eranos-Jb 56 ('Wegkreuzungen' 1987) 105-131.

h301 *Beitzel* Barry J.,   How to draw ancient highways on biblical maps: BR 4,5 (1988) 36-43.

h302 *Blakely* Jeffrey A.,   *Sauer* James A.,   The road to Wadi al-Jubah; archaeology on the ancient spice route in Yemen: Expedition 27,1 (Ph 1985) 2-9; 15 fig.

h303 *Botha* Lorraine,   The Asiatic campaign of Agesilaus — the topography of the route from Ephesus to Sardis: Acta Classica 31 (Pretoria 1988) 71-80.

h304 *Bulow-Jacobsen* Adam,   Mons Claudianus, Roman granite-quarry and station on the road to the Red Sea: → 733, Acta Hyperborea 1987/8, 159-165; 2 fig.

h305 *Dorsey* D. A.,   Travel, transportation: → 801, ISBEnc³ 4 (1988) 891-7.

h306 **Gounaropoulou** L.,   *Hatzopoulos* M. B.,   Les milliaires de la voie egnatienne 1985 → 3,f703:   ᴿGnomon 60 (1988) 241-5 (Anna *Aichinger*).

h307 **Halfmann** Helmut,   Itinera principum; Geschichte und Typologie der Kaiserreisen im Römischen Reich: Heid. Althist. Beiträge 2.   Stu 1986, Steiner.   271 p. – ᴿClasR 102 (1988) 333s (W. *Williams*); Gnomon 60 (1988) 131-7 (A. *Winterling*).

h308 **Heinz** Werner,   Strassen und Brücken im Römischen Reich: AntWelt Sondernummer 2, 1988. 72 p.; 94 fig.

h309 **Kennedy** D. L.,   Archaeological... Roman frontier NE Jordan... road-network: BAR-Int 134, 1982 → 65,d56: ᴿBInstArch 25 (1988) 128s (Margaret *Roxan*).

h310 *Kleiss* Wolfram,   Safavidische und Qadjarische Brücken in Iran II: ArchMIran 19 (1986) 312-338; 38 (foldout) fig.; pl. 35-46.

h311 *Kleiss* Wolfram, *a*) Karawanenwege in Iran (Stand der Forschung 1986); – *b*) Brücken aus Safavidischer und Qadjarischer Zeit in Südwest- und in Nordiran: ArchMIran 20 (1987) 323-330; 2 maps / 331-343; 22 (foldout) fig.; pl. 41-42.

h312 *Koch* Heidemarie,   Die achämenidische Poststrasse von Persepolis nach Susa: ArchMIran 19 (1986) 133-147; map.

h313 *Sevin* Veli,   The oldest highway; between the regions of Van and Elaziğ in eastern Anatolia: Antiquity 62 (1988) 547-551; 4 fig.

h314 *Speidel* Michael,   The Roman road to Dumata (Jawf in Saudi Arabia) and the frontier strategy of *praetensione colligare*:   Historia 36 (1987) 213-221; 1 fig.; 1 pl.; map.

h315 *Staccioli* Romolo A.,   Le grandi strade dell'Impero: Archeo 39 (1988) 49-95; color. ill.

h316 *Thiele* E. R.,   Roads, highways: → 801, ISBEnc³ 4 (1988) 199-203.

h317 **Uhlig** Helmut,   Die Seidenstrasse; antike Weltkultur zwischen China und Rom.   Bergisch Gladbach 1986, Lübbe.   288 p.; ill. – ᴿMundus 24 (1988) 126s (H. *Wilhelmy*).

h318 **Walser** Gerold, Die römischen Strassen und Meilensteine in Raetien: Itinera Romana 4. Stu 1983. 128 p.; 28 fig.; 5 maps. – [R]Archaeologia 36 (Wrocław 1985) 187s (J. *Wielowiejski*).

h319 *a*) *Walser* Gérold, Les bornes milliaires du Proche-Orient dans le cadre de CIL XVII; – *b*) *Bauzou* Thomas, Les voies romaines entre Damas et Amman; – *c*) *Gawlikowski* Michel, La route de l'Euphrate d'IsIDORE [de Charax] à Julien: → 706, Géographie 1985/8, 289-291 / 292-300; fig. 77-98; map 76.

h320 *Zahrnt* Michael, Die frühesten Meilensteine Britanniens und ihre Deutung (mit einem Ausblick auf einige Hadrianische Meilensteine aus dem gallisch-germanischen Raum): ZPapEp 73 (1988) 195-9.

h321 *Zertal* Adam, ⊕ 'From watchtowers to fortified cities' — on the history of highway forts in the Israelite kingdom: Qadmoniot 21 (1988) 82-86.

U5   *Ethnographia*, **Sociologia** [servitus → G6.5].

h322 **Aguirre** Rafael, Del movimiento de Jesús a la iglesia cristiana; ensayo de exégesis sociológica del cristianismo primitivo 1987 → 3,f712: [R]CiTom 115 (1988) 394 (J. L. *Espinel*).

h323 **Alföldy** Géza, Die römische Gesellschaft 1986 → 3,177: [R]Eirene 25 (1988) 127s (P. *Oliva*).

h324 *a*) *Archi* Alfonso, Zur Organisation der Arbeit in Ebla; – *b*) *Biga* Maria Giovanna, Frauen in der Wirtschaft von Ebla; – *c*) *Pomponio* Francesco, Gli ugula [controllore, spesso in relazione con nomi di animali] nell'amministrazione di Ebla: → 707, Wirtschaft 1986/8, 131-8 / 159-171 / 317-323.

h325 *Atkins* Robert A., Three problems in using sociological methodologies on New Testament materials and their solution using grid-group analysis: ProcGLM 8 (1988) 35-48.

h326 *Barbaglio* Giuseppe, Rassegna di studi di storia sociale e di ricerche di sociologia sulle origini cristiane I - II: RivB 36 (1988) 377-410. 495-520 [*Elliott* J., *Meeks* W. ...].

h327 *Bard* Kathryn A., The geography of excavated predynastic sites and the rise of complex society: JAmEg 6 (1988) 81-94.

h328 *Beal* Richard H., The [GIS]TUKUL in second-millennium Ḫatti: AltOrF 15 (1988) 269-305: 'men who worked for the government or others and received their pay in the form of land whose produce supported them'.

h329 **Berlev** O. D., ⊕ Obščestvennye... Social relations in Egypt of the epoch of the Middle Empire... *ḥmww*. Moskva 1978, Nauka. 367 p.

h330 *Bettenzoli* G., [AT; *Oberlinner* L. NT], Älteste: → 804, NBL, Lfg 1 (1988) 49s [50-52].

h331 **Bettini** Maurizio, Antropologia e cultura romana; parentela, tempo, immagini dell'anima: Studi Superiori 19. R 1986, Nuova Italia Scientifica. 271 p. Lit. 32.000. – [R]ClasR 102 (1988) 432 (A. *Douglas*: style lively, even jaunty; the symbols of the soul are bats, bees-hornets, and butterflies-moths).

h332 **Blasi** Anthony J., Early Christianity as a social movement: Toronto Studies in Religion 5. NY 1988, Lang. 240 p. 0-8204-0581-7.

h333 *a*) *Blok* Josine, Sexual asymmetry; a historiographical ssay; – *b*) *Versnel* H. S., Wife and helpmate; women of ancient Athens in anthropological perspective; – *c*) *Bremmer* Jan N., The old women of ancient Greece: → 437, Asymmetry 1987, 1-57 / 59-86 / 191-215.

h334 *a) Campiche* Roland J., Une approche sociologique du champ religieux; – *b) Gilliéron* Edmond, Le phénomène religieux; une approche psychodynamique de sa composante collective: RTPhil 120 (1988) 123-136 / 137-146.

h335 *Chicideanu* Ion, (roum.) Recherches sur la sociologie des nécropoles et l'idéologie funéraire: Studii ... IsVArh 39 (Bucureşti 1988) 413s.

h336 *Čipirova* L. A., ❸ Les rapports fonciers dans la commune familiale d'après l' 'obélisque à Maništušu': VDI 79,185 (1988) 3-33; franç. 34.

h337 **Collins** Randall, Weberian sociological theory. C 1986, Univ. xi-356 p. – ᴿArchScSocRel 65 (1988) 189-201 (J. *Séguy*).

h337* *Coninck* Frédéric de, Changer les choses? Une confrontation de la sociologie de la production de la société et du donné biblique: Hokhma 38 (1988) 1-22.

h338 *a) Deininger* J., Die politischen Strukturen des mittelmeerisch-vorderorientalischen Altertums in Max WEBERS Sicht; – *b) Breuer* S., Stromuferkultur und Küstenkultur; geographische und ökologische Faktoren in Max Webers 'ökonomischer Theorie der antiken Staatenwelt': → 498, ᴱ*Schluchter* W., Max Webers Sicht 1985, 72-110 / 111-150.

h339 *de Silva* Willie R., Religion a fundamental element in the societal analysis of Karl MARX and Max WEBER; a comparative study: JDharma 12 (1987) 266-288.

h340 **Dixon** Suzanne, The Roman mother. L 1988, Croom Helm. 286 p.; 10 phot. 0-7099-4511-6. – ᴿRELat 66 (1988) 337s (N. *Boëls-Janssen*).

h340* **Douglas** Mary, How institutions think ['they create shadowed places in which nothing can be seen and no questions asked (but) make other areas show finely discriminated detail', JTS 40, 493]: Abrams Lectures. Syracuse 1986, Univ. 160 p. $11. 0-8156-0206-5.

h341 *Downey* Michael, Status inconsistency and the politics of worship [*Meeks* W., First urban Christians 1983; social-unifying function of liturgy today]: Horizons 15 (1988) 64-76.

h342 **Ebertz** M. N., Das Charisma des Gekreuzigten; zur Soziologie der Jesusbewegung: WUNT 45, 1987 → 3,f733: ᴿTsTNijm 28 (1988) 307 (S. van *Tilborg*).

h343 *Elliott* John H., Patronage and clientism in early Christian society, a short reading guide: Forum 3,4 (Sonoma 1987) 39-48 [< ZIT 88,537].

h344 *Fellermayr* Josef, Hereditas: → 807, RAC 14,108s (1988) 626-648.

h345 *Fenn* Richard K., Sociology and social history; a preface to a sociology of the New Testament: JPseud 1 (1987) 95-114.

h346 **Fenton** Steve, *al.*, DURKHEIM and modern sociology 1984 → 65,d84: ᴿBijdragen 49 (1988) 228 (H. *Goddijn*).

h347 *Ferenczy* Endre, Die Freigelassenen und ihre Nachkommen im öffentlichen Leben des republikanischen Rom: Klio 70 (1988) 468-476.

Fichter Joseph H., A sociologist looks at religion: Theology and Life 23, 1988 → 189.

h348 *a) Foley* Helena P., Women in Greece; – *b) Henderson* Jeffrey, Greek attitudes toward sex; – *c) Pomeroy* Sarah B., Greek marriage; – *d) Dickson* Sheila K., Women in Rome; – *e) Hallett* Judith P., Roman attitudes toward sex; – *f) Treggiari* Susan, Roman marriage: → 444, Mediterranean 1988, 1301-1317 / 1249-1263 / 1333-1342 / 1319-1332 / 1265-1278 / 1343-1354.

h349 *a) Foraboschi* Daniele, Movimenti e tensioni sociali nell'Egitto romano; – *b) Pomeroy* Sarah B., Women in Roman Egypt; a preliminary study based on papyri: → 782, ANRW 2,10,1 (1988) 807-840 / 708-723.

h350 *a) Foraboschi* Daniele, L'ideologia della ricchezza in Aristea; – *b) Gara* Alessandra, Schiavi e soldati nella lettera di Aristea: ➤ 464, Stud. Ellenistici II (1987) 63-74 / 75-89.

h351 *Foster* James D., *Ledbetter* Mark F., Christian anti-psychology and the scientific method: JPsy&T 15 (1987) 10-18.

h352 *a)* **Fox** Robin, Kinship and marriage; an anthropological perspective. C 1983, Univ. 273 p. £15. – *b)* **Frayser** Suzanne G., Varieties of sexual experience; an anthropological perspective on human sexuality. NHv 1985, 'HRAF'. xii-546 p. $25. – ᴿAnthropos 83 (1988) 251 (Ann Marie *Powers*) / 251-3 (A. *Bruck*).

h353 *Freyne* Seán, Bandits in Galilee; a contribution to the study of social conditions in first-century Palestine: ➤ 77, ᶠKEE H., Social world 1988, 50-68.

h354 **Gardner** Jane F., Women in Roman law and society 1986 ➤ 3,f740: ᴿAmHR 92 (1987) 1185s (Mary R. *Lefkowitz*); Arctos 22 (1988) 233s (O. *Salonies*); ClasPg 83 (1988) 263-5 (R. P. *Saller*); HZ 245 (1987) 682s (Helga *Botermann*, auch über POMEROY S. 1985); Latomus 47 (1988) 459s (R. *Sotty*); RelStR 14 (1988) 155 (R. S. *Kraemer*).

h355 *Gardner* Jane F., Proofs of status in the Roman world: BInstClas 33 (1986) 1-14.

h356 **Giddens** A., Social theory and modern sociology. 1987, Polity [IrBSt 10 (1988) 182.190 'Giddens', 190s 'Gidden'].

h357 *Gill* David W. J., Expressions of wealth; Greek art and society: Antiquity 62 (1988) 735-743.

h358 ᴱ**Gill** Robin, Theology and sociology, a reader [28 extracts from WEBER, DURKHEIM ...]. L/NY 1987, Chapman/Paulist. vi-424 p. $15 [TDig 36,88].

h359 **Goudriaan** Koen, Ethnicity in Ptolemaic Egypt: Dutch MgAHA 5. Amst 1988, Gieben. 174 p. 90-5063-022-7.

h360 *Graham* Helen R., A sociological study of the Old Testament: Landas 1 (Manila 1987) 256-263 [TKontext 10/1,72].

h361 **Hallett** Judith P., Fathers and daughters in Roman society 1984 ➤ 1,f82 ... 3,f750: ᴿEirene 25 (1988) 129s (J. *Kepartová*).

h362 *Helm* Peyton R., Races and physical types in the classical world: ➤ 444, Miditerranean 1 (1988) 137-154.

h363 *Heltzer* Michael, Die Entwicklung des Handwerks vom Dienstsystem zum selbständigen Produzenten im östlichen Mittelmeergebiet (1500-500 v.u. Z.): AltOrF 15 (1988) 124-132.

h364 *a) Hermanns* Manfred, Romano GUARDINI und die Soziologie; – *b) Degkwitz* Rudolf, Abgrenzung und Zuordnung von Theologie und Psychologie: Renovatio 44 (Köln 1988) 65-81 / 88-102 [< ZIT 88,525].

h365 **Hervieu-Léger** Danièle, (*Champion* Françoise), Vers un nouveau christianisme? Introduction à la sociologie du christianisme occidental: Sciences humaines et religion. P 1986, Cerf. 395 p. – ᴿRHPR 68 (1988) 522-4 (J.-P. *Willaime*).

h366 **Hesberg-Tonn** Bärbel von, Coniunx carissima; Untersuchungen zum Normcharakter im Erscheinungsbild der römischen Frau [Diss. Stuttgart]. Stu 1983, Univ. Hist. Inst. iii-250 p.; 68 p. notes. – ᴿGnomon 60 (1988) 170-2 (P. *Guyot*).

h367 **Hirschhorn** Monique, Max WEBER et la sociologie française. P 1988, Harmattan. 229 p. – ᴿArchScSocRel 65 (1988) 195-7 (J. *Séguy*).

h368 *Hooff* Anton J. L. van, Ancient robbers; reflections behind the facts: AncS 19 (1988) 105-124.

h369 **Hopkins** Keith,   Death and renewal; sociological studies in Roman history 2, 1983 ➤ 65,d99 ... 2,b890:   ᴿAncSRes 17 (1987) 58-61 (Beryl *Rawson*: good on wealthy women's increased sexual, social. and financial freedom; but marriage-age put too low).

h370 *Hudson* Winthrop S.,   The WEBER thesis reexamined: ChH Centennial Sup (1988) 56-67.

h371 **Istas** Michel,   Les morales selon Max WEBER: Histoire de la morale 2, 1986 ➤ 3,f753:   ᴿNRT 110 (1988) 276 (J. *Javaux*); Salesianum 50 (1988) 247 (G. *Abbà*); StMoralia 26 (1988) 304s (B. *Häring*).

h372 ᴱ**Khalidi** Tarif,   Land tenure and social transformation in the Middle East [since 4th millennium, 6 papers (medieval-later, 26)] 1983/4 ➤ 1,432: ᴿBO 45 (1988) 525s.

   ᴱ**Köcka** J., Max WEBER 1985/6 ➤ 688.

h373 *Koppe* Renate,   Die Analyse antiker Gesellschaften in der marxistischen Geschichtswissenschaft der UdSSR und der DDR, ein Überblick: MünstHand 7,1 (1988) 1-29.

h374 *Koptev* A.V., ❺ L'attachement des esclaves ruraux au domaine dans l'Empire romain (Les monuments du droit romain en tant que sources historiques):   VDI 186 (1988) 30-49; franç. 49.

h375 *Košak* Silvan,   Ein hethitischer Königserlass über eine gesellschaftliche und wirtschaftliche Reform: ➤ 112*, ᶠOTTEN H., Documentum 1988, 195-202.

h376 **Kyrtatas** Dimitris J.,   The social structure of the early Christian communities [diss. Brunel, 1980, ᴰ*Hopkins* K.]. L 1987, Verso. xiv-224 p. $40. 0-86091-163-2 [NTAbs 32,392]. – ᴿJRS 78 (1988) 251s (W.A. *Meeks*).

h377 *a) LaBianca* Øystein S.,   Sociocultural anthropology and Syro-Palestinian archaeology; – *b) Mattingly* Gerald L.,   Settlement patterns and sociocultural reconstruction: ➤ 20, ᶠCALLAWAY J., Benchmarks 1988, 369-387 / 389-415.

h378 **Lampe** Peter,   Die stadtrömischen Christen... [Diss. Bern ᴰ*Luz* U.]: WUNT 2/18, 1987 ➤ 3,f759:   ᴿRelStR 14 (1988) 255 (J.H. *Elliott*: impressive; first in 50 years... [who then?]).

h379 *Lang* Bernhard,   Theokratie; Geschichte und Bedeutung eines Begriffs in Soziologie und Ethnologie: ➤ 421, ᴱ*Taubes* Jacob, Religionstheorie 3. Theokratie 1987, 11-29 [ArBegG 30 (1986s) 259s (ipse)].

h380 *Lapointe* Roger,   DURKHEIM socio-religiologue;   SR 17 (1988) 279-290.

h381 *Lee* A.D.,   Close-kin marriage in late antique Mesopotamia: GRByz 29 (1988) 403-413.

h382 **Lepenies** Wolf,   Die drei Kulturen; Soziologie zwischen Literatur und Wissenschaft.   Münster 1985, Hanser.   563 p. *f* 89,10.   3-446-14204-5. – ᴿBijdragen 49 (1988) 353 (H. *Goddijn*).

h383 *Lieu* J.M.,   The social world of the New Testament: EpworthR 14,3 (1987) 47-53 [NTAbs 32,209].

h384 **Lightstone** Jack N.,   Society, the Sacred, and Scripture in ancient Judaism; a sociology of knowledge: StChrJud 3.   Waterloo ON 1988, W. Laurier Univ.   xiii-126 p.   0-88920-795-8.

h385 **Liverani** Mario,   Antico Oriente; storia, società, economia.   R 1988, Laterza.   x-1031 p.   88-420-3266-2.

h386 *Luthy* Herbert,   Variations on a theme by Max WEBER: ➤ 405, International Calvinism 1985, 369-390 [< LuJb 54, p. 179].

   MacDonald Margaret Y.,   The Pauline churches, a socio-historical study of institutionalization 1988 ➤ 5296.

h387 **MacMullen** Ramsey, Les rapports entre les classes sociales dans l'Empire romain (50 av. J.-C. – 284 apr. J.-C.) [1974],[T]. P 1986, Seuil. 185 p. F 89. – [R]RHR 205 (1988) 96-98 (M. *Royo*).

h388 *Maekawa* Kazuya, New texts on the collective labor service of the Erin-people of Ur III Girsu: AcSum 10 (1988) 37-73; 74-85, tables; 86-94 facsimiles.

h389 *Malamat* A., Pre-monarchical social institutions in Israel in the light of Mari: → 482, VTS 40, Jerusalem congress 1986/8, 165-176.

h390 **Malina** Bruce J., Christian origins and cultural anthropology; practical models for biblical interpretation 1986 → 2,b901; 3,f769: [R]JBL 107 (1988) 532-4 (Susan R. *Garrett*: to remedy 'impressionistic individualistic intuition' of current exegesis); JPsy&T 15 (1987) 91 (P. G. *Hiebert*); Salesianum 50 (1988) 426 (R. *Vicent*).

h391 *Mayes* A. D. H., Sociology and the study of the Old Testament; some recent writing [*Herion* G., *Gideon* A. ...]: → 148, [F]WEINGREEN J. = IrBSt 10,4 (1988) 178-191.

h392 *Mayes* Andrew D. H., Idealism and materialism in WEBER and GOTTWALD: PrIrB 11 (1988) 44-58.

h393 **Meeks** Wayne A., The moral world of the first Christians 1986 → 2,b908; 3,f770: [R]Interpretation 42 (1988) 413-5 (L. M. *White*).

h394 [*Menu* B., secrétaire, Association internationale pour l'étude du droit de l'Égypte ancienne; réunion 19.XII.1987, Paris Centre Glotz:] *a*) *Barbotin* Christophe, Aspects juridiques et économiques de l'offrande au Nouvel Empire; – *b*) *Nibbi* Alessandra (1983 Paris colloquium), Evidence for the *rhj.t* people as permanent foreigners in ancient Egypt: DiscEg 9 (1987) 69-78 / 79-96; 21 fig.

h395 **Meslin** Michel, L'expérience humaine du divin; fondements d'une anthropologie religieuse. P 1988, Cerf. 421 p. F 179 [TS 50, 809-11, J. F. *Russell*].

h396 **Meštrović** Stjepan G., Émile DURKHEIM and the reformation of sociology. Totowa NJ 1988, Rowan & L. xi-156 p. $28.50 [RelStR 15,343, I. *Strenski*: maverick].

h397 **Morris** Brian, Anthropological studies of religion, an introductory text. C 1987, Univ. x-369 p. £9.50. – [R]Anthropos 83 (1988) 623-5 (T. O. *Beidelman*: inadequate).

h398 **Munch** Richard, Understanding modernity; toward a new perspective beyond DURKHEIM and WEBER [the other half of the German original is Theory of Action... beyond PARSONS 1987]. L 1988, Routledge-KP. x-358 p. $75 [RelStR 15,342, W. R. *Garrett*).

h399 *a*) *Ota* Hidemichi, The ancient Mediterranean world structure and resistance movements therein; – *b*) *Maezawa* Nobuyuki, Slave societies in Greco-Roman antiquity; – *c*) *Bieżuńska-Małowist* Iza, Formes de résistance dans l'Égypte grecque et romaine et l'attitude du gouvernement: → 702, Control 1986/8, 9-15 / 16-18 / 239-245.

h400 *Otto* Eckart, Biblische Wurzeln moderner Rationalität?; Zu Max WEBERs Religionssoziologie: EvKomm 21 (1988) 85-88.

h401 **Perepelkin** J. J., Privateigentum in der Vorstellung der Ägypter des Alten Reichs, [TE]Müller-Wollermann R., 1986 → 2,d1: [R]BO 45 (1988) 316s (N. *Kanawati*); DiscEg 6 (1986) 55-65 (S. *Allam*).

h402 **Perkins** Richard, Looking both ways... Christianity and sociology 1987 → 3,f783: [R]AndrUnS 26 (1988) 199-202 (Sara M. K. *Terian*).

h403 *Quirke* Stephen, State and labour in the Middle Kingdom; a reconsideration of the term *ḥnrt*: ⇒ 119, Mém. POSENER G., RÉgp 39 (1988) 83-106.

h404 *Rantz* Berthe, Aperçu sur la situation de la femme à Rome: ÉtClas 56 (1988) 285-299.

h405 *Rasmussen* Tarald, Max WEBERs idealtypebegrep: ⇒ 97*, ᶠLØNNING I., NorTTs 89 (1988) 67-77.

h406 ᴱ**Rawson** Beryl, The family in ancient Rome 1986 ⇒ 3,507.f787; also Ithaca NY, Cornell Univ.; $27.50: ᴿAmHR 92 (1987) 108s (Sarah B. *Pomeroy*); ClasPg 83 (1988) 265-9 (R.P. *Saller*); ÉchMClas 32 (1988) 78-83 (M. *Golden*).

h407 **Raynaud** Philippe, Max WEBER et les dilemmes de la raison moderne. P 1987, PUF. 217 p. – ᴿArchScSocRel 65 (1988) 197s (J. *Séguy*).

h408 *Ricœur* Paul, La crise; un phénomène spécifiquement moderne [doctorat d'honneur Neuchâtel 1986]: RTPhil 120 (1988) 1-19.

h409 *Rogerson* J.W., Anthropology and the OT 1984 = 1978 ⇒ 60,8503 ... 2,b923: ᴿOrAnt 27 (1988) 153s (M. *Liverani*).

h410 *Sajko* E.V., *Jankovskaja* N.B., ⊕ Le type artisanal d'organisation du travail au Proche-Orient aux IV-IIᵉᵐᵉ millénaires avant n.è.: VDI 186 (1988) 3-18; franç. 18.

h410* **Saldarini** Anthony J., Pharisees, scribes and Sadducees in Palestinian society; a sociological approach. Wilmington 1988, Glazier. x-326 p. $30 [JBL 108,381].

h411 **Samuel** Alan E., From Athens to Alexandria; Hellenism and social goals in Ptolemaic Egypt 1983 ⇒ 64,d734; 3,f783: ᴿClasR 102 (1988) 91s (J.D. *Thomas*).

h412 **Schöllgen** G., Ecclesia sordida? soziale Schichtung... TERTULLIAN 1984 ⇒ 65,d154... 3,f795: ᴿRHE 83 (1988) 681-5 (P.-A. *Deproost*); RHR 205 (1988) 212s (P. *Nautin*).

h413 *Schöllgen* Gregor, Auf der Suche nach dem 'Menschentum' im Labyrinth der neueren Max-WEBER-Forschung: HZ 246 (1988) 365-384.

h414 *Séguy* Jean, De WEBER à MARX et retour [6 livres, infra]: ArchScSocRel 65,2 (1988) 195-206.

h415 *Seidlmayer* Stephan J., Funerärer Aufwand und soziale Ungleichheit: GöMiszÄg 104 (1988) 25-51 [89s, *Guksch* Helke].

h416 *Soggin* J.A., Ancient Israel; an attempt at a social and economic analysis of the available data: ⇒ 47, ᶠFENSHAM F., Text 1988, 201-8.

h417 **Stambaugh** J., *Balch* D., The NT in its social environment 1986 ⇒ 3,f801*b*: ᴿCBQ 50 (1988) 147-9 (H.C. *Kee*: weak on Judaism and archeology); Interpretation 42 (1988) 93-94 (D.M. *Rhoads*: identity of the Zealots ignored); JAAR 56 (1988) 358-360 (J.H. *Elliott*: naïve); RB 95 (1988) 471s (J. *Murphy-O'Connor*: some vivid parts, some ill-organised or misleading).

h418 *Stoddart* Simon, *Whitley* James, The social context of literacy in Archaic Greece and Etruria: Antiquity 62 (1988) 761-772.

h419 **Tainter** Joseph A., The collapse of complex societies. C 1988, Univ. xiii-250 p.; 40 fig. £27.50. 0-521-34092-0. – ᴿAntiquity 62 (1988) 798s (D. *Whitehouse*).

h420 *Theissen* Gerd, Vers une théorie de l'histoire sociale du christianisme primitif: ÉTRel 63 (1988) 199-225.

h421 **Thiel** W., Die soziale Entwicklung Israels in vorstaatlicher Zeit 1985 ⇒ 1,f148; 2,b939: ᴿProtestantesimo 43 (1988) 116 (J.A. *Soggin*).

h422 **Todd** Emmanuel, The explanation of ideology; family structures and social systems, ᵀ*Garrioch* David. Ox 1985, Blackwell. [... Mediterranean area: BibTB 18,119].

h423 *Tvarnø* Henrik, Roman social structure; different approaches for different purposes: ➤ 142*, ᶠTHOMSEN R. 1988, 114-123; 1 fig.

Vanderbroeck Paul J., Popular leadership and collective behavior in the late Roman Republic (ca. 80-50 B.C.) 1987 ➤ d555.

h425 *Venit* Marjorie S., The Caputi hydria and working women in classical Athens: ClasW 81 (1987s) 265-272.

h426 *Waetzoldt* Hartmut, Die Situation der Frauen und Kinder anhand ihrer Einkommensverhältnisse zur Zeit der III. Dynastie von Ur: AltOrF 15 (1988) 30-44.

h427 **Walzer** Michael, La révolution des saints [c. 1975]. P 1987, Belin. 409 p. – ᴿArchScSocRel 65 (1988) 201-5 (V. *Séguy*: ligne WEBER-MARX].

h428 **Wengst** Klaus, Humility; solidarity of the humiliated; the transformation of an attitude and its social relevance in Graeco-Roman, Old Testament-Jewish and early Christian tradition [Demut 1987 ➤ 3,f811], ᵀ*Bowden* John. L 1988, SCM. ix-96 p. £6.50 pa. 0-334-02067-0.

h429 **Whitehead** David, The demes of Attica 508/7-ca. 250 B.C.; a political and social study. Princeton 1986, Univ. xxvii-485 p.; 3 fig.; map. 0-691-09412-8. – ᴿAntClas 57 (1988) 499-502 (D. *Viviers*).

h430 *Wickert-Micknat* Gisela, Die Tochter in der frühgriechischen Gesellschaft: Gymnasium 94 (1987) 193-217; pl. I-VI.

h431 ᴱ**Wiley** Norbert, The MARX-WEBER debate. Beverly Hills 1987, Sage. – ᴿArchScSocRel 65 (1988) 198s (J. *Séguy*).

h432 *Will* Édouard, Pour une 'anthropologie coloniale' du monde hellénistique: ➤ 138, ᶠSTARR C., Craft 1985, 273-301.

h433 **Winniczuk** L., ❷ *Ludzie...* People and customs of ancient Greece and Rome. Wsz 1983, PWN. 763 p. – ᴿVDI 184 (1988) 245s (I. A. *Lisovoj*).

h434 **Zeitlin** Irving M., Ancient Judaism... WEBER 1984 ➤ 65,d173 ... 3,f813: ᴿAmHR 91 (1986) 364s (J. *Van Seters*); JAOS 108 (1988) 160-2 (Christa *Schäfer-Lichtenberger*); JJS 39 (1988) 116s (J. *Hughes*); JRelHist 14 (1986s) 444s (A. D. *Crown*); JTS 39 (1988) 212s (J. W. *Rogerson*: unsuccessful).

U5.3 **Commercium**, *oeconomia*.

h435 *Alizadeh* Abbas, Socio-economic complexity in southwestern Iran during the fifth and fourth millennia B.C.; the evidence from Tall-i Bakun A: Iran 26 (1988) 17-34; 6 fig.; pl. I.

h436 *a*) *Altman* Amnon, Trade between the Aegean and the Levant in the Late Bronze Age; some neglected questions; – *b*) *Buchholz* Hans-Günter, Der Metallhandel des zweiten Jahrtausends im Mittelmeer; – *c*) *Heltzer* Michael, The Late Bronze Age service system and its decline: ➤ 742, Society 1985/8, 229-237 / 187-228; 14 fig. / 7-18.

h437 **Andreau** Jean, La vie financière dans le monde romain; les métiers de manieurs d'argent (IVᵉ siècle av. J.-C. – IIIᵉ siècle ap. J.-C.): BÉF 265. R 1987, École Française. viii-792 p. – ᴿRÉLat 66 (1988) 329s (J.-l. *Ferrary*).

h438 ᴱ**Archi** A., Circulation of goods in non-palatial context in the Ancient Near-East 1981/4 ➤ 65,694 ... 3,f814: ᴿJAOS 108 (1988) 660s (N. *Yoffee*); JNES 47 (1988) 133s (D. C. *Snell*).

h439 **Ashtor** Eliyahu, Levant trade in the later Middle Ages 1983 ➤ 1,f354: ᴿEngHR 102 (1987) 193-5 (J. *Riley-Smith*); Studi Medievali 28 (1987) 775-9 (A. *Grohmann*).

h440 *Avram* Alexandru, Zu den Handelsbeziehungen zwischen Histria und der Insel Thasos im Lichte der Amphorenstempel: Klio 70 (1988) 404-411.

h441 **Bagnall** Roger S., Currency and inflation in fourth century [A.D.] Egypt 1985 ➤ 2,b951; 3,f815: ᴿGnomon 60 (1988) 425-430 (H. *Brandt*).

h442 *Blakely* Jeffrey A., Ceramics and commerce; amphorae from Caesarea Maritima: BASOR 271 (1988) 31-50; 9 fig.

h443 *Bleiberg* Edward, The redistributive economy in New Kingdom Egypt; an examination of *b3kw(t)*: JAmEg 25 (1988) 157-168.

h444 *Boardman* John, Trade in Greek decorated pottery: OxJArch 7 (1988) 27-33; p. 369s, corrections by *Gill* David W. J.; 371-3 rejoinder.

h445 *Bogaert* Raymond, *a)* Liste chronologique des banquiers royaux thébains 255-84 avant J.-C.; ZPapEp 75 (1988) 11-5-138; – *b)* Les opérations en nature des banques en Égypte gréco-romaine: AncS 19 (1988) 213-224.

h446 **Boochs** W., Die Finanzverwaltung im Altertum 1985 ➤ 1,f181; 3,f821: ᴿArEspArq 61 (1988) 349 (A. J. *Dominguez Monedero*); Eos 76 (1988) 380-3 (M. *Żyromski*).

h447 *Boochs* Wolfgang, Fiskaldelikte: DiscEg 10 (1988) 9-19.

h448 *Botto* Massimo, L'attività economica dei Fenici in Oriente tra il IX e la prima metà dell'VIII sec. a. C.: EgVO 11 (1988) 117-154.

h449 **Bru** Patrice, Eisphora, syntaxis, stratiotika; recherches sur les finances militaires d'Athènes au IVᵉ siècle av. J.-C.: Centre RechHistAnc 50, 1983 ➤ 2,b957; 2-251-60284-4: ᴿAntClas 57 (1988) 507s (H. *Verdin*).

h450 *Choksy* Jamsheed K., Loan and sales contracts in ancient and early medieval Iran: IndIranJ 31 (1988) 191-218.

h451 *Clarysse* Willy, The financial problems of the beer-seller Ameneus: Enchoria 16 (1988) 11-21; pl. 2-3.

h452 *Cornelius* Izak, The commercial relations of Canaan in the second millenium BC — a discussion of the cuneiform texts from Mari and Ugarit: ➤ 499, Holy Land 1986/8, 14-32.

h453 **Cozzo** Andrea, *Kerdos* [... profit]; semantica, ideologia e società nella Grecia antica: Filologia e critica 56. R 1988, Ateneo. 166 p.

h454 **Crawford** Michael H., Coinage and money under the Roman republic; Italy and the Mediterranean economy 1985 ➤ 1,f185 ... 3,f829: ᴿNumC 148 (1988) 241-3 (P. *Kinns*); RNum 30 (1988) 280s (J.-B. *Giard*).

h455 *a) Deger-Jalkotzy* Sigrid, Landbesitz und Sozialstruktur im mykenischen Staat von Pylos; – *b) Hiller* Stefan, Dependent personnel in Mycenaean texts; – *c) Uchitel* Alexander, The archives of Mycenaean Greece and the Ancient Near East: ➤ 742, Society 1985/8, 31-52 / 53-68 / 19-30.

h456 **De Hoff** Sharon L., The ivory trade in the Eastern Mediterranean Bronze Age; background and preliminary investigation: diss. Minnesota. Minneapolis 1988. 274 p. 88-15272. – DissA 49 (1988s) 1922-A.

h457 **De Martino** Francesco, Wirtschaftsgeschichte des alten Rom 1985 ➤ 1,f190 ... 3,f832: ᴿBonnJbb 188 (1988) 574-8 (L. *Wierschowski*).

h458 **Ditz** Gerhard W., *a)* [Adam] SMITH and [John M.] KEYNES; religious differences in economic philosophy: Bijdragen 49 (1988) 58-86; – *b)* Smith et Keynes; la religion dans la philosophie économique: Cahiers Internationaux de Sociologie 33 (P 1987) 307-336 [< RSPT 72,342].

h459 *a) Drexhage* Hans-Joachim, Zur Preisentwicklung im römischen Ägypten von ca. 260 n. Chr. bis zum Regierungsantritt Diokletians; – *b) Winter* Engelbert, Handel und Wirtschaft in sāsānidisch-(ost-)römischen

Verträgen und Abkommen: MünstHand 6,2 (1987) 30-44; Eng. franç. 45 / 46-72; Eng. franç. 73.

h460 *a*) *Drexhage* Hans-Joachim, ... scimus, quam varia sint pretia rerum per singulas civitates regionesque ... Zu den Preisvariationen im römischen Ägypten; – *b*) *Haider* Peter W., Zu den ägyptisch-ägäischen Handelsbeziehungen zwischen ca. 1370 und 1200 v. Chr., I. Das Handelssystem: MünstHand 7,2 (1988) 1-10; Eng. 10; franç. 11 / 12-24, 4 maps; Eng. franç. 25.

h461 *Engels* Johannes, Anmerkungen zum 'Ökonomischen Denken' im 4. Jahrh. v. Chr. und zur wirtschaftlichen Entwicklung des Lykurgischen Athen: MünstHand 7,1 (1988) 90-131; Eng. 132s; franç. 133s.

h462 *Finkelstein* Israel, Arabian trade and socio-political conditions in the Negev in the twelfth-eleventh centuries B.C.E.: JNES 47 (1988) 241-252.

h463 **Finley** Moses I., *a*) Économie et société en Grèce ancienne; – *b*) Sur l'histoire ancienne; ᵀ*Carlier* Jeannie: Textes à l'appui. P 1984/7, Découverte. 322 p.; F 134 / 215 p.; F 89. 2-7071-1476-6; 712-9. – ᴿAntClas 57 (1988) 514s (G. *Raepsaet*).

h464 **Gabba** Emilio, Del buon uso della ricchezza; saggi di storia economica e sociale del mondo antico: Saggi 7. Mi 1988, Guerini. 235 p. 88-7802-043-5. 16 reprints.

h465 **Gassner** Verena, Die Kaufläden in Pompeii: Diss. Wien 178, 1986 ➤ 3,f837: ᴿMitt.Österr.Num.Ges. 27 (1987) 44.

h466 **Glotz** Gustave, Ancient Greece at work; an economic history of Greece from the Homeric period to the Roman conquest. Hildesheim 1987 = 1926, Olms. xii-402 p.; 49 fig.

h467 *Goedicke* Hans, *a*) Bilateral business in the Old Kingdom ['Pharaonic Law'; contributions from 'A.I.D.E.A.']; – *b*) The expression *ini r isw* [Contributions from the Association Internationale pour l'Étude du Droit de l'Égypte Ancienne, College de France, Paris]: DiscEg 5 (1986) 73-101 / 6 (1986) 67-78.

h468 **Gras** Michel, Trafics tyrrhéniens archaïques 1985 ➤ 2,b970; 3,f840: ᴿAntClas 57 (1988) 588-592 (R. Van *Compernolle*: 'Quel beau livre! Et quelle riche idée ...:' titre 'trafics' au lieu de 'commerce'); ClasR 102 (1988) 113s (D. *Ridgway*).

h469 **Green** Henry A., The economic and social origins of Gnosticism [St. Andrews 1982] SBL diss. 77, 1985 ➤ 1,f212 ... 3,f842: ᴿJBL 107 (1988) 156-8 (J. D. *Turner*); JPseud 1 (1987) 116-9 (W. *Adler*); ScotJT 41 (1988) 555s (S. N. C. *Lieu*).

h470 **Greene** Kevin, The archaeology of the Roman economy. L/Berkeley 1986, Batsford/ Univ. California. 192 p. incl. 73 pl. $30. /0-5200-5915-8. – ᴿClasW 82 (1988s) 58s (Phyllis *Culham*); MünstHand 7,2 (1988) 95-101 (G. *Prachner*).

h471 *a*) *Günther* Wolfgang, 'Vieux et inutilisable' dans un inventaire inédit de Milet; – *b*) *Linders* Tullia, The purpose of inventories; a close reading of the Delian inventories of the Independence; – *c*) *Manganaro* Giacomo, Le tavole finanziarie di Tauromenion: ➤ 698, Comptes 1986/8, 215-237; 2 fig. / 37-47 / 155-190; 11 fig.

h472 *Harding* Anthony F., Fernhandel in der Bronzezeit; Analyse und Interpretation: Saeculum 38 (1987) 297-311.

h473 **Harrauer** Hermann, Neue Papyri zum Steuerwesen im 3 Jh. v. Chr.: Corpus Raineri 13, Griechische Texte IX. W 1987, Hollinek. 278 p., vol. of pl. – ᴿCdÉ 63 (1988) 173-7 (J. *Bingen*).

h474 *Heltzer* Michael, Sinaranu, son of Siginu, and the trade-relations between Ugarit and Crete: Minos 23 (1988) 7-13.

h475 *a) Klengel* Horst, Ebla im Fernhandel des 3. Jahrtausends; – *b) Pinnock* Frances, Observations on the trade of lapis lazuli in the IIIrd millenium B.C.: ➤ 707, Wirtschaft 1986/8, 245-251 / 107-110.

h476 *Kolb* Anne, *Ott* Joachim, Ein 'collegium negotiatorum cisalpinorum et transalpinorum' in Augusta Rauricorum [Museum Augst, Schweiz]: ZPapEp 73 (1988) 107-110; 1 fig.

h477 *Kracht* Peter, Die handelsgeschichtliche Bedeutung der Stadt Sybaris [Unteritalien, Küste] bis zu ihrer Zerstörung im Jahre 510 v. Chr.: MünstHand 7,1 (1988) 30-44; 5 fig.; Eng. franç. 45.

h478 **Kreissig** Heinz, Wirtschaft und Gesellschaft im Seleukidenreich 1978 ➤ 60,y31 ... 62,k664: [R]OLZ 83 (1988) 141-6 (J. *Oelsner*).

h479 *Liesker* W. H. M., *Sijpesteijn* P. J., Un cas de faux en écriture à la Banque Royale thébaine en 131 avant J.-C.; CdÉ 63,125 (1988) 145-156.

h480 *Limet* H., Les paroles et les écrits; note sur les contrats d'époque paléo-babylonienne: ➤ 101, Mém. MARÇAIS P. 1985, 75-89.

h481 *a) Limet* Henri, Complexité salariale et complexité sociale à l'époque néo-sumérienne; – *b) Veenhof* Klaas R., Prices and trade; the Old Assyrian evidence; – *c) Zaccagnini* Carlo, On prices and wages at Nuzi; – *d) Dandamayev* Muhammad A., Wages and prices in Babylonia in the 6th and 5th centuries B.C.; – *e) Klengel* Horst, Einige Bemerkungen zu Löhnen und Preisen im hethitischen Anatolien; – *f) Janssen* J. J., On prices and wages in ancient Egypt; – *g) Helck* Wolfgang, Das Problem der Löhne und Preise im Alten Reich Ägyptens: AltOrF 15 (1988) 231-242 / 243-263 / 45-52 / 53-58 / 76-81 / 10-33 / 3-9.

h482 *a) Lipiński* Edward, The socio-economic condition of the clergy in the kingdom of Ugarit; – *b) Vargyas* P., Stratification sociale à Ugarit; – *c) Skaist* Aaron, A unique closing formula in the contracts from Ugarit; – *d) Izre'el* Shlomo, When was the 'General's Letter' from Ugarit written?: ➤ 742, Society 1985/8, 125-150 / 111-123 / 151-9 / 160-175.

h483 **Lowry** S. T., The archaeology of economic ideas: The classical Greek tradition. Durham NC 1987, Duke Univ. xvii-366 p. £51.30 [GreeceR 36,110, P. J. *Rhodes*].

h484 **McCann** Anna M., *al.*, The Roman port and fishery of Cosa; a center of ancient trade 1987 ➤ 3,f863: [R]AJA 92 (1988) 301s (G. E. *Rickman*).

h485 *Mehl* Andreas, Der Überseehandel von Pontos: ➤ 764, Hist. Geographie 1980/7, 103-186 [187-212, 213-232, *Olshausen* E., *Biller* J. über Pontos].

h486 *Menu* Bernadette, Les actes de vente en Égypte ancienne, particulièrement sous les rois Kouchites et Saïtes: JEA 74 (1988) 165-181; Eng. 165.

h487 **Migeotte** Léopold, L'emprunt public dans les cités grecques [diss. Lyon 1978] 1984 ➤ 2,b994; 3,f870: [R]AntClas 57 (1988) 477s (A. *Martin*); Latomus 47 (1988) 477 (J. *Schwartz*).

h488 [E]**Moxnes** H., Urkristendommen: Projekthefter, 1 (29 p.), 2 (61 p. on economics of surrounding world in Luke by Moxnes, and in general by B. J. *Malina*, from Interpretation 41,354-367; both in English). Oslo 1987, Universitet. [NTAbs 32,236.358].

h489 *Muhly* J. D., The role of Cyprus in the economy of the Eastern Mediterranean during the second millennium B.C.: ➤ 749, Cyprus between, 1985/6, 45-62.

h490 *a) Oates* John F., The quality of life [= coinage and taxes?] in Roman Egypt; – *b) Gara* Alessandra, Aspetti di economia monetaria dell'Egitto romano: ➤ 782, ANRW 2,10,1 (1988) 799-806 / 912-951.

h491 **Ørsted** Peter, Roman imperial economy and Romanization... Danube provinces A.D. K 1985, MusTusc. 415 p.; 2 maps. – ᴿBonnJbb 188 (1988) 621-3 (T. *Pekáry*).

h492 *Osborne* Robin, Social and economic implications of the leasing of land and property in classical and Hellenistic Greece: Chiron 18 (1988) 279-323.

h493 *Padró* Josep, Le rôle de l'Égypte dans les relations commerciales d'Orient et d'Occident au premier millénaire [av. J.-C.]: ➤ 127, ᶠṢALEḤ A., ASAE 71 (1987) 213-222.

h494 *a) Panitschek* Peter, Zur Entstehung des Athenischen Handels mit dem Schwarzmeerraum im 6. Jahrhundert; – *b) Bounegru* Octavian, Bemerkungen zu den römischen Importen in Scythia Minor (1.-3. Jh. n. Chr.): MünstHand 7,2 (1988) 27-42; Eng. 42s; franç. 43s / 70-85, map; Eng. 85s; franç. 86.

h495 **Peacock** D. P. S., *Williams* D. F., Amphorae and the Roman economy 1986 ➤ 2,b999; 3,f874: ᴿAntClas 57 (1988) 611 (G. *Raepsaet*); JRS 78 (1988) 241-4 (J. J. *Paterson*: also on Peacock's 'brilliant' 1982 Pottery... ethnoarchaeological); RArchéol (1988) 423 (J.-Y. *Empereur*: 'an introduction guide').

h496 **Peruzzi** E., Money in early Rome: Acad. F Colombaria Studi 73, 1985 ➤ 1,e268.f240; 3,f875: ᴿÉtClas 56 (1988) 125s (N. *Golvers*).

h497 **Puskás** Ildikó, Trade contacts between India and the Roman Empire: ➤ 42, ᶠEGGERMONT P., 1987, 141-156.

h498 ᴱ**Rouillard** Pierre, *Villanueva-Puig* Marie C., Grecs et Ibères au IVᵉ siècle avant Jésus-Christ; commerce et iconographie: Table Ronde CNRS, Bordeaux 16-18 décembre 1986 = RÉAnc 89,3s (1987) 428 p. 16 art.; *Descat* R., Économie... d'Athènes, p. 239-252.

h499 **Schmitz** Winfried, Wirtschaftliche Prosperität, soziale Integration und die Seebundpolitik Athens [Diss.]: Quellen und Forschungen zur Antiken Welt 1. Mü 1988, TUDUV. 396 p. DM 65 [Gymnasium 96, 558-560, K.-W. *Welwei*].

h500 **Serrao** Feliciano, Diritto privato, economia e società nella storia di Roma I 1984 ➤ 3,f883; Lit. 27.000: ᴿLatomus 47 (1988) 456-9 (R. *Sotty*: 'economia/società' superfluo nel titolo).

h501 *Shiff* Laurence, Neo-Babylonian 'interest-free' promissory notes: JCS 40 (1988) 187-194.

h502 **Sidebotham** Steven E., Roman economic policy in the [Indian Ocean, Persian Gulf, (and)] Erythra Thalassa 30 B.C. – A.D. 217: Mnemosyne Sup. 91. Leiden 1986, Brill. 226 p. ƒ85. – ᴿArctos 22 (1988) 237s (K. *Karttunen*); ClasR 102 (1988) 101-4 (G. W. *Bowersock*).

Sigrist Marcel, Textes économiques néo-sumériens de l'Université de Syracuse: RCivMém 29, 1983 ➤ g111.

h504 *Sigrist* Marcel, *Butz* Kilian, Wirtschaftliche Beziehungen zwischen der Susiana und Südmesopotamien in der Ur-III-Zeit: ArchMIran 19 (1986) 27-31.

h505 **Sijpesteijn** P. J., Customs duties in Graeco-Roman Egypt: StAmstEpg 17. Zutphen 1987, Terra. 90-6255-332-X [OIAc D88].

h506 **Silver** Morris, Economic structures of the Ancient Near East 1985 ➤ 1,f247; 3,f887: ᴿAmHR 93 (1988) 123s (B. R. *Foster*); BAR-W 14,3 (1988) 6. 57 (B. *Rosen*).

h507 **Smith** Thyrza R., Mycenaean trade and interaction in the West Central Mediterranean, 1600-1000 B.C.: BAR-371. Ox 1987. vii-189 p.; ill.

h508 *Snell* Daniel C., The allocation of resources in the Umma silver account system: JESHO 31 (1988) 1-13.

h509 *Steinkeller* Piotr, The administrative and economic organization of the Ur III state; the core and the periphery: → 738, Power 1983/7, 19-41.

h510 **Stenger** Werner, 'Gebt dem Kaiser, was des Kaisers ist!' Eine sozialgeschichtliche Untersuchung zur Besteuerung Palästinas in neutestamentlicher Zeit: BoBB 68. Fra 1988, Athenäum. 281 p.; ill. DM 78. – RBiKi 43 (1988) 181s (H. *Frankemölle*).

h511 **Stolper** M. W., Entrepreneurs and empire; the Murašu archive, the Murašu firm, and Persian rule in Babylonia [diss. Michigan, AA 1974]. Leiden 1985, Ned. Instituut Nab. Oosten. xxi-324 p. 90-6258-054-8 [BL 89,127, G. H. *Jones*].

h512 *Tate* Georges, Mutabilité des économies antiques; l'exemple de la Syrie du nord (IVe-VIe siècles): → 706, Géographie 1985/8, 249-256.

h513 **Teixidor** Javier, Un port romain du désert, Palmyre... 1984 → 1,f253... 3,f891: RLatomus 47 (1988) 454s (J. *Schwartz*).

h514 **Torrence** Robin, Production and exchange of stone tools; prehistoric obsidian in the Aegean [diss.]: New Studies in Archaeology 1986 → 3,f892: RBInstArch sup. 24 (1987) 14s (F. *Healy*).

h515 *Tréheux* Jacques, a) Une nouvelle lecture des inventaires d'Apollon à Délos; – b) Observations sur les inventaires du 'Brauronion' de l'Acropole d'Athènes: → 698, [FTréheux] Comptes 1986/8, 29-35 / 347-355.

h516 a) *Tsirkin* Yu. B., The economy of Carthage; – b) *Picard* Colette, L'essor de Carthage aux VIIe et VIe siècles: → 754, Carthago 1986/8, 125-135 / 43-50; 7 fig.

h517 **Wierschowski** Lothar, Heer und Wirtschaft 1984 → 1,f258; 3,f896: RLatomus 47 (1988) 226s (B. *Dobson*).

h518 *Willetts* R. F., Economy and society (with particular reference to western Crete): Cretan 1 (1988) 257-269.

U5.7 **Nomadismus; ecology.**

h519 **Bradley** Rebecca, A model for pastoralism in the Meroitic Butana: → 750, Nubian V, 1982/6, 25-29; 4 fig.

h520 **Briant** Pierre, Rois, tributs et paysans 1982 → 63,e125... 65,d229: RGnomon 60 (1988) 33-35 (J. *Wiesehöfer*).

h521 *Briant* P., Le nomadisme du Grand Roi: → 4, FAMIET P. = IrAnt 33 (1988) 253-273.

h522 *Compagnoni* Pia, La tenda nel deserto e nelle pagine bibliche: TerraS 64 (1988) 244-9.

h523 *Rosen* Steven A., Finding evidence of ancient nomads: BAR-W 14,5 (1988) 46-53 . 58s; ill.

U5.8 **Urbanismus.**

h524 **Ahern** Geoffrey, *Davie* Grace, Inner city God; the nature of belief in the inner city; foreword *Sheppard* David; C. S. Lewis Centre: L 1987, Hodder & S. 160 p. £8. – RRHPR 68 (1988) 524s (J.-P. *Willaime*); Themelios 14 (1988s) 111s (W. D. J. *McKay*).

h525 **Bernhardt** Rainer, Polis und römische Herrschaft in der späten Republik 1985 → 2,d29; 3,f907: RAntClas 57 (1988) 527s (Marie-Thérèse *Raepsaet-Charlier*); RBgPg 66 (1988) 156-8 (P. *Salmon*).

h526 *Bintliff* John, *Snodgrass* Anthony,   Mediterranean survey and the city: Antiquity 62 (1988) 57-71; 10 fig.

h527 *Boyd* Thomas D.,   Urban planning: ↠ 444, Mediterranean 3 (1988) 1691-1700.

h527* ᴱ**Brüschweiler** Françoise, *al.*, La ville dans le Proche-Orient ancien 1979/83 ↠ 1,840: ᴿOLZ 83 (1988) 394s (C. *Tietze*).

h528 **Corsini** E., *Braccesi* L., present.,   La polis e il suo teatro: Saggi e materiali universitari. Padova 1986, Programma. 222 p. – ᴿAtenRom 33 (1988) 178s (Lucia *Ronconi*).

h529 *Deckers* Johannes,   Tradition und Adaption; Bemerkungen zur Darstellung der christlichen Stadt: MiDAI-R 95 (1988) 305-382; 11 fig.; pl. 118-136.

h530 *Demand* Nancy, HERODOTUS and *metoikēsis* in the Persian wars [voluntary relocation of a city, surprisingly frequent in the Greek world]: AmJPg 109 (1988) 416-423.

h531 **Falconer** Steven E.,   Heartland of villages; reconsidering early urbanism in the southern Levant [Mesopotamia; Jordan valley]: diss. Arizona, ᴰ*Yoffee* N. 1987. 364 p. 88-05515. – DissA 49 (1988s) 532-A.

h532 **Gawantka** Wilfried,   Die sogenannte Polis 1985 ↠ 1,f278 … 3,f915: ᴿAmHR 93 (1988) 396 (L. A. *Orin*).

h533 *Geus* Cornelius H. J. de,   The new city in ancient Israel; two questions concerning the reurbanization of ʼEreṣ Yiśraʼel in the tenth century B.C.E.: ↠ 469, Wünschet 1986/8, 105-112; 133, 2 fig.

h534 *Gschnitzer* Fritz,   Die Stellung der polis in der politischen Entwicklung des Altertums: OrAnt 27 (1988) 287-302.

ᴱ**Hägg** R., *Konsola* D.,   Early Helladic architecture and urbanization 1985/6 ↠ d873.

h535 **Herman** Gabriel,   Ritualised friendship and the Greek city 1987 ↠ 3,f917; £25: ᴿArctos 22 (1988) 232s (M. *Kaimio*).

h536 *Herrmann* P.,   Zur Selbstdarstellung der Polis in hellenistischer Zeit: ↠ 684*, ᶠHEUSS A., 1984/6, 39s.

h537 **Hoepfner** Wolfram, *Schwandner* Ernst-Ludwig,   Haus und Stadt im klassischen Griechenland: Wohnen in der klassischen Polis 1, DAI, 1986 ↠ 3,f918: ᴿBonnJbb 188 (1988) 560-2 (H. *Knell*); Gymnasium 95 (1988) 174-6 (J. *Raeder*); RArchéol (1988) 395-7 (J.-F. *Bommelaer*).

h538 *Isaac* Benjamin, ⊕ Roman administration and urbanization: CHistEI 48 (1988) 9-16; Eng. 194.

h539 **Kleinow** Hans Georg,   Die Überwindung der Polis im frühen 4. Jahrhundert v.Chr.; Studien zum epigraphischen Tatenkatalog und zu den panhellenischen Reden bei LYSIAS, PLATON und ISOKRATES; Diss. Erlangen-Nürnberg 1981. 318 p. – ᴿGnomon 60 (1988) 680-4 (G. *Dobesch*).

h540 **Kolb** Frank,   Die Stadt im Altertum 1984 ↠ 65,d248 … 3,f921: ᴿPhoenix 42,1 (Toronto 1988) 85s (M. *Woloch*).

h541 **Lampe** P.,   Die stadtrömischen Christen … WUNT 2/18, 1987 ↠ 3,f759: ᴿHeythJ 29 (1988) 359s (R. E. *Brown*: adds non-literary data to Brown's in Antioch and Rome).

h542 *Lasserre* François, PLATON, HOMÈRE et la cité: ↠ 91, ᶠLABARBE J., Stemmata 1987, 3-14.

h542* *Léon-Dufour* X.,   La presenza nel mondo della città ideale secondo la Bibbia: ↠ h562, La città ideale 1985/7 … [Maia 40 (1988) 296 (L. *Robertini*)].

h543 *Lim* D. S.,   The city in the Bible: EvRT 12,2 (Exeter 1988) 138-156 [< NTAbs 32,341].

h544 *Lorenz* Thuri, Römische Städte: Grundzüge 66. Da 1987, Wiss. x-205 p. DM 37; sb. 29 [AnzAltW 41,254]. 3-534-02162-2.

h545 *Loucas* I., Aux origines de la cité-État; sôphrosynè sociale et politique religieuse nationale: → 693, Actes = Kernos 1 (1988) 141-150.

h546 **Martin** Roland, Architecture et urbanisme; préf. *Pouilloux* Jean, *Vallet* Georges: Coll. 99. R 1987, Éc. Française. x-624 p.; ill.

h547 **Mason** Peter, The city of men; ideology, sexual politics and the social formation: Mg 4. Gö 1984, Herodot. 167 p. – [R]Gnomon 60 (1988) 756s (W. *Nippel*: too technical for an interdisciplinary goal).

h547* *Meeks* Wayne A., St. Paul of the cities: → 3,640, [E]*Hawkins* P., Civitas 1982/6, 15-23 [< JBL 108,179].

h548 *Musti* Domenico, Recenti studi sulla regalità greca; prospettive sull'origine della città [*Drews* R. 1983; *Carlier* P. 1984]: RivFgIC 116 (1988) 99-121.

h549 **Osborne** Robin, Classical landscape with figures; the ancient Greek city and its countryside 1987 → 3,f927: [R]AJA 92 (1988) 295s (V. *Hanson*); Antiquity 62 (1988) 189 (B. *Jones*); ClasR 102 (1988) 312-4 (Ronald A. *Knox*: unrelated to identical title of Sir Osbert LANCASTER); ClasW 82 (1988s) 120s (J. E. *Ziolkowski*).

h550 *Owens* E., The development of Roman town planning: AncHRes 18 (1988) 156-169; 9 fig.

h551 **Pelletier** A., L'urbanisme romain sous l'Empire 1982 → 64,d831 ... 2,d60: [R]RStorAnt 16 (1986) 210-6 (G. A. *Mansuelli*).

h552 **Polignac** François de, La naissance de la cité grecque 1984 → 2,d62; 3,f930: [R]AmHR 91 (1986) 1168s (T. J. *Figueira*); AntClas 57 (1988) 569s (D. *Viviers*); RHR 205 (1988) 94-96 (F. *Jouan*).

h553 *Reviv* Hanoch, Kidinnu; observations on privileges of Mesopotamian cities: JESHO 31 (1988) 286-298.

h554 **Rhodes** P. J., The Greek city states; a source book 1986 → 2,d63; £20; pa. £10: [R]EchMClas 32 (1988) 414s (K. H. *Kinzl*); Gnomon 60 (1988) 543s (M. *Stahl*).

h555 *Scully* Stephen, Cities in Italy's golden age: Numen 35 (1988) 69-78.

h556 Sociétés Urbaines en Égypte et au Soudan [nouveau titre de] Cahiers de Recherches CRIPEL 7. Lille 1985. 135 p.; 16 pl. F 180. – [R]JAmEg 24 (1987) 144-6 (K. *Grzymski*: despite change of title, this volume remains a collection of papers on different subjects).

h557 **Stambaugh** John E., The ancient Roman city. Baltimore 1988, Johns Hopkins. 395 p.; 29 fig.; 31 pl. £19; pa. £8.50. 0-8018-3574-7; 692-1 [Antiquity 63,100].

h558 **Starr** Chester G., Individual and community; the rise of the polis 800-500 B.C. 1986 → 2,d67; 3,f936: [R]ClasW 30 (1986s) 451 (W. *Donlan*).

h559 *a*) *Teixidor* Javier, Le territoire urbain dans les textes sémitiques d'époque séleucide; – *b*) *Chuvin* Pierre, Les fondations syriens de Séleucos Nicator dans la Chronique de Jean MALALAS; – *c*) *Frézouls* Edmond, Fondations et refondations dans l'Orient syrien; problèmes d'identification et d'interprétation: → 706, Géographie 1985/8, 41-45 / 99-110 / 111-131.

h560 *Theobald* Michael, 'Wir haben hier keine bleibende Stadt, sondern suchen die Zukunftige' (Hebr 13,14); die Stadt als Ort der frühen christlichen Gemeinde: TGL 78 (1988) 16-40.

h562 [E]**Uglione** R., La Città ideale nella tradizione classica e biblica-cristiana 1985/7 → 3,774: [R]ClasR 102 (1988) 73s (J. *Ferguson*, whose 1975 Utopias got justice without sympathy from Moses FINLEY; at Turin the Bible was treated by X. *Léon-Dufour* and P. *Rossano*); Orpheus 9 (1988) 109-113 (B. *Clausi*).

h563 ᴱWeiss Harvey, The origins of cities in dry-farming Syria and Mesopotamia 1984/6 ➤ 2,d69: ᴿArOr 56 (1988) 185-7 (B. *Hruška*: sehr geglückt); BO 45 (1988) 698-700 (P. J. *La Placa*); RAss 82 (1988) 184s (D. *Charpin*); WeltOr 19 (1988) 179-181 (W. *Röllig*).

h564 *Welwei* Karl W., Ursprünge genossenschaftlicher Organisationsformen in der archaischen Polis: Saeculum 39 (1988) 12-23.

h565 *a*) *Will* Édouard, Poleis hellénistiques; deux notes; – *b*) *Kinzl* K. H., GAWANTKA's Sogenannte Polis and some thoughts à propos; – *c*) *Saradi-Mendelovici* H., The demise of the ancient city and the emergence of the mediaeval city in the eastern Roman Empire: ÉchMClas 32 (1988) 329-352 / 403-412 / 365-401.

h566 *Wilson* Robert R., The city in the OT: ➤ 3,640, Civitas 1982/6, 3-13.

h567 *a*) *Young* T. C.ᴶ, The origin of the Mesopotamian city; – *b*) *Levine* Louis D., Cities as ideology; the Neo-Assyrian centres of Ashur, Nimrud and Nineveh: CanadMesop 11 (1986) 3-9 / 12 (1986) 1-7.

h568 *Zaccagnini* Carlo, L'origine delle città [Mesopotamia; Ebla ...]: Archeo 41 (1988) 46-87; color. ill.

U5.9   Demographia, **population-statistics.**

h569 **Casarico** Loisa, Il controllo delle popolazioni nell'Egitto romano I, 1985 ➤ 2,d72; 3,f943: ᴿGnomon 60 (1988) 370s (C. *Wehrli*).

h570 *Figueira* Thomas J., Population patterns in late archaic and classical Sparta: AmPgTr 116 (1986) 165-213.

h571 *Gophna* Ram, *Portugali* Juval, Settlement and demographic processes in Israel's coastal plain from the chalcolithic to the Middle Bronze age: BASOR 269 (1988) 11-28.

h572 **Hansen** Mogens H., Demography and democracy; the number of Athenian citizens in the fourth century B.C. [30,000 + (? several) hundred thousand slaves] 1986 ➤ 3,f947: ᴿMnemosyne 41 (1988) 461-5 (L. de *Blois*, W. van *Loon*).

h573 *Hansen* Mogens H., Demography and democracy once again: ZPapEp [72 (1988) 139s, *Rauschenbusch* E., Athens citizen population 21,000 in 322 B.C.] 75 (1988) 189-193.

h574 *Hansen* Mogens H., Three studies in Athenian demography: Vidensk. Selskab. Meddelelser fg. 56. K 1988, Munksgaard. 28 p.

h575 *Hershkovitz* Israel, The Tell Maḥrad population in southern Sinai [wadi Feiran] in the Byzantine era: IsrEJ 38 (1988) 47-58; 3 fig.; pl. 10-11.

h576 **Roger** Gary L., Studies in the demography and economy of Delos in the third century B.C.: diss. Wisconsin, ᴰ*Glover* M. Madison 1987. 814 p. 88-00380. – DissA 49 (1988s) 130s-A.

h577 **Morris** Ian, Burial [does not warrant demography-conclusions] and ancient society; the rise of the Greek city-state: New Studies in Archeology. C 1987, Univ. x-262 p.; 62 fig. £27.50. 0-521-32660-X. – ᴿAntiquity 62 (1988) 410-412 (R. *Bradley*); BInstArch 25 (1985) 146s (A. *Johnston*).

h578 **Osborne** R., Demos; the discovery of classical Attika 1985 ➤ 2,d77: ᴿJHS 108 (1988) 251-3 (R. K. *Sinclair*).

h579 *a*) *Strouhal* Eugen, Demography of the Late Roman-Early Byzantine cemetery at Wadi Qitna; – *b*) *Rösing* Friedrich W., *al.*, Die 'Giza-Rasse'

und der Paradigmenwandel in der Anthropologie: → 770, Äg. Kong.
IV-1, 1985/8, 329-349 / 317-326.

U6 **Narrationes peregrinorum et exploratorum;** *Loca sancta.*

h579* **Artola** A. M., La Tierra, el Libro, el Espíritu 1986 → 2,d83; 3,f951:
RCompostellanum 33 (1988) 305s (J. *Precedo*).

h580 **Busse** Heribert, *Kretschmar* Georg, Jerusalemer Heiligtumstraditionen
in altkirchlicher und frühislamischer Zeit: Abh DPV. Wsb 1988, Harrassowitz. vi-111 p.; 4 fig. DM 52 [JTS 40, 631-4, E. J. *Yarnold*].

h580* **Chelini** Jean, *Branthomme* Henry, Histoire des pèlerinages [(I.)
chrétiens 1982; (II.):] non-chrétiens; entre magie et sacré; le chemin des
dieux. P 1987, Hachette. 538 p. – RSpiritus 29 (1988) 107s (H. *Maurier*).

h581 **Dunne** John S., The homing spirit; a pilgrimage of the mind, of the
heart, of the soul [also of the body three times to Jerusalem — Christian,
Jewish, Muslim]. NY 1988, Crossroad. viii-132 p. $13 [TDig 35,162].

h582 *Dupriez* Christian, Un homme d'esprit en Égypte au XVIIIᵉ siècle; le
voyage du Comte D'ENTRAIGUES au pays des Mamelouks: → 50,
FFONTINOY C. 1988, 113-120.

h583 **Dupront** Alphonse, Du Sacré, croisades et pèlerinages; images et langues. P 1987, Gallimard. 540 p. – RSpiritus 29 (1988) 108 (H. *Maurier*).

h584 Égérie, itinéraire; congrès international, Arezzo 23-25 oct. 1987 [MondeB
52 (1988) 49].

h585 **Firby** Nora K., European travellers and their perception of Zo-
roastrians in the 17th and 18th centuries [diss. Manchester 1984; J.
Chardin; A. H. *Anquetil du Perron*...]: ArchMIran Egb. 14. B 1988,
Reimer. 246 p. 5 fig. 3-496-00857-1.

h586 *a) Grabois* Aryeh, Medieval pilgrims, the Holy Land and its image
in European civilisation; – *b) Olivier* Hannes, Nineteenth-century
travelogues and the Land of Moab; – *c) Nethersole* Reingard, Mark
TWAIN in the Holy Land: → 499, Holy Land 1986/8, 65-79 / 80-95 /
96-104.

h587 **Klatzker** David E., American Christian travelers to the Holy Land,
1821-1939: diss. Temple, DLittell F. Ph 1987. 88-03821. – DissA 49
(1988s) 100-A.

h588 *Klatzker* David, rabbi, American Catholic travelers to the Holy Land
1861-1929: CathHR 74 (1988) 55-74.

h589 **Kristeller** Paul O., Iter italicum... alia itinera; A finding list of un-
catalogued or incompletely catalogued humanistic manuscripts of the
Renaissance in Italian and other libraries. L 1977s, Warburg Inst. – I.
Italy (A-Novara) 1977 (= ¹1963) xxviii-533 p.; II. Italy (Orvieto –
Vatican), 1977 = 1967; xv-736 p.; III. Australia to Germany 1983;
xxxix-747; IV. Great Britain to Spain, 1989; xxv-812 p. [ISBN III-IV only]
90-04-06925-9; 7719-7.

h590 **Magdalena Nom de Déu** J. R., Relatos de viajes y epístolas de peregrinos
judíos a Jerusalén (1481-1523): OrBarc 3. Sabadell 1987, AUSA. 217 p. –
RSefarad 48 (1988) 435 (C. *Alonso Fontela*).

h591 *Manns* Frédéric, Une tradition judéo-chrétienne mentionnée par Égérie
[jeûne de la semaine entière pendant le carême]: Henoch 10 (1988)
283-290; ital. 291.

h592 **Maraval** Pierre, Lieux saints et pèlerinages d'Orient 1985 → 1,f342;
3,f977: RÉglT 18 (1987) 361-3 (L *Laberge*); HZ 247 (1988) 389s (E.
Rotter); TR 84 (1988) 300s (B. *Kötting*).

h593 *Maraval* Pierre, Les pèlerinages du IVe au VIe siècles: MondeB 52 (1988) 5-15 [39s *Mora* V.].

h594 *Mathieu* Bernard, Le voyage de PLATON en Égypte: ➤ 127, ᴱṢALEḤ A., ASAE 71 (1987) 153-167; map.

h595 *Miles* Margaret, Pilgrimage as metaphor in a nuclear age: TTod 45 (1988) 166-179.

h596 ᴱ**Padovese** Luigi, *Dalbesio* Anselmo, Turchia, i luoghi delle origini cristiane 1987 ➤ 3,f983: ᴿCiuD 201 (1988) 688 (J. *Gutiérrez*); ParVi 33 (1988) 239s (F. *Mosetto*).

h597 ᵀᴱ**Schmitz** R. P., BENJAMIN von Tudela, Buch der Reisen (Sefār ha-Massa'ot), I. Text: JudUmw 22. Fra 1988, Lang. 82 p. Fs 24. 3-8204-1442-8 [BL 89, 129, S. C. *Reif*].

h598 *Sivan* Hagith, *a)* Holy Land pilgrimage and western audiences; some reflections on Egeria and her circle: ClasQ 82 (1988) 528-535; – *b)* Who was Egeria? Piety and pilgrimage in the age of Gratian: HarvTR 81 (1988) 59-72.

h599 **Staid** Ennio, Nel paese di Gesù [diario di viaggio]: Dimensione religiosa. Mi 1988, Rusconi. 160 p. Lit. 22.000. – ᴿCiVit 43 (1988) 570s (B. *Farnetani*).

h600 **Stoneman** Richard, Land of the lost gods; the search for classical Greece [early travelers since 1204 and 15th cent. CYRIAC of Ancona] 1987 ➤ 3,b192; 0-8061-2052-5: ᴿClasW 82 (1988s) 138s (J. E. *Ziolkowski*).

h601 **Väänänen** Veikko, Le journal-épître d'Égérie, étude linguistique 1987 ➤ 3,f964: ᴿRÉLat 65 (1987) 289-292 (F. *Biville*).

h602 **Zachariä** Karl Eduard, Reise in den Orient [... Saloniki, Athos, Trapezunt] 1837-8. Fra 1985 = (Gothic type) 1840, Lövenklau. – ᴿRÉByz 46 (1988) 277 (J. *Wolinsky*).

h603 **Zink** Jörg, Tief ist der Brunnen der Vergangenheit; eine Reise durch die Ursprungsländer der Bibel. Stu 1986, Kreuz. 396 p. DM 78. 3-7831-9037-X. – ᴿNatGrac 35 (1988) 441s (R. *Robles*).

U7 *Crucigeri* – The Crusades.

h604 **Burns** Robert I., Muslims, Christians, and Jews in the Crusader kingdom of Valencia 1984 ➤ 65,d303; 2,d121*: ᴿJRAS (1988) 177s (J. D. *Latham*).

h605 **Chazan** Robert, European Jewry and the First Crusade 1987 ➤ 3,g1: ᴿAmHR 93 (1988) 1031s (J. *Cohen*); CathHR 74 (1988) 335s (J. *Riley-Smith*); JAAR 56 (1988) 564-6 (D. E. *Timmer*); JEcuSt 25 (1988) 464s (T. *Morrissey*); Zion 53 (1988) 323-7 (A. *Grabois* ❶).

h606 **Edbury** Peter W., *Rowe* John G., WILLIAM of Tyre; historian of the Latin East [Historia ierosolymitana, known as Historia rerum in partibus transmarinis gestarum]. C 1988, Univ. x-187 p. £22.50. – ᴿRHE 83 (1988) 827 (N. *Spencer*).

h607 *Ehrenkreutz* Andrew S., Saladin: ➤ 792, DMA 10 (1988) 624-7.

h608 *Friedman* Mordechai A., Geniza sources for the Crusader period and for MAIMONIDES and his descendants: ➤ 3,62*, ᶠGratz College 1987 ...

h609 *Kötzsche* Lieselotte, Zwei Jerusalemer Pilgerampullen aus der Kreuzfahrerzeit: Zts Kunstgeschichte 51,1 (Mü 1988) 13-32; 24 fig.

h610 **Maalouf** Amin, The Crusades through Arab eyes, ᵀ*Rothschild* Jon 1984 ➤ 3,g12: ᴿJNES 47 (1988) 149s (J. A. *Brundage*).

h611 **Mayer** Hans E., Geschichte der Kreuzzüge[6rev]: Urban Tb 86. Stu 1985, Kohlhammer. 293 p. DM 28 pa. 3-17-008780-0. – [R]TPQ 136 (1988) 297 (F. *Schragl*).

h612 **Mayer** Hans E., The Crusades[2] [c.1965; Eng. [1]c.1975]. Ox 1988, UP. xii-354 p.; 3 maps. £27.50. – [R]RHE 83 (1988) 827 (D. *Bradley*).

h613 *Patri* S., La relation russe de la Quatrième Croisade: Byzantion 58 (1988) 461-501.

h614 **Prawer** Joshua, Crusader Institutions 1980 ➤ 62,270…1,f381. 0-19-822536-9: [R]ZDPV 104 (1988) 184-8 (C. H. *Brooker*, E. A. *Knauf*).

h615 [F]PRAWER Joshua: Outremer, [E]**Kedar** B. Z., *al*. 1982 ➤ 63,133: [R]ZDPV 104 (1988) 188s (G. *Prinzing*).

h616 *Reynaud* Georges, Observations sur l'idée de croisade au XVe siècle: BLitEc 89 (1988) 274-290; Eng. 242.

h617 **Riley-Smith** Jonathan, The First Crusade and the idea of crusading 1986 ➤ 2,d141; 3,g15: [R]AmHR 93 (1988) 133 (J. *Brundage*); Speculum 63 (1988) 714-7 (J. *Gilchrist*).

h618 *Riley-Smith* Jonathan, The Latin clergy and the settlement in Palestine and Syria, 1098-1100: CathHR 74 (1988) 539-557.

h619 *Schragl* Friedrich, Die Kreuzzüge — ein unheiliges Experiment?: TPQ 136 (1988) 203-232.

h620 **Siberry** Elizabeth, Criticism of Crusading, 1095-1274: 1985 ➤ 2,d147; 3,g19: [R]AmHR 92 (1987) 936s (M. *Gervers*); JEH 39 (1988) 297s (L. *Schmugge*).

h621 *Vermeulen* U., Le traité d'armistice entre le sultan Baybars et les hospitaliers de Hiṣn al-Akrad et al-Marqab: OrLovPer 19 (1988) 189-195.

h622 [E]**Zacour** N. P., *Hazard* H. W., The impact of the Crusades on the Near East: Hist. Crusades 5, 1985 ➤ 2,d146; 3,g24: [R]AmHR 93 (1988) 134 (R. B. *Patterson*).

U8 *Communitates Terrae Sanctae* – **The Status Quo.**

h623 **Anschütz** Helga, Die syrischen Christen vom Tur 'Abdin 1985 ➤ 65,d933…3,g27: [R]Irénikon 61 (1988) 145 (E. *Lt*.); RThom 88 (1988) 343s (J. *Jomier*).

h624 **Betts** Robert B., The Druze. NHv 1988, Yale. 161 p. – [R]PrOrChr 38 (1988) 401s (F. *Gruber*).

h625 [E]**Brinner** William M., *Rischin* Moses, Like all the nations? The life and legacy of Judah L. MAGNES. Albany 1987, SUNY. 241 p.; ill. [RelStR 15,177, J. D. *Sarna*].

h626 *Brock* Sebastian P., Syrian Christianity: ➤ 792, DMA 11 (1988) 562-7.

h627 **Buber** Martin, Sion; storia di un'idea [Israel und Palästina, zur Geschichte einer Idee],[T]; pref. *Poma* Andrea. Genova 1987, Marietti. xiv-184 p. Lit. 25.000. – [R]CC 139 (1988,3) 309 (S. M. *Katunarich*).

h628 **Cohen** Amnon, [➤ e652] Jewish life under Islam; Jerusalem in the sixteenth century 1984 ➤ 65,d341…3,g36: [R]JJS 39 (1988) 126-8 (D. *Wasserstein*).

h629 [E]**Cohen** Richard I., Vision and conflict in the Holy Land. NY/J 1987, St. Martin's/Yad Ben Zvi. vii-311 p.; ill. $30 [RelStR 15,175, J. S. *Migdal*].

h630 **Colbi** Saul P., A history of the Christian presence in the Holy Land. Lanham MD 1988, UPA. xiv-377 p. $28.50 [CBQ 51,187].

h631 *Colbi* Paolo S., Chiesa della Giorgia in Terra Santa: TerraS 64 (1988) 50-52.

h631* *David* Abraham, Safed, foyer du retour au Judaïsme de *conversos* au XVIᵉ siècle: RÉJ 146 (1987) 63-83.

h632 *a*) *Dupret* Baudouin, Les Chrétiens Coptes d'Égypte; – *b*) *Kochassarly* Khalil, Église et communauté islamique: Solidarité Orient 165 (1988,1) 9-21 / 166 (1988,2) 8-15 [< TKontext 10/1,109s].

h633 **Facchini** Augusto, Le processioni praticate dai Frati Minori nei santuari di Terra Santa; studio storico-liturgico: Studia Or.-Chr. Mg 19. Cairo-Mousky/J 1986, Centre Franciscain. v-230 p. $20. – ᴿColcFr 58 (1988) 197 (I. de *Villapadierna*).

h634 *a*) *Ferré* André, Chrétiens de Syrie et de Mésopotamie aux deux premiers siècles de l'Islam; – *b*) *Makdissi* Antoine, Les chrétiens et la renaissance arabe: Islamochristiana 14 (1988) 71-106 / 107-126.

h634* **Frangieh** Rassam K., The theme of alienation in the novel of Palestine: diss. Georgetown. Wsh 1986. 202 p. 87-26454. – DissA 48 (1987s) 2351-A.

h635 **Gerber** Haim, Ottoman rule in Jerusalem 1890-1914: Islamkundliche Untersuchungen 101, 1985 → 2,d166; 3,g46; 3-922-968-46-5: ᴿBO 45 (1988) 750s (M. H. *Şakiroğlu*).

h636 **Gil** Moshe, ❿ Palestine during the first Muslim period (634-1090). TA 1983, Univ. xxiv-688+762+742 p. – ᴿTarbiz 57 (1987s) 123-149. 281-308; Eng. VI (J. *Blau*).

h637 *Gordis* Robert, *al.*, The Arab-Israeli conflict — are these the solutions? [14 signed 'options']: Judaism 37 (1988) 391-445.

h638 *Grego* Igino, La laura di San Saba in Terra Santa, un'oasi dell'ortodossia e una cittadella dello spirito: Asprenas 35 (1988) 215-232.

h639 **Irani** George E., The papacy and the Middle East... Arab-Israeli conflict 1986 → 3,g54; 0-268-01560-0: ᴿCC 139 (1988,2) 411s (G. *Rulli*); HolyL 8 (1988) 219s (F. *Nahum*).

h640 *Khoury* Rafiq, Chrétiens arabes de la Terre Sainte: Études 369 (1988) 395-408.

h641 ᴱ**Kushner** David, Palestine in the Late Ottoman period; political, social and economic transformation. J/Leiden 1986, BenZvi/Brill. – ᴿZion 53 (1988) 75s (J. *Barnai*).

h642 ᴱ**Laqueur** Walter, *Rubin* Barry, The Israeli-Arab reader; a documentary history of the Middle East conflict⁴ʳᵉᵛ [³1976]. Hmw 1984, Pelican. xi-704 p. £6. – ᴿHZ 245 (1987) 211s (H. *Mejcher*).

h643 **Lewis** Bernard, The Jews of Islam 1984 → 65,8735...3,g63: ᴿJNES 47 (1988) 72s (N. A. *Stillman*); ScrMedit 89 (1987s) 103-5 (Maya *Shatzmiller*).

h644 **Lewis** Bernard, Die Juden in der islamischen Welt; vom frühen Mittelalter bis ins 20. Jahrhundert. Mü 1987, Beck. 216 p. DM 48.

h645 **McCarthy** Justin, Muslims and minorities; the population of Ottoman Anatolia at the end of the empire. NY 1983, NY Univ. xii-248 p. $45.50. 0-8147-5390-6. – ᴿBO 45 (1988) 748-750 (E. J. *Zürcher*).

h645* **McDowall** David, The Palestinians; pref. *Palley* Claire. L 1988, Minority Rights Group. £1.80. – ᴿTablet 242 (1988) 1277-9 (E. *Mortimer*).

h646 **Moosa** Matti, The Maronites in history. Syracuse NY 1986, Univ. 391 p. $35. – ᴿJAOS 108 (1988) 314s (R. M. *Haddad*: monophysite rather than orthodox origins).

h647 *Neudeck* Rupert, Tabgha; Zeichen zwischen Palästina und Israel: Orientierung 52 (1988) 250-3.

h648 [*Nientiedt* K.], Unbeirrt; die Ernennung eines Palästinensers zum neuen lateinischen Patriarchen von Jerusalem [Sᴀʙʙᴀʜ M.]: HerdKorr 42 (1988) 60.

h649 **Palumbo** Michael,   The Palestinian catastrophe; the 1948 expulsion of a people from their homeland.   L 1987, Faber & F.   xix-233 p.; 4 fig. £13. – ᴿDLZ 109 (1988) 956-8 (M. *Robbe*).

h650 *Pernigotti* Sergio,   Nella valle dei Copti; il cristianesimo sul Nilo: Archeo 37 (1988) 32-35; ill.

h650* **Pohl-Schöberlein** Monika,   Die schiitische Gemeinschaft des Südlibanon (Ǧabal ʿĀmil) innerhalb des libanesischen konfessionellen Systems [Diss. Heid]:   Islamkundliche Untersuchungen 117.   B 1986, Schwarz.   x-254 p. DM 78. – ᴿMundus 24 (1988) 35s (H. *Müller*).

h651 **Rabinovich** Abraham,   Jerusalem, the measure of the year [photos of its various populations by Uli Boecker].   J 1985, Carta.   160 p.   965-220-081-6. – ᴿHolyL 8 (1988) 100 . 110 (M. *Ghirlando*).

h651* **Rahe** Thomas,   Frühzionismus und Judentum; Untersuchungen zu Programmatik und historischem Kontext des frühen Zionismus bis 1897: JudUmw 21. Fra 1988, Lang.   435 p. Fs 75. – ᴿJudaica 44 (1988) 179s (P. *Maser*).

h652 **Remaud** Michel,   Cristiani di fronte a Israele.   Brescia 1986, Morcelliana. 205 p. Lit. 16.000. – ᴿParVi 33 (1988) 72s (M. *Perani*).

h652* **Rokach** Livia,   The Catholic Church and the question of Palestine; afterword (after her suicide 1984) 1982-7 by *Graham-Brown* Sarah.   L 1987, Saqi.   229 p. $45 [TDig 35,286].

h653 **Stemberger** Günter,   Juden und Christen im Heiligen Land; Palästina unter Konstantin und Theodosius.   Mü 1987, Beck.   298 p. DM 45. 3-406-32303-0. – ᴿBijdragen 49 (1988) 449s (M. *Parmentier*: encyclopedic).

h654 **Timm** Stefan,   Das christlich-koptische Ägypten in arabischer Zeit [I. 1984 → 65,d376] 4, M-P: TAVO B-41.   Wsb 1988, Reichert. – ᴿOLZ 83 (1988) 282-5 (P. *Grossmann*).

h655 *Zananiri* G.,   Le patriarcat latin de Jérusalem [M. Sᴀʙʙᴀʜ, 6 janv. 1988]: EsprVie 98 (1988) *jaune* 85s.

h656 *a) Zanelli* Claudio,   I Drusi; – *b) Iñiguez* I.,   Gli Aloiti [intorni di Ras Šamra (Ugarit)]: TerraS 64 (1988) 309-314 / 199-205.

XX. Historia Scientiae Biblicae

Y1   History of Exegesis .1 General.

h657 **Aland** Kurt,   History of Christianity [I, 1985 → 1,1432 ... 3,g77]; II. From the Reformation to the present, ᵀ*Schaaf* James L.   P 1986, Fortress.   618 p. – ᴿChH 57 (1988) 259s (C. *Lindberg*, 2); Interpretation 42 (1988) 328 (Rebecca H. *Weaver*, 2); Horizons 14 (1987) 380 (R. E. *McLaughlin*: unfavorable, 2).

h658 **Bartelink** G. J. M.,   Het vroege christendom en de antieke cultuur. Muiderberg 1986, Coutinho.   188 p. ƒ 29,50.   90-6283-660-7. – ᴿNedTTs 42 (1988) 163s (P. W. van der *Horst*).

h659 **Bernardi** Jean,   Les premiers siècles de l'Église.   P 1987, Cerf. 180 p. F 80. – ᴿSpiritus 29 (1988) 325s (F. *Nicolas*); VSp 142 (1988) 146s (T. *Camelot*).

h660 **Brown** Harold O. J.,   Heresies; the image of Christ in the mirror of heresy and orthodoxy from the Apostles to the present.   GR 1988, Baker. 486 p. (pa. ed.) [GraceTJ 9,303].

h661 **Brox** Norbert, Storia della Chiesa I. Epoca antica [➤ 65,d382; ²1986], ᵀᴱ*Mezzadri* Luigi. Brescia 1988, Queriniana. 190 p. Lit. 20.000. – ᴿETL 64 (1988) 468s (A. de *Halleux*).

h662 *Burini* Clara, 'Biblioteca patristica'; l'affermata originalità di una collezione: Benedictina 35 (1988) 567-575 [fino a 12. Gerolamo, Gli uomini illustri 1988].

h663 **Chaunu** P., L'apologie par l'histoire. P 1988, OEIL / Téqui. 618 p. – ᴿArTGran 51 (1988) 383s (A. S. *Muñoz*).

h664 **Davis** Leo D., The first seven ecumenical councils (325-787), their history and theology: Theology and Life 21. Wilmington 1987, Glazier. 342 p. $18 [CBQ 50,559].

h665 ᶠDÖRRIE Heinrich: Platonismus und Christentum, ᴱ**Blume** H.-D., *Mann* F., JbAC Egb 10, 1983 ➤ 64,28: ᴿAnzAltW 41 (1988) 129-135 (M. *Erler*: tit. pp.; compendia).

h666 **Engels** Friedrich, Sulle origini del cristianesimo [tre saggi 1883-1895 già pubblicati in italiano e con la stessa prefazione 1953 di *Donini* Ambrogio]: Universale idee 179. R 1986, Riuniti. 76 p. – ᴿSalesianum 50 (1988) 221s (E. *dal Covolo*).

h667 **Frede** H.J., Kirchenschriftsteller, Aktualisierungsheft [I. 1984 ➤ 65,d390] II. 1988: Vetus Latina 1/1B. FrB 1988, Herder. 100 p. [ZAW 101,314].

h668 **Frend** W.H.C., The rise of Christianity² 1984 ➤ 65,d191...3,g86: ᴿGnomon 60 (1988) 725-738 (P. *Habermehl*, also on his 1985 Saints and sinners).

h669 *Geerlings* Wilhelm, Apologetik und Fundamentaltheologie in der Väterzeit: ➤ 800, HbFT 4 (1988) 317-333.

h670 **Gnilka** C., Chresis 1984 ➤ 65,d393 ... 3,g87: ᴿNZMissW 43 (1987) 149s (K. J. *Rivinius*); StPatav 35 (1988) 200s (A. *Moda*).

h671 **Grossi** Vittorino [➤ 810*], *Siniscalco* Paolo, La vita cristiana nei primi secoli: La spiritualità cristiana 2. R 1988, Studium. 315 p. Lit 23.000. 88-382-3564-3.

h672 *Grossi* Vittorino, Cristianesimo e cultura nei primi secoli: Studium 84 (R 1988) 57-84.

h673 *Hann* Robert R., Post-apostolic Christianity as a revitalization movement; accounting for innovation in early patristic tradition: JRelSt 14,1s (Cleveland 1986s) 60-75 [< ᴢɪᴛ 88,720].

h674 *Horbury* William, OT interpretation in the writings of the Church Fathers: ➤ 317, Mikra 1988, 727-787.

h675 **Kelly** J.N.D., I simboli di fede nella Chiesa antica [Early Christian creeds]. N 1987, Dehoniane. xxxi-467 p. Lit. 30.000. [Asprenas 36,95, L. *Fatica*].

h676 **Köpf** Ulrich, Dogmengeschichte oder Theologiegeschichte?: ZTK 85 (1988) 455-473.

h676* **Kraus** H.J., Geschichte der historisch-kritischen Erforschung des ATs³ 1982 ➤ 63,e466...65,d402: ᴿProtestantesimo 43 (1988) 43s (J. A. *Soggin*).

h677 ᴱ**Lenzenweger** Josef, *al.*, Geschichte der katholischen Kirche, ein Grundkurs 1986 ➤ 3,430: ᴿTLZ 113 (1988) 121 (H. *Kirchner*).

h678 **Moda** Aldo, Il cristianesimo nei primi secoli. Bari 1986, Ecumenica. 126 p. – ᴿHenoch 10 (1988) 402s (P. *Sacchi*: di valore, ma dovrebbe chiarire meglio l'accettazione di SORDI M., 'sin da Tiberio il cristianesimo era una forma del giudaismo più accetto ai romani').

h679 **Mondésert** C., Pour lire les Pères de l'Église dans la collection 'Sources Chrétiennes'² [prenant en compte les 83 numéros parus après 1978]: Foi Vivante 230. P 1988, Cerf. 118 p.; 4 maps.

h681 *Pelland* Gilles,   Que faut-il attendre de l'histoire de l'exégèse ancienne?:
Gregorianum 69 (1988) 617-628; Eng. 628.

h682 **Pierini** Franco,   Alla ricerca dei Padri; introduzione e metodologia
generale: Mille anni di pensiero cristiano; le letterature e i monumenti dei
Padri I. CinB 1988, Paoline. 320 p. Lit. 22.000 [CC 139/2, dopo 416].

h683 **Placher** William C.,   A history of Christian [thought ➤ 1,f465] theology;
an introduction 1983: ᴿSWJT 31,2 (1988s) 58 (J. L. *Garrett*).

h684 **Ramsey** Boniface,   Beginning to read the Fathers 1985 ➤ 1,f467 ...
3,g108: ᴿScotJT 41 (1988) 427s (D. F. *Wright*).

h685 *Roberts* R. H.,   History without interpretation? [ᴱ*Andresen* C., HbDTG
1-3, 1980-4, aims to represent Protestant, Catholic, and Orthodox thought
wthout degrading any one strand; on the whole successfully, though
forcing comparison with HARNACK's Lehrbuch]: JTS 39 (1988) 460-476.

h686 **Robinson** Thomas A.,   The BAUER thesis examined; the geography of
heresy in the early Christian Church: StBEC 11. Lewiston NY 1988,
Mellen. xi-248 p. $50. 0-88946-611-4 [TDig 36,180].

h687 **Rogerson** John [OT], *Rowland* Christopher [intertestamental], *Lindars*
Barnabas [NT],   The study and use of the Bible: History of Christian
Theology 2 [1. was The Science of Theology] Basingstoke/GR 1988,
Marshall Pickering / Eerdmans. 415 p. $15 pa. /0-8028-0196-X [TDig
36,181].

  Rowland C.,   Christian origins; from messianic movement to Christian
religion 1985 ➤ 4265*.

h689 **Rudnick** Milton L.,   Speaking the Gospel through the ages; a history of
evangelism 1984 ➤ 1,f469 ... 3,g113: ᴿMissiology 15 (1987) 389s (R. V.
Peace: replaces standard Paulus SCHARPPF).

h690 ᴱ**Sadowski** Frank,   The Church Fathers on the Bible 1987 ➤ 3,g114:
ᴿNewTR 1,3 (1988) 99s (A. *Chirovsky*).

h691 **Sawicki** Marianne,   The Gospel in history; portrait of a teaching
Church; the origins of Christian education. NY 1988, Paulist. iv-298 p.
$13 [RelStR 15,58, P. C. *Hodgson*]. 0-8091-2954-X.

h692 **Saxer** Victor, Bible et hagiographie; Textes et thèmes bibliques dans les
Actes des martyrs ... 1986 ➤ 3,g115; 3-261-03469-6; Fs 90: ᴿNedTTs 42
(1988) 345s (A. *Hilhorst*).

h693 **Schneemelcher** W.,   Il cristianesimo delle origini 1987 ➤ 3,g117; Lit.
18.000: ᴿProtestantesimo 43 (1988) 217 (V. *Subilia*).

h694 *Selge* Kurt-Victor,   Die Kirchengeschichte in Sammelwerken und Ge-
samtdarstellungen: TRu 53 (1988) 201-222.

h695 **Sieben** Hermann J.,   Exegesis patrum 1983 ➤ 64,858* ... 3,g118: ᴿSvEx
53 (1988) 146-9 (A. *Ekenberg*).

h696 **Simonetti** M.,   Lettera e/o allegoria 1985 ➤ 1,f473; 3,g120: ᴿRivStoLR
24 (1988) 131-6 (Giuliana *Iacopino*); VigChr 42 (1988) 192-4 (G. J. M.
Bartelink).

h697 *Siniscalco* Paolo,   La riscoperta dei Padri: Studium 83 (R 1987)
185-195.

h698 *Stander* H. F.,   Patristiek en die studie van die Nuwe Testament:
HervTSt 42 (Pretoria 1986) 729-735 [< NTAbs 32,359].

h699 **Stead** Christopher,   Substance and illusion in the Christian Fathers [16
reprints 1961-83] 1985 ➤ 2,222: ᴿJEH 39 (1988) 627s (R. *Williams*); TPhil
63 (1988) 270s (A. *Grillmeier*).

h700 **Stevenson** J.,   A new Eusebius; documents illustrating the history of the
Church to AD 337 [c. 1957], ²ʳᵉᵛ *Frend* W.H.C. L 1987, SPCK. 404 p.
£12.50. – ᴿThemelios 14 (1988s) 31 (D. F. *Wright*).

h701 **Trigg** Joseph W., Biblical interpretation: Message of the Fathers 9. Wilmington 1988, Glazier. 304 p. 0-89453-349-5.

h702 **Vallin** Pierre, I cristiani e la loro storia [1985 ➤ 2,d238],[T]. Brescia 1987, Queriniana. 330 p. Lit. 30.000. – [R]CC 139 (1988,3) 443 (G. *Mellinato*).

h703 **Verbraken** P., De eerste eeuwen van het christendom, van de apostelen tot Karel de Grote. [Les premiers siècles chrétiens[2] 1984 ➤ 1,f476],[T]. Bonheiden 1986, Abdij Betlehem. 159 p. Fb 475. – [R]CollatVL 18 (1988) 246s (J. *Bonny*).

h704 **Vilanova** Evangelista, Historia de la teología cristiana I, 1987 ➤ 3,g125 [II. infra ➤ k128]: [R]ArTGran 51 (1988) 350s (A. *Segovia*); Carthaginensia 4 (1988) 295s (V. *Sánchez*); ComSev 21 (1988) 102-4 (M. *Sánchez Sánchez*); EstE 63 (1988) 119 (R. *Franco*); LumenVr 37 (1988) 91s (F. *Ortiz de Urtaran*); NatGrac 35 (1988) 247s (A. *Villalmonte*).

Walsh M., The triumph of the meek; why early Christianity succeeded 1986 ➤ d559.

h705 **Walton** Robert C., Chronological background charts of Church History. GR 1986, Zondervan. [xxi-] 84 charts. $9 pa. – [R]AndrUnS 26 (1988) 102-4 (K. A. *Strand*: not for beginners).

[E]**Woodbridge** John D., Great leaders of the Christian church [... apostles, Fathers] 1988 ➤ 428.

		Y1.4 *Patres apostolici et saeculi II* – **First two centuries.**

h707 *Bastit-Kalinowska* Agnès, Esquisse d'une histoire de l'exégèse des Évangiles jusqu'à Origène: ➤ 486, Traduction 1986/8, 151-161; Eng. 151.

h708 **Grant** Robert M., Greek apologists of the second century. L 1988, SCM. 254 p. £10.50. 0-334-00535-3.

h709 *Grant* Robert T., The Apostolic Fathers' first thousand years: ChH 57 Sup (1988) 20-28 [NTAbs 32,226].

h710 **Orbe** A., Introducción a la Teología de los siglos II y III: AnGreg 248 / Verdad e Imagen 103, 1987 ➤ 3,g128: [R]ArTGran 51 (1988) 339s (A. *Segovia*); ETL 64 (1988) 471s (A. de *Halleux*); Irénikon 61 (1988) 581s (E. L.); NatGrac 35 (1988) 237s (A. *Villalmonte*); QVidCr 144 (1988) 150s (C. *Pifarrè*); RET 48 (1988) 101-9 (E. *Romero-Pose*).

h711 CLEMENS A.: **Galloni** Matteo, Cultura, evangelizzazione e fede nel 'Protrettico' di Clemente Alessandrino: Verba Seniorum 10, 1986 ➤ 3,g133: [R]RÉByz 46 (1988) 253s (A. *Failler*).

h712 *Halton* Tom, Clement of Alexandria and ATHENAEUS (Paed III. 4,26): SecC 6 (1987s) 193-202.

Hoek Annewies van den, Clement of Alexandria and his use of Philo in the Stromateis; an early Christian reshaping of a Jewish model: VetChr Sup 3, 1988 ➤ a982.

h713 [E]**Nardi** Carlo, Clemente Alessandrino, Estratti profetici (Eclogae propheticae): BiblPatr 4, 1985 ➤ 1,f485*; 3,g134: [R]Salesianum 50 (1988) 233 (S. *Felici*); Teresianum 39 (1988) 206s (M. *Diego Sánchez*: 'ecglogae').

h714 *Places* Édouard des, Les citations profanes du IVe Stromate de Clément d'Alexandrie: RÉAnc 90 (1988) 389-397; Eng. 389.

h715 **Wyrwa** Dietmar, Die christliche PLATONaneignung ... Clemens A.: ArbKG 53, 1983 ➤ 64,d986 ... 2,d255: [R]ÉTRel 63 (1988) 126s (J.-D. *Dubois*).

h716 CLEMENS R.: **Bowe** Barbara E., A church in crisis; ecclesiology and paraenesis in Clement of Rome: Harvard Dissertations in Religion 23. Minneapolis 1988, Fortress. xvi-158 p. 0-8006-7077-9.

h717 **Herron** Thomas J., The dating of the First Epistle of Clement to the Corinthians; the theological basis of the majoral view [diss. Pont. Univ. Gregoriana 1987 ➤ 3,g140]. R 1988, Domenici-Pécheux. viii-151 p.

h718 *Simonetti* Manlio, Sulla datazione della traduzione latina della lettera di Clemente Romano: RivFgIC 116 (1988) 203-211.

h719 ᴱ**Strecker** Georg, Die Pseudoklementinen III. Konkordanz ... 1. Lateinisches Wortregister: GCS, 1986 ➤ 2,d259: ᴿTLZ 113 (1988) 34s (W. *Wiefel*).

h720 *a) Cirillo* L., Le baptême, remède à la concupiscence, selon la catéchèse ps.-clémentine de Pierre, Hom. XI 26 (Réc. VI 9; IX 7); – *b) Broek* Roelof van den, Der Brief des Jakobus an Quadratus und das Problem der judenchristlichen Bischöfe von Jerusalem (EUSEBIUS, HE IV,5,1-3): ➤ 85, ᶠKLIJN A., Text 1988, 79-90 / 56-65.

h721 **Van Voorst** Robert E., The Ascents of James; history and theology of a Jewish-Christian community as reflected in the Pseudo-Clementine Recognitions 1:33-71: diss. Union Theol. Sem. NY 1987. 302 p. 88-22289. – DissA 49 (1988s) 2271-A; RelStR 15,191.

h722 CONST. AP.: **Metzger** Marcel, Les Constitutions Apostoliques: SChr 320.329.336: I (1-2) 1985 ➤ 1,f494; II (3-6) 1986 ➤ 2,d264; III (7-8) 1983 ➤ 3,g141: ᴿJTS 39 (1988) 611-8 (T. A. *Kopeček,* 2s: fine and needed, though claim of superseding FUNK is queried); NRT 110 (1988) 761 (V. *Roisel,* 2s); RBén 98 (1988) 223s [L. *Wankenne,* 3]; RÉAug 34 (1988) 199s (J. *Doignon,* 1); RÉByz 45 (1987) 235s (J. *Darrouzès,* 1s) & 46 (1988) 239s (J. *Darrouzès,* 3); RHE 83 (1988) 522-5 (A. de *Halleux,* 3); RevSR 62 (1988) 306-312 (*ipse*); RHR 205 (1988) 214s (P. *Nautin,* 1-3); RivStoLR 24 (1988) 164 (F. *Trisoglio,* 3); ScEspr 40 (1988) 125-7 (L. *Sabourin*).

h723 DIDACHE: **Wengst** K., Didache, Barnabas, 2Klemens, Diognet 1984 ➤ 1,f495; 2,d262. – ᴿCrNSt 9 (1988) 174-6 (P. F. *Beatrice*).

h724 AD DIOGNETUM: *Baumeister* Theofried, Zur Datierung der Schrift an Diognet: VigChr 42 (1988) 105-111.

h725 *Rizzi* Marco, Per un approccio metodologico nuovo alla questione dell'autenticità dei capp. 11-12 dell''Ad Diognetum': Orpheus 9 (1988) 198-218.

h726 HERMAS: [➤ h945] *Hilhorst* A., Hermas: ➤ 807, RAC 14,108s (1988) 682-701.

h727 **Jeffers** James S., Social foundations of early Christianity at Rome; the congregations behind 1 Clement and the Shepherd of Hermas: diss. California, ᴰ*Frank* R. Irvine 1988. 355 p. 88-20214. – DissA 49 (1988s) 2268-A.

h728 *Miller* Patricia C., 'All the words were frightful'; salvation by dreams in the Shepherd of Hermas: VigChr 42 (1988) 327-338.

h729 IGNATIUS A.: *Lucchesi* Enzo, Le recueil copte des lettres d'Ignace d'Antioche; nouvelle glanure (Paris, B. N. 131°, 87 – Leiden, Insinger 90); VigChr 42 (1988) 313-317.

h730 **Schoedel** W., Ignatius ... letters 1985 ➤ 1,f502 ... 3,g147: ᴿSecC 6,1 (1987s) 46-49 (R. A. *Greer*).

h731 IRENAEUS: **Greer** Rowan A., Broken lights and mended lives 1986 ➤ 2,d276; 3,g155: ᴿJEH 39 (1988) 234s (G. *Bonner*); ScotJT 34 (1988) 142s (A. *Louth*).

h732 **Orbe** Antonio, Teologia di San Ireneo [Haer. V; I. 1985 ➤ 2,d278], II: BAC (25) 29. M 1985, Católica. 559 p. – ᴿRivStoLR 24 (1988) 353-366 (E. *Norelli*); TR 84 (1988) 374s (H.-J. *Jaschke*).

h733 *Osborn* Eric, Irenaeus; recapitulation and the beginning of Christian humour: ➤ 554, Salvation 1986/8, 64-76.

h734 JUSTINUS M.: ᵀᴱ**Bartelink** G. J. M., Twee apologeten uit het vroege christendom, Justinus en Athenagoras: Na de Schriften 1. Kampen 1986, Kok. 187 p. ƒ 35,25. – ᴿGerefTTs 88 (1988) 55s (J. den *Boeft*).

h735 *Munier* C., À propos des apologies de Justin / La méthode apologétique de Justin: RevSR 61 (1987) 177-186 / 62 (1988) 90-100, 227-239.

h736 *Price* R. M., 'Hellenization' and Logos doctrine in Justin Martyr: VigChr 42 (1988) 18-23.

h737 **Skarsaune** O., Proof from prophecy ... Justin 1987 ➤ 3,g166: ᴿChH 57 (1988) 216s (R. M. *Grant*); JEcuSt 25 (1988) 627s (Patricia *DeLeeuw*).

h738 *Skarsaune* Oskar, Justin der Märtyrer: ➤ 813, TRE 17 (1988) 471-8 [p. 478 (ZKG 8) 1885 nicht 1985].

h739 **Skarsaune** O., Da skriften ble åpnet; den første kristne tolkning av Det gamle testamente [Justin]: Sjalombøkene 19. Oslo 1987, Israelmisjon. 151 p. – ᴿTsTKi 59 (1988) 312s (Terje *Stordalen*).

h740 *Syme* Ronald, The date of Justin and the discovery of Trogus: Historia 37 (1988) 358-371.

h741 **Wartelle** André, Saint Justin, Apologies 1987 ➤ 3,g167; 2-85121-083-1: ᴿBijdragen 49 (1988) 335 (P. *Smulders*); JTS 39 (1988) 238-242 (D. *Minns*: not enough advance on the unsatisfactory GOODSPEED edition of 1915); RICathP 27 (1988) 147; RSPT 72 (1988) 615s (G.-M. de *Durand*); TPhil 63 (1988) 598s (H. J. *Sieben*).

h742 ᵀᴱ**Visonà** Giuseppe, Giustino, Dialogo con Trifone: Letture cristiane del primo millennio 5. Mi 1988, Paoline. 414 p.

h743 MELITO: *Grant* Robert M., Five apologists [Melito *al.* shortly after 175] and Marcus Aurelius: VigChr 42 (1988) 1-17.

h744 PAPIAS: **Kürzinger** J., Papias 1983 ➤ 65,e26 ... 2,d290: ᴿVigChr 42 (1988) 401-6 (B. *Dehandschutter*, aussi sur KÖRTNER U. 1983).

h745 **Körtner** Ulrich H. J., Papias 1983 ➤ 64,e25 ... 3,g168: ᴿTsTKi 59 (1988) 69-71 (R. *Hvalvik*, auch über KÜRZINGER J.).

h746 *Schmidt* Hermann H., Semitismen bei Papias: TZBas 44 (1988) 135-146.

Y1.6 Origenes.

h747 **Crouzel** Henri, Origène 1985 ➤ 1,516 ... 3,g171: ᴿJTS 39 (1988) 242-6 (Frances M. *Young*: fine but too reluctant to criticize Origen); RThom 88 (1988) 656-663 (M.-V. *Leroy*); TAth 54 (1988) 195-9 (E. D. *Moutsoulas* ⑤); TGegw 30 (1987) 217s (R. *Medisch*).

h748 **Crouzel** Henri, Origene 1986 ➤ 3,g172: ᴿCC 139 (1988,2) 402s (E. *Cattaneo*).

h749 *Crouzel* Henri, a) Chronique origénienne: BLitEc 89 (1988) 138-145; – b) The literature on Orígen 1970-1988: TS 49 (1988) 499-516.

h750 *Crouzel* Henri, Theological construction and research; Origen on free-will: ➤ 60, ᶠHANSON R., Scripture 1988, 239-265.

h751 **Dechow** Jon F., Dogma and mysticism in early Christianity; EPIPHANIUS of Cyprus and the legacy of Origen: NAmPatr Mg 13. Macon 1988, Mercer Univ. x-584 p. $25. 0-86554-311-9 [TDig 36,153].

h752 *Eijk* P. J. van der, Origenes' Verteidigung des freien Willens in De Oratione 6,1-2: VigChr 42 (1988) 339-351.

h753 **Falla** Claire,   L'apologie d'Origène par Pierre HALLOIX (1648): Univ.
Liège, Fac. ph/lett 238.   P 1983, BLettres.   xxx-194 p. – ᴿOnsGErf 62
(1988) 278-280 (J. *Andriessen*).

h754 **Harl** Marguerite, Origène, Philocalie 1-20, sur les Écritures [+ *Lange* N.
de, Suzanne]: SChr 302, 1983 ➤ 64,e18 ... 2,d305:   ᴿRThom 88 (1988)
665-7 (M.-V. *Leroy*).

h755 *Hauck* Robert J.,   'They saw what they said they saw'; sense knowledge
in early Christian polemic [CELSUS, Origen]: HarvTR 81 (1988) 239-249.

h756 **Hoffmann** R. J., CELSUS, on the true doctrine 1987 ➤ 3,g174:   ᴿChH 57
(1988) 353s (J. W. *Trigg*: tendentious 'translations').

h757 ᵀ**Kalinkowski** S.,   Orygenes, Homilie o Jer Lam Sam Reg [1983], Liczb,
Jos, Judic [1986 ➤ 3,2513], Łukasz [1986 ➤ 3,4947]:   ᴿTLZ 113 (1988)
826-8 (J. *Rohde*).

h758 ᴱ**Lies** L.,   Origeniana Quarta 1985/7 ➤ 3,664b: ᴿRSPT 72 (1988) 609
(G.-M. de *Durand*); TPhil 63 (1988) 263 (H. J. *Sieben*).

h759 **Monaci Castagno** Adèle,   Origene predicatore e il suo pubblico [300
sermons (21 in the original Greek) survive, as against only 6 before him].
Mi 1987, F. Angeli. 282 p. – ᴿRHE 83 (1988) 832 (H. *Crouzel*).

Mosetto Francesco, I miracoli ... dibattito tra Celso e Origene 1986 ➤ 4660.

h760 **Neuschäfer** Bernhard,   Origenes als Philologe: SchwBeiAltW 18/1, 1987
➤ 3,g177:   ᴿMusHelv 45 (1988) 255s (H. *Marti*).

h761 **Pietras** Henryk,   L'amore in Origene: Studia Eph. AugR 28.   R 1988,
Inst. Patristicum 'Augustinianum'.   191 p.

h762 **Rowe** J. Nigel,   Origen's doctrine of subordination; a study in Origen's
Christology [diss. Leeds 1982]: EurUnivSt 23/272.   NY 1987, Lang.
xxiv-315 p.   Fs 59,50 [TDig 35,286].

h763 **Torjesen** Karen Jo,   Hermeneutical procedure and theological method in
Origen's exegesis 1986 ➤ 2,d316; 3,g183:   ᴿBijdragen 49 (1988) 214s (M.
Parmentier); BO 45 (1988) 242-4 (K.-H. *Uthemann*); CrNSt 9 (1988) 483s
(D. *Pazzini*); OrChrPer 54 (1988) 260s (E. *Cattaneo*).

h764 *a) Vogt* Hermann-J.,   The later exegesis of Origen; – *b) Junod* Éric,
BASILE de Césarée et GRÉGOIRE de Nazianze sont-ils les compilateurs de
la Philocalie d'Origène? ...: ➤ 56, Mém. GRIBOMONT J. 1988, 583-591 /
349-360.

y1.8   **Tertullianus.**

h765 *Burrows* Mark S.,   Christianity in the Roman Forum; Tertullian and the
apologetic use of history: VigChr 42 (1988) 209-235.

h766 *Frend* W. H. C.,   Montanism, a movement of prophecy and regional
identity in the early Church: BJRyL 70,3 ('Sects and new religious
movements' 1988) 25-34.

Hallonsten Gösta,   Meritum / satisfactio bei Tertullian 1985/4 ➤ 8745s.

h767 **Heck** Eberhard L.,   *Mē theomacheîn*; Untersuchungen zur Bekämpfung
römischer Religion bei Tertullian, CYPRIAN und LAKTANZ: StKlasPg 24.
Fra 1987, Lang.   257 p.   [AnzAltW 41,121]:   ᴿClasR 102 (1988) 164s
(R.P.C. *Hanson*).

h768 **Hoppe** H.,   Sintassi e stile di Tertulliano [1903]ᵀ 1985 ➤ 1,f540 ...
3,g191:   ᴿRivStoLR 24 (1988) 136-9 (R. *Uglione*).

h769 ᵀᴱ**Mattei** Paul,   Tertullien, Le mariage unique (De monogamia): SChr
343.   P 1988, Cerf.   419 p.

h770 *a) May* Gerhard,   MARCION in contemporary views; results and open
questions; – *b) Drijvers* Han J. W.,   Marcionism in Syria; principles,

problems, polemics; – c) *Hofmann* R. Joseph, How then know this troublous teacher? Further reflections on Marcion and his church: SecC 6,3 (1988) 129-151 / 153-172 / 173-191.

h771 **Quellet** H., Concordance verbale du De cultu feminarum, de Tertullien: Alpha-Omega A-60. Hildesheim 1986, Olms. 382 p. – ᴿArTGran 51 (1988) 308s (A. *Segovia*).

h772 ᵀᴱ**Scarpat** Giuseppe, Q.S.F. TERTULLIANO. Contro Prassea[2]: Corona Patrum 12,1985 → 3,g194: ᴿLatomus 47 (1988) 209s (J.-C. *Frédouille*).

h773 ᴱ**Turcan** M., TERTULLIEN, Les spectacles: SChr 332, 1986 → 2,d326: ᴿRÉLat 65 (1987) 311-3 (R. *Braun*).

Viciano Alberto, ... soteriología de Tertuliano 1986 → 8772.

Y2 *Patres graeci* – The Greek Fathers.

h774 *Beierwaltes* Wernes, PLOTINS Erbe: MusHelv 45 (1988) 75-97.

h775 *Carcione* Filippo, La politica religiosa di Giustiniano nella fase conclusiva della 'seconda controversia origenista' (543-553); gli intrecci con la controversia sui Tre Capitoli: StRicOrCr 9 (1986) 131-147 [10 (1987) 37-51, VIGILIO].

h776 **Davis** Leo D., The first seven ecumenical councils (325-787); their history and theology. Wilmington 1987, Glazier. 304 p. $13. – ᴿAndr-UnS 26 (1988) 186s (B. *Norman*).

h777 **Dawson** John D., Ancient Alexandrian interpretation of Scripture: diss. Yale. – RTLv 20,544 sans date.

h778 *D'Souza* Denis, PLOTINUS and Indian thought: IndTSt 25 (1988) 253-9.

h779 *Fabricius* Cajus, Zu den Aussagen der griechischen Kirchenväter über PLATON: VigChr 42 (1988) 179-187.

h780 **Geerard** M., *Glorie* F., Clavis Patrum graecorum 5. indices, initia, concordantiae 1987 → 3,g202: ᴿArTGran 51 (1988) 306 (A. *Segovia*).

h780* **Gunton** Colin, The transcendent Lord: the Spirit and the Church in Calvinist and Cappadocian. L 1988, Congregational Memorial. 20 p. £1 [JTS 40,743].

h781 **Kinneavy** James L., Greek rhetorical origins of Christian faith; an inquiry 1987 → 3,g205: ᴿTTod 45 (1988s) 356. 358. 360 (N. R. *Petersen*).

h782 *a) Kretschmar* Georg, Die Wahrheit der Kirche im Streit der Theologen; Überlegungen zum Verlauf des Arianischen Streites; – *b) Mühlenberg* Ekkehard, Dogmatik und Kirchengeschichte: → 114, ꟳPANNENBERG W., Vernunft 1988, 289-321 / 436-453.

h783 **Le Boulluec** Alain, Notion d'hérésie I-II 1985 → 1,f554 ... 3,g206: ᴿCrNSt 9 (1988) 624s (A. *Benoit*); Gregorianum 69 (1988) 574 (A. *Orbe*); JTS 39 (1988) 236-8 (R. L. *Wilken*); VigChr 42 (1988) 188-192 (D. T. *Runia*).

h784 *Lilla* Salvatore, La teologia negativa dal pensiero greco classico a quello patristico e bizantino: Helikon 22-27 (1982-7) 211-279; 28 (1988) 203-279 ...

h785 **Meijering** E. P., Die Hellenisierung des Christentums ... HARNACK 1985 → 1,f557 ... 3,g208: ᴿIstina 33 (1988) 86s (B. *Dupuy*).

h786 ᴱ**Mondésert** C., Le monde grec ancien et la Bible: BTT 1, 1984 → 1,299; 2,d338: ᴿÉglT 17 (1986) 395s (L. *Laberge*); Judaica 44 (1988) 52-54 (M. *Petit*); RÉJ 146 (1987) 166s (G. *Dorival*).

h787 *Oliva* Pavel, SOLON bei den frühchristlichen Autoren: SborBrno 33 (1988) 57-62; deutsch 62.

h788 **Pépin** Jean, De la philosophie ancienne à la théologie patristique [16 art. 1956-82] 1986 → 3,275; £32: ᴿJTS 39 (1988) 590s (A. *Meredith*: elegance and enormous erudition).

h789 *Tetz* Martin, Ein enzyklisches Schreiben der Synode von Alexandrien (362): ZNW 79 (1988) 262-281.

h790 *Treu* Kurt, 'Die Griechischen Christlichen Schriftsteller der ersten Jahrhunderte' 1966-1987: TLZ [91 (1966) 391s updated] 113 (1988) 475-8.

h791 **Weltin** E. G., Athens and Jerusalem 1987 → 3,g212*: ᴿAnglTR 70 (1988) 365s (F. W. *Norris*).

---

h792 Aʀɪᴜs: *Mara* Maria G., Arriani, Arrius [aber im deutschen immer Arianismus]: → 783, AugL 1,3 (1988) 450-459.

h793 *Norderval* Øyvind, The emperor Constantine and Arius; unity in the Church and unity in the empire: ST 42 (1988) 113-150.

h794 **Williams** Rowan, Arius 1987 → 3,g216: ᴿJEH 39 (1988) 235-7 (R. P. C. *Hanson*); Month 249 (1988) 600s (R. *Butterworth*); NBlackf 69 (1988) 199s (D. *Minns*); RSPT 72 (1988) 611-3 (G.-M. de *Durand*); Tablet 242 (1988) 1017 (E. *Yarnold*); Themelios 14 (1988s) 75 (R. *Bauckham*); TLond 91 (1988) 430s (A. *Louth*); TsTNijm 28 (1988) 88s (F. van de *Paverd*).

h795 *Sidorov* A. I., ❻ L'arianisme à la lumière des recherches modernes: VDI 79,185 (1988) 86-97; franç. 97.

h796 Aᴛʜᴀɴᴀsɪᴜs: *Cunningham* Agnes, Athanasius gegen die griechische Weisheit: IkaZ 16 (1987) 491-4.

h797 *Kannengiesser* Charles, Athanasius of Alexandria, a paradigm for the Church of today: Pacifica 1,1 (1988) 85 ... [< ᴢɪᴛ 89,309].

h798 *Lorenz* Rudolf, Eine Pierius-Menoria [sic p. 87, 89, 91; but p. II has Pierus-Memoria, without *i* but with *Mem*-; concerning Athanasius Easter-letter 39] in Alexandrien: ZKG 99 (1988) 87-92.

h799 *Louth* Andrew, Athanasius and the Greek Life of Antony: JTS 39 (1988) 504-9.

h800 **Riall** Robert A., Athanasius bishop of Alexandria; the politics of spirituality: diss. ᴰ*Sage* M. Cincinnati 1987, 439 p. 88-09980. – DissA 49 (1988s) 919-A.

h801 *Stead* Christopher, Athanasius' earliest written work [Alexander's letter *Henòs sōmatos* was drafted by Athanasius, as held by J. *Möhler* and J. *Newman* (it seems implied that 'authorship' of a presidential or papal document is normally attributed to the drafter)]: JTS 39 (1988) 76-91.

h802 Bᴀsɪʟɪᴏ di Cesarea, la sua età 1979/83 → 1,539 ... 3,g222: ᴿLatomus 47 (1988) 718s (H. *Savon*).

h803 *Basarab* Mircea, Der heilige Basilius als Ausleger der Schrift: Orthodoxes Forum 1 (Mü 1987) 19-32.

h804 **Gain** B. L'église de Cappadoce ... Basile 1985 → 2,d353; 3,g223: ᴿÉglT 18 (1987) 365-8 (G. *Hudon*); HeythJ 29 (1988) 516s (D. A. *Sykes*).

h805 *Girardi* Mario, Bibbia e agiografia nell'omiletica sui martiri di Basilio di Cesarea: VetChr 25 (1988) 451-486.

h806 *Maraval* Pierre, La date de la mort de Basile de Césarée: RÉAug 34 (1988) 25-38.

h807 *Naumowicz* Józef, Studia J. Gʀɪʙᴏᴍᴏɴᴛᴀ nad św. Bazylim Wielkim: ColcT 58,1 (1988) 127-131.

h808 CHRYSOSTOMUS J.:   *Hill* Robert C.,   Chrysostom as OT commentator:
a) Prudentia 20,1 (Auckland 1988) 44-56; – b) EstBíb 46 (1988) 61-77;
castellano 61.

h809 *Leroux* Jean-Marie, Johannes Chrysostomus, ᵀ*Schäferdiek* K.: ➤ 813,
TRE 17 (1987) 118-127.

h810 **Gärtner** Michael, Die Familienerziehung in der Alten Kirche ...
Chrysostomus 1985 ➤ 1,f577: ᴿJbAC 31 (1988) 211-4 (E. *Dassmann*).

h811 *Hunter* David G., Borrowings from Libanius in the Comparatio regis et
monachi of St. John Chrysostom: JTS 39 (1988) 525-531.

h812 **Malingrey** Anne-Marie, (*Leclercq* Philippe) PALLADIOS, Dialogue sur
la vie de Jean Chrysostome, I. Intr. texte, tr., notes; II. Histoire du
texte, index, appendices: SChr 341s. P 1988, Cerf. 451 p.; 343 p.
F 332 + 218.

h813 *Pasquato* Ottorino, Eredità giudaica e famiglia cristiana; la testimonianza di Giovanni Crisostomo: Lateranum 54 (1988) 58-91.

h814 a) *Pasquato* Ottorino, Rapporto tra genitori e figli; eredità giudaica in
Giovanni Crisostomo: – b) *Leloir* Louis, Les Pères du Désert à l'école de
leurs ancêtres juifs: ➤ 570, AugR 28 (1988) 391-404 / 405-428.

h815 **Zincone** Sergio, Studi sulla visione dell'uomo in ambito antiocheno
(DIODORO, Crisostomo, TEODORO, TEODORETO): SMSR Quad NS 1.
L'Aquila 1988, Japadre. 115 p. 88-7006-155-8.

h816 *Padovese* Luigi, Riflessi della polemica anticristiana nella predicazione
di Giovanni Crisostomo: Laurentianum 29 (1988) 63-111.

h817 *Roldanus* J., Johannes Chrysostomos over de vreemdelingschap van de
christen: KerkT 39 (1988) 23-39.

h818 CYRILLUS H.: *Janeras* Sebastià, À propos de la catéchèse XIVᵉ de
Cyrille de Jérusalem: EcOrans 3 (1986) 307-318.

h819 **Piédagnel** Auguste, (ᵀ*Paris* P.) Cyrille de Jérusalem, Catéchèses
mystagogiques²ʳᵉᵛ: SChr 126bis. P 1988, Cerf. 224 p. F 164. 2-204-
02925-4.

h820 DAMASCENUS J.:   *Kotter* Bonifatius †, Johannes von Damaskus:
➤ 813, TRE 17 (1987) 127-132.

h821 EPIPHANIUS: **Dechow** J. F., Dogma and mysticism in early Christianity
[Epiphanius on Origen]. Macon 1988, Mercer Univ. x-584 p. $25. –
ᴿSWJT 31,2 (1988s) 67 (E. E. *Ellis*).

h822 *Lieu* J. M., Epiphanius on the Scribes and Pharisees (Pan. 15.1-16.4):
JTS 39 (1988) 509-524.

h823 *Riggi* Calogero, a) Comprensione umana nella Bibbia secondo Epifanio
(Panarion LIX) [< ᶠ*Cataudella* Q. (1972) 2,607-615]; – b) Epifanio e il
biblico dialogo coi non cristiani nella cornice del 'Panarion' [< Salesianum 36 (1974) 231-260]; – c) Nouvelle lecture du Panarion LIX,4;
Épiphane et le divorce [< StPatr 12 (1975) 129-134]: ➤ 251, Epistrophe
1985, 720-748 / 755-783 / 749-754.

h824 ᵀᴱ**Williams** Frank, The Panarion of Epiphanius of Salamis I (Sects
1-46): NHS 35. Leiden 1987, Brill. XXX-359 p. – ᴿVigChr 42 (1988)
301-3 (A. F. J. *Klijn*).

h825 EUSEBIUS: ᵀᴱ**Forrat** Marguerite, texte *Places* Édouard des, Eusèbe de
Césarée, Contre Hiéroclès: SChr 333, 1986 ➤ 2,d364; 3,g235: ᴿAnClas 57
(1988) 439 (R. *Joly*: texte critique par des Places 'une avancée décisive'
'plus fidèle aux manuscrits' que Kayser 1870 = 1844); MélSR 45 (1988)
111s (P.-M. *Hombert*); NRT 110 (1988) 113 (V. *Roisel*); RÉAnc 90 (1988)
223s (J. *Bernardi*); RÉByz 46 (1988) 233 (J. *Wolinski*); RHPR 68 (1988)

360s (P. *Maraval*); RivStoLR 24 (1988) 586s (J. *Mallet*); RTAM 55 (1988) 241 (G. *Michiels*); TAth 54 (1988) 402s (E. D. *Moutsoulas* ⊕); TS 49 (1988) 163s (R. J. *Daly*); VigChr 42 (1988) 202s (J. C. M. van *Winden*).

h826 *Junod* Eric, Polémique chrétienne contre Apollonius de Tyane [(ou bien?) Eusèbe, (Contre la) Vie d'Apollonius de Tyane par Philostrate ... (comme dans les manuscrits grecs) devait être le titre de SChr 333 au lieu de Contre Hiéroclès]: RTPhil 120 (1988) 475-482.

h827 **Places** Édouard des, Eusèbe de Césarée, La préparation évangélique XIV-XV: SChr 228, 1987 ➤ 3,g240: Irénikon 61 (1988) 140 (E. L.); RÉAnc 90 (1988) 221-3 (Monique *Alexandre*, XIIs); RÉByz 46 (1988) 233 (A. *Failler*); RivStoLR 24 (1988) 588-590 (J. *Mallet*); VigChr 42 (1988) 299s (J. C. M. van *Winden*).

h828 *Dal Covolo* Enrico, La filosofia tripartita nella 'Praeparatio evangelica' di Eusebio di Cesarea: RivStoLR 24 (1988) 515-523.

h829 *Drake* H. A., What Eusebius knew; the genesis of the Vita Constantini: ClasPg 83 (1988) 20-41.

h830 **Gödecke** Monika, Geschichte als Mythos; Eusebs Kirchengeschichte: EurHS 23/307, 1987 ➤ 3,g237: ᴿJTS 39 (1988) 599-601 (R. M. *Grant*: well-worked, incisive); RHE 83 (1988) 686s (P.-T. *Camelot*); TS 49 (1988) 577 (J. T. *Lienhard*); TLZ 113 (1988) 828-830 (H. *Zimmermann*); TPQ 136 (1988) 296s (J. *Speigl*).

h831 *Junod* Éric, [Eusèbe ...] Naissance de la pratique synodale et unité de l'Église au IIᵉ siècle: RHPR 68 (1988) 163-180.

h832 *Smith* Mark, A hidden use of PORPHYRY's history of philosophy in Eusebius' Praeparatio evangelica: JTS 39 (1988) 494-504.

h833 **Verheyden** Jozef, De vlucht van de christenen naar Pella; onderzoek van het getuigenis van Eusebius en EPIPHANIUS: AcWet, lett 50,127. Bru 1988, Academiën. 285 p. 90-6569-398-X.

h834 GREGORIUS NAZ.: *Norderval* Øyvind, Keiser og kappadokier; forståelsen av forholdet mellom kristendom og antikk kultur hos keiser Julian og Gregor av Nazianz: NorTTs 89 (1988) 93-113.

h834* **Kurmann** Alois, Gregor von Nazianz, Oratio 4, gegen Julian; ein Kommentar: SchwBeitAltW 19. Ba 1988 Reinhardt. iv-421 p. Fs 90 [JTS 40,618, R. van *Dam*].

h835 *Trisoglio* Francesco, Figurae sententiae e ornatus nei Discorsi di Gregorio di Nazianzo: Orpheus 7 (1987) 71-86.

h836 GREGORIUS NYSS.: **Apostolopoulos** Charalambos, Phaedo Christianus; Studien zur Verbindung und Abwägung des Verhältnisses zwischen dem platonischen 'Phaidon' und dem Dialog Gregors von Nyssa 'Über die Seele und die Auferstehung': EurHS 20/188, 1986 ➤ 2,d372: ᴿJTS 39 (1988) 258-260 (A. *Meredith*).

h837 **Canevet** Mariette, Grégoire de Nysse et l'herméneutique biblique 1983 ➤ 64,e73 ... 2,d374: ᴿLatomus 47 (1988) 719s (R. *Joly*).

h838 **Altenburger** Margarete, **Mann** Friedhelm, Bibliographie zu Gregor von Nyssa; Editionen, Übersetzungen, Literatur. Leiden 1988, Brill. xxiii-395 p. 90-04-07286-1.

h838* **Klock** Christoph, Untersuchungen zu Stil und Rhythmus bei Gregor von Nyssa; ein Beitrag zum Rhetorikverständnis der griechischen Väter: BeitKlPg 173. Fra 1987, Athenäum x-334 p. DM 68 [JTS 40,256, A. *Meredith*].

h839 GREGORIUS T.: *Simonetti* Manlio, Una nuova ipotesi su Gregorio il Taumaturgo: RivStoLR 24 (1988) 17-41.

h840 MAXIMUS: **Blowers** Paul M., Exegesis and spiritual pedagogy in the 'Quaestiones ad Thalassium' of Maximus the Confessor: diss. ND 1988. – RelStR 15,193.

h841 **Thunberg** Lars, Man and the cosmos; the vision of St. Maximus the Confessor; foreword *Allchin* A. M. Crestwood NY 1985, St. Vladimir. 184 p. $9. – ᴿSpeculum 63 (1988) 237-240 (J. E. *Rexine*).

h843 PAULUS SAMOSAT: *Fischer* J. A., Die antiochenischen Synoden gegen Paul von Samosata: AnHistConc 18 (1986) 9-30.

h844 *Simonetti* Manlio, Per la rivalutazione di alcune testimonianze su Paolo di Samosata: RivStoLR 24 (1988) 177-210.

h845 ROMANOS M.: *Arranz* Miguel, Romanos le mélode: → 791, DictSpir XIII, 89s (1988) 898-909.

h846 *Barkhuizen* J. H., Association of ideas as a principle of composition in Romanos [the poet]: Ellinika 39 (1988) 18-24.

h846* SYNESIUS: **Roques** Denis, Synésios de Cyrène et la Cyrénaïque du Bas-Empire: ÉtAntAfr. P 1987, CNRS. 492 p.; 15 fig. F 550 [JTS 40,620, L. R. *Wickham*].

h847 THEODORUS M.: *Guida* Augusto, La rinunzia evangelica ai beni; la polemica di Giuliano e la replica di Teodoro di Mopsuestia: → 8, ᶠBARIGAZZI A. (= Sileno 1984) 1986, 277-287.

h848 THEOPHILUS A.: *Curry* Carl, The theogony of Theophilus [of Antioch, Christian apologist]: VigChr 42 (1988) 318-326.

Y2.4 **Augustinus.**

h849 *a) Bartelink* Gerard J. M., Die Beeinflussung Augustins durch die griechischen Patres; – *b) Bastiaensen* Antoon A. R., Augustin et ses pré-décesseurs latins chrétiens: → 516, Aug. Traiectina 1986/7, 9-24 / 25-57.

h850 ᵀᴱ**Bavel** T. J. van, 'Veel te laat heb ik jou liefgekregen'; bij het zestiende eeuwfeest van Augustinus' bekering [Anthologie:] Leven en werk van Augustinus van Hippo. Heverlee 1986, Augustijns Hist. Inst. 227 p. Fb 700. 90-6831-060-7. – ᴿTsTNijm 28 (1988) 89 (L. *Goosen*).

h851 **Bonner** Gerald, St. Augustine of Hippo; life and controversies²ʳᵉᵛ [= ¹1963 + preface, appendix, bibliography supplement]. Norwich 1986, Canterbury. 430 p. £10. – ᴿScotJT 41 (1988) 428s (L. R. *Wickham*).

h852 **Bonner** Gerald, God's decree and man's destiny; studies in the thought of Augustine of Hippo 1987 → 3,193: ᴿChH 57 (1988) 524s (D. W. *Johnson*).

h853 **Chadwick** Henry, Augustine: Past Masters, 1986 → 2,387; 3,g271: ᴿAncHRes 18 (1988) 188-190 (B. *Brennan*); Gnomon 60 (1988) 209-213 (P. *Habermehl*); ScotJT 41 (1988) 290s (D. F. *Wright*); Thomist 52 (1988) 347-350 (G. C. *Berthold*).

h854 **Chadwick** H., Augustin, ᵀ*Spiess* A. 1987 → 3,g272: ᴿRÉLat 65 (1987) 399 (H. *Zehnacker*: F 74, Eng. F 30; 'l'anglais est volontiers une langue malicieuse'); RSPT 72 (1988) 625 (G.-M. de *Durand*).

h855 *Corcoran* Gervase, Saint Augustine and his influence: MilltSt 19s ('Sixteen-handre[d]th anniversary of the conversion' 1987) 123-133.

h856 *Fontaine* Jacques, Augustin penseur chrétien du temps: BBudé (1988) 53-71.

h857 *Kobler* Gerald, *Leinsle* Ulrich, Gemeinschaft und Philosophie in der Frühschriften des Hl. Augustinus: AnPraem 62 (1986) 133-149.

h858 **Kriegbaum** Bernhard, Kirche der Traditoren oder Kirche der Märtyrer; die Vorgeschichte des Donatismus: InnsbTSt 16, ᴰ1986 → 3,g286: ᴿChH

57 (1988) 523s (J.T. *Lienhard*); RivStoLR 24 (1988) 590-3 (Clementina *Mazzucco*); TPhil 63 (1988) 264-6 (H.J. *Sieben*); TüTQ 168 (1988) 165s (H.J. *Vogt*).

h859 ᴱ**La Bonnardière** Anne-Marie, Saint Augustin et la Bible 1986 → 2,391; 3,g287: ᴿChH 57 (1988) 77 (E. *Te Selle*); CiuD 201 (1988) 493 (J. *Gutiérrez*).

h860 *La Piana* Lillo, L'unità strutturale del 'De civitate Dei' di sant'Agostino: Salesianum 50 (1988) 345-365.

h861 **Leclercq** Jean, *al.* [12 art.], St. Augustine's conversion: Word & Spirit 9 (1987). vi-156 p. $7 pa. [TDig 35,388].

h862 *Locher* Gottlieb F.D., Die Beziehung der Zeit zur Ewigkeit bei Augustin: TZBas 44 (1988) 147-167.

h863 *Lohse* Bernhard, Die Bedeutung Augustins für den jungen LUTHER [< KerDo 11 (1965) 116-135]: → 224, Evangelium 1988, 11-30.

h864 **Maier** Jean-Louis, Le dossier du Donatisme i. Des origines à la mort de Constance II: TU 134. B 1987, Akademie. 331 p. DM 98. – ᴿMusHelv 45 (1988) 261s (H. *Marti*); RÉLat 66 (1988) 37-42 (S. *Lancel*).

h865 **Marafioti** D., L'uomo tra legge e grazia ᴰ1983 → 65,d536 ... 3,g290: ᴿAngelicum 65 (1988) 477s (R. *Kaczynski*).

h866 **Marrou** H.I., S. Agostino e la fine della cultura antica [1936], ᵀᴱ*Marabelli* C., *Tombolini* A., 1987 → 3,g292; Lit. 55.000: ᴿRasT 29 (1988) 307 (R. *Maisano*).

h867 **Mondin** Battista, Il pensiero di Agostino; filosofia, teologia, cultura. R 1988, Città Nuova. 370 p. Lit. 28.000. – ᴿCC 139 (1988,4) 300-2 (J. de *Finance*).

h868 *Nuvolone* G., *al.* Pélage: → 791, DictSp 12 (1986) 2889-2942.

h869 *Oort* J. van, Jeruzalem en Babylon; een onderzoek van Augustinus De stad van God en de bronnen van zijn leer der twee steden (rijken) ᴰ1986 → 2,d403: ᴿTR 84 (1988) 377-381 (B. *Studer*).

h870 *Poland* Lynn M., Augustine, allegory, and conversion: LitTOx 2,1 (1988) 37-48 [< ZIT].

h871 **Poque** Suzanne, Le langage symbolique dans ... Augustin 1984 → 1, f622; 2,d405: ᴿBTAM 14 (1988) 438-440 (G. *Mathon*).

h872 **Przywara** Erich, Augustin, Passions et destins de l'Occident [1934], ᵀ*Secretan* Philibert: La nuit surveillée 1987 → 3,g399: ᴿRThom 88 (1988) 506-8 (H.-F. *Rovarino*).

h873 **Rees** B.R., PELAGIUS, a reluctant heretic. Wolfeboro NH 1988, Boydell & B. xiv-176 p. $55. [TS 50,398, B. *Ramsey*].

h874 *Smalbrugge* M.A., L'emploi de la théologie apophatique chez Augustin; une question à l'historiographie: RTPhil 120 (1988) 263-274.

h875 **Solignac** Aimé, La double tradition augustinienne ['lumineuse', 'ombreuse']: Anthropologie et humanisme [Cah. Fontenay 39s. Fontenay-aux-Roses 1985, Ec. Norm. Sup.] 67-77 [< BTAM 14 (1988) 434s (H. *Silvestre*)].

h876 ᵀ**Sulowski** J., ᴱ*Myszor* W., ❷ Św. Augustyn, Pisma egzegetyczne przeciw Manichejczykom: Pisma starochrześcijańskich Pisarzy 25, 1980 → 62,m79: ᴿTLZ 113 (1988) 826 (J. *Rohde*).

h877 **Tavard** Georges, Les jardins de saint Augustin; lecture des 'Confessions'. Montréal/P 1988, Bellarmin/Cerf. 134 p. – ᴿEsprVie 98 (1988) 683s (J. *Pintard*).

h878 **Trapè** Agostino, Saint Augustin, l'homme, le pasteur, le mystique [1976], ᵀ*Arminjon* Victor. P 1988, Fayard. 334 p. – ᴿEsprVie 98 (1988)

319s (J. *Pintard*); RThom 88 (1988) 668s (M.-M. *Labourdette*: la biographie de P. Brown est inoubliable).

h879 **Trapè** Agostino, Aurelius Augustinus, ein Lebensbild [1976, ³1979], T*Brehme* Uta. Mü 1988, Neue Stadt. 272 p. – ᴿTGL 78 (1988) 433s (H. R. *Drobner*).

h880 **Verheijen** Luc, Saint Augustin raconte sa conversion [1985; ᴱ*Picoux* Cécile], Sint Augustinus verhaalt zijn bekering, Zuid-Duits handschrift c.1430. Bloemendaal 1986, Gottmer. 64 p.; ill. 90-257-2020-X. – ᴿBijdragen 49 (1988) 100 (M. *Schrams*).

h881 *Zumkeller* Adolar, Der Terminus 'sola fides' bei Augustinus: ➤ 23, ꜰCHADWICK H. 1988, 87-100

Y2.5 **Hieronymus.**

h882 *Cannon* Stephen, The Jerome-Augustine correspondence: WSpirit 9 (1987) 35-45.

h883 **Ceresa-Gastaldo** Aldo, Gerolamo, Gli uomini illustri; de viribus illustribus: Biblioteca patristica 12. F 1988, Nardini. 367 p. 88-404-2012-6.

h884 **Degórski** Remigiusz, Edizione critica della 'Vita sancti Pauli primi eremitae' di Girolamo diss. Pont. Univ. Lateranensis. R 1987. 206 p. (excerpt.) – ᴿVoxPa 12s (1987s) 475-7 (H. *Pietras*).

h885 *Godin* André, ÉRASME biographe patristique; Hieronymi Stridonensis vita: BibHumRen 50 (1988) 691-706.

h886 ᴱ**Lardet** Pierre, JÉRÔME, Apologie contre Rufin: SChr 303, 1983 ➤ 64,e134 ... 3,g316: ᴿRBgPg 66 (1988) 146 (W. *Evenepoel*).

h887 *Nees* L., Image and text; excerpts from Jerome's 'De Trinitate' and the 'Maiestas Domini' of miniature of the Gundohinus Gospels: Viator 18 (1987) 1-21 [< BStLat 18,279].

h888 **Russo** Daniel, S. Jérôme en Italie, étude d'iconographie et de spiritualité, XIIᵉ-XVᵉ s. P/R 1987, Découverte/Éc. Franç. 299 p.; 58 fig. – ᴿRHE 83 (1988) 704-7 (Thérèse *Poilvache-Lambert*).

h889 *Simonetti* Manlio, Due passi della prefazione di Girolamo alla traduzione del 'De Spiritu Sancto' di DIDIMO [*Doutreleau* L. in ꜰ*Mondésert* C. 1987]: RivStoLR 24 (1988) 28-30.

Y2.6 **Patres Latini** alphabetice.

h890 ᴱ**Di Berardino** Angelo, Patrology 4, 1986 [= the Italian 3 having combined 2 volumes of QUASTEN 1977] 4. The golden age of Latin patristic literature, T*Solari* Placid, 1986 ➤ 3,g321: ᴿJTS 39 (1988) 247-9 (A. *Louth*: splendid tool, marvelous to have in English).

h891 *May* Gerhard, Lateinische Patristik; Hilfsmittel, Handbücher, Literatur- und Auslegungsgeschichte: TRu 53 (1988) 250-276.

h892 *Schäferdiek* Knut, Das gotische liturgische Kalenderfragment — Bruchstück eines Konstantinopeler Martyrologs: ZNW 79 (1988) 116-137.

h893 **Simonetti** Manlio, La produzione letteraria latina fra romani e barbari (secoli V-VIII): Sussidi Patristici 3. R 1986, Ist. Augustinianum. 246 p. – ᴿAsprenas 35 (1988) 277-9 (L. *Fatica*); RÉAnc 90 (1988) 247-9 (J.-P. *Weiss*); ScripTPam 19 (1987) 944-6 (C. *Basevi*).

h894 AMBROSIUS: *Gori* Franco, Appunti su esegesi biblica e composizione del De virginitate di Ambrogio: ➤ 472, AnStoEseg 5 (1988) 201-214.

h895 *Sordi* Marta, I rapporti fra Ambrogio e il panegirista Pacato: Rendiconti Ist Lombardo let/mor/st 122 (1988) 93-100.

h896 CAESARIUS A.: ᵀᴱ**Delage** Marie-José, Césaire d'Arles, Sermons au peuple 3. Sermons 56-80: SChr 330. P 1986, Cerf. 318 p. F 208. – ᴿGnomon 60 (1988) 537-9 (O. *Hiltbrunner*).

h897 CHROMATIUS: **Truzzi** Carlo, ZENO, GAUDENZIO e Cromazio 1985 → 2,d434; 3,g330: ᴿCrNSt 9 (1988) 631s (C. *Kannengiesser*); Latomus 47 (1988) 473 (P. *Tordeur*); RBgPg 66 (1988) 146-9 (J. *Schamp*); TR 84 (1988) 30s (T. *Baumeister*).

h898 CYPRIANUS: ᵀᴱ**Clarke** G. W., Letters of St. Cyprian I-III, 1984-6 → 65,d562 ... 3,g332: ᴿRTLv 19 (1988) 204-7 (P.-A. *Deproost*, 1).

h899 GREGORIUS M.: **Baasten** Matthew, Pride according to Gregory the Great; a study of the Moralia: Studies in the Bible and Early Christianity 7. Lewiston NY 1986, Mellen. 206 p. $50. – ᴿZKG 99 (1988) 410 (G. R. *Evans*, Eng., 'This has the makings of a useful book, but the style is laboured and ... there is little evidence of any real grasp of the period').

h900 *Boesch Gajano* Sofia, Agiografia e geografia nei dialoghi di Gregorio Magno: → 629, ᴱ*Pricoco* S., Storia 1986/8, 209-220.

h901 **Clark** Francis, The pseudo-Gregorian dialogues 1987 → 3,g342: ᴿRÉ-Anc 90 (1988) 238-240 (P. *Cazier*).

h902 *Engelbert* Pius, Hat Papst Gregor der Grosse die 'Dialoge' geschrieben?: ErbAuf 64 (1988) 255-265.

h903 *Godding* Robert, Les Dialogues ... de Grégoire le Grand [*Clark* F. 1987]: AnBoll 106 (1988) 201-229.

h903* **La Piana** L., Teologia e ministero della parola in S. Gregorio Magno. Palermo 1987, Oftes. 208 p. Lit. 20.000 [NRT 111,306s].

h904 *Meyvaert* Paul, The enigma of Gregory the Great's dialogues; a response to Francis CLARK: JEH 39 (1988) 335-381.

h905 *Verbraken* P., Les dialogues de saint Grégoire le Grand sont-ils apocryphes? [*Clark* F.]: RBén 98 (1988) 272-7.

h906 *Vogüé* Adalbert de, Grégoire le Grand et ses 'Dialogues' d'après deux ouvrages récents [Actes Chantilly 1982/6; contre CLARK F. 1987 → 3,g342]: RHE 83 (1988) 281-348.

h907 **Evans** G. R., The thought of Gregory the Great 1986 → 2,d439: ᴿChH 57 (1988) 79 (T. F. X. *Noble*); NBlackf 68 (1987) 463s (E. *John*: very indifferent); Speculum 63 (1988) 654s (Carole *Straw*); TS 49 (1988) 382 (D. J. *Grimes*).

h908 ᴱ**Fontaine** J., *al.*, Grégoire le Grand 1982/6 → 2,433*: ᴿRÉAnc 90 (1988) 240-2 (A. *Godin*).

h909 **Petersen** Joan M., The dialogues of Gregory ... [ᴰ1981] 1984 → 1,f657 ... 3,g340: ᴿAmHR 92 (1987) 110s (R. *VanDam*); RivStoLR 24 (1988) 140-3 (G. *Cracco*).

h910 **Straw** Carole E., Gregory the Great; perfection in imperfection: Transformation of the classical heritage 14. Berkeley 1988, Univ. California. xiv-295 p. $35 [TDig 36,86].

h911 HILARIUS P.: *Doignon* Jean, Du nouveau dans l'exploration de l'œuvre d'Hilaire de Poitiers (1983-1988); recension critique de six ouvrages [*Anyanwu* A., *Durst* M. ... *Ladaria* L.]: RÉAug 34 (1988) 93-105.

h912 ᴱ**Rocher** André, Hilaire de Poitiers, Contre Constance; text stemma, *Doutreleau* L.: SChr 334. P 1987, Cerf. 275 p. F 195. 2-204-01718-9. – ᴿBijdragen 49 (1988) 337s (P. *Smulders*, Eng.); JTS 39 (1988) 609-611 (T. D. *Barnes*: origin-theory ampler and exegetical notes briefer than needed); RÉAug 34 (1988) 101-4 (J. *Doignon*); RÉLat 65 (1987) 313s (Y.-M. *Duval*).

h913 HIPPOLYTUS: *Frickel* J., Zum 'Elenchos' des Hippolyt von Rom; Kirchliches Credo oder Glaubensverweis für Heiden (El X 30-34)?: ZkT 110 (1988) 129-138.

h914 *Gelston* A., A note on the text of the Apostolic Tradition of Hippolytus: JTS 39 (1988) 112-7: post-baptismal prayer [117-9, *Cuming* G.].

h915 *Magne* Jean, En finir avec la 'Tradition' d'Hippolyte: BLitEc 89 (1988) 5-22; Eng. p. 4, 'Sett[l]ing once for all the question', against A.-G. *Martimort* and B. *Botte*.

h916 **Marcovich** Miroslav, Hippolytus, Refutatio omnium haeresium: PatrTSt 25, 1986 → 2,d447, 3,g344: RClasR 102 (1988) 149s (J. N. *Birdsall*); JHS 108 (1988) 243 (R. W. *Sharples*: 'lonely schismatic bishop crying out for recognition' p. 41); RHE 83 (1988) 96 (P.-T. *Camelot*); TR 84 (1988) 207s (H. R. *Drobner*).

h917 *Metzger* Marcel, Nouvelles perspectives pour la prétendue Tradition apostoloque [Hippolyte de Rome]: EcOrans 5 (1988) 241-259.

h918 **Osborne** Catherine, Rethinking early Greek philosophy; Hippolytus of Rome and the Presocratics. L 1987, Duckworth. viii-383 p. – RVigChr 42 (1988) 295-7 (J. C. M. van *Winden*).

h918* **Visonà** Giuseppe, Pseudo-Ippolito, In sanctum Pascha, studio edizione commento: StPatrMediolan 15. Mi 1988, ViPe. 548 p. 88-343-0172-2; pa. 3-0.

h919 LACTANTIUS: *McGuckin* John A., Does Lactantius denigrate Cyprian? [at least he has a radically different theological view]: JTS 39 (1988) 119-124.

h920 **Monat** P., Lactance Institutions I: SChr 326, 1986 → 2,d449; 3,g347: RJTS 39 (1988) 601-4 (O. *Nicholson*).

h921 NILUS R.: *Otranto* Giorgio, Tra Bibbia e agiografia; note sull'esegesi scritturistica di Nilo di Rossano: → 246, VetChr 25 (1988) 567-584.

h922 PHOEBADIUS: EDemeulenaere R., *al.*, Scriptores minores Galliae s. IV-V: Foebadius ... V. [LERINENSIS], *al.*: CCLat 64 [7 microfiches lexicologica A-28], 1985 → 1,f651; 3,g334: RJTS 39 (1988) 265-272 (J.H.A. van *Banning*); Latomus 47 (1988) 210 (Y.-M. *Duval*).

h923 PRUDENTIUS: *Buchheit* Vinzenz, Prudentius über Christus als *duplex genus* und *conditor* (cath. 11. 13-24): WienerSt 101 (1988) 297-312.

h924 SEDULIUS: **Springer** Carl P. E., The gospel as epic in late antiquity; the Paschale Carmen of Sedulius: VigChr Sup 2. Leiden 1988, Brill. xi-168 p. 90-04-08691-9.

Y2.8 Documenta orientalia.

h925 **Beulay** Robert, La lumière sans forme; introduction à l'étude de la mystique chrétienne syro-orientale: L'Esprit et le Feu. Chevetogne 1987. 358 p. – RRThom 88 (1988) 340s (D. *Cerbelaud*).

h926 TEBrock S. P., *Harvey* Susan A., Holy women of the Syrian Orient: Transf.Clas.Heritage 13, 1987 → 3,g352: ROrChrPer 54 (1988) 264s (V. *Poggi*).

h926* *Brock* Sebastian P., Two recent editions of Syrian Orthodox anaphoras: EphLtg 102 (1988) 436-445.

h927 *Bundy* David, MARCION and the Marcionites in early Syriac apologetics: Muséon 101 (1988) 21-32.

h928 **Gamber** Klaus, Die Liturgie der Goten und der Armenier; Versuch einer Darstellung und Hinführung: StPatrLtg Beih 21. Rg 1988, Pustet. 100 p.; ill. 3-7917-1190-3.

h929 *Leloir* Louis, L'humour au service d'un message spirituel; les Pères du désert: → 50, ᶠFONTINOY C. 1988, 83-91.

h930 *Lusini* Gianfrancesco, Appunti sulla patristica greca di tradizione etiopica: StClasOr 38 (1988) 469-493.

h931 **McCullough** W. Stewart, A short history of Syriac Christianity to the rise of Islam 1982 → 63,e665 .. 1,f672: ᴿÉglT 18 (1987) 139s (J. K. *Coyle*); JNES 47 (1988) 233-5 (F. M. *Donner*: some minor shortcomings).

h932 *Sauget* Joseph-Marie, Pour une interprétation de la structure de l'homéliaire syriaque; Ms. British Library Add. 12165: EcOrans 3 (1986) 121-146.

h933 *Schneider* Roger, Nouveaux témoins du texte éthiopien des Règles de l'Église [*Griaule* M. 1932]: JAs 276 (1988) 71-95; Eng. 96.

h934 **Vööbus** Arthur † 26.IX.1988, History of asceticism in the Syrian Orient; a contribution to the history of culture in the Near East 3: CSCOr 500, subs. 81. Lv 1988, Peeters, xliii-464 p. 0070-0444.

---

h935 APHRAATES: ᵀᴱ**Pierre** Marie-Joseph, Aphraate le Sage Persan, Les exposés I (exp. 1-10): SChr 349. P 1988, Cerf. 518 p. 2-204-03051-1.

h936 ATHANASIUS: **Lorenz** Rudolf, Der zehnte Osterbrief des Athanasius von Alexandrien; Text, Übersetzung, Erläuterungen: BZNW 49, 1986 → 3,g364: ᴿJTS [37 (1986) 584, a unity despite the three instalments in Syriac] 39 (1988) 249s (T. D. *Barnes*).

h937 BARHEBRAEUS: *Colless* Brian E., The mysticism of [Grigor abu-1-Faraj] Bar Hebraeus: OrChrPer 54 (1988) 153-173.

h938 DIONYSIUS TM: **Witakowski** Witold, The Syriac chronicle of Pseudo-Dionysius of Tel-Maḥrē; a study in the history of historiography: AcU, Semitica 9, 1987 → 3,g367: ᴿRÉByz 46 (1988) 276s (B. *Flusin*); RHE 83 (1988) 418-421 (J. M. *Fiey*); VigChr 42 (1988) 308-310 (J. den *Heijer*).

h939 'ENĀNĪŠŌ': ᴱ**Sauget** Joseph-Marie, Une traduction arabe de la collection d'Apophthegmata Patrum de 'Enānīšō'; étude du ms. Paris arabe 253 et des témoins parallèles: CSCOr 495, subs. 78. Lv 1987, Peeters. 204 p. 0070-0436.

h940 EUTYCHIUS: ᵀᴱ**Pirone** Bartolomeo, Eutichio patriarca di Alessandria (877-940), Gli Annali: Studia Orientalia Christiana mg 1. Cairo 1987, Franciscan Center of Christian Oriental Studies. 536 p. – ᴿSBFLA 38 (1988) 527-530 (M. *Piccirillo*).

h941 GANNAT BUSSAME: **Reinink** G. J., Die Adventssontage: CSCOr 501s, Syri 211s. Lv 1988, Peeters. I. 117 p. IIᵀ. 167 p. 0070-0452.

h942 GREGORIUS NAZ.: **Bregadze** T'amara M., Grigol Nazianzelis ... Works, description of the Georgian manuscripts. Tbilisi 1988, Mec'niereba. 328 p.

h943 GREGORIUS NYSS.: *Bonanni* Anna, La versione siriaca del 'De opificio hominis' di Gregorio di Nissa, capitolo XXIII (greco XXII): StRicOrCr 10 (1987) 140-162; testo greco 163-6; francese *Laplace* J. 167-170.

h944 *Parmentier* M. F. G., A Syriac commentary on Gregory of Nyssa's Contra Eunomium: Bijdragen 49 (1988) 2-17.

h945 HERMAS: *a*) *Beylot* Robert, Hermas, le Pasteur; quelques variantes inédites de la version éthiopienne; – *b*) *Renoux* Charles, ATHANASE d'Alexandrie dans le florilège arménien Galata 54 (Ire partie): ➤ 59, FGUILLAUMONT A. 1988, 155-162 / 163-171.

h946 ISAACUS N.: **Hansbury** M. Teresa, Evidence of Jewish influence in the writings of Isaac of Nineveh; translation [six Syriac discourses] and commentary: diss. Temple, DSloyan G. Ph 1987. 255 p. 88-03815. – DissA 49 (1988s) 846-A.

h947 LEBNA-DENGEL † 1540: TEKropp Manfred, Die Geschichte des Lebna-Dengel, Claudius und Minās: CSCOr 403s, Aethiopici 83s. Lv 1988, Peeters, 72 p.; 70 p. 0070-0398.

h948 MĒNA: TEBell David N., Mena of Nikiou, The life of Isaac of Alexandria & the Martyrdom of Saint Macrobius: CistStud 107. Kalamazoo 1988, Cistercian. vi-147 p. 0-87907-407-8; pa. 607-0.

h949 MOYSES C.: Zekiyan Boghos L., Ellenismo, ebraismo e cristianesimo in Mosé di Corene (Movses Xorenac'i); elementi per una teologia dell'etnia: ➤ 570, AugR 28 (1988) 381-390.

h950 PACHOMIUS: **Goehring** James E., The letter of Ammon and Pachomian monasticism: PatrTSt 27. B 1986, de Gruyter. xi-307 p. DM 178. – RCrNSt 9 (1988) 629-631 (T. Orlandi); JTS 39 (1988) 606-8 (K. Ware).

h951 **Rousseau** Philip, Pachomius 1985 ➤ 1,f683; 3,g386: RAmHR 92 (1987) 1186s (R. F. Sullivan); ClasPg 83 (1988) 377-9 (E. Pagels); JTS 39 (1988) 604-6 (K. Ware).

h952 PAULUS B.: **Khalil Samir**, Traité de Paul de Būš sur l'Unité et la Trinité, l'Incarnation et la vérité du christianisme 1983 ➤ 1,f694: ROLZ 83 (1988) 456-8 (T. Nagel).

h953 THEOPHILUS A.: Urbaniak-Walczak Katarzyna, Zwei verschiedene Rezensionen der [koptischen] Homilie über die Auferstehung der Jungfrau Maria von Theophilus von Alexandrien: GöMiszÄg 101 (1988) 73s.

h954 [YŪHĀNNĀN Dārāyâ] MARON Jean: Exposé de la foi et autres opuscules, TEBreydy Michel: CSCOr 497s, Syri 209s. Lv 1988, Peeters. 142 p.; 77 p. 0070-0452.

Y3 **Medium aevum,** generalia.

h955 Amigo Lorenzo, El cultismo léxico en la biblia medieval romanceada: Helmantica 118s (1988) 111-152.

h956 EAston T. H., The history of the University of Oxford [vol. 3 & 5, 1986 ➤ 2,d736] 1. ECatto J. I. (Evans R.) The early Oxford schools. Ox 1984, Clarendon. xliv-684 p., ill. £55. – RHZ 245 (1987) 698s (K. Schnith) [664-6, N. Hammerstein].

h957 **Bredero** Adriaan H., Christenheid en Christendom in de Middeleeuwen; over de verhouding van godsdienst, kerk en samenleving. Kampen 1986, Kok Agora. 358 p. f 50. 90-242-7530-X. – RBTAM 14 (1988) 473 (G. Hendrix); NedTTs 42 (1988) 164s (M. B. Pranger).

h958 Brooke Martin, Interpretatio christiana; imitation and polemic in late antique epic: ➤ 17, FBRAMBLE J. 1987, 285-295.

h959 **Brundage** James A., Law, sex, and Christian society in medieval Europe. Ch 1987, Univ. xxvi-646 p. $45. 0-226-07783-7. – RTS 49 (1988) 763-6 (L. Orsy).

h960 a) Bussmann Magdalene, 'Man muss Gott mehr gehorchen als den Menschen!' Der Konflikt um Amt und Charisma in der mittealterlichen Kirche; – b) Thomas Jean, Ist das Geld des Teufels?: Diakonia 19,4 ('Geld und Geist in der Kirche' 1988) 245-250 / 230-5 [< ZIT 88,557].

h961 **D'Alatri** Mariano, Eretici e inquisitori in Italia; Studi e documenti, I. Il Duecento; II. Il Tre e il Quattrocento: Bibliotheca seraphico-capuccina 31s. R 1986s, Ist.Stor.Cappuccini. 352 p.; 308 p.; ciascuno Lit. 30.000. – [R]ColcFr 58 (1988) 137-143 (M. *Bartoli*).

h962 [E]**Elder** E. Rozanne, The roots of the modern Christian tradition 1982/4 → 2,d484: [R]HeythJ 29 (1988) 488-490 (M. J. *Clayton*).

h963 **Ennen** Edith, Frauen im Mittelalter 1984 → 65,d596 ... 3,g393: [R]ZKG 99 (1988) 112-4 (E. *Meuthen*).

h964 **Ferruolo** Stephen C., The origins of the university; the schools of Paris and their critics, 1100-1215, 1985 → 3,g396: [R]RHE 83 (1988) 207s (P. H. *Daly*).

h965 *Frazee* Charles A., The origins of clerical celibacy in the western church: ChH Centennial Sup (1988) 108-126.

h966 *Gibson* Margaret, The study of the Bible in the Middle Ages [[F]SMALLEY B.; BTT 4]: JEH 39 (1988) 230-2.

h967 *Gies* Frances & Joseph, Marriage and the family in the Middle Ages. NY 1987, Harper & R. 372 p. $22.50. – [R]TS 49 (1988) 784 (L. *Orsy*).

h968 *Gössmann* E., *al.,* Frau: → 803, LexMA IV, 4 (1988) 852-874.

h969 **Gold** Penny S., The lady and the virgin 1985 → 2,d487; 3,g400: [R]HeythJ 29 (1988) 524s (K. W. *Woods*); JIntdis 18 (1987s) 361-4 (F. L. *Cheyette*); RBgPg 66 (1988) 474s (H. *Platelle*).

h970 **Guidi** Remo L., La morte nell'età umanistica: Aspetti religiosi nella letteratura del 1400,[5]. Vicenza 1983, LIEF. 712 p. Lit. 35.000. – [R]ÉglT 17 (1986) 249-251 (P. *Hurtubise*).

h971 *Hausherr* Reiner, Über die Auswahl des Bibeltextes in der Bible moralisée: Zts Kunstgeschichte 51,1 (Mü 1988) 126-146; 15 fig.

h971* [E]**Herren** Michael W. (*Brown* Shirley A.), The sacred nectar of the Greeks; the study of Greek in the West in the early Middle Ages. L 1988, King's College. xii-313 p. £15 [JTS 40,747].

h972 **Herrin** Judith, The formation of Christendom [transit from classical to medieval world]. Ox 1987, Blackwell. x-530 p. £29.50. – [R]TLond 91 (1988) 536-8 (L. N. *Wood*).

h973 *Jiménez Forcada* Sixto J., El manuscrito escurialense I-J-4 [versión del AT casi completa] y las biblias medievales romanceadas: Helmantica 118s (1988) 223-230.

h974 *Kelly* Henry A., Inquisition and the prosecution of heresy; misconceptions and abuses: ChH 58 (1989) 439-451.

h975 **Labarge** Margaret W., A small sound of the trumpet; women in medieval life. Boston 1986, Beacon. xiv-271 p. $30. – [R]AmHR 93 (1988) 400 (Susan M. *Stuard*).

h976 *Larcher* Gerhard, Modelle fundamentaltheologischer Problematik im Mittelalter: → 800, HbFT 4 (1988) 334-346.

h977 [E]**Le Goff** Jacques, L'uomo medievale. Bari 1987, Laterza. 424 p. Lit. 30.000. – [R]ViPe 71 (1988) 392-6 (Alessandra *Tarabochia Canavero*).

h978 *Light* Laura, The new thirteenth-century Bible and the challenge of heresy [thin parchment, minute bookhand pocket Bibles in England and France 1230-1240]: Viator 18 (1987) 275-288 [< BTAM 14 (1988) 523 (C. *Mews*)].

h979 [E]**Makdisi** G., [cf. → 1,610*] *al.,* La notion de liberté au Moyen Âge; Islam, Byzance, Occident [Paris/Dumbarton Oaks colloquium, 12-15.X. 1982]. P 1985, BLettres, 287 p. F 220. – [R]CrNSt 9 (1988) 188-191 (A. *Rigo*).

h980 *Meyendorff* John, Is 'hesycasm' the right word? [*hēsychía*, contemplative monasticism]; remarks on religious ideology in the fourteenth century: → 134, ᶠSEVČENKO I., Okeanos 1983, 447-456.

h981 *Meyvaert* Paul, Medieval forgers and modern scholars; tests of ingenuity: → 681, Book 1982/6, I, 83-96 [< BTAM 14 (1988) 449s (H. *Silvestre*)].

h982 *Milo* Daniel, L'an mil; un problème d'historiographie moderne: Hist-Theor 27 (1988) 261-281 [his pivotal dates include 476 but not c. 330].

h983 *Mojsisch* Burkhard, Dietrich von FREIBERG [c. 1300, Opera 1977-85; 'einer der ohne Zweifel originellsten Denker des Mittelalters überhaupt']: TLZ 113 (1988) 871-7.

h984 **Mollat** M., The poor in the Middle Ages; an essay in social history, ᵀ*Goldhammer* Arthur. NHv 1986, Yale Univ. viii-336 p. $30. – ᴿCath-HR 74 (1988) 321s (D. *Flood*).

h985 ᴱNí Chatháin Próinséas, *Richter* Michael, Irland und die Christenheit, Bibelstudien und Mission: Europacentrum, Kult-W. Reihe. Tü 1987. xii-523 p. DM 64 [Bijdragen 49,475].

h986 **Olsen** Birger M., L'étude des auteurs classiques latins aux XIᵉ et XIIᵉ siècles, III/1, Les classiques dans les bibliothèques médiévales. P 1987, CNRS. 381 p. – ᴿRPLH 62,1 (1988) 157s (É. des *Places*).

h987 **Orabona** L., La Chiesa dell'anno mille; spiritualità tra politica ed economia nell'Europa medievale: La spiritualità cristiana, Studi e testi 6. R 1988, Studium. 241 p. Lit. 18.000. – ᴿRasT 29 (1988) 605s (A. *Marranzini*).

h988 **Paul** J., L'Église et la culture en Occident, 1. La sanctification de l'ordre temporel et spirituel; 2. L'éveil évangélique et les mentalités religieuses: Nouvelle Clio 15. P 1986, PUF. 793 p. [2 vol. F 145 chaque]. – ᴿRSPT 72 (1988) 177 (L. J. *Bataillon*).

h989 **Pelikan** Jaroslav, The excellent empire; the fall of Rome and the triumph of the Church [Colgate-Rochester Rauschenbusch lectures 1984 on GIBBON E.]. SF 1988, Harper & R. xiii-133 p. $19 [TDig 35,197].

h990 *a)* ᴱPetroff Elizabeth A., Medieval women's visionary literature. Ox 1986, UP. 402 p. 0-19-503712-X. – *b)* ᴱ**Harley** Marta P., A revelation of Purgatory by an unknown fifteenth-century woman visionary: Studies in Women and Religion 1985. Lewiston NY 1985, Mellen. 149 p. $50. – ᴿZKG 99 (1988) 110s / 112 (P. *Dinzelbacher*).

h991 ᴱRiché P., *Lobrichon* G., Le Moyen Âge et la Bible: Bible de tous les temps 1984 → 1,306.d605 ... 3,g417: ᴿRÉJ 146 (1987) 446-8 (D. *Tollet*); RSPT 72 (1988) 443-5 (Nicole *Bériou*).

h992 **Roberts** Michael, Biblical epic and rhetorical paraphrase in late antiquity 1985 → 1,b719 ... 3,g419: ᴿJTS 39 (1988) 589s (Judith *McClure*: on hexameter versions of OT & NT texts); Latomus 47 (1988) 175s (J. *Meyers*).

h993 *Santiago-Otero* H., Comentarios bíblicos en lengua vernácula (siglos XII-XV); → 111*, ᶠORLANDIS R., J., Hispania christiana 1988, 351-364 [< RHE 83,369*].

h994 **Sieben** Hermann J., Die Konzilsidee des lateinischen Mittelalters (847-1378) 1984 → 1,f721 ... 3,g420: ᴿCarthaginensia 4 (1988) 199s (V. *Sánchez*).

h995 SMALLEY Beryl mem., The Bible in the medieval world, ᴱ**Walsh** K., *Wood* D. 1985 → 1,131; 3,g422: ᴿCathHR 73 (1987) 262s (W. J. *Courtenay*); ColcFr 57 (1987) 133-5 (O. *Schmucki*); HeythJ 29 (1988) 124s (O. *Lewry* †); Thomist 51 (1987) 186-8 (E. Ann *Matter*).

h996 **Smalley** Beryl, The Gospels in the Schools, c. 1100 – c. 1280 [4 reprints + 1 ineditum] 1985 ➤ 3,299: ᴿBTAM 14 (1988) 488s (H. *Silvestre*).

h997 **Stiefel** Tina, The intellectual revolution in twelfth century Europe 1985 ➤ 3,g423: ᴿBTAM 14 (1988) 482s (H. *Silvestre*).

h998 **Stroll** Mary, The Jewish pope; ideology and politics in the papal schism of 1130: Studies in Intellectual History 8. Leiden 1987, Brill. 205 p. $49. – ᴿJEcuSt 25 (1988) 465 (G. *MacGregor*).

h999 **Vauchez** André, Les laïcs au Moyen Âge; pratiques et expériences religieuses: Histoire. P 1987, Cerf. 312 p. F 165. – ᴿOrientierung 52 (1988) 180-3 (R. *Imbach*); RHR 205 (1988) 305-8 (M. *Zimmermann*).

k1 *Wieck* Roger S., The Book of Hours, the medieval best seller [illuminated prayer books; exhibit in Baltimore Walters Art Gallery April-July 1988]: BR 4,2 (1988) 22-27; ill.

Y3.4 **Exegetae mediaevales** (hebraei ➤ K7).

k2 ALEXANDER H.: **Fornaro** I., La teologia dell'immagine nella Glossa di Alessandro d'Hales. Vicenza 1985, L.I.E.F. 324 p. Lit. 17.000. – ᴿStPatav 35 (1988) 669-673 (A. *Jori*).

k3 AQUINAS: *Dubois* Marcel, Mystical and realistic elements in the exegesis and hermeneutics of Thomas Aquinas: ➤ 505, Creative 1985/8, 39-54 (203-211).

k4 **Eco** Umberto, The aesthestics of Thomas Aquinas, ᵀ*Bredin* Hugh. CM 1988, Harvard Univ. xi-287 p. $30. 0-674-00675-5 [TDig 36,157].

k5 *García Tato* I., Ortodoxía luterana y Escolástica medieval; Juan Jorge DORSCH y su interpretación de Tomás de Aquino: DiálEc 22 (1987) 5-26 [< RET 48,120].

k6 **Pesch** Otto H., Thomas von Aquin; Grenze und Grosse mittelalterlicher Theologie. Mainz 1988, Grünewald. 452 p. [TS 50, 796, G. A. *McCool*].

k7 *Schönborn* Christoph, Die Autorität des Lehrers nach Thomas von Aquin: ➤ 23, ᶠCHADWICK H., 1988, 101-126.

k8 *Tiebey* Simon, L'épistémologie néothomiste en U.R.S.S. [... 'la génie de s. Thomas d'Aquin est reconnu en U.R.S.S.' (*Rahner/Coreth*...) base de la critique de la philosophie bourgeoise]: RHPR 68 (1988) 209-215.

k9 *Weier* Reinhold, Das Evangelium als 'neues Gesetz'; Überlegungen zu einem umstrittenen Begriff bei Thomas von Aquin: TrierTZ 97 (1988) 39-51.

k10 **Wohlman** Avital, Thomas d'Aquin et MAIMONIDE, un dialogue exemplaire: Patrimoines. P 1988, Cerf. 417 p. 2-204-02938-6.

k11 BEDA: **Brown** George H., Bede the Venerable: English Authors 443. Boston 1987, Twayne. viii-153 p. $20. – ᴿChH 57 (1988) 222s (W. T. *Foley*).

BERNARDUS: **Leclercq** Jean, Recueil d'études sur ∼ 1987 ➤ 216.

k12 BONAVENTURA: **Reist** Thomas, Saint Bonaventure as a biblical commentator [Lk 18,14-19,42] ᴰ1985 ➤ 3,g434: ᴿWissWeis 50 (1987) 73s (H.-J. *Klauck*).

k13 CATHARINA S.: *O'Driscoll* Mary, Catherine [of Siena] the theologian: SpTod 40 (1988) 4-17.

k14 CUSANUS N.: **Manno** A. G., Il problema di Dio in Nicolò Cusano: Il problema di Dio nei grandi pensatori 3. Cassino-Frosinone 1986, Sangermano. 210 p. Lit. 30.000. – ᴿRasT 29 (1988) 106-8 (G. *Bergamaschi*).

k15 DAMIANUS P.: *Resnick* Irven M., Peter Damian on the restoration of virginity; a problem for medieval theology (AQUINAS did not uphold JEROME's claim that God cannot restore a woman's virginity; but the question then touches on the Virgin Birth]: JTS 39 (1988) 125-134.

k16 DIONYSIUS PS.-A.: *Evans* David B., Pseudo-Dionysius the Areopagite: → 792, DMA 10 (1988) 203s.

k17 *Kremer* Klaus, ['Bonum est diffusivum sui' ANRW 2/36/2 (1987) 994-1032] Dionysius Pseudo-Areopagita oder GREGOR von Nazianz? Zur Herkunft der Formel: TPhil 63 (1988) 579-585.

k18 ᵀ*Luibheid* Colm, Ps.-Dionysius 1987 → 3,g437: ᴿNewTR 1,2 (1988) 120s (Z. *Hayes*); SixtC 19 (1988) 723s (C.-G. *Nauert*); SpTod 40 (1988) 86-88 (B.-M. *Ashley*).

k19 **Rorem** Paul, Biblical and liturgical symbols within the Pseudo-Dionysian synthesis 1984 → 65,d617...3,g438: ᴿChH 57 (1988) 78 (F. *Tobin*); Parabola 13,1 (1988) 127-9 (P. *Jordan-Smith*); ZKG 99 (1988) 411s (W. *Beierwaltes*).

k21 ECKHART: *Carabine* Deirdre, Apophasis East and West [SYMEON/ Eckhart]: RTAM 55 (1988) 5-29.

k22 *Monteil* Michèle, Eckhart et LUTHER, thème usé ou sous-estimé?: PosLuth 36 (1988) 3-14 [ZIT].

k23 ERIUGENA: **O'Meara** John J., Eriugena [...with the first English translation of the influential Homily on Jn-Prologue]. Ox 1988, Clarendon. x-237 p. $65 [TS 50, 793, D. F. *Duclow*].

k24 GERSON: **Burger** Christoph, Aedificatio, fructus, utilitas; Johannes Gerson als Professor der Theologie und Kanzler der Universität Paris [Hab. Tü]: BeiHistT 70. Tü 1986, Mohr. xii-226. DM 116. 3-16-145046-9. – ᴿGregorianum 69 (1988) 796-8 (J. *Wicks* supplies more correct view of doctrinal vs. papal authority).

k25 **Burrows** Mark S., Jean Gerson and De consolatione theologiae (1418); the consolation of a biblical and reforming theology for a disordered age: diss. Princeton Theol. Sem. 1988. – RelStR 15,193.

k26 GROSSETESTE: **Southern** R. W., Robert Grosseteste; the growth of an English mind in medieval Europe. Ox 1986, Clarendon. xii-337 p. £30. 0-19-826450-X. – ᴿBijdragen 49 (1988) 102s (B. *Leurink*).

k26* *Lértora Mendoza* Celina A., Una propuesta lingüística para la exegesis en la escuela de Oxford; Grosseteste y BACON: RBibArg 30s (1988) 97-124.

k27 ISIDORUS H.: ᵀᴱ**Marshall** Peter K., Isidore of Seville, Etymologies; Book 2, Rhetoric: Auteurs Latins du Moyen Âge. P 1983, BLettres. 183 p. – ᴿGnomon 60 (1988) 653-5 (O. *Hiltbrunner*).

k28 JOACHIM F.: *Lerner* Robert E., Joachim von Fiore, ᵀ*Schäferdiek* K.: → 813, TRE 17 (1987) 84-88.

k29 **Reeves** Marjorie, *Gould* Warwick, Joachim of Fiore and the myth of the eternal evangel in the nineteenth century 1987 → 3,g448: ᴿJTS 39 (1988) 328s (T. R. *Wright*); TLond 91 (1988) 70-72 (S. *Prickett*).

k30 **West** Delno C., *Zimdars-Swartz* Sandra, Joachim of Fiore 1983 → 65,d626...2,d528: ᴿZKG 99 (1988) 121-3 (E. *Pältz*).

k31 JULIAN N.: **Jantzen** Grace M., Julian of Norwich, mystic and theologian. L 1987, SPCK. x-230 p. £9 pa. – ᴿTLond 91 (1988) 356-361 (Ann *Loades*).

k32 ᴱ**Llewellyn** R., Julian woman of our day 1985 → 2,d531: ᴿNewTR 1,2 (1988) 118-120 (D. V. *Monti*).

k33 MANETTI: **Dröge** G., Gianozzo Manetti [1396-1459] als Denker und Hebraist [Latin psalm-translation; Diss. Bonn 1983]: JudUmw 20. Fra 1987, Lang. x-234 p. Fs 52. 3-8204-9127-9 [BL 89,13].

k34 OLIVI: *Burr* David, Olivi; apocalyptic expectation and visionary experience: Traditio 41 (1985) 273-288 [BTAM 14 (1988) 539 (C. *Mews*)].

k35 PELHART: *Kosztolnyik* Z. J., Some Hungarian theologians in the late Renaissance [... Pelhart of Temešvar 1483]: ChH 57 (1988) 5-18.

k36 RABAN(us) MAUR(us): → 786, Catholicisme 12,55 (1988) 416s (J.-P. *Bouhot*).

k37 RUPERTUS T.: **Barrachina** A., La espiritualidad trinitaria de Ruperto de Deutz. Valencia 1983, Fac. S.V. Ferrer. 137 p. – ᴿSalmanticensis 35 (1988) 449s (D. de *Pablo Marcos*).

k38 SAVONAROLA: *Pinchard* Bruno, Jérôme Savonarole entre la scolastique et l'humanisme; les doutes d'un prophète: RSPT 72 (1988) 227-240; Eng. 240 'Key words: Cajetan, doubt, church, Florence, habitus, humanism, prophecy, Rome, Savonarola, scholastic'.

k39 SCOTUS [→ k23]: **Manno** A. G., Il volontarismo teologico, etico e antropologico di G. Duns Scoto: Il problema di Dio nei grandi pensatori 2. Cassino-Frosinone 1986, Sangermano. 214 p. Lit. 30.000. – ᴿRasT 29 (1988) 105 (G. *Lauriola*).

k40 SYMEON: **Fraigneau-Julien** B. [† 1982], Les sens spirituels et la vision de Dieu selon Syméon...: THist 67, 1985 → 3,1260.g457: ᴿContacts-Orthodoxe 40 (1988) 314-6 (J. M.); ÉglT 18 (1987) 369-371 (G. *Hudon*); JTS 39 (1988) 628s (K. *Ware*).

Y4.1 **Luther.**

k41 **Bach** Heinrich, Handbuch der Luthersprache; Laut- und Formenlehre in Luthers Wittenberger Drucken bis 1545 [1. 1974], 2. Druckschwache Silben, Konsonantismus 1985 → 1,f757; 2,d542: ᴿLutherJb 54 (1987) 121s (H. *Junghans*).

k42 *a) Blocher* Henri, Luther et la Bible; – *b) Daumas* Jean-Marc, Karl BARTH, Jean CALVIN et la connaissance de Dieu; filiation ou trahison?: → 28*, ᶠCOURTHIAL P., Dieu parle! 1984, 127-141 / 142-158.

k43 **Brecht** Martin, Martin Luther I. 1981, ²1983; II. 1986 → 3,g642; – III. Die Erhaltung der Kirche 1532-1546. Stu 1987, Calwer. 520 p.; 14 fig. 20 pl. DM 48. 3-7668-0825-7. – ᴿDLZ 109 (1988) 305-8 (G. *Wendelborn*, 2); Luther 19 (1988) 145-9 (H. *Düfel*).

k44 *Brosseder* Johannes, La imagen protestante y católica de Lutero en la actual investigación sobre el reformador: → 604, Lutero, jornadas 1983/4, 185-210.

k45 ᴱ**Cavallotto** Stefano, Martin Lutero, Scritti pastorali minori. N 1987, Dehoniane. lxxii-328 p. Lit. 24.000. – ᴿCC 139 (1988,4) 514 (P. *Vanzan*).

k46 *Corrington* Robert S., Being and faith; Sein und Zeit and Luther: AnglTR 70 (1988) 16-31.

k47 ᴱ**Delius** Hans-Ulrich, *al.*, Luther: Studienausgabe 4, 1986 → 3,g466: ᴿLutherJb 55 (1988) 122-5 (H. *Junghans*).

k48 **Diwald** H., Lutero [1982, anche francese], ᵀ. Mi 1986, Rizzoli. 437 p. Lit. 30.000. – ᴿProtestantesimo 43 (1988) 181s (E. *Campi*: errori non solo di traduzione assai infelici).

k49 *Ebeling* Gerhard, Das rechte Unterscheiden [Geist/Buchstabe; Gesetz/Evangelium...]; Luthers Anleitung zu theologischer Urteilskraft: ZTK 85 (1988) 219-258.

k50 **Fabisch** Peter, *Iserloh* Erwin, Dokumente zur Causa Lutheri (1517-1521),
I. Das Gutachten des Prierias und weitere Schriften gegen Luthers
Ablassthesen (1517-1518): Corpus Catholicorum 41. Münster 1988,
Aschendorff. 459 p.; ill. 3-402-03455-7.

k51 *Forsberg* Juhani, Lutherin raamattukäsitys ja raamatuntulkinta sekä
niiden merkitys tänään (Luthers Bibelauffassung und Bibelauslegung in
ihrer heutigen Bedeutung): Teologinen Aikakauskirua 91 (Helsinki 1986)
226-234 [< LuJb 55,164].

k52 *a) Greiner* Albert, Luther commentateur de l'Ave Maria; – *b) Bénédicte*
sr., Le jugement de Luther sur les vœux monastiques; – *c) Dautry* Michel,
Philippe MÉLANCHTHON et la primauté du pape: PosLuth 36,1 (1988)...
[< RHPR 68/3].

k53 **Junghans** Helmar, Der junge Luther und die Humanisten 1985
➤ 1,f777 ... 3,g481: ᴿKerkT 39 (1988) 81 (W. *Nijenhuis*).

k54 **Kittelson** James M., Luther the Reformer; the story of the man and his
career 1986 ➤ 3,g484: ᴿSixtC 19 (1988) 284 (M. U. *Edwards*).

k55 *Lamparter* Helmut, Martin Luthers Stellung zur Heiligen Schrift: ➤ 368,
Teresa - Luther 1983, 112-9 [< LuJb 54,172].

k56 *Leinhard* Marc, Martin Luther im Spannungsfeld der deutsch-franzö-
sischen Beziehungen im 19. und 20. Jahrhundert: Luther 19 (1988) 45-52.

k57 **Loewenich** Walter von, Martin Luther, the man and his work [1982],
ᵀ*Denef* Lawrence A., 1986 ➤ 3,g487: ᴿInterpretation 42 (1988) 305
(J. A. *Nestingen*: 'one book too many' [H. OBERMAN harshly] from the
author of a 1927 classic; calls 1939 studies 'recent' and fails to cope).

k58 **Lohse** Bernhard, Martin Luther, an introduction to his life and work
[1980], ᴿ*Schultz* R. C. 1986 ➤ 3,g488: ᴿCurrTM 15 (1988) 453s (K. S.
Hendel); RefTR 47 (1988) 24s (R. C. *Doyle*: useful but too general and
flat); Themelios 14 (1988s) 75 (J. *Atkinson*: not really an introduction, but
critical evaluation of a corpus of writings which would take 8 hours a day
for 25 years to read through).

k59 *a) Lohse* Bernhard, Luther und die Autorität Roms im Jahre 1518; – *b)*
Wicks Jared, The Lutheran *forma ecclesiae* in the colloquy at Augsburg,
August 1530; – *c) Yarnold* Edward, Duplex iustitia; the sixteenth century
and the twentieth: ➤ 23, ᶠCHADWICK H., Christian authority 1988,
138-159 / 160-203 / 204-223.

k60 **Luther** M., Werke: **61** [repertorio] 1983 ➤ g468: ᴿProtestantesimo 43
(1988) 52s (P. *Ricca*). – **63:** Personen- und Zitatenregister zur Abteilung
Schriften Band 1-60s. Weimar 1987, Böhlau. x-607 p. – ᴿRHE 83 (1988)
743 (J.-F. *Gilmont*: références structurées: Marie 26 colonnes avec des
subdivisions fines; Augustin 68 colonnes; contemporains de Luther moins,
environ 6).

k61 Luther 2000, 1ᵉʳ recueil, textes choisis de Martin Luther: Si c'était vrai?
21. Champigny c. 1987, Concordia. 145 p. F 39. – ᴿEsprVie 98 (1988)
86s (P. *Jay*: 66 extraits, dont un seul, comparé avec une autre traduction,
prouve que 'nous sommes ici en présence d'un autre texte que celui de
Luther').

k62 **Manns** Peter, *Loose* Helmuth N., M. Luther; Vorw. *Lohse* E. 1982
➤ 64,e255; 2,d563: ᴿLuther 19 (1988) 107 (H. *Düfel*: Meilenstein katholischer Lutherliteratur).

k63 ᴱ**Manns** Peter, Zur Bilanz des Lutherjahres 1986 ➤ 3,671*: ᴿChH 57
(1988) 256 (R. *Kolb*); Gregorianum 69 (1988) 172s (J. E. *Vercruysse*).

k64 *Martikainen* Eeva, Die finnische Lutherforschung seit 1934: TRu 53
(1988) 371-387.

k65 **Monteil** Michèle, M. Luther, la vie oui 1983 → 64,e261 ... 1,f792: ᴿÉglT 18 (1987) 253-5 (P. *Hurtubise*).

k66 *Oberman* Heiko, Teufelsdreck; eschatology and scatology in the 'Old' Luther: SixtC 19 (1988) 435-450.

k67 *Rasmussen* Tarald, Lutherforskning og historisk metode [til O. J. JENSENS diss. 1988]: NorTTs 89 (1988) 237-248.

k68 *Richter* Horst, Martin Luther and the development of the German language: → 1,575, ᴱFURCHA E., Encounters with Luther 1983/4, 186-215 [LuJb 55 (1988) 165].

k69 *Schilling* Johannes, Latinistische Hilfsmittel zum Lutherstudium: LutherJb 55 (1988) 83-101.

k70 **Schwarz** Reinhard, Luther: Die Kirche in ihrer Geschichte 3, 1986 → 3,g500: ᴿLutherJb 55 (1988) 118s (B. *Lohse*); TLZ 113 (1988) 832-4 (E. W. *Gritsch*).

k71 *Schwarz* Reinhard, Luther's inalienable inheritance of monastic theology: AmBenR 39 (1988) 430-450.

k72 *Scribner* Robert W., 'Incombustible Luther'; the image of the Reformer in early modern Germany: Past and Present 110 (Oxford 1986) 38-68 [< LuJb 54,180].

k73 *Shestov* Leon, Luther et l'Église; sola fide [Tolko veroi 1911-14; German translation noted in ᴱ*Martin* Bernard, A Shestov anthology (Athens 1970, Ohio Univ.) 322-8, list of Shestov works]. P. 1983, Le Sycomore. – ᴿCurrTM 15 (1988) 431-7 (E. *Kallas*).

k74 *Steinmetz* David C., Luther in context 1986 → 2,d571; 3,g501: ᴿAndrUnS 26 (1988) 98s (K. A. *Strand*); CurrTM 15 (1988) 282s (T. C. *Thomas*).

k75 *Thomas* Terry C., Luther's canon; Christ against Scripture [redimensioned]: WWorld 8 (1988) 141-9 [< OTAbs 11,299].

k76 *Tonkin* John, A Reformation miscellany; some [7] recent books on Luther and the Reformation. [*Atkinson* J., *McGrath* A., *al.*]: JEH 39 (1988) 445-454.

k77 **Wolf** Herbert, Germanistische Luther-Bibliographie; M. Luthers deutsches Sprachschaffen im Spiegel des internationalen Schrifttums der Jahre 1880-1980: Germanistische Bibliothek NF 6, 1985 → 3,1074: ᴿDLZ 109 (1988) 33-35 (H.-U. *Delius*); LutherJb 54 (1987) 116s (M. *Beyer*).

k78 ᴱ**Yule** George, Luther, theologian for Catholics and Protestants 1985 → 1,413 ... 3,g503: ᴿHeythJ 29 (1988) 526s (J. *Wicks*).

Y4.3 Exegesis et controversia saeculi XVI.

k79 ᴱ**Anderson** Robert A., Frühneuhochdeutsches Wörterbuch, Lfg. 1s, ᴱ*Reichmann* Oskar, Einleitung, Quellenverzeichnis, Literaturverzeichnis, A-action. B 1986, de Gruyter. 285 p. + 608 col. – ᴿLutherJb 55 (1988) 129-131 (H. *Junghans*: 10 volumes awaited).

k80 **Barnes** Robin B., Prophecy and gnosis; apocalypticism in the wake of the Lutheran Reformation. Stanford 1988, Univ. viii-371 p. $39.50. 0-8047-1405-3 [TDig 36,148]. – ᴿCathHR 74 (1988) 501-3 (J. M. *Headley*).

k81 **Baroni** Victor, La contre-reforme devant la Bible; la question biblique; Supplément, Du XVIIIᵉ siècle à nos jours. Genève 1986 = 1943, Slatkine. 555 p. 2-05-100721-7.

k82 *Barthel* Pierre, Du salut par la foi, mais non point sans les œuvres; notes concernant la naissance de l'Orthodoxie 'raisonnée' réformée, de langue française, au début du XVIIIe siècle I: Zwingliana 17 (1988) 497-511.

k83 **Baubérot** Jean, *Willaime* Jean-Paul, Le protestantisme. Le monde de ... P 1987, MA éd. 207 p. – ᴿRHPR 68 (1988) 531 (*Willaime*).

k84 ᴱ**Bianco** Cesare, [Oeconomia christiana, in olandese 1523]. Il Sommario della Sacra Scrittura e l'ordinario dei Cristiani; intr. *Trapman* J. T 1988, Claudiana. 206 p. Lit. 16.500. – ᴿCiVit 43 (1988) 417s (A. *Pellegrini*).

k85 *Blaser* K., L'Écriture, son rôle et son interprétation selon la Dispute de Lausanne: ➤ 586, Dispute de Lausanne (1536) 1986/8, 49-60.

k86 **Bujanda** J. M., Index des livres interdits 1984-6 ➤ 2,d581; 3,g511: ᴿArTGran 51 (1988) 255s (A. *Segovia*, 2-3).

k87 *McCuaig* William, Franz H. REUSCH e 'L'indice dei libri proibiti' [Index 1883-5]: RivStoLR 24 (1988) 569-583 [à propos *Bujanda* J. de, 1984].

k88 **Bush** Sargent ᴶ, *Rasmussen* Carl J., The library of Emmanuel College, Cambridge, 1584-1637 [66% theology, 6% philology largely Hebrew]. C 1986, Univ. x-223 p. £37.50. – ᴿJTS 39 (1988) 310-2 (C.N.L. *Brooke*).

k89 **Cameron** Euan, The reformation of the heretics; the Waldenses of the Alps 1480-1580: 1984 ➤ 3,g512: ᴿScotJT 41 (1988) 559s (H. R. *Sefton*).

k90 *Christophe* Paul, Les pauvres et la pauvreté. II. du XVIᵉ s. à nos jours: Bibliothèque de l'histoire du Christianisme 12. P 1987, Desclée. 196 p. F 98. – ᴿRHE 83 (1988) 810s (P. H. *Daly*).

k91 *Crimanda* Thomas J., Two French views of the Council of Trent [*Moulin* C. de 1564; *Grégoire* P. 1583]: SixtC 19 (1988) 169-186.

k92 **Dickens** A., *Tonkin* J., The Reformation in historical thought 1985 ➤ 3,g512: ᴿCathHR 74 (1988) 491-4 (L. W. *Spitz*); ChH 57 (1988) 90s (P. I. *Kaufman*). RelStR 14 (1988) 384 (S. H. *Hendrix*: slights theologians).

k93 **Dumas** André, Protestants. P 1987, Bergers / Mages. 69 p. F 50. 2-85304-072-0. – ᴿÉTRel 63 (1988) 324s (A. *Gounelle* 'yields to the temptation' of comparing it with his own Les grands principes du protestantisme); RHPR 68 (1988) 480s (R. *Mehl*).

k94 **Ebel** Jobst C., Wort und Geist bei den Verfassern der Konkordienformel; eine historisch-systematische Untersuchung: BeiEvT 89. Mü 1981, Kaiser. 333 p. DM 60. – ᴿZKG 99 (1988) 238-244 (T. *Mahlmann*).

k95 **Estep** William E., Renaissance and Reformation 1986 ➤ 2,d587; 3,g518: ᴿRefTR 46 (1987) 21s (S. D. *Gill*).

k96 **Estié** Paul, Het vluchtige bestaan van de eerste Nederlandse Lutherse gemeente, Antwerpen 1566-1567. Amst 1986. – ᴿNedTTs 42 (1988) 166s (C. C. *Visser*).

k97 **Evans** G. R., The language and logic of the Bible [II.] The road to Reformation 1985 ➤ 1,f811 ... 3,g519: ᴿCîteaux 39 (1988) 200s (Benedicta *Ward*); JAAR 56 (1988) 328s (S. R. *Gordy*); Speculum 63 (1988) 391s (T. *Reist*).

k98 ᴱ**Fatio** O., *Widmer* G., Confessions et catéchismes de la foi réformée 1986 ➤ 3,g521: ᴿProtestantesimo 43 (1988) 55s (F. *Ferrario*).

k99 *Ferrario* Fulvio, L'anabattismo delle origini e il problema ermeneutico: RasT 29 (1988) 382-400: 'La Bibbia è un boomerang' p. 399.

k100 **Ford** Alan, The Protestant Reformation in Ireland, 1590-1641: Studies in the Intercultural History of Christianity 34. Bern 1985, Lang. 316 p. Fs 65. – ᴿHeythJ 29 (1988) 369s (J. *Morrill*).

k101 **Frank** I. W., Toleranz am Mittelrhein [Worms 12.-13.IV. 1983, 500ᵉ anniversaire de la naissance de Luther]: Quellen und Abhandlungen zur mittelrheinischen Kirchengeschichte 50. Mainz 1984. 138 p. – ᴿRHE 83 (1988) 746s (A. *Minke*).

k102 **George** Timothy, Theology of the reformers. Nv 1988, Broadman. 337 p. $22 [TDig 36,60].

k103 *Honée* Eugène, De reformatie in romeinse ogen; reacties van de pauselijke curie en haar gezanten op de geloofsverdeeldheid in het duitse rijk (1521-1555): TsTNijm 28 (1988) 335-348; Eng. 348.

k104 ^E**Iserloh** E., Katholische Theologen der Reformationszeit I, 1984 ↠ 1,362 ... 3,g529: ^RLtgJb 37 (1987) 253 (A. *Heinz*).

k105 *a) Iserloh* Erwin, Reformationsgeschichte als Aufgabe des katholischen Kirchenhistorikers; – *b) Widmer* Gabriel-P., Bemerkung zur reformierten Theologie der Bilder: ↠ 53, ^FGANOCZY A., Creatio 1988, 291-9 / 329-337.

k106 **Lottin** A., Lille citadelle de la Contre-Réforme? 1598-1668. Westhoek 1984, Beffrois. 517 p. – ^RCahHist 30 (1985) 356s (J.-P. *Gutton*).

k107 **McGrath** Alister, The intellectual origins of the European reformation 1987 ↠ 3,g536: ^RJTS 39 (1988) 294s (G. R. *Evans*: 'it is easy to carp'); TLond 91 (1988) 431-3 (G. *Leff*); TS 49 (1987) 745-7 (J. *Wicks*).

k107* **McGrath** Alister E., Reformation thought; an introduction. Ox 1988, Blackwell. xi-212 p. £27.50; pa. £8 [JTS 40,362].

k108 **Maurer** Wilhelm, Historical commentary on the Augsburg Confession [1978]. ^T*Anderson* H. George. Ph 1986, Fortress. xi-434 p. – ^RChH 57 (1988) 229s (G. G. *Krodel*).

k109 *Muller* Frank, Une visualisation de la leçon luthérienne; le 'Bom des glaubens' [arbre de la foi, gravure mais 90% remplie de textes] d'Heinrich VOGTHERR l'Ancien: RHPR 68 (1988) 181-193.

k110 **Oberman** Heiko A., The dawn of the Reformation 1986 ↠ 3,g542: ^REvQ 60 (1988) 88s (A. S. *Wood*); TLond 91 (1988) 229-232 (G. *Leff*).

k111 **Oberman** Heiko A., Die Reformation, von Wittenberg nach Genf [13 essays, 3 same as in Dawn 1986] 1986 ↠ 3,268: ^RGregorianum 69 (1988) 379s (J. E. *Vercruysse*).

k112 ^E**Peter** R., *Roussel* B., Le livre et la Réforme. Bordeaux 1987, Soc. Bibliophiles Guyenne. 278 p.; 20 facsim. F 190 [RHE 83,418*].

k113 *Peyronel Rambaldi* Susanna, Itinerari italiani di un libretto riformato 'Sommario della Sacra Scrittura' [< olandese 1523]: Bollettino Soc. Studi Valdesi 160 (1987) 3-18.

k114 **Raitt** Jill, Christian spirituality ... Reformation 1987 ↠ 3,862.g545: ^RNewTR 1,2 (1988) 101-3 (Elizabeth *Dreyer*); Speculum 63 (1988) 988s (A. E. *McGrath*); SpTod 40 (1988) 81-83 (T. D. *McGonigle*); TS 49 (1988) 535 (D. F. *Duclow*).

k115 **Raitt** Jill, Shapers of religious traditions in Germany, Switzerland, and Poland 1560-1600: 1981 ↠ 63,e794: ^RZwingliana 16 (1985) 67s (P. *Fraenkel*).

k116 **Rausch** David A., *Voss* Carl H., Protestantism — its modern meaning. Ph 1987, Fortress. x-211 p. $13 pa. [TDig 35,284].

k117 **Rodríguez** Pedro, *Lanzetti* Raúl, El manuscrito original del Catecismo Romano... del concilio de Trento. Pamplona 1985, Univ. Navarra. 173 p. – ^RTPhil 63 (1988) 276s (M. *Sievernich*).

k118 *a) Roussel* Bernard, De Strasbourg à Bâle et Zurich; une 'école rhénane' d'exégèse (ca 1525 - ca 1540) – *b) Rott* Jean, Les relations extérieures de la faculté de théologie de Strasbourg de 1570 à 1658 d'après les correspondances passives de Jean PAPPUS et de Jean SCHMIDT: RHPR 68 (1988) 19-39 / 41-53.

k119 **Russell** Paul A., Lay theology in the Reformation; popular pamphleteers in southwest Germany 1521-1525: 1986 ↠ 2,d603; 3,g548: ^RJTS 39 (1988) 298s (P. N. *Brooks*).

k120 *Saxer* Ernst, Die Verurteilung der Täufer in den reformierten Bekenntnisschriften: Zwingliana 17 (1988) 121-137.

k121 **Scribner** R.W., The German Reformation. L 1986, Macmillan. x-78 p. £4 pa. – ᴿTLond 91 (1988) 149-152 (Ruth *Chavasse*, mostly on DICKENS-TOMKIN).

k122 *Sladeczek* Franz-J., 'Die götze in miner herren chilchen sind gerumpt!'; von der Bilderfrage der Berner Reformation und ihren Folgen für das Münster und sein Hauptportal: TZBas 44 (1988) 289-311; 10 fig.

k123 *Smolinsky* Heribert, The Bible and its exegesis in the controversies about reform and reformation: ➤ 505, Creative 1985/8, 115-130.

k124 **Spitz** L., The Protestant Reformation 1985 ➤ 1,f832: 2,d607: ᴿHorizons 15 (1988) 162s (G. *Macy*).

k125 **Spitz** Lewis W., The Renaissance and Reformation movements²ʳᵉᵛ [¹1971]. St. Louis 1987, Concordia, xiv-614 p. – ᴿSixtC 19 (1988) 705s (J.W. *Baker*).

k126 **Stauffer** R., Interprètes de la Bible 1980 ➤ 61,y36; 62,m239...: ᴿZwingliana 17 (1988) 80-82 (E. *Saxer*).

k127 *Vázquez Janeiro* Isaac, Cultura y censura en el siglo XVI; a propósito de la edición de 'Index des livres interdits' [SHERBROOKE]: Antonianum 63 (1988) 26-73.

k128 **Vilanova** E., Historia de la teología cristiana [I ➤ h704] II. Pre-reforma, reformas, contrareforma: Col. S. Paciá 36, 1986 ➤ 3,g553: ᴿEstFranc 89 (1988) 675-8 (A. *Bosch i Veciana*).

k129 *Wenz* Gunther, Sola scriptura? Erwägungen zum reformatorischen Schriftprinzip: ➤ 114, ᶠPANNENBERG W., Vernunft 1988, 540-567.

Y4.4 Periti aetatis reformatoriae.

k130 AGRICOLA: **Kjeldegaard-Pedersen** Steffen, Gesetz, Evangelium und Busse; theologiegeschichtliche Studien zum Verhältnis zwischen dem jungen Johann Agricola (Eisleben) und Martin LUTHER: AcDan 16, 1983 ➤ 64,e248 ... 3,g558: ᴿTLZ 112 (1987) 823-5 (B. *Hägglund*).

k131 BELLARMINUS: **Lujambio Arias** Leonardo, Origen y destinación de la copiosa declaración de la doctrina cristiana de Roberto Belarmino: diss. Pont. Univ. Salesiana, ᴰ*Braido* P. R 1987. – Salesianum 50 (1988) 473.

k132 BEZA: ᴱ**Dufour** Alain, *al.*, Correspondance de Bèze 10, 1980; 11, 1983 [➤ 65,d712]. Genève 1986, Droz. – ᴿZwingliana 17 (1988) 451-5 (F. *Büsser*, 12); 478s (10s).

k133 BOSCH: *Baaren* Th. P. van, Jeroem Bosch [Hieronymus c.1500], katholiek of ketter?: NedTTs 42 (1988) 42-59; Eng. 67.

k134 BUCER: *Kroon* Marijn de, Martin Bucer and the problem of tolerance: SixtC 19 (1988) 157-168.

k135 BUGENHAGEN: *Beintker* Horst J.E., Fortsetzung und Festigung der Reformation; Neuordnung in evangelischen Kirchen unter Bugenhagens Anleitung mittels seiner Braunschweiger Kirchenordnung von 1528: TZBas 44 (1988) 1-31.

k136 BULLINGER: *Büsser* Fritz, Bullinger et CALVIN: ÉTRel 63 (1988) 31-52.

k137 **Bullinger** Heinrich, Exegetische Schriften aus den Jahren 1525-26, ᴱ*Berg* Hans G. vom, *Hausammann* Susi: Werke 3/1. Z 1983, Theol.-V. 287 p. Fs 80 – ᴿZwingliana 17 (1988) 348s (W. E. *Meyer*).

k138 *Döring* Detlef, Eine bisher unbekannte Handschrift mit dem Text von Heinrich Bullingers 'Ratio Studiorum' in der Leipziger Universitätsbibliothek: Zwingliana 17 (1988) 27-32.

k139 CAJETANUS; *Lohse* Bernhard, Cajetan und LUTHER; zur Begegnung von Thomismus und Reformation [< KerDo 32 (1986) 150-169]: → 224, Evangelium 1988, 44-63.

k140 CALVIN: **Bell** M. Charles, Calvin snd Scottish theology; the doctrine of assurance [D1982] 1985 → 3,g568: RCalvinT 23 (1988) 66s (R. C. *Gamble*: better title, 'Calvin against the Scottish Calvinists'); JEH 39 (1988) 308s (B. R. *White*).

k141 **Bouwsma** William J., John Calvin; a sixteenth century portrait. NY 1988, Oxford-UP.   viii-310 p. $23. – RSixtC 19 (1988) 485s (W. F. *Graham*); TTod 45 (1988s) 335s (Jane D. *Douglass*).

k142 EChaunu Pierre, L'aventure de la Réforme; le monde de Jean Calvin [*Ganoczy* A. sur Calvin...] 1986 → 2,283: RRThom 88 (1988) 161 (B. *Montagnes*).

k143 EFurcha E. J., In honour of John Calvin. 3d Symposium Montréal 1986. Montréal 1987, McGill Univ. x-386 p. – RRefTR 47 (1988) 21 (R. *Swanton*); SR 17 (1988) 492-4 (J. H. *Bratt*).

k144 *Gamble* Richard C., Calvin as theologian and exegete; is there anything new?: CalvinT 23 (1988) 178-194.

k145 **Ganoczy** Alexandre, The young Calvin, TFoxgrover David, *Provo* Wade, 1987 → 3,g571: RTS 49 (1988) 747s (D. *McKim*).

k145* **Ganoczy** A, *Scheld* S., Die Hermeneutik Calvins 1983 → 65,d719... 2,d626: RZwingliana 17 (1988) 72-76 (E. *Saxer*).

k146 *McNeill* John T., Calvin as an ecumenical churchman: ChH 57-Sup (1988) 43-55.

k147 **Perrot** A., Le visage humain de Jean Calvin [...'uno degli uomini più diffamati della storia' p. 9]. Genève 1986, Labor et Fides. 248 p. Fs 28. – RProtestantesimo 43 (1988) 123 (V. *Subilia*).

k148 **Selinger** Suzanne, Calvin against himself... 1984 → 2,d630; 3,g577: RNedTTs 42 (1988) 83-85 (W. *Nijenhuis*).

k149 **Szabó** L., ⓂAz igehirtedő Kalvin (preacher of the Word). Budapest 1986, Református Egyház. 188 p. – RProtestantesimo 43 (1988) 226s (A. B. *Dezsö*).

k150 *Szücs* Ferenc, ⓂChances and limits of Christian freedom in Calvin: Theologiai Szemle 31 (1988) 85-90.

k151 **Torrance** Thomas F., The hermeneutics of John Calvin: ScotJT Mg. E 1988, Scottish Academic. 198 p. £17.50. 0-7073-0553-5 [ScotJT 41,484].

k152 *Vercruysse* Jos E., 'Nous ne sommes point nostres...?' La spiritualité de Jean Calvin: Gregorianum 69 (1988) 279-296; Eng. 297.

k153 **Wallace** Ronald S., Calvin, Geneva and the Reformation; a study of Calvin as social reformer, churchman, pastor and theologian. GR 1988, Baker. 310 p. – RTrinJ 9 (1988) 221-3 (M. J. *Klauber*).

k154 DUNGERSHEIM: EFreudenberger Theobald, Hieronymus Dungersheim [1465-1540], Schriften gegen LUTHER: CCath 39, 1987 → 3,g587: TPQ 136 (1988) 297s (R. *Bäumer*).

k155 ERASMUS: **Delcourt** Marie, Érasme [5 art. 1936] Bru 1986, Labor. 162 p. – RBibHumRen 50 (1988) 221s (Erika *Rummel*).

k156 **DeMolen** Richard L., The spirituality of Erasmus of Rotterdam [eight articles already published]. Nieuwkoop 1987, De Graaf. xviii-224 p. – RBibHumRen 50 (1988) 477s (Erika *Rummel*); RHE 83 (1988) 711s (L.-E. *Halkin*).

k157 **Krüger** Friedhelm, Humanistische Evangelienauslegung... Erasmus: Bei- HistT 68, 1986 → 3,g591: RTR 84 (1988) 475-7 (H. *Feld*).

k158 *Lohse* Bernhard,   Marginalien zum Streit zwischen Erasmus und LUTHER [< Luther 46 (1975) 5-24]: ➤ 224, Evangelium 1988, 118-137.
k159 *Lukens* Michael B., WITZEL and Erasmian irenicism in the 1530s: JTS 39 (1988) 134-6.
 Margolin Jean-Claude,   Érasme, le prix des mots et de l'homme [12 reprints 1964-83] 1986 ➤ 229.
k160 **Rummel** Erika,   Erasmus as translator of the classics: Erasmus Studies 7. Toronto 1985, Univ.   191 p. $30.   0-8020-5653-9. – ᴿClasR 102 (1988) 134-6 (M. *Lowry*).
k161 **Rummel** Erika (➤ 4389),   Erasmus' annotations on the NT; from philologist to theologian 1986 ➤ 2,d650:   ᴿJEH 39 (1988) 486 (B. *Bradshaw*).
k162 *Rummel* Erika,   An open letter to boorish critics; Erasmus' Capita argumentorum contra morosos quosdam indoctos: JTS 39 (1988) 438-459.
k163 **Seidel Menchi** Silvana,   Erasmo in Italia 1520-1580.   T 1987, Bollati Boringhieri.   530 p.   Lit. 50.000. – ᴿProtestantesimo 43 (1988) 192-5 (S. *Caponetto*: non esattamente nello stile di BATAILLON Marcel, Érasme et l'Espagne 1937).
k164 *a*) *Sider* Robert D.,   'In terms quite plain and clear?'; the exposition of grace in the New Testament paraphrases of Erasmus; – *b*) *Bateman* John J.,   From soul to soul; persuasion in Erasmus' Paraphrases on the New Testament: Erasmus in English Newsletter 15 (Toronto 1987s) 16-25 / 7-16.
k165 *Stupperich* Robert,   Erasmus von Rotterdam in seiner persönlichen und wissenschaftlichen Entwicklung: ZKG 99 (1988) 47-62.
k166 FLACIUS: ᴱ**Keller** Rudolf,   Der Schlüssel zur Schrift; die Lehre vom Wort Gottes [von] M. Flacius Illyricus: ArbGTLuth 5, ᴰ1984 ➤ 2,d653: ᴿSixtC 19 (1988) 502 (F. *Posset*).
k167 GIUSTINIANI: *Massa* Eugenio,   Paolo Giustiniani [c. 1513] e Gasparo CONTARINI [c. 1521]; la vocazione al bivio del neoplatonismo e della teologia biblica: Benedictina 35 (1988) 429-474.
k168 HOFFMAN: **Deppermann** Klaus,   Melchior Hoffman; social unrest and apocalyptic visions in the age of the reformation [1979], ᵀ*Wren* Malcolm, ᴱ*Drewery* Benjamin, 1987 ➤ 3,g600:   ᴱExpTim 99 (1987s) 346s (W.M.S. *West*); RefTR 47 (1988) 20 (S. D. *Gill*).
k169 HOOGSTRATEN: *Ickert* Scott S.,   Catholic controversialist theology and Sola Scriptura; the case of Jacob van Hoogstraten [o.p., c. 1460-1527]: CathHR 74 (1988) 13-33.
k170 HUSS: **Bartoš** František M.,   The Hussite revolution 1424-1437, ᵀ*Klassen* John M.: East European Mg. 203.   NY 1986, Columbia Univ.   xx-204 p. $25.   0-88033-097-X. – ᴿJEH 39 (1988) 147s (Anne *Hudson*).
k171 LA CEPPÈDE: **Quenot** Yvette,   Jean de la Ceppède, poète de l'Église tridentine [diss. Paris XII, 1984]; Les lectures de La Ceppède [... L'imitation de la pénitence de David]: TravHumRen 210.   Genève 1986, Droz.   265 p. – ᴿRHE 83 (1988) 852 (M. *Veissière*: p. 169-173, La Ceppède et la Bible, trop bref).
k172 LATIMER: **Stuart** Carla H.,   Latimer, apostle to the English.   GR 1986, Zondervan.   348 p. – ᴿGraceTJ 9 (1988) 298 (J. E. *McGoldrick*: not for scholars).
k173 LEFÈVRE: *Bedouelle* Guy,   Lefèvre d'Étaples et ses disciples: Bulletin de la Société de l'Histoire du Protestantisme Français 134,4 (1988) 669-672 [this issue contains a bibliography of Richard STAUFFER (1921-1984,

historien de la Réforme) and several articles by and about him: ZIT 89, 106]: *Lienhard* M. p. 673-681.

k174 **Hughes** Philip E. Lefèvre [d'É] 1984 → 1,f857... 3,g603: ᴿHeythJ 29 (1988) 368s (A. *Hamilton*); JEH 39 (1988) 148s (P. *Burke*); RTLv 19 (1988) 95-97 (J.-F. *Gilmont*).

k175 LUIS DE GRANADA: *García Trapiello* J., Un substrato ideológico en Fray Luis de Granada [† 1588]: los himnos de la Biblia: Angelicum 65 (1988) 504-520 [– 599, *al.*, sobre LG].

k176 MALDONADO: **Schmitt** Paul, La Réforme catholique... Maldonat 1985 → 1,f589... 3,g604: ᴿHeyth J 29 (1988) 527s (Mary P. *Shorter*).

k177 MELANCHTHON: *Bellucci* Dino, Melanchthon et la défense de l'astrologie: BibHumRen 50 (1988) 587-622.

k178 ᴱScheible Heinz, Melanchthons Briefwechsel, 5. (mit *Thüringer* Walter) Registen 4530-5707 (1547-9). Stu-Bad Cannstatt 1987, Frommann-Holzboog. 551 p. 3-7728-1148-5. – ᴿÉTRel 63 (1988) 470-2 (A. *Grenier*).

k179 *Collange* J.-F., Philippe Mélanchthon et Jean STURM, humanistes et pédagogues de la Réforme: RHPR 68 (1988) 5-18.

k180 SCHATZGEYER: ᴱSchäfer Philip, Kaspar Schatzgeyer, Von der waren Christlichen und Evangelischen freyheit; De vera libertate evangelica [München 1527]: CCath 40. Münster 1987, Aschendorff. xxviii-126 p.; 2 pl. – ᴿMiscFranc 88 (1988) 239-241 (T. *Mrkonjic*).

k181 SCHWENCKFELD: **McLaughlin** R. Emmet, Caspar Schwenckfeld, reluctant radical; his life to 1540 [< diss. Yale 1980]: Hist. Publ.Misc. 134, 1986 → 2,d664; 3,g611: ᴿHorizons 15 (1988) 163s (J. H. *Yoder*); RelStR 14 (1988) 76 (N. *Minnich*).

k182 STAUPITZ: ᴱWetzel Richard, Johann von Staupitz, Lateinische Schrifen 1. Tübinger Predigten: Sämtliche Schriften 1/Spätmittelalter und Reformation 13. B 1987, de Gruyter. xiii-367 p. DM 258. – ᴿJTS 39 (1988) 629-631 (A. *McGrath*: his Libellus of 1517 appeared in this series in 1979).

k183 TYNDALE: **Smeeton** Donald D., Lollard themes in the Reformation theology of William Tyndale 1986 → 3,g613. ᴿRefTR 46 (1987) 56s (D. B. *Knox*).

URSINUS Z., 1983 conference ᴱVisser D. 1986 → 663.

k184 VADIAN: *Rüsch* Ernst G., [Joachim] Vadians reformatorisches Bekenntnis: Zwingliana 17 (1988) 33-47.

k185 VERMIGLI: **Santini** Luigi, Umanesimo e teologia biblica nel primo catechismo della Riforma in Italia [P. M. Vermigli 1544]: Protestantesimo 43 (1988) 2-18.

k186 VILLANOVA: *Llín Chafer* Arturo, La Biblia en un testigo del Siglo de Oro español [S. Tomás de Villanueva: *a*) AnVal 14,27 (1988) 77-97; – *b*) RET 48 (1988) 193-211 [in indice 'Antonio'].

k187 WYCLIF: **Kenny** Anthony, Wyclif: Past Masters, 1985 → 1,f870... 3,g618: ᴿHeythJ 29 (1988) 523s (N. *Tanner*).

k188 *Nolcken* Christina von, Notes on Lollard citation of John Wyclif's writings [< Kalamazoo 1984 Medieval Studies congress]: JTS 39 (1988) 411-437.

k188* **Hudson** Anne, The premature Reformation; Wycliffite texts and Lollard history. Ox 1988, Clarendon. xii-556 p. £48 [JTS 40, 665, G. R. *Evans*].

k189 ZWINGLI: *Christ* Christine, Das Schriftverständnis von Zwingli und ERASMUS im Jahre 1522: Zwingliana 16 (1985) 111-125.

k190 ᵀCourvoisier Jacques, Huldrych Zwingli, Le Berger [Der Hirt 1523]: TextesDD 9. P 1984 Beauchesme. 91 p. F 60. – ᴿÉglT 17 (1986) 245 (A. *Peelman*).

k191 *Ferrario* Fulvio, La teologia del sinodo di Berna; note in margine: Protestantesimo 43 (1988) 93-109.

k192 ᵀᴱFurcha E, *Pepkin* H., H. Zwingli, selected writings I. Pittsburgh 1984, Pickwick. $20. 0-915138-58-1. – ᴿZwingliana 17 (1988) 435s (U. *Gäbler*).

k193 **Gäbler** U., H. Zwingli, Einführung 1983 ➤ 2,d670: ᴿZwingliana 17 (1988) 341s (H. *Meyer*).

k194 **Gäbler** Ulrich, Huldrych Zwingli; his life and work [1983] 1986 ➤ 2,d671; 3,g620: ᴿJAAR 56 (1988) 157s (D.G. *Danner*); JEH 39 (1988) 310 (A. *Pettegree*); RefTR 46 (1987) 51s (S. *Gill*).

k195 *Pipkin* H. Wayne, A Baptist perspective on Zwingli: Zwingliana 16 (1985) 239-246.

k196 **Stephens** W.P., The theology of Huldrych Zwingli 1986 ➤ 2,d674; 3,g623: ᴿNedTTs 42 (1988) 350s (U. *Gäbler*); WestTJ 50 (1988) 362-4 (R.C. *Gamble*).

k197 *Stephens* W. Peter, Huldrych Zwingli, the Swiss Reformer: ScotJT 41 (1988) 27-47.

k198 **Ziegler** Albert, Zwingli, katholisch gesehen, ökumenisch befragt. Z 1984, 'NZN'. 96 p. – ᴿZwingliana 17 (1988) 178-180 (W.J. *Hollenweger*).

ʏ4.5 *Exegesis post-reformatoria* – **Historical criticism to 1800.**

k199 *Albertan-Coppola* Sylviane, L'apologétique catholique française à l'age des lumières: RHR 205 (1988) 151-189; Eng. 151.

k200 **Andrés Martínez** Melquiades, Historia de la Teología II. Desde fines del siglo XVI hasta la actualidad. M 1987, Fund. Universitaria Esp. 986 p. – ᴿETL 64 (1988) 478 (J.E. *Vercruysse*).

k201 *Barnard* Leslie W., The use of the patristic tradition in the late seventeenth and early eighteenth centuries: ➤ 60, ꜰHANSON R., Scripture 1988, 174-203.

k202 ᴱBelaval Y., *Bourel* D., Le siècle des lumières et la Bible: Bible de tous les temps 7, 1986 ➤ 2,237; 3,g624: ᴿCrNSt 9 (1988) 640-4 (B. *Bianco*); IndTSt 25 (1988) 194-7 (L. *Legrand*) [291 on the Augustine volume]; MélSR 45 (1988) 35s (*Tran Van Toàn*); TPhil 63 (1988) 280s (H.J. *Sieben*); TR 84 (1988) 477-9 (P. *Schäfer*).

k203 *Chedozeau* Bernard, Aux sources éloignées de la révolution; les laïcistes doctrinaux et la lecture de la Bible (XVIIIᵉ siècle): RSPT 72 (1988) 517-539; Eng. 540.

k204 ᴱDal Corso M., *Borghi Cedrini* L., Vertuz e altri scritti (manoscritto GE 206) [valdese Univ. Ginevra]. T 1984, Claudiana. lxxiii-174 p. Lit. 23.000. – ᴿProtestantesimo 43 (1988) 51s (G. *Gonnet*).

k204* **Dippel** Stewart A., A study of religious thought at Oxford and Cambridge, 1590-1640. Lanham MD 1987, UPA. xiii-142 p. $19.25; pa. $9.75 [JTS 40,361]. – ᴿSixtC 19 (1988) 270s (C.M.N. *Eire*).

k205 **Funkenstein** Amos, Theology and the scientific imagination. Princeton 1986, Univ. 435 p. $47.50. 0-691-08408-4. – ᴿJAAR 56 (1988) 741-750 (Sandra R. *Luft*: 'secular theology' in the modern age).

k206 *Howe* Daniel W., The Cambridge Platonists of Old England [c. 1650] and the Cambridge Platonists of New England [Unitarians c. 1850]: ChH 57 (1988) 470-485.

k206* **Jacoby** Michael, Bibeltradition und Bibelsprache zwischen Mittelalter und 20. Jahrhundert im nordgermanischen Raum; der Einfluss der Scholastik aus Paris und der Lutherbibel 2. Fra 1988, Lang. 333 p.; 9 facsim. Fs 59 [JTS 40,743].

k207 *Lambe* Patrick J., Critics and skeptics in the seventeenth-century republic of letters [intramural Protestant histories of biblical criticism make Reformation and Enlightenment its two mainsprings]: HarvTR 81 (1988) 271-296.

k208 **Laplanche** François, L'Écriture, le sacré et l'histoire; érudits et politiques protestants devant la Bible en France du XVIIᵉ siècle 1986 → 2,d684; 90-302-1012-5: ᴿÉTRel 63 (1988) 131s (H. *Bost*).

k209 *Miele* M., Bibbia, clero e popolo nei concili provinciali posttridentini del Mezzogiorno (1565-1729): AnnHistConc 18 (1986) 144-162.

k210 **Muller** Richard A., Post-Reformation Reformed dogmatics, I. Prolegomena to theology. GR 1987, Baker. 365 p. $13 pa. – ᴿTrinJ 9,1 (1988) 115-8 (M. I. *Klauber*: first of three volumes updating HEPPE H., Reformed Dogmatics).

k211 **Podskalsky** Gerhard, Griechische Theologie in der Zeit der Türkenherrschaft 1988 → 3,g633: ᴿIrénikon 61 (1988) 304s (E. L.).

k212 **Sher** Richard B., Church and University in the Scottish Enlightenment; the moderate literati of Edinburgh. E 1985, Univ. xix-390 p. £ 30. 0-85224-504-1. – ᴿScotBEv 6 (1988) 61-63 (D. E. *Bebbington*).

---

k212* BACH: ᴱ**Petzoldt** Martin, Bach als Ausleger der Bibel 1985 → 1,304; 2,d695: ᴿTZBas 44 (1988) 274 (K. *Hammer*).

k213 BENGEL: **Hermann** Karl, Johann A. Bengel, der Klosterpräzeptor von Denkendorf; sein Werden und Werken nach handschriftlichen Quellen dargestellt. Stu 1987 = 1937, Calwer. 488 p.; 30 fig.; 12 pl. DM 48. – ᴿBiKi 43 (1988) 90 (P.-G. *Müller*).

k214 COCCEJUS: **Asselt** W. J. van, 'Amicitia Dei'; een onderzoek naar de structuur van de theologie van Johannes Coccejus (1603-1669): diss. Utrecht 1988, ᴰ*Graafland* C. – TsTNijm 28 (1988) 297s.

k215 DANNHAUER: *Wallmann* Johannes, Strassburger lutherische Orthodoxie im 17. Jahrhundert; Johann Conrad Dannhauer, Versuch einer Annäherung [... premier théologien systématique proprement dit du luthéranisme]: RHPR 68 (1988) 56-71.

k216 EDWARDS: **Jenson** Robert W., America's theologian; a recommendation of Jonathan Edwards. NY 1988, Oxford-UP. xii-224 p. [TS 50, 616, K. P. *Minkema*].

k217 *Weddle* David L., The melancholy saint; Jonathan Edwards's interpretation of David BRAINERD as a model of evangelical spirituality: HarvTR 81 (1988) 297-318.

k218 ERSKINE: *Sell* Alan P. F., The message of the Erskines [Ebenezer & Ralph, secession Presbyterians before 1782]: EvQ 60 (1988) 299-316.

k219 FOUCAULT: *Clark* Elizabeth A., Foucault, the Fathers, and sex: JAAR 56 (1988) 619-641.

k220 GERUNDIO: *Precedo Lafuente* Manuel J., Citas bíblicas en los sermones de Fray Gerundio de Campazas [1703-1781]: Compostellanum 33 (1988) 247-279.

k221 GROTIUS: *Reventlow* Henning, Humanistic exegesis; the famous Hugo Grotius [commentary on the whole Bible begun 1619]: → 505, Creative 1985/8, 175-191.

k222 HAMANN: **Büchsel** Elfriede, Biblisches Zeugnis und Sprachgestalt bei J. G. Hamann; Untersuchungen zur Struktur von Hamanns Schriften auf dem Hintergrund der Bibel [Diss. Göttingen 1953]. Giessen 1988, Brunnen. x-284 p. 3-7655-9336-2.

k223 HERDER: *Timm* Hermann, Geerdete Vernunft; Johan G. Herder als Vordenker der Lebenswelttheologie in Deutschland: → 114, [F]PANNENBERG W., Vernunft 1988, 357-376.

k224 *Whitton* Brian J., Herder's critique of the Enlightenment; cultural community versus cosmopolitan rationalism: HistTheory 27 (1988) 146-168.

k225 JANSENIUS: **Ceyssens** L., *Tans* J.A.G., Autour de l'Unigenitus; recherches sur la genèse de la Constitution [14 depuis 1981 dont 3 par les deux]: BiblETL 76, 1987 → 3,g648: [R]ETL 64 (1988) 478-480 (B. *Neveu*); JEH 39 (1908) 476-8 (J. *McManners*); NRT 110 (1988) 451 (N. *Plumat*); RHE 83 (1988) 393-403 (M. G. *Spiertz*); RHPR 68 (1988) 372s (M. *Chevallier*); RThom 88 (1988) 672 (B. *Montagnes*); TsTNijm 28 (1988) 187 (etiam M. G. *Spiertz*).

k226 *Ceyssens* Lucien, Autour de la bulle Unigenitus; *a*) le Cardinal de Bissy (1657-1737): Antonianum 63 (1988) 74-115; Eng. 74; – *b*) le Cardinal d'Alsace (1679-1759): RBgPg 66 (1988) 792-838.

k227 *Gres-Gayer* Jacques M., The Unigenitus of Clement XI [1713 against 101 'Jansenist' propositions]; a fresh look at the issues: TS 49 (1988) 259-282.

k227* [E]**Stella** P., Atti e decreti del Concilio Diocesano di Pistoia dell'anno 1786; I. Ristampa dell'edizione Bracali; II. Introduzione storica e documenti inediti: Biblioteca storica toscana 2/9. F 1986, Olschki. xxiv-255 + 143 + 31 p.; vi-697 p. Lit. 125.000. [NRT 111, 268-270, N. *Plumat*].

k228 JUNG-STILLING: *Schwinge* Gerhard, Jung-Stilling [Johann H., 1777-1817] und seine Beziehungen zur Basler Christentumsgesellschaft: TZBas 44 (1988) 32-53; p. 192, correction of footnote-reference to other footnotes.

k228* KANT: **Loades** A. L., Kant and Job's comforters. Newcastle 1985, Avero. vi-174 p. [JTS 40, 310 D. M. *MacKinnon* nowhere mentions anything about Job].

k229 LA PEYRÈRE: **Popkin** Richard H., Isaac La Peyrère (1596-1676); his life, work, and influence: Studies in Intellectual History. Leiden 1987, Brill. 241 p. *f* 127. 90-04-08157-7. – [R]ÉTRel 63 (1988) 435-440 (H. *Bost*).

k230 LESSING: **Michalson** Gordon E., Lessing's 'Ugly Ditch'... 1985 → 1,f906; 2,d717: [R]HeythJ 29 (1988) 474 (G. *Vallée*).

k231 *Van Den Hengel* John, Reason and revelation in Lessing's Enlightenment: ÉglT 17 (1986) 171-194.

k232 MEIJER: *Bonola* Gianfranco, La proposta ermeneutica radicale di Lodewijk Meijer [Philosophia S. Scripture interpres 1666]: → 472, AnStoEseg 5 (1988) 261-296.

k233 MEYFART: **Trunz** E., Johann Matthäus Meyfart, Theologe und Schriftsteller in der Zeit des dreissigjährigen Krieges. Mü 1987, Beck. 461 p.; 30 fig. DM 98 [Gymnasium 96, 266-8, U. *Müller*].

k234 MÜHLENBERG: [E]**Aland** Kurt, Die Korrespondenz Heinrich Melchior Mühlenbergs [1711-87]; aus der Anfangszeit des deutschen Luthertums in Nordamerika. B 1986s, de Gruyter. I. (1740-52) xx-573 p.; II. (1753-62) xxxiv-623 p. DM 295 + 328. – [R]TLZ 113 (1988) 126-8 (H. *Winde*).

k235 Néercassel: *Chedozeau* Bernard, Port-Royal et la Bible; le refus de la Regula IV de l'Index romain chez Jean de Néercassel et Guillaume Le Roy: RSPT 72 (1988) 427-434; Eng. 435.

k236 Pastor: *Corsani* Bruno, Uso e interpretazione della Bibbia nel Manuel du vray chrétien de Daniel Pastor ... (Genève 1652): Bollettino Soc. Studi Valdesi 161 (1987) 19-25; Eng. 69s.

k237 Reimarus: E**Stemmer** P., Reimarus H. S., Vindicatio doctorum VT in Novo allegatorum, Text der Pars I und Conspectus der Pars II, 1983 → 64,e384; DM 56: RTLZ 113 (1988) 199-204 (G. *Mühlpfordt*).

k238 *a) Reventlow* Henning, 'Sullo scopo di Gesù e dei suoi discepoli'; il contributo di H. S. Reimarus all'indagine del NT, T*Coppellotti* F.; – *b) Gericke* Wolfgang, H. S. Reimarus e la letteratura underground del suo tempo, T*Coppellotti*; – *c) Reventlow*, La critica biblica dell'illuminismo e il suo significato attuale, T*Russo* E.; – *d) Sparn* Walter, Critica biblica come progresso religioso; l'antagonismo fra storia e dogma nell'illuminismo teologico, T*Russo*: → 495*, Gesù storico 1985/8, 97-110/111-123/125-139/141-157.

k239 Simon: **Le Brun** J., *Woodbridge* J. D., Simon R., Additions à Brerewood 1983 → 64,e385 ... d,723: RRBgPg 66 (1988) 914s (J.-P. *Massaut*).

k239* *Schwarzbach* Bertram E., La fortune de Richard Simon au XVIIIe siècle [... Renan E., Revue des deux mondes 1965]: RÉJ 146 (1987) 225-239.

k240 Spinoza: *Secretan* Philibert, Zum Fall Spinoza; Emanzipation der Vernunft und politischer Gehorsam: FreibZ 35 (1988) 107-123.

k241 Wesley: *Carile* Sergio, [Wesley J.] Il metodismo, espressione teologicamente significativa: Protestantesimo 43 (1988) 130-6.

k242 *Giffin* John, Scriptural standards in religion; John Wesley's letters to William Law and James Hervey: StudiaBT 16 (1988) 143-168.

k243 Warburton William, [Divine Legation of Moses demonstrated (per la prima volta in italiano) 4/4:] Scrittura e civiltà; saggio sui geroglifici egiziani, TE*Verri* Antonio: Agorà 12. Ravenna 1986, Longo. 174 p. – RSalesianum 50 (1988) 637 (B. *Amata*).

Y5 *Saeculum XIX – Exegesis –* **19th Century.**

k244 *Dolan* Jay P., The immigrants and their gods; a new perspective in American religious history: ChH 57 (1988) 61-72.

k245 **Fogarty** Gerald P., American Catholic biblical scholarship; a history from the early republic to Vatican II. SF c.1988, Harper & R. 400 p. $33 [CouStR 18,28 adv.].

k246 **Gundert** W., Geschichte der deutschen Bibelgesellschaften im 19. Jahrhundert: Texte und Arbeiten zur Bibel 3, 1987 → 3,g686; RTR 84 (1988) 213s (P.-G. *Müller*).

k248 **Hughes** Richard T., *Allen* C. Leonard, Illusions of innocence; Protestant primitivism in America. Ch 1988, Univ. xviii-296 p. $30 [TS 50, 800, C. *Welch*].

k249 *Kulisz* Józef, ❷ Indywidualna interpretacja Ewangelii jako źródło dziewiętnastowiecznego [19th cent.] racjonalismu: ColcT 58,3 (1988) 63-76; franç. 76s.

k250 *Landau* Jacob M., The United States and the Holy Land in the nineteenth century: → 499, Holy Land 1986/8, 273-280.

k251 *Larsson* Edvin, [Norw.] The theology of the 19th century and its effect upon modern New Testament research: TsTKi 59 (1988) 1-14; Eng. 14.

k252 ᴱ**Lüdemann** G., *Schröder* M., Die religionsgeschichtliche Schule in Göttingen, eine Dokumentation 1987 → 3,g691: ᴿNRT 110 (1988) 112s (A. *Toubeau*).

k253 *Madden* Edward H., Holiness [Movement c. 1800] Thought and the moral image of man: AsbTJ 43,2 (1988) 45-61.

k254 **Marty** Martin E., Modern American religion I, 1983-1919: 1986 → 2,d739; 3,g693: ᴿChH 57 (1988) 395-7 (W. R. *Hutchison*); CCurr 23 (1988s) 115s (D. *Downey*); ÉglT 18 (1987) 409-416 (D. M. *Schlitt*); Horizons 15 (1988) 167 (R. *Van Allen*); Interpretation 42 (1988) 416. 418.420 (D. *Jodock*: 'the irony of it all' = 'the power of unintended consequences' but also 'tendency to fall into adversaries' categories'); JRel 68 (1988) 116-8 (P. A. *Carter*); TLond 91 (1988) 434-6 (D. *Martin*); TorJT 4 (1988) 152s (R. T. *Handy*); TS 49 (1988) 174s (J. E. *Wilson*); TTod 45 (1988s) 125-7 (J. M. *Mulder*).

k254* **Mead** S. E., Das Christentum in Nordamerika; Glaube und Religionsfreiheit in vier Jahrhunderten [1963], ᵀᴱ*Henning* J., *Penze(l)* K. Gö 1987, Vandenhoeck & R. 275 p. [NRT 111, 297, N. *Plumat*: 'Kl Penze' ou 'K. Penzel'?].

k255 **Reardon** Bernard M. G., Religion in the age of romanticism 1985 → 1,f929 ... 3,g696: ᴿJAAR 56 (1988) 174-6 (T. H. *Foreman*).

k256 **Rogerson** J. P., OT criticism ... 19th c., 1984 → 65,d784 ... 3,g700: ᴿHeythJ 29 (1988) 343s (R. N. *Whybray*).

k257 **Savart** Claude, Les catholiques en France au XIXᵉ siècle; le témoignage du livre religieux: THist 73, 1985 → 3,g701: ᴿRHR 205 (1988) 326-328 (F. *Laplanche*); Salesianum 50 (1988) 409 (P. *Braido*).

k258 ᴱ**Smart** Ninian, *al.*, Nineteenth century religious thought in the West I-III, 1985 → 1,399.f934; 3,g702: ᴿHeythJ 29 (1988) 530-3 (A. E. *McGrath*); ModT 4 (1987s) 404s (P. *Avis*, 1); ScotJT 41 (1988) 130-5 (R. H. *Roberts*).

k259 **Sykes** Stephen, The identity of Christianity ... Schleiermacher to Barth 1984 → 65,d786 ... 3,g704: ᴿHeythJ 29 (1988) 105-9 (J. *Thiel*: holds conflict intrinsic); ModT 4 (1987s) 99-102 (C. *Schwöbel*).

k260 **Taylor** Marion A., The Old Testament in the Old Princeton school: diss. Yale. NHv 1988. – RelStR 15,193, RTLv 20,541.

k261 *Wagner* Volk, Zur Theologiegeschichte des 19. und 20. Jahrhunderts: TRu 53 (1988) 113-200.

k262 **Welch** Claude, Protestant thought in the nineteenth century II. 1870-1914: 1985 → 2,d794; 3,g705: ᴿChH 57 (1988) 394s (Marcia *Bunge*); TTod 44 (1987s) 259-262 (M. K. *Taylor*).

---

k263 ARNOLD: *Prickett* Stephen, Biblical prophecy and nineteenth century historicism; the Joachimite Third Age in Matthew and Mary Augusta Arnold: Literature and Theology 2 (Ox 1988) 219-236 (< ZIT 88, 742].

k264 BAUR: **Kaufman** Frank F., Foundations of modern church history; a comparative structural analysis of writings from August NEANDER and Ferdinand C. Baur: diss. Vanderbilt. Nv 1988. – RelStR 15,194.

k265 BELL: *Sell* Alan P. F., God, grace and the Bible in Scottish Reformed theology [Bell M., TUTTLE G., RIESEN R.]: IrTQ 54 (1988) 66-71.

k266 BOSCO: *Schepens* Jacques, L'activité littéraire de Don Bosco au sujet de la Pénitence et de l'Eucharistie: Salesianum 50,1 ('Pensiero e prassi di Don Bosco nel 1º centenario della morte' 1988) 9-50 [–214, al.].

k267 COLANI: *Encrevé* André, Les hésitations de [Timothée] Colani dans la Revue de Strasbourg entre 1850 et 1855 [...passe progressivement de l'exégèse NT à la christologie et ensuite à la morale]: RHPR 68 (1988) 83-96.

k268 DREY: **Kustermann** Abraham P. M., Die Apologetik J. S. Dreys (1777-1853); kritische, historische und systematische Untersuchungen zu Forschungsgeschichte, Programmentwicklung, Status und Gehalt: Diss. ᴰ*Seckler*. Tü 1987s. – TR 84 (1988) 513.

k269 **Harskamp** A. van., Theologie; tekst in context; op zoek naar de methode van ideologiekritische analyse van de theologie, geillustreerd aan werk van Drey, MÖHLER en STAUDENMAIER 1986 → 2,d756; ƒ35; 90-9001-274-5; 2-9: ᴿTsTNijm 28 (1988) 299-304 (R. J. *Schreiter*: 'ideologie onderkennen in de theologie').

k270 **McCready** Douglas, The Christology of the Catholic Tübingen school, from Drey to KASPER: diss. Temple, ᴰ*Swidler* L. Ph 1987. 526 p. 88-03829. – DissA 49 (1988s) 103s-A; RelStR 14,187.

k271 FINNEY Charles G., Principles of sanctification [1840, nine lectures < Oberlin Evangelist], ᴱ*Parkhurst* Louis C. Minneapolis 1986, Bethany. 204 p. $6. – ᴿBS 145 (1988) 108 (K. L. *Sarles*: principles of discipleship / obedience, 1840/1s, awaited).

k272 FRANZELIN: **Walter** Peter, Johann B. Franzelin (1816-1886), Jesuit, Theologe, Kardinal, ein Lebensbild 1987 → 3,g714; Lit. 14.000. 88-7014-438-0: ᴿETL 64 (1988) 223s (R. *Boudens*); Gregorianum 69 (1988) 580s (M. *Chappin*: a workaholic); TPhil 63 (1988) 281 (K. *Schatz*); ZkT 110 (1988) 251s (K. H. *Neufeld*).

k273 GIFFORD: **Jaki** Stanley L., Lord Gifford and his Lectures; a centenary retrospect 1986 → 3,g687: ᴿTLZ 113 (1988) 97 (E. *Geldbach*).

k274 HEGEL: *Coda* Piero, *a*) Hegel e la teologia oggi; *b*) La presenza di Cristo fra i suoi e la dialettica hegeliana dell'intersoggettività: NuovaUm 9,49 (1987) 113-124 / 9,50 (1987) 11-37.

k275 *Kowalczyk* Stanisław, ❸ Elements of Hegelian philosophy of man: ColcT 58,3 (1988) 49-62; Eng. 62.

k276 HORT: **Patrick** Graham A., F.J.A. Hort, eminent Victorian [and real editor of 'Westcott-Hort']: Historic Texts and Interpreters in Biblical Scholarship. Sheffield 1988, Almond. 127 p. £21.50. 1-85075-098-X; pa. 7-9. – ᴿExpTim 99 (1987s) 384 (C. S. *Ross*).

k277 JONES: **Knight** George R., From 1888 to apostasy; the case of Alonzo T. Jones [Adventist leader]. Wsh 1987, Review & H. 288 p. $17. – ᴿAndrUnS 26 (1988) 187-190 (B. *McArthur*).

k278 JOWETT: **Hinchliff** Peter, Benjamin Jowett and the Christian religion. Ox 1987, Clarendon. ix-243. £25. – ᴿAnglTR 70 (1988) 273-5 (D. F. *Winslow*); JTS 39 (1988) 636-8 (I. *Ellis*: some innuendos about Florence Nightingale *al*.); TLond 91 (1988) 542-5 (S. *Gilley*).

k279 KÄHLER Martin (1835-1912): → 813, TRE 17 (1988) 511-5 (H.-J. *Kraus*).

k280 KIERKEGAARD: **Rest** Walter, Kierkegaard für Christen, eine Herausforderung; Einleitung und Textauswahl: Bücherei 1389. FrB 1987, Herder. 221 p. DM 11. – ᴿOrientierung 52 (1988) 105-8 (W. *Dirks*).

k281 KUYPER: *Ladányi* Sándor, Ⓜ Abraham Kuyper; brief retrospection to the past two centuries of the Reformed Church in the Netherlands...: Theologiai Szemle 31 (1988) 98-100.

k282 MIGNE: ᴱMandouze A., Migne et le renouveau des études patristiques 1975/85 ➤ 1,611...3,g724: ᴿBLitEc 89 (1988) 150s (H. *Crouzel*); CahHist 31 (1986) 69s (J. *Rougé*); CrNSt 9 (1988) 217s (C. *Truzzi*); ÉglT 18 (1987) 373s (É. *Lamirande*); RTAM 55 (1988) 243s (H. *Sonneville*).

k283 MÖHLER: **Geisser** Hans F., Die methodischen Prinzipien des Symbolikers Johann Adam Möhler: TüTQ 168 (1988) 83-97 [153-8, *Rieger* Reinhold, Unbekannte Texte, Bericht über eine Edition].

k284 *a*) *Stockmeier* Peter, Johann Adam MÖHLER und der Aufbruch der wissenschaftlichen Kirchengeschichtsschreibung; – *b*) *Müller* Gerhard L., Die Suche J.A. Möhlers nach der Einheit von geschichtlicher und theologischer Vernunft; – *c*) *Weitlauff* Manfred, Kirche und Theologie in der ersten Hälfte des 19. Jahrhunderts: MüTZ 39 (1988) 181-194/195-206/155-180.

k285 *Petri* Heinrich, Katholizität in der Sicht J.A. Möhlers und ihre Bedeutung für den ökumenischen Dialog: Catholica 92 (1988) 92-107.

k286 NIETZSCHE: *Moroney* Patrick, Nietzsche; anti-Christendom, not anti-Christian: IrTQ 54 (1988) 302-312.

k287 **Ledure** Yves, Lectures 'chrétiennes' de Nietzache [par de LUBAC, *al.*] 1984 ➤ 2,d778: ᴿHeythJ 29 (1988) 391s (B. R. *Brinkman*).

k288 PALMER: **White** Charles E., The beauty of holiness; Phoebe Palmer as theologian, revivalist, feminist, and humanitarian; pref. *Smith* Timothy L. GR 1986, Asbury Zondervan. xxi-330 p. $17 [RelStR 15, 89, D. G. *Roebuck*].

k289 SCHEEBEN M.J., *a*) Teologo cattolico; nel centenario della morte: Divinitas numéro spécial 1988. 521 p. 31 art. [➤ 8179] – *b*) M.J. Scheeben teologo cattolico d'ispirazione tomista. R 1988, Accademia Pontificia di S. Tommaso. – ᴿEsprVie 98 (1988) 674s (P. *Jay*: la même chose); CC 139 (1988,3) 434-6 (J. de *Finance*).

k290 SCHLEIERMACHER: ᴱClements Keith W., F. Schleiermacher, pioneer of modern theology [selections]: Making of Modern Theology, 1987 ➤ 3, g731: ᴿCurrTM 15 (1988) 451s (R. *Busse*).
Birkner H. J., *al.*, Schleiermacher e la modernità 1984/6 ➤ 637.

k291 **Gerrish** B.A., A prince of the Church 1984 ➤ 65,d811...2,d784: ᴿHeythJ 29 (1988) 259s (J. E. *Thiel*).

k292 ᴱ**Jasper** David, The interpretation of belief; COLERIDGE, Schleiermacher and romanticism 1986 ➤ 3,645: ᴿTLond 91 (1988) 48-50 (J. S. *Beer*).

k293 *Pröpper* Thomas, Schleiermachers Bestimmung des Christentums und der Erlösung; zur Problematik der transzendental-anthropologischen Hermeneutik des Glaubens: TüTQ 168 (1988) 193-214.

k294 *Sandys-Wunsch* John, A tale of two critics [*Ammon* Christof F. 1792, foe of Schleiermacher; *Hanson* P. 1982]: a hermeneutical story with a moral for those born since 1802: ➤ 29, Mem. CRAIGIE P., Ascribe 1988, 545-555.

k295 **Sorrentino** Sergio, Ermeneutica...di Schleiermacher 1986 ➤ 3,g740: ᴿCC 139 (1988,2) 404 (P. *Vanzan*).

k296 SMITH: **Riesen** Richard A., Criticism and faith in late Victorian Scotland...DAVIDSON, W. R. & G. A. Smith 1985 ➤ 1,f930...3,g710: ᴿBL (1988) 88s (W. *McKane*); ScotJT 41 (1988) 291-4 (D. M. *Murray*).

k297 STRAUSS: **Lawler** Edwina G., D. F. Strauss 1986 ➤ 2,d795; 3,g741: ᴿChH 57 (1988) 244s (D. *Jodock*).

k298 **Madges** William,   The core of Christian faith; D. F. Strauss and his
Catholic critics: AmerUnivStudies 7/38.   NY 1987, Lang.   214 p. – ᴿCBQ
50 (1988) 724s (D. J. *Harrington*).

k299 Johann B. HIRSCHER: *a) Greinacher* Norbert, [1788-1865] – Reform der
Kirche damals und heute [GROSS W.,... und Messfeier]; – *b) Wolfinger*
Franz,   Glaube und Geschichte bei Johannes Evangelist KUHN; – *c)*
Reinhardt Rudolf,   D. F. Strauss und [Preisschrift über] die Auferstehung
der Töten [Zwei (damit unverwandte) Briefe Peter SCHLEYERS 1833/4]:
TüTQ 168 (1988) 98-115 (–126) / 126-138 / 150-3 [139-149].

k300 STUART: **Giltner** John H.,   Moses Stuart, the father of biblical science
in America: SBL Biblical Scholarship in North America 14.   Atlanta
1988, Scholars.   viii-158 p.; portr. $20.   1-55540-104-X; pa. 5-8.

k301 TALAMO: **Piolanti** Antonio,   La filosofia cristiana in Mons. Salvatore
Talamo ispiratore della 'Aeterni Patris' [Leone XIII 1879]: Studi Tomistici
29.   Vaticano 1986, Pont. Accad. di S. Tommaso e di Religione Cattolica.
136 p. Lit. 14.000. – ᴿGregorianum 69 (1988) 777-9 (R. *Fisichella*: 'non
esistono prove storiche... ma, come ogni prova storica, questa tesi può
essere ben condivisa... fino a quando non verrà comprovato il contrario').

k302 WOODWORTH-ETTER: **Warner** Wayne E.,   The woman evangelist; the
life and times of charismatic evangelist Maria B. Woodworth-Etter:
Studies in Evangelicalism 8.   Metuchen NJ 1986, Scarecrow.   xxii-340 p.;
ill. $32.50 [RelStR 15, 90, D. G. *Roebuck*]. 0-8108-1912-0.

Y5.5   *Crisis modernistica* – **The Modernist era.**

k303 **Botti** Alfonso,   La Spagna e la crisi modernista; cultura, società civile e
religiosa tra Otto e Novecento: BiblStorContemporanea.   Brescia 1987,
Morcelliana.   304 p. – ᴿScriptTPamp 20 (1988) 855-8 (A. M. *Pazos*).

k304 **Chenu** M. D.,   Une école... Le Saulchoir 1985   ➤ 1,g41... 3,g747:
ᴿÉglT 17 (1986) 112-4 (B. *Garceau*).

k305 *Daoust* J.,   Un mouvement intégriste au début du siècle; La Sapinière
[< *Desreumaux* Roger, Ensemble 3 (sept. 1987) 'association de défense
contre le modernisme... devenue symbole de l'exagération']: EsprVie 98
(1988) 312-4.

k306 *Echlin* Edward P.,   Modernists and the modern environmental crisis
[RATZINGER (undocumented): 'The crisis of the present is the long
deferred resumption of the crisis of modernism']: NBlackf 69 (1988) 526-9.

k307 **Gough** Austin,   Paris and Rome; the Gallican church and the
ultramontane campaign 1848-1853: 1986 ➤ 3,g750:   ᴿChH 57 (1988)
243s (M. Patricia *Dougherty*); JTS 39 (1988) 326s (Frances *Lannon*).

k308 *Guarino* Thomas,   The truth-status of theological statements; analogy
revisited [... Modernism; response to it ...]: IrTQ 54 (1988) 140-155.

k309 **Kurtz** Lester R.,   The politics of heresy 1986 ➤ 2,d806; 3,g751:   ᴿCCurr
23 (1988s) 231-4 (M. J. *Kerlin*: half is a sociological case study, not
organized into the fairly adequate history of modernism).

k310 **O'Gara** Margaret,   Triumph in defeat; infallibility, Vatican I, and the
French minority bishops [22 who absented themselves from the final
ballot, besides Jean DEVOUCOUX who 'blessed God for calling me to
himself before the definition']. Wsh 1988, Catholic Univ. xxii-296 p. $49
[TS 50, 599, J. T. *Ford*].

k311 **Poulat** Émile,   Liberté, laïcité; la guerre des deux France et le principe de
la modernité: Éthique et société. P 1987, Cerf/Cujas. 440 p. – ᴿRevSR
62 (1988) 316-320 (A. *Faivre*); RHPR 68 (1988) 528-530 (J.-P. *Willaime*).

k312 *Poulat* Émile, La crise du modernisme dans l'Église catholique: SuppVSp 165 (1988) 57-74.

k313 **Stephenson** Alan M. G., The rise and decline of English modernism 1984 ➤ 1,f989: ᴿHeythJ 29 (1988) 261s (S. *Gilley*).

k314 Acton: **Dahlberg-Acton** John E. E., ᴱ*Fears* J. Rufus, Essays in the history of liberty / in the study and writing of history: Selected writings of Lord Acton. Indianapolis 1986, Liberty Classics. xxix-557 p.; xxv-580 p.; lviii-716 p. $15 each; pa. $7.50. – ᴿHomP 88,3 (1987s) 71s.74s (J. V. *Schall*); SWJT 31,2 (1988s) 67s (E. E. *Ellis*); Tablet 242 (1988) 1277 (R. *Hill*).

k315 **Nurser** John, The reign of conscience; individual, church, and state in Lord Acton's history of liberty: Modern European history dissertations. NY 1987, Garland. 220 p. $40 [TDig 36,72].

k316 Blondel: *Henrici* Peter, Blondel und Loisy in der modernistischen Krise: IkaZ 16 (1987) 513-530.

k317 *Izquierdo* Cesar, Presupuestos filosóficos del acceso histórico a Jesús según M. Blondel: CiTom 115 (1988) 153-9.

k317* **Porter** Lawrence B., Poetry, evolution and the unconscious in 'L'Action 1893'; an introduction to the thought of M. Blondel for the student of theology: diss. Vanderbilt. ᴰ*Te Selle* E. Nv 1988. – 283 p. 88-27290. – DissA 49 (1988s) 3064-A.

k318 *Sullivan* John, [Blondel] 'L'Action' and living truth: TLond 91 (1988) 209-216.

k319 Briggs: *Massa* Mark S., 'Mediating modernism'; Charles Briggs, Catholic modernism, and an ecumenical 'plot': HarvTR 81 (1988) 413-430.

k320 Curci: **Mucci** Giandomenico, C. M. Curci il fondatore della CC 1988 ➤ 2,d821; 3,g768: ᴿCC 139 (1988,4) 511s (F. *Molinari*).

k321 Döllinger: *Conzemius* Victor, Die Kirchenkrise Ignaz von Döllingers; deutsche gegen römische Theologie: HistJb 108 (1988) 406-429.

k322 Lamennais: *a) Le Guillou* Louis, Actualité de Lamennais; – *b) Poulat* Émile, La postérité de Lamennais; – *c) Costigan* Richard F., Lamennais and Rohrbacher and the Papacy: RUnivOtt 57 (1987) 11-22 / 23-37 / 53-65.

k323 LeRoy: **Mansini** Guy, 'What is a dogma?' The meaning and truth of dogma in Édouard Le Roy and his scholastic opponents [diss. 1983] 1985 ➤ 1,g2 ... 3,g772: ᴿComSev 21 (1986) 261s (V. J. *Ansede*); RTLv 19 (1988) 376s (Monique *Foket*: conclusions courageuses).

k324 Loisy: **Talar** C. J. T., Metaphor and modernist — the polarization of Alfred Loisy and his Neo-Thomist critics. Lanham MD 1988, UPA. 194 p. £19.50 [PrPeo 2,266]. – Ts 49 (1988) 781 (J. J. *Heaney*).

k325 *Goichot* Émile, Anamorphoses; le modernisme [Loisy 1902, Pascendi 1907] aux miroirs du roman [*Bourget* P. 1914; *Malègue* J. 1933]: RHPR 68 (1988) 435-459.

k326 **Loisy** A. F., The Gospel and the Church [1902 reply to Harnack's 1900 Wesen]: Classics of Biblical Criticism. Buffalo 1988, Prometheus. 268 p. $21. 0-87975-438-8 [NTAbs 32,373].

k327 Newman, Oxford Movement: *Armour* Leslie, Newman, Arnold and the problem of particular Providence: RelSt 24 (1988) 173-187.

k328 *a) Bedouelle* G., Pusey Edward B., 22.VIII.1800-16.IV.1882: ➤ 786, Catholicisme 12,55 (1988) 320-2; – *b) Townsend* R. D., Pusey: ➤ 791, DictSpir 12 (1986) 2678-2681.

k329 **Bouyer** Louis, Newman's vision of faith. SF 1986, Ignatius. 210 p. $11. – ᴿHomP 88,2 (1987s) 72.74 (R. J. *Fuhrman*).

k330 **Chadwick** Owen, From Bossuet to Newman² [¹1957 + 20 p. introd.; possibility of development of doctrine]. NY 1987, Cambridge-UP. xxxii-253 p. $44.50; pa. $15 [TDig 35,263].

k331 *Chitarin* Luigi, Annotazioni Newmaniane sulla predicazione universitaria: StPatav 35 (1988) 133-8; Eng. 138.

k332 **Crumb** L. N., The Oxford Movement and its leaders; a bibliography of secondary and lesser primary sources: ATLA 24. Metuchen NJ 1988, Scarecrow. xxviii-706 p. $62.50 [RHE 83,349*].

k333 **Ferreira** M. Jamie, Scepticism and reasonable doubt; the British naturalist tradition in [John] Wilkins, Hume, [Thomas] Reid, and Newman. Ox 1986, Univ. Press. xii-255 p. $40 [RelStR 15,57, S. *Satris*].

k334 *Gaffney* James, Newman on the common roots of morality and religion: JRelEth 16 (1988) 143-159.

k335 **Gauthier** Pierre, Newman et Blondel; tradition et développement du dogme [< diss. Strasbourg, ᴰ*Nédoncelle* M.]. P 1988, Cerf. 553 p. F 242 [TS 50, 377, A. *Dulles*].

k336 ᴱ**Jay** Elizabeth, The evangelical and Oxford movements: English Prose Texts. C 1983, Univ. x-219 p. – ᴿCathHR 74 (1988) 633s (T. *Bokenkotter*).

k337 *a) Mashburn* T. J., The categories of development; an overlooked aspect of Newman's theory of doctrinal development; – *b) Ferreira* M. Jamie, Newman and William James on religious experience; the theory and the concrete; – *c) Hammond* David M., Imagination in Newman's phenomenology of cognition: HeythJ 29 (1988) 33-43 / 44-57 / 21-32.

k338 *Morales* José, Semblanza religiosa y significado teológico del Movimiento de Oxford: TBraga 20 (1985) 147-186.

k339 ᴱ**Rowell** Geoffrey, Tradition renewed; the Oxford Movement conference papers [1983] 1986 ➤ 3,711: ᴿRThom 88 (1988) 511-3 (G.-T. *Bedouelle*).

k340 **Stuart** E. B., The Roman Catholic reaction to the Oxford movement and Anglican schemes for reunion 1833; the condemnation of Anglican Orders in 1896: diss. Oxford 1988. – RTLv 20,566.

k341 *a) Stuart* Elizabeth, The condemnation of Anglican Orders in the light of the Roman Catholic reaction to the Oxford Movement; – *b) Gaffney* James, Newman's criticism of the Church; lessons and object lessons; – *c) L'Estrange* Peter, Newman's relations with the Jesuits: HeythJ 29 (1988) 86-98 / 1-20 / 58-85.

k342 *Young* Frances, The critic and the visionary [Newman, Idea of a University, 1960 ed.]: ScotJT 41 (1988) 297-312.

---

k343 Renan: *Kaplan* F., Du Dieu d'Abraham, d'Isaac et de Jacob au Dieu en devenir [Renan E.]: Revue philosophique FÉ 112,4 ('Taine et Renan' 1987) 403-423 [425-447, *Marquet* J.-F.].

k344 Rosmini: *Staglianò* Antonio, Rosmini tra tradizione e modernità; a cento anni dalla condanna: TItSett 13 (1988) 250-256.

k345 **Lorizio** Giuseppe, Eschaton e storia nel pensiero di Antonio Rosmini; genesi e analisi della 'Teodicea' in prospettiva teologica: Aloisiana

21. R/Brescia 1988, Gregorian University / Morcelliana. 357 p. Lit. 42.000. – [R]CC 139 (1988,4) 606s (N. *Galantino*).

k346 **Rosmini** A., The five wounds of the Church. L c. 1988, Fowler Wright. 257 p. £9 [TLond 91,566]. 0-85244-713-4.

k347 SCALABRINI: *Bedeschi* Lorenzo, Il vescovo Scalabrini, il modernismo e il liberalcattolicesimo: HumBr 43 (1988) 75-89.

k348 SULLIVAN: *Appleby* R. Scott, Modernism as the final phase of Americanism; William L. Sullivan, American Catholic apologist, 1899-1910 [Paulist; afterward became Unitarian]: HarvTR 81 (1988) 171-192.

k349 TYRRELL: **Krasevac** Edward L., Revelation and experience; an analysis of the theology of George Tyrrell, Karl RAHNER, Edward SCHILLEBEECKX and Thomas AQUINAS: diss. Graduate Theological Union. Berkeley 1986. – RTLv 20,553; RelStR 14,187.

k350 *Leonard* Ellen, Other modernisms; Maude PETRE and the place of dissent [... Tyrrell's funeral]: 249 (1988) 1008-1015; 2 phot.

k351 WISEMAN: **Schiefen** Richard J., Nicholas Wiseman and the transformation of English Catholicism 1984 ➤ 1,g50; 2,d853: [R]HeythJ 29 (1988) 136-8 (S. *Gilley*).

Y6 *Saeculum XX* – 20th **Century Exegesis.**

k352 *Merrill* John L., The Bible and the American temperance movement; text, context, and pretext: HarvTR 81 (1988) 145-170.

k353 **Sylvester** Nigel, La Parole de Dieu dans notre monde [histoire de la Ligue pour la Lecture de la Bible]. Guebwiller 1987, LigueLB. F 59. 2-85031-138-3. – [R]ÉTRel 63 (1988) 622 (A. G. *Martin*: agréable, mais plutôt du mauvais journalisme que de l'histoire).

k354 *Trocmé* Étienne, Le Nouveau Testament à la Faculté de théologie protestante [Strasbourg] de 1870 à 1956: RHPR 68 (1988) 113-120.

k355 BEA: **Schmidt** S., A. Bea, il cardinale dell'unità 1987 ➤ 3,g812: [R]CC 139 (1988,2) 472-485 (G. *Caprile*: 'Al servizio di quattro Papi').

k356 BLOCH Ernst, The principle of hope. Ox 1986, Blackwell. 1600 p. (3 vol.) £120. – [R]ScotJT 41 (1988) 247-252 (D. M. *MacKinnon*).

k356* BROWN: **Kelly** George A., The new biblical theorists, R. E. Brown and beyond 1985 ➤ 1,g58: [R]ScripTPamp 19 (1987) 929-931 (T. J. *McGovern*).

k357 BUBER: **Friedman** Maurice, Martin Buber's life and work; the early years, 1878-1923. Detroit 1988, Wayne State Univ. [= 1981, Dutton]. xxiii-455 p.; portr. 0-8143-1944-0.

k358 Martin Buber centenary, [E]**Gordon** H., *Bloch* J. 1984 ➤ 1,457 ... 3,g817: [R]HeythJ 29 (1988) 380s (U. *Simon*).

k359 *Kepnes* Steven D., Buber as hermeneut; relations to DILTHEY and GADAMER: HarvTR 81 (1988) 193-213.

k360 **Oesterreicher** John M., The unfinished dialogue; M. Buber and the Christian Way 1986 ➤ 2,d862: [R]JEcuSt 25 (1988) 466s (M. *Fishbane*).

k360* *a) Shapira* Avraham, Bubers Platz in der jüdischen Kultur der Gegenwart; – *b) Amir* Yehoshua, Der Durchbruch des dialogischen Denkens bei Buber; – *c) Münster* Arno, Die Wurzeln der Ich-Du-Philosophie Martin Bubers: Judaica 44 (1988) 67-79 / 80-90 / 91-106.

k361 *Uffenheimer* Benjamin, Some reflections on modern Jewish biblical research [i.e. Israeli: KAUFMANN Y., Buber M.]: ➤ 505, Creative 1985/8, 161-174.

k362 **Vermes** Pamela, Buber: Jewish Thinkers, 1988 ➤ 3,g819; £11; pa. £6: ᴿJJS 39 (1988) 287-9 (P. *Mendes-Flohr*).

k363 *Werblowsky* R.J. Zwi, Reflections on Martin Buber's 'Two types of faith' [< unduly delayed German edition]: JJS 39 (1988) 92-101.

k364 BULTMANN: **Boschini** P., Eschatologia senza storia; storicismo e antistoricismo nel pensiero di R. Bultmann. Bo 1988, CLUEB. 179 p. Lit. 20.000 [CC 139/3, dopo 344].

k365 **Evang** Martin, Rudolf Bultmann in seiner Frühzeit: BeiHistT 74. Tü 1988, Mohr. viii-364 p. 3-16-145316-6.

k366 **Jüngel** Eberhard, Glauben und Verstehen; zum Theologiebegriff R. Bultmanns 1985 ➤ 1,g83; 3,g824: ᴿJTS 39 (1988) 132s (R. *Morgan*).

k367 **Johnson** Roger, [texts of] Rudolf Bultmann; interpreting faith for the modern era. SF 1987, Collins. 345 p. $20 [TS 50, 206, R. L. *Maddox*].

k368 *a*) *Mueller* David L., The whale and the elephant; BARTH and Bultmann in dialogue; – *b*) *Barnes* Elizabeth, A response to the 'Barth-Bultmann' dialogue: PerspRelSt 15 (1988) 197-214 / 215-7.

k369 *Gagnebin* Laurent, Sentiment religieux [= précompréhension de Bultmann, contre BARTH et BONHOEFFER], aliénation et aliénation religieux: ÉTRel 63 (1988) 547-560.

k370 CADBURY: **Bacon** Margaret H., Let this life speak ... H.J. Cadbury 1987 ➤ 3,g827: ᴿAmHR 93 (1988) 513s (T.D. *Hamm*: she does not ask the right questions of her sources); ChH 57 (1988) 113s (R.E. *Selleck*).

k371 FRIDRICHSEN: *Beijer* Erik, Anton Fridrichsen [born 1888] som akademisk lärare till kyrkans tjänst: SvEx 53 (1988) 88-109.

k372 **HARNACK** Adolf von, What is Christianity? [Wesen 1900, ᵀ*Saunders* Thomas B. 1901; *Bultmann* R., introduction 1950] 1986 = 1957 ➤ 3,g830: ᴿRelStR 14 (1988) 143 (C.E. *Hester*).

k373 HARPER: **Wind** James P., The Bible and the university ... W.R. Harper 1987 ➤ 3,g832: ᴿAustralBR 36 (1988) 58s (J.W. *Roffey*: notes without agreeing critics of Harper's league with Rockefeller in creating Chicago University architecture, but scarcely shows his importance as a Hebrew-Bible teacher); BL (1988) 27 (G.W. *Anderson*); VT 38 (1988) 254 (J.A. *Emerton*).

k374 HESCHEL: **Merkle** John C., The genesis of faith; the depth theology of A.J. Heschel 1985 ➤ 2,d877; 3,g834: ᴿCalvinT 23 (1988) 244-7 (D. *Sanders*: signal service by Roman Catholic prof.); HeythJ 29 (1988) 496s (Diane M. *Brewster*).

k374* MACHEN: **Chrisope** Terry A., The Bible and historical scholarship in the early life and thought of J. Gresham Machen, 1881-1915; diss. Kansas State, ᴰ*Lindner* R. Manhattan 1988. 311 p. 89-01139. – DissA 49 (1987s) 3057-A.

k375 MOULTON: *Wakefield* G.S., Ministerial training; James H. Moulton (1863-1917): EpworthR 15,1 (1988) 45-51 [NTAbs 32,140].

PERRIN: **Mercer** C., Norman Perrin's interpretation of the NT 1987 ➤ 4349.

k377 RAD Gerhard von, 21.X.1901-31.X.1971, théologie biblique AT: ➤ 786, Catholicisme 12,55 (1988) 431-3 (L. *Derousseaux*).

k378 ROBINSON: **James** Eric, A life of Bishop John A.T. Robinson, scholar, pastor, prophet 1987 ➤ 3,g839: ᴿAnglTR 70 (1988) 386s (M.F. *Wiles*); Tablet 242 (1988) 13 (N. *Lash*); TLond 91 (1988) 325-7 (A. *Kee*).

k379 **Robinson** John A.T., Where three ways meet [theology, revelation, social responsibility; remote reference to where Oedipus unwittingly killed his father]; last essays and sermons, ᴱ*James* Eric. L 1987, SCM. xiii-210 p. £9 pa. – ᴿTLond 91 (1988) 328s (R. *Godsall*).

k380 **Kee** Alistair, The roots of Christian freedom; the theology of John A. T. Robinson. L 1988, SPCK. xx-191 p. £9 pa. – ᴿTablet 242 (1988) 1128 (J. *Todd*); TLond 91 (1988) 323-5 (J. *Macquarrie*).

k381 ROSENZWEIG: *Friedmann* Friedrich G., 'Neues Denken' und Wendung zur Sprache; zu Grundmotiven der Offenbarungsphilosophie F. Rosenzweigs: Orientierung 52 (1988) 99-102.

k382 *Moses* Stéphane, Franz Rosenzweig; le Je et le Tu dans l'expérience de la Révélation: RICathP 28 (1988) 31-44.

k382* **Zak** Adam, Vom reinen Denken zur Sprachvernunft; Über die Grundmotive der Offenbarungsphilosophie Franz Rosenzweigs. Stu 1987, Kohlhammer. 224 p. – ᴿJudaica 44 (1988) 62s (F. von *Hammerstein*).

k383 *Neuer* W., Bibelausleger zwischen theologischen Fronten [Schlatter A. 1852-1938]: RefFor 2,2 (1988) 11-14 [NTAbs 32,139].

k384 SCHLIER: *Masini* Mario, Teologia biblica, un maestro, Heinrich Schlier: PalCl 65-66 (1987) 5-13.

k385 TRAINA: *McKenna* David L., Tribute to Robert A. Traina: AsbTJ 43,1 (issue 'dedicated to' Traina, 1988) 7-9.

Y6.4 **Theologi influentes** *in exegesim saeculi XX.*

k386 *Albanese* Catherine L., Religion and the American experience [*Schaff* P. 1875]: ChH 57 (1988) 337-351.

k388 ᴱ**Bauer** Johannes B., Entwürfe der Theologie 1985 ➤ 1,323; 2,d897: ᴿTR 84 (1988) 388s (S. *Wiedenhofer*).

k389 *a*) **Chidester** David, Salvation and suicide; an interpretation of Jim Jones, the People's Temple and Jonestown. Bloomington 1988, Indiana Univ. 190 p. $19. – *b*) **Hall** John R., Gone from the promised land; Jonestown in American cultural history. New Brunswick NJ 1987, Transaction. 381 p. $30 [RelStR 15, 32-37, T. *Robbins*].

k390 **Clements** Keith W., Lovers of discord; twentieth-century theological controversies in England. L 1988, SPCK. x-261 p. £9 pa. – ᴿNBlackf 69 (1988) 349 (M. *Wiles*); TLond 91 (1988) 329-331 (A. *Hastings*: rightly suggests lack of a sense of history, even very recent history; the ghost at the feast is TYRRELL, greatest and most cruelly treated of 20th century British religious controversialists).

k391 **Congar** Yves, [conversations with *Lauret* Bernard], Fifty years of Catholic theology, ᵀ*Bowden* John. Ph 1988, Fortress. 87 p. $7. 0-8006-2303-7 [TDig 36,150].

k391* **Deedy** John, American Catholicism and now where? NY 1987, Plenum. $19. 0-306-42706-0. – ᴿTablet 242 (1988) 441s (R. *Drinan*: very unfavorable on JOHN PAUL II; pessimistic but less sure of himself about the condition of the American church).

k392 **Kent** John, The unacceptable face; the modern Church in the eyes of the historian [i.e. Christian violence, war, executions] 1987 ➤ 3,g852: ᴿJEH 39 (1988) 323s (J. *Drury*); LvSt 13 (1988) 379-381 (R. *Boudens*); NBlackf 69 (1988) 149s (A. *Hastings*); PrPeo 2 (1988) 115-7 (J. P. *Marmion*); TLond 91 (1988) 152-5 (J. *Morrill*: bitter and confusing); TorJT 4 (1988) 126 (Joanne *McWilliam*).

k392* **Scholder** Klaus, The churches and the Third Reich. I. 1918-1934, ᵀ*Bowden* John. L 1987, SCM. 717 p. £35. 0-334-01922-2. – ᴿExpTim 99 (1987s) 379s (E. *Robertson*).

k393 ᴱ**Strecker** G., Theologie im 20. Jahrhundert 1983 ➤ 64,e524: ᴿProtestantesimo 43 (1988) 56s (V. *Subilia*).

---

k394 ADAM: **Kreidler** Hans, Eine Theologie des Lebens; Grundzüge im theologische Denken Karl Adams [1876-1966]. Mainz 1988, Grünewald. 344 p. DM 48 [TS 50, 805-7, J. P. *Galvin*].

k395 ASMUSSEN: *Konukiewitz* Enno, Leben und Werk von Hans Asmussen: BTZ 5 (1988) 85-102 (103-123, gegen K. BARTH: *Besier* G.).

k396 BALTHASAR: *Biser* Eugen, Dombau oder Triptychon? Zum Abschluss der Trilogie Hans Urs von Balthasars: TR 84 (1988) 177-184.

k397 *Dupré* Louis, Hans Urs von Balthasar's theology of aesthetic form: TS 49 (1988) 299-318.

k398 **Godenir** J., Jésus, l'unique; introduction a la théologie de H. U. von Balthasar: Sycomore 19, 1984 ➤ 2,d911: ᴿNRT 110 (1988) 752 (C. *Dumont*).

k399 *Narcisse* Gilbert, De la beauté humaine à la gloire de Dieu; aperçu sur l'esthétique théologique de Hans Urs von Balthasar: Carmel 45 (1987) 96-98.

 Nadevilekut James, Christus der Heilsweg; Soteria als Theodrama im Werk Balthasars: Diss. 1987 ➤ 8756*.

k401 ᴱ**Riches** John, The analogy of beauty... Balthasar 1986 ➤ 3,g858: ᴿScotJT 41 (1988) 411-4 (Francesca *Murphy*: PLATO and ARISTOTLE giving way to Greek drama).

k402 **Roberts** Louis, The theological aesthetics of H. U. v. Balthasar 1987 ➤ 3,g861: ᴿTLond 91 (1988) 551-7 (B. L. *Horne*); TS 49 (1988) 555s (J. R. *Sachs*).

k403 **Schrijver** G. de, Le merveilleux accord... Balthasar 1983 ➤ 65,d963 ...2,d913: ᴿNRT 110 (1988) 750s (C. *Dumont*).

k404 *Takayanagi* Shunichi, ❶ The theology of salvation history as dramaturgy — considerations about the 'Theodramatik' of Hans Urs von Balthasar: KatKenk 27,54 (1988) 23-48 = 209-234; Eng. iv-vi.

k405 **Vignolo** Roberto, H. U. von Balthasar; estetica e singolarità 1983 ➤ 65,d965; 1,g139: ᴿNRT 110 (1988) 751s (C. *Dumont*).

k406 **Balthasar** Hans Urs von, Theologik 1. Wahrheit der Welt; 2. Wahrheit Gottes 1985 ➤ 2,d909: ᴿTS 49 (1988) 355-8 (J. R. *Sachs*).

k407 **Balthasar** Hans Urs von, Theologik 3: Der Geist der Wahrheit + Epilog. Einsiedeln 1987, Johannes. 421 + 98 p. DM 50 + 18, [TS 50, 807-9, J. R. *Sachs*].

k408 **Balthasar**, The glory of the Lord 2s, clerical/lay styles 1984/6 ➤ 2,d908; 3,g864: ᴿIrTQ 54 (1988) 315s (N. D. *O'Donoghue*, 3); JTS 39 (1988) 339s (D. M. *MacKinnon*); MilltSt 22 (1988) 111-7 (G. *O'Hanlon*, Christian state of life 1983); Thomist 51 (1987) 178-186.710-4 (D. J. *Keefe*).

k409 **Balthasar** H. v. La dramatique divine, II. Les personnes du drame: 1. L'homme en Dieu 1986 ➤ 3,g865: ᴿNRT 110 (1988) 749s (C. *Dumont*).

k409* **Balthasar** H. v., Dramatique II/2 Les personnes dans le Christ. P/Namur 1988, Lethielleux/Culture et V. 436 p. F 250.

k410 **Balthasar** Hans Urs von, Gloria, una estética teológica [I. 1985 ➤ 3,g866]; II, M 1986s, Encuentro. 348 p.; 516 p. – ᴿComSev 21 (1988) 133 (M. *Sánchez*, 2s); EstTrin 20 (1986) 401s (N. *Silanes*, 1s).

k411 **Balthasar** Hans Urs von. Homo creatus est; Skizzen zur Theologie V,

1986 ➤ 3,184. 3-265-10310-2. 31 art. – ᴿActuBbg 25 (1988) 241s (J. *Boada*).

---

k412 BARTH: **Bächli** O., Das AT in der KD von Karl Barth 1987 ➤ 3,g868: ᴿÉTRel 63 (1988) 616s (J. *Rennes*).

k413 *Bächli* Otto, Das Alte Testament in der Passions- und Osterzeit 1931; zu Karl Barths Andachten, ein Beitrag zur Hermeneutik: TZBas 44 (1988) 54-78.

k414 **Barnes** Elizabeth B., An affront to the Gospel? The radical Barth and the Southern Baptist convention [diss.] Atlanta 1987, Scholars. 149 p. $15. 1-55540-101-5. – ᴿRExp 85 (1988) 355s (D. L. *Mueller*: Before writing Church Dogmatics, Barth saw the Gospel as more bound up with social justice praxis).

k415 **Barth** K., Preghiere, ᵀ*Pons* E. T 1987, Claudiana. 104 p. Lit. 14.000. – ᴿRasT 29 (1988) 610 (A. *Cavadi*).

k416 **Becker** Dieter, Karl Barth und Martin BUBER — Denker in dialogischer Nachbarschaft? Zur Bedeutung Martin Bubers für die Anthropologie Karl Barths: ForSysÖkT 51, 1986 ➤ 2,d919; DM 48: ᴿTZBas 44 (1988) 188s (O. *Bächli*).

k417 **Blaser** Klauspeter, Karl Barth, 1886-1986; combats, idées, reprises. Bern 1987, Lang. xii-233 p. Fs 40. 3-261-03788-1. – ᴿÉTRel 63 (1988) 305s (A. *Gounelle*).

k418 *Blaser* Klauspeter, Une année jubilaire, 1986 (K Barth. [100ᵉ anniv. de naissance, aussi de TILLICH P.] D. BONHOEFFER [80ᵉ]): RTPhil 120 (1988) 317-327.

k419 **Busch** Eberhard, Glaubensheiterkeit; Karl Barth, Erfahrungen und Begegnungen⁴. Neuk 1986. 96 p. 3-7887-1206-6. – ᴿEstE 63 (1988) 253-6 (J. J. *Alemany*: también sobre 7 otros Barthiana).

k420 *Collins* Alice, Barth's relation to SCHLEIERMACHER; a reassessment: SR 17 (1988) 213-224.

k421 **Davaney** Sheila G., Divine power... Barth, HARTSHORNE ᴰ1986 ➤ 2, d925: ᴿJAAR 56 (1988) 139-142 (P. E. *Devenish*).

k422 **Delhougne** H., Karl Barth et la rationalité; période de la Dogmatique (diss. Strasbourg): Atelier Thèses Lille, 1983 ➤ 64,e548; 65,d974: ᴿSt-Patav 35 (1988) 220s (A. *Moda*).

k423 *Dulk* M. den, ... Als twee die spreken (een manier om de heiligingsleer van Karl Barth te lezen). Haag 1987, Boekencentrum. 244 p. ƒ45. – ᴿGerefTTs 88 (1988) 116-8 (M. E. *Brinkman*).

k424 **Fisher** Simon, Revelatory positivism? Barth's earliest theology and the Marburg school [*Cohen* H., *Hermann* W. ...]. Ox/NY 1988, Oxford-UP. xv-348 p. £35/$69. 0-19-826725-8 [TDig 36,159].

k424* **Frey** Christofer [JTS 40,742], Die Theologie Karl Barths; eine Einführung. Fra 1988, Athenäum. 312 p. DM 48.

k425 ᴱ**Gisel** Pierre, ᵀ*Corset* Pierre, K. Barth, genèse et réception 1987 ➤ 3,g888: ᴿEsprVie 98 (1988) 86 (P. *Jay*); ETL 64 (1988) 488s (E. *Brito*); Gregorianum 69 (1988) 788 (E. *Farahian*); RHPR 68 (1988) 479s (F. *Lienhard*).

k427 *Hegstad* Harald, [Norw.] Leiv AALEN and Karl Barth; on the question of Barth's influence upon Norwegian theology: TsTKi 59 (1988) 241-258.

k428 *Hoogstraten* H. D. van, [Boeken] Bij de honderdste geboortedag van Karl Barth: TsTNijm 28 (1988) 401-3.

k428* **Gollwitzer** H.,   Liberazione e solidarietà [1978] 1986 ➤ 3,8471:   ᴿProtestantesimo 43 (1988) 241s (F. *Ferrario*: dialogo con Barth).

k429 **Jüngel** Eberhard,   Karl Barth — a theological legacy [1982],   ᵀ*Paul*
Garrett E.,   1986 ➤ 2,d934; 3,g887:   ᴿCalvinT 23 (1988) 80-82 (G. J.
Spykman); Interpretation 42 (1988) 324-6 (D. P. *Henry*).

k430 *a*) *Klaer* Ingo,   Überlegungen zum Offenbarungsbegriff Karl Barths; – *b*)
Gestrich Christof,   Die hermeneutische Differenz zwischen Barth und
Luther angesichts der neuzeitlichen Situation; – *c*) *Beintker* Michael,   Das
Krisis-Motiv der Römerbriefphase als Vorstufe von Barths Zuordnung
von Gesetz und Evangelium: ➤ 591*, ᴱ*Köckert* H., *Krötke* W., Theologie
als Christologie 1986/8, 90-105 / 38-55 / 56-70.

k431 **Laurenzi** Maria Cristina,   Esperienza e rivelazione; la ricerca del giovane
Barth (1909-1921): Dabar 3, 1983 ➤ 65,d980:   ᴿStPatav 35 (1988) 219s
(A. *Moda*).

k432 **Leuba** Jean-Louis,   Études barthiennes 1986 ➤ 3,g892:   ᴿRHPR 68
(1988) 478 (M.-J. *Koenig*).

k433 ᴱ**McKim** Donald K.,   How Karl Barth changed my mind [26
testimonies] 1986 ➤ 3,434:   ᴿEvQ 60 (1988) 346s (C. *Brown*); PerspRelSt
15 (1988) 184-6 (A. J. *McKelway*); RExp 84 (1987) 740-2 (T. *George*);
TLond 91 (1988) 218s (C. *Schwoebel*, also on JÜNGEL); WestTJ 60 (1988)
127-130 (R. A. *Muller*).

k434 *Mottu* Henry,   La lumière et les lumières; Christ et le monde selon le
dernier Barth: ➤ 150, ᶠWIDMER G.-P.: BCentProt 40 (1988) 39-54.

k434* *Muller* Richard A.,   The place and importance of Karl Barth in the
twentieth century; a review essay [... *Jüngel* E.; *Paul* G.]: WestTJ 50
(1988) 127-156.

k435 *Rohkrämer* Martin,   Karl Barth in der Herbstkrise 1938 [... Brief an J.
Hromádka]: EvT 48 (1988) 521-545.

k436 *a*) *Rohls* Jan,   Credo ut intelligam; Karl Barths theologisches Programm
und sein Kontext; – *b*) *Fries* Heinrich,   Fides quaerens intellectum: ➤ 114,
ᶠPANNENBERG W., Vernunft 1988, 406-435 / 93-108.

k437 ᴱ**Schwöbel** C.,   K. Barth - M. RADE Briefwechsel 1981 ➤ 64,e555:
ᴿZwingliana 16 (1985) 179-181 (H. *Stickelberger*).

k438 **Smend** R.,   Karl Barth als Ausleger der Heiligen Schrift: ➤ 591*,
ᴱ*Köckert* H., Theologie als Christologie... Barth 1988, 9-37 [< ZAW
101,328].

k439 *Winzeler* Peter,   Der Sozialismus Karl Barths in der neuesten Kritik
[... *Marquardt* F. 1972 ³1985]: EvT 48 (1988) 262-272.

k440 **Wissink** J. B. M.,   De inzet... K. Barths strijd tegen de natuurlijke
theologie 1983 ➤ 1,g163:   ᴿNedTTs 42 (1988) 87s (N. T. *Bakker*).

---

k441 BONHOEFFER: **Lange** F. de,   *a*) Grond onder de voeten; burgerlijkheid
bij D. Bonhoeffer. Kampen 1985. – *b*) Een burger op zijn best, D.
Bonhoeffer. Baarn 1986. – ᴿNedTTs 42 (1988) 169-171 (H. D. van
Hoogstraten).

k442 **Bonhoeffer** D.,   ᴱ*Bethge* E.   Resistencia y sumisión² [¹1951], ᵀ*Alemany*
J. J.: El peso de los días 18. Salamanca 1983, Sígueme. 299 p. – ᴿCiTom
114 (1987) 170s (L. *Lago Alba*).

k443 **Bonhoeffer** D.,   El precio de la gracia; el seguimiento³, ᵀ*Sicré* José L.:
Verdad e imagen 95. Salamanca 1986, Sígueme. 216 p. – ᴿCiTom 114
(1987) 171s (L. *Lago Alba*).

k444 ᴱde Gruchy John, [texts of] Dietrich Bonhoeffer, witness to Jesus Christ. SF 1988, Collins. x-308 p. $20 [TS 50, 205, J. D. *Godsey*].

k445 **Morris** Kenneth E., Bonhoeffer's ethic of discipleship; a study in social psychology, political thought, and religion. University Park 1986, Penn State Univ. xi-180 p. $18. – ᴿCalvinT 23 (1988) 251-4 (D. J. *Schuurman*).

k446 **Robertson** Edwin, The shame of the sacrifice [title from B's 1944 poem, The Death of Moses]; the life and preaching of Dietrich Bonhoeffer. L 1987, Hodder & S. £8. – ᴿTLond 91 (1988) 232-4 (H. *Lockley*).

k447 *Staats* Reinhart, Das patristische Erbe in der Theologie Dietrich Bonhoeffers: BTZ 5 (1988) 178-201.

k448 **Wendel** Ernst G., Studien zur Homiletik Dietrich Bonhoeffers [nebst BETHGES Rekonstruktion]; Predigt — Hermeneutik — Sprache: Hermeneutische Untersuchungen zur Theologie 21, 1985 ➤ 1,g176: ᴿTLZ 113 (1988) 850-2 (P. C. *Bloth*).

k449 *Wolf* Martin, Das Gebet bei D. Bonhoeffer: Laurentianum 29 (1988) 35-62.

────────────

k450 BUTTURINI G.: **Costantini** Celso: Butturini Giuseppe, Alle origini del Concilio Vaticano secondo; una proposta di ~ [désitalianisation de la Curie ...]: Storia cultura arte economia 10. Pordenone 1988, Concordia Sette. 349 p. Lit. 35.000. – ᴿRSPT 72 (1988) 667 (Y. *Congar*: 'Ah! s'il avait été le Préfet [de Propaganda] pendant le concile, à la place de celui que nous avons eu!').

k451 CASALIS: *Girardet* Giorgio, La teologia induttiva di Georges Casalis [1916-1987]: Protestantesimo 43 (1988) 137-152.

k452 CASEL: **Krahe** Maria Judith, Der Herr ist der Geist; Studien zur Theologie Odo Casels, I. Das Mysterium Christi; II. Das Mysterium vom Pneuma Christi, 1986 ➤ 3,g926: ᴿZkT 110 (1988) 478 (H. B. *Meyer*).

k453 *Klöckener* Martin, Odo Casel — Christ und Theologe für unsere Zeit; zu neuen Studien über die Mysterientheologie: TR 84 (1988) 1-18.

k454 **Gozier** André, La porte du ciel; ré-actualiser le mystère avec Odon Casel. P 1987, OEIL. 192 p. – ᴿEsprVie 98 (1988) 46-48 (J.-C. D.).

k455 CHENU: *Arnal* Oscar L., Theology and commitment: Marie-Dominique Chenu: CCurr 23 (1988s) 64-75.

k456 COGGAN: **Pawley** Margaret, [10 years York, 5 years Canterbury: Archbishop] Donald Coggan, servant of Christ 1987 ➤ 3,g929: ᴿTLond 91 (1988) 339-341 (H. *Montefiore*).

k457 CONGAR: **Henn** William, The hierarchy of truths according to Yves Congar: AnGreg 246, 1987. – ᴿEsprVie 98 (1988) 348 (G.-M. *Oury*).

k458 **Congar** Yves, [*Lauret* B.] Herbstgespräche; Erinnerungen und Anstösse [1987 ➤ 3,g930],ᵀ. Mü 1988, Neue Stadt. 136 p. DM 15,80. – ᴿHerdKorr 42 (1988) 301s (U. *Ruh*).

k459 DANIÉLOU: **Veliath** Dominic, Theological approach and understanding of religions; Jean Daniélou and Raimundo PANIKKAR; a study in contrast. Bangalore 1988, Kristu Jyoti. xiv-407 p. $22. – ᴿJDharma 13 (1988) 413s (J. *Kuttianimattathil*).

k460 EBELING: *White* Graham, Theology and logic; the case of Ebeling: ModT 4 (1987s) 17-34.

k461 **Ebeling** Gerhard, Dogmatik des christlichen Glaubens² I-III. Tü 1982 [¹1979], Mohr. xxviii-418 p.; xvi-547 p.; xix-585 p. je DM 48. – ᴿRelStR 14 (1988) 30-37 (S. *Grenz*).

k462 FREIRE: *Blackwood* Vernon, Historical and theological foundations of Paulo Freire's educational praxis [... 'one of the most widely discussed educators alive']: TrinJ 8 (1987) 201-232.

k463 GOGARTEN: *Geisser* Hans F., Theologie zwischen den Zeiten; zum Gedenken an Friedrich Gogarten (13.1.1887-16.10.1967): ZTK 85 (1988) 77-97.

k464 *Hübner* Hans, Das Neue Testament im theologischen Denken Friedrich Gogartens; Rückblick auf einen Abschnitt Göttinger Theologiegeschichte: NTS 34 (1988) 431-441.

k465 GUITTON Jean (avec *Doré* J.), Le Christ de ma vie: JJC Résonances 1. P 1987, Desclée. 298 p. – ᴿEsprVie 98 (1988) 262-4 (P. *Jay*).

k466 HEIDEGGER: *Greisch* Jean, Études heideggériennes: RSPT 72 (1988) 579-604...

k467 HIRSCH: *Herms* Eilert, Emanuel Hirsch — zu Unrecht vergessen?: Luther 19 (1988) 111-121.

k468 **Ericksen** Robert P., Theologians under Hitler... 1985 → 1,g11...3,g952: ᴿTrinJ 9,1 (1988) 110-2 (S. *McKnight*).

k469 **Schottroff** Willy, Theologie und Politik bei Emanuel Hirsch; zur Einordnung seines Verständnisses des Alten Testaments: KIsr 2 (1987) 24-49.137-158.

k470 JOHANNES XXIII: *Alberigo* Giuseppe, Johannes XXIII (Papst 1958-1963), ᵀ*Wirsching* Rosemarie: → 813, TRE 17 (1987) 113-8.

k471 ᴱ**Alberigo** G., Papa Giovanni [XXIII; colloquio Bergamo 1986] 1987 → 3,577: ᴿCrNSt 9 (1988) 225-9 (D. *Menozzi*); RivStoLR 24 (1988) 122-9 (P. *Scoppola*).

k472 **Hebblethwaite** Peter, Jean XXIII, le Pape du Concile [1984 → 2,d993], ᵀ*Feisthauer* Joseph. P 1987, Centurion. 598 p. F 170. – ᴿCrNSt 9 (1988) 653-5 (A. *Melloni*); EsprVie 98 (1988) 543s (P. G.: peu sur la nonciature à Paris); Études 368 (1988) 280s (J. *Thomas*); VSp 142 (1988) 298s (J. *Bonduelle*).

k473 JOHANNES PAULUS II: *Ciccone* Lino, Uomo-donna; l'amore umano nel piano divino; la grande catechesi del mercoledì di Giovanni Paolo II. T-Leumann 1986, LDC. 213 p. – ᴿClaretianum 27 (1987) 390-2 (J. *Rovira*); DocCom 40 (1987) 215s (D. *Composta*).

k474 *a)* *Giovanni Paolo II*, Lettera enciclica 'Sollicitudo rei socialis' [...30.XII.1987]: CC 139 (1988,1) 459-503; – *b)* *Coste* René, L'encyclique de Jean-Paul II sur la question sociale: EsprVie 98 (1988) 161-174.

k475 ᴱ**Valette** René, Jean-Paul II, Lettre encyclique 'Sollicitudo rei socialis', la question sociale. P 1988, Centurion. 106 p. F 28. – ᴿEsprVie 98 (1988) 174s (E. *Vauthier*).

k476 *Martini* Carlo M., Il disegno delle tre grandi encicliche nel pontificato di Giovanni Paolo II: CC 139 (1988,4) 114-127.

k477 *Szlaga* Jan, ❷ De Sacra Scriptura in magisterio Ioannis Pauli II: → 475, RuBi 41 (1988) 75-84.

k478 **Del Rio** Domenico, *Accattoli* Luigi, Wojtyła, il nuovo Mosè. Mi 1988, Mondadori.

k479 **Kalinowski** Georges, Autour de 'Personne et Acte' de Karol Cardinal Wojtyła; articles et conférences sur une rencontre du thomisme avec la phénoménologie. Aix-en-Provence 1987, Presses Univ. 160 p. – ᴿRThom 88 (1988) 315-9 (J.-Y. *Lacoste*).

k480 *Gałkowski* Jerzy W., The place of Thomism in the anthropology of K. Wojtyła: Angelicum 65 (1988) 181-194.

k481 *Montalbo* Melchior,   Karol Wojtyła's philosophy of the acting person: PhilipSa 23 (1988) 333-386.

k482 **Quiles** Ismael,   Filosofia de la persona según Karol Wojtyła (Estudio comparado con la antropología in-sistencial).   Buenos Aires 1987, Depalma.   ix-148 p. – ᴿCC 139 (1988,2) 610s (G. *Rulli*).

k483 **Woznicki** Andrew N.,   The dignity of man as a person; [his own] essays on the Christian humanism of His Holiness John Paul II.   SF 1987, Society of Christ.   xv-170 p. $5 [TDig 36,95].

k484 **Hogan** Richard M., *Levoir* John M.,   Faith for today; John Paul II's catechetical teaching.   NY 1988, Doubleday.   xviii-294 p. $17 [CBQ 51,401].

k485 JÜNGEL: **Webster** J. B.,   Eberhard Jüngel; an introduction to his theology 1986 ➤ 2,e9; 3,g964:   ᴿAnglTR 70 (1988) 276s (D. A. *Scott*); RExp 85 (1988) 381 (D. *Mueller*: model of lucidity, brevity, and balanced judgment); WestTJ 50 (1988) 230s (R. C. *Gamble*).

k486 **Jüngel** Eberhard,   Verweigertes Geheimnis? Bemerkungen zu einer unevangelischen Sonderlehre [*Lønning* Per (nicht Inge!) 1986 gegen Jüngel und PANNENBERG]: ➤ 114, ᶠPANNENBERG W., Vernunft 1988, 488-501.

k487 JUNGMANN: *Meyer* Hans B.,   Jungmann, Josef Andreas (1889-1975): ➤ 813, TRE 17 (1988) 465-7.

k488 KÄSEMANN Ernst,   What I have unlearned in 50 years as a German theologian: CurrTM 15 (1988) 325-335.

k489 KING: *Molla* Serge,   L'actualité de Martin Luther King, Jr.:   RTPhil 120 (1988) 329-338.

k490 KRAEMER: *a) Houwert* F.,   Hendrik Kraemer [1888-1965] en het réveil in de Hervormde Kerk, 1937-1947; – *b) Frei* Fritz,   Die katholische Stellung zu Hendrik Kraemers Werk: NedTTs 42 (1988) 275-287 / 288-306; Eng. 330.

k491 KÜNG: **Espinosa** C. Enrique,   Orthodoxy and heresy in Hans Küng; an analysis and critique of his criteria and norms of Christian truth and error: diss. Andrews, ᴰ*Dederen* R.   Berrien Springs 1988.   457 p. – RTLv 20,566.

k492 **Huovinen** Eero,   Idea Christi; die idealistische Denkform und Christologie in der Theologie Hans Küngs.   Hannover 1985. ... 159 p. – ᴿZKG 99 (1988) 286 (H. G. *Pöhlmann*).

k493 **Küng** Hans,   Teologia in cammino, un'autobiografia spirituale: Saggi.   Mi 1987, Mondadori. – ᴿQVidCr 142 (1988) 129 (P. *Busquets*).

k494 **Küng** Hans,   Pourquoi suis-je encore chrétien? [1985 ➤ 3,g968], ᵀ*Feisthauer* J.   P 1988, Centurion.   96 p. F 49 [RTLv 19,505].

k495 KUYPER: **Stellingwerff** J.,   Dr. Abraham Kuyper en de Vrije Universiteit.   Kampen 1987, Kok.   365 p. A$ 54. – ᴿRefTR 47 (1988) 62 (A. M. *Harman*).

k496 LEWIS: **Barratt** David C.,   C. S. Lewis [1898-1963] and his world.   GR 1987, Eerdmans.   46 p.; 48 color. phot. $10 [TDig 35,259].

k497 *Fernández* I.,   Un rationalisme chrétien; le cas de C. S. Lewis (1898-1963): Revue philosophique FÉ 113 (1988) 3-17 [< RSPT 72,497].

k498 **Griffin** William,   Clive Staples Lewis, a dramatic life.   SF 1986, Harper & R.   xxvi-507 p. – ᴿSalesianum 50 (1988) 393 (G. *Abbà*).

k499 LØGSTRUP: *Christoffersen* Svein A.,   Skapelsesteologi eller skapelsesfilosofi? [Løgstrup K. E.; KÄSEMANN-BONHOEFFER mellom BARTH-BULTMANN og WINGREN-EBELING]: ➤ 99*, ᶠLØNNING I., NorTTs 89 (1988) 3-17.

k500 LONERGAN: Collected works 4²ʳᵉᵛ, ᴱCrowe Frederick E., Doran Robert M. Toronto 1988, Univ. xviii-349 p.

k501 **Gregson** Vernon, Lonergan, spirituality, and the meeting of religions. Lanham MD 1985, UPA. 154 p. $10.75. – ᴿJAAR 56 (1988) 159s (Nancy C. Ring).

k502 Sala Giovanni B., B. Lonergans Methode der Theologie: TPhil 63 (1988) 34-59.

k503 Shea William M., Horizons on Bernard Lonergan: Horizons 18 (1988) 77-107.

k504 DE LUBAC: McPartlan Paul, Eucharist and Church; the contribution of Henri de Lubac: Month 249 (1988) 847-859.

k505 **Lubac** H. de, Lettres de GILSON 1986 ⇒ 2,e31; 3,g975: ᴿAngelicum 65 (1988) 148-151 (D. Ols); BLitÉc 89 (1988) 74s (B. de Guibert).

k506 **Lubac** Henri de, Letters of Étienne Gilson to / annotated by ∼. SF 1988, Ignatius. 247 p.

k507 **Lubac** H. de, The Christian faith: a) [1969 French ed.] ᵀArnandez Richard. SF 1986, Ignatius. 353 p. £9.25. – Month 249 [wrongly numbered 259 on p. 485] (1988) 525 (A. Meredith). – b) [1970 2d French edition], ᵀTrethowan Illtyd, Saward John. L 1987, Chapman [Month 249, 601: 'the only edition available outside US-Canada'].

k508 LUSTIGER J.-M., [Missika Jean-Louis, Wolton Dominique, entretiens], Le choix de Dieu. P 1987, de Fallois. 477 p. F 120. – ᴱÉtudes 368 (1988) 406s (P. Valadier); NRT 110 (1988) 97-100 (D. Dideberg).

k509 MASTON: **Martin** Earl R., Passport to servanthood; the life and missionary influence of T. B. Maston. Nv 1988, Broadman. 190 p. – ᴿSWJT 31,1 (1988s) 45 (J. C. Anderson).

k510 MEN: **Graaf** J. de, Traditie en aktuele kontext in de theologie van Alexander Men [b. 1935; Ellis Jane, The Russian Orthodox Church, a contemporary history, L 1986]: NedTTs 42 (1988) 307-316; Eng. 330.

k511 MERTON: a) Tastard Terry, Anglicanism and the conversion of Thomas Merton; – b) Leech Kenneth, Thomas Merton as a theologian of resistance: TLond 91 (1988) 17-44 / 464-473.

k512 MOLTMANN: **Bauckham** Richard, Moltmann, Messianic theology in the making. L 1987, Marshall Pickering. x-175 p. £10. – ᴿThemelios 14 (1988s) 76 (L. H. Osborn).

k513 Bauckham R., Theodicy from Ivan Karamazov to Moltmann: ModT 4 (1987s) 83-97.

k514 Moda Aldo, Sentieri nuovi eppure antichi nella teologia di J. Moltmann: StPatav 35 (1988) 197-615.

k514* MONTGOMERY: **Liefeld** David R., Lutheran orthodoxy and evangelical ecumenicity in the writings of John Warwick Montgomery [< diss. Westminster 1986]: WestTJ 50 (1988) 103-126.

k515 **NEWBIGIN** Lesslie, Unfinished agenda 1985 ⇒ 2,e35: ᴿJEcuSt 25 (1988) 306-8 (R. T. Handy).

k516 NIEBUHR: Feenstra Ronald J., Reassessing the thought of Reinhold Niebuhr: CalvinT 23 (1988) 142-160.

k517 **Fox** R., R. Niebuhr 1985 ⇒ 2,a39; 3,g981: ᴿChH 57 (1988) 251-3 (J. F. Wilson).

k518 **Benne** Robert, Ordinary saints; an introduction to the Christian life [... iii. as in the Niebuhrs]. Ph 1988, Fortress. x-214 p. [RelStR 15,62, G. Meilaender].

k519 Lovin Robin W., Reinhold Niebuhr, past and future [Fox R. 1985]: RelStR 14 (1988) 97-103.

k520 *Rasmussen* Larry,   Reinhold Niebuhr, public theologian [6 books]: CCurr 23 (1988s) 198-210.

k521 PANNENBERG: *Accordini* Giuseppe, Linguaggio, logica ed epistemologia nel pensiero di W. Pannenberg — dal realismo dell'ermeneutica storica al criticismo dell'epistemologia teologica [< diss. Venezia 1987, ᴰ*Petterlini* A]: StPatav 35 (1988) 575-592; Eng. 595; 593-5 risposta di Pannenberg a 8 domande.

k522 *Bradshaw* Timothy, God's relationship to history in Pannenberg: ➤ 114, Issues 1987/9, 48-67.

k523 **Pannenberg** Wolfhart, Metaphysik und Gottesgedanke: V-Reihe 1532. Gö 1988, Vandenhoeck & R. 100 p. DM 15,80. – ᴿTR 84 (1988) 274-6 (G. L. *Müller*).

k524 PAULUS VI: **Busquets i Sindreu** Joan, La libertad en los textos de Pablo VI y sus fundamentos: diss. Inst. Cath., ᴰ*Vidal* M. P 1988. 232 p.; 220 p. – RICathP 25 (1988) 102s.

k525 ᴱ**Vallet** G., *Piétri* C., Paul VI et la modernité dans l'Église 1983/4 ➤ 1,660; 3,g986: ᴿRBgPg 66 (1988) 907-910 (Anne *Morelli*).

k525* PELIKAN Jaroslav, The melody of theology; a philosophical dictionary. CM 1988, Harvard. x-274 p. $20 [JTS 40,747].

k526 PIE X (A. *Niers*), XI (A. *Boland*), XII (M. *O'Carroll*): DictSp 12 (1986) 1429-1432-1438-1442.

k527 PINNOCK: **Price** Robert M., Clark H. Pinnock, conservative and contemporary: EvQ 60 (1988) 157-183 [summary in BS 145 (1988) 454s (J. A. *Witmer*)].

k528 RAHNER: **Ackley** John B., The Church of the Word; a comparative study of Word, Church and office in the thought of Karl Rahner and Gerhard EBELING: diss. Catholic Univ., ᴰ*Dulles* A. Wsh 1988. 551 p. 88-14930. – DissA 49 (1988s) 1491s-A.

k529 **Callahan** Annice, Karl Rahner's spirituality of the pierced heart, ᴰ1985 ➤ 2,e62: ᴿSR 17 (1988) 496s (N. *King*).

k530 *Molnar* Thomas, La pensée et la popularité de Karl Rahner [lucky the simple faithful can't understand him]: PenséeC 233 (1988) 86-88.

k531 *Doré* J., Rahner, Karl: ➤ 786, Catholicisme 12,55 (1988) 445-456 (444s, Rahner, Hugo, G.-H. *Baudry*).

k532 *Neufeld* Karl, Rahner, Karl: ➤ 791, DictSpir XIII,86 (1987) 45-48 [... Hugo, 43-45].

k533 **Sheehan** Thomas, Karl Rahner; the philosophical foundations [Geist in Welt]. Athens OH 1987, Athens Univ. xi-320 p. $25 [TS 50, 382, T. F. *O'Meara*: high praise].

k534 **Vorgrimler** H., Understanding Karl Rahner 1986 ➤ 2,e70; 3,g998: ᴿPrPeo 2 (1988) 40s (P. *Phillips*); RRel 46 (1987) 787s (G. F. *Finnegan*).

k535 **Vorgrimler** H., Comprendere Karl Rahner; introduzione alla sua vita e al suo pensiero 1987 ➤ 3,g299: ᴿRasT 29 (1988) 104s (P. *Vanzan*).

k536 **Vorgrimler** Herbert, Entender a Karl Rahner; introducción a su vida y su pensamiento, ᵀ*Villanueva Salas* Marciano. Barc 1988, Herder. 267 p. pt. 1200. 84-254-1574-8. – ᴿActuBbg 25 (1988) 252 (J. *Boada*); ArTGran 51 (1988) 351s (J. A. *Estrada*).

k537 RAMSEY: *Wakefield* Gordon S., Michael Ramsey; a theological appraisal: TLond 91 (1988) 455-464 [the one undoubted theologian Archbishop of Canterbury this century, though 'no Barth or Balthasar, Rahner or Schillebeeckx'].

k538 RATZINGER: **Nichols** Aidan, The theology of J. Ratzinger; an introductory study. E 1988, Clark. vii-338 p. £10. 0-567-29148-0. – ᴿNRT
110 (1988) 754 (R. *Escol*); PrPeo 2 (1988) 302s (F. J. *Selman*); RivScR 2
(1988) 401-9 (R. *Stork*); Tablet 242 (1988) 117 (N. *Lash*).

k539 *Nichols* Aidan, Joseph Ratzinger's theology of political ethics [Kirche,
Ökumene 1987 3d part: 'a powerful and original theological mind ... alien
to scholasticism']: NBlackf 68 (1987) 380-392.

k540 **Rollet** Jacques, Le cardinal Ratzinger et la théologie contemporaine:
Apologétique. P 1988, Cerf. 134 p. F 66. – ᴿÉtudes 369 (1988) 137s (R.
Marlé).

k540* RAUSCHENBUSCH: **Minus** Paul M., Walter Rauschenbusch, American
reformer. NY/L 1988 Macmillan / Collier. xii-243 p.; 8 pl. $20 [JTS
40,742].

k541 SCHAEFFER: ᴱ**Ruegsegger** Ronald W., Reflections on Francis Schaeffer [evangelist 1968-84; 10 essays by Clark *Pinnock*, *al.*]. GR 1986,
Zondervan. xvi-320 p. $14. – ᴿAndrUnS 26 (1988) 97s (G. *Land*: zeal
largely based on newspaper clippings).

k542 SCHAFF: **Schriver** George H., Philip Schaff, Christian scholar and
ecumenical prophet [director of Revised Version and Lange's Com-
mentary-US]. Macon 1987, Mercer Univ. xii-138 p. $20. – ᴿAndrUnS 26
(1988) 206s (G. R. *Knight*).

k543 SCHILLEBEECKX: **Callewaert** Janet M., The role of a creation theology
in the contemporary soteriology of Edward Schillebeeckx: diss. Catholic
Univ., ᴰ*Loewe* W. Wsh 1988. 261 p. 88-14938. – DissA 49 (1987s)
1492-A.

k544 *Hilkert* M. Catherine, Hermeneutics of history; the theological method
of Edward Schillebeeckx: Thomist 51 (1987) 97-145.

k545 ᴱ**Schoof** Ted, The Schillebeeckx case 1984 ⇒ 65,e63; 2,e86: ᴿChH 57
(1988) 115s (J. P. *Gaffey*).

k546 SCHLATTER: **Bock** Ernst, Adolf-Schlatter-Archiv, Inventar. Stu 1988,
Landeskirchliches Archiv. xxi-248 p. [JBL 107,785].

k547 SCHWEITZER: *Körtner* Ulrich H. J., Ehrfurcht vor dem Leben —
Verantwortung für das Leben; Bedeuting und Problematik der Ethik
Albert Schweitzers [... mehr gelobt als gelesen]: ZTK 85 (1988) 329-348.

k548 SIRI Giuseppe, card. [⇒ 264], La strada passa per Cristo, ᴱ*Lanzi* N.; I.
Lettere 1949-82; 416 p. – II. Studi Sociali. Pisa 1985s, Giardini. Lit. 28.000
ciascuno. – ᴿDocCom 40 (1987) 296-8 (A. *Coccia*).

k549 SMITH: **Clements** Keith W., The theology of Ronald G. Smith 1986
⇒ 2,e87: ᴿRelStR 14 (1988) 238 (D. R. *Boone*).

k550 STOTT: **Edwards** David L., Essentials; a liberal-evangelical dialogue
[with/on John Stott]. L 1988, Hodder & S. xii-348 p. £7 pa. – ᴿTLond 91
(1988) 344s (D. *Stacey*).

k551 VAN TIL: **Robbins** John W., Cornelius Van Til, the man and the myth.
Jefferson MD 1986, Trinity Fd. 45 p. $2.45. – ᴿBS 145 (1988) 351 (F. R.
Howe: dubious 'full-orbed attack').

k552 TILLICH: *Abel* Olivier, Les formes du combat rationaliste chez Paul
Tillich: RHPR 68 (1988) 461-476.

k553 **Albrecht** Renate, *Schüssler* Werner, *al.*, Paul Tillich, sein Werk 1986
⇒ 2,d93; 3,h22: ᴿZkT 110 (1988) 189s (E. *Sturm*: als Band II zur
Biographie von PAUCK W. & M.).

k554 *a) Clayton* John, Tillich, TROELTSCH and the dialectical theology:
ModT 4 (1987s) 323-344; – *b) Ruddies* Hartmut, Ernst Troeltsch und

Paul Tillich; eine theologische Skizze: ➤ 140, ᶠSTOODT D., Unterwegs 1987, 409-422.

k555 *Coêlho Pires* José Luis, Razón y religión; el legado de Paul Tillich [< 'una alternativa frente a la teología liberal y la neo-ortodoxía de Karl BARTH', diss. Vítoria 1987]: LumenVr 37 (1988) 1-23.

k556 **Nuovo** Victor, Visionary science; a translation of Tillich's 'On the idea of a theology of culture' [lecture to Kant-Gesellschft 1919], with an interpretative essay. Detroit 1987, Wayne State Univ. 194 p. $27.50 [TDig 36,89].

k557 *Petit* Jean-Claude, Croire et douter; un aspect fondamental de l'éxpérience religieuse moderne selon Paul Tillich: ÉTRel 63 (1988) 17-29.

k558 *Rössler* Andreas, Paul Tillich; towards an evangelical catholicity [< ÖkRu 35 (1986) 415-427], ᵀ*Asen* B. A.: TDig 35 (1988) 123-7.

k559 *Schüssler* Werner, Paul Tillich and 'God above God' [= the God of the non-religious: StiZt 112 (1987) 765-772]; ᵀᴱ*Asen* B. A.: TDig 35 (1988) 251-5.

k560 TOMKINS: *Rodger* Patrick C., Ecumenists of our time; Oliver Stratford Tomkins: Mid-Stream 27 (1988) 227-236.

k561 TROELTSCH: **Dietrich** Wendell S., COHEN and Troeltsch; ethical monotheistic religion and theory of culture: BrownJudSt 120. Atlanta 1986, Scholars. xi-100 p. $24; pa. $19. 1-55540-0175; 8-3. – ᴿHenoch 10 (1988) 119-121 (A. *Poma*).

k562 *Liebersohn* Harry, The Utopian forms of religious life; Ernst Troeltsch's 'The social teachings of the Christian Church': ArchScSocRel 65,1 (1988) 121-144.

k563 **Yasukuta** Toshimasa, Ernst Troeltsch; systematic theologian of radical historicality 1986 ➤ 3,h34: ᴿTS 49 (1988) 781s (Diane *Yaeger*).

k564 VINCENT: *Héring* Jean, *Hauter* C.: Gilbert Vincent, la Faculté de théologie protestante et l'accueil de la phénoménologie dans l'entre-deux guerres: RHPR 68 (1988) 121-132.

k565 VISSER 'T HOOFT W. A., Memoirs. Geneva 1987, WCC. x-379 p. $20 [RelStR 15, 346, J. T. *Ford*].

k565* WILES: **Rothuizen** Gerard, Apologetics in Oxford; the theology of M. F. Wiles. Kampen 1987, Kok. 94 p. ƒ94. 90-242-4381-5. – ᴿExpTim 99 (1987s) 349s (T. *Gorringe*).

k566 WITTGENSTEIN: *Browarzik* Ulrich, Der grundlose Glaube; Wittgenstein über Religion: NSys 30 (1988) 72-100; Eng. 100.

k567 **Kerr** Fergus, Theology after Wittgenstein 1986 ➤ 2,e102; 3,h37: ᴿNBlackfr 68 (1987) 153-5 (Janet M. *Soskice*); RelSt 24 (1988) 267-9 (K. *Ward*); RSPT 72 (1988) 508-510 (D. *Bourg*); ScotJT 34 (1988) 135-7 (D. *Evans*).

Y6.8   *Tendentiae exeuntis saeculi XX* – **Late 20th Century Movements.**

k568 ᴱ**Alberigo** G., *Jossua* J. P., Vaticano II / La réception 1985 ➤ 1,g279*ab* ... 3,h38s: ᴿRHE 83 (1988) 265-7 (R. *Aubert*).

k568* ᴱ**Alberigo** G., *Jossua* J. P., ᵀᴱ*Komonchak* J., The reception of Vatican II. Wsh 1987, Catholic University of America. x-363 p. £20 [HeythJ 30,179-183, E. *Lord*].

k569 **Balasuriya** Tissa, Planetary theology 1984 ➤ 1,8032.8218; 2,e106: ᴿÉglT 17 (1986) 403s (R. P. *Hardy*: tremendous value and impact).

k570 *Barreda* J. A., Una nueva evangelización para un hombre nuevo: Studium 28 (M 1988) 3-34.

k571 *Barrett* David B., Forecasting the future in world mission: Missiology 15 (1987) 433-450 (*al.* 451-471).

k572 *Baubérot* Jean. Le Protestantisme dans une société postsécularisée: RTPhil 120 (1988) 41-61.

k573 **Beeck** Frans J. Van, Catholic identity after Vatican II; three types of faith in the one Church 1985 → 2,e107: ᴿTR 84 (1988) (W. *Beinert*).

k574 *Bianchi* Enzo, Vingt ans après le Concile; lumières et ombres: VieCons 60 (1988) 67-88.

k575 **Biser** Eugen, Die glaubensgeschichtliche Wende 1986 → 3,b43; 3-222-11721-7: ᴿActuBbg 25 (1988) 79s (J. *Boada*); TGegw 30 (1987) 143 (B. *Hidber*).

k576 *Borobio* Dionisio, La recepción del Concilio por diversos movimientos cristianos postconciliares en España: → 568, Iglesia 1987, Salmanticensis 35 (1988) 29-59 [-314, *al.*].

k577 **Bühlmann** Walbert, The Church of the future 1986 → 2,e112; 3,h45: ᴿColcFuJen 75 (1988) 143-6 (L. *Gutheinz* ☉); Gregorianum 69 (1988) 358s (J. *Dupuis*: favorable); Missiology 15,1 (1987) 127s (E. L. *Copeland*: splendid); NedTTs 42 (1988) 269s (F. O. van *Gennep*).

k578 **Cox** Harvey, Religion in the secular city; toward a post-modern theology 1984 → 65,e73 ... 3,h47: ᴿIstina 33 (1988) 93-95 (B. *Dupuy*).

k579 **Cox** Harvey, The silencing of Leonardo Boff; the Vatican and the future of world Christianity. Bloomington IN 1988, Meyer-Stone. 208 p. $10 pa. 0-940989-35-2 [CCurr 23/2 adv.].

k580 **Cupitt** Don, Lifelines [... postmodern religion] 1986 → 2,5240: ᴿNBlackf 68 (1987) 363s (G. *Turner*); TLond 91 (1988) 133-5 (P. *Baelz*: Cupitt finds value in analyzing pluralistic spiritualities even though the pilgrimage is never-ending).

k581 **Davis** Charles, What is living, what is dead ...? 1986 → 2,e117; 3,h47: ᴿÉglT 19 (1988) 299-302 (R. W. *Kropf*); Horizons 18 (1988) 180-2 (W. M. *Thompson*); JRel 68 (1988) 129s (R. *Haight*); Worship 62 (1988) 83-85 (A. *Dulles*).

k582 **Deedy** John, American Catholicism; and now where? NY 1987, Plenum. $19. – ᴿCCurr 23 (1988s) 108s (R. *Van Allen*: journalistic but not merely).

k583 **Denis** Henri, Église, qu'as-tu fait de ton concile? P 1985, Centurion. 248 p. – ᴿRHE 83 (1988) 818 (R. *Aubert*).

k584 **Drummond** Richard H., Toward a new age in Christian theology: American Society of Missiology series, 8, 1985 → 1,g291 ... 3,h52: ᴿNedTTs 42 (1988) 172s (E. J. *Schoonhoven*).

k585 **Edwards** David L., The futures of Christianity 1987 → 3,h53: ᴿTLond 91 (1988) 68-70 (P. *Coleman* is reminded of Ozymandias: 'round the decay of that colossal wreck, the lone and level sands stretch far away': the 1500 million Christians are a wreck of 20,000 denominations).

k586 ᴱ**Galantino** N., Il Concilio venti anni dopo; 3. Il rapporto chiesa-mondo. R 1986, AVE. 240 p. Lit. 16.500. – ᴿProtestantesimo 43 (1988) 238s (F. *Ferrario*).

k587 **Gill** Robin, Beyond decline [of the mainline churches]; a challenge to the churches. L 1988, SCM. 146 p. £6. 0-334-00097-1. – ᴿExpTim 99,12 2d-top choice (1987s) 354s (C. S. *Rodd*); Themelios 14 (1988s) 114 (D. J. *Tidball*).

k588 **Giussani** Luigi, entretiens avec *Ronza* Robi, Le mouvement Communion et Libération [1987], ᵀ*Piétri* Sophie: Des Chrétiens. P 1988, Sarment-Fayard. 226 p. – ᴿRThom 88 (1988) 684-6 (G.-M. *Marty*).

k589 **Giussani** Luigi [fondateur de Comunione e Liberazione 1970], Le sens religieux, ᵀ*Cierniewski* Colette. P 1988, Fayard. 258 p. – ᴿRThom 88 (1988) 682-4 (G.-M. *Marty*).

k590 *Göpfert* Michael, Zwischen Christianopolis und Hure Babylon — Perspektiven kirchlicher Praxis in der Stadt von morgen: TPrac 23 (Mü 1988) 233-249 [< ᴢɪᴛ 89,126].

k591 *a*) *Gössmann* E., Hoffnung auf eine Zukunft der Theologie; – *b*) *Metz* J.-B., Unterwegs zu einer nachidealistischen Theologie; – *c*) *Schoonenberg* P., Rückkehr zur Vergangenheit; Weg in die Zukunft? Prolegomena zu einem Entwurf der Theologie; – *d*) *Bauer* J.B., Theologie zwischen Dynamik und Erstarrung: TJb (Lp 1988) 67-79 / 80-97 / 28-39 / 14-19.

k592 *Graf* Friedrich W., Konservatives Kulturluthertum, ein theologiege-schichtlicher Prospekt: ZTK 85 (1988) 31-76.

k593 **Groos** Helmut, Christlicher Glaube und intellektuelles Gewissen; Christentumskritik am Ende des zweiten Jahrtausends 1987 ⇥ 3,h55: ᴿTGL 78 (1988) 278s (W. *Beinert*).

k594 **Hanson** A.T. & R.P.C., The identity of the Church 1987 ⇥ 3,h56: ᴿTLond 91 (1988) 140-2 (J. *Tiller*: too readily links 'scholars/saints' and 'superiors/ignorant').

k595 **Hodgson** Peter C., Revisioning the Church; ecclesial freedom in the new paradigm. Ph 1988, Fortress. 128 p. $9 pa. [TDig 36,63].

k596 *Höhn* Hans-Joachim, Ende oder Wende der Moderne?: Orientierung 52 (1988) 114-7.

k597 **Hoffman** Virginia, Birthing a living Church. NY 1988, Crossroad. xiv-183 p. $17 [TS 50,620, J.L. *Empereur*: Catholic but applicable also elsewhere].

k598 **Hopper** Jeffery, Understanding modern theology, I. Cultural revolutions and new worlds 1987 ⇥ 3,h61: ᴿTLZ 113 (1988) 220 (F. *Wagner*); TS 49 (1988) 205s (R.F. *Scuka*).

k599 **Hopper** Jeffery, Understanding modern theology, II. Reinterpreting Christian faith for changing worlds. Ph 1987, Fortress. viii-158 p. $13. – ᴿNewTR 1,4 (1988) 80-82 (S. *Bevans*).

k600 **Hunter** James D. Evangelicalism; the coming generation 1987 ⇥ 3,h62: ᴿBS 145 (1988) 472s (K.O. *Gangel*: sociologist queries D. Kᴇʟʟᴇʏ's 1972 classic); CCurr 23 (1988s) 116s (J.A. *Varacalli*); GraceTJ 9 (1988) 155s (R.T. *Clutter*: 'it is difficult to define evangelicalism').

k601 **Kaufman** G., Una teologia per l'era nucleare: GdT 179. Brescia 1988, Queriniana. 112 p. Lit. 11.000. – ᴿRasT 29 (1988) 213s (G. *Mattai*).

k602 *Kealy* Seán P., The Church of the future [*Bühlmann* W. 1986]: DocLife 37 (1987) 331-341.

k603 **Kennedy** Eugene, Tomorrow's Catholics, yesterday's Church; the two cultures of American Catholicism. NY 1988, Harper & R. xvi-208 p. $18 [CBQ 51,401].

k604 **Kobler** John F., Vatican II and phenomenology; reflections on the life-world of the Church 1985 ⇥ 3,h66: ᴿRTPhil 120 (1988) 116 (J.-E. *Bertholet*: no phenomenology, just triumphalism).

k605 *Koranyi* Max, Du bereitest vor mir einen Tisch im Angesicht meiner Feinde; biblisch-theologische Überlegungen und historische Anmerkungen zum 'Sanctuary Movement' in den USA: Junge Kirche 49 (Bremen 1988) 117s.

k606 ᴱ**Küng** Hans, *Swidler* Leonard, The Church in anguish; has the Vatican betrayed Vatican II? [1986 ⇥ 3,407],ᵀ. SF 1987, Harper & R. xi-324 p.

$17. - RHomP 89,4 (1988s) 70-72 (John M. *Grondelski*: 'It would, if it followed the suggestions of this book').

k607 **Küng** Hans, Theology for the third millennium; an ecumenical view [mostly reprints], TParis *Heinegg* Peter. NY 1988, Doubleday. xvi-315 p. $25. [TS 50, 585, R. L. *Maddox*].

k608 *Labbé* Yves, Réceptions théologiques de la 'postmodernité' [*Lafont* G. 1986; *Chauvet* L. 1987]: RSPT 72 (1988) 397-425; Eng. 426.

ELatourelle René, Vatican II 1988 → 379 Bilan, 380 Assessment.

k608* ELatourelle René, Vaticano II, bilancio e prospettive, venticinque anni dopo (1962-1987). Assisi ²1988, Cittadella. 1600 p. (2 vol.). Lit. 80.000. – RCC 139 (1988,2) 558-567 (G. P. *Salvini*: spagnuolo pronto); RClerIt 69 (1988) 384-6 (C. *Ghidelli*).

k609 *Légaut* Marcel, ¿ Se puede creer en la Iglesia del porvenir? [QVidCr 131s (1986) 153-173], TEMelero Domingo: SelT 26 (1987) 143-186.

k610 **Lindbeck** George, The nature of doctrine; religion and theology in a postliberal age 1984 → 1,g303 ... 3,h70: RHeythJ 29 (1988) 107-9 (J. E. *Thiel*); NedTTs 42 (1988) 173s (D. G. *Murphy*); TR 84 (1988) 47-49 (S. *Wiedenhofer*).

k611 **Mackey** James, Modern theology; a sense of direction. Ox 1987, UP. v-200 p. £13; pa. £5. – RTLond 91 (1988) 418s (B. L. *Horne*: clever and careless by turns, aims at a radical reformation of the Christian tradition).

k612 *a) Mardones* José M., Fe y religión en la Iglesia, hoy; hacia un cristianismo universal y policéntrico; – *b) Panikkar* Raimundo, La religión del futuro; crisis de un concepto y religiosidad humana: BibFe 14 (1988) 100-116 / 117-141.

k613 *Mattam* J., The lost God and the Church to be; two images of God and of the Church: Vidyajyoti 52 (1988) 495-505.

k614 *Morgan* Robert, A decade of theology: TLond 91 (1988) 274-283.

k615 *Nesti* Arnaldo, Il festivo e la modernizzazione: RasT 29 (1988) 166-190 . 265-280.

k615* **Neuhaus** Richard, The Catholic moment; the paradox of the Church in the postmodern world 1987 → 3,h74: RAmerica 159 (1988) 14-18 (G. G. *Higgins*).

k616 EO'Connell Timothy E., Vatican II and its documents; an American reappraisal 1986 → 2,e145: RCurrTM 15 (1988) 371s (M. *Root*).

k617 *Pizzuti* Giuseppe M., Processo al Concilio Vaticano II; la sfida di Mons. Marcel LEFEBVRE: Asprenas 35 (1988) 509-518.

k618 ERichard Lucien, Vatican II, the unfinished agenda 1987 → 3,h81: RHomP 89,3 (1988s) 71-73 (J. P. *Sheets*: good; some reserves).

k620 *Ruhbach* Gerhard, Frömmigkeit und Religiosität im ausgehenden 20. Jahrhundert: VerkFor 33 (1988) 43-71.

k621 ESavart C., *Aletti* J.-N., Le monde contemporain et la Bible: BTT 8, 1985 → 1,311 ... 3,h84: RRThom 88 (1988) 162s (B. *Montagnes*).

k622 **Sartori** L. present., Essere teologi oggi . CasM 1986, Marietti. 218 p. Lit. 25.000. – RProtestantesimo 43 (1988) 113-5 (E. *Stretti*: 'teologia italiana post-conciliare').

k623 **Saward** Michael, Evangelicals on the move. L 1987, Mowbray. xii-100 p. £5 pa. – RTLond 91 (1988) 338s (D. *Coggan*).

k624 *Seeber* David A., The future of Christianity in Europe [Einheit und Vielheit in der Weltkirche; Zeugnis Europa: Ordens-Korrespondenz 28,1 (1987) 31-41], TEAsen B. A.: TDig 35 (1988) 130s.

k625 *Sine* Tom, Shifting Christian mission to the future tense: Missiology 15,1 (1987) 15-23.

k626 **Stacpoole** Alberic, Vatican II by those who were there 1986 ➤ 2,341; 3,h87: ᴿRHE 83 (1988) 550 (G. *Temple*).

k627 **Thils** Gustave, Présence et salut de Dieu chez les 'non-chrétiens'... de l'an 2000: RTLv Cah 18, 1987 ➤ 3,h93: ᴿMélSR 45 (1988) 40s (M. *Huftier*).

k628 **Winling** Raymond, La teología del siglo XX, la teología contemporanea (1945-1980) ᵀ*Ortiz García* A. [< franç. 1983 ➤ 64,e649]: El peso de los días 23, Salamanca 1987 ➤ h99s: ᴿLumenVr 37 (1988) 89s (F. *Ortiz de Urtaran*).

Y7   (*Acta*) *Congressuum*   .2 *biblica:* **nuntii,** *rapports, Berichte.*

k629 *Agua* Agustín del, 42º Congreso internacional de la 'Studiorum Novi Testamenti Societas' (SNTS), Göttingen 24/27 agosto 1987: EstBíb 46 (1988) 253-7.

k630 *Atal* Sa Angang, Le troisième Congrès des Biblistes catholiques africains [Yaoundé 27.VII.–1.VIII.1987]: RAfT 11 (1987) 251-3.

k631 *Bitoto Abeng* Nazaire, Der Apostel Paulus und die Kirchen; Dritter Internationaler Kongress afrikanischer Exegeten; Yaoundé, Kamerun, Juli 1987: TKontext 9,1 (1988) 121.

k632 *Boccaccini* Gabriele, Seminario di Jacob NEUSNER a Bologna (13-16 marzo 1988) [nel conferire la laurea honoris causa]: RivB 36 (1988) 535s.

k633 *Borgonovo* Gianantonio, Israele alla ricerca di identità tra il II sec. a.C. e il I sec. d.C.; V Convegno di Studi Veterotestamentari, Bressanone, 7-9 settembre 1987: ScuolC 116 (1988) 79-86.

k634 *Calloud* Jean, Une session de sémiotique en Bretagne: SémBib 47 (1987) 44-48.

k635 *Catchpole* David R., Studiorum Novi Testamenti societas; the forty-second general meeting, 24-28 August 1987: NTS 34 (1988) 293s; 295-319, membership list.

k636 *Chmiel* Jerzy, ✪ *a*) Processus Iesu — traditio et historia; sessio in Graz 1987; – *b*) Iudaei et Christiani in dialogo; colloquium Cracoviae et in Tyniec 1988: RuBi 41 (1988) 233s / 231s.

k637 *Cohen* Martine, Un colloque sur les 'études juives', Paris 17-18 avril 1988: ArchScSocRel 66,2 (1988) 215-7.

k638 *Collins* R. F., *a*) The Thessalonian correspondence, Colloquium Biblicum Lovaniense XXXVIII (1988): ETL 64 (1988) 505-7. – *b*) Colloquium biblicum lovaniense 38 [Aug. 16-18, 1988]: LvSt 13 (1988) 361s.

k639 *Focant* Camille, *a*) Les épîtres aux Thessaloniciens; colloquium biblicum lovaniense XXXVIII [16-18 août 1988]: RTLv 19 (1988) 511-4; – *b*) Les paraboles évangéliques (A.C.F.E.B. 1987): RTLv 19 (1988) 120-2.

k640 *Kapera* Zdzisław, ✪ First international Qumranological congress in Poland: PrzOr (1988,2) 169-176.

k641 *Karavidopoulos* I. D., ⊜ *a*) SNTS meeting, Cambridge 1988; – *b*) 38 Colloquium Biblicum Lovaniense 1988: DeltioVM 17,2 (1988) 87-93-100.

k642 *Karukayil* Joseph, VI all-India biblical meeting, 4th to 8th December, 1987; a report: Word and Worship 21 (Bangalore 1988) 12-15 [< TKontext 10/1,53].

k643 *a*) *Klauck* H.-J., 42. Meeting der Studiorum NT Societas vom 24.-28. August 1987 in Göttingen; – *b*) *Söding* Thomas, Tagung der deutschsprachigen kath. Neutestamentler in Graz vom 6. bis 11.IV.1987: BZ 32 (1988) 165-7 / 162-5.

k644 *Loza* José, XII Congreso de la I.O.S.O.T. [Jerusalén 24-29.VIII.1986]: EfMex 5,13 (1987) 134-143.

k645 *Mazzucco* Clementina, Simposio per il XL [quarantesimo anniversario] dell'Associazione Biblica Italiana (Milano, 2-4 giugno 1988) [con l'Univ. Cattolica e la Facoltà Teologica dell'Italia Settentrionale]: RivB 36 (1988) 531-540.

k646 *Puthanangady* Paul, First All-Oceania workshop on biblical apostolate: Word and Worship 21 (Bangalore 1988) 137-141 (171-7) [< TKontext 10/1,54].

k647 *Salzano* Teresa, 'Venite, torniamo al Signore' (Os 6,1); VIII colloquio ebraico-cristiano, Camaldoli (Arezzo), 4/8 dic. 1987: StPatav 35 (1988) 245-252; Eng. 253.

k648 [*Sardini* Fausto] L'arte e la Bibbia; immagine come esegesi biblica: convegno internazionale promosso da Biblia (F-Settimello) [e] Fondazione G. Cini, Venezia 14-16 ott. 1988: BbbOr 30 (1988) 62.

k648* *Schreiner* Stefan, Erstes internationales jüdisch-christliches Gespräch in Kraków [5./6. Nov. (? 1987)]: Judaica 44 (1988) 47s.

k649 *Segalla* Giuseppe, *a*) 42° congresso internazionale della SNTS, Göttingen 24-27 agosto 1987: RivB 36 (1988) 127-130; – *b*) 48° congresso, giubilare (1938-1988) della SNTS a Cambridge (8-11 agosto 1988): StPatav 35 (1988) 759-763.

k650 *Shanks* Hershel, A wild, wonderful academic circus: [AAR-SBL-ASOR 1987 meeting in Boston]: BAR-W 14,2 (1988) 52-57.

k651 *Testa* Giuseppe, XXX settimana biblica nazionale; la missione nel mondo antico e nella Bibbia [Roma 12-16.IX.1986]: DivThom 91 (1988) 170-180.

k652 *Trebolle Barrera* Julio, Congreso de la Society of Biblical Literature: EstBíb 46 (1988) 121-4.

k653 *a*) *Verheyden* Jozef, Bijbelse Studiendagen te Leuven [38e, 16-18.VIII. 1988]: TsTNijm 28 (1988) 393s; – *b*) *Schwank* Benedikt, Cambridge und Leuven im August 1988: ErbAuf 64 (1988) 396-401.

k654 *Vincent* David, Culture, Bible and communication [Christian seminar in Papua New Guinea 13-18.III.1988]: Catalyst 18 (Goroke 1988) 84-95 [< TKontext 10/1,78].

k655 *Walsh* Jerome T., Report of the Fifty-first General Meeting of the Catholic Biblical Association of America [August 15-18, 1988, Santa Clara Univ.]: CBQ 50 (1988) 664-671.

Y7.4 (*Acta*) *theologica:* nuntii.

k656 *Althausen* Johannes, 'Christliche Mission auf dem Weg ins dritte Jahrtausend; das Evangelium der Hoffnung', VII. IAMS [International Association for Mission Studies]-Kongress, Rom 29.VI-5.VII.1988: ZMissRW 72 (1988) 306-9.

k657 *a*) *Bandera* Armando, Congreso mariológico-mariano en Kevelaer [11-20 sept. 1987]; – *b*) *Lago Alba* Luis, Salamanca en sínodo (XVI conversaciones de San Esteban): CiTom 115 (1988) 371-381 / 383-394.

k658 *Bitoto Abeng* Nazaire, Identität und Strukturen von SECAM; Reflexionen über die Zukunft der christlichen Mission in Afrika: Achte Vollversammlung vom Symposium of Episcopal Conferences of Africa and Madagascar; Lagos 12-19.VII.1987: TKontext 9,1 (1988) 120s.

k659 *Böhlig* A., 'First international conference on Manichaeism' in Lund 5.-9. August 1987: OrChr 72 (1988) 208-210.

k660 *Bossard* Alphonse [chronique] / *Molette* Charles [introduction], 44e-45e Session de la Société Française d'Études Mariales [Pontmain 5-7 sept. 1988]: Marianum 50 (1988) 576-580 / 580-9.

k661 *Carle* Paul-Laurent, Le colloque du Collège de France des 2 et 4 octobre pour préparer le XIIème centenaire de Nicée (787-1987): Divinitas 32 (1988) 565-594.

k662 *Carroll* Eamon R., *a*) International ecumenical conference, Mary woman for all Christians [Univ. SF, June 17-21, 1988]; – *b*) The 39th annual convention of the Mariological Society of America [East Aurora NY, June 1-2, 1986]: Marianum 50 (1988) 567s / 561s.

k663 *Castiau* Claude, Compte rendu de la session théologique 1988; réincarnation, immortalité, résurrection: CahSPR 3 (Bru 1988) 107-122.

k664 *Comba* Augusto, XXVII Convegno di studi sulla Riforma e i movimenti religiosi in Italia: Bollettino di Studi Valdesi 161 (1987) 61-68.

k665 *Deproost* P.-A., XIIe Congrès international de l'Association Guillaume Budé, Bordeaux 17-21 août 1988, 'Les écrivains et le sacré'; 'la vigne et le vin dans la littérature': RHE 83 (1988) 732s.

k666 *Espeja* Jesús, Simposio de Cristología [Madrid dic. 1987]: CiTom 115 (1988) 521-5.

k667 *Evers* Georg, Sozio-kulturelle Analyse in der Theologie; Zehnte Jahresversammlung der Indischen Theologischen Vereinigung, Mangalore 28.-31.XII.1986: TKontext 9,1 (1988) 122.

k668 *Evers* Georg, Theologie des interreligiösen Dialogs: Zweites Kolloquium der Theologischen Beratungskommission innerhalb der FABC (Vereinigung Asiatischer Bischofskonferenzen), Singapur 21.-27.IV.1987: TKontext 9,1 (1988) 124-6.

k669 *Evers* Georg, Leben und Arbeiten mit den Schwestern und Brüdern aus anderen Religionen, Gemeinsame Konsultation der Christlichen Konferenz von Asien CCA und der Vereinigung Asiatischer Bischofskonferenzen (FABC), Singapur 5.-10.VII.1987: TKontext 9,1 (1988) 126-9.

k670 *Fisher* Eugene J., International Jewish-Christian conference in Vienna [Nov. 27-30, 1988]: JEcuSt 25 (1988) 702-5.

k671 *a*) *Fuss* Michael, Internationale Konferenz über buddhistisch-christlichen Dialog, Berkeley/Kalifornien [10.-15. Aug. 1987]; – *b*) *Neuner* Joseph, 'Communicatio in sacris'; ein Seminar über das Selbstverständnis der Kirche im religiösen Pluralismus Indiens, Bangalore 20.-25. Januar 1988: ZMissRW 72 (1988) 66s / 240-8.

k672 *Gamberini* Paolo, La conferenza di [525 vescovi della Comunione anglicana] Lambeth '88: CC 139 (1988,4) 473-480.

k673 *a*) *Gambero* Luigi, Il X Congresso mariologico e il XVII Congresso mariano internazionale di Kevelaer; – *b*) *Napiórkowski* S.C., IIe symposium polonais sur le renouveau du culte marial; – *c*) *Carroll* E.R., The 38th annual convention of the Mariological Society of America; – *d*) *Meaolo* Gaetano, XXVI Settimana di Studi Mariani (Pompei 22-26.VI.1987): Marianum 39 (1987) 478-510 / 591-3 / 594s / 600-3.

k674 *Garstecki* Joachim, Erste Schritte auf dem gemeinsamen Weg; Tagung der ökumenischen Versammlung in der DDR (12.-15. Februar 1988): Orientierung 52 (1988) 89-93.

k675 *Gasbarro* Rosanna, Da Roma alla Terza Roma; VI Seminario Internazionale di Studi Storici [Roma-Mosca apr. magg. 1986]: StRicOrCr 10 (1987) 53-58 [141-5, *Garzaniti* Marcello, VII Sem. Roma 21-23 apr. 1987].

k676 *Gill* Theodor, 4. Vollversammlung der Karibischen Kirchenkonferenz (CCC) vom 4. bis 9. September 1986: ÖkRu 36 (1987) 96-98.

k677 *Hagedorn* Klaus,   Ökumenisches   Treffen   Assisi   [6.-12.VIII]   '88: Orientierung 52 (1988) 196-8.

k678 *Hageman* M.J.M.,   Tweede europese conferentie over 'Science and Religion' ['One world — changing perspectives on reality' 10-13.III. 1988, Twente]: TsTNijm 28 (1988) 175s.

k679 *Hoogen* T. van den,   Studiebijeenkomsten WKTN [Werkgenootschap van katholieke theologen in Nederland] over katholieke moraal en sociale verantwoordelijkheid [11.XI.1987], en over 'Vrouw en kerk' [i.e. 'Vrouwen als kerk' 16.I.1988]: TsTNijm 28 (1988) 173-5.

k680 *Jung* Hans-G.,   Bericht über die Tagung des Joint Committee der Konferenz Europäischer Kirchen, Bossey vom 26. bis 31. März 1987: ÖkRu 36 (1987) 357-361.

k681 Konferenzenberichte / Reports of conferences, by continent: [TKontext 9s =] TContext 5s (1988s).

k682 *a) Koperek* Stefan,   ❷ XI Kongres 'Societas Liturgica' [Internationalis, Brixen (Italia) 17-22.VIII] (1987); – *b) Rojewski* Andrzej, Relatio de XXIII symposio liturgico Cracoviae 1987:   RuBi 41 (1988) 442-7 / 440-2.

k683 *Lemieux* Raymond,   Un événement; le symposium 'Psychose, langage et sacré', Hammamet [Tunisie], 20-24 avril 1987: ArchScSocRel 65 (1988) 207-210.

k684 *a) Maimela* Simon S.,   Report on the Second General Assembly of the Ecumenical Association of Third World Theologians (EOTWOT), Oaxtepec Mex. 7-14.XII.1986; – *b) Mofokeng* Takatso,   Report; Black Theology consultation in New York 1-3.XII.1986: JBlackT 1,1 (1987) 54-59 / 53s [< TKontext 10/1,23s].

k685 *Marra* Bruno,   Etica ed economia [nelle società industriali dell'occidente, XIII Congresso Nazionale ATI-SM, Trento 5-8.IV.1988]: RasT 29 (1988) 483-7.

k686 *Mattai* Giuseppe,   In margine al convegno nazionale 'Uomini, nuove tecnologie, solidarietà; il servizio della Chiesa italiana' (Roma, 17-21 novembre 1987): RasT 29 (1988) 78-85.

k687 *Meaolo* Gaetano,   Convegno mariano nazionale XXVII sul tema 'conoscere, celebrare, affidarsi a Maria' (Loreto, 7-10 luglio 1988): Marianum 50 (1988) 573-5.

k688 *a) Moutsoulas* Elias D.,   ❻ Chronicles of conferences [3d Internat. Orthodox Theol. Schools, Brookline, MA Sept. 1987; 10th Patristic, Oxford 24-29 Aug. 1987]; – *b) Karathanasis* Athanasios E.,   ❻ The conference on 'Thessaloniki and the Paleologian period', Vlatadon 29-31.X.1987]; – *c) Papademetriou* George, (Eng.) The third international symposium of Orthodox theological schools: TAth 54 (1988) 377-382 / 383-9 / 390-5.

k689 *a) Naumowicz* Józef,   ❷ Anniversary of the baptism of St. Augustine, colloquium Milan 22-24.IV.1987; – *b) Jeuté* Piotr, ❷ Eastern Christian monasticism; 3d Symposium of Christian Archeology, Warszawa 27.IV.1987:   ColcT 58,4 (1988) 139-142 / 142-4.

k690 *a) Naumowicz* Józef,   ❷ Kolokwium o Soborze Nicejskim II, Paryż, 2-4.X.1986; – *b) Sondej* sr. Margarita,   ❷ Eucharystia źródłem odnowy życia chrześcijańskiego; Sprawozdanie z XVIII sympozjum w Między-zakonnym Wyższym Institucie Katechetycznym w Krakowie: ColcT 58,1 (1988) 134-6 / 99-106.

k691 *Oosterveen* Leo,   Symposium te Nijmegen over westeuropese bevrij-dingstheologie [12-13.XI.1987]:   TsTNijm 28 (1988) 75s.

k692 *Peitz* Marietta,   Die mutigen Frauen Lateinamerikas; Beobachtungen bei einem Menschenrechtskongress in San Salvador [20. Nov. 1987]: Orientierung 52 (1988) 14-17.

k693 *Pintard* J., Échos du Congrès de Toulouse sur saint Augustin [Actes = BLitEc 88,3s (1987)]: EsprVie 98 (1988) 426-8.

k694 *Pirotte* J., CREDIC (Centre de recherches et d'échanges sur la diffusion et l'inculturation du christianisme hors d'Europe, 9e session annuelle, Nimègue 14-17 juin 1988, 'L'appel à la mission; formes et évolution du XIXe s. à nos jours': RHE 83 (1988) 733-5.

k695 *Poupard* Paul, Le Synode des Évêques sur la vocation et la mission des laïcs dans l'Église et dans le monde vingt ans après le Concile Vatican II (1er-30e octobre 1987): EsprVie 98 (1988) 12-16.

k696 *Radano* John A., Symposium on Cardinal BEA [presentation of biography by S. *Schmidt*, Rome 12.II.1988]: Mid-Stream 27 (1988) 327-332.

k697 *Reina* Mario, Danaro e coscienza cristiana [convegno Bologna 10-11 aprile 1987): CC 139 (1988,1) 361-8.

k698 *Ries* J., *al.*, [Lv trois congrès 1988] Ve symposium syriacum 28-31 août; III Conference on Christian Arabic studies, 1-3 sept.; IVe Congrès international des Études coptes, 5-10 sept.: RHE 83 (1988) 777-9.

k699 *Ruiz Verdú* Pedro, XXIII Simposio de Teología Trinitaria (Salamanca 17-19.X.1988): Carthaginensia 4 (1988) 357-9.

k700 *a)* *Rusecki* Marian, ℗ Die wissenschaftliche Tagung der polnischen Fundamentaltheologen [23-24.IV.1987, Nysa]; – *b)* *Kubik* Władysław, ℗ IV. Niemiecki Kongres Katechetyczny – München [8-11.VI] 1987; – *c)* *Gliściński* Jan, ℗ Crescita dell'uomo; sympozjum patrystyczne Rzym 20-21 marca 1987 r.; – *d)* *Kołosowski* Tadeusz, ℗ Sympozjum patrystyczne 1600 r. S. Augustyna, 24-25.IV.1987, Lublin: ColcT 58,2 (1988) 167-173 / 89-93 / 147-150 / 150-152.

k701 *Schouppe* J.-P., Église universelle et Églises particulières, IXe Symposium international de théologie Pamplona [sans date]: ETL 64 (1988) 509-511.

k702 *Theodorou* Evangelos D., Ⓖ The inter-Orthodox conference on the place of women in the Orthodox church [Rhodes 30 Oct.-8 Nov. 1988]: TAth 54 (1988) 747-759 [595-600 → 9917].

k703 *a)* *Tóth* Károly, Ⓜ Opening address; towards a theology of peace, International Seminar, Budapest Raday College, Dec. 14-19, 1987; – *b)* *Moltmann* Jürgen, Ⓜ Justice creates peace, TE*Karasszon* István: Theologiai Szemle 31 (1988) 103-5 / 106-110.

k704 *Vincent* Gilbert, Œcuménisme; déclin, stagnation...? Colloque 'Les œcuménismes chrétiens', Strasbourg, 8-10 octobre 1987: ArchScSocRel 65 (1988) 211-215.

Y7.6 *Acta congressuum philologica:* **nuntii.**

k705 *Arcellaschi* A., [secr.] Compte rendu des séances de la Société des Études Latines: RÉLat [65 (1987) 1-23] 66 (1988) 1-17; liste des membres, ix-xxix; 11 thèses soutenues, p. [24] 20.

k706 *Arcoleo* Santo, Il 2o convegno di studi su PLUTARCO [Ferrara 2-3.IV.1987]: Maia 40 (1988) 84-87.

k707 *Bartoněk* Antonin, The eighth international colloquium on Mycenaean studies, Ochrid 16-22.IX.1985: SborBrno 33 (1988) 191-4 [Berlin 11.-15.VIII.1986 p. 194s].

k708 *Calder* William M.III, The Eduard MEYER symposium, Bad Homburg 10-14.XI.1987; program: Gnomon 60 (1988) 668s.

k710 ^E*Ermatinger* Charles J.,   The fourteenth Saint Louis conference on manuscript studies [Oct. 16-17, 1987], abstracts of papers: Manuscripta 32 (1988) 3-19.

k711 *Ieraci Bio* Anna Maria,   GALENO, obra, pensamiento e influencia; Madrid 22-25 marzo 1988: Koinonia 12 (1988) 83.

k712 *Motte* André,   Chronique des rencontres scientifiques: Kernos 1 (Liège 1988) 245-8.

k713 *Olshausen* Eckart, 3. Historisch-geographisches Kolloquium, Stuttgart 6.-10. Mai 1987, 'Raum und Bevölkerung in der antiken Stadtkultur': Gnomon 60 (1988) 95s.

k714 *Weijers* Olga,   Vocabulaire du livre et de l'écriture au moyen âge (Paris, 24-26 Septembre 1987): Studi Medievali 28 (1987) 1011-4.

Y7.8   *Acta congressuum orientalistica et archaeologica:* **nuntii.**

k715 *Ankum* Hans,   La XXXXIe [41st] session de la Société internationale 'F. De Visscher' pour l'histoire des droits de l'Antiquité, Saint-Sebastien et Vitoria, 22-25 septembre 1987: RIDA 35 (1988) 311-343.

k716 *Brice* William C.,   The sixth international colloquium on Aegean prehistory, at Athens [Aug. 1987]: Kadmos 27 (1988) 87s.

k717 Bulletin de la société française d'archéologie classique 20 (1986-1987): RArchéol (1988) 199-200 ► e946; g403.

k718 *Ghiberti* Giuseppe, *Alliata* Eugenio,   Trent'anni di archeologia in Terra Santa; Lo Studio Biblico Francescano di Gerusalemme al Congresso di Torino (24-26 settembre 1987): TerraS 64 (1988) 53-55. ► e638.

k719 *Gignoux* P. (en français),   First European conference of Iranian studies, Turin 7-11 sept. 1987: StIran 17 (1988) 117.

k720 *Gran-Aymerich* Jean,   Les Phéniciens à Rome et à Venise [Congrès Cons. Naz. Ric., Ist. Civiltà Fenicia, nov. 1987]: Archéologia 2,32 (Dijon 1988) 72-75; ill.

k721 *a) Herrenschmidt* Clarisse,   Le sixième atelier d'histoire achéménide, Groningen 30-31.V.1986; – *b) Richard* Francis,   Les journées de codicologie et de paléographie islamique, Istanbul 26-28 mai 1986: StIran 16 (1987) 269-271 / 267s.

k722 [*Homès-Fredericq* Denyse],   La XXXIVe Rencontre Assyriologique internationale (Istanbul); Liste alphabetique des orateurs et titre / Résumé des communications faites par des Belges / La 'Coopération' [work in progress]: Akkadica 57 (1988) 8-12-14-31.

k723 *a)* International workshop on Coptic and Nubian pottery, Nieborow, Poland, Aug. 29-31, 1988; – *b)* Fifth international congress of Egyptology (Cairo Oct. 29-Nov. 3, 1988): BLCéramÉg 13 (1988) 51s/53 (titles without comment).

k724 *Kontoyiannos* Spyridon D.,   Ⓖ Everyday life in Byzantium [— Cross-sections and continuity in the Hellenistic and Roman traditions; First International Byzantinological symposium, Athens 15-17 Sept. 1988]: TAth 54 (1988) 880-8.

k725 *Malagola* Marco,   Archeologia in Terra Santa, convegno Torino 24-26 settembre 1987: ParVi 33 (1988) 72-75; 3 fig.

k726 ^E*Pergola* Philippe,   Archeologia e cultura della tarda antichità e dell'alto medioevo, Resoconto delle sedute 1986s: RivArCr 62 (1988) 361-393.

k727 *Ries* Julien,   Le quatrième congrès international des études coptes, LvN 5-10 sept. 1988: ► d702, Monde Copte 14s (1988) 3.

k728 Société Asiatique, séances 1987s: JAs 276 (1988) 383-393; liste des membres, 395-417.

k729 *a) Stjernquist* Berta,   Den internationella arkeolog-kongressen i Mainz; – *b) Olausson* Deborah,   Symposium report 'Experimental archaeology — method and future', Gällö 24-25 Sept. 1986: Fornvännen 83 (1988) 114-6 / 112-4.

k730 *Wilding* L. S.,   The Indian Ocean in antiquity; 4th-8th July 1988, The British Museum: CanadMesop 16 (1988) 35s.

Y8   *Periti,* Scholars, personalia, organizations.

k731 *Buscemi* A. M.,   Studium Biblicum Franciscanum, cronaca 1987-8: SBFLA 38 (1988) 537-552; 539, 5 tesi di licenza [1 di laurea supra].

k732 *a) Caquot* André,   Hébreu et araméen; – *b) Leclant* Jean,   Égyptologie; – *c) Garelli* Paul,   Assyriologie; – *d) Hadot* Pierre,   Histoire de la pensée hellénistique et romaine: Annuaire du Collège de France (1987/8) 563-573 / 535-547 / 549-562 / 401-5.

k733 *Citrini* Tullio,   I venti anni della Facoltà Teologica dell'Italia Settentrionale: TItSett 13 (1988) 283-290.

k734 *Conti* Martino, *al.*,   Chronica Pontificii Athenaei Antoniani 1988-9: Antonianum 63 (1988) 621-679.

k735 E[*Crocker* John, segr., *Valentino* Carlo, assist.] Acta Pontificii Instituti Biblici 9,5 (1988s) p. 327-427.

k736 **Danker** Frederick W.,   A century of Greco-Roman philology, featuring the American Philological Association and the Society of Biblical Literature: SBL Biblical Scholarship in North America 12.   Atlanta 1988, Scholars. xvii-299 p. $27. 0-89130-986-1.

k737 GROSCHE Robert, zum hundertsten Geburtstag [Begründer 1932]: Catholica 42 (1988) 157-169 (H. *Fries*).

k738 **Handy** Robert T.,   A history of Union Theological Seminary in NY 1987 ► 3,h265:   RAndrUnS 26 (1988) 199s (G. R. *Knight*); ChH 57 (1988) 253s (C. C. *Goen*); TTod 45 (1988s) 214-7 (J. M. *Mulder*, also on MARSDEN's Fuller); WestTJ 50 (1988) 378-380 (W. M. *Brailsford*; p. 370-4, W. S. *Barker* on Marsden's Fuller).

k739 *Hinson* E. Glenn,   Dale MOODY,   Bible teacher extraordinaire: PerspRelSt 14,4 (1987) 3-18 [81-138, *al.*; 139s, bibliog.; response by Moody, 15,1 (1988) 5-16: ZIT 88,448].

k740 Historical Society of Israel and Zalman Shazar center, report of activities, 1987-8:   Zion 53 (1988) 455-469 **ⓗ**.

k741 *Irmscher* Johannes, Johannes MEWALDT, 29.IV.1880 - 1.V.1964: Helikon 28 (1988) 381-3.

k742 *Jurić* Stipe,   Dominicani et Biblia: BogSmot 58 (1988) 86-108; franç. 108s.

k743 *Leclant* Jean,   Une tradition; l'épigraphie à l'Académie des Inscriptions et Belles-Lettres: CRAI (1988) 714-732.

k744 *Garbini* G. [p. 7-24, 'Il semitista'], *al.*,   LEVI DELLA VIDA Giorgio, nel centenario della nascita (1886-1967): StSemitici NS 4. R 1988, Univ. 97 p.

k745 ENatalini Terzo,   Cento anni di cammino; Scuola Vaticana di Paleografia, Diplomatica e Archivistica (1884-1984). Vaticano 1986. 342 p. – RCC 139 (1988,1) 205s (G. *Caprile*).

k746 *Okawa* K., **ⓞ** The Bible in the interpretations of recent Oxford scholars [*Abraham* W., *Barr* J., *Muddiman* J.]: Kirisutokyo Gaku (Christian

Studies, St. Paul/Rikkyo Univ.) NS 26 (1984)... [BL 89,19; 206 p. in that issue].

k746* **Pazmiño** Robert W., The seminary in the city; a study of NY Theological Seminary. Lanham MD 1988, UPA. x-135 p. $20.50; pa. $10.25 [JTS 40,741].

k747 **Poulat** E., Liberté laïcité [1987 → k311 supra]: Ch. XI, p. 285-334, L'institution des 'Sciences Religieuses' [5ᵉ section de l'ÉPHÉ, créée à la suite de la fermeture de la Faculté de Théologie de la Sorbonne 1886, 'dont Mgr. MARET avait si longtemps maintenu l'existence contre vents et marées', EsprVie 98 (1988) 259 (É. *Cothenet*)].

k748 The Princeton Seminary Catalogue 21,2 (July 1988). 232 p.

k748* **Rousseau** L., *Despland* M., Les sciences religieuses au Québec depuis 1972: Sciences Religieuses au Canada 2. Waterloo ON 1988, W. Laurier Univ. 158 p. C$16 [NRT 111,474].

k749 Sbor Brno: Sborník praci filozoficke fakulty Brněnské University; Brno.

k749* a) *Silva* Moisés, A half-century of Reformed scholarship; – b) *Ferguson* Sinclair B., The whole counsel of God; fifty years of theological studies; – c) *Noll* Mark, The Princeton Review: WestTJ 50,2 (anniversary issue, 1988) 247-256 / 257-281 / 283-304.

k750 *Turasiewicz* Romuald, Profesor Tadeusz SINKO, 1877-1966: Eos 76 (1988) 199-209; lat. 210; bibliog. 211-5 (M. T. *Szerszeń*).

Y8.5 *Periti*, in memoriam.

k751 Obituaries, nécrologes: AntiqJ 68 (1988) 389-399; ETL 64 (1988) 85*-88*; KirSef 62 (1988s); REB 48 (1988) 227-233 . 484-497 . 742-8 . 1005-1013; RHE 83 (1988) 129*-131* . 303*-305* . 426*s.

k752 Abramowicz, Zofia, 1906 - 29.V.1988: Meander 43 (1988) 283s (-286), phot.

k752* Abramowitz, Chaim I., d. 1987; asst. ed.: Dor 16 (1987s) 1; phot.

k753 Alfonsi, Luigi, 12.XI.1917-20.I.1987: BStLat 17 (1987) 3s (G. *Aricò*).

k754 Alfrink, Bernard, kard., 1900 - 17.XII.1987: ETL 64 (1988) 243 (J. F. *Lescrauwaet*); Orientierung 52 (1988) 3s (W. *Goddijn*, ᵀ*Senn* F.).

k755 Alpatov, Michail Vladimirovič, aet. 84, † 1986: StRicOrCr 10 (1987) 103s (P. *Cazzola*).

k756 Altmann, Alexander, → 3,h289; 16.IV.1906-6.VI.1987: Zeitschrift für philosophische Forschung 42 (1988) 134-8 (M. *Albrecht*).

k757 Anthes, Rudolf → 2,e313; 1.III.1896-5.I.1985: Expedition 27,1 (Ph 1985) 34-36; 2 phot. (D. *O'Connor*).

k758 Backmund, Norbert [Wilhelm], OPraem., [→ 3,h295 Bakmund] 23.IX. 1907-1.II.1987: AnPraem 63 (1987) 259-267 (L. *Horstkötter*).

k759 Baer, Klaus, → 3,h292; 22.I.1930-14.V.1987: JAmEg 25 (1988) 2s (J. L. *Foster*).

k760 Bakhuizen van den Brink, Jan Nicolaas, → 3,h293; 1896 -5.XI.1987: NedTTs 42 (1988) 328s (O. J. de *Jong*); RHE 83 (1988) 279s (J. *Trapman*).

k761 Balthasar, Hans Urs von, card. design., 12.VIII.1905-26.VI.1988: America 159 (1988) 36-38 (E. T. *Oakes*); ETL 64 (1988) 512s; GeistL 61 (1988) 321-3; HerdKorr 42 (1988) 396; LavalTP 44 (1988) 275-8 (J.-G. *Page*).

k762 Baly, A. Denis, 24.IV.1913-27.VII.1987; geography of the Bible: BASOR 271 (1988) 1-3, phot. (A. D. *Tushingham*).

k763 Barrois Georges A., 17.II.1898-27.VIII.1987: SVlad 31 (1987) 283-5 (J. *Meyendorff*).

k764 Basham, Arthur Llewellyn, ➤ 3,h299; 24.V. [not VI. as some] 1914
-27.I.1986; Indologist: ZDMG 138 (1988) 17-23, phot.
k765 Basmatchi, Faraj, d. 5.VII.1987: Sumer 44 (1985s) 272; phot.
k766 Bauer, Gerhard, aet. 58, 9.XII.1986; KIsr 2 (1987) 3-5 (M. *Stöhr*: 'ein
Schüler und Lehrer der Bibel').
k766* Bausani, Alessandro, 1921-1988, islamologo: RSO 62 (1988) 135-8
(Biancamaria *Scarcia Amoretti*).
k767 Beek, Martinus Adrianus ➤ 3,h301; 1909 - 31.VII.1987; Assyriologie:
PhoenixEOL 33,2 (1987) 3-5, phot. (P. *Houwink ten Cate*).
k768 Bellens, August, C.I.C.M., aet. 74, 9.X.1988: AcPIB 9,5 (1988s) 421.
k769 Bennett, Crystal-M., ➤ 3,h304; 1918 - 12.VIII.1987: AntiqJ 68 (1988)
391; Levant 20 (1988) 1 [19 (1987) 1s (Geraldine *Talbot*)].
k770 Benoit, Pierre Maurice, o.p. ➤ 3,h305; 3.VIII.1906-23.IV.1987; dir. École
Biblique: DeltioVM 17,1 (1988) 69 (D. *Kaimakis*, Ⓖ); PEQ 120 (1988)
75s (J. P. *Kane*); TAth 59 (1988) 372-6 (C. S. *Vlachos* Ⓖ).
k771 Béranger, Jean, 1903 - 13.IX.1988: RÉLat 66 (1988) 18s (F. *Paschoud*).
k772 Bertetto, Domenico, † 18.VIII.1988: Salesianum 50 (1988) 650.
k773 Bogdanoff Pierre de, † c. 1987; directeur: Le Monde Copte 12 (1987) 3;
phot. (O. V. *Volkoff*).
k774 Bourguet, Pierre du, S.J., 1910 - 30.XII.1988; art paléochrétien et
égyptien: Textiles anciens 66 (1988) 77 (Marie-Hélène *Rutschowscaya*).
k775 Bride, André, mgr. 1899 - 21.II.1988, sacrements, droit: EsprVie 98
(1988) 198 (M. *Noirot*).
k776 Brown, Frank Edward, 24.V.1908-28.II.1988; long with American
Academy in Rome: AJA 92 (1988) 577-9; phot. (R. T. *Scott*).
k777 Brzuski, Witold Kazimierz, 6.IX.1935-13.XI.1987: PrzOr (1988,1) 79s
(Joanna *Mantel-Niećko*; bibliog.).
k777* Bussagli, Mario, 1917 - VIII.1988; Magi: RSO 62 (1988) 139-141 (L.
Petech).
k778 Callaway, Joseph A., ➤ 20 supra: 1920 - 23.VIII.1988, excavator of Ai:
BA 51 (1988) 67 (J. F. *Drinkard*); BAR-W 14,6 (1988) 24; phot. (H.
Shanks).
k779 Callender, John Bryan ➤ 3,h314; 11.VI.1940-16.IX.1987; Coptic:
BSocFrÉg 111 (1988) 5s (L. *Palà*).
k780 Carena, Omar, † 24.VIII.1988: AcPIB 9,5 (1988s) 420.
k781 Cejpek, Jiří, 20.II.1921-18.IV.1986; linguistic geography: ArOr 56 (1988)
62-64 (J. *Bečka*).
k782 Cerulli, Enrico, aet. 91, 19.IX.1988; Les Éthiopiens en Palestine...:
CRAI (1988) 540s (J. *Pouilloux*).
k783 Charbel, António: 10.IX.1911-7.I.1988; prof. VT: RCuBíb 11,43 (1987!)
236-243 (J. *Salvador*).
k784 Cherniss, Harold F., 11.III.1904-18.VI.1987; (Nyssa) Platonism: Gnomon 60 (1988) 665-7 (L. *Tarán*).
k785 Chiappero, Pier Giorgio, msgr., 19.III.1910-15.VII.1963; vicario patriarcale di Gerusalemme: TerraS 64 (1988) 274s (P. S. *Colbi*).
k786 Clavier, Henri, 1892-1987, un des fondateurs de la SNTS: RHPR 68
(1988) 153s (É. *Trocmé*).
k787 Clement, Paul August, 1906 - 30.VI.1986; UCLA; numismatist, Olyn-
thus excavator; member DAI: Gnomon 60 (1988) 83s (Anastasia N.
Dinsmoor).
k788 Clift, Evelyn Holst, 1910 - 9.X.1986: ClasW 80 (1986s) 204s.
k789 Condurachi, Emil, 1912 - 16.VIII.1987: Studii... IsVArh 39 (1988) 199-
201, phot. (A. *Barnea*).

k790 Cuming, Geoffrey, 1917 - 25.III.1988: Worship 62 (1988) 366.

k791 David, Martin, 3.VII.1898-9.IV.1986: Keilschriftrecht; collaboratore: Ivra 37 (1986) 207-212 (H. *Ankum*); ZSav-R 105 (1988) 989-997 (H. *Petschow*, H. *Ankum*).

k792 Devisch, Michel, aet. 49, 28.VII.1988: Q-hypothèse: ETL 64 (1988) 508s (F. *Neirynck*).

k793 D'Incerti, Vico, 1902 - 14.III.1988: RitNum 90 (1988) 605s (G. *Tabarroni*).

k794 Donoghue C. Eileen, 1905-1988: classics teacher: ClasW 82 (1988s) 115 (G. J. *Tiene*).

k795 Dresden, Mark Jan, 26.IV.1911 - 1986: StIran 16 (1987) 261-3 (R. N. *Frye*).

k796 Drexler, Hans, 11.III.1895-10.IV.1984, klass. Philologie: Gnomon 60 (1988) 188-191 (H.-U. *Berner*; 20 Schriften erwähnt).

k797 Dumézil, Georges, ⇥ 2,e353; 3,h327; 1899-1986: StIran 17 (1988) 95-97 (J. *Duchesne-Guillemin*).

k798 Dunand, Maurice, ⇥ 3,h328; 4.III.1898-29.III.1987; fouilleur de Byblos: Gnomon 60 (1988) 287 (R. A. *Stucky*).

k799 Ebner, Pietro, 13.II.1904-11.VI.1988: RitNum 90 (1988) 607-9 (G. *Libero Mangieri*).

k800 Ettinger, Shmuel, 24.VI.1919-22.IX.1988; co-editor: Zion 53 (1988) 423-440 (L. *Amnon, al.* ❿); phot. 239.

k801 Finley, Moses I., sir, 20.V.1912-23.VI.1986: HZ 244 (1987) 750-3 (W. *Nippel*).

k802 Foresti, Fabrizio, O.C.D., ⇥ 3,h335; 1.XI.1944-14.IX.1987: RivB 36 (1988) 134 (A. *Bonora*).

k803 Fuchs, Harald, 10.IX.1900-28.X.1985: lat. Philologie Basel: Gnomon 60 (1988) 80-82 (J. *Delz*).

k804 Fülep, Ferenc, ⇥ 3,h339; 5.VIII.1919-8.V.1986: Museum-Direktor: ActArchH 40 (1988) 317-9, phot. (E. *Tóth*; 317-9 bibliog., M. *Nagy*).

k805 Furstenberg Maximilien de, card. 23.X.1904-22.IX.1988; préf. Congr. Eccl. Or.: ETL 64 (1988) 508.

k806 Gätje, Helmut, ⇥ 3,h340; 16.XI.1927-8.III.1986; Arabist (syr.-aram. ...); ZDMG 138 (1988) 1-11, phot. (H. *Daiber*; 11-16 Bibliog.).

k807 Galling, Kurt, 8.I.1900-12.VII.1987; AT, Archäologie: ZDPV 104 (1988) 190-4, phot. (M. *Weippert*).

k808 Gelsi, Daniel, O.S.B., 3.III.1940-24.III.1988: Irénikon 61 (1988) 152; EcOrans 3 (1988) 97.99.

k809 Gómez Nogales, Salvador, 22.X.1913-2.XI.1987; arabista: BAsEspOr 23 (1987) 401s (F. de *Agreda*).

k810 Goodyear, Francis R. D.: 2.II.1936-24.VII.1987: Tacitus, unfinished; Gnomon 60 (1988) 763-5 (H. D. *Jocelyn*).

k811 Grimes, W. F. ('Peter') 31.X.1905-25.XII.1988, dir.: BInstAr 25 (1988) V, phot.

k812 Gross, Walter Hatto ⇥ 2,e377; 30.III.1913-24.XII.1984; klass. Archäologie: JbAkadGö (1987) 74-79 (J. *Bleicken*).

k813 Guéraud, Octave, 30.I.1901-22.IX.1987; papyrus de Toura: Aegyptus 68 (1988) 199-204 (J. *Scherer*).

k814 Halkin, François, S. J., 1.VII.1901-25.VII.1988; bollandiste: AnBoll 106,3s (1988) V-XL [P. *Devos*; XLI-XLIV bibliog. continuing 100 (1982) XIX-XXX]; RHE 83 (1988) 509s (J. van der *Straeten*).

k815 Hari, Robert, 1922-1988: BSocÉg 12 (1988) 5-7, phot.; BSocFrÉg 111 (1988) 5 (M. *Patané*).

k816 Havener, Ivan, O.S.B., 1943 - 24.IV.1988; associate editor: BToday 26 (1988) 222s (D. *Durken*).

k817 Herrmann, Johannes, 25.III.1918-8.IV.1987: Aegyptus 68 (1988) 195-8 (H.-A. *Rupprecht*); juristische Papyrologie: ZSav-R 105 (1988) 998-1002 (auch H.-A. *Rupprecht*).

k818 Herter, Hans, ➤ 1,g417; 8.VI.1899-7.XI.1984; Priapus; Plato: Gnomon 60 (1988) 473-9; portr. (E. *Vogt*).

k819 Heubeck, Alfred, 20.VII.1914-24.V.1987; Homer in Nürnberg: Gnomon 60 (1988) 283-5 (W. *Burkert*).

k820 Higounet, Charles, † 8.IV.1988: CRAI (1988) 233-5 (J. *Pouilloux*).

k821 Hockey, Stanley F., dom, aet 81, 8.IV.1988: AntiqJ 68 (1988) 394.

k822 Höffner, Josef, Kard.; ➤ 3,h362; † 16.X.1987: TrierTZ 97 (1988) 1-8 (E. *Nawroth*).

k823 Horn, Rudolf, 10.IX.1903-27.I.1984; klass. Kunst: JbAkadGö (1987) 67-73 (P. *Zanker*).

k824 Hotta, Benedict, O. F. M., aet. 57, 28.VII.1988: AcPIB 9,5 (1988s) 421.

k825 Jordahn, Bruno, aet. 79, 3.I.1988: JbLtgHymn 31 (1987s) vi.

k826 Kalousek, František, 20.XII.1901-5.IV.1988: SborBrno 33 (1988) 155-8 (V. *Podborský*).

k827 Karyszkowskij, Piotr Iosifovit, 12.III.1921-6.III.1988: VDI 186 (1988) 209s (Yu. G. *Vinozradoye*; bibliog. 211-215).

k827* Katzoff, Louis, d. 21.VII.1987; founder/editor: Dor 16 (1987s) 71s; phot. (S. *Bakon*).

k828 Kessler, Peter Josef, 25.IX.1905-4.VII.1988; droit canon: RHE 83 (1988) 748 (G. *Fransen*).

k829 Köbert, Raimund, S.J., 6.III.1903-27.IX.1987; Arabist: Orientalia 57 (1988) 212-7; portr. (W. R. *Mayer*, H. *Quecke*).

k830 Kononov, Andrej Nikolaevič, 1906-1986: AcAntH 41 (1987) 321s (A. *Róna-Tas*).

k831 Kornfeld, Walter, † 11.XI.1988: ZAW 101,172.

k832 Kustár, Péter, 1938-1987, Bible translator and expositor: Theologiai Szemle 31 (1988) 63 (C. *Fekete*, Ⓜ).

k833 Lacko, Michał, S.J. ➤ 65,e191; 19.I.1920-21.III.1982: Istina 33 (1988) 37-39 (B. *Dupuy*, bibliog.).

k834 Lentz, Otto Helmut Wolfgang, 23.II.1900-8.XII.1986; Turfan Manichean texts: StIran 16 (1987) 259s (R. N. *Frye*).

k835 Ligeti, Lájos, ➤ 3,h382; X.1902-24.V.1987; sinologue; JAs 276 (1988) 1-22 (Françoise *Aubin*).

k836 Liubinas, Bronisław, 8.VIII.1988, S. S. L.: AcPIB 9,5 (1988s) 421.

k837 Lourdaux, Willem, 31.V.1923-13.I.1988, collaborateur: RHE 83 (1988) 780s (J. M. *De Smet*).

k838 McGrath, Brendan, O.S.B., 19.II.1914-30.III.1988; CBA president: CBQ 50 (1988) 663s (C. J. *Peifer*).

k839 Mallwitz, Alfred, 2.X.1919-17.III.1986; Olympia-Ausgräber: AntWelt 19,2 (1988) 43-45.

k840 Manzini, Raimondo, 1901 - 14.I.1988; dir. OssRom 1960-1978: ETL 64 (1988) 237.

k841 Marsili, Salvatore, 10.VIII.1910-27.XI.1983: RivPastLtg 22 (1984) 86 (E. *Lodi*).

k842 Masse, André, S.J., 1940-1987: RICathP 25 (1988) 109-111 (D. *Maugenet*).

k843 Masson, Mikhail Evgenevič, 21.XI.1897-2.XI.1986: Turkménistan, archéologie: SovArch (1987,3) 282s, phot. (B. V. *Lurin*); StIran 17 (1988) 243-6, phot. (P. *Bernard*).

k844 Maurer, Joseph Abele, 29.IX.1911-1.IV.1987: ClasW 30 (1986s) 431s; phot. (Edna *Deangeli*).

k845 Maximenkov, Gleb Alekseyevitch, 26.VI.1930-10.IX.1986: SovArch (1988,3) 304 (V. A. *Semenov* ®).

k846 Michalski, Marian, 25.II.1900-18.I.1987; Patrolog: VoxPa 12s (1987s) 545s (E. *Staniek*).

k847 Moberg, Carl-Axel, 21.II.1915-3.IV.1987; statistical archeology: Fornvännen 83 (1988) 52-56, phot. (Berta *Stjernquist*).

k848 Mócsy, András, → 3,h393; 1929 - 20.I.1987: Archäologie, Budapest: Gnomon 60 (1988) 285s (T. *Pekáry*).

k849 Mohrmann, Christine, aet. 84, 13.VII.1988: VigChr 42 (1988) before p. 313; phot.

k850 Momigliano, Arnaldo Dante → 3,h396; 1908 - 1.IX.1987: Gnomon 60 (1988) 571-5, portr. (K. *Christ*).

k851 Moraux, Paul, aet. 66, 26.IX.1985; Aristotelismus: Gnomon 60 (1988) 380-2; phot. (J. *Wiesner*).

k852 Moreau, Joseph, 14.II.1900-19.XI.1988: CRAI (1988) 761s; RÉAnc 90 (1988) 301-3 (J.-C. *Fraisse*).

k853 Moser, Georg, 10.VI.1923-9.V.1988, Bischof-Protektor des Bibelwerks: BiKi 43 (1988) 93-95 (P.-G. *Müller*).

k854 Mrozek, Bernard, S.J., 25.VIII.1903-29.VIII.1987; 50 anni bibliotecario del Pont. Ist. Orientale: OrChrPer 54 (1988) 5-7 (V. *Poggi*).

k855 Mylonas, George, † 15.IV.1988: Mycenae: AntiqJ 68 (1988) 389s; Kernos 1 (1988) 6 [2,9-13, É. *Moutspoulos*].

k856 Needler, Winifred, aet. 84, 5.IX.1987: JAmEg 25 (1988) 1 (R. J. *Williams*).

k857 Nims, Charles Francis, 1906 - 19.XI.1988; Luxor epigraphic survey director: VarAeg 4 (1988) 191 (C. *Van Siclen*).

k858 Oberem, Udo, 11.XII.1923-24.XI.1986: BeiVgArch 8 (1986) 1-6 (W. W. *Wurster*).

k859 O'Donnell, J. Reginald, C. S. B., 1907-1988: MedSt 50 (1988) vii-x (J. A. *Raftis*).

k860 Ornella, Antonio, 1929 - 28.XI.1987; lasciati incompiuti commentari su Luca e Salmo 121: RivB 36 (1988) 135 (G. *Scarpat*).

k861 Palanque, Jean-Rémy, aet. 91, † 1988; Pères, S. Ambroise...: CRAI (1988) 428-431 (J. *Pouilloux*).

k862 Pellegrino, Michele, card. Torino → 2,e434; 3,h407; 25.IV.1903-10.X.1986; cristianesimo primitivo, co-fondatore RivStoLR [RHE 83,580, R. *Aubert*].

k863 Petráček, Karel, 6.II.1926-1.VII.1987, South-Semitic, Arabist: ArOr 56 (1988) 159-163 (P. *Vavroušek*, J. *Oliverius*; bibliog. p. 163-171 . 257-266).

k864 Plé, Albert, o.p., 23.III.1909-20.II.1988: fondateur: SuppVSp 164 (1988) 1s, phot.

k865 Pocquet du Haut-Jussé, Barthélemy, aet. 97: CRAI (1988) 522s (J. *Pouilloux*).

k866 Pokora, Timoteus, 26.VI.1928-11.VII.1985: AcOrH 40 (1986) 199 (F. *Tőkei*).

k867 Pol W. H. van de, 1897-1987, Fenomenologie van het Protestantisme; ETL 64 (1988) 243 (J. F. *Lescrauwaet*).

k868 Popescu, Dorin, 1904 - 27.V.1987: St... IsVArh 39 (1988) 73-78, phot., bibliog. (S. *Morintz*).

k869 Posener, Georges, 12.IX.1906-15.V.1988: BSocFrÉg 112 (1988) 4-10 (J. *Assmann*); 11-22, 'Découverte de l'ancienne Égypte', son discours pour le doctorat honoris causa, Heidelberg 26.X.1986; BIFAO 88 (1988) vii-xv; 3

phot. (J. *Yoyotte*); xvi-xxviii bibliog. (O. *Perdu*); CRAI (1988) 357-360 (J. *Pouilloux*).

k870 Poupé, Jean, 28.VI.1919-15.II.1988; histoire religieuse: RTLv 19 (1988) 253-5 (R. *Gryson*).

k871 Puech, Henri-Charles, ⇥ 2,e438; 3,h412; 20.VII.1902-11.I.1986: ⇥ 786, Catholicisme 12,55 (1988) 284s (J. *Ries*); CRAI (1988) 764-776, portr. (A. *Guillaumont*).

k872 Quasten, Johannes, msgr. ⇥ 3,h413; 3.V.1900-10.III.1987; patrologie: ⇥ 786, Catholicisme 12,55 (1988) 346s (A.-G. *Hammann*).

k873 Quigley, James M., S.J., 13.I.1929-7.VIII.1988; nuper bibliothecarius periodicorum P. Inst. Biblici et sic hujus Elenchi collaborator validus.

k874 Raes, Alphonse, 1896-1983: Istina 33 (1988) 34-37 (B. *Dupuy*, bibliog.).

k875 Ramsey, Michael, 1905 - 23.IV.1986: ETL 64 (1988) 512.

k876 Ranson, Charles Wesley, 15.VI.1903-23.I.1988, secretary of International Missionary Council: IntRMiss 77 (1988) 172.

k877 Reicke, Bo ⇥ 3,h414; 1914 - 17.V.1987: SvEx 53 (1988) 85-87 (H. *Riesenfeld*).

k878 Reindl, Joseph, 2.V.1931-24.IX.1986: ⇥ 328, ᴱ*Wallis* G., Zwischen Gericht und Heil 1987, 7.

k879 Reyero Martínez, Salustiano, o.p., 1.III.1906-13.VIII.1988; biblista: Studium 28 (M 1988) 511s (L. *López de las Heras*).

k880 Riefstahl, Elizabeth T., 8.III.1889-15.IX.1986; ed. secretary: JAmEg 24 (1987) 1 (R. S. *Bianchi*).

k881 Riposati, Benedetto, prof. mons., ⇥ 3,h416; 14.III.1903-3.IX.1986; storia della letteratura latina; Univ. cattolica Milano: Gnomon 60 (1988) 82s (Maria Grazia *Bajoni*).

k882 Ruiz González, Gregorio ⇥ 2,e443; 3,h421; aet. 49, 29.VIII.1987: BAsEspOr 23 (1987) 402s (M. de *Epalza*).

k883 Salamon, Ágnes, 14.IX.1923-18.VI.1986: Roman archeology: AcArchH 40 (1988) 319s (J. *Fitz*; 320-2, bibliog., M. *Fejér*).

k884 Salmon, Edward Togo, 1905 - 11.V.1988; Samnite history: ÉchMClas 32 (1988) 443 (A. G. *McKay*).

k885 Šašel, Jaroslav, aet. 64, 25.III.1988; epigraphist: AntiqJ 68 (1988) 390.

k886 Schachermeyr, Fritz, 10.I.1895-26.XII.1987: AnzAltW 41 (1988) 125-8 (Sigrid *Deger-Jalkotzy*).

k886* Scheiber Alexander, 1913 - 3.III.1985: RÉJ 146 (1987) 201s (Gabrielle *Sed-Rajna*).

k887 Schelkle, Karl Hermann, 3.IV.1908-9.III.1988, Mitherausgeber: TüTQ 168 (1988) 179-181 [234-6, Bibliog. (seit ᶠWort Gottes) 1973-1988, *Feld* H.]; BiKi 43 (1988) 74 (O. B. *Knoch*); BZ 32 (1988) 312.

k888 Seidl, Erwin, 6.XI.1905-4.IV.1987; droit ancien: Aegyptus 68 (1988) 204s (J. *Mélèze-Modrzejewski*).

k889 Şemriyon, Şemaḥ, 1920-1988: BethM 34,116 (1988s) 1-3 (J. *Hookerman*).

k890 Shiloh, Yigal, ⇥ 3,h428; 1937 - 13.XI.1987; Jerusalem excavator: IsrEJ 38 (1988) 92s; BAngIsr 8 (1988s) 77 (Jane M. *Cahill*, Alon de *Groot*); MondeB 53 (1988) 61, phot. (J. *Briend*).

k891 Shipton, Geoffrey M., 1910 - X.1987; Megiddo pottery expert, then business man: BASOR 272 (1988) 1s; photo (R. *Braidwood*, D. *Esse*).

k892 Simonetta, Bono, 1903 - 28.X.1987: RitNum 90 (1988) 610 (A. M.).

k893 Skowroński, Zygmunt, 14.X.1909-2.XII.1986: VoxPa 12s (1987s) 546s (J. *Slomka*).

k894 Škrinjar, Albin, S.J., aet. 92, 31.VII.1988; S. S. L., prof. S. Scr.: AcPIB 9,5 (1988s) 421.

k895 Skrzypczak, Otto, mons., 30.VII.1914-   : RCuBib 45s (1988) 184-7 (B. *Kipper*).

k896 Sourdive, Claude † 1987: BSocFrÉg 111 (1988) 4s.

k897 Starcky, Jean, 3.II.1909-9.X.1988; Petra, Palmyra: ADAJ 32 (1988) 9-11, phot. (F. *Zayadine*); 12-14 bibliog.; MondeB 56 (1988) 58s; phot. ['10.X.1988' < Jordan Times 14.X.1988, *al.*]; RICathP 28 (1988) 175-9 (D. *Pézeril*).

k898 Stratanovskij, Georgi Andreyevič, 21.V.1901-3.XI.1986: VDI 185 (1988) 254 (A. I. *Zajcev, al.*).

k899 Subilia, Vittorio, 5.VIII.1911-12.IV.1988; dir.: Protestantesimo 43 (1988) 65s.

k900 Tchalenko, Georges   → 3,h435; 23.VII.1905-5.VIII.1987; Beirut Institut Français architect: Gnomon 30 (1988) 667s (Christine *Strube*).

k901 Thiele, Edwin R., † 1987 (JAOS 108,211).

k902 Thomas, Elizabeth, → 3,h348; 29.III.1907-28.XI.1986; Thebes research: JAmEg 24 (1987) 1s (Rita E. *Freed*).

k903 Trapè Agostino, 9.I.1915-14.VI.1987:   VoxPatrum 12s (1987s) 547-9 (T. *Kaczmarek*).

k904 Urdánoz, Teófilo, o.p., 6.II.1912-8.VI.1987; dogma, moral: CiTom 114 (1987) 357-366 (R. *Hernández*; 366-9, bibliog.).

k905 Vindenas, Johanne, 28.IV.1899-21.X.1988, Chicago Oriental Institute librarian: OIAc (Oc 1988) end (R. *Wadsworth*).

k906 Vandier-Nicolas, Nicole, 1908 - 1.III.1987; art chinois: JAs 276 (1988) 23-25 (M. *Soymié*).

k907 Verheijem, Luc, O.S.A., 29.III.1917-21.IX.1987: RICathP 25 (1985) 107s (V.-S. *Arminjon*).

k908 Verlet, Pierre, aet. 79, 9.XII.1987; art historian: AntiqJ 68 (1988) 390.

k909 Vidal, Jacques, O. F. M., 4.VII.1925-26.IX.1987; religions comparées: RICathP 25 (1988) 113-6 (M. *Delahoutre*).

k910 Vööbus, Arthur † 26.IX.1988 → h934, History of Asceticism 1988, ii.

k911 Volbach, Wolfgang Fritz, 18.VIII.1892-23.XII.1988; art chrétien: Textiles anciens 66 (1988) 74-76 (Ruth *Grönwoldt*, also Eng.).

k912 Volk, Hermann, Kardinal, 27.XII.1903-1.VII.1988:   Catholica 42 (1988) 322-8 (A. *Klein*); HerdKorr 42 (1988) 395s.

k913 Weninger, Margarete, 1895-1987: Mitt. Anthrop. Ges. Wien 117 (1987) 179-182, phot. (H. *Seidler*).

k914 Ziegler, Joseph, 15.III.1902-1.X.1988: Septuaginta: ZAW 101, 1-3 (J. *Schreiner*).

k915 Zsindele, Endre, 4.V.1929-25.IV.1986:   Zwingliana 17 (1988) 139, phot. (R. *Schnyder*).

Index Alphabeticus: Auctores – *Situs (omisso al-, tell, abu, etc.)*
ᴰdiss./dir. ᴱeditor ᶠFestschrift ᴹmentio, de eo ᴿrecensio ᵀtranslator † in mem.

ᴰdiss./dir. ᴱeditor ᶠFestschrift ᴹmentio, de eo ᴿrecensio ᵀtranslator † in mem. Sub **de, van** etc.: cognomina *americana* (post 1979) et *italiana* (post 1984); **non** reliqua.

ᴰdiss./dir. ᴱeditor ᶠFestschrift ᴹmentio, de eo ᴿrecensio ᵀtranslator † in mem.
Sub **de, van** etc.: cognomina *americana* (post 1979) et *italiana* (post 1984); **non** reliqua.

Ddiss./dir. Eeditor FFestschrift Mmentio, de eo Rrecensio Ttranslator † in mem.
Sub de, van etc.: cognomina americana (post 1979) et italiana (post 1984); non reliqua.

Cognomina **italiana** et **americana** *sola* sub praefixo separato *da* etc.

Cognomina **italiana** et **americana** *sola* sub praefixo separato *da* etc.

Cognomina **italiana** et **americana** *sola* sub praefixo separato *da* etc.

Cognomina **italiana** et **americana** *sola* sub praefixo separato *da* etc.

Cognomina **italiana** et **americana** *sola* sub praefixo separato *da* etc.

ᴰdiss./dir. ᴱeditor ᶠFestschrift ᴹmentio, de eo ᴿrecensio ᵀtranslator † in mem.
Sub **de, van** etc.: cognomina *americana* (post 1979) et *italiana* (post 1984); **non** reliqua.

Ddiss./dir. Eeditor FFestschrift Mmentio, de eo Rrecensio Ttranslator † in mem.
Sub **de, van** etc.: cognomina *americana* (post 1979) et *italiana* (post 1984); **non** reliqua.

Ddiss./dir. Eeditor FFestschrift Mmentio, de eo Rrecensio Ttranslator † in mem.
Sub **de**, **van** etc.: cognomina *americana* (post 1979) et *italiana* (post 1984); **non** reliqua.

ᴰdiss./dir. ᴱeditor ᶠFestschrift ᴹmentio, de eo ᴿrecensio ᵀtranslator † in mem.
Sub **de, van** etc.: cognomina *americana* (post 1979) et *italiana* (post 1984); **non** reliqua.

Ddiss./dir. Eeditor FFestschrift Mmentio, de eo Rrecensio Ttranslator † in mem.

Sub **de**, **van** etc.: cognomina *americana* (post 1979) et *italiana* (post 1984); **non** reliqua.

Ddiss./dir. Eeditor FFestschrift Mmentio, de eo Rrecensio Ttranslator † in mem.
Sub **de, van** etc.: cognomina *americana* (post 1979) et *italiana* (post 1984); **non** reliqua.

ᴰdiss./dir. ᴱeditor ꜰFestschrift ᴹmentio, de eo ᴿrecensio ᵀtranslator † in mem.
Sub **de, van** etc.: cognomina *americana* (post 1979) et *italiana* (post 1984); **non** reliqua.

Cognomina **americana** *sola* ponuntur sub praefixo separato *van, von*

ᴰdiss./dir. ᴱeditor ᶠFestschrift ᴹmentio, de eo ᴿrecensio ᵀtranslator † in mem.
Sub **de, van** etc.: cognomina *americana* (post 1979) et *italiana* (post 1984); **non** reliqua.

VOCES

ordine **graeco**

1054 – Johannes

11,1-12-19:
 5588*ab*
11: 5589-5592
11,33: 5593
11,44: 5594
12: 5475
12,1-11: 5595
12,1-8: 5596
12,40: 5597
13-17: 5599a 5600
13: 5601
13,1-20: 5598
13,1-3: 5601 5602
13,1: 4831*a*
13,6: 5603
13,26s: 5604
14-17: 5605
14,2s: 5606
14,2: 2553
14,26: 5607
17: 5609* 5610
17,11-16: 5612
18s: 5599*b*
18,36: 5618
19,1-6: 5620
19,5: 5621
19,23: 3241
19,25-27: 5552*b*
19,28-37: 5622
19,30: 5623
19,32-35: 5624
19,39: 5626
20,1-18: 5627 5628
20,1-9: 5629
20,3-10: 5630
20,7: 5594
20,11-16: 5631
20,16: 5632
20,22: 5633
20,23: 4743
20,29: 5634
21: 5635
21,14: 5636

Actus Apostolorum

–: 5079-5116 5224-
 5317
1-15: 8942*e*
1-12: 5235
1s: 5318
1,2: 5323
1,4: 5324
1,14: 5325
1,21: 5326

1,24: 5327
2: 5329 5330
2,4: 5328
2,10: 5331
2,42: 1772
2,47: 5333
3,1-10: 5335
3,22-26: 5336
5,1-11: 5338
6,1-5: 6325
6,5: 5339
6,8-8,3: 5340
6,11: 5373
6,14: 5341
7,2-53: 5342
7,43: 3972
7,55s: 5343
8,4-25: 5344
8,17: 5339
8,26-39: 5345
8,37: 5346
9,1-29: 5348*a*
9,2: 5347
9,3-8: 5349
9,22-26: 5351
9,31: 6264
9,37: 5352
10: 5355
10,1: 5356
10,15: 5353
10,34-43: 5354
10,34-38: 5357*a*
10,35: 5358
11,9: 5353
11,18: 5359
11,27-30: 9210
14,21-23: 9210
15: 6184
16,1-33: 5370
15,1-23: 9210
15,8: 5327
16,1-3: 5371
16,11-40: 5372
17: 5355 5374
17,1-10: 5375
17,16-34: 5376
17,16-31: 5377
17,23: 5378
18,7: 5356
18,11.16: 5378*
19: 5378*
20,9: 5380
20,17-38: 9210
20,18-35: 5381
 5382
22,6-21: 5383

22,8-10: 5796*b*
25,21: 3557
26,2-23: 5384
26,12-18: 5349
27s: 5385
27: 5386
28,1-6: 5387
28,1: 5388

Ad Romanos

–: 5902-5926
 k430*c*
1: 5927
1,5: 5928 5929
1,11-11,36: 5930
1,14: 5931
1,18-3,20: 5933
1,18-2,29: 5932
2,7: 5358
2,14-16: 5934
3,1-8: 5936
3,4: 5935
3,19-31: 5937
3,27-30: 5938
4: 5939
4,5: 5941
4,15.22: 5935
5-8: 5942
5: 6115
5,12-21: 5943
7: 5948 5949
7,14-25: 5950
7,14: a683
8,9-39; 6155
8,14: 5951
8,15s: 5952
8,15.23: 5953
8,17: 5954
8,21: 5955
8,24: 8733
8,26.27: 5956
8,31-39: 5957
 5958
9-11: 5959-5981
 5990*bc*
9: 5982
9,1-23: 5983
9,3: 5960*b*
9,17: 5935
9,24-33: 5984
9,27: 5985
10,4-15: 5986
10,4: 5987 5988
10,8: 5989
11,5: 5985
11,7-10: 6140

11,18; 381
11,25-32: 5990*a*
11,26: 5992
11,30-32: 4778
12: 5993
12,1s: 5994
12,2: 5995
12,8: 5996
12,14-21: 5888
13: 5997 5999
13,1-7: 6000-6002
13,3s: 6003
14s: 6004
15,20: 6264
15,24: 6005*a*
16,1s: 6007
16,1: 6005*a* 6006
16,26: 5928 5929
16,27: 6008

1 Ad Corinthios

–: 6009-6032
1-4: 6033
1s: 6034
1,18-31: 6036
1,20: 6037
1,21: 6038*a*
2,2: a170
2,5: 6037
2,6-16: 6039
2,6-9: 6040
2,11s: 6041
3: 6042
3,1: a683
3,11: 8133
4,9-13: 6043
5s: 6044
5,5: 6045
6,12-7,39: 6046
6,12-20: 5888
7: 6038*b* 6048
7,1-7; 5888
7,1: 6053
7,8: 6050
7,12-16: 4768
7,25: 6051
7,29-31: 6052
7,35: 6053
7,39: 6054
8,1-11,1: 6055
8,4-6: 6056
8,6: 8680
9: 6057 6058*a*
9,1: 6117
9,19-23: 6059
10,1: 6384

ISBN 88-7653-594-2